Curriculum principles
and social trends

Teaching materials for the ten-year-olds of the nuclear era. (*Courtesy Greensboro (N.C.) Public Schools, Brooks School.*)

Curriculum Principles and Social Trends

THIRD EDITION

by J. MINOR GWYNN

Professor of Education, University of North Carolina

THE MACMILLAN COMPANY, New York

to Janie

PREFACE

Crucial educational events in the 1950's have led to a careful re-examination of the public school curriculum. Is our educational program on both elementary and secondary schools levels carrying out our purposes? In what respects is the curriculum soundly based and effectively taught? In what ways must improvement take place for this age of automation? This third edition of *Curriculum Principles and Social Trends* seeks to answer these important questions, insofar as is possible in this rapidly changing world. Thinking and practice with regard to the school curriculum have changed so much recently that preparing a revision has involved actually rewriting the greater part of the book and the addition of entirely new chapters.

The newer emphases of the third edition cluster around five major areas:

1. The curriculum for the nuclear age, the age of automation.
2. Curricular provisions for the atypical child, provisions as adequate for the gifted and talented child as for the slow-learning pupil.
3. The relationships of the pupil's readiness to learn and his interest(s) in learning to curricular scope and sequence at various grade levels.
4. The development by the junior high school of its own curriculum, centered around the needs and interests of early adolescents, with special guidance for pupils through "core" or "block" work or unit teaching.
5. Critical curriculum problems needing satisfactory solutions, problems caused primarily by new social legislation, the teacher shortage, the growing school-age population and lack of classroom space, special national defense needs, and desegregation.

The changes and additions from previous editions of this book are many. For example, there have been new controversies in regard to the use of texts and materials which require analysis. Reading readiness has taken on new meaning in the difference of opinion over the educational implications of phonics, of individualized reading, and the influence of the "comic" book. The guidance of youth has been accepted as a more important goal of both the elementary and secondary school. The "unit" around a center of interest has been developed more thoroughly, both as a resource and teaching tool. The controversies over religious education and federal aid to education have been blended. Other developments have taken place in regard to grouping, promotion and evaluation, and "moving up" curricular scope and sequence in the elementary school; for example, pupils are getting science concepts now at the age of ten which they did not acquire formerly until about the age of twelve. The growth of the junior high school as a special organizational level for the children of the intermediate grades has warranted an entirely new chapter devoted to its curricular growth. New proposals of a striking nature have been made for the secondary school, too, with regard to the "core" curriculum and "general" or "basic" education on the one hand, and "specialized" education and acceleration on the other.

New problems have risen also in regard to teacher education and supply, two factors which vitally affect the curriculum. New developments in community and regional planning have provided new curricular materials through cooperative participation by both lay and professional groups; at the same time, they have raised the question of how far cooperative curriculum planning can go without undue pressures from lay groups on curricular effectiveness. There has been a deluge of materials and data on intercultural and racial aspects as factors in curriculum revision. New concepts of curriculum planning and organization are implicit in the new movement labeled "group dynamics," or "cooperative group planning" for curriculum work. All of these problems and developments have been given new attention in this revision.

What are some of the types of problems that must be solved in this evolving curriculum in the public schools? For example, what should be the scope and the duration of "general" education? Can an activity curriculum be as effective as the subject-centered program? How can the teaching of democracy be incorporated best in the curriculum? How can we educate the gifted more adequately? On what bases should vocational training, guidance, and placement be established in the program of the secondary school? What emphasis in curriculum work should be placed upon the development of desirable attitudes, habits, and ideals? How can teachers in service keep abreast of new developments in the curriculum? Will teachers continue in the profession who have to attempt a curriculum more suitable for delinquents in a correctional institution than for a public school? What relationship should there be, if any, between the school and the church in the fostering of religious education for children and youth? Should the public junior college, or community institute supported by public taxation, become a permanent part of the expanding public educational structure? If so, should its program include adult education on an extensive scale? So important are these kinds of problems that a new chapter is devoted to them.

Despite the importance of new emphases, the basic approach of the earlier editions of this book remains the same. Conflicting educational theories have stimulated wide study and re-examination of the purposes of education. Another factor focusing attention upon the curricular program has been the extension of public education into areas of training formerly cared for by the home, the church, and other agencies of the community. The cumulative effects of long-continued studies of the growth and development of the individual pupil comprise a third major movement, one which is forcing adjustments to be made in the curriculum. Finally, the conditions which have followed World War II and the Korean War have made curriculum readjustments absolutely necessary. Therefore, this volume has the following purposes:

1. *To show that personal experiencing is the only way by which real improvement in the curriculum can be effected.* Each person involved in curriculum construction has to solve his own problems. Regardless of the source and the intrinsic value of any new idea, the idea is of little worth to the teacher, administrator, supervisor, or other educational employee unless it is tried out and its value is

learned by actual experience. In this volume, therefore, all of the curricular approaches which have been used successfully by educational employees are presented in the hope that the prospective experiencer will find in them many suggestions that will help him to solve his own curricular problems. Source materials and bibliographies likewise contribute to this fund of suggestions, and are generously included in the book.

2. *To evince that educational growth is and should be an evolutionary process, and that such evolution is strongly stimulated and conditioned by changes in the social, economic, and cultural life of a nation.* In order to understand this evolution and its implications for the curriculum, educational employees must know those factors which have operated to make the curriculum what it is today, as well as the new influences at work. This requires a comprehensive grasp of the purposes and structure of the *total* school curriculum; mere knowledge of the aims and the structure on one school level will not suffice.

3. *To demonstrate that teaching methods cannot be divorced from the curriculum.* Educators established the purposes of education; then they established the curriculum as the means of attaining those purposes. Teaching methods are merely other means of attaining the same purposes through the teaching process. Just as methods of teaching cannot be effectively presented to anyone without using the curriculum, so the curriculum cannot be adequately presented without considering teaching methods. The chief methods employed in teaching are therefore presented here, especially as they affect and illustrate the curriculum.

Following an historical sketch of the development of the curriculum in the schools of the United States, the book is divided into six parts: I, Factors in Curriculum Development; II, The Modern Movement for Curriculum Revision; III, The Elementary-School Curriculum; IV, The Secondary-School Curriculum; V, Other Influences on Curriculum Changes; and VI, Looking to the Future in Curriculum Revision.

Pertinent to both elementary and secondary levels are chapters on conflicting educational theories, child growth and development, sociological and economic factors, teacher education, curricular aids, influence of the textbook, development of the unit technique, the community approach to the curriculum, national and international movements, propaganda and the curriculum, and the curriculum crisis at midcentury.

At the close of each chapter there are problems for individual work and for class discussion. These problems are followed by carefully selected lists of annotated references. There is a special bibliography on general and specific aspects of the elementary-school curriculum at the end of Chapter 11, and one on the secondary-school curriculum at the end of Chapter 13. An extensive index with cross-references makes the volume readily and easily adaptable for reference, as well as for class use.

In the preparation of this book, the author is grateful to many persons for their assistance. He is particularly indebted to the students in his classes at the University of North Carolina, whose cooperation made possible a thorough trial of both the newer and older materials; to his colleagues who read the manuscript; and to Elizabeth M. Holbrook, who made many valuable suggestions as to form and content in her critical reading of the manuscript. The author wishes also to express his gratitude to those persons who generously supplied many of the illustrations for the volume, and to those authors and publishers who graciously gave their permission for the use of quoted materials. Special acknowledgment for this assistance is made at appropriate places in the book.

J. Minor Gwynn

Chapel Hill, North Carolina

CONTENTS

Chapter 1. An overview of the evolution of the curriculum   1

1. The Religious Motive (1635–1770)   1
2. The Political Motive (1770–1860)   5
3. The Utilitarian Motive (1860–1890)   13
   Earlier Influence: 1860–1890   14
   Later Developments: 1890–1920   19
4. The Motive of Mass Education (1920–Date)   34

Part I
NEW FACTORS IN CURRICULUM DEVELOPMENT

Chapter 2. Conflicting educational theories   41

Equalization of Educational Opportunity   41
The Modern Conflict in Educational Theory   42
The Relationship of the School to Other Social Agencies 47

Chapter 3. Curriculum problems concerned with child growth and development   60

The Purposes of Educational Psychology   60
Theories and Principles of Learning   63
Newer Experiments in Child Growth and Development   71
Teacher Behavior and Development and Mental Health   78

Chapter 4. Sociological and economic factors in curriculum work   85

Basic Agencies in the Educative Process   85
Leisure-time Agencies   95
   Commercial Types   95
   Noncommercial Types   101
The Relation of the School to Other Social Agencies   104

Chapter 5. National and international movements   113

Controlling Factors in the Extension of Education   113
New Social and Economic Policies   117
Regional and State Planning in National Development   126
Problems of a Racial and International Character   130

Part II
THE MODERN MOVEMENT FOR CURRICULUM REVISION

*Chapter 6. Stages of growth in the modern curriculum move-
    ment*   143

Genesis of the Movement   143
The "Aims-and-Objectives" Stage and Activity Analysis   144
The Survey Movement in Curriculum Revision   149
Development in Unit Technique   157
System-wide Curriculum Revision   157
The Core-curriculum Movement and the Large-unit Procedure,
    Including the Fusion Movement   161
The Activity Movement   171

Chapter 7. The development of the unit technique   178

Origin and Growth of the Unit Plan   178
1. Comparison of the Morrison Plan with the Herbartian Method   179
2. Growth of the Morrison Plan Since 1926   185
3. Psychologically Sound Features of the Morrison Technique   192
The Activity Movement and Teaching Technique   195
Relationship Between Methods and the Curriculum   199
Characteristics of the Unit   201

Chapter 8. The influence of the textbook   206

Position of the Textbook in American Education   206
Changes in Series of Textbooks in Reading, Language and Grammar,
    and Literature   222
Changes in the Rugg Series of Social Science (Studies) Textbooks 230
Guiding Principles for the Use of Textbooks in Curriculum Work   233

Chapter 9. The technical vocabulary of the curriculum   238

Part III
THE ELEMENTARY-SCHOOL CURRICULUM

Chapter 10. Curriculum building in the elementary school   249

The Elementary-school Situation   249
The Interests and Attitudes of Children in the Elementary School 251
Significant Conditioning Factors in Curriculum Revision   258
Types of Curriculum Approach in the Elementary Schools   267
1. The Textbook Approach   267
2. Curriculum Revision Based on Subject-matter or Subject-area Units 268
3. The Activity or "Fusion" Approach   269
4. The Plan for Larger Centers of Interest with Scope and Sequence 273

Part VI
LOOKING TO THE FUTURE IN CURRICULUM REVISION

Chapter 19. Propaganda and the curriculum **579**

Problems of Indoctrination and Propaganda 579
Samples of Propaganda Analysis in Teaching 582
ILLUSTRATION I. Consumer Education: Advertising as an Example 582
    1. Through the Press 582
    2. Through Radio and Television 587
    3. Through the Screen 592
ILLUSTRATION II. Problems of Democracy: Pressure Groups: The American Legion as an Example 592
The Techniques of Propaganda 597
Mechanics of Modern Propaganda Techniques 601
Propaganda Channels in the Schools 605
Summary 609

Chapter 20. The community approach to the curriculum **615**

The Local Pattern in American Education 615
The Community as the Center of National Planning 617
Curriculum Experiments in Local Communities 620
The State as the Larger Community 627
The Regional Approach to the Curriculum 631
The United States as the National Community 634
Implications of the Community Approach for Curricular Development 636

Chapter 21. The curriculum crisis at midcentury **643**

Past National Emergencies and Curricular Progress 643
The Present Curriculum Crisis 649
Developing Curricular Trends 669
Implications for the Future 670

Index **679**

TABLES

1. Types of schools developed in the United States, 1750 to 1860   8
2. Types of elementary school subjects—about 1900   18
3. New high-school subjects accepted for college entrance, 1860–1890   19
4. Course of study of the Chicago English High and Manual Training School, 1891–1892   20
5. Course of instruction of the high school, of Pratt Institute (Brooklyn, New York), 1891–1892   21
6. The evolution of our elementary-school curriculum, and of methods of teaching   23
7. Development of high-school subjects of study   22
8. Subjects of study in public high schools, 1891   24
9. Curricula of the Charlotte (N.C.) high school, 1914–1915   26
10. Major changes in curricular offerings, 1860–1920   33
11. Individual growth and adjustment check-list   80
12. Changes in types of moving pictures, 1920–1957   96
13. Plan of basic or core courses, California Cooperating Schools, 1936   163
14. The social-living programs in the California Cooperating Schools, 1939   164
15. Changes in the Elson series of readers, 1920 to 1957   224
16. Changes in the Elson language (grammar) series, 1917 to 1927   225
17. Changes in the Ward Sentence and Theme series, 1917 to 1929   228
18. Changes in the Literature and Life series, 1922 to 1948, and in America Reads series, 1952 to 1957   229
19. Changes in the Rugg series of social science textbooks, 1920 to 1938   232
20. Framework of the social studies program   276
21. Comparison of the different conceptions of secondary education, 1918–1952   358
22. Types of curriculum approach   409
23. Junior high-school program of study, Detroit, Mich., 1923   436

FIGURES

Teaching materials for the ten-year-olds of the nuclear age   *frontispiece*

1. Foundation stone and steps of formal education in the pre-national period   4
2. New England as a type of public school development—its curriculum, 1860   9
3. Curriculum of the academy-subjects usually given, about 1840   10
4. Evolution of high-school subject-matter fields, 1893 to date   25
5. Evolution of parallel high-school curricula, 1893–1925   28
6. Should adult education be a part of the school program?   49
7. Differences between boys and girls in physical growth   62
8. We grow faster some times than at others   69
9. We don't grow "all of a piece"   71
10. We don't all begin at the same time and we don't all end at the same time   75
11. One may be a little boy with a little boy's interests; another may be thinking and feeling like a man; all in the same classroom   77
12. The summer camp for children   87
13. Social recreation for students around a student-constructed replica of an old southern mansion   106
14. Citizenship training   116
15. Irrigation: a means of resettlement   125
16. The eleven-year-olds study   133
17. Cooperative planning   160
18. Writing the group story: Grade One   170
19. Fifth-graders proving space age facts   184
20. A tree fell. They love it. Hence, the nature trail   197
21. There can be texts other than books   216
22. Teaching speech in high school   231
23. The baby goat visits the first grade farm   264
24. The whole second grade works on an activity after planning together   270
25. The nine-year-olds experiment with sound   298
26. Utilization of pupil leadership in a learning process. Learning to read   314
27. Drill is still a part of school!   323
28. Using community resources in curriculum work   366
29. Bringing the extra-curriculum into the curriculum   374
30. Boys working in the graphic arts area in industrial arts. Graphic arts include letter press and silk screen printing, book binding, and mechanical drawing   407
31. The problems approach in teaching   414
32. An exploratory and appreciation subject in junior high school   434

33. The basic learnings are stressed in the junior high school curriculum   438
34. An algebra class for superior students   443
35. The student council as a part of the curricular program   457
36. A home project in agriculture—student being taught how to caponize
    chickens   489
37. Library facilities serve pupil needs   495
38. Arts and crafts works at Montevallo   501
39. Modern teachers have to learn to use many new tools   524
40. Turning the county-wide teachers' meeting into a workshop experi-
    ence: Visiting the Durham County (N.C.) Tuberculosis Sanatorium   531
41. The Curriculum Laboratory: Another way to enrich curricular mate-
    rials in modern education   554
42. The staff of the Materials Bureau checking in materials   559
43. Students use radio in their work   589
44. The working of the democratic process   600
45. Cooperative curriculum planning   619
46. What kinds of machine shop practices are needed for the nuclear age?   628
47. Cannery is operated by students as a service to the community   637
48. Health development through physical education—eighth and ninth
    graders   651
49. A Sociogram (7th grade in a southern town)   665
50. Fifth graders learn by doing in a space age   668
51. Using student leaders   670

Curriculum principles
and social trends

CHAPTER 1　An overview of
the evolution of the curriculum

Four outstanding motives have dominated the development of the curriculum of the schools of the United States. These motives are: (1) the Religious, (2) the Political, (3) the Utilitarian, and (4) the motive of Mass Education. With equal power, the philosophies behind the motives have influenced the changes in the curricular offerings of all school levels. The college, the secondary school, and the elementary school alike have given evidence of the impacts of these influences. Persistent refusal to recognize the existence of these motives and philosophies has at times brought catastrophe upon an existing form of the educational structure; such catastrophe is shown, for example, by the replacement of the Latin grammar school by the academy, which in turn was superseded by the high school.

To relate the story of the full development and influences of these motives is a problem for the educational historian, and cannot be attempted in this volume. Only those events and influences which provide bases for an understanding of the present structure of the school curriculum will be sketched here.

1. THE RELIGIOUS MOTIVE (1635–1770)

The transplanting of a people involves the transplanting of a culture. If one searches carefully, it is discovered that the four main elements of a culture comprise *religious, political, economic,* and *social* heritages. All of these heritages were prominent among the early settlers of America. With some, the religious heritage was predominant and controlling, as witness the Puritans who settled the rock-studded coast of New England with its stern climate. With other groups, the other heritages ruled; for example, the pioneers who settled Maryland and the southern colonies were looking for

1

gold, but they found wealth in another form, namely, in tobacco and cotton.

The historian E.P. Cubberley [1] states that the following types of education were transplanted to America, each type according to the culture from which the colonists came: (1) the church-state type, found in New England; (2) the parochial school conception, well illustrated in Protestant Pennsylvania and Catholic Maryland; and (3) charity, or philanthropic education, except collegiate education, found in Virginia and the Carolinas. The second and third might be said to represent only one type—a type fostered by the church and encouraged by the English government, with some payment for such education being made by the upper and the middle classes of society.

An analysis of the cultures which produced these educational types shows that one common factor was operating for almost a century and a half: all three types stemmed from the church, whether the church was Catholic or Protestant and whether the educational institution was operated by a private individual or by an organization. Although it was necessary for the settlers to wrest a livelihood from the new soil, it was also of paramount importance that the religion which each group professed should be perpetuated. The long-continued and bitter wars of the Reformation period (1546–1668) were fresh in the minds of the first generations of colonists. It is small wonder, then, that even the hardships of pioneer life faded into insignificance when compared with the difficulty of securing and guarding those religious principles for which the colonists had fought. After homes were constructed, the next building to be erected was the church, usually followed in short order by the schoolhouse.

In spite of their common interest in religion and education, sharp differences in educational emphasis were evident among the denominational groups which settled in various sections of the new country. Coming from England, where they were revolters against the church-state, the Puritans set about constructing and attempting to perpetuate the very influence against which they had protested

[1] *Public Education in the United States* (rev.), Boston, Houghton Mifflin Company, 1934, Chap. II.

and fought in England. Among the Puritans, the state was the church, the ministers were the social and political leaders, and for the most part the ministers were the teachers. To the Puritans, the welfare and perpetuity of the state demanded two things: (1) a ministry which knew the Bible, which could not be deceived, and which could continue to indoctrinate and to lead the people in the true faith as generation succeeded generation; and (2) a people well enough educated to read and understand the Bible. Only by the satisfactory achievement of these two aims did the Puritans feel that posterity would be secure in this world and in the life beyond. With these two aims in view, the New England colonies generally established the writing (common or elementary) school, the Latin grammar (secondary) school, and the college.

In the Middle colonies, there was no church-state, nor was one possible, because both Protestants and Catholics were found there. In those colonies, the people established schools as a part of their religious institutions, with the colonial governments taking no active part. The emphasis in subject matter was upon religion and the "three R's." Girls were educated as well as boys, in contradistinction to the compulsory church-state educational laws for boys passed in Massachusetts at the middle of the seventeenth century. The parochial type of school predominated, but there were other types of private schools.

In the plantation culture which was developed in the Southern colonies, education was almost wholly a private affair to be provided, if at all, by each family. The only public attention given to education in those colonies is found in the legislation relating to the education of orphans (mostly apprenticeship) and of children of the poor in religion and learning to conform to their estate. The church gave indifferent attention to education, the state gave even less and the individual family gave only as much as its social and financial background compelled or enabled it to give. Private tutors, small private schools, and parochial and church "charity" schools predominated. The state was interested only in higher education, and was concerned with it chiefly for the preparation of ministers and for other religious purposes.

Fig. 1 shows the types of schools transplanted from the fatherlands of the early colonists. It shows also the curricula found in each type of school.

The dame and writing schools soon combined, and by 1700 they became the usual type of school; but the only change in the curriculum was that of calling "counting" or "reckoning" arithmetic. Textbooks were published in England, but they were not plentiful;

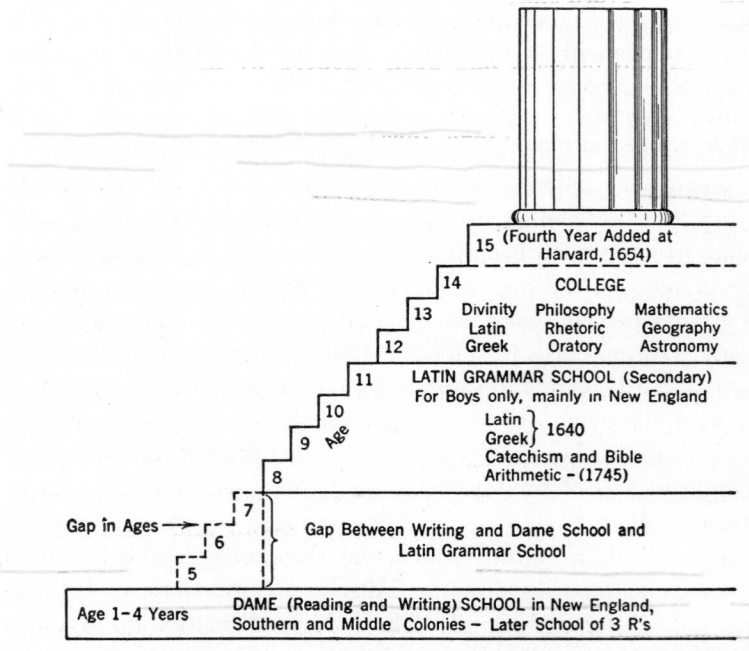

FIG. 1   *Foundation stone and steps of formal education in the pre-national period*

hence, *memoriter* teaching by drill became the vogue. Religious matter usually comprised the only reading material, except in the Latin grammar school where religious training was stressed but not to the exclusion of other subjects. The first American secular textbook did not appear until about the time of the Revolutionary War [2] (1775–1782).

In this period, schools were essentially class institutions, as is well

[2] *Ibid.*, p. 42.

illustrated by the roster of Harvard University; there students were listed according to social standing. Girls could secure only rudimentary training until the academy appeared. To anyone studying the early history of the curriculum one fact stands out, namely, that there was little fundamental change during the colonial period in the curricula of the beginner's school, the Latin grammar school, and the college. Harvard started in 1636 with a three-year course, which was lengthened to four years in 1654. By 1780 this four-year pattern, which still persists, had been adopted by most of the other eight colonial colleges.

2. THE POLITICAL MOTIVE (1770–1860) *(national emergence)*

Though the curriculum of the schools did not change appreciably during the first century and a half of the life of the nation, changes in economy, social life, political beliefs, and educational practice were going on steadily, especially in the last fifty years of the period. Even in religious thought, the second and third generations were showing signs of change.

Trade and commerce were coming to occupy a prominent place in the new country, yet the existing schools were not attempting to prepare their students for such work. Pioneer life did not contribute to the maintenance of the old "class society" system of Europe, especially when free land was to be had for the taking and when persons who became large landowners qualified automatically for the right to vote. Ownership of land by anyone who could take it, hold it against the Indians, and wrest a living from it became a powerful stimulus for men to change their ideas of government and economy. In the old country, the fathers of these settlers had not had any ownership of the soil, unless they had been born to that privilege. This factor combined with others equally powerful, but probably less discernible, to prepare the ground for revolutionary, and thoroughly indigenous, developments in education as well as in politics.

Other factors contributing to educational changes in the early national period included the following: (1) the French and Indian Wars, which left New England economically prostrate, that being the section where the greatest progress had been made in education, and where the most rigid school system had been developed; (2)

the beginning of the decline of the religious motive in controlling all life, including education, as colonization became more widespread and as the new settlements in the interior became more distantly separated from the mother settlements; (3) the development of varying sectional economies or "cultures" among the colonists, such as the free-labor West, the "class" society in the South with its indentured and slave labor, and the commercial East; (4) urban growth, with its accompanying problems of labor, poverty, and mass education; (5) dissatisfaction with the existing types of education, which did not meet the new and rapidly changing needs of the settlers; and (6) lack of provision for the education of girls.

Several fundamental innovations in schools resulted from the factors just mentioned. First, the district school system became established in New England in place of the "town" school. Second, the reading and writing schools were generally combined in smaller places, as schools of the "three R's." Third, the dame school definitely began to be adopted for the beginners, and later it became the primary school of the educational ladder. Fourth, the Latin grammar school, which was established to train only a select number of boys to become religious leaders, was unwilling to alter its curriculum to train a larger group in more effective fashion for the changing needs of the people it served; the result of this unwillingness was that two new types of secondary schools, namely, the English grammar school and the academy, were established and eventually forced the Latin grammar school out of existence. Fifth, new colleges, which began to depart from the primary purpose of the instruction of religious leaders, were established.

Internal changes taking place in America toward the end of the colonial period indicate the fundamental differences which were developing between the colonies and England in regard to ways of thinking and of living. Until the Revolutionary War, the development of schools in the colonies had continued to parallel to a great extent school development in England. The new country, however, had many problems different from those of England; for example, different methods of earning a livelihood required changes in education to meet these needs. "Educational changes to meet changing needs caused by economic and social developments" has been a powerful slogan for many generations, although modern educational leaders have unknowingly emphasized this platitude as a challenge peculiar to the present generation.

Though the war with England came to a successful conclusion for the colonies from a political point of view, its results from an educational point of view were temporarily disastrous. With the acquisition of independence came the loss of the mother country's support in educational matters. For example, textbooks which had been supplied from abroad now had to be produced at home; the Crown's support of colleges ceased; and in great part the financing of parochial and charity schools had to be taken over by the colonists without hope of much, if any, support from abroad. If one adds to these factors the shattered economic condition of the new country at the end of the Revolutionary War and the uncertainty concerning the new national structure until after the ratification of the Federal Constitution in 1789, the desperate straits in which the new nation found itself become immediately apparent. This situation gave rise to the second dominating motive in American education—the *political*.

The Constitution of the United States did not mention education. But the Ordinance of 1785, which was enacted by the Continental Congress prior to the adoption of the Constitution, provided that Section 16 of each congressional township in the Northwest Territory should be reserved for the support of schools. As new states were admitted to the Union, this policy of reserving at least one section of each congressional township for the maintenance of public schools was, with a few exceptions, confirmed by Congress. In the rapid settlement of the new territory, the district school was transplanted from New England and came to be the pattern in the new states, except where those states were settled by colonists from the South.

Whereas in the colonial period the leaders had emphasized literacy of the common people as a sure means of perpetuating religious freedom, the leaders of the early national era emphasized it for the preservation of liberty and the new democratic form of government. This political motive was reinforced by two movements which early became, and still are, fundamental in American life, namely, (1) the extension to all citizens of the right to vote, and (2) the development of "rugged individualism." Those persons who fought for universal suffrage in the United States attained their first real success in 1828 with the election of Andrew Jackson as president. In succeeding years, the ownership of property as a requisite for voting was gradually eliminated in the several states. The movement for universal suffrage has operated in modern times in the extension to women of the right to vote and to hold office. "Rugged individualism" was likewise a by-product of the pioneer days of free land and of decentralized political control. At first a by-product, rugged individualism soon became a controlling factor in American life; it made America in those days the "land of opportunity" for anyone who had the courage, the fortitude, the intelligence, and the spirit to conquer.

These main forces, with the help of large immigration, gradual industrialization, and increasing urbanization, developed a new political spirit and sectional pride which gradually forced the religious motive into the background. The fight for the free, publicly supported common school followed. Beginning in earnest around 1820, this struggle was not definitely decided in favor of free education at public expense until after the middle of the nineteenth century; of course, the issue was fought over and decided by the individual states at varying times. The conflict to *control* the state systems of common schools often continued for a time, with the separation of church and state as the fundamental issue.

The changes in the types of schools which evolved in the early national period are indicated in Table 1 and in Figs. 2 and 3.

TABLE 1   Types of schools developed in the United States, 1750 to 1860

Elementary		Secondary	Collegiate
From	*To*		
Dame School	Primary School	Academy	Extension of
Writing	School of 3 R's	English	Academy and
Schools		Grammar / High } School	Seminary
Reading	Grammar School		Upward to
Intermediate School		Latin Grammar School	College
		—a Holdover from	
		Colonial Period	

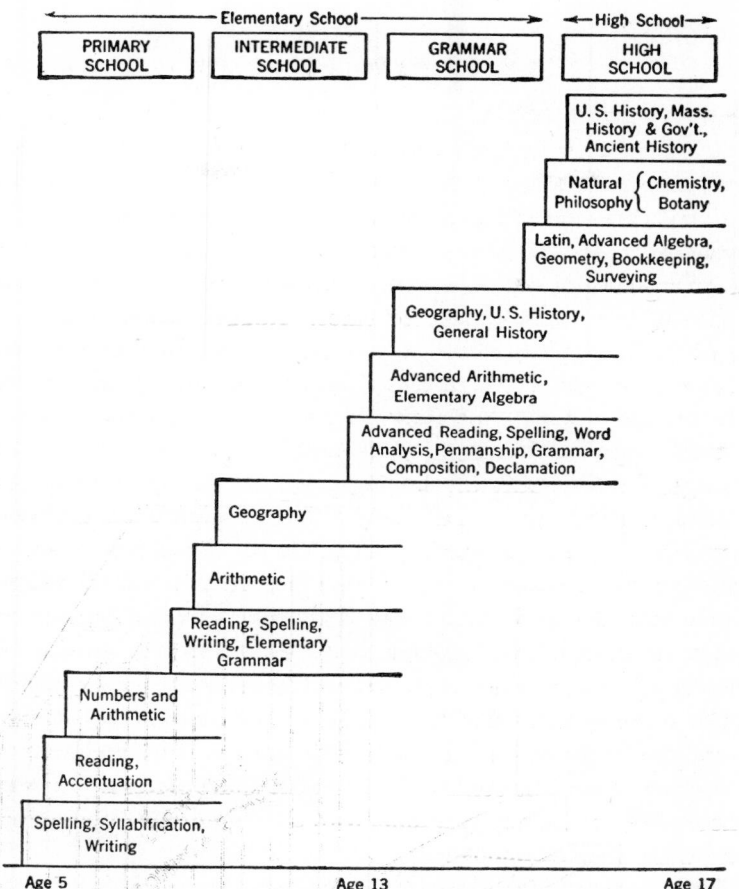

FIG. 2   *New England as a type of public school development—its curriculum, 1860*

Note 1   The high school curriculum in general over the country was three years in length until 1890, and in the South three years until the twentieth century.

Note 2   New England curriculum commonly developed as eight- or nine-year elementary school program, first; later this was shortened to the standard eight years.

Note 3   Each step represents one year in comparison with steps of the graduated educational stairway of today. The child's program could lead naturally and easily from the beginning school to the highest school (or academy).

Note 4   The high school curriculum frequently had a "Classical curriculum" and an "English curriculum," the Classical representing an evolution from the old Latin Grammar School.

Note 5   Larger towns were supposed to offer in addition on the higher level: Greek, more History, Rhetoric and Logic, French, Astronomy, Geology, Intellectual and Mental Science, and Political Economy.

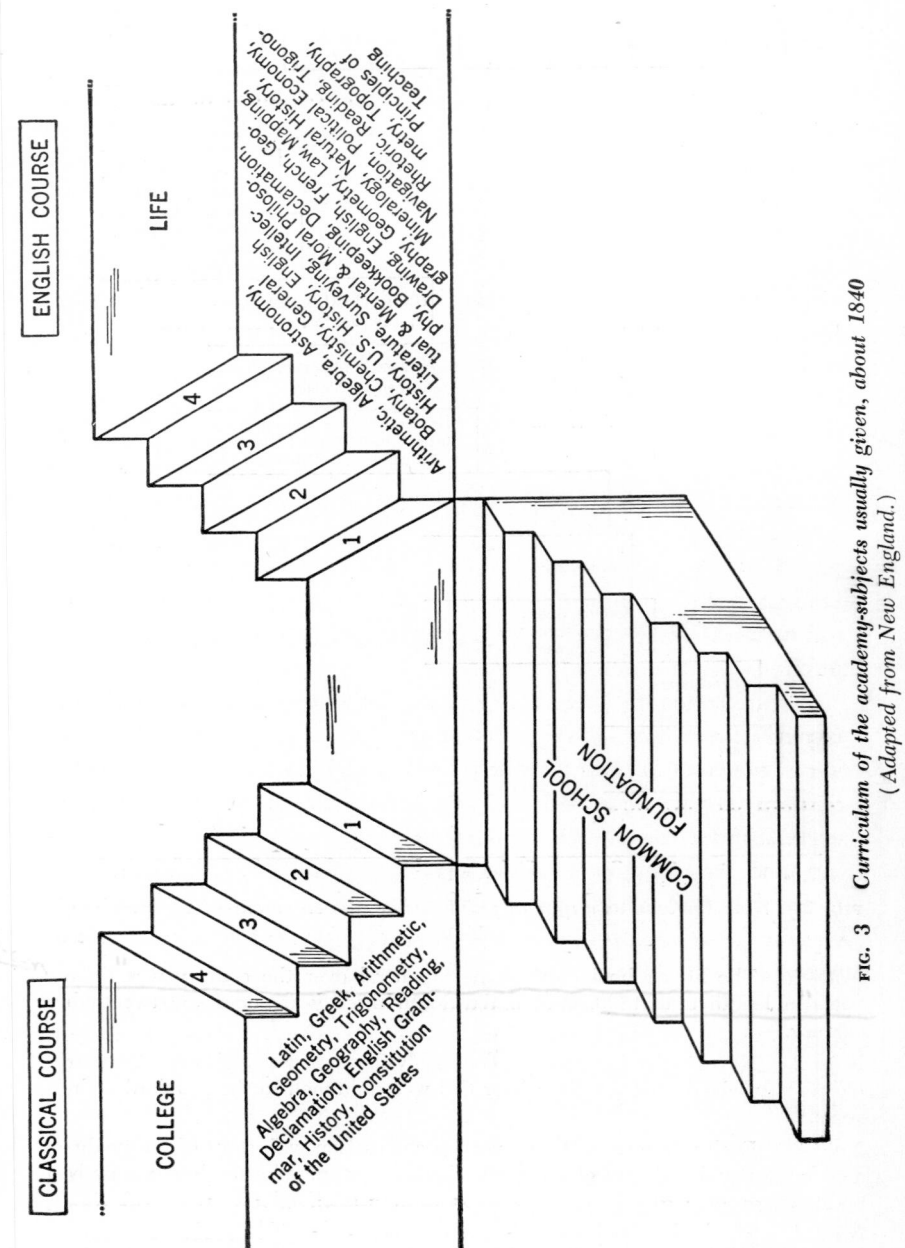

FIG. 3 *Curriculum of the academy-subjects usually given, about 1840*
(*Adapted from New England.*)

10

A description of the expansion of the curriculum of the schools during the early years of the United States as a nation would not be complete without a list of those new subjects in the secondary schools which the colleges began to accept for the admission of students. The growth of collegiate institutions of learning was phenomenal in the early part of the national period; many of the academies then established grew into colleges. By 1860, arithmetic, geography, English grammar, algebra, geometry, and ancient history came generally to be accepted as college-entrance subjects. This was a significant advance, especially since the college curriculum continued to be the most conservative of all. The records show that the American college until 1860 was primarily under religious control and that it possessed a traditional curriculum composed of the classics, mathematics, natural philosophy (science), history, and mental and moral philosophy. It is also significant that most colleges followed the New England pattern, just as the other sections of the country have usually followed the leadership of New England in the development of the public-school system on all levels.

A word in regard to the secondary and collegiate education of girls is pertinent here. Almost from their beginnings, many academies were open to boys and girls alike. Many girls pursued the same curriculum as the boys; others took differentiated courses provided especially for them, such as music, embroidery, painting, bookkeeping, and dancing. Some of the academies for girls emphasized entirely the more social accomplishments of the day, and were not equal in standard to boys' academies; they might be called the "finishing schools" of their time. Troy Female Seminary (1821) and Mt. Holyoke Seminary (1837) started higher education for women. In 1833, Oberlin College opened its doors as the first coeducational college, and it was soon followed by others of this type. This attention given to the education of women had a powerful influence upon the introduction of new studies and teaching methods into the schools.

In many ways, the growth of education in the early national period of the United States presents rather strikingly a development peculiar to the new nation; in other respects, it shows clearly the retention of traditional forms in the curriculum. The "common school" evolved into the distinct pattern of the modern graded, elementary school; in it, the "three R's," geography, history, and grammar became fixed in the curriculum. This evolution furnished for the first time in the history of education an educational stairway by which the child could start at the age of five or six, finish the common school, be promoted to the academy or high school and there prepare himself for college, then enter and finish college. On the level of secondary education, the academies and English (high) schools still required the classics for those students who were preparing for college; mathematics was added as the other required subject in this classical curriculum. English grammar and history were introduced as new courses for the classical course of study; however, these new subjects received scant encouragement and made slow progress in attaining recognition as required subjects in the college preparatory department.

For students not going to college the academy made the largest contribution to the curriculum, offering a tremendous number of new subjects of a practical type which aimed at fitting the student for more effective living. It was in these new courses that new methods were more frequently tried out and developed, since there were no college entrance examinations requiring extensive learning of a *memoriter* nature. The English classical school, which was later to become the English high school, was the father of the high school as we know it today. This type of school, as started in New England, became the prototype for the nation. Taking heed of educational needs, these new high schools usually offered the following kinds of curricula: (1) the "Classical Department" for students planning to go to college, and (2) the "English Department" for students not planning to attend college. Owing to the lack of accurate figures upon enrollment in these two departments, it is not possible to state whether the classical course was more "respectable" than the English. If the relative emphasis upon these two parallel courses in the colleges from 1860 to 1920 is any criterion, the classical course must have continued to be more acceptable.

The academy passed the peak of its growth and influence about 1850. Among the more important of its contributions were broader secondary school curricula, including the beginnings of vocational education for both girls and boys. Because of its lack of standards, its failure to become a truly public instead of a private or denominational institution, and its failure to equalize educational opportunity, the academy was eventually replaced in the educational structure by the public high school.

Alexander Inglis pointed out a significant fact in the development of the curriculum on the secondary school level, namely, that almost every new movement in secondary education has started in a private or quasi-private school before it has been taken over by the public high school. As examples in proof of this statement, Inglis cites the manual training movement, vocational education and guidance, commercial education, and the six-year high-school plan.[3]

The political motive was dominant in educational development from 1770 to 1860. Each state grew educationally at its own pace, so that the pattern of education early became that of the individual state, not a national one. The principle of free common schools had been established, as had the principles of coeducation and education for citizenship. Little change took place in the curriculum of the college from the colonial period to the Civil War (1861–1865), although the colleges grew rapidly in number and in enrollment. New textbooks were written for all subjects and grades. The introduction of these new textbooks into the elementary and secondary schools stimulated curriculum development and the adoption of new subjects of study.

3. THE UTILITARIAN MOTIVE (1860–1920)

When a period of educational development is tagged "from 1860 to 1920," or by any other dates, it is understood that such a time limitation is somewhat arbitrary. The main purpose of any such allocation is to call to attention the factors operating primarily for change in a particular era. It is admitted freely that it would be impossible to state that the utilitarian motive in American education first became manifest exactly in the year 1860. As a matter of fact, the academy had been established a hundred years before with that as one of its aims. It was only since 1860 that the cumulative force of the vocational idea began to focus attention upon the utilitarian

[3] *Principles of Secondary Education*, Boston, Houghton Mifflin Company, 1918, p. 184.

function of the curriculum. Various influences at home and from
abroad combined to bring this utilitarian motive rapidly to the front.

Earlier Influences (1860–1890)

GENERAL ACCEPTANCE OF THE PUBLIC HIGH SCHOOL.   From 1860 to
1890, the second major struggle was going on for the establishment
of free schools at public expense in the United States. Now that the
public elementary school had been generally accepted, the battle
was waged for the upward extension of the common school to include the high-school level. As the public elementary schools grew,
there arose, especially from the middle classes, a demand for a
wider educational opportunity for their children. The people felt
that they were unable to pay privately for a wider educational opportunity even when the academies offered it.

Despite the critical period for twenty years after the Civil War,
during which the evolution of the high school was retarded, the
decision in the Kalamazoo (Michigan) case in 1874 legalized the
right of local communities to establish high schools at public expense
as a part of the "common school" system. This decision set the prece-
dent for legalization of the public high school in many other states.
It was 1890, however, before the establishment of public secondary
schools was stimulated generally by state legislation or by state aid.
At first designed for a period of instruction beyond the elementary
level to fit students more fully for life, the high school soon came to
be the only avenue of preparation for a large number of youths who
wished to attend college. Thus the stage was set for the contest between the proponents of the "finishing" (preparation for life) function and those of the "fitting" (preparation for college) function of
the high school.

FEDERAL GRANTS FOR EDUCATION.   The Morrill Act of 1862 granted
to each of the states large tracts of land, or the equivalent in land scrip,
for the endowment of colleges of agriculture and mechanic arts. The
Federal government strengthened the establishment of these colleges by granting additional monetary aid to them through the second Morrill Act (1890). The establishment of these land-grant colleges laid emphasis upon new subjects of study which formerly had

not been considered socially acceptable or "respectable" for college entrance. The development of parallel curricula in these new institutions was an illustration of the type of solution offered to meet a practical need. Since the existing colleges were unwilling to grant the A.B. degree for work in agriculture and the mechanic arts, the B.S. degree was introduced to take care of the situation. The most significant effect which the establishment of these new colleges had upon the public high schools was the opportunity granted them to continue to broaden their curricula. Since many secondary schools were as adamant as the traditional colleges regarding any change in the classical curriculum, the solution was hit upon of building separate high schools of specialized types in large communities. For example, the *classical* high schools prepared youth primarily for college, while the *technical* and *commercial* high schools trained youth especially for their life work. In some cities, such schools are still administered in this way. In the specialized school, the opportunity was granted frequently to develop new curricula containing new subjects deemed necessary in particular fields of preparation.

IMMIGRATION, INDUSTRIALIZATION, AND IMPROVEMENT IN TRANSPORTATION AND COMMUNICATION. Between 1860 and 1890 the population of the nation doubled. It almost doubled again between 1890 and 1920. In view of the abundance of free land which needed development, it seemed wise to the government to encourage immigration. New settlers from many lands came in hordes. Their coming gave rise to new problems, such as Americanization and literacy, congested urban conditions, and religious freedom. The United States began to tap and to exploit its vast natural resources while this unrestricted immigration was swelling its population. The gradual industrialization of the nation followed, and this industrialization focused attention upon the problems of child and woman labor, social change, and the gradual rise of the standard of living. More rapid means of transportation and communication hastened the building of industry; they helped also to develop a national unity, an easier exchange of common experience, and a wider cultural and political heritage to stimulate the expansion of education at public expense.

EFFECTS OF THE CIVIL WAR. Other stimuli to educational growth, which operated strongly as a result of the War between the States, included the following: (1) the entrance of women into industry, a movement interfering with the solidarity and self-contained nature of the home and marking the first shift of some aspects of home training to the school; (2) the organization of labor, which brought a force to be reckoned with in education; (3) a brief pause in the rapid development of public education, caused by the exhausted economic condition of the country, which gave time for a re-examination of the school structure and for the introduction of new methods of instruction; and (4) the economic prostration of the South, a condition which retarded its educational development for more than a generation.

THE KINDERGARTEN.   Borrowed from Germany in 1855, the kindergarten found a warm welcome in America. The first public-school kindergarten was opened in St. Louis in 1873, and by 1890 the city schools began to adopt this new school as a part of the public-school system. Along with the kindergarten came manual training, which originated in the Scandinavian countries. Manual training was taught first in the elementary school, but it was later introduced into the secondary school as an upward extension of constructive handwork.

THE NORMAL-SCHOOL INFLUENCE.   After twenty-five years of struggle for its very existence, the state normal school began about 1865 that remarkable growth which has continued until the present. It has contributed much to the improvement of methods of teaching and to the enrichment of the school curriculum. It took over the function of teacher training, which previously had been exercised by the academy, and thus it accelerated the academy's decline. Primarily through the efforts of Edward A. Sheldon and his associates at the Oswego (New York) Normal School, the "oral instruction" and "object teaching" of Pestalozzi became known and widely adopted in the schools. Prior to this time, education had been primarily a process of "reciting" by memory from the textbook, which was usually written on a question-and-answer basis. The Pestalozzian principles of instruction—sense perception, reasoning, and individual judgment—changed "school keeping" into "school teaching." Through these new principles of teaching, oral language work, mental arithmetic, and object teaching developed; object teaching eventually grew into elementary science and home geography.

Taking up where Pestalozzi had left off, the German philosopher Herbart formulated a new educational psychology. Rousseau had contributed the idea that education was an individual development based on the growth of natural capacities. Pestalozzi accepted Rousseau's theory, but he added to it and formulated the "faculty" psychology of education. This "faculty theory" of education assumed that each individual possessed various faculties or talents of mind, such as reasoning, memory, and music. In line with this theory, Pestalozzi and the faculty-psychologists believed that education should strive for the equitable development of these faculties of the mind. Herbart accepted all of the methods and subjects of instruction developed by Rousseau and Pestalozzi, but he rejected their concepts of the aims of education; he believed that the chief aim of education should be the preparation of people to live a good moral life in organized society. Herbart held that man's main interests were of two kinds: (1) his touch with things in his environment, and (2) his contact with human beings, i.e., social intercourse. For the first group of man's interests he accepted Pestalozzi's group of subjects which he had developed; for the second, he added to the oral language of Pestalozzi the subjects of literature and history, with special emphasis upon the social aspects of history as revealing human relationships.

To achieve these educational aims, Herbart contended that *interest* on the part of the pupil was a first requirement for good instruction. He formulated the doctrine of "apperception," that is, the grasping and mastering of new knowledge in terms of the knowledge already acquired. The five Herbartian "steps" were developed as a system of methodology for the attainment of this "building up of concepts" in the minds of pupils. These steps were: (1) preparation; (2) presentation; (3) comparison and abstraction; (4) generalization; and (5) application. Their formalizing effects on teaching and their full implications for the curriculum will be considered in Chapter 7, where they are compared with the Morrison steps concerning the "unit." One of the main influences upon the curriculum of these five Herbartian steps was the development of the new idea of the correlation of subject matter and the unity of the learning process. These were the beginnings of the "core curriculum," one might say.

Herbart died in 1841, but it was not until half a century later that American students brought back his ideas from abroad and put them into operation in this country. The National Herbart Society, founded in 1892, still exists as a powerful research organization under the name of The National Society for the Study of Education. The Herbartian movement spread rapidly, and the normal schools introduced new courses of study in which subjects for the elementary schools were divided into *drill subjects, content subjects,* and *expression* (motor-activity) *subjects,* as indicated in Table 2.

TABLE 2   **Types of elementary school subjects—about 1900** *

Drill Subjects	Content Subjects	Expression Subjects
Reading	Literature	Kindergarten Work
Writing	Geography	Music
Spelling	History	Drawing
Language	Social Studies	Manual Arts
Arithmetic	Manners and Conduct	Domestic Arts
	Science	Plays and Games
	Agriculture	School Gardening
		Vocational Subjects

* E.P. Cubberley, *Public Education in the United States* (rev.), Boston, Houghton Mifflin Company, 1934, p. 518 (adapted in tabular form).

THE SCIENTIFIC MOVEMENT IN EDUCATION.   During the nineteenth century another German influence was at work upon American ideas concerning education. A host of American scholars invaded the colleges and universities of Europe, studied there, and returned home to institute the "scientific" approach to study. Louis Agassiz and Charles W. Eliot of Harvard University are two examples from this group who established in American colleges the teaching of science and the use of the scientific method in all studies. The curriculum of the high school reflected this influence by the introduction of laboratory courses in science and in the modern foreign languages. E.P. Cubberley gives an interesting tabulation of the studies which were introduced into the high school during the last half of the nineteenth century; he lists them in the order in which they were granted credit for admission to college (Table 3).

The first manual training high school was established at St. Louis in 1880, and the first cooking and sewing high school was opened at Toledo in 1886. The types of programs developed in those schools are illustrated in Tables 4 and 5.

TABLE 3   New high-school subjects accepted for college entrance, 1860–1890 *

Subject	Date	College First Accepting
Modern (U. S.) History	1869	Michigan
Physical Geography	1870	Michigan and Harvard
English Composition	1870	Princeton
Physical Science	1872	Harvard
English Literature	1874	Harvard
Modern Languages	1875	Harvard

* Cubberley, *ibid.*, adapted from p. 315.

By 1890 to 1900, the decade during which the United States became a world power, the educational ladder as it exists today in the public schools was complete in framework, running from the kindergarten through the state university. The typical curricula which had developed in the elementary school and in the secondary school are shown in Tables 6–8.

Later Developments (1890–1920)

That there was no uniformity among the subjects taught in the public high school in 1892 may be seen from the list of subjects in Table 8. In an address, President Charles W. Eliot of Harvard University presented this list to the National Education Association after he had made a canvass of all the subjects from which public high-school programs were then commonly made up.

Eliot's address stimulated the National Education Association to appoint the famous "Committee of Ten" (Committee on Secondary School Studies). Originally organized in 1857, the National Education Association was reorganized in 1870 with the departments of (1) School Superintendence, (2) Normal Schools, (3) Elementary

Schools, and (4) Higher Education. The memorable Report of the Committee of Ten (1893) started the movement which Cubberley terms "Reforming the Curriculum Through National Committees." A factor conducive to this new type of cooperation on a national scale was the rise of the United States to a position of world power in the last decade of the nineteenth century, culminating in her colonial expansion as a result of the Spanish-American War.

Since the reports of five of these national committees were the primary influences in setting the patterns of formalized education

TABLE 4   Course of Study of the Chicago English High and Manual Training School, 1891–1892 *

FIRST YEAR

First Term	Second Term	Third Term
Algebra	Algebra	Algebra
First part of natural philosophy	Physical geography, with primary principles of geology	Physical geography, with primary principles of astronomy

English and business letter writing throughout the year
Freehand and mechanical drawing one hour a day for three terms

Carpentry and joinery	Wood turning	Pattern and cabinet making

Twelve lectures on wood as material for building and manufactures

SECOND YEAR

Plane geometry	Solid geometry	Conic sections or commercial arithmetic
General history	General history	General history

English and general composition, three terms
Chemistry or bookkeeping, three terms
Mechanical drawing, one hour a day throughout the year

Moulding and casting	Forging and welding	Tempering, soldering, and brazing

Twelve lectures on metals as material for building and manufactures

* From the 8th Annual Report of the Commissioner of Labor (1892), *Industrial Education*, Washington, United States Government Printing Office, 1893, p. 3. Reproduced by permission of the Bureau of Labor Statistics, United States Department of Labor.

TABLE 4   Course of Study of the Chicago English High and Manual Training School, 1891–1892 °   *Continued*

THIRD YEAR

Descriptive geometry or bookkeeping	Trigonometry or bookkeeping	Surveying or bookkeeping
Natural philosophy or commercial arithmetic	Light and electricity or commercial law	Review of the sciences or commercial law
English literature	English literature	English literature
Civil government	Political economy	Political economy
Machine drawing	Architectural drawing	Typographical drawing
Machine shop work	Construction of machines	Running and care of engines
	Twelve lectures on machinery and power	

After the first year pupils may elect the commercial or scientific course, and the chemical in place of the metal laboratory work.
Stenography and typewriting are elective after the second year.

TABLE 5   Course of instruction of the high school, of Pratt Institute (Brooklyn, New York), 1891–1892 °

FIRST YEAR

English language and rhetoric	(Manual Work)
Algebra and geometry	Boys:
Physiology and physical geography	Bench work in wood
Vocal music	Wood turning
⎰Free-hand and instrumental	Pattern making
⎱Model and cast drawing	Principles of moulding
Clay modeling	Girls:
	Serving
	Hygiene
	Home nursing

SECOND YEAR

General history and English history, or Latin	(Manual work)
	Boys:
Essay writing	Foundry moulding
Geometry	Forging
Trigonometry	Tinsmithing
Bookkeeping	Girls:
Physics	Dressmaking

TABLE 5   Course of instruction of the high school, of Pratt Institute
(Brooklyn, New York), 1891–1892 *   *Continued*

SECOND YEAR

Vocal music   Wood carving
Perspective
Architectural drawing
Elements of design
Mechanical drawing

SENIOR YEAR

English literature   (Manual work)
Civil government   Boys:
Political science   Machine shop and bench work
French or Latin   Machine tool work construction
Essay writing   Girls:
Principles of construction   Cooking
Chemistry and metallurgy   Millinery
Vocal music   Dressmaking
Mechanical drawing
Problems in construction

* From the 8th Annual Report of the Commissioner of Labor (1892), *Industrial Education,* Washington, United States Government Printing Office, 1893, p. 58. Reproduced by permission of the Bureau of Labor Statistics, United States Department of Labor.

TABLE 7   Development of high-school subjects of study ‡

Before 1800	1800 to 1850	1860 to 1875
Latin (1640)	Geography (1870)	Modern History (1869)
Greek (1640)	English Grammar (1819)	Physical Geography (1870)
Arithmetic	Algebra (1820)	English Composition (1870)
(1745)	Geometry (1844)	Physical Science (1872)
	Ancient History (1847)	English Literature (1874)
		Modern Languages (1875)

‡ Adapted from Cubberley, *Public Education in the United States* (rev.), 1934, p. 315, and *An Introduction to the Study of Education and to Teaching,* 1925, p. 274.

which one finds generally today in the elementary and secondary schools, a brief account of their curricular contributions is given herewith.

TABLE 6 The evolution of our elementary-school curriculum, and of methods of teaching [1]

1775	1825	1850	1875	1900
READING	READING *	READING	READING	READING *
Spelling	Declamation	DECLAMATION	Literary Selections	LITERATURE *
Writing	SPELLING *	SPELLING	SPELLING	Spelling
Catechism	Writing	WRITING	PENMANSHIP *	Writing *
BIBLE	Good Behavior	Manners	Conduct	......
	Manners & Morals	Conduct		
Arithmetic	ARITHMETIC *	MENTAL ARITH. *	PRIMARY ARITH.	ARITHMETIC
		CIPHERING	ADVANCED ARITH. *	
	Bookkeeping	Bookkeeping	......	
	GRAMMAR	Elem. Language	Oral Language *	ORAL LANGUAGE
		GRAMMAR	GRAMMAR	Grammar
	Geography	Geography	Home Geography *	Home Geography
			TEXT GEOGRAPHY	TEXT GEOGRAPHY *
		History U. S.	U. S. HISTORY	History Stories *
			Constitution	TEXT HISTORY *
		Object Lessons	Object Lessons *	Nature Study *
			Elementary Science *	Elem. Science
			Drawing *	Drawing *
			Music *	Music *
			Physical Exercises	Play
				Physical Training *
				Sewing
	Sewing and Knitting		......	Cooking
		......		Manual Training

CAPITALS = Most important subjects.
Italics = Subjects of medium importance.

ROMAN = Least important subjects.
* = New methods of teaching now employed.

[1] Taken from Cubberley, E.P., An Introduction to the Study of Education and to Teaching, Boston, Houghton Mifflin Company, 1925, p. 17. Reprinted by permission.

23

TABLE 8   Subjects of study in public high schools, 1891 *

1. English, including both Literature and Composition and the elements of Rhetoric	15. Geology
	16. Botany
	17. Zoology
2. History (Ancient, Medieval, and Modern)	18. Physiology
	19. Physics
3. Civil Government	20. Chemistry
4. French	21. Astronomy
5. German	22. Psychology
6. Latin	23. Moral Philosophy
7. Greek	24. International Law
8. Arithmetic	25. Political Economy
9. Algebra	26. Science of Education
10. Plane Geometry	27. Music
11. Solid Geometry	28. Drawing
12. Trigonometry	29. Stenography
13. Analytic Geometry	30. Bookkeeping
14. Physical Geography	

* C.W. Eliot, "Undesirable and Desirable Uniformity in Schools," *Addresses and Proceedings of the National Education Association* (October, 1892), p. 93.

1. *Report of the Committee of Ten on Secondary School Studies* (1893). Treating mainly of the subjects on the level of the secondary school, this committee formed the secondary-school pattern in two curricular respects. It established the following:

1. *A quantitative measure of secondary education,* based on the equivalence of studies. I.L. Kandel points out [4] that on this basis the whole problem of the educational value of respective subjects ceased to exist. The principle primarily involved was that any subject taught for an equal length of time, equally intensively, and under equally competent instruction was of as much value as any other subject. One can see how the universal adoption of such an educational idea gave eventually almost a death blow to the classics and other traditional subjects in high school.

2. *Four different curricula,* any one of which could lead to graduation from high school. These were: (1) the Classical; (2) the Latin-Scientific; (3) the Modern Language; and (4) the English. The nine subject-matter fields reported on in full as to content, method, and time to be spent upon them are shown diagrammatically with the present-day subjects into which they evolved (Figure 4).

[4] *History of Secondary Education,* Boston, Houghton Mifflin Company, 1930, p. 475.

Subjects Listed by Committee of Ten	The Standard Subject-matter Fields into Which They Developed

Latin ——————————————— Latin (4 years)
Greek ———————————————

English ——————————————— English (4 years)

Other Modern Languages ———— French
Spanish
German

Arithmetic
Mathematics ———————— Algebra
Plane Geometry
Solid Geometry and Trigonometry

Physics, Astronomy, and Chemistry ——— Physics
Chemistry

Natural History (Biology, including Botany, Zoology, and Physiology) ——— Biology

Geography (Physical Geography, Geology, and Meteorology) ——— General Science

Civics (Citizenship)
Medieval and Modern History (World History)
History, Civil Government, and Political Economy ——— English History
American History
Sociology and Economics
Problems of American Democracy

FIG. 4. *Evolution of high-school subject-matter fields, 1893 to date*

TABLE 9   Curricula of the Charlotte (N.C.) high school, 1914–1915

A. ACADEMIC COURSE

First Year

English
Arithmetic
Algebra
History
Latin or Science
Domestic Science or Manual Training *
Writing and Drawing
Music

Second Year

English
Arithmetic and Penmanship
Algebra
History
Latin or Physical Geography
Domestic Science or Manual Training
Music

Third Year

English
Algebra
Geometry
History
Latin or Chemistry
Domestic Science or Manual Training
Music

Fourth Year

Required:
English
Music
    Select three:
Latin
Algebra
Solid Geometry and Plane Trigonometry
French
German
Physics
Manual Training or Domestic Science
U.S. History

B. COMMERCIAL COURSE †

First Year

English
Arithmetic
Algebra or History
Bookkeeping
Business Methods
Writing and Drawing
Music

Second Year

English
Arithmetic
Penmanship
Bookkeeping
Business Methods
Drawing
Domestic Science or Manual Training

* Required in both academic and commercial courses.

† These courses were taken from "By-Laws and Rules of the Board of School Commissioners of the City of Charlotte for 1914–15," Charlotte, N.C., Queen City Printing Company, 1914, pp. 54–55.

TABLE 9   Curricula of the Charlotte (N.C.) high school, 1914–1915
Continued

First Year	*Second Year*
Domestic Science or Manual Training	Music
	Two of the following:
	Latin
	History
	Algebra
	Physical Geography

Third Year	*Fourth Year*
English	English
Domestic Science or Manual Training	Stenography
Stenography	Typewriting or Advanced Bookkeeping
Typewriting or Advanced Bookkeeping	Music
Business Methods	Select two:
Office Practice	Latin
Two of the following:	French
Latin, Chemistry	German
Algebra	Physics
Geometry	Mathematics
	Manual Training or Domestic Science, or Domestic Science with U.S. History

A good illustration of how the four types of curricula recommended by the Committee of Ten swept over the country is presented in Table 9.

Two other recommendations of the Report of the Committee of Ten were important in curriculum development, namely, (1) that there be some sort of uniformity in college admission requirements, and (2) that a six-year course of high-school study be provided. This second recommendation was to lead to the beginning of the junior-high-school movement.

2. *Report of the Committee of Fifteen on Elementary Education* (1895). This report dealt with school organization, the correlation of the elementary school subjects, and the preparation of teachers. The emphasis placed upon the concentration, coordination, and correlation of subjects showed the influence of the Herbartian school of thought and crystallized sentiment for the Herbartian method of teaching.

3. *Report of the Committee on College Entrance Requirements* (1899). From the report of this committee, certain uniform standards or principles for high schools became firmly established, among them being the following:

1. That the principle of restricted election on the high-school level be recognized, with the following "constants" or required subjects:

Subject	Units	
Foreign Language	4	(No language in
Mathematics	2	less than 2 units)
English	2	
History	1	
Science	1	

2. That gifted students be encouraged to complete the preparatory course in less time than required of most students.
3. That a year's work in high school in any subject, four periods a week, be accepted as counting toward college entrance credit. This was the formal beginning of counting high-school credits in terms of "units."
4. That the high-school course be extended to six years, a reiteration of the feature found in the Report of the Committee of Ten.

These three reports, all made in the 1890's were dominated by subject-matter specialists, who disagreed to a certain extent among themselves as to the "mental discipline" that a student might obtain from the study of a given subject. The recommendations of these reports influenced the curriculum of the secondary school in two ways during the next thirty years. In the first place, more and more subjects of a practical nature were admitted to the secondary school curriculum, with the accompanying feature of much free election. In the second place, the four parallel curricula recommended by the Committee of Ten did not retain their expected degree of "respectability"; hence the four curricula merged into two, as found in Fig. 5.

1. Classical
2. Latin-Scientific ——————> College Preparatory
3. Modern Language
4. English   Vocational Curricula

FIG. 5   *Evolution of parallel high-school curricula, 1893–1925*

From 1890 to 1920 the fight continued apace between educational leaders who thought that the main function of the secondary school was to prepare for college and other leaders who thought that its main purpose was to prepare for life.[5] Although the struggle had been decided in principle in favor of the "finishing" function by 1910, full victory for the utilitarians was not achieved until later when experimental practices in psychology and education shifted the emphasis from subject matter to the child.

4. *The Committee on the Economy of Time in Education* (1911). Twenty years after the appointment of the Committee of Ten, the National Education Association made the first real effort on a national scale to employ scientific methods to determine curricular materials of real value, to place the materials properly by school grades, and to eliminate subject matter of little or no worth. For the first time, tests were used to measure teaching effectiveness, and textbooks and existing curricula were examined extensively. Psychological principles and other criteria were employed in an attempt to discover what knowledges and skills were most worth while to society, and a beginning was made in studying the problems of contemporary life in America. These beginnings of the use of scientific educational techniques were significant.

The reports of the Committee on the Economy of Time in Education over a period of ten years laid the foundations for the intense curriculum study which has been carried on since. Probably the outstanding contribution of the committee was its advocacy of a change in educational philosophy—a change whereby the individual child would become the center of the educational stage. Whereas before this time teachers had been interested primarily in the child's intellectual development, the work of Dewey, Thorndike, Judd, Terman, and other persons focused attention on the appreciative, the emotional, the social, and the religious nature of the pupil. In line with this new concept of human development, there was a concerted effort to introduce subjects of study which would contribute naturally and normally to the total development of the child. Therefore, such sub-

[5] W.S. Monroe and M.E. Herriott, *Reconstruction of the Secondary School Curriculum: Its Meaning and Trends,* University of Illinois, Bureau of Educational Research, 1928, Chaps. I–III.

jects as music, art, handicrafts, and physical education and hygiene were instituted on both the elementary- and secondary-school levels.

5. *The Commission on the Reorganization of Secondary Education* (1918). The *Cardinal Principles of Secondary Education* were set forth in the general report of this commission. The following seven objectives of the curricula of the high school were recommended:

1. Health
2. Command of Fundamental Processes
3. Worthy Home Membership
4. Vocation
5. Civic Education
6. Worthy Use of Leisure
7. Ethical Character.

Although these seven "cardinal principles" were accepted immediately and were approved universally, they did not achieve their purpose of interrelating subject matter and stimulating an integrated and continuous educational process. The reasons for this failure are found in certain hampering factors which were strongly operative.

FACTORS HAMPERING CHANGES IN THE CURRICULUM. The extension of compulsory school attendance was one factor which slowed up curriculum change. Massachusetts is credited with the passage in 1852 of the first law concerning compulsory school attendance. By 1897, thirty states had compulsory school attendance statutes. Today all states require children to remain in school until at least fourteen years of age, and the average for all states runs above the age of sixteen. Thus the United States has committed itself to the education of all children through at least the junior high-school grades. During such rapid expansion of school opportunities, the wonder is not that there has been so little curriculum change, but that there has been so much. The task of organizing and administering such an enlarged program has been stupendous. School officials and employees were too busy with the construction of schools, with securing and training teachers, and with financing their programs to devote as much time to what was being taught as that aspect warranted.

The swift development of a mechanized industry which emphasized the interdependence of society was another factor that hindered rapid change in the curriculum. The average citizen thought that he saw the avenue to economic success and a better social position through successful completion of the school curriculum as already established. This attitude was connected with the gradual breakdown of the home as the primary economic and social factor in American life. For example, in a North Carolina home, as late as 1908, practically all food, with the exception of sugar, salt, coffee, and tea, was raised on the farm; three-fourths of the clothes worn by the family were made in the home; there was no public school; and the family was an independent and self-contained social unit. By 1920, none of these things was true of this same family. The rapid rise of mechanized industry was coupled with the modern miracle of rapid communication and transportation to make man's world one of more comfort, more leisure, more urbanization, and more interdependence. In quick succession, movements which had been struggling for years found themselves and became articulate. Labor organizations asserted their power; the working hours of women and children in industry became the object of legislation; and women were granted the right of suffrage. All of these changes enlarged the responsibility of the school in training the child for the complex responsibilities of modern life. In fact, so many additional responsibilities in the training of children were placed upon the school that the school found itself almost baffled regarding how to change its curriculum to meet the situation.

Ironically enough, a liberal innovation which began in the Middle West proved to be one of the most powerful movements in standardizing the curriculum of the secondary school after 1900. Near the close of the nineteenth century, the North Central Association of Colleges and Secondary Schools, the Southern Association, and the Middle Atlantic States Association were formed. Through the years, the standards established by these regional groups for the accrediting of secondary schools have been pointed primarily toward college entrance. These associations were responsible for introducing the method of admission to college by certificate from their accredited secondary schools. Of even greater significance for the curriculum, however, has been the fact that many states have used the requirements of these accrediting agencies in establishing their systems of standards for their secondary schools. The result has been that a standardized system has evolved: the elementary school has prepared pupils for a secondary school, where the student in turn finds that a college preparatory curriculum is predominant, especially since the typical secondary school is small in size and does not offer diversified programs. This situation has tended to keep saddled upon the secondary school a curriculum much more rigid than that of the elementary school. At the same time, it can be truly said that the elementary school and the secondary school have become the open door to education and to economic success.

FACTORS STIMULATING CURRICULUM CHANGE. The junior high school developed primarily as a result of the movement toward economy of time in education. It soon established itself as a desirable school level for the purposes of bridging the gap between the elementary school and the secondary school, of providing for the needs of early adolescence, and of permitting exploratory work as a form of educational guidance. The freedom which was granted to it to develop its own curriculum permitted experiments in new types of courses on the level of the secondary school. The success of some of these curricular experiments raised a serious question as to the real value of certain subjects which were taught intensively and in succession in both the seventh and eighth grades of the old 8–4 type of organization. Many persons attribute better methods of teaching elementary science and social science (geography and history) in part to the stimulation of the junior high-school organization. However, distinct curricular patterns had not developed in the junior high school by 1920; these patterns will be presented and compared in Chapter 14.

Through their study of children, the psychologists made notable contributions to the curriculum. The psychology of individual differences was formulated during the second decade of the twentieth century. The study of children's traits, instincts, abilities, and responses continued, resulting in various theories of how one learns. The full force of the contributions of psychology was to be felt in the years following 1920.

Federal aid for vocational education operated as another powerful factor for bringing additions to the curriculum in the early years of the twentieth century. In 1917 the Federal Congress, through the

Smith-Hughes Act, *1917* stimulated tremendously the development of vocational education on the secondary school level; it did this by granting aid to the individual states for the promotion of courses in

TABLE 10   Major changes in curricular offerings, 1860–1920

Elementary School Subjects		Secondary School Subjects	
ADDED	DROPPED	ADDED	DROPPED OR REDUCED IN AMOUNT FOR GRADUATION
Literature	Declamation	Modern Foreign	Greek
Social Studies	General History	Languages	Latin
Science	Advanced Arith-	Literature:	Mental and Moral
Music	metic	English	Philosophy
Drawing	Elementary	American	Rhetoric and
Kindergarten	Algebra	English:	Logic
Work		History	Political Economy
Oral Language		Composition	Geology
Plays and Games		U.S. History	Astronomy
Vocational		Civics (Civil Gov-	Surveying
Subjects:		ernment)	Botany
Manual Arts		Medieval and	Zoology
Domestic Arts		Modern History	Physiology
Agriculture		Economics	Physical Science
School Garden-		Science:	Ancient History
ing		Physical	Declamation
		Geography	Pedagogy (Science
		Biology	of Teaching, or
		General	Education)
		Science	Psychology
		Commercial	
		Arithmetic	
		Music	
		Drawing	
		Vocational	
		Subjects:	
		Manual Arts	
		Home Econom-	
		ics	
		Agriculture	
		Commercial	
		Work	
		Industrial and	
		Technical	
		Work	
		Physical Educa-	
		tion	

agriculture, trades and industries, and home economics. This act gave concrete evidence on a national scale of the increasing emphasis being placed upon the utilitarian values of education.

Looking back on the development of the American school curriculum from 1860 to 1920, the *utilitarian* motive is found to be predominant in education. Ample evidence of this is found in (1) the establishment of the high school at public expense, with emphasis upon its function of preparation for life as well as preparation for college; (2) Federal grants to the several states for vocational education on both collegiate and secondary school levels; (3) the establishment of specialized schools, such as commercial and technical high schools, to prepare boys and girls for life; and (4) the emphasis upon economy of time in education, pointed toward training youth effectively for life work in a shorter period of time. Table 10 shows in compact form the cumulative changes in the pattern of the American school curriculum on various educational levels from 1860 to 1920.

4. THE MOTIVE OF MASS EDUCATION (1920 to DATE)

The mass education motive has been the controlling influence in the development of American education since about 1920. This motive and its implications for the curriculum are set forth in the remaining chapters of this volume.

Each motive which has been a primary factor in the determination of the curriculum of the schools during one period or another of American history has left its imprint. Latin and Greek in the secondary school, and reading, writing, and arithmetic in the elementary school, were inherited from the colonial schools, even though the *religious* motive of the colonial schools ceased to be a primary factor by 1850.

Although the *political* motive was predominant in the early national period, geography, history, and grammar were added to the subjects of the elementary school during that period. On the secondary school level, both the academies and early high schools offered the first types of vocational education through courses in bookkeeping, surveying, navigation, drawing, and household arts. At the same time they began to stress United States and state history, political economy, rhetoric and logic, intellectual and mental philosophy, natural philosophy (science), higher mathematics, and English grammar.

Parallel curricula or courses of study, which were begun in the secondary school in the early years of the nineteenth century, became the usual device by 1920 for attempting to prepare boys and girls either for college or for life. From 1900 to well past 1920 the *utilitarian* factor operated so strongly that the general public, parents, and pupils came to believe that graduation from secondary school and college meant a "white-collar" job, a larger income, and a better social position. Bitter experiences of graduates during the depression years of the 1930's proved the falseness of this view. Yet the trend was exemplified by the rapid addition on all school levels of vocational and appreciative subjects, and of modern foreign languages in the secondary school while the classics gradually declined.

Of the four motives which have dominated the development of the school curriculum in the United States, the *religious* motive is the only one which was almost entirely inoperative for many years, but has now become again a major factor today. The *political* motive continues as an important force, as is evidenced by the enlargement of the social studies offerings in schools. For example, following World War II and the Korean War, the teaching of "democracy" and "Americanism" became as important as the *mass education* motive which is predominant. The *utilitarian* influence is, and is likely to continue to be, a powerful factor in the development of the curriculum of the secondary school, especially in conjunction with the efforts (1) to equalize educational opportunity for all children of all the nation, (2) to provide adequate guidance for youth, and (3) to produce more scientists for America's survival in the nuclear age.

PROBLEMS FOR INDIVIDUAL STUDY
AND CLASS DISCUSSION

1. Was the early elementary (common) school wise in its emphasis upon the teaching of grammar? Should the fundamentals of formal English grammar be taught today in the elementary school or in the secondary school? Support your view.

2. Take the catalogue of your college for the years 1890, 1920, and

today; examine carefully the college entrance requirements for each of these dates. Can you give satisfactory explanations for the different entrance standards that you find?

3. Can you give reasons for the fact that the curricula of the American college up to 1860 were less susceptible to change than were secondary school curricula?

4. In the colonial curriculum, can you explain the gap in preparation between the dame school and the Latin grammar school?

5. Was there any real difference between the English grammar school and the academy?

6. Give three instances prior to 1920 of educational changes made to meet changing needs caused by economic and social developments.

7. Have the private schools made any contributions to curriculum evolution? Give reasons and illustrations to prove your point of view.

8. Why did the academy supplant the Latin grammar school, and why was it displaced in turn by the high school?

9. What bases or standards do you believe should be employed to distinguish between "drill," "content," and "expression" subjects on the elementary school level? If you believe that no such distinctions should be made, support your point of view.

10. Make a list of all the subjects commonly offered in the high school today; then take French's or Inglis' list of those offered in the heyday of the academy. Which met the needs of youth better for its period?

11. It is a fact that there have been fewer changes in the elementary than in the secondary curriculum in the history of American curriculum development. Why?

ADDITIONAL ANNOTATED REFERENCES
FOR PROBLEM OR UNIT STUDY

NOTE: This historical sketch of the American school curriculum is based primarily upon the research of such well known writers as E.E. Brown, E.P. Cubberley, F.P. Graves, E.D. Grizzell, Alexander Inglis, I.L. Kandel, E.W. Knight, Colyer Meriwether, E.H. Reisner, Harold Rugg, L.F. Snow, D.G. Tewksbury, and C.F. Thwing (cf. *Curriculum Principles and Social Trends*, rev. ed., 1950, pp. 38–40). Therefore, the additional references listed here are limited to more recent books which illuminate curriculum development up to around 1920.

Briggs, T.H., Leonard, J.P., and Justman, J., *Secondary Education* (rev. ed.), New York, The Macmillan Company, 1950.
    Chapters I and II give a comprehensive sketch of the growth of the secondary-school curriculum to about 1930.
Butts, R.F., *A Cultural History of Western Education: Its Social and*

Intellectual Foundations (2nd ed.), New York, McGraw-Hill Book Company, 1955.

The author traces in this volume the patterns of education from which our schools and curricular programs developed.

Butts, R.F., and Cremin, L.A., *A History of Education in American Culture*, New York, Henry Holt and Company, 1953.

The development of typical patterns of education and curricula for different educational levels to 1918 are set forth in Chapters iv, viii, and xii.

Drake, W.E., *The American School in Transition*, New York, Prentice-Hall, 1955.

The author presents main curricular trends in "Education for Salvation," in Chapter ii, "Education for Enlightenment," in Chapter iv, and "Education in the 19th Century Era of Transition," in Part iii.

French, W.M., *American Secondary Education*, New York, The Odyssey Press, 1957.

Primarily a history of secondary education, this book is valuable for curricular trends in Chapters i–xii.

Gilchrist, R.S., Dutton, W.H., and Wrinkle, W.L., *Secondary Education for American Democracy* (rev. ed.), New York, Rinehart and Company, 1957.

A good résumé of the history of the secondary school and its curricular changes is found in Chapter iv.

Good, H.G., *A History of American Education*, New York, The Macmillan Company, 1956.

Curricular changes to 1920 are discussed especially in Chapters ii, vi–viii; later curriculum trends are found in Chapters xiv and xv.

Leonard, J.P., *Developing the Secondary School Curriculum* (rev. ed.), New York, Rinehart and Company, 1953.

One of the best accounts of how the modern secondary-school curriculum developed is found in the first six chapters of this book.

Meyer, A.E., *An Educational History of the American People*, New York, McGraw-Hill Book Company, 1957.

Curricula, teaching methods and practices, and other significant trends are given in Chapters ii, vi, vii, and x.

Noble, S.G., *A History of American Education* (rev. ed.), New York, Rinehart and Company, 1954.

The author throughout this book discusses the religious, the utilitarian, and mass education motives in the development of American education, with much similarity to the factors discussed in this chapter.

Ragan, W.B., *Modern Elementary Curriculum*, New York, The Dryden Press, 1953.

An interesting résumé of elementary curriculum development is presented in Chapter i, with comparison by periods.

Romine, S.A., *Building the High School Curriculum,* New York, The Ronald Press Company, 1954.

Chapter III describes the evolution of the secondary-school curriculum.

Ryan, W.C., Gwynn, J.M., and King, A.K., *Secondary Education in the South,* Chapel Hill, The University of North Carolina Press, 1946.

This volume now makes available in written form the history of secondary education in the region which was the last to establish public high schools.

Williams, L.A., *Secondary Schools for American Youth,* New York, American Book Company, 1948.

The first three chapters trace the factors which operated historically to develop the unique American public high schools.

PART ONE Factors in curriculum development

CHAPTER 2 Conflicting educational theories

EQUALIZATION OF EDUCATIONAL OPPORTUNITY

The dominating factor in educational philosophy in the United States today is the desire to secure the equalization of educational opportunity for all children of all the nation. Though faced with one national emergency after another, the American people have proved the truth of this statement by enlarging educational provisions for children from six to eighteen years of age.

During recent years, "equalization" of educational opportunity has come to have two distinct meanings which are closely interrelated. To most people, equalization of educational opportunity means equalization of the length of the school term, of school facilities, and of good instruction for all children by properly qualified teachers. This interpretation of equalization has been stressed in the public press and among professional educators.

A specific example will make clear the inequalities in education existing among the various regions of the United States. The South has one-third of the country's children to educate, but it has only one-sixth of the school revenues of the nation. This is true in spite of the fact that the southern states devote a larger share of their tax income to education than does any other region of the United States. Many educational leaders maintain, therefore, that the Federal government should give aid from national revenues to all states on two bases: (1) in proportion to the number of children to be educated in each state; and (2) in proportion to the economic ability of each state to meet the costs of schools. On these two bases, the richer states would contribute more in taxes to support all of the agencies

41

of the national government, but they would receive proportionately from the Federal treasury far less in return for the support of their educational programs than the poorer states would receive. The 1938 plan of the President's Advisory Committee on Education established the basic principles for Federal aid to general education; the states lacking in financial ability to pay for schools would receive proportionately more than the richer states for certain school purposes. These purposes were set forth as (1) the lengthening of the school term; (2) an increase in the salaries of teachers; (3) the construction, consolidation, and maintenance of schools; (4) adult education; and (5) improvements in rural education. Expenditures for these purposes by the Federal government would attempt to secure equalization of educational opportunity for all children by means of equalization of the teaching personnel and of the physical and administrative facilities of the schools.

THE MODERN CONFLICT IN EDUCATIONAL THEORY

Some educational leaders have given a broader meaning to the term, "equalization of educational opportunity." These leaders define it as the attempt of educators to widen the horizon and extend the base of the curriculum. They believe that each child should have the opportunity under competent guidance to develop fully and richly as an individual and as a cooperating member of an interdependent society full of manifold social, religious, economic, community, and governmental agencies. These educators maintain that the present school curriculum is "subject-centered," whereas it should be "child-centered"; that it fails to educate adequately either the bright or the dull pupil; and that equalization of educational facilities for all children will not bring about equalization of educational opportunity until all curriculum work is centered around the child instead of the subject. Those educators who upheld this concept were named "Progressives." Their opponents were called "Traditionalists" or "Essentialists."

Between the Progressives and the Traditionalists a crucial struggle has gone on for more than thirty years. There were sharp differences between them in regard to educational theory as well as to practice.

THE "PROGRESSIVES" AND THE "ESSENTIALISTS." J.S. Brubacher [1] has presented an excellent analysis of these two conflicting educational philosophies. His groupings are as follows:

Progressivism, which includes *pragmatism* and *naturalism.*
Essentialism, or *Traditionalism,* which comprises also *idealism* and *realism.*

In order that we may be better able to understand these opposing concepts of education, we might well ask ourselves why the following characteristics and persons were associated with each concept:

Progressive Education

Characteristics	Educators
Freedom	John Dewey
Independent thinking	Boyd Bode
Initiative	W.H. Kilpatrick
Self-reliance	Carleton Washburne
Interests, urges, and needs	Carson Ryan
Social orientation	Sidney Hook
Social organization and shared experience	James Tippett
	Caroline Zachry
Problem solving	E.L. Thorndike
Activity	Harold Rugg
Individuality	George Counts
Self-expression	Murray and Dorris Lee
Purposeful learning	Alice Keliher
Connection with normal life outside of school	Harold Hand
	William Van Til
Center of interest in teaching	Alice Miel
	H. Gordon Hullfish
	Harold Taylor

Pupil {

Guiding principles of Progressivist

1. Guidance of the child
2. Development of the "whole" child
3. Democratic sharing between pupil and teacher
4. Individual differences
5. Change and novelty
6. No final or fixed values in advance
7. Constant revision of aims
8. Experimental techniques of learning and teaching
9. Education as reconstructor of society

[1] *Modern Philosophies of Education,* New York, McGraw-Hill Book Company, 1939, Chap. XIV.

The Essentialist (Traditional) Movement in Education

Characteristics	Educators
Pupil { Freedom as a social privilege	W.C. Bagley
Freedom as an outcome, not as a means of education	H.H. Horne
	M. Demiashkevich
Discipline, as needed in life	T.H. Briggs
Learning as a realization, not a creation	H.C. Morrison
	Franklin Bobbitt
Initiative as self-disciplining activity	I.L. Kandel
Interests as a part of law and order in the universe	Harold L. Clapp
	Arthur Bestor
Intellectual development and mental training	Paul Woodring
	Robert M. Hutchins
Learning for future use	Mortimer Smith
Gap between school life and the outside world	

Education as eternal striving for the perfect or absolute
Training of the child for adaptation to the mores of society
Certain fixed educational values
Set curriculum
Minimum essentials which all must learn, such as the classics in literature, mathematics, history, and science
Education as conformity to the laws of the universe
Education as creature, not creator of society
Education as the process of transmission of the heritage and culture of the race.

The objection will be made immediately that Briggs, Bobbitt, and Morrison were leaders in the curriculum revision movement, that Woodring advocated radical changes in teacher education, and that they should certainly have been placed among the Progressives. Yes, these lists give point to the mistake commonly made by labeling a movement or a person. There were as many types of Progressives as there were Traditionalists; these ranged from the extreme "right" to the extreme "left." Both the Pragmatists and the Essentialists claim, each with good reasons, that they provide amply for individual differences in children, for mastery of essential facts, and for education for democracy. Yet, in the struggle, certain educational leaders have become associated in the minds of educators and the general public with one movement or the other.

The Progressives made their greatest imprint upon the school curriculum from 1900 to 1950. They had vigorous leadership and secured large subventions from the educational foundations for experiments to improve the school program. Even the depression of the 1930's aided them in their experiments because of the general reexamination which was being made of the weaknesses of the curriculum. At midcentury the Progressives prepared to dissolve the Progressive Education Association, since they felt that their task of stimulating newer curricular approaches was completed. After long-drawn out legal technicalities involved in the dissolution, the PEA ceased to exist in 1955.

On the other hand, the Essentialists had just started a real counterattack against the Progressive movement when World War II began. After 1946, powerful support for the Essentialist point of view came from the subject-matter departments of the colleges and the secondary schools and from those in the elementary schools who held their point of view. Arthur Bestor has led the Traditionalists since 1952, and his efforts resulted in the establishment of the Council for Basic Education in 1956.[2]

The conflict between the Progressive and the Essentialist theories of education spread to the general public. Articles in popular magazines discussed the pros and cons of the issue.[3]

Clinton R. Prewett has presented clearly a summary of the main criticisms of the public school by the Essentialists:

> For just a moment let us look at a bit of history of these last ten years of mounting criticism of public education. The first phase of the battle centered around the notion that the schoolman's plea for increased financial support for education, for additional buildings, teaching facilities and teaching personnel was unrealistic. This assertion began to give ground before concerted counterattacks from professional personnel and parents generally, since it was relatively easy to refute, requiring only a simple

[2] For a complete picture of what the Council for Basic Education believes and plans, examine its monthly *CE Bulletin,* Washington 5, D.C.; for reactions to the Council's points of view and defense of its policies, read *Educational Leadership,* vol. xv, "The Importance of People" column, for October, 1957, and for January, 1958, and *Phi Delta Kappan,* xl (December, 1958), editorial, "The Editor Learns a Lesson," pp. 113–14.

[3] The *pros* and *cons* of the argument in both popular and professional magazines will be found in representative articles listed in the annotated bibliography at the end of this chapter.

counting operation to determine if the number of desks in a given school building exceeded the number of pupils seeking to enroll in that school. When this was found to be the case in so many instances-throughout the United States, it became quite obvious that the need for increased school buildings was actually genuine and a "cease and desist" policy became operative as far as this idea was concerned.

Sternly rebuked on their first major category of criticisms, the critics began to rally around another charge that caught on quickly. Quite impressively they thundered that our schools were failing to teach children the fundamentals. "Why Johnnie Can't Read" became an outstanding bestseller, when evaluated in terms of the number of copies sold. Most of the criticisms of the nature of "Quackery In Our Schools" and the above-mentioned, "Why Johnnie Can't Read" actually, deep down in the fine print, contain many truthful observations about our schools, principally, to the point that a great, great, number of children are taught to read and that an overwhelming percentage of our schools are actually doing a good job. Nevertheless, the main damage was done by the titles; a tribute to shrewd salesmanship rather than useful documents of research in educational matters.

Opportunists to the core, the critics chose this moment to resurrect another fearsome goblin with a widely discussed past: It was the "Progressive Taint" that had captured our school systems all across the land. Without bothering with defining terms or pointing out schools that were operating under such a nefarious ideology, the critics increased their broadsides against education. All instances of poor teaching were thus attributable to this sinister influence of "Progressivism" and a change was necessary.[4]

The real differences between the two groups seem less clear-cut now. W.W. Brickman[5] made an analysis of the first decade of Essentialism (1938–1948). He quoted I.L. Kandel for the Essentialist position, who believed that the chief contribution of the Progressives had been in improving methods of instruction. Perhaps the fairest analysis of "Progressive Education" has been made by Frederick L. Redefer,[6] formerly Executive Secretary of the Progressive Education

---

[4] "The Attacks Continue," *The High School Journal*, vol. XLI (November, 1957), p. 35. Quoted by permission. For an analysis of the attacks by the National Education Association, read "Ten Criticisms of Public Education," *NEA Research Bulletin*, vol. xxxv, No. 4 (December, 1957), pp. 131–74.

[5] "Essentialism Ten Years After," *School and Society*, LXVII (May 15, 1948), pp. 361–65. This article includes also in its footnotes a complete bibliography on the two theories, *pro* and *con.*

[6] "What Has Happened to Progressive Education?" *School and Society*, LXVII (May 8, 1948), pp. 345–49.

Association (later called American Education Fellowship). He gives credit to "Progressive" education also for improved methods of teaching, centered primarily around development of the whole child in a natural learning situation.[7]

In these times of stress it seems particularly wise for teachers and administrators to study carefully both the Progressive theory and the Essentialist philosophy in order that (1) each educator may decide more definitely what he thinks our educational aims should be, and that (2) the synthesis of the two concepts eventually arrived at may be for the best interests of the children and the nation. James Bryant Conant pointed this up well when he said recently:

And, to all the members of the college faculties, particularly the members of the faculties of liberal arts, I would venture to repeat what I have said on more than one occasion; namely, "In the name of the welfare of American youth, call a truce to the warfare among educators." The time is long overdue for the professors of the liberal arts and of education to join forces and work together to solve the emergency problems and to improve our schools.[8]

THE RELATIONSHIP OF THE SCHOOL TO OTHER SOCIAL AGENCIES

To what extent should the schools take over the functions of other agencies of society? Should the schools give children training in good manners and social courtesy? In personal hygiene? In consumer education? In public and private health? In occupations and vocational apprenticeship? In religious matters? In character education? In sex education and marriage? In child care, both pre- and post-natal, and in parenthood? In safety education? In driver education? In leisure- and vacation-time experiences? In participation in community life? In nursery education? Formerly all of these areas of

---

[7] Chapters x and xxi also discuss improvements in the schools which may be due in a greater or less degree to the outcomes of the clash between the "Progressives" and the "Essentialists."

[8] "The Unique Features of Our American Schools," *The Bulletin of the National Association of Secondary-School Principals,* xl (May, 1956), p. 7. Quoted by permission. *Cf.* also "An Evaluation of the Second Bowling Green Conference," by T. M. Stinnett, *Phi Delta Kappan,* xl (December, 1958), pp. 125–29.

training were within the province and the responsibility of the three
great social institutions—the Family, the Church, and the Community. Of course, in the process of acquiring such training the child
often got as much or more of it from his play group, or his age-level
group, as from these three agencies.

At one extreme are the proponents of the expansion of the American school system to care for these additional responsibilities of a
social and economic nature. They argue that the home, the church,
and the community are no longer giving this training effectively. At
the other extreme are found those persons who believe that the
school should not enlarge its curriculum in vocations and social
living. They claim that the school cannot take over the functions and
responsibilities of other social agencies, and that no further impetus
should be given to the disintegration of family and community life
and of the influence of the church. Between these two extremes will
be found the thinking of the remainder of the people.

It is not difficult to discover the factors which have caused the conflict between those who believe that the schools should take over
the functions of other agencies of society and those who believe
that they should not. Important in such a list of factors are the following: (1) improvement of means of communication and transportation; (2) mechanization of production; (3) urbanization of
much of the population; (4) immigration, accompanied by problems
of racial amalgamation, racial minorities and desegregation; (5) uncontrolled exploitation of national resources; (6) improvement in
labor conditions and regulations; (7) the position of woman as a
wage earner; (8) the interdependence of modern society; (9) extension of the public services rendered by the government; and (10)
the operation of the theory of "rugged individualism."

Not so easy to recognize are the reasons why the operation of these
factors has caused important alterations in the three primary social
agencies. Has the church failed in its religious, moral, and spiritual
task? Does it fail to appeal to children any more? If it has failed,
should any or all of its functions be taken over by the school? What
is "weekday" religious education and has it significance as a movement? Is the home outmoded? What are the chief causes of broken
homes? What pattern of experiences could be set up for the child in

school to take the place of those experiences which he should get normally in his family? Perhaps it is wiser for the school, the church, the home, and the community to cooperate to make of themselves better social institutions, instead of the school's attempting to extend its work to supplant some or all of them.

What has tended to destroy community solidarity and community thinking in American life? It is a fact that Adult Education is now tremendously concerned with attempting to rebuild these pre-

FIG. 6   *Should adult education be a part of the school program?*
Textile Chemistry for Adults. (*Courtesy Greenville (S.C.) High School. Photo by Lindsay Boozer, Jr.*)

cious intangible assets in each community by means of community forums, round-table discussions, community coordinating councils, and town meetings. Is it possible that the consolidation of local school districts has operated to eliminate the local school as a community center. What technical and commercial inventions have raised the standard of living and narrowed the distinctions between rural and urban living conditions? Is it wise to seek to eliminate the rural school by consolidation of units? Or is it wiser to attempt consciously to improve the rural school, in view of the fact that some 50 percent of all elementary-school pupils live in the open country or in villages, and approximately 70 per cent reside in rural districts or in towns of 10,000 or less population?

There are many good samples of educational thought on these questions. One is the various *White House Conferences on Children in a Democracy*. (The Midcentury Conference in 1950 and the special Conference on Education in 1955.) Another comprises the publications of the Educational Policies Commission of the American Association of School Administrators and the National Education Association. The problem of forming a national organization of all of the country's school forces was referred to this newly formed Educational Policies Commission in 1936 by the Department of Superintendence of the National Education Association.[9] This proposed organization was to "be representative of the full scope of public education in this country"[10] in its aims, structure, and activities.

The doubt of the general public about the wisdom of extending the functions of the school into areas normally cared for by other agencies of society was strikingly substantiated as far back as 1938 by the findings of the *Regents' Inquiry into the Character and Cost of Public Education in the State of New York*. The following are among the significant recommendations of that investigation concerning the extended vocational training which some educators are advocating in the modern school:

Among boys and girls who have not yet had successful vocational experience under adult working conditions, the secondary school should not seek to develop a higher degree of specialized vocational skills than the minimum needed to get and to hold such jobs as normally may be open locally to beginners in their chosen field. For example, the secondary school should not train vocationally inexperienced pupils to be specialists in electric welding, though it may train them as electricians' helpers; nor should it seek to train such pupils to be cafeteria or tearoom managers, though it may train them for counter-service or as waitresses. . . .

There is no need for the vocational institute to give up-grading work of a type that can readily be obtained through employment itself. It should, however, give instruction when such work is not otherwise avail-

---

[9] Now known as the American Association of School Administrators.
[10] *A National Organization for Education*, National Education Association, Educational Policies Commission, 1937, p. 3.

able. . . . types of work change, and, furthermore, employees cannot obtain all the needed training in grades 10 through 12. . . .[11]

Many educators, including instructors in vocational education, believe that the principles set forth here are as sound today for "work programs" in secondary schools as they were twenty years ago.

If the school should take over the major responsibility for the child's education in such areas as public recreation, health, and vocational training, how much more money would have to be provided for the work to be well done? Formal education on all levels now costs over eight billion dollars annually. Most school plants remain closed for approximately three months each year, yet such a huge capital investment ought to pay dividends to the communities the year around. Could provision be made for more adequate use of these school facilities on a year-round basis, without duplication of the work of other agencies and without adding enormously to the amount spent for schools?

THE ROLE OF THE CURRICULUM

What is the place of the curriculum in the modern school? What is its purpose? What task is it supposed to perform? The following statements should help to answer these questions.

1. *The curriculum is the means of attaining the aims or philosophy of education.* Being the means to this end, and not an end in itself, it usually follows and reflects educational trends and changes in philosophy.

2. *Curriculum change is a slow development over a period of years, not a mushroom growth of short duration.* Just as modifications in educational philosophy take place slowly over a long period of years, so do the practices resulting from those changes develop slowly. Curricular alterations usually take place no faster than the changing mores of a community.

3. *The curriculum shows, and should continue to show, evidence of conflicting educational theories.* Arguments and evidence from both the Progressives and the Essentialists are but the promising signs of a healthy

[11] T.L. Norton, *Education for Work*, copyright 1938 by McGraw-Hill Book Company, pp. 144–45, 148, and used by permission of the publisher. The "vocational institute" was generally considered as the special vocational or technical high school.

situation among educators—namely, an attitude of self-examination and self-criticism. From both schools of thought came values—from the Progressives, new ideas and suggestions for improvement; from the Essentialists, primarily an influence restraining too rapid change. Each group has at heart the best interests of the children. From each, after careful study, those curricular materials should be adopted which will serve the best interests of the children.

4. *The wider variance in needs, skills, and abilities of a school population which is tremendously larger and more heterogeneous than in the past, and which is required by compulsory school laws to remain in school longer will require gradual curricular changes for some time to come.* If the emphasis upon the equalization of educational opportunity for all children continues, this problem may cause school administrative changes as well as curricular alterations.

5. *The curriculum belongs to the public, not primarily to the professional educators.* School administrators and teachers are not wise enough to determine the curriculum by themselves. One prime reason for the existence of school boards is to bring the experience and knowledge of the layman to bear in the "thinking through" of school problems. Only through the help of laymen of all types can a careful study be made of the relations of the school to other agencies of society. Only by this approach can wise decisions be arrived at as to whether certain activities should be added to or taken from the school program.

6. *If normal development takes place, the curriculum cannot be the same in each school.* Each community has its own peculiar individuality, environment, customs, and needs. The cooperation of all community agencies with the school is necessary in building a program to meet the needs of the children and of the local social, economic, and religious structure. Such cooperation will result in a curriculum satisfactory to that community, but not fitted exactly to the needs of another school.

7. *Curricular experiments sometimes indicate the need for some sort of change, or the fact that curricular change did not harm the learner or cause him to learn less.* In these respects, the curriculum itself may help to crystallize sentiment for change.

PROBLEMS FOR INDIVIDUAL STUDY
AND CLASS DISCUSSION

1. What is a "child-centered" school? Can you describe an elementary school of this type? A secondary school of this kind?
2. Can you take from this chapter the two different lists of characteristics generally associated with "Progressive Education" and "Traditional

Education" and make a composite list of your own of those characteristics which you think both schools of thought would agree upon?

3. Make a list of the functions and responsibilities of the home in child training in 1890; in this list star (°) those items which today are primarily the function of the school instead of the home. In each case, why has the transfer taken place?

4. What is meant by "minimum" national standards for schools? How would such standards affect the equalization of educational opportunity?

5. Write a definition of education, limiting it to fifty words or less. Then define elementary education; secondary education.

6. What are two major contributions which you believe that John Dewey has made to the philosophy of American education? Support your position.

7. Why have modern conditions and regulations in regard to labor been primary factors forcing the schools to take over some of the functions of other agencies of society?

8. Make a study and report on the activities and influence of the Council for Basic Education on the school curriculum; of the Progressive Education Association on the school curriculum.

9. Does the small or the large school have a better opportunity to improve its curricular offering? Why?

10. What workable plan could you propose for the utilization during the whole year of school plans? Should school employees be expected to work on a twelve-month basis? Why or why not?

11. Is the theory of "equalization of educational opportunity" conducive to the development and training of leaders?

12. In what respects should the curricular program in a rural school be similar to that in a city school? In what respects different? Give reasons.

13. If you had a choice as a parent of sending your child as he began school to a "progressive" or "traditional" elementary school, which would you select, and why?

ADDITIONAL ANNOTATED REFERENCES
FOR PROBLEM OR UNIT STUDY

Adams, F., *Educating America's Children* (2nd ed.), New York, The Ronald Press Company, 1954.
The criticism, tasks, and responsibilities of the elementary schools are presented in Chapters I–IV.
Anderson, V.E., *Principles and Procedures of Curriculum Improvement*, New York, The Ronald Press Company, 1956.
This book is designed to help educators change from a curriculum

centered around subjects to one centered around experiences, in which the goal is change in behavior. Chapter VII takes up criticism and attacks on schools, and community attitudes.

Attacks on public education:

Perhaps the fairest compendium of representative articles from both popular magazines and professional journals (1940–1952) is found in *Public Education Under Criticism,* edited by C. Winfield Scott and Clyde M. Hill, New York, Prentice Hall, 1954. Two other sources supplement the work of Scott and Hill without much overlapping: *Crucial Issues in Education: An Anthology,* edited by Henry Ehlers, New York, Henry Holt and Company, 1955, and a kit of critical reprints and pamphlets prepared and distributed by the Commission for the Defense of Democracy Through Education, N.E.A. For samples of more extensive criticism of public education or of longer analyses of controversies over the public schools, the following books are representative of the various types: Arthur Bestor, *Educational Wastelands,* Urbana, University of Illinois Press, 1953; R.F. Butts, *The American Tradition in Religion and Education,* Boston, The Beacon Press, 1950; Percy B. Caley, *A Teacher's Answer: A Reply to Critics of Our Public Schools,* New York, Vantage Press, 1955; J.L. Childs, *Education and Morals,* New York, Appleton-Century-Crofts, 1950; Earl Conrad, *The Public School Scandal,* New York, The John Day Company, 1951; Edward Darling, *How We Fought for Our Schools,* New York, W.W. Norton and Company, 1954; Rudolph Flesch, *Why Johnny Can't Read—And What You Can Do About It,* New York, Harper and Brothers, 1955; David Hulburd, *This Happened in Pasadena,* New York, The Macmillan Company, 1951; H. Gordon Hullfish (Ed.), *Educational Freedom in an Age of Anxiety,* New York, Harper and Brothers, 1953; Albert Lynd, *Quackery in The Public Schools,* Boston, Little, Brown and Company, 1953; Mortimer Smith (Ed.), *The Public Schools in Crisis,* Chicago, Henry Regnery Company, 1956; Paul Woodring, *Let's Talk Sense About Our Schools,* New York, McGraw-Hill Book Company, 1953; and Hollis L. Caswell, *The Attack on American Schools,* Teachers College, Columbia University, 1958.

Beck, R.H., Cook, W.W., and Kearney, N.C., *Curriculum in The Modern Elementary School,* New York, Prentice-Hall, 1953.

This text, based on principles of psychology and the social sciences, attempts to relate these principles to the learning of children. Part I traces the growth of the elementary school curriculum and presents the factors conditioning and causing curriculum change.

Brameld, T., *Philosophies of Education in Cultural Perspective,* New York, The Dryden Press, 1955.

Deals in detail with the philosophies of education denominated as progressivism, essentialism, and perennialism.

Butler, J.D., *Four Philosophies and Their Practice in Education and Religion* (rev. ed.), New York, Harper and Brothers, 1957.
The four are naturalism, idealism, realism, and pragmatism.

Butts, R.F., *A Cultural History of Western Education* (2nd ed.), New York, McGraw-Hill Book Company, 1955.
The aims of education in America in their historical development are given in Chapters XIV–XVII.

Childs, J.L., *American Pragmatism and Education*, New York, Henry Holt and Company, 1956.
Sets forth the author's thesis with evidence that the influence of the pragmatists has been a revolutionary factor causing changes in the curriculum.

Clapp, E.R., *The Use of Resources in Education*, New York, Harper and Brothers, 1952.
Describes two important educational experiments, one in Kentucky and one in West Virginia, where curricula were built from the beginning around community needs and resources.

Conant, J.B., *Education and Liberty*, Cambridge, Harvard University Press, 1953.
The monograph describes the role of free schools in a democracy.

Counts, G.S., *The Challenge of Soviet Education*, New York: McGraw-Hill Book Company, 1957.
The historical evolution and current status of education in the U.S.S.R.

Educating for American Citizenship, 32nd Yearbook, American Association of School Administrators, Washington, 1954.
Citizenship as our aim of American education, and promising practices in teaching it.

Educational Differences Among the States, Washington, National Education Association, 1954.
The Research division presents the differences in educational opportunities among the various states.

Federal Funds for Education, 1954–55 and 1955–56, Washington, U.S. Department of Health, Education, and Welfare, Bulletin 1956, No. 5.
Shows how over one and a half billion dollars in Federal funds are allocated.

Federal Responsibility in the Field of Education, Washington, Commission on Intergovernmental Relations, 1955.
A controversial committee report of the Study Committee on Federal responsibility in education.

Forces Affecting American Education, 1953 Yearbook, Washington Association for Supervision and Curriculum Development, N.E.A.
Takes up the culture, the groups, and the communications affecting education.

French, W., and Associates, *Behavioral Goals of General Education in High School*, New York, Russell Sage Foundation, 1957.
Goals and expectations from general education.

French, W.M., *American Secondary Education*, New York, The Odyssey Press, 1957.
The old, the existing, and the future high school and its program are described in Chapters i, vi–ix, and xx–xxi.

Frontiers of Elementary Education I [1954] and *Frontiers of Secondary Education I* [1956], Syracuse, Syracuse University Press.
The elementary monograph presents discussions of free public schools and of the future of progressive education. The secondary monograph discusses freedom and issues in secondary education.

Good, H.G., *A History of American Education*, New York, The Macmillan Company, 1956.
Chapters xii–xiv discuss conflicting educational theories.

Gross, N., *Who Runs Our Schools?* New York, John Wiley and Sons, 1958.
Analyses by research methods showing who promotes or blocks public education and the pressures that operate on decision makers.

Hechinger, F.M., *An Adventure in Education*, New York, The Macmillan Company, 1956.
Report of Connecticut's Fact-Finding Commission, and their discovery that children need *both* skills and general knowledge.

Hollingshead, B.S., "Is European Education Better?" American Council on Education, reprint from the April 1958 issue of *The Educational Record*.
Perhaps the best-balanced analysis by an American who has lived abroad.

Kilpatrick, W.H., *Philosophy of Education*, New York, The Macmillan Company, 1951.
A critical synthesis of the chief issues of educational theory.

Mathewson, R.H., *A Strategy for American Education*, New York, Harper and Brothers, 1957.
The existing situation in society and education, and discussion of the main issues in education with suggestions for their solution.

Meier, A.R., *et al.*, *A Curriculum for Citizenship: A Total School Approach to Citizenship Education*, Detroit, Wayne University Press, 1952.
The Citizenship Education Study from 1945 to 1950, to find better ways of accomplishing one of the school's main purposes with boys and girls.

Meyer, A.E., *Education for a New Morality*, New York, The Macmillan Company, 1957.
Presents briefly and clearly the main issues of education and contemporary society.

Modern Philosophies and Education, 54th Yearbook, National Society for the Study of Education, Part I, Chicago, University of Chicago Press, 1955.
The major schools of thought in modern philosophy, and their contributions to educational philosophy.

Noble, S.G., *A History of American Education* (rev. ed.), New York, Rinehart and Company, 1954.
The different philosophies in their historical context are given in Chapters II, IV, VI, XIV, XVI, and XIX–XX.

Overstreet, H.A., *The Mature Mind,* New York, W.W. Norton and Company, 1949.
How the school can stimulate maturity in thinking and acting.

Park, J. (Ed.), *Selected Readings in the Philosophy of Education,* New York, The Macmillan Company, 1958.
Pragmatism, idealism, realism, and the philosophies of Catholics, Protestants, and Jews.

Progressive Education: representative articles by various authors

PROS AND CONS IN THE POPULAR MAGAZINES:

The American Magazine: March, 1955, pp. 24–25, 80–86. *The Atlantic:* April, 1953, pp. 29–34; May, 1954, pp. 35–38; October, 1954, pp. 57–62; December, 1954, pp. 55–57; December, 1955, pp. 69–71; and September, 1956, pp. 33–37. *Collier's:* February 5, 1954, pp. 23–28; March 19, 1954, pp. 34–40. *Good Housekeeping:* February, 1939, 24–25, 62, 64, 66, 68–70. *The Key Reporter:* January, 1956, pp. 2–3, 6. *Ladies' Home Journal:* October, 1954, pp. 53–57, 184–87, *Newsweek:* December 5, 1955, pp. 55–62, 67. *Parents Magazine:* March, 1954, pp. 46–47, 81–85; June, 1955, pp. 42, 102–4; and October, 1958, pp. 43–120. *Reader's Digest:* June, 1956, pp. 41–46; and October, 1958, pp. 49–52. *The Saturday Evening Post:* March 16, 1940, pp. 29, 105–6; March 6, 1954, pp. 26–27, 111–14; and March 17, 1956, pp. 25, 104, 107. *Saturday Review:* September 11, 1954, pp. 11–13, 47. *U.S. News and World Report:* November 30, 1956, pp. 68–72, 74, 79, 80, 82–86, 89; March 15, 1957, pp. 38–44, 122–26; June 7, 1957, pp. 120–30; June 21, 1957, pp. 114–21.

PROS AND CONS IN THE PROFESSIONAL EDUCATION MAGAZINES:

Progressive Education, the official magazine of the Progressive Education Association from 1920 to 1955, is one of the best sources of information on the movement. Other good examples include: *Bulletin of the American Association of University Professors,* Summer, 1957, pp. 266–79. *California Journal of Secondary Education,* April, 1955, pp. 227–34. *Classical Journal,* November, 1953, pp. 71–78. *Clearing*

House, December, 1939, pp. 202–4. *The Educational Forum,* May, 1953, pp. 395–400. *Educational Leadership,* January, 1955, pp. 194–230, *Educational Research Bulletin,* November, 1955, pp. 197–202. *NEA Journal,* November, 1955, pp. 474–76. *The Nation's Schools,* May, 1957, pp. 54–56, and September, 1957, pp. 44–47. *Phi Delta Kappan,* May, 1957, 309–13, and November, 1957, pp. 65–69 and pp. 73–74. *School and Society,* October 27, 1951, pp. 262–69; January 31, pp. 68–70; September 3, 1955, pp. 68–70; and February 4, 1956, pp. 39–43. *Teacher's College Record,* January, 1957, pp. 198–206.

Rugg, H., and Withers, W., *Social Foundations of Education,* Englewood Cliffs, Prentice-Hall, 1955.

A survey of the social issues of this age and a charter for education through the cultural and interdisciplinary approach.

Sayers, E.V., and Madden, W., *Education and the Democratic Faith,* New York, Appleton-Century-Crofts, 1959.

Do we have clear directives in education? This book is organized around the main philosophical issues in American education.

Saylor, J.G., and Alexander, W.M., *Curriculum Planning for Better Teaching and Learning,* New York, Rinehart and Company, 1954.

Part I presents basic issues in the curriculum and current curriculum practices in American schools.

Smith, B.O., *et al., Fundamentals of Curriculum Development* (rev. ed.), Yonkers-on-Hudson, World Book Company, 1957.

The factors causing curriculum change and conflicting curriculum issues are found in Parts I and V.

Stoddard, A.J., *Schools for Tomorrow,* New York, The Fund for the Advancement of Education, 1957.

Concerned with the size of the educational job, adequate school personnel, and the use of TV in education.

Thut, I.N., *The Story of Education,* New York, McGraw-Hill Book Company, 1957.

A critique of the main philosophies of education.

What Shall the High School Teach? Washington, Association for Supervision and Curriculum Development, N.E.A., 1956 Yearbook, 1956.

Discusses the issues and factors involved in reappraisal of the secondary school and its curriculum, including what the high schools are now teaching and differences between general, special, and vocational education.

Woodring, Paul, *A Fourth of a Nation,* New York, McGraw-Hill Book Company, 1957.

A good presentation of the complications in education because of the prolongation of school age; the classic and the pragmatic concepts of education; the aims and needs of modern education, and new directions in teacher education to effect them.

Year Round Schools. This movement's trends can be identified in "For a 210-Day School Year," by V.R. Cardozier, *Phi Delta Kappan,* XXXVIII (March, 1952), 240–42; "Keeping Schools Open All Year," by V.D. MacPherson, *The Nation's Schools,* LVI (September, 1955), 51–54; "Community Use of School Facilities Made Easy," by M. Soso, *The School Executive,* LXXVII (December, 1956), 43–44; from two articles in *U.S. News and World Report,* March 1, 1957, pp. 32–34 and August 2, 1957, pp. 48–51; and "Shall We Change the School Calendar?" *National Parent–Teacher,* LII (October, 1957), 12–14, 35.

CHAPTER 3 Curriculum problems concerned with child growth and development

THE PURPOSES OF EDUCATIONAL PSYCHOLOGY

In recent years much of the attention of educators has been centered upon the individual child and his development in the group. Historically, educational psychology developed as a branch of applied psychology in order that teachers and prospective teachers might learn more about human behavior, especially as it affected the educational life and growth of the school child. A rapid development of instruments of measurement in education accompanied this study of the pupil. Measuring instruments were formulated for ascertaining not only the child's mental capacity but also his progress in school. These experiments in measurement have produced intelligence tests, tests of achievement, diagnostic and remedial tests, interest and aptitude tests, and prognostic tests. They have also produced a mass of educational statistics.

This emphasis upon tests and measurement in education stimulated the attempt to apply the "scientific method" of study to education; more and more attention was centered upon the scientific approach to the behavior of children. For example, the Watsonian school of educational psychology believed that the principles of human behavior in learning should be established only on the basis of proof from tests and objective experiments. To date, the educational psychologists have not agreed among themselves as to exactly how children learn. As a result, educators have wondered at times whether the child was being lost sight of in the ever-expanding in-

Child Growth and Development

troduction of new types of tests and scales which were supposed to measure his reactions more accurately.

More recently the attention of the psychologists has been focused upon the fact that the child is five or six years of age before he enters the school doors, and the question has been raised as to what attitudes, habits, and emotional traits have developed and become set in his mind and actions before he comes under the influence of the school. In fact, the first grader is already aware of group differences and particular religious practices; he is a holder of definite notions about other groups, he is able to generalize, and he thinks in terms of stereotypes of groups; he is affected by marital problems in the home, and by the world's social conflict; and he has learned how to reject and be rejected because of membership in a particular group.[1] The studies of such men as Arnold Gesell,[2] and George D. Stoddard and his associates at the University of Iowa [3] opened the eyes of educators to the powerful influence which environment has had upon a child before he enters school, and how it continues to influence him. Along lines somewhat similar to these studies, other persons have either started investigations or are completing them in the area now known as "child growth and development." Some of the most significant work that has been done involves children of secondary-school age.[4]

Some of these studies of child development have been completed and are available; others are "longitudinal" studies of children, i.e., studies of individuals over a period of years, and have not been completed yet. Enough data have been published to give educational employees a fairly definite idea of the normal behavior of children under varying circumstances. Normal child behavior cannot be

[1] Cf. "Early Childhood Airs its Views," by Helen Trager and Marian Radke, *Educational Leadership*, IV (October, 1947), pp. 16–24.
[2] Cf. Frances L. Ilg and Louise B. Ames, *Child Behavior*, 1955; Arnold Gesell, *et al.*, *The Child From Five to Ten*, 1946; *The First Five Years of Life*, 1940, New York, Harper and Bros., *passim; Biographies of Child Development*, New York, Paul B. Hoeber, Inc., 1939, *passim.*
[3] "Intelligence: Its Nature and Nurture," 39th Yearbook, National Society for the Study of Education, Public School Publishing Company, 1940, Part I, pp. 21–40, 405–42; Part II, pp. 281–308, 377–99.
[4] Arnold Gesell, *et al.*, *Youth: The Years from Ten to Sixteen*, New York, Harper and Brothers, 1956, and Robert J. Havighurst, *Human Development and Education*, New York, Longmans, Green and Company, 1953, *passim.*

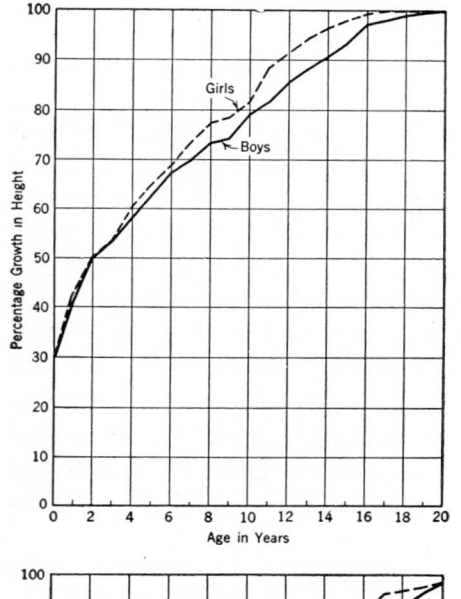

"We all know that boys usually are taller and weigh more than girls of the same age during the early years of life. However, some girls will weigh more than some boys of the same age. This is because there are great individual differences."

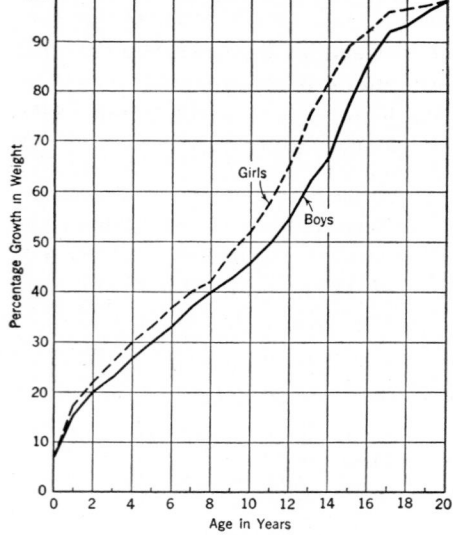

"'Girls obtain their growth earlier than boys. At any age they are farther along toward their maximum physical growth than boys of the same age. By four years of age girls have gained 60 per cent of their total height, while boys have gained only about 57 per cent. Girls are sometimes more precocious than boys because of this faster development. Boys will catch up after fourteen years of age."

FIGS. 7A and B   *Differences between boys and girls in physical growth*

These charts and the data accompanying them are reproduced by permission in modified and enlarged form from p. 9 of *Your Child's Development and Guidance Told in Pictures*, by Lois Hayden Meek, Philadelphia, J.B. Lippincott Company, 1940. The original charts were prepared by Dr. Herbert R. Stolz, Oakland (Calif.) Public Schools.

understood unless *typical* child behavior is understood. Much of the investigation that has heretofore been carried on has not been pointed toward assembling data which would show what sorts of behavior are typical of the school child. As more information on typical behavior becomes available, teachers can come to understand better the special behavior of individual children in all sorts of situations.

THEORIES AND PRINCIPLES OF LEARNING

In spite of differing ideas among educational psychologists concerning how we learn, investigations have proceeded far enough for the theories of learning to emerge distinctly. These would probably be grouped today under two main categories, with their related concepts:

Association Theories	*Field Theories*
Trial and Error, with the concept that when this kind of learning is unsuccessful, the problems were not suited to the individual's level of maturity.	*Learning by Insight*. Gestalt Theory, in which experiences, information, and activities group themselves in a pattern or field new to the learner, forming a configuration or gestalt. This theory emphasizes "wholes," i.e., the grasping of the whole field or idea and its surroundings. The parts get meaning from membership in the whole. As such, it is an extension and elaboration of John Dewey's learning by reconstruction of experience.
Behaviorism	
Situation and Connected Response. Continuous association stimulates response; and immediate reward or satisfaction reduces the need and hastens the learning.	

For all practical purposes in teaching the curriculum, the educational employee must be familiar with three well known theories of learning. These are: (1) the theory of learning by trial and error; (2) the theory of learning by insight; and (3) the theory of learning by conditioned response. J.F. Dashiell [5] gave the clearest and briefest

[5] "Contributions to Education of Scientific Knowledge about the Psychology of Learning," Part II, 37th Yearbook, National Society for the Study of Education, *The Scientific Movement in Education*, Public School Publishing Company, 1938, pp. 393–403. For a comparison of these three theories with the modern

exposition of these psychological conceptions of learning. Starting with the thesis that *education is guided habit forming*, he stated, *"Any well-learned performance remains a variable and adaptable performance."* [6]

1. THE TRIAL-AND-ERROR PRINCIPLE.   A good illustration of learning by trial and error is found in the attempt of a child to spell correctly the word "house." In the beginning he spells it "hous," omitting the final "e." He has tried to spell it and he has made an error, which is called to his attention by his teacher. The next time he spells the word, he makes the same mistake—he leaves off the "e." This time the teacher requires the child to write the word ten times correctly, and this procedure emphasizes in his mind the fact that he has made an error. By spelling the word "house" he finds that he gets out of school with the other children and does not have to "stay in" in order to rewrite the word. By this trial-and-error method he presumably achieves the proper solution, and thereafter he makes the proper adjustment in spelling the word "house." This method of learning is time-consuming and wasteful, but it is possibly one of the ways in which all individuals learn certain things. Persons who believe in this method of learning place "an extreme emphasis upon the *random, hit-or-miss, trial-and-error, unanalytic* character of the learning." [7]

2. LEARNING BY INSIGHT.   In the last three decades many experiments with other types and ways of learning have tended to disprove in part the findings of Thorndike and his group in regard to learning by trial and error. One of these other types or ways of learning is by *insight*. If one uses the same illustration given above for the trial-and-error method, the child would see a picture of a house. He would hear the word "house" repeated many times in different ways and would learn to know what "house" meant. Likewise there would be available to him the word "house" written out in many connections and at various places. The child would come gradually to have

---

conceptions of educational psychologists, consult Chaps. v and vi of A.M. Jordan's *Educational Psychology* (4th ed.), New York, Henry Holt and Company, 1956, and Chaps. iii and iv of Lee J. Cronbach's *Educational Psychology*, New York, Harcourt, Brace and Company, 1954.

[6] *Ibid.*, p. 394. Quoted by permission of the Society.
[7] *Ibid.*, p. 395. Quoted by permission of the Society.

a concept of certain important relationships in which the word "house" was used. He might even draw a picture, or several pictures, of a house, and he would see the word "house" spelled and written correctly many times. Eventually the child would write the word "house" correctly; and he would be in almost the same position as the ancient Archimedes, who exclaimed, after he had worked for a long time on a scientific problem, "Eureka!" meaning, "I have found it!" The child would have arrived eventually at an *insight* into the word "house"; the procedure by which he reached it might be termed the "problem-solving" method of learning.

In this type of learning one can easily see the reason for such a device as original problems in mathematics, in sharp contrast to the formal rules and drill work that are used generally with the multiplication table. Problems in social studies, in literature, and in English would be of the same kind. The child is supposed to bring his former experience and all of his resources to bear gradually upon a new problem and to arrive eventually at an insight into the solution of the problem. By this method he is learning new relationships through analytic examination. Learning by insight has been termed by certain German psychologists "configuration," or the *gestalt* theory. If this theory of learning for children is accepted, teachers will understand clearly why certain educational leaders insist upon setting up problems or activities for children to solve.

3. LEARNING AS A CONDITIONED RESPONSE. There seems to be a sound biological basis for belief in this third theory of learning, since the experiments of many psychologists indicate that certain habits can be implanted in children or can be eliminated from them by a *conditioning* process. Learning as a conditioned response rests upon the belief that every response by the human being is occasioned by a stimulus; the stimulus may be a complex group of stimuli or one stimulus, and the results may be almost reflex action or a combination of more complex reactions in the human being. According to this view, the child would acquire a new "stimulus-response" pattern when he learns to say "house" after seeing that word printed on the board or on a card. He has learned something new and he is delighted to repeat it over and over, especially if he is between the ages of four and eight. Observant parents have noticed that a child

repeats a new word over and over in a low tone, out loud, until the word becomes thoroughly fixed in his usage.

A large, open office filled with many clerical employees furnishes a good example of learning through conditioned response in an out-of-school situation. Each employee is working at his own particular task without regard for the noise made by typewriters and machines operated by other persons in the same office. When the new secretary or stenographer goes into that office for her first work experience, it is very annoying to her to try to answer the telephone on her desk and to hear with any degree of clarity the instructions given to her. After an experience of two weeks in the office, that same person will pick up the telephone and hear distinctly every spoken word. Most persons can become conditioned to working under any circumstances in a fairly satisfactory manner. If the teacher accepts this type of learning as possible, he begins to understand why certain children might have a fear of tests or examinations, or why certain children dislike certain noises in the classroom: there may have been in the past history of those children certain situations in which those sounds or those activities were most unpleasant, or unsatisfactory, or fearsome to them.

COMMON FACTORS IN LEARNING.   In each of these proposed theories of learning it should be noted that certain factors are present. There are: (1) motivation or a stimulus to learn, (2) reward or satisfaction when one has learned something, and (3) the neurons which bear impulses to and from the brain and central nervous system in order to produce action.

Of marked significance for curriculum work are the aims or goals of the student. In learning, natural motivation is much more effective than artificial stimulation. Teachers frequently give pupils rewards for learning and punishments for failure to learn. Experiments show that rewards lead to repetition of the response which has been rewarded, but that punishments have little value as a learning stimulus. These results tend to indicate that Thorndike's theory of the satisfaction of the individual with something that he has learned, or pleasure or reward from mastery of it, seems to fit materially into the learning process. At the same time, these results should raise in the mind of the teacher the question whether artificial rewards, such as medals, prizes, and grades, should be used if natural rewards can be used as effectively. In regard to the neurons which conduct stimuli to the central nervous system and reconduct responses back in the form of reactions, it seems safe for the curriculum worker to conclude that every child is a biological organism existing in its own environment or culture, and that he will learn most effectively when he has aims or goals in view. For example, the boy who desires to build a radio learns certain principles of physics through the actual planning and building of that radio set more effectively than he could learn them through routine classroom work.

Economy in Learning. Since teaching is usually done in large groups, it is necessary for the teacher to know that certain principles for economy in learning have been fairly well established by psychological experimentation. The most important of these principles are the following:

1. The more lifelike the learning situation is, the more effective the learning is likely to be. This principle throws into bold relief the difference between teaching isolated subject matter to children and associating this subject matter with specific situations that are lifelike, or that resemble lifelike situations. As an illustration of the application of this principle, schools have developed student-council activities and discussions in which the principles of democratic government are learned at first hand by the students. The fields of social studies and science adapt themselves more easily to this type of lifelike situation than certain other subject-matter areas.

2. Repetition and drill for the complete mastery of new principles or knowledge are more effectively accomplished if the practice of the student is spread over separate intervals instead of concentrated. The teacher's application of this principle calls for many brief tests and drills, rather than one long quiz covering the whole field.

3. The more the student is urged to reproduce consciously what he is memorizing, the better the results will be. That bane of every child's existence, the multiplication table, may be taken as a good example. If the child attempts repeatedly to reproduce the *results* of his memorization of these key numbers, the more rapidly and the more consciously will he master the full implications of memorization of the table.

4. The use of the creative urge within each child is highly efficient in the repetition or the reading of what he has begun to master. Illustrations

of this principle are numerous, from the drawing of pictures of houses, machines, and maps to the use of poetry or music in aspects of drill. Creativeness and learning go hand in hand.

TRANSFER OF TRAINING.   On the transfer aspect of learning there is little agreement among psychologists. Their experiments indicate that transfer does occur frequently, but there is disagreement as to why it takes place under one set of circumstances and not under another. What Dashiell said twenty years ago would still probably get general agreement. He declared:

> . . . a beneficial effect of training in a given school subject upon one's work in learning other subjects resides not in any peculiar and inscrutable potency within the subject matter itelf, nor in any strengthening of the student's power of memory-in-general or attention-in-general or reasoning-in-general; it resides solely in those habits of responding in this or that way to this or that aspect or detail that are common to both situations.[8]

For work in the curriculum it is important to note that conscious effort must be made by the teacher to have such a transfer take place, to have the student notice principles or elements that are identical or common to both situations. Greater transfer will occur also if teaching in each subject is focused on actual living and the present.[9] Unless this is done, teachers cannot hope for much automatic transfer to occur.

INDIVIDUAL DIFFERENCES.   In the praiseworthy attempt to care for the individual differences among school children, two false assumptions have developed. The first of these involves a misconception of common factors in learning. Teachers have been more concerned with those factors which indicate what the *average* accomplishment of the child should be at a specific age and grade level, than with what the child himself can do *in spite* of his handicaps and these factors. The experts in intelligence and achievement testing have

[8] "Contributions to Education of Scientific Knowledge about the Psychology of Learning," Part II, 37th Yearbook, copyright 1938 by the National Society for the Study of Education, *The Scientific Movement in Education*, Public School Publishing Company, p. 401. Quoted by permission of the Society.
[9] *Cf.* L.J. Cronbach, *op. cit.*, Chap. IX, A.M. Jordan, *op. cit.*, Chap. VII, and B.S. Hollingshead, "Is European Education Better?", a reprint by the American Council on Education of an article in the April, 1958, issue of *The Educational Record*, in which he points out clearly that Americans do not accept the idea of the superior discipline of some subjects that are studied over others.

quite properly developed a norm, or the average score that a child should make on each test in comparison with other children of the same age and state of educational progress. Such a test of information is indeed valuable for diagnostic and comparative purposes. But

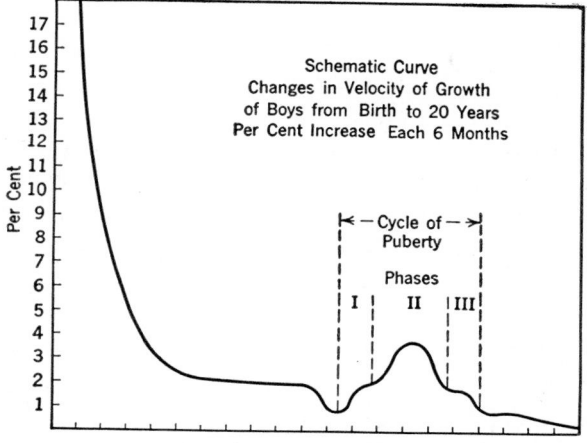

FIG. 8   *We grow faster some times than at others*

Reproduced by permission in enlarged and modified form from *Human Development in Review*, "Patterns of Growth During Adolescence With Implications for School Procedures." Discussion by Lois Hayden Meek of the research findings of Herbert R. Stolz, *Progressive Education*, Vol. XVIII, No. 1, January, 1941, p. 42. This chart and those used in Figures 9, 10, and 11 were prepared by Herbert R. Stolz from data collected at the University of California. Stolz' study was made of approximately 100 boys and 100 girls over a seven-year period, beginning when the children were in the fifth and sixth grades of the Oakland Public Schools. Cf. also Herbert R. Stolz, M.D., "A Condensed Description of the Data and the Findings Concerning Some Physical Aspects of Development," and "An Atlas of Specimen Photographs and Graphs," prepared for the use of the Division of Child Development and Teacher Personnel of the Commission on Teacher Education, American Council on Education. On file, Division of Child Development, University of Chicago and Institute of Child Welfare, University of California.

teachers have interpreted this average as a standard, with the purpose in view of pulling every child up to it if possible. On the other hand, they have not taken into account that these test norms were established in terms of those knowledges and skills which we ourselves have established arbitrarily as standards for ourselves and our children. In short, teachers have frequently used these results to standardize the educational products of the schools, rather than to individualize them. One bad result of this procedure has been the neglect with which the brighter pupils in the schools have been treated; the major effort has been made to pull up to the norm as far as possible those pupils who were duller, or who indicated less capacity according to an intelligence scale. It is unwise for educators to be concerned primarily with the average and subnormal at the expense of the brighter pupils.

The second false assumption that educators have made is found in the widespread practice of making allowance for individual differences in the children in the schools. This procedure is dangerous also. For example, when a student rates no more than 88 on an intelligence scale, the teacher is prone to conclude that he is not capable of passing certain subjects, or of profiting from the study of these subjects. Therefore the student is put to work on other subjects or areas of study that are considered less difficult. Many pupils who are less able mentally have been found to be more able manually or in creative activities such as drawing, the building of machines, and the understanding of human nature and society. One extreme result of the acceptance of this doctrine of making allowance for individual differences has been that many schools insist upon the automatic promotion of pupils from one grade or course to the succeeding grade or class each year, regardless of whether the students have mastered the work or not. It is beside the point to say that much of the teaching and much of the work being done in those grades is not suited to the children involved; the fact remains that allowance is being made for these weaknesses or supposed weaknesses of certain students on the basis of a testing scale which was not established primarily for that purpose. From another angle this practice is likewise questionable, namely, that training in social efficiency may be endangered. An important part of the social efficiency of each individual comes from his successful experiences and his mastery of learning materials in a group of his peers. A child may have an I.Q. of only 88, but he may come from a socioeconomic environment which makes his contribution to his school group potentially rich. The school is losing a real opportunity when it does not capitalize upon the contribution this child can make to the class, and upon the growth he can achieve from mastering normal activities in a group of his peers.

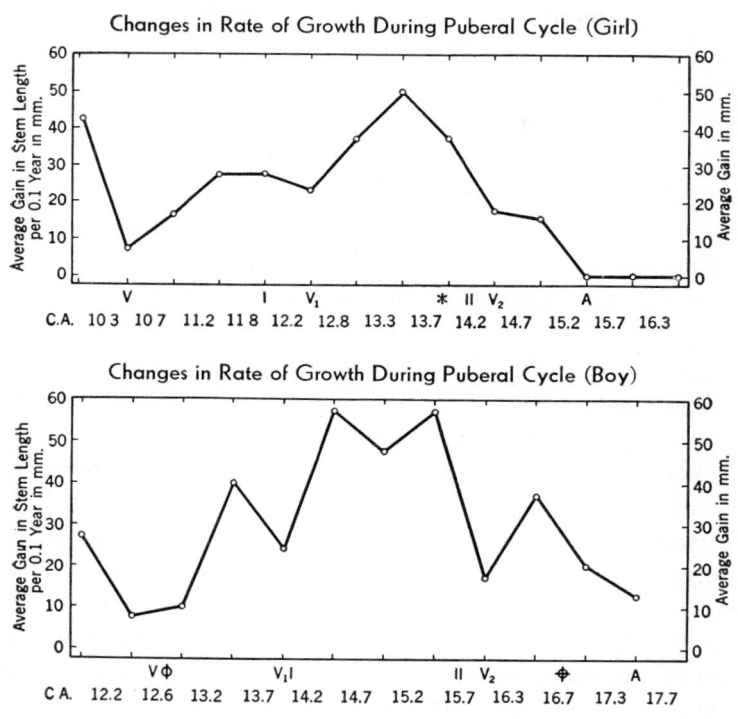

FIG. 9   *We don't grow "all of a piece"*

Reproduced by permission from *Human Development in Review*, "Patterns of Growth During Adolescence With Implications for School Procedures.'" Discussion by Lois Hayden Meek of the research findings of Herbert R. Stolz, *Progressive Education*, Vol. XVIII, No. 1, January, 1941, p. 43. Charts prepared by Herbert R. Stolz, M.D.

NEWER EXPERIMENTS IN CHILD GROWTH AND DEVELOPMENT

A newer trend in the study of individual differences has recently been developing. This trend was well illustrated by the work of the Commissions of the Progressive Education Association during the late thirties, and of Prescott [10] and his group at the University of Chicago in connection with the program of the American Council on Education through its Commission on Teacher Education. Attention is being focused more and more upon the child's *emotions* and the factors that influence his social development; studies have been made both of the physiological development of children and of the influences which the family, the community, the school, the play group, and other social agencies have upon their growth and actions.

Arnold Gesell and his group of experts [11] in child growth at Yale University have studied for many years the following areas of development in the first sixteen years of child life:

1. Motor characteristics, comprising coordination, skill, posture, etc.
2. Adjustive behavior, adjustments which indicate the child's ability to initiate and profit from the past.
3. Language, expression in dramatic forms, in communication, and in comprehension.
4. Personal-social behavior, including the child's reactions to other people, his adaptation to home life, social groups, his peers, property, and the like.

The results of these studies, many of which are available in printed form, give to teachers a fuller realization of the complex and conflicting influences that operate upon the child not only before he enters school, but thereafter. For example, there is the memorable report of the Commission on Teacher Education of the American Council on Education, *Helping Teachers Understand Children.* [12] This report presented detailed descriptions of the individual behavior of numbers of school children, both boys and girls; many of these pupils who were observed were developing into adolescence, a period of child growth which warrants special investigation of the

[10] *Helping Teachers Understand Children,* 1945, and D.A. Prescott's *Emotion and the Educative Process,* 1938, American Council on Education; Caroline B. Zachary's and Margaret Lighty's *Emotion and Conduct in Adolescence,* 1940, D. Appleton-Century Company; and the study by Lois Meek and others, *The Personal-Social Development of Boys and Girls with Implications for Secondary Education,* 1940, Progressive Education Association, Committee on Workshops.

[11] *Youth: The Years from Ten to Sixteen,* 1956, *The Child From Five to Ten,* 1946, and *The First Five Years of Life,* 1940, Harper and Bros., *passim; Biographies of Child Development,* New York, Paul B. Hoeber, Inc., 1939, *passim.*

[12] *Op. cit., passim.*

changes in the emotional and social growth of boys and girls. All of these studies put major emphasis upon giving assistance to the individual pupil in developing satisfactory relations with his play group, with his parents, and with other groups and organizations. If this approach to the revision of the curriculum is taken, the effects on the school curriculum will be significant, especially as teachers come to realize more and more distinctly the needs and the problems which children have.

THE CONTROVERSY OVER THE INTELLIGENCE QUOTIENT. "There are no 'dumb' children, there are merely children with different capacities and different possibilities," says Dr. Edward Liss, pediatrician and psychiatrist; and he adds, "Probably the most abused words in our vocabulary are 'dumb' and 'lazy'." [13] Liss states that a child may be as sick from discouragement or fear as from some physical ailment. In like vein is the following opinion of William H. Brown, a clinical psychologist at the Utah Child Guidance Center, concerning testing for intelligence:

. . . The teacher, through a wise use of the data from standardized tests and with the many opportunities for observation of thinking behavior in daily classroom situations, has an excellent basis for making very sound inferences about the personalities of each of his pupils. From his continuing contacts with each pupil, the teacher can achieve a knowledge and an understanding which will far surpass that obtainable from any test battery no matter how it is administered. With this understanding, the teacher is in the most effective position to bring to realization the intellectual potential of each child.

In spite of their vastly superior position for understanding their pupils, teachers often behave as if they have no such knowledge. They tend to accept the scores or the reports of the psychologist as absolute. The greatest danger in testing programs and procedures, whether group or individual, lies in this tendency of many persons to sanctify intelligence or personality measuring devices. There is nothing sacred or inviolate about any of the business of measuring the intellect of human beings. A score or a report upon a test is something sterile. Grave consequences can stem from accepting mental measurement as the last word. [14]

. . . .

Make the tester prove the score. Insist that he describe the pupil's pat-

[13] *Cf.* Catherine Mackenzie, *Parent and Child,* New York, William Sloane Associates, 1949, p. 254 (reprinted by permission).

[14] William H. Brown, "Behind the Test Score," *Educational Leadership,* 15:162, December, 1957 (reprinted by premission).

tern of intellectual functioning. This understanding of a child's intellectual development, coupled with the teacher's great advantage of daily observations, will enable the teacher to arrive at those rare common sense solutions to many of the learning problems of his pupils.[15]

These striking statements by Liss and Brown point up the continuing controversy over the Intelligence Quotient (I.Q.) of the child. The psychologists are still at variance among themselves concerning the I.Q., one group maintaining that there is a constancy of the I.Q. within rather narrow limits and the other group claiming that intelligence can be educated.[16] In this connection, the reports in the *1940 Yearbook* of the National Society for the Study of Education have marked significance for the curriculum as well as for teaching. Seven of the ten research centers which reported in this *Yearbook* demonstrated that children attending preschool tend to gain in I.Q., while the average gain in I.Q. is not reported in the case of three centers. It is to be noted that these data deal primarily with the nursery or preschool period of training. The studies have shown that a gain in I.Q. resulting from a change in environmental factors is much more likely to take place in the preschool years of a child's life than in the case of the student who is placed in a home of better social and economic circumstances after the ninth or twelfth year of age. Later evidence from longitudinal studies indicates that (1) the gain or loss in I.Q. may be conditioned sharply by the strains and stresses which an individual is experiencing at a particular time, (2) the score is likely to differ considerably from one test to another, as different tests are employed, and (3) some persons continue to develop in intelligence until the fifties or later, a finding at variance with the older

---

[15] *Ibid.,* p. 165 (reprinted by permission). *Cf.* also "What Do Intelligence Tests Test?" by Earl W. Kooker and Chester S. Williams, *The High School Journal,* xxxix (March, 1956), pp. 333–39 and "Don't Fall for the New I.Q. Fad," by J. K. Lagenann, *This Week Magazine,* May 25, 1958, pp. 12, 25.

[16] In addition to the 1940 Yearbook of the National Society for the Study of Education, the following summarize more recent findings: Lee. J. Cronbach, *op. cit.,* Chap. vii; Raymond G. Kuhlen and George G. Thompson (Eds.), *Psychological Studies of Human Development,* New York, Appleton-Century-Crofts, 1952, Chap. v, "Reading," pp. 20–23; A.M. Jordan, *op. cit.,* Chap. xii; and *Review of Educational Research,* xxv (December, 1955), Chap. ii.

concept that the I.Q. begins to decline after the early twenties.[17]
This controversy over whether intelligence is educable is important
to all persons who have to deal with the education of children. Many
of the devices and techniques that have been established in the

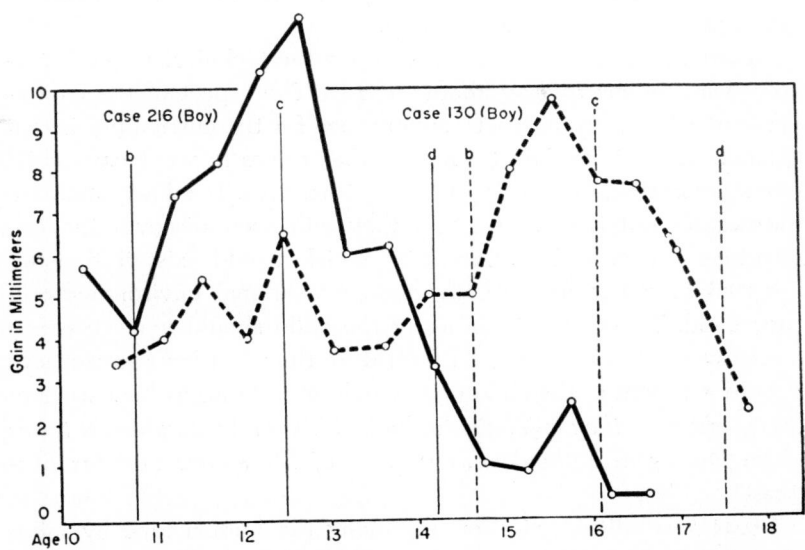

FIG. 10   *We don't all begin at the same time and we don't all end at the
same time*

Height growth curves for two boys, illustrating early and late development.
Case 216 was one of the most precocious in beginning and ending the puberal
growth period. Case 130 was the latest among the 67 cases. (From H.R. Stolz
and L.M. Stolz, *Somatic Development of Adolescent Boys,* Copyright 1951, p.
61. Used with permission of The Macmillan Company.)

school organization in order to take care of certain individual differences which were thought permanent may have to be revised. For
example, homogeneous grouping on the basis of the I.Q. was begun
in order to eliminate the wide range of ability in a school group or

[17] *Cf.* Nancy Bailey, "Consistency and Variability in the Growth of Intelligence
from Birth to Eighteen Years," *Journal of Genetic Psychology,* LXXV (1949), pp.
165–96, and Nancy Bailey and Melita H. Oden, "The Maintenance of Intellectual Ability in Gifted Adults," *Journal of Gerontology,* X (January, 1955), pp.
91–107.

class. In the light of recent experiments, we are now faced with the problem of whether we shall discard such homogeneous grouping or retain it. Whatever differences exist in the average of the hereditary capacities in different socioeconomic groups, such differences seem less than the differences in hereditary capacities known to exist between individuals in the same group.

No attempt is made here to pass upon the technical questions involved in the controversy about the I.Q. The aspect of the controversy which is of tremendous significance for the curriculum is that teachers are being asked to interest themselves in what each child *can do,* rather than in what he *cannot* perform. If educational employees set out from this point, they will soon discover the tremendous educational opportunities which would exist if they attempted to create a more favorable educational environment for each child. These recent studies of the child should make teachers more aware of the fact that in the future they will have to consider the environment of the child of as much importance as his nature or his inheritance; *they will have to think of him and study him in terms of eugenics and euthenics, as well as of his nature and his nurture.*[18]

Great possibilities exist for improving the human race by influences other than those of heredity. Not only is there a lack of information among people generally, especially among parents, concerning what characteristics human beings can inherit; there is also an alarming lack of knowledge among a large proportion of teachers in the schools concerning what is involved in heredity. For instance, few teachers can answer correctly all of the following questions: Can a child inherit tuberculosis? cancer? arthritis? syphilis? polio? Will a child fathered by a man who has been broken in mind inherit insanity? Can a man who becomes a father at sixty transmit to his child the same characteristics which he could transmit to him if he had become his father at the age of twenty? Such questions raise the larger question of whether teachers as well as parents should have a simple course in eugenics. If one is to believe the evidence in articles appearing from time to time in popular periodicals,

[18] *Cf.* Ruth Strang, *An Introduction to Child Study* (3rd ed.), The Macmillan Company, 1951, Chap. III.

the public is becoming somewhat concerned about these controversies over the *nature* and the *nurture* of the child.[19]

Compulsory education has recently brought into the school for a longer period of time many children who formerly remained in

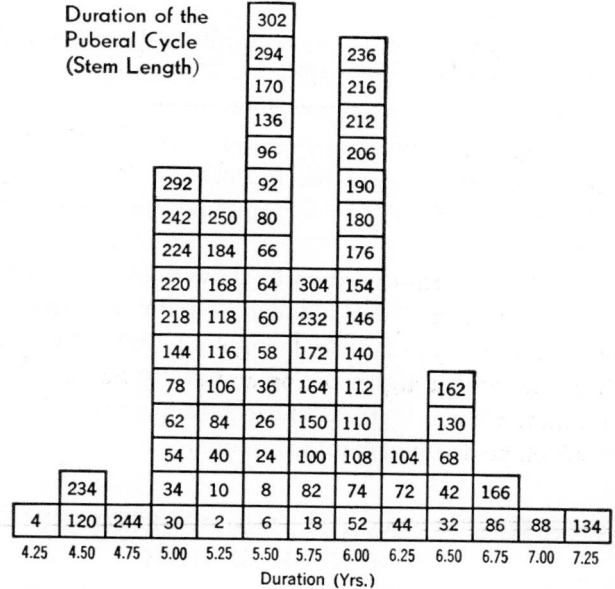

FIG. 11   *One may be a little boy with a little boy's interests; another may be thinking and feeling like a man; all in the same classroom*

The numbers in squares are identification numbers of individual cases. (Reproduced by permission from *Human Development in Review*, "Patterns of Growth During Adolescence With Implications for School Procedures." Discussion by Lois Hayden Meek of the research findings of Herbert R. Stolz, *Progressive Education*, Vol. XVIII, No. 1, January, 1941, p. 44. Chart prepared by Herbert R. Stolz, M.D.)

school for only a few years. This large and heterogeneous group embraces wide ranges in stages of growth, native ability, and scholastic accomplishment. Faced with this problem, school administrators

[19] As samples, *cf.* Catherine Mackenzie, *op. cit.*, and her weekly page in the *New York Times;* in *Good Housekeeping*, J.L. Block, "What I.Q. Means" (August, 1945), pp. 41, 68, 70; and J. Roswell Gallagher, "Why Boys Fail," *The Atlantic Monthly*, vol. 185, No. 5 (May, 1950), pp. 49–52.

have used every means at their disposal to offer better educational opportunities to all children. The measurement facilities of the educational experts were at hand for use, and the administrators are not to be blamed if they have used these devices in attempting to solve this major problem. In the light of recent psychological experiments, however, school employees should put more emphasis in the future upon the use of tests of intelligence and achievement for the purposes of diagnosis, prognosis, and placement, rather than for the purpose of attempting to segregate children in order to make them reach the average of achievement. Not to be overlooked is the proper use which should be made of the newer techniques of testing in evaluating the work of the teacher and the outcomes of the curriculum.

In general, it is doubtful wisdom to show the child's score on his intelligence test to him.[20] No influence on the sensitive, growing child can be more harmful than being told that he is dull. Conversely, the child with a high score on an intelligence test frequently uses his reputation for brightness to excuse any undesirable traits he may have which he does not want to eliminate.

TEACHER BEHAVIOR AND DEVELOPMENT AND MENTAL HEALTH

This section would not be complete without some notice of the unpredictable behavior of teachers, as well as of children. In the past, teachers have spent much time attempting to understand the behavior of children, whereas they themselves were just as unpredictable in their behavior and in many respects just as unreasonable. What are our own attitudes as teachers? Are we intolerant? Are we narrow and bigoted? What are our habits? Are they such in their entirety as we would like to have our pupils imitate? What about our educational practices? Do we feel that we know what is good for the child, regardless of what his background, his problems, and his

[20] Pullias, E.V., "Should an Individual Know His Own I.Q.? A Mental Health Problem," *Elementary School Journal*, XL (December, 1939), pp. 277–83; Robert L. Ebel, "Using Tests for Evaluation," *The National Elementary Principal* XXXV (December, 1955), pp. 29–31, 35; and William M. Brown, *op. cit.*, pp. 161–65.

interests are? Do we sometimes think that his needs are those we *believe* he should have, instead of those he *actually* has? How many teachers have stood a mental test within the last ten years? If so, were they allowed to know the findings? If they learned what marks they made upon that test, did it affect them in any way? Such questions as these are pertinent when the teacher considers tests and measurements for the children under his charge.

From all the evidence available, to distinguish between the influence of the teacher's personality and that of his method is impossible.[21] "Style is the man." It is just as true that the ranks of teachers contain individuals who are unstable in personality as it is true that there has been no effort to organize and administer schools in a way to help teachers to make the most satisfactory personal adjustments in life.

The maladjustments of teachers have a real and inescapable effect upon pupils. Their fears, loves, likes, dislikes and hates, jealousies, prejudices, and ambitions will be reflected in the behavior of their pupils. Teachers are more prone to respond promptly and with severity to the aggressive action of children than they are to the timid, withdrawing attitude of pupils who may be even more maladjusted. A critical attitude on the part of each teacher toward himself in and out of the classroom will aid him in the acquisition and maintenance of better mental health. Only through his own wholesome mental hygiene can the teacher be of real service to pupils in attaining well-balanced mental health.

The ideal teacher should be a well-adjusted, healthy, tolerant person with a broad background, well-rounded interests, excellent training, and a happy emotional and intellectual life. While teachers are working toward this ideal for themselves, they will find a simple device, such as a check-sheet in regard to pupil growth and development, of great value to them in their curricular approach; such a check-sheet is shown in Table 11.

As the teacher studies his record of John White's development to date, he cannot but be struck with certain items which seem con-

[21] *The Teacher and Society,* 1st Yearbook of the John Dewey Society, New York, D. Appleton-Century Company, 1937, Chap. iv; and *The Teacher's Role in American Society,* 14th Yearbook, edited by L.J. Stiles, New York, Harper and Brothers, 1957, Parts i and ii.

TABLE 11   Individual growth and adjustment check-sheet

(Based on Teacher's Impersonal Observation and Study)

January 7, 1959	*7th*	*White, John*
(Date)	(Grade or Class)	(Name of Pupil)

ASSETS	LIABILITIES
Cheerful	Overgrown
Truthful	Awkward
Possesses qualities of leadership	Shy
Interested in building model airplanes	Unwashed and careless in dress
Courteous	Prone to resent the leadership of others
Shows no racial or social prejudices	Not always fair in play—prone to take advantage
Ambitious	
Much interested in reading in many areas	Prone to put tasks off to the last minute
Prone to like "the center of the stage"	Shows lack of cooperation in group and class activities
Fair in physical and athletic activities	Full of good excuses for lack of performance of work
Possesses sound health and good ability	
Of good family with good social-economic status	

tradictory. For example, why is John shy, and yet desirous of holding the center of the stage? Careful thought and continued study may show that these are complementary, not contradictory, characteristics. From these written observations, as impartial as he can make them, with conscious and continuous effort to omit all of his prejudices and preconceived opinions about John, the teacher is now in a position to use this significant information in helping John to adjust himself more rapidly and satisfactorily to his curricular work. In at least the following ways, the instructor can approach John with high hopes of success: (1) through his airplane hobby; (2) through his interest in reading; (3) through his ambitions; (4) through his inconsistency in being *truthful,* and yet at times being *unfair in play.*

In the long run, there is no effective substitute for the teacher's knowledge of child growth and behavior. The teacher may be well trained, enthusiastic about his work, and desirous of helping children in their development; but without constant enlargement of his knowledge of how children grow—physically, mentally, and emotionally —he cannot be as successful a teacher as he should be.

PROBLEMS FOR INDIVIDUAL STUDY AND CLASS DISCUSSION

1. What are the effects of rewards and punishments on learning? Which is more effective? Support your position.

2. What real difference is there to you between the trial-and-error learning principle and learning through conditioned response?

3. What behavior patterns are typical of the pupil of eight years of age? Ten? Of the adolescent at thirteen years? At sixteen years?

4. How would you go about compiling a list of the emotional characteristics of a normal high-school boy of fourteen years of age? Or of a high-school girl of fourteen years of age? Of what value would such a list be to you in your curricular work?

5. Can you present a practical illustration of a lifelike learning situation in the elementary school? In the secondary school?

6. Would the study of Latin in the secondary school enable a student to spell more accurately those English words of Latin origin? Give reasons for your stand on this aspect of the transfer of training.

7. What I.Q. is considered average, or the norm for all children? Why?

8. Is homogeneous grouping of pupils on the elementary-school level a primary factor in improvement of the curriculum? On the secondary-school level? Give reasons for your answer.

9. Which of your beliefs about the growth and development of children did you modify after reading Baruch's *How to Live with Your Teenager,* Cutts' and Moseley's *Better Home Discipline,* Gesell's *Youth: The Years from Ten to Sixteen,* Hymes' *Understanding Your Child,* or Prescott's *The Child in the Educative Process?*

10. Should parents be told their child's score on an intelligence test? Why? Should the pupil himself be told his score? Support your position.

11. Why might marked improvement in the social and economic environment of a child tend to improve his I.Q.?

12. Make two lists, one containing those diseases and physical defects that a child can inherit, and another containing those he cannot inherit.

13. What factors might cause an adult to continue to develop in intelligence? Why?

14. Would cumulative records of scholastic achievement be fairer

standards by which to estimate the general mental ability of a pupil than an intelligence test? Defend your position.

15. Do you know of any standards, or can you formulate any, whereby you as a teacher might discover the needs of your pupils, instead of believing that you know or guessing at what those needs are?

ADDITIONAL ANNOTATED REFERENCES
FOR PROBLEM OR UNIT STUDY

Almy, M., *Child Development*, New York, Henry Holt and Company, 1955.
  Actual descriptions of child behavior, case studies, through succeeding age periods of six young people from birth to eighteen years of age.
Association for Supervision and Curriculum Development, N.E.A., Washington.
  Fostering Mental Health in Our Schools. 1950 yearbook, devoted to children's problems of mental health in the total process of growth and development.
Baruch, D.W., *How to Live with Your Teenager*, New York, McGraw-Hill Book Company, 1953.
  A companion volume to her *New Ways in Discipline*, this authority in the field presents case histories and anecdotes from real life, emphasizing understanding between parent and child.
Beck, R.H., *et al.*, *Curriculum in the Modern Elementary School*, New York, Prentice-Hall, 1953.
  Part I presents the practical implications of research in the curriculum on the motivation, personality, and learning of children.
Bernard, H.W., *Psychology of Learning and Teaching*, New York, McGraw-Hill Book Company, 1954.
  Parts II and III present learning and the nature of the learner in a psychology oriented in social groupings.
Blair, A.W., and Burton, W.H., *Growth and Development of the Preadolescent*, New York, Appleton-Century-Crofts, 1951.
  A compilation and critical analysis of research in the neglected field of the psychology of the preadolescent.
Britton, E.C., and Winans, J.M., *Growing from Infancy to Adulthood*, New York, Appleton-Century-Crofts, 1958.
  A summary of the changing characteristics of children and youth.
Cunningham, R., New York, Teachers College, Columbia University, *The Importance of People*, 1957, expresses the concern that we should have for the people who work with children in our schools. *Understanding Group Behavior of Boys and Girls* (with Associates, 1951) gives many illustrations of how to work effectively with children in group situations.

Cutts, N.E., and Moseley, N., *Better Home Discipline*, New York, Appleton-Century-Crofts, 1952.

A survey of home discipline in 6,000 families, giving *verbatim* parents' experiences in disciplining children.

Eye, G.G., and Lane, W.R., *The New Teacher Comes to School*, New York, Harper and Brothers, 1956.

The peculiar problems, special needs, and self-analysis of the new teacher are found in Chapters ii, iii, and ix.

Havighurst, R.J., *Human Development and Education*, New York, Longmans, Green and Company, 1953.

"Developmental tasks" concept of educational tasks of early childhood, of middle childhood, of adolescence, and of adulthood and old age, including longitudinal studies of tasks of youth from 10 to 16 years of age.

————, and Neugarten, B.L., *Society and Education*, Boston, Allyn and Bacon, 1957.

The teacher as the crucial person in the interaction between child, society, and the school is presented in Part Four, with the social origins of the teacher, his roles, and his career.

Hilgard, E.R., *Theories of Learning* (2nd ed.), New York, Appleton-Century-Crofts, 1956.

Presents each of the major learning theories—connectionism, conditioning, systematic behavior, sign learning, gestalt, field theory, psychodynamics, and functionalism.

Hurlock, E.B., *Child Development* (3rd ed.), New York, McGraw-Hill Book Company, 1956.

The development of the normal child and the role culture plays in it.

Hymes, J.L., Jr., *Understanding Your Child*, New York, Prentice-Hall, 1952.

Four big ideas about dealing with youngsters—children grow, there is a plan to the way they grow, they want things out of life, and there is some reason why. Primarily for parents, but most valuable for teachers.

Jersild, A.T., *In Search of Self*, New York, Teachers College, Columbia University, 1952.

Young people described what they liked and disliked about themselves, contrasted with what the teachers thought they would say—with interesting results.

Jones, H.E., *et al.*, *Development in Adolescence*, New York, D. Appleton-Century Company, 1943.

One of the first case histories of a youth over a period of years (Longitudinal Study).

Kuhlen, R.G., *The Psychology of Adolescent Development*, New York, Harper and Brothers, 1952.

Has adolescence been a phase of growth and development much overemphasized? Is it unusually "stressful," or not? Or are its developmental problems typical of those that occur in the second decade of life? A view of biological change in a cultural context.

Lieberman, M., *Education as a Profession,* Englewood Cliffs, Prentice-Hall, 1956.

A clear presentation of teachers and their characteristics and their economic and their occupational status in Chapters VIII, XII, and XIV.

Morse, W.C., and Wingo, G.M., *Psychology and Teaching,* Chicago, Scott, Foresman and Company, 1955.

A classroom-centered description of psychology and how it affects teaching, full of shorter case studies, well written.

National Society for the Study of Education, Chicago, University of Chicago Press:

Mental Health in Modern Education, 54th Yearbook, Part II, presents the facts concerning mental health coming of age in education, and its significance for improving classroom methods and practices.

Prescott, D.A., *The Child in the Educative Process,* New York, McGraw-Hill Book Company, 1957.

Report on sixteen years of experimentation with ways to help teachers to attain an adequate understanding of individual children in the classroom. Rich source of examples of case studies, impersonally recorded.

Redl, F., and Wattenberg, W.W., *Mental Hygiene in Teaching,* New York, Harcourt, Brace and Company, 1951.

The influence of the personality of the teacher, principles of mental health essential to creative teaching, how the teacher can come to understand his own limitations, along with vivid case data.

Strang, R., *The Adolescent Views Himself,* New York, McGraw-Hill Book Company, 1957.

How youth see themselves, their world, and growing up through youth's own statements of their attitudes, values, activities and relationships.

Stratemeyer, F.B., *et al., Developing a Curriculum for Modern Living* (2nd ed.), New York, Teachers College, Columbia University, 1957. An attempt to base the curriculum on the needs of children in our society, centered around the "persistent life situations" concept; pp. 51–332 are pertinent here.

Terman, L.M., and Oden, M.H., *et al., The Gifted Child Grows Up,* Vol. IV, Genetic Studies of Genius, Stanford University Press, 1947.

The famous twenty-five-year follow-up study of a superior group.

Yauch, W.A., *et al., The Beginning Teacher,* New York, Henry Holt and Company, 1955.

Chapters II, IX, XI, and XVI present characteristics and qualifications of well-balanced teachers.

CHAPTER 4 Sociological and economic factors in curriculum work

BASIC AGENCIES IN THE EDUCATIVE PROCESS

Education is much more comprehensive than the skills, attitudes, and knowledges which are attained in the school. In the educative process, five agencies other than the school make major contributions to the growth and development of the school child. Influence is brought to bear in different ways and with great force by (1) the family, (2) the church, (3) the play group, (4) economic agencies, and (5) noncommercial community agencies. The cumulative impacts upon the child of these five areas of social, economic, and religious life leave imprints which must be carefully considered in the formulation of the curriculum.

1. THE FAMILY. The home is still the main institution affecting the life and growth of the child. In the Maryland study almost one-third of the youth between the ages of sixteen and twenty-four came from broken homes.[1] The North Carolina study of 45,000 children from the ages of six to twenty-four showed that one-fourth of the white youth and slightly less than one-half of the Negro youth came from homes broken by death, separation, or divorce.[2] Later large-scale studies of youth show about the same situation.[3] This disrup-

---

[1] Cf. H.M. Bell, *Youth Tell Their Story: A Study of the Conditions and Attitudes of Young People in Maryland Between the Ages of 16 and 24*, American Council on Education, 1938, pp. 19–20.

[2] Gordon W. Lovejoy (coordinator), *Paths to Maturity: Findings of the North Carolina Youth Survey*, 1938–1940; Cooperative Personnel Study, University of North Carolina, 1940, p. 25 (mimeographed).

[3] For example, read A.B. Hollingsworth, *Elmtown's Youth: The Impact of Social Classes on Adolescents*, New York, John Wiley and Sons, 1949, and W.L. Warner *et al.*, *Social Class in America*, Chicago, Science Research Associates, 1949.

85

tion of normal family life could account for a large part of the mal-adjustment among children of all ages.

A study of the family at close range reveals much information for a more complete and sympathetic understanding of children. From the child's earliest age a feeling of "oneness," of identification with the family group, is naturally instilled; even before he begins the first grade of school many of his patterns of living, of conduct, of emotions and attitudes, and of ideals are already set.[4] In one family, swift and sure obedience is absolutely required; in another home it is understood that the occupation of the son or the daughter shall be decided by the parents; in still another family, the child is taught "to be seen and not heard"; and in still another, much freedom and choice may be permitted the child. Neatness and cleanliness in the home are likely to be reflected in the appearance and dress of the child; and the language habits of the parents appear in marked form in their children. Respect for and obedience to adults, respect for the property and rights of others, race prejudice, social stratification—these are but a few of the *mores* and attitudes which the child absorbs more frequently and fundamentally outside school walls than within them.

The studies of Hartshorne and May[5] illustrate well some of the influences of the home which contribute to the development of character. Brown and Havighurst and Neugarten[6] show clearly some of the types of home training which cause friction between parents and children. As boys and girls grow older, friction is especially likely to arise between parents and adolescents because the training which the adolescent has received in the family begins to clash with the customs of the "gang" or of the community.

The American family is changing in its size, its stability, and its

---

[4] Cf. Arnold Gesell, *et al.*, *The First Five Years of Life*, 1940, and *Studies in Child Development*, 1948, New York, Harper and Brothers, *passim*.

[5] H. Hartshorne, and M.A. May, *et al.*, *Studies in the Nature of Character: I, Studies in Deceit*, 1928; *II, Studies in Service and Self-Control*, 1929; *III, Studies in the Organization of Character*, 1930; New York, The Macmillan Company.

[6] F.J. Brown, *Educational Sociology* (2nd ed.), 1954, Chaps. ix, x, and *Sociology of Childhood*, 1939, pp. 107–56, New York, Prentice-Hall; R.J. Havighurst and B.L. Neugarten, *Society and Education*, Boston, Allyn and Bacon, 1957, Chaps. i, iv and v.

FIG. 12   *The summer camp for children*

An important educational agency which seeks to recreate the atmosphere of the home. (*Courtesy Gay Valley, Mary Gwynn's Camp, Brevard, N.C.*)

neighborhood culture. The school cannot take the place of the family and is not expected to do so. But how can the *mores,* the traditions, the training, and the ideals of the family be used effectively in dealing with children and their problems? There is [7] a growing emphasis in the schools upon the family and the child's relation to it. In this connection one is prone to wonder whether an individual's happiness in adult life is conditioned to a great extent by a happy, homey, congenial, understanding atmosphere in the family in which he was reared. Such factors as the type of punishment the child receives at home, and the strength or weakness of the affection he has for his parents, may be the key to an understanding of the child's reactions toward his teachers in school.

Sumner distinguished between two classes of customs which regulate human behavior; (1) the *folkways,* which he designated as the simple customs; and (2) the *mores,* which he designated as customs that are established for the group welfare and are supported by strong group agreement.[8] Now we have Odum's *techniways;* this term is used to describe ways in which the modern world reflects the technical and non-folk. For example, the use of electrical devices or switches is a techniway. Any of our ways or customs of doing things which have been developed through technology are techniways.[9] If these three definitions are accepted, individuals formulate what is right and wrong primarily in terms of the customs of the group to which they happen to belong. Children are constantly learning new things about the *mores.* In order to lead a normal life, they must learn how to live within these *mores* or how to make satisfactory adjustments to them.

The task of the teacher as a counselor to the child who is making adjustments to the *mores* is made more difficult because of the fact that the *mores* change constantly. Witness the changes in public opinion about the use of alcoholic liquors, and about the use of tobacco by women! Consider the remarkable difference in public

[7] *Cf. Family Life Sourcebook* by Oliver E. Byrd, Stanford, Stanford University Press, 1956, a collection of 400 articles from 1945-55 on family life education.

[8] Willard Waller, "Counseling and the Mores," *Journal of the National Association of Deans of Women,* III (January, 1940), pp. 51-54.

[9] H.W. Odum, *The Way of the South,* New York, The Macmillan Company, 1947, pp. 54, 73, 274.

opinion now about mental illness.[10] Look at the shift in public opinion about divorce! How many parents or teachers realize how divorce affects the social and emotional growth of the child? When a child has lost one parent by death, it is difficult enough for him to make all of the necessary adjustments without a normal family life. How much more difficult is it for him to make those adjustments when he is emotionally upset and continually troubled by the fact that his parents are divorced or separated, although both are still alive? Another striking illustration of how the *mores* change can be drawn from the customs of courtship as contrasted with the code of the past. Formal introductions are no longer necessary, and petting on dates is a general practice. No longer does the young gentleman have to pay all the expenses of the date; formal chaperones are no longer required; and it is much more common for the couple to go out for their amusement than for them to spend the evening at home.

More attention is now being devoted in the schools to aspects of the home and of family life. Courses in homemaking are found frequently on both the secondary-school and the collegiate levels, and courses in marriage and family relationships and in sex education are given on both levels. In the curriculum of the secondary school, new courses in "social living" and "social problems" are often centered around family life.

2. THE CHURCH. More than 250 denominations in the United States exert a large influence upon the homes and the children in the homes of the nation. Each of twenty-four of these denominations has as many as 200,000 members or more. Most churches have subsidiary organizations for young people.

Hartshorne and May's study [11] still provides the most exhaustive research on how "right conduct" in use is correlated with religious ideas and attitudes. The indoctrination of children in a religion does not necessarily result in a significant increase in their approved behavior. From an early age, most children come in contact with a social institution, the Church, which tends to require group action of a certain pattern in regard to personal attitudes, beliefs, wishes, and

---

[10] *Mental Health in Modern Education*, 54th Yearbook of the National Society for the Study of Education, Part II, Chicago, 1955, Chaps. I–IV.
[11] *Studies in the Organization of Character, op. cit.*

aspirations. Adolescents are especially troubled by problems of church authority, concepts of God, and ideas of Sabbath observance. If their parents are of different religious faiths, they are likely to be troubled over this difference.

Beginning as early as the age of two, the child acquires from his church and his parents certain ideas of God, of spiritual rewards and punishments, of moral right and wrong. He usually accepts these concepts with unquestioning faith until he approaches the adolescent period of life, which is youth's time for challenging everything. The loss of relatives and dear friends, changes in social environment, the sight of injustice or needless suffering—all these are causes for more or less inner conflict in most youth during the adolescent period of life. Perhaps cooperative experience, the mixed groups of society, community contacts, religious education, and parent education can help the adolescent even more than the schools to make satisfactory adjustments in his spiritual and religious life. But the teacher must understand the influence of the church on the child, and he must be prepared to help the child in those adjustments which relate to the church and its moral standards.

3. THE PLAY GROUP. During the adolescent period, the play group is more frequently termed the "group of peers," the "gang," or the "activity group." Before reaching the age when pubertal changes begin to work within him, the child is as likely to be loyal to his family, his church, or his school as to his gang. On the other hand, the secondary-school student is more likely to be loyal to his play group than to any other group. That group demands loyalty of him; it constitutes part of an unwritten code which is not violated with impunity. The imaginative, interest-shifting, neighborhood play group of early childhood was based primarily on *individual activity.* The gang of the adolescent has its own sense of unity, based on *cooperative* activity, through which the club or gang itself becomes the basis for the conduct of each member as well as the very motivation of the organization. Certain standards and activities for the adolescent are definitely fixed and rigidly required. Obedience to these gang rules is of paramount importance, and punishment is swift for the offender.

Conflicts arise among adolescents in these groups or gangs. The following main types of conflict emerge from time to time: (1) conflict in the group itself; (2) conflict between the group and other groups; (3) conflict with organized agencies of authority, such as the home, the church, and the police.[12] Through these conflicts the growing child seeks escape from a restricted home environment, the routine of everyday life, or the authority of agencies which he thinks are too cramping or dominant. Why is the "tattletale" ostracized? Why will a girl of a poor family steal to treat her friends? Why does a boy try his first cigarette or his first drink of liquor? In whom does the boy or girl confide? If the teacher can obtain satisfactory answers to such questions as these, he will have a better understanding of the problems of children in general and of adolescents in particular. The teacher must remember always that each of a child's problems is of tremendous size and perplexity to him.

4. SIGNIFICANT ECONOMIC INFLUENCES. *Child Labor.* There has been more than a half century [13] of strife over the movement to eliminate labor harmful to the child in industrial and economic life. The depression of the 1930's operated to give fresh impetus to the several states in their efforts to prevent children from taking part in industry before a reasonable age is reached. As more and more state laws were enacted to prevent the child from beginning work before the ages of sixteen or eighteen, more and more were the schools and other agencies of society supposed to help care for these children until they reached the legal age for entering industry.

As well-meaning as the labor unions are in their effort to raise the legal age at which youth can enter industry, some of the results of this policy of compulsory legislation are alarming. While the unions have labored strenuously to protect the health and growth of youth and to make more jobs available for adults who really need work in order to support their families, two aspects of the complex problem have been almost entirely overlooked. In the first place, neither the schools, the homes, nor other community agencies are now in a position to continue to train youth between the ages of sixteen and twenty in profitable ways, if youth are not allowed by law to enter

[12] R.J. Havighurst and B.L. Neugarten, *op. cit.*, Chap. v.
[13] *Labor and Education, A Brief Outline of the Resolutions and Pronouncements of the American Federation of Labor . . . from 1881–1938*, American Federation of Labor, 1939, *passim*.

industry when they finish school. Few types of apprenticeship have been established which are acceptable both to labor and to industry, and which gradually induct youth into profitable employment after they have finished their school careers. At the present time the main courses of this kind which the schools have developed have been "diversified occupations," "distributive education," and similar part-time "work programs." [14]

The second aspect of this complex problem of the legal age at which a youth can begin his life work is involved with the question of whether a person who has done no work until he is eighteen years of age will ever do any work satisfactorily. From the age of five or six, every child has as one of his ambitions the earning of some money entirely his own. If this ambition is thwarted in the child, if no opportunity or training in economic independence is given to him, his energy and his ambitions are liable to be turned in other and much less desirable directions. Each year in America over two and a quarter million arrests are made for major offenses. Of those arrested, about 47 per cent are persons under eighteen years of age. The Federal Bureau of Investigation reports that juvenile crime has increased steadily since 1950, much more in proportion than the juvenile population increase in the ages between ten and seventeen years.

Child labor decreased sharply during the operation of the National Recovery Act (1933–1935), while employment of adults showed an upward trend during the same period. Today the United States through its Social Security Act (1935) has the problem of unemployment insurance on both a national and state scale as a factor complicating the induction of youth into labor. It is doubtful whether the state should exert its protective rights over the child at the risk of developing in him habits of laziness and a dislike for real work. Consider the fact that over a million and a half boys and girls between fourteen and seventeen are usually both enrolled in school and also employed on a part-time basis. If apprenticeship composed of part-time school in conjunction with part-time work is to be one of the

[14] K.B. Haas, *Distributive Education: Organization and Administration,* United States Office of Education, Vocational Division, *Bulletin No. 211,* 1940; C.E. Rakestraw, *Training High-School Youth for Employment,* Chicago, American Technical Society, 1947; and W.H. Ivins and W.B. Runge, *Work Experience In High School,* New York, The Ronald Press Company, 1951.

satisfactory solutions for this problem of child labor, curriculum employees in the schools have their task well defined for them for the next few years. The Federal Fair Labor Standards Act (1938) limited hours of labor and established minimum standards of pay for workers in various fields. If children between the ages of fifteen and eighteen are to be inducted gradually into a vocation, better arrangements will have to be made whereby their wages and hours will be in conformity with the regulations of this act and will be agreeable both to labor and to industry. Unless community agencies and the schools work together on this vital question, youth behavior problems will undoubtedly tend to increase because of conflicts with the law when young people cannot make proper adjustments to their work environment and work world.[15]

Juvenile Delinquency. Child welfare has come to be recognized as the responsibility of the state. Much of the legislation placed upon the statute books concerning the welfare of children has been of a *corrective* nature, rather than of a *preventive* nature, as it should have been. Not only should local welfare officers be concerned with juvenile delinquency and relief; they should also make it their responsibility to attempt by proper organization to prevent children from coming to grips with the law later in life. Such prevention cannot be accomplished by one agency alone; it can only be accomplished by all social agencies working together for a common purpose. When youth is given hope, an opportunity to go forward to make a living for himself, and a chance to establish himself in the eyes of his comrades and his community, the so-called problems of youth usually take care of themselves.

The negative approach to the solution of youth's problems is to bemoan youth's delinquencies after they have occurred; to excuse them for their wrongdoing, to "bail them out" or "buy them out" of trouble by paying their fines. The frequent result of this approach is the development in youth of a defensive or combative attitude toward adult help in solving their problems, or reliance upon the

---

[15] *Cf.* E.L. Cohen and L. Rosenblum, "Are Jobs the Answer to Delinquency?" *School and Society,* 86 (May 10, 1958), pp. 215–16; M.R. Katz, "No Time for Youth," NEA Journal, xlvi (November, 1957), pp. 531–32, and W.G. Katz, "Let's Allow Our Teen-Agers to Work," *The Reader's Digest,* Vol. 68, No. 405 (January, 1956), pp. 71–74.

leniency of adults and judges in making allowance for their mis-
deeds. The positive approach is to sit down with youth and plan intelligently for the future. He needs to be shown his responsibilities
that accompany his freedoms, the rewards that will come to him
from right conduct and the punishments that society eventually
metes out to those who disregard or flout its customs and its laws.
Youth must be helped as well as disciplined. The strongest single
deterrent of juvenile delinquency is the sureness and the swiftness
of justice, not the severity of the punishment.[16]

5. NONCOMMERCIAL COMMUNITY AGENCIES. A multitudinous
number of community agencies operate to influence and condition
the school child. In this connection there come to mind, first of all,
the service clubs, e.g., Rotary, Kiwanis, Civitan, and Lions. A second
type of organization includes quasi-school agencies such as Parent-
Teacher Associations, the Junior Red Cross, the Tuberculosis Seal
organization, and the Hi-Y and Tri-Hi-Y Clubs. A third type comprises such groups as the American Legion and the American Legion
Auxiliary, the community club, the garden club, book clubs, united
community services, and the Junior Chamber of Commerce. Some
of these organizations are local, others national, in character; among
those of national prominence are Boy and Girl Scouts, Camp Fire
Girls, 4-H clubs and the Red Cross. A fourth kind of organization
might be classed as that which is supported by a particular church
or social group, such as the Baptist Student Union, the community

---

[16] There is disagreement as to the schools' responsibility for combating
juvenile delinquency, and its relation to discipline in the school. Representative
samples of the differences of opinion are found in the following: Ruth Doyle,
"What Nobody Knows about Juvenile Delinquency," *Harper's Magazine*, Vol.
213 (August, 1956), pp. 47–50; Louise E. Goeden, "You Can Hurt Them with
Happiness," *The American Legion Magazine*, January, 1957, pp. 22–23, 45–47;
Robert J. Havighurst, "The Functions of Successful Discipline," *Understanding
the Child*, xxi (April, 1952), pp. 35–38; J. Edgar Hoover, "Punish the Parent?"
The Rotarian, October, 1956, pp. 24–26; Joseph D. Lohman, "A Sociologist-
Sheriff Speaks out about Juvenile Delinquency," *Phi Delta Kappan*, xxxix
(February, 1958), pp. 206–14; Gertrude Samuels, "Youths Who Don't Make
Headlines," *The New York Times Magazine*, June 23, 1957, pp. 16–18; Sybil K.
Richardson's revision of *Discipline for Today's Children and Youth* by G.V.
Sheviakov and F. Redl, Association for Supervision and Curriculum Develop-
ment, 1956, *passim;* "Teacher Opinion on Pupil Behavior, 1955–56," *NEA Re-
search Bulletin*, Vol. xxxiv, No. 2 (April, 1956), *passim;* and William Van Til,
"Combating Juvenile Delinquency through Schools," *Educational Leadership*,
xiv (March, 1956), pp. 362–67.

theater, and dance clubs. All of these agencies contribute to and affect the lives of various children from the time they enter school until they finish. Proper connection must be made by the curriculum worker with these agencies as they can be used and as they are needed in his work.

Leisure-time Agencies

Leisure-time agencies are of two kinds, *commercial* and *noncommercial*. The chief difference between them is that the commercial agency is run for gain or profit, and the noncommercial agency is not. Under the head of commercial agencies come the screen, the radio, television, children's literature, private camps for children, dramatic and musical entertainments of many kinds, and newsstand publications. Noncommercial leisure-time agencies include libraries and museums, community theater groups, social group organizations such as dance and card clubs, community recreation centers and groups, and youth-serving organizations of both a governmental and nongovernmental character.

COMMERCIAL TYPES

1. THE SOUND PICTURE AND TELEVISION. The distinctive impact of the talking picture upon the boy and girl of school age is just beginning to be realized by educators. The changes in the types of pictures produced from 1920 through 1957 are shown in Table 12.

Which of these types of pictures are suitable for small children? For adolescents? What trends are discernible, and are the trends healthy? How many pictures does the child in the elementary school see each week, and how many should he see? What about the high-school child? Does the movie industry or the television industry establish any standards to determine which pictures are suitable for children? Do other organizations formulate such standards? How much of what a child sees and hears in a picture does he remember? What learning possibilities are there in pictures? Do children tend to accept as true, information which is sometimes false? Are there "locality" differences, that is, will children from one neighborhood observe and remember certain items in a sound picture which were unnoticed by children from another neighborhood? What educational film services are available? Are sound picture machines and television sets for schools "sound" investments?

TABLE 12   Changes in types of moving pictures, 1920–1957 [1]

Type of Picture	Percentage of Output			
	1920	1935	1947	1957
Crime	24.0	14.4	10.0	9.6
Sex	13.0	5.6	—	—
Love	44.6	34.0	8.1	10.3
Mystery	3.2	13.0	10.1	8.0
War	2.0	2.4	0.7	5.5
Children	0.4	3.0	1.9	5.5
History	0.0	2.8	2.9	7.6
Travel	0.2	1.2	—	—
Comedy	11.8	22.8	20.0	9.6
Social Propaganda	0.8	0.8	14.9	13.0
Western	—	—	21.5	18.0
Biography	—	—	—	4.0
Horror	—	—	—	2.4
Space and Science Fiction	—	—	—	1.9
Animal and Nature	—	—	—	2.4

[1] Figures for 1920 and 1935 adapted from L.A. Cook, *Community Backgrounds of Education*, New York, McGraw-Hill Book Company, 1938, p. 219; for 1947, from tabulation of feature length films of the Motion Picture Association of America; for 1957, from tabulation and analysis of *Joint Estimates of Current Entertainment Films* by the Film Estimate Board of National Organizations, New York, and from Catherine C. Edwards' analysis, "Family Movie Guide," published each month in *Parents' Magazine*. Classification changes account for discrepancies in 1947 and 1957 figures.

The "informal school system" of the radio, television, the movies, and the press presents a picture about like this, in summary:[17]

(1) The motion picture audience is composed mostly of young people, a third of them seventeen years of age and under. Though reliable evidence is scanty, TV has reduced attendance somewhat at theatrical motion picture theaters. For both elementary-school

[17] This summary is based on *Mass Media and Education*, 53rd Yearbook, National Society for the Study of Education, Part II, 1954; A.P. Sterner, *Radio, Motion Picture, and Reading Interests: A Study of High School Pupils*, Teachers College, Columbia University, 1947, Chap. I; and Paul Witty, "A Sixth Report on TV," *School and Society*, LXXXIII (May 12, 1956), pp. 166–68.

pupils (twenty hours per week) and secondary-school students (fourteen hours per week) television is a major leisure-time activity; in addition, most children listen to favorite radio programs for an additional five to six hours. The hours when one would expect children to see most of their TV programs still contain more programs involving violent acts than the programs for the rest of the week. (2) The adolescent gets much of his education from eight leisure language activities, namely, motion pictures, the radio, television, comic strips, funny books, magazines, newspapers, and books; often he spends as much time on these interests as he spends in the school classroom.

Undoubtedly the movie has been the primary factor in the recent movement toward more visual education in the schools. It has stimulated greatly the use of other visual aids. While the film may be used to supplement only, it has greatly enlarged the scope of visual teaching. It should be used to do what the other forms of pictures cannot do well; there should be no conflict between films and other visual materials. Each of the visual aids can serve a distinct purpose for which no other aid can serve equally well.

The child frequently absorbs from the commercial motion picture and motion picture "shorts" or from the 16–mm television kinescope more information, attitudes, and patterns of conduct than he gets from the school. American motion pictures, at their best, have great value in entertainment, in instruction, and in desirable effects upon mental attitudes and ideals; at their worst, they have equally great undesirable effects. In the field of the commercial motion picture, spectator adaptation, or "the spectator attitude," is the dominant characteristic. The observer takes in the whole panorama of life and the behavior of the characters, good or bad. Spectator adaptation calls for an awakened social consciousness which will consider the potentialities in the movies for both beneficial and harmful influences, in order that the growth of the child in the formative stage may be safeguarded.

2. The Radio. Though disagreement exists as to the extent to which the radio helps to develop desirable attitudes and ideals in children, there is unanimity of opinion that this new gadget is a powerful educational agency. The radio is available as a noncom-

mercial form of entertainment in practically all American homes, and
it can be used at all hours. Since it is closely connected with the fast-
moving tempo of events of modern life and possesses tremendous
dramatic potentialities, its influence upon children must be taken
into account. The radio stations of America have almost unlimited
choice in regard to the types of programs they present; this freedom
has resulted in a democratic presentation of matters of national and
local import, as well as of other kinds of features strictly of an entertainment nature.

Radio and TV programs prepared especially for children are a
comparatively recent development. Products advertised range all
the way from cereals to toys; the offers made to children vary from
club memberships and puzzles to rewards for carton tops. These
programs are varied in nature. Popular songs and music, comic-
strip characters, and space adventures lead in favor among the children. Classical music, which used to be last, has moved up in popularity since the advent of the high fidelity recording machine. What
particular programs do children listen to most? What are their likes
and dislikes? How can their activities be used to advantage in understanding them and their work in school? [18]

Of as much importance in informal education as special programs
for children are the other kinds of programs that are broadcast. Especially is this true for adolescents. To say that the school teacher has
nothing to do with the types of programs presented over radio and
TV is begging the question. The emotional life of the child, especially during his formative years, is of such significance in education
that the school cannot disclaim any interest in, or responsibility for,
the type of informal education which a child receives over these
media. The creative urge within the child tends to make him follow
creative drama with eager interest, regardless of whether that drama
is good or bad, or whether it is productive of good attitudes or poor
ones.

3. CHILDREN'S LITERATURE, THE NEWSPAPERS, AND NEWSSTAND PUB-
LICATIONS.   The leisure-time reading of children can be of tremen-

---

[18] *Cf.* Edgar Dale, *Audio-Visual Methods in Teaching* (rev. ed.), New
York, The Dryden Press, 1954, Chaps. xiv–xv, xvii and *Mass Media and Education, op. cit.,* Chaps. viii–ix.

dous value in education. Do the community conditions and home background of the child influence and direct his reading? If so, how? Many boys and girls in the United States read more of the newspaper than their parents, and many of them read the newspaper before they come to school in the morning. A new type of "picture magazine" has come into existence recently, exemplified by such publications as *Life, Look*, the picture newspaper, and others. These picture magazines are certainly of educational significance for the child, since the eye is put to work as well as the ability to read. Certain conditions, which are similar to those existing when he is observing a moving-talking picture, are present when the child is reading a picture magazine. It is a well-established fact that what one both sees and hears as well as reads is likely to remain longer in the mind than what one reads only.

It is important for the teacher to note the types of books which adolescents read. The reading interests of children seem to remain basically the same for all generations.[19] The Horatio Alger, George Henty, and Merriwell books and the "Dime Novel" contained the same kinds of stories that children enjoy now.

Tales of mystery, of adventure, of the triumph of right over wrong, of rise to fame and wealth, of success, and of strange places and strange lands continue to appeal to all youth. When *Snow White and the Seven Dwarfs* was made into a movie headliner by the drawings of Walt Disney and his group of technicians, we were given ample evidence that most adults still like fairy stories. Boys and girls like to undergo by proxy the experiences of others just as adults do; undergoing such adventures through reading or looking at a movie is called *vicarious experience*. Because all people enjoy vicarious experiences, the newsstand is a fertile ground for the informal education of all boys and girls.

[19] *Cf.* Lauretta Bender, "The Psychology of Children's Reading and the Comics," *The Journal of Educational Sociology*, xviii (December, 1944), pp. 223–31; Jean Betzer, *Exploring Literature With Children*, Teachers College, Columbia University, 1943, *passim;* Guy L. and Eva Bond, *Developmental Reading in High School*, New York, The Macmillan Company, 1941, pp. 131–45; A.M. Jordan, *Educational Psychology* (4th ed.), New York, Henry Holt and Company, 1956, pp. 234–53; Paul Witty and David Kopel, *Reading and the Educative Process*, Boston, Ginn and Company, 1939, Chap. ii; and Paul Witty, *Reading in Modern Education*, Boston, D.C. Heath & Company, 1949, Chap. ii

Have you ever stopped at a newsstand and watched for an hour the different people that came there to buy or to look or to read? The author has carried out this experiment many times within the last few years, and he has sampled the offerings of different newsstands in both small and large communities. The results of this sampling are in many respects pleasing and in many others somewhat alarming. For example, it makes no difference to the high-school boy whether certain material would be best for his age status or not. He reads it just the same; if he does not read it and it is a picture magazine and well illustrated, he looks at the pictures and reads the captions. The third-grader and the seventh-grader alike, in company with the high-school freshman and senior and the college sophomore, read the so-called "comic" action magazines, a mushroom growth of recent years. Fifty million of these comic serials are sold every month and are probably more widely read by all ages than any other newsstand publications, except the picture-magazine types. Although perhaps little real harm is done to children by their reading of *Superman* and *Wonder Woman*, the type of material found in them is a far cry from that found in *Donald Duck, Rex Morgan, M.D., Tim Tyler, Little Orphan Annie, Gasoline Alley,* and *Out Our Way: the Willetts.* The controversy over the vices and virtues of some 250 periodicals of the action-comic type on the newsstands resulted in 1948 and 1954 in the "Comics Code" of the Association of Comics Magazine Publishers; [20] this is an attempt at self-regulation and self-censorship of the comic magazines. Newsstand publications certainly appeal to the interests of all boys and girls. A careful survey of the types of literature read by and sold to school children would make an excellent starting point for curricular work which is based primarily on reading.

Excellent as the American press is, the informal education which children secure from it is at times far from what good modern journalism would desire. Newspapers range in quality from the sen-

[20] Examples of public opinion include action at national meetings of the American Legion, the PTA, the Junior Chamber of Commerce, and the General Federation of Women's Clubs. *Cf.* also *Newsweek,* XXXII (December 20, 1948), pp. 54, 56–57; *Reader's Digest,* February, 1956, pp. 105–8; and Fredric Wertham, *Seduction of the Innocent,* New York, Rinehart and Company, 1953. See Chapter 11 for a fuller discussion of readiness and interest factors in the comics.

sation-arousing tabloid to superb examples of journalism. People have to depend upon the American press, as upon the radio, for the dissemination of news and for information concerning the availability and sale of products and merchandise. As a rule, newspapers are owned or controlled by politicians or private interests which seek to advance their own businesses and purposes; therefore the point of view of the newspaper owner is often the controlling factor in determining how the news shall be treated in that particular paper. It is a debatable question whether genuine freedom of the press in its large sense exists in this country, when six large chain organizations control one-fifth of the newspaper circulation of the United States. Norman Woelfel says that unless professionally trained editors and reporters do a really honest job of following, interpreting and reporting the local, national, and international situation, freedom of the press is really not existent.[21]

Since all children read newspapers and magazines of some sort, it is of paramount importance for educators to study what the child finds of most interest in them, what type of articles or page or section he spends most time upon, and how these interests and educative experiences can be used effectively in his education at school.

NONCOMMERCIAL TYPES

Youth-serving organizations outside of school are an important factor in American life. From the number of these organizations in existence it would seem that Americans are constitutionally and characteristically "joiners" of organizations of all types, such as clubs, fraternities, and social and political groups.

The fact that two or three million children of school age go to camps each summer presents a challenge to all teachers.[22] The boards

---

[21] "The Fourth and Fifth Estate," *Frontiers of Democracy*, VII (January 15, 1941), pp. 112–15. Read also *Mass Media and Education, op. cit.*, Chaps. VII and X.

[22] *Camping and Outdoor Experiences in the School Program*, Bulletin, No. 4, Federal Security Agency, Office of Education, 1947; *Toward a New Curriculum*, 1944 Yearbook, Department of Supervision and Curriculum Development, N.E.A., Part II; and *School Camping: A Frontier of Curriculum Improvement*, by J.W. Gilliland, Association for Supervision and Curriculum Development, 1954.

of education in many cities now sponsor camp projects. In other cities there are varying degrees of cooperation between community agencies and the board of education to provide camp experiences for children. Educational opportunities of this type have been more available to undernourished and handicapped children than to normal children. In spite of this fact, it is clear that there is a growing interest in camps connected with school work, as well as in camps sponsored by private means and by various agencies in the community. The private summer camp for children has long been one of the agencies by which parents could bring their children into contact with nature and with certain activities which they are unable to get during the school year and in the existing school program.

Types of children's camps which have been experimented with are day camps, camps for a week, and camps for two weeks or longer. Since the number of hours in the normal working day for adults has been reduced, camps run by various community agencies and by the schools give promise of being as valuable to adults as to school children. They present an informal situation in which adult and child alike develop new relationships, new understandings, and new interests. Such experiences are as valuable for the teacher, through presenting a different approach to the education of the child, as for the child and his opportunities for growth. Social and community agencies that have sponsored camps for children in the summer time include the Young Men's Christian Association and the Young Women's Christian Association, community and service clubs, churches, Boy and Girl Scouts, and whole communities. Some of the camps are free to children, except for the expenses for bedding and clothing. Other camps charge a nominal fee for board and other incidentals. Still others charge the child at least part of the cost of running the camp.

Playgrounds and other recreation centers in the community furnish another type of noncommercial leisure-time agency. A good illustration of this kind of recreational program for youth can be found in the Springfield (Missouri) plan, which has been in operation for many years.[23] As additional legislation is passed forbidding children

---

[23] Elizabeth Cadle, "A Community Recreational Program for Youth," *Curriculum Journal*, XI (January, 1940), pp. 23–26.

to work in industry until the age of eighteen, some provision will have to be made for recreational facilities for them through a carefully planned program during the summer months, or during their out-of-school time.

The 1940 White House Conference on *Children in a Democracy* considered play and the constructive use of leisure time of such educational importance that it gave substantial recognition to it in its recommendations. Among the suggestions made were the following: the placing upon the communities, the state, and the Federal government the responsibility for the provision of recreational facilities and services; the survey of local recreational facilities and services and the systematic planning of such; the provision of adequate equipment, facilities, and trained personnel; the collaboration of social organizations and entertainment industries in the provision of adequate programs for the sound development of children in out-of-school times; and the equalization of opportunities available for certain neglected groups of children. The Midcentury White House Conference on Children and Youth in 1950 and The White House Conference on Education in 1955 reiterated most of these recommendations.[24]

Libraries and museums are other places where individuals can spend their leisure time without expense. These facilities, along with those furnished by dramatic and art groups, can give powerful stimulation to children in out-of-school as well as in school hours.

Finally, organizations of social groups furnish another kind of informal education; examples of these are card clubs, dancing clubs, radio clubs, and social parties of adolescent youth who visit night clubs. Community *mores* have changed so much in the last fifty years that dance and card clubs are generally as acceptable today as rook clubs and camp meetings were acceptable to previous generations. In spite of the fast-moving age of the automobile and airplane, it should be important to both the parents and the teacher for the child to hold his parties, his dances, and his social gatherings at home rather than in a night club.

[24] *General Report* adopted by the White House Conference on Children in a Democracy, January 19, 1940, pp. 37–41; *Midcentury White House Conference on Children and Youth*, 1951, and *The White House Conference on Education,* 1956, Washington, U.S. Government Printing Office, *passim.*

The big problem which faces educational employees is how out-of-school organizations can be used to advantage by the school. Should the school, using its teachers as counselors, extend its program into the months of the summer vacation and provide some of the recreation for children at that time? Would this plan be practicable? Such a program would eliminate the idleness of school plants for two or three months each year, plants in which billions of dollars have been invested. The educational possibilities of the summer use of school plants and staffs are limitless and have been scarcely scratched.

The Relation of the School to Other Social Agencies

ATTITUDES TOWARD EDUCATION.   A discussion of the social and economic factors which operate in curriculum change would not be complete without considering the opinions and attitudes of secondary-school pupils and the public in regard to education. Research and articles in the educational literature furnish this kind of comparative summary of what parents want and what pupils want the schools to teach (arranged in descending order of agreement).

"They Agree on These"

What Both Parents and Pupils Want

Development of a sense of individual belonging and security.

Acquisition of skills and tools of learning, especially the 3 R's and communication skills.

How to get along with others.

Adequate vocational education and development of ability to make a living.

Adequate preparation for advanced education.

Citizenship—including current events, participation in school and community activities, discussion opportunities, social and extracurricular experiences and adjustment.

Development of ability to read, discuss, and form sound judgments individually.

Well-equipped, comfortable, and cheerful school surroundings.

Good teachers.

Adult control and discipline of the pupil.

"They Differ on These"

<u>What Parents Want</u>	*What Pupils Want*

Health education.

Development of good morals and standards.

Discipline, as training and punishment.

History of our country and our state.

Understanding teachers.

Provisions for handicapped children.

Training in worthy use of leisure and recreation.

+ Memorization of details.

Fuller information on the progress of the child at school.

More information on what the school expects of the child and of the parent.

More homework.

What Pupils Want

Home and family life education (including etiquette, consumer education, marriage and sex education).

Typing, as a skill.

Opportunity to help in planning their own work, developing independence.

Sharing (experiences, reading, collections of hobbies, etc.)

Discussion of controversial topics.

Guidance—help to pupils to learn what they can do best.

More creative work, such as found in mechanical arts or shop work, arts and crafts, drawing, science and nature study, homemaking and sewing, art, music, and athletics.[25]

The first nation-wide survey of the opinions of the public about education was published in 1940. That survey, entitled "What People

[25] This comparative summary is based primarily upon the following studies and articles: *Educational Leadership*, Vol. I, (May, 1944), devoted to "Listen—They Speak: Children Appraise Education," pp. 447–85; B. Goodykoontz, "Matter for Young Minds," *National Parent-Teacher*, XLVIII (March, 1954), pp. 14–16, 37, and "Parents Know What They Want for Their Children," *Educational Leadership*, VII (February, 1950), pp. 286–91; D.H. Jenkins and R. Lippett, *Interceptual Perceptions of Teachers, Students, and Parents*, Research Training Action Series No. 1, Division of Adult Education Service, N.E.A., 1951, *passim;* E.L. Jones, "High-School Graduates Speak Their Minds," *School Executive*, LXVII (December, 1947), pp. 23–24; L. Monash, "What Makes Children Like or Dislike School?" *Understanding the Child*, XVI (June, 1947), pp. 67–70; R.J. Ojemann and L. Fatland, "What the Parent Expects of the School," *National Parent-Teacher*, XL (September, 1945), pp. 20–23; V.L. Replogle, "What Kinds of Schools Do Pupils Want?" *Educational Leadership*, VIII (April, 1951), pp. 406–12; and 1956 Yearbook, Association for Supervision and Curriculum Development, *What Shall the High Schools Teach?* N.E.A., *passim.*

/ 1940)

Think About Youth and Education," gave the results of a poll made by the Gallup Institute of Public Opinion at the request of several cooperating educational agencies.[26] The survey corroborated some of the opinions of the parents and pupils which have just been cited. Studies on more specific aspects of pupil opinion are contained in "The Interests of Scouts and Non-Scouts," [27] "Controversial Ques-

FIG. 13 *Social recreation for students around a student-constructed replica of an old southern mansion.*

(*Courtesy Walter M. Williams High School, Burlington, N.C. Photo submitted by Mrs. June Stone Byrd.*)

tions in One High School," [28] and "Attitudes of High School Seniors Toward Education." [29]

It is extremely difficult to tell what the public wants in education. An attempt made by the Cooperative Study of Secondary School Standards (1935–1938) to discover what parents desire in the type of education in the secondary school was inconclusive; no data from this source were included in the final criteria for discovering what progress each secondary school was making in attaining its aims.

[26] *National Education Association Research Bulletin,* Vol. XVIII, No. 5 (November, 1940).
[27] By L.E. Abt, P. Mendenhall, and E.D. Partridge, *Journal of Educational Sociology,* XIV (November, 1940), pp. 178–82.
[28] By J.H. Harris, *The School Review,* XLVIII (January, 1940), pp. 49–54.
[29] By P.W. Harnley, *The School Review,* XLVII (September, 1939), pp. 501–9.

Quite a few public opinion polls have been taken on education since the first study conducted by the Gallup Poll, "What People Think About Youth and Education"; and none of them has been any more definite or conclusive than the first. For example, the special Gallup school poll in 1958, reported in newspapers of April 9, listed these as major concerns of parents: rundown school buildings, overcrowded classrooms, and lack of discipline. Parental concern over school curricula was of secondary importance. Special surveys of state or local school systems likewise report public opinion in general rather than specific terms.[30]

Channing Pollock, in a leading short article for *This Week Magazine*, discussed from many angles "What the Public Wants." [31] He set forth the thesis that in his forty years of writing and lecturing he had learned that the widest response comes when appeal is made to the *best* in man's nature. He pointed out that the radio network has created demand for good music, that good plays succeed in spite of the frown and disapproval of theatrical producers, and that truly great screen productions remain in the eyes of the public for years. He said:

> No public can be expected to want what is not made readily available, and all progress in civilization is attributable to the men who supply the superior things—merchants and manufacturers as well as artists and scientists. We climb because there are stairs ahead of us.[32]

CURRICULAR IMPLICATIONS. The school does not work in a vacuum, but has to operate in cooperation with the home, the church, and all other agencies of society which influence the development of the child. One of the primary tasks of the teacher is to use the curriculum to help the pupil make satisfactory adjustments to these sociological and economic factors; this task is impossible unless the school employee understands well the phenomena of family, church, gang, economics, leisure time, and community life.

[30] For example, *Education In North Carolina Today and Tomorrow*, The Report of the State Education Commission, The United Forces for Education, 1948, Chap. IV.

[31] *This Week Magazine*, April 28, 1940, p. 2.

[32] Channing Pollock, "What the Public Wants," *This Week Magazine*, April 28, 1940, p. 2. Copyright 1942 by the United Newspapers Magazine Corporation. Reprinted by permission. This article by Pollock will also be found in *Guide Posts in Chaos*, New York, The Thomas Y. Crowell Company, 1942.

Family solidarity and stability as well as size have changed rapidly during the last fifty years, while many of the functions of the home in child training have been supplemented by the school. As more states enact legislation preventing the child from beginning gainful work before the age of sixteen or eighteen, more responsibility is placed upon the home, the school, and other social agencies to care for youth until they reach that age.

What particular implications exist for the teacher and the child's curriculum in this situation? They may be summarized thus:

1. A good understanding of the various aspects of home and family life must be possessed by the teacher before he can assist his pupils to make satisfactory adjustments. It must be remembered that the school should supplement, not supplant, the training of the home.

2. The teacher should have a wide knowledge of people's religious beliefs and *mores*, since the conduct and beliefs of children are strongly conditioned by those of the family and the church.

3. The introduction of school courses or activities in "Family Living" and "Home Life" requires that the school know more than ever about the home. This movement has gained much momentum and shows evidence of continued expansion.

4. The determination of additional activities and courses of study for those between sixteen and eighteen who are prohibited by law from going into a life work can be accomplished satisfactorily only when the school understands thoroughly the sociological and economic conditions which those pupils are facing and will face in the future.

5. The school system and the school teacher which fail to employ the child's informal educational experiences and interests as points of departure or motivating forces in their curricular work are neglecting a natural approach to learning and life. A pupil's attitude toward an adult, a peer, a social or economic agency, or a leisure-time activity will be more truly represented by his unrestrained reaction in enjoying a movie, the radio, television, a magazine or book, or some other form of entertainment. His reaction to the same sort of person or situation at school occurs in an artificial atmosphere, no matter how hard one attempts to make it lifelike.

PROBLEMS FOR INDIVIDUAL STUDY
AND CLASS DISCUSSION

1. Of the movies that you have seen in the last three months, which would you recommend for children in the primary grades? For children

in grades four to six? For secondary-school students? Give reasons for your recommendations.

2. Should courses in homemaking be included in the school curriculum? Support your point of view.

3. Should time out of the regular school day be granted to children to receive religious education from their church organizations? Why or why not? Should school credit be granted for such work?

4. Why do movies like the Martin and Lewis shows and the Bing Crosby and Bob Hope films appeal so strongly to adolescent boys and girls? Explain.

5. What changes in American family life make it practically impossible for approximately one-half of the children today to be trained in work habits involving manual labor?

6. Why do many parents express themselves as dreading the summer vacation months for their children?

7. Make a comprehensive list of the conflicts of opinion which arise between adolescents and parents, such as conflict over use of the family auto, etc. Which of these conflicts are of *major* and which of *minor* import to the adolescent?

8. What are the curricular implications of the child-labor legislation in your state?

9. After making a survey of the noncommercial educational agencies in your community, in what ways do you find that they could assist the school more adequately in its curriculum work?

10. For how long each day and to what types of radio or television programs does the child of eleven listen? The secondary-school boy or girl?

11. Stop at the most popular newsstand in your community some day when the children are getting out of school; remain there for two or three hours and list the types of newsstand publications which they spend their time reading and examining; then check with the proprietor on what types he finds most popular with them. What are your findings, and what suggestions do they have for your curricular work?

12. What types of radio and television programs prepared specially for children are on the air each day in your community, and at what times?

13. What is the difference between comic magazines and action-comic magazines? Is either type harmful to growing children?

14. Make out a checklist of twenty-five attitudes which you consider desirable for children to acquire in school, such as *respect for older people, tolerance for racial or minority groups, social equality,* and the like. Then give this list to your class to check; have a class committee distribute and collect the unsigned papers, tabulate the results, destroy

the individual answers, and turn the summary of opinions over to you. What did you learn?

15. If you discover a pupil reading a copy of *True Confessions* or *Mr. District Attorney* in your class, what will you do, and why?

ADDITIONAL ANNOTATED REFERENCES
FOR PROBLEM OR UNIT STUDY

Anderson, V.E., *Principles and Procedures for Curriculum Improvement*, New York, The Ronald Press Company, 1956.
Social and cultural changes are considered in Chapters ii, iv–vii, and ix.

Brookover, W.B., *A Sociology of Education*, New York, American Book Company, 1955.
Education in the social order comprises Part ii, and Part v takes up the school in the community.

Chambers, M.M., *Youth-Serving Organizations: National Non-Governmental Associations* (3rd ed.), Washington, American Council on Education, 1948.

"The Changing American Family: Implications for Secondary Schools," *California Journal of Secondary Education*, xxxi (April, 1956).
A symposium on the changing American family and teaching about the family is given on pp. 230–47.

The Community School, 52nd Yearbook of The National Society for the Study of Education, Part ii, 1953.
Presents community-school concepts, American communities, community-school ways of working, and types of programs.

Cook, L.A., and Cook, E.F., *A Sociological Approach to Education* (2nd ed.), New York, McGraw-Hill Book Company, 1957.
This volumes presents the nature of communities, the community and the child and the school, social class structure, delinquent gangs, and school and community coordination.

Cutts, N.E., and Moseley, N., *Better Home Discipline*, New York, Appleton-Century-Crofts, 1952.
Presents parents' experiences in disciplining their children and in bringing them up.

Dahlke, H.O., *Values in Culture and Classroom*, New York, Harper and Brothers, 1958.
Parts i and ii give the meaning of culture and the sociocultural background of the school and education, religion, laws, and the community's role in education.

Federal Responsibility in the Field of Education, A Study Committee

Report, submitted to the Commission on Intergovernmental Relations, Washington, U.S. Government Printing Office, 1955.
A report that shows clearly that many people are strongly opposed to any more governmental aid to education, and, in part, why.

Foshay, A.W., *et al.*, *Children's Social Values—An Action Research Study*, New York, Teachers College, Columbia University, 1954.
A careful study in Springfield (Mo.) of social atittudes of children, and attitudes and understanding of teachers of these social values.

Levy, A.V., *Other People's Children*, New York, The Ronald Press Company, 1956.
Excellent court cases that give a well-rounded picture of juvenile delinquency.

Meltzer, B.N., Doby, H.R., and Smith, P.M., *Education in Society: Readings*, New York, Thomas Y. Crowell Company, 1958.
Parts 1 to 6 present the points of view of different authorities on such sociological aspects as cultural change, the social functions and control of education, and the school and the community.

Mercer, B.E., and Carr, E.R., *Education and The Social Order*, New York, Rinehart and Company, 1957.
This book gives in Part i readings in culture, socialization, social intercourse, social change, and social disorganization. Part ii takes up the school in American society.

Moore, C.B., and Cole, W.E., *Sociology in Educational Practice*, Boston, Houghton Mifflin Company, 1952.
The family, children and groups, the church and education, and education and its relation to the economic system, leisure, and community relationships are found in Chapters i–viii.

Newsstand Publications. At practically any stand the teacher can sample the various types, such as popular weeklies like *The Saturday Evening Post;* popular monthlies like *Good Housekeeping, Better Homes and Gardens,* and *Redbook;* news magazines like *Time* and *Newsweek;* western and sports magazines; TV, radio, Hi-Fi, and camera magazines; more serious publications such as *The Atlantic* and *Field and Stream;* all kinds of "pulp" publications, running usually from ten to fifty cents in price, such as *True Confessions;* science fiction such as *Amazing Science Fiction Stories, Fantastic,* and *Science Fiction;* "action comics" and comic magazines; *Laff, Dolls and Gags, Man,* and *Adam* as samples of "girlie mags"; *True, Argosy,* and *Stag; Glamour* and *Seventeen; Esquire; The New Yorker;* and *Sexology.*

Olsen, E.G. (Ed.), *The Modern Community School*, New York, Appleton-Century-Crofts, 1953.
Principles and practices in the "community-school" approach to the school program.

Recreation in the Age of Automation, The Annals of the American Academy of Political and Social Science, Vol. 313 (September, 1957).
  A modern analysis and discussion of modern practices in planned recreation and leisure activities.
Redl, F., and Wattenberg, W.W., *Mental Hygiene in Teaching*, New York, Harcourt, Brace and Company, 1951.
  Social and personality influences that shape lives in Chapters v and vi; adjustment and maturity in Chapter vii; and working with parents in Chapter xv—all simply told.
Smith, B.O., *et al.*, *Fundamentals of Curriculum Development* (rev. ed.), Yonkers-on-Hudson, World Book Company, 1957.
  With strong emphasis upon the sociological factors that condition curriculum change, this text presents social bases in both Parts One and Five.
Stiles, L.J. (Ed.) *The Teachers' Role in American Society*, New York, Harper and Brothers, 1957.
  Part iii analyzes changes in family life, social relationships, moral values, and mass media of communications.

CHAPTER 5 National
and international movements

CONTROLLING FACTORS IN THE EXTENSION
OF EDUCATION

THE BIRTH RATE. When the factors are enumerated which will strongly affect education in the United States for the next few decades, the birth rate must be listed at or near the top. In 1933–1934 the public school enrollment in elementary and secondary schools reached the highest enrollment in history, with a total of 26,434,193. After 1934 and until 1945, the decline in total enrollment was slight, but steady, due to a gradually decreasing birth rate in the United States. 1946 was the first year to show a slight increase. Since 1947 there has been a heavy increase, to 28,400,000 in 1950, and to 35,000,000 in 1955. By 1960 a total school enrollment of some 43,000,000 is expected, and this will increase to 47,000,000 by 1965.

Population changes and trends can be shown in another way in the table on p. 114.[1]

There were two main causes for the sharp increase in the birth rate: (1) war, which always causes the birth rate to jump; and (2) "boom times," a period during and following World War II of unusual economic prosperity. The large cities which had shown only

---

[1] Data for this section on population and school enrollment and needs are based on P. K. Whelpton, *et al.*, *Forecasts of the Population of the United States, 1945–1975*, and *Statistical Abstract of the United States*, 1947, United States Department of Commerce. Bureau of the Census, United States Government Printing Office, 1947, *passim; Bienniel Surveys of Education* and Releases, United States Office of Education, Federal Security Agency and U.S. Department of Health, Education, and Welfare; *The Annals of the American Academy of Political and Social Science*, January, 1945, "World Population in Transition," pp. 1–21, 45–63, 112–22, 142–51, 193–203 and March, 1958, "A Crowding Hemisphere; Population Changes in the Americas," pp. 1–10; U.S. Bureau of the Census, *U.S. Census of Population*, 1950, Vol. II, and *Current Population Reports* from 1950 through 1957; and *Manpower and Education,* Educational Policies Commission, N.E.A. and A.A.S.A., 1956, *passim.*

Year	% Registered Births per 1,000 Population	
1921	24.2	
1933	16.6	
1934	17.2	
1935	16.9	Depression
1936	16.7	Years
1937	17.1	
1941	18.9	
1942	20.9	
1943	21.5	War Years
1944	20.2	
1945	19.6	
1946	23.3	
1947	25.3	
1948	24.9	Postwar
1949	24.8	Years
1950	24.7	
1951	25.0	
1952 to 1958	25.0	Average (Figure for 1958 is estimated).

slight population increases from 1930 to 1940 began to grow larger again. The number of babies arriving each year jumped from approximately 2,000,000 to over 4,000,000. Accompanying this increase were significant shifts in population from one section of the country to another; for example, California gained heavily and both California and Pennsylvania joined New York in the 10,000,000 class for the first time, with Texas close behind; Florida, Delaware, Arizona, and Nevada also had heavy increases. On the other hand, Arkansas, Mississippi, Vermont, and West Virginia lost population.

These sharp fluctuations in the birth rate of the United States since 1920 have posed major educational problems to be solved. The depression decade (1930–1939) with its declining birth rate presented a situation which prophesied little need for additional buildings and staff during the 1940's; it also presented larger opportunity for enrichment of the existing school program, and for the extension of that program downward to the preschool years and upward toward the public junior college. In contrast, the sharp upturn in the birth rate from 1940 to the present called for a tremendous expansion of both school facilities and staff for the 1950–1970 period; this expansion was made more difficult than usual because of the losses in teaching personnel to other professions, the inflated costs of building construction, and the steady rise in the cost of living.

This increase in the national birth-rate was reflected more and more in the elementary schools from 1947 to 1958, since more than 95 per cent of the children of elementary school age are in school.  The increase in population is also being reflected now in the high-school enrollment, where close to 80 per cent of the children of secondary-school age are enrolled today. The teen-age population will increase 70 per cent more by 1965. Since 1936 the secondary school has graduated more than 1,000,000 pupils a year. These figures indicate that more and more pupils are now being retained through successive secondary-school years.

Estimates and projections of total school enrollments for the future show these increases:

Year	Elementary (Grades 1–8)	Secondary (Grades 9–12)	Total
1955	27,738,000	7,422,000	35,160,000
1960	33,650,000	9,168,000	42,818,000
1965	35,000,000	12,000,000	47,000,000

In order to meet the need for more qualified teachers for this increased enrollment in the next decade, the estimates call for about 1,250,000 additional elementary teachers and more than 450,000 additional high-school teachers; these estimates are based upon a 1 to 27 ratio of teachers to pupils.

EDUCATIONAL LEADERSHIP. Educators cannot disregard the implications of these figures for the future. The schools cannot do a better job of education on the same amount of money that they are now receiving. The average pupil-teacher load in the United States sounds remarkably reasonable around 24.5 pupils in average daily attendance per teacher in 1956. The average, though, is misleading; many sections of the country, *e.g.*, the South, have a very high teacher load.[2] Taking into consideration all of the factors involved in educa-

[2] *Cf. Educational Differences Among the States*, N.E.A. Research Division, March, 1954, *passim*.

tion today, is it reasonable to assume that a teacher can do effective work in the classroom with a pupil load of more than 25? Per pupil costs of the schools have increased from $17.23 in 1890 to $295.00 in 1956. At present a little more than 20 per cent of the teachers in the United States are men. Americans have begun to question the wisdom of putting such a limit on school salaries that men have little or

FIG. 14   *Citizenship training*

A high-school senior appears before the Public Utilities Commission at the hearing on tramway rates. (*Courtesy Denver Public Schools.*)

no desire to enter the teaching field. The thoughtful citizen must also wonder whether it is a wise policy for children throughout their school careers to be taught almost entirely by women.

Information from the American Association of Junior Colleges shows that enrollments in these colleges doubled from 1937 to 1942, and almost doubled again by 1948; they now enroll some 900,000 students. Junior colleges themselves number over 650, an increase of more than 250 since 1929. Of marked significance for public education in the future is the fact that of these junior colleges, more than

50 per cent are publicly financed and controlled and comprise over 75 per cent of the total enrollment. The movement for the establishment and maintenance of the junior college of two years in length at public expense adds to the complexity of the problem of the future direction of the growth of public education. What types of curricula are to be established for these public junior colleges? Are they to be of the same kind as those established for the freshmen who are annually admitted to the American colleges? What aspects of them are to be duplications or continuations of the secondary-school course? Which of them are to be technical or vocational in nature?

The following five factors prophesy the continued expenditure in the future of a much larger amount of money for public education than is spent at the present time: (1) the marked increase in enrollment for the next decade because of the increase in the birth rate in the 1940's and 1950's; (2) the necessity both for increasing teachers' salaries and for employing more teachers to handle the increased enrollments; (3) the extension of state compulsory school laws beyond the age of sixteen, and the extension of education at public expense downward to the kindergarten in more states; (4) the acceptance of the principle of the establishment of public junior colleges at the expense of the state; and (5) provisions, all of them expensive, for the atypical child—both for the slow learner and for the talented pupil. The curriculum implications of such possible growths in education are large indeed.

NEW SOCIAL AND ECONOMIC POLICIES

FARM YOUTH AND THE FUTURE. The rural youth runs up against formidable barriers whenever he plans to return to the farm for his life work after he has completed his education. Youngsters on the farm are swayed strongly as to their choice of a life work by three powerful influences: (1) the regular hours and "time-and-a-half for overtime" pay of labor jobs in industry; the farm has little or no "time-and-a-half for overtime," and has irregular hours in and out of season; (2) the lack of modern living conveniences and devices on the farm for comfortable living, in contrast to such conveniences in the towns, cities, and urban fringe areas; for example, many farms lack electricity, running water, and adequate heating facilities, even though such conveniences have been brought to many other farm homes through the work of the Rural Electrification Authority and the farmers' cooperatives; and (3) the difficulty of obtaining from the Department of Agriculture an allotment of "money crops" adequate enough for an even chance in farming; as an illustration, if a landowner of 500 acres in South Carolina wished to will to his son upon the latter's marriage one half of his acreage, he could do so; but the allotment for tobacco, cotton, or peanut acreage would have to be subtracted from the father's original allotment, and this subtraction might leave both father and son without enough allotment for "money crops" to make the chance an even one that either could succeed in "money crop" farming.

As a result of this lack of desirable opportunities for rural youth to return to the farm after they finish their education, more and more farm boys and girls are going to the urban and industrial centers for jobs; and there is less labor available for the farms. As a matter of fact, if modern technology through its inventions in machinery had not made the American farmer able to produce more with less human help, the nation would be in dire want today. The average size of commercial farms has increased from 220 acres in 1940 to 336 in 1955. Less than 50 per cent of the country's people live in population centers of 2,500 or more; and the country is gradually becoming less rural and more urban.

NEGATIVE POLICIES CONCERNING INDUCTION OF YOUTH INTO LABOR'S RANKS.　During the "depression decade" (1930–1939), adults perhaps had some justification for their policy of preferring to award to other adults the jobs that were available. Many adults had families to support; without jobs to support them, they were forced on "relief." "Relief" was akin to charity, in the eyes of many, and was frequently accompanied by the loss of self-respect on the part of the laborer. Under such conditions of economic depression, there was no great stimulus to provide adequately for the induction of youth into the ranks of labor; as a matter of fact, under such adverse economic conditions, many prominent people thought that the longer it was that youth was delayed from entering the highly competitive labor market, the better it was for all concerned.

On the other hand, the "boom" period of World War II and the years following it, made one fact clear to thinking educators and social workers: *under labor laws as they exist at present in America, it is inexcusable for labor, industry, and the school to turn youth loose to find their own level on the labor mart without an adequate induction program which has been agreed upon by both labor and industry.* For example, most of the induction programs for youth between the ages of sixteen and twenty have been carried on by the schools in their "D. O." (Diversified Occupations) and "D. E." (Distributive Education) programs. These programs are under the direction of coordinators who work closely with both labor and industry in an apprenticeship program for youth; these programs involve part-time work and part-time schooling in related fields; and these two programs are part of the Federal plan for assistance to secondary schools in the fields of vocational education under the Smith-Hughes and George-Reed Acts.

In the past, youth has too often been exploited by capital (industry) in its ruthless rise to wealth and power. As a result, the Wages and Hours Act had as one of its purposes the protection of youth in industry. But social legislation of the Federal government now tends towards extending to eighteen the age at which youth can enter the ranks of regular labor. Therefore, provisions for apprenticeship and easy entrance into the ranks of labor must be worked out by labor, industry, and perhaps the school in adequate apprenticeship programs.[3]

Census figures of 1940 indicated that there were about 101,000,000 persons fourteen years of age or over. Of these, some 45,000,000 were employed in private jobs or in nonemergency government work. Slightly over 2,250,000 were employed on public emergency projects such as the Works Progress Administration, the National Youth Administration, and the Civilian Conservation Corps. And 5,000,000 persons were without jobs of any kind and looking for work. In the boom year of 1948, employment set a record level of about 60,000,000; those unemployed numbered around 2,000,000. In

---

[3] *Cf.* Mark Starr, *Labor Looks at Education* (The Inglis Lecture, 1946), Harvard University Press, 1947, *passim,* and Public Affairs Pamphlets No. 151 and No. 262, Public Affairs Committee, 1957.

1956, 66,000,000 were employed, and about 3,500,000 were unemployed.[4] From these comparative figures, one comprehends readily why economists estimate that from 3,500,000 to 5,000,000 persons are unemployed in every normal year; of these, approximately one half are youth.

For centuries the care of the poverty-stricken in the United States has been primarily the responsibility of local communities. Only since the world-wide depression era have state and Federal governments come to be the major contributors and participators in the financing of relief. What started as "emergency" relief has become a constituent part of the budgets of the nation and of each state. To the person who desires to work, there is no adequate substitute for a job, whether it be direct relief or "government-made" work.

WORLD MARKETS AND THE LIMITATION OF PRODUCTION.   Another strange development resulted from the panic era of 1930–1938. This development was the failure on the part of economists and other leaders to consider the effects of world markets as well as American markets upon national growth in the future. A nation cannot live unto itself in this interdependent world. The teacher finds it most difficult to explain this contradiction to the children, if he can explain it at all: that the reduction in American production tends to keep prices for products high, and that at the same time many millions of people suffer from want of those same articles of which production is curtailed. The student naturally asks the question: "Why do we not go ahead and produce much more, and make the price cheaper for all?"

School children also do not understand why America has tended to give up her world markets and has not made a fight to retain them for her products. They will argue with you that the rest of the world intends to trade with the United States and that the United States must trade with the rest of the world; they sometimes ask point-blank whether the United States would not be committing national suicide by giving up her world bases and markets without a struggle. The curricula in the schools in recent years have put much emphasis

[4] *The Annual Economic Report* (to the President), Council of Economic Advisers, *The U.S. News and World Report* (January 14, 1949), pp. 68–95 and *Manpower and Education, op. cit.,* Chap. III.

upon the teaching of national and international relations and democracy. Is it to be wondered that the pupil of secondary-school age has
connected the unsettled economic conditions in the rest of the world
with certain factors concerning the relinquishing of world markets
by the United States? Americans, with their high standards of living
and tendencies toward buying on the installment plan, are prone to
live beyond their means; they must therefore (1) increase their
production, or (2) add to the number of new products which they
manufacture, or (3) reduce their standard of living as their income
is curtailed and their credit is restrained. All of these aspects of life
become serious problems to boys and girls as they reach the adolescent age, and there is a heavy strain upon the teacher who attempts
to guide and counsel them at this time.

THE EFFECTS OF CHANGES IN OUR NATIONAL POLICIES. When their
elders, through lack of foresight and leadership, fail to provide adequate opportunities for youth to bridge the gap between school and
life, the effects upon the aspirations and morale of growing youth
are incalculable. The student is taught how taxes now take approximately a fourth of all payrolls, not to mention a much higher percentage of all incomes of $1,200 or over a year. He expects as a mat-
ter of course more public parks, playgrounds, recreational facilities,
and swimming pools. He is taught that public health, sanitation,
police and fire protection, social security, and old-age retirement are
things to which he should look forward in this democracy. He knows
that in most states he cannot do any gainful work before the age of
sixteen, and that he cannot engage in any work in a hazardous occupation until he is eighteen years of age. He wants to marry early the
girl of his choice, build a home of his own, and have his children
while he is still young. Later his wife expects to return to the ranks
of those regularly employed. This youth knows little or nothing
about intelligent consumer education, how to buy, and cooperative
buying and selling. He has had years of education in democracy and
citizenship and he hears much about education for the defense,
preservation, and spread of democratic ideals; he desires vocational
training of some sort; and in general, he knows little about what he
should inherit from education. He is ignorant of the fact that America has come to the end of an economic era, to the parting of the

ways as regards exploitation and conservation, to a bloodless revolution concerning the conception of man and land.

THE SHIFT IN EMPHASIS FROM INDIVIDUAL TO GROUP DEVELOPMENT. From the time that America was first settled, the emphasis has been upon the development of the individual; in the early days, land was cheap, manhood was scarce. In this new country the prospect of free land made a man and a woman stand side by side as partners in the development of its natural resources. This was in contradistinction to the view held in Europe, where one who owned land usually possessed it because of the accident of birth. Land was so scarce there and men were so numerous that the emphasis was upon the conservation of land, not upon the conservation of manhood. At the beginning of the twentieth century, the "pioneer frontier" and free public lands ceased to exist in the United States. It has taken America fifty years to realize that she is faced now, to some extent at least, with the age-old problem of Europe. In which direction shall America go? Can she conserve both her human resources and her land? What development will she choose which will continue to dignify both man and his democracy? Or shall she decide upon some type of totalitarian or labor state? [5] These are not academic questions.

Permanent solutions to our social problems concerning health, education, labor, business management, and our developing children involve the effects of (1) the shift in population from rural areas to the cities; (2) the steady increase in the number of women in the ranks of labor; (3) the sharp increase in early marriages; (4) the gradual extension of the compulsory school age from fifteen to eighteen (at present the school-leaving age is fifteen in two states, sixteen in thirty-six, seventeen in three, and eighteen in five); (5) the decline in the number of men of ages twenty-five to fifty-four in the labor force from 1955 to 1965, because the "Depression Decade" produced markedly fewer adult workers for today; and (6) how to increase the average income of workers in the poorer states and poorer groups.

[5] Harold Rugg, *Foundations for American Education*, Yonkers, World Book Company, 1947, Part III; and *Social Foundations of Education* (with William Withers), New York, Prentice-Hall, 1955; Lawrence G. Thomas, *The Occupational Structure and Education*, Englewood Cliffs, Prentice-Hall, 1957; and Public Affairs Pamphlets Nos. 230 and 151, 1957.

In regard to this economic crisis, which is of particular significance to youth, the professional educators themselves are by no means without blame for lack of satisfactory solutions. Harold Hand, writing on "What Prospects for Democracy in Our World of Educational Make-Believe?" has described our failure in long-term educational planning for the nuclear age: [6]

Nowhere is the character of educational magic more clearly portrayed than in the reams which have been written about, and in the tub-thumping orgies which have been devoted to, educational objectives. Here the Good Life is delineated in a manner which satisfies the cravings of the faithful for a spiritual grounding in "sound principles." The conflict occasioned by the fact that the life and program of the school frequently reflect these objectives very little if at all is usually covered up by the ritual of an educational conference or by the ceremony of printing and broadcasting the approved objectives. Or the conflicts may be effectively removed from consciousness by the elaborate dramatization afforded by a curriculum revision program. The fact that, in spite of the consequent clouds of incense, practices in the classroom seem to go on about as before seems to escape the attention of all but a few of the more thoughtful. Consequently, nearly everybody is satisfied and happy, but the pupil remains relatively unaffected. The psychological need for "doing something" has been satisfied—the educational gods have been propitiated, and all is well. There is thus no motivating force to drive the teacher actually "to do"—the conflict has been driven out of her consciousness, and her equilibrium has been restored by the soul-satisfying excursion into the wordy world of educational make-believe.

Every wide-awake teacher of long experience has seen this happen time and time again. That it is now happening with reference to "Democracy and Education" there is little reason to doubt. A recognition of the danger, however, will help us to avoid it—and avoid it we must, for our schools are desperately in need of more democratic procedures, realistically rooted in the real problems of democratic living.

Under these conditions of economic instability and conflict in the United States, it is not strange that the conventions of the American Association of School Administrators have reflected the concern of school leaders for the security of democratic institutions. Teachers have been flooded with publications concerning education and social

[6] Editorial in *The High School Journal*, xxiii (February, 1940), pp. 49–50; *cf.* also "The Educator's World of Make-Believe," *Educational Leadership*, v (May, 1948), pp. 550–51.

change, why social change is necessary, and the crisis of education during the changing process. One solution suggested for this so-called crisis in education is the insistent demand from educators that Federal aid should be applied quite generally to the support, but not to the control of the system of public education. All these movements are but evidences of the vague realization that the United States is stepping forth as a world-leading nation into a new era in which careful planning must be done in advance for education and the curriculum, if teachers are to help satisfactorily in the training of children.[7]

That Federal aid will be given for general education without some aspects of Federal control can scarcely be expected to take place. In the opinion of many of our citizens it would not be wise for the Federal government to supply school aid to the various states and localities without requiring that each state and locality spend a reasonable amount of its own tax funds for the same purpose. The government's recent assumption of services formerly carried on by the family, by the informal social agencies of the community, or by the state has added to the need for a coordinated plan of social service and for close administrative relationships between different social agencies. The shifting of the personnel of social work from private to public authority has had a tremendous influence upon the development and practice of social work during the last two decades. Likewise, the survey of the school community and the investigation of the educational resources of the community have become major factors since 1930 in attempting to meet the needs of children and youth. From such surveys sentiment has grown for speech education in every school; for various types of vocational education in every school; for more effective counseling and guidance practices in every school; for a broader program of student activities in every school; and for the experiment in many schools of having the students assist in planning their activities and educational experiences.

---

[7] For various views on these aspects, see the American Association of School Administrators, 23rd Yearbook, *Paths to Better Schools* (1945), 25th Yearbook, *Schools for a New World* (1947), 26th Yearbook, *The Expanding Role of Education* (1948), 32nd Yearbook, *Educating for American Citizenship* (1954), and 36th Yearbook, *The High School in a Changing World* (1958), *passim;* and the NEA *Journal*, 1936–1958, Vols. xxv–xlvii, *passim.*

THE PUBLIC DOMAIN AND RESETTLEMENT. A survey of the public domain of the United States shows that almost 400,000,000 acres of land still belong to the Federal government.[8] Most of this real estate is on the western side of the continental divide; half the land in the eleven states of the Far West is the property of the United States

FIG. 15 *Irrigation: a means of resettlement*

Filling bolsa with stream run-off at Rock Point Irrigation Project. This flooding was the only available water to mature the corn crop during the summer of 1939. Navajo Indian Agency, Window Rock, Arizona. (*Courtesy United States Indian Service.*)

government. The general land office of the Federal government supervises this land, millions of acres of which are open to homesteading. If a wise program for the development of this public land were planned and carried out over a period of years, it was the

[8] R.L. Neuberger, *Our Natural Resources—and Their Conservation,* Public Affairs Pamphlet, No. 230, 1957, and J.F. Dewhurst, *et al., America's Needs and Resources: A New Survey,* New York, Twentieth Century Fund, 1955, *passim.*

opinion of the old National Resources Committee that more than
2,500,000 new people could be settled in the Pacific Northwest within
a generation. More than 20,000,000 acres of this land are irrigated,
and 1,000,000 people now live on it. When the water is available,
another 20,000,000 acres can be reclaimed for settlement as a frontier
for tomorrow. Of these nearly 400,000,000 acres of public land, approximately 165,000,000 acres are now grazing districts and unappro-
priated public land, which may be used for settlement or resettlement
purposes as reclamation and irrigation provide. Congress passed the
Great Plains Ten-Year program in 1956, designed to cut down great
drought losses in the "dust bowl" and stabilize farming in ten states
east of the Rockies. Since the Tennessee Valley Authority completed
its project for control of the Tennessee River, there has been no
major flood in that region. If the valley of the Missouri River is likewise controlled, enough water will be available in addition to irrigate
other millons of acres of productive soil. The development of this
remaining frontier of the country offers some hope of permanent
settlement for those people who love the land and wish to make their
living by cultivating it. Such problems as reclamation, drainage,
irrigation, reforestation, and soil conservation point the way for types
of activities in the school curriculum which can render a service of
real value to boys and girls as they prepare for life.

REGIONAL AND STATE PLANNING
IN NATIONAL DEVELOPMENT

REGIONALISM.   Closely allied to the problem of the remaining
public domain of the United States is the movement which has been
under way in certain sections to study the various regions of the
country in order that the whole nation may profit. Among the pioneers in this work, with a record of more than a quarter century of
service behind them, were Howard Odum and his group of associates of the Institute for Research in Social Science at the University
of North Carolina.[9] Their particular interest has been to study the
southern region, with its many assets, liabilities, and possibilities.
Tenant farming, motherhood and population trends, the Negro,

[9] For fuller information concerning their achievements, turn to Chap. 20.

worn-out land, the problem of the one-crop system, the problems of industry in the South, and social aspects and implications of the southern region have been typical of their research projects.

The Council of Economic Advisers, under the direction of the Federal government, compiles data of all sorts upon the nation and its various regions.[10] It submits its findings of facts, and makes suggestions for a long-range program for the future. The importance of these types of studies cannot be overestimated. For example, the South has by far the largest surplus population, which in the past has been migrating to other sections of the country to make a livelihood. One state in the South, North Carolina, showed this situation: [11]

Natural Population Increase

April 1, 1950, to July 1, 1956		530,201
Less Loss to Armed Forces	33,000	
Less Loss by Migration	181,201	214,201
Net Gain in Population		316,000

If the South, with its three fundamental assets of good climate, wealth of natural resources, and plenty of children, can plan and put into operation a program whereby all of these assets can be used, then the problems attendant on the education of these children as well as on their future will begin to be solved. Harold Rugg [12] called attention to the fact that American civilization had violated the "sustained-yield" principle of economy, namely, such treatment of its soil and resources and people that a sustained yield is provided for in the future. He said that the building of soil is a lesson which the human being has never been able to learn in the history of man.

The annual conference of the governors of the southern states has been engaged for years in study of the possibilities for growth and development in the southern regions. Most of these states have state departments of conservation and development, to which are dele-

[10] For the Annual Economic Report (to the President), Council of Economic Advisers, refer to *U.S. News and World Report* from time to time.

[11] Adapted from U.S. Department of Commerce, Bureau of the Census, *Current Population Reports, op. cit.*, Series P–25, No. 165, November 4, 1957.

[12] *Now Is the Moment*. New York, Duell, Sloan and Pearce, 1943, Chaps. II and III.

gated the responsibilities for the conservation and use of the state's resources; some have planning boards or commissions on resource-use education, or both. Through state, regional, and national action, the groundwork is being laid for building a better civilization in the several regions. In the construction of this improved type of civilization, the schools will be forced to have a major part, especially in the adaptation of their curricular offerings to meet the needs of their region.

STATE TRADE BARRIERS AND "FAIR TRADE" LEGISLATION. Another aspect of regional development which is not so promising is the undeclared and mostly unnoticed "war between the states," which has been going on in various sections of the nation for a quarter of a century. It is a sad fact that among the fifty states many are busy levying import taxes on one another's goods in interstate commerce. State trade laws have been established and discriminations have been made by certain states against others.[13] Such state trade barriers are operating directly at present to eliminate the greatest *free* market in the world. This free market may be defined as a wide national market among the states, in which an effective system of transportation, abundant resources, and specialization in products by various regions have made possible the American high standard of living. Whenever state and local laws are set up which prevent the free movement of goods and services from one state and community to another, then trade laws come into effect like those which operate in all of the nations of the world. In Europe, for example, import or export duties must be paid whenever one moves a hundred, two hundred, or three hundred miles with most types of products or goods. During the "depression decade," import-tax legislation among the states increased sharply, probably more because the states were faced with a sharp decline in revenue and needed more taxes to meet their expenses, than because the states consciously wished to erect picayune trade barriers.

One strange outgrowth of the depression years has had a hectic career since 1938. This is the so-called "fair trade" legislation, which in reality meant price-fixing laws, requiring the retailer to maintain

[13] *Cf.* Gardiner Harding, "War Between the States," *This Week Magazine, New York Herald Tribune,* April 7, 1940, pp. 4, 29.

the sales price set by the manufacturer before he sold an article. Analysis of these price-fixing laws seems to indicate that their real purpose was to achieve a greater or less degree of "competition-free" control in business.[14] Forty-five of the states had "fair trade" laws by 1938, and Congress had passed the Miller-Tydings Act, which in effect exempted the companies who fixed prices from the anti-trust laws. Big department stores, super markets, and discount houses have fought such legislation primarily through the state courts. Adverse decisions by state and Federal courts on one aspect or another of the fair trade laws changed the picture by 1958, when state after state court had weakened or thrown them out; however, thirty states still have fairly effective fair trade acts.

As a matter of fact, the United States Constitution does not allow the states to place a tax on imports or exports, or to make a distinction between commerce shipped to citizens of other states as compared with that sent to citizens of their own state. Within its constitutional control over interstate commerce, the Congress of the United States can construct a national policy in this matter which will be fair both to the states and to the Federal government. But the states have managed in many ways to get around the constitutional provision of the Federal government which prevents them from levying import and export duties. Some states have bought altogether homemade products for the consumption of state agencies and institutions; some require that only legal residents shall be on their payrolls; some award printing contracts only to resident printing firms; some give preference to local contractors in the award of contracts for construction and other public work; some require textbooks for the public schools to be printed within the state; some prohibit the export of hydroelectric power; and some tax outsiders for the use of highways within the state. In all these fights among the states over import and export duties, the consumer pays "through the nose." Although these state trade barriers benefit some interested groups and individuals, they serve to hurt many more home producers than they help in view of the fact that retaliations are often made by other states, or citizens refuse to buy their own state products.

On he other hand, one should note that the consumer profits from

[14] *Consumer Reports*, Vol. xxiii (May, 1958), pp. 239–43, 282.

state and Federal laws that protect his food, his health, and his ease of transportation from one state to another. Such sound legislation is that controlling the purity of foods, the sale of narcotics, the clear labeling of patent medicines, and rates in interstate transportation.

The remedy for state trade barriers exists both within the states and in the Federal government. If the Federal government has to take action, it is usually taken after a case has been brought up through lower courts to the Supreme Court. Changing the type of legislation within a state is likewise a slow process. So citizens are left with a situation in which education must take a hand in order to make clear the implications of state trade barriers and laws, and the steps which must be taken in order to eliminate them and to maintain free trade in this nation. In this process of education, the school will have to take its part. The free movement of services, goods, and labor in free competition must continue to exist if the nation plans to prosper and to remain democratic.

PROBLEMS OF A RACIAL AND INTERNATIONAL CHARACTER

THE PROBLEM OF RACIAL MINORITIES.   As one result of the worldwide conflict which started in Europe and Asia, the United States has begun to think about and to make adequate provision for its racial minorities. Should not citizenship requirements be the same for these minorities? How can they be given equal education, and what efforts should be made to break up or to recast their racial heritage and outlook? These are two of the problems concerned with racial groups which must be carefully worked out by educators and statesmen.[15] With the exception of the Negro, most of these minorities chose America for their home. Not only should all racial minorities be given a fair chance to become real Americans in every sense of the term; they should be given more than a fair chance. The immigration laws, as now formulated, have blocked the wholesale entry of undesirable aliens into America. On the other hand, we have

[15] Many books and countless articles have been written on these problems since 1946. Consult Chapter 21 for fuller references on racial problems; also helpful are Public Affairs Pamphlets Nos. 85, 95, 233, 244, 245, and 255.

today a different kind of intramigration between the states or territories of minority groups. The largest of these groups now are the Negroes and the Puerto Ricans. Is it fair to these migrants to allow them to congregate in urban centers in localities containing only the population groups of their own race? Or is it wise to force them by economic necessity to remain, grow, and develop in slum sectors, where there is the minimum opportunity for them and for their children to become more accustomed to American ways and ideals?

One of the inner sources of strength of the democracy of the United States has been the protection of minority groups from the very beginning of the existence of the nation. Frequently these minority groups have become majority groups after the passage of four, six, eight, or some other number of years, and the former majority group thus became a minority. This type of protection for minorities and the interchange of frank opinion among all groups have been saving factors in the preservation of our democratic form of government and way of life. It is all the more pertinent, therefore, that both statesmen and educational employees should take this into careful account in establishing the framework, administration, curriculum, and teaching methods of the schools. The responsibility rests with the majority group to allow a chance for improvement and growth to the minority groups; only in this way can real adjustments in democratic life and thought be made.

INTERNATIONAL IDEOLOGIES. World War II drove home the fact that national and international ideologies which differ must inevitably clash. Whether the solution to these clashes is determined around the council table or by war depends upon the philosophy of these nations as developed over a period of years by their educational agencies of a formal and informal nature. In the totalitarian nations, the cry has been that the democratic form of organization and government has failed to provide for the common man, as well as for the more fortunate classes of society. The totalitarian state therefore insists that government control, and in most respects government ownership, of all utilities, industries, and individuals (including their private lives) is necessary to achieve this desirable goal. In the democracies there is an overwhelming opinion that the totalitarian regime is repugnant both in basic theory and in practice to the development of the individual as well as of society; and the democracies are willing to fight just as fiercely for their beliefs as the totalitarian states for theirs.

In such a momentous struggle, all types of devices and arguments are used by both sides to sway others to their point of view. When a person is in a calm, reflective mood and is not influenced by his emotions, he instantly recognizes that to attempt to settle the conflict between these two ideologies in the heat of batle is a very poor way to resolve the difficulties and differences. In the final analysis, world-wide peace will come only when one side or the other is exhausted. Even then there is the probability that the sensible training which has been given to these nations in their varied educational experiences will be so tempered by their upset emotional outlook that the peace which is arrived at will not be any more lasting, just, or satisfactory than was the treaty of Versailles, the Yalta pact, or the Korean armistice.

Countless pages have been written about the school's relation to the preservation of democracy and to the defense of its form of government.[16] It is doubtful whether schools are the *first* line of American defense, as many educators have claimed; but it can be said without fear of contradiction that they are *one* of the lines of defense for democracy. More fundamental than aid to other democracies, than schools for the defense of democracy, than the teaching of citizenship, than the limits of nationalism or Americanism or Europeanism or Communism, than propaganda, even than revolution, is the struggle for the priceless values of civilization, the love of knowledge, of humanity, of right thinking and acting, and of decency, whose capstone is the dignity of the human individual. In such a conflict, the elimination or subjugation of the middle classes of any nation leads inevitably to a state-type of government of a totalitarian character.

It is pertinent to ask the following question: *What have we as educators done or attempted to do which would inculcate in the chil-*

[16] An excellent illustration of this is found in the publications of one group alone, the Educational Policies Commission of the National Education Association and the American Association of School Administrators; many monographs and books and various pamphlet and bulletin materials have been published on these topics from 1936 to the present.

Current Affairs

Map Making

FIG. 16   *The eleven-year-olds study*
(*Courtesy Oak Lane Country Day School, Philadelphia. Photographs by Mary Merritt Lang.*)

dren under our care the eternal values? In training children to read, to write, to figure, to master certain subject-matter fields or areas of knowledge, teachers have all too often emphasized with the individual child and with the group that this particular skill or knowledge "will assist you to make a better living," to secure a "white-collar job," to gain a better economic and social status. Is education only for the *material* side of life? Is it to disregard the fact that the individual, both as a child and later as an adult, has ample leisure time today, and that improper use of that leisure time will be more destructive than constructive of democracy? Having advanced far toward the development of what might be called a materialistic system of education in this country, educators have been confronted recently with certain questionings of their product as they have turned it out. Many students have shown an alarming lack of interest in leisure-time activities, such as reading and hobbies; in habits of thrift; in consideration for their neighbors and associates; and in a desire to improve themselves and continue their growth. In part, the responsibility for this failure of education to carry over into life rests upon the home, and upon other social agencies; but the schools cannot escape a large share of the blame in the matter.

In attempting to correct through the schools some of the weaknesses in education which have become apparent through the years, our people seem to have turned to "revival" methods. For example, they have tried to do it through various national weeks: American Education Week, Children's Book Week, National Music Week, Good Health Week, National Thrift Week, and others. Even though each one comes once a year, the sad part about these national weeks is that all of the work cannot be done within such a short time. High ideals and good habits can be inculcated in children only by means of a sustained effort which permeates all educational activities and is extended over many years.

EFFECTS OF NATIONAL AND INTERNATIONAL MOVEMENTS ON THE SCHOOL CURRICULUM. At the close of World War II, there were millions of "D. P.'s" (displaced persons) in Europe; entire groups or races had been transported from their own countries to work in the victor countries. The homes of many of these had been destroyed during the struggle, and they were without any homes of their own when they returned to their own lands; others did not wish to return to their own countries. Confronted with the problem of relocating literally millions of these persons, the United States agreed to admit several hundred thousands of them.

As these D. P.'s came, here are the implications of this international movement for education in America. Most of these displaced persons (1) are full of race prejudices and hatreds, (2) are prone to take advantage of minority groups, (3) do not know the meaning of the word "democracy" in the sense in which it is lived in this country, (4) think that most Americans are wealthy, and (5) keep asking what will be required of them in the way of payment for the privilege of participating in group activities.

The problem of educating or re-educating these new immigrants from a war-torn, European, class civilization is both as old and as new as America's history for the last 150 years. The types of curriculum that will be required will probably range from the well-known classes in Americanization and literacy to the more recent enrichment types of adult and continuation education. It remains to be seen whether the structure of the existing curriculum can meet this emergency adequately. Certainly the larger the number of students and teachers involved each year in international educational exchange programs, the better understanding of other cultures will be developed.

Faced with problems of the new jet and nuclear age on both national and international levels, science alone cannot preserve us and our education.[17] Neither can our curricular goal be the encyclopedic mass of facts and information which have been acquired by the photographic mind of an adult or a ten-year-old.[18] Our goal must be the education of thinking men who know human relations, of men of big ideas who dare to use them in world organization and in building a lasting peace both for today and tomorrow. In such an educational system, we have to synthesize in American society four different philosophies of education, namely, (1) preparation for life in a fast-moving scientific world, (2) intel-

---

[17] "Science Will Not Save Us," editorial by Norman Cousins in *The Saturday Review*, December 14, 1957, p. 20.
[18] Cf. "Getting Rich on TV," *Newsweck*, March 25, 1957, pp. 63–65.

lectual development of a high order, (3) education for life in a democracy, and (4) continual development of high moral and ethical values.[19]

Movements of national and international scope tend to be reflected in gradual changes in the school curriculum. In addition to the three R's and scientific and mathematical education, the evolving school curriculum in the 1960's, by virtue of such movements, will probably have in it much more about the following problems: Land conservation and use; irrigation; crop control and rotation; natural and regional resources; racial minorities and proper provisions for them; wise choice of a life work; free trade among the several states; subsistence agriculture, as compared to strictly vocational agriculture; markets and fashions specially designed for teen-agers; problems of population mobility and urban-fringe development; changes in the labor force; medical and health insurance; part-time work programs; the displacement of population and how to care for it; national ideologies and international responsibility for law and order; leisure-time activities; and the interdependence of the modern, mechanized world. The challenge and the responsibility for the school in this situation are clearly defined.

PROBLEMS FOR INDIVIDUAL STUDY
AND CLASS DISCUSSION

1. What is a reasonable teacher-pupil load in the elementary school? In the secondary school? Explain.

2. Make a survey of population trends and school enrollments in your community for the last decade. What curricular implications do you draw from your survey?

3. If you made a list, ranking the factors operating now to retain more students of secondary-school age in school, how high on this list would you place the holding power of the secondary-school curriculum, and why?

4. What arguments can you give for the establishment of the kindergarten as an integral part of the public school system? What type of curriculum would you institute there?

[19] For a discussion of the complications involved in such a curricular program, read the 57th Yearbook of the National Society for the Study of Education, Part III, *The Integration of Learning Experiences*, 1958, *passim*.

5. If the junior college were adopted as part of the public secondary-school system, what kind of curriculum should it offer to its students?

6. How many parents of children in your school are under thirty years of age, and what special problems arising from their situation face you for solution?

7. What action would you take if a sixteen-year-old boy in your class were not interested in his school work, were interested in going to work regularly, yet his parents insisted upon his finishing high school?

8. If you taught in a rural community, how would you proceed in making a study of how crop control through the Agricultural Adjustment Act affects the ideas, attitudes, and economic life of your community and pupils?

9. Can you explain satisfactorily to a pupil the curtailment of production when millions of people are going hungry? Support the position you take.

10. Is there any relationship between the high standard of living in America and the early age at which many young people marry? Explain.

11. What curricular problems arise because of migration from one state or region of the country to another? Why?

12. Should the teaching of democracy be a part of the school curriculum? If so, can you present several practical methods of teaching it effectively?

13. If your school decided that conservation of resources should become a part of its curricular work, with what existing course or area would you teach it, and why? Or would you make a new course of it? Why?

ADDITIONAL ANNOTATED REFERENCES
FOR PROBLEM OR UNIT STUDY

American Council on Education, Washington 6.

The Council has pioneered experiments in intergroup education since 1945. *Elementary Curriculum in Intergroup Relations* (1950) and *Intergroup Education in Public Schools* (1952) give good examples of successful practices that were developed.

American Journal of Sociology, Chicago 37, frequently devotes a whole issue to one or more of the problems presented in this Chapter.

Anderson, V.E., *Principles and Procedures of Curriculum Improvement*, New York, The Ronald Press Company, 1956.

Chapter ii is on human relationships, v on social and cultural values, and vii on the attitudes and values of the community.

The Annals of the American Academy of Political and Social Science, Philadelphia 4.

"Metropolis in Ferment," November issue, 1957, presents the changes
taking place in urban, urban-fringe, and large metropolitan centers.
Association for Supervision and Curriculum Development, N.E.A., Washington 6.

A Look at Continuity in the School Program. 1958 Yearbook. One of
the best analyses, from a study of 3,000 children's experiences, of
teaching, guidance, curriculum, and adminstrative practices in terms
of what is to be learned.

Educational Leadership, ASCD's magazine, consistently devotes a
whole issue to a problem area, such as the education of migrant
children, social change and the curriculum, human relations, international and intercultural experiments in the schools, and crowding in
classrooms.

Barron, M.L. (Ed.), *American Minorities,* New York, Alfred A. Knopf,
1957.

A textbook of readings in intergroup relations, showing the various
positions and points of view.

Brookover, W.B., *A Sociology of Education,* New York, American Book
Company, 1955.

A valuable reference to many aspects of society and culture as related
to our national school problems.

Childs, John L., *American Pragmatism and Education,* New York, Henry
Holt and Company, 1956.

The author shows how American pragmatism has had a revolutionary
effect upon curriculum trends both at home and in foreign lands, and
develops the idea that "experiencing" is a necessary training for constructive leadership.

Clapp, E.R., *The Use of Resources in Education,* New York, Harper and
Brothers, 1952.

A recent account of the development of community curriculum programs in The Ballard Memorial (Ky.) and Arthurdale (W.Va.) schools.

Colegrove, K., *Democracy vs Communism,* Princeton, D. Van Nostrand
Company, 1957.

The Institute of Fiscal and Political Education prepared this analysis
of the conflict between communism and democracy for young Americans. A fair presentation of a most controversial issue.

Cook, L.A. and E.F., *A Sociological Approach to Education* (2nd ed.),
New York, McGraw-Hill Book Company, 1957.

Parts i and ii are background material on the nature of communities
in our national life.

Everett, S., and Arndt, C.O. (Eds.), *Teaching World Affairs in American
Schools,* New York, Harper and Brothers, 1956.

This is a case book for teaching about world affairs in elementary,
junior high, and senior high schools.

French, Will, and Associates, *Behavioral Goals of General Education in High School*, New York, Russell Sage Foundation, 1957.
A study and presentation of conflicting opinions as to what should constitute general education, especially in regard to youth's behavioral choices.

Gittler, J.B. (Ed.), *Understanding Minority Groups*, New York, John Wiley and Sons, 1956.
Presents discussions and data on the American Indian, the Jew, the Negro, the Japanese, the Puerto Rican, and the Catholic.

Hartford, E.F., *Moral Values in Public Education*, New York, Harper and Brothers, 1958.
The book tells how one state, Kentucky, is attempting to meet the demand of the public for more emphasis on the teaching of ethical values in the public school.

Havighurst, R.J., *Human Development and Education*, New York, Longmans, Green and Company, 1953.
Interesting results of experimental studies of the developmental tasks of humans during infancy and early childhood, middle childhood, adolescence, and adulthood and old age.

————, and Neugarten, B.L., *Society and Education*, Boston, Allyn and Bacon, 1957.
Part i for social structure and bases in America, Part iii for aspects of population change(s), intergroup and social integration, and international understanding.

Marden, C.F., *Minorities in American Education*, New York, American Book Company, 1952.
Analyzes "native-foreigner," "white-colored," and "ward-wardship" relations, along with religious difference and minority status.

Mercer, B.E., and Carr, E.R., *Education and the Social Order*, New York, Rinehart and Company, 1957.
Especially valuable are Chapters ii on the culture concept, vi on education and social change, and xiii–xiv on the school and democracy and what we expect of the schools.

Moore, C.B., and Cole, W.E., *Sociology in Educational Practice*, Boston, Houghton Mifflin Company, 1952.
Chapters ix–xiv analyze implications of population change, minority groups and intergroup education, and education in a national and international setting.

National Association of Secondary School Principals, Washington 6.
The Bulletin, Vol. xl (December, 1956) is devoted to "International Understanding Through The Secondary School Curriculum," pp. 3–247.

National Society for the Study of Education, 52nd Yearbook, Part ii, 1953, *The Community School*.

Examines and defines the community school and its program, staff, buildings, organization and administration; it also gives samples of programs on both smaller and larger scales.

Olsen, E.G. (Ed.), *The Modern Community School*, New York, Appleton-Century-Crofts, 1953.

Describes the community approach to education, the enlarged concept involving total community planning and use of resources. Samples of programs.

Pierce, T.R., *et al.*, *White and Negro Schools in The South*, Englewood Cliffs, Prentice-Hall, 1955.

The historical record of biracial education in the South, the problems and progress in regional desegregation, and a redefinition of the issues.

Smith, B.O., *et al.*, *Fundamentals of Curriculum Development* (rev. ed.), Yonkers-on-Hudson, World Book Company, 1957.

Takes up culture, technological changes and social perspective in the curriculum in Chapters i–iii; curriculum objectives, society and its demands, and the social problem approach in Part v.

Southern Education Reporting Service, Nashville 12.

Southern School News is perhaps the most complete, accurate, objective reporting of the progress (or lack of progress) in desegregation of schools in the South. Their collection of documents on microfilm is also quite extensive.

U.S. Government Printing Office, Washington.

Resources for Freedom. Vol. i. "Foundations for Growth and Security." A report to the president by the President's Materials Policy Commission, June, 1952. America's resources and how to use them intelligently.

U.S. Office of Education, U.S. Department of Health, Education, and Welfare, Washington.

Offerings and Enrollments in High School Subjects, 1948–1949. Published every fifteen years (this published in 1951).

The State and Nonpublic Schools, 1958. Has particular reference to responsibilities of State Departments of Education.

PART TWO The modern movement for curriculum revision

CHAPTER 6 Stages of growth in the modern curriculum movement

GENESIS OF THE MOVEMENT

EARLIER INVESTIGATIONS. Although the movement for the reorganization of the curriculum began as far back as 1890, and scientific investigations of curriculum construction began to get under way around 1910, it was not until 1920 that these movements began perceptibly to affect curriculum revision. E.M. Draper says:

> . . . as late as 1918, the organization of general aims or principles of learning was regarded as sufficient for the guidance of teachers in the development of learning experiences and activities for the pupils in the classroom. In the last few years, educators have generally agreed that it is essential for teachers and administrators to extend their activities in this field to the development of the specific objectives of the course of study in which they are interested.[1]

An analysis of life's needs as a basis for determining curriculum content began in 1911 with the work of the Committee on the Economy of Time in Education of the National Education Association. Other early studies of life activities included E.L. Thorndike's investigations of handwriting in 1910; the first school surveys in Baltimore, Cleveland, Portland, and Salt Lake City between 1912 and 1915; the analysis of the content of history books by W.C. Bagley and Harold Rugg in 1916; W.N. Anderson's spelling vocabulary based on actual correspondence in 1917; E.L. Thorndike's word list in 1921; the investigations by J.R. Clark and Harold Rugg of socially worth-while elements in algebra, geometry, and arithmetic, between 1915 and

[1] *Principles and Techniques of Curriculum Making*, New York, D. Appleton-Century Company, 1936, p. VII.

143

1918; and the group of job analyses by W.W. Charters from 1923 to 1927.[2]

FIVE STAGES OF GROWTH.   In the development of the curriculum of the modern school in the last four decades, the steps progressively are now fairly well defined in the form of five movements: (1) the "aims-and-objectives" stage; (2) the survey movement; (3) the development of the unit technique; (4) system-wide curriculum revision; and (5) the core curriculum and large unit procedures, including the fusion movement. Of these, the development of the unit technique is so important that the following chapter is entirely devoted to it. The others will be considered briefly here.

THE "AIMS-AND-OBJECTIVES" STAGE
AND ACTIVITY ANALYSIS

BOBBITT'S EARLIER STUDIES.   As early as 1918, Franklin Bobbitt advocated "activity analysis" as a basis for determining curriculum objectives.[3] He defined the curriculum as the entire range of consciously directed training experiences that the schools must use for completing and protecting the unfoldment of the abilities of the individual. He stated that this total range of human activities for which education should prepare should be discovered by "analytic surveys."[4] In 1922 Bobbitt reported[5] on the use of this method in the Los Angeles schools. Twelve hundred high-school teachers were given an extensive list of general objectives in education which had been compiled by graduate students working under Bobbitt at the University of Chicago. This list was submitted to the different departments of the high schools, and the departments were asked to check those objectives which they thought their department might help the pupils to achieve. A list of fundamental objectives for pupil activity necessary to achieve these general objectives was also submitted to the departments for checking. The lists included the gen-

---

[2] Data on these aspects are taken primarily from Harold Rugg's articles in the 26th Yearbook of the National Society for the Study of Education (1927), Part I, Chaps. I–V.

[3] *The Curriculum*, Boston, Houghton Mifflin Company, 1918, p. 42.

[4] *Ibid.*, p. 43.

[5] *Curriculum Making in Los Angeles*, The University of Chicago Press, 1922.

eral educational objectives, and also those objectives which each high-school department considered it was in its special province to promote.

CHARTERS' CONTRIBUTIONS. In 1923 another investigator, W.W. Charters, made a significant contribution to the activity-analysis theory as a basis for curriculum materials. He stated:

> . . . those who have formulated the aims of education have not taken into account the activities which individuals carry on. Rather have they laid stress merely upon ideals from which a curriculum can be derived. . . .[6]

Charters believed that the aim of all activity was to secure satisfaction, and that an objective statement of satisfactory types of activity comprises what we call *ideals*. The activity which brings the most satisfaction in the long run is determined by the consensus of expert opinion as it judges from the history of the race. These ideas of Charters were in line with one of the theories of learning set forth by Thorndike, namely, that the more satisfying the response is to any stimulus, the faster the response is mastered and the more desirous one is of repeating the experience. From these concepts of human activity, Charters formulated the following rules for curriculum construction:

FIRST, determine the major objectives of education by a study of the life of man in his social setting.

SECOND, analyze these objectives into ideals and activities and continue the analysis to the level of working units.

THIRD, arrange these in the order of importance.

FOURTH, raise to positions of higher order in this list those ideals and activities which are high in value for children but low in value for adults.

FIFTH, determine the number of the most important items of the resulting list which can be handled in the time allotted to school education, after deducting those which are better learned outside of school.

SIXTH, collect the best practices of the race in handling these ideals and activities.

[6] *Curriculum Construction,* New York, copyright 1938 by The Macmillan Company, p. 4. This and the following quotations used by permission of the publisher.

SEVENTH, arrange the materials so obtained in proper instructional order, according to the psychological nature of children.[7]

Since there is still today a sharp conflict among educational authorities in regard to curriculum revision, it is profitable for the curriculum employee to note that both Bobbitt and Charters called attention to the division of opinion existing thirty years ago among educators in regard to the curriculum. Bobbitt says:

> Current discussion of education reveals the presence . . . of two antagonistic schools of educational thought. On the one hand are those who look primarily to the subjective results: the enriched mind, quickened appreciation, refined sensibilities, discipline, culture.
> . . . On the other hand there are those who hold that education is to look primarily and consciously to efficient practical action in a practical world. . . .[8]

Charters makes the following significant statements:

> The standards of our day demand that our courses of study be derived from objectives which include both ideals and activities, that we should frankly accept *usefulness* as our aim rather than *comprehensive knowledge*, and that no fictitious emphasis should be placed upon the value of formal discipline.[9]
> While writers on the curriculum have begun with the statement of aims, none has been able to derive a curriculum logically from his statement of aim. In every case he has made an arbitrary mental leap from the *aims* to the *subject matter*, without providing us with adequate principles such as would bridge the gap. . . .[10]

This last quotation from Charters presents the crux of the matter in regard to the "aims-and-objectives" stage of curriculum development. Curriculum workers had not yet been able to get out of the aims-and-objectives stage, or to carry those aims and objectives over so that they worked in the curriculum as then established and administered. A careful study of Charters' book leaves the reader in a state of uncertainty as to whether Charters made the transition which he said he planned to make in this work.

BOBBITT'S LATER STUDIES.   By 1924 Bobbitt had advanced so far in

[7] *Ibid.*, p. 102.
[8] *The Curriculum, op. cit.*, p. 3.
[9] *Op. cit.*, p. 4.
[10] *Ibid.*, pp. 6–7.

his plan of activity analysis for the determination of the curriculum that he was able to divide the broad range of human experience into ten major fields, as follows:

1. Social Intercommunication
2. Maintenance of Physical Efficiency
3. Efficient Citizenship
4. General Social Contacts and Relationships
5. General Mental Efficiency
6. Leisure Occupations
7. Religious Attitudes and Activities
8. Parental Responsibilities
9. Unspecialized Practical Activities
10. Occupational Activities.[11]

The first nine of these fields were supposed to include all of those experiences which it was desirable for all normal people to have, whereas the last objective varied according to the particular occupation chosen by the individual.

Bobbitt then went a step further and set up techniques for learning, composed of general and specific types of activities for pupils. Those techniques included the following:

1. Observation, the undirected type being considered most beneficial
2. Performance, which stressed the importance of practice
3. Reading
4. Oral reports
5. Pictures
6. Prolonging, repeating, and intensifying one's experiences
7. Problem solving
8. Generalization.

In using these techniques, emphasis was to be laid on pupil "doing and experiencing." Bobbitt maintained that training should be non-specialized and uniform for all pupils until the end of the secondary school, or possibly of the junior college. This concept bears a remarkable similarity to the concept of "general" education as emphasized today. He contended that no specialized training should be undertaken until general training had been completed, except in the cases

---

[11] *How to Make a Curriculum*, Boston, Houghton Mifflin Company, 1924, pp. 11–31.

of dull pupils showing aptitude along special lines, bright pupils who could carry specialized courses in addition to general courses, and pupils who were forced to leave school and go to work.

In 1926 Bobbitt's *Curriculum Investigations* [12] carried still further his aim of analyzing the activities of those persons who come nearest to living life as it should be lived. In order to find out what activities people perform to prepare themselves for mature (adult) functioning, and on this basis to determine the curriculum, he proposed to analyze exhaustively the activities of adults in the ten major fields of experience set forth in his *How to Make a Curriculum*. His *Curriculum Investigations* reported extensive studies which were carried out in fourteen major areas of human activity. To discover these major fields of human activity, evidence was compiled from the following sources:

From periodical literature.

From newspapers.

From the *Encyclopedia Britannica*.

From language (Thorndike's *The Teacher's Word Book*).

From the *Literary Digest*.

From public opinion, as represented by leaders of current thought in the editorials of newspapers and in special articles in magazines, and from 111 leaders of thought, mostly in Chicago.

From civic and social shortcomings as curriculum indices, in which editorials of nine newspapers over a period of three months were consulted.

From social problems of the labor group, in which ten well-known books dealing with labor problems were analyzed.

From quality of conduct in the analysis of eighteen books, such as Bacon's and Carlyle's *Essays*, etc.

From social behavior, in which eleven books were analyzed, and 123 articles in the *American Magazine* were studied.

From shortcomings in the written English of adults through a representative sampling of letters addressed to an open-forum column of the *Chicago Daily Tribune*.

From the mathematics used in popular science, in which science articles in a random sampling of five magazines and three books were analyzed.

From play activities of persons of different ages.

From the placement of poems in the grades.

[12] The University of Chicago Press, 1926.

CONTRIBUTIONS OF HARAP AND UHL. In 1924 another contribution was made to the activity-analysis procedure, when Henry Harap collected data on the habits of living and standards of consumption of the population.[13] He used a variety of sources such as bulletins of government bureaus, census reports, and investigations of private companies. His study was concerned with the fundamental elements of effective social life; it covered a wide range of activities in the economic life of the people, such as food consumption, housing, household materials, household fuel consumption, and the consumption of clothing. At the end of each section, objectives for the curriculum are given, but the specific methods for teaching these objectives are not indicated. In *The Education of the Consumer*, Harap did not make the transition from the aims-and-objectives stage to the actual incorporating of the material into the curriculum of the school, but in his later work he did.[14] Harap's book on the technique of curriculum making and W.L. Uhl's *Secondary School Curricula*[15] were evidently the first books to bridge the gap from "objectives" to actual curriculum activities, teaching units, or phases of curriculum activity. The illustrations of teaching activities in these two books show the first carry-over of activity analysis into the materials of the curriculum. In Chapters ix and x of his book, Uhl gives the best presentation of objectives and of how objectives affect curricula. Of course, Uhl's book deals with the curriculum of the secondary school, but the analysis which it gives is of value to the curriculum maker on any school level.

THE SURVEY MOVEMENT IN CURRICULUM REVISION

THE FORMULATION OF AIMS BY NATIONAL COMMITTEES. During the same time that the curriculum workers were attempting to discover those activities which should go into the curriculum, national committees representing different groups of educators in general and the subject-matter fields in particular were going into the business of

[13] *The Education of the Consumer*, New York, The Macmillan Company, 1924.
[14] *The Technique of Curriculum Making*, New York, The Macmillan Company, 1929.
[15] New York, The Macmillan Company, 1927.

curriculum study on a broad scale. The Commission on the Reorganization of Secondary Education in 1920 was composed of ten committees, each working on some separate subject. Although the remaking of the curriculum through the surveys of national committees began as early as 1892, the *Twenty-sixth Yearbook* of the National Society for the Study of Education stated that these investigators lacked interest and training in the professional field of curriculum making:

> . . . the members of these national committees [1892–1926] have used subjective and *a priori* methods in arriving at their recommendations and, with two recent exceptions, have ignored the results of curricular research. . . .
>
> . . . Careful search of their [national committee] reports . . . fails to reveal a single instance in which the committee set up experimental and scientific studies to aid them in their choice of recommended content, grade-placement, and organization of the materials of the curriculum.[16]

The vast extent of the survey movement is indicated by the following representative studies, all of which were made and published between 1920 and the present:

The Classical Investigation, conducted by the Advisory Committee of the American Classical League. Part i, *General Report*. Part iii, *The Classics in England, France, and Germany*. Published in 1924 and 1925 by the Princeton University Press.

The Modern Foreign Language Study. Publication of the American and Canadian Committees on Modern Languages, Volumes 1–17, covering the results of inquiries carried on by the study from 1924 to 1927, and formulating the conclusions of the committee on investigation as they related to the entire field of modern language teaching in the secondary school and the corresponding courses in modern languages in college. Covers exhaustively the objectives of teaching, the content of courses, and the organization of classes and methods of instruction. Published by The Macmillan Company, New York, 1928–1930.

Report of the Commission on the Social Studies of the American Historical Association, Parts 1–16. Embraces comprehensive findings on the aims and objectives of the social studies, the various areas of the social studies, curriculum making, methods of instruction, social foundations of education, tests and measurements, and other organizations opera-

---

[16] Part i, *The Foundations and Technique of Curriculum Construction* (1927): Harold Rugg, "Three Decades of Mental Discipline: Curriculum-Making *via* National Committees," Chap. iii, pp. 63–64. Quoted by permission of the Society.

tive in the civic training of youth. Published from 1934 to 1941 by Charles Scribner's Sons, New York.

The National Survey of Secondary Education. The United States Department of the Interior, Office of Education, Bulletin No. 17 (1932), Monographs Nos. 1–28. Covers a careful examination over a three-year period of reorganized schools in the United States, in regard to the organization and administration, the curriculum, extra-curriculum, pupil population, supervisory problems, personnel, and activities of the secondary schools. Published by the United States Government Printing Office in 1933.

Reports of the Curriculum Commission and Committee on Correlation of the National Council of Teachers of English: *An Experience Curriculum in English,* and *A Correlated Curriculum,* English Monographs Nos. 4 and 5 of the National Council of Teachers of English. These studies, together with *Conducting Experiences in English,* English Monograph No. 8, are cumulative results of work from 1929 to 1935 on the so-called "experience curriculum" in English. Published by D. Appleton-Century Company, New York, in 1935, 1936, and 1939, respectively.

Curriculum Making in Business Education: The Second Yearbook of the Eastern Commercial Teachers Association. Published by the Eastern Commercial Teachers Association, New York, 1929.

Special studies and reports of the National Education Association and of the American Association of School Administrators by their Educational Policies Commission on different aspects of the school curriculum: *Learning the Ways of Democracy: A Case Book of Civic Education,* 1940; *Education for All American Youth,* 1944, and *Education for All American Youth—A Further Look,* 1952; *Education Services for Younger Children,* 1945; and *Education for All American Children,* 1948.

After a careful examination of these representative surveys, one must take exception to the foregoing quotation from the *Twenty-sixth Yearbook* of the National Society for the Study of Education to the effect that these reports prior to 1926 failed to reveal a single instance in which the committee organized experimental and scientific studies to aid it in its choice of recommended content, grade placement, and organization of materials for curricula. The earliest of these surveys, the *Classical Investigation,* used 1,313 secondary schools in which approximately 150,000 pupils were tested. The total number of individual tests given was approximately 750,000.[17] Excel-

[17] Part I, *General Report,* p. 13.

lent illustrations of the controlled studies of an experimental nature which were organized by the *Classical Investigation* include the related work of A.A. Hamblen [18] and R.I. Haskell [19] in the Philadelphia high schools in teaching English derivatives from Latin.

It is clear that it was not the failure to use scientific methods in so far as they had been developed at that time which was lacking in the *Classical Investigation,* as much as it was a failure to make a constructive interpretation of the results obtained. Such a constructive interpretation of results should have translated the general and specific recommendations into practical samples of activities to be carried on in the Latin classroom.

The cumulative evidence from these national surveys shows gradual progress in curriculum construction. First, each survey gives evidence of thought and some experimental work upon the objectives of the curriculum and upon the methods to be employed in attaining those objectives. Secondly, as these surveyors have had access to experimental and research work which has already been completed, they have advanced progressively toward a carry-over into actual work in the curriculum of the "aims and objectives" which they have stated. For example, if the *Classical Investigation* is compared with the series of reports at a later date of the Commission on the Social Studies of the American Historical Association, or with the Studies of the Educational Policies Commission, the conclusion must be reached that some of the evidences of the excellent work found in the later reports are due probably as much to improved methods of discovering what the aims and objectives should be and how they should be attained through curriculum materials and methods, as they are due to advanced thought and more efficient work of an experimental nature in the survey.

All of these surveys have had a tremendous influence upon the school curriculum. For example, the *Classical Investigation* gave

[18] *An Investigation to Determine the Extent to Which the Effect of the Study of Latin upon a Knowledge of English Derivatives Can Be Increased by Conscious Adaptations of Content and Method to the Attainment of This Objective,* University of Pennsylvania, 1925.

[19] *A Statistical Study of the Comparative Results Produced by Teaching Derivation in the Ninth Grade English Classes of Non-Latin Pupils in Four Philadelphia High Schools,* University of Pennsylvania, 1923 (Ph.D. thesis).

impetus to several new series of textbooks for the teaching of Latin in line with the recommendations of the investigation; the teaching of Latin in secondary schools has unquestionably profited much from the study, in spite of the limitations of the study.

SCIENTIFIC SURVEYS. Another type of national survey is well illustrated by the various publications of the National Society for the Study of Education from 1920 to the present. The list of investigations which follows [20] was selected from the studies of this nationally recognized research body as significant samples of the more scientific approach to the reorganization and rebuilding of the curriculum.

19th Yearbook, 1920, Part I: *New Materials of Instruction.*
20th Yearbook, 1921, Part I: *New Materials of Instruction;* Part II: *Report of the Society's Committee on Silent Reading.*
22nd Yearbook, 1923, Part I: *English Composition: Its Aims, Methods, and Measurements;* Part II: *The Social Studies in the Elementary and Secondary School.*
23rd Yearbook, 1924, Part II: *Vocational Guidance and Vocational Education for Industries.*
24th Yearbook, 1925, Part I: *Report of the National Committee on Reading.*
25th Yearbook, 1926, Part I: *The Present Status of Safety Education.*
26th Yearbook, 1927, Part I: *Curriculum Making: Past and Present;* Part II: *The Foundations of Curriculum-Making.*
29th Yearbook, 1930, Parts I and II: *Report of the Society's Committee on Arithmetic* (Part I, *Some Aspects of Modern Thought on Arithmetic;* Part II, *Research in Arithmetic*).
31st Yearbook, 1932, Part I: *A Program for Teaching Science.*
32nd Yearbook, 1933: The Teaching of Geography.
35th Yearbook, 1936, Part II: *Music Education.*
36th Yearbook, 1937, Part I: *Second Report on Reading.*
38th Yearbook, 1939, Part I: *Child Development and the Curriculum.*
40th Yearbook, 1941: Art in American Life and Education.
42nd Yearbook, 1943, Part I: *Vocational Education.*
43rd Yearbook, 1944, Part II: *Teaching Language in the Elementary School.*
46th Yearbook, 1947, Part I: *Science Education in American Schools.*
47th Yearbook, 1948, Part II: *Reading in the High School and College.*
48th Yearbook, 1949, Part II: *Reading in the Elementary School.*
50th Yearbook, 1951, Part II: *The Teaching of Arithmetic.*

[20] Now published by the National Society for the Study of Education.

52nd Yearbook, 1953, Part i: *Adapting the Secondary-School Program to the Needs of Youth.*
56th Yearbook, 1957, Part ii: *Social Studies in the Elementary Schools.*
57th Yearbook, 1958, Part i: *Basic Concepts in Music Education.*

A careful examination of these successive reports reveals the fact that it was approximately 1930 before broad aims and objectives in education began to be carried over into actual activities and experiences for the child in the classroom.

GENERAL SURVEYS AND INVESTIGATIONS. Although not compiled with the same scientific approach as that used by the National Society for the Study of Education, the yearbooks and reports of special groups and educational organizations within the last thirty years have considered various aspects of the curriculum and have contributed much of value to curriculum revision. Among the surveys of this type will be found the yearbooks and reports of the following Departments or Divisions of the National Education Association: the American Association of School Administrators (formerly the Department of Superintendence); Elementary School Principals; the Association (formerly the Department) of Secondary-School Principals; the Association for Supervision and Curriculum Development (formerly the Department of Supervisors and Directors of Instruction and the independent Society for Curriculum Study); the National Council for the Social Studies; and the Research Division of the National Education Association.[21]

[21] Samples of the special studies of these groups are as follows:

American Association of School Administrators:

4th Yearbook, 1926: The Nation at Work on the Public School Curriculum.
5th Yearbook, 1927: The Junior High School Curriculum.
6th Yearbook, 1928: The Development of the High-School Curriculum.
14th Yearbook, 1936: The Social Studies Curriculum.
16th Yearbook, 1938: Youth Education Today.
19th Yearbook, 1941: Education for Family Life.
20th Yearbook, 1942: Health In Schools (rev., 1951).
29th Yearbook, 1951: Conservation Education in American Schools.
31st Yearbook, 1953: American School Curriculum.
36th Yearbook, 1958: The High School in a Changing World.

Department of Elementary School Principals:

17th Yearbook, 1938: Newer Practices in Reading in the Elementary School.
18th Yearbook, 1939: Enriching the Curriculum for the Elementary School Child.

DIFFERENCE BETWEEN "CONTROLLED" AND "GENERAL" EXPERI-MENTATION. In attempting to draw conclusions concerning the survey movement, one must be careful in one's understanding of the terms involved. Controlled experimentation has generally been referred to as the "scientific approach," in which the experimenters attempt to hold all factors constant except the one factor which they are trying to measure or to discover something about. By the employment of such control techniques in scientific experimentation, the investigators try to eliminate inaccuracies and outside influences, and thus arrive at results that are significant for all education.

On the other hand, much more experimentation of a general nature without any type of comparative safeguards is prevalent, and this is

20th Yearbook, 1941: Language Arts In the Elementary School.
The Role of Speech In the Elementary School, 1946.
29th Yearbook, 1950: Health in the Elementary School.
31st Yearbook, 1952: Bases for Effective Learning.
32nd Yearbook, 1953: Science for Today's Children.
34th Yearbook, 1954: Reading for Today's Children.

National Association of Secondary-School Principals:

Bulletin No. 59, 1936: Issues of Secondary Education.
Bulletin No. 64, 1937: Functions of Secondary Education.
Bulletin No. 145, 1947: The Imperative Needs of Youth of Secondary-School Age.
Bulletin No. 215, 1955: Framework for Family Life Education.
Bulletin No. 229, 1957: Outdoor Education for American Youth.

National Council for the Social Studies:

4th Yearbook, 1934: The Social-Studies Curriculum.
17th Yearbook, 1947: The Study and Teaching of American History.
25th Yearbook, 1954: Approaches to an Understanding of World Affairs.
27th Yearbook, 1956: Science and the Social Studies.

Association for Supervision and Curriculum Development:

9th Yearbook, 1936: The Development of a Modern Program in English.
The Changing Curriculum, 1937.
The Community School, 1938, and The Modern Community School, 1953.
1944 Yearbook: Toward a New Curriculum.
1953 Yearbook: Forces Affecting American Education.
1956 Yearbook: What Shall the High Schools Teach?
1958 Yearbook: A Look at Continuity in the School Program.

National Education Association Research Bulletins:

Vol. XIII, No. 5, 1935, *Better Reading Instruction.*
Vol. XV, No. 5, 1937, *Improving Social-Studies Instruction.*
Vol. XX, No. 1, 1942, *Reading Instruction In Secondary Schools.*

equally valuable for the curriculum worker. Here the experimenter is attempting to assist the growth of a particular pupil in a group or a class, or to help his own growth. For instance, controlled experiments organized to discover whether children learn better in a life-like situation aim only at accumulating evidence enough to inform educators whether children do learn better in such a situation; on the other hand, a nonscientific experiment by a teacher in his own classroom on the same problem may enable him to meet the interests and needs of his pupils more effectively, or to adapt his work more specifically to their problems. In general the yearbooks of the National Society for the Study of Education present more of the "controlled" experiments; and the special reports and yearbooks of other educational groups represent more of the second type of "general" experimentation by individual teachers or schools. The point to be emphasized here is that both types of experiment are extremely valuable; it is only as the individual teacher experiments in some teaching area or with some group that he grows and enlarges his vision and teaching effectiveness.

When interpreted in the light of these two definitions, most of the surveys of a national character concerning the curriculum have conformed more to the general experimental approach than to the controlled experimental approach. This general experimental approach includes (1) a survey of the situation, (2) an analysis of the data which have been collected, and (3) recommendations for improvement or change. These three fundamental processes may or may not be supplemented by the giving of tests and the use of measurements, or by accompanying investigations of the controlled experimental type; they may be, and usually are, accompanied by the ideas and opinions of the people in the field of the survey. Thus it is seen that philosophical concepts based on opinion still exist in curriculum revision and are made use of in curriculum construction.

It is a significant fact that curriculum surveys in the 1920's, the 1940's, and the 1950's were paralleled by *administrative* surveys of schools. These administrative surveys made a careful examination of sites, buildings, equipment, finances, playgrounds, organization and administration, and other factors. The reports of the surveys usually contained information and recommendations about the curriculum of the school system, and thus they frequently stimulated efforts at curricular improvements.

SYMPOSIA OF EXPERIMENTAL CURRICULAR PRACTICES. The latest development in the survey movement in curriculum-building involves analyses of valuable experimental practices which have developed in various sections of the country. The earlier publications of this type for the use of curriculum workers were by Wrightstone and Spears; the more recent publications are the results of system-wide studies of the Horace Mann-Lincoln Institute of School Experimentation at Teachers College, Columbia University. Significant experiments which have been in operation in both elementary and secondary schools have been collected and analyzed with constructive comments and suggestions regarding their contributions to education.[22] This is a most practical approach to the actual introduction of new methods among school teachers, and other publications of this type will likewise prove valuable as time goes on.

DEVELOPMENT OF THE UNIT TECHNIQUE

The reader is referred to Chapter 7 for a full discussion of the unit technique.

SYSTEM-WIDE CURRICULUM REVISION

TYPES.   Since its beginning about 1924, curriculum revision on a system-wide basis has grown by leaps and bounds. Some states, such as Alabama and Virginia, have been at work for many years on such

---

[22] As good samples over a period of years, compare these: J.W. Wrightstone, *Appraisal of Experimental High School Practices*, 1936, and *Appraisal of Newer Elementary School Practices*, 1938, Teachers College, Columbia University; Harold Spears, *The Emerging High-School Curriculum and Its Direction*, 1948, New York, American Book Company, and *Curriculum Planning Through In-Service Programs*, Englewood Cliffs, Prentice-Hall, 1957, *passim;* J.P. Leonard, *Developing the Secondary-School Curriculum*, 1946, (rev., 1953), New York, Rinehart and Company, Chaps. IV–XII; and H. L. Caswell, *et al.*, *Curriculum Improvement in Public School Systems*, 1951, and F. B. Stratmeyer, *et al.*, *Developing a Curriculum for Modern Living*, 1947 (rev., 1957), Teachers College, Columbia University. A more detailed account of the experiments and contributions of the Horace Mann-Lincoln Institute of School Experimentation will be found in Chapter 21.

programs; other states also have promulgated a study of their curricula in the light of investigations and modern changes. Perhaps the most outstanding system-wide movement in curriculum revision was that which was in operation from 1919 at Winnetka, Illinois, under Superintendent Carleton Washburne. He and his board of education and teaching staff attempted to arrive at some sort of working procedure which would capitalize on their child-centered philosophy of education.[23] The Denver, Detroit, Los Angeles, St. Louis, and Long Beach school systems give other good illustrations of the earlier and the later stages of this movement among city school systems.[24] Montgomery County, Maryland, and Santa Barbara County and San Diego County in California are good examples of the operation of this movement in county school systems.

The modern curriculum movement did not get well under way on a statewide scale until 1931, when the Virginia curriculum study under the direction of H.L. Caswell and D.S. Campbell was started.[25] Among the statewide attempts at curriculum revision, the following have probably received the most notice: the Alabama program, started in 1935; the Georgia program, 1935; the California program, 1934; the Florida program, 1938; the Wisconsin program, 1944; and the Illinois program, 1947.

TRENDS IN STATE CURRICULUM PROGRAMS. Two different trends are discernible in the statewide programs. One trend emphasizes that the whole state should take part in curriculum revision, or, if it does not take part, should at least follow the revision which has been suggested. The procedure in Virginia and Florida over a long period of years illustrates this first trend rather well.[26] The other trend

[23] *Cf.* Carleton Washburne, *A Living Philosophy of Education,* New York, The John Day Company, 1940.

[24] *Cf.* J.W. Wrightstone, *Appraisal of Newer Elementary School Practices, op. cit.,* Chap. I.

[25] *Cf. Brief Description of Virginia Program for Improving Instruction,* Vol. XXI, No. 4 (January, 1939); *Tentative Course of Study for Virginia Elementary Schools, Grades I–VII,* 1934; *Course of Study for Virginia Elementary Schools, Grades I–VII,* 1943; and *Tentative Course of Study for the Core Curriculum of Virginia Secondary Schools,* 1934, all published by the State Board of Education.

[26] *Cf. The Tentative Courses of Study for Virginia, op. cit.;* and the *Florida Curriculum Bulletins No. 1, Source Materials for the Improvement of Instruction,* 1938, and *No. 2, Ways to Better Instruction in Florida Schools,* 1939, fol-

emphasizes the attempt to develop experimental procedures and suggestive materials of a source nature. This type of curriculum procedure encourages the teachers in the state to participate in the program by starting small changes of their own in their own school situations. Alabama, through its curriculum bulletins progressively leading up to procedures in large unit teaching,[27] and California, through its child development series and studies made by its state teacher groups,[28] give excellent illustrations of this trend. There is much to be said for this broad and stimulative approach, which operates through urging and not superimposing changes in the curriculum upon the schools and the teachers. In so far as one can gather from written reports and an examination of course of study bulletins, large-unit or large-area teaching in certain Alabama schools, and the fusion and core-curriculum developments in certain schools of California, have been outstanding.[29]

The development of the Virginia study of the curriculum since 1931 gives an excellent illustration of the impact of various movements upon curriculum revision on a statewide scale. The Virginia study went rather extensively into formulating the aims and objectives to be attained; then the usual compromise developed, in which an attempt was made to adapt these aims and objectives to a core curriculum, consisting on the secondary-school level of social studies, language arts, science, and general mathematics. "Centers of interest" adapted to the "major functions of social life" were selected for each year; one might call these centers of interest the forerunner of the

---

lowed by separate course of study *Bulletins* on practically all aspects of the curriculum in both the elementary and secondary schools from 1940 to 1959.

[27] Alabama, State Board of Education, in cooperation with the Alabama Education Association, *Curriculum Bulletins*, Nos. 1–9, 1936–1941, and *Course of Study and Guide for Teachers, Grades 1–12*, Division of Instruction, Instructional Series, Bulletin No. 11, 1950.

[28] California State Department of Education, *Teachers' Guide to Child Development in the Primary Grades*, 1930, and *Teachers' Guide to Child Development in the Intermediate Grades*, 1936; for the latest information on California procedures, consult two recent State Department publications, *Teachers' Guide to Education in Early Childhood*, 1956, and *Teachers' Guide to Education in Later Childhood*, 1957.

[29] Cf. Spears, *op. cit.*, 1948, Chaps. VI, XII and pp. 322–27; and H.E. Herriott, "Creative Administration," *The Bulletin of the National Association of Secondary School-Principals*, XXIX (April, 1945), p. 53.

so-called "large unit" of today. In both the elementary and the secondary schools, the organization of teaching was effected in terms of the center of interest which was selected for each grade or school year. Finally, there is discernible in the Virginia study the attempt to reinterpret the whole curriculum in terms of the activity movement;

FIG. 17   *Cooperative Planning*

Pupils and teacher discuss questions which they have formulated and which give direction to the classroom instruction. (*Courtesy Denver Public Schools.*)

in addition to the primary center of interest, there is a section on "general activities" for each grade or year for the cultural and recreational development of the child. The Virginia course of study suggestions were so soundly worked out that little basic change took place in them for over twenty years. Virginia's excellent project calls attention to the type of hybrid development which the curriculum is undergoing, whether one agrees with the procedures followed or not.[30]

THE CORE-CURRICULUM MOVEMENT AND THE LARGE-UNIT PROCEDURE, INCLUDING THE FUSION MOVEMENT

THE CORE CURRICULUM. Many educators maintain that the development in the pupil of the feeling of *social solidarity* should be one of the most important purposes of the school. Acquisition of this social solidarity would require that the child be made conscious of such things as his social duties, interests, usages, and problems, not only from an individual but also from a societal and national viewpoint. In order to achieve this so-called "social integration," these educators propose the *core curriculum*. This core would be centered around a certain area or areas of study, such as the social studies, for example, and would be required of all pupils in order to give them further light upon the common problems of citizenship in this country. Another purpose of the core curriculum would be to develop school programs in terms of the social and individual needs and interests of pupils. In conjunction with the study of the life problems of youth and of the problems and resources of local communities, the development of social living is important.[31]

[30] *Course of Study for Virginia Elementary Schools*, Grades i–vii (1943), *op. cit.*, *Tentative Course of Study for the Core Curriculum of Virginia Secondary Schools, op. cit.*, Grade viii, Sections i, ii, *passim* and Section iv. Compare also *Manual of Administration for the High Schools of Virginia*, 1942 (reprinted 1948), Chap. ii, esp. pp. 39–40 and 59–61. Few basic changes took place in these courses of study for years, as one may see from reading the *Richmond Times Dispatch*, March 10, 1955, "Revision of Manual for Teachers is Ordered," pp. 1–2.

[31] For fuller discussions of the earlier core curriculum, compare A.A. Douglass, *Modern Secondary Education*, Boston, Houghton Mifflin Company, 1938, pp. 240, 333–34, 356 *ff.*, 700–711; *Thirty Schools Tell Their Story*, New York, Harper and Brothers, 1943, pp. 146–262, 638–59; J.P. Leonard, *Developing the Secondary-School Curriculum*, New York, Rinehart and Company, 1946, Chaps. viii–xii; H.B. Alberty, *Reorganizing The High-School Curriculum*, New York, The Macmillan Company, Chaps. vi–vii; and H. N. Rivlin, *Teaching Adolescents in Secondary Schools*, New York, Appleton-Century-Crofts, 1948, pp. 47–56. For later discussions of the core curriculum, contrast the revisions of Leonard's book (1953) and Alberty's book (1953) with R.C. Faunce and N.L. Bossing, *Developing the Core Curriculum* (1951 and 1958 editions), New York, Prentice-Hall; L.L. Lurry and E.J. Alberty, *Developing a High School Core Program*, New York, The Macmillan Company, 1957; and G. Noar, *The Junior High School—Today and Tomorrow*, New York, Prentice-Hall, 1953, *passim*.

Although various approaches to the core curriculum have been made, the development over a period of years in California will be taken as typical.[32] In Los Angeles the term "core" has been used to designate the program common to all. In the junior high schools of Los Angeles, the following six major blocks of interrelated experiences were recommended for the core program:

1. Six semesters of double-period social living.
2. Four semesters of mathematics.
3. Two semesters of general science, plus related science in practical arts and science emphasis in seventh- and eighth-grade social living.
4. Three semesters of fine arts activities.
5. Three semesters of practical arts activities.
6. Six semesters of physical education.[33]

The real core of the Los Angeles program for junior high schools was the lengthened-period social living course, which included experiences formerly a part of such fields as the social studies, the sciences, language arts, and pupil guidance. In four of the six grades of the high school, the course was two periods in length.[34]

In 1934, eleven high schools in California were given special permission by the colleges of the state to experiment in curriculum revision without specific regard for the college-entrance requirements then in effect.[35] Although no two schools in this experiment followed the same line of reorganization of the curriculum, the trend was toward some form of the core curriculum. Generally speaking, the plans of the Cooperating Schools tended to ignore subject-matter lines and "to set up a required core around those experiences generally common to social interaction."[36] Because they illustrate so well the different directions that forms of the core have taken today, the plan of the basic or core courses in the California Cooperating Schools in 1936 and in 1939 are given for comparative purposes in Tables 13 and 14.

[32] H. Spears, *The Emerging High-School Curriculum and Its Direction*, New York, American Book Company, 1948, Chap. XII; a comparison of this 1939 program with that of 1945 in H.E. Herriott, *op. cit.*, and with later curriculum bulletins shows no major changes.

[33] Spears, *loc. cit.*, p. 221.

[34] *Cf.* Spears, p. 221 and Herriott, p. 53.

[35] Spears, *ibid.*, pp. 230–42.

[36] *Ibid.*, p. 232.

TABLE 13   Plan of basic or core courses, California Cooperating Schools, 1936 [1]

School	Courses, by Grades and Number of Periods a Week		
	GRADE X	GRADE XI	GRADE XII
Burbank Senior High School	World Culture....10 Survey of Science. 5	American Life or..10 Modern Science.10	American Problems 5
David Starr Jordan High School	Social Culture....10	Social Culture....10	Social Problems... 5
Eagle Rock Junior-Senior High School	World Culture....10 Physical Universe ......2 or 3	American Social Development ..10	Social Science, Literature, Oral and Written English 5
Benjamin Franklin High School °	Social Understanding 10	Social Understanding 10	
James A. Garfield High School †	Social Studies, English, Science, Social Arts, Art, Music 15	American Life and Institutions 10	Economics, Social Arts 5
Manual Arts High School ‡	Social Studies—English 10	Social Studies—English 10	
Fremont High School	Core course has not been developed. Modifications occur within the usual courses, especially science, social studies, consumers' economics, and coeducational social experience.		
University High School	First semester: Personal Management ...... 5 Second semester: Social Living .. 5	First semester: American Institutions .... 5 Second semester: Social Problems. 5 or Political Problems or Business of Living 5	First semester: Personal Management .... 5 Second semester: Social Living .. 5
Pasadena Senior High School and Junior College §	Biological Science. 5	First semester: Humanities Survey .... 5 Second semester: Physical Science Survey 5	First semester: Social Science Survey .... 5 Second semester: Home Economics Survey 5
Sequoia Union High School °°	Social Living 10	United States History 5	Social and Economic Problems. 5
Santa Monica High School	English, Social Science, Science.15	English, Social Science, Science. 15	English, Social Science, Science. 15

° Included, in the ninth grade, Social Understanding, 10 semester periods. A required course in Personal Orientation contemplated for Grade XII.

† Courses for the twelfth grade in process of formulation.

‡ It is expected that Social Studies—English will be extended to Grade XII.

§ The tenth grade is a part of the junior high school.

°° In the ninth grade the core consisted of Social Living, 10 semester periods, and Home Arts and Applied Science, 5 semester periods.

[1] State of California, Department of Education Bulletin, *Recent Developments in Secondary Education in California*, "A Preliminary Report of the Cooperating Schools," October 1, 1936, p. 17. This Table is also reproduced in Harold Spears' *The Emerging High School Curriculum and Its Direction*, New York, copyright 1940, 1948 by American Book Company, pp. 233–34. Reprinted by permission.

TABLE 14 The social-living programs in the California Cooperating Schools, 1939 [1]

Senior High Schools	Low 10	High 10	Low 11	High 11	Low 12	High 12
Los Angeles City Schools	World Cultures or Orientation (English skills emphasized) Art, Music Appreciation Practical Art †		AMERICAN INSTITUTIONS *		Senior Problems Laboratory Science (if not taken previously)	
Eagle Rock, Junior-Senior High School	SOCIAL LIVING		SOCIAL LIVING		SOCIAL LIVING	
	(sections kept intact over two-year intervals: 7–8, 9–10, and 11–12)					
Garfield and Manual Arts Senior High Schools	BASIC COURSE Social Arts	Biology	BASIC COURSE (Physical) Science Survey		Senior Problems (Consumer Economics)	(Home and Family)
Burbank Senior High School	BASIC COURSE (Orientation, Music and Art Appreciation) Biology or Science Survey		BASIC COURSE (Current Problems of American Democracy)		Basic Course (International Problems)	(Vocations and Family Relations)
David Starr Jordan High School, Long Beach	CULTURES AND INSTITUTIONS (Orientation)		CULTURES AND INSTITUTIONS (American Institutions)		Current Problems	Home and Family

164

			Humanities Physical Science Orientation		Social Studies American Family (for girls)	
Pasadena District Junior College						
University Senior High School, Oakland	Personal Management	Social Living	Am. History, Am. Civilization, Am. Problems, Am. Life, or Modern History	Political Problems, Social Problems, or Economic Problems	English, Consumer Education, or Elementary Psychology	English Business Problems, or Home Problems (for girls)
Four-year High Schools	9	10	11	12		
Carpinteria Union High School	FOUNDATIONS (Orientation)	Foundations	HUMAN RELATIONS	HUMAN RELATIONS (Social Graces)		
Sequoia Union High School, Redwood City	SOCIAL LIVING Home Arts and Applied Science (boys and girls segregated)	SOCIAL LIVING	English Social Studies or American History	English Senior Problems		
Yuba City Union High School	CORE COURSE	English World Cultures	English United States History and Civics			

* In this chart, double-period courses are indicated by capital letters.

† Much of the required art and music appreciation is related to the basic course work in grades ten and eleven.

¹ From the *Bulletin of the California State Department of Education*, No. 3 (May, 1939), "Programs of the Cooperating Secondary Schools in California," pp. 56–57.

According to the programs of the California Cooperating Schools, the social studies took the stage as the particular center around which materials from other fields were brought into play; English and science were the other areas used for the core. Although three high schools withdrew, and two new ones were added during the experiment, the trends are clearly discernible from the eight which remained for the entire time. In most of the schools, the core occupied the school time of two periods a day. Orientation was emphasized as a feature of the core course for new pupils, and there was a tendency for the teachers of the basic courses in these schools to take over more and more of the pupil guidance responsibilities. A good illustration of the development of the core curriculum in an entire city system was furnished by the Denver public schools from the 1930's to 1950.[37]

THE LARGE-UNIT PROCEDURE. The presentation of large units of teaching materials is primarily a teaching device centered around the "activity" concept of education. One of the sanest approaches to the large-unit technique is found in the curriculum bulletins of the division of instruction of the State Department of Education in Alabama.[38] In summary form, the characteristics of large-unit teaching are set forth as follows:

1. The unit should be meaningful to children, and should grow from their interests and needs in connection with some vital aspect of present-day living.
2. In all phases the children should have a major part in the making of plans, in assuming responsibilities, and in the evaluation.
3. First-hand experiences and varied types of direct activities on the part of the children, and the reading of books which are rich in vicarious experiences characterize good unit teaching.
4. Children should engage in cooperative activities in the classroom through which they work together in groups, develop common

---

[37] Spears, *op. cit.*, 1948, Chap. XIII. Compare *Thirty Schools Tell Their Story*, New York, Harper and Brothers, 1943, pp. 146–212; and G. Saylor, "Core Programs in American Secondary Schools," *Educational Leadership*, VI. (February, 1949), 332; and I.J. Quillen and L. Hanna, *Education for Social Competence*, Chicago, Scott, Foresman and Company, 1948, pp. 88–89, 102–3. For more recent core programs, turn to Chapter 13.

[38] *Procedures in Large Unit Teaching: Suggestions for Improving Instruction*, 1937, p. 17, and *Course of Study and Guide for Teachers, Grades 1–12*, 1950, *op. cit.*, Chap. VII.

interests, and share purposes, ideas, and materials in order to build desirable social habits and ideals.
5. Unit teaching coordinates the work in the various areas of learning in a meaningful way, and provides vital purposes in these different areas.

The following types of units were set forth in clear fashion in the Alabama program: (1) the experience or center-of-interest units; (2) the subject-matter units with the experience approach; and (3) the subject-matter units from the subject-matter approach. In planning the large unit at the beginning of the year, the program recommended that the teacher study his pupils to discover their past experience, their interests, their abilities, their progress and problems in previous school work, and their needs; that he make a study of the community in order to be familiar with its resources and materials for study, its opportunities for amplifying pupil experiences, and its problems; that he formulate the aims of education to help in defining possible areas of activity and leads to units of experience; and that he examine and list the instructional materials available in the school.

From the foregoing suggestions in the Alabama program, it is seen that the teacher is expected to know much about the needs, interests, aptitudes, and problems of his pupils before he starts; with this knowledge acquired in advance, he will have a fairly shrewd idea of the various "areas of interest" which may develop in cooperative planning with the students throughout the year. In this way, a large amount of the background work for the units that may be selected is done in advance, and references and sources of materials are already located, listed, and made available.

SCOPE AND SEQUENCE.   The scope and sequence of the materials to be covered must be clearly outlined in both the core curriculum and the large-unit work. This aspect was worked out carefully in the Alabama program. Some large center of human interest from the major areas of living was set up for each two or three grades. Around each of these centers of interest the grades concerned were to develop their curriculum, the interests and abilities of the children, and the areas of living. For example, look at these centers of interest for 1937 and 1950.

1937		1950	
Grades		*Grades*	
1–3	Life in the Immediate Environment	1–2	The Immediate Community
		3–4	The Community and its Relationship to Other Communities
4–6	Exploration and Discovery in an Expanded Environment	5–6	Community, State, and Nation and Relationships to Other Countries
7–9	Adjustment to Natural and Social Forces	7–9	Adjustment to Natural and Social Forces
10–12	Individual and Group Control of Modern Problems	10–12	Individual and Group Control of Modern Problems

As time passed, the core curriculum in Alabama secondary schools, working through the *large-unit* procedure, came to include these aspects: [39]

1937	1950
The Core Curriculum, or Basic Socializing Experiences	The Core Curriculum, or Basic Socializing Experiences
The Pursuit of Special Interests	Special Interests
Work in the Basic Skills and Techniques	Skills
	Recreational and Creative Abilities.

The basic socializing experiences, or areas of living with which every pupil should be familiar are home life, recreation (including creative interests), production and consumption, transportation and communication, and citizenship. In the junior high school grades, the subjects which are usually provided for in the core are English, social studies, art, music, general science, mathematics, physical education, health education, and recreational activities. In the senior high school

[39] For the earlier core curriculum, see *Planning a Core Curriculum in the Secondary School, Bulletin No. 7,* 1939; for later modification, consult *Program of Studies and Guide to the Curriculum for Secondary Schools, Bulletin No. 9,* 1941 and *Course of Study and Guide for Teachers, Grades 1–12,* 1950; for large-unit teaching, see *Procedures in Large-Unit Teaching: Suggestions for Improving Instruction,* 1937 and the 1950 bulletin, Chap. VII.

the core is composed of English and social studies. Scope and sequence continue to be cared for adequately in the entire program, and the freedom and responsibility for secondary schools in working out their own programs are stressed. For this purpose, two plans for organization of the curriculum of the high school have been offered, (1) the Core Curriculum and (2) the Modified Subject-Matter Organization. In the modified subject-matter plan, the main difference between that and the old-time subject-matter organization seems to be that the program is arranged more by *groups* of subjects; these groups work to prevent extreme departmentalization.

For comparison with the Alabama program, here is the scope and sequence in the Virginia core curriculum: [40]

	Grade(s)	Center of Interest
Elementary School	1 and 2	Home, School, and Community Life
	3 and 4	Life Adaptations to Natural Environments and Physical Frontiers
	5 and 6	Effect on Our Living of Inventions, Discoveries, and Machine Production
	7 and 8	Social Provision for Cooperative Living
High School	9	How Inventions and Discoveries Affect Basic Human Needs
	10	How Agrarianism and Industrialism Affect Our Living
	11 and 12	Effects of Democracy Upon Human Relationships

The prospect is promising for the enrichment of the whole curriculum through the growth of the core curriculum and the large unit or "center of interest." These forms are becoming bases for further curriculum development to meet pupil needs.

FUSION. Further examination of the programs of the California Cooperating Schools (Table 14) shows the development within the core curriculum of what is called "fusion." [41] Fusion means the teaching of two or more different subjects together, without regard for

[40] Adapted from *Course of Study for Virginia Elementary Schools*, 1943, Section v, especially pp. 523–31; and *Suggestions for the Inauguration of a Twelve Year School System* (mimeographed), Part I, February, 1946, p. 14.
[41] Spears, *The Emerging High-School Curriculum and Its Direction*, New York, American Book Company, 1940, 1948, pp. 58–64 and Chap. XII.

subject-matter lines; that is, the subjects are fused into a core course
or large center of interest. Approximately half of the Cooperating
Schools give evidence of the fusion of courses which were formerly

FIG. 18   *Writing the group story: Grade One*
(*Courtesy Greensboro* (*N.C.*) *Public Schools, Brooks School.*)

taught separately as English, social studies, science, and so on. An
extreme example of a fused curriculum was found in the 1940's in the
Parker district of Greenville, South Carolina, in the eighth grade.
The teacher handled all subjects in the eighth grade with large
centers of interest, just as all subjects are handled on the elementary-

school level. In this case, fusion had become the same thing as the core curriculum. There was also fusion of social studies with English and languages for a double period in grades nine, ten, eleven, and twelve in the Parker District High School. Fusion on the secondary-school level usually means only the fusing of two or more subjects, not the fusing of student activities and interests. Many junior and senior high schools attempt to give both teachers and pupils freedom from the strict confines of the subject-matter departments through fusion or "problem" teaching, in order to promote teacher-pupil planning and a more personal program for each student. These schools also provide for special-interest groups.

SOURCE MATERIALS. Of course, the development and preparation of source materials for use in the core curriculum and in large units of teaching are necessary. Such materials have been prepared in a variety of ways. Some states and systems prepare regularly resource unit materials for teacher use. In addition, many texts today are written in the form of resource units, large subject-matter units, or fused materials. In a system-wide program of curriculum revision, the special bulletins of the Florida, Long Beach, California, and Illinois public schools are outstanding as source materials for teachers.[42] School systems and individual teachers develop their own source materials as they progress in their programs. *In the final analysis, there can be little real curriculum improvement unless there is experimentation and development by the individual teacher.*

THE ACTIVITY MOVEMENT

THE RELATION OF THE ACTIVITY MOVEMENT TO MODERN CURRICULUM REVISION. The "activity" movement cannot be designated accu-

---

[42] As samples, materials in Florida and Long Beach are given here; Illinois materials will be given in Chapter 20.

Florida teachers had these resource materials available from over a hundred separate bulletins published from 1936 to 1957:
Conservation: Minerals, 1936.
        Geography, 1936.
        Sea Resources, 1936.
        Forestry, 1937.
Bulletin No. 1, Source materials for the Improvement of Instruction, 1938.
Bulletin No. 6, Planning Curriculum Study with Local Groups, 1939.
Bulletin No. 2, Ways to Better Instruction in Florida Schools, 1939.

Avenues of Understanding, 1940.
Physical Fitness Guide, 1942.
Bulletin No. 5, Source Materials for Physical Education in Secondary Schools, 1942.
Bulletin No. 29, Everyday Living, 1942.
They Work for Victory, 1943.
Bulletin No. 43, Back to School, Homemaking Education for Adults and Out-of-School Youth, 1943.
Bulletin No. 44, Lessons from Life: Survey of Some Visual Education Opportunities in the Florida Curriculum, 1943.
Bulletin No. 30, Social Studies in the Elementary School, 1944.
Bulletin No. 51, Developing Understandings for Living in an Air Age, 1946.
Bulletin No. 53, Guide to Child Development Through Beginning School Years, 1946.
Bulletin No. 223, The Audio-Visual Way, 1948.
Bulletin No. 11, A Brief Guide to Teaching Business Education in the Secondary Schools, rev., 1948.
Bulletin No. 28, A Guide for the Teaching of Social Studies in the Secondary Schools, 1948.
Bulletin No. 37, Arts in the Lives of Florida Children, 1950.
Bulletin No. 4B, A Guide to Teaching Effective Living (a course in health and safety education for senior high schools), 1950.
Bulletin No. 10A, A Suggested Program of Study for Florida Secondary Schools, September, 1952.
Bulletin No. 4D, A Program of Health Services for Florida Schools, 1953.
Bulletin No. 34A, A Guide to Teaching Speech in Florida Secondary Schools, 1954.
Bulletin No. N40, Music for Florida Children, 1954.
Bulletin No. 53A, A Guide for Organizing and Developing a Kindergarten Program in Florida, January, 1955.
Bulletin No. 23, Florida Homemaking Education, 1955.
Bulletin No. 36, Functional Mathematics in the Secondary Schools, 1955.
Bulletin No. 22C, The Materials Center, 1955.
Bulletin No. 4E, Better Health for Florida's Children, 1957.

For over thirty years the Long Beach schools have been publishing curriculum bulletins, teachers' guides, courses of study, and units for use in the system. Since 1927 more than 250 of these publications have been prepared, used, and revised as revision was necessary. In this representative sampling of resource materials, the items which are starred (*) have been withdrawn from circulation, usually because later revisions replaced them, occasionally because the work was no longer offered:

* *Learning to Make Clothing,* Grade 6A, 1931.
* *Police Protection,* Grade 2, 1932–1933.
* *Proper and Safe Operation of Motor Vehicles,* Junior High School, 1936.
* *Children of Japan,* Grade 3, 1936.
* *Junior High School Material for Use in Home Rooms or Social Studies—English Classes,* 1937.
* *Star Land,* Grade 6, 1937.
* *Telling School Children About Social Work,* All Grades, 1938.
* *Library Practice Course of Study for Senior High Schools,* 1941.
* *Getting Acquainted with our Southern Neighbors—Latin America,* Sample Unit, Grade 9, 1941.
* *Science of the Out-of-Doors,* Grade 9, 1942.

* *Guide for Chart Making and Chart Stories* (General Material), 1943, rev. 1948.
* *Resource Units for Seventh Grade Social Living Classes,* 1945, rev. 1946 (5 Vols.) I, *Our School,* II, *Our Families,* III, *Our Town,* IV, *Our State,* V, *Our Country.*
* *Occupations: Today's Consumer* (2 Resource Units—12th Grade Social Studies), 1945.
* *Community Life: A Unit of Work for 1st Year Children,* 1945.
* *Life in a Mexican Village,* Unit of work for Grade 4, 1945.
* *Ships, Harbor, and Cargoes,* Unit for Grade 3, 1946.
Pioneers of the West, Unit for Grade 5, 1947.
Life in Early California, Unit for Grade 5, 1948.
Guide to Art in the Junior High School, Junior High School, 1950.
Guide to the Teaching of Spelling, Grades 2–6, 1951.
The Very Superior Pupil; a Tentative Plan: Elementary, Elementary, 1952.
* *The Very Superior Pupil; a Tentative Plan,* Junior High, 1952.
Guide to the Teaching of Reading in the Intermediate Grades, Grades 4–6, 1952.
Physical Education, A Course of Study for Junior High School Boys, 1953.
The Long Beach Story, Grade 11, 1954.
* *Suggestions for the Integration of English Usage with History and Literature in the Tenth Grade* (Tentative), 1954.
A Teacher's Guide for Kindergarten Education, Kindergarten, 1954.
Water Transportation—How Changes in Travel on Water Affect the Way People Live, Grade 6, 1955.
* *A Supplement to the United Nations; a Teacher's Handbook,* Secondary Schools, 1955.
Guide to the Teaching of Arithmetic Grades 1 and 2 (Tentative), Grades 1 and 2, 1956.
Guide to the Teaching of Safety in the Elementary Schools, Elementary, 1956.
Guide to the Teaching of Seventh Grade Social Living (Tentatively ed.), Grade 7, 1956.
Milestones in American History, Grade 11, 1956.
The United Nations; a Teacher's Handbook, Secondary Schools, 1956.
Democracy versus Totalitarianism (a teaching unit), Grade 11, 1957.
Guide to the Teaching of Eighth Grade Social Living, Grade 8, 1957.
An Introductory Unit for General Music Classes in Junior High Schools, Grades 7–9, 1956.
Outline Course of Study for Foreign Languages, First and Second Years— French, German, Spanish, and Latin, Secondary, 1958.
Units for Various Grades:
  Airplanes and Airports, Grade 2, 1953.
  The Farm, Grade 2, 1951.
  Navaho Indians, Grade 3, 1956.
  Life in China, Grade 4, 1957.
  Life in Mexico, Grade 4, 1958.
  Life in Colonial America, Grade 5, 1954.
  Westward Movement, Grade 5, 1953.
  How Air Transportation Affects Social Living, Grade 6, 1952.
  How Changes in Communication Affect People's Lives (Tentative), Grade 6, 1957.
  How Record Keeping Has Helped Man's Progress (Tentative), Grade 6, 1956.

rately as one of the stages of curriculum development. More truly it must be called a dominating concept of method, which has accompanied each of the five steps in the growth of the modern curriculum.

The aims-and-objectives stage in curriculum revision was based upon determining the purposes and philosophy of the curriculum by activity analysis. In logical sequence, the investigators then attempted to bring into the curriculum those activities which their studies indicated were the most valuable experiences for children in preparation for adult life. The survey movement in curriculum development built upon the activity concept, first by examining in detail desirable child experiences in special subject-matter fields, and then by investigating child activities which overlapped subject-matter areas.

With the advent of system-wide curriculum revision, many additions were made to the types of activities suggested for pupils, with the view of meeting both individual and community needs more adequately. By this time the activity idea had become well established as an effective *method* of attaining curricular objectives. The core curriculum, large-unit procedures, and the fusion movement are frankly based upon the activity philosophy as the most efficient teaching method for the school.

Since the activity method of teaching has influenced modern curricular change continuously and in progressively growing degree, it will be considered in detail in the next chapter in connection with the unit method, of which it is rightfully a component part.

SUMMARY

What are the developing trends in curriculum change in our schools? Are we able to discern any emerging patterns of curriculum growth? Are patterns of curriculum revision desirable in a democracy? Or is it wiser for each state, each county, and each local community to proceed to improve its own curricular program at its own pace and in its own way to meet its own needs?

One fact emerges clearly from a study of the curricular changes in the schools within the last fifty years. That one fact is that the curricular program today in almost every school and in almost every school room shows a marked growth over the curricular program which was in operation in that same school over a quarter of a century ago. There has been general acceptance of the concept of the curriculum as including all the experiences through which children and youth go under the supervision of the school. New areas or subjects of study have been added; new methods of teaching are being employed which meet the needs of the individual or the group better; community and home life have been hooked up more closely to the work of the school; on the whole, better educated teachers are in charge; pupil activities which formerly were considered without the province of the school, have been incorporated naturally into the curricular program; and teachers and pupils, or teachers and administrators, or school and community personnel, plan cooperatively for the work of the school.[43]

PROBLEMS FOR INDIVIDUAL STUDY AND CLASS DISCUSSION

1. Assume that your school is to undertake a revision of its curriculum. What plan of organization do you think should be pursued by your school staff?

2. How would you proceed if you wanted to discover the real, everyday, life activities of the boys and girls in a class of yours?

3. What real difference is there between the core curriculum and fusion? Illustrate how each would work in a class.

4. List the aims and objectives which you think that your teaching in the social studies or in some other subject area should accomplish. What outline of activities, or what curricular program, would you formulate through which you feel you could attain those aims?

5. Of what value would it be to you in your curriculum work if you knew definitely in what types of activities adults engaged in their leisure time? Explain.

6. What is the difference between a community survey and a curriculum survey? Explain.

7. How would you organize and control a scientific experiment on "Do Pupils Learn Faster by the Recitation or the Unit Method of Teaching?"

8. If you have not had any experience with a core curriculum and

[43] Adapted from J.M. Gwynn, "Curriculum Experimentation," *The High School Journal*, xxix (November–December, 1946), 235–40.

you have accepted a position in a school where such a curriculum is in use, what steps would you take to prepare yourself for effective teaching?

9. Describe the method of teaching which you are now employing in one class; then outline some general experimental departure which you wish to try out next year and present it to the class for comment and criticism.

10. Is the core curriculum broader than the activity movement in teaching? Support your point of view.

11. Suppose that as a teacher of English and History in a secondary school you are asked by the principal to "fuse" these two subjects into one double teaching period for the next year. What plans would you make to do this successfully?

12. Can you illustrate *scope* and *sequence* in large-unit teaching of "Social Living" in grade 9? In grade 7?

13. How can the teacher develop any plans in advance for areas of interest or centers of interest which are selected and planned coopera- tively by teacher and pupils?

14. What are the different kinds of "source-unit" materials, and where can they be found?

15. Do you think that a textbook can be used successfully in core-curriculum teaching? Support your position.

ADDITIONAL SOURCE REFERENCES FOR PROBLEM OR UNIT STUDY

NOTE: The extensive reference materials given in the body of this chap- ter are not repeated here. The best source of information on current developments in the curriculum and on curricular publications in state and individual systems is *Educational Leadership,* published by the Asso- ciation for Supervision and Curriculum Development, 1201 Sixteenth Street, N.W., Washington 6, D.C. Rather complete sample titles of mate- rials and teacher guides (in systems other than those discussed in this chapter) which have been prepared since World War II and which are in current use are found in special lists published periodically by this same Association; three recent examples are *Current Curriculum Mate- rials from Representative School Publications,* 1957, *Recent Curriculum Materials,* 1958, and *Curriculum Materials,* 1959.

State School Surveys also influence curriculum change strongly; these surveys are carried out by different states as they feel the need for them. Two good examples of comprehensive surveys by different groups within the last decade are:

Education in North Carolina Tcday and Tomorrow (the Report of the

State Education Commission), Raleigh, the United Forces for Education, December, 1948.

Public Education in Tennessee: Grades 1 Through 12, a report to the Education Survey Subcommittee of the Tennessee Legislative Council, November 18, 1957, Nashville, State Department of Education.

Cities and counties likewise make curriculum and general school surveys as they need them, and these are usually available for distribution upon payment of the cost of the publication.

CHAPTER 7 The development
of the unit technique

ORIGIN AND GROWTH OF THE UNIT PLAN

During the last half century probably the greatest single effect on the method and technique of teaching was produced by H.C. Morrison's book, *The Practice of Teaching in the Secondary School.*[1] The "Morrison" or "unit" method of teaching is generally known and widely used—at least in name. The National Survey of Secondary Education reported that 737 schools, or nearly 9 per cent of the 8,594 schools which were investigated, indicated some use of the Morrison plan.[2] These findings are supported by the following statement:

It [the unit assignment] is a prominent characteristic of at least eleven plans, methods, or techniques which have been allotted extended space in educational literature and which, considered collectively, are widely practiced. . . .[3]

On the other hand, considerable difference of opinion exists concerning what constitutes a unit of learning material, and there is still greater variation in the techniques of the teaching procedure termed "the unit method." Francis D. Curtis [4] cited the National Survey of Secondary Education as reporting the following ten plans in use which were characterized by the unit assignment: (1) the project method, (2) the problem method, (3) differentiated assignments, (4) long-unit assignments, (5) the contract plan, (6) the laboratory

---

[1] Chicago, The University of Chicago Press, 1926.
[2] Cited by Francis D. Curtis, *et al.*, in "The Morrison Plan in Science," *Clearing House*, ix (May, 1935), pp. 547–54.
[3] "The Unit Assignment in Actual Practice" (an editorial), *School Review,* xl (May, 1932), p. 321.
[4] "The Unit Assignment," *Clearing House,* ix (May, 1935), pp. 543–46.

plan, (7) individualized instruction, (8) some modification of the Morrison plan, (9) the Dalton plan or some modification, and (10) the Winnetka technique or some modification. He stated that all of these plans "are one and the same thing, differentiated only in name." [5] He went on to say, however:

Granted, after consideration of . . . convincing evidence, that the terminology used in common practice to designate different types and modifications of unit teaching is meaningless, the fact remains that the use of unit assignments in one form or another, designated by one name or another, has been and is rapidly spreading in our secondary schools. . . .

After discussing arguments for and against the unit plan, he concluded that:

. . . the use of the unit assignments has become a widely established practice, and . . . is likely to continue its spread. . . . Therefore, unit teaching commands intensive study by educators who must strive to capitalize optimally on its merits and to reduce to the minimum the potential dangers and disadvantages inherent in its use.[6]

The Morrison plan commands intensive study, because it involves essentially the correct psychological approach to learning and a highly efficient method of curriculum organization. Therefore, the purposes of this chapter are:

1. To compare the Morrison plan with the Herbartian method by an examination of the aims and techniques of each.

2. To trace the growth of the Morrison plan since the publication of *The Practice of Teaching in the Secondary School.*

3. To show how the Morrison plan involves the essential features of sound method in education, both in curriculum organization and in teaching technique.

1. COMPARISON OF THE MORRISON PLAN WITH HERBARTIAN METHOD

During the last part of the nineteenth and the first part of the twentieth century, the psychology of Herbart was dominant in the field of education. Herbart's "five steps" were widely followed. Because of the later formalization of the Herbartian procedure and because of the rise of popularity of Thorndike's psychology of the

[5] *Ibid.*, p. 543.
[6] *Ibid.*, p. 546.

learning process, Herbartianism fell into disfavor. Recently, the theory of learning by insight has been accepted by many educators; this *Gestalt* psychology has supported the essential validity of Herbart's conception of the self as a unit and his idea of the necessity for the establishment of an apperceptive mass in learning. As a consequence, the modern "activity movement" tends to reconstruct method along lines similar to Herbart's technique. It is to show this similarity that the following comparative summary is made of some of the chief educational precepts of Herbart and of Morrison. A fuller analysis of the Morrisonian method is given later.

A. *Aims of Education*

Herbart	*Morrison*
1. Moral character.	1. Attainment of the basic functions of social intercourse.
2. Well-balanced and many-sided interests.	2. Attainment of intellectual, vocational, and conduct responsibility.
	3. Attainment of the fundamental methods of thinking and the sustaining cultural interests which make a self-governing intellectual and social being.

B. *Technique of Teaching*

Herbart	*Morrison*
1. Preparation for receiving new ideas.	1. Exploration of the field to be studied.
2. Clear presentation of ideas.	2. Presentation of findings.
3. Association of ideas.	3. Assimilation.
4. Classification of ideas.	4. Organization of material.
5. Application of ideas.	5. Recitation.[7]

HERBART'S THEORY OF EDUCATION.   As Herbart saw it, the aim of education was primarily the development of moral character. Two quotations from his work, *The Application of Psychology to the Science of Education*,[8] will clarify this attitude.

---

[7] For the learning of appreciations, Morrison offers a slightly different technique which will be discussed later.

[8] Cited by J.P. Wynne, *The Teacher and the Curriculum*, 1937, p. 66. *Cf.* also *Philosophies of Education*, New York, Prentice-Hall, 1947, pp. 29–31, 237, 239, and Chap. XIV.

First:

Morality is universally acknowledged as the highest aim of humanity, and consequently of education. . . .

Secondly, and this may be taken as instrumental to the realization of the first:

The end of education is to produce a well-balanced and many-sided interest. . . .

Herbart believed that the moral aim of education could be attained through correct teaching. In accordance with this belief, he formulated what has since proved substantially to be a correct analysis of the learning process. For his analysis, he chose materials for teaching which he conceived to be in line with the proper development of the child. He did not envision training children to become critical of the existing forms of society under which they lived,[9] but he did desire to train them to become useful and well-adjusted citizens. Wynne has translated Herbart's aims into modern terms as follows:

. . . every individual should learn to (1) submit himself to the ideal state that is revealed to him through intuition; (2) assume responsibility for the advancement of human culture; (3) contribute to the welfare of good government of the whole; (4) support the system of rewards and punishments; and (5) assume responsibility for a law-abiding society.[10]

If one adds to Herbart's aims in education the modern emphases on the training of children to become *progressive* members of society and *critical* of outmoded customs and institutions, one has essentially a modern attitude toward the purposes of education. Little more needs to be said about the comparison of Herbart's aims in education with those stated by Morrison. Herbart was definitely on the road toward a modern interpretation of educational objectives, and Morrison's aims may be taken as a logical extension of the movement begun by the educational renaissance of the sixteenth and seventeenth centuries.

THE HERBARTIAN FIVE STEPS. In comparing the teaching tech-

---

[10] *Ibid.*

[9] Wynne says that the principles of Herbart represented the needs of men in an aristocratic German state of the early nineteenth century: "They are stated in terms of the obligation of the individual to an established social order. *On the basis of our criteria they should be stated in terms of the mutual obligations of individuals and institutions in an emerging social order.* . . ." *Ibid.*, p. 67.

niques of Herbart and Morrison, it should be borne in mind that
Herbart did not set forth his steps primarily as a teaching technique;
he developed them as the general psychological procedure whereby
learning occurs. Herbart emphasized four steps: clearness, association, system, and method. His followers elaborated these into the
familiar "Herbartian five steps":

1. *Preparation.* In this step related subject matter which has been
learned previously is recalled. This involves Herbart's main psychological
principle—the law of apperception. He held that the mind is simply one's
previous experiences, and that new experiences must be related to past
experiences in order to become a part of one's self. When new experiences
are so related, they can be consciously perceived, or apperceived.
Herbart is making this point when he speaks of "apperceptive mass";
hence, the first step in teaching new material is to relate the material to
something previously known.

2. *Presentation.* Here the new material is presented for observation.

3. *Association.* The new material is compared with the old, and like-
nesses and differences are noted.

4. *Generalization (Classification).* The differences are given statement in definite form.

5. *Application.* Practical application must be made in order to con-
summate the process.

Herbart's followers held that all learning occurs through these
steps.

MORRISON'S AIMS AND FIELDS OF LEARNING.   Like the earlier analysis of Herbart, Morrison's plan is not primarily a specific teaching
technique. In the Preface of his book, Morrison says:

The book is . . . not . . . an exhibit of method—although it brings
together a great many phases of method which seem to have adequate
foundation in fact and in principle—but rather an analysis of teaching
procedure. . . .[11]

From these statements, it is seen that the plans of both Herbart
and Morrison are primarily analyses of *how* teaching can be accomplished, not primarily methodologies. Since Herbart's five steps and
Morrison's five steps have both been hailed as containing basically
sound principles in teaching methodology, it seems wise to compare

[11] *The Practice of Teaching in the Secondary School,* The University of
Chicago Press (rev. ed.), 1931, p. v. Hereafter this work will be referred to as
"Morrison."

them.[12] It will first be necessary, however, to distinguish the fields of learning as conceived by Morrison. He classified all of the subjects taught in the secondary schools into three general divisions:

1. The *science type*, in which the objectives are "adaptations . . . in understandings of principles . . . in the relation of cause and effect. . . ." [13] Under this division would come mathematics, "the grammar of all languages," the physical, biological, and social sciences, the theory of the fine arts, the commercial field, and the like.

2. The *practical-arts type*, which has as its objective "learnings which lead to the intelligent manipulation of appliances and molding of materials, and thence to adjustment to the mechanical environment. . . ." [14] This type includes shop courses in the mechanical arts, cooking, sewing, and the household arts.

3. The *appreciation type*, which involves attitudes of value. Such fields as the appreciation of the fine arts, religion, and ethics come under this division.

COMPARISON OF THE MORRISONIAN AND THE HERBARTIAN STEPS. As an analysis of the procedure applicable to the science-type subject, and with modifications to the practical-arts type, Morrison offers five steps (see page 180). The first, or *exploratory* step, serves to determine just what basis the pupil has upon which to build, and to orient him to the problem at hand. The second step consists in the *presentation* of the gist of the new material to the pupil. In the third step, *assimilation*, the definite learning takes place. The fourth step, *organization* of materials, serves to assure a grasp of the essential points covered. *Recitation*, the fifth step, serves as a check on what has been accomplished.

Here exploration and presentation correspond substantially to the Herbartian preparatory step. In these steps, a basis is laid for further work. Morrison's assimilative step involves the essential function of

---

[12] Morrison disclaims copying Herbart in this procedure: ". . . be it noted . . . that this five-step procedure is not an application of the Herbartian five steps. . . ," p. 256. However, there is a difference of opinion. Bossing says, "Closely akin to the Herbartian formal steps is the *cycle plan of teaching* as applied by Morrison to what he calls the science type learning. It may be taken to represent . . . a reconstruction of the Herbartian formal steps. . . ."—N.L. Bossing, *Progressive Methods of Teaching in Secondary Schools*, (rev. ed.) Boston, Houghton Mifflin Company, 1942, p. 544.

[13] Morrison, p. 92.

[14] *Ibid.*, p. 94.

Herbart's second, or presentation, step, and some phases of the Herbartian association step. Morrison's fourth, or organization, step corresponds to some of Herbart's association step, but largely to his

FIG. 19   *Fifth-graders proving space age facts.*
(*Courtesy Greensboro (N.C.) Public Schools, Brooks School.*)

generalization step, where the test of mastery is made. The Morrison recitation and the Herbartian practical-application steps serve substantially the same function.[15]

The methods of Herbart and Morrison agree on at least the following basic principles:

1. Preparation of the pupil's mind for the reception of new experi-

[15] *Cf.*, Bossing, *op. cit.*, pp. 541–46.

ences, whether by recall of previous experience or through research by the student.

2. The importance of the teacher in presenting and clarifying the material in hand.
3. The learning by the student.
4. Fixing of the learning through organization of the material by the student, or through practical application of what was learned.

For the appreciation type of subject in the secondary school, Morrison provides the following steps: (1) exploratory testing to ascertain the level of the pupil's apperceptive ability; (2) "illumination" of the field by the teacher; (3) class discussion; (4) individual reports; (5) notation of results by observing the pupil's own selection of subject matter for reading, hearing, or in some way enjoying; (6) voluntary projects; and (7) study and correction of problem cases. These seven steps contain essentially the same principles as the five steps, except that the objective is *appreciations*, instead of understandings of scientific data or the acquisition of manipulative skills.

2. GROWTH OF THE MORRISON PLAN SINCE 1926

DEFINITIONS OF THE UNIT TECHNIQUE. Before discussing the attitudes of various writers, it is necessary to have a tentative definition of the unit method. A final clarification of the term will be attempted in a later part of this chapter. Five definitions by curriculum writers in the last thirty years include the essential ideas involved in the conception of a unit. First, here is Morrison's own definition:

A unit is *a comprehensive and significant aspect of the environment, of an organized science, of an art, or of conduct, which being learned results in adaptation in personality. . . .*[16]

W.C. Ruediger defines a unit as

. . . any division of subject matter, large or small, that, when mastered, gives one an insight into, an appreciation of, or a mastery over some aspect of life. . . .[17]

Lorena B. Stretch suggests this definition:

Units . . . are organized subject matter and experiences, broken up into large comprehensive divisions, brought together because of relation-

[16] Pp. 24–25.
[17] *Teaching Procedures*, Boston, Houghton Mifflin Company, 1932, p. 244.

ships, and presented to the pupils in such a manner as to develop within them the right attitudes, abilities, and skills. . . .[18]

Vernon Anderson says:

. . . a unit is an organization of experiences and information around some problem or goal to aid the pupil in integrating his learning.[19]

In their book devoted entirely to *Unit Teaching in the Elementary School,* Lavone Hanna, Gladys Potter, and Neva Hagaman define the unit in a way remarkably similar to Morrison's definition of twenty-five years ago:

A unit, or a unit of work, can be defined as a purposeful learning experience focused upon some socially significant understanding which will modify the behavior of the learner and enable him to adjust to a life situation more effectively.[20]

In short, *the unit method is an attempt so to integrate and arrange the curriculum that the child can achieve mastery of the desired objectives in education in a meaningful and permanent manner.* Morrison believed that this mastery of educational objectives could be accomplished best through a division of the fields of subject matter and experiences into comprehensive units, presented in general accordance with the procedure outlined in his five steps. Units may or may not cut across the traditional subject-matter lines. More than likely they will. Morrison's belief was that the curriculum should be so ordered that the units of learning will correspond with those adaptations that a person must make in order to be a successful member of society. He believed further that, having determined what these units should be, there is no such thing as partial mastery of a unit. Mastery involves an "adaptation in personality," and the adaptation must be either made or not made; it cannot be partially made.

1. *Attitudes of Authors on the Unit Method (1930–1935).* Repre-

---

[18] *The Curriculum and the Child,* Minneapolis, Educational Publishers, 1939, p. 71. *Cf.* with this concept the subject-matter and experience units of William H. Burton, *The Guidance of Learning Activities,* New York, D. Appleton-Century Company, 1944, Chap. IX.

[19] Vernon E. Anderson, *Principles and Procedures of Curriculum Improvement,* Copyright 1956, New York, The Ronald Press Company, 1956, p. 362. Reprinted by permission.

[20] New York, Rinehart and Company, 1955, p. 101. Reprinted by permission.

sentative of the attitude of curriculum writers during the 1930's are the presentation and analysis of the unit method in *Curriculum Development.*[21] Caswell and Campbell's discussion (Chapter xv) is summarized here to show how far unit development had progressed by 1935, and to give a basis for comparison of further developments since that date.

As is customary, they devote several pages to an attempt to rescue the term "unit plan" from the ambiguity into which it has fallen. Their analysis represents a progressive development of the unit-plan idea. They conclude that the plan cannot be identified with any particular method such as the Dalton plan or the Winnetka technique, because practically all current teaching techniques profess to make use in some way of the unit method.

These authors state that the term "unit" implies some fundamental idea which serves to integrate either a segment of subject matter or a group of experiences. They see any unit as falling under one of the following types (p. 406):

    I. Subject Matter
       A. Topical unit
       B. Generalization unit
       C. Unit based on significant aspect of environment or culture
    II. Experience
       A. Unit based on center of interest
       B. Unit based on pupil purpose
       C. Unit based on pupil need

Organization around a "topical" unit really represents in most cases only a rejuggling of the chapter headings of a book or some other treatise. The "generalization" unit has long been used in physics and in some of the other natural sciences, and represents nothing new except possibly in its application to the social sciences; it is essentially a subject-matter unit. These authors believe that the unit "based on significant aspects of environment or culture" received particular emphasis from H.C. Morrison, saying (pp. 411–12):

This type of unit has significant merits not possessed by the other types of subject matter units. The basis of organization is the significance of

[21] By H.L. Caswell and D.S. Campbell, New York, American Book Company, 1935.

the material in explaining contemporary life. If well selected it is almost certain that the unit may be brought to have real meaning to a majority of learners. . . .

This type of unit organization is the most significant and forward looking of the three types classified under the subject matter heading. Reorganization of instruction on this basis has done much to vitalize teaching. . . .

The chief objection to the subject-matter units seems to be that the things-to-be-learned receive primary attention rather than the learner.

The unit "based on a center of interest" furnishes an excellent basis for motivation; the chief objection to it is that continuity and long-time integration are difficult when pupils are allowed to select what interests them most for their study. Units "based on pupil purpose" flourished during the heyday of the project method; they give bases for motivation, but tend to become essentially like units based on centers of interest. Units "based on pupil need" offer a practical basis for organization, and one which relates the curriculum to life; this basis for organization is the most strongly advocated today.

Caswell and Campbell provide criteria for evaluating units, and methods for developing units. The impetus given by Morrison is evident throughout their treatise. These authors assume that teaching in the future will be organized around the unit method.

Most authors on curriculum and methods of teaching from 1935 to 1950 also have devoted space to the unit method of teaching. Among these were the following leaders in curriculum improvement: [22]

[22] Cf. E.M. Draper, *Principles and Techniques of Curriculum Making*, New York, D. Appleton-Century Company, 1936; J.P. Wynne, *The Teacher and the Curriculum*, New York, Prentice-Hall, 1937; A.G. Melvin, *The Activity Program* (1936), *Activated Curriculum* (1939), and *Method for New Schools* (1941), all published by The John Day Company, New York; J.M. and D.M. Lee, *The Child and His Curriculum* (1940), rev. ed. (1950), New York, D. Appleton-Century Company; W.H. Burton, *The Guidance of Learning Activities*, New York, D. Appleton-Century Company, 1944; Faye Adams, *Educating America's Children*, New York, The Ronald Press Company, 1946; J.P. Leonard, *Developing the Secondary School Curriculum*, New York, Rinehart and Company, 1946; Harold Alberty, *Reorganizing the High School Curriculum*, New York, The Macmillan Company, 1947; F.B. Stratemeyer, *et al.*, *Developing a Curriculum for Modern Living*, New York, Teachers College, Columbia University, 1947; and I.N. Thut and J.R. Gerberich, *Foundations of Method for Secondary Schools*, New York, McGraw-Hill Book Company, 1949.

E.M. Draper (1936); J.P. Wynne (1937); and A.G. Melvin (1936 to 1941), who refused to use the word "unit" and definitely rejected textbooks and scheduled class periods in favor of "experiences" as a type of organization for teaching. Yet the specific techniques presented are based upon the *unitary* character of personal experience and learning: Murray and Dorris Lee (1940 and 1950); W.H. Burton (1944); Faye Adams and J.P. Leonard (1946); Harold Alberty and Florence Stratemeyer and her associates (1947); and I.N. Thut and J.R. Gerberich (1949).

The reader should note, however, that most authors on method do not anticipate any complete abandonment of textbooks and class periods, at least at an early date. Consequently the majority of them advocate the use of the unit method, meaning in general the organization of activities and subject matter in more closely related units around a center of interest.

SINCE 1950. Even more emphasis has been placed upon unit teaching around a center of interest since 1950. Factors contributing to this increased stress upon the unit method include more emphasis upon general education, the development of the core curriculum, and planning for teaching around larger blocks or centers of interest having close relationships to more than one subject-matter field. However, Clinton R. Prewett seems to have placed his finger upon the main reason:

. . . The first three decades of the twentieth century were replete with plans and proposals concerning educational method and procedure; such has not been the case since 1926. It is true that there has been much activity in the area of the curriculum, but it is significant to point out that no radically different major plan was suggested relating to curriculum organization during all this time. The attention of the curriculum theorists seems to have been directed towards the improvement of the content which was to be taught within the unit framework. Of course, unit teaching is concerned with both content and methodology, but the assumption seems to be sound that the unit was adequate as a framework if the proper content could be found . . .[23]

Specific evidence of the continued stress today upon the unit

[23] *The Development of the Unit Method of Teaching from the Herbartian Movement to the Present*, unpublished doctor's thesis, University of North Carolina 1950, pp. 232–33.

method of teaching comes from several sources. In the first place the revised editions of the works of these authors who have already been listed (ante, p. 189) stress the unit: W.H. Burton (2nd ed., 1952); Harold Alberty (rev. ed., 1953); J.P. Leonard (rev. ed., 1953); Faye Adams (2nd ed., 1954); and F.B. Stratemeyer, *et al.* (2nd ed., 1957). In the second place, newer authors of curriculum textbooks place emphasis on the unit method. B. Othanel Smith and his associates devote a large section of their book [24] to the unit and the activity curriculum. Galen Saylor and William Alexander likewise discuss unit teaching and planning at length.[25] On the high-school level Stephen Romine also selects the unit method as the structural organization for the curriculum.[26] Beatrice Hurley believes in organizing the elementary-school curriculum experiences around the needs of children in their community.[27] Such experiences by their very nature include the unit around a center of interest or the activity approach.

Writers of books on general and specific methods range from the larger amount of space devoted to the unit method in *Methods in Secondary Education* [28] to the smaller space on it found in *Techniques of Secondary School Teaching* [29] and *Effective Teaching in Secondary Schools.*[30]

Finally, whole books have been written on the unit method in the last decade. Two good examples are *Freedom to Live and Learn: Techniques for Selecting and Developing Units of Learning in the Modern Classroom* [31] and *Unit Teaching in the Elementary School.*[32] Other writers on the core curriculum and the junior high school use

[24] *Fundamentals of Curriculum Development* (1950, and rev. ed., 1957), Yonkers-on-Hudson, World Book Company.

[25] *Curriculum Planning,* New York, Rinehart and Company, 1954.

[26] *Building the High School Curriculum,* New York, The Ronald Press Company, 1954.

[27] *Curriculum for Elementary School Children,* New York, The Ronald Press Company, 1957, Chap. v.

[28] By J.D. Grambs and W.J. Iverson, New York, The Dryden Press, 1952 (revised with help also of F.K. Patterson, 1958).

[29] By Ralph K. Watkins, New York, The Ronald Press Company, 1958.

[30] By W.A. Alexander and P.M. Halverson, New York, Rinehart and Company, 1956.

[31] By Gertrude Noar, Philadelphia, Franklin Publishing Company, 1948.

[32] By Lavone Hanna, *et al., op. cit.* (1955).

the unit or center of interest as the teaching technique through which to attain the core or general education.[33]

2. *Evidence from School Texts and Guides.* An examination of a random sampling of school textbooks on both the elementary and secondary school levels has already been made from the period for 1930 to 1950.[34] It revealed a steadily growing trend toward texts written from the point of view of the resource unit or a larger block of text material around a central theme or problem. This trend has continued since 1950. Texts in the social studies seem to show the greatest imprint of the unit method of teaching; however, the unit approach is also found in textbooks in the language arts and English, science, health, and more recently in mathematics, literature anthologies, and grammars.

Curriculum guides and bulletins in state, county, and city school systems show in like manner the influence of the unit method. The George Peabody College surveys of curriculum and teaching guides [35] note that more than 60 per cent of the guides in 1950 and more than 50 per cent in 1953 were organized into clearly defined units of work.

A word of caution is pertinent here. A large number of the school textbooks show evidence in some measure of the effect of the activity movement in education. The more recent ones make specific attempts at adaptation to the unit method of teaching. It should be remembered that simply because a text is divided into units does not mean that it can be used effectively in the unit method of teaching. However, the recognition given to the unit method in texts is indicative of the prevailing influence of this method with textbook authors and publishers.

3. *Types of Units.* This section would not be complete without

---

[33] *Cf.* Gertrude Noar, *The Junior High School—Today and Tomorrow,* New York, Prentice-Hall, 1953, Parts III and IV, and Lucile L. Lurry and Elsie Alberty, *Developing a High School Core Program,* New York, The Macmillan Company, 1957, Chaps. VI–VIII and Appendix One.

[34] *Cf.* J. Minor Gwynn, *Curriculum Principles and Social Trends,* New York, The Macmillan Company, 1943 and 1950 editions, Chap. VII.

[35] *Trends in Production of Teaching Guides (1948–1950)* and *Trends in Production of Curriculum Guides (1951–1953),* 1955 both by Eleanor Merritt and Henry Harap.

an identification of the main kinds of units in use today in teaching. Perhaps this can be done most simply thus

Kinds of Units

Resource Units   *Teaching Units*

Constructed by one, two, or more people, in reality larger blocks of interrelated materials, resources, suggested methods, and ways of evaluating.

from which teachers or teachers and pupils

→ Plan

Which may be
(1) *Subject Matter Units*
or
(2) *Experience* or *Center-of-Interest Units*

3. PSYCHOLOGICALLY SOUND FEATURES OF THE MORRISON TECHNIQUE

It is now necessary to look a little more closely at Morrison's conception of the learning process. This is best presented in the following outline: [36]

1. *What Is Learning?*   The school curriculum was traditionally divided into segments of years. Learning was regarded as time to be spent in various courses. "Seldom," says Morrison, "has the factor of attainment quite independent of time-to-be-spent been brought into the problem. . . ." [37] Morrison regards school training as "mastery" in certain fields of social functioning. There is no question of mastering 70 per cent of a skill or an attitude and passing. The function of the primary grades is to enable the child to master the basic functions—reading, writing, ciphering, respect for authority, ability to get along with others, and ability to take care of the body. Until the child has mastered these aspects of life, he is still on the primary level. The function of the secondary school is to advance these primary adaptations to the point where the child can go on learning by himself; when he can do this, he is ready for the university. There is no such thing as partial mastery, any more than there are degrees in one's being on the second floor of a house, or degrees in being entirely across a river.

[36] Taken *passim* from Morrison's book, *The Practice of Teaching in the Secondary School* (rev. ed.), The University of Chicago Press, 1931.
[37] *Ibid.*, p. 5.

"Learning," Morrison states, "is always expressed either as a change in the attitude of the individual or as the acquisition of a special ability or as the attainment of some form of skill in manipulating instrumentalities or materials. . . ."[38] Nothing has really been learned until some adaptation of personality has taken place, and when once learned, cannot be forgotten. Morrison would agree with Briggs that there was never a more fallacious idea than that "education is what is left when we have forgotten all that we have learned."[39]

Every learning function implies something to be learned. This objective aspect Morrison calls a learning unit. His definition of a serviceable unit is:

> . . . *a comprehensive and significant aspect of the environment, of an organized science, of an art, or of conduct, which being learned results in an adaptation in personality. . . .*[40]

By environment, Morrison means not only the external universe, but bodies, and all the aspects involved in social inheritance. At the level of the secondary school, units of work will be drawn from various subject-matter fields, physical development, and conduct control. Pupil progress will be by mastery of units.

2. *Kinds of Learning.* As has already been indicated, Morrison distinguishes three fundamental types of learning: (1) the science type, in which the objectives are adaptations in the form of understanding principles and processes in cause-and-effect relationships; (2) the appreciation type, which involves adaptations in terms of value attitudes; and (3) the practical-arts type, in which field the adaptations are in the form of abilities to manipulate and form materials.

3. *Fundamental Principles of Operative Technique.* Underlying all types of operative technique are the following six fundamental principles:

1. The learning cycle. Morrison says that all learning at the human level occurs through the process of stimulus, assimilation, and reaction.

[38] *Ibid.*, p. 17.
[39] T.H. Briggs, *Improving Instruction,* New York, The Macmillan Company, 1938, p. 41.
[40] Morrison, pp. 24–25.

2. Initial diffuse movements.

3. Necessity for identification of the teaching objectives.

4. Direct teaching. This involves pupil activity aimed directly at the problem in hand.

5. Study.

6. The establishment of an "adequate apperceptive mass," the "piecing of new learning to the old." [41]

4. *Teaching Procedure.* (1) For the science type of subject and, with modifications, for the practical-arts type of subjects:

a. Exploration. The purpose here is economy of time, through the establishment of "apperceptive sequence" and orientation. In this introductory stage the teacher learns what level of achievement the child has reached, by the use of a pretest; the teacher then introduces him to the unit in hand by connecting the new material with something previously learned.

b. Presentation. The teacher gives the pupils the gist of the new material. A check test is given at the close of the presentation, not for grading, but to make sure that the pupils have grasped in outline the new material.

c. Assimilation. In this step, the class is formed into a study group, a laboratory, or into that type of organization deemed best for the purpose or purposes in view. The pupil "makes the new understanding his own by prolonged contact with the assimilative material." [42] At the close, a test is given to check mastery.

d. Organization. Without help, the pupils make an outline of the unit under study, perhaps in the form of a syllabus.

e. Recitation. Different pupils present orally to the class their understandings of the unit; others write papers.

(2) For the appreciation type of subject: This division of subjects includes conduct, religion, literature, music, and art. For these, Morrison offers a somewhat different technique. While the appreciative branches of human experience are radically different from the science type, nevertheless they must involve the following objectives and methods for learning to take place:

a. The first essential is to establish within the child some basis upon which to build appreciation. Then materials best suited to the

[41] Morrison, p. 172.
[42] *Ibid.*, p. 282.

level of appreciation which the pupil has attained must be selected.

b. The teacher should "illumine" the field by various methods. Nowhere is the ingenuity of the teacher so taxed as at this stage.

c. Class discussion may serve to clarify points and arouse interests.

d. Individual reports will serve to check the progress of the pupil.

e. The real test of mastery of an appreciation is in the observation of the choices of literature, and in the exhibitions of attitudes or ideals, when the pupil is not under school control.

f. To assure increased progress in appreciation, the pupil should be led to do voluntary projects.

g. Finally, problem cases should be given careful attention.

THE ACTIVITY MOVEMENT AND TEACHING TECHNIQUE

What Is an Activity Curriculum? Now that Morrison's conception of the learning process has been presented, the essentials involved in modern teaching procedures will be considered briefly. In 1934 the National Society for the Study of Education reported on its study of the Activity Movement.[43] One of the results was the discovery that there is no definite agreement on what constitutes an activity program. This report pointed out that for hundreds of years the idea of pupil activity as essential to learning has been abroad, but that only within the past fifty years has much progress been made in applying this principle. Changes in the curriculum resulted as the realization came that pupils must participate in real-life situations in order to learn. Attempts were made to reorganize the traditional curriculum of subject matter into units of meaningful activities. Subsequently many teaching techniques were developed by experimental schools, and these techniques were advanced as correct methods in harmony with the new psychology of learning. Methods ranged, and still range, all the way from a strict adherence to the Herbartian five steps to a loosely organized program of pupil activi-

[43] Thirty-third Yearbook, National Society for the Study of Education, Part II, Public School Publishing Company, 1934.

ties. According to Thomas Woody, all of these sought to base themselves on the "psychological notion of growth through self-activity." [44]

From a battery of definitions of the activity movement collected by William H. Kilpatrick for the National Society for the Study of Education, the following conceptions were indicated most frequently as characteristic of the activity curriculum.[45]

1. Activities
2. Experiences
3. Units
4. Projects
5. Problems
6. Enterprises
7. Centers of interest
8. Central theme.

The general attitude was that learning occurs through directed pupil activity, and that the activities should be planned by teacher and pupil together. There is a difference of opinion on whether traditional divisions of subject matter can be followed or not. The leading emphasis is placed on the belief that the whole curriculum is divided into pieces of human experience and not into pieces of formal knowledge.[46] A summary definition of the activity curriculum is pertinent and is quoted herewith from William H. Kilpatrick:

. . . an activity curriculum organizes its work on a flexible program providing definitely for periods of discussion and planning of both group and individual tasks; periods of both individual and group constructive and creative work; periods for reports of progress and for criticism and evaluation of work in progress; periods of drill upon skills needed to make the work go more rapidly and effectively; periods of individual study, research, information-gathering or constructive or creative effort; periods for the sharing of results of accomplishment with other members of the group or with other groups in the school. . . .[47]

BASIC PRINCIPLES UNDERLYING METHOD. A.A. Douglass [48] says

---

[44] *Ibid.*, p. 40. Quoted by permission of the Society.
[45] *Ibid.*, p. 47. Quoted by permission of the Society.
[46] Thirty-third Yearbook, National Society for the Study of Education, Part II, Public School Publishing Company, 1934, p. 61.
[47] *Ibid.* Quoted by permission of the Society.
[48] *Modern Secondary Education,* Boston, Houghton Mifflin Company, 1938, pp. 630–36.

that from all the literature on method, certain principles are now accorded general acceptance. These are:

1. The student must have a conscious goal toward which to work.
2. Interest conditions learning.
3. Concrete experiences are essential. Some kind of adjustment is necessary on the part of the pupil.

FIG. 20   *A tree fell. They love it. Hence, the nature trail*
(*Courtesy Greensboro (N.C.) Public Schools, Brooks School.*)

4. Some kind of plan must be evolved in order to carry out any given learning unit.
5. The procedure must be flexible.
6. Results must in some way be evaluated.

Wynne observes that many teaching procedures are similar, although they have different names:

A startling fact about the . . . long unit assignments, individualized instruction, contract plan, laboratory plan, problem method, and project method, is that detailed analysis of practices in schools reporting to use them with unusual success finds these practices to be essentially identical, no matter what name is applied. . . .[49]

To summarize, the unit method advocated by Morrison for the organization and presentation of learning activities incorporates all the essentially sound psychological procedures and techniques of modern methods as listed by the National Society for the Study of Education, by Douglass, by Wynne, and by recent sources and authors.[50]

In order to have clearly in view the essential elements of organization of the modern curriculum and modern methods, they are listed here in summary form:

Curriculum Organization

1. Units
2. Projects
3. Problems
4. Centers of interest
5. Divisions into human experience, not pieces of formal knowledge.

Method

1. Pupil interest
2. Definite goal
3. Teacher supervision and direction
4. Teacher-pupil cooperation in planning
5. Pupil activity in real-life situations
6. Periods of discussion, group and individual
7. Gathering of data
8. Constructive and creative work
9. Reports of progress for criticism
10. Evaluational tests
11. Individual study
12. Group sharing of results
13. Drill.

---

[49] *Op. cit.*, pp. 175–76.
[50] *Cf.* Thirty-third Yearbook, National Society for the Study of Education, *op. cit.*, pp. 45–64; Douglass, *op. cit.*, pp. 629–43; Wynne, *op. cit.*, pp. 172–80; Draper, *op. cit.*, pp. 505–8; and attitudes of authors since 1930.

RELATIONSHIP BETWEEN METHODS AND THE CURRICULUM

It is practically impossible for a teacher to make a clean-cut distinction between the *methods* and the *materials* of instruction. Likewise, it is difficult for a teacher to disassociate his educational philosophy from his teaching methods. Both Herbart and Morrison contended that their "steps" were not a teaching technique. The former maintained that his was a learning procedure; the latter, an analysis of teaching procedure. Careful examination of their plans reveals that each represented a philosophy or theory of learning interwoven with the materials of the curriculum and with methods of instruction. Yet to most educators both the Herbartian and the Morrisonian plans represent primarily methods of teaching. After many experiments, most institutions for the training of teachers have combined courses in "Materials and Methods," thus indicating that there is no known place at which materials end and methods of teaching begin.

The modern emphasis on the organization and construction of the curriculum has been steadily away from the use of textbooks as content-to-be-memorized, and toward the organization of pupil activities around meaningful experiences. Some educators would go so far as to abandon entirely all scheduled class periods and the organization of the curriculum around subject-matter fields. It is probable, however, that some form of scheduled class periods and some kind of subject organization will continue. All activity movements stress the organization of the curriculum into some kind of units; *whatever appreciation, attitude, or skill is to be learned, that is the unit.* Any kind of coordinated activity will be centered around some significant field of human experience, and Morrison calls this field the learning unit. That the mastery of these units may sometimes involve projects, problems, and all other techniques listed in the organization of the modern curriculum is evident.

The chief objection to the curriculum organization advocated by Morrison is that, after all, the unit method is still subject-centered and not child-centered. This objection is based on a misunderstanding of terms. Any activity must be some kind of activity, and the kind of activity it is comprises the subject. Certainly any meaningful activity would involve much content, but no one today would advocate centering attention on the content rather than on the activity of the child. Morrison says: " '. . . learning unit' is a program term. It calls for the organization of the program . . . in units rather than in informational subject-matter content. . . ." [51] Since the unit may include child activities and experiences, subject matter and various kinds of teaching methods, it accepts the "activity concept" as its basis and may be said to embrace that movement.

Another objection frequently urged against the unit is that units prepared in advance tend to become stereotyped; and further, that units which are meaningful for one student in one environment may not be applicable to another student in a different place. Of course, it would be inadvisable to attempt to establish a uniform curriculum of prepared units for all schools of the country. It would seem possible, however, to anticipate the needs and interests of the children in any given locality, and on this basis to set up resource units of work in flexible outline form. It would be indeed an overemphasis on individual differences to suppose that all of the interests and needs of every child are so radically different from those of other children that provision to meet them cannot be made in advance.

The chief characteristic of the modern organization of the curriculum, then, is the integration of learning matter into comprehensive units. The problem method, the project method, and other approaches have been advocated, the underlying idea of each being to organize the curriculum into meaningful areas of activity. This same idea is behind Morrison's reason for offering the unit plan of development.

On the side of method, the leading modern conceptions are all involved in Morrison's approach through the unit.

Herbart conceived two essentially correct ideas in regard to learning: (1) the human being acts as a unit; and (2) the acquisition of new knowledge is dependent on the establishment of an "apperceptive mass." On these bases, the Herbartian technique is fundamentally correct. Morrison has given these ideas a thoroughly modern application through his development of the unit technique.

[51] Morrison, p. 26.

Practically every objection to the unit method of teaching can be answered by Morrison's warning, as follows:

> Those readers . . . who are looking for a plan which can confidently be put in operation and prove to be a solution of the perplexities of the schoolroom will be disappointed. No such plan can be written, for teaching is not an activity which is susceptible of that kind of guidance. The analysis of the teaching process which is here presented is intended to serve as a coherent, intelligible, and reliable basis from which school people may be helped in thinking out pedagogical problems in the immense variety of schoolroom situations in which the latter are found.[52]

H.C. Morrison's last book on the curriculum [53] added nothing new to the principles involved.

A recent writer, J.C. Peel,[54] has pointed out startlingly a truth that all school personnel should realize, namely, that teaching by the unit method is one of the most complex and important teaching techniques that the teaching profession has yet evolved; and it is still evolving, being added to, being improved.

CHARACTERISTICS OF THE UNIT

The study and analysis of the unit in this chapter make it possible to set forth the framework of the unit, whether of subject-matter type or of experience type:

1. *The unit has a central theme, around which class work and activities revolve.* Some authors believe that a unit is a unit only when it is unitary to the student; that is, when the student sees the objective clearly, and understands how his activity leads to the accomplishment of that objective.

2. By its very nature, the unit *implies the use of more than one method of teaching;* every method which is employed is used for the achievement of the objective of the central theme. Therefore, one may find in a typical unit anywhere from three to five or more individual methods of teaching. Generally, the longer the unit, the more numerous are the methods that are employed by the teacher at one time or another.

3. *The unit makes use of different kinds of learning activity on the part of the pupil through provision for well-balanced*

[52] Morrison, Preface, p. vii.

[53] *The Curriculum of the Common School,* The University of Chicago Press, 1940.

[54] "The Ubiquitous Unit," Phi Delta Kappan, xxxvii (December, 1955), pp. 119–21.

a. Large Group activity ⎫
b. Small Group activity ⎬ in classroom work.
c. Individual activity ⎭

4. *It has these common characteristics in its structure:*

   a. A pretest, which seeks to ascertain what the pupil already knows about the unit, so that the teacher can guide him onward from the point of his knowledge and achievement.
   b. An "overview," or introduction, which indicates the scope and purpose(s) of the unit.
   c. A final test to discover the amount of progress which the pupil has made. In units which run for longer than two weeks, a check-test is frequently administered at about the middle of the unit to check pupil progress.
   d. On the part of the individual pupil, a synthesis, or at least a summary of some significant aspect(s) of the unit.

5. *It requires careful preparation in advance by the teacher;* this preplanning must provide ample, definite supplementary references for the pupils, as well as definite textbook sources and page references.

6. *It requires that ample supplementary reference and source materials be available for pupil use* in either the school library or in the classroom, or in the community.

7. *It employs many types of visual and audio-visual aids and materials.*

One who wishes to compare this analysis of the characteristics of the unit might look at those found in *Unit Teaching in the Elementary School.*[55] These authors state, in summary, that the unit (1) has wholeness, or cohesion; (2) cuts over subject-matter lines; (3) is based on the sound modern concept of how learning occurs; (4) is based on the needs and development of pupils, social and personal; (5) requires a larger block of time; (6) is life-centered; (7) uses the normal interests and drives of pupils; (8) is based on the level of maturity of the child; (9) emphasizes problem solving; and (10) is planned cooperatively by pupils and the teacher.

PROBLEMS FOR INDIVIDUAL STUDY AND CLASS DISCUSSION

1. Why can the project method in teaching be called a variation of the unit method?

[55] By Lavone Hanna, *et al., op. cit.,* Chap. v.

2. Could you develop a unit on "Transportation" for pupils in the fifth grade, using the five Morrison steps? For pupils in Civics in the first year of high school?

3. What standards can you establish by which to test accurately whether a textbook has been organized according to the unit method of teaching?

4. In the exploratory step of a new unit on "Our Community," assume that you desire to use a pretest as an aid in discovering what knowledge your pupils already have about the unit. Make out such a pretest of twenty-five items for fourth-grade work; for a class in Sociology at the twelfth-grade level.

5. Investigate the Winnetka plan of instruction and compare it with the Morrison unit method. What similarities do you find?

6. Why are there so many different conceptions of the unit technique among teachers?

7. Construct a check-test of fifteen to twenty items to be given to your group to check the adequacy of your presentation of a new unit.

8. Do you see any real distinction between Morrison's teaching procedure for "science-type" and "appreciation-type" subjects? Support your position.

9. Is it possible for pupils' evaluations of a unit to be worth-while? Could you make out a form for such pupil evaluation?

10. Can units planned cooperatively by teacher and pupils be prepared for in advance by the teacher? Give reasons for your position.

11. Is the original Morrison unit technique based on "subject-matter" or "experience" units? Explain.

12. Compare a unit in Morrison's *Practice of Teaching in the Secondary School* with a resource unit in *Unit Teaching in the Elementary School*, by Lavone Hanna, *et al.* What difference is there, if any?

13. Is the unit method really a type of "activity" technique? Support your position.

14. Make out a resource unit for your social studies in the sixth grade. For your Biology class in the tenth grade.

ADDITIONAL ANNOTATED REFERENCES
FOR PROBLEM OR UNIT STUDY

Adams, F., *Educating America's Children* (2nd ed.), New York, The Ronald Press Company, 1954.

Chapter v and sample units or activities centered around health, science, the social studies, reading and language arts, arithmetic, music, art, and dramatic play.

Alberty, H.B., *Reorganizing the High School Curriculum* (rev. ed.), New York, The Macmillan Company, 1953.
Chapters xiv–xv for resource units.

Anderson, V.E., *Principles and Procedures of Curriculum Improvement*, New York, The Ronald Press Company, 1956.
Part v for definition, types, cooperative planning, and evaluating the unit.

Beck, R.H., Cook, W.W., and Kearney, N.C., *Curriculum in the Modern Elementary School*, New York, Prentice-Hall, 1953.
Chapters xii, xiii, and xv for the use of teaching and resource units.

Burton, W.H., *The Guidance of Learning Activities* (2nd ed.), New York, Appleton-Century-Crofts, 1952.
Chapters xii–xiv for the unit method, planning and developing units, and analysis of a unit.

Flaum, L.S., *The Activity High School*, New York, Harper and Brothers, 1953.
Chapters i–ii for point of view, iii–iv for the activity class and unit, and types of units in subject-matter fields in Chapters viii–xi.

Hanna, L.A., Potter, G.L., and Hagaman, N., *Unit Teaching in the Elementary School*, New York, Rinehart and Company, 1955.
Parts Two and Three, and Appendix i, for characteristics of the unit, preplanning for unit teaching, resource and teaching units, and teaching the unit.

Leonard, J.P., *Developing the Secondary School Curriculum* (rev. ed.), New York, Rinehart and Company, 1953.
Chapter x for topical, cultural and problems types, Chapter xi for correlation and fusion, Chapter xiv on core courses, Chapters xv–xvii on developing and organizing various types of units.

Lurry, L.L., and Alberty, E.J., *Developing a High School Core Program*, New York, The Macmillan Company, 1957.
Chapter vi for learning units and Chapter iii for large-unit ideas.

Macomber, F.G., *Teaching in the Modern Secondary School*, New York, McGraw-Hill Book Company, 1952.
Chapters iii–vi for bases for organizing instruction around centers of interest and planning and guiding units.

Noar, G., *The Junior High School—Today and Tomorrow*, New York, Prentice-Hall, 1953.
Chapter xii for techniques in developing teaching and resource units, and Chapter xvi for resource unit outlines.

Quillen, I.J., and Hanna, L.A., *Education for Social Competence*, Chicago, Scott, Foresman and Company, 1948.
Chapter v for organization of learning experiences, Chapters vi–vii for chronological, topical, and problems approaches to units, pre-

planning and unit development in Chapters VII and VIII, and samples of resource and teaching units in Appendices.

Ragan, W.B., *Modern Elementary Curriculum*, New York, The Dryden Press, 1953.
Chapter VI and some other chapters for the unit concept and examples of types.

Romine, S.A., *Building the High Scool Curriculum*, New York, The Ronald Press Company, 1954.
Chapters IX–XI for definitions, types, building and planning units, and their use in the core curriculum.

Saylor, J.G., and Alexander, W.M., *Curriculum Planning for Better Teaching and Learning*, New York, Rinehart and Company, 1954.
Chapters XII–XIV for resource units and unit plans and planning units with pupils.

Smith, B.O., Stanley, W.O., and Shores, J.H., *Fundamentals of Curriculum Development* (rev. ed.), Yonkers-on-Hudson, World Book Company, 1957.
Chapters XII–XIII, XVI for practices in the activity concept and centers of interest, and Chapters XIV–XV for units and practices in the core curriculum.

Stratemeyer, F.B., *et al.*, *Developing a Curriculum for Modern Living* (2nd ed.), New York, Teachers College, Columbia University, 1957.
Chapters V–VI for life situations that learners face and developing curriculum from them, Chapter VIII for cooperative planning with pupils, and Part IV for samples of elementary and high school teacher-pupil planning.

Thut, I.N., and Gerberich, J.R., *Foundations of Method for Secondary Schools*, New York, McGraw-Hill Book Company, 1949.
Part II, B and C for methods based on the subject-matter and experience units.

The Unit in Curriculum Development and Instruction, Curriculum Research Report, Bureau of Curriculum Research, Board of Education of the City of New York, Aug. 20, 1956 (reprinted, 1957).
Includes the teaching unit and how it is planned and developed, the resource unit, and resources for unit teaching.

Unstattd, J.G., *Secondary School Teaching* (3rd ed.), Boston, Ginn and Company, 1953.
Division II for the development features, planning, and implementation of the unit and activity plans of teaching.

Wesley, E.B., and Wronski, S.P., *Teaching Social Studies in High Schools* (4th ed.), Boston, D.C. Heath and Company, 1958.
Chapters XIX–XXVIII for development of teaching methods and of the unit as a culmination of that development.

CHAPTER 8 The influence of the textbook

POSITION OF THE TEXTBOOK IN AMERICAN EDUCATION

The textbook is firmly entrenched in the schools of the United States. Its influence on the curriculum is powerful, and meets generally with public approval. Therefore, in this chapter a careful analysis will be made of the textbook as a factor in curriculum revision.

Two authors of methods texts on the teaching of the social studies summarized many years ago most aspects of the textbook situation which still exist today. E.B. Wesley stated:

The textbook reflects and establishes standards. It indicates, all too frequently perhaps, what the teacher is required to know and what the pupils are supposed to learn. By its teaching and learning aids it markedly affects methods and reflects the rising standards of scholarship. It expands its scope and size to meet the changing conception of what is considered educationally sound and desirable. Thus it sometimes leads and sometimes follows the educational procession, but it is always a significant factor.[1]

T.H. Schutte said:

. . . various pressure groups are constantly fighting for particular ideas, interpretations, and interests, active in their antagonism to the teaching of anything which does not agree with their preconceived notions. This has been pursued to such an extent that it has very largely made our social studies textbooks meaningless and futile compendiums. However, we need not despair of the situation, for there are definite indications of improvement. . . .[2]

---

[1] *Teaching the Social Studies* (2nd ed.), Boston, D.C. Heath and Company, 1942, p. 375. Wesley makes the same statement in his third edition, 1950, p. 299.

[2] *Teaching the Social Studies on the Secondary School Level*, New York, Prentice-Hall, 1938, pp. 289–90.

Whether curricular procedure is based upon the recommendation of national committees or upon an analysis of textbooks and courses of study makes but little difference. Textbooks and courses of study tend to adopt the recommendations of such committees. Moreover, the writers of textbooks are not always conversant with the conditions in the schools. Many of them are so absorbed in their particular subject matter that they do not reveal the relation between the subjects and what transpires in the social order generally. Their books, in turn, influence local, and even national, committees.[3]

Schutte advanced the argument that textbooks gain much of their present unpopularity because of faulty use. He believed that the textbook is an indispensable tool to most teachers, primarily because teachers lack knowledge of other materials and because other teaching materials are not available in many schools.

Whether or not society could afford to provide for sufficient library materials for the education of the young is beside the point. The fact is that in ages past it has not done so, and neither will it do so for a long time to come. To dispense with the textbook, then, is nothing short of folly, and to continue argument against its use is an educational fallacy. . . .[4]

Modern writers on the curriculum agree with many of the points emphasized years ago by Wesley and Schutte. For example, Galen Saylor and William Alexander think that good teachers would consider the textbook of today as an assistant teacher in printed form, and Vernon Anderson emphasizes the use of the textbook as a resource, as a common base for study and investigation.[5] The stress is upon the *proper* use of the textbook, even though a particular text at times will be inadequate as a *sole* source of information for teacher or pupils. The textbook continues as the main source of vicarious experience available to school personnel.

On the elementary as well as the secondary-school level, there is

---

[3] *Teaching the Social Studies on the Secondary School Level,* New York, Prentice-Hall, 1938, p. 294; compare also "Why and How Do Textbooks Get Bigger?" by John A. Nietz, *The Phi Delta Kappan,* xxxiii (January, 1952), pp. 252–53.

[4] *Ibid.,* pp. 333–34.

[5] *Cf. Curriculum Planning,* by J. Galen Saylor and William M. Alexander, New York, Rinehart and Company, 1954, pp. 485–86 and Chap. xiv, and *Principles and Procedures for Curriculum Improvement* by Vernon E. Anderson, New York, The Ronald Press Company, 1956, pp. 349–54.

ample evidence that another complaint concerning textbooks is justified. The authors of textbooks disagree widely about content, the
aims to be achieved, the placement of material, and the drill to be
devoted to specific aspects of learning. Douglas E. Lawson analyzed
thirty-five textbooks, Grades 5–8, for determination of content, and
fifty-three texts for identification of the authors' objective in teaching
the language arts.[6]

Lawson came to the conclusion that, for all practical purposes,
there was almost no agreement among authors of these elementary
language textbooks about what materials should be taught, how they
should be taught, or the objectives to be sought by the lessons which
were presented.

There is additional proof of the dissatisfaction of teachers with the
inadequacies and deficiencies of textbooks. Criticisms of school textbooks and the authors who write them are substantiated by the
Fourth Yearbook of the National Council for the Social Studies
(1934), by Blair (1933), by the Fourteenth Yearbook of the Department of Superintendence (1936), by Watt (1921), by the Twenty-
sixth (Parts I and II), Thirtieth (Part II), Thirty-third (Part II),
Thirty-sixth (Part I), and Fifty-sixth (Part II) Yearbooks of the
National Society for the Study of Education.

Four main problems concerning the textbook are of significance in
curriculum work. In the following paragraphs, those problems will
be considered carefully for the purpose of discovering whether they
help or hinder curriculum revision.

1. IS THE TEXTBOOK A PRIMARY FACTOR IN TEACHING IN THE SCHOOLS
   OF AMERICA, AND WILL IT CONTINUE TO BE A PRIMARY FACTOR?

All the evidence points to the fact that for a long time to come the
textbook will be one of the primary tools in use by teachers in curriculum work. Regardless of whether some school systems or some
teachers supplement the textbook with library materials, or dispense
with one textbook in favor of the use of specific references by students of various ages, the textbook is still the main tool employed by

---

[6] Read Mildred E. Dawson, "Elementary-School Language Textbooks," *Ele-
mentary English Review,* xv (November, 1938), p. 276, and Richard E. Gross,
"American History Teachers Look at the Book," *The Phi Delta Kappan,* xxxiii
(January, 1952), pp. 290–91.

teachers. The American public has not yet been convinced that the textbook should be discarded in curriculum work. Ample proof of the attitude of the public is present in many states in the form of state- or system-wide adoption of multiple or basal lists of textbooks for use in the public schools. The following statement by Ernest Horn seems to sum up the textbook situation which confronts the modern curriculum worker:

Most discussions of the use of the textbook assume that there is a close relationship between it and the course of study and that instruction follows the order of the topics in the textbook rather systematically. Under these conditions, which undoubtedly hold in the majority of schools, there are several potential contributions that the text, at its best, can make.[7]

2. IS THE COMPLAINT OF TEACHERS AND WRITERS JUSTIFIED, THAT THE TEXTBOOK TENDS TO SET STANDARDS FOR BOTH THE CONTENT AND THE METHOD OF WHAT IS TO BE TAUGHT TO THE CHILD?

The evidence which has already been presented shows that textbooks are a major factor in the formation of the curriculum. They tend to set the standards of the curriculum and the methods of teaching on all school levels.

3. TO WHAT EXTENT SHOULD "PRESSURE GROUPS" INFLUENCE THE WRITING, ADOPTION, AND USE OF SCHOOL TEXTBOOKS?

In considering this matter, one runs across a struggle by no means new in the annals of American education. Educators in some southern states recall the fight, in the early 1920's, of the United Daughters of the Confederacy against the history of the United States written by David S. Muzzey; the "Daughters" believed that the book was anti-southern and that it used the wrong terms in describing the "Civil War," which to them should have been described as the "War Between the States." As long ago as 1926, Harold Rugg stated that textbooks determined the dominant aims of instruction for many years in the American school curriculum, and that one reason for the conservatism of the curriculum was the entrench-

---

[7] *Methods of Instruction in the Social Studies*, New York, Charles Scribner's Sons, 1937, p. 218. *Cf.* also E.B. Wesley and M.A. Adams, *Teaching Social Studies In Elementary Schools*, Boston, D.C. Heath and Company, 1946, p. 221.

ment in the schools of the private interests of both publishers and authors.[8] Ten years later Rugg reiterated his statement, contending that a policy of laissez faire in textbook writing was equivalent to a policy of laissez faire in curriculum-making; that the school did not determine the curriculum, but that textbook writers did.[9] H.K. Beale [10] wrote of politicians and pressure groups who influence curricula and textbooks, citing specific instances and textbooks. A survey at midcentury of American history teaching in 100 senior high schools in California disclosed anew that textbooks compose the majority of most United States history courses.[11]

The perennial dispute over the textbooks used in the schools has broken out anew on a somewhat broader basis than has been in evidence for many years. Various pressure groups waged a fight for many years upon the "Social Science Series" of textbooks which were written by Harold Rugg. The publication in 1941 of the investigation by the National Association of Manufacturers of textbooks in the field of the Social Studies drew sharp attention again to pressure groups as shapers of curriculum policy, as did the *Chicago Tribune's* survey of texts in 1947. More recently there have been the controversies over *Building America* in California and the banning of certain books and magazines in school libraries in other sections of the country.

THE CONTROVERSY OVER THE RUGG TEXTBOOKS. Millions of copies of Rugg's books were sold during the thirty-five years since he began writing them, and his books went through many revisions during that time. Professor Rugg was fortunate to escape for so long the attacks which are generally made upon a successful publisher of texts in any field where controversy is likely to arise, such as the social sciences. The fight against his series went on for more than a

---

[8] Twenty-sixth Yearbook, National Society for the Study of Education, *Foundations and Techniques of Curriculum Building,* Part I, Public School Publishing Company, 1926, pp. 27–32.

[9] *American Life and the School Curriculum,* Boston, Ginn and Company, 1936, pp. 126–31.

[10] E. Ellis (Ed.), *Education Against Propaganda,* Seventh Yearbook, National Council for the Social Studies, 1937, pp. 107–9. *Cf.* also H.K. Beale, *Are American Teachers Free?* New York, Charles Scribner's Sons, 1936, Chap. XI.

[11] *Cf.* Richard E. Gross, "American History Teachers Look at the Book," *op. cit.*

dozen years; attacks on it were made in Montana, Illinois, Indiana, Massachusetts, New Jersey, New York, Pennsylvania, Ohio, California, Washington, Georgia, and the District of Columbia. Groups of national prominence taking part in the fight have been the American Legion, the Veterans of Foreign Wars, the National Association of Manufacturers, the American Federation of Advertisers, the American Newspaper Publishers' Association, the New York State Economic Council, and Friends of the Public Schools of America (Chicago).

No pressure group, however, was more effective in its attack upon the Rugg books than Professor Rugg was in their defense. Many educators and other people who believed in the right of free speech and of freedom of teaching in the schools assisted in Rugg's defense. The primary purpose here is not to trace the fight for or against Rugg and his series of books, but to emphasize the fact that school textbooks are subject to the influences of pressure groups in state, regional, and national movements at various times which may or may not be of benefit to the children in the schools.[12]

THE NATIONAL ASSOCIATION OF MANUFACTURERS AND SOCIAL STUDIES TEXTS, 1941. Of far more potential significance than the Rugg controversy to school people and the public was the investigation of textbooks in the social studies made by R.W. Robey for the National Association of Manufacturers. Robey and a staff of three assistants examined more than five hundred textbooks on economics,

---

[12] For the development of the struggle between Professor Rugg and various pressure groups the reader is referred to the following: "Propaganda Over the Schools," *Propaganda Analysis*, IV (February 25, 1941), pp. 1–12; H. Rugg, *That Men May Understand: An American in the Long Armistice*, Doubleday, Doran and Company, 1941, Chaps. VII, VIII; H. Rugg, "This Has Happened Before." *Frontiers of Democracy*, VII (January 15, 1941), pp. 105–8; A.F. Myers, "The Attacks on the Rugg Books," *Frontiers of Democracy*, VII (October 15, 1940), pp. 17–22; M.K. Hart, "Let's Discuss This on the Merits," *Frontiers of Democracy*, VII (December 15, 1940), pp. 82–87; *Social Education*, February, 1941, issue and January, 1941, issue (pp. 9–14) for statements pro and con; M.J. Brown, "A Layman Speaks About the Rugg Books," *Frontiers of Democracy*, VII (February 15, 1941), pp. 153–55; H. Hicks, "Ours to Reason Why," *American Legion Magazine*, XXX (May, 1941), pp. 5–7, 50–56; W.D. Lewis, "The Battle of the Textbooks," *School and Society*, LIV (September 27, 1941), pp. 229–31; *Propaganda in U.S. School Books*, reprinted from the *Chicago Tribune*, October, November, 1947, "Anti-American Rugg Books in Many Schools" by Frank Hughes, third of a series (October 9, 1947); "Subversive Textbooks" (editorial), *The New Age*, LVI (May, 1948), p. 259.

sociology, civics, history, and geography. Abstracts were made of important points of view in the textbooks as they relate to American government and the business system; these were prepared for distribution.

The National Association of Manufacturers did not take any controversial position on the abstracts of these books. It disclaimed any attempt to impose its ideas on the schools, and it publicly repudiated the statements of Professor Robey that a substantial proportion of the social-science textbooks used in the secondary schools tended to criticize adversely the American form of government and to hold in contempt its system of private enterprise. Yet the implications and results of such studies may be far-reaching. On the one hand, persons using such abstracts without the context of the rest of the book might attempt to prove that certain texts should not be used in the public schools; still, these particular texts in their entirety might be just as good as those which have been in use for twenty-five or thirty years. On the other hand, professional educators became agitated immediately over the study of textbooks by the American manufacturers, and many jumped into the fight without thinking. They attacked the study as an unwarranted fight on the schools and textbooks, as an affront to the integrity of textbook writers, and as an action hostile to freedom of teaching and of thought.[13]

SURVEY OF TEXTS AND MATERIALS BY THE CHICAGO TRIBUNE, 1947. The *Tribune* survey included over fifty textbooks and some guides for teachers, pamphlets, newspapers for pupils, and other materials for schools. A series of articles by Frank Hughes in the *Chicago Tribune* gave the findings of this survey.[14]

All of the materials in the survey came from schools in the southern part of Wisconsin.

[13] "The Manufacturers' Association Abstracts Textbooks," *Social Education,* v (February, 1941), pp. 134–40; *cf.* also pp. 87–90.

[14] *Propaganda in U.S. School Books,* reprinted from the *Chicago Tribune,* October, November, 1947, The Tribune Company. (Six articles in a series on October 7, 8, 9, 10, 11, and 13; and three other articles by Frank Hughes: "Unesco Drafts Plan to Revise Schools' Books," "Strange Story of British Aim to Degrade U.S.," and "British-Rooted Bodies Seek to Win Americans"). *Cf.* also the *Chicago Tribune:* cartoon, October 9, "Revising the Late Edition"; editorial, October 11, "Exposing the N.E.A."; "Hunt Outlines Schools' Plans to Combat Isms," October 14; and "Praise *Tribune* for Exposé of Red Textbooks," October 16.

Analysis of Hughes' series of six articles in the *Tribune* revealed that only six of the fifty textbooks were labeled by author and/or title as subversive; three of the teachers' guides were so labeled; and one booklet, one bulletin, and three pamphlets (resource units for teachers) were estimated to be subversive.[15] The series of articles named the textbooks or materials, and quoted subversive passages. These excerpts were mostly isolated passages without the full context of the rest of the book, as was true in regard to the abstracts of the Robey investigation for the National Association of Manufacturers in 1941.[16] The real issues involved in the *Tribune* survey, as in pre-

---

[15] The texts and teachers' guides that were named were:

H. Rugg: Social Science Series, Boston, Ginn and Company
    Our Country and Our People (Teacher's Guide only)
    Changing Countries and Changing Peoples
    The Conquest of America (Teacher's Guide only)
    America's March Toward Democracy (Text and Teacher's Guide)

M.A. Stewart, St. Louis, The Webster Publishing Company:
    Boys and Girls of the Orient
    Land of the Soviets

M.G. Kelley,
    Life in Modern America

R. and O. Goslin and H.F. Storen, New York, Harcourt, Brace and Company:
    American Democracy Today and Tomorrow

The booklet that was identified was:

    Education and the People's Peace, Washington, Educational Policies Commission

The Bulletin and the three pamphlets that were named were:

    "The Constitution Up To Date," Washington, National Council for the Social Studies

    "Problems in American Life" series, published by the National Association of Secondary-School Principals and the National Council for the Social Studies:

        No. 10: *Economic Problems of the Post-War World,* by A.H. Hansen and L.E. Leamer.
        No. 15: *International Organization After the War,* by Max Lerner, Edna Lerner, and H.J. Abraham.
        No. 20: *The American Way of Business,* by Oscar Lange, A.P. Lerner, and A.W. Troelstrup.

[16] This same technique of quoting excerpts without the context of the rest of the book was used by the American Legion against Harold Rugg and his texts in 1941–1942; compare "Rugg Philosophy Analyzed," Vols. i, ii, iii, and iv, prepared (or reprinted) and distributed by National Americanism Commission, the American Legion (Indianapolis).

vious investigations, were: (1) *Who* shall examine and pass judgment on texts and materials for use in the public schools and (2)
Shall the public schools take up *both* sides of controversial issues? [17]

ATTACKS ON *Building America* AND OTHER PERIODICALS, 1947–1949.
These years saw a steady increase in activity in regard to the removal
from schools and libraries of books and reading material which were
considered "objectionable" or "subversive" by some groups or people.

In California, *Building America* was under fire for several years
as to its suitability for use in the schools; a local chapter of a patriotic
group, the Sons of the American Revolution, led the attack upon it.
In Birmingham, Alabama, *Senior Scholastic* was banned from all
schools, apparently upon racial grounds. *The Nation* was banned
from school libraries in Newark, New Jersey, and in New York
City; it was also banned in Massachusetts from all teachers' colleges,
but the State Board of Education later lifted this ban; in the New
York case the claim was made that religious pressure was at work.
Other magazines which were under attack were *New Republic,
Survey Graphic, Commonweal, In Fact,* the *United Nations Bulletin,*
and *Life.*[18]

---

[17] Two differing views of the *Tribune* survey are illustrated by articles in
School and Society, LXVII: D.L. Geyer, "An Attack on Social-Studies Textbooks"
(March 6, 1948), pp. 187–88; and O.F. Galloway, " 'Subversive' Social-Studies
Textbooks" (June 5, 1948), p. 428. (For more complete information on propa-
ganda analysis, the reader is referred to Chap. XVIII.)

[18] For more detailed information and opinion on these aspects, the reader is
referred to these selected references: the November issue, Vol. VI, No. 2, 1948,
of *Educational Leadership,* devoted to "Looking at Controversial Issues" (especially D.K. Berninghausen, "On Keeping Our Reading Free," pp. 104–8, and
Kimball Wiles, "Building America: A Case in Point," pp. 108–14); "An Appeal
to Reason and Conscience In Defense of the Right of Freedom of Inquiry in the
United States," Ad Hoc Committee to Lift Ban on *The Nation,* Archibald Mac-
Leish (Chmn.), 20 Vesey Street, New York 7; William Jansen, "Should Re-
ligious Beliefs Be Studied and Criticized in an American Public High School?"
October 10, 1948, Office of Superintendent of Schools, New York City; J.H.
Holmes, "Sensitivity as Censor," *Saturday Review of Literature,* XXXII (February
26, 1949), pp. 9–10, 23; and A.W. Anderson, "The Nation Case," *Progressive
Education,* XXVI (March, 1949), pp. 151–57.

Editorials, news reports, and articles on various aspects of literary censorship
and book banning have been so numerous all over the nation that it is impossible to include a complete bibliography here. In addition to the references in
this chapter and in Chapter XIX on propaganda, the interested reader might get
a fair cross-section of opinion, *pro* and *con,* by reading some such list as the
following: *American Library Association Bulletin* (1948), pp. 57–59 and 204–7;
Everybody's, June, 1948, p. 5; *Library Journal* (1948), pp. 149 and 791–92;

The method of attack upon *Building America* in California presents an illustration of how a particular group in the United States can bring pressure to bear for the elimination of teaching materials in the schools.

Building America was originally (1935) a periodical, sponsored by the Society for Curriculum Study and published eight times a year (October to May); each monthly issue was intended to be a complete pictorial study unit of one modern problem. The study units were designed primarily for the junior and senior high school level and for adult study. In 1943 the Society for Curriculum Study and the Department of Supervisors and Directors of Instruction of the National Education Association were combined to form the Department of (now Association for) Supervision and Curriculum Development, which continued the policy and publication of *Building America*. In all, eighty-nine of these pictorial studies of modern problems were published from 1935 to 1946; they were available as a new unit monthly, or could be purchased as a volume of eight units yearly.

In 1946, thirty of these units of *Building America* were recommended as supplementary texts by the California Curriculum Commission to the State Board of Education; these units were to be revised and brought up to date, and were to be bound in one volume for grade seven and in two volumes for grade eight. After examination of the units, the State Superintendent, the California Parent-Teacher Association, and the Committee on Intellectual Freedom of the California Library Association recommended them. So *Building America* was adopted unanimously by the State Board early in 1947.

But appropriations were held up on account of the filing of a complaint to the California Legislature by the Sons of American Revolu-

The Nation, July 3, 1948, p. 4; *New York Herald Tribune,* February 4, 1948, and June 27, 1948, Section ii, p. 5; *New York Post,* March 9, 1948, p. 30; *The New York Times* (1948), June 15, p. 29, and June 20, p. 89, and (1947) May 22, p. 8; *Publishers' Weekly* (1948) for March 13, April 3, 10, and 17, May 8 and 29, June 26, and July 3; and *The New Age* (1948), pp. 259, 399–400, and 458–59. Recently two anthologies have brought together representative samples of *pros* and *cons* on censorship of textbooks, namely, *Public Education Under Criticism,* by C.W. Scott and C.M. Hill, New York, Prentice-Hall, 1954, Chap. vi and pp. 322–38, and *Crucial Issues in Education,* edited by Henry Ehlers, New York, Henry Holt and Company, 1955, pp. 67–117.

tion.[19] The Legislature appointed a Senate Investigating Committee on Education; this Committee tied by a vote of four to four on the problem of whether *Building America* was "subversive." An interim committee was then appointed to carry on the work of the Senate

FIG. 21   *There can be texts other than books*

This is a television science class session of approximately 150 pupils.
(*Courtesy Charlotte (N.C.) City Schools, Sedgefield Junior High School.*)

Investigating Committee until 1949; and this interim committee of five reported to the State Senate on March 27, 1948, that *Building America* was unfit for use in the schools.[20]

The staff of the San Bernardino County Free Library issued an

[19] "The Betrayal of America," complaint to California Legislature in re "Subversive Textbooks and Curriculum Practices in Public Schools," presented by Trustees of Americanism Fund, California Society, Sons of American Revolution, 926 De Young Building, San Francisco, California.

[20] *Cf. Third Report: Senate Investigating Committee on Education, Textbooks,* California Legislature, 1948 Regular Session, Sacramento (pp. 1–120); and *NEA Journal,* "News and Trends," xxxvii (May, 1948).

analysis of the criticisms of the Senate Investigating Committee's Report. They placed side by side the criticisms of the Report and their own critical estimate of the same volume.[21] Their comparisons of these two different estimates but tend to emphasize again two important points in regard to the evaluation of materials for use in the classroom: (1) Sentences or statements which are lifted out of the context frequently lose their meaning or are changed in intent; and (2) the purposes or objectives of a textbook have to be set forth before instruments can be established in order to evaluate those texts fairly.

CONFLICTS CONCERNING RACE, CREED, AND SUBVERSIVE INFLUENCES. The 1949–1952 controversy in Scarsdale, New York, is a good illustration of all three of these conflicts. Before the Board of Education issued its summary of principles in April, 1952, the attackers had (1) attempted to ban Dickens' *Oliver Twist*, Shakespeare's *Merchant of Venice*, Boak, *et al.*, *World History*, Harlow's *Story of America*, and Goslin, *et al.*, *American Democracy Today and Tomorrow;* and (2) tried to exclude from the library books by Howard Fast, Louis Untermeyer, Shirley Graham, Anna Louise Strong, and Herbert Aptheker on the grounds primarily that they were subversive, pro-Russian, or anti-American.[22] Another outstanding example of legal action to ban textbooks on grounds of the Communist connections of the author(s) was the censorship act of the Alabama legislature in 1953, later declared unconstitutional (1955).[23]

WHO SHOULD FORMULATE THE SCHOOL CURRICULUM? It is unfortunate that some professional educators take extreme stands at times against textbook surveys by laymen and the reports of the findings of these surveys, without first obtaining and reading the various abstracts of the textbooks and the textbooks themselves in their entirety. *In a democracy, educators as a group cannot expect to be wise enough to formulate the policies for the schools without the assist-*

---

[21] "The Right to Find Out: An Analysis of the Criticisms of Building America," issued by the California Library Committee on Intellectual Freedom, 1948; *cf.* also Kimball Wiles, *op. cit.*
[22] *Cf.* Kenneth M. Gould, "The Scarsdale Story," *The Humanist*, 1952, No. 4; C.W. Scott and C.M. Hill, *op. cit.*, pp. 322–36; and Henry Ehlers (ed.), *op. cit.*, II.
[23] Cited also in Ehlers, *op. cit.*, pp. 107–8.

ance of other groups. Much more healthy was the attitude of four-teen members of the Harvard Graduate School of Education when the results of the investigation of social studies texts by the National Association of Manufacturers were published; they issued a state-ment to the effect that they welcomed this wider interest in schools by every type of sincere citizens; they pointed out, however, the possibility of improper use of the abstracts.[24]

More constructive approaches have been taken recently by some outside organizations to analysis of texts and materials used in the schools. The National Conference of Christians and Jews sponsored studies in intergroup relations, among them an impartial analysis of *Intergroup Relations in Teaching Materials.*[25] They examined and analyzed 315 textbooks and course-of-study outlines used in ele-mentary, junior and senior high schools, and the first two years of college. The National Citizens' Commission for the Public Schools prepared its "Working Guide No. 8," *How Good Are Our Teaching Materials?* as an aid to citizen understanding of the problem.[26] The Council on Advancement of Secondary Education has made two careful studies in its "Study on Economic Education." The first is an analysis of basic economic areas and topics thought necessary for sound judgments and decisions. The second [27] gives the results of a survey of magazines and newspapers for economic terms. The Coun-cil is now engaged in preparing teaching-learning units on these basic economic topics.

There is real danger to the schools and to the curriculum in the "closed-mind" attitude of some educators, who seem to feel that lay-men have little knowledge of, and perhaps less interest in, the schools and the teaching materials which are used in them. It is doubtful wisdom to leave the determination of the curriculum en-tirely to the educators. In spite of the fact that special groups or individuals occasionally obtain the adoption of certain textbooks for

---

[24] "The Manufacturers' Association Abstracts Textbooks," *Social Education,* v (February, 1941).

[25] American Council on Education, 1949.

[26] Obtainable from the National Citizens' Committee for Public Schools, 2 West 45th St., New York 36 (1955).

[27] *Key Understandings in Economics,* The Council, 1956, and *Economics in The Press,* 1956, Washington 6, 1201 Sixteenth St., N.W.

their own interests or because of lack of educational foresight, the public has the final responsibility for determining the content of the curriculum. The public exercises this right to express itself through state and local legislation. And the public exercises this right without really harming textbook writers of integrity. Witness the continuing success of D.S. Muzzey,[28] who was so savagely attacked by pressure groups thirty-five years ago!

It is well known that the textbooks in totalitarian countries are written to interpret the history and the national aspirations of those countries in the light of what the officials in charge desire to be presented.[29] The possibility that such a procedure might take place in American education is repugnant to all lovers of democracy. It is patently impossible for any author to write a textbook in a living, changing field—as that of the social studies is today—without offending some special interests in this American democracy, if he tells the truth and is accurate in his presentation. A question more important than the right of any pressure group to survey school textbooks is whether the educators and textbook writers have determined accurately the degree of maturity of pupils and their stages of growth. If the writers of textbooks understand well the stages of child growth and development, then pupils on the various school levels will be able to understand progressively the conflicting theories and ideas in a democratic form of government, which preserves and defends the rights of minority groups to express their opinions.

However, the right of minority groups to express their opinions freely does not include also the right to proscribe what the majority shall read. The basic problem is well analyzed in this editorial:

Of all the mixed-up thinking on the race problem, none strikes us as being more ridiculous than the New York City Board of Education's dropping of Mark Twain's *The Adventures of Huckleberry Finn* from its approved textbook lists.

[28] E.P. Smith, D.S. Muzzey, and M. Lloyd, *World History: The Struggle for Civilization*, Boston, Ginn and Company, 1946.

[29] F. Lilge, "The Political Control of History Texts in the Soviet Union," *School and Society*, lxvii (May 29, 1948), pp. 393–97; R.W. Burkhardt, "The Soviet Union in American School Textbooks," *The Public Opinion Quarterly*, xi (Winter, 1947–1948), pp. 567–71; and G.S. Counts, "The Second World War in a Soviet High-School History," *Social Education*, x (December, 1946), pp. 345–47.

Newsday, from its vantage seat alongside what has happened, finds that "apparently the only reason is because some of its passages are derogatory to Negroes." *Newsday* sets forth its own views:

Huck Finn is an American classic. Mark Twain has been described as the "Lincoln of Literature," and "Huck" was his greatest work. If we are to seek to destroy our history, heritage and culture by censoring every book that contains Negro dialect, we shall soon antisepticize our schools and our libraries. And if we have to drop books about Negroes, what about Jews, Irish, Italians, any nationality?

Mark Twain used dialect because that was the way the Negroes along the Mississippi talked in 1840. Our great books explain American life, our energies, capacities, cultures. They were written to be read and reread—by children of any color.

With that view we are in complete accord. The reasoning—rather we'd prefer to say the lack thereof—behind the New York school board's action is similar to that which has cried for revision of such classic songs as *Old Black Joe.* It would throw *The Merchant of Venice* out of Shakespeare's repertoire because of Shylock's role. Any book which cast any member of a specific race in an unfavorable light would, by the same token, be taken out of our libraries and schools. The dialect of Uncle Remus and Mr. Dooley would undoubtedly be proscribed. If there is any logic, the ultimate follow-through would be denunciation of villains in general; and heaven knows our literature includes more who belong to the Caucasian race than all other combined.

A fine state of affairs it will be for literature, civilization and all races when we kick out folklore, ban reality or lose our sense of humor. Surely we have not become so sensitive or so foolish that we can take only a literary diet of pabulous pollyannaism. . . .[30]

The advantages of buying school books in bulk on a statewide or system-wide basis are too numerous for anyone to expect school systems to do away with textbooks. Such being the case, one of the biggest problems of the educational employee who is at work on curriculum improvement is to make certain that both pupils and teachers are supplied with supplementary materials of a source nature. Whether these materials are source units or textbooks makes little difference; by means of them, a better type of teaching can be done *in spite of* the handicaps of the textbook, as well as *with* the full use of it.

[30] *Greensboro* (N.C.) *Daily News,* September 20, 1957, p. 7 (editorial). Reprinted by permission.

4. **ARE NEW TRENDS, NEW AIMS, AND NEW PROCEDURES AND PRACTICES IN INSTRUCTION AVAILABLE IN THE TEXTBOOKS IN ORDER THAT THEY MAY BE MADE USE OF?**

Do the authors of school books supply adequately a wide enough range of teaching material? ample variation of materials to allow for individual rates of progress by different pupils? a vocabulary range adapted to the age and grade level intended? an amount of subject matter sufficient for systematic review? materials derived from scientific experiments which have been made concerning pupil growth, learning, interests, and progress? Let us assume that the same textbook is in use in a school system for a period of years, for example; what adjustments will the teacher who is interested in continuing his own growth have to make, in order to adapt that older textbook to newer methods of teaching or curriculum development, such as the large-unit plan or the core-curriculum approach? Is the textbook sometimes behind and sometimes in advance of educational movements and trends, as Wesley says? Or is it usually some distance behind?

In order to arrive at some valid conclusions about this aspect of the influence of the textbook, the writer has made a careful examination of textbook series in English and the social studies over a long period of years. These two subject areas of the curriculum were chosen as illustrations because they are generally required for all pupils from grades one to twelve. Those series were selected for examination which have gone through several revisions; many are still in use in one edition or another; therefore, reasonable comparisons can be made of the introduction of new methods, the inclusion of new aims, and the change in educational thought. Certain significant movements in education were used as criteria or standards for this examination. These movements have already been presented and analyzed in Chapters 6 and 7; at one time or another, during the last twenty years, they have been predominant or have been specially emphasized in education. These six movements are: (1) the Aims-and-Objectives Movement; (2) the Scientific Movement in Education; (3) Unit Organization; (4) the Activity Movement; (5) Integration; and (6) the "Large-Unit" Trend.

CHANGES IN SERIES OF TEXTBOOKS IN READING, LANGUAGE AND GRAMMAR, AND LITERATURE

ELSON SERIES OF READERS.   William H. Elson, chief author of the *Elson Grammar School Readers,* was largely responsible for this series for elementary schools from 1910 up to the present. The latest edition, 1956–1957, is known as the *New Basic Readers.* In 1919 these books were extended into the grades of the junior high school by the publication of *Junior High School Literature* by Elson and his collaborators. These textbooks are termed "basic" in the sense that they are designed primarily for the study of English by children in the elementary school. In another sense, they are called basic as compared to auxiliary readers of a supplementary nature, for the purpose of integrating reading with all other subjects in the elementary school. In recent years the trend has developed rapidly to include such auxiliary readers in the elementary school as materials parallel to the basal reading course.

The *New Basic Readers* are designed now for grades one to eight of the elementary school. Junior High School Literature has been discontinued, but will be replaced by seventh and eighth grade anthologies in 1959 and the *America Reads* series (four books, replacing the *Literature and Life Series*) is planned to carry the pupil on through the four years of high school. The *New Basic Readers* include the following twenty-three books: three reading readiness books, two preprimers, two primers, and two readers for the first grade; and two readers for each of the grades from two through eight. The principle of integration of the basic reading work with other studies in the elementary school is emphasized by the publishers in their auxiliary series of readers, as follows: "number stories" (two books); "science" series (nine books); "health and personal development" series (ten books); "social studies" series (six books); and "reading for independence" series (three books). The publishers advertise the claim that these auxiliary readers, integrating reading with mathematics, health, science, and social studies, are related to the basic readers in vocabulary and word-attack materials.

This entire series of readers, "basic" and "auxiliary," comprise the

"Curriculum Foundation Series," published by Scott, Foresman and Company, Chicago. They were published at the following dates:

Elson Grammar School Readers, 1910
The Elson Readers, 1920–1921
The Elson-Gray Basic Readers, 1931–1936 [31]
Basic Readers: Curriculum Foundation Series (a revision of *The Elson-Gray Basic Readers,* 1944 to 1948)
The New Basic Readers: Curriculum Foundation Series (1951 and 1957 revisions of *The Basic Readers*).

Covering the period from the first grade of the elementary school to the high school, the Elson series illustrate the main changes in reading textbooks for the period from 1910 to 1957. Since the concern here is with the influence derived from educational movements following about 1918 or 1920, the comparisons of the various series will begin with the *Elson Readers* (1920–1921), rather than with the earlier *Elson Grammar School Readers.* This analysis is given in Table 15. From the data here it is seen that the Elson readers from 1920 to 1957 exhibit tendencies toward changes which reflect the influence of various movements in education upon the textbooks for the elementary-school grades and the early secondary-school grades. Change is especially noticeable in respect to the scientific movement, unit organization, the activity movement, and the movement toward an integrated core curriculum.

ELSON LANGUAGE (GRAMMAR) SERIES. Beginning in 1917, and with reprints in 1921 and 1927, *Good English* was published as a foundation series of textbooks in grammar for elementary schools. The author, William H. Elson, collaborated with other specialists in the field of English to provide these texts, which in general represent an effort to present an introduction for elementary-school pupils to their later grammar work in the secondary school. The books were planned for use in the following grades:

Book One—Grade Three (Not included in the study).
Book Two—Grades Four and Five.
Book Three—Grades Six and Seven.

Thus the series leads up to the level of grammar instruction pre-

[31] *A Teacher's Guidebook* has been available since 1932 to accompany each book in the series.

TABLE 15 Changes in the Elson series of readers, 1920 to 1957
(Elementary School)

Evidence of Educational Movements Used as Criteria from

Editions	AIMS-AND-OBJECTIVES MOVEMENT	SCIENTIFIC MOVEMENT	UNIT ORGANIZATION	ACTIVITY MOVEMENT	INTEGRATION	LARGE-UNIT TREND
Elson Readers 1920–1921	*None* Two aims: citizenship, and learning to read	*None*	*Some* According to types of literature to be read	*Much* As individual and group "projects," antedating the more recent modern "Activity Movement"	*None*	*None*
Elson-Gray Basic Readers 1931–1936	*Some* Interest added to informational aim	*Much* Objective lesson exercises; graded vocabulary; systematic review aids *Teachers' Guidebook*	*Much* According to grouping of interests	*Much* Adds library extension reading and suggested activities for each unit	*Much* Through *auxiliary* readers in the "Curriculum Foundation Series"	*None*
Basic Readers 1944–1948 and *New Basic Readers* 1951 and 1957	*Much* Added to previous aims: reading for independence, in understanding self and world, in adapting to wider horizons, for extending interests and for special adjustment	*Much* Adds *Think-and-Do Book* for pupils to arouse interests and develop abilities; special Basic Reading Tests for evaluation of achievements of each child: Diagnostic Survey Charts to help teachers discover individual, class, and group needs; speech improvement cards; and record albums for phonics and poetry	*Much* *Teachers' Guidebooks* and Editions use the unit as the basis of approach and lesson planning	*Much* *Think-and-Do Book* for each pupil provides carefully prepared exercises and activities for large groups, small groups, and individual pupils	*Much* Effort to integrate new experiences with previous (past): vocabulary of *Basic Readers* keyed closely to vocabulary and word development in auxiliary readers in Curriculum Foundation Series	*Some* *E.g.*, there are ten units for grade 1, eight for grade 5, and eight for grade 8 in the latest revision

224

TABLE 16 · **Changes in the Elson language (grammar) series, 1917 to 1927**

(Elementary School)

Evidence of Educational Movements Used as Criteria from

Editions	AIMS-AND-OBJECTIVES MOVEMENT	SCIENTIFIC MOVEMENT	UNIT ORGANIZATION	ACTIVITY MOVEMENT	INTEGRATION	LARGE-UNIT TREND
Good English 1917	*None*	*None*	*None*	*Much* Though based mostly on the textbook, activities were good, antedating Modern Activity Movement	*None*	*None*
Good English 1921	*None*	*Some* In adoption of various National Committee Reports	*None*	*Much* As in 1917 edition	*None*	*None*
Good English 1927	*Slight* Emphasis upon oral English	*Some* Same as in 1921 edition	*None*	*Much* Similar to 1917 and 1921 editions	*None*	*None*

requisite to the use of *Sentence and Theme,* a high-school grammar published by the same textbook firm, Scott, Foresman and Company.

Good English has not been revised as recently as have some other series, and consequently its revisions may not be compared in terms of the evidences reflecting the influence of educational movements observable in textbooks which have such later editions. Yet it offers interesting analyses and may be compared with the textbooks of other more recent series. Especially interesting contrasts may be obtained from a study of the *Good English* Series [32] or *English Is Our Language* Series.[33] The Elson language texts appear in one respect to antedate the educational movements themselves, namely, in the "activity" approach (Table 16).

WARD'S SENTENCE AND THEME (GRAMMAR) SERIES. As a further example of the influence of educational movements upon school textbooks, Ward's *Sentence and Theme* may be cited. This was an English grammar for secondary-school use. Although it was intended at first as a grammar textbook for rapid review in either secondary-school or early college years, the subsequent revisions have shown a tendency to adapt the original material for secondary-school use by simplification. In general, however, it is likely that other English grammars for the secondary school will reflect more pronounced alterations than those apparent in the revisions of this series of grammar texts. Although changes are apparent, it must be borne in mind that the author was associated with a private school of a college-preparatory nature; therefore, he may not have felt the pressure of changing emphases to the same extent as authors more intimately connected with the public schools. This particular series was examined, however, to provide for a continuity of samples of textbook series published by the same firm.

C.H. Ward, master at the Taft School in Watertown. Connecticut, wrote the original edition of *Sentence and Theme* in 1917. The book reflected the classroom practices of the writer—practices suitable primarily for students preparing for college. A revision, published in 1923, seemed to ignore the emphasis then prevalent upon "aims and

[32] By H.G. Shane, F.K. Ferris, and E.E. Keener, River Forest (Ill.), Laidlaw Brothers (1952–1956) (seven books, for grades two through eight).

[33] E.L. Sterling, H.M. Lindahl, and K. Koch, Boston, D.C. Heath and Company, 1950 (six books, for grades three through eight).

objectives" of instruction, although concessions to the scientific movement and the activity movement are evident; a rearrangement of the material according to a loose unit plan is also noticeable in this edition. The third edition (1929) has not been revised recently to show the full impact of modern educational thought upon textbook construction, but it does show several changes in emphasis. The 1929 edition shows the author's realization that there had been a decrease in average ability among secondary-school pupils in recent decades; he made efforts in this edition to simplify the material and the general treatment (Table 17).

LITERATURE AND LIFE AND AMERICA READS SERIES (LITERATURE). The effects of the influence of the various movements in professional education upon school textbooks are shown clearly by the *Literature and Life* (now the *America Reads*) series. This series is composed of four graded textbooks in literature for English classes in the senior high school, and it is likewise published by Scott, Foresman and Company. These books may be considered as an extension of the *Elson Readers* for the elementary-school grades, since the authors of both series collaborated to some extent. Most of the literature included in these textbooks is fairly well standardized for English classes, but the kind of literature included, organization of the material, suggestions for activities, and introductory materials furnish indices which reflect the various changes in emphasis.

Edwin Greenlaw collaborated with William H. Elson (author of the Elson series of elementary-school readers) and Christine M. Keck to edit the first edition of these textbooks (1922–1924). Beginning in 1933, the whole series has been revised at least once; Book Three was revised twice, as Book III, Special Edition (1929) and again in the revision of 1933–1936. In 1931 (Book III) and 1932 (Book II), *Student Guides* were written to accompany the textbooks, somewhat in the manner of workbooks; these are available for all of the revised volumes. There are four recent revisions; in 1940–1943 (not included in this study), in 1947–1948, in 1951, and in 1957.

The contents of a textbook in literature are essentially stable, and literary selections tend to adhere to classical types. Yet the revisions of these textbooks in the *Literature and Life* and *America Reads* series display many features indicative of attention to movements in

TABLE 17   Changes in the Ward Sentence and Theme series, 1917 to 1929
(High School)

Evidence of Educational Movements Used as Criteria from

Editions	AIMS-AND-OBJECTIVES MOVEMENT	SCIENTIFIC MOVEMENT	UNIT ORGANIZATION	ACTIVITY MOVEMENT	INTE-GRATION	LARGE-UNIT TREND
Sentence and Theme 1917	*None*	*None*	*None*	*None*	*None*	*None*
Sentence and Theme 1923	*None*	*Slight* Some provision for differentiated courses, and a *Sentence Book* to accompany the text	*Slight* Loose unit plan discernible, from *words* to all types of *themes*	*Slight* *Sentence Book* with suggested auxiliary exercises	*None*	*Slight* Loose division into four large units, mostly only in name
Sentence and Theme 1929	*Slight* In simplification of material	*Slight* Same as 1923 edition, and better gradation of material	*Some* Improved grouping of material by "Topics" in daily lessons; and suggested "contract" units	*Some* Same as 1923 edition, and additional activities suggested in *Pilot Book* for teachers	*None*	*Slight* Same as 1923 edition

TABLE 18   Changes in the Literature and Life series, 1922 to 1948, and in America Reads series, 1952 to 1957 (High School)

Evidence of Educational Movements Used as Criteria from

Editions °	AIMS-AND-OBJECTIVES MOVEMENT	SCIENTIFIC MOVEMENT	UNIT ORGANIZATION	ACTIVITY MOVEMENT	INTEGRATION	LARGE-UNIT TREND
Literature and Life 1922–1924	*None*	*None*	*Slight* Loosely organized by units of literary interest	*None*	*None*	*None*
Literature and Life 1933–1936	*Some* In addition of definite appreciation and correlation aims	*Some* In *Student Guidebook* or *Workbook*, which included objective testing, graded vocabulary studies, and drills	*Some* Well-knit units, still of literary type	*Much* Extended activities of many types at end of chapters and some of the reading selections	*Some* Especially in Book Three; correlation of American Literature with American History	*None*
Literature and Life 1947–1948	*Much* Same as 1933–1936 edition, plus citizenship, preparation for life, reading for understanding, appreciation, and imaginative aims; interpretation through own experiences	*Much* Same as 1933–1936 edition; also use of national and systematic courses of study, systematic, provocative review questions and aids	*Much* Still based on literary type, but also tuned to adolescent interest, with larger and smaller units or contracts, built on good scope and sequence	*Much* In general, same as 1933–1936 edition, though more extensive provision for individual and group activities through *Students Guide*	*Much* Includes selections high in interest value related to the world of the past, of today, of science, industry, and human action; and Books III and IV based on periods of American and English History	*Some* Divided into four to six main parts or centers of interest, *e.g.,* Adventure, Spirit of Exploration, Heritage of the Past, and Challenge of the Present in Book I
America Reads 1951–1957	*Much* Same as 1947–1948, plus oral interpretation, creative expression, and developing modern communication skills	*Much* Same as 1947–1948, plus *Think-It Through Book* for interpretation skills and attack on new words; special testbooks for evaluation; and teachers' *Guidebook*	*Much* Teachers' *Guidebooks* use the unit as the basis of approach and lesson planning; some units are more of literary type, but tuned to adolescent interests with good scope and sequence	*Much* In general, same as 1947–1948 edition, though more carefully prepared activities for individual, small-group, and large-group work	*Much* Same as 1947–1948 in general	*More* Each divided into from about nine to sixteen units or centers of interest, with large-unit development emphasized, for example, in Book Two in such units as "Along My Way," "Out of This World," and "The American Scene"

° Special edition of Books II and III were published in 1929, primarily as a result of the "Integration" movement; Book III was revised to include some of the material formerly included in Book III, while Book III was thoroughly changed to include American Literature only, with a conscious attempt to correlate the material with American History in the same year.

educational thought. Like the *Elson Readers* for the elementary-school level, the succeeding revisions of *Literature and Life* give special evidence of (1) attention to scientific studies, (2) attention to activities, and (3) efforts at integration with the social studies. The later revisions of the series offer conclusive proof of the impact of all six of the movements in education upon its materials and organization.

CHANGES IN THE RUGG SERIES OF SOCIAL SCIENCE (STUDIES) TEXTBOOKS

The Rugg series, now out of print, gave an unusually good example of the changes in textbooks which came about gradually through the influence of different educational emphases. The whole series was dominated by one man, and went through enough revisions to reflect such changes as might be expected. In its most recent revision it furnished textbooks for both the elementary school and the junior high school.

"An engineer who got interested in social sciences when he began asking himself why the World War happened, in 1920 began writing and publishing his own 'pamphlets' (300 pages long on the average) that wrapped scattered fragments of history, economics, and geography into 'integrated' textbooks." [34] The First Experimental Edition was published in mimeographed form (1920–1922) for use in only 100 schools. The Second Experimental Edition was likewise published by the author, and was sold to other schools besides those using it in the official experiment from 1922 to 1923. The Second Edition of the Experimental Series (really a third edition, but actually the second published edition) was published from 1923 to 1926; it comprised three volumes of four pamphlets each, each volume covering a year of work in the junior high school.

More than 600,000 copies of the "Social Science Pamphlets" were used between 1923 and 1929, when Ginn and Company took over the publication on a commercial basis. This company employed the experimental use of the earlier editions as a basis for revisions. From

[34] "Professor H. O. Rugg on Carpet in Row Over 'Radical' Texts," *Newsweek*, XIV (December 4, 1939), pp. 47–48.

1929 to 1932, six new volumes of civics textbooks, or rather, social studies textbooks, appeared; two books constituted the course for each year's work in each of the three grades of the junior high school. Between 1936 and 1938, the "Rugg-Krueger Social Science Series" was published in eight volumes for use in the elementary school, two volumes for each grade from the third through the sixth. Finally, in

FIG. 22 *Teaching speech in high school*

Skills of effective speech are being developed as students record their voices and plan self-improvement. (*Courtesy Denver Public Schools.*)

1937 and 1938, the series for the junior high school was revised. When Ginn and Company took over the publication of the Rugg books, workbooks were prepared to accompany all editions for the purpose of providing activities in connection with the class work.

In contrast to most of the textbooks in the other series which have been examined, the Rugg books illustrate extremely well that textbook authors at times may be in advance of educational movements. Certainly Harold Rugg's series led the way in crystallizing sentiment

TABLE 19 Changes in the Rugg series of social science textbooks, 1920 to 1938

(Elementary and Junior High Schools)

Evidence of Educational Movements Used as Criteria from

Editions	AIMS-AND-OBJECTIVES MOVEMENT	SCIENTIFIC MOVEMENT	UNIT ORGANIZATION	ACTIVITY MOVEMENT	INTEGRATION	LARGE-UNIT TREND
First Experimental Edition 1920–1922 (Mimeographed)	*Some* Somewhat on pattern of the "seven cardinal principles"	*Much* Used experimentally in 100 schools, 1920–1922; in this respect these textbooks were leaders in this movement	*Much evidence* that Rugg's Series was the forerunner of the Unit Organization Movement from 1923, when the word "section" was used instead of "chapter"; from 1929 on, the revisions used the term "unit"	*Much evidence* that the series was also a forerunner of the Modern Activity Movement; activities of some kind were suggested in the Pamphlets from the start, and later volumes stressed this more than ever. The last two editions cared for these in a work-book to accompany each volume	*Much evidence* that the series has played an important role in the integration movement towards a core curriculum centered around the Social Studies. From the first edition emphasis was placed upon a course combining history with reading, civics, geography, and economics. Latest edition takes in more aspects of subject matter	*None*
Second Experimental Edition 1923–1926 (Pamphlets)	*Some* Same as first experimental edition, with citizenship and fundamental processes stressed	*Much* Objective tests added at ends of all chapters; still experimental				*None*
Rugg Social Science Series 1929–1932	*Much* In addition to aims of earlier editions, reading mastery and mastery of historical facts are emphasized	*Much* Over previous experiments there is gradation of vocabulary based on research; and analyses of social studies textbooks				*Slight* Perhaps unintentional
Rugg-Krueger Social Science Series 1936–1938	*Much* Added to previous aims is broadening of citizenship objective	*Much* Another addition is planned repetition of material, based on previous editions				*Slight* The large unit conception may have governed the rearrangement of material

232

for the practicable use of the scientific, unit, activity, and integration movements in the writing of textbooks for the school (Table 19).

The examination of these series of textbooks in English and the social studies illustrates one fact extremely well. The new movements in education creep into professional discussions and are reflected gradually in the materials and the organization of textbooks. Subsequent editions of these and other textbooks keep changing to meet the new emphases, retaining the valuable part of the preceding movements as a residue which perhaps justifies the emphasis accorded any particular movement for its relatively short period of acclaim. In some instances, the authors of textbooks are in advance of general acceptance by educators of the new aims, trends, and practices, as was Rugg.

GUIDING PRINCIPLES FOR THE USE OF TEXTBOOKS IN CURRICULUM WORK

The following list of suggestions concerning the selection and use of textbooks should prove helpful to both teachers and administrators in any program of curriculum improvement and organization: [35]

1. Those textbooks should be selected which are in line with the aims and philosophy of the school expecting to use them.

2. Each teacher should be allowed and encouraged to choose those books which conform to his methods of teaching and arrangement of materials.

3. If system- or state-wide adoptions of textbooks preclude unrestricted choice by the individual school and teacher, provision for supplementary textbooks should be made by the school for the use of pupils and teachers. On the elementary-school level, sets of fifteen or twenty supplementary texts can be provided at small expense, placed in a classroom for a reasonable period of time, and then used by other teachers who have children of similar age and grade levels in their class groups. This same procedure can be followed in the high school, or the

[35] Those who want suggestive standards for the selection of texts can consult E.B. Wesley and S.P. Wronski, *Teaching Social Studies in High Schools* (4th ed.), 1958, *op. cit.*, Chaps. v and xiii; C.E. Blanchard, "Tentative Criteria for the Selection of Textbooks," *The High School Journal*, xxxviii (May, 1953), pp. 293–96; and H.R. Douglass (Ed.), *The High School Curriculum* (2nd ed.), New York, The Ronald Press Company, 1956, pp. 161–64.

supplementary texts may be placed on reference in the library for use by various departments.

4. Each teacher should have available on his desk, or in his private library, at least four or five different textbooks for each of his classes, each book presenting a different curricular approach. By means of such aids he can prepare and test out new curricular departures much more effectively and quickly, as well as adapt the regular textbooks to his own way of teaching with a minimum of difficulty.

5. Every modern textbook can be helpful in curriculum revision. Each will have types of material or an approach which will fit in with some aspects of a program of curriculum improvement. There is no real cause for the complaint of teachers that their textbooks do not permit them to attempt curricular change; rather, this is the excuse for not undertaking it.

6. Textbooks should be used in the advance planning of curriculum work. Too many teachers rely upon the textbook to do the major part of their work, rather than employing it in the light of its true function—a guide to enrich the curriculum and to stimulate both teacher and pupil to further exploration. The textbook can be made the tool which it is intended to be only by means of preparation in advance by the teacher.

7. It is doubtful wisdom to load the school library with supplementary texts for library extension reading by children. Such a procedure runs counter to the stimulation of "free reading," one of the main purposes of a library.

8. Few teachers on any educational level can make successfully the abrupt transition from teaching with a textbook and without one. For one who desires to begin to teach without a set text, the following three steps are wise: (1) teaching with two texts or reference books; (2) teaching with four or five texts and reference works; and (3) teaching without a set text. In any case, careful preplanning and outline work are imperative, to prevent students from becoming lost or losing time.

9. Teachers and school officials should welcome the interest and questions of their public in the textbooks which they are using. The school is a cooperative enterprise, in need of constant questioning by its constituency in order that its task may be done better in the midst of school-community solidarity, not in spite of disagreement.

10. Primary criteria in the selection of a textbook should include (a) the philosophy set forth, (b) the range of materials, (c) variation for rates of individual pupil progress, (d) suitable vocabulary gradation for the age and grade level intended, (e) adequate drill and review matter, and (f) adequate attention to pupil growth, learning, readiness, interests, and progress.

PROBLEMS FOR INDIVIDUAL STUDY
AND CLASS DISCUSSION

1. What is the difference between a basal and a multiple adoption of textbooks? Illustrate.

2. In selecting a basal textbook or supplementary text for the third grade, what standards would you set up in order to secure one suitable in vocabulary and material for the age and grade level involved? What standards for an English textbook for the first year of high school? For a physics textbook for the eleventh grade?

3. In your class, have one student make an abstract of a textbook, and ask another student to study this abstract in comparison with the total text and its purposes. Is the abstract in or out of line with the general principles and point of view of the author?

4. What are five common faults of teachers in the use of textbooks? Illustrate each.

5. Are most school texts written by teachers of the elementary and the secondary schools? Should they be? Why, or why not?

6. If an attack were made by certain people in your community on the social studies series of texts in use in your school, what steps would you take to make a fair and impartial study of the books?

7. In your teaching assume that you have decided not to use a basic textbook with your class, but five or six texts as source references for your group. After selecting five or six for class use from the textbooks in that field, give your reasons for your choices.

8. Would it be wise for the authors and publishers of textbooks to attempt to revise them every time a new educational movement became popular, such as the core-curriculum movement, for example? Give reasons for your answer.

9. What obstacles stand in the way of abolishing the use of the textbook in school classes?

10. Why do textbook authors frequently disagree as to the content and grade placement of subject-matter materials? Is this trend healthy?

11. Assume that the present textbook in your social-studies or economics class was published in 1950. What areas of study and what social agencies have developed since that date upon which you would have to furnish your class more recent material for the satisfactory development of a unit on "Our Community"?

12. By whom should school textbooks be selected? By state textbook commissions? By school administrators? By teachers? By other groups? Give reasons for your stand.

13. Can the use of the textbook broaden the teacher? Support your position.

14. What is a workbook? Is the trend toward "workbooks" and "skill texts" to accompany textbooks of value? Support your point of view.

SELECTED BASIC REFERENCES FOR FURTHER STUDY OF THE TEXTBOOK

NOTE: The purpose of this highly selective list is to help the research student to investigate the textbook further. It does not duplicate the supporting references necessary for documentation in the body of this Chapter.

The American Council on Education, The Canada-United States Committee on Education, Publication No. 2, June, 1947, *A Study of National History Textbooks Used in the Schools of Canada and the United States.*

American History in Schools and Colleges, The Report of the Committee on American History in Schools and Colleges, New York, The Macmillan Company, 1944, *passim* (the answer to "Do Americans know their own history?").

The American Library Association (50 East Huron Street, Chicago, Ill.) has been prominent in fighting the censorship of books and printed materials. The student can secure much data from them on these aspects.

Anderson, Vernon E., *Principles and Procedures of Curriculum Improvement,* New York, The Ronald Press Company, 1956, pp. 129–38 and Chap. XIV.

Association for Supervision and Curriculum Development, N.E.A., 1953 Yearbook, *Forces Affecting American Education,* Chaps. II–IV.

Baker, E.W., *The Development of Elementary English Language Textbooks in the United States,* Nashville, George Peabody College for Teachers, Contributions to Education No. 45, 1929.

Beale, H.K., *A History of Freedom of Teaching in American Schools,* New York, Charles Scribner's Sons, 1941, *passim.*

———, *Are American Teachers Free?* New York, Charles Scribner's Sons, 1936, Chaps. XI–XII.

Carr, W.G., "Evolution of the Junior High School Textbook in English," *English Journal,* XVI (February, 1927), pp. 119–28.

Clement, J.A., *Manual for Analyzing and Selecting Textbooks,* Champaign (Ill.), the Garrard Press, 1942.

Cronbach, L.J. (Ed.), *Text Materials in Modern Education,* Urbana, University of Illinois Press, 1955, *passim.*

Ehlers, H. (Ed.), *Crucial Issues in Education: An Anthology*, New York, Henry Holt and Company, 1955, Parts ii and v.

Intergroup Relations in Teaching Materials, Report of the Committee on the Study of Teaching Materials in Intergroup Relations, Washington, American Council on Education, 1949, *passim*.

Lyman, R.L., "A Study of Twenty-Four Recent Seventh- and Eighth-Grade Language Texts," *Elementary School Journal*, xxiv (February, 1924), pp. 440–52.

National Association of Manufacturers (14 West 49th Street, New York), 1941. Abstracts of 563 social science textbooks were prepared by R.W. Robey for the Association. *The New York Times* (February 22, 1941) printed passages from the abstracts of those texts which Robey cited as derogatory of our type of government and critical of free enterprise.

National Education Association: The National Commission for the Defense of Democracy through Education (Washington 6) notes carefully and reports from time to time in its "Defense Bulletin" on attacks on textbooks by different groups of individuals.

Phi Delta Kappan, Vol. xxxiii, No. 5 (January, 1952), is devoted entirely to "Textbooks and Schools," and has a bibliography for the last two decades, pp. 241–302.

Pierce, B.L., *Civic Attitudes in American School Textbooks*, Chicago, The University of Chicago Press, 1930.

Quillen, I.J., *Textbook Improvement and International Understanding*, Washington, American Council on Education, 1948, *passim*.

Robinson, R.R., *Two Centuries of Change in the Content of School Readers*, Nashville, George Peabody College for Teachers, Contributions to Education No. 59, 1930.

Scott, C.W., and Hill, C.M., *Public Education Under Criticism*, New York, Prentice-Hall, 1954, Chaps. iv, vi, viii, and x.

Textbooks in Education: A Report from the American Textbook Publishers Institute, New York, 1949.

The Yearbook of Education, 1958, *The Secondary School Curriculum*, Yonkers-on-Hudson, World Book Company, 1958, pp. 286–96, 321–25, 357–60, and 467–76.

CHAPTER 9 The technical
vocabulary of the curriculum

To the uninitiated, the technical vocabulary used by writers in the field of education is difficult to understand at times. Even among the educators themselves, one frequently finds some confusion because of different interpretations of technical terms, such as "correlation" and "integration"; these two terms are used interchangeably by many workers in the field of education, as well as by many writers. On the other hand, there is just as much chance for confusion and perplexity to arise in the mind of the curriculum worker if certain terms are defined too narrowly or are allotted a technical meaning too limited. For example, it is confusing to find the word "curriculum" meaning both "the program of studies" and also the "curriculum" in the elementary school, but meaning only a particular combination of subjects with a particular purpose on the secondary-school level. In order to clear up some of this uncertainty and confusion about the use of educational terms and the technical vocabulary of the curriculum, some definitions and general concepts are presented in this chapter.

THE CURRICULUM. If the college student is asked what the *curriculum* is, he will usually give one of two replies: either he will state that he is taking the A.B. course, or he will want to know whether you mean by "curriculum" what course of study he is taking. When you ask the same question of the boy or girl in the secondary school, the answer will probably be one of these two: "I am taking the commercial course," or, "I am taking English, French, Physics, and American History." If the child on the elementary-school level is asked what curriculum he is taking, he is likely not to know what you are talking about, and you will be forced to explain yourself in terms of, "What subjects are you studying?" These illustrations from the three levels of education should make curriculum employees think carefully about what the term "curriculum" means to the student, as well as to the teacher.

If one wished to carry this experiment further, one might ask the teacher in the secondary school what the difference is between a "curriculum" and a "course of study." The teacher would probably answer that curriculum and course of study are terms which may be used interchangeably on the secondary-school level to denote one of the following:

1. A combination of subjects for groups of pupils which will lead to graduation from the secondary school and preparation for a particular purpose, such as college entrance or a vocation; examples of this use of the term are "the general curriculum," "the agriculture curriculum," and the academic curriculum."

2. The particular subjects which a child is taking during a particular year, without regard for a total program of studies for the four-year period; for instance, John's curriculum for this year is composed of Mathematics, Latin, English, and Civics.

3. The total program of studies which the secondary school offers in all fields; in this sense of the term, the "curriculum" would be the same as the "program of studies" of the secondary school.

4. The "course of study" in its narrow sense, such as the work offered in the English department.

The teacher who is asked to state what the curriculum is in the elementary school usually answers that it is composed of the activities and experiences of children, or that it is composed of subjects which children study under the direction of the school throughout the elementary school. From these illustrations, it is seen that there is a difference of opinion among teachers as to what the curriculum means.

A research group was engaged for more than five years in determining some evaluative standards to enable the secondary school to discover where it stands in its program and in what areas it should work to improve itself. This group has presented a definition of the curriculum which helps to clarify the conflicting ideas about it. In the section on the "Curriculum" of the *Evaluative Criteria*, the following definition was presented:

The *curriculum* may be defined as all the experiences which pupils have while under the direction of the school; thus defined it includes both classroom and extra-classroom activities. All such activities should therefore promote the needs and welfare of the individual and of society. *Courses of study* may be defined as that part of the curriculum which is organized for classroom use. They suggest content, procedures, aids and materials for the use and guidance of teachers, pupils, and administrators. Thus considered they contain only part of the individual pupil's curriculum. The curriculum and courses of study should be chiefly concerned with the orientation, guidance, instruction, and participation of youth in those significant areas of living for which education should supplement the work of other social institutions.

The results of the learning process should include (1) factual information or knowledge; (2) meaning and understanding; (3) abilities to do—knowledge and understanding combined with skill; (4) desirable attitudes—scientific, social, moral, and others; (5) worthy ideals, purposes, appreciations, and interests; and (6) resultant intelligent participation in general life activities.

Because change is universal, constant adaptation and development of the curriculum is necessary. This should be a cooperative enterprise engaging all staff members, carried on under competent leadership, and using all available resources. Carefully conducted and supervised experimentation for curriculum development is particularly valuable. Pupils should be prepared not only to understand the culture of the past; they should also be prepared for participation and leadership in present and future situations and activities.[1]

Although this statement is formulated for the secondary-school level, any teacher on any school level could take these guiding principles as a basic definition for the curriculum. It is the trend among thoughtful educators and laymen to consider the curriculum as being made up of all the experiences, both curricular and extracurricular, which children have under the administration of the school. Interpreted in the light of the definition just quoted, the program of studies of the school would also be the curriculum; the term "program of studies" could likewise be used at any time to indicate the particular program of activities which any child was carrying in order to pass the grade or to graduate, whether he was in the elementary or the secondary school. "Courses of study" would retain the meanings which they now have for most pupils and teachers; those meanings are particular *classroom subjects* in various subject-

---

[1] Cooperative Study of Secondary School Standards, *Evaluative Criteria*, 1940 edition, Washington, American Council on Education, p. 31. *Cf.* also *Evaluative Criteria*, 1950 edition, pp. 40 and 57.

matter areas, or the particular program of studies which one is taking to graduate from secondary school. Throughout this volume the term "curriculum" is used in the sense in which it has been defined here, and in general the words "course of study" and "curriculum" are not used interchangeably.[2]

THE CORE CURRICULUM. When this term first began to be employed in education, it was defined as "the common, integrating materials which have been accepted as fundamental in the education of American youth at all levels of the school system."[3] According to this definition, all children should be taught something about this nation's government, history, institutions, way of life, ideals, and democratic concepts; *e.g.*, those materials which the child should be taught as a core should certainly include the study of English expression, both oral and written, the social studies, and some mathematics. Instead of the term "core," some schools use other terms, such as "unified studies," "common learnings," "social living" courses, "integrating" courses, or "stem" courses.

About 1940 the core curriculum came to have another meaning. A.A. Douglass referred to it as "a projection of the basic, general training of the elementary school."[4] This definition is not necessarily at variance with the first one given above. On the levels of both the secondary school and the lower college, the development in recent years has been distinctly toward "general courses." These general

---

[2] For the benefit of those who wish to go more deeply into the earlier aspects of curricular definitions, the following discussions by competent authorities are listed: H.B. Alberty, *Reorganizing the High School Curriculum*, New York, The Macmillan Company, 1947, *passim*; "Designing Programs to Meet the Common Needs of Youth," 52nd Yearbook, National Society for the Study of Education, *Adapting the Secondary School Program to the Needs of Youth*, Part I, 1953, Chap. VII; H.L. Caswell and D.S. Campbell, *Curriculum Development*, New York, American Book Company, 1935, Chap. IV; E.M. Draper, *Principles and Techniques of Curriculum Making*, New York, D. Appleton-Century Company, 1936, Chap. I; J.M. Lee and D.M. Lee, *The Child and His Curriculum*, New York, D. Appleton-Century Company, 1940, Part II, esp. pp. 165–66; J.P. Leonard, *Developing the Secondary School Curriculum*, New York, Rinehart and Company, 1946, *passim.*; J.K. Norton and M.A. Norton, *Foundations of Curriculum Building*, Boston, Ginn and Company, 1936, Chap. XVII; and F.B. Stratemeyer, *et al.*, *Developing a Curriculum For Modern Living*, New York, Teachers College, Columbia University, 1947, pp. 78–120.

[3] See Draper, *op. cit.*, p. 20.

[4] *The Modern Secondary School*, Boston, Houghton Mifflin Company, 1938, p. 709.

courses are supposed to give the student basic information to prepare him for life, rather than for further educational training of a formal or professional nature. In this sense, one must conceive of the core curriculum as Draper defined it as being *the means* of attaining that "general education" to which Douglass refers.

More recently the core has come to have a meaning associated primarily with meeting the *needs* of pupils. Lucile Lurry and Elsie Alberty [5] define the core, in essence, as broad problem areas which the faculty outlines in order to meet the social and personal problems, needs, and interests of adolescents in American society. In somewhat like manner, Roland Faunce and Nelson Bossing use the core to meet needs common to all pupils. To do this, they designate the core as part of an "experience curriculum," composed of activities and experiences necessary for all pupils, in order that they may become competent for living effectively in American society. [6]

From another angle the term "core curriculum" has become confusing. This may be called the angle of usage. For example, certain teachers and administrators will explain to you that they are experimenting with a core curriculum built around the social studies in the elementary school or in the secondary school; they say that they use this "core" for the "center of interest," around which they group all other aspects of learning activities which the child should be undergoing at the same time. Let us suppose that full freedom were given to each teacher in his subject-matter area on the secondary-school level to formulate such a procedure as that just described. One might use Latin as the core around which the teacher brought in the other subject-matter aspects of English, history, and science; the Latin teacher would be likely to find certain basic materials and experiences in his subject which he thought all children should have, and he would use these as the core for the learning activities of pupils. In this particular example, the "core" would be confused with "fusion" of subject matter.

For the sake of clarity, the term "core curriculum" will be used

[5] *Developing a High School Core Program*, New York, The Macmillan Company, 1957, Chap. II.
[6] *Cf. Developing The Core Curriculum* (2nd ed.), Englewood Cliffs, Prentice-Hall, 1958, pp. 49 and 54. These authors also give and discuss in Chap. III many definitions of the core.

here in the sense in which Draper and Faunce and Bossing define it, that is, as those basic materials and experiences which have been accepted as fundamental for the education of all children at all levels of education. It is close kin to "general" education on the secondary-school level, and is one means for achieving general education.

INTEGRATION. The term "integration" came into general use as psychological studies were made available which showed clearly that the child did not develop in parts, but as a whole. Studies of "the whole child" and his development thus gave rise to the use of the term "integration," to indicate the formulation, development, and union of the child's activities into one "whole" growth and personality. (Child growth and theories of learning were discussed in Chapter 3.) Of all the more recent terms in the technical vocabulary of education, "integration" has been the most abused and the most misused. It has been confused with, or used interchangeably with, "correlation," "interrelation," and "fusion." Integration has been employed in two senses, one referring to *the growth of the whole child* and the other referring to the *uniting of subject matter*. At the present time there is no clear understanding among many teachers as to whether integration and fusion are one and the same thing; among other teachers, integration and correlation are used interchangeably with the same meaning.

In considering the curriculum, "integration" should be used primarily as it applies to the individual, and not as it applies to the uniting or fusing of subject matter. In accordance with this concept, Douglass' definition will be accepted; he states that integration consists of

. . . the processes which occur within the mind of the individual when he establishes a close relationship among facts, principles, and patterns of behavior . . . a unit of instruction may bring together or "correlate" such facts and processes, but . . . unified mental life, or integration, is dependent in the last analysis upon the reactions of the individual.[7]

CORRELATION AND INTERRELATION. Since "correlation" and "interrelation" mean practically the same thing, these terms can be used interchangeably and will be so employed. Both mean the establish-

[7] *The Modern Secondary School,* Boston, Houghton Mifflin Company, 1938, p. 693.

ment of the mutual relationships which exist between two things. For example, one may correlate the lesson today with the lesson of yesterday or of a week or month ago, or one may correlate Latin with English. The teacher may do the correlating himself in his own classes, or he may invite the teacher of another subject or a specialist in another field to come in because he feels that the visitor can do a better job of correlating the two fields or areas of study. Correlation is not a new term; the Herbartians, at the end of the nineteenth century, put emphasis upon the correlation of other subjects with the study of history, which was used as the "core" subject.

Fusion. In recent years a tendency has developed among educators to confuse *fusion* with integration. There is some reason for this confusion, since fusion actually would be a cementing together of materials, facts, and principles which were necessary in the understanding of an issue or the solving of a problem.[8] To put it another way, fusion would be to the uniting of subject matter what integration would be to the uniting and growth of the whole child. Simply stated, fusion is a disregard of subject-matter lines; it involves the teaching of two or more closely related subject-matter areas together in one class in which composite activities of all sorts are used without differentiation or special regard for the old subject-matter lines.

Fusion is also related to the core curriculum in some respects, especially when the core is used as a center of interest around which all activities of the children are focused. In the thinking of many people, fusion actually takes place in the work of pupils around "centers of interest" in the elementary school. The teaching together of English and social studies in one class on the secondary-school level, with activities centered around the English-social studies area, would be called "fusion." In most places where fusion occurs on the secondary-school level, the classes in two different fields are combined into one class of double length. The work grows out of the activities of the student centered around both areas, without regard to subject-matter lines.

If carried to its logical conclusion, the principle of fusing classes in the secondary school would eventually amount to the student's fusing the areas of his interest. The student would then bring to bear

[8] *Ibid.*

upon that big center of interest all subject-matter areas which he needed for the solution of problems. This extreme type of fusion would in effect become the pupil's "experience curriculum."

AIMS, PURPOSES, AND OBJECTIVES. These terms are used interchangeably in this volume. They include both the basic principles of educational philosophy and the specific purposes which individual teachers and administrators have in view. They should not be confused with the *outcomes* or *results* of the educational process. The aims, purposes, and objectives set up *what we plan to do;* the outcomes or results indicate *what we actually did.*

OTHER TERMS. "Experiences" and "activities" are used interchangeably. "Subject matter" is used in terms of subject-matter areas, and "subjects" usually refer to those curricular experiences in organized form in the classroom which traditionally have been thought of as being such fields as history, social studies, geography, and mathematics.

The terms "constants" or "requireds" are used to indicate those materials or subjects of study on the secondary-school level which a pupil must finish satisfactorily in order to graduate.

SUMMARY. The term "curriculum" here includes all activities of children which take place under the direction of the school, whether those activities are curricular or extracurricular, inside the classroom or outside it. "Courses of study" refer primarily to that part of the curriculum which is organized for classroom use. The "core curriculum" means the common materials and experiences which have come to be accepted as basic in the education of children on all educational levels. "Integration" refers primarily to the growth and development of the child; "fusion" means a disregard of subject-matter lines, and a fusing together of knowledge and principles necessary to the understanding of an issue or the solving of a problem. "Correlation" and "interrelation" refer to the mutual relationships existing between two different things. "Aims," "purposes," and "objectives" are interchangeable terms referring to those goals which teachers and educators establish for children as well as for themselves. "Outcomes" and "results" refer to the progress which teachers and students have made in accomplishing or achieving the objectives formulated at the beginning of their work.

PART THREE **The elementary-school curriculum**

CHAPTER 10 Curriculum building in the elementary school

If the educational employee is seeking the greatest amount of light upon curriculum revision, the best place to go is to a good elementary school. There is general agreement among the curriculum experts that the elementary school has made the greatest strides in rebuilding the curriculum to meet the needs of the pupils. Of course, there are many traditional elementary schools, and there is much teaching of the traditional type in them all over the country. Yet at least one teacher can be found in every fairly large elementary school who has made considerable progress in improving the curriculum offerings in his grade.

THE ELEMENTARY-SCHOOL SITUATION

THE FUNCTIONS OF THE ELEMENTARY SCHOOL. The elementary school has been considered traditionally as the school of the "three R's," where the child is supposed to receive the fundamentals of education, and where he is expected to master the tools for further education. People formerly thought that all of the *basic, formal* education was included in its grades, namely, that education which *all* children were supposed to need and to get for carrying on in life. This was the main reason for calling the elementary school the "common school" until fifty years ago.

This conception of the elementary school as the school of the fundamental processes has not altered radically, even with the coming of rapid changes in social, economic, and political life. The elementary-school level embraces in effect those materials, skills, and knowledges which the public as a whole considers it essential for every child to acquire. The public believes also that the child should develop desirable attitudes, ideals, and social contacts with other children during his experience in the elementary school. It is in regard to the development of desirable attitudes, ideals, social contacts, group living, and individual growth that the elementary school has broadened most in its curriculum within the last few years. In these areas, and from the ideas which involve these areas, great changes have taken place in the type of teaching and of curriculum materials in the elementary school.

Instead of changes in the functions of the elementary school, one finds changes in methods which are rapidly making it become a "child-centered" school. Instead of only drill and rote learning in fundamental subjects, it is discovered that the elementary school is effectively accomplishing the same purposes through a new approach to teaching, namely, the approach through the child and the group. There are no signs of the development in American life of another agency in formal education which is attempting to give the same training as that given by the elementary school. This is a clear indication that the elementary school is rapidly adapting itself, as it has in the past, to meet the changes which occur in national life insofar as they affect young children. Other evidence of this adaptation is seen in the fact that most children of elementary-school age are enrolled and are in attendance in schools, whether the school laws concerning compulsory attendance in certain states are strictly enforced or not.

PUPIL-TEACHER RELATIONSHIP. In the primary and grammar grades there is another factor which operates to offer a most favorable opportunity for experimentation and revision in the curriculum. The teacher in those grades is usually with the children in her room for almost the whole day. Most writers call this the "self-contained classroom" situation, as contrasted with the departmentalized situation which the children face in the high school. Of course, in many school systems certain specialists assist the regular grade teacher in such activities as physical education, music, art, and handwork, but the major portion of the day is spent by each child under the direction and guidance of one teacher. Under these conditions, unparalleled opportunities are presented to the teacher to know each child exeremely well and to study him throughout each school day. The teacher is not hindered by having the child for such a limited time that he cannot become acquainted with him, and at the same time, the pupil is not disturbed by having to make adjustments to four or five or six different teaching personalities during each school day.

A teaching situation in which one teacher has almost complete charge of the pupil for the whole day offers excellent opportunities for curriculum experimentation and development along the lines of the interests of both pupil and teacher. Outside of administrative control and restrictions in some instances and at some times, the teacher has complete direction of the child's learning program and can have a rather free hand in attempts at improving the program. No strict departmental areas are established in the elementary school, which occupy certain portions of the student's time to a greater or less degree because some other teacher demands it; few inter-scholastic contests or extracurricular activities of an interschool nature operate to divorce the child from his interest, the interests of the group, and the interests of the school; except for a few major group activities, such as an operetta in which most of the children or representatives of children from all grades take part, all activities stem from the smaller group and are headed up within it. The teacher can combine subject-matter areas as he sees fit. The child has a limit-less opportunity for real living in a child community, for the develop-ment of social responsibility and attitudes within that small group, for living life actually as it should be lived among his contempo-raries, and for learning how to adjust himself to outside influences, adults, activities, and situations.

THE INTERESTS AND ATTITUDES OF CHILDREN IN THE ELEMENTARY SCHOOL

As a child becomes older, he learns that certain actions are pro-hibited; he becomes *conditioned* against certain behavior, because he has been told or has been taught that it is wrong. As a result of this conditioning process, the child becomes much more reserved about telling his real interests than he is when he enters the elementary school. Generally speaking, the child through grades one to six is prone to be enthusiastic, more uncontrolled in the expression of his real thoughts and interests, eager to learn for the sake of the mastery of something new, more trustful of his teacher and other adults, and less prone to withdraw into a shell of indifference and solitude.

THE FIRST-GRADER.   After the normal child has been prepared carefully for the first grade and has been introduced properly to it, it is seldom that he misses a day of school without regret. He is learning something new each day; his interests are still more those of the individual child in his play and attitude, and less those of one who has become accustomed to playing in a group. During his first year of school his biggest problem is usually to make satisfactory adjustments to the group; as a matter of fact, upon this proper adjustment alone may rest his success or failure in the first grade. His interest span is short at this age, and his mind and energies do not like to remain focused for a great length of time upon any one activity or task. It is better for him if he has a wise teacher who recognizes this, and who varies the work throughout the day so that he never becomes weary of one thing before he is introduced to the next. Persons who have observed a first grade in action, but who have never taught there, marvel at the success with which a good teacher helps these children to make adjustments at this crucial stage in their lives and school careers. Until after he becomes fairly well adjusted to the group and the activities of the group, the child in the first grade frequently is not required to return to school in the afternoons, or to remain in school for as long hours as pupils in the other grades.

THE SECOND-GRADER.   When the child reaches the second grade, he soon begins to show those attributes which one might call characteristic of the "gang-buster" type. During this year the child may be "a little angel" in the classroom; yet he may be the leader of a little gang on the playground which does everything from throwing rocks at another gang to imitating the *Lone Ranger* or bringing air rifles to school and playing Dick Tracy, "cowboys and Indians," or "cops and robbers." In this grade, certain drills on fundamental processes must be made to appear to the child as a necessary responsibility if he is to make the transition successfully to the rest of the work of the elementary school. He must be taught the fundamental idea that he must respect the rights of the group.

The second-grader is at the stage where he will come home and tell his father and mother freely all that happened at school and on the playground; he will give all of this information without restraint, provided he has not been disciplined by his parents for talking freely to them about the teacher, the happenings in the schoolroom, or the occurrences on the playground. He is usually unaffected in his behavior, and he is intensely interested in every new development. Sometimes, even at this early age, the normal child will express the wish for a club house or a "club" for himself and his comrades. He does not want to remain at home alone without playmates, and he should not be without playmates for a large portion of his time. He starts to read the comics and various types of literature for himself; he begins to be more selective about his TV and radio programs, and learns avidly from them; he will absorb a tremendous amount of information at home if his interests as they evidence themselves are cared for by his parents, or if these interests are met by his parents because the teacher noticed them and suggested that they be cared for. Children of this age will even go through many sections of the *World Almanac* and *The National Geographic*, or other magazines. In this way they learn new things voluntarily, they become interested in new matters, they master new words for their vocabulary, and they become accustomed to using more effectively a varied vocabulary of both good and bad words.

THE THIRD-GRADER. Upon advancing to the third grade, the child is in the year in which he starts to grow out of the primary stage. He now begins to become somewhat secretive about events that happen in school and on the playground. In the first and second grades he frequently cried when he had a fight or was imposed upon, or when he continued what some of his comrades considered his "babyish" ways. In contrast to this, in the third grade, he begins to acquire that attitude which is characteristic of him throughout the rest of his life, namely, the attitude that he is not a "cry baby." During this year he comes to be influenced tremendously by the customs and habits of his playmates. If his friends with whom he plays go to the movies two or three times during the week or month, he feels that he should be permitted to do the same; if they are allowed to stay up until nine o'clock at night while he is compelled to go to bed at eight, he feels that he is not being treated fairly; if they wear long pants to school and his mother sends him in a snow-suit or short trousers, he is highly insulted—as a matter of fact he will refuse very soon to wear at all either of these articles of clothing; if his comrades attend Sunday school regularly, he is more likely to wish to attend.

At the same time, he is becoming less apt to believe every wild story which his comrades or adults tell him; he is not so gullible as he had been up to this time. This does not mean that he has lost faith in his comrades or in adults—it simply is a sign that he is coming to the age where he can begin to distinguish between those happenings which are possible and probable and those happenings which he thinks from his experience and reading and knowledge are not to be believed. If he has not had a bicycle, he will be very desirous at this age to own one. After he gets out of school, his afternoons are full; he has a "lot of business" to look after, ranging in type from collecting rusty nails and rigging up a water spout in the back yard to planting a flower or vegetable garden in the spring or playing sandlot football in the fall. If given the opportunity and encouraged to do so, he reads avidly, *provided* he has mastered the fundamental techniques of reading. Neither is he choice in his reading materials; he will read almost anything that is strange, or new, or of interest to him. The child has so much to do at this age that he begins to show signs of that complex which is the bane of every mother's existence, namely, the desire to avoid a bath or washing his hands. Actually he is too busy to "wash up" during the daytime, because he has so many other things that he wants to do; when night comes, he is so tired that he really does not feel equal to the washing-up process, although he would never admit it to his mother or to any one else—on the contrary, he would go to sleep sitting up before he would confess that he was worn out.

THE FOURTH-GRADER. When the child reaches the fourth grade, several factors show unmistakably that he is rapidly becoming far removed from the world of the primary child of which he was so recently a part. Although the boy had played with both boys and girls during the first three years of his school life without much differentiation or protest, he now begins to develop the idea that a girl is a "sissy" and boys are "men." Another evidence of his growth is observed in his determination to play with boys of his own age and group, whereas in the past he might have been content to play with younger children when older ones were not around. Another change in the fourth-grader is seen in his attitude toward his younger brothers and sisters; instead of taking good care of them when they are left in his care, he becomes impatient if he is required to look after them, or if they "tag along" after him in his activities. His craftsmanship in those projects which he undertakes to build or to make begins to show some differentiation between a good job and a poor one.

In other ways, too, the child in the fourth grade is very different from what he was a year ago. For example, he will work for hours on airplane models, a task which would drive many adults to distraction because of its intricacy and its tax on one's patience and powers of concentration. He will spend endless time on constructing a kite, attempting to fly it, and then reconstructing it after he found out why it would not fly. His interest in the radio, which probably began when he was in the second grade, has increased remarkably. He listens to radio programs a great deal now, as well as TV, and he has certain programs of which he is very fond; he is beginning to branch out from Dick Tracy and the Lone Ranger to take in such characters as Jack Benny and Ed Sullivan and a good orchestra or two—"good" to his way of thinking, at any rate. He would rather ride to school on his "bike" in the rain than be taken in the car, because he would thus be free to come and go about his business to and from the school and at the school without interference from his parents. He stops at the newsstand, and he reads all types of literature which interest him as well as the more recent so-called "action thrillers." He cannot be kept away from any football games in his community to which he can gain access, or from baseball games and other contests of all sorts and descriptions. Athletes frequently become his heroes at this stage of his life, and they may remain so even through the adolescent period. All in all, he is beginning to develop into a "real boy," with a differentiation of types of interests. Although he is still careless about cleanliness, he is not oblivous to what boys of his age group usually wear and like.

THE CHILD IN THE FIFTH AND SIXTH GRADES. During the fifth and sixth grades, certain interests and characteristics of the child which were noticeable for the first time in the fourth grade become emphasized and enlarged. If the boy has not had a room of his own at home prior to this time, now will come the demand that he have one where he can keep all of his "things" and can arrange them as he wants them. He begins to desire a radio or television set of his own, pictures of his own; at times, he even makes his room a workshop. If he has been guided properly by his parents and his teachers, this room of his will be a liberal education to any one who enters it and goes through it carefully to discover what his interests are. He is still likely to fill his pockets with odds and ends from trash cans and with a strange assortment of items collected from hither and yon, such as old radio or TV tubes, transistor sets, files, screwdrivers, knives, rocks, even dirt of different kinds. Instead of leaving his pockets for his mother to clear out every time that his clothes are to be cleaned, he frequently transfers the contents of his pockets to various places in his room where he keeps his materials in apparently nondescript order. He may continue to spend hours with a chemistry set or with a construction kit, with the building of airplane models, or with the collection of stamps, postmarks, match cases, jokers from decks of playing cards, and bottle caps. The urge which he got during the first or second grade to earn some money of his own has never left him. In all probability he will manage to become a paper boy for an hour or two in the late afternoon; when he reaches grade seven he may even acquire a short paper route for himself under the direction of another person. He has a great yen for making his own money and spending it for those things which he desires. He is as likely to save his money over a period in order to invest in some highly coveted possession as he is to spend it for shows, toys, sweets, and other treats. His ideas about playing with girls and taking care of younger children are even stronger than they were during the period when he was in the fourth grade. Strange as it seems, he may even wish to stay at home when his parents go on some extended trip, if he has some particular interest or business of his own which he is working on at that time.

A special transformation which takes place in the child when he is in the fifth and sixth grades is that which concerns the customs and manners of the group with which he plays, namely, the group of his "peers." For the first time he learns the following lessons well: that a tattle-tale is a contemptible person not to be tolerated by the rest of the group; that certain things that happen with the crowd are not talked about at home; that it is not right for a larger or older and stronger boy to impose upon children in the primary grades; that it is proper for each boy to learn to play the various sports and games in season, regardless of whether he wishes to learn how to play them or not; that it is the mark of a coward when one does not take a "dare"; that little sisters and little brothers are a necessary evil one has to put up with, but a responsibility which one can "get around" if he uses his head; that parents will not be worried by happenings of which they do not know; and that some teachers make school a necessary evil and others make it a joy, though they (the pupils) always pretend that it is a necessary evil.

THE CHILD IN THE SEVENTH AND EIGHTH GRADES. Approximately half of the boys and girls are beginning adolescent changes when they reach the seventh and eighth grades. This situation causes the development in *all* children of certain attitudes and ideals which accompany pubertal growth. The most important attitude developed is concerned with the maturing of the gang idea; it involves absolute adherence to the code of the play group. Those children in these grades who are not undergoing physiological and emotional changes are afraid not to subscribe to the code, while those who are going through these changes naturally expect everyone to adhere to their code. As a result, all children subscribe to the gang code. This code conditions and controls the conduct of adolescents upon the secondary-school level more than any other single factor or agency. The type of voluntary activity in which the child engages shifts suddenly from the *individual activity* in which he was engaged primarily in the previous years of his elementary school work; *group activity* now exerts primary control over him. Examples of these types of group activity are the work of the Boy and Girl Scouts or Campfire Girls, and parties with mixed groups. Other changes in interests begin to be noted in the types of movies which children like to attend, and in the kinds of radio and TV programs and public entertainments which they prefer.

If the teacher has had children of his own and has watched them grow up, he has an unparalleled opportunity to take full advantage of their interests and their stages of growth and development in his teaching. Since many teachers have not had this experience, it is of paramount importance that they study the interests and attitudes of the child as they prepare to teach on the elemenary-school level.

SIGNIFICANT CONDITIONING FACTORS
IN CURRICULUM REVISION

THE INTEREST SPAN OF THE ELEMENTARY-SCHOOL CHILD.   Often the teacher does not realize that the "concentration time" of the child in the elementary school differs with each grade. When a child enters school at the beginning of the first grade, it is doubtful whether he can concentrate effectively on any one activity for more than ten minutes at one time. When he has reached the fourth grade, he may be able to concentrate for fifteen minutes with full effect, but with less and less effect thereafter; by the time he has reached the seventh grade, this concentration span may have been raised to twenty minutes. In each of these instances, "concentration time" means that duration of time in which the child is able to work effectively at top speed and to acquire maximum results from his work; after that time has elapsed, the results obtained are usually in a rapidly decreasing ratio to the amount of time spent. Therefore it is of prime importance that each teacher realize that school work should be so arranged that the child has a varied program, in which this primary principle is used.

Careful planning and careful timing by the teacher will send the child naturally from one activity to another, with ample opportunity in the transition for the child to adjust himself to a new situation and therefore be fresh to concentrate again. Here the teacher in the elementary school has an advantage over the teacher in the secondary school in regard to teaching techniques; he controls the total teaching situation for the elementary pupils, and in arranging his work is able to make the most effective use of the interest span of the children. Society's idea of the "economy of time" in education has encouraged the violation of the principle of the interest span of children. Society believes that so much has to be learned by the child in the formal agency called the school, within a limited time and at a reasonable expenditure of funds, that it demands that students be taught in groups; society also demands that those experiences and types of knowledge should be emphasized which will give to the pupils those fundamentals which people should know, experience, and acquire. This effort at the economy of time and money in education has had too great an influence upon most teachers, especially in regard to the amount of sustained effort which teachers have required of their students in the schoolroom without regard for any variety or change of tempo in that work.

SOCIAL MATURITY. There has been much discussion of social maturity in recent years, and some attempts have been made to group children according to its standards. *Social maturity* means the ability of the child to get along with other children in his group and with other people in his group. In some school systems this type of grouping has prevailed to such an extent that the school authorities insist that pupils be promoted from one grade to another each year, regardless of whether they have mastered those skills and acquired that knowledge which would prepare them for effective work upon the next grade level. The argument for this arbitrary type of grouping has been that the child gets more from his association and contacts with his own social group of about his same age and maturity than he would get from remaining behind for a year to acquire those fundamental skills and knowledges which he has not yet mastered.

There are good arguments for grouping children according to their social maturity. Studies of human behavior, of child development, and of the environment in which children live offer evidence in favor of it. On the other hand, many teachers in the elementary school have accomplished the same purpose by rearranging their work to meet the individual needs of their pupils; by this rearrangement, those children who were not as socially mature as others have been able to make progress, and to make their adjustments throughout the school years in the various grades. These teachers have graded pupils in their work on the basis of *how far* they have come from *where they were when they started* in that grade, rather than on the basis of the *average* or the *brightest* or the *dullest* in that grade. Elementary-school teachers are on the way toward making a real contribution to this phase of school work; their centering of work around children and the activities and interests of children has resulted to a great extent in a different grading system, based upon the individual progress of students rather than upon averages or comparative marks. Of course, it takes hard work and careful planning on the part of the teacher to be able to give oral or written pretests to children to find out where they are in comparison with the point from which they started in a particular grade in the elementary school. But the good teacher is able to work out this problem satisfactorily, so that he can help all of his children to make their adjustments during their work in that grade.

ENTHUSIASM OF THE ELEMENTARY-SCHOOL PUPIL. As a rule, the child in the elementary school in grades one to four delights to come to school and cannot get enough of it. However, the higher he goes in school, the less enthusiastic he is about it; from the fifth grade on, he appears progressively to develop the idea that school is not such a delightful place to go. The teacher is indeed to be pitied who does not realize that the elementary-school child or the secondary-school child will remain enthusiastic about going to school if he has something really to work for and to master. The child of six, seven, or eight years of age can memorize quickly and retain in his memory many things which the adult cannot retain; the teacher who does not encourage and train that ability in the child is derelict in his duty. Some children graduate from the elementary school to the secondary school with this rapid retentive ability still intact, but they are few and far between. It would be impossible to say at the present time whether this apparent loss of the rapid ability to memorize is caused by the kind of training which is given to children, or whether it is caused by the physiological and emotional changes which take place in him. At any rate, it is a fact that the higher a child goes in the school, the less enthusiasm and natural motivation he has for his school work. How can this enthusiasm which the child possesses when he starts his school career be retained throughout the school levels?

In connection with the child's progressive decline in enthusiasm for school work, certain comments of Joseph S. Butterweck in regard to the secondary-school curriculum are still significant.[1] Butterweck maintained that the four weaknesses of the secondary-school curriculum are: (1) that it is authoritative, in that it is a body of knowledge which it is thought that the adult must have in order to be considered educated; (2) that the approach to the curriculum is analytic, dealing with knowledge apart from its functional setting, whereas dealing in wholes is natural and stimulative, but dealing in parts without some conception of the whole is uninteresting and unnatural; (3) that we have an unwillingness to let pupils make mistakes, whereas in the making of mistakes real education takes place for the child, just as it takes place in real life; and (4) that the program of the secondary schools kills initiative and does not give to the learner the sense and purpose of the whole process, whereas this program results in the curriculum's having to be strengthened by prizes and awards for proper performance, instead of working toward those natural awards that come from the *satisfaction* which a child gets from individual achievement and mastery.

These weaknesses, which Butterweck considered outstanding in the curriculum of the secondary school, are valuable here for comparison with the curriculum as found in the elementary school, where some of these weaknesses have been overcome or are not in operation. Certainly the making of mistakes is education itself for every person, whether he is in school or out, whether he is a child or an adult. Just as true is Butterweck's statement that the satisfaction which comes from real achievement and mastery is worth much more to any individual than the mere mastery of material for some extraneous reward. For example, it is a poor policy of motivation for a parent to promise to give his child a quarter or a dollar if his grades are "B" or better on his report card for the next month. The monetary reward is distinctly artificial, because it is not based upon the real satisfaction which would come from the mastery of the material being studied.

ADMINISTRATIVE LIMITATIONS. Another factor which operates to some extent in dampening the enthusiasm and ardor of the school

---

[1] "Curriculum Revision in the Secondary Field," *California Journal of Secondary Education*, XII (May, 1937), pp. 279–83.

child is the arbitrary administrative device whereby a grade level is set up for each step in achievement in the schools. Some administrative machinery in schools is necessary. But arbitrary standards for grade achievement which are based upon the *average* performance of *all* students are not always satisfactory in stimulating pupils to retain their interest in school work; neither do such standards encourage teachers to care for individual differences as they should on the various grade levels. R.H. Lane, an authority in the field of elementary education two decades ago, believed that the standardized organization of the elementary school does tend to hinder desirable child growth. He even went so far as to suggest establishing a "lower school" in place of the present organization of nursery school, kindergarten, and first, second, and third grades; transfer between these groups would be easy as a child needs it, and the organization and grade standards would be supplanted by the best environment in each room for each group which is being taught.[2] There has been a steady growth since 1938 in replacing several grades by divisions such as Lane suggested.[3]

When young children are carefully studied, many of their activities which are meaningless to adults are found to be very interesting and educative for them.[4] These children are engaged in a normal process, that of exploring their own environment and broadening their experience naturally. Similarly, educative procedures in school should be those that will stimulate the interest and enthusiasm of the child, and not those that make it difficult for him to broaden his experience naturally as he advances progressively through school. The teacher must recognize that those elements which go to make up a child's interests are determined and guided primarily by his environment. When this environmental factor is recognized and accepted, the teacher begins to see the school as a miniature social institution for the child; in school he can develop those broader relationships which

[2] "Blueprint for the Lower School," *Progressive Education,* xv (October (1938), pp. 489–92. *Cf.* also H.A. Lane, "Moratorium on Group Grading," *Educational Leadership,* iv (March, 1947), pp. 385–95.

[3] Read *A Look at Continuity in The School Program,* 1958 Yearbook, Association for Supervision and Curriculum Development, N.E.A., Chap. xiii.

[4] *Organizing the Elementary School for Living and Learning,* 1947 Yearbook, Association for Supervision and Curriculum Development, N.E.A., Chaps. i–ii, esp. insert opposite p. 68.

are characteristic of the larger social groups in which he will move later. The approach here is through the child's natural interest and experience with his environment. It is the psychological and normal approach, and it should be used to its fullest and richest extent; if necessary, it should be used without regard for certain formal regulations in effect in some systems and states, which require that so many minutes or hours be spent per week or day upon reading, spelling, arithmetic, geography, and other subjects.

CREATIVE URGES IN THE ELEMENTARY-SCHOOL CHILD. No matter what their I.Q., normal children have creative urges and express them much more freely and openly during their earlier years than later after teachers have had an opportunity to "spoil" them. The picture of a boat which the kindergarten child draws may not look like a boat to an adult, but it looks like a boat to him; if the child is encouraged to continue to draw and if he is given assistance through models which he may look at and study, the teacher will be surprised at the talent or ability which he may develop.

Another child in the first grade may be interested in the heavenly bodies, the stars, and the skies; he may listen to his mother or to his teacher read to him about them, he may go to a planetarium to see them, and he may draw pictures showing his conception of these natural marvels. In drawing illustrations of these phenomena, he at first conceives of the world as flat; this conception is apt to persist and to cause a development which will not be accurate and representative of the real situation, unless the child is shown a globe or has a globe of his own upon which he can see these heavenly bodies. From this globe he can ascertain where these bodies are located and how they influence the other heavenly bodies on the earth. His pictures of the stars or planets or comets may not seem at first to the teacher to be good representations, but to him they are; and with continued practice, his drawings may become extraordinarily good as he continues his growth and development.

Still another child may take his Tinker Toy set and make an airplane according to the diagram which illustrates it in the set of instructions. When he has completed the building of this airplane, he gets the idea of adding to it something which will indicate the place where a bomb is carried—for he wants the airplane to be a bomber.

He adds an apparatus or appendage which to him is a bomb carrier, or a conveyance for carrying the bomb in the air before it is dropped, although to the teacher it may not look like the bomb-carrying part of a plane. If he is given the opportunity and the proper models, he may continue to construct planes and to improve his work to such a

FIG. 23   *The baby goat visits the first grade farm*

In their study of farm life the children cooperatively built the barn seen in the background. Just inside the barn door you can see an incubator that the children used to hatch out over two dozen chickens. Several of the wooden animals constructed are seen in the foreground. (*Courtesy The University School, Ohio State University.*)

point that his product really looks like a bomber to the teacher also.

The same creative instinct operates in the child in the field of music. The child likes to sing. And he can be started early to learn an instrument with teaching by means of numbers before he can even read. With this early start, he is likely to develop not only a love for music but a proficiency in playing an instrument or in recognizing notes and octaves. Music becomes a means of expression to him, and he may even compose music at a tender age when the adult thinks that it is almost impossible for him to do so. This is but another illustration of how creative urges in young children should be encouraged, and should be developed all the way through the formal agency called the school.

In thinking about the creative urges of children, one should take into account the hurry and bustle with which some parents attempt to put their children through the schools. For example, each year many children are prohibited from entering the public schools until they reach a specified legal age. The parents of many of these children make a serious mistake in their ambition for their offspring. They insist that their children be taught privately during that year in order that they may enter the second grade, or may enter the first grade instead of the kindergarten. The chances are that the child is not any more mature socially as a result of this extra training; in fact, he may be less able to adapt himself to the social group in grade two than he would be if he were with the group in grade one with which he normally would have gone to school. Why are people in such a hurry to shove children through the school grades, anyway? Even if they graduate at sixteen and go out into life looking for work, the child labor laws in most states will not allow their regular employment. The development of creative urges in youth is not possible when the child is rushed, or when these urges are subordinated to the push and bustle of a forced march through the educational process.[5]

THE AREAS OF CONSCIOUS INTEREST OF THE MODERN ELEMENTARY-SCHOOL CHILD. The modern child is definitely *time-conscious*. He frequently inquires, "How long?" or "When?" If he listens to the radio or looks at TV and learns that he receives the sunrise service on Easter morning from a California town at ten o'clock by his clock, he immediately has the question on the tip of his tongue, "Why is that true?" In this day of radio, TV, airplanes, streamliners, and ship-to-

---

[5] For fuller treatment of creative urges in children, read *Fostering Mental Health in Our Schools* (1950 Yearbook) Chaps. I, VI–IX and *Creating a Good Environment for Learning* (1954 Yearbook), Chaps. I–III and VII, both published by the Association for Supervision and Curriculum Development, N.E.A.; and "Bases for Effective Learning," by Winifred E. Bain, pp. 12–17 in 31st Yearbook, Department of Elementary School Principals, N.E.A., 1952.

shore telephones, the teacher does not need to build up interest in this time-consciousness of the child. But the teacher does need to do a great deal of thinking and planning if he wants the child to develop an accurate time-sense that will help him to understand the true import of what he hears and reads and learns about time and its application in his own life. It is comparatively easy for the teacher, by means of careful preplanning in his curriculum work, to help the children develop a unit on "Time."

Another aspect of life of which the child today is ever conscious is the *motor age*. Most of the tempo of modern life is centered around faster and faster means of transportation and communication, based primarily now upon the internal-combustion engine, in the future upon jet propulsion. The child already has an interest in this motor age, and the teacher should use this interest as a motivating factor in curricular work; the teacher should plan carefully for the child to study the motor age in comparison with the growth of means of transportation and communication in other ages. In this way the child comes to understand more clearly the influence of the motor age upon his life, his work, and his future plans.

Other areas in which the child is already conscious of interest are those of the *motion picture,* the *radio,* and *TV.* The rapid improvements in these devices of entertainment have helped to effect a much more interdependent society in many ways, a society in which the modern individual cannot live apart from the rest of the world. Waiting at the teacher's hand are these devices in which children are interested; it is his task to prepare materials, and to help, guide, and direct the children, so that their learning from these fields of conscious interest will be the more productive and more useful for the individual and for the group.

Other areas of activities of which the child is already conscious include the growth of plants and animals; the growth of human beings; the construction of buildings and bridges; the care of pets and animals; machines which serve mankind; other peoples and races; pictures; museums; music and the arts; recreation and play of all types; newsstands and newsstand literature; and the care of the body and the prevention of disease.

TYPES OF CURRICULUM APPROACH IN THE ELEMENTARY SCHOOLS

In the struggle for curriculum revision, many different approaches have been used more or less successfully. After a careful survey of these approaches, five types appear to have been developed far enough to be easily recognizable, and they are of sufficient importance to be described and studied.

1. *The Textbook Approach*

This is the oldest and still the most widely used of the procedures for curriculum-building in both the elementary school and the secondary school. Basic to the textbook approach is the idea that the textbook is the indispensable tool around which most teaching should center; hence this method is comparatively easy of application and does not require extended study and careful work in evaluating the outcomes of new procedures.

The textbook approach to revision of the curriculum usually consists of: (1) a briefer or fuller study of the existing subject-matter areas and the texts in use; (2) the conclusion from this study that the textbooks in use can be replaced by better ones, which are both more up-to-date and more adapted to effective use by the teacher and by the children; and (3) the adoption of a new text or series of texts to replace the old in order to obtain better results from teaching. For example, after careful study a school may decide that in the field of the social studies it would be wise to replace the textbooks in use in grades four to six with the "Unified Social Studies" series in order to improve its curriculum. Many teachers, administrators, and school boards see the following advantages in this type of curriculum revision: there is less chance of offending the public by new procedures or methods; there is some enrichment of the existing curriculum; much less of the faculty's time is taken up in studying the problem; and there is less opportunity for a division of opinion and effort, such as might occur in an attempt to develop a new curriculum with the help of all the members of the school staff.

Considered in its entirety, the textbook approach is connected with curriculum change on the elementary-school level, but it is not to be placed in the same class with the other types of curriculum revision which are also described here. It does not belong with these others because it does not involve a real study of what the child needs, how the teacher should go about meeting those needs, and what experiences and activities are valuable for the child in his total school and home environment. The textbook approach places more emphasis upon the content-to-be-mastered than upon the child-to-be-taught.

2. *Curriculum Revision Based on Subject-Matter or Subject-Area Units*

Most of the more advanced curriculum experiments which are being conducted today had their origin in this type of curriculum-building. In this approach, the teacher, either through fear of becoming bewildered or through the pressure of school authorities, decides to stick to the textbook or books he is now using with his pupils, in spite of the fact that he wishes to emphasize the material along lines which are more compatible with the interests, natural experiences and activities, and needs of his pupils.

As an illustration of how this type of program of enrichment can take place, the teacher in grade four might tell his children that he thinks it would be interesting for them to study how the Indians lived and what has happened to them. So he organizes a unit for the pupils based to a great extent upon the textbook, which tells them in simple language the story of man and the races of the world, but he and his students develop particular aspects on Indian life, customs, habitats, and ideas. With all children taking part together, they draw on paper with colored chalk a frieze which depicts Indian life as lived among various tribes, their types of homes, how they hunted and lived, their marriage ceremonies, their wartime practices, and their locations. In addition, each child may be assigned a problem to study and report on to the group, for example, the history and fate of a certain tribe such as the Navajos or the Cherokees. Another variation would be to assign to certain children the making of simple three- or four-page notebooks with pictures drawn to represent the habits and customs of a particular tribe or the mode of life of an

Indian woman or warrior. Through these teacher-stimulated, teacher-controlled, and teacher-assigned plans, a unit of work is developed which supplements and ties into the work of the textbook.

Another approach to this same kind of unit based upon subject-matter areas is found. For example, the pupils suggest that they make a study of the Indians, or one pupil suggests this. The teacher accepts the suggestion, but he outlines and directs the work primarily himself, while the child does only a minimum or a small part of it on his own initiative and from the angle of his own greatest interest. This variation of curriculum revision based on subject units is valuable for the teacher as well as for the child, but it is more stimulating to the teacher than to the pupil in that he learns more about the activities and aspects of life in which children are interested.

In general, the curriculum approach based on subject-matter or subject-area units usually contributes more to the growth of the teacher than it does to the growth of the child in the way of stimulating and sustaining his enthusiasms and interests. It has its place as one step in curriculum revision, and it is an excellent method that can be suggested to those teachers who are hesitant about breaking in any respect with the textbook tradition.

3. The Activity or "Fusion" Approach

The activity approach is logically the next step in the evolution from the unit based upon subject-matter areas to the unit based upon the activities of children. This approach attempts to care for the varied interests of all members of the group, rather than for the particular interests of some; it also uses to greater advantage and in many ways the different talents of the children. For example, some children have aptitude for drawing, others are more creative in music and dramatic expression, and still others are skillful in construction work. Why should not all of these natural aptitudes be utilized by the teacher in helping the pupils to attain a comprehensive and creative concept of the Indians and their place in the growth of the United States?

In the development of this kind of curriculum work, it is a natural transition to "fuse" the major work of the whole group of children in one grade around an activity which might last anywhere from two to four or six weeks. The length of time devoted to the activity depends upon the interests of the children and the many aspects which could and would be drawn naturally into the work to be mastered by them as part of the activity or of the larger fused unit.

FIG. 24   *The whole second grade works on an activity after planning together.*
(*Courtesy Greensboro (N.C.) Public Schools, Brooks School.*)

Two distinct types of the activity approach have developed. In the first place, there is the *teacher-planned activity*, in which the major activities or teaching units for the year are made out in advance by the teacher and are taken up with the children according to the special interests expressed by them at a particular time in one unit or another. This type of procedure assumes that there are certain subject areas and certain kinds of knowledge which the children must master during the year's time, and that it is up to the teacher to see that they attain these objectives. The second type of activity approach is that in which *pupil and teacher plan the work cooperatively*, with each suggesting and all finally agreeing together upon what they should do. Good illustrations of teacher-pupil planning can be observed any day in the classrooms of teachers trained and experienced in this technique in schools all over the country. After the unit is selected through the cooperative decision of the teacher and the pupils, the teacher then brings in resource materials which have been prepared beforehand; the children use these materials in their start to develop the various kinds of work which they desire to do in the unit. For example, the unit for this kind of activity approach might be "Transportation and Communication," "Our World Today," "The Community in Which We Live," or "Where We Get Our Food." The main handicap to the teacher in carrying through this venture in cooperative planning is that he may have to work overtime to supply enough materials for the children to do effective work upon the unit which they have selected. Unless he knows rather accurately what kinds of units or activities the children are likely to select at that grade and age level, he will fail to supply the *variety* of materials needed for their effective work. Another problem which faces the teacher here is how to make a satisfactory evaluation of the progress of individual pupils in the activity in which they all agreed to engage as a group. The activity approach places upon the teacher at all times the responsibility of stimulating his pupils *to retain their interest and master their materials* throughout the period during which the activity takes place.

New York City's Experiment With the Activity Program. From 1935 to 1940, the New York City schools experimented with the "activity program" in sixty-nine elementary schools involving some 75,000 children. This program, as planned by the Division of Elementary Schools, attempted to provide for the following: socialized recitation in place of teacher domination; purposeful planning in place of formal recitation of subject matter; individual guidance in place of mass instruction; an enriched curriculum in place of formal courses of study; significant child experiences in place of drill and verbalism. A broad plan of research and evaluation was instituted in order to discover whether the children in these sixty-nine experimental schools learned more than the children in the regularly constituted, formal, elementary schools in New York City.

One may not agree with the concept that all of the teachers in these experimental schools should be compelled to follow a different curricular approach and a different type of teaching whether they were trained for them or not, but the experiment was of significance in several ways. Certainly some of the other elementary schools and teachers of New York City profited, in that they made their teaching more informal and better adapted to the experiences and enthusiasms of childhood. Probably another healthy result was that teachers acquired new ideas and broadened their own training in order to be able to meet better the needs of their children. However, there was a lack of agreement among educators as to whether the comparisons of the traditional schools with the experimental schools in this large-scale experiment really produced significant results.

Though the research findings of this large-scale study were not conclusive, the writer must agree with B. Othanel Smith and his co-authors [6] that it was one of the important investigations in recent years of curricular method and organizational technique. It was a carefully planned study and left its imprint upon curriculum growth and development.[7]

---

[6] Cf. B.O. Smith, W.O. Stanley, and J.H. Shores, *Fundamentals of Curriculum Development* (rev. ed.), Yonkers-on-Hudson, World Book Company, 1957, pp. 396–99.

[7] For more detailed information upon the New York City experiment see J.J. Loftus, "The Activity Program in New York City," *Curriculum Journal*, VIII (October, 1937), pp. 245–48; Jack Steele, "Progressive Education to Start Last Year of 6-Year Trial with Banners Flying Proudly," *New York Herald Tribune*, December 31, 1939, Sec. II, p. 5; A.T. Jersild, *et al.*, "An Evaluation of Aspects of the Activity Program in the New York City Public Elementary Schools" and "A Further Comparison of Pupils in Activity and Non-Activity Schools," *Journal of Experimental Education*, Vol. VIII (December, 1939), pp. 166–207, and Vol. IX (June, 1941), pp. 303–9, respectively; J.C. Morrison, *The Activity Program: A Curriculum Experiment*, Report of Survey by the New York State Department of Education, 1941, *passim;* "The Activity Program in New York City Schools," A symposium on various aspects, *The Journal of Educational Sociology*, XVII, No. 2 (October, 1943), pp. 65–123.

4. The Plan for Larger Centers of Interest with Scope and Sequence

School systems which have been working on curricular revision for many years have finally come to the conclusion that the unit approach with activities and large "centers of interest" is desirable, provided plans are made in advance for the *scope* and *sequence* to be discovered and followed. A practical illustration of the difficulties which these systems encountered was that the children in grade five, for example, might decide to study "Transportation and Communication," and a year later in grade six many or most of them would desire to study the same unit again. To both teachers and administrators it was patently a duplication of effort and certainly some waste of time to study the same unit on successive grade levels, even though the approach was different in each case. Therefore the scope to be involved and the sequence to be followed have been worked out in certain schools, so that these large centers of interest may not duplicate the curriculum work in succeeding years. Santa Barbara (California) at midcentury gave a good example of scope and sequence in a county school system; the program agreed upon nine basic functions of human living as the *scope* of the (core) curriculum for all grades:

I. Developing, conserving, and utilizing human resources
II. Developing, conserving, and utilizing nonhuman resources
III. Producing, distributing, and consuming goods and services
IV. Communicating
V. Transporting
VI. Recreation and playing
VII. Expressing and satisfying spiritual and aesthetic needs
VIII. Organizing and governing
IX. Providing education.

The sequence of integrating themes for the various grades in the Santa Barbara County Program was established as follows: [8]

---

[8] The *scope* was summarized from *Santa Barbara County Curriculum Guide for Teachers in Secondary Schools,* Vol. 4, the Schauer Printing Company, pp. 38–39; the *sequence* was summarized for the high-school grades from this same volume, but for the elementary grades (1–8), the summary was taken from *Manual of Information for the Santa Barbara County Schools,* Board of Education, 1948–1949, pp. 5–8.

For Kindergarten: How to live with others in social groups in a desirable, experiential situation.

For Grades One and Two: Guiding the growth of children toward more effective living in the Home, Neighborhood, School and Community.

For Grades Three and Four: Guiding the growth of children toward more effective living through understanding of adaptations of man's life to natural environmental forces and to advancing physical frontiers.

For Grades Five and Six: Guiding the growth of children toward more effective living through understanding of how man controls nature through technological pioneering.

For Grades Seven and Eight: Guiding the growth of children toward more effective living through understanding of how the social institutions—the home, the church, the club, the community, the government, and the school—can meet our human needs better through improved social controls.

For Grades Nine and Ten: Planning for educational, vocational, personal, and social goals; understanding of relationships between the problems of the individual and those of the school, community, state, and nation.

For Grades Eleven and Twelve: Understanding of how man has met and is meeting his major problems—with emphasis upon solutions now being proposed and the historical foundations of our present problems.

For Grades Thirteen and Fourteen: Development in understanding democratic ideals and their implications for social organization.

Through this type of program, Santa Barbara County attempted to look after both the scope and the sequence of the curriculum so as to avoid duplication and wasted time and effort; at the same time, it attempted to use the social studies as large areas of interest (or the core) for the development of the natural interests and enthusiasms of the child.

It is important for the curriculum worker to realize the difference between the fused and the core curriculums. The "core" curriculum is centered around those basic knowledges, skills, and experiences which the school has decided that every student should have throughout the succeeding years of his school career. The "fused" curriculum, as it has usually developed, differs fundamentally from this in one respect, namely, that the pupil's work is fused or centered around subjects or activities for a part or the whole of one year only without regard for scope and sequence in the other years or grades.

The reader should compare the scope and sequence of the present Long Beach program (Table 20) with Santa Barbara's Scope and sequence in the state programs of Virginia and Alabama have been previously referred to in Chapter 6.

5. *The Experience Curriculum Approach*

Much more progress with the "experience" approach has been made in the elementary school than in the secondary school. When this approach is used, the *first step* involves the pupil's own choice of an activity or area of interest on which he desires to work. The *second step* takes place when the child confers with the teacher and tells him what he wants to do; it is the teacher's responsibility to bring the pupil to a realization of the scope of the area selected, of his responsibilities, and of the kinds and amount of labor which will be involved. The *third step* is an exploration by the child of the materials he will need, both those of a subject-matter nature and those of an experiencing and observational character, such as a visit to a dairy or spending three or four days on a farm. During this step, the teacher suggests and supplies, and refers the student to different kinds of materials. In the *fourth step* the pupil "fuses" his experiences and activities, intellectual and otherwise, into the acquisition and mastery of his chosen area of interest. He clarifies his concepts, works out solutions for his problem. For the *final step* the child has to exhibit and explain clearly the results of his "experience," make an oral or a written illustrated report of it, take a standard or teacher-made test upon "core" aspects, or do two or more of these satisfactorily as evidence of his progress.

Since the experience curriculum is the closest approach to individual instruction which has yet evolved, it should be the ideal to be worked for by every teacher. The two fundamental obstacles to its universal adoption on all school levels are (1) the large pupil-teacher ratio, which of necessity limits the amount of time which can be devoted to each student, and (2) the kind of teacher education which emphasizes special training in subject-matter fields at the expense of the broad background necessary for the successful handling of this type of curriculum approach. One should note that the *teacher-pupil planned activity approach* in the hands of a well-prepared and effective teacher comes close to the experience curriculum approach in

TABLE 20. Framework of the social studies program [*]

Includes: Geography, History, Civics, Economics

Long Beach Unified School District Long Beach, California

LIVING IN THE COMMUNITY				LIVING IN CONTRASTING CULTURES			LIVING IN EARLY AMERICA
The Local Community		The Expanding Community		Life Studies in Primitive Cultures and in Selected Cultures			Development of the United States
Kindergarten	First Year	Second Year	Third Year	Third Year	Fourth Year		Fifth Year
			Unit Group A	*Unit Group B*	*Unit Group A*	*Unit Group B*	
Airplanes Bakeries Buses Farms Gas Stations Harbor Homes Lumberyards Oil Fields Ships Stores Trains Trucks Other phases of community life	General study of community life in Long Beach which may start with transportation as it affects general living in the community Bakeries Fire Stations Harbor Homes Hotels Markets Oil Fields Parks Post Office Stores Theaters Other phases of community life	Airplanes and Airports Bakery The Dairy Farm The Farm Wholesale and Retail Markets	Carrying the Mail Ships, Harbor, and Cargoes Trains	Navaho Indians Pueblo Indians	Life in Early California Life in Mexico	Life in China Life in Switzerland	Life in Colonial America Westward Movement

EXPLANATORY NOTES

Kindergarten: A number of short units lasting one day to three weeks are taught.

First Grade: Community life in its various aspects is taught during the first year.

Second Grade: Either *two* or *three* of the units listed may be taught. A teacher should not use both *The Farm* unit and *The Dairy Farm* unit during the same year.

Third Grade: *Two* of the units listed should be taught. The teacher should select one unit from each group.

Fourth Grade: Either *two* or *three* units may be taught. The teacher should select at least one unit from each group. If a third unit is taught it should be selected from Unit Group B.

276

IMPROVING WAYS OF LIVING	ADJUSTING TO THE CULTURAL AND PHYSICAL ENVIRONMENT			UNDERSTANDING CURRENT PROBLEMS		
Inventions & Technical Discoveries as They Affect Life Today	Emphasis on Personal Problems, Geography, History, and Government					
Sixth Year	Seventh Year	Eighth Year	Ninth Year	In Our World / Tenth Year	In Our Country / Eleventh Year	In Our Social and Economic Relationships / Twelfth Year
Unit Group A How Changes in Communication Affect People's Lives How Record Keeping Has Helped Man's Progress *Unit Group B* How Air Transportation Affects Social Living How Improved Land Transportation Has Influenced Man's Progress How Changes in Travel on Water Affect the Way People Live	Ourselves at School and at Home Our Community Our State Our Nation Contributions from Early Civilizations	Our Nation is Born Our Nation Becomes the United States of America Our Nation Is Tested Our Nation Meets Home Problems Our Nation Accepts World Responsibilities Personal Problems of Boys and Girls	Resources of the World—distribution, conservation, world trade Problems of Youth—Personal, Social, Vocational Our American Neighbors—climate, geography, resources; peoples; common problems	Orientation Driver Education Contemporary World Problems Great Britain and the British Empire France and French Africa, the Low Countries, and the Iberian Peninsula Germany, Italy, and the Scandinavian Countries Russia, Buffer States, and the Middle East Asia International Problems	The People of the United States The Development of Political Democracy and Nationalism in the United States The Economic Development of the United States The United States, a World Power Social Development of the United States Government Services in the United States	Social Problems Your Personality Development Your Family Relationships Choosing Your Marriage Partner Looking Forward to Your Marriage and Parenthood Your Family and the Community Economic Problems Occupations Today's Consumer

Sixth Grade: Either *two* or *three* units may be taught. The teacher should select at least one unit from each group. Transportation units should be selected to avoid duplication of experiences provided in grade two by the unit, *Airplanes and Airports*, and in grade three by the units, *Trains*, or *Ships, Harbors, and Cargoes.*

Seventh-Twelfth Grades: Each unit in each grade is taught. The units under each grade are listed in the order recommended for effective teaching; however, circumstances may arise which necessitate a change in the order of presentation.

Office of Curriculum Development
January, 1957

* (Reproduced by permission)

much *individual* work with pupils. The fusion of subject areas with the experiences of children is presented more fully in Chapter 11.

All of these methods of approach to curriculum improvement on the elementary-school level will make faster progress only as the teachers and administrators involved improve their training while in service. Such training should help them to understand better what the enthusiasms, interests, and needs of children are, what kinds of activities children engage in naturally, and what materials and resources are necessary for each approach.

CURRICULUM ORGANIZATION AND ADMINISTRATION IN THE ELEMENTARY SCHOOL

LEADERSHIP AND TRAINING.   Without constructive leadership and without constructive in-service training of educational employees, there is no real hope for curriculum improvement on a system-wide scale in a community. Teachers may desire to improve their work; they may be eager to meet and to carry on the interests and enthusiasms of their students; but without guidance and training, without facilities for discovering where materials are which they can use and how they may get them, without the arrangement of these materials in some sort of order and availability, they may be unable to make real progress in curriculum experimentation and revision. The same holds true of the school administrator, whether he be superintendent or principal. Those school systems have made the most progress in curriculum improvement where the administrators and the teaching staff have worked constructively hand in hand, while they all had the help of additional training while they were in service, and where they used all types of materials in order to be able to accomplish their purposes.

ORGANIZATION AND ADMINISTRATION.   The organization which should be established for curriculum revision or curriculum change is not something to stagger the imagination, nor is it something to be afraid of. The first step is usually the most difficult to take, namely, that of making an investigation of one's own system, one's own curriculum, and one's own teaching. Only through such an investigation can one discover objectively what one's purposes are, what one is doing to attain them, what one's weaknesses consist of, and how one may work cooperatively to remedy those weaknesses and to strengthen the program for the children under one's care. The traditional organization by grades in the elementary school has been one of the initial stumbling blocks to every administrator and teacher when curriculum improvement has been considered. Because of their training and practice, educational employees have developed the attitude that those procedures which they have followed for years within a certain framework and within a certain setting are necessary for the continued and satisfactory functioning of the school program. There is nothing sacred about these grade levels which have been established, if the teacher really wants to overcome any handicaps which they impose upon him in attempting to improve the curriculum for the children in his charge.

When the educational employee begins to investigate what other schools and other communities have done that is outstanding in curricular revision, the name of Carleton Washburne and his school board and teaching staff at Winnetka, Illinois, comes to mind. Many other school systems have for many years been working cooperatively in a similar way on curriculum improvement, though not for quite so long as Washburne and his colleagues. For example, not far from Winnetka, Paul Misner and his group have been striving for years to improve their curriculum. As early as 1939 they minimized the importance of the grade organization, which is found in most schools, by substituting the following levels: Kindergarten; First and Second Levels; Third Level; Fourth and Fifth Levels; Sixth Level; and Seventh and Eighth Levels.[9] In their organization, subject-matter areas were broadened to include suggestive experiences in living and learning, in accord with the major integrative theme that democratic education consists in making a community in which children cannot help being democratic, intelligent, reverent, and eager. In line with this same concept of organization is the Milwaukee Ungraded Primary Plan in operation since 1942, the Park Forest (Ill.) plan, and others.[10]

[9] P.J. Misner, "Curriculum-Building as Group Thinking," *Curriculum Journal,* x (February, 1939), p. 57.

[10] *Cf. A Look at Continuity in the School Program,* 1958 Yearbook, *op. cit.,* pp. 207–14; R.H. Anderson, "Ungraded Primary Classes," *Understanding the*

There is a distinct trend toward classification of pupils into broader "divisions" or "levels," instead of into traditional grades in the elementary school. By 1950 surveys of city schools showed that 17 per cent of the 1,600 systems practiced it to a greater or less extent.[11] Whenever a system starts to eliminate grade lines, the elimination usually takes place first in the primary grades; then the tendency is to extend the plan later further up the grades in the pattern of school organization. Three out of every four cities which had begun to replace their grades with levels or divisions reported that this practice was growing in their systems.

In contrast to this suggested simplification of the present grade system there is the view which has long been held and which has been presented by L.B. Wheat and others of grouping all children according to reading age and mental maturity. Instead of the three-grade spread of the primary school as traditionally organized, there would be as many different classes or levels of progress as the children's learning experiences require.[12]

THE EVALUATION OF CURRICULUM DEVELOPMENT

CHANGING CONCEPTIONS OF PUPIL PROGRESS. A program of curriculum revision is incomplete without standards for evaluating the progress which is made by each pupil. Of fundamental importance in this process of evaluation is the elimination of a grading system whereby children are graded in comparison with the *average* of the grade in which they are, or in which the brightest and dullest are compared.

Of course, it is difficult for the teacher to discover the stage of

---

Child, xxiv (June, 1955), pp. 66–72; and J.W. Wrightstone, *Class Organization for Instruction,* Department of Classroom Teachers and American Education Research Association, N.E.A., 1957, *passim.*

[11] "Trends in City-school Organization: 1938–1948," *National Education Association Research Bulletin,* xxvii, No. 1 (February, 1949), pp. 8–9, 16–19, 20–22; "We Look at Grouping," *Educational Leadership,* iv, No. vi (March, 1947), pp. 354–402; and "The Ungraded Primary School as a Contribution to Improved School Practices," *Frontiers of Elementary Education,* ii, Syracuse University Press, 1955, pp. 28–39.

[12] "The Flexible Progress Group System," *Elementary School Journal,* xxxviii (November, 1937), pp. 175–83; and H.M. Buckley, "Levels Instead of Grades," *School Management,* xv (May, 1946), pp. 482–83.

development of each child when he comes to that particular grade and to that particular teacher. Regardless of the school framework within which the teacher is laboring, if he can discover *the point of progress and the type of achievement which the individual child has attained when he comes to him,* he is able to do an effective job with the pupil in terms of the pupil's progress from that point. The teacher can work just as effectively with him in the traditional organization of eight grades as he can in a new organization of four or five levels, or twenty-four levels. The main point is that he must look at that child in relation to his progress individually, and also in relation to his ability to adapt and adjust himself to the group and to become a working and cooperating member of that group.

Therefore, the teacher needs at least two types of tests which he should give and should use for diagnostic and remedial purposes in studying and helping that child: (1) a pretest of some sort, written or oral, whether based entirely upon subject matter or including also certain attitudes and habits; (2) tests by which he can tell what progress the child has made in acquiring knowledge, skills, attitudes, ideals, interests, and enthusiasms. Without following these two simple, yet vital, steps in evaluation, the teacher is unable to do for each child what he hopes to be able to do. The question will naturally be asked where the teacher can secure this kind of evaluative material, or how he is to go about formulating it. Both of these questions can be answered satisfactorily from a study of those experiments which have been made along these lines.

TYPES OF TESTS.   We shall consider first the types of tests which have been constructed and perfected by other persons for use in pretesting, diagnosing, and measuring achievement. Practically all teachers are aware of the fact that excellent standard achievement tests covering the basic subject areas and skills in the elementary schools have been developed. Illustrative of these are the *New Stanford Achievement Test,* the *Metropolitan Achievement Tests* and the *California Achievement Tests.* Such tests as these should be used mainly as diagnostic instruments, though they can also be used to discover whether a particular group of children is making progress comparable to the achievement of other groups of children. In addition to these standard achievement tests, which might be called "batteries" and which test both skills and knowledges, special tests in various subject areas such as reading, number work and arithmetic, and the social studies have been prepared for diagnostic and achievement purposes. Samples of tests of this type are the following:

> Gates: *Primary Reading Test,* Grades 1–2; *Silent Reading Test,* Grades 3–8.
> *Iowa Silent Reading Test* and *Every Pupil Tests of Basic Study Skills. Cooperative Social Studies Test,* Grades 6–9.

In considering the importance of testing for curriculum purposes, it would be wise for the curriculum worker to look at some carefully carried out, controlled experiment which would give him a good example of the procedure he might employ to arrive at his particular aims through testing. Such a study in arithmetic on the third-grade level was made by W.A. Brownell, and it offers excellent ideas to any teacher who wishes to follow a reasonably accurate and safe procedure in this work.[13] Brownell's experiment showed that the following types of tests might be wisely used upon each unit, center of interest, or activity which is undertaken: (1) a pretest; (2) a test administered in the middle of the unit; (3) a final test; and (4) a retention test given some time after the unit or activity is completed.

Another kind of test which may be used for informative purposes, but not as a *sine qua non,* is the mental or intelligence test. The differences of opinion concerning intelligence testing and its value to the teacher in curriculum making have already been discussed under "Child Growth and Development" (Chapter 3). It would be well for the teacher to know about the background which this type of test presumes to show; most of them have a large section devoted to number relationships and arithmetic reasoning and spatial relationships. At the same time the teacher should not put so much weight on the intelligence test score that he is unable to conceive that the child might make some progress individually and in the group in his school work. The results from such a mental test will serve at least as confirmatory or additional evidence, and not as a primary base upon which the teacher should work with the child in all aspects of his school activities.

[13] *Learning as Reorganization: An Experimental Study in Third Grade Arithmetic,* Duke University Press, 1939.

A different type of test has recently been developed and is of great value to the curriculum worker—the test of interests. Samples of this type of test are the following:

> Wood: *Behavior Preference Record,* Elementary Form A for Grades 4–6, and Intermediate Form A for Grades 7–9.
> Haggerty-Olson-Wickman: Behavior Rating Scales.
> California Test of Personality.

Reading readiness tests, another valuable aid, will be discussed in Chapter 11.

NEW CONCEPTS OF EVALUATION. New concepts of evaluation have been developed during the last decade, and these promise significant help in curriculum improvement. Tyler, Eurich, Wrightstone, and Wrinkle led the experimenters in evaluation.[14] These educators insist that a program of evaluation should serve in general the following purposes: (1) to provide a check on the effectiveness of the school and indicate the points which should be improved; (2) to consolidate the philosophy or the purposes on or for which the school operates; (3) to provide information basic to the individual guidance of pupils; and (4) to provide a sound basis for public relations.

Wrightstone says that the average teacher can do the following things about evaluation: (1) determine or identify the major objective of the curriculum; (2) use informal methods of evaluation; and (3) use formal methods of evaluation by a careful selection of existing objective tests which measure various aspects of learning. His suggested methods of evaluating important objectives of elemen-

---

[14] *Cf.* R.W. Tyler, "The Place of Evaluation in Modern Education," *Elementary School Journal,* XLI (September, 1940), pp. 19–27; A.C. Eurich, "Approach to the Evaluation of the Outcomes of Instruction," *National Society of College Teachers of Education Yearbook,* XXVII, pp. 208–26; J.W. Wrightstone, *Appraisal of Newer Elementary School Practices,* Teachers College, Columbia University, 1938, Chaps. I–III, VIII–XIV; W.L. Wrinkle, *Improving Marking and Reporting Practices,* New York, Rinehart and Company, 1947, Chaps. I, IV, VIII–IX. For more recent opinion on purposes of an evaluation program, turn to H.H. Remmers and N.L. Gage, *Educational Measurement and Evaluation* (rev. ed.), New York, Harper and Brothers, 1955, Chap. I; J.W. Wrightstone, *et al., Evaluation in Modern Education,* New York, American Book Company, 1956, Part I; G.S. Adams and T.L. Torgerson, *Measurement and Evaluation for the Secondary School Teacher,* New York, The Dryden Press, 1956, Part I; and Victor H. Noll, *Introduction to Educational Measurement,* Boston, Houghton Mifflin Company, 1957, Chap. I.

tary school education are rich in ideas for every teacher on that level.[15]

The experts in test making and measurement in education also have had a variance of opinion concerning the formulation, construction, and use of objective methods of testing. Some contend that these tests measure only achievement in subject matter, and others contend that this is not so.[16] In the final analysis, no one technique of measurement can be adequate in appraising all directions of growth and experience in pupils. Unless a school, or the individual teacher within the school, has formulated the purposes of the instruction which it or he is attempting to give, there is no hope of being able to formulate any evaluation program which will show what is being done. If the school and the teacher have formulated such objectives, then the test of both the problem and the objective type can be of great value in discovering what progress is being made.

Self-evaluation by teachers and pupils is equally important in the organization and administration of an evaluative program in curriculum work. Even in the elementary school, pupils are capable of examining and appraising their own courses of action and activities in terms of standards which have been established by them or which they have accepted as their own. Pupils as well as teachers should participate in such evaluative procedures. The results of the pupil's appraisal of a unit of work or an area of interest upon which he has been engaged may be of great value in directing his further work; the self-appraisal may stimulate his enthusiasm for learning more than any set of standard or special tests which the experts may be

[15] *Evaluation in Modern Education, op. cit.,* Chap. II, and *Appraisal of Newer Elementary School Practices, op. cit., passim.*

[16] *Cf.* E.O. Melby, "A Comprehensive Concept of Evaluation," *Curriculum Journal,* x (November, 1939), pp. 300–303; P.R. Grim, "A Comprehensive Concept of Evaluation—A Reply," *Curriculum Journal,* xi (January, 1940), pp. 32–35; and A.E. Traxler, "Planning and Administering a Testing Program," *The School Review,* xlviii (April, 1940), pp. 253–67. More recent views are found in the April, 1947, issue of *Educational Leadership* (Vol. iv, No. 7): J. M. Lee, "Basketball Victories—Or Child Development?" pp. 426–28; G.M. Wilson, "Shall Tests Go Out of the Window?" pp. 456–60; K.L. Bean, *Construction of Educational and Personnel Tests,* New York, McGraw-Hill Book Company, 1953, Chaps. i and v; and J.M. Bradfield and H.S. Moredock, *Measurement and Evaluation in Education,* New York, The Macmillan Company, 1957, Chaps. iv and ix.

able to construct within the years to come. If the teacher in the elementary school does not know in which direction he is planning to lead his pupils, it is impossible for him to evaluate what his pupils are doing. Conversely, the evaluation which he receives cannot be of maximum worth unless he knows the point of achievement and progress at which his pupils were when they started their work with him.

The parent-teacher conference has grown rapidly in recent years as a means of evaluating a pupil's progress in school and of supplementing the written report card. Two systems that have refined this technique are Great Neck, Long Island (N.Y.) and Long Beach, California.[17]

PRINCIPLES OF EVALUATION. If the following three principles are used as guides, adequate evaluation of curriculum work can be attained. The first principle consists in the elimination of a grading system whereby children are graded in contrast with the average, or with the brightest or dullest. It is comparatively easy for an intelligent teacher to discover the achievement and attitudes of the child when he first comes to him and when he leaves him, thereby measuring his growth in terms of this progress. An intelligent use of standard and teacher-made measuring instruments will give a good picture of the pupil; pretests, midtests, final tests, and recall tests should be employed to ascertain growth in subject-matter achievement, development of attitudes and interests, and mental ability. Chapter 15 gives in some detail ways of collecting such data through use of the "Teacher-Pupil Individual Folder for Evaluation" (p. 466).

---

[17] For earlier examples of parent and pupil participation in evaluating, consult two issues of *Educational Leadership*, II, No. 7 (April, 1945), "Reports and Records of Student Growth," pp. 290–99; and IV, No. 7 (April, 1947), "Teachers Evaluate," pp. 429–32, 435–41, and 464–68. The Montclair (N.J.) Public Schools developed an interesting plan of evaluation in which the pupil, the teacher, and the parent took part in "My Growth Plan," which was employed in grades four, five, and six. The 1949 Yearbook of the Association for Supervision and Curriculum Development, N.E.A., *Toward Better Teaching*, has two good chapters on pupil evaluation, VI and VIII, and their 1954 Yearbook, *Creating a Good Environment for Learning*, has another illustrative chapter, X. Later samples of pupil and parent participation include "Reflections of a Sixth Grade," by E. Johnson, *Educational Leadership*, XI (April, 1954), pp. 418–23; and "A Parent Speaks," in Bulletin No. 62 of the Association for Childhood Education International, *Reporting on the Growth of Children*, pp. 10–12. Long Beach has a *Handbook for Parent-Teacher Conferences* (1955).

Secondly, the major purposes of the curriculum should be determined in advance. The third principle involves the use of informal evaluative measures such as pupil and teacher opinions, parents' opinions, criticisms, and suggestions for improvement, in addition to the employment of modern devices in measurement to discover whether the major objectives have been attained.

PROBLEMS FOR INDIVIDUAL STUDY AND CLASS DISCUSSION

1. Is there any difference between a unit on "The Farm" and an activity for the grade called "The Store"? Explain.

2. How could you discover what interests and attitudes are common to both boys and girls on the second-grade level? On the fifth-grade level? On the seventh-grade level?

3. Does "unit" teaching or the "activity" procedure care more adequately for the "interest" or concentration" span of children than straight textbook teaching? Give reasons for your answer.

4. Is the system of grading children by comparison with the average unfair? Support your position.

5. Make a list of the experiences and things that you have always dreamed of having. Compare it with those things you have experienced or acquired. Did the making of this list help you to understand any better the enthusiasm and dreams of children?

6. If you have no music teacher in your elementary school, and certain of your children in grade three want to learn about music and how to express themselves through it, what would you do to give them this experience?

7. What kinds of items or questions would you use in a pretest to discover the attitudes of your children when they first come to you in the third grade? When they enter your fifth grade? Can you formulate a tentative test of this kind, composed of twenty to thirty items?

8. In the sixth grade, John Black is considered a bright, but "problem," child. Assume that you know that John will be in your grade next year; what steps will you take to secure adequate information about him before he joins your grade?

9. Assume that you have decided that the only fair way in which you can evaluate your children's progress in your "unit" or "activity" teaching this year is to keep a cumulative, individual folder record of the contributions of each pupil. What materials would you place in each folder from time to time?

10. When a pupil is promoted from the second grade to you as teacher of the third grade, can you take for granted that he is prepared to do third-grade work? Why or why not?

11. Make out a clear and comprehensive list of your curricular objectives for the first grade. For the fifth grade.

12. Take the list you made out in Problem 11 and from close observation try to discover the interests, enthusiasms, activities, and creative urges of the children of that grade and age group which you might employ to advantage in motivating your curricular program.

13. Can children through failure learn the satisfaction that comes from mastery or achievement of some task or problem? Explain.

14. Is there any difference between a "center of interest" and a "unit"? Explain.

15. What is meant by "scope and sequence" in the planning of large-unit curricular work? Illustrate the principle in a center of interest for grades five and six.

16. Make out an evaluation sheet to be used by your pupils in evaluating a unit on "Transportation" which you planned and carried out cooperatively in grade five. In grade seven.

ADDITIONAL ANNOTATED REFERENCES
FOR PROBLEM OR UNIT STUDY

American Association of School Administrators, N.E.A., *American School Curriculum*, 31st Yearbook, 1953.

Chapters ii on learning and growth, iii on curriculum organization, v on curriculum development in the elementary school, and xi on evaluation.

Anderson, V.E., *Principles and Procedures of Curriculum Improvement*, New York, The Ronald Press Company, 1956.

Describes the learner in Chapter vi, organization and planning of the curriculum in Part iv, and organization of classroom experiences and evaluation in Part v.

Association for Supervision and Curriculum Development, N.E.A., *Reporting Is Communicating*, 1956.

A realistic description of a critical approach to evaluation and marking in a school system.

Baxter, Bernice, *et al.*, *The Role of Elementary Education*, Boston, D.C. Heath and Company, 1952.

Based on the idea that learning experiences should meet the different stages of growth and needs of children, the authors describe planning for teaching in Part iii, and life in the nursery school, the kindergarten, and in the primary, intermediate, and upper grades in Part iv.

Bean, K.L., *Construction of Educational and Personnel Tests,* New York, McGraw-Hill Book Company, 1953.
Gives valuable illustrations of objective-test items in Chapters III and IV, sane help in essay-type tests in Chapter V, and example of a performance test in Appendix C.

Beck, R.H., *et al., Curriculum in the Modern Elementary School,* New York, Prentice-Hall, 1953.
Description of the elementary-school child in Chapter III, evaluation in Chapter X, and curriculum structure and planning in Chapters XII and XIII.

Buros, O.K. (Ed.), *The Fourth Mental Measurement Yearbook,* New Brunswick, Rutgers University Press, 1953.
A comprehensive list and evaluative reviews of tests of all types and descriptions.

Caswell, H.L., and Foshay, A.W., *Education in the Elementary School* (3rd ed.), New York, American Book Company, 1957.
Characteristics of a good elementary school in Chapter III, of younger children in Chapter V, curriculum organization in Chapter X, and pupil appraisal in Chapter XIII.

Educational Policies Commission, N.E.A., and A.A.S.A.:

Education for All American Children, 1948   } Suggested policies, and practices recommended for carrying them out.
Educational Services for Younger Children, 1945

Gerberich, J.R., *Specimen Objective Test Items,* New York, Longmans, Green and Company, 1956.
A guide to construction of achievement tests, with objective items classified by form, type, and variety, and also by elementary and secondary subjects.

Gesell, A., *et al., Youth: The Years from Ten to Sixteen,* New York, Harper and Brothers, 1956.
Chapters IV–VII present excellent, detailed descriptions of child characteristics, years 10–13.

Greene, H.A., *et al., Measurement and Evaluation in the Elementary School* (2nd ed.), New York, Longmans, Green and Company, 1953.
Long a standard source for evaluation, it gives the classroom teacher aid on a multitude of measurement problems.

Hanna, L.A., *et al., Unit Teaching in the Elementary School,* New York, Rinehart and Company, 1955.
Presents bases for unit teaching, how to develop the unit, evaluating results of unit teaching, and sample resource and teaching units.

Herrick, V.E., *et al., The Elementary School,* Englewood Cliffs, Prentice-Hall, 1956.

Chapter v gives excellent description of characteristics of elementary-school children; Chapter vi, the planning and organization of the curriculum.

Klausmeier, H. J., *et al.*, *Teaching in the Elementary School*, New York, Harper and Brothers, 1956.
Types of curriculum organization and planning for class instruction in Chapters iv and v, reporting pupil progress and parent-teacher conferences in Chapter xvi.

Lambert, H.M., *Teaching the Kindergarten Child*, New York, Harcourt, Brace and Company, 1958.
How four- and five-year-olds grow and learn.

Langdon, G., and Stout, I.W., *Teacher-Parent Interviews*, New York, Prentice-Hall, 1954.
Discusses thoroughly this newer development in analysis and evaluation.

Miel, A., *et al.*, *Cooperative Procedures in Learning*, New York, Teachers College, Columbia University, 1952.
Concrete examples of teacher-pupil planning, including evaluation.

Nesbitt, M., *A Public School for Tomorrow*, New York, Harper and Brothers, 1953.
Describes a modern, community-backed elementary-school curriculum in an old building.

Otto, H.J., *et al.*, *Principles of Elementary Education* (rev. ed.), New York, Rinehart and Company, 1955.
Gives descriptions of typical, modern, elementary schools in Chapter i and the environment and characteristics of young children in Chapters ii and iii.

Rasey, M.I., and Menge, J.W., *What We Learn from Children*, New York, Harper and Brothers, 1956.
Accounts of children who have overcome a wide variety of difficulties at Rayswift Gables, home for exceptional children in Detroit, with important implications for teachers in public schools.

Saylor, J.G., and Alexander, W.M., *Curriculum Planning*, New York, Rinehart and Company, 1954.
Chapter v for developmental characteristics of children, Part iii for curriculum approaches and organization, and Part v for evaluation.

Smith, B.O., *et al.*, *Fundamentals of Curriculum Development* (rev. ed.), Yonkers-on-Hudson, World Book Company, 1957.
Part ii for principles and procedures in curricular development, Part iii for types of curricular organization.

Stratemeyer, F.B., *et al.*, *Developing a Curriculum for Modern Living* (2nd ed.), New York, Teachers College, Columbia University, 1957.
Chapter vi for persistent life situations faced by youngsters, viii–ix for teacher-pupil planning, xii for a description of a year's work in Grade 5, and xiv for Grade 10.

Thomas, R.M., *Ways of Teaching in Elementary Schools*, New York, Longmans, Green and Company, 1955.

Section I for descriptions of today's elementary schools, characteristics of young children, and ways of planning teaching, and Chapter xx for evaluating and reporting progress.

Torgerson, T.L., and Adams, G.S., *Measurement and Evaluation for the Elementary-School Teacher*, New York, The Dryden Press, 1954.

Defines measurement and evaluation in Part I, and gives help to teachers in construction and use of tests for classroom use in the subject-matter areas in Part III.

CHAPTER 11

Promising practices
in elementary-school
curriculum work

Significant practices in curriculum work on the elementary-school level will be noted in this chapter, practices which may indicate both the limitations and the possibilities of further improvement. Curricular experiments are so widespread and so numerous throughout the nation that no attempt will be made either to sample these experiments or to present illustrative units or work outlines of the teachers and schools which are engaged upon them. Many excellent examples of these curriculum materials have been prepared and published; a representative source list of these is given here in order that those teachers desiring full descriptions of special procedures may have access to them with a minimum amount of effort in locating them.

REPRESENTATIVE SAMPLES OF UNITS, CORE-CURRICULUM PROCEDURES, SCOPE AND SEQUENCE PLANS, AND OTHER DETAILED CURRICULAR PROCEDURES AND PRACTICES

Adams, F., *Educating America's Children: Elementary School Curriculum and Methods* (2nd ed.), New York, The Ronald Press Company, 1954, Chaps. v–xv. With the major objective of developing good citizens through practice in citizenship, it takes the child, the teacher and the curriculum as the broader view of teaching method, and uses the unit as the basis of approach and learning; presents classroom organization; techniques of pupil guidance; units of work in various school subject areas, designated as mental and physical health, science, social

studies, reading and thinking, talking and writing, number, music and
rhythm, art, and dramatic play.

Beck, R.H., *et al.*, *Curriculum in the Modern Elementary School*, New
York, Prentice-Hall, 1953, Chaps. v, ix, xiii–xvii, xix–xx. With the concept of social learning in the curriculum on the sound basis of proved
principles of learning, it describes the use of units, the subjects and
basic skills, teaching about the physical world and the earth sciences,
and art; two descriptions of individual teachers, one of how a fourth-
grade teacher developed units of work and how a man operated successfully in teacher-pupil planning in the sixth grade.

Caswell, H.L., and Campbell, D.S., *Curriculum Development*, New York,
American Book Company, 1935, esp. Chaps. ix and xv. Gives interpretation of various types of activities, and illustrations of teacher activities
that have to do with the study of the environment and the study of
pupils; classification of units, with illustrations.

Cole, L., *The Elementary School Subjects*, New York, Rinehart and
Company, 1946, Chaps. ii–iv, vii, x, xiii, xx. Presents for the teacher
in easily understandable form the extensive research of the last forty
years in reading, arithmetic, spelling, handwriting, geography and
social studies, and language, with special emphasis upon and plans for
remedial work in these areas.

Draper, E.M., *Principles and Techniques of Curriculum-Making*, New
York, D. Appleton-Century Company, 1936, Chaps. iv–v, vii–xiv. Presents the determination of education objectives from primary and secondary sources; learning activities and teaching materials, especially
with reference to standards for the selection of content when teaching
materials are organized in advance; course of study units of work, units
as centers of interest, units of work for individualized learning, child-
centered units of work, and procedures for units of work; and instructional aids in academic and nonacademic units, all well illustrated.

Hanna, L.A., *et al.*, *Unit Teaching in the Elementary School*, New York,
Rinehart and Company, 1955, *passim*. Gives the psychological bases
for unit teaching and unit selection and development, describes the unit
of work, how to develop resource and teaching units, problem solving,
construction activities, how to develop concepts and generalizations,
and sources of materials.

Hurley, B.D., *Curriculum for Elementary School Children*, New York,
The Ronald Press Company, 1957, Parts ii–iii. Using the self-contained
classroom-unit plan of curriculum organization with specialists as "col-
laborating teachers," it suggests how to guide children's growth in
language and the communication arts, social studies, science, arithmetic, arts and crafts, music and rhythms.

Indianapolis Public Schools, Indianapolis (Ind.). The use of the unit and
the problem-solving approach in grades seven to nine is well illustrated

in a recent series of "Guides for Teachers" (1954–1957) in the subject areas of the language arts, mathematics, science, social studies, health and safety, industrial arts, music, art, and the family-centered home economics program.

Lee, J.M., and Lee, D.M., *The Child and His Curriculum* (2nd ed.), New York, Appleton-Century-Crofts, 1950, Chaps. vi–xiv. Well treated and illustrated are passages on guiding life in the schools through the curriculum, units of work, and sources of materials and experiences in the different school subject areas, classified as language experiences, social experiences, number experiences, scientific experiences, healthful experiences, and creative experiences.

National Education Association:

ASSOCIATION FOR SUPERVISION AND CURRICULUM DEVELOPMENT: *1944 Yearbook, Toward a New Curriculum, passim;* describes new kinds of educational experiences, extension of the school day and year, schools and camping, preschool and adult education. *1945 Yearbook, Group Planning in Education, passim;* defines and clarifies teacher-pupil planning, presents many samples of such planning on the various grade levels, and describes how the teacher can learn to plan by planning. *1947 Yearbook, Organizing the Elementary School for Living and Learning,* Chaps. i and ii; focus is on the child; his growth and development, characteristics and needs are the guides for organizing the school (age-levels for this analysis are approaching 5; 5–6–7; 8–9–10; 11–12–13; and 14–15–16 years). *1949 Yearbook, Toward Better Teaching, passim;* this report of current practices includes examples of teaching procedures pointed toward fostering security, satisfaction, self-direction, creativity, cooperative learning, and opportunities for developing values, for social action, and for evaluating learning. *1954 Yearbook, Creating a Good Environment for Learning,* Chaps. i–iv; emphasis is on the processes by which a good learning atmosphere may be obtained by teachers at different grade levels. *1958 Yearbook, A Look At Continuity in the School Program, passim;* gives children's opinions upon continuity or lack of it in a study of the experiences of 3,000 pupils in regard to articulation or inarticulation between grade or school levels, and within the classroom.

DEPARTMENT OF ELEMENTARY SCHOOL PRINCIPALS: *23rd Yearbook, Creative Schools,* 1944, *passim;* the examples of current practices include units, projects, activities and experiences for pupils ranging in age from the kindergarten through the elementary grades. *31st Yearbook, Bases for Effective Learning,* 1952, *passim.* Attention is specially directed to characteristics of "good life" in the elementary school, to the adjustment and mental health of the teacher, and adjustment of methods to children's needs.

EDUCATIONAL POLICIES COMMISSION: *Education for* ALL *American Chil-*

dren, 1948, Part II; describes excellent practices and new departures in elementary schools.

Ragan, W.B., *Modern Elementary Curriculum,* New York, The Dryden Press, 1953, Chaps. V–XIII. Emphasizing the unified program with the unit of work, it suggests classroom organization, and how to plan work in the communication-language arts area, the social studies, arithmetic, science, health and physical education, and the arts and crafts.

Stratemeyer, F.B., *et al., Developing a Curriculum for Modern Living* (2nd ed.), New York, Teachers College, Columbia University, 1957, Chaps. V–VI and Part IV. The curriculum is centered around the life situations that learners face, with purposes, scope and sequence for these situations calling for growth in individual capacities, in social participation, and in ability to deal with environmental factors and forces; the four age-levels which are provided for are early childhood, later childhood, youth, and adulthood; illustrations of how these life situations may be built upon are given for a first grade, a fifth grade, and a tenth grade.

Teachers' Guide to Education in Early Childhood and *Teachers' Guide to Education in Later Childhood,* Sacramento, California State Department of Education, 1956 and 1957, respectively. Presents for teachers the stimulative approach to curriculum revision from kindergarten through grade six.

Wrightstone, J.W., *Appraisal of Newer Elementary School Practices,* Teachers College, Columbia University, New York, 1938, *passim.* Considers the development of newer practices, the identification of the bases of the newer trends, and the formulation of tentative objectives for the emerging elementary curriculum; there is also an excellent evaluation of conventional and experimental practices.

Of course, the curriculum employee should keep in mind that the various bulletins published in connection with the programs of Alabama, Florida, and Long Beach, which were mentioned in Chapter 6, and those of Illinois in Chapter 20, would also be of great value here. Detroit (Mich.), Oakland (Cal.), and Louisville (Ky.) public schools also have issued new series of teachers' guides and courses of study.

FUSION OF SUBJECT AREAS WITH THE ENVIRONMENT OF CHILDREN

How Fusion Developed. One of the most significant developments in the curriculum of the elementary school has been the fusing of subject matter with the activities of the pupils. Those teachers who have been bold enough to experiment with fusion of subject areas have come to the conclusion that the fusing of two or more subjects without the motivating influence of the child's interest is probably as unsatisfactory in teaching as was the old method of teaching entirely by subject divisions, such as geography, history, and reading and language. Individual subject areas may have interests in themselves, but there is seldom a time when these are not interrelated or interwoven with other interests and experiences of children which take them outside of a particular subject field. When a fifth- or sixth-grade child begins to figure the prices of foods and food items as a part of his regular work in arithmetic, he is led naturally into another field of his interest, namely, those experiences which involve buying and selling, profits, consumer education, and family budgeting.

One of the best expositions of the fusion of subject matter with the experiences of children has been given by California school personnel, first through their State Scope and Sequence Committee in its work in elementary education, and more recently through the California Curriculum Commission. Connor expressed their position with regard to the organization of school experience.[1] He said that the work of the elementary school might be divided into two parts, the first dealing with the tool subjects, and the second dealing with socializing and orientation experiences. The fields of history, geography, science, health and safety education, and language and the fine arts made up most of the socializing experiences. During the last two decades there has been a growing tendency to group instruction in these subject areas around centers of child experience. Such an organization represents a method of instruction much better suited to the age and level of development of young pupils, and it offers a satisfactory solution to the troublesome administrative problem of attempting to arrange satisfactorily arbitrary divisions of clock time for each subject-matter area.

---

[1] For earlier trends, read *Current Curricular Trends in Elementary Education,* *9th Yearbook*, California Elementary School Principals' Association, 1937, Part III, "Some Basic Considerations for the Revision of Curricula in the Elementary Schools," pp. 117–26. For latest developments, compare *Teachers' Guide to Education in Early Childhood* (1956) and *Teachers' Guide to Education in Later Childhood* (1957), California State Department of Education.

The earlier efforts to solve the problem of teaching these socializing experiences for pupils took the form of attempts at fusing the subjects of geography and history. When this was done, the social studies remained essentially history and geography. The instruction tended to be merely a succession of units in history or geography, because the unifying central factor for each unit was sought within the field of the subject matter itself, rather than within the broader scope of the child's interest, enthusiasm, and experience. In its suggestions to teachers today, the California Curriculum Commission suggests the "integrated" curriculum unit, organized around a significant aspect of social living.[2]

RECENT TRENDS.   If successful experimentation without regard to the boundaries of traditional subject-matter areas is any indication, the study of significant aspects of pupil environment on the elementary-school level is due in time to supplant these traditional subject-matter divisions. When a child has a feeling for his work, and a sense of unity and a satisfaction in it because it brings him more and more into contact with his own world of reality and meaning, as well as with his world of the imagination, the school education of the child becomes and remains of social utility and meaning; it is then in accord with basic principles of learning in the growth of the individual.

Under ideal conditions of learning, the teacher is aware of the fact that child enthusiasm and child interest go hand in hand with a situation of experiencing, not necessarily with a situation involving only artificial divisions of subject matter. This method of the fusion of subject matter with the experiences of children has been called also the "integration" of subject matter. Without some conception of the difference between the fusing of subject matters merely as such and the fusing of subject areas primarily for the purpose of broadening the experiences of children, the teacher is frequently muddled concerning what he is trying to do, or he is working at cross purposes and upon false assumptions. Illustrative of the swing from fused subject-area units to broader units of child experience are the following: from "The Store" unit to a unit on "The Family—How It Lives"; from a unit on "Our Milk Supply" to the larger one of "How

[2] *Teachers' Guide to Education in Later Childhood, op. cit.*, pp. 152–60.

Our Community Lives"; from "The Farm" as a unit to "The Rural Community"; or from a unit on "The Circus" to the broader type of child-experience unit called "Our Recreation and Amusements and How They Are Brought to Us."

CHILDREN'S SPECIAL INTERESTS

WHAT ARE THE SPECIAL INTERESTS OF CHILDREN? Accompanying the broadening of the "unit" or "center of interest" for enriched experiences for the pupil, there has come the development of techniques for discovering the types of children's special interests and enthusiasms. We mean here more particularly the *special areas* of interests of children, rather than their interests in general. One child may be particularly interested in music; another may be especially proficient in using his hands to draw and otherwise to express himself artistically; another may be especially adept in number work; and still another may like to build and be efficient at it. It looks comparatively simple for the teacher to be able to discover these interests of children in special areas. But modern society, with its many mechanical appliances and inventions, has given children access to many types of experiences—e.g., the movies, radio and TV, and the automobile—which stimulate interests that may not be as apparent as some others which the teacher can detect readily.

If the teacher is going to attempt to meet the enthusiasm and ambitions of his children for broader experiences in their school life, he has to discover various ways of ascertaining these special interests and enthusiasms and using them as motivating forces in the work which he and the pupils do together. This is particularly true if the teacher is attempting to work out a center of interest or a unit which involves the experiences of children in broad aspects, because this unit may include many or most of the subject areas as they have generally been known in the past. For example, in teaching, it is important for the teacher to know what kinds of reading the pupil does at home as well as at school; what types of moving pictures and concerts and entertainments he attends; what TV and radio programs are his favorites; what facilities he has in his home for the development of some of those interests and enthusiasms which he indicates during the time he is with the teacher; what projects or hobbies he is engaged upon outside of school hours, as well as in school; and what contacts and associations he has with adults and

FIG. 25   *The nine-year-olds experiment with sound.*
(*Courtesy Greensboro (N.C.) Public Schools, Brooks School.*)

children outside of school as well as in, and how he reacts to them.

THE CALIFORNIA STUDY OF SPECIAL INTERESTS. Schools are now developing techniques to be used in discovering the special interests and activities in which the child engages. In this respect, California was again among the leaders. In the Twelfth Yearbook of its

Elementary School Principals' Association,[3] careful consideration was given to the *arithmetic* interests, the *reading* interests, the *social studies* and *science* interests, and the *rhythmic expression* and *radio* interests of children on the elementary-school level. The special articles by different writers offered to the teacher in the elementary school valuable suggestions on how he might discover the special interests of his pupils about many subject areas. Many of the techniques used in these investigations corresponded closely to what is coming to be known as the "pretest" of children before they start a certain grade or a certain unit of work. Of special note were Culver's studies of children's interests in arithmetic.[4] Culver presented a table showing the frequency of children's questions, problems, and comments, classified according to content under the various chronological age levels of the children. The studies of children's radio interests which were made by Hockett and Fick, and by the Parent-Teacher Association of California,[5] respectively, were also significant forerunners of later studies.

SCHOOL WORK CENTERED ABOUT CHILDREN'S SPECIAL INTERESTS. The Twenty-third Yearbook of the Department of Elementary School Principals,[6] *Creative Schools,* followed the California study of special interests and presented a rich variety of school practices which have been accepted by teachers as bases for centers of interest. Included in the reports from teachers are these types of special interests which were used as centers of work: (1) reading interests, through the class newspaper; (2) creative writing interests, through poetry and play writing; (3) seasonal holiday or festival interests, by means of such programs as those for Easter or May Day; (4) TV, radio, and special listening interests, through preparation of TV and radio programs or interclassroom broadcasts; (5) music interests, by means of the orchestra or rhythm band; (6) natural science interests through the beginning of a school museum, midcentury adding of the nature trail, camping, and the science fair to these interests; (7) construction or handwork interests, through the making and operation

[3] *Children's Interests: Elementary School Level,* 1940. *Cf.* also "Children's Interests," by Harold Shane, *NEA Journal,* XLVI (April, 1957), pp. 237–39.
[4] *Ibid.,* pp. 60–70.
[5] *Ibid.,* pp. 128–37.
[6] National Education Association, 1944.

of marionettes and airplanes; (8) art interests, through panels or friezes and room decorations; (9) interpretative sociodramatic interests, through rhythmics, self-interpretative rhythms, and drama skits unplanned in advance; and (10) aviation and air-age interests.

Other good studies of the areas of special interests of children are *Science and the Social Studies,* Twenty-seventh Yearbook (1956) of the National Council for the Social Studies and *Science for Today's Children,* Thirty-second Yearbook (1953), Department of Elementary School Principals.[7]

PROBLEMS INVOLVED IN READING INTERESTS. Much has happened in the field of reading since the report of the Second Annual Conference on Reading two decades ago gave evidence of changes taking place.[8] Three more recent reports on reading of the National Society for the Study of Education [9] confirm and add to this summary: (1) reading is valuable for general education; (2) the development of sound basic reading habits and attitudes is important; (3) there is need for the improvement of reading in various subjects; (4) reading interests and tastes have to be cultivated to serve more effectively as means of personal development and social experiencing; (5) growth in reading should be a continuous process through the elementary school, the secondary school, college, and into adult life; (6) more adults between twenty-one and twenty-nine years of age are regular readers today than people over fifty years of age; (7) the poor readers will always pose teaching problems; and (8) the library can be a most effective aid in reading and learning.

It is a significant fact that the modern curriculum with its changes calls for a larger amount of reading serving a much wider variety of purposes, such as reading for understanding, for locating and utilizing needed information, for securing data to solve problems, and for increasing one's technical skills. This summary furnishes illustrations of how (1) reading is a problem in child development, (2) how

[7] Both obtainable from the N.E.A., Washington.
[8] W.S. Gray (Ed.), *Recent Trends in Reading,* the University of Chicago Press, 1939.
[9] 48th Yearbook, 1949, Part II, *Reading in the Elementary School;* 47th Yearbook, 1948, Part II, *Reading in the High School and College;* and 55th Yearbook, 1956, Part II, *Adult Reading.*

reading must be coordinated with the total school program for best results to be obtained.

The study of children's problems of a general and specific nature in reading has grown tremendously in recent years. Parts of the Eighteenth, the Twenty-fourth, the Thirty-sixth, the Forty-seventh, the Forty-eighth, and Fifty-fifth Yearbooks of the National Society for the Study of Education have been devoted to reading problems. All types of problems of reading have been investigated—problems involved in the great increase in reading done by the general public, problems of reading in the elementary school, in the secondary school, and in college, and problems of technical reading difficulties and of adult reading. Since 1925 thousands of studies have been published on reading. It is especially encouraging to find the experts in the reading problems of children turning their attention especially to the difficulty involved in the larger amount of reading required for the child in the revised curriculum of the modern school.

READING READINESS. Since Lucile Harrison's *Reading Readiness* was first published in 1936,[10] there has been a steady succession of publications which describe the factors which influence and control the pupils' readiness to read. In summary form, here are those factors, according to authorities [11] in the field of reading (without regard to any order of importance):

Mental age or maturity	Mastery of language, or linguistic
Physical maturity	maturity
Visual perception or readiness	Memory or retention span
Cultural level of child's home	Association of ideas, or readiness in
or background	the perception of relationships
Emotional stability	Informational background

[10] Boston, Houghton Mifflin Company.

[11] *Cf.* E.A. Betts, *Foundations of Reading Instruction* (rev. ed.), New York, American Book Company, 1957, Parts III and IV; Luella Cole, *The Elementary School Subjects,* New York, Rinehart and Company, 1946, Chaps. IV–VI; D.D. Durrell, *Improving Reading Instruction,* Yonkers-on-Hudson, World Book Company, 1956, Chaps. III–IV; A.J. Harris, *How to Increase Reading Ability* (3rd ed.), New York, Longmans, Green and Company, 1956, Chaps. I–III; J.L. Hymes, Jr., *Before the Child Reads,* Evanston, Row, Peterson and Company, 1958, *passim;* M. Monroe, *Growing into Reading,* Chicago, Scott, Foresman and Company, 1951, *passim;* Paul Witty, *Reading in Modern Education,* D.C. Heath and Company, 1949, Chaps. I–III; and 48th Yearbook, Part II, *op. cit.,* Chaps. II, IV, and 43rd Yearbook, Part II, 1944, *Teaching Language in the Elementary School,* National Society for the Study of Education, Chaps. III–V.

Social maturity
Interest (s)
Hearing (listening) or auditory
    readiness
Sex differences
Attitude toward reading
Self-reliance

Color discrimination
Motor skills, or manual competence
Responsiveness to books and story
    telling

The teacher should realize that the typical six-year-old has a vocabulary of from 2,500 to 5,000 words when he enters the first grade; that this vocabulary is made up partly of symbols, partly of concepts or meanings associated with objects, persons, occupations, or ideas; and that the child's readiness may have already been developed for reading, or it may have to be stimulated and developed under the direction of the teacher. Many authors of books on reading instruction and language indicate that the mastery of language (linguistic concepts) is dependent primarily upon intelligence, listening or auditory readiness, and home environment. If reading readiness has to be developed, the teacher has at hand today ample materials with which to do this, ranging from reading-readiness books and story telling to records, tape recordings, film strips, pictures, and picture-story books. The more recent books on the teaching of reading give many illustrations of how reading readiness may be fostered and developed. For our purposes here, the "comics" books will be discussed as one reading-readiness device for many different grade levels.

THE COMICS.   Books and magazines have increased in production markedly since World War II. Magazines have increased especially in number, with corresponding increases in both the number and type of the comics. Witty makes the point that one of the really significant developments of the last twenty years is the increase in popularity of the comic magazine, with its universality of appeal because of its type of presentation. With their pictures of action and with the colors which are involved, the comics appeal to the eye and to the interest of all humans, not to children alone. Therefore, any publications that use these media or forms of expression have a place in the informal education of all; especially is this true, since the reading of the comics is a favorite leisure-time activity among children of all social classes and age levels, regardless of their intelligence.[12]

1. *Definitions and History of the Comics.* The comic magazines today are misnamed; the great majority of them do not describe comic or humorous situations. A more accurate name for them would be "action comics," since most of them tell a story of action or adventure or fantasy in pictures, with accompanying words, phrases, or sentences. Many of the comics magazines started as comic strips in the newspapers, such as *Dick Tracy, Little Orphan Annie, Buck Rogers, Blondie, Mutt and Jeff,* and *Walt Disney's Comics.* The history of the various types and kinds of comic strips is found in two books, *Comics and Their Creators* [13] and *The Comics.*[14] Both books are fair and comprehensive, and both are well illustrated; taken together, they give parent, teacher, and pupil the background for a critical study of the comics.

2. *Extent of the Comic Magazine Industry.* At the close of 1956 the Comics Magazine Association of America estimated that the different titles that were active during the year sold over 600,000,000 copies. These figures are an estimate only, since precise figures are not available. Some magazines were discontinued; many appear only occasionally, for example, quarterly; new titles are continually being added.

Some of the publishers of the comics produce a series of comic magazines, edited to appeal to various age ranges. One of the best known is a group published by *Parents' Magazine.* The current series comprises four titles for different age groups: *Humpty Dumpty's Magazine for Little Children; Children's Digest; Calling All Girls* (formerly *Polly Pigtails*); and *Compact: The Teen-Age Digest.* The advisory editors for these publications have included from time to time the names of such well-known educators as Arthur T. Jersild, George Johnson, D.C. Knowlton, David S. Muzzey, and Bernice Baxter.

Another large group of some thirty different comics magazines is

[12] Witty, *op. cit.,* p. 250; Cole, *op. cit.,* pp. 120–21; *Reading in the Elementary School, op. cit.,* pp. 226–28; and Witty, *op. cit.,* pp. 37–40.
[13] By Martin Sheridan, Boston, Ralph T. Hale and Company, 1942.
[14] By Coulton Waugh, New York, The Macmillan Company, 1947.

published by the National Comics Publications, 480 Lexington Avenue, New York 17, N.Y. They are called the DC Publications, because each one has a DC round seal upon it. Their advisory editorial board has listed at various times these prominent educators: R.L. Thorndike, Lauretta Bender, Josette Frank, and W.W.D. Sones.

Some fourteen publishers produce the majority of the comic books. Those with the larger numbers also include the Dell comics, the Harvey comics, and the Classics comics (including *Classics Illustrated Junior*). Gilberton Publications, of Classics comics, also publishes illustrated stories from the Bible, such as "The Ten Commandments"; and, in cooperation with the Boy Scouts of America, publishes the "Best from Boys' Life Comics."

The publishers of these larger groups of comics magazines claim that they are prepared and edited from the viewpoint of the interests, vocabulary, and normal reading progress of children.

3. *What Information Have We from Research and Study of the Comics?* The answer is, "All too little." Since 1940, there have been probably more studies of the comics than were made in all previous years. But the number of comic magazines has increased so rapidly that the study and analysis of the comics has become a stupendous job. Dora Smith in the Forty-eighth Yearbook of the National Society for the Study of Education devoted two pages to "The Question of the Comics." [15] She presented the need for analysis of the content of the comics, the lack of adequate evidence of the effects of the comics upon individual children, the wide differences among comic magazines, the comics in a total program of reading for the child, and the need for intelligent guidance.

Luella Cole's statements still hold true: [16] (1) that the vocabulary of the comics is of the difficulty of about the fifth or sixth grades; (2) that each comic book contains approximately 10,000 words, of which about 1,000 are beyond the Thorndike Word Book's first 1,000 words; (3) that the slang in them does not exceed 5 per cent of the total reading content; (4) that most of the conversation is printed in

[15] Part II, *op. cit.*, Chap. x, pp. 226–28.
[16] *The Elementary School Subjects,* New York, Rinehart and Company, 1946, pp. 120–21.

capital letters, instead of in type; (5) that children probably learn many new words through their comics' reading; and (6) that interviews with children indicate that the comics appeal to the love of the child for adventure, mystery, excitement, sports, humor, fantasy, and desire to acquire knowledge. Paul Witty and his associates were among the earlier investigators of interests and motivation of children in the reading process. His books on reading [17] give these additional facts: (1) elementary school pupils read the comics widely; among middle grade children this is the preferred reading; (2) comic magazine reading is a major activity in lower grades, and is a favorite leisure activity, through high school; (3) the children in grades four, five, and six read regularly comic magazines, comic strips, and frequently enjoy making their own comics; (4) in the high school, comics accounted for one-fourth of the total number of magazines that were read; and (5) reading comics, looking at TV, listening to the radio, and going to the motion pictures are exciting and adventurous activities. The solution to the problem of achieving balance in the child's participation in these activities necessitates that the teacher *first* make a study of the total pattern of *each* child's interests to see what each is contributing to his development; *secondly*, the pupil should be offered a variety of good reading material, which includes ample action, adventure, suspense, surprise, and excitement.

Harris' findings [18] are similar to those of Witty and Smith. He stresses (1) that, since it is futile to try to prevent the reading of comics by children, teachers should concentrate on helping pupils establish good standards for comics, so that they themselves will discriminate between the poorer and the better ones; (2) that the better comics, such as *True Comics,* can be used to advantage in the library of the classroom; and (3) that teachers should plan consciously to lead excessive readers of the comics first into such adven-

[17] *Cf.* Paul Witty and David Kopel, *Reading and the Educative Process,* Boston, Ginn and Company, 1939, Chaps. I–II; and Paul Witty, *Reading in Modern Education,* Boston, D.C. Heath and Company, 1949, pp. 37–40; and "Some Results of Eight Yearly Studies of TV," *School and Society,* Vol. 86 (June 21, 1958), pp. 288–89.

[18] A.J. Harris, *How to Increase Reading Ability* (3rd ed.), New York, Longmans, Green and Company, 1956, pp. 472–74.

ture tales as those of Tom Swift and Tarzan, and then from those into the tales of Jules Verne, H.G. Wells, and H. Rider Haggard.

4. *A New Approach to Analysis of the Comics.* Recently, educational research has taken a little different approach to a study of the comics. This approach by three people attempted an impartial study in terms of the following questions: [19]

(1) What are the reading interests of children at various ages which we can take as standards for measurement of the content of comics magazines? (2) What other standards for magazines, books, and picture story magazines are usually set up which are good, and which we may use for judging whether the format and the art work of these picture magazines are good or not? (3) In the light of these standards which we have discovered concerning children's interests in reading and concerning good form and color for picture stories, which comic magazines of the forty-four which were examined could be approved for children? Which ones did not meet the standards? (4) Is there any way of "bridging the gap" between "comic book literature," if it might be termed such, and classics in our own literature in adventure, fantasy, mystery, and the like?

It is noteworthy that these three investigators, using rather stringent standards for these comic magazines, decided that only six of the forty-four magazines in the 1940's were found not to meet these standards.

These three investigators read and drew together what the studies of psychologists, educational psychologists, and specialists in child growth and development had shown to be the reading interests of children at various ages. There are some differences between boys and girls, especially as they grow older, but there is no need to delineate them here. Briefly summarized, these elements or types of reading material appeal most to children:

Adventure	War
Mystery	Fantasy
Heroism	Animals

[19] *Cf.* Betty Bridgeforth, "Do Comic Magazines Have Educational Values?" 1945; Thos. L. White, "A Critical Study of the Educational Values of The DC Publications," 1946; and Hatcher P. Story, "Comic Books—A Type of High School Reading in North Carolina," 1947 (unpublished Master's thesis, University of North Carolina, Chapel Hill, N.C.).

Family Life

Travel

History or Real People in History

Humor

Present World Events

Romance

Politicians

Science and Mechanics

Religion or Spiritual Aspects

Sacrifice

Morality

These seventeen types of interests are characteristic of growing children; and the studies have shown that adults find their major reading interests in these seventeen classifications, too.[20]

Hatcher Story sampled the high schools in North Carolina to discover whether any comics magazines were used in school libraries and school work. He received a representative list of replies from librarians and principals of these schools. His findings show that twenty-five different comics magazines were used in these various libraries in North Carolina to a greater or less degree. Story's study also showed that there was considerable difference of opinion among school principals and school librarians as to which magazines were valuable, and whether they should be used with regular school work.[21]

5. *"Bridging the Gap" between Comics Reading and Classics in Literature.* Of all the studies of the comic magazines, that of Story [22] perhaps contributed most to constructive suggestions for leading comics readers from their favorite comic magazines into good children's books based on the same kind of reading interest. Story was a teacher of English in high school, and he analyzed both (1) the comic books in various classifications, and (2) children's books which corresponded to the children's reading interests in these classifications. Here are examples of his suggestions for "bridging the gap": [23]

[20] *Cf.* Jean Betzner, *Exploring Literature With Children in the Elementary School,* Teachers College, Columbia University, 1943, *passim;* Guy L. Bond and Eva Bond, *Developmental Reading in High School,* New York, The Macmillan Company, 1941, Chap. VI; A.J. Harris, *How to Increase Reading Ability* (3rd ed.), *op. cit.,* Chap. XVII; A.M. Jordan, *Educational Psychology* (4th ed.), New York, Henry Holt and Company, 1956, pp. 234–45; Paul Witty and David Kopel, *Reading and the Educative Process, op. cit.,* Chap. II; and Lauretta Bender, "The Psychology of Children's Reading and the Comics," *The Journal of Educational Sociology,* XVIII (December, 1944), pp. 223–31.

[21] Hatcher P. Story, *op. cit.,* Chaps. I, IV–VII.

[22] *Ibid.,* pp. 98–109.

[23] *Loc. cit.*

FROM COMIC BOOKS CENTERED AROUND	TO GOOD CHILDREN'S BOOKS IN THE SAME CATEGORY
Animals	*Call of the Wild*, by London *White Fang*, by London *My Friend Flicka*, by O'Hara *The Yearling*, by Rawlings *Where the Blue Begins*, by Morley *Archie and Mehitabel*, by Marquis
Heroism	*Tarzan*, by Burroughs *Brave Men*, by Pyle *Up Front*, by Mauldin
Family Life	*Swiss Family Robinson*, by Wyss *The Vanishing Virginian*, by Williams *Carry Me Back*, by Williams *Little Women*, by Alcott *Little Men*, by Alcott *Heidi*, by Spyri
Romance or Home	*Seventeen*, by Tarkington *The Good Earth*, by Buck *The Scarlet Letter*, by Hawthorne *The Light That Failed*, by Kipling *Mr. Pim*, by Milne *Jane Eyre*, by Bronte
Adventure	*The Jungle Books*, by Kipling *I Married Adventure*, by Johnson *Treasure Island*, by Stevenson *Robinson Crusoe*, by Defoe *Mutiny on the Bounty*, by Nordoff & Hall *The Mysterious Island*, by Verne *Captain Blood* and *The Sea Hawk*, by Sabatini *Three Musketeers*, by Dumas
War	*Brave Men*, by Pyle *Malta Spitfire*, by Buerling and Roberts *Guadalcanal Diary*, by Tregaskis *A Bell for Adano*, by Hersey *Rabble in Arms*, by Roberts *They Were Expendable*, by White
Fantasy	*The War of the Worlds*, by Wells *When the Sleeper Awakes*, by Wells

From the Earth to the Moon, by Verne
Alice in Wonderland, by Carroll

**Mechanics and
  Science**
All About Electricity, by Knox
Man the Unknown, by Carrel

**History and Real
  People in History**
Thomas Jefferson, by Van Loon
Life of Pasteur, by Radot
Connie Mack, by Lieb
Simon Bolivar, by Waugh
Knute Rockne, by Stuhldreher
Men Against Death, by De Kruif
Up From Slavery, by Washington
Horse and Buggy Doctor, by Hertzler

Humor
Connecticut Yankee, by Clemens
  (Mark Twain)
See Here, Private Hargrove, by Hargrove
Soap Behind the Ears, by Skinner
The Iron Man and the Tin Woman, by Leacock
Jeeves, by Wodehouse
Penrod, by Tarkington
Tom Sawyer and *Huckleberry Finn,* by Clemens
  (Mark Twain)
The Egg and I, by McDonald

Mystery
Little Caesar, by Burnett
The Reader Is Warned, by Carr
Adventures of Sherlock Holmes, by Doyle

**Religion or the
  Spiritual Aspect**
The Robe, by Douglas
Magnificent Obsession, by Douglas
Poetry, by Millay

Politics
Abe Lincoln, by Sandburg

Sacrifice
A Tale of Two Cities, by Dickens

6. *What Aspects of Reading Readiness Are Found in the Comics?*
The foregoing analysis of the comics and their characteristics shows rather definitely that these "action" comic magazines possess to a greater or less degree all of these factors that influence and control the pupils' readiness to read:

Story Telling
Word Concepts
Pictures $\begin{cases} \text{action} \\ \text{still} \\ \text{color} \end{cases}$ leading to visual perception
Reading interests
Environment concepts
Charts
Memory or retention span
Association of ideas; perception of relationships
Informational background

Any medium of learning which contains as many factors as these *that relate to readiness to learn at various age- and grade-levels should be studied, analyzed, and employed by every teacher to advantage in guiding the learning and experiences of children.*

In a manner similar to this analysis of the comics and their informal and formal uses in education, the instructor should study and establish standards for use of the theatrical motion picture, the radio, TV, and other types of newsstand publications. Two of these studies of these media, those by Alice Sterner [24] and Josette Frank [25] offer further evidence of the necessity for this approach by the teacher to these informal educational agencies. Miss Sterner's report involved a careful research study of seven leisure language activities of high-school pupils. Miss Frank's pamphlet presents in form for popular reading the implications of comics, radio, TV, and movies in the informal education of children.

THE COMICS CODE.   Since 1947 there have been two controversies over whether comic magazines were harmful to the morals, ideals, habits, and growth and development of children.[26] During that time, hundreds of articles were published concerning the comics and their faults and virtues. More than half of these articles were published in

[24] *Radio, Motion Picture, and Reading Interests: A Study of High School Pupils,* Teachers College, Columbia University, 1947.

[25] *Comics, TV, Radio, Movies,* Public Affairs Pamphlet No. 148, 1957.

[26] For data on the 1947–1948 controversy and the comics code established then, see *Curriculum Principles and Social Trends* (rev. ed.), by J. Minor Gwynn, New York, The Macmillan Company, 1950, pp. 332–34. The attack on undesirable kinds of comics was led both times by Fredric Wertham, formerly senior psychiatrist for the Department of Hospitals in New York City. For a fuller exposition of his point of view, read his book, *Seduction of the Innocent,* New York, Rinehart and Company, 1953.

popular magazines, such as *Time, Newsweek,* and *The Saturday Review;* others were published in educational magazines and in the trade journals. Much misinformation, as well as some accurate information, was published in these articles.

These controversies, coupled with the fact that the publication of the comics has become a large business, led to the formation of two different organizations of the comic-magazine publishers to set up standards for good comics and to enforce them. The present organization, Comics Magazine Association of America, was set up in 1954. Since that time they have approved over 5,000 comic books. In 1958, 90 per cent of all publishers, distributors, printers, and engravers belonged to the Association and subscribed to its code. All magazines meeting the code bear the "Seal of Approval" of the Association, a seal with these words "Approved by the Comics Code Authority."

The Code completely banned all "horror" and "terror" comics and all material which may in any manner be immoral, objectionable, or in poor taste. It fosters respect for parents, police, judges, and other governmental officials. It forbids profanity, obscenity, vulgarity; it requires that females be drawn realistically "without exaggeration of any physical qualities." Advertising for the sale of knives, or realistic gun facsimiles, is prohibited, as is all questionable merchandise. Each of its forty-one provisions is a bulwark against the inclusion in comic books of any material which may be undesirable for exposure to youthful readers.[27]

READING READINESS TESTS. This section in regard to reading readiness would not be complete without samples of reading readiness tests that can be used by the educational employee as they are needed. During the last twenty-five years, psychologists and experts in child growth and development have made remarkable progress in the formulation and perfection of testing instruments for diagnostic use by the teacher. These tests have been devised primarily to help

[27] Reprinted with permission from "Facts about The Comic Code," sent to the author by Leonard Darvin, Executive Secretary. The full code can be obtained from the Association, 300 Park Ave. So., New York 10, N.Y. Teachers and parents interested in other standards for evaluating comic books can write to the Committee on Evaluation of Comic Books, Cincinnati Reports, Box No. 1486, Cincinnati, Ohio. This citizens' group has been a pioneer in evaluation for some ten years now. For some years its annual report has been printed in an issue of *Parents' Magazine.*

us to learn more about these areas of the child's life: (1) intelligence; (2) personality; (3) achievement; (4) attitudes; (5) interest(s); and (6) readiness for learning.

Samples of satisfactory tests for most of these areas have already been listed in Chapter 10. The following are typical tests of reading readiness, to be given as needed to pupils, particularly at the start of school:

Metropolitan Reading Readiness Tests
Lee-Clark Reading Readiness Tests
Stevens' Reading Readiness Tests
Marion Monroe Reading Aptitude Tests
Gates Reading Readiness Tests.

SMALL GROUPS AND COMMITTEE WORK

Attention has already been called [28] to the division of the regular grade group into smaller groups for organizational purposes, in order that the teacher may meet the group needs and differences of his pupils in better fashion. This device may be also used for another purpose in the elementary grades, particularly in grades three to eight; the teacher may divide the pupils into various groups or "committees" according to their special interests, in order that they may all contribute more effectively to one large activity or one unit of work.

For example, take "Transportation and Communication" as a unit in grade six. Certain of the children will be especially interested in ancient methods of transportation and a comparison of these with modern means. Other pupils will be equally desirous of attempting to depict by drawings or by construction projects the growth and development of transportation through the centuries. Another group will want to go more carefully and deeply into how certain modern means of transportation are established, controlled, and run. Still other children will wish to work on special aspects of communication. The wise teacher in recent years has approached the solution to this problem by dividing the children into small groups according to their special interests; these groups or "committees" are to work on

[28] Chap. 10.

certain aspects of the unit, and they are to fit those aspects into the total experience of the whole group when the culmination of the unit or center of interest is reached. This procedure develops at the same time in all of the children a fuller appreciation of the total group activity or unit.

This technique of division into small groups may be used also for the development of special skills, or for the accomplishment of remedial work with different children. Good illustrations of the various types of group activity that can be employed in the elementary school are described by the Stratemeyer group.[29]

Committee grouping as a teaching departure in the elementary school has too many possibilities for effective use to be overlooked by the teacher who is striving to improve his own work and the curriculum for his pupils. Such grouping is sound because most of the work in a real democracy is done through smaller groups or committees who report back to the whole group. In some respects, committee work is wasteful of time and is a procedure which may take more time than it appears wise to take with young children—but that is the way both life and democracy really work. It is advisable for the teacher to place the children in situations which will be similar to those which they will confront when they get out of school and into adult life.

PUPIL GUIDANCE IN THE ELEMENTARY SCHOOL

Pupil Participation in School Administration. Pupil participation in school affairs has received much attention in recent years. There is a wide variety of opinion concerning the extent to which pupil guidance and pupil participation should be employed consciously on either the elementary- or the secondary-school level. Pupil participation in school administration means that pupils take part in various school activities and help to organize and direct certain activities which go toward making the school situation and the

---

[29] Part IV, "Teachers and Learners at Work," *Developing a Curriculum for Modern Living* (2nd ed.), New York, Bureau of Publications, Teachers College, Columbia University, 1957, pp. 521–77; pp. 432–85 describe activities for a fifth grade; and pp. 616–57 present typical activities and group work in grade 10.

school community as nearly as possible like the adult situation and the adult community which the child will face later. The use of the term does not mean "self-government," nor does it mean the assumption on the part of the pupils of the discipline and management of the school. Responsibility for the control of the pupils rests primarily upon the school principal and the teachers, and this responsibility

FIG. 26   *Utilization of pupil leadership in a learning process. Learning to read*
(*Courtesy Denver Schools, Alcott School.*)

should not be transferred to the pupils. Through pupil participation in school administration in its broader sense, pupils come to have a better knowledge of the school system and what it is established for; of its organization and administration, and the limitations inherent in its framework; and of efforts and means by which their own activities may be improved and enriched within that existing framework.

GUIDANCE ASPECTS. In pupil participation in school activities, the sponsorship of the activity and the guidance of the pupils are of paramount importance. H.C. McKown [30] was the pioneer in covering rather thoroughly all of the existing practices in such activities in the elementary school, and he made suggestions of a constructive nature concerning other activities which might be stimulated and organized.

Evidence from the recent reports and practices that have already been discussed in this chapter shows that we have begun to adapt pupil activities of what used to be called an "extracurricular" nature to the needs, enthusiasms, and experiences of the child in the elementary school. Teachers used to believe that the high school was the place for these extracurricular experiences, and that they were not in existence to any marked degree on the elementary-school level. Modern teachers, however, are beginning to discover that such pupil activities have been in existence in the elementary school for some time; many schools have even incorporated extracurricular activities in their regular program as an integral part of the school program.

THE SOCIOGRAM. Since the publication of *Group Experience* [31] rapid progress has been made in the study and analysis of group processes and group interaction. Baxter and Cassidy believed (1) that the individual and the environment of the individual compose a total unit of interaction; and (2) that one's environment includes all people, events and experiences, and physiological and psychological states, past and present. They helped us to a more accurate study and understanding of individuals by (1) observation and modified case study of individuals in groups; and (2) the charting or diagramming of relationships in the groups. This chart of relationships and inter-

[30] *Activities in the Elementary School,* New York, McGraw-Hill Book Company, 1938, *passim.* In addition to McKown's book, the elementary-school teacher who desires a background of the development of guidance in the elementary school is referred to three books: H.F. Cottingham, *Guidance in Elementary Schools: Principles and Practices,* Bloomington (Ill.), McKnight and McKnight Publishing Company, 1956; E.W. and M.F. Detjen, *Elementary School Guidance,* New York, McGraw-Hill Book Company, 1952; and R.D. Willey, *Guidance in Elementary Education,* New York, Harper and Brothers, 1952. These books discuss guidance to meet physical, emotional, environmental, social, and intellectual needs; techniques of understanding children and securing information on them; guidance of the atypical; and organization for better guidance and guidance services.

[31] By Bernice Baxter and Rosalind Cassidy, New York, Harper and Brothers, 1943.

relationships has come to be known as the *sociogram*. The main purposes of the sociogram are the analysis of group structure and organization and the relationship of any one pupil to the group as a whole.[32] A teacher who understands accurately the behavior of his group can plan more effectively for both group and individual work with his class. An illustration of a sociogram will be found in Chapter 21 where the broader implications of group dynamics in curriculum-building are discussed.

TYPES OF "PUPIL-PARTICIPATION" ACTIVITIES IN THE ELEMENTARY SCHOOL. Every teacher in the elementary school should consider the following pupil activities as part of his curriculum work: the home-room organization and activities, and pupil participation in the direction of these; school clubs of one sort or another, such as the junior Red Cross, the tuberculosis and Easter seal organizations, library and museum groups, and garden clubs; the school assembly and the participation of this group in it from time to time; physical recreation and activities, such as games, play, and intramural activities among groups and grades, without the evils attendant upon interscholastic competition; [33] school trips, tours, and journeys; school camping; [34] music and dramatic activities of a creative nature; manners and courtesy and social events; training in thrift; school publications; special drives and campaigns, with the promotional events and activities which accompany them; and miscellaneous school activities of all sorts such as Eighth-Grade Day or High-School Day, cooperation with the U.D.C., the D.A.R., or the American Legion, hobby and pet exhibits and tournaments, and relations with the Parent-Teacher Association and other quasi-school organizations.

A rich field for the development of pupils along lines of their own interests and aptitudes is furnished by the stimulation and proper sponsorship of pupil activities. Closely allied to these activities is the elementary-school library, which is rapidly becoming the center

[32] *Understanding Group Behavior of Boys and Girls,* by Ruth Cunningham, *et al.,* New York, Teachers College, Columbia University, 1951, Chap. v.

[33] *Cf. Desirable Athletic Competition for Children,* Report of the Joint Committee on Athletic Competition for Children of Elementary and Junior High School Age, American Association for Health, Physical Education, and Recreation, N.E.A., 1952.

[34] *School Camping,* by John W. Gilliland, Association for Supervision and Curriculum Development, 1954.

around which worth-while teaching is being done in the elementary school. Two excellent publications have been prepared by Lucile F. Fargo on the library and the school, namely, *Activity Book, No. 2: Library Projects for Children and Young People*, and *The Library in the School*.[35] They offer suggestions for the fuller utilization of the elementary-school library; they suggest ways for the elementary-school teacher to go about stimulating his students to use the library more; and they indicate how the teacher can help to add to the resources of the library for the types of work which he is doing with his pupils. Another activity of the library can be the annual Book Fair, which exhibits new and favorite books for children.

To the uninitiated, the elementary-school newspaper is a rarity and a plaything. To the up-to-date teacher in the elementary school, such a newspaper is an activity which has developed rapidly into one of the main avenues of experience through which children learn more about written and spoken English. Through the school newspaper, pupils develop a more critical attitude toward the reading of newspapers and magazines than through any other one method that is employed today. Most school newspapers are mimeographed, although in many of the larger schools there are printing sets or presses which the children use for their publication. The newspaper in the elementary school is but another sample of the type of departure which the alert teacher is taking to enrich the curriculum for the pupils. Mimeograph paper is cheap, the experience of producing the newspaper is valuable, and through this medium children inevitably express frankly their feelings and beliefs.

MISCELLANEOUS EXPERIMENTS OF SIGNIFICANCE IN THE ELEMENTARY SCHOOL

Whether all school teachers and administrators agree with them or not, certain experiments and ideas are so thought-provoking and interest-compelling that they should be considered here. No attempt has been made to glean from the educational literature the experiments of specific types which are being carried on; on the contrary,

[35] Published in new editions from time to time by the American Library Association, Chicago.

the main purpose is to provoke further thought and planning on the part of elementary-school teachers for the education of the child.

TEACHER PROMOTION WITH THE GRADE. Newer trends in grouping in the elementary school by levels or divisions were presented in Chapter 10. Along with the trend to group all children in the first three grades into the Primary Level, for example, has come the national trend to retain the same teacher for the same group for the three primary years. This practice offers to the teacher a rich opportunity to become so familiar with every pupil in his group of some thirty persons, that he can be of maximum assistance in fuller development and growth of each child. Of course, provision in this type of organization should also be made for easy transfer of a child from one group to another when a strong personality clash develops between an occasional pupil and some particular teacher.

ECONOMIC AND CONSUMER EDUCATION. For many generations, the study of geography in the elementary school has given economics a place in the curriculum, although it would be difficult to prove whether this type of economic education ever made any difference to the child or to the society in which he lived. Under the cloak of science, industrial arts, social studies, health education, arithmetic, or allied subject areas, economic education is gaining its place in the curriculum today slowly but inevitably, in a different sense and with a different approach. One might say that consumer education is a "broad-experience area" for which the child learns through arithmetic about the family budget and how buying and selling takes place; through social studies, how public services are established and purchased by the government; and through a study of reading and the newspaper, how advertisements are necessary in order for one to know something of the manufactured products and how to evaluate the advertisements which describe and promote certain products. Whereas some experts say that adults have only recently become "consumer-conscious," the child has been consumer-conscious all of the time, and still is. How far should consumer and economic education go upon the elementary-school level? What approach should be taken to it? How can the teacher find ample and accurate materials upon which the children may base such a study and such an experience? In this connection, certain source materials are necessary for the teacher, and a certain point of view must be developed; with this in mind, the following specific references are given:

"Consumer Education Series," Units 1–10. Consumer Education Study, National Association of Secondary School Principals, 1945–1947 (for upper grades and Junior High School).

Social Education of Young Children, Kindergarten-Primary Grades (2nd rev. ed.), 1956, and *A Teacher's Guide to Economic Security for Americans*, Economic Life Series No. 3, Bulletin No. 30, 1955, both published by the National Council for the Social Studies.

SCIENCE STUDY. With the advent of new series of interesting science texts for the elementary school, the normal science interests of children are beginning to get the attention that they deserve. The range of science study now varies on different grade levels from the elementary study of foods and diet to interesting, controlled experimentation in regard to plant and animal growth. For example, science interests of the first grade include pets, trips to the farm, the dairy, and the zoo, and the manipulation of construction experiments with blocks and building materials. Seven-year-olds are interested in how people live and what they do, in seasonal changes, the heavens and the stars, rocks, simple machinery, and adaptations of animal and plant life. The eight-year-old enjoys studies of winds and weather, and simple experiments with electricity and magnets; he begins now to get knowledge of science also from books and magazines, and to revel in new experiences and in new knowledge of man and nature.

Other aspects of science and the applications of science and nature study in the elementary school include units in conservation of resources, safety education, health education, heating of homes and buildings, fire prevention, how our bodies work, disease prevention, the effects of alcohol and drugs, antiseptics, science the preserver of life, and science through the nature trail. There are ample aids to such science instruction in the form of pictures, texts, books, films, tapes, charts, and field trips.

Science is seldom taught as a separate subject in grades one to six of the elementary school. Usually the work is woven skillfully by the teacher into a type of fused unit that may take in aspects of the social studies and reading. In such teaching, it is significant that children at an early age are beginning to develop concepts in physical science. For example, the auto or truck with which the pupil plays in grade one has wheels. What do the wheels do? They go around (revolve) and make the car go. In like manner, the airplane with which the pupil works has wings. Why? What do the wings do? They help to lift the plane and keep it up, like the wings of a bird.

As a matter of fact, modern means of mass communication, such as TV and radio, prepare young children for experiences in science much further advanced than some texts offer at a particular grade level. Even some teachers do not realize how much science knowledge many young children possess today. This growth in science knowledge may force quite a few changes in the scope and sequence of the elementary science program within the next decade.[36]

CHILD STUDY OF SCHOOL BUILDINGS AND GROUNDS AND THEIR IM-PROVEMENT. The study by pupils of their school buildings and grounds is nothing new in curriculum work, but the ways in which this kind of study is developing upon a broader scale of child experience rather than upon a narrow scale of subject matter units are significant. Projects are numerous, each growing out of its own need and its own planning. The studies were broader than a mere unit on building or on improvements; each experiment involved all of the experiences and all of the problems which arose as the study was carried out. Each study included evaluation of the work by both the teacher and the pupils.[37]

FOREIGN LANGUAGES IN ELEMENTARY SCHOOL. Such teaching is not new. As long ago as 1922 foreign language teaching in the elementary grades was started on a large scale in Cleveland under E.B.

[36] Cf. "Science in the Elementary Grades," Chap. I, pp. 311–28, and "Mathematics in the Elementary Grades," Chap. II, pp. 329–42, respectively, of the *Review of Educational Research*, XXVII (October, 1957); *Conservation Experiences for Children*, U.S. Department of Health, Education and Welfare, Bulletin 1957, No. 16; *Science in the Elementary School*, Bulletin No. 12 of "What Research Says to the Teacher," Department of Classroom Teachers and American Educational Research Association, N.E.A.; and "Guideposts in Science Education: A Report on a Survey of Trends at the Elementary and Secondary Levels," by Sam S. Blanc, *The Science Teacher*, XXV (March, 1958), pp. 82–83, 109–12.

[37] *Creative Schools*, 23rd Yearbook, Department of Elementary School Principals, N.E.A., 1944, pp. 86–90; *Toward Better Teaching*, 1949 Yearbook, pp. 193–94, 195, 197, 209–10, and *Creating a Good Environment for Learning*, 1954 Yearbook, Chaps. III–IV, both published by Association for Supervision and Curriculum Development, N.E.A.

de Sauzé.[38] Following World War II, however, there has been an unusual growth; by 1956 there were programs in some 350 school systems in forty-four states and the District of Columbia. Programs start all the way from the first to the sixth grade, some continue from grade one through grade six. French and Spanish are given more frequently, though a few schools give German and Latin.

The *method* most frequently employed is the aural-oral method for teaching pupils how to speak, understand, and read a modern foreign language. The period of instruction varies in length and in number of days in the week. More emphasis is placed upon dialogue, games, songs, and activities centered around the life of the people who use the language. The in-service workshop is a favored method of preparing elementary-school teachers for this work.

In addition to Cleveland, San Diego and Los Angeles in California have operated such programs for a long time. These systems have experimented with and developed outstanding materials and courses of study.[39]

WORLD AND INTERCULTURAL UNDERSTANDINGS. As the jet and nuclear age have made world communication faster, there has been a greater need for teaching an understanding of world affairs and different cultures in our schools. This emphasis has grown in the elementary school since the end of World War II and the Korean conflict. Usually teachers have combined real study of these issues with units or larger problems fused with the interests of children. For example, one could be "The U.N. and the U.S.," another, "Ways of Living Around the World," others, "Poverty and Plenty in the World" and "The World's Value Systems." There are good materials available as resources.[40]

[38] See his article, " 'The Cleveland Plan': The Multiple Approach in Language Teaching," *The Classical Journal*, xviii (April, 1948), pp. 433–38. For an accurate summary of the status and practices in the grades, read *Foreign Language Teaching in Elementary Schools*, by Elizabeth E. Thompson and Arthur E. Hamalainen, 1958, Association for Supervision and Curriculum Development, N.E.A.

[39] *Cf.* also *The Teaching of Foreign Languages in the Elementary School*, by T. Andersson, Boston, D.C. Heath and Company, 1953, and *Teaching Spanish in the Grades*, by M.W. MacRae, Boston, Houghton Mifflin, 1957.

[40] For example, see *Introducing Children to the World*, by L.S. Kenworthy, 1957, *Teaching World Affairs in American Schools*, edited by S. Everett and C.O. Arndt, 1956, both published by Harper and Brothers, New York; and the

HOMEWORK. There is still a dearth of research on how pupils study, how effectively they study, and what conditions are most conducive to effective study. The problem is so complex, having so many factors involved, that research on it is difficult. There is still disagreement also among school personnel as to when homework in the grades should begin. Again, do pupils in small classes do more studying than those in large classes? More homework? Some light has been shed on these problems recently, which may help the teacher to set up a suitable atmosphere for study, regular study times, opportunity for independent study under supervision, and rules and principles for note-taking, outlining, and skimming and review.[41]

SHOULD THE ELEMENTARY SCHOOL BE CONCERNED WITH THESE? Some interesting experiments and studies have been made recently which pose some questions for elementary school personnel. Experiments with television in public schools (discussed more fully in Chapter 19) raise the question whether some teaching of concepts, principles, and problems cannot be done just as effectively by one teacher for large groups as for the usual smaller group of pupils. In this connection "team teaching" has been suggested by some educational leaders.[42] The pupils in each grade would remain with the homeroom teacher for one-half day devoted to reading and the language arts, and to the social studies. The rest of the day's work would be under team-teaching by specialists in mathematics, science, music, arts and crafts, health and recreation.

Recent experiments and studies of special programs for gifted children have opened up many possibilities and methods for effective teaching.[43] In this connection Paul Woodring [44] advocates a drastic

Intergroup Education publications of the American Council on Education, Washington.

[41] Read *Guided Study and Homework*, by Ruth Strang, No. 8 in the series "What Research Says to the Teacher," Department of Classroom Teachers and American Educational Research Association, N.E.A., 1955, and the special *NEA Journal* feature, "Homework," Vol. XLVI (September, 1957), pp. 365–74.

[42] *Cf.* Paul Woodring, *A Fourth of a Nation*, New York, McGraw-Hill Book Company, 1957, p. 241, and George D. Stoddard in *School and Society*, "Team-Teaching in the Grades," Vol. 86, March 1, 1958.

[43] The 57th Yearbook of the National Society for the Study of Education, Part II, *Education for the Gifted*, Section III, gives many kinds of programs that have been tried.

[44] *Op. cit.*, pp. 143–58.

reorganization of elementary education to shorten this period of schooling for the faster and more talented pupils.

Advertisements, especially on television, have made young children alert to styles in clothes and mechanical products and aware of

FIG 27   *Drill is still a part of school!*

First grade pupil checking bulletin board review. (*Courtesy Greensboro (N.C.) Public Schools, Brooks School.*)

the appeal of brands of foods and products. Shall education for wise choices in buying be expanded in the elementary grades?

Another intriguing problem for the elementary teacher is how much to try to teach children about the American system of values, about status, and emotional and social security.

In another direction some states are taking long strides, namely, in studying how to adapt the new elementary-school plant better to the newer curricular program.[45]

ARE THERE STANDARDS FOR EVALUATION OF ELEMENTARY SCHOOLS? The Cooperative Study of Secondary School Standards [46] established standards by which both local school staff and visiting experts could tell *how good a high school was, where it was weak, and in what aspects it was strong.* The Cooperative study accomplished this primarily (1) by means of an extensive number of check-list items and (2) by means of a large number of evaluations based on the answers to the check-list items.

Recent investigations have resulted in standards which can be employed to discover whether an elementary school is good or not. The most ambitious, and perhaps the most comprehensive was that evolved by the Southern Association of Colleges and Secondary Schools through its Cooperative Study in Elementary Education. Begun in 1947, the study was completed by 1952. Schools in fourteen states in 1949–1950 tried out tentative evaluative instruments, the *Elementary Evaluative Criteria* (Vols. I and II). From these were developed the final instrument, *Evaluating the Elementary School: A Guide for Cooperative Study.*[47] Basically this evaluative instrument of over 300 pages has five sections: Section A, "Viewpoint"; Section B, "Functions"; Section C, "Program"; Section D, "Resources"; and Section E, "Planning." Each school which uses these criteria first states its viewpoint and its purposes; then the curricular program of the school is evaluated in terms of these aims.

A different kind of instrument has been developed by the School of Education at Boston University, *Elementary Evaluative Criteria.*[48] These standards are patterned after the *Evaluative Criteria,* 1950 edition, and in like manner attempt to evaluate the school's program in the light of the school's particular objectives.

---

[45] *Curriculum and the Elementary School Plant,* by Helen Hefferman and Charles Bursch, Association for Supervision and Curriculum Development, N.E.A., 1958.

[46] This Study is discussed in Chapter 12.

[47] Published by the Commission on Research and Service of the Association in 1951.

[48] Boston 15, Mass., 1953.

A set of standards for the layman to use is suggested by Wilbur A. Yauch in *How Good Is Your School?* [49] It is a handbook to help parents judge how good their school is; however, more check-list items are devoted to buildings, grounds, classrooms, the teacher, and the principal than to the fundamentals of the curricular program.

It is doubtful wisdom for any school to use these types of evaluative instruments for accrediting purposes by a state or regional authority. Their real value lies in the stimulation for self-improvement that such a survey brings.

It is a fact that the public is much concerned today about the kind of school which it is getting for the money that it is spending. Whether it is possible for standards to be evolved that can be used equally effectively in all sizes of schools and types of communities is a debatable question. It is possible that all of the factors mentioned by these experimenters could be used to advantage in any evaluation of the elementary school.

SUMMARY

In spite of some rather severe attacks by a few people upon elementary education at midcentury, the curricular program of the modern elementary school continues to improve and to give evidence of promising practices in teaching.[50]

Experimental practices in curriculum work on the elementary-school level are widespread and extremely varied; this is indeed a healthy situation. Regimentation in curriculum work, as in other aspects of human existence, seldom stimulates profitable growths. Of special significance for the future are the trends toward the emphasis on child intercommunication with important aspects of his environment and with adult groups.

[49] New York, Harper and Brothers, 1951.
[50] For the main attack, that by Rudolph Flesch on the teaching of reading, turn to his *Why Johnny Can't Read—and What You Can Do About It*, New York, Harper and Brothers, 1955. For a summary of how the fundamentals are being taught and of what research reveals about this teaching, read *The Three R's in the Elementary School*, Association for Supervision and Curriculum Development, N.E.A., 1952, and *Research in the Three R's*, edited by C.W. Hunnicutt and W.G. Iverson, New York, Harper and Brothers, 1958.

PROBLEMS FOR INDIVIDUAL STUDY
AND CLASS DISCUSSION

1. Assume that next year you plan to fuse your geography and history in the sixth grade into one area of experiences for your group. Can you outline in advance the various units or activities into which you would divide the work for the first semester? Support your position.

2. Assume that your fourth grade is studying "Our Recreation and Amusements." What kind of plan would you adopt for dividing your class into groups or committees for more effective work on this?

3. What is the difference between the "core curriculum" and the "fusion" of subject areas with the experiences of children?

4. Using entirely your own ideas and various source materials, construct a unit for your grade group on "The Family"; then compare your unit with one which you find in the references suggested for you in this chapter. Upon what aspects did you do a satisfactory job? Upon which were your plans weak?

5. In what school activities should pupils participate other than the routine study of books? Why?

6. How would you go about discovering the special radio interests of your pupils? Movie interests? Reading interests? Television interests?

7. What should be your responsibility as an elementary-school teacher for the selection of books and materials for the library? Support the position which you take.

8. Assume that your children desire to produce a newspaper in your grade. What preliminary steps would you take to prepare materials and to guide this activity?

9. Assume that your state recently required by law that the evil effects of alcohol and narcotic drugs should be taught in the seventh grade. As the seventh-grade teacher, what types of activities would you take up, and would they be separate from or a part of other activities or subjects?

10. What definite aspects of consumer education should be taught in grade three? In grade six?

11. How would you as a teacher go about planning the grade's work cooperatively with your pupils? Illustrate by outlining a definite plan.

12. What guiding principles would you set up for a type of "grade-room organization" for maximum pupil participation in the activities of this small school-community group?

13. Can a teacher be mistaken in thinking that he knows what a pupil's special interests are? If so, how can he check to make sure?

14. Does teacher-pupil planning make allowance for the acquiring of those fundamental knowledges and processes which you believe that every child should get? Support your stand.

15. What standards would you as a teacher employ to evaluate a radio program? A theatrical movie? A children's book?

SPECIAL BIBLIOGRAPHY ON ELEMENTARY EDUCATION FOR THE CURRICULUM WORKER AND FOR THE ELEMENTARY TEACHER

Anderson, V.A., *Improving the Child's Speech*, New York, Oxford University Press, 1953.

Andersson, T., *The Teaching of Foreign Languages in the Elementary School*, Boston, D.C. Heath and Company, 1953.

Arbuthnot, M.H., *Children and Books*, Chicago, Scott, Foresman and Company, 1957.

Archer, C.P., *Elementary Education in Rural Areas*, New York, The Ronald Press Company, 1958.

Banks, J. H., *Learning and Teaching Arithmetic*, Boston, Allyn and Bacon, 1959.

Barr, J.A., *The Elementary Teacher and Guidance*, New York, Henry Holt and Company, 1958.

Beck, R.H. (Ed.), *The Three R's Plus: What Today's Schools Are Trying To Do—and Why*, Minneapolis, University of Minnesota Press, 1956.

Benson, K.R., *Creative Crafts for Children*, Englewood Cliffs, Prentice-Hall, 1958.

Bernard, H.W., *et al.*, *Guidance Services in Elementary Schools*, New York, Chartwell House, 1954.

Betts, E.A., *Foundations of Reading Instruction* (rev. ed.), New York, American Book Company, 1957.

Blough, G.O., and Campbell, M.H., *Making and Using Classroom Science Materials in the Elementary School*, New York, The Dryden Press, 1954.

Blough, G.O., *et al.*, *Elementary School Science and How to Teach It*, (rev. ed.), New York, The Dryden Press, 1958.

————, and A.J. Huggett, *Methods and Activities in Elementary-School Science*, New York, The Dryden Press, 1951.

Brandwein, P.F., *The Gifted Student As Future Scientist*, New York, Harcourt, Brace and Company, 1955.

Breckenridge, M.E., and Vincent, E.L., *Child Development* (3rd ed.), Philadelphia, W.B. Saunders Company, 1955.

Brogan, P., and Fox, L.K., *Helping Children Learn*, Yonkers-on-Hudson, World Book Company, 1955.

Brueckner, L.J., and Grossnickle, F.E., *How to Make Arithmetic Meaningful*, Philadelphia, the John C. Winston Company, 1947.

Bucher, C.A., and Reade, E.M., *Physical Education in the Modern Elementary School*, New York, The Macmillan Company, 1958.

Burnett, R.W., *Teaching Science in the Elementary School*, New York, Rinehart and Company, 1953.

Burrows, A.T., *Teaching Children in the Middle Grades*, Boston, D.C. Heath and Company, 1952.

Burrows, A.T., *et al.*, *They All Want to Write: Written English in The Elementary School*, New York, Prentice-Hall, Inc., 1952.

Burton, W.H., *Reading in Child Development*, Indianapolis, The Bobbs-Merrill Company, 1956.

Byrd, O.E. (Compiler), *School Health Sourcebook*, Stanford, Stanford University Press, 1955.

Cantor, N., *The Teaching-Learning Process*, New York, The Dryden Press, 1953.

Carter, H.L.J., and McGinnis, D.J., *Learning to Read: A Handbook for Teachers*, New York, McGraw-Hill Book Company, 1953.

Cassidy, R., *Curriculum Development in Physical Education*, New York, Harper and Brothers, 1954.

Caswell, H.L., and Foshay, A.W., *Education in the Elementary School* (3rd ed.), New York, American Book Company, 1957.

Causey, O.S., (Ed.), *The Reading Teacher's Reader*, New York, The Ronald Press Company, 1958.

Children in Focus: Their Health and Activity, 1954 Yearbook, American Association for Health, Physical Education, and Recreation, Washington, N.E.A.

Clark, J.R., and Eads, L.K., *Guiding Arithmetic Learning*, Yonkers-on-Hudson, World Book Company, 1954.

Cole, L., *The Elementary School Subjects*, New York, Rinehart and Company, 1946.

Cottingham, H.F., *Guidance in Elementary Schools: Principles and Practices*, Bloomington, Illinois, McKnight and McKnight Publishing Company, 1956.

Craig, G.S., *Science for The Elementary-School Teacher* (2nd ed.), Boston, Ginn and Company, 1958.

Culkin, M.L., *Teaching the Youngest*, New York, The Macmillan Company, 1949.

Cunningham, Ruth, *et al.*, *Understanding Group Behavior of Boys and Girls*, New York, Teachers College, Columbia University, 1951.

Cutts, N.E., and Moseley, N., *Better Home Discipline*, New York, Appleton-Century-Crofts, Inc., 1952.

―――, *Teaching the Bright and Gifted*, Englewood Cliffs, Prentice-Hall, Inc., 1957.

Dawson, M.A., and Bamman, H.A., *Reading in The Elementary School*, New York, Longmans, Green and Company, Inc., 1958.

Dawson, M.A., and Zollinger, M., *Guiding Language Learning*, Yonkers-on-Hudson, World Book Company, 1957.

Detjen, E.W., and Detjen, M.F., *Elementary School Guidance*, New York, McGraw-Hill Book Company, 1952.

Dolch, E.W., *Methods in Reading*, Champaign, Illinois, Garrard Press, 1955.

Durrell, D.D., *Improving Reading Instruction*, Yonkers-on-Hudson, World Book Company, 1956.

East, M., and Dale, E. (Eds.), *Display for Learning: Making and Using Visual Materials*, New York, The Dryden Press, 1952.

Elementary Evaluative Criteria, Boston, Boston University, 1953.

Erdt, M.H., *Teaching Art in the Elementary School: Child Growth Through Art Experiences*, New York, Rinehart and Company, 1954.

Freeman, K., *et al.*, *Helping Children Understand Science*, Philadelphia, the John C. Winston Company, 1954.

Gaitskell, C.D., *Children and Their Art*, New York, Harcourt, Brace and Company, 1958.

Gates, Doris, *Helping Children Discover Books*, Chicago, Science Research Associates, Inc., 1956.

Godshall, F.R., *Nutrition in the Elementary School*, New York, Harper and Brothers, 1958.

Grant, P., *Music for Elementary Schools*, New York, Appleton-Century-Crofts, 1951 (text to accompany study of materials and methods by prospective general elementary-school teacher).

Gray, Lillian, *Teaching Children to Read* (2nd ed.), New York, The Ronald Press Company, 1957.

Gray, W.C., *On Their Own in Reading*, Chicago, Scott, Foresman and Company, 1948.

Gray, W.S., and Rogers, Bernice, *Maturity in Reading*, Chicago, University of Chicago Press, 1956.

Greenlee, J., *Teaching Science to Children* and *Better Teaching Through Elementary Science*, both published by Wm. C. Brown Company, Dubuque, 1951 and 1954, respectively.

Grout, R.E., *Health Teaching in Schools* (3rd ed.), Philadelphia, W.B. Saunders Company, 1958.

Hanna, L.A., *et al.*, *Unit Teaching in the Elementary School*, New York, Rinehart and Company, 1955.

Harris, A.J., *How to Increase Reading Ability* (3rd ed.), New York, Longmans, Green and Company, Inc., 1956.

Harrison, R.H., and Gowin, L.E., *The Elementary Teacher in Action*, San Francisco, Wadsworth Publishing Company, 1958.

Hartford, E.J., *Moral Values in Public Education*, New York, Harper and Brothers, 1958.

Hatchett, E.L., and Hughes, D.H., *Teaching Language Arts in Elementary Schools*, New York, The Ronald Press Company, 1956.

Herrick, V.E., and Jacobs, L.B. (Eds.), *Children and the Language Arts,* New York, Prentice-Hall, Inc., 1955.

Heffernan, H. (Ed.), *Guiding the Young Child:* Kindergarten to Grade Three (2nd Ed.), Boston, D.C. Heath and Company, 1959.

Hester, K.B., *Teaching Every Child to Read,* New York, Harper and Brothers, 1955.

Hickerson, J.A., *Guiding Children's Arithmetic Experiences,* Englewood Cliffs, Prentice-Hall, Inc., 1952.

Hildreth, G., *Readiness for School Beginners,* Yonkers-on-Hudson, World Book Company, 1950.

————, *Teaching Spelling: A Guide to Basic Principles and Practices,* New York, Henry Holt and Company, 1955.

Hollister, G.E., and Gunderson, A.G., *Teaching Arithmetic in Grades I and II,* Boston, D.C. Heath and Company, 1954.

Huber, M.B. (Ed.), *Story and Verse for Children,* New York, The Macmillan Company, 1958.

Hubler, Clark, *Working With Children in Science,* Boston, Houghton Mifflin Company, 1957.

Huggett, A.J., and Millard, C.V., *Growth and Learning in the Elementary School,* Boston, D.C. Heath and Company, 1946.

Humphrey, J.H., *Elementary School Physical Education,* New York, Harper and Brothers, 1958.

Hunnicutt, C.W., and Iverson, W.J. (Eds.), *Research in the Three R's,* New York, Harper and Brothers, 1958.

Hymes, Jr., J.L., *A Child Development Point of View,* New York, Prentice-Hall, Inc., 1955.

————, *Behavior and Misbehavior: A Teacher's Guide to Action,* New York, Prentice-Hall, Inc., 1955.

Imhoff, M.M., *Early Elementary Education,* New York, Appleton-Century-Crofts, 1959.

Jarolimek, J., *Social Studies in Elementary Education,* New York, The Macmillan Company, 1959.

Jones, Edwina, *et al., Methods and Materials in Elementary Physical Education* (new ed.), Yonkers-on-Hudson, World Book Company, 1957.

Kearney, N.C., *Elementary School Objectives,* New York, Russell Sage Foundation, 1953.

Kellner, B.C., *How to Teach in the Elementary School,* New York, McGraw-Hill Book Company, 1958.

Klausmeier, H.J., *et al., Teaching in the Elementary School,* New York, Harper and Brothers, 1956.

Kraus, Richard, *Play Activity For Boys and Girls,* New York, McGraw-Hill Book Company, 1957.

Kyte, G.C., *The Elementary School Teacher at Work,* New York, The Dryden Press, 1957.

Lambert, Hazel M., *Teaching the Kindergarten Child,* New York, Harcourt, Brace and Company, 1958.

Lane, Howard, and Beauchamp, Mary, *Human Relations in Teaching,* New York, Prentice-Hall, Inc., 1955.

LaSalle, Dorothy, *Guidance of Children Through Physical Education* (2nd ed.), New York, The Ronald Press Company, 1957.

Laybourn, K., and Bailey, C.H., *Teaching Science to the Ordinary Pupil,* New York, Philosophical Library, 1958.

Leavitt, J.E., *Nursery-Kindergarten Education,* New York, McGraw-Hill Book Company, 1958.

Leonard, E.M., *et al., Counseling With Parents In Early Childhood Education,* New York, The Macmillan Company, 1954.

Lindsey, Margaret, and Gruhn, W.T., *Student Teaching in the Elementary School,* New York, The Ronald Press Company, 1957.

Logan, F.M., *Growth of Art in American Schools,* New York, Harper and Brothers, 1955.

Lowenfeld, V., *Your Child and His Art,* New York, The Macmillan Company, 1954.

McDonald, Blanche, *Methods That Teach,* Dubuque, Wm. C. Brown Company, 1958.

McKee, P., *The Teaching of Reading in the Elementary School,* Boston, Houghton Mifflin Company, 1948.

McKim, M.G., *Guiding Growth in Reading In the Modern Elementary School,* New York, The Macmillan Company, 1955.

McKim, M.G., *et al., Learning to Teach in the Elementary School,* New York, The Macmillan Company, 1959.

McNamee, M.B., *Reading For Understanding* (rev. ed.), New York, Rinehart and Company, 1958.

Macomber, F.G., *Principles of Teaching in the Elementary School,* New York, American Book Company, 1954.

MacRae, M.W., *Teaching Spanish in the Grades,* Boston, Houghton Mifflin Company, 1957.

Marks, J.L., and Purdy, C.R., *Teaching Arithmetic for Understanding,* New York, McGraw-Hill Book Company, 1958.

Martin, W. E., and Stendler, C. B., *Child Behavior and Development,* New York, Harcourt, Brace and Company, 1959.

Martinson, R.A., and Smallenburg, H., *Guidance in Elementary Schools,* Englewood Cliffs, Prentice-Hall, Inc., 1958.

Mathews, P.W., *You Can Teach Music,* New York, E.P. Dutton and Company, 1953.

Mehl, M.A., *et al., Teaching in Elementary School* (2nd ed.), New York, The Ronald Press Company, 1958.

Michaelis, J.U., *Social Studies for Children in a Democracy* (2nd ed.), Englewood Cliffs, Prentice-Hall, Inc., 1956.

Miel, A., and Associates, *Cooperative Procedures in Learning*, New York, Teachers College, Columbia University, 1952.

Miller, I., *et al.*, *Guidebook for Elementary Student Teachers*, Appleton-Century-Crofts, 1958.

Moffatt, M.P., and Howell, H.W., *Elementary Social Studies Instruction*, New York, Longmans, Green and Company, Inc., 1952.

Moore, S.B., and Richards, P., *Teaching in the Nursery School*, New York, Harper and Brothers, 1959.

Monroe, Marion, *Growing Into Reading*, Chicago, Scott, Foresman and Company, 1951.

Mueller, F.J., *Arithmetic: Its Structure and Concepts*, Englewood Cliffs, Prentice-Hall, Inc., 1956.

Myers, L.K., *Teaching Children Music in the Elementary School* (2nd ed.), New York, Prentice-Hall, Inc., 1956.

Nelson, L.W., and Lorbeer, G.C., *Science Activities for Elementary Children*, Dubuque, Wm. C. Brown Company, 1952.

Nesbitt, M., *A Public School for Tomorrow: A Description of the Matthew F. Maury School, Richmond, Va.*, New York, Harper and Brothers, 1953.

Nielson, N.P., and Van Hagan, W., *Physical Education for Elementary Schools*, New York, A.S. Barnes and Company, 1954.

Nye, R.E., and Bergethon, B., *Basic Music for Classroom Teachers*, Englewood Cliffs, Prentice-Hall, 1954.

Oglivie, M., *Speech in the Elementary School*, New York, McGraw-Hill Book Company, 1954.

Otto, H.J., *Social Education in Elementary Schools*, New York, Rinehart and Company, 1956.

Otto, H.J., *et al.*, *Principles of Elementary Education* (rev. ed.), New York, Rinehart and Company, 1955.

Parker, B.M., *Science Experiences: Elementary School*, Evanston, Row, Peterson and Company, 1952.

Petty, W.T., and Greene, H.A., *Developing Language Skills in the Elementary School*, Boston, Allyn and Bacon, 1959.

Preston, R.C., *Teaching Social Studies in the Elementary School*, New York, Rinehart and Company, 1958.

Roberts, C., *Teachers Guide to Word Attack: A Way to Better Reading*, New York, Harcourt, Brace and Company, 1956.

Roberts, N.H., *et al.*, *Physical Education Handbook for Elementary Teaching*, San Antonio, Texas, the Naylor Company, 1957.

Russell, K.V., *et al.*, *Developing Spelling Power*, Yonkers-on-Hudson, World Book Company, 1957.

Siks, G.B., *Creative Dramatics: An Art for Children*, New York, Harper and Brothers, 1958.

Spitzer, H.F., *The Teaching of Arithmetic* (2nd ed.), Boston, Houghton Mifflin Company, 1954.

Stendler, C.B., *Teaching in the Elementary School*, New York, Harcourt, Brace and Company, 1958.

Stokes, C.N., *Teaching the Meanings of Arithmetic*, New York, Appleton-Century-Crofts, 1951.

Stone, C.R., *Progress in Primary Reading*, St. Louis, Webster Publishing Company, 1950.

Strang, Ruth, and Bracken, D.K., *Making Better Readers*, Boston, D.C. Heath and Company, 1957.

Strickland, R.G., *The Language Arts in the Elementary School* (2nd ed.), Boston, D.C. Heath and Company, 1957.

Swain, R.L., *Understanding Arithmetic*, New York, Rinehart and Company, 1957.

Thomas, R.M., *Ways of Teaching in the Elementary School*, New York, Longmans, Green and Company, Inc., 1955.

Thralls, Z.A., *The Teaching of Geography*, New York, Appleton-Century-Crofts, Inc., 1958.

Tidyman, W.F., and Butterfield, M., *Teaching the Language Arts*, New York, McGraw-Hill Book Company, 1951.

Tinker, M.A., *Teaching Elementary Reading*, New York, Appleton-Century-Crofts, 1952.

Tooze, R., *Your Children Want to Read: A Guide for Parents and Teachers*, Englewood Cliffs, Prentice-Hall, 1957.

Tooze, R., and Krone, B.P., *Literature and Music as Resources for Social Studies*, New York, Prentice-Hall, Inc., 1955.

Van Riper, C., and Butler, K.G., *Speech in the Elementary Classroom*, New York, Harper and Brothers, 1955.

Vergara, W.E., *Science in Everyday Things*, New York, Harper and Brothers, 1958.

Walker, Herbert, *Health in the Elementary School*, New York, The Ronald Press Company, 1955.

Warner, Ruby H., *The Child and His Elementary School World*, Englewood Cliffs, Prentice-Hall, Inc., 1958.

Wesley, E.B., and Adams, M.R., *Teaching Social Studies in Elementary Schools* (rev. ed.), Boston, D.C. Heath and Company, 1952.

Wheat, H.G., *How to Teach Arithmetic*, Evanston, Row, Peterson, and Company, 1956.

Wickiser, R.L., *An Introduction to Art Education*, Yonkers-on-Hudson, World Book Company, 1957.

Willey, R.D., *Guidance in Elementary Education*, New York, Harper and Brothers, 1952.

Willgoose, C.E., *Health Education in the Elementary School*, Philadelphia, W.B. Saunders Company, 1959.

Witty, P., *How to Improve Your Reading*, Chicago, Science Research Associates, 1956.

―――, *Reading in Modern Education*, Boston, D.C. Heath and Company, 1949.

Woolf, M.D., and J.A., *Remedial Reading: Teaching and Treatment*, New York, McGraw-Hill Book Company, 1957.

Yoakam, G.A., *Basal Reading Instruction*, New York, McGraw-Hill Book Company, 1955.

PART FOUR The
secondary-school
curriculum

CHAPTER 12 The changing conception of the aims and functions of secondary education

Intensive investigation of the curriculum in the secondary schools of the United States has been under way for nearly three decades. This investigation has principally taken the form of state and national surveys and experiments, with special emphasis upon youth and its problems, its aspirations and opportunities, its growth and development, its needs, and its relation to the existing structure of the secondary school. There are sharply differing ideas of secondary education. Some educators hold the view that the existing organization of secondary education is doing a good job, and that it is capable of expansion to meet the changing needs of youth. Other educators believe that the secondary school as now organized and administered, and as its subjects are organized, is distinctly out of line with the needs of the present changing society; they maintain that the secondary school should be reorganized thoroughly, and that it should be supplemented by other types of agencies.

It has been true in the past that any secondary-school organization which did not meet the needs of youth was supplanted in time by another type of organization which seemed better fitted to meet those needs. The Latin grammar school, which was established primarily to train boys for the ministry and to which girls were not admitted, gave way during the early national period in American education to the new school known as the academy. The academy attempted to train both boys and girls and to give them an education for life as well as some preparation for college. In its turn, the academy declined and gave way to the high school, because the academy failed to meet the needs of education on a level higher than the common school.

The questions now at issue in secondary education are whether the existing structure of the secondary school can be expanded to meet the educational needs of boys and girls in society under present conditions, or whether it is to be supplanted by some or all of the educational agencies which are growing up side by side with it to meet the needs of youth. In this situation of confusion, perplexity, and indecision as to the aims and functions of the secondary school, it is necessary to take stock of two aspects: (1) the changing conception of the aims of secondary education, as exhibited in various studies and surveys; and (2) the problems peculiar to the secondary school in curriculum development.

STUDIES IN SECONDARY EDUCATION

1. *The Issues and Functions of Secondary Education, 1932–1937.* The Department (now the Association) of Secondary-School Principals of the National Education Association at its meeting in 1932 authorized the appointment of a committee for the purpose of studying and restating the principles and objectives of secondary education. After the committee had made a preliminary investigation and recommendations, the Carnegie Foundation for the Advancement of Teaching and the Department of Secondary-School Principals furnished jointly the funds for the study over a three-year period. A permanent committee was established with T.H. Briggs of Teachers College, Columbia University, as chairman. The work was completed and the findings were published by 1937. The following two significant publications grew out of the work of this committee: *The Issues of Secondary Education* (*Bulletin No. 59,* January, 1936) and *The Functions of Secondary Education* (*Bulletin No. 64,* January, 1937), both published by the Department of Secondary-School Principals of the National Education Association, Washington.

The reports on the issues and the functions of secondary education were intended to direct the thinking of secondary-school teachers and administrators toward some of the fundamental problems in the education of youth. By sampling secondary-school principals and professors of secondary education, the committee gathered a fairly representative body of opinion as to what were the issues of secondary education. The following ten *Issues* were set forth:

1. Shall secondary education be provided at public expense for all normal adolescents or only for a limited number?
2. Shall secondary education continue at public expense for all adolescents as long as they elect to attend school or be limited at the discretion of school authorities?
3. Shall secondary education be concerned only with the welfare and progress of the individual or with these as they promise a profitable contribution to the supporting social and political organizations —*i.e.*, school district, county, or state?
4. Shall secondary education provide a common curriculum or differentiated offerings?
5. Shall secondary education provide vocational education or only general education?
6. Shall secondary education primarily have in mind preparation for advanced studies or be primarily concerned with the value of its own courses regardless of the student's future academic aspirations?
7. Shall secondary education consist of unit courses usually of one year or one semester in length, each with its terminal examinations, or of interwoven courses, with periodic comprehensive examinations covering cumulative interrelated knowledge and the ability to apply it?
8. Shall secondary education seek merely adjustments of students to common life practices or the improvement of these practices?
9. Shall secondary education present merely organized knowledge or also assume responsibility for attitudes and ideals?
10. Shall secondary education be merely a part of a "gradual, continuous, unitary process" or a distinct and closely articulating part of the entire educational program with peculiarly emphasized functions of its own?

In considering these issues, it is unfortunate that they were so phrased that they mean *either* one *or* the other, because many people believe that secondary education should be concerned with *both* alternatives. For example, in Issue No. 4, many educators believe that secondary education should provide both a common curriculum and differentiated offerings; and in Issue No. 5, they believe that secondary education should give vocational training as well as general education. An analysis of this list of issues shows that there were fundamental differences of opinion in the 1930's among secondary-school principals and professors of secondary education in regard to unit courses, vocational education, general education, integration, the development of attitudes and ideals, and the gap between the education of youth in secondary school and his securing a job.

After obtaining a statement of these issues, the committee formulated the *Functions* of secondary education. These functions might be termed those purposes which the committee thought should be cared for specially by the level of secondary education, namely:

1. To continue by a definite program, though in a diminishing degree, the integration of students. This should be on an increasingly intellectual level until the desired common knowledge, appreciations, ideals, attitudes, and practices are firmly fixed.

2. To satisfy the important immediate and probable future needs of the students in so far as the maturity of the learner permits, guiding the behavior of youth in the light of increasingly remote, but always clearly perceived and appreciated, social and personal values.

3. To reveal higher activities of an increasingly differentiated type in the major fields of the racial heritage of experience and culture, their significant values for social living, the problems in them of contemporary life, the privileges and duties of each person as an individual and as a member, of social groups; to make these fields satisfying and desired by those gifted for successful achievement and to give information as to requirements for success in these fields and information as to where further training may be secured.

4. To explore higher and increasingly specialized interests, aptitudes, and capacities of students, looking toward the direction of them into avenues of study and of work for which they have manifested peculiar fitness.

5. To systematize knowledge previously acquired or being acquired in course in such ways as to show the significance both of this knowledge and especially of the laws and principles, with understanding of wider ranges of application than would otherwise be perceived.

6. To establish and to develop interests in the major fields of human activity as means to happiness, to social progress, and to continued growth.

7. To guide pupils, on the basis of exploratory and revealing courses

and of other information gathered from personnel studies, as wisely as possible into wholesome and worth-while social relationships, maximum personality adjustment, and advanced study of vocations in which they are most likely to be successful and happy.

8. To use in all courses as largely as possible methods that demand independent thought, involve the elementary principles of research, and provide intelligent and somewhat self-directed practice, individual and cooperative, in the appropriate and desirable activities of the educated person.

9. To begin and gradually to increase differentiated education on the evidence of capacity, aptitudes, and interests demonstrated in earlier years. Care must be taken to provide previous to and along with differentiation as balanced and extended a general education as is possible and profitable.

10. To retain each student until the law of diminishing returns begins to operate, or until he is ready for more independent study in a higher institution; and when it is manifest that he cannot or will not materially profit from further study of what can be offered, to eliminate him promptly, as wisely as possible directing him into some other school or into work for which he seems most fit.

As broad and general as these suggested functions were twenty years ago, they illustrate clearly the type of compromise which is still going on in the secondary school in regard to its purposes and its curricula. In effect, these functions recommend the following: (1) the continuation of general education and the introduction of differentiated education; (2) education both for the present and for the future of youth; (3) special attention to the gifted person; (4) the exploration and guidance of pupils along the lines of their specialized interests, aptitudes, and capacities; (5) emphasis on problem solving and systematic thinking; (6) assisting pupils in wholesome and worthwhile social relationships, personality adjustments, and life ambitions; and (7) connecting the school in as effective a way as possible with other agencies which may take care of certain needs of youth, if the secondary school as regularly organized is unable to do so.

Like the issues formulated by the same group, this list of functions called attention sharply to certain areas in the training of youth in which the organization of the secondary school had been deficient. The practical ways in which educators can go about remedying these deficiencies have in part been explored by this same national group in its later studies on guidance, counseling, promising practices in secondary education, and the occupational adjustment of youth.[1]

The investigation by the Department of Secondary-School Principals of the issues and functions of secondary education had significance for the curriculum. In the first place, this group led the way in being willing to make a serious study of its own organization and curriculum. Secondly, its studies caused many of the teaching personnel of the secondary school to stop and consider what they were doing, and whether they were doing for youth what should be done. Its work gave impetus to several other studies which accompanied or have followed its investigations.

2. *The National Survey of Secondary Education, 1928–1933.* The idea of making a survey of secondary education in the United States was initiated by the North Central Association of Colleges and Secondary Schools in 1928. The idea was adopted by the United States Office of Education, and the survey was carried out under the auspices of this office, with Leonard V. Koos as the active director of the survey. The findings were published in 1933 as *Bulletin No. 17, 1932, The National Survey of Secondary Education,* Monographs Nos. 1–28. The survey included various aspects of secondary education, *e.g.:* organization; population; reorganization; legal provisions; articulation; administration and supervision; selection and appointment of teachers; provisions for individual differences; programs of guidance, research, and public relations; the secondary-school library; and the subject-matter fields in the secondary-school curriculum.

Although this survey was centered primarily around reorganized secondary schools, there were certain general implications for the curriculum. Five hundred and fifty schools in forty-one states and the District of Columbia were selected for the study—schools which were engaged in outstanding practices in their work. An intensive examination of these practices was made, including visitation of the schools, and the resultant information was then tabulated and di-

---

[1] Consult the *Bulletin of the National Association of Secondary-School Principals,* 1939–1948, *passim,* for a list of these studies, conducted primarily by the Implementation Committee of the Association of Secondary-School Principals.

gested. The following findings of the survey were significant for curriculum study:

1. The large-scale comparison of selected small high schools with unselected small schools showed that small unselected high schools could be much better than they are through administrative leadership.

2. The study of state control of secondary schools as to legal and regulatory provisions brought the recommendation that there should be fewer regulatory and statutory provisions: and that the discretionary powers of state school officials should be extended in order that more flexible and adaptable programs in secondary schools could be experimented with.

3. The trend in institutions of higher education was toward an increase in the number of ways by which students might gain admission to college, and toward the improvement of the articulation between secondary school and college through studying the problems of more favorable adjustment.

4. A great confusion of terminology existed in the plan characterized by the "unit" assignment; it was confused variously with the project, the problem, the differentiated assignment, the long-unit assignment, the contract method, the laboratory method, individualized instruction, the Winnetka technique, the Dalton plan, the Morrison plan, or modifications of the last-named three.

5. In programs of curriculum revision, school authorities expressed the belief that the professional growth of teachers is particularly the one thing of greatest benefit.

6. A consideration of curriculum trends led to the conclusion that advocates of curriculum reform typically would approve the *scope* and *direction* of the changes being made, but would be impatient at the *rate* of change.

7. At the junior-high-school level, offerings showed a marked tendency toward "general" courses and away from special aspects of different subject-matter groups, especially in general mathematics, English, social studies, and science. The senior high school was less affected by this trend.

8. Homogeneous groupings, special classes for gifted and slow pupils, and classes characterized by the unit plan were three unifying elements in a typically successful program to provide for individual differences.

9. The prediction was made that the school library will soon be one of the central features of modern secondary education, on the basis of the provisions and practices found in schools with outstanding library service.

Monographs Nos. 18–28 of this survey were devoted to procedures in curriculum-making; the program of studies; and instruction in the individual subject-matter fields of English, the social studies, science, mathematics, foreign language, music and art, extracurricular activities and interscholastic activities, and health and physical education.

Antedating by four years the study of the Department of Secondary-School Principals on Issues and Functions, the National Survey of Secondary Education had a different purpose. The *Survey* tried to discover where we were in secondary education by an examination of those secondary schools which seemed to have promise as being outstanding in their practices and provisions; the *Issues* and *Functions*, on the other hand, were an attempt to discover where the philosophy of secondary education stood in relation to its practices. Both approaches are valuable and necessary for the curriculum worker.

3. *The Progressive Education Association's Eight-Year Experimental Study of Secondary Education, 1933–1941.* The Commission on the Relation of School and College of the Progressive Education Association was established in 1930. After careful planning and study, this commission submitted to certain representative colleges in 1932 a proposal for an experimental study to be carried on over a period of eight years. The plan provided that a small group of secondary schools throughout the country should be permitted by these colleges to engage in experimental work; the graduates of these schools would be accepted by the colleges for a period of five years beginning in 1936, without regard to the traditional course and unit requirements or entrance examinations generally required for all students. Almost all of the colleges agreed to admit candidates from these experimental schools on the bases of the statement of the principal of the school, a careful history of the student's school activities, life, and interests, and the results of various types of examinations and scores on scholastic, aptitude, and other diagnostic tests given to him throughout his course in secondary school. More than 250 American colleges and universities approved the plan and gave their official cooperation to the schools engaging in the study.[2]

[2] The participating secondary schools in this study were as follows: Altoona Senior High School, Altoona, Pa.; the Baldwin School, Bryn Mawr, Pa.; Beaver

By 1941, approximately 10,000 graduates from the thirty schools had been admitted to these 250 colleges. About 1,500 of these graduates from the experimental schools were studied carefully over a period of five years by a competent staff of four men chosen from college faculties. The first class in the Eight-Year Study entered college in September, 1936, and graduated in June, 1940. The fifth class began their college careers in September, 1940. Various types of higher institutions are represented in the study—men's colleges, women's colleges, private institutions, state universities, and coeducational institutions.

The study involved a comparison of the 1,500 graduates of experimental schools with the graduates of traditional secondary schools which prescribed a definite number of units of credit in specified courses for entrance to college. In order to make a valid comparison, each experimental-school graduate of the study was matched with another graduate from a traditional secondary school who was of the same sex, age, home and community background, scholastic aptitude, and vocational preference, in so far as possible. The graduates of the traditional schools had followed the general pattern of subjects usually prescribed for admission to the different colleges. The following interesting results of the study were reported by the chairman: [3]

Country Day School, Chestnut Hill, Mass.; Bronxville High School, Bronxville, N.Y.; Cheltingham Township High School, Elkins Park, Pa.; Dalton Schools, N.Y.; Denver Junior and Senior High Schools, Denver, Colo.; Des Moines Senior and Junior High Schools, Des Moines, Ia.; Eagle Rock High School, Los Angeles, Calif.; Fieldston School, N.Y.; Francis W. Parker School, Chicago, Ill.; Friends Central School, Overbrook, Pa.; George School, Pa.; Germantown Friends School, Germantown, Pa.; Horace Mann School, N.Y.; John Burroughs School, Clayton, Mo.; Lincoln School of Teachers College, N.Y.; Milton Academy, Milton, Mass.; New Trier Township High School, Winnetka, Ill.; North Shore Country Day School, Winnetka, Ill.; Pelham Manor High School, Pelham Manor, N.Y.; Radnor High School, Wayne, Pa.; Shaker Heights Senior High School, Shaker Heights, O.; Tower Hill School, Wilmington, Del.; Tulsa Senior and Junior High Schools, Tulsa, Okla.; University High School, Chicago, Ill.; University High School, Oakland, Calif.; University School, Columbus, O.; Winsor School, Boston, Mass.; Wisconsin High School, Madison, Wis. From this list it is seen that the thirty school *systems* actually comprised some *sixty* different schools, both public and private.

[3] *Cf.* "Adventure in American Education Series," New York, Harper and Brothers: Vol. i, 1942, *The Story of the Eight-Year Study with Conclusions and Recommendations,* by W.M. Aikin; Vol. ii, 1942, *Exploring the Curriculum,* by H.H. Giles, *et al.*; Vol. iii, 1942, *Appraising and Recording Student Progress*

1. On the basis of grades, students from the thirty schools did fully as well as those with whom they were compared except in foreign languages. Whatever difference there was in grades was in favor of the students in the study, but the difference might not be statistically significant.

2. The students from the six schools which departed most markedly from the conventional curriculum made decidedly better grades than their matchees.

3. Forty-six students who had no mathematics in the secondary school beyond the ninth grade did better than their matchees in all subjects, including mathematics.

4. There was no discoverable relationship between the pattern of subjects taken in school and student success in college.

5. The evidence indicated clearly that if the secondary school knows its students well, counsels them wisely, gives them, in and out of the classroom, experiences which promote their growth and meet their needs, those who go on to college will do well.

6. Without competence in the use of the English language in reading, speaking, and writing, the student cannot do college work satisfactorily. This is the one ability clearly essential, but conventional secondary-school English courses seldom develop that ability fully.

The achievements of these graduates from the experimental schools in terms of other than scholastic records were also reported upon by the special college staff. Here the results of this controlled experiment indicated that: (1) the graduates from the thirty experimental schools liked and participated more freely in a wider range of organized campus activities than graduates from the other secondary schools; (2) they were more active in intellectual hobbies, creative and appreciative experiences, and strictly social pastimes; (3) they were able to organize their time better; (4) they listened to more worthwhile radio programs; (5) they read more widely; (6) they felt more frequently a lack of preparation in English composition; and (7) in general, they showed themselves well prepared for success in their college pursuits.

There has been remarkably little criticism [4] of the Study when one

by E.R. Smith, R.W. Tyler, *et al.;* Vol. IV, 1942, *Did They Succeed in College?* by Dean Chamberlain, *et al.;* and Vol. V, 1943, *Thirty Schools Tell Their Story.*

[4] *Cf. School and Society,* W.H. Lancelot, "A Close-up of the Eight-Year Study," LVIII (December, 1943), pp. 449–51, and "The Eight-Year Study Still Awaits Fair Appraisal," LXII (November, 1945), pp. 281–82; H.G. Johnson,

considers its magnitude and the significance of its implications. Thirty schools were given a free rein to modify the types of curricula to which they should expose their students, and at least six of these changed their curricula so radically that in many respects the matter studied departed broadly from the traditional pattern of subject-matter areas and courses for college entrance. *Yet the graduates of these six schools seem to have done just as well scholastically in college as the graduates of those schools where the traditional curriculum still held sway, and where the students took the regular college preparatory courses in number of units and amount of work. One significant fact established as a result of the Eight-Year Study is that radical changes in the curriculum of the secondary school do not hinder the success of its graduates in their college work.* The secondary schools can be trusted to formulate new curricula satisfactory for college preparatory students, whether they know what constitutes student success in college or not.

The Eight-Year Study has also had a tremendous influence upon the secondary-school curriculum in another direction. From it, an improved program developed for the in-service training of teachers, to prepare them to experiment successfully with the curricula in these thirty schools without harm to the students under their charge. Soon after the Commission of the Progressive Education Association received the approval of the colleges and the secondary schools concerned, and the program was put into effect, serious limitations to the Study arose because of the lack of training among teachers for the experimental work. Faced with this situation, the commission used some of the funds granted to it for the Study in the establishment of Summer Workshops. These workshops were of six or more weeks in length, and they were instituted at first only for the teachers of those schools which were engaged in the Eight-Year Study. Groups of teachers from the various schools would come to the work-

"Weakness in the Eight-Year Study," LXIII (June 15, 1946), pp. 417–19; G.E. Jensen, "Basic Questions for an Evaluation of the Eight-Year Study," LXIV (November 16, 1946), pp. 348–50; R.W. Tyler, "A Comment on Professor Lancelot's Criticism of the Eight-Year Study," LIX (June 3, 1944), p. 396; *Curriculum Journal,* C.O. Houle, "Evaluation in the Eight-Year Study," XIV (January, 1943), pp. 18–21; *School Review,* "The Story of the Eight-Year Study," L (May, 1942), pp. 326–28; and *Time,* "Tomorrow's High School," XXXIX (February 16, 1942), pp. 53–54.

shops with the problems upon which they wanted to work during the summer, in order that they might successfully introduce new procedures to their pupils during the regular term. The implications of this workshop procedure for the better training of teachers in service are great. These implications will be discussed more fully in Chapter 17, where the relation of teacher training to the curriculum is considered.

4. *The Southern Study, 1938–1945.* Stimulated by the Eight-Year Study of the Progressive Education Association, the Association of Colleges and Secondary Schools of the Southern States requested and received financial assistance from the General Education Board in 1937 for an experimental study of a somewhat similar nature to be carried on in selected secondary schools of eleven southern states, three from each state.[5] In general, the same procedures as in the Eight-Year Study seem to have been followed by these schools, both in their experimental programs and in their summer workshops for the teachers in the participating secondary schools. Perhaps because their program was interrupted by the war, the findings of the Southern Study were not so clear-cut and significant as the results of the Eight-Year Study. Contributions of the study lay more in the successful development of programs for individual schools than in contributions which were applicable to all schools.[6]

[5] Participating schools were: *Alabama,* Tuscaloosa, Montevallo, and Holtsville High of Deatsville; *Florida,* Dixie County at Cross City, Miama Beach, and St. Petersburg; *Georgia,* University Demonstration School at Athens, Moultrie, and Peabody Training School at Millegeville; *Kentucky,* Frankfort, Lafayette at Lexington, and Benham; *Louisiana,* Campti, Minden, and E.E. Lyon at Covington; *Mississippi,* Canton, Okolona, and Meridian; *North Carolina,* Goldsboro, Greenville, and Lee Edwards High of Asheville; *South Carolina,* Sumter, Dreher of Columbia, and Parker of Greenville; *Tennessee,* Norris, Colliersville, and Peabody Demonstration School at Nashville; *Texas,* Edinburg, Highland Park at Dallas, and Thomas Jefferson at Port Arthur; *Virginia,* Waynesboro, Radford, and Cradock of Portsmouth, Frank C. Jenkins, Wesley Hall, Nashville, Tenn., was the coordinator for the Commission of the Association in its experimental work. The official report is *The Southern Study: Cooperative Study for the Improvement of Education,* prepared by F.C. Jenkins, *et al.,* Durham, Duke University Press, 1947 (reprinted from the *Southern Association Quarterly,* x, February and August, 1946).

[6] Reports of individual schools present good samples of the results of the Study. The official report in 1948 on later developments in this Study is contained in *Proceedings of the Fifty-third Annual Meeting of the Southern Association of Colleges and Secondary Schools,* Memphis, December, 1948, pp. 187–206, "What Has Happened in the Southern Study Schools," by Ellis F. Hartford.

5. *The Cooperative Study of Secondary School Standards, 1933–1939, 1950.* The various regional associations of colleges and secondary schools have had a powerful influence upon the development of secondary education since the turn of the present century. They have been effective agencies in establishing and maintaining high standards of teacher preparation, in improving the curriculum, buildings and equipment, library service, and teaching conditions, and in the standardization of secondary schools. Each of these associations has a Commission on Secondary Schools representing the viewpoints of both the colleges and the secondary schools. After preliminary work from 1928 to 1933, a conference of representatives of the six regional associations in the United States drew up proposals for a "Cooperative Study of Secondary School Standards and Accrediting Procedures." They outlined a plan of organization for the study, with the following purposes in view:

1. What are the characteristics of a good secondary school?
2. What practicable means and methods may be employed to evaluate the effectiveness of a school in terms of its objectives?
3. By what means and processes does a good school develop into a better one?
4. How can regional associations stimulate secondary schools to continuous growth? [7]

All of the regional associations of colleges and secondary schools cooperated in this study, namely, the New England Association, the Middle States Association, the North Central Association, the Southern Association, the Northwest Association, and the Western Association. Monetary grants from the General Education Board made possible a careful study of an experimental nature. An administrative committee carried on from 1933 to 1935, when it was deemed wise to obtain a coordinator and to open a main office in Washington for the work. W.C. Eells was selected to coordinate the study, and other specialists were engaged to assist him in carrying it out. From 1934 to 1936 the time was spent in a careful examination of the areas in which standards or criteria seemed desirable. During the second period of the study, 1936–1937, more than 200 secondary schools of

---

[7] *How to Evaluate a Secondary School,* 1940 edition, Cooperative Study of Secondary School Standards, 1939, p. 1.

a wide variety of types were invited to participate in the trial program and were visited by the four committees established for that purpose; these schools included both private and public, large and small, urban and rural, accredited and nonaccredited. During 1937–1938 the interpretation of the work of the Cooperative Study to the educational public was carried on. At the same time, the research specialists were tabulating the trial data on the standards which had been established and used in the 200 cooperating experimental schools. The first edition of the standards which had been worked out was called *Evaluative Criteria*, and it was published in 1938. As these criteria were used and tried out more fully, the administrative committee felt that the results were not yet satisfactory in certain areas, so further experiments were carried on in those areas. Following this, a revision of *Evaluative Criteria* appeared in 1939, called the 1940 Edition; this edition was revised again in 1950. Originally the Cooperative Study sent out trained field workers to give assistance to the states and the associations when they began trying out these standards in their schools.

The publications of the Cooperative Study, and the criteria which have been formulated, involve practically all aspects of the secondary school. These aspects include the philosophy and objectives in terms of the needs of youth, the pupil population and the school community, the curriculum and courses of study, the pupil activity program, library services, guidance services, instruction, the outcomes of the educational program, the school plant, and school administration.[8]

The sections of the *Evaluative Criteria* which are of special importance to the curriculum are Section C on philosophy and objectives, in terms of the "Educational Needs of Youth," and Sections D to D-16 on "Educational Program: Program of Studies." All activities and work of a particular secondary school are supposed to be evaluated according to the philosophy and objectives of that school as they have been determined cooperatively by the faculty and

---

[8] The full list of publications is as follows: *Evaluation of Secondary Schools, General Report*, 1939; *Evaluation of Secondary Schools: Supplementary Reprints*, 1939; *Evaluative Criteria and Educational Temperatures*, 1939; *How to Evaluate a Secondary School*, 1939 (1940 editions); and *Evaluative Criteria* (1950 edition). The next edition is planned for 1960.

administration. Each section of the *Criteria* contains certain check-list items which are statements of opinion upon aspects which the Cooperative Study deems vital to schools and their programs; each section is supposed to have at least four or five evaluations from different individuals, so that a clear view may be obtained of con-flicting opinions or of opinions which agree. No school can be evalu-ated impartially, even by the use of these extensive standards and check-lists, unless it has outside evaluators come in to pass judgment.

The main purpose of these *Criteria* is that the individual secondary school use them to discover *where it is* in regard to its program, curriculum, activities, plant, administration, supervision, and teach-ing personnel. The use of them for any other purpose, such as accrediting schools in the regional associations or attempting to find out where an individual high school stands in comparison with some others, is questionable.

Section D of the *Evaluative Criteria*, "Program of Studies," is a good example of the materials in the Cooperative Study which are valuable in curriculum work. This section has a brief statement of "guiding principles," followed by check-lists of from fifteen to twenty-three items on "General Principles and Curriculum Develop-ment." There is a page devoted to the *extent* of offerings in the curriculum; another page is devoted to the *content* of the offerings and the program in existence; two pages inquire into the *general outcomes* of the program of studies; and one page is prepared for listing the *special characteristics* of the curriculum and courses of study, on which questions are asked as to what are the best elements, which are least adequate, in what respects the curriculum and courses of study have been improved recently, and what studies of the curriculum are being made now.

If used properly, the two sections of the *Evaluative Criteria* on the philosophy and objectives and on the curriculum and the outcomes of instruction can be as valuable to a corps of secondary-school teachers as any work which they might undertake for a year or more in a cooperative study of the curriculum of their school. For this proper use, the following procedures must be followed: (1) The school's philosophy and objectives (Section C) must be formulated cooperatively, as well as checked individually by each member of the faculty, before any of the other sections concerned with the program of studies can be evaluated properly. (2) At least three individual evaluations and checkings without collaboration must be done by people in the school in a position to know something about the aspects of the program; and at least three evaluations from educational experts not connected with the school must be secured and used along with the evaluations made by the staff of the school itself. (3) Those engaged in the evaluation must understand the limitations of a technique which attempts to turn subjective judgments into figures which may be used statistically, a procedure which is practically impossible; but the subjective judgments alone will be enough to show a school where it stands, its strong points and its weak points, if a fair sampling of various opinions has been secured.

    6. *The Youth Commission of the American Council on Education,* 1935–1943. Through a different kind of approach, the American Youth Commission made its own peculiar contribution to the study  of the secondary-school curriculum. Established in 1935 by the American Council on Education to conduct a full investigation of the problems facing youth in this country, the commission finished its work in 1943. Its investigations and publications have been of value to the high-school teacher in the following ways: (1) they provided well-sampled, accurate studies of young people, their work, their problems, and their life; and (2) in the light of these comprehensive studies, further suggestions were made as to how the school through its curriculum may adapt its program to meet the needs and problems of youth today. The youth problem and the work of the American Youth Commission will be described more fully in Chapter 16.

When the American Youth Commission started its work in the depths of the business depression of the 1930's, it was considered wise to tackle the problems of youth and the unemployment situation immediately. As its work progressed through the years, the commission realized that to find out merely that certain problems of youth were not being studied or met was not sufficient—it was necessary also to make investigations to determine what adjustments could be made, and how the problems and needs of youth could be met. In making studies of possible adjustments for youth, the commission has really opened up an area needing further investigation, namely, the area concerned with the growth and development of the adolescent in the actual situations in which he is. Folsom's study on *Youth, Family and Education* was one of this type, as were many of the studies of Negro youth which were published by the commission.

The three contributions of the American Youth Commission to the secondary-school curriculum have been: (1) factual material which shows that the secondary school is not meeting enough of the needs of youth in training them for life and for making a living; (2) evidence that the public in general, as well as school administrators and teachers, have not been giving this problem enough thought; and (3) recommendations that concerted action should be taken by all agencies, including the school, in order to solve the problems of youth and to make them realize that their future is of supreme import to the country as well as to themselves.

7. *The Commissions on Secondary School Curriculum and on Human Relations of the Progressive Education Association, 1932– 1942.* An exploratory step in a new direction was made by these two commissions and by certain special committees of the Progressive Education Association. The Commission on Human Relations was established for the specific purpose of assisting young people with their personal and social problems. The Commission on Secondary School Curriculum was appointed frankly with a new purpose in view, namely, that of reorganizing secondary education in the light of the meaning and function of progressive education on the level of the secondary school; it was to survey the problems that might arise as connected with such a proposal.

The Commission on Secondary School Curriculum prepared and published two significant types of suggestive and vital material: (1) studies grouped around "general education" in the secondary school; and (2) studies of the adolescents who make up the secondary-school population. Its published studies comprised the following:

GENERAL EDUCATION

Language in General Education, 1940.
Mathematics in General Education, 1940.

Reader's Guide to Prose Fiction: Bibliographies of 1500 Novels, by Elbert Lenrow, 1940.

Reorganizing Secondary Education, by V.T. Thayer, C.B. Zachry, and Ruth Kotinsky, 1939.

Science in General Education, 1938.

The Social Studies in General Education, 1940.

Teaching Creative Writing, by L.H. Conrad, 1937.

The Visual Arts in General Education, 1940.

STUDIES OF ADOLESCENTS

Emotion and Conduct in Adolescence, by C.B. Zachry and Margaret Lighty, 1940.

The Adolescent Personality: A Study of Individual Behavior, by Peter Blos, 1941.

The following are some of the studies which were prepared and published by the Commission on Human Relations:

Life and Growth, by Alice V. Keliher, 1938.

The Family: Past and Present, by B.J. Stern, 1938.

An examination of these volumes reveals the fact that these two commissions of the Progressive Education Association discovered that it was impossible to study the curriculum without studying the adolescent for whom the curriculum is established. The titles by Zachry and Blos of the Commission on Secondary School Curriculum really belong in the field of Human Relations, just as those two by Stern and Keliher belong properly with a study of the secondary-school curriculum.

Another publication by the Committee on Workshops of the Progressive Education Association, although prepared primarily for the Eight-Year Study, belongs rightly, by virtue of its contents, with this group of studies of adolescents. It is:

The Personal-Social Development of Boys and Girls with Implications for Secondary Education, by L.H. Meek (Chairman), *et al.,* 1940.

8. *The Regents' Inquiry into the Character and Cost of Public Education in the State of New York, 1935–1939.* The Inquiry was organized late in 1935 to examine the educational enterprise of the State of New York and to analyze its methods, costs, and outcomes; it was to undertake a critical review of the work which was under way in the schools. In addition, it was to consider policies and pro-

grams for dealing with pressing problems and issues and recommend long-range objectives for the state school system. The Regents' Committee was primarily interested in ". . . isolating major issues and in hammering away at the problems which presented themselves in order to find a reasonable comprehensive solution which would commend itself to the forward-minded people of the State of New York." [9] Most of the publications of the Inquiry were limited to those staff studies which bore directly upon secondary education. Curriculum workers find the following reports [10] of value:

High School and Life, by Francis T. Spaulding, 1938.
Motion Pictures and Radio: Modern Techniques for Education, by Elizabeth Laine, 1938.
When Youth Leave School, by Ruth E. Eckert and Thomas O. Marshall, 1938.
School and Community: A Study of the Demographic and Economic Background of Education in the State of New York, by Julius B. Maller, 1938.
Education for Work, by Thomas L. Norton, 1938.
Education for Citizenship, by Howard E. Wilson, 1938.

The significance of these studies on a statewide scale lies primarily in the attempt of the educational authorities concerned to discover the exact situation, purposes, and progress of their school system. On the secondary-school level, for example, one of the problems studied was the hampering effects of the Regents' examination system upon school curricula, from the standpoints both of difficulty of change and of strict adherence to textbook and rote teaching. Another problem involved vocational education on an extensive and highly technical scale; the Inquiry concluded that making provision for such specialized vocational training was not so much the duty of the secondary school as of the secondary school in cooperation with other agencies of the community and of industry. The Regents' Reports showed clearly that the secondary-school curriculum is much broader than the mere curricular subjects or subject areas which are being taught; they showed that the curriculum includes also the effect of motion pictures and the radio, citizenship and

---

[9] *High School and Life: Report of the Regents' Inquiry,* by F.T. Spaulding, New York, McGraw-Hill Book Company, 1938, pp. ix–x.
[10] All published by the McGraw-Hill Book Company.

social problems, education and preparation for life's work, the problems of youth when they leave school, and the school and its relation to the community.

9. *Education for All American Youth, 1944, and Education for All American Youth—A Further Look, 1952.*[11] This study of the Educational Policies Commission is the story of the school systems in two fictitious communities, Farmville and American City, U.S.A. These two communities were regarded as typical of all American communities. The details of organization and program are presented as models or samples, rather than as definite plans to be used in actual school systems. It was hoped by the Commission that the descriptions would stimulate and aid in the planning and action which were already under way in many communities and states. Many of the plans discussed are departures from common practices in schools, such as (1) the extension of the public school to fourteen grades, which would include nursery school, kindergarten, elementary and secondary school; and (2) the establishment of a free public community institute to offer continued general education and vocational training for youth who want to prepare for occupations requiring limited training beyond the senior secondary school.

The Commission proposed that the goals of secondary education be established in terms of *ten imperative needs of youth.*[12] Table 21 lists these ten "imperative educational needs" and compares them with the aims or functions of secondary education as they have been formulated by various groups or individuals from 1918 to 1952. The most significant conclusion to be drawn from this table is that there has been little fundamental change in the purposes of secondary education during the last forty years. Regardless of whether these

[11] The 1952 edition adds no fundamental changes to the concepts presented in 1944, though it adds discussions of problems and issues currently important to American secondary education.

[12] Summarized from *Education for All American Youth,* Educational Policies Commission, 1944 and 1952. Table 21 is adapted from data in: *Education For All American Youth; Cardinal Principles of Secondary Education, Bulletin No. 35,* 1918, United States Bureau of Education; *Principles of Secondary Education,* by Alexander Inglis, Boston, Houghton Mifflin Company, 1918; *Issues and Functions of Secondary Education, ante,* pp. 359–61; *The Purposes of Education in American Democracy,* Educational Policies Commission, 1938; and *Reorganizing Secondary Education,* by V.T. Thayer, *et al.,* New York, D. Appleton-Century Company, 1939, Chaps. IV–IX.

purposes were expressed in terms of the activities of normal individuals, of issues and functions, of principles and objectives, or of the needs of youth, there have been only two actual additions to these purposes in the 1944 and 1952 pronouncement of the Educational Policies Commission; these two new ones are (1) opportunity to develop creative urges and (2) opportunity to develop scientific understanding of the world and man. The need of youth to learn how to become an intelligent consumer was expressed in 1918 by Alexander Inglis in his "economic-vocational" aim. Another significant contribution is that the Commission frankly hoped that their suggestions about the curriculum for these two fictitious communities would stimulate the complete reorganization of the secondary-school curriculum which is under way in the United States.

10. *The Secondary School Study, 1940–1947.* In 1940, the Commission on Secondary Schools of the Association of Colleges and Secondary Schools for Negroes requested and received a grant from the General Education Board for a service study of Negro high schools in the South.[13] During the first three years of the Study, an intensive cooperative study with a selected group of sixteen high schools was conducted. Each of the schools was free to organize in its own way. Visiting consultants were available to the schools; a rich collection of professional materials was distributed to the teachers and principals. In the summers, workshops were held in the region in cooperation with the various colleges; these afforded teachers and principals the opportunity to do more detailed planning and wide reading.

After the Study had gotten under way, the Commission realized that the progress made in the few schools could not influence all schools throughout the region. Thus, efforts were made to extend the Study to other high schools. The colleges of the region aided the Commission in identifying pressing problems of the high schools. During the last years of the Study, principals and teachers wrote up

[13] W. Carson Ryan, J. Minor Gwynn, and A.K. King (Eds.), *Secondary Education in the South*, "Experimental Programs in the Southern Association," by V.M. Sims, E.A. Waters, and W.A. Robinson, University of North Carolina Press, 1946, pp. 140–66.

TABLE 21. Comparison of the different conceptions of secondary education, 1918–1952

Commission on Reorganization of Secondary Education, 1918 (principles)	Inglis' Aims of Secondary Education, 1918 (aims)	Issues & Functions of Secondary Education, 1932–1936 (issues & functions)	Purposes of Education in American Democracy, 1938 (purposes)°	Education for All American Youth, 1944 and 1952 (needs of youth)
Health				Good health and physical fitness
Command of fundamental processes		Common curriculum and general education	Self-Realization †	
Worthy home membership			Human Relationship	Significance of family for the individual and society
Vocation	Economic-vocational	Vocational education		Development of salable skills; supervised work experience in occupations
Citizenship	Social-civic	Social living and individual responsibility as a member of society	Civic Responsibility	Rights and duties of citizen in a democratic society
Worthy use of leisure time	Individualistic-avocational	Values of social living		Good use of leisure time
Ethical character		Attitudes and ideals		Respect for others; growth of ethical values and principles
			Economic Efficiency †	Consumer education
		Systematization of knowledge previously acquired and being acquired		Critical and analytic ability
				Creative urges
				Scientific basis of world and man

° One might compare these purposes with those in *Reorganizing Secondary Education*, Chaps. IV–IX.

† When used broadly, the term "self-realization" includes health, worthy use of leisure time, and ethical character; "economic efficiency" includes vocation also.

in pamphlet form the progress that their schools had made. Two such examples were *The Evolution of Susan Prim* [14] and *Miss Parker: The New Teacher*.[15]

Ending officially in 1947, the Study has stimulated many high schools to improve their facilities so that they could become accredited regionally. On the whole, the Secondary-School Study was a strong incentive for the improvement of standards for Negro high schools. This improvement of standards has led to a careful examination and study of the curricular programs in many schools on both the elementary and high school levels.

11. *State-wide Experimental Programs.* Stimulated by the many experiments in secondary education, some states initiated state-wide curricular programs of an experimental nature, covering a greater or smaller number of years. One of the most ambitious of these secondary-school experiments was the Michigan Study of the Secondary-School Curriculum, which began in 1936; it was planned to extend for twelve years, but continued longer as the Michigan Secondary-School-College Agreement.[16] The study was sponsored and financed by the Michigan Department of Public Instruction, the General Education Board, and the McGregor Fund. A committee of seven school people was appointed to direct the study. In the fifty-four participating secondary schools, the emphasis was upon changes in secondary education in order (1) to contribute more effectively to meeting the needs of all pupils, whether they are going to college or not, and (2) to contribute to the improvement of the community. Existing agencies and resources were utilized in the experiment to the greatest possible extent; care was taken to explore carefully, and then to evaluate a limited number of specific modifications of the program of the secondary school.

In 1941 the Texas Study of Secondary Education was initiated.

[14] Developed by the Lincoln High and Elementary School Faculties (Tallahassee) in cooperation with the staff of the Secondary School Study of the Association of Colleges and Secondary Schools for Negroes, 1944.

[15] Developed by the Faculty of the Moultrie High and Elementary School (Moultrie, Ga.) in cooperation with the staff of the Secondary School Study of the Association of Colleges and Secondary Schools for Negroes, 1946.

[16] L.S. Waskin, "The Michigan Secondary-School-College Agreement," *The Bulletin of the National Association of Secondary-School Principals*, xxxiii (January, 1949), pp. 49–64.

The study was sponsored by the State Department of Education and conducted under the direction of the Department of Curriculum and Instruction of the University of Texas and with the cooperation of the Texas Association of Secondary School Principals. The main purpose of the program was to stimulate and aid the high schools in a study of their own problems. The high schools of Texas were helped in three main ways by this Study organization: (1) consultation, (2) conference, and (3) publications. As a result, practically all of the member schools pursued one or more activities which may be classified as follows: [17] (1) studies of student bodies and their communities, and the needs of both, and/or (2) direction of the school program to satisfy those needs in such ways as studying nutritional problems, minority groups and their problems, curricular adjustments, and postwar problems.

The Illinois Secondary School Curriculum Program was launched in 1947 as a cooperative study sponsored by the State Superintendent. Business and industry, labor, agriculture, and lay and professional groups were cooperating organizations, as well as all of the public and many of the private colleges. The main purposes were (1) to conduct local research studies basic to curriculum improvement, (2) to encourage "developmental" curriculum projects, (3) to train personnel and organize, statewide, for curriculum development, (4) to cooperate with higher educational institutions in planning modifications of college entrance requirements, and (5) to prepare and distribute publications for the study.

The outstanding contribution of the Illinois study by 1952 was the preparation and testing out of instruments for *basic* studies of the school program, as follows:

How to Conduct the Holding Power Study, Bulletin No. 3, 1949.
How to Conduct the Participation in Extra-Class Activities Study, Bulletin No. 5, 1949.
How to Conduct the Hidden Tuition Costs Study, Bulletin No. 4, 1949.

[17] Elenora Albrecht, "The First Five Years of the Texas Study of Secondary Education," 1942–1947, *The High School Journal,* xxxi (May, 1948), pp. 136–42. The influence of the Study was still observable in 1957, when *Developmental Reading in Texas Secondary Schools,* by R.D. Thornton, was published, Austin, Texas Study of Secondary Education.

How to Conduct the Study of the Guidance Services of the School, Bulletin No. 6, 1949.
How to Conduct the Follow-Up Study, Bulletin No. 11, 1950.[18]

The experimental programs in Michigan, Texas, and Illinois are important movements in curriculum revision. These states gave a free hand to the individual schools to develop and broaden their programs in accordance with the needs of their own communities and their own pupils; they did not hamper the schools in their experiments by regulatory provisions. Of similar nature was the California experiment with the Cooperating Schools, which was described in Chapter 6.

12. *Miscellaneous Studies and Experiments.* There have been studies of general education on both secondary-school and college levels for many years. Harvard at the middle of the century has led the way and is continuing this study.[19] Both the Russell Sage Foundation and the Carnegie Corporation have made recent grants to study general education and the comprehensive American high school. *Behavioral Goals of General Education in High School* is the product of the Russell Sage Study;[20] it lists three maturity goals and four areas of behavioral competence, all based primarily upon the four purposes of education set up by the Educational Policies Commission in 1938 (set forth on p. 358, *ante*). James B. Conant, formerly president of Harvard, made the Carnegie Study of the American high school.[21] For almost two years Conant and his collaborators were at work, visiting fifty high schools in seventeen states. They questioned administrative personnel, thousands of teachers and hundreds of pupils in small groups. These fifty schools

<hr/>

[18] For an impartial account of the first five years of the Illinois Study, read "The Illinois Secondary School Curriculum Program," by C.W. Sanford and W.B. Spalding, *California Journal of Secondary Education*, xxvii (January, 1952), pp. 28–35.

[19] *Cf. General Education in a Free Society:* Report of the Harvard Committee, 1945; *General Education in School and College*, 1952; and *Education and Liberty*, by James B. Conant, 1953, all published by the Harvard University Press. Read also the 51st Yearbook, Part i, of the National Society for the Study of Education, *General Education*, 1952.

[20] By Will French and Associates, New York, Russell Sage Foundation, 1957.

[21] *The American High School Today*, New York, McGraw-Hall Book Company, 1959.

were "comprehensive" high schools in communities serving 10,000 to 100,000 inhabitants. The term "comprehensive," as used here, means that these high schools provide college preparatory, vocational, and general programs for all the youth of a community whose parents differ in their ambitions for their children.

In effect, Conant's study showed that these comprehensive high schools in different sections of the nation (1) could (some do) provide satisfactory programs for citizenship, for vocational education for many, and for challenging work for the more able student; and (2) their successful practices can be adapted to other comprehensive high schools that are inadequate in some respect(s). However, for a comprehensive high school to meet these varying needs of its constituency, it must have a sound, effectively working guidance program to help students to take advantage of their opportunities.

Conant's specific recommendations for the identification, guidance, and effective programs for the "academically talented" are interesting, and capable of incorporation into the administrative structure of any high school. These gifted students comprise about 15 per cent of the high-school population on a national basis. He suggests for these a program for graduation of four years of English, three or four years of history and other social studies, at least three years of mathematics, at least two years of science, three years of one foreign language, a choice of another year of mathematics, and a stiff course in physics *or* three years of a second foreign language—a total of seventeen or eighteen units; and at least five subjects each year would require homework of some fifteen or more hours a week.

In order to accomplish this program, there would be necessary a school day of eight forty-five-minute periods, a schedule which some very good schools already have in operation. Placement tests in subject-matter areas would be used to sectionize the academically talented; for example, it would be possible for a boy, who is very good in English, to be in a faster section in English, but to be in a slower mathematics section because he is not so far advanced in mathematics.

Two results of the Conant study offer a lot of food for thought. First, bright girls are not going into science and math programs. Secondly, few schools offer more than *two* years of a specific foreign language; this situation makes it hard for a student to get three years of one foreign language, much less two sequences of three years in each of *two* foreign languages.

Another interesting series of studies has been devoted to experiments with different curricular programs for the talented, the creative, the gifted pupil. Implications of some of these programs will be discussed in Chapter 21.[22]

PROBLEMS PECULIAR TO THE SECONDARY SCHOOL IN CURRICULUM DEVELOPMENT

Is PUBLIC SECONDARY EDUCATION "FREE"?   If one begins really to study the public secondary schools in the United States, he soon discovers that the "free and universal" system of "tax-supported" secondary education is an anomaly, much to his surprise. Paul Jacobson  was one of the first to set this forth very clearly.[23] The secondary schools are not really free institutions in the sense that it costs children nothing or next to nothing to attend them. The evidence which Jacobson presented showed that the lower the economic status of the child's family, the less is the likelihood that the child will ever get into or complete secondary school. Information for the study was gathered from 134 high schools and from over 19,000 students. The schools which participated in the study were located in ten of the twelve regions into which the Federal Security Agency divided the United States. Only New York, Texas, Louisiana, New Mexico, and Arizona did not have schools in this study.

The study showed that the average amount of money spent by each student in connection with his attendance at a public secondary school in 1942 ran from as low as $19 to as high as $152 annually; the average yearly expenditure per pupil in these 134 schools was around

---

[22] One of the best accounts of these experiments is *Education for the Gifted*, Part II of the 57th Yearbook of the National Society for the Study of Education, 1958.

[23] "The Cost of Attending High School," *The Bulletin of the National Association of Secondary-School Principals*, XXVIII (January, 1944), pp. 3–28. *Cf.* also H.C. Hand, "For Whom Are High Schools Designed?" *Educational Leadership*, VI (March, 1949), pp. 359–65, and "Hidden Tuition Charges in High School Subjects . . . in Extra-Class Activities," *Educational Forum*, XIII (May, 1949), pp. 441–48, and XIV (November, 1949), pp. 95–103, respectively.

$75. (Of course, the amounts spent now would be much higher.[24]) Of interest here is that the range of expenditures *within* schools was much greater than *among* schools. Girls spend more than boys; this difference can be due almost entirely to clothing. There was a gradual increase from grade nine through grade twelve, which might reflect in part the fact that more students from the low-income groups, with less money to spend, dropped out of school, and so the average expenditures increased. The data presented in the study do not indicate *why* the expenditures increased from grade to grade; they indicate only that the expenditures did increase in the higher grades.

Activities and articles for which the students have to spend this extra money include special and general fees of all kinds—for musicals, dramatics, and general performances; for club and class dues; for supplementary books and materials or for the library; for interscholastic contests and student activities; for laboratory supplies and materials; for publications and for class rings; for social functions and parties; for excursions and graduation costs; and for many other items. School organizations which require special fees for their support have multiplied so rapidly that even the small secondary school may handle thousands of dollars annually for these accounts. The cost to the individual student for his secondary-school education is inevitably forcing many students out of school, because the lower economic status of their families makes it impossible for them to maintain a social position in school anywhere near that of their comrades from more fortunate economic groups.

The condition just described is but one evidence of many factors which operate to limit curriculum revision in the secondary school. The secondary school has become a miniature college, and to a large extent is modeled upon the activities of the college in both its extracurricular and social aspects; it likewise apes the college in its sacred regard for departmental lines and subject-matter divisions and fields.

ARTICULATION WITH OTHER EDUCATIONAL LEVELS AND AGENCIES. For many years teachers and principals have complained that col-

[24] A recent study confirming these general findings was made in 1955–1956 in North Carolina. Read "Out-of-Pocket Expenditures, Made by High School Students," by Frank Nania, the *Bulletin of the National Association of Secondary-School Principals,* XLI (December, 1957), pp. 48–55.

lege-entrance requirements precluded their making fundamental changes in the curricular offerings of the secondary school. Prior to 1915 there was some justification for this position, but from that date to 1955 persons who advocated that the secondary school should be a *finishing school for life* rather than primarily a *fitting school for college* have held the upper hand, and the colleges rapidly modified and broadened their admission requirements. It is true that the small school with a limited staff has been unable to give quite so diversified a program of study as the larger school; therefore it has been prone to offer more of the traditional, academic type of work than the larger school. On the other hand, the experimental studies discussed in the first part of this chapter offer ample evidence that any school which is determined to try to improve its curriculum, or to change it to meet the needs of its students and its community, will get backing and permission to take those steps. Now again requirements for admission to college strongly condition the curricular program of the high school; this has been caused because the first of the children of the increased birth rate of the early 1940's are now coming to college. The colleges are limited in facilities to care for them, and many institutions have begun to require examinations for entrance.

The colleges and the secondary schools have cooperated in recent years to give better guidance and better orientation to secondary-school pupils who plan to enter an institution of higher learning. Tests of scholastic aptitude and placement tests of different kinds have been used to good effect; and programs for the counseling of students who are entering college have assisted secondary-school graduates materially in making the transition to the college without too great an emotional upset or too sharp a break.

On the other hand, the secondary school is supposed to be articulated with the elementary school, too, and material progress is beginning to be made in regard to this transition from the elementary school to the secondary school. Where a junior-high-school organization exists within a school system, the transition is usually much better cared for than in a system where the 8–4 or 7–5 organization prevails. The junior high school contains many courses of an exploratory, orientation, and general nature which make for easy articulation with the previous work which the child has had in the elementary school. Other methods used for better orientation of those pupils who are entering high school for the first time include pre-high-school "guidance" or "days," or "weeks"; student handbooks; student and faculty advisors for pupils in the last year of elementary school in order to acquaint them with the procedures and ideals and functions of the high school; and the preregistration of high-school students.

The point at which the secondary school has been most ineffective

FIG 28   *Using community resources in curriculum work*

Junior high-school pupils and their teacher interview the city's Manager of Improvements and Parks. Other department managers were visited by similar committees. (*Courtesy Denver Public Schools.*)

in its articulation in the past has been its relation to other educational agencies of an informal or formal nature in the community. The student from the secondary school comes under the direct influence of those community agencies when he stops school, or when he graduates and does not go to college. Examples of these community organizations are labor and industry, social and welfare agencies, and recreational and youth-serving groups not under the control of the school, such as recreation centers, playgrounds and parks, and libraries. For example, when a boy stops school in the tenth grade to secure work to help support the family, or because he is tired of school and wishes to go to work, he quickly becomes aware of the fact that much of his secondary-school curriculum was not connected in any way with these other community agencies of an informal or formal type. The more he tramps the streets inquiring for work, the more there is borne home to him the fact that the school program which he followed could have had a much closer relationship to his need of getting a job and making enough money to keep him from being hungry.

A summary of the articulation which exists between the secondary school and other institutional agencies and levels would be fairly expressed in the following manner: a fairly good job is being done in articulating the secondary school with institutions of higher education in which students wish to continue formal education; not so good a job is being done in articulation with the elementary school; and little is being done in the vital area of articulation with community and youth-serving agencies, to which most pupils must turn when they leave school.

DEPARTMENTALIZATION IN THE SECONDARY SCHOOL. The vested interests of subject-matter departments tend to perpetuate themselves. For instance, the teacher of mathematics in the secondary school is prone to be suspicious of any new type of course suggested in mathematics which might result in its becoming an elective subject. The teacher of biology and physics looks with distrust upon any attempt to remove either of these subjects from the required list, and insists upon keeping them as "constants" for all students, regardless of whether certain students need them or not. The teacher of foreign languages opposes any movement which would result in a pupil's being able to graduate from secondary school without any foreign language; he often takes this stand more because he fears that his vested interests will not be perpetuated than because he believes that all children in the secondary school should study a foreign language. English is required during all four years of the 8–4 school program, or in all six years of the junior- and senior-high-school period of study; by virtue of this requirement, the English teacher tends to feel that the English courses which have been established for students to master, and which all are expected to master, compose the best type of program for the students, regardless of what they plan to do in life and regardless of the fact that some 60 per cent of them never will darken the entrance door of a college.

Some subject-matter departments in the secondary schools have placed more emphasis upon their vested interests than upon the welfare of their students; they rival the subject-matter departments of the colleges in the number and variety of the courses which they offer. Yet the colleges are duplicating many of the subjects which were given to the student in his secondary-school days because they say that the secondary school has not done its work efficiently.

Colleges frequently administer placement tests to students who are entering college for the first time. These tests often place freshmen in college courses which are similar in content and difficulty to the courses they took in the secondary school. At the present time, French, Spanish, Latin, English, Geometry and Trigonometry, and various sciences are offered upon the college level in courses which correspond almost exactly or closely to those which the student had in the secondary school. Much of this duplication of effort and expense is undesirable.

The departmentalization of subject matter in the curriculum of the secondary school is undoubtedly the greatest obstruction which the educational employee finds in his way when he suggests modifications and changes in the program to meet the needs of youth. The subject-matter specialists in both colleges and secondary schools have analyzed and subdivided English, the sciences, mathematics, and the social sciences into so many courses that when the child enters the four-year secondary school today he is confronted with a most perplexing problem; he wonders what he should take in his total program from among the multitudinous offerings in the various subjects. For example, in a secondary school which enrolls some 800 students, such courses as civics, world history, ancient and medieval history, American history, problems of American democracy, sociology, economics, and geography are usually given in the social studies. Which of these courses should the student take? Which should he omit? There is a serious doubt in the minds of many educators whether the social studies should be subdivided into so many separate subjects, especially when all aspects of social science are so closely related.

There is usually little effort made by the different subject-matter departments in the secondary school to interrelate or correlate their materials and their teaching with the experiences of the pupil. As a result of this lack of cooperation and coordination, each subject-matter specialist feels that his material is so valuable that the child must master it. During the school day, the child is divided in effect into his English personality, his Latin personality, his mathematics personality, and his science personality; he is taught apart from his total experience and his total personality, which really learns as a unit, and not in segments of specialized subject matter. This statement does not mean that the secondary school should not offer to the pupil the opportunity for specializing in the areas of his greatest interest. On the contrary, the areas of the student's greatest interest can be served best when the departments and subject-matter specialists realize that learning takes place as a "whole" experience, not in "subject-matter" parts. For example, home economics and home-making cannot be taught effectively without touching upon the realms of science which pertain to diet, growth, biological development, sanitation, hygiene, and public health. The main scientific manifestations with which the pupil is familiar, and with which he will have to deal in his future life, are not concerned primarily so much with *pure* science as with the *applied* sciences, such as chemical engineering, refrigeration, air conditioning, food dehydration, the manufacture of radios and TV sets, the workings of the gasoline, diesel, and jet engines, photography, the production of motion pictures, and sanitation. Health and physical education for children are inevitably connected with personal hygiene, a knowledge of diet and foods, public recreation and public sanitation, public health, and the development of good personal habits.

Until the teacher in the secondary school recognizes that the field of his particular subject is but part and parcel of a total program of school offerings which should touch the vital areas of experience and knowledge for all adolescent children, there will be little change for the better in his conception of the curriculum and in his methods of teaching.

ACCREDITING AGENCIES, STATE AND REGIONAL.   In the discussion of the Cooperative Study of Secondary School Standards, certain influences of regional accrediting agencies were set forth as they affected the curriculum of the secondary school. The individual states have accepted many of the standards which have been established by the regional associations for the accrediting of secondary schools. The state board of education or the state department of public instruction, through the exercise of its supervisory powers, has established certain standards which must be met by secondary schools if they expect to be accepted as standard by the state. If they fulfill those standards, their better graduates usually will be admitted to the state colleges upon certification by the principal that they have completed the proper program in the secondary school which is specified for college entrance. In the rapid growth of secondary schools in the United States, many problems arose owing to the differing quality of their products. Among these problems was the lack of any standards for graduation which were uniform enough for the student to transfer successfully from one secondary school to another, or to enter one college or another. Because of the variation among the states and the higher institutions as to what constituted a good school, the regional agencies came into existence to secure the required recognition of certain standards for the accrediting of schools. E.D. Grizzell[25] has shown that the accrediting of secondary schools has served the following important purposes: (1) it has provided a substitute for the intricate process of individual examination of all candidates for admission to college; and (2) it has standardized practice in secondary education in the selection of students for admission to college.

The standardizing of secondary schools has hindered curriculum revision because no major changes in the scope and emphasis of the standards established by the regional and state agencies have occurred in the last generation. Specific, objective criteria have been added primarily in regard to teacher preparation, pupil-teacher load,

[25] "Accrediting of Secondary Schools," *High School Journal* (November, 1940), pp. 324–29. For the picture today, read *State Accreditation of High Schools—Practices and Standards of State Agencies,* by Grace S. Wright, U.S. Department of Health, Education, and Welfare, Office of Education Bulletin 1955, No. 5.

type of equipment and building, library facilities, and teaching conditions; but the only standards which have been developed and which have really stimulated curriculum improvement are those of the Cooperative Study.

Instead of having as their main purpose the maintenance of minimum standards, the main function of accrediting agencies should come to be that of the stimulation and encouragement of continuous improvement in the secondary school. The National Survey of Secondary Education showed clearly that the schools in its study, which were not hampered by the standards and regulations of state and regional groups, were doing much better work; they were making more effective progress in curriculum improvement than other schools where standardizing factors were operative. Therefore, programs should be encouraged which stimulate the more able students to take advanced work when they go to college, and enable the less able pupils to round out a broad general education with vocational competencies.

THE JUNIOR-SENIOR HIGH SCHOOL AND THE JUNIOR COLLEGE. In the reorganization of secondary education since 1910, the junior high school has come to occupy a prominent place. Some educational experts believe that secondary education ought to include also the junior college, with its functions of "general" education and "terminal" education, or preparation for life. Both the junior high school and the junior college are pointed more than the senior high school toward general education, the acquisition of those common knowledges, skills, attitudes, and ideals which all students are supposed to gain for successful living in a democracy. As a result of being concerned more specifically with general education, both the junior high school and the junior college have given evidence of rather remarkable strides in the direction of curriculum experimentation. These experiments have centered teaching materials around "general courses," rather than around specific subject areas or subject-matter fields.

There are two types of junior college, the public and the private. Likewise there are two types of programs in the junior colleges: one type of program aims to make the two first years of college a "general" course giving a general education; the other type aims only to prepare students for admission to a senior college and for specific individual study in the subject-matter areas. Some educators see the eventual extension of the secondary-school curriculum to include the two years of junior college, or what would now be considered the first two years of the regular four-year college course.

There is a question as to what school level should mark the end of "common" or "general" education. If general education for all students should stop at the end of the junior high school, then the present departmentalization, specialization, and differentiation in the senior high school may be justified as long as the interrelationships of subjects are taken into account more than they have been in the past. If general education is to continue through the first two years of the junior college, then the senior high school with its highly specialized and differentiated courses in the subject-matter areas is an anomaly between the lower and upper levels which comprise the continuation of this common or general education.

ADOLESCENT ATTITUDES AND GROWTH. Strangely enough, the stage of development through which the adolescent passes has contributed largely to the intensification and general acceptance of the departmentalized, subject-matter organization of the curriculum in the secondary school. During the age of puberty the child is characteristically most sensitive, most loyal to the gang, most secretive, most prone to withdraw from adult guidance and to be controlled by the play group, and most eager to avoid differences of opinion with his elders. Far be it from the child at this age to upset the *status quo* as long as it does not upset his own plans and purposes! Unless any experiment to gain the child's opinion regarding the curriculum and his teachers is most carefully controlled, so that the information will not get back to those with whom he has to deal, it is almost impossible to secure an honest opinion from him. Thus, the reticence of the adolescent in expressing his opinion frankly about school affairs tends to give educational employees few suggestions as to improvements that might be made in the curriculum.

THE EXTRACURRICULUM. Though the traditional secondary school has made little progress in unifying and interrelating the different subject-matter fields, it has grown remarkably in the absorption into the curriculum of certain student activities which were formerly considered to be strictly "extracurricular." In the last two decades, student activities such as bands, orchestras, chorus and glee club work, dramatics, journalism, radio and TV clubs, science clubs, health and physical educatiton, and art have been taken into the regular curriculum of the high school; in many instances, graduation credit has been given for these activities, which have been assigned regular periods in the school schedule. To date, no satisfactory arrangement has been made whereby interscholastic activities and contests can be taken over as a part of the regular curriculum; these types of activities include interscholastic debating, athletics, dramatics, music, and journalism.

In still another direction, rapid growth has taken place in absorbing certain student activities into the regular curriculum. Student council work and organizations have come in general to occupy a place of prominence in the training of students. In a great number of schools, such activities have brought about the participation of students in the administration, and even in the control, of the secondary school; those activities have frequently been organized in such a way that they have taken their regular place in the curriculum. In this one respect at least, the secondary school has shown a development favorably comparable to that of the elementary school. It has proceeded to establish its miniature society in the school—a society composed of equals who are trained to recognize the rights of others, at the same time that they are engaged in their own activities and their individual growth and development.

THE DIFFICULTY OF THE EVALUATION OF NONTANGIBLES. There has been a slow growth in the development of instruments to measure intangibles such as emotions, attitudes, and ideals. Therefore, it has been difficult for the curriculum worker to "get across" to his comrades on the secondary-school level the belief that the development of attitudes and ideals and the emotional life of the student is as important as the acquisition of knowledges and specific study skills. Every person has to solve problems, whether he is a child, an adolescent, or an adult. In the solving of these problems, it is seldom that attitudes and emotions are separable from purely intellectual thought and analysis. Racial animosities, fear, anger, and jealousy will operate in one case or another as the deciding factor in solving the problem. Without concrete proof that these intangible factors do operate, it is exceedingly difficult for the teacher to see that they are

FIG. 29 *Bringing the extra-curriculum into the curriculum*

A scene from *The Ivory Door.* (*Courtesy Clifford J. Scott High School, East Orange, New Jersey.*)

as important as the subject-matter heritage which he believes that every child should acquire.

If the teacher could be convinced that the heritage of the race includes the pupil's attitudes, ideals, and emotions as primary factors along with knowledge in the major areas of human experience in the past and present, the improvement of the secondary-school curriculum would be assured. Some such concept as this must be realized and become prevalent among the teaching staffs of the secondary schools; for if this concept is not grasped, there is the possibility that other agencies which parallel the secondary school and which serve informally at the present time in the education of youth may supplant the traditional secondary school.

A CRITICAL RÉSUMÉ OF FACTORS FORCING CHANGE IN THE AIMS AND FUNCTIONS OF SECONDARY EDUCATION

Nationally, the conception of the aims and functions of secondary education has been changing since the business depression that started in 1930. The majority of the movements which have had marked influence on secondary education started during or shortly before this era of economic disarrangement. The contributions and weaknesses of the significant investigations, studies, and surveys may be summarized as follows:

1. *The Issues and Functions of Secondary Education* was carried out by the National Department of Secondary-School Principals of the National Education Association. They sampled the opinion of administrators and professors of secondary education in regard to the outstanding issues of secondary education; on the basis of these and other data they set forth ten functions and purposes of secondary education. Their work was valuable, provocative, and stimulative, in spite of the fact that they took a too limited sampling of opinion on the issues; certainly secondary-school teachers and selected groups of laymen should have been sampled, too. Their main contribution was to the philosophy of secondary education.

2. *The National Survey of Secondary Education* attempted to discover what promising practices for secondary education were in use in certain reorganized schools. It attempted in effect to show by a sampling of 550 schools where we were in regard to promising or progressive practices in secondary education. The job was well done in spite of not having comparative data from all types of school organizations, so that a more accurate validation of the results could be made. It is significant that the survey discovered noticeable effects of the Classical Investigation, and the Modern Foreign Language Study, and other national studies and investigations on teaching in special subject-matter fields.

3. *The Eight-Year Study of the Progressive Education Association* showed that (1) radical change in traditional college-entrance subjects

studied, and in methods of organizing secondary-school material in various
courses, did not handicap the secondary-school graduate in his future
college work; and (2) when released for the promotion of experimental
programs, some secondary schools took full advantage of their freedom
and some did not.

4. *The Cooperative Study of Secondary School Standards* aimed to find
what made a secondary school good—its weak and strong points. In spite
of subjective opinions treated statistically, and the use of these criteria
for comparing one school with another and for the accrediting of schools
by the regional and state standardizing agencies, the study contributes
valuable aid in that it enables a school group and staff to discover definitely
their weaknesses and their strengths, especially in regard to their philosophy and objectives, their curriculum, and their outcomes of instruction.

5. *Studies of the American Youth Commission of the American Council
on Education* have contributed much material of importance to the
curriculum, namely, the study of youth and its problems, the people with
whom the high school has to deal. The work of this commission is significant in that it sought through its studies to show how the school might
adapt its curriculum more adequately to meet the needs of youth, and
how youth actually grows and develops in a survey situation.

6. *The Commissions on Human Relations and Secondary-School Curriculum of the Progressive Education Association* made three curricular
contributions: (1) theirs was the first frank study of the secondary-school
curriculum with the idea of reorganizing secondary education; (2) their
publications put the greatest emphasis upon, and gave the greatest help
in, the consideration of aspects of "general education" on the secondary-
school level; and (3) their studies of child growth and development
placed emphasis upon the personality that the secondary school has to deal
with. Some of their volumes exhibit the characteristic weaknesses of committee reports—they are repetitious in regard to *general* principles, and
lacking in *specific* applications and examples.

7. *The Regents' Inquiry* was a statewide survey to discover where a
state was in regard to its school program and expenditures. It is valuable
for the significant facts revealed as regards the practices in a large statewide system, with statewide examinations.

8. *The Southern Study*'s main contribution was the successful development of individual programs for schools, rather than implications applicable to all schools.

9. *Education For All American Youth* is the story of the school systems
in two fictitious communities, one rural and one urban; it projects two
ideal school programs. One of the greatest contributions from the study
is the "ten imperative needs of youth." Like the Commissions on Human
Relations and Secondary-School Curriculum of the Progressive Education

Changing Conception of Aims and Functions   377

Association, this group faced frankly the idea of a thorough reorganization of secondary education.

10. *The Secondary School Study* was a strong incentive for the improvement of standards for Negro high schools in the South. This examination of standards led to a study of the curricular implications in many schools on both the elementary- and secondary-school levels.

11. *The Michigan, California, Texas,* and *Illinois Cooperative Secondary-School Studies* are significant for the curriculum worker in regard to: (1) freedom granted to the cooperating and contributing schools to experiment without being hampered or controlled by state standardizing agencies; (2) encouragement from both higher institutions and state departments of public instruction to set up and carry out such experiments— a practical acknowledgment that there was much work to be done in the study and improvement of the secondary-school curriculum in those states; and (3) the development of better instruments for making basic studies of the secondary-school program.

12. *Significant Experiments and Studies Under Way Now.* The continuing studies of general education in the high school and college by the Harvard University groups, coupled with the recent Russell Sage study of behavioral goals in general education, suggest promising ways by which agreement may be reached by educators on what general education in the secondary school should consist of. The study of the "comprehensive" high school made by James B. Conant showed (1) that the high school could give satisfactorily varying kinds of programs under effective guidance to meet the needs of *all* pupils in a community; (2) that programs for the academically talented can be effectively worked out under the present administrative structure of the high school; (3) that foreign-language programs are not adequate in amount and length of offerings; and (4) that few bright girls are preparing for work in science, mathematics, and industry.

A highly encouraging sign in all of those factors operating for an examination of the aims and the curriculum of the secondary school is that more of these studies have originated with the secondary-school people themselves than have been forced upon them from outside. By this process of self-appraisal, most secondary-school staffs have become aware of the large number of perplexing problems facing them, a necessary first step if they are to go about solving them satisfactorily. On the other hand, enough studies and experiments have been carried on by agencies not directly connected with secondary education for impartial data to be obtained for study, comparison, and utilization.

PROBLEMS FOR INDIVIDUAL STUDY AND CLASS DISCUSSION

1. What implications for the secondary-school curriculum do you find in *Education for All American Youth?* In *Education for all American Youth—A Further Look?*

2. To what extent should the secondary school attempt to turn out skilled workers for the vocations? Support your point of view.

3. What curricular functions should a secondary-school "guidance" program perform? Explain.

4. Should school credit be given to students for participation in student activities? Defend your position.

5. Can change and experimentation in the curriculum take place more easily in the large or the small secondary school? Why?

6. Could a more normal and more effective curricular program be offered in the secondary school if it had the same type of grade and subject organization, with one regular teacher for each grade, as the elementary school? Give reasons for your answer.

7. What is "general education" on the secondary-school level, and what types of specific courses are set up for this particular purpose?

8. What activities formerly considered "extracurricular" have been taken over into the school program with regular class periods devoted to them? What reasons are there for these changes?

9. What is the difference between the purposes of "general," "exploratory," and "orientation" courses on the secondary-school level?

10. Make a list of the different curricula which your secondary school offers, each leading to graduation and a diploma. Under each "curriculum" (such as "college preparatory," "general," etc.) write down (1) the required subjects, (2) the restricted elective subjects, and (3) the free "electives." From your analysis, is the curricular offering broad or narrow? Why?

11. If you are employed in a secondary school, take sections C and D of the *Cooperative Study of Secondary School Standards,* and fill in all the information asked for in the light of what your secondary school is doing. Did this give you a better idea of where your curricular practices are in relation to your philosophy and objectives of secondary education?

12. What various methods are in use today to help the graduate's transition from secondary school to college?

13. What are the purposes to be accomplished for adolescents by the total secondary-school program of studies?

14. Do state- or district-wide contests of an interscholastic nature in music, journalism, and dramatics have curricular value? Why or why not?

ADDITIONAL ANNOTATED REFERENCES
FOR PROBLEM OR UNIT STUDY

Adler, I., *What We Want of Our Schools,* New York, The John Day Company, 1957.
> Presents well the idea of the "open mind" as the objective of public education. Chapters VIII on progressive education and X on secondary and vocational education.

Alberty, H., *Reorganizing the High School Curriculum* (rev. ed.), New York, The Macmillan Company, 1953.
> Chapters I–VIII present his basic plan of reorganization in the light of the evolution of the secondary school curriculum.

American Association of School Administrators, N.E.A.
> 32nd Yearbook, 1954, *Educating for American Citizenship,* has this purpose for schools and presents promising practices in citizenship education in schools.
> 36th Yearbook, 1958, *The High School in a Changing World,* presents the main issues in Chapters I–VI and XII–XIII.

Association for Supervision and Curriculum Development, N.E.A.
> 1956 Yearbook, *What Shall the High School Teach?* presents brief, historical résumé in Chapter I, what courses are being taught today in III, and general, special, and vocational education in V and VI.

Bent, R.K., and Kronenberg, *Principles of Secondary Education* (3rd ed.), New York, McGraw-Hill Book Company, 1955.
> History, purposes and services, and relationships to other educational levels in Chapters I–III, V–VI; trends and issues in X and XIX.

Briggs, T.H., *et al., Secondary Education* (rev. ed.), New York, The Macmillan Company, 1950.
> Chapters I–VIII give a good history of American secondary education, its bases, its functions, adolescent needs, and articulation problems. The mores, youths' interests, and basic problems in secondary education comprise Chapters XIII–XIX.

Caswell, H.L. (Ed.), *The American High School,* New York, Harper and Brothers, 1946.
> This yearbook of the John Dewey Society presents the issues, factors influencing the high school, the problems of youth, and the responsibilities of the school for an adequate curriculum for the future.

Chamberlain, E.B., *Our Independent Schools,* New York, American Book Company, 1944.
> The private school in American secondary education, its historic roles, its characteristics, its adaptations, and its future responsibilities.

Educational Policies Commission, N.E.A. and A.A.S.A.

School Athletics: Problems and Policies, 1954, looks at a phase of school life that needs careful control, and recommendations are made for this.

Franzen, C.G.F., *Foundations of Secondary Education,* New York, Harper and Brothers, 1955.
The background and forces affecting the public high school in Chapters I–V and the objectives in X–XI.

French, W.M., *American Secondary Education,* New York, The Odyssey Press, 1957.
Secondary education's heritage in Chapters I–VII, the present confusion and crisis in I and VIII–IX, articulation in X, private and parochial schools in XI–XII, and the future in XX–XXI.

Gesell, A., *et al., Youth: The Years from Ten to Sixteen,* New York, Harper and Brothers, 1956.
The descriptions of the preadolescent and the adolescent in this monumental work pinpoint his needs and many of the kinds of educational activities which can be based on his interests.

Gilchrist, R.S., *et al., Secondary Education for American Democracy* (rev. ed.), New York, Rinehart and Company, 1957.
Chapter I for problems of the next twenty-five years, IV for secondary education's past, and III for its job today.

Havemann, E., and West, P.S., *They Went to College: The College Graduate in America Today,* New York, Harcourt, Brace and Company, 1952.
Based on a survey of college graduates by *Time* magazine, this volume is an interesting compendium of knowledge on how successful college graduates are; it also shows that graduates change with the times.

Havighurst, R.J., *Human Development and Education,* New York, Longmans, Green and Company, 1953.
The new concept of developmental tasks is presented here, tasks for adolescence are presented in detail in Part III and Part V.

Koos, L.V., *Integrating High School and College,* New York, Harper and Brothers, 1946.
Describes the 6-4-4 plan at work.

Latimer, J.F., *What's Happened to Our High Schools?* Washington, Public Affairs Press, 1958.
The point of view of a classicist concerning the purposes of the modern high school in the light of the development of the curriculum in the past.

Leonard, J.P., *Developing the Secondary School Curriculum* (rev. ed.), New York, Rinehart and Company, 1953.
Chapters I–IX trace historically the purposes of secondary education, the curricula established to carry them out, and theories of secondary education today.

MacConnell, C.M., *et al., New Schools for a New Culture* (rev. ed.), New York, Harper and Brothers, 1953.

The story of the Evanston Township high school core program, with its action program.

National Association of Secondary-School Principals, N.E.A.

What Should We Expect of Education? by H.T. Rosenberger presents in Chapter i basic issues and theories, published in *The Bulletin* of the Association, Vol. xl, February, 1956.

National Society for the Study of Education, Chicago.

52nd Yearbook, Part i, 1953, *Adapting the Secondary-School Program to the Needs of Youth*, devotes its careful analysis and planning to the "youth-needs" motive.

Romnie, S.A., *Building the High School Curriculum*, New York, The Ronald Press Company, 1954.

The evolution, bases, and purposes of the high school in Chapters ii–iv and vii, and the curriculum of the future in xvii.

Sexson, J.A., and Harbeson, J.W., *The New American College*, New York, Harper and Brothers, 1946.

The 4-year junior college, grades 11–14, organized and administered as one unit, as illustrated over a period of twenty-five years in the Pasadena Junior College.

CHAPTER 13 Trends in
curriculum development in the
secondary school

CURRICULAR PATTERNS

In order to get a clear view of the situation, it is necessary to look briefly at the existing curricular patterns in the secondary school. Therefore, the minimum requirements for graduation from secondary school which exist in three different states and in one city in widely separated areas in the United States are listed here.

North Carolina. The standards for graduation from the high schools of North Carolina are as follows: [1]

Subject	Units
English	4
Mathematics	1
Social Studies	2
Science	2
Physical Education and Health	1
Electives	6
Total	16

English—Required in each year of high school.
Mathematics—Required in the ninth year, either course A, General Mathematics, or course B, Algebra.
Social Studies—American History and one additional unit.
Science—Biology and one additional unit of science. The additional unit may be waived for students who complete the two-year course in Business Education, in Distributive Education, or Diversified Occupations.

[1] *Handbook for Elementary and Secondary Schools*, Publication No. 235, State Superintendent of Public Instruction, 1953, pp. 94–95.

Physical Education and Health—One unit in Physical Education and Health is required in the ninth grade. Additional work is recommended for other high school years.

Electives—The six elective units are provided for in terms of the possible offerings in a given school. All electives are to be selected upon the advice of principals and advisers and in terms of the educational objectives of the student. This makes a program of educational guidance imperative in every school.

Minimum offerings

All schools should provide for offering the following: English, 4 units; Mathematics, 3 units; Science, 4 units; Social Studies including Geography, 5 units; Physical and Health Education, 1 unit; and Foreign Language, 2 units. Three and four teacher high schools may find it necessary to limit the offerings for a given year by combining third- and fourth-year students in certain subjects offered in alternate years.[2]

Ohio. In the state of Ohio, these requirements prevail:

Graduation Requirements. The graduation requirements for any approved first-grade high school shall be the completion of sixteen units. One of these units must be American history and government. (Section 3313.60 R.C.) While the one unit in American history and government is a legal requirement, the State Department of Education has encouraged schools to require of all pupils one full unit of American history and in addition one-half unit of civics or a unit of problems in American government. The completion of health and physical education to the equivalent of one unit in the four years of high school may be either added to, or included within, the sixteen units required for graduation.

Minimum Quantitative Requirements. The minimum quantitative requirements for graduation from a four-year high school are sixteen units including:

English	3 units
Social Studies	2 units
Science	1 unit
Mathematics	1 unit
Health and Physical Education	1 unit

Not more than one unit within the required sixteen may be made up of quarter units. Schools desiring to do so may by board of education resolution require seventeen or eighteen units for graduation. In such cases, the one or two additional units may be made up of fractional units in such work as religious education and other work carried under private instruction.

[2] *Ibid.,* p. 129.

In addition to the major of three units in English, each graduate shall have completed one other major of three units and in addition to the minor in social studies, one other minor of two units.

. . . .

Guidance. The election of fields of study should be so guided and directed that each graduate will have completed a well-rounded program of studies consistent with his needs.[3]

Graduation Requirements, High Schools of El Paso ° ° °

Noncollege Route	College Route	Engineering Route
(18 units required for graduation)	(20 units required for graduation)	(20 units required for graduation)
°English—3 units	°English—4 units	°English—4 units
Math—2 units (Gen. Math and Bus. Arith. acceptable)	Math—3 units (Gen. Math and Bus. Arith. not acceptable)	Math—4 units (Gen. Math and Bus. Arith. not acceptable)
Soc. Stud.—3 units (same as college)	Soc. Stud.—3 units (1 unit Amer. History, ½ unit Civics, ½ unit	Mech. Draw.—1 unit Soc. Stud.—3 units, same as college
° °Science—2 units	Modern Problems, 1 unit World History)	Science—3 units, in-
P.E., Girls—2 units (4 years)	Foreign Language—2 units (must be taken	cluding Physics and Chemistry
P.E. and/or ROTC, Boys—2 units (4 years)	in consecutive semes- ters)	P.E., Girls—2 units (4 years)
Electives—6 units	Lab Science—2 units	P.E. and/or ROTC,
	P.E., Girls—same as noncollege (4 years)	Boys—2 units (4 years)
	P.E., and/or ROTC, Boys—same as non- college (4 years)	Electives—3 units
		NOTE: It is highly recom- mended that engineering students take two or more units of foreign language.

° Students must be registered in a Language Arts course at all times until they have completed four units or unless they are enrolled in the T. & I. course (see last paragraph).

° ° Two years of vocational courses or two years of foreign language may be substituted for one year of science. The remaining year of science must be Chemistry, Physics, Biology, or Applied Science.

T. & I. courses are offered at Tech only. They may be begun in the sophomore year and each such subject will allow the student to earn one solid credit plus ¼ light credit each semester.   •

° ° ° Adopted by the Board of Education, April 8, 1958. Reproduced with some abbreviations by permission of the Board.

---

[3] *Ohio High School Standards,* 1947, *Administration,* State of Ohio, Department of Education, 1947, pp. 67, 68, and Revised Code (1958).

El Paso.   The situation in the secondary schools of El Paso, Texas, can be summarized as follows:

The six high schools of El Paso, including El Paso Technical High School, offer more than 100 different courses. To fit their students' needs better, El Paso has three "routes" for graduation: (1) the College Preparatory Route, (2) the Engineering, and (3) the Noncollege Route.

In all three routes to graduation there are "solid" and "light" credits. Eighteen to twenty units are required for graduation, thus offering able pupils in the college preparatory routes ample opportunity for both enrichment and taking additional solid courses for advanced standing in college.

New York State.   Peculiar to New York State alone are the Regents Examinations, based on the core curriculum and elective subjects offered in the high schools. All students in approved high schools in all curricula must earn a minimum of sixteen units, as follows:

English	4 units
Citizenship Education (including American History)	3 units
Science	1 unit
Health	½ unit

> or the equivalent

A Major Sequence of 3 units from *one* of these fields: Mathematics; foreign language; science; music, art, business subjects; practical arts or vocational subjects

Electives   4½ units

Mathematics in the ninth year is strongly recommended for all pupils.

The Regents Examinations are statewide in scope and are formulated each year by classroom teachers working as Regents Question Committees under the State Examinations Board; the State Education Department, the higher institutions, secondary-school principals, and superintendents are represented on this State Board. The question committees are supervised by the Department subject specialists; all examinations are reviewed by the Regents Revision Committee composed of secondary-school administrators under the direction of the Director of Secondary Education. An analysis of the use of these examinations shows:[5]

At one time the Regents Examinations did set the standards for graduation from high school. Though they may indirectly affect the graduation standards for all pupils today, they actually affect only certain types of

[5] The data for New York State are based on 1958 Regulations of the Board of Regents and upon correspondence with the State Department.

pupils. Secondary schools with approved courses, and whose examinations in those courses have been approved by the State Department in place of the Regents, do not use the Regents; instead, they issue their own diplomas based on these approved standards. The State Department still issues state diplomas based on the Regents examinations.

It should be noted that these Regents Examinations for graduation from secondary school stress the passing of statewide tests in the last two years of the pupil's program. In these years, examinations are held in practically every field in the secondary school in which instruction is offered; these fields include both the regular secondary-school subjects and subjects in the special fields of music, industrial and technical work, commercial work, fine arts, home economics, and agriculture. Every pupil is not tested every year, and the examinations are frequently so framed as to be applicable to the cumulative work of two, three, or four years, rather than to the work of the one year which the pupil has just completed and with which he should still be reasonably familiar.

CURRICULAR IMPLICATIONS OF STANDARDIZATION. An analysis of the standards for graduation from secondary schools in these four different sections of the nation shows that *in general, three or four units of English are required, two or three units of social studies, one or two units of science, and some health and physical education or safety work.* Localities and states vary in their requirements as to what shall be taught in the secondary school. For example, Ohio laws require American history and government and physical education; North Carolina specifies Biology as one of the science units, and requires teaching of the evil effects of alcohol and narcotic drugs in the eighth grade; El Paso allows two units of ROTC for all boys; and New York and Ohio require one *additional subject-field sequence of at least three units.*

Certain implications for the curriculum can be drawn from this study of various school systems. *First,* the standards established by the state boards of education or by the state legislatures for accredited secondary schools are responsible in large measure for the similarity of pattern which exists all over the country today. *Secondly,* this similarity of minimum requirements for graduation exists in general for all types of separate and specialized programs of study for students; the pattern operates to hinder trial and experimentation in the curriculum of the secondary school. *Thirdly,* the institution of new courses of study in both the secondary and the elementary schools by legislative action in various states has marked influence toward standardizing the curriculum for all children, regardless of local needs and community situations. Unless such compulsory statutes concerning the curriculum are formulated broadly, experimentation cannot be carried on or progress made even in the more effective teaching of those subjects so required by law.

The sampling which has been given of the standards for graduation from secondary school indicates the patterns which one will find in operation to a greater or less extent all over the country, no matter where one goes. These patterns operate strongly to maintain the *status quo* in the subject areas, to perpetuate strict departmentalization, and to add new subjects to the curriculum rather than to subtract any from it. Only those schools which were, or are now in the experimental groups which have already been described, such as the Eight-Year Study, the Michigan Study, or the Illinois Study (Chapter 12), are really free of state or local regulation in order to experiment fully with procedures and practices which may be productive of improvement. Under these conditions, it is usually only the bold school administrator, or one who is secure in his tenure, who will take the risk and responsibility of experimenting thoroughly with the existing curricular structure of the secondary school.

PARALLEL CURRICULA AND PARALLEL AGENCIES FOR SECONDARY EDUCATION

PARALLEL CURRICULA. For many years, the secondary schools have attempted to improve their curricula within the existing administrative framework by the addition of new and parallel programs of study. Since the schools felt that they were prevented in many cases from reorganizing their curricula thoroughly because of state and regional standards for graduation, they have taken the same way out which the colleges took when they ran up against a similar problem more than fifty years ago. About 1880, the institutions of higher education in this country were beginning to be influenced by the establishment of mechanical and technical colleges which gave what was then considered a "vocational" type of education. Most of the older colleges and universities were loath to consider the curricula in agriculture and mechanic arts as "respectable" as the regular A.B. curriculum; they refused, therefore, to give the A.B. degree for these vocational courses, and insisted that such special programs lead to a degree of Bachelor of Science, or Bachelor of Philosophy, or Bachelor of Pedagogy in the case of teachers. In this way, many parallel "curricula" developed in the colleges, leading to specific degrees in special fields; and many new courses in subject matter were introduced into these fields to meet the needs of the students who took these curricula. Certain curricula, like those leading to the degree of Bachelor of Pedagogy or the degree of Bachelor of Philosophy, did not attract enough students; as a result, these particular curricula eventually disappeared from most of the college offerings.

In the meantime, a gradual change took place over a period of some fifty years in the college's conception of requirements for the A.B. degree. The classics were gradually eliminated from 1914 to 1928, first with Greek going out as a requisite and then with Latin following along. From a close examination of college catalogues today in comparison with those of fifty years ago, it is evident that certain changes were gradually forced on those persons who were in charge of requirements for the A.B. degree. Those requirements today are remarkably similar in many respects to the requirements for what used to be called the Bachelor of Philosophy or the B.S. degree, twenty, thirty, or fifty years ago; this is certainly true in so far as the requirements in the classics, mathematics, and philosophy are concerned.[6]

In many respects, the situation in curriculum growth in the secondary school today parallels the development which took place in the colleges from 1880 to 1935. Even in the smaller secondary school of from 100 to 400 pupils one will find as many as two, and frequently three, different curricular programs, each leading to graduation, with a diploma, such as *the college preparatory curriculum, the general curriculum, and the business or commercial curriculum.* In the secondary schools of larger size there may be as

---

[6] J.M. Gwynn, *Changes in the College Curriculum: 1890–1934,* unpublished doctor's thesis, Yale University, 1935, *passim.*

many as six or seven different "curricula"; each curriculum has its array of new subject-matter courses of a special nature for the benefit of students in that particular program, and each curriculum is parallel to other curricula in that it leads to the coveted diploma upon satisfactory completion of the program.

There is some reorganization of the subject-matter fields which tends to break the pattern of parallel curricula for high school graduation. H.R. Douglass, a well-known authority in many areas of secondary education, has stated that core-curriculum or "unified-studies" programs are one promising development, cutting across departmental lines.[7] The other trend to which Douglass refers is a sound one, toward a "single" curriculum of required and elective courses, or a "constants-with-variables" curriculum in place of the old multiple or parallel curricula.

GROWTH OF AGENCIES PARALLEL TO THE SECONDARY SCHOOL FOR THE TRAINING OF YOUTH. It is doubtful whether the secondary school has yet worked out its problem as satisfactorily as did the college, though the colleges still differ among themselves in their practices. Certain higher institutions give only the A.B. and B.S. degrees, whereas others offer five, six, seven, or even eight special degrees upon the undergraduate level, such as the B.S. in Engineering, the B.S. in Mathematics, the B.S. in Geology, the A.B. in Journalism, the straight A.B. degree, the straight B.S. degree, the B.S. in Medicine, and the B.S. in Civil Engineering. In solving their problem and in making adjustments, the colleges did not really change until forced to do so by circumstances and conditions which threatened their very existence. Certain of the older state universities and private institutions discovered that the newly established land-grant colleges for engineering, agriculture, and mechanic arts were beginning to take their student enrollment away from them; this factor caused them to act in order to compete more successfully with those newly established institutions. It would be unfortunate for the secondary schools to wait until they are forced by circumstances and the growth of parallel agencies to change their curricula to meet the changing needs of the student and the community

[7] "The Modern High-School Curriculum," *The School Review*, LXIII (January, 1955), pp. 16–24.

population. The educational activities of the National Youth Administration, the Civilian Conservation Corps, and the Works Progress Administration during the 1930's challenged certain aspects of training which were being administered ineffectively by the secondary school. For example, in 1941 the National Youth Administration was offering training in arts and crafts on a wide scale.[8] In the NYA service training centers, in connection with the national defense program, youth were being trained in as short a time as possible for metal work, carpentry, plumbing, welding, elementary auto mechanics and other types of mechanics, the use of die tools, masonry, and other occupations.

It is interesting to speculate about what changes would have been forced upon the curriculum of the public high school, if the National Youth Administration and the Civilian Conservation Corps had not been abolished in 1942. Disregarding speculation, it is certain that the era of the NYA and the CCC had one salutary result. The thoughtful school administrator and teacher began to ask themselves these questions: (1) Why should these parallel agencies arise so quickly in a time of emergency to train youth of secondary-school age? (2) To what extent are we in the secondary school duplicating training for youth that other agencies are providing? (3) To what extent are agencies other than the schools paralleling educational and vocational training that we are giving? and (4) How can we plan cooperatively with other agencies so that we do not attempt to duplicate expensive machinery and training for the same purpose(s)? The wise educator sees that the development of parallel agencies may inevitably take over some of the functions which the secondary school is attempting to perform at the present; and that in some respects and for many youth, they may assume the entire job of the education of adolescents, unless the secondary school is willing to study its own curriculum and the purposes for which it is established, and to work toward a much more effective program.

An educational philosopher, B. Othanel Smith, recently stated in startling terms the issue and the challenge that face the secondary school and its curriculum. He sees as the issue whether the sec-

[8] Lou Block, "Hand Skills in Crafts and Defense," *The High School Journal,* xxiv (March, 1941), pp. 111–18.

ondary school should become the custodian, in plain terms, of all youth, thus becoming responsible for their growth and for their welfare.[9] With this as the issue, of what character should the secondary-school program be? Some say that it should be composed largely of theoretical knowledge; others of practical facts and knowledge. In meeting this issue, the high-school organization will probably have to contain a synthesis of both kinds of knowledge.

The type of secondary-school organization which has been in operation in certain places in California for some years may prove to be part of the solution for the educational employee. This organization is the 6–4–4 plan, which includes six years of elementary school, four years of junior high school, and four years of what used to be called senior high school and junior college education, making a total school training of fourteen years in length.[10] The secondary school as now organized may find itself in the position of taking over and being responsible for the four years of junior-high-school work; this work would be centered around "general education" and those common ideals and attitudes and knowledges which all people believe that every child should have before he finishes school and goes out into life. The expansion of the secondary school, namely, the junior colleges and the community or technical institutes, may have to assume the further training of youth for vocations and life after these four years of school work along the lines of general education.

REMAKING THE SECONDARY-SCHOOL CURRICULUM BY ADDING NEW AND PARALLEL COURSES

A study of the practices of secondary schools in regard to curriculum revision shows that most of them, even during the depression years, added a large number of new subject-matter courses to

[9] "Basic Issues in American Secondary Education—1956," in *Frontiers of Secondary Education*, i, Syracuse University Press, 1956, pp. 17–30.
[10] *Cf.* L.V. Koos, *Integrating High School and College*, 1946, and J.A. Sexson and J.W. Harbeson, *The New American College*, 1946, both published by Harper and Brothers, New York; and *Education for All American Youth—A Further Look*, Educational Policies Commission, N.E.A., 1952, Chaps. vi–viii.

the curriculum, while they dropped comparatively few existing courses from their offerings. Studies of what the schools are teaching since 1930 show this. Hotz made a study for the North Central Association,[11] and another was made recently by the Association for Supervision and Curriculum Development.[12] During this twenty-five-year span, the only subject-matter courses showing significant losses in being dropped from the secondary-school offerings were the following: Latin, French, and Spanish in the *foreign-language group;* ancient and medieval and modern history in the *social-studies area;* botany and zoology in the *science group,* replaced by biology; and normal training and penmanship and spelling in the *miscellaneous group* of subjects. On the other hand, both investigations showed noteworthy additions to the curriculum in these secondary schools in the form of new courses in mathematics, English, the social studies, science, core courses, commercial subjects, agriculture, industrial arts, music, art, health, safety, driver, and physical education.

The following three influences have been at work to cause so many recent additions to the secondary-school curriculum: (1) the realization that some 60 per cent of the children who graduate from secondary school do not go to college; this has resulted in the attempt to provide courses in the secondary school for this 60 per cent which will prepare them for effective living both as individuals and as co-operating members of society; (2) the need for training a majority of adolescents for a vocation when they complete their secondary-school course, or when they drop out of school; and (3) legislative provisions of some states which recently have compelled the secondary schools to teach certain subjects which formerly had not been generally taught, such as health and physical education, driver education, safety education, state history, conservation education, the effect of alcohol and narcotics, and civic education.

The new subject-matter courses or courses necessary for new "programs of study" or "curricula" leading to secondary-school graduation are summarized in the following paragraphs.

[11] "Five Year Trends in the Development of North Central Association High Schools, 1930–1935," *North Central Association Quarterly,* x (April, 1936), pp. 412–21.
[12] *What Shall the High School Teach?* 1956 Yearbook, Chap. iii.

1. *Adult Education.* Although not strictly a part of the secondary-school program for adolescents, adult education is being given by many school systems throughout the forty-eight states, with an enrollment of more than 4,000,000. In San Francisco Schools, for example, the Adult Education Division offers hundreds of classes which are connected with family life and with problems of a state, national, or international nature. New York State has increased widely the extent and range of its program in the last ten years.[13] Kalamazoo, Michigan,[14] has had adult education classes for almost half a century; it offers a good example of a program that changed to meet the changing needs of adults in a community. Until recent years, adult education was organized and administered with the main idea of teaching adults to read and write who did not have that much formal education. Now adult education includes a varied list of activities, ranging from a study of home and family living to civic, international, and consumer education. In view of the fact that there is a tremendous number of youth between the ages of sixteen and twenty-four who are no longer in school and yet who desire and need further education, the secondary school is beginning to turn its attention to courses and plans for school work to fit their needs more effectively. Evidence of the importance of this new field is found in the publication of promising textbooks in the field of adult education.

2. *Character and Religious Education.* Another newcomer to the secondary-school field is character education, which assumes various guises and is fostered by different departments in different secondary schools. Some educators have contended that character education should be a by-product of the child's general education, coming through precept and example of the teacher and through association with and adjustment to the child group, as well as to the adult community. Therefore character education is found in the social-

[13] Robert A. Luke, "The Cost of Adult Under-Education," *NEA Journal*, XLV (October, 1956), pp. 428–29.

[14] *Toward a New Curriculum, 1944 Yearbook*, Department of Supervision and Curriculum Development, pp. 129–31 (and Chap. IX for an overview of the extension of adult education). For recent trends, read "Some Trends in Adult Education" by Irene Patterson, *Journal of Home Economics*, XLV (June, 1953), pp. 383–86, and *Learning Comes of Age*, by J.W. Powell, New York, Association Press, 1956.

studies department of many schools as part and parcel of citizen-ship or civics education. In other schools, character education has been thought of as part of the growth which goes hand in hand with the child's development in the family, the school, and the community; therefore, character education has been sandwiched in, or made a unit in the course in social living, or in home and family relationships, or in human relations.[15]

Religious education on school time is no new departure in certain New England centers; Bridgeport, Connecticut, has had such instruction for years. The New York state legislature enacted into its statutes a law whereby children may be freed from school attendance for one hour each week to receive religious instruction and training; the city of New York also adopted such a plan. Thus the problem of religious instruction, either by the schools or on school time, has come sharply to public attention. Many secondary schools in all parts of the country have given a course in the Bible for years, and this new emphasis upon religious instruction is but another evidence of the change in conception of the function of the secondary school.[16]

3. *Conservation Education.* A new subject in the secondary-school curriculum, conservation education has not usually been placed in charge of the agriculture department, but has been assigned to the social-studies or science areas. A wealth of material is being developed rapidly for this field; there are specific publications of the United States Office of Education, of the Soil Conservation Service of the United States Department of Agriculture, in certain regions, and of many states, such as Florida and Washington. The study of conservation of natural resources, of the management and improvement of the soil, of the prevention of erosion, and of the need for flood control and proper water usage are aspects of national life which have grown in importance; the nation has at last begun to realize that our national resources are not limitless, and that they must be preserved for use over a long period of years. In the secondary school, conservation courses range in length from

---

[15] *Cf.* "McGuffey vs the Moderns in Character Training," by Paul S. Anderson, *Phi Delta Kappan*, xxxviii (November, 1956), pp. 53–58.

[16] Chapter 21 presents the more recent controversy over religious education in the public schools.

a unit in some social science or science course, such as economics or general sciences, to a course of a semester or more in length.

4. *Consumer Education.* This is another course which has been introduced into the secondary school primarily in connection with new courses in the social studies, or as a part of an existing course. It will be found occasionally under the head of business or socio-business courses, or under the department of home economics or homemaking. Some educators contend now that it belongs properly with "distributive" education, which means a study of those distributive occupations in which workers are employed in the exchanges necessary for making available to consumers the goods and the services which have been produced by others. Regardless of where it has been located in the secondary-school curriculum, consumer education is one of the newer subjects which is destined to receive more and more emphasis as the years go by. When placed with the social studies, it is combined frequently with economics, where that course is given as a full year's work; it is occasionally found as a unit or units in sociology, where economics is not offered; and sometimes it is a full year's course called "Social Science."

Advertising, buying and selling, borrowing and lending, budgeting, the study of products, insurance, and the protection which the Federal and state governments give the consumer usually comprise the course. The Consumer Education Study [17] made one of the most careful studies of this area for secondary-school students; this group added to consumer education the aspects of wise use of health and leisure time. New textbooks for this course are being produced rapidly. Certain publications prepared by the Public Affairs Committee and by the Consumer Division of the Department of Labor give additional source material of a helpful nature, as do the monthly reports of Consumers' Union [18] and Consumers' Research.[19]

5. *Newcomers to the Subject-field of English.* Although English Courses I–IV remain primarily obligatory for students in the second-

---

[17] "The Consumer Education Series," Teaching-Learning Units for Secondary-School Students, Nos. 1–10, National Association of Secondary-School Principals, 1945–1947.

[18] In *Consumer Reports,* Mt. Vernon, N.Y.

[19] In *Consumer Bulletin,* Washington, N.J.

ary school, variations in this requirement have occurred and many new courses have been added to the area. One variation was introduced in North Carolina, for example, where it is permissible for a secondary school to allow a student to substitute dramatics or journalism for the fourth-year course in English. Public speaking, journalism, debating, dramatics, creative writing, contemporary literature, radio, TV, motion pictures, remedial English, and library science comprise new course offerings in English. It is to be noted that some of these new courses, such as journalism and dramatics, were formerly considered extracurricular in nature. The prevalence and influence of the motion picture, TV, and the radio on child life have caused the expansion of a study of these as subjects on the secondary-school level.[20]

6. *The Broadening of the Home Economics Field.* Among the more significant developments in this area in the last decade has been the extension of the base of the old home economics course to include the newer conception of homemaking for adolescents, both boys and girls. "Homemaking" courses have been stimulated in part by the George-Deen home economics teachers, who are supposed to spend ten months in the field and to relate the home economics program to the home and the family. The new emphasis on the training of adolescents in home and family life and in human relations has broadened the work in homemaking to include study of personal and social manners and customs, boy and girl problems, and questions of budgeting and child care. These new courses in homemaking have emphasized the close interrelationship which should exist between the homemaking and home economics courses, the science work, and the social studies. Many administrators and teachers maintain that this area should care for the courses in pupil guidance which have developed rapidly and extensively in the secondary school since about 1930. The type of work which is given varies from study based on textbooks, such as *Personal Adjustment, Marriage and Family Living,*[21] to a unit for girls on personal-social problems, or to a unit for both boys and girls on social living, cus-

[20] For a more recent summary, turn to "National Trends in Teaching High School English" by Arno Jewett, *The English Journal,* XLVI (September, 1957), pp. 326–29.

[21] By J.C. and M.G. Landis (2nd ed.), New York, Prentice-Hall, 1955.

toms, and problems of boys and girls. Still another approach to homemaking which is taken on the level of the junior high school is that of centering activities around those duties, responsibilities, jobs, and chores which the boy or girl has at home and should know how to perform.

7. *Trends in Foreign Languages.* The foreign languages have been losing ground steadily on the secondary-school level, as has been shown by Hotz's study and by figures on enrollments from the reports of the United States Office of Education. These data indicate that there will probably be less and less foreign language offered to and taken by students in the secondary school. Although they do not appear to be a significant addition to the foreign-language offering, courses in "general language" are being offered and textbooks for this work are available. Foreign-language teaching has grown rapidly in the elementary schools (Chapter 11), but foreign languages in high school have profited least by the addition of new subjects to the curriculum, and the reasons for this have been well summarized by Thornton Blayne and Walter V. Kaulfers.[22]

8. *Pupil Guidance.* When information from studies of youth in the depression era showed youth's lack of preparation for life and inability to get work, many educational leaders struck while the iron was hot and brought to popular attention that broad term called "guidance." One characteristic of all movements in education in the United States has been that when a workable remedy has been proposed for existing weaknesses, it has been adopted enthusiastically. The guidance movement profited by this characteristic. There is probably no secondary school, no matter how small, which has not heard of guidance, and which does not have one or more teachers who have taken special work in guidance.

There have been, and still are, differing views of guidance. In one group, the opinion is held that guidance is a function which should be performed by every teacher with his class and with his students individually. Another group holds that guidance is something which

---

[22] "College-Entrance Language Requirements and the High Schools," *The Modern Language Journal,* xxxvi (April, 1953), pp. 195–97.

can be given successfully in courses, such as those in "occupations," "vocations," or in "orientation." [23]

As a result of these conflicting views, the teacher will find guidance handled one way in one school and another way in another. For example, he will find courses in guidance in one department in one place, but in another school he will find guidance organized as a part of the program of student activities. The Providence, Rhode Island, schools have been at work since 1928 on the problem of the proper guidance of students. They have had the advantages of a faculty which has not had a large turnover in personnel each year, and of competent and constructive educational leadership. Their guidance curriculum for the junior high schools is still centered on the "Curriculum in Civics for Group Guidance Purposes." They make use of case conferences, charts, debates, displays, personal contacts, radio presentations and programs, speakers, tests, visits, and visual aids in their work. They attempt to assist the student in his introduction and orientation to secondary-school work in learning how to study, and in acquiring a survey of occupational fields; they make him aware of the need for efficient citizens, of industries and services, of the significance of transportation and communication, of trade and its commercial occupations, of civil service, of the proper selection and preparation for pupil choices in senior high school, of how the government is run, and of recreational possibilities of an educational nature.

Though the junior high schools have frequently incorporated guidance into the regular program of class work, the senior high schools have more frequently handled it as just described under Homemaking (see p. 396). They also stress student activities as an important part of guidance. [24]

9. *Physical and Health Education.*   In this area, a few states and local school systems have required the teaching of safety, hygiene, first aid, and automobile driver education along with health and

---

[23] *Cf.* "High School Courses in Occupations," by N.D. Stevens and Robert Hoppock, *The Personnel and Guidance Journal,* xxxiv (December, 1955), pp. 213–16.

[24] The Bulletin of the National Association of Secondary-School Principals, Vol. xxxvi, No. 184, *Vitalizing Student Activities in the Secondary School* (February, 1952), pp. 1–229.

physical education. Certain school systems print courses of study which include all of these different aspects of education under one teaching field. Elementary schools have had types of physical education and health programs in operation for many years, but in the secondary school the expansion of this kind of teaching has been so rapid, and the knowledges required of the teacher have been so many and widespread, that the schools have been able only recently to get enough qualified instructors. In order to furnish trained teachers for this area, many institutions of higher education have developed departments of physical education and health; some of these departments train teachers of physical education and of health for both the elementary and secondary schools and the colleges.

The attitude of persons who train teachers for the elementary school has been that each teacher in each grade should know a good deal about the activities which should constitute the program in physical education and health, in safety and safety education, and in personal hygiene. The belief is that these aspects of education should accompany the normal growth and development of each child. The secondary school is gradually coming to that same conception of physical education; however, it is a slow process to lessen emphasis on interscholastic sports and competition, and to place the main stress on the development of group and individual activities in physical education and healthy growth for all students.[25]

From trends in this area, two conclusions are justified: (1) physical and health education is so interwoven with other subject areas in the secondary school—*e.g.*, science, home economics, and the social studies—that it will be necessary for persons in charge of this work to coordinate it closely with the other courses already existent in the subject-matter fields for effective teaching; (2) the implications in the program of health and physical education in the secondary school are most promising for pupils; through a well-balanced program of this sort they can learn more about public health, the care of children, personal hygiene and sex education, diet, biological growth, and the varied activities of the individual, the group,

[25] *Cf. Health Education, a Guide for Teachers and a Text for Teacher Education* (4th ed.) and *Healthful School Living*, both published by the National Education Association. 1948 and 1958, respectively.

and the community. Many schools have combined with health and physical education the teaching of safety education and driver education—aspects which are really units of the broader work in the social studies having to do with communication and transportation, and with living in the home and the family and the community.[26]

10. *Mathematics.* In spite of a decline in emphasis in the secondary school upon advanced mathematics, especially upon algebra and geometry, a few new courses have been added to this area. "General" or "practical" mathematics is the particular newcomer which has swept the field; these general courses take the place of the year which used to be devoted to advanced arithmetic and the introduction to elementary algebra. In addition, "senior mathematics" or advanced general mathematics, socio-business arithmetic, and business mathematics have been instituted for boys and girls who are about ready to graduate from secondary school. The trend has been toward more different courses and different types of mathematics to meet the changing needs of individuals, rather than in any fundamental change in the subject-matter scope of the mathematics curriculum.

11. *Military Training—The Junior R.O.T.C.* Many secondary schools have instituted a Junior Reserve Officers Training Corps, with the cooperation and financial assistance of the Federal government. The Junior R.O.T.C. is really military training for boys on the secondary-school level; it is controlled and directed by the War Department through prescribed courses and instructors furnished by the Federal government. The original Defense Act provided that the student should complete this special course when he had once entered upon it, unless the Secretary of War ruled otherwise. From this brief description of the Junior R.O.T.C., it is to be noted that the Federal government makes statutory provision for graduation from secondary school, instead of the local school board's controlling this matter in the case of the R.O.T.C. student. It is seen, moreover, that the instructors and course of study are prescribed by the Federal government, and that the type of training is fixed and cannot be changed to meet local needs.

[26] For a good idea why many physical educators are on the defensive, read "Reconstruction in Physical Education" by Morton Levitt, *School and Society,* Vol. 85 (June 22, 1957), pp. 219–21.

The establishment of these junior units created controversies in many of the school communities where they were introduced,[27] or where the proposal was made to establish them. It is true that the crises caused by World War II, the Korean War, "cold war" events since 1950, and the need for national defense possibly justified the establishment of R.O.T.C. units as an emergency measure, but it is to be doubted that universal military training in the secondary school is wise, as a substitute for a physical or recreational program, for character education, or for the normal growth and development of the adolescent.

Nevertheless, military training has obtained a foothold in the secondary schools, for better or for worse. It is questionable whether growing boys and girls should be impelled by group opinion or the lure of glamour to take part in a type of training which they may not really want, and which may not be of constructive assistance in developing most fully their personality and their normal growth. The addition of Junior R.O.T.C. units to the secondary school is a reversal of the usual process which has been taking place; in this case an existing agency, the schools, is being used by another agency, the Federal government, instead of the government's establishing a parallel organization to care for the military training of youth of secondary-school age.

12. *Music.* Music in the high school has about held its own since 1915 in the percentage of total enrollment. However, instrumental music since 1934 has dropped sharply; band is more popular than orchestra in most schools. Vocal music reaches more pupils with its chorus, public-school music, and glee club work. Newcomers are music appreciation, harmony, and theory and practice.[28]

13. *The Expansion of the Social-Studies Field.* In the secondary school, courses in the social-studies area have multiplied more than

[27] E.C. Johnson, "Main Issues in the Junior ROTC Controversy," *Harvard Educational Review*, IX (October, 1939), pp. 469–81; and F.E. Karelsen, Jr., "Do We Want Military Training in the High Schools?" *Frontiers of Democracy*, VIII (April 15, 1942), pp. 200–202.

[28] *Cf. What Shall The High Schools Teach? op. cit.,* Chap. III; *Offerings and Enrollments in High-School Subjects,* Biennial Survey of Education in the U.S., 1948–1950, Chap. v, Federal Security Agency, Office of Education, 1951, *passim* (the regular 15-year report of the U.S. Office); and "Secondary-School Music," by A.N. Jones, *Educational Music,* XXXV (November-December, 1955), pp. 10–11, 44.

courses in any other field except business education. The following
list comprises the new courses in social studies:

Civil Defense Education
Civics and Citizenship
World History
Economics
Problems of Democracy
Geography
Guidance
Latin American History
Modern and Current History
Sociology
Government
State History

Social Culture
International Relations
Contemporary Problems of Youth
Rural Economics
Radio Broadcasting
Occupations or Vocations
Orientation to School and Life
Civic Education
Home and Family Life and Consumer Education
Psychology
Public Affairs
World Government, or the U.N.

There is much truth in the contention that the teachers of the
social studies have been unusually keen to realize their opportunities and to introduce new matter into the curriculum in various ways.
For example, they have been eager to develop the modified unit
technique and "centers of interest" around which children study
transportation, communication, modern problems in public affairs,
and home and community life. On the other hand, there is a possibility that the curriculum in the social studies will become so over-
burdened with numerous *separate* courses that the prime values
which the child is supposed to get from such a basic area will be
lost sight of in the subdivision of subject matter.

So rapid has been the growth of new subjects and "source" references in the social-studies area that it is impossible to list here all
of the types of aids which have been developed.[29] The field adapts
itself rather easily to treatment through the unit or problems approach, as well as to the approach which involves the actual experiences of children in everyday life.

14. *Courses in Civil and Public Service.* These courses represent an entirely new offering in the secondary school. When, in 1935,
the Committee on Experimental Units of the North Central As-

[29] The special bibliography at the end of this chapter contains significant
references and materials of source types. For trends in the general or junior
college, read Joe Park, "Trends in Social Studies: Grades 13 and 14," *Social
Education,* XIX (April, 1955), pp. 166–70.

sociation of Colleges and Secondary Schools interested itself in presenting to secondary-school pupils a faithful picture of the way in which American government operates, it had no idea that separate courses in preparation for public service might be established in the secondary school. The committee's interest centered primarily in the preparation of units for social-studies classes on civil service, taxation, and other problems of government.[30]

The secondary schools are now beginning to give complete courses in public and civil service of one semester or a year in length; such courses have been stimulated by the tremendous growth in the number of government employees. These courses have been put under the direction and control of the social-studies department in most schools, though a few will be found as adjuncts to vocational training, or as parts of the work in vocational courses.

15. *Science Offerings.* The change in this subject area was slight until the mid-fifties and the arrival of "Sputnik," and was in the direction of substituting Junior and Senior Science and Earth Science for the well-known courses in chemistry, physics, and biology. In some schools, however, Senior Science is offered in addition to the traditional courses in science; it is a course in which the practical and applied aspects of science are stressed, rather than the principles and laws of pure science. Other newcomers to the science field are Physical Geography, which was well known in secondary schools about the turn of the century; consumer science; conservation; descriptive chemistry; aeronautics; fundamentals of electricity; advanced biology; and physical science, both for the noncollege student and for the talented pupil.[31]

16. *Courses in Social Living.* When new courses were considered in home economics and the social studies, it was pointed out that courses in "Social Living" have recently been added to the secondary-school curriculum. These courses have ranged in length from six weeks to a semester, with emphasis primarily upon living

[30] *Cf.* "Unit Studies in American Problems," prepared for the Committee on Experimental Units of the North Central Association of Colleges and Secondary Schools, 1939–1947.

[31] *Cf.* "Physical Science for the Non-College Students" by T.B. Edwards, *California Journal of Secondary Education,* xxx (November, 1955), pp. 407–9, and "The Physical Science Study," articles by leaders in the science field in *The Science Teacher,* xxiv (November, 1957), pp. 315–30.

with others and upon social manners, customs, and problems. The variation is found in some schools of combining social living with the orientation course for freshmen in the first year of high school, or with a course in guidance and counseling, or with the course in occupations. Sex education is given occasionally in courses of this type; this controversial issue in secondary education has been discussed over a period of years by various authorities here and abroad.[32]

17. *Safety and Driver Education.* Alarmed at the rate at which Americans accidentally kill themselves or their fellow men, many agencies have made a concerted effort during the last decade to make the public "safety-conscious." Safety education as a subject of study has been instituted in a large number of schools in every state of the union, and the scope of it has been broadened to include aspects other than those connected with driving a car and with transportation. Under the broad head of education for safety come training for safety in the home, in the factory, on the street and highway, and in play and recreation. Source materials of many kinds have been prepared for these courses by such agencies as the National Education Association, the American Automobile Association, and many state departments of public instruction. In some schools, safety education has been placed under the social-studies department, while in others it has been bracketed with health and physical education. This is another one of the subjects which many states are coming to require by law to be taught in the elementary and the secondary schools. Just where it belongs in the departmental organization of the curriculum of the secondary school is still a question, however, the trend is toward having it taught in a separate course or department in the high school.

18. *Vocational Education and Occupational Adjustment.* The

[32] *Cf.* B.C. Gruenberg and J.L. Kaukonen, *High Schools and Sex Education,* United States Public Health Service, 1939; J.N. Baker, *Sex Education In High Schools* (1942) and Cyril Bibby, *Sex Education: A Guide for Parents, Teachers and Youth Leaders* (1946), New York, Emerson Books, Inc.; "The Nature of Sex Education Programs in Wisconsin High Schools," a survey reported in *The High School Journal,* xxxviii (December, 1954), pp. 77–116; and the "Sex Education Series," approved by the Joint Committee on Health Problems in Education of the National Education Association and the American Medical Association, five books, published by E.P. Dutton and Company, New York, 1955.

following list of new courses in the various departments of vocational education in the secondary school shows distinctly the trends in this area:

Industrial Arts and Industrial *Education*	*Business* *Education*
Auto mechanics	General business
Radio and TV	Business correspondence
Aviation trades and Mechanics	Salesmanship
Handicrafts	Business law
Occupations	Business organization
Welding	Business economic problems
Electrical mechanics	Personal guidance
Cosmetology	Consumer education
	Consumer economics
	Store management
	Personal efficiency

Agriculture	*Diversified Occupations and* *Distributive Education*
Farm forestry	(These two are aspects of Industrial
Conservation of soils	Arts and Industrial Education,
	and of Business or Commercial
	Education, respectively.)

Some of the courses listed above are designated as "work programs" in high school. Briefly defined, such programs of "work experience" consist of part-time work and part-time school studies in related fields for each student each day. The pupil is under a coordinator or instructor (a regular faculty member) in his work at school, and under a supervisor while on the job; he is paid as a beginner or an apprentice, at the regular rate. Diversified occupations, distributive education, business education, and industrial education have developed the most effective work programs in high school.[33]

Besides adding new vocational courses, the secondary schools have devoted much time and effort in their vocational departments

[33] For good descriptions of work programs, turn to *Work Experience in High School* by W.H. Ivins and W.B. Runge, New York, The Ronald Press Company, 1951; *Training High School Youth for Employment* by C.E. Rakestraw, Chicago, American Technical Society, 1947; and "Cooperative Education in New York City" by Grace Brennan, *NEA Journal*, XLIV (May, 1955), pp. 303–4.

toward attempting to counsel their students wisely in regard to occupations of various types. These efforts at vocational counseling have taken the form of courses in "Occupations," of personal conferences and guidance, and of studies in the vocational courses by students and teachers of the different occupations which are open and for which students might prepare themselves. In all probability, this counseling service for students in the secondary school will continue to expand.

It is doubtful whether the modifications which have developed in the curriculum through the addition of new subjects and parallel courses of study will be completely satisfactory in the long run for adjusting the secondary-school curriculum adequately to the needs of pupils and of society. Many curriculum experts are convinced that more radical steps are necessary, especially in establishing the aims and purposes of secondary education in terms of the needs of pupils and society, and then modifying the curriculum to meet those needs.

CURRICULAR PLANS IN SECONDARY EDUCATION

TYPES OF APPROACH.   Historically, the results of two significant investigations of the curriculum of the secondary school furnish an excellent point of departure for the consideration of new directions and new growth. J.W. Wrightstone's study

. . . summarizes the progress that has been made in the construction and application of new measures to the curriculum experiments in several progressive high schools. It is limited to a few matched experimental and conventional secondary schools. . . . In order to measure important objectives of the new curriculum practices, new instruments of measurement have been devised, especially in the social studies, natural sciences, and language arts. . . .[34]

In contrast with Wrightstone's purposes, Harold Spears treats of the following:

. . . (1) the more general features of current instructional reorganization, the shortcomings of such reorganization, and the challenge which these shortcomings present to the principal; (2) specific steps which the

[34] *Appraisal of Experimental High School Practices*, Teachers College, Columbia University, 1936, p. iii.

principal might take to improve the school, as indicated by examples taken from schools undergoing pronounced instructional reorganization; and (3) a curriculum charter for the principal, pointing out how he can function as a leader in the reconstruction of secondary education.[35]

From the findings of authors on the curriculum and from the evolution of the elementary-school curriculum which has already been described,[36] various curriculum approaches are presented for comparative purposes in Table 22.

FIG. 30   *Boys working in the graphic arts area in industrial arts. Graphic arts include letter press and silk screen printing, book binding, and mechanical drawing. (Courtesy Charlotte (N.C.) City Schools, Sedgefield Junior High School.)*

An analysis of these plans of curriculum development shows a marked similarity between the development of the elementary-school curriculum and the growth through which the secondary-school curriculum is now going. The "subject curriculum" or the traditional plan corresponds to the "textbook approach" in the elementary-school field; the "correlated," "fused," and "broad-fields"

[35] *The Emerging High School Curriculum and Its Direction,* New York, American Book Company, 1940, p. 7.
[36] Chap. x.

curricular bear close resemblance to the development of "subject-matter" or "subject-area" units in the elementary school, and to the "activity" or "fusion" approach there; the "core curriculum" corresponds to the larger "centers of interest" development with scope and sequence; the "experience curriculum" refuses to recognize the subject-matter approach, and is similar to the organismic approach to the experience curriculum in the elementary school.

Wrightstone's "broad-fields-of-knowledge" type of curriculum plan corresponds to the same approach mentioned by Spears and Draper; Wrightstone's "individual-interests-and-needs" plan of organization is essentially the "center-of-interest" approach used by Spears and on the elementary-school level; it is also close kin to Leonard's "topical" (or unit) plan and his "problems" plan. The "cultural-epoch organization" of Wrightstone and the "cultural plan" of Leonard bear a close resemblance to the "fused" curriculum. Wrightstone found that the dominant place in the new program of the experimental schools was held by the social studies; science was likewise used to some extent as the core in the secondary schools of the Eight-Year Study; but English literature, foreign languages, and mathematics had a much less controlling position in the curriculum than formerly. This situation still prevails today.

In actual fact, the fused, correlated, and broad-fields types of curriculum plans are variations of the subject curriculum—first steps which many schools and subject departments are taking in curriculum revision. Spears calls attention to this fact. Of course, the subject-centered curriculum is well known, inasmuch as practically every teacher in the secondary school has been trained specifically to teach in a major field or an aspect of a major field. In the subject-centered curriculum the student's work, as well as that of the teacher, revolves around a single subject of study, such as history, or even around a smaller aspect of a subject-matter field, *e.g.*, American history.

Though the plan has rather wide possibilities for assisting in the development of an "experience" or "core" curriculum, the "broad-fields" approach has proved so far to be mainly a *type of curricular organization* or *reorganization* of subject-matter departments and traditional courses in the secondary school. This broad-fields plan

TABLE 22   Types of curriculum approach ‡

Types of Curriculum Plans—High School (Spears)	Types of Curriculum Plans in the P.E.A. Study—27 Experimental High Schools (Wrightstone)	Curricular Plans (Alberty)
1. The Subject Curriculum 2. The Correlated Curriculum 3. The Fused Curriculum 4. The Broad-Fields Curriculum 5. The Core Curriculum 6. The Experience Curriculum	1. The Cultural-Epoch Organization 2. Broad Fields of Knowledge 3. Individual Interests and Needs	1. Subject-Centered Curriculum 2. Experience-Centered Curriculum (Activity Program) 3. Core Curriculum

Curricular Plans (Leonard)	Trends in Curricular Organization (Draper)	Evolution of the Elementary-School Curriculum
1. Traditional Plan Subject-Matter Framework 2. Correlated (Integrated) Curriculum 3. Fusion 4. Core Curriculum 5. Topical (Unit) Plan ° 6. Cultural Plan 7. Problems Plan	1. Subject-Matter Approach 2. Fusion and Correlation † 3. Broad-Fields Curriculum 4. Core Curriculum 5. Experience Curriculum	1. The Textbook Curriculum Approach 2. Subject-Matter or Subject-Area Units 3. "Activity" or "Fusion" Approach 4. The Development of Larger "Centers of Interest," with Scope and Sequence (Core Curriculum) 5. The Experience Curriculum

‡ The data upon which this composite table is based are: Harold Spears, *The Emerging High School Curriculum and Its Direction,* New York, American Book Company, 1948, Chap. III; J.W. Wrightstone, *Appraisal of Experimental High School Practices,* Teachers College, Columbia University, 1936, Chap. II; Harold Alberty, *Reorganizing the High-School Curriculum* (rev. ed.), New York, The Macmillan Company, 1953, Chaps. V–VI, VIII; J.P. Leonard, *Developing the Secondary School Curriculum* (rev. ed.), New York, Rinehart and Company, 1953, Chaps. X–XI, XIV; H.R. Douglass (Ed.), *The High School Curriculum* (2nd ed.), New York, The Ronald Press Company, 1956, Chap. XII, and Chap. X, *ante.*

° Leonard calls these three types of curriculum reorganization of the subject curriculum rather than plans.

† The Large Unit of work is used as a special instrument in the development of all of these plans, especially in the newer ones.

would classify all subject matter into from three to six broad fields of knowledge considered essential for all pupils; each field would be arranged in a small number of broad courses, with continuous, progressive sequence from year to year. A fuller consideration of the organizational possibilities of this plan is given in Chapter 15.

In the "cultural-epoch" approach, the controlling idea is to make of each school year's study a "cultural epoch" for the student. An extreme example of this type of organization in a four-year secondary school would include "Our Heritage from Ancient Times" in grade nine; "Our Inheritance from the Middle Centuries" in grade ten; "Our Colonial Heritage" in grade eleven; and "Modern European-American Culture" in grade twelve. This plan emphasizes the study of ideas in relationship, and is close kin to the fused and experience curricula.

THE FOUR NEW CURRICULUM PLANS. After careful examination and study, the following types of curriculum approach are presented as truly representative of the new steps in curricular development which are being taken in the secondary school:

1. *The Correlated Curriculum.* This may be defined as the attempt to show the relationships between subject areas and the interrelationships of one subject with other subjects. For example, teachers of Latin and English in the first year of secondary school may attempt to correlate their work so that they take up certain fundamental questions of grammar at the same time and show the relationships and similarity; another illustration is found in the attempt to teach American literature and American history in the third year and to correlate the material and activities. The big handicap to the development of this method is the retention of subject-matter divisions and departments in the secondary school.

2. *The Fused Curriculum* combines two or more regular courses into one course of a more general and valuable nature. In the past, the first attempts at this resulted in biology taking the place of zoology and botany as a fused course; more recently, world history tries to combine ancient, medieval, and modern history—a well-nigh impossible job. Other experiments have been tried in combining the first year of social studies with the first year of English. High-school attempts at fused curricula have usually been centered on subject matter, not on the experiences of children. Real fusion in the high school usually involves a double period and the same group of children under the same teacher for this period. When actually centered around pupil experiences, the *fused* naturally evolves into the

core curriculum on the secondary level, or Wrightstone's *cultural-epoch* plan of curriculum revision.

3. *The Core Curriculum.* Spears defines this as a provision for children of a common body of growth experiences, taking for granted that certain specific types of learning experiences are fundamental for all pupils. A true core curriculum would be considered as involving three principles: (1) a longer period for classwork than the regular length; (2) the drawing of material from an area which under the old subject-matter curriculum would embrace two or as many fields as needed. Spears uses Social Living or Social Relationships as an illustration of the core curriculum, a daily course two hours long, fusing materials from the fields of English, music, art, literature, and the social studies, and (3) centering the work not on the text or on one subject-matter field alone, but on the interests, needs, and experiences of children.

4. *The Experience Curriculum.* This curricular approach is based upon the experiences which the child will be interested in normally and go through with naturally during his growth and development. It takes into account the growth of the whole individual, discarding the idea that the child can be helped to grow most effectively by treating him as one growing in mathematics for one period a day, in English for another period, in social studies for another period, etc. In this type of curriculum, the big problem for the teacher is one of planning and providing the right situation which will continue to stimulate and drive the pupil forward to active participation and learning. It is recognized that the pupil may wish at times to pursue activities and experiences which may not be most economical of time, or wisest for him to pursue; therefore, the expert teacher surveys in advance those things which children of the adolescent age at that particular grade level have as problems, interests, and needs, and is prepared in advance with materials and general outlines for those directions of growth and experiences which the children under his counseling may follow for a month, a semester, or a year. It is the teacher's responsibility both to plan in advance and to see that reasonable scope and sequence are maintained in the learning process, in order to avoid duplication of the study of the same experience (*e.g.,* Our Social Relationships) on two successive grade levels. In the *experience* approach, the student selects his activity or center of interest and then brings to bear upon it *all* subject-matter fields which he needs for the solution of problems in that activity or area. Draper contends that the main characteristic of an experience curriculum is its planlessness; that the experience curriculum for its success demands the master teacher who is well integrated himself and who understands student growth and development so well that he can plan activities with pupils on a minute's notice.[37]

[37] H.R. Douglass (Ed.), *The High School Curriculum* (2nd ed.), New York, The Ronald Press Company, 1956, pp. 210–11.

Instituting the experience curriculum on the secondary-school level is not as easily done as on the elementary level (Chapter 10). But it is not too difficult if the principal, his staff, and his community follow these guide lines: (1) All personnel must believe honestly that they can have a better curriculum for both talented and retarded students; (2) all of the teachers must be prepared in, and *want to teach in,* two or more subject-matter fields; (3) all personnel must realize that *four* fifty-minute (or longer) class periods a week will fulfill the Carnegie unit requirement of 120 clock hours, thus leaving free for each student at least *five* extra periods a week to study what he is particularly interested in; (4) all pupils would be scheduled *first* for required or "constant" subjects, for four periods a week; then each pupil would be scheduled for "special interest" or creative subjects in the extra hours of a staggered schedule; (5) when any pupil wanted advanced work or a course not offered, he would be taught in the extra periods of each week, provided the staff had a person competent to teach what he wanted, such as calculus, or organic chemistry, or music composition; and (6) evaluative procedures are agreed upon and established, so that a pupil can take tests upon work when he finishes it, and then start on another course or interest.

CURRICULAR PRACTICES OF PROMISE

THE UNIT AND THE CORE AS INSTRUMENTS IN THE ACHIEVEMENT OF GENERAL EDUCATION. One who studies the growth of the public school curriculum in American education is impressed with the influence of the "unit of work" around a center of interest in the development of correlation, fusion, the core curriculum, and the experience curriculum.

For example, the high-school teacher usually takes *the planning and teaching of a subject-matter unit as one of his first steps* in improving his work for his students; he may also *correlate* his subject-matter area with other subject-matter fields in this subject unit; or he may correlate first, and develop the subject-matter unit as the second step. The next step that the teacher usually takes involves either *fusion* of two or more subject-matter courses, or the *core* centered primarily around pupil experiences and activities. Satisfactory scope and sequence are a natural development in the planning of the work of this growing teacher, whether he uses correlation, fusion, the core, or the experience curriculum. The point should be emphasized here, however, that the *unit of work* helps this intelligent teacher to go step by step from textbook teaching to correlation; from correlation to fusion; from fusion to core planning and teaching; and eventually from successful core-work to planning for the experience curriculum.

The correlated, fused, and core-curriculum approaches to work in the secondary school have also been both teaching and administrative devices for the achievement of what has come to be known as *general* education. Perhaps the briefest definition of general education is that education that everyone must have for satisfactory and efficient living, regardless of what one plans to make his life work.[38] *Some* define the core curriculum also *in terms* of this same definition of general education; *others* indicate that the core *is the means* by which every student achieves that general education. Regardless of what point of view is taken, general education can be attained by means of an adequate correlated, fused, or core program. Other terms that one finds in the educational literature for the "core" are "unified studies," "basic socializing courses," "common learnings," "integrating courses," and "stem" courses.

HIGH SCHOOL SUBJECTS AS COMMUNICATION ARTS. A new trend of significance in the high school curriculum is the concept that many of the subjects on this level today should be primarily "communication arts" subjects. This concept, briefly defined, is that much of the work by students on this level should be devoted to learning how to use the various subjects as tools or instruments for further learning and study. For example, students in English courses should learn (1) how to communicate intelligently through oral and written practice in expression, (2) how to acquire further knowledge and leisure-time interests through the medium of reading, and (3) how to become intelligent "consumers" of newspapers and magazines, motion pictures, radio, and television through work in English classes.

Another area, that of music and the arts, offers another rich illustration of this "communication arts" concept. Through these

[38] *Cf.* Edgar Draper on general education in Chap. XII in *The High School Curriculum* and "Technical Vocabulary of the Curriculum," Chap. 9.

media, students should learn (1) how to establish standards for good music and art; (2) how to understand the creative arts through experiencing creative work in the writing of poetry, the writing and staging of drama, and in rhythmics and dancing; and (3) how to

FIG. 31   *The problems approach in teaching*

Senior high students confer on problems of world organization with a teacher of social studies in a room especially equipped for their use. (*Courtesy Denver Public Schools.*)

recognize perspective, background, harmony, and tone. Others likewise maintain that mathematics is but a necessary tool to be mastered and used in science, music, maps, charts, graphs, history, geography, consumer education, and homemaking.

Attempts have been made to inform teachers of the possibilities of the use of high-school subjects as "communication arts." [39] What has been done, coupled with the development of the core curriculum as a means of achieving general education on the junior high-school level, gives promise of further experimentation and investigation of high-school subjects as communication arts.

OTHER SOURCE MATERIALS AND PRACTICES. In addition to a study of the various types of curriculum plans, the wide-awake teacher will want to examine source materials and promising practices elsewhere which can help him to improve his work. Two new publications furnish good illustrations of the core curriculum, from definitions through to the use of correlation, fusion, unit procedures around centers of interest, and the core class in action. [40] Gertrude Noar presents the core-type curriculum for the junior high school, the curriculum areas that could be fused, and samples of resource unit outlines. [41] Though designed primarily for the grades, *Unit Teaching in the Elementary School* [42] is full of ideas and illustrations for teachers on any level.

The National Association of Secondary-School Principals in its *Bulletin* has presented new methods, departures, and experiments from time to time in music education, family life education, international understanding, home economics, outdoor education, mathematics, speech and reading, health and physical education, and science.

In a little different manner, special issues of the *California Journal of Secondary Education* have been devoted to curriculum problems in the teaching of business education, mathematics, home and family life problems, driver education, the fine arts, adult education, and that newcomer, consumer education.

Education for Social Competence [43] is a part of the Report of the

---

[39] *Cf.* the publications of the National Council of Teachers of English and *Mass Media and Education,* 53rd Yearbook, Part II, National Society for the Study of Education, 1954, *passim.*

[40] *Developing a Core Curriculum* (2nd ed.), by R.C. Faunce and N.L. Bossing, Englewood Cliffs, Prentice-Hall, 1958, and *Developing a High School Core Program,* by L.L. Lurry and E.J. Alberty, New York, The Macmillan Company, 1957.

[41] *The Junior High School—Today and Tomorrow,* New York, Prentice-Hall, 1953.

[42] By L.A. Hanna, *et al.,* New York, Rinehart and Company, 1955.

[43] I.J. Quillen and L.A. Hanna, Chicago, Scott, Foresman and Company, 1948.

Stanford Social Education Investigation from 1939 to 1943. In the investigation, thirty-one administrators and 112 classroom teachers participated; they represented eighteen different secondary schools in ten school systems in the western states.[44] Though a majority of the 112 teachers were in social studies, the investigation included some teachers from science, English, industrial arts, home economics, and other areas. The volume surveys rather completely the social-studies curriculum and trends and newer developments in this subject area. For example, these aspects are included: pre-planning, unit development and resource units, reading materials, visual and auditory aids, using community resources, persuasion materials, and evaluation techniques.

Good examples of materials in regard to reading in the secondary school are found in special guides for teachers prepared by state and city systems. These teachers' guides emphasize the importance of the teacher knowing something about reading readiness in pupils and reading in the other subject-matter fields. Also many of the states have prepared or are preparing teacher guides and materials for a real program of health education for all of the high-school grades.

THE CONFUSED CURRICULAR SITUATION IN THE SECONDARY SCHOOLS

To the student who looks without prejudice both backward and forward at the educational scene in secondary education, the following facts are inescapable:

1. The secondary school has not stated clearly its manifold aims and functions and has not agreed upon them.
2. Not having agreed upon its purposes, the curriculum in the secondary school shows a confused mixture of subjects and activities which aptly illustrate this lack of agreement.
3. The secondary school needs curricular reorganization from within, and if this is not accomplished, curriculum revision will be forced upon it from without.

Charles H. Judd, in an address before the National Association

[44] Colorado (Denver); Utah (Salt Lake City); Washington (Seattle); Oregon (Eugene); California (Fortuna, Long Beach, Los Angeles, Menlo Park, Pasadena, Redwood City).

of Secondary School Principals in 1945,[45] urged each one of the 8,000 best equipped secondary schools to start work to prepare at least one unit of instruction which departed from tradition and which included something that could contribute directly to the introduction of all pupils into adult life. His suggestion deserves careful thought today. For example, South Edgecombe High School (N.C.) and Fork Union Military Academy (Va.) have experimented successfully over a period of years with the one-subject plan of teaching.[46] Other schools could experiment on other departures.

Additional evidence of the general confusion which exists regarding the secondary-school curriculum has been shown since the successful launching of the first Russian satellite (Sputnik). Immediately those who were responsible for America's progress in keeping abreast and ahead of others in things military seemed to excuse their own inadequacy by pointing to the lack of adequate mathematics and science training of our youth. They urged a "crash" program to produce more American scientists, with emphasis upon science and mathematics to the exclusion of what they termed "unessentials" in the high-school curriculum.

On the other hand, there are persons who believe that education is a different thing from training. They believe that *education* consists in the maximum development of individual members of society for the future benefit of all, and that *training* is concerned primarily with developing members of society as tools to turn out products.[47] Those who hold to this idea maintain that there is much to be said for education as a factor in the highest development of intellectual activity and ability; they affirm that a democratic social organization and education necessarily go hand in hand, and that education should foster endless curiosity and a striving after a larger

[45] "Changes in Secondary Education Necessary for the Solution of Problems of Youth," *Bulletin of the National Association of Secondary-School Principals*, Vol. xxiv, No. 88 (February, 1940), pp. 39–52.

[46] *Cf.* "The One-Subject Plan of Teaching," by E.H. Lacy, Jr., *Bulletin of the National Association of Secondary-School Principals*, xxxix (November, 1955), pp. 58–60; and "Flexibility in Secondary Schools Through the One-Subject Plan," by S.M. Holton, *The High School Journal*, xxxii (May, 1949), pp. 113–22.

[47] *Language Study in American Education,* prepared for the Modern Language Association of America by C.C. Fries, William M. Sale, and Edwin H. Zeydel, Commission on Trends in Education of the Modern Language Association of America, 1940.

freedom which has not yet been attained. This point of view must be considered in the revamping of the secondary-school curriculum. Some compromise will have to be worked out which will be satisfactory to this group as well as to those educators who call for more emphasis upon education for scientific and economic competency.

Finally, there is another disturbing element in the situation. Why have elementary-school teachers made so much more progress than their secondary-school colleagues in *teacher-pupil planning?* Since students in secondary schools are more mature, and are engaged in curriculum work of a more specialized nature, there is no adequate excuse for lack of attention to this cooperative venture.[48]

PROBLEMS FOR INDIVIDUAL STUDY AND CLASS DISCUSSION

1. Should new work in "Social Living" in the secondary school be a new course in Social Studies or in Home Economics, or a unit of work in some course already established? Support your point of view.

2. Did the student-aid program of the National Youth Administration on the secondary-school level have any curricular implications? Give reasons for your point of view.

3. What are the required or "constant" subjects for graduation from a standard (accredited) secondary school in your state?

4. Why has the offering in the area of the social studies expanded so rapidly in the form of new and additional courses in recent years?

5. Is it really more difficult to effect revision and experimentation in the curriculum on the secondary-school level than it is in the elementary school? Give reasons for your answer.

6. Assume that your teaching has been centered around the textbook and subject matter, and that you wish to improve it by centering your teaching around the experiences of adolescents. What steps would you take in preparation for this change in the next year's work in one of your classes?

7. How should the secondary school approach the teaching of character education?

8. For what type of school community would work in "Diversified Occupations" be valuable? Explain.

[48] For a practical, modern handbook on this for the junior and senior high-school teacher, read *Teacher-Pupil Planning for Better Classroom Learning,* by L. Parrish and Y. Waskin, New York, Harper and Brothers, 1958.

9. Why has secondary-school work in "Conservation" so frequently been delegated to the Department of Social Studies instead of to the Science Department?

10. Write down in detail by years the courses required for graduation from the business (commercial) curriculum in any secondary school. Is there a good balance between the general and specialized aspects of this special curricular program?

11. Should "consumer education" be taught in the secondary school? If so, where? To what age range? How?

12. Can you distinguish clearly between a "correlated" and a "fused" curriculum on the secondary-school level?

13. Assume that the textile mills in your community have offered to your high-school facilities for an apprenticeship program for youth of part-time work and part-time school. As principal, how would you go about planning for such a new curricular program?

14. Is there any difference between "Industrial Arts" and "Industrial Education"? Business and commercial education? "Diversified occupations" and "distributive education"?

SPECIAL BIBLIOGRAPHY ON SECONDARY EDUCATION FOR THE CURRICULUM WORKER AND FOR THE SECONDARY TEACHER

Alberty, H., *Reorganizing the High-School Curriculum* (rev. ed.), New York, The Macmillan Company, 1953.

Alcorn, Marvin D., *et al.*, *Better Teaching in Secondary Schools*, New York, Henry Holt and Company, 1954.

Aldrich, J. (Ed.), *Social Studies for the Junior High School*, Curriculum Series 6 (rev. ed.), Washington, National Council for the Social Studies, 1957.

Alexander, W.M., and Halverson, P.M., *Effective Teaching in Secondary Schools*, New York, Rinehart and Company, Inc., 1956.

Anderson, R., *Romping Through Mathematics*, New York, A.A. Knopf, 1947.

Arbuckle, D.S., *Guidance and Counseling in the Classroom*, Boston, Allyn and Bacon, 1957.

Armstrong, W.H., *Study Is Hard Work*, New York, Harper & Brothers, 1956.

Baer, M.F., and Roeber, E.C., *Occupational Information*, Chicago, Science Research Associates, 1958.

Bard, Harry, *Homework: A Guide fcr Secondary School Teachers*, New York, Rinehart and Company, 1958.

Baruch, D.W., *How to Live With Your Teen-Ager*, New York, McGraw-Hill Book Company, 1953.

Baxter, E.D., *An Approach to Guidance*, New York, D. Appleton-Century Company, 1946 (technique of "the story" and "story interpretation").

Bent, R.K., and Kronenberg, H.H., *Principles of Secondary Education* (3rd ed.), New York, McGraw-Hill Book Company, 1955.

Berry, Elizabeth, *Guiding Students in the English Class*, New York, Appleton-Century-Crofts, 1957.

Bining, A.C., and Bining, D.H., *Teaching the Social Studies in Secondary Schools* (3rd ed.), New York, McGraw-Hill Book Company, 1952.

Blair, A.W., and Burton, W.H., *Growth and Development of the Preadolescent*, New York, Appleton-Century-Crofts, Inc., 1951.

Blair, G.M., *Diagnostic and Remedial Teaching* (rev. ed.), New York, The Macmillan Company, 1956.

Bond, G.L., and Tinker, M.A., *Reading Difficulties: Their Diagnosis and Correction*, New York, Appleton-Century-Crofts, 1957.

Bossing, N.L., *Principles of Secondary Education* (2nd ed.), New York, Prentice-Hall, 1955.

————, *Teaching in Secondary Schools* (3rd ed.), Boston, Houghton Mifflin Company, 1952.

Bovard, J.F., *et al.*, *Tests and Measurements in Physical Education* (3rd ed.), Philadelphia, W.B. Saunders Company, 1949.

Boyer, L.M., *An Introduction to Mathematics for Teachers* (rev. ed.), New York, Henry Holt and Company, 1956.

Brace, D.K., *Health and Physical Education for Junior and Senior High Schools*, New York, A.S. Barnes and Company, 1948.

Brewer, J.M., *et al.*, *History of Vocational Guidance*, New York, Harper and Brothers, 1942.

Briggs, T.H., *et al.*, *Secondary Education* (rev. ed.), New York, The Macmillan Company, 1950.

Brown, C.H., *The Teaching of Secondary Mathematics*, New York, Harper and Brothers, 1953.

Brown, Francis J., *Educational Sociology*, New York, Prentice-Hall, Inc., 1954.

Burnett, R.W., *Teaching Science in the Secondary School*, New York, Rinehart and Company, 1957.

Burton, W.H., *The Guidance of Learning Activities* (2nd ed.), New York, Appleton-Century-Crofts, Inc., 1952.

Butler, C.H., and Wren, F.L., *The Teaching of Secondary Mathematics* (2nd ed.), New York, McGraw-Hill Book Company, 1951.

Butler, F.A., *The Improvement of Teaching in Secondary Schools* (rev. ed.), Chicago, University of Chicago Press, 1946.

Butler, G.D., *Introduction to Community Recreation* (3rd ed.), New York, McGraw-Hill Book Company, 1954.

Byram, H.M., and Wenrich, R.C., *Vocational Education and Practical Arts in the Community School*, New York, The Macmillan Company, 1956.

Byrd, O.E. (Compiler), *School Health Sourcebook*, Stanford, Stanford University Press, 1955.

Cassidy, R.F., *Curriculum Development in Physical Education*, New York, Harper and Brothers, 1954.

Caswell, H.L. (Ed.), *et al.*, *The American High School*, New York, Harper and Brothers, 1946.

Chambers, M.M., *Youth-Serving Organizations* (3rd ed.), Washington, American Council on Education, 1948.

Chisholm, L.L., *Guiding Youth in the Secondary School*, New York, American Book Company, 1950.

Clark, L.H., and Starr, I.S., *Secondary School Teaching Methods*, New York, The Macmillan Company, 1959.

Clarke, H.H., and Eaton, M.P., *Improving Secondary-School English*, New York, Noble and Noble, 1940.

Clemensen, J.W., *et al.*, *Your Health and Safety* (4th ed.), New York, Harcourt, Brace and Company, 1957.

Cole, C.C., Jr., *Encouraging Scientific Talent*, Princeton, Educational Testing Service, 1956.

Conant, J.B., *On Understanding Science*, New Haven, Yale University Press, 1947.

Conklin, Groft (Ed.), *The Best of Science Fiction*, New York, Crown Publishers, 1947 (samples of science fiction for high-school students).

Cook, L.A., and E.F., *A Sociological Approach to Education* (2nd ed.), New York, McGraw-Hill Book Company, 1957.

Corbett, J.F., *et al.*, *Current Affairs and Modern Education*, New York, the New York Times Company, 1950.

Crawford, A.B., and Burnham, P.S., *Forecasting College Achievement*, Part I, *General Considerations in the Measurement of Academic Promise*, New Haven, Yale University Press, 1946.

Cremin, L.A., and Borrowman, M.L., *Public Schools in Our Democracy*, New York, The Macmillan Company, 1956.

Cross, E.A., and Carney, E. *Teaching English in High Schools* (rev. ed.), New York, The Macmillan Company, 1950.

Dakin, D., *How to Teach High School English*, Boston, D.C. Heath and Company, 1947.

Dale, E., *Audio-Visual Methods in Teaching* (rev. ed.), New York, The Dryden Press, 1954.

Davis, J.B., *The Saga of a Schoolmaster*, Boston, Boston University Press, 1953.

DeBoer, J.J., *et al.*, *Teaching Secondary English*, New York, McGraw-Hill Book Company, 1951.

Degrazia, J., *Math Is Fun*, New York, The Gresham Press, 1948.

Detjen, M.F., and Detjen, E.W., *Your High School Days*, New York, McGraw-Hill Book Company, 1947 (sample text for use in courses in educational and social guidance in secondary school).

Dexter, G., *Teachers' Guide to Physical Education for Girls in High School*, Sacramento, California State Department of Education, 1957 (sample of state curriculum guide).

Dimond, S.E., *Schools and the Development of Good Citizens*, Detroit, Wayne University Press, 1953.

Douglass, H.R. (Ed.), *Education for Life Adjustment*, New York, The Ronald Press Company, 1950.

————, *Modern Administration of Secondary Schools*, Boston, Ginn and Company, 1954.

Douglass, H.R. (Ed.), *et al.*, *The High School Curriculum* (2nd ed.), New York, The Ronald Press Company, 1956.

Douglass, H.R., *Secondary Education—For Life Adjustment of American Youth*, New York, The Ronald Press Company, 1952.

Edmonson, J.B., *et al.*, *The Administration of the Modern Secondary School* (4th ed.), New York, The Macmillan Company, 1951.

Eight-Year Study, "Adventure in American Education Series," Harper and Brothers: Vol. I, 1942, *The Story of the Eight-Year Study with Conclusions and Recommendations*, by W.M. Aikin; Vol. II, 1942, *Exploring The Curriculum*, by H.H. Giles, *et al.*; Vol. III, 1942, *Appraising and Recording Student Progress*, by E. R. Smith, R.W. Tyler, *et al.*; Vol. IV, 1942, *Did They Succeed in College?* by Dean Chamberlain, *et al.*; and Vol. V, 1943, *Thirty Schools Tell Their Story*.

Eisenson, J., and Ogilvie, M., *Speech Correction in the Schools*, New York, The Macmillan Company, 1957.

Eves, H., *An Introduction to the History of Mathematics*, New York, Rinehart and Company, 1953.

Fargo, L.F., *Activity Book No. 2: Library Projects for Children and Young People*, Chicago, American Library Association, 1945.

————, *The Library in the School* (4th ed.), Chicago, American Library Association, 1947.

Faunce, R.C., *Secondary School Administration*, New York, Harper and Brothers, 1955.

Faunce, R.C., and Bossing, N.L., *Developing the Core Curriculum* (2nd ed.), Englewood-Cliffs, Prentice-Hall, Inc., 1958.

Fedder, R., *Guiding Homeroom and Club Activities*, New York, McGraw-Hill Book Company, 1949.

Fehr, H.F., *Secondary Mathematics*, Boston, D.C. Heath and Company, 1951.

Fine, B., *How to be Accepted by the College of your Choice*, New York, Channel Press, Inc., 1957.

Finocchiaro, M., *Teaching English as a Second Language*, New York, Harper and Brothers, 1958.

Flaum, L.S., *The Activity High School*, New York, Harper and Brothers, 1953.

Florio, A.E., and Stafford, G.T., *Safety Education*, New York, McGraw-Hill Book Company, 1956.

Forrester, G., *Occupational Literature: An Annotated Bibliography*, New York, H.W. Wilson Company, 1958.

Foster, C.R., *Guidance for Today's Schools*, Boston, Ginn and Company, 1957.

Frank, L.K., and Frank, Mary, *Your Adolescent At Home and In School*, New York, the Viking Press, Inc., 1956.

Frederick, R.W., *The Third Curriculum: Student Activities in American Education*, New York, Appleton-Century-Crofts, 1959.

French, W.M., *American Secondary Education*, New York, The Odyssey Press, 1957.

French, W., *Behavioral Goals of General Education in High School*, New York, Russell Sage Foundation, 1957.

French, W., et al., *American High School Administration, Policy and Practice*, New York, Rinehart and Company, 1957.

Fuess, C.M., *The College Board: Its First Fifty Years*, New York, Columbia University Press, 1950.

Gesell, Arnold, et al., *Youth: The Years from Ten to Sixteen*, New York, Harper and Brothers, 1956.

Gilchrist, R.S., et al., *Secondary Education for American Democracy* (rev. ed.), New York, Rinehart and Company, 1957.

Gordon, Ira J., *The Teacher as a Guidance Worker*, New York, Harper and Brothers, 1956.

Gordon, C. Wayne, *The Social System of the High School: A Study in the Sociology of Adolescence*, Glencoe, Illinois, Free Press, 1957.

Grambs, J.D., et al., *Modern Methods in Secondary Education* (rev. ed.), New York, The Dryden Press, 1958.

Graves, A.D., *American Secondary Education*, Boston, D.C. Heath and Company, 1951.

Greene, H.A., et al., *Measurement and Evaluation in the Secondary School* (2nd ed.), New York, Longmans, Green and Company, Inc., 1955.

Grim, P.R., and Michaelis, J.W., *The Student Teacher in the Secondary School*, New York, Prentice-Hall, Inc., 1953.

Gross, R.E., and Zeleny, L.D., *Educating Citizens For Democracy*, New York, Oxford University Press, 1958.

Grout, R.E., *Health Teaching in Schools: For Teachers in Elementary and Secondary Schools* (3rd ed.), Philadelphia, W.B. Saunders and Company, 1958.

Gruber, F.C., and Beatty, T.B., *Secondary School Activities,* New York, McGraw-Hill Book Company, 1954.

Gruhn, W.T., *Student Teaching in The Secondary School,* New York, The Ronald Press Company, 1954.

Gruhn, W.T., and Douglass, H.R., *The Modern Junior High School* (2nd ed.), New York, The Ronald Press Company, 1956.

Hall, J.O., and Klinger, R.E., *Problem Solving in Our American Democracy,* New York, American Book Company, 1957 (problem solving as a basis for units and curricula).

Hamrin, S.A., and Erickson, C.E., *Guidance in the Secondary School,* New York, D. Appleton-Century Company, 1939.

Hamrin, S.A., and Paulson, B.B., *Counseling Adolescents,* Chicago, Science Research Associates, 1950.

Hansen, K.H., *High School Teaching,* Englewood Cliffs, Prentice-Hall, 1957.

Hart, F. W., *Teachers and Teaching,* New York, The Macmillan Company, 1934.

Havemann, E., and West, P.S., *They Went To College,* New York, Harcourt, Brace and Company, 1952.

Heath, H.E., Jr., and Gelfand, L., *How To Cover, Write and Edit Sports,* Ames, Iowa, the Iowa State College Press, 1951.

Hock, L.E., *Using Committees in the Classroom,* New York, Rinehart and Company, 1958.

Hoff, A.G., *Secondary-School Science Teaching,* Philadelphia, the Blakiston Company, 1947.

Hollingshead, A.B., *Elmtown's Youth,* New York, John Wiley and Sons, Inc., 1949.

Hook, J.N., *The Teaching of High School English,* Chicago, University of Illinois Press, 1950.

Hoppock, R., *Occupational Information: Where to Get It and How to Use It in Counseling and in Teaching,* New York, New York University Press, 1957.

Hunt, N.P., and Melcalf, L.E., *Teaching High School Social Studies: Problems in Reflective Thinking and Social Understanding,* New York, Harper and Brothers, 1955.

Hurlock, E.B., *Adolescent Development* (2nd ed.), New York, McGraw-Hill Book Company, 1955.

————, *Child Growth and Development* (2nd ed.), New York, McGraw-Hill Book Company, 1956 (sample of a high school text).

Ivins, W.H., and Runge, W.B., *Work Experience in High School,* New York, The Ronald Press Company, 1951.

Jennings, S.M., *Boy's Book of Modern Science,* Cleveland, World Publishing Company, 1951.

Johnson, E.S., *Theory and Practice of the Social Studies,* New York, The Macmillan Company, 1956.

Johnston, E.G., and Faunce, R.C., *Student Activities in Secondary Schools,* New York, The Ronald Press Company, 1952.

Jones, A.J., *Principles of Guidance* (4th ed.), New York, McGraw-Hill Book Company, 1951.

Kearney, N.C., *A Teacher's Professional Guide,* Englewood Cliffs, Prentice-Hall, 1958.

Keller, F.J., *Principles of Vocational Education,* Boston, D.C. Heath and Company, 1948.

————, *The Comprehensive High School,* New York, Harper and Brothers, 1955.

Kempfer, Homer, *Adult Education,* New York, McGraw-Hill Book Company, 1955.

Kerber, A.B., and Jett, T.F., Jr., *The Teaching of Creative Poetry,* Indianapolis, the Waldemar Press, Inc., 1956.

Kettelkamp, G.C., *Teaching Adolescents,* Boston, D.C. Heath and Company, 1954.

Kilzer, L.R., *et al., Allied Activities in the Secondary School,* New York, Harper and Brothers, 1956.

Kinder, J.S., *Audio-Visual Materials and Techniques,* New York, American Book Company, 1950.

Kinney, L.B., and Purdy, C.R., *Teaching Mathematics in the Secondary School,* New York, Rinehart and Company, 1952.

Kirkendall, L.A., *Understanding Sex* (Guidance Monograph), Chicago, Science Research Associates, 1947.

Kitson, H.D., *I Find My Vocation* (4th ed.), New York, McGraw-Hill Book Company, 1954 (sample of text for high-school classes in occupations and vocational guidance).

Klausmeier, H.J., *Teaching in the Secondary School,* New York, Harper and Brothers, 1958.

Koos, L.V., *Integrating High School and College,* New York, Harper and Brothers, 1946.

————, *Junior High School Trends,* New York, Harper and Brothers, 1955.

Korol, A.G., *Soviet Education for Science and Technology,* New York, John Wiley and Sons, Inc., 1957.

Kraus, R., *Recreation Leader's Handbook,* New York, McGraw-Hill Book Company, 1955.

Landis, J.T., and Landis, M.G., *Building Your Life,* Englewood Cliffs, Prentice-Hall, Inc., 1954 (sample of a high-school guidance text).

Langdon, G., and Stout, I.W., *Helping Parents Understand Their Child's School,* Englewood Cliffs, Prentice-Hall, 1957.

Laybourn, K., and Bailey, C. H., *Teaching Science to the Ordinary Pupil.* New York, Philosophical Library, 1958.

Lease, R., and Siks, G.B., *Creative Dramatics in Home, School, and Community*, New York, Harper and Brothers, 1952.

LeMasters, E.E., *Modern Courtship and Marriage*, New York, The Macmillan Company, 1958.

Leonard, J.P., *Developing the Secondary School Curriculum* (rev. ed.), New York, Rinehart and Company, 1953.

Lerrigo, M.D., and Southard, Helen, *The Dutton Series on Sex Education,* New York, E.P. Dutton and Company, 1955: *Learning About Love: Sound Facts and Healthy Attitudes Toward Sex and Marriage; Parents' Privilege: How, When and What to Tell Your Child About Sex; Sex Facts and Attitudes; A Story About You: The Facts You Want to Know About Sex; What's Happening to Me: Sex Education for the Teen-Ager.* (Approved by the Joint Committee on Health Problems in Education of the N.E.A. and the American Medical Association.)

Logasa, H., *Historical Fiction* (5th ed.), Philadelphia, McKinley Publishing Company, 1949.

Lowenfeld, V., *Creative and Mental Growth* (3rd ed.), New York, The Macmillan Company, 1957.

Lurry, L.L., and Alberty, E.J., *Developing a High-School Core Program*, New York, The Macmillan Company, 1957.

MacConnell, C.M., *et al., New Schools for a New Culture: The Story of the Evanston Township High School Core Program* (rev. ed.), New York, Harper and Brothers, 1953.

McDaniel, H.B., *Guidance in the Modern School*, New York, The Dryden Press, 1956.

McKinney, H.D., *Music and Man*, New York, American Book Company, 1948 (sample of music appreciation text for senior high school and junior college).

McKown, H.C., *Extra-Curricular Activities* (3rd ed.), New York, The Macmillan Company, 1952.

———, *The Student Council*, New York, McGraw-Hill Book Company, 1944.

McKown, H.C., and Roberts, A.B., *Audio-Visual Aids to Instruction* (2nd ed.), New York, McGraw-Hill Book Company, 1949.

Mahoney, H.J., and Engle, T.L., *Points for Decision*, Yonkers-on-Hudson, World Book Company, 1957 (sample of a guidance and psychology text for high school).

Mathews, P., *You Can Teach Music*, New York, E.P. Dutton and Company, 1953.

Mathewson, R.H., *Guidance Policy and Practice* (rev. ed.), New York, Harper and Brothers, 1955.

Matthews, R.J., *Language and Area Studies in the Armed Services: Their Future Significance,* Washington, American Council on Education, 1947.

Mays, A.B., *Principles and Practices of Vocational Education,* New York, McGraw-Hill Book Company, 1948.

Meier, A.R., *et al., A Curriculum for Citizenship,* Detroit, Wayne University Press, 1952.

Michaelis, J.U., *Social Studies for Children in a Democracy,* New York, Prentice-Hall, 1950.

Miller, F.A., *et al., Planning Student Activities,* Englewood Cliffs, Prentice-Hall, Inc., 1956.

Mills, H.H., and Douglass, H.R., *Teaching in High School* (2nd ed.), New York, The Ronald Press Company, 1957.

Mirrielees, L.B., *Teaching Composition and Literature,* New York, Harcourt, Brace and Company, 1952.

Mitchell, E.D., *Sports for Recreation* (rev. ed.), New York, A.S. Barnes and Company, 1952.

Moffatt, M.P., *Social Studies Instruction* (2nd ed.), New York, Prentice-Hall, 1954.

Morholt, E., *et al., A Sourcebook for the Biological Sciences,* New York, Harcourt, Brace and Company, 1958.

Morton, R.L., *Teaching Children Arithmetic,* New York, Silver Burdett Company, 1953.

Mulgrave, D.I., *Speech for the Classroom Teacher* (3rd ed.), New York, Prentice-Hall, 1950.

Mursell, J.L., *Education for Musical Growth,* Boston, Ginn and Company, 1948.

Myers, G.E., *Principles and Techniques of Vocational Guidance,* New York, McGraw-Hill Book Company, 1941.

Nash, J.B., *Physical Education,* New York, A.S. Barnes and Company, 1948.

Newkirk, L.V., and Johnson, W.H., *The Industrial Arts Program,* New York, The Macmillan Company, 1948.

Nicholas, F.W., *et al., Art Activities in the Modern School,* New York, The Macmillan Company, 1939.

Noar, G., *The Junior High School: Today and Tomorrow,* New York, Prentice-Hall, Inc., 1953.

Ogilvie, V., *The English Public School,* New York, The Macmillan Company, 1957.

Parrish, L., and Waskin, Y. *Teacher-Pupil Planning for Better Classroom Learning,* New York, Harper and Brothers, 1958.

Perdew, P.W., *The American Secondary School in Action,* Boston, Allyn and Bacon, 1959.

Phillips, E.L., and Gibson, J.F,. *Psychology and Personality,* Englewood Cliffs, Prentice-Hall, Inc., 1957 (example of a high-school psychology text).

Pooley, R.C., *Teaching English Grammar,* New York, Appleton-Century-Crofts, 1957.

Powell, L., *The Art Museum Comes to the School,* New York, Harper and Brothers, 1944.

Preston, R.C. (Ed.), *Teaching World Understanding,* Englewood Cliffs, Prentice-Hall, 1955.

Quillen, I.J., and Hanna, L.A., *Education for Social Competence,* Chicago, Scott, Foresman and Company, 1948.

Rakestraw, C.E., *Training High School Youth for Employment,* Chicago, American Technical Society, 1947.

Reeve, W.D., *Mathematics for the Secondary School,* New York, Henry Holt and Company, 1954.

Reimann, L.C., *The Successful Camp,* Ann Arbor, the University of Michigan Press, 1957.

Richardson, J.S., *Science Teaching in Secondary Schools,* Englewood Cliffs, Prentice-Hall, Inc., 1957.

Righter, C.B., *Success in Teaching School Orchestras and Bands,* Minneapolis, Paul A. Schmitt Music Company, 1945.

Risk, T.M., *Principles and Practices of Teaching in Secondary Schools* (3rd ed.), New York, American Book Company, 1958.

Romine, S., *Building the High School Curriculum,* New York, The Ronald Press Company, 1954.

Ryan, W.C., *et al., Secondary Education in the South,* Chapel Hill, University of North Carolina Press, 1946.

Saltzberg, G., *Knowing Your Newspaper,* Yonkers-on-Hudson, World Book Company, 1953.

Samford, C.D., and Cottle, E., *Social Studies in the Secondary School,* New York, McGraw-Hill Book Company, 1952.

Sanderson, Herbert, *Basic Concepts in Vocational Guidance,* New York, McGraw-Hill Book Company, 1954.

Sands, L.B., *Audio-Visual Procedure in Teaching,* New York, The Ronald Press Company, 1956.

Schorling, R., and Batchelder, H.T., *Student Teaching in Secondary Schools* (3rd ed.), New York, McGraw-Hill Book Company, 1956.

Schultz, G.D., *It's Time You Knew,* Philadelphia, J.B. Lippincott Company, 1955 (example of a sex education text for young teen-agers).

Schwartz, A., and Tiedeman, S.C., *Evaluating Student Progress in the Secondary School,* New York, Longmans, Green and Company, 1957.

Science Fiction. There are several series. A good recent example is the "Winston Science Fiction Series," Philadelphia, the John C. Winston Company.

Scott, H.A., *Competitive Sports in Schools and Colleges,* New York, Harper and Brothers, 1951.

Selden, S., and Sellman, H.D., *Stage Scenery and Lighting* (rev. ed.), F.S. Crofts and Company, 1947.

Sexson, J.A., and Harbeson, J.W., *The New American College,* New York, Harper and Brothers, 1946.

Simmons, M.P., *The Young Scientist: Activities for Junior High School Students,* New York, Exposition Press, 1951.

Simpson, E.A., *Helping High-School Students Read Better,* Chicago, Science Research Associates, 1954.

Smith, D.V., *Communication, the Miracle of Shared Living,* New York, The Macmillan Company, 1955.

Smith, Glenn, *Counseling in the Secondary Schools,* New York, The Macmillan Company, 1955.

Smith, J., *Student Councils for Our Times,* New York, Teachers College, Columbia University, 1951.

Sorenson, H., and Malm, M., *Psychology for Living,* New York, McGraw-Hill Book Company, 1948 (sample of a high-school psychology text).

Spears, H., *The Emerging High-School Curriculum and Its Direction and The High School for Today,* New York, American Book Company, 1948 and 1950, respectively.

Squire, R.N., *Introduction to Music Education,* Ohio, Oberlin College Press, 1952.

Stack, H.J., and Elkon, J.D., *Education for Safe Living* (3rd ed.), Englewood Cliffs, Prentice-Hall, 1957.

Stearns, G.B., *English in the Small High School,* Omaha, University of Nebraska Press, 1950.

Stewart, L.J., et al., *Improving Reading in the Junior High School,* New York, Appleton-Century-Crofts, Inc., 1957.

Strang, R., *Counseling Techniques in College and Secondary School* (rev. ed.), New York, Harper and Brothers, 1957.

————, *Educational Guidance: Its Principles and Practice,* New York, The Macmillan Company, 1947.

Struck, T.F., *Vocational Education for a Changing World,* New York, John Wiley and Sons, 1945.

Thayer, V.T., *Religion in Public Education,* New York, the Viking Press, 1947.

Thomas, C.A., *Language Power for Youth,* New York, Appleton-Century-Crofts, 1954.

Thompson, N.Z., *Vitalized Assemblies,* New York, E.P. Dutton and Company, Inc., 1952.

Thut, I.N., and Gerberich, J.R., *Foundations of Method for Secondary Schools,* New York, McGraw Hill Book Company, 1949.

Traxler, A.E., *Techniques of Guidance* (rev. ed.), New York, Harper and Brothers, 1957.

Umstattd, J.G., *Secondary School Teaching* (3rd ed.), Boston, Ginn and Company, 1953.

Vannier, M., and Fait, H., *Teaching Physical Education in Secondary Schools*, Philadelphia, W.B. Saunders Company, 1957.

Venable, T.C., *Patterns in Secondary School Curriculum*, New York, Harper and Brothers, 1958.

Vergara, W.C., *Science in Everyday Things*, New York, Harper and Brothers, 1958.

Warters, Jane, *High School Personnel Work Today* (2nd ed.), New York, McGraw-Hill Book Company, 1956.

Watkins, R.K., *Techniques of Secondary School Teaching*, New York, The Ronald Press Company, 1958.

Wells, H., *Secondary Science Education*, New York, McGraw-Hill Book Company, 1952.

Wesley, E.B., and Wronski, S.P., *Teaching Social Studies in High Schools* (4th ed.), Boston, D.C. Heath and Company, 1958.

White, D.S., *The Teaching of Latin*, Chicago, Scott, Foresman and Company, 1941.

Wiggins, S.P., *Successful High School Teachings*, Boston, Houghton Mifflin Company, 1958.

Williams, J.F., *The Principles of Physical Education* (6th ed.), Philadelphia, W.B. Saunders Company, 1954.

Williams, J.F., and Abernathy, R., *Health Education in Schools*, New York, The Ronald Press Company, 1949.

Williams, L.A., *Secondary Schools for American Youth*, New York American Book Company, 1948.

Wilson, C.C. (Ed.), *Health Education: A Guide for Teachers and a Text for Teacher Education* (4th ed.), Washington, National Education Association and American Medical Association (Joint Committee on Health Problems in Education), 1948.

———— (Ed.), *Healthful School Living*, Washington, Joint Committee of the N.E.A. and the A.M.A., 1957.

Winslow, L.L., *The Integrated School Art Program* (2nd ed.), New York, McGraw-Hill Book Company, 1949.

Wittich, W.A., and Schuller, C.F., *Audio-Visual Materials: Their Nature and Use*, New York, Harper and Brothers, 1953.

Wolfe, D.M., *Creative Ways to Teach English*, New York, The Odyssey Press, Inc., 1958.

Wrenn, C.G., and Harley, D.L., *Time on Their Hands: A Report on Leisure, Recreation, and Young People*, Washington, American Council on Education, 1941.

Wrinkle, W.L., *Improving Marking and Reporting Practices in Elementary and Secondary Schools,* New York, Rinehart and Company, 1947.

Yauch, W.A., *Improving Human Relations in School Administration,* New York, Harper and Brothers, 1949.

Zapf, R.M., *Democratic Processes in the Secondary Classroom,* Englewood Cliffs, Prentice-Hall, 1959.

Zeran, F.R., *The High School Teacher and His Job,* New York, Chartwell House, Inc., 1953.

———— (Ed.), *Life Adjustment Education in Action,* New York, Chartwell House, 1952.

CHAPTER 14   The junior
high school curriculum

The development of the junior high school illustrates well the statement generally attributed to the pioneer in education, namely, "It takes fifty years for a sound, new idea in education to achieve general acceptance." The idea of extending the high-school grades downward was first introduced by the Committee of Ten in 1893,[1] and the Committee on College Entrance Requirements in 1899 reiterated this recommendation that a six-year course of high-school study be provided. However, almost twenty years elapsed before the first public junior high schools were established at Columbus, Ohio, and Berkeley, California, in 1909–1910.

Competent educational authorities have already traced the growth and significance of the junior high school, devoting entire books to this educational level.[2] Consequently, this chapter will be limited to a brief presentation of (1) the characteristics and needs of early adolescents, who comprise the student population of the junior high school, (2) the purposes of the junior high school, (3) the types of curricular programs, (4) the changing curricular pattern(s), and (5) newer developments.

THE CHARACTERISTICS AND NEEDS OF EARLY ADOLESCENCE

Attention has already been called to the characteristics, attitudes, and needs of the pupil in grades seven and eight.[3] An outstanding

[1] See Chapter 1 for the recommendations of this Committee, of the Committee on College Entrance Requirements, and of the Committee on Economy of Time in Education.
[2] Consult the annotated bibliography at the end of this chapter for detailed information upon the junior high school. This bibliography is also the primary source for the curriculum trends noted here, unless credit is otherwise given.
[3] See Chapter 10.

change takes place there; the kind of voluntary activity in which the developing adolescent engages shifts suddenly from *individual* activities of many types to primarily *group* activity, activity controlled mainly by the play group or gang. The authorities list these characteristics at the pre- and early-adolescent ages which cause this major shift in type of activity:

Showing gradually emerging heterosexual development.
Showing the emerging of a new pattern of religious problems.
Seeking security in regard to his adult status, his own peer group or "gang," and himself.
Desiring group approval.
Being self-conscious and bashful.
Feeling a need for independence from parental authority, manifested at times by defiance toward other forms of adult authority.
Day-dreaming and proneness to emulate other personalities in the process.
Feeling more intensified emotions than adults, but for shorter periods of time.
Awkwardness.
Proneness to save face.
Widening his interests.
Self-centeredness, as evidenced by carelessness and thoughtlessness, resulting primarily from physical and emotional changes.
Tending to be overly aggressive when thwarted.
High physical resistance to disease.
Showing off, as evidenced by being faddish and boastful.

In summary, we should remember that this young adolescent is establishing himself as a young adult, desiring to establish his independence from adults, and wishing to be treated as a young adult; he is insecure in adult society, does not know exactly how to act, but decidedly does not want to act as or appear to be still a child. At this age, in the process of becoming an adult, he must establish himself in his gang or peer group, among the other boys and girls who are becoming young adults; therefore he must adhere more to the ideas, customs, and rules of the gang than to those of adult authority. He has an irregular growth pattern at this age, peculiar to himself alone; and he is particularly resistant to physical ills at this time. His normal development in early adolescence leads eventually to emerging interest in the *opposite,* not primarily in the same, sex. Since he is establishing new group standards and values at this age, he is more likely to tell his teacher the truth about himself and his actions than he is to give information or "tell" on the actions or behavior of others; his punishment by the gang if he has broken its code is usually much more severe than any punishment that the teacher might give to him under similar circumstances.

FIG. 32   *An exploratory and appreciation subject in junior high school*

A class in seventh grade general music, learning fundamentals through key board experience. (*Courtesy Charlotte (N.C.) City Schools, Sedgefield Junior High School.*)

THE PURPOSES OF THE JUNIOR HIGH SCHOOL

A side-by-side comparison of the purposes of the planners of the early junior high school with those of today's authorities is informative: [4]

---

[4] Summarized from *Journal of Proceedings and Addresses of the National Education Association,* 1907, pp. 705–10, from succeeding reports of the Committee on Economy of Time in Education, and from W.T. Gruhn and H.R. Douglass, *The Modern Junior High School* (2nd ed.), New York, The Ronald Press Company, 1956, pp. 30–32.

Department of Secondary Education, N.E.A. (1907)	Gruhn and Douglass (1956)
°Articulation between school levels	°Articulation
°Exploration	°Exploration
°General education (emphasis upon the most important subjects)	°Integration (the term used by these authors for general education)
°Differentiation, with earlier specialization	°Differentiation (meeting individual needs)
Departmentalization	Guidance
Opportunity for use of specialists in subject-matter areas	Socialization
Better preparation for college	
Economy of time in education, acceleration, and earlier graduation.	

° Indicates that the objectives were partly or approximately the same.

A careful analysis of the literature on the junior high school and of the programs and curricula of representative junior high schools leads one to the conclusion that these lists contain practically all of the purposes of the modern junior high school. In summary, the junior high school is an educational level established specially for young adolescents of the intermediate grades. It has as its special purposes in meeting the needs of this group (1) the continuation of general education and common learnings in the subject-matter fields, (2) the opportunity to explore subject areas not encountered before, (3) the opportunity to start specialization if the student is ready for it, (4) the gradual and more effective articulation for the student between educational levels, (5) introduction of the student to the different kinds of vocations and professions, and (6) introduction of the student to student activities characteristic of the adolescent peer group. To accomplish these purposes, the junior high school must have a well-planned, well-coordinated program for both individual and group guidance.

TYPES OF CURRICULAR PROGRAMS

The offerings of the early junior high school could be identified usually as a single curriculum in grade seven, and two or more curricular programs in grades eight and nine, each with required

TABLE 23. Junior high school programs of study, Detroit, Mich., 1923

Subjects	Seventh grade B	Seventh grade A	Eighth grade *General	Eighth grade Technical Boys	Eighth grade Technical Girls	Eighth grade Commercial	Ninth grade General	Ninth grade Technical Boys	Ninth grade Technical Girls	Ninth grade Commercial
Health	5	5	5	5	5	5	5	5	5	5
Social Science	5	5	5	5	5	5	5	5	5	5
English	5	4	4	4	4	4	4	4	4	4
Mathematics	4	4	3	3	2	2	3	3	2	…
General Science	3	2	2	2	2	2	2	2	2	2
Auditorium	2	2	2	2	2	2	2	2	2	2
Music	1	1	1	…	1	1	1	…	1	1
Art and Design	1	1	1	1	2	1	1	…	2	1
Foreign Language	…	…	5	…	…	…	5	…	…	…
Cooking (girls)	2	3	1	…	3	1	1	…	3	…
Sewing (girls)	2	3	1	…	3	1	1	…	3	…
Household Science (girls)	…	…	…	…	1	…	…	…	1	…
Shops (boys)	3	5	1	6	…	1	1	6	…	…
Mechanical Drawing (boys)	1	1	1	2	…	1	1	3	…	…
Bookkeeping	…	…	…	…	…	…	…	…	…	5
Business Practice	…	…	…	…	…	5	…	…	…	1
Statistics	…	…	…	…	…	…	…	…	…	2
Typewriting	…	…	…	…	…	…	…	…	…	2
Penmanship	…	…	…	…	…	1	…	…	…	…
Total (Periods a Week)	30	30	30	30	30	30	30	30	30	30

436

* The "general" curriculum was intended for those going on to senior high school and college.

and some elective subjects. The Detroit curriculum in 1923 illustrated a rather rich offering for that day.[5]

As time passed, the junior high school began to emancipate itself from the strong influence of the senior high school upon its curricular offerings. For example, the following programs show in Type I the heavy influence of the college preparatory program on grade nine; in Type II, the beginning of curricular cohesion in the junior high school without regard to Carnegie units required for high-school graduation.

TYPE I. A program for grades seven and eight of work is centered around general education; but for grade nine a program is distinctly pointed toward college preparation and toward four units of the sixteen required for graduation from high school. A typical program of this kind would be

Grades 7 and 8	Pds. per week	Grade 9	Pds. per week
English	5	*English	5
Social Studies (Geog. and U.S. History	5	*Three from:*	
		Soc. Stud. IX	
Mathematics	5	*Math. IX	
General Science (including Hygiene)	2	*For. Lang.	Each course
		Agricul. I	meets five
Health and Physical Education	2 or 3	Home Ec. I	periods
		Man. Training	per week
Music	2 or 3	Jr. Bus. Tr.	
Art or Industrial Arts (boys)	2 or 3	Typing	
Homemaking (girls)			
Home Room or Guidance	2 to 4		

* Students going to college take these.

This type of curriculum was in part a holdover from the early days of the junior high school, when the regional accrediting associations still required sixteen units (four units a year) for graduation.

[5] Taken from *Specimen Junior High School Programs of Study*, Bulletin, 1923, No. 21, Department of the Interior, Bureau of Education, p. 7.

However, all of the regional associations now have adopted the principle of accepting from their member schools for entrance to college the twelve units earned in the last three years of high school, that is, in grades ten, eleven, and twelve. Therefore, the *junior high*

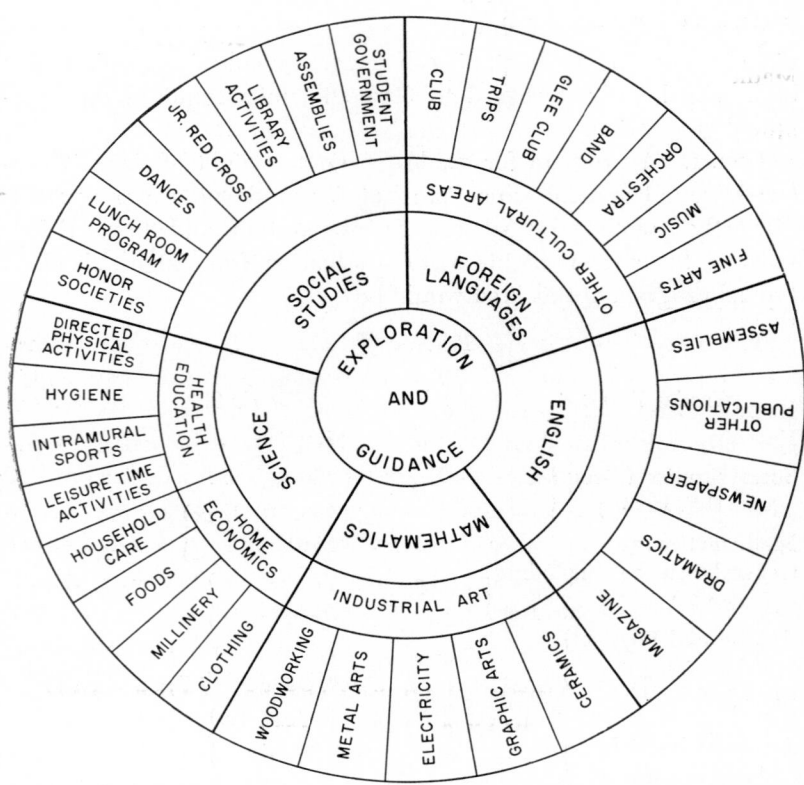

FIG. 33   *The basic learnings are stressed in the junior high-school curriculum* (Reproduced with permission from "What Educational Program Is Needed in the Junior High School?" by Joseph C. Lovetan, *The Bulletin of the National Association of Secondary-School Principals,* XLII (April, 1958), p. 43.)

school is now free to plan its work for a three-year block of time without having to point any of its work specifically toward admission to college.

TYPE II.   A program for grades seven, eight, and nine is aimed at general education. A typical curriculum program of Type II would be:

No Electives

Grade 7	Grade 8	Grade 9
English and Reading	English	*English
Art	Art	*Science
Mathematics	Science	*Social Studies
Social Studies	Mathematics	*Health and Phy. Ed.
Music	Social Studies	
Health and Phy. Ed.	Music	*Two courses from:*
Manual Training	Health and Phy. Ed.	Algebra, Gen. Math.,
Home Econ.	Manual Training	Latin, Spanish, Typing,
	Home Econ.	Art, Indus. Arts, Home-
		making, Music.

Note that the asterisk means "required."

Both Type I and Type II are found today, with variations, all over the country. Gradually elective subjects appeared in the eighth grade as well as in grade nine; slowly accredited high schools began to certificate their graduates for college on the basis of twelve units earned in the senior high school. As this occurred, more and more junior high-school staffs moved in the direction of a new approach to general education; this approach is generally termed "core" work, "unified studies," or "common learnings," with a double period block of time involved.

CHANGING CURRICULAR PATTERNS: "CORE" AND "BLOCK" PROGRAMS

Since the 1930's many experimental programs for general education have been developed.[6] As used here in connection with the junior high school, "general education" means that part of the curriculum planned to meet the general needs of all students, not their special needs or interests. Fig. 23 illustrates well the basic learnings that New York City school personnel think should meet these general needs of young adolescents.

[6] Chapters 6, 10, 12, and 13 have recounted (1) the progressive development of concepts of general education and (2) ways of attaining general education, such as through correlation, fusion, core work, and the experience curriculum.

Educators are in pretty general agreement that general education is a major function of the junior high school, but they disagree as to the ways or methods of achieving it. Roland Faunce and Nelson Bossing state the conflict briefly and clearly: [7]

On the other hand, there has been a wide divergence of judgment as to what the nature and pattern of this *general education* should be. Many writers hold to the point of view that *general education* should represent a definite pattern of subjects required of all pupils. Others would accept a minimal-essentials body of subject matter content presented in some pattern of possible broad fields organization, while still others would accept a common body of type-problem-learning experiences to which all pupils should be exposed as the meaning and form of general education. This latter concept of general education has conformed most closely to the modern *core* idea.

School personnel have experimented quite a bit before coming to what Faunce and Bossing term "the modern *core* idea." The steps which they took to go from the "required"-subjects-idea to the "core" for achieving general education are perhaps best presented by Harold Alberty in the 52nd Yearbook of the National Society for the Study of Education.[8] In summary they are:

1. Required subject-matter fields of knowledge comprised the core, taught in regular course sequence ("constant" subjects).
2. The regular subject-matter fields, some of which have close relationships to others and are consciously correlated (correlation in teaching).
3. A core from the required subject-matter fields organized around units of work, larger problems, or central themes (center-of-interest or unit teaching).
4. A core around fusion or unifying of fields of knowledge that are closely interrelated (teaching by fusion with one subject area, *e.g.*, the Social Studies, as the unifying center).
5. A core around "broad-fields" of knowledge or preplanned problem areas ("broad-fields" approach to teaching centered around learning experiences in terms of the life problems and needs of students).
6. Broad teaching units around centers of interest, planned by the teacher and pupils cooperatively in terms of the needs of the group ("core" work).

In most of the types of core described by Alberty, certainly in

[7] In *Developing the Core Curriculum* (2nd ed.), Englewood Cliffs, Prentice-Hall, copyright 1958, p. 49. (Reprinted with permission.)

[8] Part I, Chap. VII, "Designing Programs to Meet the Common Needs of Youth," 1953, pp. 118–40.

programs 3, 4, 5, and 6, a double period is commonly set aside for the work. Since examples [9] of fusion, correlation, the core curriculum, units around centers of interest or problems, and the experience curriculum approach to teaching have already been described previously, additional samples will not be included here.

Therefore, this section is concluded with a summary of the curricular plan proposed recently by the staff of a new junior high school, worked out over a two-year period [10] while the new building was being erected. They were changing from the 8–4 type of organization to the 6–3–3 plan. Note the trend toward more block work in grades eight and nine.

Curriculum Plan for the Junior High School
(6-Period Day)

7th Grade		8th Grade		9th Grade		
3-period Block of Work	Centers of Interest based on Peoples and Customs of the United States	3-period Block of Work	Centers of Interest including Science, Health, Phy. Educ.	2-period Block of Work	Our States and Community	
2-period Block of Work	Centers of Interest including Science, Health, Math, Phy. Education	2-period Block of Work	Units based on Social, Political, and Economic Forces affecting our lives	2-period Block of Work	Girls {	Math, Home-making
					Boys {	Math, Shop

1-Period: Electives to Be Chosen from These Areas (4 electives per year, 2 for each semester)

Art	Choral Music	Handicrafts
Homemaking	Instrumental Music	Exploration of foreign
Woodwork	Dramatics	languages
Nature Study	Journalism	Sports:
Stamps	Debating	Indoor
		Outdoor

[9] For examples of core or fused programs already described in this book, turn to Chapter 6 (especially pp. 161–171); Chapter 10 (especially pp. 273–278); and Chapter 13 (especially pp. 406–413).

[10] This summary was made by the author. The staff prefers that the name of the new school be omitted.

NEWER DEVELOPMENTS

Aaron Lauchner recently visited and studied [11] seventy-one "intermediate" schools over the country. Significant among his findings were: (1) A trend was noted toward having a group of pupils stay with the same teacher for two or more periods (multiple or double period) while they studied two or more subject-matter areas, a reversal of earlier practice in the junior high school; (2) the combination of subjects found most often in the multiple period was English and social studies; (3) some schools have *two* double period groupings, *e.g.*, English-social studies under one teacher and science-mathematics under another; (4) schools are learning to train their own teachers in service for core work or multiple period (block) work; and (5) schools are beginning to develop resource units and materials to help teachers in this new kind of work.

Another study confirms Lauchner's findings in some respects.[12] Over 57 per cent of 1,170 schools had block-time classes for general education, and the practice was reported from states all over the country. This study and others also showed that the commonest type of junior high school was the three-year school (grades seven, eight, and nine), reaching 84 per cent; two-year schools comprised about 14 per cent (grades seven and eight); four-year schools (grades seven, eight, nine, and ten) comprised nearly 2 per cent of the total. But one-year and five-year junior high schools were becoming scarcer.

Another trend is the basing of the whole scope and sequence in a subject-matter area, for example, the social studies, on units around centers of interest with much cooperative planning carried on by teacher and pupils.[13]

[11] "The Junior High School and the Multiple Period," *The Bulletin of the National Association of Secondary-School Principals,* xxxix (November, 1955), pp. 61–68.

[12] "The Daily Schedule in 1,250 Junior High Schools," Report of a Project of the Committee on Junior High School Education, *The Bulletin of the National Association of Secondary-School Principals,* xl (May, 1956), a preprint, pp. 1–12.

[13] A good example is found in *Social Studies, Grades 7, 8, 9: A Guide for Teachers,* City of New York, Board of Education, Curriculum Bulletin, No. 5,

It will be interesting to see whether the junior high school makes full use of its available opportunities both to enrich the program for some talented pupils and to accelerate the curricular program for others.[14] Some gifted pupils are ready socially, emotionally, and achievement-wise to be accelerated at least one year during this three-year span of education.

FIG. 34   *An algebra class for superior students*

The teacher is able to offer such a group an enriched and comprehensive elementary algebra course in the junior high school. (*Courtesy Charlotte* (*N.C.*) *City Schools, Sedgefield Junior High School.*)

These new movements in junior high school education may affect its program materially, and are worthy of mention here:

1. The preparation of teachers specially prepared to teach in the junior high school and in its "core" program. The special programs for junior high teachers at Florida, the Ohio State University, and the University of

1951–1952 Series (reprinted, 1954), *passim,* and esp. Chaps. IV–VI; and *Seventh-Grade Social Studies-Science: Tentative Outline for Areas of Study,* Oakland (Cal.), Oakland Public Schools, June 25, 1954, *passim.*

[14] Cf. "Enrichment Practices for Gifted Junior-High-School Pupils," by E.M. McWilliams, *The Bulletin of the National Association of Secondary-School Principals,* XL (September, 1946), pp. 72–81.

North Carolina are breaking new ground, as are those for the training of core teachers at Northern Illinois State College, the University of Minnesota, New York University, Temple University, Teachers College, Columbia University, Towson State Teachers College, and Troy (Alabama) State College.[15]

2. The possibility of accreditation of junior high schools by the regional accrediting associations. At its 1954 meeting, the Southern Association of Colleges and Secondary Schools authorized such accreditation. Their study, *The Junior High School Program* (1958), was a careful investigation of the purposes and status of junior high schools in the region as a preliminary move to final action.

3. The training and use of core resource teachers. St. Paul has experimented with this. As a new junior high school has been opened each year for three years, an experienced core teacher has been assigned to each school on a half-time basis as a core resource person. The experiment has worked out so well that these resource teachers at each school are now on a full-time basis.[16]

As one looks backward at the significant growth of the junior high school and forward to its curricular possibilities, he is struck with one inescapable fact—most of the mathematics, science, and health instruction required of students as a minimum for graduation is provided on this educational level. Students likewise study there art, music, and industrial arts, as well as the basic work in language arts, social studies, and the foreign languages. Therefore, a more careful study of its curricular scope and sequence is of paramount importance.

PROBLEMS FOR INDIVIDUAL STUDY AND CLASS DISCUSSION

1. As the new principal of a new junior high school, appointed a year before the school is to be opened, how would you block out plans for studying the curricular program that might be offered?

2. You are a beginning teacher in a junior high school where "core"

[15] Read *Preparation of Core Teachers for Secondary Schools*, Association for Supervision and Curriculum Development, N.E.A., 1955, *passim*, and especially Chaps. ii, iii, and v.

[16] Read "Core Resource Teacher and Coordinator Becomes an Institution in St. Paul," *The Bulletin of the National Association of Secondary-School Principals*, xlii (March, 1958), pp. 104–5.

work is carried on, and you are not trained for core work. How will you prepare yourself this summer more adequately for this new work?

3. If a junior high school has block work (or multiple-period work) in English-social studies, should it change its way of reporting to parents on the child's work in this new way of teaching? Or not? Support your point of view.

4. Does a "self-contained" classroom, with one teacher in charge of all subjects and activities for most of the day, make for a better teaching-learning situation than the departmentalized classroom? Or not? Explain.

5. Do "correlation" and "fusion" mean the same thing to you or not? Give evidence to prove your stand.

6. If your school offered you the opportunity of visiting five other junior high schools, for one day each, what standards would you use to select the five different schools you are to visit?

7. Trace historically departmentalization in the junior high school. Is it growing? Declining? Why?

8. How would you use the guidance facilities in your junior high school for better curricular opportunities for your students? Be specific, for example, as to what uses you would make of testing instruments, group guidance, and the like.

9. L.V. Koos and W.T. Gruhn have been recognized leaders in the junior high school movement. What curricular contributions has each one made? Identify these contributions in two parallel columns, starring (*) those that are the same.

10. Should one who wants to teach in the junior high school be prepared well in at least *two different* subject-matter fields or not? Support your point of view.

11. Let us assume that your school system has a policy of acceleration of well-prepared, well-balanced students in the junior high. Upon what grounds or evidences of competency would you recommend acceleration of a student?

12. "Multiple-period classes" are employed in some senior high schools, as well as in junior high. What are the different kinds of multiple-period classes (or "block work" periods) in use, and how effective are they?

ADDITIONAL ANNOTATED REFERENCES FOR PROBLEM OR UNIT STUDY

Arlington, Va., Arlington County Public Schools.
Good samples of system-wide materials resource planning in general education are found in their *Tentative Resource Units for 7th–8th–9th Grade General Education*, 1954.

Baruch, D.W., *How to Live With Your Teen-Ager*, New York, McGraw-Hill Book Company, 1953.
A rich source of information about adolescents, illustrated by what boys and girls have thought and said and done.

Bent, R.K., and Kronenberg, H.H., *Principles of Secondary Education* (3rd ed.), New York, McGraw-Hill Book Company, 1955.
General education and approaches to it in Chapters xi and xii; reorganization of secondary education in x; and curricular reorganization in xv.

Blair, A.W., and Burton, W.H., *Growth and Development of the Preadolescent*, New York, Appleton-Century-Crofts, 1951.
Opens up a new field of study, that of later childhood, with good suggestions for understanding these children.

California Journal of Secondary Education, Berkeley 4.
This educational magazine has perhaps devoted more space to the junior high school than any other journal in the last decade. For example, a recent issue is devoted mainly to "The Educational Program of the Junior High School," Vol. xxxii (October, 1957), pp. 342–81.

The Core Teacher, Temple University, Philadelphia 22.
This is the official publication of the National Core Conferences on Core Teaching, and keeps up with new practices in core work.

English in Common Learnings, Chicago, National Council of Teachers of English, 1951.
Recommendations on contributions of English to common learnings.

Faunce, R.C., and Bossing, N.L., *Developing the Core Curriculum* (2nd ed.), Englewood Cliffs, Prentice-Hall, 1958.
This book, with its first (1951) edition, is the standard source of information on the history, development, definitions and philosophy, and trends in core work.

French, Will (Ed.) *Behavioral Goals of General Education in High School*, New York, Russell Sage Foundation, 1957.
Emphasizes the improvement of student behavior as a big goal in education and subject-matter mastery as a means of learning, not the measure of learning.

Gesell, A., *et al.*, *Youth: The Years from Ten to Sixteen*, New York, Harper and Brothers, 1956.
Presents for each age maturity profile, traits, emotions, activities and interests, school life, and ethical sense.

Gruhn, W.T., and Douglass, H.R., *The Modern Junior High School* (2nd ed.), New York, The Ronald Press Company, 1956.
The standard work on the junior high school since 1947, its purposes, its program, its activities, and its place in the educational system.

Guides to Curriculum Building. Junior High School Level, Problems Ap-

proach Bulletin No. 2, Curriculum Bulletin No. 12, Wisconsin Coopera-
tive Educational Planning Program (January, 1950), Madison, State
Superintendent of Public Instruction.
The "problems approach" in place of the "pattern of subjects approach,"
especially in Chapters iv–vi.
Hanna, L., *et al.*, *Unit Teaching in the Elementary School*, New York,
Rinehart and Company, 1955.
Excellent exposition of how unit work around a center of interest has
developed. Includes developing the unit, problem solving, research pro-
cedures in the unit, and examples of resource and teaching units.
Harap, H., *Social Living in the Curriculum*, Nashville, George Peabody
College for Teachers, 1952.
A study of the core in action, Grades 1–12; general characteristics of
the core, and types of work in each grade.
The High School Journal, Chapel Hill (N.C.).
Examines periodically the junior high school, with special issues. For
example, "Planning for the Junior High School," Vol. xxxii (November-
December, 1949), pp. 225–65; "General Education in the Secondary
School," Vol. xxxvii, eight issues in 1953–1954 devoted to this theme;
and "Looking at the Junior High School," Vol. xl (December, 1956),
pp. 82–141.
Illustrative Learning Experiences, by University High School Faculty,
The Modern School Practice Series, No. 2, College of Education, Uni-
versity of Minnesota, Minneapolis, University of Minnesota Press.
Teaching units of various kinds on different grade levels.
Indianapolis, Indiana, Public Schools.
Good examples of resource materials prepared for junior high-school
teachers are their Guides for Social Studies, Music, Mathematics,
Industrial Arts, Art Experiences, Science, Health and Safety, the Lan-
guage Arts, and Home Economics, 1954–1957.
The Junior High School Program, the Southern Association of Colleges
and Secondary Schools, 1958, Atlanta 8 (Ga.).
Growth of junior high student, purposes, organization and administra-
tion, staffing.
Koos, L.V., *Junior High School Trends*, New York, Harper and Brothers,
1955.
One of the leaders describes the reorganization of secondary education,
the purposes of the junior high school, grade grouping, curriculum
organization, student activities and guidance, and coming trends.
Lurry, L.L., and Alberty, E.J., *Developing a High School Core Program*,
New York, The Macmillan Company, 1957.
Presents interestingly general education as the chief purpose of the
junior high school, defines the core program, shows by actual illustra-

tions in schools over the country how to design, develop resources, and plan cooperatively for the core.

National Education Association, Washington 6.

The Association for Supervision and Curriculum Development publishes materials on the junior high school from time to time; two examples are "The Junior High School," in *Educational Leadership*, XIV (May, 1957), pp. 461–98, and *Developing Programs for Young Adolescents*, 1954.

The Educational Policies Commission's *Education for All American Youth—A Further Look*, 1952, describes the junior high programs in Farmville and American City.

The National Association of Secondary-School Principals has devoted much of the space in its *Bulletin* for many years to the junior high school. For example, read "The Modern Junior High School," XXIX (April, 1945), pp. 4–161 and "Organizing the Junior High School," XXXV (December, 1951), pp. 5–142. The Association also prints bibliographies on the junior high school from time to time, and publishes regularly *NAASP Spotlight on Junior and Senior High Schools*.

New York, City of, Board of Education, Brooklyn 1.

Guide to Curriculum Improvement in Grades 7–8–9, Curriculum Bulletin, 1955–1956 Series, No. 10, is another example of a resource guide for teachers.

New York, State of, State Education Department, Albany.

Another good resource guide for teachers is *A Design for Early Secondary Education in New York State*, 1954. For Grades 7–8–9.

Noar, Gertrude, *Freedom to Live and Learn*, Philadelphia, Franklin Publishing and Supply Company, 1948.

Describes methods for selecting and developing teaching units.

————, *The Junior High School—Today and Tomorrow*, New York, Prentice-Hall, 1953.

A modern, constructive approach to the general education purposes of the junior high school through core work by means of unit teaching, cooperatively planned.

Stratemeyer, F.B., *et al.*, *Guides to a Curriculum for Modern Living*, New York, Teachers College, Columbia University, 1952.

Mainly paragraphic and pictorial; how to plan a curriculum centered around the persistent life situations faced by children and youth.

Stewart, L.J., *et al.*, *Improving Reading in the Junior High School*, New York, Appleton-Century-Crofts, 1957.

How a core-teacher and a librarian worked together to improve reading.

U.S. Office of Education, Washington 25.

The Office has been particularly active since 1950 in collecting and publishing information, practices, and programs in the junior high school. Samples are:

Core Curriculum Development: Problems and Practices, Bulletin 1952, No. 5.

Junior High School Facts: A Graphic Analysis, Misc. No. 21, November, 1954.

The Core Program: Abstracts of Unpublished Research, 1946–1955, Circular No. 485, June, 1956.

Block-Time Classes and the Core Program in the Junior High School, Bulletin 1958, No. 6.

CHAPTER 15 The organization,
administration, and evaluation
of secondary-school curriculum work

SPECIAL PROGRAMS OF STUDY IN THE SECONDARY SCHOOL

In considering curriculum organization and administration, one must be familiar with the use of the word "curriculum" in a special sense and with a particular meaning in the secondary school as compared with the elementary school. Secondary-school administrators commonly use the word "curriculum" to denote *a specified arrangement or combination of courses of study,* intended to meet the needs of a certain group of students and to lead to graduation if this pattern of courses is followed and completed satisfactorily by the pupil. One may find in a large secondary school several of these special "programs of study" or "curricula," each program or curriculum leading to graduation; for example, the school might have the college preparatory curriculum, the commercial curriculum, the general curriculum, the home economics curriculum, the manual training curriculum, and the industrial education curriculum. The purpose of the secondary school in offering these multiple curricula or programs of study is to meet both the common and special needs and interests of its students. Each of these curricula is in effect a specially arranged program of study *for a group* having approximately the same needs and interests.

As is true in the rest of this volume, stress is placed here on the trends in secondary-school organization and administration which allow for and encourage curricular improvements, rather than on the administrative organization *per se.* The reader may refer to other

450

writers who have treated adequately the general mechanics of organization in the secondary school.[1] The emphasis here will be directed to an analysis of the possibilities for curricular change within these existing types of organization.

TYPES OF CURRICULAR ORGANIZATION AND ADMINISTRATION

1. *Improving the Curriculum by the Addition of New Programs of Study.* A careful examination of the differentiated curricula which have been organized in the secondary school for certain groups of varying needs and interests shows that they may be divided into the following patterns:

1. The academic (college preparatory) curriculum
2. The vocational curriculum, of many and varying types
3. The general curriculum
4. The experience or individual curriculum, based on the individual needs and interests of pupils.

The subject fields of English and the social studies (*e.g.*, American history or civics and citizenship) are required in all of these specialized programs of study in the secondary school. Some science and mathematics of one type or another are requisites in the college preparatory curriculum, in the general curriculum, and in most vocational curricula.

The academic curriculum differs primarily from the others in its prescription in foreign languages and mathematics, while the commercial or business curriculum departs markedly from the rest in

---

[1] The following texts include a representative sampling of the discussion and presentation of types of curricular organization on the secondary-school level: L.L. Chisholm, *The Work of the Modern High School*, New York, The Macmillan Company, 1953, Part III; H.R. Douglass, *Modern Administration of Secondary Schools*, Boston, Ginn and Company, 1954, Chaps. VII–VIII, XXVI; H.R. Douglass (Ed.), *The High School Curriculum* (2nd ed.), 1956, Chaps. XV, XX–XXI, and W.T. Gruhn and H.R. Douglass, *The Modern Junior High School* (2nd ed.), 1956, Parts II and IV, New York, The Ronald Press Company; J.B. Edmonson, *et al.*, *The Administration of the Modern Secondary School* (4th ed.), New York, The Macmillan Company, 1953, Chaps. XVI–XVII, XXV–XXVI; J.P. Leonard, *Developing the Secondary-School Curriculum* (rev. ed.), New York, Rinehart and Company, 1953, Chaps. IX–XII; and R.K. Bent and H.H. Kronenberg, *Principles of Secondary Education* (3rd ed.), New York, McGraw-Hill Book Company, 1955, Chaps. VIII–XV.

its heavy requirements in commercial subjects. The experience, or individual, curriculum is a newcomer, and no data are yet available on it in regard to what subjects are required and what are elective.

At least two of these special curricula will usually be found even in the small secondary school with only a few teachers; the larger the school, the larger will be the number of special curricula of one type or another. The home economics curriculum, the vocational and agricultural curricula, the industrial education program, the manual training program, the business education or commercial curriculum, and the diversified occupations and distributive education "courses" are but variations in types of the vocational curriculum in the secondary school.

In a preceding chapter, it was shown that one of the ways in which curriculum change took place on the secondary-school level was through the addition of new courses in existing subject-matter fields. Here one sees that procedure carried a step further—both the old and the new courses in subject-matter fields are arranged and grouped into "programs of study" or "curricula" in special combinations for the differing needs and interests of students. Such combinations frequently require the addition of new courses to the various subject-matter fields to meet student needs more adequately in the new program. Thus the process works both ways toward curriculum growth and revision in the existing school structure: (1) new subjects of study are added in the different subject-matter fields to enrich the program, and (2) new combinations of courses into special curricula or programs of study for particular groups of students require the addition of new subject-matter courses to meet adequately the needs of these students. This procedure is essentially a step forward in the improvement of the curriculum of the secondary school, but it is not a step away from the subject-matter organization which prevails in the secondary school. New courses for these new curricula are well illustrated by the additions to the commercial curriculum; these additions include business mathematics, business English, business law, personal guidance, consumer education, socio-business courses, and general business.

The stress on general education in the secondary school has stimulated other new courses of a *general* or *survey* nature; such are the combination of zoology and botany into biology, and the telescoping of civics, government, and citizenship into a general course called "civics." More recent examples are "world history," which is an attempt to combine ancient, medieval, and modern history into one subject for one year; and "general mathematics," another newcomer, in which there are various practical aspects of mathematics from arithmetic, algebra, and geometry. This trend toward general courses in the secondary school preceded that same movement on the collegiate level, where such courses are found denominated as "contemporary civilization," "social science," "the biological sciences," and the like. One might try to predict the reconstruction of the entire curriculum of the secondary school by the addition of new subject-matter courses and special programs. Such a procedure would be dangerous and unsound. It is more important to note here that this administrative procedure is essentially a step forward in the improvement of the curriculum of the secondary school; but it is not a step away from the subject-matter organization which prevails.

2. *The "Broad Fields of Knowledge" Organization.* According to several curriculum authors,[2] the "broad-fields-of-knowledge" type of curriculum plan was prominent in the rearrangement taking place in the programs of study of the schools of the eight-year experiment of the Progressive Education Association. Wrightstone and more recent writers [3] are agreed that these broad divisions may vary from four to five or six. Wrightstone indicated the following divisions as typical:

1. The fine arts and music
2. Literature and languages
3. The social studies
4. The sciences and mathematics

[2] *Cf.* J.W. Wrightstone, *Appraisal of Experimental High School Practices,* Teachers College, Columbia University, 1936, p. 26.

[3] Edmonson, Roemer, and Bacon, *op. cit.,* p. 334, and *The High School Curriculum, op. cit.,* pp. 207–8. For more information, turn to V.E. Anderson, *Principles and Procedures of Curriculum Improvement,* New York, The Ronald Press Company, 1956, pp. 269–70, 314–15, and 322; and T.C. Venable, *Patterns in Secondary School Curriculum,* New York, Harper and Brothers, 1958, pp. 66–67, 76–77.

This procedure in curriculum revision is an attempt to replace the special subject-matter departments and their individual courses with these broad fields of knowledge; the purpose is to broaden the content and interrelate it more closely within these fields, by means of continuity and sequence throughout the various years. It is to be inferred naturally that the secondary schools have taken this idea from the colleges. The colleges have inaugurated changes in their curricula whereby they have divided knowledge into from three to five fields. In the first two college years basic training is given in such broad areas as the social sciences, the biological and natural sciences, and the arts and languages. In their last two years students are required to take a major in one of these broad areas, and a minor in a related or different field. A typical division into five areas on the college level would be the following: (1) languages and literature; (2) the arts; (3) the social sciences; (4) the biological sciences; and (5) the physical and mathematical sciences.

Under this suggested plan for the improvement of the secondary-school curriculum, an illustration of the organization in a secondary school of 1,200 pupils would be somewhat as follows:

The departments of English, French, Latin, and German would be combined into one broad field with one department head, and this field would be called Languages and Literature. The regular music and art departments would be united into one, called the Arts division. The departments of social studies and home economics would be combined under one head, and this would be called the Social Studies and Home-making area. Science and mathematics would be combined into the Mathematics and Science division with one head. The business education, industrial arts, manual training, and diversified occupations departments would be coordinated under a director into one division, called the Vocational area.

Each student in secondary school, no matter what special program or "curriculum" he was taking, would be required to take a *major* of three or four years' work in the area of languages and literature; in addition, he would be required to take *two* or more *minors* of two years each in *two* of the other different areas, with the exception of the vocational division, where he would be expected to take *one minor* and specialized courses in that particular vocational curriculum which he was pursuing.

This movement to form broad areas or fields of knowledge by

combining the subject-matter departments within the existing organization of the curriculum is promising; it tends to make secondary-school teachers more conscious of the other subjects and areas which are related to and touch closely upon their own special subject fields. It helps to break down departmental lines and to give teachers a broader view of the curriculum. It is seen, however, that this is still fundamentally an approach through the attempt to improve subject matter and subject-matter offerings, rather than an attempt to relate these subject matters seriously to the needs and the individual interests of the pupils who must take them. The "broad-fields" plan infers that the subject matter which is existent is essentially good for the child.

3. *Reorganizing the Curriculum Around the Study of Adolescent Youth.* One of the most interesting experiments in an approach to this type of curriculum organization has been going on with students in the University High School at the Ohio State University. For example, these students as long ago as 1938 described their six-year career in an experimental school, in which they started in a new building with a new type of approach to the curriculum.[4] In the seventh grade the core course was a combination of English and social studies; the other classes included mathematics, physical education, science, and a choice of the fine arts, industrial arts, or home economics. The core ran throughout the six years of high school. It was centered around the "Home" in the seventh grade, and around the "Community" in the eighth grade, where the aspects of Transportation, Communication, and Public Utilities also were studied. In the ninth grade, students and teachers chose "Governments and Their Histories" as the center of work; and in the tenth grade, the development of civilization occupied the central position of core work. In the eleventh grade, the students attempted to discover how they might understand the present world in the light of the past, one group approaching the study chronologically and the other from the standpoint of problems involved; for the twelfth grade, modern problems were the core. As in the seventh grade, the pupils had other required or elective subjects in each year in addition to this

[4] *Were We Guinea Pigs?* New York, Henry Holt and Company, 1938.

core. Lucile Lurry and Elsie Alberty describe the core program today in the University High School in a recent book.[5]

Other samples of the "core" approach and the "needs of youth" approach, and the degrees of success which have been achieved with them are reported by other writers.[6] Some aspects of this type of reorganization of the curricular structure of the secondary school in keeping with the needs of the revised curriculum have already been described.[7] In some schools the regular administrative structure has been retained with broader areas such as have already been set forth; in others, there has been almost a complete revamping of the organizational structure around the core or so-called "integrated" program, as in California and Denver. These schools and these teachers have been the educational pioneers in the reorganization and redirection of the curriculum of the secondary school. Their contributions give proof to other schools and teachers that "it can be done."

4. *The Approach through Organized Guidance.* The development of saner, more effective guidance programs in the secondary school has accompanied the addition of courses to the various subject-matter fields, the addition of parallel curricula or programs of study to the secondary-school curriculum, and the type of organization centered around a study of pupils and their interests and needs. It is not unusual to visit a small secondary school today and find a complete set of records upon each child; such records would include information on the child's past school history, his home environment, test results of many kinds, and data of a case nature. These records are the tools which the teacher and the guidance worker in the modern secondary school are begininng to use effectively in their approach to solving the educational, social, and personal problems of youth.

[5] *Developing a High School Core Program,* New York, The Macmillan Company, 1957, pp. 14–15, 20, 150–66, 203–8 and Chap. iii.
[6] *Cf. Adapting the Secondary-School Program to the Needs of Youth,* 52nd Yearbook, Part i, National Society for the Study of Education, 1953, *passim,* and especially Chap. vii; *Developing the Core Curriculum* (2nd ed.) by R.C. Faunce and N.L. Bossing, Englewood Cliffs, Prentice-Hall, 1958, Chaps. iv, vi, xiii; and *What Shall the High Schools Teach?* 1956 Yearbook, Association for Supervision and Curriculum Development, Chap. iv.
[7] Chapter 13.

Although guidance started some forty years ago as "vocational" guidance, the broader meanings of the word have become known to many teachers only within the last decade. Even staid specialists in subject matter have come to a realization that social, personal, educational, vocational, and even religious guidance and mental hygiene are aspects of education with which they should be familiar and which they should use more effectively in their work. More

FIG. 35   *The student council as a part of the curricular program*

Representatives from each homeroom and chartered organization meet weekly to plan student activities and projects. (*Courtesy Charlotte (N.C.) City Schools, Sedgefield Junior High School.*)

clearly than any other single development, the modern movement in guidance illustrates the dissatisfaction of school administrators and teachers with the organization and curriculum of the secondary school; they realized that they had to become broader than mere subject-matter specialists in order to meet the changing problems of adolescents. Most school administrators have been willing to improve the provisions for the guidance of their students, whether or not they were willing to go further in considering revision of the secondary-school curriculum. If they make a careful study of guidance, they are inevitably led to further steps towards improving the offerings in the curriculum. Curricular aspects of guidance are considered in greater detail in Chapter 16.

5. *Bringing the Extracurriculum into the Curriculum.* Thoughtful educators consider the incorporation of student activities into the regular curriculum one of the significant trends in curriculum revision in the secondary school. Student activities include journalism, radio, debating, dramatics, music, art, and physical education. Since this step seems to meet with popular approval, there is no longer reason for many of the normal activities of children to remain outside the curriculum. For many years administrators have bemoaned, and teachers have condemned and condoned, so-called "extracurricular" activities as a necessary evil, rather than encouraged and controlled them as a natural part of the activities in which children of secondary-school age wish to engage. Now that these activities are being brought into the curriculum in ever-increasing numbers, the curricular organization is expanding rapidly through this means. New school departments have even been added to teach and administer these activities, as in physical education and dramatic art.

Whatever approach to the organization and administration of the curriculum is taken, the problem of *credit* for graduation arises. The Carnegie unit was established originally in order that there might be some uniformity in the work and the credit given in the secondary schools. It was based upon *clock hours* or *number of minutes* spent in a class or subject. Under the plan of giving credits in terms of Carnegie units, a student changing from one secondary school to another, or from secondary school to college, might be expected to have spent about the same amount of time on a subject, and therefore to have mastered in that time approximately the same materials. The secondary schools usually require sixteen units for graduation, while the colleges require fifteen or sixteen units for admission. All work done by secondary-school students must be turned into these Carnegie units; and likewise all work performed by them has come to be graded upon the basis of the poorest, the best, and the average, rather than upon the basis of the progress which each individual has made in his work from the point at which he started. Under these handicaps, it is more noteworthy that the secondary school has made as much progress as it has in curriculum reorganization, than that its progress has been limited.

The reorganization of secondary education has done much to broaden the total school curriculum through the elimination of some static requirements. The junior high school has been given great freedom to experiment in curricular work; and entrance to many colleges is based now on the senior-high-school record, instead of on the four-year record.

Every organization tends to become conservative as it grows older, to make changes slowly, to become obsessed with its own ideas as to its mission and purpose, to question the wisdom of outsiders who request change within it. The secondary school is no exception to this tendency, and by virtue of it illustrates well the lag between actual cultural and social and economic development and those developments as taught and handled by the school. Add to this the fact that the secondary school is hampered also by the static requirements which it has established for graduation from it, and the situation becomes even clearer. The administrator usually thinks in terms of which new course should be considered as an elective and what, if any, credit should be granted for it—not in terms of the needs and total progress of each pupil.

THE EVALUATION OF CURRICULUM WORK IN THE SECONDARY SCHOOL

MEASUREMENTS IN TERMS OF SUBJECT MATTER. Following the evaluative procedure which the college employs, most secondary-school teachers usually think of evaluation in terms of measurement of the student's achievement in a specific subject or course. In view of the fact that testing the achievement of students is universal in formal education, it is a matter of serious concern that testing in general is so poorly done. Not only is testing of one kind or another as ancient as education itself, but the development of new test techniques in recent years has accompanied, and in many cases has motivated, curricular trends of far-reaching import on all school levels.

As has already been pointed out in Chapter 6, surveys like the Classical Investigation, the Modern Language Study, and the American Historical Association's report on the social studies have been of great value to teachers in assisting them to formulate aims in their teaching within these subject fields. In the final analysis, however, these surveys have tended to focus the attention of teachers even more sharply upon the accomplishments of certain objectives which are contained primarily within the subject-matter field itself. They have operated in the direction of more emphasis upon mastery of the subject-matter area, and have obscured the fact that the teacher must also take sharply into account the attitudes and competences which students should acquire in that area. Thus, the average secondary-school teacher has come to think of evaluation in terms of testing or examinations strictly in the subject itself. He thinks of tests in terms of finding out what the student has learned in the course, or of attempting to discover what he has learned, or of making him study in the course, or of attempting to discover the student's weaknesses in order to remedy them. There is strong cause to doubt whether the instructor uses such tests to evaluate and improve his own instruction, or to check the aims of his course; one even wonders frequently whether he employs properly the aims of his course in formulating his tests.

The classroom teacher is not to be blamed entirely for this narrow conception of "evaluation" as compared with "measurement," but he can be held responsible for a lack of mastery of the testing techniques which he does use. Numerous injustices have been done to students from time to time by well-meaning teachers, who have neither taken the time nor expended the effort necessary to achieve a mastery of testing techniques commensurate with their teaching ability and methods. It is not necessary for a teacher to give the student writer's cramp, emotional and gastronomic indigestion, and a mental set against the subject and the instructor in order for him to maintain high standards of achievement.

WHAT ARE THE PURPOSES OF THE TESTS? Teachers have been prone to overlook the fact that the experts who constructed tests and made a study of them state broad objectives for tests. The following objectives connote the broader concept of evaluation that has developed over the years, rather than the more narrow concept of measurement:

1. Pupil classification, including promotion and failure
2. The evaluation of instruction
3. Diagnosis and analysis of pupils for more efficient instruction
4. Motivation of teaching and learning situations
5. A basis for educational and vocational guidance
6. Achievement—reports to parents, pupils, and others of the quantity and quality of work being done by pupils
7. Practice in taking tests and in organizing material
8. Prognosis—to predict probable achievement or success
9. The formulation of specific standards or goals of achievement for a group, or grade, or year of work [8]

It will be noted that some overlapping occurs in these purposes, but in general the main emphases differ. The educational literature makes no distinction between tests and examinations, but uses the terms interchangeably.

An analysis of these objectives shows the enlarged scope of the testing field. This field really includes evaluation in its broad sense; and evaluation necessitates careful study for the formulation or selection of the test to meet the specific purpose which the teacher has in mind. Most teachers recognize the difference between "essay-type" and "objective" tests; yet they become more and more bewildered as they attempt to understand, or even to distinguish between, such technical terms as achievement tests, survey tests, diagnostic tests, analytic tests, prognostic tests, aptitude tests and tests of interest and skills, mental tests, placement tests, scaled tests, rate tests, power tests, cycle tests, spiral tests, and standardized tests. The newer phases in testing are valuable and are used generally now for educational placement, for vocational and educational guidance, for the supervision and evaluation of instruction, for prognosis, and for estimating mental ability. When a pupil is unable to master a subject area after constant and concentrated application, the teacher should know that it is comparatively easy to discover by the employment of proper tests whether the pupil is unable to read and comprehend, whether he is deficient mentally, or whether he

[8] *Cf.* C.W. Odell, *Educational Measurement in High School,* New York, the Century Company, 1930, pp. 4 f.; and Harry A. Greene, Albert N. Jorgensen, and J.R. Gerberich, *Measurement and Evaluation in the Secondary School* (2nd ed.), New York, Longmans, Green and Company, 1954, Chaps. i–iii, vi–xi, xxv, *passim.*

has been retarded in his development and growth in other ways.

THE SUBJECTIVITY AND VARIABILITY OF SCHOOL MARKS. Another element which has narrowed the teacher's concept of evaluation on the secondary-school level is concerned with school marks. One of the major factors which stimulated the construction of objective tests developed during the years from 1910 to 1914, when a number of studies showed that school marks as usually given, were subjective and decidedly unreliable.[9] These studies also indicated that many examinations were given without any clear conception of their function; often the examinations were more laborious than necessary for the pupil who took them, and for the teachers who scored them. B.D. Wood [10] showed that supposedly competent scorers disagree as to what are the correct answers for a test.

There are many reasons for subjectivity and variability in school marks. Different bases of marking exist even among teachers in the same school. Some teachers attempt to measure only the pupil's actual performance; others try to measure performance in the light of the pupil's ability; still other teachers take effort, attitude, and general behavior into consideration in measuring a child's performance. In some tests, stress is placed upon ability to reproduce material acquired in the course, whereas pupil initiative and ability to apply what has been learned are predominant purposes in other tests. Speed and good written English are weighted in some tests, and in other tests neither is emphasized. Other factors operating strongly in the scoring of tests pertain to the mental, emotional, and physical state of the teacher at the time of scoring, as well as to the

[9] *Cf.* W.F. Dearborn, "School and University Grades," *University of Wisconsin Bulletin,* No. 368, High School Series, No. 9, Madison, June, 1910; W.F. Johnson, "A Study of High School Grades," *School Review,* XIX (January, 1910), pp. 13–24; F.J. Kelly, *Teachers' Marks, Their Reliability and Standardization,* Teachers College Contributions to Education, Columbia University, No. 66, 1914; W.R. Miles, *Comparison of Elementary and High School Grades,* University of Iowa Studies in Education, Vol. I, No. 1, 1910; and articles by D. Starch and E.C. Elliott, in the *School Review:* "Reliability of Grading High School Work in English," XX (September, 1912), pp. 442–57; "Reliability of Grading High School Work in Mathematics," XXI (April, 1913), pp. 254–59; and "Reliability of Grading High School Work in History," XXI (December, 1913), pp. 676–81.

[10] "The Measurement of College Work," *Educational Administration and Supervision,* VII (September, 1921), pp. 301–34.

attitudes and standards which he has. There can be no doubt that poor formulation, administration, and scoring of the traditional type of examination stimulated the development of objective testing.

Both the old essay tests and the new types of objective tests can be reliable indices of pupil achievement in a special subject-matter field, provided they are properly constructed, administered, and scored. The traditional "essay" test is firmly fixed in educational practice,[11] and monthly, six-week, mid-term, and final tests are required generally upon the secondary-school level. In view of these facts, it is vitally important for the teacher to gain a broader concept of evaluation, as compared with the narrower idea of "testing" or "measurement" in subject-matter achievement only.

EVALUATION AS THE BROADER CONCEPT OF MEASUREMENT

THE THREE STEPS INVOLVED IN EVALUATION. The fundamental steps in evaluation may be briefly stated as: (1) clear and definite formulation of the aims of the work to be done with a particular group or class; (2) checking and evaluation of the methods employed by the teacher and pupils in attaining these aims; and (3) final evaluation of student outcomes, and checking of these against the aims which were formulated.

1. *Clear and Definite Formulation of Aims.* The subject-matter aims have been fairly clearly defined within the confines of the specific courses. This work on aims has been carried on primarily by the work of survey groups in the various subject fields—e.g., the Commission on the Social Studies of the American Historical Association. The secondary-school teacher should clarify these aims by the employment of two other techniques. First, by means of an oral or written pretest he should always discover as accurately as he can the stage of advancement of each individual, and the special interests and needs of his group. This involves essentially the progressive development on the part of the teacher of an improved technique of pretesting, in order that the progress of the student in that particular course may be measured from the point at which he started,

---

[11] *Cf.* Greene, *et al., op. cit.,* Chap. VI.

rather than in comparison with the average or the best achievement in the class. The second technique to be used by the teacher as he begins work with his group is the giving of a reliable test on attitudes and ideals, or aptitudes and skills; such a test will add to his knowledge of each pupil's status at the time at which he started the work.

2. *Checking and Evaluation of Teaching Techniques.* Since the methods used in this part of the evaluative process have received much of the criticism in recent years, it is well to take an example of a special course in a subject-matter field through which the evaluative procedures can be illustrated. "Problems of Democracy" is here chosen for this purpose.

Let us assume that the teacher of this class has formulated his aims for the work, has done much reading in advance, has outlined the directions which the work may take with the students in the broad units for the year, and has prepared bibliographies for the use of the students in the different units. In order to find out where his students were when they began, he has used two evaluative techniques: first, he has given the Cooperative Test in American Government [12] in order to discover what knowledge of the unit the students have when they start their work; secondly, he has given them a pretest which he himself has made out, and which is based upon the different tentative units he has outlined, such as problems of capital, problems of labor, problems of youth, problems of relief, trends in the growth of functions of the government, and international relations. From the result of these two tests, he has a more reliable idea of the point at which each student started in the course than his personal opinion would give him.

Since the class is now engaged for several weeks or months upon certain units of the course, the teacher may wish to check and evaluate the progress made and his methods of teaching as they proceed. In doing this, he may use a variety of techniques, some of which have been better developed than others. He may check on the withdrawal of books from the school library; he may require students to report on problems which he has assigned; he may stimulate students to report voluntarily on various aspects of problems which

[12] Published by Cooperative Test Division of the Educational Testing Service.

they have become interested in and have investigated; he may distribute to each student a sheet on which the student keeps a list of the materials and activities he has employed in relation to the course during a unit; he may have one or more interviews with each student in regard to his particular work and progress; he may keep an impersonal record, or "case study," of the pupil's work and attitudes and progress as they appear to him; he may arrange panel discussions and estimate the pupil's contributions to them; he may divide the class into committees and meet with these separate groups, in order to discover how his students cooperate when working with a group. All of these devices which the teacher may use, or some of which he may employ, should give him a more accurate measure of the progress of each pupil in the group; just as important, they should give him valuable suggestions on how he may improve the work, and information as to whether he is doing a good job with that class in that particular situation.

3. *Final Evaluation of Outcomes.* In making his final evaluation of the work of his students and the outcomes of the course, the teacher of the class in "Problems of Democracy" may employ the following techniques:

1. He may use the same standard achievement test which he used at the beginning to see how much progress each student has made in comparison with where he was at the start (Cooperative Test in American Government), or he may use his own teacher-made test of mastery of the subject.

2. He may give a sample problem which is concerned with the work which the students have been doing together in the course, and may require them to solve that problem in the light of the situation specifically presented, thus showing the growth and knowledge which they have attained.

3. He may require each student to make a written report upon the values which he has obtained from the course; the areas that he has become interested in, in which he was not interested before; the activities which were followed in the course which were not well done; the problems which were considered which need still further work and study upon them; and the ways by which the work in the course could be improved by both teacher and pupils.

4. He may make a list of the types of activities in which the pupils engaged in the class during the period of their work, including self-

initiated activities and voluntary contributions like clippings and reports; cooperative activities with small groups or with the class, like constructive criticisms of a report which has been presented; leadership in group or class discussion; and other performances of a miscellaneous nature.[13]

THE TEACHER-PUPIL INDIVIDUAL FOLDER
FOR EVALUATION

The teacher will have to revise his system of grading and marking pupils in the light of recent tendencies and movements in evaluation. If he is really interested in his own growth and in the maximum growth of his pupils, he will gradually develop a system of informal records which might be described as the "teacher-pupil personal folder." The teacher should file within this folder everything which the student has contributed in written form, and the impersonal comments and observations which he has made from time to time throughout the work about the student and his progress. For example, in this folder will be found the pretests and the teacher's notation of the stage of achievement at which the pupil started; the pupil's written contributions and reports in the course from time to time, with careful judgments by the teacher of the progress made, impartial comments as to growth or lack of it, and suggestions on how growth can be secured; the pupil's mid-term, monthly, or unit tests, with the written notations of the teacher; and the student's opinion of the course, the work in it, ways in which it could be improved, and other suggestions.

Such a cumulative record gives the teacher evidence of the progress of the pupil from the time that he entered the course until he finished it. The record should be equally available to the teacher and to the pupil at all times, but it should be filed in a place where other students do not have access to it. The student should be urged, and, if necessary, required to read the cumulative record of his

[13] Cf. Wrightstone, *Appraisal of Experimental High School Practices,* Teachers College, Columbia University, 1936, Chaps. ix–x; E.B. Wesley and S.P. Wronski, *Teaching the Social Studies in High Schools* (4th ed.), Boston, D.C. Heath and Company, 1958, Chaps. xxix–xxx; W.L. Wrinkle, *Improving Marking and Reporting Practices in Elementary and Secondary Schools,* New York, Rinehart and Company, 1947, Chaps. viii, xi; and A.E. Traxler, *Techniques of Guidance* (rev. ed.), New York, Harper and Brothers, 1957, Part iii.

progress from time to time as it develops; he should confer frequently with the teacher upon matters to which the teacher has called his attention, or on various ways in which he needs to grow and improve his work.

When the time comes for handing in the final grades, the teacher is able to gauge that pupil's performance on the basis of how far he has progressed from the point at which he started; he does not grade him only on the basis of his comparative standing with the rest of the group, or with the average. If this procedure is followed, the student awakens to a realization of the fact that marks as such do not control absolutely his success or failure in school, because he has before him the actual record of what he has done and how he has grown or has not developed. He begins to pay less attention to artificial awards, and more attention to the rewards and satisfaction which come from the growth which has been stimulated and which is actually shown in the form of his record. This system of record-keeping will inspire in the pupil the desire to improve himself; it develops in the teacher the realization that individual and group growth spring from the individual's development, rather than from his performance in relation to the average performance or the superior achievements of others.

RECENT DEVELOPMENTS IN EVALUATION

In addition to the testing services maintained by many college bureaus and private publishing houses for the help of the teacher, certain experiments have been made which have improved the tools and techniques that may be utilized by teachers for evaluation in the secondary school.

THE TESTS OF THE EIGHT-YEAR STUDY. Prominent among the new techniques are the types of tests developed by the Evaluation Staff of the Eight-Year Study of the Progressive Education Association.[14] This staff was established primarily to help the selected schools to evaluate their work. The instruments which were devel-

[14] Volume III of "Adventure in American Education," *Appraising and Recording Student Progress* by Eugene R. Smith, Ralph W. Tyler, and the Evaluation Staff, New York, Harper and Brothers, 1942, gives the official report on these new techniques and tests.

oped were used chiefly in these experimental schools, and were planned primarily for students on the secondary-school level; however, certain of the tests could be adapted for use in the elementary school. At the conclusion of the study, the staff made a complete report, and these instruments and techniques have helped to point the way for newer kinds of tests for the teacher to develop and use.[15] These tests, which were developed and improved during the experimental years of the Eight-Year Study, comprised the following:

Application of Principles of Science. Tests of ability to recognize *when* and *how* principles studied in general science, physical science, and biology may be applied in problem situations new to the student. These were for use in grades nine, ten, eleven, and twelve.

Social Sensitivity. These included tests on social problems and economic issues, scale of beliefs, beliefs about school life relating to school government, the curriculum, grades and awards, school spirit, pupil-teacher relations, group life, and tests of social concepts.

Interpretation of Data. These data were taken primarily from the fields of science and the social studies and were presented in paragraphs, tables, graphs, and charts; they tried to test the ability of the student to judge the soundness of interpretation from the form of statements presented in the test.

English and Literature Tests. These embraced the questionnaire on voluntary reading, literature questionnaires on the novel and the drama, literary information on English and American literature, critical-mindedness in the reading of fiction, judging the effectiveness of written composition and tests on the use of books and libraries.

Fine Arts. There was one test on certain elements in art appreciation based on seven modern paintings, and another based on forty well-known paintings.

Application of Principles of Logical Reasoning. These included tests on application of certain principles of reasoning relating to definition of terms, indirect argument, attacking the arguer rather than his argument, and "if-then" argument. Arguments were actually given from newspapers and magazines.

Nature of Proof. These tests involved analysis of argument, the situations being taken from social studies and science; they included some reports of experiments or investigations, and other reports based on opinion.

[15] For samples of some of the newer types, turn to *Measurement in Education* by A.M. Jordan, New York, McGraw-Hill Book Company, 1953, pp. 172–82, 195–205, 263–71, and Chap. xII.

Analysis of Controversial Writing. Quotations relating to social issues were given, and the students were requested to make objective judgments on the positions taken by the authors and to identify and appraise some of the propaganda techniques employed.

Interests. These included tests called the "interest indices," which attempted to find the student's likes, dislikes, or indifference in regard to 200 activities; the 200 activities in each of these forms were classified into various categories which related to personal and social areas such as the family, and social activities in and out of school; based on the items in these categories were an Interests test and two Interests and Activities tests.

An analysis of the content of these new tests reveals new trends in evaluation on the secondary-school level of great significance to the teacher in this modern age of science, automation, and need of international understanding. The tests were concerned primarily with social sensitivity, problem solving, interpretation of data, voluntary reading, interests of students, and the nature of proof and the application of principles of logical reasoning. They attempted to measure the attitudes, the reasoning and critical thinking, the ideals, and the emotional reactions of the student, as compared with types of measurement which many teachers in the past considered to be primarily concerned with the measurement of achievement in subject matter.

The teacher-parent conference is one of the newer devices for more accurate and effective evaluation of the students' work. The conference may come once or twice each semester; it supplements, but does not supplant, the report card. Two systems that have tried out this evaluative procedure and refined it are Great Neck, Long Island (N.Y.), and Long Beach, California.

CRITERIA OF THE COOPERATIVE STUDY OF SECONDARY-SCHOOL STANDARDS. The volume entitled *Evaluative Criteria* (1950 edition) contains approximately 1,500 check-list items and 500 evaluations embracing the significant phases of the modern secondary school.[16] Although these check-list and evaluative items were carefully re-

[16] The reader is referred to Chap. 12 for a fuller description of those aspects which relate to the curriculum in the Cooperative Study of Secondary School Standards. Constructive use of the *Evaluative Criteria* in various sections of the country is described in *Proceedings of the Fifty-Third Annual Meeting of the Southern Association of Colleges and Secondary Schools*, Memphis (December, 1948), pp. 119–27, 180–86, and 213–18.

fined by a group of experts through a period of fifteen years, they are being clarified further in the 1960 edition. No better device has been developed for use by the staff of a secondary school and by a staff of evaluators from outside that school for determining what the objectives of that secondary school are, what its program, curriculum, and activities are composed of, and how well they are achieving their aims and philosophy as measured by the outcomes of their instructional program. Secondary schools should use these criteria carefully over a period of years to discover exactly where they are in their curricular programs, and to make improvements from that point. Sections C, D–D16 and Y pertain especially to curriculum evaluation.

OTHER EVALUATIVE AIDS. Earlier in this chapter attention was called to two reports which present the newer approach to evaluation: *Appraisal of Experimental High School Practices* [17] and *Improving Marking and Reporting Practices in Elementary and Secondary Schools.*[18] A comparison of these two publications with *The Scientific Movement in Education* (1938), *The Measurement of Understanding* (1946),[19] and "Twenty-five Years of Educational Research" [20] gives a clearly defined picture of more recent trends in evaluation and measurement.

The Southern Association Study in Secondary Schools and Colleges developed experimental evaluative procedures in their work with thirty-three cooperating schools.[21] Provocative of thought, as well as study, are the techniques and data for evaluation which grew out of the Stanford Social Education Investigation.[22]

The Fourth Mental Measurements Yearbook [23] makes available to teachers a comprehensive list and evaluative reviews of tests of all types and descriptions. This publication will be found of value to

[17] By J.W. Wrightstone, *op. cit., passim.*
[18] By W.L. Wrinkle, *op. cit., passim.*
[19] 37th Yearbook, Part II, and 45th Yearbook, Part I, respectively, of the National Society for the Study of Education.
[20] *Review of Educational Research,* XXVI (June, 1956), Chaps. I–V.
[21] *Cooperative Study for the Improvement of Education,* the Southern Association of Colleges and Secondary Schools, 1946, Chaps. VIII–X.
[22] I.J. Quillen and L.A. Hanna, *Education for Social Competence: Curriculum and Instruction in Secondary-School Social Studies,* Chicago, Scott, Foresman and Company, 1948, Chaps. VII–VIII, XIII–XV, and Appendix III.
[23] Edited by O.K. Buros, Gryphon Press, Highland Park (N.J.), 1953.

secondary-school teachers in making a careful selection of standard tests from the hundreds of such tests on the market today.

PROBLEMS FOR INDIVIDUAL STUDY
AND CLASS DISCUSSION

1. Assume that in your secondary school there is a plan for the next school year to start regular classes with regular elective credit in Dramatics and Journalism, and that these have been extracurricular activities in the past. Under what department or subject area should they be placed, and what types of activities should be planned for each?

2. What steps as principal would you take to "fuse" a first-year, secondary-school social studies class with a first-year English class under one teacher for a double-class period?

3. Make out an "essay-type" (traditional) test for one of your classes for a six-week period; then *write out all* of the answers that could possibly be correct for each question. Does this procedure make your testing technique more accurate? Explain.

4. Should secondary-school progress and graduation be measured in terms of Carnegie units of credit? Do you know of any better method?

5. If a secondary-school pupil does not know what "curriculum" or "'program of studies" he wants to follow, what program would you as his counselor make out for him? Be specific as to subject areas and courses in your own school situation.

6. In curriculum organization, what values, if any, have resulted from replacing Ancient History with Civics? Medieval and Modern History with World History? Support your position.

7. Write out your aims for one of your classes; then prepare a final examination for the end of the year which will test whether you and your class achieved those objectives which you formulated.

8. Assume that you wish to test the attitudes and interests of one of your secondary-school classes. Of the various standard tests of this kind which have been published, which one would you recommend for use? Give reasons for your selection.

9. Is it possible under the present organization of the secondary school to arrange for "individual" curricula or programs of study for each pupil? Give reasons for your answer.

10. Assume that as an English teacher you wish to correlate your American Literature work more closely with the American History class work. How would you go about effecting this in the present departmental organization of the secondary school?

11. Could the adoption of the "core curriculum" centered around the social-studies area be effective in a secondary school with the traditional

departmental organization according to subject matter? Support your point of view.

12. Do you believe that certain subjects of study are of more inherent value than others? Explain.

13. If you were asked to list all of the subject-matter courses offered in a secondary school, and then to combine them into five "broad fields of knowledge" of more or less close relationship, what five combinations would you make? List under each combination the subject-matter courses that would fall under that area.

14. Why is student progress usually measured in terms of scholastic achievement? Should this be accepted as true, or should the development of attitudes, ideals, and emotions also be taken into account? Explain.

15. Can you make a clear distinction between achievement and diagnostic tests? Between objective and standardized test? Between prognostic tests and attitude scales? Between interest inventories and aptitude tests?

ADDITIONAL ANNOTATED REFERENCES
FOR PROBLEM OR UNIT STUDY

Adams, G.S., and Torgeson, T.L., *Measurements and Evaluation for the Secondary-School Teacher*, New York, The Dryden Press, 1956.
This text tries to "bridge the gap" between theory and practice in measurement and testing, with emphasis upon both informal and standard testing; Part III takes up evaluation in the different subject-matter fields.

Alcorn, M.D., *et al.*, *Better Teaching in Secondary Schools*, New York, Henry Holt and Company, 1954.
Section VIII is devoted to purposes, problems, planning, and administering of evaluation, including building, organizing, improving test items, and marking and reporting student achievement.

Alexander, W.M., and Halverson, P.M., *Effective Teaching in Secondary Schools*, New York, Rinehart and Company, 1956.
Organization of the program in Part II and evaluation in Part IV.

Association for Supervision and Curricular Development, N.E.A.
Toward Better Teaching, 1949 Yearbook, contains in Chapter VIII a very good description of how to help pupils evaluate their own learning.
Reporting Is Communicating, 1956, describes various approaches to evaluation and marking, including parent-teacher conferences.

Bean, K.L., *Construction of Educational and Personnel Tests*, New York, McGraw-Hill Book Company, 1953.
A book for those who need a knowledge of test construction, of both objective and essay types.

Chamberlin, Dean, *et al.*, *Did They Succeed in College?* New York, Harper and Brothers, 1942.

This is the follow-up study of some 1,500 graduates of the thirty schools in the P.E.A. Eight-Year Study. Chapters i–iii, x, and the Appendix are particularly pertinent to secondary-school evaluation. Educational Testing Service, Princeton, N.J., is the center now for objective tests of many kinds, including the Cooperative Test Division and many types of college ability and entrance tests.

Furst, E.J., *Constructing Evaluation Instruments*, New York, Longmans, Green and Company, 1958.

Designed to help the classroom teacher to construct a good classroom test. The illustrations of test items for different kinds of tests are illuminating.

Gerberich, J.R., *Specimen Objective Test Items*, New York, Longmans, Green and Company, 1956.

A guide to achievement-test construction, with Part ii containing the more valuable illustrations for the high-school teacher.

Greene, H.A., *et al.*, *Measurement and Evaluation in the Secondary School* (2nd ed.), New York, Longmans, Green and Company, 1954.

To give the young teacher a grasp in simple language of how to evaluate and test more accurately; Chapter xv–xxiv illustrate evaluation in the various subject-matter fields.

Gross, R.E., and Zeleny, L.D., *et al.*, *Educating Citizens for Democracy*, New York, Oxford University Press, 1958.

A good section on types of tests evaluating the outcomes of the social studies in the secondary school in Part v.

Gruhn, W.T., and Douglass, R.H., *The Modern Junior High School* (2nd ed.), New York, The Ronald Press Company, 1956.

The organization, administration, evaluation, and reporting of progress in the junior high school in Part iv.

Hanna, L.A., *et al.*, *Unit Teaching in the Elementary School*, New York, Rinehart and Company, 1955.

Chapter xv gives sound and definite suggestions on how to evaluate changes in behavior in unit work.

Langdon, G., and Stout, I.W., *Teacher-Parent Interviews*, New York, Prentice-Hall, 1954.

Presents in thorough fashion the strengths and weaknesses of this newer development in analysis and evaluation.

Leonard, J.P., *Developing the Secondary School Curriculum* (rev. ed.), New York, Rinehart and Company, 1953.

Chapters xiv–xv for core courses around interests and needs of youth, and xviii for evaluation of student learning.

Noar, G., *The Junior High School—Today and Tomorrow*, New York, Prentice-Hall, 1953.

The volume is devoted to a junior high-school program centered around the growth and needs of young adolescents through the core approach.

Schwartz, A., *et al.*, *Evaluating Student Progress in the Secondary School*, New York, Longmans, Green and Company, 1957.

Evaluation, with emphasis upon types of instruments that can be employed effectively, such as tests of all kinds, check-lists, inventories and questionnaires, sociometry, socio-drama, the case study, and interviews.

Thomas, R.M., *Judging Student Progress*, New York, Longmans, Green and Company, 1954.

Especially designed for junior high valuation, as well as elementary, and for diagnostic and remedial teaching, with simple illustrations, clearly presented.

Wesley, E.B., *American History in Schools and Colleges*, New York, The Macmillan Company, 1944.

This is the famous Report of the Committee on American History in Schools and Colleges. Pp. 125–45 give especially good illustrations of objective test items designed to make pupils think critically.

Wesley, E.B., and Wronski, S.P., *Teaching the Social Studies in High Schools* (4th ed.), Boston, D.C. Heath and Company, 1958.

Chapters xxix and xxx for evaluation and evaluation instruments in the social studies.

PART FIVE   Other influences on curriculum change

CHAPTER 16 Youth,
guidance and the curriculum

SIGNIFICANCE OF THE PROBLEM

Although certain aspects of the youth problem have been touched upon in preceding chapters,[1] it will be necessary in this chapter to consider in greater detail those that relate particularly to the curriculum.

In the first place, the broadening of concepts of guidance in the schools has led to a much more sympathetic understanding of the role of guidance in adjusting the curriculum of the high school to youth and also helping youth to adjust to the curriculum of the high school. The definition of guidance has both broadened and changed in the last half century. When guidance was first worked out for students in public schools in Boston, it was worked out and applied primarily in the field of vocational guidance. This definition of guidance persisted as the main definition and concept of guidance for many years; even today many school personnel think in terms of vocational guidance whenever the word "guidance" is mentioned.

However, as time went on, other aspects of guidance came to be recognized as fundamental in school work and in dealing with youth. As is true in all fields, attention is usually turned first to those particular cases that need a special kind of help; for example, guidance at first was thought of as attention and help which should be given to pupils who got into disciplinary difficulties or who failed their work in school, or who were so badly adjusted that they could not get along with other pupils. As time went on, and the psychologists studied child growth and development, the needs of all individuals for a well-rounded program were recognized. As a result, these

[1] Chaps. 5, 12, and 13.

special forms of guidance developed as aspects of a total guidance program for youth: (1) personal and social guidance; (2) educational guidance; (3) mental hygiene; and (4) vocational guidance in its manifold aspects.

It should be understood by the reader that the purpose here is to call attention to the broadening of the concept of guidance of youth, especially with respect to the total educational program within the school. It is not the purpose of this chapter to go into detail about the different types and the methods which are employed in each type of guidance.[2] An important part of the modern school's program is to educate for social, vocational, economic, group, and creative and spiritual competence. Through the guidance of youth on the secondary-school level, we attempt to achieve this particular guidance function of the school.

Another aspect of significance in youth's education is concerned with the absorption of youth into the labor market as they finish the secondary school. As has already been indicated,[3] around three million youths each year face reality in trying to get their first jobs or their first work for full financial support of themselves. In times of depression or of panic, such as the decade from 1930 to 1940, the scarcity of jobs or work opportunities for youth who had just finished their high-school education or who had just dropped out of high school before finishing their education was critical; and work of an emergency nature had to be found for them during such a period. On the other hand, in times of expansion or "boom" times, the reverse of this picture is true; many students, both boys and girls, drop out of school to take jobs or positions which may pay them

---

[2] For the student who desires several comprehensive treatments of specialized aspects of guidance, these references offer a representative sampling: L.L. Chisholm, *Guiding Youth in the Secondary School*, New York, American Book Company, 1950, *passim;* H.A. Carroll, *Mental Hygiene* (2nd ed.), New York, Prentice-Hall, 1951, *passim; Helping Teachers Understand Children*, American Council on Education, 1945, *passim;* R.H. Mathewson, *Guidance Policy and Practice* (rev. ed.), New York, Harper and Brothers, 1955, *passim;* G.E. Smith, *Counseling in the Secondary School*, New York, The Macmillan Company, 1955, *passim;* E. Stoops and G.L. Wahlquist, *Principles and Practices in Guidance*, New York, McGraw-Hill Book Company, 1958, *passim;* and Ruth Strang, *Educational Guidance: Its Principles and Practices*, New York, The Macmillan Company, 1947, *passim.*

[3] Chaps. 4 and 5.

in such times of inflation at a scale that may be larger than they will ever make again. Yet both of these types of economic periods, both the depression years and the boom years, pose the problem of the guidance of youth so that we may fit him and place him in satisfactory work upon the completion of his formal educational work in the school. In summary, it may be said that the American secondary school lags far behind many of its other accomplishments in the provisions which it makes in preparing, placing, and following up youth in jobs after they finish their high school education. The following analysis of various factors will show the situation more clearly.

THE YOUTH MOVEMENT. The important part which youth plays in the world of today may be seen by recalling some recent and tragic history. The "youth movement" which was developed in Germany laid the foundation for Hitler's use of this same youth to set the world on fire. Through the wide ramifications of these organizations for German youth, Hitler and his advisers built youth up in health for physical efficiency; through work camps and apprenticeship programs, they fulfilled their promise of work opportunities for youth. The youth of Germany gave their loyalty and support to Hitler's regime because they believed that he fulfilled the promises which he made to them.

In the United States, the American Youth Congress was formed during the depression years (1934) as a clearing center for all youth organizations, agencies, and councils. The congress eventually grew to have a delegate representation from about fifty different groups, representing a total youth membership of more than four million. The special problems of youth were discussed in this congress, and plans were laid for educating the people to the needs of youth and for persuading the government to help in the solution of their problems. The Young Communist League was an active member of the American Youth Congress, and its active and alert workers exerted far more influence than its delegate membership warranted. Under these circumstances, the American Youth Congress continued to be labeled "communistic" and "anti-American," and its potential power for great good was increasingly curtailed. Organized groups of youth can be of great help in solving all types of youth problems;

but they can also become a menace to the democratic way of life if led by persons who use youth for their own selfish purposes.[4]

Ask any young boy between the ages of sixteen and twenty-four, who is just getting out of school, whether he would rather be guaranteed some form of social security or the opportunity to work and to climb to the top of the ladder of success. Social security will be chosen by a minority. The youth problem must be considered, therefore, in its relation to the school and to other social and educational agencies paralleling the school.

STUDIES OF YOUTH AND THEIR PROBLEMS

1. The American Youth Commission

In 1935, the American Council on Education brought together sixteen people who were experts in various fields, such as education, business, and social work. These people became the American Youth Commission. The purpose of the commission was to bring attention to bear upon the problems of youth, especially of those youth between the ages of sixteen and twenty-four. As a result of its investigations, the commission came to the conclusion that manifest deficiencies in national employment, health, and education must be remedied if youth are to continue to believe in the American form of government and other American institutions.

Nongovernmental in character, the American Youth Commission received its financial support primarily from the General Education Board. Various educational institutions and Federal agencies also cooperated with it. The amount of information collected by the commission through its investigators was tremendous, and the publications that it issued to report the results of its studies were numerous; the direct and allied problems of youth which were studied in detail were comprehensive, well sampled, and well balanced. Per-

[4] For a history of the American Youth Congress, the reader is referred to *American Youth Today* by Leslie Gould, New York, Random House, 1940. For two differing viewpoints on youth and its problems prior to America's entry into World War II, the following are cited: "German Youth Will Gladly Die" by Robert L.H. Hiller, *Survey Graphic*, xxx (February, 1941), pp. 68–71, and "Neglected Youth: America's Peril" by Goodwin Watson, *The American Teacher*, xxv (November, 1940), pp. 9–14; cf. also *Youth Welfare in Germany* by John W. Taylor, Nashville (Tenn.), Baird-Ward Company, 1936.

haps the most startling contribution of the commission was the discovery that the typical American citizen knows very little about youth and its problems. Educators must, therefore, realize that some of the problems of school youth are almost as pressing for solution as the problems of youth between the ages of sixteen and twenty-four who are no longer in school.

THE MARYLAND STUDY. Among the commission's investigations, Howard M. Bell's statewide study of Maryland youth shows well both the first techniques employed and the actual information which was obtained and disseminated.[5] A representative sampling of Maryland's youth between sixteen and twenty-four years of age was taken as to age and condition—economic, social, geographical, and so on. Thirteen thousand youths were selected in this manner, and they were interviewed personally and individually. The same questions (in written form) were asked of every one, and the answers were recorded by the interviewers. The Maryland investigation discovered the following facts:

1. That large numbers of these youths were unemployed, and also in a situation where they could make no other profitable use of their time.
2. That the lower the grade at which a youth left school, the more probable it was that he might be unemployed.
3. That many of these youths were poorly adjusted to the responsibilities of citizenship.
4. That their circumstances were such that they could not solve satisfactorily the problems that confronted them.
5. That they were not well enough educated to make the best use of opportunities when they got them.
6. That the schooling of these young people had not been adequate, although the study was concerned most directly with pupils out of school.

In addition to these findings, the Maryland survey showed that one-fourth of these youths had been in school only seven years, and that 7 per cent of those who were out of school had not completed

[5] *Youth Tell Their Story: A Study of the Conditions and Attitudes of Young People in Maryland Between the Ages of 16 and 24*, American Council on Education, 1938. A complete list of the publications of the American Youth Commission is to be found in the bibliography at the end of this chapter.

the sixth grade. These figures may be compared with the country at large, where about two-thirds of the youths at that time between fourteen and eighteen years of age were in school. For many years, people have thought of the school as the primary social institution which was to prepare boys and girls for adult life. Over 60 per cent of those who graduate today from secondary school never go on to further schooling. These facts are very significant in the light of the remarkable growth since 1900 of educational opportunities at public expense throughout the nation.

The studies of the American Youth Commission, and studies conducted by various states and other groups, indicate clearly that the secondary school must prepare youth *for living*, as well as *for higher education.* These studies also indicate that the secondary school is not now doing a satisfactory job of preparing youth for living and work. Whether this task is one which the secondary school should tackle alone, or whether it is a job which the school must undertake in cooperation with other agencies, is a problem pressing for solution. This is a problem worthy of the highest type of statesmanship, and its solution will challenge many educational Solomons.

CONTRIBUTIONS OF THE AMERICAN YOUTH COMMISSION TO THE CURRICULUM. The initial survey work of the American Youth Commission was the commission's first contribution of significance for and to the curriculum. The surveys showed that secondary education, as organized and administered, was not meeting the needs of youth in regard to health, vocation, and planning problems. The earlier monograph by H.R. Douglass [6] and the later one by Newton Edwards [7] recommended a radical departure from the curricular pattern commonly formulated for the secondary school.

A second contribution of the American Youth Commission was in the form of definite information about how to make a youth and community survey. This was a new viewpoint, involving more than merely a survey of the school. There is a need for information on how to make community and youth surveys, since no two communities are alike; a revamped program for the curriculum of one school might not be adaptable to another.

[6] *Secondary Education for Youth in Modern America*, Washington, American Council on Education, 1937.
[7] *Equal Educational Opportunity for Youth: A National Responsibility*, Washington, American Council on Education, 1939.

In the meantime, the Commission extended its investigation to procure comparative data on youth and the provisions made for youth in other countries. Such a study was *Youth in European Labor Camps.*[8] This type of information furnished the third contribution of the Commission; it gave suggestions on methods in use elsewhere which might be adapted to help youth in individual communities.

The fourth contribution of the Commission embraced investigations of the Civilian Conservation Corps, the National Youth Administration, and private work camps in the United States, and their social, economic, and educational significance; and of youth employment and unemployment. These studies gave information about work provisions for youth in the United States—provisions by both emergency and private agencies.

A fifth type of contribution was the Commission's surveys of Negro youth. In making a careful study of this underprivileged racial minority, the Commission presented boldly to the American people the problems of Negro youth; it hoped that satisfactory action would be taken to meet these problems, and that the situation which faced minorities in middle Europe might not confront America. The racial minorities in various countries surrounding Germany were used by Hitler and his advisers as vehicles for stirring up dissatisfaction and disunity within those countries. Some solution must be found both in school and out for the education and satisfactory advancement of the Negro population. And the Negro problem is no longer a problem of the South; it is a problem for the whole nation.

A new step in a new direction was taken by the Commission in its studies of the education of young people for family living, leisure, and recreation. These studies showed that the influences of the student's home and of where he spends his leisure time are of paramount importance in what he decides to do, and does, in life.

2. *Emergency Agencies for Youth—The NYA (WPA) and CCC:* 1933–1942

As has been indicated already, youth had a difficult time during the depression years of the 1930's in securing jobs when they fin-

---

[8] By Kenneth Holland, Washington, American Council on Education, 1939.

484   CURRICULUM PRINCIPLES AND SOCIAL TRENDS

ished their education. Partly as a result of the studies of youth which were being made during this period and partly as a plan to furnish some sort of stop-gap work for youth during this time, the Federal government established some agencies of an emergency nature. The two agencies which were established primarily for helping youth were the National Youth Administration and the Civilian Conservation Corps.

Created in 1933, the Civilian Conservation Corps (CCC) operated almost entirely on government or public land. Its primary work was concerned with erosion control and the conservation of natural resources. Enrollees had to be between the ages of seventeen to twenty-three, although some World War I veterans were taken as an exception to this general rule. In 1938, practically two-thirds of the enrollees came from relief families; 29 per cent came from families below a normal or average standard of living; and 3 per cent had no families. The CCC was established primarily as a "relief" organization; therefore, it was hampered in its plans and work of a permanent nature by this aspect of relief or "charity." Some idea of the number of youths who were helped during the depression years by the CCC can be gathered from the fact that there were almost 325,000 junior enrollees in 1941. Youths in the CCC lived in CCC camps and learned many other aspects of vocational work in connection with the shop and the equipment which they had to use in their work. The CCC was discontinued by the Congress in 1942 after jobs become more plentiful for youth.

The National Youth Administration was established in 1935 as an agency within the Works Projects Administration. The Works Projects Administration (WPA) had been established as a "relief," not an educational, organization. Following the pattern of its parent organization, the NYA remained primarily a relief organization throughout its existence from 1935 to 1942.

THE PROGRAM OF THE NYA. The two types of projects under the program of the National Youth Administration illustrated well both the limitations and the values of the program: there were (1) student aid projects, and (2) work projects for persons who were out of school and unemployed. In this emergency Federal work program for youth who were in school, one may see the beginning of national subsidization in an emergency of educational opportunities for youth in the secondary schools and colleges. Students who had the desire and the perseverance to remain in school longer, and who were unable to do so without financial help, in effect obtained Federal aid through the NYA after their circumstances had been investigated and it had been proved that their needs were valid and that their records showed promise.

The NYA had its own administrative organization within the individual states. The distribution of funds was based on (1) the size of the youth relief population or (2) the college enrollment, in case of the college-student-aid program. Through this type of organization and administration, some opportunity was given to the several states to meet their local needs and problems in the emergency. In each of these state organizations, provision was made for the following types of services:

1. Work projects for out-of-school youth from the ages of eighteen to twenty-four.
2. Youth aid for both secondary-school and college students from the ages of sixteen to twenty-four.
3. Guidance and placement of youth, with general provisions for a hookup with the state and Federal employment agencies and presumably with the schools.
4. Negro affairs.

From 1934 to 1942, the National Youth Administration gave assistance in a single month to as many secondary-school students as 356,000, and to as many as 142,000 college students. In order to qualify for assistance through the NYA an applicant had to give verified evidence that he could not enter or remain in school without employment, that he was a citizen of the United States or had filed his intention of becoming one, that he had a good character, and that he had ability to perform good scholastic work. The aid was discontinued for those students who failed in their studies. Students who received aid had to carry three-fourths of a normal load of scholastic work.

The work program of the NYA was characterized by: (1) projects for out-of-school youth which must be of use to the community where they were initiated and carried forward; (2) experience and training in work for youth who were employed by the NYA, so as to improve their "employability" if this was possible. The age group concerned was between eighteen and twenty-four; on the out-of-school project the youth had to be out of work and unable to get a job, and must have belonged to a family whose income was insufficient for fundamental needs.

TYPES AND STUDIES OF WORK UNDER THE NYA. The NYA made quite a few studies of youth. It also cooperated with the WPA in many of its studies of youth and youth problems.[9]

The programs of the National Youth Administration were generally held in high esteem by the public. A nation-wide poll in 1940 showed that more than eight persons in every nine who were familiar with the NYA program approved of it. The types of work in which students of the secondary-school level engaged in the NYA program were primarily clerical work, library service, cafeteria work, ground and building maintenance, recreational work, and construction work. One of the potential values of the NYA program on the secondary-school level lay in the opportunities for vocational exploration and guidance, whereby the students got real practice under supervision in vocational education of many kinds.

The types of work in which students of college age engaged under the in-school program of the National Youth Administration included the following: research surveys, statistics, community service, ground and building maintenance, departmental service, library service, clerical assistance, laboratory assistance, home economics work, instruction, recreation and education, duplicating, photography, printing, art and dramatics, janitor service, bookkeeping, cataloguing, and repair work.

Out-of-school projects of the National Youth Administration furnished training and experience to youth in such work as the following: clerical and service occupations; sewing and homemaking;

[9] Cf. W. Thacher Winslow, *Youth, A World Problem*, National Youth Administration, 1937; Gordon W. Lovejoy, Coordinator, Cooperative Personnel Study, *Paths To Maturity*, University of North Carolina, 1940; *Mechanical Changes In the Cotton-Textiles Industry*, 1910–1936, The Works Projects Administration and the Bureau of Labor Statistics, United States Department of Labor; and Nettie Pauline McGill and Ellen Nathalie Mathews, *The Youth of New York City*, New York, The Macmillan Company, 1940.

public health; library service and book repair; nursery school work; serving school lunches; conservation and sanitation; the building or improvement of recreational structures and facilities; public improvements such as airports, roads, street work, bridges, parking areas, traffic line and zone painting; employment in arts and crafts work; the repair of equipment, furniture, and buildings; and the making or repairing of toys.

An analysis of the emergency program of the NYA and the CCC shows that the types of work and exploration which a student might undertake under the program were rather broad and comprehensive. The main weakness of both programs was that they were of an emergency relief nature; many deserving students who were not on relief or who did not need work were not given the opportunity to participate in the program or to improve their education from it. Whatever permanent policy is adopted eventually for the secondary school for part-time training and part-time school work for youth, it must include the basic motivation which comes from a desire to investigate and to learn about occupations, rather than the aspect of "made" work in order to keep boys and girls for a longer period of time in compulsory legal school attendance.

3. The Advisory Committee on Education

The Advisory Committee on Education was appointed by the President in 1936. It was charged with the responsibility of making a study of (1) the existent program of Federal aid for vocational education; (2) the relation of vocational training to general education and existing conditions; and (3) the extent, if any, to which an expanded program of vocational education was needed. The committee was requested to make its recommendations to the President and to the national Congress.

The general report of the committee was submitted early in 1938, and the special staff studies were published in 1938 and 1939. Some of these reports focus attention upon the youth problem and upon the system of vocational education which is operated in the individual states with the financial assistance and supervision of the Federal government. In addition to studying the vocational education program of the Federal government, the Advisory Committee considered the extent of equalization secured through state school funds, vocational rehabilitation of the physically disabled, special problems of Negro education, the National Youth Administration, educational activities of the Works Progress Administration, and educational service for Indians; all of these have implications for the curriculum of the secondary school.

The five areas of vocational education which the Federal government has subsidized in the secondary school are: (1) trades and industries; (2) home economics; (3) diversified occupations; (4) agriculture; and (5) distributive education. One of the most interesting findings of the Advisory Committee was that the arts and crafts program was the aspect of vocational education with which there was the greatest dissatisfaction.

The Advisory Committee did not try to evaluate the distributive education program, which was just starting in 1938. They found in general that the program in home economics was effective, in spite of a tendency toward the standardization of subject matter and methods and the failure to develop the program more closely in relation to a broad program of general education, with more emphasis on homemaking.

In regard to vocational agriculture, the committee discovered that a new, enriched curriculum was slowly emerging; this new program was pointed toward greater emphasis on agricultural economics, soil conservation, land management, subsistence farming, and problems of marketing, rather than on larger production, as in the past. Despite the extension of work in vocational agriculture to more schools, and despite an increase in the popularity of the courses, the program still failed to reach a large number of people who needed it. The committee recommended that a less expensive type of agricultural instruction be encouraged in the smaller rural secondary schools.

In trades and industries, the Advisory Committee stated that an all-day school program of highly specialized training in these branches has probably been of little real value to boys intending to enter trade and industrial occupations. The following weaknesses in this program seemed especially to be indicated: lack of cooperation with labor; failure to provide complete training to meet require-

FIG. 36   *A home project in agriculture—student being taught how to caponize chickens*

(*Courtesy Durham County (N.C.) Schools.*)

ments in the skilled trades; lack of careful study and survey of local conditions, and the consequent training of too many students for certain occupational fields that were already crowded; and an unfair competition resulting from a program of a type called "plant training," in which beginning workers have still been considered as "pupils" long after they have mastered the fundamentals of the trade. On the other hand, the work in part-time and evening classes in trades and industries as a whole was found excellent, especially when the instruction was limited to the kind that was supplemental to the daily employment of the person who was being trained. Most of the weaknesses of the Federally aided programs which the Committee identified are still in existence today.

4. *Other Surveys of Youth*

Stimulated in part by surveys of the American Youth Commission and other agencies, and in part by certain regional factors which had been developing in the nation, other agencies and people made excellent studies of youth. Two of these studies on a citywide or statewide basis have already been mentioned in connection with the National Youth Administration. *The Youth of New York City* sampled over 9,000 youths, including the proper percentage of Negro youth in proportion to the Negro population of the city of New York. The age range in this study was from sixteen to twenty-four. Certain aspects peculiar to metropolitan life are especially pertinent here, for employment conditions are sometimes even more difficult in a large center than in a smaller community. *Paths to Maturity* presented the findings of the North Carolina Youth Survey, which was made from 1938 to 1940 by various organizations in North Carolina with the assistance of the National Youth Administration. Some 45,000 youths from representative rural and urban areas were sampled during the period. Though many of the findings of this statewide study were remarkably similar to those of Bell's study in Maryland, the study differed in that youth were sampled from the ages of six to twenty-five years, instead of between the ages of sixteen to twenty-four only, as in the Maryland study.

Other aspects of the problems of youth were studied by other organizations and educational groups from 1936 to World War II.

The Progressive Education Association with the WPA helped to sponsor *Youth Serves the Community* by Paul Hanna with a re-search staff.[10] The Regents Inquiry investigated and reported on significant aspects of vocational education in the secondary schools of New York State in two publications in particular, *Education for Work* and *When Youth Leaves School*.[11]

The American Association of School Administrators devoted its Sixteenth Yearbook to *Youth Education Today* and to the problems which centered around youth.[12] The National Association of Secondary School Principals completed and published in 1940 a study of 914 youth who had been out of school from one and one-half to five and one-half years. This same group of administrators followed the 1940 report with two additional issues in 1941 which were devoted to a study of youth and occupations: these were *Youth at Work* and *The School Follows Through: A Post-School Adjustment of Youth*.[13] The 1940 White House Conference on Children in a Democracy devoted special sections of its report to inequalities of educational opportunities existing among certain groups; to certain aspects of compulsory school laws and their adjustment to child labor laws; to the obligation of each community to provide an educational program for all youths over sixteen years of age who are not employed or provided with work opportunities; and to programs of general secondary education based on changes in industrial life and opportunities.

Many individuals also made studies of youth and the problems of youth during the critical period of the 1930's and 1940's. Betty and Ernest Lindley gave the story of the National Youth Administration in *A New Deal for Youth*.[14] There were two significant Harvard University studies of youth. W.F. Dearborn and J.W.M. Rothney surveyed the *Scholastic, Economic, and Social Backgrounds of Unemployed Youth* in 1938. Thacher Winslow and F.P. Davidson, in *American Youth: An Enforced Reconnaisance*, considered

---

[10] New York, D. Appleton-Century Company, 1936.

[11] New York, McGraw-Hill Book Company, 1938.

[12] National Education Association, 1938.

[13] *The Bulletin of the National Association of Secondary School Principals*, *No. 93* (November, 1940), *No. 99* (May, 1941), and *No. 101* (November, 1941).

[14] New York, the Viking Press, 1938.

primarily the objectives that must be determined and accepted before youth problems can be solved satisfactorily; this study was pointed more toward the direction we should take, and toward constructive education for the future for youth. S.F. Harby made *A Study of Education in the Civilian Conservation Corps Camps of the Second Corps Area, April, 1933—March, 1937.*[15] Bruce Melvin offered a challenge in *Youth—Millions Too Many?*[16] Melvin developed the concept that youth is the determining factor in the civilization of the future, and that cooperation with youth is necessary if the nation is to succeed with the preservation of its type of government and institutions. Nels Anderson presented an interesting picture in *Men On The Move,*[17] the story of workers all over the country on the move on the road that led nowhere.

Though World War II and the Korean War interrupted research on youth problems and needs, studies have continued. The Mid-century White House Conference on Youth reiterated in its report many of the findings of the 1940 conference. The National Society for the Study of Education devoted Part I of its Yearbook to *Adapting the Secondary-School Program to the Needs of Youth.*[18] How thousands of adolescents looked at themselves and their own world during the last ten years is powerfully presented in Ruth Strang's *The Adolescent Views Himself.*[19] One of the best examples of the continuing longitudinal studies of youth is *Youth: The Years from Ten to Sixteen, by Arnold Gesell* and his associates.[20] Neither have the research people neglected to study the opportunities for youth. For example, *Manpower and Education*[21] presents the results of a careful study of manpower demands and manpower needs for modern America.

These examples of studies of youth of various kinds show the significance of the youth problem and the awareness which people have come to have of this problem during the last three decades. Studies of youth and their problems became so significant and so

---

[15] Ann Arbor (Mich.), Edwards Brothers, 1938.
[16] New York, Association Press, 1940.
[17] The University of Chicago Press, 1940.
[18] Chicago, 1953.
[19] New York, McGraw-Hill Book Company, 1957.
[20] New York, Harper and Brothers, 1956.
[21] Washington, Educational Policies Commission, 1956.

popular that in some institutions whole courses were formulated and taught with such titles as "Youth Problems" or the "Youth Movement." One of the textbooks at midcentury for a course in the principles of secondary education had the title *Secondary Schools for American Youth.*[22] This continuing study of the problems of youth, with especial emphasis upon the articulation of the secondary school and its educational program with life and industry and vocation, is perhaps one of the most significant developments of recent years. It bears witness to the fact that those who are engaged in education and the employment of youth are giving detailed study to the problems which are involved.

WORK OPPORTUNITIES AND OPENINGS FOR YOUTH

It is a well-known fact that adolescent youths are not always sure about the occupation which they want to enter. At the age of sixteen, approximately one-third of them may know quite definitely what they want for their life work, and they may be making their plans to carry out their ambitions. The other two-thirds are usually of two types: one group is composed of youths who have not thought seriously about what they want to do, even though they do not plan to attend college after they finish secondary school; the other group is made up of those who are undecided about what they want to do. This is a normal situation for the growing child, and it is not one about which anybody should become unduly alarmed. On the other hand, it is a situation in which teachers and administrators in the secondary school should be well prepared to offer counsel to these youths concerning the all-important problem of choosing a life work. It will, therefore, be the purpose of this section to indicate briefly certain lines of work which offer rather wide opportunities for youth today, as compared with the stereotyped and familiar kinds of semiskilled and skilled labor; suggestions will be made also on how the secondary-school counselor may use this and allied information in assisting youth to make satisfactory vocational decisions.

THE OCCUPATIONAL AND MANPOWER PICTURE. In the first place,

[22] I.A. Williams, New York, the American Book Company, 1948.

industry will likely have need of increasing numbers of workers.[23] Secondly, changes in methods of production, processing, and distribution of goods will increasingly make use of automation and people who can devise and use it effectively. Automation may be defined as the use of mechanical or electronic devices to control and direct the machinery in a process of production; at times, the action of one machine may call into operation the action of another. Peter Drucker made this observation recently, with which most technical and manpower authorities seem to agree: [24]

Mass production upgraded the unskilled laborer of yesterday into the semiskilled machine operator of today—and in the process multiplied both his productivity and his income. In just the same way, automation will upgrade the semiskilled machine operator of today into a highly skilled and knowledgeable technician—multiplying his income again. . . .

In the third place, the day of the skilled worker has arrived. The semiskilled workers outnumber the unskilled by three to one, and skilled workers outnumber them two to one. Fourth, the number of women workers (and married women workers) has increased sharply and is continuing to increase. Fifth, "white-collar" occupations have been growing faster than manual occupations, though the number of manual and service workers has doubled along with the population; farm workers, with a decrease from eleven to seven million, is the only major occupation to show a big drop in the last half century.

Critical manpower shortages will probably develop in the next decade in the areas of scientific research, technology and engineering, health work and services, supervisory and executive positions, education, and some semiprofessional fields, like those of dental hygienists, engineering aides, irrigation specialists, draftsmen, and other kinds of technicians.

As one looks at the manpower and occupational picture today, he is struck forcibly with the fact that most of today's occupations

[23] The data for this section were taken primarily from *U.S. Census of Population,* 1950, Vol. II, Part I, *Current Population Reports,* U.S. Bureau of the Census; *Manpower and Education, op. cit.;* and *Occupational Outlook Handbook,* 1957, Bureau of Labor Statistics, U.S. Department of Labor.

[24] "The Promise of Automation," *Harper's Magazine,* April, 1955, p. 44, reproduced with permission from *Manpower and Education,* p. 23.

demand more education and expert guidance of the student into a satisfactory life work.

TYPES OF LIFE WORK.   In the matter of a life work, the statement is usually made that there are two major fields or large areas open to youth: (1) the vocations and (2) the professions. The *professions*

FIG. 37   *Library facilities serve pupil needs*

Pupils use library resources as one means of exploring problems. (*Courtesy Denver Public Schools.*)

are usually thought of as teaching, medicine, dentistry, law, the ministry, engineering, and other highly specialized fields of work which require a large amount of technical training in the college or university. In contrast with the professions, the *vocations* have been considered as unskilled, semiskilled, skilled, and semiprofessional occupations in which a person could make a living in a more or less satisfactory manner. Attention is focused here not so much on the professions as on the areas or types usually called "vocational"; and the secondary school is conceived of as an institution which should help prepare the majority of youth for a life work upon their leaving or graduating from it, rather than as an institution established primarily for the preparation of students for higher education in specialized and technical schools.

SEASONAL OCCUPATIONS. Work in the occupations may be generally divided into two kinds, namely, "seasonal" and "permanent," either one of which may require unskilled, or semiskilled, or skilled labor. The seasonal occupations furnish work to certain people for only certain parts or months of the year, while the permanent occupations give opportunities for work of a steady nature in normal times. In the area of the seasonal occupations, for example, the following have been judged to be seasonal by the wage-hour administration: the buying, handling, stemming, and redrying of leaf tobacco; tobacco warehousing; natural ice harvesting; the pulpwood sap peeling branch of the lumber industry; ice and snow hauling of lumber in northeastern and Lake states; raw fur receiving; the buying, stripping, sizing, and packing of cigar leaf tobacco; open-cut mining of placer gold in Alaska and western states; open-cut mining of sand and gravel in northern states; spring freshet driving of lumber; the manufacture of brick in Maine, New Hampshire, and Vermont; the processing of hybrid seed corn; cane sugar processing in Louisiana; the harvesting, preparing, and processing of evergreens for the Christmas season; the curing and packing of Virginia Smithfield-cured meats; the cleaning and processing of red-top seed; the cleaning, bagging, and handling in cleaning plants of sugar beet seeds; the cleaning and preparing of garden seed and seed corn. Other seasonal occupations would include strawberry, cherry, and peanut harvesting; grain harvesting in the grain belt; cotton picking; the harvesting of peaches and apples and sugar beets; and the preserving and canning of certain kinds of fruits and vegetables.

Many of these occupations pay well, rewarding the skilled worker with top wages at the height of the season; yet they are also the types of work into which it is hardly wise to guide a secondary-school student, unless he is made to realize that such work must be supplemented by another occupation for the remainder of his time after the seasonal rush is over and there is no longer a demand for his services. There is a good possibility that some seasonal workers might be trained to follow three or four different kinds of seasonal occupations, which offer work opportunities at different times of the year. Through this kind of training, these workers may become more independent and self-sufficient members of society, instead of a burden on society for part of the year when they are unable to secure employment.

New Openings for Youth. Through new inventions, labor-saving machinery, and the consequent introduction of new industries and articles of commerce, many new lines of permanent work have been developed in recent years. Although it is true that the machine tends to throw more people out of work as its labor-saving force is brought into play, it is also true that the machine tends to create new jobs and work opportunities for mankind. Typical illustrations of some of these new jobs are given here.

Civil Aeronautics. The Federal Aviation Agency, formerly the Civil Aeronautics Administration, has furnished many jobs to trained men in caring for its ever-expanding program of emergency and permanent landing fields. Such men must be able to read the signs of the weather and interpret them correctly, learn to send and to receive messages by code, radio and radar, man the landing fields at all hours of the day and night, and attend to the thousand and one details connected with the safe flying of airships of all descriptions. So great was the need in 1940 that the Civil Aeronautics Authority was willing to take men without any training or with very little training, train them on the job while paying them a living wage, and allow them to stand for their examinations while learning on the job. The need for this type of trained person in the future will probably increase rather than diminish, if the expanding use of the airplane for all manner of purposes is any indication. Here is a promising field into which young men can go, if they get the proper training in the secondary school.

Public and Social Service. Four other newer areas in which there is a real opportunity for youth are public service, social-service work, health services, and the atomic-age professional military services. The organization of new activities and bureaus in both Federal and state governments has grown enormously since 1934. The rapid expansion of the social service of government has resulted in a shortage of trained workers, who can go into civil service positions and into positions requiring a special type of training for social and health work. Public welfare, public health, public recreation, state and Federal social security organizations, state and Federal employment services, and the growth of the Federal agencies concerned with the Agricultural Adjustment Administration, the Rural Electrification Authority, and the conservation program are calling for a large number of trained workers, of whom there has been no adequate supply. Of course, politics is involved to a certain extent in securing a position in these types of work, but a well-prepared person who stands a good examination and who has a good record will find himself able to enter these fields sooner or later.

PLASTICS. Rayon, a popular modern fabric, is a plastic material which is made from cotton, or from the fiber of wood which furnishes a pure cellulose. Rayon is a result of a process called "chemurgy." So are nylon, orlon, and dacron. In the field of plastics, hundreds of new products are made largely from cotton. Research chemistry has come to be a very important part of big business today, as its task is to develop and find new markets for chemical raw materials which are thrown away at present, or which are used only in the making of a few products. Research laboratories are being built in great industries to investigate and discover other uses for farm crops and farm wastes. Men must be specially trained in chemistry in this field of "chemurgy," for it is a chemical industry. The plastics industries demand a new type of trained operative, and they offer new opportunities for youth. The boundaries of chemurgy are limitless; by means of its development we eat the soy bean today in many forms, we get starch from the sweet potato, and we use cellophane made from cotton. The types of "ersatz" or synthetic products which have been developed through chemurgy are new, and few courses have been developed yet in which young men and women can secure the specialized training which is needed for the work. In this field the first essential is a well-rounded education, which includes a thorough general knowledge of chemistry, physics, and applied mechanics or mechanical engineering.

PLUMBING. Rather broad opportunities for young people are offered by the plumbing trade. Almost any householder will tell you there are few good plumbers, but plenty of indifferent "plumbers' helpers." Because of the addition of new legal requirements in regard to public health and sanitation, and because of the rapid advances in automatic heating, refrigeration, home appliances, and air conditioning, the task of the plumber is taking on added importance. Plumbing is a work at which a person cannot become skilled overnight. Most plumbing concerns combine work in heating with plumbing, and thus the apprentice must learn both trades. This vocation is notorious for the number of plumbers who forget their tools and have to go back to the shop for them, for workmen who stop a leak or repair a furnace and have to be called back the next day to do the same job over, and for mechanics who run pipes indiscriminately around obstacles of all types, regardless of the principles which should be employed in the standard installation of heating and plumbing systems. Plumbing pays well, and the field is wide open for boys who have a serious desire to make good pay with reasonable hours for work.

RADIO AND TV REPAIR WORK. Radio and television, with many attachments and widespread use, have brought new employment opportunities for youth. Good repairmen are as hard to find as good plumbers. There is a demand for workers who are willing to learn how a radio or a television set is made, how it should be serviced, how it should be installed, and how it should be treated. The training which is required consists of a fairly long apprenticeship, but the pay is well worth the preparation. There is no telling what television and radar will bring in the way of added work opportunities for youth, but it is safe to say that they will be extensive. For example, transistor radio sets are already in common use.

AVIATION. In aviation there is a demand for two types of workers, namely, (1) the airplane mechanic who is well trained and efficient, and (2) the worker in aviation production who is willing to be careful and painstaking in his task, and to learn how to master new automatic and electronic devices and machinery run by them. Both of these positions require some technical training, and both pay well.

ARTS AND CRAFTS. There is ample opportunity for youth in the field of creative art, as well as in the creating of a new industry. The arts and crafts industry in the United States is a comparative newcomer, especially as it relates to the making of toys and objects of superb craftsmanship and creative design representative of various periods in history, or typical of various regional conditions and products. America is far behind most nations in this type of industry; the stores are full of toys and objects of art and craftsmanship made in all nations under the sun with the exception of the United States. As capital has become interested in this industry, more and more chances for employment have opened up for youth who are willing to prepare themselves, who are creative in design, and who are faithful and patient in executing and reproducing that design. Illustrative of what man can do along this line is the story of Max Fleischer; he upset an inkwell on a rug thirty odd years ago and continued to "pour" from the inkwell a host of movie stars which included, among others, Popeye and Gulliver. Out of this same inkwell, he manufactured jobs for 200 specialists, for 80 animators, for other specialists who supply the voices and music for his characters, and for colorists, mechanics, cameramen, and minor workers. Walt Disney has built an industry of the same kind.

GROWING PULP PINE FOR NEWSPAPERS AND INDUSTRY. The discovery that newsprint paper could be manufactured from the pulp of the "field" pine has opened up a new kind of work for many rural youth in the South. The careful growth and cutting of these pines for this industry and the conservation of this supply of wood pulp is work which many youths can practice on their farms; many can even go into this as their vocation. The Agricultural Adjustment Act has reduced the production of the money crops, namely, cotton and tobacco, and has forced the rebuilding of the land through such steps as reforestation and the prevention of soil erosion. This limitation of the normal production of crops has worked also to limit the opportunities which youths have to start a career as a farmer. The farm youth now has a new opportunity in the

Weaving   Mosaic Work

Pottery

FIG. 38   *Arts and crafts works at Montevallo*
(*Photographs courtesy Montevallo (Ala.) High School.*)

South to develop a money-making business from the farm and from one of its natural products, namely, the forest.

OTHER WORK OPPORTUNITIES. The development of electric refrigeration and air conditioning has really just started. From year to year, these industries are requiring more and more skilled workers in their service work alone.

The greatest problem in securing the materiel for World War II proved to be the lack of skilled "die-tool" workers, men who are trained carefully over a period of years to make the dies or tools from which are manufactured the cannon, the shells, and the innumerable other parts of war machinery. The die-tool industry requires a long apprenticeship, but the work pays well after a person is fully trained.

Cosmetology is a new business and a rapidly growing one, employing thousands of young women each year. Schools of "beauty culture" sprang up overnight in all the states of the Union. The courses of training to prepare girls as beauty specialists range in length from some months to a year and a half or more.

Ask any old and established jewelry firm what the opportunities are in the field of engraving and handwork in silver, and it will tell you that most of the older craftsmen are dying out and that there are not enough young ones applying to learn the trade, which pays a trained person from $350 to $600 a month. Here, then, is another avenue open for the creative urge which youth has and wishes to express, and for those students who are adept with their hands and desirous of a good occupation.

A remarkable mechanical development of the last decade has been the high fidelity ("hi-fi") recording business, with its long-playing records and albums, its delicate machines with automatic controls, and the incorporation of the modern radio in its structure. This industry alone has created new jobs for thousands, and has opened up new vocational opportunities for high-school graduates.

Another field of personal service in which there is always a demand for trained people is that of housekeeper or maid. Maids who have had adequate training and who can do a good job can make an excellent living.

THE SECONDARY-SCHOOL CURRICULUM AND THE
GUIDANCE OF YOUTH

Looking back upon the various aspects of the youth problem and upon the opportunities for youth in the world of work, certain facts strike us with sharp impact. In the first place, about three million youths are unemployed yearly even in normal times. Also, each year now some three million youths come out of the high school and seek employment. These figures alone and the implications which they involve present the first problem which the program of the secondary school has to consider, namely, how can the secondary school help this many secondary-school youth find satisfactory work situations?

From the number and diversity of the studies of youth which have been carried on by national, regional, and local groups, the country has become conscious of the problems of youth and concerned about the training of youth for vocations, home and family living, and participation in individual activities of citizenship. The results of many of the studies of youth show that there is little articulation in many school systems, even in their vocational programs, between the training which the school gives for vocations and the industries and labor groups to which the student will graduate. New industries and new types of training are being developed, in many ways in various sections, and youth are not being sufficiently encouraged by the schools, by industry, or by labor to train for the new industries which require skilled workmen.

In view of all of these facts, what should be the task of the school in preparing youth for both life work and individual and group participation in community activities and home life? Should the school be responsible for intensified, specialized training in the vocations? Or should industry be responsible for such specialized training in trades and in the other vocations? Should the school attempt to give practical training in home and family living, and in the mechanics of group participation in a democracy? What should be the types of cooperation existing between the school and other formal and informal agencies which are concerned with the training and placement of youth in occupations? Should the public school institute and carry on a placement and follow-up service for youth? In the educational program of the school, what are the guidance functions of the teachers and of the curriculum?

TYPES OF GUIDANCE. If guidance is classified according to the people who make up society, there are two types: (1) group and (2) individual guidance. The difference between the two types is the difference between giving help to a larger or smaller group who can all profit from the same information and activities, and giving individual help to one person who needs aid and whose case does not resemble, or is not similar to, any other individual's. For example, it is customary in school to establish types of organizations which take care of both group and individual guidance. A course in "occupations" is one illustration of group guidance organized in the form of a regular course. The students take the work for a half year or a longer period of time; and, as a group, they learn through their own exploration about many aspects and many businesses in which they can find an occupation satisfactory to themselves if they are properly qualified. Another type of group guidance in pupil activities on the secondary-school level is found in the student council. This organization attempts to set up for students in their own school community a clearing-house and governing body for their own varied types of student activities. Through the work of the council and as individuals working with smaller and larger groups, pupils become more responsible citizens and learn more about group participation in democratic procedure. Still another illustration of group guidance is found in the organization of the dramatics club, or the journalism club, or the dance club. Students who have similar interests in any of these areas group themselves together; under faculty supervision and sponsorship, they learn more in groups about the particular field of their interest.

In contrast to group guidance which can be given to many who have the same interest at one time, individual guidance is a personal matter. It is a well-established fact that all individuals differ from other individuals, both as to rate of maturation, readiness for learning and speed in learning, and the like. Since this is a fact, any aspects of training and learning in which the individual engages require individual help and guidance from the teacher. A survey of the literature in the field of guidance seems to indicate that the following four aspects of guidance are of enough importance to be studied by the teacher so that he can help pupils satisfactorily: (1) personal-social guidance; (2) educational guidance; (3) vocational guidance; and (4) mental hygiene and emotional guidance.

The next question which one asks is, "What is the school doing to meet the need of its students for guidance? Are the program and the curriculum of the school organized so that they meet adequately the needs of its pupils in regard to guidance?" In answer to this question, these statements can be made in regard to the ways by which the school at present is attempting to meet these guidance needs:

1. There are courses in Guidance in the schools; as has just been stated, these may come under the head of courses in "occupations" or in courses in "vocations." These courses are primarily established for exploratory work in the area of *vocational* guidance.

2. There are also courses in "home and family living" or in "home-making," or in "home economics." These courses in home and family living and homemaking are outgrowths on the junior high-school level, and sometimes in the last year of high school, of the old home economics course. They are pointed more toward the problems of home and family living and consumer education than toward the older aspects of home economics called "cooking" and "sewing."

3. Courses in health education and in hygiene and physical education are being given on the high-school level; this work is pointed toward making the youngster more cognizant of good health and hygiene in making a success of life.

4. There are many types of vocational courses and vocational curricula in the high schools today. Most prominent among a list of these are home economics, agriculture, business education or commercial work, manual training, trades and industries, and diversified occupations and distributive education. These courses are primarily concentrated on a series of related experiences which consciously train boys and girls when they finish high school to go out and be successful in these areas. The teachers and instructors in these areas on the whole do a good job of advising and guiding youth in regard to their particular vocational fields.

5. A newcomer to the courses in the high school has been organized work in safety and driver education. Stimulated by the tremendous mortal-

ity in highway fatalities, the study of safety education has developed rapidly; in some states, it is required by law that it be taught.

6. Recently courses in "boy and girl problems" or in social problems, in consumer education and in sex education, have been added in some high schools. These courses aim primarily at training boys and girls to meet problems at home and in family living, and to learn how to become intelligent consumers. The publication of texts for this new field has added materially to the prospect that work in it will increase.

7. Group guidance in student activities has been another step that the schools have taken in order to give adequate guidance to their student personnel. In addition to the illustrations which were given at the first of this section in regard to the student council, student clubs, and special courses, these group activities vary widely from school to school and from community to community. Such activities include: Social groups and clubs; athletic clubs; hobbies or speciality clubs; subject-matter or subject-area clubs, such as the Latin club, the science club, the 4-H club, and the dramatics club; construction clubs, such as the airplane club, the boat club, or the photography club; and community service groups, such as the junior garden club, the Junior Red Cross, and the Boy or Girl Scouts.

The schools have made much progress within the last twenty years in putting to intelligent use the diagnostic instruments which are now available for helping with both group and individual guidance. By "diagnostic instruments" are meant those tests, scales, and inventories which give the teacher or the guidance expert more definite information upon the abilities, interests, aptitudes, and attitudes of the pupils with whom he is dealing. As a matter of fact, intelligent work in attempting to help students to choose a vocation is seldom done most successfully if these diagnostic instruments are not used intelligently. For example, a boy who has facility and dexterity with his fingers, yet is slow in working out problems with his mind, should be handled carefully in regard to suggestions of his choice or choices of life work.

A recent development in high school has been the introduction of trained counselors in the schools of medium and small size. This new development was made possible by the George-Barden Act (1946), under which the Federal government gave aid to the various states for the adequate training of counselors for guidance work in high schools. Standards for the training of these counselors are being established rapidly in the various states. It was the intent of the original bill, which may perhaps be fulfilled at a later date, that such Federal assistance in guidance of youth should be established on the same bases by which the Federal government gives aid to home economics, agriculture, trades and industries, and distributive education. It will be interesting to see whether this development works out. At any rate, the fact that more trained counselors are being educated for this work augurs well for a more careful study and evaluation of the principles of guidance in school for work and life.

Although these measures which have just been enumerated are those which are being taken by the schools in their curricular programs for the guidance of youth, this section would not be complete without more specific consideration of the studies which have been made during the last twenty years concerning the guidance, placement, and follow-up of youth. Such a consideration follows in the next section.

PRINCIPLES FOR THE GUIDANCE, PLACEMENT, AND FOLLOW-UP OF YOUTH. An earlier research study gave some suggestions on how the secondary school can solve these problems; they were presented comprehensively in *Matching Youth and Jobs*.[25] The approaches recommended in this study were based on research carried out in four metropolitan areas and four suburban and rural areas of the nation—eight representative areas in all. Many of these recommendations were confirmed by studies of the National Association of Secondary School Principals and by the findings of the Regents' Inquiry in New York State.

Many of the principles which are summarized below are based on the research studies of the American Youth Commission and *Education for All American Youth—A Further Look*.[26] If followed, these principles will furnish any secondary school with a workable plan for coordinating its curriculum with the vocational guidance which is necessary for youth. The principles are:

1. Proper pupil guidance by well-trained counselors in the secondary school is a crying need which should be filled. Such guidance should attempt to direct secondary-school students into the field of their interests

[25] Howard M. Bell, American Council on Education, 1940.
[26] Educational Policies Commission, 1952, Chaps. IV–X, *passim*.

and aptitudes through the use of all techniques of guidance which are available, such as aptitude and interests tests and tests of skills, "case" histories with personal and family backgrounds, and frequent conferences. The attempt should be made to open up possibilities in various occupational areas to the students, and care should be taken to counsel youth against entering occupations which are crowded. The technique to be used here should be in the direction of opening up and suggesting new fields which might interest the student and for which he might be fitted, and in which he might render a broader service, rather than in the way of telling him that he is not fitted for such work.

2. There are reasonable limitations upon the school's responsibility for training for occupations. In general, vocational education should be included in the program of all secondary schools if such is possible; but these vocational courses should lay emphasis on broad vocational training and on attaining the concepts involved in various types of vocational training, rather than on the development of specialized skills and specialized training for trades and industries. The guidance program in the secondary school should be linked closely with the placement of its students in further training or in agencies for further training. The guidance program should have as part of its responsibility a follow-up plan, whereby it can be of service to youth after they leave school if they are not employed, or if they need additional assistance; in these respects, close cooperation should be maintained with local, state, and Federal employment agencies, with industry, and with labor.

3. Training by industry is a responsibility of industry, and likewise it is the method which industry prefers for the training of skilled workers in specialized fields. By keeping in close touch with industry, secondary-school guidance officials will be able to do a much more satisfactory job.

4. For a successful guidance program of this type, there must be adequate knowledge of the community, of the effect of population changes, of the local labor market, and of changing occupational patterns. The community's occupational pattern should be discovered, and cooperative planning should take place between the school, labor, and industry.

5. The individual community should be considered as the basis for action in regard to vocational work in a particular secondary school, and the joint project of furnishing advice and help to the student in regard to an occupation should be developed with community committees and assistance. It is important that the home, the school, and the employment office should all be included in this cooperative venture, as well as other community agencies, labor, and industry.

NEED FOR COORDINATION OF YOUTH-SERVING AGENCIES. Another important aspect which should be considered in connection with the placement of youth in work situations is the lack of coordination which at present exists in many states between child labor law requirements and compulsory age requirements for school attendance. If the upper limit of the compulsory school attendance law is set at sixteen and the child labor law is also set at sixteen, there is no conflict; on the other hand, if the age at which a boy may enter a hazardous occupation is eighteen and compulsory school attendance ceases at sixteen, there is a conflict. It is necessary that labor be brought into the picture in a cooperative effort to establish reasonable apprenticeship standards and pay for in-school youth, or for youth just out of school who are beginning their occupational careers.

In Diversified Occupations and Distributive Education courses in secondary schools, it has been found that labor and capital are glad to work hand-in-hand to establish types of apprenticeship training for students in these part-time educational programs.[27] The number of students in these courses is limited at the present time by a lack of qualified teachers and by the careful restrictions which have been established by the Federal government and the state divisions of vocational education; only those secondary-school students who are serious about their life occupations are accepted in the program.

There is no reason to doubt that labor will be glad to cooperate with the school and with capital to prepare the young student or the young apprentice for a job; labor will not refuse some pay to the apprentice, but that pay must be on a scale commensurate with the service which the apprentice is rendering and the training he is receiving. No youth can expect to start at the top of the ladder; the beginner cannot expect to receive top pay which is given to the skilled worker of ten, fifteen, or twenty years of experience. Neither is it wise for a person to make the top pay in his chosen vocation after a period of six months, a year, or even two, three, or five years; in that way, he hits the "ceiling" too fast, and runs into an almost intolerable situation in which he sees no hope of further advancement in pay as he becomes older. If a worker reaches the top too fast, he faces practically a "dead-end" job, even though he may be doing what he desires to do.

[27] *Cf.* C.E. Rakestraw, *Training High-School Youth for Employment,* Chicago, American Technical Society, 1947, ii–iv, vi–vii. *Cf.* also W.H. Ivins and W.B. Runge, *Work Experience in High School,* New York, The Ronald Press Company, 1951, *passim.*

Certain recommendations of the President's Advisory Committee on Education still stimulate deep thought among the employed personnel of the secondary school. If those recommendations were accepted and put into operation, the following results would be obtained:

1. A deferring of intensive vocational education until the girl or boy has entered employment.
2. The elimination of the employment of vocational education to provide a reservoir of labor, to undercut wages, and to lower labor standards.
3. The establishment of approved apprenticeship training programs in state departments of labor, with certain related instruction to be given by the secondary school.
4. The refusal of Federal funds to states which do not have labor represented on the boards which supervise vocational education in the schools.[28]

It is evident that the secondary schools have far to go in adjusting their programs to meet the guidance and occupational problems of youth. As regards vocational education, curriculum workers should be thinking in terms of a closer connection among such agencies as the school, the community, labor, capital and industry, agencies of the Federal government, state and local employment agencies, and private employment, and training agencies. The secondary school should also be thinking more directly in terms of apprenticeship training of one type or another for many school youth and out-of-school youth; these youth desire to work, but are unable to get it because they are not prepared to perform it, or because their type of job has changed or been eliminated by automation, and they need retraining for work. If one knows how to perform his work well, there is still a fine art in getting ahead on the job by doing a little more than you are paid to do, and by doing the work a little better than the other workers.

After he has studied the youth problem carefully, the educational employee is again forced to consider the possible reorganization of secondary education somewhat along the line of a 6–4–4 plan. In such a plan, the secondary school would continue "general" education, exploratory work, and counseling for the student for four years beyond the elementary school. At that point the pupil would be (1)

[28] Summarized from p. 288, Staff Study No. 8, "Vocational Education."

turned over to some special school or agency to train him for an occupation, such as the community or technical institute, or schools for apprenticeship training run cooperatively by industry and labor, or (2) directed to the proper four-year-senior-high-school-junior-college organization which would give him special training looking toward a professional or highly specialized career.

Few books have been devoted entirely to guidance and the curriculum. The points of view or approach of the more recent writers are included in the Bibliography at the end of this Chapter.

PROBLEMS FOR INDIVIDUAL STUDY
AND CLASS DISCUSSION

1. Should a secondary-school youth engaged in the "Diversified Occupations" program (part-time school and part-time work for pay) be required to join the labor union before he can participate in work? Why or why not?

2. What steps would you take to make a survey of work opportunities for youth in your community?

3. Should every secondary school attempt to give vocational training to adolescents? Support your point of view.

4. Should the secondary school have any responsibility for placing boys and girls in jobs when they leave school? Defend your position.

5. What effect does the environment of the adolescent's home and community have upon his choice of an occupation or profession?

6. Make a list of the types of educational activities of the NYA and the CCC. Which were duplicating educational activities of the public high schools, and which were not?

7. What types of courses would you recommend to the secondary-school boy who plans to become an aviation mechanic? An aviation engineer? To the girl who plans to become a cosmetologist?

8. Assume that your secondary school numbers 250 students in a strictly rural community, and that the vocational work which you offer consists of Home Economics and Agriculture. How could you discover whether these vocational programs were meeting the needs of your students?

9. As John Black's counselor in your school, assume that you discover that he has decided to become a carpenter. Your survey of work opportunities in your large industrial community has revealed that there is a large surplus of skilled carpenters, but a scarcity of brick masons, welders, plumbers, and auto mechanics. Into which of these "open" occupations would you attempt to guide John, and how would you proceed with him?

10. Make two lists of occupations, one containing those which have been eliminated and another containing those which have been opened up by new inventions, machinery, and industries in the last forty years. Did you find that youth has more work opportunities today, or fewer?

11. Take five of the monographs or pamphlets which are published by some agency for the guidance of youth, such as Science Research Associates (Chicago); analyze them; and list those aspects that would help you as a teacher in guiding youth.

12. What do you as a teacher know about the arts and crafts industry in the United States? About plastics? Where would you go to get information on the kinds of occupations in the United States?

13. Under what provisions does the Federal government give curricular aid to the secondary schools in various types of vocational education?

14. Is a modern form of youth apprenticeship possible in a democracy? Support your stand.

15. What are the functions of the United States Employment Service? Of your state employment service? What connection should there be between these agencies and the secondary school?

16. Why is the cooperation of both labor and industry of prime importance for the satisfactory solution of the vocational education problem on the secondary-school level? Explain.

17. Of what value are private employment and training agencies to the secondary school? Should the school maintain close relations with them?

SPECIAL BIBLIOGRAPHY ON GUIDANCE FOR THE CURRICULUM WORKER AND THE TEACHER

NOTE: Extensive reference materials on the development of guidance as an integral part of the curriculum have been given in the body of this Chapter. This bibliography will be restricted to viewpoints and sources other than these.

Accounts of the Historical Development of Guidance During the Last Twenty Years

The Advisory Committee on Education, Washington, United States Government Printing Office: Staff Studies:

No. 8, *Vocational Education* by J.D. Russell and associates, 1938.

No. 12, *Special Problems of Negro Education* by D.A. Wilkerson, 1939.

No. 13, *The National Youth Administration* by P.O. Johnson and O.L. Harvey, 1938.

No. 14, *Educational Activities of the Works Progress Administration* by D.S. Campbell, F.H. Bair, and O.L. Harvey, 1939.

No. 18. *Educational Service for Indians* by L.E. Blauch, 1939.

American Association of School Administrators, Washington, National Education Association, 16th Yearbook, 1938, *Youth Education Today,* Chaps. I–XI, and esp. Appendices B, D, and F.
American Council on Education, Studies of the American Youth Commission, Washington:
[BOOKS]
Secondary Education for Youth in Modern America by H.R. Douglass, 1937.
Youth Tell Their Story by H.M. Bell, 1938.
American Youth: An Annotated Bibliography by L.A. Menefee and M.M. Chambers, 1938.
Equal Educational Opportunity for Youth by Newton Edwards, 1939.
Youth in European Labor Camps by Kenneth Holland, 1939.
Guideposts for Rural Youth by E.L. Kirkpatrick, 1940.
Matching Youth and Jobs by H.M. Bell, 1940.
Youth-Serving Organizations (3rd ed.) by M.M. Chambers, 1948.
Youth, Family and Education by J.K. Folsom, 1941.
Youth Work Programs: Problems and Policies by L.L. Lorwin, 1941.
Time on Their Hands: A Report on Leisure, Recreation and Young People by C.G. Wrenn and D.L. Harley, 1941.
Youth and the Future: The General Report of the American Youth Commission, 1942.
Youth in the CCC by Kenneth Holland and F.E. Hill, 1942.
Barriers to Youth Employment by P.T. David, 1942.
Postwar Youth Employment by P.T. David, 1943.
Youth—Key to America's Future by M.M. Chambers and E. Exton, 1949.
[PAMPHLETS]
How to Make a Community Youth Survey by M.M. Chambers and H.M. Bell, 1939.
The Community and Its Young People by M.M. Chambers, 1940.
What the High Schools Ought to Teach, 1940.
Work Camps for High School Youth by Kenneth Holland and G.L. Bickel, 1941.
Work Camps for College Students by Kenneth Holland, 1941.
[STATEMENTS]
A Program of Action for American Youth, 1939.
Youth, Defense, and the National Welfare, 1940.
Community Responsibility for Youth, 1940.
The Occupational Adjustment of Youth, 1940.
The Civilian Conservation Corps, 1940.
Next Steps in National Policy for Youth, 1941.
[STUDIES OF NEGRO YOUTH]
In a Minor Key: Negro Youth in Story and Fact by I. De A. Reid, 1940.

514 CURRICULUM PRINCIPLES AND SOCIAL TRENDS

Children of Bondage: The Personality Development of Negro Youth in the Urban South by Allison Davis and John Dollard, 1940.
Negro Youth at the Crossways: Their Personality Development in the Middle States by E.F. Frazier, 1940.
Growing Up in the Black Belt: Negro Youth in the Rural South by C.S. Johnson, 1941.
Color and Human Nature: Negro Personality Development in a Northern City by W.L. Warner, B.H. Junker, and W.A. Adams, 1941.
Thus Be Their Destiny: The Personality Development of Negro Youth in Three Communities by J.H. Atwood, D.W. Wyatt, V.J. Davis, and I.D. Walker, 1941.

Brewer, J.M., *et al., History of Vocational Guidance,* New York, Harper and Brothers, 1942, *passim.*

The Bulletin of the National Association of Secondary-School Principals. Washington, National Education Association:
"Youth and Work Opportunities," Vol. xxiv, No. 90, April, 1940.
"Counseling and the Changing Secondary School Curriculum," Vol. xxiv, No. 90, May, 1940.
"Work Experience in the Secondary School," and "Secondary School or College for Our Youth," Vol. xxvii, No. 111, January, 1943.
"Work Experience in the Secondary Schools," Vol. xxviii, No. 123, May, 1944, pp. 29–40.
"The Assembly Program in the Secondary School," Vol. xxx, No. 141, November, 1946.
"The Imperative Needs of Youth of Secondary-School Age," Vol. xxxi, No. 145, March, 1947.
"Present-Day Issues in Secondary Schools," Vol. xxxii, No. 156, October, 1948.
"Using Tests in the Modern Secondary School," Vol. xxxii, No. 158, December, 1948.
"Vitalizing Student Activities in the Secondary School," Vol. xxxvi, No. 184, February, 1952.
"Counseling and Guidance in the Secondary School," Vol. xxxv, No. 175, January, 1951.
"Guidance in the Secondary School," Vol. xxxvii, No. 193, March, 1953.
"Guidance Practices in Secondary Schools," Vol. xxxviii, No. 200, February, 1954.

Hollingshead, A.B., *Elmstown's Youth: The Impact of Social Classes on Adolescents,* New York, John Wiley and Sons, 1949, Part iv.

Jones, A.M., *Leisure Time Education,* New York: Harper and Brothers, 1946, Chapters, ii–iv, vi.

Keller, F.J., *Principles of Vocational Education,* Boston, D.C. Heath and Company, 1948, *passim.*

Mays, A.B., *Principles and Practices of Vocational Education*, New York, McGraw-Hill Book Company, 1948.

Starr, M., *Labor Looks at Education* (the Inglis Lecture, 1946), Cambridge, Harvard University Press, 1947, *passim*.

Struck, F.T., *Vocational Education for a Changing World*, New York, John Wiley and Sons, 1945, *passim*.

Administration, Principles, and Point of View

Association for Supervision and Curriculum Development, N.E.A.: 1955 Yearbook, *Guidance in the Curriculum, passim*.

Detjen, E.W., and Detjen, M.F., *Elementary School Guidance*, New York, McGraw-Hill Book Company, 1952 (for upper elementary and junior high grades).

Hatch, R.N., and Stefflre, B., *Administration of Guidance Services: Organization; Supervision; Evaluation*, Englewood Cliffs, Prentice-Hall, 1958.

Kelley, J.A., *Guidance and Curriculum*, Englewood Cliffs, Prentice-Hall, 1955, *passim*.

McDaniel, H.B., *Guidance in the Modern School*, New York, The Dryden Press, 1956.

McKinney, F., *Counseling for Personal Adjustment in Schools and Colleges*, Boston, Houghton Mifflin Company, 1958.

Traxler, A.E., *Techniques of Guidance* (rev. ed.), New York, Harper and Brothers, 1957.

Bibliography and Instruments for Use in Guidance

Buros, O., *The Fourth Mental Measurements Yearbook*, Highland Park (N.J.), the Gryphon Press, 1953.

Illinois Secondary School Curriculum Program, Bulletin No. 6, *How to Conduct the Study of the Guidance Services of the School*, 1949, Springfield, Superintendent of Public Instruction.

Review of Educational Research. Issues from time to time report thoroughly on research, such as Vol. xxvi (October, 1956), "Vocational and Technical Education," pp. 345–410, and Vol. xxvii (April, 1957), "Guidance and Counseling," pp. 161–235.

Traxler, A.E., *Techniques of Guidance* (rev. ed.), New York, Harper and Brothers, 1957, Chapters iv–xii.

Community Cooperation and Surveys

Evaluative Criteria, 1950 Edition, Section B, "Pupil Population and School Community," and Section G, "Guidance Services."

Williams, H.F., Jr., *Your Career Opportunities in Evansville Industry*, the Evansville (Ind.) Manufacturers and Employers Association, 1953. An excellent illustration of a cooperative community survey of career opportunities for youth.

Occupational Guides

Job Guide for Young Workers, 1958–1959 Edition, U.S. Department of Labor, Bureau of Employment Security, U.S. Employment Service, 1958.

Occupational Outlook Handbook, 1957, issued every two years, U.S. Department of Labor, Bureau of Labor Statistics.

Opinions of Curriculum Writers on Guidance in the Curriculum

Alberty, H.B., *Reorganizing the High School Curriculum* (rev. ed.), New York, The Macmillan Company, 1953, Chapters x–xi.

Douglass, H.R. (Ed.), *The High School Curriculum* (2nd ed.), New York, The Ronald Press Company, 1956, Chapters vii–ix, xviii–xix, xxvii–xxviii, and xxx.

Faunce, R.C., and Bossing, N.L., *Developing the Core Curriculum* (2nd ed.), Englewood Cliffs, Prentice-Hall, 1958, Chapters viii–ix, xiv.

Meier, A.R., *et al.*, *A Curriculum for Citizenship*, Detroit, Wayne University Press, 1952, Part iii.

Noar, G., *The Junior High School—Today and Tomorrow*, New York, Prentice-Hall, 1953, Parts i and ii.

Romine, S.A., *Building the High School Curriculum*, New York, The Ronald Press Company, 1954, Chapters xiv–xv.

Student Activities in the Guidance Program

Fedder, R., *Guiding Homeroom and Club Activities*, New York, McGraw-Hill Book Company, 1949.

Gruber, F.C., and Beatty, T.B., *Secondary School Activities*, New York, McGraw-Hill Book Company, 1954.

Johnston, E.G., and Faunce, R.C., *Student Activities in Secondary Schools*, New York, The Ronald Press Company, 1952.

Kilzer, L.R., *et al.*, *Allied Activities in the Secondary School*, New York, Harper and Brothers, 1956.

McKown, H.C., *Extracurricular Activities* (3rd ed.), New York, The Macmillan Company, 1952.

Miller, F.A., *et al.*, *Planning Student Activities*, Englewood Cliffs, Prentice-Hall, 1956.

Smith, Joe, *Student Councils for Our Times: Principles and Practices*, Teachers College, Columbia University, 1951.

Thompson, N.Z., *Vitalized Assemblies*, New York, E.P. Dutton and Company, 1952.

Teacher as Guidance Person and Counselor

Arbuckle, D.S., *Guidance and Counseling in the Classroom*, Boston, Allyn and Bacon, 1957.

Berry, E., *Guiding Students in the English Class,* New York, Appleton-Century-Crofts, 1957.

Gordon, I.J., *The Teacher as a Guidance Worker,* New York, Harper and Brothers, 1956.

Textbooks and Materials in Guidance for High-School Students (Samples)

Beck, L.F., *Human Growth,* New York, Harcourt, Brace and Company, 1949 (a text on sex education for preteens through adolescence).

Gruenberg, S.M., *The Wonderful Story of How You Were Born,* New York, Garden City, Hanover House, 1952 (sex education for mothers and very young children).

Hurlock, E.B., *Child Growth and Development* (2nd ed.), New York, McGraw-Hill Book Company, 1956 (high-school text).

Landis, J.C., and Mary G., *Personal Adjustment, Marriage, and Family Living* (2nd ed.), New York, Prentice-Hall, 1955 (text for high-school course).

Mahoney, H.J., and Engle, T.L., *Points for Decision: A Guide to Help Youth Solve Their Problems,* Yonkers-on-Hudson, World Book Company, 1957 (text in personal guidance).

Phillips, E.L., and Gibson, J.F., *Psychology and Personality,* Englewood Cliffs, Prentice-Hall, 1957 (psychology and mental hygiene text for secondary school).

Prosser, C.A., and Sifford, C.S., *Selecting an Occupation,* Bloomington (Ill.), McKnight and McKnight, 1953 (a text for a course in "Occupations").

Science Research Associates, Chicago 10, Ill., publishes two series of pamphlets for adolescents: (1) "Life Adjustment Booklets" for high school students, some fifty-four on getting along in high school, relationships with others, understandings and solving personal problems and the world today; and (2) "Junior Life Adjustment Booklets" for youth of the intermediate grades, some thirty in number on similar problems.

CHAPTER 17 How teacher training affects curriculum change

Because they are closely interwoven, it is almost impossible to treat teacher growth and curriculum improvement separately. Not only is it necessary to train teacher candidates so that they may have the opportunity for continued growth; it is also important to assist teachers in service to improve their teaching, and thus to improve the curriculum. This chapter is dedicated to the belief that every teacher, new and old, must experience in order to grow, must experiment for himself, if only on a minor scale, in order to improve his teaching. Every teacher must go through the process of experimenting with some problem, or unit, or teaching procedure in order to better his teaching; this experimental work must be of a nature which he considers promising and superior to what he has been doing.

THE DEVELOPMENT OF STATE STANDARDS
FOR TEACHING

School authorities have established many regulations which handicap the teacher and make it difficult for him to go through this experiencing for the improvement of his teaching. Between 1890 and 1930 compulsory school legislation went into effect in state after state with such rapidity that it was almost impossible for the normal schools and colleges to train enough teachers to fill the new positions which were opened in the classrooms, much less to select and choose from among the candidates who stated that they wished to teach. During this time, the normal schools trained most of the teachers for the elementary schools, and the normal schools or teachers' colleges and colleges today still prepare the majority of teachers for both elementary and secondary schools. Until recently, it was the rule rather than the exception for teachers in the elementary schools to be certificated upon the basis of two or three years of normal-school work, although four years of normal-school or college work were usually required for teaching in the secondary school. Both the general population and school enrollments were increasing by leaps and bounds from 1890 to 1930; the schools were fortunate if a minimum training could be given to teachers, in order that one might be available for each schoolroom.

During the first quarter of the twentieth century, state boards of education and local school systems started the requirement of minimum essentials in both subject-matter courses and in courses in professional education for teachers. The requirements for anyone who wished to teach in the public schools were raised gradually in state after state. First, a longer peroid of preservice training was instituted step by step and year by year, until now a great number of states require that a candidate for teaching must have completed four years of college, have a college degree, and be properly prepared as to courses in both subject matter and in professional education. Secondly, the states established progressively more specific prescriptions in professional and content courses for those desiring to teach on any level of the public school. Thirdly, specialized professional courses in materials and methods of the subjects to be taught came to be one of the important requisites for those who desired to teach. In the fourth place, practically all states came to require a period of preservice teaching or apprenticeship under actual classroom conditions; this was called "practice" or "student" or "cadet" teaching.

GROWTH OF CONTENT AND PROFESSIONAL REQUIREMENTS. Much improvement has been made in both the quality and quantity of teacher training in this broad development of higher standards for those who plan to teach in the public schools. On the other hand, the prescription of an ever-increasing number of courses in the highly specialized field of professional education has tended in part toward the education of a narrowly specialized type of teacher. For example, the requirements in some states of special courses in professional education for prospective teachers run from six to nine courses out of a total of thirty-six; such a prescription results in a top-heavy training in education at the expense of training which teachers should be obtaining in the fundamental, broad areas of human knowledge and experience.

In addition to this type of *specialization in professional education*, another factor has operated in many of the colleges which train teachers to narrow the *specialization in subject matter* or content material still further; this is the practice in the traditional colleges whereby a teacher must take "double" courses as "foundation material" for more advanced content courses. For example, the teacher-candidate in science may have to take Botany 1-2, Zoology 1-2, Chemistry 1-2, and Physics 1-2, in order to get the elementary subject matter which is required for the beginning of his specialization in science. After mastering these eight double courses in science, the teacher candidate is about ready, in the opinion of these college departments, to take the advanced courses in science which he should have in order to teach successfully in the secondary schools. The specialists in science in college do not seem to realize that the science teacher in the secondary school is usually expected to be prepared to teach any kind of course in science; and that science courses in the secondary school more often are "general" or "survey" courses, such as General Science and Biology, than they are specialized courses like Chemistry or Physics. The colleges are coming around gradually to the idea of offering "general" courses in these special areas of science for those who are preparing to teach, but it is a slow process to persuade them to do so.

THE IMPROVEMENT OF TEACHER EDUCATION THROUGH COLLEGES AND STATE DEPARTMENTS OF EDUCATION

SPRAGUE'S STUDY. Since the state teachers' colleges (now renamed in many states as "state" colleges) still prepare the largest number of teachers for the public schools, we should look briefly at their progress in the preparation of teachers. H.A. Sprague [1] examined the

---

[1] *A Decade of Progress in the Preparation of Secondary School Teachers: A Study of Curriculum Requirements in Fifty-Five State Teachers Colleges in 1928 and 1938,* Teachers College, Columbia University, 1940, *passim.*

practices in the preparation of secondary-school teachers in fifty-five state teachers' colleges for the period from 1928 to 1938; these colleges represented thirty different states. Among the more significant of his findings were the following:

1. In broad orientation or survey courses and in functional courses the prescription for the prospective teacher had been increased, while in traditional academic courses the prescription had been decreased.
2. The number of electives allowed in the field of professional education decreased during the period, and the electives allowed in the background fields decreased also.
3. The requirements in professional education had been reduced, while requirements in background and specialization fields had increased.
4. Major and minor fields of specialization increased both in number and in type, owing to additional state requirements established.[2]
5. There was an increase in nearly every subject-matter field in the semester-hour requirements for a major.
6. In 1928, there was more prescription of skill courses and purely academic courses, whereas in 1938 the emphasis in requirements was more upon survey and functional courses.
7. The most common practice among these teachers' colleges in 1938 was to require a major and two minors; this resulted generally in an increase in required courses and a decrease in free electives.

Although Sprague's study covered the preparation of secondary-school teachers, certain trends which he found in operation in the secondary school would probably be true of the training of candidates for teaching in the elementary school. One of the most significant findings of Sprague's study concerned the increased prescription of broad survey or functional courses, and the corresponding decrease in the number of electives allowed to the candidate in the background fields. This seeming paradox is explained by the fact that the usual requirement for a teacher's certificate in the secondary school is preparation in one major teaching field and/or in one or more minor teaching fields; this requirement forces the candidate to prepare in two or more specialized fields of subject matter, where elementary courses in each field are considered necessary for him in order that he may obtain a solid foundation before he takes advanced

---

[2] In 1938, thirty-six states required a major field of specialization; twenty-two required a minor; six, a second minor; and ten, specific cultural subjects, according to Sprague, *op. cit.*, p. 121.

courses in those areas. High degrees of specialization in subject-matter areas such as English, mathematics, and science may be considered desirable for the better preparation and training of teachers for those subjects; but such prescriptions preclude the orientation and training of teachers in the broader cultural fields of art, music, philosophy, sociology, and consumer economics. More important still, this narrow, specialized training operates in the direction of making the student candidate more "subject-conscious" and less "student-conscious"; it tends to make him such a specialist in a field or a few fields that he is prone to overlook the interrelationships between subject matters and between subject matter and human experience.

THE ARMSTRONG-STINNETT STUDY. This study in 1955 gave a clear picture of certification requirements for teachers in the United States.[3] There are still great differences among the states in their course requirements for teachers, both in content courses in the subject-matter fields and in professional education. This diversity has led to differences of opinion among college faculties over the amount of professional education that should be required; the controversy has even spread to the general public in this time of critical shortage of teachers.[4] The requirements of professional courses in education do hinder the teacher-candidate from getting as broad a training as he needs for his work. As an extreme illustration, when the prospective elementary-school teacher has completed the state requirements in the professional areas of special methods in arithmetic, health and physical education, science and nature study, social studies, and reading and language, along with work in educational psychology and directed teaching, he is more likely to be narrow than broad, more prepared for static teaching of subject matter than

---

[3] *A Manual on Certification Requirements for School Personnel in the United States,* 1955 Edition, National Commission on Teacher Education, N.E.A., *passim.*
[4] For an impartial account of the problems involved in the training of teachers, read *Professional Problems of Teachers* by A.J. Huggett and T.M. Stinnett, New York, The Macmillan Company, 1956, Chaps. II, IV, XV, and XVI. For a good illustration of the *pros* and *cons* in the popular press, read *The Atlantic,* April, 1958, "What Strangles American Teaching: The Certification Racket" by Lydia Stout, pp. 59–63, and July, 1958, "The Certification Racket: Florida and Elsewhere" by Daniel Tanner and others, pp. 34–39.

for the wise guidance of children whose lives cut across all subject matter. Of course, no state has such rigid requirements as those which have just been mentioned, but certification standards generally include educational psychology or child growth and development; special methods in two elementary-school subjects; a course in elementary education or in general methods; educational measurements, or the history and philosophy of education; special work in practice teaching; and an elective in education. In the training of teachers for the secondary school, a teaching major in a subject-matter field may require from fifteen to thirty semester hours, whereas a minor may run from twelve to eighteen. Professional courses in education required of teacher-candidates for the secondary school usually include some educational psychology; the principles or problems or methods of secondary education; an introductory course in education or a course in the history of education; special materials and methods in one subject-matter field; and intensive work in observation and directed or "student" teaching.

TEACHER SUPPLY AND DEMAND. In the days when it was almost impossible to get enough people who were even partially prepared to teach the children in each schoolroom, training standards could not be high; there would not have been enough teachers. As more and more people began to prepare for teaching, standards for teachers gradually were raised. They became relatively higher because there was a larger supply of teachers than formerly. Most states by 1940 had reached the point where the supply of adequately trained teachers was beginning to exceed the demand. As a result, (1) standards were raised still further, and (2) procedures for the selection of teachers were established that had not even been considered seriously before that time.

The situation in regard to teacher supply and demand has been reversed in the last two decades. During and following World War II, over 350,000 teachers left the profession for war work or better paying positions. At the same time, most youth went into service or war work, and fewer new teachers were trained. In 1939–1940 the United States Office of Education reported 911,000 teachers, principals, and supervisors in the public schools. In 1947–1948 the total number was about 883,000; of these school employees, *over 100,000 were "emergency" teachers,* that is, teachers who were issued temporary licenses because they did not meet the certification requirements of the various states. In 1954–1955 the total number was about 1,110,000; of these, over 80,000 were teaching on substandard certificates. There have been shortages of teachers on both levels, but the

FIG. 39   *Modern teachers have to learn to use many new tools*

The teacher prepares the class for drill with a tachistoscope, an instrument which helps pupils improve reading skills by reducing the number of eye fixations per line. (*Courtesy Denver Public Schools.*)

critical shortage was in the elementary schools to 1958. Now there is a shortage on both levels, except in a few high-school subject areas. Conservative estimates place the demand at more than 125,000 new teachers annually for the next decade, to care for the sharp increase in school enrollment resulting from the increased birth rate from 1941 to 1958.[5]

[5] For detailed information on various complicating factors in this teacher shortage, the student can compare: *The Education of Teachers—As Viewed by the Profession* (official Group Reports of the Bowling Green Conference, National Commission on Teacher Education and Professional Standards), National

Faced with this critical situation, the various states and cities have taken more or less energetic action to train and secure more teachers. Such action included: (1) the raising of teachers' salaries; most school systems have taken this action; (2) establishment of scholarships for candidates who elect to prepare for teaching, or for "refresher" work for qualified teachers who wish to re-enter the profession; (3) recruitment plans, starting as far down as the high-school grades, through the Future Teachers of America clubs in high school and chapters of the National Student Education Association for colleges; and (4) reciprocity among the states in teacher certification.

One of the most serious aspects of the teacher shortage in regard to curriculum development is that the improvement of in-service teacher education is slowed up. A teacher with a temporary certificate and a temporary job lacks natural incentives to self-improvement. In the second place, a beginning teacher has to work with teachers who are not so well qualified as he is; and this situation is not conducive to improvement in service. Thirdly, mobility of teaching personnel today handicaps a sound, continuing, stimulating in-service program.

TENURE AND TEACHER GROWTH. Legal provisions for teacher tenure operate in many states as a major influence upon the selection of teachers for the public schools. Tenure laws tend to keep teachers in service and to give preference to the teacher in service who has achieved tenure upon good behavior and fairly efficient teaching. School administrators and school boards are, therefore, becoming much more careful in their selection of teachers. They are paying more attention to the general as well as the specific qualifications of applicants, to their capacity to assist in normal child growth and development, and to their ability to fit into the life of the community. Such an interest on the part of school administrators and school

Education Association, 1948, pp. 73–89; L.M. Thurston and W.H. Roe, *State School Administration*, New York, Harper and Brothers, 1957, Chap. xii; A.J. Huggett and T.M. Stinnett, *op. cit.*, Chaps. ii, xv–xvi; and *NEA Research Bulletin*, Vol. xxv, No. 1 (February, 1957), "The Status of the American Public School Teacher" and No. 3 (October, 1957), "The Post-War Struggle to Provide Competent Teachers," respectively, and Vol. xxxvi, No. 1 (February, 1958), "Statistics for 1957–1958," pp. 9–11.

boards in the qualifications of the teacher will demand and will gain improvements in the higher institutions in their programs of teacher education. The colleges will be forced to train their student candidates for more effective work, or pay the penalty of not being able to place their graduates in teaching positions.

The *preservice training* of teachers is not the only problem which has relation to curriculum improvement. The *in-service growth* of teachers is just as important, and in some ways more important, because the teacher in service is usually looked to by the younger teacher for leadership and suggestions for improvement. As the various states raise their certification standards for teachers to require the bachelor's degree for teaching, the old-fashioned summer school for the purpose of acquiring additional credits for the raising of a certificate, or for the purpose of extending the certificate in force by mere course credits, will become a thing of the past. Wide-awake directors of summer schools in the colleges are spending much time in planning areas of work and experience which will be conducive to wider growth and development in the teacher through his own curricular planning and experimentation. Many school boards are coming to look upon summer-school work for their teachers as a period of necessary planning in advance for the work of the next school year; in some instances, school trustees have used school funds to defray a part or all of the expenses of their teachers to attend certain summer schools or workshops for such constructive study and planning.

TRENDS TOWARD ADDITIONAL STATIC REQUIREMENTS FOR TEACHER CERTIFICATION

For several years, state and local school boards have been taking measures to encourage their teaching staffs to improve themselves while in service. These measures have resulted in the following two types of development which have as many possibilities for narrowing as they have for broadening the training of teachers: (1) national teacher examinations and (2) graduate degree requirements for teaching.

NATIONAL TEACHER EXAMINATIONS. In 1937 a group of school

superintendents asked the assistance of the American Council on Education in ascertaining the intellectual and cultural background of teacher candidates; they felt that they needed help, because the higher institutions which prepared their teachers operated on extremely variable standards. For example, some of the best graduates of some institutions were poorer than the poorest graduates of some other institutions. As a matter of fact, the heightened interest in these variable standards of teacher preparation probably grew out of the results of the Pennsylvania Study of High School and College.

The American Council on Education established a national committee on teacher examinations, and the committee started its work in 1939. The first edition of its teacher examinations "battery" was given in March, 1940, in some twenty centers over the country. The committee insisted upon the following: (1) that the examinations should be made out by cooperative effort and should be scored in a central location by impartial scorers so that results would be comparable; (2) that local autonomy in the selection of teachers should be preserved and protected at all costs; (3) that the national examinations should be an aid of a voluntary sort to superintendents, who are under no compulsion to use them; and (4) that the examinations should not be the sole basis for the selection or promotion of teachers, or even a major basis for these purposes. These national examinations are specially designed to measure certain abilities and knowledges of candidates for teaching on a nation-wide, comparable scale. Each year new editions are made out and administered in various centers. Recently a companion Teacher Education Examination Program (TEEP) has been added, not to serve school systems, but to serve institutions offering an accredited program in teacher education.

Examinations for candidates who desire to obtain teaching positions are nothing new. New York City is an outstanding example of a school system which has had such a plan in operation for many years. South Carolina years ago instituted a statewide plan of examinations as one factor in certification.

A candidate who takes these national examinations in any one year may have his performance on them forwarded to any superintendent to whom he is applying for a position; his performance is a private record, and is available to the administrator only upon the request of the candidate. If such a plan for teacher examinations on a national scale should gain much headway, the following handicaps to teacher growth and improvement might result:

1. The examinations might engender a uniformity of preparation among teacher-training institutions, which would be unfortunate and undesirable.
2. The examinations might become the sole standard of teacher selection, in spite of the warnings of the committee.
3. Higher institutions which train teachers might become more or less schools which "prep" for the passing of these examinations.
4. The use of these examinations might take away from local school boards and authorities their warm personal interest in the selection of teachers.[6]

Since these national examinations for teachers are based primarily upon *knowledges* which the teacher has acquired, they are likely to operate to magnify in the mind of the teacher this aspect of teaching, and to minimize the attention which should be given to the child and the study which should be made of him.

GRADUATE DEGREE REQUIREMENTS. The acquisition of a graduate degree as a qualification for teaching is nothing new; but the possession of a graduate degree seems likely to become a *requirement* for teaching in the elementary and secondary schools, just as it has become necessary for teaching on the collegiate level. Following the new standards of the regional accrediting associations, some state and local school systems have required of their administrative officials that they have a master's degree in order to qualify for those positions; to date, superintendents, principals, and supervisors are the administrative officers who have been most affected by these rulings. These school officials have been required to take graduate courses in school administration, supervision, and the curriculum, and in addition, they must have a specified number of years of experience for the work.

New York and California are examples of states which have extended their teacher-training courses to a period of five years. The length of this period of preservice training conceivably might allow

---

[6] *Cf.* "The Proposed Teacher Examination Service" by A.L. Rowland, *Harvard Educational Review*, x (May, 1940), pp. 283–88. Data on the National Teacher Examinations and the TEEP can be obtained from Educational Testing Service, Princeton, N.J.

teacher-candidates to secure both the A.B. and the A.M. degrees, since the A.M. usually requires an additional year of work beyond the four years for the A.B. The belief seems to be growing that both the preservice and in-service training of teachers will be improved by a requirement that teachers should take graduate work, or should experience a longer period of training before starting the actual work of teaching. There has been a feeling among many school officials and other workers in the field of education that the apprenticeship period of teaching for those who are candidates for teaching positions should be lengthened; that four years is too short a time for the teacher-candidate to get a broad cultural education along with the specific professional and practice training which is needed for effective work in teaching. However, the existing shortage of qualified teachers now will probably preclude such a lengthening for some time to come.

The question at once arises of what this type of graduate training for teachers in service and for teachers who are preparing to serve should consist of. If the graduate training is to be composed of more specific courses in subject-matter majors and minors, and in fields of professional education subdivided according to administration, secondary education, elementary education, psychology, pupil guidance, tests and measurements and statistics, it is doubtful whether the graduate work will be the best means of improving teacher growth. It is true that the certification regulations which exist in most states would probably point the graduate work in the direction of specific prescriptions in various fields, rather than toward broader general requirements to stimulate the growth of each particular person who is teaching or is preparing to teach.

For the teacher who is already in service, such graduate work should probably embrace the study of specific problems which he is attempting to solve in the schoolroom, and plans which he is making for the improvement of his work in the broadening of the child's curriculum. For the person who is preparing to teach, the graduate study should consist in part of apprenticeship or probationary teaching, and in part of laboratory courses leading toward a better mastery of both experimental and well-known methods of teaching. It is doubtful whether graduate work based particularly upon further mastery of a specific subject-matter field or area would be an incentive to the broadening of the teacher or of the teacher-candidate. The belief that the possession of an A.M. degree would necessarily improve one's teaching has just as much false basis as the notion that the possession of a good-looking automobile will improve one's position and standing in the community.

SIGNIFICANT EXPERIMENTS IN TEACHER EDUCATION

Two cooperative experiments have awakened all persons interested in teacher education to a realization of many deficiencies in the present system of teacher training. Out of the Eight-Year Study of the Progressive Education Association has developed the "summer workshop." Out of the cooperative study of the Commission on Teacher Education of the American Council on Education have come continuing experiments which point to the possibilities of an improved type of education for teachers in service and for teacher-candidates. These two developments will be discussed in the following paragraphs.

1. *Summer Workshops for Experienced Teachers*

When the Eight-Year Study of the Progressive Education Association began, the experimental work was hindered at first because of the difficulty of providing time for proper consultation among the teachers of the schools involved. Because of pressure of their regular duties, these teachers lacked adequate time to plan and to work together on the problems which arose in their experimental programs. In order to overcome this, the suggestion was made that part of the summer be employed by the staff of the Eight-Year Study and by the teachers of the cooperating schools in working together on their problems. This procedure was tried out for a six-week period in 1936 at the Ohio State University, with thirty-five teachers who had been carefully selected from the schools. Each participant in the workshop brought a problem to which he devoted his attention during the entire six weeks, with the help of the evaluation staff and of various specialists and consultants. In view of the success of this first experimental workshop, a larger workshop was held at Sarah Lawrence

College in Bronxville, New York, in the summer of 1937. One hundred and twenty-six teachers from a wider range of subject-matter fields came as delegations of key teachers, some with part of their expenses paid by their school; they spent their time in planning and preparing for experimental changes in their work for the following year.

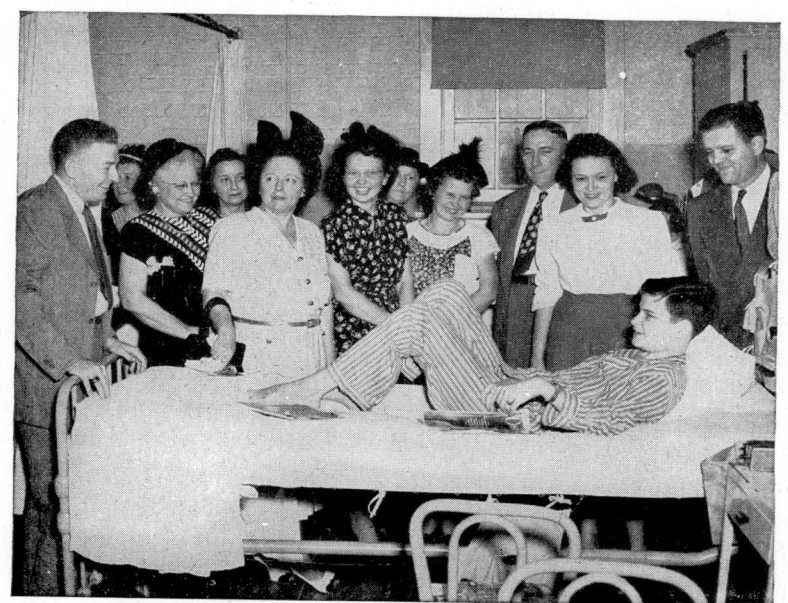

FIG. 40   *Turning the county-wide teachers' meeting into a workshop experience: Visiting the Durham County (N.C.) Tuberculosis Sanatorium*
(*Photo courtesy Durham County Schools.*)

The Eight-Year Study extended the scope of its workshop in 1938. Twenty-three faculty members from sixteen different institutions of higher education were admitted in addition to the teachers from the experimental schools. Out of the work of these college faculty members grew the Cooperative Study in General Education of the American Council on Education, which held a workshop at the University of Chicago in 1940. During the years following the summer of 1938, the workshop technique and service were broadened. The Committee on Workshops of the Progressive Education

Association offered its services to a group of cooperating universities which were willing to experiment with the new type of teacher education; the committee had the possibility in mind of incorporating the workshop approach into the teacher-training programs of these institutions as a permanent part of their summer-school work.

The summer workshop for teachers was developing also at the same time in the experimental area served by the Southern Association of Colleges and Secondary Schools. The three workshops of this association were held at Vanderbilt University, the University of North Carolina, and Eastern Kentucky State Teachers College.[7]

FEATURES OF THE WORKSHOP APPROACH. These are the essential characteristics of the workshop program as developed by the Committee on Workshops of the Progressive Education Association: (1) the outlining by the participant (teacher) of the specific problem upon which he wishes to work during the period, and the sharing by the participant in the planning of individual and group activities to meet his needs and those of his fellow students; (2) the provision of services of staff members who are specially trained to give all kinds of assistance; (3) the association of the participant in formal and informal situations with other students (teachers) of all kinds of backgrounds, to stimulate his thinking, to broaden him professionally, and to give him experiences in cooperative activities; (4) provisions to stimulate the participant to consider the growth and development of the whole child, the whole community, and the whole school; (5) provision for the participant's experiences in the workshop in the solution of his problems to help him in the solution of other professional problems in the future; and (6) provision for

---

[7] By 1940, the Progressive Education Association Workshop Committee had served and cooperated with the following institutions and educational organizations, either in their experimental programs or in the form of advisory, conference, or training program work: the University of Chicago, Claremont Colleges, Colorado State College of Education, University of Denver, Harvard University, University of Idaho, Northwestern University, Ohio State University, University of Oregon, University of Pennsylvania, Pennsylvania State College, University of Pittsburgh, Stanford University, Syracuse University, Teachers College of Columbia University, University of Washington, University of Wisconsin, Milwaukee State Teachers College, the Commission on Secondary Schools of the Southern Association of Colleges and Secondary Schools, the Michigan Study of the Secondary School Curriculum, and the Commission on Resources and Education.

balanced living for the participant in the group and individually during the period.[8]

POSSIBILITIES OF THE WORKSHOP TECHNIQUE. So successful did the Commission on Teacher Education consider the experimental program of the Committee on Workshops of the Progressive Education Association that it combined the work under the auspices of the commission as a Committee on Workshops of the Commission on Teacher Education. This committee continued the practice of holding summer workshops, where teachers in service could work cooperatively and individually on problems and procedures which they wished to put into effect in their schools. The implications of such a program of living together, working together, and solving actual curricular problems together are important for teacher education, especially for teachers in service. Instead of set courses and college credits in terms of semester hours, the teacher is really working on problems which are of vital concern to him and to his pupils. He is getting a new viewpoint, is doing that experiencing which is necessary for his growth and for the improvement of the curriculum, and is developing a broader conception of the meaning of his job.

Whether the workship technique can be organized so that graduate schools in universities will give credit for the experience and the work is another question. Certain universities have been experimenting and have found the workshop reasonably satisfactory. In all parts of the country, workshops modeled upon those started by the Progressive Education Association will be found in the higher institutions of learning. A word of caution is necessary: in order for a real workshop experience to be successful, it is necessary that it be full-time work for a period of from two to five or six weeks. In any shorter length of time, it is impossible for the individual participants and for the group to clarify their thinking, to make real progress upon their individual and group problems, and to make tentative plans of a source and organizational nature which will be of value in the solution of their problems. The workshops of the Southern Association developed a unique feature by having school groups meet together

[8] For accounts of the earlier workshops, *cf.* K.L. Heaton, *et al., Professional Education for Experienced Teachers: The Program of the Summer Workshop,* the University of Chicago Press, 1940, pp. 21–43. *Cf.* also *The Workshop* by P.B. Diederich and W. Van Til, New York, Hinds, Hayden and Eldredge, 1945.

to work on problems common to their school; each group included both the school administrator and selected teachers. This approach has much to commend it, and has been adopted by many school systems; the planning is cooperative so far as the school is concerned and is not done without the assistance and approval of the persons in authority.

The workshop should not be confused with the "work conference" or a two- or three-day "work institute." A work conference can be valuable for intensive study of a problem already defined, but is not the comprehensive and long-continued work, planning, and interaction of a group who tackle a common problem.[9]

If properly organized and carried out, the workshop procedure tends to help the teacher in experiencing in the following ways. (1) Since teachers usually teach as they have been taught, the workshop practice of providing teachers with better examples of good teaching is a rare and valuable experience for them—good teaching in which the student-teacher participates cooperatively in planning the purposes, the materials, and the procedures of the course. (2) The student-teacher in the workshop participates individually in direct learning experiences such as he would like his pupils to participate in; this direct participation opens the eyes of the student-teacher to many procedures which he has been carrying on and which he would like to improve.

2. The Commission on Teacher Education

The American Council on Education appointed the Commission on Teacher Education early in 1938 for a period of five years of work, and charged it to make a nation-wide study of the problems in the education of teachers. In its work, the commission was to use, as largely as possible, the experience of such institutions and associations as were already active in the field of teacher education. The commission started with a liberal subsidy from the General Education Board. It worked primarily through and with agencies which

---

[9] To understand the modern workshop, read *Workshops for Teachers* by M.A. O'Rourke and W.H. Burton, New York, Appleton-Century-Crofts, 1957, and *The Workshop Way of Learning* by E.C. Kelley, New York, Harper and Brothers, 1951.

existed already for teacher education; it stimulated cooperative approaches of an experimental nature to problems of teacher education in institutions which were associated with the commission; and it encouraged the cooperating groups to evaluate their programs for teacher education. Its study was a *cooperative* one in the strictest sense of the word; in this venture, the cooperating groups were represented by six universities, five liberal arts colleges, seven state teachers' colleges, two Negro colleges, and fourteen public school systems from all sections of the country.

Not only within the institutions and schools cooperating with this commission was work going on to study and to improve teacher education. An intensive approach was also made to the teacher-education interests of certain entire states. Virginia, North Carolina, Georgia, Mississippi, Kentucky, Louisiana, Florida, Arkansas, and West Virginia represented regional activities on a statewide basis.

The commission reported that the most highly developed state programs in the study of teacher education in 1940 were in Michigan, Georgia, and upper New York. The procedures in these states were in general similar to those of the national cooperative study of teacher education sponsored by the commission. In both Georgia and Michigan, the competent body which cooperated with the Commission on Teacher Education was an agency of the state department of public instruction, and consisted of a teacher-education committee representing all of the state institutions of higher learning and the school systems concerned with the improvement of teaching. Each state had a program coordinator, who worked in collaboration with a directing or steering committee. In New York, the cooperative teacher-education study was sponsored by the Association of Colleges and Universities of the state, and was under a special committee on teacher education; the Regents' Inquiry of 1938 into the character and cost of public education in the state of New York raised certain questions to which this committee especially directed its attention.

Stimulated by the work of the Commission on Teacher Education, statewide studies of teacher education were undertaken all over the country. For example, the Cooperative Commission for the Study of Teacher Education in Pennsylvania was organized with representatives from the Association of College Presidents of Pennsylvania, the Board of Teachers' College Presidents of Pennsylvania, the Pennsylvania Department of Public Instruction, the Pennsylvania State Education Association, and the Association of Liberal Arts Colleges for the Advancement of Teaching. The Pennsylvania Commission started work in 1939; it worked with school administrators, teachers, and the public in its purposes of identifying and finding possible solutions to problems in the field on a cooperative basis.

To summarize, the work of the Commission on Teacher Education was primarily concerned with helping states, colleges, and local school systems in the promotion of promising activities already under way in regard to teacher education; with assisting them in solving their problems; and with pointing out implications of their studies for the purposes of effective example and demonstration. In order to accomplish these purposes, the commission provided consultation services; it promoted intervisitation and special conferences or workshops; it gathered information and called attention to promising programs existing elsewhere; it assisted with procedures for evaluation; and it helped by making types of materials generally available. Special services were provided by the commission through its Division on Child Growth and Teacher Personnel and in evaluation.

The commission, with the help of prominent institutions of higher education, sponsored six workshops in the summer of 1941. The commission also furnished a workshop advisory service and other miscellaneous services and activities. One of the most interesting outcomes of the commission's work was the development of the program and workshops in General Education; these were for teachers on the collegiate level, who did the training of teachers in content subjects before they got to the professional courses in education.[10]

[10] The Reports of the Commission on Teacher Education of the American Council on Education comprised eight volumes. 1944—*Teachers for Our Times*, *Evaluation in Teacher Education*. *Teacher Education In Service*, and *The College and Teacher Education;* 1945—*Helping Teachers Understand Children* and *Toward Improving Ph.D. Programs;* 1946—*State Programs for the Improvement of Teacher Education*, *The Improvement of Teacher Education: Final Report of the Commission*.

STUDIES AND EXPERIENCES UNDER WAY IN TEACHER EDUCATION

It is all right to talk in broad terms of experiments in teacher education, but actual illustrations of the types of approach are necessary if the curriculum worker is to understand the implications. A few illustrations are, therefore, presented herewith.

THE PLAN AT THE OHIO STATE UNIVERSITY.　Their program has been evolving for a period of almost twenty years. The College of Education of the Ohio State University is a four-year school which controls the curriculum of its students from the time they enter upon their formal college training. Fundamental to its experimental work is the faculty's acceptance of the belief that a much more effective plan of teacher training can be instituted within the present administrative organization than has been operative in the past. The faculty believes in the formulation and actual practice of a modern philosophy of education and of teacher training—a philosophy that motivates and guides the faculty in its work as a team, rather than merely as individuals. Characteristic of this philosophy are the following points of view:

1. Teacher preparation depends not on courses taken and credits accumulated, but on the attainment of definite "factors of competency" in sufficient measure to give a real preparation for the work. The faculty has tentatively formulated these factors of competency or these qualifications for teachers, and these are taken as a working basis for the entire preparation of teacher-candidates.

2. The best way to obtain knowledge is through concrete experience. The acceptance of this point of view commits the college to the laboratory approach in teacher training from start to finish.

3. The best teaching consists of working and planning with the student as an individual: first, through an extensive set of tests and interviews to aid him in discovering his own strengths and weaknesses; secondly, through helping him secure experiences in line with his personal needs; and thirdly, through aiding in continued evaluation and planning in the light of his condition and stage of progress at the time. This means constant and detailed personnel work with students all through the four years, evaluating the abilities, skills, and attitudes attained, as well as subject-matter achievement. The evaluation of psychological tests (*e.g.*, interpretation of data, nature of proof, reading abilities) is largely made not on

the basis of total scores, but on the basis of scores on separate parts designed to evaluate different factors, such as consistency, uncertainty, and conservatism.

4. A good teacher is first of all a well-rounded and broadly experienced individual, sensitive to his physical and social environment, tolerant and adaptable. The freshman orientation course, and much of the work that follows in the first two years, is designed to give experiences less in school situations than in social situations generally.

5. The present program is kept in an evolving status; it is *not* considered as fully developed. Joint student-faculty study and planning are continually being applied as much to the improvement of the university program as to the problems of the individual student.

6. It is the responsibility of the student to *plan* and *evaluate for himself*, with the help of his advisers. Sometimes he has a share in grading himself. On the basis of what he discovers about himself, he is led often to withdraw voluntarily from training for teaching, in which case the College of Education feels its responsibility for helping him toward more appropriate placement for his life work, either outside or within some other college curriculum.

In the light of these guiding principles at the Ohio State University, it is seen that complete records on student-candidates must be maintained; and these records must be kept available for each student, beginning with the admission blanks and freshman-week tests and continuing throughout the period of preparation. Except for data that might influence the student emotionally to his disadvantage. the student is given a copy of his record and is trained to evaluate it for himself in terms of the factors of "competency" which have been formulated. The only aspects of his record which are withheld from the student would be comparable to what a physician might withhold from a patient in studying his case. The completeness of the student's record, and the constancy with which this record is available to both advisers and students and is kept in use, are important points in the continuous experimental program under way in the training of teachers.

The freshman-week checkup is most thorough, and the breadth of the orientation study includes a survey course for freshmen. There are regular conferences with the adviser in small groups throughout the year.

As a result of an effective effort to let the faculty have the major role in this organization for teacher education, there is a multiplicity and interfunctioning of faculty committees. This feature aims at the actual practice of democracy, rather than the vesting of all authority in a small number of administrative officers of the college.

A willingness to change in the light of new developments is evident. When either a student or a teacher brings in a suggestion, the first question is, "How does it relate to our accepted philosophy?" If this point is settled favorably, the next question is, "How can it be done?" Both students and faculty members seem willing to devote long periods of extra time to serious conferences about concrete problems connected with themselves, their experiences, and their work as a whole, especially for planning ahead. This type of labor and interrelationship between the faculty and the student makes for a general feeling of close fellowship. Classes are conducted informally, largely in the way of discussion of experiences which have been used as media to get students to have something to discuss and to think about. Students participate, rather than merely listen to lectures.

The "September experience" has been a unique feature of the Ohio State University plan. Because of the values that may accrue from it, other colleges have adopted the "September experience" feature. The student is placed in a regular school system for the two or three weeks of September before the university opens. During that time, he participates in any duties that may need to be done; the work is not mere observation, and it is not alike for all. The intention is to have students undergo this September experience during their last three years, preferably each year under different conditions; it was first carried out by candidates who were working for "degrees with distinction." This experience involves practical work from preparing supplies or answering office phones to actual teaching in some cases, perhaps as a substitute for a teacher who is sick and absent. Meanwhile the students, using suggestions which were prepared and given to them in advance, are studying that school and that community. The students have also had a part in planning these suggestions in advance, prior to the time of their September experience.

At the Ohio State University, the University School is available as a laboratory or experimental school. The high-school division of the University School was one of the secondary schools engaged in the Eight-Year Study of the Progressive Education Association. The unified program of the University School, extending from the kindergarten to the university with the same director in charge, offers excellent opportunities for visitation and observation to students in the College of Education preparing to teach in both elementary and secondary schools. An experimental core program in grades seven to twelve provides many opportunities for teachers in training to gain insight into the general education role of a teacher, whatever his major field. Courses in core teaching are offered to those who wish further specialization.

A promising development at Ohio State was the establishment in 1958 of a Department of School Experimentation with the University School as a pilot school within that organization. In this way, the teacher, in his preservice program and later in his in-service training, is able to see and to participate in a field laboratory in which action research on school problems is undertaken. Schools in the field will affiliate with the new unit, creating thereby an agency which permits important feedback between the teacher training institution and field situations.[11]

THE FORD FUND'S PROJECTS IN TEACHER EDUCATION. Since 1951, the Ford Foundation's Fund for the Advancement of Education has supported substantially experimental teacher-education programs in more than twenty-five colleges and universities. The amount of the subsidies for these projects has totaled millions of dollars, and the experiments have been going on in many different sections of the country.[12]

---

[11] The data for the Ohio State University program were taken from *The College and Teacher Education, op. cit.*, Chaps. VII and VIII; and A.J. Klein (Ed.), *Adventures in the Reconstruction of Education,* Ohio State University, 1941, Chaps. I–V, VII, X, and from personal correspondence with Paul R. Klohr, Assistant Dean, College of Education.

[12] For a concise report on these experiments to 1957, read *New Directions in Teacher Training,* the Fund for the Advancement of Education, New York 22, 1957, and *A Fourth of a Nation,* New York, McGraw-Hill Book Company, 1957, both by Paul Woodring. The basic data in this description were summarized primarily from these reports.

The experimental projects have generally been of three types:

1. *Five-year and fifth-year programs for liberal arts graduates and for older, mature college graduates,* respectively, who have not had or would not have any professional education in the undergraduate program, and who would have little or no subject-matter or content education during the graduate year. The much discussed University of Arkansas experiment, and the ones at Temple University, Cornell, University of Louisville, Goucher, and Harvard are samples of the five-year professional programs for liberal arts graduates, which may lead in some institutions to a master's degree. The fifth-year experimental programs are well illustrated by the four California experiments at the University of Southern Cailfornia in cooperation with Los Angeles' district schools, in the San Francisco Unified School District in cooperation with San Francisco State College, in the San Diego Schools and State College, and in the Claremont Colleges in cooperation with fourteen Southern California elementary schools; those who complete these programs receive generally the teaching certificate appropriate for their training, but no further college or graduate degree.

2. *The Master of Arts in Teaching,* a five-year program generally leading both to a master's degree and a teacher's certificate. Two different plans for this program are found. Harvard University, which has had the M.A.T. degree in existence since 1937, illustrates both plans well. Under Plan A, a person with his bachelor's degree can work in an apprenticeship program on a scholarship; his first semester is devoted to full work in courses and observation in schools, his second to apprenticeship teaching for the morning in local schools and for the afternoon in course work. Plan B is an internship program; the local school pays each intern $1,500 for one-half of a year of full-time teaching; it takes *two* interns in the same subject area to replace one beginning teacher in a school. Each intern thus teaches *one* semester, has a full load of course work the other semester, and can also use the following summer to finish his course work if he needs it. Yale, Duke, and Vanderbilt-Peabody programs offer good examples of the different practices.

3. *Four-Year Programs Combining Professional with Liberal Education.* These experiments have been planned primarily to restudy the possibilities for better teacher education *within* the accepted pattern, especially by liberal-arts colleges. The programs at Swarthmore, Carleton, Bernard, and Wilson colleges are of this kind.

In all of the Ford Foundation experiments, the emphasis has been upon four closely related parts of teacher education:

1. Liberal, or general education
2. Mastery of the subject-area to be taught

3. Professional knowledge
4. Classroom skills, working with children, and supervision of the apprentice.

From these experiments have come already such results as tapping a reservoir of mature people for teaching who have finished college; different kinds of internship programs; "team" teaching; and the idea of "teacher aides."

Since cadet or "practice teaching" for full time for a quarter or semester is already required of teacher-candidates by many institutions and some states, perhaps we can glean from the results of these programs more ideas for a permanent plan for such internship in teaching.

OTHER STUDIES AND TRENDS.   Experiments other than those stimulated by the Commission on Teacher Education and the Fund for The Advancement of Education have also been made. Syracuse University by 1940 had worked out a cooperative plan of teacher preparation in an all-university, interdepartmental School of Education. For twenty-five years, the Parker School District of Greenville, South Carolina, conducted its own summer or preschool study program for teachers in preparation for the work of the following school year.[13] The Mobile, Alabama, schools instituted an in-service study program in 1947–1948.[14] For a good example of a county-wide project in a rural section, one can turn to the Alamance County, North Carolina, in-service program. This work has been going on for almost two decades; the techniques that have been used range from the county summer workshop with visiting consultants for six weeks to intervisitation and studies of county resources and community problems.

After pioneering in summer workshops for several years, the State of Florida took a new step in teacher education. After careful study by a Citizens' Committee from 1945 to 1947,[15] Florida established a Foundation Program for its schools which included these new

---

[13] Sallie K. Mims, *The In-Service Program: Teachers of Parker School District,* Parker School District, 1948.

[14] *In-Service Education: A Program of the Mobile Public Schools,* Board of School Commissioners, 1947–1948.

[15] *Education and the Future of Florida,* Florida Citizens' Committee on Education, 1947.

features in teacher education: (1) A ten-months' program for teachers, nine teaching and the other month to be spent in study and planning for the work of the next year. This study and planning took the form in many of the counties of the state of three-week (all-day) workshops in the early or late part of the summer. (2) Scholarships for in-service teachers, both to attend summer school and workshops. The 1949 school machinery act of the North Carolina legislature gave the State Board of Education permissive power to establish a ten-month school year of a similar type, if it was deemed wise. The Florida experiment was significant; it marked the first step on a statewide scale to pay teachers to teach for nine months and to pay them to plan their work in another month. If this trend grows, the whole plan of in-service training for teachers may be changed from the campus to the field where the teachers work. The University of Florida cooperates with the state in this program in the field, and gives credit to those properly qualified to receive it if they do satisfactory work.

Among the national organizations, the John Dewey Society has featured teacher education in three of its yearbooks, *The Teacher and Society, Teachers for Democracy,* and *The Teacher's Role in American Society.*[16] In 1940 and 1950, the White House Conferences on Children and Youth in a Democracy stated that the professional training of teachers should be enriched by the study of principles of child growth and development, the place of education in a changing social order, and the significance of democratic procedures in school life and environment. The conferences emphasized also in the education of teachers the importance of guidance and counseling techniques, civic responsibilties, and cooperation with other community institutions and agencies that serve the child. The American Youth Commission presented in many of its studies the need in teacher education for better preparation for the guidance and understanding of youth and its problems, particularly as they relate to the adjustment of youth to other individuals, to society, to work, and to youth's own ambitions.

[16] First and Fourth Yearbooks, New York, D. Appleton-Century Company, 1937 and 1940, respectively, and Fourteenth Yearbook, New York, Harper and Brothers, 1957.

The Department of Supervisors and Directors of Instruction of the National Education Association (now the Association for Supervision and Curriculum Development) prepared as its Thirteenth Yearbook a careful study of *Mental Health in the Classroom.* Other yearbooks of this group which consider various aspects of preservice and in-service education are: 1944 Yearbook, *Toward a New Curriculum;* 1945 Yearbook, *Group Planning in Education;* 1946 Yearbook, *Leadership Through Supervision;* 1949 Yearbook, *Toward Better Teaching: A Report of Current Practices;* 1950 Yearbook, *Fostering Mental Health in Our Schools;* 1954 Yearbook, *Creating a Good Environment for Learning;* and 1955 Yearbook, *Guidance in the Curriculum.* The Department of Rural Education of the National Education Association has been studying the special competencies needed by teachers in rural communities. Since 1946 the National Commission on Teacher Education and Professional Standards of the National Education Association has been studying the problem.

In some states, special requirements have been established for the education and certification of teachers in guidance and counseling. Other sections of the country and many institutions of higher education are looking at this problem of training teachers for guidance work.

It is still too early to predict what effect closed-circuit television and the widespread use of television will have upon teacher education, but it may be far-reaching. In the experiment at the University of Minnesota in 1957–1958, for example, observation of classroom teaching by TV was used.

Experiments with "teacher aides" in the classrooms have been under way. Until final evaluation of the use of teacher aides, judgment must be withheld as to their effectiveness. Perhaps the best known of these experiments was the Bay City-Central Michigan College Plan, designed to test out this kind of assistance over the five-year period from 1952 to 1957. The first year was spent in analysis of the teacher's job; the aides were used to relieve regular teachers of nonprofessional tasks and duties so that they could concentrate on essential teaching. The plan has given rise to quite a controversy over turning the child over to untrained personnel and over the distinct possibility of increasing the pupil-teacher load.[17]

It is interesting to note that the colleges, in cooperation with state departments of education, are establishing broader preservice programs of professional education. Two examples of this trend are: North Carolina with adequate training required in the broad areas of (1) the child, (2) the school, and (3) teaching and practicum; and in New York, the Oneonta Program for educating elementary teachers in (1) child development, (2) the child and the curriculum, and (3) the practicum in student teaching and the seminar in education. Other interesting experiments, departures, and changes in teacher-education programs are reported from time to time in *The Newsletter of The Council on Cooperation in Teacher Education.*[18]

THE EFFECT OF TEACHER EDUCATION UPON THE CURRICULUM

The kind of preparation received by the teacher-candidate or the teacher in service practically predetermines whether the teacher will take an active and intelligent part in curriculum improvement; though this is a broad statement, all evidence from the studies of teacher education tends to confirm it. Since teacher growth depends primarily upon this factor, any well-planned and well-balanced program of teacher education for a school system should make adequate provision for the following:

1. The continuing development of a sound philosophy of teacher education, with purposes clearly defined, with determination of the competencies and experiences, as well as the qualifications, which a successful teacher should have.

---

[17] The purposes of the experiment and samples of opinion on it *pro* and *con* can be found in *Report of the First Two Years of the Study* (commonly called the *Second Report*), "The Superintendent," Bay City, Michigan; "The Bay City Project," by Dorothy McCuskey, *NEA Journal*, May, 1956, pp. 284–85; and *Schools for Tomorrow*, by A.J. Stoddard, New York 21, Fund for the Advancement of Education, 1957, pp. 19–24.

[18] The Council, Washington 6, D.C.

2. The opportunity for the *experience* approch in training, whereby the teacher-candidate or the teacher in service goes through with those activities, experiences, and procedures which should be used with children; such would certainly include cooperative (student-teacher) planning between student candidates or teachers and instructors, "group thinking," and self-evaluation.

3. The opportunity for teacher-candidates of apprenticeship and exploration of community life and school situations of types additional and supplementary to mere "practice teaching" of subject-matter, with emphasis upon the teacher's obligation to the community and to society as well as to the pupil.

4. The realization of more adequate opportunities and laboratory study for teachers in the areas of child growth and development, guidance, and the functions of other agencies which work side by side with the school in the community for the education of children.

5. Careful selection, case study, placement, and follow-up of teacher-candidates.

6. Continued leadership, stimulation, and encouragement for growth while the teacher is "on the job."

PROBLEMS FOR INDIVIDUAL STUDY AND CLASS DISCUSSION

1. Why do the personal qualifications which a teacher possesses have importance for his curricular work? Explain.

2. What specific types of community experience should a teacher-candidate have before he enters into regular teaching? Why?

3. What content or subject-matter collegiate courses should an elementary-school teacher have in preparation for teaching? Give reasons for your decisions.

4. Would you approve national teacher examinations as one test of your fitness for teaching? Support your point of view.

5. Assume that you have an opportunity to attend a five-weeks workshop for teachers in service. In what form would you present a clear statement of the particular problem upon which you desire to work during that period of study?

6. Assume that you teach in the city of Tinville, where the school board has ruled that all teachers must have an A.M. degree by the end of the next three years. What type of graduate program would be of maximum benefit to you in your teaching? Could you secure such a program in any graduate institution today?

7. If your state extended its period of preservice training for teachers

to five years instead of its present four-year program which requires a college degree and practice teaching, what additional experiences would you place in the program of the teacher-candidate? Give specific types and approximate duration of these additional activities.

8. What values do general and special educational conferences possess for the in-service improvement of teachers in curriculum work?

9. Should the beginning teacher be required to undergo a period of probationary or "cadet" teaching at a lower salary scale before he is given a permanent certificate at the lowest regular salary rate? Support your position.

10. What types of curriculum work and curriculum courses do you believe that summer schools should provide for teachers in service?

11. Assume that you plan to have a panel discussion in your secondary-school class. After stating the topic, how would you assign special aspects to the five participating members? Prepare a list of source materials for them to use in their panel study.

12. Assume that the next unit which your class will undertake is "Our Reading Interests." What plan would you devise for dividing the class of thirty into six groups or committees for more effective work and report to the entire group?

13. Can a fifth-grade teacher give adequate art or music instruction to his pupils unless he is specially trained in those fields? Support your point of view.

14. Is it possible for a secondary-school teacher, under the existing certification requirements in your state, to be well trained in more than two subject-matter fields? Explain why or why not.

15. Should teachers be employed on a year-round basis and required during two of the summer months to plan together for improved teaching in their school for the next year? Give reasons for your stand.

16. If you had your choice, which of the professional education courses would you take in preparation for your teaching? Why?

17. What standards would you establish for the selection of those high school and college students who should prepare for teaching?

18. Should practice teaching be done by a teacher-candidate in an *ideal* teaching situation or in a *typical* situation? Support your position.

19. In what ways do the social and economic status and the social, political, economic, and religious beliefs of a group of teachers influence their curricular work?

20. Should the college program of preparation for the junior high-school teacher be the same as that of the teacher for the senior high school? Or not? Explain.

21. Are certification requirements in your state too high? Too low? About right? Support your decision with evidence.

ADDITIONAL ANNOTATED REFERENCES FOR
PROBLEM OR UNIT STUDY

Anderson, V.E., et al., Principles and Practices of Secondary Education, New York, The Ronald Press Company, 1951.
Part v presents the preservice, in-service education, and the responsibilities of the secondary-school teacher.

Association for Supervision and Curriculum Development, N.E.A.
From time to time this group published special bulletins or issues of its periodical, Educational Leadership, such as, Vol. IX (October, 1951), "In-Service Programs," pp. 2–44, and Vol. xv (February, 1958), "Continuing Education for the Teaching Profession," pp. 270–305. See also Helping the New Teacher, 1956, and Children's Social Learning, 1958, by Edna Ambrose and Alice Miel, Chapter III.

Beck, R.H., et al., Curriculum in the Modern Elementary School, New York, Prentice-Hall, 1953.
Part III describes fully the experiences of a beginning teacher of promise, of a man elementary teacher, and of a supervisor who helped teachers.

Brown, E.J., Managing The Classroom, New York, The Ronald Press Company, 1952.
Presented from the standpoint of the teacher's part in school administration.

Chamberlain, L.M., and Kindred, L.W., The Teacher and School Organization (3rd ed.), Englewood Cliffs, Prentice-Hall, 1958.
Presents to the teacher his place in the modern school and his relationships to the various community and political organizations.

Cunningham, R., and Associates, Understanding Group Behavior of Boys and Girls, New York, Teachers College, Columbia University, 1951.
How elementary and secondary-school teachers can work more effectively with boys and girls in group situations, with emphasis upon cooperative planning.

Ehlers, H. (Ed.), Crucial Issues in Education, New York, Henry Holt and Company, 1955.
An anthology, with Part I devoted to freedom for teachers, and Part v to classroom materials and methods.

Eye, G.G., and Lane, W.R., The New Teacher Comes to School, New York, Harper and Brothers, 1956.
Problems of new teachers and ways of adaption to school and community.

Films on Teacher Education, New York, McGraw-Hill Book Company.
Text-films on (1) "Learning to Understand Children," Parts I and II; (2) "Maintaining Classroom Discipline"; and (3) "Broader Concept of Method," Parts I and II.

Gould, G., and Yoakam, G.A., *The Teacher and His Work* (2nd ed.), New York, The Ronald Press Company, 1954.
Chapters I–VI look at teaching as a career, the qualifications and welfare of the teacher, his professional relationships, and his relationships with children; xv considers the teacher and the community.

Gruhn, W.T., *Student Teaching in the Secondary School*, New York, The Ronald Press Company, 1954.
A sound account of problems from preservice into service.

Hart, F.W. (Ed.), *Teachers and Teaching*, New York, The Macmillan Company, 1934.
Ten thousand high-school seniors describe their best, their best-liked, and their most ineffective teacher.

Kearney, N.C., *A Teacher's Professional Guide*, Englewood Cliffs, Prentice-Hall, 1958.
Practical advice from one who has passed that way on the personal and professional problems of teachers.

Langdon, G., and Stout, I.W., *Helping Parents Understand Their Child's School*, Englewood Cliffs, Prentice-Hall, 1957.
A handbook for teachers, which helps both to anticipate and answer questions of parents.

Lieberman, M., *Education as a Profession*, Englewood Cliffs, Prentice-Hall, 1956.
An interesting account of the professionalization of the teaching field.

Miel, A., and Associates, *Cooperative Procedures in Learning*, New York, Teachers College, Columbia University, 1952.
Actual accounts of successful teacher-pupil and teacher-teacher planning.

Muldoon, M., *Learning to Teach*, New York, Harper and Brothers, 1958.
A handbook for beginning teachers.

National Council for the Social Studies, N.E.A.
The Teacher of the Social Studies, 23rd Yearbook, 1952. Includes both elementary and secondary-school teachers and their work.

National Society for the Study of Education, Chicago.
Mental Health in Modern Education, 54th Yearbook, Part II. Sections IV and V take up the teacher's mental health.

Noar, G., *The Junior High School—Today and Tomorrow*, New York, Prentice-Hall, 1953.
Teacher education in Chapter v, and other aspects in Part II.

Parrish, L., and Waskin, Y., *Teacher-Pupil Planning*, New York, Harper and Brothers, 1958.
Illustrates cooperative planning for classroom learning by actual situations in junior and senior high schools.

Review of Educational Research, American Educational Research Association, N.E.A.

Vol. xxviii, No. 3, June, 1958, gives the latest in research on aspects of teacher personnel, including extensive bibliographies.

Richey, R.W., *Planning for Teaching* (2nd ed.), New York, McGraw-Hill Book Company, 1958.
Part i for planning for teaching, ii for the work of the teacher, and iii for economic aspects of teaching.

Scott, C.W., and Hill, C.M. (Eds.), *Public Education Under Criticism,* Englewood Cliffs, Prentice-Hall, 1954.
An anthology, including "Teacher Education and Teachers" in Chapter vii and "How to Handle Criticisms" in x.

Stoddard, A.J., *Public Schools for Tomorrow*, New York, the Fund for the Advancement of Education, 1957.
A blueprint for meeting the critical shortage of teachers and buildings, including descriptions of training teachers by television, the experiment in employing of teacher aides, and teaching pupils in large numbers by "teaching teams" on television.

Teaching as a Career. Good books on teaching as a career are numerous, and some of them have been best sellers. A representative list would include:

B.S. Aldrich, *Miss Bishop*
G.H. Carroll, *Christmas Without Johnny*
G. Chase, *Four Young Teachers*
M.E. Chase, *A Goodly Fellowship*
A. De Lima, *The Little Red Schoolhouse*
J. Hilton, *Goodby, Mr. Chips*
A.L. Humphreys { *Angels in Pinafores* / *Heaven in Thy Hand* }

M.F. Kennedy and A.F. Harlow, *Schoolmaster of Yesterday*
D. McCuskey, *Bronson Alcott, Teacher*
F.G. Patton, *Good Morning, Miss Dove*
B. Perry, *And Gladly Teach*
J. Stuart, *The Thread That Runs So True*
E.G. Vining, *Windows for the Crown Prince*
J. Weber, *My Country School Diary*

Woellner, R.C., and Wood, M.A., *Requirements for Certification of Teachers and Administrators for Elementary Schools, Secondary Schools, Junior Colleges* (latest edition, usually published annually), Chicago, University of Chicago Press.

Yale Fairfield Study of Elementary Teaching, Abridged Edition of the Report of 1954–1955, New Haven, Department of Education, Yale University, 1956.
An examination of the existing school pattern, how to use elementary teachers' time to best advantage, and how to make load and work of the elementary teacher more effective and attractive.

Yauch, W.A., *et al.*, *The Beginning Teacher*, New York, Henry Holt and Company, 1955.

Addressed to graduating seniors in teacher education, the book tries to orient new teachers to their first group of learners.

Yeager, W.A., *Administration and the Teacher*, New York, Harper and Brothers, 1954.

An excellent book on the administration of staff personnel, centered around the individual teacher.

CHAPTER 18 Curricular aids

THE ENRICHMENT OF THE CURRICULUM

A veritable mine of curricular material lies within the reach of every teacher who wishes to enrich his work. Teaching confined narrowly to one textbook is a relic of the past for the wide-awake, cultured teacher of today. With few exceptions, the subject-matter areas and pupil activities are concerned directly or indirectly with fast-moving developments of a technological, economic, or social nature. As an example, a textbook in sociology or government for secondary-school youth which was written in 1958 may be out of date or lacking in information on important matters in 1960 or 1961. Since that textbook was adopted for use, important changes may have occurred and new social responsibilities and functions of government may have been added, which must be brought into the course work by the teacher from supplementary sources. Source materials have to be brought in also to supplement the texts in science and applied science, language, reading and literature, geography and history and other social studies, homemaking and home economics, shop work and industrial arts and education, business and distributive education, agriculture, health and hygiene and physical education, and diversified occupations. Because of alterations in the maps and national characters of Russia, Germany, Japan, China, and other nations, even the modern foreign languages are not exempt from changes which require supplementary materials.

When the teacher considers curricular aids, the following problems confront him: (1) What are the types of aids? (2) Where and how may these aids be obtained? (3) How should the aids be used? It is the primary purpose of this chapter to attempt to give information about curricular aids to the teacher so that he may solve these problems. It should be held in mind that this volume is primarily a handbook for curriculum workers, and that it furnishes representative bibliographies and references to teaching aids of all types.

ORGANIZED SCHOOL AGENCIES FOR ENRICHING THE CURRICULUM

1. *The Library*

The development of adequate library service on all school levels has paralleled curriculum improvement during the last twenty-five years. No longer is it necessary to convince school officials of the need for school libraries, because state and regional accrediting agencies have thrown their influence so strongly in favor of adequate facilities that most schools are being compelled gradually to provide adequate libraries and library service if they wish to meet the criteria for standardization.

Teachers and administrators are coming more and more to think of the library as that agency within the school which should serve as a central source of supply of all sorts of materials to both pupils and teachers. Broader opportunities for full use of school libraries are at hand, because many states now require that a person trained in library work should be in charge of the school library. Poorly lighted and inadequately ventilated rooms with rows of glass-enclosed bookcases and uncomfortable chairs are giving way to attractive, well-lighted, centrally located library rooms with open book shelves and comfortable seating facilities. Since one of the main purposes of the library is to encourage children to grow voluntarily in reading, this is as it should be.

The library should be by all odds the most attractive room in the school building, with easy chairs, attractive posters and notices of new materials, and cases of excellent books open and easily accessible to all for browsing and exploration. The practice in many schools of combining study halls with libraries is unsound psychologically, and it may even operate in the case of a poorly controlled study-hall situation to set the student against reading on his own initiative.

THE SELECTION OF BOOKS AND MATERIALS. Through custom and

tradition, it has become the practice in most schools for the responsibility for the selection of library books and materials of all kinds to be placed entirely upon the librarian. Although tradition is hard to break down, many schools are now thinking in new terms of the joint responsibility which rests upon the entire staff for the provision of materials for this central source of supply. No matter how well

FIG. 41   *The Curriculum Laboratory: Another way to enrich curricular materials in moden education*
(*Chapel Hill (N.C.), Bob Brooks Photo.*)

trained the school librarian may be, it is impossible for her to be the most competent judge of what every teacher needs in the way of materials.

If the sixth-grade teacher, for example, happens to be working with his group on a large unit involving both the geography and the history of certain European nations, the librarian will not be able to give the best service unless she is informed by the teacher of the types of materials which are needed for effective teaching. The materials which the sixth-grade teacher needs may include current maps showing the rapid changes in the face of Europe since World War II; charts, diagrams, and articles upon the geography and economy of these European nations at present; and recent books on travel or of a reference nature which can help to clarify the situation as it is today. The old method which might have been used by the sixth-grade teacher in handling this unit is no longer entirely satisfactory, because the series of geographical, historical, economic, and political maps which he has been using are not accurate now in many respects owing to the war and international changes which have been taking place in Europe; if he is using a basic textbook, it likewise will show big gaps in regard to modern happenings. As a matter of fact, the teacher cannot do an effective job on this unit with respect to the last few years, in particular, unless he has the cooperation of the librarian in securing and making available current materials which may be used in the classroom as well as in the library. In the solution of this curriculum problem, the librarian and the teacher must work hand in hand. The librarian must keep abreast of those types of materials which may be of value to the sixth-grade teacher; and the teacher should assist, both by telling the librarian what kinds of materials he needs and by gathering them in part himself from various sources and bringing them to the librarian for indexing, filing, and servicing.

The illustration which has just been given was taken from the elementary-school level. The same methods of securing supplementary materials should hold true more particularly for the secondary school, where departmentalization and subject-matter specialization make it a physical impossibility for the librarian to cover enough ground in her reading and study to keep up with all the subject areas. Teachers in the secondary school should be aware of the fact that the librarian cannot have a knowledge of all the new materials in the subject-matter fields; they should be eager, therefore, to supplement the librarian's information by means of their own reading and study, so that they may secure jointly those types of materials which are necessary for the most effective teaching.

GUIDES FOR THE USE OF THE LIBRARY. No teacher should be without a knowledge of the following books, written by Lucile Fargo:

The Library in the School, latest edition.
Activity Book for School Libraries.
Activity Book No. 2: Library Projects for Children and Young People.[1]

These publications discuss the purposes, materials and equipment, personnel and management, organization and administration, and the activities and curriculum-subject activities of an effective, modern school library. Of course, trained school librarians are familiar with these publications, but it has been a shock to the author to discover in his work with teachers in service on the graduate level, and with teacher-training candidates in the junior and senior classes, that no more than a fifth of educational employees were familiar with these books.

THE RESPONSIBILITY OF THE TEACHER. If a teacher of American history in the secondary school wishes to make out a well-balanced, interesting list of historical and biographical fiction, to what sources would he go for help? Should he take his problem to the school librarian with the request that she make out such a list? The librarian does not know exactly what will be included in the course, and in what way the material will be handled, nor does she know the problems upon which stress will be placed and the problems which will be touched upon only lightly. Neither can the librarian be expected to know the contents of all the books which she might secure from the various lists at her disposal. In addition, there are probably several books in the field of the social studies of such recent publication that the librarian is not familiar with them. At the least, the teacher of American history should be familiar with, and should consult, the following references: the *Wilson Standard Catalog for High School Libraries*, with its annual supplements; the *Booklist, Library Journal,* and *Junior Libraries* of the American Library Association, published monthly or semimonthly; Logasa's *Historical Fiction;* the book lists of the National Council for the Social Studies; the reading lists of the National Council of Teachers of English; and the current book review section of a good newspaper, such the *Christian Science Monitor*, the *New York Times*, or the *New York Herald Tribune*. The teacher should also consult the state-approved library list, if there is one in his state;

[1] All published by the American Library Association, Chicago.

and he should be a subscriber to *Social Education,* where he will find reviews and announcements each month of the new books in the social studies. In this particular situation, the knowledge of the expert librarian is added to the knowledge of the American history teacher; teacher and librarian thus produce jointly a well-balanced list of historical and biographical fiction which the library might work toward building up as a permanent service to the department of social studies for its students over a period of years. Only through such cooperative action and study on the part of librarians and teachers can books and other materials be carefully selected, supplied, and made easily available to students and teachers. Such materials can be used only when they are available.

In addition to the "Aids in Book Selection" given by Fargo,[2] the following book lists should be known to teachers on their respective teaching levels:

A Basic Book Collection: *For Elementary Grades* ⎫ Latest editions of the
For Junior High Schools ⎬ American Library
For High Schools ⎭ Association

Booklists of the Secondary Education Board.
Children's Catalog, of the H.W. Wilson Company, with its regular supplements.
Booklists of the National Council of Teachers of English.
Booklists of the National Council for the Social Studies.
Lists of books in the special bulletins of the Association for Childhood Education.

2. *The Materials Bureau*

A step forward in enlarging the service of the school library has been taken in some school systems by the formation of a bureau of materials of a rich and interesting nature. The Parker School District of Greenville, South Carolina, was one of the leaders in this movement.[3] The Materials Bureau for the Parker Schools served as a central distributing agency among the fifteen elementary schools and the high school in the district; it was located centrally, and had a weekly truck service for the distribution and collection of mate-

---

[2] *The Library in the School, op. cit.,* pp. 168–73.
[3] Sallie K. Mims, *The In-Service Program: Teachers of Parker School District,* 1948, *passim.*

rials. The bureau gathered a large store of books for units of work, of pictures, special books, posters, charts, maps, pamphlets, slides, stereographs, films and strip films, supplementary readers, and records of units of work. Under the direction of the trained librarian, this material was catalogued and filed appropriately in the bureau, primarily by means of the Dewey decimal system.

Both the teachers and the director of a materials bureau are always on the lookout for material coming out in pamphlet form and in periodicals which might help teachers and pupils. For example, the Eastern Air Lines printed an advertising feature called "Sky Pictures: the Story of a Great Airline"; this contained maps of the territory covered by the airline, a history of its formation and progress to date, valuable information on the men who run the planes and service them, aids to air navigation, the use of the radio in air transportation, and pictorial representations of aspects of air transportation. "Jets," a pictorial elementary booklet published by the National Aviation Education Council, is another illustration of material in pamphlet form. Although these brochures are primarily advertisements of air lines, they have valuable material of a source nature for children who are interested in learning more about this type of public transportation.

"CONSUMABLE" MATERIALS.   There are many illustrations of valuable materials which are printed in newspapers, magazines, and pamphlets, and which are frequently discarded by teachers after they have read them. Typical examples include the following: Goodyear Rubber Company advertisements upon the use of rubber and synthetic products in modern life; maps and charts of all kinds from daily newspapers and from weekly news and picture magazines; pamphlets and bulletins from the Metropolitan Life Insurance Company; advertisements and bulletins from the Association of American Railroads, the Aluminum Company of America, General Electric, Dupont, the Institute of Life Insurance, the Better Vision Institute, *Time*, and the *National Geographic Magazine;* and special guides for teachers published by the Motion Picture Association of America, by the radio network chains, General Mills, the American Iron and Steel Institute, the National Association of Manufacturers, the American Association of Advertising Agencies, and the publishers of encyclopedias and dictionaries.

Much of this material has a high propaganda content, since it is a form of advertising for a certain product or a certain line of business. On the other hand, the child and the adult are exposed at all times to such advertising, and it is part of the training which a child

FIG. 42   *The staff of the Materials Bureau checking in materials*
(Courtesy Parker (S.C.) School District.)

should receive in school to learn to analyze propaganda of this sort and to sift facts from unjustifiable claims. Teachers in many communities are overlooking some of the most valuable materials which they could be using for supplementary work, in that they frequently do not even investigate the huge concerns of national prominence which operate in their midst and which print a large amount of material concerning their business and its products. Many of the materials which would be filed in a materials bureau are also "consumable"; they are frequently of little value after a period of two or three years. That does not alter the fact that these materials are valuable, timely, and more accurate in many instances during the life of their use, even though they have to be discarded after use. These consumable items, pictures, and diagrams can be used in their original clippings or bulletin form, or they can be mounted on an inexpensive form of mounting board or cardboard; this makes them available when they are needed, and does not result in much waste when certain items have to be dispensed with after their period of usefulness is over.

TRENDS IN THE GROWTH OF MATERIALS BUREAUS. A variation of the type of service called the "materials bureau" is to be found in some schools, where the librarian and teachers work cooperatively to collect and classify these materials for a vertical file in the library. The librarian catalogues them and has them available for the use of teachers upon loan for periods ranging from a day to a week. The pictures, maps, charts, pamphlets, slides, and stereographs are distributed to a teacher for only two weeks and may not be renewed; but books which are to be used in units of work and which are available in sufficient number go out for periods as long as two to twelve weeks at a time.

There is distinctly a new trend toward broadening the services and facilities of the school library through some variation of the plan for a materials bureau. Some larger schools are building their own materials bureaus in a central location, and are attempting to service the whole system. Frequently stored, serviced, and distributed are slides, films, film strips, tape recordings, and other audio-visual materials and equipment. A newer trend since World War II has been the development of the film library or "audio-visual depository." In some places, the film library has been combined with the curriculum laboratory or the materials bureau, or both. On the other hand, in some smaller schools, classroom teachers on the elementary-school level have been encouraged to start building their own materials bureaus within their own homerooms; these teachers thus develop gradually over a period of years a tremendous amount of vertical file material for use on different units around which they build their work. Current and consumable materials which can be used effectively to supplement the textbook should be collected and catalogued properly in each school system; they should be serviced from either the library or a materials or audio-visual curriculum division, so that teachers may have access to many more aids than they have been able to obtain in the past.

3. *Curriculum Laboratories*

The development of the curriculum laboratory accompanied the movement for curriculum revision in public schools. The curriculum laboratory is a place where curriculum materials are gathered for use by the teachers in the school system. The materials in the laboratory may include such items as the following: (1) courses of study from other states and local school systems; (2) course-of-study-construction pamphlets and bulletins of all types; (3) courses of study developed within the local system; (4) source materials and units for the use of teachers within the system; and (5) textbooks and special books on various aspects of the curriculum. "Curriculum library" and "curriculum workshop" are other terms which are employed to describe the place where these teaching aids are made available. Although many states and communities have had curriculum laboratories for some time, the colleges and universities have gone into the development of this sort of organization rather extensively in recent years.[4]

TYPES. The curriculum laboratories vary in type. One type might be called a "library," in which curriculum materials of various kinds are stored for reference use by teachers. Another type is that in which curriculum materials have been assembled and then loaned to teachers for use in school units in other localities. The curriculum laboratory at Teachers College, Columbia University, was one of the first; under the direction of Bruner, it was for a time outstanding for its work in attempting to evaluate different kinds of courses of study over a period of years.[5] In other colleges, the laboratory is used as a practical workroom for teacher-candidates who are doing their practice teaching, or who are engaged in curriculum planning

[4] *Cf.* Francis L. Drag, "What Is a Curriculum Laboratory?" *Educational Leadership*, v (January, 1948), pp. 235–40; for earlier developments, read Bernice E. Leary, *Curriculum Laboratories and Divisions*, United States Office of Education, *Bulletin No. 7*, 1938, *passim.*

[5] H.B. Bruner, *et al.*, *What Our Schools Are Teaching*, Teachers College, Columbia University, 1941.

under professional guidance. Still other institutions use the curriculum laboratory as a center for curriculum planning for both in-service and summer school and workshop groups.

PURPOSES. All of these curriculum laboratories or special organizations are pointed primarily toward assisting the teacher-candidates or the teachers in training to do the following: (1) to become acquainted with the many types of curricular materials which are in existence; (2) to employ these materials wisely; (3) to develop their own materials which will further their own plans and experiments most adequately; and (4) to continue their growth. A slowly improving feature of curriculum laboratory work has been individual and group development of *source* materials of all types; it has been difficult for the teachers of teachers and for teachers themselves to get away from borrowing materials from other courses of study in other communities. Yet, it is seldom that a course of study which was prepared for a group of children in a school in one community can be adapted satisfactorily to the needs of another group of students and another teacher in another school.

Audio-visual Aids

Although audio-visual instruction has been used in teaching for centuries, it is only within the last three decades that the talking picture, the radio, television and the phonograph have been highly enough developed to expand this type of supplementary instruction enormously.

McKown and Roberts in earlier years and Edgar Dale more recently have led the way in compiling complete studies of audio-visual aids; [6] and they give valuable suggestions on the extent to which these aids can be employed effectively on the various grade levels and in the various subject-matter areas. They emphasize the utilization of audio-visual materials as *supplementary* instead of *substitutionary* aids to instruction; and they present exhaustive data on the selection, cost, and cooperative use of such aids in the school.

[6] H.C. McKown and A.B. Roberts, *Audio-Visual Aids to Instruction*, 1940 and 1949, New York, McGraw-Hill Book Company, and Edgar Dale, *Audio-Visual Methods in Teaching*, 1946 and rev. ed., 1954, New York, The Dryden Press.

The following is the list of the aids which they find most commonly employed in teaching:

Blackboard and bulletin board; duplicating devices; tack board or felt board and display.

Visual symbols: cartoons; drawings and sketches; posters; diagrams; flat maps; charts; graphs; comic strips; pictorial statistics.

Dramatics: pantomime; playlet; pageant; puppet shows; shadow play.

Still pictures: (1) flat photographs, prints, and postcards; (2) projected—opaque and daylight; slides—glass, cellophane, filmstrip, strip film, microprojection and microfilm; tachistoscope; (3) stereoscopes and stereographs.

Models and mockups: globes; objects; specimens; exhibits; museums; planetarium; demonstrations; dioramas; sand tables; miniatures and miniature sets; flash cards.

Motion pictures—silent and sound; television; films—educational, theatrical, documentary.

Phonographs and recorders: records, recordings, transcriptions.

Radio, television, dictaphone, loud speaker (public address and intercommunicating).

Trips, journeys, tours, visits, community study.

Certain aspects of visual aids are of such significance for curricular developments in the future that they will be considered briefly in the following paragraphs.

1. *The Motion Picture.* Since projectors and screens are now available in most schools, the educational uses to which the "still" movie or the talking motion picture may be put are broadened extensively. Many investigations have been made of the movies, and much material has been published on the subject of educational films. Many film libraries have been built up by schools for educational use on a system-wide basis. Colleges and state departments of education have instituted extension or service bureaus which rent films to schools that are unable to buy them. In general, two types of films are suitable for school use, the "educational" film and the "theatrical" film.

The educational film is prepared primarily for school use by private companies, the Federal government, or the school system. Good samples of films prepared by private concerns are "The Living Earth Series" [7] and "Alaska's Silver Millions" [8] on conservation. "The

[7] Encyclopaedia Britannica Films, Inc.
[8] American Can Company.

River," "Rain on the Plains," and "Forests Forever" are excellent educational films produced by the Federal government. Examples of theatrical films which are suitable for school use are "Little Women," "David Copperfield," "Helen of Troy," and "The Ten Commandments."

The teacher who wishes to supplement his curricular work with movies should certainly be familiar with the following regular sources of information concerning them:

Educational Film Guide and Filmstrip Guide of the H.W. Wilson Company, with its supplementary service, New York.

Educational Screen and *Audio-Visual Guide*, which includes each year the "Blue Book of Audio-Visual Materials," usually in the December issue, Educational Screen, Inc., Chicago.

Educators' Guide to Free Films, Educators' Guide to Free Slide-Films, and Educators' Guide to Free Tapes, Scripts, and Transcriptions, Educators' Progress Service, Randolph, Wisconsin (annual lists).

The News Letter, the Bureau of Educational Research, the Ohio State University, Columbus.

Two important principles should be followed in all educational work with motion pictures: (1) no film should be shown without careful preparation in advance by both teacher and pupil for the maximum benefit which might be derived from its showing; and (2) no teacher should select a theatrical film or commercial "short" for showing without first having seen the picture himself.

2. *The Radio and Television.* Through central program-distribution sound systems, the radio has now come to be generally accepted as an educational aid in schools. Electrical transcription and sound-recording devices have made it possible for a school to record broadcasts directly from the air, and to play these recorded programs at any time which seems appropriate. This teaching improvement bids fair to make radio one of the most valuable of supplementary educational aids, which it could not be until improved recording devices made possible this rebroadcasting of a program at the time and place that the class needed it. Now television has arrived to supplement the radio.

Much material has been published in the last decade in regard to the practical uses to which radio and television may be put in the schools. The Department of Elementary School Principals of the National Education Association published *The Audio-Visual Program in the Elementary School* in 1947–1948. The Department of Classroom Teachers and the American Educational Research Association followed with *Audio-Visual Instruction* in 1957. These bulletins include such topics as radio and TV in the schools, the use of radio and TV in education, classroom use of broadcasts, how to make successful school broadcasts, pupil growth through radio use, recordings, kinesthetic materials, radio and music education, and the educational evaluation of radio and TV programs.

At times educational journals devote an entire issue to audio-visual aids, or to radio and television; "Audio-Visual Aids in the Secondary Schools" is an example.[9] Suggestive radio and television series for schools are available from publishers; *This Is Educational Television*[10] and *Teaching Through Radio and Television*[11] are good examples of these series for teachers and school employees. *Television in Education,* a recent publication of the U.S. Department of Health, Education, and Welfare, explains the possibilities of this new medium, with ways of enriching school programs in science, languages, and other fields.[12] *The Public Opinion Quarterly*[13] has always devoted part of its space to the radio, its development, and possible usages, and to the other mass media of communication.

Ohio State University was a pioneer in the effort to use the radio with the curriculum (1929).[14] Wisconsin's School of the Air with its programs throughout the school year has offered for years a good example of coordination of the radio with the curriculum in various subjects and studies. In addition to audio-visual centers at colleges and state departments of education, the Joint Council on Educational Television stimulates TV education. The large radio networks, such as Columbia and the National Broadcasting Company, make recordings and transcriptions of outstanding radio and

[9] *The High School Journal,* xl (March, 1957), No. 6.
[10] By W.K. Cumming, Michigan State College, Department of Journalism, 1954.
[11] By W.B. Levenson and E. Stasheff, New York, Rinehart and Company, 1952.
[12] *Bulletin,* 1957, No. 21.
[13] Princeton University Press, Princeton.
[14] Ohio School of the Air.

television programs and songs, which may be secured for use in schools.

Other Types of Audio-Visual Aids. In addition to the representative lists of sources and material and equipment, given by McKown and Roberts [15] and Dale,[16] and other writers, *Educators' Guide to Free Films* and *Elementary Teachers Guide to Free Curriculum Materials* [17] are valuable for the teacher. Of similar types are *Free and Inexpensive Learning Materials.*[18]

"Picture Fact Books" present another kind of visual instruction. Earlier series of these books included the series by Alice Keliher and her associates [19] and the pictorial study units of *Building America.*[20] The technique of the picture fact book has been adopted universally by the textbook publishers; it is found most frequently in textbooks for the primary grade levels, where the story is told in whole or in great part in pictures.

SOURCE MATERIALS AND AIDS

When the teacher comes to consider and appraise source materials, he is confronted with the task of sifting those which are most valuable from the great mass of materials which are available.[21] These materials fall naturally into four groups, as follows:

1. *Textbooks and General Reference Books.* Textbooks for use in school classes are many, and they vary widely in their organization and content. It is not unusual to discover on the desk of a good

[15] H.C. McKown and A.B. Roberts, *Audio-Visual Aids to Instruction* (2nd ed.), *op. cit.*, Chap. XVI.

[16] Edgar Dale, *Audio-Visual Methods in Teaching* (rev. ed), *op. cit.*, Parts II–III.

[17] Educators' Progress Service, Randolph, Wisconsin. These lists are revised annually.

[18] Division of Surveys and Field Services, George Peabody College for Teachers, Nashville, Tennessee (published periodically).

[19] Published at various times by Harper and Brothers, Hinds, Hayden and Eldredge, and Johnson Publishing Company, 1940 to 1946.

[20] Association for Supervision and Curriculum Development, National Education Association, Washington.

[21] Throughout this volume carefully selected source materials of this type have been given in the bibliographies at the end of each chapter. These will not be repeated here, but the reader is advised to consult them for specific source materials on the various aspects of the curriculum.

teacher many different textbooks in the area in which he is teaching. Such a variety furnishes to him and to his students supplementary materials of a well-illustrated nature which are valuable in many ways.

2. *Government Publications (Federal and State).* The Federal government prints a tremendous number of works of a source nature, and many of these can be of great help to the teacher and the pupil in their work. In like manner, most states issue publications concerning such topics as conservation, fire protection, farming, labor, and industries. Which of these publications can be used effectively by the children on the elementary-school level? Which can be used by those on the secondary-school level? Which can be used by teachers? These questions point to the fact that teachers need some help in the selection of materials which they can use to enrich their work.

Certain standard publications are sources to assist the teacher materially in such a selective process. *United States' Government Publications* [22] furnishes an invaluable guide to teachers and librarians on how to acquire and use government publications. It is the only book which discusses in comprehensive fashion all types of government publications, and their classification and availability. It also includes information on maps and on technical and departmental publications.

Of another type is *Independent Commissions in the Federal Government.*[23] This book presents studies of the Interstate Commerce Commission, the Federal Communications Commission, the Security and Exchange Commission, the Federal Power Commission, the Federal Trade Commission, the National Bituminous Coal Commission, the National Labor Relations Board, the United States Maritime Commission, the Board of Governors of the Federal Reserve System, the Employees' Compensation Commission, the Social Security Board, the National Mediation Board, and the United States Tariff Commission. Especially valuable to the teacher are the explanations of the powers and duties of these independent commissions in the national government. Supplementing and bring-

---

[22] By A.M. Boyd and R.E. Rips, New York, H.W. Wilson Company, 1949.
[23] By Wilson K. Doyle, University of North Carolina Press, 1939.

ing one up-to-date on these commissions and government publications is *The United States Government Organization Manual*. It is the official handbook of the Federal government, published annually. It includes information on the branches of the government, on the quasi-official agencies, and a list of representative publications of agencies and departments of the Federal government.

Special bulletins or leaflets on government publications and their use are issued from time to time by the United States Office of Education.

In regard to the publications of state governments, the *Monthly Checklist of State Publications* of the United States Library of Congress is very valuable; it gives the titles and summarizes the contents of those state publications which it receives. Sometimes the teacher and the librarian have to secure the pamphlets or publications themselves and examine them to determine their value for effective schoolroom use. Like the publications of the Federal government, many of these state publications may be of help to the teacher, but they may be too difficult for pupils to use effectively. Valuable materials of a source nature are found in many of the state "Guides" which have been published. The "Rivers of America" series and the "American Lake" series are other valuable resource materials for both the teacher and the pupil.[24]

3. *Source Materials of Special Educational Groups.* These types are usually prepared by experts in the field of education, and they are pointed particularly toward practical problems with which teachers are confronted in the classroom. These source materials are generally a part of the educational service which is given to those teachers who affiliate themselves with the various local, state, regional, and national groups which are engaged in the same type of work which they themselves are doing. The materials can be grouped under three divisions: (1) yearbooks; (2) bulletins and special reports; and (3) professional magazines or periodicals.

Professional educational organizations which publish annually one or more of these types of materials include the following:

American Association for Adult Education
American Association of School Administrators

[24] Consult the bibliography at the end of this chapter.

American Classical League
American Council on Education
American Educational Research Association
American Personnel and Guidance Association
Association for Childhood Education
Association for Supervision and Curriculum Development
The Council of State Governments
Department of Audio-Visual Instruction of the National Education Association
Department of Classroom Teachers of the National Education Association
Department of Elementary School Principals of the National Education Association
Department of Rural Education of the National Education Association
Educational Policies Commission of the National Education Association and the American Association of School Administrators
Joint Committee on Educational Television
National Association of Secondary-School Principals
National Council for the Social Studies
National Council of Teachers of English
National Council of Teachers of Mathematics
National Education Association
National Science Teachers Association
National Society for the Study of Education
National Vocational Guidance Association
State Education Associations
United States Atomic Energy Commission
United States Office of Education

Membership in most of these professional bodies usually brings to the member the magazine or periodical published by the group. It frequently gives the member special reports, bulletins, and year-books without additional charge.

4. *Source Materials Issued by Private Groups and Businesses.* Many of the source materials issued privately are discussed at length in the two succeeding chapters. An example of one of the best and most extensive groups of publications of this kind is furnished by the Public Affairs Pamphlets, prepared and published for more than twenty years by the Public Affairs Committee, Inc. These pamphlets are revised frequently and kept up-to-date. For example, there were more than 100 titles in this series in 1958, dealing with the following areas of American life and affairs: *Social Prob-*

lems, Family Relations, Health and Science, and *Intergroup Relations.*

Of the types of materials printed by private businesses and concerns, "Quiz" on railroads and railroading by the Association of American Railroads, and the materials of the Better Vision Institute are samples. The *New York Times* frequently publishes aids to teachers for the use of this newspaper in social-studies classes, while the Motion Picture Association of America issues study outlines of motion pictures for the use of teachers and pupils. In the area of the weekly news magazines, both *Time* and *Newsweek* issue special classroom editions for school use. Among the monthly magazines, the *Atlantic* is an illustration of one which supplies special study plans for its use by high-school students.

In attempting to use these supplementary materials which are issued by private businesses, the only safe procedure for the teacher is to write for them, examine them, and then make use of them or not as his judgment dictates.

PRINCIPLES FOR THE USE OF CURRICULAR AIDS

The writers in the field of audio-visual education have set forth repeatedly in detail the precautions which should be taken for the proper use of audio-visual aids.[25] Only when definite principles are followed will the employment of extracurricular aids be most effective. The following principles are suggested for the guidance of the teacher:

The aid must suit the age level and experience of the pupil.

The aid must bring realities to the pupil.

The aid must build upon the pupil's previous experience.

The introduction of the aids should be carefully prepared for in advance by the teacher and by the pupil through study and investigation.

The aids must contribute to the learning process; they must not be allowed to become substitutes for it.

The aid should take up a reasonable amount of time.

The use of more than one aid at the same time is of doubtful value.

[25] For example, consult H.C. McKown and A.B. Roberts, *Audio-Visual Aids to Instruction* (2nd ed.), New York, McGraw-Hill Book Co., 1949, Chaps. II–III; and Edgar Dale, *Audio-Visual Methods in Teaching* (rev. ed.), New York, The Dryden Press, 1954, pp. 57–105.

The effectiveness of the use of the aids should be evaluated by both teacher and pupils.

The use of aids should be well balanced, with one type of aid being used at one time and another at another.

The aids must give an air of reality, not an artificial setting which cannot be understood by the pupils.

The objectives of instruction in each case must have been determined in advance before the aids will be of maximum value to the learner.

Aids must be used which take into account the differences in children, where one pupil sees a relationship much more quickly than another, and yet all pupils see some relationship.

Attention should be called to the fact that inexpensive aids can be just as effective at times as the more expensive types. For example, the student-constructed water wheel can illustrate certain principles of physics just as well as the more expensive model. Excursion trips to observe some activity at first hand do not always have to be long and costly. For some purposes, stereopticon pictures can be as effective as a more expensive kind of aid.

As each teacher develops his teaching techniques and plans, he should be adding to his store of curricular aids month by month and year by year; he should file these either in his own classroom or in the library. Only through experiencing can the teacher actually develop that habit of keeping "on the lookout" for new and valuable materials as aids to instruction.

PROBLEMS FOR INDIVIDUAL STUDY
AND CLASS DISCUSSION

1. What new books in your teaching field have been published in the last year which will be valuable for you as source materials in your teaching? Give reasons for your choices.

2. Assume that you plan to show the educational film, "The River," to your class. What advance preparation should you and your group undertake before it is shown?

3. In what ways can the blackboard be used as a visual aid? The bulletin board? The textbook? Illustrate.

4. Should such a newspaper as the *New York Times* be available in an elementary-school library? *Life?* Why or why not?

5. Which of the Public Affairs Pamphlets do you believe should be in your secondary-school library? Give reasons for choices.

6. What types of commercial radio broadcasts would you deem it wise to record and reproduce for class work? State specific programs, and give reasons for your selections.

7. Should a school which has a modern moving picture sound machine present commercial (theatrical) films once a week to its student body, charging admission? Support your position.

8. How would you go about the wise selection of United States government publications for your secondary-school library? For your elementary-school library?

9. What implications for your curriculum work did you obtain from your reading of *Teaching Through Radio and Television* or *This Is Educational Television?*

10. What stimulation might be given to the teachers of your school if a curriculum laboratory or curriculum library were established for their use?

11. Should the school librarian be responsible for the storing, distribution, and care of such audio-visual materials as stereographs and the stereoscope, the movie projector and films and film strips, maps and charts, slides and pictures? Give reasons for your point of view.

12. What fifty educational films would you list as valuable for use in both secondary-school and elementary-school work?

13. What standards can you mention which would enable you to decide definitely when a historical novel or a biography is true to the era and characters that it presents?

14. From current television programs, which would you select for use in your science classes? English classes? Social Studies' work? Why?

ADDITIONAL ANNOTATED REFERENCES
FOR PROBLEM OR UNIT STUDY

"American Commonwealth Series."
    In this series reputable authors describe the administration and government of particular states. Already published are those on Florida, Mississippi, New York, North Carolina, and Wyoming; in preparation are those on Georgia, Iowa, Montana, and Ohio.
"American Lake" Series, published by Bobbs-Merrill Company; good examples are *Lake Superior, Lake Champlain* and *Lake George, The Great Salt Lake*, and *Lake Okeechobee.*
American Library Association, Chicago.
    Important reading lists are:
    By Way of Introduction (2nd ed.) (recreational reading list for high school)

Periodicals for Small and Medium-sized Libraries ⎤
Subject Index to Books for Intermediate Grades,
   First Supplement ⎥ Latest
Subject Index to Books for Primary Grades, ⎥ Editions
   First Supplement ⎦

America's Education Press, N.E.A., Washington.

A classified list of educational periodicals in all subject-matter and educational fields. Issued annually.

Arbuthnot, M.H., *Children and Books* (rev. ed.), Chicago, Scott, Foresman and Company, 1957.

Well known and up-to-date, comprehensive guide to children's literature for teachers. Includes also the role of television, radio, movies, and comics in childrens' lives.

Birkmaier, E.M. (Ed.), *Illustrative Learning Experiences*, Minneapolis, University of Minnesota Press, 1952.

Illustrative subject-matter and experience teaching units in various high-school subjects.

Callahan, J.W., *Television in School, College, and Community*, New York, McGraw-Hill Book Company, 1953.

The book describes education by television in elementary, junior high, senior high schools, and colleges for children and adults; includes programming and TV writing production techniques.

Corbett, J.F., *et al.*, *Current Affairs in Modern Education*, New York, the *New York Times*, 1950.

A survey of the methods of teaching of current events in the schools of the nation.

Cronbach, L.J. (Ed.), *Text Materials in Modern Education*, Urbana, University of Illinois Press, 1955.

Explains the place and purpose of text materials, and text production, selection, and use.

Douglas, M.P., *The Teacher-Librarian's Handbook* (2nd ed.), Chicago, American Library Association, 1949.

Long a standard resource for the teacher who is also the librarian on organization and management.

East, M., *Display for Learning*, New York, The Dryden Press, 1952.

Shows how to make and use visual materials; is especially good in its suggestions for poor schools which have to produce their own.

Everett, S., and Arndt, C.O., *Teaching World Affairs in American Schools*, New York, Harper and Brothers, 1956.

A case book that shows what schools in the U.S. are offering in their courses on world affairs, and how they are doing it, on various grade levels, in school and out-of-school activities and in communities through adult education.

Falconer, V.M., *Filmstrips*, New York, McGraw-Hill Book Company, 1948.
A descriptive index and user's guide up to that date.

Haas, K.B., and Packer, H.G., *Preparation and Use of Audio-Visual Aids* (3rd ed.), New York, Prentice-Hall, 1955.
A recent revision of a sound text in the audio-visual field, with emphasis upon "home-made" materials.

Hubbell, R., *Television: Programming and Production* (3rd ed.), New York, Rinehart and Company, 1956.
Presents the nature and characteristics of television, the theatre, motion pictures, and radio in relation to TV, the camera, video technique, the audio, and programming. There is a good historical sketch of television's growth from 1945 to 1956.

Kieffer, R. de, and Cochran, L.W., *Manual of Audio-Visual Techniques*, New York, Prentice-Hall, 1955.
A good handbook for the teacher and curriculum worker.

Kinder, J.S., *Audio-Visual Materials and Techniques*, New York, American Book Company, 1950.
Modern theory and practice in the use of the newer and more varied materials of audio-visual instruction.

National Education Association, Washington.
American Association of School Administrators: the 29th Yearbook, 1951, is devoted to *Conservation Education in American Schools,* and a revision of another is on *Health in Schools;* they give examples of practices and promising programs.

American Educational Research Association and Department of Classroom Teachers, N.E.A., "What Research Says to the Teacher": pamphlets on reading, writing, spelling, mathematics, science, and other aspects of curricular work.

Association for Supervision and Curriculum Development: this group is a continuing source of curriculum materials, bibliographies and special studies or reports valuable for the teacher. Especially valuable are its annual lists of recent curriculum materials and selected bibliographies for curriculum workers.

Department of Elementary School Principals: the 35th Yearbook, *Instructional Materials for Elementary Schools,* 1956, describes the selection, use, and management of various kinds of materials.

National Association of Secondary School Principals: the Association has sponsored recently (with the Better Business Bureau) teaching-learning units in economic education, produced by the Council for Advancement of Secondary Education. This "Economic Literacy Series," just getting under way, has produced already *Economics in the Press, Key Understandings in Economics,* and *Modern Capitalism, an Introduction for Young Citizens.*

National Council for the Social Studies: the 18th Yearbook, 1947, is devoted to *Audio-Visual Materials and Methods in the Social Studies.*
National Society for the Study of Education, Chicago.

48th Yearbook, Part I, 1949, *Audio-Visual Materials of Instruction;* audio-visual instruction up to that date.

53rd Yearbook, Part II, 1954, *Mass Media and Education;* gives the investigator more recent data and developments in regard to the motion picture, the press, television, and other forms.

Perry, G.S., *Cities of America*, New York, McGraw-Hill Book Company, 1947.

A type of good resource material.

Peterson, T., *Magazines in the Twentieth Century*, Urbana, University of Illinois Press, 1956.

The book covers the major trends in the magazine industry since 1900 and attempts to identify the economic and social forces that helped to shape them and their impact on our society.

Resources for Citizenship, Citizenship Education Project, Teachers College, Columbia University, 1955.

A guide to selection of teaching materials, containing annotations of more than 700 books, pamphlets, and audio-visual materials.

Resource Units.

Good samples can be examined in "Consumer Education Series" (1945–1948), units for high-school students, and "The Living Democracy Series" (1955–1957), of the Tufts Civic Education Center (resource pamphlets), both series sponsored by the National Association of Secondary-School Principals, N.E.A.

"Economic Life Series," teachers' guides, prepared by the National Council for the Social Studies, N.E.A., with teaching aids.

Hanna, L., *et al.*, *Unit Teaching in the Elementary School*, New York, Rinehart and Company, 1955.

Lurry, L.L., and Alberty, E.J., *Developing a High School Core Program*, New York, The Macmillan Company, 1957.

Noar, G., *The Junior High School—Today and Tomorrow*, New York, Prentice-Hall, 1953.

Quillen, I.J., and Hanna, L.A., *Education for Social Competence*, Chicago, Scott, Foresman and Company, 1948.

"Rivers of America" Series, published by Rinehart and Company (formerly Farrar and Rinehart); such rivers as the Tennessee, the Chicago, the Missouri, and Powder are good samples.

Sands, L.B., *Audio-Visual Procedures in Teaching*, New York, The Ronald Press Company, 1956.

Gives a description and understanding of the different audio-visual methods for each educational level.

Saylor, J.G., and Alexander, W.M., *Curriculum Planning*, New York, Rinehart and Company, 1954.

Chapter XIV treats of selection and use of resources for the curriculum, with a specially good section on use of resource personnel of all kinds.

Siepmann, C.A., *TV and Our School Crisis*, New York, Dodd, Mead and Company, 1958.

Treats of television's birth, role in the schools, channels of communication, and findings and opinions on its use in a time of educational crisis.

Sources of Free and Inexpensive Materials, Chicago, Field Enterprises, 1955.

A source list for teachers, librarians, and school personnel; it is indexed both by *sources* and by *subject index.*

State "Guide" Series.

There are many of these, published from time to time. Earlier State Guides were published more frequently by Oxford University Press, Dodd, Mead and Company, Harcourt, Brace and Company, and the Viking Press. Later ones seem to be published more generally by the University presses.

Stimpson, G.A., *A Book About a Thousand Things*, New York, Harper and Brothers, 1946.

A sample of a modern resource book of a new type.

U.S. Government Printing Office.

Bulletin 1951, No. 21 of the Office of Education, is *3434 U.S. Government Films*. Includes motion pictures, filmstrips, sets of slides available for public use. Each item is annotated.

Wittich, W.A., and Schuller, C.F., *Audio-Visual Materials*, New York, Harper and Brothers, 1953.

Deals with the nature and use of audio-visual materials of various kinds and gives case examples of their use and source lists.

PART SIX   Looking
to the future
in curriculum revision

CHAPTER 19 Propaganda
and the curriculum

PROBLEMS OF INDOCTRINATION AND PROPAGANDA

THE ISSUES INVOLVED. Should the schools teach propaganda analysis? Should the teachers indoctrinate children in democracy? Is it possible to teach democracy effectively to students through the curriculum as it is organized at present?

After a cursory consideration of these questions, both the typical citizen and the typical educator answer "Yes"; but a more careful examination of the problems of propaganda and indoctrination reveals many difficulties. When the teacher starts to teach propaganda analysis or to indoctrinate his pupils, certain complicating factors not obvious at the start become increasingly apparent and even more complex as the attempt is made to achieve these aims. For example, may propaganda be *good* as well as *bad?* To what extent shall teacher and pupils go into the workings of private and public pressure groups? Can democracy be taught without a natural situation in which to practice its principles? If indoctrination for democracy is proper, where shall the line be drawn in regard to religious and racial questions? How deeply should the class go into national and international propaganda, aspects which the use of television and the radio has made potentially more powerful? What devices are used by propagandists to further their causes, and into how much detail should the teacher go to make students aware of the techniques of propagandists?

The extent to which pupils should be indoctrinated, or exposed to indoctrination, is an issue which has been heatedly discussed for years. An illustration of evidence of this dispute was furnished by the furor over the examination of social-studies textbooks used in the schools, which was sponsored by the National Association of Manufacturers in 1940–1941. The abstracts of these textbooks, which were made during this examination, emphasized important points of view related to American government and the business system.[1]

Another issue must now be added to this perennial issue of indoctrination in the schools, namely, *the teaching of propaganda analysis*. Propaganda analysis is closely related to indoctrination, especially on the level of the secondary school. Courses in propaganda analysis have slipped in through the back door of the curriculum, so to speak, under the head of "Consumer Economics," "Consumer Education," and "Socio-Business." This trend toward consumer education for youth of secondary-school age has been encouraged by the increasing number of special textbooks which have been published for juvenile consumption and for schoolroom reading.

WHAT IS PROPAGANDA? Propaganda is an effort to "put something across," whether it be for good or evil. As commonly understood, propaganda is "any organized movement for promoting particular doctrines or principles." If its Latin origin is held to closely, the word carries strongly with it the idea of multiplying, propagating, growing. According to this definition, propaganda automatically becomes the world's biggest business, for advertising, and advertisements of all descriptions fall into the class of legitimate propaganda. To advertise means to call to public attention, particularly by printed or spoken announcement. Advertisements are used to "put across" to others the products, businesses, plans, campaigns, and programs of an individual or a group. Hence, courses in consumer education have to deal with an analysis of advertising, in order that the student may become trained for intelligent purchasing. This is but another way of saying that courses in consumer education must contain an impartial analysis of propaganda, because advertising is but one of the many types of propaganda.

In the secondary school, the teacher is confronted with the problem of another type of propaganda analysis in such courses as "Civics," "Citizenship," "Problems of Democracy," "Sociology," "Contemporary Problems of Youth," and "Public Affairs." In what

[1] *Cf.* Chap. 8 for an analysis of this and later controversies.

ways can the normal and legitimate operation of pressure groups in a democracy be fairly presented? It is not as difficult to show the significance of the pressure of political party organizations as it is to make a fair and impartial study of business and partisan pressure groups which operate through well-planned lobbies to attain their own promotion and advancement.

WHAT PRINCIPLES SHOULD TEACHERS APPLY TO PROPAGANDA ANALYSIS AND INDOCTRINATION? The satisfactory solution to the closely related problems of propaganda analysis and indoctrination in curriculum work requires intensive study, wide reading, and a truly constructive attitude on the part of the teacher. Most of the school courses which deal with problems of propaganda and indoctrination are newcomers to the curriculum, such as "Modern Problems" and "Problems of American Democracy." "Civics" is an illustration of an existing course which has been broadened to include aspects of propaganda and indoctrination. Under the circumstances, it is not strange that many teachers are at a loss to know how to proceed, and how far they should go in a study of highly controversial issues; teacher education usually has not prepared them to do this work effectively and fairly. Teacher-candidates in some institutions for teacher training are even advised to leave controversial matters entirely out of their curricular activities.

Propaganda analysis and indoctrination in the school curriculum should not be attempted at all unless they are handled wisely. Such wise treatment must include the following:

1. Careful advance study and mastery by the teacher of all aspects of the issue, both good and evil.
2. A critical, tolerant, constructive attitude on the part of the teacher toward the problem under investigation; this is necessary if the pupils are to develop this same kind of attitude.
3. The subordination of all personal, racial, religious, and other emotional prejudices to an impartial consideration of the issue at hand.
4. A method of approach which will gain the cooperation and approval of local and national pressure groups rather than their antagonism.
5. Evaluation of the outcomes of the work primarily in the form of group and individual solutions to actual problems in a natural, experiential situation; outcomes should not be evaluated primarily on the basis of *knowledges* acquired from books.

SAMPLES OF PROPAGANDA ANALYSIS IN TEACHING

In order that teachers may realize the dangers as well as the possibilities involved in teaching propaganda analysis, two illustrations commonly found in secondary-school courses are presented in the detail with which a teacher should be familiar before he begins work in the classroom.

Illustration I. Consumer Education: Advertising as an Example

Advertising means calling to public attention, especially by printed or oral announcement. It is *paid* publicity, and it is usually labeled as such so that people can know and recognize it. Advertisements are of many kinds and are presented in many ways.

1. *Through the Press.* Perhaps the most powerful medium of advertising today is the press. The press is not to be confused with the editorship, which is obviously inspired by ownership and control, especially in instances of large newspaper chains. Approximately 75 per cent of all newspaper income is derived from advertising and 25 per cent from sales and subscriptions. Thus it is seen that newspapers are no longer only news organs; they are big business enterprises as well. The magazine which does not carry any advertisements is a rarity; professional, trade, and popular periodicals support themselves to a large extent by carrying advertising of various kinds.

Investigations and reports from time to time by the Federal Trade Commission have shown that certain advertisements are forthrightly untruthful or, at least, misleading.[2] Yet the public is largely dependent upon advertising in order to keep abreast of changes in the production and sale of articles. The shrewd consumer will not allow the campaign to "debunk" advertising to cause him

[2] For good samples of earlier studies, *cf.* T.S. Harding, *The Joy of Ignorance*, New York, William Godwin, Inc., 1932; James Rorty, *Our Master's Voice: Advertising*, New York, The John Day Company, 1934; and Blake Clark, *The Advertising Smoke Screen*, New York, Harper and Brothers, 1944. A good example of periodic reports from the Federal Trade Commission was that printed generally as a news article by most papers on October 10, 1958, setting up a new set of rules for distinguishing between legal advertising and fictitious bargain claims.

to lose faith in *all* advertisements. In the final analysis, brands or trade names are as reputable and substantial as the companies which own them.

FEDERAL AND STATE LEGISLATION RELATING TO ADVERTISING. The exposés of advertising rackets in America have undoubtedly had an influence upon the eventual passage by Congress of two laws which affect vitally this type of propaganda. One of these laws is the Food, Drug, and Cosmetics law, enacted in 1938. No food to be sold in interstate commerce can now be misbranded; likewise, no poisonous cosmetics or those usually injurious can be sold across state lines. If any drug is to be shipped from one state into another, it either must meet standard specifications established by the Department of Agriculture or must bear a label to show how it deviates from those standards. The drug section of the act is rather inclusive, because it provides protection for the buyer by means of labels regarding use, misuse, danger, deterioration, and percentages of ingredients.

The second Federal law relates to false advertising. The Federal Trade commission was the outgrowth of a demand by manufacturers for protection from unfair types of competition. Complaints about unfair practices in restraint of trade are administered by this commission. The amendment to this Act in 1938 provided for Federal jurisdiction over false advertising. It is now unlawful for an advertiser to circulate false advertising to persuade one to buy foods, drugs, cosmetics, or other goods, or to take part in any other unfair means of competition. The Federal Trade Commission has the power to investigate complaints, call hearings, institute cease and desist orders, and bring legal action.

Both of these Federal acts apply only to products manufactured for interstate trade. Twenty-five states have passed excellent laws against dishonest advertising.[3] Seventeen of the remaining states have relatively ineffective laws about false advertising, and six states have no laws of this type. In general, the evidence shows that

[3] Alabama, Colorado, Idaho, Illinois, Indiana, Iowa, Kansas, Kentucky, Louisiana, Michigan, Minnesota, Missouri, Nebraska, Nevada, New Jersey, New York, North Dakota, Ohio, Oklahoma, Oregon, Rhode Island, Virginia, Washington, Wisconsin, and Wyoming. The famous *Printers' Ink Statute* was the model for these state statutes.

thirty-eight states have statutes forbidding dishonest advertisements in practically any form concerning securities, merchandise, and service. In contrast to this apparently healthy situation, tangible evidence is lacking on whether these state laws are being enforced. Thus, the buyer is thrown back upon his own judgment as to what should be accepted and what should be rejected in this type of propaganda called *advertising*.

A recent and careful check of the metropolitan papers has shown that the Federal Trade Commission is active in its work against false advertising. An examination of the Food and Drug Administration's notices of judgment proves that this Federal agency likewise is enforcing the regulations against the misbranding and adulteration of foods, drugs, and cosmetics. By agreement when possible, and by legal action when necessary, these commissions are forcing honesty in advertising and in labeling certain products for interstate trade. When a person buys a candy bar now, he will usually find its ingredients stated on the wrapper; if he does not find such a statement, he would perhaps be wise to choose another brand.

TYPES OF ADVERTISING THROUGH THE PRESS. In spite of rapidly growing competition from radio and television, the newspaper is still the largest and the most effective agency for advertising. Free advertising may be given through the editorial columns, in the "Letters to the Editor" section, or in expository news articles presumably of public news interest. Paid advertising is generally found in the form of classified advertising. A few popular magazines almost rival the newspaper in their amount of paid advertising. The *Saturday Evening Post, Parents' Magazine, Good Housekeeping, Life,* and many other magazines are of this type.

Paid advertising is admittedly legal, both in the sense that it is allowed by statute and in the sense that it is generally accepted and approved. The question whether propaganda of this type is of genuine public service has stimulated the consumer education movement.

ADVERTISING "SEALS"; THE WORK OF THE AMERICAN MEDICAL ASSOCIATION. Seals of "acceptance" or "approval" are now found frequently on advertised products. Among the groups issuing such seals are *Good Housekeeping* and *Parents' Magazine,* the National

Retail Dry Goods Association through its Better Fabrics Testing Bureau, and the Better Hosiery Council.

The American Medical Association was a leader in this movement. Its Councils on Pharmacy and Chemistry, on Physical Medicine, and on Foods and Nutrition started the practice of issuing "Seals of Acceptance" of products or devices which conformed to the rules and regulations and general decisions of the councils. For example, the Councils on Foods and Nutrition, established in 1929, had as one of its main purposes the prevention of false advertising of food products. This body, as a general practice, will not consider individual brands of natural foods, such as eggs, fresh vegetables, and butter. Nor will it consider fundamental bakery products, sausage, carbonated drinks, dyes for food coloring, ice cream products, condiments and sauces, candy for which no health claims are made, plain salt, chemicals used in the preparation of food, or tomato juice bottled and distributed by dairies. It will review and report on these products as to their nutritional claims when it is considered best for the public interest to do so. The seal of acceptance used to be for a two-year period. During the early 1950's, they discontinued the issuance of "seals of acceptance." However, the Council continues to review claims made for foods; these reviews are reported in *Today's Health* from the A.M.A.'s Bureau of Health Education and in advertisements in the magazine.

For many years, the American Medical Association has led the fight for the protection of the public against quack medicines, and it has championed more stringent regulation of advertising to effect this protection. It has confined itself to the fields of medicines, drugs, and foods, areas in which it is the highest authority. From time to time it issues special publications along these lines, such as *Accepted Foods, General Decisions on Foods and Food Advertising,* and *Official Rules* of the Councils. If any consumer is interested in an article or product in the areas in which the councils of the American Medical Association pass judgment, an inquiry to the council which deals with that product will bring a prompt response and an unbiased opinion.

WHAT SEALS MEAN. Here is what the "Commendation Seal" of *Parents' Magazine* means. Their technical staff and/or consultants in medicine have studied the products and the claims made for them. They employ a well-known testing company on a yearly retainer basis to do what testing is necessary. Its Consumer Service Bureau awards the "seal" only after their investigations show that the product is as advertised.

When a study group or a consumer wishes to know definitely what a certain seal signifies, inquiry should be made directly to the agency which issues it. If the agency or company refuses to comply with the request, or places obstacles in the way of discovering the truth, it should be distrusted and its seals viewed with suspicion.

CONSUMER ORGANIZATIONS AND PUBLICATIONS. There are many organizations and publications which assist in the study of advertising and consumer education. They range all the way from consumer groups and counsel established in the Federal government to professedly nonprofit, private organizations with all sorts of testing facilities.

An illustration of the nonprofit type of private organization is the Consumers' Union, which is a nonprofit membership organization designed to furnish consumers with information and a guidance-in-buying service. It employs many of its own technicians and also uses the services of numerous consultants. This organization tests various products and gives purportedly an unbiased report and rating of each of those tested. Thousands of members pay an annual fee each year for Consumers' Union information. *Consumer Reports,* its monthly publication which rates products, is sold at newsstands. Of the same general type as Consumers' Union is Consumers' Research, an older and more conservative organization. Its monthly magazine is *Consumer Bulletin,* available only to subscribing members. *Popular Science Monthly* also has a regular feature on "Consumer News" or "Shopping Reports."

Among the books on consumer education, *Your Life in the Country* [4] is particularly attractive. A textbook on consumer education for students in rural schools, it is rich in ideas and types of information, as well as in reference sources and materials. Another approach is exemplified by the "Consumer Education Series" of the Consumer Education Study. This series has ten teaching-learning units for

[4] Effie G. Bathurst, New York, McGraw-Hill Book Company, 1948.

high-school students on advertising, standards and labels, consumer credit, investing in life insurance, health, leisure time, education, managing money, and the consumer and the law.[5]

A full picture of the vast power of the press for advertising propaganda cannot be presented without some reference to the unique possibilities of new inventions, such as the telephoto, the use of more than one color in advertising, and the growth of comic sections in various publications. The picture newsmagazine, with its possibilities for propaganda, is as much in its infancy now as the first tabloid (the *Daily News*) was some thirty-five years ago. *Life, Look,* and a host of other picture news-magazines led the way for the widespread use of the picture magazine or brochure for "putting over" an idea. More widespread use of these facilities in publications will probably increase the power of the press for propagandizing, in spite of the competition which TV and radio will continue to offer.

2. *Through the Radio and Television.* An infant in 1920, radio, with the help of its relative, TV, has now grown to the size of a giant. Like electricity and nuclear energy, the uses to which it may be harnessed are just being realized. As man taps its possib'lities, the existing social order of the world as it is known today may be changed so as to be unrecognizable tomorrow. For example, history will probably record that Hitler was the first man to use the radio to maximum advantage on both a national and an international scale.

ADVERTISING AS THE BASIS OF THE RADIO-TV INDUSTRY. Advertising practically supports the TV-radio industry in the United States. In contrast to this situation here, the governments of the other large nations of the world largely subsidize their telecasting and broadcasting. A British lecturer who was speaking before the American Association of School Administrators several years ago presented clearly the results of radio control in the two countries. When he had his first listening experience over the American radio, he stated that he was irritated (as many Americans still are) by the constant interruptions advertising everything "from soup to nuts." After a time, however, he began to conclude that there was something vigorous and youthfully vital about American radio programs; in

[5] National Association of Secondary-School Principals, 1945–1948.

contrast to those of his own England, they gave the opportunity for individuality in creation, and stimulated efforts to develop a point of view distinctly American and representative of American life.

THE POSSIBILITIES OF RADIO-TV AS AN ADVERTISING MEDIUM. Just how much conscious or subconscious effect the unceasing repetition of advertisements on the radio or television has upon the average listener is a debatable question. Harry Hansen in his column, "The First Reader," said that though he listened to certain favorite programs, he had never once used or purchased the products which they advertise. On the other hand, the advertising of "BC" headache powders has become so well known in certain states that in the sports section of the newspaper, as well as in popular conversation, one who may run into anxiety or trouble is advised to "take a BC with him."

A few significant figures will make clear the vast possibilities for the use of the radio and TV in advertising. It is now a four-billion-dollar business in total annual volume in advertising, sales of "time" to advertisers, and servicing. There are three types of broadcasting stations: (1) standard (amplitude modulation, or AM) stations, of which about 3,000 are licensed or under construction; (2) FM (frequency modulation) stations, with some 600 in operation or under construction; and (3) television (TV or "video") stations, of which around 500 are on the air, 100 more are under construction, and 150 have applications pending.[6] There are four national networks, the National Broadcasting Company (NBC), the Columbia Broadcasting System (CBS), the Mutual Broadcasting System (MBS), and the American Broadcasting Company (ABC). The great majority of the local radio stations in the United States are affiliated with one or more of these great networks.

The radio reaches almost all American homes (98 per cent), and there is at least one television set in 84 per cent of our homes. The average family has the radio or TV on from three to seven hours a day, depending upon the day of the week and the season of the year. In regard to the size of the listening or viewing audience, the

---

[6] These figures for 1956–1957 were furnished to the author by the Federal Communications Commission. Consult also the Annual Reports of the Federal Communications Commission.

evening furnishes the largest, the afternoon next, and the morning the smallest. Of marked significance for propaganda purposes is the fact that the lower-income groups have ample access to the radio.

A large number of these radio stations are controlled or owned by newspapers. Life insurance companies, corporations, and individuals control others. More than 90 per cent of the stations are

FIG. 43   *Students use radio in their work*

Radio speech class broadcasts drama to entire school over public address system.
(*Courtesy Denver Public Schools.*)

"commercial," although there are some "educational" stations owned by chambers of commerce, educational institutions, cities, religious organizations, and other groups.

TYPES OF PROGRAMS.   Radio and television programs are in general of two types: (1) commercial (advertising) and (2) "of public interest." Commercial programs fill time purchased for advertising propaganda, and usually consist of types of popular entertainment and news. Educational programs are given free of charge to broadcast matters of "public interest, necessity, or convenience," as stated in the Federal act (1934) which created the Federal Communications Commission to oversee the broadcasting system. The Commission licenses stations for a period of time, reissues or refuses licenses, indicates the frequencies and power that may be employed by a station, and designates the hours in which it can broadcast. Outside of the prohibition that profane and indecent language cannot be used, the Commission has not yet drawn up a code of ethics for radio or TV advertising.

Over the network of a national system, advertisers may pay thousands of dollars per hour for time between 6:00 P.M. and 11:00 P.M. during the week. The types of business that are buying most radio time over the four national networks are: (1) foods and food products; (2) drugs and toilet articles; (3) soaps and kitchen supplies; (4) tobacco products; and (5) automobile companies.

PROGRAMS FOR CHILDREN. As was true in the growth of radio, special programs for children are the most recent and rapidly growing feature of television. The New York metropolitan area had three radio programs of this type in 1928, fifty-two in 1934, and double this number of radio and TV childrens' programs today.[7]

Of marked import for advertising (propaganda) purposes are two facts: (1) Boys and girls normally spend as much time listening to the radio and television each week as they do in school; this is the favorite leisure-time activity of the typical child. (2) Program likes and dislikes have great possibilities for effective propagandizing.[8] The boys in Eisenberg's investigation voted first place by a wide margin to Wild West, detectives, humor, sports, and adventures in strange lands. The girls voted first place to romantic adventures, stories of sentiment, popular songs, dance programs, and family life. These children preferred men as announcers, and adults as program performers. Children like and listen regularly to programs which have sustained interest, adventure, and excitement.

It has been discovered that a child's or an adult's social life and

---

[7] Chap. 4 discusses the types of programs for children. For earlier developments, read A.L. Eisenberg, *Children and Radio Programs*, Columbia University Press, 1936. *Cf.* also *Education on the Air*, 17th Yearbook, Institute of Education by Radio, "Children's Programs," pp. 297–334; and Alice P. Sterner, *Radio, Motion Picture and Reading Interests*, Teachers College, Columbia University, 1947, Chaps. III and IV.

[8] *Education on the Air*, 17th Yearbook, *op. cit.*, p. 29; and Eisenberg, *op. cit.*

experiences may stimulate him to listen avidly to certain types of radio programs, or cause him to have little interest in other kinds. As an illustration, on both the screen and the radio, children from one neighborhood may see or hear and retain certain items which were unnoticed by the children from another locality.

A recent development has been tried out in advertising on the screen and in television; it is called "subliminal advertising," a result of motivational research. The name of a product, for example, is flashed on the screen for 1/3000th of a second, during a program; it may be flashed as frequently as once every five seconds. Preliminary tests of advertising of a product in this unconscious or subliminal way showed that the sales of the products went up in that area where the program was shown.[9] If this kind of advertising becomes general, there will be more need than ever for careful analysis of the ads.

The National Association of Broadcasters recognizes the power of advertising and the need for a code of ethics to prevent false claims for products or goods. They have worked out standards for this; for radio, they are called "Standards of Good Practice for Radio Broadcasters," and for television the title is "Seal of Good Practice: Television Code."[10] These self-regulating codes, if faithfully followed, will help, particularly as parents and children are now faced with special markets and goods designed solely to appeal to children and teen-agers, as in certain clothes and fashions, record players and music albums, hi-fi sets, and foods.

The radio, television, and the newspaper frequently work hand in hand in advertising. The newspaper may carry such a notation as the following on an advertisement: "Listen to the ——— program on ——— every Tuesday and Thursday." In the final analysis, the same fundamental, simple test can be applied to radio-TV advertising that should be applied to newspaper advertisements. That test is: "Are the claims made for this product sane and credible, or are they extravagant and impossible of fulfillment?" If the claims made

[9] Read "The Ad and the Id," *Reader's Digest* (November, 1957), pp. 118–21; "The Invisible Invader," *Newsweek* (September 23, 1957), p. 70; and "The Little Ad that Isn't There," *Consumer Reports* (January, 1958), pp. 7–10.
[10] Copies are available from the National Association of Broadcasters, 1771 N Street, N.W., Washington 6, D.C.

are sane and credible, a fair trial will prove the merit the product possesses; if the claims made are as doubtful as the following sample, it is necessary to question them: "Come to ———'s, where prices are lower and quality is better."

3. *Through the Screen.*   The possibilities of the screen for advertising propaganda had been relatively undeveloped until the subliminal tests just described. Brief, animated cartoons and movie-talkie "shorts" were the extent to which the screen had been used for advertising purposes among some 85,000,000 people who buy admission each week to the 16,000 theatres in 9,000 American communities. One factor which has prevented much use of the screen for advertising has been the atmosphere of entertainment, in which such advertising features are not welcomed enthusiastically. Double-feature movie shows, of a length frequently exceeding four hours, have likewise tended to hinder such a development of advertising. Yet an opportunity exists here for the exercise of a tremendous propagandizing influence through the combined medium of the eye and the ear in moving-talking pictures.

Illustration 11. Problems of Democracy; Pressure Groups: The American Legion as an Example

Pressure groups may be narrowly defined as organized minorities which maintain lobbies for the purpose of influencing legislation. The lobbyists may be paid propagandists, or they may be backing personally certain principles and causes in which they believe thoroughly. Private property and its interests hire most of the "pressure boys," but labor organizations are not far behind.[11] The lobbyist follows legislation closely, estimates how it will affect his client, and takes steps to check, amend, or defeat it, as the interests of his group dictate.

An important feature of a democratic society is the simultaneous operation of numerous pressure groups to obtain political and financial favor with the general public. Various methods of propaganda are employed, and pressure is applied by above-board or under-

---

[11] "Unofficial Government: Pressure Groups and Lobbies," *The Annals of the American Academy of Political and Social Science,* September, 1958, pp. ix–x, 1. For earlier developments read K.G. Crawford, *The Pressure Boys: The Inside Story of Lobbying in America,* New York, Julian Messner, Inc., 1939.

handed methods. Many organizations have demonstrated their aptitude for exerting pressure in the interests of relatively small groups through publications, the radio and television, lobbying, public speeches, and personal agents; these groups range in type from the American Legion and the Associated Farmers to the life insurance companies and other big-business corporations, which depend a great deal upon lobbying practices for favor and gain through legislation. Lobbying and the employment of publicity agents are characteristic of the democratic organization in the United States. The chief protection of the populace from exploitation by powerful pressure groups lies in an increased understanding of the methods and motives of these various groups. If these methods and motives are understood adequately by the *buying* public, the *listening* public, and the *voting* public, the relative merits and demerits of the cases as they are presented will eventually settle the degree of gain for each.

ORGANIZATION AND PURPOSES OF THE AMERICAN LEGION. Over a period of years, the American Legion has been one of the best examples of a pressure group which has backed principles in which it believes firmly. It is an organization of ex-service men of the United States army, dating its formation from shortly after the Armistice which ended World War I. Its influence is very strong, owing to a highly centralized organization for the dissemination of propaganda. In general, the Legion advertises its patriotic purposes as "defense of the Constitution" and "Americanism."

These purposes were questioned in 1938 by William Gellermann.[12] Gellermann concluded that the American Legion (1) was one of the most powerful of pressure groups; (2) was an instrument of a privileged group; (3) had been most active when the capitalistic system was most seriously challenged; (4) did not promote peace; (5) actively promoted "Americanism"; (6) sought to maintain the *status quo* in the present economic system; (7) promoted extra-school activities which contribute to military preparedness; and (8) sought by its program to imprint upon youth's mind certain symbols and attitudes which the Legion promotes.

[12] *The American Legion as Educator*, Teachers College, Columbia University, Contributions to Education, No. 743, 1938.

EDUCATIONAL ACTIVITIES OF THE LEGION. The American Legion carries on a program of activities for childhood and youth both within and outside the schools, all in support of its program of Americanism. Activities sponsored within the schools include the following:

1. Recommended school activities, such as flag drills; instruction conducted entirely in English; requirement of American history and civics instruction for graduation; physical education programs to improve fitness for military service; and occupational guidance.
2. American Education Week, in cooperation with the National Education Association, the United States Office of Education, and the National Congress of Parents and Teachers.
3. Essay and oratorical contests with school awards on topics related to the Legion and its Americanism program.
4. Flag education.
5. Observance of patriotic holidays.
6. Support of the Constitution.
7. Civic instruction.
8. Safety and driver education.
9. Spiritual training.

Educational activities of the Legion outside the school have included the following:

1. Junior Baseball Leagues.
2. Boy Scouts.
3. Girl Scouts, Camp Fire Girls, Y-Teens.
4. Citizens' Military Training Camps.
5. Reserve Officers' Training Corps.
6. Boys' and Girls' State, and Boys' Nation, leadership training for boys and girls in the secondary school.
7. Child welfare program.
8. Summer camps and activities for sons of American Legion members.

ACHIEVEMENTS OF THE LEGION. Disregarding for the moment World War II and the Korean conflict and their effects upon the nation, the following are the biggest victories which this typical American pressure group has achieved or helped to achieve over the years:

1. Passage of the veterans' bonus legislation (both the national act and various state acts).

2. Veterans' compensation and hospitalization for disability, whether incurred as a result of war service or not.
3. Defeat of the Supreme Court "packing" bill.
4. Organization of Citizens' Military Training Camps and Reserve Officers' Training Corps units in colleges and secondary schools.
5. Fight on subversive elements, resulting in Federal control of "racketeering" and in Federal investigations, such as that of the Dies (House Un-American) Committee.
6. The Universal Draft Act preceding and following World War II.
7. Passage of the Reserve Military Acts.

Some citizens believe that not all of these achievements are good. Others feel that all of these projects are worthy, worth fighting for, and in the best interests of the United States.

On the credit side of the ledger, anyone closely connected with school work will have to admit in all fairness that both youth and the cause of education have been aided by the American Legion Junior Baseball Leagues, by American Education Week, and by improved programs of health and physical education in the schools. A majority of school officials and employees have opposed the establishment of R.O.T.C. units in secondary schools, a provision made possible several years ago by a rider attached to an appropriations bill of the national Congress; but at present many citizens are demanding that this type of training be made compulsory in both secondary schools and colleges.

SHIFTS IN PUBLIC OPINION ABOUT PRESSURE GROUPS. The startling changes which can be brought about in public opinion in a few years are clearly etched in a consideration of the American Legion as a pressure group. In 1937–1938, there were rumors of war, but no world war was in progress; "Americanism" then was "nationalism," not democracy, and America was the last powerful, self-sufficient stronghold of that way of life; "isolation" was a term at that time to conjure with; "fifth columnists" and "subversive" elements connoted persecution, not dangers to the preservation of the nation; and preparedness for defense and war was held then to be militarism, and a threat to world peace.

With the growth of a fanatical, brutal ideology in many nations that the collectivist state is the remedy for society's ills, has the American Legion (with *its* ideology so tenaciously and persistently promoted) developed a reputation as a prophet? To say the least, many Americans today are thankful that the Legion has been so active and powerful in propagandizing for certain military legislation in the United States.

TECHNIQUES EMPLOYED BY THE LEGION. The American Legion furnishes an excellent study as a sample of the pressure of a minority group in still another way. The organization has an abundance of material which is frankly printed and boldly distributed to attain its purposes. Of marked educational significance is *The American Legion Magazine,* a regular publication of the Legion. Seldom does the magazine fail to have in each issue one or more suggested programs for activities of the local post for youth and the community, programs outlined primarily by the National Americanism Commission of the Legion. The magazine continually calls attention to the varied types of "assistance programs" begun and carried out in the schools. The wide extent to which the Legion's activities are planned for the schools may be shown by an examination of the many state and local Legion magazines published over the country.

LEGISLATION CONCERNING LOBBYING. At midcentury, twelve states had no laws controlling lobbying activities; fourteen other states had "corrupt-practices" provisions that were aimed at lobbying. Professional lobbyists were required to register in twenty-two states, and in sixteen of these complete financial statements were demanded from the employers of lobbyists.

The Federal government, on the other hand, has no statutes against lobbying, though some red tape is involved for lobbyists in having to register before a few executive agencies such as the Securities and Exchange Commission or the Maritime Commission. Since 1913, Congress has made various lobby investigations, and these have been followed by the introduction of anti-lobby bills. The compromise Black-Smith Bill in 1936 came close to passage; it would have required all lobbyists to register and to state the source of their income, even of contributions as small as ten dollars. The Federal Regulation of Lobbying Act finally was passed in 1946; but it only required lobbyists to register and report on their activities.

THE TECHNIQUES OF PROPAGANDA

In analyzing propaganda from any source, the teacher is confronted with a variety of techniques or devices which operate to achieve the aim of the propagandist. Some of these devices have been thoroughly described by informed analysts; [13] others have been added by the author. The devices include the following: (1) name-calling; (2) glittering generalities; (3) the device of transfer; (4) the device of testimonial; (5) the device of plain folks; (6) card-stacking; (7) the band-wagon device; (8) the "boring-from-within" technique; (9) the "investigation" device; and (10) the false front.

1. *Name-Calling.* "Name-calling" refers to the effort to discountenance and derogate another person, race, creed, political party, nation, or competing commercial product by applying a bad name ("smear words") to the opposition. In World War I, the name applied by the Allies to Germans was "Hun." In World War II, the Germans called Winston Churchill "German-baiter"; Prime Minister Chamberlain called Hitler a "wild beast." More recently, the term applied to those who favor school desegregation is "integrationist" or "desegregationist." It is necessary to examine the motives of the name-caller before accepting at face value the fitness of the term.

2. *The Glittering Generality.* Glittering generalities consist of good names and phrases seeking to identify a person, race, creed, party, nation, or commercial product with things bearing pleasant connotations. Thus, we have all heard such terms as the "New Deal," the "free enterprise system," "democracy," "free speech," "friend of the people," and "the Great Commoner." Well known to the psychologist, this trick of association is more difficult to spot than is the name-calling device, since the rosy glow surrounding generalities puts the reader or listener off guard.

3. *The Device of Transfer.* "Transfer" also makes use of the trick of association. The well-established prestige, glory, respect, and

---

[13] *Cf.* Alfred M. and Elizabeth B. Lee (Eds.), New York, *The Fine Art of Propaganda,* Harcourt, Brace and Company, 1939, Chaps. IV–X; Clyde R. Miller, *The Process of Persuasion,* New York, Crown Publishers, 1946, Part II; and V.O. Key, Jr., *Politics, Parties and Pressure Groups,* New York, Thomas Y. Crowell, 1952, *passim.*

authority of certain institutions, or the reverse of these attributes, are transferred by reference to some not-so-well-established cause, institution, or purpose at hand. The United States is symbolized by cartoons depicting Uncle Sam; John Bull is similarly significant to the British Empire. "Blitzkrieg" referred to a type of lightning warfare associated with the German war machine. In World War I, the German slogan came to be "Gott mit uns"; the British war-cry was "For God, for King and Country." Sometimes this device is called the "stereotype."

4. *The Testimonial Device.* Testimonial devices have been used with great effect in newspaper, magazine, and radio advertising. For some people, the beautiful girl smoking a cigarette is enough inducement to indicate the benefit to be derived from a particular brand of cigarette. Ministers refer constantly to the deeds of great men, especially of those identified with religious leadership. Politicians seek to identify their causes with those of established leaders, statesmen, or predecessors.

A careful scrutiny of testimonials often reveals that the cigarette-girl's testimonial is biased; perhaps she received $1,000 for her picture and signed statement. Political endorsements are frequently rewarded by patronage. Germany, a nation at war, published only such quoted testimonials as served her selfish interest. Analysis of propaganda must examine the motives behind the testimony.

5. *Plain Folks.* The "plain folks" device is particularly useful in politics and government. Huey Long and his "share-the-wealth" program testified to its successful employment. The late Eugene Talmadge of Georgia, famed for his "grass-roots" background, gained much political support from the display of his well-worn suspenders. Adolf Hitler cemented his leadership foundation in the Reich when he declared before the Reichstag at the beginning of the Polish campaign (September 1, 1939) that he would be "the first soldier of the Reich." Two well-known, wealthy campaigners in New York State, Nelson Rockefeller and Averell Harriman, identified themselves recently with the "plain folks" by their pizza pie exploits.

6. *Card-Stacking.* The "card-stacking" technique refers simply to purposeful lying; in it, the cards are stacked against the truth in the effort to conceal the truth. The famous Bryce Report of World War

I was a studied effort to stack the cards against the Central Powers; however, we know now that there was no "corpse-boiling soap factory" in Germany then. In World War II, the British Blue Book, the German White Book, Von Ribbentrop's timely statements of "documents" found in Poland, then in Norway and Denmark, then in Holland and Belgium, all tried to stack the cards in favor of the side that did the stacking. Hitler's announced view in *Mein Kampf* was to the effect that a lie should be complete and unequivocal in order to get the best propaganda effect.[14] "Tell 'em big, and tell 'em often" was Hitler's technique.

7. *The Band-Wagon Device.* This device derives its name from the cry, "Let's get on the band wagon!" The implication is that a certain course should be followed, a certain product should be purchased and used, or a certain candidate should be supported simply because "everybody else is doing it." The device was used effectively in Germany by the Nazis to gain converts; eventually, all persons who failed to join one of the government-sponsored organizations were branded as non-Aryans or Jews. Parades, pageantry, rallies, and other emotional outbursts are a part of this technique. In the midst of such emotional expression, it would be well for every person to pause and examine the motives behind such high-powered salesmanship.

8. *Boring from Within.* The "boring-from-within" technique has always been used most effectively by propagandists; it consists of having members of the propagandist group join bona-fide organizations of repute, where they bore from within to influence the reputable organization to their own purposes. The Communist party is well known for its perfection of this method; members of the party join other parties, bore from within, and eventually persuade the organization to approve their course of action, or take over power in the party by a coup or by force. Reputable organizations of all kinds have found this propaganda device at work in their ranks sooner or later, from the Parent-Teachers' Association and other educational associations to Chambers of Commerce and service clubs.

9. *The "Investigation" Device.* This technique has developed rapidly since 1920 as a propagandistic tool. It was stimulated first by

[14] New York, Reynal and Hitchcock, 1939, pp. 230–37.

government scandals, and then by legislative post-mortems on calamities growing out of the business depression. In the Federal and state governments, the legislative investigation of the activities of certain groups is the pattern; all too often some legislator, official, or group has a private propagandistic axe to grind by means of the

FIG. 44   *The working of the democratic process*

The Tens and Elevens meet for discussion and committee or group assignments. (*Courtesy Erie Day School, Erie, Pennsylvania.*)

power granted to subpoena witnesses, inquire into one's public and private life, and commandeer private correspondence. In local communities and political subdivisions, this device is frequently employed through agreement to have a community or school survey made; from the operations and findings of such a survey, certain individuals or groups hope to place some official or office "on the spot."

10. *The False Front.* The "false-front" technique makes use of

both the transfer trick of association and the boring-from-within mechanism. A false name of a specious-sounding type covers the activities of an organization which actually exists for an entirely different purpose. Such noble-sounding names as the following were discovered after World War II to hide the Communist activities of groups in the United States: "American Youth Congress," "Congress of American Women," "People's Educational Association," and "Labor Research Association, Inc." Of different names and adopted for doubtful purposes are some local "Taxpayers" and "Economy" Leagues.

Clyde R. Miller, one of the leaders in the movement of propaganda analysis in education, has reduced these ten techniques of propaganda to four: (1) the acceptance or "virtue" device, similar to the "glittering generality" and the "transfer" device; (2) the rejection or "poison" device (compare "name-calling"); (3) the testimonial device; and (4) the "together" device, which applies to any or all other devices through group pressure or mass action or emotion. He maintains that all aspects of persuasion are contained in these four categories.[15]

MECHANICS OF MODERN PROPAGANDA TECHNIQUES

TYPES OF MECHANICS. Modern propaganda reaches its objectives by mechanics and methods undreamed of only a generation ago. Among these are the talking picture, improved news coverage by newspapers, photography, books, the pulp magazines, attractive news weeklies, the comics, and radio and television. New channels for the dissemination of propaganda and refinements of the older channels are important in that they affect one insidiously. People are slow to become aware of the effect of these methods and mechanics, but the propagandist looks for them and uses them first.

Movies are now used to advertise almost everything. "Tobaccoland" is a talking picture of the South, especially of North Carolina, intended to advertise a certain tobacco product; "Clouds," a picture showing the significance of clouds in forecasting weather, is distributed by the United States Department of Agriculture; "Man

[15] *Cf. The Process of Persuasion, op. cit.,* Chaps. VIII–XII.

Against Microbe," which illustrates 300 years of progress in the control of disease, is a good-will effort of a life insurance company; "Frankfort-on-Main" was distributed by German railroads, and was intended to induce tourists to spend some time and money in Germany. A campaign movie entitled "A New Tomorrow" was released by the Republican party in April, 1940, to help its election prospects in November; it was made available free of charge to all civic clubs and other organizations which would give it an audience.

Improved news coverage, a large number of correspondents everywhere, the advent of wire-photo service, and more newspapers have combined to make extensive propaganda not only more possible, but also inevitable. News and picture magazines, some with color photography, can make propaganda vivid and bring it home quickly; *Time, Newsweek, Life, Look,* and numerous other current periodicals present a panorama of events almost as soon as they happen. Commercial advertisements, political campaigns, and movements for various causes come in for their share of pictorial space and editorial comment.

THE PUBLIC OPINION POLL. An unusually promising kind of machinery for propaganda on a large scale has been developed in the last decades. This is the public opinion poll. Based on as accurate a sampling as possible of the opinions of people in all walks of American life, these polls are the nearest approach yet devised to an attempt to secure a fair and impartial cross-section of public opinion on various issues and problems.

One kind of poll attempts to obtain an accurate picture of public opinion on national and international issues. Reports of the American Institute of Public Opinion (Gallup Poll) give weekly samples of these. The *Fortune* poll was of the same general type. Because of the careful selection of their cross-sections of the population and the impartial phrasing of their questions, both the Gallup and *Fortune* polls were remarkably accurate, in contrast to some of those of former years conducted by the *Literary Digest.* Even in the national election of 1948, the admitted margin of error would have cared for an outcome either way. Gallup claimed twenty years ago [16]

---

[16] G. Gallup and S.F. Rae, *The Pulse of Democracy: The Public Opinion Poll and How It Works,* New York, Simon and Schuster, 1940.

that his scientific system of polling the opinion of the rank and file of people eliminated the possibility of the abuse of the machinery; this probably accounts in part for the continuing uncanny accuracy of the Institute's poll. The newspapers are the primary support of Gallup's Institute, as most of them subscribe regularly to the releases on the polls. Such an organization as Gallup's could, however, be used by selfish groups to exploit the public through "loading" of the sampling, and the asking of leading questions. A newcomer to the polls of the same type is Trendex News Poll. One of the more popular polls of youth's ideas, concepts, and likes is the Gilbert Youth Research Company poll.

A poll on a smaller scale has been employed by the Consumer Research Staff of General Motors Corporation. This research body attempts, through a poll of automobile owners and drivers, to learn the public's viewpoint toward current and new trends in automobile design; the purpose is to give this public reaction to the engineering staff and the designers of General Motors' automobiles. One series of questions dealt with headlights, running boards, gearshift controls, automatic choke, windshield defrosters, and directional signal lights. No driver has to give his name or address, or the make of the car which he drives. Return postage on the inquiry booklet is paid by General Motors. All in all, the General Motors poll seems soundly constructed and fairly cross-sectioned; and the information gathered from it in recent years appears to have had an influence upon the design of new cars. Other businesses now employ polling services extensively.

THE COMICS. Among the mechanics for the spread of propaganda, the use of the "comics" must not be overlooked. This strictly American institution reaches practically all of the population of all ages. For many years, "Dick Tracy" has served as a medium for propaganda against crime and racketeering; "Jane Arden," "Kerry Drake," and a host of other comics have sprung up to serve the same purpose. The work of the Federal Bureau of Investigation has undoubtedly stimulated this type of comic. American family life is another favorite theme of the comics, with its trials and tribulations, its joys, its problems, and its types. "Gasoline Alley" and "Corky" (both by King) are perhaps the best all-round characterizations of family life; others of this kind include "Out Our Way: the Willetts," "Bringing Up Father," "Pa's Son-in-Law," "The Gumps," and "Blondie." Another type of comic includes a description of typical American adolescents and how they act; of these, "Penny," "Our Bill," "Winnie Winkle," "The Jackson Twins," and "Harold Teen" are samples.

Over a period of years, the greatest propagandist of the comics on a diversified scale has been Harold Gray in his "Little Orphan Annie." In step with current events, he propagandized during the 1930 business depression against fastening the stigma of "pauper" permanently on a person through relief and public charity. Time and again he has illustrated through his characters that there is opportunity in America for each one to make good if he has the will, the courage, the initiative, and the stamina. He has called attention to the fact that modern inventions which conquer time and space have brought nations so near to each other that differing ideologies must clash. He has played up the "honesty-is-the-best policy" theme, through gangster episodes of varying types. This series had as one of its central themes the idea that American gangsters are to be preferred to fifth columnists and imported agents of totalitarian states. Gray calls attention constantly to the American virtues which have made this nation great, even at the risk of preaching at times, and he warns against moral and spiritual bankruptcy.

THE RADIO AND TV. While the newspaper, the screen, magazines, pulp prints, and comics constitute increasingly effective propaganda media, the radio and television offer the most direct appeal because of (1) their immediacy, (2) their independence of literacy, and (3) the value of the spoken word over the written word. President Truman's "State of the Nation" talks and President Eisenhower's "Reports to the Nation," the annual money campaigns of the American National Red Cross, political appeals, and commercial advertisements offer, through the medium of radio-TV, the dramatic appeal entirely absent on the printed page. The background available through broadcasting is also important; commercially sponsored radio programs find that the cheering, clapping, enthusiastic studio audience lends to the appeal of the product. Political campaigners prefer an audience situation to a studio performance.

From the standpoint of driving a point home, another important factor in radio-TV propaganda has been the refinement of transcription and tape recording processes for phonographic or recorder reproduction. This is especially important in broadcasting, since stations do most of the transcribing and reproduce programs through this medium. Some commercial advertisements are thus repeated as often as twenty-five times in a single day over some radio stations; and a political broadcast at an inconvenient lunch hour can be repeated to a larger audience at night. All these possibilities are actualities, and the impact afforded by repetition is an influence of importance to analysts of propaganda.

PROPAGANDA CHANNELS IN THE SCHOOLS

Since free propagandizing is a part of the democratic system of government, it is apropos at this time to discuss certain channels through which propaganda has free entry directly into the schools.

RELIGIOUS PRESSURE. A questionnaire on propaganda in the schools, sent out by the Institute for Propaganda Analysis in 1939, elicited the information that school administrators cited religious groups most often among those pressure groups operating in the schools.[17] This still holds true today. Catholics like to have their children excused from classes for part of a day every week for religious instruction; Christian Scientists discourage hygiene courses; religious organizations, especially ministerial councils, encourage enactment of local and statewide legislation requiring the reading of the Bible in school assemblies, and Bible instruction in classes. Catholics complain of Protestant Biblical interpretation; Jews often object to religion in the schools, since it is the Christian religion that is taught. School administrators are wary of religious pressure and propaganda, and tend to avoid this issue entirely.

PATRIOTIC PRESSURE. There are many patriotic organizations in the United States which have used the schools for the dissemination of propaganda and the exertion of external pressure, *e.g.*, the American Legion, the G.A.R., the D.A.R., the U.D.C., the V.F.W., and others. The most active among the patriotic organizations is the

[17] "Propaganda in the Schools," *Propaganda Analysis*, II (May 1, 1939, p. 2.

American Legion, whose educational activities have already been discussed in detail. For many years, a strictly fraternal organization, the Junior Order of United American Mechanics, has propagandized for liberty through the public schools in a dignified and effective manner by means of the presentation of Bibles and of the American flag, and of special patriotic programs. It is difficult for the schools to withstand the pressure and the propagandistic efforts of such powerful, well-organized groups. As in the case of religious pressures and propaganda, teachers should consider the dangers as well as the advantages of propaganda sponsored by patriotic organizations.

PRESSURE BY CIVIC ORGANIZATIONS AND GOVERNMENT AGENCIES. Numerous civic organizations, such as businessmen's clubs, Civitan, Lions, Kiwanis, and Rotary, have evinced an interest in assisting in the work of the public schools. Educators usually consider this to be a hopeful sign of renewed public interest in the school program, and they welcome the cooperation of such groups. For example, Kiwanis International is especially interested in providing occupational information and pamphlets for the use of schools in their vocational guidance for young people. Kiwanis also makes it a practice to promote good citizenship by the selection of "Junior Kiwanians"; these selections are based upon factors of good school citizenship. Likewise welcome to school officials are the educational efforts of local, state, and Federal agencies, such as fire departments, police and safety officials, health, social, and conservation authorities. These agencies can cooperate with the schools to train youth for more effective citizenship.

Other organizations propagandizing in the interest of the public welfare include the National League of Women Voters, the Children's Bureau, the Brookings Institution, the American Academy of Political and Social Science, the National Safety Council, the American Library Association, the Parent-Teachers' Association, and the American Civil Liberties Union. Of similar character over the years have been such radio or television presentations as America's Town Meeting of the Air, The American Forum of the Air, the People's Platform, the University of Chicago Round Table, Youth Wants to Know, and Meet the Press.

On the other hand, there is evidence that some organizations pro- mote selfish propaganda, usually in the form of essay contests. The reader should be again reminded that "all that glitters is not gold."

COMMERCIAL ADVERTISEMENTS IN THE SCHOOLS. Commercial or- ganizations and manufacturers are always eager to get favorable publicity for their products through the channels afforded by the needs of school children and teachers. Free blotters, calendars, rulers, movies, handbooks, and catalogues are fairly common as advertising media. In so far as such free materials are usable and worthy, school officials do not usually object to their distribution to school children. There is, in fact, considerable evidence that school principals welcome some printed materials and other aids which are provided for the schools as publicity materials. Some administra- tors even consider much of the commercial publicity superior to materials prepared by school people themselves.

Companies providing a variety of materials include the nation's largest manufacturers: *e.g.*, Ford Motor Company (movies); Gen- eral Motors Corporation (movies); American Automobile Associa- tion (pamphlets); Metropolitan Life Insurance Company (health pamphlets); Pennsylvania Railroad (movies and pamphlets); Proc- ter and Gamble (soap sculpture competition with prizes, pam- phlets); Eastman Kodak (handbooks and pamphlets); and the National Association of Manufacturers (series of pamphlets). The Pennsylvania Railroad has produced a film, "On to Washington," a vivid portrayal of the nation's capital; it is an effective method of promoting good will for the railroad, especially when the movie is accompanied by an advertising brochure which can be taken home to the parents. A more subtle, but no less effective method, is that of the Procter and Gamble Soap Company, which sponsors the National Soap Sculpture Committee. This committee promotes a soap sculpture contest among school children every spring, furnish- ing free descriptions and lessons in soap sculpture; and incidentally, it builds the contest around the sculpturing possibilities which are latent in Ivory Soap.

Obviously, the propaganda content is considerable in all of these commercial advertisements. These materials should be analyzed thoroughly before they are submitted to immature minds. The criteria for such an analysis might well be the following, which were suggested by the National Education Association's Committee on Propaganda in the Schools: [18]

Whether the agency competes with a local concern.
Whether the agency is of the social welfare type.
Whether the agency is a "substantial" as opposed to a "fugitive" organization.
Whether the motion is selfish or altruistic.
Whether the motive is patriotic or otherwise.
Whether the agency has political connections.
Whether the agency is local or national.
Whether the aims of the agency concur with the aims of the school.
Whether the agency seeks to create a market for "staples" or "luxuries."
Whether the agency is locally popular or unpopular.

PROPAGANDA BY PROFESSIONAL EDUCATION GROUPS. In contrast to propaganda carried into the schools by outside groups, numerous strictly educational organizations are at work providing material similar to some of the commercial propaganda material, but free of any taint of commercialism. This tendency is obviously a healthy one, since these educational groups should be expected to have sympathy with the general aims of the schools, in contrast to the more self-interested motives of many of the extra-school propaganda agencies.

The American Council on Education is a noteworthy case in point. Two types of their publications attempt to present impartial studies of the accuracy and/or bias in textbooks: *A Study of National History Textbooks Used in the Schools of Canada and the United States* (1947) and their intergroup teaching materials (1948–1955).

The National Education Association is another important contributor of school materials. The Safety Education Exhibit of the American Association of School Administrators of the National Education Association has coordinated the safety contributions and efforts of many extra-school organizations, including the manufacturers. The Educational Policies Commission, another subsidiary organization of the National Education Association, not only has provided publications of interest to teachers and school administrators, but also has sought to influence boards of education and the general public

[18] Cited in *Propaganda Analysis,* Vol. II, No. 8.

through these publications. Illustrative of the efforts of this group are its reports, *Education for All American Youth* (1944), *Education for All American Children* (1948), and *Education for All American Youth—A Further Look* (1952).

Other professional education groups have likewise prepared materials of a propagandistic nature for schools.[19]

Not only organizations, but individuals as well, are permitted to propagandize somewhat freely within the schools. Several persons have made investigations regarding the propaganda and pressure brought to bear upon school pupils through textbooks; samples of these studies are those of Bessie Pierce [20] and Howard Beale.[21] Another type of propaganda is that affecting the teachers directly and the pupils indirectly, such as George S. Counts' *The Schools Can Teach Democracy.*[22] This booklet presents Counts' thesis that the schools should be the instrument for shaping the new, and presumably democratic, society. The analysis of such propaganda is directly the task of teachers and school administrators, who are often not well enough informed to evaluate the propaganda properly.[23]

SUMMARY

The welfare of a democratic social order is dependent upon freedom of speech, of assembly, of religion, and of the press, with their propaganda of all descriptions. There is propaganda exerted by large and small groups in the interest of the majority; there is also propaganda intended to benefit only a small or minority group, or individuals; there is partisan propaganda used for the advancement of national and even international power; and war propaganda of all kinds has been and is now rife.

That educational employees are vitally concerned with learning how to analyze propaganda in issues political, economic, social, and

[19] See the Bibliography of this Chapter for samples.
[20] *Civic Attitudes in American School Textbooks,* the University of Chicago Press, 1930.
[21] *Are American Teachers Free?* New York, Charles Scribners' Sons, 1936, Chap. XI, pp. 261–319.
[22] The John Day Company, 1939.
[23] Chap. 20 presents illustrations of good propaganda on state, regional, and national scales.

religious is increasingly apparent. Organized groups of students are actually participating in propaganda analysis through widely scattered parts of the nation.

Objective evidence from different sources indicates that schools should encourage students to analyze propaganda. In a nation-wide poll conducted by Gallup's American Institute of Public Opinion in 1936, this question was asked: "Should schools teach the facts about all forms of government including Communism, Fascism and Socialism?" The vote was 62 per cent to 38 per cent in favor of teaching *the facts* about the forms of government in question. Since 1954 both the American Bar Association and the American Legion have voiced approval of the teaching of the facts about the theory and practice of Communism.

In 1937 a group of Columbia and New York University professors surveyed the opinions of 500 teachers, representing all states of the union and coming from all types of schools, in regard to propaganda analysis by students in secondary schools and colleges. This study found that 98 per cent advocated a critical study of propaganda analysis in the school.[24] Quillen and Hanna [25] devoted a whole chapter to "The Use of Persuasion Materials" as a natural step in helping students to develop critical thinking. Other writers recognize the same responsibility.[26]

Whether a person is talking to another individual or to a group, is writing to a relative, to a friend, or to his congressman, is listening to a speech or to the radio, is attending a movie or an opera, is being solicited by a salesman or by letter, is reading or thinking, propaganda is at work on him and through him. The impact of various pressures upon him, and the influence of his opinions upon other persons, are part and parcel of his education and his development. Propaganda as a term narrowly connoting only the promotion of schemes of an undesirable type is a misnomer. In a democratic society, propaganda is interwoven with the education of each individual. Only through the development of clear-thinking and critical

[24] *Propaganda Analysis,* I (October, 1937), 3.
[25] *Education for Social Competence: Curriculum and Instruction in Secondary-School Social Studies,* Chicago, Scott, Foresman and Company, 1948, Chap. XII.
[26] *Cf.* H.B. Alberty, *Reorganizing the High School Curriculum* (rev. ed.), New York, The Macmillan Company, 1953, Chap. XII.

individuals can society, economy, and government be improved. If fear of propaganda closes one's mind to any *facts* which the propagandist has to present, society and the individual are the losers for such caution. It is the obligation of every person to learn how to judge which of the aspects presented by the propagandist are fact and which are fiction or untested theory.

PROBLEMS FOR INDIVIDUAL STUDY
AND CLASS DISCUSSION

1. Is the *NEA Journal* (magazine) a propaganda organ for a group of teachers? Is it valuable or not? Give reasons.

2. Listen to the radio or television programs for a week over a particular station at a certain time each day; make a list of the talks and of the companies and products advertised, inducements offered, and values claimed for the products. What types of propaganda did you encounter?

3. If a movie manager in your community asked permission to distribute handbills in your school advertising a forthcoming film attraction, what would you do? Give reasons for your action.

4. On what bases would you decide whether to use the periodical, *The Reader's Digest,* as source material for your students in their study?

5. Does your state have any legislation governing lobbying, or false advertising, or advertising by means of highway signs? Is that particular legislation wise or not? Give reasons for your opinion.

6. What are the possibilities of using polls of public opinion effectively in curriculum work? (*Cf.* Gallup and Rae's book, *The Pulse of Democracy,* and Gallup, *A Guide to Public Opinion Polls.*)

7. After reading the Standards of Good Practice for Radio Broadcasters or the standards set up in the Seal of Good Practice: Television Code, of the National Association of Broadcasters, how could you determine whether the broadcasting stations are living up to these standards?

8. To what list of films, or to what authorities, would you go to get an impartial opinion as to the educational use of certain films produced by private business concerns such as the American Can Company, the Ford Motor Company, and the Shell Oil Company?

9. How is the "name-calling" device of propaganda used daily by children in their school life? Illustrate.

10. What types of violations of the Federal laws relating to false advertising did you find in a regular report of the decisions and rulings of the Federal Food and Drug Administration?

11. What was the propaganda content, if any, of a recent novel or book of nonfiction which you have read?

12. What limitations, if any, should be placed upon the employment of the "testimonial" device in advertising? Support your position.

13. Do children realize the propaganda content of many of the Sunday comic supplements? Do adults? Support your point of view.

14. Have you read any book on World War II which was free of propagandistic bias?

15. Should the teacher propagandize for democracy? Why or why not?

16. Are indoctrination and propaganda the same or not? Prove your point of view.

ADDITIONAL ANNOTATED REFERENCES
FOR PROBLEM OR UNIT STUDY

Alberty, H.B., *Reorganizing the High-School Curriculum* (rev. ed.), New York, The Macmillan Company, 1953.

Chapter xɪɪ presents well the types of controversial issues which should be dealt with in the classroom, and the ways of discussing them.

Allport, G.W., and Postman, L., *The Psychology of Rumor*, New York, Henry Holt and Company, 1947.

Still one of the best analyses.

The Annals of the American Academy of Political and Social Science. Vol. 319, September, 1958, pp. 1–157, is devoted to "Unofficial Government; Pressure Groups and Lobbies"; it identifies the pressure groups, discusses the "big three" of industry, farmers, and labor, how pressure groups operate, regulations concerning them, and American and foreign pressure politics.

Bogart, L., *The Age of Television*, New York, Frederick Ungar Publishing Company, 1956.

The significant findings of a large number of research studies of television, its history, audience, its appeal, its effects on its viewers, and its future.

Cantril, H., *et al.*, *Gauging Public Opinion*, Princeton, Princeton University Press, 1944.

The mechanics of the public opinion poll.

Colegrove, K., *Democracy vs. Communism*, Princeton, D. Van Nostrand Company, 1957.

Analysis of the contrast and conflict between communism and democracy for young Americans, prepared by the Institute of Fiscal and Political Education.

Ehlers, H. (Ed.), *Crucial Issues in Education*, New York, Henry Holt and Company, 1955.

An anthology on contemporary problems of loyalty, censorship, religious education, racial segregation, and progressive education—*pro* and *con*.

The High School Journal, Vol. xli, No. 5 (February, 1958).

"Television in the Schools" is a good example of special issues which educational periodicals publish from time to time on controversial issues and propaganda techniques.

Huggett, A.J., and Stinnett, T.M., *Professional Problems of Teachers*, New York, The Macmillan Company, 1956.

Chapter ix for professional working conditions and academic freedom for teachers and x for ethics for the teaching profession.

Hullfish, H.G. (Ed.), *Educational Freedom in an Age of Anxiety*, New York, Harper and Brothers, 1953.

This Twelfth Yearbook of the John Dewey Society presents freedom of inquiry and of teaching and community pressures on teachers.

Marden, C.F., *Minorities in American Society*, New York, American Book Company, 1952.

An approach to this large problem in terms of the relations or interaction between the minority and the majority; included are native-for-eigner relations, white-colored relations, ward-wardship relations, and religious difference and minority status.

Miller, C.R., *The Process of Persuasion*, New York, Crown Publishers, 1946.

This book by one of the pioneers in propaganda analysis is still a basic reference for those who study persuasion techniques and mechanics.

National Citizens Committee for the Public Schools, New York 36, New York.

This group issues "Guides" for citizens to use in improving their public schools. *How Good Are Our Teaching Materials?* Working Guide No. 8, 1955, is concerned with problems, propaganda, and controversial issues.

National Education Association, Washington.

Recent examples of good propaganda, of discussion of controversial issues in education, and of sources of research in these areas are the following:

American Association of School Administrators, *Health in Schools* (rev. ed.), 1952, and *Educating for American Citizenship*, 1954.

American Educational Research Association, Vol. xxvi (April, 1956), "Instructional Materials," a special issue of the *Review of Educational Research* on the latest studies and findings about motion pictures, television, and radio as teaching instruments.

Association for Supervision and Curriculum Development, *Forces Affecting American Education*, 1953 Yearbook; and two issues of *Educational Leadership* devoted to "Issues in Education" (April, 1957) and "Curriculum and Survival" (October, 1958).

National Association of Secondary-School Principals, "CASE Economic Literacy Series" of the Council for Advancement of Secondary Education.

National Society for the Study of Education, Chicago 37.

    Mass Media and Education, 53rd Yearbook, Part II, takes up the role of mass communication, how it works, and media such as the press, motion pictures, radio, and television in teaching.

Pittinger, B.F., *Indoctrination for American Democracy*, New York, The Macmillan Company, 1941.

    Still the standard work on indoctrination.

The Public Opinion Quarterly, Princeton, Princeton University.

    This is the publication devoted to public opinion study and research in such areas as public opinion polls, merchandizing, radio, television, the press, status and class stereotypes, and the like.

Quillen, I.J., and Hanna, L.A., *Educat'on for Social Competence*, Chicago, Scott, Foresman and Company, 1948.

    Report of the Stanford Social Education Investigation, especially valuable in Chapters IX–XII for visual and auditory aids, reading and persuasion materials, and community resources.

Romine, S.A., *Building the High School Curriculum*, New York, The Ronald Press Company, 1954.

    Chapter XIII for controversial issues, texts, audio-visual materials.

Scott, C.W., and Hill, C.M., *Public Education Under Criticism*, Englewood Cliffs, Prentice-Hall, 1954.

    An anthology on critical issues, *pro* and *con.*, including philosophy, progressive education, the fundamentals, religion in public education, the social studies, teacher education and teachers; and analyses of criticisms and how to handle them.

Stiles, L.J. (Ed.), *The Teacher's Role in American Society*, New York, Harper and Brothers, 1957.

    This 14th Yearbook of the John Dewey Society analyzes the situation, job, and position of the teacher, his conflicts and problems, and his legal status.

U.S. Department of Health, Education, and Welfare, Office of Education, Washington.

    Television in Education, Bulletin 1957, No. 21, gives information on educational TV for children in schools, and for adults.

Wood, J.P., *Magazines in the United States*, New York, The Ronald Press Company, 1949.

    The social and economic influence of our magazines.

CHAPTER 20

The community
approach to the curriculum

THE LOCAL PATTERN IN AMERICAN EDUCATION

Throughout the development of the American school system, a fundamental policy has been pursued whereby the major support and control of the system have been considered the prime responsibility of the local district. So generally has this policy been pursued that it has become a tradition in school affairs that the local community should retain these prerogatives because it is best informed as to the educational needs which should be met. The legal pattern which was established in the Massachusetts Colony in early colonial days has been followed with few exceptions and few additions until the present.

In contrast to every other large nation in the world, the American school system is not a *national* school system; it is a composite of fifty-one different systems which comprise the fifty states and the District of Columbia. As each state developed and established its statewide system of schools, the pattern which originated in Massachusetts came to be followed generally. Even the Federal government conformed to this pattern when it began to take a part in stimulating certain types of vocational education through the Morrill Acts of 1862 and 1890, and through the Smith-Hughes Act of 1917. One of the guiding principles which Congress adopted for the stimulation of vocational training in the nation required the various states and local communities to match the amount of Federal funds which was granted to them. This Federal policy emphasized again another concept which has also become almost traditional in American education—that the local community should furnish as great a portion of the funds for school support as it is able to do, before it can receive any state funds raised for the same purpose. The equalizing funds of the several states for the last four decades have been distributed generally on the basis of this concept of maximum local support of schools. A good sample of a law in respect to this stimulation and responsibility of local districts is found in the present statutes of New York State, which require that local districts tax themselves in proportion to their resources before they can participate in state funds.

Only two states have departed from this traditional procedure of vesting support and control in the local school board. North Carolina and Delaware have attempted to take over the major support of all public schools within their borders; in those states, the funds are handled by a state board of education and are allotted to the various local systems. Therefore, financial control of the schools in these two states has passed in great part from the local board to the state governing body, although in other respects a local board has control of the school program. Except for meeting the minimum requirements of state laws or the regulations of the state board of education, even in North Carolina and Delaware the curricular program is left primarily to the local boards to formulate and administer.

During all the recent agitation for Federal aid for general education, one principle has been reiterated, namely, that the control of the schools should be left in the hands of state and local authorities, as has been the custom in the past. Most educators believe that no central authority is able to know in detail all of the complicating factors which make each school situation and each local community different from all other communities. Of course, a certain amount of Federal control has always followed Federal aid.

LACK OF A NATIONAL PATTERN A STIMULUS TO CURRICULUM DEVELOPMENT. Two communities may have apparently the same conditions, they may have the same number of children in school, and they may seem to be alike in all respects; yet those two communities will differ in many ways in regard to their philosophy of education, their *mores* and manners of living, and their standards of achievement. The type of school organization and program which may fit one community very well may not fit the other satisfactorily. With regard to the organization of both the elementary and the secondary schools, it has already been pointed out that uniformity in school administration and organization is desirable and necessary only in so far as such uniformity will enable pupils to transfer from one school system to another without loss of time. Uniformity and standardization in the development of the school curriculum are neither desirable nor profitable; it has been primarily through the freedom which has been granted to individual school systems to improve and develop their own programs of study that the rest of the schools have made progress.

For example, assume that a large city like Baltimore has been granted permission by the legislature of Maryland to levy an additional tax for school support, in order that she might improve her system for schools and offer a better curriculum. Baltimore's experiment with such a program may result in such marked improvement that other cities and districts may wish to follow suit and develop more suitable curricula for their individual communities. From this illustration, it is seen that local freedom to experiment in school affairs in order to meet local needs more effectively is absolutely necessary if progress is to be made in improving curricular programs.

THE COMMUNITY AS THE CENTER OF NATIONAL PLANNING

Small-Town Characteristics of American Life. The great majority of Americans are "small-towners"; most of us were reared in a community of 10,000 population or less, or in a rural section, and we tend to retain those small-town characteristics. Some of those characteristics are a sense of neighborliness; a feeling of neighborhood unity, even though we may be in the heart of a big city; freedom to express ourselves about the community services and schools, as well as about all other matters; an interest in local doings and in local people; and a desire to have a hand in the making of community policies and in the governing of the community.

Because of the enlarged scope of the social functions of government in recent years, there has been a sharp trend toward the centralization of power and control over certain functions and responsibilities which formerly were considered to be peculiarly within the province of the local community. Illustrations of this trend are the following: the centralized distribution of welfare or relief funds; the control of public health and sanitation; the organization of public recreation; the administration of social security; crop control; and the regulation of wages and hours in industry. It would be unfortunate if this tendency toward centralization should take away from individual communities their sense of responsibility for certain functions of local government. When a community is not forced to contribute financially to the support of its own local institutions and government, it quickly loses the incentive and the desire to control and improve these services.

THE COMMUNITY APPROACH TO THE CURRICULUM. The community approach to curriculum improvement is based on sound psychological principles. If the standards of living in a particular community are low, is it the duty of the state or the national government to attempt to raise these standards of living by imposing a special type of educational organization on that community? Would such a procedure take into account the peculiar needs of that community? Would it stimulate the people of that community to make their own achievements, based on their own responsibilities, plans, and ambitions? Does the individual community have a responsibil'ty to itself and its own development, to the cooperative solution of its own problems, to meeting its own needs? Does each community have a "community individuality," just as each individual has his individuality?

In the final analysis, the school is engaged in the most comprehensive form of social work which exists; this social work is the development and guidance of individuals for the types of work for which they are best fitted, and in which they will be happiest and most successful. Here there is no production pattern or model, as is possible in the machine production of automobiles or airplanes, for example. Each individual is an organism existing in a local culture or environment called the local community. This local community is in turn a part of the larger community called the state;

the state in turn is a part of a still larger community called the nation, which finally is a part of the even larger organization called the world. Individual teaching and counseling, therefore, do not call for mass production, but for individual guidance—a process which cannot be adapted to the methods of mass production.

SCHOOL-COMMUNITY INTERDEPENDENCE. School administrators have recognized at last that the consolidation of school districts

FIG. 45   *Cooperative curriculum planning*
Parents, pupils, and teachers engage in discussion of general education. (*Courtesy Denver Public Schools.*)

alone will not of itself solve the problem of a better educational program for all of the children who are involved. A new concept of school consolidation has emerged, which is based on the idea of school-community interdependence;[1] the limits for this type of consolidation should be the area in which people every day associate naturally in their social and economic life. This interdependence of community and school calls for the solution of problems both of the consumer and of the producer, a mutual understanding of the prob-

---

[1] *Education in Rural Communities*, 51st Yearbook, Part II, National Society for the Study of Education, 1952, Chap. IV, and *School District Organization*, Report of the Commission on School District Reorganization, 1958, *passim*, published by the American Association of School Administrators.

lems concerned, a working out of problems on a cooperative basis, and the formulation of a school program which will assist materially in accomplishing these purposes.

This new concept of school-community interdependence is essentially the same as that of "regional development," a movement to which attention has been directed nationally for some time. It is operative also in the new idea of the "balanced state," where the state concerned is essentially of homogeneous population and has the same climate, good resources, and production and consumption problems of a similar nature. On a national scale, this same concept of interdependence is evident in the attempt to strike a happy balance between the production and consumption of raw materials and finished products—a "balanced economy." So important is this new philosophy of local, state, regional, and national community development that we include here some illustrations of it as it affects the school curriculum.

CURRICULUM EXPERIMENTS IN LOCAL COMMUNITIES

EXPERIMENTS IN KENTUCKY AND WEST VIRGINIA. *The Use of Resources in Education* [2] gives the history of the operation of two experimental rural schools in their relation to the community. The first of these experimental schools was developed in the Roger Clark Ballard Memorial School in Jefferson County, Kentucky, from 1929 to 1934. A group of parents and the Board of Education of Jefferson County sponsored the experiment. The Ballard Memorial School began their program by attempting to answer the community's needs and by using its facilities for this purpose. Health and physical care for children and adults were developed; sanitation was taught and practiced; agriculture and household crafts were part of the regular work; recreation, parent education, and civic responsibility were promoted as part of the usual task of the school in cooperation with the community and the parents.

The second community school which Miss Clapp described was located in Arthurdale, West Virginia. This school was in a home-

[2] By Elsie Ripley Clapp, New York, Harper and Brothers, 1952.

stead community, sponsored and subsidized by the Federal government. The school staff in this resettlement experiment cooperated with the state and county authorities to organize a curriculum adapted to the community's needs. Formal courses of study and standardized grading were not present to hamper the school program. The community became the working laboratory of the pupils; pupil experiences were based primarily upon the community and the vocational life of the pupils. The Arthurdale health problem, a nursery school, recreation, adult education, summer activities, and school and community living were tackled. After continuing two years, this school was transferred to the regular direction of the county and state school authorities; but the West Virginia Advisory School Committee voted unanimously to consider Arthurdale as a community school and to carry on the work which had been started so well.

FIVE-YEAR COMMUNITY HIGH SCHOOLS IN ATLANTA. The Atlanta (Georgia) city school system after World War II made a forward-looking step toward the correlation of school and community in an urban environment. In September, 1947, this system was changed from a plan with large citywide, non-coeducational high schools to a plan consisting of coeducational high schools located in the various "communities" over the city. Study in preparation for this reorganization program was begun at the close of 1946, when the Atlanta Board of Education directed the Superintendent of Schools to conduct a curriculum study.[3] The study was planned in two parts: (1) development of a program of studies for the new "five-year community high schools" and (2) the implementation phase, a continuing study and adaptation of the curriculum to fit into changing needs as the program progressed and the situations changed. The following were responsible for the development of the program: The Superintendent of Atlanta Public Schools, the Atlanta Board of Education, the Education Committee of the Atlanta Chamber of Commerce, laymen, civic organizations, regular professional school personnel, and some consultants.

The program of studies was developed by committees in the

---

[3] *Five-Year Community High Schools of Atlanta*, a Report to the Superintendent and to the Board of Education, May, 1947, p. 1.

subject-matter areas, a steering committee, a committee on guidance and evaluation, and an administrative committee. The administrative committee reviewed and coordinated the reports and recommendations of the subcommittees; the final program which was proposed was the result of the analysis by this committee of the preliminary committee reports. This program of studies was published as the report of the Coordinator to the Superintendent and Board of Education.

The implementation phase of the curriculum study consisted of a continuing emphasis on improving means and methods of making an effective program. Many of the same committees and some new ones have continued to work on this phase of the study. The Atlanta Area Teacher Education Service in its in-service training program through local teacher training institutions is correlated with this work. Thus, teachers may improve their understandings and competencies for the new program while directing it to utilize better the community approach.

The scope of civic interest in the new five-year community high-school program is seen in the production of a social-studies textbook, *Building Atlanta's Future.*[4] It was produced at the direction of the Board of Education and under the guidance of an advisory committee of Atlanta business and civic leaders. This social science textbook was designed to fill the need for local material in the Community Citizenship course prescribed for the eighth grade. It emphasizes the importance of the community in the lives of people; it sets forth a framework for the improvement of community, city, region, nation, and world through citizen cooperation; and it is itself an example of cooperative effort.

The Atlanta program was unique in that its approach to the curriculum was through local communities within a metropolitan district. Continued effort is being put forth to improve coordination between the city system and the surrounding county and suburban systems.

EFFORTS OF THE W.K. KELLOGG FOUNDATION IN THE DEVELOPMENT

[4] John E. Ivey, Jr., N.J. Demerath, and Woodrow Breland, University of North Carolina Press, 1948. This publication was prepared in collaboration with the Institute for Research in Social Science of the University of North Carolina.

OF COMMUNITY HEALTH AND EDUCATION PROJECTS. The W.K. Kellogg Foundation was established in 1930 for the purpose of promoting the health, education, and welfare of mankind, particularly of children.

During the first twelve years of its existence the Foundation's operations were largely local and regional. A large part of its expenditures were made for programs within Michigan. The Foundation's chief interest at this time was a long-term program for the improvement of living conditions in rural areas, known as the Michigan Community Health Project. This program involved seven counties in southwestern Michigan with a total population of approximately 220,000 people. The principal aspects of this program included: [5] (1) the subsidizing of county health departments, medical and dental services for children, the postgraduate education of physicians, dentists, teachers, clergymen, and other professional and lay groups; (2) the promotion of community organization for health services, of camping, and other leisure activities; and (3) aid in the development of local libraries, in the construction of hospitals and consolidated schools, in the improvement of small rural schools, and in the improvement of medical diagnostic facilities and other hospital services.

When the United States entered World War II, the Foundation revised its program to direct as large a part of its resources as possible to national defense. Grants were made to professional schools to provide loan and scholarship funds for students preparing for military or civilian health services. During these years there was developed also a program of international scholarships, providing graduate and postgraduate study in the United States and Canada for members of the health professions in other countries, chiefly from Central and South America.

The W.K. Kellogg Foundation began the extension of programs in community health and education on a national scale in 1945. Since then it has assisted about half the states in subsidizing and developing programs similar to the original Michigan Community

---

[5] The early activities of the Foundation were described in *W.K. Kellogg Foundation, The First Eleven Years, 1930–41,* 1942, pp. 1–151; see also *The First Twenty-Five Years: The Story of a Foundation,* 1955, Chaps. II–V, both published by W.K. Kellogg Foundation, Battle Creek.

Health Project, most of them for a three-year period only. For example, Alabama is one of the states that received a grant-in-aid for scholarships from the W.K. Kellogg Foundation in developing their school and community health education program.[6] After the expiration of these three-year programs, five states were selected to be assisted for a further period of five years. However, no attempt to impose any pattern of development was made in these states; these programs took many different turns in the various states as their needs dictated.

In general education, the Foundation has had three chief interests: (1) the development of health education in the public schools through cooperation with the state departments of health and education, especially in the training of health educators; (2) the general improvement of rural schools; and (3) school camping as a function of public education. A special feature of the original Michigan Community Health Project was three camp schools for children, completely equipped, which operated both winter and summer. The Foundation granted funds for integration of camping and outdoor education into school programs in Michigan, California, New York, and Washington, resulting in the Foundation being labeled frequently as "the father of school camping." Since 1950 the Foundation has focused its attention primarily on the improvement of school administration through better-trained leaders.

OTHER COMMUNITY EXPERIMENTS. School administrators and teachers are familiar with the work of a broad community nature which was carried on by Superintendent Carleton Washburne, his staff, and his community at Winnetka, Illinois, over a period of twenty-five years. Other earlier experiments in community approach to the curriculum have been the following: the programs in the rural communities of Big Lick Community, Tennessee, and Pine Mountain in Harlan County, Kentucky; the Glencoe Community Coordinating Council in Glencoe, Illinois; the Dowagiac Community Plan at Dowagiac, Michigan;[7] the Community Councils of

[6] *Healthful Living in School and Community, Bulletin No. 3*, 1946, Division of Instruction, State Board of Education, Montgomery, Alabama, 1946, p. vii.
[7] Cf. the following issues of the *Curriculum Journal*: Vol. xi (March, 1940), pp. 110–14; Vol. x (April, 1939), pp. 161–63; Vol. x (November, 1939), pp. 317–19; and Vol. x (October, 1939), pp. 273–74.

Pittsburgh and Allegheny County, Pennsylvania; [8] and the "Citizens Councils" of Connecticut.[9] Reports of more recent experiments in community approach to the curriculum are described in *The Community School*, Part II of the Fifty-second Yearbook of the National Society for the Study of Education and in *The Modern Community School*.[10]

FAMILY LIFE EDUCATION. Recently much emphasis in the schools has been placed on family living. Educators in the field of family life education have become conscious of the fact that training for family life cannot be promoted adequately in the schools alone. Over the country various educators have attempted to make family life education functional by using the community as a laboratory in an effort to study cooperatively family life problems and needs, and the resources that could be mobilized to meet these problems and needs.

In 1938 the United States Office of Education, recognizing the need for controlled experimentation and evaluation of certain aspects of community organization, sponsored four experimental programs in family life education.[11] The areas selected were Obion County, Tennessee; Box Elder County, Utah; Wichita, Kansas; and Toledo, Ohio. The main purpose of these experiments was to bring about richer and more realistic programs of education for family living through the cooperative efforts of school and community agencies. Each program was a local enterprise, directed and controlled by its own administration and community circumstances; however, special consultant services were offered to these centers by the United States Office of Education.

As a result of the progress shown by these four experimental community programs, the United States Office of Education in 1941

[8] William Bacon, "When Neighbors Get Together," *Educational Leadership,* II (December, 1944), pp. 111–14.

[9] "Citizens' Councils Help in Connecticut" by Helen F. Storen in *Laymen Help Plan the Curriculum,* Association for Supervision and Curriculum Development, National Education Association, 1946, p. 26.

[10] E.G. Olsen (Ed.), New York, Appleton-Century-Crofts, 1953, Chaps. III–V.

[11] *Cf. With Focus on Family Living* by Muriel W. Brown, Federal Security Agency, Office of Education, Home Economics Education Series No. 28, 1953, *passim.*

offered vocational funds to states for the promotion of similar programs. For example, through the Division of Vocational Education
of the State Department of Public Instruction in North Carolina,
funds were offered to local urban centers to employ a person qualified in techniques of community organization and family life education as a coordinator.[12] This person was to take the leadership in
helping the community to plan and evolve a community program of
family life education. Such programs were established in the urban
areas of Raleigh, Wilmington, and Greensboro, North Carolina, and
are still operating effectively.

In addition to the establishment of these family life education
centers, a conference on family living was held in Raleigh, North
Carolina, in the fall of 1948. The conference was conducted by the
State Department with the help of some fifty agencies and organizations of the state interested in family living. The purposes of the
conference were: (1) to point up the strengths and problems of
North Carolina families and (2) to develop means for using resources for better family living in North Carolina.

Education of this type for family living is carried on by both
governmental and nongovernmental agencies and organizations. At
a national level, there are family life specialists giving service to
the states in the Extension Service of the United States Department
of Agriculture, in the United States Office of Education, and in the
Children's Bureau of the Department of Health, Education, and
Welfare. Some national agencies and organizations specializing in
family life education include (1) the General Federation of
Women's Clubs, (2) the American Association of University
Women, (3) the National Council of Family Relations, (4) the
National Committee on Parent Education, (5) the National Con-
gress of Parents and Teachers, and (6) the Association for Family
Living.[13]

On the state level, state governments are broadening their offerings in family life education through state departments of health,

[12] *Cf.* Virginia Ward, Mary E. York, and Mrs. Jessie S. Grigg, "Community
Organization for Family Life Education," *North Carolina Education,* x (April,
1944), pp. 392–94, 406.
[13] M. L. Ely (Ed.), *Handbook on Adult Education in the United States,* Institute of Adult Education, Teachers College, Columbia University, 1948.

education, and welfare, and through the Cooperative Extension Services. A few state departments of public instruction have specialists in parent education or family living on their staffs. All the states have supervisors of vocational home economics, who give full time to homemaking programs. As for the local level, agencies and organizations at work on family life education are many. Home demonstration agents in the counties and city centers concern themselves with home interests in their work with adults. Teachers under the Federal vocational acts conduct similar programs in family living in communities in which they teach.

THE STATE AS THE LARGER COMMUNITY

CITIZENS' FACT-FINDING MOVEMENT OF GEORGIA. Significant progress has been made in centering curricular problems around the state. One of the first illustrations of this type of curriculum approach was the work which was done in Georgia by the Citizens' Fact-Finding Movement. This organization was begun in 1937. By the end of World War II it was composed of more than 250,000 citizens who represented seventeen statewide organizations and their 5,000 affiliated local units, working and thinking together on Georgia's problems. In the beginning years of the Movement, ten to twelve pamphlets were issued annually as factual reports on Georgia. Among these pamphlets were three series; these dealt with Georgia's historical background, its natural resources, agriculture, industry and commerce, health, education, public welfare, penal system, political system, tax system, Federal activity in Georgia, and the state's religious, civic, and social forces.

The Fact-Finding Movement published a comprehensive source book on Georgia, *Georgia Facts in Figures* in 1946. This book was designed to facilitate comparisons of Georgia with the nation; thus, not only facts and figures about Georgia were given, but also a comparison of those in Georgia with those in the nation as a whole.

The Citizens' Fact-Finding Movement in Georgia is generally referred to by writers on the community school as one of the first fact-finding survey groups.[14]

[14] *Cf. The Modern Community School*, Part II, 52nd Yearbook of the National Society for the Study of Education, 1953, pp. 84–86.

STATE CITIZENS' COUNCILS. A fast-growing movement at the state level has been the formation of citizens' committees for the public schools. Connecticut (1937), Alabama (1938), North Caro-

FIG. 46   *What kinds of machine shop practice are needed for the nuclear age?*
(Courtesy Charlotte (N.C.) College, 1958.)

lina (1942), Florida (1945), and Delaware (1946) were leaders, each operating independently to organize citizens' groups for better public schools. For example, a Connecticut's citizens' council was organized by the commissioner of education to advise him and his State Board on educational policies; in 1952 this council organized the Connecticut Citizens' Commission for Public Schools, with sixty charter members, whose purpose is to secure cooperation of citizens to support and improve the schools.

This kind of organization in North Carolina took a little different approach. It is called the United Forces for Education, a state committee representative of seven different citizens' groups: (1) Congress of Parents and Teachers; (2) North Carolina Education Association; (3) the Grange; (4) Federation of Women's Clubs; (5) North Carolina Farm Bureau; (6) Junior Chamber of Commerce; and (7) State School Board Association. They plan and work to promote progressive school legislation at both local and state levels.

Though these state organizations have usually as their major purpose the promotion of better schools through legislative channels, their influence tends to be powerful in regard to curricular matters. For example, in Florida and Utah, comprehensive studies of the public school system and curricular programs came out of the cooperative work of their committees; and a comprehensive state curricular study is under way in North Carolina with the aid of these seven groups and special citizens' committees for the schools at the local level.[15]

THE ILLINOIS SECONDARY-SCHOOL CURRICULUM PROGRAM. This statewide program for the improvement of secondary education was planned as a cooperative effort sponsored by the State Superintendent of Public Instruction; statewide groups representing industry, business, agriculture, and labor; other professional educational groups, such as the Illinois Secondary-School Principals' Association, institutions of higher learning; and cooperating schools and school systems on a voluntary basis. In all, thirty-two different lay and professional organizations took part.[16] Started in 1947, a Steering Committee from these various groups guided the Study. It was financed primarily by the state, with higher institutions and individual participating schools also contributing for their parts in the cooperative enterprise.

[15] Turn to *Citizen Cooperation for Better Public Schools*, Part I, 53rd Yearbook of the National Society for the Study of Education, for a fuller account of this important movement on local, state, regional, and national levels.

[16] A brief account of the first five years of the study is found in Vol. xxvii of the *California Journal of Secondary Education*, "The Illinois Secondary School Curriculum Program," by C.W. Sanford and W.B. Spalding, January, 1952, pp. 28–35.

The Illinois program (commonly referred to as the ISSCP) had six main purposes which can be summarized thus:

1. To coordinate on a statewide level and on a particular local level all the persons or agencies who are or should be interested in and concerned with the secondary-school curriculum.
2. To sponsor studies and research basic to revision of the curriculum.
3. To encourage experimental curriculum projects.
4. To conduct workshops for principals and teachers.
5. To prepare and distribute publications and studies.
6. To establish relationships with colleges looking toward modification of college admission requirements.

In the first five years of the ISSCP, 1947–1952, the main emphasis was upon statewide study of the high school. Since then, enlargement of the program took place, bringing study also of the elementary-school curriculum.

Many bulletins and guides to curriculum building were published from time to time by the Office of the Illinois Superintendent of Public Instruction (Springfield). The range of these publications is all the way from research studies which developed instruments for assessment of the guidance program, extracurricular activities, and holding power of the school to human relations in curriculum change and curriculum guides. Titles of representative types of publications are:

Basic Studies of the Curriculum Program

How to Conduct the Holding Power Study, Bulletin No. 3, 1949
How to Conduct the Participation in Extra-Class Activities Study, Bulletin No. 5, 1949
How to Conduct the Hidden Tuition Costs Study, Bulletin No. 4, 1949
How to Conduct the Study of the Guidance Services of the School, Bulletin No. 6, 1949.
How to Conduct the Follow-Up Study, Bulletin No. 11, 1950

Curriculum Guides

Guide to the Study of the Curriculum in the Secondary Schools of Illinois, Curricular Series A, No. 51, Bulletin No. 1, 1948
Guides to Curriculum Planning—The Junior High School Level, Bulletin No. 8, 1949
Educating the Mentally Handicapped in the Secondary Schools, Bulletin No. 12, 1951

A Study of Practices and Opinions in Physical Education, Health, and Safety, Bulletin No. 14, 1951

What Do You Think of Our School's Family Living Program? Inventory A, Local Area Consensus Study No. 2, 1951

Miscellaneous

Human Relations in Curriculum Change, Bulletin No. 7, 1949

New College Admission Requirements Recommended, Bulletin No. 9, 1950

The Story in Nineteen Schools, Bulletin No. 10, 1950

The Schools and National Security, Bulletin No. 16, 1951

Index to Reading Materials in Use in Human Relations Programs in Secondary Schools, 1952

Resource Materials for Unit on Magazines in the Secondary School, 1952

THE REGIONAL APPROACH TO THE CURRICULUM

Newer developments prophesy more and more curriculum activity which will be centered around the region. The work and stimulation coming from such widely different groups as the Institute for Research in Social Science at the University of North Carolina and the Southern Regional Education Board have resulted in a new kind of approach to problems which has broad implications for curriculum work. This regional approach is wider than the boundaries of any one state; it takes into account the many similar problems confronting natural geographic, social, and economic areas as well as political divisions. Educational institutions and organizations, large and small private groups, and governmental agencies are engaged now in trying to solve the problems of the various regions in the United States.

THE WORK OF ODUM'S GROUP IN REGIONALISM. The Institute for Research in Social Science at the University of North Carolina has been the pioneer in the study of regional development. This institute is administered under a board of governors which represents university schools and departments and other units allied with social sciences. An executive committee of eight board members acts for the Board between meetings. It was founded in 1924 by Howard W. Odum, who served as Director for the first twenty years.

Major functions of the Institute are (1) to encourage and stimu-

late research in the social sciences at the University of North Carolina and to map out a coordinated and integrated research program;
(2) to serve as a center for discovering and developing personnel
in social science research; (3) to serve as a center for cooperation
with other agencies toward the development and testing of
procedures for making social science research of more functional
value.

Regionalism and achieving an understanding of the state and the
South have been dominant themes in the research program. During
the past decade, however, the Institute has added a widening variety
of behavioral science research financed largely by foundation grants
and by Federal agencies. Current research may be grouped under
communication, community, complex social organization, demog-
raphy, economic behavior, folk cultures, human relations in industry, land-use patterns, marriage and the family, mental health,
personality, political behavior, public opinion, race relations, small-
group behavior, social aspects of health and medical care, southern
regional and North Carolina studies (culture, history, industrial
development, regional development, rural life), survey research,
and urban studies.

In recent years, the Institute has extended its program and has
developed several specific focal areas of research, namely, an
Organization Research Group which carries on research in small-
group dynamics and complex organizations; an area which concen-
trates on the social science aspects of health and the health professions; a group concentrating on the study of political behavior;
and an Urban Studies Program, which centers around the "urban
development in the Piedmont Industrial Crescent, a regional cluster
of cities and towns located along the railway and superhighway system which forms the corridor through the Piedmont connecting
Washington with Atlanta." Although in this program major attention is focused on the Piedmont Industrial Crescent, much of the
research is organized so as to permit comparative studies with
established metropolitan areas such as Atlanta. This program is also
an excellent example of the interdisciplinary nature of the research
carried on by the Institute, since staff members from anthropology,

city and regional planning, economics, law, political science, social psychology, and sociology are participating and cooperating in studying this subregion. In addition, the following facilities are offered by the Institute: a Small-Group Laboratory with facilities for observation and a Social Science Statistical Laboratory.

The Institute is supported by funds from private sources, government contracts, and University appropriations. Since 1924, it has published more than 200 books and monographs, 700 articles, and 1,000 manuscripts, by more than 350 authors.

For example, a current publication by S.H. Hobbs, Jr., research professor in the Institute, is *North Carolina: An Economic and Social Profile.* This is a source book which brings together a vast fund of information on North Carolina's human and natural resources, economic progress, and institutions. The text is supplemented by 19 maps and figures and 124 tables. The Institute has also sponsored a series of field studies in the modern culture of the South under the direction of John P. Gillin, research professor in the Institute. Two recent publications in this series are *Blackways of Kent* by Hylan Lewis and *Millways of Kent* by J. Kenneth Morland. Each of these is a study of a subculture of a small southern Piedmont town designated as Kent. One presents the structure and content of the culture of the Negro; the other is a cultural study of the white population who work in the textile mills. A third volume, *The Townways of Kent,* by Ralph Patrick, Jr., a study of the old aristocracy, the middle class, and the newly rich collectively, will complete the trilogy and round out the picture.

Other recent volumes on the southern regions by the Institute staff include *The Urban South,* edited by Rupert B. Vance and N.J. Demerath, a series of fourteen papers on various aspects of the urbanization of the South by leading authorities in the field; *Community Power Structure* by Floyd Hunter, a study of power leaders in a southern community called "Regional City"; and *The Cokers of Carolina,* a biography of five generations of the distinguished Coker family, by George L. Simpson, Jr.

THE NORTHWEST REGIONAL COUNCIL. In the Pacific Northwest, the Northwest Regional Council pioneered in cooperation with the

Seattle schools in developing curricular materials on the resources of this region. The Council, privately financed by civic and business leaders, has had the specific purpose of helping to bring to teachers, in an attractive and reliable form, the best information and research on their regional problems. The first educational materials which were developed by the Council included "Know Your Northwest Series" and *Caravans to the Northwest*.[17]

SOUTHERN REGIONAL EDUCATION BOARD. This Board is a cooperative agency of sixteen southern states. Established and approved by legislative action, its primary purpose is to help the states by sharing their resources for higher education. The governors of the states are ex-officio members, and each appoints four representatives; one of these four is usually the state superintendent of public instruction. An offshoot from its parent body, the annual Southern Governors' Conference, this group has been powerful in educational planning on a region-wide basis. The Board now has an annual budget of close to $1,000,000, a large part of it given by private foundations to finance research projects.

Two other groups in the South have worked closely with the Southern Regional Education Board. These are the annual Southern Conference on Business and Industry and the Southern States Work Conference on Educational Problems.[18]

THE UNITED STATES AS THE NATIONAL COMMUNITY

Since 1931 the Federal government has paid markedly increased attention to the development of the nation through a study of the resources and problems of the regions of the country. Both in terms of the contribution to the total welfare of the nation and in terms of long-term economic planning on a national scale, such Federal regional study is important. Typical of this emphasis of the government on regional growth, as a component part of national progress,

---

[17] John Blanchard, Boston, Houghton Mifflin Company, 1940. For a later guidebook, read *Sawdust Empire* by Howard M. Brier, New York, Alfred A. Knopf, 1958.
[18] For an example of their work, read *Rural Education in the South,* a Report of the Southern States Work Conference on Educational Problems, 1954–1957, State Department of Education, Tallahassee (Fla.).

are the curricular bulletins of the United States Office of Education on the conservation of national resources; of the vocational division of the United States Department of Agriculture on soil adaptation and land planning; and of the Soil Conservation Division on soil erosion and conservation of natural resources. Other publications with emphasis on the United States as a national community have been reports of various councils and commissions to the President or to the Federal government, such as the Annual Economic Reports of the Council of Economic Advisers to the President and *Higher Education for American Democracy*.[19] In addition to the publications mentioned above, there have been those by various educational organizations and groups stressing the development of the nation through study of its resources and problems; for example, *School Boards in Action, Schools for a New World, The Expanding Role of Education, American School Curriculum, Education for American Citizenship*, and *The High School in a Changing World;* [20] *Community Living and the Elementary School;* [21] *Juvenile Delinquency and the Schools* and *The Community School;* [22] and *Large Was Our Bounty* and *What Shall The High School Teach?* [23]

One of the most important and serious problems which the regions of the nation face is that of the displacement of people because of changes in the type of agriculture or use of the land, or the introduction of new labor-saving machinery, or both. For example, from Tennessee through Mississippi to Alabama in the old Black Prairie Belt, cotton has been rapidly replaced by dairy farming and cattle raising, occupations in which a few workmen can take care of hundreds of acres. In the days when cotton reigned supreme, these same hundreds of acres were occupied by 75 to 100 families and furnished work and subsistence to them. How are these people

[19] *A Report of the President's Commission on Higher Education,* New York, Harper and Brothers, 1948.

[20] American Association of School Administrators, National Education Association, 24th (1946), 25th (1947), 26th (1948), 31st (1953), 32nd (1954), and 36th (1955) Yearbooks, respectively.

[21] 24th Yearbook, Department of Elementary School Principals, National Education Association, 1945.

[22] 47th and 52nd Yearbooks, National Society for the Study of Education, 1948 and 1953.

[23] Association for Supervision and Curriculum Development, National Education Association, 1948 and 1956 Yearbooks, respectively.

who have been displaced by this change in the use of the land going to be provided for, going to be resettled, going to be prevented from becoming wanderers over the face of the earth looking for work of the type which they can do?

PLANNING BOARDS. Planning boards on national, regional, state, and local levels have also stimulated community-wide educational planning. On a national level an early example was the National Resources Planning Board, which functioned from 1939 to 1944. Good examples of national planning groups today are the Education Policies Commission,[24] the National Citizens' Council for Better Schools,[25] and the National School Boards Association. The Tennessee Valley Authority's Advisory Panel furnished a good sample of the regional type. During and directly after World War II, many states established state planning boards; some of these were organized on a permanent basis, while others were temporary organizations for postwar planning and reconversion. These state planning boards varied as to purposes and functions; most of them concerned themselves with all sorts of problems and needs of the state as a whole, including educational needs. At the local level there has been much stimulation of town and city planning boards since 1944. There were several causes for this: (1) necessity for new public buildings which were held in abeyance during the war period; (2) the relocation of many industries and the reconversion of others; (3) the rapid development of (unplanned) urban-fringe areas; and (4) the demand for increased social services at public expense, such as hospitals and health services and extension of recreational facilities.

IMPLICATIONS OF THE COMMUNITY APPROACH FOR CURRICULAR DEVELOPMENT

As he considers the development and growth of the community idea in education and in American life, the following questions naturally come to the mind of the teacher: (1) What are the values

[24] Of the N.E.A. and A.A.S.A.
[25] New York 16, N.Y.

Preparing to Can

FIG. 47 *Cannery is operated by students as a service to the community*
(Photographs courtesy Montevallo (Ala.) High School.)

of this approach for the curriculum? (2) What are the values for the community? (3) What are the values for teacher education?

The answers to these questions have become pretty plain as a result of the progress made during the last thirty years in planning both for the community school and for using community resources in teaching. In the first place, the modern curriculum has a large part of its work embedded in home-school-community relationships. For example, the study of housing and the home, consumer education, applied economics and applied science, and courses in social living for children are being added to or incorporated as a part of the school curriculum as never before. In the second place, the values to be attained by children from such studies will remain more potential than real unless there is cooperative school-community planning. Third, by far the largest number of Americans live in communities of 10,000 or less population. Community planning for our fast-growing population has become a major task, and citizens of each community have become cognizant of the need for it. In addition, the American citizen today takes a more active part than he ever did in cooperative efforts for better schools and a better curricular program. Therefore the community idea cannot and will not be abandoned. Finally, the alert teacher in a fast-changing subject-matter field, such as the social studies or science, simply cannot afford not to make use of community resources in his teaching—his work would be incomplete without the reality of the field trip, the resource person from industry or labor, or the history and use of the products being manufactured under his nose.

Whether the community or the school takes the lead in organizational and survey work for the community approach to the curriculum is immaterial; both approaches have been successful, and instruments and methods for carrying on such work are many, and available. One of the trends in curriculum growth is already clearly defined—that of closer school-community action in providing for children a program which gives them a better understanding of their region and their world and a more adequate preparation for living happily and efficiently in it.

PROBLEMS FOR INDIVIDUAL STUDY
AND CLASS DISCUSSION

1. If you wanted to make a survey of your community to discover its resources for enriching your curriculum work, how would you go about it?

2. If your community decided to make year-round use of its school plants for a community recreation program, what changes would you contemplate in your present school curriculum looking toward that end?

3. What factors make for school-community solidarity and cooperation?

4. Assume that your community wishes to establish a Planning Council for community betterment, and that as a teacher in the school you are appointed to that body. What plans would you suggest for building the school curriculum more closely around community activities and needs?

5. Should the school serve as a clearing house for sentiment on community matters? Support your position.

6. Select any community mentioned in *Education in Rural Communities* (51st Yearbook, N.S.S.E.). What curricular activities that were centered around the life of this community could be used profitably in your own community? Explain.

7. How would you proceed to gather as complete a list as possible of the source materials on your state and its industries for use in enriching your class work?

8. If you had the task of dividing up the United States into "regions" for national planning, how many regions would you make and what states would you list in each? Why?

9. What should you attempt to teach your pupils about your community law enforcement agencies, warrants, and local, state and Federal jurisdiction?

10. How could you use your particular community as a source of materials for your French teaching? For your English work? For your health and physical education curriculum?

11. Should the school foster the community chest campaign? Why or why not?

12. Assume that the churches in your community have agreed to engage and pay a teacher of the Bible for the schools. Should this teacher be under the direction of the school superintendent, responsible to him, and should school credit for graduation be given for the work? Support your position.

13. Should each school system have its own public health service, or

should it be served by the community public health authorities? Support your stand.

14. Select any state "guide" book, either of your own state or one from your general geographical region. Which of the materials in it could you use effectively in your class work?

ADDITIONAL ANNOTATED REFERENCES FOR PROBLEM OR UNIT STUDY

Campbell, B., *Sixty-Three Tested Practices in School-Community Relations*, New York, Metropolitan School Study Council (525 W. 120th St.), 1954.

Twenty-five school superintendents here identify and describe a large number of successful public-relations practices.

Campbell, R.F., and Ramseyer, J.A., *The Dynamics of School-Community Relationships*, New York, Allyn and Bacon, 1955.

Gives the background for the public unrest about educational problems, clarifies the controversial issues, and offers principles and guides for better working understanding between citizens and school personnel.

Cook, L.A., and E.F,. *A Sociological Approach to Education* (2nd ed.), New York, McGraw-Hill Book Company, 1957.

The third edition of one of the standard casebooks in the study of American community life, and how cooperative action through the schools can help to solve many community problems.

Hamlin, H.M., *Citizens' Committees in the Public Schools*, Danville (Ill.), the Interstate Printers and Publishers, 1952.

A veteran in this field, he identifies citizen participation, the types, activities, and ways of organization; he also points out dangers as well as strong points, and covers the literature on the movement.

Hollingshead, A.B., *Elmtown's Youth*, New York, John Wiley and Sons, 1949.

Its subtitle explains this research study of the youth of a community, that is, the impact of social classes on adolescents.

Lynd, R.S. and H.M., *Middletown* and *Middletown in Transition*, New York, Harcourt, Brace and Company, 1929 and 1937, respectively.

The two well-known pioneer studies of a community over a period of years.

Melby, E.O., *Administering Community Education*, New York, Prentice-Hall, 1954.

Shows the background of the concept, the sources, and applications of a dynamic community-centered educational administration.

Menge, J.W., and Faunce, R.C., *Working Together for Better Schools*, New York, American Book Company, 1958.

Explains clearly how to arouse the interest of the general public in the schools and how to implement citizen participation in planning curricula and activities.

Moehlman, A.B., and Van Zwoll, J.A., *School Public Relations*, New York, Appleton-Century-Crofts, 1957.

A solid book on public opinion, propaganda, criticism of the schools; factors basic to good school-public relations, including the importance of the school survey; and the institutional and community agencies that are connected with public relations and how they operate.

National Education Association, Washington 6.

Department of Elementary School Principals, *Parents and the Schools*, 36th Yearbook, 1957; describes patterns of responsibility and authority, cultural influences, how to work with parent groups, teacher-parent conferences, and discussion groups and advisory committees.

Department of Rural Education, *Rural Education—A Forward Look*, 1955 Yearbook; gives an account of rural education and its school as a community institution.

Educational Policies Commission; shows how planning can take place in *Education for All American Children*, 1948, and *Education for All American Youth—A Further Look*, 1952.

National School Public Relations Association publishes both a magazine and special bulletins from time to time on how to carry on good public relations and how to work with parent-citizen groups.

National Society for the Study of Education, University of Chicago.

Part I of its 58th Yearbook (1959) is devoted to *Community Education*.

Odum, H.W., *The Way of the South Toward the Regional Balance of America*, New York, The Macmillan Company, 1947.

The classic in setting forth the importance of cooperative regional study and planning.

Olsen, E.G., *et al.*, *School and Community* (rev. ed.), New York, Prentice-Hall, 1954.

Gives the seven basic characteristics of the community school and illustrations.

——— (Ed.), *School and Community Programs*, New York, Prentice-Hall, 1949.

Called a "casebook" of successful practices from kindergarten through college and adult education.

Pierce, T.M., *et al.*, *Community Leadership for Public Education*, New York, Prentice-Hall, 1955.

How individuals make communities, sample communities, the patterns of community forces and status groups, decision-making in school and community.

Punke, H.H., *Community Uses of Public School Facilities*, New York, King's Crown Press, 1951.

The kinds of uses that are in practice now, the law(s) concerning them, and tort or legal liability of school districts in connection with community use.

Stearnes, H.L., *Community Relations and the Public Schools*, New York, Prentice-Hall, 1955.

The educator and school-community-citizenship relations, including problems concerned with parents, labor, industry, the churches, race and nationality, and media of mass communication.

Sumption, M.R., *How to Conduct a Citizens' School Survey*, New York, Prentice-Hall, 1952.

Sane approach to community organization to obtain the data needed for sound, long-range educational planning.

Surveys, school. There are good instruments available for obtaining basic data for cooperative educational planning. Good samples are:

Elementary Evaluative Criteria, School of Education, Boston University, 1953.

Evaluating the Elementary School: A Guide for Cooperative Study, Southern Association of Colleges and Secondary Schools, Atlanta, 1951.

Evaluative Criteria, 1950 Edition, Washington, Cooperative Study of Secondary School Standards. For high schools.

Improving Public Education Through Citizen Participation by M.J. Thomas, University of Pittsburgh, 1954.

Whitelaw, J.B., *The School and its Community* (2nd ed.), Baltimore, the Johns Hopkins Press, 1951.

A revision of his guide for the development of school-community relations.

Yauch, W.A., *How Good Is Your School?* New York, Harper and Brothers, 1951.

A handbook designed specially to help parents, ending with a simple, well-balanced check-list instrument.

Yeager, W.A., *School-Community Relations,* New York, The Dryden Press, 1951.

The standard work in this area, detailed in suggestions and recording of practices.

CHAPTER 21 The curriculum crisis at midcentury

If past history can be used as any indication of what may happen in the future, the existing national and international crisis will improve our school curriculum. National emergencies of all sorts have furthered the cause of education in the United States. After the emergency has been met, an educational residue of some type has resulted in each instance; this residue has improved the curriculum and has advanced the schools a little further in their educational program. This has been true regardless of whether the emergency has been of an international or national nature, whether it has involved a war or merely a business depression. "Sweet are the uses of adversity."

PAST NATIONAL EMERGENCIES AND CURRICULAR PROGRESS [1]

THE MORRILL ACT AND HOAR AND BLAIR BILLS. While the war between the states was in progress, Congress passed the first Morrill Act (1862), from which we developed our colleges of agriculture and mechanic arts; these became known later as "A. and M." colleges, or "land grant" colleges. The Hoar (1870) and Blair (1881) Bills were introduced during the bitter Reconstruction period after the Civil War, proposing Federal assistance for schools; though designed primarily to assist in general education for the southern region, they were the forerunners of the bills introduced perennially in Congress to the present for Federal aid to the various states for general education.

[1] For a more complete account of the curricular changes resulting from changes caused by wars and other national emergencies to 1950, read the revised edition (1950) of this book, *Curriculum Principles and Social Trends*, pp. 705–13.

FEDERAL AID FOR VOCATIONAL EDUCATION, REHABILITATION, AMER-
ICANIZATION, AND ADULT EDUCATION. Again during a war period
the curriculum was strongly affected, and eventually improved, by
Federal legislation. The Smith-Hughes Act (1917) for the further-
ance of vocational education was passed by Congress during World
War I; this act provided for Federal-state cooperation for vocational
education in agriculture, trades and industries, and home economics,
and for the training of teachers for these vocational education fields.
Complementing this action, the Smith-Sears Act (1918) and the
Vocational Rehabilitation Act of 1920 established rehabilitation education for those physically disabled by service in certain branches of
the government during the war; later the Social Security Act of
1935 embraced this responsibility, and still later the Veterans Administration took over this task. About the same time, 1918, two other
types of education emerged distinctly as a result of World War I,
and both have developed rapidly: (1) adult education and (2)
education for Americanization. The draft service of World War I
brought forcibly to the attention of American educators a fact which
census figures had been showing for some time, namely, that many
grown citizens were illiterate altogether, or they possessed only a
meager ability to use the English language. Although most of the
people of foreign birth had become naturalized citizens, it was discovered that many of them knew little and cared less for our democratic institutions and way of life. World War I, through its series
of strikes, propaganda campaigns among the foreign-born, and the
compilation of data on the lack of Americanization of great numbers
of the foreign-born population, jolted America into a realization of a
weakness in its educational structure. As a result, many classes in
adult education were established in an effort to eliminate adult
illiteracy, to acquaint foreign-born persons with American institutions, and to make English the common tongue for all Americans.

From these beginnings, both adult education and education for
Americanization grew rapidly throughout the country. More recently,
Americanization classes have largely taken over the task of preparing foreign-born individuals to meet the requirements for naturaliza-
tion in this country. On the other hand, adult education has
developed far beyond the purpose of reducing illiteracy among the

population; few states fail to make provisions today for adult education along broader lines, such as studies of communities, the discussion of public questions through public forums, clubs, recreation and health activities, and even intellectual pursuits and hobbies of many types.

HAPPENINGS IN THE DEPRESSION DECADE. During the "Great Depression" of the 1930's, events took place and studies were made which resulted in careful study of the school curriculum. President Franklin D. Roosevelt's Advisory Committee on Education made an exhaustive study of all aspects of vocational education and the Federal government's relation to them. The Report showed that the problems of vocational education were interwoven with the larger question of Federal aid to general education; and its recommendations were so conclusive and sweeping that they resulted in stronger pressure than ever for some form of Federal aid to the states for general education. The Report also recommended a rethinking of the program in trades and industries, with better articulation between the school, industry, and labor in "work programs" for youth, that is, part-time work in school and part-time work in industry learning a trade at apprenticeship wages under proper supervision. This recommendation was largely responsible later for the rapid growth of Diversified Occupations (D.O.) courses in the high schools. During the depression, Congress took further action to aid schools to establish work programs for youth with Federal aid. The George-Deen Act (1936) gave assistance to secondary schools for "Distributive Education" (D.E.) programs, under cooperative financial arrangements with the states similar to those of the Smith-Hughes Act. Though much of the Federal appropriation for D.E. work was discontinued about 1950, the individual states, once started on a good thing, took over most of the support of them. Three movements of an emergency nature which have significance for education were started by the Federal government during the most critical years of the business depression in the 1930's. Economic conditions in many rural areas became so critical that those areas were unable to keep their schools open without assistance; for these submarginal districts during 1934 and 1935, government aid was extended from relief funds in the amount of about $22,000,000. This action by the government, although of an emergency character, was an implied recognition for the first time in the history of the United States of the fact that the Federal legislature has an obligation to maintain at least a minimum standard of educational opportunity throughout the country. The second type of activity which was instituted by the national Congress during the depression developed in the form of emergency relief agencies and activities, most of which were interested to a greater or less extent in the extension of educational opportunities for persons in economic distress. These agencies included the Civilian Conservation Corps, the Works Progress Administration, the National Youth Administration, and the Public Works Administration; they and their implications for the curriculum have been discussed in a previous chapter.[2]

The third emergency activity in which the Federal government engaged in the 1930's was assisting in the furnishing of free or low-cost lunches for children in school whose level of living was so sub-marginal that they were being undernourished. This movement grew into a permanent activity, the Federal school lunch program, to which the Federal agencies contribute heavily in the form of food surpluses whose prices the government has to support in the form of minimum price subsidies. Though not directly related to the curriculum, the Federal school lunch program causes school authorities who participate to serve simple, well-balanced meals at a minimum cost, and helps to train children to appreciate and to identify well-balanced diets.

EMERGENCIES SINCE THE SECOND WORLD WAR. During World War II, Congress expanded its appropriations for aid to education for towns and school administrative units that were strongly affected by Federal troop installations, camps, or special government projects. This aid goes more frequently for school buildings, but a large part of it is direct financial aid that may be used to supplement both the equipment and teaching services in such areas.

The George-Barden Act was passed just after World War II (1946), to provide aid to the various states for the training of counselors for guidance work in high schools. Recently, under the pressure of the startling advances made by Russia since 1950 in science,

[2] Chap. 16.

The Curriculum Crisis at Midcentury

economics, and industry, the 85th Congress passed the National Defense Education Act (1958). This act appropriates money for 1958 through 1966, and authorizes through 1966 such appropriations as may be necessary to carry out the program for (1) loans to college undergraduate students, (2) graduate fellowships, (3) guidance, counseling, and testing, primarily on the secondary-school level, (4) science, mathematics, and foreign languages, including equipment, laboratory centers, and language and area centers under contract to train individuals in languages needed by the Federal government or by business or education.

Though the regulations concerning the administration of the National Defense Education Act have not been fully worked out yet, the impact of this act may be tremendous, insofar as it may cause the spending of close to a billion dollars upon special curricular areas in the next eight years. Obviously, the major changes that may take place will be upon the levels of secondary and collegiate education.

The brief historical sketch which has just been given shows that significant Federal legislation relating to education has grown out of war or national emergencies in the past history of the United States. From the results of that Federal legislation, public education has gained and retained in its curricula certain activities and types of programs which have helped to round out the total offerings in the public schools and colleges. However, a careful study of the expenditures of the various Federal agencies for education [3] will convince the thoughtful educator that *the limited Federal aid that is already in operation to improve educational facilities all over the country is being spent primarily on high-school and college programs, not on education in the elementary school.* In addition, *Federal control does go with Federal aid.* For example, the President's Advisory Committee on Education in 1938 reported these findings concerning the areas of vocational educatiton which the Federal government subsidizes in the secondary school: (1) though effective, the home economics program tended toward a standardization of subject-matter and methods and failure to develop the program more closely

---

[3] *Federal Funds for Education: 1954–55 and 1955–56*, U.S. Department of Health, Education, and Welfare, Office of Education, Bulletin, 1956, No. 5, *passim*, and especially pp. 11–15 and 18–19.

in relation to the schools' broad program of general education; (2) the program in vocational agriculture was still failing to meet the large number of people who needed it, due to its standardization, and a less expensive type of agricultural instruction for smaller schools was recommended; and (3) the highly specialized regular program in trades and industries had been of little real value to boys planning to enter trade and industrial occupations.

Another illustration of the effect of standardization of the Federally aided programs was the recent statement of a southern governor of a predominantly rural state.[4] In effect, he stated that people of vision in education and vocational education would have to rethink the objectives of vocational agriculture courses; that conditions in agriculture had changed radically since World War II, with fewer and fewer boys going into, and needing, such training; and yet more and more boys and girls who lived on the farm would in the future continue to live there, but work in near-by industrial plants and cities, and that these pupils needed instruction in *subsistence* agriculture rather than *vocational agriculture.* Anyone who advocates Federal support of general education, without Federal control, should read the full text of the 1958 National Defense Education Act, with its restrictions and matching provisions; they are remarkably similar to such provisions in special education acts passed by Congress in the past. People in this country are far from agreement upon the need for Federal aid to education.[5]

The prospects for the continuation and extension of Federal aid *to all types of general education* were bright until the sectarian and racial issues entered the picture in the late 1940's. These issues have had such significant curricular implications that their injection into the battle for Federal aid undoubtedly will influence the final decision.[6]

[4] See daily newspapers in North Carolina of November 7, 1958. Governor Luther H. Hodges spoke before the North Carolina State School Board Association.

[5] *Cf. Federal Responsibilty in the Field of Education,* a Study Committee Report submitted to the Commission on Intergovernmental Relations, June, 1955, Washington, U.S. Government Printing Office. Has dissenting views or additional statements by some of the Commission members.

[6] For a brief account of the curricular implications of these issues to 1950, turn again to the revised edition of *Curriculum Principles and Social Trends*

THE PRESENT CURRICULUM CRISIS

This crisis has not been caused by any *one* movement, pressure, or happening, but by a combination of movements and events. This complex crisis for our public educational program, which will be identified later in this chapter, was pointed up by three different groups within the last decade.

THE CRITICS. The *first* group might be called those who set themselves up as self-appointed critics of the public school and its program. Within this group would fall such leaders in broadside attacks upon the public schools [7] as Arthur Bestor in his book, *Educational Wastelands*, in his numerous interviews in *U.S. News and World Report*, and in his work as a leading founder of the Council for Basic Education; Rudolf Flesch in his popular book, *Why Johnny Can't Read and What You Can Do About It*; Albert Lynd in his book, *Quackery in the Public Schools*; and Mortimer Smith in his collection of essays, *The Public Schools in Crisis*. These critics attack public education for not teaching the fundamentals, yet in their writings refer to only a few or no research studies in the teaching of reading, vocabulary, and arithmetic; and these research studies of teaching the three R's show clearly that the schools are doing a better job here than with a much more unselected school population fifty years ago. [8] These same attackers of the public schools seem not to have done research enough on the "straw men" that they set up to knock down, to discover that the "Progressive Education Association," which they hold responsible for "progressive" education, was disbanded after 1950 following achievement of its purposes (and was finally declared legally dead in 1955 after long-drawn-out legal technicalities had

---

(1950), pp. 713–26. For the current curriculum problems concerned with desegregation in public schools, read Problems Four and Five, *post.*, pp. 655–659. The controversy over teaching religion and spiritual values remains about the same, and the bibliography at the end of this chapter will bring the reader up to date on its aspects.

[7] *Cf.* Chapter 2 for a discussion of the "traditionalists" and "progressives" as sources for curriculum building, with detailed references to the attacks *pro* and *con* on public education in its bibliography.

[8] *Cf.* C.W. Hunnicutt and W.J. Iverson (Eds.), *Research in the Three R's*, New York, Harper and Brothers, 1958, *passim*.

been met). In similar vein, these critics do not seem to know that the "Life Adjustment Education" movement, started in 1945 to enrich basic high-school education, was liquidated in 1953 after it had accomplished its aims—and that its aims had more to do with "basic" or "general" education than with special-interest fields. Again, they do not show much knowledge of the fact that teaching spelling—and reading—by phonics is not a new method, but one that has been in use as *one* of the ways of teaching reading since 1930.

However, these critics have served a useful purpose in that they have made us re-examine our school programs, reassess our curricula, plan anew for a better-balanced program in an age of anxiety both in education and world affairs.

The *second* group which has helped materially to point up our curriculum crisis is composed of those people in both public and private life who had to have a "whipping boy" when the Russians forged ahead of our scientific development by launching the first earth satellite or "sputnik." Really, the Federal government was responsible for this scientific lag behind the Soviet accomplishment, in that it (1) cut back funds for our research teams to work with and forbade a branch of the armed services to go further with such experimentation, and (2) was unsuccessful in keeping confidential information about our atomic and nuclear developments from falling into Russian hands, hands that immediately set to work to carry these scientific developments forward much further than we had.

It is common practice for a person or a group that has made a mistake to attempt to place the blame elsewhere; the bigger the mistake, as in this case, the more the tendency to shift the blame. The public schools had already been under attack from some sources as being remiss in teaching the three R's, in disciplining children and youth, in maintaining a high standard of work of pupils, and in not requiring "hard" subjects for high-school graduation. Therefore the politicians, the armed services, and even some of the scientists immediately laid the blame upon the public schools for our failure to keep up with Russia in the world scientific race. People made brief visits to Russia and brought back the word that the Russian system of education was vastly superior to ours, comparisons were made, usually derogatory to American public education, of Russian and

European schools with ours; our system of secondary education was publicly declared to be inadequate for the "space age," and in particular these critics called for more adequate science programs throughout the public schools.

The clamor of the opinions of these individuals and groups was so influential that many sober, clear-thinking American citizens who

FIG. 48   *Health development through physical education—eighth and ninth graders*
(*Courtesy Charlotte (N.C.) City Schools, Sedgefield Junior High School.*)

were genuinely proud of the accomplishments of the free, public American schools became uncertain about the value of the curricular program. They were not told many facts by these critics that they ought to know. For example, Europeans and Russians establish and organize education for purposes fundamentally different from ours; they have "common" or basic schooling for all children for ten or eleven years; then their purpose is to educate intensively only 10 to 12 per cent of the pupils of high-school age, primarily for leadership roles.[9] Another kind of accurate information was not furnished to the American citizen and taxpayer who supports our educational system; this involved enrollments in science, mathematics, and other subjects in our schools, and the kinds of science programs that we have in our good elementary as well as in our secondary schools.[10] Still another set of facts was not given to the American parent, namely, that comparisons of the American school program of fifty years ago with that of today must have the *same bases*, such as percentages of total enrollment, number of children of school age in school, and total number graduating from high school.

The *third* group of critics of the public school and its curriculum might be called the "constructive critics," persons and groups genuinely interested in and striving for the continuation and improvement of free, publicly supported education in the United States. Typical individuals who have taken outstanding roles in this group are such men as James B. Conant, former President of Harvard University and world-famous in educational circles; and Paul Woodring, a psychologist and educator well known for his constructive criticism of education and his work in exploring new approaches to teacher education.[11] Groups which have worked at constructive criticism are exemplified by the American Association of School Administrators, the Association for Supervision and Curriculum Development, and the Educational Policies Commission.[12]

[9] For a fuller presentation of differing ideas, read "Is European Education Better?" by Byron S. Hollinshead, *The Educational Record*, April, 1958, pp. 1–8; "Those Good Soviet Schools—Not for All," *U.S. News and World Report*, December 13, 1957, pp. 86–87; "Sputnik II: The Surge of Soviet Science," and "Young Soviet Minds," *Newsweek*, November 11, 1957, pp. 73–76 and December 18, 1957, p. 85, respectively; "Observing Soviet Schools," *School and Society*, Vol. 86, October 25, 1958, p. 386; and George S. Counts, *The Challenge of Soviet Education*, New York, McGraw-Hill Book Company, 1957.

[10] The U.S. Office of Education issues every fifteen years a detailed *Offerings and Enrollments in High School Subjects* (latest edition, 1948–49), with supplements from time to time. With such data available, there is no reason for incorrect figures on subject-matter enrollments, such as are referred to by Harold C. Hand in "Black Horses Eat More Than White Horses," *Bulletin of the American Association of University Professors*, XLIII (Summer, 1957), pp. 266–79.

[11] Cf. *Let's Talk Sense About Our Schools*, 1953, and *A Fourth of a Nation*, 1957, both published by the McGraw-Hill Book Company, New York.

[12] For examples turn to *The High School in a Changing World*, 1958 (A.A.S.A.), *What Shall the High Schools Teach?* 1956 (A.S.C.D., and *Education and The Future of America*, 1955 (E.P.C.), all published by the National Education Association.

From the criticisms of these groups during the decade from 1948 to 1958, the problems have emerged slowly which constitute *in toto* a crucial curriculum crisis for our schools. These problems are ten in number; to the thinking educator no one of them is more important than any other, and many of them are closely related. It is the purpose of the writer here to identify these ten problems, not to solve them; the solution will have to come in the next twenty-five years as we steadily work on them.[13]

Problem One. Shall public education and its curricular program for all children be continued at the secondary-school level, or shall secondary education become again highly selective as it was until about 1920? This problem is a very serious one, since about 50 per cent of those who enter high school do not finish and over 60 per cent of those who graduate from high school today do not go into college. Also, many industrial firms and occupations today require graduation from high school as a work prerequisite. At stake likewise is the concept that the high school should attempt to meet the needs of each adolescent, whether he is going to finish high school or not, whether he will go to college or not. Can the high school continue this policy successfully? What little evidence we have seems to point to an affirmative answer. Students from public high schools entering Harvard have done as well scholastically over a period of years as students entering from preparatory schools. Scholarship-winning students competing in the National Merit Scholarship program came in much larger numbers from the public high schools than from the private or preparatory schools. At the University of Kansas, a study was made to ascertain how many of its 1955 graduates would have been denied entrance to Kansas University had the lower 50 per cent (on test scores) been eliminated; 208 of the 1,006 would have been denied admission, and among these would have been 40 teachers, 22 engineers, 7 lawyers, 7 doctors, and 7 pharmacists.[14]

[13] Experiments, and some suggestions for the solution of some of these problems, have been described in many of the preceding chapters of this book. If a problem has not been treated previously, brief consideration will be given to its scope in this chapter.

[14] See "Who Would be Eliminated—A Study of Selective Admission to College," University of Kansas; "Grades—Excellent," *Newsweek*, October 21, 1957, p. 75; and "Super High Schools," by H.G. Rickover, *This Week Magazine*, February 16, 1958, pp. 11, 36.

Therefore, as we study this problem, the problem of standards for admission to our colleges as they are constituted today grows bigger. Is the high-school diploma rapidly becoming a kind of "union card" for admission to work in skilled and semiprofessional areas of work, as well as for college entrance?

Problem Two. Shall we add to the fundamentals of the elementary school, that is, to the three R's, the continuation of "basic" or "general" education on the junior and senior high-school levels? Most phases of this developing trend have already been presented. However, three recent studies throw more light on both disagreement and agreement with general education as a major function of the high school. Jointly the Russell Sage Foundation, the National Association of Secondary School Principals, and the Educational Testing Service sponsored a study of the *Behavioral Goals of General Education in High School* in 1956–1957.[15] The Conference on the American High School at the University of Chicago in late 1957, sponsored jointly by the National Citizens Council for Better Schools and the University presented *The High School in a New Era*, a series of thirty-eight papers centered around both general and special education.[16] The third report was submitted by James B. Conant in 1959, the results of a two-year study of the American high school.

Problem Three. Shall the emerging junior high-school curriculum be freed to perform the special functions for which it has been established? Dominated by the curriculum and demands of the senior high school since its creation, this special educational level for young adolescents in the intermediate grades is beginning at last to realize its particular curricular purposes, namely, (1) to continue general education and skill subjects for a large portion of the unselected high-school population; (2) to enrich the program for many brighter pupils who do not desire to be or should not be accelerated in school; (3) to accelerate a small percentage of those students who are mature enough and advanced enough in their subject-matter fields to do successful work; and (4) to encourage pupils under wise guidance to explore new subject fields and new interests which may

[15] By Will French and Associates, New York, Russell Sage Foundation, 1957.
[16] Edited by F.S. Chase and H.A. Anderson, University of Chicago Press, 1958.

lead either to judicious choice of a life's work or the development of special interests and hobbies that give satisfaction to the individual and assist him in the maintenance of good mental health.

Problem Four. What shall comprise the curriculum for more effective work in international and intercultural education? The bitter racial and cultural conflicts of World War II brought home to Americans with striking force (1) their lack of adequate understanding of other national groups and ideologies and (2) their lack of knowledge of the special problems of the minority groups within their own borders. These problems of human relations and intergroup understanding have been examined and studied intensively by various groups; the aspects which have been covered range from civil rights and our racial and minority groups to intercultural education in the schools.

A great number of organizations are engaged in projects concerning human relations and intergroup understanding. Some of these agencies are: (1) the American Council on Race Relations, (2) the Association for the Study of Negro Life and History, (3) the National Conference of Christians and Jews, (4) the Southern Regional Council, (5) the Public Affairs Committee, (6) the United Nations and UNESCO, (7) the American Council on Education, (8) the Council Against Intolerance in America, (9) the Federal Council of Churches of Christ in America, and (10) the National Association for the Advancement of Colored People.[17]

THE INTERGROUP EDUCATION PROJECT. An illustration of two projects which have resulted in concrete curriculum suggestions on intercultural education have been "Intergroup Education in Cooperating Schools" and "Studies in Intergroup Relations." The first project was sponsored from 1945 through 1948 by the American Council on Education and financed by the National Conference of Christians and Jews. It was a joint undertaking by the project staff and the teachers in certain cooperating public schools.[18] The domi-

[17] *Intergroup Relations Bibliography*, published by the Connecticut State Inter-Racial Commission in 1948, listed twenty-nine independent organizations and eleven state agencies engaged in some phase of intergroup activity.

[18] *The Bulletin of the National Association of Secondary-School Principals*, Vol. 33, No. 160 (February, 1949), issue on "Curriculum in Intergroup Education: Case Studies in Instruction for Secondary Schools," describes this project.

nant objectives of this project were (1) improving human relations and (2) fostering intergroup understanding through the development of new materials, techniques, approaches, and ways of mobilizing school and community resources.

In carrying out this project in intergroup education, the teachers of the cooperating schools developed several ways of (1) discovering the special needs of pupils in group relations and (2) diagnosing and meeting those needs. Though general in nature, these principles might be used in any project which involves intergroup or intercultural relations. In summary form, these principles involved the following questions:

1. What are the association patterns in peer groups, and on what social values are they based?
2. What traditions, customs, and feelings prevail in the home and in the community?
3. What is the quality, kind, and level of pupil concepts, attitudes, and insights?
4. In selection and organization of content materials for courses and activities:
   a. What is the main idea which the unit is meant to teach?
   b. What are the areas or subtopics to be studied to provide *the facts* as the basis for ideas to be developed?
   c. What comparative or contrasting details are needed to be developed under each subtopic?
   d. In what sequence should the units and subtopics be handled?
5. What special provision should be made for such selection and organization of learning activities that changing attitudes of the group can be cared for?
6. What face-to-face contacts should be provided for the learner, so that he may develop the sensitivity necessary to an understanding of new people and new situations?
7. Are there adequate provisions for repetition (of performance), so that mastery of skills involving group relations are well established?
8. In attempting to create a favorable classroom atmosphere for intergroup development and learning:
   a. What methods will yield emotional satisfactions to both pupils and teachers?
   b. What methods will emphasize group productivity and the effectiveness of group learning?
   c. What methods will be most effective for acquisition of facts, ways of thinking, and sensitiveness?

Teachers of the cooperating schools and members of the project staff developed materials to be used by teachers. All published by the American Council on Education, these are briefly listed as follows:

Literature for Human Understanding by the staff. How to use books as a motivator in building attitudes in behavior, 1948.

Sociometry in Group Relations: A Work Guide for Teachers by H.H. Jennings, *et al.*, 1948.

Elementary Curriculum in Intergroup Relations: Case Studies in Instruction by the staff, 1950.

With Focus on Human Relations: A Story of an Eighth Grade by H. Taba and D. Elkins, 1950.

Intergroup Education in Public Schools by H. Taba, *et al.* A systematic guide to curriculum development, classroom techniques, and community cooperation, 1952.

Reading Ladders for Human Relations (rev.) by L.M. Heaton and H.B. Lewis. An annotated list of 650 books for children's reading.

The second project was carried on at the University of Chicago and was sponsored by the Center for Intergroup Education. Its publication of helpful materials include (all published likewise by the American Council on Education):

Diagnosing Human Relations Needs by H. Taba, *et al.*, especially in social learning, 1951.

Leadership Training in Intergroup Education by H. Taba, 1953.

School Culture: Studies of Participation and Leadership by H. Taba, 1955.

With Perspective on Human Relations: A Study of Peer Group Dynamics in an Eighth Grade by H. Taba.

In addition to earlier intergroup studies,[19] other persons and groups have prepared materials of value. Lloyd A. and Elaine F. Cook wrote two books: *School Problems in Human Relations* and *Intergroup Education,* a systematic study of the tensions and conflicts resulting from intergroup and interpersonal relations.[20]

The John Dewey Society recently sponsored a study of *Teaching World Affairs in American Schools: A Case Book,* edited by Samuel

---

[19] Refer to *Curriculum Principles and Social Trends* (rev. ed.), 1950, for a description of these, pp. 720–26.

[20] Both published by the McGraw-Hill Book Company, New York.

Everett and Christian O. Arndt.[21] They give illustrations of class-room teaching and learning in public schools, in-school and out-of-school activities, community services, and college, teacher, and adult education.

All of these studies of the last decade point to a greater emphasis in the curriculum upon problems of human relations, intergroup education, international and intercultural education, and the under-standing of the ideas, attitudes, patterns of conduct, and hopes and ideals of minority groups.

Problem Five. How can we meet the grave curricular issues which face us as desegregation takes place in the public schools? This problem is closely related to all facets of the intercultural problem, but it poses specific curricular questions to which we must find satisfactory answers. For example, here are some of the curricular difficulties which Washington (D.C.), the first metropolitan, desegregated school system, had to try to solve: [22]

1. According to the results of the Stanford achievement tests, after two years of integration white pupils in the third grade were on a level with the national norm, but Negro pupils were already one full grade below the national average.
2. Achievement test results likewise showed that the higher the grade, the wider is the disparity between the white and Negro pupils in educational achievement.
3. A tremendous number of Negro pupils in senior high school, far more in proportion to their numbers than white pupils, could read only on the third, fourth, or fifth grade level.
4. Integration had resulted in the lowering of educational standards in schools where there were large numbers of Negroes, who had come from formely all-Negro schools and who were mostly unprepared to carry on their studies in the regular grades to which they had been assigned.

In working toward a solution of these curricular difficulties, the Congressional subcommittee and the School Superintendent recommended several approaches, some of which are being carried out:

[21] Harper and Brothers, New York, 1956.
[22] From a report on integration of public schools in Washington, made by a subcommittee of the House Committee on the District of Columbia, released December 28, 1956. The summary here is from *U.S. News and World Report,* January 4, 1957, pp. 93–100.

(1) different kinds of grouping, according to achievement in basic subject-matter areas; this would automatically make some schoolrooms in a building again all-Negro; (2) creation of separate continuation and trade schools for pupils of low mental ability who are incapable of scholastic achievement at the high-school level; (3) establishment of special, separate schools, with adequately trained personnel, for teaching atypical students; (4) the creation of a citywide technical high school of high standards; (5) the keeping of records on Washington school children by sex and race; and (6) the employment of several hundred additional teachers who are trained for and will do only remedial work with retarded pupils.

Other studies and reports have been made that also can help us. *A Citizen's Guide to Desegregation: A Study of Social and Legal Change in American Life* offers one kind of aid in approaching the problem of working together to get desegregation effected.[23] Of similar nature is Phi Delta Kappa's handbook for schools faced with desegregation, *Action Patterns in School Desegregation* (1959). A very good overview of all types of problems involved in racial desegregation is found in "Racial Desegregation and Integration," published in *The Annals of the American Academy of Political and Social Science*.[24] From time to time *Educational Leadership* has devoted whole issues particularly to the curriculum difficulties.[25] *Southern School News* is perhaps the most factual and impartial source of information on desegregation and integration. It is published monthly by Southern Education Reporting Service, a factfinding agency established by southern newspaper editors and educators.

The exhaustive studies which have been made of the Negro as a minority racial group in the United States also could be of value in meeting curricular problems. Adequate provision for this large minority group in educational advancement, vocational opportunity, and successful living in a democratic framework is fundamental if America is not to fall a prey, as did European nations, to disintegration and dissension among its own citizens because of the inequalities

[23] By H. Hill and J. Greenberg, Boston, the Beacon Press, 1955.
[24] March, 1956, pp. 1–143.
[25] For a recent sample, see Vol. xv (May, 1958), "Experiences in Cultural Integration," pp. 462–500.

existing among its racial minorities. The same should be said too of the large Puerto Rican minority now settling in America.

Problem Six. How and where shall we include in our curriculum the problems and knowledge of the nuclear age, which were not even in existence a little more than a decade ago? For example, we have to teach children today about radioactive materials and fallout, about the missile age, jet and rocket propulsion, satellites, the possibility of space and interplanetary travel. There are also the peaceful uses of the atomic and nuclear age, such as the atomic-powered submarine, the atomic cocktail, radioactive isotopes and their uses, the limitless possibilities of harnessing atomic energy for power to run our industries and heat our homes, and even the possibilities of perpetual refrigeration and industry run mostly by automation.

The hue and cry for more and better mathematics and science teachers in our schools in order to turn out more scientists at a faster rate may have a more far-reaching effect than we think—it may make us reassess our twelve-year programs in each of these subject-matter fields and come up with some experiments that may develop some of our more able students more quickly than we had ever dreamed.

Problem Seven. Shall public education devote as much attention to curricular programs for the talented or gifted as it does for the normal and slow learners? This is a very important question. For many years our experts in psychology have experimented with methods and materials of teaching the slower or less gifted pupil; out of these experiments have come programs for the slow-learning child upon which the schools have spent very large sums of money, both for the programs and for teachers specially trained to teach effectively in them. Now we are faced with the development of effective materials and methods for teaching the faster, the more gifted pupil—and we find that we have few suggestions for the teachers of these talented boys and girls.

We have made a start at this since 1950. The Fifty-Seventh Yearbook of the National Society for the Study of Education (Part II) is devoted to *Education for the Gifted*. It presents the need for special attention to this group, ways of identifying them, their kinds of giftedness, their motivation and creativity, the enrichment of education for the gifted, programs for them in elementary and secondary schools and in college, guidance for them, training of teachers for such programs, and community factors in the education of the gifted.

In his preliminary report on his two-year study of the American high school, James B. Conant emphasized that the academically talented, about 15 per cent of the high-school population, should be given special attention and work tailored to their abilities in the comprehensive American high school.[26]

The Horace Mann-Lincoln Institute of School Experimentation at Teachers College, Columbia University, started its Talented Youth Project in 1953. A. Harry Passow has directed this project, and perhaps knows firsthand—from visits to schools—more about different curricular experiments for the talented than any other one individual.[27] He reported at the annual Meeting of the Association for Supervision and Curriculum Development in March, 1958, that the experiments were interesting, varied, and for different purposes with different types of "giftedness" or "talent." He also emphasized the great need for more research and experimentation in this area.

It is a well-known fact that over a period of years the academically talented student who was admitted early to college has done well. Such recent cooperative efforts as *The Identification and Education of the Academically Talented Student in the American High School* [28] should continue as we tackle this knotty problem.

Problem Eight. How can we make maximum effective use of newer methods, newer media, new departures in teaching? When radio was invented, the public schools never made maximum use of this supplementary aid to teaching. Now television is common in almost all American homes; from it and from the radio, the motion picture, newsstand publications, magazines and newspapers, the child acquires about half of his education—half of it *outside* of

[26] Address delivered before the National School Boards Association's 18th Annual Convention, April 17–19, 1958.

[27] *Cf.* his article, "The Talented Youth Project: A Report on Research Under Way," *Educational Research Bulletin,* xxxvi (September 11, 1957), pp. 199–206.

[28] The Report of an N.E.A.-Carnegie Corporation Conference by James B. Conant, N.E.A., 1958.

school. Recent experiments with teaching larger groups of children by television show some preliminary results that further research may verify, and may make television eventually an integral part of certain kinds of teaching. Socio-drama and role-playing are well known as kinds of teaching and learning devices, yet we train teachers inadequately in these, as in the use of other techniques such as teacher-pupil planning and group dynamics.

For example, we have learned a great deal about cooperative curriculum planning and "group dynamics." One of the most interesting trends in curriculum-building has been the development of instruments and methods for getting maximum results in group discussion and planning. These group processes have come to be known by the term "group dynamics." Cecil Parker and William Golden in effect defined group processes as those methods and steps which are taken by a group of persons in planning, talking, arguing, deciding, and evaluating so that they arrive at the best solution for their common problem.[29]

L. Thomas Hopkins' *Interaction: The Democratic Process* [30] was followed soon by Bernice Baxter and Rosalind Cassidy's careful study of *Group Experience: The Democratic Way.*[31] These pioneer studies of social interaction, group work, and group workers in education were soon supplemented by other studies and publications in this area.[32] Principles and characteristics of cooperative group work include:

[29] *Group Processes in Supervision,* Association for Supervision and Curriculum Development, National Education Association, 1948, pp. 27–28.

[30] Boston, D.C. Heath and Company, 1941.

[31] Published by Harper and Brothers, 1943.

[32] *Cf.* H.H. Giles, *Teacher-Pupil Planning,* New York, Harper and Brothers, 1941; Bernice Baxter, *Teacher-Pupil Relationships,* New York, The Macmillan Company, 1941; H.J. Otto, *Elementary School Organization and Administration* (2nd ed.), New York, D. Appleton-Century Company, 1944, Chap. v; Alice Miel, *Changing the Curriculum: A Social Process,* New York, D. Appleton-Century Company, 1946; Association for Supervision and Curriculum Development: *Discipline for Today's Children and Youth* by G.V. Sheviakov and Fritz Redl, 1944 (revised in 1957); *Laymen Help Plan the Curriculum* by Helen F. Storen, 1946; 1945 Yearbook, *Group Planning in Education; Group Processes in Supervision,* 1948; 1949 Yearbook, *Toward Better Teaching,* Chap. iii; *Children's Social Learning* by Edna Ambrose and Alice Miel, 1958; G.L. Coyle, *Group Work With American Youth,* New York, Harper and Brothers, 1948; and Louise Parrish and Yvonne Waskin, *Teacher-Pupil Planning for Better Learning,* New York, Harper and Brothers, 1958.

1. Goals which are formulated by the group are ones that group activity can attain more quickly than individuals could by themselves.
2. There is a "belongingness" to the group in which all share.
3. Social control is accepted by the group—they accept majority action and group discipline.
4. The work and standards of achievement are in terms of the standards of the group, not of an individual.
5. Activities, after goals or aims are established, include (1) means for achieving goals, (2) action in putting them into effect, and (3) appraisal of results.
6. There is free opportunity to discover each other's thinking at all stages of cooperative action, and to influence the thinking of others.
7. Cooperative final decisions are sought—which all can subscribe to and support.

THE HORACE MANN-LINCOLN INSTITUTE OF SCHOOL EXPERIMENTATION. Organized in 1943, the Institute conceived of curriculum experimentation broadly, that is, as experimentation in a variety of school situations with a variety of types of schools. They wished to discover both *what changes occur* and *what brings about these changes.* In starting this study of curriculum design for children and youth, the staff of the Institute investigated and analyzed three basic problems: (1) the relation of child growth and development to the curriculum; [33] (2) what constitutes the social bases of the curriculum; and (3) a design for a curriculum built on our knowledge of child growth and development and on the social bases of the curriculum. [34]

After this preliminary groundwork had been accomplished, "associated schools" were selected which were representative of typical conditions of organization throughout the United States. These associated schools took part in five major areas of experimentation: (1) the general design of the curriculum; (2) education for economic competence; (3) cooperative planning (group dynamics); (4) health; and (5) children's needs and interests. In order to carry

---

[33] The results of this study are found in *Child Development and the Curriculum* by A.T. Jersild and others (1946). All publications of the Institute have been issued by the Bureau of Publications, Teachers College, Columbia University.

[34] This design is set forth in *Developing a Curriculum for Modern Living* by F.B. Stratemeyer, *et al.*, 1947 (rev. ed., 1958).

out experimentation and research along these lines, the Institute selected both generalists and specialists for its staff.

The associated schools included three large city systems—Denver, Kansas City, and New York City; three smaller urban centers—Battle Creek (Michigan), Glencoe (Illinois), and Springfield (Missouri); two combined rural and suburban systems—Bucks County (Pennsylvania) and Montgomery County (Maryland); and schools associated with two teacher-education institutions—Radford College (Virginia) and Tuskegee Institute (Alabama). The experiment was organized first on a five-year basis, from 1943 to 1948.

The following list of publications is indicative of the scope of the work undertaken by the Horace Mann-Lincoln Institute and the associated schools during this period:

Volumes Published

1. Stratemeyer, *et al., Developing a Curriculum for Modern Living*
2. Jersild, *et al., Child Development and the Curriculum*
3. Staff, *The Teacher's Role in Teacher-Pupil Planning* (Bulletin)
4. Staff, *Cooperative Planning in Education* (Bulletin)
5. Staff, *How to Construct a Sociogram* (Bulletin)
6. Jersild, *et al., Children's Interests*
7. Jersild, *et al., Joys and Problems of Child Rearing*
8. Del Solar, *Parents and Teachers View the Child*
9. Cunningham, *et al., Understanding Group Behavior of Boys and Girls*
10. Miel, *et al., Cooperative Procedures in Learning*

Films Produced

1. *Learning Through Cooperative Planning* (released January, 1948)
2. *We Learn Together* (released July, 1948)

In the second period of experimentation, beginning in September, 1949, the Institute focused its major energies upon the cooperative study of problems in general education at the secondary-school level. In 1953, it started its Talented Youth Project.

THE SOCIOGRAM. The sociogram has been employed as a sociometric technique to show (in diagram form) the interpersonal relationships within a given group. The Horace Mann-Lincoln Institute of School Experimentation studied the group behavior of boys and girls through (1) the use of the *Classroom Social Distance Scale* and

(2) constructing sociograms based on that scale.[35] The possibilities for developing better group activities within the classroom can be grasped more clearly by analysis of a simple sociogram (Fig. 49).

The basic data for this sociogram were secured from unsigned responses of the boys and girls to this question: "Who are your best friends in this grade?" A partial interpretation of the sociogram

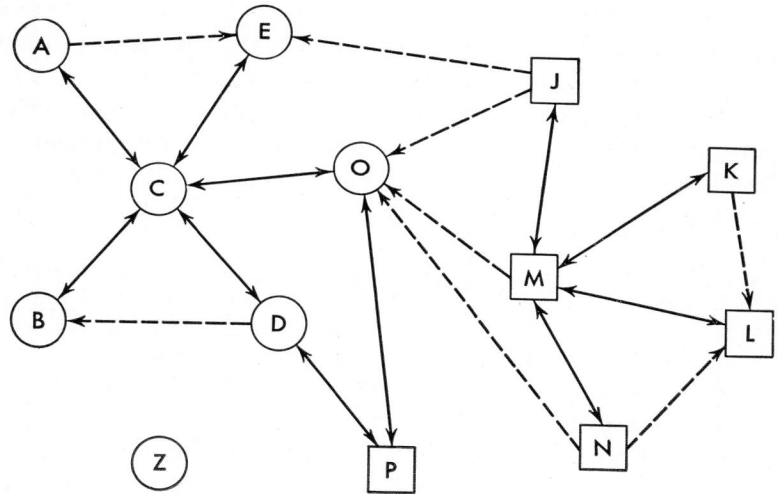

FIG. 49   *A Sociogram (7th grade in a southern town)*

NOTE: The circles represent girls and the squares represent boys. Solid arrows pointing in both directions (⟷) indicate mutual attraction; a broken arrow pointing in one direction (← or →) indicates that one pupil likes the other pupil toward which the arrow is pointing. There were actually 30 pupils in the grade, 15 boys and 15 girls. The responses of only 6 boys and 7 girls are diagrammed, in order that the principle of constructing a sociogram may be easy to grasp.

would be as follows: *Among the girls: C* is liked best by other girls, and likes most of them, but she is not interested in the boys yet; *O* attracts the interest of the boys, but likes only one boy, *P*; poor *Z* has no friends among either girls or boys, and is isolated from all of the group. *Among the boys: M* is the best liked, and likes all of the

[35] *Cf.* Cunningham, *et al., op. cit.,* Appendix. *Cf.* also *Sociometry in the Classroom,* by N.E. Gronlund, New York, Harper and Brothers, 1959.

boys except one, *P; P* is isolated from the boys, but likes and is liked by two girls, *O* and *D*. In summary, four of the six boys are beginning to show an interest in girls, and two of seven girls have boys as best friends; the teacher will have to work hard to get Z into some group activity where she can win friendship, and will have to keep a watchful eye on *P*'s lack of comradeship with boys, to see whether it is temporary or permanent.

Through a study of group interaction and through cooperative planning with their students, alert teachers in the modern school use their curriculum materials and methods to stimulate their pupils to grow in civic, group, and individual responsibility. In addition to the materials of the Horace Mann-Lincoln Institute of School Experimentation, the Association for Supervision and Curriculum Development of the National Education Association has studied group planning and has published materials on many aspects of it.

Problem Nine. How can we provide an adequate program of general and specialized education for ALL *children when our school-age population is growing so fast that we cannot build additional schools fast enough to house them and our population has become so mobile that 20 per cent of the people in most communities change schools each year?* This problem has been attacked from several directions. One solution, usually considered temporary, has been to institute "double" school sessions; this arrangement makes full use of the existing school plants, with two different sets of teachers. Fast-growing urban-fringe and metropolitan centers have had to run double sessions for many years; examples are Great Neck, Long Island, and many cities in California. Though the school day is shorter for most pupils, the double session has one virtue; teachers have to be available for a minimum workday, and during their free time before or after their session they are available to give individual help to pupils who need it—and are also available.

Another suggestion has been tried out. It may take three forms: (1) the year-round school for all children, which is one of the provisions Russia uses, and which this writer does not favor, since all children would have to go to school for twelve months, a procedure out of line with our knowledge of child growth; or (2) we can (a) utilize our school plants on a year-round basis, with a nine-months' term for the typical pupil, furnishing additional recreation activities and/or part-time work programs for him as needed, and (b) provide more school time each year to accelerate the gifted or give more help to the retarded; or (3) the school system operating on a year-round basis, with staff employed for the year except for one month of vacation or leave with pay, while sufficient personnel will be employed to run the schools for nine months for all pupils, of whom some, perhaps the larger number, will attend from September through May, some will enter in January and finish the year in September, and still others will enter in March and finish at Christmas time. This third plan utilizes plant and staff fully and also keeps a continuing program in operation for the increasingly mobile population that we have today.

Problem Ten.   How can the schools, labor, and industry cooperate to start cooperative "work programs" for youth as early as the junior high-school grades? Experts on child development tell us that the urge to work, to make their own money, is a characteristic of early adolescents. Yet both compulsory school legislation and the legislation concerning child labor prevent most youths from obtaining the discipline, satisfaction, and even interest that real work experience can furnish to them. In a nonwork atmosphere, complicated by early school leavers and juvenile delinquents, how can we help youth to develop sound values, good judgment, and a desire to work? If we study this knotty problem hard enough, we may emerge with a better-balanced secondary-school program that places greater emphasis upon subject-matter mastery and real work experience, and relatively less emphasis upon student activities and interscholastic participation.

THE VALUE OF CRISES TO EDUCATION.   The emphasis in America has been shifting gradually from individual development to group development, from rugged individualism to cooperative societal action, from the exploitation of natural resources to conservation, from the individual as the primary significant factor in national growth and development to the land and its resources and the group as the primary influences. In the years ahead, adjustments must be made to these changing conceptions of life in the United States. Education has an important part to play in this adjustive process, both in preserving the proper balance and in conserving from the present structure of American life those values which are necessary for our continued growth and wise development.

FIG. 50   *Fifth graders learn by doing in a space age*
(*Courtesy Greensboro (N.C.) Public Schools, Brooks School.*)

It has been said truly that most organizations fail to take stock of themselves unless they are forced to do so by circumstances which confront them in a crisis. This statement has also been true of education; until the crisis caused by the business depression of the 1930's, educators were too busy, or too self-satisfied, to turn their attention to taking a really good look at themselves in order to find out where they were and to evaluate what they were doing. Crises undoubtedly encourage pause for thought and self-survey, two processes which are necessary if those activities are to be eliminated which are no longer valuable and if new procedures are to be instituted which may assist in improving the work. For example, both the depression and the national emergency of World War II made Americans pause to consider their neighbors on the other continents, to think in terms of cooperation with them, and to plan for future action with them in regard to those factors which fundamentally affect them and the United States in an interdependent society. Another illustration comes from the field of natural resources, which the nation has failed to conserve; as a result of the depression and of World War II, the Federal government and many states have passed legislation and have instituted measures looking toward long-term planning in the preservation of natural resources, so that the nation may continue to prosper and to grow in the years to come.

DEVELOPING CURRICULAR TRENDS

There are indications throughout this volume of growth and improvement in the curriculum. Several favorable factors usually operate to stimulate this growth. In the first place, the more favorable the environment for learning, the greater the stimulation for curricular improvement. For example, the environment for learning will be more favorable in a school building or system which has: (1) better-qualified teachers, who remain year after year with the system and plan and grow with it; (2) close articulation of school activities with home and community life; (3) pupil activities incorporated naturally in the curricular program; (4) easily adjustable physical facilities and equipment; and (5) teachers, pupils, and administrators who plan their school work cooperatively.

A second favorable factor for curriculum development is concerned with whether the school encourages teachers toward pre-planning of their work, and makes time available for this planning in advance. One of the strong arguments for the teacher "workshop" is that it makes provision for this cooperative planning of the work of the next year. Many school boards and systems have encouraged this type of in-service education by paying the expenses of teachers to workshops, or by furnishing funds in the budget for a staff for "on-going" workshops in their systems throughout the year.

A third factor operating to stimulate curriculum improvement has been the steady stream of new curriculum materials flowing out from

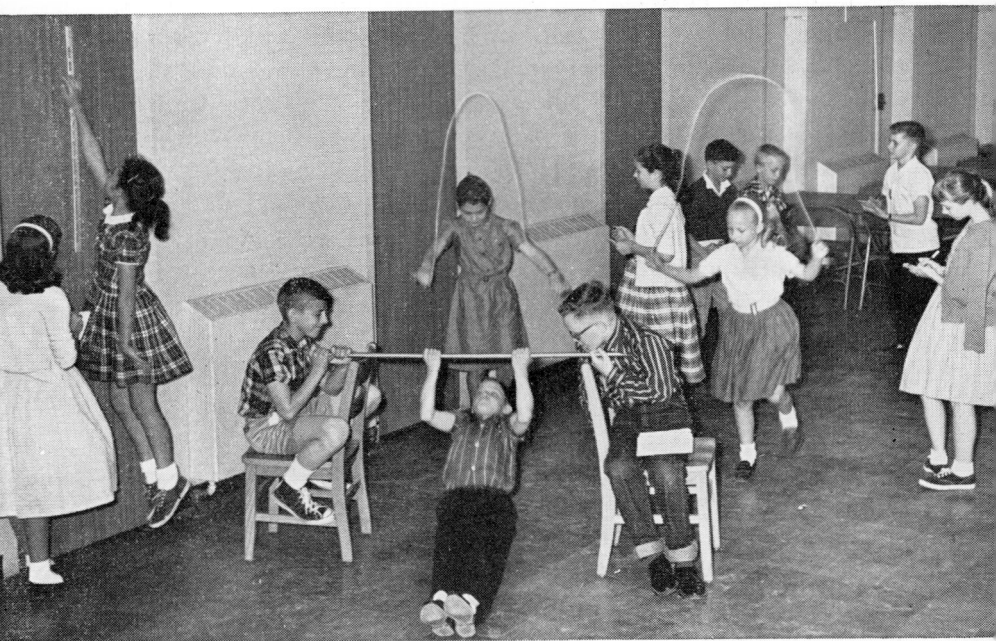

FIG. 51   *Using student leaders*

Leaders from the sixth grade; pupils in fourth grade physical education class. (*Courtesy Greensboro (N.C.) Public Schools, Brooks School.*)

all types of sources to the educational employee. Among the most obvious of these are resource units, pamphlets, motion pictures, picture-fact books, radio, TV, slides, recordings, charts, maps, objects and specimens, and popular reading materials.

IMPLICATIONS FOR THE FUTURE

The developing public school program in the United States shows steady progress, both in regard to general education and specialized education. A summary of implications for the future would include:

1. More adult education, with special attention to home and family living, mental health, the development of wide reading interests, community cooperation, and studies of cooperatives and consumer education.

2. More adequate curricular provisions for health education, including public health information, recreation, sex education, aspects of medical care and forms of socialized medicine, disease control, and effects of alcohol and drugs on humans.

3. More satisfactory provision for the education in as normal a situation as possible of those children needing special education, such as spastics, those with speech defects, and those hard of hearing.

4. Better provision for acquiring knowledge in school of consumer education, housing, and aspects of government's social services for its people.

5. More emphasis in school upon conservation of our natural resources.

6. More adequate curriculum materials in and emphasis upon science and mathematics and the newer aspects of scientific development, such as rockets, satellites and guided missiles, nuclear physics and atomic energy, jet propulsion, electronics and radar and television on all school levels.

7. More materials and units about labor, labor organizations, and labor's place in our economy.

8. More materials and work centered around community and regional study.

9. More preschool education, probably in the form of both nursery school and kindergarten education.

10. More work and materials in safety education and driver education.

11. More provision for activities in the school in fine, plastic, and applied arts.

12. More activities centered around those materials which children read naturally at certain age levels.

13. More provisions for camping experiences for youth in public education as a part of the curriculum.

14. Additional provision for part-time work and part-time school experiences for older adolescents.

15. The growth of teacher workshops, or preplanning periods for the next year's work.

WHAT OF THE FUTURE? There has emerged in the educational literature and in the teaching materials prepared for these times of emergency an awareness of the need for training pupils in practical thinking, keen analysis, and the subordination of hysteria to common sense and unemotional consideration of the facts in a situation. This trend in the direction of propaganda analysis is important, for propaganda can be clothed in such forms and disguised in so many ways that it is extremely difficult at times to recognize it. As a result of this period of national emergency under "cold war" conditions, it is not improbable that courses in propaganda analysis of all types may be emphasized more in the public schools.

It is not possible for anyone to predict what residue will accrue to the curriculum from the broader and more narrowly educational aspects of the manifold measures made necessary by national emergencies. If the history of the past is any standard for judgment, the curriculum of the schools will contain many things which it did not contain before, and the schools will be doing some things in ways different from those of former years. The future is heavy with responsibility—there will have to be reconstruction of production with the use of automation in industry, and remedies for economic maladjustment, along with political readjustment. Real freedom cannot continue to exist without the shouldering of corresponding responsibility. In this situation, however, curriculum change should continue to be a slow evolution, not a revolution.

PROBLEMS FOR INDIVIDUAL STUDY
AND CLASS DISCUSSION

1. Would you change your teaching of the social studies because of a national war program? If so, in what ways?

2. From consideration of the economic and social changes which are taking place, national and international, do you believe that the United States is facing the end of an old era and the beginning of a new one? Give reasons for your stand.

3. What should the public schools do in regard to instruction in civil rights?

4. How would you go about a study of the *pros* and *cons* of teaching the Bible in the public schools?

5. Why have some states required by law that "conservation education" be added to the elementary- or secondary-school curriculum?

6. Would you place in the curriculum of the schools any special work

on Latin America, or "Understanding Our Neighbors of the Western Hemisphere"? Support your position.

7. Are there sound reasons for placing more emphasis upon science and mathematics in the schools? Support your point of view.

8. Through what grade level should general education extend, and why?

9. Why should every teacher, whether in the secondary or the elementary school, have a knowledge and understanding of the entire curriculum of the school?

10. As a teacher in service or a teacher-candidate, what steps would you recommend that the schools take to help the United States keep a reservoir of trained men for service in the army and navy in an emergency?

11. If Federal aid to general education were granted to your state, in what particular ways would that money be expended for *curriculum improvement,* if any?

12. What types of curricular work are being given in adult education in your state?

13. What, if any, new curricular work should be added concerning Social Security, labor legislation and collective bargaining, state and United States employment services, the Rural Electrification Administration, the Agricultural Adjustment Administration, the Federal Housing Administration, and Federal Flood control? Give reasons for your answer.

14. Your school wants to make special provisions for its talented (or gifted) pupils. What methods of doing this would you suggest? Explain.

ADDITIONAL ANNOTATED REFERENCES FOR PROBLEM OR UNIT STUDY

Adult Education Association, Chicago 11.
The "Leadership Pamphlets Series" has six on how to lead groups: No. 1, *How to Lead Discussions;* 2, *Planning Better Programs;* 3, *Taking Action in the Community;* 4, *Understanding How Groups Work;* 5, *How to Teach Adults;* and 6, *How to Use Role Playing.*
Alberty, H.B., *Reorganizing the High School Curriculum* (rev. ed.), New York, The Macmillan Company, 1953.
Chapter xvi presents a plan for curriculum reorganization in the future.
The American Academy of Political and Social Science, Philadelphia 4.
Metropolis in Ferment, November, 1957, pp. 1–164; *Recreation in the Age of Automation,* September, 1957, pp. 1–147; and *Highway Safety and Traffic Control,* November, 1958, pp. 1–141.
American Council on Education, Washington 6.
The Study of Religion in the Public Schools: An Appraisal is a sym-

posium on the place of religion in a public school by authorities on various religions.

Associated Public School Systems, New York 27.

This nation-wide group of school systems, founded in 1949, publishes a national magazine, *Know-How,* and swaps accounts of better school practices and experiments.

Brookover, W.B., *A Sociology of Education,* New York, American Book Company, 1955.

In addition to a presentation of the problems and practices in the field, suggestions are offered as to how to use the tools of sociology and psychology in analysis of the educational system and processes.

California Journal of Secondary Education, Vol. xxxi (January, 1956), has a significant symposium on "Education of the 'Non-Academic' Pupil in Secondary Schools," pp. 45–61.

Caswell, H.L., *The Attack on American Schools,* New York, Teachers College, Columbia University, 1958.

A fair and scholarly presentation from his Annual Report to the Trustees, 1957–1958.

Conant, J.B., *The American High School Today: First Report to Interested Citizens,* New York, McGraw-Hill Book Company, 1959.

The report on his intensive survey of American high schools, a penetrating look at curriculum and teaching methods, at the "comprehensive" high school, and at the need for provisions for the exceptional student.

————, *Education and Liberty,* Cambridge, Harvard University Press, 1953.

The role of public schools in a modern democracy, and a suggested program for the future, especially for "general education."

Counts, G.S., *American Education Through the Soviet Looking Glass,* New York, Teachers College, Columbia University, 1951, and *The Challenge of Soviet Education,* New York, McGraw-Hill Book Company, 1957.

These companion volumes give one a comprehensive insight into the historical evolution and current status of U.S.S.R. education, and a clear picture of how Russia conceives of American education.

Cutts, N.W., and Moseley, N., *Better Home Discipline,* New York, Appleton-Century-Crofts, 1952.

An actual account of parents' experience (6,000 families) in disciplining their children.

Education in the USSR, by Division of International Education, Bulletin 1957, No. 14, 1957, Washington 25.

An account of Soviet education, planning and administration, the various levels, vocational and semiprofessional, training, higher education, and teacher training.

Ehlers, H. (Ed.), *Crucial Issues in Education: An Anthology,* New York, Henry Holt and Company, 1955.
A well-selected anthology, *pro* and *con,* on criticisms of and controversies over public education.

Freeman, R.A., *School Needs in the Decade Ahead,* Washington, The Institute for Social Science Research, 1958.
The report of the Reln Foundation Study by the Austrian-born Freeman, who came to this country about 1940. This controversial report questions constantly rising school costs in relation to enrollment and building needs.

Fund for the Advancement of Education, New York 21.
Schools for Tomorrow by A.J. Stoddard (1957) is called an "educator's blueprint" for education in this time of crisis and teacher shortages.

Gross, N., *Who Runs Our Schools?* New York, John Wiley and Sons, 1958.
Who supports and who blocks the public schools, what kinds of pressures operate, with documentation by sampling of superintendency positions.

Hand, H.C., *Principles of Public Secondary Education,* New York, Harcourt, Brace and Company, 1958.
Part iv is devoted to constructive analysis of the accomplishments and prospects of the public high school.

Hartford, E.F., *Moral Values in Public Education,* New York, Harper and Brothers, 1958.
The Kentucky Movement, and lessons to be gained from their experimental work in this area.

Havemann, E., and West, P.S., *They Went to College,* New York, Harcourt, Brace and Company, 1952.
One of the first complete studies of college graduates, their opinions, politics, marriages, religious activities, and success.

Havighurst, R.J., and Neugarten, B.L., *Society and Education,* Boston, Allyn and Bacon, 1957.
Social structure, population mobility, social bases of education, and consideration of the child's social environment, the school, and the teacher in relationships to these.

Hechinger, F.M., *An Adventure in Education,* New York, The Macmillan Company, 1956.
An interesting account of how Connecticut citizens studied their schools, made recommendations for their growth, and pointed out sound principles and practices already in use.

The High School Journal from time to time points up new teaching practices and departures; illustrative are special issues on "Audio-Visual Aids In the Secondary School," xl (March, 1957); "Improved Reading Practices and Programs," xxxix (October, 1955); and "Television in the Schools," xli (February, 1958).

Hullfish, H.G. (Ed.), *Educational Freedom in an Age of Anxiety,* New York, Harper and Brothers, 1953.

This 12th Yearbook of the John Dewey Society points up the fundamental freedom, and right to teach, in our educational system.

The Independent School Bulletin for January, 1958, has an excellent account of the Advanced Placement Program of the College Entrance Examination Board, based on replies from 166 independent and 28 public schools.

Latimer, J.F., *What's Happened to Our High Schools?* Washington, Public Affairs Press, 1958.

The point of view of a classicist concerning the failure of the secondary-school program to meet our national security needs.

Marden, C.F., *Minorities in American Society,* New York, American Book Company, 1952.

A careful study and analysis of minorities, "native"-foreigner, white-colored, ward-wardship relations, and religious differences and minority status.

Mathewson, R.H., *A Strategy for American Education,* New York, Harper and Brothers, 1957.

An inquiry into the feasibility of education for individual and social development.

Metropolitan School Study Council, New York 27, a cooperative organization of seventy school communities in and around New York City, publishes *Exchange* and other bulletins, which describe practices and promising trends in education.

Moehlman, C.H., *The Wall of Separation between Church and State,* Boston, the Beacon Press, 1951.

A historical study of recent controversy and criticism of the religious provisions of the First Amendment.

National Education Association, Washington 6, and its various Departments and Divisions carry on research and put out publications which describe new and promising practices and identify trends in education. Pertinent here are:

N.E.A. Research Division: *Educational Differences Among the States,* March, 1954; *The Status of Driver Education in Public High Schools,* 1952–1953, April, 1954; *The State and Sectarian Education,* December, 1956; *Ten Criticisms of Public Education,* December, 1957; *Can Our Schools Get by With Less? A Critical Review* of Roger A. Freeman's *School Needs in the Decade Ahead,* October, 1958; "Public Opinion on Education" and "Corporal Punishment" in October, 1958, *Research Bulletin,* pp. 75 and 88, respectively; and "Plaintiffs and Defendants" and "The Courts Decide," in April, 1958 *Research Bulletin,* pp. 58–62.

Association for Supervision and Curriculum Development: *Forces Affecting American Education,* 1953 Yearbook; *Education for American*

Freedom, 1954; *Research Helps in Teaching the Language Arts*, 1955; *Action Research*, 1957; *Juven le Delinquency: Research, Theory, and Comment*, 1958; *A Look at Continuity in the School Program*, 1958 Yearbook; and *What Does Research Say About Arithmetic* (rev. ed.), 1958.

Department of Classroom Teachers and American Educational Research Association, *Juvenile Delinquency* (a research study), 1958 (No. 10) in "What Research Says to the Teacher" series.

Educational Policies Commission: *Manpower and Education*, 1956, and *The Contemporary Challenge to American Education*, 1958.

NEA Journal: Special features on "Science, Mathematics, and the Humanities: Let's Balance the Program," February, 1958, pp. 79–90, and on "Reading," March, 1958, pp. 159–69.

National Science Teachers Association: Special features in *The Science Teacher* on "The Physical Science Study: Building a New Structure," November, 1957, pp. 315–30, and on trends at the elementary and secondary levels, "Guideposts in Science Education," by Sam S. Blanc, March, 1958, pp. 82–83, 109–112.

National Society for the Study of Education: 54th Yearbook, Part II, 1955, *Mental Health in Modern Education;* 55th Yearbook, Part II, 1956, *Adult Reading;* and 58th Yearbook, Part I, 1959, *Community Education.*

Nesbitt, M., *A Public School for Tomorrow*, New York, Harper and Brothers, 1953.
How a new, constructive elementary program developed in an old school in Richmond, Virginia.

Parents' Magazine: Special issue on "U.S. Schools: A Report on the Progress and Problems of Education," October, 1958, pp. 43–77, and *passim.*

The Public Opinion Quarterly, Princeton (N.J.).
The only professional magazine devoted entirely to the mass media of communication and learning, to the polling and analysis of public opinion, and to the development of better instruments and techniques for public opinion analysis.

Reutter, E.E., Jr., *The School Administrator and Subversive Activities*, New York, Teachers College, Columbia University, 1951.
A study of cases and action in restraint of public school personnel in regard to alleged subversive activities.

Romine, S.A., *Building the High School Curriculum*, New York, The Ronald Press Company, 1954.
Chapter XVII for the secondary-school curriculum of the future.

School and Society: Special reports at intervals on the yearly studies of TV and its effects on children (*e.g.*, Paul Witty, June 21, 1958, pp. 287–89); and on state, church, and school trends (*e.g.*, W.W. Brickman, October 25, 1952, pp. 262–67 and April 13, 1957, pp. 122–27).

Scott, C.W., and Hill, C.M. (Eds.), *Public Education Under Criticism,* Englewood Cliffs, Prentice-Hall, 1954.
An anthology, well selected for both *pros* and *cons* on each issue, with suggestions as to how to evaluate critics and handle criticisms.

The Secondary School Curriculum, the Yearbook of Education, 1958, Yonkers-on-Hudson, World Book Company, 1958.
A presentation by a host of American and British authorities which covers all kinds of curricular programs.

Shoemaker, Don (Ed.), *With All Deliberate Speed,* New York, Harper and Brothers, 1957.
One of the most complete studies of desegregation in seventeen states and the District of Columbia.

Spurlock, C., *Education and the Supreme Court,* Urbana, University of Illinois Press, 1955.
The effect of thirty-seven selected decisions of the U.S. Supreme Court upon students, parents, teachers, and administrators.

Thayer, V.T., *The Attack Upon The American Secular School,* Boston, the Beacon Press, 1951.
Analysis of the attacks and opposition to the secular school, separation of church and state, whether there should be public support of non-public schools, and how religion is taught in secular schools.

U.S. Office of Education, Washington 25.
Collections of information about public schools and special reports are issued from time to time on trends; for example, *Education Beyond the High School: Needs and Resources,* 1956; *Schools at Work in 48 States: A Study of Elementary School Practices,* Bulletin 1952, No. 13; and *The 2-Year Community College: An Annotated List of Studies and Surveys,* Bulletin 1958, No. 14.

Woodring, P., *New Directions in Teacher Education,* New York 22, the Fund for the Advancement of Education, 1957.
A report of interesting experiments in teacher education and recruiting, including professional programs for liberal arts graduates, for older college graduates, the Master of Arts in Teaching (M.A.T.), and four-year programs combining professional with liberal education.

INDEX

Academic curriculum, 432
Academy, development of, 1, 8, 10–13.
   See also Schools, evolution of types
   of
Accrediting, high schools, 386–387;
   agencies, 31–32; 370–371; of secondary schools, 31–32
Activities, definition of, 245
Activity analysis, in curriculum revision, 144
Activity concept, 171–174; movement,
   in curriculum, 180, 195–196; activity (fusion) approach to curriculum revision, 269–272; program,
   experiment in New York City, 271–
   272; as standard for textbooks,
   221 f
Adams, F., 189, 190
Administration, of curriculum, of secondary-school curriculum work,
   450–474; special programs of study,
   450–451; types of curriculum organization and administration, 451–
   459; addition of new programs of
   study, 451–453; broad-fields of
   knowledge organizations, 453–455;
   reorganizing the curriculum around
   study of youth, 455–456; approach
   through organized guidance, 456–
   457; bringing the extracurriculum
   into the curriculum, 458–459
Adolescence, as period of child growth
   and development, 61–63; 71–73; attitudes of, and growth, 372–373;
   organizing curriculum around, 455–
   456
Adult education, 393
Advertising, in consumer education
   and propaganda analysis, 580, 582–
   592, 607–608
Advisory Committee on Education,
   President's, 42, 487–490, 645
Agassiz, L., 18

Agriculture, subsistence, 648
Agricultural Adjustment Administration, 498
Agriculture, work in, 487–490; education in, and mechanic arts, 643,
   647–648
Aid, Federal. *See* Federal Aid
Aids, curricular and teaching, 552–
   571; the library, 553–557; materials
   bureau, 557–561; curriculum lab-
   oratories, 561–562; audio-visual,
   562–566; principles for use of aids,
   570–571
Aims, purposes and objectives, of cur-
   riculum, definition of, 245
Aims-and-objectives stage, in modern
   curriculum movement, 144
Aims of education, comparison of
   Herbart's with Morrison's, 180
Alabama curriculum revision program,
   294
Alberty, Elsie, 242, 456
Alberty, H., 189, 190, 440
Alexander, Wm., 190, 207
American Association of Junior
   Colleges, 116–117
American Association of School Ad-
   ministrators, 491, 652
American Automobile Association,
   404
American Council on Education, 72,
   608, 655
American Council on Race Relations,
   655
American Education Fellowship,
   47
American Education Week, 134
American Educational Research As-
   sociation, 565
American Federation of Advertisers,
   211
American Historical Association, 150,
   459–460

American Legion, the, 211, 593–596, 605–606; as pressure group, 593–596
American Library Association, publications, 556
American Medical Association, 584–585
American Newspaper Publishers' Association, 211
American Youth Commission, 352–353, 480–483, 507
American Youth Congress, 479–480
Americanism, teaching of, 35
Americanization, 644
Anderson, Nels, 492
Anderson, Vernon, 186, 207
Anderson, W. N., 143
Apperception, of Herbart, 17–18, 179–183, 199–200
Appreciation-type, field of learning, 182–183, 194–195
Apprenticeship, 3
Armstrong-Stinnett Study, 522–523
Arndt, C. D., 658
Arthurdale, community school experiment, 620–621
Articulation, of secondary school with other levels and agencies, 364–367
Association for Childhood Education, book lists of, 556
Association for Study of Negro Life and History, 655
Association for Supervision and Curriculum Development, 215, 392, 544, 652, 666
Association of Colleges and Secondary Schools for Negroes, 357–359
Association of Comics Magazine Publishers, 100
Association of Secondary-School Principals, 338
Associative Junior Work Camps, 101–102
Atlanta, Five-Year Community High Schools, 621–622
Attitudes toward education, 104–107; what parents and pupils want, 104–105
Audio-visual aids, in curriculum work, 562–566; list of types, 563; principles for use of, 570–571

Awards, in education, artificial, 462–466

Bagley, W. C., 44, 143
Ballard Memorial school experiment, in community school, 620
Band-wagon device, 599
Banning, of textbooks and periodicals, 209–220
Basic agencies in educative process, 85–112; the family, 85–89; the church, 89–90; the play group, 90–91; economic influences, 91–93; noncommercial community agencies, 94–95; leisure time, 95–104; relation of school to other social agencies, 104–108
Basic (socializing) coures, 413; basic education, 45, 650, 654. See also Core curriculum
Baxter, B., 303, 315, 662
Beale, H. K., 210
Behavior, in teachers, and mental health, 78–81
Behavior Rating Scales, 283
Bell, H. M., 481
Bell Study, of youth, in Maryland, 85
Bender, L., 304
Bestor, A., 44, 45, 649
Birth rate, national, and effect on education, 113
Black-Smith Bill, 596
Blair Bill, 643
Blair, J. L., 208
Blayne, Thornton, 397
Block system, in junior high, 439–44?
Blos, P., 353–354
Bobbitt, F., 44, 144, 146, 147, 148
Bode, B., 43
Boring-from-within device, 599
Bossing, Nelson, 242, 243, 440
Boy and girl problems, courses in, 396–397
Boy Scouts, 102
Brickman, W. W., 46
Briggs, T. H., 44, 193, 338
Broadcasting, and implications for curriculum, 604–605
Broad-fields curriculum, 406–410; as type of organization of curriculum, 453
Brown, F. J., 86

Brown, W. H., 73, 74
Brownell, W. A., 282
Brubacher, J. S., 43
Building America, and textbook controversy, 214–216
Burton, W. W., 189, 190
Butterweck, J. S., 260–261

CCC. See Civilian Conservation Corps
California controversy, over textbooks, 214 f
California Cooperating Schools, 162–166, 169–171, 377, program of curriculum revision, 215
California Study of Special Interests, of children, 298–299; State Scope and Sequence Committee, 215, 295; Test of Personality, 283, Achievement Tests, 281
Campbell, D. S., 158, 187, 188
Campfire Girls, 257
Camps, and camping, as educational factors, 101–102, 624
Cardinal principles (7) of Secondary Education, 30
Card-stacking device, 598
Carnegie Corporation, 361
Carnegie unit, 437, 458
Cassidy, R., 315, 662
Caswell, H. L., 158, 187, 188
Census, school. See Birthrate
Census figures, and employment and unemployment, 117–120
Center(s) of Interest, 187–188, 198, 242; approach, to curriculum revision, 273–275
Certification, of teachers, 518–524; supply and demand, 523–524
Changes in textbooks, over a period of years, 224, 225
Character education, 393
Charity education, 2; schools, 2–3
Charters, W. W., 144, 145, 146
Checklists, of *Evaluative Criteria*, 469–470
Chicago Tribune's, survey of textbooks, 212
Child growth and development, 60–85; newer experiments and studies, 71–78; and educational psychology, 60–63; theories of learning, 63–71; controversy over the I.Q., 73–78;

heredity and environment, 74–77; teacher behavior and development and mental health, 78–79; teacher knowledge of child development, 80–81
Child labor, implications of, for curriculum, 91–94
Children's literature, as informal educational agent, 98–101; Book Week, 134; programs, on radio, 97–98, 590
Church, the, as a social agency, 89–90; as basic agency in educative process, 89–90
Church-state, type of school, 2–3
Citizens Fact-Finding Movement of Georgia, 627
Civil service, courses in, 402–403
Civilian Conservation Corps, 390, 484, 646
Clapp, H. L., 44
Clark, J. R., 143
Classical high school, 15
Classroom Social Distance Scale, 664–665
Code, comics, 310–311
Code (Standard of Practices), of National Association of Broadcasters, 591
Cole, L., 304
College, Development of, Chap. I, *passim*
College entrance (admission) subjects, 28, 387–389
Comic action magazines. See Comics
Comics, the, as reading readiness device, 302–311; code of ethics, 310–311; history of, 303; bridging gap between comics reading and classics in literature, 307–308; new approach to analysis of, 306–307; as a mechanic of propaganda, 603–604
Comics Magazine Association of America, 303
Commission of Reorganization of Secondary Education, 30
Commission on Human Relations, 353
Commission on Relation of School and College, 344
Commission on Secondary School Curriculum, 353–354

Commission on the Social Studies, of American Historical Association, 150
Commission on Teacher Education, 72, 533, 534–536
Committee of Fifteen, 27
Committee of Ten, 24–25, 27, 28, 432
Committee on College Entrance Requirements, 28–29, 432
Committee on Economy of Time in Education, 29–30
Committee on Secondary School Studies. See Committee of Ten
Committee on Southern Regional Studies and Education, 634
Committee work, in elementary school, 312–313
Common factors, in learning, 66–67
Common learnings, 413
Common school. See Schools, evolution of types of
Communication arts, high school subjects as, 413–414
Communism, 132
Community, a social agency, Chap. V, passim
Community agencies, in educative process, leisure-time, 94–104; noncommercial, 94–95, 101–104; commercial, 95–101
Community approach, to curriculum revision, 615–638; local pattern in American education, 615–617; community as center of national planning, 617–620; curriculum experiments in local communities, 620-627; state as the larger community, 627–631; regional approach to the curriculum, 631–634; the United States as the national community, 634–636; implications of community approach for curriculum development, 636–638
Conant, J. B., 47, 361–363, 652, 654, 661
Conditioned response, learning by, 65–66
Conference on the American High School, 1957, 654
Configuration, in learning, 65
Conflict, modern, in educational theory, 42–47; among adolescents, 90–91
Conservation education, 394–395
Constants, 245
Consumable materials, 558–560
Consumer education, 149, 582–592, 595; in elementary school, 318–319; in high school, 395
Consumers Research, 586
Consumers Union, 586
Content (subject-matter) requirements, for teaching, 519–523
Contract plan (method), 178
Cook, L. A., and Elaine F., 657
Cooperative curriculum planning, and group dynamics, 312, 662–666
Cooperative Social Studies Test, 282
Cooperative Study in Elementary Education, 324
Cooperative Study of General Education, 531
Cooperative Study of Secondary School Standards, 106, 324, 349–352, 469
Core curriculum, 244, 245, 273, 274, 389, 411, 440–441; definitions of, 241–242, 245; movement, 161; procedures, in elementary curriculum, 291–294; in junior high, 432–439
Correlated curriculum, high school, 410
Correlation, of subject matter, early developments, 244, 245; later, 441
Costs, school, pupil, 115-116, 363–364
Council Against Intolerance in America, 655
Council for Basic Education, 45, 649
Council on Advancement of Secondary Education, 218
Counts, G., 43
Course of study, definitions of, 238–239, 240, 245
Creative urges, in elementary-school child, 263–265
Crisis. See Curriculum Crisis
Criteria, for textbook selection, 234; for analysis of propaganda, 581, 582 f
Critics, constructive, of school program, 652–653
Critics, of public schools and curriculum, 649–653

Cubberley, E. P., 2, 18
Curricula, high school, parallel, 28–29; typical early high school, 20–22, 24, 26–27
Curricular materials, new, 670
Curriculum, in secondary schools, changing conception of, 337–377; studies in secondary education, 338–363; problems, peculiar to, 363–375; résumé of factors forcing changes in, 375–377; curricular patterns, 382–387; in North Carolina, 382–383; in Ohio, 383–384; in El Paso, 384–385; in New York State, 385–386; implications of, 386–387
Curriculum building, in elementary school, 249–289; elementary-school situation, 249–251; interests and attitudes of children, 251–258; conditioning factors in revision, 258–266; types of curriculum approach (plans), 267–278; organization and administration, 278–280; evaluation of curriculum development, 280–286; curriculum planning, with community as center, 617–620; experiments in local communities, 620–627; state as larger center, 627–631; regional planning, 631–634; national, 634–636
Curriculum Crisis, at midcentury, 643–672; past national emergencies and curricular progress, 643–649; present curricular crisis, 648–669; developing curricular trends, 669–672
Curriculum laboratories, 561–562
Curriculum movement, stages of growth in modern, 143–175; genesis of, 143–144; aims-and-objectives stage, 144–145; activity analysis, 144–149; survey movement, 149–156; development of unit technique, Chap. VII; system-wide curriculum revision, 157–161; Core curriculum, 161–166; large-unit procedure, 166–167; scope and sequence, 167–169; fusion, 169–171; source materials, 171–173; relation of activity movement to, 196; administration of, 278 f, 451–459; definitions of curriculum, 196, 238–239, 245; four plans (approaches), in secondary school, 406–412
Curtis, F. D., 178

D. E. See Distributive education
D. O. See Diversified occupations
D. P.'s. See Displaced persons
Dale, E., 562, 566
Dalton plan, 179, 187, 343
Dame Schools, 1, 4, 6
Dashiell, J. F., 63, 68
Davidson, F. P., 491
de Sauzé, E. B., 320–321
Dearborn, W. F., 491
Demerath, N. J., 633
Demiashkevich, M., 44
Democracy, teaching of, 35
Denver, curriculum development in, 158
Department of Classroom Teachers, 565
Department of Elementary School Principals, 565
Department of Rural Education, N.E.A., 544
Department of Secondary School Principals. See National Association of Secondary School Principals.
Department of Superintendence, N.E.A., 50, 208
Department of Supervisors and Directors of Instruction. See Association for Supervision and Curriculum Development
Departmentalization, Secondary school, 367–369
Depression Decade, happenings in, 645–646
Desegregation, curricular issues of, 658–660
Detroit, curriculum development in, 158
Dewey, J., 29, 43, 543
Diagnostic, instruments, in guidance, 506
Differences, individual. See Individual differences
Differentiated assignment, 178
Disney, W., 99
Displaced persons, 134
District School System, 6
Distributive education, 92, 395, 509

Diversified occupations, 92, 509
Douglass, A. A., 196, 198, 241, 243
Douglass, H. R., 389, 482
Draper, E. M., 143, 189, 243, 408
Driver education, 398, 404
Drucker, Peter, 494

Economic factors, in curriculum work, 91–94; policies, new, and effect on education, 117–126
Economy, principles for, in learning, 29, 67–68
Education for All American Youth, 356–357
Educational guidance. See Guidance
Educational leadership, as factor in extension of education, 115
Educational Policies Commission, 50, 356–357, 608–609, 652
Educational Testing Service, 654
Edwards, N., 482
Eells, W. C., 349
Eight-year Study, P.E.A., 387, 408, 467–469
Eighth-grader, the, 257
El Paso, high school standards, 385
Elementary school, functions of, 249–250. For curriculum building, see Curriculum building; for evolution of types of, see Schools, evolution of
Elementary school subjects, types of, about 1900, 18
Eliot, C. W., 18, 19
Elson, W. H., 223, 227
Elson Readers, 222–227
Emergency Agencies for Youth, 483–487; CCC, 484; NYA, 484–487; WPA, 484
Emergency educational measures, of depression decade, 480–492
Emergency teachers, 523–524
English, new courses in, 395–396
English classical (high) school, 12
English Grammar School, 6, 8
Enrichment of the curriculum, 552–566
Enrollment, school, 113
Environment, of children, fusion of subject-areas with, 295. See also Heredity
Equalization, of educational oppor-

tunity, philosophy behind, 41–44, 47–51
Essentialists, and their theory, 42–47
Eugenics. See Heredity, and environment
Eurich, A. C., 283
Evaluation, of curriculum work, secondary, 459–463; measurements in terms of subject-matter, 459–460; purposes of tests, 460–462; subjectivity and variability of school marks, 462–463; evaluation as broader concept of measurement, 463–466; teacher-pupil individual folder for evaluation, 466–467; recent developments, 467–471. Evaluation, of elementary school curriculum work, new concepts in evaluation, 283–285; principles for evaluation, 285–286; standards for, of elementary schools, 324–325; of nontangibles, 373–375
Evaluative Criteria, 469–470
Everett, S., 657–658
Every Pupil Tests of Basic Study Skills, 282
Examinations, national, for teachers, 527 f
Expenditures, by pupils, in public high schools, 363–364
Experience curriculum, 244, 411; curriculum approach, elementary school, 275, 278
Experimental curricular practices, symposia of, 157
Experiments, curricular, in elementary schools, 317–325
Exploratory courses, 365
Extracurriculum, bringing into the curriculum, 458–459; activities, in elementary school, 251

Factors, in curriculum change, early to 1920, 1, 32 f
Faculty psychology of education, 17
Fair Trade Legislation, 128
False front, as a device in propaganda, 600–601
Family, the, as a social agency, 85–87; as basic agency in education process, 85–89

Family life education, 625–627; North Carolina, as a sample of a state, 626–627
Fargo, L. F., 555, 557
Farm youth and policies, and education, 117
Faunce, Roland, 242, 243, 440
Federal aid for vocational education, 644; rehabilitation, 644; Americanization, 644–645; adult education, 644–645; for emergencies during 1930's, 645–646
Federal Aviation Agency, 497
Federal Communications Commission, 589–590
Federal Council of Churches of Christ, 655
Federal Fair Labor Standards Act, 93
Federal Food and Drugs Act, 583
Federal Security Agency, 363
Federal Trade Commission, 582, 583
Fifth-grader, the, 255–257
First-grader, the, 252
Five formal steps, of Herbart. See Herbartian plan (method)
Fleisher, M., 500
Flesch, R., 649
Florida experiment in teacher education, program of curriculum revision, 294
Folkways, the, 88
Food and Drug Administration, 583
Ford Fund's Projects in Teacher Education, 540–542
Foreign languages, trends in, 397
Formulation of Aims by National Committees, 149
Fourth-grader, the, 254
Frank, J., 304, 310
Free, is public secondary education?, 363
French, instruction of, in elementary, 321
Friends of Public Schools of America, 211
Functions, of secondary education, 337–341
Fused curriculum, high school, 410
Fusion, 161, 169–171, 244, 245, 269–270, 294–297, 441

Gang, the, as an agency in educative process, 90–91
Gellerman, W., 593
General courses, 241, 365–366, 371–372, 452–453; general curriculum, 388
General education, 391, 405, 412–413, 437–439, 650, 654
General Education Board, 534–535
General Motors Poll, 603
George-Barden Act, 506
George-Deen Act, 396, 645
George-Reed Act, 119
Georgia Citizens' Council, 627
Gerberick, J. R., 189
German, instruction of, in elementary, 321
Gesell, A., 61, 72, 492
Gestalt theory, of learning, 64–65, 180
Gifted, education of and curriculum for, 660–661
Gilbert Youth Research Poll, 603
Gillin, John P., 633
Girl Scouts, 102, 257
Glittering generality, the, 597
Golden, W., 662
Good Health Week, 134
Graduate degree, requirements for teaching, 528–530
Graduation requirements, high school, 382–386
Grammar (English), School, 6, 8
Grammar School, 8, 9
Gray, Harold, 604
Greenlaw, E., 227
Grizzell, E. D., 370
Group development, shift in emphasis from individual to, 122
Group dynamics, 662–666; group work, small, 312–313; the sociogram, 315–316
Group planning, 662
Grouping, by social maturity, 259–260
Growth (child) and adjustment checksheet, 80
Gruhn, W. T., 435
Guidance of youth, and the curriculum, 477–516; definition and types of guidance, 477–478; curricular provisions for, 503–511; placement and follow-up, 507–508. Guidance,

pupil in elementary school, 313–317; guidance week, 366; organizing curriculum around, 456–457

Hagaman, Neva, 186
Hamblen, A. A., 152
Hand, H., 43, 123
Hanna, L., 186
Hanna, P., 491
Hansen, Harry, 588
Harap, H., 149
Harby, S. F., 492
Harris, A. J., 304
Harrison, L., 301
Hartshorne, H., 86, 89
Harvard, early curriculum, 218, 361
Haskell, R. I., 152
Havighurst, R. J., 86
Health education courses, 398–400
Herbart, 17–18, 179, 180, 181, 182; plan (method), and comparison with Morrison (unit) method, 180; steps, 17–18, 27, 181–182
Heredity, and environment, in child growth, 72–77
High school, evolution of to 1920, 9
High school, public, 14–15, 19–33, passim
Hoar Bill, 643
Hobbs, S. H., Jr., 633
Home, the, as an agency in educative process, 86–89
Home and family living, courses in, 505–506
Home Economics, 396–397, 505
Homemaking courses, 396–397, 505
Homework, in elementary school, 322
Hook, S., 43
Hopkins, L. T., 662
Horace Mann-Lincoln Institute of School Experimentation, 661, 663–666
Horn, E., 209
Horne, H. H., 44
Hotz, 392
Hughes, F., 212, 213
Hullfish, H. G., 43
Hunter, Floyd, 633
Hurley, Beatrice, 190
Hutchins, R. M., 44

I.Q., in planning for individual differences, 70; controversy over, 73–78
Idealism. See Essentialists
Ideals, as an aim in curriculum making, 145
Ideologies, international, 131–136
Individual curriculum. See Experience curriculum
Individual differences, in growth and learning, 68–71
Individualized instruction, 178–179
Indoctrination, in schools, 579–581, 582 f
Industry, and induction of youth into, 117–128, 507–511
Inglis, A., 13, 357
Insight, learning by, 64–65
Institute (Gallup) of Public Opinion, 106, 107, 602–603
Institute for Research in Social Science, 631 f
Intangibles, attempts to measure, 462, 467–477
Integrating courses. See Core curriculum
Integration, 243, 245; as standard for textbooks, 221, and 224–232, passim. Integrating courses. See Core curriculum
Intelligence Quotient. See I. Q.
Interaction. See Group dynamics
Intercultural education, 655–658
Intercultural groups, movement for better understanding of, 321
Interest span, 258
Interests, and attitudes, of elementary-school child, special, of children, 251–258; reading, of children, 297–311; areas of, urges and enthusiasm of children, 259–261
Intergroup relations, in teaching materials, 655–658; intergroup education project, 655–657; other intergroup studies, 655–658
Intermediate School, 8, 9
International education, 655–658
International movements, effect of, on curriculum, 113–117, 119, 123, 125, 127, 129, 135; ideologies, 131
Interrelation, 243–244
Investigation device, 599–600

Iowa Silent Reading Test, 282
Irrigation, and resettlement as factors in education, 125–126
ISSCP, Illinois Program, 630
Issues, of secondary education, 338 f

Jacobson, P., 363
Jersild, A. T., 303
John Dewey Society, 657
Johnson, George, 303
Joint Council on Educational Television, 565
Jones, W. W. D., 304
Judd, C. H., 29, 416
Junior college, number, size, and enrollments, 371–372
Junior High school, early influences, 27, 32; curriculum, the, 432–449; purposes, 434–435; types of curricula, 435–439, 654–655; new developments, 442–445
Juvenile delinquency, 93–94

Kalamazoo Case, 14
Kandel, I. L., 44, 46
Kaulfers, Walter V., 397
Keck, C. M., 227
Keliher, A., 43, 566
Kellogg (W. K.) Foundation, efforts in community health and education projects, 622–624
Kentucky (Sloan) Experiment, 620
Kilpatrick, W. H., 43, 196
Kindergarten, development of, 16
Knowlton, D. C., 303
Koos, L. V., 342

Labor, and induction of youth into ranks of, 117–128; and work for youth, 493–511, passim
Laboratory, curriculum, and plans (method), 557–562, passim
Ladder, educational: prenational period, 4; 1840 for academy, 10–11; 1775–1900 (elem.), 23; 1893–1920 (high school), 33
Land-grant college, 389
Lane, R. H., 262
Large-Unit, procedure, 161, 166
Latin, instruction of, in elementary, 321
Latin Grammar School, 4, 6, 8, 337

See also Evolution of types of, prior to 1920, 1–17
Lauchner, Aaron, 442
Lawson, D. E., 208
Learning, Morrison concept, 193
Lee, Dorris, 43, 189
Lee, Murray, 43, 189
Legal status, of religious education in public schools, 657
Leisure-time agencies, in educative process, 95–104; the sound picture and television, 95–97; the radio, 97–98; children's literature, the newspaper and newsstands publications, 98–101; camps and playgrounds and other types, 101–104
Leonard, J. P., 189, 190, 408
Levels, or divisions, in elementary-school organization, 278–280
Lewis, Hylan, 633
Library, the curricular aid, 553–557; responsibility of teacher in library materials, 556–557; guides for use of, 555–557
Life Adjustment Education, 650
Lindley, B. and E., 491
Liss, E., 73, 74
Lobbying Act, legislation concerning, 596
Long Beach, curriculum development in, 275, 294
Long-unit assignments, 178
Lunch program, Federal School, 646
Lurry, Lucile, 242, 456
Lynd, A., 649

McKown, H. C., 315, 562, 566
Marks, school, variability of, 462–463
Maryland Study, of Youth, 85, 481–482
Mastery method. See Unit, (Morrison) technique
Materials bureau, the, 557–561
Materials, curricular. See Aids, curricular
Mathematics, high school courses in, 400
May, M. A., 86, 89
Measurement in education, instruments of, 463–465; variability of school marks, 462–463

Mechanics, of modern propaganda, 601 ff
Melvin, A. G., 189
Melvin, Bruce, 492
Mental hygiene, 478, 504–507; health, and behavior, in teachers, 78–81
Metropolitan Achievement Tests, 281
Michigan Community Health Project, 623–624
Michigan study, of secondary-school curriculum, 359, 387
Midcentury White House Conference on Children and Youth, 103, 492
Middle States Association, 349
Miel, Alice, 43
Military training. See R.O.T.C.
Miller, C. R., 600
Minority groups, as factor in development in America, 130 ff; movement for better understanding of, 665–666
Misner, P., 279
Modern Foreign Language Study, the, 150
Montgomery County (Md.), curriculum development in, 158
Mores, the, 88–89, 103
Morland, J. Kenneth, 633
Morrill Acts, 14–15, 615, 643
Morrison, H. C., 44, 178, 181, 183, 187, 188, 192, 198, 199, 201, 343. Morrison steps in technique of teaching, 180
Morrison method (plan). See Unit technique
Morrison unit. See Unit technique
Motivation, in learning, 66–67
Motives, dominating curriculum development, 1; religious, 1–5; political, 5–13; utilitarian, 14–34; mass education, 34–35
Moving (sound) picture, in informal education of youth, 95–97; changes in types of, 1920–1947, 96; as curricular aids, 563–564; in advertising, 601 ff
Muzzey, D. S., 209, 219, 303

NDEA, 646
NRA, 92
NYA, 646

Name-calling, 597
National Association for the Advancement of Colored People, 655
National Association of Manufacturers, and examination of textbooks, 210, 211, 212, 213, 218
National Association of Secondary School Principals, 415, 654
National Citizens' Commission for the Public Schools, 218
National Citizens' Council for Better Schools, 654
National Conference of Christians and Jews, 218, 655
National Council for the Social Studies, 208, 300, 556, 557
National Council of Teachers of English, commissions on curriculum, 556, 557
National Defense Education Act, 647
National Education Association, 19 f, 50, 565
National emergencies, and curricular trends, 643–648; post-war emergencies and advancement of curriculum, effects of other types of emergencies, 643–646; movement for better understanding of intercultural, racial, and minority groups, 655–660; federal aid for general education, 643–645, 647; developing curricular trends, 649–667; implications for the future, 667–668
National Merit Scholarships, 653
National movements, effect of, on curriculum, 113–117, 119, 123, 125, 127, 129, 135
National Music Week, 134
National Recovery Act (NRA), 92
National Retail Dry Goods Association, 584–585
National (Herbart) Society, for the Study of Education, 18, 74, 195, 196, 198, 208, 300–301, 440, 492, 660
National Survey of Secondary Education, 178, 342–343
National teachers exams, 526–528
National Thrift Week, 134
National Youth Administration, 390, 484–487, 646
Nationalism. See Progressives

Nature, and nurture. *See* Heredity, and environment

Nature Study, 319 f

Negro, Youth, 490; desegregation, 655 f and 658 ff

Neugarten, B. L., 86

Neurones, in learning, 66–67

New Stanford Achievement Test, 281

New York, state, high school standards, 385–386

New York City Experiment, Activity Program, 271–272

New York City Youth Survey, 480

New York State Economic Council, 211

Newspaper, as a mechanic of modern propaganda, in elementary school, 601–605; as informal educational agent, 98, 100–101

Newsstand publications, as educational agent, 98–101

Noar, Gertrude, 415

Normal school, influence of, on curriculum, 16–18

North Carolina study of youth, 85, 490; high school standards, 382–383

North Central Association, 342, 392

Northwest Association, 349

Northwest Regional Council, the, 633–634

Nuclear age, curricular problem of, 660

Nurture. *See* Heredity, and environment

Object teaching, 16–17

Objectives-and-aims stage in modern curriculum movement, 144–149

Occupations, seasonal, 496–497; work opportunities for youth, 494–502; courses in, 404–405

Odum, H. W., 88, 126, 631

Ohio, high school standards, 383–384

Ohio State University, experiments in teacher education, 537–540

Oneonta program, teacher training, 545

Oral instruction, 16

Ordinance of 1785, 7

Organization, in elementary-school, of curriculum, 278–280

Orientation, in high school, 364–367; courses, 305–306

Oswego Normal School, 16

P.E.A., Eight-Year Study, 344–348

P.T.A., 316

PWA, 646

Parallel curricula and agencies in secondary schools, 387–391; new and parallel courses, 391–406

Parents Magazine, 303, 585

Parker, C., 662

Parker District Schools, 542

Parochial school, development of type of, 2–3

Participation, pupil, in school administration, 316–317

Part-time programs, 119, 487–490, 503 ff, 507 ff

Passow, A. H., 661

Patrick, Ralph, Jr., 633

Patriotic pressure, on schools, 605–606

Peel, J. C., 201

Pennsylvania Study of High School and College, 527; of Teacher Education, 535

Periodicals, attacks on, as text materials, 214–217

Personal guidance. *See* Guidance

Pestalozzi, 16–17

Phi Delta Kappa, 659

Philosophies, conflicting educational, Chap. II, *passim*

Physical education, courses, 398–400

Picture magazine (newspaper), 98–100

Placement tests, 367–368

Plain folks device, 598

Planning, cooperative, for school program, 669–670

Planning boards, 636

Plastics, 498–499

Playgrounds, as sociological factor in education, 102–103

Play group, the, as basic agency in educative process, 90–91

Poison device, 601

Pollock, C., 107

Polls, of public opinion, 602–603

Population changes. *See* Birthrate

Potter, Gladys, 186

Practical-arts type, field of learning, 183, 194–195
Practices, promising, in elementary curriculum work, 291–325
Pragmatists. See Progressives
Preplanning, of curricular work, 669–670
Prescott, D. A., 72
President's Advisory Committee on Education, 510, 647
Press, the, as informal educational agent, 98–101, 582
Pressure groups, and textbooks, 209, 592–593; pressure, on schools, 597–601; religious, 605; patriotic, 605–606; civic organizations and agencies, 606–607; commercial, 607
Pretest, 183–185, 194, 202, 299
Prewett, Clinton R., 45–46, 189
Primary School, 8, 9
Principles of Learning. See Theories of learning
Problem method, 178, 196
Problem solving, in learning, 62, 64–65
Problems, curricular, for schools in next twenty-five years, 653–667
Professional requirements, for teaching, 519–520; graduate, 528–530; teacher exams, 526–528
Professions, the, definitions of, 495–496
Program of study, 239, 240–241; secondary, addition of new, 450, 451–453
Progressive education. See Progressives
Progressive Education Association, 71, 453, 491, 649
Progressive Education Association Eight-Year Study. See Eight-Year Study
Progressives, and their theory, 42–47
Project Method, 178, 196
Promising practices, in elementary school curriculum, 291–325; samples of units, core curriculum procedures, 291; scope and sequence plans, 291; fusion of subject-areas with experiences of children, 294–297; children's special interests, 297–298; reading interests and readiness, 300–302; comics, 302–311; small groups and committee work, 312–

313; pupil guidance, 313–316; miscellaneous experiments, 317–325
Promotion, teacher with grade, 318
Propaganda, and the curriculum, 579–609; problems of indoctrination and of, 579–581; definition of, 580–581; teaching of propaganda analysis, 582–596; samples in analysis of, 582–596; techniques of, 597–605; mechanics of, 601–605; propaganda channels in schools, 597–609; summary, 609–611; in textbook selection, 608–609
Psychology, educational, purposes of, 60–63
Public Affairs Committee, 655
Public domain, and resettlement, 125
Public land. See Public domain
Public service, courses in, 402–403; work in, 497–498
Public Works Administration, 646
Pupil costs, 115–116
Pupil guidance. See Guidance
Pupil-teacher load, 115–116
Pupil-teacher relationship, in elementary school, 250
Puritans, 1–3
Puritans, schools of, 2–7

R.O.T.C., Junior, in high school, 386, 400–401
Racial minorities, problem of, 130; movement for better understanding of, 130 f
Radio, the, as informal educational agency, 97–98; as curricular aid, 564–566; in advertising and propaganda, 587–592; types of programs, 589–590; programs for children, 97–98, 590–591; Code of National Association of Broadcasters, 588; device of propaganda, 604–605
Reading, interests, of children, 300–301; readiness, 301–302; factors controlling and influencing pupils, 301, 309–310; samples of tests of, 311–312
Reading School, 6
Realism. See Essentialists
Red Cross, 316
Redefer, F. L., 46
Regents Examinations, 385–386, 535

Regents Inquiry (N.Y.), 50–51, 354–356, 491, 507
Regional, approach to curriculum, 631; Odum's group, 631–633; subregional laboratory, 632–633; Urban Studies Program, 632; materials for education, 632–633
Regional accrediting agencies. See Accrediting agencies
Regionalism, as factor in education, 126
Rejection device, 601
Relationships, of school to other social agencies, 47–51
Relief, youth and labor. See Labor, induction of youth into
Religious education, 393–394; in public schools, 35, 648–649
Religious pressure, on schools, 605
Requireds, 245
Resettlement, as factor in expansion of education, 125
Roberts, A. B., 562, 566
Robey, R. W., 211, 212, 213
Rommie, Stephen, 190
Roosevelt, F. D., 645
Rothney, J. W. M., 491
Rousseau, 17
Ruediger, W. C., 185
Rugg, H. 43, 127, 143, 209, 210; controversy over texts of, 210–211
Rural Electrification Authority, 498
Rural youth, and education. See Farm youth
Russell Sage Foundation, 361, 654
Ryan, Carson, 43

Safety education, 398, 404
St. Louis, curriculum development in, 158
Santa Barbara, curriculum development in, 273
Saylor, Galen, 190, 207
School census. See Birthrate
School-community interdependence, 619–620
Schools, fight for, 8; evolution of types of prior to 1920, 11–12; church-state type, 2, 3; parochial, 2–3; charity, 2–3; dame, reading and writing and 3R's, 1, 4, 6; Latin Grammar, 4, 6, 8, 337; college, 1, passim; English

Grammar School, 6–8; academy, 1, 8, 10–13; high school, 9; elementary (common) schools, 249; junior high school, 27–32
Schutte, T. H., 206, 207
Science, courses, in high schools, 403; science and nature study, elementary school, 319 f
Science education, as motive in curricular development, 35; recent emphasis on, 650–652
Science-type, field of learning, 183, 194
Scientific movement in education, 18–19
Scope and sequence, 167–169, 442; elementary, planning with centers of interest, 273–275
Scott, Foresman and Company, 223, 226, 227
Seals, of approval or acceptance, in advertising, 585–586
Seasonal occupations, 496–497
Second-grader, the, 252
Secondary School Study, the, 357–358
Securities Exchange Commission, 596
Selective Secondary education, 653
Self-government, by pupils, 336
Seminary, 8
Senior high schools, 371–372
September experience, in teacher education, 539
Sequence. See Scope and sequence
Seven Cardinal Principles. See Cardinal Principles
Seventh-grader, the, 257
Sex education, 403–404
Sheldon, E. A., 16
Simpson, George L., Jr., 633
Six-four-four plan, 391
Sixth-grader, the, 255–257
Small-town, characteristics of American life, 617–618
Smith, B. O., 190, 272, 390
Smith, Dora, 314
Smith, M., 44
Smith-Hughes Act, 33, 615, 644, 645
Smith-Sears Act, 644
Social agencies, relationship of school to in educational theory, 47–51

Social guidance. *See* Guidance
Social living courses. *See* Core curriculum
Social maturity, 259–260
Social Security Act, 92, 644
Social service, growth of, 123–124
Social studies work, in high school, 401–402
Society for Curriculum Study, 215
Socio-business courses, 395
Sociogram, the, 315, 664–666
Sociological factors, in curriculum work, basic agencies in the educative process, 85–108; leisure-time agencies, 95–104; relation of school to other social agencies, 104–108
Soil Conservation Service, 394
Sons of American Revolution, 215–216
Sound picture. *See* Moving picture
Source materials and aids, for teaching, 566–570; texts and reference books, 566–567; Federal and State publications, 567–568; of special educational groups, 568–569; of private groups, 569–570; source materials, for high school, 415–416; source materials for teachers, in curriculum movement, 566–570
Southern Association of Colleges and Secondary Schools, 324, 444
Southern Education Reporting Service, 659
Southern Regional Council, 655
Southern Regional Education Board, 634
Southern-States Work Conference, 634
Southern Study, the, 348
Spanish, instruction in elementary, 321
Spears, H., 157, 406
Special interests, areas, in junior high school, 297–312
Specialized high schools, 34
Spectator attitude, 97
Sprague, H. A., 520; study of teacher preparation, 520–522
Sputnik, 403, 646, 650
Standardization, of high schools, 382–387; of schools, 31–32; implications of, 386–387

Standards of Practice, in radio, 591
Stanford Social Education Investigation, 416
State, as larger community, 627–630
State Citizens Councils, 628–630; Connecticut as example, 628–629
State-wide experimental programs, in secondary education, Michigan, 359; Texas, 359–360; California, 361; summary of, 361–363
Stem courses, 241. *See also* Core curriculum
Sterner, A., 310
Stinnett, T. M., 522
Stoddard, G. D., 61
Story, H. P., 307
Strang, Ruth, 492
Stratemeyer, F. B., 189, 190
Stretch, L. B., 185
Student activities, as form of group guidance, 506
Studies, and experiments, in teacher education, 537–544
Studies, in secondary education, 338–363
Studies of adolescents, 353–354; studies of youth, American Youth Commission, 352–353; Emergency Agencies (NYA, WPA, CCC), 483–487; Advisory Committee on Education, 487–490; other surveys of youth, 490–493; guidance, placement, and followup, 507–511
Subject matter, and subjects, definition of, 245; subject curriculum, high school, 407–409; subject-matter (-area) unit approach to curriculum revision, 268–269
Supply and demand, for teachers, 548
Survey courses, 523–525
Surveys, administrative, of schools, 124, 156–157; survey movement, in modern curriculum movement, 149; surveys, scientific, 153–154
Surveys of youth. *See* Studies of adolescents
Syracuse (University) Study of teacher education, 542
System-wide curriculum revision, in modern curriculum movement, 157–161

Talented Youth Project, 661
Taylor, H., 43
Teacher education. *See* Teacher training
Teacher load. *See* Pupil-teacher load
Teacher-pupil individual folder, for evaluation, 466–467; teacher-pupil planning, 269–272, 275–278; relationships, in elementary school, 250–252
Teacher training, and curriculum changes, 518–549; state standards for teaching, 519–520; improvement of teacher education, 520–526; preservice training, 526; national teacher examinations, 526–527; graduate degree requirements, 528–529; significant experiments and studies in teacher education, 530–536; workshops, 347–348, 530–534; Commission on Teacher Education, 533–536; effect upon the curriculum, 545–546
Teaching unit. *See* Unit technique
Techniques, of propaganda, 597–601, 601 ff
Technical high school, 15
Techniways, the, 88
Television, as curricular aid, 564–566, 587–590, 604–605; types of programs, 589–590; in advertising and propaganda, 587–592; teaching by, 661–662
Tennessee Valley Authority, 12
Tenure, of teachers, and teacher growth, 525–526
Terman, L., 29
Terminal education, 371
Testimonial device, 598
Testing, in secondary curriculum work, 459–463; purposes of, 460–462; variability of school marks, 462–463
Tests, for elementary schools, 281–282
Texas Study of Secondary Education, 359–360
Textbook controversy. *See* Textbooks, influence of
Textbooks, influence of, on curriculum, 206–235; position of textbook, 206–208; standard setting of, 206–221; influence of pressure

groups on, 209–220; new trends, aims, and procedures in, 221–233; guiding principles for use of, 233–235; analysis of, in light of new trends and practices, 221 ff; approach to curriculum revision, 267; examination for evidences of unit method, 221 ff; conflicts concerning race, creed, and subversive influences, 217
Texts. *See* Textbooks
Theories of learning, 63–66; trial-and-error, 64; insight, 64–65; conditioned response, 65–66; common factors in, 66–67; economy in, 67–68; transfer of training, 68; individual differences, 68–71; conflicting educational, Chap. II
Third-grader, the, 253
Thorndike, E. L., 29, 43, 64, 143, 304
3R's, school of, 3, 6, 8, 249; research in, 649
Thut, I. N., 189
Tippett, J. S., 43
"Together" device, in propaganda, 601
Town School, 4, 6
Trade barriers, state, 128–130
Trades and industries, work in, 488 ff
Traditionalism. *See* Essentialists
Traditionalists, and their theory, 42–47
Transfer device, in propaganda, 597–598
Transfer of training, 68
Trendex News Poll, 603
Trends, in curriculum development, in secondary school, 382–419; curricular patterns, state, and local, 382–387; parallel curricula and agencies, 387–391; remaking the curriculum by adding new and parallel courses, 391–406; curricular plans (approaches), 406–412; practices of promise, 413–416; source materials, 416 ff; confused curricular situation, 416–417
Trends, in state curriculum programs, 158–160
Trial-and-error, learning by, 64
Tyler, R. W., 283

UNESCO, 655

Uhl, W. L., 149
Unemployment, figures, 119–120
Unified studies, 439. *See also* Core curriculum
Unit, definitions of, 185, 186, 187; characteristics of a teaching, 202; as instrument in general education, 412–413; organizational, as standard for texts, 221 ff
Unit technique, development of, 157, 178–202; origin of, 178; comparison of Morrison and Herbartian methods, 179–185; growth of Morrison plan since 1926, 185–186; attitudes of five authors on unit method, 186–190; evidence in textbooks of unit method of organization, 191; psychologically sound features of Morrison (unit) technique, 192–195; activity movement and teaching (unit) technique, 195–199; relationship between methods and the curriculum, 199–201; characteristics of the unit, 201–202
United Daughters of the Confederacy, 209
United Nations, 655
United States as the national community, 634 ff
Units, of credit, early development of, 28–29, 347
Units, samples of, in elementary school, 291–294
Units, subject-matter to units of child experience, 273–275, 295–297
U. S. Department of Health, Education, and Welfare, 565

Van Til, W., 43
Vance, R. B., 633
Veterans of Foreign Wars, 211
Vicarious experience, 99
Virginia curriculum revision program, 158–161
Virtue device, 601
Vocabulary, technical, of the curriculum, 238–245; extent of child's, 302
Vocational courses, 404–405; courses in vocations, 493–502
Vocational education, federal aid for, 644–645; curriculum, 451; trends in, 404–405
Vocational guidance. *See* Guidance
Vocational Rehabilitation Act, 1920, 644

WPA, 646
Wages and Hours Act, 119
Ward, C. H., 226
Washburne, C., 43, 158, 279
Watt, H. A., 208
Wesley, E. B., 206, 207, 221
Western Association, 349
Wheat, L. B., 280
White House Conference on Children in a Democracy, 50, 103, 491
White House Conference on Education, 103
Winnetka Plan (technique), 187, 279, 343
Winslow, T., 491
Wisconsin Cooperative Educational Planning Program, 158
Witty, P., 305
Woelfel, N., 101
Wood, B. D., 462
Woodring, P., 44, 322, 652
Woody, T., 196
Work programs, 50–51, 405, 667
Works Progress Administration, 636
Workshops, in Eight-Year Study, 348; for teachers, 530–533
World markets, as factor in extension of education, 120
Wrightstone, J. W., 157, 283, 406, 453
Wrinkle, W. L., 283
Writing School, 4, 6, 8
Wynne, J. P., 189, 197, 198

Yauch, W. A., 325
Year-Round School, for children, 666–667
Youth, guidance, and the curriculum, 477–516; significance of the problem, 477–480; studies of youth and their problems, 480–493; work opportunities and openings for youth, 493–502; secondary-school curriculum and the guidance of youth, 503–511; placement and followup of youth, 507–508; need for coordi-

nation of youth-serving agencies, 508–511

Youth Movement, 479

Youth problems, 667

Youth-serving agencies, need for co-ordination of, 508–511

Zachry, C., 43

Critical Values of t

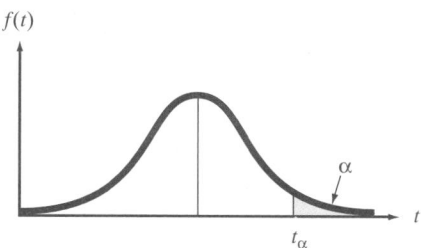

ν	$t_{.100}$	$t_{.050}$	$t_{.025}$	$t_{.010}$	$t_{.005}$	$t_{.001}$	$t_{.0005}$
1	3.078	6.314	12.706	31.821	63.657	318.31	636.62
2	1.886	2.920	4.303	6.965	9.925	22.326	31.598
3	1.638	2.353	3.182	4.541	5.841	10.213	12.924
4	1.533	2.132	2.776	3.747	4.604	7.173	8.610
5	1.476	2.015	2.571	3.365	4.032	5.893	6.869
6	1.440	1.943	2.447	3.143	3.707	5.208	5.959
7	1.415	1.895	2.365	2.998	3.499	4.785	5.408
8	1.397	1.860	2.306	2.896	3.355	4.501	5.041
9	1.383	1.833	2.262	2.821	3.250	4.297	4.781
10	1.372	1.812	2.228	2.764	3.169	4.144	4.587
11	1.363	1.796	2.201	2.718	3.106	4.025	4.437
12	1.356	1.782	2.179	2.681	3.055	3.930	4.318
13	1.350	1.771	2.160	2.650	3.012	3.852	4.221
14	1.345	1.761	2.145	2.624	2.977	3.787	4.140
15	1.341	1.753	2.131	2.602	2.947	3.733	4.073
16	1.337	1.746	2.120	2.583	2.921	3.686	4.015
17	1.333	1.740	2.110	2.567	2.898	3.646	3.965
18	1.330	1.734	2.101	2.552	2.878	3.610	3.922
19	1.328	1.729	2.093	2.539	2.861	3.579	3.883
20	1.325	1.725	2.086	2.528	2.845	3.552	3.850
21	1.323	1.721	2.080	2.518	2.831	3.527	3.819
22	1.321	1.717	2.074	2.508	2.819	3.505	3.792
23	1.319	1.714	2.069	2.500	2.807	3.485	3.767
24	1.318	1.711	2.064	2.492	2.797	3.467	3.745
25	1.316	1.708	2.060	2.485	2.787	3.450	3.725
26	1.315	1.706	2.056	2.479	2.779	3.435	3.707
27	1.314	1.703	2.052	2.473	2.771	3.421	3.690
28	1.313	1.701	2.048	2.467	2.763	3.408	3.674
29	1.311	1.699	2.045	2.462	2.756	3.396	3.659
30	1.310	1.697	2.042	2.457	2.750	3.385	3.646
40	1.303	1.684	2.021	2.423	2.704	3.307	3.551
60	1.296	1.671	2.000	2.390	2.660	3.232	3.460
120	1.289	1.658	1.980	2.358	2.617	3.160	3.373
∞	1.282	1.645	1.960	2.326	2.576	3.090	3.291

Source: This table is reproduced with the kind permission of the Trustees of Biometrika from E. S. Pearson and H. O. Hartley (eds.), *The Biometrika Tables for Statisticians*, Vol. 1, 3d ed., Biometrika, 1966.

A First Course in
BUSINESS STATISTICS

Seventh Edition

James T. McClave
Info Tech, Inc.
University of Florida

P. George Benson
Graduate School of Management
Rutgers University

Terry Sincich
University of South Florida

Prentice Hall
Upper Saddle River, New Jersey 07458

Library of Congress Cataloging-in-Publication Data
McClave, James T.
    A first course in business statistics / James T. McClave, P. George Benson,
Terry Sincich. — 7th ed.
        p.   cm.
    Includes bibliographical references and index.
    ISBN 0-13-836446-X
    ISBN 0-13-095201-X (Annotated Instructor's Edition)
    1. Commercial statistics.   2. Statistics—Data processing.   3. Commercial statistics—
Case studies.   I. Benson, P. George, 1946– .   II. Sincich, Terry.   III. Title.
HF1017.M358   1998
519.5—dc21   97-44372
                                                                                        CIP

Executive Editor: Ann Heath
Editorial Director: Tim Bozik
Editor-in-Chief: Jerome Grant
Assistant Vice President of Production and Manufacturing: David W. Riccardi
Development Editor: Millicent Treloar
Cover and Text Design/Project Management/Composition: Elm Street Publishing Services, Inc.
Managing Editor: Linda Mihatov Behrens
Executive Managing Editor: Kathleen Schiaparelli
Marketing Manager: Melody Marcus
Creative Director: Paula Maylahn
Manufacturing Buyer: Alan Fischer
Manufacturing Manager: Trudy Pisciotti
Editorial Assistant: Mindy Ince McClard
Interior Photos: David W. Hamilton/Image Bank
Cover Photo: Chuck Pefley/Tony Stone Images

© 1998 by Prentice-Hall, Inc.
Simon & Schuster / A Viacom Company
Upper Saddle River, NJ 07458

Printed in the United States of America
10   9   8   7   6   5   4

ISBN 0-13-836446-X

Prentice-Hall International (UK) Limited, *London*
Prentice-Hall of Australia Pty. Limited, *Sydney*
Prentice-Hall Canada, Inc., *Toronto*
Prentice-Hall Hispanoamericano, S.A., *Mexico*
Prentice-Hall of India Private Limited, *New Delhi*
Prentice-Hall of Japan, Inc., *Tokyo*
Simon & Schuster Asia Pte. Ltd., *Singapore*

CONTENTS

Preface   *vii*

CHAPTER 1   **Statistics, Data, and Statistical Thinking**   **1**
1.1   The Science of Statistics   **2**
1.2   Types of Statistical Applications in Business   **2**
1.3   Fundamental Elements of Statistics   **4**
1.4   Processes (Optional)   **9**
1.5   Types of Data   **12**
STATISTICS IN ACTION 1.1   Quality Improvement: U.S. Firms Respond to the Challenge from Japan   **13**
1.6   Collecting Data   **15**
1.7   The Role of Statistics in Managerial Decision-Making   **17**
STATISTICS IN ACTION 1.2   A 20/20 View of Survey Results: Fact or Fiction?   **18**
Quick Review   **21**

CHAPTER 2   **Methods for Describing Sets of Data**   **25**
2.1   Describing Qualitative Data   **26**
STATISTICS IN ACTION 2.1   Pareto Analysis   **31**
2.2   Graphical Methods for Describing Quantitative Data   **35**
2.3   The Time Series Plot (Optional)   **49**
2.4   Summation Notation   **52**
2.5   Numerical Measures of Central Tendency   **53**
2.6   Numerical Measures of Variability   **63**
2.7   Interpreting the Standard Deviation   **69**
2.8   Numerical Measures of Relative Standing   **76**
2.9   Quartiles and Box Plots (Optional)   **83**
2.10   Graphing Bivariate Relationships (Optional)   **90**
2.11   Distorting the Truth with Descriptive Techniques   **93**
STATISTICS IN ACTION 2.2   *Car & Driver's* "Road Test Digest"   **93**
Quick Review   **98**
SHOWCASE   The Kentucky Milk Case—Part I   **107**
INTERNET LAB   Accessing and Summarizing Business and Economic Data
Maintained by the U.S. Government   **109**

CHAPTER 3   **Probability**   **111**
3.1   Events, Sample Spaces, and Probability   **112**
STATISTICS IN ACTION 3.1   Game Show Strategy: To Switch or Not to Switch   **122**
3.2   Unions and Intersections   **126**
3.3   Complementary Events   **128**
3.4   The Additive Rule and Mutually Exclusive Events   **129**

3.5   Conditional Probability   **135**

3.6   The Multiplicative Rule and Independent Events   **138**

3.7   Random Sampling   **148**

STATISTICS IN ACTION 3.2   Lottery Buster   **151**

Quick Review   **153**

CHAPTER 4   **Random Variables and Probability Distributions**   **161**

4.1   Two Types of Random Variables   **162**

4.2   Probability Distributions for Discrete Random Variables   **165**

4.3   The Binomial Distribution   **174**

STATISTICS IN ACTION 4.1   The Space Shuttle *Challenger*: Catastrophe in Space   **183**

4.4   The Poisson Distribution (Optional)   **186**

4.5   Probability Distributions for Continuous Random Variables   **191**

4.6   The Uniform Distribution (Optional)   **192**

4.7   The Normal Distribution   **196**

STATISTICS IN ACTION 4.2   IQ, Economic Mobility, and the Bell Curve   **206**

4.8   The Exponential Distribution (Optional)   **209**

4.9   Sampling Distributions   **214**

4.10   The Sampling Distribution of the Sample Mean   **221**

STATISTICS IN ACTION 4.3   The Insomnia Pill   **227**

Quick Review   **230**

SHOWCASE   The Furniture Fire Case   **236**

INTERNET LAB   Analyzing Monthly Business Start-ups   **237**

CHAPTER 5   **Inferences Based on a Single Sample: Estimation with Confidence Intervals**   **239**

5.1   Large-Sample Confidence Interval for a Population Mean   **240**

5.2   Small-Sample Confidence Interval for a Population Mean   **248**

STATISTICS IN ACTIONS 5.1   Scallops, Sampling, and the Law   **254**

5.3   Large-Sample Confidence Interval for a Population Proportion   **259**

5.4   Determining the Sample Size   **265**

STATISTICS IN ACTION 5.2   Is Caffeine Addictive?   **269**

Quick Review   **272**

CHAPTER 6   **Inferences Based on a Single Sample: Tests of Hypothesis**   **277**

6.1   The Elements of a Test of Hypothesis   **278**

STATISTICS IN ACTION 6.1   Statistics Is Murder!   **282**

6.2   Large-Sample Test of Hypothesis About a Population Mean   **284**

STATISTICS IN ACTION 6.2   Statistical Quality Control, Part I   **288**

6.3   Observed Significance Levels: p-Values   **292**

6.4   Small-Sample Test of Hypothesis About a Population Mean   **298**

6.5   Large-Sample Test of Hypothesis About a Population Proportion   **305**

STATISTICS IN ACTION 6.3   Statistical Quality Control, Part II   **309**

6.6   A Nonparametric Test About a Population Median (Optional)   **312**
Quick Review   **317**

CHAPTER 7   **Comparing Population Means**   **323**
7.1   Comparing Two Population Means: Independent Sampling   **324**
STATISTICS IN ACTION 7.1   The Effect of Self-Managed Work Teams on Family Life   **334**
7.2   Comparing Two Population Means: Paired Difference Experiments   **342**
7.3   Determining the Sample Size   **353**
STATISTICS IN ACTION 7.2   Unpaid Overtime and the Fair Labor Standards Act   **355**
7.4   Testing the Assumption of Equal Population Variances (Optional)   **357**
7.5   A Nonparametric Test for Comparing Two Populations: Independent Sampling (Optional)   **364**
7.6   A Nonparametric Test for Comparing Two Populations: Paired Difference Experiments (Optional)   **372**
STATISTICS IN ACTION 7.3   Taxpayers Versus the IRS: Selecting the Trial Court   **377**
7.7   Comparing Three or More Population Means: Analysis of Variance (Optional)   **380**
Quick Review   **394**
SHOWCASE   The Kentucky Milk Case—Part II   **402**
INTERNET LAB   Choosing Between Economic Indicators   **403**

CHAPTER 8   **Comparing Population Proportions**   **405**
8.1   Comparing Two Population Proportions: Independent Sampling   **406**
8.2   Determining the Sample Size   **413**
8.3   Comparing Population Proportions: Multinomial Experiment (Optional)   **415**
8.4   Contingency Tables Analysis (Optional)   **423**
STATISTICS IN ACTION 8.1   Ethics in Computer Technology and Use   **430**
Quick Review   **437**
SHOWCASE   Discrimination in the Workplace   **444**
INTERNET LAB   Sampling and Analyzing NYSE Stock Quotes   **446**

CHAPTER 9   **Simple Linear Regression**   **447**
9.1   Probabilistic Models   **448**
9.2   Fitting the Model: The Least Squares Approach   **451**
9.3   Model Assumptions   **462**
9.4   An Estimator of σ^2 **463**
9.5   Assessing the Utility of the Model: Making Inferences About the Slope β_1 **469**
STATISTICS IN ACTION 9.1   New Jersey Banks—Serving Minorities?   **472**
9.6   The Coefficient of Correlation   **479**
9.7   The Coefficient of Determination   **482**
9.8   Using the Model for Estimation and Prediction   **490**

STATISTICS IN ACTION 9.2 Statistical Assessment of Damage to Bronx Bricks   **496**

    9.9   Simple Linear Regression: An Example   **502**

    9.10   A Nonparametric Test for Correlation (Optional)   **505**

    Quick Review   **514**

CHAPTER 10   **Introduction to Multiple Regression**   **525**

    10.1   The General Linear Model   **526**

    10.2   Fitting the Model: The Least Squares Approach   **527**

    10.3   Model Assumptions   **530**

    10.4   Inferences About the β Parameters   **532**

    10.5   Checking the Usefulness of a Model: R^2 and the Global F-Test   **544**

    10.6   Using the Model for Estimation and Prediction   **558**

    10.7   Residual Analysis: Checking the Regression Assumptions   **560**

STATISTICS IN ACTION 10.1   Predicting the Price of Vintage Red Bordeaux Wine   **561**

    10.8   Some Pitfalls: Estimability, Multicollinearity, and Extrapolation   **573**

STATISTICS IN ACTION 10.2   "Wringing" *The Bell Curve*   **576**

    Quick Review   **585**

SHOWCASE   The Condo Sales Case   **596**

INTERNET LAB   Using the Consumer Price Index in Business Forecasts of Labor, Wages, and Compensation   **598**

CHAPTER 11   **Basic Methods for Quality Improvement**   **599**

    11.1   Quality, Processes, and Systems   **600**

STATISTICS IN ACTION 11.1   Deming's 14 Points   **604**

    11.2   Statistical Control   **606**

    11.3   The Logic of Control Charts   **614**

    11.4   A Control Chart for Monitoring the Mean of a Process: The $\bar{x}$-Chart   **618**

    11.5   A Control Chart for Monitoring the Variation of a Process: The R-Chart   **635**

    11.6   A Control Chart for Monitoring the Proportion of Defectives Generated by a Process: The p-Chart   **644**

    Quick Review   **653**

SHOWCASE   The Gasket Manufacturing Case   **659**

INTERNET LAB   Quality Management Outside of Manufacturing Operation   **663**

APPENDIX A   **Basic Counting Rules**   **665**

APPENDIX B   **Tables**   **669**

APPENDIX C   **Calculation Formulas for Analysis of Variance**   **700**

    Answers to Selected Exercises   **701**

References   **708**

Index   **712**

PREFACE

This seventh edition of *A First Course in Business Statistics* has been extensively revised to stress the development of statistical thinking, the assessment of credibility and value of the inferences made from data, both by those who consume and those who produce them. This is an introductory text emphasizing inference, with extensive coverage of data collection and analysis as needed to evaluate the reported results of statistical studies and make good business decisions. It assumes a mathematical background of basic algebra.

A more comprehensive version of this book, *Statistics for Business and Economics*, 7/e, is available for two-term courses or those that include more extensive coverage of special topics.

NEW IN THE SEVENTH EDITION

MAJOR CONTENT CHANGES

- Chapter 1 has been entirely rewritten to emphasize the science of statistics and its role in business decisions. Coverage of process and quality control is expanded (Section 1.4). Data collection from published sources, designed experiments, surveys, and observations are introduced in a new section (Section 1.6). Special attention is given to statistical thinking and issues of statistical ethics (Section 1.7).

- Chapter 2 now more thoroughly covers descriptive analytical tools that are useful in examining assumptions about data. A new introductory section (Section 2.1) presents both graphical and numerical methods for summarizing qualitative data. Time series plots and the graphing of bivariate data relationships are introduced in optional sections (Sections 2.3 and 2.10). There is a greater focus throughout on variability (Section 2.7). The discussion of statistical ethics is continued in Section 2.11.

- Chapter 5 has been extensively rewritten to emphasize confidence interval estimation procedures and their interpretation. The approach to small-sample confidence intervals is motivated by pharmaceutical testing requirements (Section 5.2).

- Chapter 7 has been reorganized to present inference in the context of the experimental design used for data collection (Sections 7.1, 7.2, and 7.3).

- Chapter 9 includes an expanded coverage of correlation, which continues the emphasis from Chapter 2 on bivariate linear relationships. Where appropriate, the emphasis has shifted from the discussion of formulas to the interpretation of computer output, including Excel spreadsheets.

- A complete chapter on multiple regression has been added to the seventh edition. Chapter 10 incorporates extensive computer output. Inferences about the beta parameters include new material on confidence intervals.

NEW PEDAGOGICAL FEATURES

- **Statistics in Action**—two or three features per chapter examine high-profile business, economic, government, and entertainment issues. Questions prompt the students to form their own conclusions and to think through the statistical issues involved.

- **Examples and Exercises**—More than 60% are new or revised, featuring real business data from 1990 to 1996.
- **Quick Review**—Each chapter ends with a list of key terms and formulas, with reference to the page number where they first appear.
- **Language Lab**—Following the Quick Review is a pronunciation guide to Greek letters and other special terms. Usage notes are also provided.
- **Showcases**—Six extensive business problem-solving cases, with real data and assignments, are now included in the text. Each case serves as a good capstone and review of the material that has preceded it.
- **Internet Labs**—This is a new feature to this edition. The Labs are designed to instruct the student in retrieving and analyzing raw data downloaded from the Internet.

TRADITIONAL STRENGTHS

We have maintained the features of *A First Course in Business Statistics* that we believe make it unique among business statistics texts. These features, which assist the student in achieving an overview of statistics and an understanding of its relevance in the business world and in everyday life, are as follows:

THE USE OF EXAMPLES AS A TEACHING DEVICE

Almost all new ideas are introduced and illustrated by real data-based applications and examples. We believe that students better understand definitions, generalizations, and abstractions *after* seeing an application.

MANY EXERCISES—LABELED BY TYPE

The text includes more than 1,000 exercises illustrated by applications in almost all areas of research. Because many students have trouble learning the mechanics of statistical techniques when problems are couched in terms of realistic applications, all exercise sections are divided into two parts:

Learning the Mechanics. Designed as straightforward applications of new concepts, these exercises allow students to test their ability to comprehend a concept or a definition.

Applying the Concepts. Based on applications taken from a wide variety of journals, newspapers, and other sources, these exercises develop the student's skills at comprehending real-world problems that describe situations to which the techniques may be applied.

NONPARAMETRIC TOPICS INTEGRATED

In a one-term course it is often difficult to find time to cover nonparametric techniques when they are relegated to a separate chapter at the end of the book. Consequently, we have integrated the most commonly used techniques in optional sections as appropriate.

EXTENSIVE COVERAGE OF MULTIPLE REGRESSION ANALYSIS

This topic represents one of the most useful statistical tools for the solution of applied problems. Although an entire text could be devoted to regression modeling, we believe we have presented coverage that is understandable, usable, and more comprehensive than the presentations in other brief introductory statistics texts. We devote two chapters to discussing the major types of inferences that can be derived from a regression analysis, showing how these results appear in computer printouts and, most important, selecting multiple regression models to be used in an analysis. Thus, the instructor has the choice of a one-chapter coverage of simple regression or a two-chapter treatment of simple and multiple regression.

FOOTNOTES

Although the text is designed for students with a non-calculus background, footnotes explain the role of calculus in various derivations. Footnotes are also used to inform the student about some of the theory underlying certain results. The footnotes allow additional flexibility in the mathematical and theoretical level at which the material is presented.

SUPPLEMENTS FOR THE INSTRUCTOR

The supplements for the seventh edition have been completely revised to reflect the extensive revisions of the text. Each element in the package has been accuracy checked to ensure adherence to the approaches presented in the main text, clarity, and freedom from computational, typographical, and statistical errors.

NEW! *ANNOTATED INSTRUCTOR'S EDITION* (AIE) (ISBN 0-13-095201-X)

Marginal notes placed next to discussions of essential teaching concepts include:

- Teaching Tips—suggest alternative presentations or point out common student errors

- Exercises—reference specific section and chapter exercises that reinforce the concept

- 💾 —identify data sets and file name of material found on the data disks.

- Short Answers—section and chapter exercise answers are provided next to the selected exercises.

INSTRUCTOR'S NOTES BY MARK DUMMELDINGER (ISBN 0-13-891243-2)

This new printed resource contains suggestions for using the questions at the end of the Statistics in Action boxes as the basis for class discussion on statistical ethics and other current issues, solutions to the Showcases, a complete short answer book with letter of permission to duplicate for student use, and many of the exercises and solutions that were removed from the sixth edition of this text.

INSTRUCTOR'S SOLUTIONS MANUAL BY NANCY S. BOUDREAU (ISBN 0-13-836818-X)

Solutions to all of the even-numbered exercises are given in this manual. Careful attention has been paid to ensure that all methods of solution and notation are consistent with those used in the core text. Solutions to the odd-numbered exercises are found in the *Student's Solutions Manual.*

TEST BANK BY MARK DUMMELDINGER (ISBN 0-13-836768-X)

Entirely rewritten, the *Test Bank* now includes more than 1,000 problems that correlate to problems presented in the text.

WINDOWS PH CUSTOM TEST (ISBN 0-13-768979-9)

Incorporates three levels of test creation: (1) selection of questions from a test bank; (2) addition of new questions with the ability to import test and graphics files from WordPerfect, Microsoft Word, and Wordstar; and (3) inclusion of algorithmic capabilities. PH Custom Test has a full-featured graphics editor supporting the complex formulas and graphics required by the statistics discipline.

POWERPOINT PRESENTATION TOOL (ISBN 0-13-671116-2)

This versatile Windows-based tool may be used by professors in a number of different ways:

- Slide show in an electronic classroom
- Printed and used as transparency masters
- Printed copies may be distributed to students as a convenient note-taking device.

Included are learning objectives, thinking challenges, concept presentation slides, and examples with worked-out solutions. The PowerPoint Presentation disk may be downloaded from the FTP site found at the McClave Web site.

DATA DISK (ISBN 0-13-836883-X)

The data for all exercises containing 20 or more observations are available on a 3½" diskette in ASCII format. When a given data set is referenced, a disk symbol and the file name will appear in the text near the exercise.

NEW YORK TIMES SUPPLEMENT (ISBN 0-13-689531-X)

Copies of this supplement may be requested from Prentice Hall by instructors for distribution in their classes. This supplement contains high interest articles published recently in *The New York Times* that relate to topics covered in the text.

McCLAVE INTERNET SITE (http://www.prenhall.com/mcclave)

This site is a work in progress that will be updated throughout the year as new information, tools, and applications become available. The site will contain information about the book and its supplements as well as FTP sites for downloading the Powerpoint Presentation Disk and the Data Files. Teaching tips and student help will be provided as well as links to useful sources of data and information such as the Chance Database, the STEPS project (interactive tutorials developed by the University of Glasgow), and a site designed to help faculty establish and manage course home pages.

SUPPLEMENTS AVAILABLE FOR PURCHASE BY STUDENTS

STUDENT'S SOLUTIONS MANUAL BY NANCY S. BOUDREAU (ISBN 0-13-746116-X)

Fully worked-out solutions to all of the odd-numbered exercises are provided in this manual. Careful attention has been paid to ensure that all methods of solution and notation are consistent with those used in the core text.

STUDENT VERSIONS OF SPSS AND SYSTAT

Student versions of SPSS, the award-winning and market-leading commercial data analysis package, and SYSTAT are available for student purchase. Details on all current products are available from Prentice Hall or via the SPSS website at http://www.spss.com.

LEARNING BUSINESS STATISTICS WITH MICROSOFT ®EXCEL BY JOHN L. NEUFELD (ISBN 0-13-234097-6)

The use of Excel as a data analysis and computational package for statistics is explained in clear, easy-to-follow steps in this self-contained paperback text.

A MINITAB GUIDE TO STATISTICS BY RUTH MEYER AND DAVID KRUEGER
(ISBN 0-13-784232-5)
This manual assumes no prior knowledge of MINITAB. Organized to correspond to the table of contents of most statistics texts, this manual provides step-by-step instruction to using MINITAB for statistical analysis.

CONSTATS BY TUFTS UNIVERSITY (ISBN 0-13-502600-8)
ConStatS is a set of Microsoft Windows based programs designed to help college students understand concepts taught in a first-semester course on probability and statistics. ConStatS helps improve students' conceptual understanding of statistics by engaging them in an active, experimental style of learning. A companion ConStatS workbook (ISBN 0-13-522848-4) that guides students through the labs and ensures they gain the maximum benefit is also available.

ACKNOWLEDGMENTS
This book reflects the efforts of a great many people over a number of years. First we would like to thank the following professors, whose reviews and feedback on organization and coverage, contributed to the seventh and previous editions of the book.

REVIEWERS INVOLVED WITH THE SEVENTH EDITION
Atul Agarwal, GMI Engineering and Management Institute; Mohamed Albohali, Indiana University of Pennsylvania; Lewis Coopersmith, Rider University; Bernard Dickman, Hofstra University; Jose Luis Guerrero-Cusumano, Georgetown University; Paul Guy, California State University-Chico; Judd Hammack, California State University-Los Angeles; P. Kasliwal, California State University-Los Angeles; Tim Krehbiel, Miami University of Ohio; David Krueger, St. Cloud State University; Mabel T. Kung, California State University-Fullerton; Jim Lackritz, San Diego State University; Leigh Lawton, University of St. Thomas; Peter Lenk, University of Michigan; Benjamin Lev, University of Michigan-Dearborn; Benny Lo; Brenda Masters, Oklahoma State University; William Q. Meeker, Iowa State University; Ruth Meyer, St. Cloud State University; Edward Minieka, University of Illinois at Chicago; Rebecca Moore, Oklahoma State University; June Morita, University of Washington; Behnam Nakhai, Millersville University; Rose Prave, University of Scranton; Beth Rose, University of Southern California; Lawrence A. Sherr, University of Kansas; Toni M. Somers, Wayne State University; Kim Tamura, University of Washington; Bob VanCleave, University of Minnesota; Michael P. Wegmann, Keller Graduate School of Management; Gary Yoshimoto, St. Cloud State University; Doug Zahn, Florida State University

REVIEWERS OF PREVIOUS EDITIONS
Gordon J. Alexander, University of Minnesota; Richard W. Andrews, University of Michigan; Larry M. Austin, Texas Tech University; Golam Azam, North Carolina Agricultural & Technical University; Donald W. Bartlett, University of Minnesota; Clarence Bayne, Concordia University; Carl Bedell, Philadelphia College of Textiles and Science; David M. Bergman, University of Minnesota; William H. Beyer, University of Akron; Atul Bhatia, University of Minnesota; Jim Branscome, University of Texas at Arlington; Francis J. Brewerton, Middle Tennessee State University; Daniel G. Brick, University of St. Thomas; Robert W. Brobst, University of Texas of Arlington; Michael Broida, Miami University of

Ohio; Glenn J. Browne, University of Maryland, Baltimore; Edward Carlstein, University of North Carolina at Chapel Hill; John M. Charnes, University of Miami; Chih-Hsu Cheng, Ohio State University; Larry Claypool, Oklahoma State University; Edward R. Clayton, Virginia Polytechnic Institute and State University; Ronald L. Coccari, Cleveland State University; Ken Constantine, University of New Hampshire; Robert Curley, University of Central Oklahoma; Joyce Curley-Daly, California Polytechnic State University; Jim Daly, California Polytechnic State University; Jim Davis, Golden Gate University; Dileep Dhavale, University of Northern Iowa; Mark Eakin, University of Texas at Arlington; Rick L. Edgeman, Colorado State University; Carol Eger, Stanford University; Robert Elrod, Georgia State University; Douglas A. Elvers, University of North Carolina at Chapel Hill; Iris Fetta, Clemson University; Susan Flach, General Mills, Inc.; Alan E. Gelfand, University of Connecticut; Joseph Glaz, University of Connecticut; Edit Gombay, University of Alberta; Paul W. Guy, California State University, Chico; Michael E. Hanna, University of Texas at Arlington; Don Holbert, East Carolina University; James Holstein, University of Missouri, Columbia; Warren M. Holt, Southeastern Massachusetts University; Steve Hora, University of Hawaii, Hilo; Petros Ioannatos, GMI Engineering & Management Institute; Marius Janson, University of Missouri, St. Louis; Ross H. Johnson, Madison College; Timothy J. Killeen, University of Connecticut; David D. Krueger, St. Cloud State University; Richard W. Kulp, Wright-Patterson AFB, Air Force Institute of Technology; Martin Labbe, State University of New York College at New Paltz; James Lackritz, California State University at San Diego; Philip Levine, William Patterson College; Eddie M. Lewis, University of Southern Mississippi; Fred Leysieffer, Florida State University; Pi-Erh Lin, Florida State University; Robert Ling, Clemson University; Karen Lundquist, University of Minnesota; G. E. Martin, Clarkson University; Brenda Masters, Oklahoma State University; Ruth K. Meyer, St. Cloud State University; Paul I. Nelson, Kansas State University; Paula M. Oas, General Office Products; Dilek Onkal, Bilkent University, Turkey; Vijay Pisharody, University of Minnesota; P.V. Rao, University of Florida; Don Robinson, Illinois State University; Jan Saraph, St. Cloud State University; Craig W. Slinkman, University of Texas at Arlington; Robert K. Smidt, California Polytechnic State University; Donald N. Steinnes, University of Minnesota at Duluth; Virgil F. Stone, Texas A & M University; Katheryn Szabet, La Salle University; Alireza Tahai, Mississippi State University; Chipei Tseng, Northern Illinois University; Pankaj Vaish, Arthur Andersen & Company; Robert W. Van Cleave, University of Minnesota; Charles F. Warnock, Colorado State University; William J. Weida, United States Air Force Academy; T.J. Wharton, Oakland University; Kathleen M. Whitcomb, University of South Carolina; Edna White, Florida Atlantic University; Steve Wickstrom, University of Minnesota; James Willis, Louisiana State University; Douglas A. Wolfe, Ohio State University; Gary Yoshimoto, St. Cloud State University; Fike Zahroom, Moorhead State University; Christopher J. Zappe, Bucknell University

Special thanks are due to our ancillary authors, Nancy Shafer Boudreau and Mark Dummeldinger, and to typist Brenda Dobson, who have worked with us for many years; and to John McGill, who prepared the PowerPoint Presentation disk. Carl Richard Gumina has done an excellent job of accuracy checking the seventh edition and has helped us to ensure a highly accurate, clean text. The Prentice Hall staff of Ann Heath, Millicent Treloar, Mindy Ince McClard, Melody Marcus, Jennifer Pan, Linda Behrens, and Alan Fischer, and Elm Street Publishing Services' Martha Beyerlein, Barb Lange, Sue Langguth, and Cathy Ferguson helped greatly with all phases of the text development, production, and marketing effort. We also thank Rutgers Ph.D. students Xuan Li and Zina Taran for helping us to identify new exercise material, and we particularly thank Professor Lei Lei of Rutgers for her assistance in exercise development. Our thanks to Jane Benson for managing the exercise development process. Finally, we owe special thanks to Faith Sincich, whose efforts in preparing the manuscript for production and proofreading all stages of the book deserve special recognition.

For additional information about texts and other materials available from Prentice Hall, visit us on-line at http://www.prenhall.com.

How to Use This Book

To the Student

The following four pages will demonstrate how to use this text in the most effective way—to make studying easier and to understand the connection between statistics and your world.

Chapter Openers Provide a Road Map

- **Where We've Been** quickly reviews how information learned previously applies to the chapter at hand.

- **Where We're Going** highlights how the chapter topics fit into your growing understanding of statistical inference.

CHAPTER 5

INFERENCES BASED ON A SINGLE SAMPLE
Estimation with Confidence Intervals

CONTENTS

5.1   Large-Sample Confidence Interval for a Population Mean
5.2   Small-Sample Confidence Interval for a Population Mean
5.3   Large-Sample Confidence Interval for a Population Proportion
5.4   Determining the Sample Size

STATISTICS IN ACTION
5.1   Scallops, Sampling, and the Law
5.2   Is Caffeine Addictive?

Where We've Been

We've learned that populations are characterized by numerical descriptive measures (called *parameters*) and that decisions about their values are based on sample statistics computed from sample data. Since statistics vary in a random manner from sample to sample, inferences based on them will be subject to uncertainty. This property is reflected in the sampling (probability) distribution of a statistic.

Where We're Going

In this chapter, we'll put all the preceding material into practice; that is, we'll estimate population means and proportions based on a single sample selected from the population of interest. Most importantly, we use the sampling distribution of a sample statistic to assess the reliability of an estimate.

239

SECTION 1.5   Types of Data   **13**

STATISTICS IN ACTION

1.1 QUALITY IMPROVEMENT: U.S. FIRMS RESPOND TO THE CHALLENGE FROM JAPAN

Over the last two decades, U.S. firms have been seriously challenged by products of superior quality from overseas. For example, from 1984 to 1991, imported cars and light trucks steadily increased their share of the U.S. market from 22% to 30%. As a second example, consider the television and VCR markets. Both products were invented in the United States, but as of 1995 not a single U.S. firm manufactures either. Both are produced exclusively by Pacific Rim countries, primarily Japan.

To meet this competitive challenge, more and more U.S. firms—both manufacturing and service firms—have begun quality-improvement initiatives of their own. Many of these firms now stress the management of quality in all phases and aspects of their business, from the design of their products to production, distribution, sales, and service.

Broadly speaking, quality-improvement programs are concerned with (1) finding out what the customer wants, (2) translating those wants into a product design, and (3) producing and delivering a product or service that meets or exceeds the specifications of the product design. In all these areas, but particularly in the third, *improvement of quality requires improvement of processes*—including production processes, distribution processes, and service processes.

But what does it mean to say that a process has been improved? Generally speaking, it means that the customer of the process (i.e., the user of the output) indicates a greater satisfaction with the output. Frequently, such increases in satisfaction require a reduction in the variation of one or more process variables. That is, a reduction in the variation of the output stream of the process is needed.

produced by a given machine are the same; no two transactions performed by a given bank teller are the same. He also recognized that variation could be understood, monitored, and controlled using statistical methods. He developed a simple graphical technique—called a **control chart**—for determining whether product variation is within acceptable limits. This method provides guidance for when to adjust or change a production process and when to leave it alone. It can be used at the end of the production process or, most significantly, at different points within the process. We discuss control charts and other tools for improving processes in Chapter 13.

In the last decade, largely as a result of the Japanese challenge to the supremacy of U.S. products, control charts and other statistical tools have gained widespread use in the United States. As evidence for the claim that U.S. firms are responding well to Japan's competitive challenge, consider this: The most prestigious quality-improvement prize in the world that a firm can win is the Deming Prize. It has been awarded by the Japanese since the 1950s. In 1989 it was won for the first time by an American company—Florida Power and Light Company. Other evidence of the resurgence of U.S. competitiveness includes a turnaround in market share for U.S. automakers: imports' share of the U.S. market decreased from a high of 30% in 1991 to 25% in 1995.

Focus

a. Identify two processes that are of interest to you.

b. For each process, part **a**, identify a variable that could be used to monitor the quality of the output

"Statistics in Action" Boxes Explore High-Interest Issues

- Highlight controversial, contemporary issues that involve statistics.

- Work through the **"Focus"** questions to help you evaluate the findings.

Computer Output Integrated Throughout

- Statistical software packages such as SPSS, MINITAB, SAS, and the spreadsheet package, EXCEL, crunch data quickly so you can spend time analyzing the results. Learning how to interpret statistical output will prove helpful in future classes or on the job.

- When computer output appears in examples, the solution explains how to read and interpret the output.

Interesting Examples with Solutions

- Examples, with complete solutions and explanations, illustrate every concept and are numbered for easy reference.

- Work through the solution carefully to prepare for the section exercise set.

- The end of the solution is clearly marked with a ■ symbol.

---

244 CHAPTER 5 Inferences Based on a Single Sample: Estimation with Confidence Intervals

FIGURE 5.6
MINITAB printout for the confidence intervals in Example 5.1

	N	MEAN	STDEV	SE MEAN	90.0 PERCENT C.I.
NoSeats	225	11.6	4.1	0.273	(11.15, 12.05)

EXAMPLE 5.1 Unoccupied seats on flights cause airlines to lose revenue. Suppose a large airline wants to estimate its average number of unoccupied seats per flight over the past year. To accomplish this, the records of 225 flights are randomly selected, and the number of unoccupied seats is noted for each of the sampled flights. The sample mean and standard deviation are

$$\bar{x} = 11.6 \text{ seats} \qquad s = 4.1 \text{ seats}$$

Estimate μ, the mean number of unoccupied seats per flight during the past year, using a 90% confidence interval.

SOLUTION
The general form of the 90% confidence interval for a population mean is

$$\bar{x} \pm z_{\alpha/2}\sigma_{\bar{x}} = \bar{x} \pm z_{.05}\sigma_{\bar{x}} = \bar{x} \pm 1.645\left(\frac{\sigma}{\sqrt{n}}\right)$$

For the 225 records sampled, we have

$$11.6 \pm 1.645\left(\frac{\sigma}{\sqrt{225}}\right)$$

Since we do not know the value of σ (the standard deviation of the number of unoccupied seats per flight for all flights of the year), we use our best approximation—the sample standard deviation s. Then the 90% confidence interval is, approximately,

$$11.6 \pm 1.645\left(\frac{4.1}{\sqrt{225}}\right) = 11.6 \pm .45$$

or from 11.15 to 12.05. That is, at the 90% confidence level, we estimate the mean number of unoccupied seats per flight to be between 11.15 and 12.05 during the sampled year. This result is verified on the MINITAB printout of the analysis shown in Figure 5.6.

We stress that the confidence level for this example, 90%, refers to the procedure used. If we were to apply this procedure repeatedly to different samples, approximately 90% of the intervals would contain μ. We do not know whether this particular interval (11.15, 12.05) is one of the 90% that contain μ or one of the 10% that do not. ■

The interpretation of confidence intervals for a population mean is summarized in the accompanying box.

Interpretation of a Confidence Interval for a Population Mean
When we form a $100(1 - \alpha)$% confidence interval for μ, we usually express our confidence in the interval with a statement such as, "We can be $100(1 - \alpha)$% confident that μ lies between the lower and upper bounds of the confidence interval," where for a particular application, we substitute the appropriate numerical values for the confidence

---

Shaded Boxes Highlight Important Information

- Definitions, Strategies, Key Formulas, and other important information are highlighted.

- Prepare for quizzes and tests by reviewing the highlighted information.

Lots of Exercises for Practice

- Every section in the book is followed by an Exercise Set divided into two parts.

- **Learning the Mechanics** has straightforward applications of new concepts. Test your mastery of definitions, concepts, and basic computation. Make sure you can answer all of these questions before moving on.

- **Applying the Concepts** tests your understanding of concepts and requires you to apply statistical techniques in solving real-world problems.

Real Data

- Most of the exercises contain data or information taken from newspaper articles, magazines, and journals published since 1990. Statistics are all around you.

---

88   CHAPTER 2   Methods for Describing Sets of Data

EXERCISES   2.87–2.96

Note: Exercises marked with 💾 *contain data available for computer analysis on a 3.5" disk (file name in parentheses).*

Learning the Mechanics

2.87 Define the 25th, 50th, and 75th percentiles of a data set. Explain how they provide a description of the data.

2.88 Suppose a data set consisting of exam scores has a lower quartile $Q_L = 60$, a median $m = 75$, and an upper quartile $Q_U = 85$. The scores on the exam range from 18 to 100. Without having the actual scores available to you, construct as much of the box plot as possible.

2.89 MINITAB was used to generate the following horizontal box plot. (*Note:* The hinges are represented by the symbol "I".)

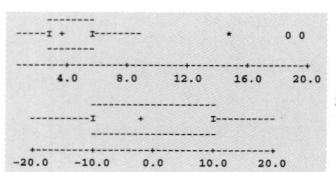

  a. What is the median of the data set (approximately)?
  b. What are the upper and lower quartiles of the data set (approximately)?
  c. What is the interquartile range of the data set (approximately)?
  d. Is the data set skewed to the left, skewed to the right, or symmetric?
  e. What percentage of the measurements in the data set lie to the right of the median? To the left of the upper quartile?

2.90 MINITAB was used to generate the horizontal box plots below. Compare and contrast the frequency distributions of the two data sets. Your answer should include comparisons of the following characteristics: central tendency, variation, skewness, and outliers.

2.91 (X02.091) Consider the following two sample data sets:

Sample A			Sample B		
121	171	158	171	152	170
173	184	163	168	169	171
157	85	145	190	183	185
165	172	196	140	173	206
170	159	172	172	174	169
161	187	100	199	151	180
142	166	171	167	170	188

  a. Use a statistical software package to construct a box plot for each data set.
  b. Using information reflected in your box plots, describe the similarities and differences in the two data sets.

Applying the Concepts

2.92 (X02.092) The table contains the top salary offer (in thousands of dollars) received by each member of a sample of 50 MBA students who graduated from the Graduate School of Management at Rutgers, the state university of New Jersey, in 1996.

61.1	48.5	47.0	49.1	43.5
50.8	62.3	50.0	65.4	58.0
53.2	39.9	49.1	75.0	51.2
41.7	40.0	53.0	39.6	49.6
55.2	54.9	62.5	35.0	50.3
41.5	56.0	55.5	70.0	59.2
39.2	47.0	58.2	59.0	60.8
72.3	55.0	41.4	51.5	63.0
48.4	61.7	45.3	63.2	41.5
47.0	43.2	44.6	47.7	58.6

Source: Career Services Office, Graduate School of Management, Rutgers University.

  a. The mean and standard deviation are 52.33 and 9.22, respectively. Find and interpret the z-score associated with the highest salary offer, the lowest salary offer, and the mean salary offer. Would you consider the highest offer to be unusually high? Why or why not?
  b. Use a statistical software package to construct a box plot for this data set. Which salary offers (if any) are potentially faulty observations? Explain.

2.93 Refer to the *Financial Management* (Spring 1995) study of 49 firms filing for prepackaged bankruptcies, Exercise 2.22. Recall that three types of "prepack" firms exist: (1) those who hold no prefiling vote; (2) those who vote their preference for a joint solution; and (3) those who vote their pref-

---

Computer Output

- Computer output screens appear in the exercise sets to give you practice in interpretation.

End of Chapter Review

- Each chapter ends with information designed to help you check your understanding of the material, study for tests, and expand your knowledge of statistics.

- **Quick Review** provides a list of key terms and formulas with page number references.

- **Language Lab** helps you learn the language of statistics through pronunciation guides, descriptions of symbols, names, etc.

- **Supplementary Exercises** review all of the important topics covered in the chapter.

Exercises marked with 💾 require a computer for solution.

Data sets for use with the 💾 problems are available on disk.

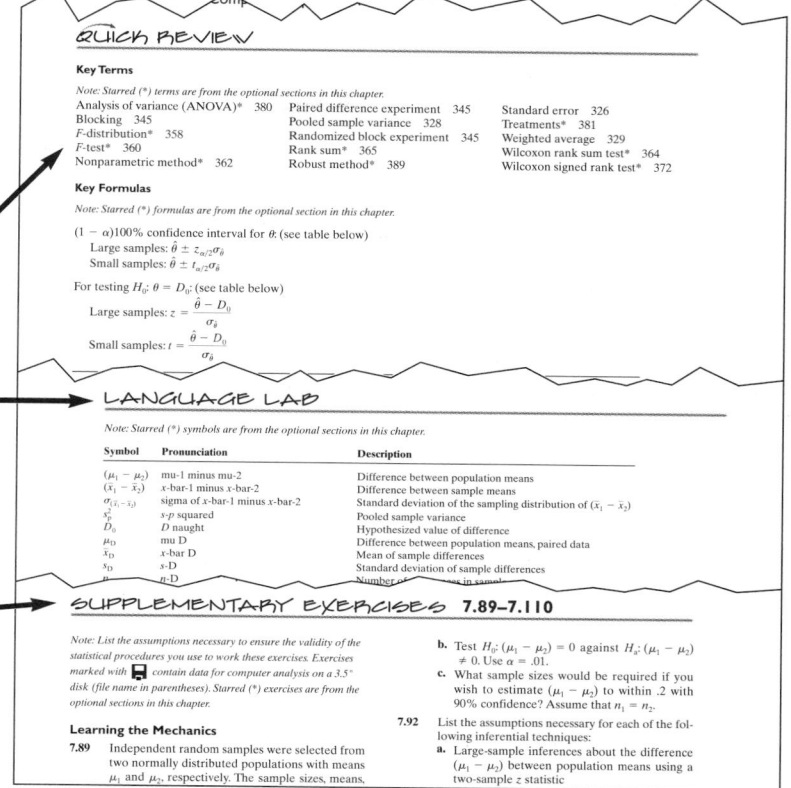

QUICK REVIEW

Key Terms

Note: Starred (*) terms are from the optional sections in this chapter.

Analysis of variance (ANOVA)* 380	Paired difference experiment 345	Standard error 326
Blocking 345	Pooled sample variance 328	Treatments* 381
F-distribution* 358	Randomized block experiment 345	Weighted average 329
F-test* 360	Rank sum* 365	Wilcoxon rank sum test* 364
Nonparametric method* 362	Robust method* 389	Wilcoxon signed rank test* 372

Key Formulas

Note: Starred (*) formulas are from the optional section in this chapter.

$(1 - \alpha)100\%$ confidence interval for θ: (see table below)
　Large samples: $\hat{\theta} \pm z_{\alpha/2}\sigma_{\hat{\theta}}$
　Small samples: $\hat{\theta} \pm t_{\alpha/2}\sigma_{\hat{\theta}}$

For testing $H_0: \theta = D_0$: (see table below)
　Large samples: $z = \dfrac{\hat{\theta} - D_0}{\sigma_{\hat{\theta}}}$
　Small samples: $t = \dfrac{\hat{\theta} - D_0}{\sigma_{\hat{\theta}}}$

LANGUAGE LAB

Note: Starred (*) symbols are from the optional sections in this chapter.

Symbol	Pronunciation	Description
$(\mu_1 - \mu_2)$	mu-1 minus mu-2	Difference between population means
$(\bar{x}_1 - \bar{x}_2)$	x-bar-1 minus x-bar-2	Difference between sample means
$\sigma_{(\bar{x}_1 - \bar{x}_2)}$	sigma of x-bar-1 minus x-bar-2	Standard deviation of the sampling distribution of $(\bar{x}_1 - \bar{x}_2)$
s_p^2	s-p squared	Pooled sample variance
D_0	D naught	Hypothesized value of difference
μ_D	mu D	Difference between population means, paired data
$\bar{x}_D$	x-bar D	Mean of sample differences
s_D	s-D	Standard deviation of sample differences
n	n-D	Number of cases in sample

SUPPLEMENTARY EXERCISES 7.89–7.110

Note: List the assumptions necessary to ensure the validity of the statistical procedures you use to work these exercises. Exercises marked with 💾 contain data for computer analysis on a 3.5" disk (file name in parentheses). Starred (*) exercises are from the optional sections in this chapter.

Learning the Mechanics

7.89 Independent random samples were selected from two normally distributed populations with means μ_1 and μ_2, respectively. The sample sizes, means,

b. Test $H_0: (\mu_1 - \mu_2) = 0$ against $H_a: (\mu_1 - \mu_2) \neq 0$. Use $\alpha = .01$.

c. What sample sizes would be required if you wish to estimate $(\mu_1 - \mu_2)$ to within .2 with 90% confidence? Assume that $n_1 = n_2$.

7.92 List the assumptions necessary for each of the following inferential techniques:
a. Large-sample inferences about the difference $(\mu_1 - \mu_2)$ between population means using a two-sample z statistic

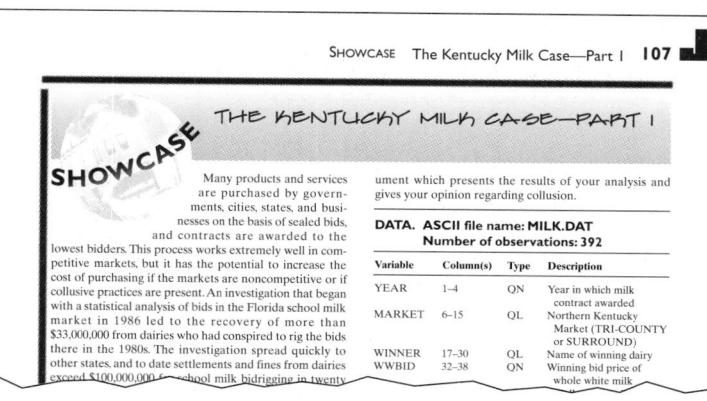

SHOWCASE　The Kentucky Milk Case—Part I　**107**

THE KENTUCKY MILK CASE—PART I

SHOWCASE

Many products and services are purchased by governments, cities, states, and businesses on the basis of sealed bids, and contracts are awarded to the lowest bidders. This process works extremely well in competitive markets, but it has the potential to increase the cost of purchasing if the markets are noncompetitive or if collusive practices are present. An investigation that began with a statistical analysis of bids in the Florida school milk market in 1986 led to the recovery of more than $33,000,000 from dairies who had conspired to rig the bids there in the 1980s. The investigation spread quickly to other states, and to date settlements and fines from dairies exceed $100,000,000 for school milk bidrigging in twenty

ument which presents the results of your analysis and gives your opinion regarding collusion.

DATA. ASCII file name: MILK.DAT
Number of observations: 392

Variable	Column(s)	Type	Description
YEAR	1–4	QN	Year in which milk contract awarded
MARKET	6–15	QL	Northern Kentucky Market (TRI-COUNTY or SURROUND)
WINNER	17–30	QL	Name of winning dairy
WWBID	32–38	QN	Winning bid price of whole white milk

- **Showcase** Six real-business cases put you in the position of the business decision maker or consultant. Use the data provided and the information you have learned in preceding chapters to reach a decision and support your arguments about the questions being asked.

INTERNET LAB　Accessing and Summarizing Business and Economic Data　**109**

www.int.com
www.int.com
INTERNET LAB
www.int.com

ACCESSING AND SUMMARIZING BUSINESS AND ECONOMIC DATA MAINTAINED BY THE U.S. GOVERNMENT

A vital underpinning of statistical analysis and interpretation of results is the information value of the data used. Data collection is often an expensive undertaking and many studies begin with an examination of external data; that is, data routinely collected and maintained by credible sources. Various government agencies play a major role in producing data across many areas of business and economics. These data constitute a primary starting point for obtaining external data.
Here we will visit an important U.S. government

10. Save the data set of interest to your statistical applications software (e.g., MINITAB) data files.
11. Summarize and describe the data using your statistical software.

SITE 1: LOCATE GROSS DOMESTIC PRODUCT (GDP) DATA
These data are produced by the U.S. Department of Commerce, located at *http://www.doc.gov/*

- **Internet Labs** follow the Showcase and are designed to help you retrieve and download raw data from the Internet for analysis. Knowing how to mine the Internet for reliable data, analyze it appropriately, and draw useful conclusions are important job skills for the 21st century.

CHAPTER 1

STATISTICS, DATA, AND STATISTICAL THINKING

CONTENTS

1.1 The Science of Statistics
1.2 Types of Statistical Applications in Business
1.3 Fundamental Elements of Statistics
1.4 Processes (Optional)
1.5 Types of Data
1.6 Collecting Data
1.7 The Role of Statistics in Managerial Decision-Making

STATISTICS IN ACTION

1.1 Quality Improvement: U.S. Firms Respond to the Challenge from Japan
1.2 A *20/20* View of Survey Results: Fact or Fiction?

Where We're Going

Statistics? Is it a field of study, a group of numbers that summarizes the state of our national economy, the performance of a stock, or the business conditions in a particular locale? Or, as one popular book (Tanur *et al.,* 1989) suggests, is it "a guide to the unknown"? We'll see in Chapter 1 that each of these descriptions is applicable in understanding what statistics is. We'll see that there are two areas of statistics: *descriptive statistics,* which focuses on developing graphical and numerical summaries that describe some business phenomenon, and *inferential statistics,* which uses these numerical summaries to assist in making business decisions. The primary theme of this text is inferential statistics. Thus, we'll concentrate on showing how you can use statistics to interpret data and use them to make decisions. Many jobs in industry, government, medicine, and other fields require you to make data-driven decisions, so understanding these methods offers you important practical benefits.

1.1 THE SCIENCE OF STATISTICS

What does statistics mean to you? Does it bring to mind batting averages, Gallup polls, unemployment figures, or numerical distortions of facts (lying with statistics!)? Or is it simply a college requirement you have to complete? We hope to persuade you that statistics is a meaningful, useful science whose broad scope of applications to business, government, and the physical and social sciences is almost limitless. We also want to show that statistics can lie only when they are misapplied. Finally, we wish to demonstrate the key role statistics play in critical thinking—whether in the classroom, on the job, or in everyday life. Our objective is to leave you with the impression that the time you spend studying this subject will repay you in many ways.

The *Random House College Dictionary* defines *statistics* as "the science that deals with the collection, classification, analysis, and interpretation of information or data." Thus, a statistician isn't just someone who calculates batting averages at baseball games or tabulates the results of a Gallup poll. Professional statisticians are trained in *statistical science*. That is, they are trained in collecting numerical information in the form of **data**, evaluating it, and drawing conclusions from it. Furthermore, statisticians determine what information is relevant in a given problem and whether the conclusions drawn from a study are to be trusted.

> **DEFINITION 1.1**
> **Statistics** is the science of data. It involves collecting, classifying, summarizing, organizing, analyzing, and interpreting numerical information.

In the next section, you'll see several real-life examples of statistical applications in business and government that involve making decisions and drawing conclusions.

1.2 TYPES OF STATISTICAL APPLICATIONS IN BUSINESS

Statistics means "numerical descriptions" to most people. Monthly unemployment figures, the failure rate of a new business, and the proportion of female executives in a particular industry all represent statistical descriptions of large sets of data collected on some phenomenon. Often the data are selected from some larger set of data whose characteristics we wish to estimate. We call this selection process *sampling*. For example, you might collect the ages of a sample of customers at a video store to estimate the average age of *all* customers of the store. Then you could use your estimate to target the store's advertisements to the appropriate age group. Notice that statistics involves two different processes: (1) describing sets of data and (2) drawing conclusions (making estimates, decisions, predictions, etc.) about the sets of data based on sampling. So, the applications of statistics can be divided into two broad areas: *descriptive statistics* and *inferential statistics*.

> **DEFINITION 1.2**
> **Descriptive statistics** utilizes numerical and graphical methods to look for patterns in a data set, to summarize the information revealed in a data set, and to present the information in a convenient form.

> **DEFINITION 1.3**
> **Inferential statistics** utilizes sample data to make estimates, decisions, predictions, or other generalizations about a larger set of data.

Although we'll discuss both descriptive and inferential statistics in the following chapters, the primary theme of the text is **inference**.

Let's begin by examining some business studies that illustrate applications of statistics.

Study 1 "Discrimination in the Workplace" (*USA Today*, Aug. 15, 1995).

According to *USA Today*, a record number of job discrimination cases—158,612—were filed with federal or state civil rights agencies in 1994. *USA Today* obtained information on each case from the Equal Employment Opportunity Center (EEOC). Then researchers at this national newspaper determined the basis of each of the 158,612 claims. They reported the results in the graph shown in Figure 1.1. The graph provides an effective summary of the 158,612 claims, clearly depicting that race and sex discrimination are the two most common bases for job discrimination complaints. Thus, Figure 1.1 is an example of *descriptive statistics*.

Study 2 "The Executive Compensation Scoreboard" (*Business Week*, Apr. 22, 1996).

How much are the top corporate executives in the United States being paid and are they worth it? To answer these questions, *Business Week* magazine compiles its "Executive Compensation Scoreboard" each year based on a survey of executives at the highest-ranking companies listed in the *Business Week 1000*. The average* total pay of chief executive officers (CEOs) at 362 companies sampled in the 1995 scoreboard was $3.75 million—an increase of 30% over the previous year.

To determine which executives are worth their pay, *Business Week* also records the ratio of total shareholder return (measured by the dollar value of a $100 investment in the company made 3 years earlier) to the total pay of the CEO (in thousand dollars) over the same 3-year period. For example, a $100 investment in Walt Disney Corporation in 1993 was worth $139 at the end of 1995. When this shareholder return ($139) is divided by CEO Michael Eisner's total 1993–1995 pay of $228.4 million, the result is a return-to-pay ratio of only .0006, one of the lowest among all other chief executives in the survey.

An analysis of the sample data set reveals that CEOs in the industrial high-technology industry have the highest average return-to-pay ratio (.048) while the

FIGURE 1.1
Basis of workplace discrimination claims filed in 1994
Source: *USA Today*, August 15, 1995, p. 10A. Copyright 1995 USA TODAY. Reprinted with permission.

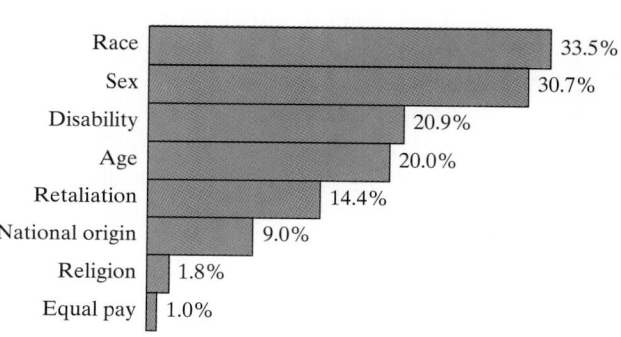

Race	33.5%
Sex	30.7%
Disability	20.9%
Age	20.0%
Retaliation	14.4%
National origin	9.0%
Religion	1.8%
Equal pay	1.0%

*Although we will not formally define the term *average* until Chapter 2, *typical* or *middle* can be substituted here without confusion.

TABLE 1.1 Average Return-to-Pay Ratios of CEOs, by Industry

Industry	Average Ratio
Industrial High-Tech	0.048
Utilities	0.046
Telecommunications	0.042
Services	0.036
Resources	0.028
Transportation	0.028
Financial	0.027
Industrial Low-Tech	0.025
Consumer Products	0.023

Source: Analysis of data in "Executive Compensation Scoreboard," *Business Week,* April 22, 1996, pp. 107–122.

CEOs in the consumer products industry have the lowest average ratio (.023). (See Table 1.1.) Armed with this sample information *Business Week* might *infer* that, from the shareholders' perspective, typical chief executives in consumer products are overpaid relative to industrial high-tech CEOs. Thus, this study is an example of *inferential statistics*.

Study 3 "The Consumer Price Index" (U.S. Department of Labor).

A data set of interest to virtually all Americans is the set of prices charged for goods and services in the U.S. economy. The general upward movement in this set of prices is referred to as *inflation;* the general downward movement is referred to as *deflation*. In order to *estimate* the change in prices over time, the Bureau of Labor Statistics (BLS) of the U.S. Department of Labor developed the Consumer Price Index (CPI). Each month, the BLS collects price data about a specific collection of goods and services (called a *market basket*) from 85 urban areas around the country. Statistical procedures are used to compute the CPI from this sample price data and other information about consumers' spending habits. By comparing the level of the CPI at different points in time, it is possible to *estimate* (make an inference about) the rate of inflation over particular time intervals and to compare the purchasing power of a dollar at different points in time.

One major use of the CPI as an index of inflation is as an indicator of the success or failure of government economic policies. A second use of the CPI is to escalate income payments. Millions of workers have *escalator clauses* in their collective bargaining contracts; these clauses call for increases in wage rates based on increases in the CPI. In addition, the incomes of Social Security beneficiaries and retired military and federal civil service employees are tied to the CPI. It has been estimated that a 1% increase in the CPI can trigger an increase of over $1 billion in income payments. Thus, it can be said that the very livelihoods of millions of Americans depend on the behavior of a statistical estimator, the CPI.

Like Study 2, this study is an example of *inferential statistics*. Market basket price data from a sample of urban areas (used to compute the CPI) is used to make inferences about the rate of inflation and wage rate increases.

These studies provide three real-life examples of the uses of statistics in business, economics, and government. Notice that each involves an analysis of data, either for the purpose of describing the data set (Study 1) or for making inferences about a data set (Studies 2 and 3).

1.3 FUNDAMENTAL ELEMENTS OF STATISTICS

Statistical methods are particularly useful for studying, analyzing, and learning about **populations**.

> **DEFINITION 1.4**
> A **population** is a set of units (usually people, objects, transactions, or events) that we are interested in studying.

For example, populations may include (1) *all* employed workers in the United States, (2) *all* registered voters in California, (3) *everyone* who has purchased a particular brand of cellular telephone, (4) *all* the cars produced last year by a particular assembly line, (5) the *entire* stock of spare parts at United Airlines' maintenance facility, (6) *all* sales made at the drive-through window of a

McDonald's restaurant during a given year, and (7) the set of *all* accidents occurring on a particular stretch of interstate highway during a holiday period. Notice that the first three population examples (1–3) are sets (groups) of people, the next two (4–5) are sets of objects, the next (6) is a set of transactions, and the last (7) is a set of events. Also notice that each set includes all the units in the population of interest.

In studying a population, we focus on one or more characteristics or properties of the units in the population. We call such characteristics *variables*. For example, we may be interested in the variables age, gender, income, and/or the number of years of education of the people currently unemployed in the United States.

DEFINITION 1.5
A **variable** is a characteristic or property of an individual population unit.

The name "variable" is derived from the fact that any particular characteristic may vary among the units in a population.

In studying a particular variable it is helpful to be able to obtain a numerical representation for it. Often, however, numerical representations are not readily available, so the process of measurement plays an important supporting role in statistical studies. **Measurement** is the process we use to assign numbers to variables of individual population units. We might, for instance, measure the preference for a food product by asking a consumer to rate the product's taste on a scale from 1 to 10. Or we might measure workforce age by simply asking each worker how old she is. In other cases, measurement involves the use of instruments such as stopwatches, scales, and calipers.

If the population we wish to study is small, it is possible to measure a variable for every unit in the population. For example, if you are measuring the starting salary for all University of Michigan MBA graduates last year, it is at least feasible to obtain every salary. When we measure a variable for every unit of a population, the result is called a **census** of the population. Typically, however, the populations of interest in most applications are much larger, involving perhaps many thousands or even an infinite number of units. Examples of large populations include those following Definition 1.4, as well as all invoices produced in the last year by a *Fortune* 500 company, all potential buyers of a new fax machine, and all stockholders of a firm listed on the New York Stock Exchange. For such populations, conducting a census would be prohibitively time-consuming and/or costly. A reasonable alternative would be to select and study a *subset* (or portion) of the units in the population.

DEFINITION 1.6
A **sample** is a subset of the units of a population.

For example, suppose a company is being audited for invoice errors. Instead of examining all 15,472 invoices produced by the company during a given year, an auditor may select and examine a sample of just 100 invoices (see Figure 1.2). If he is interested in the variable "invoice error status," he would record (measure) the status (error or no error) of each sampled invoice.

FIGURE 1.2
A sample of all
company invoices

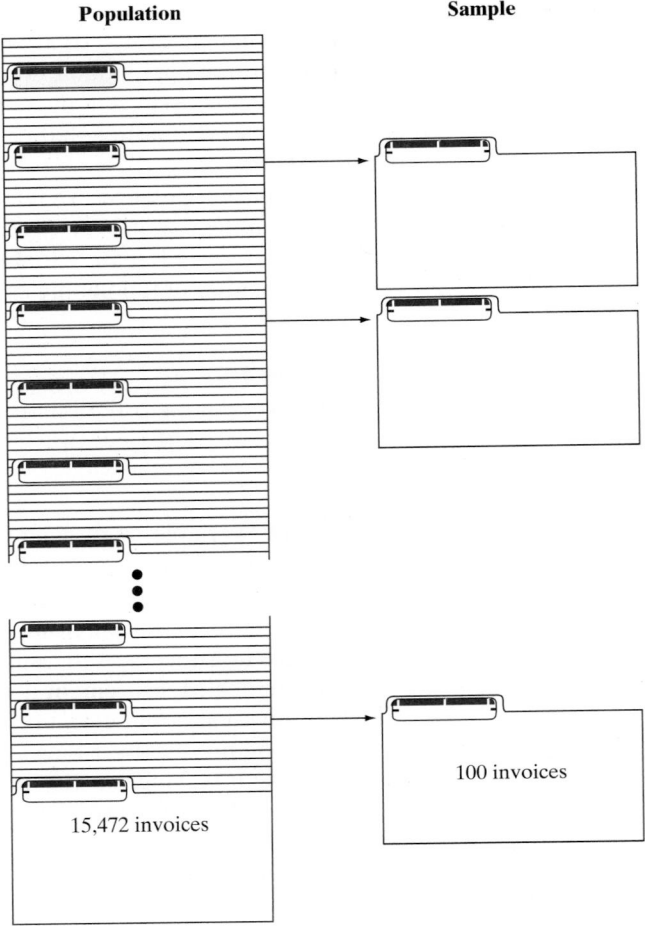

15,472 invoices

100 invoices

After the variable(s) of interest for every unit in the sample (or population) is measured, the data are analyzed, either by descriptive or inferential statistical methods. The auditor, for example, may be interested only in *describing* the error rate in the sample of 100 invoices. More likely, however, he will want to use the information in the sample to make *inferences* about the population of all 15,472 invoices.

DEFINITION 1.7
A **statistical inference** is an estimate or prediction or some other generalization about a population based on information contained in a sample.

That is, we use the information contained in the sample to learn about the larger population.* Thus, from the sample of 100 invoices, the auditor may estimate the total number of invoices containing errors in the population of 15,472 invoices. The auditor's inference about the quality of the firm's invoices can be used in deciding whether to modify the firm's billing operations.

*The terms *population* and *sample* are often used to refer to the sets of measurement themselves, as well as to the units on which the measurements are made. When a single variable of interest is being measured, this usage causes little confusion. But when the terminology is ambiguous, we'll refer to the measurements as *population data sets* and *sample data sets,* respectively.

EXAMPLE 1.1

A large paint retailer has had numerous complaints from customers about under-filled paint cans. As a result, the retailer has begun inspecting incoming shipments of paint from suppliers. Shipments with underfill problems will be returned to the supplier. A recent shipment contained 2,440 gallon-size cans. The retailer sampled 50 cans and weighed each on a scale capable of measuring weight to four decimal places. Properly filled cans weigh 10 pounds.

   a. Describe the population.

   b. Describe the variable of interest.

   c. Describe the sample.

   d. Describe the inference.

SOLUTION

   a. The population is the set of units of interest to the retailer, which is the shipment of 2,440 cans of paint.

   b. The weight of the paint cans is the variable the retailer wishes to evaluate.

   c. The sample is a subset of the population. In this case, it is the 50 cans of paint selected by the retailer.

   d. The inference of interest involves the *generalization* of the information contained in the weights of the sample of paint cans to the population of paint cans. In particular, the retailer wants to learn about the extent of the under-fill problem (if any) in the population. This might be accomplished by finding the average weight of the cans in the sample and using it to estimate the average weight of the cans in the population.   ▙

EXAMPLE 1.2

"Cola wars" is the popular term for the intense competition between Coca-Cola and Pepsi displayed in their marketing campaigns. Their campaigns have featured movie and television stars, rock videos, athletic endorsements, and claims of consumer preference based on taste tests. Suppose, as part of a Pepsi marketing campaign, 1,000 cola consumers are given a blind taste test (i.e., a taste test in which the two brand names are disguised). Each consumer is asked to state a preference for brand A or brand B.

   a. Describe the population.

   b. Describe the variable of interest.

   c. Describe the sample.

   d. Describe the inference.

SOLUTION

   a. The population of interest is the collection or set of all consumers.

   b. The characteristic that Pepsi wants to measure is the consumer's cola preference as revealed under the conditions of a blind taste test, so cola preference is the variable of interest.

   c. The sample is the 1,000 cola consumers selected from the population of all cola consumers.

   d. The inference of interest is the *generalization* of the cola preferences of the 1,000 sampled consumers to the population of all cola consumers. In particular, the preferences of the consumers in the sample can be used to *estimate* the percentage of all cola consumers who prefer each brand.   ▙

The preceding definitions and examples identify four of the five elements of an inferential statistical problem: a population, one or more variables of interest, a sample, and an inference. But making the inference is only part of the story. We also need to know its **reliability**—that is, how good the inference is. The only way we can be certain that an inference about a population is correct is to include the entire population in our sample. However, because of *resource constraints* (i.e., insufficient time and/or money), we usually can't work with whole populations, so we base our inferences on just a portion of the population (a sample). Consequently, whenever possible, it is important to determine and report the reliability of each inference made. Reliability, then, is the fifth element of inferential statistical problems.

The measure of reliability that accompanies an inference separates the science of statistics from the art of fortune-telling. A palm reader, like a statistician, may examine a sample (your hand) and make inferences about the population (your life). However, unlike statistical inferences, the palm reader's inferences include no measure of reliability.

Suppose, as in Example 1.1, we are interested in estimating the average weight of a population of paint cans from the average weight of a sample of cans. Using statistical methods, we can determine a *bound on the estimation error*. This bound is simply a number that our estimation error (the difference between the average weight of the sample and the average weight of the population of cans) is not likely to exceed. We'll see in later chapters that this bound is a measure of the uncertainty of our inference. The reliability of statistical inferences is discussed throughout this text. For now, we simply want you to realize that an inference is incomplete without a measure of its reliability.

> **DEFINITION 1.8**
> A **measure of reliability** is a statement (usually quantified) about the degree of uncertainty associated with a statistical inference.

Let's conclude this section with a summary of the elements of both descriptive and inferential statistical problems and an example to illustrate a measure of reliability.

FOUR ELEMENTS OF DESCRIPTIVE STATISTICAL PROBLEMS

1. The population or sample of interest
2. One or more variables (characteristics of the population or sample units) that are to be investigated
3. Tables, graphs, or numerical summary tools
4. Conclusions about the data based on the patterns revealed

FIVE ELEMENTS OF INFERENTIAL STATISTICAL PROBLEMS

1. The population of interest
2. One or more variables (characteristics of the population units) that are to be investigated
3. The sample of population units
4. The inference about the population based on information contained in the sample
5. A measure of reliability for the inference

EXAMPLE 1.3

Refer to Example 1.2, in which the cola preferences of 1,000 consumers were indicated in a taste test. Describe how the reliability of an inference concerning the preferences of all cola consumers in the Pepsi bottler's marketing region could be measured.

SOLUTION

When the preferences of 1,000 consumers are used to estimate the preferences of all consumers in the region, the estimate will not exactly mirror the preferences of the population. For example, if the taste test shows that 56% of the 1,000 consumers chose Pepsi, it does not follow (nor is it likely) that exactly 56% of all cola drinkers in the region prefer Pepsi. Nevertheless, we can use sound statistical reasoning (which is presented later in the text) to ensure that our sampling procedure will generate estimates that are almost certainly within a specified limit of the true percentage of all consumers who prefer Pepsi. For example, such reasoning might assure us that the estimate of the preference for Pepsi from the sample is almost certainly within 5% of the actual population preference. The implication is that the actual preference for Pepsi is between 51% [i.e., $(56 - 5)$%] and 61% [i.e., $(56 + 5)$%]—that is, (56 ± 5)%. This interval represents a measure of reliability for the inference.

1.4 PROCESSES (OPTIONAL)

Sections 1.2 and 1.3 focused on the use of statistical methods to analyze and learn about populations, which are sets of *existing* units. Statistical methods are equally useful for analyzing and making inferences about **processes**.

> **DEFINITION 1.9**
>
> A **process** is a series of actions or operations that transforms inputs to outputs. A process produces or generates output over time.

The most obvious processes that are of interest to businesses are production or manufacturing processes. A manufacturing process uses a series of operations performed by people and machines to convert inputs, such as raw materials and parts, to finished products (the outputs). Examples include the process used to produce the paper on which these words are printed, automobile assembly lines, and oil refineries.

Figure 1.3 presents a general description of a process and its inputs and outputs. In the context of manufacturing, the process in the figure (i.e., the transformation process) could be a depiction of the overall production process or it could be a depiction of one of the many processes (sometimes called subprocesses) that exist within an overall production process. Thus, the output shown could be finished goods that will be shipped to an external customer or merely the output of one of

FIGURE 1.3
Graphical depiction of a manufacturing process

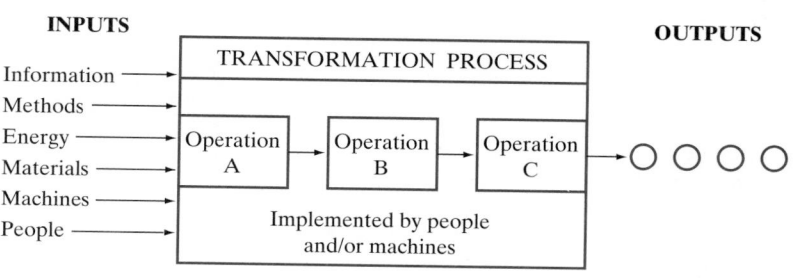

the steps or subprocesses of the overall process. In the latter case, the output becomes input for the next subprocess. For example, Figure 1.3 could represent the overall automobile assembly process, with its output being fully assembled cars ready for shipment to dealers. Or, it could depict the windshield assembly subprocess, with its output of partially assembled cars with windshields ready for "shipment" to the next subprocess in the assembly line.

Besides physical products and services, businesses and other organizations generate streams of numerical data over time that are used to evaluate the performance of the organization. Examples include weekly sales figures, quarterly earnings, and yearly profits. The U.S. economy (a complex organization) can be thought of as generating streams of data that include the Gross Domestic Product (GDP), stock prices, and the Consumer Price Index (see Section 1.2). Statisticians and other analysts conceptualize these data streams as being generated by processes. Typically, however, the series of operations or actions that cause particular data to be realized are either unknown or so complex (or both) that the processes are treated as **black boxes**.

DEFINITION 1.10

A process whose operations or actions are unknown or unspecified is called a **black box**.

Frequently, when a process is treated as a black box, its inputs are not specified either. The entire focus is on the output of the process. A black box process is illustrated in Figure 1.4.

In studying a process, we generally focus on one or more characteristics, or properties, of the output. For example, we may be interested in the weight or the length of the units produced or even the time it takes to produce each unit. As with characteristics of population units, we call these characteristics **variables**. In studying processes whose output is already in numerical form (i.e., a stream of numbers), the characteristic, or property, represented by the numbers (e.g., sales, GDP, or stock prices) is typically the variable of interest. If the output is not numeric, we use **measurement processes** to assign numerical values to variables.* For example, if in the automobile assembly process the weight of the fully assembled automobile is the variable of interest, a measurement process involving a large scale will be used to assign a numerical value to each automobile.

As with populations, we use sample data to analyze and make inferences (estimates, predictions, or other generalizations) about processes. But the concept of a sample is defined differently when dealing with processes. Recall that a population is a set of existing units and that a sample is a subset of those units. In the case

FIGURE 1.4
A black box process
with numerical output

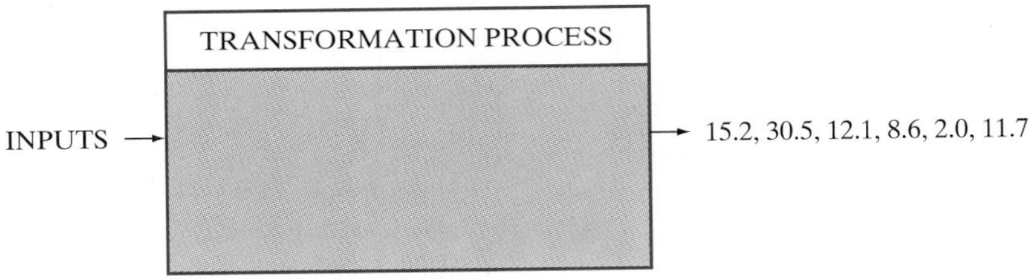

INPUTS → TRANSFORMATION PROCESS → 15.2, 30.5, 12.1, 8.6, 2.0, 11.7

---

*A process whose output is already in numerical form necessarily includes a measurement process as one of its subprocesses.

of processes, however, the concept of a set of existing units is not relevant or appropriate. Processes generate or create their output *over time*—one unit after another. For example, a particular automobile assembly line produces a completed vehicle every four minutes. We define a sample from a process in the box.

DEFINITION 1.11

Any set of output (objects or numbers) produced by a process is called a **sample**.

Thus, the next 10 cars turned out by the assembly line constitute a sample from the process, as do the next 100 cars or every fifth car produced today.

EXAMPLE 1.4

A particular fast-food restaurant chain has 6,289 outlets with drive-through windows. To attract more customers to its drive-through services, the company is considering offering a 50% discount to customers who wait more than a specified number of minutes to receive their order. To help determine what the time limit should be, the company decided to estimate the average waiting time at a particular drive-through window in Dallas, Texas. For 7 consecutive days, the worker taking customers' orders recorded the time that every order was placed. The worker who handed the order to the customer recorded the time of delivery. In both cases, workers used synchronized digital clocks that reported the time to the nearest second. At the end of the 7-day period, 2,109 orders had been timed.

a. Describe the process of interest at the Dallas restaurant.

b. Describe the variable of interest.

c. Describe the sample.

d. Describe the inference of interest.

e. Describe how the reliability of the inference could be measured.

SOLUTION

a. The process of interest is the drive-through window at a particular fast-food restaurant in Dallas, Texas. It is a process because it "produces," or "generates," meals over time. That is, it services customers over time.

b. The variable the company monitored is customer waiting time, the length of time a customer waits to receive a meal after placing an order. Since the study is focusing only on the output of the process (the time to produce the output) and not the internal operations of the process (the tasks required to produce a meal for a customer), the process is being treated as a black box.

c. The sampling plan was to monitor every order over a particular 7-day period. The sample is the 2,109 orders that were processed during the 7-day period.

d. The company's immediate interest is in learning about the drive-through window in Dallas. They plan to do this by using the waiting times from the sample to make a statistical inference about the drive-through process. In particular, they might use the average waiting time for the sample to estimate the average waiting time at the Dallas facility.

e. As for inferences about populations, measures of reliability can be developed for inferences about processes. The reliability of the estimate of the average waiting time for the Dallas restaurant could be measured by a bound on the error of estimation. That is, we might find that the average waiting time is 4.2 minutes, with a bound on the error of estimation of .5 minute. The implication would be that we could be reasonably certain that the true average waiting time for the Dallas process is between 3.7 and 4.7 minutes.

Notice that there is also a population described in this example: the company's 6,289 existing outlets with drive-through facilities. In the final analysis, the company will use what it learns about the process in Dallas and, perhaps, similar studies at other locations to make an inference about the waiting times in its populations of outlets.

Note that output already generated by a process can be viewed as a population. Suppose a soft-drink canning process produced 2,000 twelve-packs yesterday, all of which were stored in a warehouse. If we were interested in learning something about those 2,000 packages—such as the percentage with defective cardboard packaging—we could treat the 2,000 packages as a population. We might draw a sample from the population in the warehouse, measure the variable of interest, and use the sample data to make a statistical inference about the 2,000 packages, as described in Sections 1.2 and 1.3.

In this optional section we have presented a brief introduction to processes and the use of statistical methods to analyze and learn about processes. In Chapter 10 we present an in-depth treatment of these subjects.

1.5 TYPES OF DATA

You have learned that statistics is the science of data and that data are obtained by measuring the values of one or more variables on the units in the sample (or population). All data (and hence the variables we measure) can be classified as one of two general types: *quantitative data* and *qualitative data*.

Quantitative data are data that are measured on a naturally occurring numerical scale.* The following are examples of quantitative data:

1. The temperature (in degrees Celsius) at which each unit in a sample of 20 pieces of heat-resistant plastic begins to melt
2. The current unemployment rate (measured as a percentage) for each of the 50 states
3. The scores of a sample of 150 MBA applicants on the GMAT, a standardized business graduate school entrance exam administered nationwide
4. The number of female executives employed in each of a sample of 75 manufacturing companies

*Quantitative data can be subclassified as either *interval data* or *ratio data*. For ratio data, the origin (i.e., the value 0) is a meaningful number. But the origin has no meaning with interval data. Consequently, we can add and subtract interval data, but we can't multiply and divide them. Of the four quantitative data sets listed, (1) and (3) are interval data, while (2) and (4) are ratio data.

STATISTICS IN ACTION

1.1 QUALITY IMPROVEMENT: U.S. FIRMS RESPOND TO THE CHALLENGE FROM JAPAN

Over the last two decades, U.S. firms have been seriously challenged by products of superior quality from overseas. For example, from 1984 to 1991, imported cars and light trucks steadily increased their share of the U.S. market from 22% to 30%. As a second example, consider the television and VCR markets. Both products were invented in the United States, but as of 1995 not a single U.S. firm manufactures either. Both are produced exclusively by Pacific Rim countries, primarily Japan.

To meet this competitive challenge, more and more U.S. firms—both manufacturing and service firms—have begun quality-improvement initiatives of their own. Many of these firms now stress the management of quality in all phases and aspects of their business, from the design of their products to production, distribution, sales, and service.

Broadly speaking, quality-improvement programs are concerned with (1) finding out what the customer wants, (2) translating those wants into a product design, and (3) producing and delivering a product or service that meets or exceeds the specifications of the product design. In all these areas, but particularly in the third, *improvement of quality requires improvement of processes*—including production processes, distribution processes, and service processes.

But what does it mean to say that a process has been improved? Generally speaking, it means that the customer of the process (i.e., the user of the output) indicates a greater satisfaction with the output. Frequently, such increases in satisfaction require a reduction in the variation of one or more process variables. That is, a reduction in the variation of the output stream of the process is needed.

But how can process variation be monitored and reduced? In the mid-1920s, Walter Shewhart of the Bell Telephone Laboratories made perhaps the most significant breakthrough of this century for the improvement of processes. He recognized that variation in process output was inevitable. No two parts produced by a given machine are the same; no two transactions performed by a given bank teller are the same. He also recognized that variation could be understood, monitored, and controlled using statistical methods. He developed a simple graphical technique—called a **control chart**—for determining whether product variation is within acceptable limits. This method provides guidance for when to adjust or change a production process and when to leave it alone. It can be used at the end of the production process or, most significantly, at different points within the process. We discuss control charts and other tools for improving processes in Chapter 11.

In the last decade, largely as a result of the Japanese challenge to the supremacy of U.S. products, control charts and other statistical tools have gained widespread use in the United States. As evidence for the claim that U.S. firms are responding well to Japan's competitive challenge, consider this: The most prestigious quality-improvement prize in the world that a firm can win is the Deming Prize. It has been awarded by the Japanese since the 1950s. In 1989 it was won for the first time by an American company—Florida Power and Light Company. Other evidence of the resurgence of U.S. competitiveness includes a turnaround in market share for U.S. automakers: imports' share of the U.S. market decreased from a high of 30% in 1991 to 25% in 1995.

Focus

a. Identify two processes that are of interest to you.

b. For each process, part **a**, identify a variable that could be used to monitor the quality of the output of the process.

c. Walter Shewhart understood that variation is an inherent characteristic of the output of every process. Describe the possible variation over time in the output variables you identified in part **b**.

DEFINITION 1.12

Quantitative data are measurements that are recorded on a naturally occurring numerical scale.

In contrast, qualitative data cannot be measured on a natural numerical scale; they can only be classified into categories.* Examples of qualitative data are:

1. The political party affiliation (Democrat, Republican, or Independent) in a sample of 50 chief executive officers
2. The defective status (defective or not) of each of 100 computer chips manufactured by Intel
3. The size of a car (subcompact, compact, mid-size, or full-size) rented by each of a sample of 30 business travelers
4. A taste tester's ranking (best, worst, etc.) of four brands of barbecue sauce for a panel of 10 testers

Often, we assign arbitrary numerical values to qualitative data for ease of computer entry and analysis. But these assigned numerical values are simply codes: They cannot be meaningfully added, subtracted, multiplied, or divided. For example, we might code Democrat = 1, Republican = 2, and Independent = 3. Similarly, a taste tester might rank the barbecue sauces from 1 (best) to 4 (worst). These are simply arbitrarily selected numerical codes for the categories and have no utility beyond that.

> **DEFINITION 1.13**
> **Qualitative data** are measurements that cannot be measured on a natural numerical scale; they can only be classified into one of a group of categories.

EXAMPLE 1.5

Chemical and manufacturing plants sometimes discharge toxic-waste materials such as DDT into nearby rivers and streams. These toxins can adversely affect the plants and animals inhabiting the river and the river bank. The U.S. Army Corps of Engineers recently conducted a study of fish in the Tennessee River (in Alabama) and its three tributary creeks: Flint Creek, Limestone Creek, and Spring Creek. A total of 144 fish were captured and the following variables measured for each:

1. River/creek where fish was captured
2. Species (channel catfish, largemouth bass, or smallmouth buffalofish)
3. Length (centimeters)
4. Weight (grams)
5. DDT concentration (parts per million)

Classify each of the five variables measured as quantitative or qualitative.

SOLUTION

The variables length, weight, and DDT are quantitative because each is measured on a numerical scale: length in centimeters, weight in grams, and DDT in parts per million. In contrast, river/creek and species cannot be measured quantitatively: They can only be classified into categories (e.g., channel catfish, largemouth bass,

---

*Qualitative data can be subclassified as either *nominal data* or *ordinal data*. The categories of an ordinal data set can be ranked or meaningfully ordered, but the categories of a nominal data set can't be ordered. Of the four qualitative data sets listed above, (1) and (2) are nominal and (3) and (4) are ordinal.

and smallmouth buffalofish for species). Consequently, data on river/creek and species are qualitative.   **⌐**

As you would expect, the statistical methods for describing, reporting, and analyzing data depend on the type (quantitative or qualitative) of data measured. We demonstrate many useful methods in the remaining chapters of the text. But first we discuss some important ideas on data collection.

1.6   COLLECTING DATA

Once you decide on the type of data—quantitative or qualitative —appropriate for the problem at hand, you'll need to collect the data. Generally, you can obtain the data in four different ways:

1. Data from a *published source*
2. Data from a *designed experiment*
3. Data from a *survey*
4. Data collected *observationally*

Sometimes, the data set of interest has already been collected for you and is available in a **published source**, such as a book, journal, or newspaper. For example, you may want to examine and summarize the unemployment rates (i.e., percentages of eligible workers who are unemployed) in the 50 states of the United States. You can find this data set (as well as numerous other data sets) at your library in the *Statistical Abstract of the United States,* published annually by the U.S. Department of Commerce. Similarly, someone who is interested in monthly mortgage applications for new home construction would find this data set in the *Survey of Current Business,* another government publication. Other examples of published data sources include *The Wall Street Journal* (financial data), *The Sporting News* (sports information), and America Online (accessed over the Internet).*

A second method of collecting data involves conducting a **designed experiment**, in which the researcher exerts strict control over the units (people, objects, or events) in the study. For example, a recent medical study investigated the potential of aspirin in preventing heart attacks. Volunteer physicians were divided into two groups—the *treatment* group and the *control* group. In the treatment group, each physician took one aspirin tablet a day for one year, while each physician in the control group took an aspirin-free placebo (no drug) made to look like an aspirin tablet. The researchers, not the physicians under study, controlled who received the aspirin (the treatment) and who received the placebo. As you will learn in Chapter 15, a properly designed experiment allows you to extract more information from the data than is possible with an uncontrolled study.

Surveys are a third source of data. With a **survey**, the researcher samples a group of people, asks one or more questions, and records the responses. Probably the most familiar type of survey is the political polls conducted by any one of a number of organizations (e.g., Harris, Gallup, Roper, and CNN) and designed to

---

*With published data, we often make a distinction between the *primary source* and a *secondary source.* If the publisher is the original collector of the data, the source is primary. Otherwise, the data are secondary source data.

predict the outcome of a political election. Another familiar survey is the Nielsen survey, which provides the major television networks with information on the most watched TV programs. Surveys can be conducted through the mail, with telephone interviews, or with in-person interviews. Although in-person interviews are more expensive than mail or telephone surveys, they may be necessary when complex information must be collected.

Finally, observational studies can be employed to collect data. In an **observational study**, the researcher observes the experimental units in their natural setting and records the variable(s) of interest. For example, a company psychologist might observe and record the level of "Type A" behavior of a sample of assembly line workers. Similarly, a finance researcher may observe and record the closing stock prices of companies that are acquired by other firms on the day prior to the buyout and compare them to the closing prices on the day the acquisition is announced. Unlike a designed experiment, an observational study is one in which the researcher makes no attempt to control any aspect of the experimental units.

Regardless of the data collection method employed, it is likely that the data will be a sample from some population. And if we wish to apply inferential statistics, we must obtain a *representative sample*.

DEFINITION 1.14
A **representative sample** exhibits characteristics typical of those possessed by the target population.

For example, consider a political poll conducted during a presidential election year. Assume the pollster wants to estimate the percentage of all 120,000,000 registered voters in the United States who favor the incumbent president. The pollster would be unwise to base the estimate on survey data collected for a sample of voters from the incumbent's own state. Such an estimate would almost certainly be *biased* high.

The most common way to satisfy the representative sample requirement is to select a random sample. A **random sample** ensures that every subset of fixed size in the population has the same chance of being included in the sample. If the pollster samples 1,500 of the 120,000,000 voters in the population so that every subset of 1,500 voters has an equal chance of being selected, he has devised a random sample. The procedure for selecting a random sample is discussed in Chapter 3. Here, however, let's look at two examples involving actual sampling studies.

EXAMPLE 1.6

In the 1970s and early 1980s, state lotteries became commonplace in the United States. In 1985, the *Journal of the Institute for Socioeconomic Studies* (Sept. 1985) reported on a study designed to estimate the proportion of state lottery winners who quit their jobs within one year of striking it rich. Questionnaires were mailed to all 2,000 lottery winners who won at least $50,000 over the 10-year period 1976–1985. Of the 576 who responded, 11% indicated they had quit their jobs.

a. Identify the data collection method.

b. Are the sample data representative of the target population?

SOLUTION

a. The data collection method is a mail survey since questionnaires were mailed to lottery winners to elicit their job status (quit job within one year or not).

b. Because the data (576 responses to the job status question) clearly make up a subset of the target population (all 2,000 lottery winners), they do form a sample. But whether or not the sample is representative is unclear, since we are given no information on the 576 lottery winners who responded to the survey. However, mail surveys (and surveys in general) often suffer from *nonresponse bias*. The fact that only about one-fourth of the 2,000 lottery winners responded to the survey may indicate apathy on the part of lottery winners. A proportion much larger than 11% may have actually quit their jobs but were too busy enjoying their newfound fortune to bother responding to the survey.

EXAMPLE 1.7

Many business decisions are made because of offered incentives that are intended to make the decision-maker "feel good." Researchers at the Ohio State University conducted a study to determine how such a positive effect influences the risk preference of decision-makers (*Organizational Behavior and Human Decision Processes*, Vol. 39, 1987). Each in a random sample of 24 undergraduate business students at the university was assigned to one of two groups. Each student assigned to the "positive affect" group was given a bag of candies as a token of appreciation for participating in the study; students assigned to the "control" group did not receive the gift. All students were then given 10 gambling chips (worth $10) to bet in the casino game of roulette. The researchers measured the win probability (i.e., chance of winning) associated with the riskiest bet each student was willing to make. The win probabilities of the bets made by two groups of students were compared.

a. Identify the data collection method.

b. Are the sample data representative of the target population?

SOLUTION

a. The researchers controlled which group—"positive affect" or "control"—the students were assigned to. Consequently, a designed experiment was used to collect the data.

b. The sample of 24 students was randomly selected from all business students at the Ohio State University. If the target population is *all Ohio State University business students,* it is likely that the sample is representative. However, the researchers warn that the sample data should not be used to make inferences about other, more general, populations.

1.7   THE ROLE OF STATISTICS IN MANAGERIAL DECISION-MAKING

According to H. G. Wells, author of such science fiction classics as *The War of the Worlds* and *The Time Machine,* "*Statistical thinking* will one day be as necessary for efficient citizenship as the ability to read and write." Written more than a hundred years ago, Wells' prediction is proving true today.

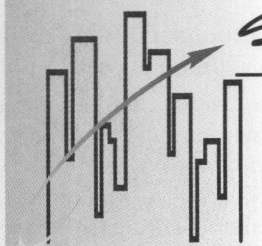

STATISTICS IN ACTION

1.2 A 20/20 VIEW OF SURVEY RESULTS: FACT OR FICTION?

Did you ever notice that, no matter where you stand on popular issues of the day, you can always find statistics or surveys to back up your point of view—whether to take vitamins, whether day care harms kids, or what foods can hurt you or save you? There is an endless flow of information to help you make decisions, but is this information accurate, unbiased? John Stossel decided to check that out, and you may be surprised to learn if the picture you're getting doesn't seem quite right, maybe it isn't.

Barbara Walters gave this introduction to a March 31, 1995, segment of the popular prime-time ABC television program *20/20*. The story is titled "Facts or Fiction?—Exposés of So-Called Surveys." One of the surveys investigated by ABC correspondent John Stossel compared the discipline problems experienced by teachers in the 1940s and those experienced today. The results: In the 1940s, teachers worried most about students talking in class, chewing gum, and running in the halls. Today, they worry most about being assaulted! This information was highly publicized in the print media—in daily newspapers, weekly magazines, Ann Landers' column, the *Congressional Quarterly,* and *The Wall Street Journal,* among others—and referenced in speeches by a variety of public figures, including former first lady Barbara Bush and former Education secretary William Bennett.

"Hearing this made me yearn for the old days when life was so much simpler and gentler, but was life that simple then?" asks Stossel. "Wasn't there juvenile delinquency [in the 1940s]? Is the survey true?" With the help of a Yale School of Management professor, Stossel found the original source of the teacher survey—Texas oilman T. Colin Davis—and discovered it wasn't a survey at all! Davis had simply identified certain disciplinary problems encountered by teachers in a conservative newsletter—a list he admitted was not obtained from a statistical survey, but from Davis' personal knowledge of the problems in the 1940s ("I was in school then") and his understanding of the problems today ("I read the papers").

Stossel's critical thinking about the teacher "survey" led to the discovery of research that is misleading at best and unethical at worst. Several more misleading (and possibly unethical) surveys were presented on the ABC program. Listed here, most of these were conducted by businesses or special interest groups with specific objectives in mind.

The *20/20* segment ended with an interview of Cynthia Crossen, author of *Tainted Truth,* an exposé of misleading and biased surveys. Crossen warns: "If everybody is misusing numbers and scaring us with numbers to get us to do something, however good [that something] is, we've lost the power of numbers. Now, we know certain things from research. For example, we know that smoking cigarettes is hard on your lungs

---

The growth in data collection associated with scientific phenomena, business operations, and government activities (quality control, statistical auditing, forecasting, etc.) has been remarkable in the past several decades. Every day the media present us with the published results of political, economic, and social surveys. In the increasing government emphasis on drug and product testing, for example, we see vivid evidence of the need to be able to evaluate data sets intelligently. Consequently, each of us has to develop a discerning sense—an ability to use rational thought to interpret and understand the meaning of data. This ability is essential for making intelligent decisions, inferences, and generalizations.

DEFINITION 1.15
Statistical thinking involves applying rational thought and the science of statistics to critically assess data and inferences. Fundamental to the thought process is that variation exists in populations and process data.

and heart, and because we know that, many people's lives have been extended or saved. We don't want to lose the power of information to help us make decisions, and that's what I worry about."

Focus

a. Consider the false March of Dimes report on domestic violence and birth defects. Discuss the type of data required to investigate the impact of domestic violence on birth defects. What data collection method would you recommend?

b. Refer to the American Association of University Women (AAUW) study of self-esteem of high school girls. Explain why the results of the AAUW study are likely to be misleading. What data might be appropriate for assessing the self-esteem of high school girls?

c. Refer to the Food Research and Action Center study of hunger in America. Explain why the results of the study are likely to be misleading. What data would provide insight into the proportion of hungry American children?

Reported Information (Source)	Actual Study Information
Eating oat bran is a cheap and easy way to reduce your cholesterol count. (Quaker Oats)	Diet must consist of nothing but oat bran to achieve a slightly lower cholesterol count.
150,000 women a year die from anorexia. (Feminist group)	Approximately 1,000 women a year die from problems that were likely caused by anorexia.
Domestic violence causes more birth defects than all medical issues combined. (March of Dimes)	No study—false report.
Only 29% of high school girls are happy with themselves, compared to 66% of elementary school girls. (American Association of University Women)	Of 3,000 high school girls 29% responded "Always true" to the statement, "I am happy the way I am." Most answered, "Sort of true" and "Sometimes true."
One in four American children under age 12 is hungry or at risk of hunger. (Food Research and Action Center)	Based on responses to the questions: "Do you ever cut the size of meals?" "Do you ever eat less than you feel you should?" "Did you ever rely on limited numbers of foods to feed your children because you were running out of money to buy food for a meal?"

To gain some insight into the role statistics plays in **critical thinking**, let's look at a recent *AmStat News* article. This article describes how a group of 27 mathematics and statistics teachers, attending an American Statistical Association course called "Chance," used statistical thinking to evaluate the results of a study. Consider the following excerpt from the article.

There are few issues in the news that are not in some way statistical. Take one. Should motorcyclists be required by law to wear helmets?... In "The Case for No Helmets" (*New York Times*, June 17, 1995), Dick Teresi, editor of a magazine for Harley-Davidson bikers, argued that helmets may actually kill, since in collisions at speeds greater than 15 miles an hour the heavy helmet may protect the head but snap the spine. [Teresi] citing a "study," said "nine states without helmet laws had a lower fatality rate (3.05 deaths per 10,000 motorcycles) than those that mandated helmets (3.38)," and "in a survey of 2,500 [at a rally], 98% of the respondents opposed such laws."

[The course instructors] asked: After reading this [*New York Times*] piece, do you think it is safer to ride a motorcycle without a helmet? Do you think 98% might be a valid estimate of bikers who oppose helmet laws? What further statistical information would you like? [From Cohn, V. "Chance in college curriculum," *AmStat News,* Aug.–Sept. 1995, No. 223, p. 2.]

You can use several of the key ideas presented in this chapter to help you think statistically about the problem presented in this article. For example, before you can evaluate the validity of the 98% estimate, you would want to know how the data were collected for the study cited by the editor of the biker magazine. If a survey was conducted, it's possible that the 2,500 bikers in the sample were not selected at random from the target population of all bikers, but rather were "self-selected." (Remember, they were all attending a rally—a rally likely for bikers who oppose the law.) If the respondents were likely to have strong opinions regarding the helmet law (e.g., strongly oppose the law), the resulting estimate is probably biased high. Also, if the biased sample was intentional, with the sole purpose to mislead the public, the researchers would be guilty of **unethical statistical practice**.

You'd also want more information about the study comparing the motorcycle fatality rate of the nine states without a helmet law to those states that mandate helmets. Were the data obtained from a published source? Were all 50 states included in the study? That is, are you seeing sample data or population data? Furthermore, do the helmet laws vary among states? If so, can you really compare the fatality rates?

These questions led the Chance group to the discovery of two scientific and statistically sound studies on helmets. The first, a UCLA study of nonfatal injuries, disputed the charge that helmets shift injuries to the spine. The second study reported a dramatic *decline* in motorcycle crash deaths after California passed its helmet law.

Successful managers rely heavily on statistical thinking to help them make decisions. The role statistics can play in managerial decision-making is displayed in the flow diagram in Figure 1.5. Every managerial decision-making problem begins

FIGURE 1.5
Flow diagram showing the role of statistics in managerial decision-making
Source: Chervany, Benson, and Iyer (1980)

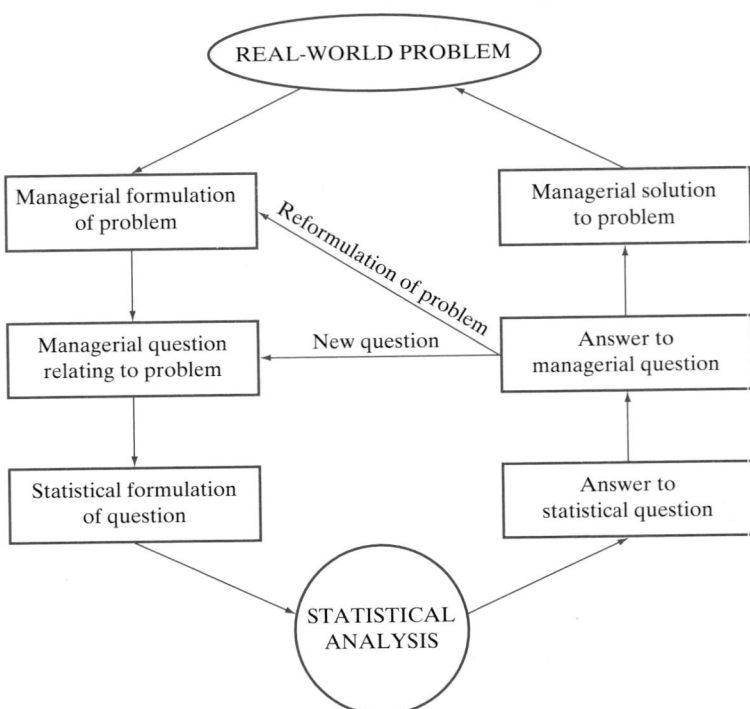

with a real-world problem. This problem is then formulated in managerial terms and framed as a managerial question. The next sequence of steps (proceeding counterclockwise around the flow diagram) identifies the role that statistics can play in this process. The managerial question is translated into a statistical question, the sample data are collected and analyzed, and the statistical question is answered. The next step in the process is using the answer to the statistical question to reach an answer to the managerial question. The answer to the managerial question may suggest a reformulation of the original managerial problem, suggest a new managerial question, or lead to the solution of the managerial problem.

One of the most difficult steps in the decision-making process—one that requires a cooperative effort among managers and statisticians—is the translation of the managerial question into statistical terms (for example, into a question about a population). This statistical question must be formulated so that, when answered, it will provide the key to the answer to the managerial question. Thus, as in the game of chess, you must formulate the statistical question with the end result, the solution to the managerial question, in mind.

In the remaining chapters of the text, you'll become familiar with the tools essential for building a firm foundation in statistics and statistical thinking.

QUICK REVIEW

Key Terms

Note: Starred (*) terms are from the optional section in this chapter.

Black box* 10	Inferential statistics 3	Qualitative data 14	Statistical thinking 18
Census 5	Measure of reliability 8	Quantitative data 13	Statistics 2
Critical thinking 19	Measurement 5	Random sample 16	Survey 15
Data 2	Observational study 16	Reliability 8	Unethical statistical
Descriptive statistics 2	Population 4	Representative sample 16	practice 20
Designed experiment 15	Process* 9	Sample 5	Variable 5
Inference 3	Published source 15	Statistical inference 6	

EXERCISES 1.1–1.30

Note: Starred (*) exercises are from the optional section in this chapter.

Learning the Mechanics

1.1 What is statistics?

1.2 Explain the difference between descriptive and inferential statistics.

1.3 List and define the four elements of a descriptive statistics problem.

1.4 List and define the five elements of an inferential statistical analysis.

1.5 List the four major methods of collecting data and explain their differences.

1.6 Explain the difference between quantitative and qualitative data.

1.7 Explain how populations and variables differ.

1.8 Explain how populations and samples differ.

1.9 What is a representative sample? What is its value?

1.10 Why would a statistician consider an inference incomplete without an accompanying measure of its reliability?

*1.11 Explain the difference between a population and a process.

1.12 Define statistical thinking.

1.13 Suppose you're given a data set that classifies each sample unit into one of four categories: A, B, C, or D. You plan to create a computer database consisting of these data, and you decide to code the data as A = 1, B = 2, C = 3, and D = 4. Are the data consisting of the classifications A, B, C, and D qualitative or quantitative? After the data are input as 1, 2, 3, or 4, are they qualitative or quantitative? Explain your answers.

Applying the Concepts

1.14 Consider the set of all students enrolled in your statistics course this term. Suppose you're interested in learning about the current grade point averages (GPAs) of this group.
   a. Define the population and variable of interest.
   b. Is the variable qualitative or quantitative?
   c. Suppose you determine the GPA of every member of the class. Would this represent a census or a sample?
   d. Suppose you determine the GPA of 10 members of the class. Would this represent a census or a sample?
   e. If you determine the GPA of every member of the class and then calculate the average, how much reliability does this calculation have as an "estimate" of the class average GPA?
   f. If you determine the GPA of 10 members of the class and then calculate the average, will the number you get necessarily be the same as the average GPA for the whole class? On what factors would you expect the reliability of the estimate to depend?
   g. What must be true in order for the sample of 10 students you select from your class to be considered a random sample?

1.15 Pollsters regularly conduct opinion polls to determine the popularity rating of the current president. Suppose a poll is to be conducted tomorrow in which 2,000 individuals will be asked whether the president is doing a good or bad job. The 2,000 individuals will be selected by random-digit telephone dialing and asked the question over the phone.
   a. What is the relevant population?
   b. What is the variable of interest? Is it quantitative or qualitative?
   c. What is the sample?
   d. What is the inference of interest to the pollster?
   e. What method of data collection is employed?
   f. How likely is the sample to be representative?

1.16 Colleges and universities are requiring an increasing amount of information about applicants before making acceptance and financial aid decisions. Classify each of the following types of data required on a college application as quantitative or qualitative.
   a. High school GPA
   b. High school class rank
   c. Applicant's score on the SAT or ACT
   d. Gender of applicant
   e. Parents' income
   f. Age of applicant

1.17 Classify the following examples of data as either qualitative or quantitative:
   a. The depth of tread remaining on each of 137 randomly selected automobile tires after 20,000 miles of wear

   b. The occupation of each of 200 shoppers at a supermarket
   c. The employment status of each adult living on a city block
   d. The time (in months) between auto maintenance for each of 100 used cars

1.18 A food-products company is considering marketing a new snack food. To see how consumers react to the product, the company conducted a taste test using a sample of 100 randomly selected shoppers at a suburban shopping mall. The shoppers were asked to taste the snack food and then fill out a short questionnaire that requested the following information:
   (1) What is your age?
   (2) Are you the person who typically does the food shopping for your household?
   (3) How many people are in your family?
   (4) How would you rate the taste of the snack food on a scale of 1 to 10, where 1 is least tasty?
   (5) Would you purchase this snack food if it were available on the market?
   (6) If you answered yes to part (5), how often would you purchase the product?
   a. Identify the data collection method.
   b. Classify the data generated for each question as quantitative or qualitative. Justify your classifications.

1.19 All highway bridges in the United States are inspected periodically for structural deficiency by the Federal Highway Administration (FHWA). Data from the FHWA inspections are compiled into the National Bridge Inventory (NBI). Several of the nearly 100 variables maintained by the NBI are listed below. Classify each variable as quantitative or qualitative.
   a. Length of maximum span (feet)
   b. Number of vehicle lanes
   c. Toll bridge (yes or no)
   d. Average daily traffic
   e. Condition of deck (good, fair, or poor)
   f. Bypass or detour length (miles)
   g. Route type (interstate, U.S., state, county, or city)

1.20 Refer to Exercise 1.19. The most recent NBI data were analyzed and the results published in the *Journal of Infrastructure Systems* (June 1995). Using the FHWA inspection ratings, each of the 470,515 highway bridges in the United States was categorized as structurally deficient, functionally obsolete, or safe. About 26% of the bridges were found to be structurally deficient, while 19% were functionally obsolete.
   a. What is the variable of interest to the researchers?
   b. Is the variable of part **a** quantitative or qualitative?

c. Is the data set analyzed a population or a sample? Explain.

d. How did the researchers obtain the data for their study?

1.21 The *Journal of Retailing* (Spring 1988) published a study of the relationship between job satisfaction and the degree of *Machiavellian orientation*. Briefly, the Machiavellian orientation is one in which the executive exerts very strong control, even to the point of deception and cruelty, over the employees he or she supervises. The authors administered a questionnaire to each in a sample of 218 department store executives and obtained both a job satisfaction score and a Machiavellian rating. They concluded that those with higher job satisfaction scores are likely to have a lower "Mach" rating.

a. What is the population from which the sample was selected?

b. What variables were measured by the authors?

c. Identify the sample.

d. Identify the data collection method used.

e. What inference was made by the authors?

1.22 Media reports suggest that disgruntled shareholders are becoming more willing to put pressure on corporate management. Is this an impression caused by a few recent high-profile cases involving a few large investors, or is shareholder activism widespread? To answer this question the Wirthlin Group, an opinion research organization in McLean, Virginia, sampled and questioned 240 large investors (money managers, mutual fund managers, institutional investors, etc.) in the United States. One question they asked was: Have you written or called a corporate director to express your views? They found that a surprisingly large 40% of the sample had (*New York Times*, Oct. 31, 1995).

a. Identify the population of interest to the Wirthlin Group.

b. Based on the question the Wirthlin Group asked, what is the variable of interest?

c. Describe the sample.

d. What inference can be made from the results of the survey?

1.23 *Corporate merger* is a means through which one firm (the bidder) acquires control of the assets of another firm (the target). During 1995 there was a frenzy of bank mergers in the United States, as the banking industry consolidated into more efficient and more competitive units. The number of banks in the United States has fallen from a high of 14,496 in 1984 to just under 10,000 at the end of 1995 (*Fortune*, Oct. 2, 1995).

a. Construct a brief questionnaire (two or three questions) that could be used to query a sample of bank presidents concerning their opinions of why the industry is consolidating and whether it will consolidate further.

b. Describe the population about which inferences could be made from the results of the survey.

c. Discuss the pros and cons of sending the questionnaire to all bank presidents versus a sample of 200.

*1.24 Coca-Cola and Schweppes Beverages Limited (CCSB), which was formed in 1987, is 49% owned by the Coca-Cola Company. According to *Industrial Management and Data Systems* (Vol. 92, 1992), CCSB's Wakefield plant can produce 4,000 cans of soft drink per minute. The automated process consists of measuring and dispensing the raw ingredients into storage vessels to create the syrup, and then injecting the syrup, along with carbon dioxide, into the beverage cans. In order to monitor the subprocess that adds carbon dioxide to the cans, five filled cans are pulled off the line every 15 minutes and the amount of carbon dioxide in each of these five is measured to determine whether the amounts are within prescribed limits.

a. Describe the process studied.

b. Describe the variable of interest.

c. Describe the sample.

d. Describe the inference of interest.

e. *Brix* is a unit for measuring sugar concentration. If a technician is assigned the task of estimating the average brix level of all 240,000 cans of beverage stored in a warehouse near Wakefield, will the technician be examining a process or a population? Explain.

1.25 *Job-sharing* is an innovative employment alternative that originated in Sweden and is becoming very popular in the United States. Firms that offer job-sharing plans allow two or more persons to work part-time, sharing one full-time job. For example, two job-sharers might alternate work weeks, with one working while the other is off. Job-sharers never work at the same time and may not even know each other. Job-sharing is particularly attractive to working mothers and to people who frequently lose their jobs due to fluctuations in the economy. In a survey of 1,035 major U.S. firms, approximately 22% offer job-sharing to their employees (*Entrepreneur*, Mar. 1995).

a. Identify the population from which the sample was selected.

b. Identify the variable measured.

c. Identify the sample selected.

d. What type of inference is of interest to the government agency?

1.26 The People's Republic of China with its 1.2 billion people is emerging as the world's biggest cigarette market. In fact, China's cigarette industry is the central government's largest source of tax revenue. To better understand Chinese smokers and the potential public health disaster they represent, door-to-door interviews of 3,423 men and 3,593 women were conducted in the Minhang District, a suburb of 500,000 people near Shanghai. The study concluded that "people in China, despite their modest incomes, are willing to spend an average of 60 percent of personal income and 17 percent of household income to buy cigarettes" (*Newark Star-Ledger*, Oct. 19, 1995).

a. Identify the population that was sampled.

b. How large was the sample size?

c. The study made inferences about what population?

d. Explain why different answers to parts **a** and **c** might affect the reliability of the study's conclusions.

1.27 Windows is a computer software product made by Microsoft Corporation. In designing Windows 95, Microsoft telephoned thousands of users of Windows 3.1 (an older version) and asked them how the product could be improved. Assume customers were asked the following questions:

    I. Are you the most frequent user of Windows 3.1 in your household?

    II. What is your age?

    III. How would you rate the helpfulness of the tutorial instructions that accompany Windows 3.1, on a scale of 1 to 10, where 1 is not helpful?

    IV. When using a printer with Windows 3.1, do you most frequently use a laser printer or another type of printer?

    V. If the speed of Windows 3.1 could be changed, which one of the following would you prefer: slower, unchanged, or faster?

    VI. How many people in your household have used Windows 3.1 at least once?

Each of these questions defines a variable of interest to the company. Classify the data generated for each variable as quantitative or qualitative. Justify your classification.

1.28 To assess how extensively accounting firms in New York State use sampling methods in auditing their clients, the New York Society of CPAs mailed a questionnaire to 800 New York accounting firms employing two or more professionals. They received responses from 179 firms of which four responses were unusable and 12 reported they had no audit practice. The questionnaire asked firms whether they use audit sampling methods and, if so, whether or not they use random sampling (*CPA Journal*, July 1995).

a. Identify the population, the variables, the sample, and the inferences of interest to the New York Society of CPAs.

b. Speculate as to what could have made four of the responses unusable.

c. In Chapters 6–9 you will learn that the reliability of an inference is related to the size of the sample used. In addition to sample size, what factors might affect the reliability of the inferences drawn in the mail survey described above?

*1.29 The Wallace Company of Houston is a distributor of pipes, valves, and fittings to the refining, chemical, and petrochemical industries. The company was a recent winner of the Malcolm Baldrige National Quality Award. According to *Small Business Reports* (May 1991), one of the steps the company takes to monitor the quality of its distribution process is to send out a survey twice a year to a subset of its current customers, asking the customers to rate the speed of deliveries, the accuracy of invoices, and the quality of the packaging of the products they have received from Wallace.

a. Describe the process studied.

b. Describe the variables of interest.

c. Describe the sample.

d. Describe the inferences of interest.

e. What are some of the factors that are likely to affect the reliability of the inferences?

1.30 The employment status (employed or unemployed) of each individual in the U.S. workforce is a set of data that is of interest to economists, businesspeople, and sociologists. These data provide information on the social and economic health of our society. To obtain information about the employment status of the workforce, the U.S. Bureau of the Census conducts what is known as the *Current Population Survey*. Each month approximately 1,500 interviewers visit about 59,000 of the 92 million households in the United States and question the occupants over 14 years of age about their employment status. Their responses enable the Bureau of the Census to *estimate* the percentage of people in the labor force who are unemployed (the *unemployment rate*).

a. Define the population of interest to the Census Bureau.

b. What variable is being measured? Is it quantitative or qualitative?

c. Is the problem of interest to the Census Bureau descriptive or inferential?

d. In order to monitor the rate of unemployment, it is essential to have a definition of "unemployed." Different economists and even different countries define it in various ways. Develop your own definition of an "unemployed person." Your definition should answer such questions as: Are students on summer vacation unemployed? Are college professors who do not teach summer school unemployed? At what age are people considered to be eligible for the workforce? Are people who are out of work but not actively seeking a job unemployed?

CHAPTER 2

METHODS FOR DESCRIBING SETS OF DATA

CONTENTS

2.1   Describing Qualitative Data

2.2   Graphical Methods for Describing Quantitative Data

2.3   The Time Series Plot (Optional)

2.4   Summation Notation

2.5   Numerical Measures of Central Tendency

2.6   Numerical Measures of Variability

2.7   Interpreting the Standard Deviation

2.8   Numerical Measures of Relative Standing

2.9   Quartiles and Box Plots (Optional)

2.10   Graphing Bivariate Relationships (Optional)

2.11   Distorting the Truth with Descriptive Techniques

STATISTICS IN ACTION

2.1   Pareto Analysis

2.2   *Car & Driver's* "Road Test Digest"

Where We've Been

In Chapter 1 we looked at some typical examples of the use of statistics and we discussed the role that statistical thinking plays in supporting managerial decision-making. We examined the difference between descriptive and inferential statistics and described the five elements of inferential statistics: a population, one or more variables, a sample, an inference, and a measure of reliability for the inference. We also learned that data can be of two types—quantitative and qualitative.

Where We're Going

Before we make an inference, we must be able to describe a data set. We can do this by using graphical and/or numerical methods, which we discuss in this chapter. As we'll see in Chapter 5, we use sample numerical descriptive measures to estimate the values of corresponding population descriptive measures. Therefore, our efforts in this chapter will ultimately lead us to statistical inference.

Suppose you wish to evaluate the managerial capabilities of a class of 400 MBA students based on their Graduate Management Aptitude Test (GMAT) scores. How would you describe these 400 measurements? Characteristics of the data set include the typical or most frequent GMAT score, the variability in the scores, the highest and lowest scores, the "shape" of the data, and whether or not the data set contains any unusual scores. Extracting this information by "eye" isn't easy. The 400 scores may provide too many bits of information for our minds to comprehend. Clearly we need some formal methods for summarizing and characterizing the information in such a data set. Methods for describing data sets are also essential for statistical inference. Most populations are large data sets. Consequently, we need methods for describing a sample data set that let us make descriptive statements (inferences) about the population from which the sample was drawn.

Two methods for describing data are presented in this chapter, one **graphical** and the other **numerical**. Both play an important role in statistics. Section 2.1 presents both graphical and numerical methods for describing qualitative data. Graphical methods for describing quantitative data are presented in Section 2.2 and optional Sections 2.3, 2.9, and 2.10; numerical descriptive methods for quantitative data are presented in Sections 2.4–2.8. We end this chapter with a section on the *misuse* of descriptive techniques.

2.1 DESCRIBING QUALITATIVE DATA

Recall the "Executive Compensation Scoreboard" tabulated annually by *Business Week* (see Study 2 in Section 1.2). *Forbes* magazine also conducts a salary survey of chief executive officers each year. In addition to salary information, *Forbes* collects and reports personal data on the CEOs, including level of education. Do most CEOs have advanced degrees, such as masters degrees or doctorates? To answer this question, Table 2.1 gives the highest college degree obtained (bachelors, masters, doctorate, or none) for each of the 25 best-paid CEOs over the 5-year period 1990–1994.

For this study, the variable of interest, highest college degree obtained, is qualitative in nature. Qualitative data are nonnumerical in nature; thus, the value of a qualitative variable can only be classified into categories called *classes*. The possible degree types—bachelors, masters, doctorate, and none—represent the classes for this qualitative variable. We can summarize such data numerically in two ways: (1) by computing the *class frequency*—the number of observations in the data set that fall into each class; or (2) by computing the *class relative frequency*—the proportion of the total number of observations falling into each class.

DEFINITION 2.1
A **class** is one of the categories into which qualitative data can be classified.

DEFINITION 2.2
The **class frequency** is the number of observations in the data set falling into a particular class.

DEFINITION 2.3
The **class relative frequency** is the class frequency divided by the total number of observations in the data set.

TABLE 2.1 Data on 25 Best-Paid Executives

CEO	Company	Highest College Degree Obtained
1. M. Eisner	Walt Disney	Bachelors
2. S. Weill	Travelers	Bachelors
3. A. O'Reilly	HJ Heintz	Doctorate
4. S. Hilbert	Consecto	None
5. B. Schwartz	Loral	Bachelors
6. H. Solomon	Forest Labs	Doctorate
7. L. Coss	Green Tree Financial	None
8. R. Goizueta	Coca-Cola	Bachelors
9. W. Sanders	Advanced Micro	Bachelors
10. S. Wynn	Mirage	Bachelors
11. J. Mellor	General Dynamics	Masters
12. R. Roberts	Comcast	Bachelors
13. P. Thomas	First Financial Mgmt.	Masters
14. R. Mark	Colgate-Palmolive	Masters
15. R. Manoogian	Masco	Bachelors
16. R. Richey	Torchmark	Doctorate
17. J. Donald	DSC Communications	Masters
18. J. Welch	General Electric	Doctorate
19. J. Hyde	Auto Zone	Bachelors
20. S. Walske	Parametric Tech	Masters
21. K. Lay	Enron	Doctorate
22. R. Araskog	ITT	Bachelors
23. D. Fuente	Office Depot	Masters
24. D. Tully	Merrill Lynch	Bachelors
25. C. Sanford	Bankers Trust NY	Masters

Source: Forbes, Vol. 155, No. 11, May 22, 1995.

Examining Table 2.1, we observe that 2 of the 25 best-paid CEOs did not obtain a college degree, 11 obtained bachelors degrees, 7 masters degrees, and 5 doctorates. These numbers—2, 11, 7, and 5—represent the class frequencies for the four classes and are shown in the summary table, Table 2.2.

Table 2.2 also gives the relative frequency of each of the four degree classes. From Definition 2.3, we know that we calculate the relative frequency by dividing the class frequency by the total number of observations in the data set. Thus, the relative frequencies for the four degree types are

$$\text{None:} \quad \frac{2}{25} = .08$$

$$\text{Bachelors:} \quad \frac{11}{25} = .44$$

TABLE 2.2 Summary Table for Data on 25 Best-Paid CEOs

CLASS Highest Degree Obtained	FREQUENCY Number of CEOs	RELATIVE FREQUENCY Proportion
None	2	.08
Bachelors	11	.44
Masters	7	.28
Doctorate	5	.20
Totals	25	1.000

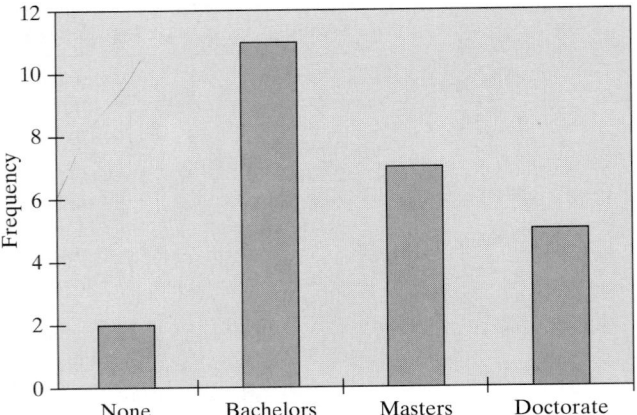

FIGURE 2.1

Bar graph for data on 25 CEOs

$$\text{Masters:} \quad \frac{7}{25} = .28$$

$$\text{Doctorate:} \quad \frac{5}{25} = .20$$

From these relative frequencies we observe that nearly half (44%) of the 25 best-paid CEOs obtained only their bachelors degree.

Although the summary table of Table 2.2 adequately describes the data of Table 2.1, we often want a graphical presentation as well. Figures 2.1 and 2.2 show two of the most widely used graphical methods for describing qualitative data—**bar graphs** and **pie charts**. Figure 2.1 shows the frequencies of "highest degree obtained" in a *bar graph* created using the EXCEL software package. Note that the height of the rectangle, or "bar," over each class is equal to the class frequency. (Optionally, the bar heights can be proportional to class relative frequencies.) In contrast, Figure 2.2 (also created using EXCEL) shows the relative frequencies of the four degree types in a *pie chart*. Note that the pie is a circle (spanning 360°) and the size (angle) of the "pie slice" assigned to each class is proportional to the class relative frequency. For example, the slice assigned to bachelors degree is 44% of 360°, or (.44)(360°) = 158.4°.

Let's look at a practical example that requires interpretation of the graphical results.

FIGURE 2.2

Pie chart for data on 25 CEOs

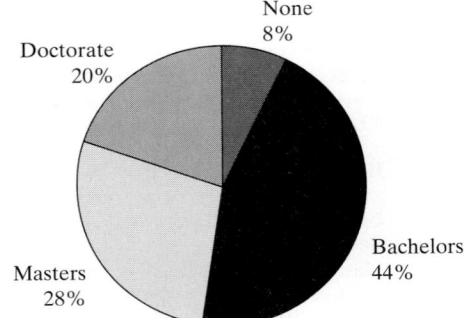

EXAMPLE 2.1

A group of cardiac physicians in southwest Florida have been studying a new drug designed to reduce blood loss in coronary artery bypass operations. Blood loss data for 114 coronary artery bypass patients (some who received a dosage of the drug and others who did not) were collected and are made available for analysis.* Although the drug shows promise in reducing blood loss, the physicians are concerned about possible side effects and complications. So their data set includes not only the qualitative variable, DRUG, which indicates whether or not the patient received the drug, but also the qualitative variable, COMP, which specifies the type (if any) of complication experienced by the patient. The four values of COMP recorded by the physicians are: (1) redo surgery, (2) post-op infection, (3) both, or (4) none.

a. Figure 2.3, generated using SAS computer software, shows summary tables for the two qualitative variables, DRUG and COMP. Interpret the results.

b. Interpret the SAS graph and summary tables shown in Figure 2.4.

SOLUTION

a. The top table in Figure 2.3 is a summary frequency table for DRUG. Note that exactly half (57) of the 114 coronary artery bypass patients received the drug and half did not. The bottom table in Figure 2.3 is a summary frequency table for COMP. The class relative frequencies are given in the **Percent** column. We see that 75.5% of the 114 patients had no complications, leaving 24.5% who experienced either a redo surgery, a post-op infection, or both.

b. At the top of Figure 2.4 is a side-by-side bar graph for the data. The first four bars represent the frequencies of COMP for the 57 patients who did not receive the drug; the next four bars represent the frequencies of COMP for the 57 patients who did receive a dosage of the drug. The graph clearly shows that patients who got the drug suffered more complications. The exact percentages are displayed in the summary tables of Figure 2.4. About 30% of the patients who got the drug had complications, compared to about 17% for the patients who got no drug.

Although these results show that the drug may be effective in reducing blood loss, they also imply that patients on the drug may have a higher risk

FIGURE 2.3
SAS summary tables for DRUG and COMP

DRUG	Frequency	Percent	Cumulative Frequency	Cumulative Percent
NO	57	50.0	57	50.0
YES	57	50.0	114	100.0

COMP	Frequency	Percent	Cumulative Frequency	Cumulative Percent
1:REDO	12	10.5	12	10.5
2:INFECT	12	10.5	24	21.0
3:BOTH	4	3.5	28	24.5
4:NONE	86	75.5	114	100.0

*The data for this study are real. For confidentiality reasons, the drug name and physician group are omitted.

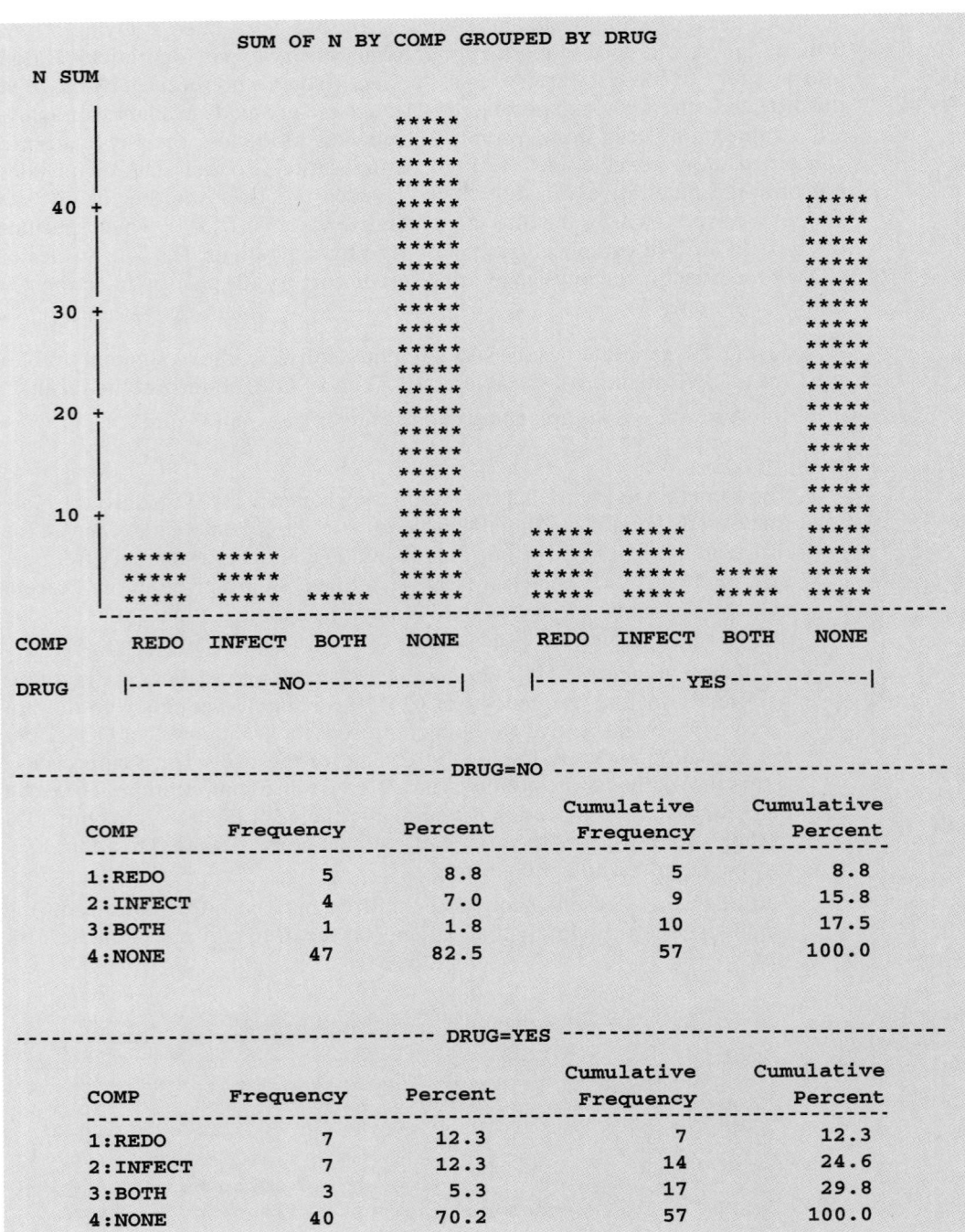

FIGURE 2.4 SAS bar graph and summary tables for COMP by DRUG

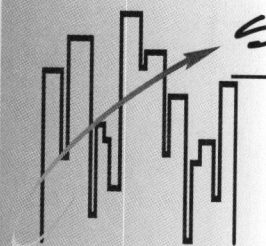

STATISTICS IN ACTION

2.1 PARETO ANALYSIS

Vilfredo Pareto (1843–1923), an Italian economist, discovered that approximately 80% of the wealth of a country lies with approximately 20% of the people. V. E. Kane, in his book *Defect Prevention* (New York: Marcel Dekker, 1989), noted similar findings in other areas: 80% of sales are attributable to 20% of the customers; 80% of customer complaints result from 20% of the components of a product; 80% of defective items produced by a process result from 20% of the types of errors that are made in production. These examples illustrate the idea of "the vital few and the trivial many," the **Pareto principle**. As applied to the last example, a "vital few" errors account for most of the defectives produced. The remaining defectives are due to many different errors, the "trivial many."

In general, **Pareto analysis** involves the categorization of items and the determination of which categories contain the most observations. These are the "vital few" categories. Pareto analysis is used in industry today as a problem-identification tool. Managers and workers use it to identify the most important problems or causes of problems that plague them. Knowledge of the "vital few" problems permits management to set priorities and focus their problem-solving efforts.

The primary tool of Pareto analysis is the **Pareto diagram**. The Pareto diagram is simply a frequency or relative frequency bar chart, with the bars arranged in descending order of height from left to right across the horizontal axis. That is, the tallest bar is positioned at the left and the shortest is at the far right. This arrange-

ment locates the most important categories—those with the largest frequencies—at the left of the chart. Since the data are qualitative, there is no inherent numerical order: They can be rearranged to make the display more useful.

Focus

a. Consider the following example from the automobile industry (adapted from Kane, 1989). All cars produced on a particular day were inspected for defects. The defects were categorized by type as follows: body, accessories, electrical, transmission, and engine. The resulting Pareto diagram for these qualitative data is shown in Figure 2.5(a) on page 32. Use the diagram to identify the most frequently observed type of defect.

b. Sufficient data were collected when the cars were inspected to take the Pareto analysis one step farther. All 70 body defects were further classified as to whether they were paint defects, dents, upholstery defects, windshield defects, or chrome defects. All 50 accessory defects were further classified as to whether they were defects in the air conditioning (A/C) system, the radio, the power steering, the cruise control, or the windshield (W/S) wipers. Two more Pareto diagrams were constructed from these data. They are shown in panels (b) and (c) of Figure 2.5. This decomposition of the original Pareto diagram is called **exploding the Pareto diagram**. Interpret the exploded diagrams. What types of defects should be targeted for special attention by managers, engineers, and assembly-line workers?

of complications. But before using this information to make a decision about the drug, the physicians will need to provide a measure of reliability for the inference. That is, the physicians will want to know whether the difference between the percentages of patients with complications observed in this sample of 114 patients is generalizable to the population of all coronary artery bypass patients. Measures of reliability will be discussed in Chapters 5–8. �!.

FIGURE 2.5
Pareto diagrams
(Statistics in
Action 2.1)

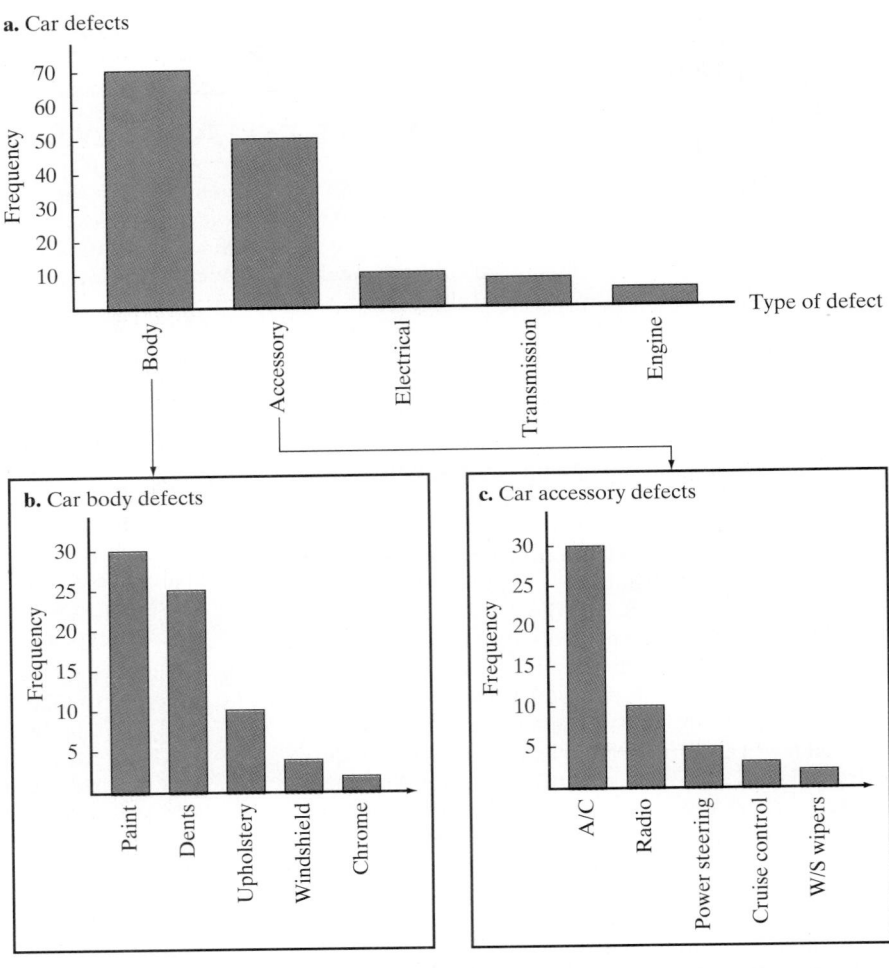

a. Car defects

b. Car body defects

c. Car accessory defects

EXERCISES 2.1–2.11

Note: Exercises marked with 💾 contain data available for
computer analysis on a 3.5" disk (file name in parentheses).

Learning the Mechanics

2.1 Complete the following table.

Grade on Business Statistics Exam	Frequency	Relative Frequency
A: 90–100		.08
B: 80–89	36	
C: 65–79	90	
D: 50–64	30	
F: Below 50	28	
Total	200	1.00

2.2 A qualitative variable with three classes (X, Y, and Z) is measured for each of 20 units randomly sampled from a target population. The data (observed class for each unit) are listed below.

```
Y  X  X  Z  X  Y  Y  Y  X  X  Z  X
Y  Y  X  Z  Y  Y  Y  X
```

a. Compute the frequency for each of the three classes.
b. Compute the relative frequency for each of the three classes.
c. Display the results, part a, in a frequency bar graph.
d. Display the results, part b, in a pie chart.

Applying the Concepts

2.3 Disgruntled shareholders who put pressure on corporate management to make certain financial decisions are referred to as shareholder activists. In Exercise 1.22 we described a survey of 240 large investors designed to determine how widespread shareholder activism actually is. One of several questions asked was: If the chief executive officer and the board of directors differed on company strategy, what action would you, as a large investor of the firm, take? (*New York Times,* Oct. 31, 1995) The responses are summarized in the table.

Response	Number of Investors
Seek formal explanation	154
Seek CEO performance review	49
Dismiss CEO	20
Seek no action	17
Total	240

   a. Construct a relative frequency table for the data.
   b. Display the relative frequencies in a graph.
   c. Discuss the findings.

2.4   According to Topaz Enterprises, a Portland, Oregon-based airfare accounting firm, "more than 80% of all tickets purchased for domestic flights are discounted" (*Travel Weekly,* May 15, 1995). The results of the accounting firm's survey of domestic airline tickets are summarized in the accompanying table.

Domestic Airline Ticket Type	Proportion
Full coach	.005
Discounted coach	.206
Negotiated coach	.425
First class	.009
Business class	.002
Business class negotiated	.001
Advance purchase	.029
Capacity controlled discount	.209
Nonrefundable	.114
Total	1.000

   a. Give your opinion on whether the data described in the table are from a population or a sample. Explain your reasoning.
   b. Display the data with a bar graph. Arrange the bars in order of height to form a Pareto diagram. Interpret the resulting graph.
   c. Do the data support the conclusion reached by Topaz Enterprises regarding the percentage of tickets purchased that are discounted?

   [*Note:* Advance purchase and negotiated tickets are considered discounted.]

2.5   "Reader-response cards" are used by marketers to advertise their product and obtain sales leads. These cards are placed in magazines and trade publications. Readers detach and mail in the cards to indicate their interest in the product, expecting literature or a phone call in return. How effective are these cards (called "bingo cards" in the industry) as a marketing tool? Performark, a Minneapolis business that helps companies close on sales leads, attempted to answer this question by responding to 17,000 card-advertisements placed by industrial marketers in a wide variety of trade publications over a 6-year period. Performark kept track of how long it took for each advertiser to respond. A summary of the response times, reported in *Inc.* magazine (July 1995), is given in the table.

Advertiser's Response Time	Percentage
Never responded	21
13–59 days	33
60–120 days	34
More than 120 days	12
Total	100

   a. Describe the variable measured by Performark.
   b. *Inc.* displayed the results in the form of a pie chart. Reconstruct the pie chart from the information given in the table.
   c. How many of the 17,000 advertisers never responded to the sales lead?
   d. Advertisers typically spend at least a million dollars on a reader-response card marketing campaign. Many industrial marketers feel these "bingo cards" are not worth their expense. Does the information in the pie chart, part **b**, support this contention? Explain why or why not. If not, what information can be gleaned from the pie chart to help potential "bingo card" campaigns?

2.6   *Choice* magazine, a publication for the academic community, provides new-book reviews in each issue. Many librarians rely on these reviews to determine which new books to purchase for their library. A thorough study of the contents of the book reviews published in *Choice* was conducted (*Library Acquisitions: Practice and Theory,* Vol. 19, 1995). A random sample of 375 book reviews in American history, geography, and area studies was selected and the "overall opinion" of the book stated in each review was ascertained. Overall opinion was coded as follows: 1 = would not recommend, 2 = cautious or very little recommendation, 3 = little or no preference, 4 = favorable/recommended, 5 = outstanding/significant contribution. A summary of the data is provided in the bar graph on page 34.
   a. Interpret the bar graph.
   b. Comment on the following statement extracted from the study: "A majority (more than 75%) of books reviewed are evaluated favorably and recommended for purchase."

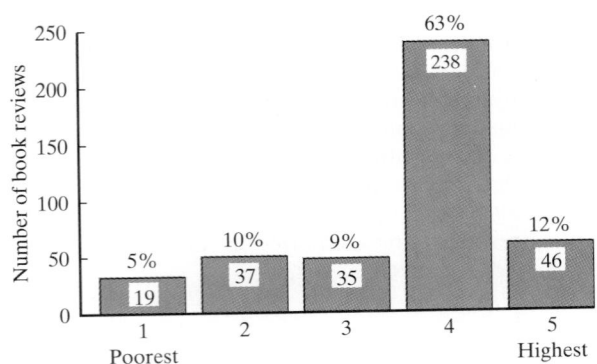

Source: Reprinted from *Library Acquisitions: Practice and Theory,* Vol. 19, No. 2, P. W. Carlo and A. Natowitx, "Choice Book Reviews in American History, Geography, and Area Studies: An Analysis for 1988–1993," p. 159. Copyright 1995, with kind permission from Elsevier Science Ltd, The Boulevard, Langford Lane, Kidlington OX5 1GB, UK.

2.7 The Internet and its World Wide Web provide computer users with a medium for both communication and entertainment. However, many businesses are recognizing the potential of using the Internet for advertising and selling their products. *Inc. Technology* (Sept. 12, 1995) conducted a survey of 2,016 small businesses (fewer than 100 employees) regarding their weekly Internet usage. The survey found 1,855 small businesses that do not use the Internet, 121 that use the Internet from one to five hours per week, and 40 that use the Internet six or more hours per week.

    a. Identify the variable measured in the survey.

    b. Summarize the survey results with a graph.

    c. What portion of the 2,016 small businesses use the Internet on a weekly basis?

2.8 Each week, *USA Today* reports on how much consumers like a major advertising campaign and how effective they think the ad is in helping the company sell its product. The topic of an August 1995 report was the "Obey your thirst" ad campaign for Sprite, a lemon-lime soft drink manufactured by Coca-Cola. A *USA Today*/Harris poll of 1,005 adults, selected nationwide, were asked, "Do you like the campaign?" and "How effective is the campaign?" The results are shown in the graphs below.

    a. What type of graphical method is used to describe the data?

    b. Interpret the results for the question: "Do you like the campaign?"

    c. Interpret the results for the question: "How effective is the campaign?"

2.9 Transgenic plants are plants that have been genetically modified using current gene technology. For example, biologists have recently developed a transgenic tomato with improved storage properties. The *Journal of Experimental Botany* (May 1995) reported on the current level of experimentation with genetically modified plants. Each experiment was identified by its trait. The accompanying bar graph describes the number of approved trials of transgenic plants worldwide, by trait, from 1990–1992.

    a. Estimate the number of transgenic plant trials approved for herbicide tolerance over this period.

    b. Estimate the number of transgenic plant trials approved for developing virus-resistant crops over this period.

    c. Modify the bar graph to show relative frequencies rather than frequencies.

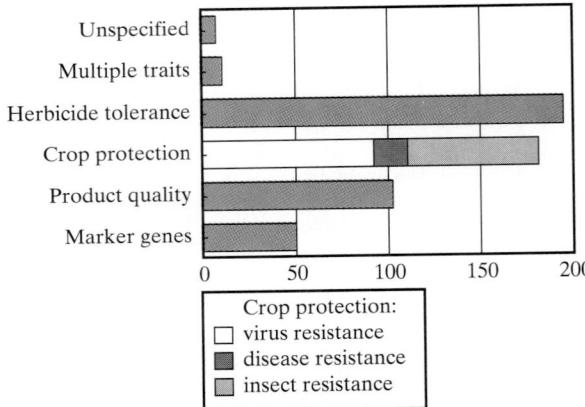

2.10 (X02.010) Owing to several major ocean oil spills by tank vessels, Congress passed the 1990 Oil Pollution Act, which requires all tankers to be designed with thicker hulls. Further improvements

Do you like the campaign?

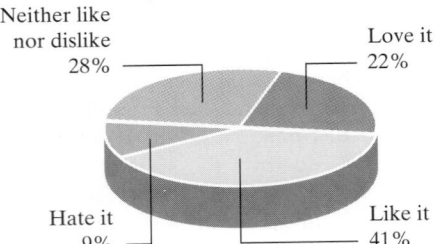

How effective is the campaign?

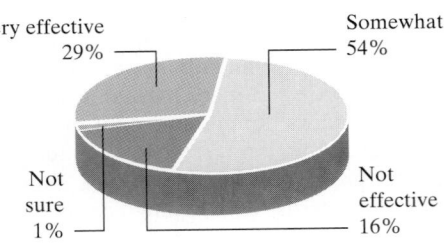

in the structural design of a tank vessel have been implemented since then, each with the objective of reducing the likelihood of an oil spill and decreasing the amount of outflow in the event of hull puncture. To aid in this development, J. C. Daidola reported on the spillage amount and cause of puncture for 50 recent major oil spills from tankers and carriers. The data are reproduced on page 36 (*Marine Technology,* Jan. 1995).

a. Use a graphical method to describe the cause of oil spillage for the 50 tankers.

b. Does the graph, part **a**, suggest that any one cause is more likely to occur than any other? How is this information of value to the design engineers?

2.11 Since opening its doors to Western investors in 1979, the People's Republic of China has been steadily moving toward a market economy. However, because of the considerable political and economic uncertainties in China, Western investors remain uneasy about their investments in China. In 1995 an agency of the Chinese government surveyed 402 foreign investors to assess their concerns with the investment environment.

Each was asked to indicate their most serious concern. The results appear below.

Investor's Concern	Frequency
Communication infrastructure	8
Environmental protection	13
Financial services	14
Government efficiency	30
Inflation rate	233
Labor supply	11
Personal safety	2
Real estate prices	82
Security of personal property	4
Water supply	5

Source: Adapted from *China Marketing News,* No. 26, November 1995.

a. Construct a Pareto diagram for the 10 categories.

b. According to your Pareto diagram, which environmental factors most concern investors?

c. In this case, are 80% of the investors concerned with 20% of the environmental factors as the Pareto principle would suggest? Justify your answer.

2.2   GRAPHICAL METHODS FOR DESCRIBING QUANTITATIVE DATA

Recall from Section 1.5 that quantitative data sets consist of data that are recorded on a meaningful numerical scale. For describing, summarizing, and detecting patterns in such data, we can use three graphical methods: dot plots, stem-and-leaf displays, and histograms.

For example, suppose a financial analyst is interested in the amount of resources spent by computer hardware and software companies on research and development (R&D). She samples 50 of these high-technology firms and calculates the amount each spent last year on R&D as a percentage of their total revenues. The results are given in Table 2.3. As numerical measurements made on the

TABLE 2.3   Percentage of Revenues Spent on Research and Development

Company	Percentage	Company	Percentage	Company	Percentage	Company	Percentage
1	13.5	14	9.5	27	8.2	39	6.5
2	8.4	15	8.1	28	6.9	40	7.5
3	10.5	16	13.5	29	7.2	41	7.1
4	9.0	17	9.9	30	8.2	42	13.2
5	9.2	18	6.9	31	9.6	43	7.7
6	9.7	19	7.5	32	7.2	44	5.9
7	6.6	20	11.1	33	8.8	45	5.2
8	10.6	21	8.2	34	11.3	46	5.6
9	10.1	22	8.0	35	8.5	47	11.7
10	7.1	23	7.7	36	9.4	48	6.0
11	8.0	24	7.4	37	10.5	49	7.8
12	7.9	25	6.5	38	6.9	50	6.5
13	6.8	26	9.5				

Tanker	Spillage (metric tons, thousands)	Collision	Grounding	Fire/ Explosion	Hull Failure	Unknown
Atlantic Empress	257	X				
Castillo De Bellver	239			X		
Amoco Cadiz	221				X	
Odyssey	132			X		
Torrey Canyon	124		X			
Sea Star	123	X				
Hawaiian Patriot	101				X	
Independento	95	X				
Urquiola	91		X			
Irenes Serenade	82			X		
Khark 5	76			X		
Nova	68	X				
Wafra	62		X			
Epic Colocotronis	58		X			
Sinclair Petrolore	57			X		
Yuyo Maru No 10	42	X				
Assimi	50			X		
Andros Patria	48			X		
World Glory	46				X	
British Ambassador	46				X	
Metula	45		X			
Pericles G.C.	44			X		
Mandoil II	41	X				
Jacob Maersk	41		X			
Burmah Agate	41	X				
J. Antonio Lavalleja	38		X			
Napier	37		X			
Exxon Valdez	36		X			
Corinthos	36	X				
Trader	36				X	
St. Peter	33			X		
Gino	32	X				
Golden Drake	32			X		
Ionnis Angelicoussis	32			X		
Chryssi	32				X	
Irenes Challenge	31				X	
Argo Merchant	28		X			
Heimvard	31	X				
Pegasus	25					X
Pacocean	31				X	
Texaco Oklahoma	29				X	
Scorpio	31		X			
Ellen Conway	31		X			
Caribbean Sea	30				X	
Cretan Star	27					X
Grand Zenith	26				X	
Athenian Venture	26			X		
Venoil	26	X				
Aragon	24				X	
Ocean Eagle	21		X			

Source: Daidola, J. C. "Tanker structure behavior during collision and grounding." *Marine Technology*, Vol. 32, No. 1, Jan. 1995, p. 22 (Table 1). Reprinted with permission of The Society of Naval Architects and Marine Engineers (SNAME), 601 Pavonia Ave., Jersey City, NJ 07306, USA, (201) 798-4800. Material appearing in The Society of Naval Architect and Marine Engineers (SNAME) publications cannot be reprinted without obtaining written permission.

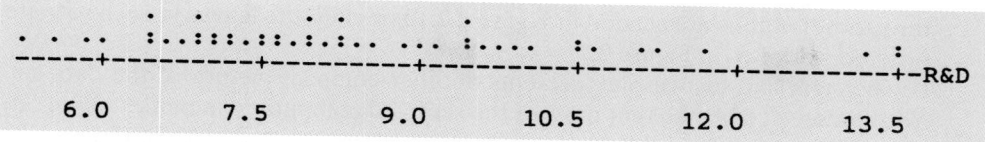

FIGURE 2.6 A MINITAB dot plot for the 50 R&D percentages

sample of 50 units (the firms), these percentages represent quantitative data. The analyst's initial objective is to summarize and describe these data in order to extract relevant information.

A visual inspection of the data indicates some obvious facts. For example, the smallest R&D percentage is 5.2% and the largest is 13.5%. But it is difficult to provide much additional information on the 50 R&D percentages without resorting to some method of summarizing the data. One such method is a dot plot.

DOT PLOTS

A computer generated (MINITAB) **dot plot** for the 50 R&D percentages is shown in Figure 2.6. The horizontal axis of Figure 2.6 is a scale for the quantitative variable, percent. The numerical value of each measurement in the data set is located on the horizontal scale by a dot. When data values repeat, the dots are placed above one another, forming a pile at that particular numerical location. As you can see, this dot plot shows that almost all of the R&D percentages are between 6% and 12%, with most falling between 7% and 9%.

STEM-AND-LEAF DISPLAY

Another graphical representation of these same data, a **stem-and-leaf display**, is shown in Figure 2.7. In this display the *stem* is the portion of the measurement (percentage) to the left of the decimal point, while the remaining portion to the right of the decimal point is the *leaf*.

The stems for the data set are listed in a column from the smallest (5) to the largest (13). Then the leaf for each observation is recorded in the row of the display corresponding to the observation's stem. For example, the leaf 5 of the first observation (13.5) in Table 2.3 is written in the row corresponding to the stem 13. Similarly, the leaf 4 for the second observation (8.4) in Table 2.3 is recorded in the row corresponding to the stem 8, while the leaf 5 for the third observation (10.5) is recorded in the row corresponding to the stem 10. (The leaves for these first

FIGURE 2.7
A stem-and-leaf display for the 50 R&D percentages

Stem	Leaf
5	2 6 9
6	0 5 5 5 6 8 9 9 9
7	1 1 2 2 4 5 5 7 7 8 9
8	0 0 1 2 2 2 4 5 8
9	0 2 4 5 5 6 7 9
10	1 5 5 6
11	1 3 7
12	
13	2 5 5

Key: Leaf units are tenths.

three observations are shaded in Figure 2.7.) Typically, the leaves in each row are ordered as shown in Figure 2.7.

The stem-and-leaf display presents another compact picture of the data set. You can see at a glance that most of the sampled computer companies (37 of 50) spent between 6.0% and 9.9% of their revenues on R&D, and 11 of them spent between 7.0% and 7.9%. Relative to the rest of the sampled companies, three spent a high percentage of revenues on R&D—in excess of 13%.

The definitions of the stem and leaf for a data set can be modified to alter the graphical description. For example, suppose we had defined the stem as the tens digit for the R&D percentage data, rather than the ones and tens digits. With this definition, the stems and leaves corresponding to the measurements 13.5 and 8.4 would be as follows:

Stem	Leaf		Stem	Leaf
1	3		0	8

Note that the decimal portion of the numbers has been dropped. Generally, only one digit is displayed in the leaf.

If you look at the data, you'll see why we didn't define the stem this way. All the R&D measurements fall below 13.5, so all the leaves would fall into just two stem rows—1 and 0—in this display. The resulting picture would not be nearly as informative as Figure 2.7.

HISTOGRAMS

A **relative frequency histogram** for these 50 R&D percentages is shown in Figure 2.8. The horizontal axis of Figure 2.8, which gives the percentage spent on R&D for each company, is divided into **intervals** commencing with the interval from (5.15–6.25) and proceeding in intervals of equal size to (12.85–13.95) percent. (The procedure for creating the class intervals will become clear in Example 2.2.) The vertical axis gives the proportion (or **relative frequency**) of the 50 percentages that fall in each interval. Thus, you can see that nearly a third of the companies spent between 7.35% and 8.45% of their revenues on research and development. This interval contains the highest relative frequency, and the intervals tend to contain a smaller fraction of the measurements as R&D percentage gets smaller or larger.

By summing the relative frequencies in the intervals 6.25–7.35, 7.35–8.45, 8.45–9.55, 9.55–10.65, you can see that 80% of the R&D percentages are between 6.25 and 10.65. Similarly, only 6% of the computer companies spent over 12.85

FIGURE 2.8
Histogram for the 50 computer companies' R&D percentages

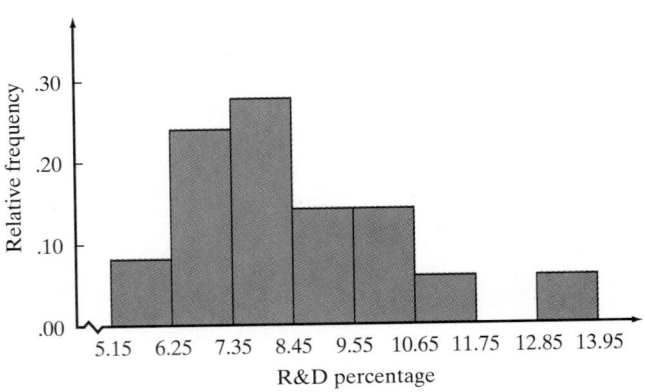

TABLE 2.4   Measurement Classes, Frequencies, and Relative Frequencies for the R&D Percentage Data

Class	Measurement Class	Class Frequency	Class Relative Frequency
1	5.15–6.25	4	$4/50 = .08$
2	6.25–7.35	12	$12/50 = .24$
3	7.35–8.45	14	$14/50 = .28$
4	8.45–9.55	7	$7/50 = .14$
5	9.55–10.65	7	$7/50 = .14$
6	10.65–11.75	3	$3/50 = .06$
7	11.75–12.85	0	$0/50 = .00$
8	12.85–13.95	3	$3/50 = .06$
Totals		50	1.00

percent of their revenues on R&D. Many other summary statements can be made by further study of the histogram.

Dot plots, stem-and-leaf displays, and histograms all provide useful graphic descriptions of quantitative data. Since most statistical software packages can be used to construct these displays, we will focus on their interpretation rather than their construction.

Histograms can be used to display either the frequency or relative frequency of the measurements falling into specified intervals known as **measurement classes**. The measurement classes, frequencies, and relative frequencies for the R&D percentage data are shown in Table 2.4.

By looking at a histogram (say, the relative frequency histogram in Figure 2.8), you can see two important facts. First, note the total area under the histogram and then note the proportion of the total area that falls over a particular interval of the horizontal axis. You'll see that the proportion of the total area above an interval is equal to the relative frequency of measurements falling in the interval. For example, the relative frequency for the class interval 7.35–8.45 is .28. Consequently, the rectangle above the interval contains .28 of the total area under the histogram.

Second, you can imagine the appearance of the relative frequency histogram for a very large set of data (say, a population). As the number of measurements in a data set is increased, you can obtain a better description of the data by decreasing the width of the class intervals. When the class intervals become small enough, a relative frequency histogram will (for all practical purposes) appear as a smooth curve (see Figure 2.9).

While histograms provide good visual descriptions of data sets—particularly very large data ones—they do not let us identify individual measurements. In contrast, each of the original measurements is visible to some extent in a dot plot and clearly visible in a stem-and-leaf display. The stem-and-leaf display arranges

FIGURE 2.9
Effect of the size of a data set on the outline of a histogram

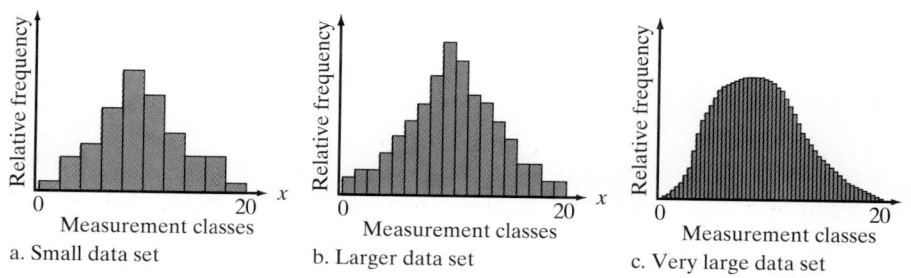

a. Small data set   b. Larger data set   c. Very large data set

the data in ascending order, so it's easy to locate the individual measurements. For example, in Figure 2.7 we can easily see that three of the R&D measurements are equal to 8.2, but we can't see that fact by inspecting the histogram in Figure 2.8. However, stem-and-leaf displays can become unwieldy for very large data sets. A very large number of stems and leaves causes the vertical and horizontal dimensions of the display to become cumbersome, diminishing the usefulness of the visual display.

EXAMPLE 2.2

A manufacturer of industrial wheels suspects that profitable orders are being lost because of the long time the firm takes to develop price quotes for potential customers. To investigate this possibility, 50 requests for price quotes were randomly selected from the set of all quotes made last year, and the processing time was determined for each quote. The processing times are displayed in Table 2.5, and each quote was classified according to whether the order was "lost" or not (i.e., whether or not the customer placed an order after receiving a price quote).

a. Use a statistical software package to create a frequency histogram for these data. Then shade the area under the histogram that corresponds to lost orders.

b. Use a statistical software package to create a stem-and-leaf display for these data. Then shade each leaf of the display that corresponds to a lost order.

c. Compare and interpret the two graphical displays of these data.

SOLUTION

a. We used SAS to generate the frequency histogram in Figure 2.10. SAS, like most statistical software, offers the user the choice of accepting default class

TABLE 2.5   Price Quote Processing Time (Days)

Request Number	Processing Time	Lost?	Request Number	Processing Time	Lost?
1	2.36	No	26	3.34	No
2	5.73	No	27	6.00	No
3	6.60	No	28	5.92	No
4	10.05	Yes	29	7.28	Yes
5	5.13	No	30	1.25	No
6	1.88	No	31	4.01	No
7	2.52	No	32	7.59	No
8	2.00	No	33	13.42	Yes
9	4.69	No	34	3.24	No
10	1.91	No	35	3.37	No
11	6.75	Yes	36	14.06	Yes
12	3.92	No	37	5.10	No
13	3.46	No	38	6.44	No
14	2.64	No	39	7.76	No
15	3.63	No	40	4.40	No
16	3.44	No	41	5.48	No
17	9.49	Yes	42	7.51	No
18	4.90	No	43	6.18	No
19	7.45	No	44	8.22	Yes
20	20.23	Yes	45	4.37	No
21	3.91	No	46	2.93	No
22	1.70	No	47	9.95	Yes
23	16.29	Yes	48	4.46	No
24	5.52	No	49	14.32	Yes
25	1.44	No	50	9.01	No

FIGURE 2.10
SAS frequency histogram for the quote processing time data

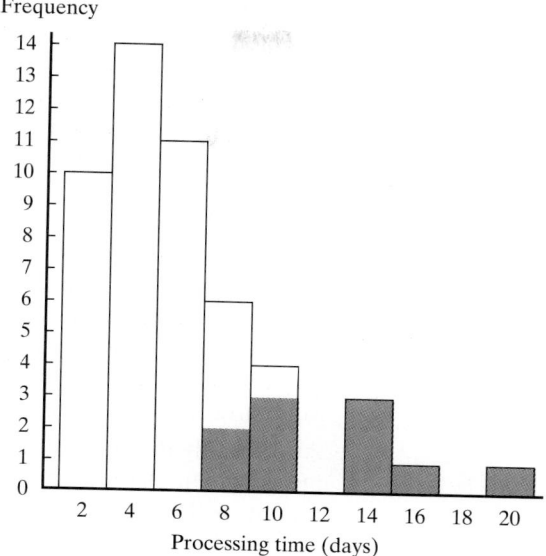

intervals and interval widths, or the user can make his or her own selections. After some experimenting with various numbers of class intervals and interval widths, we used 10 intervals. SAS then created intervals of width 2 days, beginning at 1 day, just below the smallest measurement of 1.25 days, and ending with 21 days, just above the largest measurement of 20.2 days. Note that SAS labels the midpoint of each bar, rather than its endpoints. Thus, the bar labeled "2" represents measurements from 1.00 to 2.99, the bar labeled "4" represents measurements from 3.00 to 4.99, etc. This histogram clearly shows the clustering of the measurements in the lower end of the distribution (between approximately 1 and 7 days), and the relatively few measurements in the upper end of the distribution (greater than 12 days). The shading of the area of the frequency histogram corresponding to lost orders clearly indicates that they lie in the upper tail of the distribution.

b. We used SPSS to generate the stem-and-leaf display in Figure 2.11. Note that the stem consists of the number of whole days (units and tens digits),

FIGURE 2.11
SPSS stem-and-leaf display for the quote processing time data

```
Frequency        Stem & Leaf
    5.00            1 .  24789
    5.00            2 .  03569
    8.00            3 .  23344699
    6.00            4 .  034469
    6.00            5 .  114579
    5.00            6 .  01467
    5.00            7 .  24557
    1.00            8 .  2
    3.00            9 .  049
    1.00           10 .  0
     .00           11 .
     .00           12 .
    1.00           13 .  4
    4.00 Extremes        (14.1), (14.3), (16.3), (20.2)
Stem width:        1.00
Each leaf:            1 case(s)
```

and the leaf is the tenths digit (first digit after the decimal) of each measurement.* The hundredths digit has been dropped to make the display more visually effective. SPSS also includes a column titled **Frequency** showing the number of measurements corresponding to each stem. Note, too, that instead of extending the stems all the way to 20 days to show the largest measurement, SPSS truncates the display after the stem corresponding to 13 days, labels the largest four measurements (shaded) as **Extremes**, and simply lists them horizontally in the last row of the display. Extreme observations that are detached from the remainder of the data are called **outliers**, and they usually receive special attention in statistical analyses. Although outliers may represent legitimate measurements, they are frequently mistakes: incorrectly recorded, miscoded during data entry, or taken from a population different from the one from which the rest of the sample was selected. Stem-and-leaf displays are useful for identifying outliers.

c. As is usually the case for data sets that are not too large (say, fewer than 100 measurements), the stem-and-leaf display provides more detail than the histogram without being unwieldy. For instance, the stem-and-leaf display in Figure 2.11 clearly indicates not only that the lost orders are associated with high processing times (as does the histogram in Figure 2.10), but also exactly which of the times correspond to lost orders. Histograms are most useful for displaying very large data sets, when the overall shape of the distribution of measurements is more important than the identification of individual measurements. Nevertheless, the message of both graphical displays is clear: establishing processing time limits may well result in fewer lost orders.   ▟

*In the examples in this section, the stem was formed from the digits to the left of the decimal. This is not always the case. For example, in the following data set the stems could be the tenths digit and the leaves the hundredths digit: .12, .15, .22, .25, .28, .33.

EXERCISES   2.12–2.25

Note: Exercises marked with 💾 contain data available for computer analysis on a 3.5" disk (file name in parentheses).

Learning the Mechanics

2.12 Graph the relative frequency histogram for the 500 measurements summarized in the accompanying relative frequency table.

Measurement Class	Relative Frequency
.5–2.5	.10
2.5–4.5	.15
4.5–6.5	.25
6.5–8.5	.20
8.5–10.5	.05
10.5–12.5	.10
12.5–14.5	.10
14.5–16.5	.05

2.13 Refer to Exercise 2.12. Calculate the number of the 500 measurements falling into each of the

measurement classes. Then graph a frequency histogram for these data.

2.14 SAS was used to generate the stem-and-leaf display shown here. Note that SAS arranges the stems in descending order.

Stem	Leaf
5	1
4	4 5 7
3	0 0 0 3 6
2	1 1 3 4 5 9 9
1	2 2 4 8
0	0 1 2

a. How many observations were in the original data set?
b. In the bottom row of the stem-and-leaf display, identify the stem, the leaves, and the numbers in the original data set represented by this stem and its leaves.

c. Re-create all the numbers in the data set and construct a dot plot.

2.15 MINITAB was used to generate the following histogram:

MIDDLE OF INTERVAL	NUMBER OF OBSERVATIONS	
20	1	*
22	3	***
24	2	**
26	3	***
28	4	****
30	7	*******
32	11	***********
34	6	******
36	2	**
38	3	***
40	3	***
42	2	**
44	1	*
46	1	*

a. Is this a frequency histogram or a relative frequency histogram? Explain.

b. How many measurement classes were used in the construction of this histogram?

c. How many measurements are there in the data set described by this histogram?

2.16 The graph summarizes the scores obtained by 100 students on a questionnaire designed to measure managerial ability. (Scores are integer values that range from 0 to 20. A high score indicates a high level of ability.)

a. Which measurement class contains the highest proportion of test scores?

b. What proportion of the scores lie between 3.5 and 5.5?

c. What proportion of the scores are higher than 11.5?

d. How many students scored less than 5.5?

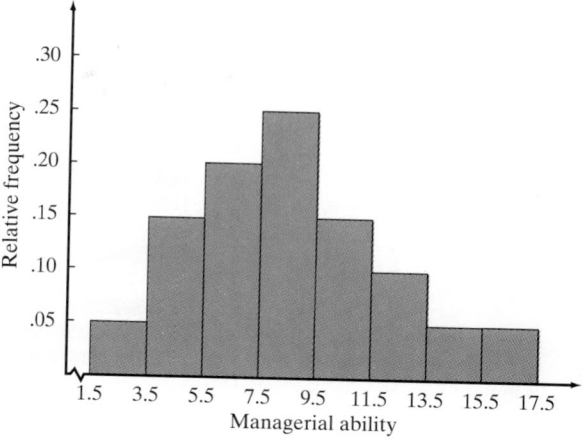

Applying the Concepts

2.17 (X02.017) Bonds can be issued by the federal government, state and local governments, and U.S. corporations. A *mortgage bond* is a promissory note in which the issuing company pledges certain real assets as security in exchange for a specified amount of money. A *debenture* is an unsecured promissory note, backed only by the general credit of the issuer. The bond price of either a mortgage bond or debenture is negotiated between the asked price (the lowest price anyone will accept) and the bid price (the highest price anyone wants to pay). (Alexander, Sharpe, and Bailey, *Fundamentals of Investments,* 1993.) The accompanying table contains the bid prices on May 31, 1996, for a sample of 30 publicly traded bonds issued by utility companies.

a. A frequency histogram was generated using SPSS and is shown on page 44. Note that SPSS labels the midpoint of each measurement class

Utility Company	Bid Price
Gulf States Utilities	$102\frac{3}{8}$
Northern States Power	$99\frac{1}{2}$
Indiana Gas	$102\frac{7}{8}$
Appalachian Power	$97\frac{3}{8}$
Empire Gas Corp.	70
Wisconsin Electric Power	$87\frac{1}{4}$
Pennsylvania Electric	$99\frac{7}{8}$
Commonwealth Edison	$89\frac{1}{8}$
El Paso Natural Gas	$105\frac{1}{4}$
Montana Power Co.	$100\frac{3}{8}$
Elizabethtown Water	$103\frac{5}{8}$
Tennessee Gas Pipeline	$82\frac{1}{2}$
Western Mass. Electric	$99\frac{5}{8}$
Carolina P&L	$99\frac{7}{8}$
Hartford Electric Lt.	$100\frac{1}{8}$

Utility Company	Bid Price
Indiana & Michigan Electric	$100\frac{1}{8}$
Toledo Edison Co.	$92\frac{7}{8}$
Dayton Power and Light	$99\frac{1}{2}$
Atlantic City Electric	$100\frac{3}{8}$
Long Island Lighting	$91\frac{5}{8}$
Portland General Electric	100
Boston Gas	$102\frac{7}{8}$
Duquesne Light Co.	73
General Electric Co.	$93\frac{1}{8}$
Ohio Power Co.	$99\frac{7}{8}$
Texas Utilities Electric	$100\frac{5}{8}$
Central Power and Light	$100\frac{1}{8}$
Boston Edison	$99\frac{3}{8}$
Philadelphia Electric	99
Colorado Interstate Gas	$114\frac{1}{4}$

Source: Bond Guide (a publication of the Standard & Poor Corporation), June 1996.

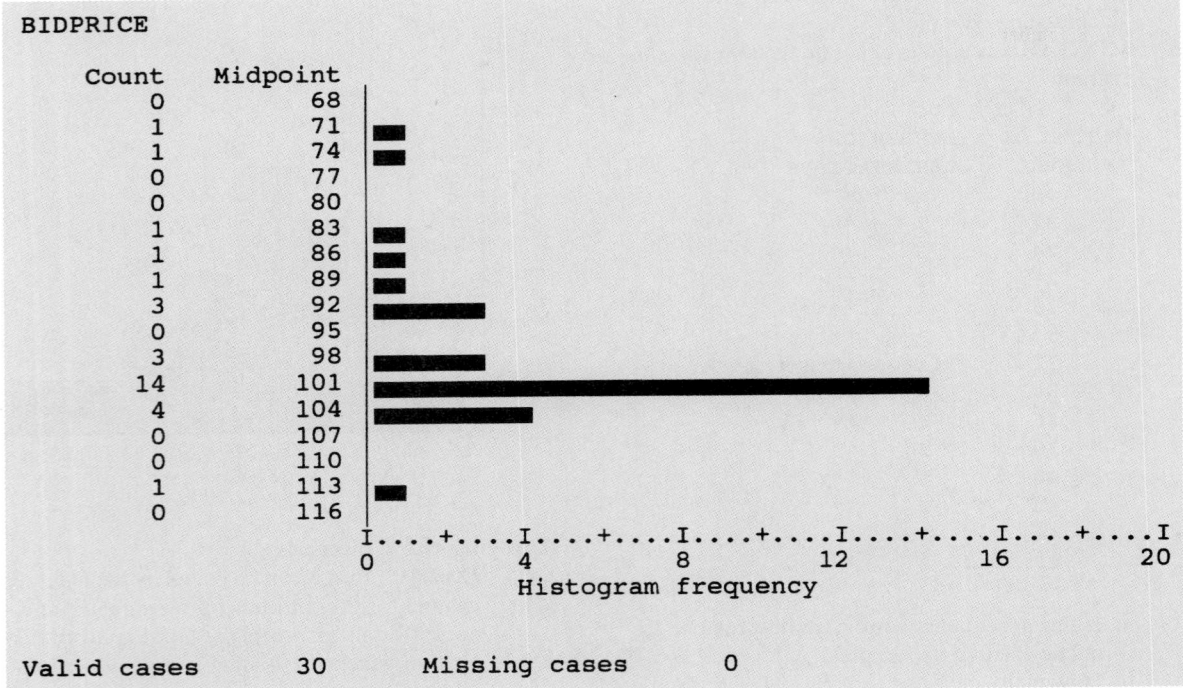

BIDPRICE

Count	Midpoint
0	68
1	71
1	74
0	77
0	80
1	83
1	86
1	89
3	92
0	95
3	98
14	101
4	104
0	107
0	110
1	113
0	116

Histogram frequency

Valid cases   30   Missing cases   0

rather than the two endpoints, and plots the bars horizontally rather than vertically. Interpret the histogram.

b. Use the histogram to determine the number of bonds in the sample that had a bid price greater than $96.50. What proportion of the total number of bonds is this group?

c. Shade the area under the histogram that corresponds to the proportion in part **b**.

2.18 Production processes may be classified as *make-to-stock processes* or *make-to-order processes*. Make-to-stock processes are designed to produce a standardized product that can be sold to customers from the firm's inventory. Make-to-order processes are designed to produce products according to customer specifications. The McDonald's and Burger King fast-food chains are classic examples of these two types of processes. McDonald's produces and stocks standardized hamburgers; Burger King—whose slogan is "Your way, right away"—makes hamburgers according to the ingredients specified by the customer (Schroeder, *Operations Management,* 1993). In general, performance of make-to-order processes is measured by delivery time—the time from receipt of an order until the product is delivered to the customer. The following data set is a sample of delivery times (in days) for a particular make-to-order firm last year. The delivery times marked

by an asterisk are associated with customers who subsequently placed additional orders with the firm.

50* 64* 56* 43* 64* 82* 65* 49* 32* 63* 44* 71
54* 51* 102 49* 73* 50* 39* 86   33* 95   59* 51*
68

The MINITAB stem-and-leaf display of these data is shown here.

```
Stem-and-leaf of Time        N = 25
Leaf Unit = 1.0

         3      3 239
         7      4 3499
        (7)     5 0011469
        11      6 34458
         6      7 13
         4      8 26
         2      9 5
         1     10 2
```

a. Circle the individual leaves that are associated with customers who did not place a subsequent order.

b. Concerned that they are losing potential repeat customers because of long delivery times, the management would like to establish a guideline for the maximum tolerable delivery time. Using the stem-and-leaf display, suggest a guideline. Explain your reasoning.

Company Identification Number	Penalty	Law*
01	$ 930,000	CERCLA
02	10,000	CWA
03	90,600	CAA
04	123,549	CWA
05	37,500	CWA
06	137,500	CWA
07	2,500	SDWA
08	1,000,000	CWA
09	25,000	CAA
09	25,000	CAA
10	25,000	CWA
10	25,000	RCRA
11	19,100	CAA
12	100,000	CWA
12	30,000	CWA
13	35,000	CAA
13	43,000	CWA
14	190,000	CWA
15	15,000	CWA

Company Identification Number	Penalty	Law*
16	90,000	RCRA
17	20,000	CWA
18	40,000	CWA
19	20,000	CWA
20	40,000	CWA
21	850,000	CWA
22	35,000	CWA
23	4,000	CAA
24	25,000	CWA
25	40,000	CWA
26	30,000	CAA
27	15,000	CWA
28	15,000	CAA
29	105,000	CAA
30	20,000	CWA
31	400,000	CWA
32	85,000	CWA
33	300,000	CWA/RCRA/CERCLA
34	30,000	CWA

*CAA: Clean Air Act; CERCLA: Comprehensive Environmental Response, Compensation, and Libility Act; CWA: Clean Water Act; RCRA: Resource Conservation and Recovery Act; SDWA: Safe Drinking Water Act.

Source: Tabor, R. H., and Stanwick, S. D. "Arkansas: An environmental perspective." *Arkansas Business and Economic Review,* Vol. 28, No. 2, Summer 1995, pp. 22–32 (Table 4).

2.19 **(X02.019)** Any corporation doing business in the United States must be aware of and obey both federal and state environmental regulations. Failure to do so may result in irreparable damage to the environment and costly financial penalties to guilty corporations. Of the 55 civil actions filed against corporations within the state of Arkansas by the U.S. Department of Justice on behalf of the Environmental Protection Agency, 38 resulted in financial penalties. These penalties along with the laws that were violated are listed in the table above. (*Note:* Some companies were involved in more than one civil action.)

a. Construct a stem-and-leaf display for all 38 penalties.

b. Circle the individual leaves that are associated with penalties imposed for violations of the Clean Air Act.

c. What does the pattern of circles in part **b** suggest about the severity of the penalties imposed for Clean Air Act violations relative to the other types of violations reported in the table? Explain.

2.20 **(X02.020)** In a manufacturing plant a *work center* is a specific production facility that consists of one or more people and/or machines and is treated as one unit for the purposes of capacity requirements planning and job scheduling. If jobs arrive at a particular work center at a faster rate than they depart, the work center impedes the overall production process and is referred to as a *bottleneck* (Fogarty, Blackstone, and Hoffmann, *Production and Inventory Management,* 1991). The data in the table below were collected by an operations manager for use in investigating a potential bottleneck work center.

MINITAB dot plots for the two sets of data are shown at the top of page 46. Do the dot plots suggest that the work center may be a bottleneck? Explain.

Number of Items Arriving at Work Center per Hour											
155	115	156	150	159	163	172	143	159	166	148	175
151	161	138	148	129	135	140	152	139			

Number of Items Departing at Work Center per Hour											
156	109	127	148	135	119	140	127	115	122	99	106
171	123	135	125	107	152	111	137	161			

```
              .           .     . .:  .    :..:  .. . :. . .   . .    . .
    -----+---------+---------+---------+---------+---------+-ARRIVE

         .     : . .    .   . ... :       :. .       . .    . .    .        .
    -----+---------+---------+---------+---------+---------+-DEPART
        105       120       135       150       165       180
```

2.21 **(X02.021)** The ability to fill a customer's order on time depends on being able to estimate how long it will take to produce the product in question. In most production processes, the time required to complete a particular task will be shorter each time the task is undertaken and, in most cases, the task time will decrease at a decreasing rate. Thus, in order to estimate how long it will take to produce a particular product, a manufacturer may want to study the relationship between production time per unit and the number of units that have been produced. The line or curve characterizing this relationship is called a *learning curve* (Adler and Clark, *Management Science,* Mar. 1991). Twenty-five employees, all of whom were performing the same production task for the tenth time, were observed. Each person's task completion time (in minutes) was recorded. The same 25 employees were observed again the 30th time they performed the same task and the 50th time they performed the task. The resulting completion times are shown in the table at right.

a. Use a statistical software package to construct a frequency histogram for each of the three data sets.

b. Compare the histograms. Does it appear that the relationship between task completion time and the number of times the task is performed is in agreement with the observations noted above about production processes in general? Explain.

2.22 **(X02.022)** Financially distressed firms can gain protection from their creditors while they restructure by filing for protection under U.S. Bankruptcy Codes. In a *prepackaged bankruptcy,* a firm negotiates a reorganization plan with its creditors prior to filing for bankruptcy. This can result in a much quicker exit from bankruptcy than traditional bankruptcy filings. Brian Betker conducted a study of 49 prepackaged bankruptcies that were filed between 1986 and 1993 and reported the results in *Financial Management* (Spring 1995). The table at the top of page 47 lists the time in bankruptcy (in months) for these 49 companies. The table also lists the results of a vote by each company's board of directors concerning their preferred reorgani-

| | PERFORMANCE | | |
Employee	10th	30th	50th
1	15	16	10
2	21	10	5
3	30	12	7
4	17	9	9
5	18	7	8
6	22	11	11
7	33	8	12
8	41	9	9
9	10	5	7
10	14	15	6
11	18	10	8
12	25	11	14
13	23	9	9
14	19	11	8
15	20	10	10
16	22	13	8
17	20	12	7
18	19	8	8
19	18	20	6
20	17	7	5
21	16	6	6
22	20	9	4
23	22	10	15
24	19	10	7
25	24	11	20

zation plan. (*Note:* "Joint" = joint exchange offer with prepackaged bankruptcy solicitation; "Prepack" = prepackaged bankruptcy solicitation only; "None" = no pre-filing vote held.)

a. Construct a stem-and-leaf display for the length of time in bankruptcy for all 49 companies.

b. Summarize the information reflected in the stem-and-leaf display, part **a**. Make a general statement about the length of time in bankruptcy for firms using "prepacks."

c. Select a graphical technique that will permit a comparison of the time-in-bankruptcy distributions for the three types of "prepack" firms: those who held no pre-filing vote; those who voted their preference for a joint solution; and those who voted their preference for a prepack.

d. The companies that were reorganized through a leveraged buyout are identified by an aster-

Company	Pre-filing Votes	Time in Bankruptcy (months)
AM International	None	3.9
Anglo Energy	Prepack	1.5
Arizona Biltmore*	Prepack	1.0
Astrex	None	10.1
Barry's Jewelers	None	4.1
Calton	Prepack	1.9
Cencor	Joint	1.4
Charter Medical*	Prepack	1.3
Cherokee*	Joint	1.2
Circle Express	Prepack	4.1
Cook Inlet Comm.	Prepack	1.1
Crystal Oil	None	3.0
Divi Hotels	None	3.2
Edgell Comm.*	Prepack	1.0
Endevco	Prepack	3.8
Gaylord Container	Joint	1.2
Great Amer. Comm.*	Prepack	1.0
Hadson	Prepack	1.5
In-Store Advertising	Prepack	1.0
JPS Textiles*	Prepack	1.4
Kendall*	Prepack	1.2
Kinder-Care	None	4.2
Kroy*	Prepack	3.0
Ladish*	Joint	1.5
LaSalle Energy*	Prepack	1.6

Company	Pre-filing Votes	Time in Bankruptcy (months)
LIVE Entertainment	Joint	1.4
Mayflower Group*	Prepack	1.4
Memorex Telex*	Prepack	1.1
Munsingwear	None	2.9
Nat'l Environmental	Joint	5.2
Petrolane Gas	Prepack	1.2
Price Communications	None	2.4
Republic Health*	Joint	4.5
Resorts Int'l*	None	7.8
Restaurant Enterprises*	Prepack	1.5
Rymer Foods	Joint	2.1
SCI TV*	Prepack	2.1
Southland*	Joint	3.9
Specialty Equipment*	None	2.6
SPI Holdings*	Joint	1.4
Sprouse-Reitz	Prepack	1.4
Sunshine Metals	Joint	5.4
TIE/Communications	None	2.4
Trump Plaza	Prepack	1.7
Trump Taj Mahal	Prepack	1.4
Trump's Castle	Prepack	2.7
USG	Prepack	1.2
Vyquest	Prepack	4.1
West Point Acq.*	Prepack	2.9

*Leveraged buyout.

Source: Betker, B. L. "An empirical examination of prepackaged bankruptcy." *Financial Management,* Vol. 24, No. 1, Spring 1995, p. 6 (Table 2).

isk (*) in the table. Identify these firms on the stem-and-leaf display, part **a**, by circling their bankruptcy times. Do you observe any pattern in the graph? Explain.

2.23 **(X02.023)** While producing many economic benefits to the state of Florida, gypsum and phosphate mines also produce a harmful by-product: radiation. It has been known for a number of years that the mine tailings (waste) contain radioactive radon 222. In fact, new housing complexes built over the leveled piles of residue have shown disturbing radiation levels within the houses. The radiation levels in waste gypsum and phosphate mounds in Polk County, Florida, are regularly monitored by the Eastern Environmental Radiation Facility (EERF) and by the Polk County Health Department (PCHD), Winter Haven, Florida. The table below lists the measurements of the exhalation rate (a measure of radiation) of soil samples taken on waste piles in Polk County, Florida. They represent part of the data contained in a report by Thomas R. Horton of EERF.

SPSS was used to generate the first stem-and-leaf printout at the top of page 48. [*Note:* To save space, SPSS places the leaves for two consecutive stems into a single stem row.]

a. Interpret the display. Which digit(s) was used for the stem and which for the leaf? Find the largest measurement in the data set and locate it in the display.

b. Note that the presence of a measurement well removed from the main body of data somewhat distorts the display, since most of the data

Exhalation Rate of Soil Samples

1,709.79	4,132.28	2,996.49	2,796.42	3,750.83	961.40	1,096.43	1,774.77
357.17	1,489.86	2,367.40	11,968.23	178.99	5,402.35	2,315.52	2,617.57
1,150.94	3,017.48	599.84	2,758.84	3,764.96	1,888.22	2,055.20	205.84
1,572.69	393.55	538.37	1,830.78	878.56	6,815.69	752.89	1,977.97
558.33	880.84	2,770.23	1,426.57	1,322.76	1,480.04	9,139.21	1,698.39

Source: Horton, T. R. "A preliminary radiological assessment of radon exhalation from phosphate gypsum piles and inactive uranium mill tailings piles." EPA–520/5–79–004. Washington D.C.: Environmental Protection Agency, 1979.

```
Stem-and-leaf display for variable . . EXHLRATE
    0 . 22445668990123455677889
    2 . 013468880088
    4 . 14
    6 . 8
    8 . 1
   10 .
   12 . 0
```

```
Stem-and-leaf display for variable . . EXHLRATE
    0 . 2244566899
    1 . 0123455677889
    2 . 01346888
    3 . 0088
    4 . 1
    5 . 4
    6 . 8
    7 .
    8 .
    9 . 1
```

set is compressed into a small portion of it. The largest measurement was removed from the data set, and a new SPSS stem-and-leaf display was generated, the second printout shown above. Interpret this display, identifying the stem and leaf used. Using both displays, give a verbal description of the data.

2.24 It's not uncommon for hearing aids to malfunction and cancel the desired signal. *IEEE Transactions on Speech and Audio Processing* (May 1995) reported on a new audio processing system designed to limit the amount of signal can-

cellation that may occur. The system utilizes a mathematical equation that involves a variable, V, called a *sufficient norm constraint*. A histogram for realizations of V, produced using simulation, is shown below.

a. Estimate the percentage of realizations of V with values ranging from .425 to .675.

b. Cancellation of the desired signal is limited by selecting a norm constraint V. Find the value of V for a company that wants to market the new hearing aid so that only 10% of the realizations have values below the selected level.

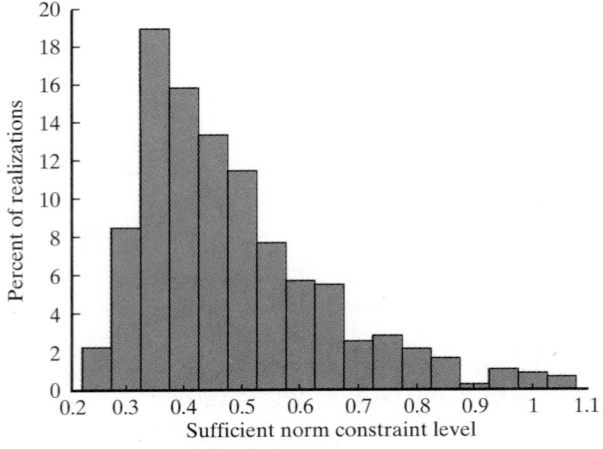

Source: Hoffman, M. W., and Buckley, K. M. "Robust time-domain processing of broadband microphone array data." *IEEE Transactions on Speech and Audio Processing*, Vol. 3, No. 3, May 1995, p. 199 (Figure 4). © 1995 IEEE.

2.25 **(X02.025)** Typically, the more attractive a corporate common stock is to an investor, the higher the stock's price-earnings (P/E) ratio. For example, if investors expect the stock's future earnings per share to increase, the price of the stock will be bid up and a high P/E ratio will result. Thus, the level of a stock's P/E ratio is a function of both the current financial performance of the firm and an investor's expectation of future performance. The table contains samples of P/E ratios from manufacturing firms and holding companies for the last day of March 1996.

a. Compare the P/E ratio distributions of manufacturing and holding firms using a graphical method.

b. What do your graphs suggest about the level of the P/E ratios of firms in the manufacturing business as compared to firms in the holding business? Explain.

MANUFACTURING FIRMS		HOLDING COMPANIES	
Company	P/E Ratio	Company	P/E Ratio
Block Drug	9	EMC Ins. Group	8
Daig Corp.	38	First Essex Bancorp	9
Modtech Inc.	31	MLG Bancorp	14
Guest Supply	16	State Auto Financial	10
Astro Systems Inc.	36	Boston Bancorp	6
Fischer Imaging	33	Cellular Communications	48
Casino Data Systems	74	Anderson Group	5
Data Key Inc.	69	Provident Bancorp	12
Network Peripherals	23	Pubco Corp.	4
Brenco, Inc.	12	Condor Services	16
Day Runner	16	Eselco Inc.	16
Safeskin Corp.	16	Mesaba	2
Marisa Christina	14	Keystone Financial	13
Merix Corp.	17	JSB Financial	16
Cognex Corp.	39	Argonaut Group	14
FLIR Systems	17	ONBANCorp	12
Stant Corp	11	Great Amer. Mgmt. Invst.	3
Grief Bros. Corp.	13	CPB, Inc.	12
Computer Identics	37	GBC Bancorp	18
PRI Automation	14	California Bancshares	16

Source: Standard & Poor's NASDAQ and Regional Exchange Profiles, Mar. 1996.

2.3   THE TIME SERIES PLOT (OPTIONAL)

Each of the previous sections has been concerned with describing the information contained in a sample or population of data. Often these data are viewed as having been produced at essentially the same point in time. Thus, time has not been a factor in any of the graphical methods described so far.

Data of interest to managers are often produced and monitored over time. Examples include the daily closing price of their company's common stock, the company's weekly sales volume and quarterly profits, and characteristics—such as weight and length—of products produced by the company.

DEFINITION 2.4

Data that are produced and monitored over time are called **time series data**.

Recall from Section 1.4 that a process is a series of actions or operations that generates output over time. Accordingly, measurements taken of a sequence of units produced by a process—such as a production process—are time series data. In general, any sequence of numbers produced over time can be thought of as being generated by a process.

When measurements are made over time, it is important to record both the numerical value and the time or the time period associated with each measurement. With this information a **time series plot**—sometimes called a **run chart**—can be constructed to describe the time series data and to learn about the process that

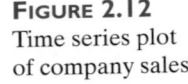

FIGURE 2.12
Time series plot
of company sales

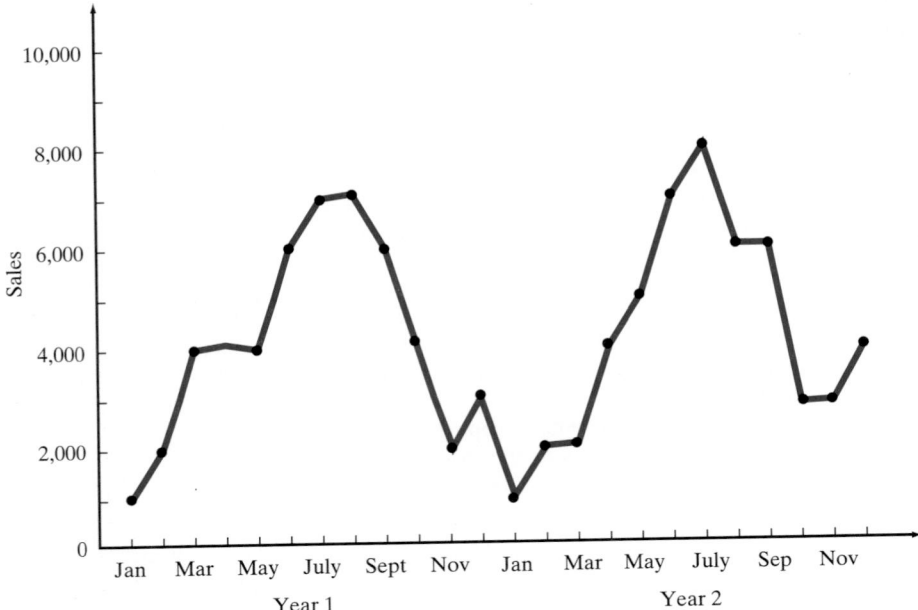

generated the data. A time series plot is a graph of the measurements (on the vertical axis) plotted against time or against the order in which the measurements were made (on the horizontal axis). The plotted points are usually connected by straight lines to make it easier to see the changes and movement in the measurements over time. For example, Figure 2.12 is a time series plot of a particular company's monthly sales (number of units sold per month). And Figure 2.13 is a time series plot of the weights of 30 one-gallon paint cans that were consecutively filled by the same filling head. Notice that the weights are plotted against the

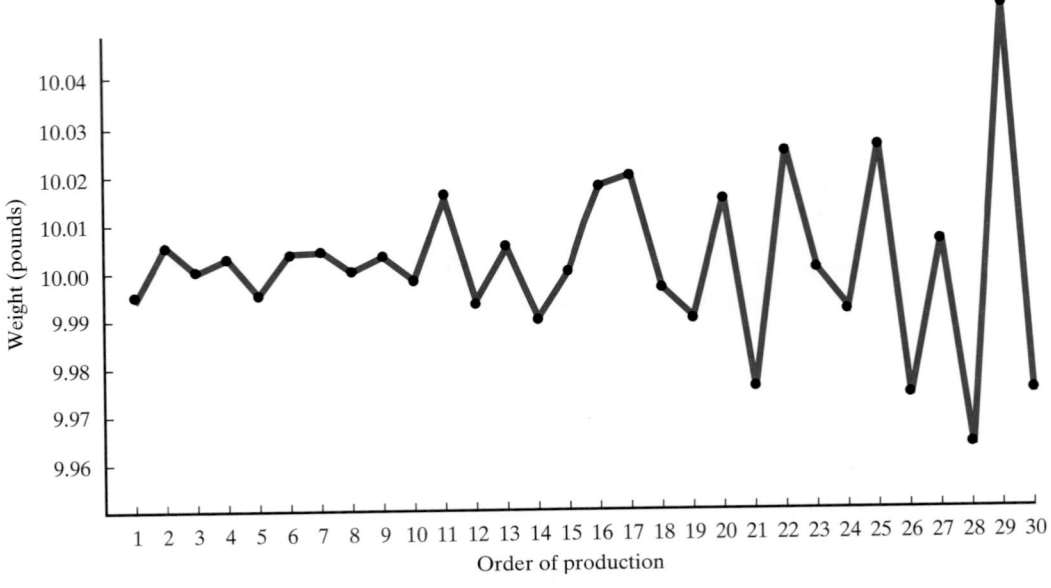

FIGURE 2.13   Time series plot of paint can weights

order in which the cans were filled rather than some unit of time. When monitoring production processes, it is often more convenient to record the order rather than the exact time at which each measurement was made.

Time series plots reveal the movement (trend) and changes (variation) in the variable being monitored. Notice how sales trend upward in the summer and how the variation in the weights of the paint cans increases over time. This kind of information would not be revealed by stem-and-leaf displays or histograms, as the following example illustrates.

EXAMPLE 2.3

W. Edwards Deming was one of America's most famous statisticians. He was best known for the role he played after World War II in teaching the Japanese how to improve the quality of their products by monitoring and continually improving their production processes. In his book *Out of the Crisis* (1986), Deming warned against the knee-jerk (i.e., automatic) use of histograms to display and extract information from data. As evidence he offered the following example.

Fifty camera springs were tested in the order in which they were produced. The elongation of each spring was measured under the pull of 20 grams. Both a time series plot and a histogram were constructed from the measurements. They are shown in Figure 2.14, which has been reproduced from Deming's book. If you had to predict the elongation measurement of the next spring to be produced (i.e., spring 51) and could use only one of the two plots to guide your prediction, which would you use? Why?

SOLUTION

Only the time series plot describes the behavior *over time* of the process that produces the springs. The fact that the elongation measurements are decreasing over time can only be gleaned from the time series plot. Because the histogram does not reflect the order in which the springs were produced, it in effect represents all observations as having been produced simultaneously. Using the histogram to predict the elongation of the 51st spring would very likely lead to an overestimate.

The lesson from Deming's example is this: For displaying and analyzing data that have been generated over time by a process, the primary graphical tool is the time series plot, not the histogram.

FIGURE 2.14
Deming's time series plot and histogram

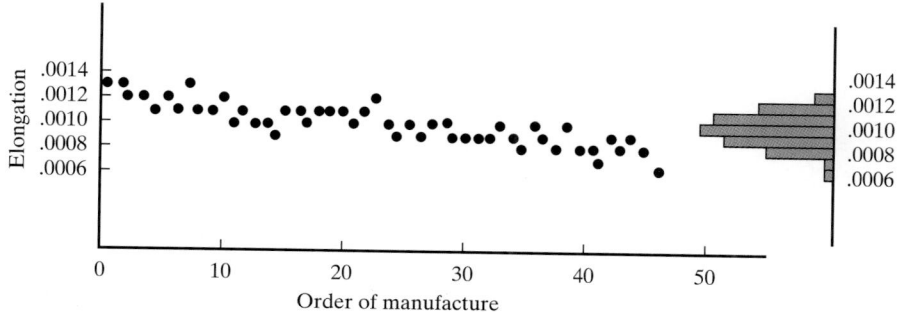

2.4 SUMMATION NOTATION

Now that we've examined some graphical techniques for summarizing and describing quantitative data sets, we turn to numerical methods for accomplishing this objective. Before giving the formulas for calculating numerical descriptive measures, let's look at some shorthand notation that will simplify our calculation instructions. Remember that such notation is used for one reason only—to avoid repeating the same verbal descriptions over and over. If you mentally substitute the verbal definition of a symbol each time you read it, you'll soon get used to it.

We denote the measurements of a quantitative data set as follows: $x_1, x_2, x_3, \ldots,$ x_n where x_1 is the first measurement in the data set, x_2 is the second measurement in the data set, x_3 is the third measurement in the data set, $\ldots$, and x_n is the nth (and last) measurement in the data set. Thus, if we have five measurements in a set of data, we will write x_1, x_2, x_3, x_4, x_5 to represent the measurements. If the actual numbers are 5, 3, 8, 5, and 4, we have $x_1 = 5, x_2 = 3, x_3 = 8, x_4 = 5,$ and $x_5 = 4$.

Most of the formulas we use require a summation of numbers. For example, one sum we'll need to obtain is the sum of all the measurements in the data set, or $x_1 + x_2 + x_3 + \cdots + x_n$. To shorten the notation, we use the symbol Σ for the summation. That is, $x_1 + x_2 + x_3 + \cdots + x_n = \sum_{i=1}^{n} x_i$. Verbally translate $\sum_{i=1}^{5} x_i$ as follows: "The sum of the measurements, whose typical member is x_i, beginning with the member x_1 and ending with the member x_n."

Suppose, as in our earlier example, $x_1 = 5, x_2 = 3, x_3 = 8, x_4 = 5,$ and $x_5 = 4$. Then the sum of the five measurements, denoted $\sum_{i=1}^{5} x_i$, is obtained as follows:

$$\sum_{i=1}^{5} x_i = x_1 + x_2 + x_3 + x_4 + x_5$$
$$= 5 + 3 + 8 + 5 + 4 = 25$$

Another important calculation requires that we square each measurement and then sum the squares. The notation for this sum is $\sum_{i=1}^{n} x_i^2$. For the five measurements above, we have

$$\sum_{i=1}^{5} x_i^2 = x_1^2 + x_2^2 + x_3^2 + x_4^2 + x_5^2$$
$$= 5^2 + 3^2 + 8^2 + 5^2 + 4^2$$
$$= 25 + 9 + 64 + 25 + 16 = 139$$

In general, the symbol following the summation sign Σ represents the variable (or function of the variable) that is to be summed.

The Meaning of Summation Notation $\sum_{i=1}^{n} x_i$

Sum the measurements on the variable that appears to the right of the summation symbol, beginning with the 1st measurement and ending with the nth measurement.

EXERCISES 2.26–2.29

Learning the Mechanics

Note: In all exercises, Σ represents $\sum\limits_{i=1}^{n}$.

2.26 A data set contains the observations 5, 1, 3, 2, 1. Find:
  a. Σx **b.** Σx^2 **c.** $\Sigma(x-1)$
  d. $\Sigma(x-1)^2$ **e.** $(\Sigma x)^2$

2.27 Suppose a data set contains the observations 3, 8, 4, 5, 3, 4, 6. Find:
  a. Σx **b.** Σx^2 **c.** $\Sigma(x-5)^2$
  d. $\Sigma(x-2)^2$ **e.** $(\Sigma x)^2$

2.28 Refer to Exercise 2.26. Find:
  a. $\Sigma x^2 - \dfrac{(\Sigma x)^2}{5}$ **b.** $\Sigma(x-2)^2$ **c.** $\Sigma x^2 - 10$

2.29 A data set contains the observations 6, 0, −2, −1, 3. Find:
  a. Σx **b.** Σx^2 **c.** $\Sigma x^2 - \dfrac{(\Sigma x)^2}{5}$

2.5 NUMERICAL MEASURES OF CENTRAL TENDENCY

When we speak of a data set, we refer to either a sample or a population. If statistical inference is our goal, we'll wish ultimately to use sample numerical descriptive measures to make inferences about the corresponding measures for a population.

As you'll see, a large number of numerical methods are available to describe quantitative data sets. Most of these methods measure one of two data characteristics:

1. The **central tendency** of the set of measurements—that is, the tendency of the data to cluster, or center, about certain numerical values (see Figure 2.15a).

2. The **variability** of the set of measurements—that is, the spread of the data (see Figure 2.15b).

In this section we concentrate on measures of central tendency. In the next section, we discuss measures of variability.

The most popular and best-understood measure of central tendency for a quantitative data set is the **arithmetic mean** (or simply the **mean**) of a data set.

> **DEFINITION 2.5**
> The **mean** of a set of quantitative data is the sum of the measurements divided by the number of measurements contained in the data set.

In everyday terms, the mean is the average value of the data set and is often used to represent a "typical" value. We denote the **mean of a sample** of measurements by $\bar{x}$ (read "x-bar"), and represent the formula for its calculation as shown in the box.

FIGURE 2.15
Numerical descriptive measures

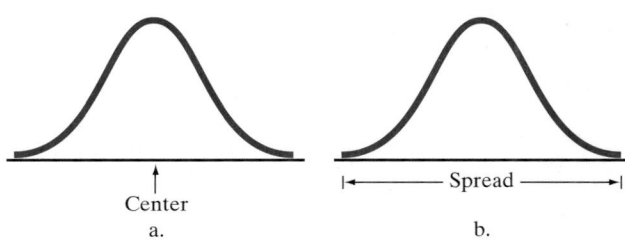

Center
a.

Spread
b.

> **Calculating a Sample Mean**
>
> $$\bar{x} = \frac{\sum_{i=1}^{n} x_i}{n}$$

EXAMPLE 2.4

Calculate the mean of the following five sample measurements: 5, 3, 8, 5, 6.

SOLUTION
Using the definition of sample mean and the summation notation, we find

$$\bar{x} = \frac{\sum_{i=1}^{5} x_i}{5} = \frac{5 + 3 + 8 + 5 + 6}{5} = \frac{27}{5} = 5.4$$

Thus, the mean of this sample is 5.4.*

EXAMPLE 2.5

Calculate the sample mean for the R&D expenditure percentages of the 50 companies given in Table 2.3.

SOLUTION
The mean R&D percentage for the 50 companies is denoted

$$\bar{x} = \frac{\sum_{i=1}^{50} x_i}{50}$$

Rather than compute $\bar{x}$ by hand (or calculator), we entered the data of Table 2.3 into a computer and employed SPSS statistical software to compute the mean. The SPSS printout is shown in Figure 2.16. The sample mean, highlighted on the printout, is $\bar{x} = 8.492$.

Given this information, you can visualize a distribution of R&D percentages centered in the vicinity of $\bar{x} = 8.492$. An examination of the relative frequency histogram (Figure 2.8) confirms that $\bar{x}$ does in fact fall near the center of the distribution.

```
      RDEXP

Valid cases:          50.0   Missing cases:     .0   Percent missing:     .0

Mean        8.4920   Std Err     .2801   Min     5.2000   Skewness     .8546
Median      8.0500   Variance   3.9228   Max    13.5000   S E Skew     .3366
5% Trim     8.3833   Std Dev    1.9806   Range   8.3000   Kurtosis     .4193
                                         IQR     2.5750   S E Kurt     .6619
```

FIGURE 2.16 SPSS printout of numerical descriptive measures for 50 R&D percentages

*In the examples given here, $\bar{x}$ is sometimes rounded to the nearest tenth, sometimes the nearest hundredth, sometimes the nearest thousandth, and so on. There is no specific rule for rounding when calculating $\bar{x}$ because $\bar{x}$ is specifically defined to be the sum of all measurements divided by n; that is, it is a specific fraction. When $\bar{x}$ is used for descriptive purposes, it is often convenient to round the calculated value of $\bar{x}$ to the number of significant figures used for the original measurements. When $\bar{x}$ is to be used in other calculations, however, it may be necessary to retain more significant figures.

The sample mean $\bar{x}$ will play an important role in accomplishing our objective of making inferences about populations based on sample information. For this reason we need to use a different symbol for the **mean of a population**—the mean of the set of measurements on every unit in the population. We use the Greek letter μ (mu) for the population mean.

Symbols for the Sample and Population Mean

In this text, we adopt a general policy of using Greek letters to represent population numerical descriptive measures and Roman letters to represent corresponding descriptive measures for the sample. The symbols for the mean are:

$\bar{x}$ = Sample mean

μ = Population mean

We'll often use the sample mean, $\bar{x}$, to estimate (make an inference about) the population mean, μ. For example, the percentages of revenues spent on R&D by the population consisting of *all* U.S. companies has a mean equal to some value, μ. Our sample of 50 companies yielded percentages with a mean of $\bar{x} = 8.492$. If, as is usually the case, we don't have access to the measurements for the entire population, we could use $\bar{x}$ as an estimator or approximator for μ. Then we'd need to know something about the reliability of our inference. That is, we'd need to know how accurately we might expect $\bar{x}$ to estimate μ. In Chapter 5, we'll find that this accuracy depends on two factors:

1. The *size of the sample*. The larger the sample, the more accurate the estimate will tend to be.

2. The *variability,* or *spread, of the data*. All other factors remaining constant, the more variable the data, the less accurate the estimate.

Another important measure of central tendency is the **median**.

DEFINITION 2.6

The **median** of a quantitative data set is the middle number when the measurements are arranged in ascending (or descending) order.

The median is of most value in describing large data sets. If the data set is characterized by a relative frequency histogram (Figure 2.17), the median is the point on the x-axis such that half the area under the histogram lies above the median and half lies below. [*Note:* In Section 2.2 we observed that the relative frequency associated with a particular interval on the horizontal axis is proportional to the amount of area under the histogram that lies above the interval.] We denote the *median* of a *sample* by m.

FIGURE 2.17
Location of the median

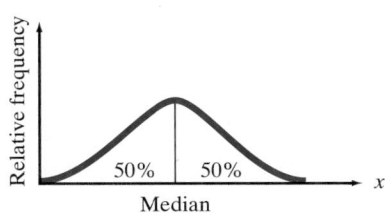

> **Calculating a Sample Median, m**
> Arrange the n measurements from smallest to largest.
> **1.** If n is odd, m is the middle number.
> **2.** If n is even, m is the mean of the middle two numbers.

EXAMPLE 2.6

Consider the following sample of $n = 7$ measurements: 5, 7, 4, 5, 20, 6, 2.

    a. Calculate the median m of this sample.

    b. Eliminate the last measurement (the 2) and calculate the median of the remaining $n = 6$ measurements.

SOLUTION

    a. The seven measurements in the sample are ranked in ascending order: 2, 4, 5, 5, 6, 7, 20

    Because the number of measurements is odd, the median is the middle measurement. Thus, the median of this sample is $m = 5$.

    b. After removing the 2 from the set of measurements, we rank the sample measurements in ascending order as follows: 4, 5, 5, 6, 7, 20

    Now the number of measurements is even, so we average the middle two measurements. The median is $m = (5 + 6)/2 = 5.5$.

In certain situations, the median may be a better measure of central tendency than the mean. In particular, the median is less sensitive than the mean to extremely large or small measurements. Note, for instance, that all but one of the measurements in part **a** of Example 2.6 center about $x = 5$. The single relatively large measurement, $x = 20$, does not affect the value of the median, 5, but it causes the mean, $\bar{x} = 7$, to lie to the right of most of the measurements.

As another example of data from which the central tendency is better described by the median than the mean, consider the salaries of professional athletes (e.g., National Basketball Association players). The presence of just a few athletes (e.g., Michael Jordan, Shaquille O'Neal) with very high salaries will affect the mean more than the median. Thus, the median will provide a more accurate picture of the typical salary for the professional league. The mean could exceed the vast majority of the sample measurements (salaries), making it a misleading measure of central tendency.

EXAMPLE 2.7

Calculate the median for the 50 R&D percentages given in Table 2.3. Compare the median to the mean computed in Example 2.5.

SOLUTION

For this large data set, we again resort to a computer analysis. The SPSS printout is reproduced in Figure 2.18, with the median highlighted. You can see that the median is 8.05. This value implies that half of the 50 R&D percentages in the data set fall below 8.05 and half lie above 8.05.

Note that the mean (8.492) for these data is larger than the median. This fact indicates that the data are **skewed** to the right—that is, there are more extreme measurements in the right tail of the distribution than in the left tail (recall the histogram, Figure 2.8).

In general, extreme values (large or small) affect the mean more than the median since these values are used explicitly in the calculation of the mean. On the other hand, the median is not affected directly by extreme measurements,

```
      RDEXP

Valid cases:            50.0   Missing cases:      .0   Percent missing:      .0

Mean        8.4920   Std Err      .2801   Min     5.2000   Skewness      .8546
Median      8.0500   Variance    3.9228   Max    13.5000   S E Skew      .3366
5% Trim     8.3833   Std Dev     1.9806   Range   8.3000   Kurtosis      .4193
                                          IQR     2.5750   S E Kurt      .6619
```

FIGURE 2.18   SPSS printout of numerical descriptive measures for 50 R&D percentages

since only the middle measurement (or two middle measurements) is explicitly used to calculate the median. Consequently, if measurements are pulled toward one end of the distribution (as with the R&D percentages), the mean will shift toward that tail more than the median.

A comparison of the mean and median gives us a general method for detecting skewness in data sets, as shown in the next box.

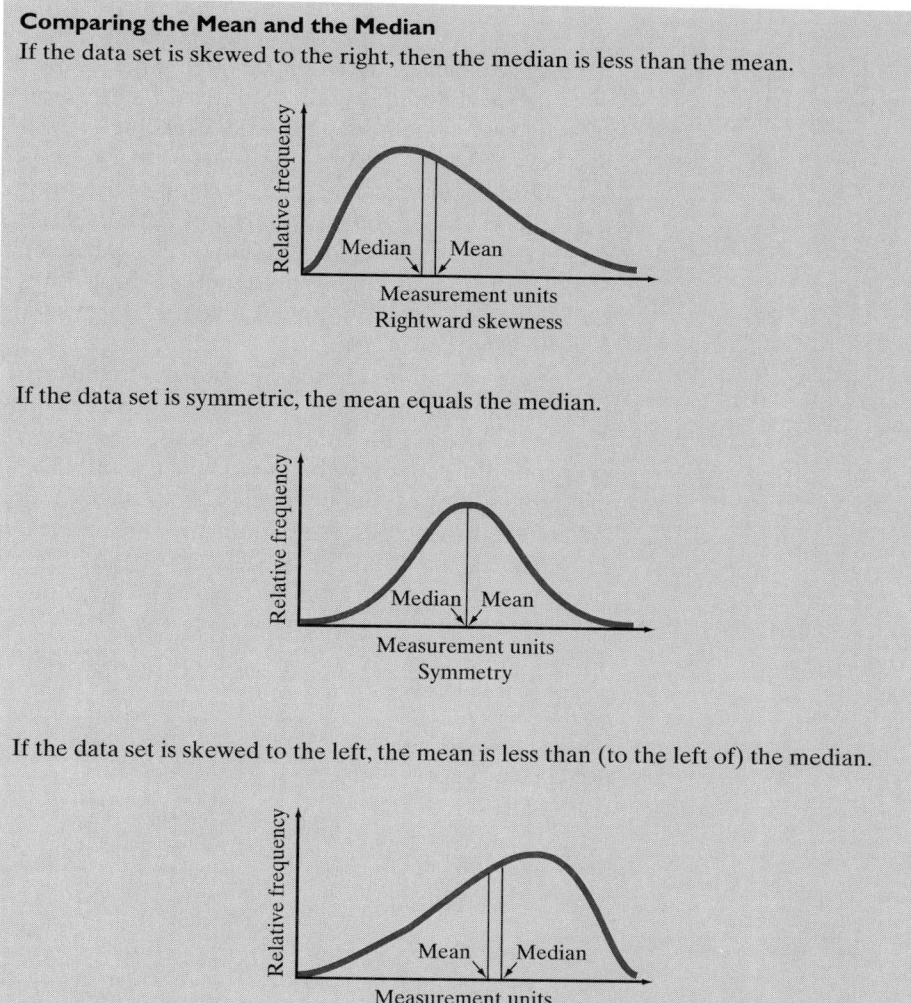

Comparing the Mean and the Median

If the data set is skewed to the right, then the median is less than the mean.

If the data set is symmetric, the mean equals the median.

If the data set is skewed to the left, the mean is less than (to the left of) the median.

A third measure of central tendency is the **mode** of a set of measurements.

> **DEFINITION 2.7**
> The **mode** is the measurement that occurs most frequently in the data set.

Therefore, the mode shows where the data tend to concentrate.

EXAMPLE 2.8

Each of 10 taste testers rated a new brand of barbecue sauce on a ten-point scale, where 1 = awful and 10 = excellent. Find the mode for the ten ratings shown below.

8   7   9   6   8   10   9   9   5   7

SOLUTION

Since 9 occurs most often, the mode of the ten taste ratings is 9.

Note that the data in Example 2.8 are actually qualitative in nature (e.g., "awful," "excellent"). The mode is particularly useful for describing qualitative data. The modal category is simply the category (or class) that occurs most often. Because it emphasizes data concentration, the mode is also used with quantitative data sets to locate the region in which much of the data is concentrated. A retailer of men's clothing would be interested in the modal neck size and sleeve length of potential customers. The modal income class of the laborers in the United States is of interest to the Labor Department.

For some quantitative data sets, the mode may not be very meaningful. For example, consider the pecentages of revenues spent on research and development (R&D) by 50 companies, Table 2.3. A reexamination of the data reveals that three of the measurements are repeated three times: 6.5%, 6.9%, and 8.2%. Thus, there are three modes in the sample and none is particularly useful as a measure of central tendency.

A more meaningful measure can be obtained from a relative frequency histogram for quantitative data. The measurement class containing the largest relative frequency is called the **modal class**. Several definitions exist for locating the position of the mode within a modal class, but the simplest is to define the mode as the midpoint of the modal class. For example, examine the relative frequency histogram for the R&D expenditure percentages, reproduced below in Figure 2.19. You can see that the modal class is the interval 7.35—8.45. The mode (the midpoint) is 7.90. This modal class (and the mode itself) identifies the area in

FIGURE 2.19
Relative frequency histogram for the computer companies' R&D percentages: The modal class

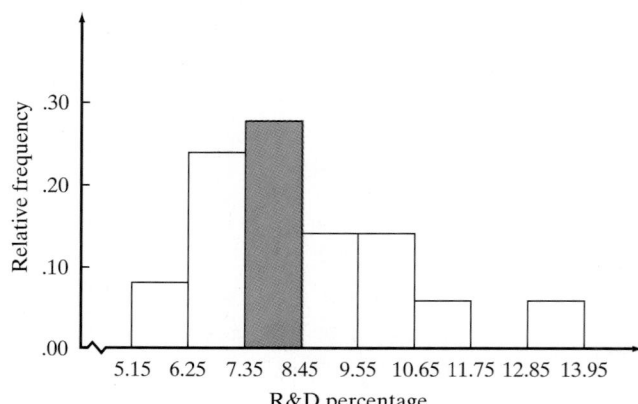

which the data are most concentrated, and in that sense it is a measure of central tendency. However, for most applications involving quantitative data, the mean and median provide more descriptive information than the mode.

EXERCISES   2.30–2.46

Note: Exercises marked with 💾 *contain data available for computer analysis on a 3.5" disk (file name in parentheses).*

Learning the Mechanics

2.30 Calculate the mode, mean, and median of the following data:

18 10 15 13 17 15 12 15 18 16 11

2.31 Calculate the mean and median of the following grade point averages:

3.2   2.5   2.1   3.7   2.8   2.0

2.32 Explain the difference between the calculation of the median for an odd and an even number of measurements. Construct one data set consisting of five measurements and another consisting of six measurements for which the medians are equal.

2.33 Explain how the relationship between the mean and median provides information about the symmetry or skewness of the data's distribution.

2.34 Calculate the mean for samples where
 a. $n = 10, \Sigma x = 85$ b. $n = 16, \Sigma x = 400$
 c. $n = 45, \Sigma x = 35$ d. $n = 18, \Sigma x = 242$

2.35 Calculate the mean, median, and mode for each of the following samples:
 a. $7, -2, 3, 3, 0, 4$ b. $2, 3, 5, 3, 2, 3, 4, 3, 5, 1, 2, 3, 4$
 c. $51, 50, 47, 50, 48, 41, 59, 68, 45, 37$

2.36 Describe how the mean compares to the median for a distribution as follows:
 a. Skewed to the left b. Skewed to the right
 c. Symmetric

Applying the Concepts

2.37 The market value of a company varies from day to day depending on the price of the company's common stock and the number of shares of stock that are held by investors. The market value is determined by multiplying the share price by the number of shares outstanding. The table below lists the market value (in millions of dollars) for the ten most valuable health care firms and the ten most valuable banks.
 a. Calculate the mean and median for each data set.
 b. What do the mean and median indicate about the skewness of each data set?
 c. In part **a**, neither median is equal to a value in its data set. Is this true for all data sets? Explain.
 d. Based on your answer to part **a** and a visual inspection of the data sets, compare and contrast the market values of the ten most valuable health care firms and the ten most valuable banks.

2.38 **(X02.038)** The Superfund Act was passed by Congress to encourage state participation in the implementation of laws relating to the release and cleanup of hazardous substances. Hazardous waste sites financed by the Superfund Act are called Superfund sites. A total of 395 Superfund sites are operated by waste management companies in Arkansas (Tabor and Stanwick, *Arkansas Business and Economic Review,* Summer 1995). The number of these Superfund sites in each of Arkansas' 75 counties is shown in the table at the top of page 60. Numerical descriptive measures for the data set are provided in the EXCEL printout below the table.

HEALTH CARE		BANKS	
Company	**Market Value**	**Company**	**Market Value**
Merck	$81,613	Citicorp	$33,329
Johnson & Johnson	60,564	Bankamerica	26,181
Bristol-Myers Squibb	43,008	Nationsbank	20,227
Pfizer	41,907	Chemical	17,942
Eli Lilly	33,437	First Union	16,810
Abbott Laboratories	33,072	J.P. Morgan	15,320
American Home Products	30,730	Banc One	15,235
Columbia/HCA	23,582	First Chicago	13,674
Pharmacia & Upjohn	21,215	Chase	13,216
Schering-Plough	20,441	Norwest	12,877

Source: "Business Week 1000." Business Week, March 25, 1996, p. 88.

3	3	2	1	2	0	5	3	5	2	1	8	2
12	3	5	3	1	3	0	8	0	9	6	8	6
2	16	0	6	0	5	5	0	1	25	0	0	0
6	2	10	12	3	10	3	17	2	4	2	1	21
4	2	1	11	5	2	2	7	2	3	1	8	2
0	0	0	2	3	10	2	3	48	21			

Source: Tabor, R. H., and Stanwick, S. D. "Arkansas: An environmental perspective." *Arkansas Business and Economic Review,* Vol. 28, No. 2, Summer 1995, pp. 22–32 (Table 1).

SITES	
Mean	5.24
Standard Error	0.836517879
Median	3
Mode	2
Standard Deviation	7.244457341
Sample Variance	52.48216216
Kurtosis	16.41176573
Skewness	3.468289878
Range	48
Minimum	0
Maximum	48
Sum	393
Count	75
Confidence Level(95.000%)	1.639542488

a. Locate the measures of central tendency on the printout and interpret their values.

b. Note that the data set contains at least one county with an unusually large number of Superfund sites. Find the largest of these measurements, called an **outlier**.

c. Delete the outlier, part **b**, from the data set and recalculate the measures of central tendency. Which measure is most affected by the elimination of the outlier?

2.39 Demographics play a key role in the recreation industry. According to D. A. Bergin (*Journal of Leisure Research,* Vol. 23, 1991), difficult times lay ahead for the industry. Bergin reports that the median age of the population in the United States was 30 in 1980, but will be about 36 by the year 2000.

a. Interpret the value of the median for both 1980 and 2000 and explain the trend.

b. If the recreation industry relies on the 18–30 age group for much of its business, what effect will this shift in the median age have? Explain.

2.40 (X02.040) Platelet-activating factor (PAF) is a potent chemical that occurs in patients suffering from shock, inflammation, hypotension, and allergic responses as well as respiratory and cardiovascular disorders. Consequently, drugs that effectively inhibit PAF, keeping it from binding to human cells, may be successful in treating these disorders. A bioassay was undertaken to investigate the potential of 17 traditional Chinese herbal drugs in PAF inhibition (H. Guiqui, *Progress in Natural Science,* June 1995). The prevention of the PAF binding process, measured as a percentage, for each drug is provided in the accompanying table.

Drug	PAF Inhibition (%)
Hai-feng-teng (Fuji)	77
Hai-feng-teng (Japan)	33
Shan-ju	75
Zhang-yiz-hu-jiao	62
Shi-nan-teng	70
Huang-hua-hu-jiao	12
Hua-nan-hu-jiao	0
Xiao-yie-pa-ai-xiang	0
Mao-ju	0
Jia-ju	15
Xie-yie-ju	25
Da-yie-ju	0
Bian-yie-hu-jiao	9
Bi-bo	24
Duo-mai-hu-jiao	40
Yan-sen	0
Jiao-guo-hu-jiao	31

Source: Guiqui, H. "PAF receptor antagonistic principles from Chinese traditional drugs." *Progress in Natural Science,* Vol. 5, No. 3, June 1995, p. 301 (Table 1).

a. Construct a stem-and-leaf display for the data.

b. Compute the median inhibition percentage for the 17 herbal drugs. Interpret the result.

c. Compute the mean inhibition percentage for the 17 herbal drugs. Interpret the result.

d. Compute the mode of the 17 inhibition percentages. Interpret the result.

e. Locate the median, mean, and mode on the stem-and-leaf display, part **a**. Do these measures of central tendency appear to locate the center of the data?

2.41 Would you expect the data sets described below to possess relative frequency distributions that are symmetric, skewed to the right, or skewed to the left? Explain.

a. The salaries of all persons employed by a large university

b. The grades on an easy test

c. The grades on a difficult test

d. The amounts of time students in your class studied last week

e. The ages of automobiles on a used-car lot

f. The amounts of time spent by students on a difficult examination (maximum time is 50 minutes)

2.42 The salaries of superstar professional athletes receive much attention in the media. The multimillion-dollar long-term contract is now commonplace among this elite group. Nevertheless, rarely does a season pass without negotiations between one or more of the players' associations and team owners for additional salary and fringe benefits for *all* players in their particular sports.

a. If a players' association wanted to support its argument for higher "average" salaries, which measure of central tendency do you think it should use? Why?

b. To refute the argument, which measure of central tendency should the owners apply to the players' salaries? Why?

2.43 Refer to the *Financial Management* (Spring 1995) study of prepackaged bankruptcy filings, Exercise 2.22. Recall that each of 49 firms that negotiated a reorganization plan with its creditors prior to filing for bankruptcy was classified in one of three categories: joint exchange offer with prepack, prepack solicitation only, and no pre-filing vote held. An SPSS printout of descriptive statistics for the length of time in bankruptcy (months), by category, is shown below.

a. Locate the measures of central tendency on the printout and interpret their values.

b. Is it reasonable to use a single number (e.g., mean or median) to describe the center of the time-in-bankruptcy distributions? Or should

three "centers" be calculated, one for each of the three categories of prepack firms? Explain.

2.44 Major conventions and conferences attract thousands of people and pump millions of dollars into the local economy of the host city. The decision as to where to hold such conferences hinges to a large extent on the availability of hotel rooms. The table, extracted from *The Wall Street Journal* (Nov. 17, 1995), lists the top ten U.S. cities ranked by the number of hotel rooms.

City	No. of Rooms	No. of Hotels
Las Vegas	93,719	231
Orlando	84,982	311
Los Angeles–Long Beach	78,597	617
Chicago	68,793	378
Washington, D.C.	66,505	351
New York City	61,512	230
Atlanta	58,445	370
San Diego	44,655	352
Anaheim–Santa Ana	44,374	351
San Francisco	42,531	294

Source: Smith Travel Research, September 1995.

a. Find and interpret the median for each of the data sets.

b. For each city, calculate the ratio of the number of rooms to the number of hotels. Then find

```
     TIME
By  CATEGORY   Joint

Valid cases:            11.0   Missing cases:          .0    Percent missing:         .0

Mean       2.6545   Std Err      .5185   Min        1.2000   Skewness        .7600
Median     1.5000   Variance    2.9567   Max        5.4000   S E Skew        .6607
5% Trim    2.5828   Std Dev     1.7195   Range      4.2000   Kurtosis     -1.4183
                                         IQR        3.1000   S E Kurt      1.2794

--------------------------------------------------------------------------------

     TIME
By  CATEGORY   None

Valid cases:            11.0   Missing cases:          .0    Percent missing:         .0

Mean       4.2364   Std Err      .7448   Min        2.4000   Skewness       1.8215
Median     3.2000   Variance    6.1025   Max       10.1000   S E Skew        .6607
5% Trim    4.0126   Std Dev     2.4703   Range      7.7000   Kurtosis      2.6270
                                         IQR        1.6000   S E Kurt      1.2794

--------------------------------------------------------------------------------

     TIME
By  CATEGORY   Prepack

Valid cases:            27.0   Missing cases:          .0    Percent missing:         .0

Mean       1.8185   Std Err      .1847   Min        1.0000   Skewness       1.4539
Median     1.4000   Variance     .9216   Max        4.1000   S E Skew        .4479
5% Trim    1.7372   Std Dev      .9600   Range      3.1000   Kurtosis       .9867
                                         IQR         .9000   S E Kurt       .8721
```

the average number of rooms per hotel in each city.

c. Re-rank the cities based on your answer to part **b**.

2.45 **(X02.045)** According to the U.S. Energy Information Association, the average price of regular unleaded gasoline in the United States in 1993 was 89.6 cents including excise taxes. The table lists the average prices (in cents) in each of a sample of 20 states.

State	Price	State	Price
Arkansas	88.3	New Hampshire	93.2
Connecticut	104.3	New Jersey	88.1
Delaware	91.7	New York	78.5
Hawaii	119.0	North Dakota	91.0
Louisiana	89.8	Oklahoma	85.1
Maine	95.4	Oregon	102.9
Massachusetts	94.3	Pennsylvania	79.2
Michigan	83.2	Texas	90.0
Missouri	79.9	Wisconsin	94.4
Nevada	103.6	Wyoming	87.9

Source: Statistical Abstract of the United States: 1995. U.S. Energy Information Association, *Petroleum Marketing Monthly.*

a. Calculate the mean, median, and mode of this data set.

b. Eliminate the highest price from the data set and repeat part **a**. What effect does dropping this measurement have on the measures of central tendency calculated in part **a**?

c. Arrange the 20 prices in order from lowest to highest. Next, eliminate the lowest two prices and the highest two prices from the data set and calculate the mean of the remaining prices. The result is called an 80% **trimmed mean**, since it is calculated using the central 80% of the values in the data set. An advantage of the trimmed mean is that it is not as sensitive as the arithmetic mean to extreme observations in the data set.

2.46 **(X02.046)** In recent years, the compensation of CEO's, entertainers, and professional athletes has been seriously questioned and often criticized by politicians, the media, and the general public. The table lists the total payroll (in millions of dollars) for active players for each major league baseball team in 1992 and 1995. Numerical descriptive measures for the two sets of data are shown in the MINITAB printouts at the bottom of the page.

Team	1995	1992
New York Yankees	$58.1	$34.9
Baltimore	48.7	24.0
Cincinnati	47.4	35.4
Atlanta	46.4	35.9
Toronto	42.1	49.2
Chicago White Sox	40.7	30.2
Cleveland	39.5	9.3
Boston	38.1	42.1
Colorado	38.0	*
Seattle	37.7	26.4
Chicago Cubs	36.8	32.4
Los Angeles	36.7	42.1
Texas	35.7	26.2
California	33.9	32.6
San Francisco	33.7	23.2
Houston	33.5	15.0
Oakland	33.4	48.0
Kansas City	31.2	32.0
Philadelphia	30.3	25.5
St. Louis	28.7	28.7
Detroit	28.7	28.2
San Diego	24.9	27.7
Florida	23.0	*
Pittsburgh	7.7	36.2
Milwaukee	17.1	30.0
Minnesota	15.4	27.3
Montreal	13.1	16.1
New York Mets	13.1	44.0

*Colorado and Florida joined the league in 1993.

Source: Newark Star-Ledger, December 4, 1995.

a. Find the mean team payroll in 1992 and interpret its value.

b. Find the median team payroll in 1992 and interpret its value.

```
Descriptive Statistics

Variable      N       N*      Mean    Median   Tr Mean   StDev   SE Mean
Sal92         26      2       30.87   30.10    31.00     9.59    1.88

Variable      Min     Max     Q1      Q3
Sal92         9.30    49.20   26.02   35.97

Descriptive Statistics

Variable      N       Mean    Median   Tr Mean   StDev   SE Mean
Sal95         28      32.63   33.80    32.61     11.80   2.23

Variable      Min     Max     Q1      Q3
Sal95         7.70    58.10   25.85   39.15
```

c. Repeat parts **a** and **b** for the 1995 team payrolls.

d. What do your answers to part **c** indicate about the skewness of the 1995 payroll data set?

e. Construct a relative frequency histogram for the 1995 team payrolls. Indicate the location of the mean, the median, and the modal class on your histogram.

2.6 NUMERICAL MEASURES OF VARIABILITY

Measures of central tendency provide only a partial description of a quantitative data set. The description is incomplete without a measure of the variability, or spread, of the data set. Knowledge of the data's variability along with its center can help us visualize the shape of a data set as well as its extreme values.

For example, suppose we are comparing the profit margin per construction job (as a percentage of the total bid price) for 100 construction jobs for each of two cost estimators working for a large construction company. The histograms for the two sets of 100 profit margin measurements are shown in Figure 2.20. If you examine the two histograms, you will notice that both data sets are symmetric with equal modes, medians, and means. However, cost estimator A (Figure 2.20a) has profit margins spread with almost equal relative frequency over the measurement classes, while cost estimator B (Figure 2.20b) has profit margins clustered about the center of the distribution. Thus, estimator B's profit margins are *less variable* than estimator A's. Consequently, you can see that we need a measure of variability as well as a measure of central tendency to describe a data set.

Perhaps the simplest measure of the variability of a quantitative data set is its *range*.

> **DEFINITION 2.8**
> The **range** of a quantitative data set is equal to the largest measurement minus the smallest measurement.

The range is easy to compute and easy to understand, but it is a rather insensitive measure of data variation when the data sets are large. This is because two data sets can have the same range and be vastly different with respect to data variation. This phenomenon is demonstrated in Figure 2.20. Although the ranges

FIGURE 2.20
Profit margin histograms for two cost estimators

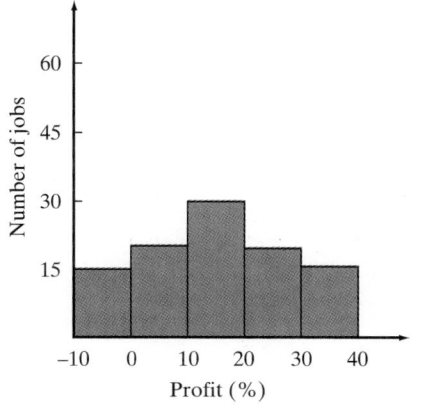

a. Cost estimator A

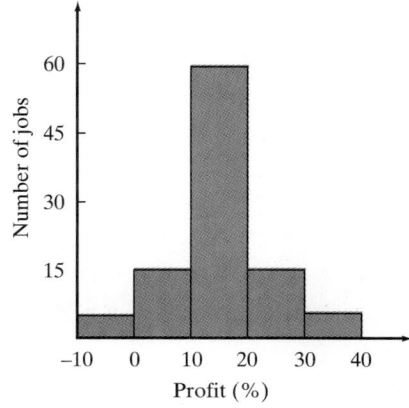

b. Cost estimator B

TABLE 2.6 Two Hypothetical Data Sets

	Sample 1	Sample 2
Measurements	$1, 2, 3, 4, 5$	$2, 3, 3, 3, 4$
Mean	$\bar{x} = \dfrac{1 + 2 + 3 + 4 + 5}{5} = \dfrac{15}{5} = 3$	$\bar{x} = \dfrac{2 + 3 + 3 + 3 + 4}{5} = \dfrac{15}{5} = 3$
Distances of measurement values from $\bar{x}$	$(1 - 3), (2 - 3), (3 - 3), (4 - 3),$ $(5 - 3)$ or $-2, -1, 0, 1, 2$	$(2 - 3), (3 - 3), (3 - 3), (3 - 3),$ $(4 - 3)$ or $-1, 0, 0, 0, 1$

are equal and all central tendency measures are the same for these two symmetric data sets, there is an obvious difference between the two sets of measurements. The difference is that estimator B's profit margins tend to be more stable—that is, to pile up or to cluster about the center of the data set. In contrast, estimator A's profit margins are more spread out over the range, indicating a higher incidence of some high profit margins, but also a greater risk of losses. Thus, even though the ranges are equal, the profit margin record of estimator A is more variable than that of estimator B, indicating a distinct difference in their cost estimating characteristics.

Let's see if we can find a measure of data variation that is more sensitive than the range. Consider the two samples in Table 2.6: Each has five measurements. (We have ordered the numbers for convenience.)

Note that both samples have a mean of 3 and that we have also calculated the distance, or **deviation**, between each measurement and the mean. What information do these distances contain? If they tend to be large in magnitude, as in sample 1, the data are spread out, or highly variable. If the distances are mostly small, as in sample 2, the data are clustered around the mean, $\bar{x}$, and therefore do not exhibit much variability. You can see that these distances, displayed graphically in Figure 2.21, provide information about the variability of the sample measurements.

The next step is to condense the information in these distances into a single numerical measure of variability. Averaging the distances from $\bar{x}$ won't help because the negative and positive distances cancel; that is, the sum of the deviations (and thus the average deviation) is always equal to zero.

Two methods come to mind for dealing with the fact that positive and negative distances from the mean cancel. The first is to treat all the distances as though they were positive, ignoring the sign of the negative distances. We won't pursue this line of thought because the resulting measure of variability (the mean of the absolute values of the distances) presents analytical difficulties beyond the scope of this text. A second method of eliminating the minus signs associated with the distances is to square them. The quantity we can calculate from the squared distances will provide a meaningful description of the variability of a data set and presents fewer analytical difficulties in inference-making.

To use the squared distances calculated from a data set, we first calculate the *sample variance.*

FIGURE 2.21
Dot plots for two data sets

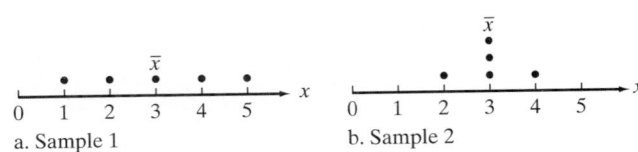

a. Sample 1

b. Sample 2

DEFINITION 2.9

The **sample variance** for a sample of n measurements is equal to the sum of the squared distances from the mean divided by $(n - 1)$. In symbols, using s^2 to represent the sample variance,

$$s^2 = \frac{\sum_{i=1}^{n}(x_i - \bar{x})^2}{n - 1}$$

Note: A shortcut formula for calculating s^2 is

$$s^2 = \frac{\sum_{i=1}^{n}x_i^2 - \dfrac{\left(\sum_{i=1}^{n}x_i\right)^2}{n}}{n - 1}$$

Referring to the two samples in Table 2.6, you can calculate the variance for sample 1 as follows:

$$s^2 = \frac{(1 - 3)^2 + (2 - 3)^2 + (3 - 3)^2 + (4 - 3)^2 + (5 - 3)^2}{5 - 1}$$

$$= \frac{4 + 1 + 0 + 1 + 4}{4} = 2.5$$

The second step in finding a meaningful measure of data variability is to calculate the *standard deviation* of the data set.

DEFINITION 2.10

The **sample standard deviation**, s, is defined as the positive square root of the sample variance, s^2. Thus, $s = \sqrt{s^2}$.

The population variance, denoted by the symbol σ^2 (sigma squared), is the average of the squared distances of the measurements on *all* units in the population from the mean, μ, and σ (sigma) is the square root of this quantity. Since we never really compute σ^2 or σ from the population (the object of sampling is to avoid this costly procedure), we simply denote these two quantities by their respective symbols.

Symbols for Variance and Standard Deviation
s^2 = Sample variance
s = Sample standard deviation
σ^2 = Population variance
σ = Population standard deviation

Notice that, unlike the variance, the standard deviation is expressed in the original units of measurement. For example, if the original measurements are in dollars, the variance is expressed in the peculiar units "dollar squared," but the standard deviation is expressed in dollars.

You may wonder why we use the divisor $(n - 1)$ instead of n when calculating the sample variance. Wouldn't using n be more logical, so that the sample variance would be the average squared distance from the mean? The trouble is, using n tends to produce an underestimate of the population variance, σ^2. So we use $(n - 1)$ in the denominator to provide the appropriate correction for this tendency.* Since sample statistics like s^2 are primarily used to estimate population parameters like σ^2, $(n - 1)$ is preferred to n when defining the sample variance.

EXAMPLE 2.9   Calculate the variance and standard deviation of the following sample: $2, 3, 3, 3, 4$.

SOLUTION

As the number of measurements increases, calculating s^2 and s becomes very tedious. Fortunately, as we show in Example 2.10, we can use a statistical software package (or calculator) to find these values. If you must calculate these quantities by hand, it is advantageous to use the shortcut formula provided in Definition 2.9. To do this, we need two summations: Σx and Σx^2. These can easily be obtained from the following type of tabulation:

x	x^2
2	4
3	9
3	9
3	9
4	16
$\Sigma x = 15$	$\Sigma x^2 = 47$

Then we use†

$$s^2 = \frac{\sum_{i=1}^{n}x_i^2 - \frac{\left(\sum_{i=1}^{n}x_i\right)^2}{n}}{n - 1} = \frac{47 - \frac{(15)^2}{5}}{5 - 1} = \frac{2}{4} = .5$$

$$s = \sqrt{.5} = .71$$

EXAMPLE 2.10   Use the computer to find the sample variance s^2 and the sample standard deviation s for the 50 companies' percentages of revenues spent on R&D.

SOLUTION
The SAS printout describing the R&D percentage data is displayed in Figure 2.22. The variance and standard deviation, highlighted on the printout, are: $s^2 = 3.922792$ and $s = 1.980604$.

You now know that the standard deviation measures the variability of a set of data and how to calculate it. But how can we interpret and use the standard deviation? This is the topic of Section 2.7.

---

*"Appropriate" here means that s^2 with the divisor of $(n - 1)$ is an **unbiased estimator** of σ^2. We define unbiased estimators in Chapter 4.

†When calculating s^2, how many decimal places should you carry? Although there are no rules for the rounding procedure, it's reasonable to retain twice as many decimal places in s^2 as you ultimately wish to have in s. If you wish to calculate s to the nearest hundredth (two decimal places), for example, you should calculate s^2 to the nearest ten-thousandth (four decimal places).

FIGURE 2.22
SAS printout of
numerical descriptive
measures for 50 R&D
percentages

```
                              UNIVARIATE PROCEDURE
      Variable=RDPCT

                                    Moments
              N                 50   Sum Wgts            50
              Mean           8.492   Sum              424.6
              Std Dev     1.980604   Variance      3.922792
              Skewness    0.854601   Kurtosis      0.419288
              USS          3797.92   CSS           192.2168
              CV          23.32317   Std Mean        0.2801
              T:Mean=0    30.31778   Prob>|T|        0.0001
              Sgn Rank       637.5   Prob>|S|        0.0001
              Num ^= 0          50

                             Quantiles(Def=5)

              100% Max       13.5    99%            13.5
               75% Q3         9.6    95%            13.2
               50% Med       8.05    90%            11.2
               25% Q1         7.1    10%             6.5
                0% Min        5.2     5%             5.9
                                     1%             5.2

              Range           8.3
              Q3-Q1           2.5
              Mode            6.5
```

EXERCISES 2.47–2.58

Note: Exercises marked with ▨ contain data available for computer analysis on a 3.5" disk (file name in parentheses).

Learning the Mechanics

2.47 Answer the following questions about variability of data sets:
  a. What is the primary disadvantage of using the range to compare the variability of data sets?
  b. Describe the sample variance using words rather than a formula. Do the same with the population variance.
  c. Can the variance of a data set ever be negative? Explain. Can the variance ever be smaller than the standard deviation? Explain.

2.48 Calculate the variance and standard deviation for samples where
  a. $n = 10, \Sigma x^2 = 84, \Sigma x = 20$
  b. $n = 40, \Sigma x^2 = 380, \Sigma x = 100$
  c. $n = 20, \Sigma x^2 = 18, \Sigma x = 17$

2.49 Calculate the range, variance, and standard deviation for the following samples:
  a. 4, 2, 1, 0, 1   **b.** 1, 6, 2, 2, 3, 0, 3
  c. 8, −2, 1, 3, 5, 4, 4, 1, 3, 3
  d. 0, 2, 0, 0, −1, 1, −2, 1, 0, −1, 1, −1, 0, −3, −2, −1, 0, 1

2.50 Calculate the range, variance, and standard deviation for the following samples:
  a. 39, 42, 40, 37, 41   **b.** 100, 4, 7, 96, 80, 3, 1, 10, 2
  c. 100, 4, 7, 30, 80, 30, 42, 2

2.51 Compute $\bar{x}, s^2$, and s for each of the following data sets. If appropriate, specify the units in which your answer is expressed.
  a. 3, 1, 10, 10, 4   **b.** 8 feet, 10 feet, 32 feet, 5 feet
  c. −1, −4, −3, 1, −4, −4
  d. ⅕ ounce, ⅕ ounce, ⅕ ounce, ⅖ ounce, ⅕ ounce, ⅘ ounce

2.52 Using only integers between 0 and 10, construct two data sets with at least 10 observations each so that the two sets have the same mean but different variances. Construct dot plots for each of your data sets and mark the mean of each data set on its dot diagram.

2.53 Using only integers between 0 and 10, construct two data sets with at least 10 observations each that have the same range but different means. Construct a dot plot for each of your data sets, and mark the mean of each data set on its dot diagram.

2.54 Consider the following sample of five measurements: 2, 1, 1, 0, 3
  a. Calculate the range, s^2, and s.
  b. Add 3 to each measurement and repeat part **a**.
  c. Subtract 4 from each measurement and repeat part **a**.
  d. Considering your answers to parts **a**, **b**, and **c**, what seems to be the effect on the variability of a data set by adding the same number to or subtracting the same number from each measurement?

Applying the Concepts

2.55 **(X02.055)** The Consumer Price Index (CPI) measures the price change of a constant market basket of goods and services. The Bureau of Labor Statistics publishes a national CPI (called the U.S. City Average Index) as well as separate indexes for each of 32 different cities in the United States. The national index and some of the city indexes are published monthly; the remainder of the city indexes are published semiannually. The CPI is used in cost-of-living escalator clauses of many labor contracts to adjust wages for inflation (*Bureau of Labor Statistics Handbook of Methods*, 1992). For example, in the printing industry of Minneapolis–St. Paul, hourly wages are adjusted every six months (based on October and April values of the CPI) by 4¢ for every point change in the Minneapolis–St. Paul CPI. The table below lists the published values of the U.S. City Average Index and the Chicago Index during 1994 and 1995.

Month	U.S. City Average Index	Chicago
January 1994	146.2	146.5
February	146.7	146.8
March	147.2	147.6
April	147.4	147.9
May	147.5	147.6
June	148.0	148.1
July	148.4	148.3
August	149.0	149.8
September	149.4	150.2
October	149.5	149.4
November	149.7	150.4
December	149.7	150.5
January 1995	150.3	151.8
February	150.9	152.3
March	151.4	152.6
April	151.9	153.1
May	152.2	153.0
June	152.5	153.5
July	152.5	153.6
August	152.9	153.8
September	153.2	154.0
October	153.7	154.3
November	153.6	154.0
December	153.5	153.8

Source: CPI Detailed Report, Bureau of Labor Statistics, Jan. 1994–Dec. 1995.

a. Calculate the mean values for the U.S. City Average Index and the Chicago Index.
b. Find the ranges of the U.S. City Average Index and the Chicago Index.
c. Calculate the standard deviation for both the U.S. City Average Index and the Chicago Index over the time period described in the table.
d. Which index displays greater variation about its mean over the time period in question? Justify your response.

2.56 To set an appropriate price for a product, it's necessary to be able to estimate its cost of production. One element of the cost is based on the length of time it takes workers to produce the product. The most widely used technique for making such measurements is the **time study**. In a time study, the task to be studied is divided into measurable parts and each is timed with a stopwatch or filmed for later analysis. For each worker, this process is repeated many times for each subtask. Then the average and standard deviation of the time required to complete each subtask are computed for each worker. A worker's overall time to complete the task under study is then determined by adding his or her subtask-time averages (Gaither, *Production and Operations Management*, 1996). The data (in minutes) given in the table are the result of a time study of a production operation involving two subtasks.

	WORKER A		WORKER B	
Repetition	Subtask 1	Subtask 2	Subtask 1	Subtask 2
1	30	2	31	7
2	28	4	30	2
3	31	3	32	6
4	38	3	30	5
5	25	2	29	4
6	29	4	30	1
7	30	3	31	4

a. Find the overall time it took each worker to complete the manufacturing operation under study.
b. For each worker, find the standard deviation of the seven times for subtask 1.
c. In the context of this problem, what are the standard deviations you computed in part **b** measuring?
d. Repeat part **b** for subtask 2.
e. If you could choose workers similar to A or workers similar to B to perform subtasks 1 and 2, which type would you assign to each subtask? Explain your decisions on the basis of your answers to parts **a**–**d**.

2.57 The table lists the 1995 profits (in millions of dollars) for a sample of seven airlines.

Airline	Profit
Southwest	182.6
Continental	226.0
Northwest	342.1
Delta	510.0
U.S. Air	119.3
United	378.0
America West	54.8

Source: "Business Week 1000." *Business Week*, March 25, 1996, p. 90.

a. Calculate the range, variance, and standard deviation of the data set.

b. Specify the units in which each of your answers to part **a** is expressed.

c. Suppose America West had a loss of $50 instead of a profit of $54.8 million. Would the range of the data set increase or decrease? Why? Would the standard deviation of the data set increase or decrease? Why?

2.58 The U.S. Federal Trade Commission has recently begun assessing fines and other penalties against weight-loss clinics that make unsupported or misleading claims about the effectiveness of their programs. Suppose you have brochures from two weight-loss clinics that both advertise "statistical evidence" about the effectiveness of their programs. Clinic A advertises that the *mean* weight loss during the first month is 15 pounds, while clinic B advertises a *median* weight loss of 10 pounds.

a. Assuming the statistics are accurately calculated, which clinic would you recommend if you had no other information? Why?

b. Upon further research, the median and standard deviation for Clinic A are found to be 10 pounds and 20 pounds, respectively, while the mean and standard deviation for clinic B are found to be 10 and 5 pounds, respectively. Both are based on samples of more than 100 clients. Describe the two clinics' weight-loss distributions as completely as possible given this additional information. What would you recommend to a prospective client now? Why?

c. Note that nothing has been said about how the sample of clients upon which the statistics are based was selected. What additional information would be important regarding the sampling techniques employed by the clinics?

2.7 INTERPRETING THE STANDARD DEVIATION

We've seen that if we are comparing the variability of two samples selected from a population, the sample with the larger standard deviation is the more variable of the two. Thus, we know how to interpret the standard deviation on a relative or comparative basis, but we haven't explained how it provides a measure of variability for a single sample.

To understand how the standard deviation provides a measure of variability of a data set, consider a specific data set and answer the following questions: How many measurements are within 1 standard deviation of the mean? How many measurements are within 2 standard deviations? For a specific data set, we can answer these questions by counting the number of measurements in each of the intervals. However, if we are interested in obtaining a general answer to these questions, the problem is more difficult.

Tables 2.7 and 2.8 give two sets of answers to the questions of how many measurements fall within 1, 2, and 3 standard deviations of the mean. The first, which applies to *any* set of data, is derived from a theorem proved by the Russian mathematician P. L. Chebyshev (1821—1894). The second, which applies to mound-shaped, symmetric distributions of data (where the mean, median, and mode are all about the same), is based upon empirical evidence that has accumulated over the years. However, the percentages given for the intervals in Table 2.8 provide remarkably good approximations even when the distribution of the data is slightly skewed or asymmetric. Note that both rules apply to either population data sets or sample data sets.

TABLE 2.7   An Aid to Interpretation of a Standard Deviation: Chebyshev's Rule

---

Chebyshev's Rule applies to any data set, regardless of the shape of the frequency distribution of the data.

a. No useful information is provided on the fraction of measurements that fall within 1 standard deviation of the mean, i.e., within the interval $(\bar{x} - s, \bar{x} + s)$ for samples and $(\mu - \sigma, \mu + \sigma)$ for populations.

continued

b. At least $\frac{3}{4}$ will fall within 2 standard deviations of the mean, i.e., within the interval $(\bar{x} - 2s, \bar{x} + 2s)$ for samples and $(\mu - 2\sigma, \mu + 2\sigma)$ for populations.

c. At least $\frac{8}{9}$ of the measurements will fall within 3 standard deviations of the mean, i.e., within the interval $(\bar{x} - 3s, \bar{x} + 3s)$ for samples and $(\mu - 3\sigma, \mu + 3\sigma)$ for populations.

d. Generally, for any number k greater than 1, at least $1 - 1/k^2$ of the measurements will fall within k standard deviations of the mean, i.e., within the interval $(\bar{x} - ks, \bar{x} + ks)$ for samples and $(\mu - k\sigma, \mu + k\sigma)$ for populations.

**TABLE 2.8   An Aid to Interpretation of a Standard Deviation:
The Empirical Rule**

The **Empirical Rule** is a rule of thumb that applies to data sets with frequency distributions that are mound-shaped and symmetric, as shown below.

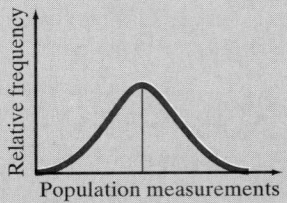

a. Approximately 68% of the measurements will fall within 1 standard deviation of the mean, i.e., within the interval $(\bar{x} - s, \bar{x} + s)$ for samples and $(\mu - \sigma, \mu + \sigma)$ for populations.

b. Approximately 95% of the measurements will fall within 2 standard deviations of the mean, i.e., within the interval $(\bar{x} - 2s, \bar{x} + 2s)$ for samples and $(\mu - 2\sigma, \mu + 2\sigma)$ for populations.

c. Approximately 99.7% (essentially all) of the measurements will fall within 3 standard deviations of the mean, i.e., within the interval $(\bar{x} - 3s, \bar{x} + 3s)$ for samples and $(\mu - 3\sigma, \mu + 3\sigma)$ for populations.

EXAMPLE 2.11

The 50 companies' percentages of revenues spent on R&D are repeated here:

13.5	9.5	8.2	6.5	8.4	8.1	6.9	7.5	10.5	13.5
7.2	7.1	9.0	9.9	8.2	13.2	9.2	6.9	9.6	7.7
9.7	7.5	7.2	5.9	6.6	11.1	8.8	5.2	10.6	8.2
11.3	5.6	10.1	8.0	8.5	11.7	7.1	7.7	9.4	6.0
8.0	7.4	10.5	7.8	7.9	6.5	6.9	6.5	6.8	9.5

We have previously shown that the mean and standard deviation of these data (rounded) are 8.49 and 1.98, respectively. Calculate the fraction of these measurements that lie within the intervals $\bar{x} \pm s, \bar{x} \pm 2s$, and $\bar{x} \pm 3s$, and compare the results with those predicted in Tables 2.7 and 2.8.

SOLUTION
We first form the interval

$$(\bar{x} - s, \bar{x} + s) = (8.49 - 1.98, 8.49 + 1.98) = (6.51, 10.47)$$

A check of the measurements reveals that 34 of the 50 measurements, or 68%, are within 1 standard deviation of the mean.

The next interval of interest

$$(\bar{x} - 2s, \bar{x} + 2s) = (8.49 - 3.96, 8.49 + 3.96) = (4.53, 12.45)$$

contains 47 of the 50 measurements, or 94%.

Finally, the 3-standard-deviation interval around $\bar{x}$,

$$(\bar{x} - 3s, \bar{x} + 3s) = (8.49 - 5.94, 8.49 + 5.94) = (2.55, 14.43)$$

contains all, or 100%, of the measurements.

In spite of the fact that the distribution of these data is skewed to the right (see Figure 2.8), the percentages within 1, 2, and 3 standard deviations (68%, 94%, and 100%) agree very well with the approximations of 68%, 95%, and 99.7% given by the Empirical Rule (Table 2.8). You will find that unless the distribution is extremely skewed, the mound-shaped approximations will be reasonably accurate. Of course, no matter what the shape of the distribution, Chebyshev's Rule (Table 2.7) assures that at least 75% and at least 89% ($\frac{8}{9}$) of the measurements will lie within 2 and 3 standard deviations of the mean, respectively. ▪

EXAMPLE 2.12

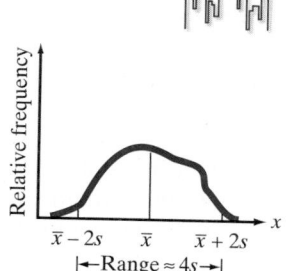

Chebyshev's Rule and the Empirical Rule are useful as a check on the calculation of the standard deviation. For example, suppose we calculated the standard deviation for the R&D percentages (Table 2.3) to be 3.92. Are there any "clues" in the data that enable us to judge whether this number is reasonable?

SOLUTION

The range of the R&D percentages in Table 2.3 is $13.5 - 5.2 = 8.3$. From Chebyshev's Rule and the Empirical Rule we know that most of the measurements (approximately 95% if the distribution is mound-shaped) will be within 2 standard deviations of the mean. And, regardless of the shape of the distribution and the number of measurements, almost all of them will fall within 3 standard deviations of the mean. Consequently, we would expect the range of the measurements to be between 4 (i.e., $\pm 2s$) and 6 (i.e., $\pm 3s$) standard deviations in length (see Figure 2.23).

For the R&D data, this means that s should fall between

$$\frac{Range}{6} = \frac{8.3}{6} = 1.38 \quad \text{and} \quad \frac{Range}{4} = \frac{8.3}{4} = 2.08$$

In particular, the standard deviation should not be much larger than $\frac{1}{4}$ of the range, particularly for the data set with 50 measurements. Thus, we have reason to believe that the calculation of 3.92 is too large. A check of our work reveals that 3.92 is the variance s^2, not the standard deviation s (see Example 2.10). We "forgot" to take the square root (a common error); the correct value is $s = 1.98$. Note that this value is between $\frac{1}{6}$ and $\frac{1}{4}$ of the range. ▪

In examples and exercises we'll sometimes use $s \approx$ range/4 to obtain a crude, and usually conservatively large, approximation for s. However, we stress that this is no substitute for calculating the exact value of s when possible.

Finally, and most importantly, we will use the concepts in Chebyshev's Rule and the Empirical Rule to build the foundation for statistical inference-making. The method is illustrated in Example 2.13.

FIGURE 2.23
The relation between the range and the standard deviation

EXAMPLE 2.13

A manufacturer of automobile batteries claims that the average length of life for its grade A battery is 60 months. However, the guarantee on this brand is for just 36 months. Suppose the standard deviation of the life length is known to be 10 months, and the frequency distribution of the life-length data is known to be mound-shaped.

a. Approximately what percentage of the manufacturer's grade A batteries will last more than 50 months, assuming the manufacturer's claim is true?

b. Approximately what percentage of the manufacturer's batteries will last less than 40 months, assuming the manufacturer's claim is true?

c. Suppose your battery lasts 37 months. What could you infer about the manufacturer's claim?

SOLUTION

If the distribution of life length is assumed to be mound-shaped with a mean of 60 months and a standard deviation of 10 months, it would appear as shown in Figure 2.24. Note that we can take advantage of the fact that mound-shaped distributions are (approximately) symmetric about the mean, so that the percentages given by the Empirical Rule can be split equally between the halves of the distribution on each side of the mean. The approximations given in Figure 2.24 are more dependent on the assumption of a mound-shaped distribution than those given by the Empirical Rule (Table 2.8), because the approximations in Figure 2.24 depend on the (approximate) symmetry of the mound-shaped distribution. We saw in Example 2.11 that the Empirical Rule can yield good approximations even for skewed distributions. This will *not* be true of the approximations in Figure 2.24; the distribution *must* be mound-shaped and approximately symmetric.

For example, since approximately 68% of the measurements will fall within 1 standard deviation of the mean, the distribution's symmetry implies that approximately ½(68%) = 34% of the measurements will fall between the mean and 1 standard deviation on each side. This concept is illustrated in Figure 2.24. The figure also shows that 2.5% of the measurements lie beyond 2 standard deviations in each direction from the mean. This result follows from the fact that if approximately 95% of the measurements fall within 2 standard deviations of the mean, then about 5% fall outside 2 standard deviations; if the distribution is approximately symmetric, then about 2.5% of the measurements fall beyond 2 standard deviations on each side of the mean.

a. It is easy to see in Figure 2.24 that the percentage of batteries lasting more than 50 months is approximately 34% (between 50 and 60 months) plus 50% (greater than 60 months). Thus, approximately 84% of the batteries should have life length exceeding 50 months.

b. The percentage of batteries that last less than 40 months can also be easily determined from Figure 2.24. Approximately 2.5% of the batteries should fail prior to 40 months, assuming the manufacturer's claim is true.

c. If you are so unfortunate that your grade A battery fails at 37 months, you can make one of two inferences: either your battery was one of the approximately 2.5% that fail prior to 40 months, or something about the manufacturer's claim is not true. Because the chances are so small that a battery fails

FIGURE 2.24
Battery life-length distribution: Manufacturer's claim assumed true

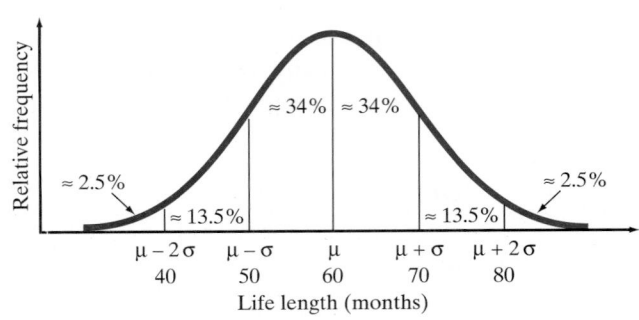

before 40 months, you would have good reason to have serious doubts about the manufacturer's claim. A mean smaller than 60 months and/or a standard deviation longer than 10 months would both increase the likelihood of failure prior to 40 months.*

Example 2.13 is our initial demonstration of the statistical inference-making process. At this point you should realize that we'll use sample information (in Example 2.13, your battery's failure at 37 months) to make inferences about the population (in Example 2.13, the manufacturer's claim about the life length for the population of all batteries). We'll build on this foundation as we proceed.

*The assumption that the distribution is mound-shaped and symmetric may also be incorrect. However, if the distribution were skewed to the right, as life-length distributions often tend to be, the percentage of measurements more than 2 standard deviations *below* the mean would be even less than 2.5%.

EXERCISES 2.59–2.74

Note: Exercises marked with ▣ contain data available for computer analysis on a 3.5" disk (file name in parentheses).

Learning the Mechanics

2.59 To what kind of data sets can Chebyshev's Rule be applied? The Empirical Rule?

2.60 The output from a statistical software package indicates that the mean and standard deviation of a data set consisting of 200 measurements are $1,500 and $300, respectively.
  a. What are the units of measurement of the variable of interest? Based on the units, what type of data is this: quantitative or qualitative?
  b. What can be said about the number of measurements between $900 and $2,100? Between $600 and $2,400? Between $1,200 and $1,800? Between $1,500 and $2,100?

2.61 For any set of data, what can be said about the percentage of the measurements contained in each of the following intervals?
  a. $\bar{x} - s$ to $\bar{x} + s$ b. $\bar{x} - 2s$ to $\bar{x} + 2s$
  c. $\bar{x} - 3s$ to $\bar{x} + 3s$

2.62 For a set of data with a mound-shaped relative frequency distribution, what can be said about the percentage of the measurements contained in each of the intervals specified in Exercise 2.61?

2.63 The following is a sample of 25 measurements:

7 6 6 11 8 9 11 9 10 8 7 7
5 9 10 7 7 7 7 9 12 10 10 8 6

  a. Compute $\bar{x}, s^2$, and s for this sample.
  b. Count the number of measurements in the intervals $\bar{x} \pm s, \bar{x} \pm 2s, \bar{x} \pm 3s$. Express each count as a percentage of the total number of measurements.
  c. Compare the percentages found in part **b** to the percentages given by the Empirical Rule and Chebyshev's Rule.
  d. Calculate the range and use it to obtain a rough approximation for s. Does the result

compare favorably with the actual value for s found in part **a**?

2.64 Given a data set with a largest value of 760 and a smallest value of 135, what would you estimate the standard deviation to be? Explain the logic behind the procedure you used to estimate the standard deviation. Suppose the standard deviation is reported to be 25. Is this feasible? Explain.

Applying the Concepts

2.65 Refer to the *Marine Technology* (Jan. 1995) data on spillage amounts (in thousands of metric tons) for 50 major oil spills, Exercise 2.10. An SPSS histogram for the 50 spillage amounts is shown at the top of page 74.
  a. Interpret the histogram.
  b. Descriptive statistics for the 50 spillage amounts are provided in the SPSS printout. Use this information to form an interval that can be used to predict the spillage amount for the next major oil spill.

2.66 (X02.066) As a result of government and consumer pressure, automobile manufacturers in the United States are deeply involved in research to improve their products' gasoline mileage. One manufacturer, hoping to achieve 40 miles per gallon on one of its compact models, measured the mileage obtained by 36 test versions of the model with the following results (rounded to the nearest mile for convenience):

43 35 41 42 42 38 40 41 41 40 40 41
42 36 43 40 38 40 38 45 39 41 42 37
40 40 44 39 40 37 39 41 39 41 37 40

The mean and standard deviation of these data are shown in the SAS printout at the bottom of page 74.
  a. Find the mean and standard deviation on the printout and give the units in which they are expressed.

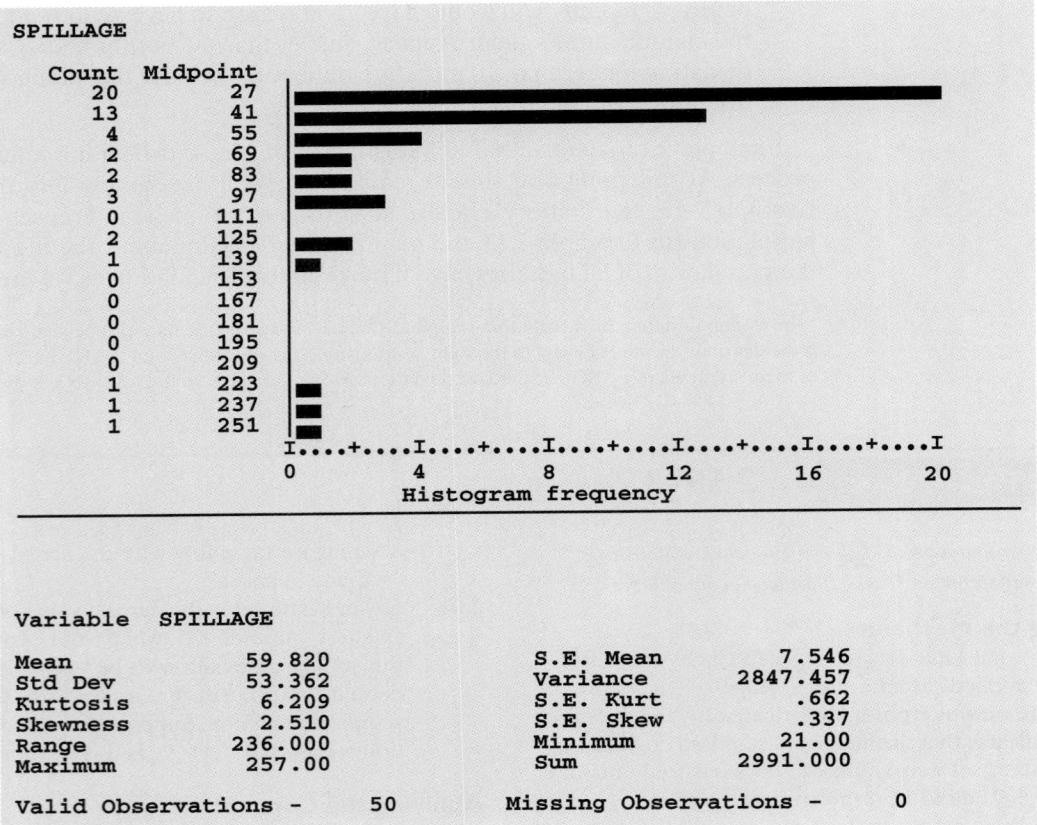

```
SPILLAGE

    Count  Midpoint
       20        27
       13        41
        4        55
        2        69
        2        83
        3        97
        0       111
        2       125
        1       139
        0       153
        0       167
        0       181
        0       195
        0       209
        1       223
        1       237
        1       251
            I....+....I....+....I....+....I....+....I....+....I
            0         4         8        12        16        20
                         Histogram frequency
```

```
Variable    SPILLAGE

Mean              59.820          S.E. Mean           7.546
Std Dev           53.362          Variance         2847.457
Kurtosis           6.209          S.E. Kurt            .662
Skewness           2.510          S.E. Skew            .337
Range            236.000          Minimum            21.00
Maximum          257.00           Sum              2991.000

Valid Observations -     50       Missing Observations -      0
```

b. If the manufacturer would be satisfied with a (population) mean of 40 miles per gallon, how would it react to the above test data?

c. Use the information in Tables 2.7–2.8 to check the reasonableness of the calculated standard deviation $s = 2.2$.

d. Construct a relative frequency histogram of the data set. Is the data set mound-shaped?

e. What percentage of the measurements would you expect to find within the intervals $\bar{x} \pm s$, $\bar{x} \pm 2s$, $\bar{x} \pm 3s$?

f. Count the number of measurements that actually fall within the intervals of part **e**. Express each interval count as a percentage of the total number of measurements. Compare these results with your answers to part **e**.

2.67 Refer to the *Financial Management* (Spring 1995) study of 49 firms filing for prepackaged bankruptcy, Exercise 2.22. Recall that the variable of interest was length of time (months) in bankruptcy for each firm.

a. A histogram (produced by MINITAB for Windows) for the 49 bankruptcy times is displayed on page 75. Comment on whether the Empirical Rule is applicable for describing the bankruptcy time distribution for firms filing for prepackaged bankruptcy.

b. Numerical descriptive statistics for the data set are shown in the MINITAB printout on page 75. Use this information to construct an interval that captures at least 75% of the bankruptcy times for "prepack" firms.

c. Refer to the data listed in Exercise 2.22. Count the number of the 49 bankruptcy times that fall within the interval, part **b**, and convert the result to a percentage. Does the result agree with Chebyshev's Rule? The Empirical Rule?

d. A firm is considering filing a prepackaged bankruptcy plan. Estimate the length of time the firm will be in bankruptcy.

2.68 Refer to the *Arkansas Business and Economic Review* (Summer 1995) study of the number of

```
Analysis Variable : MPG

N Obs    N       Minimum         Maximum            Mean           Std Dev
-----------------------------------------------------------------------------
   36   36    35.0000000      45.0000000      40.0555556        2.1770812
-----------------------------------------------------------------------------
```

```
Descriptive Statistics
Variable       N      Mean    Median    Tr Mean     StDev   SE Mean
Time          49     2.549     1.700      2.333     1.828     0.261

Variable     Min      Max        Q1         Q3
Time       1.000   10.100     1.350      3.500
```

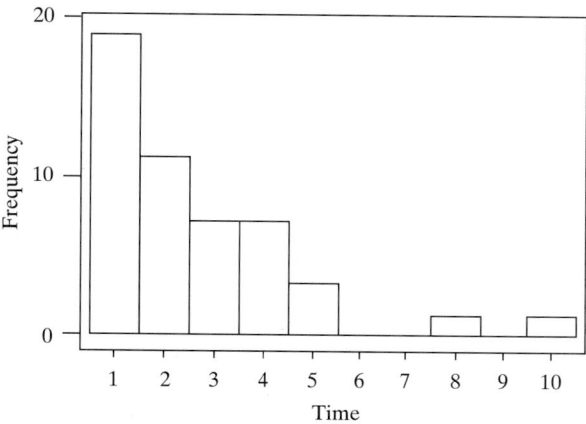

Superfund hazardous waste sites in Arkansas counties, Exercise 2.38. The data and EXCEL numerical descriptive statistics printout are reproduced below.

Calculate the percentage of measurements in the intervals $\bar{x} \pm s, \bar{x} \pm 2s$, and $\bar{x} \pm 3s$. Check the agreement of these percentages with both Chebyshev's Rule and the Empirical Rule.

SITES	
Mean	5.24
Standard Error	0.836517879
Median	3
Mode	2
Standard Deviation	7.244457341
Sample Variance	52.48216216
Kurtosis	16.41176573
Skewness	3.468289878
Range	48
Minimum	0
Maximum	48
Sum	393
Count	75
Confidence Level(95.000%)	1.639542488

2.69 The *American Rifleman* (June 1993) reported on the velocity of ammunition fired from the FEG P9R pistol, a new 9mm gun manufactured in Hungary. Field tests revealed that Winchester bullets fired from the pistol had a mean velocity (at 15 feet) of 936 feet per second and a standard deviation of 10 feet per second. Tests were also conducted with Uzi and Black Hills ammunition.
  a. Describe the velocity distribution of Winchester bullets fired from the FEG P9R pistol.
  b. A bullet, brand unknown, is fired from the FEG P9R pistol. Suppose the velocity (at 15 feet) of the bullet is 1,000 feet per second. Is the bullet likely to be manufactured by Winchester? Explain.

2.70 For each day of last year, the number of vehicles passing through a certain intersection was recorded by a city engineer. One objective of this study was to determine the percentage of days that more than 425 vehicles used the intersection. Suppose the mean for the data was 375 vehicles per day and the standard deviation was 25 vehicles.
  a. What can you say about the percentage of days that more than 425 vehicles used the intersection? Assume you know nothing about the shape of the relative frequency distribution for the data.
  b. What is your answer to part **a** if you know that the relative frequency distribution for the data is mound-shaped?

2.71 A buyer for a lumber company must decide whether to buy a piece of land containing 5,000 pine trees. If 1,000 of the trees are at least 40 feet tall, the buyer will purchase the land; otherwise, he won't. The owner of the land reports that the height of the trees has a mean of 30 feet and a standard deviation of 3 feet. Based on this information, what is the buyer's decision?

2.72 A chemical company produces a substance composed of 98% cracked corn particles and 2% zinc phosphide for use in controlling rat populations in sugarcane fields. Production must be carefully

3	3	2	1	2	0	5	3	5	2	1	8	2	12	3	5	3	1	3
0	8	0	9	6	8	6	2	16	0	6	0	5	5	0	1	25	0	0
0	6	2	10	12	3	10	3	17	2	4	2	1	21	4	2	1	11	5
2	2	7	2	3	1	8	2	0	0	0	2	3	10	2	3	48	21	

Source: Tabor, R. H., and Stanwick, S. D. "Arkansas: An environmental perspective." *ArkansasBusiness and Economic Review,* Vol. 28, No. 2, Summer 1995, pp. 22–32 (Table 1).

controlled to maintain the 2% zinc phosphide because too much zinc phosphide will cause damage to the sugarcane and too little will be ineffective in controlling the rat population. Records from past production indicate that the distribution of the actual percentage of zinc phosphide present in the substance is approximately mound-shaped, with a mean of 2.0% and a standard deviation of .08%.

a. If the production line is operating correctly, approximately what proportion of batches from a day's production will contain less than 1.84% of zinc phosphide?

b. Suppose one batch chosen randomly actually contains 1.80% zinc phosphide. Does this indicate that there is too little zinc phosphide in today's production? Explain your reasoning.

2.73 Many of the nation's largest newspapers have sharply raised prices to offset the increasing cost of newsprint, while others want to increase their circulation's share of revenue relative to advertising's share of revenue. Consequently, these newspapers have experienced a decline in daily circulation. The table lists the percentage change in daily circulation from 1994 to 1995 for 11 of the largest newspapers in the United States.

Newspaper	Percent Change
Wall Street Journal	−1.0
USA Today	+3.9
New York Times	−2.9
Los Angeles Times	−4.7
Washington Post	−2.1
New York Daily News	−2.0
Chicago Tribune	+0.9
Newsday	−8.5
Dallas Morning News	+1.8
Boston Globe	−1.5
San Francisco Chronicle	−4.0

Source: Audit Bureau of Circulations, *New York Times,* October 31, 1995.

a. Compute the mean and standard deviation of the percentage changes in daily circulation for the 11 newspapers.

b. Assume the data in the table are representative of changes in daily circulation of all large U.S. newspapers. Use the results, part **a**, to sketch the relative frequency distribution of the 1994 to 1995 percentage change in daily circulation.

c. One of the nations largest newspapers, the *Houston Chronicle*, increased daily circulation by 32.4% from 1994 to 1995. Based on the distribution, part **b**, would you expect to observe a +32.4% change in daily circulation? Explain. [*Note:* Between 1994 and 1995, the *Houston Post* closed, leaving the city with only one large newspaper, the *Chronicle.*]

2.74 (X02.074) When it is working properly, a machine that fills 25-pound bags of flour dispenses an average of 25 pounds per fill; the standard deviation of the amount of fill is .1 pound. To monitor the performance of the machine, an inspector weighs the contents of a bag coming off the machine's conveyor belt every half-hour during the day. If the contents of two consecutive bags fall more than 2 standard deviations from the mean (using the mean and standard deviation given above), the filling process is said to be out of control and the machine is shut down briefly for adjustments. The data given in the table are the weights measured by the inspector yesterday. Assume the machine is never shut down for more than 15 minutes at a time. At what times yesterday was the process shut down for adjustment? Justify your answer.

Time	Weight (pounds)	Time	Weight (pounds)
8:00 A.M.	25.10	12:30 P.M.	25.06
8:30	25.15	1:00	24.95
9:00	24.81	1:30	24.80
9:30	24.75	2:00	24.95
10:00	25.00	2:30	25.21
10:30	25.05	3:00	24.90
11:00	25.23	3:30	24.71
11:30	25.25	4:00	25.31
12:00	25.01	4:30	25.15
		5:00	25.20

2.8 NUMERICAL MEASURES OF RELATIVE STANDING

We've seen that numerical measures of central tendency and variability describe the general nature of a quantitative data set (either a sample or a population). In addition, we may be interested in describing the *relative* quantitative location of a particular measurement within a data set. Descriptive measures of the relation-

FIGURE 2.25
Location of 90th percentile for yearly sales of oil companies

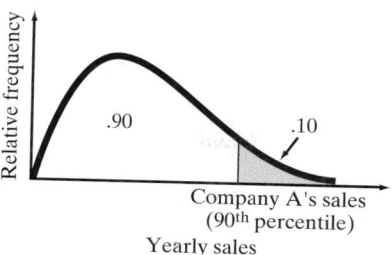

ship of a measurement to the rest of the data are called **measures of relative standing**.

One measure of the relative standing of a measurement is its **percentile ranking**. For example, if oil company A reports that its yearly sales are in the 90th percentile of all companies in the industry, the implication is that 90% of all oil companies have yearly sales *less* than company A's, and only 10% have yearly sales exceeding company A's. This is demonstrated in Figure 2.25. Similarly, if the oil company's yearly sales are in the 50th percentile (the median of the data set), 50% of all oil companies would have lower yearly sales and 50% would have higher yearly sales.

Percentile rankings are of practical value only for large data sets. Finding them involves a process similar to the one used in finding a median. The measurements are ranked in order and a rule is selected to define the location of each percentile. Since we are primarily interested in interpreting the percentile rankings of measurements (rather than finding particular percentiles for a data set), we define the *pth percentile* of a data set as shown in Definition 2.11.

DEFINITION 2.11

For any set of n measurements (arranged in ascending or descending order), the *p*th **percentile** is a number such that $p\%$ of the measurements fall below the *p*th percentile and $(100 - p)\%$ fall above it.

Another measure of relative standing in popular use is the *z*-score. As you can see in Definition 2.12, the *z*-score makes use of the mean and standard deviation of the data set in order to specify the relative location of a measurement:

DEFINITION 2.12

The **sample *z*-score** for a measurement x is

$$z = \frac{x - \bar{x}}{s}$$

The **population *z*-score** for a measurement x is

$$z = \frac{x - \mu}{\sigma}$$

FIGURE 2.26
Annual income
of steelworkers

| $18,000 | | $22,000 | $24,000 | | $30,000 |
| $\bar{x} - 3s$ | | Joe Smith's income | $\bar{x}$ | | $\bar{x} + 3s$ |

Note that the z-score is calculated by subtracting $\bar{x}$ (or μ) from the measurement x and then dividing the result by s (or σ). The final result, the z-score, represents the distance between a given measurement x and the mean, expressed in standard deviations.

EXAMPLE 2.14

Suppose 200 steelworkers are selected, and the annual income of each is determined. The mean and standard deviation are $\bar{x} = \$24,000$ and $s = \$2,000$. Suppose Joe Smith's annual income is $22,000. What is his sample z-score?

SOLUTION
Joe Smith's annual income lies below the mean income of the 200 steelworkers (see Figure 2.26). We compute

$$z = \frac{x - \bar{x}}{s} = \frac{\$22,000 - \$24,000}{\$2,000} = -1.0$$

which tells us that Joe Smith's annual income is 1.0 standard deviation *below* the sample mean, or, in short, his sample z-score is -1.0.

The numerical value of the z-score reflects the relative standing of the measurement. A large positive z-score implies that the measurement is larger than almost all other measurements, whereas a large negative z-score indicates that the measurement is smaller than almost every other measurement. If a z-score is 0 or near 0, the measurement is located at or near the mean of the sample or population.

We can be more specific if we know that the frequency distribution of the measurements is mound-shaped. In this case, the following interpretation of the z-score can be given.

Interpretation of z-Scores for Mound-Shaped Distributions of Data

1. Approximately 68% of the measurements will have a z-score between -1 and 1.
2. Approximately 95% of the measurements will have a z-score between -2 and 2.
3. Approximately 99.7% (almost all) of the measurements will have a z-score between -3 and 3.

Note that this interpretation of z-scores is identical to that given by the Empirical Rule for mound-shaped distributions (Table 2.8). The statement that a measurement falls in the interval $(\mu - \sigma)$ to $(\mu + \sigma)$ is equivalent to the statement that a measurement has a population z-score between -1 and 1, since all measurements between $(\mu - \sigma)$ and $(\mu + \sigma)$ are within 1 standard deviation of μ. These z-scores are displayed in Figure 2.27.

FIGURE 2.27

Population z-scores for a mound-shaped distribution

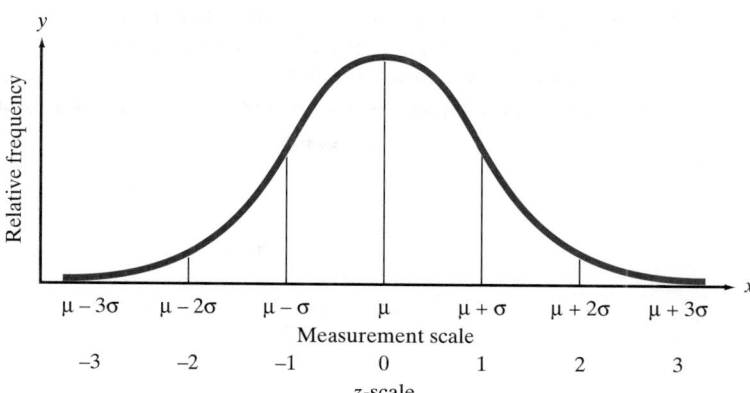

We end this section with an example that indicates how z-scores may be used to accomplish our primary objective—the use of sample information to make inferences about the population.

EXAMPLE 2.15 Suppose a female bank employee believes that her salary is low as a result of sex discrimination. To substantiate her belief, she collects information on the salaries of her male counterparts in the banking business. She finds that their salaries have a mean of $34,000 and a standard deviation of $2,000. Her salary is $27,000. Does this information support her claim of sex discrimination?

SOLUTION

The analysis might proceed as follows: First, we calculate the z-score for the woman's salary with respect to those of her male counterparts. Thus,

$$z = \frac{\$27{,}000 - \$34{,}000}{\$2{,}000} = -3.5$$

The implication is that the woman's salary is 3.5 standard deviations *below* the mean of the male salary distribution. Furthermore, if a check of the male salary data shows that the frequency distribution is mound-shaped, we can infer that very few salaries in this distribution should have a z-score less than -3, as shown in Figure 2.28. Therefore, a z-score of -3.5 represents either a measurement from a distribution different from the male salary distribution or a very unusual (highly improbable) measurement for the male salary distribution.

Which of the two situations do you think prevails? Do you think the woman's salary is simply unusually low in the distribution of salaries, or do you think her

FIGURE 2.28

Male salary distribution

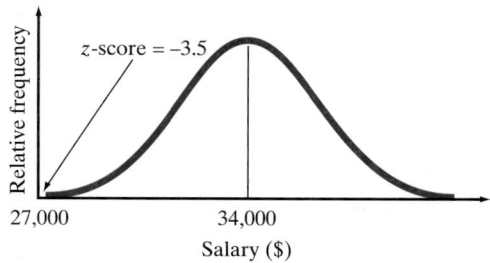

claim of sex discrimination is justified? Most people would probably conclude that her salary does not come from the male salary distribution. However, the careful investigator should require more information before inferring sex discrimination as the cause. We would want to know more about the data collection technique the woman used and more about her competence at her job. Also, perhaps other factors such as length of employment should be considered in the analysis.   ▙

Examples 2.13 and 2.15 exemplify an approach to statistical inference that might be called the **rare-event approach**. An experimenter hypothesizes a specific frequency distribution to describe a population of measurements. Then a sample of measurements is drawn from the population. If the experimenter finds it unlikely that the sample came from the hypothesized distribution, the hypothesis is concluded to be false. Thus, in Example 2.15 the woman believes her salary reflects sex discrimination. She hypothesizes that her salary should be just another measurement in the distribution of her male counterparts' salaries if no discrimination exists. However, it is so unlikely that the sample (in this case, her salary) came from the male frequency distribution that she rejects that hypothesis, concluding that the distribution from which her salary was drawn is different from the distribution for the men.

This rare-event approach to inference-making is discussed further in later chapters. Proper application of the approach requires a knowledge of probability, the subject of our next chapter.

EXERCISES   2.75–2.86

Learning the Mechanics

2.75 Compute the z-score corresponding to each of the following values of x:
a. $x = 40, s = 5, \bar{x} = 30$
b. $x = 90, \mu = 89, \sigma = 2$
c. $\mu = 50, \sigma = 5, x = 50$
d. $s = 4, x = 20, \bar{x} = 30$
e. In parts **a–d**, state whether the z-score locates x within a sample or a population.
f. In parts **a–d**, state whether each value of x lies above or below the mean and by how many standard deviations.

2.76 Give the percentage of measurements in a data set that are above and below each of the following percentiles:
a. 75th percentile   b. 50th percentile
c. 20th percentile   d. 84th percentile

2.77 What is the 50th percentile of a quantitative data set called?

2.78 Compare the z-scores to decide which of the following x values lie the greatest distance above the mean and the greatest distance below the mean.
a. $x = 100, \mu = 50, \sigma = 25$
b. $x = 1, \mu = 4, \sigma = 1$
c. $x = 0, \mu = 200, \sigma = 100$

d. $x = 10, \mu = 5, \sigma = 3$

2.79 At one university, the students are given z-scores at the end of each semester rather than the traditional GPAs. The mean and standard deviation of all students' cumulative GPAs, on which the z-scores are based, are 2.7 and .5, respectively.
a. Translate each of the following z-scores to corresponding GPA: $z = 2.0, z = -1.0, z = .5, z = -2.5$.
b. Students with z-scores below -1.6 are put on probation. What is the corresponding probationary GPA?
c. The president of the university wishes to graduate the top 16% of the students with *cum laude* honors and the top 2.5% with *summa cum laude* honors. Where (approximately) should the limits be set in terms of z-scores? In terms of GPAs? What assumption, if any, did you make about the distribution of the GPAs at the university?

2.80 Suppose that 40 and 90 are two elements of a population data set and that their z-scores are -2 and 3, respectively. Using only this information, is it possible to determine the population's mean and standard deviation? If so, find them. If not, explain why it's not possible.

Applying the Concepts

2.81   The U.S. Environmental Protection Agency (EPA) sets a limit on the amount of lead permitted in drinking water. The EPA *Action Level* for lead is .015 milligrams per liter (mg/L) of water. Under EPA guidelines, if 90% of a water system's study samples have a lead concentration less than .015 mg/L, the water is considered safe for drinking. I (co-author Sincich) received a 1994 report on a study of lead levels in the drinking water of homes in my subdivision. The 90th percentile of the study sample had a lead concentration of .00372 mg/L. Are water customers in my subdivision at risk of drinking water with unhealthy lead levels? Explain.

2.82   In *Fortune's* ranking of the 500 largest industrial corporations in the United States, Dell Computer ranked 490th in terms of 1991 sales. In 1996, it ranked 250th. Use percentiles to describe Dell Computer's position in each year's sales distribution.

2.83   In 1994 the United States imported merchandise valued at $664 billion and exported merchandise worth $513 billion. The difference between these two quantities (exports minus imports) is referred to as the *merchandise trade balance*. Since more goods were imported than exported in 1994, the merchandise trade balance was a *negative* $151 billion. The accompanying table lists the U.S. exports to and imports from a sample of ten countries in 1994 (in millions of dollars).

Country	Exports	Imports
Brazil	8,118	8,708
China	9,287	38,781
Egypt	2,844	548
France	13,622	16,775
Italy	7,193	14,711
Japan	53,481	119,149
Mexico	50,840	49,493
Panama	1,276	323
Sweden	2,520	5,044
Singapore	13,022	15,361

Source: Statistical Abstract of the United States: 1995, pp. 819–822.

   a. Calculate the U.S. merchandise trade balance with each of the ten countries. Express your answers in billions of dollars.
   b. Use a z-score to identify the relative position of the U.S. trade balance with Japan within the data set you developed in part **a**. Do the same for the trade balance with Egypt. Write a sentence or two that describes the relative positions of these two trade balances.

2.84   The accompanying table lists the unemployment rate in 1993 for a sample of nine countries.

Country	Percent Unemployed
Australia	10.9
Canada	11.2
France	11.8
Germany	5.8
Great Britain	10.4
Italy	10.5
Japan	2.5
Sweden	8.1
United States	6.8

Source: Statistical Abstract of the United States: 1995, p. 862.

The mean and standard deviation of the nine countries' unemployment rates are 8.67 and 3.12, respectively.
   a. Calculate the z-scores of the unemployment rates of the United States, France, and Japan.
   b. Describe the information conveyed by the sign (positive or negative) of the z-scores you calculated in part **a**.

2.85   Refer to the *Arkansas Business and Economic Review* (Summer 1995) study of hazardous waste sites in Arkansas counties, Exercise 2.38. A SAS descriptive statistics printout for the number of Superfund waste sites in each of the 75 counties is displayed on page 82.
   a. Find the 10th percentile of the data set on the printout. Interpret the result.
   b. Find the 95th percentile of the data set on the printout. Interpret the result.
   c. Use the information on the SAS printout to calculate the z-score for an Arkansas county with 48 Superfund sites.
   d. Based on your answer to part **c**, would you classify 48 as an extreme number of Superfund sites?

2.86   One of the ways the federal government raises money is through the sale of securities such as **Treasury bonds, Treasury bills (T-bills)**, and **U.S. savings bonds**. Treasury bonds and bills are marketable (i.e., they can be traded in the securities market) long-term and short-term notes, respectively. U.S. savings bonds are nonmarketable notes; they can be purchased and redeemed only from the U.S. Treasury. On July 5, 1996, the interest rate on three-month T-bills was 5.3%. Periodically *The Wall Street Journal* samples economists and asks them to forecast the interest rate of three-month T-bills. (T-bills are offered for sale weekly by the government, and their interest rates typically vary with each offering.) The forecasts for Sept. 30, 1996, are listed in the table at the bottom of page 82. The mean and standard deviation of the 17 forecasts are 5.4% and .60%, respectively.

```
                         UNIVARIATE  PROCEDURE
Variable=NUMSITES
                             Moments
          N                    75  Sum Wgts            75
          Mean                5.24  Sum                393
          Std Dev         7.244457  Variance      52.48216
          Skewness         3.46829  Kurtosis      16.41177
          USS                 5943  CSS            3883.68
          CV               138.253  Std Mean      0.836518
          T:Mean=0        6.264062  Prob>|T|        0.0001
          Sgn Rank            1008  Prob>|S|        0.0001
          Num ^=0               63

                         Quantiles(Def=5)

          100%   Max          48       99%            48
           75%   Q3            6       95%            21
           50%   Med           3       90%            12
           25%   Q1            1       10%             0
            0%   Min           0        5%             0
                                       1%             0

          Range              48
          Q3-Q1               5
          Mode                2

                             Extremes

          Lowest    Obs        Highest     Obs
               0(      68)        17(        47)
               0(      67)        21(        52)
               0(      66)        21(        75)
               0(      39)        25(        36)
               0(      38)        48(        74)
```

a. Calculate the z-scores of Economist #1's forecast and Economist #17's forecast. What do the z-scores tell you about their forecasts relative to the forecasts of the other economists?

b. Write a sentence or two that summarizes the 17 forecasts. In your summary, use a measure of central tendency and a measure of variability.

Economist	Interest Rate Forecast
1	5.2
2	5.25
3	5.85
4	4.30
5	5.85
6	4.75
7	5.70
8	4.23
9	5.0
10	5.0
11	6.0
12	5.0
13	5.2
14	5.5
15	5.65
16	5.75
17	6.50

2.9 QUARTILES AND BOX PLOTS (OPTIONAL)

The **box plot**, a relatively recent introduction to the methodology of descriptive measures, is based on the **quartiles** of a data set. Quartiles are values that partition the data set into four groups, each containing 25% of the measurements. The lower quartile Q_L is the 25th percentile, the middle quartile is the median m (the 50th percentile), and the upper quartile Q_U is the 75th percentile (see Figure 2.29).

> **DEFINITION 2.13**
> The **lower quartile Q_L** is the 25th percentile of a data set. The **middle quartile m** is the median. The **upper quartile Q_U** is the 75th percentile.

A box plot is based on the *interquartile range (IQR)*, the distance between the lower and upper quartiles:

$$IQR = Q_U - Q_L$$

> **DEFINITION 2.14**
> The **interquartile range (IQR)** is the distance between the lower and upper quartiles:
> $$IQR = Q_U - Q_L$$

The box plot for the 50 companies' percentages of revenues spent on R&D (Table 2.3) is given in Figure 2.30. It was generated by the MINITAB for Windows statistical software package.* Note that a rectangle (the **box**) is drawn, with the top and bottom sides of the rectangle (the **hinges**) drawn at the quartiles Q_L and Q_U. By definition, then, the "middle" 50% of the observations—those between Q_L and Q_U—fall inside the box. For the R&D data, these quartiles appear to be at (approximately) 7.0 and 9.5. Thus,

$$IQR = 9.5 - 7.0 = 2.5 \text{ (approximately)}$$

The median is shown at about 8.0 by a horizontal line within the box.

To guide the construction of the "tails" of the box plot, two sets of limits, called **inner fences** and **outer fences**, are used. Neither set of fences actually appears on the box plot. Inner fences are located at a distance of 1.5(IQR) from the hinges. Emanating from the hinges of the box are vertical lines called the **whiskers**. The two whiskers extend to the most extreme observation inside the inner fences. For

FIGURE 2.29
The quartiles for
a data set

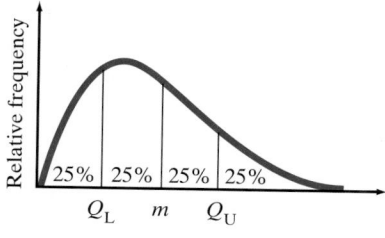

*Although box plots can be generated by hand, the amount of detail required makes them particularly well suited for computer generation. We use computer software to generate the box plots in this section.

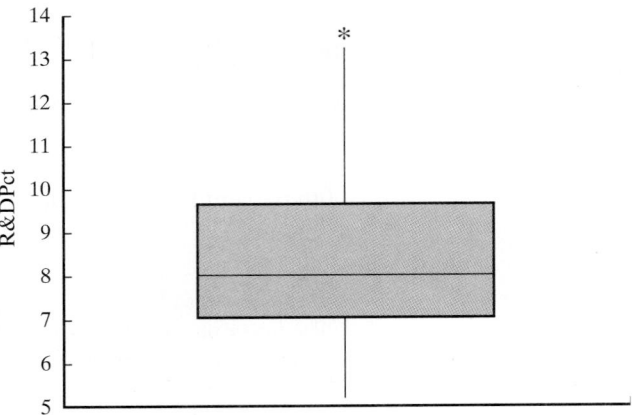

FIGURE 2.30
MINITAB box plot for R&D percentages

example, the inner fence on the lower side (bottom) of the R&D percentage box plot is (approximately)

Lower inner fence = Lower hinge − 1.5(IQR)

$\approx 7.0 - 1.5(2.5)$

$= 7.0 - 3.75 = 3.25$

The smallest measurement in the data set is 5.2, which is well inside this inner fence. Thus, the lower whisker extends to 5.2. Similarly, the upper whisker extends to about (9.5 + 3.75) = 13.25. The largest measurement inside this fence is the third largest measurement, 13.2. Note that the longer upper whisker reveals the rightward skewness of the R&D distribution.

Values that are beyond the inner fences receive special attention because they are extreme values that represent relatively rare occurrences. In fact, for mound-shaped distributions, fewer than 1% of the observations are expected to fall outside the inner fences. Two of the 50 R&D measurements, at 13.5, fall outside the upper inner fence. These measurements are represented by an asterisk (*) and they further emphasize the rightward skewness of the distribution. Note that the box plot does not reveal that there are *two* measurements at 13.5, since only a single symbol is used to represent both observations at that point.

The other two imaginary fences, the outer fences, are defined at a distance 3(IQR) from each end of the box. Measurements that fall beyond the outer fences are represented by 0s and are very extreme measurements that require special analysis. Less than one-hundredth of 1% (.01% or .0001) of the measurements from mound-shaped distributions are expected to fall beyond the outer fences. Since no measurement in the R&D percentage box plot (Figure 2.30) is represented by a 0, we know that no measurements fall outside the outer fences.

Generally, any measurements that fall beyond the inner fences—and certainly any that fall beyond the outer fences—are considered potential **outliers**. Outliers are extreme measurements that stand out from the rest of the sample and may be faulty: They may be incorrectly recorded observations, members of a population different from the rest of the sample, or, at the least, very unusual measurements from the same population. For example, the two R&D measurements at 13.5 (identified by an asterisk) may be considered outliers. When we analyze these measurements, we find that they are correctly recorded. However, it turns out that both represent R&D expenditures of relatively young and fast-growing companies. Thus, the outlier analysis may have revealed important factors that relate to the R&D expenditures of high-tech companies: their age and rate of growth.

Outlier analysis often reveals useful information of this kind and therefore plays an important role in the statistical inference-making process.

The elements (and nomenclature) of box plots are summarized in the next box. Some aids to the interpretation of box plots are also given.

Elements of a Box Plot

1. A rectangle (the **box**) is drawn with the ends (the **hinges**) drawn at the lower and upper quartiles (Q_L and Q_U). The median of the data is shown in the box, usually by a line or a symbol (such as "+").

2. The points at distances 1.5(IQR) from each hinge mark the **inner fences** of the data set. Horizontal lines (the **whiskers**) are drawn from each hinge to the most extreme measurement inside the inner fence.

3. A second pair of fences, the **outer fences**, appear at a distance of 3 interquartile ranges, 3(IQR), from the hinges. One symbol (usually "*") is used to represent measurements falling between the inner and outer fences, and another (usually "0") is used to represent measurements beyond the outer fences. Thus, outer fences are not shown unless one or more measurements lie beyond them.

4. The symbols used to represent the median and the extreme data points (those beyond the fences) will vary depending on the software you use to construct the box plot. (You may use your own symbols if you are constructing a box plot by hand.) You should consult the program's documentation to determine exactly which symbols are used.

Aids to the Interpretation of Box Plots

1. Examine the length of the box. The IQR is a measure of the sample's variability and is especially useful for the comparison of two samples (see Example 2.17).

2. Visually compare the lengths of the whiskers. If one is clearly longer, the distribution of the data is probably skewed in the direction of the longer whisker.

3. Analyze any measurements that lie beyond the fences. Fewer than 5% should fall beyond the inner fences, even for very skewed distributions. Measurements beyond the outer fences are probably outliers, with one of the following explanations:

   a. The measurement is incorrect. It may have been observed, recorded, or entered into the computer incorrectly.

   b. The measurement belongs to a population different from the population that the rest of the sample was drawn from (see Example 2.17).

   c. The measurement is correct *and* from the same population as the rest. Generally, we accept this explanation only after carefully ruling out all others.

EXAMPLE 2.16

In Example 2.2 we analyzed 50 processing times for the development of price quotes by the manufacturer of industrial wheels. The intent was to determine whether the success or failure in obtaining the order was related to the amount of time to process the price quotes. Each quote that corresponds to "lost" business was so classified. The data are repeated in Table 2.9. Use a statistical software package to draw a box plot for these data.

SOLUTION

The SAS box plot printout for these data is shown in Figure 2.31. SAS uses a horizontal dashed line in the box to represent the median, and a plus sign (+) to represent the mean. (SAS shows the mean in box plots, unlike many other statistical programs.) Also, SAS uses the symbol "0" to represent measurements between

TABLE 2.9   **Price Quote Processing Time (Days)**

Request Number	Processing Time	Lost?	Request Number	Processing Time	Lost?
1	2.36	No	26	3.34	No
2	5.73	No	27	6.00	No
3	6.60	No	28	5.92	No
4	10.05	Yes	29	7.28	Yes
5	5.13	No	30	1.25	No
6	1.88	No	31	4.01	No
7	2.52	No	32	7.59	No
8	2.00	No	33	13.42	Yes
9	4.69	No	34	3.24	No
10	1.91	No	35	3.37	No
11	6.75	Yes	36	14.06	Yes
12	3.92	No	37	5.10	No
13	3.46	No	38	6.44	No
14	2.64	No	39	7.76	No
15	3.63	No	40	4.40	No
16	3.44	No	41	5.48	No
17	9.49	Yes	42	7.51	No
18	4.90	No	43	6.18	No
19	7.45	No	44	8.22	Yes
20	20.23	Yes	45	4.37	No
21	3.91	No	46	2.93	No
22	1.70	No	47	9.95	Yes
23	16.29	Yes	48	4.46	No
24	5.52	No	49	14.32	Yes
25	1.44	No	50	9.01	No

the inner and outer fences and "*" to represent observations beyond the outer fences (the opposite of MINITAB).

Note that the upper whisker is longer than the lower whisker and that the mean lies above the median; these characteristics reveal the rightward skewness of

FIGURE 2.31
SAS box plot for
processing time data

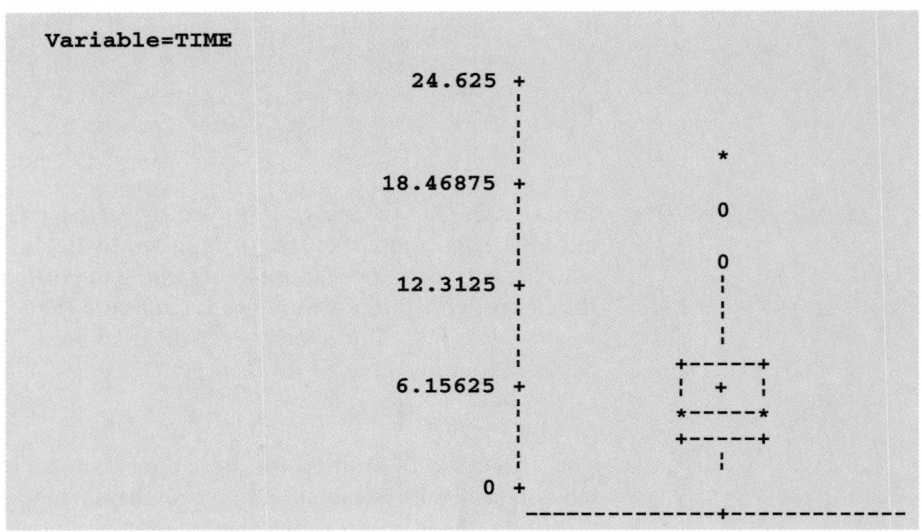

the data. However, the most important feature of the data is made very obvious by the box plot: There are at least two measurements between the inner and outer fences (in fact, there are three, but two are almost equal and are represented by the same "0") and at least one beyond the outer fence, all on the upper end of the distribution. Thus, the distribution is extremely skewed to the right, and several measurements need special attention in our analysis. We offer an explanation for the outliers in the following example.

EXAMPLE 2.17

The box plot for the 50 processing times (Figure 2.31) does not explicitly reveal the differences, if any, between the set of times corresponding to the success and the set of times corresponding to the failure to obtain the business. Box plots corresponding to the 39 "won" and 11 "lost" bids were generated using SAS, and are shown in Figure 2.32. Interpret them.

SOLUTION

The division of the data set into two parts, corresponding to won and lost bids, eliminates any observations that are beyond inner or outer fences. Furthermore, the skewness in the distributions has been reduced, as evidenced by the facts that the upper whiskers are only slightly longer than the lower, and that the means are closer to the medians than for the combined sample. The box plots also reveal that the processing times corresponding to the lost bids tend to exceed those of the won bids. A plausible explanation for the outliers in the combined box plot (Figure 2.31) is that they are from a different population than the bulk of the times. In other words, there are two populations represented by the sample of processing times—one corresponding to lost bids, and the other to won bids.

The box plots lend support to the conclusion that the price quote processing time and the success of acquiring the business are related. However, whether the visual differences between the box plots generalize to inferences about the populations corresponding to these two samples is a matter for inferential statistics, not graphical descriptions. We'll discuss how to use samples to compare two populations using inferential statistics in Chapter 7.

FIGURE 2.32
Box plots of processing time data: Won and lost bids

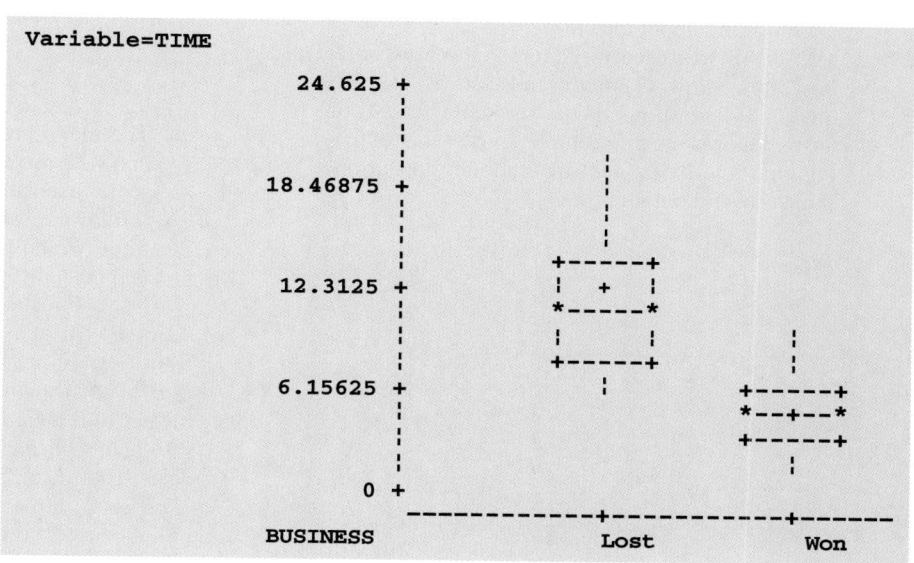

EXERCISES   2.87–2.96

Note: Exercises marked with 💾 *contain data available for computer analysis on a 3.5" disk (file name in parentheses).*

Learning the Mechanics

2.87 Define the 25th, 50th, and 75th percentiles of a data set. Explain how they provide a description of the data.

2.88 Suppose a data set consisting of exam scores has a lower quartile $Q_L = 60$, a median $m = 75$, and an upper quartile $Q_U = 85$. The scores on the exam range from 18 to 100. Without having the actual scores available to you, construct as much of the box plot as possible.

2.89 MINITAB was used to generate the following horizontal box plot. (*Note:* The hinges are represented by the symbol "I".)

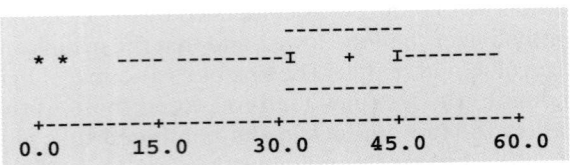

a. What is the median of the data set (approximately)?
b. What are the upper and lower quartiles of the data set (approximately)?
c. What is the interquartile range of the data set (approximately)?
d. Is the data set skewed to the left, skewed to the right, or symmetric?
e. What percentage of the measurements in the data set lie to the right of the median? To the left of the upper quartile?

2.90 MINITAB was used to generate the horizontal box plots below. Compare and contrast the frequency distributions of the two data sets. Your answer should include comparisons of the following characteristics: central tendency, variation, skewness, and outliers.

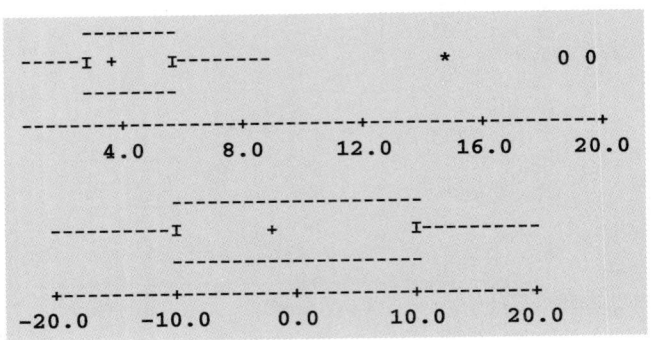

2.91 (X02.091) Consider the following two sample data sets: 💾

Sample A			Sample B		
121	171	158	171	152	170
173	184	163	168	169	171
157	85	145	190	183	185
165	172	196	140	173	206
170	159	172	172	174	169
161	187	100	199	151	180
142	166	171	167	170	188

a. Use a statistical software package to construct a box plot for each data set.
b. Using information reflected in your box plots, describe the similarities and differences in the two data sets.

Applying the Concepts

2.92 (X02.092) The table contains the top salary offer (in thousands of dollars) received by each member of a sample of 50 MBA students who graduated from the Graduate School of Management at Rutgers, the state university of New Jersey, in 1996.

61.1	48.5	47.0	49.1	43.5
50.8	62.3	50.0	65.4	58.0
53.2	39.9	49.1	75.0	51.2
41.7	40.0	53.0	39.6	49.6
55.2	54.9	62.5	35.0	50.3
41.5	56.0	55.5	70.0	59.2
39.2	47.0	58.2	59.0	60.8
72.3	55.0	41.4	51.5	63.0
48.4	61.7	45.3	63.2	41.5
47.0	43.2	44.6	47.7	58.6

Source: Career Services Office, Graduate School of Management, Rutgers University.

a. The mean and standard deviation are 52.33 and 9.22, respectively. Find and interpret the z-score associated with the highest salary offer, the lowest salary offer, and the mean salary offer. Would you consider the highest offer to be unusually high? Why or why not?
b. Use a statistical software package to construct a box plot for this data set. Which salary offers (if any) are potentially faulty observations? Explain.

2.93 Refer to the *Financial Management* (Spring 1995) study of 49 firms filing for prepackaged bankruptcies, Exercise 2.22. Recall that three types of "prepack" firms exist: (1) those who hold no pre-filing vote; (2) those who vote their preference for a joint solution; and (3) those who vote their preference for a prepack. Box plots, constructed using MINITAB for Windows, for the time in bankruptcy (months) for each type of firm are shown below.

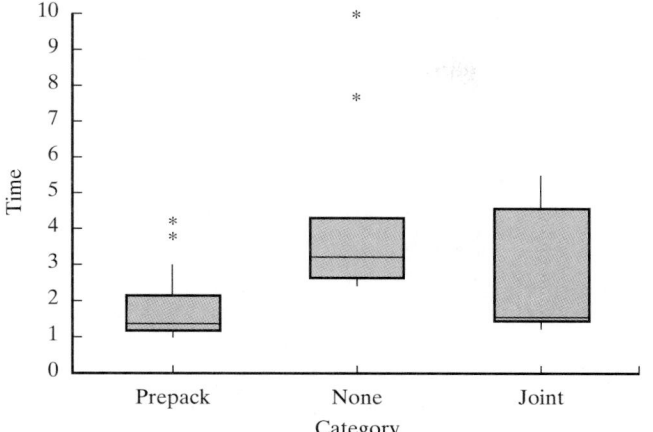

a. How do the median bankruptcy times compare for the three types? [*Hint:* Recall that MINITAB for Windows uses a horizontal line through the box to represent the median.]

b. How do the variabilities of the bankruptcy times compare for the three types?

c. The standard deviations of the bankruptcy times are 2.47 for "none," 1.72 for "joint," and 0.96 for "prepack." Do the standard deviations agree with the interquartile ranges (part **b**) with regard to the comparison of the variabilities of the bankruptcy times?

d. Is there evidence of outliers in any of the three distributions?

2.94 A firm's earnings per share (E/S) of common stock is a measure used by investors to monitor the financial performance of a firm. Thirty firms were sampled from *Fortune's* 1996 listing of the 500 largest corporations in the United States, and their earnings per share for 1995 are recorded in the table (above, to the right).

a. **(X02.094)** Use a statistical software package to construct a box plot for this data set. Identify any outliers that may exist in this data set.

b. For each outlier identified in part **a**, determine how many standard deviations it lies from the mean of the E/S data set.

2.95 A manufacturer of minicomputer systems is interested in improving its customer support services. As a first step, its marketing department has been charged with the responsibility of summarizing the extent of customer problems in terms of system down time. The 40 most recent customers were surveyed to determine the amount of down time (in hours) they had experienced during the previous month. These data are listed in the table to the right.

Firm	E/S
Illinois Tool Works	3.29
Sara Lee	1.62
Reynolds Metals	5.35
Nike	5.44
Phelps Dodge	10.65
Centex	3.04
Avery Dennison	2.70
Warner-Lambert	5.48
Maytag	−0.19
General Electric	3.90
Cooper Industries	0.84
Lockheed	3.28
Kellogg	2.24
FMC	5.72
Hasbro	1.76
Dow Chemical	7.72
Olin	5.50
Avon Products	3.76
Bear Stearns	1.70
American Stores	2.16
Humana	1.17
Asarco	4.00
Office Depot	0.85
DANA	2.84
Exxon	5.18
Georgia-Pacific	11.29
Crown Cork & Seal	0.83
DuPont (E.I.) de Nemours	5.61
McDonald's	1.97
UAL	20.01

Source: Fortune, April 29, 1996, pp. F1–F20.

Customer Number	Down Time	Customer Number	Down Time	Customer Number	Down Time
230	12	244	2	258	28
231	16	245	11	259	19
232	5	246	22	260	34
233	16	247	17	261	26
234	21	248	31	262	17
235	29	249	10	263	11
236	38	250	4	264	64
237	14	251	10	265	19
238	47	252	15	266	18
239	0	253	7	267	24
240	24	254	20	268	49
241	15	255	9	269	50
242	13	256	22		
243	8	257	18		

a. **(X02.095)** Use a statistical software package to construct a box plot for these data. Use the information reflected in the box plot to describe the frequency distribution of the data set. Your description should address central tendency, variation, and skewness.

b. Use your box plot to determine which customers are having unusually lengthy down times.

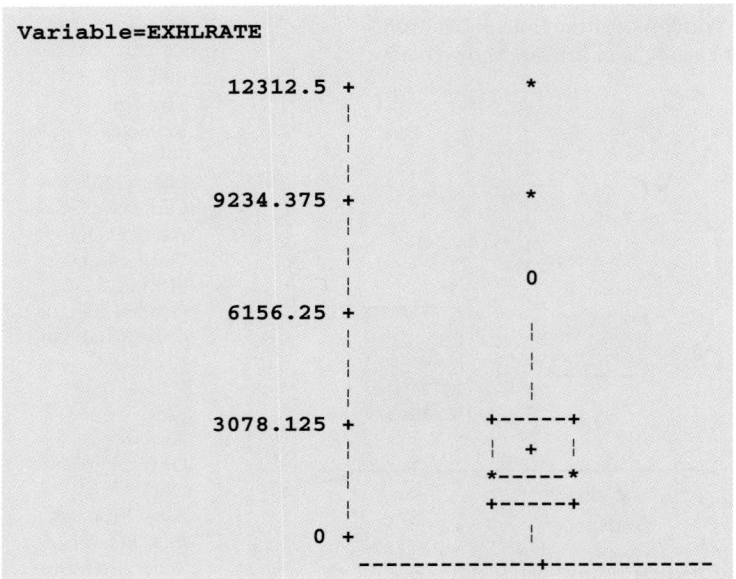

c. Find and interpret the z-scores associated with customers you identified in part **b**.

2.96   In Exercise 2.23 we constructed a stem-and-leaf display for 40 radiation (exhalation rate) measurements on waste gypsum and phosphate mounds in Florida. The figure above, constructed using SAS, is a box plot for the same data.

a. Use the box plot to estimate the lower quartile, median, and upper quartile of these data.

b. Does the distribution appear to be skewed? Explain.

c. Are there any outliers among these data? Explain.

d. Examine the stem-and-leaf display for these data in Exercise 2.23, and the box plot here. Which do you prefer as a description of these radiation measurements?

2.10   GRAPHING BIVARIATE RELATIONSHIPS (OPTIONAL)

The claim is often made that the crime rate and the unemployment rate are "highly correlated." Another popular belief is that the Gross Domestic Product (GDP) and the rate of inflation are "related." Some people even believe that the Dow Jones Industrial Average and the lengths of fashionable skirts are "associated." The words "correlated," "related," and "associated" imply a relationship between two variables—in the examples above, two *quantitative* variables.

One way to describe the relationship between two quantitative variables—called a **bivariate relationship**—is to plot the data in a **scattergram** (or **scatterplot**). A scattergram is a two-dimensional plot, with one variable's values plotted along the vertical axis and the other along the horizontal axis. For example, Figure 2.33 is a scattergram relating (1) the cost of mechanical work (heating, ventilating, and plumbing) to (2) the floor area of the building for a sample of 26 factory and warehouse buildings. Note that the scattergram suggests a general tendency for mechanical cost to increase as building floor area increases.

When an increase in one variable is generally associated with an increase in the second variable, we say that the two variables are "positively related" or "positively correlated."* Figure 2.33 implies that mechanical cost and floor area are positively correlated. Alternatively, if one variable has a tendency to decrease as

*A formal definition of correlation is given in Chapter 9.

FIGURE 2.33
Scattergram of cost vs.
floor area

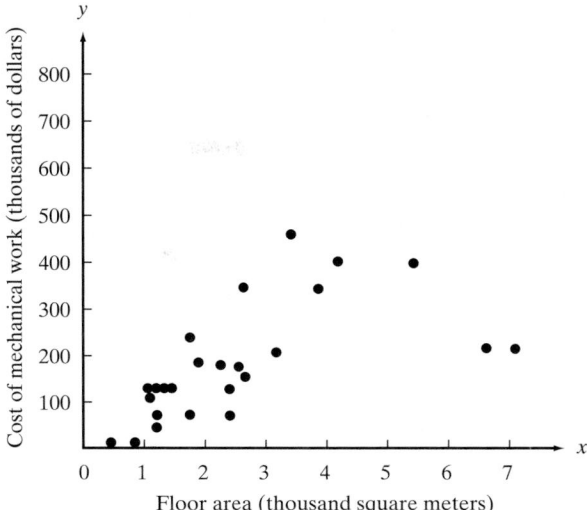

the other increases, we say the variables are "negatively correlated." Figure 2.34 shows several hypothetical scattergrams that portray a positive bivariate relationship (Figure 2.34a), a negative bivariate relationship (Figure 2.34b), and a situation where the two variables are unrelated (Figure 2.34c).

EXAMPLE 2.18

A medical item used to administer to a hospital patient is called a **factor**. For example, factors can be intravenous (IV) tubing, IV fluid, needles, shave kits, bedpans, diapers, dressings, medications, and even code carts. The coronary care unit at Bayonet Point Hospital (St. Petersburg, Florida) recently investigated the relationship between the number of factors administered per patient and the patient's length of stay (in days). Data on these two variables for a sample of 50 coronary care patients are given in Table 2.10. Use a scattergram to describe the relationship between the two variables of interest, number of factors and length of stay.

SOLUTION
Rather than construct the plot by hand, we resort to a statistical software package. The SPSS plot of the data in Table 2.10, with length of stay (LOS) on the vertical axis and number of factors (FACTORS) on the horizontal axis, is shown in Figure 2.35.

As plotting symbols, SPSS uses numbers. Each symbol represents the number of sample points, (e.g., patients) plotted at that particular coordinate. Although the plotted points exhibit a fair amount of variation, the scattergram clearly shows an

FIGURE 2.34
Hypothetical bivariate
relationship

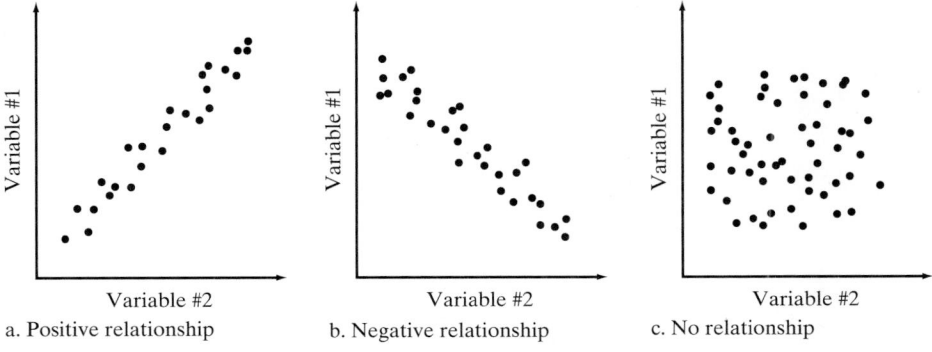

TABLE 2.10   Data on Patient's Factors and Length of Stay

Number of Factors	Length of Stay (days)	Number of Factors	Length of Stay (days)
231	9	354	11
323	7	142	7
113	8	286	9
208	5	341	10
162	4	201	5
117	4	158	11
159	6	243	6
169	9	156	6
55	6	184	7
77	3	115	4
103	4	202	6
147	6	206	5
230	6	360	6
78	3	84	3
525	9	331	9
121	7	302	7
248	5	60	2
233	8	110	2
260	4	131	5
224	7	364	4
472	12	180	7
220	8	134	6
383	6	401	15
301	9	155	4
262	7	338	8

Source: Bayonet Point Hospital, Coronary Care Unit.

increasing trend. It appears that a patient's length of stay is positively correlated with the number of factors administered to the patient. Hospital administrators may use this information to improve their forecasts of lengths of stay for future patients.

FIGURE 2.35
SPSS scatterplot of data in Table 2.10

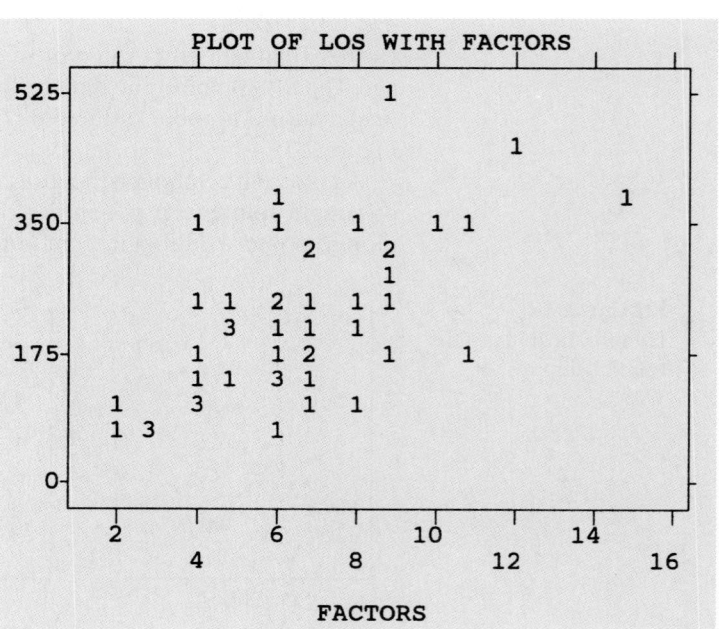

STATISTICS IN ACTION

2.2 CAR & DRIVER'S "ROAD TEST DIGEST"

Periodically, *Car & Driver* magazine conducts comprehensive road tests on all new car models. The results of the tests are reported in *Car & Driver's* "Road Test Digest." The "Road Test Digest" includes the following variables for each new car tested:

1. Model
2. List price ($)
3. Elapsed time from 0 to 60 mph (seconds)
4. Elapsed time for ¼ mile at full throttle (seconds)
5. Maximum speed (mph)
6. Braking distance from 70 to 0 mph (feet)
7. EPA-estimated city fuel economy (mpg)
8. Road-holding (grip) during cornering (gravitational force, in g's)

Focus

The "Road Test Digest" data from the August 1995 issue of *Car & Driver* is available in ASCII format on a 3.5" diskette that accompanies this text. The name of the file containing the data is CAR.DAT. Your assignment is to completely describe the data for *Car & Driver* magazine. Are there any trends in the data? What are typical values of these variables that a new car buyer can expect? Are there any new car models that have exceptional values of these variables? Are there any relationships among the variables? Your summary results will be reported in a future issue of the magazine.

The scattergram is a simple but powerful tool for describing a bivariate relationship. However, keep in mind that it is only a graph. No measure of reliability can be attached to inferences made about bivariate populations based on scattergrams of sample data. The statistical tools that enable us to make inferences about bivariate relationships are presented in Chapter 9.

2.11   DISTORTING THE TRUTH WITH DESCRIPTIVE TECHNIQUES

A picture may be "worth a thousand words," but pictures can also color messages or distort them. In fact, the pictures in statistics (e.g., histograms, bar charts, time series plots, etc.) are susceptible to distortion, whether unintentional or as a result of unethical statistical practices. In this section, we will mention a few of the pitfalls to watch for when interpreting a chart, graph, or numerical descriptive measure.

One common way to change the impression conveyed by a graph is to change the scale on the vertical axis, the horizontal axis, or both. For example, Figure 2.36 is a bar graph that shows the market share of sales for a company for each of the years 1990 to 1995. If you want to show that the change in firm A's market share over time is moderate, you should pack in a large number of units per inch on the vertical axis—that is, make the distance between successive units on the vertical scale small, as shown in Figure 2.36. You can see that a change in the firm's market share over time is barely apparent.

If you want to use the same data to make the changes in firm A's market share appear large, you should increase the distance between successive units on the vertical axis. That is, stretch the vertical axis by graphing only a few units per inch as in Figure 2.37. A telltale sign of stretching is a long vertical axis, but this is often hidden by starting the vertical axis at some point above 0, as shown in the time

FIGURE 2.36

Firm A's market share from 1990 to 1995—packed vertical axis

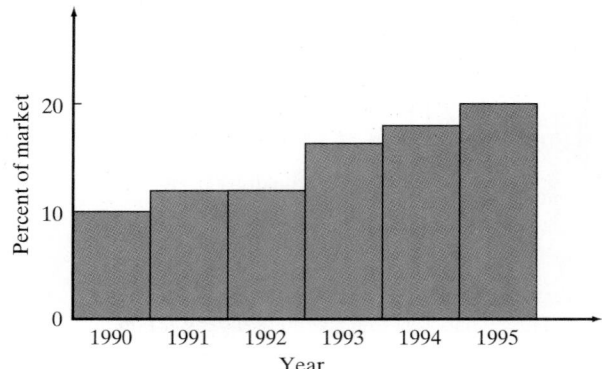

series plot, Figure 2.38a. The same effect can be achieved by using a broken line—called a *scale break*—for the vertical axis, as shown in Figure 2.38b.

Stretching the horizontal axis (increasing the distance between successive units) may also lead you to incorrect conclusions. For example, Figure 2.39a depicts the change in the Gross Domestic Product (GDP) from the first quarter of 1993 to the last quarter of 1994. If you increase the size of the horizontal axis, as in Figure 2.39b, the change in GDP over time seems less pronounced.

The changes in categories indicated by a bar graph can also be emphasized or deemphasized by stretching or shrinking the vertical axis. Another method of achieving visual distortion with bar graphs is by making the width of the bars proportional to the height. For example, look at the bar chart in Figure 2.40a, which depicts the percentage of a year's total automobile sales attributable to each of the four major manufacturers. Now suppose we make both the width and the height grow as the market share grows. This change is shown in Figure 2.40b. The reader may tend to equate the *area* of the bars with the relative market share of each manufacturer. But in fact, the true relative market share is proportional only to the *height* of the bars.

Sometimes we do not need to manipulate the graph to distort the impression it creates. Modifying the verbal description that accompanies the graph can change the interpretation that will be made by the viewer. Figure 2.41 provides a good illustration of this ploy.

Although we've discussed only a few of the ways that graphs can be used to convey misleading pictures of phenomena, the lesson is clear. Look at all graphical descriptions of data with a critical eye. Particularly, check the axes and the size

FIGURE 2.37

Firm A's market share from 1990 to 1995—stretched vertical axis

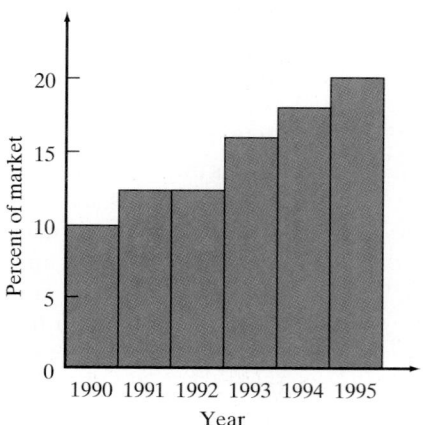

FIGURE 2.38
Changes in money
supply from
January to June

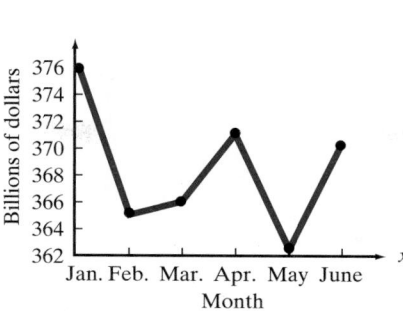

a. Vertical axis started at a point greater
than zero

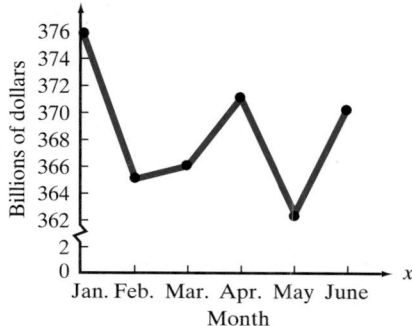

b. Gap in vertical axis

of the units on each axis. Ignore the visual changes and concentrate on the actual
numerical changes indicated by the graph or chart.

The information in a data set can also be distorted by using numerical descriptive measures, as Example 2.19 indicates.

EXAMPLE 2.19

Suppose you're considering working for a small law firm—one that currently has
a senior member and three junior members. You inquire about the salary you
could expect to earn if you join the firm. Unfortunately, you receive two answers:

Answer A: The senior member tells you that an "average employee" earns
$67,500.

Answer B: One of the junior members later tells you that an "average
employee" earns $55,000.

Which answer can you believe?

SOLUTION

The confusion exists because the phrase "average employee" has not been clearly defined. Suppose the four salaries paid are $55,000 for each of the three junior members and $105,000 for the senior member. Thus,

$$\text{Mean} = \frac{3(\$55,000) + \$105,000}{4} = \frac{\$270,000}{4} = \$67,500$$

$$\text{Median} = \$55,000$$

FIGURE 2.39
Gross National
Product from 1993
to 1994

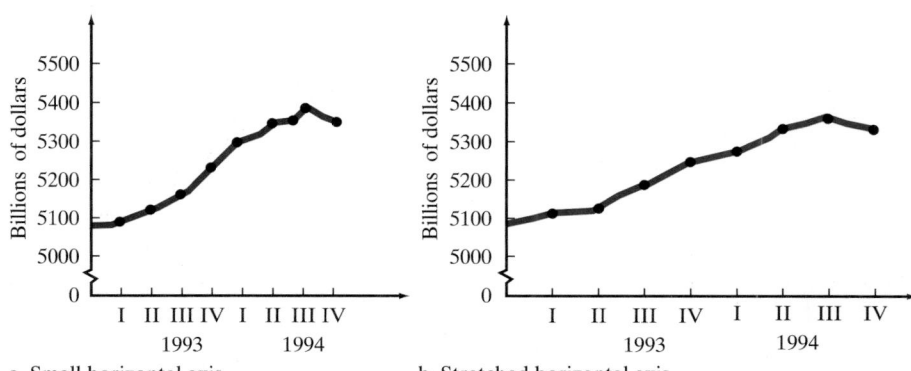

a. Small horizontal axis   b. Stretched horizontal axis

FIGURE 2.40
Relative share of the automobile market for each of four major manufacturers

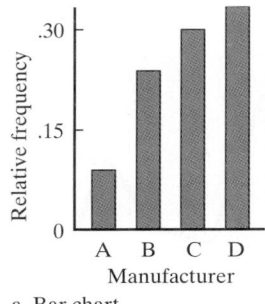

a. Bar chart

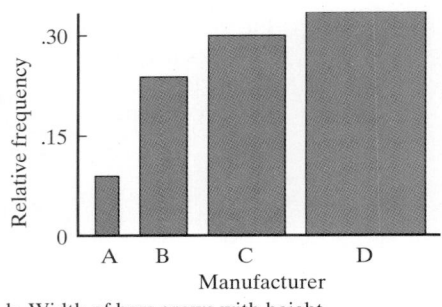

b. Width of bars grows with height

You can now see how the two answers were obtained. The senior member reported the mean of the four salaries, and the junior member reported the median. The information you received was distorted because neither person stated which measure of central tendency was being used. ▪.

Another distortion of information in a sample occurs when *only* a measure of central tendency is reported. Both a measure of central tendency and a measure of variability are needed to obtain an accurate mental image of a data set.

Suppose you want to buy a new car and are trying to decide which of two models to purchase. Since energy and economy are both important issues, you decide to purchase model A because its EPA mileage rating is 32 miles per gallon in the city, whereas the mileage rating for model B is only 30 miles per gallon in the city.

FIGURE 2.41
Changing the verbal description to change a viewer's interpretation
Source: Adapted from Selazny, G. "Grappling with Graphics," *Management Review,* Oct. 1975, p. 7.

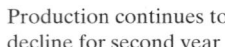
Production continues to decline for second year

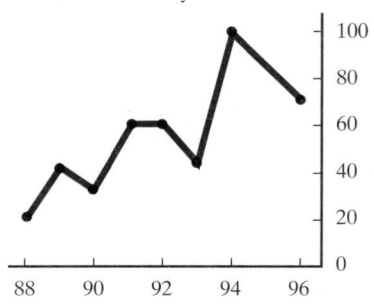

For our production, we need not even change the chart, so we can't be accused of fudging the data. Here we'll simply change the title so that for the Senate subcommittee, we'll indicate that we're not doing as well as in the past...

1996: 3rd best year for production

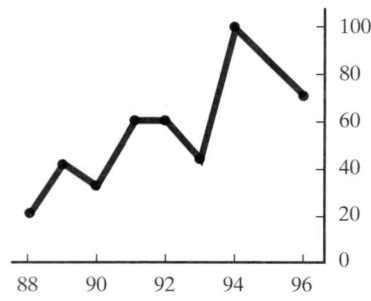

whereas for the general public, we'll tell them that we're still in the prime years.

FIGURE 2.42
Mileage distributions
for two car models

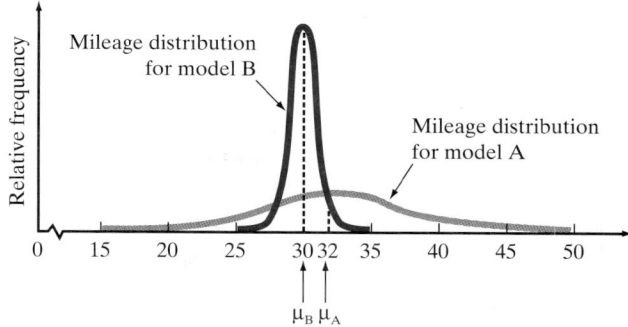

However, you may have acted too quickly. How much variability is associated with the ratings? As an extreme example, suppose that further investigation reveals that the standard deviation for model A mileages is 5 miles per gallon, whereas that for model B is only 1 mile per gallon. If the mileages form a mound-shaped distribution, they might appear as shown in Figure 2.42. Note that the larger amount of variability associated with model A implies that more risk is involved in purchasing model A. That is, the particular car you purchase is more likely to have a mileage rating that will greatly differ from the EPA rating of 32 miles per gallon if you purchase model A, while a model B car is not likely to vary from the 30-miles-per-gallon rating by more than 2 miles per gallon.

We conclude this section with another example on distorting the truth with numerical descriptive measures.

EXAMPLE 2.20

Children Out of School in America is a report on delinquency of school-age children prepared by the Children's Defense Fund (CDF), a government-sponsored organization. Consider the following three reported results of the CDF survey.

Reported result 1: 25 percent of the 16- and 17-year-olds in the Portland, Maine, Bayside East Housing Project were out of school. Fact: *Only eight children were surveyed; two were found to be out of school.*

Reported result 2: Of all the secondary school students who had been suspended more than once in census tract 22 in Columbia, South Carolina, 33% had been suspended two times and 67% had been suspended three or more times. Fact: *CDF found only three children in that entire census tract who had been suspended; one child was suspended twice and the other two children, three or more times.*

Reported result 3: In the Portland Bayside East Housing Project, 50% of all the secondary school children who had been suspended more than once had been suspended three or more times. Fact: *The survey found two secondary school children had been suspended in that area; one of them had been suspended three or more times.*

Identify the potential distortions in the results reported by the CDF.

SOLUTION

In each of these examples the reporting of percentages (i.e., relative frequencies) instead of the numbers themselves is misleading. No inference we might draw from the cited examples would be reliable. (We'll see how to measure the reliability of estimated percentages in Chapter 5.) In short, either the report should state the numbers alone instead of percentages, or, better yet, it should state that the numbers were too small to report by region. If several regions were combined, the numbers (and percentages) would be more meaningful. **L.**

QUICK REVIEW

Key Terms

Note: Starred (*) terms are from the optional sections in this chapter.

Bar graph   28
Bivariate relationship*   90
Box plots*   83
Chebyshev's Rule   69
Class frequency   26
Class relative frequency   26
Classes   26
Dot plot   37
Empirical Rule   70
Hinges*   83
Histogram   38
Inner fences*   83
Interquartile range*   83
Lower quartile*   83

Mean   53
Measurement classes   39
Measures of central tendency   53
Measures of relative standing   77
Measures of variation or spread   53
Median   55
Mode   58
Numerical descriptive measures   53
Outer fences*   83
Outliers*   84
Percentile   77
Pie chart   28
Quartiles*   83
Range   63

Rare-event approach   80
Relative frequency histogram   38
Scattergram*   90
Skewness   56
Standard deviation   65
Stem-and-leaf display   37
Time series data*   49
Time series plot*   49
Upper quartile*   83
Variance   65
Whiskers*   83
z-score   77

Key Formulas

$$x = \frac{\sum_{i=1}^{n} x_i}{n}$$

Sample mean   54

$$s^2 = \frac{\sum_{i=1}^{n}(x_i - \bar{x})^2}{n-1} = \frac{\sum_{i=1}^{n}x_i^2 - \frac{\left(\sum_{i=1}^{n}x_i\right)^2}{n}}{n-1}$$

Sample variance   65

$$s = \sqrt{s^2}$$

Sample standard deviation   65

$$z = \frac{x - \bar{x}}{s}$$

Sample z-score   77

$$z = \frac{x - \mu}{\sigma}$$

Population z-score   77

$$IQR = Q_U - Q_L$$

Interquartile range   83

LANGUAGE LAB

Symbol	Pronunciation	Description
Σ	sum of	Summation notation; $\sum_{i=1}^{n} x_i$ represents the sum of the measurements $x_1, x_2, ..., x_n$
μ	mu	Population mean
$\bar{x}$	x-bar	Sample mean
σ^2	sigma squared	Population variance
σ	sigma	Population standard deviation
s^2		Sample variance
s		Sample standard deviation
z		z-score for a measurement
m		Median (middle quartile) of a sample data set
Q_L		Lower quartile (25th percentile)
Q_U		Upper quartile (75th percentile)
IQR		Interquartile range

SUPPLEMENTARY EXERCISES 2.97–2.123

Note: Exercises marked with 💾 *contain data available for computer analysis on a 3.5" disk (file name in parentheses). Starred (*) exercises are from the optional sections in this chapter.*

Learning the Mechanics

2.97 Construct a relative frequency histogram for the data summarized in the accompanying table.

Measurement Class	Relative Frequency	Measurement Class	Relative Frequency
.00–.75	.02	5.25–6.00	.15
.75–1.50	.01	6.00–6.75	.12
1.50–2.25	.03	6.75–7.50	.09
2.25–3.00	.05	7.50–8.25	.05
3.00–3.75	.10	8.25–9.00	.04
3.75–4.50	.14	9.00–9.75	.01
4.50–5.25	.19		

2.98 Discuss the conditions under which the median is preferred to the mean as a measure of central tendency.

2.99 Consider the following three measurements: 50, 70, 80. Find the z-score for each measurement if they are from a population with a mean and standard deviation equal to
a. $\mu = 60, \sigma = 10$ **b.** $\mu = 60, \sigma = 5$
c. $\mu = 40, \sigma = 10$ **d.** $\mu = 40, \sigma = 100$

2.100 If the range of a set of data is 20, find a rough approximation to the standard deviation of the data set.

2.101 For each of the following data sets, compute $\bar{x}, s^2$, and s:
a. $13, 1, 10, 3, 3$ **b.** $13, 6, 6, 0$
c. $1, 0, 1, 10, 11, 11, 15$ **d.** $3, 3, 3, 3$

2.102 For each of the following data sets, compute $\bar{x}, s^2$, and s. If appropriate, specify the units in which your answers are expressed.
a. $4, 6, 6, 5, 6, 7$ **b.** $-\$1, \$4, -\$3, \$0, -\$3, -\$6$
c. $\frac{3}{5}\%, \frac{4}{5}\%, \frac{2}{5}\%, \frac{1}{5}\%, \frac{1}{16}\%$
d. Calculate the range of each data set in parts **a–c.**

2.103 Explain why we generally prefer the standard deviation to the range as a measure of variability for quantitative data.

Applying the Concepts

2.104 U.S. manufacturing executives frequently complain about the high cost of labor in this country. While it may be high relative to many Pacific Rim and South American countries, the table at right indicates that among Western countries, U.S. labor costs are relatively low.

Country	Hourly Manufacturing Labor Rates (in German marks)
Germany	43.97
Switzerland	41.47
Belgium	37.35
Japan	36.01
Austria	35.19
Netherlands	34.87
Sweden	31.00
France	28.92
United States	27.97
Italy	27.21
Ireland	22.17
Britain	22.06
Spain	20.25
Portugal	9.10

Source: The New York Times, October 15, 1995, p. 10.

a. What percentage of countries listed in the table have a higher wage rate than the United States? A lower wage rate than the United States?
b. As of July 5, 1996, one German mark was worth .65 U.S. dollars (*The Wall Street Journal,* July 8, 1996). Convert the data set to U.S. dollars and use the data set to answer the remaining parts of this exercise.
c. What is the mean hourly wage for the 13 Western countries listed in the table? For all 14 countries?
d. Find s^2 and s for all 14 countries.
e. According to Chebyshev's Rule, what percentage of the measurements in the table would you expect to find in the intervals $\bar{x} \pm .75s, \bar{x} \pm 2.5s, \bar{x} \pm 4s$?
f. What percentage of measurements actually fall in the intervals of part **e**? Compare your results with those of part **e**.

2.105 The sequence of pie charts on page 100 portrays the evolution of the structure of the top 500 firms in the United States and the top 200 firms in the United Kingdom over the period 1950–1980.
a. Describe the trends that are revealed by these pie charts.
b. Using your answer to part **a**, draw pie charts for the United Kingdom and the United States that forecast diversification in 2000.

2.106 *Consumer Reports* is a magazine that contains ratings and reports for consumers on goods, services, health, and personal finances. It is published by Consumers Union, a nonprofit organization established in 1936. Consumers Union reported on the testing of 46 brands of toothpaste (*Consumer Reports,* Sept. 1992). Each was rated on: package

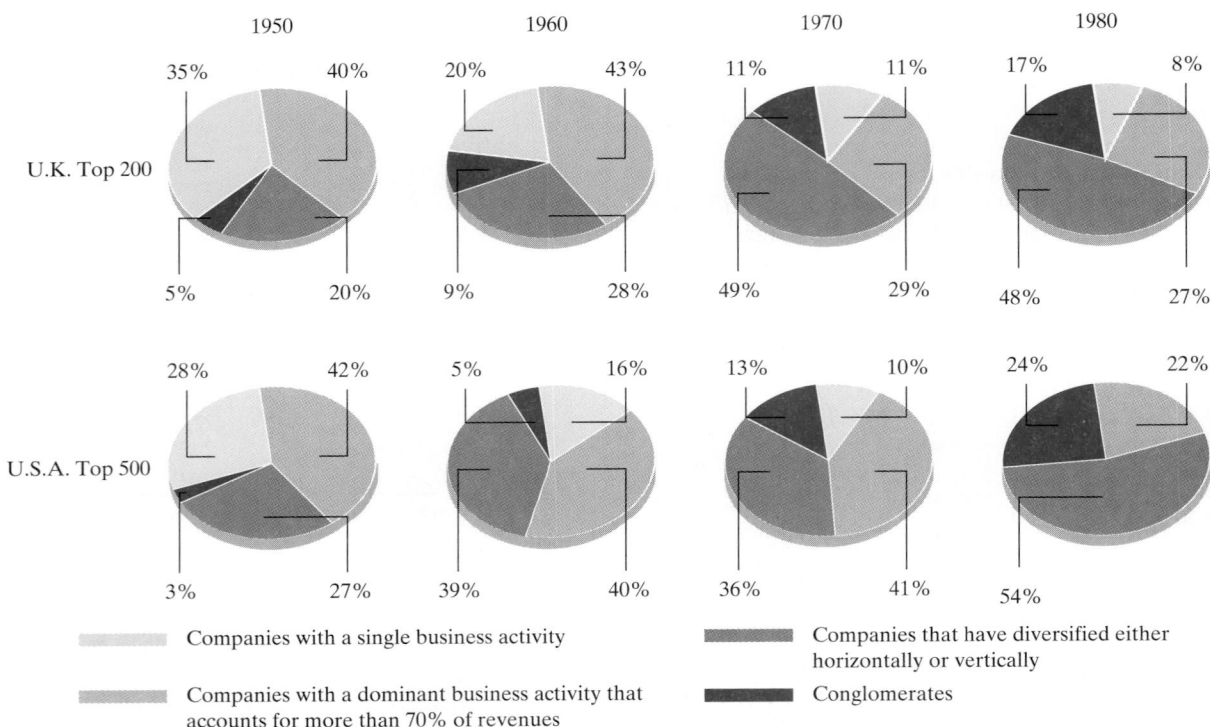

Growth of Diversification of Large Companies

Companies with a single business activity

Companies with a dominant business activity that accounts for more than 70% of revenues

Companies that have diversified either horizontally or vertically

Conglomerates

Source: Adapted and reprinted from *Long Range Planning,* Vol. 19, No. 1, pp. 52–60, Copyright 1986, with kind permission from Elsevier Science Ltd., The Boulevard, Langford Lane, Kidlington OX5 1GB UK.

design, flavor, cleaning ability, fluoride content, and cost per month (a cost estimate based on brushing with half-inch of toothpaste twice daily). The data below are costs per month for the 46 brands. Costs marked by an asterisk represent those brands that carry the American Dental Association (ADA) seal verifying effective decay prevention.

a. **(X02.106)** Use a statistical software package to construct a stem-and-leaf display for the data.

b. Circle the individual leaves that represent those brands that carry the ADA seal.

c. What does the pattern of circles suggest about the costs of those brands approved by the ADA?

2.107 **(X02.107)** A manufacturer of industrial wheels is losing many profitable orders because of the long time it takes the firm's marketing, engineering, and accounting departments to develop price quotes for potential customers. To remedy this problem the firm's management would like to set guidelines for the length of time each department should spend developing price quotes. To help develop these guidelines, 50 requests for price quotes were randomly selected from the set of all price quotes made last year; the processing time was determined for each price quote for each department. These times are displayed in the table on page 101. The price quotes are also classified by whether they were "lost" (i.e., whether or not the customer placed an order after receiving the price quote).

.58	.66	1.02	1.11	1.77	1.40	.73*	.53*	.57*	1.34
1.29	.89*	.49	.53*	.52	3.90	4.73	1.26	.71*	.55*
.59*	.97	.44*	.74*	.51*	.68*	.67	1.22	.39	.55
.62	.66*	1.07	.64	1.32*	1.77*	.80*	.79	.89*	.64
.81*	.79*	.44*	1.09	1.04	1.12				

PRICE QUOTE PROCESSING TIMES (IN DAYS)

Request Number	Marketing	Engineering	Accounting	Lost?	Request Number	Marketing	Engineering	Accounting	Lost?
1	7.0	6.2	.1	No	26	.6	2.2	.5	No
2	.4	5.2	.1	No	27	6.0	1.8	.2	No
3	2.4	4.6	.6	No	28	5.8	.6	.5	No
4	6.2	13.0	.8	Yes	29	7.8	7.2	2.2	Yes
5	4.7	.9	.5	No	30	3.2	6.9	.1	No
6	1.3	.4	.1	No	31	11.0	1.7	3.3	No
7	7.3	6.1	.1	No	32	6.2	1.3	2.0	No
8	5.6	3.6	3.8	No	33	6.9	6.0	10.5	Yes
9	5.5	9.6	.5	No	34	5.4	.4	8.4	No
10	5.3	4.8	.8	No	35	6.0	7.9	.4	No
11	6.0	2.6	.1	No	36	4.0	1.8	18.2	Yes
12	2.6	11.3	1.0	No	37	4.5	1.3	.3	No
13	2.0	.6	.8	No	38	2.2	4.8	.4	No
14	.4	12.2	1.0	No	39	3.5	7.2	7.0	Yes
15	8.7	2.2	3.7	No	40	.1	.9	14.4	No
16	4.7	9.6	.1	No	41	2.9	7.7	5.8	No
17	6.9	12.3	.2	Yes	42	5.4	3.8	.3	No
18	.2	4.2	.3	No	43	6.7	1.3	.1	No
19	5.5	3.5	.4	No	44	2.0	6.3	9.9	Yes
20	2.9	5.3	22.0	No	45	.1	12.0	3.2	No
21	5.9	7.3	1.7	No	46	6.4	1.3	6.2	No
22	6.2	4.4	.1	No	47	4.0	2.4	13.5	Yes
23	4.1	2.1	30.0	Yes	48	10.0	5.3	.1	No
24	5.8	.6	.1	No	49	8.0	14.4	1.9	Yes
25	5.0	3.1	2.3	No	50	7.0	10.0	2.0	No

a. MINITAB stem-and-leaf displays for each of the departments and for the total processing time are shown below and shown on page 102. Note that the units of the leaves for accounting and total processing times are units (1.0), while the leaf units for marketing and engineering processing times are tenths (.1). Shade the leaves that correspond to "lost" orders in each of the displays, and interpret each of the displays.

b. Using your results from part **a**, develop "maximum processing time" guidelines for each department that, if followed, will help the firm reduce the number of lost orders.

```
Stem-and-leaf of MKT        N = 50
Leaf Unit = 0.10

    6      0  112446
    7      1  3
   14      2  0024699
   16      3  25
   22      4  001577
  (10)     5  0344556889
   18      6  0002224799
    8      7  0038
    4      8  07
    2      9
    2     10  0
    1     11  0
```

```
Stem-and-leaf of ENG        N = 50
Leaf Unit = 0.10

    7      0  4466699
   14      1  3333788
   19      2  12246
   23      3  1568
   (5)     4  24688
   22      5  233
   19      6  01239
   14      7  22379
    9      8
    9      9  66
    7     10  0
    6     11  3
    5     12  023
    2     13  0
    1     14  4
```

```
Stem-and-leaf of ACC        N = 50
Leaf Unit = 1.0
    (31)    0  0000000000000000000000000001111
     19     0  22223333
     11     0  5
     10     0  67
      8     0  89
      6     1  0
      5     1  3
      4     1  4
      3     1
      3     1  8
      2     2
      2     2  2
      1     2
      1     2
      1     2
      1     3  0
```

```
Stem-and-leaf of TOTAL      N = 50
Leaf Unit = 1.0
      4     0  1334
     17     0  5666677888999
    (15)    1  000033333444444
     18     1  555566778999
      6     2  0344
      2     2
      2     3  0
      1     3  6
```

2.108 Refer to Exercise 2.107. Summary statistics for the processing times are given in the MINITAB print-out below.

a. Calculate the z-score corresponding to the maximum processing time guideline you developed in Exercise 2.107 for each department, and for the total processing time.

b. Calculate the maximum processing time corresponding to a z-score of 3 for each of the departments. What percentage of the orders exceed these guidelines? How does this agree with Chebyshev's Rule and the Empirical Rule?

c. Repeat part **b** using a z-score of 2.

d. Compare the percentage of "lost" quotes with corresponding times that exceed at least one of the guidelines in part **b** to the same percentage using the guidelines in part **c**. Which set of guidelines would you recommend be adopted? Why?

	N	MEAN	MEDIAN	TRMEAN	STDEV	SEMEAN
MKT	50	4.766	5.400	4.732	2.584	0.365
ENG	50	5.044	4.500	4.798	3.835	0.542
ACC	50	3.652	0.800	2.548	6.256	0.885
TOTAL	50	13.462	13.750	13.043	6.820	0.965

	MIN	MAX	Q1	Q3
MKT	0.100	11.000	2.825	6.250
ENG	0.400	14.400	1.775	7.225
ACC	0.100	30.000	0.200	3.725
TOTAL	1.800	36.200	8.075	16.600

*2.109 A time series plot similar to the one shown here appeared in a recent advertisement for a well-known golf magazine. One person might interpret the plot's message as the longer you subscribe to the magazine, the better golfer you should become. Another person might interpret it as indicating that if you subscribe for 3 years, your game should improve dramatically.

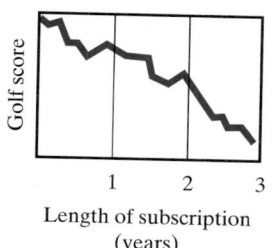

Length of subscription
(years)

a. Explain why the plot can be interpreted in more than one way.

b. How could the plot be altered to rectify the current distortion?

2.110 A company has roughly the same number of people in each of five departments: Production, Sales, R&D, Maintenance, and Administration. The following table lists the number and type of major injuries that occurred in each department last year.

Type of Injury	Department	Number of Injuries
Burn	Production	3
	Maintenance	6
Back strain	Production	2
	Sales	1
	R&D	1
	Maintenance	5
	Administration	2
Eye damage	Production	1
	Maintenance	2
	Administration	1
Deafness	Production	1
Cuts	Production	4
	Sales	1
	R&D	1
	Maintenance	10
Broken arm	Production	2
	Maintenance	2
Broken leg	Sales	1
	Maintenance	1
Broken finger	Administration	1
Concussion	Maintenance	3
	Administration	1
Hearing loss	Maintenance	2

a. Construct a Pareto diagram to identify which department or departments have the worst safety record.

b. Explode the Pareto diagram of part **a** to identify the most prevalent type of injury in the department with the worst safety record.

2.111 In some locations, radiation levels in homes are measured at well above normal background levels in the environment. As a result, many architects and builders are making design changes to ensure adequate air exchange so that radiation will not be "trapped" in homes. In one such location, 50 homes' levels were measured, and the mean level was 10 parts per billion (ppb), the median was 8 ppb, and the standard deviation was 3 ppb. Background levels in this location are at about 4 ppb.

a. Based on these results, is the distribution of the 50 homes' radiation levels symmetric, skewed to the left, or skewed to the right? Why?

b. Use both Chebyshev's Rule and the Empirical Rule to describe the distribution of radiation levels. Which do you think is most appropriate in this case? Why?

c. Use the results from part **b** to approximate the number of homes in this sample that have radiation levels above the background level.

d. Suppose another home is measured at a location 10 miles from the one sampled, and has a level of 20 ppb. What is the z-score for this measurement relative to the 50 homes sampled in the other location? Is it likely that this new measurement comes from the same distribution of radiation levels as the other 50? Why? How would you go about confirming your conclusion?

2.112 The 1995 Salary Survey by *Working Women* magazine (Jan. 1996) reports that over the 15-year period that ended in 1993, pay for female managers and executives climbed 18.3%, while their male colleagues gained only 1.7%. However, a gap still remains between the genders. For example, they report the median salaries for senior vice presidents/account managers in the advertising field are $122,000 for women and $145,000 for men. These medians were determined from sample data. They are estimates of the medians of their respective populations.

a. Describe the two populations.

b. Is it possible to determine the exact medians of these populations? Explain in detail.

c. Interpret the values of the reported medians.

2.113 Part-time and temporary workers have always represented a large share of employment in Japan. The need for less costly labor and protection against fluctuations in labor demand over the past decade in Japan have raised the number of part-time and temporary workers there. The table on page 104, extracted from *Monthly Labor*

U.S. Peanut Production*
(in billions of pounds)

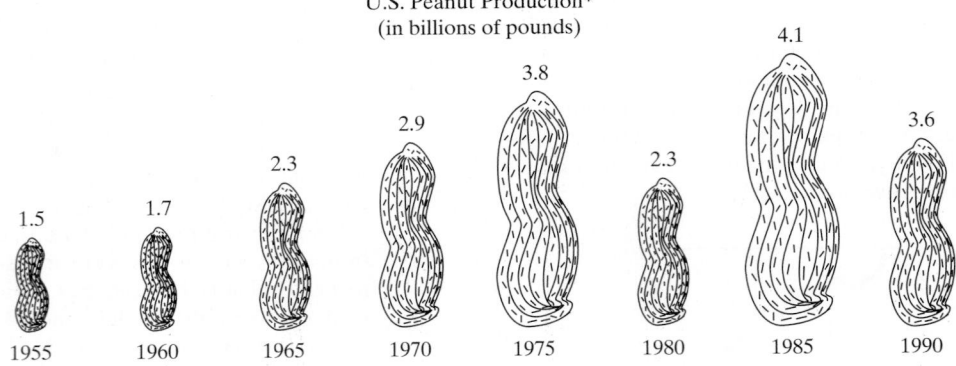

Review (Oct. 1995), gives the percentages of all paid employees in Japan in the different job categories for 1982 and 1992. Use a graphical method to demonstrate the increase in part-time and temporary workers in Japan from 1982 to 1992.

Job Category	PERCENT OF TOTAL NUMBER OF PAID WORKERS	
	1982	**1992**
Regular full-time	72.7	68.8
Part-time	11.0	16.1
Temporary	7.9	8.4
Day laborer	3.6	2.8
Other nonregular	4.8	3.9
Totals	100.0	100.0

*2.114 If not examined carefully, the graphical description of U.S. peanut production shown at the top of the page can be misleading.

   a. Explain why the graph may mislead some readers.

   b. Construct an undistorted graph of U.S. peanut production for the given years.

2.115 In experimenting with a new technique for imprinting paper napkins with designs, names, etc., a paper-products company discovered that four different results were possible:

   (A) Imprint successful
   (B) Imprint smeared
   (C) Imprint off-center to the left
   (D) Imprint off-center to the right

To test the reliability of the technique, the company imprinted 1,000 napkins and obtained the results shown in the graph in the next column.

   a. What type of graphical tool is the figure?

   b. What information does the graph convey to you?

   c. From the information provided by the graph, how might you numerically describe the reliability of the imprinting technique?

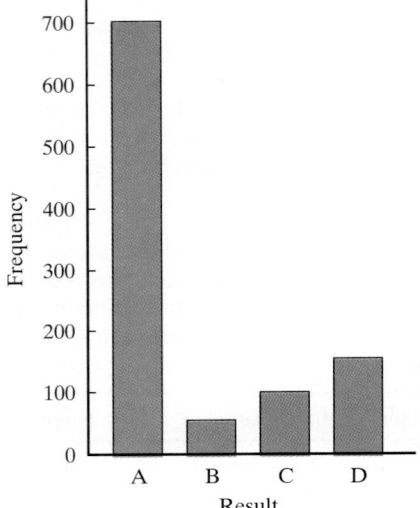

2.116 The data in the table below describe the distribution of rent amounts paid by U.S. apartment dwellers in 1993. Use a relative frequency histogram to describe the data.

Rent (in dollars)	Percent of Renters in Rent Class
Less than $100	2.0
$100–$199	7.0
$200–$299	10.0
$300–$399	15.0
$400–$499	18.0
$500–$599	16.0
$600–$699	12.0
$700–$799	8.0
$800–$899	4.0
$900–$999	3.0
$1000 or more	5.0
Total	100.0

Source: U.S. Bureau of the Census, *Statistical Abstract of the United States: 1995*, p. 738.

2.117 A study by the U.S. Public Research Interest Group found that in Massachusetts bank customers were charged lower fees than the national average for regular checking accounts, NOW accounts, and savings accounts. For regular checking accounts the Massachusetts mean was $190.06 per year, while the national mean was $201.94 (*Boston Globe*, Aug. 9, 1995). The referenced article did not explain how these averages were determined other than to say the national average was estimated from a sample of 271 banks in 25 states. Prepare a report that explains in detail how Massachusetts' mean could have been estimated. There are 245 banks in Massachusetts. Your answer should include a sampling plan, a measurement plan, and a calculation formula.

2.118 Polychlorinated biphenyls (PCBs), considered to be extremely hazardous to humans, are often used in the insulation of large electric transformers. The *Gainesville Sun* (Mar. 24, 1984) reported on the discovery of a particularly high PCB count at a salvage company in Clay County, Florida. The company, which salvaged the copper in electrical transformers, allowed oil contaminated with PCBs to seep into the soil in and around the salvage site. One soil sample in the vicinity registered 200 parts per million (ppm) of PCBs, four times the safe limit established by the Florida Department of Environmental Regulation. Suppose that the PCB count in samples of soil in the vicinity of the salvage operation has a distribution with mean equal to 25 ppm and standard deviation equal to 5 ppm of PCBs. Would a soil sample showing 200 ppm be classified as an extreme observation? Explain.

2.119 The table lists the average inflation rates between 1985 and 1993 for two samples of countries, those with high Gross National Products (GNP) per capita and low GNP per capita.

	High GNP		Low GNP
United States	3.5	China	8.1
Sweden	6.3	India	9.7
Germany	3.2	Egypt	16.9
Spain	6.8	Ethiopia	380.0
France	3.0	Ghana	29.4
Italy	6.5	Vietnam	118.7
Japan	1.4	Sudan	55.3
Australia	4.6	Pakistan	8.4

Source: The World Bank Atlas, 1995.

a. For each sample, characterize the magnitude and variability of the inflation rates using appropriate numerical descriptive measures.

b. Justify the measures you used in part **a**. For example, is the mean, median, or mode the most appropriate measure of magnitude?

c. Notice that there is variation in the inflation rates both within each sample and between the samples. Is this surprising? Why or why not?

2.120 The Age Discrimination in Employment Act mandates that workers 40 years of age or older be treated without regard to age in all phases of employment (hiring, promotions, firing, etc.). Age discrimination cases are of two types: *disparate treatment* and *disparate impact*. In the former, the issue is whether workers have been intentionally discriminated against. In the latter, the issue is whether employment practices adversely affect the protected class (i.e., workers 40 and over) even though no such effect was intended by the employer (Zabell, 1989). During the recession of the early 1990s, a small computer manufacturer laid off 10 of its 20 software engineers. The ages of all the engineers at the time of the layoff are shown in the table.

| Not laid off: | 34 | 55 | 42 | 38 | 42 | 32 | 40 | 40 | 46 | 29 |
| Laid off: | 52 | 35 | 40 | 41 | 40 | 39 | 40 | 64 | 47 | 44 |

Analyze the data to determine whether the company may be vulnerable to a disparate impact claim.

*2.121 A national chain of automobile oil-change franchises claims that "your hood will be open for less than 12 minutes when we service your car." To check their claim, an undercover consumer reporter from a local television station monitored the "hood time" of 25 consecutive customers at one of the chain's franchises. The resulting data follow. Construct a time series plot for these data and describe in words what it reveals.

Customer Number	Hood Open (Minutes)	Customer Number	Hood Open (Minutes)
1	11.50	14	12.50
2	13.50	15	13.75
3	12.25	16	12.00
4	15.00	17	11.50
5	14.50	18	14.25
6	13.75	19	15.50
7	14.00	20	13.00
8	11.00	21	18.25
9	12.75	22	11.75
10	11.50	23	12.50
11	11.00	24	11.25
12	13.00	25	14.75
13	16.25		

2.122 The table on page 106 reports the year-to-date automobile sales in the United States (in thousands of cars) for the "Big Three" U.S. manufacturers (Ford, General Motors, and Chrysler), European manufacturers, and Japanese manufacturers.

a. Construct a relative frequency bar graph for these data.

Manufacturer	November 1995
General Motors	229.7
Ford	131.2
Chrysler	58.3
Japanese	192.6
European	37.0
Total	648.8

Source: Wall Street Journal, December 6, 1995, p. B5.

b. *Stacking* is the combining of all bars in a bar graph into a single bar, by drawing one on top of the other and distinguishing one from another by the use of colors or patterns. Stack the relative frequencies of the five car manufacturers for November 1995.

c. What information about the U.S. automobile market is reflected in your graph of part **a**?

d. What share of the U.S. automobile market has been captured by U.S. manufacturers?

2.123 Computer anxiety is defined as "the mixture of fear, apprehension, and hope that people feel when planning to interact, or when interacting with a computer." Researchers have found computer anxiety in people at all levels of society, including students, doctors, lawyers, secretaries, managers, and college professors. One profession for which little is known about the level and impact of computer anxiety is secondary technical education (STE), since STE teachers have just recently begun to participate in the high-tech computer revolution. The extent of computer anxiety among STE teachers was investigated by H. R. D. Gordon in the *Journal of Studies in Technical Careers* (Vol. 15, 1995). A sample of 116 teachers were administered the Computer Anxiety Scale (COMPAS) designed to measure level of computer anxiety. Scores, ranging from 10 to 50, were categorized as follows: very anxious (37–50); anxious/tense (33–36); some mild anxiety (27–32); generally relaxed/comfortable (20–26); very relaxed/confident (10–19). A summary of the COMPAS anxiety levels for the sample is provided in the following table.

Category	Score Range	Frequency	Relative Frequency
Very anxious	37–50	22	.19
Anxious/tense	33–36	8	.07
Some mild anxiety	27–32	23	.20
Generally relaxed/ comfortable	20–26	24	.21
Very relaxed/confident	10–19	39	.33
Totals		116	1.00

Source: Gordon, H. R. D. "Analysis of the computer anxiety levels of secondary technical education teachers in West Virginia." *Journal of Studies in Technical Careers,* Vol. 15, No. 2, 1995, pp. 26–27 (Table 1).

a. Graph and interpret the results.

b. One of the objectives of the research is to compare the computer anxiety levels of male and female STE teachers. Use the summary information in the following table to make the comparison.

	Male Teachers	Female Teachers	All Teachers
n	68	48	116
$\bar{x}$	26.4	24.5	25.6
s	10.6	11.2	10.8

Source: Gordon, H. R. D. "Analysis of the computer anxiety levels of secondary technical education teachers in West Virginia." *Journal of Studies in Technical Careers,* Vol. 15, No. 2, 1995, pp. 26–27 (Table 2).

SHOWCASE THE KENTUCKY MILK CASE—PART I

Many products and services are purchased by governments, cities, states, and businesses on the basis of sealed bids, and contracts are awarded to the lowest bidders. This process works extremely well in competitive markets, but it has the potential to increase the cost of purchasing if the markets are noncompetitive or if collusive practices are present. An investigation that began with a statistical analysis of bids in the Florida school milk market in 1986 led to the recovery of more than $33,000,000 from dairies who had conspired to rig the bids there in the 1980s. The investigation spread quickly to other states, and to date settlements and fines from dairies exceed $100,000,000 for school milk bidrigging in twenty other states. This case concerns a school milk bidrigging investigation in Kentucky.

Each year, the Commonwealth of Kentucky invites bids from dairies to supply half-pint containers of fluid milk products for its school districts. The products include whole white milk, low-fat white milk, and low-fat chocolate milk. In 13 school districts in northern Kentucky, the suppliers (dairies) were accused of "price-fixing," that is, conspiring to allocate the districts, so that the "winner" was predetermined. Since these districts are located in Boone, Campbell, and Kenton counties, the geographic market they represent is designated as the "tri-county" market. Between 1983 and 1991, two dairies—Meyer Dairy and Trauth Dairy—were the only bidders on the milk contracts in the school districts in the tri-county market. Consequently, these two companies were awarded all the milk contracts in the market. (In contrast, a large number of different dairies won the milk contracts for the school districts in the remainder of the northern Kentucky market–called the "surrounding" market.) The Commonwealth of Kentucky alleged that Meyer and Trauth conspired to allocate the districts in the tri-county market. To date, one of the dairies (Meyer) has admitted guilt, while the other (Trauth) steadfastly maintains its innocence.

The Commonwealth of Kentucky maintains a database on all bids received from the dairies competing for the milk contracts. Some of these data have been made available to you to analyze to determine whether there is empirical evidence of bid collusion in the tri-county market. The data, available in ASCII format on a 3.5" diskette, is described in detail below. Some background information on the data and important economic theory regarding bid collusion is also provided. Use this information to guide your analysis. Prepare a professional document which presents the results of your analysis and gives your opinion regarding collusion.

DATA. ASCII file name: MILK.DAT
Number of observations: 392

Variable	Column(s)	Type	Description
YEAR	1–4	QN	Year in which milk contract awarded
MARKET	6–15	QL	Northern Kentucky Market (TRI-COUNTY or SURROUND)
WINNER	17–30	QL	Name of winning dairy
WWBID	32–38	QN	Winning bid price of whole white milk (dollars per half-pint)
WWQTY	40–46	QN	Quantity of whole white milk purchased (number of half-pints)
LFWBID	48–53	QN	Winning bid price of low-fat white milk (dollars per half-pint)
LFWQTY	55–62	QN	Quantity of low-fat white milk purchased (number of half-pints)
LFCBID	64–69	QN	Winning bid price of low-fat chocolate milk (dollars per half-pint)
LFCQTY	71–78	QN	Quantity of low-fat chocolate milk purchased (number of half-pints)
DISTRICT	80–82	QL	School district number
KYFMO	84–89	QN	FMO minimum raw cost of milk (dollars per half-pint)
MILESM	91–93	QN	Distance (miles) from Meyer processing plant to school district
MILEST	95–97	QN	Distance (miles) from Trauth processing plant to school district
LETDATE	99–106	QL	Date on which bidding on milk contract began (month/day/year)

BACKGROUND INFORMATION

Collusive Market Environment. Certain economic features of a market create an environment in which collusion may be found. These basic features include:

1. *Few sellers and high concentration.* Only a few dairies control all or nearly all of the milk business in the market.

2. *Homogeneous products.* The products sold are essentially the same from the standpoint of the buyer (i.e., the school district).

3. *Inelastic demand.* Demand is relatively insensitive to price. (Note: The quantity of milk required by a school district is primarily determined by school enrollment, not price.)

4. *Similar costs.* The dairies bidding for the milk contracts face similar cost conditions. (Note: Approximately 60% of a dairy's production cost is raw milk, which is federally regulated. Meyer and Trauth are dairies of similar size and both bought their raw milk from the same supplier.)

Although these market structure characteristics create an environment which makes collusive behavior easier, they do not necessarily indicate the existence of collusion. An analysis of the actual bid prices may provide additional information about the degree of competition in the market.

Collusive Bidding Patterns. The analyses of patterns in sealed bids reveal much about the level of competition, or lack thereof, among the vendors serving the market. Consider the following bid analyses:

1. *Market shares.* A market share for a dairy is the number of milk half-pints supplied by the dairy over a given school year, divided by the total number of half-pints supplied to the entire market. One sign of potential collusive behavior is stable, nearly equal market shares over time for the dairies under investigation.

2. *Incumbency rates.* Market allocation is a common form of collusive behavior in bidrigging conspiracies. Typically, the same diary controls the same school districts year after year. The incumbency rate for a market in a given school year is defined as the percentage of school districts that are won by the same vendor who won the previous year. An incumbency rate that exceeds 70% has been considered a sign of collusive behavior.

3. *Bid levels and dispersion.* In competitive sealed bid markets vendors do not share information about their bids. Consequently, more dispersion or variability among the bids is observed than in collusive markets, where vendors communicate about their bids and have a tendency to submit bids in close proximity to one another in an attempt to make the bidding appear competitive. Furthermore, in competitive markets the bid dispersion tends to be directly proportional to the level of the bid: When bids are submitted at relatively high levels, there is more variability among the bids than when they are submitted at or near marginal cost, which will be approximately the same among dairies in the same geographic market.

4. *Price versus cost/distance.* In competitive markets, bid prices are expected to track costs over time. Thus, if the market is competitive, the bid price of milk should be highly correlated with the raw milk cost. Lack of such a relationship is another sign of collusion. Similarly, bid price should be correlated to the distance the product must travel from the processing plant to the school (due to delivery costs) in a competitive market.

5. *Bid sequence.* School milk bids are submitted over the spring and summer months, generally at the end of one school year and before the beginning of the next. When the bids are examined in sequence in competitive markets, the level of bidding is expected to fall as the bidding season progresses. (This phenomenon is attributable to the learning process that occurs during the season, with bids adjusted accordingly. Dairies may submit relatively high bids early in the season to "test the market," confident that volume can be picked up later if the early high bids lose. But, dairies who do not win much business early in the season are likely to become more aggressive in their bidding as the season progresses, driving price levels down.) Constant or slightly increasing price patterns of sequential bids in a market where a single dairy wins year after year is considered another indication of collusive behavior.

6. *Comparison of average winning bid prices.* Consider two similar markets, one in which bids are possibly rigged and the other in which bids are competitively determined. In theory, the mean winning price in the "rigged" market will be significantly higher than the mean price in the competitive market for each year in which collusion occurs. ▲

www.int.com
www.int.com
INTERNET LAB
www.int.com

ACCESSING AND SUMMARIZING BUSINESS AND ECONOMIC DATA MAINTAINED BY THE U.S. GOVERNMENT

A vital underpinning of statistical analysis and interpretation of results is the information value of the data used. Data collection is often an expensive undertaking and many studies begin with an examination of external data; that is, data routinely collected and maintained by credible sources. Various government agencies play a major role in producing data across many areas of business and economics. These data constitute a primary starting point for obtaining external data.

Here we will visit three important U.S. government sites, all of which provide data for examining business and economic conditions. Our initial focus is to become acquainted with locating prominent data published by these three agencies and to learn about the variety of different data each of these sources produces. In the process of examining these sites, you will notice links to other government sites where yet other data reside. Visiting these three sites will not give you an exhaustive overview of either U.S. government or Internet resources but hopefully will provide you with a structured introduction to the vast resources available. Later labs will examine in further detail data selections from these three sites, among others.

For each site, perform the following tasks:

1. Note the type of data (quantitative or qualitative) available.

2. Note the format of the data set of interest (ASCII, HTML, SAS, SPSS, etc.) and read any associated notes about downloading and/or formatting the data.

3. Are there subscription fees or other conditions or restrictions on obtaining the data? If so, note what those are.

4. Write down the direct URL address of the requested data.

5. List three or more other major data series available from the parent agency.

6. Are there special formats, subscriptions, and so forth associated with any of these other data sets?

7. Name some other agencies or organizations to which this site provides links.

8. Leave the site completely by typing in the home page address of your school in your address location area (use: *http://www.prenhall.com* if you do not know the school's address).

9. Now type in the direct address of the requested data from step 4. Are you able to locate the data in one step?

10. Save the data set of interest to your statistical applications software (e.g., MINITAB) data files.

11. Summarize and describe the data using your statistical software.

SITE 1: LOCATE GROSS DOMESTIC PRODUCT (GDP) DATA

These data are produced by the U.S. Department of Commerce, located at *http://www.docgov/*

- At the Department of Commerce home page, click on: **U.S. Department of Commerce Agencies**
- At this location, click on: **Bureau of Economic Analysis** (BEA)
- From the main BEA page, click on: **BEA Data and Methodology**
- Here, scroll down to the heading "Please select one of BEA's three program areas," click on: **National**
- From BEA National programs, scroll to the heading/subheading "Data—National Income and Product Accounts," click on: **4. Time Series**
- On the page of Frequently Requested NIPA Data: History, click on: **Real GDP, GNP, and final sales. Annually**

SITE 2: LOCATE UNEMPLOYMENT STATISTICS

These data are produced by the U.S. Department of Labor, Bureau of Labor Statistics, located at *http://stats.bls.gov:80/*

- From the Bureau of Labor Statistics site, click on: **Data**
- Then click on: **Most Requested Series**
- Next, click on: **Overall BLS Most Requested Data**
- Here, scroll down through the selections

SITE 3: LOCATE DATA ON NEW BUSINESS START-UPS

These data are made available from the Federal Reserve Bank of Kansas City, located at *http://www.kc.frb.org/*

- From the Federal Reserve Board of Kansas City home page, click on: **Contents**
- Scroll down to the heading "Special features …," click on: **Regional historical economic data**
- Here, click on: **business activity**

As a final task, pick key words of the requested data set from any of sites 1, 2, or 3. Use those key words in the *Net Search* area of your browser. Try out four or five of the search engines (Yahoo!, Excite, Alta Vista, and so forth). Which of the search engines directs you to the data in the first 25 selections? ○

CHAPTER 3

PROBABILITY

CONTENTS

3.1   Events, Sample Spaces, and Probability

3.2   Unions and Intersections

3.3   Complementary Events

3.4   The Additive Rule and Mutually Exclusive Events

3.5   Conditional Probability

3.6   The Multiplicative Rule and Independent Events

3.7   Random Sampling

STATISTICS IN ACTION

3.1   Game Show Strategy: To Switch or Not to Switch

3.2   Lottery Buster

Where We've Been

We've identified inference, from a sample to a population, as the goal of statistics. And we've seen that to reach this goal, we must be able to describe a set of measurements. Thus, we explored the use of graphical and numerical methods for describing both quantitative and qualitative data sets.

Where We're Going

We now turn to the problem of making an inference. What is it that permits us to make the inferential jump from sample to population and then to give a measure of reliability for the inference? As you'll see, the answer is *probability*. This chapter is devoted to a study of probability—what it is and some of the basic concepts of the theory behind it.

Recall that one branch of statistics is concerned with decisions about a population based on sample information. You can see how this is accomplished more easily if you understand the relationship between population and sample—a relationship that becomes clearer if we reverse the statistical procedure of making inferences from sample to population. In this chapter then, we assume that the population is *known* and calculate the chances of obtaining various samples from the population. Thus, we show that probability is the reverse of statistics: In probability, we use the population information to infer the probable nature of the sample.

Probability plays an important role in inference-making. Suppose, for example, you have an opportunity to invest in an oil exploration company. Past records show that out of 10 previous oil drillings (a sample of the company's experiences), all 10 came up dry. What do you conclude? Do you think the chances are better than 50:50 that the company will hit a gusher? Should you invest in this company? Chances are, your answer to these questions will be an emphatic No. If the company's exploratory prowess is sufficient to hit a producing well 50% of the time, a record of 10 dry wells out of 10 drilled is an event that is just too improbable.

Or suppose you're playing poker with what your opponents assure you is a well-shuffled deck of cards. In three consecutive five-card hands, the person on your right is dealt four aces. Based on this sample of three deals, do you think the cards are being adequately shuffled? Again, your answer is likely to be No because dealing three hands of four aces is just too improbable if the cards were properly shuffled.

Note that the decisions concerning the potential success of the oil drilling company and the adequacy of card shuffling both involve knowing the chance—or probability—of a certain sample result. Both situations were contrived so that you could easily conclude that the probabilities of the sample results were small. Unfortunately, the probabilities of many observed sample results aren't so easy to evaluate intuitively. For these cases we will need the assistance of a theory of probability.

3.1 EVENTS, SAMPLE SPACES, AND PROBABILITY

Let's begin our treatment of probability with simple examples that are easily described. With the aid of simple examples, we can introduce important definitions that will help us develop the notion of probability more easily.

Suppose a coin is tossed once and the up face is recorded. The result we see and record is called an *observation,* or *measurement,* and the process of making an observation is called an *experiment.* Notice that our definition of experiment is broader than the one used in the physical sciences, where you would picture test tubes, microscopes, and other laboratory equipment. Among other things, statistical experiments may include recording a customer's preference for one of two computer operating systems (DOS or Macintosh), recording a change in the Dow Jones Industrial Average from one day to the next, recording the weekly sales of a business firm, and counting the number of errors on a page of an accountant's ledger. The point is that a statistical experiment can be almost any act of observation as long as the outcome is uncertain.

DEFINITION 3.1
An **experiment** is an act or process of observation that leads to a single outcome that cannot be predicted with certainty.

Consider another simple experiment consisting of tossing a die and observing the number on the up face. The six basic possible outcomes to this experiment are:

1. Observe a 1
2. Observe a 2
3. Observe a 3
4. Observe a 4
5. Observe a 5
6. Observe a 6

Note that if this experiment is conducted once, *you can observe one and only one of these six basic outcomes, and the outcome cannot be predicted with certainty*. Also, these possibilities cannot be decomposed into more basic outcomes. Because observing the outcome of an experiment is similar to selecting a sample from a population, the basic possible outcomes to an experiment are called *sample points*.*

> **DEFINITION 3.2**
> A **sample point** is the most basic outcome of an experiment.

EXAMPLE 3.1

Two coins are tossed, and their up faces are recorded. List all the sample points for this experiment.

SOLUTION
Even for a seemingly trivial experiment, we must be careful when listing the sample points. At first glance, we might expect three basic outcomes: Observe two heads, Observe two tails, or Observe one head and one tail. However, further reflection reveals that the last of these, Observe one head and one tail, can be decomposed into two outcomes: Head on coin 1, Tail on coin 2; and Tail on coin 1, Head on coin 2.† Thus, we have four sample points:

1. Observe *HH*
2. Observe *HT*
3. Observe *TH*
4. Observe *TT*

where *H* in the first position means "Head on coin 1," *H* in the second position means "Head on coin 2," and so on.

We often wish to refer to the collection of all the sample points of an experiment. This collection is called the *sample space* of the experiment. For example, there are six sample points in the sample space associated with the die-toss experiment. The sample spaces for the experiments discussed thus far are shown in Table 3.1.

---

*Alternatively, the term "simple event" can be used.
†Even if the coins are identical in appearance, there are, in fact, two distinct coins. Thus, the designation of one coin as coin 1 and the other coin as coin 2 is legitimate in any case.

TABLE 3.1   Experiments and Their Sample Spaces

Experiment: Observe the up face on a coin.
Sample space: 1. Observe a head
2. Observe a tail
This sample space can be represented in set notation as a set containing two sample points:

$$S: \{H, T\}$$

where H represents the sample point Observe a head and T represents the sample point Observe a tail.

Experiment: Observe the up face on a die.
Sample space: 1. Observe a 1
2. Observe a 2
3. Observe a 3
4. Observe a 4
5. Observe a 5
6. Observe a 6
This sample space can be represented in set notation as a set of six sample points:

$$S: \{1, 2, 3, 4, 5, 6\}$$

Experiment: Observe the up faces on two coins.
Sample space: 1. Observe HH
2. Observe HT
3. Observe TH
4. Observe TT
This sample space can be represented in set notation as a set of four sample points:

$$S: \{HH, HT, TH, TT\}$$

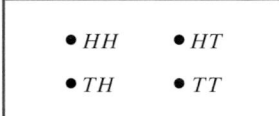

a. Experiment: Observe the up face on a coin

b. Experiment: Observe the up face on a die

c. Experiment: Observe the up faces on two coins

FIGURE 3.1
Venn diagrams for the three experiments from Table 3.1

> **DEFINITION 3.3**
> The **sample space** of an experiment is the collection of all its sample points.

Just as graphs are useful in describing sets of data, a pictorial method for presenting the sample space will often be useful. Figure 3.1 shows such a representation for each of the experiments in Table 3.1. In each case, the sample space is shown as a closed figure, labeled S, containing all possible sample points. Each sample point is represented by a solid dot (i.e., a "point") and labeled accordingly. Such graphical representations are called **Venn diagrams**.

Now that we know that an experiment will result in *only one* basic outcome—called a sample point—and that the sample space is the collection of all possible sample points, we're ready to discuss the probabilities of the sample points. You've undoubtedly used the term *probability* and have some intuitive idea about its meaning. Probability is generally used synonymously with "chance," "odds," and similar concepts. For example, if a fair coin is tossed, we might reason that both the sample points, Observe a head and Observe a tail, have the same *chance* of occurring. Thus, we might state that "the probability of observing a head is 50%" or "the odds of seeing a head are 50:50." Both of these statements are based on an informal knowledge of probability. We'll begin our treatment of probability by using such informal concepts and then solidify what we mean later.

The probability of a sample point is a number between 0 and 1 that measures the likelihood that the outcome will occur when the experiment is performed. This number is usually taken to be the relative frequency of the occurrence of a sample

FIGURE 3.2
The proportion of
heads in N tosses
of a coin

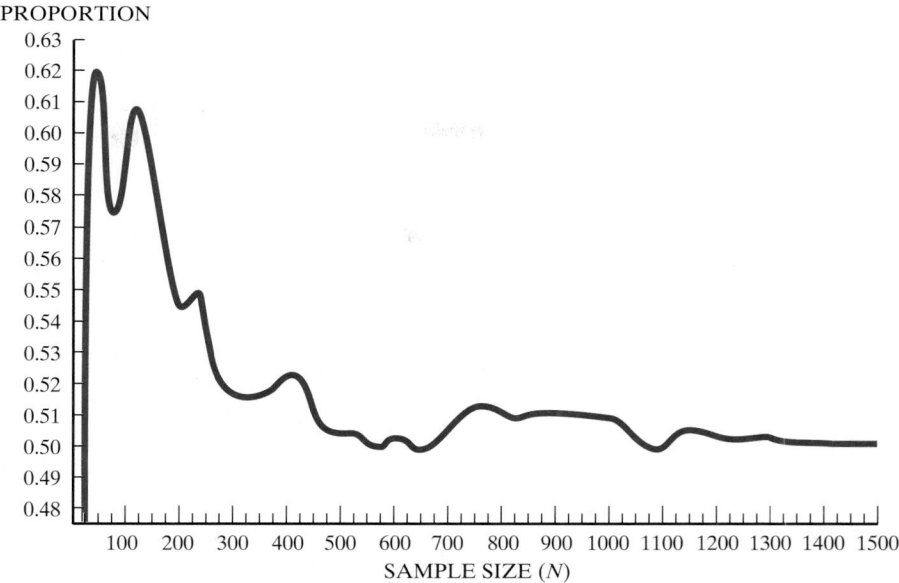

point in a very long series of repetitions of an experiment.* For example, if we are assigning probabilities to the two sample points in the coin-toss experiment (Observe a head and Observe a tail), we might reason that if we toss a balanced coin a very large number of times, the sample points Observe a head and Observe a tail will occur with the same relative frequency of .5.

Our reasoning is supported by Figure 3.2. The figure plots the relative frequency of the number of times that a head occurs when simulating (by computer) the toss of a coin N times, where N ranges from as few as 25 tosses to as many as 1,500 tosses of the coin. You can see that when N is large (i.e., $N = 1,500$), the relative frequency is converging to .5. Thus, the probability of each sample point in the coin-tossing experiment is .5.

For some experiments, we may have little or no information on the relative frequency of occurrence of the sample points; consequently, we must assign probabilities to the sample points based on general information about the experiment. For example, if the experiment is to invest in a business venture and to observe whether it succeeds or fails, the sample space would appear as in Figure 3.3. We are unlikely to be able to assign probabilities to the sample points of this experiment based on a long series of repetitions since unique factors govern each performance of this kind of experiment. Instead, we may consider factors such as the personnel managing the venture, the general state of the economy at the time, the rate of success of similar ventures, and any other pertinent information. If we finally decide that the venture has an 80% chance of succeeding, we assign a probability of .8 to the sample point Success. This probability can be interpreted as a measure of our degree of belief in the outcome of the business venture; that is, it is a subjective probability. Notice, however, that such probabilities should be based on expert information that is carefully assessed. If not, we may be misled on any

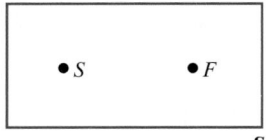

FIGURE 3.3
Experiment: Invest in a
business venture and
observe whether it
succeeds (S) or fails (F)

---

*The result derives from an axiom in probability theory called the **Law of Large Numbers**. Phrased informally, this law states that the relative frequency of the number of times that an outcome occurs when an experiment is replicated over and over again (i.e., a large number of times) approaches the theoretical probability of the outcome.

decisions based on these probabilities or based on any calculations in which they appear. [*Note:* For a text that deals in detail with the subjective evaluation of probabilities, see Winkler (1972) or Lindley (1985).]

No matter how you assign the probabilities to sample points, the probabilities assigned must obey two rules:

Probability Rules for Sample Points

1. All sample point probabilities *must* lie between 0 and 1.
2. The probabilities of all the sample points within a sample space *must* sum to 1.

Assigning probabilities to sample points is easy for some experiments. For example, if the experiment is to toss a fair coin and observe the face, we would probably all agree to assign a probability of $\frac{1}{2}$ to the two sample points, Observe a head and Observe a tail. However, many experiments have sample points whose probabilities are more difficult to assign.

EXAMPLE 3.2

A retail computer store sells two basic types of personal computers (PCs): standard desktop units and laptop units. Thus the owner must decide how many of each type of PC to stock. An important factor affecting the solution is the proportion of customers who purchase each type of PC. Show how this problem might be formulated in the framework of an experiment with sample points and a sample space. Indicate how probabilities might be assigned to the sample points.

SOLUTION

If we use the term *customer* to refer to a person who purchases one of the two types of PCs, the experiment can be defined as the entrance of a customer and the observation of which type of PC is purchased. There are two sample points in the sample space corresponding to this experiment:

D: {The customer purchases a standard desktop unit}

L: {The customer purchases a laptop unit}

The difference between this and the coin-toss experiment becomes apparent when we attempt to assign probabilities to the two sample points. What probability should we assign to the sample point *D*? If you answer .5, you are assuming that the events *D* and *L* should occur with equal likelihood, just like the sample points Heads and Tails in the coin-toss experiment. But assignment of sample point probabilities for the PC purchase experiment is not so easy. Suppose a check of the store's records indicates that 80% of its customers purchase desktop units. Then it might be reasonable to approximate the probability of the sample point *D* as .8 and that of the sample point *L* as .2. Here we see that sample points are not always equally likely, so assigning probabilities to them can be complicated—particularly for experiments that represent real applications (as opposed to coin- and die-toss experiments).

Although the probabilities of sample points are often of interest in their own right, it is usually probabilities of collections of sample points that are important. Example 3.3 demonstrates this point.

EXAMPLE 3.3 A fair die is tossed, and the up face is observed. If the face is even, you win $1. Otherwise, you lose $1. What is the probability that you win?

SOLUTION
Recall that the sample space for this experiment contains six sample points:

$$S: \{1, 2, 3, 4, 5, 6\}$$

Since the die is balanced, we assign a probability of $\frac{1}{6}$ to each of the sample points in this sample space. An even number will occur if one of the sample points, Observe a 2, Observe a 4, or Observe a 6, occurs. A collection of sample points such as this is called an *event*, which we denote by the letter A. Since the event A contains three sample points—each with probability $\frac{1}{6}$—and since no sample points can occur simultaneously, we reason that the probability of A is the sum of the probabilities of the sample points in A. Thus, the probability of A is $\frac{1}{6} + \frac{1}{6} + \frac{1}{6} = \frac{1}{2}$. This implies that, *in the long run*, you will win $1 half the time and lose $1 half the time.

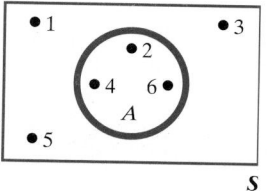

FIGURE 3.4
Die-toss experiment with event *A:* Observe an even number

Figure 3.4 is a Venn diagram depicting the sample space associated with a die-toss experiment and the event A, Observe an even number. The event A is represented by the closed figure inside the sample space S. This closed figure A contains all the sample points that comprise it.

To decide which sample points belong to the set associated with an event A, test each sample point in the sample space S. If event A occurs, then that sample point is in the event A. For example, the event A, Observe an even number, in the die-toss experiment will occur if the sample point Observe a 2 occurs. By the same reasoning, the sample points Observe a 4 and Observe a 6 are also in event A.

To summarize, we have demonstrated that an event can be defined in words or it can be defined as a specific set of sample points. This leads us to the following general definition of an event:

DEFINITION 3.4
An **event** is a specific collection of sample points.

EXAMPLE 3.4 Consider the experiment of tossing two coins. Suppose the coins are *not* balanced and the correct probabilities associated with the sample points are given in the table. [*Note:* The necessary properties for assigning probabilities to sample points are satisfied.]

Consider the events

$A:$ {Observe exactly one head}
$B:$ {Observe at least one head}

Calculate the probability of A and the probability of B.

Sample Point	Probability
HH	$\frac{4}{9}$
HT	$\frac{2}{9}$
TH	$\frac{2}{9}$
TT	$\frac{1}{9}$

SOLUTION

Event *A* contains the sample points *HT* and *TH*. Since two or more sample points cannot occur at the same time, we can easily calculate the probability of event *A* by summing the probabilities of the two sample points. Thus, the probability of observing exactly one head (event *A*), denoted by the symbol *P(A)*, is

$$P(A) = P(\text{Observe } HT) + P(\text{Observe } TH) = \tfrac{2}{9} + \tfrac{2}{9} = \tfrac{4}{9}$$

Similarly, since *B* contains the sample points *HH, HT,* and *TH*,

$$P(B) = \tfrac{4}{9} + \tfrac{2}{9} + \tfrac{2}{9} = \tfrac{8}{9}$$

The preceding example leads us to a general procedure for finding the probability of an event *A:*

> The probability of an event *A* is calculated by summing the probabilities of the sample points in the sample space for *A*.

Thus, we can summarize the steps for calculating the probability of any event, as indicated in the next box.

Steps for Calculating Probabilities of Events
1. Define the experiment; that is, describe the process used to make an observation and the type of observation that will be recorded.
2. List the sample points.
3. Assign probabilities to the sample points.
4. Determine the collection of sample points contained in the event of interest.
5. Sum the sample point probabilities to get the event probability.

EXAMPLE 3.5

Diversity training of employees is the latest trend in U.S. business. *USA Today* (Aug. 15, 1995) reported on the primary reasons businesses give for making diversity training part of their strategic planning process. The reasons are summarized in Table 3.2. Assume that one business is selected at random from all U.S. businesses that use diversity training and the primary reason is determined.

a. Define the experiment that generated the data in Table 3.2, and list the sample points.

TABLE 3.2 Primary Reasons for Diversity Training

Reason	Percentage
Comply with personnel policies (CPP)	7
Increase productivity (IP)	47
Stay competitive (SC)	38
Social responsibility (SR)	4
Other (O)	4
Total	100%

Source: USA Today, August 15, 1995.

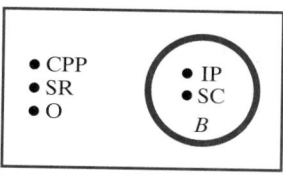

FIGURE 3.5
Venn diagram for
diversity training survey

**TABLE 3.3 Sample
Point Probabilities
for Diversity
Training Survey**

Sample Point	Probability
CPP	.07
IP	.47
SC	.38
SR	.04
O	.04

b. Assign probabilities to the sample points.

c. What is the probability that the primary reason for diversity training is business related; that is, related to competition or productivity?

d. What is the probability that social responsibility is not a primary reason for diversity training?

SOLUTION

a. The experiment is the act of determining the primary reason for diversity training of employees at a U.S. business. The sample points, the simplest outcomes of the experiment, are the five response categories listed in Table 3.2. These sample points are shown in the Venn diagram in Figure 3.5.

b. If, as in Example 3.1, we were to assign equal probabilities in this case, each of the response categories would have a probability of one-fifth ($\frac{1}{5}$), or .20. But, by examining Table 3.2 you can see that equal probabilities are not reasonable here because the response percentages were not even approximately the same in the five classifications. It is more reasonable to assign a probability equal to the response percentage in each class, as shown in Table 3.3.*

c. Let the symbol B represent the event that the primary reason for diversity training is business related. B is not a sample point because it consists of more than one of the response classifications (the sample points). In fact, as shown in Figure 3.5, B consists of two sample points, IP and SC. The probability of B is defined to be the sum of the probabilities of the sample points in B:

$$P(B) = P(IP) + P(SC) = .47 + .38 = .85$$

d. Let NSR represent the event that social responsibility is not a primary reason for diversity training. Then NSR consists of all sample points except SR, and the probability is the sum of the corresponding sample point probabilities:

$$P(NSR) = P(CPP) + P(IP) + P(SC) + P(O)$$
$$= .07 + .47 + .38 + .04 = .96$$

EXAMPLE 3.6

You have the capital to invest in two of four ventures, each of which requires approximately the same amount of investment capital. Unknown to you, two of the investments will eventually fail and two will be successful. You research the four ventures because you think that your research will increase your probability of a successful choice over a purely random selection, and you eventually decide on two. What is the lower limit of your probability of selecting the two best out of four? That is, if you used none of the information generated by your research, and selected two ventures at random, what is the probability that you would select the two successful ventures? At least one?

SOLUTION

Denote the two successful enterprises as S_1 and S_2 and the two failing enterprises as F_1 and F_2. The experiment involves a random selection of two out of the four ventures, and each possible pair of ventures represents a sample point. The six sample points that make up the sample space are

*The response percentages were based on a sample of U.S. businesses; consequently, these assigned probabilities are estimates of the true population-response percentages. You'll learn how to measure the reliability of probability estimates in Chapter 7.

1. (S_1, S_2)
2. (S_1, F_1)
3. (S_1, F_2)
4. (S_2, F_1)
5. (S_2, F_2)
6. (F_1, F_2)

The next step is to assign probabilities to the sample points. If we assume that the choice of any one pair is as likely as any other, then the probability of each sample point is $\frac{1}{6}$. Now check to see which sample points result in the choice of two successful ventures. Only one such sample point exists—namely, (S_1, S_2). Therefore, the probability of choosing two successful ventures out of the four is

$$P(S_1, S_2) = \frac{1}{6}$$

The event of selecting at least one of the two successful ventures includes all the sample points except (F_1, F_2).

$$P(\text{Select at least one success}) = P(S_1, S_2) + P(S_1, F_1) + P(S_1, F_2) + P(S_2, F_1)$$
$$+ P(S_2, F_2)$$

$$= \frac{1}{6} + \frac{1}{6} + \frac{1}{6} + \frac{1}{6} + \frac{1}{6} = \frac{5}{6}$$

Therefore, the worst that you could do in selecting two ventures out of four may not be too bad. With a random selection, the probability of selecting two successful ventures will be $\frac{1}{6}$ and the probability of selecting at least one successful venture out of two is $\frac{5}{6}$. ∎

The preceding examples have one thing in common: The number of sample points in each of the sample spaces was small; hence, the sample points were easy to identify and list. How can we manage this when the sample points run into the thousands or millions? For example, suppose you wish to select five business ventures from a group of 1,000. Then each different group of five ventures would represent a sample point. How can you determine the number of sample points associated with this experiment?

One method of determining the number of sample points for a complex experiment is to develop a counting system. Start by examining a simple version of the experiment. For example, see if you can develop a system for counting the number of ways to select two ventures from a total of four (this is exactly what was done in Example 3.6). If the ventures are represented by the symbols V_1, V_2, V_3, and V_4, the sample points could be listed in the following pattern:

(V_1, V_2) (V_2, V_3) (V_3, V_4)
(V_1, V_3) (V_2, V_4)
(V_1, V_4)

Note the pattern and now try a more complex situation—say, sampling three ventures out of five. List the sample points and observe the pattern. Finally, see if you can deduce the pattern for the general case. Perhaps you can program a computer to produce the matching and counting for the number of samples of 5 selected from a total of 1,000.

A second method of determining the number of sample points for an experiment is to use **combinatorial mathematics**. This branch of mathematics is concerned with developing counting rules for given situations. For example, there is a simple rule for finding the number of different samples of five ventures selected from 1,000. This rule, called the **combinations rule**, is given by the formula

$$\binom{N}{n} = \frac{N!}{n!(N-n)!}$$

where N is the number of elements in the population; n is the number of elements in the sample; and the factorial symbol (!) means that, say,

$$n! = n(n-1)(n-2) \cdots (3)(2)(1)$$

Thus, $5! = 5 \cdot 4 \cdot 3 \cdot 2 \cdot 1$. (The quantity 0! is defined to be equal to 1.)

EXAMPLE 3.7

Refer to Example 3.6 in which we selected two ventures from four in which to invest. Use the combinatorial counting rule to determine how many different selections can be made.

SOLUTION

For this example, $N = 4, n = 2$, and

$$\binom{4}{2} = \frac{4!}{2!2!} = \frac{4 \cdot 3 \cdot 2 \cdot 1}{(2 \cdot 1)(2 \cdot 1)} = 6$$

You can see that this agrees with the number of sample points obtained in Example 3.6.

EXAMPLE 3.8

Suppose you plan to invest equal amounts of money in each of five business ventures. If you have 20 ventures from which to make the selection, how many different samples of five ventures can be selected from the 20?

SOLUTION

For this example, $N = 20$ and $n = 5$. Then the number of different samples of 5 that can be selected from the 20 ventures is

$$\binom{20}{5} = \frac{20!}{5!(20-5)!} = \frac{20!}{5!15!}$$

$$= \frac{20 \cdot 19 \cdot 18 \cdot \cdots \cdot 3 \cdot 2 \cdot 1}{(5 \cdot 4 \cdot 3 \cdot 2 \cdot 1)(15 \cdot 14 \cdot 13 \cdot \cdots \cdot 3 \cdot 2 \cdot 1)} = 15,504$$

The symbol $\binom{N}{n}$, meaning the **number of combinations of N elements taken n at a time,** is just one of a large number of counting rules that have been developed by combinatorial mathematicians. This counting rule applies to situations in which the experiment calls for selecting n elements from a total of N elements, without replacing each element before the next is selected. If you are interested in learning other methods for counting sample points for various types of experiments, you will find a few of the basic counting rules in Appendix A. Others can be found in the chapter references.

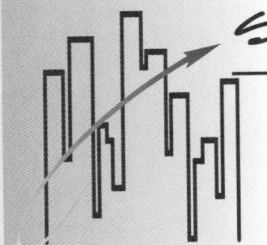

STATISTICS IN ACTION

3.1 GAME SHOW STRATEGY: TO SWITCH OR NOT TO SWITCH?

Marilyn vos Savant, who is listed in *Guinness Book of World Records Hall of Fame* for "Highest IQ," writes a monthly column in the Sunday newspaper supplement, *Parade Magazine*. Her column, "Ask Marilyn," is devoted to games of skill, puzzles, and mind-bending riddles. In one issue, vos Savant posed the following question:

Suppose you're on a game show, and you're given a choice of three doors. Behind one door is a car; behind the others, goats. You pick a door—say, #1—and the host, who knows what's behind the doors, opens another door—say #3—which has a goat. He then says to you, "Do you want to pick door #2?" Is it to your advantage to switch your choice?

Vos Savant's answer: "Yes, you should switch. The first door has a ⅓ chance of winning [the car], but the second has a ⅔ chance [of winning the car]." Predictably, vos Savant's surprising answer elicited thousands of critical letters, many of them from Ph.D. mathematicians, who disagreed with her. Some of the more interesting and critical letters, which were printed in her next column (*Parade Magazine*, Feb. 24, 1991) are condensed below:

- "May I suggest you obtain and refer to a standard textbook on probability before you try to answer a question of this type again?" (University of Florida)

- "Your logic is in error, and I am sure you will receive many letters on this topic from high school and college students. Perhaps you should keep a few addresses for help with future columns." (Georgia State University)

- "You are utterly incorrect about the game-show question, and I hope this controversy will call some public attention to the serious national crisis in mathematical education. If you can admit your error you will have contributed constructively toward the solution of a deplorable situation. How many irate mathematicians are needed to get you to change your mind?" (Georgetown University)

- "I am in shock that after being corrected by at least three mathematicians, you still do not see your mistake." (Dickinson State University)

- "You are the goat!" (Western State University)

- "You're wrong, but look on the positive side. If all the Ph.D.'s were wrong, the country would be in serious trouble." (U.S. Army Research Institute)

The logic employed by those who disagree with vos Savant is as follows: Once the host shows you door #3 (a goat), only two doors remain. The probability of the car being behind door #1 (your door) is ½; similarly, the probability is ½ for door #2. Therefore, in the long run (i.e., over a long series of trials) it doesn't matter whether you switch to door #2 or keep door #1. Approximately 50% of the time you'll win a car, and 50% of the time you'll get a goat.

Who is correct, the Ph.D.s or vos Savant? By answering the following series of questions, you'll arrive at the correct solution.

Focus

a. Before the show is taped, the host randomly decides the door behind which to put the car; then the goats go behind the remaining two doors. List the sample points for this experiment.

b. Suppose you choose at random door #1. Now, for each sample point in part a, circle door #1 and put an X through one of the remaining two doors that hides a goat. (This is the door that the host shows—always a goat.)

c. Refer to the altered sample points in part b. Assume your strategy is to keep door #1. Count the number of sample points for which this is a "winning" strategy (i.e., you win the car). Assuming equally likely sample points, what is the probability that you win the car?

d. Repeat part c, but assume your strategy is to always switch doors.

e. Based on the probabilities of parts c and d, is it to your advantage to switch your choice?

EXERCISES 3.1–3.15

Learning the Mechanics

3.1 An experiment results in one of the following sample points: E_1, E_2, E_3, E_4, or E_5.
   a. Find $P(E_3)$ if $P(E_1) = .1, P(E_2) = .2, P(E_4) = .1$, and $P(E_5) = .1$.
   b. Find $P(E_3)$ if $P(E_1) = P(E_3), P(E_2) = .1$, $P(E_4) = .2$, and $P(E_5) = .1$.
   c. Find $P(E_3)$ if $P(E_1) = P(E_2) = P(E_4) = P(E_5) = .1$.

3.2 The accompanying diagram describes the sample space of a particular experiment and events A and B.

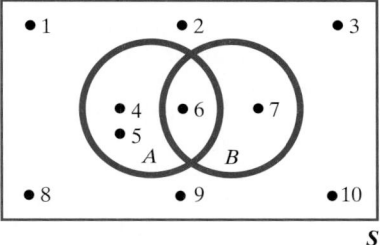

   a. What is this type of diagram called?
   b. Suppose the sample points are equally likely. Find $P(A)$ and $P(B)$.
   c. Suppose $P(1) = P(2) = P(3) = P(4) = P(5) = \frac{1}{20}$ and $P(6) = P(7) = P(8) = P(9) = P(10) = \frac{3}{20}$. Find $P(A)$ and $P(B)$.

3.3 The sample space for an experiment contains five sample points with probabilities as shown in the table. Find the probability of each of the following events:

Sample Points	Probabilities
1	.05
2	.20
3	.30
4	.30
5	.15

   A: {Either 1, 2, or 3 occurs}
   B: {Either 1, 3, or 5 occurs}
   C: {4 does not occur}

3.4 Compute each of the following:
   a. $\binom{9}{4}$ **b.** $\binom{7}{2}$ **c.** $\binom{4}{4}$ **d.** $\binom{5}{0}$ **e.** $\binom{6}{5}$

3.5 Two marbles are drawn at random and without replacement from a box containing two blue marbles and three red marbles. Determine the probability of observing each of the following events:
   A: {Two blue marbles are drawn}
   B: {A red and a blue marble are drawn}
   C: {Two red marbles are drawn}

3.6 Simulate the experiment described in Exercise 3.5 using any five identically shaped objects, two of which are one color and three, another. Mix the objects, draw two, record the results, and then replace the objects. Repeat the experiment a large number of times (at least 100). Calculate the proportion of time events A, B, and C occur. How do these proportions compare with the probabilities you calculated in Exercise 3.5? Should these proportions equal the probabilities? Explain.

Applying the Concepts

3.7 *Total Quality Management* (TQM) has been defined as responsive customer service through continuously improved and redesigned work processes (*Quality Progress*, July 1995). However, as its usage has grown it has been called different names by different organizations. At the University of North Carolina in Charlotte (UNCC), where TQM implementation began in 1992, it is called Continuous Quality Improvement (CQI). In evaluating perceptions of CQI, UNCC professors K. Buch and J. W. Shelnutt asked 159 employees to indicate how strongly they agreed or disagreed with a series of statements including: "I believe that management is committed to CQI." The following responses were received:

Strongly agree	Agree	Neither agree nor disagree	Disagree	Strongly disagree
30	64	41	18	6

Source: Buch, K., and Shelnut, J. W. "UNC Charlotte measures the effects of its quality initiative." *Quality Progress*, July 1995, p. 75 (Table 2).

   a. Define the experiment and list the sample points.
   b. Assign probabilities to the sample points.
   c. What is the probability that an employee agrees or strongly agrees with the above statement?

d. What is the probability that an employee does not strongly agree with the above statement?

3.8 Communications products (telephones, fax machines, etc.) can be designed to operate on either an analog or a digital system. Because of improved accuracy, a digital signal will soon replace the current analog signal used in telephone lines. The result will be a flood of new digital products for consumers to choose from (*Newsweek,* Nov. 16, 1992). Suppose a particular firm plans to produce a new fax machine in both analog and digital forms. Concerned with whether the products will succeed or fail in the marketplace, a market analysis is conducted that results in the sample points and associated probabilities of occurrence listed in the table (S_a: analog succeeds, F_a: analog fails, etc.). Find the probability of each of the following events:

A: {Both new products are successful}

B: {The analog design is successful}

C: {The digital design is successful}

D: {At least one of the two products is successful}

Sample Points	Probabilities
S_aS_d	.31
S_aF_d	.10
F_aS_d	.50
F_aF_d	.09

3.9 Of six cars produced at a particular factory between 8 and 10 A.M. last Monday morning, test runs revealed three of them to be "lemons." Nevertheless, three of the six cars were shipped to dealer A and the other three to dealer B. Dealer A received all three lemons. What is the probability of this event occurring if, in fact, the three cars shipped to dealer A were selected at random from the six produced?

3.10 Carbon monoxide (CO) is an odorless, colorless, highly toxic gas which is produced by fires as well as by motor vehicles and appliances that use carbon-based fuels. The *American Journal of Public Health* (July 1995) published a study on unintentional CO poisoning of Colorado residents for the years 1986–1991. A total of 981 cases of CO poisoning were reported during the six-year period. Each case was classified as fatal or nonfatal and by source of exposure. The number of cases occurring in each of the categories is shown in the accompanying table. Assume that one of the 981 cases of unintentional CO poisoning is randomly selected.

a. List all sample points for this experiment.

Source of Exposure	Fatal	Nonfatal	Total
Fire	63	53	116
Auto exhaust	60	178	238
Furnace	18	345	363
Kerosene or spaceheater	9	18	27
Appliance	9	63	72
Other gas-powered motor	3	73	76
Fireplace	0	16	16
Other	3	19	22
Unknown	9	42	51
Total	174	807	981

Source: Cook, M. C., Simon, P. A., and Hoffman, R. E. "Unintentional carbon monoxide poisoning in Colorado, 1986 through 1991." *American Journal of Public Health,* Vol. 85, No. 7, July 1995, p. 989 (Table 1). American Public Health Association.

b. What is the set of all sample points called?

c. Let *A* be the event that the CO poisoning is caused by fire. Find $P(A)$.

d. Let *B* be the event that the CO poisoning is fatal. Find $P(B)$.

e. Let *C* be the event that the CO poisoning is caused by auto exhaust. Find $P(C)$.

f. Let *D* be the event that the CO poisoning is caused by auto exhaust and is fatal. Find $P(D)$.

g. Let *E* be the event that the CO poisoning is caused by fire but is nonfatal. Find $P(E)$.

3.11 The credit card industry depends heavily on mail solicitation to attract new customers. In 1994, the industry sent out 2.4 billion pieces of mail and incurred postage costs of nearly $500 million (*Forbes,* Sept. 11, 1995). The table on page 125 lists the number of credit card accounts outstanding on June 30, 1995, for the top 15 credit card companies. One of these 177.5 million accounts is to be selected at random and the credit card company holding the account is to be identified.

a. List or describe the sample points in this experiment.

b. Find the probability of each sample point.

c. What is the probability that the account selected belongs to a nontraditional bank? A traditional bank?

3.12 *Consumer Reports* magazine annually asks readers to evaluate their experiences in buying a new car during the previous year. More than 120,000 questionnaires were completed for the 1994 sales year. Analysis of the questionnaires revealed that readers' were most satisfied with the following three dealers (in no particular order): Infiniti, Saturn, and Saab (*Consumer Reports,* Apr. 1995).

a. List all possible sets of rankings for these top three dealers.

b. Assuming that each set of rankings in part **a** is equally likely, what is the probability that

	Number of Accounts (in millions)
Citibank	24.3
Discover/Novus*	33.6
MBNA*	12.1
First USA*	7.8
First Chicago	13.2
AT&T Universal*	16.2
Household International*	12.2
Chase Manhattan	9.8
Chemical Bank	6.7
Capital One*	5.8
Bank of America	9.3
Bank One	9.7
Advanta*	4.9
Bank of New York	5.9
Optima (American Express)*	6.0
Total	177.5

*Not a traditional bank

Source: RAM Research Corp./Capital One Financial Corp.

Secondary Source: Novack, J. "The data edge." *Forbes,* September 11, 1995, p. 148.

readers ranked Saturn first? That readers ranked Saturn third? That readers ranked Saturn first and Infiniti second (which is, in fact, what they did)?

3.13 Often, probabilities are expressed in terms of **odds**, especially in gambling settings. For example, handicappers for greyhound races express their belief about the probabilities that each greyhound will win a race in terms of odds. If the probability of event E is $P(E)$, then the *odds in favor of E* are $P(E)$ to $1 - P(E)$. Thus, if a handicapper assesses a probability of .25 that Oxford Shoes will win its next race, the odds in favor of Oxford Shoes are $^{25}/_{100}$ to $^{75}/_{100}$, or 1 to 3. It follows that the *odds against E* are $1 - P(E)$ to $P(E)$, or 3 to 1 against a win by Oxford Shoes. In general, if the odds in favor of event E are a to b, then $P(E) = a/(a + b)$.

a. A second handicapper assesses the probability of a win by Oxford Shoes to be $^{1}/_{3}$. According to the second handicapper, what are the odds in favor of Oxford Shoes winning?

b. A third handicapper assesses the odds in favor of Oxford Shoes to be 1 to 1. According to the third handicapper, what is the probability of Oxford Shoes winning?

c. A fourth handicapper assesses the odds against Oxford Shoes winning to be 3 to 2. Find this handicapper's assessment of the probability that Oxford Shoes will win.

3.14 The Value Line Survey, a service for common stock investors, provides its subscribers with up-to-date evaluations of the prospects and risks associated with the purchase of a large number of common stocks. Each stock is ranked 1 (highest) to 5 (lowest) according to Value Line's estimate of the stock's potential for price appreciation during the next 12 months. Suppose you plan to purchase stock in three electrical utility companies from among seven that possess rankings of 2 for price appreciation. Unknown to you, two of the companies will experience serious difficulties with their nuclear facilities during the coming year. If you randomly select the three companies from among the seven, what is the probability that you select:

a. None of the companies with prospective nuclear difficulties?

b. One of the companies with prospective nuclear difficulties?

c. Both of the companies with prospective nuclear difficulties?

3.15 *Sustainable development* or *sustainable farming* means "finding ways to live and work the Earth without jeopardizing the future" (Schmickle, *Minneapolis Star Tribune*, June 20, 1992). Studies were conducted in five midwestern states to develop a profile of a sustainable farmer. The results revealed that farmers can be classified along a sustainability scale, depending on whether they are likely or unlikely to engage in the following practices: (1) Raise a broad mix of crops; (2) Raise livestock; (3) Use chemicals sparingly; (4) Use techniques for regenerating the soil, such as crop rotation.

a. List the different sets of classifications that are possible.

b. Suppose you are planning to interview farmers across the country to determine the frequency with which they fall into the classification sets you listed for part **a**. Since no information is yet available, assume initially that there is an equal chance of a farmer falling into any single classification set. Using that assumption, what is the probability that a farmer will be classi-

fied as unlikely on all four criteria (i.e., classified as a nonsustainable farmer)?

c. Using the same assumption as in part **b**, what is the probability that a farmer will be classified as likely on at least three of the criteria (i.e., classified as a near-sustainable farmer)?

3.2 UNIONS AND INTERSECTIONS

An event can often be viewed as a composition of two or more other events. Such events, which are called **compound events**, can be formed (composed) in two ways, as defined and illustrated here.

DEFINITION 3.5

The **union** of two events A and B is the event that occurs if either A or B or both occur on a single performance of the experiment. We denote the union of events A and B by the symbol $A \cup B$. $A \cup B$ consists of all the sample points that belong to A or B or both. (See Figure 3.6a.)

DEFINITION 3.6

The **intersection** of two events A and B is the event that occurs if both A and B occur on a single performance of the experiment. We write $A \cap B$ for the intersection of A and B. $A \cap B$ consists of all the sample points belonging to *both A and B*. (See Figure 3.6b.)

EXAMPLE 3.9

Consider the die-toss experiment. Define the following events:

> A: {Toss an even number}
> B: {Toss a number less than or equal to 3}

a. Describe $A \cup B$ for this experiment.

b. Describe $A \cap B$ for this experiment.

c. Calculate $P(A \cup B)$ and $P(A \cap B)$ assuming the die is fair.

SOLUTION

Draw the Venn diagram as shown in Figure 3.7

a. The union of A and B is the event that occurs if we observe either an even number, a number less than or equal to 3, or both on a single throw of the die. Consequently, the sample points in the event $A \cup B$ are those for which A occurs, B occurs, or both A and B occur. Checking the sample points in the

FIGURE 3.6
Venn diagrams for union and intersection

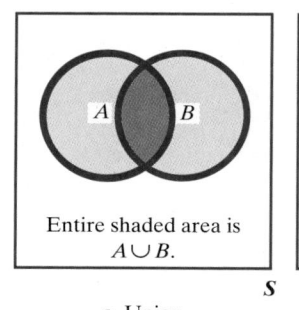

Entire shaded area is
$A \cup B$.

a. Union

Shaded area is
$A \cap B$.

b. Intersection

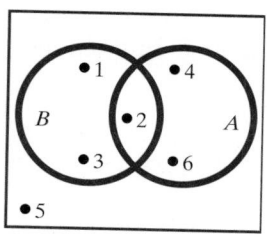

FIGURE 3.7
Venn diagram for die toss

entire sample space, we find that the collection of sample points in the union of A and B is

$$A \cup B = \{1, 2, 3, 4, 6\}$$

b. The intersection of A and B is the event that occurs if we observe *both* an even number and a number less than or equal to 3 on a single throw of the die. Checking the sample points to see which imply the occurrence of *both* events A and B, we see that the intersection contains only one sample point:

$$A \cap B = \{2\}$$

In other words, the intersection of A and B is the sample point Observe a 2.

c. Recalling that the probability of an event is the sum of the probabilities of the sample points of which the event is composed, we have

$$P(A \cup B) = P(1) + P(2) + P(3) + P(4) + P(6)$$
$$= \tfrac{1}{6} + \tfrac{1}{6} + \tfrac{1}{6} + \tfrac{1}{6} + \tfrac{1}{6} = \tfrac{5}{6}$$

and

$$P(A \cap B) = P(2) = \tfrac{1}{6}$$

EXAMPLE 3.10

Many firms undertake direct marketing campaigns to promote their products. The campaigns typically involve mailing information to millions of households. The response rates are carefully monitored to determine the demographic characteristics of respondents. By studying tendencies to respond, the firms can better target future mailings to those segments of the population most likely to purchase their products.

Suppose a distributor of mail-order tools is analyzing the results of a recent mailing. The probability of response is believed to be related to income and age. The percentages of the total number of respondents to the mailing are given by income and age classification in Table 3.4.

Define the following events:

A: {A respondent's income is more than $50,000}
B: {A respondent's age is 30 or more}

a. Find $P(A)$ and $P(B)$.
b. Find $P(A \cup B)$.
c. Find $P(A \cap B)$.

SOLUTION

Following the steps for calculating probabilities of events, we first note that the objective is to characterize the income and age distribution of respondents to the mailing. To accomplish this, we define the experiment to consist of selecting a

TABLE 3.4 Percentage of Respondents in Age-Income Classes

Age	INCOME		
	<$25,000	$25,000–$50,000	>$50,000
< 30 yrs	5%	12%	10%
30–50 yrs	14%	22%	16%
> 50 yrs	8%	10%	3%

respondent from the collection of all respondents and observing which income and age class he or she occupies. The sample points are the nine different age-income classifications:

$$E_1: \{<30 \text{ yrs}, <\$25,000\}$$
$$E_2: \{30–50 \text{ yrs}, <\$25,000\}$$
$$\cdot$$
$$\cdot$$
$$\cdot$$
$$E_9: \{>50 \text{ yrs}, >\$50,000\}$$

Next, we assign probabilities to the sample points. If we blindly select one of the respondents, the probability that he or she will occupy a particular age-income classification is just the proportion, or relative frequency, of respondents in the classification. These proportions are given (as percentages) in Table 3.4. Thus,

$$P(E_1) = \text{Relative frequency of respondents in age-income class}$$
$$\{<30 \text{ yrs}, <\$25,000\} = .05$$

$$P(E_2) = .14$$

and so forth. You may verify that the sample points probabilities add to 1.

a. To find $P(A)$, we first determine the collection of sample points contained in event A. Since A is defined as $\{>\$50,000\}$, we see from Table 3.4 that A contains the three sample points represented by the last column of the table. In words, the event A consists of the income classification $\{>\$50,000\}$ in all three age classifications. The probability of A is the sum of the probabilities of the sample points in A:

$$P(A) = .10 + .16 + .03 = .29$$

Similarly, B consists of the six sample points in the second and third rows of Table 3.4:

$$P(B) = .14 + .22 + .16 + .08 + .10 + .03 = .73$$

b. The union of events A and B, $A \cup B$, consists of all the sample points in *either A or B or both*. That is, the union of A and B consists of all respondents whose income exceeds $50,000 *or* whose age is 30 or more. In Table 3.4 this is any sample point found in the third column *or* the last two rows. Thus,

$$P(A \cup B) = .10 + .14 + .22 + .16 + .08 + .10 + .03 = .83$$

c. The intersection of events A and B, $A \cap B$, consists of all sample points in *both A and B*. That is, the intersection of A and B consists of all respondents whose income exceeds $50,000 *and* whose age is 30 or more. In Table 3.4 this is any sample point found in the third column *and* the last two rows. Thus,

$$P(A \cap B) = .16 + .03 = .19$$

3.5 COMPLEMENTARY EVENTS

A very useful concept in the calculation of event probabilities is the notion of **complementary events**:

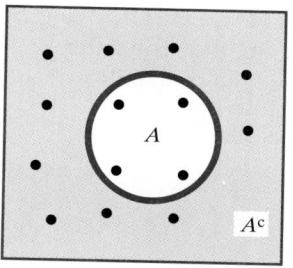

FIGURE 3.8
Venn diagram of
complementary events

> **DEFINITION 3.7**
> The **complement** of an event A is the event that A does *not* occur—that is, the event consisting of all sample points that are not in event A. We denote the complement of A by A^c.

An event A is a collection of sample points, and the sample points included in A^c are those not in A. Figure 3.8 demonstrates this idea. Note from the figure that all sample points in S are included in *either* A or A^c and that *no* sample point is in both A and A^c. This leads us to conclude that the probabilities of an event and its complement *must sum to 1*:

> The sum of the probabilities of complementary events equals 1; i.e., $P(A) + P(A^c) = 1$.

In many probability problems, calculating the probability of the complement of the event of interest is easier than calculating the event itself. Then, because

$$P(A) + P(A^c) = 1$$

we can calculate $P(A)$ by using the relationship

$$P(A) = 1 - P(A^c).$$

EXAMPLE 3.11   Consider the experiment of tossing two fair coins. Use the complementary relationship to calculate the probability of event A: {Observing at least one head}.

SOLUTION
We know that the event A: {Observing at least one head} consists of the sample points

A: {HH, HT, TH}

The complement of A is defined as the event that occurs when A does not occur. Therefore,

A^c: {Observe no heads} = {TT}

This complementary relationship is shown in Figure 3.9. Assuming the coins are balanced,

$$P(A^c) = P(TT) = \tfrac{1}{4}$$

and

$$P(A) = 1 - P(A^c) = 1 - \tfrac{1}{4} = \tfrac{3}{4}.$$

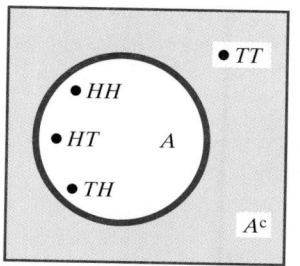

FIGURE 3.9
Complementary events
in the toss of two coins

3.4   THE ADDITIVE RULE AND MUTUALLY EXCLUSIVE EVENTS

In Section 3.2 we saw how to determine which sample points are contained in a union and how to calculate the probability of the union by adding the probabilities of the sample points in the union. It is also possible to obtain the probability of the union of two events by using the **additive rule of probability**.

The union of two events will often contain many sample points, since the union occurs if either one or both of the events occur. By studying the Venn diagram in

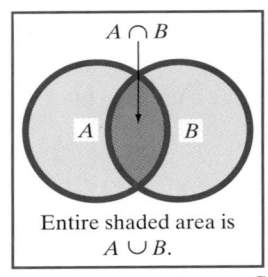

Entire shaded area is
$A \cup B$.

FIGURE 3.10
Venn diagram of union

Figure 3.10, you can see that the probability of the union of two events, A and B, can be obtained by summing $P(A)$ and $P(B)$ and subtracting the probability corresponding to $A \cap B$. Therefore, the formula for calculating the probability of the union of two events is given in the next box.

Additive Rule of Probability

The probability of the union of events A and B is the sum of the probability of events A and B minus the probability of the intersection of events A and B, that is,

$$P(A \cup B) = P(A) + P(B) - P(A \cap B)$$

EXAMPLE 3.12

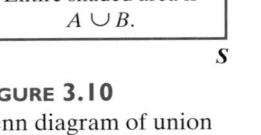

Hospital records show that 12% of all patients are admitted for surgical treatment, 16% are admitted for obstetrics, and 2% receive both obstetrics and surgical treatment. If a new patient is admitted to the hospital, what is the probability that the patient will be admitted either for surgery, obstetrics, or both? Use the additive rule of probability to arrive at the answer.

SOLUTION

Consider the following events:

A: {A patient admitted to the hospital receives surgical treatment}

B: {A patient admitted to the hospital receives obstetrics treatment}

Then, from the given information,

$$P(A) = .12$$
$$P(B) = .16$$

and the probability of the event that a patient receives both obstetrics and surgical treatment is

$$P(A \cap B) = .02$$

The event that a patient admitted to the hospital receives either surgical treatment, obstetrics treatment, or both is the union $A \cup B$. The probability of $A \cup B$ is given by the additive rule of probability:

$$P(A \cup B) = P(A) + P(B) - P(A \cap B) = .12 + .16 - .02 = .26$$

Thus, 26% of all patients admitted to the hospital receive either surgical treatment, obstetrics treatment, or both. ∎

A very special relationship exists between events A and B when $A \cap B$ contains no sample points. In this case we call the events A and B *mutually exclusive events*.

DEFINITION 3.8

Events A and B are **mutually exclusive** if $A \cap B$ contains no sample points, that is, if A and B have no sample points in common.

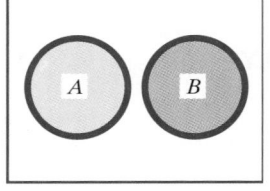

FIGURE 3.11
Venn diagram of
mutually exclusive events

Figure 3.11 shows a Venn diagram of two mutually exclusive events. The events A and B have no sample points in common, that is, A and B cannot occur simultaneously, and $P(A \cap B) = 0$. Thus, we have the important relationship given in the box.

> If two events A and B are *mutually exclusive,* the probability of the union of A and B equals the sum of the probabilities of A and B; that is, $P(A \cup B) = P(A) + P(B)$

Caution: The formula shown above is *false* if the events are *not* mutually exclusive. In this case (i.e., two nonmutually exclusive events), you must apply the general additive rule of probability.

EXAMPLE 3.13 Consider the experiment of tossing two balanced coins. Find the probability of observing *at least* one head.

SOLUTION
Define the events

$A:$ {Observe at least one head}

$B:$ {Observe exactly one head}

$C:$ {Observe exactly two heads}

Note that

$$A = B \cup C$$

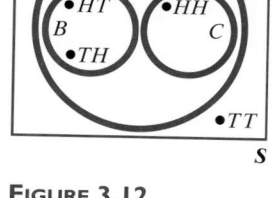

and that $B \cap C$ contains no sample points (see Figure 3.12). Thus, B and C are mutually exclusive, so that

$$P(A) = P(B \cup C) = P(B) + P(C) = \tfrac{1}{2} + \tfrac{1}{4} = \tfrac{3}{4}$$

FIGURE 3.12
Venn diagram for
coin-toss experiment

Although Example 3.13 is very simple, it shows us that writing events with verbal descriptions that include the phrases "at least" or "at most" as unions of mutually exclusive events is very useful. This practice enables us to find the probability of the event by adding the probabilities of the mutually exclusive events.

EXERCISES 3.16–3.31

Learning the Mechanics

3.16 A fair coin is tossed three times and the events A and B are defined as follows:

$A:$ {At least one head is observed}

$B:$ {The number of heads observed is odd}

    a. Identify the sample points in the events A, B, $A \cup B$, A^c, and $A \cap B$.

    b. Find $P(A), P(B), P(A \cup B), P(A^c)$, and $P(A \cap B)$ by summing the probabilities of the appropriate sample points.

    c. Find $P(A \cup B)$ using the additive rule. Compare your answer to the one you obtained in part **b**.

    d. Are the events A and B mutually exclusive? Why?

3.17 What are mutually exclusive events? Give a verbal description, then draw a Venn diagram.

3.18 A pair of fair dice is tossed. Define the following events:

$A:$ {You will roll a 7} (i.e., the sum of the dots on the up faces of the two dice is equal to 7)

$B:$ {At least one of the two dice shows a 4}

    a. Identify the sample points in the events A, B, $A \cap B$, $A \cup B$, and A^c.

    b. Find $P(A), P(B), P(A \cap B), P(A \cup B)$, and $P(A^c)$ by summing the probabilities of the appropriate sample points.

    c. Find $P(A \cup B)$ using the additive rule. Compare your answer to that for the same event in part **b**.

    d. Are A and B mutually exclusive? Why?

3.19 Consider the accompanying Venn diagram, where $P(E_1) = P(E_2) = P(E_3) = \tfrac{1}{5}$, $P(E_4) = P(E_5) = \tfrac{1}{20}$, $P(E_6) = \tfrac{1}{10}$, and $P(E_7) = \tfrac{1}{5}$. Find each of the following probabilities:

a. $P(A)$ **b.** $P(B)$ **c.** $P(A \cup B)$ **d.** $P(A \cap B)$
e. $P(A^c)$ **f.** $P(B^c)$ **g.** $P(A \cup A^c)$ **h.** $P(A^c \cap B)$

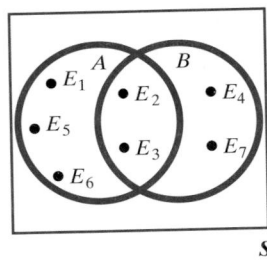

3.20 Consider the accompanying Venn diagram, where $P(E_1) = .10$, $P(E_2) = .05$, $P(E_3) = P(E_4) = .2$, $P(E_5) = .06$, $P(E_6) = .3$, $P(E_7) = .06$, and $P(E_8) = .03$. Find the following probabilities:
a. $P(A^c)$ **b.** $P(B^c)$ **c.** $P(A^c \cap B)$ **d.** $P(A \cup B)$
e. $P(A \cap B)$ **f.** $P(A^c \cup B^c)$
g. Are events A and B mutually exclusive? Why?

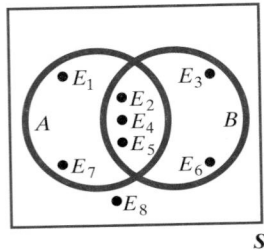

3.21 The following table describes the adult population of a small suburb of a large southern city. A marketing research firm plans to randomly select one adult from the suburb to evaluate a new food product. For this experiment the nine age-income categories are the sample points. Consider the following events:

A: {Person is under 25}

B: {Person is between 25 and 45}

C: {Person is over 45}

D: {Person has income under \$20,000}

E: {Person has income of \$20,000–\$50,000}

F: {Person has income over \$50,000}

Convert the frequencies in the table to relative frequencies and use them to calculate the following probabilities:

	INCOME		
Age	<\$20,000	\$20,000–\$50,000	>\$50,000
<25	950	1,000	50
25–45	450	2,050	1,500
>45	50	950	1,000

a. $P(B)$ **b.** $P(F)$ **c.** $P(C \cap F)$ **d.** $P(B \cup C)$
e. $P(A^c)$ **f.** $P(A^c \cap F)$
g. Consider each pair of events (A and B, A and C, etc.) and list the pairs of events that are mutually exclusive. Justify your choices.

3.22 Refer to Exercise 3.21. Use the same event definitions to do the following exercises.
a. Write the event that the person selected is under 25 with an income over \$50,000 as an intersection of two events.
b. Write the event that the person selected is age 25 or older as the union of two mutually exclusive events and as the complement of an event.

Applying the Concepts

3.23 A state energy agency mailed questionnaires on energy conservation to 1,000 homeowners in the state capital. Five hundred questionnaires were returned. Suppose an experiment consists of randomly selecting and reviewing one of the returned questionnaires. Consider the events:

A: {The home is constructed of brick}

B: {The home is more than 30 years old}

C: {The home is heated with oil}

Describe each of the following events in terms of unions, intersections, and complements (i.e., $A \cup B$, $A \cap B$, A^c, etc.):
a. The home is more than 30 years old and is heated with oil.
b. The home is not constructed of brick.
c. The home is heated with oil or is more than 30 years old.
d. The home is constructed of brick and is not heated with oil.

3.24 Corporate downsizing in the United States has caused a significant increase in the demand for temporary and part-time workers. In Japan a similar increase in demand has been fueled by the need for less costly labor and protection against variation in labor demand. The distribution (in percent) of nonregular workers in Japan in 1992 (by age) is provided in the table on page 133 (adapted from *Monthly Labor Review*, Oct. 1995). Column headings are defined below the table.

Suppose a nonregular worker is to be chosen at random from this population. Define the following events:

A: {The worker is 40 or over}

B: {The worker is a teenager and part-time}

C: {The worker is under 40 and either arubaito or dispatched}

D: {The worker is part-time}

a. Find the probability of each of the above events.
b. Find $P(A \cap D)$ and $P(A \cup D)$.

Age	Part-Time	Arubaito	Temporary and Day	Dispatched	Totals
15–19	.3	3.7	2.3	.2	6.5
20–29	3.4	7.8	6.1	4.7	22.0
30–39	8.4	1.6	4.5	2.7	17.2
40–49	15.6	1.6	7.3	1.4	25.9
50–59	9.4	1.1	5.8	.6	16.9
60 and over	4.3	1.8	4.8	.6	11.5
Totals	41.4	17.6	30.8	10.2	100.0

Part-time: Work fewer hours per day or days per week than regular workers; *arubaito:* someone with a "side" job who is in school or has regular employment elsewhere; *temporary:* employed on a contract lasting more than one month but less than one year; *day:* employed on a contract of less than one month's duration; *dispatched:* hired from a temporary-help agency.

Source: Houseman, S., and Osawa, M. "Part-time and temporary employment in Japan." *Monthly Labor Review,* October 1995, pp. 12–13 (Tables 1 and 2).

c. Describe in words the following events: A^c, B^c, and D^c.

d. Find the probability of each of the events you described in part **c**.

3.25 A buyer for a large metropolitan department store must choose two firms from the four available to supply the store's fall line of men's slacks. The buyer has not dealt with any of the four firms before and considers their products equally attractive. Unknown to the buyer, two of the four firms are having serious financial problems that may result in their not being able to deliver the fall line of slacks as soon as promised. The four firms are identified as G_1 and G_2 (firms in good financial condition) and P_1 and P_2 (firms in poor financial condition). Sample points identify the pairs of firms selected. If the probability of the buyer's selecting a particular firm from among the four is the same for each firm, the sample points and their probabilities for this buying experiment are those listed in the following table.

Sample Points	Probability
$G_1 G_2$	$\frac{1}{6}$
$G_1 P_1$	$\frac{1}{6}$
$G_1 P_2$	$\frac{1}{6}$
$G_2 P_1$	$\frac{1}{6}$
$G_2 P_2$	$\frac{1}{6}$
$P_1 P_2$	$\frac{1}{6}$

We define the following events:

A: {At least one of the selected firms is in good financial condition}

B: {Firm P_1 is selected}

a. Define the event $A \cap B$ as a specific collection of sample points.

b. Define the event $A \cup B$ as a specific collection of sample points.

c. Define the event A^c as a specific collection of sample points.

d. Find $P(A)$, $P(B)$, $P(A \cap B)$, $P(A \cup B)$, and $P(A^c)$ by summing the probabilities of the appropriate sample points.

e. Find $P(A \cup B)$ using the additive rule. Are events A and B mutually exclusive? Why?

3.26 *Roulette* is a very popular game in many American casinos. In roulette, a ball spins on a circular wheel that is divided into 38 arcs of equal length, bearing the numbers 00, 0, 1, 2, ..., 35, 36. The number of the arc on which the ball stops is the outcome of one play of the game. The numbers are also colored in the following manner:

Red: 1, 3, 5, 7, 9, 12, 14, 16, 18, 19, 21, 23, 25, 27, 30, 32, 34, 36
Black: 2, 4, 6, 8, 10, 11, 13, 15, 17, 20, 22, 24, 26, 28, 29, 31, 33, 35
Green: 00, 0

Players may place bets on the table in a variety of ways, including bets on odd, even, red, black, high, low, etc. Define the following events:

A: {Outcome is an odd number (00 and 0 are considered neither odd nor even)}

B: {Outcome is a black number}

C: {Outcome is a low number (1–18)}

a. Define the event $A \cap B$ as a specific set of sample points.

b. Define the event $A \cup B$ as a specific set of sample points.

c. Find $P(A)$, $P(B)$, $P(A \cap B)$, $P(A \cup B)$, and $P(C)$ by summing the probabilities of the appropriate sample points.

d. Define the event $A \cap B \cap C$ as a specific set of sample points.

e. Find $P(A \cup B)$ using the additive rule. Are events A and B mutually exclusive? Why?

f. Find $P(A \cap B \cap C)$ by summing the probabilities of the sample points given in part **d**.

g. Define the event $(A \cup B \cup C)$ as a specific set of sample points.

h. Find $P(A \cup B \cup C)$ by summing the probabilities of the sample points given in part **g**.

3.27 After completing an inventory of three warehouses, a manufacturer of golf club shafts described its stock of 20,125 shafts with the percentages given in the table. Suppose a shaft is selected at random from the 20,125 currently in stock and the warehouse number and type of shaft are observed.

		TYPE OF SHAFT		
		Regular	Stiff	Extra Stiff
Warehouse	1	41%	6%	0%
	2	10%	15%	4%
	3	11%	7%	6%

a. List all the sample points for this experiment.
b. What is the set of all sample points called?
c. Let C be the event that the shaft selected is from warehouse 3. Find $P(C)$ by summing the probabilities of the sample points in C.
d. Let F be the event that the shaft chosen is an extra-stiff type. Find $P(F)$.
e. Let A be the event that the shaft selected is from warehouse 1. Find $P(A)$.
f. Let D be the event that the shaft selected is a regular type. Find $P(D)$.
g. Let E be the event that the shaft selected is a stiff type. Find $P(E)$.

3.28 Refer to Exercise 3.27. Define the characteristics of a golf club shaft portrayed by the following events, and then find the probability of each. For each union, use the additive rule to find the probability. Also, determine whether the events are mutually exclusive.
a. $A \cap F$ **b.** $C \cup E$ **c.** $C \cap D$
d. $A \cup F$ **e.** $A \cup D$

3.29 The types of occupations of the 123,060,000 employed workers (age 16 years and older) in the United States in 1994 are described in the table, and their relative frequencies are listed. A worker is to be selected at random from this population and his or her occupation is to be determined. (Assume that each worker in the population has only one occupation.)
a. What is the probability that the worker will be a male service worker?
b. What is the probability that the worker will be a manager or a professional?
c. What is the probability that the worker will be a female professional or a female operator/fabricator/laborer?
d. What is the probability that the worker will not be in a technical/sales administrative occupation?

Occupation	Relative Frequency
Male Worker	.54
Managerial/professional	.14
Technical/sales/administrative	.11
Service	.06
Precision production, craft, and repair	.10
Operators/fabricators/laborers	.11
Farming, forestry, and fishing	.02
Female Worker	.46
Managerial/professional	.13
Technical/sales/administrative	.19
Service	.08
Precision production, craft, and repair	.01
Operators/fabricators/laborers	.04
Farming, forestry, and fishing	.01

Source: Statistical Abstract of the United States: 1995, p. 411.

3.30 The long-run success of a business depends on its ability to market products with superior characteristics that maximize consumer satisfaction and that give the firm a competitive advantage (Kotler, *Marketing Management*, 1994). Ten new products have been developed by a food-products firm. Market research has indicated that the 10 products have the characteristics described by the Venn diagram shown here.

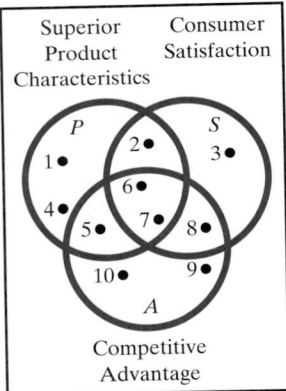

a. Write the event that a product possesses all the desired characteristics as an intersection of the events defined in the Venn diagram. Which products are contained in this intersection?
b. If one of the 10 products were selected at random to be marketed, what is the probability that it would possess all the desired characteristics?
c. Write the event that the randomly selected product would give the firm a competitive advantage or would satisfy consumers as a union of the events defined in the Venn diagram. Find the probability of this union.

d. Write the event that the randomly selected product would possess superior product characteristics and satisfy consumers. Find the probability of this intersection.

3.31 Identifying managerial prospects who are both talented and motivated is difficult. A human-resources director constructed the following two-way table to define nine combinations of talent-motivation levels. The number in a cell is the director's estimate of the probability that a managerial prospect will fall in that category. Suppose the director has decided to hire a new manager. Define the following events:

A: {Prospect places in high-motivation category}

B: {Prospect places in high-talent category}

C: {Prospect is medium or better in both categories}

D: {Prospect places low in at least one category}

E: {Prospect places highest in both categories}

	TALENT		
Motivation	High	Medium	Low
High	.05	.16	.05
Medium	.19	.32	.05
Low	.11	.05	.02

a. Does the sum of the cell probabilities equal 1?

b. List the sample points in each of the events described above and find their probabilities.

c. Find $P(A \cup B)$, $P(A \cap B)$, and $P(A \cup C)$.

d. Find $P(A^c)$ and explain what this means from a practical point of view.

e. Consider each pair of events (*A* and *B*, *A* and *C*, etc.). Which of the pairs are mutually exclusive? Why?

3.5 CONDITIONAL PROBABILITY

The event probabilities we've been discussing give the relative frequencies of the occurrences of the events when the experiment is repeated a very large number of times. Such probabilities are often called **unconditional probabilities** because no special conditions are assumed, other than those that define the experiment.

Often, however, we have additional knowledge that might affect the outcome of an experiment, so we need to alter the probability of an event of interest. A probability that reflects such additional knowledge is called the **conditional probability** of the event. For example, we've seen that the probability of observing an even number (event *A*) on a toss of a fair die is $\frac{1}{2}$. But suppose we're given the information that on a particular throw of the die the result was a number less than or equal to 3 (event *B*). Would the probability of observing an even number on that throw of the die still be equal to $\frac{1}{2}$? It can't be, because making the assumption that *B* has occurred reduces the sample space from six sample points to three sample points (namely, those contained in event *B*). This reduced sample space is as shown in Figure 3.13. Because the sample points for the die-toss experiment are equally likely, each of the three sample points in the reduced sample space is assigned an equal *conditional probability* of $\frac{1}{3}$. Since the only even number of the three in the reduced sample space *B* is the number 2 and the die is fair, we conclude that the probability that *A* occurs *given that B occurs* is $\frac{1}{3}$. We use the symbol $P(A|B)$ to represent the probability of event *A* given that event *B* occurs. For the die-toss example $P(A|B) = \frac{1}{3}$.

To get the probability of event *A* given that event *B* occurs, we proceed as follows. We divide the probability of the part of *A* that falls within the reduced sample space *B*, namely $P(A \cap B)$, by the total probability of the reduced sample space, namely, $P(B)$. Thus, for the die-toss example with event *A:* {Observe an even number} and event *B:* {Observe a number less than or equal to 3}, we find

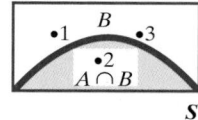

FIGURE 3.13

Reduced sample space for the die-toss experiment given that event *B* has occurred

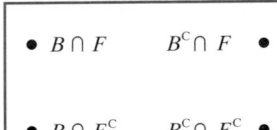

$$P(A|B) = \frac{P(A \cap B)}{P(B)} = \frac{P(2)}{P(1) + P(2) + P(3)} = \frac{\frac{1}{6}}{\frac{3}{6}} = \frac{1}{3}$$

FIGURE 3.14
Sample space for contacting a sales product

The formula for $P(A|B)$ is true in general:

> To find the *conditional probability that event A occurs given that event B occurs*, divide the probability that *both A* and *B* occur by the probability that *B* occurs, that is,
>
> $$P(A|B) = \frac{P(A \cap B)}{P(B)} \qquad [\text{We assume that } P(B) \neq 0.]$$

This formula adjusts the probability of $A \cap B$ from its original value in the complete sample space S to a conditional probability in the reduced sample space B. If the sample points in the complete sample space are equally likely, then the formula will assign equal probabilities to the sample points in the reduced sample space, as in the die-toss experiment. If, on the other hand, the sample points have unequal probabilities, the formula will assign conditional probabilities proportional to the probabilities in the complete sample space. This is illustrated by the following examples.

 **3.14**

Suppose you are interested in the probability of the sale of a large piece of earth-moving equipment. A single prospect is contacted. Let F be the event that the buyer has sufficient money (or credit) to buy the product and let F^c denote the complement of F (the event that the prospect does not have the financial capability to buy the product). Similarly, let B be the event that the buyer wishes to buy the product and let B^c be the complement of that event. Then the four sample points associated with the experiment are shown in Figure 3.14, and their probabilities are given in Table 3.5.

Find the probability that a single prospect will buy, given that the prospect is able to finance the purchase.

SOLUTION
Suppose you consider the large collection of prospects for the sale of your product and randomly select one person from this collection. What is the probability that the person selected will buy the product? In order to buy the product, the customer must be financially able *and* have the desire to buy, so this probability would correspond to the entry in Table 3.5 below {To buy, B} and next to {Yes, F}, or $P(B \cap F) = .2$. This is called the **unconditional probability** of the event $B \cap F$.

In contrast, suppose you know that the prospect selected has the financial capability for purchasing the product. Now you are seeking the probability that the customer will buy given (the condition) that the customer has the financial ability to pay. This probability, the **conditional probability** of B given that F has occurred and denoted by the symbol $P(B|F)$, would be determined by considering

TABLE 3.5 Probabilities of Customer Desire to Buy and Ability to Finance

		DESIRE	
		To Buy, B	Not to Buy, B^c
Able to Finance	Yes, F	.2	.1
	No, F^c	.4	.3

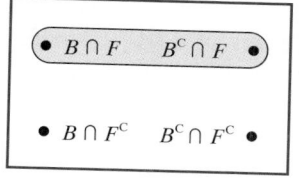

FIGURE 3.15
Subspace (shaded)
containing sample points
implying a financially
able prospect

only the sample points in the reduced sample space containing the sample points $B \cap F$ and $B^c \cap F$—i.e., sample points that imply the prospect is financially able to buy. (This subspace is shaded in Figure 3.15.) From our definition of conditional probability,

$$P(B|F) = \frac{P(B \cap F)}{P(F)}$$

where $P(F)$ is the sum of the probabilities of the two sample points corresponding to $B \cap F$ and $B^c \cap F$ (given in Table 3.5). Then

$$P(F) = P(B \cap F) + P(B^c \cap F) = .2 + .1 = .3$$

and the conditional probability that a prospect buys, given that the prospect is financially able, is

$$P(B|F) = \frac{P(B \cap F)}{P(F)} = \frac{.2}{.3} = .667$$

As we would expect, the probability that the prospect will buy, given that he or she is financially able, is higher than the unconditional probability of selecting a prospect who will buy.

Note in Example 3.14, that the conditional probability formula assigns a probability to the event $(B \cap F)$ in the reduced sample space that is proportional to the probability of the event in the complete sample space. To see this, note that the two sample points in the reduced sample space, $(B \cap F)$ and $(B^c \cap F)$, have probabilities of .2 and .1, respectively, in the complete sample space S. The formula assigns conditional probabilities $2/3$ and $1/3$ (use the formula to check the second one) to these sample points in the reduced sample space F, so that the conditional probabilities retain the 2 to 1 proportionality of the original sample point probabilities.

EXAMPLE 3.15

The investigation of consumer product complaints by the Federal Trade Commission (FTC) has generated much interest by manufacturers in the quality of their products. A manufacturer of an electromechanical kitchen utensil conducted an analysis of a large number of consumer complaints and found that they fell into the six categories shown in Table 3.6. If a consumer complaint is received, what is the probability that the cause of the complaint was product appearance given that the complaint originated during the guarantee period?

SOLUTION
Let A represent the event that the cause of a particular complaint is product appearance, and let B represent the event that the complaint occurred during the guarantee period. Checking Table 3.6, you can see that $(18 + 13 + 32)\% = 63\%$ of the complaints occur during the guarantee period. Hence, $P(B) = .63$. The

TABLE 3.6 Distribution of Product Complaints

	REASON FOR COMPLAINT			
	Electrical	Mechanical	Appearance	Totals
During Guarantee Period	18%	13%	32%	63%
After Guarantee Period	12%	22%	3%	37%
Totals	30%	35%	35%	100%

percentage of complaints that were caused by the appearance and occurred during the guarantee period (the event $A \cap B$) is 32%. Therefore, $P(A \cap B) = .32$.

Using these probability values, we can calculate the conditional probability $P(A|B)$ that the cause of a complaint is appearance given that the complaint occurred during the guarantee time:

$$P(A|B) = \frac{P(A \cap B)}{P(B)} = \frac{.32}{.63} = .51$$

Consequently, we can see that slightly more than half the complaints that occurred during the guarantee period were due to scratches, dents, or other imperfections in the surface of the kitchen devices.

You will see in later chapters that conditional probability plays a key role in many applications of statistics. For example, we may be interested in the probability that a particular stock gains 10% during the next year. We may assess this probability using information such as the past performance of the stock or the general state of the economy at present. However, our probability may change drastically if we assume that the Gross Domestic Product (GDP) will increase by 10% in the next year. We would then be assessing the *conditional probability* that our stock gains 10% in the next year given that the GDP gains 10% in the same year. Thus, the probability of any event that is calculated or assessed based on an assumption that some other event occurs concurrently is a conditional probability.

3.6   THE MULTIPLICATIVE RULE AND INDEPENDENT EVENTS

The probability of an intersection of two events can be calculated using the multiplicative rule, which employs the conditional probabilities we defined in the previous section. Actually, we have already developed the formula in another context. You will recall that the formula for calculating the conditional probability of B given A is

$$P(B|A) = \frac{P(A \cap B)}{P(A)}$$

If we multiply both sides of this equation by $P(A)$, we get a formula for the probability of the intersection of events A and B:

> **Multiplicative Rule of Probability**
> $P(A \cap B) = P(A)P(B|A)$ or, equivalently, $P(A \cap B) = P(B)P(A|B)$

The second expression in the box is obtained by multiplying both sides of the equation $P(A|B) = P(A \cap B)/P(B)$ by $P(B)$.

EXAMPLE 3.16   An investor in wheat futures is concerned with the following events:

> B: {U.S. production of wheat will be profitable next year}
> A: {A serious drought will occur next year}

Based on available information, the investor believes that the probability is .01 that production of wheat will be profitable *assuming* a serious drought will occur in the same year and that the probability is .05 that a serious drought will occur. That is,

$$P(B|A) = .01 \text{ and } P(A) = .05$$

Based on the information provided, what is the probability that a serious drought will occur *and* that a profit will be made? That is, find $P(A \cap B)$, the probability of the intersection of events A and B.

SOLUTION

We want to calculate $P(A \cap B)$. Using the formula for the multiplicative rule, we obtain:

$$P(A \cap B) = P(A)P(B|A) = (.05)(.01) = .0005$$

The probability that a serious drought occurs *and* the production of wheat is profitable is only .0005. As we might expect, this intersection is a very rare event. ▐▌

Intersections often contain only a few sample points. In this case, the probability of an intersection is easy to calculate by summing the appropriate sample point probabilities. However, the formula for calculating intersection probabilities is invaluable when the intersection contains numerous sample points, as the next example illustrates.

EXAMPLE 3.17

A county welfare agency employs ten welfare workers who interview prospective food stamp recipients. Periodically the supervisor selects, at random, the forms completed by two workers to audit for illegal deductions. Unknown to the supervisor, three of the workers have regularly been giving illegal deductions to applicants. What is the probability that both of the two workers chosen have been giving illegal deductions?

SOLUTION

Define the following two events:

> *A:* {First worker selected gives illegal deductions}
> *B:* {Second worker selected gives illegal deductions}

We want to find the probability of the event that both selected workers have been giving illegal deductions. This event can be restated as: {First worker gives illegal deductions *and* second worker gives illegal deductions}. Thus, we want to find the probability of the intersection, $A \cap B$. Applying the multiplicative rule, we have

$$P(A \cap B) = P(A)P(B|A)$$

To find $P(A)$ it is helpful to consider the experiment as selecting one worker from the ten. Then the sample space for the experiment contains ten sample points (representing the ten welfare workers), where the three workers giving illegal deductions are denoted by the symbol I (I_1, I_2, I_3), and the seven workers not giving illegal deductions are denoted by the symbol N ($N_1, \ldots, N_7$). The resulting Venn diagram is illustrated in Figure 3.16. Since the first worker is selected at random from the ten, it is reasonable to assign equal probabilities to the 10 sample points. Thus, each sample point has a probability of $\frac{1}{10}$. The sample points in event A are $\{I_1, I_2, I_3\}$—the three workers who are giving illegal deductions. Thus,

$$P(A) = P(I_1) + P(I_2) + P(I_3) = \frac{1}{10} + \frac{1}{10} + \frac{1}{10} = \frac{3}{10}$$

FIGURE 3.16
Venn diagram for finding $P(A)$

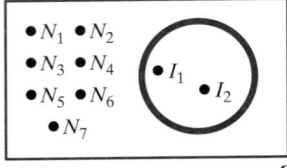

FIGURE 3.17
Venn diagram for
finding $P(B|A)$

To find the conditional probability, $P(B|A)$, we need to alter the sample space S. Since we know A has occurred, i.e., the first worker selected is giving illegal deductions, only two of the nine remaining workers in the sample space are giving illegal deductions. The Venn diagram for this new sample space is shown in Figure 3.17. Each of these 9 sample points are equally likely, so each is assigned a probability of $1/9$. Since the event $(B|A)$ contains the sample points $\{I_1, I_2\}$, we have

$$P(B|A) = P(I_1) + P(I_2) = \tfrac{1}{9} + \tfrac{1}{9} = \tfrac{2}{9}$$

Substituting $P(A) = 3/10$ and $P(B|A) = 2/9$ into the formula for the multiplicative rule, we find

$$P(A \cap B) = P(A)P(B|A) = (\tfrac{3}{10})(\tfrac{2}{9}) = \tfrac{6}{90} = \tfrac{1}{15}$$

Thus, there is a 1 in 15 chance that both workers chosen by the supervisor have been giving illegal deductions to food stamp recipients.

The sample space approach is only one way to solve the problem posed in Example 3.17. An alternative method employs the concept of a **tree diagram**. Tree diagrams are helpful for calculating the probability of an intersection.

To illustrate, a tree diagram for Example 3.17 is displayed in Figure 3.18 The tree begins at the far left with two branches. These branches represent the two possible outcomes N (no illegal deductions) and I (illegal deductions) for the first worker selected. The unconditional probability of each outcome is given (in parentheses) on the appropriate branch. That is, for the first worker selected, $P(N) = 7/10$ and $P(I) = 3/10$. (These can be obtained by summing sample point probabilities as in Example 3.17.)

The next level of the tree diagram (moving to the right) represents the outcomes for the second worker selected. The probabilities shown here are conditional probabilities since the outcome for the first worker is assumed to be known. For example, if the first worker is giving illegal deductions (I), the probability that the second worker is also giving illegal deductions (I) is $2/9$ since of the nine workers left to be selected, only two remain who are giving illegal deductions. This

FIGURE 3.18
Tree diagram for
Example 3.17

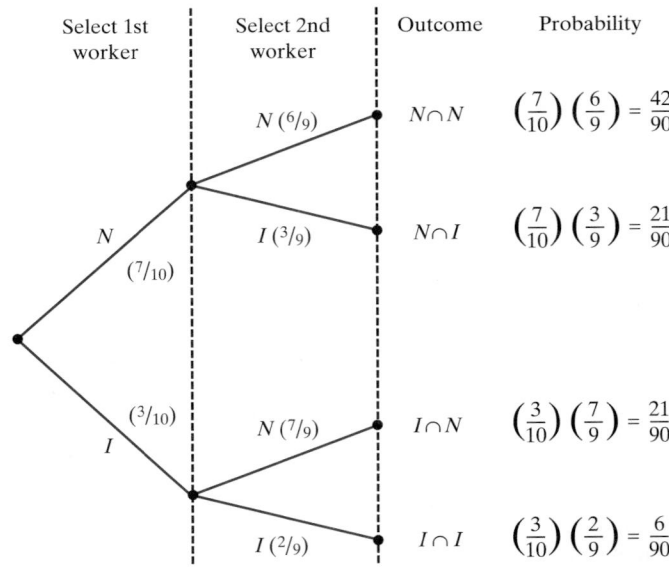

conditional probability, $\frac{2}{9}$, is shown in parentheses on the bottom branch of Figure 3.18.

Finally, the four possible outcomes of the experiment are shown at the end of each of the four tree branches. These events are intersections of two events (outcome of first worker *and* outcome of second worker). Consequently, the multiplicative rule is applied to calculate each probability, as shown in Figure 3.18. You can see that the intersection $\{I \cap I\}$, i.e., the event that both workers selected are giving illegal deductions, has probability $\frac{6}{90} = \frac{1}{15}$—the same value obtained in Example 3.17.

In Section 3.5 we showed that the probability of an event A may be substantially altered by the knowledge that an event B has occurred. However, this will not always be the case. In some instances, the assumption that event B has occurred will *not* alter the probability of event A at all. When this is true, we call events A and B **independent**.

DEFINITION 3.9

Events A and B are **independent events** if the occurrence of B does not alter the probability that A has occurred; that is, events A and B are independent if

$$P(A|B) = P(A)$$

When events A and B are independent, it is also true that

$$P(B|A) = P(B)$$

Events that are not independent are said to be **dependent**.

EXAMPLE 3.18   Consider the experiment of tossing a fair die and let

A: {Observe an even number}
B: {Observe a number less than or equal to 4}

Are events A and B independent?

SOLUTION

The Venn diagram for this experiment is shown in Figure 3.19. We first calculate

$$P(A) = P(2) + P(4) + P(6) = \frac{1}{2}$$

$$P(B) = P(1) + P(2) + P(3) + P(4) = \frac{2}{3}$$

$$P(A \cap B) = P(2) + P(4) = \frac{1}{3}$$

Now assuming B has occurred, the conditional probability of A given B is

$$P(A|B) = \frac{P(A \cap B)}{P(B)} = \frac{\frac{1}{3}}{\frac{2}{3}} = \frac{1}{2} = P(A)$$

Thus, assuming that event B does not alter the probability of observing an even number, it remains $\frac{1}{2}$. Therefore, the events A and B are independent. Note that if we calculate the conditional probability of B given A, our conclusion is the same:

$$P(B|A) = \frac{P(A \cap B)}{P(A)} = \frac{\frac{1}{3}}{\frac{1}{2}} = \frac{2}{3} = P(B)$$

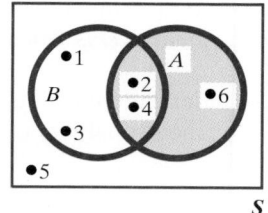

FIGURE 3.19
Venn diagram for die-toss experiment

EXAMPLE 3.19

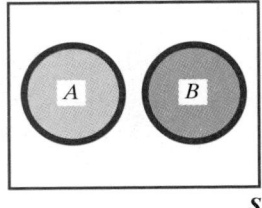

Refer to the consumer product complaint study in Example 3.15. The percentages of complaints of various types during and after the guarantee period are shown in Table 3.6. Define the following events:

A: {Cause of complaint is product appearance}

B: {Complaint occurred during the guarantee term}

Are A and B independent events?

SOLUTION

Events A and B are independent if $P(A|B) = P(A)$. We calculated $P(A|B)$ in Example 3.15 to be .51, and from Table 3.6 we see that

$$P(A) = .32 + .03 = .35$$

Therefore, $P(A|B)$ is not equal to $P(A)$, and A and B are dependent events.   ∎

To gain an intuitive understanding of independence, think of situations in which the occurrence of one event does not alter the probability that a second event will occur. For example, suppose two small companies are being monitored by a financier for possible investment. If the businesses are in different industries and they are otherwise unrelated, then the success or failure of one company may be *independent* of the success or failure of the other. That is, the event that company A fails may not alter the probability that company B will fail.

As a second example, consider an election poll in which 1,000 registered voters are asked their preference between two candidates. Pollsters try to use procedures for selecting a sample of voters so that the responses are independent. That is, the objective of the pollster is to select the sample so the event that one polled voter prefers candidate A does not alter the probability that a second polled voter prefers candidate A.

We will make three final points about independence. The first is that the property of independence, unlike the mutually exclusive property, cannot be shown on or gleaned from a Venn diagram. This means *you can't trust your intuition.* In general, the only way to check for independence is by performing the calculations of the probabilities in the definition.

The second point concerns the relationship between the mutually exclusive and independence properties. Suppose that events A and B are mutually exclusive, as shown in Figure 3.20, and both events have nonzero probabilities. Are these events independent or dependent? That is, does the assumption that B occurs alter the probability of the occurrence of A? It certainly does, because if we assume that B has occurred, it is impossible for A to have occurred simultaneously. That is, $P(A|B) = 0$. Thus, *mutually exclusive events are dependent events* since $P(A) \neq P(A|B)$.

The third point is that the probability of the intersection of independent events is very easy to calculate. Referring to the formula for calculating the probability of an intersection, we find

$$P(A \cap B) = P(A)P(B|A)$$

FIGURE 3.20
Mutually exclusive events are dependent events

Thus, since $P(B|A) = P(B)$ when A and B are independent, we have the following useful rule:

> *If events A and B are independent,* the probability of the intersection of A and B equals the product of the probabilities of A and B; that is,
>
> $$P(A \cap B) = P(A)P(B)$$
>
> The converse is also true: If $P(A \cap B) = P(A)P(B)$, then events A and B are independent.

In the die-toss experiment, we showed in Example 3.18 that the events A: {Observe an even number} and B: {Observe a number less than or equal to 4} are independent if the die is fair. Thus,

$$P(A \cap B) = P(A)P(B) = (\tfrac{1}{2})(\tfrac{2}{3}) = \tfrac{1}{3}$$

This agrees with the result that we obtained in the example:

$$P(A \cap B) = P(2) + P(4) = \tfrac{2}{6} = \tfrac{1}{3}$$

EXAMPLE 3.20

Almost every retail business has the problem of determining how much inventory to purchase. Insufficient inventory may result in lost business, and excess inventory may have a detrimental effect on profits. Suppose a retail computer store owner is planning to place an order for personal computers (PCs). She is trying to decide how many IBM PCs and how many IBM compatibles to order.

The owner's records indicate that 80% of the previous PC customers purchased IBM PCs and 20% purchased compatibles.

a. What is the probability that the next two customers will purchase compatibles?

b. What is the probability that the next ten customers will purchase compatibles?

SOLUTION

a. Let C_1 represent the event that customer 1 will purchase a compatible and C_2 represent the event that customer 2 will purchase a compatible. The event that *both* customers purchase compatibles is the intersection of the two events, $C_1 \cap C_2$. From the records the store owner could reasonably conclude that $P(C_1) = .2$ (based on the fact that 20% of past customers have purchased compatibles), and the same reasoning would apply to C_2. However, in order to compute the probability of $C_1 \cap C_2$, we need more information. Either the records must be examined for the occurrence of consecutive purchases of compatibles, or some assumption must be made to allow the calculation of $P(C_1 \cap C_2)$ from the multiplicative rule. It seems reasonable to make the assumption that the two events are independent, since the decision of the first customer is not likely to affect the decision of the second customer. Assuming independence, we have

$$P(C_1 \cap C_2) = P(C_1)P(C_2) = (.2)(.2) = .04$$

b. To see how to compute the probability that ten consecutive purchases will be compatibles, first consider the event that three consecutive customers purchase compatibles. If C_3 represents the event that the third customer purchases a compatible, then we want to compute the probability of the intersection $C_1 \cap C_2$ with C_3. Again assuming independence of the purchasing decisions, we have

$$P(C_1 \cap C_2 \cap C_3) = P(C_1 \cap C_2) \, P(C_3) = (.2)^2(.2) = .008$$

Similar reasoning leads to the conclusion that the intersection of ten such events can be calculated as follows:

$$P(C_1 \cap C_2 \cap \cdots \cap C_{10}) = P(C_1)P(C_2) \cdots P(C_{10}) = (.2)^{10} = .0000001024$$

Thus, the probability that ten consecutive customers purchase IBM compatibles is about 1 in 10 million, assuming the probability of each customer's purchase of a compatible is .2 and the purchase decisions are independent. ▙

EXERCISES   3.32–3.51

Learning the Mechanics

3.32 An experiment results in one of three mutually exclusive events, A, B, or C. It is known that $P(A) = .30$, $P(B) = .55$, and $P(C) = .15$. Find each of the following probabilities:
   a. $P(A \cup B)$ **b.** $P(A \cap C)$
   c. $P(A|B)$ **d.** $P(B \cup C)$
   e. Are B and C independent events? Explain.

3.33 Consider the experiment depicted by the Venn diagram, with the sample space S containing five sample points. The sample points are assigned the following probabilities: $P(E_1) = .20$, $P(E_2) = .30$, $P(E_3) = .30$, $P(E_4) = .10$, $P(E_5) = .10$.

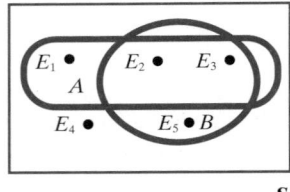

S

   a. Calculate $P(A)$, $P(B)$, and $P(A \cap B)$.
   b. Suppose we know that event A has occurred, so that the reduced sample space consists of the three sample points in A—namely, E_1, E_2, and E_3. Use the formula for conditional probability to adjust the probabilities of these three sample points for the knowledge that A has occurred [i.e., $P(E_i|A)$]. Verify that the conditional probabilities are in the same proportion to one another as the original sample point probabilities.
   c. Calculate the conditional probability $P(B|A)$ in two ways: (1) Add the adjusted (conditional) probabilities of the sample points in the intersection $A \cap B$, since these represent the event that B occurs given that A has occurred; (2) Use the formula for conditional probability:

$$P(B|A) = \frac{P(A \cap B)}{P(A)}$$

Verify that the two methods yield the same result.
   d. Are events A and B independent? Why or why not?

3.34 Three fair coins are tossed and the following events are defined:

   A: {Observe at least one head}
   B: {Observe exactly two heads}
   C: {Observe exactly two tails}
   D: {Observe at most one head}

   a. Sum the probabilities of the appropriate sample points to find: $P(A)$, $P(B)$, $P(C)$, $P(D)$, $P(A \cap B)$, $P(A \cap D)$, $P(B \cap C)$, and $P(B \cap D)$.
   b. Use your answers to part **a** to calculate $P(B|A)$, $P(A|D)$, and $P(C|B)$.
   c. Which pairs of events, if any, are independent? Why?

3.35 An experiment results in one of five sample points with the following probabilities: $P(E_1) = .22$, $P(E_2) = .31$, $P(E_3) = .15$, $P(E_4) = .22$, and $P(E_5) = .1$. The following events have been defined:

   A: $\{E_1, E_3\}$
   B: $\{E_2, E_3, E_4\}$
   C: $\{E_1, E_5\}$

   Find each of the following probabilities:
   a. $P(A)$ **b.** $P(B)$ **c.** $P(A \cap B)$
   d. $P(A|B)$ **e.** $P(B \cap C)$ **f.** $P(C|B)$
   g. Consider each pair of events: A and B, A and C, and B and C. Are any of the pairs of events independent? Why?

3.36 Two fair dice are tossed, and the following events are defined:

   A: {Sum of the numbers showing is odd}
   B: {Sum of the numbers showing is 9, 11, or 12}

   Are events A and B independent? Why?

3.37 A sample space contains six sample points and events A, B, and C as shown in the Venn diagram. The probabilities of the sample points are

$P(1) = .20, P(2) = .05, P(3) = .30, P(4) = .10,$
$P(5) = .10, P(6) = .25.$

S

a. Which pairs of events, if any, are mutually exclusive? Why?

b. Which pairs of events, if any, are independent? Why?

c. Find $P(A \cup B)$ by adding the probabilities of the sample points and then by using the additive rule. Verify that the answers agree. Repeat for $P(A \cup C)$.

3.38 Defend or refute each of the following statements:

a. Dependent events are always mutually exclusive.

b. Mutually exclusive events are always dependent.

c. Independent events are always mutually exclusive.

3.39 For two events, *A* and *B*, $P(A) = .4$ and $P(B) = .2$.

a. If *A* and *B* are independent, find $P(A \cap B)$, $P(A|B)$, and $P(A \cup B)$.

b. If *A* and *B* are dependent, with $P(A|B) = .6$, find $P(A \cap B)$ and $P(B|A)$.

Applying the Concepts

3.40 "Go" is one of the oldest and most popular strategic board games in the world, especially in Japan and Korea. This two-player game is played on a flat surface marked with 19 vertical and 19 horizontal lines. The objective is to control territory by placing pieces called "stones" on vacant points on the board. Players alternate placing their stones. The player using black stones goes first, followed by the player using white stones. [*Note:* The University of Virginia requires MBA students to learn Go to understand how the Japanese conduct business.] *Chance* (Summer 1995) published an article that investigated the advantage of playing first (i.e., using the black stones) in Go. The results of 577 games recently played by professional Go players were analyzed.

a. In the 577 games, the player with the black stones won 319 times and the player with the white stones won 258 times. Use this information to assess the probability of winning when you play first in Go.

b. Professional Go players are classified by level. Group C includes the top-level players followed by Group B (middle-level) and Group A (low-level) players. The table below describes the number of games won by the player with the black stones, categorized by level of the black player and level of the opponent. Assess the probability of winning when you play first in Go for each combination of player and opponent level.

c. If the player with the black stones is ranked higher than the player with the white stones, what is the probability that black wins?

d. Given the players are of the same level, what is the probability that the player with the black stones wins?

3.41 Businesses that offer credit to their customers are inevitably faced with the task of collecting unpaid bills. A study of collection remedies used by creditors was published in the *Journal of Financial Research* (Spring 1986). As part of the study, creditors in four states were asked about how they deal with past-due bills. Their responses are tallied in the table on page 146. "Tough actions"

Black Player Level	Opponent Level	Number of Wins	Number of Games
C	A	34	34
C	B	69	79
C	C	66	118
B	A	40	54
B	B	52	95
B	C	27	79
A	A	15	28
A	B	11	51
A	C	5	39
Totals		319	577

Source: J. Kim, and H. J. Kim. "The advantage of playing first in Go." *Chance,* Vol. 8, No. 3, Summer 1995, p. 26 (Table 3).

	Wisconsin	Illinois	Arkansas	Louisiana
Take tough action early	0	1	5	1
Take tough action later	37	23	22	21
Never take tough action	9	11	6	15

included filing a legal action, turning the debt over to a third party such as an attorney or collection agency, garnishing wages, and repossessing secured property. Suppose one of the creditors questioned is selected at random.

a. What is the probability that the creditor is from Wisconsin or Louisiana?

b. What is the probability that the creditor is not from Wisconsin or Louisiana?

c. What is the probability that the creditor never takes tough action?

d. What is the probability that the creditor is from Arkansas and never takes tough action?

e. What is the probability that the creditor never takes tough action, given that the creditor is from Arkansas?

f. If the creditor takes tough action early, what is the probability that the creditor is from Arkansas or Louisiana?

g. What is the probability that a creditor from Arkansas never takes tough action?

3.42 In the last decade, increasingly more employees have been offered a variety of health care plans to choose from. This is a direct result of the growing prevalence of preferred provider organizations (PPOs) and health maintenance organizations (HMOs). PPOs permit employees to choose their health care provider, but offer financial incentives when designated doctors and hospitals are chosen. HMOs offer prepaid health care from a particular set of providers (*Monthly Labor Review,* Oct. 1995). A survey of 100 large, 100 medium, and 100 small companies that offer their employees HMOs, PPOs, and fee-for-service plans was conducted; each firm provided information on the plans chosen by their employees. These companies had a total employment of 833,303 people. A breakdown of the number of employees in each category by firm size and plan is provided in the table.

Company Size	Fee-for-Service	PPO	HMO	Totals
Small	1,808	1,757	1,456	5,021
Medium	8,953	6,491	6,983	22,382
Large	330,419	241,770	233,711	805,900
Totals	341,180	250,018	242,105	833,303

Source: Adapted from Bucci, M., and Grant, R. "Employer-sponsored health insurance: What's offered; what's chosen?" *Monthly Labor Review,* October 1995, pp. 38–43.

One employee from the 833,303 total employees is to be chosen at random for further analysis. Define the events A and B as follows:

A: {Observe an employee that chose fee-for-service}

B: {Observe an employee from a small company}

a. Find $P(B)$. **b.** Find $P(A \cap B)$.

c. Find $P(A \cup B)$. **d.** Find $P(A|B)$.

e. Are A and B independent? Justify your answer.

3.43 Refer to the *American Journal of Public Health* study of unintentional carbon monoxide (CO) poisonings in Colorado, Exercise 3.10. The 981 cases were classified in a table, which is reproduced below. A case of unintentional CO poisoning is chosen at random from the 981 cases.

Source of Exposure	Fatal	Nonfatal	Total
Fire	63	53	116
Auto exhaust	60	178	238
Furnace	18	345	363
Kerosene or spaceheater	9	18	27
Appliance	9	63	72
Other gas-powered motor	3	73	76
Fireplace	0	16	16
Other	3	19	22
Unknown	9	42	51
Total	174	807	981

Source: Cook, M. C., Simon, P. A., and Hoffman, R. E. "Unintentional carbon monoxide poisoning in Colorado, 1986 through 1991." *American Journal of Public Health,* Vol. 85, No. 7, July 1995, p. 989 (Table 1). American Public Health Association.

a. Given that the source of the poisoning is fire, what is the probability that the case is fatal?

b. Given that the case is nonfatal, what is the probability that it is caused by auto exhaust?

c. If the case is fatal, what is the probability that the source is unknown?

d. If the case is nonfatal, what is the probability that the source is not fire or a fireplace?

3.44 Physicians and pharmacists sometimes fail to inform patients adequately about the proper application of prescription drugs and about the precautions to take in order to avoid potential side effects. This failure is an ongoing problem in the United States. One method of increasing patients' awareness of the problem is for physicians to provide Patient Medication Instruction (PMI) sheets. The American Medical Association, however, has found that only 20% of the doctors who prescribe drugs frequently distribute PMI sheets to their patients. Assume that 20% of all patients receive the PMI sheet with their prescriptions and that 12% receive the PMI sheet and are hospitalized because of a drug-related problem. What is the probability that a person will be hospitalized for a drug-related problem given that the person has received the PMI sheet?

3.45   A soft-drink bottler has two quality control inspectors independently check each case of soft drinks for chipped or cracked bottles before the cases leave the bottling plant. Having observed the work of the two trusted inspectors over several years, the bottler has determined that the probability of a defective case getting by the first inspector is .05 and the probability of a defective case getting by the second inspector is .10. What is the probability that a defective case gets by both inspectors?

3.46   The table describes the 63.1 million U.S. long-form federal tax returns filed with the Internal Revenue Service (IRS) in 1992 and the percentage of those returns that were audited by the IRS.

Income	Number of Tax Filers (millions)	Percentage Audited
Under $25,000	18.7	.6
$25,000–$49,999	27.5	.6
$50,000–$99,999	13.7	1.0
$100,000 or more	3.2	4.9

Source: Statistical Abstract of the United States: 1995, p. 344.

   a. If a tax filer is randomly selected from this population of tax filers (i.e., each tax filer has an equal probability of being selected), what is the probability that the tax filer was audited?

   b. If a tax filer is randomly selected from this population of tax filers, what is the probability that the tax filer had an income of $25,000–$49,999 in 1992 *and* was audited? What is the probability that the tax filer had an income of $50,000 or more in 1992 *or* was not audited?

3.47   "Channel One" is an education television network that is available to all secondary schools in the United States. Participating schools are equipped with TV sets in every classroom in order to receive the Channel One broadcasts. According to *Educational Technology* (May–June 1995), 40% of all U.S. secondary schools subscribe to the Channel One Communications Network (CCN). Of these subscribers, only 5% never use the CCN broadcasts, while 20% use CCN more than five times per week.

   a. Find the probability that a randomly selected U.S. secondary school subscribes to CCN but never uses the CCN broadcasts.

   b. Find the probability that a randomly selected U.S. secondary school subscribes to CCN and uses the broadcasts more than five times per week.

3.48   In October 1994, a flaw was discovered in the Pentium chip installed in many new personal computers. The chip produced an incorrect result when dividing two numbers. Intel, the manufacturer of the Pentium chip, initially announced that such an error would occur only once in 9 billion divides, or "once in every 27,000 years" for a typical user; consequently, it did not immediately replace the chip. Assume the probability of a divide error with the Pentium chip is, in fact, $1/9,000,000,000$.

   a. For a division performed using the flawed Pentium chip, what is the probability that no error will occur?

   b. Consider two successive divisions performed using the flawed chip. What is the probability that neither result will be in error? (Assume that any one division has no impact on the result of any other division performed by the chip.)

   c. Depending on the procedure, statistical software packages may perform an extremely large number of divisions to produce the required output. For heavy users of the software, 1 billion divisions over a short time frame is not unusual. Calculate the probability that 1 billion divisions performed using the flawed Pentium chip will result in no errors.

   d. Use the result, part **c**, to compute the probability of at least one error in the 1 billion divisions. [*Note:* Two months after the flaw was discovered, Intel agreed to replace all Pentium chips free of charge.]

3.49   The genetic origin and properties of maize (modern-day corn), a domestic plant developed 8,000 years ago in Mexico, was investigated in *Economic Botany* (Jan.–Mar. 1995). Seeds from maize ears carry either single spikelets or paired spikelets, but not both. Progeny tests on approximately 600 maize ears revealed the following information. Forty percent of all seeds carry single spikelets, while 60% carry paired spikelets. A seed with single spikelets will produce maize ears with single spikelets 29% of the time and paired spikelets 71% of the time. A seed with paired spikelets will produce maize ears with single spikelets 26% of the time and paired spikelets 74% of the time.

   a. Find the probability that a randomly selected maize ear seed carries a single spikelet and produces ears with single spikelets.

   b. Find the probability that a randomly selected maize ear seed produces ears with paired spikelets.

3.50 A particular automatic sprinkler system for high-rise apartment buildings, office buildings, and hotels has two different types of activation devices for each sprinkler head. One type has a reliability of .91 (i.e., the probability that it will activate the sprinkler when it should is .91). The other type, which operates independently of the first type, has a reliability of .87. Suppose a serious fire starts near a particular sprinkler head.

a. What is the probability that the sprinkler head will be activated?

b. What is the probability that the sprinkler head will not be activated?

c. What is the probability that both activation devices will work properly?

d. What is the probability that only the device with reliability .91 will work properly?

3.51 One definition of *Total Quality Management* (TQM) was given in Exercise 3.7. Another definition is a "management philosophy and a system of management techniques to improve product and service quality and worker productivity." TQM involves such techniques as teamwork, empower-ment of workers, improved communication with customers, evaluation of work processes, and statistical analysis of processes and their output (Benson, *Minnesota Management Review,* Fall 1992). One hundred U.S. companies were surveyed and it was found that 30 had implemented TQM. Among the 100 companies surveyed, 60 reported an increase in sales last year. Of those 60, 20 had implemented TQM. Suppose one of the 100 surveyed companies is to be selected at random for additional analysis.

a. What is the probability that a firm that implemented TQM is selected? That a firm whose sales increased is selected?

b. Are the two events {TQM implemented} and {Sales increased} independent or dependent? Explain.

c. Suppose that instead of 20 TQM implementers among the 60 firms reporting sales increases, there were 18. Now are the events {TQM implemented} and {Sales increased} independent or dependent? Explain.

3.7 RANDOM SAMPLING

How a sample is selected from a population is of vital importance in statistical inference because the probability of an observed sample will be used to infer the characteristics of the sampled population. To illustrate, suppose you deal yourself four cards from a deck of 52 cards and all four cards are aces. Do you conclude that your deck is an ordinary bridge deck, containing only four aces, or do you conclude that the deck is stacked with more than four aces? It depends on how the cards were drawn. If the four aces were always placed at the top of a standard bridge deck, drawing four aces is not unusual—it is certain. On the other hand, if the cards are thoroughly mixed, drawing four aces in a sample of four cards is highly improbable. The point, of course, is that in order to use the observed sample of four cards to draw inferences about the population (the deck of 52 cards), you need to know how the sample was selected from the deck.

One of the simplest and most frequently employed sampling procedures is implied in many of the previous examples and exercises. It is called **random sampling** and produces what is known as a *random sample.*

DEFINITION 3.10

If *n* elements are selected from a population in such a way that every set of *n* elements in the population has an equal probability of being selected, the *n* elements are said to be a **random sample**.*

If a population is not too large and the elements can be numbered on slips of paper, poker chips, etc., you can physically mix the slips of paper or chips and remove *n* elements from the total. The numbers that appear on the chips selected would indicate the population elements to be included in the sample. Since it is

---

*Strictly speaking, this is a **simple random sample**. There are many different types of random samples. The simple random sample is the most common.

often difficult to achieve a thorough mix, such a procedure only provides an approximation to random sampling. Most researchers rely on **random number generators** to automatically generate the random sample. Random number generators are available in table form and they are built into most statistical software packages.

EXAMPLE 3.21

Suppose you wish to randomly sample five households from a population of 100,000 households to participate in a study.

  a. How many different samples can be selected?

  b. Use a random number generator to select a random sample.

SOLUTION

  a. To determine the number of samples, we'll apply the combinatorial rule of Section 3.1. In this case, $N = 100{,}000$ and $n = 5$. Then,

$$\binom{N}{n} = \binom{100{,}000}{5} = \frac{100{,}000!}{5!\,99{,}995!}$$

$$= \frac{100{,}000 \cdot 99{,}999 \cdot 99{,}998 \cdot 99{,}997 \cdot 99{,}996}{5 \cdot 4 \cdot 3 \cdot 2 \cdot 1}$$

$$= 8.33 \times 10^{22}$$

Thus, there are 83.3 billion trillion different samples of five households that can be selected from 100,000.

  b. To ensure that each of the possible samples has an equal chance of being selected, as required for random sampling, we can employ a **random number table**, as provided in Table I of Appendix B. Random number tables are constructed in such a way that every number occurs with (approximately) equal probability. Furthermore, the occurrence of any one number in a position is independent of any of the other numbers that appear in the table. To use a table of random numbers, number the N elements in the population from 1 to N. Then turn to Table I and select a starting number in the table. Proceeding from this number either across the row or down the column, remove and record n numbers from the table.

To illustrate, first we number the households in the population from 1 to 100,000. Then, we turn to a page of Table I, say the first page. (A partial reproduction of the first page of Table I is shown in Table 3.7.) Now, we arbitrarily select a starting number, say the random number appearing in the third row, second column. This number is 48,360. Then we proceed down the second column to obtain the remaining four random numbers. In this case we have selected five random numbers, which are shaded in Table 3.7. Using the first five digits to represent households from 1 to 99,999 and the number 00000 to represent household 100,000, we can see that the households numbered

48,360

93,093

39,975

6,907

72,905

should be included in our sample. *Note:* Use only the necessary number of digits in each random number to identify the element to be included in the sample. If, in

TABLE 3.7   Partial Reproduction of Table I in Appendix B

Row \ Column	1	2	3	4	5	6
1	10480	15011	01536	02011	81647	91646
2	22368	46573	25595	85393	30995	89198
3	24130	48360	22527	97265	76393	64809
4	42167	93093	06243	61680	07856	16376
5	37570	39975	81837	16656	06121	91782
6	77921	06907	11008	42751	27756	53498
7	99562	72905	56420	69994	98872	31016
8	96301	91977	05463	07972	18876	20922
9	89579	14342	63661	10281	17453	18103
10	85475	36857	53342	53988	53060	59533
11	28918	69578	88231	33276	70997	79936
12	63553	40961	48235	03427	49626	69445
13	09429	93969	52636	92737	88974	33488

the course of recording the n numbers from the table, you select a number that has already been selected, simply discard the duplicate and select a replacement at the end of the sequence. Thus, you may have to record more than n numbers from the table to obtain a sample of n unique numbers.

Can we be perfectly sure that all 83.3 billion trillion samples have an equal chance of being selected? That fact is, we can't; but to the extent that the random number table contains truly random sequences of digits, the sample should be very close to random. ⌐

Table I in Appendix B is just one example of a random number generator. For most scientific studies that require a large random sample, computers are used to generate the random sample. The SAS and MINITAB statistical software packages both have easy-to-use random number generators.

For example, suppose we required a random sample of $n = 50$ households from the population of 100,000 households in Example 3.21. Here, we might employ the SAS random number generator. Figure 3.21 shows a SAS printout listing 50 random numbers (from a population of 100,000). The households with these identification numbers would be included in the random sample.

FIGURE 3.21
SAS-generated random sample of 50 households

OBS	HOUSENUM	OBS	HOUSENUM	OBS	HOUSENUM	OBS	HOUSENUM
1	47122	14	47271	27	17098	40	4260
2	94231	15	3642	28	23259	41	58140
3	95531	16	7611	29	30512	42	22903
4	41445	17	81646	30	91548	43	65959
5	80287	18	92158	31	7673	44	13962
6	11731	19	36667	32	68549	45	25819
7	47523	20	71811	33	85433	46	66497
8	84847	21	78988	34	5231	47	79559
9	69822	22	3819	35	13455	48	87017
10	18270	23	21873	36	71666	49	28483
11	52636	24	74938	37	66280	50	91806
12	21750	25	23635	38	66210		
13	63363	26	35807	39	21998		

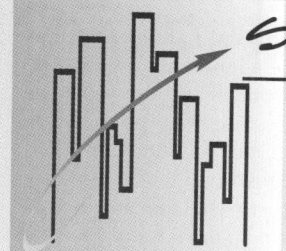

STATISTICS IN ACTION

3.2 LOTTERY BUSTER

"Welcome to the Wonderful World of Lottery Bu$ters." So begins the premier issue of *Lottery Buster*, a monthly publication for players of the state lottery games. *Lottery Buster* provides interesting facts and figures on the nearly 40 state lotteries currently operating in the United States and purported "tips" on how to increase a player's odds of winning the lottery.

New Hampshire, in 1963, was the first state in modern times to authorize a state lottery as an alternative to increasing taxes. (Prior to this time, beginning in 1895, lotteries were banned in America for fear of corruption.) Since then, lotteries have become immensely popular for two reasons. First, they lure you with the opportunity to win millions of dollars with a $1 investment; second, when you lose, at least you know your money is going to a good cause.

The popularity of the state lottery has brought with it an avalanche of self-proclaimed "experts" and "mathematical wizards" (such as the editors of *Lottery Buster*) who provide advice on how to win the lottery—for a fee, of course! These experts—the legitimate ones, anyway—base their "systems" of winning on their knowledge of probability and statistics.

For example, more experts would agree that the "golden rule" or "first rule" in winning lotteries is *game selection*. State lotteries generally offer three types of games: Instant (scratch-off) tickets, Daily Numbers (Pick-3 and Pick-4), and the weekly Pick-6 Lotto game.

The Instant game involves scratching off the thin, opaque covering on a ticket to determine whether you have won or lost. The cost of a ticket is 50¢, and the amount to be won ranges from $1 to $100,000 in most states, while it reaches $1 million in others. *Lottery Buster* advises against playing the Instant game because it is "a pure chance play, and you can win only by dumb luck. No skill can be applied to this game."

The Daily Numbers game permits you to choose either a three-digit (Pick-3) or four-digit (Pick-4) number at a cost of $1 per ticket. Each night, the winning number is drawn. If your number matches the winning number, you win a large sum of money, usually $100,000. You do have some control over the Daily Numbers game (since you pick the numbers that you play) and, consequently, there are strategies available to increase your chances of winning. However, the Daily Numbers game, like the Instant game, is not available for out-of-state play. For this reason, and because the payoffs are relatively small, lottery experts prefer the weekly Pick-6 Lotto game.

To play Pick-6 Lotto, you select six numbers of your choice from a field of numbers ranging from 1 to N, where N depends on which state's game you are playing. For example, Florida's Lotto game involves picking six numbers ranging from 1 to 49 (denoted 6/49) as shown on the Florida Lotto ticket, Figure 3.22. Delaware's Lotto is a 6/30 game, and Pennsylvania's is a 6/40 game. The cost of a ticket is $1 and the payoff, if your six numbers match the winning numbers drawn at the end of each week, is $6 million or more, depending on the number of tickets purchased. (To date, Pennsylvania has had the largest weekly payoff of $97 million.) In addition to the grand prize, you can win second-, third-, and fourth-prize payoffs by matching five, four, and three of the six numbers drawn, respectively. And you don't have to be a resident of the state to play the state's Lotto game. Anyone can play by calling a toll-free "hotline" number.

Focus

a. Consider Florida's 6/49 Lotto game. Calculate the number of possible ways in which you can choose the six numbers from the 49 available. If you purchase a single $1 ticket, what is the probability that you win the grand prize (i.e., match all six numbers)?

b. Repeat part **a** for Delaware's 6/30 game.

c. Repeat part **a** for Pennsylvania's 6/40 game.

d. Since you can play any state's Lotto game, which of the three, Florida, Delaware, or Pennsylvania, would you choose to play? Why?

e. One strategy used to increase your odds of winning a Lotto is to employ a *wheeling system*. In a complete wheeling system, you select more than six numbers, say, seven, and play every combination of six of those seven numbers. Suppose you choose to "wheel" the following seven numbers in a 6/40 game: 2, 7, 18, 23, 30, 32, 39. How many tickets would you need to purchase to have every possible combination of the seven numbers? List the six numbers on each of these tickets.

continued

f. Refer to part **e.** What is the probability of winning the 6/40 Lotto when you wheel seven numbers? Does the strategy, in fact, increase your odds of winning?

g. Consider the strategy of playing **neighboring pairs**. Neighboring pairs are two consecutive numbers that come up together on the winning ticket. In one state lottery, for example, 79% of the winning tick-ets had at least one neighboring pair. Thus, some "experts" feel that you have a better chance of winning if you include at least one neighboring pair in your number selection. Calculate the probability of winning the 6/40 Lotto with the six numbers: 2, 15, 19, 20, 27, 37. [*Note:* 19, 20 is a neighboring pair.] Compare this probability to the one in part **c.** Comment on the neighboring pairs strategy.

FIGURE 3.22
Reproduction of Florida's 6/49 Lotto ticket (Statistics in Action 3.2)

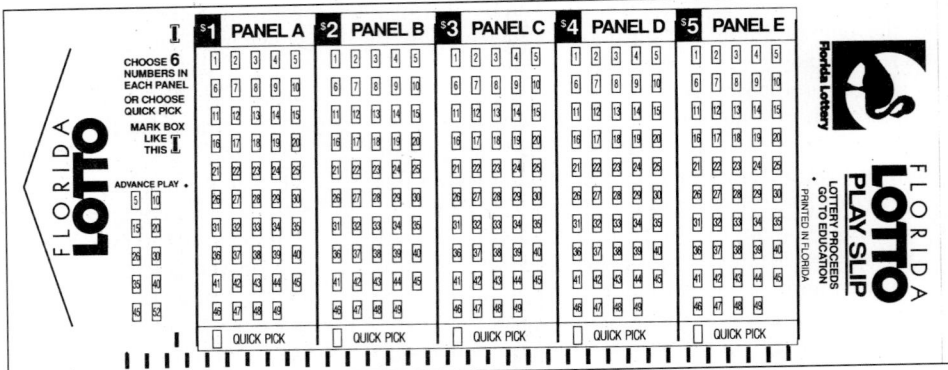

EXERCISES   3.52–3.58

Learning the Mechanics

3.52 Suppose you wish to sample $n = 2$ elements from a total of $N = 10$ elements.

a. Count the number of different samples that can be drawn, first by listing them, and then by using combinatorial mathematics. (See Section 3.1.)

b. If random sampling is to be employed, what is the probability that any particular sample will be selected?

c. Show how to use the random number table, Table I in Appendix B, to select a random sample of 2 elements from a population of 10 elements. Perform the sampling procedure 20 times. Do any two of the samples contain the same 2 elements? Given your answer to part **b,** did you expect repeated samples?

3.53 Suppose you wish to sample $n = 3$ elements from a total of $N = 600$ elements.

a. Count the number of different samples by using combinatorial mathematics (see Section 3.1).

b. If random sampling is to be employed, what is the probability that any particular sample will be selected?

c. Show how to use the random number table, Table I in Appendix B, to select a random sample of 3 elements from a population of 600 elements. Perform the sampling procedure 20 times. Do any two of the samples contain the same three elements? Given your answer to part **b,** did you expect repeated samples?

d. Use a computer to generate a random sample of 3 from the population of 600 elements.

3.54 Suppose that a population contains $N = 200{,}000$ elements. Use a computer or Table I of Appendix B to select a random sample of $n = 10$ elements from the population. Explain how you selected your sample.

Applying the Concepts

3.55 In auditing a firm's financial statements, an auditor will (1) assess the capability of the firm's accounting system to accumulate, measure, and synthesize transactional data properly, and (2) assess the operational effectiveness of the accounting system. In performing the second assessment, the auditor frequently relies on a random sample of actual transactions (Stickney and Weil, *Financial Accounting: An Introduction to Concepts, Methods, and Uses,* 1994). A particular firm has 5,382 customer accounts that are numbered from 0001 to 5382.

a. One account is to be selected at random for audit. What is the probability that account number 3,241 is selected?

b. Draw a random sample of ten accounts and explain in detail the procedure you used.

c. Refer to part **b.** The following are two possible random samples of size ten. Is one more likely to be selected than the other? Explain.

Sample Number 1

5011	0082	0963	0772	3415
2663	1126	0008	0026	4189

Sample Number 2

0001	0003	0005	0007	0009
0002	0004	0006	0008	0010

3.56 To ascertain the effectiveness of their advertising campaigns, firms frequently conduct telephone interviews with consumers. They may use random samples of telephone numbers that are arbitrarily or systematically selected from telephone directories, or they may employ an innovation called *random-digit dialing*. In this approach, a random number generator mechanically creates the sample of phone numbers to be called. An advantage of random-digit dialing is that it can obtain a representative sample from the population of *all* households with telephones, whereas telephone-directory sampling obtains a sample only from the population of households with *listed* telephone numbers.

a. Explain how the random number table (Table I of Appendix B, or a computer) could be used to generate a sample of 7-digit telephone numbers.

b. Use the procedure you described in part **a** to generate a sample of ten 7-digit telephone numbers.

c. Use the procedure you described in part **a** to generate five 7-digit telephone numbers whose first three digits are 373.

3.57 When a company sells shares of stock to investors, the transaction is said to take place in the *primary market*. To enable investors to resell the stock when they wish, *secondary markets* called *stock exchanges* were created. Stock exchange transactions involve buyers and sellers exchanging cash for shares of stock, with none of the proceeds going to the companies that issued the shares (Radcliffe, *Investment: Concepts, Analysis, Strategy*, 1994). The results of the previous business day's transactions for stocks traded on the New York Stock Exchange (NYSE) and five regional exchanges—the Midwest, Pacific, Philadelphia, Boston, and Cincinnati stock exchanges—are summarized each business day in the NYSE–Composite Transactions table in *The Wall Street Journal*.

a. Examine the NYSE–Composite Transactions table in a recent issue of *The Wall Street Journal* and explain how to draw a random sample of stocks from the table.

b. Use the procedure you described in part **a** to draw a random sample of 20 stocks from a recent NYSE–Composite Transactions table. For each stock in the sample, list its name (i.e., the abbreviation given in the table), its sales volume, and its closing price.

3.58 In addition to its decennial enumeration of the population, the U.S. Bureau of the Census regularly samples the population to estimate level of and changes in a number of other attributes, such as income, family size, employment, and marital status. Suppose the bureau plans to sample 1,000 households in a city that has a total of 534,322 households. Show how the bureau could use the random number table in Appendix B or a computer to generate the sample. Select the first 10 households to be included in the sample.

QUICK REVIEW

Key Terms

Additive rule of probability   130
Combinations rule   121
Combinatorial mathematics   121
Complementary events   128
Compound event   126
Conditional probability   135
Event   117

Experiment   112
Independent events   141
Intersection   126
Multiplicative rule   138
Multiplicative rule of probability   138
Mutually exclusive events   130
Probability rules   116

Random number generator   149
Random sample   148
Sample point   113
Sample space   114
Tree diagram   140
Union   126
Venn diagram   114

Key Formulas

$P(A) + P(A^c) = 1$

$P(A \cup B) = P(A) + P(B) - P(A \cap B)$

$P(A \cap B) = 0$

$P(A \cup B) = P(A) + P(B)$

$P(A|B) = \dfrac{P(A \cap B)}{P(B)}$

$P(A \cap B) = P(A)P(B|A) = P(B)P(A|B)$

$P(A|B) = P(A)$

$P(A \cap B) = P(A)P(B)$

$\dbinom{N}{n} = \dfrac{N!}{n!(N-n)!}$

where $N! = N(N-1)(N-2)\cdots(2)(1)$

Complementary events   129
Additive rule   130
Mutually exclusive events   130
Additive rule for mutually exclusive events   131

Conditional probability   136

Multiplicative rule   138
Independent events   141
Multiplicative rule for independent events   143

Combinatorial rule   121

LANGUAGE LAB

Symbol	Pronunciation	Description
S		Sample space
$S: \{1, 2, 3, 4, 5\}$		Set of sample points, 1, 2, 3, 4, 5, in sample space
$A: \{1, 2\}$		Set of sample points, 1, 2, in event A
$P(A)$	Probability of A	Probability that event A occurs
$A \cup B$	A union B	Union of events A and B (either A or B or both occur)
$A \cap B$	A intersect B	Intersection of events A and B (both A and B occur)
A^c	A complement	Complement of event A (the event that A does not occur)
$P(A|B)$	Probability of A given B	Conditional probability that event A occurs given that event B occurs
$\dbinom{N}{n}$	N chose n	Number of combinations of N elements taken n at a time
$N!$	N factorial	Multiply $N(N-1)(N-2)\cdots(2)(1)$

SUPPLEMENTARY EXERCISES   3.59–3.88

Learning the Mechanics

3.59   What are the two rules that probabilities assigned to sample points must obey?

3.60   Are mutually exclusive events also dependent events? Explain.

3.61   Given that $P(A \cap B) = .4$ and $P(A|B) = .8$, find $P(B)$.

3.62   Which of the following pairs of events are mutually exclusive? Justify your response.
  a. {The Dow Jones Industrial Average increases on Monday}, {A large New York bank decreases its prime interest rate on Monday}
  b. {The next sale by a PC retailer is an IBM compatible microcomputer}, {The next sale by a PC retailer is an Apple microcomputer}
  c. {You reinvest all your dividend income for 1997 in a limited partnership}, {You reinvest all your dividend income for 1997 in a money market fund}

3.63   The accompanying Venn diagram illustrates a sample space containing six sample points and three events, A, B, and C. The probabilities of the sample points are: $P(1) = .3, P(2) = .2, P(3) = .1, P(4) = .1, P(5) = .1,$ and $P(6) = .2$.

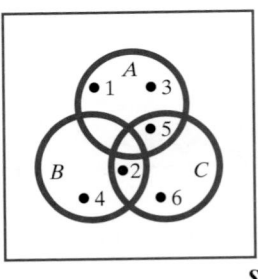

S

  a. Find $P(A \cap B), P(B \cap C), P(A \cup C), P(A \cup B \cup C), P(B^c), P(A^c \cap B), P(B|C),$ and $P(B|A)$.
  b. Are A and B independent? Mutually exclusive? Why?

c. Are B and C independent? Mutually exclusive? Why?

3.64 Two events, A and B, are independent, with $P(A)$ = .3 and $P(B)$ = .1.
   a. Are A and B mutually exclusive? Why?
   b. Find $P(A|B)$ and $P(B|A)$.
   c. Find $P(A \cup B)$.

3.65 Find the numerical value of:
   a. $6!$ **b.** $\binom{10}{9}$ **c.** $\binom{10}{1}$ **d.** $\binom{6}{3}$ **e.** $0!$

3.66 A random sample of five graduate students is to be selected from 50 MBA majors for participation in a case competition.
   a. In how many different ways can the sample be drawn?
   b. Show how the random number table, Table I of Appendix B, can be used to select the sample of students.

Applying the Concepts

3.67 A research and development company surveyed all 200 of its employees over the age of 60 and obtained the information given in the table below. One of these 200 employees is selected at random.
   a. What is the probability that the person selected is on the technical staff?
   b. If the person selected has over 20 years of service with the company, what is the probability that the person plans to retire at age 68?
   c. If the person selected is on the technical staff, what is the probability that the person has been with the company less than 20 years?
   d. What is the probability that the person selected has over 20 years with the company, is on the nontechnical staff, and plans to retire at age 65?
   e. Consider the events A: {Plan to retire at age 68} and B: {On the technical staff}. Are events A and B independent? Explain.
   f. Consider the event D: {Plan to retire at age 68 *and* on the technical staff}. Describe the complement of event D.
   g. Consider the event E: {On the nontechnical staff}. Are events B and E mutually exclusive? Explain.

3.68 Many U.S. manufacturers are adopting the ISO 9000 series of standards for setting up and documenting quality systems, processes, and procedures. However, it is not generally known how managers who have led or participated in the implementation of the standards view them or how the standards were achieved. A sample of 40 ISO 9000–registered companies in Colorado was selected and the manager most responsible for ISO 9000 implementation was interviewed (*Quality Progress*, 1995). The following are some of the data obtained by the study:

Level of Top Management Involvement in the ISO 9000 Registration Process	Frequency
Very involved	9
Moderate involvement	16
Minimal involvement	12
Not involved	3

Length of Time to Achieve ISO 9000 Registration	Frequency
Less than 1 year	5
1–1.5 years	21
1.6–2 years	9
2.1–2.5 years	2
More than 2.5 years	3

Source: Weston, F. C., "What do managers really think of the ISO 9000 registration process?" *Quality Progress*, October 1995, p. 68–69 (Tables 3 and 4).

Suppose one of the 40 managers who were interviewed is to be randomly selected for additional questioning. Consider the events defined below:

A: {The manager was involved in the ISO 9000 registration}

B: {The length of time to achieve ISO 9000 registration was more than 2 years}

   a. Find $P(A)$.
   b. Find $P(B)$.
   c. Explain why the above data are not sufficient to determine whether events A and B are independent.

3.69 The table on page 156 lists the overall percentage of domestic flights of major U.S. airlines that arrived on time during June 1995.
   a. One of these ten airlines is to be selected at random. What is the probability that Southwest is selected? That Continental is selected?
   b. If one of Continental's domestic flights during June 1995 were randomly selected, what is the

	UNDER 20 YEARS WITH COMPANY		OVER 20 YEARS WITH COMPANY	
	Technical Staff	Nontechnical Staff	Technical Staff	Nontechnical Staff
Plan to Retire at Age 65	31	5	45	12
Plan to Retire at Age 68	59	25	15	8

Carrier	Percent Arriving on Time
Southwest	82.9
American	78.5
Northwest	78.4
USAir	77.0
America West	75.8
United	75.4
Delta	74.3
TWA	72.9
Alaska	70.0
Continental	64.1

Source: Aviation Daily, August 7, 1995.

probability that the flight arrived on time? Was late?

c. These data are reported each month by the airlines to the U.S. Department of Transportation. Consequently, some experts question their accuracy. With this in mind, would you recommend that these percentages be treated as upper or lower bounds for the actual on-time percentages? Explain.

3.70 The state legislature has appropriated $1 million to be distributed in the form of grants to individuals and organizations engaged in the research and development of alternative energy sources. You have been hired by the state's energy agency to assemble a panel of five energy experts whose task it will be to determine which individuals and organizations should receive the grant money. You have identified 11 equally qualified individuals who are willing to serve on the panel. How many different panels of five experts could be formed from these 11 individuals?

3.71 A manufacturer of electronic digital watches claims that the probability of its watch running more than 1 minute slow or 1 minute fast after 1 year of use is .05. A consumer protection agency has purchased four of the manufacturer's watches with the intention of testing the claim.

a. Assuming that the manufacturer's claim is correct, what is the probability that none of the watches are as accurate as claimed?

b. Assuming that the manufacturer's claim is correct, what is the probability that exactly two of the four watches are as accurate as claimed?

c. Suppose that only one of the four tested watches is as accurate as claimed. What inference can be made about the manufacturer's claim? Explain.

d. Suppose that none of the watches tested are as accurate as claimed. Is it necessarily true that the manufacturer's claim is false? Explain.

3.72 The corporations in the highly competitive razor blade industry do a tremendous amount of advertising each year. Corporation G gave a supply of three top name brands, G, S, and W, to a consumer and asked her to use them and rank them in order of preference. The corporation was, of course, hoping the consumer would prefer its brand and rank it first, thereby giving them some material for a consumer interview advertising campaign. If the consumer did not prefer one blade over any other, but was still required to rank the blades, what is the probability that:

a. The consumer ranked brand G first?

b. The consumer ranked brand G last?

c. The consumer ranked brand G last and brand W second?

d. The consumer ranked brand W first, brand G second, and brand S third?

3.73 Two marketing research companies, Richard Saunders International and Marketing Intelligence Service, joined forces to create a consumer preference poll called Acupoll. Acupoll is used to predict whether newly developed products will succeed if they are brought to market. The reliability of the Acupoll has been described as follows: The probability that Acupoll predicts the success of a particular product, given that later the product actually is successful, is .89 (*Minneapolis Star Tribune,* Dec. 16, 1992). A company is considering the introduction of a new product and assesses the product's probability of success to be .90. If this company were to have its product evaluated through Acupoll, what is the probability that Acupoll predicts success for the product and the product actually turns out to be successful?

3.74 Use your intuitive understanding of independence to form an opinion about whether each of the following scenarios represents an independent event.

a. The results of consecutive tosses of a coin

b. The opinions of randomly selected individuals in a preelection poll

c. A major league baseball player's results in two consecutive at-bats

d. The amount of gain or loss associated with investments in different stocks if these stocks are bought on the same day and sold on the same day one month later

e. The amount of gain or loss associated with investments in different stocks that are bought and sold in different time periods, five years apart

f. The prices bid by two different development firms in response to a building construction proposal

3.75 A local country club has a membership of 600 and operates facilities that include an 18-hole championship golf course and 12 tennis courts. Before deciding whether to accept new members, the club president would like to know how many members regularly use each facility. A survey of the membership indicates that 70% regularly use the golf course, 50% regularly use the tennis courts, and 5% use neither of these facilities regularly.

a. Construct a Venn diagram to describe the results of the survey.

b. If one club member is chosen at random, what is the probability that the member uses either the golf course or the tennis courts or both?

c. If one member is chosen at random, what is the probability that the member uses both the golf and the tennis facilities?

d. A member is chosen at random from among those known to use the tennis courts regularly. What is the probability that the member also uses the golf course regularly?

3.76 Insurance companies use *mortality tables* to help them determine how large a premium to charge a particular individual for a particular life insurance policy. The accompanying table shows the probability of survival to age 65 for persons of the specified ages.

Age	Probability of Survival to Age 65
0	.72
10	.74
20	.74
30	.75
35	.76
40	.77
45	.79
50	.81
55	.85
60	.90

a. For a person 20 years old, what is the probability that he or she will die before age 65?

b. Describe in words the trend indicated by the increasing probabilities in the second and fourth columns.

3.77 "What are the characteristics of families with young children (under age 6)?" This was one of several questions posed by a University of Michigan researcher in *Children and Youth Services Review* (Vol. 17, 1995). Using data obtained from the National Child Care Survey,

the income distribution and employment status of these families are summarized in the table below:

a. Find the probability that a randomly selected family with young children has an income above the poverty line, but less than $25,000.

b. Find the probability that a randomly selected family with young children has unemployed parents or no parents.

c. Find the probability that a randomly selected family with young children has an income below the poverty line.

3.78 All-terrain vehicles (ATVs) came under fire in the 1980s owing to the high number of injuries and deaths attributed to these machines. In response, manufacturers agreed to provide extensive safety warnings to owners, to develop a media safety-awareness program, and to implement a nationwide training program. The *Journal of Risk and Uncertainty* (May 1992) published an article investigating the relationship of injury rate to a variety of factors. One of the more interesting factors studied, age of the driver, was found to have a strong relationship to injury rate. The article reports that prior to the safety-awareness program, 14% of the ATV drivers were under age 12; another 13% were 12–15, and 48% were under age 25. Suppose an ATV driver is selected at random prior to the installation of the safety-awareness program.

a. Find the probability that the ATV driver is 15 years old or younger.

b. Find the probability that the ATV driver is 25 years old or older.

c. Given that the ATV driver is under age 25, what is the probability the driver is under age 12?

d. Are the events Under age 25 and Under age 12 mutually exclusive? Why or why not?

e. Are the events Under age 25 and Under age 12 independent? Why or why not?

3.79 The probability that an Avon salesperson sells beauty products to a prospective customer on the first visit to the customer is .4. If the salesperson fails to make the sale on the first visit, the probability that the sale will be made on the second visit is .65. The salesperson never visits a prospective customer more than twice. What is the probability

Income Characteristic	Percentage
No parent	1
Below poverty line; not employed	7
Below poverty line; employed	7
Above poverty line, but less than $25,000; not employed	2
Above poverty line, but less than $25,000; employed	22
$25,000 or more	61
Total	100

A System Comprised of Three Components in Series

Input ⟶ (#1) ⟶ (#2) ⟶ (#3) ⟶ Output

that the salesperson will make a sale to a particular customer?

3.80 The performance of quality inspectors affects both the quality of outgoing products and the cost of the products. A product that passes inspection is assumed to meet quality standards; a product that fails inspection may be reworked, scrapped, or reinspected. Quality engineers at Westinghouse Electric Corporation evaluated performances of inspectors in judging the quality of solder joints by comparing each inspector's classifications of a set of 153 joints with the consensus evaluation of a panel of experts. The results for a particular inspector are shown in the accompanying table.

	INSPECTOR'S JUDGMENT	
Committee's Judgment	**Joint Acceptable**	**Joint Rejectable**
Joint acceptable	101	10
Joint rejectable	23	19

Source: Meagher, J. J., and Scazzero, J. A. "Measuring inspector variability." *39th Annual Quality Congress Transactions,* May 1985, pp. 75–81, American Society for Quality Control.

One of the 153 solder joints is to be selected at random.
a. What is the probability that the inspector judges the joint to be acceptable? That the committee judges the joint to be acceptable?
b. What is the probability that both the inspector and the committee judge the joint to be acceptable? That neither judge the joint to be acceptable?
c. What is the probability that the inspector and the committee disagree? Agree?

3.81 The figure shown above is a schematic representation of a system comprised of three components. The system operates properly only if all three components operate properly. The three components are said to operate *in series*. The components could be mechanical or electrical; they could be work stations in an assembly process; or they could represent the functions of three different

departments in an organization. The probability of failure for each component is listed in the table. Assume the components operate independently of each other.

Component	Probability of Failure
1	.12
2	.09
3	.11

a. Find the probability that the system operates properly.
b. What is the probability that at least one of the components will fail and therefore that the system will fail?

3.82 The figure below is a representation of a system comprised of two subsystems that are said to operate *in parallel*. Each subsystem has two components that operate in series (refer to Exercise 3.81). The system will operate properly as long as at least one of the subsystems functions properly. The probability of failure for each component in the system is .1. Assume the components operate independently of each other.
a. Find the probability that the system operates properly.
b. Find the probability that exactly one subsystem fails.
c. Find the probability that the system fails to operate properly.
d. How many parallel subsystems like the two shown here would be required to guarantee that the system would operate properly at least 99% of the time?

3.83 Consider the population of new savings accounts opened in one business day at a bank, as shown in the table. Suppose you wish to draw a random sample of two accounts from this population.

Account Number	0001	0002	0003	0004	0005
Account Balance	$1,000	$12,500	$850	$1,000	$3,450

A System Comprised of Two Parallel Subsystems

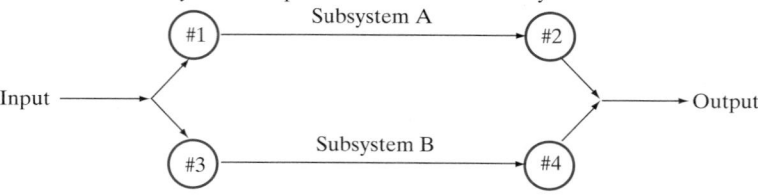

Subsystem A
Input ⟶ (#1) ⟶ (#2) ⟶ Output
Subsystem B
(#3) ⟶ (#4)

a. List all possible different pairs of accounts that could be obtained.

b. What is the probability of selecting accounts 0001 and 0004?

c. What is the probability of selecting two accounts that each have a balance of $1,000? That each have a balance other than $1,000?

3.84 Two hundred shoppers at a large suburban mall were asked two questions: (1) Did you see a television ad for the sale at department store X during the past two weeks? (2) Did you shop at department store X during the past two weeks? The responses to these questions are summarized in the table. One of the 200 shoppers questioned is to be chosen at random.

	Shopped at X	Did Not Shop at X
Saw ad	100	25
Did not see ad	25	50

a. What is the probability that the person selected saw the ad?

b. What is the probability that the person selected saw the ad and shopped at store X?

c. Find the conditional probability that the person shopped at store X given that the person saw the ad.

d. What is the probability that the person selected shopped at store X?

e. Use your answers to parts **a**, **b**, and **d** to check the independence of the events {Saw ad} and {Shopped at X}.

f. Are the two events {Did not see ad} and {Did not shop at X} mutually exclusive? Explain.

3.85 The National Resident Matching Program (NRMP) is a service provided by the Association of American Medical Colleges to match graduating medical students with residency appointments at hospitals. After students and hospitals have evaluated each other, they submit rank-order lists of their preferences to the NRMP. Using a matching algorithm, the NRMP then generates final, nonnegotiable assignments of students to the residency programs of hospitals (*Academic Medicine,* June 1995). Assume that three graduating medical students (#1, #2, and #3) have applied for positions at three different hospitals (A, B, and C), where each hospital has one and only one resident opening.

a. How many different assignments of medical students to hospitals are possible? List them.

b. Suppose student #1 prefers hospital B. If the NRMP algorithm is entirely random, what is the probability that the student is assigned to hospital B?

3.86 A small brewery has two bottling machines. Machine A produces 75% of the bottles and machine B produces 25%. One out of every 20 bottles filled by A is rejected for some reason, while one out of every 30 bottles from B is rejected. What proportion of bottles is rejected? What is the probability that a randomly selected bottle comes from machine A, given that it is accepted?

3.87 Suppose there are 500 applicants for five equivalent positions at a factory and the company is able to narrow the field to 30 equally qualified applicants. Seven of the finalists are minority candidates. Assume that the five who are chosen are selected at random from this final group of 30.

a. In how many different ways can the selection be made?

b. What is the probability that none of the minority candidates is hired?

c. What is the probability that no more than one minority candidate is hired?

3.88 A fair coin is flipped 20 times and 20 heads are observed. In such cases it is often said that a tail is due on the next flip. Is this statement true or false? Explain.

CHAPTER 4

RANDOM VARIABLES AND PROBABILITY DISTRIBUTIONS

CONTENTS

4.1 Two Types of Random Variables

4.2 Probability Distributions for Discrete Random Variables

4.3 The Binomial Distribution

4.4 The Poisson Distribution (Optional)

4.5 Probability Distributions for Continuous Random Variables

4.6 The Uniform Distribution (Optional)

4.7 The Normal Distribution

4.8 The Exponential Distribution (Optional)

4.9 Sampling Distributions

4.10 The Sampling Distribution of the Sample Mean

STATISTICS IN ACTION

4.1 The Space Shuttle *Challenger:* Catastrophe in Space

4.2 IQ, Economic Mobility, and the Bell Curve

4.3 The Insomnia Pill

Where We've Been

We saw by illustration in Chapter 3 how probability would be used to make an inference about a population from data contained in an observed sample. We also noted that probability would be used to measure the reliability of the inference.

Where We're Going

Most of the experimental events we encountered in Chapter 3 were events described in words and denoted by capital letters. In real life, most sample observations are numerical—in other words, they are numerical data. In this chapter, we learn that data are observed values of random variables. We study several important random variables and learn how to find the probabilities of specific numerical outcomes.

161

FIGURE 4.1
Venn diagram for coin-tossing experiment

You may have noticed that many of the examples of experiments in Chapter 3 generated quantitative (numerical) observations. The Consumer Price Index, the unemployment rate, the number of sales made in a week, and the yearly profit of a company are all examples of numerical measurements of some phenomenon. Thus, most experiments have sample points that correspond to values of some numerical variable.

To illustrate, consider the coin-tossing experiment of Chapter 3. Figure 4.1 is a Venn diagram showing the sample points when two coins are tossed and the up faces (heads or tails) of the coins are observed. One possible numerical outcome is the total number of heads observed. These values (0, 1, or 2) are shown in parentheses on the Venn diagram, one numerical value associated with each sample point. In the jargon of probability, the variable "total number of heads observed in two tosses of a coin" is called a **random variable**.

DEFINITION 4.1
A **random variable** is a variable that assumes numerical values associated with the random outcomes of an experiment, where one (and only one) numerical value is assigned to each sample point.

The term *random variable* is more meaningful than the term *variable* because the adjective *random* indicates that the coin-tossing experiment may result in one of the several possible values of the variable—0, 1, and 2—according to the *random* outcome of the experiment, *HH, HT, TH,* and *TT*. Similarly, if the experiment is to count the number of customers who use the drive-up window of a bank each day, the random variable (the number of customers) will vary from day to day, partly because of the random phenomena that influence whether customers use the drive-up window. Thus, the possible values of this random variable range from 0 to the maximum number of customers the window could possibly serve in a day.

We define two different types of random variables, *discrete* and *continuous,* in Section 4.1. Then we spend the remainder of this chapter discussing specific types of random variables and the aspects that make them important in business applications.

4.1 TWO TYPES OF RANDOM VARIABLES

Recall that the sample point probabilities corresponding to an experiment must sum to 1. Dividing one unit of probability among the sample points in a sample space and consequently assigning probabilities to the values of a random variable is not always as easy as the examples in Chapter 3 might lead you to believe. If the number of sample points can be completely listed, the job is straightforward. But if the experiment results in an infinite number of numerical sample points that are impossible to list, the task of assigning probabilities to the sample points is impossible without the aid of a probability model. The next three examples demonstrate the need for different probability models depending on the number of values that a random variable can assume.

EXAMPLE 4.1

A panel of 10 experts for the *Wine Spectator* (a national publication) is asked to taste a new white wine and assign a rating of 0, 1, 2, or 3. A score is then obtained by adding together the ratings of the 10 experts. How many values can this random variable assume?

SOLUTION

A sample point is a sequence of 10 numbers associated with the rating of each expert. For example, one sample point is

$$\{1, 0, 0, 1, 2, 0, 0, 3, 1, 0\}.$$

The random variable assigns a score to each one of these sample points by adding the 10 numbers together. Thus, the smallest score is 0 (if all 10 ratings are 0) and the largest score is 30 (if all 10 ratings are 3). Since every integer between 0 and 30 is a possible score, the random variable denoted by the symbol x can assume 31 values. Note that the value of the random variable for the sample point above is $x = 8$.*

This is an example of a **discrete random variable**, since there is a finite number of distinct possible values. Whenever all the possible values a random variable can assume can be listed (or counted), the random variable is discrete. ◣

EXAMPLE 4.2

Suppose the Environmental Protection Agency (EPA) takes readings once a month on the amount of pesticide in the discharge water of a chemical company. If the amount of pesticide exceeds the maximum level set by the EPA, the company is forced to take corrective action and may be subject to penalty. Consider the following random variable:

Number, x, of months before the company's discharge
exceeds the EPA's maximum level

What values can x assume?

SOLUTION

The company's discharge of pesticide may exceed the maximum allowable level on the first month of testing, the second month of testing, etc. It is possible that the company's discharge will *never* exceed the maximum level. Thus, the set of possible values for the number of months until the level is first exceeded is the set of all positive integers

$$1, 2, 3, 4, \ldots$$

If we can list the values of a random variable x, even though the list is never-ending, we call the list **countable** and the corresponding random variable *discrete*. Thus, the number of months until the company's discharge first exceeds the limit is a *discrete random variable*. ◣

EXAMPLE 4.3

Refer to Example 4.2. A second random variable of interest is the amount x of pesticide (in milligrams per liter) found in the monthly sample of discharge waters from the chemical company. What values can this random variable assume?

---

*The standard mathematical convention is to use a capital letter (e.g., X) to denote the theoretical random variable. The possible values (or realizations) of the random variable are typically denoted with a lowercase letter (e.g., x). Thus, in Example 4.1, the random variable X can take on the values $x = 0, 1, 2, \ldots, 30$. Since this notation can be confusing for introductory statistics students, we simplify the notation by using the lowercase x to represent the random variable throughout.

SOLUTION

Unlike the *number* of months before the company's discharge exceeds the EPA's maximum level, the set of all possible values for the *amount* of discharge *cannot* be listed—i.e., is not countable. The possible values for the amounts of pesticide would correspond to the points on the interval between 0 and the largest possible value the amount of the discharge could attain, the maximum number of milligrams that could occupy 1 liter of volume. (Practically, the interval would be much smaller, say, between 0 and 500 milligrams per liter.) When the values of a random variable are not countable but instead correspond to the points on some interval, we call it a **continuous random variable**. Thus, the *amount* of pesticide in the chemical plant's discharge waters is a *continuous random variable*. ◾

DEFINITION 4.2
Random variables that can assume a *countable* number of values are called **discrete**.

DEFINITION 4.3
Random variables that can assume values corresponding to any of the points contained in one or more intervals are called **continuous**.

Several more examples of discrete random variables follow:

1. The number of sales made by a salesperson in a given week: $x = 0, 1, 2, \ldots$
2. The number of consumers in a sample of 500 who favor a particular product over all competitors: $x = 0, 1, 2, \ldots, 500$
3. The number of bids received in a bond offering: $x = 0, 1, 2, \ldots$
4. The number of errors on a page of an accountant's ledger: $x = 0, 1, 2, \ldots$
5. The number of customers waiting to be served in a restaurant at a particular time: $x = 0, 1, 2, \ldots$

Note that each of the examples of discrete random variables begins with the words "The number of ..." This wording is very common, since the discrete random variables most frequently observed are counts.

We conclude this section with some more examples of continuous random variables:

1. The length of time between arrivals at a hospital clinic: $0 \leq x < \infty$ (infinity)
2. For a new apartment complex, the length of time from completion until a specified number of apartments are rented: $0 \leq x < \infty$
3. The amount of carbonated beverage loaded into a 12-ounce can in a can-filling operation: $0 \leq x \leq 12$
4. The depth at which a successful oil drilling venture first strikes oil: $0 \leq x \leq c$, where c is the maximum depth obtainable
5. The weight of a food item bought in a supermarket: $0 \leq x \leq 500$ [*Note:* Theoretically, there is no upper limit on x, but it is unlikely that it would exceed 500 pounds.]

Discrete random variables and their probability distributions are discussed in Sections 4.2–4.4. Continuous random variables and their probability distributions are the topic of Sections 4.5–4.10.

EXERCISES   4.1–4.10

Applying the Concepts

4.1   What is a random variable?

4.2   How do discrete and continuous random variables differ?

4.3   Security analysts are professionals who devote full-time efforts to evaluating the investment worth of a narrow list of stocks. For example, one security analyst might specialize in bank stocks while another specializes in evaluating firms in the computer or pharmaceutical industries. The following variables are of interest to security analysts (Radcliffe, *Investments: Concepts, Analysis and Strategy*, 1994). Which are discrete and which are continuous random variables?
a. The closing price of a particular stock on the New York Stock Exchange.
b. The number of shares of a particular stock that are traded each business day.
c. The quarterly earnings of a particular firm.
d. The percentage change in yearly earnings between 1996 and 1997 for a particular firm.
e. The number of new products introduced per year by a firm.
f. The time until a pharmaceutical company gains approval from the U.S. Food and Drug Administration to market a new drug.

4.4   Which of the following describe continuous random variables, and which describe discrete random variables?
a. The number of newspapers sold by the *New York Times* each month
b. The amount of ink used in printing a Sunday edition of the *New York Times*
c. The actual number of ounces in a one-gallon bottle of laundry detergent
d. The number of defective parts in a shipment of nuts and bolts
e. The number of people collecting unemployment insurance each month

4.5   Give two examples of a business-oriented discrete random variable. Do the same for a continuous random variable.

4.6   Give an example of a discrete random variable that would be of interest to a banker.

4.7   Give an example of a continuous random variable that would be of interest to an economist.

4.8   Give an example of a discrete random variable that would be of interest to the manager of a hotel.

4.9   Give two examples of discrete random variables that would be of interest to the manager of a clothing store.

4.10   Give an example of a continuous random variable that would be of interest to a stockbroker.

4.2   PROBABILITY DISTRIBUTIONS FOR DISCRETE RANDOM VARIABLES

A complete description of a discrete random variable requires that we *specify the possible values the random variable can assume and the probability associated with each value.* To illustrate, consider Example 4.4.

EXAMPLE 4.4

Recall the experiment of tossing two coins (Section 4.1), and let x be the number of heads observed. Find the probability associated with each value of the random variable x, assuming the two coins are fair.

SOLUTION

The sample space and sample points for this experiment are reproduced in Figure 4.2. Note that the random variable x can assume values 0, 1, 2. Recall (from Chapter 3) that the probability associated with each of the four sample points is $\frac{1}{4}$. Then, identifying the probabilities of the sample points associated with each of these values of x, we have

$$P(x = 0) = P(TT) = \frac{1}{4}$$
$$P(x = 1) = P(TH) + P(HT) = \frac{1}{4} + \frac{1}{4} = \frac{1}{2}$$
$$P(x = 2) = P(HH) = \frac{1}{4}$$

Thus, we now know the values the random variable can assume (0, 1, 2) and how the probability is *distributed over* these values ($\frac{1}{4}, \frac{1}{2}, \frac{1}{4}$). This completely describes the random variable and is referred to as the *probability distribution,*

```
┌─────────────────────────┐
│  HH            HT        │
│  •             •         │
│  x = 2         x = 1     │
│                          │
│                          │
│  TH            TT        │
│  •             •         │
│  x = 1         x = 0     │
│                          │
└─────────────────────────┘
                         S
```

FIGURE 4.2
Venn diagram for the two-coin-toss experiment

TABLE 4.1 Probability Distribution for Coin-Toss Experiment: Tabular Form

x	$p(x)$
0	$\frac{1}{4}$
1	$\frac{1}{2}$
2	$\frac{1}{4}$

FIGURE 4.3
Probability distribution for coin-toss experiment: Graphical form

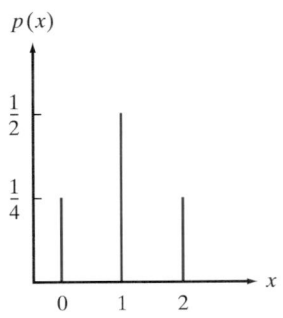

a. Point representation of $p(x)$

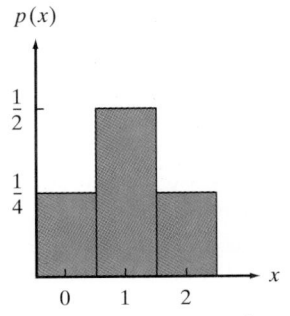

b. Histogram representation of $p(x)$

denoted by the symbol $p(x)$.* The probability distribution for the coin-toss example is shown in tabular form in Table 4.1 and in graphic form in Figure 4.3. Since the probability distribution for a discrete random variable is concentrated at specific points (values of x), the graph in Figure 4.3a represents the probabilities as the heights of vertical lines over the corresponding values of x. Although the representation of the probability distribution as a histogram, as in Figure 4.3b, is less precise (since the probability is spread over a unit interval), the histogram representation will prove useful when we approximate probabilities of certain discrete random variables in Section 4.4.

We could also present the probability distribution for x as a formula, but this would unnecessarily complicate a very simple example. We give the formulas for the probability distributions of some common discrete random variables later in this chapter.

DEFINITION 4.4
The **probability distribution** of a discrete random variable is a graph, table, or formula that specifies the probability associated with each possible value the random variable can assume.

Two requirements must be satisfied by all probability distributions for discrete random variables.

Requirements for the Probability Distribution of a Discrete Random Variable, x

$p(x) \geqslant 0$ for all values of x

$$\sum p(x) = 1$$

where the summation of $p(x)$ is over all possible values of x.†

Example 4.4 illustrates how the probability distribution for a discrete random variable can be derived, but for many practical situations the task is much more difficult. Fortunately, many experiments and associated discrete random variables observed in business possess identical characteristics. Thus, you might observe a random variable in a marketing experiment that would possess the same charac-

---

*In standard mathematical notation, the probability that a random variable X takes on a value x is denoted $P(X = x) = p(x)$. Thus, $P(X = 0) = p(0)$, $P(X = 1) = p(1)$, etc. In this introductory text, we adopt the simpler $p(x)$ notation.
†Unless otherwise indicated, summations will always be over all possible values of x.

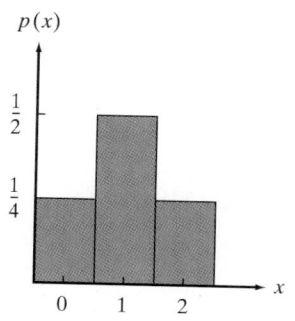

$p(x)$

FIGURE 4.4
Probability distribution
for a two-coin toss

teristics as a random variable observed in accounting, economics, or management. We classify random variables according to type of experiment, derive the probability distribution for each of the different types, and then use the appropriate probability distribution when a particular type of random variable is observed in a practical situation. The probability distributions for most commonly occurring discrete random variables have already been derived. This fact simplifies the problem of finding the appropriate probability distributions for the business analyst.

Before we present some important types of discrete random variables (Sections 4.3 and 4.4), we discuss some descriptive measures of these sometimes complex probability distributions.

If a discrete random variable x were observed a very large number of times and the data generated were arranged in a relative frequency distribution, the relative frequency distribution would be indistinguishable from the probability distribution for the random variable. Thus, the probability distribution for a random variable is a theoretical model for the relative frequency distribution of a population. To the extent that the two distributions are equivalent (and we will assume they are), the probability distribution for x possesses a mean μ and a variance σ^2 that are identical to the corresponding descriptive measures for the population. We illustrate the procedure for finding the mean and variance of x with an example.

Examine the probability distribution for x (the number of heads observed in the toss of two fair coins) in Figure 4.4. Try to locate the mean of the distribution intuitively. We may reason that the mean μ of this distribution is equal to 1 as follows: In a large number of experiments, $\frac{1}{4}$ should result in $x = 0$, $\frac{1}{2}$ in $x = 1$, and $\frac{1}{4}$ in $x = 2$ heads. Therefore, the average number of heads is

$$\mu = 0(\tfrac{1}{4}) + 1(\tfrac{1}{2}) + 2(\tfrac{1}{4}) = 0 + \tfrac{1}{2} + \tfrac{1}{2} = 1$$

Note that to get the population mean of the random variable x, we multiply each possible value of x by its probability $p(x)$, and then sum this product over all possible values of x. The *mean of x* is also referred to as the *expected value of x,* denoted $E(x)$.

DEFINITION 4.5
The **mean**, or **expected value**, of a discrete random variable x is

$$\mu = E(x) = \sum x p(x)$$

The term *expected* is a mathematical term and should not be interpreted as it is typically used. Specifically, a random variable might never be equal to its "expected value." Rather, the expected value is the mean of the probability distribution or a measure of its central tendency. You can think of μ as the mean value of x in a *very large* (actually, *infinite*) number of repetitions of the experiment.

EXAMPLE 4.5

Suppose you work for an insurance company, and you sell a $10,000 whole-life insurance policy at an annual premium of $290. Actuarial tables show that the probability of death during the next year for a person of your customer's age, sex, health, etc. is .001. What is the expected gain (amount of money made by the company) for a policy of this type?

SOLUTION
The experiment is to observe whether the customer survives the upcoming year. The probabilities associated with the two sample points, Live and Die, are .999 and .001, respectively. The random variable you are interested in is the gain x, which can assume the values shown in the following table.

Gain, x	Sample Point	Probability
$290	Customer lives	.999
$290–$10,000	Customer dies	.001

If the customer lives, the company gains the $290 premium as profit. If the customer dies, the gain is negative because the company must pay $10,000, for a net "gain" of $(290 − 10,000). The expected gain is therefore

$$\mu = E(x) = \sum_{\text{all } x} xp(x)$$

$$= (290)(.999) + (290 − 10,000)(.001) = \$280$$

In other words, if the company were to sell a very large number of one-year $10,000 policies to customers possessing the characteristics described above, it would (on the average) net $280 per sale in the next year.

Example 4.5 illustrates that the expected value of a random variable x need not equal a possible value of x. That is, the expected value is $280, but x will equal either $290 or −$9,710 each time the experiment is performed (a policy is sold and a year elapses). The expected value is a measure of central tendency—and in this case represents the average over a very large number of one-year policies—but is not a possible value of x.

We learned in Chapter 2 that the mean and other measures of central tendency tell only part of the story about a set of data. The same is true about probability distributions. We need to measure variability as well. Since a probability distribution can be viewed as a representation of a population, we will use the population variance to measure its variability.

The **population variance** σ^2 is defined as the average of the squared distance of x from the population mean μ. Since x is a random variable, the squared distance, $(x − \mu)^2$, is also a random variable. Using the same logic used to find the mean value of x, we find the mean value of $(x − \mu)^2$ by multiplying all possible values of $(x − \mu)^2$ by $p(x)$ and then summing over all possible x values.* This quantity,

$$E[(x − \mu)^2] = \sum_{\text{all } x} (x − \mu)^2 p(x)$$

is also called the **expected value of the squared distance from the mean**; that is, $\sigma^2 = E[(x − \mu)^2]$. The standard deviation of x is defined as the square root of the variance σ^2.

DEFINITION 4.6
The **variance** of a random variable x is

$$\sigma^2 = E[(x − \mu)^2] = \sum (x − \mu)^2 p(x)$$

---

*It can be shown that $E[(x − \mu)^2] = E(x^2) − \mu^2$ where $E(x^2) = \sum x^2 p(x)$. Note the similarity between this expression and the shortcut formula $\sum (x − \bar{x})^2 = \sum x^2 − \left(\sum x\right)^2/n$ given in Chapter 2.

FIGURE 4.5

Shapes of two probability distributions for a discrete random variable x

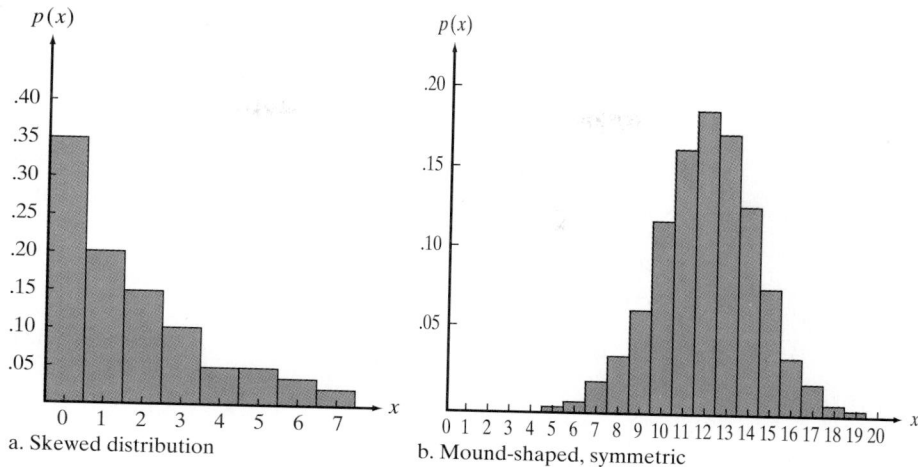

a. Skewed distribution

b. Mound-shaped, symmetric

DEFINITION 4.7

The **standard deviation** of a discrete random variable is equal to the square root of the variance, i.e., $\sigma = \sqrt{\sigma^2}$.

Knowing the mean μ and standard deviation σ of the probability distribution of x, in conjunction with Chebyshev's Rule (Table 2.7) and the Empirical Rule (Table 2.8), we can make statements about the likelihood that values of x will fall within the intervals $\mu \pm \sigma$, $\mu \pm 2\sigma$, and $\mu \pm 3\sigma$. These probabilities are given in the box.

Chebyshev's Rule and Empirical Rule for a Discrete Random Variable

Let x be a discrete random variable with probability distribution $p(x)$, mean μ, and standard deviation σ. Then, depending on the shape of $p(x)$, the following probability statements can be made:

	Chebyshev's Rule	**Empirical Rule**
	Applies to any probability distribution (see Figure 4.5a)	Applies to probability distributions that are mound-shaped and symmetric (see Figure 4.5b)
$P(\mu - \sigma < x < \mu + \sigma)$	≥ 0	$\approx .68$
$P(\mu - 2\sigma < x < \mu + 2\sigma)$	$\geq \frac{3}{4}$	$\approx .95$
$P(\mu - 3\sigma < x < \mu + 3\sigma)$	$\geq \frac{8}{9}$	≈ 1.00

EXAMPLE 4.6

Suppose you invest a fixed sum of money in each of five business ventures. Assume you know that 70% of such ventures are successful, the outcomes of the ventures are independent of one another, and the probability distribution for the number, x, of successful ventures out of five is:

x	0	1	2	3	4	5
$p(x)$	.002	.029	.132	.309	.360	.168

a. Find $\mu = E(x)$. Interpret the result.

b. Find $\sigma = \sqrt{E[(x - \mu)^2]}$. Interpret the result.

c. Graph $p(x)$. Locate μ and the interval $\mu \pm 2\sigma$ on the graph. Use either Chebyshev's Rule or the Empirical Rule to approximate the probability that x falls in this interval. Compare this result with the actual probability.

d. Would you expect to observe fewer than two successful ventures out of five?

SOLUTION

a. Applying the formula,

$$\mu = E(x) = \sum xp(x) = 0(.002) + 1(.029) + 2(.132) + 3(.309) \\ + 4(.360) + 5(.168) = 3.50$$

On average, the number of successful ventures out of five will equal 3.5. Remember that this expected value only has meaning when the experiment—investing in five business ventures—is repeated a large number of times.

b. Now we calculate the variance of x:

$$\sigma^2 = E[(x - \mu)^2] = \sum (x - \mu)^2 p(x)$$

$$= (0 - 3.5)^2(.002) + (1 - 3.5)^2(.029) + (2 - 3.5)^2(.132)$$

$$+ (3 - 3.5)^2(.309) + (4 - 3.5)^2(.360) + (5 - 3.5)^2(.168)$$

$$= 1.05$$

Thus, the standard deviation is

$$\sigma = \sqrt{\sigma^2} = \sqrt{1.05} = 1.02$$

This value measures the spread of the probability distribution of x, the number of successful ventures out of five.

c. The graph of $p(x)$ is shown in Figure 4.6 with the mean μ and the interval $\mu \pm 2\sigma = 3.50 \pm 2(1.02) = 3.50 \pm 2.04 = (1.46, 5.54)$ shown on the graph. Note particularly that $\mu = 3.5$ locates the center of the probability distribu-

FIGURE 4.6
Graph of $p(x)$ for Example 4.6

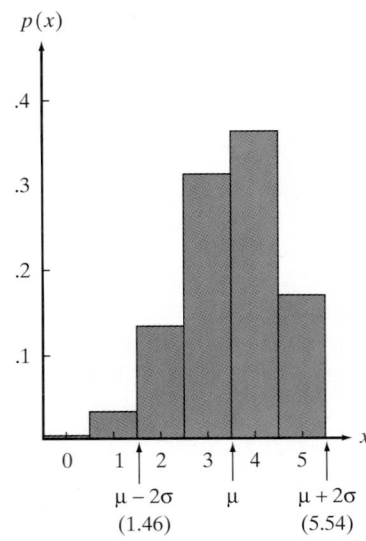

tion. Since this distribution is a theoretical relative frequency distribution that is moderately mound-shaped (see Figure 4.6), we expect (from Chebyshev's Rule) at least 75% and, more likely (from the Empirical Rule), approximately 95% of observed x values to fall in the interval $\mu \pm 2\sigma$—that is, between 1.46 and 5.54. You can see from Figure 4.6 that the actual probability that x falls in the interval $\mu \pm 2\sigma$ includes the sum of $p(x)$ for the values $x = 2, x = 3, x = 4$, and $x = 5$. This probability is $p(2) + p(3) + p(4) + p(5) = .132 + .309 + .360 + .168 = .969$. Therefore, 96.9% of the probability distribution lies within 2 standard deviations of the mean. This percentage is consistent with both Chebyshev's Rule and the Empirical Rule.

d. Fewer than two successful ventures out of five implies that $x = 0$ or $x = 1$. Since both these values of x lie outside the interval $\mu \pm 2\sigma$, we know from the Empirical Rule that such a result is unlikely (approximate probability of .05). The exact probability, $P(x \leqslant 1)$, is $p(0) + p(1) = .002 + .029 = .031$. Consequently, in a single experiment where we invest in five business ventures, we would not expect to observe fewer than two successful ones. ▎

EXERCISES   4.11–4.25

Learning the Mechanics

4.11 Toss three fair coins and let x equal the number of heads observed.
  a. Identify the sample points associated with this experiment and assign a value of x to each sample point.
  b. Calculate $p(x)$ for each value of x.
  c. Construct a probability histogram for $p(x)$.
  d. What is $P(x = 2 \text{ or } x = 3)$?

4.12 Explain why each of the following is or is not a valid probability distribution for a discrete random variable x:

a.
x	0	1	2	3
$p(x)$	.1	.3	.3	.2

b.
x	−2	−1	0
$p(x)$	.25	.50	.25

c.
x	4	9	20
$p(x)$	−.3	.4	.3

d.
x	2	3	5	6
$p(x)$	.15	.15	.45	.35

4.13 A die is tossed. Let x be the number of spots observed on the upturned face of the die.
  a. Find the probability distribution of x and display it in tabular form.
  b. Display the probability distribution of x in graphical form.

4.14 The random variable x has the following discrete probability distribution:

x	1	3	5	7	9
$p(x)$	.1	.2	.4	.2	.1

  a. Find $P(x \leqslant 3)$. b. Find $P(x < 3)$.
  c. Find $P(x = 7)$. d. Find $P(x \geqslant 5)$.
  e. Find $P(x > 2)$. f. Find $P(3 \leqslant x \leqslant 9)$.

4.15 Consider the probability distribution for the random variable x shown here.

x	10	20	30	40	50	60
$p(x)$	.05	.20	.30	.25	.10	.10

  a. Find μ, σ^2, and σ. b. Graph $p(x)$.
  c. Locate μ and the interval $\mu \pm 2\sigma$ on your graph. What is the probability that x will fall within the interval $\mu \pm 2\sigma$?

4.16 Consider the probability distribution shown here.

x	−4	−3	−2	−1	0	1	2	3	4
$p(x)$	.02	.07	.10	.15	.30	.18	.10	.06	.02

  a. Calculate μ, σ^2, and σ.
  b. Graph $p(x)$. Locate μ, $\mu - 2\sigma$, and $\mu + 2\sigma$ on the graph.
  c. What is the probability that x is in the interval $\mu \pm 2\sigma$?

x	5	6	7	8	9	10	11	12	13	14	15
$p(x)$	.01	.02	.03	.05	.08	.09	.11	.13	.12	.10	.08

x	16	17	18	19	20	21
$p(x)$	.06	.05	.03	.02	.01	.01

Source: Ford, R., Roberts, D., and Saxton, P. *Queuing Models.* Graduate School of Management, Rutgers University, 1992.

Applying the Concepts

4.17 In a study of tax write-offs by the affluent, Peter Dreier of Occidental College (Los Angeles) compiled the relative frequency distribution shown below. The distribution below describes the incomes of all households in the United States that filed tax returns in 1995. A household is to be randomly sampled from this population.

   a. Explain why the percentages in the table can be interpreted as probabilities. For example, the probability of selecting a household with income under $10,000 is .185.

   b. Find the probability that the selected household has income over $200,000; over $100,000; less than $100,000; between $30,000 and $49,999.

   c. Together, the income categories (1, 2, 3, ...) and the percentages form a discrete probability distribution. Graph this distribution.

   d. What is the probability that the randomly selected household will fall in income category 6? In income category 1 or 9?

Income Category	Household Income	Percentage of Households
1	Under $10,000	18.5
2	$10,000 to $19,999	19.0
3	$20,000 to $29,999	15.9
4	$30,000 to $39,999	12.8
5	$40,000 to $49,999	9.1
6	$50,000 to $74,999	13.8
7	$75,000 to $99,999	5.7
8	$100,000 to $199,999	4.1
9	$200,000 and over	1.1

Source: Johnston, D. C. "The Divine Write-off." *New York Times,* January 12, 1996, p. D1.

4.18 A team of consultants studied the service operation at the Wendy's Restaurant in the Woodbridge Mall, Woodbridge, NJ. They measured the time between customer arrivals to the restaurant over the course of a day and used those data to develop a probability distribution to characterize x, the number of customer arrivals per 15-minute period. The distribution is shown at the top of the page.

   a. Does this distribution meet the two requirements for the probability distribution of a discrete random variable? Justify your answer.

   b. What is the probability that exactly 16 customers enter the restaurant in the next 15 minutes?

   c. Find $p(x \leq 10)$.   **d.** Find $p(5 \leq x \leq 15)$.

4.19 Many real-world systems (e.g., electric power transmission, transportation, telecommunications, and manufacturing systems) can be regarded as capacitated-flow networks, whose arcs have independent but random capacities. A team of Chinese university professors investigated the reliability of several flow networks in the journal *Networks* (May 1995). One network examined in the article, and illustrated on page 173, is a bridge network with arcs a_1, a_2, a_3, a_4, a_5, and a_6. The probability distribution of the capacity x for each of the six arcs is provided below.

   a. Verify that the properties of discrete probability distributions are satisfied for each arc capacity distribution.

   b. Find the probability that the capacity for arc a_1 will exceed 1.

   c. Repeat part **b** for each of the remaining five arcs.

   d. One path from the source node to the sink node is through arcs a_1 and a_2. Find the probability that the system maintains a capacity of

Arc	Capacity (x)	$p(x)$		Arc	Capacity (x)	$p(x)$
a_1	3	.60		a_4	1	.90
	2	.25			0	.10
	1	.10				
	0	.05				
a_2	2	.60		a_5	1	.90
	1	.30			0	.10
	0	.10				
a_3	1	.90		a_6	2	.70
	0	.10			1	.25
					0	.05

Source: Lin, J., *et al.* "On reliability evaluation of capacitated-flow network in terms of minimal pathsets." *Networks,* Vol. 25, No. 3, May 1995, p. 135 (Table 1), 1995, John Wiley and Sons.

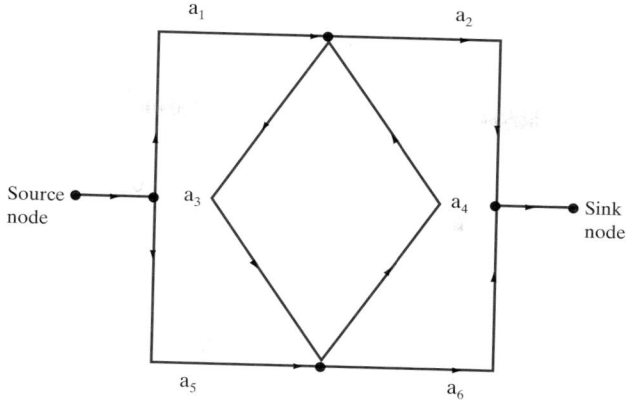

more than 1 through the a_1–a_2 path. (Recall that the arc capacities are independent.)

4.20 Refer to Exercise 4.19. Compute the mean capacity of each of the six areas. Interpret the results.

4.21 The analysis of the risk of a portfolio of financial assets is sometimes called *investment risk* (Radcliffe, 1994). In general, investment risk is typically measured by computing the variance or standard deviation of the probability distribution that describes the decision-maker's potential outcomes (gains or losses). This follows from the fact that the greater the variation in potential outcomes, the greater the uncertainty faced by the decision-maker; the smaller the variation in potential outcomes, the more predictable the decision-maker's gains or losses. The two discrete probability distributions given in the table were developed from historical data. They describe the potential

total physical damage losses next year to the fleets of delivery trucks of two different firms.

a. Verify that both firms have the same expected total physical damage loss.

b. Compute the standard deviation of each probability distribution, and determine which firm faces the greater risk of physical damage to its fleet next year.

4.22 A team of consultants working for a large national supermarket chain based in the New York metropolitan area developed a statistical model for predicting the annual sales of potential new store locations. Part of their analysis involved identifying variables that influence store sales, such as the size of the store (in square feet), the size of the surrounding population, and the number of checkout lanes. They surveyed 52 supermarkets in a particular region of the country and constructed the relative frequency distribution shown below to describe the number of checkout lanes per store, x.

a. Why do the relative frequencies in the table represent the approximate probabilities of a randomly selected supermarket having x number of checkout lanes?

b. Find $E(x)$ and interpret its value in the context of the problem.

c. Find the standard deviation of x.

d. According to Chebyshev's Rule (Chapter 2), what percentage of supermarkets would be expected to fall within $\mu \pm \sigma$? Within $\mu \pm 2\sigma$?

e. What is the actual number of supermarkets that fall within $\mu \pm \sigma$? $\mu \pm 2\sigma$? Compare your answers to those of part **d**. Are the answers consistent?

FIRM A		FIRM B	
Loss next year	**Probability**	**Loss next year**	**Probability**
$ 0	.01	$ 0	.00
500	.01	200	.01
1,000	.01	700	.02
1,500	.02	1,200	.02
2,000	.35	1,700	.15
2,500	.30	2,200	.30
3,000	.25	2,700	.30
3,500	.02	3,200	.15
4,000	.01	3,700	.02
4,500	.01	4,200	.02
5,000	.01	4,700	.01

x	1	2	3	4	5	6	7	8	9	10
Relative Frequency	.01	.04	.04	.08	.10	.15	.25	.20	.08	.05

Source: Adapted from Chow, W., *et. al.* "A model for predicting a supermarket's annual sales per square foot." Graduate School of Management, Rutgers University, 1994.

4.23 The number of training units that must be passed before a complex computer software program is mastered varies from one to five, depending on the student. After much experience, the software manufacturer has determined the probability distribution that describes the fraction of users mastering the software after each number of training units:

Number of Units	1	2	3	4	5
Probability of Mastery	.1	.25	.4	.15	.1

a. Calculate the mean number of training units necessary to master the program. Calculate the median. Interpret each.

b. If the firm wants to ensure that at least 75% of the students master the program, what is the minimum number of training units that must be administered? At least 90%?

c. Suppose the firm develops a new training program that increases the probability that only one unit of training is needed from .1 to .25, increases the probability that only two units are needed to .35, leaves the probability that three units are needed at .4, and completely eliminates the need for four or five units. How do your answers to parts **a** and **b** change for this new program?

4.24 Most states offer weekly lotteries to generate revenue for the state. Despite the long odds of winning, residents continue to gamble on the lottery each week (see Statistics in Action 3.2). The chance of winning Florida's Pick-6 Lotto game is 1 in approximately 14 million. Suppose you buy a $1 Lotto ticket in anticipation of winning the $7 million grand prize. Calculate your expected net winnings. Interpret the result.

4.25 The success of an organization is determined largely by the caliber of its employees. Thus, it is vital for any organization to have effective recruitment and selection policies. These policies must have the support of top management and be regularly evaluated (Cowling and James, *The Essence of Personnel Management and Industrial Relations,* 1994). A company is interested in hiring a person with an MBA degree and at least two years experience in a marketing department of a computer products firm. The company's personnel department has determined that it will cost the company $1,000 per job candidate to collect the required background information and to interview the candidate. As a result, the company will hire the first qualified person it finds and will interview no more than three candidates. The company has received job applications from four persons who appear to be qualified but, unknown to the company, only one actually possesses the required background. Candidates to be interviewed will be randomly selected from the pool of four applicants.

a. Construct the probability distribution for the total cost to the firm of the interviewing strategy.

b. What is the probability that the firm's interviewing strategy will result in none of the four applicants being hired?

c. Calculate the mean of the probability distribution you constructed in part **a.**

d. What is the expected total cost of the interviewing strategy?

4.3 THE BINOMIAL DISTRIBUTION

Many experiments result in *dichotomous* responses—i.e., responses for which there exist two possible alternatives, such as Yes-No, Pass-Fail, Defective-Nondefective, or Male-Female. A simple example of such an experiment is the coin-toss experiment. A coin is tossed a number of times, say 10. Each toss results in one of two outcomes, Head or Tail. Ultimately, we are interested in the probability distribution of x, the number of heads observed. Many other experiments are equivalent to tossing a coin (either balanced or unbalanced) a fixed number n of times and observing the number x of times that one of the two possible outcomes occurs. Random variables that possess these characteristics are called **binomial random variables**.

Public opinion and consumer preference polls (e.g., the Gallup and Harris polls) frequently yield observations on binomial random variables. For example, suppose a sample of 100 current customers is selected from a firm's data base and each person is asked whether he or she prefers the firm's product (a Head) or prefers a competitor's product (a Tail). Ultimately, we are interested in x, the number of customers in the sample who prefer the firm's product. Sampling 100 customers is analogous to tossing the coin 100 times. Thus, you can see that consumer preference polls like the one described here are real-life equivalents of coin-toss experiments. We have been describing a **binomial experiment**; it is identified by the following characteristics.

> **Characteristics of a Binomial Random Variable**
> **1.** The experiment consists of n identical trials.
> **2.** There are only two possible outcomes on each trial. We will denote one outcome by S (for Success) and the other by F (for Failure).
> **3.** The probability of S remains the same from trial to trial. This probability is denoted by p, and the probability of F is denoted by q. Note that $q = 1 - p$.
> **4.** The trials are independent.
> **5.** The binomial random variable x is the number of S's in n trials.

EXAMPLE 4.7

For the following examples, decide whether x is a binomial random variable.

a. You randomly select three bonds out of a possible ten for an investment portfolio. Unknown to you, eight of the ten will maintain their present value, and the other two will lose value due to a change in their ratings. Let x be the number of the three bonds you select that lose value.

b. Before marketing a new product on a large scale, many companies will conduct a consumer preference survey to determine whether the product is likely to be successful. Suppose a company develops a new diet soda and then conducts a taste preference survey in which 100 randomly chosen consumers state their preferences among the new soda and the two leading sellers. Let x be the number of the 100 who choose the new brand over the two others.

c. Some surveys are conducted by using a method of sampling other than simple random sampling (defined in Chapter 3). For example, suppose a television cable company plans to conduct a survey to determine the fraction of households in the city that would use the cable television service. The sampling method is to choose a city block at random and then survey every household on that block. This sampling technique is called **cluster sampling**. Suppose 10 blocks are so sampled, producing a total of 124 household responses. Let x be the number of the 124 households that would use the television cable service.

SOLUTION

a. In checking the binomial characteristics in the box, a problem arises with both characteristic 3 (probabilities remaining the same from trial to trial) and characteristic 4 (independence). The probability that the first bond you pick loses value is clearly $2/10$. Now suppose the first bond you picked was one of the two that will lose value. This reduces the chance that the second bond you pick will lose value to $1/9$, since now only one of the nine remaining bonds are in that category. Thus, the choices you make are dependent, and therefore x, the number of the three bonds you select that lose value, is *not* a binomial random variable.

b. Surveys that produce dichotomous responses and use random sampling techniques are classic examples of binomial experiments. In our example, each randomly selected consumer either states a preference for the new diet soda or does not. The sample of 100 consumers is a very small proportion of the totality of potential consumers, so the response of one would be, for all practical purposes, independent of another.* Thus, x is a binomial random variable.

---

*In most real-life applications of the binomial distribution, the population of interest has a finite number of elements (trials), denoted N. When N is large and the sample size n is small relative to N, say $n/N \leq .05$, the sampling procedure, for all practical purposes, satisfies the conditions of a binomial experiment.

c. This example is a survey with dichotomous responses (Yes or No to the cable service), but the sampling method is not simple random sampling. Again, the binomial characteristic of independent trials would probably not be satisfied. The responses of households within a particular block would be dependent, since the households within a block tend to be similar with respect to income, level of education, and general interests. Thus, the binomial model would not be satisfactory for x if the cluster sampling technique were employed.

EXAMPLE 4.8

A retail computer store sells desktop personal computers (PCs) and laptops. Assume that 80% of the PCs that the store sells are desktops, and 20% are laptops.

a. Use the steps given in Chapter 3 (box on page 118) to find the probability that all of the next four PC purchases are laptops.

b. Find the probability that three of the next four PC purchases are laptops.

c. Let x represent the number of the next four PC purchases that are laptops. Explain why x is a binomial random variable.

d. Use the answers to parts **a** and **b** to derive a formula for $p(x)$, the probability distribution of the binomial random variable, x.

SOLUTION

a. 1. The first step is to define the experiment. Here we are interested in observing the type of PC purchased by each of the next four (buying) customers: desktop (D) or laptop (L).

2. Next, we list the sample points associated with the experiment. Each sample point consists of the purchase decisions made by the four customers. For example, $DDDD$ represents the sample point that all four purchase desktop PCs, while $LDDD$ represents the sample point that customer 1 purchases a laptop, while customers 2, 3, and 4 purchase desktops. The 16 sample points are listed in Table 4.2.

3. We now assign probabilities to the sample points. Note that each sample point can be viewed as the intersection of four customers' decisions and, assuming the decisions are made independently, the probability of each sample point can be obtained using the multiplicative rule, as follows:

$$P(DDDD) = P[(\text{customer 1 chooses desktop}) \cap (\text{customer 2 chooses desktop})$$
$$\cap (\text{customer 3 chooses desktop}) \cap (\text{customer 4 chooses desktop})]$$

$$= P[(\text{customer 1 chooses desktop}) \times P(\text{customer 2 chooses desktop}) \times P(\text{customer 3 chooses desktop})$$
$$\times P(\text{customer 4 chooses desktop})]$$

$$= (.8)(.8)(.8)(.8) = (.8)^4 = .4096$$

TABLE 4.2   Sample Points for PC Experiment of Example 4.8

$DDDD$	$LDDD$	$LLDD$	$DLLL$	LLLL
	$DLDD$	$LDLD$	$LDLL$	
	$DDLD$	$LDDL$	$LLDL$	
	$DDDL$	$DLLD$	$LLLD$	
		$DLDL$		
		$DDLL$		

All other sample point probabilities are calculated using similar reasoning. For example,

$$P(LDDD) = (.2)(.8)(.8)(.8) = (.2)(.8)^3 = .1024$$

You can check that this reasoning results in sample point probabilities that add to 1 over the 16 points in the sample space.

4. Finally, we add the appropriate sample point probabilities to obtain the desired event probability. The event of interest is that all four customers purchase laptops. In Table 4.2 we find only one sample point, LLLL, contained in this event. All other sample points imply that at least one desktop is purchased. Thus,

$$P(\text{All four purchase laptops}) = P(LLLL) = (.2)^4 = .0016$$

That is, the probability is only 16 in 10,000 that all four customers purchase laptop PCs.

b. The event that three of the next four buyers purchase laptops consists of the four sample points in the fourth column of Table 4.2: $DLLL$, $LDLL$, $LLDL$, and $LLLD$. To obtain the event probability we add the sample point probabilities:

$P(3 \text{ of next 4 customers purchase laptops})$
$$= P(DLLL) + P(LDLL) + P(LLDL) + P(LLLD)$$
$$= (.2)^3(.8) + (.2)^3(.8) + (.2)^3(.8) + (.2)^3(.8)$$
$$= 4(.2)^3(.8) = .0256$$

Note that each of the four sample point probabilities is the same, because each sample point consists of three L's and one D; the order does not affect the probability because the customers' decisions are (assumed) independent.

c. We can characterize the experiment as consisting of four identical trials— the four customers' purchase decisions. There are two possible outcomes to each trial, D or L, and the probability of L, $p = .2$, is the same for each trial. Finally, we are assuming that each customer's purchase decision is independent of all others, so that the four trials are independent. Then it follows that x, the number of the next four purchases that are laptops, is a binomial random variable.

d. The event probabilities in parts **a** and **b** provide insight into the formula for the probability distribution $p(x)$. First, consider the event that three purchases are laptops (part **b**). We found that

$$P(x = 3) = (\text{Number of sample points for which } x = 3) \times$$
$$(.2)^{\text{Number of laptops purchased}} \times (.8)^{\text{Number of desktops purchased}}$$
$$= 4(.2)^3(.8)^1$$

In general, we can use combinatorial mathematics to count the number of sample points. For example,

Number of sample points for which $(x = 3)$
= Number of different ways of selecting 3 of the 4 trials for L purchases

$$= \binom{4}{3} = \frac{4!}{3!(4-3)!} = \frac{4 \cdot 3 \cdot 2 \cdot 1}{(3 \cdot 2 \cdot 1) \cdot 1} = 4$$

The formula that works for any value of x can be deduced as follows:

$$P(x = 3) = \binom{4}{3}(.2)^3(.8)^1 = \binom{4}{x}(.2)^x(.8)^{4-x}$$

The component $\binom{4}{x}$ counts the number of sample points with x laptops and the component $(.2)^x(.8)^{4-x}$ is the probability associated with each sample point having x laptops.

For the general binomial experiment, with n trials and probability of Success p on each trial, the probability of x Successes is

$$p(x) = \binom{n}{x} \cdot p^x(1 - p)^{n - x}$$

$\uparrow$ No. of simple events with x S's

$\uparrow$ Probability of x S's and $(n - x)$ F's in any simple event

In theory, you could always resort to the principles developed in Example 4.8 to calculate binomial probabilities; list the sample points and sum their probabilities. However, as the number of trials (n) increases, the number of sample points grows very rapidly (the number of sample points is 2^n). Thus, we prefer the formula for calculating binomial probabilities, since its use avoids listing sample points.

The binomial distribution is summarized in the box.

The Binomial Probability Distribution

$$p(x) = \binom{n}{x}p^x q^{n-x} \qquad (x = 0, 1, 2, ..., n)$$

where p = Probability of a success on a single trial
$q = 1 - p$
n = Number of trials
x = Number of successes in n trials
$\binom{n}{x} = \dfrac{n!}{x!(n - x)!}$

As noted in Chapter 3, the symbol 5! means $5 \cdot 4 \cdot 3 \cdot 2 \cdot 1 = 120$. Similarly, $n! = n(n - 1)(n - 2) \cdots 3 \cdot 2 \cdot 1$; remember, $0! = 1$.

The mean, variance, and standard deviation for the binomial random variable x are shown in the box.

Mean, Variance, and Standard Deviation for a Binomial Random Variable

Mean: $\mu = np$

Variance: $\sigma^2 = npq$

Standard deviation: $\sigma = \sqrt{npq}$

As we demonstrated in Chapter 2, the mean and standard deviation provide measures of the central tendency and variability, respectively, of a distribution. Thus, we can use μ and σ to obtain a rough visualization of the probability distribution for x when the calculation of the probabilities is too tedious. To illustrate the use of the binomial probability distribution, consider Examples 4.9 and 4.10.

EXAMPLE 4.9

A machine that produces stampings for automobile engines is malfunctioning and producing 10% defectives. The defective and nondefective stampings proceed from the machine in a random manner. If the next five stampings are tested, find the probability that three of them are defective.

SOLUTION

Let x equal the number of defectives in $n = 5$ trials. Then x is a binomial random variable with p, the probability that a single stamping will be defective, equal to .1, and $q = 1 - p = 1 - .1 = .9$. The probability distribution for x is given by the expression

$$p(x) = \binom{n}{x} p^x q^{n-x} = \binom{5}{x}(.1)^x(.9)^{5-x}$$

$$= \frac{5!}{x!(5-x)!}(.1)^x(.9)^{5-x} \qquad (x = 0, 1, 2, 3, 4, 5)$$

To find the probability of observing $x = 3$ defectives in a sample of $n = 5$, substitute $x = 3$ into the formula for $p(x)$ to obtain

$$p(3) = \frac{5!}{3!(5-3)!}(.1)^3(.9)^{5-3} = \frac{5!}{3!2!}(.1)^3(.9)^2$$

$$= \frac{5 \cdot 4 \cdot 3 \cdot 2 \cdot 1}{(3 \cdot 2 \cdot 1)(2 \cdot 1)}(.1)^3(.9)^2 = 10(.1)^3(.9)^2$$

$$= .0081$$

Note that the binomial formula tells us that there are 10 sample points having 3 defectives (check this by listing them), each with probability $(.1)^3(.9)^2$. ◾

EXAMPLE 4.10

Refer to Example 4.9 and find the values of $p(0), p(1), p(2), p(4)$, and $p(5)$. Graph $p(x)$. Calculate the mean μ and standard deviation σ. Locate μ and the interval $\mu - 2\sigma$ to $\mu + 2\sigma$ on the graph. If the experiment were to be repeated many times, what proportion of the x observations would fall within the interval $\mu - 2\sigma$ to $\mu + 2\sigma$?

SOLUTION

Again, $n = 5, p = .1$, and $q = .9$. Then, substituting into the formula for $p(x)$:

$$p(0) = \frac{5!}{0!(5-0)!}(.1)^0(.9)^{5-0} = \frac{5 \cdot 4 \cdot 3 \cdot 2 \cdot 1}{(1)(5 \cdot 4 \cdot 3 \cdot 2 \cdot 1)}(1)(.9)^5 = .59049$$

$$p(1) = \frac{5!}{1!(5-1)!}(.1)^1(.9)^{5-1} = 5(.1)(.9)^4 = .32805$$

$$p(2) = \frac{5!}{2!(5-2)!}(.1)^2(.9)^{5-2} = (10)(.1)^2(.9)^3 = .07290$$

$$p(4) = \frac{5!}{4!(5-4)!}(.1)^4(.9)^{5-4} = 5(.1)^4(.9) = .00045$$

$$p(5) = \frac{5!}{5!(5-5)!}(.1)^5(.9)^{5-5} = (.1)^5 = .00001$$

The graph of $p(x)$ is shown as a probability histogram in Figure 4.7. [$p(3)$ is taken from Example 4.9 to be .0081.]

To calculate the values of μ and σ, substitute $n = 5$ and $p = .1$ into the following formulas:

FIGURE 4.7
The binomial
distribution: $n = 5$,
$p = .1$

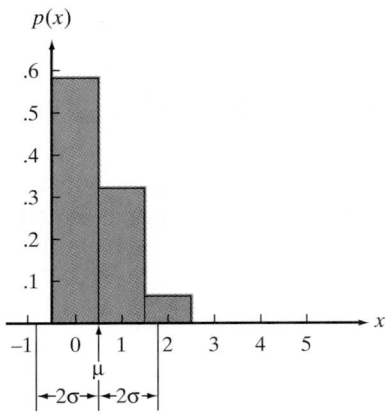

$$\mu = np = (5)(.1) = .5$$

$$\sigma = \sqrt{npq} = \sqrt{(5)(.1)(.9)} = \sqrt{.45} = .67$$

To find the interval $\mu - 2\sigma$ to $\mu + 2\sigma$, we calculate

$$\mu - 2\sigma = .5 - 2(.67) = -.84$$

$$\mu + 2\sigma = .5 + 2(.67) = 1.84$$

If the experiment were to be repeated a large number of times, what proportion of the x observations would fall within the interval $\mu - 2\sigma$ to $\mu + 2\sigma$? You can see from Figure 4.7 that all observations equal to 0 or 1 will fall within the interval. The probabilities corresponding to these values are .5905 and .3280, respectively. Consequently, you would expect .5905 + .3280 = .9185, or approximately 91.9%, of the observations to fall within the interval $\mu - 2\sigma$ to $\mu + 2\sigma$. This again emphasizes that for most probability distributions, observations rarely fall more than 2 standard deviations from μ.

USING BINOMIAL TABLES

Calculating binomial probabilities becomes tedious when n is large. For some values of n and p the binomial probabilities have been tabulated in Table II of Appendix B. Part of Table II is shown in Table 4.3; a graph of the binomial proba-

TABLE 4.3   Reproduction of Part of Table II of Appendix B: Binomial Probabilities for $n = 10$

k \ p	.01	.05	.10	.20	.30	.40	.50	.60	.70	.80	.90	.95	.99
0	.904	.599	.349	.107	.028	.006	.001	.000	.000	.000	.000	.000	.000
1	.996	.914	.736	.376	.149	.046	.011	.002	.000	.000	.000	.000	.000
2	1.000	.988	.930	.678	.383	.167	.055	.012	.002	.000	.000	.000	.000
3	1.000	.999	.987	.879	.650	.382	.172	.055	.011	.001	.000	.000	.000
4	1.000	1.000	.998	.967	.850	.633	.377	.166	.047	.006	.000	.000	.000
5	1.000	1.000	1.000	.994	.953	.834	.623	.367	.150	.033	.002	.000	.000
6	1.000	1.000	1.000	.999	.989	.945	.828	.618	.350	.121	.013	.001	.000
7	1.000	1.000	1.000	1.000	.998	.988	.945	.833	.617	.322	.070	.012	.000
8	1.000	1.000	1.000	1.000	1.000	.998	.989	.954	.851	.624	.264	.086	.004
9	1.000	1.000	1.000	1.000	1.000	1.000	.999	.994	.972	.893	.651	.401	.096

FIGURE 4.8
Binomial probability
distribution for $n = 10$
and $p = .10$; $P(x \leqslant 2)$
shaded

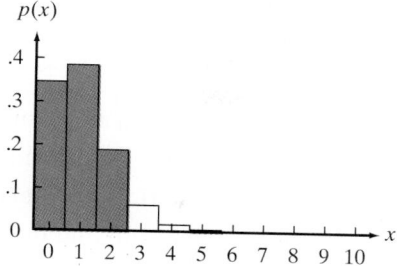

bility distribution for $n = 10$ and $p = .10$ is shown in Figure 4.8. Table II actually contains a total of nine tables, labeled (**a**) through (**i**), one each corresponding to $n = 5, 6, 7, 8, 9, 10, 15, 20,$ and 25. In each of these tables the columns correspond to values of p, and the rows correspond to values of the random variable x. The entries in the table represent **cumulative** binomial probabilities. Thus, for example, the entry in the column corresponding to $p = .10$ and the row corresponding to $x = 2$ is .930 (shaded), and its interpretation is

$$P(x \leqslant 2) = P(x = 0) + P(x = 1) + P(x = 2) = .930$$

This probability is also shaded in the graphical representation of the binomial distribution with $n = 10$ and $p = .10$ in Figure 4.8.

You can also use Table II to find the probability that x equals a specific value. For example, suppose you want to find the probability that $x = 2$ in the binomial distribution with $n = 10$ and $p = .10$. This is found by subtraction as follows:

$$P(x = 2) = [P(x = 0) + P(x = 1) + P(x = 2)] - [P(x = 0) + P(x = 1)]$$

$$= P(x \leqslant 2) - P(x \leqslant 1) = .930 - .736 = .194$$

The probability that a binomial random variable exceeds a specified value can be found using Table II and the notion of complementary events. For example, to find the probability that x exceeds 2 when $n = 10$ and $p = .10$, we use

$$P(x > 2) = 1 - P(x \leqslant 2) = 1 - .930 = .070$$

Note that this probability is represented by the unshaded portion of the graph in Figure 4.8.

All probabilities in Table II are rounded to three decimal places. Thus, although none of the binomial probabilities in the table is exactly zero, some are small enough (less than .0005) to round to .000. For example, using the formula to find $P(x = 0)$ when $n = 10$ and $p = .6$, we obtain

$$P(x = 0) = \binom{10}{0}(.6)^0(.4)^{10-0} = .4^{10} = .00010486$$

but this is rounded to .000 in Table II of Appendix B (see Table 4.3).

Similarly, none of the table entries is exactly 1.0, but when the cumulative probabilities exceed .9995, they are rounded to 1.000. The row corresponding to the largest possible value for x, $x = n$, is omitted, because all the cumulative probabilities in that row are equal to 1.0 (exactly). For example, in Table 4.3 with $n = 10$, $P(x \leqslant 10) = 1.0$, no matter what the value of p.

The following example further illustrates the use of Table II.

EXAMPLE 4.11

Suppose a poll of 20 employees is taken in a large company. The purpose is to determine x, the number who favor unionization. Suppose that 60% of all the company's employees favor unionization.

  a. Find the mean and standard deviation of x.

  b. Use Table II of Appendix B to find the probability that $x < 10$.

  c. Use Table II to find the probability that $x > 12$.

  d. Use Table II to find the probability that $x = 11$.

SOLUTION

  a. The number of employees polled is presumably small compared with the total number of employees in this company. Thus, we may treat x, the number of the 20 who favor unionization, as a binomial random variable. The value of p is the fraction of the total employees who favor unionization; i.e., $p = .6$. Therefore, we calculate the mean and variance:

$$\mu = np = 20(.6) = 12$$

$$\sigma^2 = npq = 20(.6)(.4) = 4.8$$

$$\sigma = \sqrt{4.8} = 2.19$$

  b. The tabulated value is

$$P(x \leqslant 9) = .128$$

  c. To find the probability

$$P(x > 12) = \sum_{x=13}^{20} p(x)$$

we use the fact that for all probability distributions, $\sum_{\text{All } x} p(x) = 1$. Therefore,

$$P(x > 12) = 1 - P(x \leqslant 12) = 1 - \sum_{x=0}^{12} p(x)$$

Consulting Table II, we find the entry in row $k = 12$, column $p = .6$ to be .584. Thus,

$$P(x > 12) = 1 - .584 = .416$$

  d. To find the probability that exactly 11 employees favor unionization, recall that the entries in Table II are cumulative probabilities and use the relationship

$$P(x = 11) = [p(0) + p(1) + \cdots + p(11)] - [p(0) + p(1) + \cdots + p(10)]$$

$$= P(x \leqslant 11) - P(x \leqslant 10)$$

Then

$$P(x = 11) = .404 - .245 = .159$$

The probability distribution for x in this example is shown in Figure 4.9. Note that the interval $\mu \pm 2\sigma$ is (7.6, 16.4).

FIGURE 4.9
The binomial
probability distribution
for x in Example 4.11:
$n = 20, p = .6$

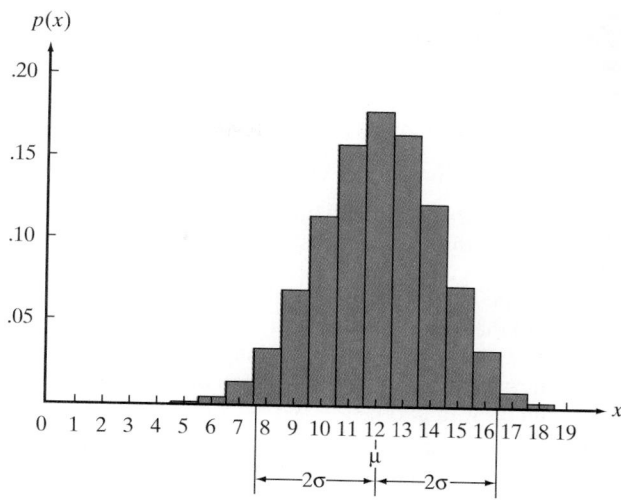

4.1 THE SPACE SHUTTLE CHALLENGER: CATASTROPHE IN SPACE

On January 28, 1986, at 11:39.13 A.M. (EST), while traveling at mach 1.92 at an altitude of 46,000 feet, the space shuttle *Challenger* was totally enveloped in an explosive burn that destroyed the shuttle and resulted in the deaths of all seven astronauts aboard. What happened? What was the cause of this catastrophe? This was the 25th shuttle mission. The preceding 24 missions had all been successful.

According to *Discover* (Apr. 1986), the report of the presidential commission assigned to investigate the accident concluded that the explosion was caused by the failure of the O-ring seal in the joint between the two lower segments of the right solid-fuel rocket booster. The seal is supposed to prevent superhot gases from leaking through the joint during the propellant burn of the booster rocket. The failure of the seal permitted a jet of white-hot gases to escape and to ignite the liquid fuel of the external fuel tank. The fuel tank fireburst destroyed the *Challenger*.

What were the chances that this event would occur? In a report made one year prior to the catastrophe, the National Aeronautics and Space Administration (NASA) claimed that the probability of such a failure was about $1/60{,}000$, or about once in every 60,000 flights. But a risk assessment study conducted for the Air Force at about the same time assessed the probability

of shuttle catastrophe due to booster rocket "burn-through" to be $1/35$, or about once in every 35 missions.

Focus

a. Assuming NASA's failure-rate estimate was accurate, compute the probability that no disasters would have occurred during 25 shuttle missions.

b. Repeat part **a**, but use the Air Force's failure-rate estimate.

c. What conditions must exist for the probabilities, parts **a** and **b**, to be valid?

d. Given the events of January 28, 1986, which risk assessment—NASA's or the Air Force's—appears to be more appropriate? [*Hint:* Consider the complement of the events, parts **a** and **b**.]

e. After making improvements in the shuttle's systems over the late 1980s and early 1990s, NASA issued a report in 1993 in which the risk of catastrophic failure of the shuttle's main engine was assessed for each mission at 1 in 120. ("Laying Odds on Shuttle Disaster," *Chance,* Fall 1993.) Use this risk assessment and the binomial probability distribution to find the probability of at least one catastrophic failure in the next 10 missions.

EXERCISES 4.26–4.40

Learning the Mechanics

4.26 Consider the following probability distribution:

$$p(x) = \binom{5}{x}(.7)^x(.3)^{5-x} \quad (x = 0, 1, 2, ..., 5)$$

a. Is x a discrete or a continuous random variable?
b. What is the name of this probability distribution?
c. Graph the probability distribution.
d. Find the mean and standard deviation of x.
e. Show the mean and the 2-standard-deviation interval on each side of the mean on the graph you drew in part c.

4.27 If x is a binomial random variable, compute $p(x)$ for each of the following cases:
a. $n = 5, x = 1, p = .2$ b. $n = 4, x = 2, q = .4$
c. $n = 3, x = 0, p = .7$ d. $n = 5, x = 3, p = .1$
e. $n = 4, x = 2, q = .6$ f. $n = 3, x = 1, p = .9$

4.28 Suppose x is a binomial random variable with $n = 3$ and $p = .3$.
a. Calculate the value of $p(x)$, $x = 0, 1, 2, 3$, using the formula for a binomial probability distribution.
b. Using your answers to part a, give the probability distribution for x in tabular form.

4.29 If x is a binomial random variable, calculate μ, σ^2, and σ for each of the following:
a. $n = 25, p = .5$ b. $n = 80, p = .2$
c. $n = 100, p = .6$ d. $n = 70, p = .9$
e. $n = 60, p = .8$ f. $n = 1,000, p = .04$

4.30 If x is a binomial random variable, use Table II in Appendix B to find the following probabilities:
a. $P(x = 2)$ for $n = 10, p = .4$
b. $P(x \leq 5)$ for $n = 15, p = .6$
c. $P(x > 1)$ for $n = 5, p = .1$
d. $P(x < 10)$ for $n = 25, p = .7$
e. $P(x \geq 10)$ for $n = 15, p = .9$
f. $P(x = 2)$ for $n = 20, p = .2$

4.31 The binomial probability distribution is a family of probability distributions with each single distribution depending on the values of n and p. Assume that x is a binomial random variable with $n = 4$.
a. Determine a value of p such that the probability distribution of x is symmetric.
b. Determine a value of p such that the probability distribution of x is skewed to the right.
c. Determine a value of p such that the probability distribution of x is skewed to the left.
d. Graph each of the binomial distributions you obtained in parts a, b, and c. Locate the mean for each distribution on its graph.
e. In general, for what values of p will a binomial distribution be symmetric? Skewed to the right? Skewed to the left?

Applying the Concepts

4.32 Lechmere, a division of Chicago-based Montgomery Ward, is a national appliance chain store. Recently, the Massachusetts Division of Standards discovered that checkout scanners at Lechmere stores in five Boston suburbs were registering the wrong price more than $1/3$ of the time for sale items (*Boston Globe*, Aug. 8, 1996). Of the 235 sale items checked by state investigators, 83 scanned incorrectly with 51 resulting in overcharges. (The problem was due to the main computer in Chicago overriding the local scanning systems.) Consider a sample of 10 sale items purchased at the Lechmere stores under investigation. Suppose we are interested in x, the number of items that register the wrong sale price when scanned at the checkout register.
a. Show that x is an approximate binomial random variable.
b. Use the information gathered by the investigators to estimate p for the binomial experiment. (Round the estimate to the nearest .05.)
c. Using the value of p, part b, what is the probability of exactly two scanning errors in the sample of 10 items? At least two?
d. Estimate the probability of observing at least two items resulting in overcharges because of scanning errors.

4.33 According to the Internal Revenue Service (IRS), the chances of your tax return being audited are about 6 in 1,000 if your income is less than $50,000; 10 in 1,000 if your income is between $50,000 and $99,999; and 49 in 1,000 if your income is $100,000 or more (*Statistical Abstract of the United States: 1995*).
a. What is the probability that a taxpayer with income less than $50,000 will be audited by the IRS? With income between $50,000 and $99,999? With income $100,000 or more?
b. If five taxpayers with incomes under $50,000 are randomly selected, what is the probability that exactly one will be audited? That more than one will be audited?
c. Repeat part b assuming that five taxpayers with incomes between $50,000 and $99,999 are randomly selected.
d. If two taxpayers with incomes under $50,000 are randomly selected and two with incomes more than $100,000 are randomly selected, what is the probability that none of these taxpayers will be audited by the IRS?
e. What assumptions did you have to make in order to answer these questions using the methodology presented in this section?

4.34 A problem of considerable economic impact on the economy is the burgeoning cost of Medicare and other public-funded medical services. One aspect of this problem concerns the high percentage of people seeking medical treatment who, in fact, have no physical basis for their ailments. One conservative estimate is that the percentage of people who seek medical assistance and who have no real physical ailment is 10%, and some doctors believe that it may be as high as 40%. Suppose we were to randomly sample the records of a doctor and found that five of 15 patients seeking medical assistance were physically healthy.

a. What is the probability of observing five or more physically healthy patients in a sample of 15 if the proportion, p, that the doctor normally sees is 10%?

b. What is the probability of observing five or more physically healthy patients in a sample of 15 if the proportion, p, that the doctor normally sees is 40%?

c. Why might your answer to part **a** make you believe that p is larger than .10?

4.35 According to the U.S. Golf Association (USGA), "The weight of the [golf] ball shall not be greater than 1.620 ounces avoirdupois (45.93 grams). …The diameter of the ball shall not be less than 1.680 inches. …The velocity of the ball shall not be greater than 250 feet per second" (USGA, 1996). The USGA periodically checks the specifications of golf balls sold in the United States by randomly sampling balls from pro shops around the country. Two dozen of each kind are sampled, and if more than three do not meet size and/or velocity requirements, that kind of ball is removed from the USGA's approved-ball list.

a. What assumptions must be made and what information must be known in order to use the binomial probability distribution to calculate the probability that the USGA will remove a particular kind of golf ball from its approved-ball list?

b. Suppose 10% of all balls produced by a particular manufacturer are less than 1.680 inches in diameter, and assume that the number of such balls, x, in a sample of two dozen balls can be adequately characterized by a binomial probability distribution. Find the mean and standard deviation of the binomial distribution.

c. Refer to part **b**. If x has a binomial distribution, then so does the number, y, of balls in the sample that meet the USGA's minimum diameter. [*Note:* $x + y = 24$.] Describe the distribution of y. In particular, what are p, q, and n? Also, find $E(y)$ and the standard deviation of y.

4.36 Suppose you are a purchasing officer for a large company. You have purchased 5 million electrical switches and your supplier has guaranteed that the shipment will contain no more than .1% defectives. To check the shipment, you randomly sample 500 switches, test them, and find that four are defective. If the switches are as represented, calculate μ and σ for this sample of 500. Based on this evidence, do you think the supplier has complied with the guarantee? Explain.

4.37 Every quarter the Food and Drug Administration (FDA) produces a report called the *Total Diet Study*. The FDA's report covers more than 200 food items, each of which is analyzed for potentially harmful chemical compounds. A recent *Total Diet Study* reported that no pesticides at all were found in 65% of the domestically produced food samples (*Consumer's Research,* June 1995). Consider a random sample of 800 food items analyzed for the presence of pesticides.

a. Compute μ and σ for the random variable x, the number of food items found that showed no trace of pesticide.

b. Based on a sample of 800 food items, is it likely you would observe less than half without any traces of pesticide? Explain.

4.38 A study conducted in New Jersey by the Governor's Council for a Drug Free Workplace concluded that 70% of New Jersey's businesses have employees whose performance is affected by drugs and/or alcohol. In those businesses, it was estimated that 8.5% of their workforces have alcohol problems and 5.2% have drug problems. These last two numbers are slightly lower than the national statistics of 10% and 7%, respectively (*Report: The Governor's Council for a Drug Free Workplace,* Spring/Summer 1995).

a. In a New Jersey company that acknowledges it has performance problems caused by substance abuse, out of every 1,000 employees, approximately how many have drug problems?

b. In the company referred to in part **a**, if 10 employees are randomly selected to form a committee to address alcohol abuse problems, what is the probability that at least one member of the committee is an alcohol abuser? That exactly two are alcohol abusers?

c. What assumptions did you have to make in order to answer part **b** using the methodology of this section?

4.39 Many firms utilize sampling plans to control the quality of manufactured items ready for shipment or the quality of incoming items (parts, raw materials, etc.) that have been purchased. To illustrate the use of a sampling plan, suppose you are shipping electrical fuses in lots, each containing 5,000 fuses. The plan specifies that you will randomly sample 25 fuses from each lot and accept (and ship) the lot if the number of defective fuses, x, in the sample is less than 3. If $x \geq 3$, you will reject the lot. Find the probability of accepting a lot ($x = 0, 1,$ or 2) if the actual fraction defective in the lot is:

a. 0   **b.** .01   **c.** .10   **d.** .30
e. .50   **f.** .80   **g.** .95   **h.** 1
i. Construct a graph showing $P(A)$, the probability of lot acceptance, as a function of the lot fraction defective, p. This graph is called the **operating characteristic curve** for the sampling plan.

4.40 Refer to Exercise 4.39. Suppose the sampling plan called for sampling $n = 25$ fuses and accepting a lot of $x \leq 3$. Calculate the quantities specified in Exercise 4.39, and construct the operating characteristic curve for this sampling plan. Compare this curve with the curve obtained in Exercise 4.39. (Note how the curve characterizes the ability of the plan to screen bad lots from shipment.)

4.4 THE POISSON DISTRIBUTION (OPTIONAL)

A type of probability distribution that is often useful in describing the number of events that will occur in a specific period of time or in a specific area or volume is the **Poisson distribution** (named after the 18th-century physicist and mathematician, Siméon Poisson). Typical examples of random variables for which the Poisson probability distribution provides a good model are

1. The number of industrial accidents per month at a manufacturing plant
2. The number of noticeable surface defects (scratches, dents, etc.) found by quality inspectors on a new automobile
3. The parts per million of some toxin found in the water or air emission from a manufacturing plant
4. The number of customer arrivals per unit of time at a supermarket checkout counter
5. The number of death claims received per day by an insurance company
6. The number of errors per 100 invoices in the accounting records of a company

Characteristics of a Poisson Random Variable

1. The experiment consists of counting the number of times a certain event occurs during a given unit of time or in a given area or volume (or weight, distance, or any other unit of measurement).
2. The probability that an event occurs in a given unit of time, area, or volume is the same for all the units.
3. The number of events that occur in one unit of time, area, or volume is independent of the number that occur in other units.
4. The mean (or expected) number of events in each unit is denoted by the Greek letter lambda, λ.

The characteristics of the Poisson random variable are usually difficult to verify for practical examples. The examples given satisfy them well enough that the Poisson distribution provides a good model in many instances. As with all probability models, the real test of the adequacy of the Poisson model is in whether it provides a reasonable approximation to reality—that is, whether empirical data support it.

The probability distribution, mean, and variance for a Poisson random variable are shown in the next box.

> **Probability Distribution, Mean, and Variance for a Poisson Random Variable***
>
> $$p(x) = \frac{\lambda^x e^{-\lambda}}{x!} \qquad (x = 0, 1, 2, \dots)$$
> $$\mu = \lambda$$
> $$\sigma^2 = \lambda$$
>
> where
>
> λ = Mean number of events during given unit of time, area, volume, etc.
>
> $e = 2.71828\dots$

The calculation of Poisson probabilities is made easier by the use of Table III in Appendix B, which gives the cumulative probabilities $P(x \le k)$ for various values of λ. The use of Table III is illustrated in Example 4.12.

EXAMPLE 4.12 Suppose the number, x, of a company's employees who are absent on Mondays has (approximately) a Poisson probability distribution. Furthermore, assume that the average number of Monday absentees is 2.6.

a. Find the mean and standard deviation of x, the number of employees absent on Monday.

b. Use Table III to find the probability that fewer than two employees are absent on a given Monday.

c. Use Table III to find the probability that more than five employees are absent on a given Monday.

d. Use Table III to find the probability that exactly five employees are absent on a given Monday.

SOLUTION

a. The mean and variance of a Poisson random variable are both equal to λ. Thus, for this example,

$$\mu = \lambda = 2.6$$
$$\sigma^2 = \lambda = 2.6$$

Then the standard deviation of x is

$$\sigma = \sqrt{2.6} = 1.61$$

Remember that the mean measures the central tendency of the distribution and does not necessarily equal a possible value of x. In this example, the mean is 2.6 absences, and although there cannot be 2.6 absences on a given Monday, the average number of Monday absences is 2.6. Similarly, the standard deviation of 1.61 measures the variability of the number of absences per week. Perhaps a more helpful measure is the interval $\mu \pm 2\sigma$, which in this case stretches from $-.62$ to 5.82. We expect the number of absences to fall in this interval most of the time—with at least 75% relative frequency (according to Chebyshev's Rule) and probably with approximately 95%

---

*The Poisson probability distribution also provides a good approximation to a binomial distribution with mean $\lambda = np$ when n is large and p is small (say, $np \le 7$).

FIGURE 4.10
Probability distribution for number of Monday absences

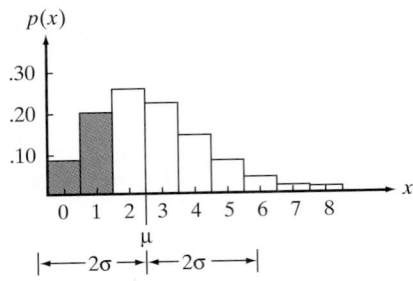

relative frequency (the Empirical Rule). The mean and the 2-standard-deviation interval around it are shown in Figure 4.10.

b. A partial reproduction of Table III is shown in Table 4.4. The rows of the table correspond to different values of λ, and the columns correspond to different values of the Poisson random variable x. The entries in the table are cumulative probabilities (much like the binomial probabilities in Table II). To find the probability that fewer than two employees are absent on Monday, we first note that

$$P(x < 2) = P(x \leq 1)$$

This probability is a cumulative probability and therefore is the entry in Table III in the row corresponding to $\lambda = 2.6$ and the column corresponding to $x = 1$. The entry is .267, shown shaded in Table 4.4. This probability corresponds to the shaded area in Figure 4.10 and may be interpreted as meaning that there is a 26.7% chance that fewer than two employees will be absent on a given Monday.

c. To find the probability that more than five employees are absent on a given Monday, we consider the complementary event

$$P(x > 5) = 1 - P(x \leq 5) = 1 - .951 = .049$$

where .951 is the entry in Table III corresponding to $\lambda = 2.6$ and $x = 5$ (see Table 4.4). Note from Figure 4.10 that this is the area in the interval $\mu \pm 2\sigma$, or $-.62$ to 5.82. Then the number of absences should exceed 5—or, equivalently, should be more than 2 standard deviations from the mean—during only about 4.9% of all Mondays. Note that this percentage agrees remarkably well with that given by the Empirical Rule for mound-shaped distributions, which tells us to expect approximately 5% of the measurements (values of the random variable) to lie farther than 2 standard deviations from the mean.

d. To use Table III to find the probability that *exactly* five employees are absent on a Monday, we must write the probability as the difference between two cumulative probabilities:

$$P(x = 5) = P(x \leq 5) - P(x \leq 4) = .951 - .877 = .074$$

Note that the probabilities in Table III are all rounded to three decimal places. Thus, although in theory a Poisson random variable can assume infinitely large values, the values of x in Table III are extended only until the cumulative probability is 1.000. This does not mean that x *cannot* assume larger values, but only that the likelihood is less than .001 (in fact, less than .0005) that it will do so.

TABLE 4.4   Reproduction of Part of Table III in Appendix B

λ \ x	0	1	2	3	4	5	6	7	8	9
2.2	.111	.355	.623	.819	.928	.975	.993	.998	1.000	1.000
2.4	.091	.308	.570	.779	.904	.964	.988	.997	.999	1.000
2.6	.074	.267	.518	.736	.877	.951	.983	.995	.999	1.000
2.8	.061	.231	.469	.692	.848	.935	.976	.992	.998	.999
3.0	.050	.199	.423	.647	.815	.916	.966	.988	.996	.999
3.2	.041	.171	.380	.603	.781	.895	.955	.983	.994	.998
3.4	.033	.147	.340	.558	.744	.871	.942	.977	.992	.997
3.6	.027	.126	.303	.515	.706	.844	.927	.969	.988	.996
3.8	.022	.107	.269	.473	.668	.816	.909	.960	.984	.994
4.0	.018	.092	.238	.433	.629	.785	.889	.949	.979	.992
4.2	.015	.078	.210	.395	.590	.753	.867	.936	.972	.989
4.4	.012	.066	.185	.359	.551	.720	.844	.921	.964	.985
4.6	.010	.056	.163	.326	.513	.686	.818	.905	.955	.980
4.8	.008	.048	.143	.294	.476	.651	.791	.887	.944	.975
5.0	.007	.040	.125	.265	.440	.616	.762	.867	.932	.968
5.2	.006	.034	.109	.238	.406	.581	.732	.845	.918	.960
5.4	.005	.029	.095	.213	.373	.546	.702	.822	.903	.951
5.6	.004	.024	.082	.191	.342	.512	.670	.797	.886	.941
5.8	.003	.021	.072	.170	.313	.478	.638	.771	.867	.929
6.0	.002	.017	.062	.151	.285	.446	.606	.744	.847	.916

Finally, you may need to calculate Poisson probabilities for values of λ not found in Table III. You may be able to obtain an adequate approximation by interpolation, but if not, consult more extensive tables for the Poisson distribution.

EXERCISES   4.41–4.53

Learning the Mechanics

4.41 Consider the probability distribution shown here:

$$p(x) = \frac{3^x e^{-3}}{x!} \qquad (x = 0, 1, 2, \ldots)$$

a. Is x a discrete or continuous random variable? Explain.
b. What is the name of this probability distribution?
c. Graph the probability distribution.
d. Find the mean and standard deviation of x.
e. Find the mean and standard deviation of the probability distribution.

4.42 Given that x is a random variable for which a Poisson probability distribution provides a good approximation, use Table III to compute the following:

a. $P(x \le 2)$ when $\lambda = 1$
b. $P(x \le 2)$ when $\lambda = 2$
c. $P(x \le 2)$ when $\lambda = 3$

d. What happens to the probability of the event $\{x \le 2\}$ as λ increases from 1 to 3? Is this intuitively reasonable?

4.43 Assume that x is a random variable having a Poisson probability distribution with a mean of 1.5. Use Table III to find the following probabilities:

a. $P(x \le 3)$ **b.** $P(x \ge 3)$ **c.** $P(x = 3)$
d. $P(x = 0)$ **e.** $P(x > 0)$ **f.** $P(x > 6)$

4.44 Suppose x is a random variable for which a Poisson probability distribution with $\lambda = 5$ provides a good characterization.

a. Graph $p(x)$ for $x = 0, 1, 2, \ldots, 15$.
b. Find μ and σ for x, and locate μ and the interval $\mu \pm 2\sigma$ on the graph.
c. What is the probability that x will fall within the interval $\mu \pm 2\sigma$?

Applying the Concepts

4.45 The Federal Deposit Insurance Corporation (FDIC), established in 1933, insures deposits of up to $100,000 in banks that are members of the Federal Reserve System (and others that voluntarily join the insurance fund) against losses due to bank failure or theft. From 1988 through 1994 the average number of bank failures per year among insured banks was approximately 128.6 (*Statistical Abstract of the United States: 1995*). Assume that x, the number of bank failures per year among insured banks, can be adequately characterized by a Poisson probability distribution with mean 128.6.

a. Find the expected value and standard deviation of x.

b. In 1993, only 41 insured banks failed. How far (in standard deviations) does $x = 41$ lie below the mean of the Poisson distribution? That is, find the z-score for $x = 41$.

c. In 1992, 122 insured banks failed. Indicate how to calculate $P(x \leq 122)$. Do not actually perform the calculation.

d. Discuss conditions that would make the Poisson assumption plausible.

4.46 As part of a project targeted at improving the services of a local bakery, a management consultant (L. Lei of Rutgers University) monitored customer arrivals for several Saturdays and Sundays. Using the arrival data, she estimated the average number of customer arrivals per 10-minute period on Saturdays to be 6.2. She assumed that arrivals per 10-minute interval followed the Poisson distribution (some of whose values are missing) shown at the bottom of the page.

a. Compute the missing probabilities.

b. Plot the distribution.

c. Find μ and σ and plot the intervals $\mu \pm \sigma$, $\mu \pm 2\sigma$, and $\mu \pm 3\sigma$ on your plot of part **b**.

d. The owner of the bakery claims that more than 75 customers per hour enter the store on Saturdays. Based on the consultant's data, is this likely? Explain.

4.47 The Environmental Protection Agency (EPA), established in 1970 as part of the executive branch of the federal government, issues pollution standards that vitally affect the safety of consumers and the operations of industry (*The United States Government Manual 1995–1996*). For example, the EPA states that manufacturers of vinyl chloride and similar compounds must limit the amount of these chemicals in plant air emissions to no more than 10 parts per million. Suppose the mean emis-

sion of vinyl chloride for a particular plant is 4 parts per million. Assume that the number of parts per million of vinyl chloride in air samples, x, follows a Poisson probability distribution.

a. What is the standard deviation of x for the plant?

b. Is it likely that a sample of air from the plant would yield a value of x that would exceed the EPA limit? Explain.

c. Discuss conditions that would make the Poisson assumption plausible.

4.48 U.S. airlines fly approximately 41 billion passenger-miles per month and average about 3.75 fatalities per month (*Statistical Abstract of the United States: 1995*). Assume the probability distribution for x, the number of fatalities per month, can be approximated by a Poisson probability distribution.

a. What is the probability that no fatalities will occur during any given month? [*Hint:* Either use Table III of Appendix B and interpolate to approximate the probability, or use a calculator or computer to calculate the probability exactly.]

b. Find $E(x)$ and the standard deviation of x.

c. Use your answers to part **b** to describe the probability that as many as 10 fatalities will occur in any given month.

d. Discuss conditions that would make the Poisson assumption plausible.

4.49 The mean number of patients admitted per day to the emergency room of a small hospital is 2.5. If, on a given day, there are only four beds available for new patients, what is the probability the hospital will not have enough beds to accommodate its newly admitted patients?

4.50 As a check on the quality of the wooden doors produced by a company, its owner requested that each door undergo inspection for defects before leaving the plant. The plant's quality control inspector found that one square foot of door surface contains, on the average, .5 minor flaw. Subsequently, one square foot of each door's surface was examined for flaws. The owner decided to have all doors reworked that were found to have two or more minor flaws in the square foot of surface that was inspected. What is the probability that a door will fail inspection and be sent back for reworking? What is the probability that a door will pass inspection?

x	0	1	2	3	4	5	6	7	8	9	10	11	12	13
$p(x)$	.002	.013	—	.081	.125	.155	—	.142	.110	.076	—	.026	.014	.007

Source: Lei, L. Dorsi's Bakery: Modeling Service Operations. Graduate School of Management, Rutgers University, 1993.

4.51   The safety supervisor at a large manufacturing plant believes the expected number of industrial accidents per month is 3.4.

   a. What is the probability of exactly two accidents occurring next month?

   b. What is the probability of three or more accidents occurring next month?

   c. What assumptions do you need to make to solve this problem using the methodology of this chapter?

4.52   The number x of people who arrive at a cashier's counter in a bank during a specified period of time often exhibits (approximately) a Poisson probability distribution. If we know the mean arrival rate λ, the Poisson probability distribution can be used to aid in the design of the customer service facility. Suppose you estimate that the mean number of arrivals per minute for cashier service at a bank is one person per minute.

   a. What is the probability that in a given minute the number of arrivals will equal three or more?

   b. Can you tell the bank manager that the number of arrivals will rarely exceed two per minute?

4.53   A large manufacturing plant has 3,200 incandescent light bulbs illuminating the manufacturing floor. If the rate at which the bulbs fail follows a Poisson distribution with a mean of three bulbs per hour, what is the probability that exactly three light bulbs fail in an hour? What is the probability that no bulbs fail in an hour? That no bulbs fail in an eight-hour shift? What assumption is required to calculate the last probability?

4.5 PROBABILITY DISTRIBUTIONS FOR CONTINUOUS RANDOM VARIABLES

Recall that a continuous random variable is one that can assume any value within some interval or intervals. For example, the length of time between a customer's purchase of new automobiles, the thickness of sheets of steel produced in a rolling mill, and the yield of wheat per acre of farmland are all continuous random variables.

The graphical form of the probability distribution for a continuous random variable x is a smooth curve that might appear as shown in Figure 4.11. This curve, a function of x, is denoted by the symbol $f(x)$ and is variously called a **probability density function**, a **frequency function**, or a **probability distribution**.

The areas under a probability distribution correspond to probabilities for x. For example, the area A beneath the curve between the two points a and b, as shown in Figure 4.11, is the probability that x assumes a value between a and b $(a < x < b)$. Because there is no area over a point, say $x = a$, it follows that (according to our model) the probability associated with a particular value of x is equal to 0; that is, $P(x = a) = 0$ and hence $P(a < x < b) = P(a \leq x \leq b)$. In other words, the probability is the same whether or not you include the endpoints of the interval. Also, because areas over intervals represent probabilities, it follows that the total area under a probability distribution, the probability assigned to all values of x, should equal 1. Note that probability distributions for continuous random variables possess different shapes depending on the relative frequency distributions of real data that the probability distributions are supposed to model.

FIGURE 4.11
A probability distribution $f(x)$ for a continuous random variable x

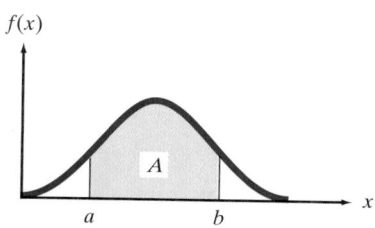

The areas under most probability distributions are obtained by using calculus or numerical methods.* Because these methods often involve difficult procedures, we will give the areas for some of the most common probability distributions in tabular form in Appendix B. Then, to find the area between two values of x, say $x = a$ and $x = b$, you simply have to consult the appropriate table.

For each of the continuous random variables presented in this chapter, we will give the formula for the probability distribution along with its mean μ and standard deviation σ. These two numbers will enable you to make some approximate probability statements about a random variable even when you do not have access to a table of areas under the probability distribution.

4.6   THE UNIFORM DISTRIBUTION (OPTIONAL)

All the probability problems discussed in Chapter 3 had sample spaces that contained a finite number of sample points. In many of these problems, the sample points were assigned equal probabilities—for example, the die toss or the coin toss. For continuous random variables, there is an infinite number of values in the sample space, but in some cases the values may appear to be equally likely. For example, if a short exists in a 5-meter stretch of electrical wire, it may have an equal probability of being in any particular 1-centimeter segment along the line. Or if a safety inspector plans to choose a time at random during the 4 afternoon work hours to pay a surprise visit to a certain area of a plant, then each 1-minute time interval in this 4-work-hour period will have an equally likely chance of being selected for the visit.

Continuous random variables that appear to have equally likely outcomes over their range of possible values possess a **uniform probability distribution**, perhaps the simplest of all continuous probability distributions. Suppose the random variable x can assume values only in an interval $c \leq x \leq d$. Then the uniform frequency function has a rectangular shape, as shown in Figure 4.12. Note that the possible values of x consist of all points in the interval between point c and point d. The height of $f(x)$ is constant in that interval and equals $1/(d - c)$. Therefore, the total area under $f(x)$ is given by

$$\text{Total area of rectangle} = (\text{Base})(\text{Height}) = (d - c)\left(\frac{1}{d - c}\right) = 1$$

FIGURE 4.12
The uniform probability distribution

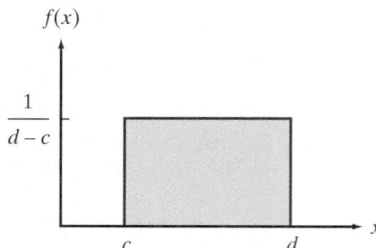

*Students with knowledge of calculus should note that the probability that x assumes a value in the interval $a < x < b$ is $P(a < x < b) = \int_a^b f(x)\, dx$, assuming the integral exists. Similar to the requirement for a discrete probability distribution, we require $f(x) \geq 0$ and $\int_{-\infty}^{\infty} f(x)\, dx = 1$.

The uniform probability distribution provides a model for continuous random variables that are *evenly distributed* over a certain interval. That is, a uniform random variable is one that is just as likely to assume a value in one interval as it is to assume a value in any other interval of equal size. There is no clustering of values around any value; instead, there is an even spread over the entire region of possible values.

The uniform distribution is sometimes referred to as the **randomness distribution**, since one way of generating a uniform random variable is to perform an experiment in which a point is *randomly selected* on the horizontal axis between the points c and d. If we were to repeat this experiment infinitely often, we would create a uniform probability distribution like that shown in Figure 4.12. The random selection of points in an interval can also be used to generate random numbers such as those in Table I of Appendix B. Recall that random numbers are selected in such a way that every number would have an equal probability of selection. Therefore, random numbers are realizations of a uniform random variable. (Random numbers were used to draw random samples in Section 3.7.) The formulas for the uniform probability distribution, its mean, and standard deviation are shown in the box.

Probability Distribution, Mean, and Standard Deviation of a Uniform Random Variable x

$$f(x) = \frac{1}{d - c} \qquad c \leqslant x \leqslant d$$

$$\mu = \frac{c + d}{2} \qquad \sigma = \frac{d - c}{\sqrt{12}}$$

Suppose the interval $a < x < b$ lies within the domain of x; that is, it falls within the larger interval $c \leqslant x \leqslant d$. Then the probability that x assumes a value within the interval $a < x < b$ is equal to the area of the rectangle over the interval, namely, $(b - a)/(d - c)$.*

EXAMPLE 4.13

Suppose the research department of a steel manufacturer believes that one of the company's rolling machines is producing sheets of steel of varying thickness. The thickness is a uniform random variable with values between 150 and 200 millimeters. Any sheets less than 160 millimeters must be scrapped because they are unacceptable to buyers.

a. Calculate the mean and standard deviation of x, the thickness of the sheets produced by this machine. Graph the probability distribution of x, and show the mean on the horizontal axis. Also show 1- and 2-standard-deviation intervals around the mean.

b. Calculate the fraction of steel sheets produced by this machine that have to be scrapped.

---

*The student with knowledge of calculus should note that

$$P(a < x < b) = \int_a^b f(x)\, d(x) = \int_a^b 1/(d - c)\, dx = (b - a)/(d - c)$$

FIGURE 4.13
Distribution for x
in Example 4.13

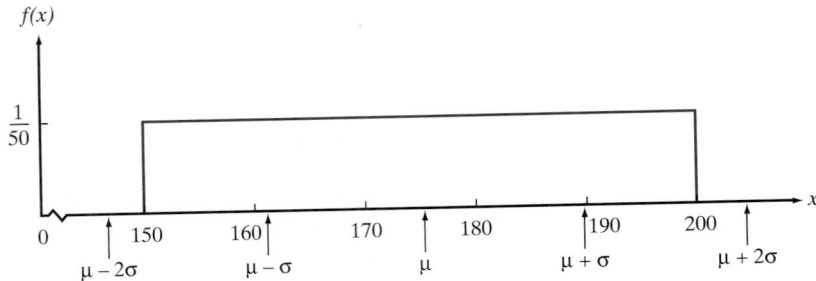

FIGURE 4.14
Probability that sheet
thickness, x, is between
150 and 160
millimeters

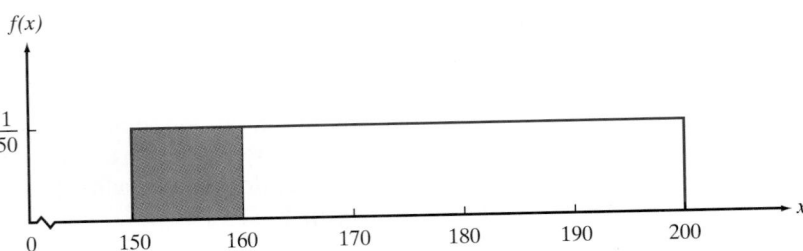

SOLUTION

a. To calculate the mean and standard deviation for x, we substitute 150 and 200 millimeters for c and d, respectively, in the formulas for uniform random variables. Thus,

$$\mu = \frac{c + d}{2} = \frac{150 + 200}{2} = 175 \text{ millimeters}$$

and

$$\sigma = \frac{d - c}{\sqrt{12}} = \frac{200 - 150}{\sqrt{12}} = \frac{50}{3.464} = 14.43 \text{ millimeters}$$

The uniform probability distribution is

$$f(x) = \frac{1}{d - c} = \frac{1}{200 - 150} = \frac{1}{50} \qquad (150 \leq x \leq 200)$$

The graph of this function is shown in Figure 4.13. The mean and 1- and 2-standard-deviation intervals around the mean are shown on the horizontal axis.

b. To find the fraction of steel sheets produced by the machine that have to be scrapped, we must find the probability that x, the thickness, is less than 160 millimeters. As indicated in Figure 4.14, we need to calculate the area under the frequency function $f(x)$ between the points $x = 150$ and $x = 160$. This is the area of a rectangle with base $160 - 150 = 10$ and height $\frac{1}{50}$. The fraction that has to be scrapped is then

$$P(x < 160) = (\text{Base})(\text{Height}) = (10)\left(\frac{1}{50}\right) = \frac{1}{5}$$

That is, 20% of all the sheets made by this machine must be scrapped.

EXERCISES   4.54–4.64

Note: Exercises marked with 💾 *contain data available for computer analysis on a 3.5" disk (file name in parentheses).*

Learning the Mechanics

4.54 Suppose x is a random variable best described by a uniform probability distribution with $c = 20$ and $d = 45$. Find the following probabilities:
  a. $P(20 \le x \le 30)$ **b.** $P(20 < x < 30)$
  c. $P(x \ge 30)$ **d.** $P(x \ge 45)$ **e.** $P(x \le 40)$
  f. $P(x < 40)$ **g.** $P(15 \le x \le 35)$
  h. $P(21.5 \le x \le 31.5)$

4.55 Suppose x is a random variable best described by a uniform probability distribution with $c = 3$ and $d = 7$.
  a. Find $f(x)$.
  b. Find the mean and standard deviation of x.
  c. Find $P(\mu - \sigma \le x \le \mu + \sigma)$.

4.56 Refer to Exercise 4.55. Find the value of a that makes each of the following probability statements true.
  a. $P(x \ge a) = .6$ **b.** $P(x \le a) = .25$
  c. $P(x \le a) = 1$ **d.** $P(4 \le x \le a) = .5$

4.57 The random variable x is best described by a uniform probability distribution with $c = 100$ and $d = 200$. Find the probability that x assumes a value
  a. More than 2 standard deviations from μ.
  b. Less than 3 standard deviations from μ.
  c. Within 2 standard deviations of μ.

4.58 The random variable x is best described by a uniform probability distribution with mean 10 and standard deviation 1. Find c, d, and $f(x)$. Graph the probability distribution.

Applying the Concepts

4.59 The manager of a local soft-drink bottling company believes that when a new beverage-dispensing machine is set to dispense 7 ounces, it in fact dispenses an amount x at random anywhere between 6.5 and 7.5 ounces inclusive. Suppose x has a uniform probability distribution.
  a. Is the amount dispensed by the beverage machine a discrete or a continuous random variable? Explain.
  b. Graph the frequency function for x, the amount of beverage the manager believes is dispensed by the new machine when it is set to dispense 7 ounces.
  c. Find the mean and standard deviation for the distribution graphed in part **b**, and locate the mean and the interval $\mu \pm 2\sigma$ on the graph.
  d. Find $P(x \ge 7)$.   **e.** Find $P(x < 6)$.

  f. Find $P(6.5 \le x \le 7.25)$.
  g. What is the probability that each of the next six bottles filled by the new machine will contain more than 7.25 ounces of beverage? Assume that the amount of beverage dispensed in one bottle is independent of the amount dispensed in another bottle.

4.60 Researchers at the University of California–Berkeley have designed, built, and tested a switched-capacitor circuit for generating random signals (*International Journal of Circuit Theory and Applications,* May–June 1990). The circuit's trajectory was shown to be uniformly distributed on the interval $(0, 1)$.
  a. Give the mean and variance of the circuit's trajectory.
  b. Compute the probability that the trajectory falls between .2 and .4.
  c. Would you expect to observe a trajectory that exceeds .995? Explain.

4.61 **(X04.061)** The data set listed below was created using the MINITAB random number generator. Construct a relative frequency histogram for the data. Except for the expected variation in relative frequencies among the class intervals, does your histogram suggest that the data are observations on a uniform random variable with $c = 0$ and $d = 100$? Explain.

38.8759	98.0716	64.5788	60.8422	.8413
88.3734	31.8792	32.9847	.7434	93.3017
12.4337	11.7828	87.4506	94.1727	23.0892
47.0121	43.3629	50.7119	88.2612	69.2875
62.6626	55.6267	78.3936	28.6777	71.6829
44.0466	57.8870	71.8318	28.9622	23.0278
35.6438	38.6584	46.7404	11.2159	96.1009
95.3660	21.5478	87.7819	12.0605	75.1015

4.62 During the recession of the late 1980s and early 1990s, many companies began tightening their reimbursement expense policies. For example, a survey of 550 companies by the Dartnell Corporation found that in 1992 about half reimbursed their salespeople for home fax machines, but by 1994 only one-fourth continued to do so (*Inc.,* Sept. 1995). One company found that monthly reimbursements to their employees, x, could be adequately modeled by a uniform distribution over the interval $\$10,000 \le x \le \$15,000$.
  a. Find $E(x)$ and interpret it in the context of the exercise.
  b. What is the probability of employee reimbursements exceeding $\$12,000$ next month?

c. For budgeting purposes, the company needs to estimate next month's employee reimbursement expenses. How much should the company budget for employee reimbursements if they want the probability of exceeding the budgeted amount to be only .20?

4.63 A tool-and-die machine shop produces extremely high-tolerance spindles. The spindles are 18-inch slender rods used in a variety of military equipment. A piece of equipment used in the manufacture of the spindles malfunctions on occasion and places a single gouge somewhere on the spindle. However, if the spindle can be cut so that it has 14 consecutive inches without a gouge, then the spindle can be salvaged for other purposes. Assuming that the location of the gouge along the spindle is best described by a uniform distribution, what is the probability that a defective spindle can be salvaged?

4.64 The **reliability** of a piece of equipment is frequently defined to be the probability, p, that the equipment performs its intended function successfully for a given period of time under specific conditions (Render and Heizer, *Principles of Operations Management*, 1995). Because p varies from one point in time to another, some reliability analysts treat p as if it were a random variable. Suppose an analyst characterizes the uncertainty about the reliability of a particular robotic device used in an automobile assembly line using the following distribution:

$$f(p) = \begin{cases} 1 & 0 \le p \le 1 \\ 0 & \text{otherwise} \end{cases}$$

a. Graph the analyst's probability distribution for p.
b. Find the mean and variance of p.
c. According to the analyst's probability distribution for p, what is the probability that p is greater than .95? Less than .95?
d. Suppose the analyst receives the additional information that p is definitely between .90 and .95, but that there is complete uncertainty about where it lies between these values. Describe the probability distribution the analyst should now use to describe p.

4.7 THE NORMAL DISTRIBUTION

One of the most commonly observed continuous random variables has a **bell-shaped** probability distribution as shown in Figure 4.15. It is known as a **normal random variable** and its probability distribution is called a **normal distribution**.

The normal distribution plays a very important role in the science of statistical inference. Moreover, many business phenomena generate random variables with probability distributions that are very well approximated by a normal distribution. For example, the monthly rate of return for a particular stock is approximately a normal random variable, and the probability distribution for the weekly sales of a corporation might be approximated by a normal probability distribution. The normal distribution might also provide an accurate model for the distribution of scores on an employment aptitude test. You can determine the adequacy of the normal approximation to an existing population by comparing the relative frequency distribution of a large sample of the data to the normal probability distribution. Tests to detect disagreement between a set of data and the assumption of normality are available, but they are beyond the scope of this book.

FIGURE 4.15
A normal probability distribution

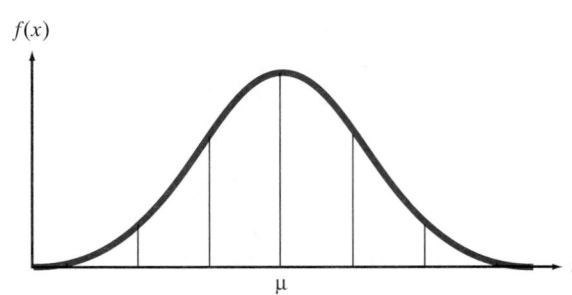

FIGURE 4.16

Several normal distributions with different means and standard deviations

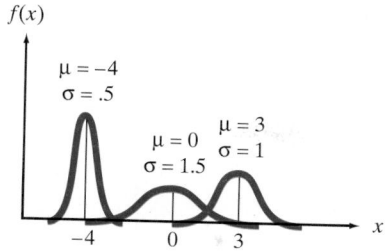

The normal distribution is perfectly symmetric about its mean μ, as can be seen in the examples in Figure 4.16. Its spread is determined by the value of its standard deviation σ.

The formula for the normal probability distribution is shown in the box. When plotted, this formula yields a curve like that shown in Figure 4.15.

Probability Distribution for a Normal Random Variable x

$$f(x) = \frac{1}{\sigma\sqrt{2\pi}} \, e^{-(1/2)[(x-\mu)/\sigma]^2}$$

where μ = Mean of the normal random variable x
σ = Standard deviation
π = 3.1416...
e = 2.71828...

Note that the mean μ and standard deviation σ appear in this formula, so that no separate formulas for μ and σ are necessary. To graph the normal curve we have to know the numerical values of μ and σ.

Computing the area over intervals under the normal probability distribution is a difficult task.* Consequently, we will use the computed areas listed in Table IV of Appendix B (and inside the front cover). Although there are an infinitely large number of normal curves—one for each pair of values for μ and σ—we have formed a single table that will apply to any normal curve.

Table IV is based on a normal distribution with mean $\mu = 0$ and standard deviation $\sigma = 1$, called a *standard normal distribution*. A random variable with a standard normal distribution is typically denoted by the symbol z. The formula for the probability distribution of z is given by

$$f(z) = \frac{1}{\sqrt{2\pi}} \, e^{-(1/2)z^2}$$

Figure 4.17 shows the graph of a standard normal distribution.

Since we will ultimately convert all normal random variables to standard normal in order to use Table IV to find probabilities, it is important that you

---

*The student with knowledge of calculus should note that there is not a closed-form expression for $P(a < x < b) = \int_{a}^{b} f(x)\, dx$ for the normal probability distribution. The value of this definite integral can be obtained to any desired degree of accuracy by numerical approximation procedures. For this reason, it is tabulated for the user.

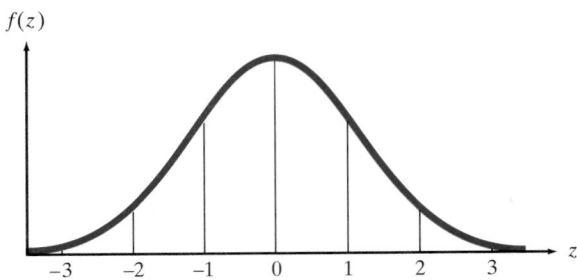

FIGURE 4.17
Standard normal
distribution: $\mu = 0$,
$\sigma = 1$

TABLE 4.5   **Reproduction of Part of Table IV in Appendix B**

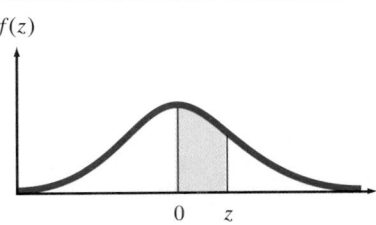

z	.00	.01	.02	.03	.04	.05	.06	.07	.08	.09
.0	.0000	.0040	.0080	.0120	.0160	.0199	.0239	.0279	.0319	.0359
.1	.0398	.0438	.0478	.0517	.0557	.0596	.0636	.0675	.0714	.0753
.2	.0793	.0832	.0871	.0910	.0948	.0987	.1026	.1064	.1103	.1141
.3	.1179	.1217	.1255	.1293	.1331	.1368	.1406	.1443	.1480	.1517
.4	.1554	.1591	.1628	.1664	.1700	.1736	.1772	.1808	.1844	.1879
.5	.1915	.1950	.1985	.2019	.2054	.2088	.2123	.2157	.2190	.2224
.6	.2257	.2291	.2324	.2357	.2389	.2422	.2454	.2486	.2517	.2549
.7	.2580	.2611	.2642	.2673	.2704	.2734	.2764	.2794	.2823	.2852
.8	.2881	.2910	.2939	.2967	.2995	.3023	.3051	.3078	.3106	.3133
.9	.3159	.3186	.3212	.3238	.3264	.3289	.3315	.3340	.3365	.3389
1.0	.3413	.3438	.3461	.3485	.3508	.3531	.3554	.3577	.3599	.3621
1.1	.3643	.3665	.3686	.3708	.3729	.3749	.3770	.3790	.3810	.3830
1.2	.3849	.3869	.3888	.3907	.3925	.3944	.3962	.3980	.3997	.4015
1.3	.4032	.4049	.4066	.4082	.4099	.4115	.4131	.4147	.4162	.4177
1.4	.4192	.4207	.4222	.4236	.4251	.4265	.4279	.4292	.4306	.4319
1.5	.4332	.4345	.4357	.4370	.4382	.4394	.4406	.4418	.4429	.4441

learn to use Table IV well. A partial reproduction of Table IV is shown in Table 4.5. Note that the values of the standard normal random variable z are listed in the left-hand column. The entries in the body of the table give the area (probability) between 0 and z. Examples 4.14–4.17 illustrate the use of the table.

EXAMPLE 4.14   Find the probability that the standard normal random variable z falls between -1.33 and $+1.33$.

SOLUTION
The standard normal distribution is shown again in Figure 4.18. Since all probabilities associated with standard normal random variables can be depicted as areas under the standard normal curve, you should always draw the curve and then equate the desired probability to an area.

FIGURE 4.18
Areas under the
standard normal curve
for Example 4.14

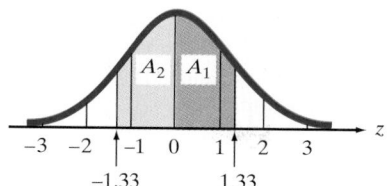

In this example we want to find the probability that z falls between -1.33 and $+1.33$, which is equivalent to the area between -1.33 and $+1.33$, shown shaded in Figure 4.18. Table IV provides the area between $z = 0$ and any value of z, so that if we look up $z = 1.33$, we find that the area between $z = 0$ and $z = 1.33$ is .4082. This is the area labeled A_1 in Figure 4.18. To find the area A_2 located between $z = 0$ and $z = -1.33$, we note that the symmetry of the normal distribution implies that the area between $z = 0$ and any point to the left is equal to the area between $z = 0$ and the point equidistant to the right. Thus, in this example the area between $z = 0$ and $z = -1.33$ is equal to the area between $z = 0$ and $z = +1.33$. That is,

$$A_1 = A_2 = .4082$$

The probability that z falls between -1.33 and $+1.33$ is the sum of the areas of A_1 and A_2. We summarize in probabilistic notation:

$$P(-1.33 < z < 1.33) = P(-1.33 < z < 0) + P(0 < z \leq 1.33)$$
$$= A_1 + A_2 = .4082 + .4082 = .8164$$

Remember that "$<$" and "$\leq$" are equivalent in events involving z, because the inclusion (or exclusion) of a single point does not alter the probability of an event involving a continuous random variable. ∎

EXAMPLE 4.15   Find the probability that a standard normal random variable exceeds 1.64; that is, find $P(z > 1.64)$.

SOLUTION
The area under the standard normal distribution to the right of 1.64 is the shaded area labeled A_1 in Figure 4.19. This area represents the desired probability that z exceeds 1.64. However, when we look up $z = 1.64$ in Table IV, we must remember that the probability given in the table corresponds to the area between $z = 0$ and $z = 1.64$ (the area labeled A_2 in Figure 4.19). From Table IV we find that $A_2 = .4495$. To find the area A_1 to the right of 1.64, we make use of two facts:

1. The standard normal distribution is symmetric about its mean, $z = 0$.
2. The total area under the standard normal probability distribution equals 1.

FIGURE 4.19
Areas under the
standard normal curve
for Example 4.15

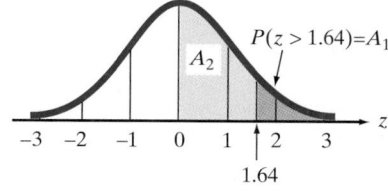

FIGURE 4.20
Areas under the
standard normal curve
for Example 4.16

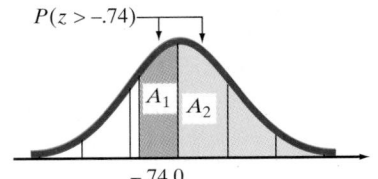

Taken together, these two facts imply that the areas on either side of the mean $z = 0$ equal .5; thus, the area to the right of $z = 0$ in Figure 4.19 is $A_1 + A_2 = .5$. Then

$$P(z > 1.64) = A_1 = .5 - A_2 = .5 - .4495 = .0505$$

To attach some practical significance to this probability, note that the implication is that the chance of a standard normal random variable exceeding 1.64 is approximately .05.

EXAMPLE 4.16 Find the probability that a standard normal random variable lies to the right of $-.74$.

SOLUTION
We want to find $P(z > -.74)$. The event is shown as the shaded area in Figure 4.20. We divide the shaded area into two parts: the area A_1 between $z = -.74$ and $z = 0$, and the area A_2 to the right of $z = 0$. We must always make such a division when the desired area lies on both sides of the mean ($z = 0$) because Table IV contains areas between $z = 0$ and the point you look up. To find A_1, we remember that the sign of z is unimportant when determining the area, because the standard normal distribution is symmetric about its mean. We look up $z = .74$ in Table IV to find that $A_1 = .2704$. The symmetry also implies that half the distribution lies on each side of the mean, so the area A_2 to the right of $z = 0$ is .5. Then,

$$P(z > -.74) = A_1 + A_2 = .2704 + .5 = .7704$$

EXAMPLE 4.17 Find the probability that a standard normal random variable exceeds 1.96 in absolute value.

SOLUTION
We want to find

$$P(|z| > 1.96) = P(z < -1.96 \text{ or } z > 1.96)$$

This probability is the shaded area in Figure 4.21. Note that the total shaded area is the sum of two areas, A_1 and A_2—areas that are equal because of the symmetry of the normal distribution.

We look up $z = 1.96$ and find the area between $z = 0$ and $z = 1.96$ to be .4750. Then the area to the right of 1.96, A_2, is $.5 - .4750 = .0250$, so that

$$P(|z| > 1.96) = A_1 + A_2 = .0250 + .0250 = .05$$

FIGURE 4.21
Areas under the
standard normal curve
for Example 4.17

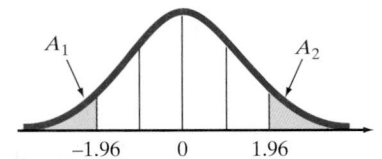

To apply Table IV to a normal random variable x with any mean μ and any standard deviation σ, we must first convert the value of x to a z-score. The population z-score for a measurement was defined (in Section 2.6) as the *distance* between the measurement and the population mean, divided by the population standard deviation. Thus, the z-score gives the distance between a measurement and the mean in units equal to the standard deviation. In symbolic form, the z-score for the measurement x is

$$z = \frac{x - \mu}{\sigma}$$

Note that when $x = \mu$, we obtain $z = 0$.

An important property of the normal distribution is that if x is normally distributed with any mean and any standard deviation, z is *always* normally distributed with mean 0 and standard deviation 1. That is, z is a standard normal random variable.

DEFINITION 4.8

The **standard normal distribution** is a normal distribution with $\mu = 0$ and $\sigma = 1$. A random variable with a standard normal distribution, denoted by the symbol z, is called a **standard normal random variable**.

Property of Normal Distributions

If x is a normal random variable with mean μ and standard deviation σ, then the random variable z, defined by the formula

$$z = \frac{x - \mu}{\sigma}$$

has a standard normal distribution. The value z describes the number of standard deviations between x and μ.

Recall from Example 4.17 that $P(|z| > 1.96) = .05$. This probability coupled with our interpretation of z implies that any normal random variable lies more than 1.96 standard deviations from its mean only 5% of the time. Compare this to the Empirical Rule (Chapter 2) which tells us that about 5% of the measurements in mound-shaped distributions will lie beyond 2 standard deviations from the mean. The normal distribution actually provides the model on which the Empirical Rule is based, along with much "empirical" experience with real data that often approximately obey the rule, whether drawn from a normal distribution or not.

EXAMPLE 4.18

Assume that the length of time, x, between charges of a pocket calculator is normally distributed with a mean of 100 hours and a standard deviation of 15 hours. Find the probability that the calculator will last between 80 and 120 hours between charges.

SOLUTION

The normal distribution with mean $\mu = 100$ and $\sigma = 15$ is shown in Figure 4.22. The desired probability that the calculator lasts between 80 and 120 hours is shaded. In order to find the probability, we must first convert the distribution to standard normal, which we do by calculating the z-score:

FIGURE 4.22
Areas under the
normal curve for
Example 4.18

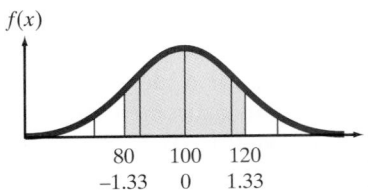

$$z = \frac{x - \mu}{\sigma}$$

The z-scores corresponding to the important values of x are shown beneath the x values on the horizontal axis in Figure 4.22. Note that $z = 0$ corresponds to the mean of $\mu = 100$ hours, whereas the x values 80 and 120 yield z-scores of -1.33 and $+1.33$, respectively. Thus, the event that the calculator lasts between 80 and 120 hours is equivalent to the event that a standard normal random variable lies between -1.33 and $+1.33$. We found this probability in Example 4.14 (see Figure 4.18) by doubling the area corresponding to $z = 1.33$ in Table IV. That is,

$$P(80 \leqslant x \leqslant 120) = P(-1.33 \leqslant z \leqslant 1.33) = 2(.4082) = .8164$$

The steps to follow when calculating a probability corresponding to a normal random variable are shown in the box.

Steps for Finding a Probability Corresponding to a Normal Random Variable

1. Sketch the normal distribution and indicate the mean of the random variable x. Then shade the area corresponding to the probability you want to find.

2. Convert the boundaries of the shaded area from x values to standard normal random variable z values using the formula

$$z = \frac{x - \mu}{\sigma}$$

Show the z values under the corresponding x values on your sketch.

3. Use Table IV in Appendix B (and inside the front cover) to find the areas corresponding to the z values. If necessary, use the symmetry of the normal distribution to find areas corresponding to negative z values and the fact that the total area on each side of the mean equals .5 to convert the areas from Table IV to the probabilities of the event you have shaded.

EXAMPLE 4.19

Suppose an automobile manufacturer introduces a new model that has an advertised mean in-city mileage of 27 miles per gallon. Although such advertisements seldom report any measure of variability, suppose you write the manufacturer for the details of the tests, and you find that the standard deviation is 3 miles per gallon. This information leads you to formulate a probability model for the random variable x, the in-city mileage for this car model. You believe that the probability distribution of x can be approximated by a normal distribution with a mean of 27 and a standard deviation of 3.

a. If you were to buy this model of automobile, what is the probability that you would purchase one that averages less than 20 miles per gallon for in-city driving? In other words, find $P(x < 20)$.

b. Suppose you purchase one of these new models and it does get less than 20 miles per gallon for in-city driving. Should you conclude that your probability model is incorrect?

SOLUTION

a. The probability model proposed for x, the in-city mileage, is shown in Figure 4.23.

We are interested in finding the area A to the left of 20 since this area corresponds to the probability that a measurement chosen from this distribution falls below 20. In other words, if this model is correct, the area A represents the fraction of cars that can be expected to get less than 20 miles per gallon for in-city driving. To find A, we first calculate the z value corresponding to $x = 20$. That is,

$$z = \frac{x - \mu}{\sigma} = \frac{20 - 27}{3} = -\frac{7}{3} = -2.33$$

Then

$$P(x < 20) = P(z < -2.33)$$

as indicated by the shaded area in Figure 4.23. Since Table IV gives only areas to the right of the mean (and because the normal distribution is symmetric about its mean), we look up 2.33 in Table IV and find that the corresponding area is .4901. This is equal to the area between $z = 0$ and $z = -2.33$, so we find

$$P(x < 20) = A = .5 - .4901 = .0099 \approx .01$$

According to this probability model, you should have only about a 1% chance of purchasing a car of this make with an in-city mileage under 20 miles per gallon.

b. Now you are asked to make an inference based on a sample—the car you purchased. You are getting less than 20 miles per gallon for in-city driving. What do you infer? We think you will agree that one of two possibilities is true:

1. The probability model is correct. You simply were unfortunate to have purchased one of the cars in the 1% that get less than 20 miles per gallon in the city.

2. The probability model is incorrect. Perhaps the assumption of a normal distribution is unwarranted or the mean of 27 is an overestimate, or the standard deviation of 3 is an underestimate, or some combination of these errors was made. At any rate, the form of the actual probability model certainly merits further investigation.

You have no way of knowing with certainty which possibility is correct, but the evidence points to the second one. We are again relying on the rare-event

FIGURE 4.23
Area under the normal curve for Example 4.19

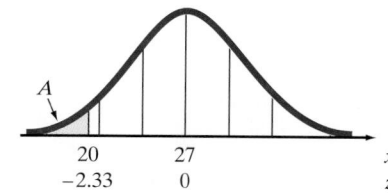

approach to statistical inference that we introduced earlier. The sample (one measurement in this case) was so unlikely to have been drawn from the proposed probability model that it casts serious doubt on the model. We would be inclined to believe that the model is somehow in error.

Occasionally you will be given a probability and will want to find the values of the normal random variable that correspond to the probability. For example, suppose the scores on a college entrance examination are known to be normally distributed, and a certain prestigious university will consider for admission only those applicants whose scores exceed the 90th percentile of the test score distribution. To determine the minimum score for admission consideration, you will need to be able to use Table IV in reverse, as demonstrated in the following example.

EXAMPLE 4.20   Find the value of z, call it z_0, in the standard normal distribution that will be exceeded only 10% of the time. That is, find z_0 such that $P(z \geqslant z_0) = .10$.

SOLUTION
In this case we are given a probability, or an area, and asked to find the value of the standard normal random variable that corresponds to the area. Specifically, we want to find the value z_0 such that only 10% of the standard normal distribution exceeds z_0 (see Figure 4.24).

We know that the total area to the right of the mean $z = 0$ is .5, which implies that z_0 must lie to the right of (above) 0. To pinpoint the value, we use the fact that the area to the right of z_0 is .10, which implies that the area between $z = 0$ and z_0 is $.5 - .1 = .4$. But areas between $z = 0$ and some other z value are exactly the types given in Table IV. Therefore, we look up the area .4000 in the body of Table IV and find that the corresponding z value is (to the closest approximation) $z_0 = 1.28$. The implication is that the point 1.28 standard deviations above the mean is the 90th percentile of a normal distribution.

EXAMPLE 4.21   Find the value of z_0 such that 95% of the standard normal z values lie between $-z_0$ and $+z_0$, i.e., $P(-z_0 \leqslant z \leqslant z_0) = .95$.

SOLUTION
Here we wish to move an equal distance z_0 in the positive and negative directions from the mean $z = 0$ until 95% of the standard normal distribution is enclosed. This means that the area on each side of the mean will be equal $\frac{1}{2}(.95) = .475$, as shown in Figure 4.25. Since the area between $z = 0$ and z_0 is .475, we look up .475 in the body of Table IV to find the value $z_0 = 1.96$. Thus, as we found in the reverse order in Example 4.17, 95% of a normal distribution lies between $+1.96$ and -1.96 standard deviations of the mean.

Now that you have learned to use Table IV to find a standard normal z value that corresponds to a specified probability, we demonstrate a practical application in Example 4.22.

FIGURE 4.24
Areas under the
standard normal curve
for Example 4.20

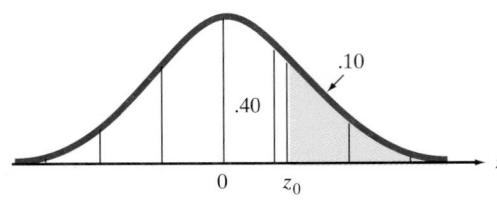

FIGURE 4.25
Areas under the
standard normal curve
for Example 4.21

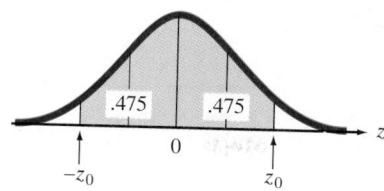

EXAMPLE 4.22 Suppose a paint manufacturer has a daily production, x, that is normally distributed with a mean of 100,000 gallons and a standard deviation of 10,000 gallons.
Management wants to create an incentive bonus for the production crew when
the daily production exceeds the 90th percentile of the distribution, in hopes that
the crew will, in turn, become more productive. At what level of production should
management pay the incentive bonus?

SOLUTION
In this example, we want to find a production level, x_0, such that 90% of the daily
levels (x values) in the distribution fall below x_0 and only 10% fall above x_0. That is,

$$P(x \leq x_0) = .90$$

Converting x to a standard normal random variable, where $\mu = 100{,}000$ and $\sigma
= 10{,}000$, we have

$$P(x \leq x_0) = P\left(z \leq \frac{x_0 - \mu}{\sigma}\right)$$

$$= P\left(z \leq \frac{x_0 - 100{,}000}{10{,}000}\right) = .90$$

In Example 4.20 (see Figure 4.24) we found the 90th percentile of the standard
normal distribution to be $z_0 = 1.28$. That is, we found $P(z \leq 1.28) = .90$.
Consequently, we know the production level x_0 at which the incentive bonus is
paid corresponds to a z-score of 1.28; that is,

$$\frac{x_0 - 100{,}000}{10{,}000} = 1.28$$

If we solve this equation for x_0, we find

$$x_0 = 100{,}000 + 1.28(10{,}000) = 100{,}000 + 12{,}800 = 112{,}800$$

This x value is shown in Figure 4.26. Thus, the 90th percentile of the production
distribution is 112,800 gallons. Management should pay an incentive bonus when
a day's production exceeds this level if its objective is to pay only when production
is in the top 10% of the current daily production distribution. ◼

FIGURE 4.26
Area under the
normal curve for
Example 4.22

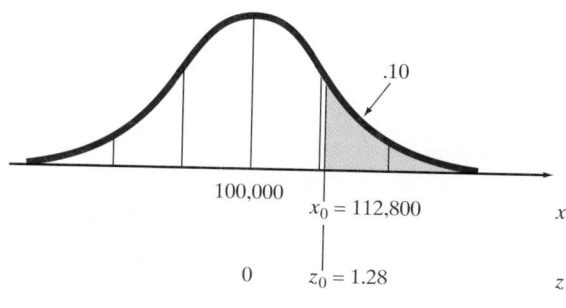

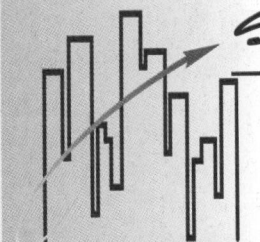

STATISTICS IN ACTION

4.2 IQ, ECONOMIC MOBILITY, AND THE BELL CURVE

In their controversial book *The Bell Curve* (Free Press, 1994), Professors Richard J. Herrnstein (a Harvard psychologist who died while the book was in production) and Charles Murray (a political scientist at MIT) explore, as the subtitle states, "intelligence and class structure in American life." *The Bell Curve* heavily employs statistical analyses in an attempt to support the authors' positions. Since the book's publication, many expert statisticians have raised doubts about the authors' statistical methods and the inferences drawn from them. (See, for example, "Wringing *The Bell Curve*: A cautionary tale about the relationships among race, genes, and IQ," *Chance*, Summer 1995.) In Statistics in Action 10.2, we explore a few of these problems.

One of the many controversies sparked by the book is the authors' tenet that level of intelligence (or lack thereof) is a cause of a wide range of intractable social problems, including constrained economic mobility.

"America has taken great pride in the mobility of generations," state Herrnstein and Murray, "but this mobility has its limits. ...The son of a father whose earnings are in the bottom five percent of the [income] distribution has something like one chance in twenty (or less) of rising to the top fifth of the income distribution and almost a fifty-fifty chance of staying in the bottom fifth. He has less than one chance in four of rising above even the median income. ...Most people at present are stuck near where their parents were on the income distribution in part because [intelligence], which has become a major predictor of income, passes on sufficiently from one generation to the next to constrain economic mobility."

The measure of intelligence chosen by the authors is the well known Intelligent Quotient (IQ). Numerous tests have been developed to measure IQ; Herrnstein and Murray use the Armed Forces Qualification Test (AFQT), originally designed to measure the cognitive ability of military recruits. Psychologists traditionally

FIGURE 4.27
The distribution of IQ
(Statistics in Action 4.2)

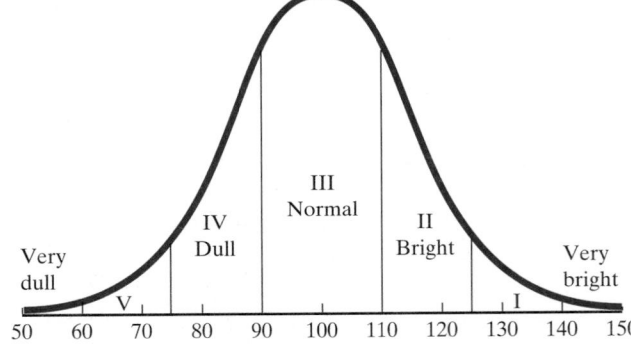

EXERCISES   4.65–4.85

Learning the Mechanics

4.65 Find the area under the standard normal probability distribution between the following pairs of z-scores:
   a. $z = 0$ and $z = 2.00$ **b.** $z = 0$ and $z = 3$
   c. $z = 0$ and $z = 1.5$ **d.** $z = 0$ and $z = .80$

4.66 Find the following probabilities for the standard normal random variable z:

   a. $P(-1 \leq z \leq 1)$ **b.** $P(-2 \leq z \leq 2)$
   c. $P(-2.16 \leq z \leq .55)$ **d.** $P(-.42 < z < 1.96)$
   e. $P(z \geq -2.33)$ **f.** $P(z < 2.33)$

4.67 Find the following probabilities for the standard normal random variable z:
   a. $P(z > 1.46)$ **b.** $P(z < -1.56)$
   c. $P(.67 \leq z \leq 2.41)$ **d.** $P(-1.96 \leq z < -.33)$
   e. $P(z \geq 0)$ **f.** $P(-2.33 < z < 1.50)$

treat IQ as a random variable having a normal distribution with mean $\mu = 100$ and standard deviation $\sigma = 15$. This distribution, or *bell curve*, is shown in Figure 4.27.

In their book, Herrnstein and Murray refer to five cognitive classes of people defined by percentiles of the normal distribution. Class I ("very bright") consists of those with IQs above the 95th percentile; Class II ("bright") are those with IQs between the 75th and 95th percentiles; Class III ("normal") includes IQs between the 25th and 75th percentiles; Class IV ("dull") are those with IQs between the 5th and 25th percentiles; and Class V ("very dull") are IQs below the 5th percentile. These classes are also illustrated in Figure 4.27.

Focus

a. Assuming that the distribution of IQ is accurately represented by the bell curve in Figure 4.27, deter-

mine the proportion of people with IQs in each of the five cognitive classes defined by Herrnstein and Murray.

b. Although the cognitive classes above are defined in terms of percentiles, the authors stress that IQ scores should be compared with z-scores, not percentiles. In other words, it is more informative to give the difference in z-scores for two IQ scores than it is to give the difference in percentiles. To demonstrate this point, calculate the difference in z-scores for IQs at the 50th and 55th percentiles. Do the same for IQs at the 94th and 99th percentiles. What do you observe?

c. Researchers have found that scores on many intelligence tests are decidedly nonnormal. Some distributions are skewed toward higher scores, others toward lower scores. How would the proportions in the five cognitive classes differ for an IQ distribution that is skewed right? Skewed left?

4.68 Find each of the following probabilities for the standard normal random variable z:
a. $P(-1 \le z \le 1)$ **b.** $P(-1.96 \le z \le 1.96)$
c. $P(-1.645 \le z \le 1.645)$ **d.** $P(-2 \le z \le 2)$

4.69 Find a value of the standard normal random variable z, call it z_0, such that
a. $P(z \ge z_0) = .05$ **b.** $P(z \ge z_0) = .025$
c. $P(z \le z_0) = .025$ **d.** $P(z \ge z_0) = .10$
e. $P(z > z_0) = .10$

4.70 Find a value of the standard normal random variable z, call it z_0, such that
a. $P(z \le z_0) = .2090$ **b.** $P(z \le z_0) = .7090$
c. $P(-z_0 \le z < z_0) = .8472$
d. $P(-z_0 \le z \le z_0) = .1664$
e. $P(z_0 \le z \le 0) = .4798$
f. $P(-1 < z < z_0) = .5328$

4.71 Suppose the random variable x is best described by a normal distribution with $\mu = 30$ and $\sigma = 4$. Find the z-score that corresponds to each of the following x values:
a. $x = 20$ **b.** $x = 30$ **c.** $x = 27.5$
d. $x = 15$ **e.** $x = 35$ **f.** $x = 25$

4.72 The random variable x has a normal distribution with $\mu = 1{,}000$ and $\sigma = 10$.

a. Find the probability that x assumes a value more than 2 standard deviations from its mean. More than 3 standard deviations from μ.
b. Find the probability that x assumes a value within 1 standard deviation of its mean. Within 2 standard deviations of μ.
c. Find the value of x that represents the 80th percentile of this distribution. The 10th percentile.

4.73 Suppose x is a normally distributed random variable with $\mu = 11$ and $\sigma = 2$. Find each of the following:
a. $P(10 \le x \le 12)$ **b.** $P(6 \le x \le 10)$
c. $P(13 \le x \le 16)$ **d.** $P(7.8 \le x \le 12.6)$
e. $P(x \ge 13.24)$ **f.** $P(x \ge 7.62)$

4.74 Suppose x is a normally distributed random variable with $\mu = 50$ and $\sigma = 3$. Find a value of the random variable, call it x_0, such that
a. $P(x \le x_0) = .8413$ **b.** $P(x > x_0) = .025$
c. $P(x > x_0) = .95$ **d.** $P(41 \le x < x_0) = .8630$
e. 10% of the values of x are less than x_0.
f. 1% of the values of x are greater than x_0.

4.75 Suppose x is a normally distributed random variable with mean 120 and variance 36. Draw a rough graph of the distribution of x. Locate μ and the interval $\mu \pm 2\sigma$ on the graph. Find the following probabilities:

a. $P(\mu - 2\sigma \leqslant x \leqslant \mu + 2\sigma)$ **b.** $P(x \geqslant 128)$
c. $P(x \leqslant 108)$ **d.** $P(112 \leqslant x \leqslant 130)$
e. $P(114 \leqslant x \leqslant 116)$ **f.** $P(115 \leqslant x \leqslant 128)$

4.76   The random variable x has a normal distribution with standard deviation 25. It is known that the probability that x exceeds 150 is .90. Find the mean μ of the probability distribution.

Applying the Concepts

4.77   It is vitally important for airlines to appropriately match aircraft to passenger demand on each flight leg. This is called the **flight assignment problem**. If the aircraft is too large, the result is empty seats and, therefore, lost revenue; if the aircraft is too small, business is lost to other airlines. **Spill** is defined as the number of passengers not carried because the aircraft's capacity is insufficient. A solution to the flight assignment problem at Delta Airlines was published in *Interfaces* (Jan.–Feb. 1994). The authors—four Delta Airlines researchers and a Georgia Tech professor (Roy Marsten)—demonstrated their approach with an example in which passenger demand for a particular flight leg is normally distributed with a mean of 125 passengers and a standard deviation of 45. Consider a Boeing 727 with a capacity of 148 passengers and a Boeing 757 with a capacity of 182.

a. What is the probability that passenger demand will exceed the capacity of the Boeing 727? The Boeing 757?
b. If the 727 is assigned to the flight leg, what is the probability that the flight will depart with one or more empty seats? Answer the same question for the Boeing 757.
c. If the 727 is assigned to the flight, what is the probability that the spill will be more than 100 passengers?

4.78   Ideally, a worker seeking a new job in a particular industry should acquire information about wage rates offered by all firms in the industry. However, workers may not find it worthwhile to search until they find the highest available wage rate. The result is that managers may not have to pay top dollar to attract workers. These factors help to explain the existing disparity in wage rates among firms. The latest government data indicate that the mean hourly wage for manufacturing workers in the United States is $13.69 (*Statistical Abstract of the United States: 1995*). Suppose the distribution of manufacturing wage rates nationwide can be approximated by a normal distribution with standard deviation $1.25 per hour. The first manufacturing firm contacted by a particular worker pays $15.00 per hour.

a. If the worker were to undertake a nationwide job search, approximately what proportion of the wage rates would be greater than $15.00 per hour?
b. If the worker were to randomly select a U.S. manufacturing firm, what is the probability the firm would pay more than $15.00 per hour?
c. The population median, call it η, of a continuous random variable x is the value such that $P(x \geqslant \eta) = P(x \leqslant \eta) = .5$. That is, the median is the value η such that half the area under the probability distribution lies above η and half lies below it. Find the median of the random variable corresponding to the wage rate and compare it to the mean wage rate.

4.79   In studying the dynamics of fish populations, knowing the length of a species at different ages is critical, especially for commercial fishermen. *Fisheries Science* (Feb. 1995) published a study of the length distributions of sardines inhabiting Japanese waters. At two years of age, fish have a length distribution that is approximately normal with $\mu = 20.20$ centimeters (cm) and $\sigma = .65$ cm.

a. Find the probability that a two-year-old sardine inhabiting Japanese waters is between 20 and 21 cm long.
b. A sardine captured in Japanese waters has a length of 19.84 cm. Is this sardine likely to be two years old?
c. Repeat part **b** for a sardine with a length of 22.01 cm.

4.80   Personnel tests are designed to test a job applicant's cognitive and/or physical abilities. An IQ test is an example of the former; a speed test involving the arrangement of pegs on a peg board is an example of the latter (Cowling and James, *The Essence of Personnel Management and Industrial Relations*, 1994). A particular dexterity test is administered nationwide by a private testing service. It is known that for all tests administered last year the distribution of scores was approximately normal with mean 75 and standard deviation 7.5.

a. A particular employer requires job candidates to score at least 80 on the dexterity test. Approximately what percentage of the test scores during the past year exceeded 80?
b. The testing service reported to a particular employer that one of its job candidate's scores fell at the 98th percentile of the distribution (i.e., approximately 98% of the scores were lower than the candidate's, and only 2% were higher). What was the candidate's score?

4.81   In baseball, a "no-hitter" is a regulation 9-inning game in which the pitcher yields no hits to the opposing batters. *Chance* (Summer 1994) reported on a study of no-hitters in Major League Baseball

(MLB). The initial analysis focused on the total number of hits yielded per game per team for all 9-inning MLB games played between 1989 and 1993. The distribution of hits/9-innings is approximately normal with mean 8.72 and standard deviation 1.10.

a. What percentage of 9-inning MLB games result in fewer than 6 hits?

b. Demonstrate, statistically, why a no-hitter is considered an extremely rare occurrence in MLB.

4.82 Before negotiating a long-term construction contract, building contractors must carefully estimate the total cost of completing the project and, thereafter, determine the price they would need to charge in order to make a reasonable profit. The process is complicated by the fact that total cost cannot be known with certainty ahead of time. Wages, salaries, the price of materials, the time to complete the job, etc. are all subject to change. Benzion Barlev of New York University proposed a model for total cost of a long-term contract based on the normal distribution (*Journal of Business Finance and Accounting,* July 1995). For one particular construction contract, Barlev assumed total cost, x, to be normally distributed with mean $850,000 and standard deviation $170,000. The revenue, R, promised to the contractor is $1,000,000.

a. The contract will be profitable if revenue exceeds total cost. What is the probability that the contract will be profitable for the contractor?

b. What is the probability that the project will result in a loss for the contractor?

c. Suppose the contractor has the opportunity to renegotiate the contract. What value of R should the contractor strive for in order to have a .99 probability of making a profit?

4.83 A machine used to regulate the amount of dye dispensed for mixing shades of paint can be set so that it discharges an average of μ milliliters (mL) of dye per can of paint. The amount of dye discharged is known to have a normal distribution with a standard deviation of .4 mL. If more than 6 mL of dye are discharged when making a certain shade of blue paint, the shade is unacceptable. Determine the setting for μ so that only 1% of the cans of paint will be unacceptable.

4.84 An important quality characteristic for soft-drink bottlers is the amount of soft drink injected into each bottle. This volume is determined (approximately) by measuring the height of the soft drink in the neck of the bottle and comparing it to a scale that converts the height measurement to a volume measurement (Montgomery, *Introduction to Statistical Quality Control,* 1991). In a particular filling process, the number of ounces injected into 8-ounce bottles is approximately normally distributed with mean 8.00 ounces and standard deviation .05 ounce. Bottles that contain less than 7.9 ounces do not meet the bottle's quality standard and are sold at a substantial discount.

a. If 20,000 bottles are filled, approximately how many will fail to meet the quality standard?

b. Suppose that, due to the failure of one of the filling system's components, the mean of the filling process shifts to 7.95 ounces. (Assume that the standard deviation remains .05 ounce.) If 20,000 bottles are filled, approximately how many will fail to meet the quality standard?

c. Suppose that a different component fails and, although the mean of the filling process remains 8.00 ounces, the standard deviation increases to .1 ounce. If 20,000 bottles are filled, approximately how many will fail to meet the quality standard?

4.85 Do security analysts do a good job of forecasting corporate earnings growth and advising their clientele? This question was addressed in an article titled "Astrology might be better" (*Forbes,* Mar. 26, 1984). The basis of the article is a study by Professors Michael Sandretto of Harvard and Sudhir Milkrishnamurthi of the Massachusetts Institute of Technology. The study surveys security analysts' forecasts of annual earnings for the (then) current year for more than 769 companies with five or more forecasts per company per year. The average forecast error for this large number of forecasts was 31.3%. To apply this information to a practical situation, suppose the population of analysts' forecast errors is normally distributed with a mean of 31.3% and a standard deviation of 10%.

a. If you obtain a security analyst's forecast for a particular company, what is the probability that it will be in error by more than 50%?

b. If three analysts make the forecast, what is the probability that at least one of the analysts will err by more than 50%?

4.8 THE EXPONENTIAL DISTRIBUTION (OPTIONAL)

The length of time between arrivals at a fast-food drive-through restaurant, the length of time between breakdowns of manufacturing equipment, and the length of time between filings of claims in a small insurance office are all business phenomena that we might want to describe probabilistically. The amount of time between

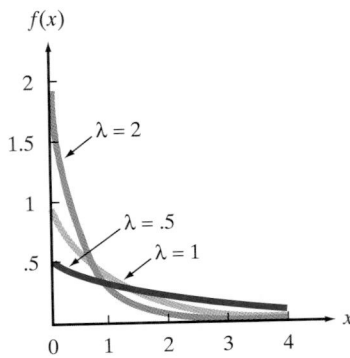

FIGURE 4.28
Exponential distributions

occurrences of random events like these can often be described by the **exponential probability distribution**. For this reason, the exponential distribution is sometimes called the **waiting time distribution**. The formula for the exponential probability distribution is shown in the box along with its mean and standard deviation.

Probability Distribution, Mean, and Standard Deviation for an Exponential Random Variable x

$$f(x) = \lambda e^{-\lambda x} \qquad (x > 0)$$

$$\mu = \frac{1}{\lambda}$$

$$\sigma = \frac{1}{\lambda}$$

Unlike the normal distribution which has a shape and location determined by the values of the two quantities μ and σ, the shape of the exponential distribution is governed by a single quantity, λ. Further, it is a probability distribution with the property that its mean equals its standard deviation. Exponential distributions corresponding to $\lambda = .5, 1,$ and 2 are shown in Figure 4.28.

To calculate probabilities for exponential random variables, we need to be able to find areas under the exponential probability distribution. Suppose we want to find the area A to the right of some number a, as shown in Figure 4.29. This area can be calculated by using the following formula:

Finding the Area A to the Right of a Number *a* for an Exponential Distribution*

$$A = P(x \geq a) = e^{-\lambda a}$$

Use Table V in Appendix B or a pocket calculator with an exponential function to find the value of $e^{-\lambda a}$ after substituting the appropriate numerical values for λ and a.

---

*For students with a knowledge of calculus, the shaded area in Figure 4.29 corresponds to the integral

$$\int_a^\infty \lambda e^{-\lambda x}\, dx = \left. -e^{-\lambda x}\right|_a^\infty = e^{-\lambda a}$$

FIGURE 4.29

The area A to the right of a number a for an exponential distribution

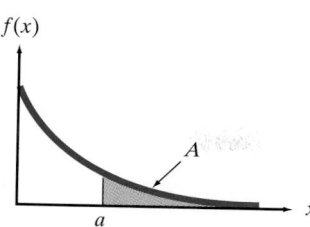

EXAMPLE 4.23

Suppose the length of time (in days) between sales for an automobile salesperson is modeled as an exponential distribution with $\lambda = .5$. What is the probability the salesperson goes more than 5 days without a sale?

SOLUTION

The probability we want is the area A to the right of $a = 5$ in Figure 4.30. To find this probability, use the formula given for area:

$$A = e^{-\lambda a} = e^{-(.5)5} = e^{-2.5}$$

Referring to Table V, we find

$$A = e^{-2.5} = .082085$$

Our exponential model indicates that the probability of going more than 5 days without a sale is about .08 for this automobile salesperson.

EXAMPLE 4.24

A microwave oven manufacturer is trying to determine the length of warranty period it should attach to its magnetron tube, the most critical component in the oven. Preliminary testing has shown that the length of life (in years), x, of a magnetron tube has an exponential probability distribution with $\lambda = .16$.

a. Find the mean and standard deviation of x.

b. Suppose a warranty period of 5 years is attached to the magnetron tube. What fraction of tubes must the manufacturer plan to replace, assuming that the exponential model with $\lambda = .16$ is correct?

c. Find the probability that the length of life of a magnetron tube will fall within the interval $\mu - 2\sigma$ to $\mu + 2\sigma$.

SOLUTION

a. For this exponential random variable, $\mu = 1/\lambda = 1/.16 = 6.25$ years. Also, since $\mu = \sigma$, $\sigma = 6.25$ years.

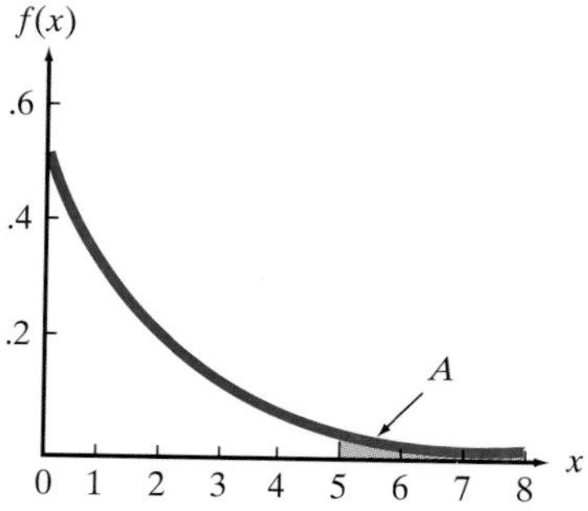

FIGURE 4.30

Area to the right of $a = 5$ for Example 4.23

FIGURE 4.31
Area to the left of
$a = 5$ for Example 4.24

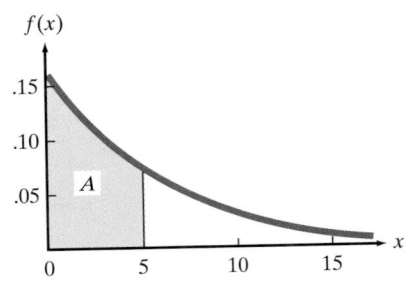

b. To find the fraction of tubes that will have to be replaced before the 5-year warranty period expires, we need to find the area between 0 and 5 under the distribution. This area, A, is shown in Figure 4.31.

To find the required probability, we recall the formula

$$P(x > a) = e^{-\lambda a}$$

Using this formula, we can find

$$P(x > 5) = e^{-\lambda(5)} = e^{-(.16)(5)} = e^{-.80} = .449329$$

(see Table V). To find the area A, we use the complementary relationship:

$$P(x \leq 5) = 1 - P(x > 5) = 1 - .449329 = .550671$$

So approximately 55% of the magnetron tubes will have to be replaced during the 5-year warranty period.

c. We would expect the probability that the life of a magnetron tube, x, falls within the interval $\mu - 2\sigma$ to $\mu + 2\sigma$ to be quite large. A graph of the exponential distribution showing the interval $\mu - 2\sigma$ to $\mu + 2\sigma$ is given in Figure 4.32. Since the point $\mu - 2\sigma$ lies below $x = 0$, we need to find only the area between $x = 0$ and $x = \mu + 2\sigma = 6.25 + 2(6.25) = 18.75$. This area, P, which is shaded in Figure 4.32, is

$$P = 1 - P(x > 18.75) = 1 - e^{-\lambda(18.75)} = 1 - e^{-(.16)(18.75)} = 1 - e^{-3}$$

Using Table V or a calculator, we find $e^{-3} = .049787$. Therefore, the probability that the life x of a magnetron tube will fall within the interval $\mu - 2\sigma$ to $\mu + 2\sigma$ is

$$P = 1 - e^{-3} = 1 - .049787 = .950213$$

FIGURE 4.32
Area in the interval
$\mu \pm 2\sigma$ for
Example 4.24

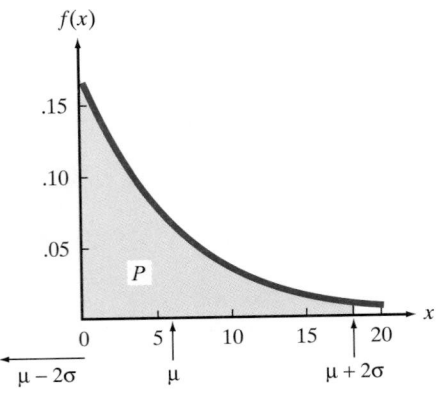

You can see that this probability agrees very well with the Empirical Rule even though this probability distribution is not mound-shaped. (It is strongly skewed to the right.)

EXERCISES 4.86–4.97

Learning the Mechanics

4.86 The random variables x and y have exponential distributions with $\lambda = 3$ and $\lambda = .75$, respectively. Using Table V in Appendix B, carefully plot both distributions on the same set of axes.

4.87 Use Table V in Appendix B to determine the value of $e^{-\lambda a}$ for each of the following cases.
   a. $\lambda = 1, a = 1$ **b.** $\lambda = 1, a = 2.5$
   c. $\lambda = 2.5, a = 3$ **d.** $\lambda = 5, a = .3$

4.88 Suppose x has an exponential distribution with $\lambda = 3$. Find the following probabilities:
   a. $P(x > 2)$ **b.** $P(x > 1.5)$ **c.** $P(x > 3)$
   d. $P(x > .45)$

4.89 Suppose x has an exponential distribution with $\lambda = 2.5$. Find the following probabilities:
   a. $P(x \leq 3)$ **b.** $P(x \leq 4)$ **c.** $P(x \leq 1.6)$
   d. $P(x \leq .4)$

4.90 Suppose the random variable x has an exponential probability distribution with $\lambda = 2$. Find the mean and standard deviation of x. Find the probability that x will assume a value within the interval $\mu \pm 2\sigma$.

4.91 The random variable x can be adequately approximated by an exponential probability distribution with $\lambda = 1$. Find the probability that x assumes a value
   a. More than 3 standard deviations from μ.
   b. Less than 2 standard deviations from μ.
   c. Within .5 standard deviation of μ.

Applying the Concepts

4.92 Cargo transported by ship is normally delivered directly to a pier in the receiving port. However, lack of port facilities or shallow water may require cargo to be transferred at sea to smaller craft that deliver the cargo to shore. This process may require the smaller craft to cycle back and forth from ship to shore many times. Queueing of these craft may occur at either the ship or the pier or both. Researchers G. Horne (Center for Naval Analysis) and T. Irony (George Washington University) developed models of this transfer process that provide estimates of ship-to-shore transfer times (*Naval Research Logistics*, Vol. 41, 1994). They modeled the time between arrivals of the smaller craft at the pier using an exponential distribution.

   a. Assume the mean time between arrivals at the pier is 17 minutes. Give the value of λ for this exponential distribution. Graph the distribution.
   b. Suppose there is only one unloading zone at the pier available for the small craft to use. If the first craft docks at 10:00 A.M. and doesn't finish unloading until 10:15 A.M., what is the probability that the second craft will arrive at the unloading zone and have to wait before docking?

4.93 In the National Hockey League (NHL), games that are tied at the end of three periods are sent to "sudden-death" overtime. In overtime, the team to score the first goal wins. An analysis of all NHL overtime games played between 1970 and 1993 showed that the length of time elapsed before the winning goal is scored has an exponential distribution with mean 9.15 minutes (*Chance*, Winter 1995).
   a. For a randomly selected overtime NHL game, find the probability that the winning goal is scored in three minutes or less.
   b. In the NHL, each period (including overtime) lasts 20 minutes. If neither team scores a goal in overtime, the game is considered a tie. What is the probability of an NHL game ending in a tie?

4.94 A part processed in a flexible manufacturing system (FMS) is routed through a set of operations, some of which are sequential and some of which are parallel. In addition, an FMS operation can be processed by alternative machines. An article in *IEEE Transactions* (Mar. 1990) gave an example of an FMS with four machines operating independently. The repair rates for the machines (i.e., the time, in hours, it takes to repair a failed machine) are exponentially distributed with means $\mu_1 = 1, \mu_2 = 2, \mu_3 = .5$, and $\mu_4 = .5$, respectively.
   a. Find the probability that the repair time for machine 1 exceeds one hour.
   b. Repeat part **a** for machine 2.
   c. Repeat part **a** for machines 3 and 4.
   d. If all four machines fail simultaneously, find the probability that the repair time for the entire system exceeds one hour.

4.95 **Product reliability** has been defined as the probability that a product will perform its intended function satisfactorily for its intended life when operating under specified conditions. The **reliabil-**

ity function, $R(x)$, for a product indicates the probability of the product's life exceeding x time periods. When the time until failure of a product can be adequately modeled by an exponential distribution, the product's reliability function is $R(x) = e^{-\lambda x}$ (Ross, *Stochastic Processes,* 1996). Suppose that the time to failure (in years) of a particular product is modeled by an exponential distribution with $\lambda = .5$.

a. What is the product's reliability function?

b. What is the probability that the product will perform satisfactorily for at least four years?

c. What is the probability that a particular product will survive longer than the mean life of the product?

d. If λ changes, will the probability that you calculated in part **c** change? Explain.

e. If 10,000 units of the product are sold, approximately how many will perform satisfactorily for more than five years? About how many will fail within one year?

f. How long should the length of the warranty period be for the product if the manufacturer wants to replace no more than 5% of the units sold while under warranty?

4.96 A taxi service based at an airport can be characterized as a transportation system with one source terminal and a fleet of vehicles. Each vehicle takes passengers from the terminal to different destinations; then it returns to the terminal after some random trip time and makes another trip. To improve the vehicle-dispatching decisions involved in such a system (e.g., How many passengers should be allocated to a waiting taxi?), a study was conducted and published in the *European Journal of Operational Research* (Vol. 21, 1985). In modeling the system, the authors assumed travel times of successive trips to be independent exponential random variables. Assume $\lambda = .05$.

a. What is the mean trip time for the taxi service?

b. What is the probability that a particular trip will take more than 30 minutes?

c. Two taxis have just been dispatched. What is the probability that both will be gone for more than 30 minutes? That at least one of the taxis will return within 30 minutes?

4.97 The importance of modeling machine downtime correctly in simulation studies was discussed in *Industrial Engineering* (Aug. 1990). The paper presented simulation results for a single-machine-tool system with the following properties:

- The interarrival times of jobs are exponentially distributed with a mean of 1.25 minutes

- The amount of time the machine operates before breaking down is exponentially distributed with a mean of 540 minutes

a. Find the probability that two jobs arrive for processing at most one minute apart.

b. Find the probability that the machine operates for at least 720 minutes (12 hours) before breaking down.

4.9 SAMPLING DISTRIBUTIONS

In previous sections we assumed that we knew the probability distribution of a random variable, and using this knowledge we were able to compute the mean, variance, and probabilities associated with the random variable. However, in most practical applications, the true mean and standard deviation are unknown quantities that would have to be estimated. Numerical quantities that describe probability distributions are called *parameters*. Thus, p, the probability of a success in a binomial experiment, and μ and σ, the mean and standard deviation of a normal distribution, are examples of parameters.

DEFINITION 4.9

A **parameter** is a numerical descriptive measure of a population. Because it is based on the observations in the population, its value is almost always unknown.

We have also discussed the sample mean $\bar{x}$, sample variance s^2, sample standard deviation s, etc., which are numerical descriptive measures calculated from the sample. We will often use the information contained in these *sample statistics* to make inferences about the parameters of a population.

> **DEFINITION 4.10**
> A **sample statistic** is a numerical descriptive measure of a sample. It is calculated from the observations in the sample.

Note that the term *statistic* refers to a *sample* quantity and the term *parameter* refers to a *population* quantity.

Before we can show you how to use sample statistics to make inferences about population parameters, we need to be able to evaluate their properties. Does one sample statistic contain more information than another about a population parameter? On what basis should we choose the "best" statistic for making inferences about a parameter? If we want to estimate, for example, the population mean μ, we could use a number of sample statistics for our estimate. Two possibilities are the sample mean $\bar{x}$ and the sample median m. Which of these do you think will provide a better estimate of μ?

Before answering this question, consider the following example: Toss a fair die, and let x equal the number of dots showing on the up face. Suppose the die is tossed three times, producing the sample measurements 2, 2, 6. The sample mean is $\bar{x} = 3.33$ and the sample median is $m = 2$. Since the population mean of x is $\mu = 3.5$, you can see that for this sample of three measurements, the sample mean $\bar{x}$ provides an estimate that falls closer to μ than does the sample median (see Figure 4.33a). Now suppose we toss the die three more times and obtain the sample measurements 3, 4, 6. The mean and median of this sample are $\bar{x} = 4.33$ and $m = 4$, respectively. This time m is closer to μ (see Figure 4.33b).

This simple example illustrates an important point: Neither the sample mean nor the sample median will *always* fall closer to the population mean. Consequently, we cannot compare these two sample statistics, or, in general, any two sample statistics, on the basis of their performance for a single sample. Instead, we need to recognize that sample statistics are themselves random variables, because different samples can lead to different values for the sample statistics. As random variables, sample statistics must be judged and compared on the basis of their probability distributions, i.e., the *collection* of values and associated probabilities of each statistic that would be obtained if the sampling experiment were repeated a *very large number of times*. We will illustrate this concept with another example.

Suppose it is known that the connector module manufactured for a certain brand of pacemaker has a mean length of $\mu = .3$ inch and a standard deviation of .005 inch. Consider an experiment consisting of randomly selecting 25 recently manufactured connector modules, measuring the length of each, and calculating the sample mean length $\bar{x}$. If this experiment were repeated a very large number of times, the value of $\bar{x}$ would vary from sample to sample. For example, the first sample of 25 length measurements might have a mean $\bar{x} = .301$, the second sample a mean $\bar{x} = .298$, the third sample a mean $\bar{x} = .303$, etc. If the sampling experiment were repeated a very large number of times, the resulting histogram of sample means would be approximately the probability distribution of $\bar{x}$. If $\bar{x}$ is a

FIGURE 4.33
Comparing the sample mean ($\bar{x}$) and sample median (m) as estimators of the population mean (μ)

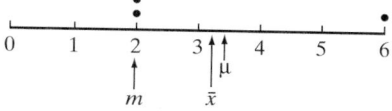

a. Sample 1: $\bar{x}$ is closer than m to μ

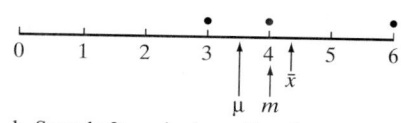

b. Sample 2: m is closer than $\bar{x}$ to μ

FIGURE 4.34
Sampling distribution
for $\bar{x}$ based on a
sample of $n = 25$
length measurements

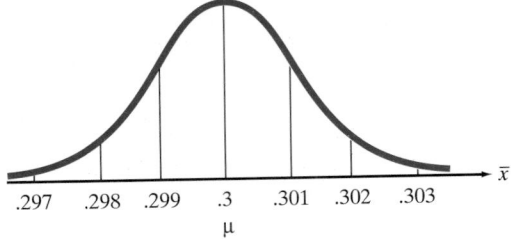

.297   .298   .299   .3   .301   .302   .303
μ

good estimator of μ, we would expect the values of $\bar{x}$ to cluster around μ as shown in Figure 4.34. This probability distribution is called a *sampling distribution* because it is generated by repeating a sampling experiment a very large number of times.

DEFINITION 4.11

The **sampling distribution** of a sample statistic calculated from a sample of n measurements is the probability distribution of the statistic.

In actual practice, the sampling distribution of a statistic is obtained mathematically or (at least approximately) by simulating the sample on a computer using a procedure similar to that just described.

If $\bar{x}$ has been calculated from a sample of $n = 25$ measurements selected from a population with mean $\mu = .3$ and standard deviation $\sigma = .005$, the sampling distribution (Figure 4.34) provides information about the behavior of $\bar{x}$ in repeated sampling. For example, the probability that you will draw a sample of 25 length measurements and obtain a value of $\bar{x}$ in the interval $.299 \leqslant \bar{x} \leqslant .3$ will be the area under the sampling distribution over that interval.

Since the properties of a statistic are typified by its sampling distribution, it follows that to compare two sample statistics you compare their sampling distributions. For example, if you have two statistics, A and B, for estimating the same parameter (for purposes of illustration, suppose the parameter is the population variance σ^2) and if their sampling distributions are as shown in Figure 4.35, you would choose statistic A in preference to statistic B. You would make this choice because the sampling distribution for statistic A centers over σ^2 and has less spread (variation) than the sampling distribution for statistic B. When you draw a single sample in a practical sampling situation, the probability is higher that statistic A will fall nearer σ^2.

Remember that in practice we will not know the numerical value of the unknown parameter σ^2, so we will not know whether statistic A or statistic B is closer to σ^2 for a sample. We have to rely on our knowledge of the theoretical

FIGURE 4.35
Two sampling
distributions for
estimating the
population variance, σ^2

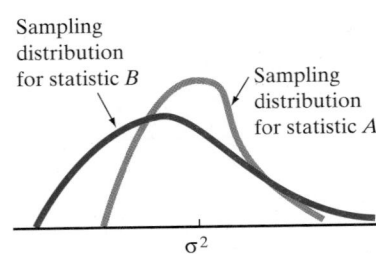

Sampling
distribution
for statistic B

Sampling
distribution
for statistic A

σ^2

TABLE 4.6   All Possible Samples of n = 3 Measurements, Example 4.25

Possible Samples	$\bar{x}$	m	Probability
0, 0, 0	0	0	$1/27$
0, 0, 3	1	0	$1/27$
0, 0, 12	4	0	$1/27$
0, 3, 0	1	0	$1/27$
0, 3, 3	2	3	$1/27$
0, 3, 12	5	3	$1/27$
0, 12, 0	4	0	$1/27$
0, 12, 3	5	3	$1/27$
0, 12, 12	8	12	$1/27$
3, 0, 0	1	0	$1/27$
3, 0, 3	2	3	$1/27$
3, 0, 12	5	3	$1/27$
3, 3, 0	2	3	$1/27$
3, 3, 3	3	3	$1/27$
3, 3, 12	6	3	$1/27$
3, 12, 0	5	3	$1/27$
3, 12, 3	6	3	$1/27$
3, 12, 12	9	12	$1/27$
12, 0, 0	4	0	$1/27$
12, 0, 3	5	3	$1/27$
12, 0, 12	8	12	$1/27$
12, 3, 0	5	3	$1/27$
12, 3, 3	6	3	$1/27$
12, 3, 12	9	12	$1/27$
12, 12, 0	8	12	$1/27$
12, 12, 3	9	12	$1/27$
12, 12, 12	12	12	$1/27$

sampling distributions to choose the best sample statistic and then use it sample after sample. The procedure for finding the sampling distribution for a statistic is demonstrated in the next example.

 **EXAMPLE 4.25**

Consider a population consisting of the measurements 0, 3, and 12 and described by the probability distribution shown here. A random sample of $n = 3$ measurements is selected from the population.

a. Find the sampling distribution of the sample mean $\bar{x}$.

b. Find the sampling distribution of the sample median m.

x	0	3	12
$p(x)$	$1/3$	$1/3$	$1/3$

SOLUTION

Every possible sample of $n = 3$ measurements is listed in Table 4.6 along with the sample mean and median. Also, because any one sample is as likely to be selected as any other (random sampling), the probability of observing any particular sample is $1/27$. The probability is also listed in Table 4.6.

a. From Table 4.6 you can see that $\bar{x}$ can assume the values 0, 1, 2, 3, 4, 5, 6, 8, 9, and 12. Because $\bar{x} = 0$ occurs in only one sample, $P(\bar{x} = 0) = 1/27$. Similarly, $\bar{x} = 1$ occurs in three samples: (0, 0, 3) (0, 3, 0), and (3, 0, 0). Therefore, $P(\bar{x} = 1) = 3/27 = 1/9$. Calculating the probabilities of the remaining values of

$\bar{x}$ and arranging them in a table, we obtain the probability distribution shown here.

x	0	1	2	3	4	5	6	8	9	12
$p(\bar{x})$	$1/27$	$3/27$	$3/27$	$1/27$	$3/27$	$6/27$	$3/27$	$3/27$	$3/27$	$1/27$

This is the sampling distribution for $\bar{x}$ because it specifies the probability associated with each possible value of $\bar{x}$.

b. In Table 4.6 you can see that the median m can assume one of the three values 0, 3, or 12. The value $m = 0$ occurs in seven different samples. Therefore, $P(m = 0) = 7/27$. Similarly, $m = 3$ occurs in 13 samples and $m = 12$ occurs in seven samples. Therefore, the probability distribution (i.e., the sampling distribution) for the median m is as shown below.

m	0	3	12
$p(m)$	$7/27$	$13/27$	$7/27$

Example 4.25 demonstrates the procedure for finding the exact sampling distribution of a statistic when the number of different samples that could be selected from the population is relatively small. In the real world, populations often consist of a large number of different values, making samples difficult (or impossible) to enumerate. When this situation occurs, we may choose to obtain the approximate sampling distribution for a statistic by simulating the sampling over and over again and recording the proportion of times different values of the statistic occur. Example 4.26 illustrates this procedure.

EXAMPLE 4.26

Suppose we perform the following experiment over and over again: Take a sample of 11 measurements from the distribution shown in Figure 4.36. This distribution, known as the **uniform distribution**, was discussed in optional Section 4.6. Calculate the two sample statistics

$$\bar{x} = \text{Sample mean} = \frac{\sum x}{11}$$

$m = \text{Median} = \text{Sixth sample measurement when the 11 measurements are arranged in ascending order}$

Obtain approximations to the sampling distributions of $\bar{x}$ and m.

$f(x)$

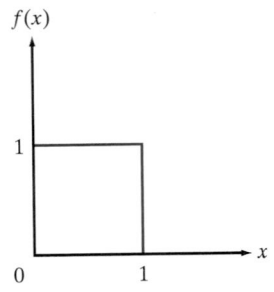

FIGURE 4.36
Uniform distribution from 0 to 1

SOLUTION
We use a computer to generate 1,000 samples, each with $n = 11$ observations. Then we compute $\bar{x}$ and m for each sample. Our goal is to obtain approximations to the sampling distributions of $\bar{x}$ and m to find out which sample statistic ($\bar{x}$ or m) contains more information about μ. [*Note:* In this particular example, we *know* the population mean is $\mu = .5$. (See optional Section 4.6.)] The first 10 of the 1,000 samples generated are presented in Table 4.7. For instance, the first computer-generated sample from the uniform distribution (arranged in ascending order) contained the following measurements: .125, .138, .139, .217, .419, .506, .516, .757, .771, .786, and .919. The sample mean $\bar{x}$ and median m computed for this sample are

TABLE 4.7   First 10 Samples of n = 11 Measurements from a Uniform Distribution

Sample	Measurements										
1	.217	.786	.757	.125	.139	.919	.506	.771	.138	.516	.419
2	.303	.703	.812	.650	.848	.392	.988	.469	.632	.012	.065
3	.383	.547	.383	.584	.098	.676	.091	.535	.256	.163	.390
4	.218	.376	.248	.606	.610	.055	.095	.311	.086	.165	.665
5	.144	.069	.485	.739	.491	.054	.953	.179	.865	.429	.648
6	.426	.563	.186	.896	.628	.075	.283	.549	.295	.522	.674
7	.643	.828	.465	.672	.074	.300	.319	.254	.708	.384	.534
8	.616	.049	.324	.700	.803	.399	.557	.975	.569	.023	.072
9	.093	.835	.534	.212	.201	.041	.889	.728	.466	.142	.574
10	.957	.253	.983	.904	.696	.766	.880	.485	.035	.881	.732

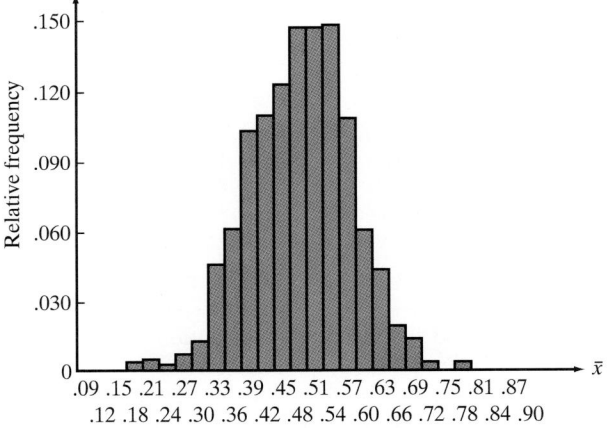

a. Sampling distribution for $\bar{x}$ (based on 1,000 samples of $n = 11$ measurements)

b. Sampling distribution for m (based on 1,000 samples of $n = 11$ measurements)

FIGURE 4.37   Relative frequency histograms for $\bar{x}$ and m, Example 4.26

$$x = \frac{.125 + .138 + \cdots + .919}{11} = .481$$

$$m = \text{Sixth ordered measurement} = .506$$

The relative frequency histograms for $\bar{x}$ and m for the 1,000 samples of size $n = 11$ are shown in Figure 4.37.

You can see that the values of $\bar{x}$ tend to cluster around μ to a greater extent than do the values of m. Thus, on the basis of the observed sampling distributions, we conclude that $\bar{x}$ contains more information about μ than m does—at least for samples of $n = 11$ measurements from the uniform distribution.   ◤

As noted earlier, many sampling distributions can be derived mathematically, but the theory necessary to do this is beyond the scope of this text. Consequently, when we need to know the properties of a statistic, we will present its sampling distribution and simply describe its properties. An important sampling distribution, the sampling distribution of $\bar{x}$, is discussed in the next section.

EXERCISES 4.98–4.104

Note: Exercises marked with 💾 *require the use of a computer.*

Learning the Mechanics

4.98 The probability distribution shown here describes a population of measurements that can assume values of 0, 2, 4, and 6, each of which occurs with the same relative frequency:

x	0	2	4	6
$p(x)$	$\frac{1}{4}$	$\frac{1}{4}$	$\frac{1}{4}$	$\frac{1}{4}$

a. List all the different samples of $n = 2$ measurements that can be selected from this population.
b. Calculate the mean of each different sample listed in part **a**.
c. If a sample of $n = 2$ measurements is randomly selected from the population, what is the probability that a specific sample will be selected?
d. Assume that a random sample of $n = 2$ measurements is selected from the population. List the different values of $\bar{x}$ found in part **b**, and find the probability of each. Then give the sampling distribution of the sample mean $\bar{x}$ in tabular form.
e. Construct a probability histogram for the sampling distribution of $\bar{x}$.

4.99 Simulate sampling from the population described in Exercise 4.98 by marking the values of x, one on each of four identical coins (or poker chips, etc.). Place the coins (marked 0, 2, 4, and 6) into a bag, randomly select one, and observe its value. Replace this coin, draw a second coin, and observe its value. Finally, calculate the mean $\bar{x}$ for this sample of $n = 2$ observations randomly selected from the population (Exercise 4.98, part **b**). Replace the coins, mix, and using the same procedure, select a sample of $n = 2$ observations from the population. Record the numbers and calculate $\bar{x}$ for this sample. Repeat this sampling process until you acquire 100 values of $\bar{x}$. Construct a relative frequency distribution for these 100 sample means. Compare this distribution to the exact sampling distribution of $\bar{x}$ found in part **e** of Exercise 4.98. [*Note:* The distribution obtained in this exercise is an approximation to the exact sampling distribution. But, if you were to repeat the sampling procedure, drawing two coins not 100 times but 10,000 times, the relative frequency distribution for the 10,000 sample means would be almost identical to the sampling distribution of $\bar{x}$ found in Exercise 4.98, part **e**.]

4.100 Consider the population described by the probability distribution shown here.

x	1	2	3	4	5
$p(x)$	.2	.3	.2	.2	.1

The random variable x is observed twice. If these observations are independent, verify that the different samples of size 2 and their probabilities are as shown here.

Sample	Probability	Sample	Probability
1, 1	.04	3, 4	.04
1, 2	.06	3, 5	.02
1, 3	.04	4, 1	.04
1, 4	.04	4, 2	.06
1, 5	.02	4, 3	.04
2, 1	.06	4, 4	.04
2, 2	.09	4, 5	.02
2, 3	.06	5, 1	.02
2, 4	.06	5, 2	.03
2, 5	.03	5, 3	.02
3, 1	.04	5, 4	.02
3, 2	.06	5, 5	.01
3, 3	.04		

a. Find the sampling distribution of the sample mean $\bar{x}$.
b. Construct a probability histogram for the sampling distribution of $\bar{x}$.
c. What is the probability that $\bar{x}$ is 4.5 or larger?
d. Would you expect to observe a value of $\bar{x}$ equal to 4.5 or larger? Explain.

4.101 Refer to Exercise 4.100 and find $E(x) = \mu$. Then use the sampling distribution of $\bar{x}$ found in Exercise 4.100 to find the expected value of $\bar{x}$. Note that $E(\bar{x}) = \mu$.

4.102 Refer to Exercise 4.100. Assume that a random sample of $n = 2$ measurements is randomly selected from the population.
a. List the different values that the sample median m may assume and find the probability of each. Then give the sampling distribution of the sample median.
b. Construct a probability histogram for the sampling distribution of the sample median and compare it with the probability histogram for the sample mean (Exercise 4.100, part **b**).

4.103 In Example 4.26 we used the computer to generate 1,000 samples, each containing $n = 11$ observations, from a uniform distribution over the interval from 0 to 1. For this exercise, generate 500 samples, each containing $n = 15$ observations, from this population.

a. Calculate the sample mean for each sample. To approximate the sampling distribution of $\bar{x}$, construct a relative frequency histogram for the 500 values of $\bar{x}$.

b. Repeat part **a** for the sample median. Compare this approximate sampling distribution with the approximate sampling distribution of $\bar{x}$ found in part **a**.

4.104 Consider a population that contains values of x equal to 00, 01, 02, 03, ..., 96, 97, 98, 99. Assume

that these values of x occur with equal probability. Generate 500 samples, each containing $n = 25$ measurements, from this population. Calculate the sample mean $\bar{x}$ and sample variance s^2 for each of the 500 samples.

a. To approximate the sampling distribution of $\bar{x}$, construct a relative frequency histogram for the 500 values of $\bar{x}$.

b. Repeat part **a** for the 500 values of s^2.

4.10   THE SAMPLING DISTRIBUTION OF THE SAMPLE MEAN

Estimating the mean useful life of automobiles, the mean monthly sales for all computer dealers in a large city, and the mean breaking strength of a new plastic are practical problems with something in common. In each case we are interested in making an inference about the mean μ of some population. As we mentioned in Chapter 2, the sample mean $\bar{x}$ is, in general, a good estimator of μ. We now develop pertinent information about the sampling distribution for this useful statistic.

EXAMPLE 4.27

Suppose a population has the uniform probability distribution given in Figure 4.38. The mean and standard deviation of this probability distribution are $\mu = .5$ and $\sigma = .29$. (See optional Section 4.6 for the formulas for μ and σ.) Now suppose a sample of 11 measurements is selected from this population. Describe the sampling distribution of the sample mean $\bar{x}$ based on the 1,000 sampling experiments discussed in Example 4.26.

SOLUTION

You will recall that in Example 4.26 we generated 1,000 samples of $n = 11$ measurements each. The relative frequency histogram for the 1,000 sample means is shown in Figure 4.39 with a normal probability distribution superimposed. You can see that this normal probability distribution approximates the computer-generated sampling distribution very well.

To fully describe a normal probability distribution, it is necessary to know its mean and standard deviation. Inspection of Figure 4.39 indicates that the mean of the distribution of $\bar{x}$, $\mu_{\bar{x}}$, appears to be very close to .5, the mean of the sampled

FIGURE 4.38
Sampled uniform population

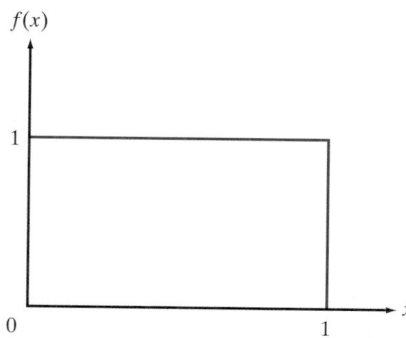

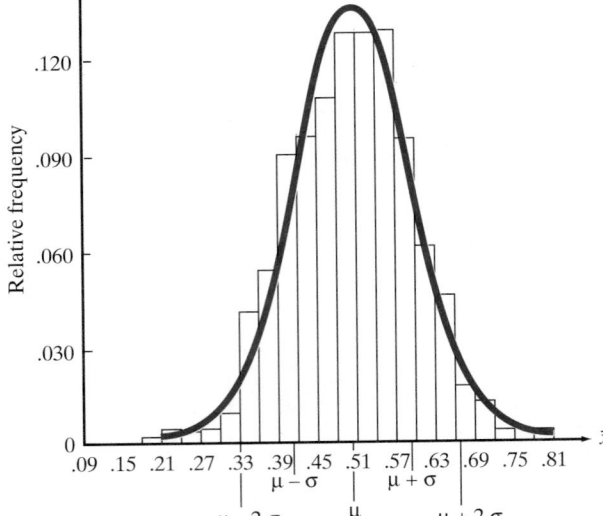

FIGURE 4.39
Relative frequency histogram for $\bar{x}$ in 1,000 samples of $n = 11$ measurements with normal distribution superimposed

uniform population. Furthermore, for a mound-shaped distribution such as that shown in Figure 4.39, almost all the measurements should fall within 3 standard deviations of the mean. Since the number of values of $\bar{x}$ is very large (1,000), the range of the observed $\bar{x}$'s divided by 6 (rather than 4) should give a reasonable approximation to the standard deviation of the sample mean, $\sigma_{\bar{x}}$. The values of $\bar{x}$ range from about .2 to .8, so we calculate

$$\sigma_{\bar{x}} \approx \frac{\text{Range of } \bar{x}\text{'s}}{6} = \frac{.8 - .2}{6} = .1$$

To summarize our findings based on 1,000 samples, each consisting of 11 measurements from a uniform population, the sampling distribution of $\bar{x}$ appears to be approximately normal with a mean of about .5 and a standard deviation of about .1.

The sampling distribution of $\bar{x}$ has the properties given in the next box, assuming only that a random sample of n observations has been selected from *any* population.

> **Properties of the Sampling Distribution of $\bar{x}$**
> **1.** Mean of sampling distribution equals mean of sampled population. That is,
> $$\mu_{\bar{x}} = E(\bar{x}) = \mu.^*$$
> **2.** Standard deviation of sampling distribution equals

*If the sampling distribution of a sample statistic has a mean equal to the population parameter the statistic is intended to estimate, the statistic is said to be an **unbiased estimate** of the parameter. Otherwise, the statistic is said to be a **biased estimate** of the parameter. Consequently, $\bar{x}$ is an unbiased estimate of μ.

$$\frac{\text{Standard deviation of sampled population}}{\text{Square root of sample size}}$$

That is, $\sigma_{\bar{x}} = \sigma/\sqrt{n}.$*
The standard deviation $\sigma_{\bar{x}}$ is often referred to as the **standard error of the mean.**

You can see that our approximation to $\mu_{\bar{x}}$ in Example 4.27 was precise, since property 1 assures us that the mean is the same as that of the sampled population: .5. Property 2 tells us how to calculate the standard deviation of the sampling distribution of $\bar{x}$. Substituting $\sigma = .29$, the standard deviation of the sampled uniform distribution, and the sample size $n = 11$ into the formula for $\sigma_{\bar{x}}$, we find

$$\sigma_{\bar{x}} = \frac{\sigma}{\sqrt{n}} = \frac{.29}{\sqrt{11}} = .09$$

Thus, the approximation we obtained in Example 6.6, $\sigma_{\bar{x}} \approx .1$, is very close to the exact value, $\sigma_{\bar{x}} = .09$.

What can be said about the shape of the sampling distribution of $\bar{x}$? Two important theorems provide this information.

Theorem 4.1

If a random sample of n observations is selected from a population with a normal distribution, the sampling distribution of $\bar{x}$ will be a normal distribution.

Theorem 4.2 (Central Limit Theorem)

Consider a random sample of n observations selected from a population (*any* population) with mean μ and standard deviation σ. Then, when n is sufficiently large, the sampling distribution of $\bar{x}$ will be approximately a normal distribution with mean $\mu_{\bar{x}} = \mu$ and standard deviation $\sigma_{\bar{x}} = \sigma/\sqrt{n}$. The larger the sample size, the better will be the normal approximation to the sampling distribution of $\bar{x}$.†

Thus, for sufficiently large samples the sampling distribution of $\bar{x}$ is approximately normal. How large must the sample size n be so that the normal distribution provides a good approximation for the sampling distribution of $\bar{x}$? The answer depends on the shape of the distribution of the sampled population, as shown by Figure 4.40. Generally speaking, the greater the skewness of the sampled population distribution, the larger the sample size must be before the normal distribution is an adequate approximation for the sampling distribution of $\bar{x}$. For most sampled populations, sample sizes of $n \geq 30$ will suffice for the normal approximation to be reasonable. We will use the normal approximation for the sampling distribution of $\bar{x}$ when the sample size is at least 30.

---

*It can be shown that $\sigma_{\bar{x}}$ is the smallest among the standard errors of all unbiased estimators of μ. Consequently, we say that $\bar{x}$ is the minimum variance unbiased estimator (MVUE) of μ. Also, if the sample size, n, is large relative to the number, N, of elements in the population, (e.g., 5% or more), $\sigma/\sqrt{n}$ must be multiplied by a finite population correction factor, $\sqrt{(N - n)/(N - 1)}$. For most sampling situations, this correction factor will be close to 1 and can be ignored.
†Moreover, because of the Central Limit Theorem, the sum of a random sample of n observations, Σx, will possess a sampling distribution that is approximately normal for large samples. This distribution will have a mean equal to $n\mu$ and a variance equal to $n\sigma^2$. Proof of the Central Limit Theorem is beyond the scope of this book, but it can be found in many mathematical statistics texts.

FIGURE 4.40
Sampling distributions of $\bar{x}$ for different populations and different sample sizes

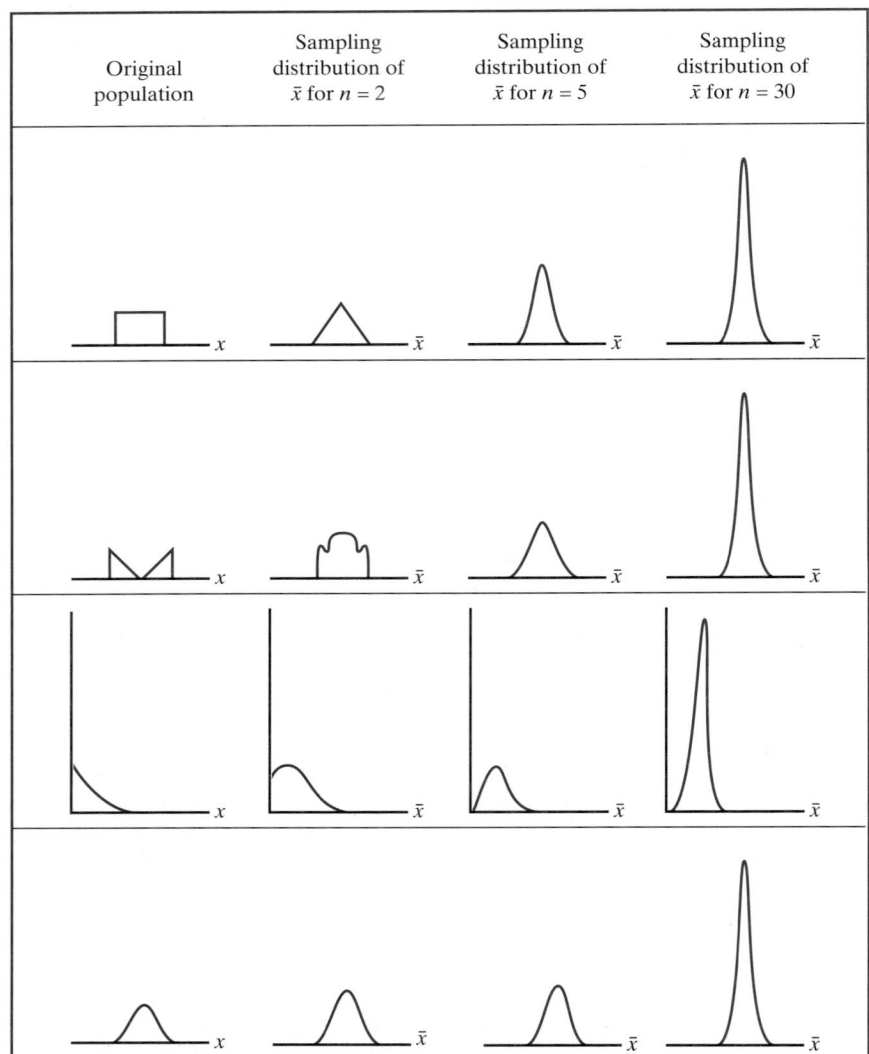

EXAMPLE **4.28**

Suppose we have selected a random sample of $n = 25$ observations from a population with mean equal to 80 and standard deviation equal to 5. It is known that the population is not extremely skewed.

    a. Sketch the relative frequency distributions for the population and for the sampling distribution of the sample mean, $\bar{x}$.

    b. Find the probability that $\bar{x}$ will be larger than 82.

SOLUTION

    a. We do not know the exact shape of the population relative frequency distribution, but we do know that it should be centered about $\mu = 80$, its spread should be measured by $\sigma = 5$, and it is not highly skewed. One possibility is shown in Figure 4.41a. From the Central Limit Theorem, we know that the sampling distribution of $\bar{x}$ will be approximately normal since the sampled population distribution is not extremely skewed. We also know that the sampling distribution will have mean and standard deviation

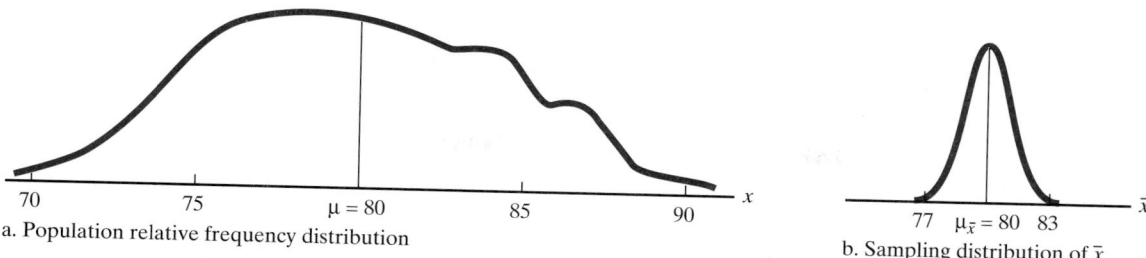

70   75   μ = 80   85   90 x

a. Population relative frequency distribution

77   $\mu_{\bar{x}} = 80$ 83 $\bar{x}$

b. Sampling distribution of $\bar{x}$

FIGURE 4.41   A population relative frequency distribution and the sampling distribution for $\bar{x}$

FIGURE 4.42
The sampling
distribution of $\bar{x}$

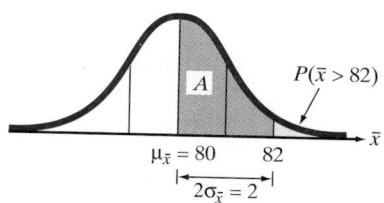

A $P(\bar{x} > 82)$

$\mu_{\bar{x}} = 80$ 82 $\bar{x}$

$2\sigma_{\bar{x}} = 2$

$$\mu_{\bar{x}} = \mu = 80 \quad \text{and} \quad \sigma_{\bar{x}} = \frac{\sigma}{\sqrt{n}} = \frac{5}{\sqrt{25}} = 1$$

The sampling distribution of $\bar{x}$ is shown in Figure 4.41b.

b. The probability that $\bar{x}$ will exceed 82 is equal to the lightly shaded area in Figure 4.42. To find this area, we need to find the z value corresponding to $\bar{x}$ = 82. Recall that the standard normal random variable z is the difference between any normally distributed random variable and its mean, expressed in units of its standard deviation. Since $\bar{x}$ is a normally distributed random variable with mean $\mu_{\bar{x}} = \mu$ and $\sigma_{\bar{x}} = \sigma/\sqrt{n}$, it follows that the standard normal z value corresponding to the sample mean, $\bar{x}$, is

$$z = \frac{\text{(Normal random variable)} - \text{(Mean)}}{\text{Standard deviation}} = \frac{\bar{x} - \mu_{\bar{x}}}{\sigma_{\bar{x}}}$$

Therefore, for $\bar{x}$ = 82, we have

$$z = \frac{\bar{x} - \mu_{\bar{x}}}{\sigma_{\bar{x}}} = \frac{82 - 80}{1} = 2$$

The area A in Figure 4.42 corresponding to $z = 2$ is given in the table of areas under the normal curve (see Table IV of Appendix B) as .4772. Therefore, the tail area corresponding to the probability that $\bar{x}$ exceeds 82 is

$$P(\bar{x} > 82) = P(z > 2) = .5 - .4772 = .0228. \quad \blacksquare$$

EXAMPLE 4.29

A manufacturer of automobile batteries claims that the distribution of the lengths of life of its best battery has a mean of 54 months and a standard deviation of 6 months. Suppose a consumer group decides to check the claim by purchasing a sample of 50 of these batteries and subjecting them to tests that determine battery life.

a. Assuming that the manufacturer's claim is true, describe the sampling distribution of the mean lifetime of a sample of 50 batteries.

FIGURE 4.43
Sampling distribution
of $\bar{x}$ in Example 4.29
for $n = 50$

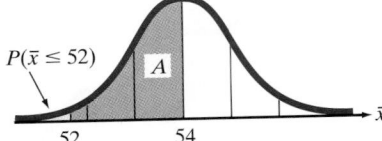

$P(\bar{x} \leq 52)$

A

52   54

$\bar{x}$

b. Assuming that the manufacturer's claim is true, what is the probability the consumer group's sample has a mean life of 52 or fewer months?

SOLUTION

a. Even though we have no information about the shape of the probability distribution of the lives of the batteries, we can use the Central Limit Theorem to deduce that the sampling distribution for a sample mean lifetime of 50 batteries is approximately normally distributed. Furthermore, the mean of this sampling distribution is the same as the mean of the sampled population, which is $\mu = 54$ months according to the manufacturer's claim. Finally, the standard deviation of the sampling distribution is given by

$$\sigma_{\bar{x}} = \frac{\sigma}{\sqrt{n}} = \frac{6}{\sqrt{50}} = .85 \text{ month}$$

Note that we used the claimed standard deviation of the sampled population, $\sigma = 6$ months. Thus, if we assume that the claim is true, the sampling distribution for the mean life of the 50 batteries sampled is as shown in Figure 4.43.

b. If the manufacturer's claim is true, the probability that the consumer group observes a mean battery life of 52 or fewer months for their sample of 50 batteries, $P(x \leq 52)$, is equivalent to the lightly shaded area in Figure 4.43. Since the sampling distribution is approximately normal, we can find this area by computing the standard normal z value:

$$z = \frac{\bar{x} - \mu_{\bar{x}}}{\sigma_{\bar{x}}} = \frac{\bar{x} - \mu}{\sigma_{\bar{x}}} = \frac{52 - 54}{.85} = -2.35$$

where $\mu_{\bar{x}}$, the mean of the sampling distribution of $\bar{x}$, is equal to μ, the mean of the lives of the sampled population, and $\sigma_{\bar{x}}$ is the standard deviation of the sampling distribution of $\bar{x}$. Note that z is the familiar standardized distance (z-score) of Section 2.7 and, since $\bar{x}$ is approximately normally distributed, it will possess the standard normal distribution of Section 4.7.

The area A shown in Figure 4.43 between $\bar{x} = 52$ and $\bar{x} = 54$ (corresponding to $z = -2.35$) is found in Table IV of Appendix B to be .4906. Therefore, the area to the left of $\bar{x} = 52$ is

$$P(\bar{x} \leq 52) = .5 - A = .5 - .4906 = .0094$$

Thus, the probability the consumer group will observe a sample mean of 52 or less is only .0094 if the manufacturer's claim is true. If the 50 tested batteries do exhibit a mean of 52 or fewer months, the consumer group will have strong evidence that the manufacturer's claim is untrue, because such an event is very unlikely to occur if the claim is true. (This is still another application of the *rare-event approach to statistical inference.*) ∎

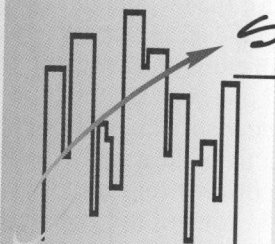

STATISTICS IN ACTION

4.3 THE INSOMNIA PILL

A research report published in the *Proceedings of the National Academy of Sciences* (Mar. 1994) brought encouraging news to insomniacs and international business travelers who suffer from jet lag. Neuroscientists at the Massachusetts Institute of Technology (MIT) have been experimenting with melatonin—a hormone secreted by the pineal gland in the brain—as a sleep-inducing hormone. Since the hormone is naturally produced, it is nonaddictive. The researchers believe melatonin may be effective in treating jet lag—the body's response to rapid travel across many time zones so that a daylight-darkness change disrupts sleep patterns.

In the MIT study, young male volunteers were given various doses of melatonin or a placebo (a dummy medication containing no melatonin). Then they were placed in a dark room at midday and told to close their eyes for 30 minutes. The variable of interest was the time (in minutes) elapsed before each volunteer fell asleep.

According to the lead investigator, Professor Richard Wurtman, "Our volunteers fall asleep in five or six minutes on melatonin, while those on placebo take about 15 minutes." Wurtman warns, however, that uncontrolled doses of melatonin could cause mood-altering side effects. (Melatonin is sold in some health food stores. However, sales are unregulated, and the purity and strength of the hormone are often uncertain.)

Focus

With the placebo (i.e., no hormone) the researchers found that the mean time to fall asleep was 15 minutes. Assume that with the placebo treatment $\mu = 15$ and $\sigma = 5$. Now, consider a random sample of 40 young males, each of whom is given a dosage of the sleep-inducing hormone, melatonin. The times (in minutes) to fall asleep for these 40 males are listed in Table 4.8.* Use the data to make an inference about the true value of μ for those taking the melatonin. Does melatonin appear to be an effective drug against insomnia?

*These are simulated sleep times based on summary information provided in the MIT study.

TABLE 4.8   Times (in Minutes) for 40 Male Volunteers to Fall Asleep (Statistics in Action 4.3)

6.4	6.0	3.2	4.4	6.2	1.7	5.1
5.9	1.6	4.4	16.2	4.8	8.3	7.5
4.8	3.3	4.0	6.2	6.3	5.0	6.3
5.1	6.4	15.6	3.4	3.1	6.1	6.0
5.0	1.8	6.1	4.5	4.5	1.5	4.7
7.6	8.2	4.9	6.1	3.9		

We conclude this section with two final comments on the sampling distribution of $\bar{x}$. First, from the formula $\sigma_{\bar{x}} = \sigma/\sqrt{n}$, we see that the standard deviation of the sampling distribution of $\bar{x}$ gets smaller as the sample size n gets larger. For example, we computed $\sigma_{\bar{x}} = .85$ when $n = 50$ in Example 4.29. However, for $n = 100$ we obtain $\sigma_{\bar{x}} = \sigma/\sqrt{n} = 6/\sqrt{100} = .60$. This relationship will hold true for most of the sample statistics encountered in this text. That is: *The standard deviation of the sampling distribution decreases as the sample size increases.* Consequently, the larger the sample size, the more accurate the sample statistic (e.g., $\bar{x}$) is in estimating a population parameter (e.g., μ). We will use this result in Chapter 5 to help us determine the sample size needed to obtain a specified accuracy of estimation.

Our second comment concerns the Central Limit Theorem. In addition to providing a very useful approximation for the sampling distribution of a sample mean, the Central Limit Theorem offers an explanation for the fact that many relative frequency distributions of data possess mound-shaped distributions. Many of the measurements we take in business are really means or sums of a large number of small phenomena. For example, a company's sales for one year are the total of the many individual sales the company made during the year. Similarly, we can view the length of time a construction company takes to build a house as the total of the times taken to complete a multitude of the distinct jobs, and we can regard the monthly demand for blood at a hospital as the total of the many individual patients' needs. Whether or not the observations entering into these sums satisfy the assumptions basic to the Central Limit Theorem is open to question. However, it is a fact that many distributions of data in nature are mound-shaped and possess the appearance of normal distributions.

EXERCISES 4.105–4.120

Note: Exercises marked with 💾 *require the use of a computer.*

Learning the Mechanics

4.105 Suppose a random sample of n measurements is selected from a population with mean $\mu = 100$ and variance $\sigma^2 = 100$. For each of the following values of n, give the mean and standard deviation of the sampling distribution of the sample mean $\bar{x}$.
a. $n = 4$ **b.** $n = 25$ **c.** $n = 100$
d. $n = 50$ **e.** $n = 500$ **f.** $n = 1,000$

4.106 Suppose a random sample of $n = 25$ measurements is selected from a population with mean μ and standard deviation σ. For each of the following values of μ and σ, give the values of $\mu_{\bar{x}}$ and $\sigma_{\bar{x}}$.
a. $\mu = 10, \sigma = 3$ **b.** $\mu = 100, \sigma = 25$
c. $\mu = 20, \sigma = 40$ **d.** $\mu = 10, \sigma = 100$

4.107 Consider the probability distribution shown here.

x	1	2	3	8
$p(x)$	.1	.4	.4	.1

a. Find μ, σ^2, and σ.
b. Find the sampling distribution of $\bar{x}$ for random samples of $n = 2$ measurements from this distribution by listing all possible values of $\bar{x}$, and find the probability associated with each.
c. Use the results of part **b** to calculate $\mu_{\bar{x}}$ and $\sigma_{\bar{x}}$. Confirm that $\mu_{\bar{x}} = \mu$ and $\sigma_{\bar{x}} = \sigma/\sqrt{n} = \sigma/\sqrt{2}$.

4.108 Will the sampling distribution of $\bar{x}$ always be approximately normally distributed? Explain.

4.109 A random sample of $n = 64$ observations is drawn from a population with a mean equal to 20 and standard deviation equal to 16.
a. Give the mean and standard deviation of the (repeated) sampling distribution of $\bar{x}$.
b. Describe the shape of the sampling distribution of $\bar{x}$. Does your answer depend on the sample size?

c. Calculate the standard normal z-score corresponding to a value of $\bar{x} = 15.5$.
d. Calculate the standard normal z-score corresponding to $\bar{x} = 23$.

4.110 Refer to Exercise 4.109. Find the probability that
a. $\bar{x}$ is less than 16 **b.** $\bar{x}$ is greater than 23
c. $\bar{x}$ is greater than 25
d. $\bar{x}$ falls between 16 and 22 **e.** $\bar{x}$ is less than 14

4.111 A random sample of $n = 100$ observations is selected from a population with $\mu = 30$ and $\sigma = 16$. Approximate the following probabilities:
a. $P(\bar{x} \geq 28)$ **b.** $P(22.1 \leq \bar{x} \leq 26.8)$
c. $P(\bar{x} \leq 28.2)$ **d.** $P(\bar{x} \geq 27.0)$

4.112 A random sample of $n = 900$ observations is selected from a population with $\mu = 100$ and $\sigma = 10$.
a. What are the largest and smallest values of $\bar{x}$ that you would expect to see?
b. How far, at the most, would you expect $\bar{x}$ to deviate from μ?
c. Did you have to know μ to answer part **b**? Explain.

4.113 💾 Consider a population that contains values of x equal to 0, 1, 2, ..., 97, 98, 99. Assume that the values of x are equally likely. For each of the following values of n, generate 500 random samples and calculate $\bar{x}$ for each sample. For each sample size, construct a relative frequency histogram of the 500 values of $\bar{x}$. What changes occur in the histograms as the value of n increases? What similarities exist? Use $n = 2, n = 5, n = 10, n = 30$, and $n = 50$.

Applying the Concepts

4.114 The *College Student Journal* (Dec. 1992) investigated differences in traditional and nontraditional students, where nontraditional students are generally defined as those 25 years or older and who are working full or part-time. Based on the study results, we can assume that the population mean and standard deviation for the GPA of all nontra-ditional students is $\mu = 3.5$ and $\sigma = .5$. Suppose that a random sample of $n = 100$ nontraditional students is selected from the population of all nontraditional students, and the GPA of each student is determined. Then $\bar{x}$, the sample mean, will be approximately normally distributed (because of the Central Limit Theorem).

a. Calculate $\mu_{\bar{x}}$ and $\sigma_{\bar{x}}$.

b. What is the approximate probability that the nontraditional student sample has a mean GPA between 3.40 and 3.60?

c. What is the approximate probability that the sample of 100 nontraditional students has a mean GPA that exceeds 3.62?

d. How would the sampling distribution of $\bar{x}$ change if the sample size n were doubled from 100 to 200? How do your answers to parts **b** and **c** change when the sample size is doubled?

4.115 Filling processes are used in the production of a wide variety of products including beverages, food, soaps, cleaners, chemicals, paints, and pharmaceuticals. They involve inserting a specific amount of a product into a container, subject to certain specifications. However, because of both the physical properties of the product and the design of the filling process, the amount of "fill" dispensed is a random variable. University of Louisville researchers J. Usher, S. Alexander, and D. Duggins examined the process of filling plastic pouches of dry blended biscuit mix (*Quality Engineering*, Vol. 9, 1996). The current fill mean of the process is set at $\mu = 406$ grams and the process fill standard deviation is $\sigma = 10.1$ grams. (According to the researchers, "The high level of variation is due to the fact that the product has poor flow properties and is, therefore, difficult to fill consistently from pouch to pouch.") Operators monitor the process by randomly sampling 36 pouches each day and measuring the amount of biscuit mix in each. Consider $\bar{x}$, the main fill amount of the sample of 36 products.

a. Describe the sampling distribution of $\bar{x}$. (Give the values of $\mu_{\bar{x}}$ and $\sigma_{\bar{x}}$, and the shape of the probability distribution.)

b. Find $P(\bar{x} \leq 400.8)$.

c. Suppose that on one particular day, the operators observe $\bar{x} = 400.8$. One of the operators believes that this indicates that the true process fill mean μ for that day is less than 406 grams. Another operator argues that $\mu = 406$ and the small value of $\bar{x}$ observed is due to random variation in the fill process. Which operator do you agree with? Why?

4.116 Last year a company began a program to compensate its employees for unused sick days, paying each employee a bonus of one-half the usual wage earned for each unused sick day. The question that naturally arises is: "Did this policy motivate employees to use fewer sick days?" *Before* last year, the number of sick days used by employees had a distribution with a mean of 7 days and a standard deviation of 2 days.

a. Assuming that these parameters did not change last year, find the approximate probability that the sample mean number of sick days used by 100 employees chosen at random was less than or equal to 6.4 last year.

b. How would you interpret the result if the sample mean for the 100 employees was 6.4?

4.117 The ocean quahog is a type of clam found in the coastal waters of New England and the mid-Atlantic states. Extensive beds of ocean quahogs along the New Jersey shore gave rise to the development of the largest U.S. shellfish harvesting program. A federal survey of offshore ocean quahog harvesting in New Jersey, conducted from 1980 to 1992, revealed an average catch per unit effort (CPUE) of 89.34 clams. The CPUE standard deviation was 7.74 (*Journal of Shellfish Research,* June 1995). Let $\bar{x}$ represent the mean CPUE for a sample of 35 attempts to catch ocean quahogs off the New Jersey shore.

a. Compute $\mu_{\bar{x}}$ and $\sigma_{\bar{x}}$. Interpret their values.

b. Sketch the sampling distribution of $\bar{x}$.

c. Find $P(\bar{x} > 88)$.   **d.** Find $P(\bar{x} < 87)$.

4.118 In determining when to place orders to replenish depleted product inventories, a retailer should take into consideration the lead times for the products. **Lead time** is the time between placing the order and having the product available to satisfy customer demand. It includes time for placing the order, receiving the shipment from the supplier, inspecting the units received, and placing them in inventory (Clauss, *Applied Management Science and Spreadsheet Modeling,* 1996). Interested in the average lead time, μ, for a particular supplier of men's apparel, the purchasing department of a national department store chain randomly sampled 50 of the supplier's lead times and found $\bar{x} = 44$ days.

a. Describe the shape of the sampling distribution of $\bar{x}$.

b. If μ and σ are really 40 and 12, respectively, what is the probability that a second random sample of size 50 would yield $\bar{x}$ greater than or equal to 44?

c. Using the values for μ and σ in part **b**, what is the probability that a sample of size 50 would yield a sample mean within the interval $\mu \pm 2\sigma/\sqrt{n}$?

4.119 A soft-drink bottler purchases glass bottles from a vendor. The bottles are required to have an internal pressure strength of at least 150 pounds per square inch (psi). A prospective bottle vendor claims that its production process yields bottles with a mean internal pressure strength of 157 psi and a standard deviation of 3 psi. The bottler strikes an agreement with the vendor that permits the bottler to sample from the vendor's production process to verify the vendor's claim. The bottler randomly selects 40 bottles from the last 10,000 produced, measures the internal pressure of each, and finds the mean pressure for the sample to be 1.3 psi below the process mean cited by the vendor.

a. Assuming the vendor's claim to be true, what is the probability of obtaining a sample mean this far or farther below the process mean? What does your answer suggest about the validity of the vendor's claim?

b. If the process standard deviation were 3 psi as claimed by the vendor, but the mean were 156 psi, would the observed sample result be more or less likely than in part **a**? What if the mean were 158 psi?

c. If the process mean were 157 psi as claimed, but the process standard deviation were 2 psi, would the sample result be more or less likely than in part **a**? What if instead the standard deviation were 6 psi?

4.120   National Car Rental Systems, Inc. commissioned USAC Properties, Inc. [the performance testing/endorsement arm of the United States Automobile Club (USAC)] to conduct a survey of the general condition of the cars rented to the public by Hertz, Avis, National, and Budget Rent-a-Car.*

USAC officials evaluate each company's cars on appearance and cleanliness, accessory performance, mechanical functions, and vehicle safety using a demerit point system designed specifically for this survey. Each car starts with a perfect score of 0 points and incurs demerit points for each discrepancy noted by the inspectors. One measure of the overall condition of a company's cars is the mean of all scores received by the company, i.e., the company's *fleet mean score*. To estimate the fleet mean score of each rental car company, 10 major airports were randomly selected, and 10 cars from each company were randomly rented for inspection from each airport by USAC officials; i.e., a sample of size $n = 100$ cars from each company's fleet was drawn and inspected.

a. Describe the sampling distribution of $\bar{x}$, the mean score of a sample of $n = 100$ rental cars.

b. Interpret the mean of $\bar{x}$ in the context of this problem.

c. Assume $\mu = 30$ and $\sigma = 60$ for one rental car company. For this company, find $P(\bar{x} \geq 45)$.

d. Refer to part **c**. The company claims that their true fleet mean score "couldn't possibly be as high as 30." The sample mean score tabulated by USAC for this company was $\bar{x} = 45$. Does this result tend to support or refute the claim? Explain.

*Information by personal communication with Rajiv Tandon, Corporate Vice President and General Manager of the Car Rental Division, National Car Rental Systems, Inc., Minneapolis, Minnesota.

QUICK REVIEW

Key Terms

Note: Starred (*) terms refer to the optional sections in this chapter.

Bell curve   196
Binomial experiment   174
Binomial random variable   174
Biased estimate   222
Central Limit Theorem   223
Continuous probability
 distribution   191
Continuous random variable   164

Cumulative binomial
 probabilities   181
Discrete random variable   164
Expected value   167
Exponential distribution*   210
Frequency function   191
Normal distribution   196
Parameter   214
Poisson random variable*   186

Probability density function   191
Probability distribution   166
Random variable   162
Sample statistic   215
Sampling distribution   216
Standard error of the mean   223
Standard normal distribution   201
Uniform distribution*   192
Waiting time distribution*   210

Key Formulas

Note: Starred (*) formulas refer to the optional sections in this chapter.

Random Variable	Probability Distribution or Density Function	Mean	Standard Deviation	
General discrete, x	$p(x)$	$\sum_{\text{all } x} xp(x)$	$\sqrt{\sum (x - \mu)^2 p(x)}$	166, 167, 168

Distribution	Probability	Mean	Standard Deviation	Page
Binomial, x	$\binom{n}{x}p^x q^{n-x}$	np	$\sqrt{npq}$	178
Poisson,* x	$\dfrac{\lambda^x e^{-\lambda}}{x!}$	λ	$\sqrt{\lambda}$	187
Uniform,* x	$\dfrac{1}{d-c},\ (c \le x \le d)$	$\dfrac{c+d}{2}$	$\dfrac{d-c}{\sqrt{12}}$	193
Normal, x	$\dfrac{1}{\sigma\sqrt{2\pi}}e^{-(1/2)[(x-\mu)/\sigma]^2}$	μ	σ	197
Standard normal, $z = \left(\dfrac{x-\mu}{\sigma}\right)$	$\dfrac{1}{\sqrt{2\pi}}e^{-(1/2)z^2}$	0	1	197
Exponential,* x	$\lambda e^{-\lambda x},\ (x>0)$	$\dfrac{1}{\lambda}$	$\dfrac{1}{\lambda}$	210
Sample mean, $\bar{x}$	Normal (for large n)	μ	$\sigma/\sqrt{n}$	222–223

LANGUAGE LAB

Symbol	Pronunciation	Description
$p(x)$		Probability distribution of the random variable x
S		The outcome of a binomial trial denoted a "success"
F		The outcome of a binomial trial denoted a "failure"
p		The probability of success (S) in a binomial trial
q		The probability of failure (F) in a binomial trial, where $q = 1-p$
λ	lambda	The mean (or expected) number of events for a Poisson random variable; parameter for an exponential random variable
e		A constant used in the Poisson probability distribution, where $e = 2.71828...$
$f(x)$	f of x	Probability density function for a continuous random variable x
θ	theta	Population parameter (general)
$\mu_{\bar{x}}$	mu of x-bar	True mean of sampling distribution of $\bar{x}$
$\sigma_{\bar{x}}$	sigma of x-bar	True standard deviation of sampling distribution of $\bar{x}$

SUPPLEMENTARY EXERCISES 4.121–4.144

Note: Starred (*) exercises refer to the optional sections in this chapter.

Learning the Mechanics

4.121 For each of the following examples, decide whether x is a binomial random variable and explain your decision:

a. A manufacturer of computer chips randomly selects 100 chips from each hour's production in order to estimate the proportion defective. Let x represent the number of defectives in the 100 sampled chips.

b. Of five applicants for a job, two will be selected. Although all applicants appear to be equally qualified, only three have the ability to fulfill the expectations of the company. Suppose that the two selections are made at random from the five applicants, and let x be the number of qualified applicants selected.

c. A software developer establishes a support hotline for customers to call in with questions regarding use of the software. Let x represent the number of calls received on the support hotline during a specified workday.

d. Florida is one of a minority of states with no state income tax. A poll of 1,000 registered voters is conducted to determine how many would favor a state income tax in light of the state's current fiscal condition. Let x be the number in the sample who would favor the tax.

4.122 Consider the discrete probability distribution shown here.

x	10	12	18	20
$p(x)$	.2	.3	.1	.4

a. Calculate μ, σ^2, and σ. **b.** What is $P(x < 15)$?
c. Calculate $\mu \pm 2\sigma$.

d. What is the probability that x is in the interval $\mu \pm 2\sigma$?

4.123 Suppose x is a binomial random variable with $n = 20$ and $p = .7$.
   a. Find $P(x = 14)$.   **b.** Find $P(x \leq 12)$.
   c. Find $P(x > 12)$.   **d.** Find $P(9 \leq x \leq 18)$.
   e. Find $P(8 < x < 18)$.   **f.** Find μ, σ^2, and σ.
   g. What is the probability that x is in the interval $\mu \pm 2\sigma$?

*4.124 Suppose x is a Poisson random variable. Compute $p(x)$ for each of the following cases:
   a. $\lambda = 2, x = 3$ **b.** $\lambda = 1, x = 4$ **c.** $\lambda = .5, x = 2$

4.125 Which of the following describe discrete random variables, and which describe continuous random variables?
   a. The number of damaged inventory items
   b. The average monthly sales revenue generated by a salesperson over the past year
   c. The number of square feet of warehouse space a company rents
   d. The length of time a firm must wait before its copying machine is fixed

4.126 Find the following probabilities for the standard normal random variable z:
   a. $P(z \leq 2.1)$ **b.** $P(z \geq 2.1)$
   c. $P(z \geq -1.65)$ **d.** $P(-2.13 \leq z \leq -.41)$
   e. $P(-1.45 \leq z \leq 2.15)$ **f.** $P(z \leq -1.43)$

*4.127 Assume that x is a random variable best described by a uniform distribution with $c = 10$ and $d = 90$.
   a. Find $f(x)$.
   b. Find the mean and standard deviation of x.
   c. Graph the probability distribution for x and locate its mean and the interval $\mu \pm 2\sigma$ on the graph.
   d. Find $P(x \leq 60)$.   **e.** Find $P(x \geq 90)$.
   f. Find $P(x \leq 80)$.
   g. Find $P(\mu - \sigma \leq x \leq \mu + \sigma)$.
   h. Find $P(x > 75)$.

4.128 The random variable x has a normal distribution with $\mu = 75$ and $\sigma = 10$. Find the following probabilities:
   a. $P(x \leq 80)$ **b.** $P(x \geq 85)$
   c. $P(70 \leq x \leq 75)$ **d.** $P(x > 80)$
   e. $P(x = 78)$ **f.** $P(x \leq 110)$

4.129 The random variable x has a normal distribution with $\mu = 40$ and $\sigma^2 = 36$. Find a value of x, call it x_0, such that
   a. $P(x \geq x_0) = .10$ **b.** $P(\mu \leq x < x_0) = .40$
   c. $P(x < x_0) = .05$ **d.** $P(x \geq x_0) = .40$
   e. $P(x_0 \leq x < \mu) = .45$

*4.130 Assume that x has an exponential distribution with $\lambda = 3.0$. Find
   a. $P(x \leq 2)$ **b.** $P(x > 3)$ **c.** $P(x = 1)$
   d. $P(x \leq 7)$ **e.** $P(4 \leq x \leq 12)$

4.131 A random sample of $n = 68$ observations is selected from a population with $\mu = 19.6$ and $\sigma = 3.2$. Approximate each of the following probabilities.

   a. $P(\bar{x} \leq 19.6)$ **b.** $P(\bar{x} \leq 19)$
   c. $P(\bar{x} \geq 20.1)$ **d.** $P(19.2 \leq \bar{x} \leq 20.6)$

4.132 A random sample of 40 observations is to be drawn from a large population of measurements. It is known that 30% of the measurements in the population are 1's, 20% are 2's, 20% are 3's, and 30% are 4's.
   a. Give the mean and standard deviation of the (repeated) sampling distribution of $\bar{x}$, the sample mean of the 40 observations.
   b. Describe the shape of the sampling distribution of $\bar{x}$. Does your answer depend on the sample size?

Applying the Concepts

4.133 The metropolitan airport commission is considering the establishment of limitations on noise pollution around a local airport. At the present time, the noise level per jet takeoff in one neighborhood near the airport is approximately normally distributed with a mean of 100 decibels and a standard deviation of 6 decibels.
   a. What is the probability that a randomly selected jet will generate a noise level greater than 108 decibels in this neighborhood?
   b. What is the probability that a randomly selected jet will generate a noise level of exactly 100 decibels?
   c. Suppose a regulation is passed that requires jet noise in this neighborhood to be lower than 105 decibels 95% of the time. Assuming the standard deviation of the noise distribution remains the same, how much will the mean level of noise have to be lowered to comply with the regulation?

4.134 The fourth *Annual Report: Florida Employer Opinion Survey* (1992) gives the results of an extensive survey of employer opinions in Florida. Each employer was asked to rate his or her satisfaction with the preparation of employees by the public education system. Responses were 1, 1.5, or 2, representing very dissatisfied, neither satisfied nor dissatisfied, and very satisfied, respectively. A sample of 651 employers was selected. Assume that the mean for all employers in Florida is 1.50 (the "dividing line" between satisfied and dissatisfied) and the standard deviation is .45.
   a. Which type of distribution describes the individual survey responses, continuous or discrete?
   b. Describe the distribution that best approximates the sample mean response of 651 employers. What are the mean and standard deviation of this distribution? What assumptions, if any, are necessary to ensure the validity of your answers?
   c. What is the approximate probability that the sample mean will be 1.45 or less?

d. The mean of the sample of 651 employers surveyed in 1992 was 1.36. Given this result, do you think it is likely that all Florida employers' opinions were evenly divided on the effectiveness of public education? That is, do you think the assumption that the population mean is 1.50 is correct? Why or why not?

4.135 To help highway planners anticipate the need for road repairs and design future construction projects, data are collected on the volume and weight of truck traffic on specific roadways (Edwards, *Transportation Planning Handbook*, 1992). Equipment has been developed that can be built into road surfaces to measure traffic volumes and to weigh trucks without requiring them to stop at roadside weigh stations. As with any measuring device, however, the "weigh-in-motion" equipment does not always record truck weights accurately. In an experiment performed by the Minnesota Department of Transportation involving repeated weighing of a 27,907-pound truck, it was found that the weights recorded by the weigh-in-motion equipment were approximately normally distributed with mean 27,315 and a standard deviation of 628 pounds (Minnesota Department of Transportation). It follows that the difference between the actual weight and recorded weight, the error of measurement, is normally distributed with mean 592 pounds and standard deviation 628 pounds.

a. What is the probability that the weigh-in-motion equipment understates the actual weight of the truck?

b. If a 27,907-pound truck were driven over the weigh-in-motion equipment 100 times, approximately how many times would the equipment overstate the truck's weight?

c. What is the probability that the error in the weight recorded by the weigh-in-motion equipment for a 27,907-pound truck exceeds 400 pounds?

d. It is possible to adjust (or *calibrate*) the weigh-in-motion equipment to control the mean error of measurement. At what level should the mean error be set so the equipment will understate the weight of a 27,907-pound truck 50% of the time? Only 40% of the time?

4.136 A large number of preventable errors are being made by doctors and nurses in U.S. hospitals. From overdoses to botched operations to misdiagnoses, many patients leave the hospital in worse condition than they entered. The on-going debate on health care in the United States has revived calls for systematic approaches for catching errors, approaches that involve management techniques and computer systems to control quality, as is

done in industry (*New York Times,* July 18, 1995). A study of a major metropolitan hospital revealed that of every 100 medications prescribed or dispensed, 1 was in error; but, only 1 in 500 resulted in an error that caused significant problems for the patient. It is known that the hospital prescribes and dispenses 60,000 medications per year.

a. What is the expected number of errors per year at this hospital? The expected number of significant errors per year?

b. Within what limits would you expect the number of significant errors per year to fall?

c. What assumptions did you need to make in order to answer these questions?

*4.137 Millions of suburban commuters are finding railroads to be a convenient, time-saving, less stressful alternative to the automobile. While generally perceived as a safe mode of transportation, the average number of deaths per week due to railroad accidents is a surprisingly high 14 (U.S. National Center for Health Statistics, *Vital Statistics of the United States, 1995*).

a. Construct arguments both for and against the use of the Poisson distribution to characterize the number of deaths per week due to railroad accidents.

b. For the remainder of this exercise, assume the Poisson distribution is an adequate approximation for x, the number of deaths per week due to railroad accidents. Find $E(x)$ and the standard deviation of x.

c. Based strictly on your answers to part **b**, is it likely that only 4 or fewer deaths occur next week? Explain.

d. Find $P(x \leq 4)$. Is this probability consistent with your answer to part **c**? Explain.

4.138 The owner of construction company A bids on jobs so that if awarded the job, company A will make a $10,000 profit. The owner of construction company B makes bids on jobs so that if awarded the job, company B will make a $15,000 profit. Each company describes the probability distribution of the number of jobs the company is awarded per year as shown in the table.

Company A		Company B	
2	.05	2	.15
3	.15	3	.30
4	.20	4	.30
5	.35	5	.20
6	.25	6	.05

a. Find the expected number of jobs each will be awarded in a year.

b. What is the expected profit for each company?

c. Find the variance and standard deviation of the distribution of number of jobs awarded per year for each company.

d. Graph $p(x)$ for both companies A and B. For each company, what proportion of the time will x fall in the interval $\mu \pm 2\sigma$?

4.139 A. K. Shah published a simple approximation for areas under the normal curve in the *American Statistician* (Feb. 1985). Shah showed that the area A under the standard normal curve between 0 and z is

$$A \approx \begin{cases} z(4.4 - z)/10 & \text{for } 0 \le z \le 2.2 \\ .49 & \text{for } 2.2 < z < 2.6 \\ .50 & \text{for } z \ge 2.6 \end{cases}$$

a. Use the approximation to find
(i) $P(0 < z < 1.2)$
(ii) $P(0 < z < 2.5)$
(iii) $P(z > .8)$
(iv) $P(z < 1.0)$

b. Find the exact probabilities in part **a**.

c. Shah showed that the approximation has a maximum absolute error of .0052. Verify this for the approximations in part **a**.

*4.140 Based on sample data collected in the Denver area, a study found that in some cases the exponential distribution is an adequate approximation for the distribution of the time (in weeks) an individual is unemployed (*Journal of Economics*, Vol. 28, 1985). In particular, the author found the exponential distribution to be appropriate for white and African American workers but not for Hispanics. Use $\lambda = 1/13$ to answer the following questions.

a. What is the mean time workers are unemployed according to the exponential distribution?

b. Find the probability that a white worker who just lost her job will be unemployed for at least 2 weeks. For more than 6 weeks.

c. What is the probability that an unemployed worker will find a new job within 12 weeks?

4.141 One measure of elevator performance is cycle time. Elevator cycle time is the time between successive elevator starts, which includes the time when the car is moving and the time when it is standing at a floor. Researchers have found that simulation is necessary to determine the average cycle time of a system of elevators in complex traffic situations. *Simulation* (Oct. 1993) published a study on the use of a microcomputer-based simulator for elevators. The simulator produced an average cycle time μ of 26 seconds when traffic intensity was set at 50 persons every five minutes. Consider a sample of 200 simulated elevator runs and let $\bar{x}$ represent the mean cycle time of this sample.

a. What do you know about the distribution of x, the time between successive elevator starts? (Give the value of the mean and standard deviation of x and the shape of the distribution, if possible.)

b. What do you know about the distribution of $\bar{x}$? (Give the value of the mean and standard deviation of $\bar{x}$ and the shape of the distribution, if possible.)

c. Assume σ, the standard deviation of cycle time x, is 20 seconds. Use this information to calculate $P(\bar{x} > 26.8)$.

d. Repeat part **c** but assume $\sigma = 10$.

4.142 Refer to the *Simulation* (Oct. 1993) study of elevator cycle times, Exercise 4.141. Cycle time is related to the distance (measured by number of floors) the elevator covers on a particular run, called *running distance*. The simulated distribution of running distance, x, during a down-peak period in elevator traffic intensity is shown in the figure at the top of page 235. The distribution has mean $\mu = 5.5$ floors and standard deviation $\sigma = 7$ floors. Consider a random sample of 80 simulated elevator runs during a down-peak in traffic intensity. Of interest is the sample mean running distance, $\bar{x}$.

a. Find $\mu_{\bar{x}}$ and $\sigma_{\bar{x}}$.

b. Is the shape of the distribution of $\bar{x}$ similar to the figure? If not, sketch the distribution.

c. During a down-peak in traffic intensity, is it likely to observe a sample mean running distance of $\bar{x} = 5.3$ floors? Explain.

4.143 The efficacy of insecticides is often measured by the dose necessary to kill a certain percentage of insects. Suppose a certain dose of a new insecticide is supposed to kill 80% of the insects that receive it. To test the claim, 25 insects are exposed to the insecticide.

a. If the insecticide really kills 80% of the exposed insects, what is the probability that fewer than 15 die?

b. If you observed such a result, what would you conclude about the new insecticide? Explain your logic.

4.144 A national study conducted by Geoffrey Alpert of the University of South Carolina found that 40% of all high-speed police chases end in accidents; 20% of all chases end in injury; and 1% in death. In trying to balance public safety, law enforcement, and liability concerns, many police departments have moved to restrict high-speed chases. One exception is the Tampa Police Department. After restricting chases for three years, management changed their policy and eased the restrictions. Prior to doing so, however, police received safety guidelines and refresher

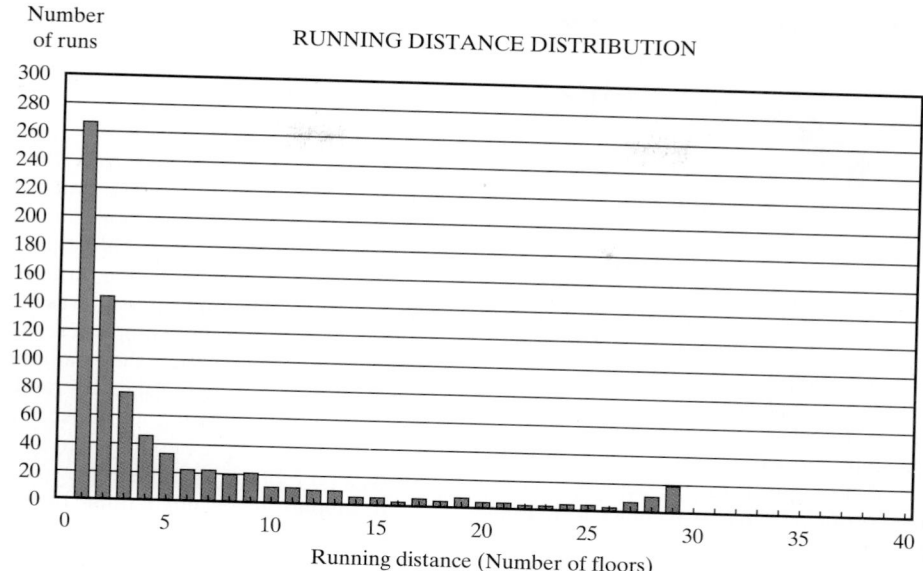

Number of runs

RUNNING DISTANCE DISTRIBUTION

Running distance (Number of floors)

Source: Siikonen, M. L. "Elevator traffic simulation." *Simulation,* Vol. 61, No. 4, Oct. 1993, p. 266 (Figure 8). Copyright © 1993 by Simulation Councils, Inc. Reprinted by permission.

safe-driving courses. The result: high-speed chases increased from 10 in the previous 5 months to 85 in the succeeding 5 months, with 29 of those resulting in accidents. But, auto thefts dropped by 51% and overall crime dropped by 25% (*New York Times,* Dec. 17, 1995). Consider a random sample of five high-speed chases.

a. Demonstrate that x, the number of chases resulting in an accident, is an approximate binomial random variable.

b. Using the Alpert statistics, what is the probability that the five high-speed chases result in at least one accident?

c. Use the Tampa data to estimate the probability of part **b**.

d. Which probability, part **b** or part **c**, best describes high-speed chases in your state? Explain.

THE FURNITURE FIRE CASE

SHOWCASE

A wholesale furniture retailer stores in-stock items at a large warehouse located in Tampa, Florida. In early 1992, a fire destroyed the warehouse and all the furniture in it. After determining the fire was an accident, the retailer sought to recover costs by submitting a claim to its insurance company.

As is typical in a fire insurance policy of this type, the furniture retailer must provide the insurance company with an estimate of "lost" profit for the destroyed items. Retailers calculate profit margin in percentage form using the Gross Profit Factor (GPF). By definition, the GPF for a single sold item is the ratio of the profit to the item's selling price measured as a percentage, i.e.,

$$\text{Item GPF} = (\text{Profit/Sales price}) \times 100$$

Of interest to both the retailer and the insurance company is the average GPF for all of the items in the warehouse. Since these furniture pieces were all destroyed, their eventual selling prices and profit values are obviously unknown. Consequently, the average GPF for all the warehouse items is unknown.

One way to estimate the mean GPF of the destroyed items is to use the mean GPF of similar, recently sold items. The retailer sold 3,005 furniture items in 1991 (the year prior to the fire) and kept paper invoices on all sales. Rather than calculate the mean GPF for all 3,005 items (the data were not computerized), the retailer sampled a total of 253 of the invoices and computed the mean GPF for these items. The 253 items were obtained by first selecting a sample of 134 items and then augmenting this sample with a second sample of 119 items. The mean GPFs for the two subsamples were calculated to be 50.6% and 51.0%, respectively, yielding an overall average GPF of 50.8%. This average GPF can be applied to the costs of the furniture items destroyed in the fire to obtain an estimate of the "lost" profit.

According to experienced claims adjusters at the insurance company, the GPF for sale items of the type destroyed in the fire rarely exceeds 48%. Consequently, the estimate of 50.8% appeared to be unusually high. (A 1% increase in GPF for items of this type equates to, approximately, an additional $16,000 in profit.) When the insurance company questioned the retailer on this issue, the retailer responded, "Our estimate was based on selecting two independent, random samples from the population of 3,005 invoices in 1991. Since the samples were selected randomly and the total sample size is large, the mean GPF estimate of 50.8% is valid."

A dispute arose between the furniture retailer and the insurance company, and a lawsuit was filed. In one portion of the suit, the insurance company accused the retailer of fraudulently representing their sampling methodology. Rather than selecting the samples randomly, the retailer was accused of selecting an unusual number of "high profit" items from the population in order to increase the average GPF of the overall sample.

To support their claim of fraud, the insurance company hired a CPA firm to independently assess the retailer's 1991 Gross Profit Factor. Through the discovery process, the CPA firm legally obtained the paper invoices for the entire population of 3,005 items sold and input the information into a computer. The selling price, profit, profit margin, and month sold for these 3,005 furniture items are available in ASCII format on a 3.5-inch diskette, as described below.

Your objective in this case is to use these data to determine the likelihood of fraud. Is it likely that a random sample of 253 items selected from the population of 3,005 items would yield a mean GPF of at least 50.8%? Or, is it likely that two independent, random samples of size 134 and 119 will yield mean GPFs of at least 50.6% and 51.0%, respectively? (These were the questions posed to a statistician retained by the CPA firm.) Use the ideas of probability and sampling distributions to guide your analysis.

Prepare a professional document that presents the results of your analysis and gives your opinion regarding fraud. Be sure to describe the assumptions and methodology used to arrive at your findings.

DATA   ASCII file name: FIRE.DAT
Number of observations: 3005

Variable	Column(s)	Type	Description
MONTH	17–19	QL	Month in which item was sold in 1991
INVOICE	25–29	QN	Invoice number
SALES	35–42	QN	Sales price of item in dollars
PROFIT	47–54	QN	Profit amount of item in dollars
MARGIN	59–64	QN	Profit margin of item = (Profit/Sales) × 100

www.int.com
www.int.com
INTERNET LAB
www.int.com

ANALYZING MONTHLY BUSINESS START-UPS

A pulse of economic health regionally, and nationally, is the rate of new business start-ups. Strategic planners follow this business activity as a guide to timing the introduction of new ventures.

Here we examine the distribution of the monthly data on business start-ups provided by the Federal Reserve Board of Kansas City: *http://www.kc.frb.org/* (refer to your notes or the Internet Lab that follows Chapter 2).

1. Obtain monthly national business start-up data for the past eight or nine full years.

2. Save the data in your statistical applications software data files.

3. Calculate the mean and standard deviation of the monthly number of start-ups over all the years of data you have. Assume these values represent the population parameters, μ and σ, respectively.

4. For each full year of data, calculate the mean number of start-ups. Also, compute the standard error for this distribution of start-ups.

5. For each month (January, February, and so forth), calculate the mean number of start-ups. Also, compare the standard error for this distribution of means.

6. Sequentially, plot the means obtained in each of steps 4 and 5. Do either or both of these distributions show evidence of bias? How might that bias be interpreted in terms of changing, seasonal, or cyclical economic activity? ○

CHAPTER 5

INFERENCES BASED ON A SINGLE SAMPLE
Estimation with Confidence Intervals

CONTENTS

5.1   Large-Sample Confidence Interval for a Population Mean

5.2   Small-Sample Confidence Interval for a Population Mean

5.3   Large-Sample Confidence Interval for a Population Proportion

5.4   Determining the Sample Size

STATISTICS IN ACTION

5.1   Scallops, Sampling, and the Law

5.2   Is Caffeine Addictive?

Where We've Been

We've learned that populations are characterized by numerical descriptive measures (called *parameters*) and that decisions about their values are based on sample statistics computed from sample data. Since statistics vary in a random manner from sample to sample, inferences based on them will be subject to uncertainty. This property is reflected in the sampling (probability) distribution of a statistic.

Where We're Going

In this chapter, we'll put all the preceding material into practice; that is, we'll estimate population means and proportions based on a single sample selected from the population of interest. Most importantly, we use the sampling distribution of a sample statistic to assess the reliability of an estimate.

The estimation of the mean gas mileage for a new car model, the estimation of the expected life of a computer monitor, and the estimation of the mean yearly sales for companies in the steel industry are problems with a common element. In each case, we're interested in estimating the mean of a population of quantitative measurements. This important problem constitutes the primary topic of this chapter.

You'll see that different techniques are used for estimating a mean, depending on whether a sample contains a large or small number of measurements. Nevertheless, our objectives remain the same: We want to use the sample information to estimate the mean and to assess the reliability of the estimate.

First, we consider a method of estimating a population mean using a large random sample (Section 5.1) and a small random sample (Section 5.2). Then, we consider estimation of population proportions (Section 5.3). Finally, we see how to determine the sample sizes necessary for reliable estimates based on random sampling (Section 5.4).

5.1 LARGE-SAMPLE CONFIDENCE INTERVAL FOR A POPULATION MEAN

We illustrate the **large-sample method** of estimating a population mean with an example. Suppose a large bank wants to estimate the average amount of money owed by its delinquent debtors—i.e., debtors who are more than two months behind in payment. To accomplish this objective, the bank plans to randomly sample 100 of its delinquent accounts and to use the sample mean, $\bar{x}$, of the amounts overdue to estimate μ, the mean for *all* delinquent accounts. The sample mean $\bar{x}$ represents a *point estimator* of the population mean μ.

DEFINITION 5.1

A **point estimator** of a population parameter is a rule or formula that tells us how to use the sample data to calculate a single number that can be used as an *estimate* of the population parameter.

How can we assess the accuracy of this point estimator?

According to the Central Limit Theorem, the sampling distribution of the sample mean is approximately normal for large samples, as shown in Figure 5.1. Let us calculate the interval

$$\bar{x} \pm 2\sigma_{\bar{x}} = \bar{x} \pm \frac{2\sigma}{\sqrt{n}}$$

FIGURE 5.1
Sampling distribution of $\bar{x}$

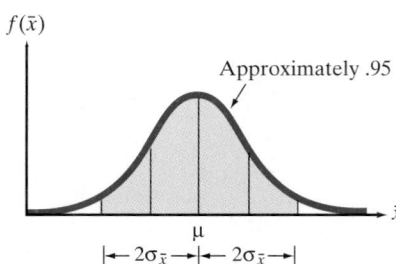

TABLE 5.1   Overdue Amounts (in Dollars) for 100 Delinquent Accounts

195	243	132	133	209	400	142	312	221	289
221	162	134	275	355	293	242	458	378	148
278	222	236	178	202	222	334	208	194	135
363	221	449	265	146	215	113	229	221	243
512	193	134	138	209	207	206	310	293	310
237	135	252	365	371	238	232	271	121	134
203	178	180	148	162	160	86	234	244	266
119	259	108	289	328	331	330	227	162	354
304	141	158	240	82	17	357	187	364	268
368	274	278	190	344	157	219	77	171	280

That is, we form an interval 4 standard deviations wide—from 2 standard deviations below the sample mean to 2 standard deviations above the mean. Prior to drawing the sample, what are the chances that this interval will enclose μ, the population mean?

To answer this question, refer to Figure 5.1. If the 100 measurements yield a value of $\bar{x}$ that falls between the two lines on either side of μ—i.e., within 2 standard deviations of μ—then the interval $\bar{x} \pm 2\sigma_{\bar{x}}$ will contain μ; if $\bar{x}$ falls outside these boundaries, the interval $\bar{x} \pm 2\sigma_{\bar{x}}$ will not contain μ. Since the area under the normal curve (the sampling distribution of $\bar{x}$) between these boundaries is about .95 (more precisely, from Table IV in Appendix B the area is .9544), we know that the interval $\bar{x} \pm 2\sigma_{\bar{x}}$ will contain μ with a probability approximately equal to .95.

For instance, consider the overdue amounts for 100 delinquent accounts shown in Table 5.1. A SAS printout of summary statistics for the sample of 100 overdue amounts is shown in Figure 5.2. From the printout, we find $\bar{x} = \$233.28$ and $s = \$90.34$. To achieve our objective, we must construct the interval

$$\bar{x} \pm 2\sigma_{\bar{x}} = 233.28 \pm 2\frac{\sigma}{\sqrt{100}}$$

But now we face a problem. You can see that without knowing the standard deviation σ of the original population—that is, the standard deviation of the overdue amounts of *all* delinquent accounts—we cannot calculate this interval. However, since we have a large sample ($n = 100$ measurements), we can approximate the interval by using the sample standard deviation s to approximate σ. Thus,

$$\bar{x} \pm 2\frac{\sigma}{\sqrt{100}} \approx \bar{x} \pm 2\frac{s}{\sqrt{100}} = 233.28 \pm 2\left(\frac{90.34}{10}\right) = 233.28 \pm 18.07$$

That is, we estimate the mean amount of delinquency for all accounts to fall within the interval \$215.21 to \$251.35.

Can we be sure that μ, the true mean, is in the interval (215.21, 251.35)? We cannot be certain, but we can be reasonably confident that it is. This confidence is derived from the knowledge that if we were to draw repeated random samples of 100 measurements from this population and form the interval $\bar{x} \pm 2\sigma_{\bar{x}}$ each time,

FIGURE 5.2
SAS summary statistics for the overdue amounts of 100 delinquent accounts

```
Analysis Variable : AMOUNT

N Obs    N      Minimum       Maximum             Mean        Std Dev
--------------------------------------------------------------------
 100    100   17.0000000   512.0000000   233.2800000    90.3398835
--------------------------------------------------------------------
```

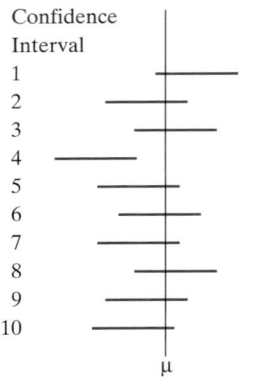

FIGURE 5.3
Confidence intervals for μ:
10 samples

approximately 95% of the intervals would contain μ. We have no way of knowing (without looking at all the delinquent accounts) whether our sample interval is one of the 95% that contain μ or one of the 5% that do not, but the odds certainly favor its containing μ. Consequently, the interval $215.21 to $251.35 provides a reliable estimate of the mean delinquency per account.

The formula that tells us how to calculate an interval estimate based on sample data is called an *interval estimator,* or *confidence interval.* The probability, .95, that measures the confidence we can place in the interval estimate is called a *confidence coefficient.* The percentage, 95%, is called the *confidence level* for the interval estimate. It is not usually possible to assess precisely the reliability of point estimators because they are single points rather than intervals. So, because we prefer to use estimators for which a measure of reliability can be calculated, we will generally use interval estimators.

DEFINITION 5.2
An **interval estimator** (or **confidence interval**) is a formula that tells us how to use sample data to calculate an interval that estimates a population parameter.

DEFINITION 5.3
The **confidence coefficient** is the probability that a confidence interval encloses the population parameter—that is, the relative frequency with which the interval encloses the population parameter when the estimator is used repeatedly a very large number of times. The **confidence level** is the confidence coefficient expressed as a percentage.

Now we have seen how an interval can be used to estimate a population mean. When we use an interval estimator, we can usually calculate the probability that the estimation *process* will result in an interval that contains the true value of the population mean. That is, the probability that the interval contains the parameter in repeated usage is usually known. Figure 5.3 shows what happens when 10 different samples are drawn from a population, and a confidence interval for μ is calculated from each. The location of μ is indicated by the vertical line in the figure. Ten confidence intervals, each based on one of 10 samples, are shown as horizontal line segments. Note that the confidence intervals move from sample to sample—sometimes containing μ and other times missing μ. If our confidence level is 95%, then in the long run, 95% of our sample confidence intervals will contain μ and 5% will not.

Suppose you wish to choose a confidence coefficient other than .95. Notice in Figure 5.1 that the confidence coefficient .95 is equal to the total area under the sampling distribution, less .05 of the area, which is divided equally between the two tails. Using this idea, we can construct a confidence interval with any desired confidence coefficient by increasing or decreasing the area (call it α) assigned to the tails of the sampling distribution (see Figure 5.4). For example, if we place area

FIGURE 5.4
Locating $z_{\alpha/2}$ on the standard normal curve

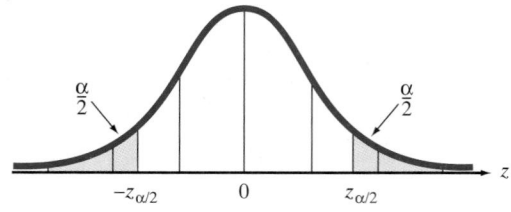

FIGURE 5.5

The z value ($z_{.05}$) corresponding to an area equal to .05 in the upper tail of the z-distribution

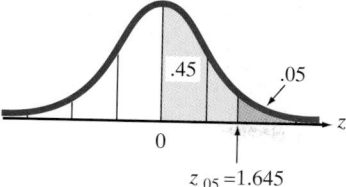

$z_{.05} = 1.645$

$\alpha/2$ in each tail and if $z_{\alpha/2}$ is the z value such that the area $\alpha/2$ lies to its right, then the confidence interval with confidence coefficient $(1 - \alpha)$ is

$$\bar{x} \pm z_{\alpha/2}\sigma_{\bar{x}}$$

To illustrate, for a confidence coefficient of .90 we have $(1 - \alpha) = .90$, $\alpha = .10$, and $\alpha/2 = .05$; $z_{.05}$ is the z value that locates area .05 in the upper tail of the sampling distribution. Recall that Table IV in Appendix B gives the areas between the mean and a specified z value. Since the total area to the right of the mean is .5, we find that $z_{.05}$ will be the z value corresponding to an area of $.5 - .05 = .45$ to the right of the mean (see Figure 5.5). This z value is $z_{.05} = 1.645$.

Confidence coefficients used in practice usually range from .90 to .99. The most commonly used confidence coefficients with corresponding values of α and $z_{\alpha/2}$ are shown in Table 5.2.

Large-Sample $100(1 - \alpha)\%$ Confidence Interval for μ

$$\bar{x} \pm z_{\alpha/2}\sigma_{\bar{x}} = \bar{x} \pm z_{\alpha/2}\frac{\sigma}{\sqrt{n}}$$

where $z_{\alpha/2}$ is the z value with an area $\alpha/2$ to its right (see Figure 5.4) and $\sigma_{\bar{x}} = \sigma/\sqrt{n}$. The parameter σ is the standard deviation of the sampled population and n is the sample size.

Note: When σ is unknown (as is almost always the case) and n is large (say, $n \geqslant 30$), the confidence interval is approximately equal to

$$\bar{x} \pm z_{\alpha/2}\left(\frac{s}{\sqrt{n}}\right)$$

where s is the sample standard deviation.

Assumptions: None, since the Central Limit Theorem guarantees that the sampling distribution of $\bar{x}$ is approximately normal.

TABLE 5.2   Commonly Used Values of $z_{\alpha/2}$

CONFIDENCE LEVEL $100(1-\alpha)$	α	$\alpha/2$	$z_{\alpha/2}$
90%	.10	.05	1.645
95%	.05	.025	1.96
99%	.01	.005	2.575

FIGURE 5.6
MINITAB printout
for the confidence
intervals in
Example 5.1

	N	MEAN	STDEV	SE MEAN	90.0 PERCENT C.I.
NoSeats	225	11.6	4.1	0.273	(11.15, 12.05)

EXAMPLE 5.1

Unoccupied seats on flights cause airlines to lose revenue. Suppose a large airline wants to estimate its average number of unoccupied seats per flight over the past year. To accomplish this, the records of 225 flights are randomly selected, and the number of unoccupied seats is noted for each of the sampled flights. The sample mean and standard deviation are

$$\bar{x} = 11.6 \text{ seats} \qquad s = 4.1 \text{ seats}$$

Estimate μ, the mean number of unoccupied seats per flight during the past year, using a 90% confidence interval.

SOLUTION

The general form of the 90% confidence interval for a population mean is

$$\bar{x} \pm z_{\alpha/2}\sigma_{\bar{x}} = \bar{x} \pm z_{.05}\sigma_{\bar{x}} = \bar{x} \pm 1.645\left(\frac{\sigma}{\sqrt{n}}\right)$$

For the 225 records sampled, we have

$$11.6 \pm 1.645\left(\frac{\sigma}{\sqrt{225}}\right)$$

Since we do not know the value of σ (the standard deviation of the number of unoccupied seats per flight for all flights of the year), we use our best approximation—the sample standard deviation s. Then the 90% confidence interval is, approximately,

$$11.6 \pm 1.645\left(\frac{4.1}{\sqrt{225}}\right) = 11.6 \pm .45$$

or from 11.15 to 12.05. That is, at the 90% confidence level, we estimate the mean number of unoccupied seats per flight to be between 11.15 and 12.05 during the sampled year. This result is verified on the MINITAB printout of the analysis shown in Figure 5.6.

We stress that the confidence level for this example, 90%, refers to the procedure used. If we were to apply this procedure repeatedly to different samples, approximately 90% of the intervals would contain μ. We do not know whether this particular interval (11.15, 12.05) is one of the 90% that contain μ or one of the 10% that do not.

The interpretation of confidence intervals for a population mean is summarized in the accompanying box.

Interpretation of a Confidence Interval for a Population Mean
When we form a $100(1 - \alpha)\%$ confidence interval for μ, we usually express our confidence in the interval with a statement such as, "We can be $100(1 - \alpha)\%$ confident that μ lies between the lower and upper bounds of the confidence interval," where for a particular application, we substitute the appropriate numerical values for the confidence

and for the lower and upper bounds. *The statement reflects our confidence in the estimation process rather than in the particular interval that is calculated from the sample data.* We know that repeated application of the same procedure will result in different lower and upper bounds on the interval. Furthermore, we know that $100(1 - \alpha)\%$ of the resulting intervals will contain μ. There is (usually) no way to determine whether any particular interval is one of those that contain μ, or one that does not. However, unlike point estimators, confidence intervals have some measure of reliability, the confidence coefficient, associated with them. For that reason they are generally preferred to point estimators.

Sometimes, the estimation procedure yields a confidence interval that is too wide for our purposes. In this case, we will want to reduce the width of the interval to obtain a more precise estimate of μ. One way to accomplish this is to decrease the confidence coefficient, $1 - \alpha$. For example, reconsider the problem of estimating the mean amount owed, μ, for all delinquent accounts. Recall that for a sample of 100 accounts, $\bar{x} = \$233.28$ and $s = \$90.34$. A 90% confidence interval for μ is

$$\bar{x} \pm 1.645\sigma/\sqrt{n} \approx 233.28 \pm (1.645)\left(90.34/\sqrt{100}\right) = 233.28 \pm 14.86$$

or ($218.42, $248.14). You can see that this interval is narrower than the previously calculated 95% confidence interval, ($215.21, $251.35). Unfortunately, we also have "less confidence" in the 90% confidence interval. An alternative method used to decrease the width of an interval without sacrificing "confidence" is to increase the sample size n. We demonstrate this method in Section 5.4.

EXERCISES   5.1–5.17

Note: Exercises marked with 💾 *contain data available for computer analysis on a 3.5" disk (file name in parentheses).*

Learning the Mechanics

5.1 Find $z_{\alpha/2}$ for each of the following:
   a. $\alpha = .10$ **b.** $\alpha = .01$ **c.** $\alpha = .05$ **d.** $\alpha = .20$

5.2 What is the confidence level of each of the following confidence intervals for μ?

   a. $\bar{x} \pm 1.96\left(\dfrac{\sigma}{\sqrt{n}}\right)$ **b.** $\bar{x} \pm 1.645\left(\dfrac{\sigma}{\sqrt{n}}\right)$

   c. $\bar{x} \pm 2.575\left(\dfrac{\sigma}{\sqrt{n}}\right)$ **d.** $\bar{x} \pm 1.282\left(\dfrac{\sigma}{\sqrt{n}}\right)$

   e. $\bar{x} \pm .99\left(\dfrac{\sigma}{\sqrt{n}}\right)$

5.3 A random sample of n measurements was selected from a population with unknown mean μ and standard deviation σ. Calculate a 95% confidence interval for μ for each of the following situations:
   a. $n = 75, \bar{x} = 28, s^2 = 12$
   b. $n = 200, \bar{x} = 102, s^2 = 22$
   c. $n = 100, \bar{x} = 15, s = .3$

   d. $n = 100, \bar{x} = 4.05, s = .83$
   e. Is the assumption that the underlying population of measurements is normally distributed necessary to ensure the validity of the confidence intervals in parts **a–d**? Explain.

5.4 A random sample of 90 observations produced a mean $\bar{x} = 25.9$ and a standard deviation $s = 2.7$.
   a. Find a 95% confidence interval for the population mean μ.
   b. Find a 90% confidence interval for μ.
   c. Find a 99% confidence interval for μ.

5.5 A random sample of 70 observations from a normally distributed population possesses a mean equal to 26.2 and a standard deviation equal to 4.1.
   a. Find a 95% confidence interval for μ.
   b. What do you mean when you say that a confidence coefficient is .95?
   c. Find a 99% confidence interval for μ.
   d. What happens to the width of a confidence interval as the value of the confidence coefficient is increased while the sample size is held fixed?

e. Would your confidence intervals of parts **a** and **c** be valid if the distribution of the original population was not normal? Explain.

5.6 Explain what is meant by the statement, "We are 95% confident that an interval estimate contains μ."

5.7 Explain the difference between an interval estimator and a point estimator for μ.

5.8 The mean and standard deviation of a random sample of n measurements are equal to 33.9 and 3.3, respectively.

a. Find a 95% confidence interval for μ if $n = 100$.

b. Find a 95% confidence interval for μ if $n = 400$.

c. Find the widths of the confidence intervals found in parts **a** and **b**. What is the effect on the width of a confidence interval of quadrupling the sample size while holding the confidence coefficient fixed?

5.9 Will a large-sample confidence interval be valid if the population from which the sample is taken is not normally distributed? Explain.

Applying the Concepts

5.10 The *Journal of the American Medical Association* (Apr. 21, 1993) reported on the results of a National Health Interview Survey designed to determine the prevalence of smoking among U.S. adults. More than 40,000 adults responded to questions such as "Have you smoked at least 100 cigarettes in your lifetime?" and "Do you smoke cigarettes now?" Current smokers (more than 11,000 adults in the survey) were also asked: "On the average, how many cigarettes do you now smoke a day?" The results yielded a mean of 20.0 cigarettes per day with an associated 95% confidence interval of (19.7, 20.3).

a. Carefully describe the population from which the sample was drawn.

b. Interpret the 95% confidence interval.

c. State any assumptions about the target population of current cigarette smokers that must be satisfied for inferences derived from the interval to be valid.

d. A tobacco industry researcher claims that the mean number of cigarettes smoked per day by regular cigarette smokers is less than 15. Comment on this claim.

5.11 (X05.011) At the end of 1992, 1993, and 1994, the average prices of a share of stock on the New York Stock Exchange (NYSE) were $34.83, $34.65, and $31.26, respectively (*Statistical Abstract of the United States: 1995*). To investigate the average share price at the end of 1995, a random sample of 30 NYSE stocks was drawn. Their closing prices on December 29, 1995, are listed (by their NYSE abbreviations) in the table. A SAS descriptive statistics printout is at the bottom of the page.

Stock	Price	Stock	Price
Litton	$44\frac{1}{2}$	MCN	$23\frac{1}{4}$
Morton	$35\frac{7}{8}$	Premdor	$7\frac{3}{4}$
Deere	$35\frac{1}{4}$	Clorox	$71\frac{5}{8}$
Tremont	$16\frac{5}{8}$	ToysRUs	$21\frac{3}{4}$
Munivest PA	$11\frac{1}{2}$	Penn Entr	$37\frac{7}{8}$
Case Cp	$45\frac{3}{4}$	Ameron	$37\frac{5}{8}$
TriMas	$18\frac{3}{4}$	MDC	$7\frac{1}{8}$
Pac Ent	$28\frac{1}{4}$	Dean Food	$27\frac{1}{2}$
Pepsi Co	$55\frac{7}{8}$	PubSvcEnt	$30\frac{5}{8}$
DeVry	27	CocaCola	$74\frac{1}{4}$
Loctite	$47\frac{1}{2}$	Morgan	$80\frac{1}{4}$
Lyondell	$27\frac{7}{8}$	Dana Cp	$29\frac{1}{4}$
Moore Cp	$18\frac{3}{4}$	CV REIT	$11\frac{1}{4}$
MrgnStnAtr	$12\frac{7}{8}$	PLC Cap MPS	$26\frac{1}{2}$
Alco Std	$45\frac{5}{8}$	Progrsv Cp	$48\frac{7}{8}$

Source: Wall Street Journal, January 2, 1996.

a. Use the information in the SAS printout below to estimate the average price of a share of stock at the end of 1995 with a 90% confidence interval.

b. Use the latest edition of the *Statistical Abstract of the United States* to find the actual average price of a stock on the NYSE at the end of 1995. Is this figure in agreement with your confidence interval? Explain. If not, provide a possible explanation for the disagreement.

5.12 Research indicates that bicycle helmets save lives. A study reported in *Public Health Reports* (May–June 1992) was intended to identify ways of encouraging helmet use in children. One of the variables measured was the children's perception of the risk involved in bicycling. A four-point scale was used, with scores ranging from 1 (no risk) to 4 (very high risk). A sample of 797 children in grades 4–6 yielded the following results on the perception of risk variable: $\bar{x} = 3.39, s = .80$.

a. Calculate a 90% confidence interval for the average perception of risk for all students in grades 4–6. What assumptions did you make to ensure the validity of the confidence interval?

b. If the population mean perception of risk exceeds 2.50, the researchers will conclude that

```
Analysis Variable : PRICE

N Obs    N       Minimum         Maximum           Mean        Std Dev
-----------------------------------------------------------------------
  30     30      7.1250000      80.2500000      33.5833333    19.1494613
-----------------------------------------------------------------------
```

students in these grades exhibit an awareness of the risk involved with bicycling. Interpret the confidence interval constructed in part **a** in this context.

5.13 An auditor was hired to verify the accuracy of a company's new billing system. The auditor randomly sampled 35 invoices produced since the system was installed. Each invoice was compared against the relevant internal records to determine by how much the invoice was in error. The amount of the error, x, was defined as $(A - I)$, where A is the actual amount owed the company and I is the amount indicated on the invoice. The auditor found that $\bar{x} = \$1$ and $s = \$124$.
  a. Identify the population the auditor studied.
  b. Describe the variable that the auditor measured.
  c. Construct a 98% confidence interval for the mean error per invoice.
  d. Interpret the confidence interval.
  e. Comment on the accuracy of the billing system.

5.14 The trade magazine *Quality Progress* randomly sampled 9,117 of its more than 100,000 subscribers and mailed them a salary questionnaire. A week after the first mailing, a postcard was sent to the same people reminding them to complete the questionnaire. Two weeks after the postcard was mailed, a duplicate questionnaire was sent to all those people who hadn't yet responded. A week later another reminder postcard was sent. In the end, 4,828 usable responses were received, yielding a response rate of 53%. (*Note:* This high response rate could not have been achieved without the extensive follow-up procedures that were employed.) The survey yielded the data shown below concerning salary and job title.
  a. The column labeled "Mean" reports point estimators for certain parameters. Carefully describe both the relevant populations and parameters.

  b. Construct and interpret a 95% confidence interval for the mean salary for managers.
  c. Repeat part **b** for vice presidents.
  d. Explain why the confidence intervals of parts **b** and **c** are preferred over the point estimates when describing the mean salaries of managers and vice presidents.

5.15 Nasser Arshadi and Edward Lawrence investigated the profiles (i.e., career patterns, social backgrounds, and so forth) of the top executives in the U.S. banking industry (*Journal of Retail Banking,* Winter 1983–1984). They sampled 96 executives and found that 80% studied business or economics and that 45% had a graduate degree. With respect to the number of years of service, x, at the same bank, the group had a mean of 23.43 years and a standard deviation of 10.82 years.
  a. Construct a 90% confidence interval for $E(x) = \mu$.
  b. Interpret your interval in the context of the problem.
  c. What assumption(s) was it necessary to make in order to construct the confidence interval of part **a**?
  d. Is your interval estimate for $E(x)$ also an interval estimate for $E(\bar{x})$? Explain. [*Hint:* See Chapter 4.]

5.16 Named for the section of the 1978 Internal Revenue Code that authorized them, 401(k) plans permit employees to shift part of their before-tax salaries into investments such as mutual funds. Employers typically match 50% of the employee's contribution up to about 6% of salary (*Fortune,* Dec. 28, 1992). One company, concerned with what it believed was a low employee participation rate in its 401(k) plan, sampled 30 other companies with similar plans and asked for their 401(k) participation rates. The rates (in percentages) shown on the next page were obtained:

Title	Sample Size	Mean	Standard Deviation
Inspector	251	26,098	7,395
Technician	397	27,384	5,956
Coordinator	176	36,919	13,178
Specialist	373	42,110	13,449
Supervisor	456	42,699	14,187
Engineer	651	46,816	12,557
Manager	1,142	55,076	17,910
Consultant (in-house)	260	60,601	20,561
Director	670	67,339	23,211
Consultant (independent)	163	69,355	26,871
Vice president	284	93,247	33,740

Source: "1994 Salary Survey." *Quality Progress,* November 1994, pp. 27–49.

Number of Valid Observations (Listwise) =				30.00	
Variable	Mean	Std Dev	Minimum	Maximum	N Label
PARTRATE	79.73	5.96	60.00	90.00	30

80	76	81	77	82	80	85	60	80	79	82	70
88	85	80	79	83	75	87	78	80	84	72	75
90	84	82	77	75	86

Descriptive statistics for the data are given in the SPSS printout at the top of the page:

a. Use the information on the SPSS printout to construct a 95% confidence interval for the mean participation rate for all companies that have 401(k) plans.

b. Interpret the interval in the context of this problem.

c. What assumption is necessary to ensure the validity of this confidence interval?

d. If the company that conducted the sample has a 71% participation rate, can it safely conclude that its rate is below the population mean rate for all companies with 401(k) plans? Explain.

e. If in the data set the 60% had been 80%, how would the center and width of the confidence interval you constructed in part **a** be affected?

5.17 Research reported in the *Journal of Psychology and Aging* (May 1992) studied the role that the age of workers has in determining their level of job satisfaction. The researcher hypothesized that both younger and older workers would have a higher job satisfaction rating than middle-age workers. Each of a sample of 1,686 adults was given a job satisfaction score based on answers to a series of questions. Higher job satisfaction scores indicate higher levels of job satisfaction. The data are given in the accompanying table, arranged by age group.

	AGE GROUP		
	Younger 18–24	Middle-Age 25–44	Older 45–64
$\bar{x}$	4.17	4.04	4.31
s	.75	.81	.82
n	241	768	677

a. Construct 95% confidence intervals for the mean job satisfaction scores of each age group. Carefully interpret each interval.

b. In the construction of three 95% confidence intervals, is it more or less likely that at least one of them will *not* contain the population mean it is intended to estimate than it is for a single confidence interval to miss the population mean? [*Hint:* Assume the three intervals are independent and calculate the probability that at least one of them will not contain the population mean it estimates. Compare this probability to the probability that a single interval fails to enclose the mean.]

c. Based on these intervals, does it appear that the researcher's hypothesis is supported? [*Caution:* We will learn how to use sample information to compare population means in Chapter 7, and will return to this exercise at that time. Here, simply base your opinion on the individual confidence intervals you constructed in part **a**.]

5.2   SMALL-SAMPLE CONFIDENCE INTERVAL FOR A POPULATION MEAN

Federal legislation requires pharmaceutical companies to perform extensive tests on new drugs before they can be marketed. Initially, a new drug is tested on animals. If the drug is deemed safe after this first phase of testing, the pharmaceutical company is then permitted to begin human testing on a limited basis. During this second phase, inferences must be made about the safety of the drug based on information in very small samples.

Suppose a pharmaceutical company must estimate the average increase in blood pressure of patients who take a certain new drug. Assume that only six patients (randomly selected from the population of all patients) can be used in the initial phase of human testing. The use of a **small sample** in making an inference about μ presents two immediate problems when we attempt to use the standard normal z as a test statistic.

Problem I. The shape of the sampling distribution of the sample mean $\bar{x}$ (and the z statistic) now depends on the shape of the population that is sampled. We can no longer assume that the sampling distribution of $\bar{x}$ is approximately normal, because the Central Limit Theorem ensures normality only for samples that are sufficiently large.

Solution to Problem 1. According to Theorem 4.1, the sampling distribution of $\bar{x}$ (and z) is exactly normal even for relatively small samples if the sampled population is normal. It is approximately normal if the sampled population is approximately normal.

Problem 2. The population standard deviation σ is almost always unknown. Although it is still true that $\sigma_{\bar{x}} = \sigma/\sqrt{n}$, the sample standard deviation s may provide a poor approximation for σ when the sample size is small.

Solution to Problem 2. Instead of using the standard normal statistic

$$z = \frac{\bar{x} - \mu}{\sigma_{\bar{x}}} = \frac{\bar{x} - \mu}{\sigma/\sqrt{n}}$$

which requires knowledge of or a good approximation to σ, we define and use the statistic

$$t = \frac{\bar{x} - \mu}{s/\sqrt{n}}$$

in which the sample standard deviation, s, replaces the population standard deviation, σ.

The distribution of the **t statistic** in repeated sampling was discovered by W. S. Gosset, a chemist in the Guinness brewery in Ireland, who published his discovery in 1908 under the pen name of Student. The main result of Gosset's work is that if we are sampling from a normal distribution, the t statistic has a sampling distribution very much like that of the z statistic: mound-shaped, symmetric, with mean 0. The primary difference between the sampling distributions of t and z is that the t statistic is more variable than the z, which follows intuitively when you realize that t contains two random quantities ($\bar{x}$ and s), whereas z contains only one ($\bar{x}$).

The actual amount of variability in the sampling distribution of t depends on the sample size n. A convenient way of expressing this dependence is to say that the t statistic has $(n-1)$ **degrees of freedom (df).** Recall that the quantity $(n-1)$ is the divisor that appears in the formula for s^2. This number plays a key role in the sampling distribution of s^2 and appears in discussions of other statistics in later chapters. In particular, the smaller the number of degrees of freedom associated with the t statistic, the more variable will be its sampling distribution.

In Figure 5.7 we show both the sampling distribution of z and the sampling distribution of a t statistic with 4 df. You can see that the increased variability of the t statistic means that the t value, t_α, that locates an area α in the upper tail of the

FIGURE 5.7
Standard normal (z)
distribution and t-
distribution with 4 df

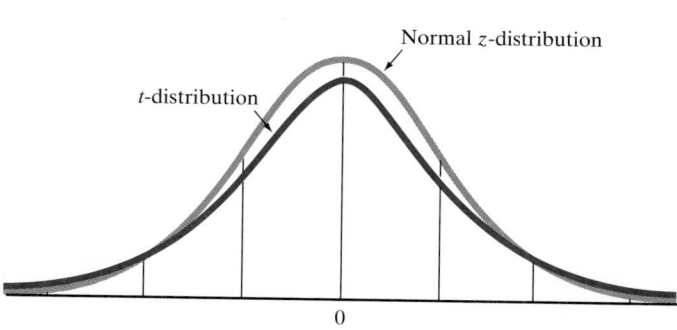

Normal z-distribution

t-distribution

0

TABLE 5.3   Reproduction of Part of Table VI in Appendix B

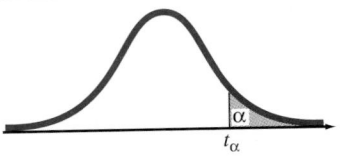

Degrees of Freedom	$t_{.100}$	$t_{.050}$	$t_{.025}$	$t_{.010}$	$t_{.005}$	$t_{.001}$	$t_{.0005}$
1	3.078	6.314	12.706	31.821	63.657	318.31	636.62
2	1.886	2.920	4.303	6.965	9.925	22.326	21.598
3	1.638	2.353	3.182	4.541	5.841	10.213	12.924
4	1.533	2.132	2.776	3.747	4.604	7.173	8.610
5	1.476	2.015	2.571	3.365	4.032	5.893	6.869
6	1.440	1.943	2.447	3.132	3.707	5.208	5.959
7	1.415	1.895	2.365	2.998	3.499	4.785	5.408
8	1.397	1.860	2.306	2.896	3.355	4.501	5.041
9	1.383	1.833	2.262	2.821	3.250	4.297	4.781
10	1.372	1.812	2.228	2.764	3.169	4.144	4.587
11	1.363	1.796	2.201	2.718	3.106	4.025	4.437
12	1.356	1.782	2.179	2.681	3.055	3.930	4.318
13	1.350	1.771	2.160	2.650	3.012	3.852	4.221
14	1.345	1.761	2.145	2.624	2.977	3.787	4.140
15	1.341	1.753	2.131	2.602	2.947	3.733	4.073
⋮	⋮	⋮	⋮	⋮	⋮	⋮	⋮
∞	1.282	1.645	1.960	2.326	2.576	3.090	3.291

t-distribution is larger than the corresponding value z_α. For any given value of α, the t value t_α increases as the number of degrees of freedom (df) decreases. Values of t that will be used in forming small-sample confidence intervals of μ are given in Table VI of Appendix B and inside the back cover of the text. A partial reproduction of this table is shown in Table 5.3.

Note that t_α values are listed for degrees of freedom from 1 to 29, where α refers to the tail area under the t-distribution to the right of t_α. For example, if we want the t value with an area of .025 to its right and 4 df, we look in the table under the column $t_{.025}$ for the entry in the row corresponding to 4 df. This entry is $t_{.025} = 2.776$, as shown in Figure 5.8. The corresponding standard normal z-score is $z_{.025} = 1.96$.

Note that the last row of Table VI, where df = ∞ (infinity), contains the standard normal z values. This follows from the fact that as the sample size n grows very large, s becomes closer to σ and thus t becomes closer in distribution to z. In fact, when df = 29, there is little difference between corresponding tabulated values of z and t. Thus, we choose the arbitrary cutoff of $n = 30$ (df = 29) to distinguish between the large-sample and small-sample inferential techniques.

FIGURE 5.8

The $t_{.025}$ value in a t-distribution with 4 df and the corresponding $z_{.025}$ value

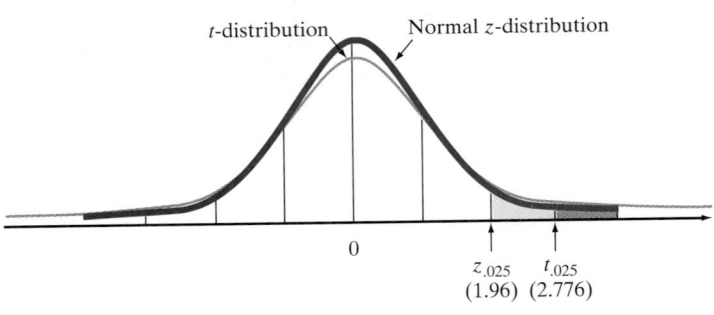

Returning to the example of testing a new drug, suppose that the six test patients have blood pressure increases of 1.7, 3.0, .8, 3.4, 2.7, and 2.1 points. How can we use this information to construct a 95% confidence interval for μ, the mean increase in blood pressure associated with the new drug for all patients in the population?

First, we know that we are dealing with a sample too small to assume that the sample mean $\bar{x}$ is approximately normally distributed by the Central Limit Theorem. That is, we do not get the normal distribution of $\bar{x}$ "automatically" from the Central Limit Theorem when the sample size is small. Instead, the measured variable, in this case the increase in blood pressure, must be normally distributed in order for the distribution of $\bar{x}$ to be normal.

Second, unless we are fortunate enough to know the population standard deviation σ, which in this case represents the standard deviation of *all* the patients' increases in blood pressure when they take the new drug, we cannot use the standard normal z statistic to form our confidence interval for μ. Instead, we must use the t-distribution, with $(n-1)$ degrees of freedom.

In this case, $n - 1 = 5$ df, and the t value is found in Table 5.3 to be $t_{.025} = 2.571$ with 5 df. Recall that the large-sample confidence interval would have been of the form

$$\bar{x} \pm z_{\alpha/2}\sigma_{\bar{x}} = \bar{x} \pm z_{\alpha/2}\frac{\sigma}{\sqrt{n}} = \bar{x} \pm z_{.025}\frac{\sigma}{\sqrt{n}}$$

where 95% is the desired confidence level. To form the interval for a small sample from *a normal distribution, we simply substitute* t *for z and* s *for* σ *in the preceding formula:*

$$\bar{x} \pm t_{\alpha/2}\frac{s}{\sqrt{n}}$$

A MINITAB printout showing descriptive statistics for the six blood pressure increases is displayed in Figure 5.9. Note that $\bar{x} = 2.283$ and $s = .950$. Substituting these numerical values into the confidence interval formula, we get

$$2.283 \pm (2.571)\left(\frac{.950}{\sqrt{6}}\right) = 2.283 \pm .997$$

or 1.286 to 3.280 points. Note that this interval agrees (except for rounding) with the confidence interval generated by MINITAB in Figure 5.9.

We interpret the interval as follows: We can be 95% confident that the mean increase in blood pressure associated with taking this new drug is between 1.286 and 3.28 points. As with our large-sample interval estimates, our confidence is in the process, not in this particular interval. We know that if we were to repeatedly use this estimation procedure, 95% of the confidence intervals produced would contain the true mean μ, *if the probability distribution of changes in blood pressure from which our sample was selected is normal.* If the distribution is nonnormal, the small-sample interval is not valid.

What price did we pay for having to utilize a small sample to make the inference? First, we had to assume the underlying population is normally distributed,

FIGURE 5.9
MINITAB analysis of six blood pressure increases

	N	MEAN	STDEV	SE MEAN	95.0 PERCENT C.I.
BPIncr	6	2.283	0.950	0.388	(1.287, 3.280)

and if the assumption is invalid, our interval might also be invalid.* Second, we had to form the interval using a t value of 2.571 rather than a z value of 1.96, resulting in a wider interval to achieve the same 95% level of confidence. If the interval from 1.286 to 3.28 is too wide to be of use, then we know how to remedy the situation: increase the number of patients sampled to decrease the interval width (on average).

The procedure for forming a small-sample confidence interval is summarized in the accompanying box.

Small-Sample Confidence Interval† for μ

$$\bar{x} \pm t_{\alpha/2}\left(\frac{s}{\sqrt{n}}\right)$$

where $t_{\alpha/2}$ is based on $(n - 1)$ degrees of freedom

Assumptions: A random sample is selected from a population with a relative frequency distribution that is approximately normal.

EXAMPLE 5.2

Some quality control experiments require *destructive sampling* (i.e., the test to determine whether the item is defective destroys the item) in order to measure some particular characteristic of the product. The cost of destructive sampling often dictates small samples. For example, suppose a manufacturer of printers for personal computers wishes to estimate the mean number of characters printed before the printhead fails. Suppose the printer manufacturer tests $n = 15$ randomly selected printheads and records the number of characters printed until failure for each. These 15 measurements (in millions of characters) are listed in Table 5.4, followed by an EXCEL summary statistics printout in Figure 5.10.

a. Form a 99% confidence interval for the mean number of characters printed before the printhead fails. Interpret the result.

b. What assumption is required for the interval, part **a**, to be valid? Is it reasonably satisfied?

SOLUTION

a. For this small sample ($n = 15$), we use the t statistic to form the confidence interval. We use a confidence coefficient of .99 and $n - 1 = 14$ degrees of freedom to find $t_{\alpha/2}$ in Table VI:

**TABLE 5.4   Number of Characters (in Millions)
for $n = 15$ Printhead Tests**

1.13	1.55	1.43	.92	1.25
1.36	1.32	.85	1.07	1.48
1.20	1.33	1.18	1.22	1.29

---

*By *invalid*, we mean that the probability that the procedure will yield an interval that contains μ is not equal to $(1 - \alpha)$. Generally, if the underlying population is approximately normal, then the confidence coefficient will approximate the probability that the interval contains μ.

$\dagger$The procedure given in the box assumes that the population standard deviation σ is unknown, which is almost always the case. If σ is known, we can form the small-sample confidence interval just as we would a large-sample confidence interval using a standard normal z value instead of t. However, we must still assume that the underlying population is approximately normal.

FIGURE 5.10
EXCEL summary
statistics printout for
data in Table 5.4

Number	
Mean	1.238667
Standard Error	0.049875
Median	1.25
Mode	#N/A
Standard Deviation	0.193164
Sample Variance	0.037312
Kurtosis	0.063636
Skewness	-0.49126
Range	0.7
Minimum	0.85
Maximum	1.55
Sum	18.58
Count	15
Confidence Level(95.000%)	0.097753

$$t_{\alpha/2} = t_{.005} = 2.977$$

[*Note:* The small sample forces us to extend the interval almost 3 standard deviations (of $\bar{x}$) on each side of the sample mean in order to form the 99% confidence interval.] From the EXCEL printout, Figure 5.10, we find $\bar{x} = 1.239$ and $s = .193$. Substituting these values into the confidence interval formula, we obtain:

$$\bar{x} \pm t_{.005}\left(\frac{s}{\sqrt{n}}\right) = 1.239 \pm 2.977\left(\frac{.193}{\sqrt{15}}\right)$$

$$= 1.239 \pm .148 \quad \text{or} \quad (1.091, 1.387)$$

Thus, the manufacturer can be 99% confident that the printhead has a mean life of between 1.091 and 1.387 million characters. If the manufacturer were to advertise that the mean life of its printheads is (at least) 1 million characters, the interval would support such a claim. Our confidence is derived from the fact that 99% of the intervals formed in repeated applications of this procedure would contain μ.

b. Since n is small, we must assume that the number of characters printed before printhead failure is a random variable from a normal distribution. That is, we assume that the population from which the sample of 15 measurements is selected is distributed normally. One way to check this assumption is to graph the distribution of data in Table 5.4. If the sample data are approximately normal, then the population from which the sample is selected is very likely to be normal. A MINITAB stem-and-leaf plot for the sample data is displayed in Figure 5.11 (page 254). The distribution is mound-shaped and nearly symmetric. Therefore, the assumption of normality appears to be reasonably satisfied. ◣

We have emphasized throughout this section that an assumption that the population is approximately normally distributed is necessary for making small-sample inferences about μ when using the t statistic. Although many phenomena do have approximately normal distributions, it is also true that many random phenomena have distributions that are not normal or even mound-shaped. Empirical evidence acquired over the years has shown that the t-distribution is

FIGURE 5.11
MINITAB stem-and-leaf display of data in Table 5.4

```
Stem-and-leaf of NUMBER     N = 15
Leaf Unit = 0.010

     1     8 5
     2     9 2
     3    10 7
     5    11 38
    (4)   12 0259
     6    13 236
     3    14 38
     1    15 5
```

rather insensitive to moderate departures from normality. That is, use of the *t* statistic when sampling from mound-shaped populations generally produces credible results; however, for cases in which the distribution is distinctly nonnormal, we must either take a large sample or use a *nonparametric method*. (A nonparametric method for making inferences from a single sample is presented in optional Section 6.6.)

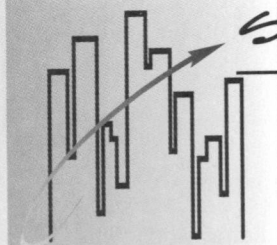

STATISTICS IN ACTION

5.1 SCALLOPS, SAMPLING, AND THE LAW

Arnold Bennett, a Sloan School of Management professor at the Massachusetts Institute of Technology (MIT), describes a recent legal case in which he served as a statistical "expert" in *Interfaces* (Mar.–Apr. 1995). The case involved a ship that fishes for scallops off the coast of New England. In order to protect baby scallops from being harvested, the U.S. Fisheries and Wildlife Service requires that "the average meat per scallop weigh at least 1/36 of a pound." The ship was accused of violating this weight standard. Bennett lays out the scenario:

The vessel arrived at a Massachusetts port with 11,000 bags of scallops, from which the harbormaster randomly selected 18 bags for weighing. From each such bag, his agents took a large scoopful of scallops; then, to estimate the bag's average meat per scallop, they divided the total weight of meat in the scoopful by the number of scallops it contained. Based on the 18 [numbers] thus generated, the harbormaster estimated that each of the ship's scallops possessed an average 1/39 of a pound of meat (that is, they were about seven percent lighter than the minimum requirement). Viewing this outcome as conclusive evidence that the weight standard had been

violated, federal authorities at once confiscated *95 percent* of the catch (which they then sold at auction). The fishing voyage was thus transformed into a financial catastrophe for its participants.

Bennett provided the actual scallop weight measurements for each of the 18 sampled bags in the article. The data are listed in Table 5.5. For ease of exposition, Bennett expressed each number as a multiple of 1/36 of a pound, the minimum permissible average weight per scallop. Consequently, numbers below one indicate individual bags that do not meet the standard.

The ship's owner filed a lawsuit against the federal government, declaring that his vessel had fully complied with the weight standard. A Boston law firm was hired to represent the owner in legal proceedings and Bennett was retained by the firm to provide statistical litigation support and, if necessary, expert witness testimony.

Focus

a. Recall that the harbormaster sampled only 18 of the ship's 11,000 bags of scallops. One of the questions the lawyers asked Bennett was: "Can a reliable estimate of the mean weight of all the scallops be obtained from a sample of size 18?" Give your opinion on this issue.

b. As stated in the article, the government's decision rule is to confiscate a scallop catch if the sample mean weight of the scallops is less than $\frac{1}{36}$ of a pound. Do you see any flaws in this rule?

c. Develop your own procedure for determining whether a ship is in violation of the minimum weight restriction. Apply your rule to the data in Table 5.5. Draw a conclusion about the ship in question.

TABLE 5.5   Scallop Weight Measurements for 18 Bags Sampled (Statistics in Action 5.1)

.93	.88	.85	.91	.91	.84	.90	.98	.88
.89	.98	.87	.91	.92	.99	1.14	1.06	.93

Source: Bennett, A. "Misapplications review: Jail terms." *Interfaces,* Vol. 25, No. 2, March–April 1995, p. 20.

EXERCISES   5.18–5.31

Note: Exercises marked with 💾 *contain data available for computer analysis on a 3.5" disk (file name in parentheses).*

Learning the Mechanics

5.18 Explain the differences in the sampling distributions of $\bar{x}$ for large and small samples under the following assumptions.
  a. The variable of interest, x, is normally distributed.
  b. Nothing is known about the distribution of the variable x.

5.19 Suppose you have selected a random sample of $n = 5$ measurements from a normal distribution. Compare the standard normal z values with the corresponding t values if you were forming the following confidence intervals.
  a. 80% confidence interval
  b. 90% confidence interval
  c. 95% confidence interval
  d. 98% confidence interval
  e. 99% confidence interval
  f. Use the table values you obtained in parts **a–e** to sketch the z- and t-distributions. What are the similarities and differences?

5.20 Let t_o be a specific value of t. Use Table VI in Appendix B to find t_o values such that the following statements are true.
  a. $P(t \geq t_0) = .025$ where df $= 11$
  b. $P(t \geq t_0) = .01$ where df $= 9$
  c. $P(t \leq t_0) = .005$ where df $= 6$
  d. $P(t \leq t_0) = .05$ where df $= 18$

5.21 Let t_o be a particular value of t. Use Table VI of Appendix B to find t_o values such that the following statements are true.
  a. $P(-t_0 < t < t_0) = .95$ where df $= 10$
  b. $P(t \leq -t_0 \text{ or } t \geq t_0) = .05$ where df $= 10$
  c. $P(t \leq t_0) = .05$ where df $= 10$
  d. $P(t \leq -t_0 \text{ or } t \geq t_0) = .10$ where df $= 20$
  e. $P(t \leq -t_0 \text{ or } t \geq t_0) = .01$ where df $= 5$

5.22 The following random sample was selected from a normal distribution: 4, 6, 3, 5, 9, 3.
  a. Construct a 90% confidence interval for the population mean μ.
  b. Construct a 95% confidence interval for the population mean μ.
  c. Construct a 99% confidence interval for the population mean μ.
  d. Assume that the sample mean $\bar{x}$ and sample standard deviation s remain exactly the same as those you just calculated but that they are based on a sample of $n = 25$ observations rather than $n = 6$ observations. Repeat parts **a–c**. What is the effect of increasing the sample size on the width of the confidence intervals?

5.23 The following sample of 16 measurements was selected from a population that is approximately normally distributed:

91 80 99 110 95 106 78 121 106 100 97 82
100 83 115 104

a. Construct an 80% confidence interval for the population mean.

b. Construct a 95% confidence interval for the population mean and compare the width of this interval with that of part **a**.

c. Carefully interpret each of the confidence intervals and explain why the 80% confidence interval is narrower.

Applying the Concepts

5.24 Health insurers and the federal government are both putting pressure on hospitals to shorten the average length of stay (LOS) of their patients. In 1993, the average LOS for men in the United States was 6.5 days and the average for women was 5.6 days (*Statistical Abstract of the United States: 1995*). A random sample of 20 hospitals in one state had a mean LOS for women in 1996 of 3.8 days and a standard deviation of 1.2 days.

a. Use a 90% confidence interval to estimate the population mean LOS for women for the state's hospitals in 1996.

b. Interpret the interval in terms of this application.

c. What is meant by the phrase "90% confidence interval"?

5.25 Accidental spillage and misguided disposal of petroleum wastes have resulted in extensive contamination of soils across the country. A common hazardous compound found in the contaminated soil is benzo(a)pyrene [B(a)p]. An experiment was conducted to determine the effectiveness of a method designed to remove B(a)p from soil (*Journal of Hazardous Materials*, June 1995). Three soil specimens contaminated with a known amount of B(a)p were treated with a toxin that inhibits microbial growth. After 95 days of incubation, the percentage of B(a)p removed from each soil specimen was measured. The experiment produced the following summary statistics: $\bar{x} = 49.3$ and $s = 1.5$.

a. Use a 99% confidence interval to estimate the mean percentage of B(a)p removed from a soil specimen in which the toxin was used.

b. Interpret the interval in terms of this application.

c. What assumption is necessary to ensure the validity of this confidence interval?

5.26 (X05.026) A *mortgage* is a type of loan that is secured by a designated piece of property. If the borrower defaults on the loan, the lender can sell the property to recover the outstanding debt. In a home mortgage, the borrower pledges the home in question as security for the loan (Alexander, Sharpe, and Bailey, 1993). A federal bank examiner is interested in estimating the mean outstanding principal balance of all home mortgages foreclosed by the bank due to default by the borrower during the last three years. A random sample of 20 foreclosed mortgages yielded the following data (in dollars):

95,982	81,422	39,888	46,836	66,899	69,110
59,200	62,331	105,812	55,545	56,635	72,123
60,044	75,267	71,490	65,273	42,871	68,100
84,525	79,006				

a. Describe the population from which the bank examiner collected the sample data. What characteristic must this population possess to enable us to construct a confidence interval for the mean outstanding principal balance using the method described in this section? Check this graphically.

b. A 90% confidence interval for the mean of interest is displayed in the MINITAB printout below. Locate the interval.

c. Carefully interpret the confidence interval in the context of the problem.

5.27 Kitchens are frequently the most expensive room for homeowners to remodel. The job requires electricians, carpenters, and plumbers and can cost as much as $600 a square foot, compared to $60 a square foot for a bedroom. The average cost of a major kitchen remodeling job in each of a sample of 11 U.S. cities is shown in the table.

City	Average Cost
Atlanta	$20,427
Boston	27,255
Des Moines	22,115
Kansas City, Mo.	23,256
Louisville	21,887
Portland, Ore.	24,255
Raleigh-Durham	19,852
Reno, Nev.	23,624
Ridgewood, N.J.	25,885
San Francisco	28,999
Tulsa	20,836

Source: Auerbach, J. "A guide to what's cooking in kitchens." *Wall Street Journal*, November 17, 1995, p. B10.

	N	MEAN	STDEV	SE MEAN	90.0 PERCENT C.I.
prinbal	20	67918.0	16552.4	3701.2	(61516.5, 74319.4)

a. Describe possible causes for the variation in the sample data.

b. Use a 95% confidence interval to estimate the mean kitchen remodeling cost per city in the United States.

c. Why are you so confident that the true mean kitchen remodeling cost per city in the United States falls within the interval, part **b**?

5.28 **(X05.028)** It is customary practice in the United States to base roadway design on the 30th highest hourly volume in a year. Thus, all roadway facilities are expected to operate at acceptable levels of service for all but 29 hours of the year. The Florida Department of Transportation (DOT), however, has shifted from the 30th highest hour to the 100th highest hour as the basis for level-of-service determinators. Florida Atlantic University researcher Reid Ewing investigated whether this shift was warranted in the *Journal of STAR Research* (July 1994). The table on page 258 gives the traffic counts at the 30th highest hour and the 100th highest hour of a recent year for 20 randomly selected DOT permanent count stations. MINITAB stem-and-leaf plots for the two variables are provided on page 258 as well as summary statistics and 95% confidence interval printouts.

a. Describe the population from which the sample data is selected.

b. Does the sample appear to be representative of the population? Explain.

c. Locate and interpret the 95% confidence interval for the mean traffic count at the 30th highest hour.

d. What assumption is necessary for the confidence interval to be valid? Does it appear to be satisfied? Explain.

e. Repeat parts **c** and **d** for the 100th highest hour.

5.29 Private and public colleges and universities rely on money contributed by individuals, corporations, and foundations for both salaries and operating expenses. Much of this money is put into a

fund called an *endowment,* and the college spends only the interest earned by the fund. A random sample of eight college endowments drawn from the list of endowments in the *Chronicle of Higher Education Almanac* (Sept. 2, 1996) yielded the following endowments (in millions of dollars): 148.6, 66.1, 340.8, 500.2, 212.8, 55.4, 72.6, 83.4. Estimate the mean endowment for this population of colleges and universities using a 95% confidence interval. List any assumptions you make.

5.30 One of the continuing concerns of U.S. industry is the increasing cost of health insurance for its workers. In 1993 the average cost of health premiums per employee was $2,851, up 10.5% from 1992 (*Nation's Business,* Feb. 1995). In 1997, a random sample of 23 U.S. companies had a mean health insurance premium per employee of $3,321 and a standard deviation of $255.

a. Use a 95% confidence interval to estimate the mean health insurance premium per employee for all U.S. companies.

b. What assumption is necessary to ensure the validity of the confidence interval?

c. Make an inference about whether the true mean health insurance premium per employee in 1997 exceeds $2,851—the 1993 mean.

5.31 **(X05.031)** The table below lists the number of full-time employees at each of 22 office furniture dealers serving Tampa, Florida, and its surrounding communities. Summary statistics for the data are provided in the SAS printout below.

a. Construct a 99% confidence interval for the true mean number of full-time employees at office furniture dealers in Tampa.

b. Interpret the interval, part **a**.

c. Comment on the assumption required for the interval to be valid.

d. The 22 dealers in the sample were the top-ranked furniture dealers in Tampa based on sales volume in 1995. How does this fact impact the validity of the confidence interval? Explain.

| 50 | 78 | 41 | 32 | 35 | 12 | 12 | 15 | 5 | 3 | 5 |
| 23 | 16 | 24 | 24 | 15 | 12 | 11 | 30 | 43 | 4 | 4 |

Source: Tampa Bay Business Journal, June 21–27, 1996, p. 27.

```
Analysis Variable : NUMEMPLY

N Obs   N      Minimum        Maximum              Mean        Std Dev
--------------------------------------------------------------------
   22  22    3.0000000     78.0000000        22.4545455     18.5182722
--------------------------------------------------------------------
```

Station	Type of Route	30th Highest Hour	100th Highest Hour
0117	small city	1,890	1,736
0087	recreational	2,217	2,069
0166	small city	1,444	1,345
0013	rural	2,105	2,049
0161	urban	4,905	4,815
0096	urban	2,022	1,958
0145	rural	594	548
0149	rural	252	229
0038	urban	2,162	2,048
0118	rural	1,938	1,748
0047	rural	879	811
0066	urban	1,913	1,772
0094	rural	3,494	3,403
0105	small city	1,424	1,309
0113	small city	4,571	4,425
0151	urban	3,494	3,359
0159	rural	2,222	2,137
0160	small city	1,076	989
0164	recreational	2,167	2,039
0165	recreational	3,350	3,123

Source: Ewing, R. "Roadway levels of service in an era of growth management."
Journal of STAR Research, Vol. 3, July 1994, p. 103 (Table 2).

```
Stem-and-leaf of Hour30     N = 20
Leaf Unit = 100

    1     0 2
    3     0 58
    6     1 044
    9     1 899
   (6)    2 011122
    5     2
    5     3 344
    2     3
    2     4
    2     4 59


Stem-and-leaf of Hour100    N = 20
Leaf Unit = 100
    1     0 2
    4     0 589
    6     1 33
   10     1 7779
   10     2 00001
    5     2
    5     3 134
    2     3
    2     4 4
    1     4 8
```

	N	MEAN	STDEV	SE MEAN	95.0 PERCENT C.I.
Hour30	20	2205.95	1223.81	273.65	(1633.05, 2778.85)
Hour100	20	2095.60	1203.12	269.02	(1532.39, 2658.81)

5.3   LARGE-SAMPLE CONFIDENCE INTERVAL FOR A POPULATION PROPORTION

The number of public opinion polls has grown at an astounding rate in recent years. Almost daily, the news media report the results of some poll. Pollsters regularly determine the percentage of people who approve of the president's on-the-job performance, the fraction of voters in favor of a certain candidate, the fraction of customers who prefer a particular product, and the proportion of households that watch a particular TV program. In each case, we are interested in estimating the percentage (or proportion) of some group with a certain characteristic. In this section we consider methods for making inferences about population proportions when the sample is large.

EXAMPLE 5.3

A food-products company conducted a market study by randomly sampling and interviewing 1,000 consumers to determine which brand of breakfast cereal they prefer. Suppose 313 consumers were found to prefer the company's brand. How would you estimate the true fraction of *all* consumers who prefer the company's cereal brand?

SOLUTION

What we have really asked is how you would estimate the probability p of success in a binomial experiment, where p is the probability that a chosen consumer prefers the company's brand. One logical method of estimating p for the population is to use the proportion of successes in the sample. That is, we can estimate p by calculating

$$\hat{p} = \frac{\text{Number of consumers sampled who prefer the company's brand}}{\text{Number of consumers sampled}}$$

where $\hat{p}$ is read "p hat." Thus, in this case,

$$\hat{p} = \frac{313}{1,000} = .313$$

To determine the reliability of the estimator $\hat{p}$, we need to know its sampling distribution. That is, if we were to draw samples of 1,000 consumers over and over again, each time calculating a new estimate $\hat{p}$, what would be the frequency distribution of all the $\hat{p}$ values? The answer lies in viewing $\hat{p}$ as the average, or mean, number of successes per trial over the n trials. If each success is assigned a value equal to 1 and a failure is assigned a value of 0, then the sum of all n sample observations is x, the total number of successes, and $\hat{p} = x/n$ is the average, or mean, number of successes per trial in the n trials. The Central Limit Theorem tells us that the relative frequency distribution of the sample mean for any population is approximately normal for sufficiently large samples. ∎

The repeated sampling distribution of $\hat{p}$ has the characteristics listed in the next box and shown in Figure 5.12.

Sampling Distribution of $\hat{p}$

1. The mean of the sampling distribution of $\hat{p}$ is p; that is, $\hat{p}$ is an unbiased estimator of p.

continued

FIGURE 5.12
Sampling distribution
of $\hat{p}$

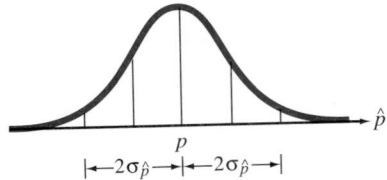

2. The standard deviation of the sampling distribution of $\hat{p}$ is $\sqrt{pq/n}$; that is, $\sigma_{\hat{p}} = \sqrt{pq/n}$, where $q = 1 - p$.
3. For large samples, the sampling distribution of $\hat{p}$ is approximately normal. A sample size is considered large if the interval $\hat{p} \pm 3\sigma_{\hat{p}}$ does not include 0 or 1.

The fact that $\hat{p}$ is a "sample mean fraction of successes" allows us to form confidence intervals about p in a manner that is completely analogous to that used for large-sample estimation of μ.

Large-Sample Confidence Interval for p

$$\hat{p} \pm z_{\alpha/2}\sigma_{\hat{p}} = \hat{p} \pm z_{\alpha/2}\sqrt{\frac{pq}{n}} \approx \hat{p} \pm z_{\alpha/2}\sqrt{\frac{\hat{p}\hat{q}}{n}}$$

where $\hat{p} = \dfrac{x}{n}$ and $\hat{q} = 1 - \hat{p}$

Note: When n is large, $\hat{p}$ can approximate the value of p in the formula for $\sigma_{\hat{p}}$.

Thus, if 313 of 1,000 consumers prefer the company's cereal brand, a 95% confidence interval for the proportion of *all* consumers who prefer the company's brand is

$$\hat{p} \pm z_{\alpha/2}\sigma_{\hat{p}} = .313 \pm 1.96\sqrt{\frac{pq}{1,000}}$$

where $q = 1 - p$. Just as we needed an approximation for σ in calculating a large-sample confidence interval for μ, we now need an approximation for p. As Table 5.6 shows, the approximation for p does not have to be especially accurate, because the value of $\sqrt{pq}$ needed for the confidence interval is relatively insensitive to changes in p. Therefore, we can use $\hat{p}$ to approximate p. Keeping in mind that $\hat{q} = 1 - \hat{p}$, we substitute these values into the formula for the confidence interval:

$$\hat{p} \pm 1.96\sqrt{\frac{pq}{1,000}} \approx \hat{p} \pm 1.96\sqrt{\frac{\hat{p}\hat{q}}{1,000}}$$

$$= .313 \pm 1.96\sqrt{\frac{(.313)(.687)}{1,000}}$$

$$= .313 \pm .029$$

$$= (.284, .342)$$

TABLE 5.6   Values of pq for Several Different Values of p

p	pq	$\sqrt{pq}$
.5	.25	.50
.6 or .4	.24	.49
.7 or .3	.21	.46
.8 or .2	.16	.40
.9 or .1	.09	.30

The company can be 95% confident that the interval from 28.4% to 34.2% contains the true percentage of *all* consumers who prefer its brand. That is, in repeated construction of confidence intervals, approximately 95% of all samples would produce confidence intervals that enclose p. Note that the guidelines for interpreting a confidence interval about μ also apply to interpreting a confidence interval for p because p is the "population mean fraction of successes" in a binomial experiment.

EXAMPLE 5.4

Many public polling agencies conduct surveys to determine the current consumer sentiment concerning the state of the economy. For example, the Bureau of Economic and Business Research (BEBR) at the University of Florida conducts quarterly surveys to gauge consumer sentiment in the Sunshine State. Suppose that BEBR randomly samples 484 consumers and finds that 257 are optimistic about the state of the economy. Use a 90% confidence interval to estimate the proportion of all consumers in Florida who are optimistic about the state of the economy. Based on the confidence interval, can BEBR infer that the majority of Florida consumers are optimistic about the economy?

SOLUTION

The number, x, of the 484 sampled consumers who are optimistic about the Florida economy is a binomial random variable if we can assume that the sample was randomly selected from the population of Florida consumers and that the poll was conducted identically for each sampled consumer.

The point estimate of the proportion of Florida consumers who are optimistic about the economy is

$$\hat{p} = \frac{x}{n} = \frac{257}{484} = .531$$

We first check to be sure that the sample size is sufficiently large that the normal distribution provides a reasonable approximation for the sampling distribution of $\hat{p}$. We check the 3-standard-deviation interval around $\hat{p}$:

$$\hat{p} \pm 3\sigma_{\hat{p}} \approx \hat{p} \pm 3\sqrt{\frac{\hat{p}\hat{q}}{n}}$$

$$= .531 \pm 3\sqrt{\frac{(.531)(.469)}{484}} = .531 \pm .068 = (.463, .599)$$

Since this interval is wholly contained in the interval $(0, 1)$, we may conclude that the normal approximation is reasonable.

We now proceed to form the 90% confidence interval for p, the true proportion of Florida consumers who are optimistic about the state of the economy:

$$\hat{p} \pm z_{\alpha/2}\sigma_{\hat{p}} = \hat{p} \pm z_{\alpha/2}\sqrt{\frac{pq}{n}} \approx \hat{p} \pm z_{\alpha/2}\sqrt{\frac{\hat{p}\hat{q}}{n}}$$

$$= .531 \pm 1.645\sqrt{\frac{(.531)(.469)}{484}} = .531 \pm .037 = (.494, .568)$$

Thus, we can be 90% confident that the proportion of all Florida consumers who are confident about the economy is between .494 and .568. As always, our confidence stems from the fact that 90% of all similarly formed intervals will contain the true proportion p and not from any knowledge about whether this particular interval does.

Can we conclude that the majority of Florida consumers are optimistic about the economy based on this interval? If we wished to use this interval to infer that a majority is optimistic, the interval would have to support the inference that p exceeds .5—that is, that more than 50% of the Florida consumers are optimistic about the economy. Note that the interval contains some values below .5 (as low as .494) as well as some above .5 (as high as .568). Therefore, we cannot conclude that the true value of p exceeds .5 based on this 90% confidence interval. �

In Example 5.4 we used the confidence interval to make an inference about whether the true value of p exceeds .5. That is, we used the sample to **test** whether p exceeds .5. When we want to use sample information to test the value of a population parameter, we usually conduct a *test of hypothesis*, the subject of Chapter 6. But first, we'll conclude Chapter 5 with a section showing how to determine the sample size necessary to estimate either a population mean or a population proportion.

EXERCISES   5.32–5.45

Note: Exercises marked with 🖫 *contain data available for computer analysis on a 3.5" disk (file name in parentheses).*

Learning the Mechanics

5.32 Describe the sampling distribution of $\hat{p}$ based on large samples of size n. That is, give the mean, the standard deviation, and the (approximate) shape of the distribution of $\hat{p}$ when large samples of size n are (repeatedly) selected from the binomial distribution with probability of success p.

5.33 For the binomial sample information summarized in each part, indicate whether the sample size is large enough to use the methods of this chapter to construct a confidence interval for p.
a. $n = 400, \hat{p} = .10$ **b.** $n = 50, \hat{p} = .10$
c. $n = 20, \hat{p} = .5$ **d.** $n = 20, \hat{p} = .3$

5.34 A random sample of size $n = 121$ yielded $\hat{p} = .88$.
a. Is the sample size large enough to use the methods of this section to construct a confidence interval for p? Explain.
b. Construct a 90% confidence interval for p.
c. What assumption is necessary to ensure the validity of this confidence interval?

5.35 A random sample of size $n = 225$ yielded $\hat{p} = .46$.
a. Is the sample size large enough to use the methods of this section to construct a confidence interval for p? Explain.
b. Construct a 95% confidence interval for p.
c. Interpret the 95% confidence interval.
d. Explain what is meant by the phrase "95% confidence interval."

5.36 A random sample of 50 consumers taste tested a new snack food. Their responses were coded (0: do not like; 1: like; 2: indifferent) and recorded as follows:

1	0	0	1	2	0	1	1	0	0
0	1	0	2	0	2	2	0	0	1
1	0	0	0	0	1	0	2	0	0
0	1	0	0	1	0	0	1	0	1
0	2	0	0	1	1	0	0	0	1

a. Use an 80% confidence interval to estimate the proportion of consumers who like the snack food.
b. Provide a statistical interpretation for the confidence interval you constructed in part **a**.

Applying the Concepts

5.37 Substance abuse problems are widespread at New Jersey businesses, according to the *Governor's Council for a Drug Free Workplace Report* (Spring/Summer 1995). A questionnaire on the issue was mailed to all New Jersey businesses that were members of the Governor's Council. Of the 72 companies that responded to the survey, 50 admitted that they had employees whose performance was affected by drugs or alcohol.
a. Use a 95% confidence interval to estimate the proportion of all New Jersey companies with substance abuse problems.
b. What assumptions are necessary to ensure the validity of the confidence interval?
c. Interpret the interval in the context of the problem.
d. In interpreting the confidence interval, what does it mean to say you are "95% confident"?
e. Would you use the interval of part **a** to estimate the proportion of all U.S. companies with substance abuse problems? Why or why not?

5.38 According to the U.S. Bureau of Labor Statistics, one of every 80 American workers (i.e., 1.3%) was fired or laid off in 1995. Are employees with cancer fired or laid off at the same rate? To answer this question, *Working Women* magazine and Amgen—a company that makes drugs to lessen chemotherapy side effects—conducted a telephone survey of 100 cancer survivors who worked while undergoing treatment (*Tampa Tribune*, Sept. 25, 1996). Of these 100 cancer patients, 7 were fired or laid off due to their illness.

a. Construct a 90% confidence interval for the true percentage of all cancer patients who are fired or laid off due to their illness.

b. Give a practical interpretation of the interval, part **a**.

c. Are employees with cancer fired or laid off at the same rate as all U.S. workers? Explain.

5.39   Past research has clearly indicated that the stress produced by today's lifestyles results in health problems for a large proportion of society. An article in the *International Journal of Sports Psychology* (July–Sept. 1992) evaluates the relationship between physical fitness and stress. Employees of companies that participate in the Health Examination Program offered by Health Advancement Services (HAS) were classified into three fitness levels: poor, average, and good. Each person was tested for signs of stress. The results for the three groups are reported below:

Fitness Level	Sample Size	Proportion with Signs of Stress
Poor	242	.155
Average	212	.133
Good	95	.108

a. Check to see whether each of these samples is large enough to construct a confidence interval for the true proportion of all employees at each fitness level exhibiting signs of stress.

b. Assuming each sample represents a random sample from its corresponding population, calculate and interpret a 95% confidence interval for the proportion of people with signs of stress within each of the three fitness levels.

c. Interpret each of the confidence intervals constructed in part **b** using the terminology of this exercise.

5.40   Obstructive sleep apnea is a sleep disorder that causes a person to stop breathing momentarily and then awaken briefly. These sleep interruptions, which may occur hundreds of times in a night, can drastically reduce the quality of rest and cause fatigue during waking hours. Researchers at Stanford University studied 159 commercial truck drivers and found that 124 of them suffered from obstructive sleep apnea (*Chest,* May 1995).

a. Use the study results to estimate, with 90% confidence, the fraction of truck drivers who suffer from the sleep disorder.

b. Sleep researchers believe that about 25% of the general population suffer from obstructive sleep apnea. Comment on whether or not this value represents the true percentage of truck drivers who suffer from the sleep disorder.

5.41   For the last five years, the accounting firm Price Waterhouse has monitored the U.S. Postal Service's performance. One parameter of interest is the percentage of mail delivered on time. In a sample of 332,000 items mailed between Dec. 10, 1994, and Mar. 3, 1995—the most difficult delivery season due to bad weather and holidays—Price Waterhouse determined that 282,200 items were delivered on time (*Tampa Tribune,* Mar. 26, 1995). Use this information to estimate with 99% confidence the true percentage of items delivered on time by the U.S. Postal Service. Interpret the result.

5.42   Family-owned companies are notorious for having difficulties in transferring control from one generation to the next. Part of this problem can be traced to lack of a well-documented strategic business plan. In a survey of 3,900 privately held family firms with revenues exceeding $1,000,000 a year, Arthur Andersen, the international accounting and consulting firm, found that 1,911 had no strategic business plan (*Minneapolis Star Tribune,* Sept. 4, 1995).

a. Describe the population studied by Arthur Andersen.

b. Assume the 3,900 firms were randomly sampled from the population. Use a 90% confidence interval to estimate the proportion of family-owned companies without strategic business plans.

c. How wide is the 90% confidence interval you constructed in part **b**? Would an 80% confidence interval be wider or narrower? Justify your answer.

5.43   Performark, Inc., a sales and marketing consulting company located in Minneapolis, Minn., provides its clients with sales programs designed to maximize efficiency and control. The sales programs are based on Performark's extensive research on product advertisements. One study, conducted over a five-year period, examined advertisements for products that cost at least $5,000. Each of these ads were in the form of inquiry cards, bingo cards, or reader-response cards (see Exercise 2.5) in which the potential buyer returns the card with the information requested. Of the 15,324 ad inquiries that were returned to the advertiser, Performark found that 3,371, or 22%, of the advertisers never bothered to respond to or contact the potential buyer (*The Current State of Inquiry Management,* Performark, Inc., 1995).

a. Describe the population of interest to Performark in this study.

b. Construct a 99% confidence interval for the true proportion of advertisers that do not respond to their own ad inquiries.

c. Interpret the interval, part **b**.

5.44   In August 1995 the Gallup organization conducted interviews with a random sample of 1,002 people who operate businesses in their homes. The most common reason given for starting a home business

Tanker	Spillage (metric tons, thousands)	CAUSE OF SPILLAGE				
		Collision	Grounding	Fire/ Explosion	Hull Failure	Unknown
Atlantic Empress	257	X				
Castillo De Bellver	239			X		
Amoco Cadiz	221				X	
Odyssey	132			X		
Torrey Canyon	124		X			
Sea Star	123	X				
Hawaiian Patriot	101				X	
Independento	95	X				
Urquiola	91		X			
Irenes Serenade	82			X		
Khark 5	76			X		
Nova	68	X				
Wafra	62		X			
Epic Colocotronis	58		X			
Sinclair Petrolore	57			X		
Yuyo Maru No 10	42	X				
Assimi	50			X		
Andros Patria	48			X		
World Glory	46				X	
British Ambassador	46				X	
Metula	45		X			
Pericles G.C.	44			X		
Mandoil II	41	X				
Jacob Maersk	41		X			
Burmah Agate	41	X				
J. Antonio Lavalleja	38		X			
Napier	37		X			
Exxon Valdez	36		X			
Corinthos	36	X				
Trader	36				X	
St. Peter	33			X		
Gino	32	X				
Golden Drake	32			X		
Ionnis Angelicoussis	32			X		
Chryssi	32				X	
Irenes Challenge	31				X	
Argo Merchant	28		X			
Heimvard	31	X				
Pegasus	25					X
Pacocean	31				X	
Texaco Oklahoma	29				X	
Scorpio	31		X			
Ellen Conway	31		X			
Caribbean Sea	30				X	
Cretan Star	27					X
Grand Zenith	26				X	
Athenian Venture	26			X		
Venoil	26	X				
Aragon	24				X	
Ocean Eagle	21		X			

Source: Daidola, J. C. "Tanker structure behavior during collision and grounding." *Marine Technology*, Vol. 32, No. 1, Jan. 1995, p. 22 (Table 1). Reprinted with permission of The Society of Naval Architects and Marine Engineers (SNAME), 601 Pavonia Ave., Jersey City, NJ 07306, USA, (201) 798-4800. Material appearing in The Society of Naval Architect and Marine Engineers (SNAME) publications cannot be reprinted without obtaining written permission.

was wanting to be one's own boss (170 respondents); being laid off was the least common reason (30 respondents) (*New York Times,* Oct. 15, 1995).

a. Describe the population of interest to the Gallup organization.

b. Is the sample size large enough to construct a valid confidence interval for the proportion of home business operators who started their business because they were laid off? Justify your answer.

c. Repeat part **b** for the proportion wanting to be their own boss.

d. Estimate the proportion referred to in part **c** using a 95% confidence interval and interpret your result.

5.45 **(X05.045)** Refer to the *Marine Technology* (Jan. 1995) study of the causes of fifty recent major oil spills from tankers and carriers, Exercise 2.10. The data is reproduced in the table on page 264.

a. Give a point estimate for the proportion of major oil spills that are caused by hull failure.

b. Form a 95% confidence interval for the estimate, part **a.** Interpret the result.

5.4 DETERMINING THE SAMPLE SIZE

Recall (Section 1.5) that one way to collect the relevant data for a study used to make inferences about the population is to implement a designed (planned) experiment. Perhaps the most important design decision faced by the analyst is to determine the size of the sample. We show in this section that the appropriate sample size for making an inference about a population mean or proportion depends on the desired reliability.

ESTIMATING A POPULATION MEAN

Consider the example from Section 5.1 in which we estimated the mean overdue amount for all delinquent accounts in a large credit corporation. A sample of 100 delinquent accounts produced the 95% confidence interval: $\bar{x} \pm 2\sigma_{\bar{x}} \approx 233.28 \pm 18.07$. Consequently, our estimate $\bar{x}$ was within $18.07 of the true mean amount due, μ, for all the delinquent accounts at the 95% confidence level. That is, the 95% confidence interval for μ was $2(18.07) = \$36.14$ wide when 100 accounts were sampled. This is illustrated in Figure 5.13a.

Now suppose we want to estimate μ to within $5 with 95% confidence. That is, we want to narrow the width of the confidence interval from $36.14 to $5, as shown in Figure 5.13b. How much will the sample size have to be increased to accomplish this? If we want the estimator $\bar{x}$ to be within $5 of μ, we must have

$$2\sigma_{\bar{x}} = 5 \quad \text{or, equivalently,} \quad 2\left(\frac{\sigma}{\sqrt{n}}\right) = 5$$

The necessary sample size is obtained by solving this equation for n. To do this we need an approximation for σ. We have an approximation from the initial sample of 100 accounts—namely, the sample standard deviation, $s = 90.34$. Thus,

$$2\left(\frac{\sigma}{\sqrt{n}}\right) \approx 2\left(\frac{s}{\sqrt{n}}\right) = 2\left(\frac{90.34}{\sqrt{n}}\right) = 5$$

$$\sqrt{n} = \frac{2(90.34)}{5} = 36.136$$

$$n = (36.136)^2 = 1{,}305.81 \approx 1{,}306$$

Approximately 1,306 accounts will have to be randomly sampled to estimate the mean overdue amount μ to within $5 with (approximately) 95% confidence. The confidence interval resulting from a sample of this size will be approximately $10 wide (see Figure 5.13b).

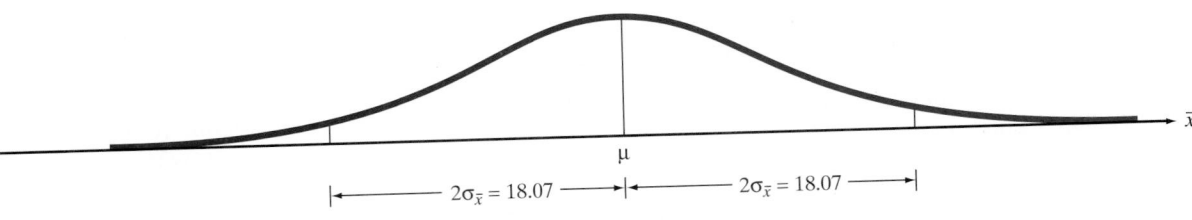

a. $n = 100$

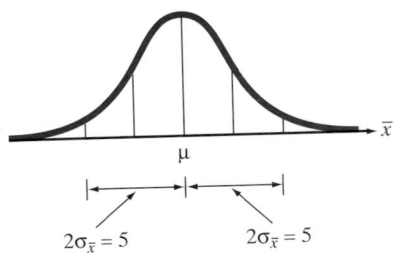

b. $n = 867$

FIGURE 5.13 Relationship between sample size and width of confidence interval: Delinquent creditors example

FIGURE 5.14
Specifying the bound
B as the half-width of
a confidence interval

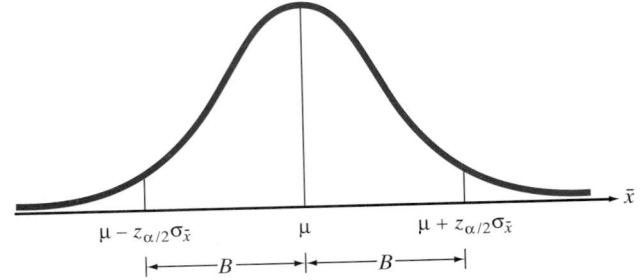

In general, we express the reliability associated with a confidence interval for the population mean μ by specifying the **bound, B**, within which we want to estimate μ with $100(1 - \alpha)\%$ confidence. The bound B then is equal to the half-width of the confidence interval, as shown in Figure 5.14.

The procedure for finding the sample size necessary to estimate μ to within a given bound B is given in the box.

Sample Size Determination for $100(1 - \alpha)\%$ Confidence Intervals for μ

In order to estimate μ to within a **bound B** with $100(1 - \alpha)\%$ confidence, the required sample size is found as follows:

$$z_{\alpha/2}\left(\frac{\sigma}{\sqrt{n}}\right) = B$$

The solution can be written in terms of B as follows:

$$n = \frac{(z_{\alpha/2})^2 \sigma^2}{B^2}$$

The value of σ is usually unknown. It can be estimated by the standard deviation, s, from a prior sample. Alternatively, we may approximate the range R of observations in the population, and (conservatively) estimate $\sigma \approx R/4$. In any case, you should round the value of n obtained *upward* to ensure that the sample size will be sufficient to achieve the specified reliability.

EXAMPLE 5.5   The manufacturer of official NFL footballs uses a machine to inflate its new balls to a pressure of 13.5 pounds. When the machine is properly calibrated, the mean inflation pressure is 13.5 pounds, but uncontrollable factors cause the pressures of individual footballs to vary randomly from about 13.3 to 13.7 pounds. For quality control purposes, the manufacturer wishes to estimate the mean inflation pressure to within .025 pound of its true value with a 99% confidence interval. What sample size should be used?

SOLUTION
We desire a 99% confidence interval that estimates μ to within $B = .025$ pound of its true value. For a 99% confidence interval, we have $z_{\alpha/2} = z_{.005} = 2.575$. To esti-mate σ, we note that the range of observations is $R = 13.7 - 13.3 = .4$ and use $\sigma \approx R/4 = .1$. Now we use the formula derived in the box to find the sample size n:

$$n = \frac{(z_{\alpha/2})^2 \sigma^2}{B^2} \approx \frac{(2.575)^2 (.1)^2}{(.025)^2} = 106.09$$

We round this up to $n = 107$. Realizing that σ was approximated by $R/4$, we might even advise that the sample size be specified as $n = 110$ to be more certain of attaining the objective of a 99% confidence interval with bound $B = .025$ pound or less.   ∎

Sometimes the formula will yield a small sample size $(n < 30)$. Unfortunately, this solution is invalid because the procedures and assumptions for small samples differ from those for large samples, as we discovered in Section 5.2. Therefore, if the formulas yield a small sample size, one simple strategy is to select a sample size $n \geq 30$.

ESTIMATING A POPULATION PROPORTION

The method outlined above is easily applied to a population proportion p. For example, in Section 5.3 a company used a sample of 1,000 consumers to calculate a 95% confidence interval for the proportion of consumers who preferred its cereal brand, obtaining the interval $.313 \pm .029$. Suppose the company wishes to estimate its market share more precisely, say to within .015 with a 95% confi-dence interval.

The company wants a confidence interval with a bound B on the estimate of p of $B = .015$. The sample size required to generate such an interval is found by solving the following equation for n:

$$z_{\alpha/2} \sigma_{\hat{p}} = B \qquad \text{or} \qquad z_{\alpha/2} \sqrt{\frac{pq}{n}} = .015 \qquad \text{(see Figure 5.15)}$$

Since a 95% confidence interval is desired, the appropriate z value is $z_{\alpha/2} = z_{.025} = 1.96 \approx 2$. We must approximate the value of the product pq before we can solve the equation for n. As shown in Table 5.6, the closer the values of p and q to .5, the larger the product pq. Thus, to find a conservatively large sample size that will generate a confidence interval with the specified reliability, we generally choose an approximation of p close to .5. In the case of the tobacco company, however, we

FIGURE 5.15
Specifying the bound B
of a confidence interval
for a population
proportion p

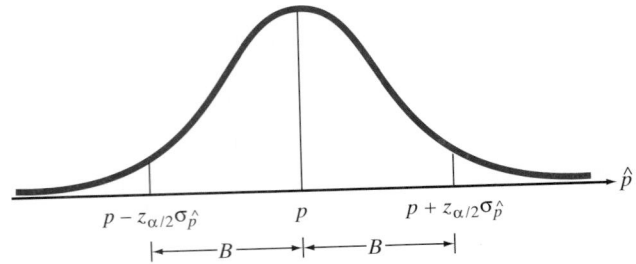

$$p - z_{\alpha/2}\sigma_{\hat{p}} \qquad p \qquad p + z_{\alpha/2}\sigma_{\hat{p}}$$

$$\longleftarrow B \longrightarrow \longleftarrow B \longrightarrow$$

have an initial sample estimate of $\hat{p} = .313$. A conservatively large estimate of pq can therefore be obtained by using, say, $p = .35$. We now substitute into the equation and solve for n:

$$2\sqrt{\frac{(.35)(.65)}{n}} = .015$$

$$n = \frac{(2)^2(.35)(.65)}{(.015)^2}$$

$$= 4,044.44 \approx 4,045$$

The company must sample about 4,045 consumers to estimate the percentage who prefer its brand to within .015 with a 95% confidence interval.

The procedure for finding the sample size necessary to estimate a population proportion p to within a given bound B is given in the box.

Sample Size Determination for $100(1 - \alpha)\%$ Confidence Interval for p

In order to estimate a binomial probability p to within a bound B with $100(1 - \alpha)\%$ confidence, the required sample size is found by solving the following equation for n:

$$z_{\alpha/2}\sqrt{\frac{pq}{n}} = B$$

The solution can be written in terms of B:

$$n = \frac{(z_{\alpha/2})^2(pq)}{B^2}$$

Since the value of the product pq is unknown, it can be estimated by using the sample fraction of successes, $\hat{p}$, from a prior sample. Remember (Table 5.6) that the value of pq is at its maximum when p equals .5, so that you can obtain conservatively large values of n by approximating p by .5 or values close to .5. In any case, you should round the value of n obtained *upward* to ensure that the sample size will be sufficient to achieve the specified reliability.

EXAMPLE 5.6

A small telephone manufacturer that entered the postregulation market too quickly has an initial problem with excessive customer complaints and consequent returns of the phones for repair or replacement. The manufacturer wants to determine the magnitude of the problem in order to estimate its warranty liability. How many telephones should the company randomly sample from its warehouse and check in order to estimate the fraction defective, p, to within .01 with 90% confidence?

FIGURE 5.16
Specified reliability
for estimate of
fraction defective
in Example 5.6

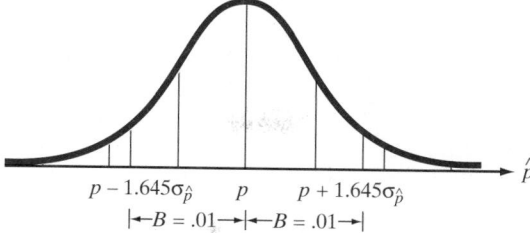

$$p - 1.645\sigma_{\hat{p}} \qquad p \qquad p + 1.645\sigma_{\hat{p}}$$

$$|{\leftarrow}B = .01{\rightarrow}|{\leftarrow}B = .01{\rightarrow}|$$

SOLUTION

In order to estimate p to within a bound of .01, we set the half-width of the confidence interval equal to $B = .01$, as shown in Figure 5.16.

The equation for the sample size n requires an estimate of the product pq. We could most conservatively estimate $pq = .25$ (i.e., use $p = .5$), but this may be overly conservative when estimating a fraction defective. A value of .1, corresponding to 10% defective, will probably be conservatively large for this application. The solution is therefore

$$n = \frac{(z_{\alpha/2})^2(pq)}{B^2} = \frac{(1.645)^2(.1)(.9)}{(.01)^2} = 2,435.4 \approx 2,436$$

Thus, the manufacturer should sample 2,436 telephones in order to estimate the fraction defective, p, to within .01 with 90% confidence. Remember that this answer depends on our approximation for pq, where we used .09. If the fraction defective is closer to .05 than .10, we can use a sample of 1,286 telephones (check this) to estimate p to within .01 with 90% confidence. ◼

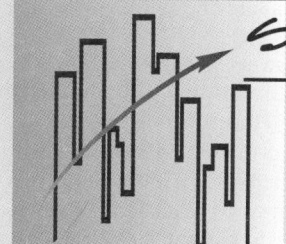

STATISTICS IN ACTION

5.2 IS CAFFEINE ADDICTIVE?

Scientific research has established that certain substances, when taken in excess, can become addictive. These substances range from heavy narcotic drugs such as heroine and cocaine to alcohol in beer and wine and nicotine in cigarettes. Media blitzes have made drug users, drinkers, and smokers well aware of the dangers of these addictions. But what about the millions of Americans who regularly drink coffee, tea, or cola products each day? Does the caffeine in coffee, tea, and cola induce an addiction similar to that induced by alcohol, tobacco, heroine, and cocaine?

In an attempt to answer this question, researchers at Johns Hopkins University recently examined 27 caffeine drinkers and found 25 who displayed some type of withdrawal symptoms when abstaining from caffeine. [*Note:* The 27 caffeine drinkers volunteered for the study.] Furthermore, of 11 caffeine drinkers who were diagnosed as caffeine dependent, 8 displayed dramatic withdrawal symptoms (including impairment in normal functioning) when they consumed a caffeine-free diet in a controlled setting.

The National Coffee Association claimed, however, that the study group was too small to draw conclusions. "It is inappropriate to overgeneralize the results of this ... study, since caffeine as normally consumed poses no health risk to the average consumer and cannot be described as a substance of dependence" (*Los Angeles Times*, Oct. 5, 1994).

Focus

Give your (supported) opinion on the issue. If the sample size is deemed satisfactory, establish confidence intervals for the parameters of interest. If not, how large a sample should be selected?

The cost of sampling will also play an important role in the final determination of the sample size to be selected to estimate either μ or p. Although more complex formulas can be derived to balance the reliability and cost considerations, we will solve for the necessary sample size and note that the sampling budget may be a limiting factor. Consult the references for a more complete treatment of this problem.

EXERCISES 5.46–5.61

Learning the Mechanics

5.46 If nothing is known about p, .5 can be substituted for p in the sample-size formula for a population proportion. But when this is done, the resulting sample size may be larger than needed. Under what circumstances will using $p = .5$ in the sample-size formula yield a sample size larger than needed to construct a confidence interval for p with a specified bound and a specified confidence level?

5.47 If you wish to estimate a population mean to within a bound $B = .3$ using a 95% confidence interval and you know from prior sampling that σ^2 is approximately equal to 7.2, how many observations would have to be included in your sample?

5.48 In each case, find the approximate sample size required to construct a 95% confidence interval for p that has bound $B = .08$.
  a. Assume p is near .2.
  b. Assume you have no prior knowledge about p, but you wish to be certain that your sample is large enough to achieve the specified accuracy for the estimate.

5.49 Suppose you wish to estimate a population mean correct to within a bound $B = .20$ with probability equal to .90. You do not know σ^2, but you know that the observations will range in value between 30 and 34.
  a. Find the approximate sample size that will produce the desired accuracy of the estimate. You wish to be conservative to ensure that the sample size will be ample to achieve the desired accuracy of the estimate. [*Hint:* Using your knowledge of data variation from Section 2.6, assume that the range of the observations will equal 4σ.]
  b. Calculate the approximate sample size making the less conservative assumption that the range of the observations is equal to 6σ.

5.50 It costs you $10 to draw a sample of size $n = 1$ and measure the attribute of interest. You have a budget of $1,500.
  a. Do you have sufficient funds to estimate the population mean for the attribute of interest with a 95% confidence interval 5 units in width? Assume $\sigma = 14$.
  b. If you used a 90% confidence level, would your answer to part **a** change? Explain.

5.51 The following is a 90% confidence interval for p: (.26, .54). How large was the sample used to construct this interval?

Applying the Concepts

5.52 The 1994 salary survey of quality professionals described in Exercise 5.14 generated responses from 1,142 quality managers. The lowest salary reported by a manager was $18,500; the highest was $167,000 ("1994 Salary Survey," *Quality Progress*, Nov. 1994).
  a. Plans are being made to repeat the survey this year. Use the above information to determine how large a sample would need to be drawn to estimate the mean income of managers to within $5,000 with 95% confidence.
  b. In the 1994 survey, the standard deviation of managers' salaries was $17,910. Use this information and recalculate the sample size asked for in part **a**.
  c. Compare your answers to parts **a** and **b**. Which sample size would you use to estimate this year's mean salary? Justify your answer.

5.53 As businesses around the world rush to cash in on the popularity of the World Wide Web (WWW), questions have arisen as to what WWW services users would be willing to pay for. In 1995, Georgia Institute of Technology's Graphics Visualization and Usability Center surveyed 13,000 WWW users and asked them about their willingness to pay fees for access to web sites. Of these, 2,938 were definitely not willing to pay such fees (*Inc. Technology*, No. 3, 1995).
  a. Assume the 13,000 users were randomly selected. Construct a 95% confidence interval for the proportion definitely unwilling to pay fees.
  b. What is the width of the interval you constructed in part **a**? For most applications, this width is unnecessarily narrow. What does that suggest about the survey's sample size?
  c. How large a sample size is necessary to estimate the proportion of interest to within 2% with 95% confidence?

5.54 Although corporate executives are probably not as highly stressed as air-traffic controllers or inner-city police, research has indicated that they are among the more highly pressured work groups. In order to estimate p, the proportion of managers who perceive themselves to be frequently under stress, one study sampled 532 managers in western Australian corporations (*Harvard Business Review*, Jan.–Feb. 1986). One hundred ninety of these managers fell into the high-stress group. Assume that random sampling was used in this study. Was the sample size large enough to estimate p to within .03 with 95% confidence? Explain.

5.55 A large food-products company receives about 100,000 phone calls a year from consumers on its toll-free number. A computer monitors and records how many rings it takes for an operator to answer, how much time each caller spends "on hold," and other data. However, the reliability of the monitoring system has been called into question by the operators and their labor union. As a check on the computer system, approximately how many calls should be manually monitored during the next year to estimate the true mean time that callers spend on hold to within 3 seconds with 95% confidence? Answer this question for the following values of the standard deviation of waiting times (in seconds): 10, 20, and 30.

5.56 According to estimates made by the General Accounting Office, the Internal Revenue Service (IRS) answered 18.3 million telephone inquiries during a recent tax season, and 17% of the IRS offices provided answers that were wrong. These estimates were based on data collected from sample calls to numerous IRS offices. How many IRS offices should be randomly selected and contacted in order to estimate the proportion of IRS offices that fail to correctly answer questions about gift taxes with a 90% confidence interval of width .06?

5.57 Refer to Exercise 5.17, in which workers' level of job satisfaction was related to age. Suppose that we want to estimate the mean job-level satisfaction for younger workers (age 18–24) to within .04 with 95% confidence. How large a sample should be selected? Recall that the standard deviation for this age group was .75.

5.58 In a survey conducted for *Money* magazine by the ICR Survey Research Group, 26% of parents with college-bound high school children reported not having saved any money for college. The poll had a "... margin of error of plus or minus 4 percentage points" (*Newark Star-Ledger*, Aug. 16, 1996).
   a. Assume that random sampling was used in conducting the survey and that the researchers

wanted to have 95% confidence in their results. Estimate the sample size used in the survey.
   b. Repeat part **a**, but this time assume the researchers wanted to be 99% confident.

5.59 The United States Golf Association (USGA) tests all new brands of golf balls to ensure that they meet USGA specifications. One test conducted is intended to measure the average distance traveled when the ball is hit by a machine called "Iron Byron," a name inspired by the swing of the famous golfer Byron Nelson. Suppose the USGA wishes to estimate the mean distance for a new brand to within 1 yard with 90% confidence. Assume that past tests have indicated that the standard deviation of the distances Iron Byron hits golf balls is approximately 10 yards. How many golf balls should be hit by Iron Byron to achieve the desired accuracy in estimating the mean?

5.60 It costs more to produce defective items—since they must be scrapped or reworked—than it does to produce nondefective items. This simple fact suggests that manufacturers should ensure the quality of their products by perfecting their production processes rather than through inspection of finished products (Deming, 1986). In order to better understand a particular metal-stamping process, a manufacturer wishes to estimate the mean length of items produced by the process during the past 24 hours.
   a. How many parts should be sampled in order to estimate the population mean to within .1 millimeter (mm) with 90% confidence? Previous studies of this machine have indicated that the standard deviation of lengths produced by the stamping operation is about 2 mm.
   b. Time permits the use of a sample size no larger than 100. If a 90% confidence interval for μ is constructed using $n = 100$, will it be wider or narrower than would have been obtained using the sample size determined in part **a**? Explain.
   c. If management requires that μ be estimated to within .1 mm and that a sample size of no more than 100 be used, what is (approximately) the maximum confidence level that could be attained for a confidence interval that meets management's specifications?

5.61 Refer to the *International Journal of Sports Psychology* study, Exercise 5.39, where a sample of 95 workers in good physical condition was used to estimate the proportion of all workers in good condition who showed signs of stress. Recall that the point estimate of the proportion was .108. How many workers from this category must be sampled to estimate the true proportion who are stressed to within .01 with 95% confidence?

QUICK REVIEW

Key Terms

Bound on the error of estimation 266

Confidence coefficient 242

Confidence interval 242

Confidence level 242

Degrees of freedom 249

Interval estimator 242

t statistic 249

Key Formulas

$\hat{\theta} \pm (z_{\alpha/2})\sigma_{\hat{\theta}}$

Large-sample confidence interval for population parameter θ where $\hat{\theta}$ and $\sigma_{\hat{\theta}}$ are obtained from the table below

Parameter θ	Estimator $\hat{\theta}$	Standard Error $\sigma_{\hat{\theta}}$	
Mean, μ	$\bar{x}$	$\dfrac{\sigma}{\sqrt{n}}$	243
Proportion, p	$\hat{p}$	$\sqrt{\dfrac{pq}{n}}$	260

$\bar{x} \pm t_{\alpha/2}\left(\dfrac{s}{\sqrt{n}}\right)$ Small-sample confidence interval for population mean μ 252

$n = \dfrac{(z_{\alpha/2})^2 \sigma^2}{B^2}$ Determining the sample size n for estimating μ 266

$n = \dfrac{(z_{\alpha/2})^2 (pq)}{B^2}$ Determining the sample size n for estimating p 268

LANGUAGE LAB

Symbol	Pronunciation	Description
θ	theta	General population parameter
μ	mu	Population mean
p		Population proportion
B		Bound on error of estimation
α	alpha	$(1 - \alpha)$ represents the confidence coefficient
$z_{\alpha/2}$	z of alpha over 2	z value used in a $100(1 - \alpha)\%$ large-sample confidence interval
$t_{\alpha/2}$	t of alpha over 2	t value used in a $100(1 - \alpha)\%$ small-sample confidence interval
$\bar{x}$	x-bar	Sample mean; point estimate of μ
$\hat{p}$	p-hat	Sample proportion; point estimate of p
σ	sigma	Population standard deviation
s		Sample standard deviation; point estimate of σ
$\sigma_{\bar{x}}$	sigma of $\bar{x}$	Standard deviation of sampling distribution of $\bar{x}$
$\sigma_{\hat{p}}$	sigma of $\hat{p}$	Standard deviation of sampling distribution of $\hat{p}$

SUPPLEMENTARY EXERCISES 5.62–5.79

Note: List the assumptions necessary for the valid implementation of the statistical procedures you use in solving all these exercises.

Exercises marked with 💾 *contain data available for computer analysis on a 3.5" disk (file name in parentheses).*

Learning the Mechanics

5.62 In each of the following instances, determine whether you would use a z or t statistic (or neither) to form a 95% confidence interval, and then look up the appropriate z or t value.

a. Random sample of size $n = 23$ from a normal distribution with unknown mean μ and standard deviation σ

b. Random sample of size $n = 135$ from a normal distribution with unknown mean μ and standard deviation σ

c. Random sample of size $n = 10$ from a normal distribution with unknown mean μ and standard deviation $\sigma = 5$

d. Random sample of size $n = 73$ from a distribution about which nothing is known

e. Random sample of size $n = 12$ from a distribution about which nothing is known

5.63 A random sample of 225 measurements is selected from a population, and the sample mean and standard deviation are $\bar{x} = 32.5$ and $s = 30.0$, respectively.

a. Use a 99% confidence interval to estimate the mean of the population, μ.

b. How large a sample would be needed to estimate μ to within .5 with 99% confidence?

c. What is meant by the phrase "99% confidence" as it is used in this exercise?

5.64 In a random sample of 400 measurements, 227 of the measurements possess the characteristic of interest, A.

a. Use a 95% confidence interval to estimate the true proportion p of measurements in the population with characteristic A.

b. How large a sample would be needed to estimate p to within .02 with 95% confidence?

Applying the Concepts

5.65 (X05.065) As part of a study of residential property values in Cedar Grove, New Jersey, the county tax assessor sampled 20 single-family

homes that sold during the first half of 1996 and recorded their sales prices (in thousands of dollars; see table below). A stem-and-leaf display and descriptive statistics for these data are shown in the MINITAB printout below.

a. On the MINITAB printout, locate a 95% confidence interval for the mean sale price of all single-family homes in Cedar Grove, New Jersey.

b. Give a practical interpretation of the interval, part **a**.

c. What is meant by the phrase "95% confidence" as it is used in this exercise?

d. Comment on the validity of any assumptions required to properly apply the estimation procedure.

5.66 The Centers for Disease Control and Prevention (CDCP) in Atlanta, Georgia, conducts an annual survey of the general health of the U.S. population as part of its Behavioral Risk Factor Surveillance System (*New York Times*, Mar. 29, 1995). Using random-digit dialing, the CDCP telephones U.S. citizens over 18 years of age and asks them the following four questions:

(1) Is your health generally excellent, very good, good, fair, or poor?

(2) How many days during the previous 30 days was your physical health not good because of injury or illness?

189.9	235.0	159.0	190.9	239.0	559.0	875.0	635.0
265.0	330.0	669.0	935.0	210.0	179.9	334.9	219.0
1,190.0	739.0	424.7	229.0				

Source: Multiple Listing Service of Suburban Essex County, May 17, 1996.

```
Stem-and-leaf of SalePric   N = 20
Leaf Unit = 10

   4     1 5789
  10     2 112336
  10     3 33
   8     4 2
   7     5 5
   6     6 36
   4     7 3
   3     8 7
   2     9 3
   1    10
   1    11 9


              N      MEAN    STDEV   SE MEAN    95.0 PERCENT C.I.
SalePric     20     440.4    303.0     67.8   (    298.6,   582.3)
```

(3) How many days during the previous 30 days was your mental health not good because of stress, depression, or emotional problems?

(4) How many days during the previous 30 days did your physical or mental health prevent you from performing your usual activities?

Identify the parameter of interest for each question.

5.67 Refer to Exercise 5.66. According to the CDCP, 89,582 of 102,263 adults interviewed stated their health was good, very good, or excellent.

a. Use a 99% confidence interval to estimate the true proportion of U.S. adults who believe their health to be good to excellent. Interpret the interval.

b. Why might the estimate, part a, be overly optimistic (i.e., biased high)?

5.68 A firm's president, vice presidents, department managers, and others use financial data generated by the firm's accounting system to help them make decisions regarding such things as pricing, budgeting, and plant expansion. To provide reasonable certainty that the system provides reliable data, internal auditors periodically perform various checks of the system (Horngren, Foster, and Datar, *Cost Accounting: A Managerial Emphasis,* 1994). Suppose an internal auditor is interested in determining the proportion of sales invoices in a population of 5,000 sales invoices for which the "total sales" figure is in error. She plans to estimate the true proportion of invoices in error based on a random sample of size 100.

a. Assume that the population of invoices is numbered from 1 to 5,000 and that every invoice ending with a 0 is in error (i.e., 10% are in error). Use a random number generator to draw a random sample of 100 invoices from the population of 5,000 invoices. For example, random number 456 stands for invoice number 456. List the invoice numbers in your sample and indicate which of your sampled invoices are in error (i.e., those ending in a 0).

b. Use the results of your sample of part a to construct a 90% confidence interval for the true proportion of invoices in error.

c. Recall that the true population proportion of invoices in error is equal to .1. Compare the true proportion with the estimate of the true proportion you developed in part b. Does your confidence interval include the true proportion?

5.69 Research reported in the *Professional Geographer* (May 1992) investigates the hypothesis that the disproportionate housework responsibility of women in two-income households is a major factor in determining the proximity of a woman's place of employment. The researcher studied the distance (in miles) to work for both men and women in two-

income households. Random samples of men and women yielded the following results:

| | CENTRAL CITY RESIDENCE | | SUBURBAN RESIDENCE | |
	Men	Women	Men	Women
Sample Size	159	119	138	93
Mean	7.4	4.5	9.3	6.6
Std. Deviation	6.3	4.2	7.1	5.6

a. For central city residences, calculate a 95% confidence interval for the average distance to work for men and women in two-income households. Interpret the intervals.

b. Repeat part a for suburban residences.

[*Note:* We will show how to use statistical techniques to compare two population means in Chapter 7.]

5.70 Refer to the *Journal of the American Medical Association* (Apr. 21, 1993) report on the prevalence of cigarette smoking among U.S. adults, Exercise 5.10. Of the 43,732 survey respondents, 11,239 indicated that they were current smokers and 10,539 indicated they were former smokers.

a. Construct and interpret a 90% confidence interval for the percentage of U.S. adults who currently smoke cigarettes.

b. Construct and interpret a 90% confidence interval for the percentage of U.S. adults who are former cigarette smokers.

5.71 A company is interested in estimating μ, the mean number of days of sick leave taken by all its employees. The firm's statistician selects at random 100 personnel files and notes the number of sick days taken by each employee. The following sample statistics are computed: $\bar{x} = 12.2$ days, $s = 10$ days.

a. Estimate μ using a 90% confidence interval.

b. How many personnel files would the statistician have to select in order to estimate μ to within 2 days with a 99% confidence interval?

5.72 In the United States, people over age 50 represent 25% of the population, yet they control 70% of the wealth. Research indicates the highest priority of retirees is travel. A study in the *Annals of Tourism Research* (Vol. 19, 1992) investigates the relationship of retirement status (pre- and post-retirement) to various items of interest to the travel industry. As one part of the study, a sample of 323 retirees was selected, and the number of nights each typically stayed away from home on trips was determined. One hundred seventy-two (172) responded that their typical stays ranged from 4 to 7 nights. Use a 90% confidence interval to estimate the true proportion of postretirement travelers who stay between 4 and 7 nights on a typical trip. Interpret the interval.

5.73 The primary determinant of the amount of vacation time U.S. employees receive is their length of service. According to data released by Hewitt Associates (*Management Review,* Nov. 1995), more than 8 of 10 employers provide two weeks of vacation after the first year. After five years, 75% of employers provide three weeks and after 15 years most provide four-week vacations. To more accurately estimate p, the proportion of U.S. employers who provide only two weeks of vacation to new hires, a random sample of 24 major U.S. companies was contacted. The following vacation times were reported (in days):

10	12	10	10	10	10
15	10	10	10	10	10
10	10	10	10	10	15
10	10	15	10	10	10

  a. Is the sample size large enough to ensure that the normal distribution provides a reasonable approximation to the sampling distribution of $\hat{p}$? Justify your answer.
  b. How large a sample would be required to estimate p to within .02 with 95% confidence?

5.74 (X05.074) One of the most important ways to measure the performance of a business is to evaluate how well it has treated its stockholders. After all, it is the stockholders who provided the capital to launch and/or expand the business; it is the stockholders who own the business. This can be done by examining the rate of return received by stockholders. To evaluate the performance of U.S. corporations in 1995 and over the five-year period 1991–1995, a random sample of 15 corporations was drawn from the 1,000 major U.S. corporations listed in *The Wall Street Journal*'s Shareholder Scoreboard (Feb. 29, 1996):

Corporation	Stockholder's Return: 1995	Stockholder's Return: 1991–1995
Andrew	9.8%	51.2%
Bank One	54.4	19.3
Gannett	18.1	14.2
Hasbro	7.5	25.4
Alco Standard	47.5	25.0
Ceridian	53.5	39.9
Teledyne	32.8	15.2
Snap-On	40.0	10.7
Salomon	−4.0	9.7
New York Times	37.0	9.9
Jostens	34.5	−2.2
Ogden	20.7	8.8
UAL	104.3	17.7
Merck	76.4	20.1
Liz Claiborne	65.4	−0.1

  a. Find point estimates for the mean rate of return of the 1,000 companies in 1995 and over the period 1991–1995.

  b. Construct 90% confidence intervals for the two parameters described in part **a** and list any assumptions that are needed to ensure the validity of the confidence intervals.
  c. Interpret the confidence intervals in the context of the problem.
  d. Which method of estimation is better, point estimation or interval estimation? Justify your answer.

5.75 *Management Accounting* (June 1995) reported the results of its sixth annual salary survey of the members of the Institute of Management Accountants (IMA). The 2,112 members responding had a salary distribution with a 20th percentile of $35,100; a median of $50,000; and an 80th percentile of $73,000.
  a. Use this information to determine the minimum sample size that could be used in next year's survey to estimate the mean salary of IMA members to within $2,000 with 98% confidence.
  b. Explain how you estimated the standard deviation required for the sample size calculation.
  c. List any assumptions you make.

5.76 For decades, U.S. companies have tied a portion of the compensation of many upper-management employees to the performance of the firm. In the last few years, however, a growing number of companies have begun offering similar performance incentives to all of their employees. What instigated this change in pay structures? Of 46 companies (surveyed by the American Compensation Association) that had modified their traditional pay structures, 26 reported making the modification in response to profound market changes in the last decade: global competition, consumer demand for high-quality goods and services, etc. They needed new ways to improve performance and cut costs (*Minneapolis Star Tribune*, June 29, 1992). For the population of U.S. firms that have switched to nontraditional pay structures, estimate the proportion that have done so in response to market forces (rather than to growth, downsizing, or some other reason). Use a 90% confidence interval and specify whatever assumptions are necessary to ensure the validity of the estimate.

5.77 In 1989, the American Society for Quality Control began publishing a journal called *Quality Engineering*. In 1994, the journal distributed a questionnaire to its 8,521 subscribers. A total of 202 replies were received. To the question "How long have you been a subscriber?" they got the responses shown on page 276.
  a. What assumption(s) would need to be made in order to apply the confidence interval methodology described in this chapter to the problem of estimating the mean subscription length for the population of 8,521 journal subscribers?

Years	1	2	3	4	5	6	7	8	9	10	11	12	No reply
No. of Responses	44	39	27	17	12	38	1	1	0	0	0	1	22

Source: Adapted from "Quality engineering reader survey." *Quality Engineering,* Vol. 7, No. 4, 1995, p. ix.

b. Use a 98% confidence interval to estimate the population mean referred to in part **a**.

5.78 Recently, a case of salmonella (bacterial) poisoning was traced to a particular brand of ice cream bar, and the manufacturer removed the bars from the market. Despite this response, many consumers refused to purchase *any* brand of ice cream bars for some period of time after the event (McClave, personal consulting). One manufacturer conducted a survey of consumers 6 months after the outbreak. A sample of 244 ice cream bar consumers was contacted, and 23 respondents indicated that they would not purchase ice cream bars because of the potential for food poisoning.

a. What is the point estimate of the true fraction of the entire market who refuse to purchase bars 6 months after the outbreak?

b. Is the sample size large enough to use the normal approximation for the sampling distribution of the estimator of the binomial probability? Justify your response.

c. Construct a 95% confidence interval for the true proportion of the market who still refuse to purchase ice cream bars 6 months after the event.

d. Interpret both the point estimate and confidence interval in terms of this application.

5.79 Refer to Exercise 5.78. Suppose it is now 1 year after the outbreak of food poisoning was traced to ice cream bars. The manufacturer wishes to estimate the proportion who still will not purchase bars to within .02 using a 95% confidence interval. How many consumers should be sampled?

CHAPTER 6

INFERENCES BASED ON A SINGLE SAMPLE
Tests of Hypothesis

CONTENTS

6.1   The Elements of a Test of Hypothesis

6.2   Large-Sample Test of Hypothesis About a Population Mean

6.3   Observed Significance Levels: *p*-values

6.4   Small-Sample Test of Hypothesis About a Population Mean

6.5   Large-Sample Test of Hypothesis About a Population Proportion

6.6   A Nonparametric Test About a Population Median (Optional)

STATISTICS IN ACTION

6.1   Statistics Is Murder!

6.2   Statistical Quality Control, Part I

6.3   Statistical Quality Control, Part II

Where We've Been

We saw how to use sample information to estimate population parameters in Chapter 5. The sampling distribution of a statistic is used to assess the reliability of an estimate, which we express in terms of a confidence interval.

Where We're Going

We'll see how to utilize sample information to test what the value of a population parameter may be. This type of inference is called a *test of hypothesis*. We'll also see how to conduct a test of hypothesis about a population mean μ and a population proportion p. And, just as with estimation, we'll stress the measurement of the reliability of the inference. An inference without a measure of reliability is little more than a guess.

Suppose you wanted to determine whether the mean waiting time in the drive-through line of a fast-food restaurant is less than five minutes, or whether the majority of consumers are optimistic about the economy. In both cases you are interested in making an inference about how the value of a parameter relates to a specific numerical value. Is it less than, equal to, or greater than the specified number? This type of inference, called a **test of hypothesis**, is the subject of this chapter.

We introduce the elements of a test of hypothesis in Section 6.1. We then show how to conduct a large-sample test of hypothesis about a population mean in Sections 6.2 and 6.3. In Section 6.4 we utilize small samples to conduct tests about means, and in optional Section 6.6 we consider an alternate nonparametric test. Large-sample tests about binomial probabilities are the subject of Section 6.5.

6.1 THE ELEMENTS OF A TEST OF HYPOTHESIS

Suppose building specifications in a certain city require that the average breaking strength of residential sewer pipe be more than 2,400 pounds per foot of length (i.e., per linear foot). Each manufacturer who wants to sell pipe in this city must demonstrate that its product meets the specification. Note that we are again interested in making an inference about the mean μ of a population. However, in this example we are less interested in estimating the value of μ than we are in testing a *hypothesis* about its value. That is, we want to decide whether the mean breaking strength of the pipe exceeds 2,400 pounds per linear foot.

The method used to reach a decision is based on the rare-event concept explained in earlier chapters. We define two hypotheses: (1) The **null hypothesis** is that which represents the status quo to the party performing the sampling experiment—the hypothesis that will be accepted unless the data provide convincing evidence that it is false. (2) The **alternative**, or **research**, **hypothesis** is that which will be accepted only if the data provide convincing evidence of its truth. From the point of view of the city conducting the tests, the null hypothesis is that the manufacturer's pipe does *not* meet specifications unless the tests provide convincing evidence otherwise. The null and alternative hypotheses are therefore

Null hypothesis (H_0): $\mu \leq 2,400$ (i.e., the manufacturer's pipe does not meet specifications)

Alternative (research) hypothesis (H_a): $\mu > 2,400$ (i.e., the manufacturer's pipe meets specifications)

How can the city decide when enough evidence exists to conclude that the manufacturer's pipe meets specifications? Since the hypotheses concern the value of the population mean μ, it is reasonable to use the sample mean $\bar{x}$ to make the inference, just as we did when forming confidence intervals for μ in Sections 5.1 and 5.2. The city will conclude that the pipe meets specifications only when the sample mean $\bar{x}$ convincingly indicates that the population mean exceeds 2,400 pounds per linear foot.

"Convincing" evidence in favor of the alternative hypothesis will exist when the value of $\bar{x}$ exceeds 2,400 by an amount that cannot be readily attributed to sampling variability. To decide, we compute a **test statistic**, which is the z value that measures the distance between the value of $\bar{x}$ and the value of μ specified in the null hypothesis. When the null hypothesis contains more than one value of μ, as in this case (H_0: $\mu \leq 2,400$), we use the value of μ closest to the values specified in the alternative hypothesis. The idea is that if the hypothesis that μ *equals* 2,400 can

FIGURE 6.1
The sampling
distribution of $\bar{x}$,
assuming $\mu = 2,400$

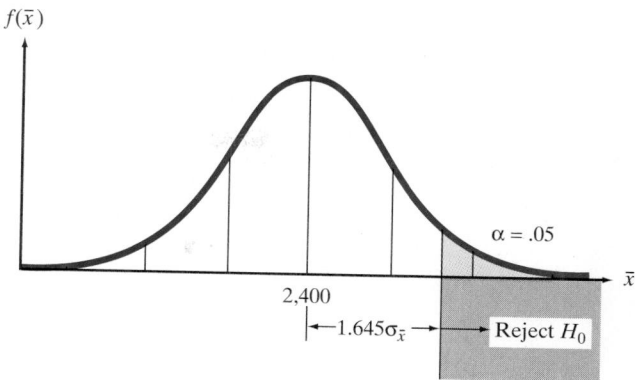

be rejected in favor of $\mu > 2,400$, then μ *less than or equal to* 2,400 can certainly be rejected. Thus, the test statistic is

$$z = \frac{\bar{x} - 2,400}{\sigma_{\bar{x}}} = \frac{\bar{x} - 2,400}{\sigma/\sqrt{n}}$$

Note that a value of $z = 1$ means that $\bar{x}$ is 1 standard deviation above $\mu = 2,400$; a value of $z = 1.5$ means that $\bar{x}$ is 1.5 standard deviations above $\mu = 2,400$, etc. How large must z be before the city can be convinced that the null hypothesis can be rejected in favor of the alternative and conclude that the pipe meets specifications?

If you examine Figure 6.1, you will note that the chance of observing $\bar{x}$ more than 1.645 standard deviations above 2,400 is only .05—*if in fact the true mean μ is 2,400.* Thus, if the sample mean is more than 1.645 standard deviations above 2,400, either H_0 is true and a relatively rare event has occurred (.05 probability) or H_a is true and the population mean exceeds 2,400. Since we would most likely reject the notion that a rare event has occurred, we would reject the null hypothesis ($\mu \leq 2,400$) and conclude that the alternative hypothesis ($\mu > 2,400$) is true. What is the probability that this procedure will lead us to an incorrect decision?

Such an incorrect decision—deciding that the null hypothesis is false when in fact it is true—is called a **Type I error**. As indicated in Figure 6.1, the risk of making a Type I error is denoted by the symbol α. That is,

$\alpha = P(\text{Type I error})$

$\quad = P(\text{Rejecting the null hypothesis when in fact the null hypothesis is true})$

In our example

$$\alpha = P(z > 1.645 \text{ when in fact } \mu = 2,400) = .05$$

We now summarize the elements of the test:

H_0: $\mu \leq 2,400$

H_a: $\mu > 2,400$

Test statistic: $z = \dfrac{\bar{x} - 2,400}{\sigma_{\bar{x}}}$

Rejection region: $z > 1.645$, which corresponds to $\alpha = .05$

Note that the **rejection region** refers to the values of the test statistic for which we will *reject the null hypothesis.*

FIGURE 6.2
Location of the test
statistic for a test of
the hypothesis
$H_0: \mu = 2{,}400$

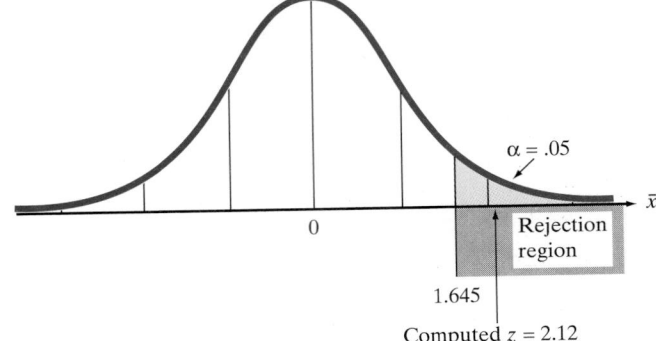

To illustrate the use of the test, suppose we test 50 sections of sewer pipe and find the mean and standard deviation for these 50 measurements to be

$$\bar{x} = 2{,}460 \text{ pounds per linear foot}$$

$$s = 200 \text{ pounds per linear foot}$$

As in the case of estimation, we can use s to approximate σ when s is calculated from a large set of sample measurements.

The test statistic is

$$z = \frac{\bar{x} - 2{,}400}{\sigma_{\bar{x}}} = \frac{\bar{x} - 2{,}400}{\sigma/\sqrt{n}} \approx \frac{\bar{x} - 2{,}400}{s/\sqrt{n}}$$

Substituting $\bar{x} = 2{,}460$, $n = 50$, and $s = 200$, we have

$$z \approx \frac{2{,}460 - 2{,}400}{200/\sqrt{50}} = \frac{60}{28.28} = 2.12$$

Therefore, the sample mean lies $2.12\sigma_{\bar{x}}$ above the hypothesized value of μ, $2{,}400$, as shown in Figure 6.2. Since this value of z exceeds 1.645, it falls in the rejection region. That is, we reject the null hypothesis that $\mu = 2{,}400$ and conclude that $\mu > 2{,}400$. Thus, it appears that the company's pipe has a mean strength that exceeds 2,400 pounds per linear foot.

How much faith can be placed in this conclusion? What is the probability that our statistical test could lead us to reject the null hypothesis (and conclude that the company's pipe meets the city's specifications) when in fact the null hypothesis is true? The answer is $\alpha = .05$. That is, we selected the level of risk, α, of making a Type I error when we constructed the test. Thus, the chance is only 1 in 20 that our test would lead us to conclude the manufacturer's pipe satisfies the city's specifications when in fact the pipe does *not* meet specifications.

Now, suppose the sample mean breaking strength for the 50 sections of sewer pipe turned out to be $\bar{x} = 2{,}430$ pounds per linear foot. Assuming that the sample standard deviation is still $s = 200$, the test statistic is

$$z = \frac{2{,}430 - 2{,}400}{200/\sqrt{50}} = \frac{30}{28.28} = 1.06$$

Therefore, the sample mean $\bar{x} = 2{,}430$ is only 1.06 standard deviations above the null hypothesized value of $\mu = 2{,}400$. As shown in Figure 6.3, this value does not fall into the rejection region ($z > 1.645$). Therefore, we know that we cannot reject H_0 using $\alpha = .05$. Even though the sample mean exceeds the city's specification of 2,400 by 30 pounds per linear foot, it does not exceed the specification by enough to provide *convincing* evidence that the *population mean* exceeds 2,400.

FIGURE 6.3
Location of test
statistic when
$\bar{x} = 2{,}430$

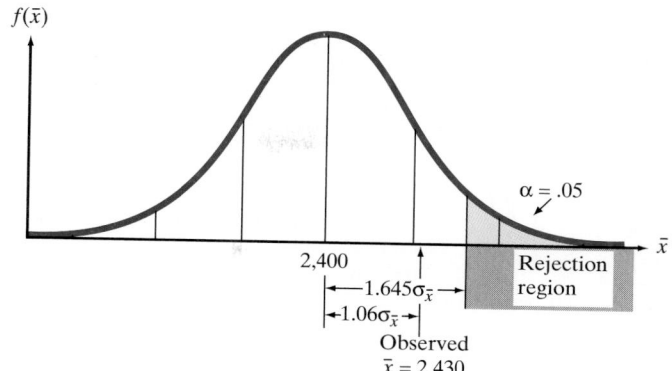

Should we accept the null hypothesis $H_0: \mu \leqslant 2{,}400$ and conclude that the manufacturer's pipe does not meet specifications? To do so would be to risk a **Type II error**—that of concluding that the null hypothesis is true (the pipe does not meet specifications) when in fact it is false (the pipe does meet specifications). We denote the probability of committing a Type II error by β. Unfortunately, β is often difficult to determine precisely. Rather than make a decision (accept H_0) for which the probability of error (β) is unknown, we avoid the potential Type II error by avoiding the conclusion that the null hypothesis is true. Instead, we will simply state that *the sample evidence is insufficient to reject H_0 at $\alpha = .05$*. Since the null hypothesis is the "status-quo" hypothesis, the effect of not rejecting H_0 is to maintain the status quo. In our pipe-testing example, the effect of having insufficient evidence to reject the null hypothesis that the pipe does not meet specifications is probably to prohibit the utilization of the manufacturer's pipe unless and until there is sufficient evidence that the pipe does meet specifications. That is, until the data indicate convincingly that the null hypothesis is false, we usually maintain the status quo implied by its truth.

Table 6.1 summarizes the four possible outcomes of a test of hypothesis. The "true state of nature" columns in Table 6.1 refer to the fact that either the null hypothesis H_0 is true or the alternative hypothesis H_a is true. Note that the true state of nature is unknown to the researcher conducting the test. The "decision" rows in Table 6.1 refer to the action of the researcher, assuming that he or she will either conclude that H_0 is true or that H_a is true, based on the results of the sampling experiment. Note that a Type I error can be made *only* when the null hypothesis is rejected in favor of the alternative hypothesis, and a Type II error can be made *only* when the null hypothesis is accepted. Our policy will be to make a decision only when we know the probability of making the error that corresponds to that decision. Since α is usually specified by the analyst, we will generally be able to reject H_0 (accept H_a) when the sample evidence supports that decision. However, since β is usually not specified, we will generally avoid the

TABLE 6.1   Conclusions and Consequences for a Test of Hypothesis

		TRUE STATE OF NATURE	
		H_0 **True**	H_a **True**
Conclusion	H_0 True	Correct decision	Type II error (probability β)
	H_a True	Type I error (probability α)	Correct decision

STATISTICS IN ACTION

6.1 STATISTICS IS MURDER!

Statistics and probability can play a key role in establishing credible evidence in a trial by jury. For example, statistics similar to those you produced for the Kentucky Milk Case (Showcase 1) ultimately led to the conviction of one dairy owner for bid collusion. Sometimes, the outcome of a jury trial defies belief from the general public (e.g., the O.J. Simpson verdict in the "Trial of the Century"). Such a verdict is more understandable when you realize that the jury trial of an accused murderer is analogous to the statistical hypothesis-testing process. Each of the elements of a test of hypothesis applies to the jury system of deciding the guilt or innocence of the accused:

1. *Null hypothesis* H_0: The null hypothesis in a jury trial is that the accused is innocent. The status quo hypothesis in the U.S. system of justice is innocence, which in a murder trial is assumed to be true until proven *beyond a reasonable doubt*.

2. *Alternative hypothesis* H_a: The alternative hypothesis is guilt, which is accepted only when sufficient evidence exists to establish its truth.

3. *Test statistic:* The test statistic in a trial is the final vote of the jury—that is, the number of the jury members who vote "guilty."

4. *Rejection region:* In a murder trial the jury vote must be unanimous in favor of guilt before the null hypothesis of innocence is rejected in favor of the alternative hypothesis of guilt. Thus, for a 12-member jury trial, the rejection region is $x = 12$, where x is the number of "guilty" votes.

5. *Assumption:* The primary assumption made in trials concerns the method of selecting the jury. The jury is assumed to represent a random sample of citizens who have no prejudice concerning the case.

6. *Experiment and calculation of the test statistic:* The sampling experiment is analogous to the jury selec-tion, the trial, and the jury deliberations. The final vote of the jury is analogous to the calculation of the test statistic.

7. *Conclusion:*

   a. If the vote of the jury is unanimous in favor of guilt, the null hypothesis of innocence is rejected and the court concludes that the accused mur-derer is guilty.

   b. Any vote other than a unanimous one for guilt results in the court's reserving judgment about the hypotheses, either by declaring the accused "not guilty," or by declaring a mistrial and repeating the "test" with a new jury. (The latter is analogous to collecting more data and repeat-ing a statistical test of hypothesis.) The court never accepts the null hypothesis; that is, the court never declares the accused "innocent." A "not guilty" verdict (as in the O. J. Simpson case) implies that the court could not find the defen-dant guilty **beyond a reasonable doubt**.

Focus

a. Define Type I and Type II errors in a murder trial.

b. Which of the two errors is the more serious? Explain.

c. The court does not, in general, know the values of α and β; but ideally, both should be small. One of these probabilities is assumed to be smaller than the other in a jury trial. Which one, and why?

d. The court system relies on the belief that the value of α is made very small by requiring a unanimous vote before guilt is concluded. Explain why this is so.

e. For a jury prejudiced against a guilty verdict as the trial begins, will the value of α increase or decrease? Explain.

f. For a jury prejudiced against a guilty verdict as the trial begins, will the value of β increase or decrease? Explain.

decision to accept H_0, preferring instead to state that the sample evidence is insuf-ficient to reject H_0 when the test statistic is not in the rejection region.

The elements of a test of hypothesis are summarized in the following box. Note that the first four elements are all specified *before* the sampling experiment is performed. In no case will the results of the sample be used to determine the hypotheses—the data are collected to test the predetermined hypotheses, not to formulate them.

Elements of a Test of Hypothesis

1. *Null hypothesis* (H_0): A theory about the values of one or more population parameters. The theory generally represents the status quo, which we adopt until it is proven false.

2. *Alternative (research) hypothesis* (H_a): A theory that contradicts the null hypothesis. The theory generally represents that which we will adopt only when sufficient evidence exists to establish its truth.

3. *Test statistic:* A sample statistic used to decide whether to reject the null hypothesis.

4. *Rejection region:* The numerical values of the test statistic for which the null hypothesis will be rejected. The rejection region is chosen so that the probability is α that it will contain the test statistic when the null hypothesis is true, thereby leading to a Type I error. The value of α is usually chosen to be small (e.g., .01, .05, or .10), and is referred to as the **level of significance** of the test.

5. *Assumptions:* Clear statement(s) of any assumptions made about the population(s) being sampled.

6. *Experiment and calculation of test statistic:* Performance of the sampling experiment and determination of the numerical value of the test statistic.

7. *Conclusion:*
   a. If the numerical value of the test statistic falls in the rejection region, we reject the null hypothesis and conclude that the alternative hypothesis is true. We know that the hypothesis-testing process will lead to this conclusion incorrectly (Type I error) only $100\alpha\%$ of the time when H_0 is true.
   b. If the test statistic does not fall in the rejection region, we do not reject H_0. Thus, we reserve judgment about which hypothesis is true. We do not conclude that the null hypothesis is true because we do not (in general) know the probability β that our test procedure will lead to an incorrect acceptance of H_0 (Type II error).*

*In many practical business applications of hypothesis testing, nonrejection leads management to behave as if the null hypothesis were accepted. Accordingly, the distinction between acceptance and nonrejection is frequently blurred in practice.

EXERCISES   6.1–6.10

Learning the Mechanics

6.1 Which hypothesis, the null or the alternative, is the status-quo hypothesis? Which is the research hypothesis?

6.2 Which element of a test of hypothesis is used to decide whether to reject the null hypothesis in favor of the alternative hypothesis?

6.3 What is the level of significance of a test of hypothesis?

6.4 What is the difference between Type I and Type II errors in hypothesis testing? How do α and β relate to Type I and Type II errors?

6.5 List the four possible results of the combinations of decisions and true states of nature for a test of hypothesis.

6.6 We (generally) reject the null hypothesis when the test statistic falls in the rejection region, but we do not accept the null hypothesis when the test statistic does not fall in the rejection region. Why?

6.7 If you test a hypothesis and reject the null hypothesis in favor of the alternative hypothesis, does your test prove that the alternative hypothesis is correct? Explain.

Applying the Concepts

6.8 In 1895 an Italian criminologist, Cesare Lombroso, proposed that blood pressure be used to test for truthfulness. In the 1930s, William Marston added the measurements of respiration and perspiration to the process, built a machine to do the measuring, and called his invention the *polygraph*, or *lie detector*. Today, the federal court system will not consider polygraph results as evidence, but nearly half the state courts do permit polygraph tests under certain circumstances. In addition, its use in screening job applicants is on the rise. Physicians Michael Phillips, Allan Brett, and John Beary subjected the polygraph to the same careful testing given to medical diagnostic tests. They found that if 1,000 people were subjected to the polygraph and 500 told the truth and 500 lied, the polygraph would indicate that approximately 185 of the truth tellers were liars and that approximately 120 of the liars were truth tellers ("Lie detectors can make a liar of you," *Discover*, June 1986).

a. In the application of a polygraph test, an individual is presumed to be a truth teller (H_0) until "proven" a liar (H_a). In this context, what is a Type I error? A Type II error?

b. According to Phillips, Brett, and Beary, what is the probability (approximately) that a polygraph test will result in a Type I error? A Type II error?

6.9 According to *Chemical Marketing Reporter* (Feb. 20, 1995), pharmaceutical companies spend $15 billion per year on research and development of new drugs. The pharmaceutical company must subject each new drug to lengthy and involved testing before receiving the necessary permission from the Food and Drug Administration (FDA) to market the drug. The FDA's policy is that the pharmaceutical company must provide substantial evidence that a new drug is safe prior to receiving FDA approval, so that the FDA can confidently certify the safety of the drug to potential consumers.

a. If the new drug testing were to be placed in a test of hypothesis framework, would the null hypothesis be that the drug is safe or unsafe? The alternative hypothesis?

b. Given the choice of null and alternative hypotheses in part **a**, describe Type I and Type II errors in terms of this application. Define α and β in terms of this application.

c. If the FDA wants to be very confident that the drug is safe before permitting it to be market-ed, is it more important that α or β be small? Explain.

6.10 One of the most pressing problems in high-technology industries is computer security. Computer security is typically achieved by use of a *password*—a collection of symbols (usually letters and numbers) that must be supplied by the user before the computer permits access to the account. The problem is that persistent hackers can create programs that enter millions of combinations of symbols into a target system until the correct password is found. The newest systems solve this problem by requiring authorized users to identify themselves by unique body characteristics. For example, a system developed by Palmguard, Inc. tests the hypothesis

H_0: The proposed user is authorized

versus

H_a: The proposed user is unauthorized

by checking characteristics of the proposed user's palm against those stored in the authorized users' data bank (*Omni*, 1984).

a. Define a Type I error and Type II error for this test. Which is the more serious error? Why?

b. Palmguard reports that the Type I error rate for its system is less than 1%, whereas the Type II error rate is .00025%. Interpret these error rates.

c. Another successful security system, the EyeDentifyer, "spots authorized computer users by reading the one-of-a-kind patterns formed by the network of minute blood vessels across the retina at the back of the eye." The EyeDentifyer reports Type I and II error rates of .01% (1 in 10,000) and .005% (5 in 100,000), respectively. Interpret these rates.

6.2 LARGE-SAMPLE TEST OF HYPOTHESIS ABOUT A POPULATION MEAN

In Section 6.1 we learned that the null and alternative hypotheses form the basis for a test of hypothesis inference. The null and alternative hypotheses may take one of several forms. In the sewer pipe example we tested the null hypothesis that the population mean strength of the pipe is less than or equal to 2,400 pounds per linear foot against the alternative hypothesis that the mean strength exceeds 2,400. That is, we tested

$$H_0: \mu \leq 2,400$$

$$H_a: \mu > 2,400$$

This is a **one-tailed** (or **one-sided**) **statistical test** because the alternative hypothesis specifies that the population parameter (the population mean μ, in this example) is strictly greater than a specified value (2,400, in this example). If the null hypothesis had been $H_0: \mu \geq 2,400$ and the alternative hypothesis had been $H_a: \mu < 2,400$, the test would still be one-sided, because the parameter is still specified to be on "one

FIGURE 6.4

Rejection regions corresponding to one- and two-tailed tests

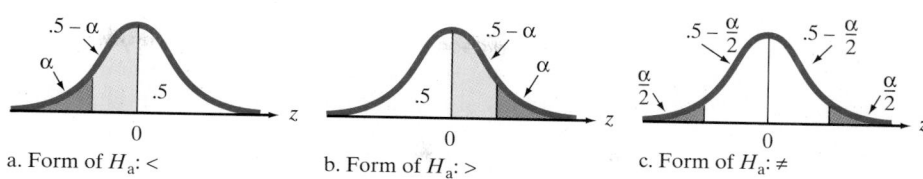

a. Form of H_a: <   b. Form of H_a: >   c. Form of H_a: $\neq$

side" of the null hypothesis value. Some statistical investigations seek to show that the population parameter is *either larger or smaller* than some specified value. Such an alternative hypothesis is called a **two-tailed (or two-sided) hypothesis**.

While alternative hypotheses are always specified as strict inequalities, such as $\mu < 2{,}400$, $\mu > 2{,}400$, or $\mu \neq 2{,}400$, null hypotheses are usually specified as equalities, such as $\mu = 2{,}400$. Even when the null hypothesis is an inequality, such as $\mu \leq 2{,}400$, we specify $H_0: \mu = 2{,}400$, reasoning that if sufficient evidence exists to show that $H_a: \mu > 2{,}400$ is true when tested against $H_0: \mu = 2{,}400$, then surely sufficient evidence exists to reject $\mu < 2{,}400$ as well. Therefore, the null hypothesis is specified as the value of μ closest to a one-sided alternative hypothesis and as the only value *not* specified in a two-tailed alternative hypothesis. The steps for selecting the null and alternative hypotheses are summarized in the accompanying box.

Steps for Selecting the Null and Alternative Hypotheses

1. Select the *alternative hypothesis* as that which the sampling experiment is intended to establish. The alternative hypothesis will assume one of three forms:

   a. One-tailed, upper-tailed   *Example: $H_a: \mu > 2{,}400$*

   b. One-tailed, lower-tailed   *Example: $H_a: \mu < 2{,}400$*

   c. Two-tailed   *Example: $H_a: \mu \neq 2{,}400$*

2. Select the *null hypothesis* as the status quo, that which will be presumed true unless the sampling experiment conclusively establishes the alternative hypothesis. The null hypothesis will be specified as that parameter value closest to the alternative in one-tailed tests, and as the complementary (or only unspecified) value in two-tailed tests.

Example: $H_0: \mu = 2{,}400$

The rejection region for a two-tailed test differs from that for a one-tailed test. When we are trying to detect departure from the null hypothesis in *either* direction, we must establish a rejection region in both tails of the sampling distribution of the test statistic. Figures 6.4a and 6.4b show the one-tailed rejection regions for lower- and upper-tailed tests, respectively. The two-tailed rejection region is illustrated in Figure 6.4c. Note that a rejection region is established in each tail of the sampling distribution for a two-tailed test.

The rejection regions corresponding to typical values selected for α are shown in Table 6.2 for one- and two-tailed tests. Note that the smaller α you select, the more evidence (the larger z) you will need before you can reject H_0.

TABLE 6.2   Rejection Regions for Common Values of α

	ALTERNATIVE HYPOTHESES		
	Lower-Tailed	**Upper-Tailed**	**Two-Tailed**
$\alpha = .10$	$z < -1.28$	$z > 1.28$	$z < -1.645$ or $z > 1.645$
$\alpha = .05$	$z < -1.645$	$z > 1.645$	$z < -1.96$ or $z > 1.96$
$\alpha = .01$	$z < -2.33$	$z > 2.33$	$z < -2.575$ or $z > 2.575$

EXAMPLE 6.1

A manufacturer of cereal wants to test the performance of one of its filling machines. The machine is designed to discharge a mean amount of $\mu = 12$ ounces per box, and the manufacturer wants to detect any departure from this setting. This quality study calls for randomly sampling 100 boxes from today's production run and determining whether the mean fill for the run is 12 ounces per box. Set up a test of hypothesis for this study, using $\alpha = .01$. (In Statistics in Action 6.2 and in Chapter 11, we describe how this problem can be addressed using control charts.)

SOLUTION

Since the manufacturer wishes to detect a departure from the setting of $\mu = 12$ in either direction, $\mu < 12$ or $\mu > 12$, we conduct a two-tailed statistical test. Following the procedure for selecting the null and alternative hypotheses, we specify as the alternative hypothesis that the mean differs from 12 ounces, since detecting the machine's departure from specifications is the purpose of the quality control study. The null hypothesis is the presumption that the fill machine is operating properly unless the sample data indicate otherwise. Thus,

$$H_0: \mu = 12$$

$$H_a: \mu \neq 12 \text{ (i.e., } \mu < 12 \text{ or } \mu > 12)$$

The test statistic measures the number of standard deviations between the observed value of $\bar{x}$ and the null hypothesized value $\mu = 12$:

$$\text{Test statistic: } \frac{\bar{x} - 12}{\sigma_{\bar{x}}}$$

The rejection region must be designated to detect a departure from $\mu = 12$ in *either* direction, so we will reject H_0 for values of z that are either too small (negative) or too large (positive). To determine the precise values of z that comprise the rejection region, we first select α, the probability that the test will lead to incorrect rejection of the null hypothesis. Then we divide α equally between the lower and upper tail of the distribution of z, as shown in Figure 6.5. In this example, $\alpha = .01$, so $\alpha/2 = .005$ is placed in each tail. The areas in the tails correspond to $z = -2.575$ and $z = 2.575$, respectively (from Table 6.2):

$$\text{Rejection region: } z < -2.575 \text{ or } z > 2.575 \qquad \text{(see Figure 6.5)}$$

Assumptions: Since the sample size of the experiment is large enough $(n > 30)$, the Central Limit Theorem will apply, and no assumptions need be made about the population of fill measurements. The sampling distribution of the sample mean fill of 100 boxes will be approximately normal regardless of the distribution of the individual boxes' fills. ■

FIGURE 6.5
Two-tailed rejection region: $\alpha = .01$

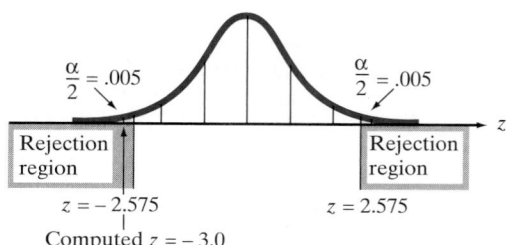

Note that the test in Example 6.1 is set up *before* the sampling experiment is conducted. The data are not used to develop the test. Evidently, the manufacturer does not want to disrupt the filling process to adjust the machine unless the sample data provide very convincing evidence that it is not meeting specifications, because the value of α has been set quite low at .01. If the sample evidence results in the rejection of H_0, the manufacturer can be 99% confident that the machine needs adjustment.

Once the test is set up, the manufacturer is ready to perform the sampling experiment and conduct the test. The test is performed in Example 6.2.

EXAMPLE 6.2   Refer to the quality control test set up in Example 6.1. Suppose the sample yields the following results:

$$n = 100 \text{ observations} \qquad \bar{x} = 11.85 \text{ ounces} \qquad s = .5 \text{ ounce}$$

Use these data to conduct the test of hypothesis.

SOLUTION

Since the test is completely specified in Example 6.1, we simply substitute the sample statistics into the test statistic:

$$z = \frac{\bar{x} - 12}{\sigma_{\bar{x}}} = \frac{\bar{x} - 12}{\sigma/\sqrt{n}} = \frac{11.85 - 12}{\sigma/\sqrt{100}}$$

$$\approx \frac{11.85 - 12}{s/10} = \frac{-.15}{.5/10} = -3.0$$

The implication is that the sample mean, 11.85, is (approximately) 3 standard deviations below the null hypothesized value of 12.0 in the sampling distribution of $\bar{x}$. You can see in Figure 6.5 that this value of z is in the lower-tail rejection region, which consists of all values of $z < -2.575$. These sample data provide sufficient evidence to reject H_0 and conclude, at the $\alpha = .01$ level of significance, that the mean fill differs from the specification of $\mu = 12$ ounces. It appears that the machine is, on average, underfilling the boxes.   **⌐**

Two final points about the test of hypothesis in Example 6.2 apply to all statistical tests:

1. Since z is less than -2.575, it is tempting to state our conclusion at a significance level lower than $\alpha = .01$. We resist the temptation because the level of α is determined *before* the sampling experiment is performed. If we decide that we are willing to tolerate a 1% Type I error rate, the result of the sampling experiment should have no effect on that decision. *In general, the same data should not be used both to set up and to conduct the test.*

2. When we state our conclusion at the .01 level of significance, we are referring to the failure rate of the *procedure,* not the result of this particular test. We know that the test procedure will lead to the rejection of the null hypothesis only 1% of the time when in fact $\mu = 12$. *Therefore, when the test statistic falls in the rejection region, we infer that the alternative $\mu \neq 12$ is true and express our confidence in the procedure by quoting the α level of significance, or the $100(1 - \alpha)\%$ confidence level.*

The setup of a large-sample test of hypothesis about a population mean is summarized in the following box. Both the one- and two-tailed tests are shown.

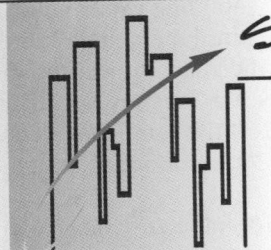

STATISTICS IN ACTION

6.2 STATISTICAL QUALITY CONTROL, PART I

A graphical device, known as a control chart, can be used in business operations to monitor the variation over time in the quality of products and services being produced. The control chart was developed by Walter A. Shewhart of Bell Telephone Laboratories in 1924 and has become a basic tool of quality control engineers and operations managers the world over. Japan's emergence as an industrial superpower is due in part to its early adoption and refinement of quality control techniques, such as the control chart (Duncan, 1986). In this Statistics in Action and Statistics in Action 6.3, we expand the discussion of control charts and demonstrate that they are simply vehicles for conducting hypothesis tests. We discuss control charts in detail in Chapter 11.

Suppose it is desired to monitor the pitch diameter of the threads on a particular aircraft fitting. When the process is in control, the pitch diameters follow a normal distribution with mean μ_0 and standard deviation σ_0. Such monitoring can be accomplished by (1) sampling n items from the production process at regular time intervals, (2) measuring the pitch diameter of each item sampled, and (3) plotting the mean diameter

of each sample, $\bar{x}$, on a control chart like that in Figure 6.6. Such a control chart is called an **$\bar{x}$-chart**. If a value of $\bar{x}$ falls above the upper control limit or below the lower control limit, there is strong evidence that the process is out of control—i.e., that the quality of the product being produced does not meet established standards. Otherwise, the process is deemed to be in control.

In effect, each time an analyst plots a sample mean on an $\bar{x}$-chart and observes where it falls in relation to the control limits, the analyst is conducting a two-tailed hypothesis test.

Focus

Describe the analyst's decision process in the language of hypothesis testing by answering the following questions.

a. What are the null and alternative hypotheses of interest?

b. What is the test statistic?

c. Specify the rejection region.

d. What is the probability of committing a Type I error?

Large-Sample Test of Hypothesis About μ

One-Tailed Test

$H_0: \mu = \mu_0{}^*$

$H_a: \mu < \mu_0$:
  (or $H_a: \mu > \mu_0$)

Test statistic: $z = \dfrac{\bar{x} - \mu_0}{\sigma_{\bar{x}}}$

Rejection region: $z < -z_\alpha$
  (or $z > z_\alpha$ when $H_a: \mu > \mu_0$)

where z_α is chosen so that
  $P(z > z_\alpha) = \alpha$

Two-Tailed Test

$H_0: \mu = \mu_0{}^*$

$H_a: \mu \neq \mu_0$

Test statistic: $z = \dfrac{\bar{x} - \mu_0}{\sigma_{\bar{x}}}$

Rejection region: $z < -z_{\alpha/2}$
  or $z > z_{\alpha/2}$

where $z_{\alpha/2}$ is chosen so that
  $P(z > z_{\alpha/2}) = \alpha/2$

Assumptions: None, since the Central Limit Theorem assures us that the sampling distribution of $\bar{x}$ (and, hence, the test statistic z) will be approximately normal.

*Note: μ_0 is the symbol for the numerical value assigned to μ under the null hypothesis.

FIGURE 6.6
$\bar{x}$-chart (Statistics in Action 6.2)

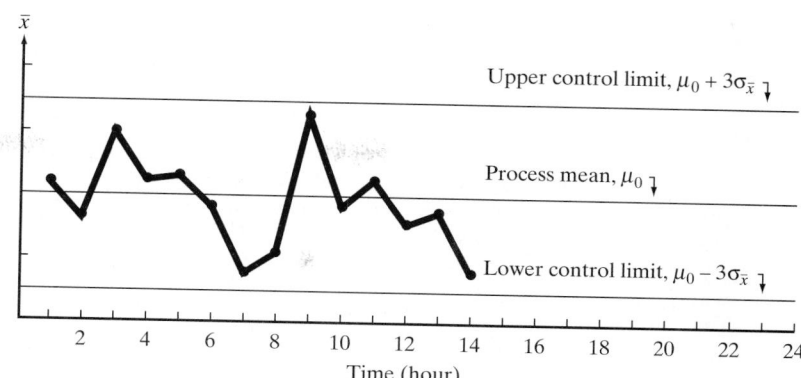

Once the test has been set up, the sampling experiment is performed and the test statistic calculated. The next box contains possible conclusions for a test of hypothesis, depending on the result of the sampling experiment.

Possible Conclusions for a Test of Hypothesis

1. If the calculated test statistic falls in the rejection region, reject H_0 and conclude that the alternative hypothesis H_a is true. State that you are rejecting H_0 at the α level of significance. Remember that the confidence is in the testing *process*, not the particular result of a single test.

2. If the test statistic does not fall in the rejection region, conclude that the sampling experiment does not provide sufficient evidence to reject H_0 at the α level of significance. [Generally, we will not "accept" the null hypothesis unless the probability β of a Type II error has been calculated. Consult the chapter references for some advanced methods of calculating β.]

EXERCISES   6.11–6.23

Note: Exercises marked with 💾 *contain data for computer analysis on a 3.5" disk (file name in parentheses).*

Learning the Mechanics

6.11 For each of the following rejection regions, sketch the sampling distribution for z and indicate the location of the rejection region.

    a. $z > 1.96$ **b.** $z > 1.645$ **c.** $z > 2.575$
    d. $z < -1.28$ **e.** $z < -1.645$ or $z > 1.645$
    f. $z < -2.575$ or $z > 2.575$
    g. For each of the rejection regions specified in parts **a–f**, what is the probability that a Type I error will be made?

6.12 Suppose you are interested in conducting the statistical test of $H_0: \mu = 255$ against $H_a: \mu > 255$, and you have decided to use the following decision rule: Reject H_0 if the sample mean of a random sample of 81 items is more than 270. Assume that the standard deviation of the population is 63.

    a. Express the decision rule in terms of z.
    b. Find α, the probability of making a Type I error, by using this decision rule.

6.13 A random sample of 100 observations from a population with standard deviation 60 yielded a sample mean of 110.

    a. Test the null hypothesis that $\mu = 100$ against the alternative hypothesis that $\mu > 100$ using $\alpha = .05$. Interpret the results of the test.
    b. Test the null hypothesis that $\mu = 100$ against the alternative hypothesis that $\mu \neq 100$ using $\alpha = .05$. Interpret the results of the test.
    c. Compare the results of the two tests you conducted. Explain why the results differ.

6.14 A random sample of 64 observations produced the following summary statistics: $\bar{x} = .323$ and $s^2 = .034$.

    a. Test the null hypothesis that $\mu = .36$ against the alternative hypothesis that $\mu < .36$ using $\alpha = .10$.

b. Test the null hypothesis that $\mu = .36$ against the alternative hypothesis that $\mu \neq .36$ using $\alpha = .10$. Interpret the result.

Applying the Concepts

6.15 Most major corporations have psychologists available to help employees who suffer from stress. One problem that is difficult to diagnose is post-traumatic stress disorder (PTSD). Researchers studying PTSD often use as subjects former prisoners of war (POWs). *Psychological Assessment* (Mar. 1995) published the results of a study of World War II aviators who were captured by German forces after they were shot down. Having located a total of 239 World War II aviator POW survivors, the researchers asked each veteran to participate in the study; 33 responded to the letter of invitation. Each of the 33 POW survivors were administered the Minnesota Multiphasic Personality Inventory, one component of which measures level of PTSD. [*Note:* The higher the score, the higher the level of PTSD.] The aviators produced a mean PTSD score of $\bar{x} = 9.00$ and a standard deviation of $s = 9.32$.

a. Set up the null and alternative hypotheses for determining whether the true mean PTSD score of all World War II aviator POWs is less than 16. [*Note:* The value, 16, represents the mean PTSD score established for Vietnam POWs.]

b. Conduct the test, part **a**, using $\alpha = .10$. What are the practical implications of the test?

c. Discuss the representativeness of the sample used in the study and its ramifications.

6.16 A study reported in the *Journal of Occupational and Organizational Psychology* (Dec. 1992) investigated the relationship of employment status to mental health. A sample of 49 unemployed men was given a mental health examination using the General Health Questionnaire (GHQ). The GHQ is a widely recognized measure of present mental health, with lower values indicating better mental health. The mean and standard deviation of the GHQ scores were $\bar{x} = 10.94$ and $s = 5.10$, respectively.

a. Specify the appropriate null and alternative hypotheses if we wish to test the research hypothesis that the mean GHQ score for all unemployed men exceeds 10. Is the test one-tailed or two-tailed? Why?

b. If we specify $\alpha = .05$, what is the appropriate rejection region for this test?

c. Conduct the test, and state your conclusion clearly in the language of this exercise.

6.17 **(X06.017)** In quality control applications of hypothesis testing (see Statistics in Action 6.2), the null and alternative hypotheses are frequently specified as

H_0: The production process is performing satisfactorily

H_a: The process is performing in an unsatisfactory manner

Accordingly, α is sometimes referred to as the **producer's risk**, while β is called the **consumer's risk** (Stevenson, *Production/Operations Management*, 1996). An injection molder produces plastic golf tees. The process is designed to produce tees with a mean weight of .250 ounce. To investigate whether the injection molder is operating satisfactorily, 40 tees were randomly sampled from the last hour's production. Their weights (in ounces) are listed in the table below. Summary statistics for the data are shown in the SAS printout that follows.

a. Do the data provide sufficient evidence to conclude that the process is not operating satisfactorily? Test using $\alpha = .01$.

b. In the context of this problem, explain why it makes sense to call α the producer's risk and β the consumer's risk.

6.18 What factors inhibit the learning process in the classroom? To answer this question, researchers at Murray State University surveyed 40 students from a senior-level marketing class (*Marketing Education Review*, Fall 1994). Each student was given a list of factors and asked to rate the extent to which each factor inhibited the learning process in courses offered in their department. A 7-point rating scale was used, where 1 = "not at all" and 7 = "to a great extent." The factor with the highest rating was instructor-related: "Professors who place too much emphasis on a single right answer rather than overall thinking and creative ideas."

.247	.251	.254	.253	.253	.248	.253	.255	.256	.252
.253	.252	.253	.256	.254	.256	.252	.251	.253	.251
.253	.253	.248	.251	.253	.256	.254	.250	.254	.255
.249	.250	.254	.251	.251	.255	.251	.253	.252	.253

```
Analysis Variable : WEIGHT

N Obs    N      Minimum         Maximum             Mean         Std Dev
-------------------------------------------------------------------------
  40    40    0.2470000       0.2560000         0.2524750       0.0022302
-------------------------------------------------------------------------
```

Summary statistics for the student ratings of this factor are: $\bar{x} = 4.70$, $s = 1.62$.

a. Conduct a test to determine if the true mean rating for this instructor-related factor exceeds 4. Use $\alpha = .05$. Interpret the test results.

b. Because the variable of interest, rating, is measured on a 7-point scale, it is unlikely that the population of ratings will be normally distributed. Consequently, some analysts may perceive the test, part **a**, to be invalid and search for alternative methods of analysis. Defend or refute this argument.

6.19 In 1993 U.S. banks handled 61 billion individual and corporate checks, compared to 46 billion ten years ago. The increase in check writing has apparently led to an increase in check fraud. An American Bankers Association 1993 survey of 50 midsized banks found a mean loss due to check fraud of $37,443 per bank (*Bank Security Report*, Feb. 1995). Losses at the 50 individual banks ranged from $208 to $400,000. Assume that ten years ago, the true mean loss per midsized bank due to check fraud was $15,100. Conduct a test at $\alpha = .10$ to determine whether the true mean loss due to check fraud of midsized banks in 1993 exceeds $15,100 per bank.

6.20 **(X06.020)** The introduction of printed circuit boards (PCBs) in the 1950s revolutionized the electronics industry. However, solder-joint defects on PCBs have plagued electronics manufacturers since the introduction of the PCB. A single PCB may contain thousands of solder joints. Current technology uses X-rays and lasers for inspection (*Quality Congress Transactions*, 1986). A particular manufacturer of laser-based inspection equipment claims that its product can inspect on average at least 10 solder joints per second when the joints are spaced .1 inch apart. The equipment was tested by a potential buyer on 48 different PCBs. In each case, the equipment was operated for exactly 1 second. The number of solder joints inspected on each run follows:

10	9	10	10	11	9	12	8	8	9	6	10
7	10	11	9	9	13	9	10	11	10	12	8
9	9	9	7	12	6	9	10	10	8	7	9
11	12	10	0	10	11	12	9	7	9	9	10

a. The potential buyer wants to know whether the sample data refute the manufacturer's claim. Specify the null and alternative hypotheses that the buyer should test.

b. In the context of this exercise, what is a Type I error? A Type II error?

c. Conduct the hypothesis test you described in part **a**, and interpret the test's results in the context of this exercise. Use $\alpha = .05$ and the SPSS descriptive statistics printout below.

6.21 A company has devised a new ink-jet cartridge for its plain-paper fax machine that it believes has a longer lifetime (on average) than the one currently being produced. To investigate its length of life, 225 of the new cartridges were tested by counting the number of high-quality printed pages each was able to produce. The sample mean and standard deviation were determined to be 1,511.4 pages and 35.7 pages, respectively. The historical average lifetime for cartridges produced by the current process is 1,502.5 pages; the historical standard deviation is 97.3 pages.

a. What are the appropriate null and alternative hypotheses to test whether the mean lifetime of the new cartridges exceeds that of the old cartridges?

b. Use $\alpha = .005$ to conduct the test in part **a**. Do the new cartridges have an average lifetime that is statistically significantly longer than the cartridges currently in production?

c. Does the difference in average lifetimes appear to be of practical significance from the perspective of the consumer? Explain.

d. Should the apparent decrease in the standard deviation in lifetimes associated with the new cartridges be viewed as an improvement over the old cartridges? Explain.

6.22 Nutritionists stress that weight control generally requires significant reductions in the intake of fat. A random sample of 64 middle-aged men on weight control programs is selected to determine whether their mean intake of fat exceeds the recommended 30 grams per day. The sample mean and standard deviation are $\bar{x} = 37$ and $s = 32$, respectively.

a. Considering the sample mean and standard deviation, would you expect the distribution for fat intake per day to be symmetric or skewed? Explain.

b. Do the sample results indicate that the mean intake for middle-aged men on weight control programs exceeds 30 grams? Test using $\alpha = .10$.

c. Would you reach the same conclusion as in part **b** using $\alpha = .05$? Using $\alpha = .01$? Why can the conclusion of a test change when the value of α is changed?

6.23 The pain reliever currently used in a hospital is known to bring relief to patients in a mean time of

Variable	Mean	Std Dev	Minimum	Maximum	N	Label
NUMBER	9.29	2.10	.00	13.00	48	

3.5 minutes. To compare a new pain reliever with the current one, the new drug is administered to a random sample of 50 patients. The mean time to relief for the sample of patients is 2.8 minutes and the standard deviation is 1.14 minutes. Do the data provide sufficient evidence to conclude that the new drug was effective in reducing the mean time until a patient receives relief from pain? Test using $\alpha = .10$.

6.3   OBSERVED SIGNIFICANCE LEVELS: P-VALUES

According to the statistical test procedure described in Section 6.2, the rejection region and, correspondingly, the value of α are selected prior to conducting the test, and the conclusions are stated in terms of rejecting or not rejecting the null hypothesis. A second method of presenting the results of a statistical test is one that reports the extent to which the test statistic disagrees with the null hypothesis and leaves to the reader the task of deciding whether to reject the null hypothesis. This measure of disagreement is called the *observed significance level* (or *p-value*) for the test.

> **DEFINITION 6.1**
> The **observed significance level**, or **p-value**, for a specific statistical test is the probability (assuming H_0 is true) of observing a value of the test statistic that is at least as contradictory to the null hypothesis, and supportive of the alternative hypothesis, as the actual one computed from the sample data.

For example, the value of the test statistic computed for the sample of $n = 50$ sections of sewer pipe was $z = 2.12$. Since the test is one-tailed—i.e., the alternative (research) hypothesis of interest is $H_a: \mu > 2,400$—values of the test statistic even more contradictory to H_0 than the one observed would be values larger than $z = 2.12$. Therefore, the observed significance level (*p-value*) for this test is

$$p\text{-value} = P(z \geq 2.12)$$

or, equivalently, the area under the standard normal curve to the right of $z = 2.12$ (see Figure 6.7).

The area A in Figure 6.7 is given in Table IV in Appendix B as .4830. Therefore, the upper-tail area corresponding to $z = 2.12$ is

$$p\text{-value} = .5 - .4830 = .0170$$

Consequently, we say that these test results are "very significant"; i.e., they disagree rather strongly with the null hypothesis, $H_0: \mu = 2,400$, and favor $H_a: \mu > 2,400$. The probability of observing a z value as large as 2.12 is only .0170, if in fact the true value of μ is 2,400.

If you are inclined to select $\alpha = .05$ for this test, then you would reject the null hypothesis because the *p-value* for the test, .0170, is less than .05. In contrast, if you choose $\alpha = .01$, you would not reject the null hypothesis because the *p-value*

FIGURE 6.7
Finding the *p-value* for an upper-tailed test when $z = 2.12$

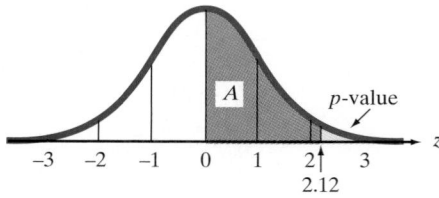

FIGURE 6.8
Finding the *p*-value for
a one-tailed test

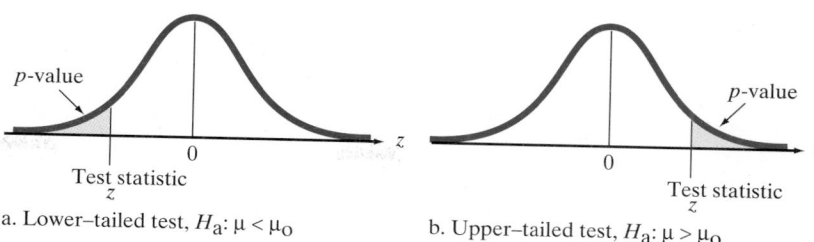

a. Lower–tailed test, H_a: $\mu < \mu_0$ b. Upper–tailed test, H_a: $\mu > \mu_0$

for the test is larger than .01. Thus, the use of the observed significance level is identical to the test procedure described in the preceding sections except that the choice of α is left to you.

The steps for calculating the *p*-value corresponding to a test statistic for a population mean are given in the next box.

Steps for Calculating the *p*-value for a Test of Hypothesis

1. Determine the value of the test statistic z corresponding to the result of the sampling experiment.

2. **a.** If the test is one-tailed, the *p*-value is equal to the tail area beyond z in the same direction as the alternative hypothesis. Thus, if the alternative hypothesis is of the form >, the *p*-value is the area to the right of, or above, the observed z value. Conversely, if the alternative is of the form <, the *p*-value is the area to the left of, or below, the observed z value. (See Figure 6.8.)

   b. If the test is two-tailed, the *p*-value is equal to twice the tail area beyond the observed z value in the direction of the sign of z. That is, if z is positive, the *p*-value is twice the area to the right of, or above, the observed z value. Conversely, if z is negative, the *p*-value is twice the area to the left of, or below, the observed z value. (See Figure 6.9.)

EXAMPLE 6.3   Find the observed significance level for the test of the mean filling weight in Examples 6.1 and 6.2.

SOLUTION

Example 6.1 presented a two-tailed test of the hypothesis

$$H_0: \mu = 12 \text{ ounces}$$

against the alternative hypothesis

$$H_a: \mu \neq 12 \text{ ounces}$$

The observed value of the test statistic in Example 6.2 was $z = -3.0$, and any value of z less than -3.0 or greater than $+3.0$ (because this is a two-tailed test) would be even more contradictory to H_0. Therefore, the observed significance level for the test is

$$p\text{-value} = P(z < -3.0 \text{ or } z > +3.0) = P(|z| > 3.0)$$

FIGURE 6.9
Finding the *p*-value for
a two-tailed test:
p-value = 2(*p*/2)

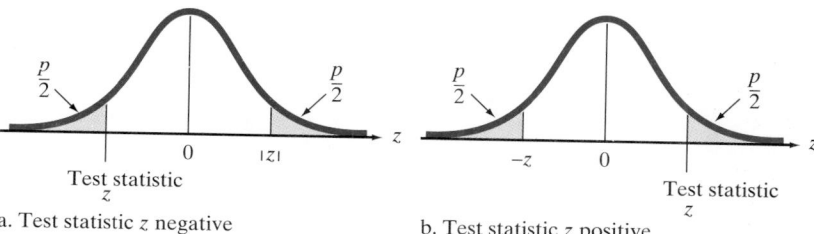

a. Test statistic z negative   b. Test statistic z positive

Thus, we calculate the area below the observed z value, $z = -3.0$, and double it. Consulting Table IV in Appendix B, we find that $P(z < -3.0) = .5 - .4987 = .0013$. Therefore, the p-value for this two-tailed test is

$$2P(z < -3.0) = 2(.0013) = .0026$$

We can interpret this p-value as a strong indication that the machine is not filling the boxes according to specifications, since we would observe a test statistic this extreme or more extreme only 26 in 10,000 times if the machine were meeting specifications ($\mu = 12$). The extent to which the mean differs from 12 could be better determined by calculating a confidence interval for μ.

When publishing the results of a statistical test of hypothesis in journals, case studies, reports, etc., many researchers make use of p-values. Instead of selecting α beforehand and then conducting a test, as outlined in this chapter, the researcher computes (usually with the aid of a statistical software package) and reports the value of the appropriate test statistic and its associated p-value. It is left to the reader of the report to judge the significance of the result—i.e., the reader must determine whether to reject the null hypothesis in favor of the alternative hypothesis, based on the reported p-value. Usually, the null hypothesis is rejected if the observed significance level is *less than* the fixed significance level, α, chosen by the reader. The inherent advantage of reporting test results in this manner are twofold: (1) Readers are permitted to select the maximum value of α that they would be willing to tolerate if they actually carried out a standard test of hypothesis in the manner outlined in this chapter, and (2) a measure of the degree of significance of the result (i.e., the p-value) is provided.

Reporting Test Results as p-values: How to Decide Whether to Reject H_0

1. Choose the maximum value of α that you are willing to tolerate.

2. If the observed significance level (p-value) of the test is less than the chosen value of α, reject the null hypothesis. Otherwise, do not reject the null hypothesis.

EXAMPLE 6.4

Knowledge of the amount of time a patient occupies a hospital bed—called length of stay (LOS)—is important for allocating resources. At one hospital, the mean length of stay was determined to be 5 days. A hospital administrator believes that the mean LOS may now be less than 5 days due to a newly adopted managed care system. To check this, the LOSs (in days) for 100 randomly selected hospital patients were recorded; these are listed in Table 6.3. Test the hypothesis that the true mean LOS at the hospital is less than 5 days, i.e.,

TABLE 6.3 Lengths of Stay for 100 Hospital Patients

2	3	8	6	4	4	6	4	2	5
8	10	4	4	4	2	1	3	2	10
1	3	2	3	4	3	5	2	4	1
2	9	1	7	17	9	9	9	4	4
1	1	1	3	1	6	3	3	2	5
1	3	3	14	2	3	9	6	6	3
5	1	4	6	11	22	1	9	6	5
2	2	5	4	3	6	1	5	1	6
17	1	2	4	5	4	4	3	2	3
3	5	2	3	3	2	10	2	4	2

FIGURE 6.10

MINITAB printout for the lower-tailed test in Example 6.4

```
TEST OF MU = 5.000 VS MU L.T. 5.000
THE ASSUMED SIGMA = 3.68
```

	N	MEAN	STDEV	SE MEAN	Z	P VALUE
LOS	100	4.530	3.678	0.368	-1.28	0.10

$$H_0\text{: } \mu = 5$$
$$H_a\text{: } \mu < 5$$

Use the data in the table to conduct the test at $\alpha = .05$.

SOLUTION

Instead of performing the computations by hand, we will use a statistical software package. The data were entered into a computer and MINITAB was used to conduct the analysis. The MINITAB printout for the lower-tailed test is displayed in Figure 6.10. Both the test statistic, $z = -1.28$, and p-value of the test, $p = .10$, are highlighted on the MINITAB printout. Since the p-value exceeds our selected α value, $\alpha = .05$, we cannot reject the null hypothesis. Hence, there is insufficient evidence (at $\alpha = .05$) to conclude that the true mean LOS at the hospital is less than 5 days. ∎

Note: MINITAB provides an option for selecting one-tailed or two-tailed tests and reports the appropriate p-value. Some statistical software packages such as SAS and SPSS will conduct only two-tailed tests of hypothesis. For these packages, you obtain the p-value for a one-tailed test as follows:

$$p = \frac{\text{Reported } p\text{-value}}{2} \quad \text{if } \begin{cases} H_a \text{ is of form} > \text{ and } z \text{ is positive} \\ H_a \text{ is of form} < \text{ and } z \text{ is negative} \end{cases}$$

$$p = 1 - \left(\frac{\text{Reported } p\text{-value}}{2}\right) \quad \text{if } \begin{cases} H_a \text{ is of form} > \text{ and } z \text{ is negative} \\ H_a \text{ is of form} < \text{ and } z \text{ is positive} \end{cases}$$

EXERCISES   6.24–6.38

Note: Exercises marked with 💾 *contain data for computer analysis on a 3.5" disk (file name in parentheses).*

Learning the Mechanics

6.24   If a hypothesis test were conducted using $\alpha = .05$, for which of the following p-values would the null hypothesis be rejected?
   a. .06   **b.** .10   **c.** .01   **d.** .001   **e.** .251   **f.** .042

6.25   For each α and observed significance level (p-value) pair, indicate whether the null hypothesis would be rejected.
   a. $\alpha = .05, p\text{-value} = .10$
   b. $\alpha = .10, p\text{-value} = .05$
   c. $\alpha = .01, p\text{-value} = .001$
   d. $\alpha = .025, p\text{-value} = .05$
   e. $\alpha = .10, p\text{-value} = .45$

6.26   An analyst tested the null hypothesis $\mu \geq 20$ against the alternative hypothesis that $\mu < 20$. The

analyst reported a p-value of .06. What is the smallest value of α for which the null hypothesis would be rejected?

6.27   In a test of H_0: $\mu = 100$ against H_a: $\mu > 100$, the sample data yielded the test statistic $z = 2.17$. Find the p-value for the test.

6.28   In a test of H_0: $\mu = 100$ against H_a: $\mu \neq 100$, the sample data yielded the test statistic $z = 2.17$. Find the p-value for the test.

6.29   In a test of the hypothesis H_0: $\mu = 50$ versus H_a: $\mu > 50$, a sample of $n = 100$ observations possessed mean $\bar{x} = 49.4$ and standard deviation $s = 4.1$. Find and interpret the p-value for this test.

6.30   In a test of the hypothesis H_0: $\mu = 10$ versus H_a: $\mu \neq 10$, a sample of $n = 50$ observations possessed mean $\bar{x} = 10.7$ and standard deviation $s = 3.1$. Find and interpret the p-value for this test.

6.31 Consider a test of H_0: $\mu = 75$ performed using the computer. SAS reports a two-tailed p-value of .1032. Make the appropriate conclusion for each of the following situations:

a. H_a: $\mu < 75$, $z = -1.63$, $\alpha = .05$
b. H_a: $\mu < 75$, $z = 1.63$, $\alpha = .10$
c. H_a: $\mu > 75$, $z = 1.63$, $\alpha = .10$
d. H_a: $\mu \neq 75$, $z = -1.63$, $\alpha = .01$

Applying the Concepts

6.32 Refer to the *Psychological Assessment* study of World War II aviator POWs, Exercise 6.15. You tested whether the true mean post-traumatic stress disorder score of World War II aviator POWs is less than 16. Recall that $\bar{x} = 9.00$ and $s = 9.32$ for a sample of $n = 33$ POWs. Compute the p-value of the test and interpret the result.

6.33 (X06.033) The one-year rate of return to shareholders in 1995 was calculated for each in a sample of 63 electric utility stocks. The data, extracted from *The Wall Street Journal* (Feb. 29, 1996), are shown in the table below.

Summary statistics for the data are computed using EXCEL. The resulting printout is given below.

Return	
Mean	31.92857143
Standard Error	1.696482051
Median	32
Mode	31.8
Standard Deviation	13.46540883
Sample Variance	181.317235
Kurtosis	5.231651006
Skewness	-1.083676944
Range	90.4
Minimum	-27.1
Maximum	63.3
Sum	2011.5
Count	63
Confidence Level(95.000%)	3.325038797

Electric Utilities	Rate of Return (%)
Pinnacle West Capital	52.4
DPL Inc	27.7
Nipsco Industries Inc	34.8
Cipsco Inc	53.8
Southern Co	30.3
DQE Inc	63.3
Scana Corp	44.4
Western Resources Inc	24.2
Portland General Corp	59.0
Peco Energy Co	30.5
Allegheny Power System	40.6
New England Electric System	31.8
Public Service Co of Colo	28.4
FPL Group Inc	38.1
CiNergy Corp	39.2
Illinova Corp	42.8
LG&E Energy Corp	21.0
Baltimore Gas & Electric	36.8
American Electric Power	31.9
Kansas City Power & Light	19.8
Boston Edison Co	32.0
General Public Utilities	38.0
Carolina Power & Light	37.5
Duke Power Co	30.4
Ohio Edison Co	35.9
KU Energy Corp	17.9
Northern States Power	18.4
Ipalco Enterprises Inc	35.3
Union Electric Co	25.9
UtiliCorp United Inc	17.8
Teco Energy Inc	32.7
Houston Industries Inc	46.1
Florida Progress Corp	25.5
Consolidated Edison of NY	32.3

Electric Utilities	Rate of Return (%)
Wisconsin Energy Corp	24.6
Potomac Electric Power	54.4
Dominion Resources Inc	22.6
Delmarva Power & Light	35.4
Northeast Utilities	20.8
Energy Corp	43.8
Central & South West Corp	31.8
Detroit Edison Co	41.2
Hawaiian Electric Inds	27.8
Public Service Entrp	24.5
Puget Sound Power & Light	25.7
Texas Utilities Co	38.8
Southwestern Public Svc Co	32.9
Idaho Power Co	37.4
PP&L Resources Inc	42.0
Oklahoma Gas & Electric	39.7
Pacific Gas & Electric	24.8
Montana Power Co	5.5
San Diego Gas & Electric	32.4
New York State Elec & Gas	44.8
Unicom Corp	44.5
MidAmerican Energy Co	31.8
PacifiCorp	23.4
SCEcorp	26.1
CMS Energy Corp	35.4
Long Island Lighting	19.0
Niagara Mohawk Power	-27.1
Centerior Energy Corp	8.6
AES Corp	22.4

```
TEST OF MU = 10.00 VS MU G.T. 10.00
THE ASSUMED SIGMA = 5.10

        N    MEAN   STDEV   SE MEAN     Z   P VALUE
GHQ    49   10.94    5.10     0.73   1.29    .0985
```

a. Specify the null and alternative hypotheses tested for determining whether the true mean one-year rate of return for electric utility stocks exceeded 30%.

b. Calculate the observed significance level of the test.

c. Interpret the result, part **b**, in the words of the problem.

6.34 Refer to Exercise 6.16, in which a random sample of 49 unemployed men were administered the General Health Questionnaire (GHQ). The sample mean and standard deviation were 10.94 and 5.10, respectively. Denoting the population mean GHQ for unemployed workers by μ, we wish to test the null hypothesis $H_0: \mu = 10$ versus the one-tailed alternative $H_a: \mu > 10$.

a. When the data are run through MINITAB, the results (in part) are as shown above. Check the program's results for accuracy.

b. What conclusion would you reach about the test based on the computer analysis?

6.35 In Exercise 5.12 we examined research about bicycle helmets reported in *Public Health Reports* (May–June 1992). One of the variables measured was the children's perception of the risk involved in bicycling. A random sample of 797 children in grades 4–6 were asked to rate their perception of bicycle risk without wearing a helmet, ranging from 1 (no risk) to 4 (very high risk). The mean and standard deviation of the sample were $\bar{x} = 3.39, s = .80$, respectively.

a. Assume that a mean score, μ, of 2.5 is indicative of indifference to risk, and values of μ exceeding 2.5 indicate a perception that a risk exists. What are the appropriate null and alternative hypotheses for testing the research hypothesis that children in this age group perceive a risk associated with failure to wear helmets?

b. Calculate the *p*-value for the data collected in this study.

c. Interpret the *p*-value in the context of this research.

6.36 In Exercise 6.17 you tested $H_0: \mu = .250$ versus $H_a: \mu \neq .250$, where μ is the population mean weight of plastic golf tees. A SAS printout for the hypothesis test is shown below. Locate the *p*-value on the printout and interpret its value.

6.37 An article published in the *Journal of the American Medical Association* (Oct. 16, 1995) calls smoking in China "a public health emergency." The researchers found that smokers in China smoke an average of 16.5 cigarettes a day. The high smoking rate is one reason why the tobacco industry is the central government's largest source of tax revenue. Has the average number of cigarettes smoked per day by Chinese smokers increased over the past two years? Consider that in a random sample of 200 Chinese smokers in 1997, the number of cigarettes smoked per day had a mean of 17.05 and a standard deviation of 5.21.

a. Set up the null and alternative hypotheses for testing whether Chinese smokers smoke, on average, more cigarettes a day in 1997 than in 1995. (Assume that the population mean for 1995 is $\mu = 16.5$.)

b. Compute and interpret the observed significance level of the test.

c. Why is a two-tailed test inappropriate for this problem?

6.38 In Exercise 6.20 you tested $H_0: \mu \geq 10$ versus $H_a: \mu < 10$, where μ is the average number of solder joints inspected per second when the joints are spaced .1 inch apart. An SPSS printout of the hypothesis test is shown on page 298.

a. Locate the two-tailed *p*-value of the test shown on the printout.

b. Adjust the *p*-value for the one-tailed test (if necessary) and interpret its value.

```
Analysis Variable : WT_250 (Test Mean Weight=.250)

N Obs        Mean          Std Dev           T    Prob>|T|
------------------------------------------------------------
  40       0.0024750      0.0022302      7.0188284    0.0001
------------------------------------------------------------
```

Variable	Number of Cases	Mean	Standard Deviation	Standard Error
NUMBER	48	9.2917	2.103	.304
MU	48	10.0000	.	.

(Difference) Mean	Standard Deviation	Standard Error	t Value	Degrees of Freedom	2-Tail Prob.
-.7083	2.103	.304	-2.33	47	.024

6.4 SMALL-SAMPLE TEST OF HYPOTHESIS ABOUT A POPULATION MEAN

A manufacturing operation consists of a single-machine-tool system that produces an average of 15.5 transformer parts every hour. After undergoing a complete overhaul, the system was monitored by observing the number of parts produced in each of seventeen randomly selected one-hour periods. The mean and standard deviation for the 17 production runs are:

$$\bar{x} = 15.42 \qquad s = .16$$

Does this sample provide sufficient evidence to conclude that the true mean number of parts produced every hour by the overhauled system differs from 15.5?

This inference can be placed in a test of hypothesis framework. We establish the preoverhaul mean as the null hypothesized value and utilize a two-tailed alternative that the true mean of the overhauled system differs from the preoverhaul mean:

$$H_0: \mu = 15.5$$

$$H_a: \mu \neq 15.5$$

Recall from Section 5.3 that when we are faced with making inferences about a population mean using the information in a small sample, two problems emerge:

1. The normality of the sampling distribution for $\bar{x}$ does not follow from the Central Limit Theorem when the sample size is small. We must assume that the distribution of measurements from which the sample was selected is approximately normally distributed in order to ensure the approximate normality of the sampling distribution of $\bar{x}$.

2. If the population standard deviation σ is unknown, as is usually the case, then we cannot assume that s will provide a good approximation for σ when the sample size is small. Instead, we must use the t-distribution rather than the standard normal z-distribution to make inferences about the population mean μ.

Therefore, as the test statistic of a small-sample test of a population mean, we use the t statistic:

$$\textit{Test statistic: } t = \frac{\bar{x} - \mu_0}{s/\sqrt{n}} = \frac{\bar{x} - 15.5}{s/\sqrt{n}}$$

where μ_0 is the null hypothesized value of the population mean, μ. In our example, $\mu_0 = 15.5$.

To find the rejection region, we must specify the value of α, the probability that the test will lead to rejection of the null hypothesis when it is true, and then con-

FIGURE 6.11

Two-tailed rejection region for small-sample *t*-test

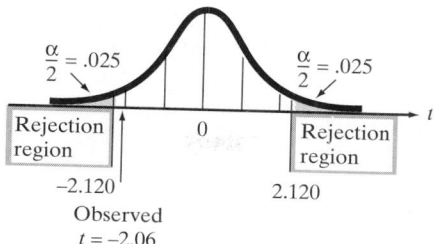

sult the *t*-table (Table VI of Appendix B). Using $\alpha = .05$, the two-tailed rejection region is

$$\text{Rejection region: } t_{\alpha/2} = t_{.025} = 2.120 \text{ with } n - 1 = 16 \text{ degrees of freedom}$$

$$\text{Reject } H_0 \text{ if } t < -2.120 \text{ or } t > 2.120$$

The rejection region is shown in Figure 6.11.

We are now prepared to calculate the test statistic and reach a conclusion:

$$t = \frac{\bar{x} - \mu_0}{s/\sqrt{n}} = \frac{15.42 - 15.50}{.16/\sqrt{17}} = \frac{-.08}{.0388} = -2.06$$

Since the calculated value of *t* does not fall in the rejection region (Figure 6.11), we cannot reject H_0 at the $\alpha = .05$ level of significance. Based on the sample evidence, we should not conclude that the mean number of parts produced per hour by the overhauled system differs from 15.5.

It is interesting to note that the calculated *t* value, -2.06, is *less than* the .05 level *z* value, -1.96. The implication is that if we had *incorrectly* used a *z* statistic for this test, we would have rejected the null hypothesis at the .05 level, concluding that the mean production per hour of the overhauled system differs from 15.5 parts. The important point is that the statistical procedure to be used must always be closely scrutinized and all the assumptions understood. Many statistical distortions are the result of misapplications of otherwise valid procedures.

The technique for conducting a small-sample test of hypothesis about a population mean is summarized in the following box.

Small-Sample Test of Hypothesis About μ

One-Tailed Test

$H_0: \mu = \mu_0$

$H_a: \mu < \mu_0$
  (or $H_a: \mu > \mu_0$)

Test statistic: $t = \dfrac{\bar{x} - \mu_0}{s/\sqrt{n}}$

Rejection region: $t < -t_\alpha$
  (or $t > t_\alpha$ when $H_a: \mu > \mu_0$)

Two-Tailed Test

$H_0: \mu = \mu_0$

$H_a: \mu \neq \mu_0$

Test statistic: $t = \dfrac{\bar{x} - \mu_0}{s/\sqrt{n}}$

Rejection region: $t < -t_{\alpha/2}$
  or $t > t_{\alpha/2}$

where t_α and $t_{\alpha/2}$ are based on $(n - 1)$ degrees of freedom

Assumption: A random sample is selected from a population with a relative frequency distribution that is approximately normal.

EXAMPLE 6.5

A major car manufacturer wants to test a new engine to determine whether it meets new air pollution standards. The mean emission μ of all engines of this type must be less than 20 parts per million of carbon. Ten engines are manufactured for testing purposes, and the emission level of each is determined. The data (in parts per million) are listed below:

15.6   16.2   22.5   20.5   16.4   19.4   16.6   17.9   12.7   13.9

Do the data supply sufficient evidence to allow the manufacturer to conclude that this type of engine meets the pollution standard? Assume that the production process is stable and the manufacturer is willing to risk a Type I error with probability $\alpha = .01$.

SOLUTION

The manufacturer wants to support the research hypothesis that the mean emission level μ for all engines of this type is less than 20 parts per million. The elements of this small-sample one-tailed test are

$$H_0: \mu = 20$$

$$H_a: \mu < 20$$

$$\text{Test statistic: } t = \frac{\bar{x} - 20}{s/\sqrt{n}}$$

Assumption: The relative frequency distribution of the population of emission levels for all engines of this type is approximately normal.

Rejection region: For $\alpha = .01$ and $df = n - 1 = 9$, the one-tailed rejection region (see Figure 6.12) is $t < -t_{.01} = -2.821$.

To calculate the test statistic, we entered the data into a computer and analyzed it using SAS. The SAS descriptive statistics printout is shown in Figure 6.13. From the printout, we obtain $\bar{x} = 17.17, s = 2.98$. Substituting these values into the test statistic formula, we get

$$t = \frac{\bar{x} - 20}{s/\sqrt{n}} = \frac{17.17 - 20}{2.98/\sqrt{10}} = -3.00$$

Since the calculated t falls in the rejection region (see Figure 6.12), the manufacturer concludes that $\mu < 20$ parts per million and the new engine type meets the pollution standard. Are you satisfied with the reliability associated with this infer-

FIGURE 6.12
A t-distribution with 9 df and the rejection region for Example 6.5

$\alpha = .01$

Rejection region

-2.821

-3.00

0

t

FIGURE 6.13
SAS descriptive statistics for 10 emission levels

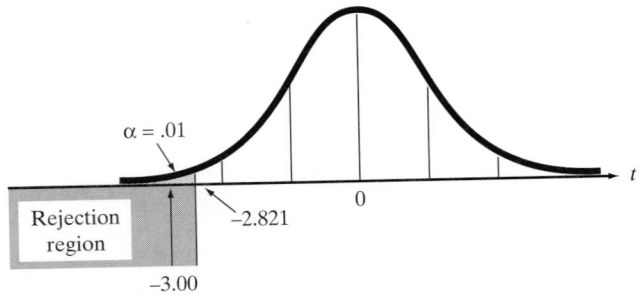

Analysis Variable : EMIT				
N Obs	N	Minimum	Maximum	Mean	Std Dev
10	10	12.7000000	22.5000000	17.1700000	2.9814426

FIGURE 6.14

The observed
significance level for
the test of Example 6.5

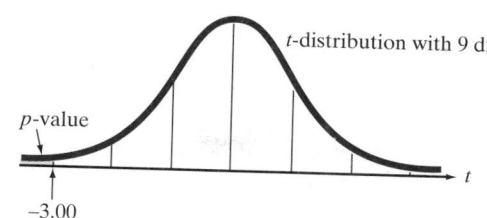

ence? The probability is only $\alpha = .01$ that the test would support the research hypothesis if in fact it were false.

EXAMPLE 6.6   Find the observed significance level for the test described in Example 6.5. Interpret the result.

SOLUTION

The test of Example 6.5 was a lower-tailed test: $H_0: \mu = 20$ versus $H_a: \mu < 20$. Since the value of t computed from the sample data was $t = -3.00$, the observed significance level (or p-value) for the test is equal to the probability that t would assume a value less than or equal to -3.00 if in fact H_0 were true. This is equal to the area in the lower tail of the t-distribution (shaded in Figure 6.14).

One way to find this area—i.e., the p-value for the test—is to consult the t-table (Table VI in Appendix B). Unlike the table of areas under the normal curve, Table VI gives only the t values corresponding to the areas .100, .050, .025, .010, .005, .001, and .0005. Therefore, we can only approximate the p-value for the test. Since the observed t value was based on 9 degrees of freedom, we use the df = 9 row in Table VI and move across the row until we reach the t values that are closest to the observed $t = -3.00$. [*Note:* We ignore the minus sign.] The t values corresponding to p-values of .010 and .005 are 2.821 and 3.250, respectively. Since the observed t value falls between $t_{.010}$ and $t_{.005}$, the p-value for the test lies between .005 and .010. In other words, $.005 < p\text{-value} < .01$. Thus, we would reject the null hypothesis, $H_0: \mu = 20$ parts per million, for any value of α larger than .01 (the upper bound of the p-value).

A second, more accurate, way to obtain the p-value is to use a statistical software package to conduct the test of hypothesis. The SAS printout for the test of $H_0: \mu = 20$ is displayed in Figure 6.15. Both the test statistic (-3.00) and p-value (.0149) are highlighted in Figure 6.15. Recall (from Section 6.3) that SAS conducts, by default, a two-tailed test. That is, SAS tests the alternative $H_a: \mu \neq 20$. Thus, the p-value reported on the printout must be adjusted to obtain the appropriate p-value for our lower-tailed test. Since the value of the test statistic is negative and H_a is of the form $<$ (i.e., the value of t agrees with the direction specified in H_a), the p-value is obtained by dividing the printout value in half:

$$\text{One-tailed } p\text{-value } = \frac{\text{Reported } p\text{-value}}{2} = \frac{.0149}{2} = .00745$$

You can see that the actual p-value of the test falls within the bounds obtained from Table VI. Thus, the two methods agree; we will reject $H_0: \mu = 20$ in favor of $H_a: \mu < 20$ for any α level larger than .01.

FIGURE 6.15
SAS test of $H_0: \mu = 20$
for Example 6.6

Analysis Variable : EMIT_20				
N Obs	Mean	Std Dev	T	Prob>|T|
10	-2.8300000	2.9814426	-3.0016495	0.0149

Small-sample inferences typically require more assumptions and provide less information about the population parameter than do large-sample inferences. Nevertheless, the t-test is a method of testing a hypothesis about a population mean of a normal distribution when only a small number of observations are available. What can be done if you know that the population relative frequency distribution is decidedly nonnormal, say highly skewed? We answer this question in optional Section 6.6.

EXERCISES   6.39–6.52

Learning the Mechanics

6.39 Under what circumstances should you use the t-distribution in testing a hypothesis about a population mean?

6.40 In what ways are the distributions of the z statistic and t-test statistic alike? How do they differ?

6.41 For each of the following rejection regions, sketch the sampling distribution of t, and indicate the location of the rejection region on your sketch:
a. $t > 1.440$ where df = 6
b. $t < -1.782$ where df = 12
c. $t < -2.060$ or $t > 2.060$ where df = 25

6.42 For each of the rejection regions defined in Exercise 6.41, what is the probability that a Type I error will be made?

6.43 A random sample of n observations is selected from a normal population to test the null hypothesis that $\mu = 10$. Specify the rejection region for each of the following combinations of H_a, α, and n:
a. $H_a: \mu \neq 10; \alpha = .05; n = 14$
b. $H_a: \mu > 10; \alpha = .01; n = 24$
c. $H_a: \mu > 10; \alpha = .10; n = 9$
d. $H_a: \mu < 10; \alpha = .01; n = 12$
e. $H_a: \mu \neq 10; \alpha = .10; n = 20$
f. $H_a: \mu < 10; \alpha = .05; n = 4$

6.44 A sample of five measurements, randomly selected from a normally distributed population, resulted in the following summary statistics: $\bar{x} = 4.8, s = 1.3$.
a. Test the null hypothesis that the mean of the population is 6 against the alternative hypothesis, $\mu < 6$. Use $\alpha = .05$.

b. Test the null hypothesis that the mean of the population is 6 against the alternative hypothesis, $\mu \neq 6$. Use $\alpha = .05$.
c. Find the observed significance level for each test.

6.45 MINITAB is used to conduct a t-test for the null hypothesis $H_0: \mu = 1,000$ versus the alternative hypothesis $H_a: \mu > 1,000$ based on a sample of 17 observations. The software's output is shown below.
a. What assumptions are necessary for the validity of this procedure?
b. Interpret the results of the test.
c. Suppose the alternative hypothesis had been the two-tailed $H_a: \mu \neq 1,000$. If the t statistic were unchanged, then what would the p-value be for this test? Interpret the p-value for the two-tailed test.

Applying the Concepts

6.46 The Cleveland Casting Plant is a large, highly automated producer of gray and nodular iron automotive castings for Ford Motor Company. Since Cleveland Casting ships 400,000 tons of iron-cast automobile parts per year, periodic monitoring of the settings for the casting process is required to achieve acceptable performance levels. Researchers B. Price and B. Barth studied process data collected at Cleveland Casting (*Quality Engineering*, Vol. 7, 1995). One process variable of interest to the researchers was the pouring temperature of the molten iron. The pouring temperatures (in degrees Fahrenheit) for a sample of 10 crankshafts are listed in the table on page 303. The

TEST OF MU = 1,000 VS MU G.T. 1,000

	N	MEAN	STDEV	SE MEAN	T	P VALUE
X	17	1020	43.54	10.56	1.894	.0382

target setting for the pouring temperature is set at 2,550 degrees. Assuming the process is stable, conduct a test to determine whether the true mean pouring temperature differs from the target setting. Test using $\alpha = .01$.

2,543	2,541	2,544	2,620	2,560	2,559	2,562
2,553	2,552	2,553				

Source: Price, B., and Barth, B. "A structural model relating process inputs and final product characteristics." *Quality Engineering,* Vol. 7, No. 4, 1995, p. 696 (Table 2).

6.47 Organochlorine pesticides (OCPs), like polychlorinated biphenyls (PCBs), are highly toxic organic compounds that are often found in fish. By law, the levels of OCPs and PCBs in fish are constantly monitored, so it is important to be able to accurately measure the amounts of these compounds in fish specimens. A new technique, called matrix solid-phase dispersion (MSPD), has been developed for chemically extracting trace organic compounds from solids (*Chromatographia,* Mar. 1995). The MSPD method was tested as follows. Uncontaminated fish fillets were injected with a known amount of OCP or PCB. The MSPD method was then used to extract the contaminant and the percentage of the toxic compound recovered was measured. The recovery percentages for $n = 5$ fish fillets injected with the OCP Aldrin are listed below:

$$99 \quad 102 \quad 94 \quad 99 \quad 95$$

Do the data provide sufficient evidence to indicate that the mean recovery percentage of Aldrin exceeds 85% using the new MSPD method? Test using $\alpha = .05$.

6.48 To instill customer loyalty, airlines, hotels, rental car companies, and credit card companies (among others) have initiated **frequency marketing programs** that reward their regular customers. In the United States alone, 30 million people are members of the frequent flier programs of the airline industry (*Fortune,* Feb. 22, 1993). A large fast-food restaurant chain wished to explore the profitability of such a program. They randomly selected 12 of their 1,200 restaurants nationwide and instituted a frequency program that rewarded customers with a $5.00 gift certificate after every 10 meals purchased at full price. They ran the trial program for three months. The restaurants not in the sample had an average increase in profits of $1,047.34 over the previous three months, whereas the restaurants in the sample had the following changes in profit:

$2,232.90	$545.47	$3,440.70	$1,809.10
$6,552.70	$4,798.70	$2,965.00	$2,610.70
$3,381.30	$1,591.40	$2,376.20	−$2,191.00

Note that the last number is negative, representing a decrease in profits. Summary statistics and

graphs for the data are given in the SPSS printout at the top of page 304.

a. Specify the appropriate null and alternative hypotheses for determining whether the mean profit change for restaurants with frequency programs is significantly greater (in a statistical sense) than $1,047.34.

b. Conduct the test of part **b** using $\alpha = .05$. Does it appear that the frequency program would be profitable for the company if adopted nationwide?

6.49 The changing ecology of the Everglades National Park in Florida, considered a national treasure by many, has been the subject of much environmental research. One water-quality parameter of concern in the park is the total phosphorus level. Suppose that the EPA makes 12 measurements in one section of the park, yielding a mean level of total phosphorus at 12.3 parts per billion (ppb) and a standard deviation of 5.4 ppb. The EPA wants to test whether the data support the conclusion that the mean level is less than 15 ppb.

a. What are the null and alternative hypotheses appropriate for the EPA's test?

b. The EPA statistician analyzed the data using SAS, with the results shown. Find and adjust (if necessary) the *p*-value of the test.

c. Interpret the results of the test.

```
Analysis Variable : PHOS_15

   N Obs          T    Prob>|T|
---------------------------------
     12      -1.732      0.1112
---------------------------------
```

6.50 The Occupational Safety and Health Act (OSHA) allows issuance of engineering standards to ensure safe workplaces for all Americans. The maximum allowable mean level of arsenic in smelters, herbicide production facilities, and other places where arsenic is used is .004 milligram per cubic meter of air. Suppose smelters at two plants are being investigated to determine whether they are meeting OSHA standards. Two analyses of the air are made at each plant, and the results (in milligrams per cubic meter of air) are shown in the table.

PLANT 1		PLANT 2	
Observation	Arsenic Level	Observation	Arsenic Level
1	.01	1	.05
2	.005	2	.09

a. What are the appropriate null and alternative hypotheses if we wish to test whether the plants meet the current OSHA standard?

```
        PROFIT
  Valid cases:          12.0   Missing cases:      .0   Percent missing:      .0

  Mean        2509.431  Std Err   620.4388  Min   -2191.00  Skewness    -.3616
  Median      2493.450  Variance  4619332   Max    6552.700  S E Skew     .6373
  5% Trim     2545.940  Std Dev   2149.263  Range  8743.700  Kurtosis    1.8750
                                            IQR    1780.025  S E Kurt    1.2322

  ------------------------------------------------------------------------------

  Frequency      Stem &  Leaf

     1.00  Extremes    (-2191)
     1.00      0 .  5
     2.00      1 .  58
     4.00      2 .  2369
     2.00      3 .  34
     1.00      4 .  7
     1.00  Extremes    (6553)

  Stem width:   1000.00
  Each leaf:       1 case(s)
  ------------------------------------------------------------------------------
```

```
   8000.00 ─

                     (O)  CASE5

   4000.00 ─  ┌───┐
              │ * │
              └───┘
      .00  ─

                     (O)  CASE12

  -4000.00 ─


  Variables        PROFIT

  N of Cases       12.00

        Symbol Key:       *   - Median    (O)  - Outlier    (E)  - Extreme
```

b. These data are analyzed by MINITAB, with the results shown below. Check the calculations of the *t* statistics and *p*-values.

c. Interpret the results of the two tests.

6.51 Periodic assessment of stress in paved highways is important to maintaining safe roads. The Mississippi Department of Transportation recently collected data on number of cracks (called *crack intensity*) in an undivided two-lane highway using van-mounted state-of-the-art video technology (*Journal of Infrastructure Systems*, Mar. 1995). The mean number of cracks found in a sample of eight 50-meter sections of the highway was $\bar{x} = .210$, with a variance of $s^2 = .011$. Suppose the American Association of State Highway and Transportation Officials (AASHTO) recommends a maximum mean crack intensity of .100 for safety purposes. Test the hypothesis that the true mean crack intensity of the Mississippi highway exceeds the AASHTO recommended maximum. Use $\alpha = .01$.

```
  TEST OF MU = 0.00400 VS MU G.T. 0.00400

               N     MEAN     STDEV    SE MEAN      T    P VALUE
  Plant1       2   0.00750   0.00354   0.00250    1.40     0.20
  Plant2       2   0.07000   0.02828   0.02000    3.30     0.094
```

6.52 One way of evaluating a measuring instrument is to repeatedly measure the same item and compare the average of these measurements to the item's known measured value. The difference is used to assess the instrument's accuracy (*Quality Progress,* Jan. 1993). To evaluate a particular Metlar scale, an item whose weight is known to be 16.01 ounces is weighed five times by the same operator. The measurements, in ounces, are as follows:

15.99   16.00   15.97   16.01   15.96

a. In a statistical sense, does the average measurement differ from 16.01? Conduct the appropriate hypothesis test. What does your analysis suggest about the accuracy of the instrument?

b. List any assumptions you make in conducting the hypothesis test.

6.5 LARGE-SAMPLE TEST OF HYPOTHESIS ABOUT A POPULATION PROPORTION

Inferences about population proportions (or percentages) are often made in the context of the probability, p, of "success" for a binomial distribution. We saw how to use large samples from binomial distributions to form confidence intervals for p in Section 5.3. We now consider tests of hypotheses about p.

For example, consider the problem of *insider trading* in the stock market. Insider trading is the buying and selling of stock by an individual privy to inside information in a company, usually a high-level executive in the firm. The Securities and Exchange Commission (SEC) imposes strict guidelines about insider trading so that all investors can have equal access to information that may affect the stock's price. An investor wishing to test the effectiveness of the SEC guidelines monitors the market for a period of a year and records the number of times a stock price increases the day following a significant purchase of stock by an insider. For a total of 576 such transactions, the stock increased the following day 327 times. Does this sample provide evidence that the stock price may be affected by insider trading?

We first view this as a binomial experiment, with the 576 transactions as the trials, and success representing an increase in the stock's price the following day. Let p represent the probability that the stock price will increase following a large insider purchase. If the insider purchase has no effect on the stock price (that is, if the information available to the insider is identical to that available to the general market), then the investor expects the probability of a stock increase to be the same as that of a decrease, or $p = .5$. On the other hand, if insider trading affects the stock price (indicating that the market has not fully accounted for the information known to the insiders), then the investor expects the stock either to decrease or to increase more than half the time following significant insider transactions; that is, $p \neq .5$.

We can now place the problem in the context of a test of hypothesis:

$$H_0: p = .5$$

$$H_a: p \neq .5$$

Recall that the sample proportion, $\hat{p}$ is really just the sample mean of the outcomes of the individual binomial trials and, as such, is approximately normally distributed (for large samples) according to the Central Limit Theorem. Thus, for large samples we can use the standard normal z as the test statistic:

$$\text{Test statistic: } z = \frac{\text{Sample proportion} - \text{Null hypothesized proportion}}{\text{Standard deviation of sample proportion}}$$

$$= \frac{\hat{p} - p_0}{\sigma_{\hat{p}}}$$

where we use the symbol p_0 to represent the null hypothesized value of p.

Figure 6.16
Rejection region for insider trading example

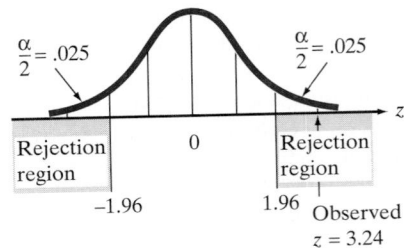

Rejection region: We use the standard normal distribution to find the appropriate rejection region for the specified value of α. Using $\alpha = .05$, the two-tailed rejection region is

$$z < -z_{\alpha/2} = -z_{.025} = -1.96 \quad \text{or} \quad z > z_{\alpha/2} = z_{.025} = 1.96$$

See Figure 6.16.

We are now prepared to calculate the value of the test statistic. Before doing so, we want to be sure that the sample size is large enough to ensure that the normal approximation for the sampling distribution of $\hat{p}$ is reasonable. To check this, we calculate a 3-standard-deviation interval around the null hypothesized value, p_0, which is assumed to be the true value of p until our test procedure indicates otherwise. Recall that $\sigma_{\hat{p}} = \sqrt{pq/n}$ and that we need an estimate of the product pq in order to calculate a numerical value of the test statistic z. Since the null hypothesized value is generally the accepted-until-proven-otherwise value, we use the value of $p_0 q_0$ (where $q_0 = 1 - p_0$) to estimate pq in the calculation of z. Thus,

$$\sigma_{\hat{p}} = \sqrt{\frac{pq}{n}} = \sqrt{\frac{p_0 q_0}{n}} = \sqrt{\frac{(.5)(.5)}{576}} = .021$$

and the 3-standard-deviation interval around p_0 is

$$p_0 \pm 3\sigma_{\hat{p}} \approx .5 \pm 3(.021) = (.437, .563)$$

As long as this interval does not contain 0 or 1 (i.e., is completely contained in the interval 0 to 1), as is the case here, the normal distribution will provide a reasonable approximation for the sampling distribution of $\hat{p}$.

Returning to the hypothesis test at hand, the proportion of the sampled transactions that resulted in a stock increase is

$$\hat{p} = \frac{327}{576} = .568$$

Finally, we calculate the number of standard deviations (the z value) between the sampled and hypothesized value of the binomial proportion:

$$z = \frac{\hat{p} - p_0}{\sigma_{\hat{p}}} = \frac{\hat{p} - p_0}{\sqrt{p_0 q_0/n}} = \frac{.568 - .5}{.021} = \frac{.068}{.021} = 3.24$$

The implication is that the observed sample proportion is (approximately) 3.24 standard deviations above the null hypothesized proportion .5 (Figure 6.16). Therefore, we reject the null hypothesis, concluding at the .05 level of significance that the true probability of an increase or decrease in a stock's price differs from .5 the day following insider purchase of the stock. It appears that an insider purchase significantly increases the probability that the stock price will increase the following day. (To estimate the magnitude of the probability of an increase, a confidence interval can be constructed.)

The test of hypothesis about a population proportion p is summarized in the next box. Note that the procedure is entirely analogous to that used for conducting large-sample tests about a population mean.

Large-Sample Test of Hypothesis About p

One-Tailed Test

$H_0: p = p_0$
  (p_0 = hypothesized value of p)

$H_a: p < p_0$
  (or $H_a: p > p_0$)

Test statistic: $z = \dfrac{\hat{p} - p_0}{\sigma_{\hat{p}}}$

Two-Tailed Test

$H_0: p = p_0$

$H_a: p \neq p_0$

Test statistic: $z = \dfrac{\hat{p} - p_0}{\sigma_{\hat{p}}}$

where, according to H_0, $\sigma_{\hat{p}} = \sqrt{p_0 q_0 / n}$ and $q_0 = 1 - p_0$

Rejection region: $z < -z_\alpha$
  (or $z > z_\alpha$ when $H_a: p > p_0$)

Rejection region: $z < -z_{\alpha/2}$
  or $z > z_{\alpha/2}$

Assumption: The experiment is binomial, and the sample size is large enough that the interval $p_0 \pm 3\sigma_{\hat{p}}$ does not include 0 or 1.

EXAMPLE 6.7

The reputations (and hence sales) of many businesses can be severely damaged by shipments of manufactured items that contain a large percentage of defectives. For example, a manufacturer of alkaline batteries may want to be reasonably certain that fewer than 5% of its batteries are defective. Suppose 300 batteries are randomly selected from a very large shipment; each is tested and 10 defective batteries are found. Does this provide sufficient evidence for the manufacturer to conclude that the fraction defective in the entire shipment is less than .05? Use $\alpha = .01$.

SOLUTION

Before conducting the test of hypothesis, we check to determine whether the sample size is large enough to use the normal approximation for the sampling distribution of $\hat{p}$. The criterion is tested by the interval

$$p_0 \pm 3\sigma_{\hat{p}} = p_0 \pm 3\sqrt{\frac{p_0 q_0}{n}} = .05 \pm 3\sqrt{\frac{(.05)(.95)}{300}}$$

$$= .05 \pm .04 \qquad \text{or} \qquad (.01, .09)$$

Since the interval lies within the interval $(0, 1)$, the normal approximation will be adequate.

The objective of the sampling is to determine whether there is sufficient evidence to indicate that the fraction defective, p, is less than .05. Consequently, we will test the null hypothesis that $p = .05$ against the alternative hypothesis that $p < .05$. The elements of the test are

$$H_0: p = .05$$

$$H_a: p < .05$$

Figure 6.17
Rejection region
for Example 6.7

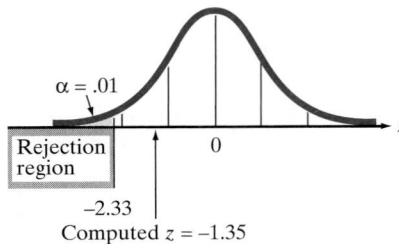

$\alpha = .01$

Rejection
region

0

z

-2.33

Computed $z = -1.35$

$$\text{Test statistic: } z = \frac{\hat{p} - p_0}{\sigma_{\hat{p}}}$$

Rejection region: $z < -z_{.01} = -2.33$ (see Figure 6.17)

We now calculate the test statistic:

$$z = \frac{\hat{p} - .05}{\sigma_{\hat{p}}} = \frac{(10/300) - .05}{\sqrt{p_0 q_0 / n}} = \frac{.033 - .05}{\sqrt{p_0 q_0 / 300}}$$

Notice that we use p_0 to calculate $\sigma_{\hat{p}}$ because, in contrast to calculating $\sigma_{\hat{p}}$ for a confidence interval, the test statistic is computed on the assumption that the null hypothesis is true—that is, $p = p_0$. Therefore, substituting the values for $\hat{p}$ and p_0 into the z statistic, we obtain

$$z \approx \frac{-.017}{\sqrt{(.05)(.95)/300}} = \frac{-.017}{.0126} = -1.35$$

As shown in Figure 6.17, the calculated z value does not fall in the rejection region. Therefore, there is insufficient evidence at the .01 level of significance to indicate that the shipment contains fewer than 5% defective batteries. ∎

EXAMPLE 6.8

In Example 6.7 we found that we did not have sufficient evidence, at the $\alpha = .01$ level of significance, to indicate that the fraction defective p of alkaline batteries was less than $p = .05$. How strong was the weight of evidence favoring the alternative hypothesis ($H_a: p < .05$)? Find the observed significance level for the test.

SOLUTION
The computed value of the test statistic z was $z = -1.35$. Therefore, for this lower-tailed test, the observed significance level is

$$\text{Observed significance level} = P(z \leq -1.35)$$

This lower-tail area is shown in Figure 6.18. The area between $z = 0$ and $z = 1.35$ is given in Table IV in Appendix B as .4115. Therefore, the observed significance level is $.5 - .4115 = .0885$. Note that this probability is quite small. Although we did not reject $H_0: p = .05$ at $\alpha = .01$, the probability of observing a z value as small as or smaller than -1.35 is only .0885 if in fact H_0 is true. Therefore, we would reject H_0 if we choose $\alpha = .10$ (since the observed significance level is less than .10), and we would not reject H_0 (the conclusion of Example 6.7) if we choose $\alpha = .05$ or $\alpha = .01$. ∎

Figure 6.18
The observed
significance level
for Example 6.8

p-value = .0885

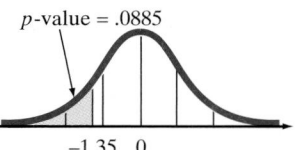

-1.35 0 z

STATISTICS IN ACTION

6.3 STATISTICAL QUALITY CONTROL, PART II

In complicated assembly operations (such as railway-car assembly), many quality variables could be measured (e.g., strength of welds, degree of corrosion, and number of paint flaws), and in principle, each could be monitored over time using control charts, as described in Statistics in Action 6.2. In some situations, however, an alternative, simpler procedure may be more appropriate. For example, n finished products could be randomly sampled at regular time intervals, inspected for defects, and simply classified as being defective or nondefective products. Then $\hat{p}$, the proportion of defectives in each sample, could be determined and plotted on a control chart called a *p*-**chart**, as illustrated in Figure 6.19. In this way, the proportion of defective products produced and, therefore, product quality and the current capability of the production process could be monitored over time (Montgomery, 1991).

In order to construct the control chart shown in Figure 6.19, it is necessary to know (i.e., have a good estimate for) p_0, the proportion of defectives produced when the process is operating properly (i.e., in control). Then, assuming n is large enough to use the normal distribution to approximate the sampling distribution of $\hat{p}$, the control limits are located $3\sigma_{\hat{p}}$ above

and below p_0. If a value of $\hat{p}$ falls above the upper limit or below the lower limit, there is strong evidence that the process is out of control.

Focus

Describe this control chart decision procedure in the language of hypothesis testing by answering the following questions:

a. What are the null and alternative hypotheses of interest?

b. What is the test statistic?

c. Specify the rejection region.

d. What is the probability of committing a Type I error?

e. If a value of $\hat{p}$ falls above the upper limit, it is a signal that the process is turning out more defectives than usual. But what is the significance of the lower control limit? Why should the manufacturer be concerned if fewer defectives than usual are being produced? [*Hint:* There are two important reasons. One is related to the problem of inspection error; the other has to do with acquiring new knowledge to improve the production process.]

Small-sample test procedures are also available for p. These are omitted from our discussion because most surveys use samples that are large enough to employ the large-sample tests presented in this section.

FIGURE 6.19
p-chart for proportion defective (Statistics in Action 6.3)

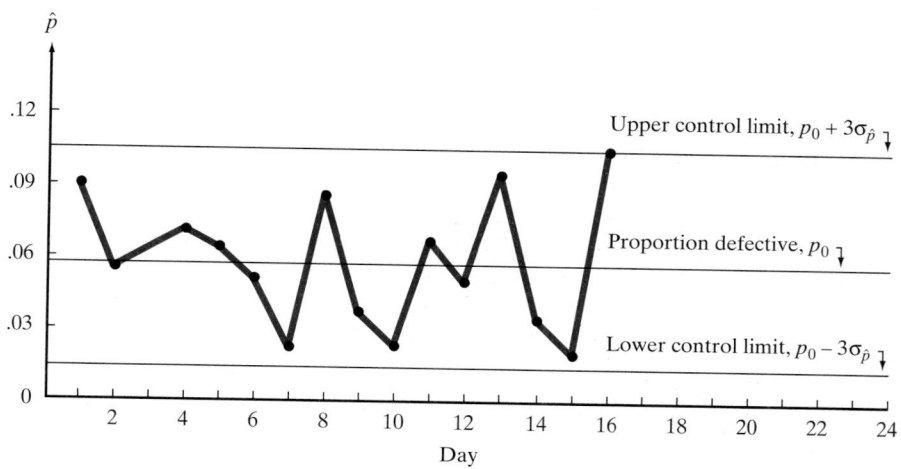

![EXERCISES] **6.53–6.64**

Note: Exercises marked with 💾 *contain data for computer analysis on a 3.5" disk (file name in parentheses).*

Learning the Mechanics

6.53 For the binomial sample sizes and null hypothesized values of p in each part, determine whether the sample size is large enough to use the normal approximation methodology presented in this section to conduct a test of the null hypothesis H_0: $p = p_0$.
  a. $n = 900, p_0 = .975$ **b.** $n = 125, p_0 = .01$
  c. $n = 40, p_0 = .75$ **d.** $n = 15, p_0 = .75$
  e. $n = 12, p_0 = .62$

6.54 Suppose a random sample of 100 observations from a binomial population gives a value of $\hat{p} = .63$ and you wish to test the null hypothesis that the population parameter p is equal to .70 against the alternative hypothesis that p is less than .70.
  a. Noting that $\hat{p} = .63$, what does your intuition tell you? Does the value of $\hat{p}$ appear to contradict the null hypothesis?
  b. Use the large-sample z-test to test H_0: $p = .70$ against the alternative hypothesis, H_a: $p < .70$. Use $\alpha = .05$. How do the test results compare with your intuitive decision from part **a**?
  c. Find and interpret the observed significance level of the test you conducted in part **b**.

6.55 Suppose the sample in Exercise 6.54 has produced $\hat{p} = .83$ and we wish to test H_0: $p = .9$ against the alternative H_a: $p < .9$.
  a. Calculate the value of the z statistic for this test.
  b. Note that the numerator of the z statistic $(\hat{p} - p_0 = .83 - .90 = -.07)$ is the same as for Exercise 6.54. Considering this, why is the absolute value of z for this exercise larger than that calculated in Exercise 6.54?
  c. Complete the test using $\alpha = .05$ and interpret the result.
  d. Find the observed significance level for the test and interpret its value.

6.56 A statistics student used a computer program to test the null hypothesis H_0: $p = .5$ against the one-tailed alternative, H_a: $p > .5$. A sample of 500 observations are input into SPSS, which returns the output shown at the bottom of the page.
  a. The student concludes, based on the p-value, that there is a 33% chance that the alternative hypothesis is true. Do you agree? If not, correct the interpretation.
  b. How would the p-value change if the alternative hypothesis were two-tailed, H_a: $p \neq .5$? Interpret this p-value.

6.57 (X06.057) Refer to Exercise 5.36, in which 50 consumers taste tested a new snack food. Their responses (where $0 =$ do not like; $1 =$ like; $2 =$ indifferent) are reproduced below.

1	0	0	1	2	0	1	1	0	0	1
0	2	0	2	2	0	0	1	1	0	0
0	1	0	2	0	0	0	1	0	0	1	0
0	1	0	1	0	2	0	0	1	1	0	0
0	1									

  a. Test H_0: $p = .5$ against H_a: $p > .5$, where p is the proportion of customers who do not like the snack food. Use $\alpha = .10$.
  b. Find the observed significance level of your test.

Applying the Concepts

6.58 In 1895, druggist Asa Candler began distributing handwritten tickets to his customers for free glasses of Coca-Cola at his soda fountain. That was the genesis of the discount coupon. In 1975 it was estimated that 69% of U.S. consumers regularly used discount coupons when shopping. Today more than 3,000 manufacturers distribute more than 310 billion coupons per year. In a 1995 consumer survey, 71% said they regularly redeem coupons (*Newark Star-Ledger*, Oct. 9, 1995). Assume the 1995 survey consisted of a random sample of 1,000 shoppers.
  a. Does the 1995 survey provide sufficient evidence that the percentage of shoppers using cents-off coupons exceeds 69%? Test using $\alpha = .05$.
  b. Is the sample size large enough to use the inferential procedures presented in this section? Explain.
  c. Find the observed significance level for the test you conducted in part **a**, and interpret its value.

```
- - - - - - - Binomial Test
        Cases

                                  Test Prop. =    .5000
          220     = 1             Obs. Prop. =    .4400
          280     = 0
           --                     Z Approximation
          500    Total            2-Tailed P =   0.3300
```

6.59 If you live in California, the decision to purchase earthquake insurance is a critical one. An article in the *Annals of the Association of American Geographers* (June 1992) investigated many factors that California residents consider when purchasing earthquake insurance. The survey revealed that only 133 of 337 randomly selected residences in Los Angeles County were protected by earthquake insurance.

    a. What are the appropriate null and alternative hypotheses to test the research hypothesis that less than 40% of the residents of Los Angeles County were protected by earthquake insurance?

    b. Do the data provide sufficient evidence to support the research hypothesis? Use $\alpha = .10$.

    c. Calculate and interpret the *p*-value for the test.

6.60 **(X06.060)** *Consumer Reports* (Sept. 1992) recently evaluated and rated 46 brands of toothpaste. (See Exercise 2.106.) One attribute examined in the study was whether or not a toothpaste brand carries an American Dental Association (ADA) seal verifying effective decay prevention. The data for the 46 brands (coded 1 = ADA seal, 0 = no ADA seal) are reproduced below.

```
0  0  0  0  0  0  1  1  1  0  0  1
0  1  0  0  0  0  1  1  1  0  1  1
1  1  0  0  0  0  0  1  0  0  1  1
1  0  1  0  1  1  1  0  0  0
```

    a. Give the null and alternative hypotheses for testing whether the true proportion of toothpaste brands with the ADA seal verifying effective decay prevention is less than .5.

    b. The data were analyzed in SPSS; the results of the test are shown in the SPSS printout below. Interpret the results.

6.61 A placebo is a pill that looks and tastes real but contains no medically active chemicals. The *placebo effect* describes the phenomenon of improvement in the condition of a patient taking placebos. For the placebo effect to occur, both doctors and patients must believe that the placebo being administered is really a drug. Such was the case at a clinic in La Jolla, California. Physicians gave what they thought were drugs to 7,000 asthma, ulcer, and herpes patients. Although the doctors later learned that the drugs were really placebos, 70% of the patients reported an improved condition (*Forbes*, May 22, 1995). Use this information to test (at $\alpha = .05$) if there is a placebo effect at the clinic. Assume that if the placebo is ineffective, the probability of a patient's condition improving is .5.

6.62 "Take the Pepsi Challenge" was a marketing campaign used recently by the Pepsi-Cola Company. Coca-Cola drinkers participated in a blind taste test where they were asked to taste unmarked cups of Pepsi and Coke and were asked to select their favorite. In one Pepsi television commercial, an announcer states that "in recent blind taste tests, more than half the Diet Coke drinkers surveyed said they preferred the taste of Diet Pepsi" (*Consumer's Research*, May 1993). Suppose 100 Diet Coke drinkers took the Pepsi Challenge and 56 preferred the taste of Diet Pepsi. Test the hypothesis that more than half of all Diet Coke drinkers will select Diet Pepsi in the blind taste test. Use $\alpha = .05$. What are the consequences of the test results from Coca-Cola's perspective?

6.63 Refer to the *Chest* (May 1995) study of obstructive sleep apnea, Exercise 5.40. Recall that the disorder causes a person to stop breathing and awaken briefly during a sleep cycle. Stanford University researchers found that 124 of 159 commercial truck drivers suffered from obstructive sleep apnea.

    a. Sleep researchers theorize that 25% of the general population suffer from obstructive sleep apnea. Use a test of hypothesis (at $\alpha = .10$) to determine whether this percentage differs for commercial truck drivers.

    b. Find the observed significance level of the test and interpret its value.

    c. In part **b** of Exercise 5.40, you used a 90% confidence interval to make the inference of part **a**. Explain why these two inferences must necessarily agree.

6.64 In gambling, a *system* is a strategy for playing a game that is thought to improve one's chances of winning. A professional gambler sells videotapes that teach his system for playing casino blackjack. His televised advertisements on late-night cable

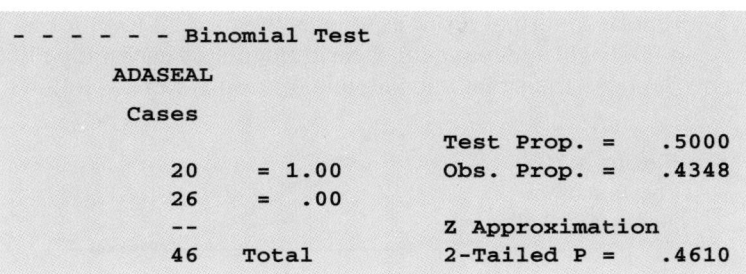

```
- - - - - - Binomial Test

    ADASEAL

    Cases
                                    Test Prop. =    .5000
            20    = 1.00           Obs. Prop. =    .4348
            26    =  .00
            --                     Z Approximation
            46    Total            2-Tailed P =    .4610
```

TV claim that the "system guarantees winning results on average." A customer who lost thousands of dollars while using the system decided to sue the professional gambler for false advertising. To test the gambler's claim, the customer's lawyer commissioned a computer simulation study. The computer "played" 1,000,000 independent games of blackjack with the "player" following the gambler's system and the "dealer" obeying the standard house rules. The "player" won 497,584 of the simulated games.

a. Letting p represent the long-run proportion of games won by players using the system, test $H_0: p \geq .50$ versus $H_a: p < .50$ using $\alpha = .01$.

b. Do the results of this test contradict the advertised claim? Explain.

c. Suppose the simulation had been run only 10,000 times. Would the results of the test be the same if the "player" won the same proportion of the simulated games (i.e., 4,976)?

d. List any assumptions that you made in answering parts **a** and **c**.

e. Find the observed significance levels for the tests you conducted in parts **a** and **c** and interpret their values.

6.6 A NONPARAMETRIC TEST ABOUT A POPULATION MEDIAN (OPTIONAL)

In Sections 6.2 through 6.4 we utilized the z and t statistics for testing hypotheses about a population mean. The z statistic is appropriate for large random samples selected from "general" populations—that is, with few limitations on the probability distribution of the underlying population. The t statistic was developed for small-sample tests in which the sample is selected at random from a *normal* distribution. The question is: How can we conduct a test of hypothesis when we have a small sample from a *nonnormal* distribution? The answer is: Use a procedure that requires fewer or less stringent assumptions about the underlying population, called a **nonparametric method**.

The **sign test** is a relatively simple nonparametric procedure for testing hypotheses about the central tendency of a nonnormal probability distribution. Note that we used the phrase *central tendency* rather than *population mean*. This is because the sign test, like many nonparametric procedures, provides inferences about the population *median* rather than the population mean μ. Denoting the population median by the Greek letter, η, we know (Chapter 2) that η is the 50th percentile of the distribution (Figure 6.20) and as such is less affected by the skewness of the distribution and the presence of outliers (extreme observations). Since the nonparametric test must be suitable for all distributions, not just the normal, it is reasonable for nonparametric tests to focus on the more robust (less sensitive to extreme values) measure of central tendency, the median.

For example, increasing numbers of both private and public agencies are requiring their employees to submit to tests for substance abuse. One laboratory that conducts such testing has developed a system with a normalized measurement scale, in which values less than 1.00 indicate "normal" ranges and values equal to or greater than 1.00 are indicative of potential substance abuse. The lab reports a normal result as long as the median level for an individual is less than 1.00. Eight independent measurements of each individual's sample are made. Suppose, then, that one individual's results were as follows:

FIGURE 6.20
Location of the population median, η

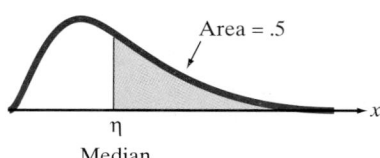

.78   .51   3.79   .23   .77   .98   .96   .89

If the objective is to determine whether the *population* median (that is, the true median level if an indefinitely large number of measurements were made on the same individual sample) is less than 1.00, we establish that as our alternative hypothesis and test

$$H_0: \eta = 1.00$$

$$H_a: \eta < 1.00$$

The one-tailed sign test is conducted by counting the number of sample measurements that "favor" the alternative hypothesis—in this case, the number that are less than 1.00. If the null hypothesis is true, we expect approximately half of the measurements to fall on each side of the hypothesized median and if the alternative is true, we expect significantly more than half to favor the alternative— that is, to be less than 1.00. Thus,

Test statistic: S = Number of measurements less than 1.00, the null hypothesized median

If we wish to conduct the test at the $\alpha = .05$ level of significance, the rejection region can be expressed in terms of the observed significance level, or p-value of the test:

Rejection region: p-value $\leq .05$

In this example, $S = 7$ of the 8 measurements are less than 1.00. To determine the observed significance level associated with this outcome, we note that the number of measurements less than 1.00 is a binomial random variable (check the binomial characteristics presented in Chapter 4), and *if* H_0 *is true*, the binomial probability p that a measurement lies below (or above) the median 1.00 is equal to .5 (Figure 6.20). What is the probability that a result is *as contrary to or more contrary to* H_0 than the one observed? That is, what is the probability that 7 *or more* of 8 binomial measurements will result in Success (be less than 1.00) if the probability of Success is .5? Binomial Table II in Appendix B (using $n = 8$ and $p = .5$) indicates that

$$P(x \geq 7) = 1 - P(x \leq 6) = 1 - .965 = .035$$

Thus, the probability that at least 7 of 8 measurements would be less than 1.00 *if the true median were* 1.00 is only .035. The p-value of the test is therefore .035.

This p-value can also be obtained using a statistical software package. The MINITAB printout of the analysis is shown in Figure 6.21, with the p-value highlighted on the printout. Since $p = .035$ is less than $\alpha = .05$, we conclude that this sample provides sufficient evidence to reject the null hypothesis. The implication of this rejection is that the laboratory can conclude at the $\alpha = .05$ level of significance that the true median level for the tested individual is less than 1.00. However, we note that one of the measurements greatly exceeds the others, with a value of 3.79, and deserves special attention. Note that this large measurement is an outlier that would make the use of a t-test and its concomitant assumption of normality dubious. The only assumption necessary to ensure the validity of the sign test is that the probability distribution of measurements is continuous.

FIGURE 6.21
MINITAB printout
of sign test

SIGN TEST OF MEDIAN = 1.000 VERSUS L.T. 1.000					
	N	BELOW	EQUAL	ABOVE	P-VALUE	MEDIAN
READING	8	7	0	1	0.0352	0.8350

The use of the sign test for testing hypotheses about population medians is summarized in the box.

Sign Test for a Population Median η

One-Tailed Test

$H_0: \eta = \eta_0$

$H_a: \eta > \eta_0$ [or $H_a: \eta < \eta_0$]

Two-Tailed Test

$H_0: \eta = \eta_0$

$H_a: \eta \neq \eta_0$

Test statistic:

S = Number of sample measurements greater than η_0 [or S = number of measurements less than η_0]

S = Larger of S_1 and S_2, where S_1 is the number of measurements less than η_0 and S_2 is the number of measurements greater than η_0

Observed significance level:

p-value $= P(x \geq S)$

p-value $= 2P(x \geq S)$

where x has a binomial distribution with parameters n and $p = .5$. (Use Table II, Appendix B.)

Rejection region: Reject H_0 if p-value $\leq .05$.

Assumption: The sample is selected randomly from a continuous probability distribution. [*Note*: No assumptions need to be made about the shape of the probability distribution.]

It can be shown (proof omitted) that the normal probability distribution provides a good approximation for the binomial distribution when the sample size is large. For tests about the median of a distribution, the null hypothesis implies that $p = .5$, and the normal distribution provides a good approximation if $n \geq 10$. (Samples with $n \geq 10$ satisfy the condition that $np \pm 3\sqrt{npq}$ is contained in the interval 0 to n.) Thus, we can use the standard normal z-distribution to conduct the sign test for large samples. The large-sample sign test is summarized in the next box.

Large-Sample Sign Test for a Population Median η

One-Tailed Test

$H_0: \eta = \eta_0$

$H_a: \eta > \eta_0$
   [or $H_a: \eta < \eta_0$]

Two-Tailed Test

$H_0: \eta = \eta_0$

$H_a: \eta \neq \eta_0$

Test statistic: $z = \dfrac{(S - .5) - .5n}{.5\sqrt{n}}$

where S is calculated as shown in the previous box, the null hypothesized mean value is $np = .5n$, and the standard deviation is

$$\sqrt{npq} = \sqrt{n(.5)(.5)} = .5\sqrt{n}$$

Rejection region: $z > z_\alpha$

Rejection region: $z > z_{\alpha/2}$

where tabulated z values can be found inside the front cover.

EXAMPLE 6.9

A manufacturer of compact disk (CD) players has established that the median time to failure for its players is 5,250 hours of utilization. A sample of 20 CDs from a competitor is obtained, and they are continuously tested until each fails. The 20 failure times range from five hours (a "defective" player) to 6,575 hours, and 14 of the 20 exceed 5,250 hours. Is there evidence that the median failure time of the competitor differs from 5,250 hours? Use $\alpha = .10$.

SOLUTION

The null and alternative hypotheses of interest are

$$H_0: \eta = 5{,}250 \text{ hours}$$

$$H_a: \eta \ne 5{,}250 \text{ hours}$$

Test statistic: Since $n \geq 10$, we use the standard normal z statistic:

$$z = \frac{(S - .5) - .5n}{.5\sqrt{n}}$$

where S is the maximum of S_1, the number of measurements greater than 5,250, and S_2, the number of measurements less than 5,250.

Rejection region: $z > 1.645$ where $z_{\alpha/2} = z_{.05} = 1.645$

Assumptions: The distribution of the failure times is continuous (time is a continuous variable), but nothing is assumed about the shape of its probability distribution.

Since the number of measurements exceeding 5,250 is $S_2 = 14$ and thus the number of measurements less than 5,250 is $S_1 = 6$, then $S = 14$, the greater of S_1 and S_2. The calculated z statistic is therefore

$$z = \frac{(S - .5) - .5n}{.5\sqrt{n}} = \frac{13.5 - 10}{.5\sqrt{20}} = \frac{3.5}{2.236} = 1.565$$

The value of z is not in the rejection region, so we cannot reject the null hypothesis at the $\alpha = .10$ level of significance. Thus, the CD manufacturer should not conclude, on the basis of this sample, that its competitor's CDs have a median failure time that differs from 5,250 hours. **⌐**

The one-sample nonparametric sign test for a median provides an alternative to the t-test for small samples from nonnormal distributions. However, if the distribution is approximately normal, the t-test provides a more powerful test about the central tendency of the distribution.

EXERCISES   6.65–6.74

Note: Exercises marked with **▣** *contain data for computer analysis on a 3.5″ disk (file name in parentheses).*

Learning the Mechanics

6.65   Under what circumstances is the sign test preferred to the t-test for making inferences about the central tendency of a population?

6.66   What is the probability that a randomly selected observation exceeds the

    a. Mean of a normal distribution?

    b. Median of a normal distribution?

    c. Mean of a nonnormal distribution?

    d. Median of a nonnormal distribution?

6.67   Use Table II of Appendix B to calculate the following binomial probabilities:

    a. $P(x \geq 7)$ when $n = 8$ and $p = .5$

    b. $P(x \geq 5)$ when $n = 8$ and $p = .5$

    c. $P(x \geq 8)$ when $n = 8$ and $p = .5$

    d. $P(x \geq 10)$ when $n = 15$ and $p = .5$. Also use the normal approximation to calculate this probability, then compare the approximation with the exact value.

e. $P(x \geq 15)$ when $n = 25$ and $p = .5$. Also use the normal approximation to calculate this probability, then compare the approximation with the exact value.

6.68 Consider the following sample of 10 measurements:

8.4 16.9 15.8 12.5 10.3 4.9 12.9 9.8 23.7 7.3

Use these data to conduct each of the following sign tests using the binomial tables (Table II, Appendix B) and $\alpha = .05$:

a. $H_0: \eta = 9$ versus $H_a: \eta > 9$

b. $H_0: \eta = 9$ versus $H_a: \eta \neq 9$

c. $H_0: \eta = 20$ versus $H_a: \eta < 20$

d. $H_0: \eta = 20$ versus $H_a: \eta \neq 20$

e. Repeat each of the preceding tests using the normal approximation to the binomial probabilities. Compare the results.

f. What assumptions are necessary to ensure the validity of each of the preceding tests?

6.69 Suppose you wish to conduct a test of the research hypothesis that the median of a population is greater than 75. You randomly sample 25 measurements from the population and determine that 17 of them exceed 75. Set up and conduct the appropriate test of hypothesis at the .10 level of significance. Be sure to specify all necessary assumptions.

Applying the Concepts

6.70 According to the National Restaurant Association, hamburgers were the number one selling fast-food item in the United States in 1996. The $39 billion market was dominated by McDonald's (42%), Burger King (19%), and Wendy's (11%) (*Newark Star-Ledger*, Mar. 17, 1997). An economist studying the fast-food buying habits of Americans paid graduate students to stand outside two suburban McDonald's restaurants near Boston and ask departing customers whether they spent more or less than $2.25 on hamburger products for their lunch. Twenty answered "less than"; 50 said "more than"; and 10 refused to answer the question.

a. Is there sufficient evidence to conclude that the median amount spent for hamburgers at lunch at McDonald's is less than $2.25?

b. Does your conclusion apply to all Americans who eat lunch at McDonald's? Justify your answer.

c. What assumptions must hold to ensure the validity of your test in part **a**?

6.71 The biting rate of a particular species of fly was investigated in a study reported in the *Journal of the American Mosquito Control Association* (Mar. 1995). Biting rate was defined as the number of flies biting a volunteer during 15 minutes of exposure. This species of fly is known to have a median biting rate of 5 bites per 15 minutes on Stanbury Island, Utah. However, it is theorized that the median biting rate is higher in bright, sunny weather. (This information is of interest to marketers of pesticides.) To test this theory, 122 volunteers were exposed to the flies during a sunny day on Stanbury Island. Of these volunteers, 95 experienced biting rates greater than 5.

a. Set up the null and alternative hypotheses for the test.

b. Calculate the approximate p-value of the test. [*Hint:* Use the normal approximation for a binomial probability.]

c. Make the appropriate conclusion at $\alpha = .01$.

6.72 (**X06.072**) Since the early 1990s many firms have found it necessary to reduce the size of their workforces in order to reduce costs. These reductions are referred to as *corporate downsizing* and *reductions in force* (RIF) by the business community and media (*Business Week*, Feb. 24, 1997). Following RIFs, companies are often sued by former employees who allege that the RIFs were discriminatory with regard to age. Federal law protects employees over 40 years of age against such discrimination. Suppose one large company's employees have a median age of 37. Its RIF plan is to fire 15 employees aged 43, 32, 39, 28, 54, 41, 50, 62, 22, 45, 47, 54, 43, 33, and 59 years.

a. Calculate the median age of the employees who are being terminated.

b. What are the appropriate null and alternative hypotheses to test whether the population from which the terminated employees were selected has a median age that exceeds the entire company's median age?

c. The test of part **b** was conducted using MINITAB. Find the significance level of the test on the MINITAB printout below and interpret its value.

d. Assuming that courts generally require statistical evidence at the .10 level of significance before ruling that age discrimination laws were violated, what do you advise the company about its planned RIF? Explain.

6.73 Airline industry analysts expect that the Federal Aviation Administration (FAA) will increase the

```
SIGN TEST OF MEDIAN = 37.00 VERSUS  G.T.  37.00

            N   BELOW  EQUAL  ABOVE   P-VALUE   MEDIAN
AGE        15     4      0     11     0.0592    43.00
```

frequency and thoroughness of its review of aircraft maintenance procedures in response to the admission by ValuJet Airlines in the summer of 1996 that it had not met some maintenance requirements. Suppose that the FAA samples the records of six aircraft currently utilized by one airline and determines the number of flights between the last two complete engine maintenances for each, with the following results: 24, 27, 25, 94, 29, 28. The FAA requires that this maintenance be performed at least every 30 flights. Although it is obvious that not all aircraft are meeting the requirement, the FAA wishes to test whether the airline is meeting this particular maintenance requirement "on average."

  a. Would you suggest the *t*-test or sign test to conduct the test? Why?
  b. Set up the null and alternative hypotheses such that the burden of proof is on the airline to show it is meeting the "on-average" requirement.
  c. What are the test statistic and rejection region for this test if the level of significance is $\alpha = .01$? Why would the level of significance be set at such a low value?
  d. Conduct the test, and state the conclusion in terms of this application.

6.74 In Exercise 5.27 the average cost of a major kitchen remodeling job in each of a sample of 11

U.S. cities was investigated. The data are reproduced below.

City	Average Cost
Atlanta	$20,427
Boston	27,255
Des Moines	22,115
Kansas City, Mo.	23,256
Louisville	21,887
Portland, Ore.	24,255
Raleigh-Durham	19,852
Reno, Nev.	23,624
Ridgewood, N.J.	25,885
San Francisco	28,999
Tulsa	20,836

Source: Auerbach, J. "A guide to what's cooking in kitchens." *The Wall Street Journal,* Nov. 17, 1995, p. B10.

  a. Under what circumstances could a *t*-test be used to determine whether the mean cost of remodeling a kitchen in the United States is greater than $25,000?
  b. What is the name of an alternative nonparametric test? Specify the null and alternative hypotheses of the test.
  c. Conduct the test of part **b** using $\alpha = .05$. Interpret your results in the context of the problem.

QUICK REVIEW

Key Terms

Note: Starred (*) terms refer to the optional section in this chapter.

Alternative (research) hypothesis 278
Conclusion 283
Level of significance 283
Lower-tailed test 285
Nonparametric method* 312

Null hypothesis 278
Observed significance level (*p*-value) 292
One-tailed test 284
Rejection region 279
Sign test* 312

Test statistic 278
Two-tailed test 285
Type I error 279
Type II error 281
Upper-tailed test 285

Key Formulas

Note: Starred (*) formulas are from the optional section in this chapter.

For testing H_0: $\theta = \theta_0$, the **large-sample test statistic** is

$$z = \frac{\hat{\theta} - \theta_0}{\sigma_{\hat{\theta}}}$$

where $\hat{\theta}$, θ_0, and $\sigma_{\hat{\theta}}$ are obtained from the table below:

Parameter, θ	Hypothesized Parameter Value, θ_0	Estimator, $\hat{\theta}$	Standard Error of Estimator, $\sigma_{\hat{\theta}}$	
μ	μ_0	$\bar{x}$	$\dfrac{\sigma}{\sqrt{n}}$	279, 288
p	p_0	$\hat{p}$	$\sqrt{\dfrac{p_0 q_0}{n}}$	307

For testing $H_0: \mu = \mu_0$, the **small-sample test statistic** is

$$t = \frac{\bar{x} - \mu_0}{s/\sqrt{n}} \qquad 299$$

*For testing $H_0: \eta = \eta_0$, the **nonparametric test statistic** is S, the number of sample measurements greater than (or less than) η_0. If the sample size is large, use the normal test statistic

$$z = \frac{(S - .5) - .5n}{.5\sqrt{n}} \qquad 314$$

LANGUAGE LAB

Symbol	Pronunciation	Description
H_0	H-oh	Null hypothesis
H_a	H-a	Alternative hypothesis
α	alpha	Probability of Type I error
β	beta	Probability of Type II error
η	eta	Population median
S		Test statistic for sign test (see Key Formulas)

SUPPLEMENTARY EXERCISES 6.75–6.97

Note: List the assumptions necessary for the valid implementation of the statistical procedures you use in solving all these exercises. Starred (*) exercises refer to the optional section in this chapter.

Learning the Mechanics

6.75 Complete the following statement: The smaller the p-value associated with a test of hypothesis, the stronger the support for the _____ hypothesis. Explain your answer.

6.76 Specify the differences between a large-sample and small-sample test of hypothesis about a population mean μ. Focus on the assumptions and test statistics.

6.77 Which of the elements of a test of hypothesis can and should be specified *prior* to analyzing the data that are to be utilized to conduct the test?

6.78 If the rejection of the null hypothesis of a particular test would cause your firm to go out of business, would you want α to be small or large? Explain.

6.79 A random sample of 20 observations selected from a normal population produced $\bar{x} = 72.6$ and $s^2 = 19.4$.
a. Test $H_0: \mu = 80$ against $H_a: \mu < 80$. Use $\alpha = .05$.
b. Test $H_0: \mu = 80$ against $H_a: \mu \neq 80$. Use $\alpha = .01$.

6.80 A random sample of $n = 200$ observations from a binomial population yields $\hat{p} = .29$.
a. Test $H_0: p = .35$ against $H_a: p < .35$. Use $\alpha = .05$.
b. Test $H_0: p = .35$ against $H_a: p \neq .35$. Use $\alpha = .05$.

6.81 A random sample of 175 measurements possessed a mean $\bar{x} = 8.2$ and a standard deviation $s = .79$.
a. Test $H_0: \mu = 8.3$ against $H_a: \mu \neq 8.3$. Use $\alpha = .05$.
b. Test $H_0: \mu = 8.4$ against $H_a: \mu \neq 8.4$. Use $\alpha = .05$.

6.82 A t-test is conducted for the null hypothesis $H_0: \mu = 10$ versus the alternative $H_a: \mu > 10$ for a random sample of $n = 17$ observations. The data are analyzed using MINITAB, with the results shown below.
a. Interpret the p-value.
b. What assumptions are necessary for the validity of this test?
c. Calculate and interpret the p-value assuming the alternative hypothesis was instead $H_a: \mu \neq 10$.

Applying the Concepts

6.83 Medical tests have been developed to detect many serious diseases. A medical test is designed to minimize the probability that it will produce a "false positive" or a "false negative." A false positive

```
TEST OF MU = 10.000 VS MU G.T. 10.000

          N      MEAN    STDEV   SE MEAN      T    P VALUE
X        17     12.50     8.78      2.13   1.174     .1288
```

refers to a positive test result for an individual who does not have the disease, whereas a false negative is a negative test result for an individual who does have the disease.

a. If we treat a medical test for a disease as a statistical test of hypothesis, what are the null and alternative hypotheses for the medical test?

b. What are the Type I and Type II errors for the test? Relate each to false positives and false negatives.

c. Which of the errors has graver consequences? Considering this error, is it more important to minimize α or β? Explain.

6.84 The Lincoln Tunnel (under the Hudson River) connects suburban New Jersey to midtown Manhattan. On Mondays at 8:30 A.M., the mean number of cars waiting in line to pay the Lincoln Tunnel toll is 1,220. Because of the substantial wait during rush hour, the Port Authority of New York and New Jersey is considering raising the amount of the toll between 7:30 and 8:30 A.M. to encourage more drivers to use the tunnel at an earlier or later time. Such peak-hour pricing is already used successfully in Paris, Singapore, and Milan (*Newark Star-Ledger,* Aug. 27, 1995). Suppose the Port Authority experiments with peak-hour pricing for six months, increasing the toll from $4 to $7 during the rush hour peak. On 10 different workdays at 8:30 A.M. aerial photographs of the tunnel queues are taken and the number of vehicles counted. The results follow:

1,260 1,052 1,201 942 1,062 999 931 849 867 735

Analyze the data for the purpose of determining whether peak-hour pricing succeeded in reducing the average number of vehicles attempting to use the Lincoln Tunnel during the peak rush hour. Utilize the information in the accompanying EXCEL printout.

Count	
Mean	989.8
Standard Error	50.81006025
Median	970.5
Mode	#N/A
Standard Deviation	160.6755184
Sample Variance	25816.62222
Kurtosis	-0.339458911
Skewness	0.276807237
Range	525
Minimum	735
Maximum	1260
Sum	9898
Count	10
Confidence Level(95.000%)	99.58574067

6.85 The trade publication *Potentials in Marketing* (Nov./Dec. 1995) surveyed its readers concerning their opinions of electronic marketing (i.e., marketing via the Internet, e-mail, CD-ROMS, etc.). A questionnaire was faxed to 1,500 randomly selected U.S. readers in August and September 1995. Of the 195 questionnaires that were returned, 37 reported that their company already has a World Wide Web site and 59 indicated that their company had plans to create one.

a. Do these data provide sufficient evidence to reject the claim by a producer of a well-known Web browser that "more than 25% of all U.S. businesses will have Web sites by the middle of 1995"?

b. Discuss potential problems associated with the sampling methodology and the appropriateness of the sample for making generalizations about all U.S. businesses.

6.86 Failure to meet payments on student loans guaranteed by the U.S. government has been a major problem for both banks and the government. Approximately 50% of all student loans guaranteed by the government are in default. A random sample of 350 loans to college students in one region of the United States indicates that 147 loans are in default.

a. Do the data indicate that the proportion of student loans in default in this area of the country differs from the proportion of all student loans in the United States that are in default? Use $\alpha = .01$.

b. Find the observed significance level for the test and interpret its value.

6.87 In order to be effective, the mean length of life of a certain mechanical component used in a spacecraft must be larger than 1,100 hours. Owing to the prohibitive cost of this component, only three can be tested under simulated space conditions. The lifetimes (hours) of the components were recorded and the following statistics were computed: $\bar{x} = 1,173.6$ and $s = 36.3$. These data were analyzed using MINITAB, with the results shown on page 320.

a. Verify that the software has correctly calculated the t statistic and determine whether the p-value is in the appropriate range.

b. Interpret the p-value.

c. Which type of error, I or II, is of greater concern for this test? Explain.

d. Would you recommend that this component be passed as meeting specifications?

6.88 A consumer protection group is concerned that a ketchup manufacturer is filling its 20-ounce family-size containers with less than 20 ounces of ketchup. The group purchases 10 family-size

```
TEST OF MU = 1100 VS MU G.T. 1100
          N      MEAN     STDEV    SE MEAN      T    P VALUE
COMP      3     1,173.6    36.3     20.96     3.512   .0362
```

bottles of this ketchup, weighs the contents of each, and finds that the mean weight is equal to 19.86 ounces, and the standard deviation is equal to .22 ounce.

a. Do the data provide sufficient evidence for the consumer group to conclude that the mean fill per family-size bottle is less than 20 ounces? Test using $\alpha = .05$.

b. If the test in part **a** were conducted on a periodic basis by the company's quality control department, is the consumer group more concerned about making a Type I error or a Type II error? (The probability of making this type of error is called the *consumer's risk.*)

c. The ketchup company is also interested in the mean amount of ketchup per bottle. It does not wish to overfill them. For the test conducted in part **a**, which type of error is more serious from the company's point of view—a Type I error or a Type II error? (The probability of making this type of error is called the *producer's risk.*)

6.89 Sales promotions that are used by manufacturers to entice retailers to carry, feature, or push the manufacturer's products are called *trade promotions.* A survey of 250 manufacturers conducted by Cannondale Associates, a sales and marketing consulting firm, found that 91% of the manufacturers believe their spending for trade promotions is inefficient (*Potentials in Marketing,* June 1995). Is this sufficient evidence to reject a previous claim by the American Marketing Association that no more than half of all manufacturers are dissatisfied with their trade promotion spending?

a. Conduct the appropriate hypothesis test at $\alpha = .02$. Begin your analysis by determining whether the sample size is large enough to apply the testing methodology presented in this section.

b. Report the observed significance level of the test and interpret its meaning in the context of the problem.

*6.90 According to the Internal Revenue Service (IRS), in 1980, 4,414 taxpayers reported earning more than \$1 million in adjusted gross income. By 1994 that number had grown to 68,064. Interestingly, as the number of millionaires rose dramatically, their charitable contributions nose-dived from a median of \$207,089 in 1980 to \$98,500 in 1994 (Internal Revenue Service, *Statistics of Income Bulletin,* Spring 1996). Will this trend continue into the late 1990s? The IRS sampled six 1997 tax returns of millionaires and found the following charitable contributions (in thousands of dollars):

91.1   103.2   62.9   150.4   209.5   31.7

Do the sample data indicate that annual charitable contributions by millionaires have increased since 1994? Conduct the test using $\alpha = .05$.

6.91 The EPA sets an airborne limit of 5 parts per million (ppm) on vinyl chloride, a colorless gas used to make plastics, adhesives, and other chemicals. It is both a carcinogen and a mutagen (New Jersey Department of Health, *Hazardous Substance Fact Sheet,* Dec. 1994). A major plastics manufacturer, attempting to control the amount of vinyl chloride its workers are exposed to, has given instructions to halt production if the mean amount of vinyl chloride in the air exceeds 3.0 ppm. A random sample of 50 air specimens produced the following statistics: $\bar{x} = 3.1$ ppm, $s = .5$ ppm.

a. Do these statistics provide sufficient evidence to halt the production process? Use $\alpha = .01$.

b. If you were the plant manager, would you want to use a large or a small value for α for the test in part **a**? Explain.

c. Find the *p*-value for the test and interpret its value.

6.92 One study (*Journal of Political Economy,* Feb. 1988) of gambling newsletters that purport to improve a bettor's odds of winning bets on NFL football games indicates that the newsletters' betting schemes were not profitable. Suppose a random sample of 50 games is selected to test one gambling newsletter. Following the newsletter's recommendations, 30 of the 50 games produced winning wagers.

a. Test whether the newsletter can be said to significantly increase the odds of winning over what one could expect by selecting the winner at random. Use $\alpha = .05$.

b. Calculate and interpret the *p*-value for the test.

6.93 The *Chronicle of Higher Education Almanac* (Sept. 2, 1996) reported that for the 1995–1996 academic year, four-year private colleges charged students an average of \$12,432 for tuition and fees, whereas at four-year public colleges the average was \$2,860. Suppose that for 1996–1997 a

```
TEST OF MU = 12432 VS MU G.T. 12432
THE ASSUMED SIGMA = 1721

                N      MEAN     STDEV    SE MEAN     Z     P VALUE
    TUITION     30     13016    1721     314.03    1.86     .0314
```

random sample of 30 private colleges yielded the following data on tuition and fees: $\bar{x} = \$13,016$ and $s = \$1,721$. Assume that $12,432$ is the population mean for 1995–1996.

a. Specify the null and alternative hypotheses you would use to investigate whether the mean amount for tuition and fees in 1996–1997 was significantly larger (in the statistical sense) than it was in 1995–1996.

b. The data are submitted to MINITAB, and the results obtained are shown above. Check these calculations, and interpret the result.

c. Explain the difference between statistical significance and practical significance in the context of this exercise.

6.94 Twenty years ago, personal computers (PCs) didn't even exist. Today they are fast becoming as common in the home as television sets and toasters. In 1995, Roper Starch Worldwide surveyed 2,000 middle-class Americans and found that 860 had used a PC in the past 12 months (*USA Today Special Newsletter Edition*, Dec. 1995). Is this sufficient evidence for Roper Starch Worldwide to claim that "one in two middle-class Americans has used a PC within the past year"? Test using $\alpha = .10$.

*6.95 Many water treatment facilities supplement the natural fluoride concentration with hydrofluosilicic acid in order to reach a target concentration of fluoride in drinking water. Certain levels are thought to enhance dental health, but very high concentrations can be dangerous. Suppose that one such treatment plant targets .75 milligrams per liter (mg/L) for their water. The plant tests 25 samples each day to determine whether the median level differs from the target.

a. Set up the null and alternative hypotheses.

b. Set up the test statistic and rejection region using $\alpha = .10$.

c. Explain the implication of a Type I error in the context of this application. A Type II error.

d. Suppose that one day's samples result in 18 values that exceed .75 mg/L. Conduct the test and state the appropriate conclusion in the context of this application.

e. When it was suggested to the plant's supervisor that a *t*-test should be used to conduct the daily test, she replied that the probability distribution of the fluoride concentrations was "heavily skewed to the right." Show graphically what she meant by this, and explain why this is a reason to prefer the sign test to the *t*-test.

6.96 The "beta coefficient" of a stock is a measure of the stock's volatility (or risk) relative to the market as a whole. Stocks with beta coefficients greater than 1 generally bear greater risk (more volatility) than the market, whereas stocks with beta coefficients less than 1 are less risky (less volatile) than the overall market (Alexander, Sharpe, and Bailey, *Fundamentals of Investments*, 1993). A random sample of 15 high-technology stocks was selected at the end of 1996, and the mean and standard deviation of the beta coefficients were calculated: $\bar{x} = 1.23, s = .37$.

a. Set up the appropriate null and alternative hypotheses to test whether the average high-technology stock is riskier than the market as a whole.

b. Establish the appropriate test statistic and rejection region for the test. Use $\alpha = .10$.

c. What assumptions are necessary to ensure the validity of the test?

d. Calculate the test statistic and state your conclusion.

e. What is the approximate *p*-value associated with this test? Interpret it.

6.97 Refer to Exercise 6.96. SAS was used to analyze the data, and the output was as follows:

```
Analysis Variable : BETA_1

  N Obs              T    Prob>|T|
-----------------------------------
    15      2.4080000     0.0304
-----------------------------------
```

a. Interpret the *p*-value on the computer output. (**Prob** $> |\mathbf{T}|$ on the SAS printout corresponds to a two-tailed test of the null hypothesis $\mu = 1$.)

b. If the alternative hypothesis of interest is $\mu > 1$, what is the appropriate *p*-value of the test?

CHAPTER 7

COMPARING POPULATION MEANS

CONTENTS

7.1   Comparing Two Population Means: Independent Sampling

7.2   Comparing Two Population Means: Paired Difference Experiments

7.3   Determining the Sample Size

7.4   Testing the Assumption of Equal Population Variances (Optional)

7.5   A Nonparametric Test for Comparing Two Populations: Independent Sampling (Optional)

7.6   A Nonparametric Test for Comparing Two Populations: Paired Difference Experiments (Optional)

7.7   Comparing Three or More Population Means: Analysis of Variance (Optional)

STATISTICS IN ACTION

7.1   The Effect of Self-Managed Work Teams on Family Life

7.2   Unpaid Overtime and the Fair Labor Standards Act

7.3   Taxpayers Versus the IRS: Selecting the Trial Court

Where We've Been

We explored two methods for making statistical inferences, confidence intervals, and tests of hypotheses in Chapters 5 and 6. In particular, we studied confidence intervals and tests of hypotheses concerning a single population mean μ and a single population proportion p. We also learned how to select the sample size necessary to obtain a specified amount of information concerning μ or p.

Where We're Going

Now that we've learned to make inferences about a single population, we'll learn how to compare two (or more) population means. For example, we may wish to compare the mean gas mileages for two models of automobiles. In this chapter we'll see how to decide whether differences exist and how to estimate the differences between population means. We learn how to compare population proportions in Chapter 8.

Many experiments involve a comparison of two population means. For instance, a consumer group may want to test whether two major brands of food freezers differ in the mean amount of electricity they use. A golf ball supplier may wish to compare the average distance that two competing brands of golf balls travel when struck with the same club. In this chapter we consider techniques for using two (or more) samples to compare the means of the populations from which they were selected.

7.1 COMPARING TWO POPULATION MEANS: INDEPENDENT SAMPLING

Many of the same procedures that are used to estimate and test hypotheses about a single parameter can be modified to make inferences about two parameters. Both the z and t statistics may be adapted to make inferences about the difference between two population means.

In this section we develop both large-sample and small-sample methodologies for comparing two population means. In the large-sample case we use the z statistic, while in the small-sample case we use the t statistic.

LARGE SAMPLES

EXAMPLE 7.1

In recent years, the United States and Japan have engaged in intense negotiations regarding restrictions on trade between the two countries. One of the claims made repeatedly by U.S. officials is that many Japanese manufacturers price their goods higher in Japan than in the United States, in effect subsidizing low prices in the United States by extremely high prices in Japan. According to the U.S. argument, Japan accomplishes this by keeping competitive U.S. goods from reaching the Japanese marketplace.

An economist decided to test the hypothesis that higher retail prices are being charged for Japanese automobiles in Japan than in the United States. She obtained random samples of 50 retail sales in the United States and 30 retail sales in Japan over the same time period and for the same model of automobile, converted the Japanese sales prices from yen to dollars using current conversion rates, and obtained the summary information shown in Table 7.1. Form a 95% confidence interval for the difference between the population mean retail prices of this automobile model for the two countries. Interpret the result.

SOLUTION

Recall that the general form of a large-sample confidence interval for a single mean μ is $\bar{x} \pm z_{\alpha/2}\sigma_{\bar{x}}$. That is, we add and subtract $z_{\alpha/2}$ standard deviations of the sample estimate, $\bar{x}$, to the value of the estimate. We employ a similar procedure to form the confidence interval for the difference between two population means.

TABLE 7.1 Summary Statistics for Automobile Retail Price Study

	U.S. Sales	Japan Sales
Sample Size	50	30
Sample Mean	$14,545	$15,243
Sample Standard Deviation	$ 1,989	$ 1,843

FIGURE 7.1
Sampling distribution
of $(\bar{x}_1 - \bar{x}_2)$

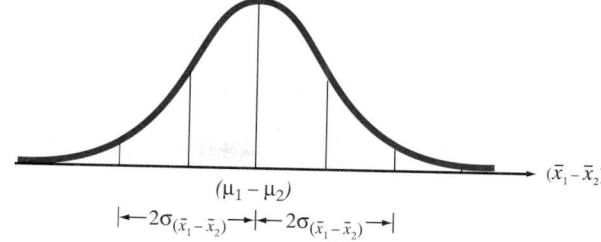

$(\mu_1 - \mu_2)$

$\leftarrow 2\sigma_{(\bar{x}_1 - \bar{x}_2)} \rightarrow \! \leftarrow 2\sigma_{(\bar{x}_1 - \bar{x}_2)} \rightarrow$

Let μ_1 represent the mean of the population of retail sales prices for this car model sold in the United States. Let μ_2 be similarly defined for retail sales in Japan. We wish to form a confidence interval for $(\mu_1 - \mu_2)$. An intuitively appealing estimator for $(\mu_1 - \mu_2)$ is the difference between the sample means, $(\bar{x}_1 - \bar{x}_2)$. Thus, we will form the confidence interval of interest by

$$(\bar{x}_1 - \bar{x}_2) \pm z_{\alpha/2}\sigma_{(\bar{x}_1 - \bar{x}_2)}$$

Assuming the two samples are independent, the standard deviation of the difference between the sample means is

$$\sigma_{(\bar{x}_1 - \bar{x}_2)} = \sqrt{\frac{\sigma_1^2}{n_1} + \frac{\sigma_2^2}{n_2}} \approx \sqrt{\frac{s_1^2}{n_1} + \frac{s_2^2}{n_2}}$$

Using the sample data and noting that $\alpha = .05$ and $z_{.025} = 1.96$, we find that the 95% confidence interval is, approximately,

$$(14{,}545 - 15{,}243) \pm 1.96\sqrt{\frac{(1{,}989)^2}{50} + \frac{(1{,}843)^2}{30}} = -698 \pm (1.96)(438.57)$$

$$= -698 \pm 860$$

or $(-1{,}558, 162)$. Using this estimation procedure over and over again for different samples, we know that approximately 95% of the confidence intervals formed in this manner will enclose the difference in population means $(\mu_1 - \mu_2)$. Therefore, we are highly confident that the difference in mean retail prices in the United States and Japan is between $-\$1{,}558$ and $\$162$. Since 0 falls in this interval, the economist cannot conclude that a significant difference exists between the mean retail prices in the two countries. ◾

The justification for the procedure used in Example 7.1 to estimate $(\mu_1 - \mu_2)$ relies on the properties of the sampling distribution of $(\bar{x}_1 - \bar{x}_2)$. The performance of the estimator in repeated sampling is pictured in Figure 7.1, and its properties are summarized in the box.

Properties of the Sampling Distribution of $(\bar{x}_1 - \bar{x}_2)$

1. The mean of the sampling distribution $(\bar{x}_1 - \bar{x}_2)$ is $(\mu_1 - \mu_2)$.

2. If the two samples are independent, the standard deviation of the sampling distribution is

$$\sigma_{(\bar{x}_1 - \bar{x}_2)} = \sqrt{\frac{\sigma_1^2}{n_1} + \frac{\sigma_2^2}{n_2}}$$

continued

where σ_1^2 and σ_2^2 are the variances of the two populations being sampled and n_1 and n_2 are the respective sample sizes. We also refer to $\sigma_{(\bar{x}_1 - \bar{x}_2)}$ as the **standard error** of the statistic $(\bar{x}_1 - \bar{x}_2)$.

3. The sampling distribution of $(\bar{x}_1 - \bar{x}_2)$ is approximately normal for *large samples* by the Central Limit Theorem.

In Example 7.1, we noted the similarity in the procedures for forming a large-sample confidence interval for one population mean and a large-sample confidence interval for the difference between two population means. When we are testing hypotheses, the procedures are again very similar. The general large-sample procedures for forming confidence intervals and testing hypotheses about $(\mu_1 - \mu_2)$ are summarized in the next two boxes.

Large-Sample Confidence Interval for $(\mu_1 - \mu_2)$

$$(\bar{x}_1 - \bar{x}_2) \pm z_{\alpha/2}\sigma_{(\bar{x}_1 - \bar{x}_2)} = (\bar{x}_1 - \bar{x}_2) \pm z_{\alpha/2}\sqrt{\frac{\sigma_1^2}{n_1} + \frac{\sigma_2^2}{n_2}}$$

Assumptions: The two samples are randomly selected in an independent manner from the two populations; the sample sizes n_1 and n_2 are large (i.e., $n_1 \geqslant 30$ and $n_2 \geqslant 30$).

Large-Sample Test of Hypothesis for $(\mu_1 - \mu_2)$

One-Tailed Test	**Two-Tailed Test**

$H_0: (\mu_1 - \mu_2) = D_0$ $\qquad\qquad\qquad$ $H_0: (\mu_1 - \mu_2) = D_0$

$H_a: (\mu_1 - \mu_2) < D_0$ $\qquad\qquad\qquad$ $H_a: (\mu_1 - \mu_2) \neq D_0$
  $\quad$[or $H_a: (\mu_1 - \mu_2) > D_0$]

where D_0 = Hypothesized difference between the means (this difference is often hypothesized to be equal to 0)

Test statistic:

$$z = \frac{(\bar{x}_1 - \bar{x}_2) - D_0}{\sigma_{(\bar{x}_1 - \bar{x}_2)}} \qquad \text{where} \quad \sigma_{(\bar{x}_1 - \bar{x}_2)} = \sqrt{\frac{\sigma_1^2}{n_1} + \frac{\sigma_2^2}{n_2}}$$

Rejection region: $z < -z_\alpha$ $\qquad\qquad\qquad$ *Rejection region:* $|z| > z_{\alpha/2}$
  $\quad$[or $z > z_\alpha$ when $H_a: (\mu_1 - \mu_2) > D_0$]

Assumptions: Same as for the large-sample confidence interval.

EXAMPLE 7.2

Refer to the study of retail prices of an automobile sold in the United States and Japan, Example 7.1. Another way to compare the mean retail prices for the two countries is to conduct a test of hypothesis. Use the summary data in Table 7.1 to conduct the test. Use $\alpha = .05$.

SOLUTION

Again, we let μ_1 and μ_2 represent the population mean retail sales prices in the United States and Japan, respectively. If the claim made by the U.S. government is

FIGURE 7.2
Rejection region
for Example 7.2

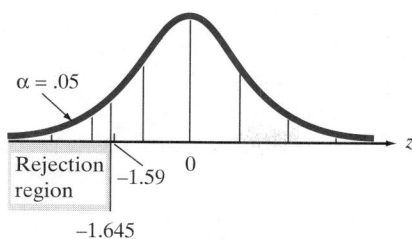

true, then the mean retail price in Japan will exceed the mean in the U.S., i.e., $\mu_1 < \mu_2$ or $(\mu_1 - \mu_2) < 0$.

Thus, the elements of the test are as follows:

H_0: $(\mu_1 - \mu_2) = 0$ (i.e., $\mu_1 = \mu_2$; note that $D_0 = 0$ for this hypothesis test)

H_a: $(\mu_1 - \mu_2) < 0$ (i.e., $\mu_1 < \mu_2$)

Test statistic: $z = \dfrac{(\bar{x}_1 - \bar{x}_2) - D_0}{\sigma_{(\bar{x}_1 - \bar{x}_2)}} = \dfrac{\bar{x}_1 - \bar{x}_2 - 0}{\sigma_{(\bar{x}_1 - \bar{x}_2)}}$

Rejection region: $z < -z_{.05} = -1.645$ (see Figure 7.2)

Substituting the summary statistics given in Table 7.1 into the test statistic, we obtain

$$z = \frac{(\bar{x}_1 - \bar{x}_2) - 0}{\sigma_{(\bar{x}_1 - \bar{x}_2)}} = \frac{(14{,}545 - 15{,}243)}{\sqrt{\dfrac{\sigma_1^2}{n_1} + \dfrac{\sigma_2^2}{n_2}}}$$

$$\approx \frac{-698}{\sqrt{\dfrac{s_1^2}{n_1} + \dfrac{s_2^2}{n_2}}} = \frac{-698}{\sqrt{\dfrac{(1{,}989)^2}{50} + \dfrac{(1{,}843)^2}{30}}} = \frac{-698}{438.57} = -1.59$$

As you can see in Figure 7.2, the calculated z value does not fall in the rejection region. Therefore, the samples do not provide sufficient evidence, at $\alpha = .05$, for the economist to conclude that the mean retail price in Japan exceeds that in the United States.

Note that this conclusion agrees with the inference drawn from the 95% confidence interval in Example 7.1.　◾

EXAMPLE 7.3 Find the observed significance level for the test in Example 7.2. Interpret the result.

SOLUTION

The alternative hypothesis in Example 7.2, H_a: $(\mu_1 - \mu_2) < 0$, required a lower one-tailed test using

$$z = \frac{\bar{x}_1 - \bar{x}_2}{\sigma_{(\bar{x}_1 - \bar{x}_2)}}$$

as a test statistic. Since the value z calculated from the sample data was -1.59, the observed significance level (p-value) for the lower-tailed test is the probability of observing a value of z at least as contradictory to the null hypothesis as $z = -1.59$; that is,

$$p\text{-value} = P(z \leqslant -1.59)$$

This probability is computed assuming H_0 is true and is equal to the shaded area shown in Figure 7.3.

FIGURE 7.3
The observed
significance level
for Example 7.2

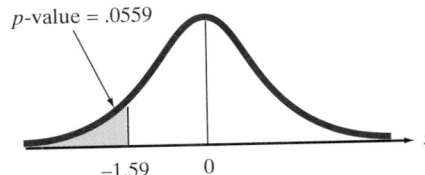

FIGURE 7.4
MINITAB printout
for the hypothesis
test of Example 7.2

```
Two sample T for US vs JAPAN
          N      Mean     StDev    SE Mean
US       50     14545     1989      281.29
JAPAN    30     15243     1843      336.48

95% CI for mu US - mu JAPAN: (-1558, 162)
T-Test mu US = mu JAPAN (vs <): T= -1.59  P=0.056  DF= 78
```

The tabulated area corresponding to $z = 1.59$ in Table IV of Appendix B is .4441. Therefore, the observed significance level of the test is

$$p\text{-value} = .5 - .4441 = .0559$$

Since our selected α value, .05, is less than this p-value, we have insufficient evidence to reject $H_0: (\mu_1 - \mu_2) = 0$ in favor of $H_a: (\mu_1 - \mu_2) < 0$.

The p-value of the test is more easily obtained from a statistical software package. A MINITAB printout for the hypothesis test is displayed in Figure 7.4. The one-tailed p-value, highlighted on the printout, is .056. [Note that MINITAB also gives a 95% confidence interval for $(\mu_1 - \mu_2)$. This interval agrees with the interval calculated in Example 7.1.]

Reminder: The SAS and SPSS software packages conduct only two-tailed hypothesis tests. For these packages, obtain the p-value for a one-tailed test as follows:

$$p = \frac{\text{Reported } p\text{-value}}{2} \quad \text{if form of } H_a \text{ (e.g., } <) \text{ agrees with sign of test statistic (e.g., negative)}$$

$$p = 1 - \frac{\text{Reported } p\text{-value}}{2} \quad \text{if form of } H_a \text{ (e.g., } <) \text{ disagrees with sign of test statistic (e.g., positive)}$$

SMALL SAMPLES

When comparing two population means with small samples (say, $n_1 < 30$ and $n_2 < 30$), the methodology of the previous three examples is invalid. The reason? When the sample sizes are small, estimates of σ_1^2 and σ_2^2 are unreliable and the Central Limit Theorem (which guarantees that the z statistic is normal) can no longer be applied. But as in the case of a single mean (Section 6.4), we use the familiar Student's t-distribution described in Chapter 5.

To use the t-distribution, both sampled populations must be approximately normally distributed with equal population variances, and the random samples must be selected independently of each other.

The normality and equal variances assumptions imply relative frequency distributions for the populations that would appear as shown in Figure 7.5.

Since we assume the two populations have equal variances ($\sigma_1^2 = \sigma_2^2 = \sigma^2$), it is reasonable to use the information contained in both samples to construct a **pooled sample estimator** of σ^2 for use in confidence intervals and test statistics.

FIGURE 7.5
Assumptions for the
two-sample t:
(1) normal populations,
(2) equal variances

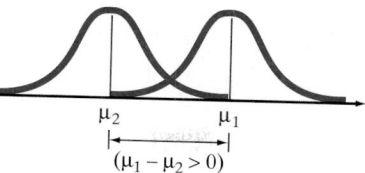

Thus, if s_1^2 and s_2^2 are the two sample variances (both estimating the variance σ^2 common to both populations), the pooled estimator of σ^2, denoted as s_p^2, is

$$s_p^2 = \frac{(n_1 - 1)s_1^2 + (n_2 - 1)s_2^2}{(n_1 - 1) + (n_2 - 1)} = \frac{(n_1 - 1)s_1^2 + (n_2 - 1)s_2^2}{n_1 + n_2 - 2}$$

or

$$s_p^2 = \frac{\overbrace{\sum(x_1 - \bar{x}_1)^2}^{\text{From sample 1}} + \overbrace{\sum(x_2 - \bar{x}_2)^2}^{\text{From sample 2}}}{n_1 + n_2 - 2}$$

where x_1 represents a measurement from sample 1 and x_2 represents a measurement from sample 2. Recall that the term *degrees of freedom* was defined in Section 7.2 as 1 less than the sample size. Thus, in this case, we have $(n_1 - 1)$ degrees of freedom for sample 1 and $(n_2 - 1)$ degrees of freedom for sample 2. Since we are pooling the information on σ^2 obtained from both samples, the degrees of freedom associated with the pooled variance s_p^2 is equal to the sum of the degrees of freedom for the two samples, namely, the denominator of s_p^2; that is, $(n_1 - 1) + (n_2 - 1) = n_1 + n_2 - 2$.

Note that the second formula given for s_p^2 shows that the pooled variance is simply a **weighted average** of the two sample variances, s_1^2 and s_2^2. The weight given each variance is proportional to its degrees of freedom. If the two variances have the same number of degrees of freedom (i.e., if the sample sizes are equal), then the pooled variance is a simple average of the two sample variances. The result is an average or "pooled" variance that is a better estimate of σ^2 than either s_1^2 or s_2^2 alone.

Both the confidence interval and the test of hypothesis procedures for comparing two population means with small samples are summarized in the accompanying boxes.

Small-Sample Confidence Interval for $(\mu_1 - \mu_2)$ (Independent Samples)

$$(\bar{x}_1 - \bar{x}_2) \pm t_{\alpha/2}\sqrt{s_p^2\left(\frac{1}{n_1} + \frac{1}{n_2}\right)}$$

where $s_p^2 = \dfrac{(n_1 - 1)s_1^2 + (n_2 - 1)s_2^2}{n_1 + n_2 - 2}$

and $t_{\alpha/2}$ is based on $(n_1 + n_2 - 2)$ degrees of freedom.

Assumptions: **1.** Both sampled populations have relative frequency distributions that are approximately normal.

2. The population variances are equal.

3. The samples are randomly and independently selected from the population.

> **Small-Sample Test of Hypothesis for $(\mu_1 - \mu_2)$ (Independent Samples)**
>
> **One-Tailed Test**
>
> $H_0: (\mu_1 - \mu_2) = D_0$
>
> $H_a: (\mu_1 - \mu_2) < D_0$
>   [or $H_a: (\mu_1 - \mu_2) > D_0$]
>
> **Two-Tailed Test**
>
> $H_0: (\mu_1 - \mu_2) = D_0$
>
> $H_a: (\mu_1 - \mu_2) \neq D_0$
>
> *Test statistic:*
>
> $$t = \frac{(\bar{x}_1 - \bar{x}_2) - D_0}{\sqrt{s_p^2\left(\dfrac{1}{n_1} + \dfrac{1}{n_2}\right)}}$$
>
> *Rejection region:* $t < -t_\alpha$
>   [or $t > t_\alpha$ when $H_a: (\mu_1 - \mu_2) > D_0$]
>
> *Rejection region:* $|t| > t_{\alpha/2}$
>
> where t_α and $t_{\alpha/2}$ are based on $(n_1 + n_2 - 2)$ degrees of freedom.
>
> *Assumptions:* Same as for the small-sample confidence interval for $(\mu_1 - \mu_2)$ in the previous box.

EXAMPLE 7.4

Behavioral researchers have developed an index designed to measure manageri-al success. The index (measured on a 100-point scale) is based on the manager's length of time in the organization and his or her level within the firm; the higher the index, the more successful the manager. Suppose a researcher wants to com-pare the average success index for two groups of managers at a large manufac-turing plant. Managers in group 1 engage in a high volume of interactions with people outside the manager's work unit. (Such interactions include phone and face-to-face meetings with customers and suppliers, outside meetings, and public relations work.) Managers in group 2 rarely interact with people outside their work unit. Independent random samples of 12 and 15 managers are selected from groups 1 and 2, respectively, and the success index of each recorded. The results of the study are given in Table 7.2.

   a. Use the data in the table to estimate the true mean difference between the success indexes of managers in the two groups. Use a 95% confidence inter-val, and interpret the interval.

   b. What assumptions must be made in order that the estimate be valid? Are they reasonably satisfied?

SOLUTION

   a. For this experiment, let μ_1 and μ_2 represent the mean success index of group 1 and group 2 managers, respectively. Then, the objective is to obtain a 95% confidence interval for $(\mu_1 - \mu_2)$.

TABLE 7.2   **Managerial Success Indexes for Two Groups of Managers**

GROUP 1						GROUP 2					
Interaction with Outsiders						Few Interactions					
65	58	78	60	68	69	62	53	36	34	56	50
66	70	53	71	63	63	42	57	46	68	48	42
						52	53	43			

FIGURE 7.6
SAS printout for
Example 7.4

```
Analysis Variable : SUCCESS
----------------------------------- GROUP=1 -----------------------------------
 N Obs   N     Minimum       Maximum               Mean      Std Dev
 ------------------------------------------------------------------------
   12    12  53.0000000   78.0000000      65.3333333   6.6103683
 ------------------------------------------------------------------------

----------------------------------- GROUP=2 -----------------------------------
 N Obs   N     Minimum       Maximum               Mean      Std Dev
 ------------------------------------------------------------------------
   15    15  34.0000000   68.0000000      49.4666667   9.3340136
 ------------------------------------------------------------------------
```

The first step in constructing the confidence interval is to obtain summary statistics (e.g., $\bar{x}$ and s) on the success index for each group of managers. The data of Table 7.2 were entered into a computer, and SAS used to obtain these descriptive statistics. The SAS printout appears in Figure 7.6. Note that $\bar{x}_1 = 65.33$, $s_1 = 6.61$, $\bar{x}_2 = 49.47$, and $s_2 = 9.33$.

Next, we calculate the pooled estimate of variance:

$$s_p^2 = \frac{(n_1 - 1)s_1^2 + (n_2 - 1)s_2^2}{n_1 + n_2 - 2}$$

$$= \frac{(12 - 1)(6.61)^2 + (15 - 1)(9.33)^2}{12 + 15 - 2} = 67.97$$

where s_p^2 is based on $(n_1 + n_2 - 2) = (12 + 15 - 2) = 25$ degrees of freedom. Also, we find $t_{\alpha/2} = t_{.025} = 2.06$ (based on 25 degrees of freedom) from Table VI of Appendix B.

Finally, the 95% confidence interval for $(\mu_1 - \mu_2)$, the difference between mean managerial success indexes for the two groups, is

$$(\bar{x}_1 - \bar{x}_2) \pm t_{\alpha/2}\sqrt{s_p^2\left(\frac{1}{n_1} + \frac{1}{n_2}\right)} = 65.33 - 49.47 \pm t_{.025}\sqrt{67.97\left(\frac{1}{12} + \frac{1}{15}\right)}$$

$$= 15.86 \pm (2.06)(3.19)$$

$$= 15.86 \pm 6.58$$

or (9.28, 22.44). Note that the interval includes only positive differences. Consequently, we are 95% confident that $(\mu_1 - \mu_2)$ exceeds 0. In fact, we estimate the mean success index, μ_1, for managers with a high volume of outsider interaction (group 1) to be anywhere between 9.28 and 22.44 points higher than the mean success index, μ_2, of managers with few interactions (group 2).

b. To properly use the small-sample confidence interval, the following assumptions must be satisfied:

1. The samples of managers are randomly and independently selected from the populations of group 1 and group 2 managers.

2. The success indexes are normally distributed for both groups of managers.

3. The variance of the success indexes are the same for the two populations, i.e., $\sigma_1^2 = \sigma_2^2$.

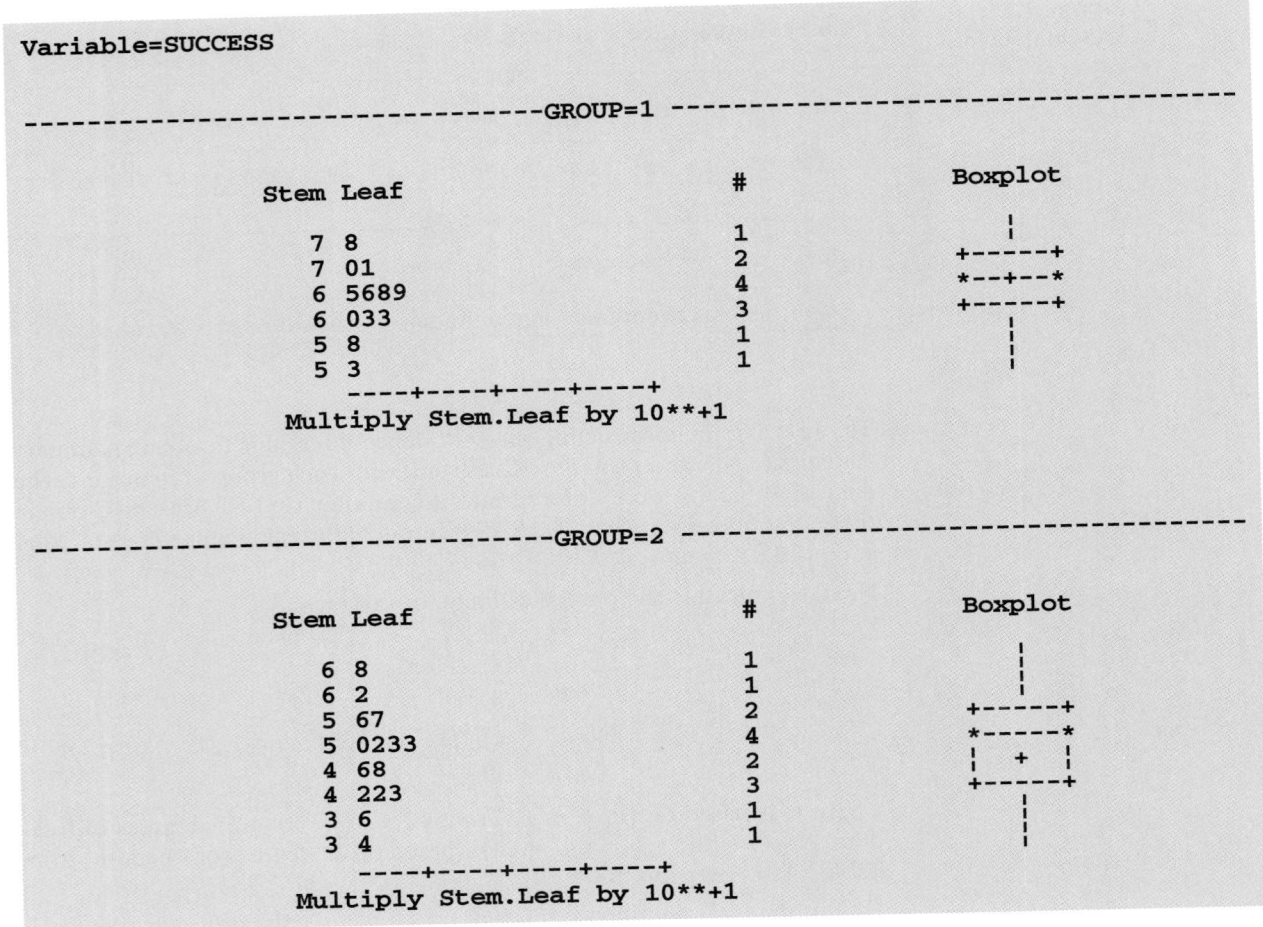

Variable=SUCCESS

```
---------------------------------GROUP=1 ----------------------------------------

              Stem Leaf                         #            Boxplot
                                                                |
                 7  8                           1              |
                 7  01                          2         +------+
                 6  5689                         4         *--+--*
                 6  033                          3         +------+
                 5  8                            1              |
                 5  3                            1              |
                    ----+----+----+----+
              Multiply Stem.Leaf by 10**+1




-----------------------------------GROUP=2 ----------------------------------------

              Stem Leaf                         #            Boxplot
                                                                |
                 6  8                           1              |
                 6  2                           1              |
                 5  67                          2         +------+
                 5  0233                         4         *------*
                 4  68                           2         |  +   |
                 4  223                          3         +------+
                 3  6                            1              |
                 3  4                            1              |
                    ----+----+----+----+
              Multiply Stem.Leaf by 10**+1
```

FIGURE 7.7 SAS graphs for Example 7.4

The first assumption is satisfied, based on the information provided about the sampling procedure in the problem description. To check the plausibility of the remaining two assumptions, we resort to graphical methods. Figure 7.7 is a portion of the SAS printout that gives stem-and-leaf displays for the success indexes of the two samples of managers. Both plots reveal distributions that are approximately mound-shaped and symmetric. Consequently, each sample data set appears to come from a population that is approximately normal.

One way to check assumption #3 is to test the null hypothesis $H_0: \sigma_1^2 = \sigma_2^2$. This test is covered in optional Section 7.4. Another approach is to examine box plots for the sample data. Figure 7.8 is a SAS printout that shows side-by-side vertical box plots for the success indexes in the two samples. Recall, from Section 2.9, that the box plot represents the "spread" of a data set. The two box plots appear to have about the same spread; thus, the samples appear to come from populations with approximately the same variance.

All three assumptions, then, appear to be reasonably satisfied for this application of the small-sample confidence interval.

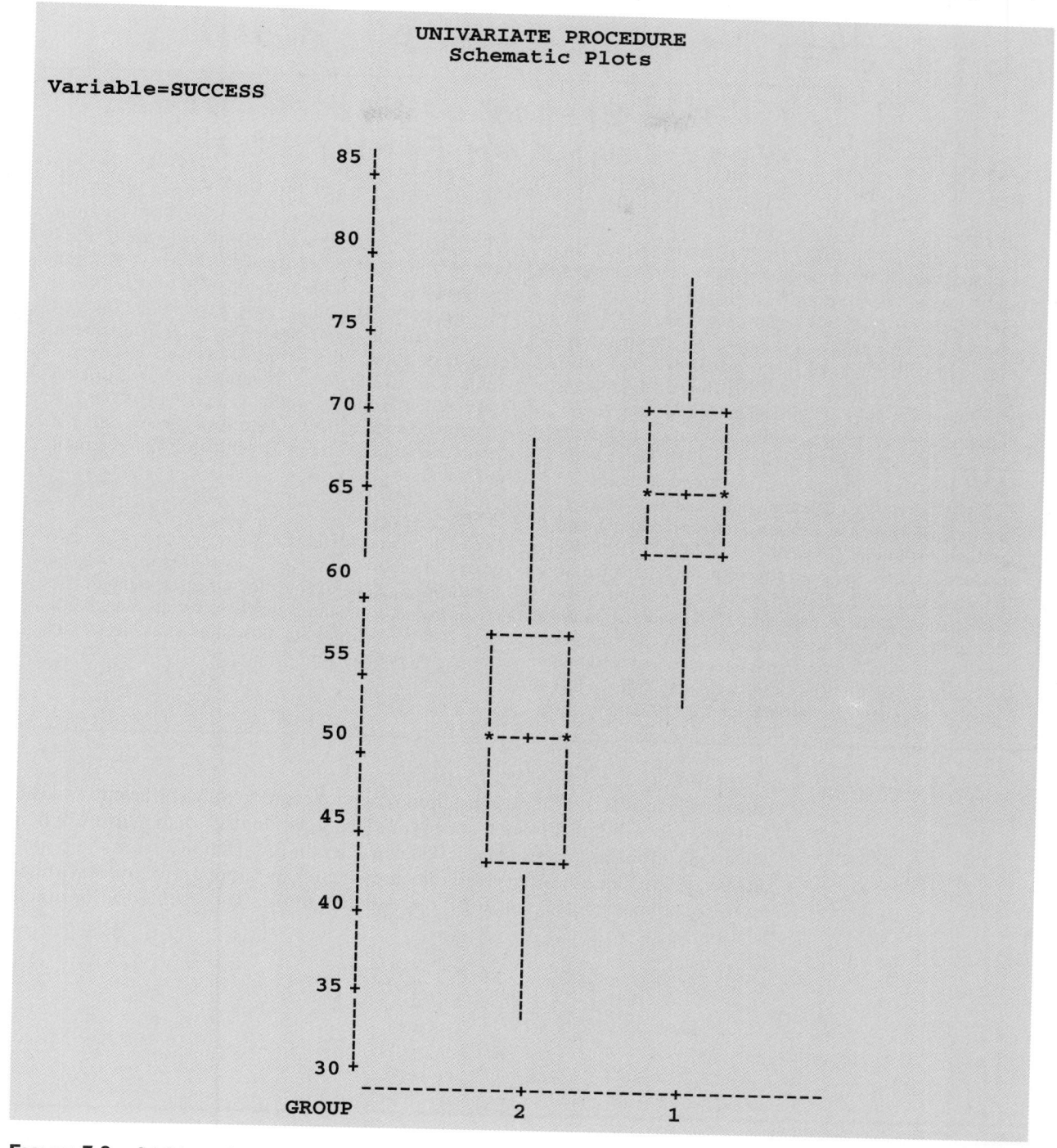

FIGURE 7.8   SAS box plots for Example 7.4

The two-sample t statistic is a powerful tool for comparing population means when the assumptions are satisfied. It has also been shown to retain its usefulness when the sampled populations are only approximately normally distributed. And when the sample sizes are equal, the assumption of equal population variances

STATISTICS IN ACTION

7.1 THE EFFECT OF SELF-MANAGED WORK TEAMS ON FAMILY LIFE

To improve quality, productivity, and timeliness, more and more American industries are adopting a new participative management style utilizing self-managed work teams (SMWTs). A team typically consists of five to 15 workers who are collectively responsible for making decisions and performing all tasks related to a particular project. For example, a SMWT may be responsible for scheduling work hours, interfacing with customers, disciplining team members, and participating in hiring. Studies reveal that SMWTs have positive impacts on both a firm's performance and employee attitudes.

SMWTs require that employees be trained in interpersonal skills such as listening, decision-making, and conflict resolution. Consequently, SMWTs can have potential positive spillover effects on a worker's family life. Researchers L. Stanley-Stevens (Tarleton State University), D. E. Yeatts, and R. R. Seward (both University of North Texas) investigated the connection between SMWT work characteristics and workers' perceptions of positive spillover into family life (*Quality Management Journal*, Summer 1995).

Survey data were collected from 114 AT&T employees who work in one of fifteen SMWTs at an AT&T technical division. The workers were divided into two groups: (1) those who reported positive spillover of work skills to family life and (2) those who did not report positive work spillover. The two groups were compared on a variety of job and demographic characteristics, several of which are shown in Table 7.3. All but the demographic characteristics were measured on a 7-point scale, ranging from 1 = "strongly disagree" to 7 = "strongly agree"; thus, the larger the number, the more of the job characteristic indicated.

Focus

For each characteristic, the sample means of the two groups are shown in Table 7.3, as well as the observed significance level (*p*-value) for a test to compare the group means. Fully interpret these results. Which job-related characteristics are most highly associated with positive work spillover?

---

can be relaxed. That is, if $n_1 = n_2$, then σ_1^2 and σ_2^2 can be quite different and the test statistic will still possess, approximately, a Student's *t*-distribution. When the assumptions are not satisfied, you can select larger samples from the populations or you can use other available statistical tests (nonparametric statistical tests). A nonparametric test for independent samples is presented in optional Section 7.5.

EXERCISES 7.1–7.22

Note: Exercises marked with 💾 *contain data for computer analysis on a 3.5" disk (file name in parentheses).*

Learning the Mechanics

7.1 The purpose of this exercise is to compare the variability of $\bar{x}_1$ and $\bar{x}_2$ with the variability of $(\bar{x}_1 - \bar{x}_2)$.

a. Suppose the first sample is selected from a population with mean $\mu_1 = 150$ and variance $\sigma_1^2 = 900$. Within what range should the sample mean vary about 95% of the time in repeated samples of 100 measurements from this distribution? That is, construct an interval extending 2 standard deviations of $\bar{x}_1$ on each side of μ_1.

TABLE 7.3 Results of Tests to Compare Two Groups of SMWT Employees (Statistics in Action 7.1)

	Characteristic	MEANS		p-Value
		No Positive Work Spillover ($n = 67$)	Positive Work Spillover ($n = 47$)	
Information Flow (7-point scale)	Use of creative ideas	4.4	5.3	$p < .001$
	Communication	3.6	4.4	$.001 < p < .01$
	Cooperation	4.6	5.5	$p < .001$
	Utilization of information	4.7	5.2	$p > .05$
Decision-Making (7-point scale)	Participation in decisions regarding personnel matters	2.7	3.3	$.01 < p < .05$
	Participation in decisions regarding work conditions	4.2	5.0	$.001 < p < .01$
Job (7-point scale)	Good use of skills	4.8	5.9	$p < .001$
	Task significance	5.3	6.0	$.001 < p < .01$
	Task identity	4.2	4.8	$.01 < p < .05$
Demographics	Age (years)	45.0	46.2	$p > .05$
	Education (years)	13.1	13.0	$p > .05$
	Gender (percent female)	12.0	17.0	$p > .05$

Source: Stanley-Stevens, L., Yeatts, D. E., and Seward, R. R. "Positive effects of work on family-life: A case for self-managed work teams." *Quality Management Journal,* Summer 1995, p. 38 (Table 1).

b. Suppose the second sample is selected independently of the first from a second population with mean $\mu_2 = 150$ and variance $\sigma_2^2 = 1{,}600$. Within what range should the sample mean vary about 95% of the time in repeated samples of 100 measurements from this distribution? That is, construct an interval extending 2 standard deviations of $\bar{x}_2$ on each side of μ_2.

c. Now consider the difference between the two sample means $(\bar{x}_1 - \bar{x}_2)$. What are the mean and standard deviation of the sampling distribution of $(\bar{x}_1 - \bar{x}_2)$?

d. Within what range should the difference in sample means vary about 95% of the time in repeated independent samples of 100 measurements each from the two populations?

e. What, in general, can be said about the variability of the difference between independent sample means relative to the variability of the individual sample means?

7.2 Independent random samples of 64 observations each are chosen from two normal populations with the following means and standard deviations:

Population 1	Population 2
$\mu_1 = 12$	$\mu_2 = 10$
$\sigma_1 = 4$	$\sigma_2 = 3$

Let $\bar{x}_1$ and $\bar{x}_2$ denote the two sample means.

a. Give the mean and standard deviation of the sampling distribution of $\bar{x}_1$.

b. Give the mean and standard deviation of the sampling distribution of $\bar{x}_2$.

c. Suppose you were to calculate the difference $(\bar{x}_1 - \bar{x}_2)$ between the sample means. Find the mean and standard deviation of the sampling distribution of $(\bar{x}_1 - \bar{x}_2)$.

d. Will the statistic $(\bar{x}_1 - \bar{x}_2)$ be normally distributed? Explain.

7.3 In order to compare the means of two populations, independent random samples of 400 observations are selected from each population, with the following results:

Sample 1	Sample 2
$\bar{x}_1 = 5{,}275$	$\bar{x}_2 = 5{,}240$
$s_1 = 150$	$s_2 = 200$

a. Use a 95% confidence interval to estimate the difference between the population means $(\mu_1 - \mu_2)$. Interpret the confidence interval.

b. Test the null hypothesis $H_0: (\mu_1 - \mu_2) = 0$ versus the alternative hypothesis $H_a: (\mu_1 - \mu_2) \neq 0$. Give the significance level of the test, and interpret the result.

c. Suppose the test in part b was conducted with the alternative hypothesis $H_a: (\mu_1 - \mu_2) > 0$. How would your answer to part b change?

d. Test the null hypothesis $H_0: (\mu_1 - \mu_2) = 25$ versus $H_a: (\mu_1 - \mu_2) \neq 25$. Give the significance level, and interpret the result. Compare your answer to the test conducted in part b.

e. What assumptions are necessary to ensure the validity of the inferential procedures applied in parts a–d?

7.4 Two populations are described in each of the following cases. In which cases would it be appropriate

```
Two sample Z for X1 vs X2
            N       Mean      StDev    SE Mean
X1         233       473        84      15.26
X2         312       485        93      17.66
Z-Test mu X1 = mu X2 (vs n.e.): T= -1.576  P=0.1150
```

to apply the small-sample t-test to investigate the difference between the population means?

a. Population 1: Normal distribution with variance σ_1^2. Population 2: Skewed to the right with variance $\sigma_2^2 = \sigma_1^2$.

b. Population 1: Normal distribution with variance σ_1^2. Population 2: Normal distribution with variance $\sigma_2^2 \neq \sigma_1^2$.

c. Population 1: Skewed to the left with variance σ_1^2. Population 2: Skewed to the left with variance $\sigma_2^2 = \sigma_1^2$.

d. Population 1: Normal distribution with variance σ_1^2. Population 2: Normal distribution with variance $\sigma_2^2 = \sigma_1^2$.

e. Population 1: Uniform distribution with variance σ_1^2. Population 2: Uniform distribution with variance $\sigma_2^2 = \sigma_1^2$.

7.5 Assume that $\sigma_1^2 = \sigma_2^2 = \sigma^2$. Calculate the pooled estimator of σ^2 for each of the following cases:

a. $s_1^2 = 120, s_2^2 = 100, n_1 = n_2 = 25$
b. $s_1^2 = 12, s_2^2 = 20, n_1 = 20, n_2 = 10$
c. $s_1^2 = .15, s_2^2 = .20, n_1 = 6, n_2 = 10$
d. $s_1^2 = 3,000, s_2^2 = 2,500, n_1 = 16, n_2 = 17$
e. Note that the pooled estimate is a weighted average of the sample variances. To which of the variances does the pooled estimate fall nearer in each of the above cases?

7.6 Independent random samples from normal populations produced the results shown below:

Sample 1	Sample 2
1.2	4.2
3.1	2.7
1.7	3.6
2.8	3.9
3.0	

a. Calculate the pooled estimate of σ^2.
b. Do the data provide sufficient evidence to indicate that $\mu_2 > \mu_1$? Test using $\alpha = .10$.
c. Find a 90% confidence interval for $(\mu_1 - \mu_2)$.
d. Which of the two inferential procedures, the test of hypothesis in part **b** or the confidence interval in part **c**, provides more information about $(\mu_1 - \mu_2)$?

7.7 Two independent random samples have been selected, 100 observations from population 1 and

100 from population 2. Sample means $\bar{x}_1 = 15.5$ and $\bar{x}_2 = 26.6$ were obtained. From previous experience with these populations, it is known that the variances are $\sigma_1^2 = 9$ and $\sigma_2^2 = 16$.

a. Find $\sigma_{(\bar{x}_1 - \bar{x}_2)}$.
b. Sketch the approximate sampling distribution for $(\bar{x}_1 - \bar{x}_2)$ assuming $(\mu_1 - \mu_2) = 10$.
c. Locate the observed value of $(\bar{x}_1 - \bar{x}_2)$ on the graph you drew in part **b**. Does it appear that this value contradicts the null hypothesis H_0: $(\mu_1 - \mu_2) = 10$?
d. Use the z-table on the inside of the front cover to determine the rejection region for the test of H_0: $(\mu_1 - \mu_2) = 10$ against H_0: $(\mu_1 - \mu_2) \neq 10$. Use $\alpha = .05$.
e. Conduct the hypothesis test of part **d** and interpret your result.

7.8 Refer to Exercise 7.7. Construct a 95% confidence interval for $(\mu_1 - \mu_2)$. Interpret the interval. Which inference provides more information about the value of $(\mu_1 - \mu_2)$—the test of hypothesis in Exercise 7.7 or the confidence interval in this exercise?

7.9 Independent random samples are selected from two populations and used to test the hypothesis H_0: $(\mu_1 - \mu_2) = 0$ against the alternative H_a: $(\mu_1 - \mu_2) \neq 0$. A total of 233 observations from population 1 and 312 from population 2 are analyzed by using MINITAB, with the results shown above.

a. Interpret the results of the computer analysis.
b. If the alternative hypothesis had been H_a: $(\mu_1 - \mu_2) < 0$, how would the p-value change? Interpret the p-value for this one-tailed test.

7.10 (X07.010) Independent random samples from approximately normal populations produced the results shown below:

Sample 1				Sample 2			
52	33	42	44	52	43	47	56
41	50	44	51	62	53	61	50
45	38	37	40	56	52	53	60
44	50	43		50	48	60	55

a. Do the data provide sufficient evidence to conclude that $(\mu_2 - \mu_1) > 10$? Test using $\alpha = .01$.
b. Construct a 98% confidence interval for $(\mu_2 - \mu_1)$. Interpret your result.

7.11 Independent random samples selected from two normal populations produced the sample means and standard deviations shown below:

Sample 1	Sample 2
$n_1 = 17$	$n_2 = 12$
$\bar{x}_1 = 5.4$	$\bar{x}_2 = 7.9$
$s_1 = 3.4$	$s_2 = 4.8$

a. The test H_0: $(\mu_1 - \mu_2) = 0$ against H_a: $(\mu_1 - \mu_2) \neq 0$ was conducted using SAS, with the results shown below. Check and interpret the results.

b. Estimate $(\mu_1 - \mu_2)$ using a 95% confidence interval.

Applying the Concepts

7.12 Some college professors make bound lecture notes available to their classes in an effort to improve teaching effectiveness. Because students pay the additional cost, educators want to know whether the students find the lecture notes to be of good educational value. *Marketing Educational Review* (Fall 1994) published a study of business students' opinions of lecture notes. Two groups of students were surveyed—86 students enrolled in a promotional strategy class that required the purchase of lecture notes, and 35 students enrolled in a sales/retailing elective that did not offer lecture notes. In both courses, the instructor used lectures as the main method of delivery. At the end of the semester, the students were asked to respond to the statement: "Having a copy of the lecture notes was [would be] helpful in understanding the material." Responses were measured on a 9-point semantic difference scale, where 1 = "strongly disagree" and 9 = "strongly agree." A summary of the results are reported in the next table.

a. Describe the two populations involved in the comparison.

b. Do the samples provide sufficient evidence to conclude that there is a difference in the mean responses of the two groups of students? Test using $\alpha = .01$.

c. Construct a 99% confidence interval for $(\mu_1 - \mu_2)$. Interpret the result.

d. Would a 95% confidence interval for $(\mu_1 - \mu_2)$ be narrower or wider than the one you found in part **c**? Why?

Classes Buying Lecture Notes	Classes Not Buying Lecture Notes
$n_1 = 86$	$n_2 = 35$
$\bar{x}_1 = 8.48$	$\bar{x}_2 = 7.80$
$s_1^2 = 0.94$	$s_2^2 = 2.99$

Source: Gray, J. I., and Abernathy, A. M. "Pros and cons of lecture notes and handout packages: Faculty and student opinions," *Marketing Education Review,* Vol. 4, No. 3, Fall 1984, p. 25 (Table 4), American Marketing Association.

7.13 **(X07.013)** Marketing strategists would like to predict consumer response to new products and their accompanying promotional schemes. Consequently, studies that examine the differences between buyers and nonbuyers of a product are of interest. One classic study conducted by Shuchman and Riesz (*Journal of Marketing Research,* Feb. 1975) was aimed at characterizing the purchasers and nonpurchasers of Crest toothpaste. Purchasers were defined as households that converted to Crest following its endorsement by the Council on Dental Therapeutics of the American Dental Association on August 1, 1960, and remained "loyal" to Crest until at least April 1963. Nonpurchasers were defined as households that did not convert to Crest during the same time period. Using demographic data collected from a sample of 499 purchasers and 499 nonpurchasers, Shuchman and Riesz demonstrated that both the mean household size (number of persons) and mean household income were significantly larger for purchasers than for nonpurchasers. A similar study utilized independent random samples of size 20 and yielded the data shown in the table (page 338) on the age of the householder primarily responsible for buying toothpaste. An analysis of the data is provided in the SAS printout on page 338.

```
Variable: X

SAMPLE    N     Mean    Std Dev       Std Error
-----------------------------------------------
   1      17    5.4      3.4            4.123
   2      12    7.9      4.8            3.464

Variances         T      DF      Prob>|T|
-----------------------------------------------
Equal           -1.646   27         .1114
```

	Purchasers						Nonpurchasers					
34	35	23	44	52	46		28	22	44	33	55	63
28	48	28	34	33	52		45	31	60	54	53	58
41	32	34	49	50	45		52	52	66	35	25	48
29	59						59	61				

```
                          TTEST PROCEDURE

Variable: AGE

BUYER        N              Mean         Std Dev         Std Error
------------------------------------------------------------------
NONPURCH     20         47.20000000    13.62119092      3.04579088
PURCHASE     20         39.80000000    10.03992032      2.24499443

Variances      T       DF     Prob>|T|
------------------------------------------------------------------
Unequal     1.9557    34.9      0.0585
Equal       1.9557    38.0      0.0579

For HO: Variances are equal, F' = 1.84   DF =  (19,19)   Prob>F' = 0.1927
```

a. Do the data present sufficient evidence to conclude there is a difference in the mean age of purchasers and nonpurchasers? Use $\alpha = .10$.

b. What assumptions are necessary in order to answer part **a**?

c. Find the observed significance level for the test on the printout, and interpret its value.

d. Calculate and interpret a 90% confidence interval for the difference between the mean ages of purchasers and nonpurchasers.

7.14 Valparaiso University professors D. L. Schroeder and K. E. Reichardt conducted a salary survey of members of the Institute of Management Accountants (IMA) and reported the results in *Management Accounting* (June 1995). A salary questionnaire was mailed to a random sample of 4,800 IMA members; 2,287 were returned and form the database for the study. The researchers compared average salaries by management level, education, and gender. Some of the results for entry level managers are shown in the following table.

a. Suppose you want to make an inference about the difference between salaries of male and female entry-level managers who earned a CPA degree, at a 95% level of confidence. Why is this impossible to do using the information in the table?

b. Make the inference, part **a**, assuming the salary standard deviation for male and female entry-level managers with CPAs are $4,000 and $3,000, respectively.

c. Repeat part **b**, but assume the male and female salary standard deviations are $16,000 and $12,000, respectively.

d. Compare the two inferences, parts **b** and **c**.

e. Suppose you want to compare the mean salaries of male entry-level managers with a CPA to the mean salary of male entry-level managers without a CPA degree. Give sample standard deviation values that will yield a significant difference between the two means, at $\alpha = .05$.

f. In your opinion, are the sample standard deviations, part **e**, reasonable values for the salary data? Explain.

7.15 When Firm A combines with Firm B and only Firm A survives, this is called a *merger*. When Firm A and Firm B combine to form Firm C, a new company, this is called a *consolidation*. A third form of business combination occurs when Firm A buys Firm B and both remain in existence.

	CPA DEGREE		BACCALAUREATE DEGREE NO CPA	
	Men	Women	Men	Women
Mean Salary	$40,084	$35,377	$39,268	$33,159
Number of Respondents	48	39	205	177

Source: Schroeder, D. L., and Reichardt, K. E. "Salaries 1994." *Management Accounting,* Vol. 76, No. 12, June 1995, p. 34 (Table 12).

	Merged Firms	Nonmerged Firms
Sample Mean	7.295	14.666
Sample Standard Deviation	7.374	16.089

Source: Wansley, J. W., Roenfeldt, R. L., and Corley, P. L. "Abnormal returns from merger profiles." *Journal of Financial and Quantitative Analysis,* Vol. 18, No. 2, June 1983, pp. 149–162.

This is called an *acquisition* (Lee, Finnerty, and Norton, *Foundations of Financial Management,* 1997). During a recent wave of merger activity, researchers compared the profiles of a sample of 44 firms that merged with those of a sample of 44 firms that did not merge. The table above displays information obtained on the firms' price-earnings ratios (P/E):

a. The analysis indicated that merged firms generally have smaller price-earnings ratios. Do you agree? Test using $\alpha = .05$.

b. Report and interpret the *p*-value of the test you conducted in part **a**.

c. Do you think that the distributions of the price-earnings ratios for the populations from which these samples were drawn are normally distributed? Why or why not? [*Hint:* Note the relative values of the sample means and standard deviations.]

d. How does your answer to part **c** impact the validity of the inference drawn from the analysis? Explain.

7.16 As a country's standard of living increases, so does its production of solid waste. The attendant environmental threat makes solid-waste management an important national problem in many countries of the world. The *International Journal of Environmental Health Research* (Vol. 4, 1994) reported on the solid-waste generation rates (in kilograms per capita per day) for samples of cities from industrialized and middle-income countries. The data are provided in the next table.

Industrialized Countries		Middle-Income Countries	
New York (USA)	2.27	Singapore	0.87
Phoenix (USA)	2.31	Hong Kong	0.85
London (UK)	2.24	Medellin (Colombia)	0.54
Hamburg (Germany)	2.18	Kano (Nigeria)	0.46
Rome (Italy)	2.15	Manila (Philippines)	0.50
		Cairo (Egypt)	0.50
		Tunis (Tunisia)	0.56

a. Based on only a visual inspection of the data, does it appear that the mean waste generation rates of cities in industrialized and middle-income countries differ?

b. Conduct a test of hypothesis (at $\alpha = .05$) to support your observation in part **a**. Use the EXCEL printout below to make your conclusion.

7.17 A recent rash of retirements from the U.S. Senate prompted Middlebury College researchers J. E. Trickett and P. M. Sommers to study the ages and lengths of service of members of Congress (*Chance,* Spring 1996). One question of interest to the researchers is: "Did the 13 senators who decided to retire in 1995–1996 begin their careers at a younger average age than did the rest of their colleagues in the Senate?"

a. The average age at which the 13 retiring senators began their service is 45.783 years; the corresponding average for all other senators is 47.201 years. Is this sufficient information to answer the researchers' question? Explain.

t-Test: Two-Sample Assuming Equal Variances		
	INDUST	MIDDLE
Mean	2.23	0.611428571
Variance	0.00425	0.029880952
Observations	5	7
Pooled Variance	0.019628571	
Hypothesized Mean Difference	0	
df	10	
t Stat	19.73017433	
P(T<=t) one-tail	1.22537E-09	
t Critical one-tail	1.812461505	
P(T<=t)two-tail	2.45073E-09	
t Critical two-tail	2.228139238	

b. The researchers conducted a two-sample *t*-test on the difference between the two means. Specify the null and alternative hypothesis for this test. Clearly define the parameter of interest.

c. The observed significance level for the test, part **b**, was reported as $p = .55$. Interpret this result.

7.18 *Sales quotas* are volume objectives assigned to specific sales units, such as regions, districts, or salespersons' territories. Sometimes to achieve manufacturing efficiency or long-term goals, sales managers set quotas for specific products at challenging levels. The underlying idea is that setting challenging quotas and attaching significant rewards will direct salespersons' efforts along desired paths (Guiltinan and Paul, 1994). The Universal Products Company (real company, fictitious name) manufactures and markets electronic and electromechanical industrial equipment. It has a sales force of over 1,000, organized in 10 districts and 135 branch offices. Salespersons have sales quotas on two specific products, Dataprinters and Micromagnetics, as well as an overall sales volume quota. Many salespersons have complained that having to make the quota on Dataprinters takes so much time that it keeps them from generating a higher overall sales volume. To determine how reducing the Dataprinter quota would affect total sales volume, the sales volumes of a sample of branch offices whose salespersons all worked under the standard quota were compared with the sales volumes of a sample of branch offices whose salespersons all were given a lower Dataprinter quota. Data were collected for a seven-month period and are reported in the next table in terms of total sales per worker-month (in thousands of dollars).

a. What are the appropriate null and alternative hypotheses for testing whether salespersons on the two types of quotas differ in their mean sales per worker-month? Define any symbols you use.

b. The data in the table are submitted to MINITAB, with results as shown below. What do you conclude about the test set up in part **a**?

c. Interpret the confidence interval. Does its width imply that little or much information

Branch	Lower Quota	Standard Quota
1		17.7
2	15.6	
3		15.1
4	14.0	
5		12.3
6		12.0
7	11.2	
8	11.0	
9		10.5
10	10.3	
11		10.0
12	9.4	

Source: Adapted from Winer, L. "The effect of product sales quotas on sales force productivity." *Journal of Marketing Research,* Vol. 10, May 1973.

about the difference in mean sales is contained in these data? How could the amount of information be increased?

7.19 Since the emergence of Japan as an industrial superpower in the 1970s and 1980s, U.S. businesses have paid close attention to Japanese management styles and philosophies. Some of the credit for the high quality of Japanese products is attributed to the Japanese system of permanent employment for their workers. In the United States, high job turnover rates are common in many industries and are associated with high product defect rates. High turnover rates mean U.S. plants have more inexperienced workers who are unfamiliar with the company's product lines than Japan has (Stevenson, *Production/Operations Management,* 1996). For example, in a study of the air conditioner industry in Japan and the United States, the difference in the average annual turnover rate of workers between U.S. plants and Japanese plants was reported as 3.1% (*Harvard Business Review,* Sept.–Oct. 1983). In a more recent study, five Japanese and five U.S. plants that manufacture air conditioners were randomly sampled; their turnover rates and a MINITAB descriptive statistics printout are shown at the top of page 341.

a. Do the data provide sufficient evidence to indicate that the mean annual percentage

```
TWOSAMPLE T FOR LOWER VS STANDARD
              N      MEAN     STDEV    SE MEAN
LOWER         6      11.92    2.38     0.97
STANDARD      6      12.93    2.94     1.2

95 PCT CI FOR MU LOWER - MU STANDARD: (-4.51, 2.5)

TTEST MU LOWER = MU STANDARD (VS NE): T= -0.66  P=0.53  DF= 9
```

```
TWOSAMPLE T FOR US VS JAPAN
              N       MEAN      STDEV    SE MEAN
    US        5       6.56      1.22      0.54
    JAPAN     5       3.12      1.23      0.55

    95 PCT CI FOR MU US - MU JAPAN: (1.62, 5.27)

    TTEST MU US = MU JAPAN (VS NE): T= 4.46   P=0.0031   DF= 7
```

U.S. Plants	Japanese Plants
7.11%	3.52%
6.06	2.02
8.00	4.91
6.87	3.22
4.77	1.92

turnover for U.S. plants exceeds the corresponding mean percentage for Japanese plants? Test using $\alpha = .05$.

b. Report and interpret the observed significance level of the test you conducted in part **a**.

c. List any assumptions you made in conducting the hypothesis test of part **a**. Comment on their validity for this application.

7.20 Suppose you manage a plant that purifies its liquid waste and discharges the water into a local river. An EPA inspector has collected water specimens of the discharge of your plant and also water specimens in the river upstream from your plant. Each water specimen is divided into five parts, the bacteria count is read on each, and the mean count for each specimen is reported. The average bacteria counts for each of six specimens are reported in the following table for the two locations.

Plant Discharge			Upstream		
30.1	36.2	33.4	29.7	30.3	26.4
28.2	29.8	34.9	27.3	31.7	32.3

a. Why might the bacteria counts shown here tend to be approximately normally distributed?

b. What are the appropriate null and alternative hypotheses to test whether the mean bacteria count for the plant discharge exceeds that for the upstream location? Be sure to define any symbols you use.

c. When the data are submitted to SPSS, part of the output is shown at the bottom of the page. Carefully interpret this output.

d. What assumptions are necessary to ensure the validity of this test?

7.21 While cable television companies in Minnesota are prohibited from holding exclusive rights to an area, the laws do not demand that a company face competition (*Minneapolis Star-Tribune*, Jan. 10, 1993). Many subscribers feel that these de facto monopolies exploit consumers by charging excessive monthly cable fees. Suppose a congressional subcommittee considering regulation of the cable industry investigates whether cable rates are higher in areas with no competition than in areas with competition. They randomly sample basic rates for six cable companies that have no competition and for six companies that face competition (but not from each other). The observed rates are shown in the table at the top of page 342.

a. What are the appropriate null and alternative hypotheses to test the research hypothesis of the subcommittee?

```
Independent samples of  LOCATION

Group 1:  LOCATION EQ        1.00              Group 2:  LOCATION EQ      2.00
t-test for:  BACOUNT

                        Number                   Standard      Standard
                      of Cases      Mean         Deviation      Error
          Group 1        6         32.1000         3.189        1.302
          Group 2        6         29.6167         2.355         .961

              Pooled Variance Estimate    Separate Variance Estimate
    F    2-Tail         t    Degrees of  2-Tail      t     Degrees of  2-Tail
  Value  Prob.       Value   Freedom      Prob.    Value    Freedom     Prob.
  1.83    .522        1.53      10         .156     1.53      9.20       .159
```

No competition	$18.44	$26.88	$22.87	$25.78	$23.34	$27.52
Competition	$18.95	$23.74	$17.25	$20.14	$18.98	$20.14

b. Conduct the test of part **a** using $\alpha = .05$. Report and interpret the approximate significance level of the test.

c. What assumptions are necessary to ensure the validity of the test? Why does it matter that none of the companies in the sample compete against each other?

7.22 Research reported in the *Professional Geographer* (May 1992) examines the hypothesis that the disproportionate housework responsibility of women in two-income households is a major factor in determining the proximity of a woman's place of employment. The distance to work for both men and women in two-income households is reported in the next table for random samples of both central city and suburban residences.

a. For central city residences, calculate a 99% confidence interval for the difference in aver-

	CENTRAL CITY RESIDENCE		SUBURBAN RESIDENCE	
	Men	Women	Men	Women
n	159	119	138	93
$\bar{x}$	7.4	4.5	9.3	6.6
s	6.3	4.2	7.1	5.6

age distance to work for men and women in two-income households. Interpret the interval.

b. Repeat part **a** for suburban residences.

c. Interpret the confidence intervals. Do they indicate that women tend to work closer to home than men?

d. What assumptions have you made to assure the validity of the confidence intervals constructed in parts **a** and **b**?

7.2   COMPARING TWO POPULATION MEANS: PAIRED DIFFERENCE EXPERIMENTS

Suppose you want to compare the mean daily sales of two restaurants located in the same city. If you were to record the restaurants' total sales for each of 12 randomly selected days during a six-month period, the results might appear as shown in Table 7.4. An SPSS printout of descriptive statistics for the data is displayed in Figure 7.9. Do these data provide evidence of a difference between the mean daily sales of the two restaurants?

TABLE 7.4   Daily Sales for Two Restaurants

Day	Restaurant 1	Restaurant 2
1 (Wednesday)	$1,005	$ 918
2 (Saturday)	2,073	1,971
3 (Tuesday)	873	825
4 (Wednesday)	1,074	999
5 (Friday)	1,932	1,827
6 (Thursday)	1,338	1,281
7 (Thursday)	1,449	1,302
8 (Monday)	759	678
9 (Friday)	1,905	1,782
10 (Monday)	693	639
11 (Saturday)	2,106	2,049
12 (Tuesday)	981	933

FIGURE 7.9
SPSS printout for daily restaurant sales

```
Number of Valid Observations (Listwise) =        12.00

Variable      Mean      Std Dev    Minimum    Maximum      N   Label

REST1       1349.00     530.07     693.00    2106.00      12
REST2       1267.00     516.04     639.00    2049.00      12
```

We want to test the null hypothesis that the mean daily sales, μ_1 and μ_2, for the two restaurants are equal against the alternative hypothesis that they differ, i.e.,

$$H_0: (\mu_1 - \mu_2) = 0$$

$$H_a: (\mu_1 - \mu_2) \neq 0$$

If we employ the t statistic for independent samples (Section 7.1) we first calculate s_p^2 using the values of s_1 and s_2 highlighted on the SPSS printout:

$$s_p^2 = \frac{(n_1 - 1)s_1^2 + (n_2 - 1)s_2^2}{n_1 + n_2 - 2}$$

$$= \frac{(12 - 1)(530.07)^2 + (12 - 1)(516.04)^2}{12 + 12 - 2} = 273{,}630.6$$

Then we substitute the values of $\bar{x}_1$ and $\bar{x}_2$, also highlighted on the printout, to form the test statistic:

$$t = \frac{(\bar{x}_1 - \bar{x}_2) - 0}{\sqrt{s_p^2\left(\dfrac{1}{n_1} + \dfrac{1}{n_2}\right)}} = \frac{(1{,}349.00 - 1{,}267.00)}{\sqrt{273{,}630.6\left(\dfrac{1}{12} + \dfrac{1}{12}\right)}} = \frac{82.0}{213.54} = .38$$

This small t value will not lead to rejection of H_0 when compared to the t-distribution with $n_1 + n_2 - 2 = 22$ df, even if α were chosen as large as .20 ($t_{\alpha/2} = t_{.10} = 1.321$). Thus, from *this* analysis we might conclude that insufficient evidence exists to infer that there is a difference in mean daily sales for the two restaurants.

However, if you examine the data in Table 7.4 more closely, you will find this conclusion difficult to accept. The sales of restaurant 1 exceed those of restaurant 2 *for every one of the randomly selected 12 days.* This, in itself, is strong evidence to indicate that μ_1 differs from μ_2, and we will subsequently confirm this fact. Why, then, was the t-test unable to detect this difference? The answer is: *The independent samples* t*-test is not a valid procedure to use with this set of data.*

The t-test is inappropriate because the assumption of independent samples is invalid. We have randomly chosen *days*, and thus, once we have chosen the sample of days for restaurant 1, we have *not* independently chosen the sample of days for restaurant 2. The dependence between observations within days can be seen by examining the pairs of daily sales, which tend to rise and fall together as we go from day to day. This pattern provides strong visual evidence of a violation of the assumption of independence required for the two-sample t-test of Section 7.1. In this situation, you will note the *large variation within samples* (reflected by the large value of s_p^2) in comparison to the relatively *small difference between the sample means.* Because s_p^2 is so large, the t-test of Section 7.1 is unable to detect a possible difference between μ_1 and μ_2.

We now consider a valid method of analyzing the data of Table 7.4. In Table 7.5 we add the column of differences between the daily sales of the two restaurants. We can regard these daily differences in sales as a random sample of all daily differences, past and present. Then we can use this sample to make inferences about the mean of the population of differences, μ_D, which is equal to the difference $(\mu_1 - \mu_2)$. That is, the mean of the population (and sample) of differences equals the difference between the population (and sample) means. Thus, our test becomes

$$H_0: \mu_D = 0 \qquad (\mu_1 - \mu_2) = 0$$

$$H_a: \mu_D \neq 0 \qquad (\mu_1 - \mu_2) \neq 0$$

TABLE 7.5   Daily Sales and Differences for Two Restaurants

Day	Restaurant 1	Restaurant 2	Restaurant 1 − Restaurant 2
1 (Wednesday)	$1,005	$ 918	$ 87
2 (Saturday)	2,073	1,971	102
3 (Tuesday)	873	825	48
4 (Wednesday)	1,074	999	75
5 (Friday)	1,932	1,827	105
6 (Thursday)	1,338	1,281	57
7 (Thursday)	1,449	1,302	147
8 (Monday)	759	678	81
9 (Friday)	1,905	1,782	123
10 (Monday)	693	639	54
11 (Saturday)	2,106	2,049	57
12 (Tuesday)	981	933	48

The test statistic is a one-sample t (Section 6.4), since we are now analyzing a single sample of differences for small n:

$$\text{Test statistic: } t = \frac{\bar{x}_D - 0}{s_D / \sqrt{n_D}}$$

where $\bar{x}_D$ = Sample mean difference

s_D = Sample standard deviation of differences

n_D = Number of differences = Number of pairs

Assumptions: The population of differences in daily sales is approximately normally distributed. The sample differences are randomly selected from the population differences. [*Note:* We do not need to make the assumption that $\sigma_1^2 = \sigma_2^2$.]

Rejection region: At significance level $\alpha = .05$, we will reject H_0 if $|t| > t_{.05}$, where $t_{.05}$ is based on $(n_D - 1)$ degrees of freedom.

Referring to Table IV in Appendix B, we find the t value corresponding to $\alpha = .025$ and $n_D - 1 = 12 - 1 = 11$ df to be $t_{.025} = 2.201$. Then we will reject the null hypothesis if $|t| > 2.201$, (see Figure 7.10). Note that the number of degrees of freedom has decreased from $n_1 + n_2 - 2 = 22$ to 11 when we use the paired difference experiment rather than the two independent random samples design.

Summary statistics for the $n = 12$ differences are shown on the MINITAB printout, Figure 7.11. Note that $\bar{x}_D = 82.0$ and $s_D = 32.0$ (rounded). Substituting these values into the formula for the test statistic, we have

FIGURE 7.10
Rejection region
for restaurant sales
example

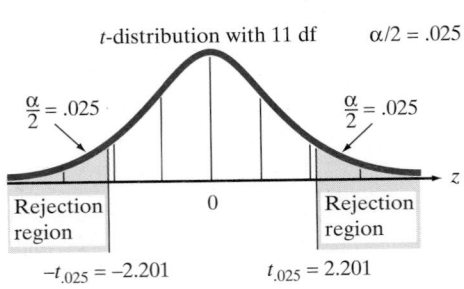

t-distribution with 11 df $\alpha/2 = .025$

$\frac{\alpha}{2} = .025$ $\frac{\alpha}{2} = .025$

Rejection region   0   Rejection region

$-t_{.025} = -2.201$ $t_{.025} = 2.201$

FIGURE 7.11
MINITAB analysis of
differences in Table 7.5

```
TEST OF MU =   0.000 VS MU N.E.   0.000

                 N        MEAN     STDEV    SE MEAN          T      P VALUE
DIFF            12      82.000    31.989      9.234       8.88       0.0000
```

$$t = \frac{\bar{x}_D - 0}{s_D / \sqrt{n_D}} = \frac{82}{32/\sqrt{12}} = 8.88$$

Because this value of t falls in the rejection region, we conclude (at $\alpha = .05$) that the difference in population mean daily sales for the two restaurants differs from 0. We can reach the same conclusion by noting that the p-value of the test, highlighted in Figure 7.11, is approximately 0. The fact that $\bar{x}_1 - \bar{x}_2 = \bar{x}_D = \$82.00$ strongly suggests that the mean daily sales for restaurant 1 exceeds the mean daily sales for restaurant 2.

This kind of experiment, in which observations are paired and the differences are analyzed, is called a **paired difference experiment**. In many cases, a paired difference experiment can provide more information about the difference between population means than an independent samples experiment. The idea is to compare population means by comparing the differences between pairs of experimental units (objects, people, etc.) that were very similar prior to the experiment. The differencing removes sources of variation that tend to inflate σ^2. For instance, in the restaurant example, the day-to-day variability in daily sales is removed by analyzing the differences between the restaurants' daily sales. Making comparisons within groups of similar experimental units is called **blocking**, and the paired difference experiment is an example of a **randomized block experiment**. In our example, the days represent the blocks.

Some other examples for which the paired difference experiment might be appropriate are the following:

1. Suppose you want to estimate the difference ($\mu_1 - \mu_2$) in mean price per gallon between two major brands of premium gasoline. If you choose two independent random samples of stations for each brand, the variability in price due to geographic location may be large. To eliminate this source of variability you could choose pairs of stations of similar size, one station for each brand, in close geographic proximity and use the sample of differences between the prices of the brands to make an inference about ($\mu_1 - \mu_2$).

2. A college placement center wants to estimate the difference ($\mu_1 - \mu_2$) in mean starting salaries for men and women graduates who seek jobs through the center. If it independently samples men and women, the starting salaries may vary because of their different college majors and differences in grade point averages. To eliminate these sources of variability, the placement center could match male and female job seekers according to their majors and grade point averages. Then the differences between the starting salaries of each pair in the sample could be used to make an inference about ($\mu_1 - \mu_2$).

3. To compare the performance of two automobile salespeople, we might test a hypothesis about the difference ($\mu_1 - \mu_2$) in their respective mean monthly sales. If we randomly choose n_1 months of salesperson 1's sales and independently choose n_2 months of salesperson 2's sales, the month-to-month variability caused by the seasonal nature of new car sales might inflate s_p^2 and prevent the two-sample t statistic from detecting a difference between

μ_1 and μ_2, if such a difference actually exists. However, by taking the difference in monthly sales for the two salespeople for each of n months, we eliminate the month-to-month variability (seasonal variation) in sales, and the probability of detecting a difference between μ_1 and μ_2, if a difference exists, is increased.

The hypothesis-testing procedures and the method of forming confidence intervals for the difference between two means using a paired difference experiment are summarized in the boxes for both large and small n.

Paired Difference Confidence Interval for $\mu_D = \mu_1 - \mu_2$

Large Sample

$$\bar{x}_D \pm z_{\alpha/2}\frac{\sigma_D}{\sqrt{n_D}} \approx \bar{x}_D \pm z_{\alpha/2}\frac{s_D}{\sqrt{n_D}}$$

Assumption: The sample differences are randomly selected from the population of differences.

Small Sample

$$\bar{x}_D \pm t_{\alpha/2}\frac{s_D}{\sqrt{n_D}}$$

where $t_{\alpha/2}$ is based on $(n_D - 1)$ degrees of freedom

Assumptions: 1. The relative frequency distribution of the population of differences is normal.
2. The sample differences are randomly selected from the population of differences.

Paired Difference Test of Hypothesis for $\mu_D = \mu_1 - \mu_2$

One-Tailed Test

$H_0: \mu_D = D_0$

$H_a: \mu_D < D_0$
[or $H_a: \mu_D > D_0$]

Two-Tailed Test

$H_0: \mu_D = D_0$

$H_a: \mu_D \neq D_0$

Large Sample

Test statistic:
$$z = \frac{\bar{x}_D - D_0}{\sigma_D/\sqrt{n_D}} \approx \frac{\bar{x}_D - D_0}{s_D/\sqrt{n_D}}$$

Rejection region: $z < -z_\alpha$
[or $z > z_\alpha$ when $H_a: \mu_D > D_0$]

Rejection region: $|z| > z_{\alpha/2}$

Assumption: The differences are randomly selected from the population of differences.

Small Sample

Test statistic:
$$t = \frac{\bar{x}_D - D_0}{s_D/\sqrt{n_D}}$$

Rejection region: $t < -t_\alpha$
[or $t > t_\alpha$ when $H_a: \mu_D > D_0$]

Rejection region: $|t| > t_{\alpha/2}$

where t_α and $t_{\alpha/2}$ are based on $(n_D - 1)$ degrees of freedom

> *Assumptions:* **1.** The relative frequency distribution of the population of differences is normal.
>
> **2.** The differences are randomly selected from the population of differences.

EXAMPLE 7.5

An experiment is conducted to compare the starting salaries of male and female college graduates who find jobs. Pairs are formed by choosing a male and a female with the same major and similar grade point averages (GPAs). Suppose a random sample of 10 pairs is formed in this manner and the starting annual salary of each person is recorded. The results are shown in Table 7.6. Compare the mean starting salary, μ_1, for males to the mean starting salary, μ_2, for females using a 95% confidence interval. Interpret the results.

SOLUTION

Since the data on annual salary are collected in pairs of males and females matched on GPA and major, a paired difference experiment is performed. To conduct the analysis, we first compute the differences between the salaries, as shown in Table 7.6. Summary statistics for these $n = 10$ differences are displayed in the MINITAB printout, Figure 7.12.

The 95% confidence interval for $\mu_D = (\mu_1 - \mu_2)$ for this small sample is

$$\bar{x}_D \pm t_{\alpha/2}\frac{s_D}{\sqrt{n_D}}$$

where $t_{\alpha/2} = t_{.025} = 2.262$ (obtained from Table VI, Appendix B) is based on $n - 2 = 8$ degrees of freedom. Substituting the values of $\bar{x}_D$ and s_D shown on the printout, we obtain

$$\bar{x}_D \pm 2.262\frac{s_D}{\sqrt{n_D}} = 400 \pm 2.262\left(\frac{434.613}{\sqrt{10}}\right)$$

$$= 400 \pm 310.88 \approx 400 \pm 311 = (\$89, \$711)$$

[*Note:* This interval is also shown on the MINITAB printout, Figure 7.12.] Our interpretation is that the true mean difference between the starting salaries of males and females falls between $89 and $711, with 95% confidence. Since the interval falls above 0, we infer that $\mu_1 - \mu_2 > 0$, that is, that the mean salary for males exceeds the mean salary for females.

To measure the amount of information about $(\mu_1 - \mu_2)$ gained by using a paired difference experiment in Example 7.5 rather than an independent samples

---

TABLE 7.6 Data on Annual Salaries for Matched Pairs of College Graduates

Pair	Male	Female	Difference (Male–Female)	Pair	Male	Female	Difference (Male–Female)
1	$29,300	$28,800	$ 500	6	$27,800	$28,000	$−200
2	31,500	31,600	−100	7	29,500	29,200	300
3	30,400	29,800	600	8	31,200	30,100	1,100
4	28,500	28,500	0	9	28,400	28,200	200
5	33,500	32,600	900	10	29,200	28,500	700

FIGURE 7.12
MINITAB analysis of differences in Table 7.6

	N	MEAN	STDEV	SE MEAN	95.0 PERCENT C.I.
DIFF	10	400.000	434.613	137.437	(89.013, 710.987)

FIGURE 7.13

MINITAB analysis of data in Table 7.6, assuming independent samples

```
TWOSAMPLE T FOR C1 VS C2
         N      MEAN      STDEV   SE MEAN
C1   10        29930      1735       549
C2   10        29530      1527       483

95 PCT CI FOR MU C1 - MU C2:  (-1136, 1936)

TTEST MU C1 = MU C2 (VS NE):  T= 0.55   P=0.59   DF=  18

POOLED STDEV =          1634
```

experiment, we can compare the relative widths of the confidence intervals obtained by the two methods. A 95% confidence interval for $(\mu_1 - \mu_2)$ using the paired difference experiment is, from Example 7.5, ($89, $711). If we analyzed the same data as though this were an independent samples experiment,* we would first obtain the descriptive statistics shown in the MINITAB printout, Figure 7.13.

Then we substitute the sample means and standard deviations shown on the printout into the formula for a 95% confidence interval for $(\mu_1 - \mu_2)$ using independent samples:

$$(\bar{x}_1 - \bar{x}_2) \pm t_{.025} \sqrt{s_p^2 \left(\frac{1}{n_1} + \frac{1}{n_2}\right)}$$

where

$$s_p^2 = \frac{(n_1 - 1)s_1^2 + (n_2 - 1)s_2^2}{n_1 + n_2 - 2}$$

MINITAB performed these calculations and obtained the interval $(-$1,136, $1,936)$. This interval is highlighted on Figure 7.13.

Notice that the independent samples interval includes 0. Consequently, if we were to use this interval to make an inference about $(\mu_1 - \mu_2)$, we would incorrectly conclude that the mean starting salaries of males and females do not differ! You can see that the confidence interval for the independent sampling experiment is about five times wider than for the corresponding paired difference confidence interval. Blocking out the variability due to differences in majors and grade point averages significantly increases the information about the difference in male and female mean starting salaries by providing a much more accurate (smaller confidence interval for the same confidence coefficient) estimate of $(\mu_1 - \mu_2)$.

You may wonder whether conducting a paired difference experiment is always superior to an independent samples experiment. The answer is: Most of the time, but not always. We sacrifice half the degrees of freedom in the t statistic when a paired difference design is used instead of an independent samples design. This is a loss of information, and unless this loss is more than compensated for by the reduction in variability obtained by blocking (pairing), the paired difference experiment will result in a net loss of information about $(\mu_1 - \mu_2)$. Thus, we should be convinced that the pairing will significantly reduce variability before performing the paired difference experiment. Most of the time this will happen.

*This is done only to provide a measure of the increase in the amount of information obtained by a paired design in comparison to an unpaired design. Actually, if an experiment is designed using pairing, an unpaired analysis would be invalid because the assumption of independent samples would not be satisfied.

Note: The pairing of the observations is determined before the experiment is performed (that is, by the *design* of the experiment). A paired difference experiment is *never* obtained by pairing the sample observations after the measurements have been acquired. Nonparametric methods are available for analyzing paired data when the assumptions are not satisfied. One such test is discussed in optional Section 7.6.

EXERCISES   7.23–7.35

Note: Exercises marked with 💾 *contain data for computer analysis on a 3.5" disk (file name in parentheses).*

Learning the Mechanics

7.23 A paired difference experiment yielded n_D pairs of observations. In each case, what is the rejection region for testing H_0: $\mu_D > 2$?
a. $n_D = 12, \alpha = .05$ **b.** $n_D = 24, \alpha = .10$
c. $n_D = 4, \alpha = .025$ **d.** $n_D = 8, \alpha = .01$

7.24 The data for a random sample of six paired observations are shown in the next table.

Pair	Sample from Population 1 Observation 1	Sample from Population 2 Observation 2
1	7	4
2	3	1
3	9	7
4	6	2
5	4	4
6	8	7

a. Calculate the difference between each pair of observations by subtracting observation 2 from observation 1. Use the differences to calculate $\bar{x}_D$ and s_D^2.
b. If μ_1 and μ_2 are the means of populations 1 and 2, respectively, express μ_D in terms of μ_1 and μ_2.
c. Form a 95% confidence interval for μ_D.

d. Test the null hypothesis H_0: $\mu_D = 0$ against the alternative hypothesis H_a: $\mu_D \neq 0$. Use $\alpha = .05$.

7.25 The data for a random sample of 10 paired observations are shown in the accompanying table.

Pair	Sample from Population 1	Sample from Population 2
1	19	24
2	25	27
3	31	36
4	52	53
5	49	55
6	34	34
7	59	66
8	47	51
9	17	20
10	51	55

a. If you wish to test whether these data are sufficient to indicate that the mean for population 2 is larger than that for population 1, what are the appropriate null and alternative hypotheses? Define any symbols you use.
b. The data are analyzed using MINITAB, with the results shown below. Interpret these results.
c. The output of MINITAB also included a confidence interval. Interpret this output.
d. What assumptions are necessary to ensure the validity of this analysis?

```
TEST OF MU = 0.000 VS MU L.T. 0.000

           N      MEAN     STDEV   SE MEAN      T     P VALUE
DIFF      10    -3.700     2.214     0.700    -5.29    0.0002
-----------------------------------------------------------
           N      MEAN     STDEV   SE MEAN    95.0 PERCENT C.I.
DIFF      10    -3.700     2.214     0.700   ( -5.284,  -2.116)
```

7.26 A paired difference experiment produced the following data:

$$n_D = 18 \quad \bar{x}_1 = 92 \quad \bar{x}_2 = 95.5 \quad \bar{x}_D = -3.5 \quad s_D^2 = 21$$

a. Determine the values of t for which the null hypothesis, $\mu_1 - \mu_2 = 0$, would be rejected in favor of the alternative hypothesis, $\mu_1 - \mu_2 < 0$. Use $\alpha = .10$.

b. Conduct the paired difference test described in part **a**. Draw the appropriate conclusions.

c. What assumptions are necessary so that the paired difference test will be valid?

d. Find a 90% confidence interval for the mean difference μ_D.

e. Which of the two inferential procedures, the confidence interval of part **d** or the test of hypothesis of part **b**, provides more information about the differences between the population means?

7.27 A paired difference experiment yielded the data shown in the next table.

Pair	x	y	Pair	x	y
1	55	44	5	75	62
2	68	55	6	52	38
3	40	25	7	49	31
4	55	56			

a. Test $H_0: \mu_D = 10$ against $H_a: \mu_D \neq 10$, where $\mu_D = (\mu_1 - \mu_2)$. Use $\alpha = .05$.

b. Report the p-value for the test you conducted in part **a**. Interpret the p-value.

Applying the Concepts

7.28 It has been estimated that U.S. companies spend more than $500 million annually on service recognition programs for their employees. Such programs reward workers for such things as years of service, attendance, high-quality work, customer service, suggestions, and safety ("Dispelling the myths about service recognition programs," *Potentials in Marketing*, Feb. 1996). Before instituting a new employee service recognition program in its manufacturing plant, a company randomly sampled eight workers and measured their productivity in terms of the number of items produced per day. A year after the start of the service recognition program the productivity of seven of these workers was reevaluated. (The eighth had been promoted in the interim.) These productivity data are shown in the next table.

a. Do these data provide evidence that the service recognition program has helped to increase worker productivity? Test using $\alpha = .10$, and clearly state any assumptions you make in conducting the test.

Employee ID Number	August 1996	August 1997
1011	10	9
0033	9	11
0998	12	14
0006	8	9
1802	10	9
0246	11	14
0777	14	—
1112	11	13

b. Discuss how the one-year gap between productivity evaluations could weaken the results of the study.

7.29 Facility layout and material flowpath design are major factors in the productivity analysis of automated manufacturing systems. Facility layout is concerned with the location arrangement of machines and buffers for work-in-process. Flowpath design is concerned with the direction of manufacturing material flows (e.g., unidirectional or bidirectional) (Lee, Lei, and Pinedo, *Annals of Operations Research*, 1997). A manufacturer of printed circuit boards (PCBs) is interested in evaluating two alternative existing layout and flowpath designs. The output of each design was monitored for eight consecutive working days.

Working Days	Design 1	Design 2
8/16	1,220 units	1,273 units
8/17	1,092 units	1,363 units
8/18	1,136 units	1,342 units
8/19	1,205 units	1,471 units
8/20	1,086 units	1,299 units
8/23	1,274 units	1,457 units
8/24	1,145 units	1,263 units
8/25	1,281 units	1,368 units

a. Construct a 95% confidence interval for the difference in mean daily output of the two designs.

b. What assumptions must hold to ensure the validity of the confidence interval?

c. Design 2 appears to be superior to Design 1. Is this confirmed by the confidence interval? Explain.

7.30 A manufacturer of automobile shock absorbers was interested in comparing the durability of its shocks with that of the shocks produced by its biggest competitor. To make the comparison, one of the manufacturer's and one of the competitor's shocks were randomly selected and installed on the rear wheels of each of six cars. After the cars had been driven 20,000 miles, the strength of each test shock was measured, coded, and recorded; results are shown in the next table.

Car Number	Manufacturer's Shock	Competitor's Shock
1	8.8	8.4
2	10.5	10.1
3	12.5	12.0
4	9.7	9.3
5	9.6	9.0
6	13.2	13.0

a. Do the data present sufficient evidence to conclude that there is a difference in the mean strength of the two types of shocks after 20,000 miles of use? Use $\alpha = .05$.

b. Find the approximate observed significance level for the test, and interpret its value.

c. What assumptions are necessary to apply a paired difference analysis to the data?

d. Construct a 95% confidence interval for $(\mu_1 - \mu_2)$. Interpret the confidence interval.

7.31 Suppose the data in Exercise 7.30 are based on independent random samples.

a. Do the data provide sufficient evidence to indicate a difference between the mean strengths for the two types of shocks? Use $\alpha = .05$.

b. Construct a 95% confidence interval for $(\mu_1 - \mu_2)$. Interpret your result.

c. Compare the confidence intervals you obtained in Exercise 7.30 and in part **b** of this exercise. Which is wider? To what do you attribute the difference in width? Assuming in each case that the appropriate assumptions are satisfied, which interval provides you with more information about $(\mu_1 - \mu_2)$? Explain.

d. Are the results of an unpaired analysis valid if the data come from a paired experiment?

7.32 (X07.032) A *pupillometer* is a device used to observe changes in pupil dilations as the eye is exposed to different visual stimuli. Since there is a direct correlation between the amount an individual's pupil dilates and his or her interest in the stimuli, marketing organizations sometimes use pupillometers to help them evaluate potential consumer interest in new products, alternative package designs, and other factors (McLaren, Fjerstad, and Brubaker, *Optical Engineering*, Mar. 1995). The Design and Market Research Laboratories of the Container Corporation of America used a pupillometer to evaluate consumer reaction to different silverware patterns for a client (McGuire, 1973). Suppose 15 consumers were chosen at random, and each was shown two silverware patterns. Their pupillometer readings (in millimeters) are shown in the table below.

a. What are the appropriate null and alternative hypotheses to test whether the mean amount of pupil dilation differs for the two patterns? Define any symbols you use.

b. The data were analyzed using MINITAB, with the results shown in the printout below. Interpret these results.

c. Is the paired difference design used for this study preferable to an independent samples design? For independent samples we could select 30 consumers, divide them into two groups of 15, and show each group a different pattern. Explain your preference.

7.33 Twice a year *The Wall Street Journal* asks a panel of economists to forecast interest rates, inflation rates, growth in Gross Domestic Product, and other economic variables. The table at the top of page 352

Consumer	Pattern 1	Pattern 2	Consumer	Pattern 1	Pattern 2
1	1.00	.80	9	.98	.91
2	.97	.66	10	1.46	1.10
3	1.45	1.22	11	1.85	1.60
4	1.21	1.00	12	.33	.21
5	.77	.81	13	1.77	1.50
6	1.32	1.11	14	.85	.65
7	1.81	1.30	15	.15	.05
8	.91	.32			

```
TEST OF MU = 0.000 VS MU N.E. 0.000

        N     MEAN    STDEV    SE MEAN      T     P VALUE
DIFF   15     .239    .161      .0415     5.76    0.0000

        N     MEAN    STDEV    SE MEAN    95.0 PERCENT CI
DIFF   15     .239    .161      .0415      (.150,  .328)
```

INFLATION FORECASTS (IN PERCENT)		
	June 1995 Forecast for 11/95	January 1996 Forecast for 11/96
Maureen Allyn	3.1	2.4
Wayne Angell	3.4	3.1
David Blitzer	3.0	3.1
Michael Cosgrove	4.0	3.5
Gail Fosler	3.7	3.8
Irwin Kellner	3.3	2.3
Donald Ratajczak	3.5	2.9
Thomas Synott	3.5	3.2
John Williams	3.3	2.6

Source: Wall Street Journal, January 2, 1996.

reports the inflation forecasts made in June 1995 and in January 1996 by nine randomly selected members of the panel.

a. As a group, were the economists more optimistic about the prospects for low inflation in late 1996 than they were for late 1995? Specify the hypotheses to be tested.

b. Conduct the hypothesis testing using $\alpha = .05$ and answer the question proposed in part **a**.

7.34 A study reported in the *Journal of Psychology* (Mar. 1991) measures the change in female students' self-concepts as they move from high school to college. A sample of 133 Boston College first-year female students was selected for the study. Each was asked to evaluate several aspects of her life at two points in time: at the end of her senior year of high school, and during her sophomore year of college. Each student was asked to evaluate where she believed she stood on a scale that ranged from top 10% of class (1) to lowest 10% of class (5). The results for three of the traits evaluated are reported in the table below.

a. What null and alternative hypotheses would you test to determine whether the mean self-concept of females decreases between the senior year of high school and the sophomore year of college as measured by each of these three traits?

b. Are these traits more appropriately analyzed using an independent samples test or a paired difference test? Explain.

c. Noting the size of the sample, what assumptions are necessary to ensure the validity of the tests?

d. The article reports that the leadership test results in a p-value greater than .05, while the tests for popularity and intellectual self-confidence result in p-values less than .05. Interpret these results.

7.35 (X07.035) Merck Research Labs conducted an experiment to evaluate the effect of a new drug using the single-T swim maze. Nineteen impregnated dam rats were captured and allocated a dosage of 12.5 milligrams of the drug. One male and one female rat pup were randomly selected from each resulting litter to perform in the swim maze. Each pup was placed in the water at one end of the maze and allowed to swim until it escaped at the opposite end. If the pup failed to escape after a certain period of time, it was placed at the beginning of the maze and given another chance. The experiment was repeated until each pup accomplished three successful escapes. The table on page 353 reports the number of swims required by each pup to perform three successful escapes. Is there sufficient evidence of a difference between the mean number of swims required

Trait	n	SENIOR YEAR OF HIGH SCHOOL $\bar{x}$	SOPHOMORE YEAR OF COLLEGE $\bar{x}$
Leadership	133	2.09	2.33
Popularity	133	2.48	2.69
Intellectual self-confidence	133	2.29	2.55

Litter	Male	Female	Litter	Male	Female
1	8	5	11	6	5
2	8	4	12	6	3
3	6	7	13	12	5
4	6	3	14	3	8
5	6	5	15	3	4
6	6	3	16	8	12
7	3	8	17	3	6
8	5	10	18	6	4
9	4	4	19	9	5
10	4	4			

Source: Thomas E. Bradstreet, Merck Research Labs, BL 3-2, West Point, PA 19486

```
TEST OF MU = 0.000 VS MU N.E. 0.000

             N      MEAN    STDEV    SE MEAN       T    P VALUE
SwimDiff    19     0.368    3.515      0.806    0.46      0.65
```

by male and female pups? Use the accompanying MINITAB printout to conduct the test (at $\alpha = $ .10). Comment on the assumptions required for the test to be valid.

7.3   DETERMINING THE SAMPLE SIZE

You can find the appropriate sample size to estimate the difference between a pair of parameters with a specified degree of reliability by using the method described in Section 5.4. That is, to estimate the difference between a pair of parameters correct to within B units with probability $(1 - \alpha)$, let $z_{\alpha/2}$ standard deviations of the sampling distribution of the estimator equal B. Then solve for the sample size. To do this, you have to solve the problem for a specific ratio between n_1 and n_2. Most often, you will want to have equal sample sizes, that is, $n_1 = n_2 = n$. We will illustrate the procedure for means with two examples.

EXAMPLE 7.6

New fertilizer compounds are often advertised with the promise of increased crop yields. Suppose we want to compare the mean yield μ_1 of wheat when a new fertilizer is used to the mean yield μ_2 with a fertilizer in common use. The estimate of the difference in mean yield per acre is to be correct to within .25 bushel with a confidence coefficient of .95. If the sample sizes are to be equal, find $n_1 = n_2 = n$, the number of one-acre plots of wheat assigned to each fertilizer.

SOLUTION

To solve the problem, you need to know something about the variation in the bushels of yield per acre. Suppose from past records you know the yields of wheat possess a range of approximately 10 bushels per acre. You could then approximate $\sigma_1 = \sigma_2 = \sigma$ by letting the range equal 4σ. Thus,

$$4\sigma \approx 10 \text{ bushels}$$

$$\sigma \approx 2.5 \text{ bushels}$$

The next step is to solve the equation

$$z_{\alpha/2}\sigma_{(\bar{x}_1 - \bar{x}_2)} = B \quad \text{or} \quad z_{\alpha/2}\sqrt{\frac{\sigma_1^2}{n_1} + \frac{\sigma_2^2}{n_2}} = B$$

for n, where $n = n_1 = n_2$. Since we want the estimate to lie within $B = .25$ of $(\mu_1 - \mu_2)$ with confidence coefficient equal to .95, we have $z_{\alpha/2} = z_{.025} = 1.96$. Then, letting $\sigma_1 = \sigma_2 = 2.5$ and solving for n, we have

$$1.96\sqrt{\frac{(2.5)^2}{n} + \frac{(2.5)^2}{n}} = .25$$

$$1.96\sqrt{\frac{2(2.5)^2}{n}} = .25$$

$$n = 768.32 \approx 769 \text{ (rounding up)}$$

Consequently, you will have to sample 769 acres of wheat for each fertilizer to estimate the difference in mean yield per acre to within .25 bushel. Since this would necessitate extensive and costly experimentation, you might decide to allow a larger bound (say, $B = .50$ or $B = 1$) in order to reduce the sample size, or you might decrease the confidence coefficient. The point is that we can obtain an idea of the experimental effort necessary to achieve a specified precision in our final estimate by determining the approximate sample size *before* the experiment is begun. ▄

EXAMPLE 7.7

A laboratory manager wishes to compare the difference in the mean readings of two instruments, A and B, designed to measure the potency (in parts per million) of an antibiotic. To conduct the experiment, the manager plans to select n_D specimens of the antibiotic from a vat and to measure each specimen with both instruments. The difference $(\mu_A - \mu_B)$ will be estimated based on the n_D paired differences $(x_A - x_B)$ obtained in the experiment. If preliminary measurements suggest that the differences will range between plus or minus 10 parts per million, how many differences will be needed to estimate $(\mu_A - \mu_B)$ correct to within 1 part per million with confidence coefficient equal to .99?

SOLUTION
The estimator for $(\mu_A - \mu_B)$, based on a paired difference experiment, is $\bar{x}_D = (\bar{x}_A - \bar{x}_B)$ and

$$\sigma_{\bar{x}_D} = \frac{\sigma_D}{\sqrt{n_D}}$$

Thus, the number n_D of pairs of measurements needed to estimate $(\mu_A - \mu_B)$ to within 1 part per million can be obtained by solving for n_D in the equation

$$z_{\alpha/2}\frac{\sigma_D}{\sqrt{n_D}} = B$$

where $z_{.005} = 2.58$ and $B = 1$. To solve this equation for n_D, we need to have an approximate value for σ_D.

We are given the information that the differences are expected to range from -10 to 10 parts per million. Letting the range equal $4\sigma_D$, we find

$$\text{Range} = 20 \approx 4\sigma_D$$

$$\sigma_D \approx 5$$

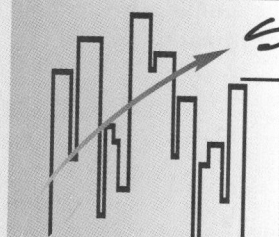

STATISTICS IN ACTION

7.2 UNPAID OVERTIME AND THE FAIR LABOR STANDARDS ACT

In 1938, Congress passed and President Roosevelt signed a wage and hour law called the Fair Labor Standards Act (FLSA). It was part of Roosevelt's "New Deal," a program aimed at ending the Great Depression. The law applies to employees of companies that do business in more than one state and have annual sales of more than $500,000. It established a minimum wage (then $.25 per hour; now $5.15 per hour); set a limit on the number of hours of labor per week per individual worker (then 44 hours; now 40 hours); and discouraged oppressive child labor practices. The act also requires employees to be paid for *overtime*—the time worked beyond the regular 40-hour work week—at a rate one and one-half times their regular hourly wage. The act has been amended many times. An amendment passed in 1963, called the Equal Pay Act, requires employers to pay men and women equally for doing equal work. The act is enforced by the U.S. Department of Labor (Twomey, *Labor and Employment Law,* 1994).

This application involves a well-known U.S. fast-food restaurant chain with 10,000 employees and restaurants in 20 midwestern and southwestern states. (For reasons of confidentiality, the name of the restaurant is withheld.) The chain has three levels of employees in its restaurants: crew, shift leaders, and managers. In early 1996, a group of 75 crew-level employees from 10 different Arizona restaurants charged that management frequently required them to work overtime without pay in order to be considered for promotion to shift leader. They filed suit under the Fair Labor Standards Act seeking an award of back wages, attorneys' fees, and other related costs. Top management at the restaurant chain strongly denied the charges.

As part of the investigation of this claim, a federal judge appointed an examiner to compare the average number of hours of unpaid overtime worked per week per employee for Arizona-based crew members to the corresponding average for Illinois-based crew members using independent random samples of crew members from both states. The examiner planned to use equal sample sizes and to depose (question under oath) each sampled employee concerning overtime worked "off the clock." These data would then be used to estimate the difference in the average number of hours of unpaid overtime worked per week per employee in the two states to within one-half hour with 95% confidence. [*Note:* Pilot samples indicated that the standard deviation for the Illinois employees was about 1.5 hours and the standard deviation for the Arizona employees was about 3.6 hours.]

Focus

a. Your goal is to develop a sampling plan for the examiner in order to achieve the objective outlined by the federal judge. The plan should address each of the following:

   1. the target population(s)

   2. the parameter of interest

   3. the desired level of confidence

   4. the required sample sizes

   5. a method of obtaining the samples

b. Due to time constraints, the examiner may only be able to depose between 60 and 80 employees, total. Develop a contingency sampling plan should this occur.

Substituting $\sigma_D = 5$, $B = 1$, and $z_{.005} = 2.58$ into the equation and solving for n_D, we obtain

$$2.58\frac{5}{\sqrt{n_D}} = 1$$

$$n_D = [(2.58)(5)]^2$$

$$= 166.41$$

Therefore, it will require $n_D = 167$ pairs of measurements to estimate $(\mu_A - \mu_B)$ correct to within 1 part per million using the paired difference experiment. **L**

The box summarizes the procedures for determining the sample sizes necessary for estimating $(\mu_1 - \mu_2)$ for the case $n_1 = n_2 = n$ and for estimating μ_D.

Determination of Sample Sizes for Comparing Two Means

Independent Random Samples

To estimate $(\mu_1 - \mu_2)$ to within a given bound B with probability $(1 - \alpha)$, use the following formula to solve for equal sample sizes that will achieve the desired reliability:

$$n_1 = n_2 = \frac{(z_{\alpha/2})^2(\sigma_1^2 + \sigma_2^2)}{B^2}$$

You will need to substitute estimates for the values of σ_1^2 and σ_2^2 before solving for the sample size. These estimates might be sample variances s_1^2 and s_2^2 from prior sampling (e.g., a pilot sample), or from an educated (and conservatively large) guess based on the range—that is, $s \approx R/4$.

Paired Difference Experiment

To estimate μ_D to within a given bound B with probability $(1 - \alpha)$, use the following formula to solve for n:

$$n = \frac{(z_{\alpha/2})^2 \sigma_D^2}{B^2}$$

You will need to substitute an estimate of σ_D^2 before solving for the sample size. This estimate might be the sample variances s_D^2 from prior sampling (e.g., a pilot study), or from an educated (and conservatively large) guess based on the range—that is, $s \approx R/4$.

EXERCISES 7.36–7.43

Learning the Mechanics

7.36 Find the appropriate values of n_1 and n_2 (assume $n_1 = n_2$) needed to estimate $(\mu_1 - \mu_2)$ with:

   a. A bound on the error of estimation equal to 3.2 with 95% confidence. From prior experience it is known that $\sigma_1 \approx 15$ and $\sigma_2 \approx 17$.

   b. A bound on the error of estimation equal to 8 with 99% confidence. The range of each population is 60.

   c. A 90% confidence interval of width 1.0. Assume that $\sigma_1^2 \approx 5.8$ and $\sigma_2^2 \approx 7.5$.

7.37 Suppose you want to estimate the difference between two population means correct to within 1.8 with a 95% confidence interval. If prior information suggests that the population variances are approximately equal to $\sigma_1^2 = \sigma_2^2 = 14$ and you want to select independent random samples of equal size from the populations, how large should the sample sizes, n_1 and n_2, be?

7.38 Enough money has been budgeted to collect independent random samples of size $n_1 = n_2 = 100$ from populations 1 and 2 in order to estimate $(\mu_1 - \mu_2)$. Prior information indicates that $\sigma_1 = \sigma_2 = 10$. Have sufficient funds been

allocated to construct a 90% confidence interval for $(\mu_1 - \mu_2)$ of width 5 or less? Justify your answer.

Applying the Concepts

7.39 Is housework hazardous to your health? A study in the *Public Health Reports* (July–Aug. 1992) compares the life expectancies of 25-year-old white women in the labor force to those who are housewives. How large a sample would have to be taken from each group in order to be 95% confident that the estimate of difference in average life expectancies for the two groups is within one year of the true difference in average life expectancies? Assume that equal sample sizes will be selected from the two groups, and that the standard deviation for both groups is approximately 15 years.

7.40 Even though Japan is an economic superpower, Japanese workers are in many ways worse off than their U.S. and European counterparts. For example, in 1991 the estimated average housing space per person (in square feet) was 665.2 in the United States, 400.4 in Germany, and only 269 in Japan (*Minneapolis Star-Tribune*, Jan. 31, 1993).

Next year a team of economists and sociologists from the United Nations plans to reestimate the difference in the mean housing space per person for U.S. and Japanese workers. Assume that equal sample sizes will be used for each country and that the standard deviation is 35 square feet for Japan and 80 for the United States. How many people should be sampled in each country to estimate the difference to within 10 square feet with 95% confidence?

7.41 In seeking a good professional football running back, a coach is looking for a player with high mean yards gained per carry and a small standard deviation. Suppose the coach wishes to compare the mean yards gained per carry for two major prospects based on independent random samples of their yards gained per carry in the early part of the coming pro football season. Suppose data from last year indicate that $\sigma_1 = \sigma_2 \approx 5$ yards. If the coach wants to estimate the difference in means correct to within 1 yard with probability equal to .9, how many runs would have to be observed for each player? (Assume equal sample sizes.)

7.42 Refer to *The Professional Geographer* (May 1992) study of the proximity of a woman's place of employment in two-income households, Exercise 7.22. Recall that one inference involved estimating the difference between the average distances to work for men and women living in suburban residences. Determine the sample sizes required to estimate this difference to within 1 mile with 99% confidence. Assume an equal number of men and women will be sampled. [Hint: Use the relevant information provided in Exercise 7.22 to obtain estimates of the population variances.]

7.43 Refer to the Merck Research Labs experiment designed to evaluate the effect of a new drug using rats in a single-T swim maze, Exercise 7.35. How many matched pairs of male and female rat pups need to be included in the experiment in order to estimate the difference between the mean number of swim attempts required to escape to within 1.5 attempts with 95% confidence? Use the value of s_D found in Exercise 7.35 in your calculations.

7.4 TESTING THE ASSUMPTION OF EQUAL POPULATION VARIANCES (OPTIONAL)

Consider the problem of comparing two population means with small (independent) samples. Recall, from Section 7.1, that the statistical method employed requires that the variances of the two populations be equal. Before we compare the means we should check to be sure that this assumption is reasonably satisfied. Otherwise, any inferences derived from the *t*-test for comparing means may be invalid.

To solve problems like these we need to develop a statistical procedure to compare population variances. The common statistical procedure for comparing population variances, σ_1^2 and σ_2^2, makes an inference about the ratio σ_1^2/σ_2^2. In this section, we will show how to test the null hypothesis that the ratio σ_1^2/σ_2^2 equals 1 (the variances are equal) against the alternative hypothesis that the ratio differs from 1 (the variances differ):

$$H_0: \frac{\sigma_1^2}{\sigma_2^2} = 1 \qquad (\sigma_1^2 = \sigma_2^2)$$

$$H_a: \frac{\sigma_1^2}{\sigma_2^2} \neq 1 \qquad (\sigma_1^2 \neq \sigma_2^2)$$

To make an inference about the ratio σ_1^2/σ_2^2, it seems reasonable to collect sample data and use the ratio of the sample variances, s_1^2/s_2^2. We will use the test statistic

$$F = \frac{s_1^2}{s_2^2}$$

To establish a rejection region for the test statistic, we need to know the sampling distribution of s_1^2/s_2^2. As you will subsequently see, the sampling distribution of s_1^2/s_2^2 is based on two of the assumptions already required for the *t*-test:

FIGURE 7.14
An *F*-distribution with 7 numerator and 9 denominator degrees of freedom

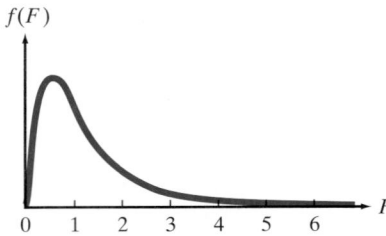

FIGURE 7.15
An *F*-distribution for $\nu_1 = 7$ and $\nu_2 = 9$ df; $\alpha = .05$

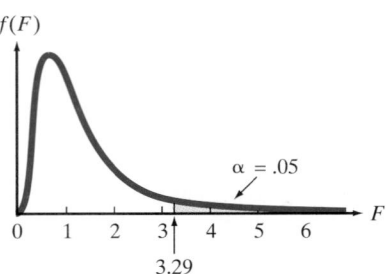

1. The two sampled populations are normally distributed.
2. The samples are randomly and independently selected from their respective populations.

When these assumptions are satisfied and when the null hypothesis is true (that is, $\sigma_1^2 = \sigma_2^2$), the sampling distribution of $F = s_1^2/s_2^2$ is the **F-distribution** with $(n_1 - 1)$ numerator degrees of freedom and $(n_2 - 1)$ denominator degrees of freedom, respectively. The shape of the *F*-distribution depends on the degrees of freedom associated with s_1^2 and s_2^2—that is, on $(n_1 - 1)$ and $(n_2 - 1)$. An *F*-distribution with 7 and 9 df is shown in Figure 7.14. As you can see, the distribution is skewed to the right, since s_1^2/s_2^2 cannot be less than 0 but can increase without bound.

We need to be able to find *F* values corresponding to the tail areas of this distribution in order to establish the rejection region for our test of hypothesis because we expect the ratio *F* of the sample variances to be either very large or very small when the population variances are unequal. The upper-tail *F* values for $\alpha = .10, .05, .025$, and $.01$ can be found in Tables VII, VIII, IX, and X of Appendix B. Table VIII is partially reproduced in Table 7.7. It gives *F* values that correspond to $\alpha = .05$ upper-tail areas for different degrees of freedom ν_1 for the numerator sample variance, s_1^2, whereas the rows correspond to the degrees of freedom ν_2 for the denominator sample variance, s_2^2. Thus, if the numerator degrees of freedom is $\nu_1 = 7$ and the denominator degrees of freedom is $\nu_2 = 9$, we look in the seventh column and ninth row to find $F_{.05} = 3.29$. As shown in Figure 7.15, $\alpha = .05$ is the tail area to the right of 3.29 in the *F*-distribution with 7 and 9 df. That is, if $\sigma_1^2 = \sigma_2^2$, then the probability that the *F* statistic will exceed 3.29 is $\alpha = .05$.

EXAMPLE 7.8

In Example 7.4 (Section 7.1) we used the two-sample *t* statistic to compare the success indexes of two groups of managers. The data are repeated in Table 7.8 followed by a SAS printout of the analysis in Figure 7.16. The use of the *t* statistic was based on the assumption that the population variances of the managerial success indexes were equal for the two groups. Check this assumption at $\alpha = .10$.

TABLE 7.7   Reproduction of Part of Table VIII in Appendix B: Percentage Points of the F-Distribution, $\alpha = .05$

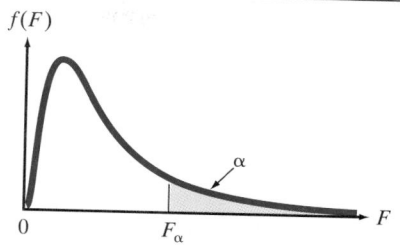

NUMERATOR DEGREES OF FREEDOM

ν_2 \ ν_1	1	2	3	4	5	6	7	8	9
1	161.4	199.5	215.7	224.6	230.2	234.0	236.8	238.9	240.5
2	18.51	19.00	19.16	19.25	19.30	19.33	19.35	19.37	19.38
3	10.13	9.55	9.28	9.12	9.01	8.94	8.89	8.85	8.81
4	7.71	6.94	6.59	6.39	6.26	6.16	6.09	6.04	6.00
5	6.61	5.79	5.41	5.19	5.05	4.95	4.88	4.82	4.77
6	5.99	5.14	4.76	4.53	4.39	4.28	4.21	4.15	4.10
7	5.59	4.74	4.35	4.12	3.97	3.87	3.79	3.73	3.68
8	5.32	4.46	4.07	3.84	3.69	3.58	3.50	3.44	3.39
9	5.12	4.26	3.86	3.63	3.48	3.37	3.29	3.23	3.18
10	4.96	4.10	3.71	3.48	3.33	3.22	3.14	3.07	3.02
11	4.84	3.98	3.59	3.36	3.20	3.09	3.01	2.95	2.90
12	4.75	3.89	3.49	3.25	3.11	3.00	2.91	2.85	2.80
13	4.67	3.81	3.41	3.18	3.03	2.92	2.83	2.77	2.71
14	4.60	3.74	3.34	3.11	2.96	2.85	2.76	2.70	2.65

DENOMINATOR DEGREES OF FREEDOM

TABLE 7.8   Managerial Success Indexes for Two Groups of Managers

GROUP 1						GROUP 2					
Interaction with Outsiders						Few Interactions					
65	58	78	60	68	69	62	53	36	34	56	50
66	70	53	71	63	63	42	57	46	68	48	42
						52	53	43			

```
                          TTEST PROCEDURE
Variable: SUCCESS

GROUP        N          Mean        Std Dev      Std Error       Minimum         Maximum
-------------------------------------------------------------------------------------------
  1         12     65.33333333    6.61036835    1.90824897    53.00000000    78.00000000
  2         15     49.46666667    9.33401358    2.41003194    34.00000000    68.00000000

Variances           T         DF      Prob>|T|
---------------------------------------------
Unequal          5.1615      24.7      0.0001
Equal            4.9675      25.0      0.0000

For HO: Variances are equal,  F' = 1.99    DF = (14,11)    Prob>F' = 0.2554
```

FIGURE 7.16   SAS F-test for the data in Table 7.8

SOLUTION

Let

$$\sigma_1^2 = \text{Population variance of success indexes for Group 1 managers}$$

$$\sigma_2^2 = \text{Population variance of success indexes for Group 2 managers}$$

The hypotheses of interest then are

$$H_0: \frac{\sigma_1^2}{\sigma_2^2} = 1 \qquad (\sigma_1^2 = \sigma_2^2)$$

$$H_a: \frac{\sigma_1^2}{\sigma_2^2} \neq 1 \qquad (\sigma_1^2 \neq \sigma_2^2)$$

The nature of the F-tables given in Appendix B affects the form of the test statistic. To form the rejection region for a two-tailed **F-test**, we want to make certain that the upper tail is used, because only the upper-tail values of F are shown in Tables VII, VIII, IX, and X. To accomplish this, *we will always place the larger sample variance in the numerator of the* F-*test statistic.* This has the effect of doubling the tabulated value for α, since we double the probability that the F-ratio will fall in the upper tail by always placing the larger sample variance in the numerator. That is, we establish a one-tailed rejection region by putting the larger variance in the numerator rather than establishing rejection regions in both tails.

From Figure 7.16, we find that $s_1 = 6.610$ and $s_2 = 9.334$. Therefore, the test statistic will be

$$F = \frac{\text{Larger sample variance}}{\text{Smaller sample variance}} = \frac{s_2^2}{s_1^2}$$

For numerator df $v_1 = n_2 - 1 = 14$ and denominator df $v_2 = n_1 - 1 = 11$, we will reject $H_0: \sigma_1^2 = \sigma_2^2$ at $\alpha = .10$ when the calculated value of F exceeds the tabulated value:

$$F_{\alpha/2} = F_{.05} = 2.74 \quad \text{(see Figure 7.17)}$$

We can now calculate the value of the test statistic and complete the analysis:

$$F = \frac{s_2^2}{s_1^2} = \frac{(9.334)^2}{(6.610)^2} = 1.99$$

When we compare this result to the rejection region shown in Figure 7.17, we see that $F = 1.99$ does not fall into the rejection region. Therefore, the data provide insufficient evidence to reject the null hypothesis of equal population variances.

FIGURE 7.17
Rejection region
for Example 7.8

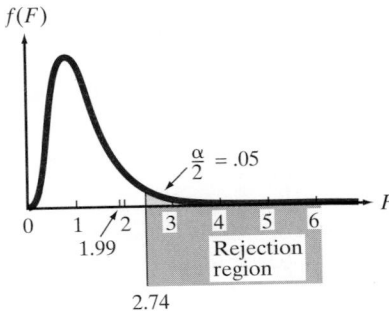

This F-test is also shown on the SAS printout, Figure 7.16. Both the test statistic, $F = 1.99$, and two-tailed p-value, .2554, are highlighted on the printout. Since $\alpha = .10$ is less than the p-value, our conclusion is confirmed: we do not reject the null hypothesis that the population variances of the success indexes are equal.

Although we must be careful not to accept H_0 (since the probability of a Type II error, β, is unknown), this result leads us to behave as if the assumption of equal population variances is reasonably satisfied. Consequently, the inference drawn from the t-test in Example 7.4 appears to be valid. ⬛

Note: Rejecting the null hypothesis H_0: $\sigma_1^2 = \sigma_2^2$ implies that the assumption of equal population variances is violated. Consequently, the small-sample procedure for comparing population means in Section 7.1 may lead to invalid inferences. In this situation, apply the nonparametric procedure for comparing two populations discussed in optional Section 7.5, or consult the references for procedures that utilize an adjusted t-statistic.

We conclude this section with a summary of the F-test for equal population variances.*

F-Test for Equal Population Variances

One-Tailed Test	**Two-Tailed Test**
H_0: $\sigma_1^2 = \sigma_2^2$	H_0: $\sigma_1^2 = \sigma_2^2$
H_a: $\sigma_1^2 < \sigma_2^2$ (or H_a: $\sigma_1^2 > \sigma_2^2$)	H_a: $\sigma_1^2 \neq \sigma_2^2$

Test statistic:

$$F = \frac{s_2^2}{s_1^2}$$

$$\left(\text{or } F = \frac{s_1^2}{s_2^2} \text{ when } H_a\text{: } \sigma_1^2 > \sigma_2^2\right)$$

Test statistic:

$$F = \frac{\text{Larger sample variance}}{\text{Smaller sample variance}}$$

$$= \frac{s_1^2}{s_2^2} \text{ when } s_1^2 > s_2^2$$

$$\left(\text{or } \frac{s_2^2}{s_1^2} \text{ when } s_2^2 > s_1^2\right)$$

Rejection region:
$$F > F_\alpha$$

Rejection region:
$$F > F_{\alpha/2}$$

where F_α and $F_{\alpha/2}$ are based on ν_1 = numerator degrees of freedom and ν_2 = denominator degrees of freedom; ν_1 and ν_2 are the degrees of freedom for the numerator and denominator sample variances, respectively.

Assumptions: **1.** Both sampled populations are normally distributed.†
                2. The samples are random and independent.

---

*Although a test of a hypothesis of equality of variances is the most common application of the F-test, it can also be used to test a hypothesis that the ratio between the population variances is equal to some specified value, H_0: $\sigma_1^2/\sigma_2^2 = k$. The test is conducted in exactly the same way as specified in the box, except that we use the test statistic

$$F = \frac{s_1^2}{s_2^2}\left(\frac{1}{k}\right)$$

†The F-test is much less robust (i.e., much more sensitive) to departures from normality than the t-test for comparing the population means (Section 7.1). If you have doubts about the normality of the population frequency distributions, use a **nonparametric method** for comparing the two population variances. A method can be found in the nonparametric statistics texts listed in the references.

EXERCISES 7.44–7.52

Note: Exercises marked with 💾 *contain data for computer analysis on a 3.5" disk (file name in parentheses).*

Learning the Mechanics

7.44 Under what conditions is the sampling distribution of s_1^2/s_2^2 an F-distribution?

7.45 Use Tables VII, VIII, IX, and X of Appendix B to find each of the following F values:
  a. $F_{.05}$ where $\nu_1 = 9$ and $\nu_2 = 6$
  b. $F_{.01}$ where $\nu_1 = 18$ and $\nu_2 = 14$
  c. $F_{.025}$ where $\nu_1 = 11$ and $\nu_2 = 4$
  d. $F_{.10}$ where $\nu_1 = 20$ and $\nu_2 = 5$

7.46 For each of the following cases, identify the rejection region that should be used to test $H_0: \sigma_1^2 = \sigma_2^2$ against $H_a: \sigma_1^2 \neq \sigma_2^2$. Assume $\nu_1 = 10$ and $\nu_2 = 12$.
  a. $\alpha = .20$ **b.** $\alpha = .10$ **c.** $\alpha = .05$ **d.** $\alpha = .02$

7.47 Independent random samples were selected from each of two normally distributed populations, $n_1 = 6$ from population 1 and $n_2 = 5$ from population 2. The data are shown in the table below, followed by an SPSS descriptive statistics printout at the bottom of the page.

Sample 1	Sample 2
3.1	2.3
4.4	1.4
1.2	3.7
1.7	8.9
.7	5.5
3.4	

  a. Test $H_0: \sigma_1^2 = \sigma_2^2$ against $H_a: \sigma_1^2 < \sigma_2^2$. Use $\alpha = .01$.
  b. Find the approximate p-value of the test.

7.48 Independent random samples were selected from each of two normally distributed populations, $n_1 = 12$ from population 1 and $n_2 = 27$ from population

2. The means and variances for the two samples are shown in the table.

Sample 1	Sample 2
$n_1 = 12$	$n_2 = 27$
$\bar{x}_1 = 31.7$	$\bar{x}_2 = 37.4$
$s_1^2 = 3.87$	$s_2^2 = 8.75$

  a. Test the null hypothesis $H_0: \sigma_1^2 = \sigma_2^2$ against the alternative hypothesis $H_a: \sigma_1^2 \neq \sigma_2^2$. Use $\alpha = .10$.
  b. Find the approximate p-value of the test.

Applying the Concepts

7.49 (X07.049) Tests of product quality can be completely automated or can be conducted using human inspectors or human inspectors aided by mechanical devices. Although human inspection is frequently the most economical alternative, it can lead to serious inspection error problems. Numerous studies have demonstrated that inspectors often cannot detect as many as 85% of the defective items that they inspect; moreover, performance varies from inspector to inspector (*Journal of Quality Technology,* Apr. 1986). To evaluate the performance of inspectors in a new company, a quality manager had a sample of 12 novice inspectors evaluate 200 finished products. The same 200 items were evaluated by 12 experienced inspectors. The quality of each item—whether defective or nondefective—was known to the manager. The next table lists the number of inspection errors (classifying a defective item as nondefective or vice versa) made by each inspector. A SAS printout with descriptive statistics for the two types of inspectors is shown at the top of page 363.

```
Summaries of    X
By levels of    SAMPLE

Variable      Value  Label                    Mean    Std Dev   Cases

For Entire Population                        3.3000    2.3656      11

SAMPLE            1.00                       2.4167    1.4359       6
SAMPLE            2.00                       4.3600    2.9729       5

   Total Cases =         11
```

```
Analysis Variable : ERRORS

--------------------------------INSPECT=EXPER--------------------------------
N Obs   N      Minimum          Maximum               Mean        Std Dev
-----------------------------------------------------------------------------
 12    12    10.0000000       31.0000000        20.5833333       5.7439032
-----------------------------------------------------------------------------

--------------------------------INSPECT=NOVICE-------------------------------
N Obs   N      Minimum          Maximum               Mean        Std Dev
-----------------------------------------------------------------------------
 12    12    20.0000000       48.0000000        32.8333333       8.6427409
-----------------------------------------------------------------------------
```

Novice Inspectors				Experienced Inspectors			
30	35	26	40	31	15	25	19
36	20	45	31	28	17	19	18
33	29	21	48	24	10	20	21

a. Prior to conducting this experiment, the manager believed the variance in inspection errors was lower for experienced inspectors than for novice inspectors. Do the sample data support her belief? Test using $\alpha = .05$.

b. What is the appropriate p-value of the test you conducted in part **a**?

7.50 A study in the *Journal of Occupational and Organizational Psychology* (Dec. 1992) investigated the relationship of employment status and mental health. A sample of working and unemployed people was selected, and each person was given a mental health examination using the General Health Questionnaire (GHQ), a widely recognized measure of mental health. Although the article focused on comparing the mean GHQ levels, a comparison of the variability of GHQ scores for employed and unemployed men and women is of interest as well.

a. In general terms, what does the amount of variability in GHQ scores tell us about the group?

b. What are the appropriate null and alternative hypotheses to compare the variability of the mental health scores of the employed and unemployed groups? Define any symbols you use.

c. The standard deviation for a sample of 142 employed men was 3.26, while the standard deviation for 49 unemployed men was 5.10. Conduct the test you set up in part **b** using $\alpha = .05$. Interpret the results.

d. What assumptions are necessary to ensure the validity of the test?

7.51 (X07.051) Following the Persian Gulf War, the Pentagon changed its logistics processes to be more corporate-like. The extravagant "just-in-case" mentality was replaced with "just-in-time" systems. Emulating Federal Express and United Parcel Service, deliveries from factories to foxholes are now expedited using bar codes, laser cards, radio tags, and databases to track supplies. The following table contains order-to-delivery times for a sample of shipments from the United States to the Persian Gulf in 1991 and a sample of shipments to Bosnia in 1995.

ORDER-TO-DELIVERY TIMES (IN DAYS)

Persian Gulf 1991	Bosnia 1995
28.0	15.1
20.0	6.4
26.5	5.0
10.6	11.4
9.1	6.5
35.2	6.5
29.1	3.0
41.2	7.0
27.5	5.5

Source: Adapted from Crock, S. "The Pentagon goes to B-school." *Business Week,* December 11, 1995, p. 98.

a. Use the SPSS printout at the top of page 364 to test whether the variances in order-to-delivery times for Persian Gulf and Bosnia shipments are equal. Use $\alpha = .05$.

b. Given your answer to part **a**, is it appropriate to construct a confidence interval for the difference between the mean order-to-delivery times? Explain.

7.52 Refer to the *International Journal of Environmental Health Research* (Vol. 4, 1994) study, Exercise 7.16, in which the mean solid-waste generation rates for middle-income and industrialized

```
Independent samples of    LOCATION
Group 1:  LOCATION   EQ      1.00          Group 2:  LOCATION   EQ        2.00
t-test for:  TIME
                      Number              Standard   Standard
                      of Cases    Mean    Deviation    Error
             Group 1     9       25.2444   10.520      3.507
             Group 2     9        7.3778    3.654      1.218
                      Pooled Variance Estimate   |  Separate Variance Estimate
        F    2-Tail       t    Degrees of 2-Tail |     t    Degrees of  2-Tail
      Value  Prob.      Value   Freedom   Prob.  |   Value   Freedom    Prob.
      8.29   .007       4.81      16      .000   |   4.81     9.90       .001
```

countries were compared. The data are reproduced in the next table.

a. In order to conduct the two-sample t-test in
Exercise 7.16, it was necessary to assume that
the two population variances were equal. Test
this assumption at $\alpha = .05$. Use the SAS printout below to conduct the test.

b. What does your test indicate about the appropriateness of applying a two-sample t-test?

Industrialized Countries		Middle-Income Countries	
New York (USA)	2.27	Singapore	0.87
Phoenix (USA)	2.31	Hong Kong	0.85
London (UK)	2.24	Medellin (Colombia)	0.54
Hamburg (Germany)	2.18	Kano (Nigeria)	0.46
Rome (Italy)	2.15	Manila (Philippines)	0.50
		Cairo (Egypt)	0.50
		Tunis (Tunisia)	0.56

```
                          TTEST PROCEDURE

Variable: WASTE

COUNTRY        N           Mean          Std Dev        Std Error
-------------------------------------------------------------------------
INDUS          5       2.23000000      0.06519202      0.02915476
MIDDLE         7       0.61142857      0.17286108      0.06533535

Variances        T     DF    Prob>|T|
-------------------------------------------------------------------------
Unequal       22.6231  8.1    0.0001
Equal         19.7302 10.0    0.0000

For HO: Variances are equal, F' = 7.03     DF = (6,4)    Prob>F' = 0.0800
```

7.5 A NONPARAMETRIC TEST FOR COMPARING TWO POPULATIONS: INDEPENDENT SAMPLING (OPTIONAL)

Suppose two independent random samples are to be used to compare two populations and the t-test of Section 7.1 is inappropriate for making the comparison.
We may be unwilling to make assumptions about the form of the underlying population probability distributions or we may be unable to obtain exact values of the
sample measurements. If the data can be ranked in order of magnitude for either
of these situations, the **Wilcoxon rank sum test** (developed by Frank Wilcoxon)
can be used to test the hypothesis that the probability distributions associated with
the two populations are equivalent.

TABLE 7.9   Percentage Cost of Living Change, as Predicted by Government and University Economists

GOVERNMENT ECONOMIST		UNIVERSITY ECONOMIST	
Prediction	**Rank**	**Prediction**	**Rank**
3.1	4	4.4	6
4.8	7	5.8	9
2.3	2	3.9	5
5.6	8	8.7	11
0.0	1	6.3	10
2.9	3	10.5	12
		10.8	13

For example, suppose six economists who work for the federal government and seven university economists are randomly selected, and each is asked to predict next year's percentage change in cost of living as compared with this year's figure. The objective of the study is to compare the government economists' predictions to those of the university economists. The data are shown in Table 7.9.

The two populations of predictions are those that would be obtained from *all* government and *all* university economists if they could all be questioned. To compare their probability distributions, we first *rank the sample observations as though they were all drawn from the same population.* That is, we pool the measurements from both samples and then rank the measurements from the smallest (a rank of 1) to the largest (a rank of 13). The ranks of the 13 economists' predictions are indicated in Table 7.9.

The test statistic for the Wilcoxon test is based on the totals of the ranks for each of the two samples—that is, on the **rank sums**. If the two rank sums are nearly equal, the implication is that there is no evidence that the probability distributions from which the samples were drawn are different. On the other hand, if the two rank sums are very different, the implication is that the two samples may have come from different populations.

For the economists' predictions, we arbitrarily denote the rank sum for government economists by T_A and that for university economists by T_B. Then

$$T_A = 4 + 7 + 2 + 8 + 1 + 3 = 25$$

$$T_B = 6 + 9 + 5 + 11 + 10 + 12 + 13 = 66$$

The sum of T_A and T_B will always equal $n(n + 1)/2$, where $n = n_1 + n_2$. So, for this example, $n_1 = 6$, $n_2 = 7$, and

$$T_A + T_B = \frac{13(13 + 1)}{2} = 91$$

Since $T_A + T_B$ is fixed, a small value for T_A implies a large value for T_B (and vice versa) and a large difference between T_A and T_B. Therefore, the smaller the value of one of the rank sums, the greater the evidence to indicate that the samples were selected from different populations.

The test statistic for this test is the rank sum for the smaller sample; or, in the case where $n_1 = n_2$, either rank sum can be used. Values that locate the rejection region for this rank sum are given in Table XII of Appendix B. A partial reproduction of this table is shown in Table 7.10. The columns of the table represent n_1, the first sample size, and the rows represent n_2, the second sample size. *The* T_L *and*

TABLE 7.10 Reproduction of Part of Table XII in Appendix B: Critical Values for the Wilcoxon Rank Sum Test

$\alpha = .025$ one-tailed; $\alpha = .05$ two-tailed

n_2 \ n_1	3 T_L	3 T_U	4 T_L	4 T_U	5 T_L	5 T_U	6 T_L	6 T_U	7 T_L	7 T_U	8 T_L	8 T_U	9 T_L	9 T_U	10 T_L	10 T_U
3	5	16	6	18	6	21	7	23	7	26	8	28	8	31	9	33
4	6	18	11	25	12	28	12	32	13	35	14	38	15	41	16	44
5	6	21	12	28	18	37	19	41	20	45	21	49	22	53	24	56
6	7	23	12	32	19	41	26	52	28	56	29	61	31	65	32	70
7	7	26	13	35	20	45	28	56	37	68	39	73	41	78	43	83
8	8	28	14	38	21	49	29	61	39	73	49	87	51	93	54	98
9	8	31	15	41	22	53	31	65	41	78	51	93	63	108	66	114
10	9	33	16	44	24	56	32	70	43	83	54	98	66	114	79	131

T_U entries in the table are the boundaries of the lower and upper regions, respectively, for the rank sum associated with the sample that has fewer measurements. If the sample sizes n_1 and n_2 are the same, either rank sum may be used as the test statistic. To illustrate, suppose $n_1 = 8$ and $n_2 = 10$. For a two-tailed test with $\alpha = .05$, we consult part **a** of the table and find that the null hypothesis will be rejected if the rank sum of sample 1 (the sample with fewer measurements), T, is less than or equal to $T_L = 54$ or greater than or equal to $T_U = 98$. The Wilcoxon rank sum test is summarized in the next box.

Wilcoxon Rank Sum Test: Independent Samples*

One-Tailed Test

H_0: Two sampled populations have identical probability distributions

H_a: The probability distribution for population A is shifted to the right of that for B

Test statistic: The rank sum T associated with the sample with fewer measurements (if sample sizes are equal, either rank sum can be used)

Rejection region: Assuming the smaller sample size is associated with distribution A (if sample sizes are equal, we use the rank sum T_A), we reject the null hypothesis if

$$T_A \geq T_U$$

where T_U is the upper value given by Table XII in Appendix B for the chosen *one-tailed* α value.

Two-Tailed Test

H_0: Two sampled populations have identical probability distributions

H_a: The probability distribution for population A is shifted to the left *or* to the right of that for B

Test statistic: The rank sum T associated with the sample with fewer measurements (if sample sizes are equal, either rank sum can be used)

Rejection region: $T \leq T_L$
  or $T \geq T_U$

where T_L is the lower value given by Table XII in Appendix B for the chosen *two-tailed* α value and T_U is the upper value from Table XII.

---

*Another statistic used for comparing two populations based on independent random samples is the **Mann-Whitney** U **statistic**. The U statistic is a simple function of the rank sums. It can be shown that the Wilcoxon rank sum test and the Mann-Whitney U-test are equivalent.

[*Note:* If the one-sided alternative is that the probability distribution for A is shifted to the *left* of B (and T_A is the test statistic), we reject the null hypothesis if $T_A \leq T_L$.]

Assumptions: **1.** The two samples are random and independent.

2. The two probability distributions from which the samples are drawn are continuous.

Ties: Assign tied measurements the average of the ranks they would receive if they were unequal but occurred in successive order. For example, if the third-ranked and fourth-ranked measurements are tied, assign each a rank of $(3 + 4)/2 = 3.5$.

Note that the assumptions necessary for the validity of the Wilcoxon rank sum test do not specify the shape or type of probability distribution. However, the distributions are assumed to be continuous so that the probability of tied measurements is 0 (see Chapter 4), and each measurement can be assigned a unique rank. In practice, however, rounding of continuous measurements will sometimes produce ties. As long as the number of ties is small relative to the sample sizes, the Wilcoxon test procedure will still have an approximate significance level of α. The test is not recommended to compare discrete distributions for which many ties are expected.

EXAMPLE 7.9

Test the hypothesis that the university economists' predictions of next year's percentage change in cost of living tend to be higher than the government economists'. Conduct the test using the data in Table 7.9 and $\alpha = .05$.

SOLUTION

H_0: The probability distributions corresponding to the government and university economists' predictions of inflation rate are identical

H_a: The probability distribution for the university economists' predictions lies above (to the right of) the probability distribution for the government economists' predictions*

Test statistic: Since fewer government economists ($n_1 = 6$) than university economists ($n_2 = 7$) were sampled, the test statistic is T_A, the rank sum of the government economists' predictions.

Rejection region: Since the test is one-sided, we consult part **b** of Table XII for the rejection region corresponding to $\alpha = .05$. We reject H_0 only for $T_A \leq T_L$, the lower value from Table XII, since we are specifically testing that the distribution of the government economists' predictions lies *below* the distribution of university economists' predictions, as shown in Figure 7.18. Thus, we reject H_0 if $T_A \leq 30$.

Since T_A, the rank sum of the government economists' predictions in Table 7.9, is 25, it is in the rejection region (see Figure 7.18). Therefore, we can conclude that the university economists' predictions tend, in general, to exceed the government economists' predictions. This same conclusion can be reached using a statistical

---

*The alternative hypotheses in this chapter will be stated in terms of a difference in the *location* of the distributions. However, since the shapes of the distributions may also differ under H_a, some of the figures (e.g., Figure 7.18) depicting the alternative hypothesis will show probability distributions with different shapes.

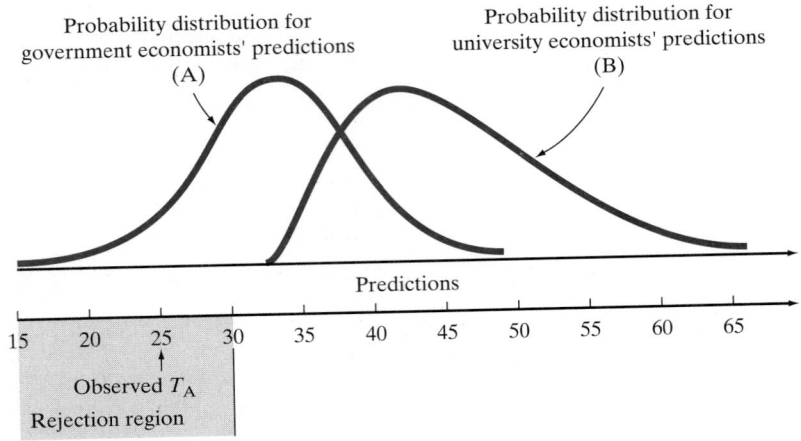

FIGURE 7.18 Alternative hypothesis and rejection region for Example 7.9

```
                     N P A R 1 W A Y   P R O C E D U R E

           Wilcoxon Scores (Rank Sums) for Variable PCTCHNG
                    Classified by Variable ECONOMST

                            Sum of      Expected        Std Dev          Mean
ECONOMST         N          Scores      Under H0        Under H0         Score

A                6            25.0          42.0             7.0     4.16666667
B                7            66.0          49.0             7.0     9.42857143

          Wilcoxon 2-Sample Test (Normal Approximation)
          (with Continuity Correction of .5)

          S=   25.0000        Z= -2.35714     Prob > |Z| = 0.0184

          T-Test approx. Significance =        0.0362

          Kruskal-Wallis Test (Chi-Square Approximation)
          CHISQ=   5.8980      DF=   1       Prob > CHISQ=     0.0152
```

FIGURE 7.19 SAS printout for Example 7.9

software package. The SAS printout of the analysis is shown in Figure 7.19. Both the test statistic ($T_A = 25$) and two-tailed p-value ($p = .0184$) are highlighted on the printout. The one-tailed p-value, $p = .0184/2 = .0092$, is less than $\alpha = .05$, leading us to reject H_0.

Table XII in Appendix B gives values of T_L and T_U for values of n_1 and n_2 less than or equal to 10. When both sample sizes n_1 and n_2 are 10 or larger, the sampling distribution of T_A can be approximated by a normal distribution with mean and variance

$$E(T_A) = \frac{n_1(n_1 + n_2 + 1)}{2} \qquad \text{and} \qquad \sigma^2_{T_A} = \frac{n_1 n_2(n_1 + n_2 + 1)}{12}$$

Therefore, for $n_1 \geqslant 10$ and $n_2 \geqslant 10$ we can conduct the Wilcoxon rank sum test using the familiar z-test of Section 7.1. The test is summarized in the next box.

Wilcoxon Rank Sum Test: Large Independent Samples

One-Tailed Test

H_0: Two sampled populations have identical probability distributions

H_a: The probability distribution for population A is shifted to the right of that for B

Two-Tailed Test

H_0: Two sampled populations have identical probability distributions

H_a: The probability distribution for population A is shifted to the left *or* to the right of that for B

Test statistic: $z = \dfrac{T_A - \dfrac{n_1(n_1 + n_2 + 1)}{2}}{\sqrt{\dfrac{n_1 n_2(n_1 + n_2 + 1)}{12}}}$

Rejection region: $z > z_\alpha$

Assumptions: $n_1 \geqslant 10$ and $n_2 \geqslant 10$

Rejection region: $|z| > z_{\alpha/2}$

Assumptions: $n_1 \geqslant 10$ and $n_2 \geqslant 10$

EXERCISES   7.53–7.63

Note: Exercises marked with 💾 *contain data for computer analysis on a 3.5" disk (file name in parentheses).*

Learning the Mechanics

7.53 Specify the test statistic and the rejection region for the Wilcoxon rank sum test for independent samples in each of the following situations:

a. $n_A = 10, n_B = 6, \alpha = .10$

H_0: Two probability distributions, A and B, are identical

H_a: Probability distribution for population A is shifted to the right or left of the probability distribution for population B

b. $n_A = 5, n_B = 7, \alpha = .05$

H_0: Two probability distributions, A and B, are identical

H_a: Probability distribution for population A is shifted to the right of the probability distribution for population B

c. $n_A = 9, n_B = 8, \alpha = .025$

H_0: Two probability distributions, A and B, are identical

H_a: Probability distribution for population A is shifted to the left of the probability distribution for population B

d. $n_A = 15, n_B = 15, \alpha = .05$

H_0: Two probability distributions, A and B, are identical

H_a: Probability distribution for population A is shifted to the right or left of the probability distribution for population B

7.54 Suppose you want to compare two treatments, A and B. In particular, you wish to determine whether the distribution for population B is shifted to the right of the distribution for population A. You plan to use the Wilcoxon rank sum test.

a. Specify the null and alternative hypotheses you would test.

b. Suppose you obtained the following independent random samples of observations on experimental units subjected to the two treatments:

Sample A: 37, 40, 33, 29, 42, 33, 35, 28, 34

Sample B: 65, 35, 47, 52

Conduct a test of the hypotheses described in part **a**. Test using $\alpha = .05$.

7.55 Explain the difference between the one-tailed and two-tailed versions of the Wilcoxon rank sum test for independent random samples.

7.56 Independent random samples are selected from two populations. The data are shown in the table.

Population 1		Population 2		
15	16	5	9	5
10	13	12	8	10
12	8	9	4	

a. Use the Wilcoxon rank sum test to determine whether the data provide sufficient evidence to indicate a shift in the locations of the probability distributions of the sampled populations. Test using $\alpha = .05$.

b. Do the data provide sufficient evidence to indicate that the probability distribution for population 1 is shifted to the right of the probability distribution for population 2? Use the Wilcoxon rank sum test with $\alpha = .05$.

Private Sector	Public Sector
2.58%	5.40%
5.05	2.55
.05	9.00
2.10	10.55
4.30	1.02
2.25	5.11
2.50	12.42
1.94	1.67
2.33	3.33

Source: Adapted from Hann, J., and Weber, R. "Information systems planning: A model and empirical tests." *Management Science,* Vol. 42, No. 2, July, 1996, pp. 1043–1064.

Applying the Concepts

7.57 **(X07.057)** University of Queensland researchers J. Hann and R. Weber sampled private sector and public sector organizations in Australia to study the planning undertaken by their information systems departments (*Management Science,* July 1996). As part of that process they asked each sample organization how much it had spent on information systems and technology in the previous fiscal year as a percentage of the organization's total revenues. The results are reported in the table.

Cities of Low-Income Countries		Cities of Middle-Income Countries	
Jakarta	.60	Singapore	.87
Surabaya	.52	Hong Kong	.85
Bandung	.55	Medellin	.54
Lahore	.60	Kano	.46
Karachi	.50	Manila	.50
Calcutta	.51	Cairo	.50
Kanpur	.50	Tunis	.56

Source: Al-Momani, A. H. "Solid-waste management: Sampling, analysis and assessment of household waste in the city of Amman." *International Journal of Environmental Health Research,* 1994, pp. 208–222.

a. Do the two sampled populations have identical probability distributions or is the distribution for public sector organizations in Australia located to the right of Australia's private sector firms? Test using $\alpha = .05$.

b. Is the *p*-value for the test less than or greater than .05? Justify your answer.

c. What assumptions must be met to ensure the validity of the test you conducted in part **a**?

7.58 **(X07.058)** In Exercise 7.16, the solid waste generation rates for cities in industrialized countries

and cities in middle-income countries were investigated. In this exercise, the focus is on middle-income countries versus low-income countries. The table, extracted from the *International Journal of Environmental Health Research* (1994), reports waste generation values (kg per capita per day) for two independent samples. Do the rates differ for the two categories of countries?

Neighborhood A		Neighborhood B	
.850	.880	.911	.835
1.060	.895	.770	.800
.910	.844	.815	.793
.813	.965	.748	.796
.737	.875		

a. Which nonparametric hypothesis-testing procedures could be used to answer the question?

b. Specify the null and alternative hypotheses of the test.

c. Conduct the test using $\alpha = .01$. Interpret the results in the context of the problem.

7.59 **(X07.059)** Are tax assessments fair? One measure of "fairness" is the ratio of a property's assessed value to its market value—or a proxy for market value such as a recent sale price (*Journal of Business and Economic Statistics,* Jan. 1985). The accompanying table lists assessment ratios for random samples of 10 properties in neighborhood A and eight properties in neighborhood B.

Station 1			Station 2		
127.96	108.91	100.85	114.79	85.54	280.55
210.07	178.21	85.89	109.11	117.64	145.11
203.24	285.37		330.33	302.74	95.36

Source: Gastwirth, J. L., and Mahmoud, H. "An efficient robust nonparametric test for scale change for data from a gamma distribution." *Technometrics,* Vol. 28, No. 1, Feb. 1986, p. 83 (Table 2).

a. Use the Wilcoxon rank sum test to investigate the fairness of the assessments between the two neighborhoods. Use $\alpha = .05$ and interpret your findings in the context of the problem.

b. Under what circumstances could the two-sample *t*-test of Section 7.1 be used to investigate the fairness issue of part **a**?

c. What assumptions are necessary to ensure the validity of the test you conducted in part **a**?

7.60 **(X07.060)** The data in the table, extracted from *Technometrics* (Feb. 1986), represent daily accumulated stream flow and precipitation (in inches) for two U.S. Geological Survey stations in Colorado. Conduct a test to determine whether the distributions of daily accumulated stream flow and precipitation for the two stations differ in location. Use

$\alpha = .10$. Why is a nonparametric test appropriate for this data?

U.S. Plants	Japanese Plants
7.11%	3.52%
6.06	2.02
8.00	4.91
6.87	3.22
4.77	1.92

7.61 **(X07.061)** Recall that the variance of a binomial sample proportion, $\hat{p}$, depends on the value of the population parameter, p. As a consequence, the variance of a sample percentage, $(100\hat{p})\%$, also depends on p. Thus if you conduct an unpaired t-test (Section 7.1) to compare the means of two populations of percentages, you may be violating the assumption that $\sigma_1^2 = \sigma_2^2$, upon which the t-test is based. If the disparity in the variances is large, you will obtain more reliable test results using the Wilcoxon rank sum test for independent samples. In Exercise 7.19, we used a Student's t-test to compare the mean annual percentages of labor turnover between U.S. and Japanese manufacturers of air conditioners. The annual percentage turnover rates for five U.S. and five Japanese plants are shown in the table. Do the data provide sufficient evidence to indicate that the mean annual percentage turnover for American plants exceeds the corresponding mean for Japanese plants? Test using the Wilcoxon rank sum test with $\alpha = .05$. Do your test conclusions agree with those of the t-test in Exercise 7.19?

Twin Blades		Single Blades	
8	15	10	13
17	10	6	14
9	6	3	5
11	12	7	7

7.62 **(X07.062)** A major razor blade manufacturer advertises that its twin-blade disposable razor "gets you lots more shaves" than any single-blade disposable razor on the market. A rival company that has been very successful in selling single-blade razors plans to test this claim. Independent random samples of eight single-blade users and eight twin-blade users are taken, and the number of shaves that each gets before indicating a preference to change blades is recorded. The results are shown in the table.

a. Do the data support the twin-blade manufacturer's claim? Use $\alpha = .05$.

b. Do you think this experiment was designed in the best possible way? If not, what design might have been better?

c. What assumptions are necessary for the validity of the test you performed in part **a**? Do the assumptions seem reasonable for this application?

7.63 **(X07.063)** A *management information system* (MIS) is a computer-based information-processing system designed to support the operations, management, and decision functions of an organization. The development of an MIS involves three stages: definition, physical design, and implementation of the system (Davis and Hamilton, 1993). The successful implementation of an MIS is related to the quality of the entire development process. It could fail due to inadequate planning by and negotiating between the designers and the future users of the system prior to construction, or simply because the users were improperly trained. Thirty firms that recently implemented an MIS were surveyed: 16 were satisfied with the implementation results, 14 were not. Each firm was asked to rate the quality of the planning and negotiation stages of the development process, using a scale of 0 to 100, with higher numbers indicating better quality. (A score of 100 indicates that all the problems that occurred in the planning and negotiation stages were successfully resolved, while 0 indicates that none were resolved.) The results obtained are shown in the table.

Firms with a Good MIS			Firms with a Poor MIS		
52	59	95	60	40	90
70	60	90	50	55	85
40	90	86	55	65	80
80	75	95	70	55	90
82	80	93	41	70	
65					

a. The Wilcoxon rank sum test was used to compare the quality of the development processes of successfully and unsuccessfully implemented MISs. The results are shown in the SAS printout at the top of page 372. Determine whether the distribution of quality scores for successfully implemented systems lies above the distribution of scores for unsuccessfully implemented systems. Test using $\alpha = .05$.

b. Under what circumstances could you use the two-sample t-test of Section 7.1 to conduct the same test?

```
                        N P A R 1 W A Y   P R O C E D U R E
               Wilcoxon Scores (Rank Sums) for Variable QUALITY
                        Classified by Variable FIRM

                        Sum of        Expected       Std Dev         Mean
      FIRM       N       Scores       Under H0       Under H0        Score

      GOOD      16     290.500000       248.0       23.9858196    18.1562500
      POOR      14     174.500000       217.0       23.9858196    12.4642857
                        Average Scores were used for Ties
            Wilcoxon 2-Sample Test (Normal Approximation)
            (with Continuity Correction of .5)

            S=  174.500       Z= -1.75103       Prob > |Z| = 0.0799

            T-Test approx. Significance =       0.0905

            Kruskal-Wallis Test (Chi-Square Approximation)
            CHISQ=  3.1396       DF=  1       Prob > CHISQ=     0.0764
```

7.6   A NONPARAMETRIC TEST FOR COMPARING TWO POPULATIONS: PAIRED DIFFERENCE EXPERIMENTS (OPTIONAL)

Nonparametric techniques can also be employed to compare two probability distributions when a paired difference design is used. For example, consumer preferences for two competing products are often compared by having each of a sample of consumers rate both products. Thus, the ratings have been paired on each consumer. Here is an example of this type of experiment.

For some paper products, softness is an important consideration in determining consumer acceptance. One method of determining softness is to have judges give a sample of the products a softness rating. Suppose each of ten judges is given a sample of two products that a company wants to compare. Each judge rates the softness of each product on a scale from 1 to 10, with higher ratings implying a softer product. The results of the experiment are shown in Table 7.11.

Since this is a paired difference experiment, we analyze the differences between the measurements (see Section 7.2). However, the nonparametric approach—called the **Wilcoxon signed rank test**—requires that we calculate the ranks of the absolute values of the differences between the measurements, that is, the ranks of the differences after removing any minus signs. *Note that tied absolute differences are assigned the average of the ranks they would receive if they were unequal but successive measurements.* After the absolute differences are ranked, the sum of the ranks of the positive differences of the original measurements, T_+, and the sum of the ranks of the negative differences of the original measurements, T_-, are computed.

We are now prepared to test the nonparametric hypotheses:

H_0: The probability distributions of the ratings for products A and B are identical

H_a: The probability distributions of the ratings differ (in location) for the two products (Note that this is a two-sided alternative and that it implies a two-tailed test.)

TABLE 7.11   Softness Ratings of Paper

Judge	PRODUCT A	PRODUCT B	DIFFERENCE (A − B)	Absolute Value of Difference	Rank of Absolute Value
1	6	4	2	2	5
2	8	5	3	3	7.5
3	4	5	−1	1	2
4	9	8	1	1	2
5	4	1	3	3	7.5
6	7	9	−2	2	5
7	6	2	4	4	9
8	5	3	2	2	5
9	6	7	−1	1	2
10	8	2	6	6	10

$$T_+ = \text{Sum of positive ranks} = 46$$
$$T_- = \text{Sum of negative ranks} = \;9$$

TABLE 7.12   Reproduction of Part of Table XIII of Appendix B: Critical Values for the Wilcoxon Paired Difference Signed Rank Test

One-Tailed	Two-Tailed	n = 5	n = 6	n = 7	n = 8	n = 9	n = 10
$\alpha = .05$	$\alpha = .10$	1	2	4	6	8	11
$\alpha = .025$	$\alpha = .05$		1	2	4	6	8
$\alpha = .01$	$\alpha = .02$			0	2	3	5
$\alpha = .005$	$\alpha = .01$				0	2	3

		n = 11	n = 12	n = 13	n = 14	n = 15	n = 16
$\alpha = .05$	$\alpha = .10$	14	17	21	26	30	36
$\alpha = .025$	$\alpha = .05$	11	14	17	21	25	30
$\alpha = .01$	$\alpha = .02$	7	10	13	16	20	24
$\alpha = .005$	$\alpha = .01$	5	7	10	13	16	19

		n = 17	n = 18	n = 19	n = 20	n = 21	n = 22
$\alpha = .05$	$\alpha = .10$	41	47	54	60	68	75
$\alpha = .025$	$\alpha = .05$	35	40	46	52	59	66
$\alpha = .01$	$\alpha = .02$	28	33	38	43	49	56
$\alpha = .005$	$\alpha = .01$	23	28	32	37	43	49

		n = 23	n = 24	n = 25	n = 26	n = 27	n = 28
$\alpha = .05$	$\alpha = .10$	83	92	101	110	120	130
$\alpha = .025$	$\alpha = .05$	73	81	90	98	107	117
$\alpha = .01$	$\alpha = .02$	62	69	77	85	93	102
$\alpha = .005$	$\alpha = .01$	55	61	68	76	84	92

Test statistic: $T = $ Smaller of the positive and negative rank sums T_+ and T_-

The smaller the value of T, the greater the evidence to indicate that the two probability distributions differ in location. The rejection region for T can be determined by consulting Table XIII in Appendix B (part of the table is shown in Table 7.12).

This table gives a value T_0 for both one-tailed and two-tailed tests for each value of n, the number of matched pairs. For a two-tailed test with $\alpha = .05$, we will

FIGURE 7.20

Rejection region for paired difference experiment

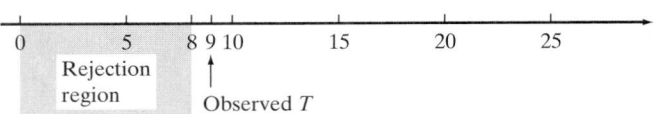

reject H_0 if $T \leq T_0$. You can see in Table 7.12 that the value of T_0 that locates the boundary of the rejection region for the judges' ratings for $\alpha = .05$ and $n = 10$ pairs of observations is 8. Thus, the rejection region for the test (see Figure 7.20) is

Rejection region: $T \leq 8$ for $\alpha = .05$

Since the smaller rank sum for the paper data, $T_- = 9$, does not fall within the rejection region, the experiment has not provided sufficient evidence to indicate that the two paper products differ with respect to their softness ratings at the $\alpha = .05$ level.

Note that if a significance level of $\alpha = .10$ had been used, the rejection region would have been $T \leq 11$ and we would have rejected H_0. In other words, the samples do provide evidence that the probability distributions of the softness ratings differ at the $\alpha = .10$ significance level.

The Wilcoxon signed rank test is summarized in the following box. Note that the difference measurements are assumed to have a continuous probability distribution so that the absolute differences will have unique ranks. Although tied (absolute) differences can be assigned ranks by averaging, the number of ties should be small relative to the number of observations to ensure the validity of the test.

Wilcoxon Signed Rank Test for a Paired Difference Experiment

One-Tailed Test

H_0: Two sampled populations have identical probability distributions

H_a: The probability distribution for population A is shifted to the right of that for population B

Test statistic: T_-, the negative rank sum (we assume the differences are computed by subtracting each paired B measurement from the corresponding A measurement)

Rejection region: $T_- \leq T_0$, where T_0 is found in Table XIII (in Appendix B) for the one-tailed significance level α and the number of untied pairs, n.

Two-Tailed Test

H_0: Two sampled populations have identical probability distributions

H_a: The probability distribution for population A is shifted to the right *or* to the left of that for population B

Test statistic: T, the smaller of the positive and negative rank sums, T_+ and T_-

Rejection region: $T \leq T_0$, where T_0 is found in Table XIII (in Appendix B) for the two-tailed significance level α and the number of untied pairs, n.

[*Note*: If the alternative hypothesis is that the probability distribution for A is shifted to the left of B, we use T_+ as the test statistic and reject H_0 if $T_+ \leq T_0$.]

Assumptions: **1.** The sample of differences is randomly selected from the population of differences.

2. The probability distribution from which the sample of paired differences is drawn is continuous.

> *Ties:* Assign tied absolute differences the average of the ranks they would receive if they were unequal but occurred in successive order. For example, if the third-ranked and fourth-ranked differences are tied, assign both a rank of $(3 + 4)/2 = 3.5$.

EXAMPLE 7.10

Suppose the U.S. Consumer Product Safety Commission (CPSC) wants to test the hypothesis that New York City electrical contractors are more likely to install unsafe electrical outlets in urban homes than in suburban homes. A pair of homes, one urban and one suburban and both serviced by the same electrical contractor, is chosen for each of ten randomly selected electrical contractors. A CPSC inspector assigns each of the 20 homes a safety rating between 1 and 10, with higher numbers implying safer electrical conditions. The results are shown in Table 7.13. Use the Wilcoxon signed rank test to determine whether the CPSC hypothesis is supported at the $\alpha = .05$ level.

SOLUTION

The null and alternative hypotheses are

H_0: The probability distributions of home electrical ratings are identical for urban and suburban homes

H_a: The electrical ratings for suburban homes tend to exceed the electrical ratings for urban homes

Since a paired difference design was used (the homes were selected in urban-suburban pairs so that the electrical contractor was the same for both), we first calculate the difference between the ratings for each pair of homes, and then rank the absolute values of the differences (see Table 7.13). Note that one pair of ratings was the same (both 8), and the resulting 0 difference contributes to neither the positive nor the negative rank sum. Thus, we eliminate this pair from the calculation of the test statistic.

Test statistic: T_+, the positive rank sum

In Table 7.13, we compute the urban minus suburban rating differences, and if the alternative hypothesis is true, we would expect most of these differences to be

TABLE 7.13   Electrical Safety Ratings for 10 Pairs of New York City Homes

	LOCATION		DIFFERENCE	
Contractor	Urban A	Suburban B	(A − B)	Rank of Absolute Difference
1	7	9	−2	4.5
2	4	5	−1	2
3	8	8	0	(Eliminated)
4	9	8	1	2
5	3	6	−3	6
6	6	10	−4	7.5
7	8	9	−1	2
8	10	8	2	4.5
9	9	4	5	9
10	5	9	−4	7.5

Positive rank sum = T_+ = 15.5

FIGURE 7.21
The alternative hypothesis for Example 7.10: We expect T_+ to be small

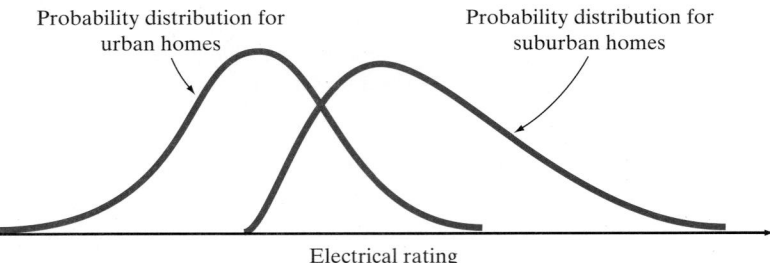

FIGURE 7.22
MINITAB printout for Example 7.10

TEST OF MEDIAN = 0.000000 VERSUS MEDIAN L.T. 0.000000					
		N FOR	WILCOXON		ESTIMATED
	N	TEST	STATISTIC	P-VALUE	MEDIAN
AminusB	10	9	15.5	0.221	−1.000

negative. Or, in other words, we would expect the *positive* rank sum T_+ to be small if the alternative hypothesis is true (see Figure 7.21).

Rejection region: For $\alpha = .05$, from Table XIII of Appendix B, we use $n = 9$ (remember, one pair of observations was eliminated) to find the rejection region for this one-tailed test: $T_+ \leqslant 8$

Since the computed value $T_+ = 15.5$ exceeds the critical value of 8, we conclude that this sample provides insufficient evidence at $\alpha = .05$ to support the alternative hypothesis. We *cannot* conclude on the basis of this sample information that suburban homes have safer electrical outlets than urban homes. A MINITAB printout of the analysis, shown in Figure 7.22, confirms this conclusion. The *p*-value of the test (highlighted) is .221, which exceeds $\alpha = .05$. ◣

As is the case for the rank sum test for independent samples, the sampling distribution of the signed rank statistic can be approximated by a normal distribution when the number n of paired observations is large (say, $n \geqslant 25$). The large-sample z-test is summarized in the next box.

Wilcoxon Signed Rank Test for a Paired Difference Experiment: Large Sample

One-Tailed Test

H_0: Two sampled populations have identical probability distributions

H_a: The probability distribution for population A is shifted to the right of that for population B

Two-Tailed Test

H_0: Two sampled populations have identical probability distributions

H_a: The probability distribution for population A is shifted to the right *or* to the left of that for population B

Test statistic: $z = \dfrac{T_+ - \dfrac{n(n+1)}{4}}{\sqrt{\dfrac{n(n+1)(2n+1)}{24}}}$

Rejection region: $z > z_\alpha$

Assumptions: $n \geqslant 25$

Rejection region: $|z| > z_{\alpha/2}$

Assumptions: $n \geqslant 25$

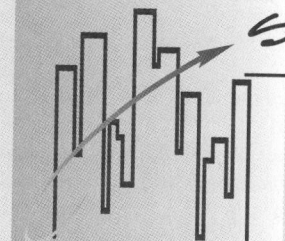

STATISTICS IN ACTION

7.3 TAXPAYERS VERSUS THE IRS: SELECTING THE TRIAL COURT

The Internal Revenue Service (IRS) is empowered by the U.S. Treasury to administer the tax laws. Because taxpayers are responsible for determining and paying their taxes, the IRS periodically audits tax returns to ensure that taxpayers are in compliance with the tax laws. The audit typically requires that the taxpayer provide detailed records and explanations to support the tax return. Most audits result in a mutual agreement between the IRS and taxpayer, usually requiring the taxpayer to pay additional taxes. If the disagreement cannot be resolved, the IRS may decide to litigate the tax dispute, that is, take the taxpayer to court.

Did you know that in litigating tax disputes with the IRS, taxpayers are permitted to choose the court forum? Three mutually exclusive trial courts are available: (1) U.S. Tax Court, (2) Federal District Court, and (3) U.S. Claims Court. Each court possesses different requirements and restrictions that make the choice an important one for the taxpayer.

For example, the U.S. Tax Court does not require prepayment of the disputed amount owed. On the other hand, District Court offers the taxpayer a trial by jury, while the Claims Court tends to favor the taxpayer when the amount disputed is high. Of course, the probability of the taxpayer winning the case in the selected court will also influence the decision.

Accounting professors B. A. Billings (Wayne State University) and B. P. Green (University of Michigan—

Dearborn), and business law professor W. H. Volz (Wayne State University) conducted a study of taxpayers' choice of forum in litigating tax issues (*Journal of Applied Business Research*, Fall 1996). The researchers collected data on litigated tax disputes that were decided in 1987, available from *The American Federal Tax Reports* (Prentice-Hall) and *United States Tax Court Reports* (U.S. Government Printing Office). A random sample of 161 court decisions were obtained for analysis. Two of the many variables measured for each case were taxpayer's choice of forum (Tax, District, or Claims Court) and tax deficiency (i.e., the disputed amount, in dollars).

One of the objectives of the study was to determine those factors that taxpayers consider important in their choice of forum. Consider the variable tax deficiency—called DEF by Billings, Green, and Volz. If DEF is an important factor, then the mean DEF values for the three tax courts should be significantly different.

Focus

a. The researchers applied a nonparametric test rather than a parametric test to compare the DEF distributions of the three tax litigation forums. Give a plausible reason for their choice.

b. Table 7.14 summarizes the data analyzed by the researchers. Conduct nonparametric tests that compare the DEF distributions for each pair of court forums. Use $\alpha = .01$ for each test.

TABLE 7.14 Summary of DEF Data (Statistics in Action 7.3)

Court Selected by Taxpayer	Sample Size	Sample Mean DEF	Rank Sum of DEF Values
Tax	67	$ 80,357	5,335
District	57	74,213	3,937
Claims	37	185,648	3,769

Source: Billings, B. A., Green, B. P., and Volz, W. H. "Selection of forum for litigated tax issues." *Journal of Applied Business Research,* Vol. 12, Fall 1996, p. 38 (Table 2).

EXERCISES 7.64–7.75

Note: Exercises marked with 🖫 *contain data for computer analysis on a 3.5" disk (file name in parentheses).*

Learning the Mechanics

7.64 Specify the test statistic and the rejection region for the Wilcoxon signed rank test for the paired difference design in each of the following situations:

a. $n = 30, \alpha = .10$

H_0: Two probability distributions, A and B, are identical

H_a: Probability distribution for population A is shifted to the right or left of probability distribution for population B

b. $n = 20, \alpha = .05$

H_0: Two probability distributions, A and B, are identical

H_a: Probability distribution for population A is shifted to the right of the probability distribution for population B

c. $n = 8, \alpha = .005$

H_0: Two probability distributions, A and B, are identical

H_a: Probability distribution for population A is shifted to the left of the probability distribution for population B

7.65 **(X07.065)** Suppose you want to test a hypothesis that two treatments, A and B, are equivalent against the alternative hypothesis that the responses for A tend to be larger than those for B. You plan to use a paired difference experiment and to analyze the resulting data using the Wilcoxon signed rank test.

a. Specify the null and alternative hypotheses you would test.

b. Suppose the paired difference experiment yielded the data in the following table. Conduct the test of part **a**. Test using $\alpha = .025$.

Pair	TREATMENT A	TREATMENT B	Pair	TREATMENT A	TREATMENT B
1	54	45	6	77	75
2	60	45	7	74	63
3	98	87	8	29	30
4	43	31	9	63	59
5	82	71	10	80	82

7.66 Explain the difference between the one- and two-tailed versions of the Wilcoxon signed rank test for the paired difference experiment.

7.67 In order to conduct the Wilcoxon signed rank test, why do we need to assume the probability distribution of differences is continuous?

7.68 Suppose you wish to test a hypothesis that two treatments, A and B, are equivalent against the alternative that the responses for A tend to be larger than those for B.

a. If the number of pairs equals 25, give the rejection region for the large-sample Wilcoxon signed rank test for $\alpha = .05$.

b. Suppose that $T_+ = 273$. State your test conclusions.

c. Find the p-value for the test and interpret it.

7.69 A paired difference experiment with $n = 30$ pairs yielded $T_+ = 354$.

a. Specify the null and alternative hypotheses that should be used in conducting a hypothesis test to determine whether the probability distribution for population A is located to the right of that for population B.

b. Conduct the test of part **a** using $\alpha = .05$.

c. What is the approximate p-value of the test of part **b**?

d. What assumptions are necessary to ensure the validity of the test you performed in part **b**?

Applying the Concepts

7.70 **(X07.070)** An atlas is a compendium of geographic, economic, and social information that describes one or more geographic regions. Atlases are used by the sales and marketing functions of businesses, local chambers of commerce, and educators. One of the most critical aspects of a new atlas design is its thematic content. In a survey of atlas users (*Journal of Geography*, May/June 1995), a large sample of high school teachers in British Columbia ranked 12 thematic atlas topics for usefulness. The consensus rankings of the teachers (based on the percentage of teachers who responded they "would definitely use" the topic) are given in the table.

Theme	RANKINGS High School Teachers	RANKINGS Geography Alumni
Tourism	10	2
Physical	2	1
Transportation	7	3
People	1	6
History	2	5
Climate	6	4
Forestry	5	8
Agriculture	7	10
Fishing	9	7
Energy	2	8
Mining	10	11
Manufacturing	12	12

Source: Keller, C. P., *et al.* "Planning the next generation of regional atlases: Input from educators." *Journal of Geography*, Vol. 94, No. 3, May/June 1995, p. 413 (Table 1).

These teacher rankings were compared to the rankings of a group of university geography alumni made three years earlier. Compare the distributions of theme rankings for the two groups with an appropriate nonparametric test. Use $\alpha = .05$. Interpret the results practically.

7.71 A study published in the *Journal of Business Communications* (Fall 1985) considered the question: "Which is the more effective means of dealing with complex group problem-solving tasks—face-to-face meetings or video teleconferencing?" Using an experiment similar to the one described below, two Stetson University researchers concluded that video teleconferencing may be the more effective method. Ten groups of four people each were randomly assigned both to a specific communication setting (face-to-face or video teleconferencing) and to one of two specific complex problems. On completion of the problem-solving task, the same groups were placed in the alternative communication setting and asked to complete the second problem-solving task. The percentage of each problem task correctly completed was recorded for each group, with the results given in the accompanying table.

Group	Face-to-Face	Video Teleconferencing
1	65%	75%
2	82	80
3	54	60
4	69	65
5	40	55
6	85	90
7	98	98
8	35	40
9	85	89
10	70	80

a. What type of experimental design was used in this study?
b. Specify the null and alternative hypotheses that should be used in determining whether the data provide sufficient evidence to conclude that the problem-solving performance of video teleconferencing groups is superior to that of groups that interact face-to-face.
c. Conduct the hypothesis test of part **b**. Use $\alpha = .05$. Interpret the results of your test in the context of the problem.
d. What is the *p*-value of the test in part **c**?

7.72 In Exercise 7.33 inflation forecasts of nine economists that were made in June 1995 and in January 1996 were reported. These forecasts are reproduced here. To determine whether the economists were more optimistic about the prospects for low inflation in late 1996 than they were for late 1995, the Wilcoxon signed rank test will be applied.

	INFLATION FORECASTS (%)	
Economist	June 1995 Forecast for 11/95	January 1996 Forecast for 11/96
Maureen Allyn	3.1	2.4
Wayne Angell	3.4	3.1
David Blitzer	3.0	3.1
Michael Cosgrove	4.0	3.5
Gail Fosler	3.7	3.8
Irwin Kellner	3.3	2.3
Donald Ratajczak	3.5	2.9
Thomas Synott	3.5	3.2
John Williams	3.3	2.6

Source: The Wall Street Journal, Jan. 2, 1996.

a. Specify the null and alternative hypotheses you would employ.
b. Conduct the test using $\alpha = .05$. Interpret your results in the context of the problem.
c. Explain the difference between a Type I and a Type II error in the context of the problem.

7.73 Traditionally, workers in the United States have had a fixed eight-hour workday. A job-scheduling innovation that has helped managers overcome motivation and absenteeism problems associated with the fixed workday is a concept called *flextime*. This flexible working hours program permits employees to design their own 40-hour work week to meet their personal needs (*New York Times,* Mar. 31, 1996). The management of a large manufacturing firm may adopt a flextime program for its administrators and professional employees, depending on the success or failure of a pilot program. Ten employees were randomly selected and given a questionnaire designed to measure their attitude toward their job. Each was then permitted to design and follow a flextime workday. After six months, attitudes toward their jobs were again measured. The resulting attitude scores are displayed in the table. The higher the score, the more favorable the employee's attitude toward his or her work. Use a nonparametric test procedure to evaluate the success of the pilot flextime program. Test using $\alpha = .05$.

Employee	Before	After	Employee	Before	After
1	54	68	6	82	88
2	25	42	7	94	90
3	80	80	8	72	81
4	76	91	9	33	39
5	63	70	10	90	93

7.74 The stocks that comprise Standard and Poor's 500 Index account for 69% of the market capitalization of all U.S. stocks. The index is a benchmark against which investors compare the performance

```
- - - - - Wilcoxon Matched-pairs Signed-ranks Test

        PCHD
with EERF

    Mean Rank      Cases

        8.40         10   - Ranks  (EERF Lt PCHD)
        7.20          5   + Ranks  (EERF Gt PCHD)
                      0     Ties   (EERF Eq PCHD)
                     --
                     15  Total

      Z = -1.3631                 2-tailed P = .1728
```

of individual stocks. A sample of eight of the manufacturing companies included in the index were evaluated for profitability in 1995 and 1996. The profitability measure used was net margin. *Net margin* is defined as net income from continuing operations before extraordinary items as a percentage of sales.

Firm	1996 Net Margin (%)	1995 Net Margin (%)
Tyco International	6.1	5.6
Applied Materials	11.6	15.6
Caterpillar	8.2	7.1
Ingersoll-Rand	5.3	4.7
Johnson Controls	2.3	2.4
3M	10.6	9.7
Black & Decker	3.2	4.5
Rubbermaid	6.5	2.6

Source: Business Week, Mar. 24, 1997, pp. 119–149.

a. Is there sufficient evidence to conclude that U.S. manufacturing firms were more profitable in 1996 than 1995? Test using $\alpha = .05$.

b. What assumptions must be met to ensure the validity of the test in part **a**?

7.75 It has been known for a number of years that the tailings (waste) of gypsum and phosphate mines in Florida contain radioactive radon 222. The radiation levels in waste gypsum and phosphate mounds in Polk County, Florida, are regularly monitored by the Eastern Environmental Radiation Facility (EERF) and by the Polk County Health Department (PCHD), Winter Haven, Florida. The following table shows measurements of the exhalation rate (a measure of radiation) for 15 soil samples obtained from waste mounds in Polk County, Florida. The exhalation rate was measured for each soil sample by both the PCHD and the EERF. Do the data provide sufficient evidence (at $\alpha = .05$) to indicate that one of the measuring facilities, PCHD or EERF, tends to read higher or lower than the other? Use the SPSS Wilcoxon signed rank printout above to make your conclusions.

Charcoal Canister No.	PCHD	EERF
71	1,709.79	1,479.0
58	357.17	257.8
84	1,150.94	1,287.0
91	1,572.69	1,395.0
44	558.33	416.5
43	4,132.28	3,993.0
79	1,489.86	1,351.0
61	3,017.48	1,813.0
85	393.55	187.7
46	880.84	630.4
4	2,996.49	3,707.0
20	2,367.40	2,791.0
36	599.84	706.8
42	538.37	618.5
55	2,770.23	2,639.0

Source: Horton, T. R. "Preliminary radiological assessment of radon exhalation from phosphate gypsum piles and inactive uranium mill tailings piles." EPA-520/5-79-004. Washington, D.C.: Environmental Protection Agency, 1979.

7.7 COMPARING THREE OR MORE POPULATION MEANS: ANALYSIS OF VARIANCE (OPTIONAL)

Suppose we are interested in comparing the means of three or more populations. For example, we could compare the mean SAT scores of seniors at three different high schools. Or, we could compare the mean income per household of residents in four census districts. Since the methods of Sections 7.1–7.6 apply to two populations only, we require an alternative technique. In this optional section, we discuss a method for comparing three or more population means based on independent random sampling, called an **analysis of variance** (**ANOVA**).

In the jargon of ANOVA, **treatments** represent the groups or populations of interest. Thus, the primary objective of an analysis of variance is to compare the treatment (or population) means. If we denote the true means of the p treatments as $\mu_1, \mu_2, \ldots, \mu_p$, then we will test the null hypothesis that the treatment means are all equal against the alternative that at least two of the treatment means differ:

$$H_0: \mu_1 = \mu_2 = \cdots = \mu_p$$

$$H_a: \text{At least two of the } p \text{ treatment means differ}$$

The μ's might represent the means of *all* high school seniors' SAT scores at three high schools or the means of *all* households' income in each of four census regions.

To conduct a statistical test of these hypotheses, we will use the means of the independent random samples selected from the treatment populations. That is, we compare the p sample means, $\bar{x}_1, \bar{x}_2, \ldots, \bar{x}_p$.

To illustrate the method in a two-sample case, suppose you select independent random samples of five female and five male high school seniors and obtain sample mean SAT scores of 550 and 590, respectively. Can we conclude that males score 40 points higher, on average, than females? To answer this question, we must consider the amount of sampling variability among the experimental units (students). If the scores are as depicted in the dot plot shown in Figure 7.23, then the difference between the means is small relative to the sampling variability of the scores within the treatments, Female and Male. We would be inclined not to reject the null hypothesis of equal population means in this case.

In contrast, if the data are as depicted in the dot plot of Figure 7.24, then the sampling variability is small relative to the difference between the two means. We would be inclined to favor the alternative hypothesis that the population means differ in this case.

You can see that the key is to compare the difference between the treatment means to the amount of sampling variability. To conduct a formal statistical test of the hypotheses requires numerical measures of the difference between the treatment means and the sampling variability within each treatment. The variation between the treatment means is measured by the **Sum of Squares for Treatments** (SST), which is calculated by squaring the distance between each treatment mean

FIGURE 7.23
Dot plot of SAT scores: Difference between means dominated by sampling variability

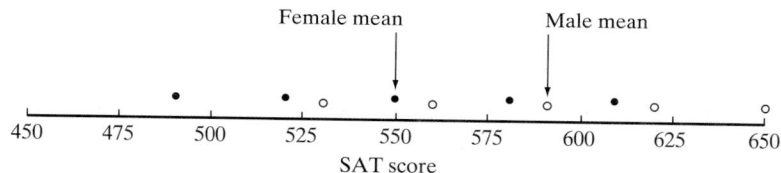

FIGURE 7.24
Dot plot of SAT scores: Difference between means large relative to sampling variability

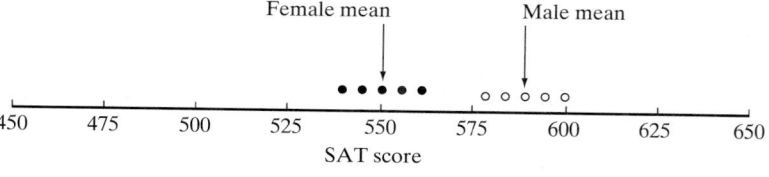

and the overall mean of *all* sample measurements, multiplying each squared distance by the number of sample measurements for the treatment, and adding the results over all treatments:

$$\text{SST} = \sum_{i=1}^{p} n_i(\bar{x}_i - \bar{x})^2 = 5(550 - 570)^2 + 5(590 - 570)^2 = 4,000$$

where we use $\bar{x}$ to represent the overall mean response of all sample measurements, that is, the mean of the combined samples. The symbol n_i is used to denote the sample size for the *i*th treatment. You can see that the value of SST is 4,000 for the two samples of five female and five male SAT scores depicted in Figures 7.23 and 7.24.

Next, we must measure the sampling variability within the treatments. We call this the **Sum of Squares for Error** (SSE) because it measures the variability around the treatment means that is attributed to sampling error. Suppose the 10 measurements in the first dot plot (Figure 7.23) are 490, 520, 550, 580, and 610 for females, and 530, 560, 590, 620, and 650 for males. Then the value of SSE is computed by summing the squared distance between each response measurement and the corresponding treatment mean, and then adding the squared differences over all measurements in the entire sample:

$$\text{SSE} = \sum_{j=1}^{n_1}(x_{1j} - \bar{x}_1)^2 + \sum_{j=1}^{n_2}(x_{2j} - \bar{x}_2)^2 + \cdots + \sum_{j=1}^{n_p}(x_{pj} - \bar{x}_p)^2$$

where the symbol x_{1j} is the *j*th measurement in sample 1, x_{2j} is the *j*th measurement in sample 2, and so on. This rather complex-looking formula can be simplified by recalling the formula for the sample variance, s^2, given in Chapter 2:

$$s^2 = \sum_{i=1}^{n} \frac{(x_i - \bar{x})^2}{n - 1}$$

Note that each sum in SSE is simply the numerator of s^2 for that particular treatment. Consequently, we can rewrite SSE as

$$\text{SSE} = (n_1 - 1)s_1^2 + (n_2 - 1)s_2^2 + \cdots + (n_p - 1)s_p^2$$

where $s_1^2, s_2^2, \ldots, s_p^2$ are the sample variances for the p treatments. For our samples of SAT scores, we find $s_1^2 = 2,250$ (for females) and $s_2^2 = 2,250$ (for males); then we have

$$\text{SSE} = (5 - 1)(2,250) + (5 - 1)(2,250) = 18,000$$

To make the two measurements of variability comparable, we divide each by the degrees of freedom to convert the sums of squares to mean squares. First, the **Mean Square for Treatments** (MST), which measures the variability *among* the treatment means, is equal to

$$\text{MST} = \frac{\text{SST}}{p - 1} = \frac{4,000}{2 - 1} = 4,000$$

where the number of degrees of freedom for the p treatments is $(p - 1)$. Next, the **Mean Square for Error** (MSE), which measures the sampling variability *within* the treatments, is

$$\text{MSE} = \frac{\text{SSE}}{n - p} = \frac{18,000}{10 - 2} = 2,250$$

Finally, we calculate the ratio of MST to MSE—an *F* statistic:

$$F = \frac{\text{MST}}{\text{MSE}} = \frac{4,000}{2,250} = 1.78$$

Values of the F statistic near 1 indicate that the two sources of variation, between treatment means and within treatments, are approximately equal. In this case, the difference between the treatment means may well be attributable to sampling error, which provides little support for the alternative hypothesis that the population treatment means differ. Values of F well in excess of 1 indicate that the variation among treatment means well exceeds that within means and therefore support the alternative hypothesis that the population treatment means differ.

When does F exceed 1 by enough to reject the null hypothesis that the means are equal? This depends on the degrees of freedom for treatments and for error, and on the value of α selected for the test. We compare the calculated F value to a table F value (Tables VII–X of Appendix B) with $v_1 = (p - 1)$ degrees of freedom in the numerator and $v_2 = (n - p)$ degrees of freedom in the denominator and corresponding to a Type I error probability of α. For the SAT score example, the F statistic has $v_1 = (2 - 1) = 1$ numerator degree of freedom and $v_2 = (10 - 2) = 8$ denominator degrees of freedom. Thus, for $\alpha = .05$ we find (Table VIII of Appendix B)

$$F_{.05} = 5.32$$

The implication is that MST would have to be 5.32 times greater than MSE before we could conclude at the .05 level of significance that the two population treatment means differ. Since the data yielded $F = 1.78$, our initial impressions for the dot plot in Figure 7.23 are confirmed—there is insufficient information to conclude that the mean SAT scores differ for the populations of female and male high school seniors. The rejection region and the calculated F value are shown in Figure 7.25.

In contrast, consider the dot plot in Figure 7.24. Since the means are the same as in the first example, 550 and 590, respectively, the variation between the means is the same, MST = 4,000. But the variation within the two treatments appears to be considerably smaller. The observed SAT scores are 540, 545, 550, 555, and 560 for females, and 580, 585, 590, 595, and 600 for males. These values yield $s_1^2 = 62.5$ and $s_2^2 = 62.5$. Thus, the variation within the treatments is measured by

$$\text{SSE} = (5 - 1)(62.5) + (5 - 1)(62.5)$$
$$= 500$$

$$\text{MSE} = \frac{\text{SSE}}{n - p} = \frac{500}{8} = 62.5$$

FIGURE 7.25
Rejection region and calculated F values for SAT score samples

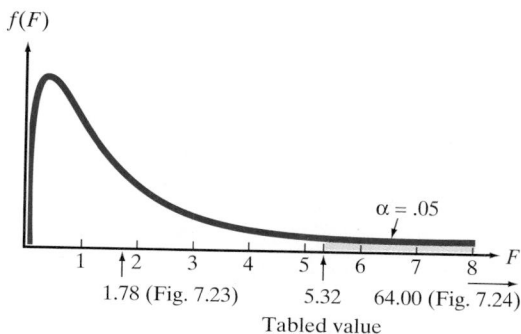

Then the F-ratio is

$$F = \frac{\text{MST}}{\text{MSE}} = \frac{4{,}000}{62.5} = 64.0$$

Again, our visual analysis of the dot plot is confirmed statistically: $F = 64.0$ well exceeds the tabled F value, 5.32, corresponding to the .05 level of significance. We would therefore reject the null hypothesis at that level and conclude that the SAT mean score of males differs from that of females.

Recall that we performed a hypothesis test for the difference between two means in Section 7.1, using a two-sample t statistic for two independent samples. When two independent samples are being compared, the t- and F-tests are equivalent. To see this, recall the formula

$$t = \frac{\bar{x}_1 - \bar{x}_2}{\sqrt{s_p^2\left(\frac{1}{n_1} + \frac{1}{n_2}\right)}} = \frac{590 - 550}{\sqrt{(62.5)\left(\frac{1}{5} + \frac{1}{5}\right)}} = \frac{40}{5} = 8$$

where we used the fact that $s_p^2 = \text{MSE}$, which you can verify by comparing the formulas. Note that the calculated F for these samples ($F = 64$) equals the square of the calculated t for the same samples ($t = 8$). Likewise, the tabled F value (5.32) equals the square of the tabled t value at the two-sided .05 level of significance ($t_{.025} = 2.306$ with 8 df). Since both the rejection region and the calculated values are related in the same way, the tests are equivalent. Moreover, the assumptions that must be met to ensure the validity of the t- and F-tests are the same:

1. The probability distributions of the populations of responses associated with each treatment must all be normal.

2. The probability distributions of the populations of responses associated with each treatment must have equal variances.

3. The samples of experimental units selected for the treatments must be random and independent.

In fact, the only real difference between the tests is that the F-test can be used to compare *more than two* treatment means, whereas the t-test is applicable to two samples only. The F-test is summarized in the accompanying box.

ANOVA Test to Compare p Treatment Means: Independent Sampling

$$H_0\text{: } \mu_1 = \mu_2 = \cdots = \mu_p$$

H_a: At least two treatment means differ

$$\text{Test statistic: } F = \frac{\text{MST}}{\text{MSE}}$$

Assumptions: 1. Samples are selected randomly and independently from the respective populations.

2. All p population probability distributions are normal.

3. The p population variances are equal.

Rejection region: $F > F_\alpha$, where F_α is based on $(p - 1)$ numerator degrees of freedom (associated with MST) and $(n - p)$ denominator degrees of freedom (associated with MSE).

TABLE 7.15   Results of Completely Randomized Design: Iron Byron Driver

	Brand A	Brand B	Brand C	Brand D
	251.2	263.2	269.7	251.6
	245.1	262.9	263.2	248.6
	248.0	265.0	277.5	249.4
	251.1	254.5	267.4	242.0
	260.5	264.3	270.5	246.5
	250.0	257.0	265.5	251.3
	253.9	262.8	270.7	261.8
	244.6	264.4	272.9	249.0
	254.6	260.6	275.6	247.1
	248.8	255.9	266.5	245.9
Sample Means	250.8	261.1	270.0	249.3

Computational formulas for MST and MSE are given in Appendix C. We will rely on some of the many statistical software packages available to compute the F statistic, concentrating on the interpretation of the results rather than their calculations.

EXAMPLE 7.11

Suppose the USGA wants to compare the mean distances associated with four different brands of golf balls when struck with a driver. A completely randomized design is employed, with Iron Byron, the USGA's robotic golfer, using a driver to hit a random sample of 10 balls of each brand in a random sequence. The distance is recorded for each hit, and the results are shown in Table 7.15, organized by brand.

a. Set up the test to compare the mean distances for the four brands. Use $\alpha = .10$.

b. Use the SAS Analysis of Variance program to obtain the test statistic and p-value. Interpret the results.

SOLUTION

a. To compare the mean distances of the four brands, we first specify the hypotheses to be tested. Denoting the population mean of the ith brand by μ_i, we test

$$H_0: \mu_1 = \mu_2 = \mu_3 = \mu_4$$

H_a: The mean distances differ for at least two of the brands

The test statistic compares the variation among the four treatment (Brand) means to the sampling variability within each of the treatments.

Test statistic: $F = \dfrac{\text{MST}}{\text{MSE}}$

Rejection region: $F > F_\alpha = F_{.10}$
with $v_1 = (p - 1) = 3$ df and $v_2 = (n - p) = 36$ df

From Table VII of Appendix B, we find $F_{.10} \approx 2.25$ for 3 and 36 df. Thus, we will reject H_0 if $F > 2.25$. (See Figure 7.26.)

The assumptions necessary to ensure the validity of the test are as follows:

1. The samples of 10 golf balls for each brand are selected randomly and independently.

FIGURE 7.26
F-Test for golf ball experiment

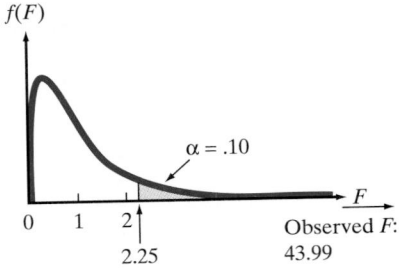

2. The probability distributions of the distances for each brand are normal.

3. The variances of the distance probability distributions for each brand are equal.

b. The SAS printout for the data in Table 7.15 resulting from this completely randomized design is given in Figure 7.27. Note that the top part of the printout is identical to that in a regression analysis. The Total Sum of Squares is designated the **Corrected Total**, and it is partitioned into the **Model** and **Error Sums of Squares**. The bottom part of the printout further partitions the **Model** component into the factors that comprise the model. In this single-factor experiment, the Model and Brand sums of squares are the same. The **Sum of Squares** column is headed **Anova SS**.

The values of the mean squares, MST and MSE (highlighted on the printout), are 931.46 and 21.18, respectively. The *F*-ratio, 43.99, also highlighted on the printout, exceeds the tabled value of 2.25. We therefore reject the null hypothesis at the .10 level of significance, concluding that at least two of the brands differ with respect to mean distance traveled when struck by the driver.

The observed significance level of the *F*-test is also highlighted on the printout: .0001. This is the area to the right of the calculated *F* value and it implies that we would reject the null hypothesis that the means are equal at any α level greater than .0001.

The results of an analysis of variance (ANOVA) can be summarized in a simple tabular format similar to that obtained from the SAS program in Example 7.11. The general form of the table is shown in Table 7.16, where the symbols df, SS, and

Analysis of Variance Procedure

Dependent Variable: DISTANCE

Source	DF	Sum of Squares	Mean Square	F Value	Pr > F
Model	3	2794.388750	931.462917	43.99	0.0001
Error	36	762.301000	21.175028		
Corrected Total	39	3556.689750			

R-Square	C.V.	Root MSE	DISTANCE Mean
0.785671	1.785118	4.601633	257.777500

Source	DF	Anova SS	Mean Square	F Value	Pr > F
BRAND	3	2794.388750	931.462917	43.99	0.0001

FIGURE 7.27 SAS analysis of variance printout for golf ball distance data

TABLE 7.16   General ANOVA Summary Table for a Completely Randomized Design

Source	df	SS	MS	F
Treatments	$p-1$	SST	$\text{MST} = \dfrac{\text{SST}}{p-1}$	$\dfrac{\text{MST}}{\text{MSE}}$
Error	$n-p$	SSE	$\text{MSE} = \dfrac{\text{SSE}}{n-p}$	
Total	$n-1$	SS(Total)		

TABLE 7.17   ANOVA Summary Table for Example 7.11

Source	df	SS	MS	F	p-Value
Brands	3	2,794.39	931.46	43.99	.0001
Error	36	762.30	21.18		
Total	39	3,556.69			

MS stand for degrees of freedom, Sum of Squares, and Mean Square, respectively. Note that the two sources of variation, Treatments and Error, add to the Total Sum of Squares, SS(Total). The ANOVA summary table for Example 7.11 is given in Table 7.17.

Suppose the F-test results in a rejection of the null hypothesis that the treatment means are equal. Is the analysis complete? Usually, the conclusion that at least two of the treatment means differ leads to other questions. Which of the means differ, and by how much? For example, the F-test in Example 7.11 leads to the conclusion that at least two of the brands of golf balls have different mean distances traveled when struck with a driver. Now the question is, which of the brands differ? How are the brands ranked with respect to mean distance?

One way to obtain this information is to construct a confidence interval for the difference between the means of any pair of treatments using the method of Section 7.1. For example, if a 95% confidence interval for $\mu_A - \mu_C$ in Example 7.11 is found to be $(-24, -13)$, we are confident that the mean distance for Brand C exceeds the mean for Brand A (since all differences in the interval are negative). Constructing these confidence intervals for all possible brand pairs will allow you to rank the brand means. A method for conducting these *multiple comparisons*—one that controls for Type I errors—is beyond the scope of this introductory text. Consult the references to learn more about this methodology.

EXAMPLE 7.12

Refer to the ANOVA conducted in Example 7.11. Are the assumptions required for the test approximately satisfied?

SOLUTION

The assumptions for the test are repeated below.

1. The samples of golf balls for each brand are selected randomly and independently.
2. The probability distributions of the distances for each brand are normal.
3. The variances of the distance probability distributions for each brand are equal.

FIGURE 7.28
MINITAB stem-
and-leaf displays
for golf ball
distance data

```
Stem-and-leaf of BrandA   N = 10
Leaf Unit = 1.0

    2    24 45
    2    24
    4    24 88
   (3)   25 011
    3    25 3
    2    25 4
    1    25
    1    25
    1    26 0

Stem-and-leaf of BrandB   N = 10
Leaf Unit = 1.0

    2    25 45
    3    25 7
    3    25
    4    26 0
   (3)   26 223
    3    26 445

Stem-and-leaf of BrandC   N = 10
Leaf Unit = 1.0

    1    26 3
    2    26 5
    4    26 67
    5    26 9
    5    27 00
    3    27 2
    2    27 5
    1    27 7

Stem-and-leaf of BrandD N = 10
Leaf Unit = 1.0

    1    24 2
    2    24 5
    4    24 67
   (3)   24 899
    3    25 11
    1    25
    1    25
    1    25
    1    25
    1    26 1
```

Since the sample consisted of 10 randomly selected balls of each brand and the robotic golfer Iron Byron was used to drive all the balls, the first assumption of independent random samples is satisfied. To check the next two assumptions, we will employ two graphical methods presented in Chapter 2: stem-and-leaf displays and dot plots. A MINITAB stem-and-leaf display for the sample distances of each brand of golf ball is shown in Figure 7.28, followed by a MINITAB dot plot in Figure 7.29.

The normality assumption can be checked by examining the stem-and-leaf displays in Figure 7.28. With only 10 sample measurements for each brand, however, the displays are not very informative. More data would need to be collected

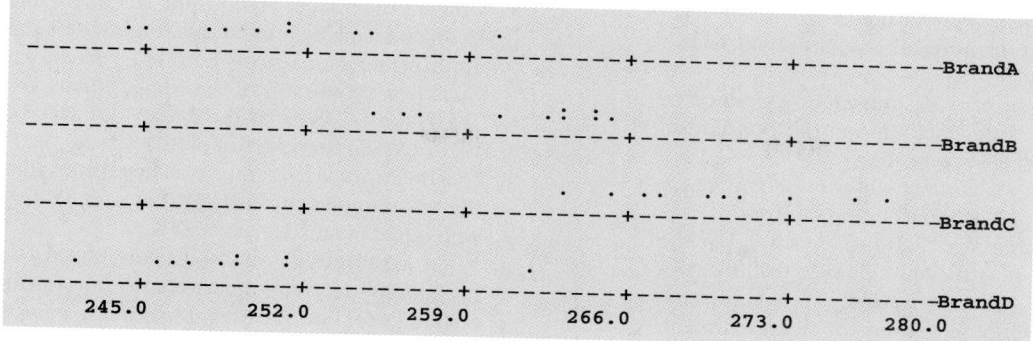

FIGURE 7.29   MINITAB dot plots for golf ball distance data

for each brand before we could assess whether the distances come from normal distributions. Fortunately, analysis of variance has been shown to be a very **robust method** when the assumption of normality is not satisfied exactly: That is, moderate departures from normality do not have much effect on the significance level of the ANOVA F-test or on confidence coefficients. Rather than spend the time, energy, or money to collect additional data for this experiment in order to verify the normality assumption, we will rely on the robustness of the ANOVA methodology.

Dot plots are a convenient way to obtain a rough check on the assumption of equal variances. With the exception of a possible outlier for Brand D, the dot plots in Figure 7.29 show that the spread of the distance measurements is about the same for each brand. Since the sample variances appear to be the same, the assumption of equal population variances for the brands is probably satisfied. Although robust with respect to the normality assumption, ANOVA is *not robust* with respect to the equal variances assumption. Departures from the assumption of equal population variances can affect the associated measures of reliability (e.g., p-values and confidence levels). Fortunately, the effect is slight when the sample sizes are equal, as in this experiment.

Although graphs can be used to check the ANOVA assumptions, as in Example 7.12, no measures of reliability can be attached to these graphs. When you have a plot that is unclear as to whether or not an assumption is satisfied, you can use formal statistical tests, which are beyond the scope of this text. (Consult the references for information on these tests.) When the validity of the ANOVA assumptions is in doubt, nonparametric statistical methods are available.

EXERCISES   7.76–7.88

Note: Exercises marked with 💾 *contain data for computer analysis on a 3.5" disk (file name in parentheses).*

Learning the Mechanics

7.76   A partially completed ANOVA table for a completely randomized design is shown here:

Source	df	SS	MS	F
Treatments	6	17.5	—	—
Error	—	—	—	
Total	41	46.5		

a. Complete the ANOVA table.

b. How many treatments are involved in the experiment?

c. Do the data provide sufficient evidence to indicate a difference among the population means? Test using $\alpha = .10$.

d. Find the approximate observed significance level for the test in part **c**, and interpret it.

e. Suppose that $\bar{x}_1 = 3.7$ and $\bar{x}_2 = 4.1$. Do the data provide sufficient evidence to indicate a difference between μ_1 and μ_2? Assume that there are six observations for each treatment. Test using $\alpha = .10$.

f. Refer to part **e**. Find a 90% confidence interval for $(\mu_1 - \mu_2)$.

g. Refer to part **e**. Find a 90% confidence interval for μ_1.

7.77 Consider dot plots **a** and **b** shown below. In which plot is the difference between the sample means small relative to the variability within the sample observations? Justify your answer.

7.78 Refer to Exercise 7.77. Assume that the two samples represent independent, random samples corresponding to two treatments in a completely randomized design.

a. Calculate the treatment means, i.e., the means of samples 1 and 2, for both dot plots.

b. Use the means to calculate the Sum of Squares for Treatments (SST) for each dot plot.

c. Calculate the sample variance for each sample and use these values to obtain the Sum of Squares for Error (SSE) for each dot plot.

d. Calculate the Total Sum of Squares [SS(Total)] for the two dot plots by adding the Sums of Squares for Treatment and Error. What percentage of SS(Total) is accounted for by the treatments—that is, what percentage of the Total Sum of Squares is the Sum of Squares for Treatment—in each case?

e. Convert the Sum of Squares for Treatment and Error to mean squares by dividing each by the appropriate number of degrees of freedom. Calculate the F-ratio of the Mean Square for Treatment (MST) to the Mean Square for Error (MSE) for each dot plot.

f. Use the F-ratios to test the null hypothesis that the two samples are drawn from populations with equal means. Use $\alpha = .05$.

g. What assumptions must be made about the probability distributions corresponding to the responses for each treatment in order to ensure the validity of the F-tests conducted in part **f**?

7.79 Refer to Exercises 7.77 and 7.78. Conduct a two-sample t-test (Section 7.1) of the null hypothesis that the two treatment means are equal for each dot plot. Use $\alpha = .05$ and two-tailed tests. In the course of the test, compare each of the following with the F-tests in Exercise 7.78:

a. The pooled variances and the MSEs

b. The t- and F-test statistics

c. The tabled values of t and F that determine the rejection regions

d. The conclusions of the t- and F-tests

e. The assumptions that must be made in order to ensure the validity of the t- and F-tests

7.80 Refer to Exercises 7.77 and 7.78. Complete the following ANOVA table for each of the two dot plots:

Source	df	SS	MS	F
Treatments				
Error				
Total				

7.81 See the MINITAB printout below for an experiment utilizing a completely randomized design. [*Note:* MINITAB uses "FACTOR" instead of "Treatments" in this printout.]

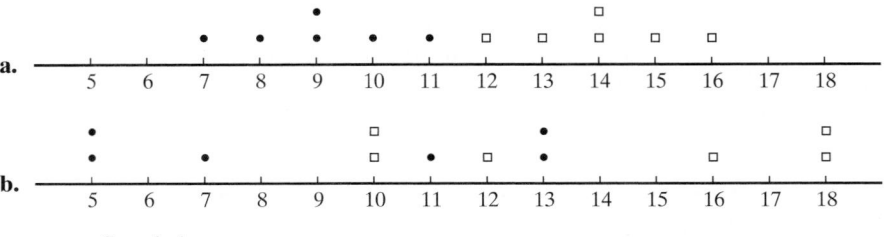

a.

```
   5   6   7   8   9   10  11  12  13  14  15  16  17  18
```

b.

```
   5   6   7   8   9   10  11  12  13  14  15  16  17  18
```

● Sample 1
□ Sample 2

ANALYSIS OF VARIANCE ON Y					
SOURCE	DF	SS	MS	F	p
FACTOR	3	57258	19086	14.80	0.002
ERROR	34	43836	1289		
TOTAL	37	101094			

a. How many treatments are involved in the experiment? What is the total sample size?

b. Conduct a test of the null hypothesis that the treatment means are equal. Use $\alpha = .10$.

c. What additional information is needed in order to be able to compare specific pairs of treatment means?

Applying the Concepts

7.82   A recent study in the *Journal of Psychology and Marketing* (Jan. 1992) investigates consumer attitudes toward product tampering. One variable considered was the education level of the consumer. Consumers were divided into five educational classifications and asked to rate their concern about product tampering on a scale of 1 (little or no concern) to 9 (very concerned). The education levels and the means are shown in the table.

Education Level	Mean	Sample Size
Non–high school graduate	3.731	26
High school graduate	3.224	49
Some college completed	3.330	94
College graduate	3.167	60
Some postgraduate work	4.341	86

a. Identify the type of ANOVA design used in this experiment. Identify the treatments in this experiment.

b. The article compared the mean concern ratings for the five education levels. The F statistic for this test was reported to be 3.298. Conduct a test of hypothesis to determine whether the mean concern ratings differ for at least two of the education levels. [*Hint:* Calculate the degrees of freedom for Treatment and Error from the information given.]

7.83   Speech recognition technology has advanced to the point that it is now possible to communicate with a computer through verbal commands. A study was conducted to evaluate the value of speech recognition in human interactions with computer systems (*Special Interest Group on Computer-Human Interaction Bulletin,* July 1993.) A sample of 45 subjects was randomly divided into three groups (15 subjects per group), and each subject was asked to perform tasks on a basic voice-mail system. A different interface was employed in each group: (1) touchtone, (2) human operator, or (3) simulated speech recognition. One of the variables measured was overall time (in seconds) to perform the assigned tasks. An analysis was conducted to compare the mean overall performance times of the three groups.

a. Identify the experimental design employed in this study.

b. The sample mean performance times for the three groups are given below. Although the sample means are different, the null hypothesis of the ANOVA could not be rejected at $\alpha = .05$. Explain how this is possible.

Group	Mean Performance Time (seconds)
Touchtone	1,400
Human operator	1,030
Speech recognition	1,040

7.84   (X07.084) An accounting firm that specializes in auditing the financial records of large corporations is interested in evaluating the appropriateness of the fees it charges for its services. As part of its evaluation, it wants to compare the costs it incurs in auditing corporations of different sizes. The accounting firm decided to measure the size of its client corporations in terms of their yearly sales. Accordingly, its population of client corporations was divided into three subpopulations:

A: Those with sales over $250 million

B: Those with sales between $100 million and $250 million

C: Those with sales under $100 million

The firm chose random samples of 10 corporations from each of the subpopulations and determined the costs (in thousands of dollars), given in the next table, from its records.

A	B	C
250	100	80
150	150	125
275	75	20
100	200	186
475	55	52
600	80	92
150	110	88
800	160	141
325	132	76
230	233	200

a. Construct a dot plot (refer to Figures 7.23 and 7.24) for the sample data, using different types of dots for each of the three samples. Indicate the location of each of the sample means. Based on the information reflected in your dot plot, do you believe that a significant difference exists among the subpopulation means? Explain.

b. SAS was used to conduct the analysis of variance calculations, resulting in the printout shown at the top of page 392. Conduct a test to determine whether the three classes of firms have different mean costs incurred in audits. Use $\alpha = .05$.

```
                      General Linear Models Procedure
     Dependent Variable: COST

                                  Sum of          Mean
     Source               DF      Squares        Square     F Value   Pr > F
     Model                 2    318861.667     159430.833     8.44    0.0014
     Error                27    510163.000      18894.926
     Corrected Total      29    829024.667

                 R-Square          C.V.      Root MSE           COST Mean
                 0.384623      72.220043      137.459          190.333333

     Source               DF   Type 1 SS  Mean Square     F Value   Pr > F
     TREATMNT              2   318861.67   159430.83          8.44    0.0014
```

c. What is the observed significance level for the test in part **b**? Interpret it.

d. What assumptions must be met in order to ensure the validity of the inferences you made in parts **b** and **c**?

7.85 The Minnesota Multiphasic Personality Inventory (MMPI) is a questionnaire used to gauge personality type. Several scales are built into the MMPI to assess response distortion; these include the Infrequency (I), Obvious (O), Subtle (S), Obvious-subtle (O-S), and Dissimulation (D) scales. *Psychological Assessment* (Mar. 1995) published a study that investigated the effectiveness of these MMPI scales in detecting deliberately distorted responses. A completely randomized design with four treatments was employed. The treatments consisted of independent random samples of females in the following four groups: nonforensic psychiatric patients ($n_1 = 65$), forensic psychiatric patients ($n_2 = 28$), college students who were requested to respond honestly ($n_3 = 140$), and college students who were instructed to provide "fake bad" responses ($n_4 = 45$). All 278 participants were given the MMPI and the I, O, S, O-S, and D scores were recorded for each. Each scale was treated as a response variable and an analysis of variance conducted. The ANOVA F-values are reported in the table.

a. For each response variable, determine whether the mean scores of the four groups completing the MMPI differ significantly. Use $\alpha = .05$ for each test.

Response Variable	ANOVA F-Value
Infrequency (I)	155.8
Obvious (O)	49.7
Subtle (S)	10.3
Obvious-subtle (O-S)	45.4
Dissimulation (D)	39.1

b. If the MMPI is effective in detecting distorted responses, then the mean score for the "fake bad" treatment group will be largest. Based on the information provided, can the researchers make an inference about the effectiveness of the MMPI? Explain.

7.86 (X07.086) Organic chemical solvents are used for cleaning fabricated metal parts in industries such as aerospace, electronics, and automobiles. These solvents, when disposed of, have the potential to become hazardous waste. The *Journal of Hazardous Materials* (July 1995) published the results of a study of the chemical properties of three different types of hazardous organic solvents used to clean metal parts: aromatics, chloroalkanes, and esters. One variable studied was sorption rate, measured as mole percentage. Independent samples of solvents from each type were tested and their sorption rates were recorded, as shown in the table on page 393. A MINITAB analysis of variance of the data is shown in the printout below.

a. Construct an ANOVA table from the MINITAB printout.

```
     Analysis of Variance for SORPRATE
     Source      DF       SS        MS        F        p
     SOLVENT      2    3.3054    1.6527    24.51    0.000
     Error       29    1.9553    0.0674
     Total       31    5.2607
```

Aromatics		Chloroalkanes		Esters		
1.06	.95	1.58	1.12	.29	.43	.06
.79	.65	1.45	.91	.06	.51	.09
.82	1.15	.57	.83	.44	.10	.17
.89	1.12	1.16	.43	.61	.34	.60
1.05				.55	.53	.17

Source: Reprinted from *Journal of Hazardous Materials,* Vol. 42, No. 2, J. D. Ortego *et al.,* "A review of polymeric geosynthetics used in hazardous waste facilities," p. 142 (Table 9), July 1995.

b. Is there evidence of differences among the mean sorption rates of the three organic solvent types? Test using $\alpha = .10$.

7.87 Industrial sales professionals have long debated the effectiveness of various sales closing techniques. University of Akron researchers S. Hawes, J. Strong, and B. Winick investigated the impact of five different closing techniques and a no-close condition on the level of a sales prospect's trust in the salesperson (*Industrial Marketing Management,* Sept. 1996). Two of the five closing techniques were the *assumed close* and the *impending event technique.* In the former, the salesperson simply writes up the order or behaves as if the sale has been made. In the latter, the salesperson encourages the buyer to buy now before some future event occurs that makes the terms of the sale less favorable for the buyer. Sales scenarios were presented to a sample of 238 purchasing executives. Each subject received one of the five closing techniques or a scenario in which no close was achieved. After reading the sales scenario, each executive was asked to rate their level of trust in the salesperson on a 7-point scale. The table reports the six treatments employed in the study and the number of subjects receiving each treatment.

Treatments: Closing Techniques	Sample Size
1. No close	38
2. Impending event	36
3. Social validation	29
4. If-then	42
5. Assumed close	36
6. Either-or	56

a. The investigator's hypotheses were

H_0: The salesperson's level of prospect trust *is not* influenced by the choice of closing method

H_a: The salesperson's level of prospect trust *is* influenced by the choice of closing method

Rewrite these hypotheses in the form required for an analysis of variance.

b. The researchers reported the ANOVA F statistic as $F = 2.21$. Is there sufficient evidence to reject H_0 at $\alpha = .05$?

c. What assumptions must be met in order for the test of part **a** to be valid?

7.88 On average, over a million new businesses are started in the United States every year. An article in the *Journal of Business Venturing* (Vol. 11, 1996) reported on the activities of entrepreneurs during the organization creation process. Among the questions investigated were what activities and how many activities do entrepreneurs initiate in attempting to establish a new business? A total of 71 entrepreneurs were interviewed and divided into three groups: those that were successful in founding a new firm (34), those still actively trying to establish a firm (21), and those who tried to start a new firm, but eventually gave up (16). The total number of activities undertaken (i.e., developed a business plan, sought funding, looked for facilities, etc.) by each group over a specified time period during organization creation was measured and the following incomplete ANOVA table produced:

Source	df	SS	MS	F
Groups	2	128.70	___	___
Error	68	27,124.52	___	

Source: Carter, N., Garner, W., and Reynolds, P. "Exploring start-up event sequences." *Journal of Business Venturing,* Vol. 11, 1996, p. 159.

a. Complete the ANOVA table.

b. Do the data provide sufficient evidence to indicate that the total number of activities undertaken differed among the three groups of entrepreneurs? Test using $\alpha = .05$.

c. What is the *p*-value of the test you conducted in part **b**?

d. One of the conclusions of the study was that the behaviors of entrepreneurs who have successfully started a new company can be differentiated from the behaviors of entrepreneurs that failed. Do you agree? Justify your answer.

QUICK REVIEW

Key Terms

Note: Starred (*) terms are from the optional sections in this chapter.

Analysis of variance (ANOVA)* 380
Blocking 345
F-distribution* 358
F-test* 360
Nonparametric method* 362

Paired difference experiment 345
Pooled sample variance 328
Randomized block experiment 345
Rank sum* 365
Robust method* 389

Standard error 326
Treatments* 381
Weighted average 329
Wilcoxon rank sum test* 364
Wilcoxon signed rank test* 372

Key Formulas

Note: Starred (*) formulas are from the optional section in this chapter.

$(1 - \alpha)100\%$ confidence interval for θ: (see table below)
Large samples: $\hat{\theta} \pm z_{\alpha/2}\sigma_{\hat{\theta}}$
Small samples: $\hat{\theta} \pm t_{\alpha/2}\sigma_{\hat{\theta}}$

For testing H_0: $\theta = D_0$: (see table below)
Large samples: $z = \dfrac{\hat{\theta} - D_0}{\sigma_{\hat{\theta}}}$

Small samples: $t = \dfrac{\hat{\theta} - D_0}{\sigma_{\hat{\theta}}}$

Parameter, θ	Estimator, $\hat{\theta}$	Standard Error of Estimator, $\sigma_{\hat{\theta}}$	Estimated Standard Error	
$(\mu_1 - \mu_2)$ (independent samples)	$(\bar{x}_1 - \bar{x}_2)$	$\sqrt{\dfrac{\sigma_1^2}{n_1} + \dfrac{\sigma_2^2}{n_2}}$	Large n: $\sqrt{\dfrac{s_1^2}{n_1} + \dfrac{s_2^2}{n_2}}$	326
			Small n: $\sqrt{s_p^2\left(\dfrac{1}{n_1} + \dfrac{1}{n_2}\right)}$	329, 330
μ_D (paired sample)	$\bar{x}_D$	$\dfrac{\sigma_D}{\sqrt{n_D}}$	$\dfrac{s_D}{\sqrt{n_D}}$	346

$s_p^2 = \dfrac{(n_1 - 1)s_1^2 + (n_2 - 1)s_2^2}{n_1 + n_2 - 2}$ Pooled sample variance 329

$n_1 = n_2 = \dfrac{(z_{\alpha/2})^2(\sigma_1^2 + \sigma_2^2)}{B^2}$ Determining the sample size for estimating $(\mu_1 - \mu_2)$ 356

$*F = \begin{cases} \dfrac{\text{larger } s^2}{\text{smaller } s^2} & \text{if } H_a: \dfrac{\sigma_1^2}{\sigma_2^2} \neq 1 \\ \dfrac{s_1^2}{s_2^2} & \text{if } H_a: \dfrac{\sigma_1^2}{\sigma_2^2} > 1 \end{cases}$ Test statistic for testing H_0: $\dfrac{\sigma_1^2}{\sigma_2^2}$ 361

$$*z = \frac{T_A - \dfrac{n_1(n_1 + n_2 + 1)}{2}}{\sqrt{\dfrac{n_1 n_2(n_1 + n_2 + 1)}{12}}}$$

Wilcoxon rank sum test (large samples)   366, 369

$$*z = \frac{T_{+-} - \dfrac{n(n + 1)}{4}}{\sqrt{\dfrac{n(n + 1)(2n + 1)}{24}}}$$

Wilcoxon signed ranks test (large sample)   374, 376

$$*F = \frac{\text{MST}}{\text{MSE}}$$

ANOVA F-test   384

LANGUAGE LAB

Note: Starred (*) symbols are from the optional sections in this chapter.

Symbol	Pronunciation	Description
$(\mu_1 - \mu_2)$	mu-1 minus mu-2	Difference between population means
$(\bar{x}_1 - \bar{x}_2)$	x-bar-1 minus x-bar-2	Difference between sample means
$\sigma_{(\bar{x}_1 - \bar{x}_2)}$	sigma of x-bar-1 minus x-bar-2	Standard deviation of the sampling distribution of $(\bar{x}_1 - \bar{x}_2)$
s_p^2	s-p squared	Pooled sample variance
D_0	D naught	Hypothesized value of difference
μ_D	mu D	Difference between population means, paired data
$\bar{x}_D$	x-bar D	Mean of sample differences
s_D	s-D	Standard deviation of sample differences
n_D	n-D	Number of differences in sample
$F_\alpha *$	F-alpha	Critical value of F associated with tail area α
$\nu_1 *$	nu-1	Numerator degrees of freedom for F statistic
$\nu_2 *$	nu-2	Denominator degrees of freedom for F statistic
$\dfrac{\sigma_1^2}{\sigma_2^2} *$	sigma-1 squared over sigma-2 squared	Ratio of two population variances
$T_A *$		Sum of ranks of observations in sample A
$T_B *$		Sum of ranks of observations in sample B
$T_L *$		Critical lower Wilcoxon rank sum value
$T_U *$		Critical upper Wilcoxon rank sum value
$T_+ *$		Sum of ranks of positive differences of paired observations
$T_- *$		Sum of ranks of negative differences of paired observations
$T_0 *$		Critical value of Wilcoxon signed ranks test
ANOVA*		Analysis of variance
SST*		Sum of Squares for Treatments (i.e., the variation among treatment means)
SSE*		Sum of Squares for Error (i.e., the variability around the treatment means due to sampling error)
MST*		Mean Square for Treatments
MSE*		Mean Square for Error (an estimate of σ^2)

SUPPLEMENTARY EXERCISES 7.89–7.110

Note: List the assumptions necessary to ensure the validity of the statistical procedures you use to work these exercises. Exercises marked with ▯ *contain data for computer analysis on a 3.5" disk (file name in parentheses). Starred (*) exercises are from the optional sections in this chapter.*

Learning the Mechanics

7.89 Independent random samples were selected from two normally distributed populations with means μ_1 and μ_2, respectively. The sample sizes, means, and variances are shown in the following table.

Sample 1	Sample 2
$n_1 = 12$	$n_2 = 14$
$\bar{x}_1 = 17.8$	$\bar{x}_2 = 15.3$
$s_1^2 = 74.2$	$s_2^2 = 60.5$

a. Test H_0: $(\mu_1 - \mu_2) = 0$ against H_a: $(\mu_1 - \mu_2) > 0$. Use $\alpha = .05$.
b. Form a 99% confidence interval for $(\mu_1 - \mu_2)$.
c. How large must n_1 and n_2 be if you wish to estimate $(\mu_1 - \mu_2)$ to within 2 units with 99% confidence? Assume that $n_1 = n_2$.

*7.90 Two independent random samples were selected from normally distributed populations with means and variances (μ_1, σ_1^2) and (μ_2, σ_2^2), respectively. The sample sizes, means, and variances are shown in the table below.

Sample 1	Sample 2
$n_1 = 20$	$n_2 = 15$
$\bar{x}_1 = 123$	$\bar{x}_2 = 116$
$s_1^2 = 31.3$	$s_2^2 = 120.1$

a. Test H_0: $\sigma_1^2 = \sigma_2^2$ against H_a: $\sigma_1^2 \neq \sigma_2^2$. Use $\alpha = .05$.
b. Would you be willing to use a t-test to test the null hypothesis H_0: $(\mu_1 - \mu_2) = 0$ against the alternative hypothesis H_a: $(\mu_1 - \mu_2) \neq 0$? Why?

7.91 Two independent random samples are taken from two populations. The results of these samples are summarized in the following table.

Sample 1	Sample 2
$n_1 = 135$	$n_2 = 148$
$\bar{x}_1 = 12.2$	$\bar{x}_2 = 8.3$
$s_1^2 = 2.1$	$s_2^2 = 3.0$

a. Form a 90% confidence interval for $(\mu_1 - \mu_2)$.

b. Test H_0: $(\mu_1 - \mu_2) = 0$ against H_a: $(\mu_1 - \mu_2) \neq 0$. Use $\alpha = .01$.
c. What sample sizes would be required if you wish to estimate $(\mu_1 - \mu_2)$ to within .2 with 90% confidence? Assume that $n_1 = n_2$.

7.92 List the assumptions necessary for each of the following inferential techniques:
a. Large-sample inferences about the difference $(\mu_1 - \mu_2)$ between population means using a two-sample z statistic
b. Small-sample inferences about $(\mu_1 - \mu_2)$ using an independent samples design and a two-sample t statistic
c. Small-sample inferences about $(\mu_1 - \mu_2)$ using a paired difference design and a single-sample t statistic to analyze the differences
*d. Inferences about the ratio σ_1^2/σ_2^2 of two population variances using an F-test.
*e. Inferences about whether three population means—μ_1, μ_2, and μ_3—are equal using an ANOVA F-test.

7.93 A random sample of five pairs of observations were selected, one of each pair from a population with mean μ_1, the other from a population with mean μ_2. The data are shown in the accompanying table.

Pair	Value from Population 1	Value from Population 2
1	28	22
2	31	27
3	24	20
4	30	27
5	22	20

a. Test the null hypothesis H_0: $\mu_D = 0$ against H_a: $\mu_D \neq 0$, where $\mu_D = \mu_1 - \mu_2$. Use $\alpha = .05$.
b. Form a 95% confidence interval for μ_D.
c. When are the procedures you used in parts **a** and **b** valid?

*7.94 Two independent random samples produced the measurements listed in the table below. Do the data provide sufficient evidence to conclude that there is a difference between the locations of the probability distributions for the sampled populations? Test using $\alpha = .05$.

Sample from Population 1		Sample from Population 2	
1.2	1.0	1.5	1.9
1.9	1.8	1.3	2.7
.7	1.1	2.9	3.5
2.5			

*7.95 A random sample of nine pairs of observations are recorded on two variables, x and y. The data are shown in the following table.

Pair	x	y	Pair	x	y
1	19	12	6	29	10
2	27	19	7	16	16
3	15	7	8	22	10
4	35	25	9	16	18
5	13	11			

Do the data provide sufficient evidence to indicate that the probability distribution for x is shifted to the right of that for y? Test using $\alpha = .05$.

*7.96 **(X07.096)** Independent random samples are utilized to compare four treatment means. The data are shown in the table below.

Treatment 1	Treatment 2	Treatment 3	Treatment 4
8	6	9	12
10	9	10	13
9	8	8	10
10	8	11	11
11	7	12	11

a. Given that SST = 36.95 and SS(Total) = 62.55, complete an ANOVA table for this experiment.

b. Is there evidence that the treatment means differ? Use $\alpha = .10$.

c. Place a 90% confidence interval on the mean response for treatment 4.

Applying the Concepts

*7.97 The *Journal of Testing and Evaluation* (July 1992) published an investigation of the mean compression strength of corrugated fiberboard shipping containers. Comparisons were made for boxes of five different sizes: A, B, C, D, and E. Twenty identical boxes of each size were tested and the peak compression strength (pounds) recorded for each box. The figure (see next column) shows the sample means for the five box types as well as the variation around each sample mean.

a. Refer to box types B and D. Based on the graph, does it appear that the mean compressive strengths of these two box types are significantly different? Explain.

b. Based on the graph, does it appear that the mean compressive strengths of all five box types are significantly different? Explain.

7.98 Was the average amount spent by firms in the pharmaceutical industry on company-sponsored research and development (R&D) higher in 1995 than in 1994? The next table lists R&D expendi-

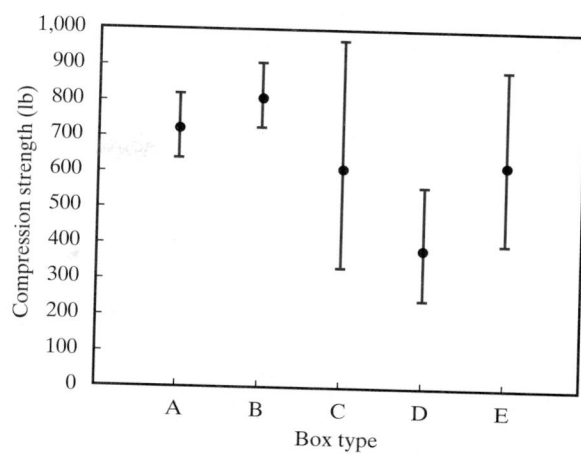

Source: Singh, S. P. , *et. al.* "Compression of single-wall corrugated shipping containers using fixed and floating test platens." *Journal of Testing and Evaluation*, Vol. 20, No. 4, July 1992, p. 319 (Figure 3). Copyright American Society for Testing and Materials. Reprinted with permission.

tures (in millions of dollars) for a sample of firms in the pharmaceutical industry.

Firm	1994	1995
Alza	18.1	20.9
American Home Products	817.1	1,355.0
Bristol Myers Squibb	1,108.0	1,199.0
Johnson and Johnson	1,278.0	1,634.0
Merck	1,230.6	1,331.4
Pfizer	1,139.4	1,442.4
Warner-Lambert	456.0	501.2

Source: Standard and Poor's Compustat 1996.

a. A securities analyst who follows the pharmaceutical industry believes that mean R&D expenditures have increased by more than $100 million per firm. Do the data support the analyst's belief? Use the EXCEL printout at the top of page 398 to answer the question.

b. What are the Type I and Type II errors associated with your hypothesis test of part **a**?

c. What assumptions must hold in order for your test of part **a** to be valid?

7.99 Refer to Exercise 7.98. Use a 95% confidence interval to estimate the mean difference between 1995 and 1994 R&D expenditures. Interpret the interval.

7.100 Nontraditional university students, generally defined as those at least 25 years old, comprise an increasingly large proportion of undergraduate student bodies at most universities. A study reported in the *College Student Journal* (Dec. 1992) compared traditional and nontraditional students on a number of factors, including grade

t-Test: Paired Two Sample for Means		
	year94	year95
Mean	863.8857143	1069.128571
Variance	220897.1748	341185.4424
Observations	7	7
Pearson Correlation	0.952837714	
Hypothesized Mean Difference	0	
df	6	
t Stat	-2.75263003	
P(T<=t) one-tail	0.016588005	
t Critical one-tail	1.943180905	
P(T<=t) two-tail	0.03317601	
t Critical two-tail	2.446913641	

point average (GPA). The table below summarizes the information from the sample.

GPA	Traditional Students	Nontraditional Students
n	94	73
$\bar{x}$	2.90	3.50
s	.50	.50

a. What are the appropriate null and alternative hypotheses if we want to test whether the mean GPAs of traditional and nontraditional students differ?

b. Conduct the test using $\alpha = .01$, and interpret the result.

c. What assumptions are necessary to ensure the validity of the test?

7.101 One theory regarding the mobility of college and university faculty members is that those who publish the most scholarly articles are also the most mobile. The logic behind this theory is that good researchers who publish frequently receive more job offers and are therefore more likely to move from one university to another. The *Academy of Management Journal* (Vol. 25, 1982) examined this relationship for persons employed in industry. Using the personnel records of a large national oil company, the researchers obtained the early career performance records for 529 of the company's employees. Of these, 174 were classified as *stayers*, those who stayed with the company; the other 355, who left the company at varying points during a 15-year period, were classified as *leavers*. Summary statistics on three variables—initial performance, rate of career advancement (number of promotions per year), and final performance appraisals—for both stayers and leavers are shown in the table at the bottom of the page. For each variable, compare the means of stayers and leavers using an appropriate statistical method. Interpret the results.

7.102 A study in the *Journal of Psychology and Marketing* (Jan. 1992) investigates the degree to which American consumers are concerned about product tampering. Large random samples of male and female consumers were asked to rate their concern about product tampering on a scale of 1 (little or no concern) to 9 (very concerned).

a. What are the appropriate null and alternative hypotheses to determine whether a difference exists in the mean level of concern about product tampering between men and women? Define any symbols you use.

b. The statistics reported include those shown in the MINITAB printout at the top of page 399. Interpret these results.

c. What assumptions are necessary to ensure the validity of this test?

7.103 Management training programs are often instituted to teach supervisory skills and thereby increase productivity. Suppose a company psychologist administers a set of examinations to each of ten

	STAYERS ($n_1 = 174$)		LEAVERS ($n_2 = 355$)	
Variable	$\bar{x}_1$	s_1	$\bar{x}_2$	s_2
Initial performance	3.51	.51	3.24	.52
Rate of career advancement	.43	.20	.31	.31
Final performance appraisal	3.78	.62	3.15	.68

```
TWOSAMPLE T FOR MSCORE VS FSCORE
             N       MEAN      STDEV    SE MEAN
MSCORE      200      3.209      2.33     0.165
FSCORE      200      3.923      2.94     0.208
TTEST MU MSCORE = MU FSCORE (VS NE): T= -2.69 P=0.0072 DF=398
```

supervisors before such a training program begins and then administers similar examinations at the end of the program. The examinations are designed to measure supervisory skills, with higher scores indicating increased skill. The results of the tests are shown in the table.

Supervisor	Pre-Test	Post-Test
1	63	78
2	93	92
3	84	91
4	72	80
5	65	69
6	72	85
7	91	99
8	84	82
9	71	81
10	80	87

a. Do the data provide evidence that the training program is effective in increasing supervisory skills, as measured by the examination scores? Use $\alpha = .10$.

b. Find and interpret the approximate p-value for the test on the MINITAB printout shown below.

7.104 Some power plants are located near rivers or oceans so that the available water can be used for cooling the condensers. Suppose that, as part of an environmental impact study, a power company wants to estimate the difference in mean water temperature between the discharge of its plant and the offshore waters. How many sample measurements must be taken at each site in order to estimate the true difference between means to within .2°C with 95% confidence? Assume that the range in readings will be about 4°C at each site and the same number of readings will be taken at each site.

*7.105 The length of time required for a human subject to respond to a new painkiller was tested in the following manner. Seven randomly selected subjects were assigned to receive both aspirin and the new drug. The two treatments were spaced in time and assigned in random order. The length of time (in minutes) required for a subject to indicate that he or she could feel pain relief was recorded for both the aspirin and the drug. The data are shown in the next table. Do the data provide sufficient evidence to indicate that the probability distribution of the times required to obtain relief with aspirin is shifted to the right of the probability distribution of the times required to obtain relief with the new drug?

Subject	Aspirin	New Drug
1	15	7
2	20	14
3	12	13
4	20	11
5	17	10
6	14	16
7	17	11

7.106 Does the time of day during which one works affect job satisfaction? A study in the *Journal of Occupational Psychology* (Sept. 1991) examined differences in job satisfaction between day-shift and night-shift nurses. Nurses' satisfaction with their hours of work, free time away from work, and breaks during work were measured. The following table shows the mean scores for each measure of job satisfaction (higher scores indicate greater satisfaction), along with the observed significance level comparing the means for the day-shift and night-shift samples:

	MEAN SATISFACTION		
	Day Shift	Night Shift	*p*-Value
Satisfaction with:			
Hours of work	3.91	3.56	.813
Free time	2.55	1.72	.047
Breaks	2.53	3.75	.0073

```
TEST OF MU = 0.000 VS MU N.E. 0.000
               N      MEAN     STDEV    SE MEAN        T     P VALUE
PRE-POST      10     -6.900    5.425     1.716      -4.02    0.0030
```

a. Specify the null and alternative hypotheses if we wish to test whether a difference in job satisfaction exists between day-shift and night-shift nurses on each of the three measures. Define any symbols you use.

b. Interpret the p-value for each of the tests. (Each of the p-values in the table is two-tailed.)

c. Assume that each of the tests is based on small samples of nurses from each group. What assumptions are necessary for the tests to be valid?

7.107 (X07.107) Independent random samples of size 36 were drawn from stocks listed on the New York Stock Exchange (NYSE), the American Stock Exchange (ASE), and NASDAQ National Market, respectively. The closing prices of all 108 stocks on March 3, 1997, are listed in the table (see next column). The data are analyzed using SAS. According to the printout at the bottom of the page, is there evidence that the mean closing price differed among the three markets? Test using $\alpha = .10$.

*7.108 When new instruments are developed to perform chemical analyses of products (food, medicine, etc.), they are usually evaluated with respect to two criteria: accuracy and precision. *Accuracy* refers to the ability of the instrument to identify correctly the nature and amounts of a product's components. *Precision* refers to the consistency with which the instrument will identify the components of the same material. Thus, a large variability in the identification of a single batch of a product indicates a lack of precision. Suppose a pharmaceutical firm is considering two brands of an instrument designed to identify the components of certain drugs. As part of a comparison of precision, 10 test-tube samples of a well-mixed batch of a drug are selected and then five are analyzed by instrument A and five by instrument B.

NYSE		ASE		NASDAQ	
$31\frac{3}{4}$	$27\frac{1}{2}$	$5\frac{3}{4}$	$5\frac{1}{2}$	$8\frac{1}{2}$	$6\frac{3}{4}$
$22\frac{1}{4}$	$36\frac{3}{4}$	$23\frac{1}{8}$	$123\frac{1}{2}$	$5\frac{1}{8}$	$21\frac{1}{2}$
$18\frac{3}{4}$	$20\frac{1}{4}$	2	23	$10\frac{1}{4}$	12
$11\frac{1}{4}$	$78\frac{3}{4}$	$11\frac{1}{4}$	$15\frac{3}{4}$	$4\frac{1}{8}$	$4\frac{3}{4}$
43	$13\frac{5}{8}$	$11\frac{3}{4}$	$5\frac{1}{4}$	$7\frac{3}{4}$	$27\frac{3}{4}$
$32\frac{7}{8}$	$12\frac{3}{4}$	$10\frac{1}{4}$	$11\frac{3}{4}$	$22\frac{3}{4}$	16
$20\frac{1}{2}$	$19\frac{3}{4}$	$15\frac{5}{8}$	$15\frac{1}{8}$	$8\frac{1}{2}$	$5\frac{7}{8}$
$3\frac{7}{8}$	$25\frac{1}{4}$	$7\frac{1}{8}$	$2\frac{1}{4}$	$18\frac{7}{8}$	$25\frac{1}{4}$
$9\frac{1}{4}$	$27\frac{1}{2}$	$5\frac{1}{2}$	$19\frac{7}{8}$	$14\frac{5}{8}$	$17\frac{1}{8}$
$11\frac{1}{8}$	$58\frac{1}{2}$	$15\frac{3}{4}$	16	10	$27\frac{3}{4}$
$25\frac{7}{8}$	$18\frac{3}{4}$	1	$7\frac{1}{8}$	$2\frac{1}{4}$	$5\frac{5}{8}$
$16\frac{3}{8}$	$13\frac{1}{8}$	5	$26\frac{1}{4}$	$55\frac{3}{4}$	$2\frac{3}{4}$
$20\frac{7}{8}$	$57\frac{5}{8}$	$30\frac{7}{8}$	$10\frac{3}{8}$	$79\frac{1}{2}$	$26\frac{3}{4}$
8	$40\frac{3}{8}$	$23\frac{3}{4}$	$9\frac{1}{4}$	$5\frac{7}{8}$	$15\frac{7}{8}$
$9\frac{5}{8}$	$21\frac{3}{4}$	$4\frac{3}{8}$	14	53	17
22	$13\frac{1}{4}$	$8\frac{1}{8}$	19	$17\frac{1}{2}$	$14\frac{1}{2}$
$37\frac{3}{4}$	32	$30\frac{3}{8}$	$5\frac{1}{4}$	$4\frac{3}{8}$	$1\frac{7}{8}$
$9\frac{3}{4}$	$38\frac{3}{8}$	$1\frac{7}{8}$	$\frac{5}{8}$	25	$18\frac{1}{4}$

Source: The New York Times, Mar. 4, 1997.

The data shown below are the percentages of the primary component of the drug given by the instruments. Do these data provide evidence of a difference in the precision of the two machines? Use $\alpha = .10$.

Instrument A	Instrument B
43	46
48	49
37	43
52	41
45	48

7.109 How does gender affect the type of advertising that proves to be most effective? An article in the *Journal of Advertising Research* (May/June 1990)

```
                    Analysis of Variance Procedure

Dependent Variable: PRICE

                                Sum of          Mean
Source                DF       Squares         Square    F Value   Pr > F

Model                  2    2082.334201    1041.167101     3.34    0.0394
Error                105   32767.348090     312.069982
Corrected Total      107   34849.682292

             R-Square            C.V.        Root MSE            PRICE Mean

             0.059752         91.93467        17.66550            19.2152778

Source                DF       Anova SS     Mean Square   F Value   Pr > F

STOCK                  2    2082.334201    1041.167101     3.34    0.0394
```

Consumer Products		Utilities	
Nike	.54	Williams	2.50
Coca-Cola	.81	Oneok	4.12
Clorox	1.92	Nicor	3.84
Russell	1.38	Unicom	7.11
Maytag	3.03	Entergy	6.76
Tandy	1.63	Enserch	.95
Seagram	1.64	Peco Energy	8.23
Stride Rite	1.67	PG&E	5.33

Source: Business Week, Mar. 24, 1997.

makes reference to numerous studies that conclude males tend to be more competitive with others than with themselves. To apply this conclusion to advertising, the author creates two ads promoting a new brand of soft drink:

Ad 1: Four men are shown competing in racquetball

Ad 2: One man is shown competing against himself in racquetball

The author hypothesized that the first ad will be more effective when shown to males. To test this hypothesis, 43 males were shown both ads and asked to measure their attitude toward the advertisement (Aad), their attitude toward the brand of soft drink (Ab), and their intention to purchase the soft drink (Intention). Each variable was measured using a 7-point scale, with higher scores indicating a more favorable attitude. The results are shown here:

	SAMPLE MEANS		
	Aad	**Ab**	**Intention**
Ad 1	4.465	3.311	4.366
Ad 2	4.150	2.902	3.813
Level of significance	$p = .091$	$p = .032$	$p = .050$

a. What are the appropriate null and alternative hypotheses to test the author's research hypothesis? Define any symbols you use.

b. Based on the information provided about this experiment, do you think this is an independent samples experiment or a paired difference experiment? Explain.

c. Interpret the p-value for each test.

d. What assumptions are necessary for the validity of the tests?

*7.110 (X07.110) Dividends are cash payments made to stockholders by the corporation. A stock's *dividend yield* is the total amount of cash paid on a single share of stock over the period of a year expressed as a percentage of the current market price of the stock (Alexander, Sharpe, and Bailey, 1993). The table above reports the dividend yields for samples of corporations in two different industries.

a. Under what circumstances would it be appropriate to use a t-test to determine whether the mean dividend yield differs among the two industries? Check this statistically.

b. Assume the circumstances of part **a** do not hold. What nonparametric test could be performed to shed light on the issue of differences in the dividend yields across the three industries?

c. Conduct the test. Use $\alpha = .05$. Interpret your results in the context of the problem.

THE KENTUCKY MILK CASE—PART II

SHOWCASE

In The Kentucky Milk Case—Part I, you used graphical and numerical descriptive statistics to investigate bid collusion in the Kentucky school milk market. This case expands your previous analyses, incorporating inferential statistical methodology. The three areas of your focus are described below. [See page 107 for the file layout of the data available on disk for analysis.] Again, you should prepare a professional document which presents the results of the analyses and any implications regarding collusionary practices in the tri-county Kentucky milk market.

1. *Incumbency rates.* Recall from Part I that market allocation (where the same dairy controls the same school districts year after year) is a common form of collusive behavior in bidrigging conspiracies. Market allocation is typically gauged by the incumbency rate for a market in a given school year—defined as the percentage of school districts that are won by the same milk vendor who won the previous year. Past experience with milk bids in a competitive market reveals that a "normal" incumbency rate is about .7. That is, 70% of the school districts are expected to purchase their milk from the same vendor who supplied the milk the previous year. In the 13-district tri-county Kentucky market, 13 vendor transitions potentially exist each year. Over the 1985–1988 period (when bid collusion was alleged to have occurred), there are 52 potential vendor transitions. Based on the actual number of vendor transitions that occurred each year and over the 1985–1988 period, make an inference regarding bid collusion.

2. *Bid price dispersion.* Recall that in competitive sealed-bid markets, more dispersion or variability among the bids is observed than in collusive markets. (This is due to conspiring vendors sharing information about their bids.) Consequently, if collusion exists, the variation in bid prices in the tri-county market should be significantly smaller than the corresponding variation in the surrounding market. For each milk product, conduct an analysis to compare the bid price variances of the two markets each year. Make the appropriate inferences.

3. *Average winning bid price.* According to collusion theorists, the mean winning bid price in the "rigged" market will exceed the mean winning bid price in the competitive market for each year in which collusion occurs. In addition, the difference between the competitive average and the "rigged" average tends to grow over time when collusionary tactics are employed over several consecutive years. For each milk product, conduct an analysis to compare the winning bid price means of the tri-county and surrounding markets each year. Make the appropriate inferences. ▲

www.int.com
www.int.com
INTERNET LAB
www.int.com

CHOOSING BETWEEN ECONOMIC INDICATORS

The Gross Domestic Product (GDP) data that was located in the Internet Lab on page 109 is a measure of all product revenues produced by U.S. business concerns, within and outside the borders of the United States. Another economic indicator, the Gross National Product (GNP), measures all product revenues produced within the borders of the United States by either domestic or foreign-owned business concerns. Prior to 1991, the United States relied on GNP information as the basis for measuring productivity growth, and many businesses used that measure in negotiating union labor contracts. A change to using GDP occurred in 1991 for two primary reasons: (1) other advanced countries in the world used GDP exclusively; and (2) some economists argued that the GNP overstated U.S. economic growth, and thus wage and price increases based on it.

Here we will examine whether these two different measures behave the same statistically or which might have the greater information value if used in business forecasting models of revenues, materials, prices, labor costs, and so forth. Data is provided by the U.S. Department of Commerce: *http://doc.gov/* (refer to your notes from the Internet Lab on page 109).

1. Obtain annual GDP and GNP data from 1980 to present.

2. Save the data in your statistical applications software data files.

3. Formulate and test the hypothesis that the average economic growth measured by the two methods over this time period is equal against the alternative hypothesis that the average GNP is higher than the average GDP. If you are able to reject the null hypothesis, what further business and economic implications do you think this would have other than the level of wage and benefits adjustments? ○

CHAPTER 8

COMPARING POPULATION PROPORTIONS

CONTENTS

8.1   Comparing Two Population Proportions:
Independent Sampling

8.2   Determining the Sample Size

8.3   Comparing Population Proportions:
Multinomial Experiment (Optional)

8.4   Contingency Table Analysis (Optional)

STATISTICS IN ACTION

8.1   Ethics in Computer Technology and Use

Where We've Been

Chapter 7 presented both parametric and nonparametric methods for comparing two or more population means.

Where We're Going

In this chapter we consider the problem of comparing two or more population proportions. The need to compare proportions arises from business and social experiments involving surveys, where categorical responses to the questions are of interest. For example, in this chapter we'll learn how to compare the proportion of consumers who prefer brand A to the corresponding proportion who prefer brand B using either a test of hypothesis or a confidence interval.

Many experiments are conducted in business and the social sciences to compare two or more population proportions. Those conducted to sample the opinions of people are called **sample surveys**. For example, a state government might wish to estimate the difference between the proportions of people in two regions of the state who would qualify for a new welfare program. Or, after an innovative process change, an engineer might wish to determine whether the proportion of defective items produced by a manufacturing process was less than the proportion of defectives produced before the change. In Section 8.1 we show you how to test hypotheses about the difference between two population proportions based on independent random sampling. We will also show how to find a confidence interval for the difference. Then, in optional Section 8.3 we will compare more than two population proportions, and in optional Section 8.4 we will present a related problem.

8.1 COMPARING TWO POPULATION PROPORTIONS: INDEPENDENT SAMPLING

Suppose a manufacturer of camper vans wants to compare the potential market for its products in the northeastern United States to the market in the southeastern United States. Such a comparison would help the manufacturer decide where to concentrate sales efforts. Using telephone directories, the company randomly chooses 1,000 households in the northeast (NE) and 1,000 households in the southeast (SE) and determines whether each household plans to buy a camper within the next five years. The objective is to use this sample information to make an inference about the difference $(p_1 - p_2)$ between the proportion p_1 of *all* households in the NE and the proportion p_2 of *all* households in the SE that plan to purchase a camper within five years.

The two samples represent independent binomial experiments. (See Section 4.3 for the characteristics of binomial experiments.) The binomial random variables are the numbers x_1 and x_2 of the 1,000 sampled households in each area that indicate they will purchase a camper within five years. The results are summarized below.

NE	SE
$n_1 = 1,000$	$n_2 = 1,000$
$x_1 = 42$	$x_2 = 24$

We can now calculate the sample proportions $\hat{p}_1$ and $\hat{p}_2$ of the households in the NE and SE, respectively, that are prospective buyers:

$$\hat{p}_1 = \frac{x_1}{n_1} = \frac{42}{1,000} = .042$$

$$\hat{p}_2 = \frac{x_2}{n_2} = \frac{24}{1,000} = .024$$

The difference between the sample proportions $(\hat{p}_1 - \hat{p}_2)$ makes an intuitively appealing point estimator of the difference between the population parameters $(p_1 - p_2)$. For our example, the estimate is

$$(\hat{p}_1 - \hat{p}_2) = .042 - .024 = .018$$

To judge the reliability of the estimator $(\hat{p}_1 - \hat{p}_2)$, we must observe its performance in repeated sampling from the two populations. That is, we need to know the sampling distribution of $(\hat{p}_1 - \hat{p}_2)$. The properties of the sampling distribution are given in the following box. Remember that $\hat{p}_1$ and $\hat{p}_2$ can be viewed as means of the number of successes per trial in the respective samples, so the Central Limit Theorem applies when the sample sizes are large.

Properties of the Sampling Distribution of $(\hat{p}_1 - \hat{p}_2)$

1. The mean of the sampling distribution of $(\hat{p}_1 - \hat{p}_2)$ is $(p_1 - p_2)$; that is,

$$E(\hat{p}_1 - \hat{p}_2) = p_1 - p_2$$

Thus, $(\hat{p}_1 - \hat{p}_2)$ is an unbiased estimator of $(p_1 - p_2)$.

2. The standard deviation of the sampling distribution of $(\hat{p}_1 - \hat{p}_2)$ is

$$\sigma_{(\hat{p}_1 - \hat{p}_2)} = \sqrt{\frac{p_1 q_1}{n_1} + \frac{p_2 q_2}{n_2}}$$

3. If the sample sizes n_1 and n_2 are large (see Section 5.3 for a guideline), the sampling distribution of $(\hat{p}_1 - \hat{p}_2)$ is approximately normal.

Since the distribution of $(\hat{p}_1 - \hat{p}_2)$ in repeated sampling is approximately normal, we can use the z statistic to derive confidence intervals for $(p_1 - p_2)$ or to test a hypothesis about $(p_1 - p_2)$.

For the camper example, a 95% confidence interval for the difference $(p_1 - p_2)$ is

$$(\hat{p}_1 - \hat{p}_2) \pm 1.96 \sigma_{(\hat{p}_1 - \hat{p}_2)} \qquad \text{or} \qquad (\hat{p}_1 - \hat{p}_2) \pm 1.96 \sqrt{\frac{p_1 q_1}{n_1} + \frac{p_2 q_2}{n_2}}$$

The quantities $p_1 q_1$ and $p_2 q_2$ must be estimated in order to complete the calculation of the standard deviation $\sigma_{(\hat{p}_1 - \hat{p}_2)}$ and hence the calculation of the confidence interval. In Section 5.3 we showed that the value of pq is relatively insensitive to the value chosen to approximate p. Therefore, $\hat{p}_1 \hat{q}_1$ and $\hat{p}_2 \hat{q}_2$ will provide satisfactory estimates to approximate $p_1 q_1$ and $p_2 q_2$, respectively. Then

$$\sqrt{\frac{p_1 q_1}{n_1} + \frac{p_2 q_2}{n_2}} \approx \sqrt{\frac{\hat{p}_1 \hat{q}_1}{n_1} + \frac{\hat{p}_2 \hat{q}_2}{n_2}}$$

and we will approximate the 95% confidence interval by

$$(\hat{p}_1 - \hat{p}_2) \pm 1.96 \sqrt{\frac{\hat{p}_1 \hat{q}_1}{n_1} + \frac{\hat{p}_2 \hat{q}_2}{n_2}}$$

Substituting the sample quantities yields

$$(.042 - .024) \pm 1.96 \sqrt{\frac{(.042)(.958)}{1,000} + \frac{(.024)(.976)}{1,000}}$$

or $.018 \pm .016$. Thus, we are 95% confident that the interval from .002 to .034 contains $(p_1 - p_2)$.

We infer that there are between .2% and 3.4% more households in the northeast than in the southeast that plan to purchase campers in the next five years.

The general form of a confidence interval for the difference $(p_1 - p_2)$ between population proportions is given in the following box.

Large-Sample $100(1 - \alpha)\%$ Confidence Interval for $(p_1 - p_2)$

$$(\hat{p}_1 - \hat{p}_2) \pm z_{\alpha/2}\sigma_{(\hat{p}_1-\hat{p}_2)} = (\hat{p}_1 - \hat{p}_2) \pm z_{\alpha/2}\sqrt{\frac{p_1 q_1}{n_1} + \frac{p_2 q_2}{n_2}}$$

$$\approx (\hat{p}_1 - \hat{p}_2) \pm z_{\alpha/2}\sqrt{\frac{\hat{p}_1\hat{q}_1}{n_1} + \frac{\hat{p}_2\hat{q}_2}{n_2}}$$

Assumptions: The two samples are independent random samples. Both samples should be large enough that the normal distribution provides an adequate approximation to the sampling distribution of $\hat{p}_1$ and $\hat{p}_2$ (see Section 6.5).

The z statistic,

$$z = \frac{(\hat{p}_1 - \hat{p}_2) - (p_1 - p_2)}{\sigma_{(\hat{p}_1-\hat{p}_2)}}$$

is used to test the null hypothesis that $(p_1 - p_2)$ equals some specified difference, say D_0. For the special case where $D_0 = 0$, that is, where we want to test the null hypothesis $H_0: (p_1 - p_2) = 0$ (or, equivalently, $H_0: p_1 = p_2$), the best estimate of $p_1 = p_2 = p$ is obtained by dividing the total number of successes $(x_1 + x_2)$ for the two samples by the total number of observations $(n_1 + n_2)$; that is

$$\hat{p} = \frac{x_1 + x_2}{n_1 + n_2} \qquad \text{or} \qquad \hat{p} = \frac{n_1\hat{p}_1 + n_2\hat{p}_2}{n_1 + n_2}$$

The second equation shows that $\hat{p}$ is a weighted average of $\hat{p}_1$ and $\hat{p}_2$, with the larger sample receiving more weight. If the sample sizes are equal, then $\hat{p}$ is a simple average of the two sample proportions of successes.

We now substitute the weighted average $\hat{p}$ for both p_1 and p_2 in the formula for the standard deviation of $(\hat{p}_1 - \hat{p}_2)$:

$$\sigma_{(\hat{p}_1-\hat{p}_2)} = \sqrt{\frac{p_1 q_1}{n_1} + \frac{p_2 q_2}{n_2}} \approx \sqrt{\frac{\hat{p}\hat{q}}{n_1} + \frac{\hat{p}\hat{q}}{n_2}} = \sqrt{\hat{p}\hat{q}\left(\frac{1}{n_1} + \frac{1}{n_2}\right)}$$

The test is summarized in the next box.

Large-Sample Test of Hypothesis About $(p_1 - p_2)$

One-Tailed Test

$H_0: (p_1 - p_2) = 0$*

$H_a: (p_1 - p_2) < 0$
  [or $H_a: (p_1 - p_2) > 0$]

Two-Tailed Test

$H_0: (p_1 - p_2) = 0$

$H_a: (p_1 - p_2) \neq 0$

Test statistic:

$$z = \frac{\hat{p}_1 - \hat{p}_2}{\sigma_{(\hat{p}_1-\hat{p}_2)}}$$

Rejection region: $z < -z_\alpha$
  [or $z > z_\alpha$ when $H_a: (p_1 - p_2) > 0$]

Rejection region: $|z| > z_{\alpha/2}$

Note: $\sigma_{(\hat{p}_1-\hat{p}_2)} = \sqrt{\dfrac{p_1 q_1}{n_1} + \dfrac{p_2 q_2}{n_2}} \approx \sqrt{\hat{p}\hat{q}\left(\dfrac{1}{n_1} + \dfrac{1}{n_2}\right)}$ where $\hat{p} = \dfrac{x_1 + x_2}{n_1 + n_2}$

*The test can be adapted to test for a difference $D_0 \neq 0$. Because most applications call for a comparison of p_1 and p_2, implying $D_0 = 0$, we will confine our attention to this case.

Assumption: Same as for large-sample confidence interval for $(p_1 - p_2)$.

EXAMPLE 8.1

A consumer advocacy group wants to determine whether there is a difference between the proportions of the two leading automobile models that need major repairs (more than \$500) within two years of their purchase. A sample of 400 two-year owners of model 1 is contacted, and a sample of 500 two-year owners of model 2 is contacted. The numbers x_1 and x_2 of owners who report that their cars needed major repairs within the first two years are 53 and 78, respectively. Test the null hypothesis that no difference exists between the proportions in populations 1 and 2 needing major repairs against the alternative that a difference does exist. Use $\alpha = .10$.

SOLUTION

If we define p_1 and p_2 as the true proportions of model 1 and model 2 owners, respectively, whose cars need major repairs within two years, the elements of the test are

$$H_0: (p_1 - p_2) = 0$$

$$H_a: (p_1 - p_2) \neq 0$$

$$\text{Test statistic: } z = \frac{(\hat{p}_1 - \hat{p}_2) - 0}{\sigma_{(\hat{p}_1 - \hat{p}_2)}}$$

Rejection region $(\alpha = .10)$: $|z| > z_{\alpha/2} = z_{.05} = 1.645$ (see Figure 8.1)

We now calculate the sample proportions of owners who need major car repairs,

$$\hat{p}_1 = \frac{x_1}{n_1} = \frac{53}{400} = .1325$$

$$\hat{p}_2 = \frac{x_2}{n_2} = \frac{78}{500} = .1560$$

Then

$$z = \frac{(\hat{p}_1 - \hat{p}_2) - 0}{\sigma_{(\hat{p}_1 - \hat{p}_2)}} \approx \frac{(\hat{p}_1 - \hat{p}_2)}{\sqrt{\hat{p}\hat{q}\left(\frac{1}{n_1} + \frac{1}{n_2}\right)}}$$

where

$$\hat{p} = \frac{x_1 + x_2}{n_1 + n_2} = \frac{53 + 78}{400 + 500} = .1456$$

FIGURE 8.1
Rejection region
for Example 8.1

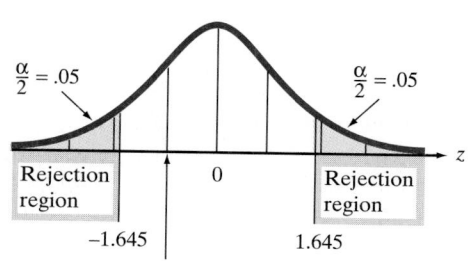

Observed
$z = -.99$

FIGURE 8.2
The observed
significance level for
the test of Example 8.1

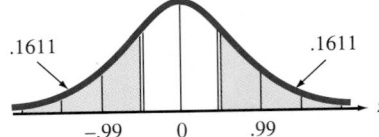

.1611   .1611

−.99   0   .99 z

Note that $\hat{p}$ is a weighted average of $\hat{p}_1$ and $\hat{p}_2$, with more weight given to the larger sample of model 2 owners.

Thus, the computed value of the test statistic is

$$z = \frac{.1325 - .1560}{\sqrt{(.1456)(.8544)\left(\dfrac{1}{400} + \dfrac{1}{500}\right)}} = \frac{-.0235}{.0237} = -.99$$

The samples provide insufficient evidence at $\alpha = .10$ to detect a difference between the proportions of the two models that need repairs within two years. Even though 2.35% more sampled owners of model 2 found they needed major repairs, this difference is less than 1 standard deviation ($z = -.99$) from the hypothesized zero difference between the true proportions. ◼

EXAMPLE 8.2   Find the observed significance level for the test in Example 8.1.

   **SOLUTION**
The observed value of z for this two-tailed test was $z = -.99$. Therefore, the observed significance level is

$$p\text{-value} = P(|z| > .99) = P(z < -.99 \text{ or } z > .99)$$

This probability is equal to the shaded area shown in Figure 8.2. The area corresponding to $z = .99$ is given in Table IV of Appendix B as .3389. Therefore, the observed significance level for the test, the sum of the two shaded tail areas under the standard normal curve, is

$$p\text{-value} = 2(.5 - .3389) = .3222$$

The probability of observing a z as large as .99 or less than $-.99$ if in fact $p_1 = p_2$ is .3222. This large p-value indicates that there is little or no evidence of a difference between p_1 and p_2. ◼

EXERCISES   **8.1–8.16**

Learning the Mechanics

8.1   Explain why the Central Limit Theorem is important in finding an approximate distribution for $(\hat{p}_1 - \hat{p}_2)$.

8.2   In each case, determine whether the sample sizes are large enough to conclude that the sampling distribution of $(\hat{p}_1 - \hat{p}_2)$ is approximately normal.
  a. $n_1 = 12, n_2 = 14, \hat{p}_1 = .42, \hat{p}_2 = .57$

  b. $n_1 = 12, n_2 = 14, \hat{p}_1 = .92, \hat{p}_2 = .86$
  c. $n_1 = n_2 = 30, \hat{p}_1 = .70, \hat{p}_2 = .73$
  d. $n_1 = 100, n_2 = 250, \hat{p}_1 = .93, \hat{p}_2 = .97$
  e. $n_1 = 125, n_2 = 200, \hat{p}_1 = .08, \hat{p}_2 = .12$

8.3   For each of the following values of α, find the values of z for which $H_0: (p_1 - p_2) = 0$ would be rejected in favor of $H_a: (p_1 - p_2) < 0$.
  a. $\alpha = .01$ **b.** $\alpha = .025$

c. $\alpha = .05$ **d.** $\alpha = .10$

8.4   Independent random samples, each containing 800 observations, were selected from two binomial populations. The samples from populations 1 and 2 produced 320 and 400 successes, respectively.

   a. Test $H_0: (p_1 - p_2) = 0$ against $H_a: (p_1 - p_2) \neq 0$. Use $\alpha = .05$.

   b. Test $H_0: (p_1 - p_2) = 0$ against $H_a: (p_1 - p_2) \neq 0$. Use $\alpha = .01$.

   c. Test $H_0: (p_1 - p_2) = 0$ against $H_a: (p_1 - p_2) < 0$. Use $\alpha = .01$.

   d. Form a 90% confidence interval for $(p_1 - p_2)$.

8.5   Construct a 95% confidence interval for $(p_1 - p_2)$ in each of the following situations:

   a. $n_1 = 400, \hat{p}_1 = .65; n_2 = 400, \hat{p}_2 = .58$

   b. $n_1 = 180, \hat{p}_1 = .31; n_2 = 250, \hat{p}_2 = .25$

   c. $n_1 = 100, \hat{p}_1 = .46; n_2 = 120, \hat{p}_2 = .61$

8.6   Sketch the sampling distribution of $(\hat{p}_1 - \hat{p}_2)$ based on independent random samples of $n_1 = 100$ and $n_2 = 200$ observations from two binomial populations with success probabilities $\hat{p}_1 = .1$ and $\hat{p}_2 = .5$, respectively.

8.7   Random samples of size $n_1 = 55$ and $n_2 = 65$ were drawn from populations 1 and 2, respectively. The samples yielded $\hat{p}_1 = .7$ and $\hat{p}_2 = .6$. Test $H_0: (p_1 - p_2) = 0$ against $H_a: (p_1 - p_2) > 0$ using $\alpha = .05$.

Applying the Concepts

8.8   Since the early 1990s marketers have wrestled with the appropriateness of using ads that appeal to children to sell adult products. One controversial advertisement campaign is Camel cigarettes' use of the cartoon character "Joe Camel" as its brand symbol. The Federal Trade Commission has considered banning ads featuring Joe Camel because they supposedly encourage young people to smoke. Lucy L. Henke, a marketing professor at the University of New Hampshire, assessed young children's abilities to recognize cigarette brand advertising symbols. She found that 15 out of 28 children under the age of 6, and 46 out of 55 children age 6 and over recognized Joe Camel, the brand symbol of Camel cigarettes (*Journal of Advertising,* Winter 1995).

   a. Use a 95% confidence interval to estimate the proportion of all children that recognize Joe Camel. Interpret the interval.

   b. Do the data indicate that recognition of Joe Camel increases with age? Test using $\alpha = .05$.

8.9   Price scanners are widely used in U.S. supermarkets. While they are fast and easy to use, they also make mistakes. Over the years, various consumer advocacy groups have complained that scanners routinely gouge the customer by overcharging. A recent Federal Trade Commission study found

that supermarket scanners erred 3.47% of the time and department store scanners erred 9.15% of the time ("Scan Errors Help Public," *Newark Star-Ledger,* Oct. 23, 1996).

   a. Assume the above error rates were determined from merchandise samples of size 800 and 900, respectively. Are these sample sizes large enough to apply the methods of this section to estimate the difference in the error rates? Justify your answer.

   b. Use a 98% confidence interval to estimate the difference in the error rates. Interpret your result.

   c. What assumptions must hold to ensure the validity of the confidence interval of part **b**?

8.10   Do you have an insatiable craving for chocolate or some other food? Since many North Americans apparently do, psychologists are designing scientific studies to examine the phenomenon. According to the *New York Times* (Feb. 22, 1995), one of the largest studies of food cravings involved a survey of 1,000 McMaster University (Canada) students. The survey revealed that 97% of the women in the study acknowledged specific food cravings while only 67% of the men did. Assume that 600 of the respondents were women and 400 were men.

   a. Is there sufficient evidence to claim that the true proportion of women who acknowledge having food cravings exceeds the corresponding proportion of men? Test using $\alpha = .01$.

   b. Why is it dangerous to conclude from the study that women have a higher incidence of food cravings than men?

8.11   Most large consumer and industrial products companies assign a *product manager* to each product/brand they sell. The overall responsibility of the product manager is to integrate the various segments of the business—including design, production, marketing, and sales—to ensure the success of the product or product line. *Industrial Marketing Management* (Vol. 25, 1996) published a study that examined the demographics, decision-making roles, and time demands of product managers. Independent samples of $n_1 = 93$ consumer/commercial product managers and $n_2 = 212$ industrial product managers took part in the study. In the consumer/commercial group, 40% of the product managers are 40 years of age or older; in the industrial group, 54% are 40 or more years old. Use the method outlined in this section to make an inference about the difference between the true proportions of consumer/commercial and industrial product managers who are at least 40 years old. Justify your choice of method (confidence interval or hypothesis test) and α level. Do industrial product managers tend to be older than consumer/commercial product managers?

8.12 Many female undergraduates at four-year colleges and universities switch from science, mathematics, and engineering (SME) majors into disciplines that are not science based, such as journalism, marketing, and sociology. When female undergraduates switch majors, are their reasons different from those of their male counterparts? This question was investigated in *Science Education* (July 1995). A sample of 335 junior/senior undergraduates—172 females and 163 males—at two large research universities were identified as "switchers," that is, they left a declared SME major for a non-SME major. Each student listed one or more factors that contributed to their switching decision.

a. Of the 172 females in the sample, 74 listed lack or loss of interest in SME (i.e., "turned off" by science) as a major factor, compared to 72 of the 163 males. Conduct a test (at $\alpha = .10$) to determine whether the proportion of female switchers who give "lack of interest in SME" as a major reason for switching differs from the corresponding proportion of males.

b. Thirty-three of the 172 females in the sample admitted they were discouraged or lost confidence due to low grades in SME during their early years, compared to 44 of 163 males. Construct a 90% confidence interval for the difference between the proportions of female and male switchers who lost confidence due to low grades in SME. Interpret the result.

8.13 Despite company policies allowing unpaid family leave for new fathers, many men fear that exercising this option would be held against them by their superiors (*Minneapolis Star-Tribune*, Feb. 14, 1993). In a random sample of 100 male workers planning to become fathers, 35 agreed with the statement, "If I knew there would be no repercussions, I would choose to participate in the family leave program after the birth of a son or daughter." However, of 96 men who became fathers in the previous 16 months, only nine participated in the program.

a. Specify the appropriate null and alternative hypotheses to test whether the sample data provide sufficient evidence to reject the hypothesis that the proportion of new fathers participating in the program is the same as the proportion that would like to participate. Define any symbols you use.

b. Are the sample sizes large enough to conclude that the sampling distribution of $(\hat{p}_1 - \hat{p}_2)$ is approximately normal?

c. Conduct the hypothesis test using $\alpha = .05$. Report the observed significance level of the test.

d. What assumptions must be satisfied for the test to be valid?

8.14 Women are filling managerial positions in increasing numbers, although there is much dissension about whether progress has been fast enough. Does marriage hinder the career progression of women to a greater degree than that of men? An article in the *Journal of Applied Psychology* (Vol. 77, 1992) investigates this and other questions relating to managerial careers of men and women in today's workforce. In a random sample of 795 male managers and 223 female managers from 20 *Fortune* 500 corporations, 86% of the male managers and 45% of the female managers were married.

a. Use a 95% confidence interval to estimate the difference between the proportions of men and women managers who are married.

b. Interpret the interval. State your conclusion in terms of the populations from which the samples were drawn.

8.15 Refer to Exercise 5.39, in which we examined data from an article in the *International Journal of Sports Psychology* (1990) studying the relationship between levels of fitness and stress among employees of companies offering health and fitness programs. Random samples of employees were selected from each of three fitness-level categories, and each was evaluated for signs of stress. The data are shown in the table below.

Fitness Level	Sample Size	Proportion with Signs of Stress
Poor	242	.155
Average	212	.133
Good	95	.108

a. What are the appropriate null and alternative hypotheses to test whether a greater proportion of employees in the poor fitness category show signs of stress than those in the average fitness category? Define any symbols you use.

b. Conduct the test constructed in part **a** using $\alpha = .10$. Interpret the result.

c. How would your null and alternative hypotheses change if you wanted to compare the proportions showing signs of stress in the poor and good fitness categories?

d. To conduct the test in part **c**, the data are analyzed by a statistical software package with the results shown below. Based on these results, state whether you would be willing to support the following statement: "Fitness level has no bearing on whether an individual shows signs of stress." Explain.

```
Z = 1.11        P-VALUE = .1335
```

8.16   When recruiting sales representatives, sales managers sometimes advertise for these positions in local newspapers, and then invite applicants to interviews which are frequently held in hotel rooms. An article in *Sloan Management Review* (Spring 1982) examined the effects of the hotel interview site on prospective sales representatives, and on women in particular. Each in a sample of 74 female college students from Rutgers University, Montclair State College, and Union College was asked whether she would agree to a job interview in a room at a local hotel; 62% said they would.

Another sample of 74 college women were asked whether they would agree to a job interview in a room of a local office building, and 98% said yes. Use this information to make an inference about $(p_1 - p_2)$, where p_1 represents the proportion of female college students who, if offered a job interview in a room of a local office building, would say they would attend the interview and p_2 represents the proportion of female college students who, if offered a job interview in a room of a local hotel, would say they would attend the interview.

8.2   DETERMINING THE SAMPLE SIZE

The sample sizes n_1 and n_2 required to compare two population proportions can be found in a manner similar to the method described in Section 7.3 for comparing two population means. We will assume equal sample sizes, i.e., $n_1 = n_2 = n$, and then choose n so that $(\hat{p}_1 - \hat{p}_2)$ will differ from $(p_1 - p_2)$ by no more than a bound B with a specified probability. We will illustrate the procedure with an example.

EXAMPLE 8.3

A production supervisor suspects that a difference exists between the proportions p_1 and p_2 of defective items produced by two different machines. Experience has shown that the proportion defective for each of the two machines is in the neighborhood of .03. If the supervisor wants to estimate the difference in the proportions to within .005 using a 95% confidence interval, how many items must be randomly sampled from the production of each machine? (Assume that the supervisor wants $n_1 = n_2 = n$.)

SOLUTION

In this sampling problem, $B = .005$, and for the specified level of confidence, $z_{\alpha/2} = z_{.025} = 1.96$. Then, letting $p_1 = p_2 = .03$ and $n_1 = n_2 = n$, we find the required sample size per machine by solving the following equation for n:

$$z_{\alpha/2}\sigma_{(\hat{p}_1 - \hat{p}_2)} = B$$

or

$$z_{\alpha/2}\sqrt{\frac{p_1 q_1}{n_1} + \frac{p_2 q_2}{n_2}} = B$$

$$1.96\sqrt{\frac{(.03)(.97)}{n} + \frac{(.03)(.97)}{n}} = .005$$

$$1.96\sqrt{\frac{2(.03)(.97)}{n}} = .005$$

$$n = 8,943.2$$

This may be a tedious sampling procedure. If the supervisor insists on estimating $(p_1 - p_2)$ correct to within .005 with 95% confidence, approximately 9,000 items will have to be inspected for each machine. ∎

You can see from the calculations in Example 8.3 that $\sigma_{(\hat{p}_1 - \hat{p}_2)}$ (and hence the solution, $n_1 = n_2 = n$) depends on the actual (but unknown) values of p_1 and p_2.

In fact, the required sample size $n_1 = n_2 = n$ is largest when $p_1 = p_2 = .5$. Therefore, if you have no prior information on the approximate values of p_1 and p_2, use $p_1 = p_2 = .5$ in the formula for $\sigma_{(\hat{p}_1 - \hat{p}_2)}$. If p_1 and p_2 are in fact close to .5, then the values of n_1 and n_2 that you have calculated will be correct. If p_1 and p_2 differ substantially from .5, then your solutions for n_1 and n_2 will be larger than needed. Consequently, using $p_1 = p_2 = .5$ when solving for n_1 and n_2 is a conservative procedure because the sample sizes n_1 and n_2 will be at least as large as (and probably larger than) needed.

The procedure for determining sample sizes necessary for estimating $(p_1 - p_2)$ for the case $n_1 = n_2$ is given in the next box.

Determination of Sample Size for Comparing Two Proportions

To estimate $(p_1 - p_2)$ to within a given bound B with probability $(1 - \alpha)$, use the following formula to solve for equal sample sizes that will achieve the desired reliability:

$$n_1 = n_2 = \frac{(z_{\alpha/2})^2 (p_1 q_1 + p_2 q_2)}{B^2}$$

You will need to substitute estimates for the values of p_1 and p_2 before solving for the sample size. These estimates might be based on prior samples, obtained from educated guesses or, most conservatively, specified as $p_1 = p_2 = .5$.

EXERCISES 8.17–8.22

Learning the Mechanics

8.17 Assuming that $n_1 = n_2$, find the sample sizes needed to estimate $(p_1 - p_2)$ for each of the following situations:

a. Bound = .01 with 99% confidence. Assume that $p_1 \approx .4$ and $p_2 \approx .7$.

b. A 90% confidence interval of width .05. Assume that there is no prior information available to obtain approximate values of p_1 and p_2.

c. Bound = .03 with 90% confidence. Assume that $p_1 \approx .2$ and $p_2 \approx .3$.

Applying the Concepts

8.18 A pollster wants to estimate the difference between the proportions of men and women who favor a particular national candidate using a 90% confidence interval of width .04. Suppose the pollster has no prior information about the proportions. If equal numbers of men and women are to be polled, how large should the sample sizes be?

8.19 After an extended period of downsizing and restructuring in which U.S. corporations laid off workers in record numbers, a 1996 national survey of 1,441 firms by the American Management Association revealed that only 20% plan to eliminate jobs within the next year, while nearly 50% plan to add jobs. They concluded that downsizing was no longer the dominant theme in the workplace (*Newark Star-Ledger,* Oct. 22, 1996). But are there regional differences in this phenomenon? Is there more growth in jobs in the Sunbelt than the Rustbelt? Assuming equal sample sizes for the two regions, how large would the samples need to be to estimate the difference in the proportion of firms that plan to add new jobs in the next year in the two regions? A 90% confidence interval of width no more than .10 is desired.

8.20 Nationally televised home shopping was introduced in 1985. Overnight it became the hottest craze in television programming. Today, nearly all cable companies carry at least one home shopping channel. Who uses these home shopping services? Are the shoppers primarily men or women? Suppose you want to estimate the difference in the proportions of men and women who say they have used or expect to use televised home shopping using an 80% confidence interval of width .06 or less.

a. Approximately how many people should be included in your samples?

b. Suppose you want to obtain individual estimates for the two proportions of interest. Will the sample size found in part a be large enough to provide estimates of each proportion correct to within .02 with probability equal to .90? Justify your response.

8.21 Rat damage creates a large financial loss in the production of sugarcane. One aspect of the problem that has been investigated by the U.S. Department of Agriculture concerns the optimal place to locate rat poison. To be most effective in reducing rat damage, should the poison be located in the middle of the field or on the outer perimeter? One way to answer this question is to determine where the greater amount of damage occurs. If damage is measured by the proportion of cane stalks that have been damaged by rats, how many stalks from each section of the field should be sampled in order to estimate the true difference between proportions of stalks damaged in the two sections to within .02 with 95% confidence?

8.22 Refer to Exercise 8.15, where we examined data relating levels of fitness and stress (*International Journal of Sports Psychology,* July–Sept. 1990). Essentially, we failed to reject the null hypothesis that those in poor physical condition exhibit signs of stress in the same proportion as those in good physical condition, even though the sample proportions differed by nearly .05. (That is, of those

sampled, almost 5% more of those in poor condition exhibited signs of stress than those in good condition.)

a. How large would the samples have to be to estimate the difference in the proportions showing signs of stress to within .04 with 95% confidence? Assume the sample sizes for the two groups will be equal, and remember that the first samples selected resulted in proportions of .155 and .108 for the poor and good fitness levels, respectively.

b. Suppose samples of the size you calculated in part **a** were selected from each group, and the sample proportions again turned out to be .155 and .108. Test the null hypothesis $H_0: (p_1 - p_2) = 0$ against the alternative $H_a: (p_1 - p_2) > 0$, where p_1 is the proportion of all employees at the poor fitness level who show signs of stress and p_2 is the proportion of all employees at the good fitness level who show signs of stress. Calculate and interpret the observed significance level.

8.3 COMPARING POPULATION PROPORTIONS: MULTINOMIAL EXPERIMENT (OPTIONAL)

In this section, we consider a statistical method to compare two or more, say k, population proportions. For example, suppose a large supermarket chain conducts a consumer preference survey by recording the brand of bread purchased by customers in its stores. Assume the chain carries three brands of bread—two major brands (A and B) and its own store brand. The brand preferences of a random sample of 150 consumers are observed, and the resulting **count data** (i.e., number of consumers in each brand category) appear in Table 8.1. Do these data indicate that a preference exists for any of the brands?

To answer this question, we have to know the underlying probability distribution of these count data. This distribution, called the **multinomial probability distribution**, is an extension of the binomial distribution (Section 4.3). The properties of the multinomial distribution are shown in the box.

TABLE 8.1
Consumer Preference Survey Results

A	B	Store Brand
61	53	36

Properties of the Multinomial Probability Distribution
1. The experiment consists of n identical trials.
2. There are k possible outcomes to each trial.
3. The probabilities of the k outcomes, denoted by $p_1, p_2, ..., p_k$, remain the same from trial to trial, where $p_1 + p_2 + \cdots + p_k = 1$.
4. The trials are independent.
5. The random variables of interest are the counts $n_1, n_2, ..., n_k$ in each of the k cells.

Note that our consumer-preference survey satisfies the properties of a **multinomial experiment**. The experiment consists of randomly sampling $n = 150$ buyers from a large population of consumers containing an unknown proportion p_1 who prefer brand A, a proportion p_2 who prefer brand B, and a proportion p_3 who prefer the store brand. Each buyer represents a single trial that can result in one of three outcomes: The consumer prefers brand A, B, or the store brand with probabilities p_1, p_2, and p_3, respectively. (Assume that all consumers will have a preference.) The buyer preference of any single consumer in the sample does not affect the preference of another; consequently, the trials are independent. And, finally, you can see that the recorded data are the number of buyers in each of three consumer-preference categories. Thus, the consumer-preference survey satisfies the five properties of a multinomial experiment. You can see that the properties of the multinomial experiment closely resemble those of the binomial experiment and that, in fact, a binomial experiment is a multinomial experiment for the special case where $k = 2$.

In the consumer-preference survey, and in most practical applications of the multinomial experiment, the k outcomes probabilities $p_1, p_2, ..., p_k$ are unknown and we want to use the survey data to make inferences about their values. The unknown probabilities in the consumer-preference survey are

p_1 = Proportion of all buyers who prefer brand A

p_2 = Proportion of all buyers who prefer brand B

p_3 = Proportion of all buyers who prefer the store brand

To decide whether the consumers have a preference for any of the brands, we will want to test the null hypothesis that the brands of bread are equally preferred (that is, $p_1 = p_2 = p_3 = \frac{1}{3}$) against the alternative hypothesis that one brand is preferred (that is, at least one of the probabilities p_1, p_2, and p_3 exceeds $\frac{1}{3}$). Thus, we want to test

$H_0: p_1 = p_2 = p_3 = \frac{1}{3}$ (no preference)

H_a: At least one of the proportions exceeds $\frac{1}{3}$ (a preference exists)

If the null hypothesis is true and $p_1 = p_2 = p_3 = \frac{1}{3}$, the expected value (mean value) of the number of customers who prefer brand A is given by

$$E(n_1) = np_1 = (n)\frac{1}{3} = (150)\frac{1}{3} = 50$$

Similarly, $E(n_2) = E(n_3) = 50$ if the null hypothesis is true and no preference exists.

The following test statistic—the **chi-square test**—measures the degree of disagreement between the data and the null hypothesis:

$$\chi^2 = \frac{[n_1 - E(n_1)]^2}{E(n_1)} + \frac{[n_2 - E(n_2)]^2}{E(n_2)} + \frac{[n_3 - E(n_3)]^2}{E(n_3)}$$

$$= \frac{(n_1 - 50)^2}{50} + \frac{(n_2 - 50)^2}{50} + \frac{(n_3 - 50)^2}{50}$$

Note that the farther the observed numbers n_1, n_2, and n_3 are from their expected value (50), the larger χ^2 will become. That is, large values of χ^2 imply that the null hypothesis is false.

We have to know the distribution of χ^2 in repeated sampling before we can decide whether the data indicate that a preference exists. When H_0 is true, χ^2 can be shown to have (approximately) a chi-square distribution. The shape of the chi-

FIGURE 8.3
Several χ^2 probability distributions

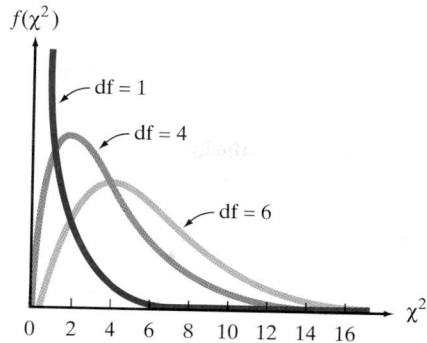

square distribution depends on the degrees of freedom (df) associated with Table 8.1. For this application, the χ^2 distribution has $(k-1)$ degrees of freedom.* The shapes of several χ^2 distributions with different degrees of freedom are shown in Figure 8.3.

Critical values of χ^2 are provided in Table XIII of Appendix B, a portion of which is shown in Table 8.2. To illustrate, the rejection region for the consumer-preference survey for $\alpha = .05$ and $k-1 = 3-1 = 2$ df is

$$\text{Rejection region: } \chi^2 > \chi^2_{.05}$$

TABLE 8.2   Reproduction of Part of Table XIII of Appendix B: Critical Values of χ^2

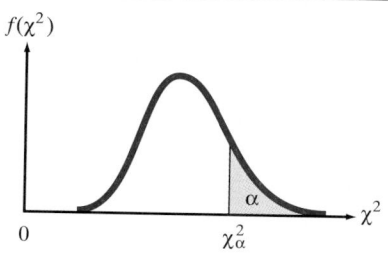

Degrees of Freedom	$\chi^2_{.100}$	$\chi^2_{.050}$	$\chi^2_{.025}$	$\chi^2_{.010}$	$\chi^2_{.005}$
1	2.70554	3.84146	5.02389	6.63490	7.87944
2	4.60517	5.99147	7.37776	9.21034	10.5966
3	6.25139	7.81473	9.34840	11.3449	12.8381
4	7.77944	9.48773	11.1433	13.2767	14.8602
5	9.23635	11.0705	12.8325	15.0863	16.7496
6	10.6446	12.5916	14.4494	16.8119	18.5476
7	12.0170	14.0671	16.0128	18.4753	20.2777
8	13.3616	15.5073	17.5346	20.0902	21.9550
9	14.6837	16.9190	19.0228	21.6660	23.5893
10	15.9871	18.3070	20.4831	23.2093	25.1882
11	17.2750	19.6751	21.9200	24.7250	26.7569

*The derivation of the degrees of freedom for χ^2 involves the number of linear restrictions imposed on the count data. In the present case, the only constraint is that $\Sigma n_i = n$, where n (the sample size) is fixed in advance. Therefore, df $= k-1$. For other cases, we will give the degrees of freedom for each usage of χ^2 and refer the interested reader to the references for more detail.

FIGURE 8.4
Rejection region for consumer-preference survey

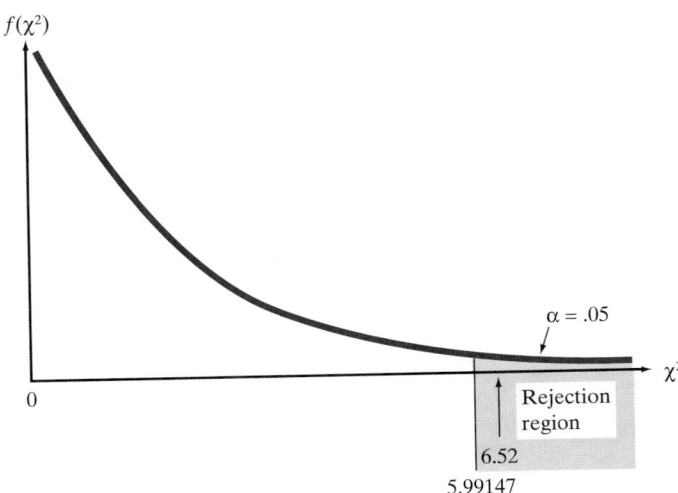

The value of $\chi^2_{.05}$ (found in Table XIII) is 5.99147. (See Figure 8.4.) The computed value of the test statistic is

$$\chi^2 = \frac{(n_1 - 50)^2}{50} + \frac{(n_2 - 50)^2}{50} + \frac{(n_3 - 50)^2}{50}$$

$$= \frac{(61 - 50)^2}{50} + \frac{(53 - 50)^2}{50} + \frac{(36 - 50)^2}{50} = 6.52$$

Since the computed $\chi^2 = 6.52$ exceeds the critical value of 5.99147, we conclude at the $\alpha = .05$ level of significance that there does exist a consumer preference for one or more of the brands of bread.

Now that we have evidence to indicate that the proportions $p_1, p_2,$ and p_3 are unequal, we can make inferences concerning their individual values using the methods of Section 6.5. [*Note:* We cannot use the methods of Section 8.1 to compare two proportions because the cell counts are dependent random variables.] The general form for a test of a hypothesis concerning multinomial probabilities is shown in the next box.

A Test of a Hypothesis About Multinomial Probabilities: One-Way Table

$$H_0: p_1 = p_{1,0}, p_2 = p_{2,0}, \dots, p_k = p_{k,0}$$

where $p_{1,0}, p_{2,0}, \dots, p_{k,0}$ represent the hypothesized values of the multinomial probabilities

H_a: At least one of the multinomial probabilities does not equal its hypothesized value

Test statistic: $\chi^2 = \sum \dfrac{[n_i - E(n_i)]^2}{E(n_i)}$

where $E(n_i) = np_{i,0}$ is the **expected cell count**, that is, the expected number of outcomes of type i assuming that H_0 is true. The total sample size is n.

Rejection region: $\chi^2 > \chi^2_\alpha$,

where χ^2_α has $(k - 1)$ df.

> *Assumptions:* **1.** A multinomial experiment has been conducted. This is generally satisfied by taking a random sample from the population of interest.
> **2.** The sample size n will be large enough so that for every cell, the expected cell count $E(n_i)$ will be equal to 5 or more.*

EXAMPLE 8.4

A large firm has established what it hopes is an objective system of deciding on annual pay increases for its employees. The system is based on a series of evaluation scores determined by the supervisors of each employee. Employees with scores above 80 receive a merit pay increase, those with scores between 50 and 80 receive the standard increase, and those below 50 receive no increase. The firm designed the plan with the objective that, on the average, 25% of its employees would receive merit increases, 65% would receive standard increases, and 10% would receive no increase. After one year of operation using the new plan, the distribution of pay increases for the 600 company employees was as shown in Table 8.3. Test at the $\alpha = .01$ level to determine whether these data indicate that the distribution of pay increases differs significantly from the proportions established by the firm.

SOLUTION
Define

$$p_1 = \text{Proportion of employees who receive no pay increase}$$
$$p_2 = \text{Proportion of employees who receive a standard increase}$$
$$p_3 = \text{Proportion of employees who receive a merit increase}$$

Then the null and alternative hypotheses are:

$H_0: p_1 = .10, p_2 = .65, p_3 = .25$

H_a: At least two of the proportions differ from the firm's proposed plan

Test statistic: $\chi^2 = \sum \dfrac{[n_i - E(n_i)]^2}{E(n_i)}$

where

$$E(n_1) = np_{1,0} = 600(.10) = 60$$
$$E(n_2) = np_{2,0} = 600(.65) = 390$$
$$E(n_3) = np_{3,0} = 600(.25) = 150$$

Rejection region: For $\alpha = .01$ and df $= k - 1 = 2$, reject H_0 if $\chi^2 > \chi^2_{.01}$, where (from Table XIII of Appendix B) $\chi^2_{.01} = 9.21034$.

We now calculate the test statistic:

$$\chi^2 = \frac{(42 - 60)^2}{60} + \frac{(365 - 390)^2}{390} + \frac{(193 - 150)^2}{150} = 19.33$$

TABLE 8.3
Distribution of Pay Increases

None	Standard	Merit
42	365	193

*The assumption that all expected cell counts are at least 5 is necessary in order to ensure that the χ^2 approximation is appropriate. Exact methods for conducting the test of a hypothesis exist and may be used for small expected cell counts, but these methods are beyond the scope of this text.

FIGURE 8.5
EXCEL analysis of
data in Table 8.3

CHI-SQUARE	P-VALUE
19.33	6.34664E-05

Since this value exceeds the table value of χ^2 (9.21034), the data provide strong evidence ($\alpha = .01$) that the company's pay plan is not working as planned.

The χ^2 test can also be conducted using an available statistical software package. Figure 8.5 is a portion of an EXCEL printout of the analysis of the data in Table 8.3; note that the p-value of the test is .0000634664. Since $\alpha = .01$ exceeds this p-value, there is sufficient evidence to reject H_0. ∎

If we focus on one particular outcome of a multinomial experiment, we can use the methods developed in Section 5.3 for a binomial proportion to establish a confidence interval for any one of the multinomial probabilities.* For example, if we want a 95% confidence interval for the proportion of the company's employees who will receive merit increases under the new system, we calculate

$$\hat{p}_3 \pm 1.96\sigma_{\hat{p}_3} \approx \hat{p}_3 \pm 1.96\sqrt{\frac{\hat{p}_3(1 - \hat{p}_3)}{n}} \quad \text{where } \hat{p}_3 = \frac{n_3}{n} = \frac{193}{600} = .32$$

$$= .32 \pm 1.96\sqrt{\frac{(.32)(1 - .32)}{600}} = .32 \pm .04$$

Thus, we estimate that between 28% and 36% of the firm's employees will qualify for merit increases under the new plan. It appears that the firm will have to raise the requirements for merit increases in order to achieve the stated goal of a 25% employee qualification rate.

*Note that focusing on one outcome has the effect of lumping the other $(k - 1)$ outcomes into a single group. Thus, we obtain, in effect, two outcomes—or a binomial experiment.

EXERCISES   **8.23–8.36**

Learning the Mechanics

8.23 Use Table XIII of Appendix B to find each of the following χ^2 values:
   a. $\chi^2_{.05}$ for df = 17   **b.** $\chi^2_{.990}$ for df = 100
   c. $\chi^2_{.10}$ for df = 15   **d.** $\chi^2_{.005}$ for df = 3

8.24 What are the characteristics of a multinomial experiment? Compare the characteristics to those of a binomial experiment.

8.25 Find the rejection region for a one-dimensional χ^2-test of a null hypothesis concerning $p_1, p_2, \ldots, p_k$ if
   a. $k = 3; \alpha = .05$
   b. $k = 5; \alpha = .10$
   c. $k = 4; \alpha = .01$

8.26 A multinomial experiment with $k = 3$ cells and $n = 320$ produced the data shown in the following table. Do these data provide sufficient evidence to contradict the null hypothesis that $p_1 = .25$, $p_2 = .25$, and $p_3 = .50$? Test using $\alpha = .05$.

	CELL		
	1	2	3
n_i	78	60	182

8.27 A multinomial experiment with $k = 4$ cells and $n = 205$ produced the data shown in the table.

	CELL			
	1	2	3	4
n_i	43	56	59	47

   a. Do these data provide sufficient evidence to conclude that the multinomial probabilities differ? Test using $\alpha = .05$.
   b. What are the Type I and Type II errors associated with the test of part **a**?

8.28   Refer to Exercise 8.27. Construct a 95% confidence interval for the multinomial probability associated with cell 3.

8.29   What conditions must n satisfy to make the χ^2-test valid?

Applying the Concepts

8.30   Data from supermarket scanners are used by researchers to understand the purchasing patterns and preferences of consumers. Researchers frequently study the purchases of a sample of households, called a *scanner panel*. When shopping, these households present a magnetic identification card that permits their purchase data to be identified and aggregated. Marketing researchers recently studied the extent to which panel households' purchase behavior is representative of the population of households shopping at the same stores (*Marketing Research*, Nov. 1996). The table below reports the peanut butter purchase data collected by A. C. Nielsen Company for a panel of 2,500 households in Sioux Falls, South Dakota, over a 102-week period. The market share percentages in the table are derived from all peanut butter purchases at the same 15 stores at which the panel shopped during the same 102-week period.

Brand	Size	Number of Purchases by Household Panel	Market Shares
Jif	18 oz.	3,165	20.10%
Jif	28	1,892	10.10
Jif	40	726	5.42
Peter Pan	10	4,079	16.01
Skippy	18	6,206	28.65
Skippy	28	1,627	12.38
Skippy	40	1,420	7.32
Total		19,115	

Source: Gupta, S., *et al.* "Do household scanner data provide representative inferences from brand choices? A comparison with store data." *Journal of Marketing Research*, Vol. 33, Nov. 1996, pp. 393 (Table 6).

a. Do the data provide sufficient evidence to conclude that the purchases of the household panel are representative of the population of households? Test using $\alpha = .05$.

b. What assumptions must hold to ensure the validity of the testing procedure you used in part **a**?

c. Find the approximate p-value for the test of part **a** and interpret it in the context of the problem.

8.31   *Inc. Technology* (Mar. 18, 1997) reported the results of the 1996 Equifax/Harris Consumer Privacy Survey in which 328 Internet users indicated their level of agreement with the following statement: "The government needs to be able to scan Internet messages and user communications to prevent fraud and other crimes." The number of users in each response category is summarized below.

Agree Strongly	Agree Somewhat	Disagree Somewhat	Disagree Strongly
59	108	82	79

a. Specify the null and alternative hypotheses you would use to determine if the opinions of Internet users are evenly divided among the four categories.

b. Conduct the test of part **a** using $\alpha = .05$.

c. In the context of this exercise, what is a Type I error? A Type II error?

d. What assumptions must hold in order to ensure the validity of the test you conducted in part **b**?

8.32   In education, the term *instructional technology* refers to products such as computers, spreadsheets, CD-ROMs, videos, and presentation software. How frequently do professors use instructional technology in the classroom? To answer this question, researchers at Western Michigan University surveyed 306 of their fellow faculty (*Educational Technology*, Mar.–Apr. 1995). Responses to the frequency-of-technology use in teaching were recorded as "weekly to every class," "once a semester to monthly," or "never." The faculty responses (number in each response category) for the three technologies are summarized in the table.

Technology	Weekly	Once a Semester/ Monthly	Never
Computer spreadsheets	58	67	181
Word processing	168	61	77
Statistical software	37	82	187

a. Determine whether the percentages in the three frequency-of-use response categories differ for computer spreadsheets. Use $\alpha = .01$.

b. Repeat part **a** for word processing.

c. Repeat part **a** for statistical software.

d. Construct a 99% confidence interval for the true percentage of faculty who never use computer spreadsheets in the classroom. Interpret the interval.

8.33   Each year, approximately 1.3 million Americans suffer adverse drug effects (ADEs), that is, unintended injuries caused by prescribed medication. A study in the *Journal of the American Medical*

Association (July 5, 1995) identified the cause of 247 ADEs that occurred at two Boston hospitals. The researchers found that dosing errors (that is, wrong dosage prescribed and/or dispensed) were the most common. The table summarizes the proximate cause of 95 ADEs that resulted from a dosing error. Conduct a test (at $\alpha = .10$) to determine whether the true percentages of ADEs in the five "cause" categories are different. Use the accompanying EXCEL printout to arrive at your decision.

Wrong Dosage Cause	Number of ADEs
(1) Lack of knowledge of drug	29
(2) Rule violation	17
(3) Faulty dose checking	13
(4) Slips	9
(5) Other	27

CAUSE	ADEs
NO KNOWLEDGE	29
RULE VIOLATE	17
FAULTY DOSE	13
SLIPS	9
OTHER	27
CHI-SQUARE	16
P-VALUE	0.003019

8.34 The threat of earthquakes is a part of life in California, where scientists have warned about "the big one" for decades. An article in the *Annals of the Association of American Geographers* (June 1992) investigated what influences homeowners in purchasing earthquake insurance. One factor investigated was the proximity to a major fault. The researchers hypothesized that the nearer a county is to a major fault, the more likely residents are to own earthquake insurance. Suppose that a random sample of 700 earthquake-insured residents from four counties is selected, and the number in each county is counted and recorded in the table at the top of the next column.

a. What are the appropriate null and alternative hypotheses to test whether the proportions of

	Contra Costa	Santa Clara	Los Angeles	San Bernardino
Number Insured	103	213	241	143

all earthquake-insured residents in the four counties differ?

b. Do the data provide sufficient evidence that the proportions of all earthquake-insured residents differ among the four counties? Test using $\alpha = .05$.

c. Los Angeles County is closest to a major earthquake fault. Construct a 95% confidence interval for the proportion of all earthquake-insured residents in the four counties that reside in Los Angeles County.

d. Does the confidence interval you formed in part **c** support the conclusion of the test conducted in part **b**? Explain.

8.35 Overweight trucks are responsible for much of the damage sustained by our local, state, and federal highway systems. Although illegal, overloading is common. Truckers may avoid weigh stations run by enforcement officers by taking back roads or by traveling when weigh stations are likely to be closed. A state highway planning agency (Minnesota Department of Transportation) monitored the movements of overweight trucks on an interstate highway using an unmanned, computerized scale that is built into the highway. Unknown to the truckers, the scale weighed their vehicles as they passed over it. Each day's proportion of one week's total truck traffic (five-axle tractor truck semitrailers) is shown in the first table below. During the same week, the number of overweight trucks per day is given in the second table.

a. The planning agency would like to know whether the number of overweight trucks per week is distributed over the seven days of the week in direct proportion to the volume of truck traffic. Test using $\alpha = .05$.

b. Find the approximate p-value for the test of part **a**.

8.36 A company that manufactures dice for gambling casinos regularly inspects its product to be sure

Monday	Tuesday	Wednesday	Thursday	Friday	Saturday	Sunday
.191	.198	.187	.180	.155	.043	.046

Monday	Tuesday	Wednesday	Thursday	Friday	Saturday	Sunday
90	82	72	70	51	18	31

that only "fair" (balanced) dice are supplied to the casinos. One die was randomly chosen from a production lot and rolled 120 times. Counts of the numbers showing face up are recorded in the table. Do the data provide sufficient evidence to indicate that the die is unbalanced? Test using $\alpha = .10$.

Numbers Face Up	1	2	3	4	5	6
Frequency	28	27	20	18	15	12

8.4 CONTINGENCY TABLE ANALYSIS (OPTIONAL)

In optional Section 8.3, we introduced the multinomial probability distribution and considered data classified according to a single criterion. We now consider multinomial experiments in which the data are classified according to two criteria, that is, *classification with respect to two factors.*

For example, high gasoline prices have made many consumers more aware of the size of the automobiles they purchase. Suppose an automobile manufacturer is interested in determining the relationship between the size and manufacturer of newly purchased automobiles. One thousand recent buyers of cars made in the United States are randomly sampled, and each purchase is classified with respect to the size and manufacturer of the automobile. The data are summarized in the **two-way table** shown in Table 8.4. This table is called a **contingency table**; it presents multinomial count data classified on two scales, or **dimensions**, of classification—namely, automobile size and manufacturer.

The symbols representing the cell counts for the multinomial experiment in Table 8.4 are shown in Table 8.5A; and the corresponding cell, row, and column probabilities are shown in Table 8.5B. Thus, n_{11} represents the number of buyers who purchase a small car of manufacturer A and p_{11} represents the corresponding cell probability. Note the symbols for the row and column totals and also the symbols for the probability totals. The latter are called **marginal probabilities** for each row and column. The marginal probability p_{r1} is the probability that a small car is purchased; the marginal probability p_{c1} is the probability that a car by manufacturer A is purchased. Thus,

$$p_{r1} = p_{11} + p_{12} + p_{13} + p_{14} \quad \text{and} \quad p_{c1} = p_{11} + p_{21} + p_{31}$$

Thus, we can see that this really is a multinomial experiment with a total of 1,000 trials, $(3)(4) = 12$ cells or possible outcomes, and probabilities for each cell as shown in Table 8.5B. If the 1,000 recent buyers are randomly chosen, the trials are considered independent and the probabilities are viewed as remaining constant from trial to trial.

Suppose we want to know whether the two classifications, manufacturer and size, are dependent. That is, if we know which size car a buyer will choose, does

---

TABLE 8.4 **Contingency Table for Automobile Size Example**

		MANUFACTURER				
		A	**B**	**C**	**D**	**Totals**
AUTO SIZE	Small	157	65	181	10	413
	Intermediate	126	82	142	46	396
	Large	58	45	60	28	191
	Totals	341	192	383	84	1,000

TABLE 8.5A   Observed Counts for Contingency Table 8.4

		MANUFACTURER				
		A	B	C	D	Totals
AUTO SIZE	Small	n_{11}	n_{12}	n_{13}	n_{14}	r_1
	Intermediate	n_{21}	n_{22}	n_{23}	n_{24}	r_2
	Large	n_{31}	n_{32}	n_{33}	n_{34}	r_3
	Totals	c_1	c_2	c_3	c_4	n

TABLE 8.5B   Probabilities for Contingency Table 8.4

		MANUFACTURER				
		A	B	C	D	Totals
AUTO SIZE	Small	p_{11}	p_{12}	p_{13}	p_{14}	p_{r1}
	Intermediate	p_{21}	p_{22}	p_{23}	p_{24}	p_{r2}
	Large	p_{31}	p_{32}	p_{33}	p_{34}	p_{r3}
	Totals	p_{c1}	p_{c2}	p_{c3}	p_{c4}	1

that information give us a clue about the manufacturer of the car the buyer will choose? In a probabilistic sense we know (Chapter 3) that independence of events A and B implies $P(AB) = P(A)P(B)$. Similarly, in the contingency table analysis, if the **two classifications are independent**, the probability that an item is classified in any particular cell of the table is the product of the corresponding marginal probabilities. Thus, under the hypothesis of independence, in Table 8.5B, we must have

$$p_{11} = p_{r1}p_{c1}$$
$$p_{12} = p_{r1}p_{c2}$$

and so forth.

To test the hypothesis of independence, we use the same reasoning employed in the one-dimensional tests of optional Section 8.3. First, we calculate the *expected, or mean, count in each cell* assuming that the null hypothesis of independence is true. We do this by noting that the expected count in a cell of the table is just the total number of multinomial trials, n, times the cell probability. Recall that n_{ij} represents the **observed count** in the cell located in the ith row and jth column. Then the expected cell count for the upper lefthand cell (first row, first column) is

$$E(n_{11}) = np_{11}$$

or, when the null hypothesis (the classifications are independent) is true,

$$E(n_{11}) = np_{r1}p_{c1}$$

Since these true probabilities are not known, we estimate p_{r1} and p_{c1} by the same proportions $\hat{p}r_1 = r_1/n$ and $\hat{p}_{c1} = c_1/n$. Thus, the estimate of the expected value $E(n_{11})$ is

$$\hat{E}(n_{11}) = n\left(\frac{r_1}{n}\right)\left(\frac{c_1}{n}\right) = \frac{r_1c_1}{n}$$

TABLE 8.6 Observed and Estimated Expected (in Parentheses) Counts

| | | MANUFACTURER | | | | |
		A	B	C	D	Totals
	Small	157	65	181	10	
		(140.833)	(79.296)	(158.179)	(34.692)	413
AUTO SIZE	Intermediate	126	82	142	46	
		(135.036)	(76.032)	(151.668)	(33.264)	396
	Large	58	45	60	28	
		(65.131)	(36.672)	(73.153)	(16.044)	191
	Totals	341	192	383	84	1,000

Similarly, for each i, j,

$$\hat{E}(n_{ij}) = \frac{(\text{Row total})(\text{Column total})}{\text{Total sample size}}$$

Thus,

$$\hat{E}(n_{12}) = \frac{r_1 c_2}{n}$$
$$\vdots \qquad \vdots$$
$$\hat{E}(n_{34}) = \frac{r_3 c_4}{n}$$

Using the data in Table 8.4, we find

$$\hat{E}(n_{11}) = \frac{r_1 c_1}{n} = \frac{(413)(341)}{1,000} = 140.833$$

$$\hat{E}(n_{12}) = \frac{r_1 c_2}{n} = \frac{(413)(192)}{1,000} = 79.296$$
$$\vdots \qquad \vdots \qquad \vdots \qquad \vdots$$
$$\hat{E}(n_{34}) = \frac{r_3 c_4}{n} = \frac{(191)(84)}{1,000} = 16.044$$

The observed data and the estimated expected values (in parentheses) are shown in Table 8.6.

We now use the χ^2 statistic to compare the observed and expected (estimated) counts in each cell of the contingency table:

$$\chi^2 = \frac{[n_{11} - \hat{E}(n_{11})]^2}{\hat{E}(n_{11})} + \frac{[n_{12} - \hat{E}(n_{12})]^2}{\hat{E}(n_{12})} + \cdots + \frac{[n_{34} - \hat{E}(n_{34})]^2}{\hat{E}(n_{34})}$$

$$= \sum \frac{[n_{ij} - \hat{E}(n_{ij})]^2}{\hat{E}(n_{ij})}$$

Note: The use of Σ in the context of a contingency table analysis refers to a sum over all cells in the table.

Substituting the data of Table 8.6 into this expression, we get

$$\chi^2 = \frac{(157 - 140.833)^2}{140.833} + \frac{(65 - 79.296)^2}{79.296} + \cdots + \frac{(28 - 16.044)^2}{16.044} = 45.81$$

Large values of χ^2 imply that the observed counts do not closely agree and hence that the hypothesis of independence is false. To determine how large χ^2 must be before it is too large to be attributed to chance, we make use of the fact that the sampling distribution of χ^2 is approximately a χ^2 probability distribution when the classifications are independent.

When testing the null hypothesis of independence in a two-way contingency table, the appropriate degrees of freedom will be $(r - 1)(c - 1)$, where r is the number of rows and c is the number of columns in the table.

For the size and make of automobiles example, the degrees of freedom for χ^2 is $(r - 1)(c - 1) = (3 - 1)(4 - 1) = 6$. Then, for $\alpha = .05$, we reject the hypothesis of independence when

$$\chi^2 > \chi^2_{.05} = 12.5916$$

Since the computed $\chi^2 = 45.81$ exceeds the value 12.5916, we conclude that the size and manufacturer of a car selected by a purchaser are dependent events.

The pattern of **dependence** can be seen more clearly by expressing the data as percentages. We first select one of the two classifications to be used as the base variable. In the automobile size preference example, suppose we select manufacturer as the classificatory variable to be the base. Next, we represent the responses for each level of the second categorical variable (size of automobile in our example) as a percentage of the subtotal for the base variable. For example, from Table 8.6 we convert the response for small car sales for manufacturer A (157) to a percentage of the total sales for manufacturer A (341). That is,

$$\left(\frac{157}{341}\right)100\% = 46\%$$

The conversions of all Table 8.6 entries are similarly computed, and the values are shown in Table 8.7. The value shown at the right of each row is the row's total expressed as a percentage of the total number of responses in the entire table. Thus, the small car percentage is $413/1{,}000(100\%) = 41\%$ (rounded to the nearest percent).

If the size and manufacturer variables are independent, then the percentages in the cells of the table are expected to be approximately equal to the corresponding row percentages. Thus, we would expect the small car percentages for each of the four manufacturers to be approximately 41% if size and manufacturer are independent. The extent to which each manufacturer's percentage departs from this value determines the dependence of the two classifications, with greater variability of the row percentages meaning a greater degree of dependence. A plot of the

TABLE 8.7 Percentage of Car Sizes by Manufacturer

		MANUFACTURER				
		A	B	C	D	All
AUTO SIZE	Small	46	34	47	12	41
	Intermediate	37	43	37	55	40
	Large	17	23	16	33	19
	Totals	100	100	100	100	100

FIGURE 8.6

Size as a percentage of manufacturer subtotals

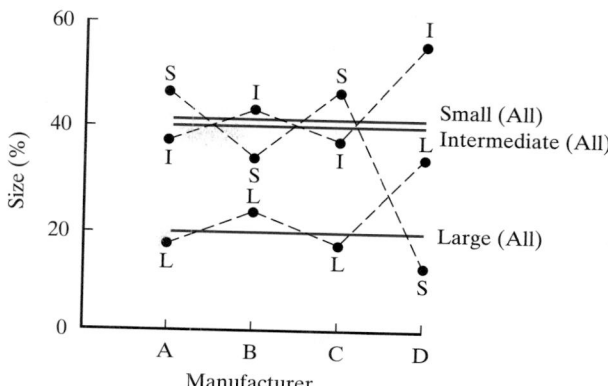

percentages helps summarize the observed pattern. In Figure 8.6 we show the manufacturer (the base variable) on the horizontal axis, and the size percentages on the vertical axis. The "expected" percentages under the assumption of independence are shown as horizontal lines, and each observed value is represented by a symbol indicating the size category.

Figure 8.6 clearly indicates the reason that the test resulted in the conclusion that the two classifications in the contingency table are dependent. Note that the sales of manufacturers A, B, and C fall relatively close to the expected percentages under the assumption of independence. However, the sales of manufacturer D deviate significantly from the expected values, with much higher percentages for large and intermediate cars and a much smaller percentage for small cars than expected under independence. Also, manufacturer B deviates slightly from the expected pattern, with a greater percentage of intermediate than small car sales. Statistical measures of the degree of dependence and procedures for making comparisons of pairs of levels for classifications are available. They are beyond the scope of this text, but can be found in the references. We will, however, utilize descriptive summaries such as Figure 8.6 to examine the degree of dependence exhibited by the sample data.

The general form of a two-way contingency table containing r rows and c columns (called an $r \times c$ contingency table) is shown in Table 8.8. Note that the observed count in the (ij) cell is denoted by n_{ij}, the ith row total is r_i, the jth column total is c_j, and the total sample size is n. Using this notation, we give the general form of the contingency table test for independent classifications in the next box.

TABLE 8.8   General $r \times c$ Contingency Table

		COLUMN				
		1	2	...	c	Row Totals
ROW	1	n_{11}	n_{12}	...	n_{1c}	r_1
	2	n_{21}	n_{22}	...	n_{2c}	r_2
	⋮	⋮	⋮		⋮	⋮
	r	n_{r1}	n_{r2}	...	n_{rc}	r_r
Column Totals		c_1	c_2	...	c_c	n

> **General Form of a Contingency Table Analysis: A Test for Independence**
>
> H_0: The two classifications are independent
>
> H_a: The two classifications are dependent
>
> Test statistic: $\chi^2 = \sum \dfrac{[n_{ij} - \hat{E}(n_{ij})]^2}{\hat{E}(n_{ij})}$
>
> where $\hat{E}(n_{ij}) = \dfrac{r_i c_j}{n}$.
>
> Rejection region: $\chi^2 > \chi^2_\alpha$, where χ^2_α has $(r-1)(c-1)$ df.
>
> Assumptions: 1. The n observed counts are a random sample from the population of interest. We may then consider this to be a multinomial experiment with $r \times c$ possible outcomes.
>
> 2. The sample size, n, will be large enough so that, for every cell, the expected count, $E(n_{ij})$, will be equal to 5 or more.

EXAMPLE 8.5

A large brokerage firm wants to determine whether the service it provides to affluent clients differs from the service it provides to lower-income clients. A sample of 500 clients are selected, and each client is asked to rate his or her broker. The results are shown in Table 8.9.

a. Test to determine whether there is evidence that broker rating and customer income are independent. Use $\alpha = .10$.

b. Plot the data and describe the patterns revealed. Is the result of the test supported by the plot?

SOLUTION

a. The first step is to calculate estimated expected cell frequencies under the assumption that the classifications are independent. Rather than compute these values by hand, we resort to a computer. The SAS printout of the analysis of Table 8.9 is displayed in Figure 8.7. Each cell in Figure 8.7 contains the observed (top) and expected (bottom) frequency in that cell. Note that $\hat{E}(n_{11})$, the estimated expected count for the Outstanding, Under $30,000 cell is 53.856. Similarly, the estimated expected count for the Outstanding, $30,000–$60,000 cell is $\hat{E}(n_{12}) = 66.402$. Since all the estimated expected cell frequencies are greater than 5, the χ^2 approximation for the test statistic is appropriate. Assuming the clients chosen were randomly selected from all clients of the brokerage firm, the characteristics of the

TABLE 8.9 Survey Results (Observed Clients), Example 8.5

		CLIENT'S INCOME			
		Under $30,000	$30,000–$60,000	Over $60,000	Totals
BROKER RATING	Outstanding	48	64	41	153
	Average	98	120	50	268
	Poor	30	33	16	79
Totals		176	217	107	500

FIGURE 8.7

SAS contingency table printout

```
                    TABLE OF RATING BY INCOME
   RATING        INCOME
   Frequency┊
   Expected  ┊UNDER30K┊30K-60K ┊OVER60K┊   Total
   ----------+--------+--------+-------+
   OUTSTAND  ┊    48  ┊    64  ┊   41 ┊    153
             ┊ 53.856 ┊ 66.402 ┊ 32.742┊
   ----------+--------+--------+-------+
   AVERAGE   ┊    98  ┊   120  ┊   50 ┊    268
             ┊ 94.336 ┊ 116.31 ┊ 57.352┊
   ----------+--------+--------+-------+
   POOR      ┊    30  ┊    33  ┊   16 ┊     79
             ┊ 27.808 ┊ 34.286 ┊ 16.906┊
   ----------+--------+--------+-------+
   Total         176      217     107      500

       STATISTICS FOR TABLE OF RATING BY INCOME
   Statistic                       DF    Value    Prob
   ------------------------------------------------------
   Chi-Square                       4    4.278    0.370
   Likelihood Ratio Chi-Square      4    4.184    0.382
   Mantel-Haenszel Chi-Square       1    2.445    0.118
   Phi Coefficient                       0.092
   Contingency Coefficient               0.092
   Cramer's V                            0.065

   Sample Size = 500
```

multinomial probability distribution are satisfied. The null and alternative hypotheses we want to test are:

H_0: The rating a client gives his or her broker is independent of client's income

H_a: Broker rating and client income are dependent

The test statistic, $\chi^2 = 4.278$, is highlighted at the bottom of the printout as is the observed significance level (p-value) of the test. Since $\alpha = .10$ is less than $p = .370$, we fail to reject H_0. This survey does not support the firm's alternative hypothesis that affluent clients receive different broker service than lower-income clients.

b. The broker rating frequencies are expressed as percentages of income category frequencies in Table 8.10. The expected percentages under the assumption of independence are shown at the right of each row. The plot of the percentage data is shown in Figure 8.8, where the horizontal lines represent the

TABLE 8.10 Broker Ratings as Percentage of Income Class

		CLIENT'S INCOME			
		Under $30,000	$30,000–$60,000	Over $60,000	Totals
BROKER RATING	Outstanding	27	29	38	31
	Average	56	55	47	54
	Poor	17	15	15	16
Totals		100	99*	100	101*

*Percentages do not add up to 100 because of rounding.

FIGURE 8.8

Plot of broker rating–customer income contingency table

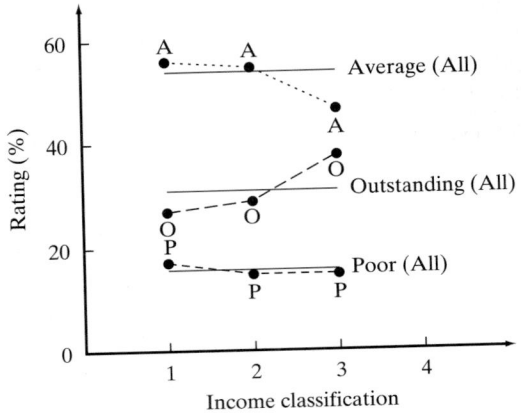

expected percentages assuming independence. Note that the response percentages deviate only slightly from those expected under the assumption of independence, supporting the result of the test in part **a**. That is, neither the descriptive plot nor the statistical test provides evidence that the rating given the broker services depends on (varies with) the customer's income.

STATISTICS IN ACTION

8.1 ETHICS IN COMPUTER TECHNOLOGY AND USE

Ethics refers to a set of rules or principles used for moral decision-making. Employees in the computer industry face ethical problems every day in the workplace. Illegal and improper actions are practiced knowingly and unknowingly by computer technology users. Some recent examples of unethical practices include Robert Morris's introduction of a "worm" into the Internet and software copyright infringements by several reputable colleges and universities.

Professors Margaret A. Pierce and John W. Henry of Georgia Southern University explored the ethical decision-making behavior of users of computers and computer technology and published their results in the *Journal of Business Ethics* (Vol. 15, 1996). Three primary influencing factors were considered by Pierce and Henry: (1) the individual's own personal code of ethics; (2) any informal code of ethical behavior that is operative in the workplace; and (3) the company's formal code of computer ethics (i.e., policies regarding computer technology).

The researchers mailed a computer ethics questionnaire to a random sample of 2,551 information systems (IS) professionals selected from members of the Data Processing Management Association (DPMA). The issues and questions addressed in the survey are given in Figure 8.9. Approximately 14% of the questionnaires were returned, yielding a total of 356 usable responses. Table 8.11 (page 432) gives a breakdown of the respondents by industry type. Tables 8.12 and 8.13 summarize the responses to two questions on the survey and their relationship to the three influencing factors identified by the researchers. (The tables show the number of responses in each category. Due to nonresponse for some questions, the sample size is less than 356.)

Focus

a. Does the existence of a company code of ethics influence computer users' perceptions of the importance of formal, informal, and personal ethics codes? If so, investigate the pattern of dependence by plotting the appropriate percentages on a graph.

b. Does the position of the computer user (professional or employee) influence the use of formal, informal, and personal ethics codes? If so, investigate the pattern of dependence by plotting the appropriate percentages on a graph.

c. With respect to industry type, is the sample of returned questionnaires representative of the 2,551 IS professionals who were mailed the survey? Explain.

Part I. Please answer the following statements/questions regarding ethics. In all parts of this survey "ethics" is defined as ethics related to computer technology/computer use. "Your company" refers to the organization or educational institution where you work.

1. Gender: Female _____ male _____
2. Your age on your last birthday. _____
3. Education
   (Please circle the highest level attained.) (1) high school (2) 2-yr college (3) 4-yr college
   (4) master's (5) doctorate
4. Circle the category which best describes your position. (1) CS/MIS educator (2) other educator (3) programmer
   (4) DP manager (5) system supervisor (6) other _____
5. Do you hold any professional certification or license? (1) no (2) yes, please specify _____
6. Number of years: (1) in profession _____ (2) with present employer _____
7. Type of company you work for: (1) Manufacture (2) Government (3) Education (4) Finance
   (Please circle one or specify.) (5) Utilities (6) Service (7) Consulting (8) Wholesale/retail
   (9) Other (specify) _____
8. Size of company (Number of employees) _____
9. Do you think of yourself as (Please circle one.) (1) DP/computer professional (2) an employee of the company
10. Circle the professional organizations listed to which you belong. (1) DPMA (2) ACM (3) IEEE-CS
11. (a) Are you familiar with any of the codes of ethics of the above professional organizations? (1) yes (2) no
    (b) If yes which one(s)? (1) DPMA (2) ACM (3) IEEE-CS
    (c) If yes do you use the code(s) to guide your own behavior? (1) yes (2) no
12. Have you had any formal study concerning theories of ethics or ethical behavior? (1) yes (2) no

---

Part II. Please respond to the following statements/questions about a formal company code of ethics (stated in writing or orally, representing the official position of the company), an informal code of ethics (ethical behavior actually practiced in the workplace), and a personal code of ethics (your own principles) related to computer use/computer technology.

1. Does your company have a formal company code of ethics? (1) yes (2) no
   (If there is a written code, please include a copy of the code.)
2. Which code of ethics is most important in guiding the behavior of employees where you work? (1) formal code (2) informal code (3) personal code
   (if there is one)
3. Which code of ethics do *you* use most frequently to guide ethical decisions? (1) formal code (2) informal code (3) personal code
   (if there is one)
4. These codes of ethics are deterrents to unethical behavior.
   a. formal company code of ethics strongly agree 1 2 3 4 5 strongly disagree
   b. informal code of ethics strongly agree 1 2 3 4 5 strongly disagree
   c. personal code of ethics strongly agree 1 2 3 4 5 strongly disagree
5. There are opportunities in my company to engage in unethical behavior. strongly agree 1 2 3 4 5 strongly disagree
6. Many people in my company engage in what I consider unethical behavior. strongly agree 1 2 3 4 5 strongly disagree
7. I am aware of the specifics of the informal company code of ethics. strongly agree 1 2 3 4 5 strongly disagree
8. I have a well-formulated personal code of ethics related to computer use/computer technology strongly agree 1 2 3 4 5 strongly disagree

FIGURE 8.9 Computer ethics questionnaire
Source: Margaret A. Pierce and John W. Henry, "Computer Ethics: the Role of Personal, Informal, and Formal Codes," *Journal of Business Ethics*, Vol. 15/4, 1996, pp. 425–437. Reprinted with kind permission of Kluwer Academic Publishers.

TABLE 8.11   **Number of Questionnaires Returned, by Industry (Statistics in Action 8.1)**

Industry Type	Number Returned	Percent in Original Sample of 2,551
Manufacturing	67	19
DP Service/Consult	57	16
Utilities	20	5.5
Wholesale/Retail	18	5
Financial/Real Estate	42	12
Education/Medical/Legal	80	22
Government	21	6
Other	51	14.5
Total	356	100.0

Source: Pierce, M. A., and Henry, J. W. "Computer ethics: The role of personal, informal, and formal codes." *Journal of Business Ethics,* Vol. 15, 1996, p. 429 (Table I).

TABLE 8.12   **What Type of Code Is Important in Making Ethical Decisions? (Statistics in Action 8.1)**

	COMPANY CODE	
Code	Yes	No
Formal	51	6
Informal	47	69
Personal	70	100

Source: Pierce, M. A., and Henry, J. W. "Computer ethics: The role of personal, informal, and formal codes." *Journal of Business Ethics,* Vol. 15, 1996, p. 431 (Table II).

TABLE 8.13   **Which Code Do You Use? (Statistics in Action 8.1)**

	POSITION	
Ethics Code	CS Professional	Employee
Formal	27	2
Informal	34	5
Personal	208	63

Source: Pierce, M. A., and Henry, J. W. "Computer ethics: The role of personal, informal, and formal codes." *Journal of Business Ethics,* Vol. 15, 1996, p. 432 (Table IV).

EXERCISES   8.37–8.49

Learning the Mechanics

8.37   Find the rejection region for a test of independence of two classifications where the contingency table contains r rows and c columns.

a. $r = 5, c = 5, \alpha = .05$
b. $r = 3, c = 6, \alpha = .10$
c. $r = 2, c = 3, \alpha = .01$

8.38   Consider the accompanying 2×3 (i.e., $r = 2$ and $c = 3$) contingency table.

a. Specify the null and alternative hypotheses that should be used in testing the independence of the row and column classifications.
b. Specify the test statistic and the rejection region that should be used in conducting the hypothesis test of part **a**. Use $\alpha = .01$.

	COLUMN		
	1	2	3
ROW 1	9	34	53
2	16	30	25

c. Assuming the row classification and the column classification are independent, find estimates for the expected cell counts.

d. Conduct the hypothesis test of part **a**. Interpret your result.

e. Convert the frequency responses to percentages by calculating the percentage of each column total falling in each row. Also convert the row totals to percentages of the total number of responses. Display the percentages in a table.

f. Create a graph with percentage on the vertical axis and column number on the horizontal axis. Showing the row total percentages as horizontal lines on the graph, plot the cell percentages from part **a** using the row number as a plotting symbol.

g. What pattern do you expect to see if the rows and columns are independent? Does the plot support the result of the test of independence, part **d**?

8.39 Test the null hypothesis of independence of the two classifications, A and B, of the 3 × 3 contingency table shown here. Test using $\alpha = .05$.

		B		
		B_1	B_2	B_3
A	A_1	40	72	42
	A_2	63	53	70
	A_3	31	38	30

8.40 Refer to Exercise 8.39. Convert the responses to percentages by calculating the percentage of each B class total falling into each A classification. Also, calculate the percentage of the total number of responses that constitute each of the A classification totals. Create a graph with percentage on

the vertical axis and B classification on the horizontal axis. Show the percentages corresponding to the A classification totals as horizontal lines on the graph, and plot the individual cell percentages using the A class number as a plotting symbol. Does the graph support the result of the test of hypothesis in Exercise 8.39? Explain.

Applying the Concepts

8.41 The *American Journal of Public Health* (July 1995) reported on a population-based study of trauma in Hispanic children. One of the objectives of the study was to compare the use of protective devices in motor vehicles used to transport Hispanic and non-Hispanic white children. On the basis of data collected from the San Diego County Regionalized Trauma System, 792 children treated for injuries sustained in vehicular accidents were classified according to ethnic status (Hispanic or non-Hispanic white) and seatbelt usage (worn or not worn) during the accident. The data are summarized in the table below.

a. Calculate the sample proportion of injured Hispanic children who were not wearing seatbelts during the accident.

b. Calculate the sample proportion of injured non-Hispanic white children who were not wearing seatbelts during the accident.

c. Compare the two sample proportions, parts **a** and **b**. Do you think the true population proportions differ?

d. Conduct a test to determine whether seatbelt usage in motor vehicle accidents depends on ethnic status in the San Diego County Regionalized Trauma System. Use $\alpha = .01$.

e. Construct a 99% confidence interval for the difference between the proportions, parts **a** and **b**. Interpret the interval.

8.42 To better understand whether and how Total Quality Management (TQM) is practiced in U.S. companies, University of Scranton researchers N. Tamimi and R. Sebastianelli interviewed one manager in each of a sample of 86 companies in Pennsylvania, New York, and New Jersey (*Production and Inventory Management Journal,* 1996). Concerning whether or not the firms were

	Hispanic	Non-Hispanic White	Totals
Seatbelts worn	31	148	179
Seatbelts not worn	283	330	613
Totals	314	478	792

Source: Matteneci, R. M. *et al.* "Trauma among Hispanic children: A population-based study in a regionalized system of trauma care." *American Journal of Public Health,* Vol. 85, No. 7, July 1995, p. 1007 (Table 2).

involved with TQM, the following data were obtained:

	Service Firms	Manufacturing Firms
Number practicing TQM	34	23
Number not practicing TQM	18	11
Total	52	34

Source: Adapted from Tamimi, N., and Sebastianelli, R. "How firms define and measure quality." *Production and Inventory Management Journal,* Third Quarter, 1996, p. 35.

a. The researchers concluded that "manufacturing firms were not significantly more likely to be involved with TQM than service firms." Do you agree? Test using $\alpha = .05$.

b. Find and interpret the approximate *p*-value for the test you conducted in part **a**.

c. What assumptions must hold in order for your test of part **a** and your *p*-value of part **b** to be valid?

8.43 Are all employees equally likely to have accidents? Are certain employee groups—say, younger employees—more prone to particular kinds of accidents? The effective implementation of hiring policies, training programs, and safety programs requires such knowledge. A study conducted to address these questions for a particular manufacturing company was published in *Professional Safety* (Oct. 1985). A portion of the research results is summarized in the accompanying contingency table.

		KIND OF ACCIDENT		
		Sprain	**Burn**	**Cut**
AGE	**Under 25**	9	17	5
	25 and Over	61	13	12

Source: Parry, A. E. "Changing assumptions about loss frequency." *Professional Safety,* Oct. 1985, pp. 39–43.

a. From the contingency table, the researcher concluded that there is a relationship between an employee's age and the kind of accident that the employee may have. Do you agree? Test using $\alpha = .05$.

b. According to the frequencies of the contingency table, which is the most frequent type of accident? Are younger or older employees more likely to have sprains? Burns? Justify your answers.

c. What assumptions must hold in order for your test of part **a** to be valid?

d. Plot the percentage of employees under 25 who are injured based on the total injuries for each kind of accident. Compare this to the percentage of the total number of employees under 25

who are injured based on the total of all kinds of accidents. What does the plot indicate about the pattern of dependence in the data?

8.44 In recent years, the accounting profession has become increasingly concerned with ethics. University of Louisville professor Julia Karcher conducted an experiment to investigate the ethical behavior of accountants (*Journal of Business Ethics,* Vol. 15, 1996). She focused on auditor abilities to detect ethical problems that may not be obvious. Seventy auditors from Big-Six accounting firms were given a detailed case study that contained several problems including tax evasion by the client. In 35 of the cases the tax evasion issue was severe; in the other 35 cases it was moderate. The auditors were asked to identify any problems they detected in the case. The table summarizes the results for the ethical issue.

	SEVERITY OF ETHICAL ISSUE	
	Moderate	**Severe**
Ethical Issue Identified	27	26
Ethical Issue Not Identified	8	9

Source: Karcher, J. "Auditors' ability to discern the presence of ethical problems." *Journal of Business Ethics,* Vol. 15, 1996, p. 1041 (Table V).

a. Did the severity of the ethical issue influence whether the issue was identified or not by the auditors? Test using $\alpha = .05$.

b. Suppose the lefthand column of the table contained the counts 35 and 0 instead of 27 and 8. Should the test of part **a** still be conducted? Explain.

c. Keeping the sample size the same, change the numbers in the contingency table so that the answer you would get for the question posed in part **a** changes.

8.45 Many companies use well-known celebrities in their ads, while other companies create their own spokesperson (such as the Maytag repairman). A study in the *Journal of Marketing* (Fall 1992) investigated the relationship between the gender of the spokesperson and the gender of the viewer in order to see how this relationship affected brand awareness. Three hundred television viewers were asked to identify the products advertised by celebrity spokespersons. See the next two tables at the top of page 435.

a. For the products advertised by male spokespersons, conduct a test to determine whether audience gender and product identification are dependent factors. Test using $\alpha = .05$.

b. Repeat part **a** for the products advertised by female spokespersons.

c. How would you interpret these results?

Male Spokesperson

	AUDIENCE GENDER		
	Male	Female	Total
Identified Product	95	41	136
Could Not Identify Product	55	109	164
Total	150	150	300

Female Spokesperson

	AUDIENCE GENDER		
	Male	Female	Total
Identified Product	47	61	108
Could Not Identify Product	103	89	192
Total	150	150	300

8.46 In recent years, corporate boards of directors have been pressed to improve their monitoring of corporate economic performance and to become more careful overseers of the activities of management. In addition, boards are being asked to guide the long-term responsiveness of their respective organizations to the economic and social climate. These pressures have forced many boards of directors to better articulate the mission and strategies of their firms. To study the extent and nature of strategic planning being undertaken by boards of directors, A. Tashakori and W. Boulton questioned a sample of 119 chief executive officers of major U.S. corporations (*Journal of Business Strategy,* Winter 1983). One objective was to determine if a relationship exists between the composition of a board—i.e., a majority of outside directors versus a majority of in-house directors—and its level of participation in the strategic planning process. To this end, the questionnaire data were used to classify the responding corporations according to the level of their board's participation in the strategic planning process:

Level 1: Board participates in formulation or implementation or evaluation of strategy

Level 2: Board participates in formulation and implementation, formulation and evaluation, or implementation and evaluation of strategy

Level 3: Board participates in formulation, implementation, and evaluation of strategy

The results obtained are shown in the next table. Of these 119 firms, 100 had boards where outside directors constituted a majority. Their levels of participation in strategic planning are shown in the second table.

  a. The researchers concluded that a relationship exists between a board's level of participation

ALL FIRMS

Level	1	2	3
Number of firms	22	37	60

OUTSIDE DIRECTED

Level	1	2	3
Number of firms	20	27	53

in the strategic planning process and the composition of the board. Do you agree? Construct the appropriate contingency table, and test using $\alpha = .10$.

  b. In the context of this problem, specify the Type I and Type II errors associated with the test of part **a**.

  c. Find the *p*-value for the test in the SAS printout on page 436. Based on the *p*-value, would the null hypothesis have been rejected at $\alpha = .05$? Explain.

  d. Construct a graph that helps to interpret the result of the test in part **a**.

8.47 Research has indicated that the stress produced by today's lifestyles results in health problems for a large proportion of society. An article in the *International Journal of Sports Psychology* (July–Sept. 1990) evaluated the relationship between physical fitness and stress. Five hundred forty-nine employees of companies that participate in the Health Examination Program offered by Health Advancement Services (HAS) were classified into three groups of fitness levels: good, average, and poor. Each person was tested for signs of stress. The table reports the results for the three groups. [*Note:* The proportions given are the proportions of the entire group that show signs of stress and fall into each particular fitness level.] Do the data provide evidence to indicate that the likelihood for stress is dependent on an employee's fitness level?

Fitness Level	Sample Size	Proportions with Signs of Stress
Poor	242	.155
Average	212	.133
Good	95	.108

8.48 In the United States, people over age 50 represent 25% of the population, yet they control 70% of the wealth. Research indicates that the highest priority of retirees is travel. A study in the *Annals of Tourism Research* (Vol. 19, 1992) investigates the relationship of retirement status (pre- and postretirement) to various items related to the travel industry. One part of the study investigated

```
                    TABLE OF LEVEL BY COMPOSIT

          LEVEL        COMPOSIT

          Frequency|
          Expected |INSIDE  |OUTSIDE |     Total
          ---------+--------+--------+
              1    |    2   |   20   |      22
                   | 3.5126 | 18.487 |
          ---------+--------+--------+
              2    |   10   |   27   |      37
                   | 5.9076 | 31.092 |
          ---------+--------+--------+
              3    |    7   |   53   |      60
                   | 9.5798 | 50.42  |
          ---------+--------+--------+
          Total        19       100         119

        STATISTICS FOR TABLE OF LEVEL BY COMPOSIT

        Statistic                    DF     Value     Prob
        ----------------------------------------------------

        Chi-Square                    2     4.976     0.083
        Likelihood Ratio Chi-Square   2     4.696     0.096
        Mantel-Haenszel Chi-Square    1     0.120     0.729
        Phi Coefficient                     0.204
        Contingency Coefficient             0.200
        Cramer's V                          0.204

        Sample Size = 119
```

the differences in the length of stay of a trip for pre- and postretirees. A sample of 703 travelers were asked how long they stayed on a typical trip. The results are shown in the table. Use the information in the table to determine whether the retirement status of a traveler and the duration of a typical trip are dependent. Test using $\alpha = .05$.

Number of Nights	Preretirement	Postretirement
4–7	247	172
8–13	82	67
14–21	35	52
22 or more	16	32
Total	380	323

8.49 According to research reported in the *Journal of the National Cancer Institute* (Apr. 1991), eating foods high in fiber may help protect against breast cancer. The researchers randomly divided 120 lab-oratory rats into four groups of 30 each. All rats were injected with a drug that causes breast cancer, then each rat was fed a diet of fat and fiber for 15 weeks. However, the levels of fat and fiber varied from group to group. At the end of the feeding period, the number of rats with cancer tumors was determined for each group. The data is summarized in the accompanying contingency table.

a. Does the sampling appear to satisfy the assumptions for a multinomial experiment (see Section 8.3)? Explain.

b. Calculate the expected cell counts for the contingency table.

c. Calculate the χ^2 statistic.

d. Is there evidence to indicate that diet and presence/absence of cancer are independent? Test using $\alpha = .05$.

e. Compare the percentage of rats on a high-fat/no-fiber diet with cancer to the percentage of rats on a high-fat/fiber diet with cancer using a 95% confidence interval. Interpret the result.

		DIET				
		High-Fat/No-Fiber	High-Fat/Fiber	Low-Fat/No-Fiber	Low-Fat/Fiber	Totals
CANCER TUMORS	Yes	27	20	19	14	80
	No	3	10	11	16	40
	Totals	30	30	30	30	120

Source: Tampa Tribune, Apr. 3, 1991.

QUICK REVIEW

Key Terms

Note: Starred (*) terms are from the optional sections in this chapter.

Chi-square test*   416
Contingency table*   423
Count data*   415
Dependence*   426
Expected cell count*   418
Independence of two classifications*   424
Marginal probabilities*   423

Multinomial experiment*   416
Multinomial probability distribution*   415
Observed cell count*   424
Population proportions   406
Sampling distribution of the difference between estimated proportions   407
Two-dimensional (two-way) table*   423

Key Formulas

Note: Starred (*) formulas are from the optional sections in this chapter.

$$(\hat{p}_1 - \hat{p}_2) \pm z_{\alpha/2} \sqrt{\frac{\hat{p}_1\hat{q}_1}{n_1} + \frac{\hat{p}_2\hat{q}_2}{n_2}}$$

Confidence interval for $(p_1 - p_2)$ 408

$$z = \frac{(\hat{p}_1 - \hat{p}_2) - 0}{\sqrt{\hat{p}\hat{q}\left(\frac{1}{n_1} + \frac{1}{n_2}\right)}}$$

Test statistic for $H_0: (p_1 - p_2) = 0$ 408

where $\hat{p} = \dfrac{x_1 + x_2}{n_1 + n_2}$

$\hat{q} = 1 - \hat{p}$

$$n_1 = n_2 = \frac{(z_{\alpha/2})^2(p_1q_1 + p_2q_2)}{B^2}$$

Sample size for estimating $(p_1 - p_2)$ 414

$$\chi^2 = \sum \frac{[n_i - E(n_i)]^2}{E(n_i)}$$

χ^2 test for one-way table*   418

where n_i = count for cell i

$E(n_i) = np_{i,0}$

$p_{i,0}$ = hypothesized value of p_i in H_0

$$\chi^2 = \sum \frac{[n_{ij} - \hat{E}(n_{ij})]^2}{\hat{E}(n_{ij})}$$

χ^2 test for two-way table*   428

where n_{ij} = count for cell in row i, column j

$\hat{E}(n_{ij}) = r_i c_j / n$

r_i = total for row i

c_j = total for column j

n = total sample size

LANGUAGE LAB

Note: Starred (*) symbols are from the optional sections in this chapter.

Symbol	Pronunciation	Description
$(p_1 - p_2)$	p-1 minus p-2	Difference between population proportions
$(\hat{p}_1 - \hat{p}_2)$	p-1 hat minus p-2 hat	Difference between sample proportions
$\sigma_{(\hat{p}_1 - \hat{p}_2)}$	sigma of p-1 hat minus p-2 hat	Standard deviation of the sampling distribution of $(\hat{p}_1 - \hat{p}_2)$
D_0	D naught	Hypothesized value of $(\hat{p}_1 - \hat{p}_2)$
$p_{i,0}$*	p-i-zero	Value of multinomial probability p_i hypothesized in H_0
χ^2*	Chi-square	Test statistic used in analysis of count data

n_i^*	$n\text{-}i$	Number of observed outcomes in cell i of one-way table
$E(n_i)^*$	Expected value of $n\text{-}i$	Expected number of outcomes in cell i of one-way table when H_0 is true
p_{ij}^*	$p\text{-}i\text{-}j$	Probability of an outcome in row i and column j of a two-way contingency table
n_{ij}^*	$n\text{-}i\text{-}j$	Number of observed outcomes in row i and column j of a two-way contingency table
$\hat{E}(n_{ij})^*$	Estimated expected value of $n\text{-}i\text{-}j$	Estimated expected number of outcomes in row i and column j of a two-way contingency table
r_i^*	$r\text{-}i$	Total number of outcomes in row i of a contingency table
c_j^*	$c\text{-}j$	Total number of outcomes in column j of a contingency table

SUPPLEMENTARY EXERCISES   8.50–8.66

Note: Exercises marked with 💾 *contain data for computer analysis on a 3.5" disk (file name in parentheses). Starred (*) exercises are from the optional sections in this chapter.*

Learning the Mechanics

8.50   Independent random samples were selected from two binomial populations. The sizes and number of observed successes for each sample are shown in the table below.

Sample 1	Sample 2
$n_1 = 200$	$n_2 = 200$
$x_1 = 110$	$x_2 = 130$

a. Test $H_0: (p_1 - p_2) = 0$ against $H_a: (p_1 - p_2) < 0$. Use $\alpha = .10$.

b. Form a 95% confidence interval for $(p_1 - p_2)$.

c. What sample sizes would be required if we wish to use a 95% confidence interval of width .01 to estimate $(p_1 - p_2)$?

*8.51   A random sample of 150 observations was classified into the categories shown in the table below.

			CATEGORY		
	1	**2**	**3**	**4**	**5**
n_i	28	35	33	25	29

a. Do the data provide sufficient evidence that the categories are not equally likely? Use $\alpha = .10$.

b. Form a 90% confidence interval for p_2, the probability that an observation will fall in category 2.

*8.52   A random sample of 250 observations was classified according to the row and column categories shown in the next table.

a. Do the data provide sufficient evidence to conclude that the rows and columns are dependent? Test using $\alpha = .05$.

b. Would the analysis change if the row totals were fixed before the data were collected?

		COLUMN		
		1	**2**	**3**
	1	20	20	10
ROW	**2**	10	20	70
	3	20	50	30

c. Do the assumptions required for the analysis to be valid differ according to whether the row (or column) totals are fixed? Explain.

d. Convert the table entries to percentages by using each column total as a base and calculating each row response as a percentage of the corresponding column total. In addition, calculate the row totals and convert them to percentages of all 250 observations.

e. Plot the row percentages on the vertical axis against the column number on the horizontal axis. Draw horizontal lines corresponding to the row total percentages. Does the deviation (or lack thereof) of the individual row percentages from the row total percentages support the result of the test conducted in part **a**?

Applying the Concepts

8.53   Advertising companies often try to characterize the average user of a client's product so ads can be targeted at particular segments of the buying community. A new movie is about to be released, and the advertising company wants to determine whether to aim the ad campaign at people under or over 25 years of age. It plans to arrange an advance showing of the movie to an audience from each group, then obtain an opinion about the movie from each individual. How many individuals should be included in each sample if the advertising company wants to estimate the difference in the proportions of viewers in each age group who will like the movie to within .05 with 90% confidence? Assume the sample size for each group will be the same and about half of each group will like the movie.

8.54 In a study of the effectiveness of a new TV commercial, shoppers were randomly selected as they entered a large Phoenix supermarket and asked their preferences for several product brands. One was brand XYZ, whose new TV commercial was the object of the study. Ostensibly in exchange for their time, the shoppers were given a packet of "cents-off" coupons for various products sold in the supermarket, including XYZ. The coupons could be used only in that store and only on that day. A second sample of 387 shoppers were given the same interview, but were also asked to watch four television commercials in a trailer parked outside the supermarket. One commercial was the newly developed ad for XYZ. Following the viewing, the shoppers were asked for their reactions to the commercials, then were given the same packet of coupons. Of the 392 shoppers not exposed to the television commercials, 57 redeemed the coupon for XYZ. Of the 387 shoppers who saw XYZ's commercial, 84 redeemed the XYZ coupon.

a. Do the sample data provide sufficient evidence to conclude that the new XYZ commercial motivates shoppers to purchase the XYZ brand? Use $\alpha = .05$.

b. Find and interpret the observed significance level for the test.

*8.55 Over the years, pollsters have found that the public's confidence in big business is closely tied to the economic climate. When businesses are growing and employment is increasing, public confidence is high. When the opposite occurs, public confidence is low. Harvey Kahalas hypothesized that there is a relationship between the level of confidence in business and job satisfaction, and that this is true for both union and nonunion workers (*Baylor Business Studies*, Feb.–Apr. 1981). He analyzed sample data collected by the National Opinion Research Center and shown in the tables below.

Kahalas concluded that his hypothesis was not supported by the data. Do you agree? Use the SPSS printouts on page 440 to conduct the appropriate tests using $\alpha = .05$. Be sure to specify your null and alternative hypotheses.

*8.56 Because shareholders control the firm, they can transfer wealth from the firm's bondholders to themselves through several different dividend strategies. This potential conflict of interest between shareholders and bondholders can be reduced through the use of debt covenants. Accountants E. Griner and H. Huss of Georgia State University investigated the effects of insider ownership and the size of the firm on the types of debt covenants required by a firm's bondholders (*Journal of Applied Business Research*, Vol. 11, 1995). As part of the study, they examined a sample of 31 companies whose bondholders required covenants based on tangible assets rather than on liquidity or net assets or retained earnings. Characteristics of those 31 firms are summarized below. The objective of the study is to determine if there is a relationship between the extent of insider ownership and the size of the firm for firms with tangible asset covenants.

		SIZE	
		Small	**Large**
INSIDE OWNERSHIP	**Low**	3	17
	High	8	3

Source: Griner, E., and Huss, H. "Firm size, insider ownership, and accounting-based debt covenants." *Journal of Applied Business Research*, Vol. 11, No. 4, 1995, p. 7 (Table 4).

a. Assuming the null hypothesis of independence is true, how many firms are expected to fall in each cell of the table?

b. The researchers were unable to use the chi-square test to analyze the data. Show why.

		JOB SATISFACTION			
		Very Satisfied	**Moderately Satisfied**	**A Little Dissatisfied**	**Very Dissatisfied**
UNION MEMBER CONFIDENCE IN MAJOR CORPORATIONS	**A Great Deal**	26	15	2	1
	Only Some	95	73	16	5
	Hardly Any	34	28	10	9

		JOB SATISFACTION			
		Very Satisfied	**Moderately Satisfied**	**A Little Dissatisfied**	**Very Dissatisfied**
NONUNION CONFIDENCE IN MAJOR CORPORATIONS	**A Great Deal**	111	52	12	4
	Only Some	246	142	37	18
	Hardly Any	73	51	19	9

```
UNIONCON  by  JOBSAT

                      JOBSAT
            Count
            Exp Val
                                                                    Row
                      Little   Moderate None      Very      Total
UNIONCON
        GreatDeal       2         15       1        26        44
                       3.9       16.3     2.1      21.7      14.0%

        HardlyAny      10         28       9        34        81
                       7.2       29.9     3.9      40.0      25.8%

        OnlySome       16         73       5        95       189
                      16.9       69.8     9.0      93.3      60.2%

        Column         28        116      15       155       314
        Total         8.9%      36.9%    4.8%     49.4%     100.0%

        Chi-Square                  Value          DF          Significance
    -------------------          ----------       ----        ------------
Pearson                          13.36744          6              .03756
Likelihood Ratio                 12.08304          6              .06014

Minimum Expected Frequency -      2.102
Cells with Expected Frequency < 5 -     3 OF      12 (25.0%)

-----------------------------------------------------------------------------

NOUNCON  by  JOBSAT

                      JOBSAT
            Count
            Exp Val
                                                                    Row
                      Little   Moderate None      Very      Total
NOUNCON
        GreatDeal      12         52       4       111       179
                      15.7       56.7     7.2      99.4      23.1%

        HardlyAny      19         51       9        73       152
                      13.4       48.1     6.1      84.4      19.6%

        OnlySome       37        142      18       246       443
                      38.9      140.2    17.7     246.1      57.2%

        Column         68        245      31       430       774
        Total         8.8%      31.7%    4.0%     55.6%     100.0%

        Chi-Square                  Value          DF          Significance
    -------------------          ----------       ----        ------------
Pearson                           9.63514          6              .14088
Likelihood Ratio                  9.55907          6              .14449

Minimum Expected Frequency -      6.088
```

c. A test of the null hypothesis can be conducted using a small-sample method known as **Fisher's exact test**. This method calculates the exact probability (*p*-value) of observing sample results at least as contradictory to the null hypothesis as those observed for the researchers' data. The researchers reported the *p*-value for this test as .0043. Interpret this result.

d. Investigate the nature of the dependence exhibited by the contingency table by plotting the appropriate contingency table percentages. Describe what you find.

8.57 An economist wants to investigate the difference in unemployment rates between an urban industrial community and a university community in the same state. She interviews 525 potential members of the work force in the industrial community and 375 in the university community. Of these, 47 and 22, respectively, are unemployed. Use a 95% confidence interval to estimate the difference in unemployment rates in the two communities.

8.58 An important interaction occurs when a consumer dissatisfied with a purchase returns to the retailer to obtain satisfaction. The action taken by the retailer, however, may not conform to the consumer's expectations, and the resulting frustration and ill will benefit neither party. In a classic study published in the *Journal of Consumer Affairs* (Summer 1975), a hypothesis test was conducted to determine whether differences exist between retailers' and consumers' perceptions regarding actions taken by retailers in market transactions. A random sample of 300 consumers selected from the Cincinnati Metropolitan Area Telephone Directory were asked via mail questionnaire to react to scenarios like the following:

- A customer calls the retailer to report that her refrigerator purchased two weeks ago is not cooling properly and all the food has spoiled.

- Action that should be taken by the retailer: The customer should be reimbursed for the value of the spoiled food.

One hundred usable questionnaires were returned. The same questionnaire was presented in person to 100 managers and assistant managers of a random sample of 40 retail establishments drawn from the yellow pages of the Cincinnati Telephone Directory. For the preceding scenario, 89 consumers agreed with the action prescribed for the retailer, 3 disagreed, and 8 had no opinion. Thirty-seven retailers (managers or assistant managers) agreed with the prescribed action, 54 disagreed, and 9 had no opinion.

a. Use a 95% confidence interval to estimate the difference in the proportions of consumers and retailers who agree with the action prescribed. Draw appropriate conclusions regarding the hypothesis of interest to the researchers.

b. What assumption(s), if any, must be made in constructing the confidence interval?

c. Discuss the implications of the composition of the sample of retailers for the validity of the conclusions you made in part **a**. How would you improve the sampling procedure?

*8.59 Many investors believe that the stock market's directional change in January signals the market's direction for the remainder of the year. This so-called January indicator is frequently cited in the popular press. But is this indicator valid? If so, the well-known *random walk and efficient markets* theories (basically postulating that market movements are unpredictable) of stock-price behavior

would be called into question. The accompanying table summarizes the relevant changes in the Dow Jones Industrial Average for the period December 31, 1927, through January 31, 1981. J. Martinich applied the chi-square test of independence to these data to investigate the January indicator (*Mid-South Business Journal*, Vol. 4, 1984).

		NEXT 11-MONTH CHANGE	
		Up	Down
JANUARY CHANGE	Up	25	10
	Down	9	9

a. Examine the contingency table. Based solely on your visual inspection, do the data appear to confirm the validity of the January indicator? Explain.

b. Construct a plot of the percentage of years for which the 11-month movement is up based on the January change. Compare these two percentages to the percentage of times the market moved up during the last 11 months over all years in the sample. What do you think of the January indicator now?

c. If a chi-square test of independence is to be used to investigate the January indicator, what are the appropriate null and alternative hypotheses?

d. Conduct the test of part **c**. Use $\alpha = .05$. Interpret your results in the context of the problem.

e. Would you get the same result in part **d** if $\alpha = .10$ were used? Explain.

*8.60 If a company can identify times of day when accidents are most likely to occur, extra precautions can be instituted during those times. A random sampling of the accident reports over the last year at a plant gives the frequency of occurrence of accidents during the different hours of the workday. Can it be concluded from the data in the table that the proportions of accidents are different for at least two of the four time periods?

Hours	1–2	3–4	5–6	7–8
Number of Accidents	31	28	45	47

*8.61 (X08.061) An economist was interested in knowing whether sons have a tendency to choose the same occupation as their fathers. To investigate this question, 500 males were polled and questioned concerning their occupation and the occupation of their father. A summary of the numbers of father-son pairs falling in each occupational category is shown in the next table. Do the data provide sufficient evidence at $\alpha = .05$ to indicate

		SON			
		Professional or Business	**Skilled**	**Unskilled**	**Farmer**
FATHER	**Professional or Business**	55	38	7	0
	Skilled	79	71	25	0
	Unskilled	22	75	38	10
	Farmer	15	23	10	32

a dependence between a son's choice of occupation and his father's occupation? Use the SAS printout below to conduct the analysis.

8.62 What makes entrepreneurs different from chief executive officers (CEOs) of *Fortune* 500 companies? The *Wall Street Journal* hired the Gallup organization to investigate this question. For the study, entrepreneurs were defined as chief executive officers of companies listed by *Inc.* magazine as among the 500 fastest-growing smaller companies in the United States. The Gallup organization sampled 207 CEOs of *Fortune* 500 companies and 153 entrepreneurs. They obtained the results shown in the table at the bottom of the page.

a. In each of the three areas—age, education, and employment record—are the sample sizes large enough to use the inferential methods of this section to investigate the differences between *Fortune* 500 CEOs and entrepreneurs? Justify your answer.

```
                TABLE OF FATHER BY SON

FATHER       SON

Frequency|
Expected |Farmer | Prof/Bus|Skill  |Unskill | Total
---------+-------+--------+-------+-------+
Farmer   |   32  |   15   |  23   |  10   |   80
         |  6.72 | 27.36  | 33.12 | 12.8  |
---------+-------+--------+-------+-------+
Prof/Bus |    0  |   55   |  38   |   7   |  100
         |  8.4  | 34.2   | 41.4  |  16   |
---------+-------+--------+-------+-------+
Skill    |    0  |   79   |  71   |  25   |  175
         | 14.7  | 59.85  | 72.45 |  28   |
---------+-------+--------+-------+-------+
Unskill  |   10  |   22   |  75   |  38   |  145
         | 12.18 | 49.59  | 60.03 | 23.2  |
---------+-------+--------+-------+-------+
Total        42      171     207     80     500

    STATISTICS FOR TABLE OF FATHER BY SON

Statistic                   DF    Value    Prob
-----------------------------------------------
Chi-Square                   9   180.874   0.000
Likelihood Ratio Chi-Square  9   160.832   0.000
Mantel-Haenszel Chi-Square   1    52.040   0.000
Phi Coefficient                   0.601
Contingency Coefficient           0.515
Cramer's V                        0.347

Sample Size = 500
```

Variable	*Fortune* 500 CEOs	Entrepreneurs
Age Under 45 years old	19	96
Education Completed 4 years of college	195	116
Employment record Have been fired or dismissed from a job	19	47

Source: Graham, E. "The entrepreneurial mystique." *Wall Street Journal,* May 20, 1985.

b. Test to determine whether the data indicate that the fractions of CEOs and entrepreneurs who have been fired or dismissed from a job differ at the $\alpha = .01$ level of significance.

c. Construct a 99% confidence interval for the difference between the fractions of CEOs and entrepreneurs who have been fired or dismissed from a job.

d. Which inferential procedure provides more information about the difference between employment records, the test of part **b** or the interval of part **c**? Explain.

*8.63 A computer used by a 24-hour banking service is supposed to assign each transaction to one of five memory locations at random. A check at the end of a day's transactions gives the following counts to each of the five memory locations:

1	2	3	4	5
90	78	100	72	85

Is there evidence to indicate a difference among the proportions of transactions assigned to the five memory locations? Test using $\alpha = .025$.

*8.64 According to the Magnuson-Moss Warranty Act (enacted by Congress in 1977 to reform consumer product warranty practices), all warranties must be designated as "full" or "limited" and must be clearly written in readily understood language. A study was undertaken to investigate consumer satisfaction with warranty practices since the advent of the Magnuson-Moss Warranty Act (*Baylor Business Studies,* Nov.–Dec. 1983). Using a mailed questionnaire, 237 midwestern consumers who had purchased a major appliance within the past 6 to 18 months were sampled. One of the questions asked of the consumers was, "Do most retailers and dealers make a conscientious effort to satisfy their customers' warranty claims?" One hundred fifty-six answered yes, 61 were uncertain, and 20 said no. The population of consumers from which this sample was drawn had also been investigated two years prior to the passage of the Magnuson-Moss Warranty Act. At that time, 37.0% of the population answered yes to the same question, 53.3% were uncertain, and 9.7% said no.

a. As reflected in the answers to the above question, have consumer attitudes toward warranties changed since the pre-Magnuson-Moss Act study? Test using $\alpha = .05$.

b. Compare the pre- and post-Magnuson-Moss Warranty Act responses, and describe the changes that have occurred.

*8.65 When a buyer charges a purchase, the seller records the sale in his or her record books under a category called *accounts receivable.* Some retailers monitor the status of their accounts receivable by regularly classifying each in one of the following categories: current, 1–30 days late, 31–60 days late, more than 60 days late, or uncollectable. Historical data indicate that the status of a particular retailer's accounts receivable can be described as follows:

Current	65%
1–30 days late	15%
31–60 days late	10%
Over 60 days late	7%
Uncollectable	3%

Six months after the interest rate charged to late accounts was increased, the status of the retailer's 200 accounts receivable was as follows:

Current	78%
1–30 days late	12%
31–60 days late	5%
Over 60 days late	2%
Uncollectable	3%

a. Is there evidence to indicate that the increase in interest rates affected the timing of buyers' payments? Test using $\alpha = .10$.

b. Find the approximate observed significance level for the test.

*8.66 Product or service quality is often defined as *fitness for use.* This means the product or service meets the customer's needs. Generally speaking, fitness for use is based on five quality characteristics: technological (e.g., strength, hardness), psychological (taste, beauty), time-oriented (reliability), contractual (guarantee provisions), and ethical (courtesy, honesty). The quality of a service may involve all these characteristics, while the quality of a manufactured product generally depends on technological and time-oriented characteristics (Schroeder, *Operations Management,* 1993). After a barrage of customer complaints about poor quality, a manufacturer of gasoline filters for cars had its quality inspectors sample 600 filters—200 per work shift—and check for defects. The data in the table resulted.

Shift	Defectives Produced
First	25
Second	35
Third	80

a. Do the data indicate that the quality of the filters being produced may be related to the shift producing the filter? Test using $\alpha = .05$.

b. Estimate the proportion of defective filters produced by the first shift. Use a 95% confidence interval.

DISCRIMINATION IN THE WORKPLACE

SHOWCASE

Title VII of the Civil Rights Act of 1964 prohibits discrimination in the workplace on the basis of race, color, religion, gender, or national origin. The Age Discrimination in Employment Act of 1967 (ADEA) protects workers age 40 to 70 against discrimination based on age. The potential for discrimination exists in such processes as hiring, promotion, compensation, and termination.

In 1971 the U.S. Supreme Court established that employment discrimination cases fall into two categories: **disparate treatment** and **disparate impact**. In the former, the issue is whether the employer intentionally discriminated against a worker. For example, if the employer considered an individual's race in deciding whether to terminate him, the case is one of disparate treatment. In a disparate impact case, the issue is whether employment practices have an adverse impact on a protected group or class of people, even when the employer does not intend to discriminate.

PART I: DOWNSIZING AT A COMPUTER FIRM

Disparate impact cases almost always involve the use of statistical evidence and expert testimony by professional statisticians. Attorneys for the plaintiffs frequently use hypothesis test results in the form of *p*-values in arguing the case for their clients.

Table C4.1 was recently introduced as evidence in a race case that resulted from a round of layoffs during the downsizing of a division of a computer manufacturer. The company had selected 51 of the division's 1,215 employees to lay off. The plaintiff's—in this case 15 of the 20 African Americans who were laid off—were suing the company for $20 million in damages.

The company's lawyers argued that the selections followed from a performance-based ranking of all employees. The plaintiffs legal team and their expert witnesses,

citing the results of a statistical test of hypothesis, argued that layoffs were a function of race.

The validity of the plaintiff's interpretation of the data is dependent on whether the assumptions of the test are met in this situation. In particular, like all hypothesis tests presented in this text, the assumption of random sampling must hold. If it does not, the results of the test may be due to the violation of this assumption rather than to discrimination. In general, the appropriateness of the testing procedure is dependent on the test's ability to capture the relevant aspects of the employment process in question (DeGroot, Fienberg, and Kadane, *Statistics and the Law*, 1986).

Prepare a document to be submitted as evidence in the case (i.e., an exhibit), in which you evaluate the validity of the plaintiff's interpretation of the data. Your evaluation should be based in part on your knowledge of the processes companies use to lay off employees and how well those processes are reflected in the hypothesis-testing procedure employed by the plaintiffs.

PART II: AGE DISCRIMINATION— YOU BE THE JUDGE

In 1996, as part of a significant restructuring of product lines, AJAX Pharmaceuticals (a fictitious name for a real company) laid off 24 of 55 assembly-line workers in its Pittsburgh manufacturing plant. Citing the ADEA, 11 of the laid-off workers claimed they were discriminated against on the basis of age and sued AJAX for $5,000,000. Management disputed the claim, saying that since the workers were essentially interchangeable, they had used random sampling to choose the 24 workers to be terminated.

Table C4.2 lists the 55 assembly-line workers and identifies which were terminated and which remained active. Plaintiffs are denoted by an asterisk. These data were used by both the plaintiffs and the defendants to determine whether the layoffs had an adverse impact on workers

TABLE C4.1 Summary of Downsizing Data for Race Case

		DECISION	
		Retained	**Laid off**
RACE	**White**	1,051	31
	Black	113	20

Source: Confidential personal communication with P. George Benson, 1997.

TABLE C4.2   Data for Age Discrimination Case

Employee	Yearly Wages	Age	Employment Status	Employee	Yearly Wages	Age	Employment Status
* Adler, C.J.	$41,200	45	Terminated	* Huang, T.J.	42,995	48	Terminated
Alario, B.N.	39,565	43	Active	Jatho, J.A.	31,755	40	Active
Anders, J.M.	30,980	41	Active	Johnson, C.H.	29,540	32	Active
Bajwa, K.K.	23,225	27	Active	Jurasik, T.B.	34,300	41	Active
Barny, M.L.	21,250	26	Active	Klein, K.L.	43,700	51	Terminated
* Berger, R.W.	41,875	45	Terminated	Lang, T.F.	19,435	22	Active
Brenn, L.O.	31,225	41	Active	Liao, P.C.	28,750	32	Active
Cain, E.J.	30,135	36	Terminated	* Lostan, W.J.	44,675	52	Terminated
Carle, W.J.	29,850	32	Active	Mak, G.L.	35,505	38	Terminated
Castle, A.L.	21,850	22	Active	Maloff, V.R.	33,425	38	Terminated
Chan, S.D.	43,005	48	Terminated	McCall, R.M.	31,300	36	Terminated
Cho, J.Y.	34,785	41	Active	* Nadeau, S.R.	42,300	46	Terminated
Cohen, S.D.	25,350	27	Active	* Nguyen, O.L.	43,625	50	Terminated
Darel, F.E.	36,300	42	Active	Oas, R.C.	37,650	42	Active
* Davis, D.E.	40,425	46	Terminated	* Patel, M.J.	38,400	43	Terminated
* Dawson, P.K.	39,150	42	Terminated	Porter, K.D.	32,195	35	Terminated
Denker, U.H.	19,435	19	Active	Rosa, L.M.	19,435	21	Active
Dorando, T.R.	24,125	28	Active	Roth, J.H.	32,785	39	Terminated
Dubois, A.G.	30,450	40	Active	Savino, G.L.	37,900	42	Active
England, N.	24,750	25	Active	Scott, I.W.	29,150	30	Terminated
Estis, K.B.	22,755	23	Active	Smith, E.E.	35,125	41	Active
Fenton, C.K.	23,000	24	Active	Teel, Q.V.	27,655	33	Active
Finer, H.R.	42,000	46	Terminated	* Walker, F.O.	42,545	47	Terminated
* Frees, O.C.	44,100	52	Terminated	Wang, T.G.	22,200	32	Active
Gary, J.G.	44,975	55	Terminated	Yen, D.O.	40,350	44	Terminated
Gillen, D.J.	25,900	27	Active	Young, N.L.	28,305	34	Active
Harvey, D.A.	40,875	46	Terminated	Zeitels, P.W.	36,500	42	Active
Higgins, N.M.	38,595	41	Active				

*Denotes plaintiffs

age 40 and over and to establish the credibility of management's random sampling claim.

Using whatever statistical methods you think are appropriate, build a case that supports the plaintiff's position. (Call documents related to this issue Exhibit A.) Similarly, build a case that supports the defendant's position. (Call these documents Exhibit B.) Then discuss which of the two cases is more convincing and why. [*Note:* The data for this case are available in ASCII format in the file described at right.] ▲

DATA   ASCII file name: DISCRIM.DAT
Number of observations: 55

Variable	Column(s)	Type
LASTNAME	1–10	QL
WAGES	15–19	QN
AGE	35–36	QN
STATUS	47	QL (A=active, T=terminated)

www.int.com
www.int.com
INTERNET LAB
www.int.com

SAMPLING AND ANALYZING NYSE STOCK QUOTES

The success of any investment in common stock depends, to a certain extent, on timing, particularly as it relates to movement and changes in the stock market and the economy. Stock market indexes, such as the Dow Jones Industrial Average, act both as indicators of stock market activity and as economic indicators. Other information on stock market behavior is available, including the Composite daily summaries of all stocks traded on the New York Stock Exchange (NYSE).

In this lab exercise we will experiment with sampling and analyzing current NYSE data. Following are relevant NYSE site addresses:

NYSE Home Page: *http://www.nyse.com/*
(Select *Data* icon)

Data Page: *http://www.nyse.com/public/data.html*
(Select *NYSE Historical Statistics Archive*)

NYSE Historical Statistics:
http://www.nyse.com/public/data/stathtoc.html

1. Obtain the daily closing prices for a random sample of 30 stocks on the last business day of 1995. Repeat for the last days of 1996 and for 1997. (Be sure that your three samples of stocks are independent.)

2. Download and save the data in your statistical applications software data files.

3. Use available statistical software to compare the closing prices for 1995, 1996, and 1997. Use both parametric and nonparametric statistical tests and compare the results. ○

CHAPTER 9

SIMPLE LINEAR REGRESSION

CONTENTS

9.1   Probabilistic Models

9.2   Fitting the Model: The Least Squares Approach

9.3   Model Assumptions

9.4   An Estimator of σ^2

9.5   Assessing the Utility of the Model: Making Inferences About the Slope β_1

9.6   The Coefficient of Correlation

9.7   The Coefficient of Determination

9.8   Using the Model for Estimation and Prediction

9.9   Simple Linear Regression: An Example

9.10   A Nonparametric Test for Correlation (Optional)

STATISTICS IN ACTION

9.1   New Jersey Banks—Serving Minorities?

9.2   Statistical Assessment of Damage to Bronx Bricks

Where We've Been

We've learned how to estimate and test hypotheses about population parameters based on a random sample of observations from the population. We've also seen how to extend these methods to allow for a comparison of parameters from two populations.

Where We're Going

Suppose we want to predict the assessed value of a house in a particular community. We could select a single random sample of n houses from the community, use the methods of Chapter 5 to estimate the mean assessed value μ, and then use this quantity to predict the house's assessed value. A better method uses information that is available to any property appraiser, e.g., square feet of floor space and age of the house. If we measure square footage and age at the same time as assessed value, we can establish the relationship between these variables—one that lets us use these variables for prediction. This chapter covers the simplest situation—relating two variables. The more complex problem of relating more than two variables is the topic of Chapter 10.

In Chapters 5–7 we described methods for making inferences about population means. The mean of a population was treated as a *constant,* and we showed how to use sample data to estimate or to test hypotheses about this constant mean. In many applications, the mean of a population is not viewed as a constant, but rather as a variable. For example, the mean sale price of residences in a large city during 1997 can be treated as a constant and might be equal to $150,000. But we might also treat the mean sale price as a variable that depends on the square feet of living space in the residence. For example, the relationship might be

$$\text{Mean sale price} = \$30{,}000 + \$60(\text{Square feet})$$

This formula implies that the mean sale price of 1,000-square-foot homes is $90,000, the mean sale price of 2,000-square-foot homes is $150,000, and the mean sale price of 3,000-square-foot homes is $210,000.

What do we gain by treating the mean as a variable rather than a constant? In many practical applications we will be dealing with highly variable data, data for which the standard deviation is so large that a constant mean is almost "lost" in a sea of variability. For example, if the mean residential sale price is $150,000 but the standard deviation is $75,000, then the actual sale prices will vary considerably, and the mean price is not a very meaningful or useful characterization of the price distribution. On the other hand, if the mean sale price is treated as a variable that depends on the square feet of living space, the standard deviation of sale prices for any given size of home might be only $10,000. In this case, the mean price will provide a much better characterization of sale prices when it is treated as a variable rather than a constant.

In this chapter we discuss situations in which the mean of the population is treated as a variable, dependent on the value of another variable. The dependence of residential sale price on the square feet of living space is one illustration. Other examples include the dependence of mean sales revenue of a firm on advertising expenditure, the dependence of mean starting salary of a college graduate on the student's GPA, and the dependence of mean monthly production of automobiles on the total number of sales in the previous month.

In this chapter we discuss the simplest of all models relating a population mean to another variable, *the straight-line model.* We show how to use the sample data to estimate the straight-line relationship between the mean value of one variable, *y,* as it relates to a second variable, *x.* The methodology of estimating and using a straight-line relationship is referred to as *simple linear regression analysis.*

9.1 PROBABILISTIC MODELS

An important consideration in merchandising a product is the amount of money spent on advertising. Suppose you want to model the monthly sales revenue of an appliance store as a function of the monthly advertising expenditure. The first question to be answered is this: "Do you think an exact relationship exists between these two variables?" That is, do you think it is possible to state the exact monthly sales revenue if the amount spent on advertising is known? We think you will agree with us that this is *not* possible for several reasons. Sales depend on many variables other than advertising expenditure—for example, time of year, the state of the general economy, inventory, and price structure. Even if many variables are included in a model (the topic of Chapter 11), it is still unlikely that we would be able to predict the monthly sales *exactly.* There will almost certainly be some variation in response times due strictly to *random phenomena* that cannot be modeled or explained.

FIGURE 9.1

Possible sales revenues, *y*, for five different months, *x*

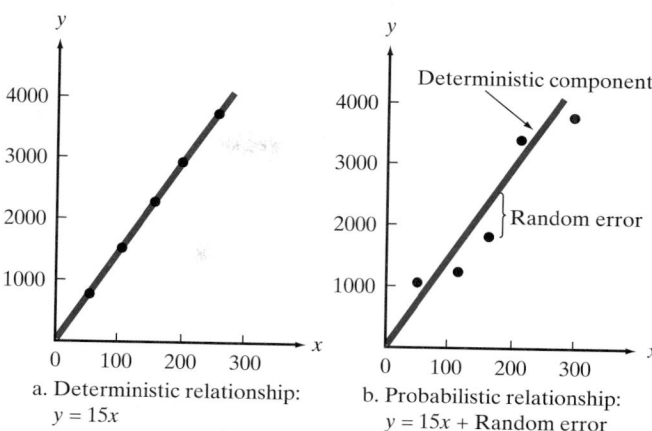

a. Deterministic relationship:
$y = 15x$

b. Probabilistic relationship:
$y = 15x + $ Random error

If we were to construct a model that hypothesized an exact relationship between variables, it would be called a **deterministic model**. For example, if we believe that *y*, the monthly sales revenue, will be exactly fifteen times *x*, the monthly advertising expenditure, we write

$$y = 15x$$

This represents a **deterministic relationship** between the variables *y* and *x*. It implies that *y* can always be determined exactly when the value of *x* is known. *There is no allowance for error in this prediction.*

If, on the other hand, we believe there will be unexplained variation in monthly sales—perhaps caused by important but unincluded variables or by random phenomena—we discard the deterministic model and use a model that accounts for this **random error**. This **probabilistic model** includes both a deterministic component and a random error component. For example, if we hypothesize that the sales *y* is related to advertising expenditure *x* by

$$y = 15x + \text{Random error}$$

we are hypothesizing a **probabilistic relationship** between *y* and *x*. Note that the deterministic component of this probabilistic model is $15x$.

Figure 9.1a shows the possible values of *y* and *x* for five different months, when the model is deterministic. All the pairs of (x, y) data points must fall exactly on the line because a deterministic model leaves no room for error.

Figure 9.1b shows a possible set of points for the same values of *x* when we are using a probabilistic model. Note that the deterministic part of the model (the straight line itself) is the same. Now, however, the inclusion of a random error component allows the monthly sales to vary from this line. Since we know that the sales revenue does vary randomly for a given value of *x*, the probabilistic model provides a more realistic model for *y* than does the deterministic model.

General Form of Probabilistic Models

$$y = \text{Deterministic component} + \text{Random error}$$

where *y* is the variable of interest. We always assume that the mean value of the random error equals 0. This is equivalent to assuming that the mean value of *y*, $E(y)$, equals the deterministic component of the model; that is

$$E(y) = \text{Deterministic component}$$

We begin with the simplest of probabilistic models—the **straight-line model**—which derives its name from the fact that the deterministic portion of the model graphs as a straight line. Fitting this model to a set of data is an example of **regression analysis**, or **regression modeling**. The elements of the straight-line model are summarized in the next box.

A First-Order (Straight-Line) Probabilistic Model

$$y = \beta_0 + \beta_1 x + \epsilon$$

where

y = *Dependent or response variable* (variable to be modeled)

x = *Independent or predictor variable* (variable used as a predictor of y)*

$E(y) = \beta_0 + \beta_1 x$ = Deterministic component

ϵ (epsilon) = Random error component

β_0 (beta zero) = *y-intercept of the line*, that is, the point at which the line intercepts or cuts through the y-axis (see Figure 9.2)

β_1 (beta one) = *Slope of the line*, that is, the amount of increase (or decrease) in the deterministic component of y for every 1-unit increase in x. [As you can see in Figure 9.2, $E(y)$ increases by the amount β_1 as x increases from 2 to 3.]

In the probabilistic model, the deterministic component is referred to as the **line of means**, because the mean of y, $E(y)$, is equal to the straight-line component of the model. That is,

$$E(y) = \beta_0 + \beta_1 x$$

Note that the Greek symbols β_0 and β_1, respectively, represent the y-intercept and slope of the model. They are population parameters that will be known only if we have access to the entire population of (x, y) measurements. Together with a specific value of the independent variable x, they determine the mean value of y, which is just a specific point on the line of means (Figure 9.2).

FIGURE 9.2
The straight-line model

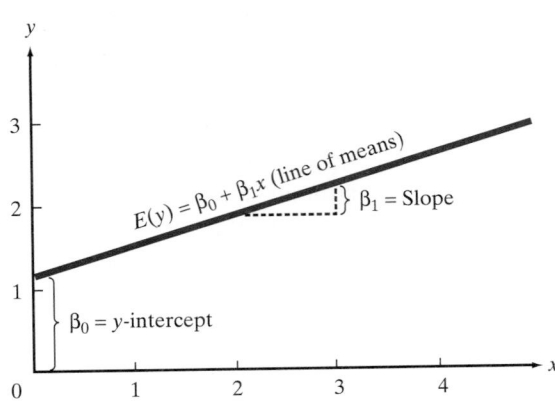

*The word *independent* should not be interpreted in a probabilistic sense, as defined in Chapter 3. The phrase *independent variable* is used in regression analysis to refer to a predictor variable for the response y.

The values of β_0 and β_1 will be unknown in almost all practical applications of regression analysis. The process of developing a model, estimating the unknown parameters, and using the model can be viewed as the five-step procedure shown in the next box.

Step 1	Hypothesize the deterministic component of the model that relates the mean, $E(y)$, to the independent variable x (Section 9.1).
Step 2	Use the sample data to estimate unknown parameters in the model (Section 9.2).
Step 3	Specify the probability distribution of the random error term and estimate the standard deviation of this distribution (Sections 9.3 and 9.4).
Step 4	Statistically evaluate the usefulness of the model (Sections 9.5, 9.6, and 9.7).
Step 5	When satisfied that the model is useful, use it for prediction, estimation, and other purposes (Section 9.8).

In this chapter only the straight-line model is discussed; more complex models are addressed in Chapter 10.

EXERCISES   9.1–9.9

Learning the Mechanics

9.1 In each case, graph the line that passes through the given points.
 a. $(1, 1)$ and $(5, 5)$ b. $(0, 3)$ and $(3, 0)$
 c. $(-1, 1)$ and $(4, 2)$ d. $(-6, -3)$ and $(2, 6)$

9.2 Give the slope and y-intercept for each of the lines graphed in Exercise 9.1.

9.3 The equation for a straight line (deterministic model) is

$$y = \beta_0 + \beta_1 x$$

If the line passes through the point $(-2, 4)$, then $x = -2, y = 4$ must satisfy the equation; that is,

$$4 = \beta_0 + \beta_1(-2)$$

Similarly, if the line passes through the point $(4, 6)$, then $x = 4, y = 6$ must satisfy the equation; that is,

$$6 = \beta_0 + \beta_1(4)$$

Use these two equations to solve for β_0 and β_1; then find the equation of the line that passes through the points $(-2, 4)$ and $(4, 6)$.

9.4 Refer to Exercise 9.3. Find the equations of the lines that pass through the points listed in Exercise 9.1.

9.5 Plot the following lines:
 a. $y = 4 + x$ b. $y = 5 - 2x$ c. $y = -4 + 3x$
 d. $y = -2x$ e. $y = x$ f. $y = .50 + 1.5x$

9.6 Give the slope and y-intercept for each of the lines defined in Exercise 9.5.

9.7 Why do we generally prefer a probabilistic model to a deterministic model? Give examples for which the two types of models might be appropriate.

9.8 What is the line of means?

9.9 If a straight-line probabilistic relationship relates the mean $E(y)$ to an independent variable x, does it imply that every value of the variable y will always fall exactly on the line of means? Why or why not?

9.2   FITTING THE MODEL: THE LEAST SQUARES APPROACH

After the straight-line model has been hypothesized to relate the mean $E(y)$ to the independent variable x, the next step is to collect data and to estimate the (unknown) population parameters, the y-intercept β_0 and the slope β_1.

TABLE 9.1 **Advertising–Sales Data**

Month	Advertising Expenditure, x ($100s)	Sales Revenue, y ($1,000s)
1	1	1
2	2	1
3	3	2
4	4	2
5	5	4

To begin with a simple example, suppose an appliance store conducts a five-month experiment to determine the effect of advertising on sales revenue. The results are shown in Table 9.1. (The number of measurements and the measurements themselves are unrealistically simple in order to avoid arithmetic confusion in this introductory example.) This set of data will be used to demonstrate the five-step procedure of regression modeling given in Section 9.1. In this section we hypothesize the deterministic component of the model and estimate its unknown parameters (steps 1 and 2). The model assumptions and the random error component (step 3) are the subjects of Sections 9.3 and 9.4, whereas Sections 9.5–9.7 assess the utility of the model (step 4). Finally, we use the model for prediction and estimation (step 5) in Section 9.8.

Step 1 *Hypothesize the deterministic component of the probabilistic model.* As stated before, we will consider only straight-line models in this chapter. Thus, the complete model to relate mean sales revenue $E(y)$ to advertising expenditure x is given by

$$E(y) = \beta_0 + \beta_1 x$$

Step 2 *Use sample data to estimate unknown parameters in the model.* This step is the subject of this section—namely, how can we best use the information in the sample of five observations in Table 9.1 to estimate the unknown y-intercept β_0 and slope β_1?

To determine whether a linear relationship between y and x is plausible, it is helpful to plot the sample data in a **scattergram** (see optional Section 2.10). The scattergram for the five data points of Table 9.1 is shown in Figure 9.3. Note that the scattergram suggests a general tendency for y to increase as x increases. If you place a ruler on the scattergram, you will see that a line may be drawn through three of the five points, as shown in Figure 9.4. To obtain the equation of this visually fitted line, note that the line intersects the y-axis at $y = -1$, so the y-intercept is -1. Also, y increases exactly 1 unit for every 1-unit increase in x, indicating that the slope is $+1$. Therefore, the equation is

$$\tilde{y} = -1 + 1(x) = -1 + x$$

where $\tilde{y}$ is used to denote the predicted y from the visual model.

FIGURE 9.3
Scattergram for data in Table 9.1

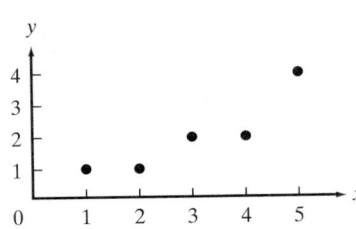

FIGURE 9.4
Visual straight
line fitted to the
data in Figure 9.3

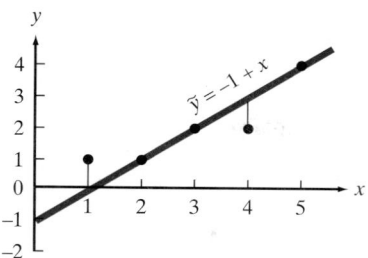

One way to decide quantitatively how well a straight line fits a set of data is to note the extent to which the data points deviate from the line. For example, to evaluate the model in Figure 9.4, we calculate the magnitude of the **deviations**, i.e., the differences between the observed and the predicted values of y. These deviations, or **errors**, are the vertical distances between observed and predicted values (see Figure 9.4). The observed and predicted values of y, their differences, and their squared differences are shown in Table 9.2. Note that the *sum of errors* equals 0 and the *sum of squares of the errors* (SSE), which gives greater emphasis to large deviations of the points from the line, is equal to 2.

You can see by shifting the ruler around the graph that it is possible to find many lines for which the sum of errors is equal to 0, but it can be shown that there is one (and only one) line for which the SSE is a *minimum*. This line is called the **least squares line**, the **regression line**, or the **least squares prediction equation**.

To find the least squares prediction equation for a set of data, assume that we have a sample of n data points consisting of pairs of values of x and y, say (x_1, y_1), (x_2, y_2), ..., (x_n, y_n). For example, the $n = 5$ data points shown in Table 9.2 are $(1, 1)$, $(2, 1)$, $(3, 2)$, $(4, 2)$, and $(5, 4)$. The fitted line, which we will calculate based on the five data points, is written as

$$\hat{y} = \hat{\beta}_0 + \hat{\beta}_1 x$$

The "hats" indicate that the symbols below them are estimates: $\hat{y}$ (y-hat) is an estimator of the mean value of y, $E(y)$, and a predictor of some future value of y; and $\hat{\beta}_0$ and $\hat{\beta}_1$ are estimators of β_0 and β_1, respectively.

For a given data point, say the point (x_i, y_i), the observed value of y is y_i and the predicted value of y would be obtained by substituting x_i into the prediction equation:

$$\hat{y}_i = \hat{\beta}_0 + \hat{\beta}_1 x_i$$

And the deviation of the ith value of y from its predicted value is

$$(y_i - \hat{y}_i) = [y_i - (\hat{\beta}_0 + \hat{\beta}_1 x_i)]$$

**TABLE 9.2   Comparing Observed and Predicted Values
for the Visual Model**

x	y	$\tilde{y} = -1 + x$	$(y - \tilde{y})$	$(y - \tilde{y})^2$
1	1	0	$(1 - 0) =$ 1	1
2	1	1	$(1 - 1) =$ 0	0
3	2	2	$(2 - 2) =$ 0	0
4	2	3	$(2 - 3) = -1$	1
5	4	4	$(4 - 4) =$ 0	0
			Sum of errors = 0	Sum of squared errors (SSE) = 2

Then the sum of squares of the deviations of the y-values about their predicted values for all the n points is

$$\text{SSE} = \sum[y_i - (\hat{\beta}_0 + \hat{\beta}_1 x_i)]^2$$

The quantities $\hat{\beta}_0$ and $\hat{\beta}_1$ that make the SSE a minimum are called the **least squares estimates** of the population parameters β_0 and β_1, and the prediction equation $\hat{y} = \hat{\beta}_0 + \hat{\beta}_1 x$ is called the *least squares line.*

DEFINITION 9.1

The **least squares line** is one that has the following two properties:

1. the sum of the errors (SE) equals 0
2. the sum of squared errors (SSE) is smaller than for any other straight-line model

---

The values of $\hat{\beta}_0$ and $\hat{\beta}_1$ that minimize the SSE are (proof omitted) given by the formulas in the box.*

Formulas for the Least Squares Estimates

Slope: $\hat{\beta}_1 = \dfrac{\text{SS}_{xy}}{\text{SS}_{xx}}$

y-intercept: $\hat{\beta}_0 = \bar{y} - \hat{\beta}_1 \bar{x}$

where $\text{SS}_{xy} = \sum(x_i - \bar{x})(y_i - \bar{y}) = \sum x_i y_i - \dfrac{\left(\sum x_i\right)\left(\sum y_i\right)}{n}$

$\text{SS}_{xx} = \sum(x_i - \bar{x})^2 = \sum x_i^2 - \dfrac{\left(\sum x_i\right)^2}{n}$

$n = $ Sample size

Preliminary computations for finding the least squares line for the advertising–sales example are presented in Table 9.3. We can now calculate

$$\text{SS}_{xy} = \sum x_i y_i - \frac{\left(\sum x_i\right)\left(\sum y_i\right)}{5} = 37 - \frac{(15)(10)}{5} = 37 - 30 = 7$$

$$\text{SS}_{xx} = \sum x_i^2 - \frac{\left(\sum x_i\right)^2}{5} = 55 - \frac{(15)^2}{5} = 55 - 45 = 10$$

Then the slope of the least squares line is

$$\hat{\beta}_1 = \frac{\text{SS}_{xy}}{\text{SS}_{xx}} = \frac{7}{10} = .7$$

---

*Students who are familiar with calculus should note that the values of β_0 and β_1 that minimize $\text{SSE} = \Sigma(y_i - \hat{y}_i)^2$ are obtained by setting the two partial derivatives $\partial\text{SSE}/\partial\beta_0$ and $\partial\text{SSE}/\partial\beta_1$ equal to 0. The solutions to these two equations yield the formulas shown in the box. Furthermore, we denote the *sample* solutions to the equations by $\hat{\beta}_0$ and $\hat{\beta}_1$, where the "hat" denotes that these are sample estimates of the true population intercept β_0 and true population slope β_1.

TABLE 9.3 Preliminary Computations for Advertising–Sales Example

	x_i	y_i	x_i^2	$x_i y_i$
	1	1	1	1
	2	1	4	2
	3	2	9	6
	4	2	16	8
	5	4	25	20
Totals	$\sum x_i = 15$	$\sum y_i = 10$	$\sum x_i^2 = 55$	$\sum x_i y_i = 37$

and the y-intercept is

$$\hat{\beta}_0 = \bar{y} - \hat{\beta}_1 \bar{x} = \frac{\sum y_i}{5} - \hat{\beta}_1 \frac{\sum x_i}{5}$$

$$= \frac{10}{5} - (.7)\left(\frac{15}{5}\right) = 2 - (.7)(3) = 2 - 2.1 = -.1$$

The least squares line is thus

$$\hat{y} = \hat{\beta}_0 + \hat{\beta}_1 x = -.1 + .7x$$

The graph of this line is shown in Figure 9.5.

The predicted value of y for a given value of x can be obtained by substituting into the formula for the least squares line. Thus, when $x = 2$ we predict y to be

$$\hat{y} = -.1 + .7x = -.1 + .7(2) = 1.3$$

We show how to find a prediction interval for y in Section 9.8.

The observed and predicted values of y, the deviations of the y values about their predicted values, and the squares of these deviations are shown in Table 9.4. Note that the sum of squares of the deviations, SSE, is 1.10, and (as we would

FIGURE 9.5
The line $\hat{y} = -.1 + .7x$
fit to the data

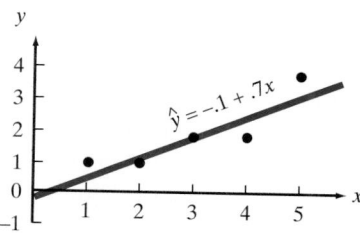

TABLE 9.4 Comparing Observed and Predicted Values for the Least Squares Prediction Equation

x	y	$\hat{y} = -.1 + .7x$	$(y - \hat{y})$	$(y - \hat{y})^2$
1	1	.6	$(1 - .6) = .4$	.16
2	1	1.3	$(1 - 1.3) = -.3$	.09
3	2	2.0	$(2 - 2.0) = 0$	.00
4	2	2.7	$(2 - 2.7) = -.7$	.49
5	4	3.4	$(4 - 3.4) = .6$	.36
			Sum of errors = 0	SSE = 1.10

Dependent Variable: Y

Analysis of Variance

Source	DF	Sum of Squares	Mean Square	F Value	Prob>F
Model	1	4.90000	4.90000	13.364	0.0354
Error	3	1.10000	0.36667		
C Total	4	6.00000			

Root MSE	0.60553	R-square	0.8167	
Dep Mean	2.00000	Adj R-sq	0.7556	
C.V.	30.27650			

Parameter Estimates

Variable	DF	Parameter Estimate	Standard Error	T for HO: Parameter=0	Prob>|T|
INTERCEP	1	-0.100000	0.63508530	-0.157	0.8849
X	1	0.700000	0.19148542	3.656	0.0354

FIGURE 9.6 SAS printout for advertising–sales regression

expect) this is less than the SSE = 2.0 obtained in Table 9.2 for the visually fitted line.

The calculations required to obtain $\hat{\beta}_0, \hat{\beta}_1$, and SSE in simple linear regression, although straightforward, can become rather tedious. Even with the use of a pocket calculator, the process is laborious and susceptible to error, especially when the sample size is large. Fortunately, the use of a statistical software package can significantly reduce the labor involved in regression calculations. The SAS output for the simple linear regression of the data in Table 9.1 is displayed in Figure 9.6. The values of $\hat{\beta}_0$ and $\hat{\beta}_1$ are highlighted on the SAS printout under the **Parameter Estimate** column in the rows labeled **INTERCEP** and **X**, respectively. These values, $\hat{\beta}_0 = -.1$ and $\hat{\beta}_1 = .7$, agree exactly with our hand-calculated values. The value of SSE = 1.10 is also highlighted in Figure 9.6, under the **Sum of Squares** column in the row labeled **Error**.

Whether you use a hand calculator or a computer, it is important that you be able to interpret the intercept and slope in terms of the data being utilized to fit the model. In the advertising–sales example, the estimated y-intercept, $\hat{\beta}_0 = -.1$, appears to imply that the estimated mean sales revenue is equal to −.1, or −$100, when the advertising expenditure, x, is equal to $0. Since negative sales revenues are not possible, this seems to make the model nonsensical. However, *the model parameters should be interpreted only within the sampled range of the independent variable*—in this case, for advertising expenditures between $100 and $500. Thus, the y-intercept—which is, by definition, at $x = 0$ ($0 advertising expenditure)—is not within the range of the sampled values of x and is not subject to meaningful interpretation.

The slope of the least squares line, $\hat{\beta}_1 = -.7$, implies that for every unit increase of x, the mean value of y is estimated to increase by .7 unit. In terms of this example, for every $100 increase in advertising, the mean sales revenue is estimated to increase by $700 *over the sampled range of advertising expenditures from $100 to $500*. Thus, the model does not imply that increasing the advertising expenditures from $500 to $1,000 will result in an increase in mean sales of $3,500, because the range of x in the sample does not extend to $1,000 ($x = 10$). Be careful to interpret the estimated parameters only within the sampled range of x.

Even when the interpretations of the estimated parameters are meaningful, we need to remember that they are only estimates based on the sample. As such, their values will typically change in repeated sampling. How much confidence do we have that the estimated slope, $\hat{\beta}_1$, accurately approximates the true slope, β_1? This requires statistical inference, in the form of confidence intervals and tests of hypotheses, which we address in Section 9.5.

To summarize, we defined the best-fitting straight line to be the one that minimizes the sum of squared errors around the line, and we called it the least squares line. We should interpret the least squares line only within the sampled range of the independent variable. In subsequent sections we show how to make statistical inferences about the model.

EXERCISES 9.10–9.21

Note: Exercises marked with ■ contain data for computer analysis on a 3.5" disk (file name in parentheses).

Learning the Mechanics

9.10 The following table is similar to Table 9.3. It is used for making the preliminary computations for finding the least squares line for the given pairs of x and y values.

x_i	y_i	x_i^2	$x_i y_i$
7	2		
4	4		
6	2		
2	5		
1	7		
1	6		
3	5		
Totals $\sum x_i =$	$\sum y_i =$	$\sum x_i^2 =$	$\sum x_i y_i =$

a. Complete the table. **b.** Find SS_{xy}.
c. Find SS_{xx}. **d.** Find $\hat{\beta}_1$.
e. Find $\bar{x}$ and $\bar{y}$. **f.** Find $\hat{\beta}_0$.
g. Find the least squares line.

9.11 Refer to Exercise 9.10. After the least squares line has been obtained, the table below (which is similar to Table 9.4) can be used for (1) comparing the observed and the predicted values of y, and (2) computing SSE.

x	y	$\hat{y}$	$(y - \hat{y})$	$(y - \hat{y})^2$
7	2			
4	4			
6	2			
2	5			
1	7			
1	6			
3	5			
			$\sum(y - \hat{y}) =$	SSE $= \sum(y - \hat{y})^2 =$

a. Complete the table.
b. Plot the least squares line on a scattergram of the data. Plot the following line on the same graph: $\hat{y} = 14 - 2.5x$
c. Show that SSE is larger for the line in part **b** than it is for the least squares line.

9.12 Construct a scattergram for the data in the following table.

x	.5	1	1.5
y	2	1	3

a. Plot the following two lines on your scattergram:

$$y = 3 - x \quad \text{and} \quad y = 1 + x$$

b. Which of these lines would you choose to characterize the relationship between x and y? Explain.
c. Show that the sum of errors for both of these lines equals 0.
d. Which of these lines has the smaller SSE?
e. Find the least squares line for the data and compare it to the two lines described in part **a**.

9.13 Consider the following pairs of measurements:

x	8	5	4	6	2	5	3
y	1	3	6	3	7	2	5

a. Construct a scattergram for these data.
b. What does the scattergram suggest about the relationship between x and y?
c. Find the least squares estimates of β_0 and β_1 on the MINITAB printout on page 458.
d. Plot the least squares line on your scattergram. Does the line appear to fit the data well? Explain.
e. Interpret the y-intercept and slope of the least squares line. Over what range of x are these interpretations meaningful?

```
The regression equation is
Y = 8.54 - 0.994 X

Predictor          Coef        Stdev        t-ratio         p
Constant          8.543        1.117           7.65     0.001
X                -0.9939       0.2208          -4.50     0.006

s = 1.069          R-sq = 80.2%        R-sq(adj) = 76.2%

Analysis of Variance

SOURCE           DF          SS           MS          F          p
Regression        1      23.144       23.144      20.25      0.006
Error             5       5.713        1.143
Total             6      28.857
```

9.14 Suppose that $n = 100$ recent residential home sales in a city are used to fit a least squares straight-line model relating the sale price, y, to the square feet of living space, x. Homes in the sample range from 1,500 square feet to 4,000 square feet of living space, and the resulting least squares equation is

$$\hat{y} = -30,000 + 70x$$

a. What is the underlying hypothesized probabilistic model for this application? What does it imply about the relationship between the mean sale price and living space?

b. Identify the least squares estimates of the y-intercept and slope of the model.

c. Interpret the least squares estimate of the y-intercept. Is it meaningful for this application? Why?

d. Interpret the least squares estimate of the slope of the model. Over what range of x is the interpretation meaningful?

e. Use the least squares model to estimate the mean sale price of a 3,000-square-foot home. Is the estimate meaningful? Explain.

f. Use the least squares model to estimate the mean sale price of a 5,000-square-foot home. Is the estimate meaningful? Explain.

[*Note:* We show how to measure the statistical reliability of these least squares estimates in subsequent sections.]

Applying the Concepts

9.15 (X09.015) Individuals who report perceived wrongdoing of a corporation or public agency are known as *whistle blowers*. Two researchers developed an index to measure the extent of retaliation against a whistle blower (*Journal of Applied Psychology*, 1986). The index was based on the number of forms of reprisal actually experienced, the number of forms of reprisal threatened, and the number of people within the organization (e.g., coworkers or immediate supervisor) who retaliated against them. The table lists the retalia-

tion index (higher numbers indicate more extensive retaliation) and salary for a sample of 15 whistle blowers from federal agencies.

Retaliation Index	Salary	Retaliation Index	Salary
301	$62,000	535	$19,800
550	36,500	455	44,000
755	21,600	615	46,600
327	24,000	700	15,100
500	30,100	650	70,000
377	35,000	630	21,000
290	47,500	360	16,900
452	54,000		

Source: Data adapted from Near, J. P., and Miceli, M. P. "Retaliation against whistle blowers: Predictors and effects." *Journal of Applied Psychology*, Vol. 71, No. 1, 1986, pp. 137–145.

a. Construct a scattergram for the data. Does it appear that the extent of retaliation increases, decreases, or stays the same with an increase in salary? Explain.

b. Use the method of least squares to fit a straight line to the data.

c. Graph the least squares line on your scattergram. Does the least squares line support your answer to the question in part **a**? Explain.

d. Interpret the y-intercept, $\hat{\beta}_0$, of the least squares line in terms of this application. Is the interpretation meaningful?

e. Interpret the slope, $\hat{\beta}_1$, of the least squares line in terms of this application. Over what range of x is this interpretation meaningful?

9.16 (X09.016) Due primarily to the price controls of the Organization of Petroleum Exporting Countries (OPEC), a cartel of crude-oil suppliers, the price of crude oil rose dramatically from the mid-1970s to the mid-1980s. As a result, motorists saw an upward spiral in gasoline prices. The data in the table on page 459 are typical prices for a gallon of regular leaded gasoline and a barrel of crude oil (refiner acquisition cost) for the indicated years.

a. Use the data to calculate the least squares line that describes the relationship between

Year	Gasoline, y (¢/gal.)	Crude Oil, x ($/bbl.)
1975	57	10.38
1976	59	10.89
1977	62	11.96
1978	63	12.46
1979	86	17.72
1980	119	28.07
1981	131	35.24
1982	122	31.87
1983	116	28.99
1984	113	28.63
1985	112	26.75
1986	86	14.55
1987	90	17.90
1988	90	14.67
1989	100	17.97
1990	115	22.23
1991	72	16.54
1992	71	15.99
1993	75	14.24

Source: U.S. Bureau of the Census, *Statistical Abstract of the United States: 1982–1995.*

Team	Games Won, y	Team Batting Average, x
Cleveland	99	.293
New York	92	.288
Boston	85	.283
Toronto	74	.259
Texas	90	.284
Detroit	53	.256
Minnesota	78	.288
Baltimore	88	.274
California	70	.276
Milwaukee	80	.279
Seattle	85	.287
Kansas City	75	.267
Oakland	78	.265
Chicago	85	.281

Source: Compiled by the Major League Baseball (MLB) Baseball Information System, 1996.

the price of a gallon of gasoline and the price of a barrel of crude oil over the period 1975–1985.

b. Construct a scattergram of *all* the data.

c. Plot your least squares line on the scattergram. Does your least squares line appear to be an appropriate characterization of the relationship between *y* and *x* over the period 1975–1985?

d. According to your model, if the price of crude oil fell to $15 per barrel, to what level (approximately) would the price of regular leaded gasoline fall? Justify your answer.

9.17 Baseball wisdom says if you can't hit, you can't win. But is the number of games won by a major league baseball team in a season related to the team's batting average? The table (upper right) shows the number of games won and the batting averages for the 14 teams in the American League for the 1996 season, for games played through September 29.

a. If you were to model the relationship between the mean (or expected) number of games won by a major league team and the team's batting average *x*, using a straight line, would you expect the slope of the line to be positive or negative? Explain.

b. Construct a scattergram of the data. Does the pattern revealed by the scattergram agree with your answer to part **a**?

c. An SPSS printout of the simple linear regression is provided at the top of page 460. Find the estimates of the β's on the printout and write the equation of the least squares line.

d. Graph the least squares line on your scattergram. Does your least squares line seem to fit the points on your scattergram?

e. Does the mean (or expected) number of games won appear to be strongly related to a team's batting average? Explain.

f. Interpret the values of $\hat{\beta}_0$ and $\hat{\beta}_1$ in the words of the problem.

9.18 (X09.018) The long jump is a track and field event in which a competitor attempts to jump a maximum distance into a sandpit after a running start. At the edge of the sandpit is a takeoff board. Jumpers usually try to plant their toes at the front edge of this board to maximize jumping distance. The absolute distance between the front edge of the takeoff board and the spot where the toe actually lands on the board prior to jumping is called "takeoff error." Is takeoff error in the long jump linearly related to best jumping distance? To answer this question, kinesiology researchers videotaped the performances of 18 novice long jumpers at a high school track meet (*Journal of Applied Biomechanics,* May 1995). The average takeoff error, *x*, and best jumping distance (out of three jumps), *y*, for each jumper are recorded in the table on page 460.

a. Propose a straight-line model relating *y* to *x*.

b. Construct a scattergram for the data. Is there visual evidence of a linear relationship between *y* and *x*?

c. A MINITAB printout of the simple linear regression analysis is given below the table. Find the estimates of β_0 and β_1 on the printout.

d. Graph the least squares line on the scattergram. Does the least squares line seem to fit the points on the scattergram?

e. Interpret the least squares intercept and slope.

9.19 A recent winner of Britain's Best Factory Award, NCR Ltd., manufactures automated teller

```
* * * *      M U L T I P L E      R E G R E S S I O N      * * * *
Equation Number 1 Dependent Variable..  WINS

Variable(s) Entered on Step Number
   1.. BATAVE

Multiple R              .78592
R Square                .61767
Adjusted R Square       .58581
Standard Error          7.21028

Analysis of Variance
                    DF        Sum of Squares          Mean Square
Regression           1          1007.85692            1007.85692
Residual            12           623.85737              51.98811

F =      19.38630         Signif F =  .0009

-------------------Variables in the Equation --------------------

Variable              B           SE B        Beta         T      Sig T

BATAVE         765.101228    173.768675    .785918      4.403    .0009
(Constant)    -131.185197     48.197286                -2.722    .0185
```

Jumper	Best Jumping Distance y (meters)	Average Takeoff Error, x (meters)	Jumper	Best Jumping Distance y (meters)	Average Takeoff Error, x (meters)
1	5.30	.09	10	5.77	.09
2	5.55	.17	11	5.12	.13
3	5.47	.19	12	5.77	.16
4	5.45	.24	13	6.22	.03
5	5.07	.16	14	5.82	.50
6	5.32	.22	15	5.15	.13
7	6.15	.09	16	4.92	.04
8	4.70	.12	17	5.20	.07
9	5.22	.09	18	5.42	.04

Source: W. P. Berg and N. L. Greer, "A kinematic profile of the approach run of novice long jumpers." *Journal of Applied Biomechanics,* Vol. 11, No. 2, May 1995, p. 147 (Table 1).

```
The regression equation is
DISTANCE = 5.35 + 0.530 TAKOFFER

Predictor       Coef        Stdev      t-ratio        p
Constant       5.3480      0.1635       32.71      0.000
TAKOFFER       0.5299      0.9254        0.57      0.575

s = 0.4115        R-sq = 2.0%       R-sq(adj) = 0.0%

Analysis of Variance

SOURCE         DF          SS          MS          F        p
Regression      1       0.0555      0.0555       0.33    0.575
Error          16       2.7091      0.1693
Total          17       2.7646
```

machines. NCR attributes its success to Total Quality Management (TQM) strategies, including reducing inventory levels through just-in-time (JIT) inventory ordering policies, instructing operators to stop the assembly line when quality problems are detected, and using only high-quality suppliers. This last strategy helped NCR cut the number of suppliers from 430 to 180 between 1980 and 1989. It saw a corresponding increase in the percentage of products that passed final

	1980	1982	1985	1987	1989
Number of Suppliers, x	430	395	360	270	180
Products Passing Inspection, y (%)	40	60	80	88	98

Source: Lee-Mortimer, A. "Best of the best." *Total Quality Management,* December 1990, p. 317.

inspection, from 40% to 98%. Data on number of suppliers x and percent of products passing inspection y for five years between 1980 and 1989 are shown in the table above.

a. Give the equation of the straight-line model relating y to x.

b. Find the least squares line.

c. Plot the data and graph the least squares line as a check on your calculations.

d. Interpret the least squares estimates $\hat{\beta}_0$ and $\hat{\beta}_1$ in the context of the problem.

9.20 Each year *Sales and Marketing Management* determines the "effective buying income" (EBI) of the average household in a state. Can the EBI be used to predict retail sales per household in the store-group category "eating and drinking places"?

a. Use the data for 13 states given in the table below to find the least squares line relating retail sales per household (y) to average household EBI (x).

b. Plot the least squares line, as well as the actual data points, on a scattergram.

c. Based on the graph, part b, give your opinion regarding the predictive ability of the least squares line.

9.21 The downsizing and restructuring that took place in corporate America during the first half of the 1990s encouraged both laid off middle managers and recent graduates of business schools to become entrepreneurs and start their own businesses. Assuming a business start-up does well, how fast will it grow? Can it expect to need 10 employees in

three years or 50 or 100? To answer these questions, a random sample of 12 firms were drawn from the *Inc. Magazine's* "1996 Ranking of the Fastest-Growing Private Companies in America." The age (in years since 1995), x, and number of employees (in 1995), y, of each firm are recorded in the table. SAS was used to conduct a simple linear regression analysis for the model, $E(y) = \beta_0 + \beta_1 x$. The printout is on page 462.

Firm	Age, x (years)	Number of Employees, y
General Shelters of Texas	5	43
Productivity Point International	5	52
K.C. Oswald	4	9
Multimax	7	40
Pay + Benefits	5	6
Radio Spirits	6	12
KRA	14	200
Consulting Partners	5	76
Apex Instruments	7	15
Portable Products	6	40
Progressive System Technology	5	65
Viking Components	7	175

Source: Inc. 500, October 22, 1996, pp. 103–132.

a. Plot the data in a scattergram. Does the number of employees at a fast-growing firm appear to increase linearly as the firm's age increases?

b. Find the estimates of β_0 and β_1 in the SAS printout. Interpret their values.

State	Average Household Buying Income ($)	Retail Sales: Eating and Drinking Places ($ per household)
Connecticut	60,998	2,553.8
New Jersey	63,853	2,154.8
Michigan	46,915	2,523.3
Minnesota	44,717	2,278.6
Florida	42,442	2,475.8
South Carolina	37,848	2,358.4
Mississippi	34,490	1,538.4
Oklahoma	34,830	2,063.1
Texas	44,729	2,363.5
Colorado	44,571	3,214.9
Utah	43,421	2,653.8
California	50,713	2,215.0
Oregon	40,597	2,144.0

Source: Sales and Marketing Management, 1995.

Dependent Variable: NUMBER

Analysis of Variance

Source	DF	Sum of Squares	Mean Square	F Value	Prob>F
Model	1	23536.50149	23536.50149	11.451	0.0070
Error	10	20554.41518	2055.44152		
C Total	11	44090.91667			

Root MSE	45.33698	R-square	0.5338	
Dep Mean	61.08333	Adj R-sq	0.4872	
C.V.	74.22152			

Parameter Estimates

Variable	DF	Parameter Estimate	Standard Error	T for H0: Parameter=0	Prob > |T|
INTERCEP	1	-51.361607	35.71379104	-1.438	0.1809
AGE	1	17.754464	5.24673562	3.384	0.0070

9.3 MODEL ASSUMPTIONS

In Section 9.2 we assumed that the probabilistic model relating the firm's sales revenue y to the advertising dollars is

$$y = \beta_0 + \beta_1 x + \epsilon$$

We also recall that the least squares estimate of the deterministic component of the model, $\beta_0 + \beta_1 x$ is

$$\hat{y} = \hat{\beta}_0 + \hat{\beta}_1 x = -.1 + .7x$$

Now we turn our attention to the random component ϵ of the probabilistic model and its relation to the errors in estimating β_0 and β_1. We will use a probability distribution to characterize the behavior of ϵ. We will see how the probability distribution of ϵ determines how well the model describes the relationship between the dependent variable y and the independent variable x.

Step 3 in a regression analysis requires us to specify the probability distribution of the random error ϵ. We will make four basic assumptions about the general form of this probability distribution:

Assumption I: The mean of the probability distribution of ϵ is 0. That is, the average of the values of ϵ over an infinitely long series of experiments is 0 for each setting of the independent variable x. This assumption implies that the mean value of y, $E(y)$, for a given value of x is $E(y) = \beta_0 + \beta_1 x$.

Assumption 2: The variance of the probability distribution of ϵ is constant for all settings of the independent variable x. For our straight-line model, this assumption means that the variance of ϵ is equal to a constant, say σ^2, for all values of x.

Assumption 3: The probability distribution of ϵ is normal.

Assumption 4: The values of ϵ associated with any two observed values of y are independent. That is, the value of ϵ associated with one value of y has no effect on the values of ϵ associated with other y values.

The implications of the first three assumptions can be seen in Figure 9.7, which shows distributions of errors for three values of x, namely, $x_1, x_2,$ and x_3. Note that the relative frequency distributions of the errors are normal with a mean of 0 and

FIGURE 9.7
The probability
distribution of ϵ

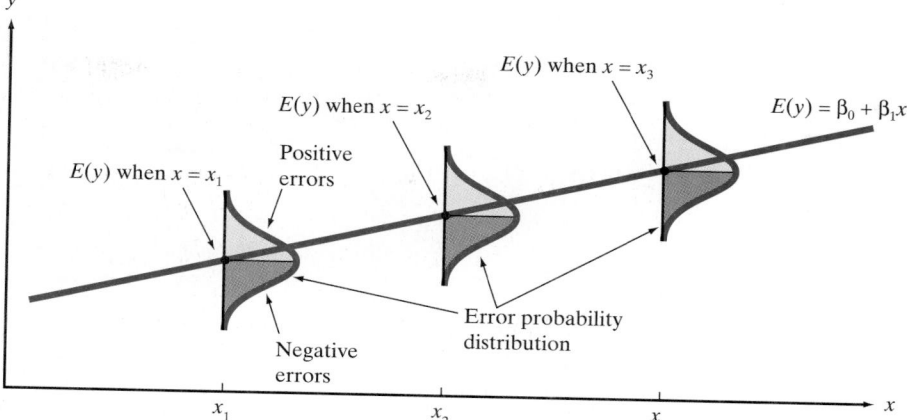

a constant variance σ^2. (All the distributions shown have the same amount of spread or variability.) The straight line shown in Figure 9.7 is the line of means. It indicates the mean value of y for a given value of x. We denote this mean value as $E(y)$. Then, the line of means is given by the equation

$$E(y) = \beta_0 + \beta_1 x$$

These assumptions make it possible for us to develop measures of reliability for the least squares estimators and to develop hypothesis tests for examining the usefulness of the least squares line. We have various techniques for checking the validity of these assumptions, and we have remedies to apply when they appear to be invalid. Several of these remedies are discussed in Chapter 10. Fortunately, the assumptions need not hold exactly in order for least squares estimators to be useful. The assumptions will be satisfied adequately for many applications encountered in practice.

9.4   AN ESTIMATOR OF σ^2

It seems reasonable to assume that the greater the variability of the random error ϵ (which is measured by its variance σ^2), the greater will be the errors in the estimation of the model parameters β_0 and β_1 and in the error of prediction when $\hat{y}$ is used to predict y for some value of x. Consequently, you should not be surprised, as we proceed through this chapter, to find that σ^2 appears in the formulas for all confidence intervals and test statistics that we will be using.

Estimation of σ^2 for a (First-Order) Straight-Line Model

$$s^2 = \frac{\text{SSE}}{\text{Degrees of freedom for error}} = \frac{\text{SSE}}{n-2}$$

where $\text{SSE} = \sum (y_i - \hat{y}_i)^2 = \text{SS}_{yy} - \hat{\beta}_1 \text{SS}_{xy}$

$$\text{SS}_{yy} = \sum (y_i - \bar{y})^2 = \sum y_i^2 - \frac{\left(\sum y_i\right)^2}{n}$$

continued

To estimate the standard deviation σ of ϵ, we calculate

$$s = \sqrt{s^2} = \sqrt{\frac{SSE}{n-2}}$$

We will refer to s as the **estimated standard error of the regression model**.

Warning: When performing these calculations, you may be tempted to round the calculated values of SS_{yy}, $\hat{\beta}_1$, and SS_{xy}. Be certain to carry at least six significant figures for each of these quantities to avoid substantial errors in calculation of the SSE.

In most practical situations, σ^2 is unknown and we must use our data to estimate its value. The best estimate of σ^2, denoted by s^2, is obtained by dividing the sum of squares of the deviations of the y values from the prediction line,

$$SSE = \sum(y_i - \hat{y}_i)^2$$

by the number of degrees of freedom associated with this quantity. We use 2 df to estimate the two parameters β_0 and β_1 in the straight-line model, leaving $(n - 2)$ df for the error variance estimation.

In the advertising–sales example, we previously calculated SSE = 1.10 for the least squares line $\hat{y} = -.1 + .7x$. Recalling that there were $n = 5$ data points, we have $n - 2 = 5 - 2 = 3$ df for estimating σ^2. Thus,

$$s^2 = \frac{SSE}{n-2} = \frac{1.10}{3} = .367$$

is the estimated variance, and

$$s = \sqrt{.367} = .61$$

is the standard error of the regression model.

The values of s^2 and s can also be obtained from a simple linear regression printout. The SAS printout for the advertising–sales example is reproduced in Figure 9.8. The value of s^2 is highlighted on the printout in the **Mean Square** column in the row labeled **Error**. (In regression, the estimate of σ^2 is called Mean Square for Error, or MSE.) The value, $s^2 = .36667$, rounded to three decimal places agrees with the one calculated by hand. The value of s is highlighted in Figure 9.8 next to the heading **Root MSE**. This value, $s = .60553$, agrees (except for rounding) with our hand-calculated value.

You may be able to grasp s intuitively by recalling the interpretation of a standard deviation given in Chapter 2 and remembering that the least squares line estimates the mean value of y for a given value of x. Since s measures the spread of the distribution of y values about the least squares line, we should not be surprised to find that most of the observations lie within $2s$, or $2(.61) = 1.22$, of the least squares line. For this simple example (only five data points), all five sales revenue values fall within $2s$ (or $1,220) of the least squares line. In Section 9.8, we use s to evaluate the error of prediction when the least squares line is used to predict a value of y to be observed for a given value of x.

Interpretation of s, the Estimated Standard Deviation of ϵ

We expect most of the observed y values to lie within $2s$ of their respective least squares predicted values, $\hat{y}$.

Dependent Variable: Y

Analysis of Variance

Source	DF	Sum of Squares	Mean Square	F Value	Prob>F
Model	1	4.90000	4.90000	13.364	0.0354
Error	3	1.10000	0.36667		
C Total	4	6.00000			

Root MSE	0.60553	R-square	0.8167	
Dep Mean	2.00000	Adj R-sq	0.7556	
C.V.	30.27650			

Parameter Estimates

Variable	DF	Parameter Estimate	Standard Error	T for HO: Parameter=0	Prob > |T|
INTERCEP	1	-0.100000	0.63508530	-0.157	0.8849
X	1	0.700000	0.19148542	3.656	0.0354

FIGURE 9.8 SAS printout for advertising expenditure–sales revenue example

EXERCISES 9.22–9.30

Note: Exercises marked with a disk icon contain data for computer analysis on a 3.5" disk (file name in parentheses).

Learning the Mechanics

9.22 Calculate SSE and s^2 for each of the following cases:
a. $n = 20, SS_{yy} = 95, SS_{xy} = 50, \hat{\beta}_1 = .75$
b. $n = 40, \Sigma y^2 = 860, \Sigma y = 50, SS_{xy} = 2{,}700, \hat{\beta}_1 = .2$
c. $n = 10, \Sigma(y_i - \bar{y})^2 = 58, SS_{xy} = 91, SS_{xx} = 170$

9.23 Suppose you fit a least squares line to 26 data points and the calculated value of SSE is 8.34.
a. Find s^2, the estimator of σ^2 (the variance of the random error term ϵ).
b. What is the largest deviation that you might expect between any one of the 26 points and the least squares line?

9.24 Visually compare the scattergrams shown below. If a least squares line were determined for each data set, which do you think would have the smallest variance, s^2? Explain.

9.25 Refer to Exercises 9.10 and 9.13. Calculate SSE, s^2, and s for the least squares lines obtained in these exercises. Interpret the standard error of the regression model, s, for each.

Applying the Concepts

9.26 Prior to the 1970s the developing countries played a small role in world trade because their own economic policies hindered integration with the world economy. However, many of these countries have since changed their policies and vastly improved their importance to the global economy (*World Economy*, July 1992). Data for investigating the relationship between developing coun-

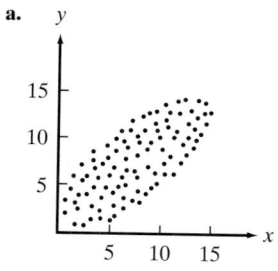
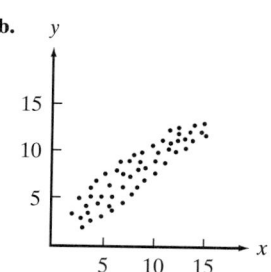
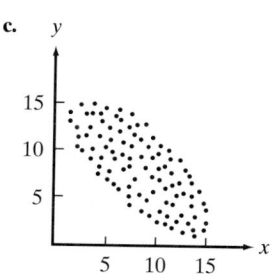

	1950	1960	1970	1980	1990
Industrial Countries' Imports, x	39.8	85.4	226.9	1,370.2	2,237.9
Developing Countries' Imports, y	21.1	40.1	75.6	556.4	819.4

tries and industrial countries in annual import levels is shown in the table above (given in billions of U.S. dollars).

a. Given that $SS_{xx} = 3,809,368.452$, $SS_{xy} = 1,419,492.796$, $SS_{yy} = 531,174.148$, $\bar{x} = 792.04$, and $\bar{y} = 302.52$, fit a least squares line to the data. Plot the data points and graph the least squares line as a check on your calculations.

b. According to your least squares line, approximately what would you expect annual imports for developing countries to be if annual imports for industrial countries were $1,600 billion?

c. Calculate SSE and s^2.

d. Interpret the standard deviation s in the context of this problem.

9.27 Refer to the simple linear regression relating games won by a major league baseball team y to team batting average x, Exercise 9.17. The SPSS printout is reproduced below.

a. Find SSE, s^2, and s on the printout.

b. Interpret the value of s.

9.28 Refer to the simple linear regression relating number of employees y to age x of a fast-growing firm, Exercise 9.21. The SAS printout is reproduced on page 467.

a. Find SSE, s^2, and s on the printout.

b. Interpret the value of s.

9.29 A much larger proportion of U.S. teenagers are working while attending high school than was the case a decade ago. These heavy workloads often result in underachievement in the classroom and lower grades. As a result, many states are imposing tighter child labor laws. A study of high school students in California and Wisconsin showed that those who worked only a few hours per week had the highest grade point averages (*Newsweek,* Nov. 16, 1992). The following table shows grade point averages (GPAs) and number of hours worked per week for a sample of five students. Consider a simple linear regression relating GPA (y) to hours worked (x).

Grade Point Average, y	2.93	3.00	2.86	3.04	2.66
Hours Worked per Week, x	12	0	17	5	21

a. Find the equation of the least squares line.

b. Plot the data and graph the least squares line.

c. Predict the grade point average of a high school student who works 10 hours per week. Repeat this for one who works 16 hours per week.

d. Compute SSE and s.

```
* * * *   M U L T I P L E    R E G R E S S I O N   * * * *

Equation Number 1      Dependent Variable..    WINS

Variable(s) Entered on Step Number
   1..      BATAVE

Multiple R              .78592
R Square                .61767
Adjusted R Square       .58581
Standard Error         7.21028

Analysis of Variance
                    DF        Sum of Squares       Mean Square
Regression           1           1007.85692        1007.85692
Residual            12            623.85737          51.98811

F =      19.38630       Signif F =    .0009

------------------ Variables in the Equation --------------------

Variable            B         SE B           Beta          T   Sig T

BATAVE       765.101228   173.768675       .785918       4.403   .0009
(Constant)  -131.185197    48.197286                    -2.722   .0185
```

Dependent Variable: NUMBER

Analysis of Variance

Source	DF	Sum of Squares	Mean Square	F Value	Prob>F
Model	1	23536.50149	23536.50149	11.451	0.0070
Error	10	20554.41518	2055.44152		
C Total	11	44090.91667			

Root MSE	45.33698	R-square	0.5338	
Dep Mean	61.08333	Adj R-sq	0.4872	
C.V.	74.22152			

Parameter Estimates

Variable	DF	Parameter Estimate	Standard Error	T for H0: Parameter=0	Prob > |T|
INTERCEP	1	-51.361607	35.71379104	-1.438	0.1809
AGE	1	17.754464	5.24673562	3.384	0.0070

e. Within what approximate distance do you expect your predictions in part **c** to fall from the student's true grade point average? [*Note:* A more precise measure of reliability for these predictions is discussed in Section 9.8.]

9.30 **(X09.030)** To improve the quality of the output of any production process, it is necessary first to understand the capabilities of the process (Gitlow, *et al., Quality Management: Tools and Methods for Improvement*, 1995). In a particular manufacturing process, the useful life of a cutting tool is related to the speed at which the tool is operated. It is necessary to understand this relationship in order to predict when the tool should be replaced and how many spare tools should be available. The data in the table below were derived from life

tests for the two different brands of cutting tools currently used in the production process.

a. Construct a scattergram for each brand of cutting tool.
b. For each brand, the method of least squares was used to model the relationship between useful life and cutting speed. Find the least squares line for each brand on the EXCEL printouts shown on page 468.
c. Locate SSE, s^2, and s for each least squares line on the printouts.
d. For a cutting speed of 70 meters per minute, find $\hat{y} \pm 2s$ for each least squares line.
e. For which brand would you feel more confident in using the least squares line to predict useful life for a given cutting speed? Explain.

	USEFUL LIFE (HOURS)	
Cutting Speed (meters per minute)	Brand A	Brand B
30	4.5	6.0
30	3.5	6.5
30	5.2	5.0
40	5.2	6.0
40	4.0	4.5
40	2.5	5.0
50	4.4	4.5
50	2.8	4.0
50	1.0	3.7
60	4.0	3.8
60	2.0	3.0
60	1.1	2.4
70	1.1	1.5
70	.5	2.0
70	3.0	1.0

EXCEL Output: Brand A

SUMMARY OUTPUT

Regression Statistics	
Multiple R	0.6737515
R Square	0.453941084
Adjusted R Square	0.411936552
Standard Error	1.210721336
Observations	15

ANOVA

	df	SS	MS	F	Significance F
Regression	1	15.84133333	15.84133333	10.80695494	0.00588884
Residual	13	19.056	1.465846154		
Total	14	34.89733333			

	Coefficients	Standard Error	t Stat	P-value	Lower 95%	Upper 95%
Intercept	6.62	1.14859111	5.763582829	6.55988E-05	4.138620245	9.101379755
Speed(x)	-0.072666667	0.022104646	-3.287393335	0.00588884	-0.120420842	-0.024912491

EXCEL Output: Brand B

SUMMARY OUTPUT

Regression Statistics	
Multiple R	0.937007633
R Square	0.877983304
Adjusted R Square	0.868597404
Standard Error	0.609728817
Observations	15

ANOVA

	df	SS	MS	F	Significance F
Regression	1	34.77633333	34.77633333	93.5427961	2.64643E-07
Residual	13	4.833	0.371769231		
Total	14	39.60933333			

	Coefficients	Standard Error	t Stat	P-value	Lower 95%	Upper 95%
Intercept	9.31	0.578439545	16.09502683	5.7707E-10	8.060357577	10.55964242
Speed(x)	-0.10766667	0.011132074	-9.67175248	2.6464E-07	-0.13171605	-0.08361729

9.5   ASSESSING THE UTILITY OF THE MODEL: MAKING INFERENCES ABOUT THE SLOPE β_1

Now that we have specified the probability distribution of ϵ and found an estimate of the variance σ^2, we are ready to make statistical inferences about the model's usefulness for predicting the response y. This is step 4 in our regression modeling procedure.

Refer again to the data of Table 9.1 and suppose the appliance store's sales revenue is *completely unrelated* to the advertising expenditure. What could be said about the values of β_0 and β_1 in the hypothesized probabilistic model

$$y = \beta_0 + \beta_1 x + \epsilon$$

if x contributes no information for the prediction of y? The implication is that the mean of y—that is, the deterministic part of the model $E(y) = \beta_0 + \beta_1 x$—does not change as x changes. In the straight-line model, this means that the true slope, β_1, is equal to 0 (see Figure 9.9). Therefore, to test the null hypothesis that the linear model contributes no information for the prediction of y against the alternative hypothesis that the linear model is useful for predicting y, we test

$$H_0: \beta_1 = 0$$

$$H_a: \beta_1 \neq 0$$

If the data support the alternative hypothesis, we will conclude that x does contribute information for the prediction of y using the straight-line model (although the true relationship between $E(y)$ and x could be more complex than a straight line). Thus, in effect, this is a test of the usefulness of the hypothesized model.

The appropriate test statistic is found by considering the sampling distribution of $\hat{\beta}_1$, the least squares estimator of the slope β_1, as shown in the following box.

Sampling Distribution of $\hat{\beta}_1$

If we make the four assumptions about ϵ (see Section 9.3), the sampling distribution of the least squares estimator $\hat{\beta}_1$ of the slope will be normal with mean β_1 (the true slope) and standard deviation

$$\sigma_{\hat{\beta}_1} = \frac{\sigma}{\sqrt{SS_{xx}}} \qquad \text{(see Figure 9.10)}$$

We estimate $\sigma_{\hat{\beta}_1}$ by $s_{\hat{\beta}_1} = \dfrac{s}{\sqrt{SS_{xx}}}$ and refer to this quantity as the estimated standard error of the least squares slope $\hat{\beta}_1$.

FIGURE 9.9
Graphing the model
$y = \beta_0 + \epsilon$ $(\beta_1 = 0)$

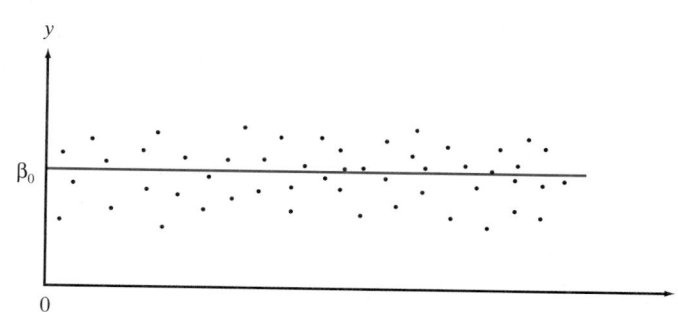

FIGURE 9.10
Sampling distribution
of $\hat{\beta}_1$

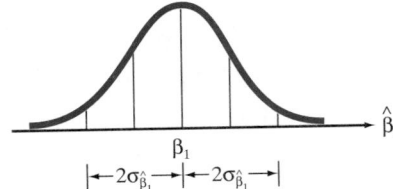

Since σ is usually unknown, the appropriate test statistic is a t statistic, formed as follows:

$$t = \frac{\hat{\beta}_1 - \text{Hypothesized value of } \beta_1}{s_{\hat{\beta}_1}} \qquad \text{where } s_{\hat{\beta}_1} = \frac{s}{\sqrt{SS_{xx}}}$$

Thus,

$$t = \frac{\hat{\beta}_1 - 0}{s/\sqrt{SS_{xx}}}$$

Note that we have substituted the estimator s for σ and then formed the estimated standard error $s_{\hat{\beta}_1}$ by dividing s by $\sqrt{SS_{xx}}$. The number of degrees of freedom associated with this t statistic is the same as the number of degrees of freedom associated with s. Recall that this number is $(n - 2)$ df when the hypothesized model is a straight line (see Section 9.4). The setup of our test of the usefulness of the straight-line model is summarized in the next box.

A Test of Model Utility: Simple Linear Regression

One-Tailed Test

H_0: $\beta_1 = 0$

H_a: $\beta_1 < 0$ (or H_a: $\beta_1 > 0$)

Test statistic:

Two-Tailed Test

H_0: $\beta_1 = 0$

H_a: $\beta_1 \neq 0$

$$t = \frac{\hat{\beta}_1}{s_{\hat{\beta}_1}} = \frac{\hat{\beta}_1}{s/\sqrt{SS_{xx}}}$$

Rejection region: $t < -t_\alpha$
  (or $t > t_\alpha$ when H_a: $\beta_1 > 0$)

Rejection region: $|t| > t_{\alpha/2}$

where t_α and $t_{\alpha/2}$ are based on $(n - 2)$ degrees of freedom

Assumptions: The four assumptions about ϵ listed in Section 9.3.

For the advertising–sales example, we will choose $\alpha = .05$ and, since $n = 5$, t will be based on $n - 2 = 3$ df and the rejection region will be

$$|t| > t_{.025} = 3.182$$

We previously calculated $\hat{\beta}_1 = .7$, $s = .61$, and $SS_{xx} = 10$. Thus,

$$t = \frac{\hat{\beta}_1}{s/\sqrt{SS_{xx}}} = \frac{.7}{.61\sqrt{10}} = \frac{.7}{.19} = 3.7$$

Since this calculated t value falls in the upper-tail rejection region (see Figure 9.11), we reject the null hypothesis and conclude that the slope β_1 is not 0. The

FIGURE 9.11

Rejection region and calculated t value for testing H_0: $\beta_1 = 0$ versus H_a: $\beta_1 \neq 0$

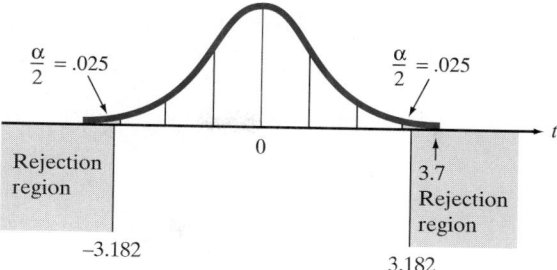

sample evidence indicates that advertising expenditure x contributes information for the prediction of sales revenue y when a linear model is used.

We can reach the same conclusion by using the observed significance level (p-value) of the test from a computer printout. The SAS printout for the advertising–sales example is reproduced in Figure 9.12. The test statistic is highlighted on the printout under the **T for HO: Parameter=0** column in the row corresponding to **X**, while the two-tailed p-value is highlighted under the column labeled **Prob >|T|**. Since the p-value = .0354 is smaller than α = .05, we will reject H_0.

What conclusion can be drawn if the calculated t value does not fall in the rejection region or if the observed significance level of the test exceeds α? We know from previous discussions of the philosophy of hypothesis testing that such a t value does *not* lead us to accept the null hypothesis. That is, we do not conclude that $\beta_1 = 0$. Additional data might indicate that β_1 differs from 0, or a more complex relationship may exist between x and y, requiring the fitting of a model other than the straight-line model. We discuss several such models in Chapter 10.

Another way to make inferences about the slope β_1 is to estimate it using a confidence interval. This interval is formed as shown in the next box.

Dependent Variable: Y

Analysis of Variance

Source	DF	Sum of Squares	Mean Square	F Value	Prob>F
Model	1	4.90000	4.90000	13.364	0.0354
Error	3	1.10000	0.36667		
C Total	4	6.00000			

Root MSE	0.60553	R-square	0.8167
Dep Mean	2.00000	Adj R-sq	0.7556
C.V.	30.27650		

Parameter Estimates

Variable	DF	Parameter Estimate	Standard Error	T for HO: Parameter=0	Prob > |T|
INTERCEP	1	-0.100000	0.63508530	-0.157	0.8849
X	1	0.700000	0.19148542	3.656	0.0354

FIGURE 9.12   SAS printout for advertising–sales example

> **A $100(1 - \alpha)$% Confidence Interval for the Simple Linear Regression Slope β_1**
>
> $$\hat{\beta}_1 \pm t_{\alpha/2} s_{\hat{\beta}_1}$$
>
> where the estimated standard error $\hat{\beta}_1$ is calculated by
>
> $$s_{\hat{\beta}_1} = \frac{s}{\sqrt{SS_{xx}}}$$
>
> and $t_{\alpha/2}$ is based on $(n - 2)$ degrees of freedom.
>
> *Assumptions:* The four assumptions about ϵ listed in Section 9.3.

For the advertising–sales example, $t_{\alpha/2}$ is based on $(n - 2) = 3$ degrees of freedom. Therefore, a 95% confidence interval for the slope β_1, the expected change in sales revenue for a $100 increase in advertising expenditure, is

$$\hat{\beta}_1 \pm t_{.025} s_{\hat{\beta}_1} = .7 \pm 3.182 \left(\frac{s}{\sqrt{SS_{xx}}} \right) = .7 \pm 3.182 \left(\frac{.61}{\sqrt{10}} \right) = .7 \pm .61$$

Thus, the interval estimate of the slope parameter β_1 is .09 to 1.31. In terms of this example, the implication is that we can be 95% confident that the *true* mean increase in monthly sales revenue per additional $100 of advertising expenditure is between $90 and $1,310. This inference is meaningful only over the sampled range of x—that is, from $100 to $500 of advertising expenditures.

Since all the values in this interval are positive, it appears that β_1 is positive and that the mean of y, $E(y)$, increases as x increases. However, the rather large width of the confidence interval reflects the small number of data points (and, consequently, a lack of information) in the experiment. Particularly bothersome is the fact that the lower end of the confidence interval implies that we are not even recovering our additional expenditure, since a $100 increase in advertising may produce as little as a $90 increase in mean sales. If we wish to tighten this interval, we need to increase the sample size.

STATISTICS IN ACTION

9.1 NEW JERSEY BANKS— SERVING MINORITIES?

Bankers and community leaders both agree that financial institutions have a legal and social responsibility to serve all communities. But is this obligation being met? Do banks adequately serve both inner city and suburban neighborhoods, both poor and wealthy communities? In New Jersey, banks have been charged with withdrawing from urban areas with a high percentage of minorities. Some surprising statistics: Three out of four minority areas in New Jersey have no bank branches whatsoever, while two out of three white areas have at least one branch.

To examine this charge, a regional New Jersey newspaper, the *Asbury Park Press*, compiled county-by-county data on (1) the number of people in each county per branch bank in the county and (2) the percentage of the population in each county that is minority. These data for each of New Jersey's 21 counties are provided in Table 9.5.

Focus

Use the methods of this chapter to determine whether these data support or refute the charge made against the New Jersey banking community. Summarize your analysis and findings in a report addressed to New Jersey's Commissioner of Banking. [*Note:* The data is available on a 3.5" disk under the file name TAB09.005.]

TABLE 9.5   Data on New Jersey Banks (Statistics in Action 9.1)

County	Number of People per Bank Branch	Percentage of Minority Population
Atlantic	3,073	23.3
Bergen	2,095	13.0
Burlington	2,905	17.8
Camden	3,330	23.4
Cape May	1,321	7.3
Cumberland	2,557	26.5
Essex	3,474	48.8
Gloucester	3,068	10.7
Hudson	3,683	33.2
Hunterdon	1,998	3.7
Mercer	2,607	24.9
Middlesex	3,154	18.1
Monmouth	2,609	12.6
Morris	2,253	8.2
Ocean	2,317	4.7
Passaic	3,307	28.1
Salem	2,511	16.7
Somerset	2,333	12.0
Sussex	2,568	2.4
Union	3,048	25.6
Warren	2,349	2.8

Source: D'Ambrosio, P., and Chambers, S. "No checks and balances." *Asbury Park Press,* September 10, 1995.

EXERCISES   9.31–9.43

Note: Exercises marked with 🖫 *contain data for computer analysis on a 3.5" disk (file name in parentheses).*

Learning the Mechanics

9.31   Construct both a 95% and a 90% confidence interval for β_1 for each of the following cases:
a. $\hat{\beta}_1 = 31, s = 3, SS_{xx} = 35, n = 10$
b. $\hat{\beta}_1 = 64, SSE = 1,960, SS_{xx} = 30, n = 14$
c. $\hat{\beta}_1 = -8.4, SSE = 146, SS_{xx} = 64, n = 20$

9.32   Consider the following pairs of observations:

x	1	4	3	2	5	6	0
y	1	3	3	1	4	7	2

a. Construct a scattergram for the data.
b. Use the method of least squares to fit a straight line to the seven data points in the table.
c. Plot the least squares line on your scattergram of part **a**.
d. Specify the null and alternative hypotheses you would use to test whether the data provide sufficient evidence to indicate that x contributes information for the (linear) prediction of y.
e. What is the test statistic that should be used in conducting the hypothesis test of part **d**? Specify the degrees of freedom associated with the test statistic.

f. Conduct the hypothesis test of part **d** using $\alpha = .05$.

9.33   Refer to Exercise 9.32. Construct an 80% and a 98% confidence interval for β_1.

9.34   Do the accompanying data provide sufficient evidence to conclude that a straight line is useful for characterizing the relationship between x and y?

y	4	2	4	3	2	4
x	1	6	5	3	2	4

9.35   Suppose that $n = 100$ recent residential home sales in a city are used to fit a least squares straight-line model relating the sale price, y, to the square feet of living space, x. Homes in the sample range from 1,500 square feet to 4,000 square feet of living space, and the resulting least squares equation is

$$\hat{y} = -30,000 + 70x$$

a. When the null hypothesis that the true slope is zero is tested, the result is a t value of 6.572. Give the appropriate p-value of this test, and interpret the result in the context of this application.
b. The 95% confidence interval for the slope is calculated to be 49.1 to 90.9. Interpret this interval in the context of this application. What can be done to obtain a narrower confidence interval?

Applying the Concepts

9.36 The U.S. Department of Agriculture has developed and adopted the Universal Soil Loss Equation (USLE) for predicting water erosion of soils. In geographical areas where runoff from melting snow is common, the USLE requires an accurate estimate of snowmelt runoff erosion. An article in the *Journal of Soil and Water Conservation* (Mar.–Apr. 1995) used simple linear regression to develop a snowmelt erosion index. Data for 54 climatological stations in Canada were used to model the McCool winter-adjusted rainfall erosivity index, *y*, as a straight-line function of the once-in-five-year snowmelt runoff amount, *x* (measured in millimeters).

a. The data points are plotted in the scattergram shown below. Is there visual evidence of a linear trend?

b. The data for seven stations were removed from the analysis due to lack of snowfall during the study period. Why is this strategy advisable?

c. The simple linear regression on the remaining $n = 47$ data points yielded the following results:

$$\hat{y} = -6.72 + 1.39x; \ s_{\hat{\beta}_1} = .06$$

Use this information to construct a 90% confidence interval for β_1.

d. Interpret the interval, part **c**.

9.37 One of the most common types of "information retrieval" processes is document-database searching. An experiment was conducted to investigate the variables that influence search performance in the Medline database and retrieval system (*Journal of Information Science,* Vol. 21, 1995).

Simple linear regression was used to model the fraction *y* of the set of potentially informative documents that are retrieved using Medline as a function of the number *x* of terms in the search query, based on a sample of $n = 124$ queries. The results are summarized below:

$$\hat{y} = .202 + .135x \qquad t \text{ (for testing } H_0\text{: } \beta_1 = 0) = 4.98$$

Two-tailed *p*-value = .001

a. Is there sufficient evidence to indicate that *x* and *y* are linearly related? Test using $\alpha = .01$.

b. If appropriate, use the model to predict the fraction of documents retrieved for a search query with $x = 3$ terms.

9.38 **(X09.038)** Successful U.S. investors, no longer focusing exclusively on U.S. securities, have developed global investment strategies. One of the most difficult tasks of developing and managing a global portfolio is assessing the risks of potential foreign investments. Duke University researcher C. R. Henry collaborated with two First Chicago Investment Management Company directors to examine the use of country credit ratings as a means of evaluating foreign investments (*Journal of Portfolio Management,* Winter 1995). To be effective, such a measure should help explain and predict the volatility of the foreign market in question. The researchers analyzed data on annualized risk (*y*) and average credit rating (*x*) for the 40 countries shown in the table on page 476. An SPSS printout for a simple linear regression analysis conducted on the data is shown at the top of page 475.

a. Locate the least squares estimates of β_0 and β_1 on the printout.

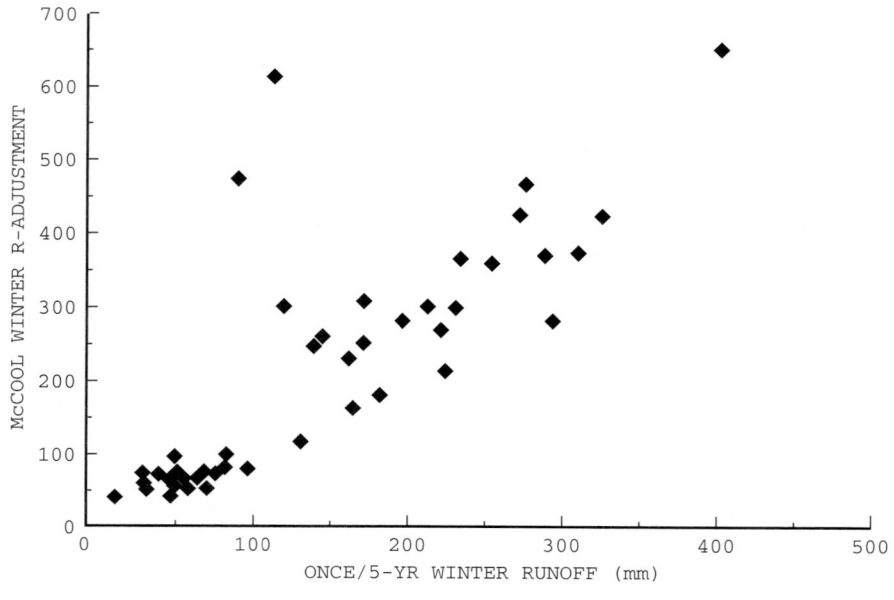

```
* * * *    M U L T I P L E    R E G R E S S I O N    * * * *
Equation Number 1      Dependent Variable..    RISK

Variable(s) Entered on Step Number
    1..      RATING

Multiple R                  .57802
R Square                    .33411
Adjusted R Square           .31658
Standard Error            12.67770

Analysis of Variance
                     DF          Sum of Squares          Mean Square
Regression            1              3064.40538          3064.40538
Residual             38              6107.51862           160.72417

F =        19.06624          Signif F =   .0001

------------------ Variables in the Equation ----------------------

Variable                  B          SE B          Beta            T      Sig T

RATING              -.399606       .091516      -.578020       -4.366    .0001
(Constant)         57.755060      6.127836                      9.425    .0000
```

```
Dependent Variable:   NUMBER

                         Analysis of Variance

                          Sum of             Mean
   Source        DF       Squares            Square       F Value      Prob>F

   Model          1    23536.50149       23536.50149       11.451       0.0070
   Error         10    20554.41518        2055.44152
   C Total       11    44090.91667

        Root MSE          45.33698      R-square          0.5338
        Dep Mean          61.08333      Adj R-sq          0.4872
        C.V.              74.22152

                         Parameter Estimates

                    Parameter          Standard        T for HO:
Variable    DF       Estimate            Error       Parameter=0     Prob > |T|

INTERCEP     1      -51.361607       35.71379104        -1.438         0.1809
AGE          1       17.754464        5.24673562         3.384         0.0070
```

b. Plot the data in a scattergram, then sketch the least squares line on the graph.

c. Do the data provide sufficient evidence to conclude that country credit risk (x) contributes information for the prediction of market volatility (y)?

d. Use the plot, part **b**, to locate any unusual data points (outliers).

e. Eliminate the outlier(s), part **d**, from the data set and rerun the simple linear regression analysis. Note any dramatic changes in the results.

9.39 Refer to Exercises 9.21 and 9.28. The SAS simple linear regression printout relating number of employees y to age of a fast-growing firm x is reproduced directly above.

a. Test to determine whether y is positively linearly related to x. Use $\alpha = .01$.

b. Construct a 99% confidence interval for β_1. Practically interpret the result.

9.40 (X09.040) H. Mintzberg's classic book, *The Nature of Managerial Work* (1973), identified the roles found in all managerial jobs. An observational study of 19 managers from a medium-sized manufacturing plant extended Mintzberg's work by investigating which activities *successful* managers actually perform (*Journal of Applied Behavioral*

Country	Annualized Risk (%)	Average Credit Rating
Argentina	87.0	31.8
Australia	26.9	78.2
Austria	26.3	83.8
Belgium	22.0	78.4
Brazil	64.8	36.2
Canada	19.2	87.1
Chile	31.6	38.6
Colombia	31.5	44.4
Denmark	20.6	72.6
Finland	26.1	76.0
France	23.8	85.3
Germany	23.0	93.4
Greece	39.6	51.9
Hong Kong	34.3	69.6
India	30.0	46.6
Ireland	23.4	66.4
Italy	28.0	75.5
Japan	25.7	94.5
Jordan	17.6	33.6
Korea	30.7	62.2
Malaysia	26.7	64.4
Mexico	46.3	43.3
Netherlands	18.5	87.6
New Zealand	26.3	68.9
Nigeria	41.4	30.6
Norway	28.3	83.0
Pakistan	24.4	26.4
Philippines	38.4	29.6
Portugal	47.5	56.7
Singapore	26.4	77.6
Spain	24.8	70.8
Sweden	24.5	79.5
Switzerland	19.6	94.7
Taiwan	53.7	72.9
Thailand	27.0	55.8
Turkey	74.1	32.6
United Kingdom	21.8	87.6
United States	15.4	93.4
Venezuela	46.0	45.0
Zimbabwe	35.6	24.5

Source: Erb, C. B., Harvey, C. R., and Viskanta, T. E. "Country risk and global equity selection." *Journal of Portfolio Management,* Vol. 21, No. 2, Winter 1995, p. 76. This copyrighted material is reprinted with permission from *The Journal of Portfolio Management,* a publication of Institutional Investor, Inc., 488 Madison Ave., New York, NY 10022.

Science, Aug. 1985). To measure success, the researchers devised an index based on the manager's length of time in the organization and his or her level within the firm; the higher the index, the more successful the manager. The table at the top of page 477 presents data (which are representative of the data collected by the researchers) that can be used to determine whether managerial success is related to the extensiveness of a manger's network-building interactions with people outside the manager's work unit. Such interactions include phone and face-to-face meetings with customers and suppliers, attending outside meetings, and doing public relations work. A MINITAB printout of the simple linear regression follows the table.

a. Construct a scattergram for the data.
b. Find the prediction equation for managerial success.
c. Find s for your prediction equation. Interpret the standard deviation s in the context of this problem.
d. Plot the least squares line on your scattergram of part **a**. Does it appear that the number of interactions with outsiders contributes information for the prediction of managerial success? Explain.

Manager	Manager Success Index, y	Number of Interactions with Outsiders, x
1	40	12
2	73	71
3	95	70
4	60	81
5	81	43
6	27	50
7	53	42
8	66	18
9	25	35
10	63	82
11	70	20
12	47	81
13	80	40
14	51	33
15	32	45
16	50	10
17	52	65
18	30	20
19	42	21

```
The regression equation is
SUCCESS = 44.1 + 0.237 INTERACT

Predictor        Coef         Stdev       t-ratio           p
Constant       44.130        9.362          4.71       0.000
INTERACT       0.2366        0.1865         1.27       0.222

s = 19.40         R-sq = 8.6%       R-sq(adj) = 3.3%

Analysis of Variance

SOURCE          DF            SS            MS          F          p
Regression      1           606.0         606.0       1.61      0.222
Error          17          6400.6         376.5
Total          18          7006.6
```

e. Conduct a formal statistical hypothesis test to answer the question posed in part **d**. Use $\alpha = .05$.

f. Construct a 95% confidence interval for β_1. Interpret the interval in the context of the problem.

9.41 The expenses involved in a manufacturing operation may be categorized as being for *raw material, direct labor,* and *overhead*. Direct labor refers to the persons employed to transform the raw materials into the finished product. Overhead refers to all expenses other than those for raw materials and direct labor that are involved with running the factory (e.g., supervisory labor, maintenance of equipment, and office supplies) (Horngren, *et al., Cost Accounting,* 1994). A manufacturer of 10-speed racing bicycles is interested in estimating the relationship between its monthly factory overhead and the total number of bicycles produced per month. The estimate will be used to help develop the manufacturing budget for next year.

The data in the table below have been collected for the previous 12 months.

Month	Production Level (1,000's of units)	Overhead ($1,000s)
1	16.9	41.4
2	15.6	35.0
3	17.4	38.3
4	11.6	29.5
5	17.7	39.6
6	17.6	37.4
7	16.3	37.5
8	15.5	37.0
9	23.4	47.9
10	28.4	55.6
11	27.1	53.1
12	19.2	40.6

a. Find the least squares prediction equation relating monthly overhead y to monthly production level x on the EXCEL printout on page 478.

SUMMARY OUTPUT

Regression Statistics

Multiple R	0.985330898
R Square	0.970876979
Adjusted R Square	0.967964677
Standard Error	1.350376282
Observations	12

ANOVA

	df	SS	MS	F	Significance F
Regression	1	607.907339	607.907339	333.3709739	5.2194E-09
Residual	10	18.23516102	1.823516102		
Total	11	626.1425			

	Coefficients	Standard Error	t Stat	P-value	Lower 95%	Upper 95%
Intercept	12.71272173	1.601544156	7.937790339	1.26074E-05	9.144258354	16.2811851
Prodlevel	1.501311598	0.08222558	18.25844938	5.2194E-09	1.318101556	1.68452164

b. Does the straight-line model contribute information for predicting overhead costs? Test at $\alpha = .05$.

c. Which of the four assumptions we make about the random error ϵ may be inappropriate in this problem? Explain.

9.42 During June, July, and early August of 1981, 10 bids were made by DuPont, Seagram, and Mobil to take over Conoco. Finally, on August 5, DuPont announced success. The total value of the offer accepted by Conoco was $7.54 billion, making it the largest takeover in the history of American business at that time. A study of the Conoco takeover used regression analysis to examine whether movements in the rate of return of the contending companies' common stock could be explained by movements in the return rate of the stock market as a whole. The model was $y = \beta_0 + \beta_1 x + \epsilon$, where y is the daily rate of return of a stock, x is the daily rate of return of the stock market as a whole (based on Standard & Poor's 500 Composite Index), and ϵ is believed to satisfy the assumptions of Section 10.3. (This model is known in the finance literature as the *market model*. Note that the parameter β_1 reflects the sensitivity of the stock's return rate to movements in the stock market as a whole.) Daily data from early 1979 through 1980 ($n = 504$) yielded the least squares lines shown in the table for the four firms in question. The t statistics and p-values associated with the values of β_1 are also shown.

Firm	Estimated Market Model	t Statistics	p-Values
Conoco	$\hat{y} = .0010 + 1.40x$	$t = 21.93$	.000
DuPont	$\hat{y} = -.0005 + 1.21x$	$t = 18.76$	.000
Mobil	$\hat{y} = .0010 + 1.62x$	$t = 16.21$	.000
Seagram	$\hat{y} = .0013 + .76x$	$t = 6.05$	.000

Source: Ruback, R. S. "The Conoco takeover and stockholder returns." *Sloan Management Review,* Vol. 23, Winter 1982, pp. 13–33.

a. For each of the models, test $H_0: \beta_1 = 0$ versus $H_a: \beta_1 \neq 0$. Use $\alpha = .01$. Draw the appropriate conclusion regarding the usefulness of the market model in each case.

b. If the rate of return of Standard & Poor's 500 Composite Index increased by .10, how much change would occur in the mean rate of return for Conoco's common stock? For Seagram's?

c. Which of the two stocks, Conoco or Seagram, appears to be more responsive to changes in the market as a whole? Explain.

9.43 Refer to Exercise 9.15, in which the extent of retaliation against whistle blowers was investigated. Since salary is a reasonably good indicator of a person's power within an organization, the data of Exercise 9.15 can be used to investigate whether the extent of retaliation is related to the power of the whistle blower in the organization. The researchers were unable to reject the hypothesis that the extent of retaliation is unrelated to power. Do you agree? Test using $\alpha = .05$.

9.6   THE COEFFICIENT OF CORRELATION

Recall (from optional Section 2.10) that a **bivariate relationship** describes a relationship between two variables, x and y. Scattergrams are used to graphically describe a bivariate relationship. In this section we will discuss the concept of **correlation** and show how it can be used to measure the linear relationship between two variables x and y. A numerical descriptive measure of correlation is provided by the *Pearson product moment coefficient of correlation, r.*

DEFINITION 9.2

The **Pearson product moment coefficient of correlation**, r, is a measure of the strength of the *linear* relationship between two variables x and y. It is computed (for a sample of n measurements on x and y) as follows:

$$r = \frac{SS_{xy}}{\sqrt{SS_{xx}SS_{yy}}}$$

Note that the computational formula for the correlation coefficient r given in Definition 9.2 involves the same quantities that were used in computing the least squares prediction equation. In fact, since the numerators of the expressions for $\hat{\beta}_1$ and r are identical, you can see that $r = 0$ when $\hat{\beta}_1 = 0$ (the case where x

FIGURE 9.13
Values of r and their
implications

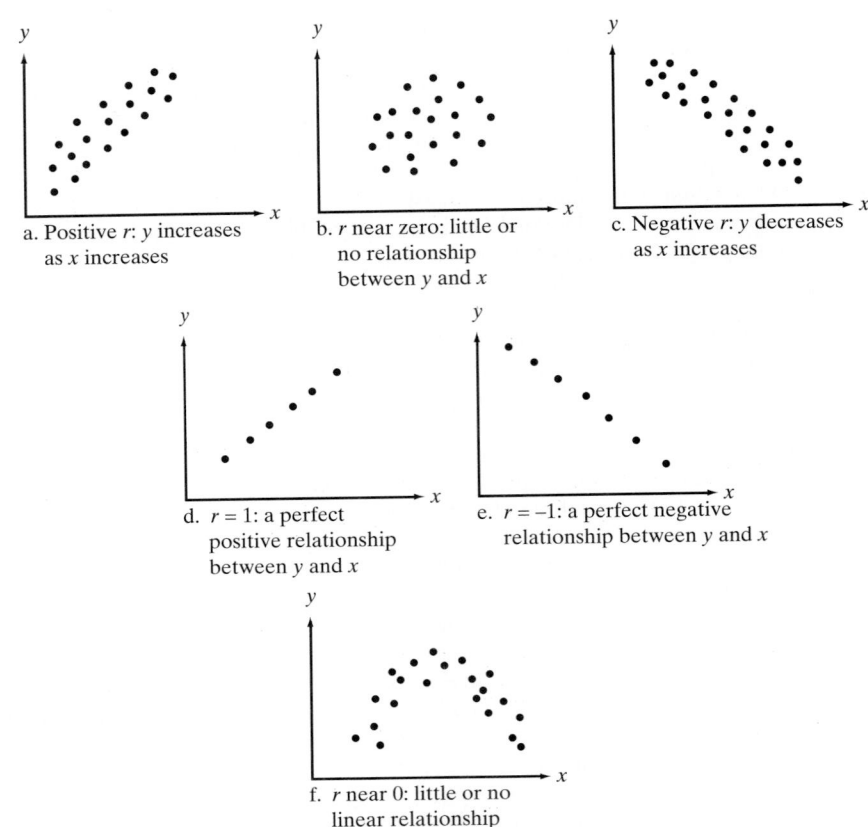

a. Positive r: y increases
as x increases

b. r near zero: little or
no relationship
between y and x

c. Negative r: y decreases
as x increases

d. $r = 1$: a perfect
positive relationship
between y and x

e. $r = -1$: a perfect negative
relationship between y and x

f. r near 0: little or no
linear relationship
between y and x

contributes no information for the prediction of y) and that r is positive when the slope is positive and negative when the slope is negative. Unlike $\hat{\beta}_1$, the correlation coefficient r is *scaleless* and assumes a value between -1 and $+1$, regardless of the units of x and y.

A value of r near or equal to 0 implies little or no linear relationship between y and x. In contrast, the closer r comes to 1 or -1, the stronger the linear relationship between y and x. And if $r = 1$ or $r = -1$, all the sample points fall exactly on the least squares line. Positive values of r imply a positive linear relationship between y and x; that is, y increases as x increases. Negative values of r imply a negative linear relationship between y and x; that is, y decreases as x increases. Each of these situations is portrayed in Figure 9.13.

We demonstrate how to calculate the coefficient of correlation r using the data in Table 9.1 for the advertising–sales example. The quantities needed to calculate r are SS_{xy}, SS_{xx}, and SS_{yy}. The first two quantities have been calculated previously and are repeated here for convenience:

$$SS_{xy} = 7 \qquad SS_{xx} = 10 \qquad SS_{yy} = \sum y^2 - \frac{\left(\sum y\right)^2}{n}$$

$$= 26 - \frac{(10)^2}{5} = 26 - 20 = 6$$

We now find the coefficient of correlation:

$$r = \frac{SS_{xy}}{\sqrt{SS_{xx}SS_{yy}}} = \frac{7}{\sqrt{(10)(6)}} = \frac{7}{\sqrt{60}} = .904$$

The fact that r is positive and near 1 in value indicates that the sales revenue y tends to increase as advertising expenditure x increases—*for this sample of five months.* This is the same conclusion we reached when we found the calculated value of the least squares slope to be positive.

EXAMPLE 9.1

Legalized gambling is available on several riverboat casinos operated by a city in Mississippi. The mayor of the city wants to know the correlation between the number of casino employees and the yearly crime rate. The records for the past 10 years are examined, and the results listed in Table 9.6 are obtained. Calculate the coefficient of correlation r for the data.

SOLUTION

Rather than use the computing formula given in Definition 9.2, we resort to a statistical software package. The data of Table 9.6 were entered into a computer and MINITAB was used to compute r. The MINITAB printout is shown in Figure 9.14.

The coefficient of correlation, highlighted on the printout, is $r = .987$. Thus, the size of the casino workforce and crime rate in this city are very highly correlated—at least over the past 10 years. The implication is that a strong positive linear relationship exists between these variables (see Figure 9.15). We must be careful, however, not to jump to any unwarranted conclusions. For instance, the mayor may be tempted to conclude that hiring more casino workers next year will increase the crime rate—that is, that there is a *causal relationship* between the two variables. However, high correlation does not imply causality. The fact is, many things have probably contributed both to the increase in the casino workforce and to the increase in crime rate. The city's tourist trade has undoubtedly grown since legalizing riverboat casinos and it is likely that the casinos have expanded both in services offered and in number. *We cannot infer a causal relationship on the basis of high sample correlation. When a high correlation is observed in the sample data, the only safe conclusion is that a linear trend may exist between* x *and* y. Another variable, such as the increase in tourism, may be the underlying cause of the high correlation between x and y.

TABLE 9.6   Data on Casino Employees and Crime Rate, Example 9.1

Year	Number of Casino Employees x, thousands	Crime Rate y, number of crimes per 1,000 population
1987	15	1.35
1988	18	1.63
1989	24	2.33
1990	22	2.41
1991	25	2.63
1992	29	2.93
1993	30	3.41
1994	32	3.26
1995	35	3.63
1996	38	4.15

FIGURE 9.14
MINITAB printout for Example 9.1

Correlation of NOEMPLOY and CRIMERAT = 0.987

FIGURE 9.15
Scattergram for
Example 9.1

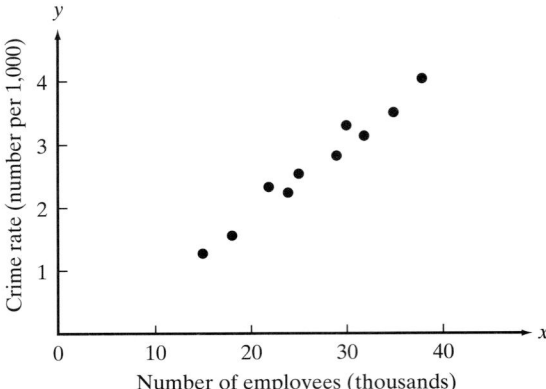

Keep in mind that the correlation coefficient r measures the linear correlation between x values and y values in the sample, and a similar linear coefficient of correlation exists for the population from which the data points were selected. The **population correlation coefficient** is denoted by the symbol ρ (rho). As you might expect, ρ is estimated by the corresponding sample statistic, r. Or, instead of estimating ρ, we might want to test the null hypothesis H_0: $\rho = 0$ against H_a: $\rho \neq 0$— that is, we can test the hypothesis that x contributes no information for the prediction of y by using the straight-line model against the alternative that the two variables are at least linearly related.

However, we already performed this *identical* test in Section 9.5 when we tested H_0: $\beta_1 = 0$ against H_a: $\beta_1 \neq 0$. That is, the null hypothesis H_0: $\rho = 0$ is equivalent to the hypothesis H_0: $\beta_1 = 0$.* When we tested the null hypothesis H_0: $\beta_1 = 0$ in connection with the advertising–sales example, the data led to a rejection of the null hypothesis at the $\alpha = .05$ level. This rejection implies that the null hypothesis of a 0 linear correlation between the two variables (sales revenue and advertising expenditure) can also be rejected at the $\alpha = .05$ level. The only real difference between the least squares slope $\hat{\beta}_1$ and the coefficient of correlation r is the measurement scale. Therefore, the information they provide about the usefulness of the least squares model is to some extent redundant. For this reason, we will use the slope to make inferences about the existence of a positive or negative linear relationship between two variables.

9.7 THE COEFFICIENT OF DETERMINATION

Another way to measure the usefulness of the model is to measure the contribution of x in predicting y. To accomplish this, we calculate how much the errors of prediction of y were reduced by using the information provided by x. To illustrate, consider the sample shown in the scattergram of Figure 9.16a. If we assume that x contributes no information for the prediction of y, the best prediction for a value of y is the sample mean $\bar{y}$, which is shown as the horizontal line in Figure 9.16b. The vertical line segments in Figure 9.16b are the deviations of the points about the mean $\bar{y}$. Note that the sum of squares of deviations for the prediction equation $\hat{y} = \bar{y}$ is

---

*The correlation test statistic that is equivalent to $t = \hat{\beta}_1/s_{\hat{\beta}_1}$ is $t = \dfrac{r}{\sqrt{(1 - r^2)/(n - 2)}}$.

FIGURE 9.16

A comparison of the sum of squares of deviations for two models

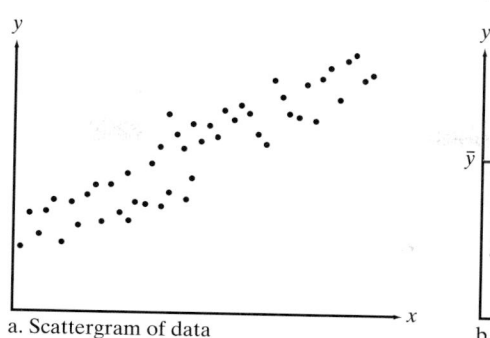

a. Scattergram of data

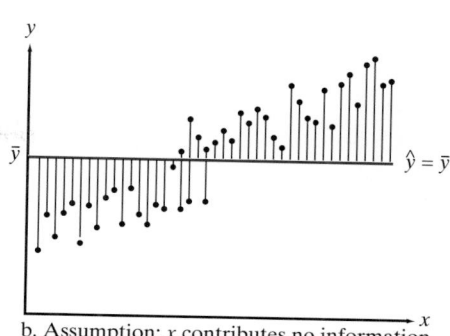

b. Assumption: x contributes no information for predicting y, $\hat{y} = \bar{y}$

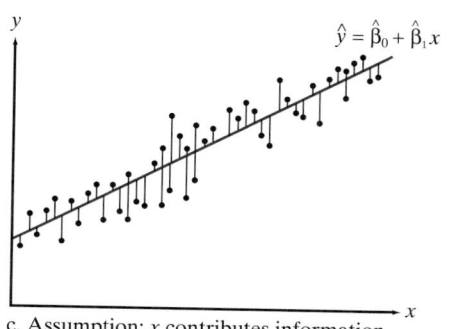

c. Assumption: x contributes information for predicting y, $\hat{y} = \hat{\beta}_0 + \hat{\beta}_1 x$

$$SS_{yy} = \sum(y_i - \bar{y})^2$$

Now suppose you fit a least squares line to the same set of data and locate the deviations of the points about the line as shown in Figure 9.16c. Compare the deviations about the prediction lines in Figures 9.16b and 9.16c. You can see that

1. If x contributes little or no information for the prediction of y, the sums of squares of deviations for the two lines,

$$SS_{yy} = \sum(y_i - \bar{y})^2 \qquad \text{and} \qquad SSE = \sum(y_i - \hat{y}_i)^2$$

will be nearly equal.

2. If x does contribute information for the prediction of y, the SSE will be smaller than SS_{yy}. In fact, if all the points fall on the least squares line, then SSE = 0.

Then the reduction in the sum of squares of deviations that can be attributed to x, expressed as a proportion of SS_{yy}, is

$$\frac{SS_{yy} - SSE}{SS_{yy}}$$

Note that SS_{yy} is the "total sample variation" of the observations around the mean $\bar{y}$ and that SSE is the remaining "unexplained sample variability" after fitting the line $\hat{y}$. Thus, the difference $(SS_{yy} - SSE)$ is the "explained sample variability" attributable to the linear relationship with x. Then a verbal description of the proportion is

$$\frac{SS_{yy} - SSE}{SS_{yy}} = \frac{\text{Explained sample variability}}{\text{Total sample variability}}$$

$$= \text{Proportion of total sample variability explained}$$
$$\text{by the linear relationship}$$

In simple linear regression, it can be shown that this proportion is equal to the square of the simple linear coefficient of correlation r (the Pearson product moment coefficient of correlation.)

DEFINITION 9.3
The **coefficient of determination** is

$$r^2 = \frac{SS_{yy} - SSE}{SS_{yy}} = 1 - \frac{SSE}{SS_{yy}}$$

It represents the proportion of the total sample variability around $\bar{y}$ that is explained by the linear relationship between y and x. (In simple linear regression, it may also be computed as the square of the coefficient of correlation r.)

Note that r^2 is always between 0 and 1, because r is between -1 and $+1$. Thus, an r^2 of .60 means that the sum of squares of deviations of the y values about their predicted values has been reduced 60% by the use of the least squares equation $\hat{y}$, instead of $\bar{y}$, to predict y.

EXAMPLE 9.2   Calculate the coefficient of determination for the advertising–sales example. The data are repeated in Table 9.7 for convenience. Interpret the result.

SOLUTION
From previous calculations,

$$SS_{yy} = 6 \quad \text{and} \quad SSE = \sum(y - \hat{y})^2 = 1.10$$

Then, from Definition 9.3, the coefficient of determination is given by

$$r^2 = \frac{SS_{yy} - SSE}{SS_{yy}} = \frac{6.0 - 1.1}{6.0} = \frac{4.9}{6.0} = .82$$

Another way to compute r^2 is to recall (Section 9.6) that $r = .904$. Then we have $r^2 = (.904)^2 = .82$. A third way to obtain r^2 is from a computer printout. This value is highlighted on the SAS printout reproduced in Figure 9.17 next to the heading

---

TABLE 9.7 Advertising Expenditure–Sales Revenue Data

Advertising Expenditure, x ($100s)	Sales Revenue, y ($1,000s)
1	1
2	1
3	2
4	2
5	4

Dependent Variable: Y

Analysis of Variance

Source	DF	Sum of Squares	Mean Square	F Value	Prob>F
Model	1	4.90000	4.90000	13.364	0.0354
Error	3	1.10000	0.36667		
C Total	4	6.00000			

Root MSE	0.60553	R-square	0.8167	
Dep Mean	2.00000	Adj R-sq	0.7556	
C.V.	30.27650			

Parameter Estimates

Variable	DF	Parameter Estimate	Standard Error	T for H0: Parameter=0	Prob > |T|
INTERCEP	1	-0.100000	0.63508530	-0.157	0.8849
X	1	0.700000	0.19148542	3.656	0.0354

FIGURE 9.17 SAS printout for advertising–sales example

R-square. Our interpretation is as follows: We know that using advertising expenditure, x, to predict y with the least squares line

$$\hat{y} = -.1 + .7x$$

accounts for 82% of the total sum of squares of deviations of the five sample y values about their mean. Or, stated another way, 82% of the sample variation in sales revenue (y) can be "explained" by using advertising expenditure (x) in a straight-line model.

Practical Interpretation of the Coefficient of Determination, r^2
About $100(r^2)\%$ of the sample variation in y (measured by the total sum of squares of deviations of the sample y values about their mean $\bar{y}$) can be explained by (or attributed to) using x to predict y in the straight-line model.

EXERCISES   9.44–9.56

Note: Exercises marked with ⬛ contain data for computer analysis on a 3.5" disk (file name in parentheses).

Learning the Mechanics

9.44 Explain what each of the following sample correlation coefficients tells you about the relationship between the x and y values in the sample:
a. $r = 1$ **b.** $r = -1$ **c.** $r = 0$
d. $r = .90$ **e.** $r = .10$ **f.** $r = -.88$

9.45 Describe the slope of the least squares line if
a. $r = .7$ **b.** $r = -.7$ **c.** $r = 0$ **d.** $r^2 = .64$

9.46 Construct a scattergram for each data set (**a–d**). Then calculate r and r^2 for each data set. Interpret their values.

a.

x	-2	-1	0	1	2
y	-2	1	2	5	6

b.

x	-2	-1	0	1	2
y	6	5	3	2	0

c.

x	1	2	2	3	3	3	4
y	2	1	3	1	2	3	2

d.

x	0	1	3	5	6
y	0	1	2	1	0

9.47   Calculate r^2 for the least squares line in each of the following exercises. Interpret their values.
a. Exercise 9.10   **b.** Exercise 9.13

Applying the Concepts

9.48   **(X09.048)** The table below reports the average daily hotel room rate and average car-rental rate during a week in October 1995 for a sample of 20 U.S. cities.

City	Daily Room Rate	Daily Car-Rental Rate
Atlanta	$118	$56
Boston	192	49
Chicago	168	57
Cleveland	77	51
Dallas	118	45
Denver	94	37
Detroit	114	53
Houston	115	62
Los Angeles	136	42
Miami	138	32
Minneapolis	98	49
New Orleans	136	55
New York	177	69
Orlando	95	41
Phoenix	135	45
Pittsburgh	133	47
St. Louis	109	77
San Francisco	181	49
Seattle	124	45
Washington, D.C.	167	53

Source: The Wall Street Journal, October 20, 1995, p. B6.

a. Construct a scatterplot for the data.
b. Based on a visual inspection of the plot, describe in words the strength of the linear relationship between the two variables.
c. Find and interpret the coefficient of correlation for these data.

9.49   Many high school students experience "math anxiety," which has been shown to have a negative effect on their learning achievement. Does such an attitude carry over to learning computer skills? A math and computer science researcher at Duquesne University investigated this question and published her results in *Educational Technology* (May–June 1995). A sample of 1,730 high school students—902 boys and 828 girls—from public schools in Pittsburgh, Pennsylvania, participated in the study. Using 5-point Likert scales, where 1 = "strongly disagree" and 5 = "strongly agree," the researcher measured the students' interest and confidence in both mathematics and computers.

a. For boys, math confidence and computer interest were correlated at $r = .14$. Fully interpret this result.
b. For girls, math confidence and computer interest were correlated at $r = .33$. Fully interpret this result.

9.50   Studies of Asian (particularly Japanese) and U.S. managers in the 1970s and 1980s found sharp differences of opinion and attitude toward quality management. Do these differences continue to exist? To find out, two California State University researchers (B. F. Yavas and T. M. Burrows) surveyed 100 U.S. and 96 Asian managers in the electronics manufacturing industry (*Quality Management Journal*, Fall 1994). The accompanying table gives the percentages of U.S. and Asian managers who agree with each of 13 randomly selected statements regarding quality. (For example, one statement is "Quality is a problem in my company." Another is "Improving quality is expensive.")

	PERCENTAGE OF MANAGERS WHO AGREE	
Statement	**United States**	**Asian**
1	36	38
2	31	42
3	28	43
4	27	48
5	78	58
6	74	49
7	43	46
8	50	56
9	31	65
10	66	58
11	18	21
12	61	69
13	53	45

Source: Yavas, B. F., and Burrows, T. M. "A comparative study of attitudes of U.S. and Asian managers toward product quality." *Quality Management Journal*, Fall 1994, p. 49 (Table 5).

a. Find the coefficient of correlation r for these data on the MINITAB printout below.

> **Correlation of USA and ASIAN = 0.570**

b. Interpret r in the context of the problem. Do U.S. and Asian managers tend to have similar attitudes toward quality and quality management?

9.51   Refer to Exercise 9.50. Using the coefficient of correlation r to make inferences about the difference in attitudes between U.S. and Asian managers regarding quality can be misleading. The value of r measures the strength of the linear relationship between two variables; it does not

Quality Statement	PERCENTAGE OF MANAGERS WHO AGREE	
	U.S.	Asian
1	20	50
2	30	65
3	40	70
4	50	80
5	55	90

account for a difference between the means of the variables. To illustrate this, consider the hypothetical data shown in the table above.

a. Show that the coefficient of correlation r is near 1.

b. Examine the hypothetical data and note that the Asian percentage is approximately 30 points higher for each quality statement. In this case, does $r = 1$ imply that the attitudes of U.S. and Asian managers are similar? Explain.

9.52 **(X09.052)** The fertility rate of a country is defined as the number of children a woman citizen bears, on average, in her lifetime. *Scientific American* (Dec. 1993) reported on the declining fertility rate in developing countries. The researchers found that family planning can have a great effect on fertility rate. The table below gives the fertility rate, y, and contraceptive prevalence, x (measured as the percentage of married women who use contraception), for each of 27 developing countries. A SAS printout of the simple linear regression analysis is on page 488.

a. According to the researchers, "the data reveal that differences in contraceptive prevalence explain about 90% of the variation in fertility rates." Do you concur?

b. The researchers also concluded that "if contraceptive use increases by 15 percent, women bear, on average, one fewer child." Is this statement supported by the data? Explain.

9.53 **(X09.053)** A negotiable certificate of deposit is a marketable receipt for funds deposited in a bank for a specified period of time at a specified rate of interest (Lee, Finnerty, and Norton, 1997). The table on page 488 lists the end-of-quarter interest rate for three-month certificates of deposit from January 1982 through December 1995 with the concurrent end-of-quarter values of Standard & Poor's 500 Stock Composite Average (an indicator of stock market activity). Find the coefficient of determination and the correlation coefficient for the data and interpret those results. Use the SPSS printout at the top of page 489 to arrive at your answer.

9.54 Refer to the *Journal of Information Science* study of the relationship between the fraction y of documents retrieved using Medline and the number x of terms in the search query, Exercise 9.37.

a. The value of r was reported in the article as $r = .679$. Interpret this result.

b. Calculate the coefficient of determination, r^2, and interpret the result.

Country	Contraceptive Prevalence, x	Fertility Rate, y
Mauritius	76	2.2
Thailand	69	2.3
Colombia	66	2.9
Costa Rica	71	3.5
Sri Lanka	63	2.7
Turkey	62	3.4
Peru	60	3.5
Mexico	55	4.0
Jamaica	55	2.9
Indonesia	50	3.1
Tunisia	51	4.3
El Salvador	48	4.5
Morocco	42	4.0
Zimbabwe	46	5.4

Country	Contraceptive Prevalence, x	Fertility Rate, y
Egypt	40	4.5
Bangladesh	40	5.5
Botswana	35	4.8
Jordan	35	5.5
Kenya	28	6.5
Guatemala	24	5.5
Cameroon	16	5.8
Ghana	14	6.0
Pakistan	13	5.0
Senegal	13	6.5
Sudan	10	4.8
Yemen	9	7.0
Nigeria	7	5.7

Source: Robey, B., *et al.* "The fertility decline in developing countries." *Scientific American,* December 1993, p. 62. [*Note:* The data values are estimated from a scatterplot.]

```
Dependent Variable: FERTRATE
                        Analysis of Variance

                             Sum of          Mean
       Source       DF      Squares         Square      F Value     Prob>F

       Model         1      35.96633       35.96633      74.309      0.0001
       Error        25      12.10033        0.48401
       C Total      26      48.06667

              Root MSE        0.69571     R-square     0.7483
              Dep Mean        4.51111     Adj R-sq     0.7382
              C.V.           15.42216

                         Parameter Estimates

                      Parameter      Standard     T for HO:
       Variable   DF   Estimate         Error    Parameter=0    Prob > |T|

       INTERCEP    1   6.731929      0.29034252     23.186        0.0001
       CONTPREV    1  -0.054610      0.00633512     -8.620        0.0001
```

Year	Quarter	Interest Rate, x	S&P 500, y	Year	Quarter	Interest Rate, x	S&P 500, y
1982	I	14.21	111.96	1989	I	10.09	294.87
	II	14.46	109.61		II	9.20	317.98
	III	10.66	120.42		III	8.78	349.15
	IV	8.66	135.28		IV	8.32	353.40
1983	I	8.69	152.96	1990	I	8.27	339.94
	II	9.20	168.11		II	8.33	358.02
	III	9.39	166.07		III	8.08	306.05
	IV	9.69	164.93		IV	7.96	330.22
1984	I	10.08	159.18	1991	I	6.71	375.22
	II	11.34	153.18		II	6.01	371.16
	III	11.29	166.10		III	5.70	387.86
	IV	8.60	167.24		IV	4.91	417.09
1985	I	9.02	180.66	1992	I	4.25	403.69
	II	7.44	191.85		II	3.86	408.14
	III	7.93	182.08		III	3.13	417.80
	IV	7.80	211.28		IV	3.48	435.71
1986	I	7.24	238.90	1993	I	3.11	451.67
	II	6.73	250.84		II	3.21	450.53
	III	5.71	231.32		III	3.12	458.93
	IV	6.04	242.17		IV	3.17	466.45
1987	I	6.17	291.70	1994	I	3.77	445.77
	II	6.94	304.00		II	4.52	444.27
	III	7.37	321.83		III	5.03	462.69
	IV	7.66	247.08		IV	6.29	459.27
1988	I	6.63	258.89	1995	I	6.15	500.71
	II	7.51	273.50		II	5.90	544.75
	III	8.23	271.91		III	5.73	584.41
	IV	9.25	277.72		IV	5.62	615.93

Source: Standard & Poor's Statistical Service, Current Statistics. Standard & Poor's Corporation, 1992, 1996.

9.55 The Minnesota Department of Transportation installed a state-of-the-art weigh-in-motion scale in the concrete surface of the eastbound lanes of Interstate 494 in Bloomington, Minnesota. After installation, a study was undertaken to determine whether the scale's readings correspond with the static weights of the vehicles being monitored. (Studies of this type are known as *calibration stud-*

```
Correlations:  SP500

   INTRATE      -.7607**

N of cases:     56          1-tailed Signif:  * - .01  ** - .001
-----------------------------------------------------------------------
          * * * *  M U L T I P L E  R E G R E S S I O N  * * * *
Equation Number 1    Dependent Variable..  SP500
Variable(s) Entered on Step Number
   1..     INTRATE

Multiple R          .76074
R Square            .57873
Adjusted R Square   .57093
Standard Error     84.49296

Analysis of Variance
                  DF      Sum of Squares          Mean Square
Regression        1          529604.21837       529604.21837
Residual         54          385509.26034         7139.06038

F =      74.18402       Signif F = .0000
------------------- Variables in the Equation --------------------

Variable              B          SE B        Beta       T    Sig T

INTRATE          -37.887641   4.398883   -.760743   -8.613  .0000
(Constant)       587.662145  33.878984             17.346  .0000
```

Trial Number	Static Weight of Truck x (thousand pounds)	Weigh-in-Motion Reading Prior to Calibration Adjustment, y_1 (thousand pounds)	Weigh-in-Motion Reading After Calibration Adjustment, y_2 (thousand pounds)
1	27.9	26.0	27.8
2	29.1	29.9	29.1
3	38.0	39.5	37.8
4	27.0	25.1	27.1
5	30.3	31.6	30.6
6	34.5	36.2	34.3
7	27.8	25.1	26.9
8	29.6	31.0	29.6
9	33.1	35.6	33.0
10	35.5	40.2	35.0

Source: Adapted from data in Wright J. L., Owen, F., and Pena, D. "Status of MN/DOT's weigh-in-motion program." St. Paul: Minnesota Department of Transportation, January 1983.

ies.) After some preliminary comparisons using a two-axle, six-tire truck carrying different loads (see the table above), calibration adjustments were made in the software of the weigh-in-motion system and the scales were reevaluated.

a. Construct two scattergrams, one of y_1 versus x and the other of y_2 versus x.

b. Use the scattergrams of part **a** to evaluate the performance of the weigh-in-motion scale both before and after the calibration adjustment.

c. Calculate the correlation coefficient for both sets of data and interpret their values. Explain

how these correlation coefficients can be used to evaluate the weigh-in-motion scale.

d. Suppose the sample correlation coefficient for y_2 and x was 1. Could this happen if the static weights and the weigh-in-motion readings disagreed? Explain.

9.56 A firm's *demand curve* describes the quantity of its product that can be sold at various prices, other things being equal (Mansfield, *Applied Microeconomics*, 1994). Over the period of a year, a tire company varied the price of a radial tire to estimate its demand curve. When the price was set very low or very high, few tires sold. The latter result the firm understood, the former it attributed to consumer misperception that low price implies poor quality. The data in the table describe the tire's sales over the experimental period. A simple linear regression analysis was conducted using MINITAB. The printout follows.

Price, x ($)	Sales, y (100s)
20	13
35	57
45	85
60	43
70	17

a. Find the least squares line to approximate the firm's demand curve.

b. Construct a scattergram and plot the least squares line on the graph.

c. Test $H_0: \beta_1 = 0$ using a two-tailed test and $\alpha = .05$. Draw the appropriate conclusion in the context of the problem.

d. Does the nonrejection of H_0 in part c imply that no relationship exists between tire price and sales volume?

e. Find the coefficient of determination for the least squares line of part a and interpret its value in the context of the problem.

f. Find the coefficient of correlation for the least squares line of part a and interpret its value in the context of the problem.

```
The regression equation is
SALES = 44.2 -  0.025 PRICE

Predictor          Coef       Stdev     t-ratio          p
Constant          44.17       42.71        1.03      0.377
PRICE           -0.0255      0.8663       -0.03      0.978

s = 34.33          R-sq = 0.0%       R-sq(adj) = 0.0%

Analysis of Variance

SOURCE          DF          SS          MS          F          p
Regression       1           1           1       0.00      0.978
Error            3        3535        1178
Total            4        3536

-------------------------------------------------------------

Correlation of PRICE and SALES = -0.017
```

9.8 USING THE MODEL FOR ESTIMATION AND PREDICTION

If we are satisfied that a useful model has been found to describe the relationship between x and y, we are ready for step 5 in our regression modeling procedure: using the model for estimation and prediction.

The most common uses of a probabilistic model for making inferences can be divided into two categories. The first is the use of the model for estimating the mean value of y, $E(y)$, for a specific value of x.

For our advertising–sales example, we may want to estimate the mean sales revenue for *all* months during which $400 ($x = 4$) is expended on advertising.

The second use of the model entails predicting a new individual y value for a given x.

That is, if we decide to expend $400 in advertising next month, we may want to predict the firm's sales revenue for that month.

In the first case, we are attempting to estimate the mean value of y for a very large number of experiments at the given x value. In the second case, we are trying to predict the outcome of a single experiment at the given x value. Which of these model uses—estimating the mean value of y or predicting an individual new value of y (for the same value of x)—can be accomplished with the greater accuracy?

Before answering this question, we first consider the problem of choosing an estimator (or predictor) of the mean (or a new individual) y value. We will use the least squares prediction equation

$$\hat{y} = \hat{\beta}_0 + \hat{\beta}_1 x$$

both to estimate the mean value of y and to predict a specific new value of y for a given value of x. For our example, we found

$$\hat{y} = -.1 + .7x$$

so that the estimated mean sales revenue for all months when $x = 4$ (advertising is $400) is

$$\hat{y} = -.1 + .7(4) = 2.7$$

or $2,700. (Recall that the units of y are thousands of dollars.) The same value is used to predict a new y value when $x = 4$. That is, both the estimated mean and the predicted value of y are $\hat{y} = 2.7$ when $x = 4$, as shown in Figure 9.18.

The difference between these two model uses lies in the relative accuracy of the estimate and the prediction. These accuracies are best measured by using the sampling errors of the least squares line when it is used as an estimator and as a predictor, respectively. These errors are reflected in the standard deviations given in the next box.

Sampling Errors for the Estimator of the Mean of y and the Predictor of an Individual New Value of y

1. The standard deviation of the sampling distribution of the estimator $\hat{y}$ of the mean value of y at a specific value of x, say x_p, is

$$\sigma_{\hat{y}} = \sigma \sqrt{\frac{1}{n} + \frac{(x_p - \bar{x})^2}{SS_{xx}}}$$

where σ is the standard deviation of the random error ϵ. We refer to $\sigma_{\hat{y}}$ as the standard error of $\hat{y}$.

2. The standard deviation of the prediction error for the predictor $\hat{y}$ of an individual new y value at a specific value of x is

$$\sigma_{(y - \hat{y})} = \sigma \sqrt{1 + \frac{1}{n} + \frac{(x_p - \bar{x})^2}{SS_{xx}}}$$

where σ is the standard deviation of the random error ϵ. We refer to $\sigma_{(y - \hat{y})}$ as the standard error of the prediction.

FIGURE 9.18
Estimated mean value and predicted individual value of sales revenue y for $x = 4$

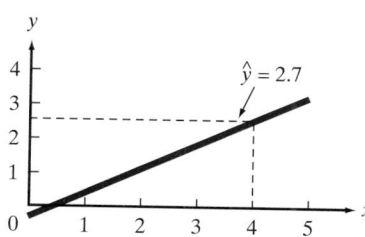

The true value of σ is rarely known, so we estimate σ by s and calculate the estimation and prediction intervals as shown in the next two boxes.

A 100$(1 - \alpha)$% Confidence Interval for the Mean Value of y at $x = x_p$

$$\hat{y} \pm t_{\alpha/2} \cdot (\text{Estimated standard error of } \hat{y})$$

or

$$\hat{y} \pm t_{\alpha/2}s \sqrt{\frac{1}{n} + \frac{(x_p - \bar{x})^2}{SS_{xx}}}$$

where $t_{\alpha/2}$ is based on $(n - 2)$ degrees of freedom.

A 100$(1 - \alpha)$% Prediction Interval* for an Individual New Value of y at $x = x_p$

$$\hat{y} \pm t_{\alpha/2} \cdot (\text{Estimated standard error of prediction})$$

or

$$\hat{y} \pm t_{\alpha/2}s \sqrt{1 + \frac{1}{n} + \frac{(x_p - \bar{x})^2}{SS_{xx}}}$$

where $t_{\alpha/2}$ is based on $(n - 2)$ degrees of freedom.

EXAMPLE 9.3 Find a 95% confidence interval for the mean monthly sales when the appliance store spends $400 on advertising.

SOLUTION
For a $400 advertising expenditure, $x = 4$ and the confidence interval for the mean value of y is

$$\hat{y} \pm t_{\alpha/2}s \sqrt{\frac{1}{n} + \frac{(x_p - \bar{x})^2}{SS_{xx}}} = \hat{y} \pm t_{.025}s \sqrt{\frac{1}{5} + \frac{(4 - \bar{x})^2}{SS_{xx}}}$$

where $t_{.025}$ is based on $n - 2 = 5 - 2 = 3$ degrees of freedom. Recall that $\hat{y} = 2.7$, $s = .61, \bar{x} = 3$, and $SS_{xx} = 10$. From Table VI in Appendix B, $t_{.025} = 3.182$. Thus, we have

$$2.7 \pm (3.182)(.61) \sqrt{\frac{1}{5} + \frac{(4 - 3)^2}{10}} = 2.7 \pm (3.182)(.61)(.55)$$

$$= 2.7 \pm (3.182)(.34)$$

$$= 2.7 \pm 1.1 = (1.6, 3.8)$$

Therefore, when the store spends $400 a month on advertising, we are 95% confident that the mean sales revenue is between $1,600 and $3,800. Note that we used a small amount of data (small in size) for purposes of illustration in fitting the least squares line. The interval would probably be narrower if more information had been obtained from a larger sample.

---

*The term *prediction interval* is used when the interval formed is intended to enclose the value of a random variable. The term *confidence interval* is reserved for estimation of population parameters (such as the mean).

EXAMPLE 9.4 Predict the monthly sales for next month, if $400 is spent on advertising. Use a 95% prediction interval.

SOLUTION

To predict the sales for a particular month for which $x_p = 4$, we calculate the 95% prediction interval as

$$\hat{y} \pm t_{\alpha/2}s\sqrt{1 + \frac{1}{n} + \frac{(x_p - \bar{x})^2}{SS_{xx}}} = 2.7 \pm (3.182)(.61)\sqrt{1 + \frac{1}{5} + \frac{(4 - 3)^2}{10}}$$

$$= 2.7 \pm (3.182)(.61)(1.14)$$

$$= 2.7 \pm (3.182)(.70)$$

$$= 2.7 \pm 2.2 = (.5, 4.9)$$

Therefore, we predict with 95% confidence that the sales revenue next month (a month in which we spend $400 in advertising) will fall in the interval from $500 to $4,900. Like the confidence interval for the mean value of y, the prediction interval for y is quite large. This is because we have chosen a simple example (only five data points) to fit the least squares line. The width of the prediction interval could be reduced by using a larger number of data points. ∎

Both the confidence interval for $E(y)$ and prediction interval for y can be obtained using a statistical software package. Figures 9.19 and 9.20 are SAS printouts showing confidence intervals and prediction intervals, respectively, for the data in the advertising–sales example.

The 95% confidence interval for $E(y)$ when $x = 4$ is highlighted in Figure 9.19 in the row corresponding to **4** under the columns labeled **Lower95% Mean** and **Upper95% Mean**. The interval shown on the printout, (1.6445, 3.7555), agrees (except for rounding) with the interval calculated in Example 9.3. The 95% prediction interval for y when $x = 4$ is highlighted in Figure 9.20 under the columns **Lower95% Predict** and **Upper95% Predict**. Again, except for rounding, the SAS interval (.5028, 4.8972) agrees with the one computed in Example 9.4.

Obs	X		Dep Var Y	Predict Value	Std Err Predict	Lower95% Mean	Upper95% Mean	Residual
1	1		1.0000	0.6000	0.469	-0.8927	2.0927	0.4000
2	2		1.0000	1.3000	0.332	0.2445	2.3555	-0.3000
3	3		2.0000	2.0000	0.271	1.1382	2.8618	0
4	4		2.0000	2.7000	0.332	1.6445	3.7555	-0.7000
5	5		4.0000	3.4000	0.469	1.9073	4.8927	0.6000

FIGURE 9.19 SAS printout giving 95% confidence intervals for $E(y)$

Obs	X		Dep Var Y	Predict Value	Std Err Predict	Lower95% Predict	Upper95% Predict	Residual
1	1		1.0000	0.6000	0.469	-1.8376	3.0376	0.4000
2	2		1.0000	1.3000	0.332	-0.8972	3.4972	-0.3000
3	3		2.0000	2.0000	0.271	-0.1110	4.1110	0
4	4		2.0000	2.7000	0.332	0.5028	4.8972	-0.7000
5	5		4.0000	3.4000	0.469	0.9624	5.8376	0.6000

FIGURE 9.20 SAS printout giving 95% prediction intervals for y

FIGURE 9.21
A 95% confidence interval for mean sales and a prediction interval for sales when $x = 4$

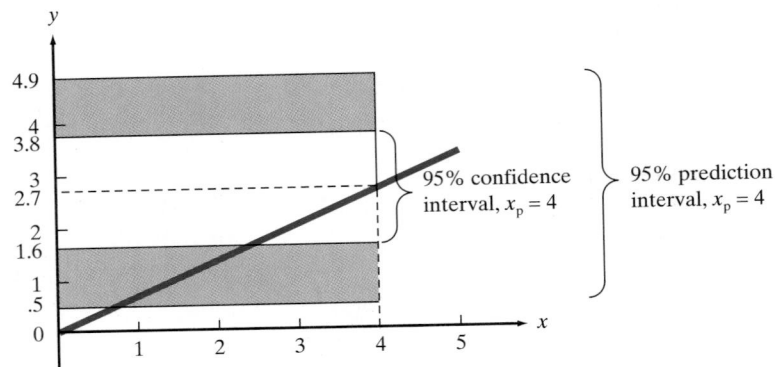

A comparison of the confidence interval for the mean value of y and the prediction interval for a new value of y when $x = 4$ is illustrated in Figure 9.21. Note that the prediction interval for an individual new value of y is always wider than the corresponding confidence interval for the mean value of y. You can see this by examining the formulas for the two intervals and by studying Figure 9.21.

The error in estimating the mean value of y, $E(y)$, for a given value of x, say x_p, is the distance between the least squares line and the true line of means, $E(y) = \beta_0 + \beta_1 x$. This error, $[\hat{y} - E(y)]$, is shown in Figure 9.22. In contrast, *the error* $(y_p - \hat{y})$ *in predicting some future value of* y *is the sum of two errors*—the error of estimating the mean of y, $E(y)$, shown in Figure 9.22, plus the random error that is a component of the value of y to be predicted (see Figure 9.23). Consequently, the error of predicting a particular value of y will be larger than the error of estimating the mean value of y for a particular value of x. Note from their formulas that both the error of estimation and the error of prediction take their smallest values when $x_p = \bar{x}$. The farther x_p lies from $\bar{x}$, the larger will be the errors of estimation and prediction. You can see why this is true by noting the deviations for different values of x_p between the line of means $E(y) = \beta_0 + \beta_1 x$ and the predicted line of means $\hat{y} = \hat{\beta}_0 + \hat{\beta}_1 x$ shown in Figure 9.23. The deviation is larger at the extremes of the interval where the largest and smallest values of x in the data set occur.

Both the confidence intervals for mean values and the prediction intervals for new values are depicted over the entire range of the regression line in Figure

FIGURE 9.22
Error of estimating the mean value of y for a given value of x

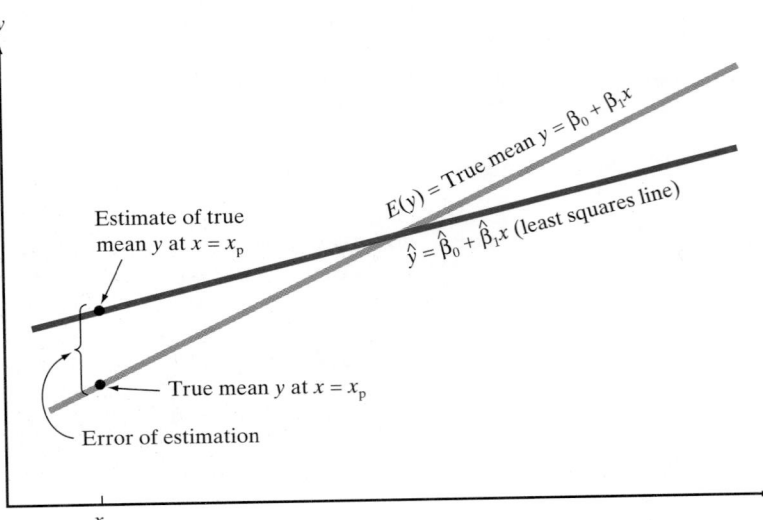

FIGURE 9.23
Error of predicting a
future value of y for a
given value of x

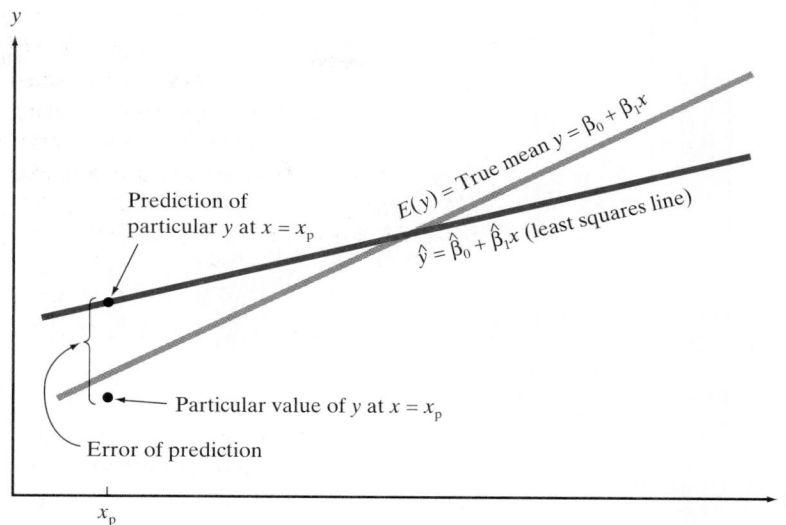

9.24. You can see that the confidence interval is always narrower than the prediction interval, and that they are both narrowest at the mean $\bar{x}$, increasing steadily as the distance $|x - \bar{x}|$ increases. In fact, when x is selected far enough away from $\bar{x}$ so that it falls outside the range of the sample data, it is dangerous to make any inferences about $E(y)$, or y.

> **Warning**
> Using the least squares prediction equation to estimate the mean value of y or to predict a particular value of y for values of x that fall *outside the range* of the values of x contained in your sample data may lead to errors of estimation or prediction that are much larger than expected. Although the least squares model may provide a very good fit to the data over the range of x values contained in the sample, it could give a poor representation of the true model for values of x outside this region.

The confidence interval width grows smaller as n is increased; thus, in theory, you can obtain as precise an estimate of the mean value of y as desired (at any given x) by selecting a large enough sample. The prediction interval for a new value of y also grows smaller as n increases, but there is a lower limit on its width.

FIGURE 9.24
Confidence intervals
for mean values and
prediction intervals for
new values

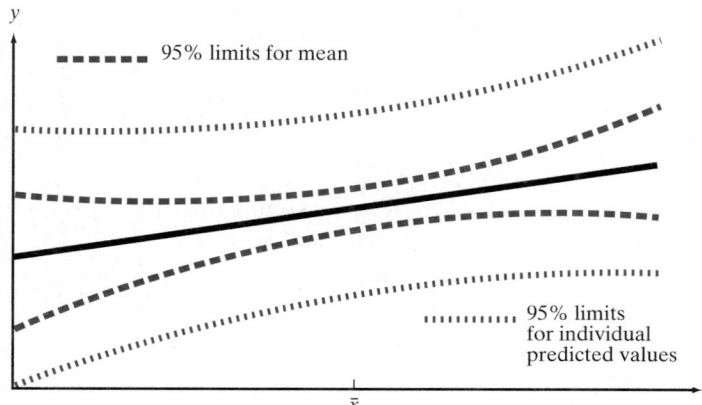

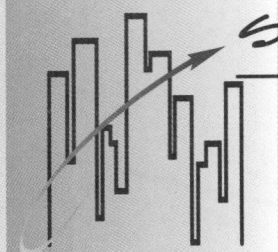

STATISTICS IN ACTION

9.2 STATISTICAL ASSESSMENT OF DAMAGE TO BRONX BRICKS

This case concerns an actual civil suit, described in *Chance* (Summer 1994), in which statistics played a key role in the jury's decision. The suit revolved around a five-building apartment complex located in the Bronx, New York. The buildings were constructed in the late 1970s from custom-designed jumbo (35-pound) bricks. Nearly three-quarters of a million bricks were used in the construction.

Over time, the bricks began to suffer *spalling* damage, i.e., separation of some portion of the face of a brick from its body. Experts agreed that the cause of the spalling was winter month freeze-thaw cycles in which water absorbed in the brick face alternates between freezing and thawing. The owner of the complex alleged that the bricks were defective. The brick manufacturer countered that poor design and shoddy management of water runoff caused the water to be trapped and absorbed in the bricks, leading to the damage. Ultimately, the suit required an estimate of the spall rate—the rate of damage per 1,000 bricks.

The owner estimated the spall rate using several *scaffold-drop* surveys. With this method, an engineer lowers a scaffold to selected places on building walls and counts the number of visible spalls for every 1,000 bricks in the observation area. The estimated spall rate is then multiplied by the total number of bricks (in thousands) in the entire complex to determine the total number of damaged bricks. When properly designed, the scaffold-drop survey, although extremely time-consuming and tedious to perform, is considered the "gold standard" for measuring spall damage. However, the owner did not drop the scaffolds at randomly selected wall areas. Instead, scaffolds were dropped primarily in areas of high spall concentration, leading to a substantially biased high estimate of total spall damage.

In an attempt to obtain an unbiased estimate of spall rate, the brick manufacturer conducted its own survey of the walls of the complex. The walls were divided into 83 wall segments and a photograph of each wall segment was taken. The number of spalled bricks that could be made out from each photo was recorded and the sum over all 83 wall segments was used as an estimate of total spall damage.

When the data from the two methods were compared, major discrepancies were discovered. At eleven locations that had been painstakingly surveyed by the scaffold drops, the spalls visible from the photos did not include all of the spalls identified on the drops. For these wall segments, the photo method provided a serious underestimate of the spall rate, as shown in Table 9.8. Consequently, the total spall damage estimated by the photo survey will also be underestimated.

In this court case, the jury was faced with the following dilemma: The scaffold-drop survey provided the most accurate estimate of spall rate in a given wall segment. Unfortunately, the drop areas were not selected at random from the entire complex; rather, drops were made at areas with high spall concentrations, leading to an overestimate of the total damage. On the other hand, the photo survey was complete in that all 83 wall segments in the complex were checked for spall damage. But the spall rate estimated by the photos, at least in areas of high spall concentration, was biased low, leading to an underestimate of the total damage.

Focus

Use the data in Table 9.8, as did expert statisticians who testified in the case, to help the jury estimate the true spall rate at a given wall segment. Then explain how this information, coupled with the data (not given here) on all 83 wall segments, can provide a reasonable estimate of the total spall damage (i.e., total number of damaged bricks). [*Note:* The data in Table 9.8 is available on a 3.5" disk in the file named TAB09.008.]

If you examine the formula for the prediction interval, you will see that the interval can get no smaller than $\hat{y} \pm z_{\alpha/2}\sigma$.* Thus, the only way to obtain more accurate predictions for new values of y is to reduce the standard deviation of the regression model, σ. This can be accomplished only by improving the model, either by

*The result follows from the facts that, for large n, $t_{\alpha/2} \approx z_{\alpha/2}$, $s \approx \sigma$, and the last two terms under the radical in the standard error of the predictor are approximately 0.

TABLE 9.8   **Comparison of Spall Rates Estimated by Two Methods (Statistics in Action 9.2)**

Drop Location	Drop Spall Rate (per 1,000 bricks)	Photo Spall Rate (per 1,000 bricks)
1	0	0
2	5.1	0
3	6.6	0
4	1.1	.8
5	1.8	1.0
6	3.9	1.0
7	11.5	1.9
8	22.1	7.7
9	39.3	14.9
10	39.9	13.9
11	43.0	11.8

Source: Fairley, W. B., *et al.* "Bricks, buildings, and the Bronx: Estimating masonry deterioration." *Chance,* Vol. 7, No. 3, Summer 1994, p. 36 (Figure 3). [*Note:* The data points are estimated from the points shown on a scatterplot.]

using a curvilinear (rather than linear) relationship with x or by adding new independent variables to the model, or both. Methods of improving the model are discussed in Chapter 10.

EXERCISES   9.57–9.66

Note: Exercises marked with 💾 *contain data for computer analysis on a 3.5" disk (file name in parentheses).*

Learning the Mechanics

9.57 Consider the following pairs of measurements:

x	−2	0	2	4	6	8	10
y	0	3	2	3	8	10	11

a. Construct a scattergram for these data.
b. Find the least squares line, and plot it on your scattergram.
c. Find s^2.
d. Find a 90% confidence interval for the mean value of y when $x = 3$. Plot the upper and lower bounds of the confidence interval on your scattergram.
e. Find a 90% prediction interval for a new value of y when $x = 3$. Plot the upper and lower bounds of the prediction interval on your scattergram.
f. Compare the widths of the intervals you constructed in parts **d** and **e**. Which is wider and why?

9.58 Consider the pairs of measurements shown in the next table.

x	4	6	0	5	2	3	2	6	2	1
y	3	5	−1	4	3	2	0	4	1	1

For these data, $SS_{xx} = 38.9000$, $SS_{yy} = 33.600$, $SS_{xy} = 32.8$, and $\hat{y} = -.414 + .843x$.

a. Construct a scattergram for these data.
b. Plot the least squares line on your scattergram.
c. Use a 95% confidence interval to estimate the mean value of y when $x_p = 6$. Plot the upper and lower bounds of the interval on your scattergram.
d. Repeat part **c** for $x_p = 3.2$ and $x_p = 0$.
e. Compare the widths of the three confidence intervals you constructed in parts **c** and **d** and explain why they differ.

9.59 Refer to Exercise 9.58.

a. Using no information about x, estimate and calculate a 95% confidence interval for the mean value of y. [*Hint:* Use the one-sample t methodology of Section 5.2.]
b. Plot the estimated mean value and the confidence interval as horizontal lines on your scattergram.
c. Compare the confidence intervals you calculated in parts **c** and **d** of Exercise 9.58 with the one you calculated in part **a** of this exercise. Does x appear to contribute information about the mean value of y?
d. Check the answer you gave in part **c** with a statistical test of the null hypothesis $H_0: \beta_1 = 0$ against $H_a: \beta_1 \neq 0$. Use $\alpha = .05$.

9.60 In fitting a least squares line to $n = 10$ data points, the following quantities were computed:

$$SS_{xx} = 32$$
$$\bar{x} = 3$$
$$SS_{yy} = 26$$
$$\bar{y} = 4$$
$$SS_{xy} = 28$$

a. Find the least squares line.
b. Graph the least squares line.
c. Calculate SSE.   d. Calculate s^2.
e. Find a 95% confidence interval for the mean value of y when $x_p = 2.5$.
f. Find a 95% prediction interval for y when $x_p = 4$.

Applying the Concepts

9.61 (X09.061) Many variables influence the sales of existing single-family homes. One of these is the interest rate charged for mortgage loans. Shown in the table below are the total number of existing single-family homes sold annually, y, and the average annual conventional mortgage interest rate, x, for 1982–1994. A MINITAB printout of the simple linear regression follows the table.

a. Plot the data points on graph paper.
b. Find the least squares line relating y to x on the printout. Plot the line on your graph from part **a** to see if the line appears to model the relationship between y and x.
c. Do the data provide sufficient evidence to indicate that mortgage interest rates contribute information for the prediction of annual sales of existing single-family homes? Use $\alpha = .05$.
d. Locate r^2 and interpret its value.
e. A 95% confidence interval for the mean annual number of existing single-family homes sold when the average annual mortgage interest rate is 10.0% is shown under **95% C.I.** on the printout. Interpret this interval.
f. A 95% prediction interval for the annual number of existing single-family homes sold when the average annual mortgage interest rate is 10.0% is shown under **95% P.I.** on the printout. Interpret this interval.
g. Explain why the widths of the intervals found in parts **e** and **f** differ.

9.62 Refer to the simple linear regression of number of employees y and age x for fast-growing firms, Exercises 9.21, 9.28, and 9.39. The SAS printout of the analysis is reproduced on page 499.

Year	Homes Sold y (1,000s)	Interest Rate x (%)	Year	Homes Sold y (1,000s)	Interest Rate x (%)
1982	1,990	15.82	1989	3,346	10.22
1983	2,719	13.44	1990	3,211	10.08
1984	2,868	13.81	1991	3,220	9.20
1985	3,214	12.29	1992	3,520	8.43
1986	3,565	10.09	1993	3,802	7.36
1987	3,526	10.17	1994	3,946	8.59
1988	3,594	10.31			

Source: U.S. Bureau of the Census, *Statistical Abstract of the United States: 1995*, pp. 529, 730.

```
The regression equation is
HOMES = 5342 - 193 INTRATE

Predictor       Coef       Stdev      t-ratio        p
Constant      5341.9      298.9        17.87     0.000
INTRATE      -192.58       27.17        -7.09     0.000

s = 227.8      R-sq = 82.0%      R-sq(adj) = 80.4%

Analysis of Variance

SOURCE         DF          SS           MS          F         p
Regression      1      2607650      2607650      50.25     0.000
Error          11       570876        51898
Total          12      3178526

        Fit   Stdev.Fit         95% C.I.           95% P.I.
     3416.2        66.4   ( 3269.9, 3562.4) ( 2893.7, 3938.6)
```

Dependent Variable: NUMBER

Analysis of Variance

Source	DF	Sum of Squares	Mean Square	F Value	Prob>F
Model	1	23536.50149	23536.50149	11.451	0.0070
Error	10	20554.41518	2055.44152		
C Total	11	44090.91667			

Root MSE	45.33698	R-square	0.5338	
Dep Mean	61.08333	Adj R-sq	0.4872	
C.V.	74.22152			

Parameter Estimates

Variable	DF	Parameter Estimate	Standard Error	T for H0: Parameter=0	Prob > |T|
INTERCEP	1	-51.361607	35.71379104	-1.438	0.1809
AGE	1	17.754464	5.24673562	3.384	0.0070

Obs	AGE	Dep Var NUMBER	Predict Value	Std Err Predict	Lower95% Predict	Upper95% Predict	Residual
1	5	43.0000	37.4107	14.840	-68.8810	143.7	5.5893
2	5	52.0000	37.4107	14.840	-68.8810	143.7	14.5893
3	4	9.0000	19.6563	17.921	-88.9672	128.3	-10.6562
4	7	40.0000	72.9196	13.547	-32.5114	178.4	-32.9196
5	5	6.0000	37.4107	14.840	-68.8810	143.7	-31.4107
6	6	12.0000	55.1652	13.204	-50.0496	160.4	-43.1652
7	14	200.0	197.2	42.301	59.0415	335.4	2.7991
8	5	76.0000	37.4107	14.840	-68.8810	143.7	38.5893
9	7	15.0000	72.9196	13.547	-32.5114	178.4	-57.9196
10	6	40.0000	55.1652	13.204	-50.0496	160.4	-15.1652
11	5	65.0000	37.4107	14.840	-68.8810	143.7	27.5893
12	7	175.0	72.9196	13.547	-32.5114	178.4	102.1
13	10	.	126.2	23.268	12.6384	239.7	.

a. A 95% prediction interval for *y* when *x* = 10 is shown at the bottom of the printout. Interpret this interval.

b. How would the width of a 95% confidence interval for $E(y)$ when *x* = 10 compare to the interval, part **a**?

c. Would you recommend using the model to predict the number of employees at a firm that has been in business two years? Explain.

9.63 (X09.063) Managers are an important part of any organization's resource base. Accordingly, the organization should be just as concerned about forecasting its future managerial needs as it is with forecasting its needs for, say, the natural resources used in its production process (Northcraft and Neale, *Organizational Behavior: A Management Challenge,* 1994). A common forecasting procedure is to model the relationship between sales and the number of managers needed, since the demand for managers is the result of the increases and decreases in the demand for products and ser-

vices that a firm offers its customers. To develop this relationship, the data shown in the table at the top of page 500 are collected from a firm's records. An SPSS printout of the simple linear regression follows the table.

a. Test the usefulness of the model. Use $\alpha = .05$. State your conclusion in the context of the problem.

b. The company projects that it will sell 39 units in May of 1997. Use the least squares model to construct a 90% prediction interval for the number of managers needed in May 1997.

c. Interpret the interval in part **b**. Use the interval to determine the reliability of the firm's projection.

9.64 The reasons given by workers for quitting their jobs generally fall into one of two categories: (1) worker quits to seek or take a different job, or (2) worker quits to withdraw from the labor force. Economic theory suggests that wages and quit rates are related. Quit rates (quits per 100 employees)

Month	Units Sold, x	Managers, y
3/92	5	10
6/92	4	11
9/92	8	10
12/92	7	10
3/93	9	9
6/93	15	10
9/93	20	11
12/93	21	17
3/94	25	19
6/94	24	21

Month	Units Sold, x	Managers, y
9/94	30	22
12/94	31	25
3/95	36	30
6/95	38	30
9/95	40	31
12/95	41	31
3/96	51	32
6/96	40	30
9/96	48	32
12/96	47	32

```
* * * *   M U L T I P L E   R E G R E S S I O N   * * * *

Equation Number 1    Dependent Variable..    MANAGERS

Variable(s) Entered on Step Number
   1..     UNITS

Multiple R            .96386
R Square              .92903
Adjusted R Square     .92509
Standard Error        2.56642

Analysis of Variance
                    DF      Sum of Squares      Mean Square
Regression           1         1551.99292       1551.99292
Residual            18          118.55708          6.58650

F =      235.63225       Signif F =  .0000

------------------ Variables in the Equation ------------------

Variable              B         SE B         Beta        T     Sig T

UNITS           .586100      .038182      .963863    15.350   .0000
(Constant)     5.325299     1.179868                  4.513   .0003
```

and the average hourly wage in a sample of 15 manufacturing industries are shown in the table below. A MINITAB printout of the simple linear regression of quit rate y on average wage x is shown on page 501.

Industry	Quit Rate, y	Average Wage, x
1	1.4	$ 8.20
2	.7	10.35
3	2.6	6.18
4	3.4	5.37
5	1.7	9.94
6	1.7	9.11
7	1.0	10.59
8	.5	13.29
9	2.0	7.99
10	3.8	5.54
11	2.3	7.50
12	1.9	6.43
13	1.4	8.83
14	1.8	10.93
15	2.0	8.80

a. Do the data present sufficient evidence to conclude that average hourly wage rate contributes useful information for the prediction of quit rates? What does your model suggest about the relationship between quit rates and wages?

b. A 95% prediction interval for the quit rate in an industry with an average hourly wage of $9.00 is given at the bottom of the MINITAB printout. Interpret the result.

c. A 95% confidence interval for the mean quit rate for industries with an average hourly wage of $9.00 is also shown on the printout. Interpret this result.

9.65 (X09.065) Managers are interested in modeling past cost behavior in order to make more accurate predictions of future costs. Models of past cost behavior are called *cost functions*. Factors that influence costs are called *cost drivers* (Horngren, Foster, and Datar, *Cost Accounting*, 1994). The cost data on page 501 are from a rug manufacturer. Indirect manufacturing labor costs consist of

```
The regression equation is
QuitRate = 4.86 - 0.347 AveWage

Predictor          Coef       Stdev      t-ratio        p
Constant         4.8615      0.5201         9.35    0.000
AveWage        -0.34655     0.05866        -5.91    0.000

s = 0.4862      R-sq = 72.9%      R-sq(adj) = 70.8%

Analysis of Variance

SOURCE          DF          SS          MS          F         p
Regression       1       8.2507      8.2507      34.90     0.000
Error           13       3.0733      0.2364
Total           14      11.3240

    Fit   Stdev.Fit         95% C.I.          95% P.I.
   1.743     0.128    ( 1.467, 2.018)   ( 0.656, 2.829)
```

machine maintenance costs and setup labor costs. The latter are the costs of preparing the machines to produce a particular carpet pattern.

Week	Indirect Manufacturing Labor Costs	Cost Driven: Machine Hours
1	$1,190	68
2	1,211	88
3	1,004	62
4	917	72
5	770	60
6	1,456	96
7	1,180	78
8	710	46
9	1,316	82
10	1,032	94
11	752	68
12	963	48

Source: Horngren, Foster, and Datar, *Cost Accounting,* 1994.

a. In developing a cost function from these data, which variable should be the dependent variable? Why?

b. Construct a scatterplot for these data. What does the scatterplot suggest about the relationship between cost and machine hours?

c. Use the method of least squares to estimate the cost function.

d. Is the least squares model statistically useful? Conduct the appropriate hypothesis test. Use $\alpha = .05$.

e. Calculate r^2 and interpret its value in the context of the problem.

f. Find a 95% prediction interval for y for a selected value of x. Interpret the interval.

9.66 The data for Exercise 9.30 are reproduced below.

a. Use a 90% confidence interval to estimate the mean useful life of a brand A cutting tool when the cutting speed is 45 meters per minute.

Cutting Speed (meters per minute)	USEFUL LIFE (HOURS)	
	Brand A	Brand B
30	4.5	6.0
30	3.5	6.5
30	5.2	5.0
40	5.2	6.0
40	4.0	4.5
40	2.5	5.0
50	4.4	4.5
50	2.8	4.0
50	1.0	3.7
60	4.0	3.8
60	2.0	3.0
60	1.1	2.4
70	1.1	1.5
70	.5	2.0
70	3.0	1.0

Repeat for brand B. Compare the widths of the two intervals and comment on the reasons for any difference.

b. Use a 90% prediction interval to predict the useful life of a brand A cutting tool when the cutting speed is 45 meters per minute. Repeat for brand B. Compare the widths of the two intervals to each other, and to the two intervals you calculated in part **a**. Comment on the reasons for any differences.

c. Note that the estimation and prediction you performed in parts **a** and **b** were for a value of x that was not included in the original sample. That is, the value $x = 45$ was not part of the sample. However, the value is within the range of x values in the sample, so that the regres-sion model spans the x value for which the esti-mation and prediction were made. In such situations, estimation and prediction represent **interpolations**. Suppose you were asked to pre-dict the useful life of a brand A cutting tool for a cutting speed of $x = 100$ meters per minute. Since the given value of x is outside the range of the sample x values, the prediction is an example of **extrapolation**. Predict the useful life of a brand A cutting tool that is operated at 100 meters per minute, and construct a 95% confidence interval for the actual useful life of the tool. What additional assumption do you have to make in order to ensure the validity of an extrapolation?

9.9 SIMPLE LINEAR REGRESSION: AN EXAMPLE

In the preceding sections we have presented the basic elements necessary to fit and use a straight-line regression model. In this section we will assemble these ele-ments by applying them in an example with the aid of a computer.

Suppose a fire insurance company wants to relate the amount of fire damage in major residential fires to the distance between the burning house and the nearest fire station. The study is to be conducted in a large suburb of a major city; a sample of 15 recent fires in this suburb is selected. The amount of damage, y, and the distance between the fire and the nearest fire station, x, are recorded for each fire. The results are given in Table 9.9.

Step 1 First, we hypothesize a model to relate fire damage, y, to the distance from the nearest fire station, x. We hypothesize a straight-line proba-bilistic model:

$$y = \beta_0 + \beta_1 x + \epsilon$$

TABLE 9.9 Fire Damage Data

Distance From Fire Station, x (miles)	Fire Damage, y (thousands of dollars)
3.4	26.2
1.8	17.8
4.6	31.3
2.3	23.1
3.1	27.5
5.5	36.0
.7	14.1
3.0	22.3
2.6	19.6
4.3	31.3
2.1	24.0
1.1	17.3
6.1	43.2
4.8	36.4
3.8	26.1

Dep Variable: Y

Analysis of Variance

Source	DF	Sum of Squares	Mean Square	F Value	Prob>F
Model	1	841.76636	841.76636	156.886	0.0001
Error	13	69.75098	5.36546		
C Total	14	911.51733			

Root MSE	2.31635		R-Square	0.9235	
Dep Mean	26.41333		Adj R-Sq	0.9176	
C.V.	8.76961				

Parameter Estimates

Variable	DF	Parameter Estimate	Standard Error	T for H0: Parameter=0	Prob > |T|
INTERCEP	1	10.277929	1.42027781	7.237	0.0001
X	1	4.919331	0.39274775	12.525	0.0001

Obs	X	Y	Predict Value	Residual	Lower95% Predict	Upper95% Predict
1	3.4	26.2000	27.0037	-0.8037	21.8344	32.1729
2	1.8	17.8000	19.1327	-1.3327	13.8141	24.4514
3	4.6	31.3000	32.9068	-1.6068	27.6186	38.1951
4	2.3	23.1000	21.5924	1.5076	16.3577	26.8271
5	3.1	27.5000	25.5279	1.9721	20.3573	30.6984
6	5.5	36.0000	37.3342	-1.3342	31.8334	42.8351
7	0.7	14.1000	13.7215	0.3785	8.1087	19.3342
8	3.0	22.3000	25.0359	-2.7359	19.8622	30.2097
9	2.6	19.6000	23.0682	-3.4682	17.8678	28.2686
10	4.3	31.3000	31.4311	-0.1311	26.1908	36.6713
11	2.1	24.0000	20.6085	3.3915	15.3442	25.8729
12	1.1	17.3000	15.6892	1.6108	10.1999	21.1785
13	6.1	43.2000	40.2858	2.9142	34.5906	45.9811
14	4.8	36.4000	33.8907	2.5093	28.5640	39.2175
15	3.8	26.1000	28.9714	-2.8714	23.7843	34.1585
16	3.5		27.4956		22.3239	32.6672

Sum of Residuals   -3.73035E-14
Sum of Squared Residuals   69.7510
Predicted Resid SS (Press)   93.2117

FIGURE 9.25   SAS printout for fire damage regression analysis

Step 2   Next, we enter the data of Table 9.9 into a computer and use a statistical software package to estimate the unknown parameters in the deterministic component of the hypothesized model. The SAS printout for the simple linear regression analysis is shown in Figure 9.25. The least squares estimate of the slope β_1 and intercept β_0, highlighted on the printout, are

$$\hat{\beta}_1 = 4.919331$$
$$\hat{\beta}_0 = 10.277929$$

and the least squares equation is (rounded)

$$\hat{y} = 10.278 + 4.919x$$

FIGURE 9.26
Least squares
model for the fire
damage data

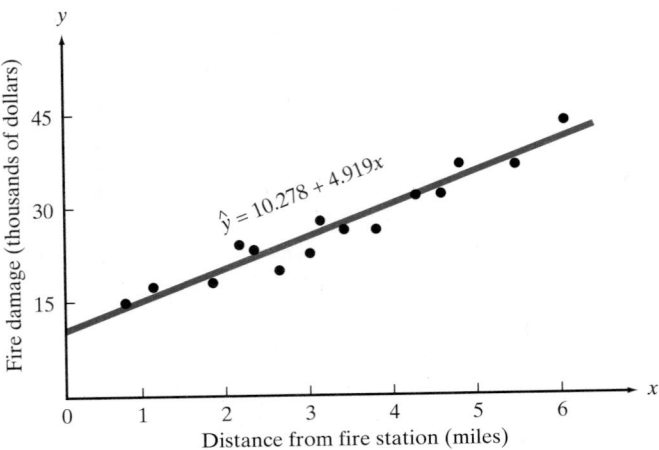

This prediction equation is graphed in Figure 9.26 along with a plot of the data points.

The least squares estimate of the slope, $\hat{\beta}_1 = 4.919$, implies that the estimated mean damage increases by \$4,919 for each additional mile from the fire station. This interpretation is valid over the range of x, or from .7 to 6.1 miles from the station. The estimated y-intercept, $\hat{\beta}_0 = 10.278$, has the interpretation that a fire 0 miles from the fire station has an estimated mean damage of \$10,278. Although this would seem to apply to the fire station itself, remember that the y-intercept is meaningfully interpretable only if $x = 0$ is within the sampled range of the independent variable, which it is not in this case.

Step 3 Now we specify the probability distribution of the random error component ϵ. The assumptions about the distribution are identical to those listed in Section 9.3. Although we know that these assumptions are not completely satisfied (they rarely are for practical problems), we are willing to assume they are approximately satisfied for this example. The estimate of the standard deviation σ of ϵ, highlighted on the printout, is:

$$s = 2.31635$$

This implies that most of the observed fire damage (y) values will fall within approximately $2s = 4.64$ thousand dollars of their respective predicted values when using the least squares line.

Step 4 We can now check the usefulness of the hypothesized model—that is, whether x really contributes information for the prediction of y using the straight-line model. First, test the null hypothesis that the slope β_1 is 0, that is, that there is no linear relationship between fire damage and the distance from the nearest fire station, against the alternative hypothesis that fire damage increases as the distance increases. We test

$$H_0: \beta_1 = 0$$
$$H_a: \beta_1 > 0$$

The observed significance level for testing $H_a: \beta_1 \neq 0$, highlighted on the printout, is .0001. Thus, the p-value for our one-tailed test is $p = .0001/2 = .00005$. This small p-value leaves little doubt that mean fire damage and distance between the fire and station are at least linearly related, with mean fire damage increasing as the distance increases.

We gain additional information about the relationship by forming a confidence interval for the slope β_1. A 95% confidence interval is

$$\hat{\beta}_1 \pm t_{.025}s_{\hat{\beta}_1}$$

where $\hat{\beta}_1 = 4.919$ and its standard error, $s_{\hat{\beta}_1} = .393$ are both obtained from the printout. The value $t_{.025}$, based on $n - 2 = 13$ df, is 2.160. Therefore, the 95% confidence interval is

$$\hat{\beta}_1 \pm t_{.025}s_{\hat{\beta}_1} = 4.919 \pm (2.160)(.393) = 4.919 \pm .849 = (4.070, 5.768)$$

We estimate that the interval from \$4,070 to \$5,768 encloses the mean increase (β_1) in fire damage per additional mile distance from the fire station.

Another measure of the utility of the model is the coefficient of determination, r^2. The value (highlighted on the printout) is $r^2 = .9235$, which implies that about 92% of the sample variation in fire damage (y) is explained by the distance (x) between the fire and the fire station.

The coefficient of correlation, r, that measures the strength of the linear relationship between y and x is not shown on the SAS printout and must be calculated. Using the facts that $r = \sqrt{r^2}$ in simple linear regression and that r and $\hat{\beta}_1$ have the same sign, we find

$$r = +\sqrt{r^2} = \sqrt{.9235} = .96$$

The high correlation confirms our conclusion that β_1 is greater than 0; it appears that fire damage and distance from the fire station are positively correlated. All signs point to a strong linear relationship between y and x.

Step 5 We are now prepared to use the least squares model. Suppose the insurance company wants to predict the fire damage if a major residential fire were to occur 3.5 miles from the nearest fire station. The predicted value (highlighted at the bottom of the printout) is $\hat{y} = 27.4956$, while the 95% prediction interval (also highlighted) is (22.3239, 32.6672). Therefore, with 95% confidence we predict fire damage in a major residential fire 3.5 miles from the nearest station to be between \$22,324 and \$32,667.

One caution before closing: We would not use this prediction model to make predictions for homes less than .7 mile or more than 6.1 miles from the nearest fire station. A look at the data in Table 9.9 reveals that all the x values fall between .7 and 6.1. It is dangerous to use the model to make predictions outside the region in which the sample data fall. A straight line might not provide a good model for the relationship between the mean value of y and the value of x when stretched over a wider range of x values.

9.10 A NONPARAMETRIC TEST FOR CORRELATION (OPTIONAL)

When the simple linear regression assumptions (Section 9.3) are violated, e.g., the random error ϵ has a highly skewed distribution, an alternative method of analysis is preferred. One technique is to apply a nonparametric test for correlation based on ranks. To illustrate, suppose 10 new car models are evaluated by two

TABLE 9.10 Brake Rankings of 10 New Car Models by Two Consumer Magazines

Car Model	PERFECT AGREEMENT		PERFECT DISAGREEMENT	
	Magazine 1	Magazine 2	Magazine 1	Magazine 2
1	4	4	9	2
2	1	1	3	8
3	7	7	5	6
4	5	5	1	10
5	2	2	2	9
6	6	6	10	1
7	8	8	6	5
8	3	3	4	7
9	10	10	8	3
10	9	9	7	4

consumer magazines and each magazine ranks the braking systems of the cars from 1 (best) to 10 (worst). We want to determine whether the magazines' ranks are related. Does a correspondence exist between their ratings? If a car is ranked high by magazine 1, is it likely to be ranked high by magazine 2? Or do high rankings by one magazine correspond to low rankings by the other? That is, are the rankings of the magazines **correlated**?

If the rankings are as shown in the "Perfect Agreement" columns of Table 9.10, we immediately notice that the magazines agree on the rank of every car. High ranks correspond to high ranks and low ranks to low ranks. This is an example of **perfect positive correlation** between the ranks. In contrast, if the rankings appear as shown in the "Perfect Disagreement" columns of Table 9.10, high ranks for one magazine correspond to low ranks for the other. This is an example of **perfect negative correlation**.

In practice, you will rarely see perfect positive or negative correlation between the ranks. In fact, it is quite possible for the magazines' ranks to appear as shown in Table 9.11. You will note that these rankings indicate some agreement between the consumer magazines, but not perfect agreement, thus indicating a need for a measure of **rank correlation**.

TABLE 9.11 Brake Rankings of New Car Models: Less Than Perfect Agreement

Car Model	MAGAZINE 1	2	DIFFERENCE BETWEEN RANK 1 AND RANK 2 d	d^2
1	4	5	−1	1
2	1	2	−1	1
3	9	10	−1	1
4	5	6	−1	1
5	2	1	1	1
6	10	9	1	1
7	7	7	0	0
8	3	3	0	0
9	6	4	2	4
10	8	8	0	0
				$\Sigma d^2 = 10$

Spearman's rank correlation coefficient, r_s, provides a measure of correlation between ranks. The formula for this measure of correlation is given in the next box. We also give a formula that is identical to r_s when there are no ties in rankings; this provides a good approximation to r_s when the number of ties is small relative to the number of pairs.

Note that if the ranks for the two magazines are identical, as in the second and third columns of Table 9.10, the differences between the ranks, d, will all be 0. Thus,

$$r_s = 1 - \frac{6\sum d^2}{n(n^2 - 1)} = 1 - \frac{6(0)}{10(99)} = 1$$

That is, *perfect positive correlation* between the pairs of ranks is characterized by a Spearman correlation coefficient of $r_s = 1$. When the ranks indicate perfect disagreement, as in the fourth and fifth columns of Table 9.10, $\sum d_i^2 = 330$ and

$$r_s = 1 - \frac{6(330)}{10(99)} = -1$$

Thus, *perfect negative correlation* is indicated by $r_s = -1$.

Spearman's Rank Correlation Coefficient

$$r_s = \frac{SS_{uv}}{\sqrt{SS_{uu}SS_{vv}}}$$

where

$$SS_{uv} = \sum(u_i - \bar{u})(v_i - \bar{v}) = \sum u_i v_i - \frac{\left(\sum u_i\right)\left(\sum v_i\right)}{n}$$

$$SS_{uu} = \sum(u_i - \bar{u})^2 = \sum u_i^2 - \frac{\left(\sum u_i\right)^2}{n}$$

$$SS_{vv} = \sum(v_i - \bar{v})^2 = \sum v_i^2 - \frac{\left(\sum v_i\right)^2}{n}$$

u_i = Rank of the ith observation in sample 1

v_i = Rank of the ith observation in sample 2

n = Number of pairs of observations (number of observations in each sample)

Shortcut Formula for r_s*

$$r_s = 1 - \frac{6\sum d_i^2}{n(n^2 - 1)}$$

where

$d_i = u_i - v_i$ (difference in the ranks of the ith observations for samples 1 and 2)

---

*The shortcut formula is not exact when there are tied measurements, but it is a good approximation when the total number of ties is not large relative to n.

For the data of Table 9.11,

$$r_s = 1 - \frac{6\sum d^2}{n(n^2 - 1)} = 1 - \frac{6(10)}{10(99)} = 1 - \frac{6}{99} = .94$$

The fact that r_s is close to 1 indicates that the magazines tend to agree, but the agreement is not perfect.

The value of r_s *always falls between* −1 *and* +1, *with* +1 *indicating perfect positive correlation and* −1 *indicating perfect negative correlation.* The closer r_s falls to +1 or −1, the greater the correlation between the ranks. Conversely, the nearer r_s is to 0, the less the correlation.

Note that the concept of correlation implies that two responses are obtained for each experimental unit. In the consumer magazine example, each new car model received two ranks (one for each magazine) and the objective of the study was to determine the degree of positive correlation between the two rankings. Rank correlation methods can be used to measure the correlation between any pair of variables. If two variables are measured on each of n experimental units, we rank the measurements associated with each variable separately. Ties receive the average of the ranks of the tied observations. Then we calculate the value of r_s for the two rankings. This value measures the rank correlation between the two variables. We illustrate the procedure in Example 9.5.

EXAMPLE 9.5

Manufacturers of perishable foods often use preservatives to retard spoilage. One concern is that too much preservative will change the flavor of the food. Suppose an experiment is conducted using samples of a food product with varying amounts of preservative added. Both length of time until the food shows signs of spoiling and a taste rating are recorded for each sample. The taste rating is the average rating for three tasters, each of whom rates each sample on a scale from 1 (good) to 5 (bad). Twelve sample measurements are shown in Table 9.12.

a. Calculate Spearman's rank correlation coefficient between spoiling time and taste rating.

b. Use a nonparametric test to find out whether the spoilage times and taste ratings are negatively correlated. Use $\alpha = .05$.

TABLE 9.12   Data and Correlations for Example 9.5

Sample	Days Until Spoilage	Rank	Taste Rating	Rank	d	d^2
1	30	2	4.3	11	−9	81
2	47	5	3.6	7.5	−2.5	6.25
3	26	1	4.5	12	−11	121
4	94	11	2.8	3	8	64
5	67	7	3.3	6	1	1
6	83	10	2.7	2	8	64
7	36	3	4.2	10	−7	49
8	77	9	3.9	9	0	0
9	43	4	3.6	7.5	−3.5	12.25
10	109	12	2.2	1	11	121
11	56	6	3.1	5	1	1
12	70	8	2.9	4	4	16
					Total =	536.5

Note: Tied measurements are assigned the average of the ranks they would be given if they were different but consecutive.

SOLUTION

a. We first rank the days until spoilage, assigning a 1 to the smallest number (26) and a 12 to the largest (109). Similarly, we assign ranks to the 12 taste ratings. [*Note:* The tied taste ratings receive the average of their respective ranks.] Since the number of ties is relatively small, we will use the shortcut formula to calculate r_s. The differences d between the ranks of days until spoilage and the ranks of taste rating are shown in Table 9.12. The squares of the differences, d^2, are also given. Thus,

$$r_s = 1 - \frac{6\sum d_i^2}{n(n^2 - 1)} = 1 - \frac{6(536.5)}{12(12^2 - 1)} = 1 - 1.876 = -.876$$

The value of r_s can also be obtained using a computer. An EXCEL printout of the analysis is shown in Figure 9.27. The value of r_s, highlighted on the printout, is $-.879$ and agrees (except for rounding) with our hand-calculated value. This negative correlation coefficient indicates that in this sample an increase in the number of days until spoilage is *associated with* (but is not necessarily the *cause of*) a decrease in the taste rating.

b. If we define ρ as the **population rank correlation coefficient** [i.e., the rank correlation coefficient that could be calculated from all (x, y) values in the population], this question can be answered by conducting the test

$H_0: \rho = 0$ (no population correlation between ranks)

$H_a: \rho < 0$ (negative population correlation between ranks)

Test statistic: r_s (the *sample* Spearman rank correlation coefficient)

To determine a rejection region, we consult Table XIV in Appendix B, which is partially reproduced in Table 9.13. Note that the left-hand column gives values of n, the number of pairs of observations. The entries in the table are values for an upper-tail rejection region, since only positive values are given. Thus, for $n = 12$ and $\alpha = .05$, the value .497 is the boundary of the upper-tailed rejection region, so that $P(r_s > .497) = .05$ if $H_0: \rho = 0$ is true. Similarly, for negative values of r_s, we have $P(r_s < -.497) = .05$ if $\rho = 0$. That is, we expect to see $r_s < -.497$ only 5% of the time if there is really no relationship between the ranks of the variables. The lower-tailed rejection region is therefore

FIGURE 9.27
EXCEL printout for
Example 9.5

Sample	Days	Taste
1	30	4.3
2	47	3.6
3	26	4.5
4	94	2.8
5	67	3.3
6	83	2.7
7	36	4.2
8	77	3.9
9	43	3.6
10	109	2.2
11	56	3.1
12	70	2.9
Spearman r(s)	-0.879160718	0.000165104

TABLE 9.13 Reproduction of Part of Table XIV in Appendix B: Critical Values of Spearman's Rank Correlation Coefficient

n	$\alpha = .05$	$\alpha = .025$	$\alpha = .01$	$\alpha = .005$
5	.900	—	—	—
6	.829	.886	.943	—
7	.714	.786	.893	—
8	.643	.738	.833	.881
9	.600	.683	.783	.833
10	.564	.648	.745	.794
11	.523	.623	.736	.818
12	.497	.591	.703	.780
13	.475	.566	.673	.745
14	.457	.545	.646	.716
15	.441	.525	.623	.689
16	.425	.507	.601	.666
17	.412	.490	.582	.645
18	.399	.476	.564	.625
19	.388	.462	.549	.608
20	.377	.450	.534	.591

Rejection region ($\alpha = .05$): $r_s < -.497$

Since the calculated $r_s = -.876$ is less than $-.497$, we reject H_0 at the $\alpha = .05$ level of significance. That is, this sample provides sufficient evidence to conclude that a negative correlation exists between number of days until spoilage and taste rating of the food product. It appears that the preservative does affect the taste of this food adversely. [*Note:* The two-tailed p-value of the test is highlighted on the EXCEL printout next to the value of r_s in Figure 9.27. Since the lower-tailed p-value, $p = .00016/2 = .00008$, is less than $\alpha = .05$, our conclusion is the same: reject H_0.]

A summary of Spearman's nonparametric test for correlation is given in the next box.

Spearman's Nonparametric Test for Rank Correlation

One-Tailed Test

$H_0: \rho = 0$

$H_a: \rho > 0$ (or $H_a: \rho < 0$)

Two-Tailed Test

$H_0: \rho = 0$

$H_a: \rho \neq 0$

Test statistic: r_s, the sample rank correlation (see the formulas for calculating r_s)

Rejection region: $r_s > r_{s,\alpha}$
(or $r_s < -r_{s,\alpha}$ when $H_a: \rho_s < 0$)

where $r_{s,\alpha}$ is the value from Table XIV corresponding to the upper-tail area α and n pairs of observations

Rejection region: $|r_s| > r_{s,\alpha/2}$

where $r_{s,\alpha/2}$ is the value from Table XIV corresponding to the upper-tail area $\alpha/2$ and n pairs of observations

Assumptions: 1. The sample of experimental units on which the two variables are measured is randomly selected.

2. The probability distributions of the two variables are continuous.

> *Ties*: Assign tied measurements the average of the ranks they would receive if they were unequal but occurred in successive order. For example, if the third-ranked and fourth-ranked measurements are tied, assign each a rank of $(3 + 4)/2 = 3.5$. The number of ties should be small relative to the total number of observations.

EXERCISES   9.67–9.76

Note: Exercises marked with 💾 *contain data for computer analysis on a 3.5" disk (file name in parentheses).*

Learning the Mechanics

9.67   Specify the rejection region for Spearman's nonparametric test for rank correlation in each of the following situations:
  a. $H_0: \rho = 0; H_a: \rho \neq 0, n = 10, \alpha = .05$
  b. $H_0: \rho = 0; H_a: \rho > 0, n = 20, \alpha = .025$
  c. $H_0: \rho = 0; H_a: \rho < 0, n = 30, \alpha = .01$

9.68   Compute Spearman's rank correlation coefficient for each of the following pairs of sample observations:

a.

x	33	61	20	19	40
y	26	36	65	25	35

b.

x	89	102	120	137	41
y	81	94	75	52	136

c.

x	2	15	4	10
y	11	2	15	21

d.

x	5	20	15	10	3
y	80	83	91	82	87

9.69   The following sample data were collected on variables x and y:

x	0	3	0	−4	3	0	4
y	0	2	2	0	3	1	2

  a. Specify the null and alternative hypotheses that should be used in conducting a hypothesis test to determine whether the variables x and y are correlated.
  b. Conduct the test of part **a** using $\alpha = .05$.
  c. What is the approximate p-value of the test of part **b**?
  d. What assumptions are necessary to ensure the validity of the test of part **b**?

Applying the Concepts

9.70   (X09.070) There has been growing recognition of and appreciation for the role that corporations play in the vitality of metropolitan economies. For example, metropolitan areas with many corporate headquarters are finding it easier to transition from a manufacturing economy to a service economy through job growth in small companies and subsidiaries that service the corporate parent. James O. Wheeler of the University of Georgia studied the relationship between the number of corporate headquarters in eleven metropolitan areas and the number of subsidiaries located there (*Growth and Change*, Spring 1988). He hypothesized that there would be a positive relationship between the variables.

Metropolitan Area	No. of Parent Companies	No. of Subsidiaries
New York	643	2,617
Chicago	381	1,724
Los Angeles	342	1,867
Dallas–Ft. Worth	251	1,238
Detroit	216	890
Boston	208	681
Houston	192	1,534
San Francisco	141	899
Minneapolis	131	492
Cleveland	128	579
Denver	124	672

Source: Wheeler, J. O. "The corporate role of large metropolitan areas in the United States." *Growth and Change*, Spring 1988, pp. 75–88.

  a. Calculate Spearman's rank correlation coefficient for these data. What does it indicate about Wheeler's hypothesis?
  b. To conduct a formal test of Wheeler's hypothesis using Spearman's rank correlation coefficient, certain assumptions must hold. What are they? Do they appear to hold? Explain.

9.71   Universities receive gifts and donations from corporations, foundations, friends, and alumni. It has long been argued that universities rise or fall depending on the level of support of their alumni.

The table below reports the total dollars raised during 1994–1995 by a sample of major U.S. universities. In addition, it reports the percentage of that total donated by alumni:

University	Total Funds Raised	Alumni Contribution
Harvard	$323,406,242	47.5%
Yale	199,646,606	54.6
Cornell	198,736,229	56.2
Wisconsin	164,349,458	17.4
Michigan	145,757,642	45.4
Pennsylvania	135,324,761	34.3
Illinois	116,578,975	36.6
Princeton	103,826,392	53.2
Brown	102,513,437	34.7
Northwestern	101,041,213	27.3

Source: The Chronicle of Higher Education, Sept. 2, 1996, p. 27.

a. Do these data indicate that total fundraising and alumni contributions are correlated? Test using $\alpha = .05$.
b. What assumptions must hold to ensure the validity of your test?

9.72 Two expert wine tasters were asked to rank six brands of wine. Their rankings are shown in the table. Do the data present sufficient evidence to indicate a positive correlation in the rankings of the two experts?

Brand	Expert 1	Expert 2
A	6	5
B	5	6
C	1	2
D	3	1
E	2	4
F	4	3

9.73 **(X09.073)** An *employee suggestion system* is a formal process for capturing, analyzing, implementing, and recognizing employee-proposed organizational improvements. (The first known system was implemented by the Yale and Towne Manufacturing Company of Stamford, Connecticut, in 1880). Using data from the National Association of Suggestion Systems, D. Carnevale and B. Sharp examined the strengths of the relationships between the extent of employee participation in suggestion plans and cost savings realized by employers (*Review of Public Personnel Administration,* Spring 1993). The data in the table are representative of the data they analyzed for 1991 for a sample of federal, state, and local government agencies. Savings are calculated from the first year measurable benefits were observed.

Employee Involvement (% of all employees submitting suggestions)	Savings Rate (% of total budget)
10.1%	8.5%
6.2	6.0
16.3	9.0
1.2	0.0
4.8	5.1
11.5	6.1
.6	1.2
2.8	4.5
8.9	5.4
20.2	15.3
2.7	3.8

Source: Data adapted from Carnevale, D. G., and Sharp, B. S. "The old employee suggestion box." Review of Public Personnel Administration, Spring 1993, pp. 82–92.

a. Explain why the savings data used in this study may understate the total benefits derived from the implemented suggestions.
b. Carnevale and Sharp concluded that a significant moderate positive relationship exists between participation rates and cost savings rates in public sector suggestion systems. Do you agree? Test using $\alpha = .01$.
c. Justify the statistical methodology you used in part **b**.

9.74 **(X09.074)** A *negotiable certificate of deposit* is a marketable receipt for funds deposited in a bank for a specified period of time at a specified rate of interest (Lee, Finnerty, and Norton, 1997). The table at the top of page 513 lists the end-of-quarter interest rate for three-month certificates of deposit from January 1982 through December 1995 with the concurrent end-of-quarter values of Standard & Poor's 500 Stock Composite Average (an indicator of stock market activity).

a. Locate Spearman's rank correlation coefficient on the SAS printout below the table on page 513. [*Note:* To compute Spearman's rank correlation coefficient, SAS first ranks the values of the two variables, then calculates Pearson's correlation coefficient for the ranked values.] Interpret the result.
b. Test the null hypothesis that the interest rate on certificates of deposit and the S&P 500 are not correlated against the alternative hypothesis that these variables are correlated. Use $\alpha = .10$.
c. Repeat parts **a** and **b** using data from 1996 through the present, which can be obtained at your library in *Standard & Poor's Current Statistics.* Compare your results for the newer data with your results for the earlier period.

Year	Quarter	Interest Rate, x	S&P 500, y	Year	Quarter	Interest Rate, x	S&P 500, y
1982	I	14.21	111.96	1989	I	10.09	294.87
	II	14.46	109.61		II	9.20	317.98
	III	10.66	120.42		III	8.78	349.15
	IV	8.66	135.28		IV	8.32	353.40
1983	I	8.69	152.96	1990	I	8.27	339.94
	II	9.20	168.11		II	8.33	358.02
	III	9.39	166.07		III	8.08	306.05
	IV	9.69	164.93		IV	7.96	330.22
1984	I	10.08	159.18	1991	I	6.71	375.22
	II	11.34	153.18		II	6.01	371.16
	III	11.29	166.10		III	5.70	387.86
	IV	8.60	167.24		IV	4.91	417.09
1985	I	9.02	180.66	1992	I	4.25	403.69
	II	7.44	191.85		II	3.86	408.14
	III	7.93	182.08		III	3.13	417.80
	IV	7.80	211.28		IV	3.48	435.71
1986	I	7.24	238.90	1993	I	3.11	451.67
	II	6.73	250.84		II	3.21	450.53
	III	5.71	231.32		III	3.12	458.93
	IV	6.04	242.17		IV	3.17	466.45
1987	I	6.17	291.70	1994	I	3.77	445.77
	II	6.94	304.00		II	4.52	444.27
	III	7.37	321.83		III	5.03	462.69
	IV	7.66	247.08		IV	6.29	459.27
1988	I	6.63	258.89	1995	I	6.15	500.71
	II	7.51	273.50		II	5.90	544.75
	III	8.23	271.91		III	5.73	584.41
	IV	9.25	277.72		IV	5.62	615.93

Source: Standard & Poor's Current Statistics. Standard & Poor's Corporation, 1992, 1996.

```
                         CORRELATION ANALYSIS

 Pearson Correlation Coefficients / Prob > |R| under Ho: Rho=0 / N = 56

                                     INTRANK            SP5RANK

        INTRANK                      1.00000           -0.79215
        RANK FOR VARIABLE INTRATE    0.0                0.0001

        SP5RANK                     -0.79215            1.00000
        RANK FOR VARIABLE SP500      0.0001             0.0
```

9.75 **(X09.075)** The decision to build a new plant or to move an existing plant to a new location involves long-term commitment of both human and monetary resources. Accordingly, such decisions should be made only after carefully considering the relevant factors at alternative sites. G. Michael Epping examined the relationship between the location factors deemed important by businesses that located in Arkansas and those that considered Arkansas but located elsewhere (*Growth and Change,* Apr. 1982). A questionnaire that asked manufacturers to rate the importance of 13 general location factors on a 9-point scale was complet-ed by 118 firms that had moved a plant to Arkansas in the period 1955–1977 and by 73 firms that had considered Arkansas but went elsewhere. Epping averaged the importance ratings and arrived at the rankings shown in the table at the top of page 514. Calculate Spearman's rank correlation coefficient and carefully interpret its value in the context of the problem.

9.76 Health maintenance organizations (HMOs) provide and monitor a variety of short-term outpatient services, including crisis intervention mental health services. To investigate the standards used by HMOs in interpreting crisis intervention, two

Location Factor	Firms Choosing Arkansas: Rank	Firms Rejecting Arkansas: Rank
Labor	1	1
Taxes	2	2
Industrial site	3	4
Information sources, special inducements	4	5
Legislative laws and structure	5	3
Utilities and resources	6	7
Transportation facilities	7	8
Raw material supplies	8	10
Community	9	6
Industrial financing	10	9
Markets	11	12
Business services	12	11
Personal preferences	13	13

researchers (Cheifetz and Salloway, 1985) conducted a comprehensive questionnaire survey of 145 national HMOs. Each HMO was asked to "write a brief, descriptive definition of situations or states you would include as qualifying for 'crisis intervention.'" The researchers sorted these situations into 10 categories and then asked three experienced clinicians to rate each category for two criteria: validity of crisis intervention (i.e., is the situation defined really a "crisis") and clarity of guidelines for offering service. A 4-point rating scale was provided for both criteria. The mean ratings for the 10 categories on both the crisis intervention and clarity scales are given in the table below. Is there evidence of a positive relationship between the mean crisis intervention and mean clarity ratings? Test using $\alpha = .05$.

Category (Situation)	Crisis Intervention Rating (1 = definitely a crisis, 4 = definitely not a crisis)	Clarity Rating (1 = very clear guideline, 4 = very unclear guideline)
Psychosis	1.31	1.33
Drug/alcohol abuse	1.33	1.29
Depression/anxiety	1.48	1.59
Emphasis on acuteness	1.76	2.50
Insistence on "short-term" response	2.48	3.22
Suicide	1.13	1.32
Family problems	2.59	2.30
Violence/harm	1.06	1.86
Miscellaneous	2.60	2.33
Nondefinition	3.57	3.57

Source: Cheifetz, D. I., and Salloway, J. C. "Crisis intervention: Interpretation and practice by HMO." *Medical Care,* Vol. 23, No. 1, Jan. 1985, pp. 89–93.

QUICK REVIEW

Key Terms

Note: Starred (*) terms are from the optional section in this chapter.

Bivariate relationship   479
Coefficient of correlation   479
Coefficient of determination   484
Confidence interval for mean of y 492
Dependent variable   450
Deterministic model   449
Independent variable   450
Least squares line   453

Line of means   450
Method of least squares   454
Pearson product moment coefficient of correlation   479
Prediction interval for y 492
Predictor variable   450
Probabilistic model   449
Random error   449
Rank correlation*   506

Regression analysis   450
Response variable   450
Scattergrams   452
Slope   450

Spearman's rank correlation coefficient*   507
Straight-line (first-order) model   450
y-intercept   450

Key Formulas

Note: Starred (*) formulas are from the optional section in this chapter.

$$\hat{\beta}_1 = \frac{SS_{xy}}{SS_{xx}}, \quad \hat{\beta}_0 = \bar{y} - \hat{\beta}_1\bar{x}$$ Least squares estimates of β's   454

where $SS_{xy} = \sum xy - \frac{(\Sigma x)(\Sigma y)}{n}$

$SS_{xx} = \sum x^2 - \frac{(\Sigma x)^2}{n}$

$$\hat{y} = \hat{\beta}_0 + \hat{\beta}_1 x$$ Least squares line   453

$$SSE = \sum(y_i - \hat{y}_i)^2 = SS_{yy} - \hat{\beta}_1 SS_{xy}$$ Sum of squared errors   463

where $SS_{yy} = \sum y^2 - \frac{(\Sigma y)^2}{n}$

$$s^2 = \frac{SSE}{n-2}$$ Estimated variance of σ^2 of ϵ 463

$$s_{\hat{\beta}_1} = \frac{s}{\sqrt{SS_{xx}}}$$ Estimated standard error of $\hat{\beta}_1$ 469

$$\hat{\beta}_1 \pm (t_{\alpha/2})s_{\hat{\beta}_1}$$ $(1-\alpha)100\%$ confidence interval for β_1 472

$$t = \frac{\hat{\beta}_1}{s_{\hat{\beta}_1}}$$ Test statistic for $H_0: \beta_1 = 0$ 470

$$r^2 = \frac{SS_{yy} - SSE}{SS_{yy}}$$ Coefficient of determination   484

$$r = \frac{SS_{xy}}{\sqrt{SS_{xx}SS_{yy}}} = \pm\sqrt{r^2} \text{ (same sign as } \hat{\beta}_1)$$ Coefficient of correlation   479

$$\hat{y} \pm (t_{\alpha/2})s\sqrt{\frac{1}{n} + \frac{(x_p - \bar{x})^2}{SS_{xx}}}$$ $(1-\alpha)100\%$ confidence interval for $E(y)$ when $x = x_p$ 492

$$\hat{y} \pm (t_{\alpha/2})s\sqrt{1 + \frac{1}{n} + \frac{(x_p - \bar{x})^2}{SS_{xx}}}$$ $(1-\alpha)100\%$ prediction interval for y when $x = x_p$ 492

$$r_s = 1 - \frac{6\sum d_i^2}{n(n^2-1)}$$ Spearman's rank correlation coefficient*   507

where d_i = difference in ranks of
x-value and y-value
for ith observation

LANGUAGE LAB

Note: Starred (*) symbols are from the optional section in this chapter.

Symbol	Pronunciation	Description
y		Dependent variable (variable to be predicted or modeled)
x		Independent (predictor) variable
$E(y)$		Expected (mean) value of y
β_0	beta-zero	y-intercept of true line

β_1	beta-one	Slope of true line
$\hat{\beta}_0$	beta-zero hat	Least squares estimate of y-intercept
$\hat{\beta}_1$	beta-one hat	Least squares estimate of slope
ϵ	epsilon	Random error
$\hat{y}$	y-hat	Predicted value of y
$(y - \hat{y})$		Error of prediction
SE		Sum of errors (will equal zero with least squares line)
SSE		Sum of squared errors (will be smallest for least squares line)
SS_{xx}		Sum of squares of x-values
SS_{yy}		Sum of squares of y-values
SS_{xy}		Sum of squares of cross-products, $x \cdot y$
r		Coefficient of correlation
r^2	R-squared	Coefficient of determination
x_p		Value of x used to predict y
r_s^*	r-s	Spearman's rank correlation coefficient

SUPPLEMENTARY EXERCISES 9.77–9.91

Note: Exercises marked with ▇ contain data for computer analysis on a 3.5" disk (file name in parentheses). Starred (*) exercises are from the optional section in this chapter.

Learning the Mechanics

9.77 In fitting a least squares line to $n = 15$ data points, the following quantities were computed: $SS_{xx} = 55$, $SS_{yy} = 198$, $SS_{xy} = -88$, $\bar{x} = 1.3$, and $\bar{y} = 35$.
  a. Find the least squares line.
  b. Graph the least squares line.
  c. Calculate SSE.
  d. Calculate s^2.
  e. Find a 90% confidence interval for β_1. Interpret this estimate.
  f. Find a 90% confidence interval for the mean value of y when $x = 15$.
  g. Find a 90% prediction interval for y when $x = 15$.

9.78 Consider the following sample data:

y	5	1	3
x	5	1	3

  a. Construct a scattergram for the data.
  b. It is possible to find many lines for which $\Sigma(y - \hat{y}) = 0$. For this reason, the criterion $\Sigma(y - \hat{y}) = 0$ is not used for identifying the "best-fitting" straight line. Find two lines that have $\Sigma(y - \hat{y}) = 0$.
  c. Find the least squares line.
  d. Compare the value of SSE for the least squares line to that of the two lines you found in part **b**. What principle of least squares is demonstrated by this comparison?

9.79 Consider the following 10 data points:

x	3	5	6	4	3	7	6	5	4	7
y	4	3	2	1	2	3	3	5	4	2

  a. Plot the data on a scattergram.
  b. Calculate the values of r and r^2.
  c. Is there sufficient evidence to indicate that x and y are linearly correlated? Test at the $\alpha = .10$ level of significance.

Applying the Concepts

9.80 (X09.080) Emotional exhaustion, or *burnout*, is a significant problem for people with careers in the field of human services. It seriously affects productivity and feelings of job satisfaction. Regression analysis was used to investigate the relationship between burnout and aspects of the human services professional's job and job-related behavior (*Journal of Applied Behavioral Science*, Vol. 22, 1986). Emotional exhaustion was measured with the Maslach Burnout Inventory, a questionnaire. One of the independent variables considered, called *concentration*, was the proportion of social contacts with individuals who belong to a person's work group. The table at the top of page 517 lists the values of the emotional exhaustion index (higher values indicate greater exhaustion) and concentration for a sample of 25 human services professionals who work in a large public hospital. An SPSS printout of the simple linear regression follows the table.
  a. Construct a scattergram for the data. Do the variables x and y appear to be related?
  b. Find the correlation coefficient for the data and interpret its value. Does your conclusion

Exhaustion Index, y	Concentration, x	Exhaustion Index, y	Concentration, x
100	20%	493	86%
525	60	892	83
300	38	527	79
980	88	600	75
310	79	855	81
900	87	709	75
410	68	791	77
296	12	718	77
120	35	684	77
501	70	141	17
920	80	400	85
810	92	970	96
506	77		

```
Correlations:    CONCEN

  EXHAUST         .7825**

N of cases:      25        1-tailed Signif:  * - .01  ** - .001

---------------------------------------------------------------------
          * * * *   M U L T I P L E   R E G R E S S I O N   * * * *
Equation Number 1    Dependent Variable..   EXHAUST

Variable(s) Entered on Step Number
   1..    CONCEN

Multiple R            .78250
R Square              .61231
Adjusted R Square     .59545
Standard Error    174.20742

Analysis of Variance
                  DF      Sum of Squares      Mean Square
Regression         1       1102408.24475    1102408.24475
Residual          23        698009.19525      30348.22588

F =      36.32529      Signif F =  .0000

-------------------- Variables in the Equation -----------------------

Variable             B         SE B      95% Confdnce Intrvl B         T    Sig T

CONCEN         8.865471    1.470948     5.822584    11.908359     6.027    .0000
(Constant)   -29.496718  106.697163  -250.216617   191.223182     -.276    .7847
```

mean that concentration causes emotional exhaustion? Explain.

c. Test the usefulness of the straight-line relationship with concentration for predicting burnout. Use $\alpha = .05$.

d. Find the coefficient of determination for the model and interpret it.

e. Find a 95% confidence interval for the slope β_1. Interpret the result.

f. Use a 95% confidence interval to estimate the mean exhaustion level for all professionals who have 80% of their social contacts within their work groups. Interpret the interval.

9.81 *Work standards* specify time, cost, and efficiency norms for the performance of work tasks. They are typically used to monitor job performance. In the distribution center of McCormick and Co., Inc., data were collected to develop work standards for the time to assemble or fill customer orders. The table at the top of page 518 contains data for a random sample of 9 orders.

a. Construct a scattergram for these data and interpret it.

b. Fit a least squares line to these data using time as the dependent variable.

Time (mins.)	Order Size (cases)
27	36
15	34
71	255
35	103
8	4
60	555
3	6
10	60
10	96

Source: Boyle, D., Ray, B. A., and Kahan, G. "Work standards—the quality way." *Production and Inventory Management Journal,* Second Quarter, 1991, p. 67.

c. In general, we would expect the mean time to fill an order to increase with the size of the order. Do the data support this theory? Test using $\alpha = .05$.

d. Find a 95% confidence interval for the mean time to fill an order consisting of 150 cases.

9.82 Common maize rust is a serious disease of sweet corn. Although fungicides are effective in controlling maize rust, the timing of the application is crucial. Researchers in New York state have developed an action threshold for initiation of fungicide applications based on a regression equation relating maize rust incidence to severity of the disease (*Phytopathology,* Vol. 80, 1990). In one particular field, data were collected on more than 100 plants of the sweet corn hybrid Jubilee. For each plant, incidence was measured as the percentage of leaves infected (x) and severity was calculated as the log (base 10) of the average number of infections per leaf (y). A simple linear regression analysis of the data produced the following results:

$$\hat{y} = -.939 + .020x$$

$$r^2 = .816$$

$$s = .288$$

a. Interpret the value of $\hat{\beta}_1$.

b. Interpret the value of r^2.

c. Interpret the value of s.

d. Calculate the value of r and interpret it.

e. Use the result, part **d**, to test the utility of the model. Use $\alpha = .05$. (Assume $n = 100$.)

f. Predict the severity of the disease when the incidence of maize rust for a plant is 80%. [*Note:* Take the antilog (base 10) of $\hat{y}$ to obtain the predicted average number of infections per leaf.]

9.83 In 1995, nearly half of all eating places in the United States were fast-food restaurants. These include nontraditional sites, such as hospitals, airports, gas stations, and department stores. For a sample of eight well-known fast-food chains, the table below reports the year each began franchising and the number of outlets each had in 1996. Is there a linear relationship between age of a fast-food chain and its number of outlets? Answer the question by conducting a complete simple linear regression analysis of the data.

*9.84 (X09.084) D. Campbell, J. Gaertner, and R. Vecchio investigated the perceptions of accounting professors with respect to the present and desired importance of various factors considered in promotion and tenure decisions at major universities (*Journal of Education,* Spring 1983). One hundred fifteen professors at universities with accredited doctoral programs responded to a mailed questionnaire. The questionnaire asked the professors to rate (1) the actual importance placed on 20 factors in the promotion and tenure decisions at their universities and (2) how they believe the factors *should* be weighted. Responses were obtained on a 5-point scale ranging from "no importance" to "extreme importance." The resulting ratings were averaged and converted to the rankings shown in the table at the top of page 519. Calculate Spearman's rank correlation coefficient for the data and carefully interpret its value in the context of the problem.

Restaurant	Year Began Franchising	Number of Outlets in 1996
McDonald's	1955	8,282
Dunkin' Donuts	1955	2,927
Wendy's	1971	3,002
Pizza Hut	1959	2,738
Taco Bell	1964	1,704
KFC	1971	5,142
TCBY	1982	1,148
Blimpie	1977	986

Source: Franchise Times, October 1996, pp. 14–55.

Factor	Actual	Ideal
I. Teaching (and related items):		
Teaching performance	6	1
Advising and counseling students	19	15
Students' complaints/praise	14	17
II. Research:		
Number of journal articles	1	6.5
Quality of journal articles	4	2
Refereed publications:		
a. Applied studies	5	4
b. Theoretical empirical studies	2	3
c. Educationally oriented	11	8
Papers at professional meetings	10	12
Journal editor or reviewer	9	10
Other (textbooks, etc.)	7.5	11
III. Service and professional interaction:		
Service to profession	15	9
Professional/academic awards	7.5	6.5
Community service	18	19
University service	16	16
Collegiality/cooperativeness	12	13
IV. Other:		
Academic degrees attained	3	5
Professional certification	17	14
Consulting activities	20	20
Grantsmanship	13	18

Source: Campbell, D. K., Gaertner, J., and Vecchio, R. P. "Perceptions of promotion and tenure criteria: A survey of accounting educators." *Journal of Accounting Education,* Vol. 1, Spring 1983, pp. 83–92.

9.85 **(X09.085)** In the late 1970s and early 1980s, the prices of single-family homes in the United States rose faster than the rate of inflation. As a result, many investors directed their funds to the housing market as a hedge against inflation. One way an investor can assess the value of a specific house is to compare it to recent sale prices for similar houses. Another popular approach is to use a regression analysis to model the relationship between price and the variables that influence price. Independent variables that could be utilized are total living area, number of rooms, number of baths, age of property, and so on. Of these factors, total living area provides the most information for determining the worth of a house. The table below lists the final selling price and total living area for a sample of 24 homes in suburban Essex county, New Jersey, that were sold during the first three months of 1996. The SAS regression printout for a straight-line model relating price to area for these data is shown on the top of page 520.

a. Construct a scattergram for the data.

b. Find the least squares line and plot it on your scattergram.

c. Find r^2 and interpret its value in the context of the problem.

d. Do the data provide evidence that living area contributes information for predicting the price of a home? Use $\alpha = .05$.

e. Find a 95% confidence interval for β_1. Does your confidence interval support the conclusion you reached in part **d**? Explain.

f. Find the observed significance level for the test in part **d**, and interpret its value.

g. Estimate the mean selling price for homes with a total living area of 3,000 square feet. Use a 95% confidence interval.

9.86 Refer to Exercise 9.40, in which managerial success, y, was modeled as a function of the number of contacts a manager makes with people outside his or her work unit, x, during a specific period of time. The data are repeated in the table on page 520, and the MINITAB simple linear regression printout is shown at the top of page 521.

Area (sq. ft.)	Price	Area (sq. ft.)	Price
2,306	$145,541	1,753	129,900
2,677	179,900	3,206	235,000
2,324	149,000	2,474	129,900
1,447	113,900	2,933	199,500
3,333	189,000	3,987	319,000
3,004	184,500	2,598	185,500
4,142	339,717	4,934	375,000
2,923	228,000	2,253	169,000
2,902	209,000	2,998	185,900
1,847	133,000	2,791	189,800
2,148	168,000	2,865	192,000
2,819	205,000	4,417	379,900

Source: Adapted from data compiled by the Multiple Listing Service, Suburban Essex County, New Jersey, 1996.

Dependent Variable: PRICE

Analysis of Variance

Source	DF	Sum of Squares	Mean Square	F Value	Prob>F
Model	1	115571437221	115571437221	194.384	0.0001
Error	22	13080132976	594551498.89		
C Total	23	128651570197			

Root MSE	24383.42673	R-square	0.8983	
Dep Mean	205623.25000	Adj R-sq	0.8937	
C.V.	11.85830			

Parameter Estimates

Variable	DF	Parameter Estimate	Standard Error	T for HO: Parameter=0	Prob > |T|
INTERCEP	1	-39001	18237.940955	-2.138	0.0438
AREA	1	84.986976	6.09567579	13.942	0.0001

Obs	AREA	Dep Var PRICE	Predict Value	Std Err Predict	Lower95% Mean	Upper95% Mean	Residual
25	3000	.	215960	5032.160	205524	226396	.

Manager	Manager Success Index, y	Number of Interactions with Outsiders, x
1	40	12
2	73	71
3	95	70
4	60	81
5	81	43
6	27	50
7	53	42
8	66	18
9	25	35
10	63	82
11	70	20
12	47	81
13	80	40
14	51	33
15	32	45
16	50	10
17	52	65
18	30	20
19	42	21

a. A particular manager was observed for two weeks, as in the *Journal of Applied Behavioral Science* (1985) study. She made 55 contacts with people outside her work unit. Predict the value of the manager's success index. Use a 90% prediction interval.

b. A second manager was observed for two weeks. This manager made 110 contacts with people outside his work unit. Give two reasons why caution should be exercised in using the least squares model developed from the given data set to construct a prediction interval for this manager's success index.

c. In the context of this problem, determine the value of x for which the associated prediction interval for y is the narrowest.

9.87 (X09.087) Firms planning to build new plants or make additions to existing facilities have become very conscious of the energy efficiency of proposed new structures and are interested in the relation between yearly energy consumption and the number of square feet of building shell. The next table lists the energy consumption in British thermal units (a BTU is the amount of heat required to raise 1 pound of water 1°F) for 22 buildings that were all subjected to the same climatic conditions. The SAS printout that fits the straight-line model relating BTU consumption, y, to building shell area, x, is on page 522.

a. Find the least squares estimates of the intercept β_0 and the slope β_1.

b. Investigate the usefulness of the model you developed in part **a**. Is yearly energy consumption positively linearly related to the shell area of the building? Test using $\alpha = .10$.

c. Calculate the observed significance level of the test of part **b** using the printout. Interpret its value.

d. Find the coefficient of determination r^2 and interpret its value.

e. A company wishes to build a new warehouse that will contain 8,000 square feet of shell area.

```
The regression equation is
SUCCESS = 44.1 + 0.237 INTERACT

Predictor        Coef        Stdev       t-ratio          p
Constant       44.130        9.362         4.71        0.000
INTERACT       0.2366        0.1865        1.27        0.222

s = 19.40          R-sq = 8.6%        R-sq(adj) = 3.3%

Analysis of Variance

SOURCE           DF          SS           MS          F          p
Regression        1        606.0        606.0       1.61      0.222
Error            17       6400.6        376.5
Total            18       7006.6
```

BTU/Year (thousands)	Shell Area (square feet)
3,870,000	30,001
1,371,000	13,530
2,422,000	26,060
672,200	6,355
233,100	4,576
218,900	24,680
354,000	2,621
3,135,000	23,350
1,470,000	18,770
1,408,000	12,220
2,201,000	25,490
2,680,000	23,680
337,500	5,650
567,500	8,001
555,300	6,147
239,400	2,660
2,629,000	19,240
1,102,000	10,700
423,500	9,125
423,500	6,510
1,691,000	13,530
1,870,000	18,860

Find the predicted value of energy consumption and a 95% prediction interval on the printout. Comment on the usefulness of this interval.

f. The application of the model you developed in part **a** to the warehouse problem of part **e** is appropriate only if certain assumptions can be made about the new warehouse. What are these assumptions?

*9.88 (X09.088) It has been conjectured that income is a primary determinant of job satisfaction. To investigate this theory, 15 employees of a particular firm are chosen at random and their gross salaries are noted. Each employee is then asked to complete a questionnaire designed to measure job satisfaction. The resulting scores (higher scores mean greater satisfaction) and gross incomes (in thousands of dollars) are given in the table at right.

a. Compute Spearman's rank correlation coefficient for these data.
b. Is there evidence that job satisfaction and income are positively correlated? Use $\alpha = .05$.
c. Is there evidence that the median job score of all employees of the firm exceeds 75? Use $\alpha = .05$.

Employee	Job Score	Income
1	92	29.9
2	51	18.7
3	88	32.0
4	65	15.0
5	80	26.0
6	31	9.0
7	38	11.3
8	75	22.1
9	45	16.0
10	72	25.0
11	53	17.2
12	43	9.7
13	87	20.1
14	30	15.5
15	74	16.5

9.89 (X09.089) *Comparable worth* is a compensation plan designed to eliminate pay inequities among jobs of similar worth. A number of state and municipal governments have adopted comparable-worth plans, and some unions have attempted to negotiate comparable-worth clauses into their contracts. To develop such a plan, a sample of benchmark jobs are evaluated and assigned points, x, based on factors such as responsibility, skill, effort, and working conditions. A market survey is conducted to determine the market rates (or salaries), y, of the benchmark jobs. A regression analysis is then used to characterize the relationship between salary and job evaluation points (*Public Personnel Management*, Vol. 20, 1991). The table at the top of page 523 gives

Dep Variable: BTU

Analysis of Variance

Source	DF	Sum of Squares	Mean Square	F Value	Prob>F
Model	1	1.658498E+13	1.658498E+13	42.028	0.0001
Error	20	7.89232E+12	394616010047		
C Total	21	2.44773E+13			

Root MSE	628184.69422	R-Square	0.6776
Dep Mean	1357904.54545	Adj R-Sq	0.6614
C.V.	46.26133		

Parameter Estimates

Variable	DF	Parameter Estimate	Standard Error	T for H0: Parameter=0	Prob > |T|
INTERCEP	1	-99045	261617.65980	-0.379	0.7090
AREA	1	102.814048	15.85924082	6.483	0.0001

Obs	AREA	BTU	Predict Value	Residual	Lower95% Predict	Upper95% Predict
1	30001	3870000	2985479	884521	1546958	4424000
2	13530	1371000	1292029	78971.2	-47949.3	2632007
3	26060	2422000	2580289	-158289	1183940	3976637
4	6355	672200	554338	117862	-810192	1918868
5	4576	233100	371432	-138332	-1005463	1748327
6	24680	218900	2438405	-2219505	1054223	3822588
7	2621	354000	170430	183570	-1222796	1563657
8	23350	3135000	2301663	833337	927871	3675455
9	18770	1470000	1830774	-360774	482352	3179196
10	12220	1408000	1157342	250658	-184021	2498706
11	25490	2201000	2521685	-320685	1130530	3912840
12	23680	2680000	2335591	344409	959345	3711838
13	5650	337500	481854	-144354	-887287	1850995
14	8001	567500	723570	-156070	-631698	2078838
15	6147	555300	532953	22347.3	-832898	1898804
16	2660	239400	174440	64959.9	-1218433	1567313
17	19240	2629000	1879097	749903	528832	3229362
18	10700	1102000	1001065	100935	-343656	2345786
19	9125	423500	839133	-415633	-511035	2189301
20	6510	423500	570274	-146774	-793294	1933842
21	13530	1691000	1292029	398971	-47949.3	2632007
22	18860	1870000	1840028	29972.3	491266	3188789
23	8000	.	723467	.	-631806	2078740

Sum of Residuals	1.6298145E-9
Sum of Squared Residuals	7.89232E+12
Predicted Resid SS (Press)	1.012747E+13

the job evaluation points and salaries for a set of 21 benchmark jobs.

a. Construct a scattergram for these data. What does it suggest about the relationship between salary and job evaluation points?

b. The SAS printout on page 524 shows the results of a straight-line model fit to these data. Identify and interpret the least squares equation.

c. Interpret the value of r^2 for this least squares equation.

d. Is there sufficient evidence to conclude that a straight-line model provides useful information about the relationship in question? Interpret the p-value for this test.

e. A job outside the set of benchmark jobs is evaluated and receives a score of 800 points.

Job Evaluation Points, x	Salary, y	
970	$15,704	Electrician
500	13,984	Semiskilled laborer
370	14,196	Motor equipment operator
220	13,380	Janitor
250	13,153	Laborer
1,350	18,472	Senior engineering technician
470	14,193	Senior janitor
2,040	20,642	Revenue agent
370	13,614	Engineering aide
1,200	16,869	Electrician supervisor
820	15,184	Senior maintenance technician
1,865	17,341	Registered nurse
1,065	15,194	Licensed practical nurse
880	13,614	Principal clerk typist
340	12,594	Clerk typist
540	13,126	Senior clerk stenographer
490	12,958	Senior clerk typist
940	13,894	Principal clerk stenographer
600	13,380	Institutional attendant
805	15,559	Eligibility technician
220	13,844	Cook's helper

Under the comparable-worth plan, what is a reasonable range within which a fair salary for this job should be found?

9.90 **(X09.090)** The table below lists the 1994 sales y (in millions of dollars) and number of employees x (in thousands) for a random sample of 20 *Fortune* 500 companies. Perform a regression analysis that follows the five steps presented in this chapter; be sure to state all assumptions you make. Give a prediction interval for a *Fortune* 500 company with 50,000 employees.

9.91 Refer to Exercise 9.65, in which a cost function for a rug manufacturer was estimated. The table below provides data on a second cost driver— "direct manufacturing labor-hours"—for this company.

Company	Sales, y (in millions of dollars)	Employees, x (in thousands)
Time Warner	7,396	28.8
AGWAY	3,017	7.9
Boeing	21,924	115.0
QVC	1,390	6.7
Fruit of the Loom	2,298	37.4
Lennar	818	1.5
ILLINOVA	1,590	4.3
Adolph Coors	1,663	6.3
Sara Lee	15,536	145.9
Bear Stearns	3,441	7.3
Hercules	2,821	11.9
Valspar	787	2.5
Teledyne	2,391	18.0
U.S. BANCORP	1,936	10.6
First Security Corp.	980	7.6
ITT	23,767	110.0
Equifax	1,422	14.2
Atlantic Energy	816	1.7
UNISYS	7,400	46.3
Detroit Edison	3,519	8.4

Source: "The Fortune 500." *Fortune,* May 15, 1995.

Week	Indirect Manufacturing Labor Costs	Machine-Hours	Direct Manufacturing Labor-Hours
1	$1,190	68	30
2	1,211	88	35
3	1,004	62	36
4	917	72	20
5	770	60	47
6	1,456	96	45
7	1,180	78	44
8	710	46	38
9	1,316	82	70
10	1,032	94	30
11	752	68	29
12	963	48	38

Source: Data and exercise adapted from Horngren, C. T., Foster, G., and Datar, S. M. *Cost Accounting,* Englewood Cliffs, N.J.: Prentice-Hall, 1994.

Your task is to estimate and compare two alternative cost functions. In the first, machine-hours is the independent variable; in the second, direct manufacturing labor-hours is the independent variable. Prepare a report that compares the two cost functions and recommends which should be used to explain and predict indirect manufacturing labor costs. Be sure to justify your choice.

Dependent Variable: Y

Analysis of Variance

Source	DF	Sum of Squares	Mean Square	F Value	Prob>F
Model	1	66801750.334	66801750.334	74.670	0.0001
Error	19	16997968.904	894629.94232		
C Total	20	83799719.238			

Root MSE	945.84879	R-square	0.7972	
Dep Mean	14804.52381	Adj R-sq	0.7865	
C.V.	6.38892			

Parameter Estimates

Variable	DF	Parameter Estimate	Standard Error	T for HO: Parameter=0	Prob > |T|
INTERCEP	1	12024	382.31829064	31.449	0.0001
X	1	3.581616	0.41448305	8.641	0.0001

Obs	X	Dep Var Y	Predict Value	Std Err Predict	Lower95% Predict	Upper95% Predict	Residual
1	970	15704.0	15497.8	221.447	13464.6	17531.0	206.2
2	500	13984.0	13814.5	236.070	11774.1	15854.9	169.5
3	370	14196.0	13348.9	266.420	11292.1	15405.6	847.1
4	220	13380.0	12811.6	309.502	10728.6	14894.6	568.4
5	250	13153.0	12919.1	300.351	10842.0	14996.2	233.9
6	1350	18472.0	16858.8	314.833	14772.4	18945.3	1613.2
7	470	14193.0	13707.0	242.349	11663.4	15750.6	486.0
8	2040	20642.0	19330.2	562.933	17026.4	21633.9	1311.8
9	370	13614.0	13348.9	266.420	11292.1	15405.6	265.1
10	1200	16869.0	16321.6	270.968	14262.3	18380.9	547.4
11	820	15184.0	14960.6	207.190	12934.0	16987.2	223.4
12	1865	17341.0	18703.4	496.193	16467.8	20938.9	-1362.4
13	1065	15194.0	15838.1	238.553	13796.4	17879.8	-644.1
14	880	13614.0	15175.5	210.818	13147.2	17203.7	-1561.5
15	340	12594.0	13241.4	274.451	11180.1	15302.7	-647.4
16	540	13126.0	13957.7	228.483	11921.1	15994.4	-831.7
17	490	12958.0	13778.6	238.109	11737.2	15820.1	-820.6
18	940	13894.0	15390.4	217.251	13359.1	17421.6	-1496.4
19	600	13380.0	14172.6	218.972	12140.6	16204.7	-792.6
20	805	15559.0	14906.9	206.741	12880.4	16933.3	652.1
21	220	13844.0	12811.6	309.502	10728.6	14894.6	1032.4
22	800	.	14888.9	206.632	12862.6	16915.3	.

CHAPTER 10

INTRODUCTION TO MULTIPLE REGRESSION

CONTENTS

10.1   The General Linear Model

10.2   Fitting the Model: The Least Squares Approach

10.3   Model Assumptions

10.4   Inferences About the β Parameters

10.5   Checking the Usefulness of a Model: R^2 and the Global F-Test

10.6   Using the Model for Estimation and Prediction

10.7   Residual Analysis: Checking the Regression Assumptions

10.8   Some Pitfalls: Estimability, Multicollinearity, and Extrapolation

STATISTICS IN ACTION

10.1   Predicting the Price of Vintage Red Bordeaux Wine

10.2   "Wringing" *The Bell Curve*

Where We've Been

In Chapter 9 we saw how to model the relationship between a dependent variable y and an independent variable x using a straight line. We fit the straight line to the data points, used r and r^2 to measure the strength of the relationship between y and $x,$ and used the resulting prediction equation to estimate the mean value of y or to predict some future value of y for a given value of x.

Where We're Going

This chapter extends the basic concept of Chapter 9, converting it into a powerful estimation and prediction device by modeling the mean value of y as a function of two or more independent variables. The techniques developed will enable you to model a response, $y,$ as a function of both quantitative and qualitative variables. As in the case of a simple linear regression, a multiple regression analysis involves fitting the model to a data set, testing the utility of the model, and using it for estimation and prediction.

10.1 THE GENERAL LINEAR MODEL

Most practical applications of regression analysis utilize models that are more complex than the simple straight-line model. For example, a realistic probabilistic model for monthly sales revenue would include more than just advertising expenditures. Factors such as season, inventory on hand, size of sales force, and price are a few of the many variables that might influence sales. Thus, we would want to incorporate these and other potentially important independent variables into the model in order to make accurate predictions.

Probabilistic models that include more than one independent variable are called **multiple regression models**. The general form of these models is

$$y = \beta_0 + \beta_1 x_1 + \beta_2 x_2 + \cdots + \beta_k x_k + \epsilon$$

Since the dependent variable y is now written as a linear function of k independent variables, $x_1, x_2, \ldots, x_k$, the model is also termed a **general linear model**. The random error term is added to make the model probabilistic rather than deterministic. The value of the coefficient β_i determines the contribution of the independent variable x_i, and β_0 is the y-intercept. The coefficients $\beta_0, \beta_1, \ldots, \beta_k$ are usually unknown because they represent population parameters.

At first glance it might appear that the general linear model shown above would not allow for anything other than straight-line relationships between y and the independent variables, but this is not true. Actually, $x_1, x_2, \ldots, x_k$ can be functions of variables as long as the functions do not contain unknown parameters. For example, the dollar sales, y, in new housing in a region could be a function of the independent variables

$$x_1 = \text{Mortgage interest rate}$$

$$x_2 = (\text{Mortgage interest rate})^2 = x_1^2$$

$$x_3 = \text{Unemployment rate in the region}$$

and so on. You could even insert a cyclical term (if it would be useful) of the form $x_4 = \sin t$, where t is a time variable. The multiple regression model is quite versatile and can be made to model many different types of response variables.

The General Linear Model

$$y = \beta_0 + \beta_1 x_1 + \beta_2 x_2 + \cdots + \beta_k x_k + \epsilon$$

where

y is the dependent variable

$x_1, x_2, \ldots, x_k$ are the independent variables

$E(y) = \beta_0 + \beta_1 x_1 + \beta_2 x_2 + \cdots + \beta_k x_k$ is the deterministic portion of the model

β_i determines the contribution of the independent variable x_i

Note: The symbols $x_1, x_2, \ldots, x_k$ may represent higher-order terms. For example, x_1 might represent the current interest rate, x_2 might represent x_1^2, and so forth.

As shown in the next box, we use the same steps to develop the multiple regression model as we used for the simple regression model.

Analyzing a Multiple Regression Model

Step 1 Hypothesize the deterministic component of the model. This component relates the mean, $E(y)$, to the independent variables $x_1, x_2, ..., x_k$. This involves the choice of the independent variables to be included in the model.

Step 2 Use the sample data to estimate the unknown model parameters $\beta_0, \beta_1, \beta_2, ..., \beta_k$ in the model.

Step 3 Specify the probability distribution of the random error term, ϵ, and estimate the standard deviation of this distribution, σ.

Step 4 Statistically evaluate the usefulness of the model.

Step 5 When satisfied that the model is useful, use it for prediction, estimation, and other purposes.

In the process of covering these five steps, we introduce several different types of multiple regression models in this chapter.

10.2 FITTING THE MODEL: THE LEAST SQUARES APPROACH

The method of fitting multiple regression models is identical to that of fitting the simple straight-line model: the method of least squares. That is, we choose the estimated model

$$\hat{y} = \hat{\beta}_0 + \hat{\beta}_1 x_1 + \cdots + \hat{\beta}_k x_k$$

that minimizes

$$\text{SSE} = \sum(y - \hat{y})^2$$

As in the case of the simple linear model, the sample estimates $\hat{\beta}_0, \hat{\beta}_1, ..., \hat{\beta}_k$ are obtained as a solution to a set of simultaneous linear equations.*

The primary difference between fitting the simple and multiple regression models is computational difficulty. The $(k+1)$ simultaneous linear equations that must be solved to find the $(k+1)$ estimated coefficients $\hat{\beta}_0, \hat{\beta}_1, ..., \hat{\beta}_k$ are difficult (sometimes nearly impossible) to solve with a calculator. Consequently, we resort to the use of computers exclusively, presenting output from the SAS, SPSS, MINITAB, and EXCEL statistical software packages. We demonstrate the SAS regression output with the following example.

In all-electric homes the amount of electricity expended is of interest to consumers, builders, and groups involved with energy conservation. Suppose we wish to investigate the monthly electrical usage, y, in all-electric homes and its relationship to the size, x, of the home. Moreover, suppose we think that monthly electrical usage in all-electric homes is related to the size of the home by the model

$$y = \beta_0 + \beta_1 x + \beta_2 x^2 + \epsilon$$

To estimate the unknown parameters β_0, β_1, and β_2, values of y and x are collected for 10 homes during a particular month. The data are shown in Table 10.1.

*Students who are familiar with calculus should note that $\hat{\beta}_0, \hat{\beta}_1, ..., \hat{\beta}_k$ are the solutions to the set of equations $\partial\text{SSE}/\partial\hat{\beta}_0 = 0$, $\partial\text{SSE}/\partial\hat{\beta}_1 = 0$, ..., $\partial\text{SSE}/\partial\hat{\beta}_k = 0$. The solution is usually given in matrix form, but we do not present the details here. See the references for details.

TABLE 10.1 **Home Size–Electrical Usage Data**

Size of Home x (sq. ft.)	Monthly Usage y (kilowatt-hours)
1,290	1,182
1,350	1,172
1,470	1,264
1,600	1,493
1,710	1,571
1,840	1,711
1,980	1,804
2,230	1,840
2,400	1,956
2,930	1,954

Notice that we include a term involving x^2 in this model because we expect curvature in the graph of the response model relating y to x. The term involving x^2 is called a **quadratic term**. Figure 10.1 illustrates that the electrical usage appears to increase in a curvilinear manner with the size of the home. This provides some support for the inclusion of the quadratic term x^2 in the model.

Part of the output from the SAS multiple regression routine for the data in Table 10.1 is reproduced in Figure 10.2. The least squares estimates of the β parameters appear in the column labeled **Parameter Estimate**. You can see that $\hat{\beta}_0 = -1,216.1, \hat{\beta}_1 = 2.3989$, and $\hat{\beta}_2 = -.00045$. Therefore, the equation that minimizes the SSE for the data is

$$\hat{y} = -1,216.1 + 2.3989x - .00045x^2$$

The minimum value of the SSE, 15,332.6, also appears (highlighted) in the printout. [*Note:* Throughout this chapter we highlight the aspects of the printout that are under discussion.]

Note that the graph of the multiple regression model (Figure 10.3, a response curve) provides a good fit to the data of Table 10.1. Furthermore, the small value of $\hat{\beta}_2$ does *not* imply that the curvature is insignificant, since the numerical value of $\hat{\beta}_2$ depends on the scale of the measurements. We will test the contribution of the quadratic coefficient $\hat{\beta}_2$ in Section 10.4.

The ultimate goal of this multiple regression analysis is to use the fitted model to predict electrical usage y for a home of a specific size (area) x. And, of course, we will want to give a prediction interval for y so that we will know how much faith we can place in the prediction. That is, if the prediction model is used to pre-

FIGURE 10.1
Scattergram of the home size–electrical usage data

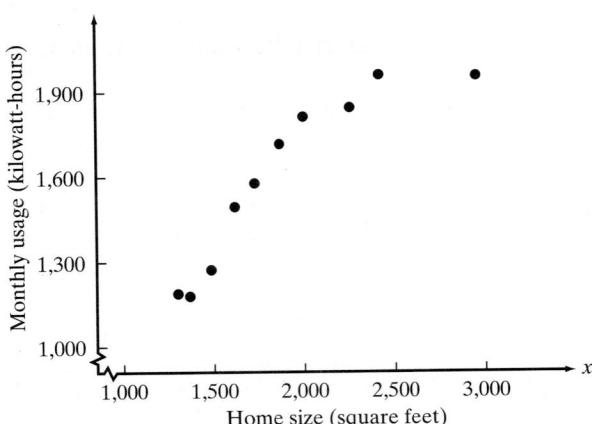

Dep Variable: Y

Analysis of Variance

Source	DF	Sum of Squares	Mean Square	F Value	Prob>F
Model	2	831069.54637	415534.77319	189.710	0.0001
Error	7	15332.55363	2190.36480		
C Total	9	846402.10000			

Root MSE	46.80133	R-square	0.9819
Dep Mean	1594.70000	Adj R-sq	0.9767
C.V.	2.93480		

Parameter Estimates

Variable	DF	Parameter Estimate	Standard Error	T for H0: Parameter=0	Prob > |T|
INTERCEP	1	-1216.143887	242.80636850	-5.009	0.0016
X	1	2.398930	0.24583560	9.758	0.0001
XSQ	1	-0.000450	0.00005908	-7.618	0.0001

FIGURE 10.2   SAS output for the home size–electrical usage data

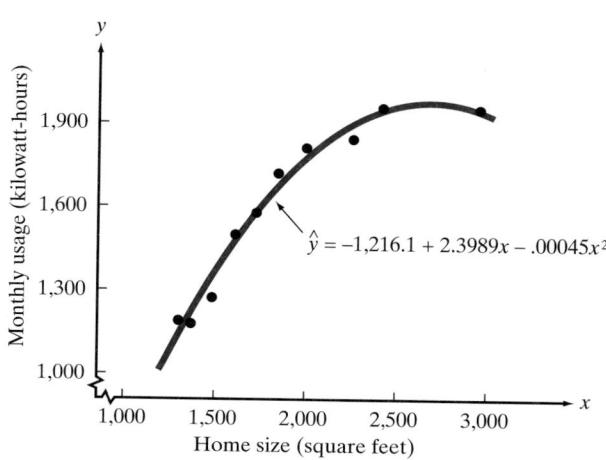

FIGURE 10.3
Least squares model for the home size–electrical usage data

$\hat{y} = -1{,}216.1 + 2.3989x - .00045x^2$

dict electrical usage y for a given size of home, x, what will be the error of prediction? To answer this question, we need to estimate σ^2, the variance of ϵ.

The interpretation of the estimated coefficients in a quadratic model must be undertaken cautiously. First, the estimated y-intercept, $\hat{\beta}_0$, can be meaningfully interpreted only if the range of the independent variables includes zero—that is, if $x = 0$ is included in the sampled range of x. In the electrical usage example, $\hat{\beta}_0 = -1{,}216.1$, which would seem to imply that the estimated electrical usage is negative when $x = 0$, but this zero point represents a home with 0 square feet. The zero point is, of course, not in the range of the sample (the lowest value of x is 1,290 square feet), and thus the interpretation of $\hat{\beta}_0$ is not meaningful.

The estimated coefficient of x is $\hat{\beta}_1$, but it no longer represents a slope in the presence of the quadratic term x^2.* The estimated coefficient of the linear term x will not, in general, have a meaningful interpretation in the quadratic model.

*For students with knowledge of calculus, note that the slope of the quadratic model is the first derivative $\partial y / \partial x = \beta_1 + 2\beta_2 x$. Thus, the slope varies as a function of x, rather than the constant slope associated with the straight-line model.

FIGURE 10.4
Potential misuse
of model

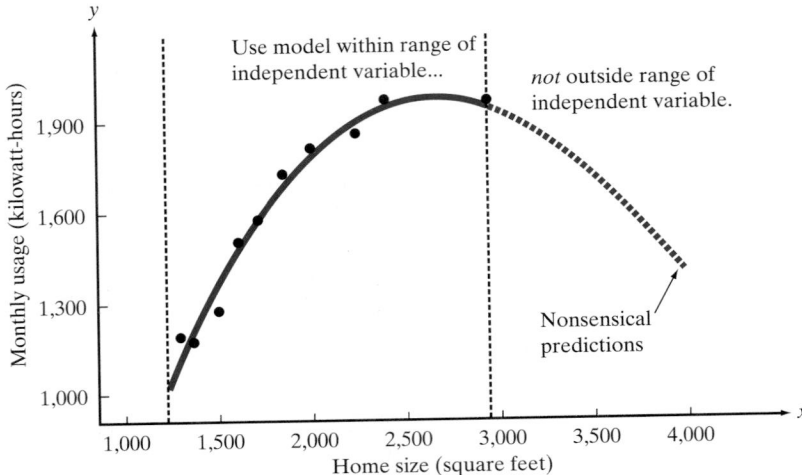

The sign of the coefficient, $\hat{\beta}_2$, of the quadratic term, x^2, is the indicator of whether the curve is concave downward (mound-shaped) or concave upward (bowl-shaped). A negative $\hat{\beta}_2$ implies downward concavity, as in the electrical usage example (Figure 10.3), and a positive $\hat{\beta}_2$ implies upward concavity. Rather than interpreting the numerical value of $\hat{\beta}_2$ itself, we utilize a graphical representation of the model, as in Figure 10.3, to describe the model.

Note that Figure 10.3 implies that the estimated electrical usage is leveling off as the home sizes increase beyond 2,500 square feet. In fact, the convexity of the model would lead to decreasing usage estimates if we were to display the model out to 4,000 square feet and beyond (see Figure 10.4). However, model interpretations are not meaningful outside the range of the independent variable, which has a maximum value of 2,930 square feet in this example. Thus, although the model appears to support the hypothesis that the *rate of increase* per square foot *decreases* for the home sizes near the high end of the sampled values, the conclusion that usage will actually begin to decrease for very large homes would be a *misuse* of the model, since no homes of 3,000 square feet or more were included in the sample.

All the interpretations of the electrical usage model were based on the sample estimates of unknown model parameters. As has been our theme throughout, we want to measure the reliability of these interpretations with regard to the real relationship between usage and home size. Additionally, we will want to use the model to estimate usage for homes not included in the sample, and to measure the reliability of these estimates. All this requires an assessment of the error in the model—that is, of the probability distribution of the random error component, ϵ. This is the subject of the next section.

10.3 MODEL ASSUMPTIONS

We noted in Section 10.1 that the multiple regression model is of the form

$$y = \beta_0 + \beta_1 x_1 + \beta_2 x_2 + \cdots + \beta_k x_k + \epsilon$$

where y is the response variable that we wish to predict; $\beta_0, \beta_1, \ldots, \beta_k$ are parameters with unknown values; $x_1, x_2, \ldots, x_k$ are information-contributing variables that are measured without error; and ϵ is a random error component. Since $\beta_0, \beta_1, \ldots, \beta_k$, and $x_1, x_2, \ldots, x_k$ are nonrandom, the quantity

$$\beta_0 + \beta_1 x_1 + \beta_2 x_2 + \cdots + \beta_k x_k$$

represents the deterministic portion of the model. Therefore, y is composed of two components—one fixed and one random—and, consequently, y is a random variable.

Deterministic portion of model	Random error

$$y = \overbrace{\beta_0 + \beta_1 x_1 + \cdots + \beta_k x_k} + \overbrace{\epsilon}$$

We will assume (as in Chapter 9) that the random error can be positive or negative and that for any setting of the x values, $x_1, x_2, \ldots, x_k$, the random error ϵ has a normal probability distribution with mean equal to 0 and variance equal to σ^2. Further, we assume that the random errors associated with any (and every) pair of y values are probabilistically independent. That is, the error, ϵ, associated with any one y value is independent of the error associated with any other y value. These assumptions are summarized in the next box.

Assumptions for Random Error ϵ

1. For any given set of values of $x_1, x_2, \ldots, x_k$, the random error ϵ has a normal probability distribution with mean equal to 0 and variance equal to σ^2.

2. The random errors are independent (in a probabilistic sense).

Note that σ^2 represents the variance of the random error, ϵ. As such, σ^2 is an important measure of the usefulness of the model for the estimation of the mean and the prediction of actual values of y. If $\sigma^2 = 0$, all the random errors will equal 0 and the predicted values, $\hat{y}$, will be identical to $E(y)$; that is $E(y)$ will be estimated without error. In contrast, a large value of σ^2 implies large (absolute) values of ϵ and larger deviations between the predicted values, $\hat{y}$, and the mean value, $E(y)$. Consequently, the larger the value of σ^2, the greater will be the error in estimating the model parameters $\beta_0, \beta_1, \ldots, \beta_k$ and the error in predicting a value of y for a specific set of values $x_1, x_2, \ldots, x_k$. Thus, σ^2 plays a major role in making inferences about $\beta_0, \beta_1, \ldots, \beta_k$ in estimating $E(y)$, and in predicting y for specific values of $x_1, x_2, \ldots, x_k$.

Since the variance, σ^2, of the random error, ϵ, will rarely be known, we must use the results of the regression analysis to estimate its value. Recall that σ^2 is the variance of the probability distribution of the random error, ϵ, for a given set of values for $x_1, x_2, \ldots, x_k$; hence it is the mean value of the deviations of the y values (for given values of $x_1, x_2, \ldots, x_k$) about the mean value $E(y)$.* Since the predicted value, $\hat{y}$, estimates $E(y)$ for each of the data points, it seems natural to use

$$\text{SSE} = \sum (y_i - \hat{y}_i)^2$$

to construct an estimator of σ^2.

For example, in the second-order (quadratic) model describing electrical usage as a function of home size, we found that SSE = 15,332.6. We now want to use this quantity to estimate the variance of ϵ. Recall that the estimator for the straight-line model is $s^2 = \text{SSE}/(n - 2)$ and note that the denominator is $(n -$ Number of

---

*Since $y = E(y) + \epsilon$, ϵ is equal to the deviation $y - E(y)$. Also, by definition, the variance of a random variable is the expected value of the square of the deviation of the random variable from its mean. According to our model, $E(\epsilon) = 0$. Therefore, $\sigma^2 = E(\epsilon^2)$.

estimated β parameters), which is $(n - 2)$ in the first-order (straight-line) model. Since we must estimate one more parameter, β_2, for the second-order model, the estimator of σ^2 is

$$s^2 = \frac{SSE}{n - 3}$$

That is, the denominator becomes $(n - 3)$ because there are now three β parameters in the model. The numerical estimate for this example is

$$s^2 = \frac{SSE}{10 - 3} = \frac{15,332.6}{7} = 2,190.36$$

In many computer printouts and textbooks, s^2 is called the **mean square for error (MSE)**. This estimate of σ^2 is shown in the column titled **Mean Square** in the SAS printout in Figure 10.2.

The units of the estimated variance are squared units of the dependent variable, y. In the electrical usage example, the units of s^2 are (kilowatt-hours)^2. This makes meaningful interpretation of s^2 difficult, so we use the standard deviation s to provide a more meaningful measure of variability. In the electrical usage example,

$$s = \sqrt{2,190.36} = 46.8,$$

which is given on the SAS printout in Figure 10.2 under **Root MSE**. One useful interpretation of the estimated standard deviation s is that the interval $\pm 2s$ will provide a rough approximation to the accuracy with which the model will predict future values of y for given values of x. Thus, in the electrical usage example, we expect the model to provide predictions of electrical usage to within $\pm 2s = \pm 93.6$ kilowatt-hours.*

For the general multiple regression model

$$y = \beta_0 + \beta_1 x_1 + \beta_2 x_2 + \cdots + \beta_k x_k + \epsilon$$

we must estimate the $(k + 1)$ parameters $\beta_0, \beta_1, \beta_2, \ldots, \beta_k$. Thus, the estimator of σ^2 is SSE divided by the quantity $(n - \text{Number of estimated } \beta \text{ parameters})$.

We will use the estimator of σ^2 both to check the utility of the model (Sections 10.4 and 10.5) and to provide a measure of reliability of predictions and estimates when the model is used for those purposes (Section 10.6). Thus, you can see that the estimation of σ^2 plays an important part in the development of a regression model.

Estimator of σ^2 for Multiple Regression Model with k Independent Variables

$$s^2 = \text{MSE} = \frac{SSE}{n - \text{Number of estimated } \beta \text{ parameters}} = \frac{SSE}{n - (k + 1)}$$

10.4 INFERENCES ABOUT THE β PARAMETERS

Sometimes the individual β parameters in a model have practical significance and we want to estimate their values or test hypotheses about them. For example, if electrical usage y is related to home size x by the straight-line relationship

$$y = \beta_0 + \beta_1 x + \epsilon$$

*The $\pm 2s$ approximation will improve as the sample size is increased. We will provide more precise methodology for the construction of prediction intervals in Section 10.6.

FIGURE 10.5
The interpretation of β_2 for a second-order model

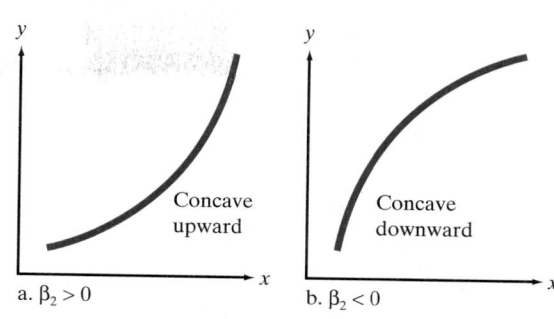

a. $\beta_2 > 0$ b. $\beta_2 < 0$

then β_1 has a very practical interpretation. That is, you saw in Chapter 9 that β_1 is the mean increase in electrical usage, y, for a 1-unit increase in home size x.

As proposed in the preceding sections, suppose that electrical usage y is related to home size x by the quadratic model

$$y = \beta_0 + \beta_1 x + \beta_2 x^2 + \epsilon$$

Then the mean value of y for a given value of x is

$$E(y) = \beta_0 + \beta_1 x + \beta_2 x^2$$

What is the practical interpretation of β_2? As noted earlier, the parameter β_2 measures the curvature of the response curve shown in Figure 10.3. If $\beta_2 > 0$, the slope of the curve will increase as x increases (upward concavity), as shown in Figure 10.5a. If $\beta_2 < 0$, the slope of the curve will decrease as x increases (downward concavity), as shown in Figure 10.5b.

Intuitively, we would expect the electrical usage, y, to rise almost proportionally to home size, x. Then, eventually, as the size of the home increases, the increase in electrical usage for a 1-unit increase in home size might begin to decrease. Thus, a forecaster of electrical usage would want to determine whether this type of curvature actually was present in the response curve or, equivalently, the forecaster would want to test the null hypothesis

$$H_0: \beta_2 = 0 \quad \text{(No curvature in the response curve)}$$

against the alternative hypothesis

$$H_a: \beta_2 < 0 \quad \text{(Downward concavity exists in the response curve)}$$

A test of this hypothesis can be performed using a t-test.

The t-test utilizes a test statistic analogous to that used to make inferences about the slope of the straight-line model (Section 9.5). The t statistic is formed by dividing the sample estimate, $\hat{\beta}_2$, of the parameter β_2 by the estimated standard deviation of the sampling distribution of $\hat{\beta}_2$:

$$\text{Test statistic: } \frac{\hat{\beta}_2}{s_{\hat{\beta}_2}}$$

We use the symbol $s_{\hat{\beta}_2}$ to represent the estimated standard deviation of $\hat{\beta}_2$. The formula for computing $s_{\hat{\beta}_2}$ is very complex and its presentation is beyond the scope of this text,* but this omission will not cause difficulty. Most computer packages list

---

*Because most of the formulas in a multiple regression analysis are so complex, the only reasonable way to present them is by using matrix algebra. We do not assume a prerequisite of matrix algebra for this text and, in any case, we think the formulas can be omitted in an introductory course without serious loss. They are programmed into almost all statistical software packages with multiple regression routines and are presented in some of the texts listed in the references.

FIGURE 10.6
Rejection region for
test of β_2

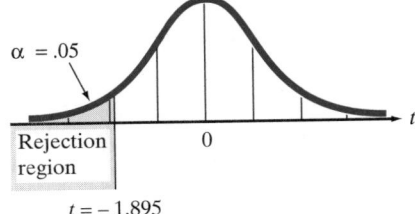

$\alpha = .05$

Rejection region

0

t

$t = -1.895$

the estimated standard deviation $s_{\hat{\beta}_i}$ for each of the estimated model coefficients $\hat{\beta}_i$. Moreover, they usually give the calculated t values for each coefficient.

The rejection region for the test is found in exactly the same way as the rejection regions for the t-tests in previous chapters. That is, we consult Table VI in Appendix B to obtain an upper-tail value of t. This is a value t_α such that $P(t > t_\alpha) = \alpha$. We can then use this value to construct rejection regions for either one-tailed or two-tailed tests. To illustrate, in the electrical usage example the error degrees of freedom is $(n - 3) = 7$, the denominator of the estimate of σ^2. Then the rejection region (shown in Figure 10.6) for a one-tailed test with $\alpha = .05$ is

$$\textit{Rejection region: } t < -t_\alpha$$

$$t < -1.895$$

In Figure 10.7, we again show a portion of the SAS printout for the electrical usage example. The following quantities are highlighted:

1. The estimated coefficients $\hat{\beta}_0, \hat{\beta}_1,$ and $\hat{\beta}_2$.
2. The SSE and MSE (estimate of σ^2, variance of ϵ)
3. The t statistic, observed significance level, and standard error of $\hat{\beta}_2$ for testing H_0: $\beta_2 = 0$

Dep Variable: Y

Analysis of Variance

Source	DF	Sum of Squares	Mean Square	F Value	Prob>F
Model	2	831069.54637	415534.77319	189.710	0.0001
Error	7	15332.55363	2190.36480		
C Total	9	846402.10000			

Root MSE	46.80133	R-square	0.9819
Dep Mean	1594.70000	Adj R-sq	0.9767
C.V.	2.93480		

Parameter Estimates

Variable	DF	Parameter Estimate	Standard Error	T for H0: Parameter=0	Prob > |T|
INTERCEP	1	-1216.143887	242.80636850	-5.009	0.0016
X	1	2.398930	0.24583560	9.758	0.0001
XSQ	1	-0.000450	0.00005908	-7.618	0.0001

FIGURE 10.7   SAS multiple regression output

The estimated standard deviations for the model coefficients appear under the column labeled **Standard Error**. The t statistics for testing the null hypothesis that the true coefficients are equal to 0 appear under the column headed **T for HO: Parameter=0**. The t value corresponding to the test of the null hypothesis H_0: $\beta_2 = 0$ is found at the bottom of that column, that is, $t = -7.618$. Since this value is less than -1.895, we conclude that the quadratic term $\beta_2 x^2$ makes a contribution to the prediction model of electrical usage.

The SAS printout shown in Figure 10.7 also lists the two-tailed significance levels for each t value under the column headed **Prob > |T|**. The significance level .0001 corresponds to the quadratic term, and this implies that we would reject H_0: $\beta_2 = 0$ in favor of H_a: $\beta_2 \neq 0$ at any α level larger than .0001. Since our alternative was one-sided, H_a: $\beta_2 < 0$, and $\hat{\beta}_2$ is negative, the significance level is half that given in the printout, that is, $\frac{1}{2}(.0001) = .00005$. Thus, there is very strong evidence that the mean electrical usage increases more slowly per square foot for large houses than for small houses.

We can also form a confidence interval for the parameter β_2 as follows:

$$\hat{\beta}_2 \pm t_{\alpha/2} s_{\hat{\beta}_2} = -.000450 \pm (2.365)(.0000591)$$

or $(-.000590, -.000310)$. Note that the t value 2.365 corresponds to $\alpha/2 = .025$ and $(n - 3) = 7$ df. This interval constitutes a 95% confidence interval for β_2 and can be used to estimate the rate of curvature in mean electrical usage as home size is increased. Note that all values in the interval are negative, reconfirming the conclusion of our test.

Note that the SAS printout in Figure 10.7 also provides the t-test statistic and corresponding two-tailed p-values for the tests of H_0: $\beta_0 = 0$ and H_0: $\beta_1 = 0$. Since the interpretation of these parameters is not meaningful for this model, the tests are not of interest.

Testing a hypothesis about a single β parameter that appears in any multiple regression model is accomplished in exactly the same manner as described for the quadratic electrical usage model. The t-test and a confidence interval for a β parameter are shown in the next two boxes.

Test of an Individual Parameter Coefficient in the Multiple Regression Model

One-Tailed Test	*Two-Tailed Test*
H_0: $\beta_i = 0$	H_0: $\beta_i = 0$
H_a: $\beta_i < 0$ (or H_a: $\beta_i > 0$)	H_a: $\beta_i \neq 0$

Test statistic: $t = \dfrac{\hat{\beta}_i}{s_{\hat{\beta}_i}}$

Rejection region: $t < t_\alpha$ (or $t > t_\alpha$ when H_a: $-\beta_i > 0$)	Rejection region: $|t| > t_{\alpha/2}$

where t_α and $t_{\alpha/2}$ are based on $n - (k + 1)$ degrees of freedom and

n = Number of observations

$k + 1$ = Number of β parameters in the model

Assumptions: See Section 10.3 for assumptions about the probability distribution for the random error component ϵ.

> **A 100(1 − α)% Confidence Interval for a β Parameter**
>
> $$\hat{\beta}_i \pm t_{\alpha/2} s_{\hat{\beta}_i}$$
>
> where $t_{\alpha/2}$ is based on $n - (k + 1)$ degrees of freedom and
>
> n = Number of observations
> $k + 1$ = Number of β parameters in the model

EXAMPLE 10.1

A collector of antique grandfather clocks knows that the price received for the clocks increases linearly with the age of the clocks. Moreover, the collector hypothesizes that the auction price of the clocks will increase linearly as the number of bidders increases. Thus, the following model is hypothesized:

$$y = \beta_0 + \beta_1 x_1 + \beta_2 x_2 + \epsilon$$

where

y = Auction price
x_1 = Age of clock (years)
x_2 = Number of bidders

A sample of 32 auction prices of grandfather clocks, along with their age and the number of bidders, is given in Table 10.2. The model $y = \beta_0 + \beta_1 x_1 + \beta_2 x_2 + \epsilon$ is fit to the data, and a portion of the MINITAB printout is shown in Figure 10.8.

a. Test the hypothesis that the mean auction price of a clock increases as the number of bidders increases when age is held constant, that is, $\beta_2 > 0$. Use $\alpha = .05$.

b. Interpret the estimates of the β coefficients in the model.

SOLUTION

a. The hypotheses of interest concern the parameter β_2. Specifically,

$$H_0: \beta_2 = 0$$
$$H_a: \beta_2 > 0$$

TABLE 10.2 Auction Price Data

Age x_1	Number of Bidders x_2	Auction Price y	Age x_1	Number of Bidders x_2	Auction Price y
127	13	$1,235	170	14	$2,131
115	12	1,080	182	8	1,550
127	7	845	162	11	1,884
150	9	1,522	184	10	2,041
156	6	1,047	143	6	845
182	11	1,979	159	9	1,483
156	12	1,822	108	14	1,055
132	10	1,253	175	8	1,545
137	9	1,297	108	6	729
113	9	946	179	9	1,792
137	15	1,713	111	15	1,175
117	11	1,024	187	8	1,593
137	8	1,147	111	7	785
153	6	1,092	115	7	744
117	13	1,152	194	5	1,356
126	10	1,336	168	7	1,262

FIGURE 10.8
MINITAB printout for
Example 10.1

```
The regression equation is
Y = -1339 + 12.7 X1 + 86.0 X2

Predictor        Coef      Stdev    t-ratio        p
Constant      -1339.0      173.8      -7.70    0.000
X1            12.7406     0.9047      14.08    0.000
X2            85.953       8.729       9.85    0.000

s = 133.5        R-sq = 89.2%        R-sq(adj) = 88.5%

Analysis of Variance

SOURCE         DF         SS         MS        F        p
Regression      2    4283063    2141532   120.19    0.000
Error          29     516727      17818
Total          31    4799789
```

FIGURE 10.9
Rejection region for
$H_0: \beta_2 = 0$

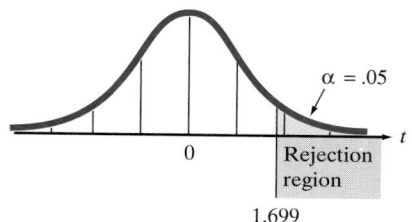

Test statistic: $t = \dfrac{\hat{\beta}_2}{s_{\hat{\beta}_2}} = 9.85$

Rejection region: For $\alpha = .05$ and $n - (k + 1) = 32 - (2 + 1) = 29$ df, reject H_0 if $t > 1.699$ (see Figure 10.9).

The calculated *t*-value, $t = 9.85$, is highlighted on the MINITAB printout, Figure 10.8. This value falls in the rejection region shown in Figure 10.9. Thus, the collector can conclude that the mean auction price of a clock increases as the number of bidders increases, when age is held constant. Note that the observed significance level (*p*-value) of the test is 0. Therefore, any nonzero α will lead us to reject H_0.

b. The values $\hat{\beta}_1 = 12.74$ and $\hat{\beta}_2 = 85.95$ (highlighted in Figure 10.8) are easily interpreted. We estimated that the mean auction price increases $12.74 per year of age of the clock (when the number of bidders is held constant), and that the mean price increases by $85.95 per additional bidder (when the age of the clock is held constant).

Be careful not to interpret the estimated intercept $\hat{\beta}_0 = -1,339$ in the same way $\hat{\beta}_1$ and $\hat{\beta}_2$ are interpreted. You might think that this negative value implies a negative price for clocks 0 years of age with 0 bidders. However, these zeros are meaningless numbers in this example, since the ages range from 108 to 194 and the number of bidders ranges from 5 to 15. Interpretations of predicted *y* values for values of the independent variables outside their sampled range can be very misleading.

The models presented so far utilized quantitative independent variables (e.g., home size, age of a clock, and number of bidders). Multiple regression models can include qualitative independent variables also. For example, suppose we want to develop a model for the mean operating cost per mile, $E(y)$, of cars as a function of the car manufacturer's country of origin. Further suppose that we are interested only in classifying the manufacturer's origin as "domestic" or "foreign." Then the manufacturer's origin is a single qualitative independent variable with two levels: domestic and foreign. Recall that with a qualitative variable, we cannot attach a meaningful quantitative measure to a given level. Consequently, we utilize a system of coding described below.

To simplify our notation, let μ_D be the mean cost per mile for cars manufactured domestically, and let μ_F be the corresponding mean cost per mile for those foreign-manufactured cars. Our objective is to write a single equation that will give the mean value of y (cost per mile) for both domestic and foreign-made cars. This can be done as follows:

$$E(y) = \beta_0 + \beta_1 x$$

where $x = \begin{cases} 1 & \text{if the car is manufactured domestically} \\ 0 & \text{if the car is not manufactured domestically} \end{cases}$

The variable x is not a meaningful independent variable as in the case of models with quantitative independent variables. Instead, it is a **dummy** (or **indicator**) **variable** that makes the model work. To see how, let $x = 0$. This condition will apply when we are seeking the mean cost of foreign-made cars. (If the car is not domestically produced, it must be foreign-made.) Then the mean cost per mile, $E(y)$, is

$$\mu_F = E(y) = \beta_0 + \beta_1(0) = \beta_0$$

This tells us that the mean cost per mile for foreign cars is β_0. Or, using our notation, it means that $\mu_F = \beta_0$.

Now suppose we want to represent the mean cost per mile, $E(y)$, for cars manufactured domestically. Checking the dummy variable definition, we see that we should let $x = 1$:

$$\mu_D = E(y) = \beta_0 + \beta_1 x = \beta_0 + \beta_1(1) = \beta_0 + \beta_1$$

or, since $\beta_0 = \mu_F$,

$$\mu_D = \mu_F + \beta_1$$

Then it follows that the interpretation of β_1 is

$$\beta_1 = \mu_D - \mu_F$$

which is the difference between the mean costs per mile for domestic and foreign cars. Consequently, at t-test of the null hypothesis $H_0: \beta_1 = 0$ is equivalent to testing $H_0: \mu_D - \mu_F = 0$. Rejecting H_0, then, implies that the mean costs per mile for domestic and foreign cars are different.

It is important to note that β_0 and β_1 in the dummy variable model above *do not* represent the y-intercept and slope, respectively, as in the simple linear regression model of Chapter 9. In general, when using the 1–0 system of coding* for a dummy variable, β_0 will represent the mean value of y for the level of the qualitative variable assigned a value of 0 (called the **base level**) and β_1 will represent a difference between the mean values of y for the two levels (with the mean of the base level always subtracted).†

*You do not have to use a 1–0 system of coding for the dummy variables. Any two-value system will work, but the interpretation given to the model parameters will depend on the code. Using the 1–0 system makes the model parameters easy to interpret.

†The system of coding for a qualitative variable at more than two, say k, levels requires that you create $k-1$ dummy variables, one for each level except the base level. The interpretation of β_i is $\beta_i = \mu_{\text{level } i} - \mu_{\text{base level}}$.

EXERCISES 10.1–10.12

Note: Exercises marked with 💾 *contain data for computer analysis on a 3.5" disk (file name in parentheses).*

Learning the Mechanics

10.1 SAS was used to fit the model $y = \beta_0 + \beta_1 x_1 + \beta_2 x_2 + \epsilon$ to $n = 20$ data points and the printout shown below was obtained.
    a. What are the sample estimates of $\beta_0, \beta_1,$ and β_2?
    b. What is the least squares prediction equation?
    c. Find SSE, MSE, and s. Interpret the standard deviation in the context of the problem.
    d. Test $H_0: \beta_1 = 0$ against $H_a: \beta_1 \neq 0$. Use $\alpha = .05$.
    e. Use a 95% confidence interval to estimate $\hat{\beta}_2$.

10.2 Suppose you fit the multiple regression model

$$y = \beta_0 + \beta_1 x_1 + \beta_2 x_2 + \epsilon$$

to $n = 30$ data points and obtain the following result:

$$\hat{y} = 3.4 - 4.6x_1 + 2.7x_2 + .93x_3$$

The estimated standard errors of $\hat{\beta}_2$ and $\hat{\beta}_3$ are 1.86 and .29, respectively.
    a. Test the null hypothesis $H_0: \beta_2 = 0$ against the alternative hypothesis $H_a: \beta_2 \neq 0$. Use $\alpha = .05$.
    b. Test the null hypothesis $H_0: \beta_3 = 0$ against the alternative hypothesis $H_a: \beta_3 \neq 0$. Use $\alpha = .05$.
    c. The null hypothesis $H_0: \beta_2 = 0$ is not rejected. In contrast, the null hypothesis $H_0: \beta_3 = 0$ is rejected. Explain how this can happen even though $\hat{\beta}_2 > \hat{\beta}_3$.

10.3 Suppose you fit the second-order model

$$y = \beta_0 + \beta_1 x + \beta_2 x^2 + \epsilon$$

to $n = 25$ data points. Your estimate of β_2 is $\hat{\beta}_2 = .47$, and the estimated standard error of the estimate is

$$s_{\hat{\beta}_2} = .15$$

    a. Test the null hypothesis that the mean value of y is related to x by the (*first-order*) linear model

$$E(y) = \beta_0 + \beta_1 x$$

($H_0: \beta_2 = 0$) against the alternative hypothesis that the true relationship is given by the (*second-order*) quadratic model

$$E(y) = \beta_0 + \beta_1 x + \beta_2 x^2$$

($H_a: \beta_2 \neq 0$). Use $\alpha = .05$.
    b. Suppose you want to determine only whether the quadratic curve opens upward; that is, as x increases, the slope of the curve increases. Give the test statistic and the rejection region for the test for $\alpha = .05$. Do the data support the theory that the slope of the curve increases as x increases? Explain.
    c. What is the value of the F statistic for testing the null hypothesis $H_0: \beta_2 = 0$ against the alternative hypothesis $H_a: \beta_2 \neq 0$?
    d. Could the F statistic in part **c** be used to conduct the test in part **b**? Explain.

10.4 💾 (X10.004) Use a computer to fit a second-order model to the following data:

x	0	1	2	3	4	5	6
y	1	2.7	3.8	4.5	5.0	5.3	5.2

Dep Variable: Y

Analysis of Variance

Source	DF	Sum of Squares	Mean Square	F Value	Prob>F
Model	2	128329.27624	64164.63812	7.223	0.0054
Error	17	151015.72376	8883.27787		
C Total	19	279345.00000			

Root MSE	94.25114	R-square	0.4594	
Dep Mean	360.50000	Adj R-sq	0.3958	
C.V.	26.14456			

Parameter Estimates

Variable	DF	Parameter Estimate	Standard Error	T for H0: Parameter=0	Prob > |T|
INTERCEP	1	506.346067	45.16942487	11.210	0.0001
X1	1	-941.900226	275.08555975	-3.424	0.0032
X2	1	-429.060418	379.82566485	-1.130	0.2743

a. Find SSE and s^2.
b. Do the data provide sufficient evidence to indicate that the second-order term provides information for the prediction of y? [*Hint:* Test $H_0: \beta_2 = 0$.]
c. Find the least squares prediction equation.
d. Plot the data points and graph $\hat{y}$. Does your prediction equation provide a good fit to the data?

Applying the Concepts

10.5 In 1995–1996, four-year private colleges charged an average of $12,432 for tuition and fees for the year; four-year public colleges charged $2,860 (*Chronicle of Higher Education Almanac,* Sept. 2, 1996). In order to estimate the difference in the mean amounts charged for the 1997–1998 academic year, random samples of 40 private colleges and 40 public colleges were contacted and questioned about their tuition structures.
a. Which of the procedures described in Chapter 7 could be used to estimate the difference in mean charges between private and public colleges?
b. Propose a regression model involving the qualitative independent variable Type of college that could be used to investigate the difference between the means. Be sure to specify the coding scheme for the dummy variable in the model.

c. Explain how the regression model you developed in part **b** could be used to estimate the difference between the population means.

10.6 (X10.006) Economists have two major types of data available to them: *time series data* and *cross-sectional data.* For example, an economist estimating a consumption function, say, household food consumption as a function of household income and household size, might measure the variables of interest for one sample of households at one point in time. In this case, the economist is using *cross-sectional data.* If instead, the economist is interested in how total consumption in the United States is related to national income, the economist probably would track these variables over time, using *time series data* (Mansfield, *Applied Microeconomics,* 1994). The data in the table below were collected for a random sample of 25 households in Washington, D.C., during 1996, and therefore are cross-sectional data.
a. It has been hypothesized that household food consumption y is related to household income x_1 and to household size x_2 as follows:

$$y = \beta_0 + \beta_1 x_1 + \beta_2 x_2 + \epsilon$$

The SPSS printout for fitting the model to the data is shown on page 541. Give the least squares prediction equation.

Household	1996 Food Consumption ($1,000s)	1996 Income ($1,000s)	Household Size (Dec. 1996)
1	4.2	41.1	4
2	3.4	30.5	2
3	4.8	52.3	4
4	2.9	28.9	1
5	3.5	36.5	2
6	4.0	29.8	4
7	3.6	44.3	3
8	4.2	38.1	4
9	5.1	92.0	5
10	2.7	36.0	1
11	4.0	76.9	3
12	2.7	69.9	1
13	5.5	43.1	7
14	4.1	95.2	2
15	5.5	45.6	9
16	4.5	78.5	3
17	5.0	20.5	5
18	4.5	31.6	4
19	2.8	39.9	1
20	3.9	38.6	3
21	3.6	30.2	2
22	4.6	48.7	5
23	3.8	21.2	3
24	4.5	24.3	7
25	4.0	26.9	5

```
* * * *   M U L T I P L E   R E G R E S S I O N   * * * *
Equation Number 1      Dependent Variable..    FOOD

Variable(s) Entered on Step Number
   1..     SIZE
   2..     INCOME

Multiple R              .90872
R Square                .82578
Adjusted R Square       .80994
Standard Error          .35014

Analysis of Variance
                  DF      Sum of Squares      Mean Square
Regression         2         12.78439           6.39219
Residual          22          2.69721            .12260

F =      52.13842      Signif F =   .0000
---------------- Variables in the Equation -------------------

Variable             B         SE B        Beta         T     Sig T

SIZE            .353964     .035183     .899604     10.061    .0000
INCOME          .009193     .003375     .243540      2.724    .0124
(Constant)     2.369646     .218135                 10.863    .0000
```

b. Do the data provide sufficient evidence to conclude that the mean food consumption increases with household income? Test using $\alpha = .01$.

c. As a check on your conclusion of part **b**, construct a scattergram of household food consumption versus household income. Does the plot support your conclusion in part **b**? Explain.

d. In Chapter 9, we used the method of least squares to fit a straight line to a set of data points that were plotted in two dimensions. In this exercise, we are fitting a plane to a set of points plotted in three dimensions. We are attempting to determine the plane, $\hat{y} = \hat{\beta}_0 + \hat{\beta}_1 x_1 + \hat{\beta}_2 x_2$, that, according to the principle of least squares, best fits the data points. Sketch the least squares plane you developed in part **a**. Be sure to label all three axes of your graph.

10.7 Location is one of the most important decisions for hotel chains and lodging firms. A hotel chain that can select good sites more accurately and quickly than its competition has a distinct competitive advantage. Researchers S. E. Kimes (Cornell University) and J. A. Fitzsimmons (University of Texas) studied the site selection process of La Quinta Motor Inns, a moderately priced hotel chain (*Interfaces*, Mar.–Apr. 1990). Using data collected on 57 mature inns owned by La Quinta, the researchers built a regression model designed to predict the profitability for sites under construction. The least squares model is:

$$\hat{y} = 39.05 - 5.41x_1 + 5.86x_2 - 3.09x_3 + 1.75x_4$$

where

y = operating margin (measured as a percentage)

$$= \frac{(\text{profit} + \text{interest expenses} + \text{depreciation})}{\text{total revenue}}$$

x_1 = state population (in thousands) divided by the total number of inns in the state

x_2 = room rate ($) for the inn

x_3 = square root of the median income of the area (in $ thousands)

x_4 = number of college students within four miles of the inn

[*Note:* All variables were "standardized" to have a mean of 0 and a standard deviation of 1.]

Interpret the β estimates of the model. Comment on the effect of each independent variable on operating margin, y. [*Note:* A profitable inn is defined as one with an operating margin of over 50%.]

10.8 Fish reared in captivity for commercial purposes must be fed a diet containing an appropriate balance of nutrients and adequate energy to permit efficient growth. The amount of nitrogen excreted through the gills of a fish is one way to measure fish energy metabolism. *Fisheries Science* (Feb. 1995) reported on a study of the variables that affect endogenous nitrogen excretion (ENE) in carp raised in Japan. Carp were divided into groups of 2 to 15 fish each according to body weight and each group placed in a separate tank. The carp were then fed a protein-free diet three times daily for a period of 20 days. One day after terminating the feeding experiment, the amount of ENE in each tank was measured. The table gives the mean body weight (in grams) and ENE amount (in milligrams per 100 grams of body weight per day) for each carp group.

Tank	Body Weight, x	ENE, y
1	11.7	15.3
2	25.3	9.3
3	90.2	6.5
4	213.0	6.0
5	10.2	15.7
6	17.6	10.0
7	32.6	8.6
8	81.3	6.4
9	141.5	5.6
10	285.7	6.0

Source: Watanabe, T., and Ohta, M. "Endogenous nitrogen excretion and non-fecal energy losses in carp and rainbow trout." *Fisheries Science,* Vol. 61, No. 1, February 1995, p. 56 (Table 5).

a. Plot the data in a scattergram. Do you detect a pattern?

b. The quadratic model, $E(y) = \beta_0 + \beta_1 x + \beta_2 x^2$, was fit to the data using MINITAB. The MINITAB printout is displayed below. Use the printout information to test $H_0: \beta_2 = 0$ against $H_a: \beta_2 \neq 0$ using $\alpha = .10$. Give the conclusion in the words of the problem.

10.9 **(X10.009)** Running a manufacturing operation efficiently requires knowledge of the time it takes employees to manufacture the product, otherwise the cost of making the product cannot be determined. Furthermore, management would not be able to establish an effective incentive plan for its employees because it would not know how to set work standards (Chase and Aquilano, *Production and Operations Management,* 1992). Estimates of production time are frequently obtained using time studies. The data in the accompanying table came from a recent time study of a sample of 15 employees performing a particular task on an automobile assembly line.

Time to Assemble, y (minutes)	Months of Experience, x
10	24
20	1
15	10
11	15
11	17
19	3
11	20
13	9
17	3
18	1
16	7
16	9
17	7
18	5
10	20

a. The SAS printout for fitting the model $y = \beta_0 + \beta_1 x + \beta_2 x^2 + \epsilon$ is shown on page 543. Find the least squares prediction equation.

b. Plot the fitted equation on a scattergram of the data. Is there sufficient evidence to support the inclusion of the quadratic term in the model? Explain.

c. Test the null hypothesis that $\beta_2 = 0$ against the alternative that $\beta_2 \neq 0$. Use $\alpha = .01$. Does the quadratic term make an important contribution to the model?

d. Your conclusion in part **c** should have been to drop the quadratic term from the model. Do so and fit the "reduced model," $y = \beta_0 + \beta_1 x + \epsilon$, to the data.

e. Define β_1 in the context of this exercise. Find a 90% confidence interval for β_1 in the reduced model of part **d**.

10.10 Empirical research was conducted to investigate the variables that impact the size distribution of

```
The regression equation is
ENE = 13.7 - 0.102 WEIGHT +0.000273 WGHTSQ

Predictor        Coef        Stdev      t-ratio        p
Constant       13.713        1.306        10.50    0.000
WEIGHT       -0.10184      0.02881        -3.53    0.010
WGHTSQ      0.0002735    0.0001016         2.69    0.031

s = 2.194      R-sq = 73.7%      R-sq(adj) = 66.2%

Analysis of Variance

SOURCE        DF          SS          MS          F        p
Regression     2      94.659      47.329       9.83    0.009
Error          7      33.705       4.815
Total          9     128.364
```

```
Dep Variable: TIME

                        Analysis of Variance

                        Sum of           Mean
     Source        DF   Squares          Square      F Value    Prob>F

     Model          2   156.11948        78.05974    65.594     0.0001
     Error         12    14.28052         1.19004
     C Total       14   170.40000

          Root MSE         1.09089       R-square    0.9162
          Dep Mean        14.80000       Adj R-sq    0.9022
          C.V.             7.37089

                        Parameter Estimates

                   Parameter        Standard      T for HO:
     Variable   DF  Estimate          Error      Parameter=0   Prob > |T|

     INTERCEP    1   20.091108       0.72470507    27.723        0.0001
     EXP         1   -0.670522       0.15470634    -4.334        0.0010
     EXPSQ       1    0.009535       0.00632580     1.507        0.1576
```

manufacturing firms in international markets (*World Development*, Vol. 20, 1992). Data collected on $n = 54$ countries were used to model a country's size distribution, y, measured as the share of manufacturing firms in the country with 100 or more workers. The model studied was $E(y) = \beta_0 + \beta_1 x_1 + \beta_2 x_2 + \beta_3 x_3 + \beta_4 x_4 + \beta_5 x_5$, where

x_1 = natural logarithm of Gross National Product (LGNP)

x_2 = geographic area per capita (in thousands of square meters) (AREAC)

x_3 = share of heavy industry in manufacturing value added (SVA)

x_4 = ratio of credit claims on the private sector to Gross Domestic Product (CREDIT)

x_5 = ratio of stock equity shares to Gross Domestic Product (STOCK)

a. The researchers hypothesized that the higher the credit ratio of a country, the smaller the size distribution of manufacturing firms. Explain how to test this hypothesis.

b. The researchers hypothesized that the higher the stock ratio of a country, the larger the size distribution of manufacturing firms. Explain how to test this hypothesis.

10.11 **(X10.011)** Many variables influence the price of a company's common stock, including company-specific internal variables such as product quality and financial performance, and external market variables such as interest rates and stock market performance. The table on page 544 contains quarterly data on three such external variables (x_1, x_2, x_3) and the price y of Ford Motor Company's

Common stock (adjusted for a stock split). The Japanese Yen Exchange Rate (the value of a U.S. dollar expressed in yen), x_1, measures the strength of the yen versus the U.S. dollar. The higher the rate, the cheaper are Japanese imports—such as the automobiles of Toyota, Nissan, Honda, and Subaru—to U.S. consumers. Similarly, the higher the deutsche mark exchange rate, x_2, the less expensive are BMW's and Mercedes Benz's to U.S. consumers. The S&P 500 Index, x_3, is a general measure of the performance of the market for stocks in U.S. firms.

a. Fit the first-order model $y = \beta_0 + \beta_1 x_1 + \beta_2 x_2 + \beta_3 x_3 + \epsilon$ to the data. Report the least squares prediction equation.

b. Find the standard deviation of the regression model and interpret its value in the context of this problem.

c. Do the data provide sufficient evidence to conclude that the price of Ford stock decreases as the yen rate increases? Report the observed significance level and reach a conclusion using $\alpha = .05$.

d. Interpret the value of $\hat{\beta}_2$ in terms of these data. Remember that your interpretation must recognize the presence of the other variables in the model.

10.12 A researcher wished to investigate the effects of several factors on production-line supervisors' attitudes toward disabled workers. A study was conducted involving 40 randomly selected supervisors. The response y, a supervisor's attitude toward disabled workers, was measured with a standardized attitude scale. Independent variables used in the study were

Date		Ford Motor Co. Common Stock y	Yen Exchange Rate x_1	Deutsche Mark Exchange Rate x_2	S&P 500 x_3
1992	I	$38\frac{3}{8}$	133.2	1.64	407.36
	II	$45\frac{7}{8}$	125.5	1.53	408.21
	III	$39\frac{1}{2}$	119.2	1.41	418.48
	IV	$42\frac{7}{8}$	124.7	1.61	435.64
1993	I	52	121.0	1.61	450.16
	II	$52\frac{1}{4}$	110.1	1.69	447.29
	III	$55\frac{1}{4}$	105.2	1.62	459.24
	IV	$64\frac{1}{2}$	111.9	1.73	465.95
1994	I	$58\frac{3}{4}$	103.2	1.67	463.81
	II	59	99.1	1.60	454.83
	III	$27\frac{3}{4}$	98.5	1.55	466.96
	IV	$27\frac{7}{8}$	99.7	1.55	455.19
1995	I	$26\frac{7}{8}$	89.4	1.38	493.15
	II	$29\frac{3}{4}$	84.6	1.38	539.35
	III	$31\frac{1}{8}$	98.3	1.42	578.77
	IV	$28\frac{7}{8}$	102.8	1.43	614.57
1996	I	$34\frac{3}{8}$	106.3	1.48	647.07
	II	$32\frac{3}{8}$	109.4	1.52	668.50

Sources: 1. International Financial Statistics, International Monetary Fund, Washington, D.C., 1993–1996, 2. Economic Indicators, Congress, Joint Economic Committee, Washington, D.C., 1992–1996, 3. Dow Jones News/Retrieval database, Dow Jones and Company, New York, 1996.

$$x_1 = \begin{cases} 1 & \text{if the supervisor is female} \\ 0 & \text{if the supervisor is male} \end{cases}$$

x_2 = Number of years of experience in a supervisory job

The researcher fit the model

$$y = \beta_0 + \beta_1 x_1 + \beta_2 x_2 + \beta_3 x_2^2 + \epsilon$$

to the data with the following results:

$$\hat{y} = 50 + 5x_1 + 5x_2 - .1x_2^2$$

a. Is there sufficient evidence to indicate that the quadratic term in years of experience, x_2^2, is useful for predicting attitude score? Use $\alpha = .05$.

b. Sketch the predicted attitude score $\hat{y}$ as a function of the number of years of experience x_2 for male supervisors ($x_1 = 0$). Next, substitute $x_1 = 1$ into the least squares equation and thereby obtain a plot of the prediction equation for female supervisors. [*Note:* For both males and females, plotting $\hat{y}$ for $x_2 = 0, 2, 4, 6, 8$, and 10 will produce a good picture of the prediction equations. The vertical distance between the males' and females' prediction curves is the same for all values of x_2.]

10.5 CHECKING THE USEFULNESS OF A MODEL: R^2 AND THE GLOBAL F-TEST

Conducting t-tests on each β parameter in a model is *not* a good way to determine whether a model is contributing information for the prediction of y. If we were to conduct a series of t-tests to determine whether the independent variables are contributing to the predictive relationship, we would be very likely to make one or more errors in deciding which terms to retain in the model and which to exclude. For example, even if all the β parameters (except β_0) are equal to 0, $100(\alpha)\%$ of the time you will reject the null hypothesis and conclude that some β parameter differs from 0. Thus, in multiple regression models for which a large number of independent variables are being considered, conducting a series of t-tests may include a large number of insignificant variables and exclude some useful ones. If we want to test the utility of a multiple regression model, we will need a **global** test (one that encompasses all the β parameters). We would also like to find some statistical quantity that measures how well the model fits the data.

We commence with the easier problem—finding a measure of how well a linear model fits a set of data. For this we use the multiple regression equivalent of r^2,

```
Dep Variable: Y

                        Analysis of Variance

                              Sum of           Mean
         Source       DF      Squares          Square      F Value    Prob>F
         Model         2   831069.54637    415534.77319    189.710    0.0001
         Error         7    15332.55363      2190.36480
         C Total       9   846402.10000

              Root MSE        46.80133     R-square      0.9819
              Dep Mean      1594.70000     Adj R-sq      0.9767
              C.V.             2.93480

                        Parameter Estimates

                      Parameter      Standard     T for HO:
      Variable   DF    Estimate         Error   Parameter=0   Prob > |T|

      INTERCEP    1  -1216.143887   242.80636850     -5.009      0.0016
      X           1      2.398930     0.24583560      9.758      0.0001
      XSQ         1     -0.000450     0.00005908     -7.618      0.0001
```

FIGURE 10.10   SAS printout for electrical usage example

the coefficient of determination for the straight-line model (Chapter 9). Thus, we define the **multiple coefficient of determination, R^2,** as

$$R^2 = 1 - \frac{\sum(y - \hat{y})^2}{\sum(y - \bar{y})^2} = 1 - \frac{\text{SSE}}{\text{SS}_{yy}} = \frac{\text{SS}_{yy} - \text{SSE}}{\text{SS}_{yy}} = \frac{\text{Explained variability}}{\text{Total variability}}$$

where $\hat{y}$ is the predicted value of y for the model. Just as for the simple linear model, R^2 represents the fraction of the sample variation of the y values (measured by SS_{yy}) that is explained by the least squares prediction equation. Thus, $R^2 = 0$ implies a complete lack of fit of the model to the data and $R^2 = 1$ implies a perfect fit with the model passing through every data point. In general, the larger the value of R^2, the better the model fits the data.

To illustrate, the value $R^2 = .9819$ for the electrical usage example is highlighted in Figure 10.10. This very high value of R^2 implies that using the independent variable home size in a quadratic model explains approximately 98% of the total **sample variation** (measured by SS_{yy}) of electrical usage y. Thus, R^2 is a sample statistic that tells how well the model fits the data and thereby represents a measure of the usefulness of the entire model.

The fact that R^2 is a sample statistic implies that it can be used to make inferences about the usefulness of the entire model for predicting the population of y values at each setting of the independent variables. In particular, for the electrical usage data, the test

$$H_0: \beta_1 = \beta_2 = 0$$

$$H_a: \text{At least one of the coefficients is nonzero}$$

would formally test the global usefulness of the model.

The test statistic used to test this hypothesis is an F statistic, and several equivalent versions of the formula can be used (although we will usually rely on the computer to calculate the F statistic):

$$\textit{Test statistic: } F = \frac{(SS_{yy} - SSE)/k}{SSE/[n - (k + 1)]} = \frac{R^2/k}{(1 - R^2)/[n - (k + 1)]}$$

Both these formulas indicate that the F statistic is the ratio of the *explained* variability divided by the error degrees of freedom. Thus, the larger the proportion of the total variability accounted for by the model, the larger the F statistic.

To determine when the ratio becomes large enough that we can confidently reject the null hypothesis and conclude that the model is more useful than no model at all for predicting y, we compare the calculated F statistic to a tabulated F value with k df in the numerator and $[n - (k + 1)]$ df in the denominator. Tabulations of the F-distribution for various values of α are given in Tables VIII, IX, X, and XI of Appendix B.

Rejection region: $F > F_\alpha$, where F is based on k numerator and $n - (k + 1)$ denominator degrees of freedom.

For the electrical usage example $[n = 10, k = 2, n - (k + 1) = 7,$ and $\alpha = .05]$, we will reject $H_0: \beta_1 = \beta_2 = 0$ if

$$F > F_{.05} = 4.74$$

From the SAS printout (Figure 10.10), we find that the computed F is 189.71. Since this value greatly exceeds the tabulated value of 4.74, we conclude that at least one of the model coefficients β_1 and β_2 is nonzero. Therefore, this global F-test indicates that the quadratic model $y = \beta_0 + \beta_1 x + \beta_2 x^2 + \epsilon$ is useful for predicting electrical usage.

The F statistic is also given as a part of most regression printouts, usually in a portion of the printout called the "Analysis of Variance." This is an appropriate descriptive term, since the F statistic relates the explained and unexplained portions of the total variance of y. For example, the elements of the SAS printout in Figure 10.10 that lead to the calculation of the F value are:

$$F \text{ Value} = \frac{\text{Sum of Squares(Model)}/\text{df(Model)}}{\text{Sum of Squares(Error)}/\text{df(Error)}} = \frac{\text{Mean Square(Model)}}{\text{Mean Square(Error)}}$$

From Figure 10.10 we see that **F Value** = 189.71. Note, too, that the observed significance level for the F statistic is given under the heading **Prob>F** as .0001, which means that we would reject the null hypothesis $H_0: \beta_1 = \beta_2 = 0$ at any α value greater than .0001.

The F-test for testing the usefulness of the model is summarized in the next box.

Testing Global Usefulness of the Model: The F-Test

$H_0: \beta_1 = \beta_2 = \cdots = \beta_k = 0$ (All model terms are unimportant for predicting y)

$H_a:$ At least one $\beta_i \neq 0$ (At least one model term is useful for predicting y)

$$\textit{Test statistic: } F = \frac{(SS_{yy} - SSE)/k}{SSE/[n - (k + 1)]} = \frac{R^2/k}{(1 - R^2)/[n - (k + 1)]}$$

$$= \frac{\text{Mean Square(Model))}}{\text{Mean Square(Error)}}$$

where n is the sample size and k is the number of terms in the model.

Rejection region: $F > F_\alpha$, with k numerator degrees of freedom and $[n - (k + 1)]$ denominator degrees of freedom.

Assumptions: The standard regression assumptions about the random error component (Section 10.3).

Caution: A rejection of the null hypothesis leads to the conclusion [with $100(1 - \alpha)\%$ confidence] that the model is useful. However, "useful" does not necessarily mean "best." Another model may prove even more useful in terms of providing more reliable estimates and predictions. This global F-test is usually regarded as a test that the model *must* pass to merit further consideration.

EXAMPLE 10.2

Refer to Example 10.1, in which an antique collector modeled the auction price y of grandfather clocks as a function of the age of the clock, x_1, and the number of bidders, x_2. The hypothesized model is

$$y = \beta_0 + \beta_1 x_1 + \beta_2 x_2 + \epsilon$$

A sample of 32 observations is obtained, with the results summarized in the MINITAB printout repeated in Figure 10.11.

  a. Find and interpret the coefficient of determination R^2 for this example.

  b. Conduct the global F-test of model usefulness at the $\alpha = .05$ level of significance.

SOLUTION

  a. The R^2 value (highlighted in Figure 10.11) is .892. This implies that the least squares model has explained about 89% of the total sample variation in y values (auction prices).

  b. The elements of the global test of the model follow:

H_0: $\beta_1 = \beta_2 = 0$ [*Note:* $k = 2$]

H_a: At least one of the two model coefficients is nonzero

Test statistic: $F = \dfrac{R^2/k}{(1 - R^2)/[n - (k + 1)]} = 120.19$ (see Figure 10.11)

Rejection region: $F > F_\alpha$

For this example, $n = 32$, $k = 2$, and $n - (k + 1) = 32 - 3 = 29$. Then, for $\alpha = .05$, we will reject H_0: $\beta_1 = \beta_2 = 0$ if $F > F_{.05}$, where F is based on $k = 2$ numerator and $n - (k + 1) = 29$ denominator degrees of freedom—that is, if $F > 3.33$. Since the computed value of the F-test statistic falls in the rejection region ($F = 120.19$

FIGURE 10.11

MINITAB printout for Example 10.2

```
The regression equation is
Y = -1339 + 12.7 X1 + 86.0 X2

Predictor        Coef        Stdev      t-ratio        p
Constant       -1339.0       173.8       -7.70      0.000
X1             12.7406       0.9047      14.08      0.000
X2             85.953        8.729        9.85      0.000

s = 133.5       R-sq = 89.2%      R-sq(adj) = 88.5%

Analysis of Variance

SOURCE          DF          SS          MS         F          p
Regression      2        4283063     2141532    120.19     0.000
Error          29         516727       17818
Total          31        4799789
```

greatly exceeds $F_{.05} = 3.33$, and $\alpha = .05$ exceeds $p = .000$), the data provide strong evidence that at least one of the model coefficients is nonzero. The model appears to be useful for predicting auction prices. ▙

Can we be sure that the best prediction model has been found if the global F-test indicates that a model is useful? Unfortunately, we cannot. The addition of other independent variables may improve the usefulness of the model, as Example 10.3 demonstrates.

EXAMPLE 10.3

Refer to Examples 10.1 and 10.2. Suppose the collector, having observed many auctions, believes that the *rate of increase* of the auction price with age will be driven upward by a large number of bidders. Thus, instead of a relationship like that shown in Figure 10.12a, in which the rate of increase in price with age is the same for any number of bidders, the collector believes the relationship is like that shown in Figure 10.12b. Note that as the number of bidders increases from 5 to 15, the slope of the price versus age line increases. When the slope of the relationship between y and one independent variable (x_1) depends on the value of a second independent variable (x_2), as is the case here, we say that x_1 and x_2 **interact**. The **interaction model** is written

$$y = \beta_0 + \beta_1 x_1 + \beta_2 x_2 + \beta_3 x_1 x_2 + \epsilon$$

Note that the increase in the mean price, $E(y)$, for each one-year increase in age, x_1, is no longer given by the constant β_1 but is now $\beta_1 + \beta_3 x_2$. *That is, the amount $E(y)$ increases for each 1-unit increase in x_1 is dependent on the number of bidders, x_2. Thus, the two variables x_1 and x_2 interact to affect y.*

The 32 data points listed in Table 10.2 were used to fit the model with interaction. A portion of the MINITAB printout is shown in Figure 10.13. Test the hypothesis that the price-age slope increases as the number of bidders increases—that is, that age and number of bidders, x_2, interact positively.

SOLUTION

The model is

$$y = \beta_0 + \beta_1 x_1 + \beta_2 x_2 + \beta_3 x_1 x_2 + \epsilon$$

and the hypotheses of interest to the collector concern the parameter β_3. Specifically,

$$H_0: \beta_3 = 0$$
$$H_a: \beta_3 > 0$$

FIGURE 10.12
Examples of no-interaction and interaction models

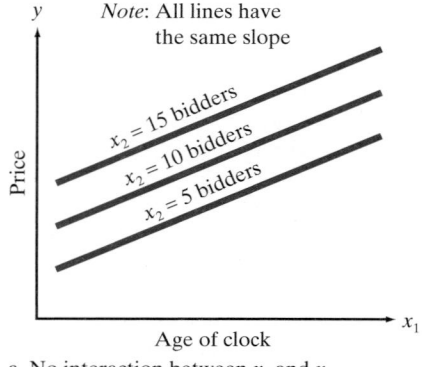

a. No interaction between x_1 and x_2

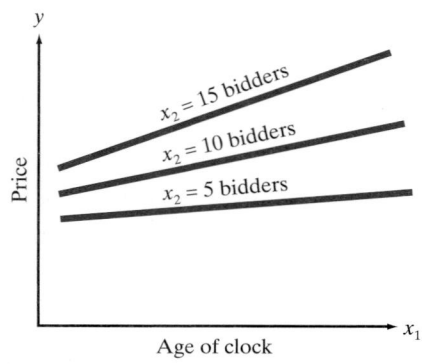

b. Interaction between x_1 and x_2

FIGURE 10.13

MINITAB printout for the model with interaction

```
The regression equation is
Y = 320 + 0.88 X1 - 93.3 X2 + 1.30 X1X2

Predictor       Coef       Stdev    t-ratio        p
Constant       320.5       295.1       1.09    0.287
X1             0.878       2.032       0.43    0.669
X2            -93.26       29.89      -3.12    0.004
X1X2          1.2978      0.2123       6.11    0.000

s = 88.91      R-sq = 95.4%      R-sq(adj) = 94.9%

Analysis of Variance

SOURCE       DF         SS          MS         F        p
Regression    3    4578428     1526142    193.04    0.000
Error        28     221362        7906
Total        31    4799789
```

$$\textit{Test statistic: } t = \frac{\hat{\beta}_3}{s_{\hat{\beta}_3}}$$

$$\textit{Rejection region: For } \alpha = .05, t > t_{.05}$$

where $n = 32$, $k = 3$, and $t_{.05} = 1.701$, based on $n - (k + 1) = 28$ df. [*Remember:* $(k + 1) = 4$ is the number of parameters in the regression model.]

The t value corresponding to $\hat{\beta}_3$ is highlighted in Figure 10.13. The value $t = 6.11$ exceeds 1.701 and therefore falls in the rejection region. Thus, the collector can conclude that the rate of change of the mean price of the clocks with age increases as the number of bidders increases; that is, x_1 and x_2 interact. (The same conclusion can be reached by noting that the p-value of the test is 0.) Thus, it appears that the interaction term should be included in the model. ∎

One note of caution: Although the coefficient of x_2 is negative ($\hat{\beta}_2 = -93.26$) in Example 10.3, this does *not* imply that auction price decreases as the number of bidders increases. Since interaction is present, the rate of change (slope) of mean auction price with the number of bidders *depends* on x_1, the age of the clock. Thus, for example, the estimated rate of change of y for a unit increase in x_2 (one new bidder) for a 150-year-old clock is

$$\text{Estimated } x_2 \text{ slope} = \hat{\beta}_2 + \hat{\beta}_3 x_1 = -93.26 + 1.30(150) = 101.74$$

In other words, we estimate that the auction price of a 150-year-old clock will *increase* by about \$101.74 for every additional bidder. Although the rate of increase will vary as x_1 is changed, it will remain positive for the range of values of x_1 included in the sample. Extreme care is needed in interpreting the signs and sizes of coefficients in a multiple regression model.

To summarize the discussion in this section, the value of R^2 is an indicator of how well the prediction equation fits the data. More importantly, it can be used in the F statistic to determine whether the data provide sufficient evidence to indicate that the model contributes information for the prediction of y. Intuitive evaluations of the contribution of the model based on the computed value of R^2 must be examined with care. The value of R^2 increases as more and more variables are added to the model. Consequently, you could force R^2 to take a value very close to 1 even though the model contributes no information for the prediction of y. In fact, R^2 equals 1 when the number of terms in the model equals the number of data points. Therefore, you should not rely solely on the value of R^2 to tell you whether the model is useful for predicting y. Use the F-test.

After we have determined that the overall model is useful for predicting y using the F-test, we may elect to conduct one or more t-tests on the individual β parameters (see Section 10.4). However, the test (or tests) to be conducted should be decided *a priori,* that is, prior to fitting the model. Also, we should limit the number of t-tests conducted to avoid the potential problem of making too many Type I errors. Generally, the regression analyst will conduct t-tests only on the "most important" β's.

Recommendation for Checking the Utility of a Multiple Regression Model

1. Conduct a test of overall model adequacy using the F-test, that is, test

$$H_0: \beta_1 = \beta_2 = \cdots = \beta_k = 0$$

If the model is deemed adequate (that is, if you reject H_0), then proceed to step 2. Otherwise, you should hypothesize and fit another model. The new model may include more independent variables or higher-order terms.

2. Conduct t-tests on those β parameters in which you are particularly interested (that is, the "most important" β's). These usually involve only the β's associated with higher-order terms ($x^2, x_1 x_2$, etc.). However, it is a safe practice to limit the number of β's that are tested. Conducting a series of t-tests leads to a high overall Type I error rate α.

EXERCISES 10.13–10.26

Note: Exercises marked with 🖫 *contain data for computer analysis on a 3.5" disk (file name in parentheses).*

Learning the Mechanics

10.13 Suppose you fit the model

$$y = \beta_0 + \beta_1 x_1 + \beta_2 x_2 + \beta_3 x_1 x_2 + \beta_4 x_1^2 + \beta_5 x_2^2 + \epsilon$$

to $n = 30$ data points and obtain

$$\text{SSE} = .46 \qquad R^2 = .87$$

a. Do the values of SSE and R^2 suggest that the model provides a good fit to the data? Explain.

b. Is the model of any use in predicting y? Test the null hypothesis that $E(y) = \beta_0$; that is, test

$$H_0: \beta_1 = \beta_2 = \cdots = \beta_5 = 0$$

against the alternative hypothesis

H_a: At least one of the parameters $\beta_1, \beta_2, \ldots, \beta_5$ is nonzero

Use $\alpha = .05$.

10.14 The model $y = \beta_0 + \beta_1 x + \beta_2 x^2 + \epsilon$ was fit to $n = 19$ data points with the results shown in the SAS printout on page 551.

a. Find R^2 and interpret its value.

b. Test the null hypothesis that $\beta_1 = \beta_2 = 0$ against the alternative hypothesis that at least one of β_1 and β_2 is nonzero. Calculate the test statistic using the two formulas given in this section, and compare your results to each other and to that given on the printout. Use $\alpha = .05$ and interpret the result of your test.

c. Find the observed significance level for this test on the printout and interpret it.

d. Test $H_0: \beta_2 = 0$ against $H_a: \beta_2 \neq 0$. Use $\alpha = .05$ and interpret the result of your test. Report and interpret the observed significance level of the test.

10.15 Suppose you fit the model

$$y = \beta_0 + \beta_1 x_1 + \beta_2 x_2 + \epsilon$$

to $n = 20$ data points and obtain

$$\sum (y_i - \hat{y}_i)^2 = 12.37 \qquad \sum (y_i - \bar{y})^2 = 23.75$$

a. Construct an analysis of variance table for this regression analysis, using the printout in Exercise 10.14 as a model. Be sure to include the sources of variability, the degrees of freedom, the sums of squares, the mean squares, and the F statistic. Calculate R^2 for the regression analysis.

b. Test the null hypothesis that $\beta_1 = \beta_2 = 0$ against the alternative hypothesis that at least one of the parameters differs from 0. Calculate the test statistic in two different ways and compare the results. Use $\alpha = .05$ to reach a conclusion about whether the model contributes information for the prediction of y.

Dep Variable: Y

Analysis of Variance

Source	DF	Sum of Squares	Mean Square	F Value	Prob>F
Model	2	24.22335	12.11167	65.478	0.0001
Error	16	2.95955	0.18497		
C Total	18	27.18289			

Root MSE	0.43008	R-square	0.8911	
Dep Mean	3.56053	Adj R-sq	0.8775	
C.V.	12.07921			

Parameter Estimates

Variable	DF	Parameter Estimate	Standard Error	T for H0: Parameter=0	Prob > |T|
INTERCEP	1	0.734606	0.29313351	2.506	0.0234
X	1	0.765179	0.08754136	8.741	0.0001
XSQ	1	-0.030810	0.00452890	-6.803	0.0001

10.16 If the global F-test leads to the conclusion that at least one of the model parameters is nonzero, can you conclude that the model is the best predictor for the dependent variable y? Can you conclude that all of the terms in the model are important for predicting y? What is the appropriate conclusion?

Applying the Concepts

10.17 External auditors are hired to review and analyze the financial and other records of an organization and to attest to the integrity of the organization's financial statements. In recent years, the fees charged by auditors have come under increasing scrutiny. S. Butterworth and K. A. Houghton, two University of Melbourne (Australia) researchers, investigated the effects of several variables on the fee charged by auditors. (*Journal of Business Finance and Accounting*, April 1995.) These variables are described at the bottom of the page. The multiple regression model, $E(y) = \beta_0 + \beta_1 x_1 + \beta_2 x_2 + \beta_3 x_3 + \cdots + \beta_7 x_7$ was fit to data collected for $n = 268$ companies. The results are summarized in the table at the top of page 552.

a. Write the least squares prediction equation.
b. Assess the overall fit of the model.
c. Interpret the estimate of β_3.
d. The researchers hypothesized the direction of the effect of each independent variable on audit fees. These hypotheses are given in the "Expected Sign of β" column in the table. (For example, if the expected sign is negative, the

$y = $ Logarithm of audit fee charged to auditee (FEE)

$x_1 = \begin{cases} 1 & \text{if auditee changed auditors after one year (CHANGE)} \\ 0 & \text{if not} \end{cases}$

$x_2 = $ Logarithm of auditee's total assets (SIZE)

$x_3 = $ Number of subsidiaries of auditee (COMPLEX)

$x_4 = \begin{cases} 1 & \text{if auditee receives an audit qualification (RISK)} \\ 0 & \text{if not} \end{cases}$

$x_5 = \begin{cases} 1 & \text{if auditee in mining industry (INDUSTRY)} \\ 0 & \text{if not} \end{cases}$

$x_6 = \begin{cases} 1 & \text{if auditor is a member of a "Big 8" firm (BIG8)} \\ 0 & \text{if not} \end{cases}$

$x_7 = $ Logarithm of dollar-value of non-audit services provided by auditor (NAS)

Independent Variable	Expected Sign of β	β Estimate	t Value	Level of Significance (p-value)
Constant	−	−4.30	−3.45	.001 (two-tailed)
CHANGE	+	−.002	−0.049	.961 (one-tailed)
SIZE	+	.336	9.94	.000 (one-tailed)
COMPLEX	+	.384	7.63	.000 (one-tailed)
RISK	+	.067	1.76	.079 (one-tailed)
INDUSTRY	−	−.143	−4.05	.000 (one-tailed)
BIG8	+	.081	2.18	.030 (one-tailed)
NAS	+/−	.134	4.54	.000 (two-tailed)

$R^2 = .712$ $F = 111.1$

Source: Butterworth, S., and Houghton, K. A. "Auditor switching: The pricing of audit services." *Journal of Business Finance and Accounting,* Vol. 22, No. 3, April 1995, p. 334 (Table 4).

alternative hypothesis is H_a: $\beta_i < 0$.) Interpret the results of the hypothesis test for β_4. Use $\alpha = .05$.

e. The main objective of the analysis was to determine whether new auditors charge less than incumbent auditors in a given year. If this hypothesis is true, then the true value of β_1 is negative. Is there evidence to support this hypothesis? Explain.

10.18 The *Journal of Quantitative Criminology* (Vol. 8, 1992) published a paper on the determinants of regional property crime levels in the United Kingdom. Several multiple regression models for property crime prevalence, y, measured as the percentage of residents in a geographic region who were victims of at least one property crime, were examined. The results for one of the models, based

on a sample of $n = 313$ responses collected for the British Crime Survey, are shown in the table below. [*Note:* All variables except Density are expressed as a percentage of the base region.]

a. Test the hypothesis that the density (x_1) of a region is positively linearly related to crime prevalence (y), holding the other independent variables constant.

b. Do you advise conducting t-tests on each of the 18 independent variables in the model to determine which variables are important predictors of crime prevalence? Explain.

c. The model yielded $R^2 = .411$. Use this information to conduct a test of the global utility of the model. Use $\alpha = .05$.

10.19 Refer to the *Interfaces* (Mar.–Apr. 1990) study of La Quinta Motor Inns, Exercise 10.7. The

Variable	$\hat{\beta}$	t	p-Value
x_1 = Density (population per hectare)	.331	3.88	$p < .01$
x_2 = Unemployed male population	−.121	−1.17	$p > .10$
x_3 = Professional population	−.187	−1.90	$.01 < p < .10$
x_4 = Population aged less than 5	−.151	−1.51	$p > .10$
x_5 = Population aged between 5 and 15	.353	3.42	$p < .01$
x_6 = Female population	.095	1.31	$p > .10$
x_7 = 10-year change in population	.130	1.40	$p > .10$
x_8 = Minority population	−.122	−1.51	$p > .10$
x_9 = Young adult population	.163	5.62	$p < .01$
x_{10} = 1 if North region, 0 if not	.369	1.72	$.01 < p < .10$
x_{11} = 1 if Yorkshire region, 0 if not	−.210	−1.39	$p > .10$
x_{12} = 1 if East Midlands region, 0 if not	−.192	−0.78	$p > .10$
x_{13} = 1 if East Anglia region, 0 if not	−.548	−2.22	$.01 < p < .10$
x_{14} = 1 if South East region, 0 if not	.152	1.37	$p > .10$
x_{15} = 1 if South West region, 0 if not	−.151	−0.88	$p > .10$
x_{16} = 1 if West Midlands region, 0 if not	−.308	−1.93	$.01 < p < .10$
x_{17} = 1 if North West region, 0 if not	.311	2.13	$.01 < p < .10$
x_{18} = 1 if Wales region, 0 if not	−.019	−0.08	$p > .10$

Source: Osborn, D. R., Tickett, A., and Elder, R. "Area characteristics and regional variates as determinants of area property crime." *Journal of Quantitative Criminology,* Vol. 8, No. 3, 1992, Plenum Publishing Corp.

researchers used state population per inn (x_1), inn room rate (x_2), median income of the area (x_3), and college enrollment (x_4) to build a first-order model for operating margin (y) of a La Quinta inn. Based on a sample of $n = 57$ inns, the model yielded $R^2 = .51$.

a. Give a descriptive measure of model adequacy.
b. Make an inference about model adequacy by conducting the appropriate test. Use $\alpha = .05$.

10.20 An important goal in occupational safety is "active caring." Employees demonstrate active caring (AC) about the safety of their coworkers when they identify environmental hazards and unsafe work practices and then implement appropriate corrective actions for these unsafe conditions or behaviors. Three factors hypothesized to increase the propensity for an employee to actively care for safety are (1) high self-esteem, (2) optimism, and (3) group cohesiveness. A study published in *Applied and Preventive Psychology* (Winter 1995) attempted to establish empirical support for the AC hypothesis by fitting the model

$$E(y) = \beta_0 + \beta_1 x_1 + \beta_2 x_2 + \beta_3 x_3,$$

where

y = AC score (measuring active caring on a 15-point scale)

x_1 = Self-esteem score

x_2 = Optimism score

x_3 = Group cohesion score

The regression analysis, based on data collected for $n = 31$ hourly workers at a large fiber-manufacturing plant, yielded a multiple coefficient of determination of $R^2 = .362$.

a. Interpret the value of R^2.
b. Use the R^2-value to test the global utility of the model. Use $\alpha = .05$.

10.21 *Trichuristrichiura*, a parasitic worm, affects millions of school-age children each year, especially children from developing countries. A study was conducted by a pharmaceutical company to determine the effects of treatment of the parasite on school achievement in 407 school-age Jamaican children infected with the disease (*Journal of Nutrition*, July 1995). About half the children in the sample received the treatment, while the others received a placebo. Multiple regression was used to model spelling test score y, measured as number correct, as a function of the following independent variables:

Treatment (T):

$$x_1 = \begin{cases} 1 & \text{if treatment} \\ 0 & \text{if placebo} \end{cases}$$

Disease Intensity (I):

$$x_2 = \begin{cases} 1 & \text{if more than 7,000 eggs per gram of stool} \\ 0 & \text{if not} \end{cases}$$

a. Propose a model for $E(y)$ that includes interaction between treatment and disease intensity.
b. The estimates of the β's in the model, part **a**, and the respective p-values for t-tests on the β's are given in the table. Is there sufficient evidence to indicate that the effect of the treatment on spelling score depends on disease intensity? Test using $\alpha = .05$.

Variable	β Estimate	p-Value
Treatment (x_1)	$-.1$	.62
Intensity (x_2)	$-.3$	.57
$T \times I$ ($x_1 x_2$)	1.6	.02

[*Note:* The actual model fit in the study included several other variables such as age, gender, and socioeconomic status.]

c. Based on the result, part **b**, explain why the analyst should avoid conducting t-tests for the treatment (x_1) and intensity (x_2) β's or interpreting these β's individually.

10.22 (X10.022) Multiple regression is used by accountants in cost analysis to shed light on the factors that cause costs to be incurred and the magnitudes of their effects. The independent variables of such a regression model are the factors believed to be related to cost, the dependent variable. Assuming no interactions between the independent variables, the estimates of the coefficients of the regression model provide measures of the magnitude of the factors' effects on cost. In some instances, however, it is desirable to use physical units instead of cost as the dependent variable in a cost analysis. This would be the case if most of the cost associated with the activity of interest is a function of some physical unit, such as hours of labor. The advantage of this approach is that the regression model will provide estimates of the number of labor hours required under different circumstances and these hours can then be costed at the current labor rate (Horngren, Foster, and Datar, 1994; Benston, 1966). The sample data shown in the table at the top of page 555 have been collected from a firm's accounting and production records to provide cost information about the firm's shipping department. The EXCEL computer printout for fitting the model $y = \beta_0 + \beta_1 x_1 + \beta_2 x_2 + \beta_3 x_3 + \epsilon$ is shown on page 554.

a. Find the least squares prediction equation.
b. Use an F-test to investigate the usefulness of the model specified in part **a**. Use $\alpha = .01$, and state your conclusion in the context of the problem.

SUMMARY OUTPUT

Regression Statistics	
Multiple R	0.87755597
R Square	0.77010448
Adjusted R Square	0.72699907
Standard Error	9.810345853
Observations	20

ANOVA

	df	SS	MS	F	Significance F
Regression	3	5158.313828	1719.437943	17.86561083	2.32332E-05
Residual	16	1539.886172	96.24288576		
Total	19	6698.2			

	Coefficients	Standard Error	t Stat	P-value	Lower 95%	Upper 95%
Intercept	131.9242521	25.69321439	5.134595076	9.98597E-05	77.45708304	186.3914211
Ship(x1)	2.72608977	2.275004884	1.198278645	0.24825743	-2.096704051	7.548883591
Truck(x2)	0.047218412	0.093348559	0.505829045	0.6198742	-0.150671647	0.245108472
Weight(x3)	-2.587443905	0.642818185	-4.025156669	0.000978875	-3.950157275	-1.224730536

Week	Labor y (hrs.)	Pounds Shipped x_1 (1,000s)	Percentage of Units Shipped by Truck x_2	Average Shipment Weight x_3 (lbs.)
1	100	5.1	90	20
2	85	3.8	99	22
3	108	5.3	58	19
4	116	7.5	16	15
5	92	4.5	54	20
6	63	3.3	42	26
7	79	5.3	12	25
8	101	5.9	32	21
9	88	4.0	56	24
10	71	4.2	64	29
11	122	6.8	78	10
12	85	3.9	90	30
13	50	3.8	74	28
14	114	7.5	89	14
15	104	4.5	90	21
16	111	6.0	40	20
17	110	8.1	55	16
18	100	2.9	64	19
19	82	4.0	35	23
20	85	4.8	58	25

c. Test $H_0: \beta_2 = 0$ versus $H_a: \beta_2 \neq 0$ using $\alpha = .05$. What do the results of your test suggest about the magnitude of the effects of x_2 on labor costs?

d. Find R^2, and interpret its value in the context of the problem.

e. If shipping department employees are paid $7.50 per hour, how much less, on average, will it cost the company per week if the average number of pounds per shipment increases from a level of 20 to 21? Assume that x_1 and x_2 remain unchanged. Your answer is an estimate of what is known in economics as the *expected marginal cost* associated with a one-pound increase in x_3.

f. With what approximate precision can this model be used to predict the hours of labor? [*Note:* The precision of multiple regression predictions is discussed in Section 10.6.]

g. Can regression analysis alone indicate what factors *cause* costs to increase? Explain.

10.23 (X10.023) Many nonprofit and public hospitals are struggling to survive in the face of the new market forces of managed health care and the extreme fiscal pressures on local governments ("Hard cases at the hospital door," *New York Times*, Sept. 17, 1995). Regression analysis was employed to investigate the determinants of survival size of nonprofit hospitals. For a given sample of hospitals, survival size, y, is defined as the largest size hospital (in terms of number of beds) exhibiting growth in market share over a specific time interval. Suppose 10 states are randomly selected and the survival size for all nonprofit hospitals in each state is determined for two

time periods five years apart, yielding two observations per state. The 20 survival sizes are listed in the table at the top of page 556, along with the following data for each state, for the second year in each time interval:

$x_1 =$ Percentage of beds that are in for-profit hospitals

$x_2 =$ Ratio of the number of persons enrolled in health maintenance organizations (HMOs) to the number of persons covered by hospital insurance

$x_3 =$ State population (in thousands)

$x_4 =$ Percentage of state that is urban

The following model characterizes the relationship between survival size and the four variables just listed:

$$y = \beta_0 + \beta_1 x_1 + \beta_2 x_2 + \beta_3 x_3 + \beta_4 x_4 + \epsilon$$

a. The model was fit to the data in the table using SAS, with the results given in the printout on page 556. Report the least squares prediction equation.

b. Find the regression standard deviation s and interpret its value in the context of the problem.

c. Use an F-test to investigate the usefulness of the hypothesized model. Report the observed significance level, and use $\alpha = .025$ to reach your conclusion.

d. Prior to collecting the data it was hypothesized that increases in the number of for-profit hospital beds would decrease the survival size of nonprofit hospitals. Do the data support this hypothesis? Test using $\alpha = .05$.

State	Time Period	Survival Size y	x_1	x_2	x_3	x_4
1	1	370	.13	.09	5,800	89
1	2	390	.15	.09	5,955	87
2	1	455	.08	.11	17,648	87
2	2	450	.10	.16	17,895	85
3	1	500	.03	.04	7,332	79
3	2	480	.07	.05	7,610	78
4	1	550	.06	.005	11,731	80
4	2	600	.10	.005	11,790	81
5	1	205	.30	.12	2,932	44
5	2	230	.25	.13	3,100	45
6	1	425	.04	.01	4,148	36
6	2	445	.07	.02	4,205	38
7	1	245	.20	.01	1,574	25
7	2	200	.30	.01	1,560	28
8	1	250	.07	.08	2,471	38
8	2	275	.08	.10	2,511	38
9	1	300	.09	.12	4,060	52
9	2	290	.12	.20	4,175	54
10	1	280	.10	.02	2,902	37
10	2	270	.11	.05	2,925	38

```
Dep Variable: Y
                      Analysis of Variance

                    Sum of          Mean
    Source    DF    Squares         Square      F Value     Prob>F

    Model      4 246537.05939   61634.26485     28.180      0.0001
    Error     15  32807.94061    2187.19604
    C Total   19 279345.00000

         Root MSE    46.76747       R-square     0.8826
         Dep Mean   360.50000       Adj R-sq     0.8512
         C.V.        12.97295

                     Parameter Estimates

                    Parameter       Standard     T for HO:
    Variable   DF   Estimate        Error        Parameter=0  Prob > |T|

    INTERCEP   1    295.327091      40.17888737      7.350      0.0001
    X1         1   -480.837576     150.39050364     -3.197      0.0060
    X2         1   -829.464955     196.47303539     -4.222      0.0007
    X3         1      0.007934       0.00355335      2.233      0.0412
    X4         1      2.360769       0.76150774      3.100      0.0073
```

10.24 Because the coefficient of determination R^2 always increases when a new independent variable is added to the model, it is tempting to include many variables in a model to force R^2 to be near 1. However, doing so reduces the degrees of freedom available for estimating σ^2, which adversely affects our ability to make reliable inferences. Suppose you want to use 18 economic indicators to predict next year's Gross Domestic Product (GDP). You fit the model

$$y = \beta_0 + \beta_1 x_1 + \beta_2 x_2 + \cdots + \beta_{17} x_{17} + \beta_{18} x_{18} + \epsilon$$

where $y =$ GDP and $x_1, x_2, ..., x_{18}$ are indicators. Only 20 years of data ($n = 20$) are used to fit the model, and you obtain $R^2 = .95$. Test to see whether this impressive-looking R^2 is large enough for you to infer that the model is useful, that is, that at least one term in the model is important for predicting GDP. Use $\alpha = .05$.

10.25 Much research—and much litigation—has been conducted on the disparity between the salary levels of men and women. Research reported in *Work and Occupations* (Nov. 1992) analyzes the salaries for a sample of 191 Illinois managers using a regression analysis with the following independent variables:

x_1 = Gender of manager = $\begin{cases} 1 \text{ if male} \\ 0 \text{ if not} \end{cases}$

x_2 = Race of manager = $\begin{cases} 1 \text{ if white} \\ 0 \text{ if not} \end{cases}$

x_3 = Education level (in years)

x_4 = Tenure with firm (in years)

x_5 = Number of hours worked per week

The regression results are shown below as they were reported in the article.

Variable	$\hat{\beta}$	p-Value
x_1	12.774	<.05
x_2	.713	>.10
x_3	1.519	<.05
x_4	.320	<.05
x_5	.205	<.05
Constant	15.491	—
$R^2 = .240$	$n = 191$	

a. Write the hypothesized model that was used, and interpret each of the β parameters in the model.

b. Write the least squares equation that estimates the model in part **a**, and interpret each of the β estimates.

c. Interpret the value of R^2. Test to determine whether the model is useful for predicting annual salary. Test using $\alpha = .05$.

d. Test to determine whether the gender variable indicates that male managers are paid more than female managers, even after adjusting for and holding constant the other four factors in the model. Test using $\alpha = .05$. [*Note:* The p-values given in the table are two-tailed.]

e. Why would one want to adjust for these other factors before conducting a test for salary discrimination?

f. Discuss how the interaction between gender (x_1) and tenure with the firm (x_4) might affect the results of the analysis.

10.26 Does extensive media coverage of a military crisis influence public opinion on how to respond to the crisis? Political scientists at UCLA researched this question and reported their results in *Communication Research* (June 1993). The military crisis of interest was the 1990 Persian Gulf War, precipitated by Iraqi leader Saddam Hussein's invasion of Kuwait. The researchers used multiple regression analysis to model the level y of U.S. public support for a military (rather than a diplomatic) response to the crisis. Values of y ranged from 0 (preference for a diplomatic response) to 4 (preference for a military response). The independent variables used in the model are described below.

x_1 = Level of TV news exposure in a selected week (number of days)

x_2 = Knowledge of seven political figures (1 point for each correct answer)

x_3 = Gender (1 if male, 0 if female)

x_4 = Race (1 if nonwhite, 0 if white)

x_5 = Partisanship (0–6 scale, where 0 = strong Democrat and 6 = strong Republican)

x_6 = Defense-spending attitude (1–7 scale, where 1 = greatly decrease spending and 7 = greatly increase spending)

x_7 = Education level (1–7 scale, where 1 = less than eight grades and 7 = college)

Data from a survey of 1,763 U.S. citizens were used to fit the model

$$E(y) = \beta_0 + \beta_1 x_1 + \beta_2 x_2 + \beta_3 x_3 + \beta_4 x_4 + \beta_5 x_5 + \beta_6 x_6 + \beta_7 x_7 + \beta_8 x_2 x_3 + \beta_9 x_2 x_4$$

The regression results are shown in the accompanying table.

Variable	β Estimate	Standard Error	Two-Tailed p-Value
TV news exposure (x_1)	.02	.01	.03
Political knowledge (x_2)	.07	.03	.03
Gender (x_3)	.67	.11	<.001
Race (x_4)	−.76	.13	<.001
Partisanship (x_5)	.07	.01	<.001
Defense Spending (x_6)	.20	.02	<.001
Education (x_7)	.07	.02	<.001
Knowledge × Gender ($x_2 x_3$)	−.09	.04	.02
Knowledge × Race ($x_2 x_4$)	.10	.06	.08

Source: Iyengar, S., and Simon, A. "News coverage of the Gulf Crisis and public opinion." *Communication Research*, Vol. 20, No. 3, June 1993, p. 380 (Table 2), Sage Publications.

a. Interpret the β estimate for the variable x_1, TV news exposure.

b. Conduct a test to determine whether an increase in TV news exposure is associated with an increase in support for a military resolution of the crisis. Use $\alpha = .05$.

c. Is there sufficient evidence to indicate that the relationship between support for a military resolution (y) and gender (x_3) depends on political knowledge (x_2)? Test using $\alpha = .05$.

d. Is there sufficient evidence to indicate that the relationship between support for a military resolution (y) and race (x_4) depends on political knowledge (x_2)? Test using $\alpha = .05$.

e. The coefficient of determination for the model was $R^2 = .194$. Interpret this value.

f. Use the value of R^2, part **e**, to conduct a global test for model utility. Use $\alpha = .05$

10.6 USING THE MODEL FOR ESTIMATION AND PREDICTION

In Section 9.8 we discussed the use of the least squares line for estimating the mean value of y, $E(y)$, for some particular value of x, say $x = x_p$. We also showed how to use the same fitted model to predict, when $x = x_p$, some new value of y to be observed in the future. Recall that the least squares line yielded the same value for both the estimate of $E(y)$ and the prediction of some future value of y. That is, both are the result of substituting x_p into the prediction equation $\hat{y} = \hat{\beta}_0 + \hat{\beta}_1 x$ and calculating $\hat{y}_p$. There the equivalence ends. The confidence interval for the mean $E(y)$ is narrower than the prediction interval for y because of the additional uncertainty attributable to the random error ϵ when predicting some future value of y.

These same concepts carry over to the multiple regression model. Suppose we want to estimate the mean electrical usage for a given home size, say $x_p = 1,500$ square feet. Assuming that the quadratic model represents the true relationship between electrical usage and home size, we want to estimate

$$E(y) = \beta_0 + \beta_1 x_p + \beta_2 x_p^2 = \beta_0 + \beta_1(1,500) + \beta_2(1,500)^2$$

Substituting into the least squares prediction equation, we find the estimate of $E(y)$ to be

$$\hat{y} = \hat{\beta}_0 + \hat{\beta}_1(1,500) + \hat{\beta}_2(1,500)^2$$
$$= -1,216.144 + 2.3989(1,500) - .00045004(1,500)^2 = 1,369.7$$

Obs	X	Dep Var Y	Predict Value	Std Err Predict	Lower95% Mean	Upper95% Mean	Residual
1	1290	1182.0	1129.6	30.072	1058.5	1200.7	52.4359
2	1350	1172.0	1202.2	25.851	1141.1	1263.3	-30.2136
3	1470	1264.0	1337.8	19.832	1290.9	1384.7	-73.7916
4	1600	1493.0	1470.0	17.392	1428.9	1511.2	22.9586
5	1710	1571.0	1570.1	17.976	1527.6	1612.6	0.9359
6	1840	1711.0	1674.2	19.919	1627.1	1721.3	36.7685
7	1980	1804.0	1769.4	21.887	1717.6	1821.2	34.5998
8	2230	1840.0	1895.5	23.348	1840.3	1950.7	-55.4654
9	2400	1956.0	1949.1	23.611	1893.2	2004.9	6.9431
10	2930	1954.0	1949.2	44.734	1843.4	2055.0	4.8287
11	1500	.	1369.7	18.892	1325.0	1414.3	.

FIGURE 10.14 SAS printout for estimated mean values and corresponding confidence intervals

FIGURE 10.15
Confidence interval
for mean electrical
usage when $x_p = 1,500$

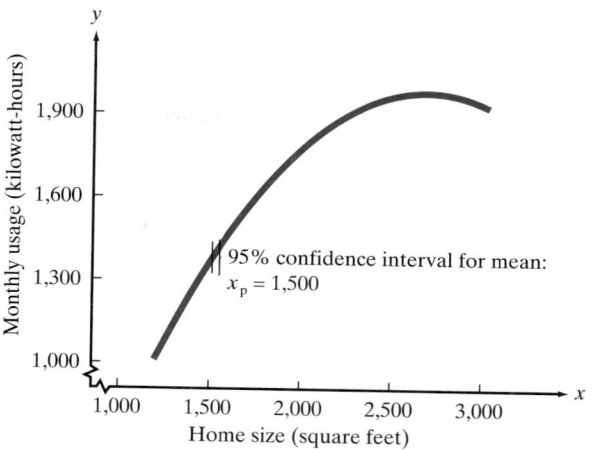

To form a confidence interval for the mean, we need to know the standard deviation of the sampling distribution for the estimator $\hat{y}$. For multiple regression models, the form of this standard deviation is rather complex. However, some regression packages allow us to obtain the confidence intervals for mean values of y for any given combination of values of the independent variables. A portion of the SAS output for the electrical usage example is shown in Figure 10.14 (page 558). The mean value and corresponding 95% confidence interval for the x-values in the sample are shown in the columns labeled **Predict Value**, **Lower95% Mean**, and **Upper95% Mean**. In the last row, corresponding to $x_p = 1,500$, we observe that $\hat{y} = 1,369.7$, which agrees with our earlier calculation. The corresponding 95% confidence interval for the true mean of y, highlighted on the printout, is 1,325.0 to 1,414.3. (This interval is shown graphically in Figure 10.15.)

If we were interested in predicting the electrical usage for a particular 1,500-square-foot home, we would use $\hat{y} = 1,369.7$ as the predicted value. However, the prediction interval for a new value of y is wider than the confidence interval for the mean value. This is reflected by the SAS printout shown in Figure 10.16, which gives the predicted values of y and corresponding 95% prediction intervals under the columns **Lower95% Predict** and **Upper95% Predict**. Note that the prediction interval for $x_p = 1,500$ (highlighted in the last row) is 1,250.3 to 1,489.0. (This interval is shown graphically in Figure 10.17.)

Obs	X	Dep Var Y	Predict Value	Std Err Predict	Lower95% Predict	Upper95% Predict	Residual
1	1290	1182.0	1129.6	30.072	998.0	1261.1	52.4359
2	1350	1172.0	1202.2	25.851	1075.8	1328.6	-30.2136
3	1470	1264.0	1337.8	19.832	1217.6	1458.0	-73.7916
4	1600	1493.0	1470.0	17.392	1352.0	1588.1	22.9586
5	1710	1571.0	1570.1	17.976	1451.5	1688.6	0.9359
6	1840	1711.0	1674.2	19.919	1554.0	1794.5	36.7685
7	1980	1804.0	1769.4	21.887	1647.2	1891.6	34.5998
8	2230	1840.0	1895.5	23.348	1771.8	2019.1	-55.4654
9	2400	1956.0	1949.1	23.611	1825.1	2073.0	6.9431
10	2930	1954.0	1949.2	44.734	1796.1	2102.3	4.8287
11	1500	.	1369.7	18.892	1250.3	1489.0	.

FIGURE 10.16   SAS printout for predicted values and corresponding prediction intervals

FIGURE 10.17
Prediction interval for electrical usage when $x_p = 1,500$

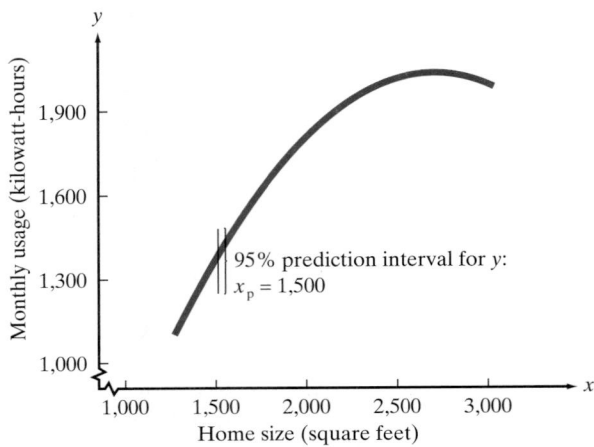

Unfortunately, not all statistical software packages have the capability to produce confidence intervals for means and prediction intervals for specific y values. This is a rather serious oversight, since the estimation of mean values and the prediction of specific values represent the culmination of our model-building efforts: using the model to make inferences about the dependent variable y.

10.7 RESIDUAL ANALYSIS: CHECKING THE REGRESSION ASSUMPTIONS

When we apply regression analysis to a set of data, we never know for certain whether the assumptions of Section 10.3 are satisfied. How far can we deviate from the assumptions and still expect regression analysis to yield results that will have the reliability stated in this chapter? How can we detect departures (if they exist) from the assumptions of Section 10.3 and what can we do about them? We provide some partial answers to these questions in this section.

Remember from Section 10.3 that

$$y = E(y) + \epsilon$$

where the expected value $E(y)$ of y for a given set of values of $x_1, x_2, \ldots, x_k$ is

$$E(y) = \beta_0 + \beta_1 x_1 + \beta_2 x_2 + \cdots + \beta_k x_k$$

and ϵ is a random error. The first assumption we made was that the mean value of the random error for *any* given set of values $x_1, x_2, \ldots, x_k$ is $E(\epsilon) = 0$. One consequence of this assumption is that the mean $E(y)$ for a specific set of values of $x_1, x_2, \ldots, x_k$ is

$$E(y) = \beta_0 + \beta_1 x_1 + \beta_2 x_2 + \cdots + \beta_k x_k$$

That is,

Mean value of y for specific values of $x_1, x_2, \ldots, x_k$		**Random error**
y =	$E(y)$ +	ϵ

The second consequence of the assumption is that the least squares estimators of the model parameters, $\beta_0, \beta_1, \beta_2, \ldots, \beta_k$, will be unbiased regardless of the

STATISTICS IN ACTION

10.1 PREDICTING THE PRICE OF VINTAGE RED BORDEAUX WINE

The vineyards in the Bordeaux region of France are known for producing excellent red wines. Wine experts agree that weather during the grape growing season is critical to producing good wines. The best vineyards in Europe are usually located near a large body of water (to delay spring frosts, prolong fall ripening, and reduce temperature fluctuations), on a slope with a southern exposure to the sun (to enhance spring ripening), and in a soil with good drainage (to overcome the dilution of the grapes that accompanies fall rains). The seaport city of Bordeaux, located on the Garonne River, meets all these desired conditions. Consequently, red Bordeaux wines are some of the most expensive wines in the world.

Usually, the more a wine ages, the more expensive it is. This is because young wines—even young wines produced from the best Bordeaux vineyards—are astringent and many wine drinkers find astringent wines unpalatable. As these wines age, they lose their astringency. Since older wines taste better than younger wines, they are deemed more valuable. Thus, both wine sellers and wine drinkers have an incentive to store young wines until they mature.

The combination of factors—the uncertainty of the weather during the growing season, the phenomenon that wine tastes better with age, and the fact that some vineyards produce better wines than others—encourages speculation concerning the value of a case of wine produced by a certain vineyard during a certain year (or vintage). As a result, many wine experts attempt to predict the auction price of a case of wine (on the London market). Trade magazines such as *Wine* and the *Wine Spectator* provide these opinions regularly, based on subjective assessments of the weather and general knowledge about the reputation of the vineyard.

Recently, a newsletter titled *Liquid Assets: The International Guide to Fine Wines* introduced a quantitative approach to predicting wine prices. The method, which employs statistics and multiple regression analysis to analyze wine prices, has sent the wine trade press into a frenzy. The front page headline in the *New York Times* (Mar. 4, 1995) read, "Wine Equation Puts Some Noses Out of Joint." In the article, the most influential wine critic in America called the approach "a Neanderthal way of looking at wine." According to Britain's *Wine* magazine, "the formula's self-evident silliness invited disrespect." Why has the use of multiple regression to predict wine prices engendered such controversy? One reason is simply that the theory behind the method is misunderstood. For example, the *Wine Spectator* condemned the multiple regression model because "the predictions come exactly true only 3 times in the 27 vintages since 1961 that were calculated, even though the formula was specifically designed to fit price data that already existed. The predicted prices are both under and over the actual prices." Obviously, the *Wine Spectator* does not understand that least squares regression proposes a probabilistic (not a deterministic) model that minimizes SSE and yields an average prediction error of 0.

The publishers of *Liquid Assets* discussed the multiple regression approach to predicting the London auction price of red Bordeaux wine in *Chance* (Fall 1995). The natural logarithm of the price y (in dollars) of a case containing a dozen bottles of red wine* was modeled as a function of weather during growing season and age of vintage using data collected for the vintages of 1952–1980.† The natural log of price, denoted $\ln(y)$, was selected in order to measure increases (or decreases) in price as a percentage. Three models were proposed:

Model 1:

$$\ln(y) = \beta_0 + \beta_1 x_1 + \epsilon,$$

where

x_1 = Age of the vintage (year)

Model 2:

$$\ln(y) = \beta_0 + \beta_1 x_1 + \beta_2 x_2 + \beta_3 x_3 + \beta_4 x_4 + \epsilon,$$

where

x_1 = Age of the vintage (year)

x_2 = Average temperature (°C) over growing season (Apr.–Sept.)

x_3 = Rainfall (cm) in September and August

x_4 = Rainfall (cm) in the months preceding the vintage (Oct.–Mar.)

*The price of a case is an index based on the wines of several Bordeaux vineyards. The bottles in the case were deliberately selected to represent the most expensive wines as well as a selection of less expensive wines.
†The 1954 and 1956 vintages were excluded because they are now rarely sold.

continued

Model 3:

$$\ln(y) = \beta_0 + \beta_1 x_1 + \beta_2 x_2 + \beta_3 x_3 + \beta_4 x_4 + \beta_5 x_5 + \epsilon,$$

where

x_1 = Age of the vintage (year)

x_2 = Average temperature (°C) over growing season (Apr.–Sept.)

x_3 = Rainfall (cm) in September and August

x_4 = Rainfall (cm) in the months preceding the vintage (Oct.–Mar.)

x_5 = Average temperature (°C) in September.

The results of the regressions are summarized in Table 10.3.

Focus

a. Which of the three models would you use to predict red Bordeaux wine prices? Explain.

b. Interpret R^2 and s for the model you selected, part **a**.

c. Conduct a t-test for each of the β parameters in the model you selected, part **a**. Interpret the results.

d. When $\ln(y)$ is used as a dependent variable, the antilogarithm of a β coefficient minus 1, that is, $e^{\beta_i} - 1$, represents the percentage change in y for every 1-unit increase in the associated x value.* Use this information to interpret the β estimates of the model you selected in part **a**.

*The result is derived by expressing the percentage change in price y as $(y_1 - y_0)/y_0$, where y_1 = the value of y when, say, $x = 1$, and y_0 = the value of y when $x = 0$. Now let $y^* = \ln(y)$ and assume the model is $y^* = \beta_0 + \beta_1 x$. Then

$$y = e^{y^*} = e^{\beta_0} e^{\beta_1 x} = \begin{cases} e^{\beta_0} & \text{when } x = 0 \\ e^{\beta_0} e^{\beta_1} & \text{when } x = 1 \end{cases}$$

Substituting, we have

$$\frac{y_1 - y_0}{y_0} = \frac{e^{\beta_0} e^{\beta_1} - e^{\beta_0}}{e^{\beta_0}} = e^{\beta_1} - 1$$

TABLE 10.3 Regression of ln(Price) of Red Bourdeaux Wine (Statistics in Action 10.1)

Independent Variables in Model	BETA ESTIMATES (STANDARD ERRORS)		
	Model 1	Model 2	Model 3
Vintage (x_1)	.0354 (.0137)	.0238 (.00717)	.0240 (.00747)
Growing season temperature (x_2)	—	.616 (.0952)	.608 (.116)
Sept./Aug. rain (x_3)	—	−.00386 (.00081)	−.00380 (.00095)
Pre-rain (x_4)	—	.0001173 (.000482)	.00115 (.000505)
Sept. temperature (x_5)	—	—	.00765 (.0565)
R^2	.212	.828	.828
s	.575	.287	.293

Source: Ashenfelter, O., Ashmore, D., and LaLonde, R. "Bourdeaux wine vintage quality and weather." *Chance,* Vol. 8, No. 4, Fall 1995, p. 116 (Table 2).

remaining assumptions that we attribute to the random errors and their probability distributions.

The properties of the sampling distributions of the parameter estimators $\hat{\beta}_0, \hat{\beta}_1, ..., \hat{\beta}_k$ will depend on the remaining assumptions that we specify concerning the probability distributions of the random errors. Recall that we assumed that for any given set of values of $x_1, x_2, ..., x_k$, ϵ has a normal probability distribution with mean equal to 0 and variance equal to σ^2. Also, we assumed that the random errors are probabilistically independent.

It is unlikely that these assumptions are ever satisfied exactly in a practical application of regression analysis. Fortunately, experience has shown that least squares regression analysis produces reliable statistical tests, confidence intervals, and prediction intervals as long as the departures from the assumptions are not too great. In this section we present some methods for determining whether the data indicate significant departures from the assumptions.

FIGURE 10.18
Actual random error
and regression
residual

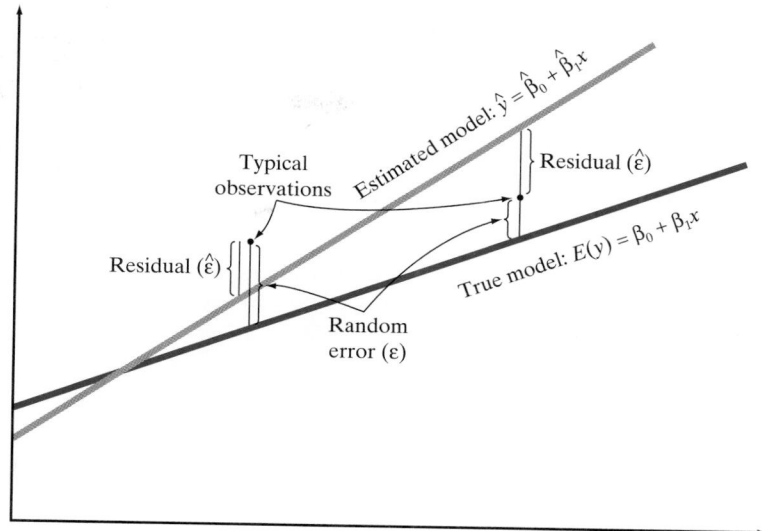

Because the assumptions all concern the random error component, ϵ, of the model, the first step is to estimate the random error. Since the actual random error associated with a particular value of y is the difference between the actual y value and its unknown mean, we estimate the error by the difference between the actual y value and the *estimated* mean. This estimated error is called the **regression residual**, or simply the **residual**, and is denoted by $\hat{\epsilon}$. The actual error ϵ and residual $\hat{\epsilon}$ are shown in Figure 10.18.

Actual random error $= \epsilon$

$$= (\text{Actual } y \text{ value}) - (\text{Mean of } y)$$
$$= y - E(y) = y - (\beta_0 + \beta_1 x_1 + \beta_2 x_2 + \cdots + \beta_k x_k)$$

Estimated random
error (residual) $= \hat{\epsilon}$

$$= (\text{Actual } y \text{ value}) - (\text{Estimated mean of } y)$$
$$= y - \hat{y} = y - (\hat{\beta}_0 + \hat{\beta}_1 x_1 + \hat{\beta}_2 x_2 + \cdots + \hat{\beta}_k x_k)$$

Since the true mean of y (that is, the true regression model) is not known, the actual random error cannot be calculated. However, because the residual is based on the estimated mean (the least squares regression model), it can be calculated and used to estimate the random error and to check the regression assumptions. Such checks are generally referred to as **residual analyses**. Some useful properties of residuals are given in the next box.

Properties of Regression Residuals

1. A residual is equal to the difference between the observed y value and its estimated (regression) mean:

$$\text{Residual } = y - \hat{y}$$

continued

2. The mean of the residuals is equal to 0. This property follows from the fact that the sum of the differences between the observed y values and their least squares predicted ($\hat{y}$) values is equal to 0.

$$\sum(\text{Residuals}) = \sum(y - \hat{y}) = 0$$

3. The standard deviation of the residuals is equal to the standard deviation of the fitted regression model, s. This property follows from the fact that the sum of the squared residuals is equal to SSE, which when divided by the error degrees of freedom is equal to the variance of the fitted regression model, s^2. The square root of the variance is both the standard deviation of the residuals and the standard deviation of the regression model.

$$\sum(\text{Residuals})^2 = \sum(y - \hat{y})^2 = \text{SSE}$$

$$s = \sqrt{\frac{\sum(\text{Residuals})^2}{n - (k + 1)}} = \sqrt{\frac{\text{SSE}}{n - (k + 1)}}$$

The following examples show how the analysis of regression residuals can be used to verify the assumptions associated with the model and to improve the model when the assumptions do not appear to be satisfied. Although the residuals can be calculated and plotted by hand, we rely on the computer for these tasks in the examples and exercises. Most statistical computer packages now include residual analyses as a standard component of their regression modeling programs.

EXAMPLE 10.4

The data for the home size–electrical usage example used throughout this chapter are repeated in Table 10.4. EXCEL printouts for a straight-line model and a quadratic model fit to the data are shown in Figures 10.19a and 10.19b, respectively. The residuals from these models are highlighted in the printouts. The residuals are then plotted on the vertical axis against the variable x, size of home, on the horizontal axis in Figures 10.20a and 10.20b (see page 567), respectively.

a. Verify that each residual is equal to the difference between the observed y value and the estimated mean value, $\hat{y}$.

b. Analyze the residual plots.

TABLE 10.4   Home Size–Electrical Usage Data

Size of Home x (sq. ft.)	Monthly Usage y (kilowatt-hours)
1,290	1,182
1,350	1,172
1,470	1,264
1,600	1,493
1,710	1,571
1,840	1,711
1,980	1,804
2,230	1,840
2,400	1,956
2,930	1,954

SUMMARY OUTPUT

Regression Statistics	
Multiple R	0.91978829
R Square	0.831705384
Adjusted R Square	0.810668557
Standard Error	133.4376805
Observations	10

ANOVA

	df	SS	MS	F	Significance F
Regression	1	703957.1834	703957.1834	39.53568581	0.000235885
Residual	8	142444.9166	17805.61457		
Total	9	846402.1			

	Coefficients	Standard Error	t Stat	P-value	Lower 95%	Upper 95%
Intercept	578.9277515	166.9680571	3.467296448	0.008476357	193.8984723	963.9570307
Size(x)	0.540304387	0.085929811	6.287740915	0.000235885	0.3214976	0.738459015

RESIDUAL OUTPUT

Observation	Predicted Usage(y)	Residuals
1	1275.920411	-93.92041138
2	1308.338675	-136.3386746
3	1373.175201	-109.1752011
4	1443.414772	49.5852285
5	1502.848254	68.15174587
6	1573.087825	137.9121755
7	1648.730439	155.2695613
8	1783.806536	56.19346438
9	1875.658281	80.3417185
10	2162.019607	-208.0196069

FIGURE 10.19A   EXCEL printout for electrical usage example: Straight-line model

SUMMARY OUTPUT						
Regression Statistics						
Multiple R	0.990901117					
R Square	0.981885024					
Adjusted R Square	0.976709317					
Standard Error	46.80133336					
Observations	10					
ANOVA						
	df	SS	MS	F	Significance F	
Regression	2	831069.5464	415534.7732	189.7103041	8.00078E-07	
Residual	7	15332.55363	2190.364804			
Total	9	846402.1				
	Coefficients	Standard Error	t Stat	P-value	Lower 95%	Upper 95%
Intercept	-1216.143887	242.8063685	-5.008698472	0.001550025	-1790.289304	-641.9984703
Size(x)	2.398930177	0.245835602	9.758269998	2.51335E-05	1.817621767	2.980238587
SizeSq(x2)	-0.00045004	5.90766E-05	-7.617907059	0.000124415	-0.000589734	-0.000310346
RESIDUAL OUTPUT						
Observation	Predicted Usage(y)	Residuals				
1	1129.564114	52.43588588				
2	1202.213554	-30.21355416				
3	1337.791566	-73.79156553				
4	1470.041437	22.95856259				
5	1570.064113	0.935886603				
6	1674.231476	36.76852434				
7	1769.400192	34.59980832				
8	1895.465406	-55.46540615				
9	1949.05688	6.943119595				
10	1949.171261	4.828738521				

FIGURE 10.19B EXCEL printout for electrical usage example: Quadratic model

FIGURE 10.20A
EXCEL residual plot for electrical usage example: Straight-line model

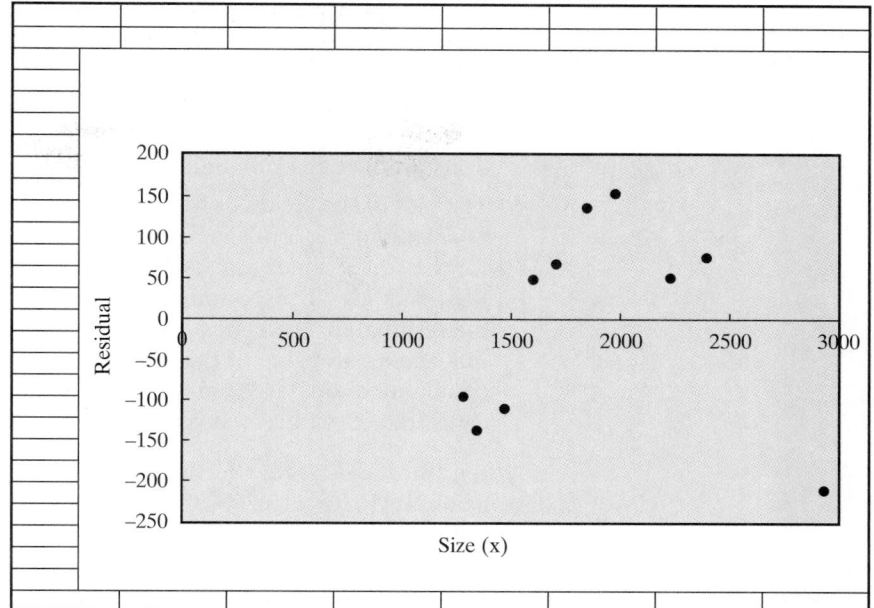

FIGURE 10.20B
EXCEL residual plot for electrical usage example: Quadratic model

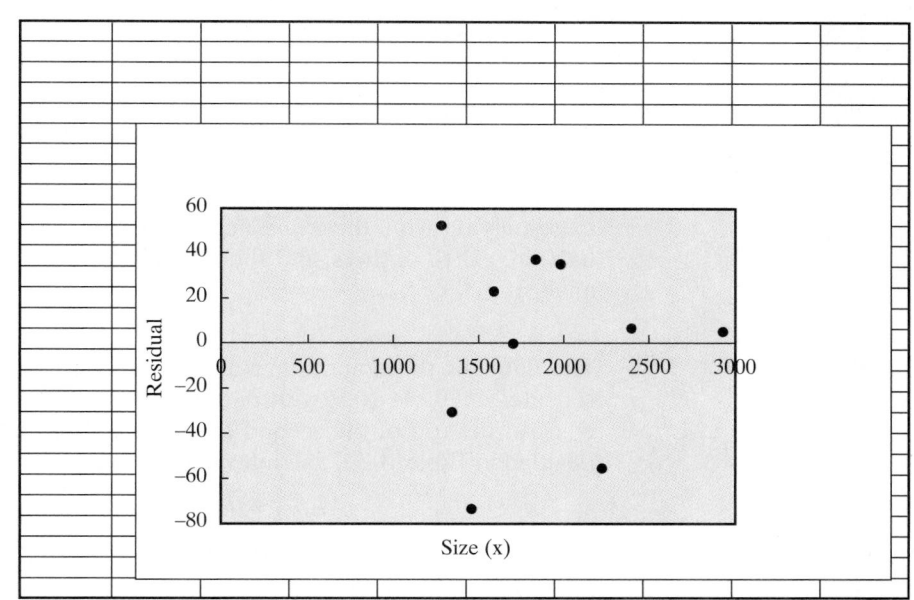

SOLUTION

a. For the straight-line model the residual is calculated for the first y value as follows:

$$\text{Residual} = (\text{Observed } y \text{ value}) - (\text{Estimated mean})$$
$$= y - \hat{y} = 1,182 - 1,275.92 = -93.92$$

where the estimated mean is the first number in the column labeled **Predicted Usage(y)** (highlighted) on the EXCEL printout in Figure 10.19a. Similarly, the residual for the first y value using the quadratic model is

$$\text{Residual} = 1,182 - 1,129.56 = 52.44$$

Both residuals agree (after rounding) with the first values given in the column labeled **Residuals** in Figures 10.19a and 10.19b, respectively. Although the residuals both correspond to the same observed y value, 1,182, they differ because the estimated mean value changes depending on whether the straight-line model or quadratic model is used. Similar calculations produce the remaining residuals.

b. The plot of the residuals for the straight-line model (Figure 10.20a) reveals a nonrandom pattern. The residuals exhibit a curved shape, with the residuals for the small values of x below the horizontal 0 (mean of the residuals) line, the residuals corresponding to the middle values of x above the 0 line, and the residual for the largest value of x again below the 0 line. The indication is that the mean value of the random error ϵ *within* each of these ranges of x (small, medium, large) may not be equal to 0. Such a pattern usually indicates that curvature needs to be added to the model.

When the second-order term is added to the model, the nonrandom pattern disappears. In Figure 10.20b, the residuals appear to be randomly distributed around the 0 line, as expected. Note, too, that the value of $2s$ for the quadratic model is $2(46.8) = 93.6$, compared to $2s = 2(133.4) = 266.8$ for the straight-line model. The implication is that the quadratic model provides a considerably better model for predicting electrical usage, verifying our conclusions from previous analyses in this chapter. ▗

Residual analyses are also useful for detecting one or more observations that deviate significantly from the regression model. We expect approximately 95% of the residuals to fall within 2 standard deviations of the 0 line, and all or almost all of them to lie within 3 standard deviations of their mean of 0. Residuals that are extremely far from the 0 line, and disconnected from the bulk of the other residuals, are called **outliers**, and should receive special attention from the regression analyst.

EXAMPLE 10.5

The data for the grandfather clock example used throughout this chapter are repeated in Table 10.5, with one important difference: The auction price of the clock at the top of the second column has been changed from \$2,131 to \$1,131 (shaded in Table 10.5). The interaction model

$$E(y) = \beta_0 + \beta_1 x_1 + \beta_2 x_2 + \beta_3 x_1 x_2$$

is again fit to these (modified) data, with the MINITAB printout shown in Figure 10.21. The residuals are shown highlighted in the printout and then plotted against the number of bidders, x_2, in Figure 10.22 (page 571). Analyze the residual plot.

SOLUTION

The residual plot dramatically reveals the one altered measurement. Note that one of the two residuals at $x_2 = 14$ bidders falls more than 3 standard deviations below 0. Note that no other residual falls more than 2 standard deviations from 0.

What do we do with outliers once we identify them? First, we try to determine the cause. Were the data entered into the computer incorrectly? Was the observation recorded incorrectly when the data were collected? If so, we correct the observation and rerun the program. Another possibility is that the observation is not representative of the conditions we are trying to model. For example, in this

TABLE 10.5   Auction Price Data

Age x_1	Number of Bidders x_2	Auction Price y	Age x_1	Number of Bidders x_2	Auction Price y
127	13	$1,235	170	14	$1,131
115	12	1,080	182	8	1,550
127	7	845	162	11	1,884
150	9	1,522	184	10	2,041
156	6	1,047	143	6	845
182	11	1,979	159	9	1,483
156	12	1,822	108	14	1,055
132	10	1,253	175	8	1,545
137	9	1,297	108	6	729
113	9	946	179	9	1,792
137	15	1,713	111	15	1,175
117	11	1,024	187	8	1,593
137	8	1,147	111	7	785
153	6	1,092	115	7	744
117	13	1,152	194	5	1,356
126	10	1,336	168	7	1,262

case the low price may be attributable to extreme damage to the clock, or to a clock of inferior quality compared to the others. In these cases we probably would exclude the observation from the analysis. In many cases you may not be able to determine the cause of the outlier. Even so, you may want to rerun the regression analysis excluding the outlier in order to assess the effect of that observation on the results of the analysis.

Figure 10.23 on page 571 shows the printout when the outlier observation is excluded from the grandfather clock analysis, and Figure 10.24 on page 572 shows the new plot of the residuals against the number of bidders. Now only one of the residuals lies beyond 2 standard deviations from 0, and none of them lies beyond 3 standard deviations. Also, the model statistics indicate a much better model without the outlier. Most notably, the standard deviation (s) has decreased from 200.6 to 85.83, indicating a model that will provide more precise estimates and predictions (narrower confidence and prediction intervals) for clocks that are similar to those in the reduced sample. But remember that if the outlier is removed from the analysis when in fact it belongs to the same population as the rest of the sample, the resulting model may provide misleading estimates and predictions.

Outlier analysis is another example of testing the assumption that the expected (mean) value of the random error component is 0, since this assumption is in doubt for the error terms corresponding to the outliers. The last example in this section checks the assumption of the normality of the random error component.

EXAMPLE 10.6

Refer to Example 10.5. Use a stem-and-leaf display (Section 2.2) to plot the frequency distribution of the residuals in the grandfather clock example, both before and after the outlier residual is removed. Analyze the plots and determine whether the assumption of normality of the error distribution is reasonable.

```
The regression equation is
PRICE = - 513 + 8.17 AGE = 19.9 BIDDERS + 0.320 AGE-BID
```

Predictor	Coef	Stdev	t-ratio	p
Constant	-512.8	665.9	-0.77	0.448
AGE	8.165	4.585	1.78	0.086
BIDDERS	19.89	67.44	0.29	0.770
AGE-BID	0.3196	0.4790	0.67	0.510

```
s = 200.6     R-sq = 72.9%   R-sq(adj) = 70.0%
```

Analysis of Variance

SOURCE	DF	SS	MS	F	p
Regression	3	3033587	1011196	25.13	0.000
Error	28	1126703	40239		
Total	31	4160289			

Obs.	AGE	PRICE	Fit	Stdev.Fit	Residual	St.Resid
1	127	1235.0	1310.4	59.3	-75.4	-0.39
2	115	1080.0	1105.9	62.1	-25.9	-0.14
3	127	845.0	947.5	61.1	-102.5	-0.54
4	150	1522.0	1322.5	37.1	199.5	1.01
5	156	1047.0	1179.5	60.3	-132.5	-0.69
6	182	1979.0	1831.9	82.9	147.1	0.81
7	156	1822.0	1598.0	61.9	224.0	1.17
8	132	1253.0	1185.8	39.7	67.2	0.34
9	137	1297.0	1178.9	39.0	118.1	0.60
10	113	946.0	913.9	58.6	32.1	0.17
11	137	1713.0	1561.0	78.4	152.0	0.82
12	117	1024.0	1072.6	53.1	-48.6	-0.25
13	137	1147.0	1115.2	44.3	31.8	0.16
14	153	1092.0	1149.2	59.0	-57.2	-0.30
15	117	1152.0	1187.2	69.7	-35.2	-0.19
16	126	1336.0	1117.6	43.4	218.4	1.12
17	170	1131.0	1914.4	116.7	-783.4	-4.80R
18	182	1550.0	1597.7	62.8	-47.7	-0.25
19	162	1884.0	1598.3	57.0	285.7	1.49
20	184	2041.0	1776.6	70.7	264.4	1.41
21	143	845.0	1048.4	58.9	-203.4	-1.06
22	159	1483.0	1421.8	40.6	61.2	0.31
23	108	1055.0	1130.7	97.9	-75.7	-0.43
24	175	1545.0	1522.7	55.4	22.3	0.12
25	108	729.0	695.5	99.6	33.5	0.19
26	179	1792.0	1642.7	57.6	149.3	0.78
27	111	1175.0	1224.0	107.2	-49.0	-0.29
28	187	1593.0	1651.3	68.6	-58.3	-0.31
29	111	785.0	781.1	80.9	3.9	0.02
30	115	744.0	822.7	75.5	-78.7	-0.42
31	194	1356.0	1480.7	133.6	-124.7	-0.83 X
32	168	1262.0	1374.0	57.7	-112.0	-0.58

```
R denotes an obs. with a large st. resid.
X denotes an obs. whose X value gives it large influence.
```

FIGURE 10.21   MINITAB printout for grandfather clock example with altered data

FIGURE 10.22
MINITAB residual plot against number of bidders

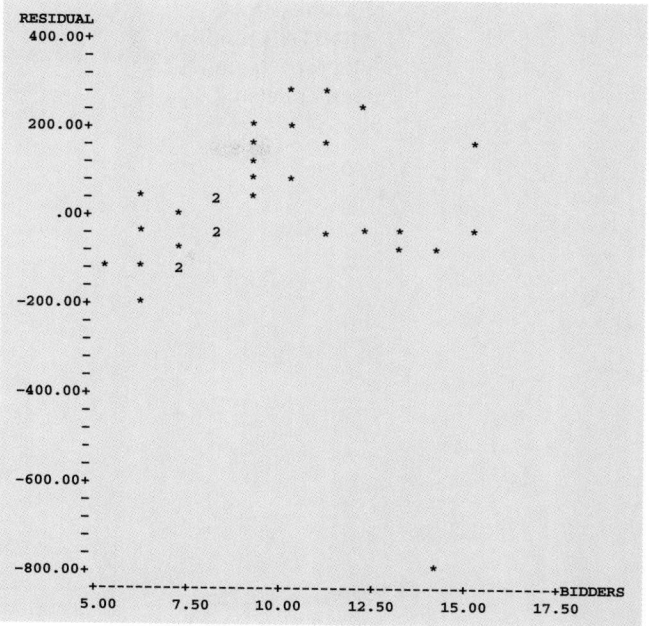

FIGURE 10.23
MINITAB printout for Example 10.5: Outlier deleted

The regression equation is
PRICE = 474 - 0.46 AGE - 114 BIDDERS + 1.48 AGE-BID

Predictor	Coef	Stdev	t-ratio	p
Constant	474.0	298.2	1.59	0.124
AGE	-0.465	2.107	-0.22	0.827
BIDDERS	-114.12	31.23	-3.65	0.001
AGE-BID	1.4781	0.2295	6.44	0.000

s = 85.83   R-sq = 95.2%   R-sq(adj) = 94.7%

Analysis of Variance

SOURCE	DF	SS	MS	F	p
Regression	3	3933417	1311139	177.99	0.000
Error	27	198897	7367		
Total	30	4132314			

SOLUTION

The stem-and-leaf displays for the two sets of residuals are constructed using MINITAB and are shown in Figure 10.25.* Note that the outlier appears to skew the frequency distribution in Figure 10.25a, whereas the stem-and-leaf display in Figure 10.25b appears to be more mound-shaped. Although the displays do not provide formal statistical tests of normality, they do provide a descriptive display. Relative frequency histograms can also be used to check the normality assumption. In this example the normality assumption appears to be more plausible after the outlier is removed. Consult the references for methods to conduct statistical tests of normality using the residuals.   **◤**

*Recall that the left column of the MINITAB printout shows the number of measurements at least as extreme as the stem. In Figure 10.25a, for example, the 6 corresponding to the STEM = −1 means that six measurements are less than or equal to −100. If one of the numbers in the leftmost column is enclosed in parentheses, the number in parentheses is the number of measurements in that row, and the median is contained in that row.

FIGURE 10.24
MINITAB residual plot for Example 10.5: Outlier deleted

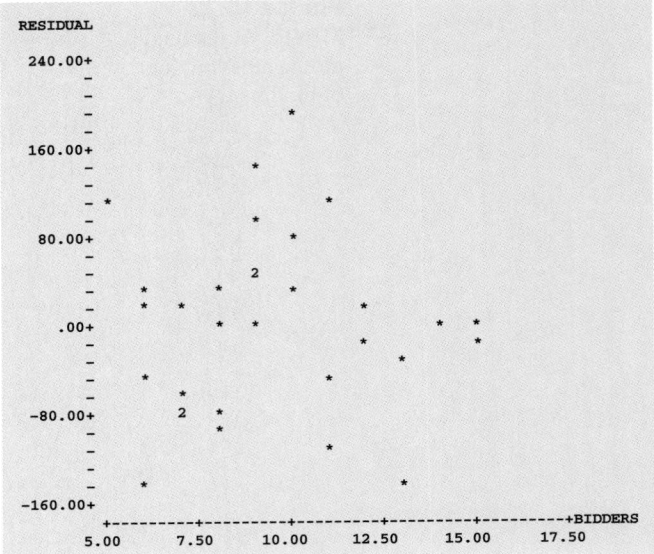

FIGURE 10.25A
MINITAB stem-and-leaf displays for grandfather clock example: Outlier included

```
STEM-AND-LEAF DISPLAY OF RESIDUAL
LEAF DIGIT UNIT =   10.0000
1 2 REPRESENTS 120.

        STEM   LEAF
    1    -7    8
    1    -6
    1    -5
    1    -4
    1    -3
    1    -2
    6    -1    93210
   16    -0    7775544432
   16     0    0233366
    9     1    14459
    4     2    1268
```

FIGURE 10.25B
MINITAB stem-and-leaf displays for grandfather clock example: Outlier excluded

```
STEM-AND-LEAF DISPLAY OF RESIDUAL
LEAF DIGIT UNIT =   10.0000
1 2 REPRESENTS 120.

    3    -1*   331
    9    -0.   987765
   (7)   -0*   4321000
   15    +0*   011223344
    6    +0.   79
    4     1*   004
    1     1.   9
```

Residual analysis is a useful tool for the regression analyst, not only to check the assumptions, but also to provide information about how the model can be improved. A summary of the residual analyses presented in this section to check the assumption that the random error ϵ is normally distributed with mean 0 is presented in the next box.

Steps in a Residual Analysis

1. Calculate and plot the residuals against each of the independent variables, preferably with the assistance of a statistical software program.

2. Analyze each plot, looking for curvature—either a mound or bowl shape. Both shapes are distinguished by groups of residuals at the low and high values of the x variable on one side of the 0 line, with the residuals for the medium x values on the opposite side of the 0 line. This shape signals the need for a curvature term in the model. Try a second-order term in the variable against which the residuals are plotted.

3. Examine the residual plots for outliers. Draw lines on the residual plots at 2- and 3-standard-deviation distances below and above the 0 line. Examine residuals outside the 3-standard-deviation lines as potential outliers, and check to see that approximately 5% of the residuals exceed the 2-standard-deviation lines. Determine whether each outlier can be explained as an error in data collection or transcription, or corresponds to a member of a population different from that of the remainder of the sample, or simply represents an unusual observation. If the observation is determined to be an error, fix it or remove it. Even if you can't determine the cause, you may want to rerun the regression analysis without the observation to determine its effect on the analysis.

4. Plot a frequency distribution of the residuals, using a stem-and-leaf display or a histogram. Check to see if obvious departures from normality exist. Extreme skewness of the frequency distribution may indicate the need for a transformation of the dependent variable. This topic is beyond the scope of this book, but you can find it in the references.

10.8 SOME PITFALLS: ESTIMABILITY, MULTICOLLINEARITY, AND EXTRAPOLATION

You should be aware of several potential problems when constructing a prediction model for some response y. A few of the most important are discussed in this section.

PROBLEM 1 PARAMETER ESTIMABILITY

Suppose you want to fit a model relating annual crop yield y to the total expenditure for fertilizer, x. We propose the first-order model

$$E(y) = \beta_0 + \beta_1 x$$

Now suppose we have three years of data and $1,000 is spent on fertilizer each year. The data are shown in Figure 10.26. You can see the problem: The parameters of the model cannot be estimated when all the data are concentrated at a single x value. Recall that it takes two points (x values) to fit a straight line. Thus, the parameters are not estimable when only one x is observed.

FIGURE 10.26
Yield and fertilizer expenditure data: Three years

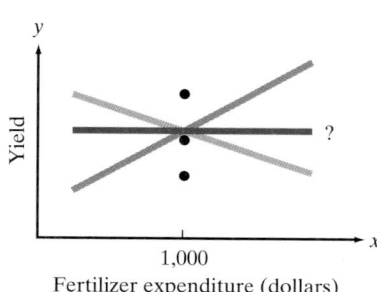

Fertilizer expenditure (dollars)

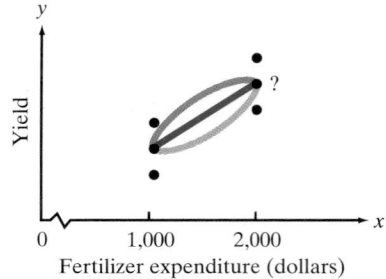

FIGURE 10.27
Only two x values
observed—quadratic
model is not estimable

A similar problem would occur if we attempted to fit the quadratic model

$$E(y) = \beta_0 + \beta_1 x + \beta_2 x^2$$

to a set of data for which only one or two different x values were observed (see Figure 10.27). At least three different x values must be observed before a quadratic model can be fit to a set of data (that is, before all three parameters are estimable). *In general, the number of levels of observed* x *values must be one more than the order of the polynomial in* x *that you want to fit.*

For controlled experiments, the researcher can select experimental designs that will permit estimation of the model parameters. Even when the values of the independent variables cannot be controlled by the researcher, the independent variables are almost always observed at a sufficient number of levels to permit estimation of the model parameters. When the computer program you use suddenly refuses to fit a model, however, the problem is probably inestimable parameters.

PROBLEM 2 MULTICOLLINEARITY

Often, two or more of the independent variables used in the model for $E(y)$ contribute redundant information. That is, the independent variables are correlated with each other. Suppose we want to construct a model to predict the gas mileage rating of a truck as a function of its load, x_1, and the horsepower, x_2, of its engine. In general, we would expect heavy loads to require greater horsepower and to result in lower mileage ratings. Thus, although both x_1 and x_2 contribute information for the prediction of mileage rating, some of the information is overlapping because x_1 and x_2 are correlated.

If the model

$$E(y) = \beta_0 + \beta_1 x_1 + \beta_2 x_2$$

were fit to a set of data, we might find that the t values for both $\hat{\beta}_1$ and $\hat{\beta}_2$ (the least squares estimates) are nonsignificant. However, the F-test for $H_0: \beta_1 = \beta_2 = 0$ would probably be highly significant. The tests may seem to produce contradictory conclusions, but really they do not. The t-tests indicate that the contribution of one variable, say $x_1 = $ Load, is not significant after the effect of $x_2 = $ Horsepower has been taken into account (because x_2 is also in the model). The significant F-test, on the other hand, tells us that at least one of the two variables is making a contribution to the prediction of y (that is, either β_1 or β_2, or both, differ from 0). In fact, both are probably contributing, but the contribution of one overlaps with that of the other.

When highly correlated independent variables are present in a regression model, the results are confusing. The researcher may want to include only one of the variables in the final model. One way of deciding which one to include is by using a technique called **stepwise regression**. In stepwise regression, all possible one-variable models of the form $E(y) = \beta_0 + \beta_1 x_i$ are fit and the "best" x_i is selected based on the t-test for β_1. Next, two-variable models of the form $E(y) = \beta_0 + \beta_1 x_1 + \beta_2 x_i$ are fit (where x_1 is the variable selected in the first step); the "second best" x_i is selected based on the test for β_2. The process continues in this fashion until no more "important" x's can be added to the model. Generally, only one of a set of multicollinear independent variables is included in a stepwise regression model, since at each step every variable is tested in the presence of all the variables already in the model. For example, if at one step the variable Load is included as a significant variable in the prediction of the mileage rating, the variable Horsepower will probably never be added in a future step. Thus, if a set of independent variables is thought to be multicollinear, some screening by stepwise regression may be helpful.

Note that it would be fallacious to conclude that an independent variable x_1 is unimportant for predicting y *only* because it is not chosen by a stepwise regression procedure. The independent variable x_1 may be correlated with another one, x_2, that the stepwise procedure did select. The implication is that x_2 contributes *more* for predicting y (in the sample being analyzed), but it may still be true that x_1 alone contributes information for the prediction of y.

PROBLEM 3   PREDICTION OUTSIDE THE EXPERIMENTAL REGION

By the late 1960s many research economists had developed highly technical models to relate the state of the economy to various economic indices and other independent variables. Many of these models were multiple regression models, where, for example, the dependent variable y might be next year's growth in GDP and the independent variables might include this year's rate of inflation, this year's Consumer Price Index (CPI), etc. In other words, the model might be constructed to predict next year's economy using this year's knowledge.

Unfortunately, these models were almost all unsuccessful in predicting the recession in the early 1970s. What went wrong? One of the problems was that many of the regression models were used for **extrapolation**, i.e., to predict y for values of the independent variables that were outside the region in which the model was developed. For example, the inflation rate in the late 1960s, when the models were developed, ranged from 6% to 8%. When the double-digit inflation of the early 1970s became a reality, some researchers attempted to use the same models to predict future growth in GDP. As you can see in Figure 10.28, the model may be very accurate for predicting y when x is in the range of experimentation, but the use of the model outside that range is a dangerous practice.

FIGURE 10.28
Using a regression model outside the experimental region

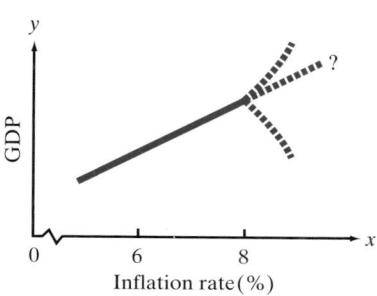

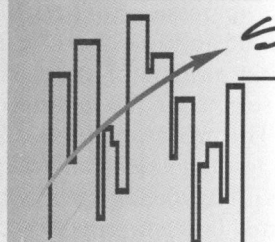

STATISTICS IN ACTION

10.2 "WRINGING" THE BELL CURVE

In Statistics in Action 4.2, we introduced *The Bell Curve* (Free Press, 1994) by Richard Herrnstein and Charles Murray, a controversial book about race, genes, IQ, and economic mobility. The book heavily employs statistics and statistical methodology in an attempt to support the authors' positions on the relationships among these variables and their social consequences. The main theme of *The Bell Curve* can be summarized as follows:

1. Measured intelligence (IQ) is largely genetically inherited.

2. IQ is correlated positively with a variety of socioeconomic status success measures, such as prestigious job, high annual income, and high educational attainment.

3. From 1 and 2, it follows that socioeconomic successes are largely genetically caused and therefore resistant to educational and environmental interventions (such as affirmative action).

With the help of a major marketing campaign, the book became a best-seller shortly after its publication in October 1994. The underlying theme of the book—that intelligence is hereditary and tied to race and class—apparently appealed to many readers. However, reviews of *The Bell Curve* in popular magazines and newspapers were mostly negative. Social critics have described the authors as "un-American" and "pseudoscientific racists," and their book as "alien and repellant." (On the other hand, there were defenders who labeled the book as "powerfully written" and "overwhelmingly convincing.") This Statistics in Action is based on two reviews of *The Bell Curve* that critique the statistical methodology employed by the authors and the inferences derived from the statistics. Both reviews, one published in *Chance* (Summer 1995) and the other in the *Journal of the American Statistical Association* (Dec. 1995), were written by Carnegie Mellon University professors Bernie Devlin, Stephen Fienberg, Daniel Resnick, and Kathryn Roeder. (Devlin, Fienberg, and Roeder are all statisticians; Resnick, a historian.)

Here, our focus is on the statistical method used repeatedly by Herrnstein and Murray (H&M) to support their conclusions in *The Bell Curve:* regression analysis. The following are just a few of the problems with H&M's use of regression that are identified by the Carnegie Mellon professors:

Problem I

H&M consistently use a trio of independent variables—IQ, socioeconomic status, and age—in a series of first-order models designed to predict dependent social outcome variables such as income and unemployment. (Only on a single occasion are interaction terms incorporated.) Consider, for example, the model

$$E(y) = \beta_0 + \beta_1 x_1 + \beta_2 x_2 + \beta_3 x_3$$

where y = income, x_1 = IQ, x_2 = socioeconomic status, and x_3 = age. H&M utilize t-tests on the individual β parameters to assess the importance of the independent variables. As with most of the models considered

PROBLEM 4   CORRELATED ERRORS

Another problem associated with using a regression model to predict a variable y based on independent variables $x_1, x_2, \ldots, x_k$ arises from the fact that the data are frequently **time series**. That is, the values of both the dependent and independent variables are observed sequentially over a period of time. The observations tend to be correlated over time, which in turn often causes the prediction errors of the regression model to be correlated. Thus, the assumption of independent errors is violated, and the model tests and prediction intervals are no longer valid. One solution to this problem is to construct a **time series model**; consult the references for this chapter to learn more about these complex, but powerful, models.

in *The Bell Curve*, the estimate of β_1 in the income model is positive and statistically significant at $\alpha = .05$, and the associated t value is larger (in absolute value) than the t values associated with the other independent variables. Consequently, *H&M claim that IQ is a better predictor of income than the other two independent variables.* No attempt was made to determine whether the model was properly specified or whether the model provides an adequate fit to the data.

Problem 2

In an appendix, the authors describe multiple regression as a "mathematical procedure that yields coefficients for each of [the independent variables], indicating how much of a change in [the dependent variable] can be anticipated for a given change in any particular [independent] variable, with all the others held constant." Armed with this information and the fact that the estimate of β_1 in the model above is positive, *H&M infer that a high IQ necessarily implies (or causes) a high income, and a low IQ inevitably leads to a low income.* (Cause-and-effect inferences like this are made repeatedly throughout the book.)

Problem 3

The title of the book refers to the normal distribution and its well-known "bell-shaped" curve. There is a misconception among the general public that scores on intelligence tests (IQ) are normally distributed. In fact, most IQ scores have distributions that are decidedly skewed. Traditionally, psychologists and psychometricians have transformed these scores so that the result-

ing numbers have a precise normal distribution. H&M make a special point to do this. Consequently, *the measure of IQ used in all the regression models is normalized (i.e., transformed so that the resulting distribution is normal), despite the fact that regression methodology does not require predictor (independent) variables to be normally distributed.*

Problem 4

A variable that is not used as a predictor of social outcome in any of the models in *The Bell Curve* is level of education. H&M purposely omit education from the models, arguing that IQ causes education, not the other way around. Other researchers who have examined H&M's data report that *when education is included as an independent variable in the model, the effect of IQ on the dependent variable (say, income) is diminished.*

Focus

a. Comment on each of the problems identified by the Carnegie Mellon University professors in their review of *The Bell Curve*. Why do each of these problems cast a shadow on the inferences made by the authors?

b. Using the variables specified in the model above, describe how you would conduct the multiple regression analysis. (Propose a more complex model and describe the appropriate model tests, including a residual analysis.)

EXERCISES   10.27–10.39

Note: Exercises marked with 💾 *contain data for computer analysis on a 3.5" disk (file name in parentheses).*

Learning the Mechanics

10.27   When a multiple regression model is used for estimating the mean of the dependent variable and for predicting a particular value of y, which will be narrower, the confidence interval for the mean or the prediction interval for the particular y value? Explain.

10.28   Refer to Exercise 10.1, in which the model

$$y = \beta_0 + \beta_1 x_1 + \beta_2 x_2 + \epsilon$$

was fit to $n = 20$ data points. The MINITAB regression printout for these data is shown on page 578. Both a confidence interval for $E(y)$ and a prediction interval for y when $x_1 = .5$ and $x_2 = .2$ are shown at the bottom of the printout.
a. Interpret the confidence interval for $E(y)$.
b. Interpret the prediction interval for y.

```
The regression equation is
Y = 508 - 942 X1 + 429 X2

Predictor        Coef       Stdev      t-ratio         p
Constant       506.35       45.17        11.21     0.000
X1            -941.9       275.11        -3.42     0.004
X2             429.1       379.80         1.13     0.252

s = 94.25        R-sq = 45.9%      R-sq(adj) = 39.6%

Analysis of Variance

SOURCE          DF          SS          MS          F          p
Regression       2      128329       64165       7.22      0.003
Error           17      151016        8883
Total           19      279345

       Fit  Stdev.Fit        95% C.I.            95% P.I.
    121.22       46.0    ( 91.7, 150.7)     ( 29.2, 213.2)
```

10.29 Refer to Exercise 10.14, in which a quadratic model was fit to $n = 19$ data points. Two SAS residual plots are shown on page 579—the top one corresponds to the fitting of a straight-line model to the data, and the other to the quadratic model fit in Exercise 10.14. Analyze the two plots. Is the need for a quadratic term evident from the residual plot for the straight-line model? Does your conclusion agree with your test of the quadratic term in Exercise 10.14?

10.30 Consider fitting the multiple regression model

$$E(y) = \beta_0 + \beta_1 x_1 + \beta_2 x_2 + \beta_3 x_3 + \beta_4 x_4 + \beta_5 x_5.$$

A matrix of correlations for all pairs of independent variables is shown in the next column. Do you detect a multicollinearity problem? Explain.

	x_1	x_2	x_3	x_4	x_5
x_1	—	.17	.02	−.23	.19
x_2		—	.45	.93	.02
x_3			—	.22	−.01
x_4				—	.86
x_5					—

Applying the Concepts

10.31 (X10.031) A Wall Street security analyst who specializes in the pharmaceutical industry is interested in better understanding the relationship between a firm's sales and its research and development (R&D) expenditures. The table below presents 1995 data on sales revenue (y), number of employees (x_1), and R&D expenditures (x_2) for a sample of 15 pharmaceutical companies.

Company	Sales y (millions of $)	Number of Employees x_1 (thousands)	R&D Expense x_2 (millions of $)
Abbott Laboratories	10,012	50.24	1,072
Alza	326	1.44	20
American Home Products Corp.	13,376	64.71	1,354
Bristol Myers Squibb	13,767	49.14	1,199
Carter-Wallace Inc.	662	3.61	26
Genentech Inc.	857	2.84	503
IVAX Corp.	1,259	7.89	64
Johnson & Johnson	18,842	82.30	1,634
Lilly (Eli) & Co.	6,763	26.80	4,239
Merck & Co.	16,681	45.20	5,269
Pharmacia & Upjohn Inc.	7,094	35.00	3,383
Pfizer	10,021	43.80	3,472
Rhone-Poulenc Roren	5,142	28.00	1,621
Schering-Plough	5,104	20.10	2,098
Warner-Lambert Co.	7,039	37.00	2,006

Source: Compuserve, 1996.

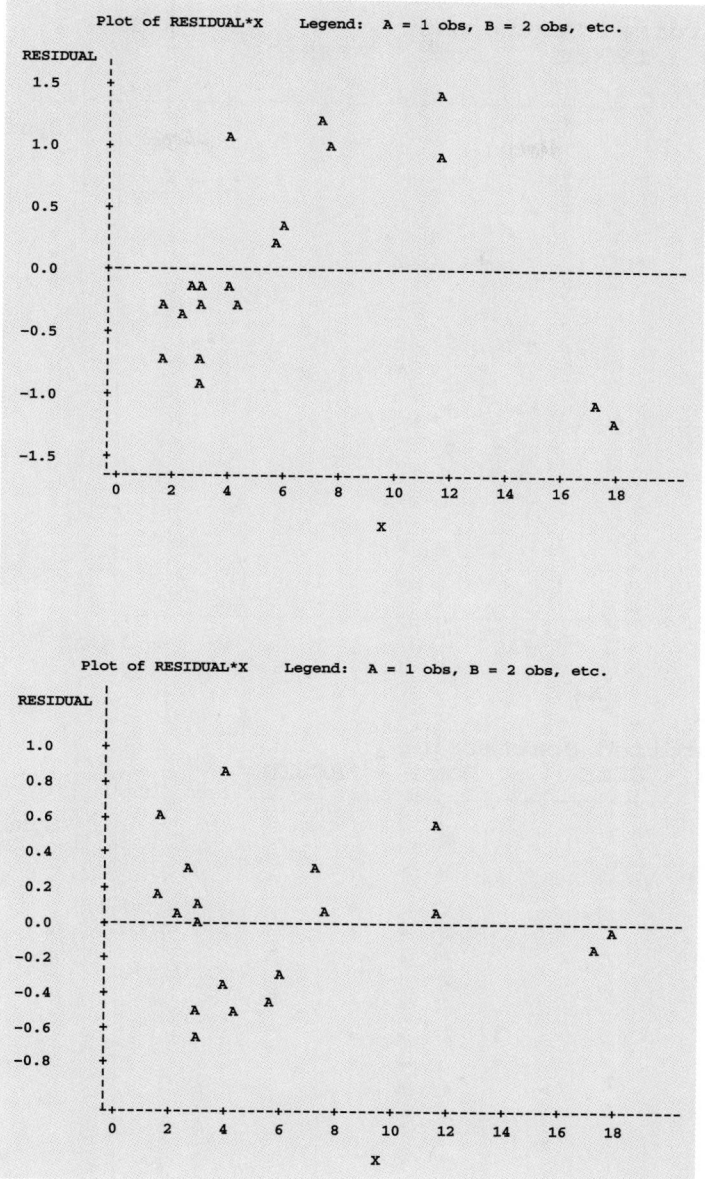

a. Fit the multiple regression model $E(y) = \beta_0 + \beta_1 x_1 + \beta_2 x_2$ to the data using a statistical software package.

b. Use the software to generate a 95% confidence interval for the mean sales revenue of companies with 1,000 employees and R&D expenditures of $500 million. Interpret the interval.

c. Do you detect any signs of multicollinearity? Explain.

d. Verify your answer to part **c** by finding the correlation between number of employees (x_1) and R&D expenditures (x_2).

10.32 Refer to Exercise 10.6, in which the 1996 food consumption expenditure y of a sample of 25 households in Washington, D.C., was related to the household income x_1 and size of household x_2 by the model

$$y = \beta_0 + \beta_1 x_1 + \beta_2 x_2 + \epsilon$$

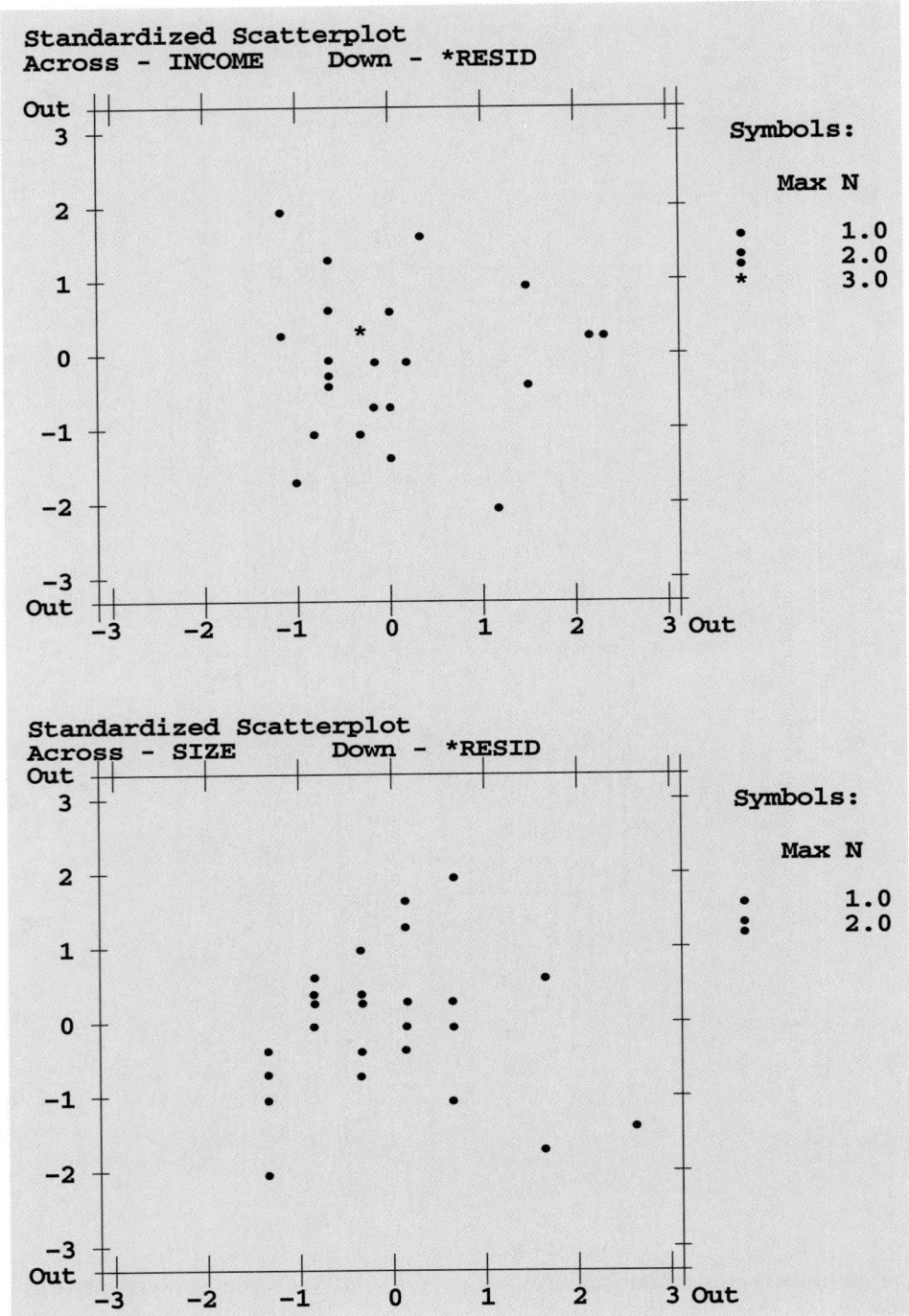

SPSS plots of the standardized residuals from this model are shown above—one versus x_1 and one versus x_2. Analyze the plots. Is there visual evidence of a need for a quadratic term in either x_1 or x_2? Explain.

10.33 Refer to Exercise 10.32. Suppose a 26th household is added to the sample, with the following characteristics:

Food consumption: 7.5
Income: 7.3
Household size: 5

```
Model: MODEL1
Dependent Variable: FOOD
                           Analysis of Variance

                           Sum of          Mean
           Source      DF  Squares        Square     F Value      Prob>F
           Model        2  12.78439       6.39219     52.138      0.0001
           Error       22   2.69721       0.12260
           C Total     24  15.48160

                Root MSE      0.35014    R-square      0.8258
                Dep Mean      4.05600    Adj R-sq      0.8099
                C.V.          8.63273

                           Parameter Estimates

                        Parameter     Standard    T for HO:
        Variable   DF    Estimate       Error     Parameter=0    Prob > |T|
        INTERCEP    1    2.369646     0.21813514    10.863        0.0001
        INCOME      1    0.009193     0.00337540     2.724        0.0124
        SIZE        1    0.353964     0.03518275    10.061        0.0001

                      Dep Var   Predict   Std Err   Lower95%   Upper95%
   Obs  INCOME  SIZE   FOOD      Value    Predict   Predict    Predict   Residual
    1    41.1    4    4.2000    4.1633    0.072     3.4219     4.9048    0.0367
```

```
Model: MODEL2
Dependent Variable: FOOD
                           Analysis of Variance

                           Sum of          Mean
           Source      DF  Squares        Square     F Value      Prob>F
           Model        2  17.79867       8.89934     22.523      0.0001
           Error       23   9.08786       0.39512
           C Total     25  26.88654

                Root MSE      0.62859    R-square      0.6620
                Dep Mean      4.18846    Adj R-sq      0.6326
                C.V.         15.00764

                           Parameter Estimates

                        Parameter     Standard    T for HO:
        Variable   DF    Estimate       Error     Parameter=0    Prob > |T|
        INTERCEP    1    2.036250     0.38272822     5.320        0.0001
        INCOME      1    0.015560     0.00584915     2.660        0.0140
        SIZE        1    0.393637     0.06238612     6.310        0.0001

                      Dep Var   Predict   Std Err   Lower95%   Upper95%
   Obs  INCOME  SIZE   FOOD      Value    Predict   Predict    Predict   Residual
    1    41.1    4    4.2000    4.2503    0.128     2.9233     5.5773   -0.0503
```

Two SAS printouts are shown above—one for the same model fit to the first 25 observations, the second fit to all 26 observations.

a. Record the least squares estimates of the model parameters for each model, and note differences in the estimates. Interpret each estimate.

b. Find and interpret the standard deviation for each model.

c. Conduct the analysis of variance F-test for each model using $\alpha = .05$.

d. Place a 95% confidence interval on the mean rate of change in food consumption per additional person in the household for each model, assuming household income is constant.

e. For each model, interpret the 95% prediction interval for y shown at the bottom of the printout.

f. According to the results of parts a–d, how much influence does the additional observation have on the model?

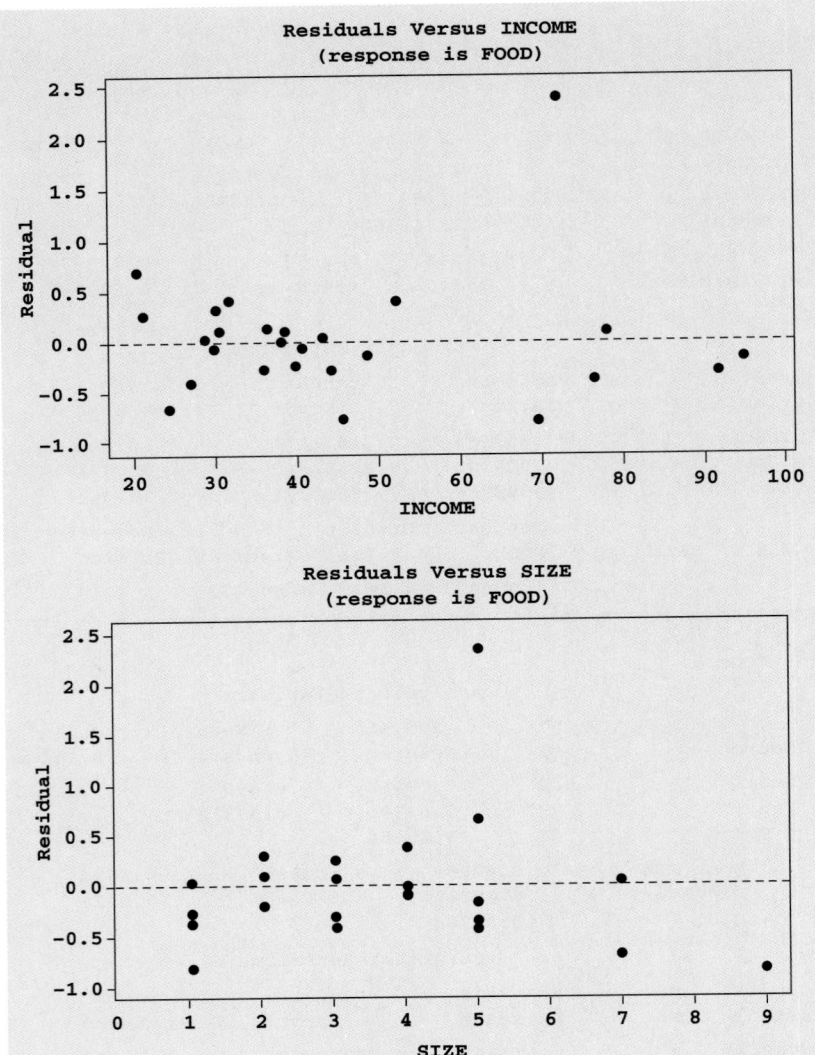

10.34 Refer to Exercises 10.32 and 10.33. MINITAB residual plots against household income and size of household for the models corresponding to 26 observations are shown above.

    a. Analyze the plots. Are there any outliers? If so, identify them.

    b. What are possible explanations for any outliers you identified in part **a**?

10.35 Refer to Exercises 10.32–10.34. The MINITAB stem-and-leaf displays shown on page 583 represent the frequency distributions of the residuals for the two data sets, one with $n = 25$ and one with $n = 26$. Analyze the displays, especially with regard to the normality assumption.

10.36 Refer to the *World Development* study of the variables impacting the size distribution of manufac-

turing firms in international markets, Exercise 10.10. Five independent variables, LGNP, AREAC, SVA, CREDIT, and STOCK, were used to model the share, y, of firms with 100 or more workers. The researchers detected a high correlation between pairs of the following independent variables: LGNP and SVA, LGNP and STOCK, and CREDIT and STOCK. Describe the problems that may arise if these high correlations are ignored in the multiple regression analysis of the model.

10.37 **(X10.037)** Passive exposure to environmental tobacco smoke has been associated with growth suppression and an increased frequency of respiratory tract infections in normal children. Is this association more pronounced in children with cystic fibrosis? To answer this question, a study

```
Stem-and-leaf of RESID25   N = 25
Leaf Unit = 0.010

     1    -6 6
     2    -5 7
     3    -4 7
     5    -3 85
     7    -2 93
     8    -1 3
    10    -0 85
    (5)    0 13468
    10     1 1147
     6     2 45
     4     3 4
     3     4 2
     2     5 3
     1     6 7
----------------------------------
Stem-and-leaf of RESID26   N = 26
Leaf Unit = 0.10

     3    -0 876
    (11)  -0 44332221000
    12     0 0000112333
     2     0 6
     1     1
     1     1
     1     2 3
```

relating y to x is shown on page 584. Examine the residuals. Do you detect any outliers?

Weight Percentile y	No. of Cigarettes Smoked per Day x
6	0
6	15
2	40
8	23
11	20
17	7
24	3
25	0
17	25
25	20
25	15
31	23
35	10
43	0
49	0
50	0
49	22
46	30
54	0
58	0
62	0
66	0
66	23
83	0
87	44

Source: Rubin, B. K. "Exposure of children with cystic fibrosis to environmental tobacco smoke." *New England Journal of Medicine,* Vol. 323, No. 12, September 20, 1990, p. 785 (data extracted from Figure 3).

was conducted on 43 children (18 girls and 25 boys) attending a two-week summer camp for cystic fibrosis patients (*New England Journal of Medicine,* Sept. 20, 1990). Researchers investigated the correlation between a child's weight percentile (y) and the number of cigarettes smoked per day in the child's home (x). The accompanying table lists the data for the 25 boys. A MINITAB printout (with residuals) for the straight-line model

10.38   Refer to Exercise 10.9, in which a quadratic model was used to relate the time to complete a task, y, to the months of experience, x, for a sample of 15 employees on an automobile assembly line. Suppose a straight-line model has been fit instead. The SPSS printout for the straight-line model is shown below. A residual plot is shown

```
Multiple R              .94886
R Square                .90033
Adjusted R Square       .89266
Standard Error         1.14301

Analysis of Variance
                  DF     Sum of Squares      Mean Square
Regression         1          153.41583        153.41583
Residual          13           16.98417          1.30647

F =    117.42733          Signif F = .0000

----------------- Variables in the Equation ------------------

Variable            B         SE B       Beta         T     Sig T

X              -.44494      .04106    -.94886    -10.836    .0000
(Constant)    19.27908      .50788                37.960    .0000
```

```
The regression equation is
WTPCTILE = 41.2 - 0.262 SMOKED

Predictor        Coef        Stdev      t-ratio          p
Constant       41.153       6.843         6.01      0.000
SMOKED        -0.2619       0.3702        -0.71      0.486

s = 24.68       R-sq = 2.1%     R-sq(adj) = 0.0%

Analysis of Variance

SOURCE          DF          SS          MS          F          p
Regression       1        304.9       304.9       0.50      0.486
Error           23      14011.1       609.2
Total           24      14316.0

Obs.    SMOKED   WTPCTILE       Fit   Stdev.Fit  Residual   St.Resid
  1       0.0       6.00      41.15       6.84     -35.15      -1.48
  2      15.0       6.00      37.22       5.00     -31.22      -1.29
  3      40.0       2.00      30.68      11.22     -28.68      -1.30
  4      23.0       8.00      35.13       6.22     -27.13      -1.14
  5      20.0      11.00      35.91       5.61     -24.91      -1.04
  6       7.0      17.00      39.32       5.38     -22.32      -0.93
  7       3.0      24.00      40.37       6.13     -16.37      -0.68
  8       0.0      25.00      41.15       6.84     -16.15      -0.68
  9      25.0      17.00      34.60       6.69     -17.60      -0.74
 10      20.0      25.00      35.91       5.61     -10.91      -0.45
 11      15.0      25.00      37.22       5.00     -12.22      -0.51
 12      23.0      31.00      35.13       6.22      -4.13      -0.17
 13      10.0      35.00      38.53       5.04      -3.53      -0.15
 14       0.0      43.00      41.15       6.84       1.85       0.08
 15       0.0      49.00      41.15       6.84       7.85       0.33
 16       0.0      50.00      41.15       6.84       8.85       0.37
 17      22.0      49.00      35.39       6.00      13.61       0.57
 18      30.0      46.00      33.29       8.06      12.71       0.54
 19       0.0      54.00      41.15       6.84      12.85       0.54
 20       0.0      58.00      41.15       6.84      16.85       0.71
 21       0.0      62.00      41.15       6.84      20.85       0.88
 22       0.0      66.00      41.15       6.84      24.85       1.05
 23      23.0      66.00      35.13       6.22      30.87       1.29
 24       0.0      83.00      41.15       6.84      41.85       1.76
 25      44.0      87.00      29.63      12.56      57.37       2.70
```

on page 585. Does the residual analysis support the statistical test you conducted in part **c** of Exercise 10.9?

10.39 *Teaching Sociology* (July 1995) developed a model for the professional socialization of graduate students working toward their doctorate. One of the dependent variables modeled was professional confidence, *y*, measured on a 5-point scale. The model included more than 20 independent variables and was fit to data collected for a sample of 309 graduate students. One concern is whether multicollinearity exists in the data. A matrix of Pearson product moment correlations for 10 of the independent variables is shown on page 585. [*Note:* Each entry in the table is the correlation coefficient *r* between the variable in the corresponding row and corresponding column.]

a. Examine the correlation matrix and find the independent variables that are moderately or highly correlated.

b. What modeling problems may occur if the variables, part **a**, are left in the model? Explain.

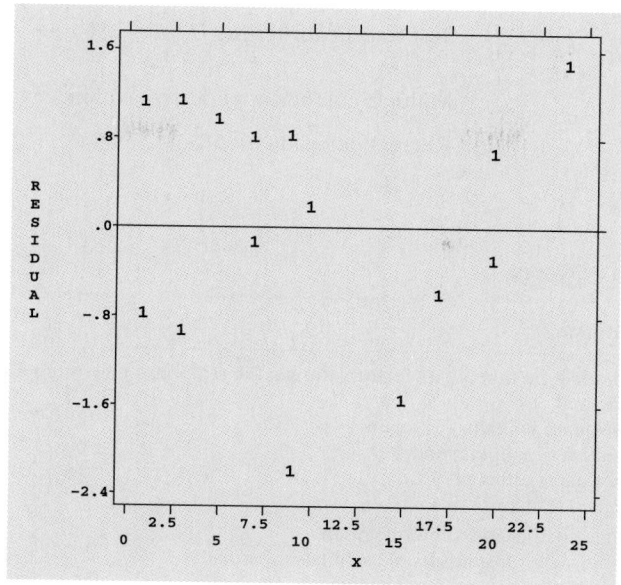

Independent Variable	(1)	(2)	(3)	(4)	(5)	(6)	(7)	(8)	(9)	(10)
(1) Father's occupation	1.000	.363	.099	−.110	−.047	−.053	−.111	.178	.078	.049
(2) Mother's education	.363	1.000	.228	−.139	−.216	.084	−.118	.192	.125	.068
(3) Race	.099	.228	1.000	.036	−.515	.014	−.120	.112	.117	.337
(4) Sex	−.110	−.139	.036	1.000	.165	−.256	.173	−.106	−.117	.073
(5) Foreign status	−.047	−.216	−.515	.165	1.000	−.041	.159	−.130	−.165	−.171
(6) Undergraduate GPA	−.053	.084	.014	−.256	−.041	1.000	.032	.028	−.034	.092
(7) Year GRE taken	−.111	−.118	−.120	.173	.159	.032	1.000	−.086	−.602	.016
(8) Verbal GRE score	.178	.192	.112	−.106	−.130	.028	−.086	1.000	.132	.087
(9) Years in graduate program	.078	.125	.117	−.117	−.165	−.034	−.602	.132	1.000	−.071
(10) First-year graduate GPA	.049	.068	.337	.073	−.171	.092	.016	.087	−.071	1.000

Source: Keith, B., and Moore, H. A. "Training sociologists: An assessment of professional socialization and the emergence of career aspirations" *Teaching Sociology,* Vol. 23, No. 3, July 1995, p. 205 (Table 1).

QUICK REVIEW

Key Terms

Correlated errors   576
Dummy variable   538
Extrapolation   575
General linear model   526
Global *F*-test   544
Interaction   548

Interaction model   548
Mean square for error   532
Multicollinearity   574
Multiple coefficient of
   determination   545
Multiple regression model   526

Outlier   568
Parameter estimability   573
Quadratic term   528
Residual   563
Residual analysis   563
Time series model   576

Key Formulas

$$s^2 = MSE = \frac{SSE}{n - (k + 1)}$$

Estimator of σ^2 for a model with k independent variables   532

$$t = \frac{\hat{\beta}_i}{s_{\hat{\beta}_i}}$$

Test statistic for testing $H_0: \beta_i = 0$ 535

$$\hat{\beta}_i \pm (t_{\alpha/2})s_{\hat{\beta}_i},$$
   where t depends on $n - (k + 1)$ df

$(1 - \alpha)$ 100% confidence interval for β_i 536

$$F = \frac{MS(Model)}{MSE} = \frac{R^2/k}{(1 - R^2)/[n - (k + 1)]}$$

Test statistic for testing $H_0: \beta_1 = \beta_2 = \cdots = \beta_k = 0$ 546

$$R^2 = \frac{SS_{yy} - SSE}{SS_{yy}}$$

Multiple coefficient of determination   545

$y - \hat{y}$

Regression residual   563

LANGUAGE LAB

Symbol	Pronunciation	Description
x_1^2	x-1 squared	Quadratic term that allows for curvature in the relationship between y and x
$x_1 x_2$	x-1 x-2	Interaction term
MSE	M-S-E	Mean square for error (estimates σ^2)
β_i	beta-i	Coefficient of x_i in the model
$\hat{\beta}_i$	beta-i-hat	Least squares estimate of β_i
$s_{\hat{\beta}_i}$	s of beta-i-hat	Estimated standard error of $\hat{\beta}_i$
R^2	R-squared	Multiple coefficient of determination
F		Test statistic for testing global usefulness of model
$\hat{\epsilon}$	epsilon-hat	Estimated random error, or residual

SUPPLEMENTARY EXERCISES 10.40–10.55

Note: Exercises marked with 💾 *contain data for computer analysis on a 3.5" disk (file name in parentheses).*

Learning the Mechanics

10.40 Suppose you used MINITAB to fit the model

$$y = \beta_0 + \beta_1 x_1 + \beta_2 x_2 + \epsilon$$

to $n = 15$ data points and you obtained the printout shown below.
a. What is the least squares prediction equation?
b. Find R^2 and interpret its value.

c. Is there sufficient evidence to indicate that the model is useful for predicting y? Conduct an F-test using $\alpha = .05$.
d. Test the null hypothesis $H_0: \beta_1 = 0$ against the alternative hypothesis $H_a: \beta_1 \neq 0$. Test using $\alpha = .05$. Draw the appropriate conclusions.
e. Find the standard deviation of the regression model and interpret it.

10.41 Suppose you fit the model

$$y = \beta_0 + \beta_1 x_1 + \beta_2 x_1^2 + \beta_3 x_2 + \beta_4 x_1 x_2 + \epsilon$$

to $n = 25$ data points and find that

```
The regression equation is
Y = 90.1 - 1.84 X1 + .285 X2

Predictor      Coef       Stdev     t-ratio        p
Constant       90.10      23.10       3.90      0.002
X1             -1.836      0.367      -5.01      0.001
X2              0.285      0.231       1.24      0.465

s = 10.68     R-sq = 91.6%      R-sq(adj) = 90.2%

Analysis of Variance

SOURCE        DF          SS          MS         F        p
Regression     2        14801        7400     64.91    0.001
Error         12         1364         114
Total         14        16165
```

$\hat{\beta}_0 = 1.26 \qquad \hat{\beta}_1 = -2.43 \qquad \hat{\beta}_2 = .05 \qquad \hat{\beta}_3 = .62$

$\hat{\beta}_4 = 1.81 \qquad \text{SSE} = .41 \qquad R^2 = .83$

$s_{\hat{\beta}_1} = 1.21 \qquad s_{\hat{\beta}_2} = .16 \qquad s_{\hat{\beta}_3} = .26 \qquad s_{\hat{\beta}_4} = 1.49$

a. Is there sufficient evidence to conclude that at least one of the parameters β_1, β_2, β_3, or β_4 is nonzero? Test using $\alpha = .05$.

b. Test H_0: $\beta_1 = 0$ against H_a: $\beta_1 < 0$. Use $\alpha = .05$.

c. Test H_0: $\beta_2 = 0$ against H_a: $\beta_2 > 0$. Use $\alpha = .05$.

d. Test H_0: $\beta_3 = 0$ against H_a: $\beta_3 \neq 0$. Use $\alpha = .05$.

10.42 Suppose you have developed a regression model to explain the relationship between y and x_1, x_2, and x_3. A set of $n = 15$ data points is used to find the least squares prediction equation. The ranges of the variables you observed were as follows: $10 \leqslant y \leqslant 100$, $5 \leqslant x_1 \leqslant 55$, $.5 \leqslant x_2 \leqslant 1$, and $1,000 \leqslant x_3 \leqslant 2,000$. Will the error of prediction be smaller when you use the least squares equation to predict y when $x_1 = 30$, $x_2 = .6$, and $x_3 = 1,300$, or when $x_1 = 60$, $x_2 = .4$, and $x_3 = 900$? Why?

10.43 Refer to Exercise 10.14, in which a quadratic model was fit to $n = 19$ data points. Two residual plots are shown—the one below corresponds to the fitting of a straight-line model to the data and the other, on page 588, to the quadratic model fit

in Exercise 10.14. Analyze the two plots. Is the need for a quadratic term evident from the residual plot for the straight-line model? Does your conclusion agree with your test of the quadratic term in Exercise 10.14?

Applying the Concepts

10.44 Since the Great Depression of the 1930s, the link between the suicide rate and the state of the economy has been the subject of much research. Research exploring this link using regression analysis was reported in an article in the *Journal of Socio-Economics* (Spring 1992). The researchers collected data from a 45-year period on the following variables:

y = Suicide rate

x_1 = Unemployment rate

x_2 = Percentage of females in the labor force

x_3 = Divorce rate

x_4 = Logarithm of Gross Domestic Product (GDP)

x_5 = Annual percent change in GDP

One of the models explored by the researchers was a multiple regression model relating y to linear terms in x_1 through x_5. The least squares

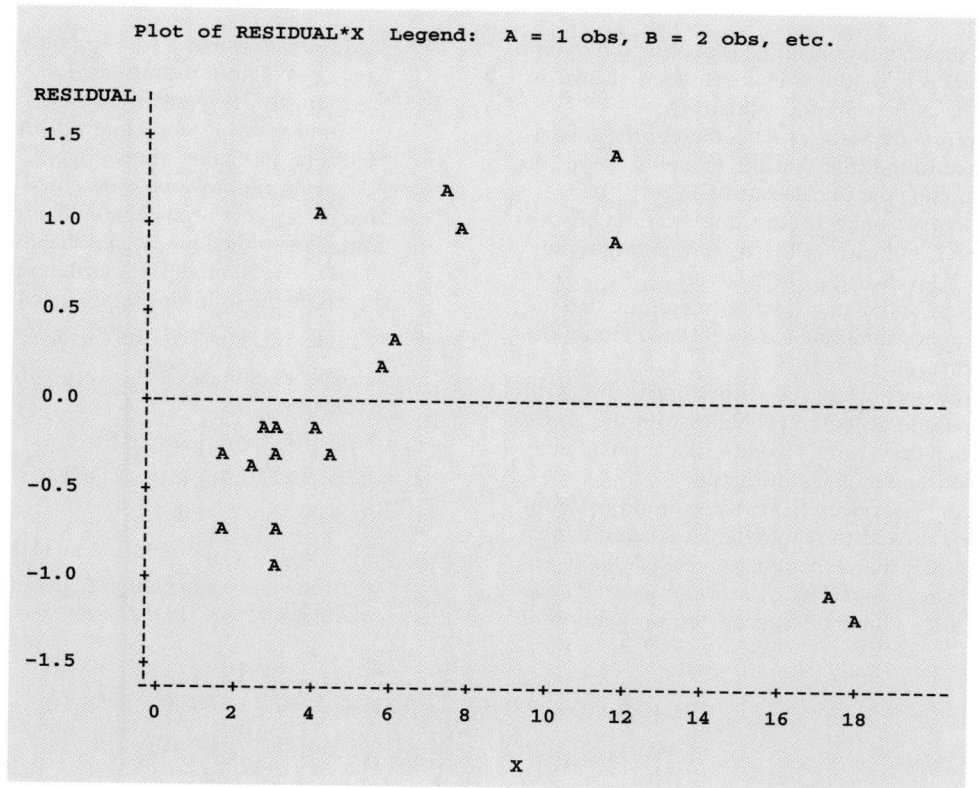

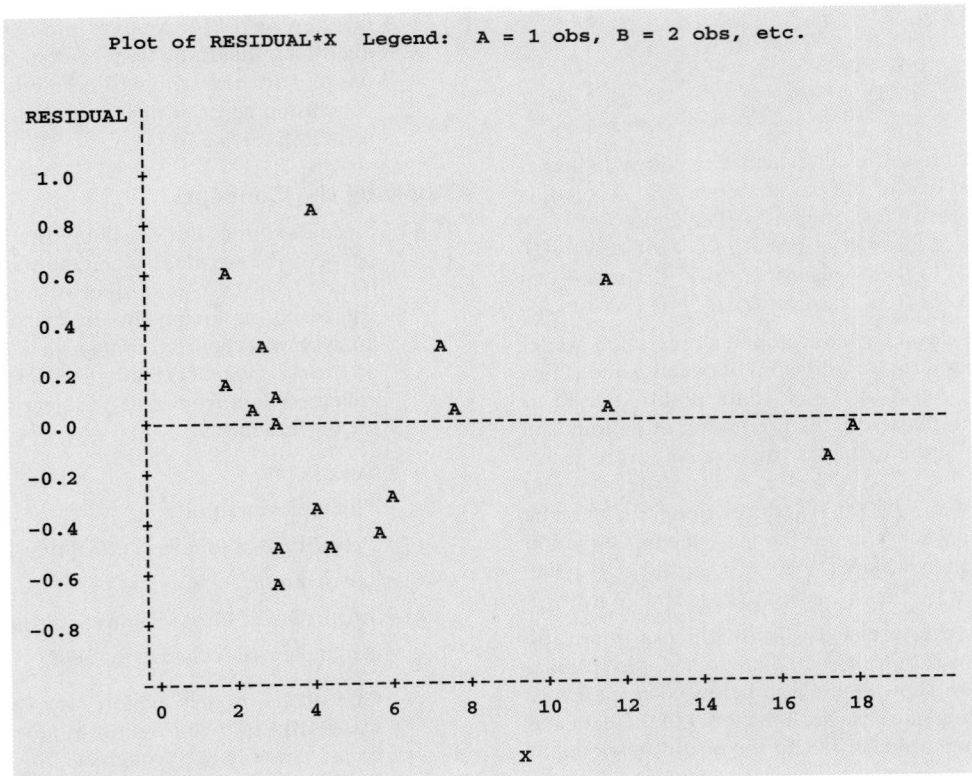

model shown below resulted (the observed significance levels of the β estimates are shown in parentheses beneath the estimates).

a. Interpret the value of R^2. Is there sufficient evidence to indicate that the model is useful for predicting the suicide rate? Use $\alpha = .05$.

b. Interpret each of the coefficients in the model, and each of the corresponding significance levels.

c. Is there sufficient evidence to indicate that the unemployment rate is a useful predictor of the suicide rate? Use $\alpha = .05$.

d. Discuss each of the following terms with respect to potential problems with the above model: curvature (second-order terms), interaction, and multicollinearity.

10.45 Emergency services (EMS) personnel are constantly exposed to traumatic situations; consequently, they may experience severe psychological stress. The *Journal of Consulting and Clinical Psychology* (June 1995) reported on a study of

EMS rescue workers who responded to the I-880 freeway collapse during the 1989 San Francisco earthquake. The goal of the study was to identify the predictors of symptomatic distress in the EMS workers. With this knowledge, EMS personnel managers can anticipate potential problems and assign workers accordingly. One of the distress variables studied was the Global Symptom Index (GSI). Several models for GSI, y, were considered based on the following independent variables:

x_1 = Critical Incident Exposure scale (CIE)

x_2 = Hogan Personality Inventory-Adjustment scale (HPI-A)

x_3 = Years of experience (EXP)

x_4 = Locus of Control scale (LOC)

x_5 = Social Support scale (SS)

x_6 = Dissociative Experiences scale (DES)

x_7 = Peritraumatic Dissociation Experiences Questionnaire, self-report (PDEQ-SR)

$$\hat{y} = .002 + .0204x_1 + (-.0231)x_2 + .0765x_3 + .2760x_4 + .0018x_5$$
$$\quad\quad\quad (.002) \quad\quad (.02) \quad\quad (>.10) \quad\quad (>.10) \quad\quad (>.10)$$

$$R^2 = .45$$

a. Write a first-order model for $E(y)$ as a function of the first five independent variables, x_1–x_5.

b. The model of part **a**, fit to data collected for $n = 147$ EMS workers, yielded the following results: $R^2 = .469$, $F = 34.47$, p-value $< .001$. Interpret these results.

c. Write a first-order model for $E(y)$ as a function of all seven independent variables, x_1–x_7.

d. The model, part **c**, yielded $R^2 = .603$. Interpret this result.

e. The t-tests for testing the DES and PDEQ-SR variables both yielded a p-value of .001. Interpret these results.

10.46 Most companies institute rigorous safety programs to ensure employee safety. Suppose accident reports over the last year at a company are sampled, and the number of hours the employee had worked before the accident occurred, x, and the amount of time the employee lost from work, y, are recorded. A quadratic model is proposed to investigate a fatigue hypothesis that more serious accidents occur near the end of workdays than occur near the beginning, but that the rate of increase of time lost with hours worked is slower near the end of day. Thus, the proposed model is

$$E(y) = \beta_0 + \beta_1 x + \beta_2 x^2$$

A total of 60 accident reports are examined and the model fit to the data. The regression results are shown here:

$$\hat{y} = 12.3 + .25x - .0033x^2 \qquad R^2 = .0430$$

$$F = 1.28\ (p\text{-value} = .8711) \qquad s_{\hat{\beta}_2} = .0469$$

a. According to the fatigue hypothesis, what is the expected sign of β_2?

b. Test the fatigue hypothesis at $\alpha = .05$.

c. Conduct a test of overall model adequacy at $\alpha = .05$.

d. Use the model to predict the number of days missed by an employee who has an accident after six hours of work.

e. Suppose the 95% prediction interval for the predicted value in part **d** is determined to be (1.35, 26.01). Interpret this interval. Does this interval support your conclusion about the model in part **c**?

10.47 To meet the increasing demand for new software products, many systems development experts have adopted a prototyping methodology. The effects of prototyping on the system development life cycle (SDLC) were investigated in the *Journal of Computer Information Systems* (Spring 1993). A survey of 500 randomly selected corporate-level MIS managers was conducted. Three potential independent variables were (1) *importance* of pro-

totyping to each phase of the SDLC; (2) degree of *support* prototyping provides for the SDLC; and (3) degree to which prototyping *replaces* each phase of the SDLC. The accompanying table gives the pairwise correlations of the three variables in the survey data for one particular phase of the SDLC. Use this information to assess the degree of multicollinearity in the survey data. Would you recommend using all three independent variables in a regression analysis? Explain.

Variable Pairs	Correlation Coefficient, r
Importance—Replace	.2682
Importance—Support	.6991
Replace—Support	−.0531

Source: Hardgrave, B. C., Doke, E. R., and Swanson, N. E. "Prototyping effects on the system development life cycle: An empirical study." *Journal of Computer Information Systems,* Vol. 33, No. 3, Spring 1993, p. 16 (Table 1).

10.48 To increase the motivation and productivity of workers, an electronics manufacturer decides to experiment with a new pay incentive structure at one of two plants. The experimental plan will be tried at plant A for six months, whereas workers at plant B will remain on the original pay plan. To evaluate the effectiveness of the new plan, the average assembly time for part of an electronic system was measured for employees at both plants at the beginning and end of the six-month period. Suppose the model proposed was

$$y = \beta_0 + \beta_1 x_1 + \beta_2 x_2 + \epsilon$$

where

$y =$ Assembly time (hours) at end of six-month period

$x_1 =$ Assembly time (hours) at beginning of six-month period

$$x_2 = \begin{cases} 1 & \text{if plant A} \\ 0 & \text{if plant B} \end{cases}$$

A sample of $n = 42$ observations yielded

$$\hat{y} = .11 + .98x_1 - .53x_2$$

where

$$s_{\hat{\beta}_1} = .231 \qquad s_{\hat{\beta}_2} = .48$$

Test to see whether, after allowing for the effect of initial assembly time, plant A had a lower mean assembly time than plant B. Use $\alpha = .01$.

10.49 Research was conducted to discover the factors in a person's education that determine future wages (*Southern Economic Journal,* Vol. 50, 1983). A first-order model was fit to a set of $n = 60$ data points and the prediction equation and t-test values were

$$\hat{y} = 0 - .0945x_1 - .032x_2 + .009x_3 - .0028x_4 + .007x_5 + .105x_6 + .469x_7$$
$$\phantom{\hat{y} = 0} (-2.61) \quad (-.96) \quad (2.74) \quad (-2.23) \quad (5.71) \quad (4.02) \quad (2.21)$$

where

y = Future wages

x_1 = Amount of business course work in high school

x_2 = Amount of college prep work in high school

x_3 = Math aptitude

x_4 = High school GPA

x_5 = Measure of socioeconomic status

x_6 = 1 if the individual is married, 0 if not

x_7 = Amount of on-the-job training

obtained (see the table above). The t values used to test the individual model parameters are shown in parentheses below their respective estimates.

a. What are the interpretations of the coefficients?

b. Are they statistically significant at the $\alpha = .01$ level?

c. The standard error for the estimate of β_5 is .001225. Use this information to construct a 99% confidence interval for β_5.

d. Interpret the interval, part c.

10.50 **(X10.050)** In Exercise 9.85 you used simple regression to model the relationship between the sales prices (y) of existing homes in suburban Essex county, New Jersey, and their square footage (x_1). These data are reproduced below along with the number of bathrooms (x_2) and yearly property taxes (x_3). Consider the multiple regression model

$$E(y) = \beta_0 + \beta_1 x_1 + \beta_2 x_2 + \beta_3 x_3 +$$
$$\beta_4 x_1 x_2 + \beta_5 x_1 x_3 + \beta_6 x_2 x_3$$

a. Use a statistical software package to fit the model to the data.

Area (sq. ft.)	Price ($)	Number of Bathrooms	1995 Property Taxes ($)
2306	145,541	1	3,611
2677	179,900	2	4,433
2324	149,000	1	4,132
1447	113,900	2	2,668
3333	189,000	3	6,089
3004	184,500	2	5,867
4142	339,717	4	5,094
2923	228,000	2	3,776
2902	209,000	3	6,200
1847	133,000	1	3,205
2148	168,000	2	6,034
2819	205,000	2	2,985
1753	129,900	1	2,586
3206	235,000	3	7,184
2474	129,900	2	3,458
2933	199,500	2	5,646
3987	319,000	3	5,669
2598	185,500	2	4,211
4934	375,000	4	9,896
2253	169,000	3	5,502
2998	185,900	1	3,962
2791	189,800	3	4,295
2865	192,000	2	4,416
4417	379,900	4	8,121

Source: Adapted from data compiled by the Multiple Listing Service, Suburban Essex County, New Jersey, 1996.

b. Is there evidence (at $\alpha = .05$) that the overall model is useful for predicting price (y)?

c. Is there evidence (at $\alpha = .05$) that the linear relationship between price (y) and square footage (x_1) is dependent on the yearly property taxes (x_3)?

d. Conduct a residual analysis for the model. Identify any outliers in the data and any assumptions that may be violated.

10.51 **(X10.051)** In the oil industry, water mixes with crude oil during production and transportation resulting in tiny oil particles suspended within the water. This water and oil (w/o) suspension is called an emulsion. Chemists have found that the oil can be extracted from the w/o emulsion electrically. Researchers at the University of Bergen (Norway) conducted a series of experiments to study the factors that influence the voltage required to separate the water from the oil in w/o emulsions (*Journal of Colloid and Interface Science*, Aug. 1995). The seven independent variables investigated in the study are described here. Each variable was measured at two levels—a "low" level and a "high" level.

x_1: Volume fraction of disperse phase (as a percentage of weight); Low = 40%, High = 80%

x_2: Salinity of emulsion (as a percentage of weight); Low = 1%, High = 4%

x_3: Temperature of emulsion (in °C); Low = 4°, High = 23°

x_4: Time delay after emulsification (in hours); Low = .25 hour, High = 24 hours

x_5: Concentration of surface-active agent, or "surfactant" (as a percentage of weight); Low = 2%, High = 4%

x_6: Ratio of two chemicals (Span and Triton) used as surfactants; Low = .25, High = .75

x_7: Amount of solid particles added (as a percentage of weight); Low = .5%, High = 2%

Sixteen w/o emulsions were prepared using different combinations of the independent variables listed above; then each emulsion was exposed to a high electric field. In addition, three w/o emulsions were tested when all independent variables were set to 0. For all 19 emulsions, the amount of voltage (Kilovolts per centimeter) where the first sign of macroscopic activity is observed was measured; this value represents the dependent variable, y. The data for the study are provided in the table below.

a. Propose a model for y as a function of all seven independent variables. Assume that a linear relationship exists between y and x_i, $i = 1, 2, ..., 7$.

b. Use a statistical software package to fit the model to the data in the table.

c. Fully interpret the results of the regression. Part of the analysis should include an interpretation of the β estimates.

Experiment Number	Voltage y	Disperse Phase Volume x_1	Salinity x_2	Temperature x_3	Time Delay x_4	Surfactant Concentration x_5	S:T Ratio x_6	Solid Particles x_7
1	.64	40	1	4	.25	2	.25	.5
2	.80	80	1	4	.25	4	.25	2
3	3.20	40	4	4	.25	4	.75	.5
4	.48	80	4	4	.25	2	.75	2
5	1.72	40	1	23	.25	4	.75	2
6	.32	80	1	23	.25	2	.75	.5
7	.64	40	4	23	.25	2	.25	2
8	.68	80	4	23	.25	4	.25	.5
9	.12	40	1	4	24	2	.75	2
10	.88	80	1	4	24	4	.75	.5
11	2.32	40	4	4	24	4	.25	2
12	.40	80	4	4	24	2	.25	.5
13	1.04	40	1	23	24	4	.25	.5
14	.12	80	1	23	24	2	.25	2
15	1.28	40	4	23	24	2	.75	.5
16	.72	80	4	23	24	4	.75	2
17	1.08	0	0	0	0	0	0	0
18	1.08	0	0	0	0	0	0	0
19	1.04	0	0	0	0	0	0	0

Source: Førdedal, H., *et al.* "A multivariate analysis of W/O emulsions in high external electric fields as studied by means of dielectric time domain spectroscopy." *Journal of Colloid and Interface Science,* Vol. 173, No. 2, August 1995, p. 398 (Table 2).

d. According to the researchers, the model predicts a negative value for the voltage y for experiment #14. Verify this result.

e. The researchers state that the result, part d, "is physically not acceptable, and a model with interaction terms must be proposed." The model the researchers selected is

$$E(y) = \beta_0 + \beta_1 x_1 + \beta_2 x_2 + \beta_3 x_5 + \beta_4 x_1 x_2 + \beta_5 x_1 x_5.$$

Note that the model includes interaction between disperse phase volume (x_1) and salinity (x_2) as well as interaction between disperse phase volume (x_1) and surfactant concentration (x_5). Discuss how these interaction terms impact the hypothetical relationship between y and x_1. Draw a sketch to support your answer.

f. Fit the interaction model, part e, to the data. Does the model appear to fit the data better than the model, part a? Explain.

g. Interpret the β estimates of the interaction model, part e.

h. The researchers concluded that "in order to break an emulsion with the lowest possible voltage, the volume fraction of the disperse phase (x_1) should be high, while the salinity (x_2) and the amount of surfactant (x_5) should be low." Use this information and the interaction model to find a 95% prediction interval for this "low" voltage y. Interpret the interval.

10.52 (X10.052) Many colleges and universities develop regression models for predicting the GPA of incoming freshmen. This predicted GPA can then be used to make admission decisions. Although most models use many independent variables to predict GPA, we will illustrate by choosing two variables:

x_1 = Verbal score on college entrance examination (percentile)

x_2 = Mathematics score on college entrance examination (percentile)

The data in the table are obtained for a random sample of 40 freshmen at one college. The SPSS printout corresponding to the model $y = \beta_0 + \beta_1 x_1 + \beta_2 x_2 + \epsilon$ is shown below.

Verbal x_1	Mathematics x_2	GPA y	Verbal x_1	Mathematics x_2	GPA y	Verbal x_1	Mathematics x_2	GPA y
81	87	3.49	83	76	3.75	97	80	3.27
68	99	2.89	64	66	2.70	77	90	3.47
57	86	2.73	83	72	3.15	49	54	1.30
100	49	1.54	93	54	2.28	39	81	1.22
54	83	2.56	74	59	2.92	87	69	3.23
82	86	3.43	51	75	2.48	70	95	3.82
75	74	3.59	79	75	3.45	57	89	2.93
58	98	2.86	81	62	2.76	74	67	2.83
55	54	1.46	50	69	1.90	87	93	3.84
49	81	2.11	72	70	3.01	90	65	3.01
64	76	2.69	54	52	1.48	81	76	3.33
66	59	2.16	65	79	2.98	84	69	3.06
80	61	2.60	56	78	2.58			
100	85	3.30	98	67	2.73			

```
Multiple R              .82527
R Square                .68106
Adjusted R Square       .66382
Standard Error          .40228

Analysis of Variance
                    DF      Sum of Squares      Mean Square
Regression           2          12.78595           6.39297
Residual            37           5.98755            .16183

F =      39.50530      Signif F =   .0000

------------------Variables in the Equation--------------------

Variable            B          SE B         Beta          T     Sig T

X1            .02573  4.02357E-03         .59719       6.395    .0000
X2            .03361  4.92751E-03         .63702       6.822    .0000
(Constant)  -1.57054       .49375                     -3.181    .0030
```

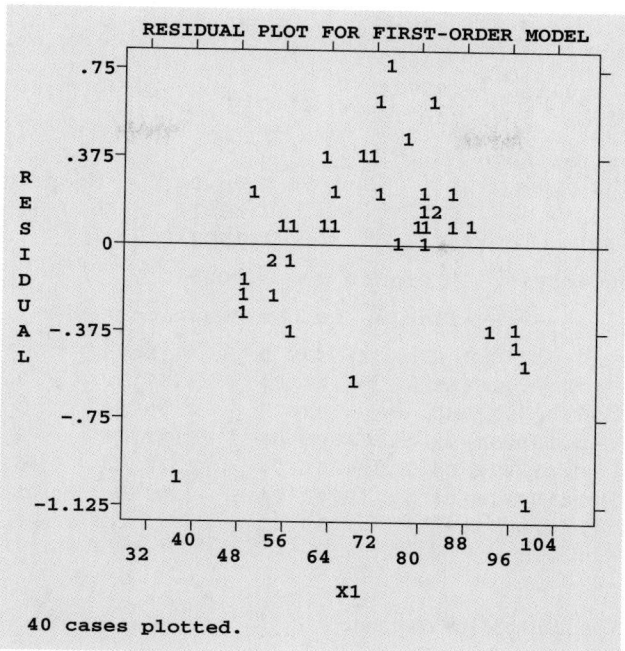

40 cases plotted.

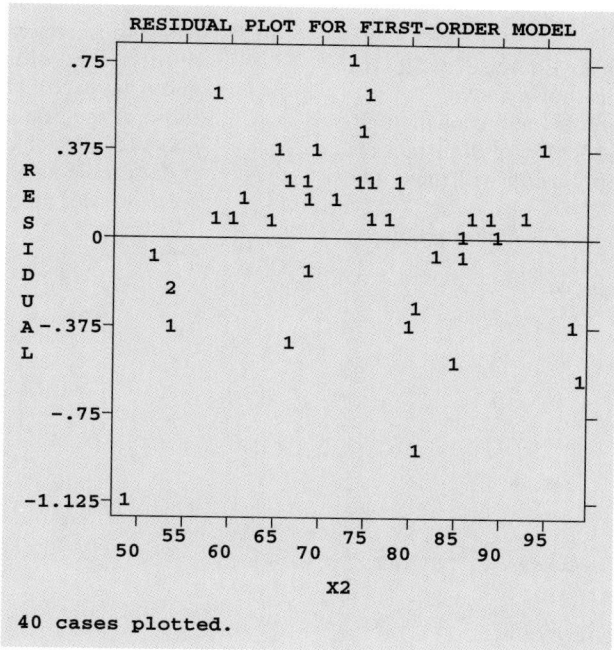

40 cases plotted.

a. Interpret the least squares estimates $\hat{\beta}_1$ and $\hat{\beta}_2$ in the context of this application.

b. Interpret the standard deviation and the coefficient of determination of the regression model in the context of this application.

c. Is this model useful for predicting GPA? Conduct a statistical test to justify your answer.

d. Sketch the relationship between predicted GPA, $\hat{y}$, and verbal score, x_1, for the following mathematics scores: $x_2 = 60, 75$, and 90.

10.53 Refer to Exercise 10.52. The residuals from the first-order model are plotted against x_1 and x_2. Analyze the two plots shown above, and determine whether visual evidence exists that curvature (a quadratic term) for either x_1 or x_2 should be added to the model.

```
Multiple R              .96777
R Square                .93657
Adjusted R Square       .92724
Standard Error          .18714

Analysis of Variance
                    DF      Sum of Squares      Mean Square
Regression           5           17.58274          3.51655
Residual            34            1.19076           .03502

F =      100.40901        Signif F =   .0000
-------------------Variables in the Equation-------------------

Variable             B            SE B          Beta          T    Sig T
X1                .16681          .02124       3.87132      7.852   .0000
X2                .13760          .02673       2.60754      5.147   .0000
X1SQ       -1.10825E-03  1.17288E-04         -3.71359     -9.449   .0000
X2SQ       -8.43267E-04  1.59423E-04         -2.37284     -5.290   .0000
X1X2        2.410891E-04 1.43974E-04           .49600      1.675   .1032
(Constant)     -9.91676        1.35441                    -7.322   .0000
```

10.54 Refer to Exercises 10.52 and 10.53. The complete second-order model

$$y = \beta_0 + \beta_1 x_1 + \beta_2 x_2 + \beta_3 x_1^2 + \beta_4 x_2^2 + \beta_5 x_1 x_2 + \epsilon$$

is fit to the data given in Exercise 10.52. The resulting SPSS printout is shown above.

a. Compare the standard deviations of the first-order and second-order regression models. With what relative precision will these two models predict GPA?

b. Test whether this model is useful for predicting GPA. Use $\alpha = .05$.

c. Test whether the interaction term, $\beta_5 x_1 x_2$, is important for the prediction of GPA. Use $\alpha = .10$.

10.55 Refer to Exercises 10.52 and 10.53. The residuals of the second-order model are plotted against x_1 and x_2 on page 595. Compare the residual plots to those of the first-order model in Exercises 10.52 and 10.53. Which of the two models do you think is preferable as a predictor of GPA: the first- or second-order model?

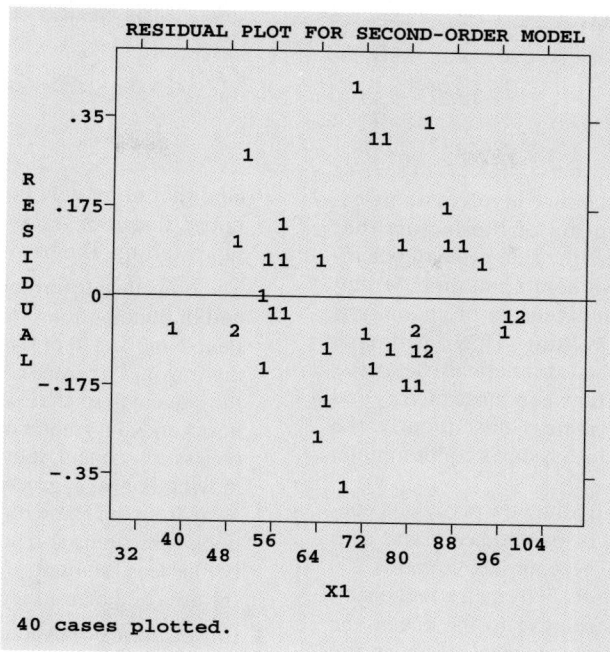

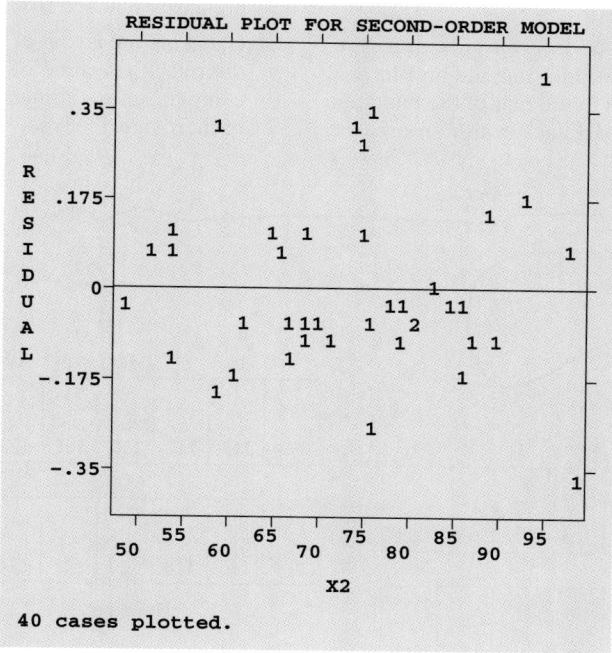

THE CONDO SALES CASE

This case involves an investigation of the factors that affect the sale price of ocean-side condominium units. It represents an extension of an analysis of the same data by Herman Kelting (1979). Although condo sale prices have increased dramatically over the past 20 years, the relationship between these factors and sale price remain about the same. Consequently, the data provide valuable insight into today's condominium sales market.

The sales data were obtained for a new oceanside condominium complex consisting of two adjacent and connected eight-floor buildings. The complex contains 200 units of equal size (approximately 500 square feet each). The locations of the buildings relative to the ocean, the swimming pool, the parking lot, etc. are shown in the accompanying figure. There are several features of the complex that you should note:

1. The units facing south, called *ocean-view,* face the beach and ocean. In addition, units in building 1 have a good view of the pool. Units to the rear of the building, called *bay-view,* face the parking lot and an area of land that ultimately borders a bay. The view from the upper floors of these units is primarily of wooded, sandy terrain. The bay is very distant and barely visible.

2. The only elevator in the complex is located at the east end of building 1, as are the office and the game room. People moving to or from the higher floor units in building 2 would likely use the elevator and move through the passages to their units. Thus, units on the higher floors and at a greater distance from the elevator would be less convenient; they would require greater effort in moving baggage, groceries, etc., and would be farther away from the game room, the office, and the swimming pool. These units also possess an advantage: there would be the least amount of traffic through the hallways in the area and hence they are the most private.

3. Lower-floor oceanside units are most suited to active people; they open onto the beach, ocean, and pool. They are within easy reach of the game room and they are easily reached from the parking area.

4. Checking the layout of the condominium complex, you discover that some of the units in the center of the complex, units ending in numbers 11 and 14, have part of their view blocked.

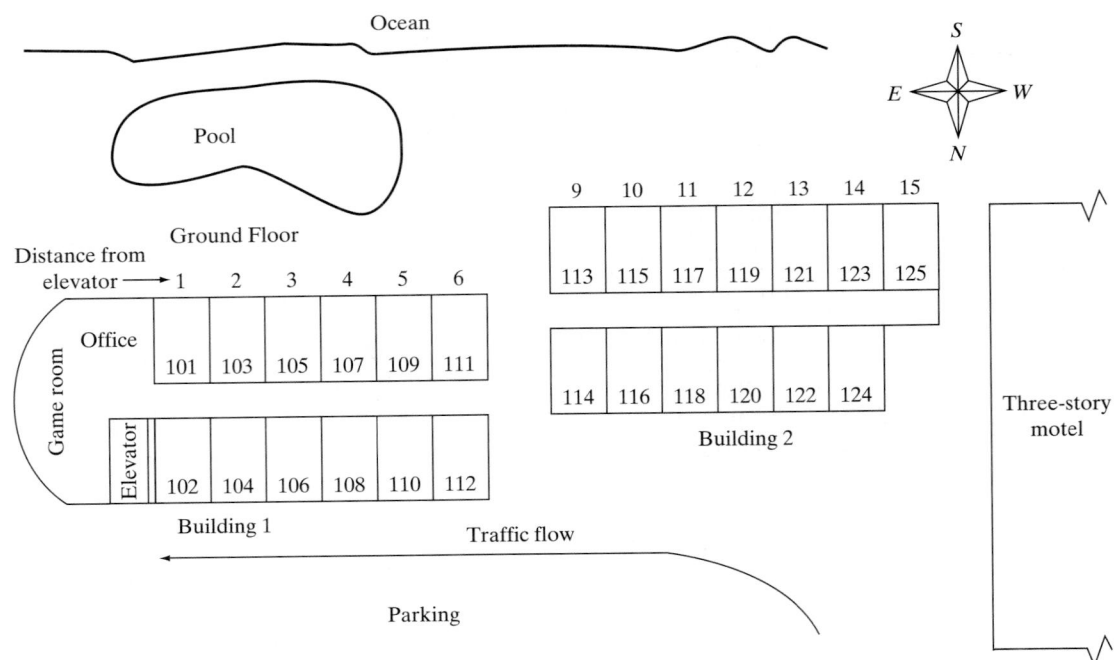

FIGURE C5.1 Layout of Condominium Complex

5. The condominium complex was completed at the time of the 1975 recession; sales were slow and the developer was forced to sell most of the units at auction approximately 18 months after opening. Consequently, the auction data are completely buyer-specified and hence consumer-oriented in contrast to most other real estate sales data which are, to a high degree, seller and broker specified.

6. Many unsold units in the complex were furnished by the developer and rented prior to the auction. Consequently, some of the units bid on and sold at auction had furniture, others did not.

This condominium complex is obviously unique. For example, the single elevator located at one end of the complex produces a remarkably high level of both inconvenience and privacy for the people occupying units on the top floors in building 2. Consequently, the developer is unsure of how the height of the unit (floor number), distance of the unit from the elevator, presence or absence of an ocean view, etc. affect the prices of the units sold at auction. To investigate these relationships, the following data were recorded for each of the 106 units sold at the auction:

1. *Sale price.* Measured in hundreds of dollars (adjusted for inflation)

2. *Floor height.* The floor location of the unit; the variable levels are 1, 2, ..., 8.

3. *Distance from elevator.* This distance, measured along the length of the complex, is expressed in number of condominium units. An additional two units of distance was added to the units in building 2 to account for the walking distance in the connecting area between the two buildings. Thus, the distance of unit 105 from the elevator would be 3, and the distance between unit 113 and the elevator would be 9. The variable levels are 1, 2, ..., 15.

4. *View of ocean.* The presence or absence of an ocean view is recorded for each unit and specified with a dummy variable (1 if the unit possessed an ocean view and 0 if not). Note that units not possessing an ocean view would face the parking lot.

5. *End unit.* We expect the partial reduction of view of end units on the ocean side (numbers ending in 11) to reduce their sale price. The ocean view of these end units is partially blocked by building 2. This qualitative variable is also specified with a dummy variable (1 if the unit has a unit number ending in 11 and 0 if not).

6. *Furniture.* The presence or absence of furniture is recorded for each unit, and represented with a single dummy variable (1 if the unit was furnished and 0 if not).

Your objective for this case is to build a regression model that accurately predicts the sale price of a condominium unit sold at auction. Prepare a professional document that presents the results of your analysis. Include graphs that demonstrate how each of the independent variables in your model affects auction price. A layout of the data file is described below.

DATA   ASCII file name: CONDO.DAT
       Number of observations: 106

Variable	Column(s)	Type
PRICE	1–3	QN
FLOOR	5	QN
DISTANCE	7–8	QN
VIEW	10	QL
ENDUNIT	12	QL
FURNISH	14	QL

www.int.com
www.int.com
INTERNET LAB
www.int.com

USING THE CONSUMER PRICE INDEX IN BUSINESS FORECASTS OF LABOR, WAGES, AND COMPENSATION

The Consumer Price Index (CPI) is one of the most used economic indicators by business and government. It measures monthly price changes for some 300 selected consumer items, including products from the categories of food, transportation, and housing, among others. Large corporations use the CPI—or the so called cost-of-living index—in forecasting revenues and profits. Staffing decisions regarding total company employment, wages, and compensation are often directly based on the CPI.

Here we will explore using the CPI in prediction models of key labor statistics.

1. Obtain annual CPI data for the past 30 years. The site address for the Bureau of Labor Statistics: *http://stats.bls.gov:80/*

   - Here, click on: **Data**
   - Then, click on: **Most Requested Series**
   - Next, scroll down to the heading "Prices and Living Conditions"
   - Select: CPI—Urban Wage Earners and Clerical Workers

2. Download and save the data in your statistical applications software data files.

3. Go back to the Bureau of Labor Statistics site: Most Requested Series

   - Here, click on: **Overall BLS Most Requested Series**

This page from Most Requested Series allows you to select and view data for a number of key labor statistics. From the categories of Employment and Compensation, view several of these variables and select three for downloading. Include one from each of the three categories: employment level, wages, and compensation.

4. For each of the variables selected, obtain the same 30 years of data as with the CPI.

5. Download and save the data in your statistical applications software data files.

6. Analyze the data you have saved:

   a. For each of the variables selected, find the correlation of the variable with CPI. Interpret the results.

   b. Select one of the three variables as the dependent variable in a regression analysis. Assuming that CPI and the other two variables will be used to model the selected variable, assess the degree of multicollinearity in the data.

   c. Conduct a complete regression analysis on the data, including model building and an analysis of residuals. Prepare a report of your findings and present the results to your class. ○

CHAPTER 11

BASIC METHODS FOR QUALITY IMPROVEMENT

CONTENTS

11.1 Quality, Processes, and Systems

11.2 Statistical Control

11.3 The Logic of Control Charts

11.4 A Control Chart for Monitoring the Mean of a Process: The $\bar{x}$-Chart

11.5 A Control Chart for Monitoring the Variation of a Process: The R-Chart

11.6 A Control Chart for Monitoring the Proportion of Defectives Generated by a Process: The p-Chart

STATISTICS IN ACTION

11.1 Deming's 14 Points

Where We've Been

In Chapters 5–8 we described methods for making inferences about populations based on sample data. In Chapters 9–10 we focused on modeling relationships between variables using regression analysis.

Where We're Going

In this chapter, we turn our attention to processes. Recall from Chapter 1 that a process is a series of actions or operations that transform inputs to outputs. This chapter introduces methods for improving processes and the quality of the output they produce.

Over the last two decades U.S. firms have been seriously challenged by products of superior quality from overseas, particularly from Japan. Japan currently produces 25% of the cars sold in the United States. In 1989, for the first time, the top-selling car in the United States was made in Japan: the Honda Accord. Although it's an American invention, virtually all VCRs are produced in Japan. Only one U.S. firm still manufactures televisions; the rest are made in Japan.

To meet this competitive challenge, more and more U.S. firms—both manufacturing and service firms—have begun quality-improvement initiatives of their own. Many of these firms now stress **Total Quality Management** (TQM), i.e., the management of quality in all phases and aspects of their business, from the design of their products to production, distribution, sales, and service.

Broadly speaking, TQM is concerned with (1) finding out what it is that the customer wants, (2) translating those wants into a product or service design, and (3) producing a product or service that meets or exceeds the specifications of the design. In this chapter we focus primarily on the third of these three areas and its major problem—product and service variation.

Variation is inherent in the output of all production and service processes. No two parts produced by a given machine are the same; no two transactions performed by a given bank teller are the same. Why is this a problem? With variation in output comes variation in the quality of the product or service. If this variation is unacceptable to customers, sales are lost, profits suffer, and the firm may not survive.

The existence of this ever-present variation has made statistical methods and statistical training vitally important to industry. In this chapter we present some of the basic tools and methods currently employed by firms worldwide to monitor and reduce product and service variation.

11.1 QUALITY, PROCESSES, AND SYSTEMS

QUALITY

Before describing various tools and methods that can be used to monitor and improve the quality of products and services, we need to consider what is meant by the term *quality*. Quality can be defined from several different perspectives. To the engineers and scientists who design products, quality typically refers to the amount of some ingredient or attribute possessed by the product. For example, high-quality ice cream contains a large amount of butterfat. High-quality rugs have a large number of knots per square inch. A high-quality shirt or blouse has 22 to 26 stitches per inch.

To managers, engineers, and workers involved in the production of a product (or the delivery of a service), quality usually means conformance to requirements, or the degree to which the product or service conforms to its design specifications. For example, in order to fit properly, the cap of a particular molded plastic bottle must be between 1.0000 inch and 1.0015 inches in diameter. Caps that do not conform to this requirement are considered to be of inferior quality. For an example in a service operation, consider the service provided to customers in a fast-food restaurant. A particular restaurant has been designed to serve customers within two minutes of the time their order is placed. If it takes more than two minutes, the service does not conform to specifications and is considered to be of inferior quality. Using this production-based interpretation of quality, well-made products are high quality; poorly made products are low quality. Thus, a well-made Rolls Royce and a well-made Chevrolet Nova are both high-quality cars.

Although quality can be defined from either the perspective of the designers or the producers of a product, in the final analysis both definitions should be derived from the needs and preferences of the *user* of the product or service. A firm that produces goods that no one wants to purchase cannot stay in business. We define quality accordingly.

DEFINITION 11.1

The **quality** of a good or service is indicated by the extent to which it satisfies the needs and preferences of its users.

Consumers' needs and wants shape their perceptions of quality. Thus, to produce a high-quality product, it is necessary to study the needs and wants of consumers. This is typically one of the major functions of a firm's marketing department. Once the necessary consumer research has been conducted, it is necessary to translate consumers' desires into a product design. This design must then be translated into a production plan and production specifications that, if properly implemented, will turn out a product with characteristics that will satisfy users' needs and wants. In short, consumer perceptions of quality play a role in all phases and aspects of a firm's operations.

But what product characteristics are consumers looking for? What is it that influences users' perceptions of quality? This is the kind of knowledge that firms need in order to develop and deliver high-quality goods and services. The basic elements of quality are summarized in the eight dimensions shown in the box.

The Eight Dimensions of Quality*

1. **Performance:** The primary operating characteristics of the product. For an automobile, these would include acceleration, handling, smoothness of ride, gas mileage, etc.

2. **Features:** The "bells and whistles" that supplement the product's basic functions. Examples include CD players and digital clocks on cars and the frequent-flyer mileage and free drinks offered by airlines.

3. **Reliability:** Reflects the probability that the product will not operate properly within a given period of time.

4. **Conformance:** The extent or degree to which a product meets preestablished standards. This is reflected in, for example, a pharmaceutical manufacturer's concern that the plastic bottles it orders for its drugs have caps that are between 1.0000 and 1.0015 inches in diameter, as specified in their order.

5. **Durability:** The life of the product. If repair is possible, durability relates to the length of time a product can be used before replacement is judged to be preferable to continued repair.

6. **Serviceability:** The ease of repair, speed of repair, and competence and courtesy of the repair staff.

7. **Aesthetics:** How a product looks, feels, sounds, smells, or tastes.

8. **Other perceptions that influence judgments of quality:** Such factors as a firm's reputation and the images of the firm and its products that are created through advertising.

In order to design and produce products of high quality, it is necessary to translate the characteristics described in the box into product attributes that can be built into the product by the manufacturer. That is, user preferences must be

* Garvin, D. *Managing Quality.* New York: Free Press/Macmillan, 1988.

interpreted in terms of product variables over which the manufacturer has control. For example, in considering the performance characteristics of a particular brand of wooden pencil, users may indicate a preference for being able to use the pencil for longer periods between sharpenings. The manufacturer may translate this performance characteristic into one or more measurable physical characteristics such as wood hardness, lead hardness, and lead composition. Besides being used to design high-quality products, such variables are used in the process of monitoring and improving quality during production.

PROCESSES

Much of this textbook focuses on methods for using sample data drawn from a population to learn about that population. In this chapter and the next, however, our attention is not on populations, but on processes—such as manufacturing processes—and the output that they generate. In general, a process is defined as follows:

> **DEFINITION 11.2**
> A **process** is a series of actions or operations that transforms inputs to outputs. A process produces output over time.

Processes can be organizational or personal in nature. Organizational processes are those associated with organizations such as businesses and governments. Perhaps the best example is a manufacturing process, which consists of a series of operations, performed by people and machines, whereby inputs such as raw materials and parts are converted into finished products (the outputs). Examples include automobile assembly lines, oil refineries, and steel mills. Personal processes are those associated with your private life. The series of steps you go through each morning to get ready for school or work can be thought of as a process. Through turning off the alarm clock, showering, dressing, eating, and opening the garage door, you transform yourself from a sleeping person to one who is ready to interact with the outside world. Figure 11.1 presents a general description of a process and its inputs.

It is useful to think of processes as *adding value* to the inputs of the process. Manufacturing processes, for example, are designed so that the value of the outputs to potential customers exceeds the value of the inputs—otherwise the firm would have no demand for its products and would not survive.

SYSTEMS

To understand what causes variation in process output and how processes and their output can be improved, we must understand the role that processes play in *systems*.

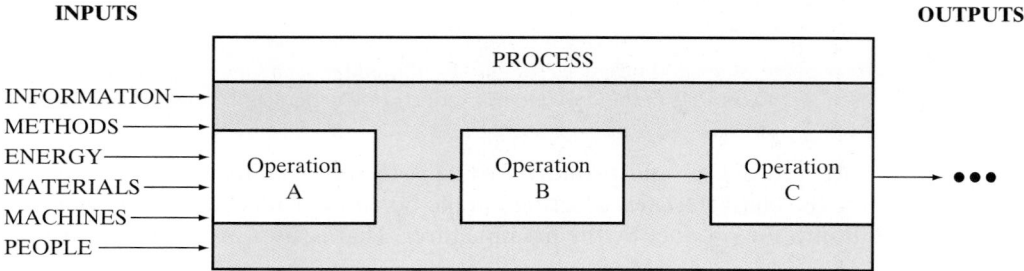

FIGURE 11.1   Graphical depiction of a process and its inputs

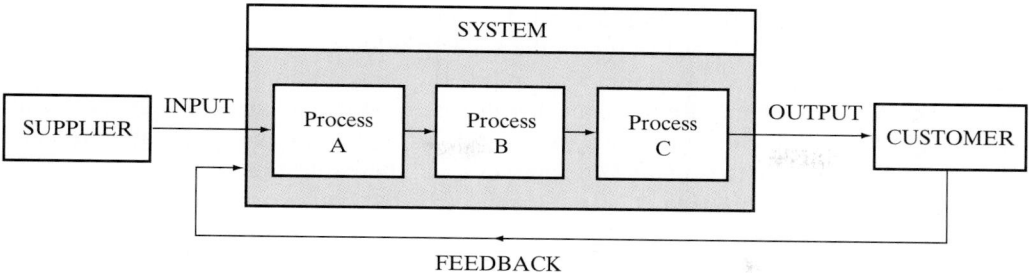

FIGURE 11.2   Model of a basic system

> **DEFINITION 11.3**
>
> A **system** is a collection or arrangement of interacting processes that has an ongoing purpose or mission. A system receives inputs from its environment, transforms those inputs to outputs, and delivers them to its environment. In order to survive, a system uses feedback (i.e., information) from its environment to understand and adapt to changes in its environment.

Figure 11.2 presents a model of a basic system. As an example of a system, consider a manufacturing company. It has a collection of interacting processes—marketing research, engineering, purchasing, receiving, production, sales, distribution, billing, etc. Its mission is to make money for its owners, to provide high-quality working conditions for its employees, and to stay in business. The firm receives raw materials and parts (inputs) from outside vendors which, through its production processes, it transforms to finished goods (outputs). The finished goods are distributed to its customers. Through its marketing research, the firm "listens" (receives feedback from) its customers and potential customers in order to change or adapt its processes and products to meet (or exceed) the needs, preferences, and expectations of the marketplace.

Since systems are collections of processes, the various types of system inputs are the same as those listed in Figure 11.1 for processes. System outputs are products or services. These outputs may be physical objects made, assembled, repaired, or moved by the system; or they may be symbolical, such as information, ideas, or knowledge. For example, a brokerage house supplies customers with information about stocks and bonds and the markets where they are traded.

Two important points about systems and the output of their processes are: (1) No two items produced by a process are the same; (2) Variability is an inherent characteristic of the output of all processes. This is illustrated in Figure 11.3. No two cars produced by the same assembly line are the same: No two windshields are the same; no two wheels are the same; no two tires are the same; no two hubcaps

FIGURE 11.3
Output variation

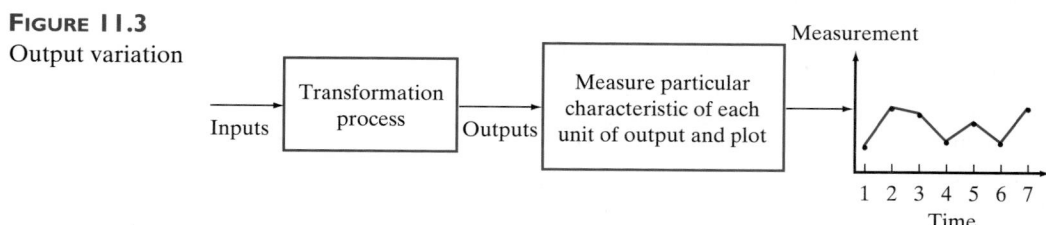

are the same. The same thing can be said for processes that deliver services. Consider the services offered at the teller windows of a bank to two customers waiting in two lines. Will they wait in line the same amount of time? Will they be serviced by tellers with the same degree of expertise and with the same personalities? Assuming the customers' transactions are the same, will they take the same amount of time to execute? The answer to all these questions is no.

In general, variation in output is caused by the six factors listed in the box.

The Six Major Sources of Process Variation
1. People
2. Machines
3. Materials
4. Methods
5. Measurement
6. Environment

Awareness of this ever-present process variation has made training in statistical thinking and statistical methods highly valued by industry. By **statistical thinking** we mean the knack of recognizing variation, and exploiting it in problem solving and decision-making. The remainder of this chapter is devoted to statistical tools for monitoring process variation.

STATISTICS IN ACTION

11.1 DEMING'S 14 POINTS

How is it that the Japanese became quality leaders? What inspired their concern for quality? In part, it was the statistical and managerial expertise exported to Japan from the United States following World War II. At the end of the war Japan faced the difficult task of rebuilding its economy. To this end, a group of engineers was assigned by the Allied command to assist the Japanese in improving the quality of their communication systems. These engineers taught the Japanese the statistical quality control methods that had been developed in the United States under the direction of Walter Shewhart of Bell Laboratories in the 1920s and 1930s. Then, in 1950, the Japanese Union of Scientists and Engineers invited W. Edwards Deming, a statistician who had studied with Shewhart, to present a series of lectures on statistical quality-improvement methods to hundreds of Japanese researchers, plant managers, and engineers. During his stay in Japan he also met with many of the top executives of Japan's largest com-

panies. At the time, Japan was notorious for the inferior quality of its products. Deming told the executives that by listening to what consumers wanted and by applying statistical methods in the production of those goods, they could export high-quality products that would find markets all over the world.

In 1951 the Japanese established the **Deming Prize** to be given annually to companies with significant accomplishments in the area of quality. In 1989, for the first time, the Deming Prize was given to a U.S. company—Florida Power and Light Company.

One of Deming's major contributions to the quality movement that is spreading across the major industrialized nations of the world was his recognition that statistical (and other) process improvement methods cannot succeed without the proper organizational climate and culture. Accordingly, he proposed 14 guidelines that, if followed, transform the organizational climate to one in which process-management efforts can flourish. These 14 points are, in essence, Deming's philosophy of management. He argues convincingly that all 14 should be implemented, not just certain subsets. We list all 14 points here, adding clarifying statements where needed. For a fuller discussion of these points, see Deming (1986), Gitlow *et al.* (1995), Walton (1986), and Joiner and Goudard (1990).

1. **Create constancy of purpose toward improvement of product and service, with the aim to become competitive and to stay in business, and to provide jobs.** The organization must have a clear goal or purpose. Everyone in the organization must be encouraged to work toward that goal day in and day out, year after year.

2. **Adopt the new philosophy.** Reject detection-rejection management in favor of a customer-oriented, preventative style of management in which never-ending quality improvement is the driving force.

3. **Cease dependence on inspection to achieve quality.** It is because of poorly designed products and excessive process variation that inspection is needed. If quality is designed into products and process management is used in their production, mass inspection of finished products will not be necessary.

4. **End the practice of awarding business on the basis of price tag.** Do not simply buy from the lowest bidder. Consider the quality of the supplier's products along with the supplier's price. Establish long-term relationships with suppliers based on loyalty and trust. Move toward using a single supplier for each item needed.

5. **Improve constantly and forever the system of production and service, to improve quality and productivity, and thus constantly decrease costs.**

6. **Institute training.** Workers are often trained by other workers who were never properly trained themselves. The result is excessive process variation and inferior products and services. This is not the workers' fault; no one has told them how to do their jobs well.

7. **Institute leadership.** Supervisors should help the workers to do a better job. Their job is to lead, not to order workers around or to punish them.

8. **Drive out fear, so that everyone may work effectively for the company.** Many workers are afraid to ask questions or to bring problems to the attention of management. Such a climate is not conducive to producing high-quality goods and services. People work best when they feel secure.

9. **Break down barriers between departments.** Everyone in the organization must work together as a team. Different areas within the firm should have complementary, not conflicting, goals. People across the organization must realize that they are all part of the same system. Pooling their resources to solve problems is better than competing against each other.

10. **Eliminate slogans, exhortations, and arbitrary numerical goals and targets for the workforce which urge the workers to achieve new levels of productivity and quality.** Simply asking the workers to improve their work is not enough; they must be shown *how* to improve it. Management must realize that significant improvements can be achieved only if management takes responsibility for quality and makes the necessary changes in the design of the system in which the workers operate.

11. **Eliminate numerical quotas.** Quotas are purely quantitative (e.g., number of pieces to produce per day); they do not take quality into consideration. When faced with quotas, people attempt to meet them at any cost, regardless of the damage to the organization.

12. **Remove barriers that rob employees of their pride of workmanship.** People must be treated as human beings, not commodities. Working conditions must be improved, including the elimination of poor supervision, poor product design, defective materials, and defective machines. These things stand in the way of workers' performing up to their capabilities and producing work they are proud of.

13. **Institute a vigorous program of education and self-improvement.** Continuous improvement requires continuous learning. Everyone in the organization must be trained in the modern methods of quality improvement, including statistical concepts and interdepartmental teamwork. Top management should be the first to be trained.

14. **Take action to accomplish the transformation.** Hire people with the knowledge to implement the 14 points. Build a critical mass of people committed to transforming the organization. Put together a top management team to lead the way. Develop a plan and an organizational structure that will facilitate the transformation.

Focus

Contact a company located near your college or university and find out how many (if any) of Deming's 14 points have been implemented at the firm. Pool your results with those of your classmates to obtain a sense of the quality movement in your area. Summarize the results.

11.2 STATISTICAL CONTROL

For the rest of this chapter we turn our attention to **control charts**—graphical devices used for monitoring process variation, for identifying when to take action to improve the process, and for assisting in diagnosing the causes of process variation. Control charts, developed by Walter Shewhart of Bell Laboratories in the mid 1920s, are the tool of choice for continuously monitoring processes. Before we go into the details of control chart construction and use, however, it is important that you have a fuller understanding of process variation. To this end, we discuss patterns of variation in this section.

As was discussed in Chapter 2, the proper graphical method for describing the variation of process output is a **time series plot**, sometimes called a **run chart**. Recall that in a time series plot the measurements of interest are plotted against time or are plotted in the order in which the measurements were made, as in Figure 11.4. Whenever you face the task of analyzing data that were generated over time, your first reaction should be to plot them. The human eye is one of our most sensitive statistical instruments. Take advantage of that sensitivity by plotting the data and allowing your eyes to seek out patterns in the data.

Let's begin thinking about process variation by examining the plot in Figure 11.4 more closely. The measurements, taken from a paint manufacturing process, are the weights of 50 one-gallon cans of paint that were consecutively filled by the same filling head (nozzle). The weights were plotted in the order of production. Do you detect any systematic, persistent patterns in the sequence of weights? For example, do the weights tend to drift steadily upward or downward over time? Do they oscillate—high, then low, then high, then low, etc.?

To assist your visual examination of this or any other time series plot, Roberts (1991) recommends enhancing the basic plot in two ways. First, compute (or simply estimate) the mean of the set of 50 weights and draw a horizontal line on the graph at the level of the mean. This **centerline** gives you a point of reference in searching for patterns in the data. Second, using straight lines, connect each of the plotted weights in the order in which they were produced. This

FIGURE 11.4

Time series plot of fill weights for 50 consecutively produced gallon cans of paint

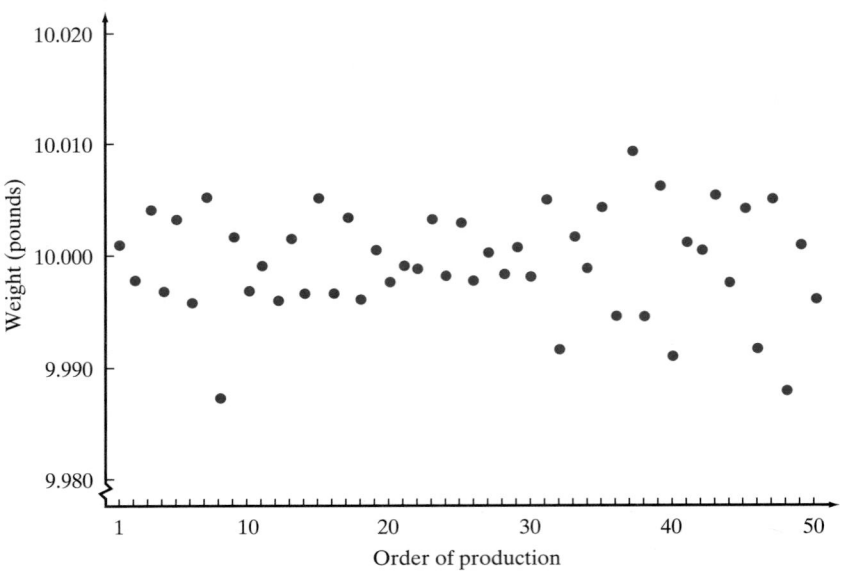

FIGURE 11.5

An enhanced version of the paint fill time series

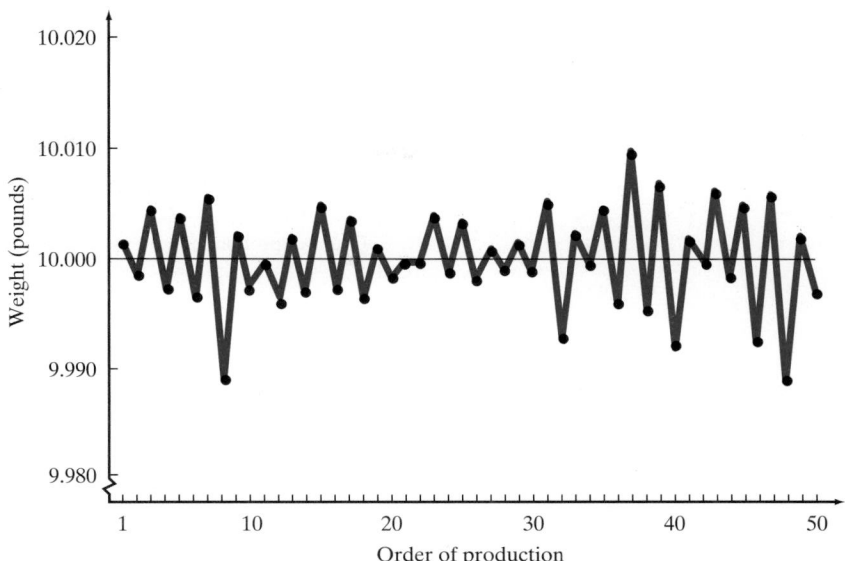

helps display the sequence of the measurements. Both enhancements are shown in Figure 11.5.

Now do you see a pattern in the data? Successive points alternate up and down, high then low, in an **oscillating sequence**. In this case, the points alternate above and below the centerline. This pattern was caused by a valve in the paint-filling machine that tended to stick in a partially closed position every other time it operated.

Other patterns of process variation are shown in Figure 11.6. We discuss several of them later.

In trying to describe process variation and diagnose its causes, it helps to think of the sequence of measurements of the output variable (e.g., weight, length, number of defects) as having been generated in the following way:

1. At any point in time, the output variable of interest can be described by a particular probability distribution (or relative frequency distribution). This distribution describes the possible values that the variable can assume and their likelihood of occurrence. Three such distributions are shown in Figure 11.7.

2. The particular value of the output variable that is realized at a given time can be thought of as being generated or produced according to the distribution described in point 1. (Alternatively, the realized value can be thought of as being generated by a random sample of size $n = 1$ from a population of values whose relative frequency distribution is that of point 1.)

3. The distribution that describes the output variable may change over time. For simplicity, we characterize the changes as being of three types: the mean (i.e., location) of the distribution may change; the variance (i.e., shape) of the distribution may change; or both. This is illustrated in Figure 11.8.

In general, when the output variable's distribution changes over time, we refer to this as a change in the *process*. Thus, if the mean shifts to a higher level, we say that the process mean has shifted. Accordingly, we sometimes refer to the distribution of the output variable as simply the **distribution of the process**, or the **output distribution of the process**.

FIGURE 11.6
Patterns of
process variation:
Some examples

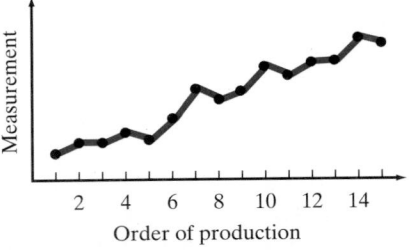

a. Uptrend

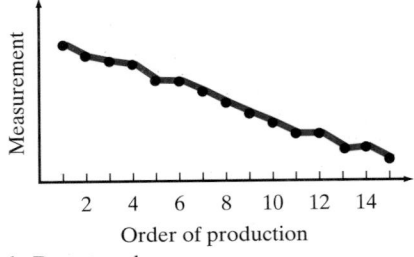

b. Downtrend

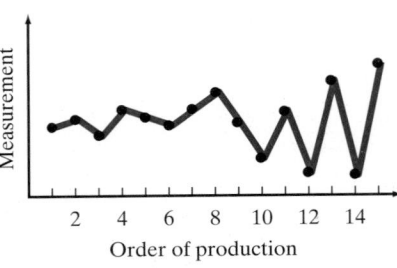

c. Increasing variance

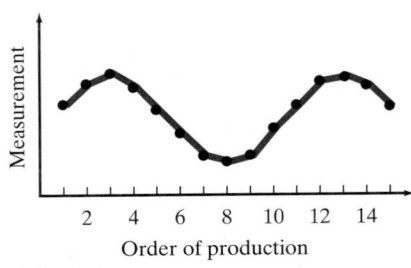

d. Cyclical

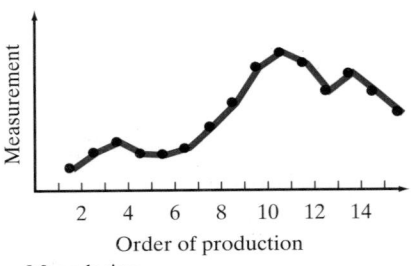

e. Meandering

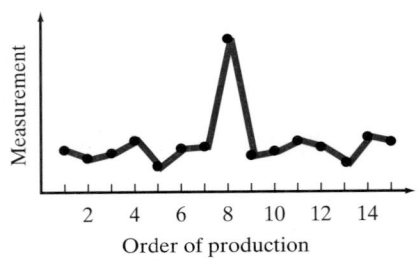

f. Shock/Freak/Outlier

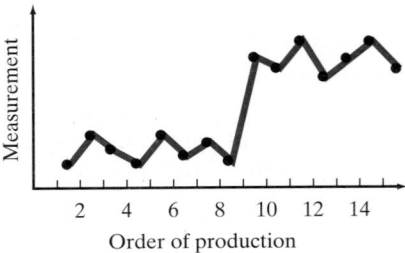

g. Level shift

FIGURE 11.7
Distributions
describing one
output variable at
three points in time

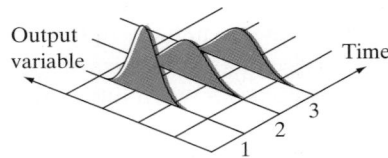

FIGURE 11.8

Types of changes in output variables

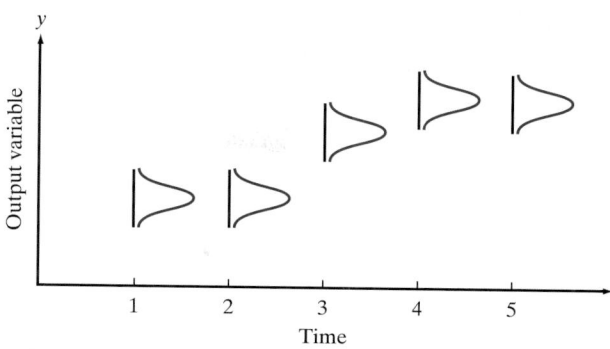

a. Change in mean (i.e., location)

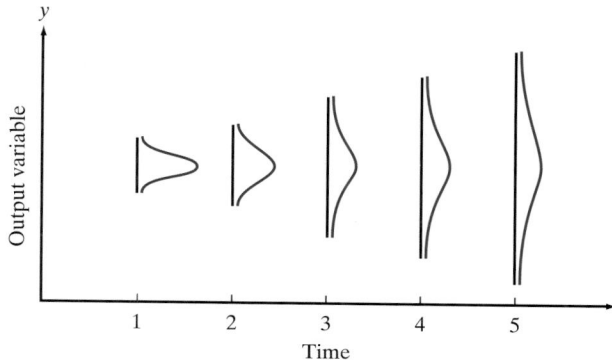

b. Change in variance (i.e., shape)

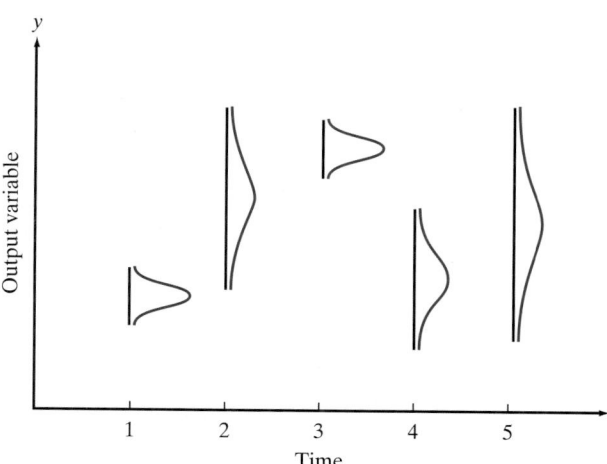

c. Change in mean and variance

Let's reconsider the patterns of variation in Figure 11.6 and model them using this conceptualization. This is done in Figure 11.9. The uptrend of Figure 11.6a can be characterized as resulting from a process whose mean is gradually shifting upward over time, as in Figure 11.9a. Gradual shifts like this are a common phenomenon in manufacturing processes. For example, as a machine wears out (e.g., cutting blades dull), certain characteristics of its output gradually change.

FIGURE 11.9
Patterns of process
variation described by
changing distributions

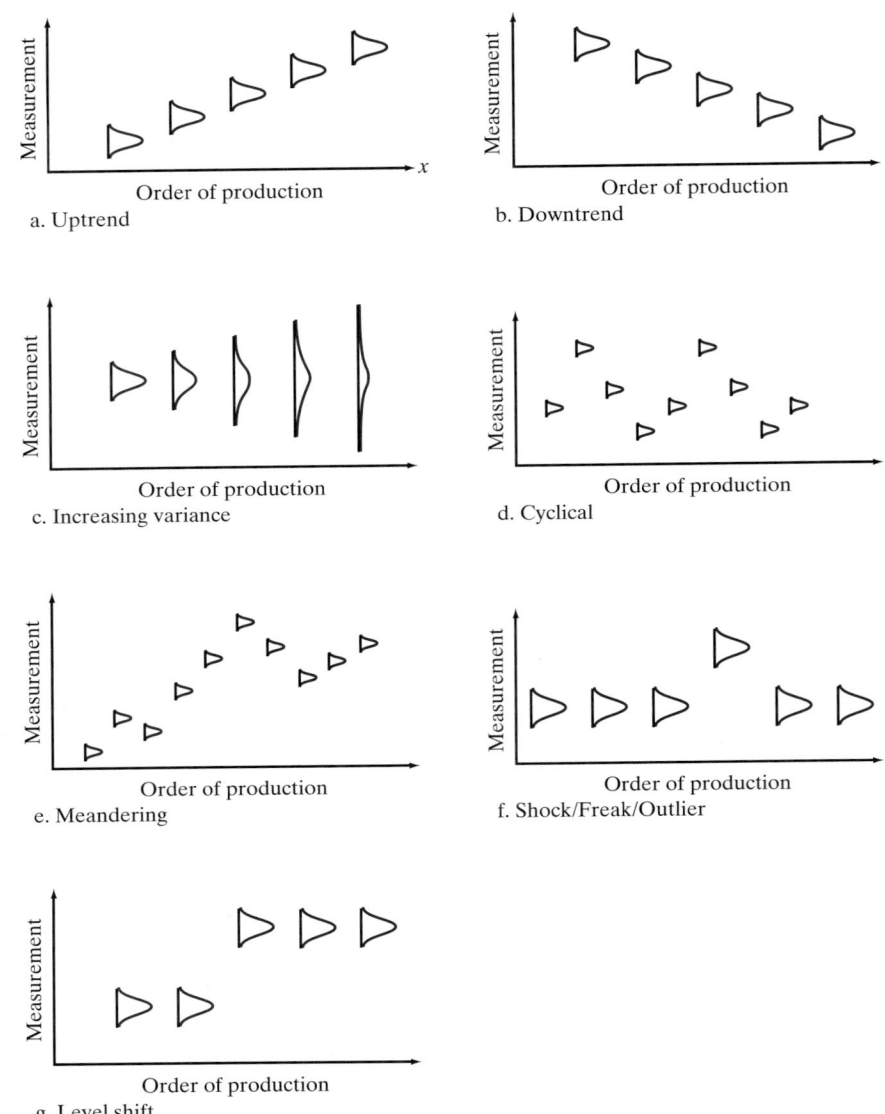

a. Uptrend

b. Downtrend

c. Increasing variance

d. Cyclical

e. Meandering

f. Shock/Freak/Outlier

g. Level shift

The pattern of increasing dispersion in Figure 11.6c can be thought of as resulting from a process whose mean remains constant but whose variance increases over time, as shown in Figure 11.9c. This type of deterioration in a process may be the result of worker fatigue. At the beginning of a shift, workers—whether they be typists, machine operators, waiters, or managers—are fresh and pay close attention to every item that they process. But as the day wears on, concentration may wane and the workers may become more and more careless or more easily distracted. As a result, some items receive more attention than other items, causing the variance of the workers' output to increase.

The sudden shift in the level of the measurements in Figure 11.6g can be thought of as resulting from a process whose mean suddenly increases but whose variance remains constant, as shown in Figure 11.9g. This type of pattern may be caused by such things as a change in the quality of raw materials used in the process or bringing a new machine or new operator into the process.

One thing that all these examples have in common is that the distribution of the output variable *changes over time*. In such cases, we say the process lacks **stability**. We formalize the notion of stability in the following definition.

DEFINITION 11.4

A process whose output distribution does *not* change over time is said to be in a state of **statistical control**, or simply **in control**. If it does change, it is said to be **out of statistical control**, or simply **out of control**.

Figure 11.10 illustrates a sequence of output distributions for both an in-control and an out-of-control process.

To see what the pattern of measurements looks like on a time series plot for a process that is in statistical control, consider Figure 11.11. These data are from the same paint-filling process we described earlier, but the sequence of measurements was made *after* the faulty valve was replaced. Notice that there are no discernible persistent, systematic patterns in the sequence of measurements such as those in Figures 11.5 and 11.6a–11.6e. Nor are there level shifts or transitory shocks as in Figures 11.6f–11.6g. This "patternless" behavior is called **random behavior. The output of processes that are in statistical control exhibits random behavior. Thus, even the output of stable processes exhibits variation.**

FIGURE 11.10

Comparison of in-control and out-of-control processes

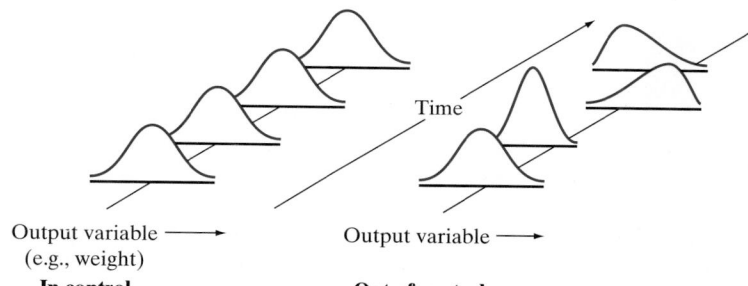

Output variable ⟶
(e.g., weight)
In control

Output variable ⟶
Out of control

FIGURE 11.11

Time series plot of 50 consecutive paint can fills collected after replacing faulty valve

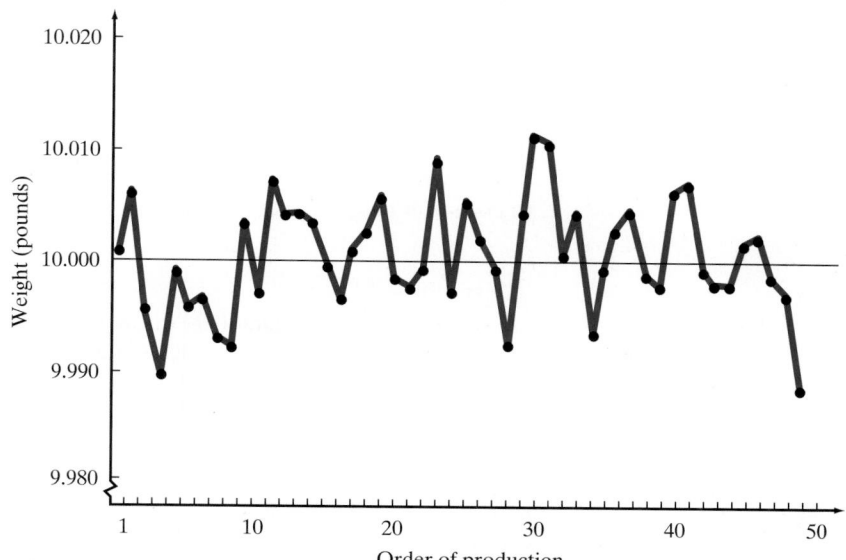

FIGURE 11.12
In-control processes
are predictable;
out-of-control
processes are not

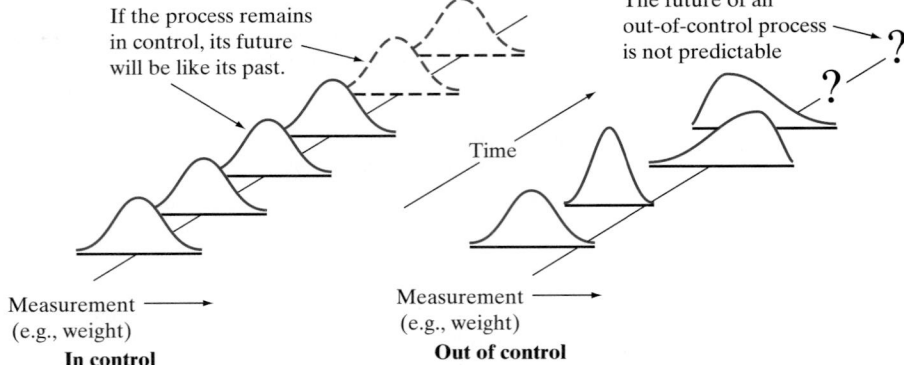

If the process remains
in control, its future
will be like its past.

The future of an
out-of-control process
is not predictable

Time

Measurement ——▶
(e.g., weight)
In control

Measurement ——▶
(e.g., weight)
Out of control

If a process is in control and remains in control, its future will be like its past. Accordingly, the process is predictable, in the sense that its output will stay within certain limits. This cannot be said about an out-of-control process. As illustrated in Figure 11.12, with most out-of-control processes you have no idea what the future pattern of output from the process may look like.* You simply do not know what to expect from the process. Consequently, a business that operates out-of-control processes runs the risk of (1) providing inferior quality products and services to its internal customers (people within the organization who use the outputs of the processes) and (2) selling inferior products and services to its external customers. In short, it risks losing its customers and threatens its own survival.

One of the fundamental goals of process management is to identify out-of-control processes, to take actions to bring them into statistical control, and to keep them in a state of statistical control. The series of activities used to attain this goal is referred to as **statistical process control**.

> **DEFINITION 11.5**
> The process of monitoring and eliminating variation in order to *keep* a process in a state of statistical control or to *bring* a process into statistical control is called **statistical process control (SPC)**.

Everything discussed in this section and the remaining sections of this chapter is concerned with statistical process control. We now continue our discussion of statistical control.

The variation that is exhibited by processes that are in control is said to be due to *common causes of variation*.

> **DEFINITION 11.6**
> **Common causes of variation** are the methods, materials, machines, personnel, and environment that make up a process and the inputs required by the process. Common causes are thus attributable to the design of the process. Common causes affect all output of the process and may affect everyone who participates in the process.

*The output variables of in-control processes may follow approximately normal distributions, as in Figures 11.10 and 11.12, or they may not. But any in-control process will follow the *same* distribution over time. Do not misinterpret the use of normal distributions in many figures in this chapter as indicating that all in-control processes follow normal distributions.

The total variation that is exhibited by an in-control process is due to many different common causes, most of which affect process output in very minor ways. In general, however, each common cause has the potential to affect every unit of output produced by the process. Examples of common causes include the lighting in a factory or office, the grade of raw materials required, and the extent of worker training. Each of these factors can influence the variability of the process output. Poor lighting can cause workers to overlook flaws and defects that they might otherwise catch. Inconsistencies in raw materials can cause inconsistencies in the quality of the finished product. The extent of the training provided to workers can affect their level of expertise and, as a result, the quality of the products and services for which they are responsible.

Since common causes are, in effect, designed into a process, the level of variation that results from common causes is viewed as being representative of the capability of the process. If that level is too great (i.e., if the quality of the output varies too much), the process must be redesigned (or modified) to eliminate one or more common causes of variation. Since process redesign is the responsibility of management, the *elimination of common causes of variation is typically the responsibility of management,* not of the workers.

Processes that are out of control exhibit variation that is the result of both common causes and **special causes of variation**.

DEFINITION 11.7

Special causes of variation (sometimes called **assignable causes**) are events or actions that are not part of the process design. Typically, they are transient, fleeting events that affect only local areas or operations within the process (e.g., a single worker, machine, or batch of materials) for a brief period of time. Occasionally, however, such events may have a persistent or recurrent effect on the process.

Examples of special causes of variation include a worker accidentally setting the controls of a machine improperly, a worker becoming ill on the job and continuing to work, a particular machine slipping out of adjustment, and a negligent supplier shipping a batch of inferior raw materials to the process.

In the latter case, the pattern of output variation may look like Figure 11.6f. If instead of shipping just one bad batch the supplier continued to send inferior materials, the pattern of variation might look like Figure 11.6g. The output of a machine that is gradually slipping out of adjustment might yield a pattern like Figure 11.6a, 11.6b, or 11.6c. All these patterns owe part of their variation to common causes and part to the noted special causes. In general, we treat any pattern of variation other than a random pattern as due to both common and special causes.* Since the effects of special causes are frequently localized within a process, *special causes can often be diagnosed and eliminated by workers or their immediate supervisor.* Occasionally, they must be dealt with by management, as in the case of a negligent or deceitful supplier.

It is important to recognize that **most processes are not naturally in a state of statistical control**. As Deming (1986, p. 322) observed: "*Stability [i.e., statistical*

*For certain processes (e.g., those affected by seasonal factors), a persistent systematic pattern—such as the cyclical pattern of Figure 11.6d—is an inherent characteristic. In these special cases, some analysts treat the cause of the systematic variation as a common cause. This type of analysis is beyond the scope of this text. We refer the interested reader to Alwan and Roberts (1988).

FIGURE 11.13
The effects of
eliminating causes
of variation

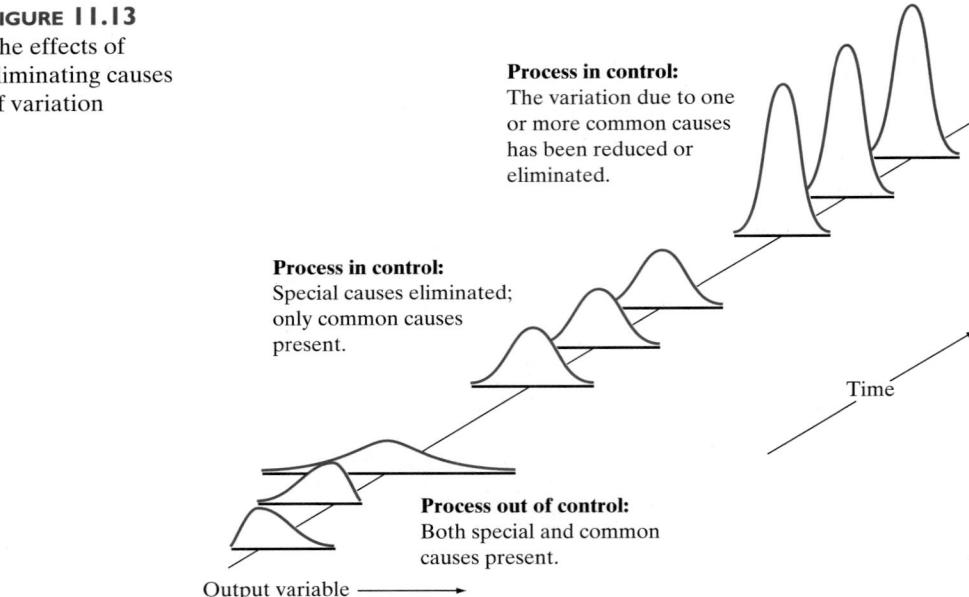

Process in control:
The variation due to one
or more common causes
has been reduced or
eliminated.

Process in control:
Special causes eliminated;
only common causes
present.

Time

Process out of control:
Both special and common
causes present.

Output variable ⟶

control] is seldom a natural state. It is an achievement, the result of eliminating
special causes one by one ... leaving only the random variation of a stable process"
(italics added).

Process improvement first requires the identification, diagnosis, and removal of
special causes of variation. Removing all special causes puts the process in a state
of statistical control. Further improvement of the process then requires the identification, diagnosis, and removal of common causes of variation. The effects on
the process of the removal of special and common causes of variation are illustrated in Figure 11.13.

In the remainder of this chapter, we introduce you to some of the methods of
statistical process control. In particular, we address how control charts help us
determine whether a given process is in control.

11.3   THE LOGIC OF CONTROL CHARTS

We use control charts to help us differentiate between process variation due to
common causes and special causes. That is, we use them to determine whether a
process is under statistical control (only common causes present) or not (both
common and special causes present). Being able to differentiate means knowing
when to take action to find and remove special causes and when to leave the
process alone. If you take actions to remove special causes that do not exist—that
is called tampering with the process—you may actually end up increasing the
variation of the process and, thereby, hurting the quality of the output.

In general, control charts are useful for evaluating the past performance of a
process and for monitoring its current performance. We can use them to determine whether a process was in control during, say, the past two weeks or to determine whether the process is remaining under control from hour to hour or minute
to minute. In the latter case, our goal is the swiftest detection and removal of any
special causes of variation that might arise. Keep in mind that **the primary goal of
quality-improvement activities is variance reduction**.

FIGURE 11.14
A control chart

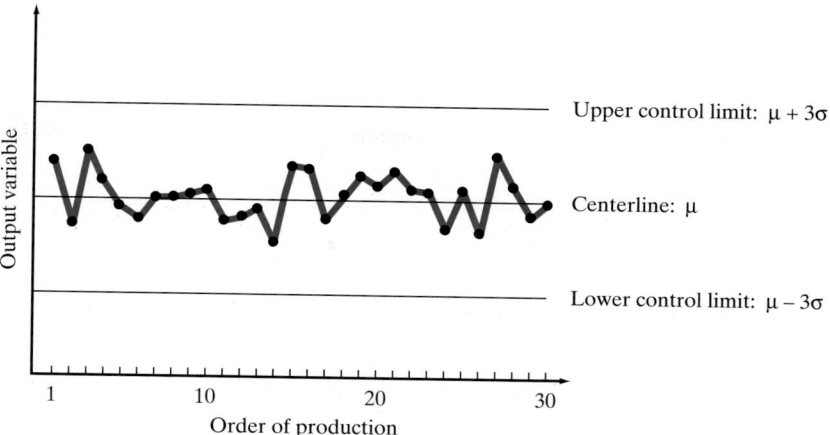

An example of a control chart is shown in Figure 11.14. A control chart is simply a time series plot of the individual measurements of a quality variable (i.e., an output variable), to which a centerline and two other horizontal lines called **control limits** have been added. The centerline represents the mean of the process (i.e., the mean of the quality variable) *when the process is in a state of statistical control*. The **upper control limit** and the **lower control limit** are positioned so that *when the process is in control* the probability of an individual value of the output variable falling outside the control limits is very small. Most practitioners position the control limits a distance of 3 standard deviations from the centerline (i.e., from the process mean) and refer to them as **3-sigma limits**. If the process is in control and following a normal distribution, the probability of an individual measurement falling outside the control limits is .0027 (less than 3 chances in 1,000). This is shown in Figure 11.15.

As long as the individual values stay between the control limits, the process is considered to be under control, meaning that no special causes of variation are influencing the output of the process. If one or more values fall outside the control

In this chapter we show you how to construct and use control charts for both quantitative and qualitative quality variables. Important quantitative variables include such things as weight, width, and time. An important qualitative variable is product status: defective or nondefective.

FIGURE 11.15
The probability of observing a measurement beyond the control limits when the process is in control

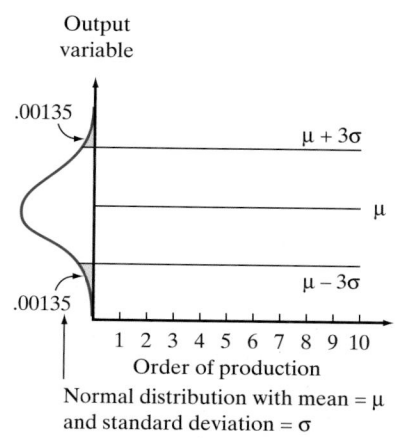

limits, either a **rare event** has occurred or the process is out of control. Following the rare-event approach to inference described earlier in the text, such a result is interpreted as evidence that the process is out of control and that actions should be taken to eliminate the special causes of variation that exist.

Other evidence to indicate that the process is out of control may be present on the control chart. For example, if we observe any of the patterns of variation shown in Figure 11.6, we can conclude the process is out of control *even if all the points fall between the control limits*. In general, any persistent, systematic variation pattern (i.e., any nonrandom pattern) is interpreted as evidence that the process is out of control. We discuss this in detail in the next section.

In Chapter 8 we described how to make inferences about populations using hypothesis-testing techniques. What we do in this section should seem quite similar. Although our focus now is on making inferences about a *process* rather than a *population*, we are again testing hypotheses. In this case, we test

$$H_0: \text{Process is under control}$$

$$H_a: \text{Process is out of control}$$

Each time we plot a new point and see whether it falls inside or outside of the control limits, we are running a two-sided hypothesis test. The control limits function as the critical values for the test.

What we learned in Chapter 6 about the types of errors that we might make in running a hypothesis test holds true in using control charts as well. Any time we reject the hypothesis that the process is under control and conclude that the process is out of control, we run the risk of making a Type I error (rejecting the null hypothesis when the null is true). Anytime we conclude (or behave as if we conclude) that the process is in control, we run the risk of a Type II error (accepting the null hypothesis when the alternative is true). There is nothing magical or mystical about control charts. Just as in any hypothesis test, the conclusion suggested by a control chart may be wrong.

One of the main reasons that 3-sigma control limits are used (rather than 2-sigma or 1-sigma limits, for example) is the small Type I error probability associated with their use. The probability we noted previously of an individual measurement falling outside the control limits—.0027—is a Type I error probability. Since we interpret a sample point that falls beyond the limits as a signal that the process is out of control, the use of 3-sigma limits yields very few signals that are "false alarms."

To make these ideas more concrete, we will construct and interpret a control chart for the paint-filling process discussed in Section 11.2. Our intention is simply to help you better understand the logic of control charts. Structured, step-by-step descriptions of how to construct control charts will be given in later sections.

TABLE 11.1 Fill Weights of 50 Consecutively Produced Cans of Paint

1. 10.0008	11. 9.9957	21. 9.9977	31. 10.0107	41. 10.0054
2. 10.0062	12. 10.0076	22. 9.9968	32. 10.0102	42. 10.0061
3. 9.9948	13. 10.0036	23. 9.9982	33. 9.9995	43. 9.9978
4. 9.9893	14. 10.0037	24. 10.0092	34. 10.0038	44. 9.9969
5. 9.9994	15. 10.0029	25. 9.9964	35. 9.9925	45. 9.9969
6. 9.9953	16. 9.9995	26. 10.0053	36. 9.9983	46. 10.0006
7. 9.9963	17. 9.9956	27. 10.0012	37. 10.0018	47. 10.0011
8. 9.9925	18. 10.0005	28. 9.9988	38. 10.0038	48. 9.9973
9. 9.9914	19. 10.0020	29. 9.9914	39. 9.9974	49. 9.9958
10. 10.0035	20. 10.0053	30. 10.0036	40. 9.9966	50. 9.9873

FIGURE 11.16
Control chart of fill weights for 50 consecutive paint can fills

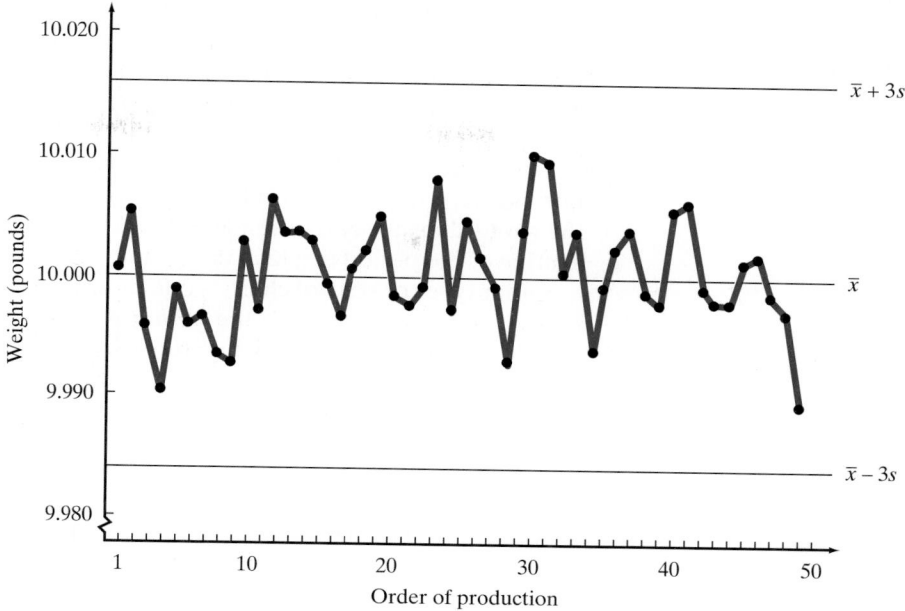

The sample measurements from the paint-filling process, presented in Table 11.1, were previously plotted in Figure 11.11. We use the mean and standard deviation of the sample, $\bar{x} = 9.9997$ and $s = .0053$, to estimate the mean and the standard deviation of the process. Although these are estimates, in using and interpreting control charts we treat them *as if* they were the actual mean μ and standard deviation σ of the process. This is standard practice in control charting.

The centerline of the control chart, representing the process mean, is drawn so that it intersects the vertical axis at 9.9997, as shown in Figure 11.16. The upper control limit is drawn at a distance of $3s = 3(.0053) = .0159$ above the centerline, and the lower control limit is $3s = .0159$ below the centerline. Then the 50 sample weights are plotted on the chart in the order that they were generated by the paint-filling process.

As can be seen in Figure 11.16, all the weight measurements fall within the control limits. Further, there do not appear to be any systematic nonrandom patterns in the data such as displayed in Figures 11.5 and 11.6. Accordingly, we are unable to conclude that the process is out of control. That is, we are unable to reject the null hypothesis that the process is in control. However, instead of using this formal hypothesis-testing language in interpreting control chart results, we prefer simply to say that the data suggest or indicate that the process is in control. We do this, however, with the full understanding that the probability of a Type II error is generally unknown in control chart applications and that we might be wrong in our conclusion. What we are really saying when we conclude that the process is in control is that *the data indicate that it is better to behave as if the process were under control than to tamper with the process.*

We have portrayed the control chart hypothesis test as testing "in control" versus "out of control." Another way to look at it is this: When we compare the weight of an *individual* can of paint to the control limits, we are conducting the following two-tailed hypothesis test:

$$H_0: \mu = 9.9997$$

$$H_a: \mu \neq 9.9997$$

where 9.9997 is the centerline of the control chart. The control limits delineate the two rejection regions for this test. Accordingly, with each weight measurement that we plot and compare to the control limits, we are testing whether the process mean (the mean fill weight) has changed. Thus, what the control chart is monitoring is the mean of the process. **The control chart leads us to accept or reject statistical control on the basis of whether the mean of the process has changed or not**. This type of process instability is illustrated in the top graph of Figure 11.8. In the paint-filling process example, the process mean apparently has remained constant over the period in which the sample weights were collected.

Other types of control charts—one of which we will describe in Section 11.5—help us determine whether the *variance* of the process has changed, as in the middle and bottom graphs of Figure 11.8.

The control chart we have just described is called an **individuals chart**, or an **x-chart**. The term *individuals* refers to the fact that the chart uses individual measurements to monitor the process—that is, measurements taken from individual units of process output. This is in contrast to plotting sample means on the control chart, for example, as we do in the next section.

Students sometimes confuse control limits with product **specification limits**. We have already explained control limits, which are a function of the natural variability of the process. Assuming we always use 3-sigma limits, the position of the control limits is a function of the size of σ, the process standard deviation.

DEFINITION 11.8

Specification limits are boundary points that define the acceptable values for an output variable (i.e., for a quality characteristic) of a particular product or service. They are determined by customers, management, and product designers. Specification limits may be two-sided, with upper and lower limits, or one-sided, with either an upper or a lower limit.

Process output that falls inside the specification limits is said to **conform to specifications**. Otherwise it is said to be **nonconforming**.

Unlike control limits, specification limits are not dependent on the process in any way. A customer of the paint-filling process may specify that all cans contain no more than 10.005 pounds of paint and no less than 9.995 pounds. These are specification limits. The customer has reasons for these specifications but may have no idea whether the supplier's process can meet them. Both the customer's specification limits and the control limits of the supplier's paint-filling process are shown in Figure 11.17. Do you think the customer will be satisfied with the quality of the product received? We don't. Although some cans are within the specification limits, most are not, as indicated by the shaded region on the figure.

11.4 A Control Chart for Monitoring the Mean of a Process: The $\bar{x}$-Chart

In the last section we introduced you to the logic of control charts by focusing on a chart that reflected the variation in individual measurements of process output. We used the chart to determine whether the process mean had shifted. The control chart we present in this section—the $\bar{x}$-chart—is also used to detect changes in the process mean, but it does so by monitoring the variation in the mean of

FIGURE 11.17
Comparison of control limits and specification limits

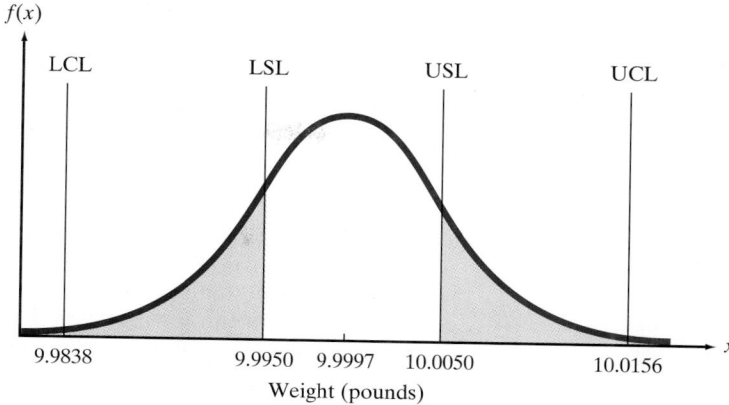

LCL = Lower control limit
UCL = Upper control limit
LSL = Lower specification limit
USL = Upper specification limit

samples that have been drawn from the process. That is, instead of plotting individual measurements on the control chart, in this case we plot sample means. Because of the additional information reflected in sample means (because each sample mean is calculated from n individual measurements), the $\bar{x}$-chart is more sensitive than the individuals chart for detecting changes in the process mean.

In practice, the $\bar{x}$-chart is rarely used alone. It is typically used in conjunction with a chart that monitors the variation of the process, usually a chart called an R-chart. The $\bar{x}$- and R-charts are the most widely used control charts in industry. Used in concert, these charts make it possible to determine whether a process has gone out of control because the variation has changed or because the mean has changed. We present the R-chart in the next section, at the end of which we discuss their simultaneous use. For now, we focus only on the $\bar{x}$-chart. **Consequently, we assume throughout this section that the process variation is stable.**[*]

Figure 11.18 provides an example of an $\bar{x}$-chart. As with the individuals chart, the centerline represents the mean of the process and the upper and lower control limits are positioned a distance of 3 standard deviations from the mean. However, since the chart is tracking sample means rather than individual measurements, the relevant standard deviation is the standard deviation of $\bar{x}$, not σ, the standard deviation of the output variable.

FIGURE 11.18
$\bar{x}$-Chart

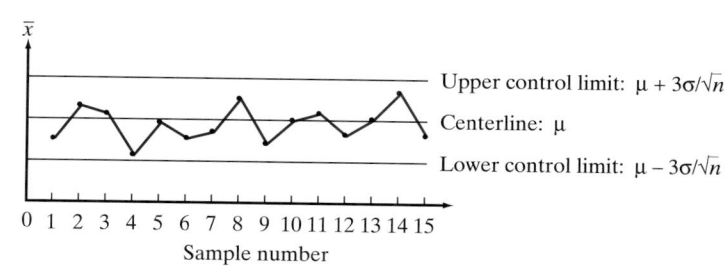

[*]*To the instructor:* Technically, the R-chart should be constructed and interpreted before the $\bar{x}$-chart. However, in our experience, students more quickly grasp control chart concepts if they are familiar with the underlying theory. We begin with $\bar{x}$-charts because their underlying theory was presented in Chapters 4–6.

If the process were in statistical control, the sequence of $\bar{x}$'s plotted on the chart would exhibit random behavior between the control limits. Only if a rare event occurred or if the process went out of control would a sample mean fall beyond the control limits.

To better understand the justification for having control limits that involve $\sigma_{\bar{x}}$, consider the following. The $\bar{x}$-chart is concerned with the variation in $\bar{x}$ which, as we saw in Chapter 4, is described by $\bar{x}$'s sampling distribution. But what is the sampling distribution of $\bar{x}$? If the process is in control and its output variable x is characterized at each point in time by a normal distribution with mean μ and standard deviation σ, the distribution of $\bar{x}$ (i.e., $\bar{x}$'s sampling distribution) also follows a normal distribution with mean μ at each point in time. But, as we saw in Chapter 4, its standard deviation is $\sigma_{\bar{x}} = \sigma/\sqrt{n}$. The control limits of the $\bar{x}$-chart are determined from and interpreted with respect to the sampling distribution of $\bar{x}$, not the distribution of x. These points are illustrated in Figure 11.19.*

In order to construct an $\bar{x}$-chart, you should have at least 20 samples of n items each, where $n \geqslant 2$. This will provide sufficient data to obtain reasonably good estimates of the mean and variance of the process. The centerline, which represents the mean of the process, is determined as follows:

$$\text{Centerline: } \bar{\bar{x}} = \frac{\bar{x}_1 + \bar{x}_2 + \cdots + \bar{x}_k}{k}$$

FIGURE 11.19
The sampling
distribution of $\bar{x}$

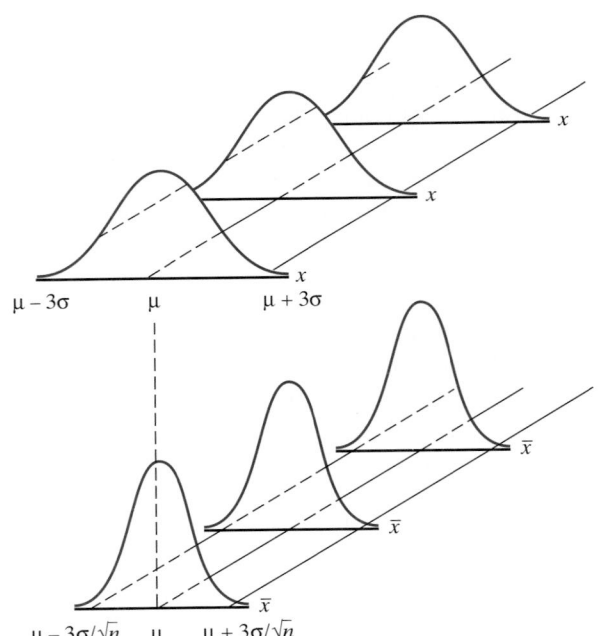

If the process is under control and follows a normal distribution with mean μ and standard deviation σ...

$\bar{x}$ also follows a normal distribution with mean μ but has standard deviation σ/√n.

*The sampling distribution of $\bar{x}$ can also be approximated using the Central Limit Theorem (Chapter 4). That is, when the process is under control and $\bar{x}$ is to be computed from a large sample from the process ($n \geqslant 30$), the sampling distribution will be approximately normally distributed with mean μ and standard deviation $\sigma/\sqrt{n}$. Even for samples as small as 4 or 5, the sampling distribution of $\bar{x}$ will be approximately normal as long as the distribution of x is reasonably symmetric and roughly bell-shaped.

where k is the number of samples of size n from which the chart is to be constructed and $\bar{x}_i$ is the sample mean of the ith sample. Thus $\bar{\bar{x}}$ is an estimator of μ.
The control limits are positioned as follows:

$$\text{Upper control limit: } \bar{\bar{x}} + \frac{3\sigma}{\sqrt{n}}$$

$$\text{Lower control limit: } \bar{\bar{x}} - \frac{3\sigma}{\sqrt{n}}$$

Since σ, the process standard deviation, is virtually always unknown, it must be estimated. This can be done in several ways. One approach involves calculating the standard deviations for each of the k samples and averaging them. Another involves using the sample standard deviation s from a large sample that was generated while the process was believed to be in control. We employ a third approach, however—the one favored by industry. It has been shown to be as effective as the other approaches for sample sizes of $n = 10$ or less, the sizes most often used in industry.

This approach utilizes the ranges of the k samples to estimate the process standard deviation, σ. Recall from Chapter 2 that the range, R, of a sample is the difference between the maximum and minimum measurements in the sample. It can be shown that dividing the mean of the k ranges, $\bar{R}$, by the constant d_2, obtains an unbiased estimator for σ. [For details, see Ryan (1989).] The estimator, denoted by $\hat{\sigma}$, is calculated as follows:

$$\hat{\sigma} = \frac{\bar{R}}{d_2} = \frac{R_1 + R_2 + \cdots + R_k}{k}\left(\frac{1}{d_2}\right)$$

where R_i is the range of the ith sample and d_2 is a constant that depends on the sample size. Values of d_2 for samples of size $n = 2$ to $n = 25$ can be found in Appendix B, Table XV.

Substituting $\hat{\sigma}$ for σ in the formulas for the upper control limit (UCL) and the lower control limit (LCL), we get

$$\text{UCL: } \bar{\bar{x}} + \frac{3\left(\dfrac{\bar{R}}{d_2}\right)}{\sqrt{n}} \qquad \text{LCL: } \bar{\bar{x}} - \frac{3\left(\dfrac{\bar{R}}{d_2}\right)}{\sqrt{n}}$$

Notice that $(\bar{R}/d_2)/\sqrt{n}$ is an estimator of $\sigma_{\bar{x}}$. The calculation of these limits can be simplified by creating the constant

$$A_2 = \frac{3}{d_2\sqrt{n}}$$

Then the control limits can be expressed as

$$\text{UCL: } \bar{\bar{x}} + A_2\bar{R}$$
$$\text{LCL: } \bar{\bar{x}} - A_2\bar{R}$$

where the values for A_2 for samples of size $n = 2$ to $n = 25$ can be found in Appendix B, Table XV.

The degree of sensitivity of the $\bar{x}$-chart to changes in the process mean depends on two decisions that must be made in constructing the chart.

The Two Most Important Decisions in Constructing an $\bar{x}$-Chart

1. The sample size, n, must be determined.

2. The frequency with which samples are to be drawn from the process must be determined (e.g., once an hour, once each shift, or once a day).

In order to quickly detect process change, we try to choose samples in such a way that the change in the process mean occurs *between* samples, not *within* samples (i.e., not during the period when a sample is being drawn). In this way, every measurement in the sample before the change will be unaffected by the change and every measurement in the sample following the change will be affected. The result is that the $\bar{x}$ computed from the latter sample should be substantially different from that of the former sample—a signal that something has happened to the process mean.

DEFINITION 11.9

Samples whose size and frequency have been designed to make it likely that process changes will occur between, rather than within, the samples are referred to as **rational subgroups**.

Rational Subgrouping Strategy

The samples (rational subgroups) should be chosen in a manner that:

1. Gives the maximum chance for the *measurements* in each sample to be similar (i.e., to be affected by the same sources of variation).

2. Gives the maximum chance for the *samples* to differ (i.e., be affected by at least one different source of variation).

The following example illustrates the concept of **rational subgrouping**. An operations manager suspects that the quality of the output in a manufacturing process may differ from shift to shift because of the preponderance of newly hired workers on the night shift. The manager wants to be able to detect such differences quickly, using an $\bar{x}$-chart. Following the rational subgrouping strategy, the control chart should be constructed with samples that are drawn *within* each shift. None of the samples should span shifts. That is, no sample should contain, say, the last three items produced by shift 1 and the first two items produced by shift 2. In this way, the measurements in each sample would be similar, but the $\bar{x}$'s would reflect differences between shifts.

The secret to designing an effective $\bar{x}$-chart is to anticipate the *types of special causes of variation* that might affect the process mean. Then purposeful rational subgrouping can be employed to construct a chart that is sensitive to the anticipated cause or causes of variation.

The preceding discussion and example focused primarily on the timing or frequency of samples. Concerning the size of the samples, practitioners typically work with samples of size $n = 4$ to $n = 10$ consecutively produced items. Using small samples of consecutively produced items helps to ensure that the measurements in each sample will be similar (i.e., affected by the same causes of variation).

Constructing an x-Chart: A Summary

1. Using a rational subgrouping strategy, collect at least 20 samples (subgroups), each of size $n \geqslant 2$.

2. Calculate the mean and range for each sample.

3. Calculate the mean of the sample means, $\bar{\bar{x}}$, and the mean of the sample ranges, $\bar{R}$:

$$\bar{\bar{x}} = \frac{\bar{x}_1 + \bar{x}_2 + \cdots + \bar{x}_k}{k} \qquad \bar{R} = \frac{R_1 + R_2 + \cdots + R_k}{k}$$

where

k = number of samples (i.e., subgroups)

$\bar{x}_i$ = sample mean for the ith sample

R_i = range of the ith sample

4. Plot the centerline and control limits:

$$Centerline: \bar{\bar{x}}$$

$$Upper\ control\ limit: \bar{\bar{x}} + A_2\bar{R}$$

$$Lower\ control\ limit: \bar{\bar{x}} - A_2\bar{R}$$

where A_2 is a constant that depends on n. Its values are given in Appendix B, Table XV, for samples of size $n = 2$ to $n = 25$.

5. Plot the k sample means on the control chart in the order that the samples were produced by the process.

When interpreting a control chart, it is convenient to think of the chart as consisting of six zones, as shown in Figure 11.20. Each zone is 1 standard deviation wide. The two zones within 1 standard deviation of the centerline are called **C zones**; the regions between 1 and 2 standard deviations from the centerline are called **B zones**; and the regions between 2 and 3 standard deviations from the centerline are called **A zones**. The box describes how to construct the *zone boundaries* for an $\bar{x}$-chart.

FIGURE 11.20
The zones of a
control chart

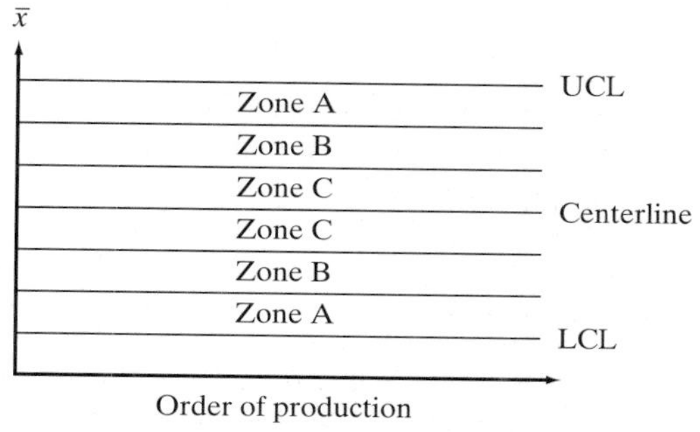

Order of production

Constructing Zone Boundaries for an $\bar{x}$-Chart

The zone boundaries can be constructed in either of the following ways:

1. Using the 3-sigma control limits:

$$\text{Upper A–B boundary: } \bar{\bar{x}} + \frac{2}{3}(A_2\bar{R})$$

$$\text{Lower A–B boundary: } \bar{\bar{x}} - \frac{2}{3}(A_2\bar{R})$$

$$\text{Upper B–C boundary: } \bar{\bar{x}} + \frac{1}{3}(A_2\bar{R})$$

$$\text{Lower B–C boundary: } \bar{\bar{x}} - \frac{1}{3}(A_2\bar{R})$$

2. Using the estimated standard deviation of $\bar{x}$, $(\bar{R}/d_2)/\sqrt{n}$:

$$\text{Upper A–B boundary: } \bar{\bar{x}} + 2\left[\frac{\left(\frac{\bar{R}}{d_2}\right)}{\sqrt{n}}\right]$$

$$\text{Lower A–B boundary: } \bar{\bar{x}} - 2\left[\frac{\left(\frac{\bar{R}}{d_2}\right)}{\sqrt{n}}\right]$$

$$\text{Upper B–C boundary: } \bar{\bar{x}} + \left[\frac{\left(\frac{\bar{R}}{d_2}\right)}{\sqrt{n}}\right]$$

$$\text{Lower B–C boundary: } \bar{\bar{x}} - \left[\frac{\left(\frac{\bar{R}}{d_2}\right)}{\sqrt{n}}\right]$$

Practitioners use six simple rules that are based on these zones to help determine when a process is out of control. The six rules are summarized in Figure 11.21. They are referred to as **pattern-analysis rules**.

Rule 1 is the familiar point-beyond-the-control-limit rule that we have mentioned several times. The other rules all help to determine when the process is out of control *even though all the plotted points fall within the control limits*. That is, the other rules help to identify nonrandom patterns of variation that have not yet broken through the control limits (or may never break through).

All the patterns shown in Figure 11.21 are **rare events** under the assumption that the process is under control. To see this, let's assume that the process is under control and follows a normal distribution. We can then easily work out the probability that an individual point will fall in any given zone. (We dealt with this type of problem in Chapter 5.) Just focusing on one side of the centerline, you can show that the probability of a point falling beyond Zone A is .00135, in Zone A is .02135, in Zone B is .1360, and in Zone C is .3413. Of course, the same probabilities apply to both sides of the centerline.

From these probabilities we can determine the likelihood of various patterns of points. For example, let's evaluate Rule 1. The probability of observing a point outside the control limits (i.e., above the upper control limit or below the lower control limit) is .00135 + .00135 = .0027. This is clearly a rare event.

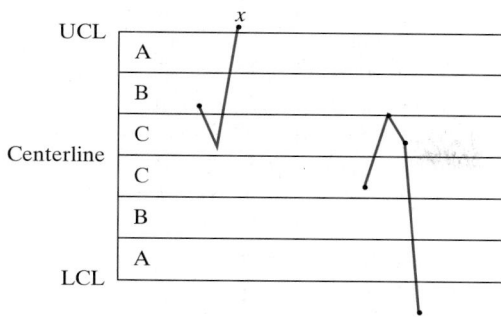

Rule 1: One point beyond Zone A

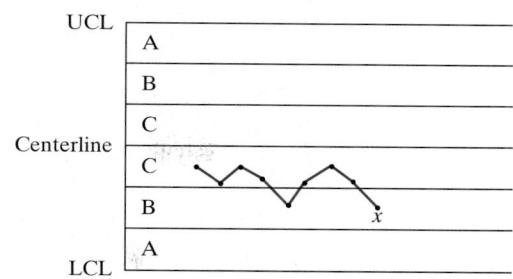

Rule 2: Nine points in a row in Zone C or beyond

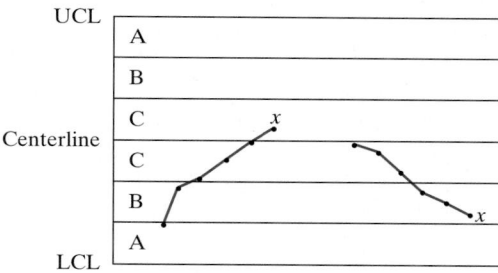

Rule 3: Six points in a row steadily increasing or decreasing

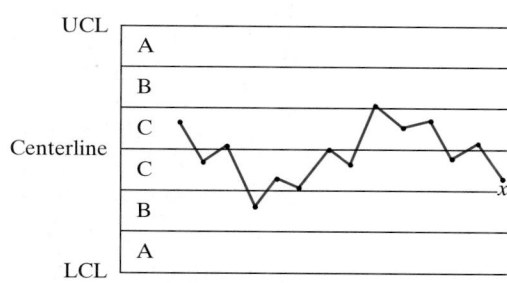

Rule 4: Fourteen points in a row alternating up and down

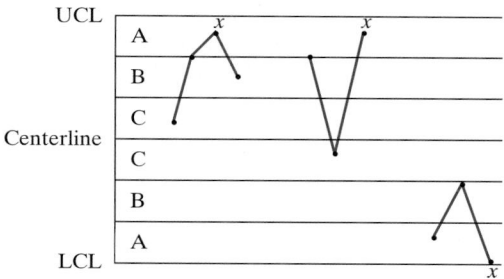

Rule 5: Two out of three points in a row in Zone A or beyond

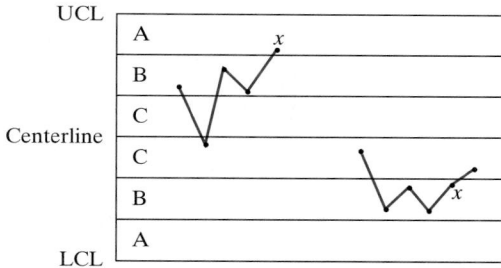

Rule 6: Four out of five points in a row in Zone B or beyond

> Rules 1, 2, 5, and 6 should be applied separately to the upper and lower halves of the control chart. Rules 3 and 4 should be applied to the whole chart.

FIGURE 11.21 Pattern-analysis rules for detecting the presence of special causes of variation

As another example, Rule 5 indicates that the observation of two out of three points in a row in Zone A or beyond is a rare event. Is it? The probability of being in Zone A or beyond is $.00135 + .02135 = .0227$. We can use the binomial distribution (Chapter 4) to find the probability of observing 2 out of 3 points in or beyond Zone A. The binomial probability $P(x = 2)$ when $n = 3$ and $p = .0227$ is $.0015$. Again, this is clearly a rare event.

In general, when the process is in control and normally distributed, the probability of any one of these rules *incorrectly* signaling the presence of special causes of variation is less than .005, or 5 chances in 1,000. If all of the first four rules are applied, the overall probability of a false signal is about .01. If all six of the rules are applied, the overall probability of a false signal rises to .02, or 2 chances in 100. These three probabilities can be thought of as Type I error probabilities. Each indicates the probability of incorrectly rejecting the null hypothesis that the process is in a state of statistical control.

Explanation of the possible causes of these nonrandom patterns is beyond the scope of this text. We refer the interested reader to AT&T's *Statistical Quality Control Handbook* (1956).

We use these rules again in the next section when we interpret the *R*-chart.

Interpreting an $\bar{x}$-Chart

1. The **process is out of control** if one or more sample means fall beyond the control limits or if any of the other five patterns of variation of Figure 11.21 are observed. Such signals are an indication that one or more special causes of variation are affecting the process mean. We must identify and eliminate them to bring the process into control.

2. The **process is treated as being in control** if none of the previously noted out-of-control signals are observed. Processes that are in control should not be tampered with. However, if the level of variation is unacceptably high, common causes of variation should be identified and eliminated.

Assumption: The variation of the process is stable. (If it were not, the control limits of the $\bar{x}$-chart would be meaningless, since they are a function of the process variation. The *R*-chart, presented in the next section, is used to investigate this assumption.)

In theory, the centerline and control limits should be developed using samples that were collected during a period in which the process was in control. Otherwise, they will not be representative of the variation of the process (or, in the present case, the variation of $\bar{x}$) when the process is in control. However, we will not know whether the process is in control until after we have constructed a control chart. Consequently, when a control chart is first constructed, the centerline and control limits are treated as **trial values**. If the chart indicates that the process was in control during the period when the sample data were collected, then the centerline and control limits become "official" (i.e., no longer treated as trial values). It is then appropriate to extend the control limits and the centerline to the right and to use the chart to monitor future process output.

However, if in applying the pattern-analysis rules of Figure 11.21 it is determined that the process was out of control while the sample data were being collected, the trial values (i.e., the trial chart) should, in general, not be used to monitor the process. The points on the control chart that indicate that the process is out of control should be investigated to see if any special causes of variation can be identified. If special causes of variation are found, (1) they should be eliminated, (2) any points on the chart determined to have been influenced by the special causes—whether inside or outside the control limits—should be discarded, and (3) *new* trial centerline and control limits should be calculated from the remaining data. However, the new trial limits may still indicate that the process is out of control. If so, repeat these three steps until all points fall within the control limits.

If special causes cannot be found and eliminated, the severity of the out-of-control indications should be evaluated and a judgment made as to whether (1) the

TABLE 11.2   Twenty-five Samples of Size 5 from the Paint-Filling Process

Sample	Measurements					Mean	Range
1	10.0042	9.9981	10.0010	9.9964	10.0001	9.99995	.0078
2	9.9950	9.9986	9.9948	10.0030	9.9938	9.99704	.0092
3	10.0028	9.9998	10.0086	9.9949	9.9980	10.00082	.0137
4	9.9952	9.9923	10.0034	9.9965	10.0026	9.99800	.0111
5	9.9997	9.9983	9.9975	10.0078	9.9891	9.99649	.0195
6	9.9987	10.0027	10.0001	10.0027	10.0029	10.00141	.0042
7	10.0004	10.0023	10.0024	9.9992	10.0135	10.00358	.0143
8	10.0013	9.9938	10.0017	10.0089	10.0001	10.00116	.0151
9	10.0103	10.0009	9.9969	10.0103	9.9986	10.00339	.0134
10	9.9980	9.9954	9.9941	9.9958	9.9963	9.99594	.0039
11	10.0013	10.0033	9.9943	9.9949	9.9999	9.99874	.0090
12	9.9986	9.9990	10.0009	9.9947	10.0008	9.99882	.0062
13	10.0089	10.0056	9.9976	9.9997	9.9922	10.00080	.0167
14	9.9971	10.0015	9.9962	10.0038	10.0022	10.00016	.0076
15	9.9949	10.0011	10.0043	9.9988	9.9919	9.99822	.0124
16	9.9951	9.9957	10.0094	10.0040	9.9974	10.00033	.0137
17	10.0015	10.0026	10.0032	9.9971	10.0019	10.00127	.0061
18	9.9983	10.0019	9.9978	9.9997	10.0029	10.00130	.0051
19	9.9977	9.9963	9.9981	9.9968	10.0009	9.99798	.0127
20	10.0078	10.0004	9.9966	10.0051	10.0007	10.00212	.0112
21	9.9963	9.9990	10.0037	9.9936	9.9962	9.99764	.0101
22	9.9999	10.0022	10.0057	10.0026	10.0032	10.00272	.0058
23	9.9998	10.0002	9.9978	9.9966	10.0060	10.00009	.0094
24	10.0031	10.0078	9.9988	10.0032	9.9944	10.00146	.0134
25	9.9993	9.9978	9.9964	10.0032	10.0041	10.00015	.0077

out-of-control points should be discarded anyway and new trial limits constructed, (2) the original trial limits are good enough to be made official, or (3) new sample data should be collected to construct new trial limits.

EXAMPLE 11.1

Let's return to the paint-filling process described in Sections 11.2 and 11.3. Suppose instead of sampling 50 consecutive gallons of paint from the filling process to develop a control chart, it was decided to sample five consecutive cans once each hour for the next 25 hours. The sample data are presented in Table 11.2. This sampling strategy (rational subgrouping) was selected because several times a month the filling head in question becomes clogged. When that happens, the head dispenses less and less paint over the course of the day. However, the pattern of decrease is so irregular that minute-to-minute or even half-hour-to-half-hour changes are difficult to detect.

a. Explain the logic behind the rational subgrouping strategy that was used.

b. Construct an $\bar{x}$-chart for the process using the data in Table 11.2.

c. What does the chart suggest about the stability of the filling process (whether the process is in or out of statistical control)?

d. Should the control limits be used to monitor future process output?

SOLUTION

a. The samples are far enough apart in time to detect hour-to-hour shifts or changes in the mean amount of paint dispensed, but the individual measurements that make up each sample are close enough together in time to ensure that the process has changed little, if at all, during the time the individual measurements were made. Overall, the rational subgrouping employed affords the opportunity for process changes to occur between samples and therefore show up on the control chart as differences between the sample means.

b. Twenty-five samples ($k = 25$ subgroups), each containing $n = 5$ cans of paint, were collected from the process. The first step after collecting the data is to calculate the 25 sample means and sample ranges needed to construct the $\bar{x}$-chart. The mean and range of the first sample are

$$\bar{x} = \frac{10.0042 + 9.9981 + 10.0010 + 9.9964 + 10.0001}{5} = 9.99995$$

$$R = 10.0042 - 9.9964 = .0078$$

All 25 means and ranges are displayed in Table 11.2.

Next, we calculate the mean of the sample means and the mean of the sample ranges:

$$\bar{\bar{x}} = \frac{9.99995 + 9.99704 + \cdots + 10.00015}{25} = 9.9999$$

$$\bar{R} = \frac{.0078 + .0092 + \cdots + .0077}{25} = .01028$$

The centerline of the chart is positioned at $\bar{\bar{x}} = 9.9999$. To determine the control limits, we need the constant A_2, which can be found in Table XV of Appendix B. For $n = 5$, $A_2 = .577$. Then,

$$\text{UCL:} \bar{\bar{x}} + A_2\bar{R} = 9.9999 + .577(.01028) = 10.0058$$

$$\text{LCL:} \bar{\bar{x}} - A_2\bar{R} = 9.9999 - .577(.01028) = 9.9940$$

After positioning the control limits on the chart, we plot the 25 sample means in the order of sampling and connect the points with straight lines. The resulting trial $\bar{x}$-chart is shown in Figure 11.22.

c. To check the stability of the process, we use the six pattern-analysis rules for detecting special causes of variation, which were presented in Figure 11.21.

FIGURE 11.22
$\bar{x}$-chart for the paint-filling process

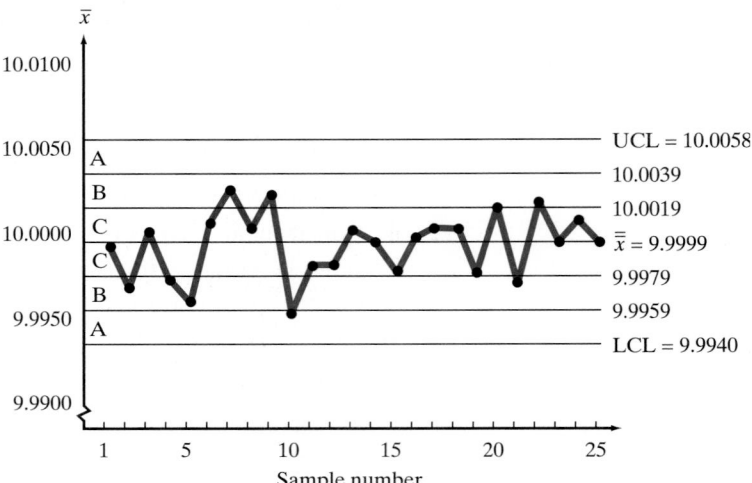

To apply most of these rules requires identifying the A, B, and C zones of the control chart. These are indicated in Figure 11.22. We describe how they were constructed below.

The boundary between the A and B zones is 2 standard deviations from the centerline, and the boundary between the B and C zones is 1 standard deviation from the centerline. Thus, using $A_2\bar{R}$ and the 3-sigma limits previously calculated, we locate the A, B, and C zones above the centerline:

$$\text{A–B boundary} = \bar{\bar{x}} + \tfrac{2}{3}(A_2\bar{R}) = 9.9999 + \tfrac{2}{3}(.577)(.01028) = 10.0039$$

$$\text{B–C boundary} = \bar{\bar{x}} + \tfrac{1}{3}(A_2\bar{R}) = 9.9999 + \tfrac{1}{3}(.577)(.01028) = 10.0019$$

Similarly, the zones below the centerline are located:

$$\text{A–B boundary} = \bar{\bar{x}} - \tfrac{2}{3}(A_2\bar{R}) = 9.9959$$

$$\text{B–C boundary} = \bar{\bar{x}} - \tfrac{1}{3}(A_2\bar{R}) = 9.9979$$

A careful comparison of the six pattern-analysis rules with the sequence of sample means yields no out-of-control signals. All points are inside the control limits and there appear to be no nonrandom patterns within the control limits. That is, we can find no evidence of a shift in the process mean. Accordingly, we conclude that the process is in control.

d. Since the process was found to be in control during the period in which the samples were drawn, the trial control limits constructed in part **b** can be considered official. They should be extended to the right and used to monitor future process output.

EXAMPLE 11.2

Ten new samples of size $n = 5$ were drawn from the paint-filling process of the previous example. The sample data, including sample means and ranges, are shown in Table 11.3. Investigate whether the process remained in control during the period in which the new sample data were collected.

SOLUTION

We begin by simply extending the control limits, centerline, and zone boundaries of the control chart in Figure 11.22 to the right. Next, beginning with sample number 26, we plot the 10 new sample means on the control chart and connect them with straight lines. This extended version of the control chart is shown in Figure 11.23.

Now that the control chart has been prepared, we apply the six pattern-analysis rules for detecting special causes of variation (Figure 11.21) to the new

TABLE 11.3   Ten Additional Samples of Size 5 from the Paint-Filling Process

Sample	Measurements					Mean	Range
26	10.0019	9.9981	9.9952	9.9976	9.9999	9.99841	.0067
27	10.0041	9.9982	10.0028	10.0040	9.9971	10.00125	.0070
28	9.9999	9.9974	10.0078	9.9971	9.9923	9.99890	.0155
29	9.9982	10.0002	9.9916	10.0040	9.9916	9.99713	.0124
30	9.9933	9.9963	9.9955	9.9993	9.9905	9.99498	.0088
31	9.9915	9.9984	10.0053	9.9888	9.9876	9.99433	.0177
32	9.9912	9.9970	9.9961	9.9879	9.9970	9.99382	.0091
33	9.9942	9.9960	9.9975	10.0019	9.9912	9.99614	.0107
34	9.9949	9.9967	9.9936	9.9941	10.0071	9.99726	.0135
35	9.9943	9.9969	9.9937	9.9912	10.0053	9.99626	.0141

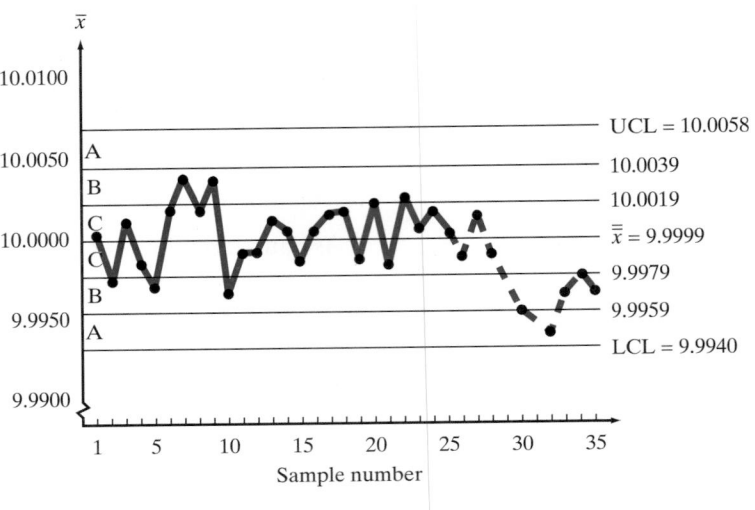

FIGURE 11.23

Extended $\bar{x}$-chart for paint-filling process

sequence of sample means. No points fall outside the control limits, but we notice six points in a row that steadily decrease (samples 27–32). Rule 3 says that if we observe six points in a row steadily increasing or decreasing, that is an indication of the presence of special causes of variation.

Notice that if you apply the rules from left to right along the sequence of sample means, the decreasing pattern also triggers signals from Rules 5 (samples 29–31) and 6 (samples 28–32).

These signals lead us to conclude that the process has gone out of control. Apparently, the filling head began to clog about the time that either sample 26 or 27 was drawn from the process. As a result, the mean of the process (the mean fill weight dispensed by the process) began to decline.

EXERCISES 11.1–11.16

Note: Exercises marked with 💾 *contain data for computer analysis on a 3.5" disk (file name in parentheses).*

Learning the Mechanics

11.1 What is a control chart? Describe its use.

11.2 Explain why rational subgrouping should be used in constructing control charts.

11.3 When a control chart is first constructed, why are the centerline and control limits treated as trial values?

11.4 Which process parameter is an $\bar{x}$-chart used to monitor?

11.5 Even if all the points on an $\bar{x}$-chart fall between the control limits, the process may be out of control. Explain.

11.6 What must be true about the variation of a process before an $\bar{x}$-chart is used to monitor the mean of the process? Why?

11.7 Use the six pattern-analysis rules described in Figure 11.21 to determine whether the process being monitored with the accompanying $\bar{x}$-chart is out of statistical control.

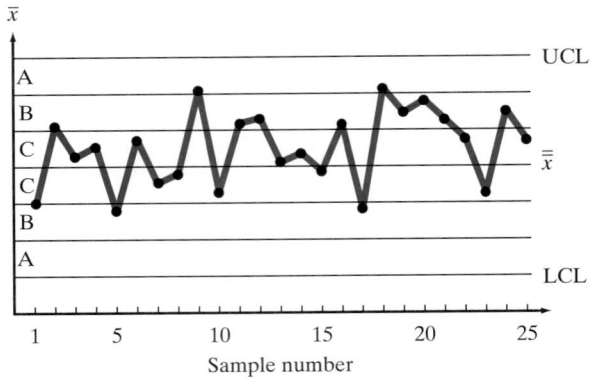

11.8 Is the process for which the accompanying $\bar{x}$-chart was constructed affected by only special causes of variation, only common causes of variation, or both? Explain.

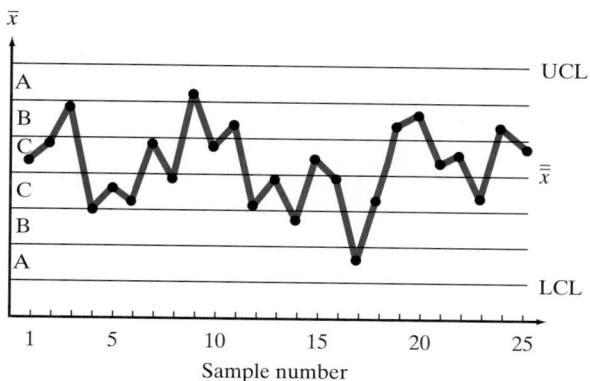

11.9 Use Table XV in Appendix B to find the value of A_2 for each of the following sample sizes.
  a. $n = 3$ **b.** $n = 10$ **c.** $n = 22$

11.10 **(X11.010)** Twenty-five samples of size $n = 5$ were collected to construct an $\bar{x}$-chart. The accompanying sample means and ranges were calculated for these data.

Sample	$\bar{x}$	R	Sample	$\bar{x}$	R
1	80.2	7.2	14	83.1	10.2
2	79.1	9.0	15	79.6	7.8
3	83.2	4.7	16	80.0	6.1
4	81.0	5.6	17	83.2	8.4
5	77.6	10.1	18	75.9	9.9
6	81.7	8.6	19	78.1	6.0
7	80.4	4.4	20	81.4	7.4
8	77.5	6.2	21	81.7	10.4
9	79.8	7.9	22	80.9	9.1
10	85.3	7.1	23	78.4	7.3
11	77.7	9.8	24	79.6	8.0
12	82.3	10.7	25	81.6	7.6
13	79.5	9.2			

  a. Calculate the mean of the sample means, $\bar{\bar{x}}$, and the mean of the sample ranges, $\bar{R}$.
  b. Calculate and plot the centerline and the upper and lower control limits for the $\bar{x}$-chart.
  c. Calculate and plot the A, B, and C zone boundaries of the $\bar{x}$-chart.
  d. Plot the 25 sample means on the $\bar{x}$-chart and use the six pattern-analysis rules to determine whether the process is under statistical control.

11.11 **(X11.011)** The data in the next table were collected for the purpose of constructing an $\bar{x}$-chart.
  a. Calculate $\bar{x}$ and R for each sample.

Sample	Measurements			
1	19.4	19.7	20.6	21.2
2	18.7	18.4	21.2	20.7
3	20.2	18.8	22.6	20.1
4	19.6	21.2	18.7	19.4
5	20.4	20.9	22.3	18.6
6	17.3	22.3	20.3	19.7
7	21.8	17.6	22.8	23.1
8	20.9	17.4	19.5	20.7
9	18.1	18.3	20.6	20.4
10	22.6	21.4	18.5	19.7
11	22.7	21.2	21.5	19.5
12	20.1	20.6	21.0	20.2
13	19.7	18.6	21.2	19.1
14	18.6	21.7	17.7	18.3
15	18.2	20.4	19.8	19.2
16	18.9	20.7	23.2	20.0
17	20.5	19.7	21.4	17.8
18	21.0	18.7	19.9	21.2
19	20.5	19.6	19.8	21.8
20	20.6	16.9	22.4	19.7

  b. Calculate $\bar{\bar{x}}$ and $\bar{R}$.
  c. Calculate and plot the centerline and the upper and lower control limits for the $\bar{x}$-chart.
  d. Calculate and plot the A, B, and C zone boundaries of the $\bar{x}$-chart.
  e. Plot the 20 sample means on the $\bar{x}$-chart. Is the process in control? Justify your answer.

Applying the Concepts

11.12 The central processing unit (CPU) of a microcomputer is a computer chip containing millions of transistors. Connecting the transistors are slender circuit paths only .5 to .85 micron wide. To understand how narrow these paths are, consider that a micron is a millionth of a meter, and a human hair is 70 microns wide (*Compute*, 1992). A manufacturer of CPU chips knows that if the circuit paths are not .5–.85 micron wide, a variety of problems will arise in the chips' performance. The manufacturer sampled four CPU chips six times a day (every 90 minutes from 8:00 A.M. until 4:30 P.M.) for five consecutive days and measured the circuit path widths. These data and MINITAB were used to construct the $\bar{x}$-chart shown on page 632.
  a. Assuming that $\bar{R} = .3162$, calculate the chart's upper and lower control limits, the upper and lower A–B boundaries, and the upper and lower B–C boundaries.
  b. What does the chart suggest about the stability of the process used to put circuit paths on the CPU chip? Justify your answer.
  c. Should the control limits be used to monitor future process output? Explain.

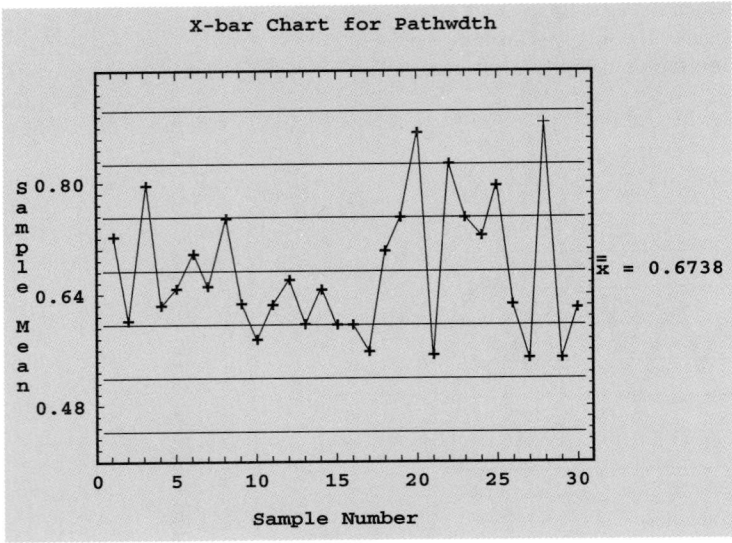

X-bar Chart for Pathwdth

11.13 (X11.013) A machine at K-Company fills boxes with bran flakes cereal. The target weight for the filled boxes is 24 ounces. The company would like to use an $\bar{x}$-chart to monitor the performance of the machine. To develop the control chart, the company decides to sample and weigh five consecutive boxes of cereal five times each day (at 8:00 and 11:00 A.M. and 2:00, 5:00, and 8:00 P.M.) for twenty consecutive days. The data are presented in the table, along with a SAS printout with summary statistics.

Day	Weight of Cereal Boxes (ounces)				
1	24.02	23.91	24.12	24.06	24.13
2	23.89	23.98	24.01	24.00	23.91
3	24.11	24.02	23.99	23.79	24.04
4	24.06	23.98	23.95	24.01	24.11
5	23.81	23.90	23.99	24.07	23.96
6	23.87	24.12	24.07	24.01	23.99
7	23.88	24.00	24.05	23.97	23.97
8	24.01	24.03	23.99	23.91	23.98
9	24.06	24.02	23.80	23.79	24.07
10	23.96	23.99	24.03	23.99	24.01
11	24.10	23.90	24.11	23.98	23.95
12	24.01	24.07	23.93	24.09	23.98
13	24.14	24.07	24.08	23.98	24.02
14	23.91	24.04	23.89	24.01	23.95
15	24.03	24.04	24.01	23.98	24.10
16	23.94	24.07	24.12	24.00	24.02
17	23.88	23.94	23.91	24.06	24.07
18	24.11	23.99	23.90	24.01	23.98
19	24.05	24.04	23.97	24.08	23.95
20	24.02	23.96	23.95	23.89	24.04

a. Construct an $\bar{x}$-chart from the given data.
b. What does the chart suggest about the stability of the filling process (whether the process is in or out of statistical control)? Justify your answer.
c. Should the control limits be used to monitor future process output? Explain.
d. Two shifts of workers run the filling operation. Each day the second shift takes over at 3:00 P.M. Will the rational subgrouping strategy used by K-Company facilitate or hinder the identification of process variation caused by differences in the two shifts? Explain.

	WEIGHT	
	MEAN	RANGE
DAY		
1	24.05	0.22
2	23.96	0.12
3	23.99	0.32
4	24.02	0.16
5	23.95	0.26
6	24.01	0.25
7	23.97	0.17
8	23.98	0.12
9	23.95	0.28
10	24.00	0.07
11	24.01	0.21
12	24.02	0.16
13	24.06	0.16
14	23.96	0.15
15	24.03	0.12
16	24.03	0.18
17	23.97	0.19
18	24.00	0.21
19	24.02	0.13
20	23.97	0.15

11.14 **(X11.014)** A precision parts manufacturer produces bolts for use in military aircraft. Ideally, the bolts should be 37 centimeters in length. The company sampled four consecutively produced bolts each hour on the hour for 25 consecutive hours and measured them using a computerized precision instrument. The data are presented below. A MINITAB printout with descriptive statistics for each hour is shown on page 634.

Hour	Bolt Lengths (centimeters)			
1	37.03	37.08	36.90	36.88
2	36.96	37.04	36.85	36.98
3	37.16	37.11	36.99	37.01
4	37.20	37.06	37.02	36.98
5	36.81	36.97	36.91	37.10
6	37.13	36.96	37.01	36.89
7	37.07	36.94	36.99	37.00
8	37.01	36.91	36.98	37.12
9	37.17	37.03	36.90	37.01
10	36.91	36.99	36.87	37.11
11	36.88	37.10	37.07	37.03
12	37.06	36.98	36.90	36.99
13	36.91	37.22	37.12	37.03
14	37.08	37.07	37.10	37.04
15	37.03	37.04	36.89	37.01
16	36.95	36.98	36.90	36.99
17	36.97	36.94	37.14	37.10
18	37.11	37.04	36.98	36.91
19	36.88	36.99	37.01	36.94
20	36.90	37.15	37.09	37.00
21	37.01	36.96	37.05	36.96
22	37.09	36.95	36.93	37.12
23	37.00	37.02	36.95	37.04
24	36.99	37.07	36.90	37.02
25	37.10	37.03	37.01	36.90

a. What process is the manufacturer interested in monitoring?

b. Construct an $\bar{x}$-chart from the data.

c. Does the chart suggest that special causes of variation are present? Justify your answer.

d. Provide an example of a special cause of variation that could potentially affect this process. Do the same for a common cause of variation.

e. Should the control limits be used to monitor future process output? Explain.

11.15 **(X11.015)** In their text, *Quantitative Analysis of Management* (1997), B. Render (Rollins College) and R. M. Stair (Florida State University), present the case of the Bayfield Mud Company. Bayfield supplies boxcars of 50-pound bags of mud treating agents to the Wet-Land Drilling Company. Mud treating agents are used to control the pH and other chemical properties of the cone during oil drilling operations. Wet-Land has complained to Bayfield that its most recent shipment of bags were underweight by about 5%. (The use of underweight bags may result in poor chemical

control during drilling, which may hurt drilling efficiency resulting in serious economic consequences.) Afraid of losing a long-time customer, Bayfield immediately began investigating their production process. Management suspected that the causes of the problem were the recently added third shift and the fact that all three shifts were under pressure to increase output to meet increasing demand for the product. Their quality control staff began randomly sampling and weighing six bags of output each hour. The average weight of each sample over the last three days is recorded in the table on page 635 along with the weight of the heaviest and lightest bag in each sample.

a. Construct an $\bar{x}$-chart for these data.

b. Is the process under statistical control?

c. Does it appear that management's suspicion about the third shift is correct? Explain?

11.16 **(X11.016)** A high-quality overnight film processing laboratory is concerned about recent processing delays that have resulted in customer complaints. The company has initiated a review of all processing steps. One step involves the evaluation of the quality of negatives. To determine if the time to complete this step is in a state of statistical control, an analyst sampled five customer orders per day for 20 working days in August, observed the processing, and obtained the following data:

Date	Sample Average (in minutes)	Sample Range (in minutes)
8/5	2.3	2.4
8/6	4.1	2.2
8/7	1.1	1.9
8/8	5.9	4.7
8/9	4.4	2.3
8/12	2.8	1.7
8/13	1.3	0.2
8/14	3.5	2.0
8/15	3.8	1.2
8/16	2.5	1.0
8/19	2.8	1.7
8/20	1.8	1.5
8/21	3.5	1.8
8/22	3.0	1.2
8/23	2.2	1.6
8/26	2.9	1.1
8/27	1.7	1.1
8/28	0.9	0.6
8/29	4.1	1.2
8/30	1.2	0.7

a. Construct an $\bar{x}$-chart for this process.

b. Is there evidence that special causes of variation are affecting the process? Explain.

c. Discuss the potential problems associated with the data collection method used to study the process.

```
Descriptive Statistics
```

Variable	HOUR	N	MEAN	MEDIAN	TR MEAN	STDEV	SE MEAN
LENGTH	1	4	36.973	36.965	36.973	0.098	0.049
	2	4	36.957	36.970	36.957	0.079	0.040
	3	4	37.067	37.060	37.067	0.081	0.040
	4	4	37.065	37.040	37.065	0.096	0.048
	5	4	36.947	36.940	36.947	0.121	0.061
	6	4	36.998	36.985	36.998	0.101	0.051
	7	4	37.000	36.995	37.000	0.054	0.027
	8	4	37.005	36.995	37.005	0.087	0.044
	9	4	37.028	37.020	37.028	0.111	0.055
	10	4	36.970	36.950	36.970	0.106	0.053
	11	4	37.020	37.050	37.020	0.098	0.049
	12	4	36.982	36.985	36.982	0.066	0.033
	13	4	37.070	37.075	37.070	0.132	0.066
	14	4	37.072	37.075	37.072	0.025	0.013
	15	4	36.993	37.020	36.993	0.069	0.035
	16	4	36.955	36.965	36.955	0.040	0.020
	17	4	37.038	37.035	37.038	0.097	0.049
	18	4	37.010	37.010	37.010	0.085	0.043
	19	4	36.955	36.965	36.955	0.058	0.029
	20	4	37.035	37.045	37.035	0.109	0.055
	21	4	36.995	36.985	36.995	0.044	0.022
	22	4	37.023	37.020	37.023	0.096	0.048
	23	4	37.003	37.010	37.003	0.039	0.019
	24	4	36.995	37.005	36.995	0.071	0.036
	25	4	37.010	37.020	37.010	0.083	0.041

Variable	HOUR	MIN	MAX	Q1	Q3
LENGTH	1	36.880	37.080	36.885	37.067
	2	36.850	37.040	36.878	37.025
	3	36.990	37.160	36.995	37.147
	4	36.980	37.200	36.990	37.165
	5	36.810	37.100	36.835	37.068
	6	36.890	37.130	36.907	37.100
	7	36.940	37.070	36.953	37.053
	8	36.910	37.120	36.927	37.092
	9	36.900	37.170	36.927	37.135
	10	36.870	37.110	36.880	37.080
	11	36.880	37.100	36.918	37.092
	12	36.900	37.060	36.920	37.043
	13	36.910	37.220	36.940	37.195
	14	37.040	37.100	37.047	37.095
	15	36.890	37.040	36.920	37.038
	16	36.900	36.990	36.913	36.987
	17	36.940	37.140	36.947	37.130
	18	36.910	37.110	36.927	37.092
	19	36.880	37.010	36.895	37.005
	20	36.900	37.150	36.925	37.135
	21	36.960	37.050	36.960	37.040
	22	36.930	37.120	36.935	37.113
	23	36.950	37.040	36.962	37.035
	24	36.900	37.070	36.922	37.058
	25	36.900	37.100	36.927	37.083

Time	Average Weight (pounds)	Lightest	Heaviest	Time	Average Weight (pounds)	Lightest	Heaviest
6:00 A.M.	49.6	48.7	50.7	6:00 P.M	46.8	41.0	51.2
7:00	50.2	49.1	51.2	7:00	50.0	46.2	51.7
8:00	50.6	49.6	51.4	8:00	47.4	44.0	48.7
9:00	50.8	50.2	51.8	9:00	47.0	44.2	48.9
10:00	49.9	49.2	52.3	10:00	47.2	46.6	50.2
11:00	50.3	48.6	51.7	11:00	48.6	47.0	50.0
12 noon	48.6	46.2	50.4	12 midnight	49.8	48.2	50.4
1:00 P.M	49.0	46.4	50.0	1:00 A.M.	49.6	48.4	51.7
2:00	49.0	46.0	50.6	2:00	50.0	49.0	52.2
3:00	49.8	48.2	50.8	3:00	50.0	49.2	50.0
4:00	50.3	49.2	52.7	4:00	47.2	46.3	50.5
5:00	51.4	50.0	55.3	5:00	47.0	44.1	49.7
6:00	51.6	49.2	54.7	6:00	48.4	45.0	49.0
7:00	51.8	50.0	55.6	7:00	48.8	44.8	49.7
8:00	51.0	48.6	53.2	8:00	49.6	48.0	51.8
9:00	50.5	49.4	52.4	9:00	50.0	48.1	52.7
10:00	49.2	46.1	50.7	10:00	51.0	48.1	55.2
11:00	49.0	46.3	50.8	11:00	50.4	49.5	54.1
12 midnight	48.4	45.4	50.2	12 noon	50.0	48.7	50.9
1:00 A.M.	47.6	44.3	49.7	1:00 P.M.	48.9	47.6	51.2
2:00	47.4	44.1	49.6	2:00	49.8	48.4	51.0
3:00	48.2	45.2	49.0	3:00	49.8	48.8	50.8
4:00	48.0	45.5	49.1	4:00	50.0	49.1	50.6
5:00	48.4	47.1	49.6	5:00	47.8	45.2	51.2
6:00	48.6	47.4	52.0	6:00	46.4	44.0	49.7
7:00	50.0	49.2	52.2	7:00	46.4	44.4	50.0
8:00	49.8	49.0	52.4	8:00	47.2	46.6	48.9
9:00	50.3	49.4	51.7	9:00	48.4	47.2	49.5
10:00	50.2	49.6	51.8	10:00	49.2	48.1	50.7
11:00	50.0	49.0	52.3	11:00	48.4	47.0	50.8
12 noon	50.0	48.8	52.4	12 midnight	47.2	46.4	49.2
1:00 P.M	50.1	49.4	53.6	1:00 A.M.	47.4	46.8	49.0
2:00	49.7	48.6	51.0	2:00	48.8	47.2	51.4
3:00	48.4	47.2	51.7	3:00	49.6	49.0	50.6
4:00	47.2	45.3	50.9	4:00	51.0	50.5	51.5
5:00	46.8	44.1	49.0	5:00	50.5	50.0	51.9

Source: Kinard, J., Western Carolina University, as reported in Render, B., and Stair, Jr., R., *Quantitative Analysis for Management,* 6th ed. Upper Saddle River, N.J.: Prentice-Hall, 1997.

11.5 A CONTROL CHART FOR MONITORING THE VARIATION OF A PROCESS: THE *R*-CHART

Recall from Section 11.2 that a process may be out of statistical control because its mean or variance or both are changing over time (see Figure 11.8). The $\bar{x}$-chart of the previous section is used to detect changes in the process mean. The control chart we present in this section—the *R*-chart—is used to detect changes in process variation.

The primary difference between the $\bar{x}$-chart and the *R*-chart is that instead of plotting *sample means* and monitoring their variation, we plot and monitor the variation of *sample ranges*. Changes in the behavior of the sample range signal changes in the variation of the process.

We could also monitor process variation by plotting *sample standard deviations*. That is, we could calculate *s* for each sample (i.e., each subgroup) and plot them

FIGURE 11.24
R-chart

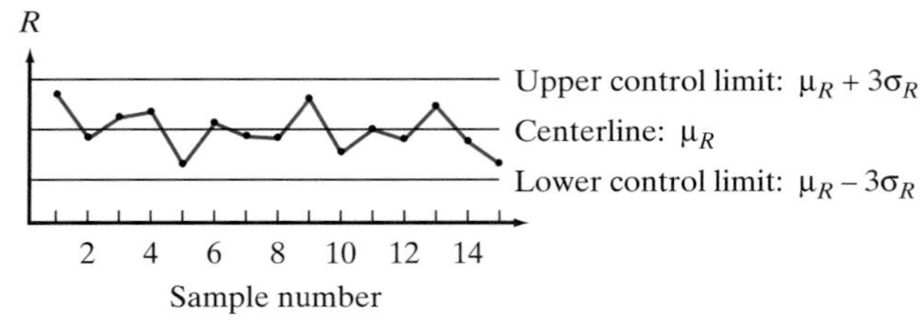

Upper control limit: $\mu_R + 3\sigma_R$
Centerline: μ_R
Lower control limit: $\mu_R - 3\sigma_R$

on a control chart known as an **s-chart**. In this chapter, however, we focus on just the *R*-chart because (1) when using samples of size 9 or less, the *s*-chart and the *R*-chart reflect about the same information, and (2) the *R*-chart is used much more widely by practitioners than is the *s*-chart (primarily because the sample range is easier to calculate and interpret than the sample standard deviation). For more information about *s*-charts, see the references at the end of the book.

The underlying logic and basic form of the *R*-chart are similar to the $\bar{x}$-chart. In monitoring $\bar{x}$, we use the standard deviation of $\bar{x}$ to develop 3-sigma control limits. Now, since we want to be able to determine when *R* takes on unusually large or small values, we use the standard deviation of *R*, or σ_R, to construct 3-sigma control limits. The centerline of the $\bar{x}$-chart represents the process mean μ or, equivalently, the mean of the sampling distribution of $\bar{x}$, $\mu_{\bar{x}}$. Similarly, the centerline of the *R*-chart represents μ_R, the mean of the sampling distribution of *R*. These points are illustrated in the *R*-chart of Figure 11.24.

As with the $\bar{x}$-chart, you should have at least 20 samples of *n* items each ($n \geqslant 2$) to construct an *R*-chart. This will provide sufficient data to obtain reasonably good estimates of μ_R and σ_R. Rational subgrouping is again used for determining sample size and frequency of sampling.

The centerline of the *R*-chart is positioned as follows:

$$Centerline: \bar{R} = \frac{R_1 + R_2 + \cdots + R_k}{k}$$

where *k* is the number of samples of size *n* and R_i is the range of the *i*th sample. $\bar{R}$ is an estimate of μ_R.

In order to construct the control limits, we need an estimator of σ_R. The estimator recommended by Montgomery (1991) and Ryan (1989) is

$$\hat{\sigma}_R = d_3\left(\frac{\bar{R}}{d_2}\right)$$

where d_2 and d_3 are constants whose values depend on the sample size, *n*. Values for d_2 and d_3 for samples of size $n = 2$ to $n = 25$ are given in Table XV of Appendix B.

The control limits are positioned as follows:

$$Upper\ control\ limit: \bar{R} + 3\hat{\sigma}_R = \bar{R} + 3d_3\left(\frac{\bar{R}}{d_2}\right)$$

$$Lower\ control\ limit: \bar{R} - 3\hat{\sigma}_R = \bar{R} + 3d_3\left(\frac{\bar{R}}{d_2}\right)$$

Notice that $\bar{R}$ appears twice in each control limit. Accordingly, we can simplify the calculation of these limits by factoring out $\bar{R}$:

$$UCL: \bar{R}\left(1 + \frac{3d_3}{d_2}\right) = \bar{R}D_4 \qquad LCL: \bar{R}\left(1 - \frac{3d_3}{d_2}\right) = \bar{R}D_3$$

where

$$D_4 = \left(1 + \frac{3d_3}{d_2}\right) \qquad D_3 = \left(1 - \frac{3d_3}{d_2}\right)$$

The values for D_3 and D_4 have been tabulated for samples of size $n = 2$ to $n = 25$ and can be found in Appendix B, Table XV.

For samples of size $n = 2$ through $n = 6$, D_3 is negative, and the lower control limit falls below zero. Since the sample range cannot take on negative values, such a control limit is meaningless. Thus, when $n \leq 6$ the *R*-chart contains only one control limit, the upper control limit.

Although D_3 is actually negative for $n \leq 6$, the values reported in Table XV in Appendix B are all zeros. This has been done to discourage the inappropriate construction of negative lower control limits. If the lower control limit is calculated using $D_3 = 0$, you obtain $D_3\bar{R} = 0$. This should be interpreted as indicating that the *R*-chart has no lower 3-sigma control limit.

Constructing an *R*-Chart: A Summary

1. Using a rational subgrouping strategy, collect at least 20 samples (i.e., subgroups), each of size $n \geq 2$.

2. Calculate the range of each sample.

3. Calculate the mean of the sample ranges, $\bar{R}$:

$$\bar{R} = \frac{R_1 + R_2 + \cdots + R_k}{k}$$

where

  k = The number of samples (i.e., subgroups)
  R_i = The range of the *i*th sample

4. Plot the centerline and control limits:

Centerline: $\bar{R}$

Upper control limit: $\bar{R}D_4$

Lower control limit: $\bar{R}D_3$

where D_3 and D_4 are constants that depend on n. Their values can be found in Appendix B, Table XV. When $n \leq 6$, $D_3 = 0$, indicating that the control chart does not have a lower control limit.

5. Plot the k sample ranges on the control chart in the order that the samples were produced by the process.

We interpret the completed *R*-chart in basically the same way as we did the $\bar{x}$-chart. We look for indications that the process is out of control. Those indications include points that fall outside the control limits as well as any nonrandom patterns of variation that appear between the control limits. To help spot nonrandom behavior, we include the A, B, and C zones (described in the previous section) on the *R*-chart. The next box describes how to construct the zone boundaries for the *R*-chart. It requires only Rules 1 through 4 of Figure 11.21, because Rules 5 and 6 are based on the assumption that the statistic plotted on the control chart follows a normal (or nearly normal) distribution, whereas *R*'s distribution is skewed to the right.*

---

*Some authors (e.g., Kane, 1989) apply all six pattern-analysis rules as long as $n \geq 4$.

Constructing Zone Boundaries for an R-Chart

The simplest method of construction uses the estimator of the standard deviation of R, which is $\hat{\sigma}_R = d_3(\bar{R}/d_2)$:

$$Upper\ A\text{–}B\ boundary{:}\ \bar{R} + 2d_3\left(\frac{\bar{R}}{d_2}\right)$$

$$Lower\ A\text{–}B\ boundary{:}\ \bar{R} - 2d_3\left(\frac{\bar{R}}{d_2}\right)$$

$$Upper\ B\text{–}C\ boundary{:}\ \bar{R} + d_3\left(\frac{\bar{R}}{d_2}\right)$$

$$Lower\ B\text{–}C\ boundary{:}\ \bar{R} - d_3\left(\frac{\bar{R}}{d_2}\right)$$

Note: Whenever $n \leq 6$ the R-chart has no lower 3-sigma control limit. However, the lower A–B, B–C boundaries can still be plotted if they are nonnegative.

Interpreting an R-Chart

1. The **process is out of control** if one or more sample ranges fall beyond the control limits (Rule 1) or if any of the three patterns of variation described by Rules 2, 3, and 4 (Figure 11.21) are observed. Such signals indicate that one or more special causes of variation are influencing the *variation* of the process. These causes should be identified and eliminated to bring the process into control.

2. The **process is treated as being in control** if none of the noted out-of-control signals are observed. Processes that are in control should not be tampered with. However, if the level of variation is unacceptably high, common causes of variation should be identified and eliminated.

As with the $\bar{x}$-chart, the centerline and control limits should be developed using samples that were collected during a period in which the process was in control. Accordingly, when an R-chart is first constructed, the centerline and the control limits are treated as **trial values** (see Section 11.4) and are modified, if necessary, before being extended to the right and used to monitor future process output.

EXAMPLE 11.3 Refer to Example 11.1.

a. Construct an R-chart for the paint-filling process.

b. What does the chart indicate about the stability of the filling process during the time when the data were collected?

c. Is it appropriate to use the control limits constructed in part **a** to monitor future process output?

SOLUTION

a. The first step after collecting the data is to calculate the range of each sample. For the first sample the range is

$$R_1 = 10.0042 - 9.9964 = .0078$$

All 25 sample ranges appear in Table 11.2.

Next, calculate the mean of the ranges:

FIGURE 11.25
R-chart for the
paint-filling process

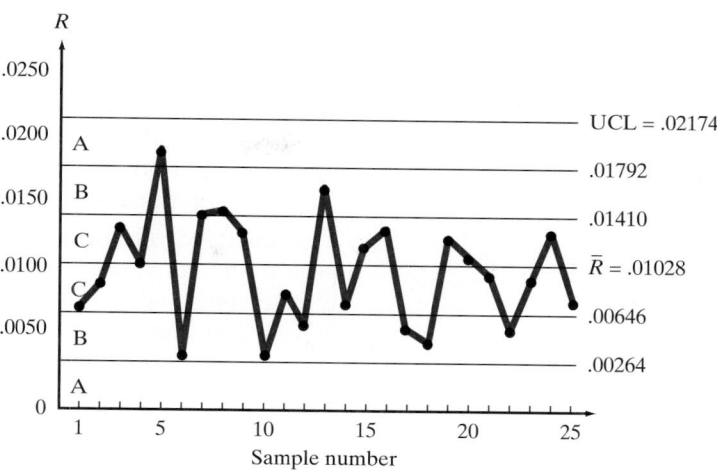

$$\overline{R} = \frac{.0078 + .0092 + \cdots + .0077}{25} + .01028$$

The centerline of the chart is positioned at $\overline{R} = .01028$. To determine the control limits, we need the constants D_3 and D_4, which can be found in Table XV of Appendix B. For $n = 5$, $D_3 = 0$, and $D_4 = 2.115$. Since $D_3 = 0$, the lower 3-sigma control limit is negative and is not included on the chart. The upper control limit is calculated as follows:

$$\text{UCL: } \overline{R}D_4 = (.01028)(2.115) = .0217$$

After positioning the upper control limit on the chart, we plot the 25 sample ranges in the order of sampling and connect the points with straight lines. The resulting trial *R*-chart is shown in Figure 11.25.

b. To facilitate our examination of the *R*-chart, we plot the four zone boundaries. Recall that in general the A–B boundaries are positioned 2 standard deviations from the centerline and the B–C boundaries are 1 standard deviation from the centerline. In the case of the *R*-chart, we use the estimated standard deviation of R, $\hat{\sigma}_R = d_3(\overline{R}/d_2)$, and calculate the boundaries:

$$\textit{Upper A–B boundary: } \overline{R} + 2d_3\left(\frac{\overline{R}}{d_2}\right) = .01792$$

$$\textit{Lower A–B boundary: } \overline{R} - 2d_3\left(\frac{\overline{R}}{d_2}\right) = .00264$$

$$\textit{Upper B–C boundary: } \overline{R} + d_3\left(\frac{\overline{R}}{d_2}\right) = .01410$$

$$\textit{Lower B–C boundary: } \overline{R} - d_3\left(\frac{\overline{R}}{d_2}\right) = .00646$$

where (from Table XV of Appendix B) for $n = 5$, $d_2 = 2.326$ and $d_3 = .864$. Notice in Figure 11.25 that the lower A zone is slightly narrower than the upper A zone. This occurs because the lower 3-sigma control limit (the usual lower boundary of the lower A zone) is negative.

All the plotted *R* values fall below the upper control limit. This is one indication that the process is under control (i.e., is stable). However, we must also look for patterns of points that would be unlikely to occur if the process were in control. To assist us with this process, we use pattern-analysis rules 1–4 (Figure 11.21). None of the rules signal the presence of special causes of variation. Accordingly, we conclude that it is reasonable to treat the process—in particular, the variation of the process—as being under control during the period in question. Apparently, no significant special causes of variation are influencing the variation of the process.

c. Yes. Since the variation of the process appears to be in control during the period when the sample data were collected, the control limits appropriately characterize the variation in R that would be expected when the process is in a state of statistical control. ◣

In practice, the $\bar{x}$-chart and the R-chart are not used in isolation, as our presentation so far might suggest. Rather, they are used together to monitor the mean (i.e., the location) of the process and the variation of the process simultaneously. In fact, many practitioners plot them on the same piece of paper.

One important reason for dealing with them as a unit is that the control limits of the $\bar{x}$-chart are a function of R. That is, the control limits depend on the variation of the process. (Recall that the control limits are $\bar{x} \pm A_2\bar{R}$.) Thus, if the process variation is out of control the control limits of the $\bar{x}$-chart have little meaning. This is because when the process variation is changing (as in the bottom two graphs of Figure 11.8), any single estimate of the variation (such as $\bar{R}$ or s) is not representative of the process. Accordingly, **the appropriate procedure is to first construct and then interpret the R-chart. If it indicates that the process variation is in control, then it makes sense to construct and interpret the $\bar{x}$-chart**.

Figure 11.26 is reprinted from Kaoru Ishikawa's classic text on quality-improvement methods, *Guide to Quality Control* (1986). It illustrates how particular changes in a process over time may be reflected in $\bar{x}$- and R-charts. At the top of the figure, running across the page, is a series of probability distributions A, B,

FIGURE 11.26

Combined $\bar{x}$- and R-chart

Source: Reprinted from *Guide to Quality Control*, by Kaoru Ishikawa, © 1986 by Asian Productivity Organization, with permission of the publisher Asian Productivity Organization. Distributed in North America by Quality Resources, New York, NY.

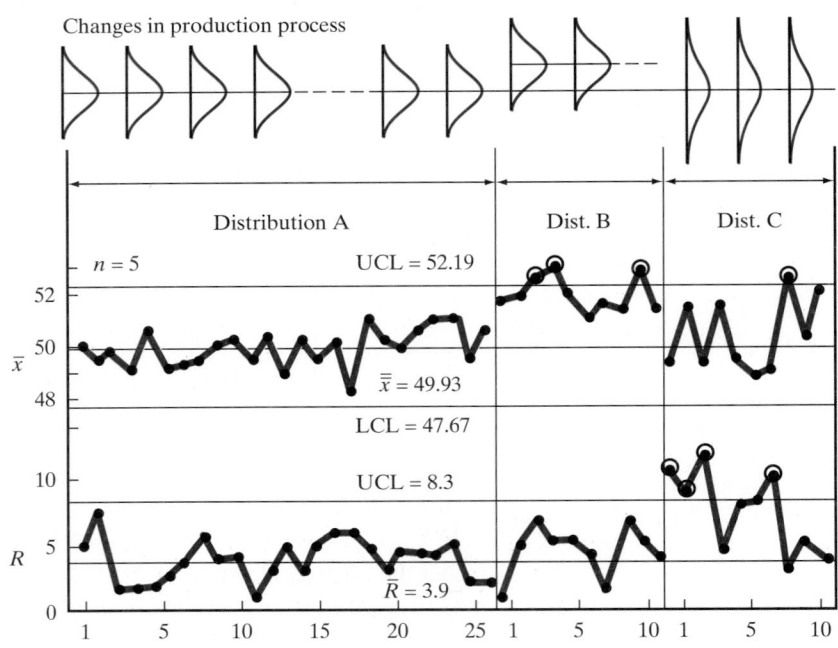

and C that describe the process (i.e., the output variable) at different points in time. In practice, we never have this information. For this example, however, Ishikawa worked with a known process (i.e., with its given probabilistic characterization) to illustrate how sample data from a known process might behave.

The control limits for both charts were constructed from $k = 25$ samples of size $n = 5$. These data were generated by Distribution A. The 25 sample means and ranges were plotted on the $\bar{x}$- and R-charts, respectively. Since the distribution did not change over this period of time, it follows from the definition of statistical control that the process was under control. If you did not know this—as would be the case in practice—what would you conclude from looking at the control charts? (Remember, always interpret the R-chart before the $\bar{x}$-chart.) Both charts indicate that the process is under control. Accordingly, the control limits are made official and can be used to monitor future output, as is done next.

Toward the middle of the figure, the process changes. The mean shifts to a higher level. Now the output variable is described by Distribution B. The process is out of control. Ten new samples of size 5 are sampled from the process. Since the variation of the process has not changed, the R-chart should indicate that the variation remains stable. This is, in fact, the case. All points fall below the upper control limit. As we would hope, it is the $\bar{x}$-chart that reacts to the change in the mean of the process.

Then the process changes again (Distribution C). This time the mean shifts back to its original position, but the variation of the process increases. The process is still out of control but this time for a different reason. Checking the R-chart first, we see that it has reacted as we would hope. It has detected the increase in the variation. Given this R-chart finding, the control limits of the $\bar{x}$-chart become inappropriate (as described before) and we would not use them. Notice, however, how the sample means react to the increased variation in the process. This increased variation in $\bar{x}$ is consistent with what we know about the variance of $\bar{x}$. It is directly proportional to the variance of the process, $\sigma_{\bar{x}}^2 = \sigma^2/n$.

Keep in mind that what Ishikawa did in this example is exactly the opposite of what we do in practice. In practice we use sample data and control charts to make inferences about changes in unknown process distributions. Here, for the purpose of helping you to understand and interpret control charts, known process distributions were changed to see what would happen to the control charts.

EXERCISES   11.17–11.27

Note: Exercises marked with 💾 *contain data for computer analysis on a 3.5" disk (file name in parentheses).*

Learning the Mechanics

11.17 What characteristic of a process is an R-chart designed to monitor?

11.18 In practice, $\bar{x}$- and R-charts are used together to monitor a process. However, the R-chart should be interpreted before the $\bar{x}$-chart. Why?

11.19 Use Table XV in Appendix B to find the values of D_3 and D_4 for each of the following sample sizes.
  a. $n = 4$ **b.** $n = 12$ **c.** $n = 24$

11.20 Construct and interpret an R-chart for the data in Exercise 11.10.

a. Calculate and plot the upper control limit and, if appropriate, the lower control limit.
b. Calculate and plot the A, B, and C zone boundaries on the R-chart.
c. Plot the sample ranges on the R-chart and use pattern-analysis rules 1–4 of Figure 11.21 to determine whether the process is under statistical control.

11.21 Construct and interpret an R-chart for the data in Exercise 11.11.
  a. Calculate and plot the upper control limit and, if appropriate, the lower control limit.
  b. Calculate and plot the A, B, and C zone boundaries on the R-chart.

Sample	Measurements							$\bar{x}$	R
	1	2	3	4	5	6	7		
1	20.1	19.0	20.9	22.2	18.9	18.1	21.3	20.07	4.1
2	19.0	17.9	21.2	20.4	20.0	22.3	21.5	20.33	4.4
3	22.6	21.4	21.4	22.1	19.2	20.6	18.7	20.86	3.9
4	18.1	20.8	17.8	19.6	19.8	21.7	20.0	19.69	3.9
5	22.6	19.1	21.4	21.8	18.4	18.0	19.5	20.11	4.6
6	19.1	19.0	22.3	21.5	17.8	19.2	19.4	19.76	4.5
7	17.1	19.4	18.6	20.9	21.8	21.0	19.8	19.80	4.7
8	20.2	22.4	22.0	19.6	19.6	20.0	18.5	20.33	3.9
9	21.9	24.1	23.1	22.8	25.6	24.2	25.2	23.84	3.7
10	25.1	24.3	26.0	23.1	25.8	27.0	26.5	25.40	3.9
11	25.8	29.2	28.5	29.1	27.8	29.0	28.0	28.20	3.4
12	28.2	27.5	29.3	30.7	27.6	28.0	27.0	28.33	3.7
13	28.2	28.6	28.1	26.0	30.0	28.5	28.3	28.24	4.0
14	22.1	21.4	23.3	20.5	19.8	20.5	19.0	20.94	4.3
15	18.5	19.2	18.0	20.1	22.0	20.2	19.5	19.64	4.0
16	21.4	20.3	22.0	19.2	18.0	17.9	19.5	19.76	4.1
17	18.4	16.5	18.1	19.2	17.5	20.9	19.6	18.60	4.4
18	20.1	19.8	22.3	22.5	21.8	22.7	23.0	21.74	3.2
19	20.0	17.5	21.0	18.2	19.5	17.2	18.1	18.79	3.8
20	22.3	18.2	21.5	19.0	19.4	20.5	20.0	20.13	4.1

c. Plot the sample ranges on the R-chart and determine whether the process is in control.

11.22 **(X11.022)** Construct and interpret an R-chart and an $\bar{x}$-chart from the sample data shown above. Remember to interpret the R-chart *before* the $\bar{x}$-chart.

Applying the Concepts

11.23 Refer to Exercise 11.12, where the desired circuit path widths were .5 to .85 micron. The manufacturer sampled four CPU chips six times a day (every 90 minutes from 8:00 A.M. until 4:30 P.M.) for five consecutive days. The path widths were

measured and used to construct the MINITAB R-chart shown.

a. Calculate the chart's upper and lower control limits.

b. What does the R-chart suggest about the presence of special causes of variation during the time when the data were collected?

c. Should the control limit(s) be used to monitor future process output? Explain.

d. How many different R values are plotted on the control chart? Notice how most of the R values fall along three horizontal lines. What could cause such a pattern?

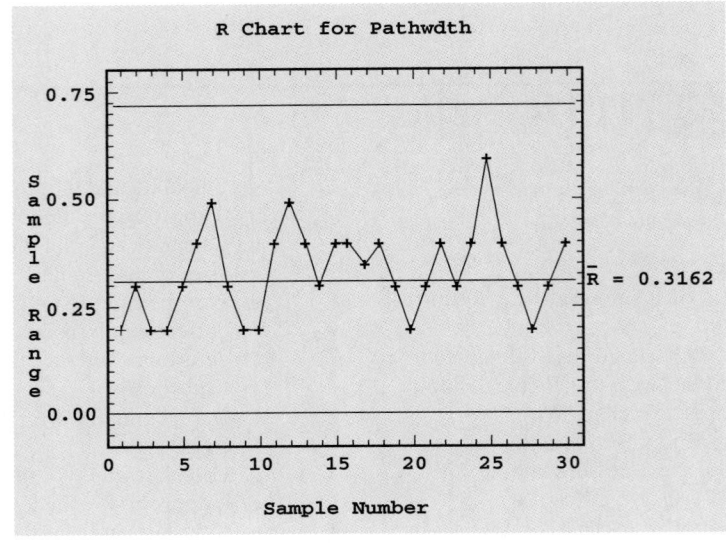

R Chart for Pathwdth

$\bar{R}$ = 0.3162

11.24 **(X11.024)** A soft-drink bottling company is interested in monitoring the amount of cola injected into 16-ounce bottles by a particular filling head. The process is entirely automated and operates 24 hours a day. At 6 A.M. and 6 P.M. each day, a new dispenser of carbon dioxide capable of producing 20,000 gallons of cola is hooked up to the filling machine. In order to monitor the process using control charts, the company decided to sample five consecutive bottles of cola each hour beginning at 6:15 A.M. (i.e., 6:15 A.M., 7:15 A.M., 8:15 A.M., etc.). The data for the first day are given at right, followed by an SPSS descriptive statistics printout.

a. Will the rational subgrouping strategy that was used enable the company to detect variation in fill caused by differences in the carbon dioxide dispensers? Explain.
b. Construct an *R*-chart from the data.
c. What does the *R*-chart indicate about the stability of the filling process during the time when the data were collected? Justify your answer.
d. Should the control limit(s) be used to monitor future process output? Explain.
e. Given your answer to part c, should an $\bar{x}$-chart be constructed from the given data? Explain.

Sample	Measurements				
1	16.01	16.03	15.98	16.00	16.01
2	16.03	16.02	15.97	15.99	15.99
3	15.98	16.00	16.03	16.04	15.99
4	16.00	16.03	16.02	15.98	15.98
5	15.97	15.99	16.03	16.01	16.04
6	16.01	16.03	16.04	15.97	15.99
7	16.04	16.05	15.97	15.96	16.00
8	16.02	16.05	16.03	15.97	15.98
9	15.97	15.99	16.02	16.03	15.95
10	16.00	16.01	15.95	16.04	16.06
11	15.95	16.04	16.07	15.93	16.03
12	15.98	16.07	15.94	16.08	16.02
13	15.96	16.00	16.01	16.00	15.98
14	15.98	16.01	16.02	15.99	15.99
15	15.99	16.03	16.00	15.98	16.01
16	16.02	16.02	16.01	15.97	16.00
17	16.01	16.05	15.99	15.99	16.03
18	15.98	16.03	16.04	15.98	16.01
19	15.97	15.96	15.99	15.99	16.01
20	16.03	16.01	16.04	15.96	15.99
21	15.99	16.03	15.97	16.05	16.03
22	15.98	15.95	16.07	16.01	16.04
23	15.99	16.06	15.95	16.03	16.07
24	16.00	16.01	16.08	15.94	15.93

SAMPLE	Variable	Mean	Range	Minimum	Maximum	N
1.00	COLA	16.006	.05	15.98	16.03	5
2.00	COLA	16.000	.06	15.97	16.03	5
3.00	COLA	16.008	.06	15.98	16.04	5
4.00	COLA	16.002	.05	15.98	16.03	5
5.00	COLA	16.008	.07	15.97	16.04	5
6.00	COLA	16.008	.07	15.97	16.04	5
7.00	COLA	16.004	.09	15.96	16.05	5
8.00	COLA	16.010	.08	15.97	16.05	5
9.00	COLA	15.992	.08	15.95	16.03	5
10.00	COLA	16.012	.11	15.95	16.06	5
11.00	COLA	16.004	.14	15.93	16.07	5
12.00	COLA	16.018	.14	15.94	16.08	5
13.00	COLA	15.990	.05	15.96	16.01	5
14.00	COLA	15.998	.04	15.98	16.02	5
15.00	COLA	16.002	.05	15.98	16.03	5
16.00	COLA	16.004	.05	15.97	16.02	5
17.00	COLA	16.014	.06	15.99	16.05	5
18.00	COLA	16.008	.06	15.98	16.04	5
19.00	COLA	15.984	.05	15.96	16.01	5
20.00	COLA	16.006	.08	15.96	16.04	5
21.00	COLA	16.014	.08	15.97	16.05	5
22.00	COLA	16.010	.12	15.95	16.07	5
23.00	COLA	16.020	.12	15.95	16.07	5
24.00	COLA	15.992	.15	15.93	16.08	5

11.25 Refer to Exercise 11.15, in which the Bayfield Mud Company was concerned with discovering why their filling operation was producing underfilled bags of mud.
   a. Construct an R-chart for the filling process.
   b. According to the R-chart, is the process under statistical control? Explain.
   c. Does the R-chart provide any evidence concerning the cause of Bayfield's underfilling problem? Explain.

11.26 Refer to Exercise 11.16, in which an overnight film processing laboratory was concerned about processing delays.
   a. Construct an R-chart for the time required to complete the evaluation of negatives.
   b. Which parameter of the evaluation process does your R-chart provide information about?
   c. What does the R-chart suggest about the presence of special causes of variation during the time when the data were collected?

11.27 **(X11.027)** American companies have been reaping the benefits of Japanese "Just-in-Time" (JIT) production methods for more than a decade. Major benefits include shorter lead times, lower defect rates, less raw material inventory, less work-in-process inventory, less finished-goods inventory, and a more flexible workforce. One problem that production managers often face in scheduling the operations of a JIT assembly process is ensuring consistent cycle times for the subassemblies. *Cycle time* is the time it takes for a workstation to complete its set of tasks. The greater the difference in cycle times, the greater the idle time at the faster workstations. This is both inefficient and can be the cause of serious morale problems at the slower workstations (Melnyk and Denzler, *Operations Management: A Value-Driven Approach*, 1996). To evaluate the cycle time of a particular workstation in a bicycle assembly process, an operations manager measured the first five cycle times of the morning shift for five consecutive days. These measurements are given in the table.

Date	Cycle Time (in minutes)
11/12/96	45
	51
	47
	49
	53
11/13/96	44
	48
	57
	54
	43
11/14/96	54
	47
	51
	50
	46
11/15/96	50
	48
	55
	59
	42
11/16/96	46
	49
	43
	52
	58

   a. Construct an R-chart and an $\bar{x}$-chart for this workstation.
   b. Which chart should be evaluated first? Why?
   c. What do the $\bar{x}$- and R-charts suggest about the stability of the process? Explain.
   d. The bicycle company operates with two work shifts five days a week and is closed on the weekends. Will the rational subgrouping strategy that was used enable the operations manager to detect variation in cycle times due to differences in work shifts? Explain.

11.6 A CONTROL CHART FOR MONITORING THE PROPORTION OF DEFECTIVES GENERATED BY A PROCESS: THE p-CHART

Among the dozens of different control charts that have been proposed by researchers and practitioners, the $\bar{x}$- and R-charts are by far the most popular for use in monitoring **quantitative** output variables such as time, length, and weight. Among the charts developed for use with **qualitative** output variables, the chart we introduce in this section is the most popular. Called the **p-chart**, it is used when the output variable is categorical (i.e., measured on a nominal scale). With the p-chart, the proportion, *p*, of units produced by the process that belong to a particular category (e.g., defective or nondefective; successful or unsuccessful; early, on-time, or late) can be monitored.

The p-chart is typically used to monitor the proportion of defective units produced by a process (i.e., the proportion of units that do not conform to specification). This proportion is used to characterize a process in the same sense that the mean and variance are used to characterize a process when the output variable is quantitative. Examples of process proportions that are monitored in industry include the proportion of billing errors made by credit card companies; the proportion of nonfunctional semiconductor chips produced; and the proportion of checks that a bank's magnetic ink character-recognition system is unable to read.

As is the case for the mean and variance, the process proportion can change over time. For example, it can drift upward or downward or jump to a new level. In such cases, the process is out of control. **As long as the process proportion remains constant, the process is in a state of statistical control**.

As with the other control charts presented in this chapter, the p-chart has a centerline and control limits that are determined from sample data. After k samples of size n are drawn from the process, each unit is classified (e.g., defective or nondefective), the proportion of defective units in each sample—$\hat{p}$— is calculated, the centerline and control limits are determined using this information, and the sample proportions are plotted on the p-chart. It is the variation in the $\hat{p}$'s over time that we monitor and interpret. Changes in the behavior of the $\hat{p}$'s signal changes in the process proportion, p.

The p-chart is based on the assumption that the number of defectives observed in each sample can be modeled as a binomial random variable (see Chapter 4). What we have called the process proportion is really the binomial probability, p. When the process is in a state of statistical control, p remains constant over time. Variation in $\hat{p}$—as displayed on a p-chart—is used to judge whether p is stable.

To determine the centerline and control limits for the p-chart we need to know $\hat{p}$'s sampling distribution. We described the sampling distribution of $\hat{p}$ in Section 5.3. Recall that

$$\hat{p} = \frac{\text{Number of defective items in the sample}}{\text{Number of items in the sample}} = \frac{x}{n}$$

$$\mu_{\hat{p}} = p$$

$$\sigma_{\hat{p}} = \sqrt{\frac{p(1-p)}{n}}$$

and that for large samples $\hat{p}$ is approximately normally distributed. Thus, if p were known, the centerline would be p and the 3-sigma control limits would be $s \pm 3\sqrt{p(1-p)/n}$. However, since p is unknown, it must be estimated from the sample data. The appropriate estimator is $\bar{p}$, the overall proportion of defective units in the nk units sampled:

$$\bar{p} = \frac{\text{Total number of defective units in all } k \text{ samples}}{\text{Total number of units sampled}}$$

To calculate the control limits of the p-chart, substitute $\bar{p}$ for p in the preceding expression for the control limits, as illustrated in Figure 11.27.

In constructing a p-chart it is advisable to use a much larger sample size than is typically used for $\bar{x}$- and R-charts. Most processes that are monitored in industry

FIGURE 11.27
p-chart

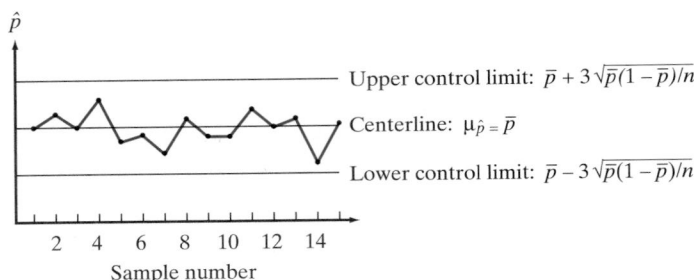

have relatively small process proportions, often less than .05 (i.e., less than 5% of output is nonconforming). In those cases, if a small sample size is used, say $n = 5$, samples drawn from the process would likely not contain any nonconforming output. As a result, most, if not all, $\hat{p}$'s would equal zero.

We present a rule of thumb that can be used to determine a sample size large enough to avoid this problem. This rule will also help protect against ending up with a negative lower control limit, a situation that frequently occurs when both *p* and *n* are small. See Montgomery (1991) or Duncan (1986) for further details.

Sample-Size Determination

Choose *n* such that $n > \dfrac{9(1 - p_0)}{p_0}$

where

n = Sample size

p_0 = An estimate (perhaps judgmental) of the process proportion *p*

For example, if *p* is thought to be about .05, the rule indicates that samples of at least size 171 should be used in constructing the *p*-chart:

$$n > \frac{9(1 - .05)}{.05} = 171$$

In the next three boxes we summarize how to construct a *p*-chart and its zone boundaries and how to interpret a *p*-chart.

Constructing a *p*-Chart: A Summary

1. Using a rational subgrouping strategy, collect at least 20 samples, each of size

$$n > \frac{9(1 - p_0)}{p_0}$$

where p_0 is an estimate of *p*, the proportion defective (i.e., nonconforming) produced by the process. p_0 can be determined from sample data (i.e., $\hat{p}$) or may be based on expert opinion.

2. For each sample, calculate $\hat{p}$, the proportion of defective units in the sample:

$$\hat{p} = \frac{\text{Number of defective items in the sample}}{\text{Number of items in the sample}}$$

3. Plot the centerline and control limits:

$$\text{Centerline: } \bar{p} = \frac{\text{Total number of defective units in all } k \text{ samples}}{\text{Total number of units in all } k \text{ samples}}$$

$$\text{Upper control limit: } \bar{p} + 3\sqrt{\frac{\bar{p}(1-\bar{p})}{n}}$$

$$\text{Lower control limit: } \bar{p} - 3\sqrt{\frac{\bar{p}(1-\bar{p})}{n}}$$

where k is the number of samples of size n and $\bar{p}$ is the overall proportion of defective units in the nk units sampled. $\bar{p}$ is an estimate of the unknown process proportion p.

4. Plot the k sample proportions on the control chart in the order that the samples were produced by the process.

Constructing Zone Boundaries for a p-Chart

$$\text{Upper A–B boundary: } \bar{p} + 2\sqrt{\frac{\bar{p}(1-\bar{p})}{n}}$$

$$\text{Lower A–B boundary: } \bar{p} - 2\sqrt{\frac{\bar{p}(1-\bar{p})}{n}}$$

$$\text{Upper B–C boundary: } \bar{p} + \sqrt{\frac{\bar{p}(1-\bar{p})}{n}}$$

$$\text{Lower B–C boundary: } \bar{p} - \sqrt{\frac{\bar{p}(1-\bar{p})}{n}}$$

Note: When the lower control limit is negative, it should not be plotted on the control chart. However, the lower zone boundaries can still be plotted if they are nonnegative.

Interpreting a p-Chart

1. The **process is out of control** if one or more sample proportions fall beyond the control limits (Rule 1) or if any of the three patterns of variation described by Rules 2, 3, and 4 (Figure 11.21) are observed. Such signals indicate that one or more special causes of variation are influencing the process proportion, p. These causes should be identified and eliminated in order to bring the process into control.

2. The **process is treated as being in control** if none of the above noted out-of-control signals are observed. Processes that are in control should not be tampered with. However, if the level of variation is unacceptably high, common causes of variation should be identified and eliminated.

As with the $\bar{x}$- and R-charts, the centerline and control limits should be developed using samples that were collected during a period in which the process was in control. Accordingly, when a p-chart is first constructed, the centerline and the control limits should be treated as *trial values* (see Section 11.4) and, if necessary, modified before being extended to the right on the control chart and used to monitor future process output.

EXAMPLE 11.4 A manufacturer of auto parts is interested in implementing statistical process control in several areas within its warehouse operation. The manufacturer wants to begin with the order assembly process. Too frequently orders received by customers contain the wrong items or too few items.

For each order received, parts are picked from storage bins in the warehouse, labeled, and placed on a conveyor belt system. Since the bins are spread over a three-acre area, items that are part of the same order may be placed on different spurs of the conveyor belt system. Near the end of the belt system all spurs converge and a worker sorts the items according to the order they belong to. That information is contained on the labels that were placed on the items by the pickers.

The workers have identified three errors that cause shipments to be improperly assembled: (1) pickers pick from the wrong bin, (2) pickers mislabel items, and (3) the sorter makes an error.

The firm's quality manager has implemented a sampling program in which 90 assembled orders are sampled each day and checked for accuracy. An assembled order is considered nonconforming (defective) if it differs in any way from the order placed by the customer. To date, 25 samples have been evaluated. The resulting data are shown in Table 11.4.

a. Construct a p-chart for the order assembly operation.

b. What does the chart indicate about the stability of the process?

c. Is it appropriate to use the control limits and centerline constructed in part **a** to monitor future process output?

TABLE 11.4 Twenty-Five Samples of Size 90 from the Warehouse Order Assembly Process

Sample	Size	Defective Orders	Sample Proportion
1	90	12	.13333
2	90	6	.06666
3	90	11	.12222
4	90	8	.08888
5	90	13	.14444
6	90	14	.15555
7	90	12	.13333
8	90	6	.06666
9	90	10	.11111
10	90	13	.14444
11	90	12	.13333
12	90	24	.26666
13	90	23	.25555
14	90	22	.24444
15	90	8	.08888
16	90	3	.03333
17	90	11	.12222
18	90	14	.15555
19	90	5	.05555
20	90	12	.13333
21	90	18	.20000
22	90	12	.13333
23	90	13	.14444
24	90	4	.04444
25	90	6	.06666
Totals	2,250	292	

SOLUTION

a. The first step in constructing the p-chart after collecting the sample data is to calculate the sample proportion for each sample. For the first sample,

$$\hat{p} = \frac{\text{Number of defective items in the sample}}{\text{Number of items in the sample}} = \frac{12}{90} = .13333$$

All the sample proportions are displayed in Table 11.4. Next, calculate the proportion of defective items in the total number of items sampled:

$$\bar{p} = \frac{\text{Total number of defective items}}{\text{Total number of items sampled}} = \frac{292}{2250} = .12978$$

The centerline is positioned at $\bar{p}$, and $\bar{p}$ is used to calculate the control limits:

$$\bar{p} \pm 3\sqrt{\frac{\bar{p}(1 - \bar{p})}{n}} = .12978 \pm 3\sqrt{\frac{.12978(1 - .12978)}{90}}$$

$$= .12978 \pm .10627$$

$$\text{UCL: .23605}$$

$$\text{LCL: .02351}$$

After plotting the centerline and the control limits, plot the 25 sample proportions in the order of sampling and connect the points with straight lines. The completed control chart is shown in Figure 11.28.

b. To assist our examination of the control chart, we add the 1- and 2-standard-deviation zone boundaries. The boundaries are located by substituting $\bar{p} = .12978$ into the following formulas:

$$\textit{Upper A–B boundary: } \bar{p} + 2\sqrt{\frac{\bar{p}(1 - \bar{p})}{n}} = .20063$$

$$\textit{Upper B–C boundary: } \bar{p} + \sqrt{\frac{\bar{p}(1 - \bar{p})}{n}} = .16521$$

$$\textit{Lower A–B boundary: } \bar{p} - 2\sqrt{\frac{\bar{p}(1 - \bar{p})}{n}} = .05893$$

$$\textit{Lower B–C boundary: } \bar{p} - \sqrt{\frac{\bar{p}(1 - \bar{p})}{n}} = .09435$$

FIGURE 11.28
p-chart for order assembly process

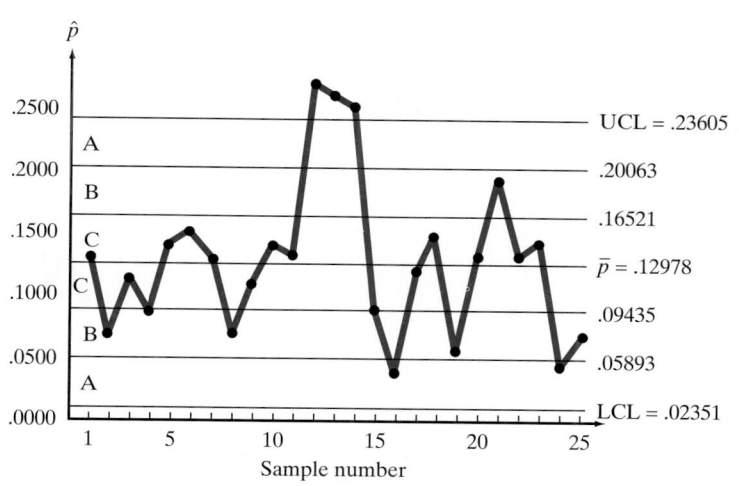

Because three of the sample proportions fall above the upper control limit (Rule 1), there is strong evidence that the process is out of control. None of the nonrandom patterns of Rules 2, 3, and 4 (Figure 11.21) are evident. The process proportion appears to have increased dramatically somewhere around sample 12.

c. Because the process was apparently out of control during the period in which sample data were collected to build the control chart, it is not appropriate to continue using the chart. The control limits and centerline are not representative of the process when it is in control. The chart must be revised before it is used to monitor future output.

In this case, the three out-of-control points were investigated and it was discovered that they occurred on days when a temporary sorter was working in place of the regular sorter. Actions were taken to ensure that in the future better-trained temporary sorters would be available.

Since the special cause of the observed variation was identified and eliminated, all sample data from the three days the temporary sorter was working were dropped from the data set and the centerline and control limits were recalculated:

$$Centerline: \bar{p} = \frac{223}{1980} = .11263$$

$$Control\ limits: \bar{p} \pm 3\sqrt{\frac{\bar{p}(1-\bar{p})}{n}} = .11263 \pm 3\sqrt{\frac{.11263(.88737)}{90}}$$

$$= .11263 \pm .09997$$

$$UCL: .21259 \qquad LCL: .01266$$

The revised zones are calculated by substituting $\bar{p} = .11263$ in the following formulas:

$$Upper\ A\text{--}B\ boundary: \bar{p} + 2\sqrt{\frac{\bar{p}(1-\bar{p})}{n}} = .17927$$

$$Upper\ B\text{--}C\ boundary: \bar{p} + \sqrt{\frac{\bar{p}(1-\bar{p})}{n}} = .14595$$

FIGURE 11.29
Revised p-chart for order assembly process

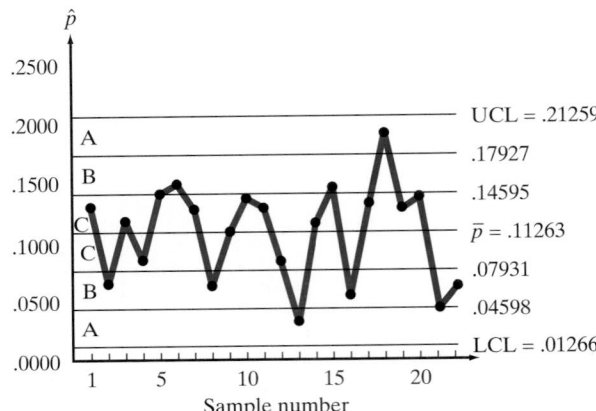

$$\text{Lower A–B boundary: } \bar{p} - 2\sqrt{\frac{\bar{p}(1-\bar{p})}{n}} = .04598$$

$$\text{Lower B–C boundary: } \bar{p} - \sqrt{\frac{\bar{p}(1-\bar{p})}{n}} = .07931$$

The revised control chart appears in Figure 11.29. Notice that now all sample proportions fall within the control limits. These limits can now be treated as official, extended to the right on the chart, and used to monitor future orders.

EXERCISES   11.28–11.36

Note: Exercises marked with 💾 contain data for computer analysis on a 3.5" disk (file name in parentheses).

Learning the Mechanics

11.28   What characteristic of a process is a *p*-chart designed to monitor?

11.29   The proportion of defective items generated by a manufacturing process is believed to be 8%. In constructing a *p*-chart for the process, determine how large the sample size should be to avoid ending up with a negative lower control limit.

11.30   💾 **(X11.030)** To construct a *p*-chart for a manufacturing process, 25 samples of size 200 were drawn from the process. The number of defectives in each sample is listed here.

Sample	Sample Size	Defectives
1	200	16
2	200	14
3	200	9
4	200	11
5	200	15
6	200	8
7	200	12
8	200	16
9	200	17
10	200	13
11	200	15
12	200	10
13	200	9
14	200	12
15	200	14
16	200	11
17	200	8
18	200	7
19	200	12
20	200	15
21	200	9
22	200	16
23	200	13
24	200	11
25	200	10

a. Calculate the proportion defective in each sample.

b. Calculate and plot $\bar{p}$ and the upper and lower control limits for the *p*-chart.

c. Calculate and plot the A, B, and C zone boundaries on the *p*-chart.

d. Plot the sample proportions on the *p*-chart and connect them with straight lines.

e. Use the pattern-analysis rules 1–4 for detecting the presence of special causes of variation (Figure 11.21) to determine whether the process is out of control.

11.31   💾 **(X11.031)** To construct a *p*-chart, 20 samples of size 150 were drawn from a process. The proportion of defective items found in each of the samples is listed in the accompanying table.

Sample	Proportion Defective	Sample	Proportion Defective
1	.03	11	.07
2	.05	12	.04
3	.10	13	.06
4	.02	14	.05
5	.08	15	.07
6	.09	16	.06
7	.08	17	.07
8	.05	18	.02
9	.07	19	.05
10	.06	20	.03

a. Calculate and plot the centerline and the upper and lower control limits for the *p*-chart.

b. Calculate and plot the A, B, and C zone boundaries on the *p*-chart.

c. Plot the sample proportions on the *p*-chart.

d. Is the process under control? Explain.

e. Should the control limits and centerline of part **a** be used to monitor future process output? Explain.

11.32   In each of the following cases, use the sample size formula to determine a sample size large enough to avoid constructing a *p*-chart with a negative lower control limit.

a. $p_0 = .01$ **b.** $p_0 = .05$ **c.** $p_0 = .10$ **d.** $p_0 = .20$

Applying the Concepts

11.33 A manufacturer produces disks for personal computers. From past experience the production manager believes that 1% of the disks are defective. The company collected a sample of the first 1,000 disks manufactured after 4:00 P.M. every other day for a month. The disks were analyzed for defects, then these data and MINITAB were used to construct the *p*-chart shown below.

a. From a statistical perspective, is a sample size of 1,000 adequate for constructing the *p*-chart? Explain.

b. Calculate the chart's upper and lower control limits.

c. What does the *p*-chart suggest about the presence of special causes during the time when the data were collected?

d. Critique the rational subgrouping strategy used by the disk manufacturer.

11.34 **(X11.034)** Goodstone Tire & Rubber Company is interested in monitoring the proportion of defective tires generated by the production process at its Akron, Ohio, production plant. The company's chief engineer believes that the proportion is about 7%. Because the tires are destroyed during the testing process, the company would like to keep the number of tires tested to a minimum. However, the engineer would also like to use a *p*-chart with a positive lower control limit. A positive lower control limit makes it possible to determine when the process has generated an unusually small proportion of defectives. Such an occurrence is good news and would signal the engineer to look for causes of the superior perfor-

mance. That information can be used to improve the production process. Using the sample size formula, the chief engineer recommended that the company randomly sample and test 120 tires from each day's production. To date, 20 samples have been taken. The data are presented here.

Sample	Sample Size	Defectives
1	120	11
2	120	5
3	120	4
4	120	8
5	120	10
6	120	13
7	120	9
8	120	8
9	120	10
10	120	11
11	120	10
12	120	12
13	120	8
14	120	6
15	120	10
16	120	5
17	120	10
18	120	10
19	120	3
20	120	8

a. Use the sample size formula to show how the chief engineer arrived at the recommended sample size of 120.

b. Construct a *p*-chart for the tire production process.

c. What does the chart indicate about the stability of the process? Explain.

d. Is it appropriate to use the control limits to monitor future process output? Explain.

e. Is the *p*-chart you constructed in part **b** capable of signaling hour-to-hour changes in *p*? Explain.

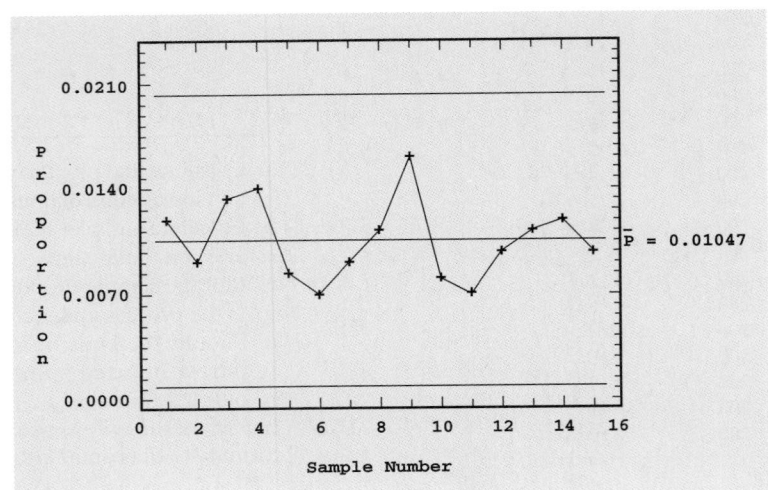

11.35 **(X11.035)** Accurate typesetting is crucial to the production of high-quality newspapers. The editor of the Morristown *Daily Tribune*, a weekly publication with circulation of 27,000, has instituted a process for monitoring the performance of typesetters. Each week 100 paragraphs of the paper are randomly sampled and read for accuracy. The number of paragraphs with errors is recorded for each of the last 30 weeks in the table.

Week	Paragraph with Errors	Week	Paragraph with Errors
1	2	16	2
2	4	17	3
3	10	18	7
4	4	19	3
5	1	20	2
6	1	21	3
7	13	22	7
8	9	23	4
9	11	24	3
10	0	25	2
11	3	26	2
12	4	27	0
13	2	28	1
14	2	29	3
15	8	30	4

Primary Source: Jerry Kinard, Western Carolina University.

Secondary Source: Render, B., and Stair, Jr., R. *Quantitative Analysis for Management,* 6th ed. Upper Saddle River, N.J.: Prentice-Hall, 1997.

a. Construct a *p*-chart for the process.
b. Is the process under statistical control? Explain.
c. Should the control limits of part **a** be used to monitor future process output? Explain.
d. Suggest two methods that could be used to facilitate the diagnosis of causes of process variation.

11.36 **(X11.036)** A Japanese floppy disk manufacturer has a daily production rate of about 20,000 high density 3.5-inch diskettes. Quality is monitored by randomly sampling 200 finished disks every other hour from the production process and testing them for defects. If one or more defects are discovered, the disk is considered defective and is destroyed. The production process operates 20 hours per day, seven days a week. The table reports data for the last three days of production.

Day	Hour	Number of Defectives	Day	Hour	Number of Defectives
1	1	13		6	3
	2	5		7	1
	3	2		8	2
	4	3		9	3
	5	2		10	1
	6	3	3	1	9
	7	1		2	5
	8	2		3	2
	9	1		4	1
	10	1		5	3
2	1	11		6	2
	2	6		7	4
	3	2		8	2
	4	3		9	1
	5	1		10	1

a. Construct a *p*-chart for the diskette production process.
b. What does it indicate about the stability of the process? Explain.
c. What advice can you give the manufacturer to assist them in their search for the special cause(s) of variation that is plaguing the process?

QUICK REVIEW

Key Terms

A zone   623
B zone   623
centerline   606
common causes of variation   612
control chart   606
control limits   615
C zone   623
in control   611
individuals chart   618
lower control limit   615
oscillating sequence   607

out of control   611
output distribution   607
p-chart   644
pattern-analysis rules   624
process   602
process variation   607
quality   601
R-chart   635
rational subgroups   622
run chart   606
s-chart   636

special (assignable) causes of
   variation   613
specification limits   618
statistical process control   612
system   603
time series plot   606
total quality management   600
trial values   626
upper control limit   615
x-chart   618
$\bar{x}$-chart   618

Key Formulas

Control Chart	Centerline	Control Limits (Lower, Upper)	A–B Boundary (Lower, Upper)	B–C Boundary (Lower, Upper)
$\bar{x}$-chart	$\bar{\bar{x}} = \dfrac{\sum\limits_{i=1}^{k} \bar{x}_i}{k}$	$\bar{\bar{x}} \pm A_2\bar{R}$	$\bar{\bar{x}} \pm \dfrac{2}{3}(A_2\bar{R})$ or $\bar{\bar{x}} \pm 2\dfrac{(\bar{R}/d_2)}{\sqrt{n}}$	$\bar{\bar{x}} \pm \dfrac{1}{3}(A_2\bar{R})$ or $\bar{\bar{x}} \pm \dfrac{(\bar{R}/d_2)}{\sqrt{n}}$
R-chart	$\bar{R} = \dfrac{\sum\limits_{i=1}^{k} R_i}{k}$	$(\bar{R}D_3, \bar{R}D_4)$	$\bar{R} \pm 2d_3\left(\dfrac{\bar{R}}{d_2}\right)$	$\bar{R} \pm d_3\left(\dfrac{\bar{R}}{d_2}\right)$
p-chart	$\bar{p} = \dfrac{\text{Total number defectives}}{\text{Total number units sampled}}$	$\bar{p} \pm 3\sqrt{\dfrac{\bar{p}(1-\bar{p})}{n}}$	$\bar{p} \pm 2\sqrt{\dfrac{\bar{p}(1-\bar{p})}{n}}$	$\bar{p} \pm \sqrt{\dfrac{\bar{p}(1-\bar{p})}{n}}$

$n > \dfrac{9(1-p_0)}{p_0}$ where p_0 estimates the true proportion defective   Sample size for p-chart   646

LANGUAGE LAB

Symbol	Pronunciation	Description
LCL	L-C-L	Lower control limit
UCL	U-C-L	Upper control limit
$\bar{\bar{x}}$	x-bar-bar	Average of the sample means
$\bar{R}$	R-bar	Average of the sample ranges
A_2	A-two	Constant obtained from Table XV, Appendix B
D_3	D-three	Constant obtained from Table XV, Appendix B
D_4	D-four	Constant obtained from Table XV, Appendix B
d_2	d-two	Constant obtained from Table XV, Appendix B
d_3	d-three	Constant obtained from Table XV, Appendix B
$\hat{p}$	p-hat	Estimated number of defectives in sample
$\bar{p}$	p-bar	Overall proportion of defective units in all nk samples
p_0	p-naught	Estimated overall proportion of defectives for entire process
SPC	S-P-C	Statistical process control

SUPPLEMENTARY EXERCISES 11.37–11.55

Note: Exercises marked with 💾 *contain data for computer analysis on a 3.5" disk (file name in parentheses).*

Learning the Mechanics

11.37 Define *quality* and list its important dimensions.

11.38 What is a system? Give an example of a system with which you are familiar, and describe its inputs, outputs, and transformation process.

11.39 What is a process? Give an example of an organizational process and a personal process.

11.40 Select a personal process that you would like to better understand or to improve and construct a flowchart for it.

11.41 Describe the six major sources of process variation.

11.42 Suppose all the output of a process over the last year were measured and found to be within the specification limits required by customers of the process. Should you worry about whether the process is in statistical control? Explain.

11.43 Compare and contrast special and common causes of variation.

11.44 Explain the role of the control limits of a control chart.

11.45 Explain the difference between control limits and specification limits.

11.46 A process is under control and follows a normal distribution with mean 100 and standard deviation 10. In constructing a standard $\bar{x}$-chart for this process, the control limits are set 3 standard deviations from the mean—i.e., $100 \pm 3(10/\sqrt{n})$. The probability of observing an $\bar{x}$ outside the control limits is .00135 + .00135 = .0027. Suppose it is desired to construct a control chart that signals the presence of a potential special cause of variation for less extreme values of $\bar{x}$. How many standard deviations from the mean should the control limits be set such that the probability of the chart falsely indicating the presence of a special cause of variation is .10 rather than .0027?

Applying the Concepts

11.47 **(X11.047)** Consider the following time series data.

Order of Production	Weight (grams)	Order of Production	Weight (grams)
1	6.0	9	6.5
2	5.0	10	9.0
3	7.0	11	3.0
4	5.5	12	11.0
5	7.0	13	3.0
6	6.0	14	12.0
7	8.0	15	2.0
8	5.0		

a. Construct a time series plot. Be sure to connect the points and add a centerline.
b. Which type of variation pattern in Figure 11.6 best describes the pattern revealed by your plot?

11.48 **(X11.048)** The accompanying length measurements were made on 20 consecutively produced pencils.

Order of Production	Length (inches)	Order of Production	Length (inches)
1	7.47	11	7.57
2	7.48	12	7.56
3	7.51	13	7.55
4	7.49	14	7.58
5	7.50	15	7.56
6	7.51	16	7.59
7	7.48	17	7.57
8	7.49	18	7.55
9	7.48	19	7.56
10	7.50	20	7.58

a. Construct a time series plot. Be sure to connect the plotted points and add a centerline.
b. Which type of variation pattern in Figure 11.6 best describes the pattern shown in your plot?

11.49 Use the appropriate pattern-analysis rules to determine whether the process being monitored by the control chart shown below is under the influence of special causes of variation.

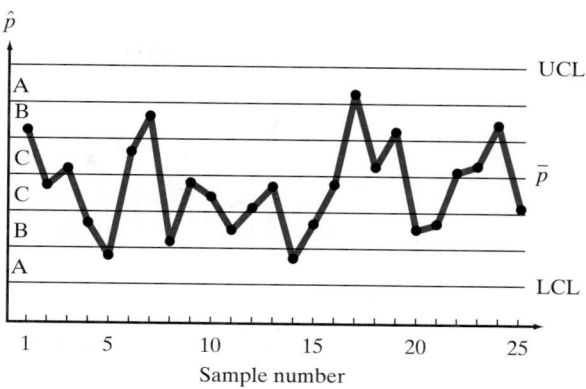

11.50 **(X11.050)** A company that manufactures plastic molded parts believes it is producing an unusually large number of defects. To investigate this suspicion, each shift drew seven random samples of 200 parts, visually inspected each part to determine whether it was defective, and tallied the primary type of defect present (Hart, 1992). These data are presented in the table at the top of page 656.
a. From a statistical perspective, are the number of samples and the sample size of 200 adequate for constructing a p-chart for these data? Explain.
b. Construct a p-chart for this manufacturing process.
c. Should the control limits be used to monitor future process output? Explain.
d. Suggest a strategy for identifying the special causes of variation that may be present.

11.51 **(X11.051)** A hospital has used control charts continuously since 1978 to monitor the quality of its nursing care. A set of 363 scoring criteria, or standards, are applied at critical points in the patients' stay to determine whether the patients are receiving beneficial nursing care. Auditors regularly visit each hospital unit, sample two patients, and evaluate their care. The auditors review patients' records; interview the patients, the nurse, and the head nurse; and observe the nursing care given (*International Journal of Quality and Reliability Management*, Vol. 9, 1992). The quality scores following part **d** were collected over a three-month period for a newly opened unit of the hospital.
a. Construct an R-chart for the nursing care process.
b. Construct an $\bar{x}$-chart for the nursing care process.
c. Should the control charts of parts **a** and **b** be used to monitor future process output? Explain.

			TYPE OF DEFECT				
Sample	Shift	# of Defects	Crack	Burn	Dirt	Blister	Trim
1	1	4	1	1	1	0	1
2	1	6	2	1	0	2	1
3	1	11	1	2	3	3	2
4	1	12	2	2	2	3	3
5	1	5	0	1	0	2	2
6	1	10	1	3	2	2	2
7	1	8	0	3	1	1	3
8	2	16	2	0	8	2	4
9	2	17	3	2	8	2	2
10	2	20	0	3	11	3	3
11	2	28	3	2	17	2	4
12	2	20	0	0	16	4	0
13	2	20	1	1	18	0	0
14	2	17	2	2	13	0	0
15	3	13	3	2	5	1	2
16	3	10	0	3	4	2	1
17	3	11	2	2	3	2	2
18	3	7	0	3	2	2	0
19	3	6	1	2	0	1	2
20	3	8	1	1	2	3	1
21	3	9	1	2	2	2	2

d. The hospital would like all quality scores to exceed 335 (their specification limit). Over the three-month periods, what proportion of the sampled patients received care that did not conform to the hospital's requirements?

Sample	Scores	Sample	Scores	Sample	Scores
1	345,341	8	344,344	15	345,329
2	331,328	9	359,334	16	358,351
3	343,355	10	346,361	17	353,352
4	351,352	11	360,355	18	334,340
5	360,348	12	325,335	19	341,335
6	342,336	13	350,348	20	358,345
7	328,331	14	336,337		

11.52 **(X11.052)** AirExpress, an overnight mail service, is concerned about the operating efficiency of the package-sorting departments at its Toledo, Ohio, terminal. The company would like to monitor the time it takes for packages to be put in outgoing delivery bins from the time they are received. The sorting department operates six hours per day, from 6 P.M. to midnight. The company randomly sampled four packages during each hour of operation during four consecutive days. The time for each package to move through the system, in minutes, is given.

a. Construct an $\bar{x}$-chart from these data. In order for this chart to be meaningful, what assump-

Sample	Transit Time (mins.)			
1	31.9	33.4	37.8	26.2
2	29.1	24.3	33.2	36.7
3	30.3	31.1	26.3	34.1
4	39.6	29.4	31.4	37.7
5	27.4	29.7	36.5	33.3
6	32.7	32.9	40.1	29.7
7	30.7	36.9	26.8	34.0
8	28.4	24.1	29.6	30.9
9	30.5	35.5	36.1	27.4
10	27.8	29.6	29.0	34.1
11	34.0	30.1	35.9	28.8
12	25.5	26.3	34.8	30.0
13	24.6	29.9	31.8	37.9
14	30.6	36.0	40.2	30.8
15	29.7	33.2	34.9	27.6
16	24.1	26.8	32.7	29.0
17	29.4	31.6	35.2	27.6
18	31.1	33.0	29.6	35.2
19	27.0	29.0	35.1	25.1
20	36.6	32.4	28.7	27.9
21	33.0	27.1	26.2	35.1
22	33.2	41.2	30.7	31.6
23	26.7	35.2	39.7	31.5
24	30.5	36.8	27.9	28.6

tion must be made about the variation of the process? Why?

b. What does the chart suggest about the stability of the package-sorting process? Explain.

c. Should the control limits be used to monitor future process output? Explain.

11.53 (X11.053) Officials at Mountain Airlines are interested in monitoring the length of time customers must wait in line to check in at their airport counter in Reno, Nevada. In order to develop a control chart, five customers were sampled each day for 20 days. The data, in minutes, are presented here.

Sample	Waiting Time (mins.)				
1	3.2	6.7	1.3	8.4	2.2
2	5.0	4.1	7.9	8.1	.4
3	7.1	3.2	2.1	6.5	3.7
4	4.2	1.6	2.7	7.2	1.4
5	1.7	7.1	1.6	.9	1.8
6	4.7	5.5	1.6	3.9	4.0
7	6.2	2.0	1.2	.9	1.4
8	1.4	2.7	3.8	4.6	3.8
9	1.1	4.3	9.1	3.1	2.7
10	5.3	4.1	9.8	2.9	2.7
11	3.2	2.9	4.1	5.6	.8
12	2.4	4.3	6.7	1.9	4.8
13	8.8	5.3	6.6	1.0	4.5
14	3.7	3.6	2.0	2.7	5.9
15	1.0	1.9	6.5	3.3	4.7
16	7.0	4.0	4.9	4.4	4.7
17	5.5	7.1	2.1	.9	2.8
18	1.8	5.6	2.2	1.7	2.1
19	2.6	3.7	4.8	1.4	5.8
20	3.6	.8	5.1	4.7	6.3

a. Construct an R-chart from these data.
b. What does the R-chart suggest about the stability of the process? Explain.
c. Explain why the R-chart should be interpreted prior to the $\bar{x}$-chart.
d. Construct an $\bar{x}$-chart from these data.
e. What does the $\bar{x}$-chart suggest about the stability of the process? Explain.
f. Should the control limits for the R-chart and $\bar{x}$-chart be used to monitor future process output? Explain.

11.54 (X11.054) Over the last year, a company that manufactures golf clubs has received numerous complaints about the performance of its graphite shafts and has lost several market share percentage points. In response, the company decided to monitor its shaft production process to identify new opportunities to improve its product. The process involves pultrusion. A fabric is pulled through a thermosetting polymer bath and then through a long heated steel die. As it moves through the die, the shaft is cured. Finally, it is cut to the desired length. Defects that can occur during the process are internal voids, broken strands, gaps between successive layers, and microcracks caused by improper curing. The company's newly formed quality department sampled 10 consecutive shafts every 30 minutes and nondestructive testing was used to seek out flaws in the shafts. The data from each eight-hour work shift were combined to form a shift sample of 160 shafts. Data on the proportion of defective shafts for 36 shift samples are presented in the table below. Data on the types of flaws identified are given in the first table on page 658. [*Note:* Each defective shaft may have more than one flaw.]

Shift Number	Number of Defective Shafts	Proportion of Defective Shafts
1	9	.05625
2	6	.03750
3	8	.05000
4	14	.08750
5	7	.04375
6	5	.03125
7	7	.04375
8	9	.05625
9	5	.03125
10	9	.05625
11	1	.00625
12	7	.04375
13	9	.05625
14	14	.08750
15	7	.04375
16	8	.05000
17	4	.02500
18	10	.06250
19	6	.03750
20	12	.07500
21	8	.05000
22	5	.03125
23	9	.05625
24	15	.09375
25	6	.03750
26	8	.05000
27	4	.02500
28	7	.04375
29	2	.01250
30	6	.03750
31	9	.05625
32	11	.06875
33	8	.05000
34	9	.05625
35	7	.04375
36	8	.05000

Source: Kolarik, W. *Creating Quality: Concepts, Systems, Strategies, and Tools.* New York: McGraw-Hill, 1995.

a. Use the appropriate control chart to determine whether the process proportion remains stable over time.
b. Does your control chart indicate that both common and special causes of variation are present? Explain.

Type of Defect	Number of Defects
Internal voids	11
Broken strands	96
Gaps between layers	72
Microcracks	150

c. To help diagnose the causes of variation in process output, construct a Pareto diagram for the types of shaft defects observed. Which are the "vital few"? The "trivial many"? (See Statistics in Action 2.1 for a description of Pareto analysis.)

11.55 (X11.055) A company called CRW runs credit checks for a large number of banks and insurance companies. Credit history information is typed into computer files by trained administrative assistants. The company is interested in monitoring the proportion of credit histories that contain one or more data entry errors. Based on her experience with the data entry operation, the director of the data processing unit believes that the proportion of histories with data entry errors is about 6%. CRW audited 150 randomly selected credit histories each day for 20 days. The sample data are presented at right.

a. Use the sample size formula to show that a sample size of 150 is large enough to prevent the lower control limit of the p-chart they plan to construct from being negative.

b. Construct a p-chart for the data entry process.
c. What does the chart indicate about the presence of special causes of variation? Explain.
d. Provide an example of a special cause of variation that could potentially affect this process. Do the same for a common cause of variation.
e. Should the control limits be used to monitor future credit histories produced by the data entry operation? Explain.

Sample	Sample Size	Histories with Errors
1	150	9
2	150	11
3	150	12
4	150	8
5	150	10
6	150	6
7	150	13
8	150	9
9	150	11
10	150	5
11	150	7
12	150	6
13	150	12
14	150	10
15	150	11
16	150	7
17	150	6
18	150	12
19	150	14
20	150	10

SHOWCASE THE GASKET MANUFACTURING CASE

The Problem. A Midwestern manufacturer of gaskets for automotive and off-road vehicle applications was suddenly and unexpectedly notified by a major customer—a U.S. auto manufacturer—that they had significantly tightened the specification limits on the overall thickness of a hard gasket used in their automotive engines. Although the current specification limits were by and large being met by the gasket manufacturer, their product did not come close to meeting the new specification.

The gasket manufacturer's first reaction was to negotiate with the customer to obtain a relaxation of the new specification. When these efforts failed, the customer-supplier relationship became somewhat strained. The gasket manufacturer's next thought was that if they waited long enough, the automotive company would eventually be forced to loosen the requirements and purchase the existing product. However, as time went on it became clear that this was not going to happen and that some positive steps would have to be taken to improve the quality of their gaskets. But what should be done? And by whom?

The Product. Figure C6.1 shows the product in question, a hard gasket. A hard gasket is comprised of two outer layers of soft gasket material and an inner layer consisting of a perforated piece of sheet metal. These three pieces are assembled, and some blanking and punching operations follow, after which metal rings are installed around the inside of the cylinder bore clearance holes and the entire outside periphery of the gasket. The quality characteristic of interest in this case is the assembly thickness.

The Process. An initial study by the staff engineers revealed that the variation in the thickness of soft gasket material—the two outer layers of the hard gasket—was large and undoubtedly responsible for much of the total variability in the final product. Figure C6.2 shows the roll mill process that fabricates the sheets of soft gasket material from which the two outer layers of the hard gasket are made. To manufacture a sheet of soft gasket material, an operator adds raw material, in a soft pelletlike form, to the gap—called the knip—between the two rolls. The larger roll rotates about its axis with no lateral movement; the smaller roll rotates and moves back and forth laterally to change the size of the knip. As the operator adds more and more material to the knip, the sheet is formed around the larger roll. When the smaller roll reaches a preset destination (i.e., final gap/sheet thickness), a bell rings and a red light goes on telling the operator to stop adding raw material. The operator stops the rolls and cuts the sheet horizontally along the larger roll so that it may be pulled off the roll. The finished sheet, called a pull, is pulled onto a table where the operator checks its thickness with a micrometer. The operator can adjust the final gap if he or she believes that the sheets are coming out too thick or too thin relative to the prescribed nominal value (i.e., the target thickness).

Process Operation. Investigation revealed that the operator runs the process in the following way. After each sheet is made, the operator measures the thickness with a micrometer. The thickness values for three consecutive sheets are averaged and the average is plotted on a piece of graph paper that, at the start of the shift, has only a solid horizontal line drawn on it to indicate the target thickness value for the particular soft gasket sheet the operator is making. Periodically, the operator reviews these evolving data and makes a decision as to whether or not the process mean—the sheet thickness—needs to be adjusted. This can be accomplished by stopping the machine, loosening some clamps on the small roll, and jogging the small roll laterally in or out by a few thousandths of an inch—whatever the operator feels is needed. The clamps are tightened, the gap is checked with a taper gage, and if adjusted properly, the operator begins to make sheets again. Typically, this adjustment process takes 10 to 15 minutes. The questions of when to make such adjustments and how much to change the roll gap for each adjustment are completely at the operator's discretion, based on the evolving plot of thickness averages.

FIGURE C6.1
A hard gasket for automotive applications

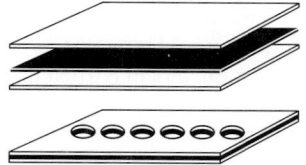

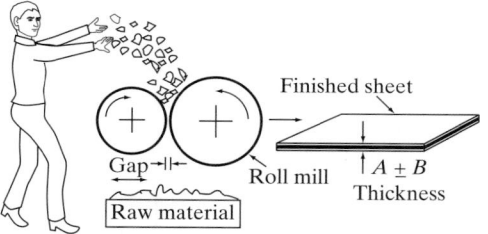

FIGURE C6.2   Roll mill for the manufacture of soft gasket material

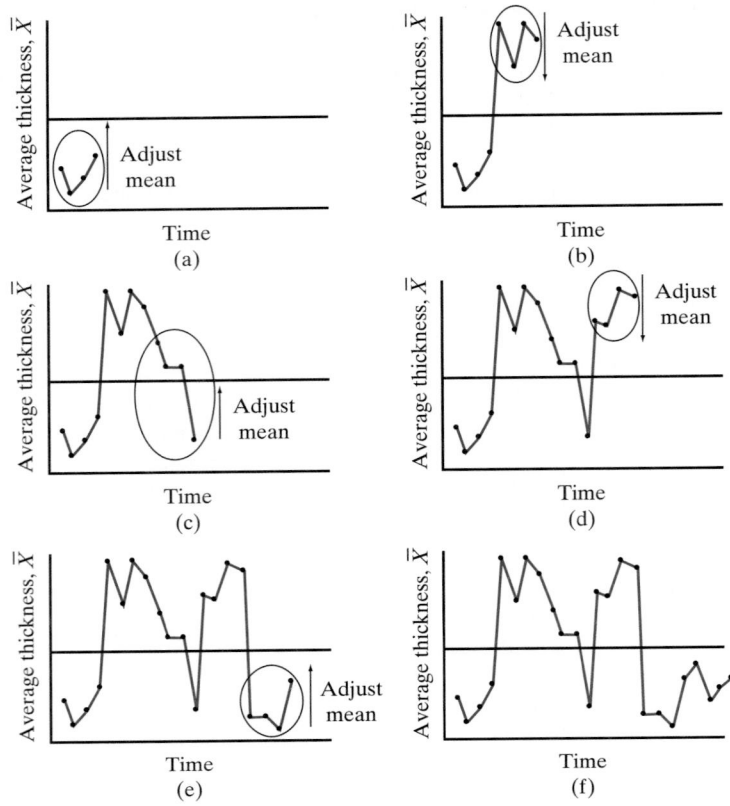

FIGURE C6.3 Process adjustment history over one shift

Figure C6.3 shows a series of plots that detail the history of one particular work shift over which the operator made several process adjustments. (These data come from the same shift that the staff engineers used to collect data for a process capability study that is described later.) Figure C6.3(a) shows the process data after the first 12 sheets have been made—four averages of three successive sheet thicknesses. At this point the operator judged that the data were telling her that the process was running below the target, so she stopped the process and made an adjustment to slightly increase the final roll gap. She then proceeded to make more sheets. Figure C6.3(b) shows the state of the process somewhat later. Now it appeared to the operator that the sheets were coming out too thick, so she stopped and made another adjustment. As shown in Figure C6.3(c), the process seemed to run well for a while, but then an average somewhat below the target led the operator to believe that another adjustment was necessary. Figures C6.3(d) and C6.3(e) show points in time where other adjustments were made.

Figure C6.3(f) shows the complete history of the shift. A total of 24 × 3, or 72, sheets were made during this shift. When asked, the operator indicated that the history of this shift was quite typical of what happens on a day-to-day basis.

The Company's Stop-Gap Solution. While the staff engineers were studying the problem to formulate an appropriate action plan, something had to be done to make it possible to deliver hard gaskets within the new specification limits. Management decided to increase product inspection and, in particular, to grade each piece of material according to thickness so that the wide variation in thickness could be balanced out at the assembly process. Extra inspectors were used to grade each piece of soft gasket material. Sheets of the same thickness were shipped in separate bundles on pallets to a sister plant for assembly. Thick and thin sheets were selected as needed to make a hard gasket that met the specification. The process worked pretty well and there was some discussion about making it permanent. However, some felt it was too costly and did not get at the root cause of the problem.

The Engineering Department's Analysis. Meanwhile, the staff engineers in the company were continuing to study the problem and came to the conclusion that the existing roll mill process equipment for making the soft gasket

TABLE C6.1   Measurements of Sheet Thickness

Sheet	Thickness (in.)	Sheet	Thickness (in.)	Sheet	Thickness (in.)
1	0.0440	25	0.0464	49	0.0427
2	0.0446	26	0.0457	50	0.0437
3	0.0437	27	0.0447	51	0.0445
4	0.0438	28	0.0451	52	0.0431
5	0.0425	29	0.0447	53	0.0448
6	0.0443	30	0.0457	54	0.0429
7	0.0453	31	0.0456	55	0.0425
8	0.0428	32	0.0455	56	0.0442
9	0.0433	33	0.0445	57	0.0432
10	0.0451	34	0.0448	58	0.0429
11	0.0441	35	0.0423	59	0.0447
12	0.0434	36	0.0442	60	0.0450
13	0.0459	37	0.0459	61	0.0443
14	0.0466	38	0.0468	62	0.0441
15	0.0476	39	0.0452	63	0.0450
16	0.0449	40	0.0456	64	0.0443
17	0.0471	41	0.0471	65	0.0423
18	0.0451	42	0.0450	66	0.0447
19	0.0472	43	0.0472	67	0.0429
20	0.0477	44	0.0465	68	0.0427
21	0.0452	45	0.0461	69	0.0464
22	0.0457	46	0.0462	70	0.0448
23	0.0459	47	0.0463	71	0.0451
24	0.0472	48	0.0471	72	0.0428

sheets simply was not capable of meeting the new specifications. This conclusion was reached as a result of the examination of production data and scrap logs over the past several months. They had researched some new equipment that had a track record for very good sheet-to-sheet consistency and had decided to write a proposal to replace the existing roll mills with this new equipment.

To strengthen the proposal, their boss asked them to include data that demonstrated the poor capability of the existing equipment. The engineers, confident that the equipment was not capable, selected what they thought was the best operator and the best roll mill (the plant has several roll mill lines) and took careful measurements of the thickness of each sheet made on an eight-hour shift. During that shift, a total of 72 sheets/pulls were made. This was considered quite acceptable since the work standard for the process is 70 sheets per shift. The measurements of the sheet thickness (in the order of manufacture) for the 72 sheets are given in Table C6.1. The engineers set out to use these data to conduct a process capability study.

Relying on a statistical methods course that one of the engineers had in college 10 years ago, the group decided to construct a frequency distribution from the data and use it to estimate the percentage of the measurements that fell within the specification limits. Their histogram is shown in Figure C6.4. Also shown in the figure are the upper and lower specification values. The dark shaded part of the histogram represents the amount of the product that lies outside of the specification limits. It is immediately apparent from the histogram that a large proportion of the output does not meet the customer's needs. Eight of the 72 sheets fall outside the specification limits. Therefore, in terms of percent conforming to specifications, the engineers estimated the process capability to be 88.8%. This was clearly unacceptable. This analysis confirmed the engineer's low opinion of the roll mill process equipment. They included it in their proposal and sent

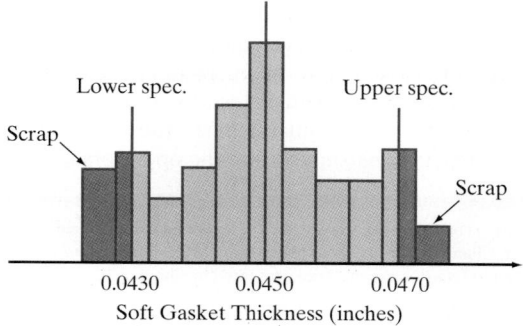

FIGURE C6.4   Histogram of data from process capability study

TABLE C6.2 **Measurements of Sheet Thickness for a Shift Run with No Operator Adjustment**

Sheet	Thickness (in.)	Sheet	Thickness (in.)	Sheet	Thickness (in.)
1	.0445	25	.0443	49	.0445
2	.0455	26	.0450	50	.0471
3	.0457	27	.0441	51	.0465
4	.0435	28	.0449	52	.0438
5	.0453	29	.0448	53	.0445
6	.0450	30	.0467	54	.0472
7	.0438	31	.0465	55	.0453
8	.0459	32	.0449	56	.0444
9	.0428	33	.0448	57	.0451
10	.0449	34	.0461	58	.0455
11	.0449	35	.0439	59	.0435
12	.0467	36	.0452	60	.0443
13	.0433	37	.0443	61	.0440
14	.0461	38	.0434	62	.0438
15	.0451	39	.0454	63	.0444
16	.0455	40	.0456	64	.0444
17	.0454	41	.0459	65	.0450
18	.0461	42	.0452	66	.0467
19	.0455	43	.0447	67	.0445
20	.0458	44	.0442	68	.0447
21	.0445	45	.0457	69	.0461
22	.0445	46	.0454	70	.0450
23	.0451	47	.0445	71	.0463
24	.0436	48	.0451	72	.0456

their recommendation to replace the equipment to the president's office.

Your Assignment. You have been hired as an external consultant by the company's president, Marilyn Carlson. She would like you to critique the engineers' analysis, conclusion, and recommendations.

Suspecting that the engineers' work may be flawed, President Carlson would also like you to conduct your own study and make your own recommendations concerning how to resolve the company's problem. She would like you to use the data reported in Table C6.1 along with the data of Table C6.2, which she ordered be collected for you. These data were collected in the same manner as the data in Table C6.1. However, they were collected during a period of time when the roll mill operator was instructed *not* to adjust the sheet thickness. In your analysis, if you choose to construct control charts, use the same three-measurement subgrouping that the operators use.

Prepare an in-depth, written report for the president that responds to her requests. It should begin with an executive summary and include whatever tables and figures are needed to support your analysis and recommendations. (A layout of the data file available for this case is described below.)

DATA ASCII file name: GASKET.DAT
Number of observations: 144

Variable	Column(s)	Type	
SHEET	1–2	QN	
THICKNSS	7–11	QN	
ADJUST	13	QL	(A=operator adjustments, N=no adjustments)

This case is based on the experiences of an actual company whose identity is disguised for confidentiality reasons. The case was originally written by DeVor, Chang, and Sutherland (*Statistical Quality Design and Control* [New York: Macmillan Publishing Co., 1992] pp. 298–329) and has been adapted to focus on the material presented in Chapter 11.

www.int.com
www.int.com
INTERNET LAB
www.int.com

QUALITY MANAGEMENT OUTSIDE OF MANUFACTURING OPERATION

Statistical quality control methods originated in manufacturing and today are being widely applied beyond it. Service operations such as marketing, sales, and customer service are benefiting from process management concepts. As you might expect, both the choice of which quality characteristic to measure and how to measure it are topics receiving much attention in these newer settings.

Here we will visit the American Productivity & Quality Center (APQC), a member-based organization that provides educational and standardization services to industry in support of quality improvement efforts.

1. The site address for the APQC is: *http://www.apqc.org/*

2. At the APQC home page, please note the variety of quality improvement applications for which the organization maintains information.

   - Click on the icon: **Measurement**

   - Next, scroll down to the heading "Publications" and click on **Measurement in Practice**, a new case study series devoted to measuring.

This case study series offers you a selection of articles that are updated biweekly. You are encouraged to review the full variety of information available here.

3. Select an article and read it on the screen or download it to your notepad or other word-processing software.

4. After reading the article, answer the following questions:

   a. What functional areas of the company are measuring the quality of their work?

   b. What company goals are being advanced by the measurement activity?

   c. Identify specific measures being used and the related data collection processes.

   d. Comment on how clearly the specific measures are related to the goals identified in part **b**.

   e. How did the company arrive at the adopted quality measures? What were the criteria for choosing them? Who is responsible for the quality monitoring process?

   f. What goals has the company met so far? What does it expect to achieve in the future?

   g. Does the company plan to revise any of its quality measurements or its monitoring processes? If so, for what reasons? ○

APPENDIX A
BASIC COUNTING RULES

Sample points associated with many experiments have identical characteristics. If you can develop a counting rule to count the number of sample points, it can be used to aid in the solution of many probability problems. For example, many experiments involve sampling n elements from a population of N. Then, as explained in Section 3.1, we can use the formula

$$\binom{N}{n} = \frac{N!}{n!(N-n)!}$$

to find the number of different samples of n elements that could be selected from the total of N elements. This gives the number of sample points for the experiment.

Here, we give you a few useful counting rules. You should learn the characteristics of the situation to which each rule applies. Then, when working a probability problem, carefully examine the experiment to see whether you can use one of the rules.

Learning how to decide whether a particular counting rule applies to an experiment takes patience and practice. If you want to develop this skill, try to use the rules to solve some of the exercises in Chapter 3. Proofs of the rules below can be found in the text by W. Feller listed in the references to Chapter 3.

Multiplicative Rule

You have k sets of different elements, n_1 in the first set, n_2 in the second set, ..., and n_k in the kth set. Suppose you want to form a sample of k elements *by taking one element from each of the* k *sets.* The number of different samples that can be formed is the product

$$n_1 \cdot n_2 \cdot n_3 \cdots n_k$$

EXAMPLE A.1   A product can be shipped by four airlines and each airline can ship via three different routes. How many distinct ways exist to ship the product?

SOLUTION

A method of shipment corresponds to a pairing of one airline and one route. Therefore, $k = 2$, the number of airlines is $n_1 = 4$, the number of routes is $n_2 = 3$, and the number of ways to ship the product is

$$n_1 \cdot n_2 = (4)(3) = 12$$

How the multiplicative rule works can be seen by using a tree diagram, introduced in Section 3.6. The airline choice is shown by three branching lines in Figure A.1.

FIGURE A.1
Tree diagram for
airline example

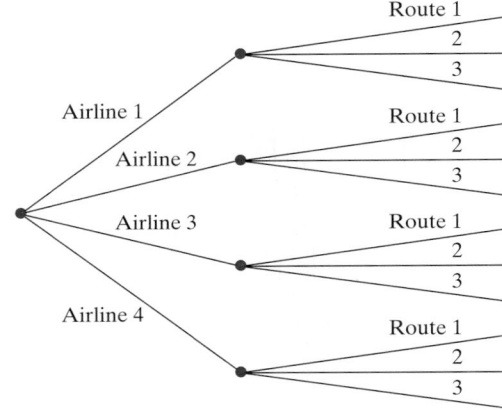

EXAMPLE A.2

You have twenty candidates for three different executive positions, E_1, E_2, and E_3. How many different ways could you fill the positions?

SOLUTION
For this example, there are $k = 3$ sets of elements:

Set 1: The candidates available to fill position E_1

Set 2: The candidates remaining (after filling E_1) that are available to fill E_2

Set 3: The candidates remaining (after filling E_1 and E_2) that are available to fill E_3

The numbers of elements in the sets are $n_1 = 20$, $n_2 = 19$, and $n_3 = 18$. Thus, the number of different ways to fill the three positions is

$$n_1 \cdot n_2 \cdot n_3 = (20)(19)(18) = 6{,}480$$

Partitions Rule
You have a *single* set of N distinctly different elements, and you want to partition it into k sets, the first set containing n_1 elements, the second containing n_2 elements, ..., and the kth containing n_k elements. The number of different partitions is

$$\frac{N!}{n_1!n_2!\cdots n_k!} \qquad \text{where } n_1 + n_2 + n_3 + \cdots + n_k = N$$

EXAMPLE A.3

You have twelve construction workers available for three job sites. Suppose you want to assign three workers to job 1, four to job 2, and five to job 3. How many different ways could you make this assignment?

SOLUTION
For this example, $k = 3$ (corresponding to the $k = 3$ job sites), $N = 12$, and $n_1 = 3$, $n_2 = 4$, $n_3 = 5$. Then, the number of different ways to assign the workers to the job sites is

$$\frac{N!}{n_1!n_2!n_3!} = \frac{12!}{3!4!5!} = \frac{12\cdot11\cdot10\cdots\cdot3\cdot2\cdot1}{(3\cdot2\cdot1)(4\cdot3\cdot2\cdot1)(5\cdot4\cdot3\cdot2\cdot1)} = 27{,}720$$

Combinations Rule
The combinations rule given in Chapter 3 is a special case ($k = 2$) of the partitions rule. That is, sampling is equivalent to partitioning a set of N elements into $k = 2$ groups: elements that appear in the sample and those that do not. Let $n_1 = n$, the number of elements in the sample, and $n_2 = N - n$, the number of elements remaining. Then the number of different samples of n elements that can be selected from N is

$$\frac{N!}{n_1!n_2!} = \frac{N!}{n!(N - n)!} = \binom{N}{n}$$

This formula was given in Section 3.1.

EXAMPLE **A.4**   How many samples of four fire fighters can be selected from a group of 10?

SOLUTION
We have $N = 10$ and $n = 4$; then,

$$\binom{N}{n} = \binom{10}{4} = \frac{10!}{4!6!} = \frac{10 \cdot 9 \cdot 8 \cdots 3 \cdot 2 \cdot 1}{(4 \cdot 3 \cdot 2 \cdot 1)(6 \cdot 5 \cdots 2 \cdot 1)} = 210$$

APPENDIX B
TABLES

Contents

TABLE I	Random Numbers
TABLE II	Binomial Probabilities
TABLE III	Poisson Probabilities
TABLE IV	Normal Curve Areas
TABLE V	Exponentials
TABLE VI	Critical Values of t
TABLE VII	Percentage Points of the F-Distribution, $\alpha = .10$
TABLE VIII	Percentage Points of the F-Distribution, $\alpha = .05$
TABLE IX	Percentage Points of the F-Distribution, $\alpha = .025$
TABLE X	Percentage Points of the F-Distribution, $\alpha = .01$
TABLE XI	Critical Values of T_L and T_U for the Wilcoxon Rank Sum Test: Independent Samples
TABLE XII	Critical Values of T_0 in the Wilcoxon Paired Difference Signed Rank Test
TABLE XIII	Critical Values of χ^2
TABLE XIV	Critical Values of Spearman's Rank Correlation Coefficient
TABLE XV	Control Chart Constants

TABLE I Random Numbers

Row \ Column	1	2	3	4	5	6	7	8	9	10	11	12	13	14
1	10480	15011	01536	02011	81647	91646	69179	14194	62590	36207	20969	99570	91291	90700
2	22368	46573	25595	85393	30995	89198	27982	53402	93965	34095	52666	19174	39615	99505
3	24130	48360	22527	97265	76393	64809	15179	24830	49340	32081	30680	19655	63348	58629
4	42167	93093	06243	61680	07856	16376	39440	53537	71341	57004	00849	74917	97758	16379
5	37570	39975	81837	16656	06121	91782	60468	81305	49684	60672	14110	06927	01263	54613
6	77921	06907	11008	42751	27756	53498	18602	70659	90655	15053	21916	81825	44394	42880
7	99562	72905	56420	69994	98872	31016	71194	18738	44013	48840	63213	21069	10634	12952
8	96301	91977	05463	07972	18876	20922	94595	56869	69014	60045	18425	84903	42508	32307
9	89579	14342	63661	10281	17453	18103	57740	84378	25331	12566	58678	44947	05585	56941
10	85475	36857	53342	53988	53060	59533	38867	62300	08158	17983	16439	11458	18593	64952
11	28918	69578	88231	33276	70997	79936	56865	05859	90106	31595	01547	85590	91610	78188
12	63553	40961	48235	03427	49626	69445	18663	72695	52180	20847	12234	90511	33703	90322
13	09429	93969	52636	92737	88974	33488	36320	17617	30015	08272	84115	27156	30613	74952
14	10365	61129	87529	85689	48237	52267	67689	93394	01511	26358	85104	20285	29975	89868
15	07119	97336	71048	08178	77233	13916	47564	81056	97735	85977	29372	74461	28551	90707
16	51085	12765	51821	51259	77452	16308	60756	92144	49442	53900	70960	63990	75601	40719
17	02368	21382	52404	60268	89368	19885	55322	44819	01188	65255	64835	44919	05944	55157
18	01011	54092	33362	94904	31273	04146	18594	29852	71585	85030	51132	01915	92747	64951
19	52162	53916	46369	58586	23216	14513	83149	98736	23495	64350	94738	17752	35156	35749
20	07056	97628	33787	09998	42698	06691	76988	13602	51851	46104	88916	19509	25625	58104
21	48663	91245	85828	14346	09172	30168	90229	04734	59193	22178	30421	61666	99904	32812
22	54164	58492	22421	74103	47070	25306	76468	26384	58151	06646	21524	15227	96909	44592
23	32639	32363	05597	24200	13363	38005	94342	28728	35806	06912	17012	64161	18296	22851
24	29334	27001	87637	87308	58731	00256	45834	15398	46557	41135	10367	07684	36188	18510
25	02488	33062	28834	07351	19731	92420	60952	61280	50001	67658	32586	86679	50720	94953
26	81525	72295	04839	96423	24878	82651	66566	14778	76797	14780	13300	87074	79666	95725
27	29676	20591	68086	26432	46901	20849	89768	81536	86645	12659	92259	57102	80428	25280
28	00742	57392	39064	66432	84673	40027	32832	61362	98947	96067	64760	64584	96096	98253
29	05366	04213	25669	26422	44407	44048	37937	63904	45766	66134	75470	66520	34693	90449
30	91921	26418	64117	94305	26766	25940	39972	22209	71500	64568	91402	42416	07844	69618
31	00582	04711	87917	77341	42206	35126	74087	99547	81817	42607	43808	76655	62028	76630
32	00725	69884	62797	56170	86324	88072	76222	36086	84637	93161	76038	65855	77919	88006
33	69011	65795	95876	55293	18988	27354	26575	08625	40801	59920	29841	80150	12777	48501
34	25976	57948	29888	88604	67917	48708	18912	82271	65424	69774	33611	54262	85963	03547
35	09763	83473	73577	12908	30883	18317	28290	35797	05998	41688	34952	37888	38917	88050

continued

TABLE I Continued

Row	1	2	3	4	5	6	7	8	9	10	11	12	13	14
36	91576	42595	27958	30134	04024	86385	29880	99730	55536	84855	29080	09250	79656	73211
37	17955	56349	90999	49127	20044	59931	06115	20542	18059	02008	73708	83517	36103	42791
38	46503	18584	18845	49618	02304	51038	20655	58727	28168	15475	56942	53389	20562	87338
39	92157	89634	94824	78171	84610	82834	09922	25417	44137	48413	25555	21246	35509	20468
40	14577	62765	35605	81263	39667	47358	56873	56307	61607	49518	89656	20103	77490	18062
41	98427	07523	33362	64270	01638	92477	66969	98420	04880	45585	46565	04102	46880	45709
42	34914	63976	88720	82765	34476	17032	87589	40836	32427	70002	70663	88863	77775	69348
43	70060	28277	39475	46473	23219	53416	94970	25832	69975	94884	19661	72828	00102	66794
44	53976	54914	06990	67245	68350	82948	11398	42878	80287	88267	47363	46634	06541	97809
45	76072	29515	40980	07391	58745	25774	22987	80059	39911	96189	41151	14222	60697	59583
46	90725	52210	83974	29992	65831	38857	50490	83765	55657	14361	31720	57375	56228	41546
47	64364	67412	33339	31926	14883	24413	59744	92351	97473	89286	35931	04110	23726	51900
48	08962	00358	31662	25388	61642	34072	81249	35648	56891	69352	48373	45578	78547	81788
49	95012	68379	93526	70765	10592	04542	76463	54328	02349	17247	28865	14777	62730	92277
50	15664	10493	20492	38391	91132	21999	59516	81652	27195	48223	46751	22923	32261	85653
51	16408	81899	04153	53381	79401	21438	83035	92350	36693	31238	59649	91754	72772	02338
52	18629	81953	05520	91962	04739	13092	97662	24822	94730	06496	35090	04822	86774	98289
53	73115	35101	47498	87637	99016	71060	88824	71013	18735	20286	23153	72924	35165	43040
54	57491	16703	23167	49323	45021	33132	12544	41035	80780	45393	44812	12512	98931	91202
55	30405	83946	23792	14422	15059	45799	22716	19792	09983	74353	68668	30429	70735	25499
56	16631	35006	85900	98275	32388	52390	16815	69290	82732	38480	73817	32523	41961	44437
57	96773	20206	42559	78985	05300	22164	24369	54224	35083	19687	11052	91491	60383	19746
58	38935	64202	14349	82674	66523	44133	00697	35552	35970	19124	63318	29686	03387	59846
59	31624	76384	17403	53363	44167	64486	64758	75366	76554	31601	12614	33072	60332	92325
60	78919	19474	23632	27889	47914	02584	37680	20801	72152	39339	34806	08930	85001	87820
61	03931	33309	57047	74211	63445	17361	62825	39908	05607	91284	68833	25570	38818	46920
62	74426	33278	43972	10110	89917	15665	52872	73823	73144	88662	88970	74492	51805	99378
63	09066	00903	20795	95452	92648	45454	09552	88815	16553	51125	79375	97596	16296	66092
64	42238	12426	87025	14267	20979	04508	64535	31355	86064	29472	47689	05974	52468	16834
65	16153	08002	26504	41744	81959	65642	74240	56302	00033	67107	77510	70625	28725	34191
66	21457	40742	29820	96783	29400	21840	15035	34537	33310	06116	95240	15957	16572	06004
67	21581	57802	02050	89728	17937	37621	47075	42080	97403	48626	68995	43805	33386	21597
68	55612	78095	83197	33732	05810	24813	86902	60397	16489	03264	88525	42786	05269	92532
69	44657	66999	99324	51281	84463	60563	79312	93454	68876	25471	93911	25650	12682	73572
70	91340	84979	46949	81973	37949	61023	43997	15263	80644	43942	89203	71795	99533	50501

TABLE I Continued

Column / Row	1	2	3	4	5	6	7	8	9	10	11	12	13	14
71	91227	21199	31935	27022	84067	05462	35216	14486	29891	68607	41867	14951	91696	85065
72	50001	38140	66321	19924	72163	09538	12151	06878	91903	18749	34405	56087	82790	70925
73	65390	05224	72958	28609	81406	39147	25549	48542	42627	45233	57202	94617	23772	07896
74	27504	96131	83944	41575	10573	08619	64482	73923	36152	05184	94142	25299	84387	34925
75	37169	94851	39117	89632	00959	16487	65536	49071	39782	17095	02330	74301	00275	48280
76	11508	70225	51111	38351	19444	66499	71945	05422	13442	78675	84081	66938	93654	59894
77	37449	30362	06694	54690	04052	53115	62757	95348	78662	11163	81651	50245	34971	52924
78	46515	70331	85922	38329	57015	15765	97161	17869	45349	61796	66345	81073	49106	79860
79	30986	81223	42416	58353	21532	30502	32305	86482	05174	07901	54339	58861	74818	46942
80	63798	64995	46583	09785	44160	78128	83991	42865	92520	83531	80377	35909	81250	54238
81	82486	84846	99254	67632	43218	50076	21361	64816	51202	88124	41870	52689	51275	83556
82	21885	32906	92431	09060	64297	51674	64126	62570	26123	05155	59194	52799	28225	85762
83	60336	98782	07408	53458	13564	59089	26445	29789	85205	41001	12535	12133	14645	23541
84	43937	46891	24010	25560	86355	33941	25786	54990	71899	15475	95434	98227	21824	19585
85	97656	63175	89303	16275	07100	92063	21942	18611	47348	20203	18534	03862	78095	50136
86	03299	01221	05418	38982	55758	92237	26759	86367	21216	98442	08303	56613	91511	75928
87	79626	06486	03574	17668	07785	76020	79924	25651	83325	88428	85076	72811	22717	50585
88	85636	68335	47539	03129	65651	11977	02510	26113	99447	68645	34327	15152	55230	93448
89	18039	14367	64337	06177	12143	46609	32989	74014	64708	00533	35398	58408	13261	47908
90	08362	15656	60627	36478	65648	16764	53412	09013	07832	41574	17639	82163	60859	75567
91	79556	29068	04142	16268	15387	12856	66227	38358	22478	73373	88732	09443	82558	05250
92	92608	82674	27072	32534	17075	27698	98204	63863	11951	34648	88022	56148	34925	57031
93	23982	25835	40055	67006	12293	02753	14827	23235	35071	99704	37543	11601	35503	85171
94	09915	96306	05908	97901	28395	14186	00821	80703	70426	75647	76310	88717	37890	40129
95	59037	33300	26695	62247	69927	76123	50842	43834	86654	70959	79725	93872	28117	19233
96	42488	78077	69882	61657	34136	79180	97526	43092	04098	73571	80799	76536	71255	64239
97	46764	86273	63003	93017	31204	36692	40202	35275	57306	55543	53203	18098	47625	88684
98	03237	45430	55417	63282	90816	17349	88298	90183	36600	78406	06216	95787	42579	90730
99	86591	81482	52667	61582	14972	90053	89534	76036	49199	43716	97548	04379	46370	28672
100	38534	01715	94964	87288	65680	43772	39560	12918	86537	62738	19636	51132	25739	56947

Source: Abridged from W. H. Beyer (ed.), CRC Standard Mathematical Tables, 24th edition. (Cleveland: The Chemical Rubber Company), 1976. Reproduced by permission of the publisher.

TABLE II Binomial Probabilities

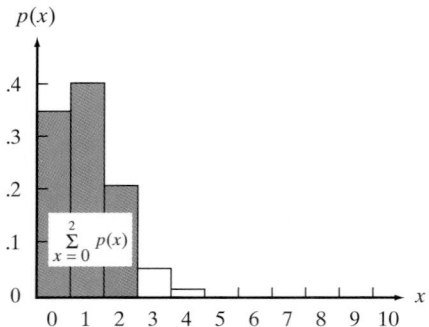

Tabulated values are $\sum_{x=0}^{k} p(x)$. (Computations are rounded at the third decimal place.)

a. $n = 5$

k	.01	.05	.10	.20	.30	.40	.50	.60	.70	.80	.90	.95	.99
0	.951	.774	.590	.328	.168	.078	.031	.010	.002	.000	.000	.000	.000
1	.999	.977	.919	.737	.528	.337	.188	.087	.031	.007	.000	.000	.000
2	1.000	.999	.991	.942	.837	.683	.500	.317	.163	.058	.009	.001	.000
3	1.000	1.000	1.000	.993	.969	.913	.812	.663	.472	.263	.081	.023	.001
4	1.000	1.000	1.000	1.000	.998	.990	.969	.922	.832	.672	.410	.226	.049

b. $n = 6$

k	.01	.05	.10	.20	.30	.40	.50	.60	.70	.80	.90	.95	.99
0	.941	.735	.531	.262	.118	.047	.016	.004	.001	.000	.000	.000	.000
1	.999	.967	.886	.655	.420	.233	.109	.041	.011	.002	.000	.000	.000
2	1.000	.998	.984	.901	.744	.544	.344	.179	.070	.017	.001	.000	.000
3	1.000	1.000	.999	.983	.930	.821	.656	.456	.256	.099	.016	.002	.000
4	1.000	1.000	1.000	.998	.989	.959	.891	.767	.580	.345	.114	.033	.001
5	1.000	1.000	1.000	1.000	.999	.996	.984	.953	.882	.738	.469	.265	.059

c. $n = 7$

k	.01	.05	.10	.20	.30	.40	.50	.60	.70	.80	.90	.95	.99
0	.932	.698	.478	.210	.082	.028	.008	.002	.000	.000	.000	.000	.000
1	.998	.956	.850	.577	.329	.159	.063	.019	.004	.000	.000	.000	.000
2	1.000	.996	.974	.852	.647	.420	.227	.096	.029	.005	.000	.000	.000
3	1.000	1.000	.997	.967	.874	.710	.500	.290	.126	.033	.003	.000	.000
4	1.000	1.000	1.000	.995	.971	.904	.773	.580	.353	.148	.026	.004	.000
5	1.000	1.000	1.000	1.000	.996	.981	.937	.841	.671	.423	.150	.044	.002
6	1.000	1.000	1.000	1.000	1.000	.998	.992	.972	.918	.790	.522	.302	.068

TABLE II Continued

d. n = 8

k \ p	.01	.05	.10	.20	.30	.40	.50	.60	.70	.80	.90	.95	.99
0	.923	.663	.430	.168	.058	.017	.004	.001	.000	.000	.000	.000	.000
1	.997	.943	.813	.503	.255	.106	.035	.009	.001	.000	.000	.000	.000
2	1.000	.994	.962	.797	.552	.315	.145	.050	.011	.001	.000	.000	.000
3	1.000	1.000	.995	.944	.806	.594	.363	.174	.058	.010	.000	.000	.000
4	1.000	1.000	1.000	.990	.942	.826	.637	.406	.194	.056	.005	.000	.000
5	1.000	1.000	1.000	.999	.989	.950	.855	.685	.448	.203	.038	.006	.000
6	1.000	1.000	1.000	1.000	.999	.991	.965	.894	.745	.497	.187	.057	.003
7	1.000	1.000	1.000	1.000	1.000	.999	.996	.983	.942	.832	.570	.337	.077

e. n = 9

k \ p	.01	.05	.10	.20	.30	.40	.50	.60	.70	.80	.90	.95	.99
0	.914	.630	.387	.134	.040	.010	.002	.000	.000	.000	.000	.000	.000
1	.997	.929	.775	.436	.196	.071	.020	.004	.000	.000	.000	.000	.000
2	1.000	.992	.947	.738	.463	.232	.090	.025	.004	.000	.000	.000	.000
3	1.000	.999	.992	.914	.730	.483	.254	.099	.025	.003	.000	.000	.000
4	1.000	1.000	.999	.980	.901	.733	.500	.267	.099	.020	.001	.000	.000
5	1.000	1.000	1.000	.997	.975	.901	.746	.517	.270	.086	.008	.001	.000
6	1.000	1.000	1.000	1.000	.996	.975	.910	.768	.537	.262	.053	.008	.000
7	1.000	1.000	1.000	1.000	1.000	.996	.980	.929	.804	.564	.225	.071	.003
8	1.000	1.000	1.000	1.000	1.000	1.000	.998	.990	.960	.866	.613	.370	.086

f. n = 10

k \ p	.01	.05	.10	.20	.30	.40	.50	.60	.70	.80	.90	.95	.99
0	.904	.599	.349	.107	.028	.006	.001	.000	.000	.000	.000	.000	.000
1	.996	.914	.736	.376	.149	.046	.011	.002	.000	.000	.000	.000	.000
2	1.000	.988	.930	.678	.383	.167	.055	.012	.002	.000	.000	.000	.000
3	1.000	.999	.987	.879	.650	.382	.172	.055	.011	.001	.000	.000	.000
4	1.000	1.000	.998	.967	.850	.633	.377	.166	.047	.006	.000	.000	.000
5	1.000	1.000	1.000	.999	.953	.834	.623	.367	.150	.033	.002	.000	.000
6	1.000	1.000	1.000	.999	.989	.945	.828	.618	.350	.121	.013	.001	.000
7	1.000	1.000	1.000	1.000	.998	.988	.945	.833	.617	.322	.070	.012	.000
8	1.000	1.000	1.000	1.000	1.000	.998	.989	.954	.851	.624	.264	.086	.004
9	1.000	1.000	1.000	1.000	1.000	1.000	.999	.994	.972	.893	.651	.401	.096

continued

Table II Continued

g. $n = 15$

k \ p	.01	.05	.10	.20	.30	.40	.50	.60	.70	.80	.90	.95	.99
0	.860	.463	.206	.035	.005	.000	.000	.000	.000	.000	.000	.000	.000
1	.990	.829	.549	.167	.035	.005	.000	.000	.000	.000	.000	.000	.000
2	1.000	.964	.816	.398	.127	.027	.004	.000	.000	.000	.000	.000	.000
3	1.000	.995	.944	.648	.297	.091	.018	.002	.000	.000	.000	.000	.000
4	1.000	.999	.987	.838	.515	.217	.059	.009	.001	.000	.000	.000	.000
5	1.000	1.000	.998	.939	.722	.403	.151	.034	.004	.000	.000	.000	.000
6	1.000	1.000	1.000	.982	.869	.610	.304	.095	.015	.001	.000	.000	.000
7	1.000	1.000	1.000	.996	.950	.787	.500	.213	.050	.004	.000	.000	.000
8	1.000	1.000	1.000	.999	.985	.905	.696	.390	.131	.018	.000	.000	.000
9	1.000	1.000	1.000	1.000	.996	.966	.849	.597	.278	.061	.002	.000	.000
10	1.000	1.000	1.000	1.000	.999	.991	.941	.783	.485	.164	.013	.001	.000
11	1.000	1.000	1.000	1.000	1.000	.998	.982	.909	.703	.352	.056	.005	.000
12	1.000	1.000	1.000	1.000	1.000	1.000	.996	.973	.873	.602	.184	.036	.000
13	1.000	1.000	1.000	1.000	1.000	1.000	1.000	.995	.965	.833	.451	.171	.010
14	1.000	1.000	1.000	1.000	1.000	1.000	1.000	1.000	.995	.965	.794	.537	.140

h. $n = 20$

k \ p	.01	.05	.10	.20	.30	.40	.50	.60	.70	.80	.90	.95	.99
0	.818	.358	.122	.012	.001	.000	.000	.000	.000	.000	.000	.000	.000
1	.983	.736	.392	.069	.008	.001	.000	.000	.000	.000	.000	.000	.000
2	.999	.925	.677	.206	.035	.004	.000	.000	.000	.000	.000	.000	.000
3	1.000	.984	.867	.411	.107	.016	.001	.000	.000	.000	.000	.000	.000
4	1.000	.997	.957	.630	.238	.051	.006	.000	.000	.000	.000	.000	.000
5	1.000	1.000	.989	.804	.416	.126	.021	.002	.000	.000	.000	.000	.000
6	1.000	1.000	.998	.913	.608	.250	.058	.006	.000	.000	.000	.000	.000
7	1.000	1.000	1.000	.968	.772	.416	.132	.021	.001	.000	.000	.000	.000
8	1.000	1.000	1.000	.990	.887	.596	.252	.057	.005	.000	.000	.000	.000
9	1.000	1.000	1.000	.997	.952	.755	.412	.128	.017	.001	.000	.000	.000
10	1.000	1.000	1.000	.999	.983	.872	.588	.245	.048	.003	.000	.000	.000
11	1.000	1.000	1.000	1.000	.995	.943	.748	.404	.113	.010	.000	.000	.000
12	1.000	1.000	1.000	1.000	.999	.979	.868	.584	.228	.032	.000	.000	.000
13	1.000	1.000	1.000	1.000	1.000	.994	.942	.750	.392	.087	.002	.000	.000
14	1.000	1.000	1.000	1.000	1.000	.998	.979	.874	.584	.196	.011	.000	.000
15	1.000	1.000	1.000	1.000	1.000	1.000	.994	.949	.762	.370	.043	.003	.000
16	1.000	1.000	1.000	1.000	1.000	1.000	.999	.984	.893	.589	.133	.016	.000
17	1.000	1.000	1.000	1.000	1.000	1.000	1.000	.996	.965	.794	.323	.075	.001
18	1.000	1.000	1.000	1.000	1.000	1.000	1.000	.999	.992	.931	.608	.264	.017
19	1.000	1.000	1.000	1.000	1.000	1.000	1.000	1.000	.999	.988	.878	.642	.182

TABLE II Continued

i. $n = 25$

k \ p	.01	.05	.10	.20	.30	.40	.50	.60	.70	.80	.90	.95	.99
0	.778	.277	.072	.004	.000	.000	.000	.000	.000	.000	.000	.000	.000
1	.974	.642	.271	.027	.002	.000	.000	.000	.000	.000	.000	.000	.000
2	.998	.873	.537	.098	.009	.000	.000	.000	.000	.000	.000	.000	.000
3	1.000	.966	.764	.234	.033	.002	.000	.000	.000	.000	.000	.000	.000
4	1.000	.993	.902	.421	.090	.009	.000	.000	.000	.000	.000	.000	.000
5	1.000	.999	.967	.617	.193	.029	.002	.000	.000	.000	.000	.000	.000
6	1.000	1.000	.991	.780	.341	.074	.007	.000	.000	.000	.000	.000	.000
7	1.000	1.000	.998	.891	.512	.154	.022	.001	.000	.000	.000	.000	.000
8	1.000	1.000	1.000	.953	.677	.274	.054	.004	.000	.000	.000	.000	.000
9	1.000	1.000	1.000	.983	.811	.425	.115	.013	.000	.000	.000	.000	.000
10	1.000	1.000	1.000	.994	.902	.586	.212	.034	.002	.000	.000	.000	.000
11	1.000	1.000	1.000	.998	.956	.732	.345	.078	.006	.000	.000	.000	.000
12	1.000	1.000	1.000	1.000	.983	.846	.500	.154	.017	.000	.000	.000	.000
13	1.000	1.000	1.000	1.000	.994	.922	.655	.268	.044	.002	.000	.000	.000
14	1.000	1.000	1.000	1.000	.998	.966	.788	.414	.098	.006	.000	.000	.000
15	1.000	1.000	1.000	1.000	1.000	.987	.885	.575	.189	.017	.000	.000	.000
16	1.000	1.000	1.000	1.000	1.000	.996	.946	.726	.323	.047	.000	.000	.000
17	1.000	1.000	1.000	1.000	1.000	.999	.978	.846	.488	.109	.002	.000	.000
18	1.000	1.000	1.000	1.000	1.000	1.000	.993	.926	.659	.220	.009	.000	.000
19	1.000	1.000	1.000	1.000	1.000	1.000	.998	.971	.807	.383	.033	.001	.000
20	1.000	1.000	1.000	1.000	1.000	1.000	1.000	.991	.910	.579	.098	.007	.000
21	1.000	1.000	1.000	1.000	1.000	1.000	1.000	.998	.967	.766	.236	.034	.000
22	1.000	1.000	1.000	1.000	1.000	1.000	1.000	1.000	.991	.902	.463	.127	.002
23	1.000	1.000	1.000	1.000	1.000	1.000	1.000	1.000	.998	.973	.729	.358	.026
24	1.000	1.000	1.000	1.000	1.000	1.000	1.000	1.000	1.000	.996	.928	.723	.222

TABLE III Poisson Probabilities

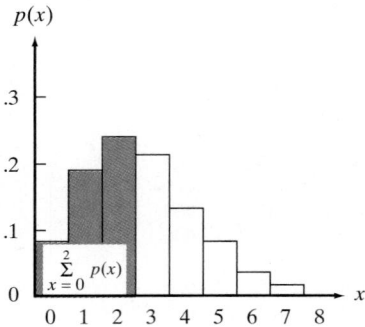

Tabulated values are $\sum_{x=0}^{k} p(x)$. *(Computations are rounded at the third decimal place.)*

λ \ x	0	1	2	3	4	5	6	7	8	9
.02	.980	1.000								
.04	.961	.999	1.000							
.06	.942	.998	1.000							
.08	.923	.997	1.000							
.10	.905	.995	1.000							
.15	.861	.990	.999	1.000						
.20	.819	.982	.999	1.000						
.25	.779	.974	.998	1.000						
.30	.741	.963	.996	1.000						
.35	.705	.951	.994	1.000						
.40	.670	.938	.992	.999	1.000					
.45	.638	.925	.989	.999	1.000					
.50	.607	.910	.986	.998	1.000					
.55	.577	.894	.982	.998	1.000					
.60	.549	.878	.977	.997	1.000					
.65	.522	.861	.972	.996	.999	1.000				
.70	.497	.844	.966	.994	.999	1.000				
.75	.472	.827	.959	.993	.999	1.000				
.80	.449	.809	.953	.991	.999	1.000				
.85	.427	.791	.945	.989	.998	1.000				
.90	.407	.772	.937	.987	.998	1.000				
.95	.387	.754	.929	.981	.997	1.000				
1.00	.368	.736	.920	.981	.996	.999	1.000			
1.1	.333	.699	.900	.974	.995	.999	1.000			
1.2	.301	.663	.879	.966	.992	.998	1.000			
1.3	.273	.627	.857	.957	.989	.998	1.000			
1.4	.247	.592	.833	.946	.986	.997	.999	1.000		
1.5	.223	.558	.809	.934	.981	.996	.999	1.000		

TABLE III   Continued

λ \ x	0	1	2	3	4	5	6	7	8	9
1.6	.202	.525	.783	.921	.976	.994	.999	1.000		
1.7	.183	.493	.757	.907	.970	.992	.998	1.000		
1.8	.165	.463	.731	.891	.964	.990	.997	.999	1.000	
1.9	.150	.434	.704	.875	.956	.987	.997	.999	1.000	
2.0	.135	.406	.677	.857	.947	.983	.995	.999	1.000	
2.2	.111	.355	.623	.819	.928	.975	.993	.998	1.000	
2.4	.091	.308	.570	.779	.904	.964	.988	.997	.999	1.000
2.6	.074	.267	.518	.736	.877	.951	.983	.995	.999	1.000
2.8	.061	.231	.469	.692	.848	.935	.976	.992	.998	.999
3.0	.050	.199	.423	.647	.815	.916	.966	.988	.996	.999
3.2	.041	.171	.380	.603	.781	.895	.955	.983	.994	.998
3.4	.033	.147	.340	.558	.744	.871	.942	.977	.992	.997
3.6	.027	.126	.303	.515	.706	.844	.927	.969	.988	.996
3.8	.022	.107	.269	.473	.668	.816	.909	.960	.984	.994
4.0	.018	.092	.238	.433	.629	.785	.889	.949	.979	.992
4.2	.015	.078	.210	.395	.590	.753	.867	.936	.972	.989
4.4	.012	.066	.185	.359	.551	.720	.844	.921	.964	.985
4.6	.010	.056	.163	.326	.513	.686	.818	.905	.955	.980
4.8	.008	.048	.143	.294	.476	.651	.791	.887	.944	.975
5.0	.007	.040	.125	.265	.440	.616	.762	.867	.932	.968
5.2	.006	.034	.109	.238	.406	.581	.732	.845	.918	.960
5.4	.005	.029	.095	.213	.373	.546	.702	.822	.903	.951
5.6	.004	.024	.082	.191	.342	.512	.670	.797	.886	.941
5.8	.003	.021	.072	.170	.313	.478	.638	.771	.867	.929
6.0	.002	.017	.062	.151	.285	.446	.606	.744	.847	.916

λ	10	11	12	13	14	15	16
2.8	1.000						
3.0	1.000						
3.2	1.000						
3.4	.999	1.000					
3.6	.999	1.000					
3.8	.998	.999	1.000				
4.0	.997	.999	1.000				
4.2	.996	.999	1.000				
4.4	.994	.998	.999	1.000			
4.6	.992	.997	.999	1.000			
4.8	.990	.996	.999	1.000			
5.0	.986	.995	.998	.999	1.000		
5.2	.982	.993	.997	.999	1.000		
5.4	.977	.990	.996	.999	1.000		
5.6	.972	.988	.995	.998	.999	1.000	
5.8	.965	.984	.993	.997	.999	1.000	
6.0	.957	.980	.991	.996	.999	.999	1.000

continued

TABLE III   Continued

λ \ x	0	1	2	3	4	5	6	7	8	9
6.2	.002	.015	.054	.134	.259	.414	.574	.716	.826	.902
6.4	.002	.012	.046	.119	.235	.384	.542	.687	.803	.886
6.6	.001	.010	.040	.105	.213	.355	.511	.658	.780	.869
6.8	.001	.009	.034	.093	.192	.327	.480	.628	.755	.850
7.0	.001	.007	.030	.082	.173	.301	.450	.599	.729	.830
7.2	.001	.006	.025	.072	.156	.276	.420	.569	.703	.810
7.4	.001	.005	.022	.063	.140	.253	.392	.539	.676	.788
7.6	.001	.004	.019	.055	.125	.231	.365	.510	.648	.765
7.8	.000	.004	.016	.048	.112	.210	.338	.481	.620	.741
8.0	.000	.003	.014	.042	.100	.191	.313	.453	.593	.717
8.5	.000	.002	.009	.030	.074	.150	.256	.386	.523	.653
9.0	.000	.001	.006	.021	.055	.116	.207	.324	.456	.587
9.5	.000	.001	.004	.015	.040	.089	.165	.269	.392	.522
10.0	.000	.000	.003	.010	.029	.067	.130	.220	.333	.458

λ	10	11	12	13	14	15	16	17	18	19
6.2	.949	.975	.989	.995	.998	.999	1.000			
6.4	.939	.969	.986	.994	.997	.999	1.000			
6.6	.927	.963	.982	.992	.997	.999	.999	1.000		
6.8	.915	.955	.978	.990	.996	.998	.999	1.000		
7.0	.901	.947	.973	.987	.994	.998	.999	1.000		
7.2	.887	.937	.967	.984	.993	.997	.999	.999	1.000	
7.4	.871	.926	.961	.980	.991	.996	.998	.999	1.000	
7.6	.854	.915	.954	.976	.989	.995	.998	.999	1.000	
7.8	.835	.902	.945	.971	.986	.993	.997	.999	1.000	
8.0	.816	.888	.936	.966	.983	.992	.996	.998	.999	1.000
8.5	.763	.849	.909	.949	.973	.986	.993	.997	.999	.999
9.0	.706	.803	.876	.926	.959	.978	.989	.995	.998	.999
9.5	.645	.752	.836	.898	.940	.967	.982	.991	.996	.998
10.0	.583	.697	.792	.864	.917	.951	.973	.986	.993	.997

λ	20	21	22
8.5	1.000		
9.0	1.000		
9.5	.999	1.000	
10.0	.998	.999	1.000

TABLE III Continued

λ \ x	0	1	2	3	4	5	6	7	8	9
10.5	.000	.000	.002	.007	.021	.050	.102	.179	.279	.397
11.0	.000	.000	.001	.005	.015	.038	.079	.143	.232	.341
11.5	.000	.000	.001	.003	.011	.028	.060	.114	.191	.289
12.0	.000	.000	.001	.002	.008	.020	.046	.090	.155	.242
12.5	.000	.000	.000	.002	.005	.015	.035	.070	.125	.201
13.0	.000	.000	.000	.001	.004	.011	.026	.054	.100	.166
13.5	.000	.000	.000	.001	.003	.008	.019	.041	.079	.135
14.0	.000	.000	.000	.000	.002	.006	.014	.032	.062	.109
14.5	.000	.000	.000	.000	.001	.004	.010	.024	.048	.088
15.0	.000	.000	.000	.000	.001	.003	.008	.018	.037	.070

λ	10	11	12	13	14	15	16	17	18	19
10.5	.521	.639	.742	.825	.888	.932	.960	.978	.988	.994
11.0	.460	.579	.689	.781	.854	.907	.944	.968	.982	.991
11.5	.402	.520	.633	.733	.815	.878	.924	.954	.974	.986
12.0	.347	.462	.576	.682	.772	.844	.899	.937	.963	.979
12.5	.297	.406	.519	.628	.725	.806	.869	.916	.948	.969
13.0	.252	.353	.463	.573	.675	.764	.835	.890	.930	.957
13.5	.211	.304	.409	.518	.623	.718	.798	.861	.908	.942
14.0	.176	.260	.358	.464	.570	.669	.756	.827	.883	.923
14.5	.145	.220	.311	.413	.518	.619	.711	.790	.853	.901
15.0	.118	.185	.268	.363	.466	.568	.664	.749	.819	.875

λ	20	21	22	23	24	25	26	27	28	29
10.5	.997	.999	.999	1.000						
11.0	.995	.998	.999	1.000						
11.5	.992	.996	.998	.999	1.000					
12.0	.988	.994	.987	.999	.999	1.000				
12.5	.983	.991	.995	.998	.999	.999	1.000			
13.0	.975	.986	.992	.996	.998	.999	1.000			
13.5	.965	.980	.989	.994	.997	.998	.999	1.000		
14.0	.952	.971	.983	.991	.995	.997	.999	.999	1.000	
14.5	.936	.960	.976	.986	.992	.996	.998	.999	.999	1.000
15.0	.917	.947	.967	.981	.989	.994	.997	.998	.999	1.000

continued

TABLE III Continued

λ \ x	4	5	6	7	8	9	10	11	12	13
16	.000	.001	.004	.010	.022	.043	.077	.127	.193	.275
17	.000	.001	.002	.005	.013	.026	.049	.085	.135	.201
18	.000	.000	.001	.003	.007	.015	.030	.055	.092	.143
19	.000	.000	.001	.002	.004	.009	.018	.035	.061	.098
20	.000	.000	.000	.001	.002	.005	.011	.021	.039	.066
21	.000	.000	.000	.000	.001	.003	.006	.013	.025	.043
22	.000	.000	.000	.000	.001	.002	.004	.008	.015	.028
23	.000	.000	.000	.000	.000	.001	.002	.004	.009	.017
24	.000	.000	.000	.000	.000	.000	.001	.003	.005	.011
25	.000	.000	.000	.000	.000	.000	.001	.001	.003	.006

λ	14	15	16	17	18	19	20	21	22	23
16	.368	.467	.566	.659	.742	.812	.868	.911	.942	.963
17	.281	.371	.468	.564	.655	.736	.805	.861	.905	.937
18	.208	.287	.375	.469	.562	.651	.731	.799	.855	.899
19	.150	.215	.292	.378	.469	.561	.647	.725	.793	.849
20	.105	.157	.221	.297	.381	.470	.559	.644	.721	.787
21	.072	.111	.163	.227	.302	.384	.471	.558	.640	.716
22	.048	.077	.117	.169	.232	.306	.387	.472	.556	.637
23	.031	.052	.082	.123	.175	.238	.310	.389	.472	.555
24	.020	.034	.056	.087	.128	.180	.243	.314	.392	.473
25	.012	.022	.038	.060	.092	.134	.185	.247	.318	.394

λ	24	25	26	27	28	29	30	31	32	33
16	.978	.987	.993	.996	.998	.999	.999	1.000		
17	.959	.975	.985	.991	.995	.997	.999	.999	1.000	
18	.932	.955	.972	.983	.990	.994	.997	.998	.999	1.000
19	.893	.927	.951	.969	.980	.988	.993	.996	.998	.999
20	.843	.888	.922	.948	.966	.978	.987	.992	.995	.997
21	.782	.838	.883	.917	.944	.963	.976	.985	.991	.994
22	.712	.777	.832	.877	.913	.940	.959	.973	.983	.989
23	.635	.708	.772	.827	.873	.908	.936	.956	.971	.981
24	.554	.632	.704	.768	.823	.868	.904	.932	.953	.969
25	.473	.553	.629	.700	.763	.818	.863	.900	.929	.950

λ	34	35	36	37	38	39	40	41	42	43
19	.999	1.000								
20	.999	.999	1.000							
21	.997	.998	.999	.999	1.000					
22	.994	.996	.998	.999	.999	1.000				
23	.988	.993	.996	.997	.999	.999	1.000			
24	.979	.987	.992	.995	.997	.998	.999	.999	1.000	
25	.966	.978	.985	.991	.991	.997	.998	.999	.999	1.000

TABLE IV   Normal Curve Areas

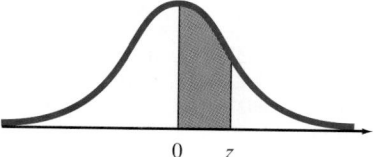

z	.00	.01	.02	.03	.04	.05	.06	.07	.08	.09
.0	.0000	.0040	.0080	.0120	.0160	.0199	.0239	.0279	.0319	.0359
.1	.0398	.0438	.0478	.0517	.0557	.0596	.0636	.0675	.0714	.0753
.2	.0793	.0832	.0871	.0910	.0948	.0987	.1026	.1064	.1103	.1141
.3	.1179	.1217	.1255	.1293	.1331	.1368	.1406	.1443	.1480	.1517
.4	.1554	.1591	.1628	.1664	.1700	.1736	.1772	.1808	.1844	.1879
.5	.1915	.1950	.1985	.2019	.2054	.2088	.2123	.2157	.2190	.2224
.6	.2257	.2291	.2324	.2357	.2389	.2422	.2454	.2486	.2517	.2549
.7	.2580	.2611	.2642	.2673	.2704	.2734	.2764	.2794	.2823	.2852
.8	.2881	.2910	.2939	.2967	.2995	.3023	.3051	.3078	.3106	.3133
.9	.3159	.3186	.3212	.3238	.3264	.3289	.3315	.3340	.3365	.3389
1.0	.3413	.3438	.3461	.3485	.3508	.3531	.3554	.3577	.3599	.3621
1.1	.3643	.3665	.3686	.3708	.3729	.3749	.3770	.3790	.3810	.3830
1.2	.3849	.3869	.3888	.3907	.3925	.3944	.3962	.3980	.3997	.4015
1.3	.4032	.4049	.4066	.4082	.4099	.4115	.4131	.4147	.4162	.4177
1.4	.4192	.4207	.4222	.4236	.4251	.4265	.4279	.4292	.4306	.4319
1.5	.4332	.4345	.4357	.4370	.4382	.4394	.4406	.4418	.4429	.4441
1.6	.4452	.4463	.4474	.4484	.4495	.4505	.4515	.4525	.4535	.4545
1.7	.4554	.4564	.4573	.4582	.4591	.4599	.4608	.4616	.4625	.4633
1.8	.4641	.4649	.4656	.4664	.4671	.4678	.4686	.4693	.4699	.4706
1.9	.4713	.4719	.4726	.4732	.4738	.4744	.4750	.4756	.4761	.4767
2.0	.4772	.4778	.4783	.4788	.4793	.4798	.4803	.4808	.4812	.4817
2.1	.4821	.4826	.4830	.4834	.4838	.4842	.4846	.4850	.4854	.4857
2.2	.4861	.4864	.4868	.4871	.4875	.4878	.4881	.4884	.4887	.4890
2.3	.4893	.4896	.4898	.4901	.4904	.4906	.4909	.4911	.4913	.4916
2.4	.4918	.4920	.4922	.4925	.4927	.4929	.4931	.4932	.4934	.4936
2.5	.4938	.4940	.4941	.4943	.4945	.4946	.4948	.4949	.4951	.4952
2.6	.4953	.4955	.4956	.4957	.4959	.4960	.4961	.4962	.4963	.4964
2.7	.4965	.4966	.4967	.4968	.4969	.4970	.4971	.4972	.4973	.4974
2.8	.4974	.4975	.4976	.4977	.4977	.4978	.4979	.4979	.4980	.4981
2.9	.4981	.4982	.4982	.4983	.4984	.4984	.4985	.4985	.4986	.4986
3.0	.4987	.4987	.4987	.4988	.4988	.4989	.4989	.4989	.4990	.4990

Source: Abridged from Table I of A. Hald, *Statistical Tables and Formulas* (New York: Wiley), 1952. Reproduced by permission of A. Hald.

TABLE V Exponentials

λ	$e^{-\lambda}$	λ	$e^{-\lambda}$	λ	$e^{-\lambda}$	λ	$e^{-\lambda}$	λ	$e^{-\lambda}$
.00	1.000000	2.05	.128735	4.05	.017422	6.05	.002358	8.05	.000319
.05	.951229	2.10	.122456	4.10	.016573	6.10	.002243	8.10	.000304
.10	.904837	2.15	.116484	4.15	.015764	6.15	.002133	8.15	.000289
.15	.860708	2.20	.110803	4.20	.014996	6.20	.002029	8.20	.000275
.20	.818731	2.25	.105399	4.25	.014264	6.25	.001930	8.25	.000261
.25	.778801	2.30	.100259	4.30	.013569	6.30	.001836	8.30	.000249
.30	.740818	2.35	.095369	4.35	.012907	6.35	.001747	8.35	.000236
.35	.704688	2.40	.090718	4.40	.012277	6.40	.001661	8.40	.000225
.40	.670320	2.45	.086294	4.45	.011679	6.45	.001581	8.45	.000214
.45	.637628	2.50	.082085	4.50	.011109	6.50	.001503	8.50	.000204
.50	.606531	2.55	.078082	4.55	.010567	6.55	.001430	8.55	.000194
.55	.576950	2.60	.074274	4.60	.010052	6.60	.001360	8.60	.000184
.60	.548812	2.65	.070651	4.65	.009562	6.65	.001294	8.65	.000175
.65	.522046	2.70	.067206	4.70	.009095	6.70	.001231	8.70	.000167
.70	.496585	2.75	.063928	4.75	.008652	6.75	.001171	8.75	.000158
.75	.472367	2.80	.060810	4.80	.008230	6.80	.001114	8.80	.000151
.80	.449329	2.85	.057844	4.85	.007828	6.85	.001059	8.85	.000143
.85	.427415	2.90	.055023	4.90	.007447	6.90	.001008	8.90	.000136
.90	.406570	2.95	.052340	4.95	.007083	6.95	.000959	8.95	.000130
.95	.386741	3.00	.049787	5.00	.006738	7.00	.000912	9.00	.000123
1.00	.367879	3.05	.047359	5.05	.006409	7.05	.000867	9.05	.000117
1.05	.349938	3.10	.045049	5.10	.006097	7.10	.000825	9.10	.000112
1.10	.332871	3.15	.042852	5.15	.005799	7.15	.000785	9.15	.000106
1.15	.316637	3.20	.040762	5.20	.005517	7.20	.000747	9.20	.000101
1.20	.301194	3.25	.038774	5.25	.005248	7.25	.000710	9.25	.000096
1.25	.286505	3.30	.036883	5.30	.004992	7.30	.000676	9.30	.000091
1.30	.272532	3.35	.035084	5.35	.004748	7.35	.000643	9.35	.000087
1.35	.259240	3.40	.033373	5.40	.004517	7.40	.000611	9.40	.000083
1.40	.246597	3.45	.031746	5.45	.004296	7.45	.000581	9.45	.000079
1.45	.234570	3.50	.030197	5.50	.004087	7.50	.000553	9.50	.000075
1.50	.223130	3.55	.028725	5.55	.003887	7.55	.000526	9.55	.000071
1.55	.212248	3.60	.027324	5.60	.003698	7.60	.000501	9.60	.000068
1.60	.201897	3.65	.025991	5.65	.003518	7.65	.000476	9.65	.000064
1.65	.192050	3.70	.024724	5.70	.003346	7.70	.000453	9.70	.000061
1.70	.182684	3.75	.023518	5.75	.003183	7.75	.000431	9.75	.000058
1.75	.173774	3.80	.022371	5.80	.003028	7.80	.000410	9.80	.000056
1.80	.165299	3.85	.021280	5.85	.002880	7.85	.000390	9.85	.000053
1.85	.157237	3.90	.020242	5.90	.002739	7.90	.000371	9.90	.000050
1.90	.149569	3.95	.019255	5.95	.002606	7.95	.000353	9.95	.000048
1.95	.142274	4.00	.018316	6.00	.002479	8.00	.000336	10.00	.000045
2.00	.135335								

TABLE VI   Critical Values of t

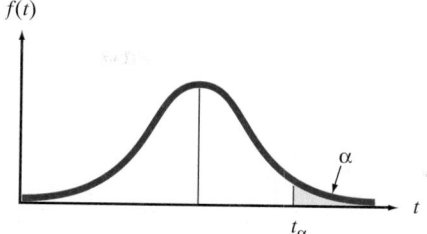

$f(t)$

v	$t_{.100}$	$t_{.050}$	$t_{.025}$	$t_{.010}$	$t_{.005}$	$t_{.001}$	$t_{.0005}$
1	3.078	6.314	12.706	31.821	63.657	318.31	636.62
2	1.886	2.920	4.303	6.965	9.925	22.326	31.598
3	1.638	2.353	3.182	4.541	5.841	10.213	12.924
4	1.533	2.132	2.776	3.747	4.604	7.173	8.610
5	1.476	2.015	2.571	3.365	4.032	5.893	6.869
6	1.440	1.943	2.447	3.143	3.707	5.208	5.959
7	1.415	1.895	2.365	2.998	3.499	4.785	5.408
8	1.397	1.860	2.306	2.896	3.355	4.501	5.041
9	1.383	1.833	2.262	2.821	3.250	4.297	4.781
10	1.372	1.812	2.228	2.764	3.169	4.144	4.587
11	1.363	1.796	2.201	2.718	3.106	4.025	4.437
12	1.356	1.782	2.179	2.681	3.055	3.930	4.318
13	1.350	1.771	2.160	2.650	3.012	3.852	4.221
14	1.345	1.761	2.145	2.624	2.977	3.787	4.140
15	1.341	1.753	2.131	2.602	2.947	3.733	4.073
16	1.337	1.746	2.120	2.583	2.921	3.686	4.015
17	1.333	1.740	2.110	2.567	2.898	3.646	3.965
18	1.330	1.734	2.101	2.552	2.878	3.610	3.922
19	1.328	1.729	2.093	2.539	2.861	3.579	3.883
20	1.325	1.725	2.086	2.528	2.845	3.552	3.850
21	1.323	1.721	2.080	2.518	2.831	3.527	3.819
22	1.321	1.717	2.074	2.508	2.819	3.505	3.792
23	1.319	1.714	2.069	2.500	2.807	3.485	3.767
24	1.318	1.711	2.064	2.492	2.797	3.467	3.745
25	1.316	1.708	2.060	2.485	2.787	3.450	3.725
26	1.315	1.706	2.056	2.479	2.779	3.435	3.707
27	1.314	1.703	2.052	2.473	2.771	3.421	3.690
28	1.313	1.701	2.048	2.467	2.763	3.408	3.674
29	1.311	1.699	2.045	2.462	2.756	3.396	3.659
30	1.310	1.697	2.042	2.457	2.750	3.385	3.646
40	1.303	1.684	2.021	2.423	2.704	3.307	3.551
60	1.296	1.671	2.000	2.390	2.660	3.232	3.460
120	1.289	1.658	1.980	2.358	2.617	3.160	3.373
∞	1.282	1.645	1.960	2.326	2.576	3.090	3.291

Source: This table is reproduced with the kind permission of the Trustees of Biometrika from E. S. Pearson and H. O. Hartley (eds.), *The Biometrika Tables for Statisticians*, Vol. 1, 3d ed., Biometrika, 1966.

TABLE VII Percentage Points of the *F*-distribution, $\alpha = .10$

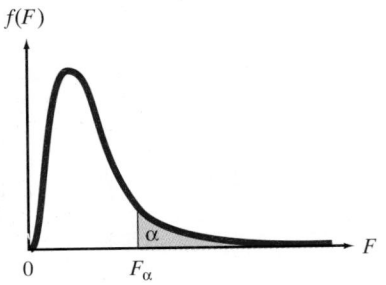

ν_1	NUMERATOR DEGREES OF FREEDOM								
ν_2	1	2	3	4	5	6	7	8	9
1	39.86	49.50	53.59	55.83	57.24	58.20	58.91	59.44	59.86
2	8.53	9.00	9.16	9.24	9.29	9.33	9.35	9.37	9.38
3	5.54	5.46	5.39	5.34	5.31	5.28	5.27	5.25	5.24
4	4.54	4.32	4.19	4.11	4.05	4.01	3.98	3.95	3.94
5	4.06	3.78	3.62	3.52	3.45	3.40	3.37	3.34	3.32
6	3.78	3.46	3.29	3.18	3.11	3.05	3.01	2.98	2.96
7	3.59	3.26	3.07	2.96	2.88	2.83	2.78	2.75	2.72
8	3.46	3.11	2.92	2.81	2.73	2.67	2.62	2.59	2.56
9	3.36	3.01	2.81	2.69	2.61	2.55	2.51	2.47	2.44
10	3.29	2.92	2.73	2.61	2.52	2.46	2.41	2.38	2.35
11	3.23	2.86	2.66	2.54	2.45	2.39	2.34	2.30	2.27
12	3.18	2.81	2.61	2.48	2.39	2.33	2.28	2.24	2.21
13	3.14	2.76	2.56	2.43	2.35	2.28	2.23	2.20	2.16
14	3.10	2.73	2.52	2.39	2.31	2.24	2.19	2.15	2.12
15	3.07	2.70	2.49	2.36	2.27	2.21	2.16	2.12	2.09
16	3.05	2.67	2.46	2.33	2.24	2.18	2.13	2.09	2.06
17	3.03	2.64	2.44	2.31	2.22	2.15	2.10	2.06	2.03
18	3.01	2.62	2.42	2.29	2.20	2.13	2.08	2.04	2.00
19	2.99	2.61	2.40	2.27	2.18	2.11	2.06	2.02	1.98
20	2.97	2.59	2.38	2.25	2.16	2.09	2.04	2.00	1.96
21	2.96	2.57	2.36	2.23	2.14	2.08	2.02	1.98	1.95
22	2.95	2.56	2.35	2.22	2.13	2.06	2.01	1.97	1.93
23	2.94	2.55	2.34	2.21	2.11	2.05	1.99	1.95	1.92
24	2.93	2.54	2.33	2.19	2.10	2.04	1.98	1.94	1.91
25	2.92	2.53	2.32	2.18	2.09	2.02	1.97	1.93	1.89
26	2.91	2.52	2.31	2.17	2.08	2.01	1.96	1.92	1.88
27	2.90	2.51	2.30	2.17	2.07	2.00	1.95	1.91	1.87
28	2.89	2.50	2.29	2.16	2.06	2.00	1.94	1.90	1.87
29	2.89	2.50	2.28	2.15	2.06	1.99	1.93	1.89	1.86
30	2.88	2.49	2.28	2.14	2.05	1.98	1.93	1.88	1.85
40	2.84	2.44	2.23	2.09	2.00	1.93	1.87	1.83	1.79
60	2.79	2.39	2.18	2.04	1.95	1.87	1.82	1.77	1.74
120	2.75	2.35	2.13	1.99	1.90	1.82	1.77	1.72	1.68
∞	2.71	2.30	2.08	1.94	1.85	1.77	1.72	1.67	1.63

Source: From M. Merrington and C. M. Thompson, "Tables of Percentage Points of the Inverted Beta (*F*)-Distribution," *Biometrika*, 1943, 33, 73–88. Reproduced by permission of the *Biometrika* Trustees.

TABLE VII   Continued

DENOMINATOR DEGREES OF FREEDOM

ν_2 \ ν_1	NUMERATOR DEGREES OF FREEDOM									
	10	**12**	**15**	**20**	**24**	**30**	**40**	**60**	**120**	**∞**
1	60.19	60.71	61.22	61.74	62.00	62.26	62.53	62.79	63.06	63.33
2	9.39	9.41	9.42	9.44	9.45	9.46	9.47	9.47	9.48	9.49
3	5.23	5.22	5.20	5.18	5.18	5.17	5.16	5.15	5.14	5.13
4	3.92	3.90	3.87	3.84	3.83	3.82	3.80	3.79	3.78	3.76
5	3.30	3.27	3.24	3.21	3.19	3.17	3.16	3.14	3.12	3.10
6	2.94	2.90	2.87	2.84	2.82	2.80	2.78	2.76	2.74	2.72
7	2.70	2.67	2.63	2.59	2.58	2.56	2.54	2.51	2.49	2.47
8	2.54	2.50	2.46	2.42	2.40	2.38	2.36	2.34	2.32	2.29
9	2.42	2.38	2.34	2.30	2.28	2.25	2.23	2.21	2.18	2.16
10	2.32	2.28	2.24	2.20	2.18	2.16	2.13	2.11	2.08	2.06
11	2.25	2.21	2.17	2.12	2.10	2.08	2.05	2.03	2.00	1.97
12	2.19	2.15	2.10	2.06	2.04	2.01	1.99	1.96	1.93	1.90
13	2.14	2.10	2.05	2.01	1.98	1.96	1.93	1.90	1.88	1.85
14	2.10	2.05	2.01	1.96	1.94	1.91	1.89	1.86	1.83	1.80
15	2.06	2.02	1.97	1.92	1.90	1.87	1.85	1.82	1.79	1.76
16	2.03	1.99	1.94	1.89	1.87	1.84	1.81	1.78	1.75	1.72
17	2.00	1.96	1.91	1.86	1.84	1.81	1.78	1.75	1.72	1.69
18	1.98	1.93	1.89	1.84	1.81	1.78	1.75	1.72	1.69	1.66
19	1.96	1.91	1.86	1.81	1.79	1.76	1.73	1.70	1.67	1.63
20	1.94	1.89	1.84	1.79	1.77	1.74	1.71	1.68	1.64	1.61
21	1.92	1.87	1.83	1.78	1.75	1.72	1.69	1.66	1.62	1.59
22	1.90	1.86	1.81	1.76	1.73	1.70	1.67	1.64	1.60	1.57
23	1.89	1.84	1.80	1.74	1.72	1.69	1.66	1.62	1.59	1.55
24	1.88	1.83	1.78	1.73	1.70	1.67	1.64	1.61	1.57	1.53
25	1.87	1.82	1.77	1.72	1.69	1.66	1.63	1.59	1.56	1.52
26	1.86	1.81	1.76	1.71	1.68	1.65	1.61	1.58	1.54	1.50
27	1.85	1.80	1.75	1.70	1.67	1.64	1.60	1.57	1.53	1.49
28	1.84	1.79	1.74	1.69	1.66	1.63	1.59	1.56	1.52	1.48
29	1.83	1.78	1.73	1.68	1.65	1.62	1.58	1.55	1.51	1.47
30	1.82	1.77	1.72	1.67	1.64	1.61	1.57	1.54	1.50	1.46
40	1.76	1.71	1.66	1.61	1.57	1.54	1.51	1.47	1.42	1.38
60	1.71	1.66	1.60	1.54	1.51	1.48	1.44	1.40	1.35	1.29
120	1.65	1.60	1.55	1.48	1.45	1.41	1.37	1.32	1.26	1.19
∞	1.60	1.55	1.49	1.42	1.38	1.34	1.30	1.24	1.17	1.00

TABLE VIII Percentage Points of the *F*-distribution, $\alpha = .05$

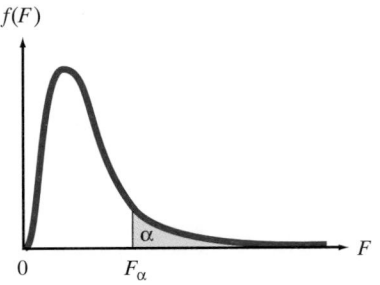

ν_1				NUMERATOR DEGREES OF FREEDOM					
ν_2	1	2	3	4	5	6	7	8	9
1	161.4	199.5	215.7	224.6	230.2	234.0	236.8	238.9	240.5
2	18.51	19.00	19.16	19.25	19.30	19.33	19.35	19.37	19.38
3	10.13	9.55	9.28	9.12	9.01	8.94	8.89	8.85	8.81
4	7.71	6.94	6.59	6.39	6.26	6.16	6.09	6.04	6.00
5	6.61	5.79	5.41	5.19	5.05	4.95	4.88	4.82	4.77
6	5.99	5.14	4.76	4.53	4.39	4.28	4.21	4.15	4.10
7	5.59	4.74	4.35	4.12	3.97	3.87	3.79	3.73	3.68
8	5.32	4.46	4.07	3.84	3.69	3.58	3.50	3.44	3.39
9	5.12	4.26	3.86	3.63	3.48	3.37	3.29	3.23	3.18
10	4.96	4.10	3.71	3.48	3.33	3.22	3.14	3.07	3.02
11	4.84	3.98	3.59	3.36	3.20	3.09	3.01	2.95	2.90
12	4.75	3.89	3.49	3.26	3.11	3.00	2.91	2.85	2.80
13	4.67	3.81	3.41	3.18	3.03	2.92	2.83	2.77	2.71
14	4.60	3.74	3.34	3.11	2.96	2.85	2.76	2.70	2.65
15	4.54	3.68	3.29	3.06	2.90	2.79	2.71	2.64	2.59
16	4.49	3.63	3.24	3.01	2.85	2.74	2.66	2.59	2.54
17	4.45	3.59	3.20	2.96	2.81	2.70	2.61	2.55	2.49
18	4.41	3.55	3.16	2.93	2.77	2.66	2.58	2.51	2.46
19	4.38	3.52	3.13	2.90	2.74	2.63	2.54	2.48	2.42
20	4.35	3.49	3.10	2.87	2.71	2.60	2.51	2.45	2.39
21	4.32	3.47	3.07	2.84	2.68	2.57	2.49	2.42	2.37
22	4.30	3.44	3.05	2.82	2.66	2.55	2.46	2.40	2.34
23	4.28	3.42	3.03	2.80	2.64	2.53	2.44	2.37	2.32
24	4.26	3.40	3.01	2.78	2.62	2.51	2.42	2.36	2.30
25	4.24	3.39	2.99	2.76	2.60	2.49	2.40	2.34	2.28
26	4.23	3.37	2.98	2.74	2.59	2.47	2.39	2.32	2.77
27	4.21	3.35	2.96	2.73	2.57	2.46	2.37	2.31	2.25
28	4.20	3.34	2.95	2.71	2.56	2.45	2.36	2.29	2.24
29	4.18	3.33	2.93	2.70	2.55	2.43	2.35	2.28	2.22
30	4.17	3.32	2.92	2.69	2.53	2.42	2.33	2.27	2.21
40	4.08	3.23	2.84	2.61	2.45	2.34	2.25	2.18	2.12
60	4.00	3.15	2.76	2.53	2.37	2.25	2.17	2.10	2.04
120	3.92	3.07	2.68	2.45	2.29	2.17	2.09	2.02	1.96
∞	3.84	3.00	2.60	2.37	2.21	2.10	2.01	1.94	1.88

DENOMINATOR DEGREES OF FREEDOM

Source: From M. Merrington and C. M. Thompson, "Tables of Percentage Points of the Inverted Beta (*F*)-Distribution." *Biometrika*, 1943, 33, 73–88. Reproduced by permission of the *Biometrika* Trustees.

TABLE VIII Continued

ν_2 \ ν_1	NUMERATOR DEGREES OF FREEDOM

ν_2	10	12	15	20	24	30	40	60	120	∞
1	241.9	243.9	245.9	248.0	249.1	250.1	251.1	252.2	253.3	254.3
2	19.40	19.41	19.43	19.45	19.45	19.46	19.47	19.48	19.49	19.50
3	8.79	8.74	8.70	8.66	8.64	8.62	8.59	8.57	8.55	8.53
4	5.96	5.91	5.86	5.80	5.77	5.75	5.72	5.69	5.66	5.63
5	4.74	4.68	4.62	4.56	4.53	4.50	4.46	4.43	4.40	4.36
6	4.06	4.00	3.94	3.87	3.84	3.81	3.77	3.74	3.70	3.67
7	3.64	3.57	3.51	3.44	3.41	3.38	3.34	3.30	3.27	3.23
8	3.35	3.28	3.22	3.15	3.12	3.08	3.04	3.01	2.97	2.93
9	3.14	3.07	3.01	2.94	2.90	2.86	2.83	2.79	2.75	2.71
10	2.98	2.91	2.85	2.77	2.74	2.70	2.66	2.62	2.58	2.54
11	2.85	2.79	2.72	2.65	2.61	2.57	2.53	2.49	2.45	2.40
12	2.75	2.69	2.62	2.54	2.51	2.47	2.43	2.38	2.34	2.30
13	2.67	2.60	2.53	2.46	2.42	2.38	2.34	2.30	2.25	2.21
14	2.60	2.53	2.46	2.39	2.35	2.31	2.27	2.22	2.18	2.13
15	2.54	2.48	2.40	2.33	2.29	2.25	2.20	2.16	2.11	2.07
16	2.49	2.42	2.35	2.28	2.24	2.19	2.15	2.11	2.06	2.01
17	2.45	2.38	2.31	2.23	2.19	2.15	2.10	2.06	2.01	1.96
18	2.41	2.34	2.27	2.19	2.15	2.11	2.06	2.02	1.97	1.92
19	2.38	2.31	2.23	2.16	2.11	2.07	2.03	1.98	1.93	1.88
20	2.35	2.28	2.20	2.12	2.08	2.04	1.99	1.95	1.90	1.84
21	2.32	2.25	2.18	2.10	2.05	2.01	1.96	1.92	1.87	1.81
22	2.30	2.23	2.15	2.07	2.03	1.98	1.94	1.89	1.84	1.78
23	2.27	2.20	2.13	2.05	2.01	1.96	1.91	1.86	1.81	1.76
24	2.25	2.18	2.11	2.03	1.98	1.94	1.89	1.84	1.79	1.73
25	2.24	2.16	2.09	2.01	1.96	1.92	1.87	1.82	1.77	1.71
26	2.22	2.15	2.07	1.99	1.95	1.90	1.85	1.80	1.75	1.69
27	2.20	2.13	2.06	1.97	1.93	1.88	1.84	1.79	1.73	1.67
28	2.19	2.12	2.04	1.96	1.91	1.87	1.82	1.77	1.71	1.65
29	2.18	2.10	2.03	1.94	1.90	1.85	1.81	1.75	1.70	1.64
30	2.16	2.09	2.01	1.93	1.89	1.84	1.79	1.74	1.68	1.62
40	2.08	2.00	1.92	1.84	1.79	1.74	1.69	1.64	1.58	1.51
60	1.99	1.92	1.84	1.75	1.70	1.65	1.59	1.53	1.47	1.39
120	1.91	1.83	1.75	1.66	1.61	1.55	1.50	1.43	1.35	1.25
∞	1.83	1.75	1.67	1.57	1.52	1.46	1.39	1.32	1.22	1.00

DENOMINATOR DEGREES OF FREEDOM

TABLE IX   Percentage Points of the *F*-distribution, $\alpha = .025$

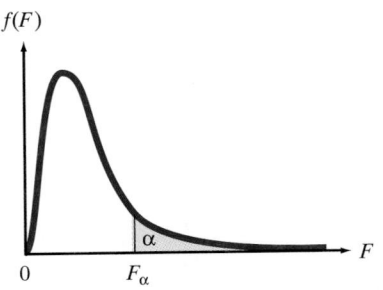

ν_2 \ ν_1	NUMERATOR DEGREES OF FREEDOM								
	1	**2**	**3**	**4**	**5**	**6**	**7**	**8**	**9**
1	647.8	799.5	864.2	899.6	921.8	937.1	948.2	956.7	963.3
2	38.51	39.00	39.17	39.25	39.30	39.33	39.36	39.37	39.39
3	17.44	16.04	15.44	15.10	14.88	14.73	14.62	14.54	14.47
4	12.22	10.65	9.98	9.60	9.36	9.20	9.07	8.98	8.90
5	10.01	8.43	7.76	7.39	7.15	6.98	6.85	6.76	6.68
6	8.81	7.26	6.60	6.23	5.99	5.82	5.70	5.60	5.52
7	8.07	6.54	5.89	5.52	5.29	5.12	4.99	4.90	4.82
8	7.57	6.06	5.42	5.05	4.82	4.65	4.53	4.43	4.36
9	7.21	5.71	5.08	4.72	4.48	4.32	4.20	4.10	4.03
10	6.94	5.46	4.83	4.47	4.24	4.07	3.95	3.85	3.78
11	6.72	5.26	4.63	4.28	4.04	3.88	3.76	3.66	3.59
12	6.55	5.10	4.47	4.12	3.89	3.73	3.61	3.51	3.44
13	6.41	4.97	4.35	4.00	3.77	3.60	3.48	3.39	3.31
14	6.30	4.86	4.24	3.89	3.66	3.50	3.38	3.29	3.21
15	6.20	4.77	4.15	3.80	3.58	3.41	3.29	3.20	3.12
16	6.12	4.69	4.08	3.73	3.50	3.34	3.22	3.12	3.05
17	6.04	4.62	4.01	3.66	3.44	3.28	3.16	3.06	2.98
18	5.98	4.56	3.95	3.61	3.38	3.22	3.10	3.01	2.93
19	5.92	4.51	3.90	3.56	3.33	3.17	3.05	2.96	2.88
20	5.87	4.46	3.86	3.51	3.29	3.13	3.01	2.91	2.84
21	5.83	4.42	3.82	3.48	3.25	3.09	2.97	2.87	2.80
22	5.79	4.38	3.78	3.44	3.22	3.05	2.93	2.84	2.76
23	5.75	4.35	3.75	3.41	3.18	3.02	2.90	2.81	2.73
24	5.72	4.32	3.72	3.38	3.15	2.99	2.87	2.78	2.70
25	5.69	4.29	3.69	3.35	3.13	2.97	2.85	2.75	2.68
26	5.66	4.27	3.67	3.33	3.10	2.94	2.82	2.73	2.65
27	5.63	4.24	3.65	3.31	3.08	2.92	2.80	2.71	2.63
28	5.61	4.22	3.63	3.29	3.06	2.90	2.78	2.69	2.61
29	5.59	4.20	3.61	3.27	3.04	2.88	2.76	2.67	2.59
30	5.57	4.18	3.59	3.25	3.03	2.87	2.75	2.65	2.57
40	5.42	4.05	3.46	3.13	2.90	2.74	2.62	2.53	2.45
60	5.29	3.93	3.34	3.01	2.79	2.63	2.51	2.41	2.33
120	5.15	3.80	3.23	2.89	2.67	2.52	2.39	2.30	2.22
∞	5.02	3.69	3.12	2.79	2.57	2.41	2.29	2.19	2.11

Source: From M. Merrington and C. M. Thompson, "Tables of Percentage Points of the Inverted Beta (*F*)-Distribution," *Biometrika*, 1943, 33, 73–88. Reproduced by permission of the *Biometrika* Trustees.

Table IX Continued

ν_2 \ ν_1	NUMERATOR DEGREES OF FREEDOM									
	10	**12**	**15**	**20**	**24**	**30**	**40**	**60**	**120**	**∞**
1	968.6	976.7	984.9	993.1	997.2	1,001	1,006	1,010	1,014	1,018
2	39.40	39.41	39.43	39.45	39.46	39.46	39.47	39.48	39.49	39.50
3	14.42	14.34	14.25	14.17	14.12	14.08	14.04	13.99	13.95	13.90
4	8.84	8.75	8.66	8.56	8.51	8.46	8.41	8.36	8.31	8.26
5	6.62	6.52	6.43	6.33	6.28	6.23	6.18	6.12	6.07	6.02
6	5.46	5.37	5.27	5.17	5.12	5.07	5.01	4.96	4.90	4.85
7	4.76	4.67	4.57	4.47	4.42	4.36	4.31	4.25	4.20	4.14
8	4.30	4.20	4.10	4.00	3.95	3.89	3.84	3.78	3.73	3.67
9	3.96	3.87	3.77	3.67	3.61	3.56	3.51	3.45	3.39	3.33
10	3.72	3.62	3.52	3.42	3.37	3.31	3.26	3.20	3.14	3.08
11	3.53	3.43	3.33	3.23	3.17	3.12	3.06	3.00	2.94	2.88
12	3.37	3.28	3.18	3.07	3.02	2.96	2.91	2.85	2.79	2.72
13	3.25	3.15	3.05	2.95	2.89	2.84	2.78	2.72	2.66	2.60
14	3.15	3.05	2.95	2.84	2.79	2.73	2.67	2.61	2.55	2.49
15	3.06	2.96	2.86	2.76	2.70	2.64	2.59	2.52	2.46	2.40
16	2.99	2.89	2.79	2.68	2.63	2.57	2.51	2.45	2.38	2.32
17	2.92	2.82	2.72	2.62	2.56	2.50	2.44	2.38	2.32	2.25
18	2.87	2.77	2.67	2.56	2.50	2.44	2.38	2.32	2.26	2.19
19	2.82	2.72	2.62	2.51	2.45	2.39	2.33	2.27	2.20	2.13
20	2.77	2.68	2.57	2.46	2.41	2.35	2.29	2.22	2.16	2.09
21	2.73	2.64	2.53	2.42	2.37	2.31	2.25	2.18	2.11	2.04
22	2.70	2.60	2.50	2.39	2.33	2.27	2.21	2.14	2.08	2.00
23	2.67	2.57	2.47	2.36	2.30	2.24	2.18	2.11	2.04	1.97
24	2.64	2.54	2.44	2.33	2.27	2.21	2.15	2.08	2.01	1.94
25	2.61	2.51	2.41	2.30	2.24	2.18	2.12	2.05	1.98	1.91
26	2.59	2.49	2.39	2.28	2.22	2.16	2.09	2.03	1.95	1.88
27	2.57	2.47	2.36	2.25	2.19	2.13	2.07	2.00	1.93	1.85
28	2.55	2.45	2.34	2.23	2.17	2.11	2.05	1.98	1.91	1.83
29	2.53	2.43	2.32	2.21	2.15	2.09	2.03	1.96	1.89	1.81
30	2.51	2.41	2.31	2.20	2.14	2.07	2.01	1.94	1.87	1.79
40	2.39	2.29	2.18	2.07	2.01	1.94	1.88	1.80	1.72	1.64
60	2.27	2.17	2.06	1.94	1.88	1.82	1.74	1.67	1.58	1.48
120	2.16	2.05	1.94	1.82	1.76	1.69	1.61	1.53	1.43	1.31
∞	2.05	1.94	1.83	1.71	1.64	1.57	1.48	1.39	1.27	1.00

DENOMINATOR DEGREES OF FREEDOM

TABLE X Percentage Points of the *F*-distribution, $\alpha = .01$

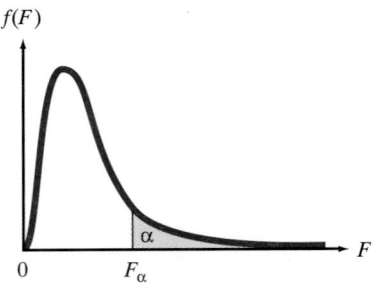

ν_2	\multicolumn{9}{c}{NUMERATOR DEGREES OF FREEDOM}

ν_2	1	2	3	4	5	6	7	8	9
1	4,052	4,999.5	5,403	5,625	5,764	5,859	5,928	5,982	6,022
2	98.50	99.00	99.17	99.25	99.30	99.33	99.36	99.37	99.39
3	34.12	30.82	29.46	28.71	28.24	27.91	27.67	27.49	27.35
4	21.20	18.00	16.69	15.98	15.52	15.21	14.98	14.80	14.66
5	16.26	13.27	12.06	11.39	10.97	10.67	10.46	10.29	10.16
6	13.75	10.92	9.78	9.15	8.75	8.47	8.26	8.10	7.98
7	12.25	9.55	8.45	7.85	7.46	7.19	6.99	6.84	6.72
8	11.26	8.65	7.59	7.01	6.63	6.37	6.18	6.03	5.91
9	10.56	8.02	6.99	6.42	6.06	5.80	5.61	5.47	5.35
10	10.04	7.56	6.55	5.99	5.64	5.39	5.20	5.06	4.94
11	9.65	7.21	6.22	5.67	5.32	5.07	4.89	4.74	4.63
12	9.33	6.93	5.95	5.41	5.06	4.82	4.64	4.50	4.39
13	9.07	6.70	5.74	5.21	4.86	4.62	4.44	4.30	4.19
14	8.86	6.51	5.56	5.04	4.69	4.46	4.28	4.14	4.03
15	8.68	6.36	5.42	4.89	4.56	4.32	4.14	4.00	3.89
16	8.53	6.23	5.29	4.77	4.44	4.20	4.03	3.89	3.78
17	8.40	6.11	5.18	4.67	4.34	4.10	3.93	3.79	3.68
18	8.29	6.01	5.09	4.58	4.25	4.01	3.84	3.71	3.60
19	8.18	5.93	5.01	4.50	4.17	3.94	3.77	3.63	3.52
20	8.10	5.85	4.94	4.43	4.10	3.87	3.70	3.56	3.46
21	8.02	5.78	4.87	4.37	4.04	3.81	3.64	3.51	3.40
22	7.95	5.72	4.82	4.31	3.99	3.76	3.59	3.45	3.35
23	7.88	5.66	4.76	4.26	3.94	3.71	3.54	3.41	3.30
24	7.82	5.61	4.72	4.22	3.90	3.67	3.50	3.36	3.26
25	7.77	5.57	4.68	4.18	3.85	3.63	3.46	3.32	3.22
26	7.72	5.53	4.64	4.14	3.82	3.59	3.42	3.29	3.18
27	7.68	5.49	4.60	4.11	3.78	3.56	3.39	3.26	3.15
28	7.64	5.45	4.57	4.07	3.75	3.53	3.36	3.23	3.12
29	7.60	5.42	4.54	4.04	3.73	3.50	3.33	3.20	3.09
30	7.56	5.39	4.51	4.02	3.70	3.47	3.30	3.17	3.07
40	7.31	5.18	4.31	3.83	3.51	3.29	3.12	2.99	2.89
60	7.08	4.98	4.13	3.65	3.34	3.12	2.95	2.82	2.72
120	6.85	4.79	3.95	3.48	3.17	2.96	2.79	2.66	2.56
∞	6.63	4.61	3.78	3.32	3.02	2.80	2.64	2.51	2.41

Source: From M. Merrington and C. M. Thompson, "Tables of Percentage Points of the Inverted Beta (*F*)-Distribution," *Biometrika,* 1943, 33, 73–88. Reproduced by permission of the *Biometrika* Trustees.

(DENOMINATOR DEGREES OF FREEDOM)

TABLE X Continued

v_2 \ v_1	10	12	15	20	24	30	40	60	120	∞
1	6,056	6,106	6,157	6,209	6,235	6,261	6,287	6,313	6,339	6,366
2	99.40	99.42	99.43	99.45	99.46	99.47	99.47	99.48	99.49	99.50
3	27.23	27.05	26.87	26.69	26.60	26.50	26.41	26.32	26.22	26.13
4	14.55	14.37	14.20	14.02	13.93	13.84	13.75	13.65	13.56	13.46
5	10.05	9.89	9.72	9.55	9.47	9.38	9.29	9.20	9.11	9.02
6	7.87	7.72	7.56	7.40	7.31	7.23	7.14	7.06	6.97	6.88
7	6.62	6.47	6.31	6.16	6.07	5.99	5.91	5.82	5.74	5.65
8	5.81	5.67	5.52	5.36	5.28	5.20	5.12	5.03	4.95	4.86
9	5.26	5.11	4.96	4.81	4.73	4.65	4.57	4.48	4.40	4.31
10	4.85	4.71	4.56	4.41	4.33	4.25	4.17	4.08	4.00	3.91
11	4.54	4.40	4.25	4.10	4.02	3.94	3.86	3.78	3.69	3.60
12	4.30	4.16	4.01	3.86	3.78	3.70	3.62	3.54	3.45	3.36
13	4.10	3.96	3.82	3.66	3.59	3.51	3.43	3.34	3.25	3.17
14	3.94	3.80	3.66	3.51	3.43	3.35	3.27	3.18	3.09	3.00
15	3.80	3.67	3.52	3.37	3.29	3.21	3.13	3.05	2.96	2.87
16	3.69	3.55	3.41	3.26	3.18	3.10	3.02	2.93	2.84	2.75
17	3.59	3.46	3.31	3.16	3.08	3.00	2.92	2.83	2.75	2.65
18	3.51	3.37	3.23	3.08	3.00	2.92	2.84	2.75	2.66	2.57
19	3.43	3.30	3.15	3.00	2.92	2.84	2.76	2.67	2.58	2.49
20	3.37	3.23	3.09	2.94	2.86	2.78	2.69	2.61	2.52	2.42
21	3.31	3.17	3.03	2.88	2.80	2.72	2.64	2.55	2.46	2.36
22	3.26	3.12	2.98	2.83	2.75	2.67	2.58	2.50	2.40	2.31
23	3.21	3.07	2.93	2.78	2.70	2.62	2.54	2.45	2.35	2.26
24	3.17	3.03	2.89	2.74	2.66	2.58	2.49	2.40	2.31	2.21
25	3.13	2.99	2.85	2.70	2.62	2.54	2.45	2.36	2.27	2.17
26	3.09	2.96	2.81	2.66	2.58	2.50	2.42	2.33	2.23	2.13
27	3.06	2.93	2.78	2.63	2.55	2.47	2.38	2.29	2.20	2.10
28	3.03	2.90	2.75	2.60	2.52	2.44	2.35	2.26	2.17	2.06
29	3.00	2.87	2.73	2.57	2.49	2.41	2.33	2.23	2.14	2.03
30	2.98	2.84	2.70	2.55	2.47	2.39	2.30	2.21	2.11	2.01
40	2.80	2.66	2.52	2.37	2.29	2.20	2.11	2.02	1.92	1.80
60	2.63	2.50	2.35	2.20	2.12	2.03	1.94	1.84	1.73	1.60
120	2.47	2.34	2.19	2.03	1.95	1.86	1.76	1.66	1.53	1.38
∞	2.32	2.18	2.04	1.88	1.79	1.70	1.59	1.47	1.32	1.00

NUMERATOR DEGREES OF FREEDOM / DENOMINATOR DEGREES OF FREEDOM

TABLE XI   Critical Values of T_L and T_U for the Wilcoxon Rank Sum Test: Independent Samples

Test statistic is the rank sum associated with the smaller sample (if equal sample sizes, either rank sum can be used).

a. $\alpha = .025$ one-tailed; $\alpha = .05$ two-tailed

n_2 \ n_1	3 T_L	3 T_U	4 T_L	4 T_U	5 T_L	5 T_U	6 T_L	6 T_U	7 T_L	7 T_U	8 T_L	8 T_U	9 T_L	9 T_U	10 T_L	10 T_U
3	5	16	6	18	6	21	7	23	7	26	8	28	8	31	9	33
4	6	18	11	25	12	28	12	32	13	35	14	38	15	41	16	44
5	6	21	12	28	18	37	19	41	20	45	21	49	22	53	24	56
6	7	23	12	32	19	41	26	52	28	56	29	61	31	65	32	70
7	7	26	13	35	20	45	28	56	37	68	39	73	41	78	43	83
8	8	28	14	38	21	49	29	61	39	73	49	87	51	93	54	98
9	8	31	15	41	22	53	31	65	41	78	51	93	63	108	66	114
10	9	33	16	44	24	56	32	70	43	83	54	98	66	114	79	131

b. $\alpha = .05$ one-tailed; $\alpha = .10$ two-tailed

n_2 \ n_1	3 T_L	3 T_U	4 T_L	4 T_U	5 T_L	5 T_U	6 T_L	6 T_U	7 T_L	7 T_U	8 T_L	8 T_U	9 T_L	9 T_U	10 T_L	10 T_U
3	6	15	7	17	7	20	8	22	9	24	9	27	10	29	11	31
4	7	17	12	24	13	27	14	30	15	33	16	36	17	39	18	42
5	7	20	13	27	19	36	20	40	22	43	24	46	25	50	26	54
6	8	22	14	30	20	40	28	50	30	54	32	58	33	63	35	67
7	9	24	15	33	22	43	30	54	39	66	41	71	43	76	46	80
8	9	27	16	36	24	46	32	58	41	71	52	84	54	90	57	95
9	10	29	17	39	25	50	33	63	43	76	54	90	66	105	69	111
10	11	31	18	42	26	54	35	67	46	80	57	95	69	111	83	127

Source: From F. Wilcoxon and R. A. Wilcox, "Some Rapid Approximate Statistical Procedures," 1964, 20–23. Courtesy of Lederle Laboratories Division of American Cyanamid Company, Madison, NJ.

TABLE XII   Critical Values of T_0 in the Wilcoxon Paired Difference Signed Rank Test

One-Tailed	Two-Tailed	$n = 5$	$n = 6$	$n = 7$	$n = 8$	$n = 9$	$n = 10$
$\alpha = .05$	$\alpha = .10$	1	2	4	6	8	11
$\alpha = .025$	$\alpha = .05$		1	2	4	6	8
$\alpha = .01$	$\alpha = .02$			0	2	3	5
$\alpha = .005$	$\alpha = .01$				0	2	3
		$n = 11$	$n = 12$	$n = 13$	$n = 14$	$n = 15$	$n = 16$
$\alpha = .05$	$\alpha = .10$	14	17	21	26	30	36
$\alpha = .025$	$\alpha = .05$	11	14	17	21	25	30
$\alpha = .01$	$\alpha = .02$	7	10	13	16	20	24
$\alpha = .005$	$\alpha = .01$	5	7	10	13	16	19
		$n = 17$	$n = 18$	$n = 19$	$n = 20$	$n = 21$	$n = 22$
$\alpha = .05$	$\alpha = .10$	41	47	54	60	68	75
$\alpha = .025$	$\alpha = .05$	35	40	46	52	59	66
$\alpha = .01$	$\alpha = .02$	28	33	38	43	49	56
$\alpha = .005$	$\alpha = .01$	23	28	32	37	43	49
		$n = 23$	$n = 24$	$n = 25$	$n = 26$	$n = 27$	$n = 28$
$\alpha = .05$	$\alpha = .10$	83	92	101	110	120	130
$\alpha = .025$	$\alpha = .05$	73	81	90	98	107	117
$\alpha = .01$	$\alpha = .02$	62	69	77	85	93	102
$\alpha = .005$	$\alpha = .01$	55	61	68	76	84	92
		$n = 29$	$n = 30$	$n = 31$	$n = 32$	$n = 33$	$n = 34$
$\alpha = .05$	$\alpha = .10$	141	152	163	175	188	201
$\alpha = .025$	$\alpha = .05$	127	137	148	159	171	183
$\alpha = .01$	$\alpha = .02$	111	120	130	141	151	162
$\alpha = .005$	$\alpha = .01$	100	109	118	128	138	149
		$n = 35$	$n = 36$	$n = 37$	$n = 38$	$n = 39$	
$\alpha = .05$	$\alpha = .10$	214	228	242	256	271	
$\alpha = .025$	$\alpha = .05$	195	208	222	235	250	
$\alpha = .01$	$\alpha = .02$	174	186	198	211	224	
$\alpha = .005$	$\alpha = .01$	160	171	183	195	208	
		$n = 40$	$n = 41$	$n = 42$	$n = 43$	$n = 44$	$n = 45$
$\alpha = .05$	$\alpha = .10$	287	303	319	336	353	371
$\alpha = .025$	$\alpha = .05$	264	279	295	311	327	344
$\alpha = .01$	$\alpha = .02$	238	252	267	281	297	313
$\alpha = .005$	$\alpha = .01$	221	234	248	262	277	292
		$n = 46$	$n = 47$	$n = 48$	$n = 49$	$n = 50$	
$\alpha = .05$	$\alpha = .10$	389	408	427	446	466	
$\alpha = .025$	$\alpha = .05$	361	379	397	415	434	
$\alpha = .01$	$\alpha = .02$	329	345	362	380	398	
$\alpha = .005$	$\alpha = .01$	307	323	339	356	373	

Source: From F. Wilcoxon and R. A. Wilcox, "Some Rapid Approximate Statistical Procedures," 1964, p. 28. Courtesy of Lederle Laboratories Division of American Cyanamid Company, Madison, NJ.

TABLE XIII   Critical Values of χ^2

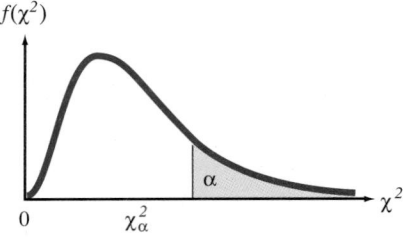

Degrees of Freedom	$\chi^2_{.995}$	$\chi^2_{.990}$	$\chi^2_{.975}$	$\chi^2_{.950}$	$\chi^2_{.900}$
1	.0000393	.0001571	.0009821	.0039321	.0157908
2	.0100251	.0201007	.0506356	.102587	.210720
3	.0717212	.114832	.215795	.351846	.584375
4	.206990	.297110	.484419	.710721	1.063623
5	.411740	.554300	.831211	1.145476	1.61031
6	.675727	.872085	1.237347	1.63539	2.20413
7	.989265	1.239043	1.68987	2.16735	2.83311
8	1.344419	1.646482	2.17973	2.73264	3.48954
9	1.734926	2.087912	2.70039	3.32511	4.16816
10	2.15585	2.55821	3.24697	3.94030	4.86518
11	2.60321	3.05347	3.81575	4.57481	5.57779
12	3.07382	3.57056	4.40379	5.22603	6.30380
13	3.56503	4.10691	5.00874	5.89186	7.04150
14	4.07468	4.66043	5.62872	6.57063	7.78953
15	4.60094	5.22935	6.26214	7.26094	8.54675
16	5.14224	5.81221	6.90766	7.96164	9.31223
17	5.69724	6.40776	7.56418	8.67176	10.0852
18	6.26481	7.01491	8.23075	9.39046	10.8649
19	6.84398	7.63273	8.90655	10.1170	11.6509
20	7.43386	8.26040	9.59083	10.8508	12.4426
21	8.03366	8.89720	10.28293	11.5913	13.2396
22	8.64272	9.54249	10.9823	12.3380	14.0415
23	9.26042	10.19567	11.6885	13.0905	14.8479
24	9.88623	10.8564	12.4011	13.8484	15.6587
25	10.5197	11.5240	13.1197	14.6114	16.4734
26	11.1603	12.1981	13.8439	15.3791	17.2919
27	11.8076	12.8786	14.5733	16.1513	18.1138
28	12.4613	13.5648	15.3079	16.9279	18.9392
29	13.1211	14.2565	16.0471	17.7083	19.7677
30	13.7867	14.9535	16.7908	18.4926	20.5992
40	20.7065	22.1643	24.4331	26.5093	29.0505
50	27.9907	29.7067	32.3574	34.7642	37.6886
60	35.5346	37.4848	40.4817	43.1879	46.4589
70	43.2752	45.4418	48.7576	51.7393	55.3290
80	51.1720	53.5400	57.1532	60.3915	64.2778
90	59.1963	61.7541	65.6466	69.1260	73.2912
100	67.3276	70.0648	74.2219	77.9295	82.3581

Source: From C. M. Thompson, "Tables of the Percentage Points of the χ^2-Distribution," *Biometrika,* 1941, 32, 188–189. Reproduced by permission of the *Biometrika* Trustees.

TABLE XIII   Continued

Degrees of Freedom	$\chi^2_{.100}$	$\chi^2_{.050}$	$\chi^2_{.025}$	$\chi^2_{.010}$	$\chi^2_{.005}$
1	2.70554	3.84146	5.02389	6.63490	7.87944
2	4.60517	5.99147	7.37776	9.21034	10.5966
3	6.25139	7.81473	9.34840	11.3449	12.8381
4	7.77944	9.48773	11.1433	13.2767	14.8602
5	9.23635	11.0705	12.8325	15.0863	16.7496
6	10.6446	12.5916	14.4494	16.8119	18.5476
7	12.0170	14.0671	16.0128	18.4753	20.2777
8	13.3616	15.5073	17.5346	20.0902	21.9550
9	14.6837	16.9190	19.0228	21.6660	23.5893
10	15.9871	18.3070	20.4831	23.2093	25.1882
11	17.2750	19.6751	21.9200	24.7250	26.7569
12	18.5494	21.0261	23.3367	26.2170	28.2995
13	19.8119	22.3621	24.7356	27.6883	29.8194
14	21.0642	23.6848	26.1190	29.1413	31.3193
15	22.3072	24.9958	27.4884	30.5779	32.8013
16	23.5418	26.2962	28.8454	31.9999	34.2672
17	24.7690	27.5871	30.1910	33.4087	35.7185
18	25.9894	28.8693	31.5264	34.8053	37.1564
19	27.2036	30.1435	32.8523	36.1908	38.5822
20	28.4120	31.4104	34.1696	37.5662	39.9968
21	29.6151	32.6705	35.4789	38.9321	41.4010
22	30.8133	33.9244	36.7807	40.2894	42.7956
23	32.0069	35.1725	38.0757	41.6384	44.1813
24	33.1963	36.4151	39.3641	42.9798	45.5585
25	34.3816	37.6525	40.6465	44.3141	46.9278
26	35.5631	38.8852	41.9232	45.6417	48.2899
27	36.7412	40.1133	43.1944	46.9630	49.6449
28	37.9159	41.3372	44.4607	48.2782	50.9933
29	39.0875	42.5569	45.7222	49.5879	52.3356
30	40.2560	43.7729	46.9792	50.8922	53.6720
40	51.8050	55.7585	59.3417	63.6907	66.7659
50	63.1671	67.5048	71.4202	76.1539	79.4900
60	74.3970	79.0819	83.2976	88.3794	91.9517
70	85.5271	90.5312	95.0231	100.425	104.215
80	96.5782	101.879	106.629	112.329	116.321
90	107.565	113.145	118.136	124.116	128.299
100	118.498	124.342	129.561	135.807	140.169

TABLE XIV Critical Values of Spearman's Rank Correlation Coefficient

The α values correspond to a one-tailed test of H_0: $\rho = 0$. The value should be doubled for two-tailed tests.

n	α = .05	α = .025	α = .01	α = .005	n	α = .05	α = .025	α = .01	α = .005
5	.900	—	—	—	18	.399	.476	.564	.625
6	.829	.886	.943	—	19	.388	.462	.549	.608
7	.714	.786	.893	—	20	.377	.450	.534	.591
8	.643	.738	.833	.881	21	.368	.438	.521	.576
9	.600	.683	.783	.833	22	.359	.428	.508	.562
10	.564	.648	.745	.794	23	.351	.418	.496	.549
11	.523	.623	.736	.818	24	.343	.409	.485	.537
12	.497	.591	.703	.780	25	.336	.400	.475	.526
13	.475	.566	.673	.745	26	.329	.392	.465	.515
14	.457	.545	.646	.716	27	.323	.385	.456	.505
15	.441	.525	.623	.689	28	.317	.377	.448	.496
16	.425	.507	.601	.666	29	.311	.370	.440	.487
17	.412	.490	.582	.645	30	.305	.364	.432	.478

Source: From E. G. Olds, "Distribution of Sums of Squares of Rank Differences for Small Samples," *Annals of Mathematical Statistics,* 1938, 9. Reproduced with the permission of the Editor, *Annals of Mathematical Statistics.*

TABLE XV   Control Chart Constants

Number of Observations in Subgroup, n	A_2	d_2	d_3	D_3	D_4
2	1.880	1.128	.853	.000	3.267
3	1.023	1.693	.888	.000	2.574
4	.729	2.059	.880	.000	2.282
5	.577	2.326	.864	.000	2.114
6	.483	2.534	.848	.000	2.004
7	.419	2.704	.833	.076	1.924
8	.373	2.847	.820	.136	1.864
9	.337	2.970	.808	.184	1.816
10	.308	3.078	.797	.223	1.777
11	.285	3.173	.787	.256	1.744
12	.266	3.258	.778	.283	1.717
13	.249	3.336	.770	.307	1.693
14	.235	3.407	.762	.328	1.672
15	.223	3.472	.755	.347	1.653
16	.212	3.532	.749	.363	1.637
17	.203	3.588	.743	.378	1.622
18	.194	3.640	.738	.391	1.608
19	.187	3.689	.733	.403	1.597
20	.180	3.735	.729	.415	1.585
21	.173	3.778	.724	.425	1.575
22	.167	3.819	.720	.434	1.566
23	.162	3.858	.716	.443	1.557
24	.157	3.895	.712	.451	1.548
25	.153	3.931	.709	.459	1.541
More than 25	$3/\sqrt{n}$				

Source: ASTM Manual on the Presentation of Data and Control Chart Analysis, Philadelphia, PA: American Society for Testing Materials, pp. 134–136, 1976.

APPENDIX C
CALCULATION FORMULAS FOR ANALYSIS OF VARIANCE: INDEPENDENT SAMPLING

$$\text{CM} = \text{Correction for mean}$$

$$= \frac{(\text{Total of all observations})^2}{\text{Total number of observations}} = \frac{\left(\sum\limits_{i=1}^{n} y_i\right)^2}{n}$$

$$\text{SS(Total)} = \text{Total sum of squares}$$

$$= (\text{Sum of squares of all observations}) - \text{CM} = \sum\limits_{i=1}^{n} y_i^2 - \text{CM}$$

$$\text{SST} = \text{Sum of squares for treatments}$$

$$= \left(\begin{array}{c}\text{Sum of squares of treatment totals with} \\ \text{each square divided by the number of} \\ \text{observations for that treatment}\end{array}\right) - \text{CM}$$

$$= \frac{T_1^2}{n_1} + \frac{T_2^2}{n_2} + \cdots + \frac{T_p^2}{n_p} - \text{CM}$$

$$\text{SSE} = \text{Sum of squares for error} = \text{SS(Total)} - \text{SST}$$

$$\text{MST} = \text{Mean square for treatments} = \frac{\text{SST}}{p-1}$$

$$\text{MSE} = \text{Mean square for error} = \frac{\text{SSE}}{n-p}$$

$$F = \text{Test statistic} = \frac{\text{MST}}{\text{MSE}}$$

where

n = Total number of observations

p = Number of treatments

T_i = Total for treatment i ($i = 1, 2, ..., p$)

ANSWERS TO SELECTED EXERCISES

CHAPTER 1

1.13 Qualitative, qualitative **1.15a.** Citizens of U.S. **b.** President's performance, qualitative **c.** 2,000 individuals **d.** 0 **e.** Survey **f.** Not likely
1.17a. Quantitative **b.** Qualitative **c.** Qualitative **d.** Quantitative
1.19a. Quantitative **b.** Quantitative **c.** Qualitative **d.** Quantitative
e. Qualitative **f.** Quantitative **g.** Qualitative **1.21a.** All department store executives **b.** Job satisfaction and Machiavellian rating **c.** 218 executives
d. Survey **1.23b.** All bank presidents in U.S. **1.25a.** All major U.S. firms
b. Job-sharing availability **c.** 1,035 firms **1.27I.** Qualitative
II. Quantitative **III.** Quantitative **IV.** Qualitative **V.** Qualitative
VI. Quantitative **1.29b.** Speed, accuracy, and packaging **c.** Total number of questionnaires received

CHAPTER 2

2.3a. .642, .204, .083, .071 **2.5a.** Length of time **c.** 3,570 **d.** No
2.7a. Length of time **c.** .08 **2.9a.** 195 **b.** 90 **c.** .016, .024, .355, .327, .187, .091 **2.11b.** Inflation rate **c.** Yes **2.13** (See figure below)
2.15a. Frequency histogram **b.** 14 **c.** 49 **2.17b.** .733 **2.21b.** Yes
2.23a. Stem: 1000's, Leaf 100's; Largest: 11,968.23 represented by 12.0
2.25b. P/E ratios in manufacturing exceed P/E ratios in holding **2.27a.** 33
b. 175 **c.** 20 **d.** 71 **e.** 1,089 **2.29a.** 6 **b.** 50 **c.** 42.8 **2.31** Mean = 2.717, median = 2.65 **2.35a.** 2.5, 3, 3 **b.** 3.08, 3, 3 **c.** 49.6, 49, 50
2.37a. Health care: mean = 38,956.9, median = 33,254.5; Banks: mean = 18,481.1, median = 16,065 **b.** Both skewed right **c.** No **2.43a.** Joint: mean = 2.6545, median = 1.5; No: mean = 4.2364, median = 3.2; Prepack: mean = 1.8185, median = 1.4 **2.45a.** Mean = 91.99, median = 90.5, mode = all values
b. Mean = 90.57, median = 90, mode = all values **c.** 80% trimmed mean = 91.175 **2.47c.** No **2.49a.** 4, 2.3, 1.52 **b.** 6, 3.619, 1.90 **c.** 10, 7.111, 2.67
d. 5, 1.624, 1.274 **2.51a.** 5.6, 17.3, 4.1593 **b.** 13.75 feet, 152.25 square feet, 12.339 feet **c.** .33 ounce, .0587 square ounces, .2422 ounce **2.53** (See figure below) **2.55a.** U.S. Index: $\bar{x}$ = 150.3042; Chicago Index: $\bar{x}$ = 150.9542

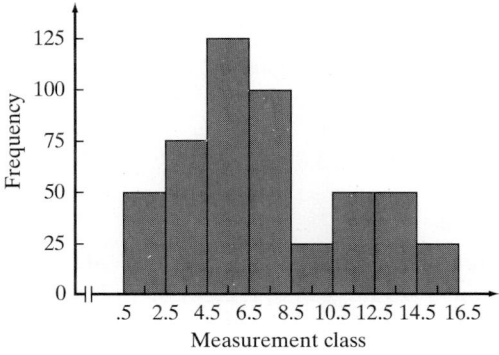

Exercise 2.13

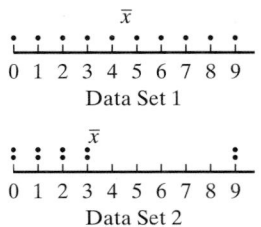

Exercise 2.53

b. U.S. Index: Range = 7.5; Chicago Index: Range = 7.8 **c.** U.S. Index: s = 2.4108; Chicago Index: s = 2.6572 **d.** Chicago Index **2.57a.** Range = 455.2, s^2 = 25,367.88238, s = 159.2730 **b.** Million dollars, million dollars squared, million dollars **c.** Increase, increase **2.59** Any data, mound-shaped and symmetric **2.61a.** Nothing **b.** At least 3/4 **c.** At least 8/9 **2.63a.** 8.24, 3.357, 1.83 **b.** 72%, 96%, 100% **c.** $s \approx 1.75$ **2.65b.** (−100.266, 219.906) **2.67a.** Not appropriate **b.** (−1.107, 6.205) **c.** 95.9% **2.69b.** No **2.71** Do not buy the land. **2.73a.** −1.83, 11.2942 **c.** No **2.75a.** 2 **b.** .5 **c.** 0 **d.** −2.5 **e.** Sample, population, population, sample **f.** Above, above, at, below **2.77** Median **2.79a.** 3.7, 2.2, 2.95, 1.45 **b.** 1.9 **c.** $z = 1, 2$; GPA = 3.2, 3.7; Assume mound-shaped **2.81** No **2.83b.** Japan: $z = 2.57$; Egypt: $z = .61$ **2.85a.** 0 **b.** 21 **c.** 5.90 **d.** Yes **2.89a.** 39 **b.** 31.5, 45 **c.** ≈ 13.5 **d.** Skewed left **e.** 50%, 75% **2.93c.** No **d.** Yes **2.95b.** 238, 268, 269, 264 **c.** 1.92, 2.06, 2.13, 3.14 **2.99a.** −1, 1, 2 **b.** −2, 2, 4 **c.** 1, 3, 4 **d.** .1, .3, .4 **2.101a.** $\bar{x} = 6, s^2 = 27, s = 5.20$ **b.** $\bar{x} = 6.25, s^2 = 28.25, s = 5.32$ **c.** $\bar{x} = 7$, $s^2 = 37.67, s = 6.14$ **d.** $\bar{x} = 3, s^2 = 0, s = 0$ **2.107b.** 6.5 days, 7.0 days, 8.5 days **2.111a.** Skewed right **b.** Chebyshev's Rule appropriate **c.** ≈ 38 homes **d.** $z = 3.333$, no **2.115a.** Frequency bar chart **c.** 70% successful **2.119a.** High GNP: $\bar{x} = 4.4125, s = 1.965$; Low GNP: Median = 23.15, $s = 127.54$ **c.** No

Chapter 3

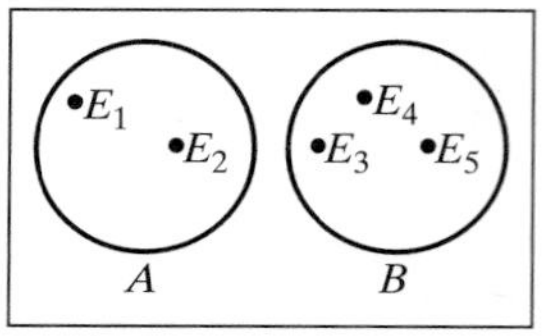

Exercise 3.17

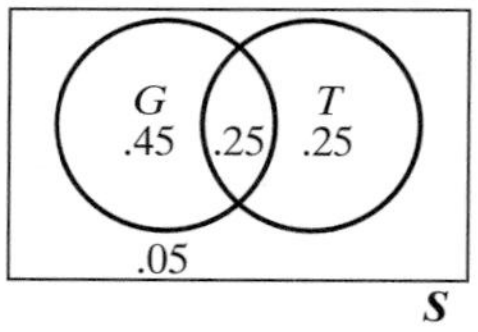

Exercise 3.75a

3.1a. .5 **b.** .3 **c.** .6 **3.3** $P(A) = .55, P(B) = .50, P(C) = .70$ **3.5** $P(A) = 1/10$, $P(B) = 3/5$, $P(C) = 3/10$ **3.7a.** Strongly agree, agree, neither, disagree, strongly disagree **b.** .189, .403, .258, .113, .038 **c.** .592 **d.** .812 **3.9** 1/20 **3.11c.** .556, .444 **3.13a.** 1 to 2 **b.** 1/2 **c.** 2/5 **3.15b.** 1/16 **c.** 5/16 **3.17** (See figure at left) **3.19a.** 3/4 **b.** 13/20 **c.** 1 **d.** 2/5 **e.** 1/4 **f.** 7/20 **g.** 1 **h.** 1/4 **3.21a.** .5 **b.** .31875 **c.** .125 **d.** .75 **e.** .75 **f.** .3125 **g.** $(A, B), (A, C), (B, C), (D, E), (D, F), (E, F)$ are mutually exclusive. **3.23a.** $B \cap C$ **b.** A^c **c.** $C \cup B$ **d.** $A \cap C^c$ **3.25d.** 5/6, 1/2, 1/3, 1, 1/6 **e.** 1, no **3.27b** Sample space **c.** .24 **d.** .10 **e.** .47 **f.** .62 **g.** .28 **3.29a.** .06 **b.** .27 **c.** .17 **d.** .70 **3.31a.** Yes **b.** .26, .35, .72, .28, .05 **c.** .56, .05, .77 **d.** .74 **e.** $C \cap D$ and $D \cap E$ contains no events **3.33a.** .8, .7, .6 **b.** .25, .375, .375 **c.** .75, .75 **d.** No **3.35a.** .37 **b.** .68 **c.** .15 **d.** .2206 **e.** 0 **f.** 0 **g.** None **3.37a.** $A \cap C$ and $B \cap C$ **b.** None **c.** $P(A \cup B) = .65, P(A \cap C) = .90$ **3.39a.** .08, .4, .52 **b.** .12, .30 **3.41a.** .550 **b.** .450 **c.** .272 **d.** .040 **e.** .182 **f.** .857 **g.** .182 **3.43a.** .543 **b.** .221 **c.** .052 **d.** .914 **3.45** .005 **3.47a.** .02 **b.** .08 **3.49a.** .116 **b.** .728 **3.51a.** .3, .6 **b.** Dependent **c.** Independent **3.53a.** 35,820,200 **b.** 1/35,820,200 **3.55a.** .000186 **c.** No **3.61** .5 **3.63a.** 0, .2, .9, 1, .7, .3, .4, 0 **b.** No, yes **c.** No, no **3.65a.** 720 **b.** 10 **c.** 10 **d.** 20 **e.** 1 **3.67a.** .75 **b.** .2875 **c.** .6 **d.** .06 **e.** No **g.** Yes **3.69a.** $P(A) = 1/10, P(B) = 1/10$ **b.** .641, .359 **c.** Upper bounds **3.71a.** .00000625 **b.** .0135 **c.** Doubt claim; $p = .000475$ **d.** Not positive, but $p = .00000625$ **3.73** .801 **3.75a.** (See figure at left) **b.** .95 **c.** .25 **d.** .5 **3.77a.** .24 **b.** .1 **c.** .14 **3.79** .79 **3.81a.** .7127 **b.** .2873 **3.83b.** 1/10 **c.** 1/10, 3/10 **3.85a.** 6 **b.** 1/3 **3.87a.** 142,506 **b.** .2361 **c.** .6711

Chapter 4

4.3a. Discrete **b.** Discrete **c.** Discrete **d.** Continuous **e.** Discrete **f.** Continuous **4.11a.** $x = 0, 1, 2, 3$ **b.** $p(3) = 1/8, p(2) = 3/8, p(1) = 3/8$, $p(0) = 1/8$ **d.** 1/2 **4.15a.** $\mu = 34.5, \sigma^2 = 174.75, \sigma = 13.219$ **c.** 1.00

Cost	p
$1,000	.25
$2,000	.25
$3,000	.50

Exercise 4.25a

4.17b. $p(x > 200,000) = .011, p(x > 100,000) = .052, p(x < 100,000) = .948$
d. $p(6) = .138, p(1 \text{ or } 9) = .196$ **4.19b.** .85 **c.** a_2: .6, a_3: 0, a_4: 0, a_5: 0, a_6: .7
d. .51 **4.21a.** $\mu_A = \mu_B = 2,450$ **b.** $\sigma_A = 661.44, \sigma_B = 701.78$ **4.23a.** $\mu = 2.9$,
median = 3 **b.** 3, 4 **c.** 3, 3 **4.25a.** (See table at left) **4.27a.** .4096 **b.** .3456
c. .027 **d.** .0081 **e.** .3456 **f.** .027 **4.29a.** $\mu = 12.5, \sigma^2 = 6.25, \sigma = 2.5$
b. $\mu = 16, \sigma^2 = 12.8, \sigma = 3.578$ **c.** $\mu = 60, \sigma^2 = 24, \sigma = 4.899$ **d.** $\mu = 63$,
$\sigma^2 = 6.3, \sigma = 2.510$ **e.** $\mu = 48, \sigma^2 = 9.6, \sigma = 3.098$ **f.** $\mu = 40, \sigma^2 = 38.4$,
$\sigma = 6.197$ **4.31a.** $p = .5$ **b.** $p < .5$ **c.** $p > .5$ **e.** $p = .5$ symmetric; $p < .5$
skewed right; $p > .5$ skewed left **4.33a.** .006, .01, .049 **b.** .0293, .0003
c. .0480, .0010 **d.** .8936 **4.35b.** $\mu = 2.4, \sigma = 1.47$ **c.** $p = .90, q = .10, n = 24$;
$\mu = 21.60, \sigma = 1.47$ **4.37a.** $\mu = 520, \sigma = 13.491$ **b.** No, $z = -8.895$ **4.39a.** 1
b. .998 **c.** .537 **d.** .009 **e.** ≈ 0 **f.** ≈ 0 **g.** ≈ 0 **h.** $= 0$ **4.41a.** Discrete
b. Poisson **d.** $\mu = 3, \sigma = 1.7321$ **e.** $\mu = 3, \sigma = 1.7321$ **4.43a.** .934 **b.** .191
c. .125 **d.** .223 **e.** .777 **f.** .001 **4.45a.** $\mu = 128.6, \sigma = 11.340$ **b.** $z = -7.72$
4.47a. $\sigma = 2$ **b.** No, $P(x > 10) = .003$ **4.49** $P(x > 4) = .1088$ **4.51a.** .193
b. .660 **4.53** $P(3) = .224, P(0) = .050, .05^8$ **4.55b.** $\mu = 5, \sigma = 1.155$
4.57a. 0 **b.** 1 **c.** 1 **4.59a.** Continuous **c.** $\mu = 7, \sigma = .2887$ **d.** .5 **e.** 0
f. .75 **g.** .0002 **4.63** .4444 **4.65a.** .4772 **b.** .4987 **c.** .4332 **d.** .2881
4.67a. .0721 **b.** .0594 **c.** .2434 **d.** .3457 **e.** .5 **f.** .9233 **4.69a.** 1.645
b. 1.96 **c.** -1.96 **d.** 1.28 **e.** 1.28 **4.71a.** -2.5 **b.** 0 **c.** $-.625$ **d.** -3.75
e. 1.25 **f.** -1.25 **4.73a.** .3830 **b.** .3023 **c.** .1525 **d.** .7333 **e.** .1314
f. .9545 **4.75a.** .9544 **b.** .0918 **c.** .0228 **d.** .8607 **e.** .0927 **f.** .7049
4.77a. .3050, .1020 **b.** .6879, .8925 **c.** .0032 **4.79a.** .5124 **b.** Yes, $p = .2912$
c. No, $p = .0027$ **4.81a.** .68% **4.83** $\mu = 5.068$ **4.85a.** .0307 **b.** .0893
4.87a. .367879 **b.** .082085 **c.** .000553 **d.** .223130 **4.89a.** .999447
b. .999955 **c.** .981684 **d.** .632121 **4.91a.** .018316 **b.** .950213 **c.** .383401
4.93a. .279543 **b.** .1123887 **4.95a.** $R(x) = e^{-.5x}$ **b.** .13535 **c.** .367879
d. No **e.** 820.85, 3,934.69 **f.** 36.5 days **4.97a.** .550671 **b.** .263597
4.101 2.7 **4.105a.** 100, 5 **b.** 100, 2 **c.** 100, 1 **d.** 100, 1.414 **e.** 100, .447
f. 100, .316 **4.107a.** $\mu = 2.9, \sigma^2 = 3.29, \sigma = 1.814$ **c.** $\mu_{\bar{x}} = 2.9, \sigma_{\bar{x}} = 1.283$
4.109a. $\mu_{\bar{x}} = 20, \sigma_{\bar{x}} = 2$ **b.** Approximately normal **c.** $z = -2.25$
d. $z = 1.50$ **4.111a.** .8944 **b.** .0228 **c.** .1292 **d.** .9699 **4.115a.** $\mu_{\bar{x}} = 406$,
$\sigma_{\bar{x}} = 1.6833$, approximately normal **b.** .0010 **c.** The first **4.117a.** $\mu_{\bar{x}} = 89.34$,
$\sigma_{\bar{x}} = 1.3083$ **c.** .8461 **d.** .0367 **4.119a.** .0031, claim is too high **b.** .2643, 0
c. 0, .0853 **4.121a.** No **b.** No **c.** Yes **d.** Yes **4.123a.** .192 **b.** .228
c. .772 **d.** .987 **e.** .960 **f.** $\mu = 14, \sigma^2 = 4.2, \sigma = 2.05$ **g.** .975
4.125a. Discrete **b.** Continuous **c.** Continuous **d.** Continuous
4.127b. $\mu = 50, \sigma = 23.094$ **d.** .625 **e.** 0 **f.** .875 **g.** .577 **h.** .1875
4.129a. 47.68 **b.** 47.68 **c.** 30.13 **d.** 41.56 **e.** 30.13 **4.131a.** .5
b. .0606 **c.** .0985 **d.** .8436 **4.133a.** .0918 **b.** 0 **c.** $\mu = 95.13$ lower 4.87
decibels **4.135a.** .8264 **b.** 17.36 times **c.** .6217 **d.** $\mu = 0, \mu = -157$
4.137b. 14; 3.742 **c.** Yes **d.** .002 **4.139a.** i. .384; ii. .49; iii. .212; iv. .84
b. i. .3849; ii. .4938; iii. .2119; iv. .8413 **c.** i. .0009; ii. .0038; iii. .0001; iv. .0013
4.141a. $\mu_x = 26, \sigma_x = \sigma$ **b.** $\mu_{\bar{x}} = 26, \mu_{\bar{x}} = \sigma/\sqrt{n}$, approximately normal
c. .2843 **d.** .1292 **4.143a.** .006 **b.** $p < .80$

CHAPTER 5

5.1a. 1.645 **b.** 2.58 **c.** 1.96 **d.** 1.28 **5.3a.** $28 \pm .784$ **b.** $102 \pm .65$
c. $15 \pm .0588$ **d.** $4.05 \pm .163$ **e.** No **5.5a.** $26.2 \pm .96$ **c.** 26.2 ± 1.26
d. Increases **e.** Yes **5.9** Yes, if $n \geq 30$ **5.11a.** 33.583 ± 5.751

5.13c. 1 ± 48.84 **e.** Not very accurate   **5.15a.** 23.43 ± 1.817 **d.** Yes
5.17a. Younger: $4.17 \pm .095$; middle-age: $4.04 \pm .057$; older: $4.31 \pm .062$
b. More likely   **5.19a.** $z = 1.28, t = 1.533$ **b.** $z = 1.645, t = 2.132$
c. $z = 1.96, t = 2.776$ **d.** $z = 2.33, t = 3.747$ **e.** $z = 2.575, t = 4.604$
5.21a. 2.228 **b.** 2.228 **c.** -1.812 **d.** 2.086 **e.** 4.032 **5.23a.** 97.94 ± 4.240
b. 97.94 ± 6.737 **5.25a.** 49.3 ± 8.60 **c.** Normal population   **5.27b.** $23,490.09$
$\pm 1,958.97$ **5.29** 184.99 ± 133.94 **5.31a.** 22.455 ± 11.177 **c.** Normal population   **d.** Assumption is suspect   **5.33a.** $.10 \pm .045$ **b.** $.10 \pm .127$ **c.** $.5 \pm .335$
d. $.3 \pm .307$ **5.35a.** Yes   **b.** $.46 \pm .065$ **5.37a.** $.694 \pm .106$ **b.** Randomly
sample   **5.39a.** All are large   **b.** Poor: $.155 \pm .046$; average: $.133 \pm .046$; good:
$.108 \pm .062$ **5.41** $.85 \pm .002$ **5.43b.** $.22 \pm .0086$ **5.45a.** $\hat{p} = .24$ **b.** $.24 \pm .118$
5.47 $n = 308$ **5.49a.** $n = 68$ **b.** $n = 31$ **5.51** $n = 34$ **5.53a.** $.226 \pm .007$
b. $.014$ **c.** $n = 1,680$ **5.55** $s = 10$: $n = 43$; $s = 20$: $n = 171$; $s = 30$: $n = 385$
5.57 $n = 1,351$ **5.59** $n = 271$ **5.61** $n = 3,701$ **5.63a.** 32.5 ± 5.16
b. $n = 23,964$ **5.65a.** $(298.6, 582.3)$ **5.67a.** $.876 \pm .003$ **5.69a.** Men: $7.4 \pm$
$.979$; women: $4.5 \pm .755$ **b.** Men: 9.3 ± 1.185; women: 6.6 ± 1.138
5.71a. 12.2 ± 1.645 **b.** $n = 167$ **5.73a.** No   **b.** $n = 1,337$ **5.75a.** $n = 191$
5.77a. Random sample   **b.** $3.256 \pm .348$ **5.79** $n = 818$

CHAPTER 6

6.1 Null; alternative   **6.3** α **6.11a.** $\alpha = .025$ **b.** $\alpha = .05$ **c.** $\alpha = .005$
d. $\alpha = .1003$ **e.** $\alpha = .10$ **f.** $\alpha = .01$ **6.13a.** $z = 1.67$, reject H_0 **b.** $z = 1.67$,
fail to reject H_0 **6.15a.** H_0: $\mu = 16$; H_a: $\mu < 16$ **b.** $z = -4.31$, reject H_0
6.17a. $z = 7.02$, reject H_0 **6.19** $z = 1.58$, reject H_0 **6.21a.** H_0: $\mu = 1,502.5$;
H_a: $\mu > 1,502.5$ **b.** $z = 3.74$, reject H_0 **c.** No   **d.** Yes   **6.23** $z = -4.34$,
reject H_0 **6.25a.** Fail to reject H_0 **b.** Reject H_0 **c.** Reject H_0 **d.** Fail to
reject H_0 **e.** Fail to reject H_0 **6.27** $p = .0150$ **6.29** $p = .9279$, fail to reject H_0
6.31a. Fail to reject H_0 **b.** Fail to reject H_0 **c.** Reject H_0 **d.** Fail to reject H_0
6.33a. H_0: $\mu = 30\%$; H_a: $\mu > 30\%$ **b.** $p = .1271$ **c.** Fail to reject H_0
6.35a. H_0: $\mu = 2.5$; H_a: $\mu > 2.5$ **b.** $p \approx 0$ **c.** Reject H_0 **6.37a.** H_0: $\mu = 16.5$;
H_a: $\mu > 16.5$ **b.** $p = .0681$ **6.43a.** $t < -2.160$ or $t > 2.160$ **b.** $t > 2.500$
c. $t > 1.397$ **d.** $t < -2.718$ **e.** $t < -1.729$ or $t > 1.729$ **f.** $t < -2.353$
6.45b. $p = .0382$, reject H_0 at $\alpha > .0382$ **c.** $p = .0764$, fail to reject H_0 at
$\alpha = .05$ **6.47** $t = 8.75$, reject H_0 **6.49a.** H_0: $\mu = 15$; H_a: $\mu < 15$ **b.** $p = .0556$
c. At $\alpha = .05$, fail to reject H_0 **6.51** $t = 2.97$, fail to reject H_0 **6.53a.** Yes
b. No   **c.** Yes   **d.** No   **e.** No   **6.55a.** $z = -2.33$ **c.** Reject H_0
d. $p = .0099$, reject H_0 **6.57a.** $z = 1.13$, fail to reject H_0 **b.** $p = .1292$
6.59a. H_0: $p = .4$; H_a: $p < .4$ **b.** $z = -.19$, fail to reject H_0 **c.** $p = .4247$, fail to
reject H_0 **6.61** $z = 33.47$, reject H_0 **6.63a.** $z = 15.61$, reject H_0 **b.** $p \approx 0$,
reject H_0 **6.67a.** $.035$ **b.** $.363$ **c.** $.004$ **d.** $.151, .1515$ **e.** $.212, .2119$
6.69 $p = .054$, reject H_0 **6.71a.** H_0: $\eta = 5$; H_a: $\eta > 5$ **b.** $p \approx 0$ **c.** Reject H_0
6.73a. Sign test   **b.** H_0: $\eta = 30$; H_a: $\eta < 30$ **c.** $s = 5$ **d.** $p = .109$, fail to
reject H_0 **6.75** Alternative   **6.79a.** $t = -7.51$, reject H_0 **b.** $t = -7.51$,
reject H_0 **6.81a.** $z = -1.67$, fail to reject H_0 **b.** $z = -3.35$, reject H_0
6.83c. Type II   **6.85a.** $z = -1.93$, reject H_0 **6.87a.** $.025 < p < .05$
b. $p = .0362$, reject H_0 at $\alpha = .0362$ **c.** Type I   **6.89a.** $z = 12.97$, reject H_0
b. $p \approx 0$, reject H_0 **c.** $\beta = .6844$ **6.91a.** $z = 1.41$, fail to reject H_0 **b.** Small
c. $p = .0793$, fail to reject H_0 **6.93a.** H_0: $\mu = 12,432$; H_a: $\mu > 12,432$
b. $z = 1.86, p = .0314$; at $\alpha = .05$, reject H_0 **6.95a.** H_0: $\eta = .75$; H_a: $\eta \neq .75$
d. p-value $= .014$, reject H_0 **6.97a.** $p = .0304$, reject H_0 at $\alpha = .10$
b. $p = .0152$

CHAPTER 7

7.1a. 150 ± 6 **b.** 150 ± 8 **c.** $\mu_{\bar{x}_1 - \bar{x}_2} = 0; \sigma_{\bar{x}_1 - \bar{x}_2} = 5$ **d.** 0 ± 10
7.3a. 35 ± 24.5 **b.** $p = .0052$, reject H_0 at $\alpha = .05$ **c.** $p = .0026$ **d.** $p = .4238$, fail to reject H_0 **7.5a.** $s_p^2 = 110$ **b.** $s_p^2 = 14.5714$ **c.** $s_p^2 = .1821$
d. $s_p^2 = 2,741.9355$ **7.7a.** $\sigma_{\bar{x}_1 - \bar{x}_2} = .5$ **d.** $z > 1.96$ or $z < -1.96$ **e.** $z = -42.2$, reject H_0 **7.9a.** $z = -1.576, p = .1150$ **b.** $p = .0575$ **7.11a.** $t = -1.646$,
$p = .1114$, fail to reject H_0 at $\alpha = .10$ **b.** -2.50 ± 3.12 **7.13a.** $t = 1.9557$,
reject H_0 **c.** $p = .0579$, reject H_0 **d.** -7.4 ± 6.382 **7.15a.** $z = -2.76$,
reject H_0 **b.** $p = .0029$ **c.** No **7.17b.** $H_0: \mu_1 - \mu_2 = 0; H_a: \mu_1 - \mu_2 < 0$
c. Fail to reject H_0 **7.19a.** $t = 4.46$, reject H_0 **b.** $p = .00155$, reject H_0
7.21a. $H_0: \mu_1 - \mu_2 = 0; H_a: \mu_1 - \mu_2 > 0$ **b.** $t = 2.616, .01 < p < .025$, reject H_0
at $\alpha = .05$ **7.25a.** $H_0: \mu_D = 0; H_a: \mu_D < 0$ **b.** $t = -5.29; p = .0002$
c. $(-5.284, -2.116)$ **7.27a.** $t = .81$, fail to reject H_0 **b.** $p > .20$, fail to reject
H_0 **7.29a.** -174.625 ± 67.666 **c.** Yes **7.31a.** $t = .40$, fail to reject H_0
b. $.4167 \pm 2.2963$ **c.** Part **b** is wider **d.** No **7.33a.** $H_0: \mu_D = 0; H_a: \mu_D > 0$
b. $t = 3.506$, reject H_0 **7.35** $t = .46, p = .65$, fail to reject H_0 **7.37** $n_1 = n_2 = 34$
7.39 $n_1 = n_2 = 1729$ **7.41** $n_1 = n_2 = 136$ **7.43** $n \approx 21$ **7.45a.** 4.10 **b.** 3.57
c. 8.805 **d.** 3.21 **7.47a.** $F = 4.29$, fail to reject H_0 **b.** $.05 < p < .10$
7.49a. $F = 2.26$, fail to reject H_0 **b.** $.05 < p < .10$ **7.51a.** $F = 8.29, p = .007$,
reject H_0 **b.** No **7.53a.** $T_B; T_B \leq 35$ or $T_B \geq 67$ **b.** $T_A; T_A \geq 43$ **c.** T_B;
$T_B \geq 93$ **d.** $z; z < -z_{\alpha/2}$ or $z > z_{\alpha/2}$ **7.57a.** $T_2 = 105$, fail to reject H_0
b. $p < .05$ **7.59a.** $T_B = 53$, reject H_0 **7.61** $T_A = 39$, reject H_0
7.63a. $z = -1.75$, reject H_0 **7.65b.** $T_- = 3.5$, reject H_0 **7.69b.** $z = 2.499$,
reject H_0 **c.** $p = .0062$ **7.71a.** Paired difference design **c.** $T_+ = 3.5$,
reject H_0 **d.** $.01 < p < .025$ **7.73** $T_+ = 2$, reject H_0 **7.75** $z = -1.3631$,
$p = .1728$, fail to reject H_0 **7.77** Diagram b **7.79c.** Plot **a:** $t = -6.12$, reject H_0;
plot **b:** $t = -2.28$, reject H_0 **7.81a.** $4, n = 38$ **b.** $F = 14.80$, reject H_0
7.83a. Completely randomized design **7.85a.** Infrequency: $F = 155.8$, reject H_0;
obvious: $F = 49.7$, reject H_0; subtle: $F = 10.3$, reject H_0; obvious-subtle: $F = 45.4$,
reject H_0; dissimulation: $F = 39.1$, reject H_0 **b.** No **7.87a.** $H_0: \mu_1 = \mu_2 = \mu_3 = \mu_4 = \mu_5 = \mu_6; H_a:$ At least two means differ **b.** Fail to reject H_0 **7.89a.** $t = .78$,
fail to reject H_0 **b.** 2.5 ± 7.5 **c.** $n_1 = n_2 = 225$ **7.91a.** $3.9 \pm .31$ **b.** $z = 20.6$,
reject H_0 **c.** $n_1 = n_2 = 345$ **7.93a.** $t = 5.73$, reject H_0 **b.** 3.8 ± 1.84
7.95 $T_- = 1.5$, reject H_0 **7.103a.** $t = -4.02$, yes **b.** $p = .0030$ **7.105** $T_- = 3$,
reject H_0 **7.107** $F = 3.34$, reject H_0

CHAPTER 8

8.3a. $z < -2.33$ **b.** $z < -1.96$ **c.** $z < -1.645$ **d.** $z < -1.28$ **8.5a.** $.07 \pm .067$
b. $.06 \pm .086$ **c.** $-.15 \pm .131$ **8.7** $z = 1.14$, fail to reject H_0 **8.9a.** Yes
b. $-.0568 \pm .0270$ **8.11** $z = -2.25$, reject H_0 **8.13a.** $H_0: p_1 - p_2 = 0$;
$H_a: p_1 - p_2 \neq 0$ **b.** Yes **c.** $z = -4.30$, reject H_0 **8.15a.** $H_0: p_1 - p_2 = 0$;
$H_a: p_1 - p_2 > 0$ **b.** $z = .664$, fail to reject H_0 **c.** $H_0: p_1 - p_3 = 0$;
$H_a: p_1 - p_3 > 0$ **d.** $z = 1.11, p = .1335$, fail to reject H_0 **8.17a.** $n_1 = n_2 = 29,954$ **b.** $n_1 = n_2 = 2,165$ **c.** $n_1 = n_2 = 1,113$ **8.19** $n_1 = n_2 = 542$
8.21 $n_1 = n_2 = 4,802$ **8.23a.** 27.5871 **b.** 70.0648 **c.** 22.3072 **d.** 12.8381
8.25a. $\chi^2 > 5.99147$ **b.** $\chi^2 > 7.77944$ **c.** $\chi^2 > 11.3449$ **8.27a.** $\chi^2 = 3.293$,
fail to reject H_0 **8.31a.** $H_0: p_1 = p_2 = p_3 = p_4 = .25; H_a:$ At least one $p \neq .25$
b. $\chi^2 = 14.805$, reject H_0 **8.33** $\chi^2 = 16, p = .003019$, reject H_0
8.35a. $\chi^2 = 12.374$, fail to reject H_0 **b.** $p < .10$ **8.37a.** $\chi^2 > 26.2962$
b. $\chi^2 > 15.9871$ **c.** $\chi^2 > 9.21034$ **8.39** $\chi^2 = 12.36$, reject H_0 **8.41a.** $\hat{p} = .901$
b. $\hat{p} = .690$ **d.** $\chi^2 = 48.191$, reject H_0 **e.** $.211 \pm .070$ **8.43a.** $\chi^2 = 20.78$,

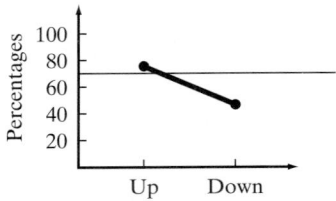

Exercise 8.59b

reject H_0 **b.** Older, younger **8.45a.** $\chi^2 = 39.22$, reject H_0 **b.** $\chi^2 = 2.84$, fail to reject H_0 **8.47** $\chi^2 = 24.524$, reject H_0 **8.49a.** No **c.** $\chi^2 = 12.9$ **d.** Reject H_0 **e.** $.233 \pm .200$ **8.51a.** $\chi^2 = 2.133$, fail to reject H_0 **b.** $.233 \pm .057$ **8.53** $n_1 = n_2 = 542$ **8.55** Union: $\chi^2 = 13.36744$, reject H_0; nonunion: $\chi^2 = 9.63514$, fail to reject H_0 **8.57** $.03 \pm .034$ **8.59a.** No **b.** (See figure above) **d.** $\chi^2 = 2.373$, fail to reject H_0 **e.** Yes **8.61** Yes, $\chi^2 = 180.874$ **8.63** $\chi^2 = 5.506$, fail to reject H_0 **8.65a.** $\chi^2 = 18.54$, reject H_0 **b.** $p < .005$

CHAPTER 9

9.3a. $y = \frac{14}{3} + \frac{1}{3}x$ **9.9** No **9.13c.** $\hat{\beta}_1 = -.9939$, $\hat{\beta}_0 = 8.543$ **d.** $\hat{y} = 8.543 - .994x$ **9.15a.** Decreases **b.** $\hat{y} = 569.58 - .00192x$ **9.17a.** Positive **c.** $\hat{y} = -131.185 + 765.101x$ **9.19a.** $y = \beta_0 + \beta_1 x + \epsilon$ **b.** $\hat{y} = 141.347 - .208x$ **9.21b.** $\hat{\beta}_0 = -51.3616$, $\hat{\beta}_1 = 17.7545$ **9.23a.** $s^2 = .3475$ **b.** 1.179 **9.27a.** SSE $= 623.857$; $s^2 = 51.988$; $s = 7.210$ **9.29a.** $\hat{y} = 3.068 - .015x$ **c.** $\hat{y}_{10} = 2.918$, $\hat{y}_{16} = 2.828$ **d.** SSE $= .01926$; $s = .0801$ **e.** $.1602$ **9.31a.** 31 ± 1.13; $31 \pm .92$ **b.** 64 ± 4.28; 64 ± 3.53 **c.** $-8.4 \pm .67$; $-8.4 \pm .55$ **9.33** 80%: $.8214 \pm .3325$; 98%: $.8214 \pm .7581$ **9.35a.** $p < .001$, reject H_0 **9.37a.** $t = 4.98$, $p = .001$, reject H_0 **b.** $\hat{y} = .607$ **9.39a.** $t = 3.384$; $p = .0035$, reject H_0 **b.** 17.754 ± 16.627 **9.41a.** $\hat{y} = 12.71 + 1.50x$ **b.** $t = 18.258$, reject H_0 **c.** Independent errors **9.43** $t = -.96$, fail to reject H_0 **9.45a.** Positive **b.** Negative **c.** 0 **d.** Positive or negative **9.47a.** $r^2 = .9438$ **b.** $r^2 = .8020$ **9.51a.** $r = .9844$ **9.53** $r^2 = .57873$ **9.55c.** $r_1 = .9653$; $r_2 = .9960$ **d.** Yes **9.57b.** $\hat{y} = 1.5 + .946x$ **c.** $s^2 = 2.221$ **d.** 4.338 ± 1.170 **e.** 4.338 ± 3.223 **f.** Prediction interval **9.59a.** 2.2 ± 1.382 **c.** Yes **d.** $t = 6.10$, reject H_0 **9.61b.** $\hat{y} = 5341.9 - 192.58x$ **c.** $t = -7.09$, reject H_0 **d.** $r^2 = .820$ **e.** $(3,269.9, 3,562.4)$ **f.** $(2,893.7, 3,938.6)$ **9.63a.** $t = 15.35$, reject H_0 **b.** 28.183 ± 4.629 **9.65a.** Indirect manufacturing cost **c.** $\hat{y} = 300.976 + 10.312x$ **d.** $t = 3.301$, reject H_0 **e.** $r^2 = .5214$ **f.** 816.596 ± 187.420 **9.67a.** $r_s > .648$ or $r_s < -.648$ **b.** $r_s > .450$ **c.** $r_s < -.432$ **9.69a.** $H_0: \rho_s = 0$; $H_a: \rho_s \neq 0$ **b.** $r_s = .745$, fail to reject H_0 **c.** $.05 < p < .10$ **9.71a.** $r_s = .491$, fail to reject H_0 **9.73b.** $r_s = .972$, reject H_0 **9.75** $r_s = .9341$ **9.77a.** $\hat{y} = 37.08 - 1.6x$ **c.** SSE $= 57.2$ **d.** $s^2 = 4.4$ **e.** $-1.6 \pm .501$ **f.** 13.08 ± 6.929 **g.** 13.08 ± 7.862 **9.79b.** $r = -.1245$, $r^2 = .0155$ **c.** $t = -.35$, fail to reject H_0 **9.81b.** $\hat{y} = 12.594 + .10936x$ **c.** $t = 3.50$, reject H_0 **d.** 28.988 ± 12.500 **9.83** $t = -1.926$, fail to reject H_0; $r^2 = .3073$ **9.85b.** $\hat{y} = -39,001.1 + 84.987x$ **c.** $r^2 = .8983$ **d.** $t = 13.942$, reject H_0 **e.** 84.987 ± 12.642 **f.** $p = .0001$, reject H_0 **g.** $(205,524, 226,396)$ **9.87a.** $\hat{\beta}_0 = -99045$, $\hat{\beta}_1 = 102.814$, **b.** $t = 6.483$, reject H_0 **c.** $p < .00005$ **d.** $r^2 = .6776$ **e.** $(-631,806, 2,078,740)$ **9.89b.** $\hat{y} = 12,024 + 3.582x$ **c.** $r^2 = .7972$ **d.** $t = 8.641$; $p = .0001$, reject H_0 **e.** $(\$12,862.60, \$16,915.30)$

CHAPTER 10

10.1a. $\hat{\beta}_0 = 506.346, \hat{\beta}_1 = -941.900, \hat{\beta}_2 = -429.060$ **b.** $\hat{y} = 506.346 - 941.900x_1 - 429.060x_2$ **c.** SSE $= 151,015$, MSE $= 8,883.3, s = 94.25$
d. $t = -3.424$, reject H_0 **e.** -429.060 ± 801.432 **10.3a.** $t = 3.133$, reject H_0
b. $t = 3.133$, reject H_0 **c.** $F = 9.816$ **d.** No **10.5a.** SSE $= .0438; s^2 = .0110$
b. $t = -13.97$, reject H_0 **c.** $\hat{y} = 1.095 + 1.636x_1 - .1595x_1^2$ **10.7** $\hat{\beta}_0 = 39.05$,
$\hat{\beta}_1 = -5.41, \hat{\beta}_2 = 5.86, \hat{\beta}_3 = -3.09, \hat{\beta}_4 = 1.75$ **10.9a.** $\hat{y} = 20.0911 - .6705x + .0095x^2$ **c.** $t = 1.51$, fail to reject H_0 **d.** $\hat{y} = 19.279 - .445x$ **e.** $-.445 \pm .0727$
10.11a. $\hat{y} = -72.558 - .058x_1 + 84.925x_2 - .022x_3$ **b.** $s = 8.563$ **c.** $t = -.293$,
fail to reject H_0 **10.13a.** Yes **b.** $F = 32.12$, reject H_0 **10.15a.** $R^2 = .4792$
b. $F = 7.82$, reject H_0 **10.17a.** $\hat{y} = -4.30 - .002x_1 + .336x_2 + .384x_3 + .067x_4 - .143x_5 + .081x_6 + .134x_7$ **b.** $F = 111.1$, reject H_0 **c.** $\hat{\beta}_3 = .384$ **d.** $t = 1.76$,
fail to reject H_0 **e.** $t = -.049$, fail to reject H_0 **10.19a.** $R^2 = .51$ **b.** $F = 13.53$,
reject H_0 **10.21a.** $E(y) = \beta_0 + \beta_1x_1 + \beta_2x_2 + \beta_3x_1x_2$ **b.** $p = .02$, reject H_0
10.23a. $\hat{y} = 295.33 - 480.84x_1 - 829.46x_2 + .0079x_3 + 2.3608x_4$ **b.** $s = 46.767$
c. $F = 28.18$, reject H_0 **d.** $t = -3.197$, reject H_0 **10.25a.** $E(y) = \beta_0 + \beta_1x_1 + \beta_2x_2 + \beta_3x_3 + \beta_4x_4 + \beta_5x_5$ **b.** $\hat{y} = 15.491 + 12.774x_1 + .713x_2 + 1.519x_3 + .32x_4 + .205x_5$ **c.** $R^2 = .240, F = 11.68$, reject H_0 **d.** $p = .025$, reject H_0
10.27 Confidence interval **10.29** Quadratics needed **10.31a.** $\hat{y} = -754.711 + 217.493x_1 + .713x_2$ **b.** $(-1,991.8, 1,630.5)$ **c.** No **d.** $r = .36332$
10.33b. $s_1 = .35014; s_2 = .62859$ **c.** $F_1 = 52.138$, reject $H_0; F_2 = 22.523$,
reject H_0 **d.** Model 1: $.354 \pm .0730$; Model 2: $.394 \pm .1291$ **f.** Large amount
10.35 26th observation skews the distribution to the right **10.37** Observation #25 is a possible outlier **10.39a.** "Year GRE taken" and "years in graduate program"; "race" and "foreign status" **10.41a.** $F = 24.41$, reject H_0
b. $t = -2.01$, reject H_0 **c.** $t = .31$, fail to reject H_0 **d.** $t = 2.38$, reject H_0
10.43 Need quadratic model **10.45a.** $E(y) = \beta_0 + \beta_1x_1 + \beta_2x_2 + \beta_3x_3 + \beta_4x_4 + \beta_5x_5$ **b.** $p < .001$, reject H_0 **c.** $E(y) = \beta_0 + \beta_1x_1 + \beta_2x_2 + \beta_3x_3 + \beta_4x_4 + \beta_5x_5 + \beta_6x_6 + \beta_7x_7$ **e.** Both are useful predictors of GSI **10.47** No
10.49b. Reject H_0 when testing $\beta_3, \beta_5,$ and β_6 **c.** $.007 \pm .0033$ **10.51a.** $E(y) = \beta_0 + \beta_1x_1 + \beta_2x_2 + \beta_3x_3 + \beta_4x_4 + \beta_5x_5 + \beta_6x_6 + \beta_7x_7$ **b.** $\hat{y} = .998 - .022x_1 + .156x_2 - .017x_3 - .010x_4 + .421x_5 + .417x_6 - .155x_7$ **c.** $F = 5.292$, reject H_0
d. $\hat{y} = -.60075$ **f.** Model has higher R^2 and lower s **h.** For obs. #14: $(-1.282, 1.218)$ **10.53** Add x_1^2 to the model **10.55** Second-order model is better

CHAPTER 11

11.7 Out of control **11.9a.** 1.023 **b.** $.308$ **c.** $.167$ **11.11b.** $\bar{\bar{x}} = 20.11625$,
$\bar{R} = 3.31$ **c.** UCL $= 22.529$, LCL $= 17.703$ **e.** In control **11.13b.** In control
c. Yes **11.15b.** Out of control **c.** No **11.17** Variation **11.19a.** $D_3 = .000$,
$D_4 = 2.282$ **b.** $D_3 = .283, D_4 = 1.717$ **c.** $D_3 = .451, D_4 = 1.548$
11.21a. UCL $= 7.553$ **c.** In control **11.23a.** UCL $= .7216$ **b.** In control
c. Yes **11.25b.** Out of control **c.** Yes **11.27b.** $\bar{R}$ chart **c.** Both suggest it
is in control **d.** No **11.29** $n \approx 104$ **11.31a.** $\bar{p} = .0575$, UCL $= .1145$,
LCL $= .0005$ **d.** No, out of control **e.** No **11.33a.** Yes **b.** UCL $= .02013$,
LCL $= .00081$ **c.** In control **11.35a.** $\bar{p} = .04$, UCL $= .099$, LCL $= -.019$
b. No **c.** No **11.47a.** $\bar{x} = 6.4$ **b.** Increasing variance **11.49** Process is out
of control **11.51a.** UCL $= 24.18$ **b.** UCL $= 358.06$, LCL $= 330.24$ **c.** No
d. $.25$ **11.53a.** UCL $= 11.532$ **b.** In control **d.** UCL $= 7.015$, LCL $= .719$
e. In control **f.** Yes **11.55a.** $n > 141$ **b.** UCL $= .123$, LCL $= .003$
c. They are present **e.** No

REFERENCES

CHAPTER 1

Careers in Statistics. American Statistical Association, Biometric Society, Institute of Mathematical Statistics and Statistical Society of Canada, 1995.

Chervany, N. L., Benson, P. G., and Iyer, R. K. "The planning stage in statistical reasoning." *American Statistician,* Nov. 1980, pp. 222–239.

Ethical Guidelines for Statistical Practice. American Statistical Association, 1995.

Tanur, J. M., Mosteller, F., Kruskal, W. H., Link, R. F., Pieters, R. S., and Rising, G. R. *Statistics: A Guide to the Unknown.* (E. L. Lehmann, special editor.) San Francisco: Holden-Day, 1989.

U.S. Bureau of the Census. *Statistical Abstract of the United States: 1995.* Washington, D.C.: U.S. Government Printing Office, 1995.

What Is a Survey? Section on Survey Research Methods, American Statistical Association, 1995.

CHAPTER 2

Adler, P. S., and Clark, K. B. "Behind the learning curve: A sketch of the learning process." *Management Science,* March 1991, p. 267.

Alexander, G. J., Sharpe, W. F., and Bailey, J. V. *Fundamentals of Investments,* 2nd ed. Englewood Cliffs, N.J.: Prentice-Hall, 1993.

Deming, W. E. *Out of the Crisis.* Cambridge, Mass: M.I.T. Center for Advanced Engineering Study, 1986.

Fogarty, D. W., Blackstone, J. H., Jr., and Hoffman, T. R. *Production and Inventory Management.* Cincinnati, Ohio: South-Western, 1991.

Gaither, N. *Production and Operations Management,* 7th ed. Belmont, Calif: Duxbury Press, 1996.

Gitlow, H., Oppenheim, A., and Oppenheim, R. *Quality Mangement: Methods for Improvement,* 2nd ed., Burr Ridge, Ill.: Irwin, 1995.

Huff, D. *How to Lie with Statistics.* New York: Norton, 1954.

Ishikawa, K. *Guide to Quality Control,* 2nd ed. White Plains, N.Y.: Kraus International Publications, 1982.

Juran, J. M. *Juran on Planning for Quality.* New York: The Free Press, 1988.

Mendenhall, W. *Introduction to Probability and Statistics,* 9th ed. North Scituate, Mass.: Duxbury, 1994.

Schroeder, R. G. *Operations Management,* 4th ed. New York: McGraw-Hill, 1993.

Wasserman, P., and Bernero, J. *Statistics Sources,* 5th ed. Detroit: Gale Research Company, 1978.

Zabel, S. L. "Statistical proof of employment discrimination." *Statistics: A Guide to the Unknown,* 3rd ed. Pacific Grove, Calif. Wadsworth, 1989.

CHAPTER 3

Benson, G. "Process thinking: The quality catalyst." *Minnesota Management Review,* University of Minnesota, Minneapolis, Fall 1992.

Feller, W. *An Introduction to Probability Theory and Its Applications,* 3rd ed., Vol. 1. New York: Wiley, 1968.

Kotler, Philip. *Marketing Management,* 8th ed. Englewood Cliffs, N.J.: Prentice-Hall, 1994.

Lindley, D. V. *Making Decisions,* 2nd ed. London: Wiley, 1985.

Parzen, E. *Modern Probability Theory and Its Applications.* New York: Wiley, 1960.

Radcliffe, R. C. *Investment: Concepts, Analysis, Strategy,* 4th ed. New York: HarperCollins College Publishers, 1994.

Scheaffer, R. L., and Mendenhall, W. *Introduction to Probability: Theory and Applications.* North Scituate, Mass.: Duxbury, 1975.

Stickney, C. P. and Weil, R. L. *Financial Accounting: An Introduction to Concepts, Methods, and Uses,* 7th ed. Fort Worth: The Dryden Press, 1994.

Williams, B. *A Sampler on Sampling.* New York: Wiley, 1978.

Winkler, R. L. *An Introduction to Bayesian Inference and Decision.* New York: Holt, Rinehart and Winston, 1972.

CHAPTER 4

Clauss, F. J. *Applied Management Science and Spreadsheet Modeling.* Belmont, Calif.: Duxbury Press, 1996.

Edwards, J. P., Jr., ed. *Transportation Planning Handbook.* Englewood Cliffs, N.J.: Prentice-Hall, 1992.

Herrnstein, R. J., and Murray, C. *The Bell Curve.* New York: The Free Press, 1994.

Hogg, R. V., and Craig, A. T. *Introduction to Mathematical Statistics,* 4th ed. New York: Macmillan, 1978.

Lindgren, B. W. *Statistical Theory,* 3rd ed. New York: Macmillan, 1976.

Mendenhall, W. *Introduction to Mathematical Statistics,* 8th ed. Boston: Duxbury, 1991.

Mendenhall, W., Wackerly, D., and Scheaffer, R. L. *Mathematical Statistics with Applications,* 4th ed. Boston: PWS-Kent, 1990.

Montgomery, D. C. *Introduction to Statistical Quality Control,* 2nd ed. New York: Wiley, 1991.

Mood, A. M., Graybill, F. A., and Boes, D. C. *Introduction to the Theory of Statistics,* 3rd ed. New York: McGraw-Hill, 1974.

Neter, J., Wasserman, W., and Whitmore, G. A. *Applied Statistics,* 4th ed. Boston: Allyn and Bacon, 1993.

Parzen, E. *Modern Probability Theory and Its Applications.* New York: Wiley, 1960.

Radcliffe, R. C. *Investments: Concepts, Analysis, Strategy,* 4th ed. New York: HarperCollins, 1994.

Render, B., and Heizer, J. *Principles of Operations Management.* Englewood Cliffs, N.J.: Prentice-Hall, 1995.

Ross, S. M. *Stochastic Processes,* 2nd ed. New York: Wiley, 1996.

CHAPTER 5

Arkin, H. *Sampling Methods for the Auditor.* New York: McGraw-Hill, 1982.

Cochran, W. G. *Sampling Techniques,* 3rd ed. New York: Wiley, 1977.

Freedman, D., Pisani, R., and Purves, R. *Statistics.* New York: Norton, 1978.

Horngren, C. T., Foster, G., and Datar, S. M. *Cost Accounting: A Managerial Emphasis,* 8th ed. Englewood Cliffs, NJ: Prentice-Hall, 1994.

Kish, L. *Survey Sampling.* New York: Wiley, 1965.

Mendenhall, W., and Beaver, B. *Introduction to Probability and Statistics,* 8th ed. Boston: PWS-Kent, 1991.

CHAPTER 6

Alexander, G. J., Sharpe, William F., and Bailey, J. *Fundamentals of Investments,* 2nd ed. Englewood Cliffs, N.J.: Prentice-Hall, 1993.

Duncan, A. J. *Quality Control and Industrial Statistics,* 5th ed. Homewood, Ill.: Richard D. Irwin, 1986.

Montgomery, D. C. *Introduction to Statistical Quality Control,* 2nd ed. New York: Wiley, 1991.

Schonberger, R. J., and Knod E. M., Jr. *Operations Management,* 5th ed. Burr Ridge, Ill.: Irwin, 1994.

Snedecor, G. W., and Cochran, W. G. *Statistical Methods,* 7th ed. Ames: Iowa State University Press, 1980.

Stevenson, W. J. *Production/Operations Management,* 5th ed. Chicago: Irwin, 1996.

CHAPTER 7

Agresti, A., and Agresti, B. F. *Statistical Methods for the Social Sciences,* 2nd ed. San Francisco: Dellen, 1986.

Conover, W. J. *Practical Nonparametric Statistics,* 2nd ed. New York: Wiley, 1980.

Davis, G. B., and Hamilton, S. *Managing Information.* Homewood, Ill.: Richard D. Irwin, Inc., 1993.

Freedman, D., Pisani, R., and Purves, R. *Statistics.* New York: W. W. Norton and Co., 1978.

Gibbons, J. D. *Nonparametric Statistical Inference,* 2nd ed. New York: McGraw-Hill, 1985.

Hollander, M., and Wolfe, D. A. *Nonparametric Statistical Methods.* New York: Wiley, 1973.

Lee, C. F., Finnerty, J. E., and Norton, E. A. *Foundations of Financial Management.* Minneapolis–St. Paul: West Publishing Co., 1997.

Lehmann, E. L. *Nonparametrics: Statistical Methods Based on Ranks.* San Francisco: Holden-Day, 1975.

McLaren, J. W., Fjerstad, W. H., and Brubaker, R. R. "New video pupillometer." *Optical Engineering,* Vol. 34, No. 3, Mar. 1, 1995.

Mendenhall, W. *Introduction to Linear Models and the Design and Analysis of Experiments.* Belmont, Calif.: Wadsworth, 1968.

Miller, R. G., Jr. *Simultaneous Statistical Inference.* New York: Springer-Verlag, 1981.

Neter, J., Wasserman, W., and Kutner, M. *Applied Linear Statistical Models,* 3rd ed. Homewood, Ill.: Richard D. Irwin, 1990.

Noether, G. E. *Elements of Nonparametric Statistics.* New York: Wiley, 1967.

Satterthwaite, F. W. "An approximate distribution of estimates of variance components." *Biometrics Bulletin,* Vol. 2, 1946, pp. 110–114.

Snedecor, G. W., and Cochran, W. *Statistical Methods,* 7th ed. Ames: Iowa State University Press, 1980.

Steel, R. G. D., and Torrie, J. H. *Principles and Procedures of Statistics,* 2nd ed. New York: McGraw-Hill, 1980.

Twomey, D. P. *Labor and Employment Law,* 9th ed. Cincinnati: South-Western Publishing Co., 1994.

Winer, B. J. *Statistical Principles in Experimental Design,* 2nd ed. New York: McGraw-Hill, 1971.

CHAPTER 8

Agresti, A., and Agresti, B. F. *Statistical Methods for the Social Sciences,* 2nd ed. San Francisco: Dellen, 1986.

Cochran, W. G. "The χ^2 test of goodness of fit." *Annals of Mathematical Statistics,* Vol. 23, 1952.

Conover, W. J. *Practical Nonparametric Statistics,* 2nd ed. New York: Wiley, 1980.

Hollander, M., and Wolfe, D. A. *Nonparametric Statistical Methods.* New York: Wiley, 1973.

Schroeder, R. G. *Operations Management,* 4th ed. New York: McGraw-Hill, 1993.

Siegel, S. *Nonparametric Statistics for the Behavioral Sciences.* New York: McGraw-Hill, 1956.

CHAPTER 9

Gitlow, H., Oppenheim, A., and Oppenheim, R. *Quality Management: Tools and Methods for Improvement,* 2nd ed. Burr Ridge, Ill.: Irwin, 1995.

Graybill, F. *Theory and Application of the Linear Model.* North Scituate, Mass.: Duxbury, 1976.

Horngren, C. T., Foster, G., and Datar, S. M. *Cost Accounting,* 8th ed. Englewood Cliffs, N.J.: Prentice-Hall, 1994.

Mendenhall, W. *Introduction to Linear Models and the Design and Analysis of Experiments.* Belmont, Calif.: Wadsworth, 1968.

Mintzberg, H. *The Nature of Managerial Work.* New York: Harper and Row, 1973.

Younger, M. S. *A First Course in Linear Regression,* 2nd ed. Boston, Mass.: Duxbury, 1985.

CHAPTER 10

Benston, G. J. "Multiple regression analysis of cost behavior." *Accounting Review,* Vol. 41, Oct. 1966, pp. 657-672.

Chase, R. B., and Aquilano, N. J. *Production and Operations Management,* 6th ed. Homewood, Ill.: Richard D. Irwin, 1992.

Chatterjee, S., and Price, B. *Regression Analysis by Example,* 2nd ed. New York: Wiley, 1991.

Devlin, B., Fienberg, S. E., Resnick, D. P., and Roeder, K. "Wringing *The Bell Curve:* A cautionary tale about relationships among race, genes, and IQ," *Chance,* Vol. 8, No. 3, Summer 1995.

Diamond, M. *Financial Accounting,* 4th ed. Cincinnati, Ohio: South-Western, 1996.

Draper, N. R., and Smith, H. *Applied Regression Analysis,* 2nd ed. New York: Wiley, 1981.

Graybill, F. *Theory and Application of the Linear Model.* North Scituate, Mass.: Duxbury, 1976.

Horngren, Charles T., Foster, G., and Datar, S. M. *Cost Accounting,* 8th ed. Englewood Cliffs, N.J.: Prentice-Hall, 1994.

Kleinbaum, D., and Kupper, L. *Applied Regression Analysis and Other Multivariable Methods.* North Scituate, Mass.: Duxbury, 1978.

Mansfield, E. *Applied Microeconomics.* New York: Norton, 1994.

Mendenhall, W. *Introduction to Linear Models and the Design and Analysis of Experiments.* Belmont, Calif.: Wadsworth, 1968.

Mendenhall, W., and Sincich, T. *A Second Course in Statistics: Regression Analysis,* 5th ed. Saddle Lake, N.J.: Prentice-Hall, 1996.

Neter, J., Wasserman, W., and Kutner, M. *Applied Linear Statistical Models,* 3rd ed. Homewood, Ill.: Richard D. Irwin, 1992.

Weisberg, S. *Applied Linear Regression,* 2nd ed. New York: Wiley, 1985.

Wonnacott, R. J., and Wonnacott, T. H. *Econometrics,* 2nd ed. New York: Wiley, 1979.

CHAPTER 11

Alwan, L., and Roberts, H. "Time-series modeling for statistical process control." *Journal of Business and Economic Statistics,* Vol. 6, 1988, pp. 87–95.

Banks, J. *Principles of Quality Control.* New York: Wiley, 1989.

Checkland, P. *Systems Thinking, Systems Practice.* New York: Wiley, 1981.

Deming, W. *Out of the Crisis.* Cambridge, Mass.: MIT Center for Advanced Engineering Study, 1986.

DeVor, R., Chang, T., and Southerland, J. *Statistical Quality Design and Control.* New York: Macmillan, 1992.

Duncan, A. *Quality Control and Industrial Statistics.* Homewood, Ill.: Irwin, 1986.

Feigenbaum, A. *Total Quality Control,* 3rd ed. New York: McGraw-Hill, 1983.

Garvin, D. *Managing Quality.* New York: Free Press/Macmillan, 1988.

Gitlow, H., et al. *Quality Management: Tools and Methods for Improvement,* 2nd ed. Burr Ridge, Ill.: Irwin, 1995.

Grant, E., and Leavenworth, R. *Statistical Quality Control,* 6th ed. New York: McGraw-Hill, 1988.

Hart, M. "Quality tools for improvement." *Production and Inventory Management Journal,* Vol. 33, No. 1, First Quarter 1992, p. 59.

Ishikawa, K. *Guide to Quality Control,* 2nd ed. White Plains, N.Y.: Kraus International Publications, 1986.

Joiner, B., and Goudard, M. "Variation, management, and W. Edwards Deming." *Quality Process,* Dec. 1990, pp. 29–37.

Juran, J. *Juran of Planning for Quality.* New York: Free Press/Macmillan, 1988.

Juran, J., and Gryna, Jr., F. *Quality Planning Analysis,* 2nd ed. New York: McGraw-Hill, 1980.

Kane, V. *Defect Prevention.* New York: Marcel Dekker, 1989.

Latzko, W. *Quality and Productivity for Bankers and Financial Managers.* New York: Marcel Dekker, 1986.

Melynk, S., and Denzler, D. *Operations Management: A Value-Driven Approach.* Chicago: Irwin, 1996.

Moen, R., Nolan, T., and Provost, L. *Improving Quality Through Planned Experimentation.* New York: McGraw-Hill, 1991.

Montgomery, D. *Introduction to Statistical Quality Control,* 2nd ed. New York: Wiley, 1991.

Nelson, L. "The Shewhart control chart—Tests for special causes." *Journal of Quality Technology,* Vol. 16, No. 4, Oct. 1984, pp. 237–239.

Roberts, H. *Data Analysis for Managers,* 2nd ed. Redwood City, Calif.: Scientific Press, 1991.

Rosander, A. *Applications of Quality Control in the Service Industries.* New York: Marcel Dekker, 1985.

Rummler, G., and Brache, A. *Improving Performance: How to Manage the White Space on the Organization Chart.* San Francisco: Jossey-Bass, 1991.

Ryan, T. *Statistical Methods for Quality Improvement.* New York: Wiley, 1989.

Statistical Quality Control Handbook. Indianapolis, Ind.: AT&T Technologies, Select Code 700-444 (inquiries: 800-432-6600); originally published by Western Electric Company, 1956.

The Ernst and Young Quality Improvement Consulting Group. *Total Quality: An Executive's Guide for the 1990s.* Homewood, Ill.: Dow-Jones Irwin, 1990.

Wadsworth, H., Stephens, K., and Godfrey, A. *Modern Methods for Quality Control and Improvement.* New York: Wiley, 1986.

Walton, M. *The Deming Management Method.* New York: Dodd, Mead, and Company, 1986.

Wheeler, D., and Chambers, D. *Understanding Statistical Process Control.* Knoxville, Tenn.: Statistical Process Controls, Inc., 1986.

INDEX

Accounts receivable, 443
Acquisitions, 339
Acupoll, 156
Additive rule, 129–30
Adverse drug effects (ADEs), 421–22
Age discrimination, 444–45
Age Discrimination in Employment
    Act, 105
All-terrain vehicles (ATVs), 157
alpha (probability of Type I error), 279
Alternative (research) hypothesis, 278,
    283, 285, 367
Analysis of variance (ANOVA), 380–93
    F-test, 546–48
    robustness of, 389
Anxiety, computer, 106
Arithmetic mean. *See* Mean(s)
Armed Forces Qualification Test (AFQT),
    206–7
Assumptions, 283
Average, weighted, 329
A zones, 623

Bankruptcy, prepackaged, 46, 88–89
Bar graphs, 28, 30, 31
Base level, 538
Bell Curve, The (Herrnstein & Murray),
    206–7, 576–77
Bell-shaped distribution. *See* Normal
    distribution
Benzo(a)pyrene [B(a)], 256
Beta coefficient of stock, 321
beta (probability of Type II error), 281
Bias, nonresponse, 17
Biased estimate, 222
Bid riggings, 107–8, 402
Binomial distribution, 178
Binomial experiment, 174
Binomial probabilities, cumulative, 181
Binomial random variables, 174–75
    binomial tables, 180–83
    characteristics of, 175
    defined, 174
    distribution of, 178
    mean, variance, and standard deviation
        for, 178
Binomial sample proportion,
    variance of, 370
Bivariate relationships, 90–93, 479
    graphing, 90–93
Black boxes, 10
Blocking, 345
Bond(s)
    government, 81
    mortgage, 43

Bordeaux wine, predicting price of,
    561–62
Bottleneck, 45
Bound B, 266
Bound on estimation error, 8
Box plots, 83–90
    interpretation of, 85
Brix, 23
Burnout, 516
Business combinations, 338–39
Business start–ups, 109–10, 237
B zones, 623

Caffeine, addictiveness of, 269
Calibration studies, 488–89
Capacitated-flow networks, 172
Carbon monoxide (CO), 124
Car & Driver's "Road Test Digest," 93
Causal relationship, 481
Cell count
    expected, 418, 424
    observed, 424
Cells. *See* Class(es)
Census, 5
Centerline, 606–7
    for p-chart, 645
    for R-chart, 636
    for $\bar{x}$-chart, 620
Central Limit Theorem, 223, 227–28, 620
Central tendency
    measures of, 53–63
    mean, 53–55, 57
    median, 55–57
    mode, 58–59
Certificate of deposit, negotiable, 487, 512
Challenger catastrophe, 183
Channel One, 147
Chebyshev, P.L., 69
Chebyshev's Rule, 69–70, 71
    for discrete random variable, 169
Children Out of School in America, 97
Children's Defense Fund (CDF), 97
Chi-square (χ^2) test, 416–20
Class(es), 26
    measurement, 39
    modal, 58–59
Class frequency, 26
Class relative frequency, 26
Cluster sampling, 175
Coefficient
    confidence, 242–43
    of correlation, 479–82
        Pearson product moment (r),
            479–81
        population (ρ), 482

    of determination (r^2), 482–90
        defined, 484
        multiple (R^2), 545–46
        practical interpretation of, 485
Combinations, business, 338–39
Combinations rule, 121
Combinatorial mathematics, 121
Common causes of variations, 612–13
Common maize rust, 518
Comparable worth, 521–23
Complementary events, 128–29
Compound events, 126
Computer anxiety, 106
Computer technology and use, ethics in,
    430–32
Conditional probability, 135–38
Condominium sale prices, 596–97
Confidence coefficient, 242–43
Confidence interval(s), 239–76
    for beta parameters in multiple
        regression model, 536
    defined, 242, 243
    for difference between population
        proportions, 408
    for difference of two population
        means, 326, 329–30
    large-sample
        for population mean, 240–48
        for population proportion, 259–65
    for mean, 492–97
    for paired difference experiments, 346
    for simple linear regression slope
        β_1, 472
    small-sample, 265–71
        for population mean, 248–58
Confidence level, 242
Conforming to specifications, 618
Consolidation, 338
Consumer Price Index (CPI), 4, 67–68
    in business forecasts, 598
Consumer Reports, 99
Consumer's risk, 290, 320
Contingency tables, 423–36
Continuous Quality Improvement
    (CQI), 123
Continuous random variable(s), 162, 164,
    191–214
    distribution for, 191–92
        exponential, 209–14
        normal. *See* Normal distribution
        uniform, 192–96
    standard, 201
Control charts, 13, 288, 614–53
    individuals chart (x-chart), 618
    logic of, 614–18

Control charts *continued*
  for monitoring mean of a process
    ($\bar{x}$-chart), 618–30
    center line and control limits in,
      620–21
    construction of, 622–23
    degree of sensitivity of, 621–22
    interpreting, 623, 624–26
    zone boundaries for, 623–24
  for monitoring process variation
    (R-chart), 635–44
    center line and control limits in,
      636–37
    construction of, 638
    interpretation of, 637–38
    zone boundaries for, 638
  for monitoring proportion of
    defectives generated by process
    (p-chart), 309, 644–51
    center line and control limits in, 645
    construction of, 645–47
    interpretation of, 647
    sample size determination for, 646
Control group, 15
Control limits, 615, 618
  for p-chart, 645
  for R-chart, 636–37
  for $\bar{x}$-chart, 621
Corporate downsizing, 316
Corporate merger, 23, 338, 339
Correlated errors, 576
Correlation
  causality and, 481
  coefficient of, 479–82
    Pearson product moment, 479–81
    population, 482
    population rank (ρ), 509
    Spearman's rank, 507–11
Cost drivers, 500
Cost functions, 500
Countable list, 163
Covenants, debt, 439
CPI. *See* Consumer Price Index (CPI)
Crack intensity, 304
Critical thinking, 19
Crossen, Cynthia, 18
Cross-sectional data, 540
Cumulative binomial probabilities, 181
Current Population Survey, 23, 24
Cycle time, 234
Cyclical variations, 608, 610
C zones, 623

Data, 2
  collecting, 15–17
  cross-sectional, 540
  ordinal, 14
  population, 6
  qualitative, 14
  quantitative, 12–13
  sample, 6
  skewed, 56
  time series. *See* Time series data

U.S. government-maintained, 109–10
Data description, 25–110
  distorting truth with, 93–97
  graphical methods of, 26, 35–53
    bar graphs, 28, 30, 31
    bivariate relationships, 90–93
    box plots, 83–90
    dot plots, 37, 39
    histograms, 38–42, 51
    pie charts, 28
    scattergrams (scatterplots),
      90–93, 452
    stem-and-leaf displays, 37–38, 39–40
    time series plot, 49–51, 606
  numerical methods of, 26, 52–90
    measures of central tendency, 53–63
    measures of relative standing,
      76–82
    measures of variability, 53, 63–76
    quartiles, 83–90
    summation notation, 52–53
Debenture, 43
Debt covenants, 439
Decision-making, managerial, 17–21
Defectives generated by process,
  monitoring. *See* p-chart
Deflation, 4
Degrees of freedom (df), 249, 329
Demand curve, 489–90
Deming, W. Edwards, 51, 604–5
Deming Prize, 13, 604
Density function, probability, 191
Dependence, 426
Dependent events, 142
Dependent variable, 450
Descriptive statistics
  defined, 2–3
  elements of problems in, 8
Designed experiments, 15
Destructive sampling, 252–53
Deterministic relationship, 449
Development, sustainable, 125
Deviation, 64–67, 453. *See also* Error(s);
    Standard deviation
Dialing, random-digital, 153
Dichotomous responses, 174
Dimensions (scales) of classification, 423
Direct labor expenses, 477
Discrete random variables, 161–99
  binomial, 174–75
    binomial tables, 180–83
    characteristics of, 175
    defined, 174
    distribution of, 178
    mean, variance, and standard
      deviation for, 178
  defined, 163
  expected values (mean) of, 167
  Poisson, 186–91
    characteristics of, 186
    mean, variance, and standard
      deviation for, 187
  probability distributions for, 165–74

standard deviation of, 169
  variance of, 168
Discrimination in workplace, 444–45
Disparate impact, 105, 444
Disparate treatment, 105, 444
Distribution(s), 191
  binomial, 178
  for continuous random variable,
    191–92, 209–14
    exponential, 209–14
    uniform, 192–96
  for discrete random variables, 165–74
  exponential, 234
  F-, 358
  mound-shaped, 69, 70, 72, 78
  multinomial, 415
  normal. *See* Normal distribution
  Poisson, 186, 187
  of the process, 607
  sampling. *See* Sampling distribution(s)
  uniform, 192–96, 218
  of uniform random variable, 193
Dividend yield, 401
Dot plots, 37, 39
Downsizing, corporate, 316
Downtrends, 608, 610
Dummy (indicator) variables, 538

Earnings per share (E/S), 89
Economic indicators, 109, 403
Economic mobility, 206–7
Effective buying income (EBI), 461
Elevator cycle time, 234
Elevator running distance, 234
Emotional exhaustion (burnout), 516
Empirical Rule, 70, 71, 201
  for discrete random variable, 169
Employee suggestion system, 512
Entrepreneurs, 442–43
Environmental Protection Agency
  (EPA), 190
Error(s), 453
  bound on estimation, 8
  correlated, 576
  mean square for (s^2), 532
  random, 449, 531
  regression residual, 563–68
  sampling, 491
  standard. *See* Standard error
  sum of (SE), 453
  sum of squares of (SSE), 453
  Type I, 279, 616
  Type II, 281, 616
Escalator clauses, 4
Estimates, unbiased and biased, 222
Estimation
  multiple regression model for,
    558–60
  simple linear regression for, 490–502
Estimation error, bound on, 8
Estimator
  point, 240
  unbiased, 66

Ethics, 20, 434
  in computer technology and use, 430–32
Event(s), 118
  complementary, 128–29
  compound, 126
  defined, 117
  dependent, 142
  independent, 141–44
  mutually exclusive, 130–31, 142
  rare, 616, 624
  simple, 113
Evidence, credibility of, 282
Expected marginal cost, 555
Expected (mean) cell count, 418, 424
Expected value(s)
  of discrete random variables, 167
  of squared distance from the mean, 168
Experiment(s), 112–13. *See also* Designed
      experiments
  binomial, 174
  multinomial, 415–23
  randomized block, 345
  sample spaces of, 114
Exploding the Pareto diagram, 31
Exponential distribution, 209–14, 234
Exponential random variable, 210
Extrapolation, 502, 575

Factors, 91. *See also* Independent
      variable(s)
Fair Labor Standards Act of 1938
      (FLSA), 355
Farming, sustainable, 125
F-distribution, 358–59
Federal Deposit Insurance Corporation
      (FDIC), 189–90
Fertility rate, 487
Filling processes, 229
First-order (straight-line) models, 450–51.
      See also Simple linear regression
Fisher's exact test, 440
Fitness for use, 443
Fleet mean score, 230
Flexible manufacturing system (FMS), 213
Flextime, 379
Flight assignment problem, 208
Forecasting, CPI in, 598. *See also* Prediction
401(k) plans, 247
Frequency
  class, 26
  class relative, 26
  relative, 38
Frequency function, 191
Frequency marketing programs, 303
F statistic, 382–83, 385
F-test, 384
  analysis of variance, 546–48
  for equal population variances, 360–62

Generalization, 7
General linear model. *See* Multiple
      regression

Go, 145
Graphs, 26, 35–53
  bar graphs, 28, 30, 31
  of bivariate relationships, 90–93
  box plots, 83–90
  dot plots, 37, 39
  histograms, 38–42, 51
  pie charts, 28
  scattergrams (scatterplots), 90–93, 452
  stem-and-leaf displays, 37–38, 39–40
  time series plot, 49–51, 606
Gross Domestic Product (GDP), 109, 403
Gross National Product (GNP), 403
Gross Profit Factor (GPF), 236

Health Maintenance Organizations
      (HMOs), 513–14
Herrnstein, Richard J., 206–7, 576–77
Hinges, 83, 85
Histograms, 38–42, 51
Hypothesis
  alternative (research), 278, 283, 285, 367
  null, 278, 283, 285
  one-tailed, 284–85, 288
  tests of. *See* Control charts; Tests of
      hypotheses
  two-tailed, 285, 288

Impact, disparate, 105, 444
Income, effective buying (EBI), 461
In control processes, 611, 612, 614
Incumbency rates, 402
Independent classifications, 424
Independent events, 141–44
Independent samples, Wilcoxon rank sum
      for, 364–72
Independent sampling
  for comparing population proportions,
      406–13
  for comparing two population means,
      324–42
    large samples, 324–28
    for small samples, 328–42
Independent variable(s), 450
Indicator (dummy) variables, 538
Individuals chart (*x*-chart), 618
Inference, 6, 111
Inferential statistics, 4
  defined, 3
  elements of problems in, 8
Inflation, 4
Inner fences, 83, 85
Insider trading, 305
Insomnia pill, 227
Instructional technology, 421
Intelligence, economic mobility and, 206–7
Intelligence quotient (IQ), 576
Interaction model(s), 548
Internal Revenue Service (IRS), 377
Internet, 34
Interpolations, 502
Interquartile range (IQR), 83, 85

Intersections, 126–28
Interval data, 12
Interval estimator. *See* Confidence
      interval(s)
Intervals, 38
Investment portfolios, 173
Investment risk, 173
Ishikawa, Kaoru, 640

January indicator, 441
Jet lag, 227
Job-sharing, 23
Just-in-Time (JIT) inventory ordering, 460
Just-in-Time (JIT) production, 644

Kentucky milk bid rigging case, 107–8, 402

Large Numbers, Law of, 115
Law of Large Numbers, 115
Lead time, 229
Learning curve, 46
Least squares approach, 453
  to linear regression, 451–62, 527
  to multiple regression, 527–30
Least squares line, 453
  sampling errors of, 491
Level of significance, 283
Level shifts, 608, 610
Lie detector (polygraph), 283–84
Linear regression. *See* Simple linear
      regression
Line of means, 450
List, countable, 163
Long jump, 459
Lotteries, 151–52
Lottery Buster, 151
Lower control limit, 615
Lower quartile, 83

Machiavellian orientation, 23
Magnuson-Moss Warranty Act, 443
Maize rust, common, 518
Make-to-order processes, 44
Make-to-stock processes, 44
Management information system
      (MIS), 371
Manager, product, 411–21
Managerial decision-making, 17–21
Mann-Whitney *U* statistic, 366
Manufacturing process, 9–10
Marginal cost, expected, 555
Marginal probabilities, 423
Market allocation, 402
Market basket, 4
Market model, 479
Markets, stock, 153
"Math anxiety," 486
Mathematics, combinatorial, 121
Matrix solid-phase dispersion (MPSD), 303
Mean(s), 53–55, 57
  for binomial random variables, 178
  confidence interval for, 492–97

Mean(s) *continued*
    defined, 53
    of discrete random variables, 167
    expected value of squared distance
        from, 168
    for exponential random variable, 210
    line of, 450
    for normal distribution, 197
    of Poisson random variables, 187
    population. *See* Population mean(s)
    of process, monitoring. *See* $\bar{x}$-chart
    sample. *See* Sample mean
    standard error of the, 223
    treatment. *See* Designed experiments
    trimmed, 62
    of uniform random variable, 193
Meandering variations, 608, 610
Mean (expected) cell count, 418, 424
Mean square for error (s^2), 382–85, 532
Mean Square for Treatments (MST),
    382–85
Measurement, 5, 112
Measurement classes, 39
Measurement processes, 10
Median, 55–57
    nonparametric tests about, 312–17
Melatonin, 227
Merchandise trade balance, 81
Mergers, corporate, 23, 338, 339
Middle quartile, 83
Milk bidrigging case, Kentucky, 107–8, 402
Minnesota Multiphasic Personality
    Inventory (MMPI), 392
Minorities, New Jersey banks and, 472–73
MIS, 371
Mobility, economic, 206–7
Modal class, 58–59
Mode, 58–59
Model(s)
    first-order, 450–51
    market, 479
    multiple regression, 526–27, 530–32
    probabilistic. *See* Probabilistic models
    stepwise regression, 575
    time series, 576
Morris, Robert, 430
Mortality tables, 157
Mortgage, 256
Mortgage bond, 43
Mound-shaped distributions, 69, 70, 72, 78
MPSD, 303
MSE, 382–85, 532
Multicollinearity, 574–75
Multinomial experiment, 415–23
Multiple coefficient of determination (R^2),
    545–46
Multiple regression, 525–98
    for estimation and prediction, 558–60
    inferences about β parameters, 532–44
    least squares approach to, 527–30
    models of, 526–27
        assumptions of, 530–32

    pitfalls of, 573–77
        correlated errors, 576
        multicollinearity, 574–75
        parameter estimability, 573–74
        prediction outside experimental
            region, 575
    procedure for, 527
    residual analysis of, 560–73
        outliers, 568
        steps in, 573
    usefulness of, 544–50
        analysis of variance F-test, 546–48
        multiple coefficient of
            determination (R^2) and,
            545–46
Multiplicative rule, 138–41
Murray, Charles, 206–7, 576–77
Mutually exclusive events, 130–31, 142

National Resident Matching Program
    (NRMP), 159
Negative correlation, perfect, 506, 507
Negotiable certificate of deposit, 487, 512
Networks, capacitated-flow, 172
New Jersey banks, minorities and, 472–73
New York Stock Exchange (NYSE), 446
Nielsen survey, 16
Nominal data, 14
Nonconforming to specifications, 618
Nonparametric statistics, 254, 362
    sign test, 312–17
    Spearman's rank correlation
        coefficient, 507–11
        formulas for, 507
    Wilcoxon rank sum test
        for independent samples, 364–72
        for paired difference experiment
            (Wilcoxon signed rank test),
            372–80
Nonresponse bias, 17
Normal distribution, 196–209
    characteristics of, 197
    economic mobility and, 206–7
    formula for, 197
    properties of, 201
    standard, 197–201
    z-score and, 201–2
Normal random variable, 196
    probability corresponding to, 202
    standard, 201
NRMP, 159
Null hypothesis, 278, 283, 285
Numerical methods of data description,
    26, 52–90
    measures of central tendency, 53–63
    measures of relative standing, 76–82
    measures of variability, 53, 63–76
    quartiles, 83–90
    summation notation, 52–53

O.J. Simpson case, 282
Observation, 112

Observational studies, 16
Observed cell count, 424
Observed significance levels (p-values),
    292–98
    calculating, 293
    recording test results as, 294
Obstructive sleep apnea, 263
Ocean quahog, 229
OCPs, 303
Odds, 125
One-tailed test(s), 284–85, 288, 299
    of beta parameters in multiple
        regression model, 535
    for comparing two population means,
        326, 330
    about population mean, 284–85,
        288, 299
    about population proportion, 307
    sign test for population median, 314
    for simple linear regression, 470
    Spearman's nonparametric test for
        rank correlation, 510–11
    Wilcoxon rank sum test for
        independent samples, 366–67,
        368–69
    Wilcoxon signed rank test, 374–75, 376
Operating characteristic curve, 186
Ordinal data, 14
Organization of Petroleum Exporting
    Countries (OPEC), 458
Organochlorine pesticides (OCPs), 303
Oscillating sequences, 607
Outer fences, 83, 85
Outliers, 42, 60, 84–85, 568, 608, 610
Out of statistical control (out of control),
    611, 612, 614
Out of the Crisis (Edwards), 51
Output distribution of the process, 607
Overhead, 477
Overtime, unpaid, 355

PAF, 60
Paired difference experiments
    for comparing two population means,
        342–53
        appropriate applications of,
            345–46
        confidence interval for, 348
    Wilcoxon rank sum for, 372–80
Parameter estimability, 573–74
Parameters, 214, 215, 239
    biased and unbiased estimates of, 222
Pareto, Vilfredo, 31
Pareto analysis, 31
Pareto diagram, 31
Pareto principal, 31
Passwords, 284
Pattern-analysis rules, 624–25
PCBs, 105
p-chart, 309, 644–51
    center line and control limits in, 645
    construction of, 645–47

p-chart *continued*
   interpretation of, 647
   sample size determination for, 646
Pearson product moment coefficient of
      correlation, 479–81
Pentium chip, 147
Percentile ranking, 77
Perfect negative correlation, 506, 507
Perfect positive correlation, 506, 507
Personnel tests, 208
Pie charts, 28
Placebo effect, 311
Plants, transgenic, 34
Platelet-activating factor (PAF), 60
Point estimator, 240
Poisson, Siméon, 186
Poisson distribution, 186, 187
Poisson random variables, 186–91
   characteristics of, 186
   mean, variance, and distribution of, 187
Polls, political, 15–16
Polychlorinated biphenyls (PCBs), 105
Polygraph (lie detector), 283–84
Pooled sample estimator, 328–29
Population(s), 6
   defined, 4
   z-score for, 77
Population correlation coefficient (ρ), 482
Population data, 6
Population mean(s), 55
   ANOVA to compare, 380–93
   comparing two, 323–403
      determining sample size for, 353–57
      independent sampling, 324–42
      paired difference experiments,
         342–53
   confidence intervals for, 240–58
      large-sample, 240–48
      small-sample, 248–58
   estimating, 265–67
   large-sample tests of hypothesis about,
      284–92
      conclusions for, 289
      one-tailed test, 284–85, 288
      two-tailed test, 285, 288
   small-sample tests of hypothesis about,
      298–305
      one-tailed test, 299
      t statistic for, 298–99, 302
      two-tailed test, 299
   as variable, 448. *See also* Simple linear
      regression
Population median, nonparametric tests
      about, 312–17
Population proportion(s)
   comparing, 405–46
      contingency table analysis, 423–36
      independent sampling for, 406–13
      multinomial experiment, 415–23
      sample size determination for,
         353–57, 413–15
   estimating, 267–70

large-sample confidence intervals for,
      259–65
large-sample tests of hypothesis about,
      305–12
   one-tailed, 307
   two-tailed, 307
   z-test for, 305–7
Population rank correlation coefficient
      (ρ), 509
Population variance(s), 65, 168
   equal, 357–64
Portfolios, investment, 173
Positive correlation, perfect, 505, 507
Post-traumatic stress disorder (PTSD), 290
Precision, 401
Prediction
   multiple regression model for, 558–60
      outside experimental region, 575
   simple linear regression for, 490–502
Prediction interval, 492–97
Prepackaged bankruptcy, 46, 88–89
Price scanners, 411
Primary market, 153
Primary source of data, 15
Printed circuit boards (PCBs), 291
Probabilistic models, 448–51
   common uses of, 490
   first-order. *See* First-order
      (straight-line) models
   general form of, 449
Probabilistic relationship, 449
Probability(ies), 111–59
   additive rule of, 129–30
   conditional, 135–38
   of events, 118
      complementary events, 128–29
      independent events, 141–44
      mutually exclusive events,
         130–31, 142
   marginal, 423
   multiplicative rule of, 138–41
   for normal random variable, 202
   random sampling and, 148–52
   of sample points, 114–21
   sample space and, 113–15
   unconditional, 135, 136
   unions and intersections, 126–28
Probability density function, 191
Probability distribution. *See* Distribution(s)
Process(es), 9–12, 602
   black boxes, 10
   defined, 9
   distribution of the, 607
   filling, 229
   manufacturing, 9–10
   measurement, 10
   production, 44
   sample and, 10–11
   stability of, 611
Producer's risk, 290, 320
Production processes, 44
Product manager, 411–21

Product reliability, 213–14
Promotions, trade, 320
Proportion, sample, 305
*p*th percentile, 77
PTSD, 290
Published sources of data, 15
Pupillometer, 351
p-values (observed significance level),
      292–98, 440
   calculating, 293
   recording test results as, 294

Quadratic term, 528
Qualitative data, 14
Quality, 600–602
   defined, 601
   dimensions of, 601
Quality control
   through control charts, 288
   with *p*-charts, 309
   Total Quality Management (TQM),
      123, 148, 433–34, 460, 600
Quality improvement, 13, 599–663. *See
      also* Control charts
   continuous (CQI), 123
   Deming's contributions to, 51, 604–5
   statistical control, 606–14
   through variance reduction, 614
Quantitative data, 12–13
Quartiles, 83–90
Quotas, sales, 340

Random behavior, 611
Random-digital dialing, 153
Random error, 449
   in multiple regression, 531
Randomized block experiment, 345
Randomness (uniform) distribution,
      192–96, 218
Random number generators, 149
Random number table, 149, 150
Random phenomena, 448
Random sample, 16, 148–52
Random variable(s)
   defined, 162
   Poisson, 186–91
   types of, 162–64. *See also* Continuous
      random variable(s); Discrete
      random variables
Range, 63–64, 266–67
   interquartile (IQR), 83, 85
Rank sums, 365
Rare-event approach, 80, 226
Rare events, 616, 624
Ratio data, 12
Rational subgroups, 622
Raw material expenses, 477
R-chart, 635–44
   center line and control limits in, 636–37
   construction of, 637
   interpretation of, 637–38
   zone boundaries for, 638

Reductions in force (RIF), 316
Regression analysis (regression
    modeling), 450. *See also* Model(s);
    Multiple regression; Simple linear
    regression
    stepwise, 575
Regression residuals, 563–68
    properties of, 563–64
Rejection region, 279–80, 283, 285,
    298–99, 306
Relative frequency, 38
Relative frequency histogram, 38
Relative standing, measures of, 76–82
    percentile ranking, 77
    z-score, 77–80, 201–2
Reliability, 196
    measure of, 8
    product, 213–14
Reliability function, 213–14
Representative sample, 16
Research (alternative) hypothesis, 278, 283,
    285, 367
Residual analysis, 560–73
    outliers, 568
    steps in, 573
Resource constraints, 8
Risk
    consumer's, 290, 320
    investment, 173
    producer's, 290, 320
"Road Test Digest," 93
Roulette, 133
Run chart (time series plot), 49–51, 606.
    See also Control charts
Running distance, elevator, 234

Sales closing techniques, 393
Sales quotas, 340
Sample, 6
    defined, 5–6
    median of, 55–56
    processes and, 10–11
    random, 16
    representative, 16
    standard deviation of, 65
    z-score for, 77
Sample data, 6
Sample mean, 53–55
    sampling distribution of, 221–30
        Central Limit Theorem and, 223,
            227–28
        properties of, 222–23
        shape of, 223–24
        standard deviation of, 227
Sample points, 113, 114–21
Sample proportion, 305
    variance of binomial, 370
Sample size, 55
    for comparing means or proportions,
        353–57
    for comparing population proportions,
        413–15

confidence intervals and, 265–71
    for p-chart, 646
Sample space, probability and, 113–15
Sample statistics, 214–15
Sample surveys, 406
Sample variance, 64–65
Sample variation, 545
Sampling, 2
    cluster, 175
    destructive, 252–53
    random, 148–52
Sampling distribution(s), 214–21
    defined, 216
    of difference between sample
        proportions, 407
    of difference of two population means,
        325–26
    of least squares estimator, 469
    of sample mean, 221–30
        Central Limit Theorem and, 223,
            227–28
        properties of, 222–23
        shape of, 223–24
        standard deviation of, 227
    of sample proportion, 259–60
    of t versus z, 250–51
Sampling errors, 491
Scaffold-drop surveys, 496
Scale break, 94
Scales (dimensions) of classification, 423
Scanner panel, 421
Scattergrams (scatterplots), 90–93, 452
S-chart, 636
Secondary markets, 153
Secondary source of data, 15
Securities and Exchange Commission
    (SEC), 305
Self-managed work teams (SMWTs),
    334–35
Shewhart, Walter, 13, 288, 604, 606
Shock/freak/outlier variations, 608, 610
Significance levels, 283
    observed (p-values), 292–98
        calculating, 293
        recording test results as, 294
Sign test, 312–17
Simple event (sample point), 113
Simple linear regression, 447–524
    assessing utility of (slope of β_1), 469–79
    assumptions of, 462–63
    coefficient of correlation, 479–82
    coefficient of determination, 482–90
    estimated standard error of, 463–68
    for estimation and prediction, 490–502
    example of, 502–5
    least squares approach to, 451–62, 527
    steps in using, 452
Simple random sample, 148
Skewed data, 56
Sleep apnea, obstructive, 263
SMWTs, 334–35
Solvents, organic chemical, 392

Spalling damage, 496–97
SPC. *See* Statistical process control (SPC)
Spearman's rank correlation coefficient,
    507–11
    formulas for, 507
Special causes of variation, 613
Specification limits, 618
Spill, 208
SSE, 382, 453
SST, 381–82
Stability of process, 611
Stacking, 106
Standard deviation, 65–67
    for binomial random variables, 178
    for discrete random variables, 169
    for exponential random variables, 210
    interpretation of, 69–76
        Chebyshev's Rule and, 69–70, 71
        Empirical Rule and, 70, 71
    for normal distribution, 197
    of random error (ϵ), 463, 464
    of sampling distribution of sample
        mean, 227
    of uniform random variable, 193
Standard error, 326
    of the mean, 223
    of regression model, 463–68
Standard normal distribution, 197–201
Standard normal random variable, 201
Standards, work, 517–18
Start-ups, business, 109–10, 237
Statistical control, 606–14
    defined, 611
Statistical inference, 6
Statistical process control (SPC), 612
Statistical thinking, 18, 604
Statistics, 1–24
    data collection and, 15–17
    data types and, 12–15
    defined, 2
    fundamental elements of, 4–9
    in managerial decision-making, 17–21
    processes and, 9–12
    science of, 2
    types of, 2–4
    unemployment, 109
Stem-and-leaf displays, 37–38, 39–40
Stepwise regression, 575
Stock
    beta coefficient of, 321
    dividend yield of, 401
    sampling and analyzing quotes, 446
Stock exchanges, 153, 446
Stossel, John, 18
Straight-line model. *See* First-order
    (straight-line) models
Stress, 263
"Sudden-death" overtime, 213
Sufficient norm constraint, 48
Summation notation, 52–53
Sum of errors (SE), 453
Sum of Squares for Error (SSE), 382, 453

Sum of Squares for Treatments (SST), 381–82
Sum of squares of errors (SSE), 453
Superfund Act, 59
Surveys
    data from, 15–16
    misleading and biased, 18–19
    sample, 406
    scaffold-drop, 496
Sustainable development, 125
Sustainable farming, 125
System, in gambling, 311–12
Systems, 602–5

Table(s)
    binomial, 180–83
    contingency, 423–36
    contingency. See Contingency tables
    mortality, 157
    random number, 149, 150
    two-way, 423
Tax disputes, litigating, 377
Technology, instructional, 421
Tests of hypotheses, 262, 277–321
    defined, 278
    about difference between population
        proportions, 408–9
    elements of, 278–84
    about multinomial probabilities, 418–19
    about population mean
        large-sample, 284–92
        more than one, 323–403
        small-sample, 298–305
    about population proportion
        large-sample, 305–12
        sample size for, 353–57
    about population variances, 357–64
    p-values, 292–98
        calculating, 293
        recording test results as, 294
Test statistic, 278, 283
Thinking
    critical, 19
    statistical, 18, 604
Time series data, 540
    correlated errors with, 576
    defined, 49
Time series model, 576
Time series plot (run chart), 49–51, 606.
        See also Control charts
Time study, 68
Total Diet Study, 185
Total Quality Management (TQM), 123,
        148, 433–34, 460, 600
Trade balance, merchandise, 81
Trade promotions, 320
Transgenic plants, 34
Treasury bills (T-bills), 81

Treasury bonds, 81
Treatment, disparate, 105, 444
Treatment group, 15
Treatment means. See Designed
        experiments
Tree diagram, 140–41
Trial values, 626, 638, 647
Trichuristrichiura, 553
Trimmed mean, 62
t statistic, 249–54, 298–99, 302
    for comparing population means, 330,
        333–34
t-test, 298–99, 302
    of beta parameters in multiple
        regression model, 533
    inappropriate application of, 343
Two-dimensional classification. See
        Contingency tables
Two-tailed hypothesis, 285, 288
Two-tailed test, 299
    of beta parameters in multiple
        regression model, 535
    for comparing two population means,
        326, 330
    about population mean, 285, 288, 299
    sign test for population median, 314
    for simple linear regression, 470
    Spearman's nonparametric test for
        rank correlation, 510–11
    Wilcoxon rank sum test for indepen-
        dent samples, 366–67, 368–69
    Wilcoxon signed rank test, 374–75, 376
Two-way table. See Contingency tables
Type I error, 279, 616
Type II error, 281, 616

Unbiased estimate, 222
Unbiased estimator, 66
Unconditional probability, 135, 136
Unemployment rate, 24
Unemployment statistics, 109
Unethical statistical practice, 20
Uniform distribution, 192–96, 218
Unions, 126–28
U.S. savings bonds, 81
Universal Soil Loss Equation (USLE), 474
Upper control limit, 615
Upper quartile, 83
Uptrends, 608, 609, 610

Variability, measures of, 53, 63–76
    deviation, 64–67, 453
    range, 63–64
    variance, 64–67
Variable(s), 10
    defined, 5
    dependent, 450
    dummy (indicator), 538

independent. See Independent
        variable(s)
    population mean as, 448
    random. See Random variable(s)
Variance(s), 64–67
    for binomial random variables, 178
    of binomial sample proportion, 370
    for discrete random variables, 168
    for Poisson random variables, 187
    population, 65, 168
        equal, 357–64
    sample, 64–65
Variation(s). See also Control charts
    causes/sources of, 604
        common, 612–13
        special, 613
    patterns of, 606–14
    sample, 545
Venn diagrams, 114
Vinyl chloride, 320
Vos Savant, Marilyn, 122

Waiting time (exponential) distribution,
        209–14
Walters, Barbara, 18
Weighted average, 329
Wells, H.G., 17
Whiskers, 83, 85
Whistle blowing, 458
Wilcoxon, Frank, 364
Wilcoxon rank sum test
    for independent samples, 364–72
    for paired difference experiment
        (Wilcoxon signed rank test),
        372–80
Work center, 45
Workplace, discrimination in, 444–45
Work standards, 517–18
Work teams, self–managed (SMWTs),
        334–35
World Wide Web, 34

x-chart, 618
x̄-chart, 288, 618–30
    center line and control limits in, 620–21
    construction of, 622–23
    degree of sensitivity of, 621–22
    interpreting, 623, 624–26
    zone boundaries for, 623–24

Yield, dividend, 401

Zone boundaries
    for R-chart, 638
    for x̄-chart, 623–24
z-score, 77–80, 201–2
z-test, 305–7